ASSOCIATION FOR CONSUMER RESEARCH

BUILDING CONNECTIONS

2011

Volume XXXIX
PROCEEDINGS

Editors
Rohini Ahluwalia
Tanya L. Chartrand
Rebecca K. Ratner

Advances in Consumer Research, Volume 39

Rohini Ahluwalia, Tanya L. Chartrand, and Rebecca K. Ratner, Editors

2012 Copyright © ASSOCIATION FOR CONSUMER RESEARCH

International Standard Book Number (ISBN): 978-0-915552-69-6

Association for Consumer Research
Labovitz School of Business & Economics
University of Minnesota Duluth
11 East Superior Street, Suite 210
Duluth, MN 55802

www.acrwebsite.org

Preface

The 39th annual North American Conference of the Association for Consumer Research was held at the Hyatt Regency St. Louis at The Arch in St. Louis, MO from Thursday, October 13 through Sunday, October 16, 2011. This volume consists of research presented during this conference. The volume is organized by type of research submission and includes the following: Special Session Summaries, Full Competitive Papers, Competitive Extended Abstracts, Film Festival Abstracts, Roundtable Summaries, and Working Paper Abstracts.

The theme of ACR 2011 was "Building Connections," reflecting the role of St. Louis as the historic Gateway to the West. The goal for the conference was to promote connections between researchers from different areas of consumer research, different theoretical perspectives and methodologies, and between academia and industry. By all accounts this goal was met; the quality of the research was exceptional and people and perspectives were brought together in many ways.

There were several changes at the 2011 conference that reflected our Building Connections theme. First, we introduced an opening Plenary Session; we kicked off the conference Thursday with a session immediately preceding the Thursday night reception. This plenary session was designed to bring the ACR community together for a lively discussion and Q&A with panelists. Second, we created a "Coffee Connections Lounge", complete with sofas, tables, and coffee, which was designed to facilitate conversation during breaks in the program. During the Long Coffee Breaks, participants were invited to connect with researchers with similar interests. Third, we added some social media in the form of Twitter. Conference attendees were encouraged to tweet about the presentations or other conference events, which appeared on a "Twitter Fountain" displayed in a central location. Finally, we introduced ACR At-A-Glance this year, which consisted of a one-page fold-out in the program that identified the session topics, time slots, and room numbers. This provided a quick way to make connections between the various topics featured at the 2011 conference, and to make it easier for attendees to find their way to the next session.

We would like to thank the generous donors who provided financial support for this year's conference. We also want to thank all the people who provided us with invaluable help with this conference. We especially want to thank the Associate Editors, the Senior AEs, the members of the ACR program committee, the working paper reviewers, film festival reviewers, and competitive paper reviewers. In addition, we owe a special thanks to all the student volunteers from University of Minnesota, Duke University, and University of Maryland who helped us tremendously. Finally, we thank Rajiv Vaidyanathan, executive director of ACR, for his support throughout the process, and to Sharon Shavitt for trusting us with this conference and giving us the opportunity to give back to the amazing community of consumer behavior researchers.

Rohini Ahluwalia, University of Minnesota
Tanya L. Chartrand, Duke University
Rebecca K. Ratner, University of Maryland

Table of Contents

Competitive Papers—Full

Competitive Papers—Extended Abstracts

Film Festival

Roundtable Summaries

Working Papers

Author Index

ACR Presidential Address 2011

What's New? Novelty in Consumer Research

Sharon Shavitt, Walter H. Stellner Professor of Marketing, University of Illinois at Urbana-Champaign, USA

This is a slightly expanded version of the address given in St. Louis, October 14, 2011

I want to talk about your next paper. The next piece of work you will submit for review. In this talk, I will address one of the most important criteria that will determine whether it is accepted or rejected. Surprisingly, it's the least understood criterion. Everyone will judge your work on it, but no one quantifies or defines it.

I'm going to talk about novelty in research. How we assess it. Why we seek it. And what are the consequences.

The topic for this talk was inspired by a review of one of my old manuscripts. Perhaps you have a review just like it – the kind that haunts you long after the paper is published. Years ago, my student and I submitted such a paper to one of our top journals. It addressed how attitudes can shift when people anticipate a group discussion. We got good feedback, but one reviewer complained that the paper lacked novelty: "The additional contribution seems marginal. We already know that reference groups influence judgments."

That review changed my view of our field. It was accurate – we do know that reference groups influence judgments. But does that mean we're finished with this entire domain? When is a topic *spent*? How do we decide if something has already been done, or if it's novel? I couldn't stop asking myself these questions.

The view of novelty in that review reminds me of the *New Yorker* cartoon where one caveman says to the other, "Og discovered fire, and Thorak invented the wheel. There's nothing left for us."

It's easy to get the feeling that it's all been done. We could have stopped with Og and Thorak. Yet, people have found ways to keep innovating. We have novelty, but we don't always recognize it.

In this address, I will describe the subjective ways we assess novelty. I will discuss our deeper motivations for seeking it. And I will propose that if we worried less about pursuing what's new, we could enhance innovation in our field.

WHO CARES ABOUT NOVELTY?

We all do. We are all judged on it. We all try to claim it for our research. Making a convincing claim is getting harder as the field rapidly grows. But it's urgent for junior scholars. They need to carve out their niche while the tenure clock is ticking. There is a lot on the line.

For us older scholars, novelty is also important. It's a way of ensuring we have made a mark. Our life's work has mattered because we did something new.

Why is novelty so important to these goals? Because, in the academic world, novelty is status. It's the Gucci, Vuitton, and Lamborghini of research -- all rolled into one. Novelty compensates for other flaws (Rozin, 2009), like Botox, smoothing out the wrinkles in our studies. Novelty assures our findings will get attention and admiring glances. If we're lucky, maybe publication in *JSSR* -- the *Journal of Short Sexy Results*. Who wouldn't want that?

Journals want novelty, too. Want it and demand it. Each editorial we read tells us to send in only our most novel work. One marketing journal's website insists that,

"All submissions must be interesting,..."
"...The editors...especially encourage research that is novel, visionary or pathbreaking."

Clearly, the bar is high for judging the novelty of your next paper.

WHAT'S NEW? DEFINING NOVELTY

Novelty can come in various forms. So, when you ask people, "what is novelty in research?" they will say: It is a new area, a new idea, a new finding or method. That is fine, but it still leaves the question – what's "new?"

The subject of novelty has been addressed in the sociology of science. Robert Merton (1973 [1942]) and others described how scientists get credit for original discoveries, and the rewards that follow from that (see Guetkow, Lamont, & Mallard, 2004, for a review). This classic work dealt with a number of issues, except what novelty actually is. What is the threshold for calling something "novel?"

There really is no authoritative work on that. The word "novel" is used – a lot— but always as if the concept is self-evident. As if everyone who looked at a piece of research would judge its novelty the same way.

The difficulty in defining novelty is immediately apparent to those who try. C.W. Park (2011), editor of the *Journal of Consumer Psychology*, offered helpful guidelines on submitting novel work to *JCP*. He acknowledged that judging novelty,

"involves a high degree of subjectivity… The bottom line is that [novel papers] …cause readers to slap their forehead, exclaiming 'Silly me, …why didn't I observe this?'"

I think this statement may be as good as it gets in defining novelty. It recognizes that novelty in research confers status and elicits envy.

When you submit your next paper, you may be told that it does not seem new, or that enough has been done on your topic. That kind of feedback can feel quite discouraging, especially if you are a young scholar eager to establish yourself. Fear not. You are in good company:

"For my annual review in 1974, the department head suggested that I move away from pricing research as I had done about all that could be done in this area."

This is Kent Monroe (2008, p. 16) speaking when he was named ACR Fellow for decades of pioneering work on pricing. I mention this quote for two reasons. One is to reassure you that the best have faced this criticism. Another is to support the plausibility of three points I want to make about novelty.

(1) Novelty is not an intrinsic attribute (of a theory, a finding, or anything else).
  An assessment of novelty is a mental construction.
  -It draws from feelings and subjective experiences.
  -And it is sensitive to context. How we judge it depends on where we're standing.

We don't have to look far to see what kinds of factors can impact judgments of novelty. We can just look at the research we conduct or cite: Research on fluency and metacognition, on thinking styles, and values. In fact,

(2)   *The way we seek novelty in research is tied to our core values.*

Because values are not universal, neither is the way we understand novelty, as we'll see. And my final point:

(3)   *Pursuing novelty in research has unintended consequences.*

Of course, we need novelty if we hope to push the boundaries of knowledge. At the same time, any criterion applied reflexively is bound to cause trouble. I will offer some reasons to loosen up when it comes to judging the novelty of each other's work.

HOW DO WE ASSESS NOVELTY?

Let's consider my first point: Novelty is a mental construction. I think that something is perceived to be novel when it,
- feels unfamiliar and surprising and
- does not appear subsumed by existing categories.

Seen-Before Judgments

For research to seem novel, it has to be experienced as unfamiliar – as something we haven't seen or learned before.

As John Lynch (1998) noted in an earlier presidential address, reviewers will often assert that a finding is already well known without providing references to back it up. In principle, if you already know something you should be able to say where you saw it. In practice, it's not so easy.

In fact, entire paradigms in psychology have been based on the fact that people are not good at judging whether they have seen or experienced something before. Consider mere exposure effects (e.g., Zajonc, 1968; Bornstein, 1989), false-fame effects (e.g., Jacoby, Kelley, Brown, and Jasechko, 1989; Jacoby, Woloshyn, & Kelley 1989), and various false memory paradigms (e.g., Koriat, Goldsmith, & Pensky, 2000; Lakshmanan & Krishnan, 2009; Rajagopal & Montgomery, 2011). Conscious recollection of past exposures is not at all accurate. This is why people can confuse fluency from an irrelevant source with familiarity.

In consumer research, as well, studies show that when something feels easy to process or when an experience evokes imagery, it creates a false sense of familiarity. People think they've already been there, done that – when they haven't, and didn't (see Rajagopal & Montgomery, 2011; also Lakshmanan & Krishnan, 2009; Mehta, Hoegg, and Chakravarti, 2011; Schlosser, 2006).

It's hard for people to remember every piece of research they've ever seen. This is especially so with increasing online exposure to science blogs, TED talks, journal feeds, etc. (see Lutz, 2011). Many assessments of novelty are probably not based on exact recall of past work. They reflect a vague sense of whether a topic feels saturated. So, if something about your next paper feels too fluent, instead of taxing their memory, people may assume it's all been done.

Feelings of Surprise

For research findings to be experienced as novel, they also need to feel somewhat surprising. But here too, as some have observed, our feelings can be misleading (Lynch, 1998; Lilienfeld, 2011).

One can fall prey to the hindsight bias – the feeling that one "knew it all along" (Fischhoff, 1975; Wood, 1978). People who know an outcome tend to overestimate its likelihood. This is one rea-

son that surveys show the general public tends to dismiss behavioral research (Lilienfeld, 2011). It *feels* like common sense.

The hindsight bias has been demonstrated many times, in many populations (Bernstein et al., 2011; Pohl, Bender, & Lachmann, 2002) and domains (see Bernstein et al., 2011, for a review). Could it also affect an expert's view of whether a research finding is surprising?

Sure. As just one example, Lily Wong (1995) in educational psychology showed people lists of findings about teaching that were either actual well-replicated findings, or their opposites. When asked to select which were the real findings about teaching, experienced teachers were no more accurate than novices – which is to say, not accurate at all. And both groups tended to rate their selected findings as obvious.

If reviewers dismiss the novelty of your next paper, saying, "it's not surprising," how much weight should we put on such feelings? Once people know your findings, they can feel obvious in an illusory way – even to experts (Wong, 1995; see also Arkes et al., 1981; Knoll, 2010).

Construal Level and Novelty Categorization

To assess whether findings are novel, we also need to consider mental representations of "what everyone already knows" (Kaufer & Geisler, 1989), and decide whether the findings can be subsumed by those categories. Recent work by psychologist Jens Förster suggests that perceived novelty is a by-product of this sort of process (Förster, Liberman, & Shapira, 2009; Förster, Marguc, & Gillebaart, 2010). Events are experienced as novel when they don't seem to fit existing categories.

But this, too, is a matter of perspective.

To understand the experience of novelty, Förster and his colleagues build on a theory that has inspired a great deal of consumer research, Construal Level Theory (e.g., Trope & Liberman, 2003). They emphasize that anything can be experienced as either novel or old: Any new town we visit could be seen as "just another city;" any new person we meet could be "just another person" (Förster, et al., 2009, 2010).

Whether we define something as "new" depends on how broad or abstract is the category we call "old." And *that* has to do with our psychological distance from it.

Distance from something leads to the use of broader categories to represent it. This makes it easy to subsume new things, making them feel old and familiar. Innovation becomes harder to appreciate.

So it is in consumer research. If someone isn't close to the subject, they tend to classify knowledge at an abstract level. They might say: *We already know that consumers link possessions to the self.* Or: *We know that messages are more persuasive when they match one's motives.* These broad categories subsume a lot of the work in our field, and probably a lot of future work, too.

As a result, if you want to increase the chance that your next paper will be seen as novel, some will tell you to go and explore a whole new area, apart from what others have done.[1]

Still, as we've seen, novelty is in the eye of the beholder. It's a mental construction. And the size of the bins we use to classify existing knowledge is arbitrary. We don't have to insist on novelty at the "never-been-done" level.

So, why do we?

WHY DO WE SEEK NOVELTY?

To answer this question, let's consider a finding in the sociology of science. A few years ago, Michele Lamont and a team of colleagues, supported by the National Science Foundation, set out to examine how scholars perceive originality (Guetzkow, Lamont, & Mallard, 2004). They were looking for variations between disciplines. So, they interviewed panelists for American fellowship competitions in social sciences and humanities. As it turns out, the most interesting thing they found isn't what differed between disciplines, but what was the same. Across disciplines, from art history to sociology, reviewers saw the originality or novelty of a proposal as a sign of the applicant's *moral character*.

People who submitted proposals seen as novel were described as courageous, independent, intellectually honest, and "thinking for themselves." They were praised and respected as authentic scholars with high integrity.

To be independent and courageous demonstrates that one is pursuing one's own authentic interests. Reviewers deeply valued these qualities and wanted to reward them (for similar perspectives, see King, 2010; Zaltman, LeMasters, & Heffring, 1985).

On the other hand, applicants whose work was seen as lacking in novelty were viewed as morally deficient. Reviewers scorned them as conformist, derivative, lazy, traditional, and "riding the bandwagon." These were not scholars who had genuine intellectual passion.

So, novelty judgments – subjective as they are – were more than an assessment of someone's ideas. They were an assessment of the person, as well.

I was fascinated by this, and wondered, why the moral meaning of novelty? Then it hit me: There is a direct line between this novelty ideal and Western values. To be admired in Western individualist societies you have to be independent, authentic, honest, and nonconforming (e.g., Markus & Kitayama, 1991; Triandis, 1995). You've got to act on your passions and pursue your own unique interests. This is the perfect model of an authentic, independent, path-breaking scholar. In other words, this is where the values of our science map onto the values of our culture.

Defining novelty as "independent and different" is ingrained in our value system. We don't question it. It's assumed that you should blaze a separate intellectual trail. A trail that sets you apart.

For those of us who are Western individualists, this model of novelty is a perfect fit. We expect the same from ideas as we do from people: to be unique and independent. We are socialized to meet these expectations. As Ashok Lalwani and I have found in our research, individualists really do strive to present themselves in these terms (Lalwani, Shavitt, & Johnson, 2006; Lalwani & Shavitt, 2009).

What's more, as Richard Nisbett and many others have shown, Westerners tend to think in ways that sharpen differences. They separate and distinguish things, disconnecting things from their context, choosing one side or the other (e.g., Nisbett, et al. 2001; Nisbett, 2003; Oyserman & Lee, 2008; see Koo & Shavitt, 2011, for a review). This *analytic thinking style* is perfectly suited to the task of differentiating oneself, and one's ideas, from others (see MacInnis, 2011).

CONSEQUENCES OF NOVELTY SEEKING

Looking at novelty through the lens of cultural values suggests some consequences, and in the last part of my talk I'd like to address them.

Novel = Different?

Our standard for novelty is about setting yourself apart. But reflecting on the values that drive our novelty standards helps us to evaluate those standards. If they reflect a cultural ideal, is it the only ideal we should pursue?

I don't think so. Consumer research is globalizing fast. New scholars around the world are ready to contribute. Many are based in non-Western cultures that are collectivistic. In their day-to-day lives, being called "unique" and "independent" is not a compliment. Conformity and interdependence are more valued (Markus & Kitayama, 1991; Kim & Markus, 1999). Relationships are valued (Triandis, 1995).

In these societies, people are socialized to think in ways that connect and integrate, putting things together instead of pulling them apart, seeking resolution instead of choosing sides (Nisbett, et al., 2001; Nisbett, 2003; Oyserman & Lee, 2008). This holistic thinking style helps one to see relationships and to integrate things into a bigger picture. And this is not only a cultural pattern – individuals also differ in the values and thinking styles they tend to adopt (Choi, Koo, & Choi, 2007).

What does this mean for consumer research? There is no doubt that scholars around the world can meet the same standards for novelty. But imposing one standard at the expense of others is a mistake. We miss opportunities to leverage relational values and skills. Relational skills help us to represent connections between ideas.

Indeed, as Debbie MacInnis (2011) points out in a recent essay, our thinking skills foster specific types of novel contributions. Analytic thinking skills foster typologies that highlight differences. It's no surprise, then, that MacInnis's analysis of our field's conceptual papers over the last 25 years reveals a clear emphasis on *differentiation*. Integration papers are rare.

Yet, those are valuable innovations. McGill, Peracchio, and Luce (2011) point out in their editorial that, from a historical standpoint, the most important breakthroughs in science have been integrations. They innovate by unifying – highlighting parallels across areas, resolving contradictions, and enhancing understanding. Classic examples include Petty & Cacioppo's (1986) Elaboration Likelihood Model, which unified distinct routes to persuasion under a common set of processing assumptions. In a current example, Press and Arnould (2011) show that identification with a firm happens in a parallel way for consumers as for employees. These are valuable innovations. We need more integration.

To get there, we need to broaden our view of novelty. We should encourage authors who have a relational view of the field, wherever they come from, to find novel connections, or to build new integrative frameworks (e.g., Deighton, et al., 2010). If your next paper does these things, we should reward that.

Fragmentation

When we mainly reward the kind of novelty that sets us apart, we don't foster integration. Instead, this fragments the field.

Consider our incentives. We reward novelty at the paper level. So, papers get published on the basis of their difference from other work, not their connection to it. Many have raised concerns about what this does to the literature (e.g., Guetzkow, et al., 2004; Hubbard & Lindsay, 2002; Wyer & Shavitt, 2005).

These incentives for novelty affect what we study. Authors are encouraged to publish one paper on a topic and then go on to something different under the assumption that follow-ups will not be published.

These incentives also impact how we write. To be seen as novel, we have to apply new labels. So, we try to "name it and claim it" or "RE-name it and claim it." This doesn't foster connection, either.

Incentives for novelty even encourage us to position our own articles as having little to do with one another, instead of building on each other. It becomes harder than it should be to grasp the big picture in the field because authors are reluctant to connect the dots.

Where's the Theory?

Finally, our novelty incentives can get in the way of original theory building (Wyer & Shavitt, 2005). The shortage of original theories within our field has been widely recognized (see Frazier, 2011; MacInnis, 2004, 2011; Yadav, 2010). Yet, few theories that have a broad impact can be delivered in one paper. Building and testing a theory takes multiple papers reporting a program of research that shows generality, boundaries, and convergence around a core insight.

Authors who try may be told, "this is not novel because it is derivable from past work." But testing an extension of a theory is, by definition, derivable from past work.

What if we changed our incentives, and worried less about whether every paper is different? We would have the scope needed to build and test our own theories. And I think we would do it. In other words, we could greatly enhance originality at the macro level by relaxing the novelty constraint at the paper level.

Reviewers – all of us – play a key role in this. So do editors and other gatekeepers. Some have signaled openness to different types of novelty (e.g., Deighton, et al., 2010; Erdem, 2010), but it would help to be more explicit, to tell reviewers: Don't just ask, is it new? Ask, what's the connection? Encourage authors to link their findings to past work, don't penalize them for it. Seek contributions that integrate and connect. Reward systematic extensions that establish new theories in our field.

CONCLUSIONS

In summary, let us approach assessments of novelty with caution. They are mental constructions, influenced by the same factors we study: fluency, hindsight, level of construal. And the way we seek novelty reflects deeply held core values.

This means that we can acknowledge the value of novelty in research without imposing one criterion uniformly (Alba, 2012). We need more than one kind of novelty – things that differentiate and things that integrate. It would make our literature more coherent and enable originality in theory building.

Our theme at ACR this year is "Building Connections." In fact, this is a frequent theme for ACR conferences, along with bridges and confluence. We seem to yearn for a more integrated field. Let's consider whether our expectations for novelty are getting in the way. We can build more connections when we're less focused on setting ourselves apart.

CODA

In closing, I want to offer an invitation and some thanks. First, I invite you to a Roundtable Session right after this luncheon. In it, we discuss recommendations by an ACR Task force appointed this year to plan for the growth and globalization of our field. This task force, chaired by Joel Huber and Don Lehmann, made several recommendations to enhance the field as it expands, including suggestions for new and existing publication outlets and conference structures. The task force charge and report can be read, and your input provided, on the ACR website at www.acrwebsite.org/ .

Finally, I want to thank several people. First, I am grateful to the present and past officers and board members of ACR, for creating and nurturing such a stimulating association.

Next, thank you to my friends who gave me such generous and helpful input. And to my students who helped with details. I am so grateful.

Last but not least, thank you to my family for all of their patience and encouragement. My parents, for believing in me always. My husband, Steve, who has been supportive and helpful beyond words. And my daughters, who found their own ways to cope with me being too busy: Arielle who worked alongside me on her homework so that we kept each other company, and Ellie who cheerfully repaid me by sneaking onto my computer to type nonsense words into this talk. I hope I found them all.

Thank you.

ENDNOTES

1 This talk focused on novelty as defined in terms of unexplored topics or areas. Although I did not have time to address it, another important type of novelty is represented by findings that challenge existing beliefs in established areas. In some scientific disciplines, publication incentives reward this type of novelty, emphasizing results that question established ideas or reverse accepted findings. Jonah Lehrer (2010) analyzed the cumulative impact of these novelty-seeking publication incentives in several scientific fields. His review shows how these incentives give rise to oscillations in the accepted knowledge base. In short, pursuing this type of novelty can also produce unintended consequences that impact the reliability and credibility of scientific knowledge.

REFERENCES

Alba, J. W. (2012). In defense of bumbling. *Journal of Consumer Research, 38,* in press.

Arkes, H. R., Wortman, R. L., Saville, P. D., & Harkness, A. R. (1981). Hindsight bias among physicians weighing the likelihood of diagnoses. *Journal of Applied Psychology, 66,* 252–254.

Bernstein, D. M., Erdfelder, E., Meltzoff, A. N., Peria, W., & Loftus, G. R. (2011). Hindsight bias from 3 to 95 years of age. *Journal of Experimental Psychology: Learning, Memory, and Cognition, 37*(2), 378-391.

Bornstein, R. F. (1989). Exposure and affect: Overview and meta-analysis of research, 1968 –1987. *Psychological Bulletin, 106,* 265–289.

Choi, I., Koo, M., & Choi, J. A. (2007). Individual differences in analytic versus holistic thinking. *Personality and Social Psychology Bulletin, 33,* 691-705.

Deighton, J., MacInnis, D., McGill, A., & Shiv, B. (2010). Broadening the scope of consumer research. *Journal of Consumer Research, 36* (6), v-vii.

Erdem, T. (2010). Spanning the Boundaries. *Journal of Marketing Research, 47* (1), 1-2.

Fischhoff, B. (1975). Hindsight ≠ foresight: The effect of outcome knowledge on judgment under uncertainty. *Journal of Experimental Psychology: Human Perception and Performance, 1,* 288 –299.

Förster, J., Liberman, N., & Shapira, O. (2009). Preparing for novel versus familiar events: Shifts in global and local processing. *Journal of Experimental Psychology: General, 138*(3), 383-399.

Förster, J., Marguc, J., & Gillebaart, M. (2010). Novelty Categorization Theory. *Social and Personality Psychology Compass, 4*(9), 736-755.

Frazier, G. L. (2011). From the incoming editor. *Journal of Marketing.* 75, (4), 1-2.

Guetzkow, J., Lamont, M., & Mallard, G. (2004). What is originality in the social sciences and the humanities? *American Sociological Review, 69,* 190–212.

Hubbard, R., & Linsay, R. M. (2002), How the emphasis on "original" empirical marketing research impedes knowledge development, *Marketing Theory, 2* (4), 381-402.

Jacoby, L. L., Kelley, C. M., Brown, J., & Jasechko, J. (1989). Becoming famous overnight: Limits on the ability to avoid unconscious influences of the past. *Journal of Personality and Social Psychology, 56,* 326 –338.

Jacoby, L. L., Woloshyn, V., & Kelley, C. M. (1989). Becoming famous without being recognized: Unconscious influences of memory produced by dividing attention. *Journal of Experimental Psychology: General, 118,* 115–125.

Kaufer, D. S., & Geisler, C. (1989). Novelty in academic writing. *Written Communication, 6* (3), 286-311.

Kim, H., & Markus, H. R. (1999). Deviance or uniqueness, harmony or conformity? A cultural analysis. *Journal of Personality and Social Psychology, 77*(4), 785-800.

King, L. A. (2010). Editorial. *Journal of Personality and Social Psychology, 98* (1), 104 –105.

Knoll, M. A. Z. M. (2010). The effects of expertise on the hindsight bias. *Dissertation Abstracts International: Section B: The Sciences and Engineering, 70* (8-B), 5213. (UMI No. AAI3368433)

Koo, M., & Shavitt, S. (2011). Cross-cultural psychology of consumer behavior. In Richard P. Bagozzi and Ayalla Ruvio (Eds.), *Consumer Behavior,* a volume in the Wiley International Encyclopedia of Marketing. New York: John Wiley and Sons. p. 125-133.

Koriat, A., Goldsmith, M., & Pansky, A. (2000). Towards a psychology of memory accuracy, *Annual Review of Psychology, 51,* 481–37.

Lakshmanan, A., & Krishnan, S. H. (2009). How Does Imagery in Interactive Consumption Lead to False Memory? A Reconstructive Memory Perspective. *Journal of Consumer Psychology, 19* (3), 451–62.

Lalwani, A.K., & Shavitt, S. (2009). The "me" I claim to be: Cultural self-construal elicits self-presentational goal pursuit. *Journal of Personality and Social Psychology, 97*(1), 88-102.

Lalwani, A., Shavitt, S., & Johnson, T.P. (2006). What is the relation between cultural orientation and socially desirable responding? *Journal of Personality and Social Psychology, 90*(1), 165-178.

Lehrer, J. (2010, December 13). The truth wears off: Is there something wrong with the scientific method? *The New Yorker.* Accessed at: www.*newyorker.com/ reporting/2010/12/13/101213fa_fact_lehrer*

Lilienfeld, S. O. (2011, June 13). Public skepticism of psychology: Why many people perceive the study of human behavior as unscientific. *American Psychologist.* Advance online publication. doi: 10.1037/a0023963.

Lutz, R. J. (2011). Marketing Scholarship 2.0. *Journal of Marketing, 75*(4), 225-234.

Lynch, J. G. (1998). Presidential address: Reviewing. In Joseph W. Alba and J. Wesley Hutchinson (Eds), *Advances in Consumer Research,* Volume 25. Provo, UT : Association for Consumer Research, p. 1-6.

MacInnis, D. (2004). Where have all the papers gone? *Association for Consumer Research Newsletter* (Spring), 1–3.

MacInnis, D. (2011). A framework for conceptual contributions in marketing. *Journal of Marketing,* 75(4), 136-154.

Markus, H. R., & Kitayama, S. (1991). Culture and the self: Implication for cognition, emotion, and motivation. *Psychological Review, 98,* 224 –253.

McGill, A., Peracchio, L., & Luce, M. F. (2011). Solidarity of purpose: Building an understanding of consumers through a community of scholars, *Journal of Consumer Research, 38* (1), ii-viii.

Mehta, R., Hoegg, J., & Chakravarti, A. (2011). Knowing too much: Expertise induced false recall effects in product comparison. *Journal of Consumer Research, 38*(3), 535-554.

Merton, R. K. (1973 [1942]). The normative structure of science. In N. W. Storer (Ed), *The Sociology of Science.* Chicago, IL: University of Chicago Press. p. 267-278.

Monroe, K. B. (2008). Fellow's address: ACR and ME. *Advances in consumer research,* Volume 35. Provo, UT: Association for Consumer Research, p. 13-17.

Nisbett, R. E., Peng, K., Choi, I., & Norenzayan, A. (2001). Culture and systems of thought:

Holistic versus analytic cognition. *Psychological Review, 108*(2), 291-310.

Nisbett, R. E. (2003). *The geography of thought: How Asians and Westerners think differently ... and why.* New York: The Free Press.

Oyserman, D., & Lee, S.W.S. (2008). A situated cognition perspective on culture: Effects of priming cultural syndromes on cognition and motivation. In R. Sorrentino & S. Yamaguchi (Eds.), *Handbook of Motivation and Cognition across Cultures.* New York: Elsevier. p. 237-265.

Park, C. W. (2011). Editorial email to *Journal of Consumer Psychology* reviewers.

Petty, R. E., & Cacioppo, J. T. (1986). *Communication and persuasion: Central and peripheral routes to attitude change.* New York: Springer-Verlag.

Pohl, R. F., Bender, M., & Lachmann, G. (2002). Hindsight bias around the world. *Experimental Psychology, 49,* 270 –282.

Press, M., & Arnould, E. J. (2011, May 11). How does organizational identification form? A consumer behavior perspective. *Journal of Consumer Research.* Advance online publication. doi: 10.1086/660699.

Rajagopal, P., & Montgomery, N. (2011). I Imagine, I Experience, I Like: The false experience effect, *Journal of Consumer Research, 38*(3), 578-594.

Rozin, P. (2009). What kind of empirical research should we publish, fund, and reward?: A different perspective, *Perspectives on Psychological Science, 4* (4), 435-439.

Schlosser, A. E. (2006). Learning through virtual product experience: The role of imagery on true versus false memories. *Journal of Consumer Research, 33* (3), 377–83.

Triandis, H. C. (1995). *Individualism and collectivism.* Boulder, CO: Westview Press.

Trope, Y., & Liberman, N. (2003). Temporal construal. *Psychological Review, 110* (3), 403-421.

Wong, L. Y. S. (1995). Research on teaching: Process-product research findings and the feeling of obviousness. *Journal of Educational Psychology, 87,* 504–511.

Wood, G. (1978). The knew-it-all-along effect. *Journal of Experimental Psychology: Human Perception and Performance, 4,* 345–353.

Wyer, R. S., & Shavitt, S. (2005). Editorial. *Journal of Consumer Psychology, 15* (4), 271-274.

Yadav, M. S. (2010). The decline of conceptual articles and implications for knowledge development. *Journal of Marketing,* 74(1), 1-19.

Zajonc, R. B. (1968). Attitudinal effects of mere exposure. *Journal of Personality and Social Psychology Monographs, 9* (2, Pt. 2), 1–27.

Zaltman, G., LeMasters, K., & Heffring, M. (1985). *Theory construction in marketing.* New York: John Wiley & Sons, Inc.

Special Session Summaries

Strategic Spending in Booms and Busts:
Surprising Effects of Economic Recessions on Consumer Behavior

Chairs: Vladas Griskevicius, University of Minnesota, USA
Kobe Millet, VU University Amsterdam, The Netherlands

Paper #1: Economic Recessions Increase Spending on Beauty Products: Experimental Evidence for the Lipstick Effect

Sarah Hill, Texas Christian University, USA
Christopher Rodeheffer, Texas Christian University, USA
Vladas Griskevicius, University of Minnesota, USA
Kristina Durante, University of Texas at San Antonio, USA

Paper #2: Paying More for "Us" In Times of Crisis: Economic Downturns Increase the Need to Belong

Jaione Yabar, Tilburg University, The Netherlands
Diederik Stapel, Tilburg University, The Netherlands
Rik Peters, Tilburg University, The Netherlands

Paper #3: Economic Recessions Release the Inner Child

Vladas Griskevicius, University of Minnesota, USA
Joshua Ackerman, MIT, USA

Paper #4: Financial Decision Making in Hard and Prosperous Times

Kobe Millet, VU University Amsterdam, The Netherlands
Lien Lamey, Lessius University College and KU Leuven, Belgium
Bram Van den Bergh, Erasmus University Rotterdam, The Netherlands

SESSION OVERVIEW

Conventional wisdom suggests that economic recessions lead consumers to decrease spending and be more cautious with their money. Consistent with previous recessionary periods, the most recent economic downturn has led consumers to downsize spending on everything ranging from groceries to homes. For example, many people are trading in their vacations for a "stay-cation," choosing to vacation in the low-cost destination of their own home.

But while aggregate spending decreases during recessions, much less is known about how economic recessions influence the specifics of consumer behavior, including the possibility that economic downturns might *increase* spending on various products. Economists have established that recessions are reliably associated with increased spending on two types of products: traditional inferior goods (e.g., spending more on tuna rather than salmon) and morale boosters (e.g., going to see a Charlie Chaplin film in the great depression). The current session presents evidence that economic downturns lead to a richer assortment of strategic spending.

The four papers in this session all present emerging research examining how economic recessions influence consumer behavior. The first two papers focus on how economic downturn cues influence desire and spending for specific product categories. The last two papers focus on how economic booms and busts influence financial decision-making. Unlike most previous research looking at recessionary spending, all four papers include studies with experimental methodologies to test the influence of economic recession cues on consumer behavior.

The first paper by **Hill, Rodeheffer, Griskevicius, and Durante** examines the "Lipstick Effect" – the notion that recessions increase spending on beauty products, such as the increase in lipstick sales during the great depression. Across a series of experiments that manipulate recession cues, they find that while recession cues decrease desire to spend on most types of products, recession cues increase women's desire to spend on beauty products, including lipstick.

The second paper by **Yabar, Stapel, and Pieters** investigates the links between economic downturns and people's need to belong. Across three experiments they find that recession cues lead consumers to desire products that facilitate social connectedness, including increasing consumers' willingness to pay for products related to affiliation.

This third paper by **Griskevicius and Ackerman** investigates whether economic uncertainty leads people to save or splurge. They find that economic uncertainty has vastly different effects depending on whether people grew up feeling poor or wealthy. Recession cues led individuals who grew up relatively wealthy to save for the future. But recession cues led individuals who grew up relatively poor to splurge on immediate rewards.

The final paper by **Millet, Lamey, and Van den Bergh** examines how financial decision-making changes in booms and busts. Using both time-series and experimental methods, they find that people are drawn toward achieving gains during economic expansions, but people are drawn toward avoiding losses during economic contractions.

Overall, this session builds connections by addressing an important theoretical and practical question—how economic recessions influence consumer behavior—from different theoretical perspectives. The papers in this session address this question by drawing on regulatory fit theory, evolutionary theory, and life history theory. Furthermore, the session presents research based on both experimental and time-series methodologies. As such, the session would be of interest to a breadth of consumer researchers, including those interested in motivation, affiliation, regulatory fit, financial decision-making, risk, intertemporal choice, and evolutionary approaches to consumer behavior.

Economic Recessions Increase Spending on Beauty Products: Experimental Evidence for the Lipstick Effect

EXTENDED ABSTRACT

The year 2007 began with what has been considered by many economists to be the worst economic recession since the great depression. Consistent with previous recessionary periods, consumers downsized spending on everything ranging from groceries to homes. Although spending on most consumer products during the recent recession has predictably declined, one class of products has fared unusually well: beauty products (Schaefer, 2008). For instance, sales figures from one of the world's biggest cosmetics companies – L'Oreal – showed that during 2008, a year when the rest of the economy was suffering record declines in sales, they experienced sales *growth* of 5.3% (Elliot, 2008). The notion that women may spend relatively more money on attractiveness-enhancing products during times of economic uncertainty has been dubbed the "Lipstick Effect" (Nelson, 2001). The lipstick effect has been observed in several recent economic downturns, and it is even believed to have occurred during the Great Depression, when sales of women's cosmetics products boomed unexpectedly.

In the current research, we experimentally examine the idea of the lipstick effect. To understand how and why economic recessions might influence consumer behavior, we draw on the framework of life history theory (Kaplan and Gangestad 2005; Stearns 1992). Life history theory is an established theoretical framework in evolutionary biology and behavioral ecology used to predict how and why organisms, including humans, allocate effort among the various tasks needed for survival and reproduction. Because energy and resources are inherently limited, life history theory highlights that organisms face important trade-offs in how they allocate resources at a given point in life.

A key tradeoff faced by all individuals is between allocating resources toward *immediate reproduction vs. future reproduction*. Resource allocation to immediate reproductive effort, such as women's allocation of resources to enhance their appearance, is predicted to be favored in environments where there is unpredictability in the availability of critical resources (Ellis et al. 2009). When the present and future are highly uncertain, individuals should invest more in immediate reproduction because this strategy enhanced reproductive fitness in uncertain environments (Ellis et al. 2009).

In three studies we manipulated perceptions of resource unpredictability by priming people with cues to an economic recession. We predicted that recession cues should decrease desire to spend on most consumer products. However, we specifically predicted that recession cues should increase women's desire to purchase products that aid in facilitating mating, such as lipstick or other beauty-enhancing products.

In Study 1, we experimentally manipulated cues to economic recessions by having people read a news article about the recent economic recession or having them read a control article. We then examine how these primes influence women's and men's desire to purchase products that can enhance beauty (e.g., clothing, make-up) and produce that cannot enhance beauty (e.g., office supplies, electronics). Findings demonstrated that the economic recession article significantly *decreased* men's and women's desire to purchase products that did not enhance physical attractiveness. However, the same recession cues significantly *increased* women's desire to purchase products that could enhance attractiveness.

In Study 2, we directly manipulated perceptions of product function by varying how the same products (e.g., jeans, boots, perfume) are advertised. Specifically, product slogans were manipulated to touted product benefits directly related to mating (e.g., the opposite sex finds it irresistible) or benefits unrelated to mating (e.g., feels great). Economic recession cues were manipulated by having women view a slideshow with visual images of economic recession or control images. Consistent with predictions, viewing images of economic uncertainty led women to desire products advertised as serving a mating function. But when the same products were advertised as serving a function not directly related to mating, economic recession cues no longer enhanced their desirability.

Study 3 examined a key individual difference moderator, which provided insight into which women drive the lipstick effect. Life history theory predicts that there are individual differences in people who prioritize immediate reproduction vs. future reproduction. This literature points to a particular individual difference: experiencing

earlier pubertal development is considered to be a physiological marker of favoring immediate over future reproduction (Ellis 2004). We therefore predicted that cues to economic uncertainty would produce the strongest lipstick effect for women who had earlier – compared to later – pubertal development.

Conceptually replicating the first study, Study 3 found that economic uncertainty led women to be *less* interested in products that do not enhance appearance. Conversely, economic uncertainly led women to be *more* interested in products that do enhance appearance. Critically, the increased desire for beauty product was driven by women experiencing earlier pubertal development. This means that women who underwent puberty at earlier ages were especially likely to respond to economic uncertainty by wanting beauty products.

These studies provide the first experimental evidence of the lipstick effect. We show that while cues to economic recessions lead to a diminished desire for most types of products, recession cues increase women's desire for products that can enhance attractiveness. This research provides novel insight into how and why economic recessions influence women's consumer preferences.

REFERENCES

Elliott, L. (2008, December, 22). Into the red: 'Lipstick effect' reveals the true face of the recession. *The Guardian*. Retrieved from http://www.guardian.co.uk

Ellis, B. J. (2004). Timing of pubertal maturation in girls: An integrated life history approach. *Psychological Bulletin, 130*, 920-958.

Ellis, B. J., Figueredo, A. J., Brumbach, B. H., et al. (2009). Fundamental dimensions of environmental risk: The impact of harsh versus unpredictable environments on the evolution and development of life history strategies. *Human Nature, 20*, 204-268.

Kaplan, H. S., & Gangestad, S. W. (2005). Life history theory and evolutionary psychology. In D. M. Buss (Ed.), *Handbook of evolutionary psychology* (pp. 68-95). New York: Wiley.

Nelson, E. (2001, November 26) "Rising Lipstick Sales May Mean Pouting Economy," *The Wall Street Journal*.

Schaefer, K. (2008, May 1). Hard times, but your lips look great. *The New York Times*. Retrieved from http://www.nytimes.com

Stearns, S. (1992). *The evolution of life histories*. Oxford, England: Oxford University Press.

Paying More for "Us" In Times of Crisis: Economic Downturns Increase the Need to Belong

EXTENDED ABSTRACT

Conventional wisdom holds that during economic downturns consumers react by economizing: they spend less and they defer expenses (Katona 1975). For instance, in times of economic crisis consumers become more price conscious, buying more private label products and discounted goods. Thus, when an economic crisis hits, governments and companies tend to focus on providing financial and economic incentives aimed at promoting consumption. During the most recent economic crisis, for example, governments subsidized housing and reduced the cost of borrowing, attempting to promote spending. Likewise, Sam's Club introduced a program to facilitate loans for shoppers of up to $25,000.

Although these economization strategies may help consumers to deal with the effects of an economic crisis on their personal finances, they do not necessarily help manage the psychological implications of a crisis, such as feelings of threat and fear. Psychological research suggests that a natural reaction to cope with the self-threatening consequences of an economic crisis is an increase in the need to be connected with others. When people feel threatened, they seek the support of others. From an evolutionary perspective, social connections are devices of self-preservation linked with an increased safety in numbers as well as with an improved ability to gather food and to obtain empathy of social groups. Given the potential advantage of sharing resources, and the competitive disadvantage of the lone individual if other people are in groups, social groups confer protection and survival benefits to their members (Kenrick et al. 2010). Consequently, threat and fear signals activate a desire for affiliation and social connectedness (Baumeister and Leary 1995). When experiencing an increased desire for connectedness, individuals tend to allocate their attention to social opportunities and try to build connections with others—both real others as well as "snack" on symbolic reminders of others (Gardner, Pickett and Knowles, 2005; Griskevicius et al. 2009).

This logic suggests that that when an economic crisis hits, the need for connectedness should increase, which should affect consumer choices. In the present research, we test the idea that cues of economic downturn might produce a higher preference and willingness to pay for products and advertisements that signal social connectedness, such as images of people or product popularity appeals. This suggests that in times of economic hardship, people might be willing to pay a premium for "we" products that signal social connectedness.

Study 1 manipulated economic recession cues by having participants read either a news story about the recent recession or a control story. Participants then indicated the attractiveness of, and their willingness to pay for, various advertised products. For half of the participants, the products were advertised with "me" slogans that focused on the consumer (e.g. "ready for you"); the other half of participants viewed ads with "we" slogans focused on social connectedness (e.g. "ready to share"). Findings showed that economic downturns led consumers to evaluated more positively slogans that positioned the product as being jointly usable instead of just for the self. Consumers were also willing to pay more for the products advertised as collectively usable.

Study 2 again primed either economic recession cues or control cues. Participants then evaluated products that were in two types of packaging: half of the packages showed multiple people, and the other half showed a single person. Findings showed that people in the economic crisis condition had a higher preference and were willing to pay more for products that featured pictorial cues of social connection (e.g. an image of multiple people) in their packaging.

Study 3 again primed either economic recession cues or control cues. Participants were then shown pictures of pairs of products together with a description about the price, quality, and percentage of consumers who preferred each of the products in the pair. In each pair the product described as preferred by a majority of consumers was also described as having a lower quality and a slightly higher price than the less popular product. Findings revealed that economic recession cues increased desire for products with popularity appeals (e.g. "60% of consumers preferred this product"), even leading people to choose the popular products when it was the most expensive and lowest quality alternative.

Taken together, these findings suggest that in times of economic crisis, consumers' need to belong is increased and therefore their preference for social connecteness products increases. A better understanding of the effect of fundamental needs, such as the need to belong, on consumer spending in face of economic contractions is important to further understand consumer reactions to economic downturns. For marketers, understanding how fundamental needs, in particular the need to belong, affect consumer spending patterns could help them sharpen and rethink the value they provide to consumers in times of economic uncertainty. Additionally, a policy-relevant insight of this research is that factors like social belonging can help promote consumer spending and thus economic recovery, while avoiding some of the risks associated with economic incentives. For example, the traditional approaches of focusing on economic incentives to stimulate the economy have the risk of slowing economic growth further if falling prices and retailer promotions lead consumers to delay purchases in the expectation of additional promotions and price cuts.

REFERENCES

Baumeister, Roy F. and Mark R. Leary (1995), "The Need to Belong: Desire for Interpersonal Attachments as a Fundamental Human Motivation," *Psychology Bulletin*, 117 (3), 497-529.

Gardner, Wendi L, Cynthia L. Pickett, and Megan L. Knowles (2005). Social snacking and shielding: Using social symbols, selves, and surrogates in the service of belonging needs. In K.D. Williams, J.P. Forgas, and W. von Hippel (Eds.), *The social outcast: Ostracism, social exclusion, rejection, and bullying* (pp. 227-241). New York, NY: Psychology Press.

Griskevicius, Vladas, Noah J. Goldstein, Chad R. Mortensen, Jill M. Sundie, Robert B. Cialdini, and Douglas T. Kenrick (2009), "Fear and loving in Las Vegas: Evolution, emotion, and persuasion," *Journal of Marketing Research,* June, 384–395.

Kenrick, D. T., Griskevicius, V., Neuberg, S. L., & Schaller, M. (2010). Renovating the pyramid of needs: Contemporary extensions built upon ancient foundations. *Perspectives on Psychological Science, 5*, 292–314

Katona, George (1975), *Psychological Economics,* New York: Elsevier.

Does Economic Uncertainty Lead People to Save or Splurge? It Depends on One's Childhood Environment

EXTENDED ABSTRACT

How do economic recessions influence desire for immediate rewards, such whether people splurge on the lottery? Examining the effect of the most recent economic downturn on U.S. state lottery sales shows mixed results, averaging to a null effect of the recession on lottery sales (Cousins 2009). Published research also paints a mixed picture. One study, for example, showed that lottery sales increase as unemployment goes up (Mikesell 1994), but another study found that unemployed individuals tend to be risk-averse (Diaz-Serrano and O'Neill 2004). Summarizing the average effect of recessions on lottery spending, Clyde Barrow, the director of the Center for Policy Analysis at the University of Massachusetts, observed in a recent interview that in economic downturns, "lottery sales are typically flat" (Saldinger 2009).

We propose that there may be more to this flat effect on lottery spending—and on intertemporal choice and financial decision-making more generally—than initially meets the eye. We examine how economic uncertainty influences intertemporal choice, saving, and borrowing. To address this question, we draw on the framework of life history theory (Stearns 1992). Life history theory (LHT) was originally developed in evolutionary biology and behavioral ecology, but is now increasing being applied to study human behavior.

According to a life history framework, individuals, including humans, can follow a variety of different life history strategies. Life history strategies exist along a slow-to-fast continuum (Promislow and Harvey 1990). Slower strategies are associated with reproducing at a later age and having fewer offspring. Faster strategies have the opposite characteristics, being associated with reproducing at an earlier age and having more offspring. In addition to reproduction, each strategy is associated with a specific type of orientation toward the world. Faster strategists tend to be opportunistic in that they take more risks and desire immediate gratification for short-term benefits. In contrast, slower strategists tend to be long-term planners who take fewer risks and delay gratification for future payoffs (Nettle 2010).

Recent research has begun to test how experimentally priming people with cues of an unpredictable environment—a key determinant of life history strategies (Ellis et al. 2009)—influences outcomes related to fast and slow life history strategies. Findings show that the salience of unpredictability produces divergent life history strategies for different groups of people (Griskevicius et al. 2010). Unpredictability cues have a different effect on people who grew up in a relatively resource-scarce environment (e.g., "I felt relatively poor when growing up") than on those who grew up in a relatively resource-plentiful environment (e.g., "I felt relatively wealthy compared to the other kids in my school"). For lower childhood SES individuals, unpredictability cues led to a preference for earlier reproduction. This suggests that unpredictability cues shift people from lower-SES childhoods toward a faster strategy. Conversely, for individuals who grew up in higher-SES environments, the same cues led to a preference to delay reproduction, consistent with shifting to a slower strategy.

The current research examine how cues to resource unpredictability (i.e., economic recessions) influence intertemporal choice. As discussed earlier, faster life history strategies are associated with desiring immediate rewards, whereas slower strategies are associate with delaying gratification for future payoffs. Thus, building on previous research highlighting the importance of childhood environment (Griskevicius et al. 2010), we predicted that individuals who grew up in relatively resource-scarce environments would respond to economic uncertainty cues by value the present. In contrast, individuals who grew up in relatively resource-plentiful environments should respond to economic uncertainty cues by valuing the future.

Study 1 examined how economic uncertainty influenced intertemporal choice. Participants read a news story about either the recent economic recession or a control story. Participants then made a series of financial choices in which they chose between receiving a reward tomorrow or receiving a larger reward in the future (e.g., $31 tomorrow vs. $50 in 2 months). The study had real monetary incentives, meaning that participants would actually receive their chose reward for one of their choices.

Findings showed that economic recession cues had a different effect on people as a function of their childhood environment. The salience of economic uncertainty led people who had higher-SES childhoods to value the future, increasing their likelihood of choosing the larger, later reward. Conversely, economic uncertainly cues led people who had lower-SES childhoods to value the present, increasing their likelihood of choosing the smaller, immediate reward.

Study 2 used a different manipulation of economic uncertainty, where people saw a slide show of images depicting a recession or a control images. Participants then indicated their desire to save money for the future and their desire to borrow money for immediate expenditures. Conceptually replicating findings from the first study, results showed that economic recession cues had diverging effects as a function of people's childhood SES environments. Economic uncertainty led people who had higher-SES childhoods to want to save money for the future and not go into debt. Conversely, eco-

nomic uncertainty cues led people who had lower-SES childhoods to decrease savings and increase desire to borrow money for immediate expenditures.

Study 3 attempted to extend the findings from the first two studies by examining the hormonal mechanism by which economic uncertainly cues influence intertemporal choice. Preliminary findings show individuals from lower-SES backgrounds respond to economic uncertainty with increases in both Testosterone and increases in Cortisol. This suggests that lower-SES childhood individuals respond to resource unpredictability by becoming both more action-focused and more anxious, consistent with desiring immediate rewards. Overall, these findings show how, when, and why economic uncertainty influences financial decisions related to intertemporal choice.

REFERENCES

Cousins, Juanita (2009). "Feeling Lucky? Many States' Lottery Sales Rising in Recession," USA Today, January 12, 2009.

Ellis, Bruce J., Aurelio J. Figueredo, et al. (2009), "Fundamental Dimensions of Environmental Risk: The Impact of Harsh Versus Unpredictable Environments on the Evolution and Development of Life History Strategies," *Human Nature,* 20, 204-268.

Griskevicius, Vladas, Andrew Delton, et al. (2010), "Environmental Contingency in Life History Strategies: The Influence of Mortality and Socioeconomic Status on Reproductive Timing," *Journal of Personality and Social Psychology.*

Mikesell, John L. (1994), "State Lottery Sales and Economic Activity," *National Tax Journal,* 47, 165-171.

Nettle, Daniel (2010), "Dying Young and Living Fast: Variation in Life History Across English Neighborhoods," *Behavioral Ecology,* 21, 387-395.

Rabin, Matthew (2000), "Risk Aversion and Expected-Utility: A Calibration Theorem," *Econometrica,* 68 (5), 1281-1292.

Stearns, Stephen C. (1992). *The evolution of life histories.* New York: Oxford University Press.

Saldinger, Adva (2009). "No Longer Recession-Proof, Lottery is Losing Sales," *Patriot Ledger,* February 14, 2009.

Financial Decision Making in Hard and Prosperous Times

EXTENDED ABSTRACT

Global and national economies alternate between hard and prosperous economic times. These business cycle fluctuations also influence individuals within the economy. For example, economic recessions are associated with poorer health (Bambra 2010). We propose that economic expansions and contractions influence consumer financial decision-making.

Financial decisions depend both on expected returns (i.e., potential benefits) and expected risks (i.e., potential costs; Mellers 2000; Raghubir & Das 2010). Although the achievement of financial benefits and avoidance of risk are often taken into account simultaneously, these concerns can be managed separately (Zhou & Pham 2004). For example, regulatory fit theory (Higgins 2000) states that individuals with a promotion focus (i.e., a self-regulatory focus on approaching desired opportunities) make decisions primarily on the basis of positive outcomes. In contrast, individuals with a prevention focus (i.e., a self-regulatory focus on the prevention of losses) make decisions based primarily on avoiding negative outcomes (Idson, Liberman, & Higgins 2004). While a promotion focus might be especially manifest itself during economic expansions, a prevention focus might be more pronounced during economic contractions.

Hence, we hypothesize that people should be predominantly drawn toward achieving gains during expansions, but especially drawn toward avoiding losses during economic contractions.

Study 1 examined whether cues to business cycle fluctuations influence likelihood estimates of financial outcomes. Participants read a short scenario describing either an economic recession, prosperity, or a control condition. Afterwards, participants indicated the perceived likelihood of positive and negative outcomes of 8 financial investment decisions (e.g. "investing 5% of your annual income in a very speculative stock"). Participants indicated for each decision the chance of both a positive and a negative outcome. Findings showed that the perceived likelihood of a negative outcome is higher in the contraction than in the expansion and the control condition. However, the perceived likelihood of a positive outcome is higher in the expansion than in the recession and the control condition.

Study 2 aimed to demonstrate behavioral consequences of business cycle fluctuations. Participants were again primed with cues to an economic recession, expansion, or control cues. Then, participants made a series of financial choices related to gains or related to losses based on Hsee and Weber (1999). Each question offered a choice between a safe and a risky option. In the gain set, participants could receive money, while in the loss set they could pay fines. Consistent with Study 1, findings showed that people became more risk-averse for losses in the contraction condition. However, people become more risk-seeking for gains in the expansion condition.

Study 3 used a time-series methodology that mirrored the experimental studies. Findings showed that consumption of financial products that are especially focused on the achievement of gains (i.e. gambling) or the prevention of losses (i.e. purchase of insurances) covaried with the business cycle in the predicted fashion. Gain achievement focused consumption is affected by expansions, but not by contractions, whereas loss prevention focused consumption is affected by contractions, but not by expansions.

In sum, the present set of studies provides support for the hypothesis that business cycle fluctuations selectively influence financial decision-making. We provide causal evidence that cues of business cycle fluctuations influence financial decision making (studies 1 and 2) and investigated the relationship between financial decision making and business cycle fluctuations over a substantial time period, making use of real consumption behavior over several business cycles (study 3). Our studies suggest that business cycle fluctuations might trigger different motivational systems that affect financial decision making.

REFERENCES

Bambra, Clare (2010), "Yesterday once more? Unemployment and health in the 21st century," *Journal of Epidemiology and Community Health*, 64 (3), 213-15.

--- (2000), "Making a good decision: Value from fit," *American Psychologist*, 55 (11), 1217-30.

Hsee, C. K., & Weber, E. U. (1999). Cross-national differences in risk preference and lay predictions. *Journal of Behavioral Decision Making, 12*(2), 165-179.

Idson, Lorraine Chen, Nira Liberman, and E. Torry Higgins (2004), "Imagining how you'd feel: The role of motivational experiences from regulatory fit," *Personality and Social Psychology Bulletin*, 30 (7), 926-37.

Mellers, Barbara A. (2000), "Choice and the relative pleasure of consequences," *Psychological Bulletin*, 126 (6), 910-24.

Raghubir, Priya and Sanjiv R. Das (2010), "The Long and Short of It: Why Are Stocks with Shorter Runs Preferred?," *Journal of Consumer Research*, 36 (6), 964-82.

Zhou, Rongrong and Michel Tuan Pham (2004), "Promotion and Prevention across Mental Accounts: When Financial Products Dictate Consumers' Investment Goals," *Journal of Consumer Research*, 31 (1), 125-35.

Sex and Money

Chairs: Vladas Griskevicius, University of Minnesota, USA
Bram Van den Bergh, Erasmus University Rotterdam, The Netherlands

Paper #1: Ovulatory Cycle Effects on Women's Financial Decisions in Economic Games

> Kristina Durante, University of Texas at San Antonio, USA
> Vladas Griskevicius, University of Minnesota, USA
> Stephanie Cantu, University of Minnesota, USA
> Jeffry Simpson, University of Minnesota, USA

Paper #2: Sex Ratio and the Financial Consequences of Too Many Men

> Vladas Griskevicius, University of Minnesota, USA
> Joshua Ackerman, MIT, USA

Paper #3: Men, Sex, and Risk: Turning Up the Heat on Men's Financial Decisions

> Bram Van den Bergh, Erasmus University Rotterdam, The Netherlands
> Kobe Millet, VU University Amsterdam, The Netherlands
> Vladas Griskevicius, University of Minnesota, USA

Paper #4: Women, Sex, and Risk: Mating Motivation and Financial Risk-Taking in Women

> Yexin Jessica Li, Arizona State University, USA
> Douglas Kenrick, Arizona State University, USA
> Steven Neuberg, Arizona State University, USA

SESSION OVERVIEW

Many marketers consider the expression "sex sells" to be a self-evident maxim. Sex and money have been a ubiquitous marketing power-pair for nearly a century. Modern consumers are inundated with sexual images and messages. From billboards to storefronts, from media advertising to media content and programming, from magazine covers to music, art, sports, and most types of entertainment, sexual cues pervade the modern world. From a marketing perspective, the connection between sex and money is not surprising: Many people are innately drawn to sexual cues, making them an effective method for attracting consumers' attention. More surprising, however, is that considering the omnipresence of sex and money in our environment, so little research has examined how sexual cues and mating concerns actually influence financial decisions.

The four papers in this session all present emerging research examining how, why, and when sex influences financial decisions. The first paper examines how women's sex hormones associated with the monthly ovulatory cycle influence economic decisions. The second paper examines how sex ratio—the ratio of men to women in the environment—influences saving, borrowing, and spending. The final two papers examine how sex cues in the environment influence financial risk-taking for men (paper 3) and for women (paper 4). Taken together, the session presents a deeper understanding of when, why, and how sex does and doesn't sell.

The first paper by **Durante, Griskevicius, Cantu, and Simpson** investigates how the monthly ovulatory cycle influences women's choices in the Dictator Game. They find that the effects of ovulation depend on whether women are playing against a man or a woman. Ovulating women gave significantly more money to attractive men, but ovulating women gave much less money when playing against attractive women.

Griskevicius and Ackerman examine how the ratio of men to women in the environment—known as sex ratio in animal behavior—influences saving, borrowing, and spending. They find that male-biased sex ratios (a scarcity of women) lead men to discount the future, decreasing savings and increasing borrowing for immediate expenditures. A scarcity of women also increased expectations that men will spend more during courtship.

Van den Bergh and Millet examine how sexual cues influence men's preferences for financial risk. They show that sexual cues produce financial risk-aversion, leading men to take a bird in the hand rather than two birds in the bush. Sex cues essentially cause men to prefer certain (but smaller) gains over uncertain (but larger) gains.

Finally, **Li, Kenrick, and Neuberg** examine how mating cues influence women's financial decisions. They find that mating cues generally don't influence women's financial risk preferences. However, mating cues do lead women to become more financially risk-seeking when the monetary choices can serve as a signal to specific audiences.

Overall, this session builds connections by addressing an important theoretical and practical question—the relationship between sex and financial decisions. Two of the papers aim to answer the basic question of how sex cues influence financial decisions for men and for women, and the two other papers elucidate on these effects by examining hormonal mechanisms and by examining more complex sex cues that include the ratio of men to women. As such, the session would be of interest to a breadth of consumer researchers, including those interested in sexual advertising, hormones, financial decision-making, risk, intertemporal choice, and evolutionary approaches to consumer behavior.

Ovulatory Cycle Effects on Women's Financial Decisions in Economic Games

EXTENDED ABSTRACT

Emerging research in evolutionary biology shows that women's psychology and behavior changes during the brief window each month when women are fertile—the days around ovulation. These hormonally-regulated shifts have traditionally been believed to be linked to mating. For instance, women's mate preferences nonconsciously shift around ovulation toward desiring men who show classic biological indicators of male genetic fitness, such as facial symmetry and social dominance (Gangestad and Thornhill 2008). Women are also more likely cheat on their relationship partner when they are ovulating (Gangestad et al. 2002).

More recent research has begun to uncover that the ovulatory cycle doesn't just influence mating. Instead, ovulation also appears to regulate behaviors linked to same-sex competition with rivals. For example, women's clothing choices non-consciously shift around ovulation toward sexier and more revealing outfits (Durante et al. 2011). This hormonally-regulated shift is not related to appearing more desirable to men, but is instead driven by trying to outcompete rival women (Durante et al. 2011). Such same-sex competition effects for ovulating women parallel findings in many non-human primates. For example, ovulation is known to lead primates to become more aggressive and competitive with other females (Wallen 1995).

The current research examined how the ovulatory cycle influences women's financial decisions in economic games. We investigated whether ovulating women might become more generous or more competitive when splitting money among themselves and another person. Given that previous research shows that the ovulatory cycle has independent effects on mating and on same-sex competition, we hypothesized that ovulation would have a different effect depending on whether women were exchanging resources with a man or with a another woman. We predicted that ovulation should lead women to be more fair and generous when splitting resources with a desirable man. In contrast, we predicted that ovulation should lead women to be more competitive and spiteful when splitting resources with an attractive woman.

Study 1examined how the ovulatory cycle influenced women's decisions between making "equitable" versus "competitive" financial offers to another person. Using a modified version of the Social Value Orientation inventory (Van Lange 1999), participants were presented with the following hypothetical options: (A) You get $480, other person gets $480; (B) You get $280, other person gets $80. Whereas option A represents an equitable split, option B represents a competitive split. Choosing option B signifies that a person is willing to take less money for themselves so that the other person receives an even lesser amount.

Participants were told that the other person is either an attractive man or an attractive woman. To determine whether women were ovulating, we used an established counting method (Haselton and Gangestad 2006). Findings showed that when the exchange partner was an attractive man, ovulating women were more likely to choose an equitable split. However, when the exchange partner was an attractive woman, ovulating women were more like to choose the competitive option. This means that ovulating women were willing to take less money for themselves as long as another attractive woman received even less money.

Study 2 extended these findings by having ovulating and non-ovulating women play the Dictator Game using real money. Using a more stringent methodology, ovulation was confirmed using urine hormone tests. Female participants were assigned to the role of Proposer in the Dictator Game. They were given $5, and their task was to dictate how to split the money between themselves and another person. The women would get to keep the amount of money they left for themselves, and this amount was not contingent on the other person, meaning that they could give as much or as little as they wanted.

Women were paired in the game either with an attractive woman or an attractive man. When women were not ovulating, they gave about 40% of their monetary endowment to the man and the woman. When women were not ovulating, women's decisions were similar regardless of whether they were playing a man or woman. However, ovulation had drastic effects. When playing with an attractive man, ovulating women's giving went up to 72% of their endowment, meaning that some women gave more than half of the money to the man. In contrast, when playing with an attractive woman, ovulating women's giving went down to 17% of their endowment. This means that while ovulating women become more generous when playing with a man, they became more spiteful when playing with an attractive woman.

These studies provide the first evidence that economic decisions are influenced by the ovulatory cycle. Results of both studies support the idea that women use financial decision both for purposes of courtship and for purposes on intra-sexual competition, become more intra-sexually competitive near ovulation.

REFERENCES
Durante, Kristina M., Vladas Griskevicius, Sarah E. Hill, Carin Perilloux, and Norman Li (forthcoming), "Ovulation, Female Competition, and Product Choice: Hormonal Influences on Consumer Behavior," *Journal of Consumer Research.*

Gangestad, Steven W. and Randy Thornhill (2008), "Human Oestrus," *Proceedings of the Royal Society B, 275,* 991-1000.
Gangestad, Steven W., Randy Thornhill, and Christine E. Garver (2002), "Changes inWomen's Sexual Interests and Their Partner's Mate-Retention Tactics across the Menstrual Cycle: Evidence for Shifting Conflicts of Interest," *Proceedings of the Royal Society of London* B, 269, 975–82.
Haselton, Martie G. and StevenW. Gangestad (2006), "Conditional Expression of Women's Desires and Men's Mate Guarding across the Ovulatory Cycle," *Hormones and Behavior*, 49 (April), 509–18.
Van Lange, Paul A. M. (1999), "The Pursuit of Joint Outcomes and Equality in Outcomes: An Integrative Model of Social Value Orientation," *Journal of Personality and Social Psychology, 77,* 337-349.
Wallen, Kim (1995), "The Evolution of Female Sexual Desire," in *Sexual Nature, Sexual Culture*, ed. P. Abramson and S. Pinkerton, Chicago: University of Chicago Press, 57–79.

The Influence of Sex Ratio on Saving, Borrowing, and Spending

EXTENDED ABSTRACT
The ratio of males to females in a population is known to be an important factor in determining animal behavior. Animal research shows that imbalanced sex ratio tends to have the strongest effects on male behavior. The most commonly observed pattern is that what females become scarce (male-biased sex ratio), males intensify competition and invest in immediate mating effort. For example, as sex ratio shifts from female-biased to male-biased, male grey mouse lemurs allocate more effort on mate search and courtship (Eberle and Kappeler 2004). Similarly, male European bitterlings intensify intra-sexual competition over mates when females become scarce (Mills and Reynolds 2003).

Sex ratio also varies in human populations. For example, whereas Las Vegas, Nevada, has 1.16 men per every woman, Birmingham, Alabama, has 0.88 men per every woman (Kruger 2009). Sex ratios can also vary between nations. Multiple Asian countries have recently become strongly male-biased. In the most striking case, China will soon have a surplus of over 40 million men, producing an adult sex ratio of over 1.2 men for every woman (Hesketh 2009).

Correlational research at the population level has begun to examine how sex ratio relates to various human behaviors (Guttentag and Secord 1983). Paralleling findings in animal behavior, a scarcity of women in human population is associated with increased competition. For example, male aggression and violence increase as populations become more male-biased (Barber 2003), whereby men amplify competition and immediate mating effort when there is a scarcity of women.

We hypothesize that sex ratio may have a much broader impact on human behavior, affecting many critically important areas of human life, including financial decision-making. Because a male-biased sex ratio is expected to shift men toward prioritizing immediate mating effort and competition, shifts in sex ratio may influence men's desire for immediate monetary resources, which can then be used for expenditures on mating effort and competition.

In Experiment 1 participants viewed photo arrays of men and women that were ostensibly indicative of the local population. The arrays were either male-skewed, female-skewed, or equal sex ratio (control). Then, participants made a series of financial choices involving real monetary incentives. For example, people chose between receiving $37 tomorrow versus $54 in 33 days. Findings showed that sex ratio had no effect on women's intertemporal choice. For men, however, sex ratio produced a large effect. As predicted, a male-biased ratio led men to opt for immediate financial rewards when compared to either a female-biased or an even sex ratio. This means that as women become scarce, men desired immediate monetary rewards.

In Experiment 2 participants read news articles describing the local population as either male-biased or female-biased. Participants then indicated how much money they would save each month from a paycheck, as well as how much money they would borrow each month for immediate expenditures. Findings showed that sex ratio again had no effect on women's financial desires. However, male-biased sex ratios led men to save less money, cutting their monthly savings by 42%. Male-biased sex ratios also led men to want to borrow 84% more money for use toward immediate expenditures.

Whereas the first two experiments examined how sex ratio influenced the desire to acquire immediate monetary resources, the third experiment investigated whether sex ratio has parallel influences on how monetary resources are spent. Recall that in both human and non-human animals, male-biased sex ratios are associated with increased investment by males in mating effort. Thus, if men value immediate financial yields under male biased sex-ratios as a means of attracting mates, then men should be expected to spend more on mating-related expenditures when the sex ratio is male-biased.

Experiment 3 examined how sex ratio influenced the amount of money people expected men to pay for three mating-related expenditures: a romantic Valentine's Day gift, an entrée for a dinner date, and an engagement ring. Because females become choosier and males invest more in mating effort under a male-biased sex ratio, we predicted that men would be expected to pay more for the same mating-related expenditures when women were scarce. Supporting predictions, findings showed that when the sex ratio was male-biased, men were expected to pay $6.01 more for a Valentine's Day gift, pay $1.51 more for an entrée on a dinner date, and pay $278 more for an engagement ring.

Our findings highlight people's sensitivity to a particular feature of the social environment—the ratio of adult men to women. Just as sex ratio has important effects on animal behavior, we find that sex ratio has theoretically consistent effects on human behavior. However, the effects of sex ratio on humans are not limited to the traditional domains of study, which include mating, parenting, and aggression. Instead, sex ratio also appears to influence other life domains that may be even more relevant to daily behavior.

REFERENCES

Barber, N. (2003). The sex ratio and female marital opportunity as historical predictors of violent crime in England, Scotland, and the United States. *Cross-Cultural Research, 37,* 373-391.

Eberle, M., & Kappeler, P. M. (2004). Sex in the dark: determinants and consequences of mixed male mating tactics in *Microcebus murinus*, a small solitary nocturnal primate. *Behavioral Ecology and Sociobiology, 57,* 77-90.

Guttentag, M., & Secord, P. F. (1983). *Too many women? The sex ratio question.* Beverly Hills, CA: Sage.

Hesketh, T. (2009). Too many males in China: The causes and consequences. *Significance, 6,* 9-13.

Kruger, D. J. (2009). Male scarcity is differentially related to male marital likelihood across the life course. *Evolutionary Psychology, 7,* 280-287.

Mills, S. C., & Reynolds, J. D. (2003). Operational sex ratio and alternative reproductive behaviours in the European bitterling, *Rhodeus sericeus. Behavioral Ecology and Sociobiology, 54,* 98-104.

Men, Sex, and Risk: Turning Up the Heat on Men's Financial Decisions

EXTENDED ABSTRACT

In this research we address a basic question: Do sexual cues lead men to prefer more financial risk or less financial risk? For example, does interacting with an alluring woman—or merely seeing an ad with a sexy model—lead men to be safer with their money or to gamble? At first glance, the answer to this question might appear obvious. Not only do sexual cues lead to impulsivity (Van den Bergh, Dewitte and Warlop 2008), but sexual arousal has been linked to risk-proneness. For instance, sexually aroused men report a greater willingness to engage in risky sexual activities (Ariely and Loewenstein 2006), and exposure to images of nude Playboy models leads men to be more willing to behave in a sexually forceful manner (Loewenstein, Nagin and Paternoster 1997).

Drawing on research on how decision-making is influenced by cold and hot psychological systems (Metcalfe and Mischel 1999), we propose that sexual cues produce a tendency to maximize the probability of monetary rewards. When the cold, cognitive system is compromised (e.g., people are unable to deliberate), people prefer smaller, certain rewards over larger, risky rewards (Whitney, Rinehart, and Hinson 2008). We hypothesize that activating the hot spots of the affective system, rather than overloading the cool nodes of the cognitive system, leads to financial risk-aversion. We therefore predict that sexual cues should not lead men to become more financially risky, but instead, cause them to become financially risk-averse.

In Experiment 1 we manipulated sex cues by having the same female research assistant wear either plain/unrevealing attire or wearing revealing/sexy attire. Participants then made a series of financial choices between safe (certain) vs. risky (uncertain) financial options. For example, do you prefer to: Receive $70 for sure or 50% to receive $200. Findings showed that men chose the certain option more often after exposure to a research assistant in sexy clothing than after exposure to the same research assistant in plain clothing.

The next study extended these findings by examining a key individual difference moderator. We hypothesize that sexual cues lead men to choose certain options because sexual cues activate a general reward-seeking system that seeks immediate gratification. If so, we predicted that the effects of sex cues should be strongest for men who have a sensitive reward system. In Experiment 2 sex cues were manipulated by having male participants inspect and touch either a T-shirt or lingerie. Then, participant engaged in a probability discounting task, allowing us to assess preferences for financial risk. The sensitivity of the general reward-seeking system was assessed via an established individual difference measure (Torrubia et al. 2001). Findings again showed that sexual cues led to a preference for smaller, certain rewards over larger, uncertain rewards. In addition, this effect was moderated by the sensitivity of people's reward system. As predicted, the effect was most pronounced among men with a sensitive reward system, but become weaker for men with a less sensitive reward system.

We hypothesize that sexual cues should produce a desire to maximize the probability of monetary rewards. This means that the sexual system should play a critical role in evaluating *certain* rewards but less so in evaluating merely *probable* rewards. In Experiment 3, sexual cues were manipulated by having male participants view photos of women who were either wearing unrevealing clothing or wearing a swimsuit/lingerie. Participants then engaged in a probability discounting task that included a safe and a risky prospect. Findings showed that exposure to bikini models led to a higher valuation of smaller monetary rewards in the certain condition, but not in the risky condition. That is, sexual cues instigate risk aversion only when a sure prospect could be obtained.

Using varied methodologies to enhance validity and generalizability, in three experiments we found that sex cues led men to be financially risk-averse. In addition, we tested two key

moderators of this predicted effect that provide insight into the underlying mechanism. This

research not only shows how, why, and when sexual cues influence risky financial decisions,

but it also contributes to a growing body of research documenting that a desire for a reward in one domain (e.g., sex) influences decisions about rewards in other domains (e.g., money).

REFERENCES

Ariely, Dan and George Loewenstein (2006), "The Heat of the Moment: The Effect of SexualArousal on Sexual Decision Making," *Journal of Behavioral Decision Making*, 19 (2),87-98.

Dahl, Darren W., Jaideep Sengupta, and Kathleen D. Vohs (2009), "Sex in Advertising:Gender Differences and the Role of Relationship Commitment," *Journal of Consumer Research*, 36 (2), 215-31

Loewenstein, George F., Daniel Nagin, and Raymond Paternoster (1997), "The Effect of Sexual Arousal on Expectations of Sexual Forcefulness," *Journal of Research in Crime and Delinquency*, 34 (4), 443-73.

Metcalfe, Janet and Walter Mischel (1999), "A Hot/Cool-System Analysis of Delay of Gratification: Dynamics of Willpower," *Psychological Review*, 106 (1), 3-19.

Torrubia, R., Avila, C., Molto, J., & Caseras, X. (2001). The Sensitivity to Punishment and Sensitivity to Reward Questionnaire (SPSRQ) as a measure of Gray's anxiety and impulsivity dimensions. Personality and Individual Differences, 31, 837–862.

Van den Bergh, Bram, Siegfried Dewitte, and Luk Warlop (2008), "Bikinis Instigate Generalized Impatience in Intertemporal Choice," *Journal of Consumer Research*, 35 (1), 85-97.

Whitney, Paul, Christa A. Rinehart, and John M. Hinson (2008), "Framing Effects under Cognitive Load: The Role of Working Memory in Risky Decisions," *Psychonomic Bulletin & Review*, 15 (6), 1179-84.

Women, Sex, and Risk: Mating Motivation and Financial Risk-Taking in Women

EXTENDED ABSTRACT

Little is known about how mating cues influence women's behavior. The current research examined how mating cues affect women's financial risk-taking. There is little reason to believe that mating cues by themselves will influence women's preferences for risk. Indeed, mating cues seldom influence female choice patterns (e.g., Wilson and Daly 2004; Roney 2003). Nevertheless, to the extent that financial decisions may function to alter others' perceptions, underlying psychological systems regulating financial decision-making may be sensitive to the presence of others (Bateson et al. 2006; Burnham and Hare 2007; Haley and Fessler 2005). The lack of effects of mating cues on female choice in prior research may therefore stem from

failing to take into account potential audience effects. The present research addresses this shortcoming by taking into account both mating motivation and audience effects among female decision-makers.

In Study 1, mating cues were manipulated by having participants read a guided visualization scenarios designed to elicit either a mating motivation or no motivation. Then, participants were assigned to one of two audience conditions. Those in the no-audience condition were told they were randomly selected not to share their answers with anyone and were reminded that their answers would be completely anonymous. Participants in the audience condition were told they were randomly selected to share their answers with two men and two women completing the same study in other rooms in the lab. Participants then made three decisions, choosing for each a sure gain (e.g., $10 for sure) or a chance of gaining more money accompanied by a risk of gaining nothing (e.g., a 90% chance of getting $15 and a 10% chance of getting nothing). Findings showed that a mating motivation did not influence women's risk when choices were anonymous. However, women became riskier in the mating condition when they thought they were going to be sharing their answers with an audience.

Because the audience condition in Study 1 involved a mixed sex audience, it is not clear for whom the participants were displaying riskiness. That is, women could have been displaying their riskiness to members of their own sex. Or, women could have been displaying riskiness to members of the opposite sex. Alternatively, it is possible that women only engage in financial risk-taking when both potential mates and competitors are present.

In Study 2, we aimed to explore this question by employing a more comprehensive array of possible audience compositions. The mating motive manipulations were the same as in Study 1 (mating versus control scenarios), but four audience manipulations were included. In the no audience condition, participants were told their answers would be completely anonymous. In the all-female condition, participants were told they would be sharing their answers with four women. In the all-male condition, participants were told they would be sharing their answers with four men. And in the mixed-sex condition, participants were told they would be sharing their answers with two men and two women. Financial risk-taking was measured using the same items as in Study 1. Results revealed that there was only one condition in which mating motives led women to take more financial risks – when they were in the presence of a mixed-sex audience.

Taken together, these studies reveal that a mating motivation by itself did not influence women's financial risk preferences. However, a mating cue in conjunction with an audience did lead women to take more financial risks. The second study revealed that an all-male or an all-female audience does not appear to elicit more risk. Instead, in both studies it was only when a mixed-sex audience was introduced that women took more risks. Therefore, the present findings suggest that two distinct processes might be driving female financial decision making: Intrasexual selection and intersexual selection. Intrasexual selection involves competition between members of the same sex for mating access to members of the opposite sex. Intersexual selection, in contrast, involves preferential choice exerted by members of one sex for members of the opposite sex. Mating motivation increased the willingness to take financial risks only when female rivals could be outdone (intrasexual selection), and at the same time mates could be secured (intersexual selection). If one of these conditions is not met (e.g., rivals cannot be outdone or opposite sex individuals are not around), women appear to adopt a risk-avoidant strategy and do not experience a need to engage in financial risk seeking.

REFERENCES

Bateson, Melissa, Daniel Nettle, and Gilbert Roberts (2006), "Cues of being watched enhance cooperation in a real-world setting," *Biology Letters*, 2 (3), 412-14.

Burnham, Terence and Brian Hare (2007), "Engineering Human Cooperation. Does Involuntary Neural Activation Increase Public Goods Contributions?," *Human Nature*, 18 (2), 88-108.

Haley, Kevin J. and Daniel M. T. Fessler (2005), "Nobody's watching?: Subtle cues affect generosity in an anonymous economic game," *Evolution and Human Behavior*, 26 (3), 245-56.

Roney, James R. (2003), "Effects of visual exposure to the opposite sex: Cognitive aspects of mate attraction in human males," *Personality and Social Psychology Bulletin*, 29 (3), 393-404.

Wilson, Margo and Martin Daly (2004), "Do pretty women inspire men to discount the future?," *Proceedings of the Royal Society of London Series B-Biological Sciences*, 271, S177-S79.

Online Word of Mouth

Chairs: Yu-Jen Chen, University of Maryland, USA
Amna Kirmani, University of Maryland, USA

Paper #1: Different Drivers of Online and Offline Word of Mouth

Jonah Berger, University of Pennsylvania, USA

Paper #2: Linguistic Mimicry in Online Word of Mouth

Sarah Moore, University of Alberta, Canada
Brent McFerran, University of Michigan, USA

Paper #3: Temporal Contiguity and the Negativity Bias in Online Reviews

Zoey Chen, Georgia Tech, USA
Nicholas Lurie, Georgia Tech, USA

Paper #4: Persuading Others Online: The Consumer as Media Planner

Yu-Jen Chen, University of Maryland, USA
Amna Kirmani, University of Maryland, USA

SESSION OVERVIEW

General orientation and objectives: Research on online WOM has shifted from a focus on the role of consumers as information providers to a focus on why consumers talk about product experiences on the Internet. We examine how motivation affects consumers' online posting decisions and how posting impacts both message posters and receivers, to better understand the new world of online interpersonal communication. The objective of this session is to study the relationship between the antecedents (e.g., motivation, consumption experience, target audience, and temporal proximity cues) and consequences of online posting on both posters' behavior (e.g., online or offline, linguistic mimicry, posting frequency, where to post) and readers' perceptions (e.g., perceived helpfulness and inferred poster's motive).

Issues and topics to be covered: All four papers share a common focus on deepening our theoretical understanding of factors that influence consumers' online posting behaviors, and how these behaviors influence downstream WOM effectiveness. Specifically, these papers focus on the role of motivation in affecting online WOM senders in terms of why they talk (papers 1, 2, 3, and 4), what they talk about (papers 2 and 3), and where they talk (paper 4). Each paper has a unique perspective on these topics.

The first paper, by Berger, examines whether there are different drivers of online and offline WOM. It proposes that online WOM requires a higher threshold for discussion, so there is a stronger link between whether something is interesting and whether it gets talked about online rather than offline. The second paper, by Moore and McFerran, introduces the notion of linguistic mimicry in online WOM and shows that copying others' language use is dependent on whom forum posters are conversing with. Specifically, posters are more likely to mimic similar forum members than dissimilar others. Similarly, the third paper, by Chen and Lurie, investigates posters' language but focuses on how readers infer posters' motives by temporal proximity cues in a review (e.g., "today" or "just got back"). They show that when these cues are present, readers may infer that poster's have a self-enhancement motive, which attenuates perceived helpfulness of a negative review. The last paper, by Chen and Kirmani, discusses how posters with an influence motive (e.g., self-enhancement or persuasion) make their decision of *where* to post on an online discussion forum. The results provide initial evidence that posters, depending on their message valence and consumption

benefit, will use persuasion knowledge in strategically choosing a forum to maximize their impact.

These papers address commonalities and differences in the antecedents and consequences of online WOM, and build connections by providing a more complete picture of online WOM. This session will benefit WOM researchers by showing why, how, and where consumers share their experiences on the Internet, and will provide suggestions for marketing practitioners for developing strategies that encourage customers to talk about their experiences.

Potential audience: The session will appeal to researchers interested in the antecedents and consequences of WOM (online and offline) and more generally, to those interested in motivation, social influence, communication, and persuasion.

Potential contribution: This session makes theoretical contributions to research on WOM communication in marketing. While these four papers all feature factors related to posters' motivation, each takes a unique perspective to explain the role of motivation in shaping diverse subsequent behaviors. Taken together, these papers substantively deepen our understanding of the role of different components in WOM and how each relates to the others.

State of completion: Data have been collected for the studies described in all four papers.

Different Drivers of Online and Offline Word of Mouth

EXTENDED ABSTRACT

Word of mouth is frequent and has an important impact on consumer behavior. Consumers talk about new running shoes, write reviews about bad hotel stays, and share information about the best way to get out tough stains. But while recent research has shown that word of mouth (WOM) impacts everything from the products consumers buy to the drugs doctors prescribe, this research has treated different types of WOM (e.g., online reviews and face-to-face discussions) as the same. But are the factors that drive people to share online WOM (e.g., reviews, blog postings, and product ratings) the same as those that drive them to have face-to-face discussions, or might there different factors drive online and offline WOM?

Looking across prior papers hints at an intriguing possibility. More interesting *New York Times* articles are more likely to make the most emailed list (Berger & Milkman 2011). In contrast, however, more interesting products do not get any more face to face word of mouth (Berger & Schwartz 2011). These two papers relied on different datasets that used different subject populations, making it hard to directly compare their results, but might it be the case that interest plays a different role in online and offline WOM?

We suggest that there are some important differences in psychological drivers of online and face-to-face WOM. In particular, we suggest that face-to-face interactions may have a lower threshold for discussion. It is awkward to have dinner with a friend in silence, or ride in a cab with a colleague without conversing, and so few things will be deemed too boring to talk about. In a sense, the outside option is to not talk at all, and talking about anything is better than that. With online WOM, however, the threshold for discussion is often higher. Most decisions to post a review or share a news article are not driven by the need to fill conversational space, but by the belief that there is useful or interesting information to be passed along. Consequently, factors like interest may have a greater impact on online transmission. While more interesting products (e.g., iPads or Hollywood movies) may get more online WOM than their less interesting counterparts (e.g., Walmart and toasters) these types of products may get similar amount of offline WOM.

Carefully studying this possibility is hampered, however, by data availability. One could imagine comparing the relationship between the amount of interest a brand evokes and the amount of WOM it receives online and offline, but aggregate data introduces selection issues. If certain types of people are more likely to share WOM online, than it might be those doing the talking, rather than the channel, that is driving any observed patterns in online vs. offline data.

We avoid this difficulty by using a unique individual level dataset from the WOM marketing firm KellerFay. It contains over 35,000 brand and product mentions from a nationally representative sample of approximately 6,000 people who recorded all the WOM they shared, as well as the channel they shared it through (e.g. face to face or online) over a one day period. By looking people that talk both online and off, and controlling for variation at the individual and product levels, we can examine the causal impact of channel (i.e., online vs. offline) on WOM.

We compiled a list of all the brands and products mentioned by the survey respondents and then had independent raters code them based on how interesting each product or brand would be to talk about (1 = not at all, 7 = extremely). Different raters' ratings were highly correlated ($r = .68$) and we averaged across raters to create a product interest score for each product. We then examined how this related to online and offline WOM.

Consistent with our theorizing, results indicate that interest plays a different role in driving online and offline WOM. While more interesting products received more WOM online than less interesting products ($p < .01$) there was no relationship between interest and face-to-face WOM ($p > .70$). Further, to ensure that our results were not driven by outside raters rating how interesting the products were, we also conducted a follow-up study (Study 2) where participants recorded what they talked about in a given day but then rated interest themselves. We find the same results. While more interesting products get more online WOM than more boring ones, there is no relationship between interest and offline WOM.

Taken together, these two studies deepen our understanding of the drivers of word of mouth. While a great deal of research has shown that WOM has important consequences, less is known about why people talk about and share certain things rather than others. Accordingly, this work shows that there are some important differences in what leads people to talk face to face versus share things online.

Linguistic Mimicry in Online Word of Mouth

EXTENDED ABSTRACT

New digital media has changed WOM radically in terms of how and with whom consumers share consumption experiences. We now converse with thousands of other consumers through online forums, email, text messages, and websites such as Amazon.com. There are documented consequences of WOM for firms and consumers (Chevalier and Mayzlin 2006). However, past work has not focused on WOM as a conversation (only as a single interaction; but see Cowley 2007) or on how *specific* language use in WOM impacts consumers (Moore 2012). We address these gaps in the literature by introducing *linguistic mimicry* to consumer research. This allows us to break down language into specific parcels and to examine how mimicking WOM language (and being mimicked) affects the flow and content of online interactions.

Linguistic mimicry measures how closely individuals match others' word use in conversation. New software can calculate linguistic mimicry between two or more individuals engaged in conversation in terms of style (e.g. article, pronoun, conjunction use) and content (e.g. use of emotional, cognitive, social words) (Pennebaker et al. 2007). As with behavioral mimicry (e.g. mannerisms, talking speed), linguistic mimicry acts as a "social glue" that both reflects and creates bonds between people. For example, higher levels of linguistic mimicry increase romantic interest between individuals who are speed dating (Ireland et al. 2011) and increase group performance and cohesion (Gonzales, Hancock, and Pennebaker 2010). However, work in this new area is largely correlational, and has examined neither the consequences of mimicry in a marketing context, nor variables that predict linguistic mimicry. Using field and experimental data, we examine the causal relations between social variables that predict mimicry, levels of linguistic mimicry, and consequences of mimicry.

We expect linguistic mimicry to be influenced by similarity; for example, forum members who live in the same location should mimic one another more than they should mimic those do not share this characteristic. In addition, mimicry should impact consumers' attitudes and behavior. Consumers should feel a greater sense of affiliation with those they mimic (Jefferis, van Baaren, and Chartrand 2003), which should increase posting frequency within a forum and information sharing outside the forum (e.g. Twitter). *Being* mimicked by others will also have important consequences. Individuals who are mimicked by similar others will likely feel more group affiliation and post more frequently, while those who are mimicked by dissimilar others will likely feel less affiliation and post less frequently. We examine these predictions in two studies, one using online forum data and a second using experimental data.

In study 1, we downloaded an entire product review forum from a parenting discussion site (1386 posts, 241 users). We coded how much personal information users disclosed about themselves (e.g. location, gender) and their children (e.g. gender, names, ages, or birthdates) in their profile, such that higher numbers indicate more disclosure. We also calculated how similar consecutive posters were to one another, personally (i.e. same gender or not) and in terms of their children (i.e. same gender or not). We then calculated mimicry of linguistic style (e.g. articles, pronouns) and content (e.g. cognitive words, emotion words) for consecutive posts; that is, how much an individual mimicked the post immediately prior to theirs. Personal similarity and self disclosure predicted mimicry. The more similar a poster was to the poster immediately preceding them, the less they mimicked this individuals' linguistic style (e.g. articles, pronouns) and cognitive word use, but the more they mimicked positive linguistic content (exclamation marks, assent words). Similar levels of self disclosure also predicted decreased mimicry of cognitive words as well as decreased mimicry of non-fluencies (e.g. uh, um).

In study 2, we extended the inquiry into a lab setting. We asked undergraduate seniors ($N = 102$) to think of a recent positive or negative visit to a well-know chain of coffee shops. Next, participants read a positive or negative online review of the chain, allegedly written by an undergraduate at another college (dissimilar) or at their college (similar); they then wrote a review of their own. In this study, participants' linguistic style and content mimicry was predicted by the interaction between similarity, participants' evaluations, and the other writer's evaluations. First, regardless of similarity, individuals were least likely to mimic linguistic style when the audience had positive but they had negative evaluations of the coffee shop. Content word use in terms of punctuation, cognitive, and social words, was predicted by similarity and evaluations. For example, participants showed less mimicry of cognitive words when they shared negative as opposed to positive evaluations with a similar audience. These differences in mimicry predicted important outcomes for participants in terms of their liking of the coffee shop and their liking of the other reviewer. Increased style mimicry increased participants' liking of their experience, while mimicry of social words decreased their liking. Most importantly, the more participants mimicked their audience's content words, the more they liked the audience.

We provide the first examination of linguistic mimicry in marketing. Using field and experimental data, we investigate the antecedents and consequences of linguistic mimicry; we find the first evidence that linguistic mimicry is predicted by whom one's audience is, and that mimicry has consequences for consumers' evaluations of their own experiences as well as their relationships with other consumers. Several other studies, involving both lab and field data, are in the planning stage. This project contributes to theory and methodology in both marketing and psychology, and will lead to important conclusions for managers as well as for consumers engaged in online WOM. Further, it should open the door for other research in this area.

Temporal Contiguity and the Negativity Bias in Online Reviews

EXTENDED ABSTRACT

Online Word-of-Mouth (WOM) is as an important information source for consumers (Chevalier and Mayzlin 2006). However, not all reviews have similar effects on consumer behavior. Although positive reviews tend to more prevalent than negative reviews (Fowler and Avila 2009), they have less impact than negative reviews on product sales (Chevalier and Mayzlin 2006) and evaluations (Herr, Kardes, and Kim 1991). While many have documented the disproportionate impact of negative information (Fiske 1980), little attention has been paid to factors that take away the negativity bias.

One explanation for a negativity bias in online reviews is that positive reviews are more likely to be seen as self-serving. In particular, readers may infer that the writers of positive reviews are trying to feel good about their purchase decisions and demonstrate their good taste. Writers of highly positive reviews may also be seen as less discerning (Schlosser 2005). In other words, positive reviews are less likely to be seen as "caused" by the product or service experience. Negative reviews, on the other hand, are more likely to be viewed as caused of the reviewer's experience since there are less self-serving reasons to write negative reviews. This suggests that cues that enhance the causal connection between product or service experiences and the review should increase the perceived usefulness of positive reviews.

Attributions of causality are often based on temporal contiguity between input and output events (Michotte 1963). For example, perception of causality between two physical events (e.g., ball A hitting ball B and ball B moves) is reduced when temporal contiguity is missing (Michotte 1963). This suggests that the presence of cues to temporal contiguity between product experience and product review will enhance the perceived usefulness of positive reviews. We test these ideas in three studies.

Study 1 examined the effect of temporal contiguity cues on the perceived usefulness of positive and negative reviews on a real website. Over 65,000 restaurant reviews were collected from the popular website Yelp. For each review, we used a computer program to determine the presence of keywords indicating temporal contigu-ity. Hand coding a sample of 500 reviews showed that the computer program correctly coded over 90% of reviews. Review valence (1-5 stars, with 5 being best) served as the other primary independent variable of interest and the number of people finding the review help-ful served as the dependent measure. In support of our predictions, a negative binomial regression shows that the presence of temporal contiguity cues moderate the relationship between review valence and usefulness. In reviews written without temporal contiguity cues, review usefulness is negatively related to review valence. However, in reviews written with temporal contiguity cues, there is a non-sig-nificant relationship between valence and usefulness.

Although the secondary data supports our predictions, one might argue that temporal contiguity cues decrease the usefulness of negative reviews rather than increase the usefulness of positive reviews as we have hypothesized. To examine this possibility, we conducted a lab study (Study 2a). Using a lab study also addresses potential self-selection issues in the secondary data. The lab study manipulated review valence at two levels (positive vs. negative) and also manipulated the presence of temporal continuity cues (present or absent) between-subjects. Participants were randomly assigned to one of the four experimental conditions in which they first read then evaluated a restaurant review. Results show that the presence of temporal contiguity cues significantly increased the usefulness of positive, but not negative, reviews. This provides evidence for the prediction that temporal contiguity cues increase the usefulness of positive reviews more than negative reviews.

An additional lab study (Study 2b) examined how temporal contiguity cues affect reader attributions. Respondents were random-ly assigned to read one of the four reviews used in study 2A. After reading the reviews, review attributions of the causes for the review were measured on Likert scales. Confirming our proposals, participants felt more strongly that positive (versus negative) reviews were caused by the reviewer. In addition, the presence of temporal conti-guity cues reduced attributions that reviews were caused by the re-viewer for positive but not negative reviews.

Although the negativity bias is well documented word-of-mouth and other contexts, this research is the first to demonstrate a way to overcome this bias by changing consumer attributions about the motivations of word-of-mouth providers. In particular, simple textual cues to temporal contiguity can remove differences in the perceived usefulness of positive and negative reviews. Our examina-tion of temporal contiguity cues in secondary data and lab studies documents and explains these effects.

Persuading Others Online: The Consumer as Media Planner

EXTENDED ABSTRACT

Although substantial research has studied *what* people post on the Internet, little attention has been paid to the question of *where* consumers post. In this paper, we examine how consumers decide where to post their consumption experience. We suggest that given the plethora of choices about where to post, consumers must become intuitive media planners for scheduling their online messages. As media planners, they must access their intuitive theories or persua-sion knowledge (Friestad &Wright, 1994) about which type of web-site or forum may allow their post to achieve maximal impact.

We examine the posting choice of consumers whose motive is to influence others, either for intrinsic reasons, such as self-enhance-ment, or for extrinsic reasons, such as being hired by a buzz agent. We expect that an influence motive activates persuasion knowledge. Within the context of an online discussion website, we focus on the decision of which specific forum to post in. We categorize forums into two groups: those with a more homogeneous audience with high brand loyalty (e.g., Nikon Forum), and those with heterogeneous audience with neutral attitude toward different brands (e.g., Digital Camera Open Forum).

We propose that consumers use persuasion knowledge to choose a forum based on two factors: valence of the post (positive or negative message) and the nature of the consumption experience (e.g., utilitarian or hedonic), both of which affect the post's ability to draw attention and convince others (Godes & Mayzlin, 2009). We propose that negative messages are likely to be more salient on homogeneous forums, while positive messages may be more salient on heterogeneous forums. In addition, the nature of the experience (hedonic vs. utilitarian) should moderate this effect. Specifically, while product evaluations that reflect utilitarian benefits are likely to focus on functional and objective attributes, product evaluations that reflect hedonic benefits are likely to focus on subjective experience (Sen & Lerman, 2007). As a result, a post of subjective but negative brand experience may be less convincing on a brand forum, where people are high in brand loyalty, than on a product category forum, where people have low brand loyalty and are more open to different opinions. Similarly, a post of subjective but positive experience may be highly supported on a brand forum rather than a product category forum.

We conducted three experiments to test our hypotheses. Study 1 tests the basic premise that influence-motivated posters will choose a different forum based on message valence after having a utilitarian consumption experience. All participants were asked to imagine they just purchased a Dell laptop with either positive or negative experience and they wanted to post their experience for one of the three types of influential motive: self-enhancement, persuasion, or reward-seeking. In the self-enhancement condition, participants were told that their goal was to choose a website such that "forum users will be interested in your post and consider you a knowledgeable expert". In the persuasion condition, the participants' goal was to choose a website such that "forum users' purchase decisions will be affected by your post". In the reward-seeking condition, participants were told that they were paid to post to make some impact. The results show that participants across all three influence motives preferred a homogeneous forum (Dell Review Forum) when posting positive experiences but preferred a heterogeneous forum (Computer Review Forum) when posting negative experiences. In addition, measures of persuasion knowledge revealed that participants made their choices based on the audience characteristics of the two forums.

Study 2 examined whether the type of consumption experience (utilitarian or hedonic) moderated the results. We assessed participants' focal consumption experience by measuring their relative interests in watching either a fun or useful cooking video. We then manipulated message valence by playing either a fun or useful video such that watching a matching video would lead to a positive review and mismatching videos would lead to a negative review. After writing the review, participants saw two forum options for posting and indicated their forum choice and relative preferences. A 2 (consumption experience) x 2 (message valence) ANOVA on relative preferences (1: Chef Forum - homogeneous; 10: General Cooking Forum - heterogeneous) revealed a significant interaction ($F(1, 130) = 8.79$, $p < .01$). Specifically, in the utilitarian conditions, the significant contrast between positive and negative valence replicated our finding in study 1 ($M_{positive} = 6.80$ vs. $M_{negative} = 5.51$; $F(1,130) = 4.49$, $p < .04$). In contrast, in the hedonic conditions, we found a significant contrast between positive and negative valence that flipped the pattern ($M_{positive} = 4.83$ vs. $M_{negative} = 6.45$; $F(1,130) = 4.43$, $p < .04$).

Study 3 further examined the process by manipulating posting motive as either to influence or to affiliate with others. The study showed that the predicted effects occurred only in the influence motive condition, suggesting that persuasion knowledge underlies these effects.

The paper makes two major contributions. First, to our knowledge, this is the first paper in the consumer behavior literature to consider where consumers post. Second, the paper demonstrates that consumers may act as intuitive media planners when posting their online messages. Thus, when they have an influence motive, they use persuasion knowledge to choose a posting forum that will be most effective in persuading others to their viewpoints. This extends the literature on persuasion knowledge to a media planning context.

REFERENCES:

Berger, Jonah & Katy Milkman (2011), "Social Transmission, Emotion, and the Virality of Online Content," *Working paper*.

Berger, Jonah & Eric Schwartz (2011), "What Do People Talk About and Why?" *Jounral of Marketing Research*, Forthcoming.

Brown, Jacqueline Johnson & Peter H. Reingen (1987), "Social Ties and Word-of-Mouth Referral Behavior," *Journal of Consumer Research*, 14 (December), 350-362.

Chevalier, Judith A. & Dina Mayzlin (2006), "The Effect of Word of Mouth on Sales: Online Book Reviews," *Journal of Marketing Research,* 43 (3), 345-354.

Cowley, Elizabeth (2007), "The Power of the Story: Word-of-Mouth and Autobiographical Memory," University of Sydney.

Feick, Lawrence F. & Linda L. Price (1987), "The Market Marven: A Diffuser of Marketplace Informaiton," *Journal of Marketing*, 51(1), 83-97.

Fowler, Geoffrey A. and Joseph De Avila (2009), "On the internet, everyone's a critic but they're not very critical," in *Wall Street Journal*, Vol. 1.

Friestad, Marian & Peter Wright (1994), "The Persuasion Knowledge Model: How People Cope with Persuasion Attempts," *Journal of Consumer Research*, 21(June), 1-31.

Godes, David & Dina Mayzlin (2009), "Firm-Created Word-of-Mouth Communication: Evidence from a Field Test," *Marketing Science*, 28(4), 721-739.

Gonzales, Amy L., Jeffrey T. Hancock, & James W. Pennebaker (2010), "Language Style Matching as a Predictor of Social Dynamics in Small Groups," *Communication Research, 31,* 3-19.

Gershoff, Andrew D., Susan M. Broniarczyk, & Patricia M. West (2001), "Recommendation or Evaluation? Task Sensitivity in Information Source Selection," *Journal of Consumer Research*, 28 (December), 418-438.

Herr, Paul M., Frank R. Kardes, & John Kim (1991), "Effects of Word-of-Mouth and Product-Attribute Information on Persuasion: An Accessibility-Diagnosticity Perspective," *Journal of Consumer Research*, 17 (March), 454-462.

Ireland, Molly E., Richard B. Slatcher, Paul W. Eastwick, Lauren E. Scissors, Eli J. Finkel & James W. Pennebaker (2011), "Language Style Matching Predicts Relationship initiation and Stability," *Psychological Science, 22*, 39-44.

Jefferis, Valerie E., Richard van Baaren, & Tanya L. Chartrand (2003), "The Functional Purpose of Mimicry for Creating Interpersonal Closeness," The Ohio State University.

Michotte, A. (1963), *The Perception of Causality*, Oxford, England: Basic Books.

Moore, Sarah G. (2012), "Some things are Better Left Unsaid: How Word of Mouth Influences the Storyteller," *Journal of Consumer Research,* forthcoming.

Pennebaker, James W., C. K. Chung, Molly E. Ireland, Amy L. Gonzales & Roger J. Booth (2007), *The development and psychometric properties of LIWC2007,* Austin, TX: LIWC.net.

Schlosser, Ann E. (2005), "Posting versus Lurking: Communicating in a Multiple Audience Context, "*Journal of Consumer Research,* 32(September), 260-265.

Sen, Shahana & Dawn Lerman (2007), "Why are you telling me this? An examination into negative consumer reviews on the Web," *Journal of Interactive Marketing,* 21(4), 76-94.

Skowronski John J. & Donal E. Carlston (1989), " Negativity and extremity biases in impression-formation - a review of explanations," *Psychological Bulletin*, 105, 131-142.

Ironic Effects on Persuasion: From Communicators to Message Characteristics

Chair: David Dubois, HEC Paris, France

Paper #1: Using Communicator Power to Foster Warmth or Competence

David Dubois, Northwestern University, USA
Derek Rucker, Northwestern University, USA
Adam Galinsky, Northwestern University, USA

Paper #2: The Artful Dodger: Answering the Wrong Question the Right Way

Todd Rogers, Harvard University and Analyst Institute, USA
Michael I. Norton, Harvard Business School, USA

Paper #3: The Persuasive Power of Contradicting Oneself

Taly Reich, Stanford University, USA
Zakary L. Tormala, Stanford University, USA

Paper #4: From Blemishing to Blossoming: The Positive Effect of Negative Information

Danit Ein-Gar, Tel-Aviv University, Israel
Baba Shiv, Stanford University, USA

SESSION OVERVIEW

This session proposes that factors traditionally thought to weaken a message's delivery or content can actually enhance its persuasive appeal under specific conditions. In particular, using a powerful individual as a spokesperson, directly addressing an audience's questions, and including consistent or favorable arguments in a message have all been suggested or alluded to increase persuasiveness (for reviews, see Petty and Wegener 1998; Dillard and Pfau 2002). In contrast to these perspectives, the present session assembles papers that demonstrate circumstances under which the opposite, and more counterintuitive, outcomes hold. Papers 1 and 2 focus on message communication and examine how a communicator who feels powerless or provides evasive answers can actually be a better persuader. Papers 3 and 4 focus on message content and investigate when including inconsistent opinions or unfavorable product features increases persuasion.

Past work has equated effective communication with high levels of power (Kipnis 1972). However, Dubois et al. demonstrate powerlessness can heighten persuasiveness– provided the context highlights warmth, and/or that recipients value warmth. In their research, persuaders experimentally made to feel powerless displayed greater warmth, which spilled over their delivery style and increased success. Moving to another facet of communication – the art of answering questions – Rogers and Norton show that dodging questions can yield greater effectiveness than merely answering the question, when speakers respond to a question with answers that *seem* to address the question (e.g., stating a similar topic).

The final two papers examine situations under which adding counter-attitudinal information to a message's content can enhance its impact. Reich and Tormala examine how conflicting evidence influences message receptivity. Their data show conflicting messages can be more effective than consistent ones, provided the arguments presented are strong and/or the source is trusted. Ein-Gar and Shiv's work shows that providing consumers with positive information followed by a minor piece of negative information appears to enhance their overall evaluations of a target relative to providing exclusively positive information, but only when processing effort is low. These effects shed new insights into the "inoculation" view of persuasion by suggesting that including negative information can ironically make positive information more salient.

This session is of interest to a broad swath of consumer researchers and of special interest to those interested in communication, information processing, persuasion and social judgment. By providing a series of thought-provoking findings of when previously documented negative influences on persuasion can actually serve as benefits to persuasion, this session offers novel insights on persuasive processes and paves the road for future research.

Using Communicator Power to Foster Warmth or Competence

EXTENDED ABSTRACT

The choice of a spokesperson to promote an idea or a product is one of the most difficult yet important choice organizations have to make. Such a choice will likely guide recipients' favorable or unfavorable responses. From simple consumers to successful CEOs, one key feature on which spokespersons differ is their level of power – defined as perceived or actual control over resources or other people (Magee and Galinsky 2008). As a central basis of social hierarchy, power deeply permeates to individuals' everyday experiences through both chronic (e.g. one's socio-economic status) and momentary (e.g. choice of options) factors.

We propose that states of powerlessness and power systematically affect communicators' delivery style of persuasive appeals along two foundational dimensions of social judgments: warmth and competence (Cuddy et al., 2008). Where warmth captures how good-natured and trustworthy a communicator is perceived to be, competence refers to perceptions of skillfulness and confidence attached to a communicator. How might power affect communicator delivery style? Given research showing powerlessness increases one's ability to take others' perspective (Galinsky et al. 2008) and compassion (Van Kleef et al. 2008), states of powerlessness might enhance communicators' warmth. In contrast, given research linking power with action-orientation (Galinsky et al. 2003 and confidence (Briñol et al. 2007), power might enhance communicators' competence. If true, powerless communicators should be more persuasive than powerful and baseline communicators when advocating "warm" products or ideas (e.g. charities, see Aaker et al. 2010). Three experiments test these hypotheses and explore consequences for persuasion. Analyses used ANOVAs and t-tests as appropriate.

Experiment 1: Can powerless communicators trump powerful ones? Participants were divided into communicators and recipients. We manipulated communicators' power through an episodic recall task (Galinsky et al. 2003). Next, communicators wrote the promotional content of an ad appeal for a charity project (funding for a community bus) promoted by a ".org". Finally, we presented the ad to recipients, and gave them the option to donate money for the project. The ad was standard, except a portion of the copy executed by communicators whose power was manipulated. An ANOVA revealed a main effect of power, $p < .01$. Recipients gave $4.30 on average to low-power communicators, but only $1.74 to high-power communicators. In addition, communicators' perceived warmth mediated the amounts donated (95% CI = -.350; .096), suggesting powerlessness can yield more effective communication than states of power.

Experiment 2: Powerless candidate, but powerful president? Experiment 2 tested whether the acquisition of power changed communicators' expressed warmth versus competence. We randomly presented undergraduates with short seconds interview excerpts of

Barak Obama with the same interviewer performed when Obama was a candidate (i.e., not in power) or the president-elect (i.e., in power). The excerpts were cut from actual interviews by a research assistant blind to the hypotheses. Importantly, any information that could allow participants to know Obama's position at the time of the interview was removed (i.e., any sentence or action mentioning or implying he was a candidate or a president at the time of the interview). After viewing a series of excerpts, participants rated Obama' warmth and competence ($\alpha = .91$ and $\alpha = .87$, respectively; items from Cuddy et al., 2008). Obama was judged warmer when candidate than when president, $p < .01$, but more competent when president than when candidate, $p < .01$ regardless of participants' political affiliations, and despite the fact participants did not know whether Obama was president or candidate when the interview was produced. Thus, powerlessness (power) might foster communicator warmth (competence).

Experiment 3: Communicator's effectiveness as a function of Recipient Power. Our last experiment provides experimental evidence of the effectiveness of powerful and powerless communicators against different populations. That is, we reasoned that changes in power may not only affect communicators but also recipients' sensitivity to certain aspects of the communication in the same direction. Put differently, what states of high (low)- power foster at the delivery stage might also be what high (low)-power recipients weigh at the reception stage. If true, powerless communicators might be more effective against powerless recipients since those are particularly sensitive to warmth. In contrast, powerful communicators might be more effective against powerful recipients since those are particularly sensitive to competence.

Undergraduates were assigned to a 3 (communicators' power: baseline, low, high) × 3 (recipients' power: baseline, low, high) between subject design. Both communicators' and recipients' power was manipulated as in experiment 1. Communicators wrote a persuasive message promoting their university. These messages were then randomly presented to recipients who judged the message on three dimensions: persuasiveness, competence, and warmth. Results revealed high-(low-) power recipients found high-(low-) power communicators more persuasive than low-power (high-power) and baseline communicators. Among baseline recipients, there was no effect of power on persuasion. In addition, regardless of recipients' power, high-power communicators were judged as more competent than both baseline and low-power communicators. In contrast, regardless of recipients' power, low-power communicators were judged as warmer than both baseline and high-power communicators. Further analyses revealed competence (95% CI = .072; .703), but not warmth (95% CI = -.051; .198) mediated the effect of communicator's power on persuasiveness. In contrast, low-power recipients found that warmth (95% CI = -.223; .152), but not competence (95% CI = -.641; -091) mediated the effect of communicator's power on persuasiveness.

Discussion. These experiments offer a framework for understanding how power affects the communication and reception of persuasive messages, and suggests temporary states of power unilaterally shift one's expression and sensitivity to competence and warmth leading powerless and powerful communicators to yield effective communication, but for different reasons. Implications for social policy and political communication will be discussed.

The Artful Dodger: Answering the Wrong Question the Right Way

EXTENDED ABSTRACT

Many in public life seek to master the artful dodge, frequently attempting to wriggle out from answering questions they would rather avoid. Though perhaps most grating when performed by politicians, question-dodging occurs in a wide array of other contexts as well: from corporate executives avoiding reporters' requests for their expectations for the next fiscal quarter, to employees sidestepping their bosses' questions as to why they are late for the third straight day, to spouses evading their partners' inquiries as to their whereabouts the previous evening. Among relevant marketing and consumer domains, consider the public relations officers who deal with tough questions from consumers, regulators, and the media in the aftermath of product-safety crises; tactics in customer relationship management (CRM) for pacifying clients even when unable to actually solve their substantive problems; or a salesperson skillfully evading questions about the true value of buying dealership rustproofing for new car, or about the accident history of a used one.

But are such attempts to dodge successful? Most importantly, what determines whether a dodge is successful – when a speaker's answer to the wrong question goes unnoticed, and therefore unpunished? In the experiments that follow we show that dodges succeed when speakers respond to a question by responding with answers that *seem* to address the question, but which in fact address an entirely different, though similar, question. For instance, a politician in a debate asked about the illegal drug problem in America whose answer stresses the need for universal healthcare has engaged in a successful dodge if listeners have both forgotten that she was even asked about drugs, and evaluate her highly. Indeed, we show that in some cases, speakers end up better off by answering the *wrong* question well than the right question poorly.

Experiment 1. We asked participants to listen to a brief excerpt from a debate between two politicians. For the second politician, we varied the question asked – about healthcare, the illegal drug problem, or the War on Terror – but this politician always gave the same answer about healthcare. Thus we varied whether the politician answered the question asked (about healthcare), a similar question (the drug problem), or a dissimilar question (the War on Terror). As predicted, results showed that when the politician answered a similar question, participants forgot the original question – a successful dodge – and rated him highly; in contrast, when the politician answered a dissimilar question, participants noticed the effort to dodge and penalized him accordingly. Overall, speakers could get away with dodging questions without punishment when answering a question similar to the one asked. In everyday life, of course, people usually attempt to dodge questions when they are not prepared with a good answer to the question asked – for example, when an employee's boss pops into her office unannounced to inquire as to her lateness, leaving her to stammer through a poorly phrased answer.

Experiment 2. In experiment 2, we compared the efficacy of dodging questions by answering a similar question to bumbling through an answer to the actual question. Results showed that providing a good answer to a similar question resulted in evaluations similar to providing a good answer to the actual question (replicating experiment 1); most interestingly, providing a good answer to a similar question resulted in *higher* interpersonal ratings than answering the actual question poorly. How might we improve people's ability to detect dodges? Interestingly, television networks have taken steps to curtail politicians' efforts to dodge questions during political debates by posting the question asked of politicians for the duration of their answers. We tested the efficacy of this procedure in the next experiment.

Experiment 3. Participants watched the same excerpt as in experiment 1; as before, we varied the question asked of the second politician – about healthcare or the illegal drug problem – and the politician always answered about healthcare. In addition, however, we also added two conditions which were identical to these, except that in both versions, the text of the question remained on the screen while the politician answered; here, we expected participants to notice the effort to dodge. As in experiments 1 and 2, without the aid of the question on the screen, dodging by answering a similar question was quite successful. In contrast, participants who were aided by having the actual question on the screen were nearly as good at remembering the actual question as those who heard the politician answer the actual question.

Discussion. These results suggest that the emerging strategy used by television networks to increase viewers' ability to recall the original question does in fact increase the detection of dodges. In many real-world situations, however, similar interventions are unlikely to be feasible: it would be difficult to ask an acquaintance or salesperson to hold up a sign indicating what question he was meant to be answering, for example. Accordingly, increasing dodge detection in everyday social and consumer interactions may be no easy task. At the same time, intervening to reduce the incidence of successful dodging is essential if we wish to reverse the results from our second experiment, and ensure that those who answer the right question with substance are preferred over those who answer the wrong question with style.

The Persuasive Power of Contradicting Oneself

EXTENDED ABSTRACT

When people seek to persuade others, or gain their support, they often do so by conveying a consistent message, or repeating their arguments and opinions. Indeed, past research suggests that, compared to stating an argument or expressing an opinion just once, repeating that argument or opinion can make it seem more valid or true (Begg et al., 1992), which can give it more persuasive impact (Moons et al., 2009). Despite the intuitive appeal of this strategy, and empirical support for its potential value, we explore the possibility that under some conditions contradicting oneself (e.g., initially opposing something and then later supporting it) can offer a persuasive advantage. In particular, we test the hypothesis that some message sources are more persuasive when they deliver conflicting rather than consistent messages. The rationale is that, assuming recipients trust the source of a message, that source can induce the perception that he or she gathered new information by contradicting him- or herself. As a consequence, message recipients can be induced to process more deeply via contradictions, which promotes persuasion in response to strong arguments. We investigate this notion across 3 experiments.

Experiment 1. Participants were randomly assigned to receive different kinds of advice. In every condition, they were told to imagine that they had sought medical advice from a friend regarding a suspicious mole on their arm. In the *conflicting advice* condition, the friend was initially reassuring (saying that there is no reason to worry), but then changed his mind a few days later (saying that on second thought, it would be a good idea to remove the mole in order to conduct a biopsy). In the *time 1 advice only* condition, the friend initially suggested that it would be a good idea to remove the mole to conduct a biopsy. In the *time 2 advice only* condition, the friend recommended the biopsy after a few days. The rationale for getting the biopsy was identical across conditions. We varied merely the timing

of this recommendation, and whether it had been preceded by different advice. Results indicated that participants found the advice more compelling and were more likely to remove the mole in the conflicting advice condition than in either of the one-time advice conditions, which did not differ from one another.

Experiment 2. Next, we sought to replicate this effect in a different setting, and explore the underlying mechanism. All participants received advice (or a persuasive recommendation) twice, but we varied whether it was consistent or conflicting. Undergraduate students read about a friend who offered his opinion about a new university policy on two different occasions. In the *consistent message* condition, the friend expressed a positive opinion on both occasions in which the topic was raised, elaborating on his opinion and the arguments in favor of the policy on the second occasion. In the *conflicting message* condition, the friend expressed an initial negative opinion followed by a change of mind a week later, at which time he elaborated on his opinion and the arguments in favor of the policy. To permit a test of processing differences, we also manipulated argument strength such that the friend offered strong or weak reasons to implement the policy on the second occasion. Results indicated a significant interaction between message consistency and argument strength on attitudes. Argument strength had a greater effect on attitudes in the conflicting message condition than in the consistent message condition, consistent with the notion that conflicting messages can stimulate greater processing. Viewed differently, under strong but not weak argument conditions, the conflicting message produced more favorable attitudes than did the consistent message. Moreover, this processing difference stemmed from participants' perception that the source of the message had gathered new information between the first and second time he offered his opinion.

Experiment 3. In experiment 3, we sought to show that a conflicting message would only foster increased processing when the source was trusted. The rationale was that only when people trust the source should they make favorable attributions (to acquiring new information) based on the contradictory messages. Here we used the same core paradigm as in experiment 2, but we manipulated the trustworthiness of the source prior to the delivery of the message. As predicted, there was a three-way interaction between message consistency, trustworthiness, and argument quality. This three-way interaction involved 2 two-way interactions of opposing patterns. Under high trust conditions, we replicated the effects from experiment 2. Under low trust conditions, we found a significant message consistency × argument quality interaction but in the opposite form. In this case, the argument quality effect was significant in the consistent message condition but not in the conflicting message condition. Thus, contradicting oneself before offering strong arguments can promote persuasion under high trust conditions, but it backfires under low trust conditions. Consistent with our information processing perspective, these effects were mediated by thought favorability.

Discussion. In summary, conventional wisdom and past research suggest that if a persuader seeks to change someone's attitude, he or she would benefit from delivering a consistent and/or repetitive message. In contrast, our research suggests that contradicting oneself, or changing one's mind, can sometimes offer a persuasive advantage. Our findings are consistent with an information processing account, suggesting that a conflicting message can grab attention and increase message processing under some conditions. This increased processing, in turn, can promote persuasion when strong arguments have been presented. Implications for understanding numerous counterintuitive means of influencing attitudes and behavior will be discussed.

From Blemishing to Blossoming:
The Positive Effect of Negative Information

EXTENDED ABSTRACT

Imagine that you are considering a new restaurant and reading reviews of it online. Most of the reviews are very good: Great food, pleasant music, relaxed atmosphere. Then you come across a review that mentions that there is no parking nearby, a piece of information that is negative but not quite central to your value proposition for restaurants. How does this small dose of negative information influence the positive impression you had begun to form of the restaurant? Could this weak piece of negative information actually enhance your positive reaction? Intuition and past research generally suggests that if weak negative information has any effect at all, it ought to be negative—that is, it should undermine the favorable impression you had begun to form. In contrast to this notion, we propose that weak negative information can sometimes bolster, or intensify, initial favorable impressions arising from positive information.

The rationale for this effect is that when consumers receive negative information after already receiving positive information, especially if that negative information is relatively minor and just "blemishes" the product, it ironically highlights or increases the salience of the positive information. This boosts the impact of the positive information and fosters more positive evaluations. Of importance, though, if true, this effect should only occur when negative information follows positive information, and when consumers' processing effort is relatively low as low processing orients consumers toward primacy effects and makes them less likely to thoughtfully consider the negative implications of subsequent negative information (Kruglanski and Webster 1996). We present four experiments investigating this *blemishing effect*.

Experiment 1. This initial experiment sought to test the hypothesis that, under conditions of low processing effort, consumers might evaluate a product more favorably when they received a weak negative piece of information about it following positive information. To test this hypothesis, we presented participants with all positive (5 positive attributes) or both positive and negative (4 positive and 1 negative attribute) information about a pair of hiking boots under high or low processing conditions, and then measured their interest in purchasing the boots. To manipulate processing effort we used a divided attention task adapted from past research (e.g., Fitzsimons and Williams 2000). Results indicated the predicted interaction, such that under low processing conditions, participants were more interested in purchasing the boots when they were presented with a weak negative attribute compared to when they were presented with only positive attributes. Under high effort conditions, this effect was reversed.

Experiment 2. This second experiment aimed to replicate the effect in a field setting. Students were approached on campus either immediately prior to taking an exam (low processing [high distraction] condition) or while they were simply walking around outside (i.e., high processing [low distraction] condition) and were offered a chocolate bar. In the *positive only condition*, the experimenter listed three positive attributes. In the *positive + weak negative condition*, the experimenter also briefly mentioned that the chocolate bar was a bit broken. We found a significant interaction, such that under low processing conditions, participants purchased more chocolate bars when a negative attribute was mentioned than when there was only positive information. By contrast, under high processing conditions, participants purchased more chocolate bars when there was only positive information presented.

Experiment 3. This experiment was designed to demonstrate the effect measuring individual differences is processing. Participants first completed a holistic-analytic processing measure (Choi, Koo, and Choi 2007) and then read a description of some champagne glasses. In the *positive only condition* just one positive attribute was featured. In the *positive + weak negative condition* the product's description included the same positive attribute along with a minor negative—that the glasses did not come in a hard box. After reading the description, participants indicated the extent to which they would be willing to try the champagne glasses. As predicted, we found an interaction on willingness to try. Holistic (low effort) thinkers reported greater willingness to try the product when its description included negative information rather than only positive information. In contrast, analytic (high effort) thinkers reported more willingness to try the product when only positive information was presented.

Experiment 4. Finally, in experiment 4 we tested the role of presentation order. Participants under high or low processing conditions (manipulated using a divided attention task) received a list of favorable attributes for a pair of hiking boots along with a picture of the boots showing damaged packaging (a slightly blemished box). We manipulated whether participants read the positive information and then saw the negative picture, or saw the negative picture and then read the positive information. As hypothesized, participants under low processing conditions evaluated the boots more favorably when they received positive and then minor negative information rather than minor negative and then positive information. Participants under high processing conditions showed no difference, evaluating the boots more moderately regardless of when the negative feature was presented. We also found mediation evidence in this experiment— low processing participants saw the positive attributes as more positive (and the negative as less negative) when the negative information followed rather than preceded the positive information, and these perceptions mediated overall product evaluations. In addition, we ruled out several competing accounts in this study—e.g., those based on two-sided message perceptions or perceived source/ information authenticity effects.

Discussion. Overall, we obtained substantial support for the blemishing effect. When processing effort is low, providing consumers with positive information followed by a minor piece of negative information appears to enhance their overall evaluations of a target relative to providing exclusively positive information. This effect stems from low-effort processors tendency toward primacy effects, which are bolstered or intensified by the later appearance of conflicting information. High-effort processors, by contrast, appear to form more modest evaluations when negative information is included, regardless of its timing. Implications for understanding other ironic effects in persuasion and choice are discussed.

REFERENCES

Aaker, Jennifer, Kathleen D. Vohs, and Casse Mogilner (2010), "Nonprofits Are Seen as Warm and for-Profits as Competent: Firm Stereotypes Matter," *Journal of Consumer Research*, 37, 224-37.

Begg, Ian M., Ann Anas, and Suzanne Farinacci (1992), "Dissociation of Processes in Belief: Source Recollection, Statement Familiarity, and the Illusion of Truth," *Journal of Experimental Psychology: General,* 121(4), 446-458.

Briñol, P., Richard E. Petty, C. Valle, and Derek D. Rucker (2007), "The Effects of Message Recipients' Power before and after Persuasion: A Self-Validation Analysis," *Journal of Personality and Social Psychology*, 93 (Dec), 1040-53.

Choi, Incheol, Minkyung Koo, and Jong An Choi (2007), "Individual Differences in Analytic Versus Holistic Thinking," *Personality and Social Psychology Bulletin*, 33 (5), 691-705.

Cuddy, Amy J. C., Susan T. Fiske, and Peter Glick (2008), "Warmth and Competence as Universal Dimensions of Social Perception: The Stereotype Content Model and the Bias Map," in *Advances in Experimental Social Psychology*, P. Zanna Mark, Ed. Vol. Volume 40: Academic Press, 61-149.

Dillard, James P., and Michael Pfau (2002). *"The persuasion handbook : developments in theory and practice, "* Thousand Oaks, Calif: Sage Publications.

Fitzsimons, Gavan J. and Patti Williams (2000), "Asking Questions Can Change Choice Behavior: Does It Do So Automatically or Effortfully?," *Journal of Experimental Psychology: Applied*, 6 (3), 195-206.

Galinsky, Adam D., Deborah H. Gruenfeld, and Joe C. Magee (2003), "From Power to Action," *Journal of Personality and Social Psychology.* 85(3), 453-466.

Galinsky, Adam D., Joe C. Magee, Deborah H. Gruenfeld, Jennifer A. Whitson, and Katie A. Liljenquist (2008), "Power Reduces the Press of the Situation: Implications for Creativity, Conformity, and Dissonance," *Journal of Personality and Social Psychology*, 95, 1450-66.

Kipnis, David (1972), "Does power corrupt? " *Journal of Personality and Social Psychology, 24*(1), 33-41.

Kruglanski, Arie W. and Donna M. Webster (1996), "Motivated Closing of The Mind: "Seizing" And "Freezing"," *Psychological Review*, 103 (2), 263-283.

Magee, Joe C. and Adam D. Galinsky (2008), *"The Self-Reinforcing Nature of Social Hierarchy: Origins and Consequences of Power and Status,"* Academy of Management Annals (Ed.) Vol. 2.

Moons, Wesley G., Diane M. Mackie, and Teresa Garcia-Marques (2009), "The impact of repetition-induced familiarity on agreement with weak and strong arguments," *Journal of Personality and Social Psychology,* 96 (1), 32-44.

Petty, Richard E., and Duane T. Wegener (1998), Attitude change: "Multiple roles for persuasion variables," In D. Gilbert, S. Fiske, & G. Lindzey (Eds.), *The handbook of social psychology* (4th ed., pp. 323-390). New York: McGraw-Hill.

Van Kleef, Gerben A., Christopher Oveis, Ilmo van der Löwe, Aleksandr LuoKogan, Jennifer Goetz, and Dacher Keltner (2008), "Power, Distress, and Compassion: Turning a Blind Eye to the Suffering of Others," *Psychological Science*, 19, 1315-22.

Achieving Our Goals: Some Tips and Tricks

Chair: Julia Belyavsky Bayuk, University of Delaware

Paper #1: A Life in Balance or a Slippery Slope?: Exploring the Use and Effectiveness of Moderation versus Avoidance Self-Control Strategies

Kelly Haws, Texas A&M University, USA
Cait Lamberton, University of Pittsburgh, USA
Hristina Dzhogleva, University of Pittsburgh, USA
Gavan Fitzsimons, Duke University, USA

Paper #2: It is Just Too Easy: Impact of Planning on Effort and Behavior

Julia Bayuk, University of Delaware, USA
Juliano Laran, University of Miami, USA

Paper #3: Consider it Done! The Cognitive Effects of Unfulfilled Goals are Eliminated by Making a Plan

E. J. Masicampo, Tufts University, USA
Roy Baumeister, Florida State University, USA

Paper #4: In Praise of Putting Things Off: Postponing Consumption Pleasures Facilitates Self-Control

Nicole Mead, Catholic University of Portugal, USA
Vanessa Patrick, University of Houston, USA

SESSION OVERVIEW

Every day, consumers strive to achieve a wide array of short-term and long-term goals. These goals range from very specific goals, such as giving up dessert at dinner, to more abstract goals, such as living a healthy lifestyle. Regardless of the type of goal, the strategies that people adopt are often maladaptive. The objective of this session is to highlight research that examines goal achievement strategies in a fresh yet rigorous manner. Together, the four papers stimulate a new understanding of when and why goal achievement strategies are effective and when they prove to be detrimental. Thus, we present some "tips and tricks" for when various strategies of goal-pursuit will be optimal for goal achievement. Together, these papers suggest that often an avoidance strategy, rather than a moderation strategy, is beneficial; it can be better not to plan rather than plan out the way to achieve our goal; plans can free thoughts and attention for unrelated tasks and goals; and postponing consumption of hedonic goods can ultimately lead to decreased consumption, and thus a greater likelihood of goal achievement.

Kelly Haws, Cait Poynor Lamberton, Hristina Dzhogleva and Gavan Fitzsimons begin the session by examining several potential strategies towards goal pursuit, and show that moderating, rather than eliminating, indulgence or exposure to temptation can prove to be an effective self-control strategy. Specifically, in three studies they find that when a self-control task is easy, a moderation strategy may be advisable, but that when a self-control task is difficult, the same person may undermine their own progress by adopting a moderation strategy. Julia Bayuk and Juliano Laran look at the effects that planning has on the likelihood of goal achievement. They find that planning can lead people to feel that the necessary steps are not very effortful, which can lead to a decreased likelihood to engage in the goal directed behavior. Hence, plans can at times backfire. E. J. Masicampo and Roy Baumeister complement that work with an examination of how planning for a goal affects other, unrelated pursuits. They show that just making a plan is enough to get people to reduce the amount of thinking and attention they dedicate to an unfulfilled goal, freeing thoughts and attention for other interests. Lastly, Nicole Mead and Vanessa Patrick look at postponement of he-

donic consumption as a strategy for goal achievement. They find that postponing consumption of a hedonic temptation to an unspecified future time reduces desire for and consumption of that hedonic item.

Together, these papers evaluate some commonly used strategies to achieve a goal, show when these strategies may actually backfire and when they can be effective, and "build connections" amongst a variety of consumer researchers. This session should be of great interest to consumer researchers studying goals or self-control, as well as to those interested in public policy. This work has many implications for consumer well-being as people often pursue, yet fail to achieve, goals such as saving money or losing weight. We truly hope that it will encourage interaction and collaboration amongst the numerous consumer researchers studying different aspects of goals–from goal selection and commitment, to goal planning and goal pursuit, to goal disengagement.

All of the papers in the session are works in progress, and have at least two studies completed.

A Life in Balance or a Slippery Slope? Exploring the Use and Effectiveness of Moderation versus Avoidance Self-Control Strategies

EXTENDED ABSTRACT

Though decades of self-control research have identified numerous techniques to help consumers better achieve their goals, we still have relatively little insight into the conditions under which specific techniques may be more or less fruitful. The present research compares the use and efficacy of two frequently utilized self-control strategies: moderation and avoidance (Hoch and Loewenstein 1991). Moderation involves the consumption of some measured quantity of pleasurable good or experience in keeping with pre-established consumption limits. By contrast, avoidance entails not consuming any of the "forbidden fruit," perhaps even going out of one's way to avoid all exposure to a potential temptation.

Clearly, in some areas of life complete avoidance is advocated. For example, alcoholics may choose to allow no alcohol in their homes or avoid circumstances where drinking is likely to occur. Apparently aware of this fact, consumers often categorize their world of options as acceptable or "off-limits" in order to facilitate goal achievement (Poynor and Haws 2009). However, research also suggests that moderation, rather than complete avoidance, may have positive outcomes. For example, "cold turkey" approaches may lead to detrimental outcomes when strict regulations backfire, prompting a desire for greater indulgence (Cochran and Tesser 1996, Finkelstein and Fishbach 2010). Incorporating some small amount of indulgence into one's life, in fact, may neither harm long-term goals nor preclude one from long-term satisfaction (Krishnamurthy and Prokopec 2010; Haws and Poynor 2008).

Such work suggests that moderating, rather than eliminating, indulgence or exposure to temptation can prove to be an effective self-control strategy. But what determines the relative use and efficacy of moderation as opposed to avoidance strategies for a given individual? We suggest that chronic or situational self-control capabilities moderate the use and effectiveness of these two approaches. Specifically, chronically good self-controllers tend to both choose to moderate more often and find more success in doing so. Further, when put in a moderation mindset, individuals with higher self-control exhibit more successful self-regulation than do lower self-control individuals. Finally, we find that within any given individual, context-specific control capabilities drive their success with moderation as opposed to avoidance strategies. Whereas self-control tasks seen as easy can be managed using either avoidance or moderation, difficult self-control tasks likely require avoidance to be successfully pursued.

In study 1, 137 consumers (41% male, M_{age} = 32.63), reported agreement with statements focused on moderation ("I try to find moderation in my life") and more extreme avoidance strategies ("I tend to think of life in terms of all or nothing."). These responses were combined to create a relative moderation focus. Respondents also provided individual self-control ratings (Tangney et al. 2004) and reported their experience with a number of life outcomes – achievement of diet goals, the presence of harmful addictions, exercise, and subjective well-being. Results showed that higher self-control individuals showed stronger moderation focus than did lower self-control individuals ($p < .001$). Importantly, individuals with a stronger moderation focus tended to achieve their diet goals, were less likely to have addiction issues, exercised more frequently, and were happier overall (all $p < .05$). As such, initial evidence suggests that moderation strategies may be more common and effective for higher as opposed to lower self-control consumers.

But can we show that use of a moderation strategy is, in fact, more successful for higher as opposed to lower self-control individuals? Study 2 followed a 2 (moderation v. avoidance prime) x continuously measured eating self-control design. Undergraduate participants (n = 114) wrote short essays about the virtues of either moderation ("everything in moderation") or avoidance ("staying away from temptation"). As part of a subsequent task participants indicated how much that they would like to eat each item on a list of snacks at that moment. Separately, we assessed individual differences in eating self-control (e.g., Giner-Sorolla 2001). Results showed that those who more easily practiced eating restraint showed a higher desire for healthy as opposed to unhealthy foods ($p < .0001$). However, a significant interaction of primed strategy and individual eating self control also emerged ($p < .0001$). Individuals primed with an avoidance strategy showed similar patterns of healthy consumption regardless of their level of self-control ($p >.8$). However, in the moderation condition, consumers high in self-control increased their tendency toward healthy consumption while those lower in self-control decreased their preference for healthy food alternatives. Here, a moderation strategy seemed to be more effective than avoidance, but *only* for consumers higher in self-control in this domain. For consumers who struggle to control their eating, a moderation mindset generated a slippery slope, prompting greater indulgence than an avoidance mindset.

Taken together, results suggest that when a self-control task is easy, a moderation strategy may be advisable, but that when a self-control task is difficult, doing so may undermine goal progress. To test this general theory, study 3 asked participants to rate a series of self-control challenges in terms of their personal difficulty. They then read a scenario presenting a self-control problem in each domain, and stated their likelihood of adopting a moderation or avoidance strategy as well as their anticipated success in each. Results indicate that individuals believe that avoidance strategies will be equally effective regardless of the difficulty of a self-control task. However, participants felt that moderation strategies would yield better results on easier as opposed to harder self-control problems, and thus, showed a higher likelihood to moderate on easy tasks. Given our prior results, these expectations are appropriate for higher self-control individuals, but suggest a reason why lower self-control

individuals, mistakenly applying moderation strategies, may fail to see progress toward their goals.

Overall, this research aims to help consumers more effectively achieve their long-term goals. While for some individuals, and in some areas, moderation strategies may lead to a happy and well-balanced life, we all have weak spots. In these domains, results suggest that avoidance, rather than moderation, is a surer path to self-control success.

REFERENCES

Cochran, Winona and Abraham Tesser (1996), "The "What the Hell" Effect: Some Effects of Goal Proximity and Goal Framing on Performance.," in *Striving and Feeling: Interactions among Goals, Affect, and Self-Regulation.*, Vol., ed. Leonard L. Martin and Abraham Tesser, Hillsdale, NJ: Lawrence Erlbaum Associates, Inc, 99-120.

Finkelstein, Stacey R. and Ayelet Fishbach (2010), "When Healthy Food Makes You Hungry," *Journal of Consumer Research*, 37 (October), In press.

Giner-Sorolla, Roger (2001), "Guilty Pleasures and Grim Necessities: Affective Attitudes in Dilemmas of Self-Control.," *Journal of Personality and Social Psychology*, 80 (2), 206-21.

Haws, Kelly L., William O. Bearden, and Gergana Y. Nenkov (2011), "Consumer Spending Self-Control Effectiveness and Outcome Elaboration Prompts," forthcoming at *the Journal of the Academy of Marketing Science*.

Haws, Kelly L. and Cait Poynor (2008), "Seize the Day! Encouraging Indulgence for the Hyperopic Consumer," *Journal of Consumer Research*, 35 (4), 680-91.

Hoch, Stephen J. and George F. Loewenstein (1991), "Time-Inconsistent Preferences and Consumer Self-Control," *Journal of Consumer Research,* 17 (March), 492-506.

Krishnamurthy, Parthasarathy and Sonja Prokopec (2010), "Resisting That Triple-Chocolate Cake: Mental Budgets and Self-Control," *Journal of Consumer Research*, 37 (June), 68-79.

Poynor, Cait and Kelly L. Haws (2009), "Lines in the Sand: The Role of Motivated Categorization in the Pursuit of Self-Control Goals," *Journal of Consumer Research*, 35 (5), 772-87.

Rozin, Paul, Kimberly Kabnick, Erin Pete, Claude Fischler, and Christy Shields (2003), "The Ecology of Eating: Smaller Portion Sizes in France Than in the United States Help Explain the French Paradox," *Psychological Science*, 14 (5), 450-54.

Shiv, Baba and Alexander Fedorikhin (1999), "Heart and Mind in Conflict: The Interplay of Affect and Cognition in Consumer Decision Making," *Journal of Consumer Research*, 26 (3), 278-92.

Tangney, June P., Roy F. Baumeister, and Angie L. Boone (2004), "High Self-Control Predicts Good Adjustment, Less Pathology, Better Grades, and Interpersonal Success," *Journal of Personality*, 72 (2), 271-324.

Wansink, Brian, Collin R. Payne, and Pierre Chandon (2007), "Internal and External Cues of Meal Cessation: The French Paradox Redux?," *Obesity*, 15 (12), 2920-24.

It is Just Too Easy: Impact of Planning on Effort and Behavior

EXTENDED ABSTRACT

Consumers live busy lives and often search for ways to simplify them. When the options available are limited, consumers are able to make decisions more easily and become more likely to purchase a product (Iyengar and Lepper 2000; Tversky and Shafir 1992). In addition, easy processing of information has been shown to affect an individual's liking for both products and advertisements (Labroo and Kim 2009; Schwarz 2004). Common sense also suggests that people would rather do things that are easy than things that require effort. Nevertheless, some research on the effect of ease of performing an action on product evaluations and goal-directed behaviors suggests that people often prefer to engage in behaviors that are more difficult and effortful to execute (Gollwitzer and Brandstatter 1997; Locke et al. 1981; Norton, Mochon, and Ariely 2010). This paper builds on this work and examines how forming a plan to perform a behavior (e.g., purchase a product, experience, or service) affects the perception of effort required to execute the behavior, and in turn, how the effort required influences the likelihood to engage in the behavior. Forming a plan and knowing what needs to be done should make it easier to execute the necessary activities. Thus, forming a plan could lead to a lower perception of effort. We propose that perceptions of higher effort increase consumers' likelihood of performing a behavior. Because forming a plan may decrease perceptions of effort associated this behavior, this may decrease consumers' likelihood of performing the behavior in certain circumstances. We test our propositions with three studies that examine the effect of planning on perceptions of effort and on behavior.

Study 1 shows that forming a plan to engage in a behavior can decrease a person's intention to engage in the behavior. The study employed a 2 (Vacation Type: related to plan vs. unrelated to plan) by 2 (Form Plan: no vs. yes) between-subjects design. All of the participants were told about a cruise vacation, and approximately half of the participants formed a plan to go on the cruise (specify how and when they would book the trip), whereas the other half did not. Results showed that participants who formed a plan to book the cruise stated that they would be less likely to go compared to those who did not form such a plan. To show that the effect is specific to the behavior for which the plan was formed, and not any related behavior, we also asked participants to estimate their likelihood to go on a trip to an alternative destination (Last Vegas), and found that the likelihood to book did not differ depending on whether or not participants formed a plan to book the cruise. Overall, this study shows that planning can lead to a decreased likelihood to engage in a behavior.

Study 2 uses real behavior to show that, when the amount of activities necessary to perform a behavior is high, the performance of a target behavior will seem more effortful for people who form a plan compared to those who do not form a plan, which will increase engagement in the behavior among people who have formed a plan. This two-part study employed a 2 (Effort: moderate vs. high) by 2 (Form Plan: no vs. yes) between-subjects design. During the first part, half of the participants formed a plan specifying how they will save money by dining out less in the upcoming weeks, whereas the other half did not. Effort was manipulated by varying how many things (e.g., going to grocery store more, purchasing groceries, cooking at home) participants were explicitly asked to consider when forming their plan. Exactly a week later, all of the participants were contacted by e-mail and asked how much they spent on dining out in the past week. We found that in the moderate effort condition, forming a plan led to significantly greater spending on dining out compared to not forming a plan. However, in the high effort condition, forming a plan led to significantly lower spending on dining out compared to not forming a plan.

Lastly, study 3 examines how a common marketing occurrence, a price change, affects an individuals' intention to engage in a behavior (purchase a product) after forming a plan to do it. It shows that

when a price increase occurs, consumers who form a plan perceive the behavior to be more effortful, and are more likely to make the purchase compared to consumers who do not form a plan. The study employed a 2 (Price Change: no vs. yes) by 2 (Form Plan: no vs. yes) between-subjects design. As in Study 2, some participants form a plan to book a trip to Brazil, whereas others do not. The key dependent variable was participant's likelihood to book the trip. When no price change occurred, participants who formed a plan were less likely to book the trip, and believed the booking process to be less effortful. When the price changed, participants who formed a plan became more likely to perform a target behavior compared to those who did not form a plan. Perceptions of effort increased among those who formed a plan, but decreased among those who did not. The effect of the interaction between price change and plan on likelihood to book the trip is fully mediated by the perceived effort required to engage in the behavior.

In summary, forming a plan is often beneficial, but primarily when engaging in the necessary behaviors seems highly effort once a plan has been made. The challenge is to teach people when planning will be beneficial, versus detrimental, to their aspirations. Making people feel like the necessary activities to perform a behavior are easy will decrease engagement in the behavior when a plan has been formed. In these cases, "not forming a plan" is the best advice people might receive.

REFERENCES

Gollwitzer, Peter M. and Veronika Brandstätter (1997), "Implementation Intentions and Effective Goal Pursuit," *Journal of Personality and Social Psychology*, 73 (July), 186–99.

Iyengar, Sheena S. and Mark R. Lepper (2000), "When Choice is Demotivating: Can One Desire

Too Much of a Good Thing?," *Journal of Personality and Social Psychology*, 79 (December), 995–1006.

Labroo, Aparna A. and Sara Kim (2009), "The 'Instrumentality' Heuristic: Why Metacognitive

Difficulty is Desirable During Goal Pursuit," *Psychological Science*, 20 (January), 127–34.

Locke, Edwin A., Karyll N. Shaw, Lise M. Saari, and Gary P. Latham (1981), "Goal Setting and

Task Performance: 1969-1980," *Psychological Bulletin*, 90 (July), 125–52.

Norton, Michael I., Daniel Mochon, and Dan Ariely (2010), "The 'IKEA Effect': When Labor

Leads to Love," Working Paper, Harvard Business School, Boston, MA.

Schwarz, Norbert (2004), "Metacognitive Experiences in Consumer Judgment and Decision

Making," *Journal of Consumer Psychology*, 14 (4), 332–48.

Tversky, Amos and Eldar *Shafir (1992),* "Choice under Conflict: The Dynamics of Deferred

Decision," *Psychological Science*, 3 (November) 358–61.

Consider it Done!:
The Cognitive Effects of Unfulfilled
Goals are Eliminated by Making a Plan

EXTENDED ABSTRACT

The human mind is remarkably well designed for goal pursuit. Attention, perception, thoughts, and attitudes all become tuned to help one pursue a goal. The mind vigorously promotes this intense focus on a goal, protecting it from distractions and resuming it after it has been interrupted. Even when one is not consciously working toward a goal, the mind keeps the goal active in the unconscious, maintaining vigilance for opportunities to fulfill it. Thus, once a goal is chosen, the mind has many processes to promote its pursuit. The standard view has held that the various cognitive processes related to unfulfilled goals cease when the goal is attained. This view has been favored in theories of goal pursuit and has found support in empirical research. However, the present investigation tested the hypothesis that many of the goal promotion processes can cease long before attainment — specifically, when a plan is made.

Planning has been studied recently in the form of implementation intentions, which are highly specific prescriptions for what to do under what circumstances (Gollwitzer, 1999). Such plans turn control of goal pursuit over to automatic, unconscious processes, which can resume goal pursuit at the appropriate time or place specified in the given plan. Once a plan is made, the unconscious knows how and when to act, and so in a sense the uncertainty of the unfinished task is resolved. The implication then is that a plan may render many of the cognitive activities related to the goal unnecessary. We predicted that contributing to goal pursuit through plan making could satisfy the various cognitive processes that usually promote goal pursuit, thereby causing them to cease.

In each of the studies reported, we activated unfulfilled goals and measured the extent to which they persisted in the mind during later tasks. In Study 1, participants selected tasks or goals from their own lives that needed to be done, and then we measured how much people's minds wandered while reading a novel that had nothing to do with the unfulfilled tasks. Unfulfilled tasks made people's minds wander, thereby reducing their ability to read and understand the novel. But participants who made a plan to get their personal tasks done were able to read with less mind wandering. Despite having had an unfulfilled goal activated, they exhibited few intrusive thoughts about their goals and were relatively well able to read and concentrate on material unrelated to their goals.

Studies 2 and 3 examined goal accessibility. In Study 2, participants reflected on an upcoming final exam, and thoughts related to doing well on the exam remained highly accessible during a later word stem completion task. This effect was eliminated, however, among participants who made a plan for when and how to study for the exam. Study 3 examined the accessibility of means of goal achievement. It used one goal that most young people embrace (to live a fit and healthy life) but that remains unfulfilled for most. Reflecting on this unfulfilled goal caused the various means of reaching it to become highly accessible, as indicated by goal-relevant answers on a word completion task. Once again, having made a plan eliminated the effect. Study 3 also showed that the various effects (persistent activation over time as well as reduced activation after planning) were obtained mainly among participants for whom the unfulfilled goal had high personal importance.

Study 4 replicated the effects of plans using an experimentally assigned task. The unfulfilled goal to do well on a later laboratory task interfered with performance on a separate, unrelated task in the interim (solving anagrams). Making a plan eliminated the interference effect as in the previous studies. More important, Study 4 showed that most participants did actually follow the plans they had made — and the degree to which they followed their plans was closely linked to the improvement in performance on the anagram task. Thus, the more people made plans that they were actually going to use, the more they were freed from intrusive thoughts about the unfulfilled goal while working on the unrelated task. To put it another way: What reduced cognitive activity from unfinished tasks

was making highly specific plans that were actually going to be used to finish those tasks.

By planning for their goals, people can better manage their multiple pursuits. It has been well documented that specific plans increase success (Gollwitzer, 1999), and they do so in part by making pursuit of the goal more automatic. When a detailed plan has been made, one no longer has to think about the goal to fulfill it (Brandstätter, Lengfelder, & Gollwitzer, 2001). Apparently, a plan can also reduce the amount of thoughts and attention that are typically recruited in service of an unfulfilled goal. Thoughts of an incomplete goal do not necessarily persist until the goal is fulfilled – making a plan is sufficient to eliminate the various cognitive effects of unfulfilled goals. Planning may therefore represent a crucial strategy for the management of multiple goals. By planning for a goal, one can free one's thoughts and attention for other pursuits.

REFERENCES

Gollwitzer, Peter M. (1999), "Implementation Intentions: Strong Effects of Simple Plans,"
American Psychologist, 54, 493-503.
Brandstätter, Veronika, Angelika Lengfelder, and Peter M. Gollwitzer (2001), "Implementation
Intentions and Efficient Action Initiation," *Journal of Personality and Social Psychology*, 81, 946-960.

In Praise of Putting Things Off: Postponing Consumption Pleasures Facilitates Self-Control

EXTENDED ABSTRACT

Many approaches to self-control assume that people have two, albeit suboptimal, options when faced with a tempting yet unwanted pleasure – *give in* to or *give up* the pleasure (Baumeister, Heatherton, and Tice 1994; Baumeister and Heatherton 1996; Giner-Sorolla 2001; Kivetz and Keinan 2006; Myrseth, Fishbach, and Trope 2009). Giving in entails a short burst of pleasure, but is quickly overrun by feelings of guilt for transgressing from long-term goals. In contrast, giving up a temptation is just plain psychologically painful and taxing. Research indicates that deprivation typically backfires, leading to increases rather than decreases in consumption (e.g., Vohs and Heatherton 2000). In the current research, we investigate a third option, postponement, which was hypothesized to facilitate self-control in the face of consumption pleasures without feelings of self-denial or loss.

Postponement entails "having it later", whereas deprivation mandates "not having it at all". Thus, although postponing means not consuming in the present, it allows people to consume, albeit at a later date. Postponement was briefly suggested as a desire-reduction strategy (Hoch and Loewenstein 1991) but to date has received scant (if any) empirical attention. In three experiments, we tested whether postponement can in fact reduce desire for a hedonic consumption pleasure, and whether this reduction in desire in turn facilitates self-control. We theorize that in the short run, postponement 1) reduces the motivational conflict associated with giving in versus giving up a tempting option, and, consequently, 2) encourages self-control by dampening the desire for the affectively powerful temptation. In the long run, we hypothesize that the lack of reinforcement helps ensure that the already weakened hedonic impulse continues to decay, thereby facilitating self-control. In all three experiments, described next, the short- and long-run consequences of postponement were compared to the two outcomes most frequently investigated in self-control research, satiation (giving in) and deprivation (giving up). In experiment 2, a delay of gratification condition (giving up on a small reward now to obtain a larger reward later) was also included.

In experiment 1, we tested the behavioral consequences of postponement for both short and long-term consumption. At time 1, participants were asked to watch a short film-clip. Ostensibly to enhance the feeling of actually being in the movies, a bowl of M&Ms was placed in front of participants. Participants randomly assigned to the *satiation* condition were allowed to eat freely. Those participants assigned to the *deprivation* condition were asked not to eat any of the M&Ms. Participants in the *postpone* condition were asked not to eat the M&Ms; instead they could have a snack later on, if they liked. At the end of the experiment, all participants were given the opportunity to eat M&Ms in private. Results indicated that participants in the postpone condition ate fewer M&Ms than participants in the deprivation condition. Consistent with work indicating that satiating the desire for a particular item reduces subsequent intake (McSweeney and Sindell 1999; Rolls, Rolls, Rowe, and Sweeney 1981), the postpone and satiate conditions were not significantly different from one another. At time 2, one day after the experiment, participants were emailed and asked to indicate their desire for M&Ms. As expected, postpone participants reported a lower desire to eat M&Ms than the other two experimental conditions. Finally, at time 3, one week after the experiment, participants indicated how much chocolate they had eaten since the experiment. Results indicated that participants in the postpone condition ate less chocolate over the course of the week, relative to the satiation and postpone conditions. Desire for chocolate 24 hours after the completion of the experiment fully mediated the effect of the manipulation on consumption over the week.

Experiments 2 and 3 were designed to assess the psychological mechanisms underlying the effect of postponement on decreased consumption. Our hypothesis was that postponement alleviates the motivational conflict between deprivation and satiation, allowing the reflective system to dominate and the impulsive system to dissipate. In experiment 2, we used an implicit measure to determine whether the hedonic or reflective system was dominant (e.g., Hofmann, Friese, and Strack 2009). Participants in the postpone condition showed heightened activation of the reflective system, whereas participants in the satiation and deprivation conditions showed heightened activation of the hedonic system. Moreover, participants in the postpone condition reported the lowest desire to eat dessert as well as the lowest levels of deprivation and loss. As expected, the delay of gratification condition mirrored the deprivation condition in terms of hedonic activation. In experiment 3, participants asked to postpone eating ice cream reported a reduced desire to eat ice cream, relative to participants assigned to the deprivation and delay of gratification conditions. Taken together, results of experiments 2 and 3 suggest

that postponement activates the reflective system, the seat of self-control, and dampens the hedonic affective response to consume the hedonic good.

In sum, results from three experiments suggest that postponing consumption activates the reflective system and reduces the affective desire for the hedonic good, enabling participants to forego consumption of hedonic pleasures, in both the short- and long-term. Theoretically, results suggest that postponement has different effects on the reflective and impulsive systems as compared to the two most common avoidance strategies – deprivation and delay of gratification. Practically, postponement seems to be a strategy that enables consumers to manage transient hedonic desires.

REFERENCES

Baumeister, Roy F., Todd F. Heatherton, and Dianne M. Tice (1994), *Losing Control: How and Why People Fail at Self-Regulation.* San Diego, CA: Academic Press.
Baumeister, Roy F. and Todd F. Heatherton (1996), "Self-Regulation Failure: An Overview," *Psychological Inquiry*, 7 (3), 1-15.
Giner-Sorolla, Roger (2001), "Guilty pleasures and grim necessities: Immediate and deliberative affective attitudes in dilemmas of self-control," *Journal of Personality and Social Psychology, 80*, 208-21.
Hoch, Stephen J. and George F. Loewenstein (1991), "Time-Inconsistent Preferences and Consumer Self-Control," *Journal of Consumer Research*, 17 (March), 492-507.
Hofmann, Wilhelm, Malte Friese, and Fritz Strack (2009), "Impulse and self-control from a dual systems perspective," *Perspectives on Psychological Science, 4(2)*, 162-76.
Kivetz, Ran and Anat Keinan (2006), "Repenting Hyperopia: An Analysis of Self-Control Regrets," *Journal of Consumer Research*, 33 (September), 273–82.
McSweeney, Frances K. and Samantha Swindell (1999), "General-Process Theories of Motivation Revisited: The Role of Habituation," *Psychological Bulletin,* 125 (4) 437-57.
Myrseth, Kristian Ove R., Ayelet Fishbach, and Yaacov Trope (2009), "Counteractive self-control: When making temptation available makes temptation less tempting," *Psychological Science, 20*, 159 – 63.
Rolls, Barbara J, Edmund T. Rolls, Edward A. Rowe, and Kevin Sweeney (1981), "Sensory Specific Satiety in Man," *Physiology & Behavior*, 27(1), 137-42.
Vohs, Kathleen D. and Todd F. Heatherton (2000), "Self-Regulation Failure: A Resource-Depletion Approach," *Psychological Science*, 11 (May), 249-54.

Disposing: Constructing and Structuring Consumption

Chair: Meltem Ture, Bilkent University, Turkey

Paper #1: An Exploration of Consumers' Use of Disposing Practices in their Daily Lives

Meltem Ture, Bilkent University, Turkey
Guliz Ger, Bilkent University, Turkey

Paper #2: Doing Family through Practices of Disposal: Enacting Affiliation and Sacrifice through the Consumption of Food Leftovers

Benedetta Cappellini, University of London, UK
Elizabeth Parsons, Keele University, UK

Paper #3: Recycling: Yes But Caring for my Loved Ones First! Exploring Identity Conflicts Amongst "Green" Working Mothers

Iain Black, The University of Edinburgh, UK
Helene Cherrier, Griffith University, Australia

SPECIAL SESSION

Consumption consists of three stages: acquisition, usage and disposition (Jacoby et al. 1977, Holbrook 1987), with the first two gaining more attention from consumer researchers. Few exceptional studies include examinations of the effects of personal and situational factors on consumers' disposition decisions (e.g. Jacoby et al. 1977) and the symbolic, emotional, and ritualistic aspects of disposition (e.g. Lastovicka and Fernandez 2005). At ACR, the sessions and papers that pertain in some way to disposing have focused on issues such as environmental concerns (Alwitt and Berger 1993), charity behavior (Lee and Strahilevitz 2004), intergenerational flow of heirlooms (Heisley 1997), or rites of passages (Ozanne 1992). These rare inquiries demonstrate how studying disposing might contribute to our understanding of consumer identity projects, charity behavior, policy making and environmentalism, and the improvement of product design processes. Nevertheless, there is still much to be discovered about disposing per se and its relationship to various consumption practices. Moreover, disposing is an important area of research, now even more so than ever, due to the increasing concerns for wasting, sustainability and over-consumption.

Mindful of this state of affairs, the *Journal of Consumer Behavior* recently published a special issue on disposing. Some of the papers in that issue indicate that disposing empowers consumers (Cherrier 2009), blurs the boundary between commodity and private possession (Denegri-Knott and Molesworth 2009), bridges the past and subsequent consumption practices (Cappellini 2009) and is embedded in individual and societal values (Albinsson et al. 2009). Moving on from that 2009 issue and broadening the conceptualizations of disposition, this session shows that disposing is actually a very rich context that sheds light on and connects various topics consumer researchers have long been fascinated with. Overall, the session aims to explore a number of questions such as: How do different disposing practices create different meanings for consumers? How does disposing help consumers negotiate and deal with various (and usually conflicting) norms and identities? How do disposing practices change with lifestyle changes? And perhaps more importantly, how and what do consumers "create" through a practice that has long been regarded as the terminal stop for objects or the end of consumption, and how do practices of disposal fold back to those of consumption?

In the first paper, Ture and Ger explore the practices and processes of disposing in their relationship to the constructions and evaluations of consumers' own consumption. The authors indicate that various manners of disposing serve consumers in dealing with the conflicting ideologies and norms: the consumerist ethos of the modern consumer society they live in and the traditional norms of sociality and caring. The second study investigates disposing in the context of food consumption and preparation. Cappellini and Parsons demonstrate how the divestment of leftovers influences the planning of the meal, cooking, and storing; and thus, reveal a hierarchical pattern of weekly meals. They indicate that disposal-consumption circularity contributes to family cohesion. The third study explains how consumers' multiple roles relate to the modification of disposal practices. Focusing on working women who attempt to adapt to a "greener" lifestyle, Black and Cherrier reveal that becoming green necessitates new disposing practices and is managed through the processes of assimilation, negotiation, and rejection. However, these practices and how they are performed are contingent upon the hierarchical nature of the conflicting identities these women juggle. For all the three studies included in the session, data collection and analyses have already been completed.

The papers presented in this session provide a cross-cultural examination of disposing in a diversity of consumption contexts. In doing so, we show that disposing, as broadly construed, constitutes a site where some of the most important topics in consumer research (e.g. family construction, identity conflict, norms of consumption) overlap and intersect. As such, this session contributes to consumer behavior by moving consumer researchers towards a more comprehensive picture of "consuming". Also, focusing on disposing as an inseparable part of the consumption cycle helps us to understand not only issues such as over-consumption but also the processes through which consumers achieve, preserve or redefine desired identities and relations with others. Furthermore, we provide implications for policy makers on topics such as prevention of wasting and promotion of recycling or increasing the sustainability of products.

The session, with its presentations drawing from a diverse range of disposing contexts, bridges important topics of consumer research and is expected to be of interest to a significant amount of ACR attendees. However, we believe that researchers particularly concerned with family and individual identity formation, waste management and sustainability, and ideological aspects of consumption will benefit from the session most. With Jonathan Schroeder, who has significant works on identity, cultural aspects of consumption and gender, as our discussant, we expect this session to nurture a lively and productive discussion environment. The last 15-20 minutes of our session will be reserved for discussions, which will be guided by Jonathan Schroeder to build connections between the papers, motivate audience-presenter dialogue and underline the overall significance of the session.

An Exploration of Consumers' Use of Disposing Practices in their Daily Lives

EXTENDED ABSTRACT

In the consumer behavior literature, disposition of possessions has mostly been studied as a process through which consumers physically and emotionally detach from their possessions (Wallendorf and Young 1989). During times of transitions, disposing helps consumers cut ties with previous roles and adjust to new roles by cleansing the person from the old self and stabilizing the new identities (Schouten 1991). In the context of old age, where consumers engage in a review of life, disposition is found to be useful in dealing with concerns for continuation of legacy and self-extension (e.g. Price et al. 2000, Marcoux 2001). These studies imply that strategic choices of when and to whom to dispose special possessions are used by consumers to create a desirable memory, gain symbolic immortality, and re-construct and legitimize their relations with certain people.

Although these studies contribute greatly to our understanding of how consumers construct meanings through disposing and use it in their identity projects, there is still much to discover about disposing. In addition to its role with special objects and/or special situations, disposing is embedded, above all, in the more mundane sphere of consumption, and is mostly employed during routine practices such as ordering of wardrobes or arranging the children's rooms (e.g. Gregson 2007). But, could such ordinary activities really have important implications for consumption studies? Recent research provides promising evidence. For example, it was found that mundane activities of domestic life are as significant as the sacred practices in creating a life history for items, moving them in an out of a network of singularized objects, and meanwhile, establishing the family identity (Epp and Price 2010). Building on these studies, we intend to explore disposing as a network of mundane practices and uncover its connections to other consumption practices as well as to consumers' identity and lifestyle construction processes. Our aim is to understand how consumers engage in and experience various processes while disposing their items, and hence to discover the consequences of these processes. With these goals in mind, we conducted in-depth interviews with 16 middle and upper-middle class men and women in Turkey, aged between 29 and 58. We also had 62 undergrad students write essays about their experiences with disposing their items. Specifically, they wrote about what items they usually dispose as well as when and how they dispose of these items. In addition, they were encouraged to reveal what motivates them to adopt certain practices of disposing over the others.

We find that disposing consists of a network of practices that are rooted simultaneously in economical, moral, social and rational domains of consumption. As such, rather than just emancipate from (Cherrier 2009) or conform to (Norris 2004) particular norms, consumers use disposing in order to negotiate conflicting norms. Both the interviews and student essays point that, living in a transitional society, our participants encounter a tension between rising consumerism and traditional social values as projected in their everyday life. They resort to disposing in order to be able to continue to consume in a relatively guilt-free manner. For example, our participants are able to un-alienate themselves by passing their items onto people in need (especially after a shopping spree) without having to compromise their consumption. That is, mundane practices of disposing serve as a bridge between the ethos of consumerism and ideals of social cooperation, solidarity, or caring for others.

Our findings also shed light on the specific ways through which disposing relates to other consumption experiences. Previous research has shown relationships between timing of disposing and the timing and financing of new acquisitions (eg. DeBell and Dardis 1979). Going beyond time and money issues, we indicate that consumers use particular manners of disposing to classify, define, and rationalize their previous or subsequent consumption. For instance, while engaging in "luxury" or "unnecessary" shopping practices, consumers predict the disposal of the items they are about to acquire, and depending on such predictions, re-define their shopping experience as "a good bargain" or even "altruistic", which facilitates the buying process. Possible discrepancies between the predicted and actual disposing episodes usually lead consumers to reflect on their past purchases and readjust their behavior at subsequent shopping trips. Consumers refer to their manners of disposing as they construct and evaluate their past consumption experiences and make decisions about the future ones.

We suggest that analyzing disposing in the realm of everyday consumption practices furnishes new insights about consumption as well as the processes and meanings of disposing. Our findings have clear implications regarding the perceived morality of consumption. In addition, our results have implications for policy makers who would like to enhance consumers' adoption of sustainable consumption and recycling activities, and for charity organizations who want to increase their donations.

Doing Family through Practices of Disposal: Enacting Affiliation and Sacrifice through the Consumption of Food Leftovers

EXTENDED ABSTRACT

This paper contributes in two key ways to our understandings of disposal. First it identifies the circularity of consumption and disposal, in particular how the meanings surrounding the processes and practices of disposal fold back into those of consumption (Thompson 1979, Gregson et al. 2007). Second, through anthropological concepts of consumption as affiliation (Douglas and Isherwood 1980) and as sacrifice (Miller 1998) it explores the ways in which the circularity of disposal contributes to family cohesion and belonging. These two aspects of disposal are investigated through an ethnographic study on everyday food consumption practices of 20 British families. The study seeks to understand how consumption of leftovers influences other consumption practices such as planning the meal, cooking and storing. It also seeks to understand how the consumption of leftovers provides a vehicle for both roles and relations in the household and the sense of family's belonging.

In general, divestment practices remain a neglected area in consumer research (Parsons and Maclaran 2009). The indifference to the topic is probably related to the marketing assumption that disposal is the last stage of goods trajectory (production-consumption-disposal) and as such it does not require particular attention (Hetherington 2004). In contradiction with this common assumption recent studies assume that disposal matters. By criticizing Douglas' (1984 [1966]) analysis of the ways in which the social world is based on binary classifications of clean-in/dirty-out and the consequences for our relative understandings of consumption/disposal, Gregson et al. (2007) point out that divestment (how, where, and when people place things) is also a consumption practice wherein "dirty" goods can be re-evaluated and re-become clean. Indeed in their divestment practices people do not simply move things out, rather they "move things along" (Gregson et al. 2007, 198) and designate them to a specific somewhere (i.e. charity shops, the street, a friend's home). Similarly Munro (1995) assumes that divestment is a consumption practice. Food disposal, which consists of multiple conduits, "has implication for the acquisition, cooking and ingestion stages in the process" (Munro 1995, 324) and as such it is part of the circularity, rather than the linearity, of food consumption. We argue here that it is through displacement that people both narrate the social order (the normative) (Gregson et al. 2007) and their belonging to it (Munro 1995). It is in fact through the continuous movement of things and owners that people materialize what such norms might be and reconstitute the self, the others and their relations with them (Gregson et al. 2007).

A first finding confirms the circularities of consumption, finding that disposal has an important impact on the entire process of food provision. In particular practices "of moving leftovers along" reveal a common hierarchical pattern of meals on a weekly basis. Leftovers are usually produced during the most important meal of the day (domestic dinner, the only cooked meal at home during working days) and they are moved to the following day's lunch or dinner. They are also usually produced during the weekend meals and moved along during the weekday dinners. Therefore the leftovers "are moved horizontally" from a weekday dinner to another weekday dinner and are "moved vertically", down, in the weekly structure of the meals from a higher position to a lower one "weekend meals-weekday dinners", "weekday dinner- weekday lunch".

A second finding confirms that disposal is an act of affiliation to the family. Participants perceive leftovers consumption as a sacrifice, a thrift practice (Miller 1998), consisting of saving resources to be donated to an object of devotion. Indeed participants describe their consumption of leftovers as a sacrifice wherein hybrid food is transformed and re-used for a meal. This concept of 'hybrid food' encapsulates food that is neither clean nor dirty (Douglas (1984 [1966]) having been displayed previously, but not yet been cast out. Consumption of this hybrid food requires a higher degree of affiliation to the family than clean food. Resources (such as time, effort and money) saved in reusing leftovers are then invested in extraordinary food consumption, such as family celebrations, wherein the family is celebrated as an object of devotion. As others point out, in such extraordinary occasions, intimate and non intimate guests are admitted to celebrate the family. What has not been underlined is that it is not only in extraordinary food consumption that family is celebrated; rather it is in the everyday sacrifice of consuming leftovers that the affiliation to the family is reinforced and perpetuated.

This paper contributes to the current consumer research on disposal in two ways. Firstly it highlights how divestment practices are incorporated in the circular process of domestic food consumption. Moving leftovers along reveals not simply the participants' weekly hierarchical pattern of the meals but also the circular process of saving resources in ordinary meals and spending such resources in extraordinary meals. Indeed the sacrifice of consuming leftovers by family members is addressed to produce excess value which will be spent in extraordinary food occasions wherein the family as a whole entity is celebrated. Secondly this paper highlights that consuming leftovers requires a high degree of affiliation to the family, and only family members are admitted to a meal based on leftovers. Thus it is not only in extraordinary food occasions that family members reaffirm their affiliation to the household, but it is also in their everyday sacrifice that they reconstitute their object of devotion, which is the family itself.

Recycling: Yes but caring for my loved ones first! Exploring Identity Conflicts amongst "Green" Working Mothers

EXTENDED ABSTRACT

Researchers have documented that professional working mothers experience conflicting personal and social expectations. On the one hand, they strive toward self-directed accomplishments such as professional development; and on the other hand, they try to preserve traditional motherhood values for care of the children (Thompson 1996). In managing these conflicting expectations, these supermothers often opt for unsustainable consumption practices such as convenience consumption (Reilly 1982; Reilly and Wallendorf 1987) or buying pre-processed foods (Thompson 1996). As these women experience accelerated time frame, they do not often have to time and energy to integrate sustainable waste management in their lifestyle (Godbey et al. 1998).

This research considers the notions of juggling lifestyles and identity conflicts for professional working mothers who, with the goal of consuming in a more sustainable fashion, had recently diminished the amount of waste they generate and had integrated recycling as their main disposal practice. This group typically has multiple roles and identities, such as mother, wife, homemaker, employee, and friend. We conducted in-depth interviews with six middle and upper class, professional working mothers, who lived in Toronto and moved away from wasteful practices, deliberately lowered their household waste generation and integrated recycling into their lives as a daily chore. By studying this group and probing on reasons for changing their practice of disposal, insights were gained into how recycling and sustainable waste management are performed and how such practices are influenced by self and social positions. Our analysis revealed how sustainable disposal (lower waste generation and recycling) is achieved by assimilation, negotiation or rejection.

It is clear that the findings can be effectively represented and understood using a framework of identity conflicts and strategies used to manage these conflicts (Swann 1987, Murray 2002, Ahuvia 2005). The mothers demonstrated a high level of knowledge and commitment to performing a wide range of sustainable behaviors. As well as being aware of the general concerns about the state of the ecosystem, they talked in detail about specific environmental issues such as greenhouse gas emissions, rubbish disposal and pollution in air, water and food. They also discussed what they saw as the consequences of these issues, with global warming and health problems attributed to specific concerns. It was also common for a clear link to be made between environmental concerns, the potential consequences of this and their motivation to act (based on their identity as mothers). Interestingly, few mentions were made about wanting to reduce overall consumption levels, though informants did want to reduce the impact of this consumer lifestyle and dispose accordingly. It was clear that the informants want to remain within the current consumerist society but also want it reformed. For the informants, one of the most accessible changes toward sustainability was to modify their practice of disposal. All informants integrated practices of recycling and reduced the household waste production. It was issues surrounding motherhood such as pregnancy, birth of a baby or pressure from their children that motivated these changes.

Each informant discussed how within their daily lives they performed several different roles; which contributed to a range of different social positions. It is conflict between the behaviors and values inherent within social positions and the subsequent management of this conflict that, it is argued here, can help explain change in disposal practices: moving from heavy waste generation and throwing away to limited waste generation and recycling. When exploring the conflicts and how these working mothers manage to integrate recycling in their daily routines, we did not find Ahuvia's (2005) "Demarcating," "Compromising" and "Synthesizing" strategies. Rather, when managing conflicting social positions between mother, professional worker and green consumer, our informants' interviews expressed an "assimilation" strategy. Sustainable disposal by "assimilation" is a process of rejecting, accepting or modifying the new disposal practice where rather than leading to the negotiated merging of the conflicting identities (as present in Ahuvia's synthesizing approach), values and meanings of sustainable disposal, are assimilated into prominent "core" identities without changing them. This allows respondents to reduce their amount of waste and the adoption of recycling to occur within personally and socially acceptable boundaries.

The respondents described how despite disposing of modes of behavior that they had performed for many years and then adopted different practices, they had not changed to become other identities such as radical conservationists nor had their identity as a mother changed. For example, Katherine talked about stopping the waste linked to using strong chemical household cleaners. In order to modify her waste production, she started using vinegar and baking soda but in doing so, the meaning of this sustainable disposal practices was assimilated into her conceptualization of herself as a mother *without* changing it. Here we have an example of sustainable disposal without disposing of the meaning of the practice; instead some of the meaning is transferred on to a new behavior that does not cause conflict between her multiple roles. Assimilation appears to occur because of the hierarchical nature of the conflicting identities and the central importance of motherhood to these women's sense of self. These properties do not exist in Ahuvia's examination of loved objects (2005) or Mick and Fournier's (1998) technical paradoxes.

REFERENCES

Ahuvia, Aaron. C. (2005), "Beyond the Extended Self: Loved Objects and Consumers' Identity Narratives," Journal of Consumer Research, vol.32, 171-84.

Albinsson, P. and B.Y. Perera (2009). "From Trash to Treasure and Beyond: The Meaning of Voluntary Disposition", Journal of Consumer Behavior, vol.8, 340-353

Alwitt, L.F. and Ida E. Berger (1993), "Special Session Summary: Consumer Behavior Processes as Bases to Segment the "Green" Marketplace: Applications to Solid Waste Disposal", Advances in Consumer Research, vol.20,188

Cappellini, B. (2009) "The Sacrifice of Re-use: The Travels of Leftovers and Family Relations", Journal of Consumer Behavior, vol.8, 365-375

Cherrier, H. (2009). "Disposal and Simple Living: Exploring the Circulation of Goods and the Development of Sacred Consumption", Journal of Consumer Behavior, vol.8, 327-339

DeBell, M. and R. Dardis (1979). "Extending Product Life: Technology isn't the Only Issue". Advances in Consumer Research. vol.6, 381-385

Denegri-Knott, J and M. Molesworth (2009)."'I'll Sell This and I'll Buy Them That': eBay and the Management of Possessions as Stock" Journal of Consumer Behavior, vol.8, 305-315

Douglas, M (1984 [1966]) Purity and Danger: an Analysis of the Concept of Pollution and Taboo, London, Routledge.

Epp, Amber M. & L.L. Price (2010). "The Storied Life of Singularized Objects: Forces of Agency and Network Transformation". Journal of Consumer Research, vol.36, 820-837

Gregson, Nicky (2007) Living with Things: Ridding, Accommodating, Dwelling. Sean Kingston Publishing: UK

Gregson N., A. Metcalfe and L. Crewe (2007) "Moving Things Along: the Conduits and Practices of Divestment in Consumption", Transactions of the Institute of British Geographers, vol.32, 187-200.

Godbey, Geoffrey, Reid Lifset, and John Robinson (1998), "No Time to Waste: An Exploration of Time Use, Attitudes toward Time, and the Generation of Municipal Solid Waste," Social Research, vol.65, 101-15.

Heisley, Deborah D. (1997), "Special Session Summary: the Intergenerational Flow of Wealth in the Family", Advances in Consumer Research, vol.24, 242-243

Hetherington K. (2004) "Secondhandedness: Consumption, Disposal and Absent Presence". Environment and Planning D: Society and Space, vol.22, 157-173.

Holbrook, M.B. (1987). "What is Consumer Research?", Journal of Consumer Research, vol.14, 128-132

Jacoby, Jacob, Carol K. Benning and T.F. Dietvorst (1977). "What about Disposition?" Journal of Marketing. vol.41, 22-28

Lastovicka, John L. and Karen V. Fernandez (2005), "Three Paths to Disposition: The Movement of Meaningful Possessions to Strangers," Journal of Consumer Research, vol.31, 813-823

Lee, S.N. and M.A. Strahilevitz (2004), "Special Session Summary: Feeling Badly Helps: Negative Affect and Giving Behavior", Advances in Consumer Research, vol.31, 27-27

Marcoux, Jean-Sebastien (2001). "The 'Casser Maison' Ritual: Constructing the Self by Emptying the Home". Journal of Material Culture. vol. 6, 213-235

Miller, D. (1998) A Theory of Shopping, Ithaca New York, Cornell University Press.

Mick, David G. and Susan Fournier (1998), "Paradoxes of Technology: Consumer Cognizance, Emotions and Coping Strategies," Journal of Consumer Research, vol.25, 123-143.

Munro R. (1995) "The Disposal of the Meal", in Food Choice and the Consumer, ed. D. Marshall, Glasgow: Chapman&Hall, 313-325.

Murray, Jeff B. (2002),"The Politics of Consumption: A Re-inquiry on Thompson and Haytko's (1997) "Speaking of Fashion", Journal of Consumer Research, vol.29, 427-440.

Norris, Lucy (2004). "Shedding Skins: The Materiality of Divestment in India", Journal of Material Culture. vol. 9, 59–71

Ozanne, Julie L. (1992), "The Role of Consumption and Disposition During Classic Rites of Passage: The Journey of Birth, Initiation, and Death," Advances in Consumer Research Volume, vol.19, 396-403.

Parsons E. and P. Maclaran (2009) "'Unpacking Disposal': Introduction to the Special Issue" Journal of Consumer Behaviour, vol.8, 301-304.

Price, Linda, E. Arnould, and C. Curasi (2000). "Older Consumers' Disposition of Valued Possessions". Journal of Consumer Research, vol.27, 179-201

Reilly, Michael D. (1982), "Working Wives and Convenience Consumption," Journal of Consumer Research, vol.8, 407-418.

Reilly, M. D. and M. Wallendorf (1987), "A Comparison of Group Differences in Food Consumption Using Household Refuse," Journal of Consumer Research, vol.14, 289-295.

Schouten, John W. (1991),"Personal Rites of Passage and The Reconstruction of Self", in Advances in Consumer Research, vol.18, 49-51.

Swann, William. B (1987), "Identity Negotiation: Where Two Roads Meet," Journal of Personality and Social Psychology, vol.53, 1038-51.

Thompson, M. (1979) Rubbish Theory, Oxford, Oxford University Press.

Thompson, Craig J. (1996), "Caring consumers: Gendered consumption meanings and the Juggling Lifestyle," Journal of Consumer Research, vol.22, 388-407.

Wallendorf, M., and Young, M. M. (1989) "Ashes to Ashes, Dust to Dust: Conceptualizing Consumer Disposition of Possessions", Marketing Theory and Practice, AMA Winter Educators Conference, 33–38

Wallendorf M. and E. Arnould (1991) "We Gather Together: Consumption and Rituals of Thanksgiving Day", Journal of Consumer Research, vol.18, 13-31.

Deciphering the Cognitive Sources of Creativity

Chairs: Haiyang Yang, INSEAD, Singapore
Amitava Chattopadhyay, INSEAD, France
Darren Dahl, University of British Columbia, Canada

Paper #1: Exploring the Role of External Rewards in Creative Cognition

Ravi Mehta, University of British Columbia, Canada
Rui (Juliet) Zhu, University of British Columbia, Canada
Darren Dahl, University of British Columbia, Canada

Paper #2: Grounded Cognition, Spatial Working Memory and Category Experience as Influencers of Creative Imagination

José Antonio Rosa, University of Wyoming, USA
Julie Ruth, Rutgers University, USA
William J. Qualls, University of Illinois at Urbana-Champaign, USA

Paper #3: Unconscious Creativity: The Impact of Deliberation-Without-Attention Duration on Creative Ingenuity

Haiyang Yang, INSEAD, Singapore
Amitava Chattopadhyay, INSEAD, Singapore
Kuangjie Zhang, INSEAD, France
Darren Dahl, University of British Columbia, Canada

SESSION OVERVIEW

From the zealous adoption of innovative products such as the iPhone and Wii, to the widespread passion for do-it-yourself goods, today's consumers not only value creative aspects of the goods they consume but also enjoy engaging in creative activities themselves (Dahl and Moreau 2007). To win the hearts of these consumers and thrive in a competitive global market, firms have to constantly innovate and develop creative products and services. Interestingly, though deciphering the sources of creative ingenuity is clearly important for both consumer satisfaction and corporate success, research on creativity within this context has been relatively limited (Burroughs and Mick 2004; Moreau and Dahl 2005). The purpose of this proposed special session is to draw the attention of consumer researchers to this domain, to present recent research findings, and to foster a discussion of potentially interesting questions regarding the cognitive mechanisms underlying creativity and thus spark future research. In the first of three research presentations, Mehta, Zhu, and Dahl investigate the interplay between motivations and cognitive mechanisms underlying creativity. Their research reconciles the disparate findings on the effects of monetary versus social rewards on creativity performance, and sheds light on how different motivations engender different cognitive processes. The second presentation by Rosa, Ruth, and Qualls examines how grounded cognition (i.e., modality-specific systems for vision, action, affect, etc.) and spatial working memory affect different aspects of creativity, and how consumer knowledge moderates these effects. Finally, the third presentation by Yang, Chattopadhyay, Zhang, and Dahl explores the impact of unconscious thought on creativity. These researchers show that longer duration of unconscious deliberation can actually harm, rather than boost, creativity, and that the superiority of unconscious thought pertains only to the novelty dimension of creativity but not the appropriateness dimension. Following the presentation of these research papers, James E. Burroughs, who has done extensive work in the area of creativity, will lead a discussion on the broad questions and issues pertaining to cognitive processes underlying creativity.

Contributions: This special session contributes to the ACR conference in several ways. Through the three presentations on different aspects of creativity and implications for consumers and firms, we bring researchers' attention to creativity research in consumer context, fostering research interests in this domain. Further, we highlight new theoretical development on the cognitive mechanisms underlying creativity, and the recent research findings on determinants and moderators of creativity. Finally, we initiate discussions among consumer researchers on the theory development and future research directions in this domain.

Likely Audience: This session would appeal to a wide range of consumer researchers, such as those interested in creativity, cognition, memory, motivation, and unconscious thought.

"Exploring the Role of External Rewards in Creative Cognition," Mehta, Zhu, & Dahl

EXTENDED ABSTRACT

Nearly three decades of research has fallen short of reaching a consensus regarding the effects of various kinds of external rewards (e.g., monetary versus social rewards such as recognition) on creativity. Some research suggests that monetary vis-à-vis social rewards reduce intrinsic motivation and are hence detrimental to creativity (Amabile 1982). While, other research suggests that monetary rewards may enhance intrinsic motivation and hence creativity, especially when the rewards are contingent on the creativity of the outcome (Eisenberger and Cameron 1996). Although, creativity is seen as a product of both motivational and cognitive processes (Runco and Chand 1995), this research has predominantly focused on motivational aspects of external rewards.

We propose that the disparate findings in the literature may stem from a limited understanding of the cognitive processes through which rewards affect creativity. Hence, in current work we address this paucity by examining the effect of rewards on cognitive processes that lead to creativity. Consistent with extant research, we focus on monetary and social-recognition rewards, and examine their impact on creativity when the contingency of the reward to the creative outcome is varied. We propose that these two rewards prompt different mental search strategies for idea generation and consequently affect creativity depending on the reward's contingency. Specifically, a social-recognition reward is likely to induce a broad and comprehensive search strategy. This is so because social rewards induce expectation of social scrutiny, which prompts individuals to engage in more broad and comprehensive information search to cover their bases (Tetlock 1983). In contrast, monetary reward induces a focused mindset and risk-seeking tendency (Eysenck and Eysenck 1982) and is hence, expected to encourage a more focused and narrower search strategy. Galileo System methodology is utilized to evaluate exploration of ideas in an individual's mental space.

Next, we propose that these alternative search strategies prompted by different rewards interact with reward contingency to jointly determine creativity. When rewards are not explicitly stated to be contingent on creativity, broader search for ideas inspired by a social-recognition reward should lead to greater creativity compared to when a monetary or no reward is offered. However, when rewards are contingent on creative performance i.e., a clear goal to be achieved is present, the focused exploration under monetary reward will occur in a domain distant from the mundane. This is because money besides prompting a focused mindset, also induces greater risk seeking tendencies (Coles, Daniel, and Naveen 2006). Thus we should observe greater creativity under monetary reward as compared to a social-recognition reward.

To test our hypotheses, we asked 146 participants to generate as many ideas as possible to reduce teenage smoking in a 3(Reward Type: Monetary vs. Social-recognition vs. No reward) x 2(Reward Contingency: Creative-outcome vs. Control) between-subjects study. The data was subject to sets of analyses to confirm our predictions. The first set of analyses examined the creativity of the ideas generated. Ratings from twelve judges on 4 items (creative, original, novel and innovative) were used to create a creativity index for each participant. ANOVA revealed that in the control condition, the ideas generated under social-recognition reward were rated as more creative than those generated under monetary or no reward conditions. No difference was observed between the latter two conditions. For contingency condition, ideas generated under monetary reward were rated as more creative than those generated under social-recognition reward which in turn was rated as more creative than those under no reward.

Next we tested respondents' ideation patterns in their mental space i.e. the underlying cognitive process that affects creativity. First, we ascertained the position of each generated idea in conceptual space using the Galileo System of multidimensional scaling. Two expert consumer judges provided distance estimates between the ideas generated by each participant. The distance estimate between any pair of ideas represents the dissimilarity between the two, such that the ideas that are more similar are closer to each-other than those that are more dissimilar. These distance estimates were submitted to the Galileo algorithm, which generated Cartesian coordinates for ideas generated within each treatment condition. An examination of the Cartesian plots and ANOVA showed that the social-recognition reward produced ideas that were more spread out i.e., the average distance between the ideas was higher as compared to monetary or no reward conditions irrespective of contingency of rewards.

Next we analyzed the location of exploration under different treatment conditions, vis-à-vis location of the most conventional idea. First, the most conventional idea was identified from the pool of all the generated ideas and then estimates were obtained for the distances between the most conventional idea and each of the other ideas generated by each participant. These estimates were input into the Galileo algorithm to obtain respective Cartesian coordinates. Analysis of the Cartesian plots and ANOVA for mean value of the distances between the most conventional idea and all other ideas generated by a participant showed that the location of exploration from the most conventional idea was farthest for the creativity contingent monetary reward as compared to all other conditions.

Thus, this work then demonstrates that although both monetary and social-recognition rewards can enhance creativity, they operate via different mechanisms: while social recognition reward encourages broader exploration leading to higher creativity, a monetary reward induces exploration within a narrow area. However, when rewards are contingent on creativity of the outcome this narrower exploration happens at a farther distance from mundane ideas leading to higher level of creativity.

"Grounded Cognition, Spatial Working Memory and Category Experience as Influencers of Creative Imagination," Rosa, Ruth, & Qualls

EXTENDED ABSTRACT

This study explores the influence of grounded cognition – modality-specific systems for vision, action, affect, etc – on the creative imagination of consumers. It has been argued that creativity, particular when it comes to products and their use, has multiple dimensions, such as functionality and novelty. It has also been argued that creativity draws on multiple mechanisms and sources, such as analogical reasoning, memory capabilities, pre-existing knowledge schemas, personal disposition, and affective state (e.g., Price and Ridgway 1982; Amabile 1996; Dahl and Moreau 2002; Burroughs and Mick 2004, Moreau and Dahl 2005, Burroughs, Moreau, and Mick 2008). The isolated influence on novelty and functionality of higher or lower levels of grounded cognition (Barsalou 1999, 2008), however, has not been explored in consumer research. Of necessity, exploring the influence of grounded cognition on creative imagination must take into account other factors likely to affect the process, such as a person's general capacity for conceptually manipulating known components into novel arrays (e.g., spatial working memory), and general knowledge of product categories that may guide creative efforts in the development of new entries to the category. Accounting for such additional factors is part of this study.

In two experiments, participants were asked to study three simple geometric shapes that were presented as either three-dimensional wood objects or line drawings of the objects. This constitutes the grounded cognition manipulation. Subsequent to studying the components for two minutes, they were asked to without access to the components, imagine product concepts that made use of all three components, draw and give names to their creations, explain how they work and briefly describe how they felt about their creations. The creative imagination outputs from participants were assessed by independent judges for novelty and functionality as indicators of creativity. Judges were also asked to assess how study participants felt about their creations from the narratives as a measure of engagement with the task. Spatial working memory capability was assessed based on gender (females typically having greater capacity) and general knowledge of product categories was controlled for by varying the categories (e.g., personal items, tools, toys) for which participants imagined product concepts in the second experiment.

Results show that higher levels of grounded cognition (e.g., greater sensory inputs gleaned from three-dimensional wood shapes) led to increased functionality in the imagined products, while the reduced level of grounded cognition from line diagrams induced higher novelty in some situations. In addition, consumers with higher spatial memory capacity (assumed in female participants) delivered products that were more novel and functional. The effects of grounded cognition and spatial working memory were moderated, however, by changes in product category, and the effects seem to be related to gender-based norms for product category familiarity. Overall the results affirm a role for grounded cognition in creative imagination among consumers, and suggest that the influence of grounded cognition and spatial working memory on creativity may be more complex than originally envisioned. Several areas for additional research were made clear by the results.

"Unconscious Creativity: The Impact of Deliberation-Without-Attention Duration on Creative Ingenuity," Yang, Chattopadhyay, Zhang, & Dahl

EXTENDED ABSTRACT

Though deciphering the sources of creative ingenuity is important for both consumer satisfaction and corporate success, research on creativity within this context has been relatively limited (Burroughs and Mick 2004; Moreau and Dahl 2005). Given the recent findings on the superior capabilities of unconscious thought (i.e., "deliberation in the absence of conscious attention directed at the problem," Dijksterhuis et al. 2006, p.1005) in processing complex information and decision making (Dijksterhuis 2004), it is reasonable to argue that unconscious deliberation has a role to play in facilitating creativity in consumer domains.

Indeed, pioneering research has found initial evidence supporting the positive impact of unconscious thought on creativity. For example, in one study (Dijksterhuis and Meurs 2006), participants were asked to list out Dutch place names starting with the letter "A" or letter "H." Whereas those who deliberated consciously generated more names of large cities and towns, those who deliberated unconsciously reported more names of small villages. This suggests that unconscious thought may have better access to unusual, prestored information. A subsequent study (Zhong et al. 2008) found that, for difficult remote association test (RAT) items, a short period of unconscious thought, as opposed to an equal duration of conscious thought, increased the speed at which participants were able to respond to the RAT items correctly. However, in this study, unconscious thought did not increase the number of correct answers provided by participants. Thus, despite encouraging findings, it is unclear how the power of unconscious thought can be adequately harnessed to improve actual creativity.

The current research seeks to fill this gap in the literature and sheds light on the conditions under which unconscious thought positively impacts creative ingenuity. We follow the conceptualization that impact of unconscious thought on creativity is a two-stage process (Zhong et al. 2008). In the first phase, unconscious deliberation generates creative ideas for the target task, resulting in "deep activation" of mental constructs representing these ideas (Wegner and Smart 1997). This deliberation is a goal-driven process (Bos et al. 2007) and is monitored unconsciously (Bongers and Dijksterhuis 2009; Moskowitz et al. 2004)—once the goal of generating creative ideas is deemed completed, the unconscious ceases to deliberate about the target task. Thus, even if an individual is allotted ample time for unconscious deliberation, that person might not deliberate unconsciously for the entire duration and could stop generating creative ideas early on. In the second phase, the fruit of the unconscious labor is outputted. Because this outputting (e.g., writing down ideas) is typically a conscious process, the deeply activated constructs need to emerge from the unconscious to the conscious to be successfully realized. However, because the activation of mental constructs decays rapidly (e.g., Kiefer and Spitzer 2000), the longer the gap between the time when the constructs were activated and the time when they are outputted, the fewer of these constructs would remain activated enough to be transferred to consciousness. Thus, the combined outcome of the goal directed generation phase of unconscious deliberation and the decay of unconsciously activated mental constructs results in an inverted-U shaped relationship between duration of unconscious thinking and creativity performance—when the duration of conscious thought is short, few constructs are generated and, thus, few constructs are available to be outputted. However, when the duration is too long, some or all of the found constructs

may no longer be sufficiently activated to be consciously realized. In contrast, conscious deliberation does not hinge on the transference of unconsciously activated mental constructs to consciousness. By definition, conscious thought makes the fruit of its labor consciously available. Further, because conscious thought operates at a significantly slower speed than unconscious thought (Dijksterhuis 2004), longer duration of conscious deliberation may be beneficial to creativity performance. Therefore, the creative output of unconscious deliberation is likely to be superior to that of conscious deliberation only when deliberation duration is moderate.

Moreover, creativity performance involves two dimensions—novelty and appropriateness (e.g., Amabile 1996). Given that unconscious thought has superior capabilities in searching and associating complex knowledge bases (Dijksterhuis et al. 2006), it is reasonable to predict that deliberation-without-attention can help identify and produce more novel ideas. However, unconscious thought theory (Dijksterhuis and Nordgren 2006) also states that conscious thought excels in precision processing and following rules and constraints, whereas unconscious thought is adept at producing rough estimates. Because appropriateness is characterized by producing solutions that meet the stringent constraints of the situation, it is thus unlikely that unconscious deliberation would lead to improvement on this dimension of creativity.

We tested these hypotheses in two experimental studies. In Experiment 1, participants were first shown the target task (i.e., write down things they can do with paperclips). Those who in the conscious-thought conditions were given one (vs. three vs. five minutes) to think about how to answer the question and then two more minutes to write down their responses. Those in the unconscious-thought conditions, however, spent the first period of time on a distraction task—a two-back lexical task; they were then given two minutes to write down their answers. Two independent judges evaluated each participant's responses in terms of novelty and appropriateness. Consistent with our predictions, a curvilinear relationship was found: The novelty rating of the ideas generated by participants, first increased with the duration of unconscious deliberation, and then decreased. Further, participants in the unconscious-thought conditions outperformed those in the conscious-thought conditions when the deliberation duration was three minutes, but not one or five minutes. Also consistent with our hypothesis, no difference on the appropriateness dimension was found between the thought conditions regardless of the deliberation duration.

Whereas Experiment 1 assessed the range and the quantity of creative ideas generated, Experiment 2 focused on investigating the impact of unconscious thought on the extent to which a *single* solution for a specific task is creative. The target task in Experiment 2, i.e., designing a toy for children, not only improved the ecological validity of our research, but also helped demonstrate the real-world implications of our findings. As expected, the results of Experiment 2 were consistent with those of Experiment1: Longer duration of unconscious deliberation actually harmed, rather than boosted, creativity performance. The creative output of unconscious thought was superior to that of conscious thought only when deliberation duration was moderate, and this superiority pertained only to the novelty dimension of creativity but not the appropriateness dimension.

REFERENCES

Amabile, Teresa M. (1982), "Children's Artistic Creativity: Detrimental Effects of Competition in a Field Setting," *Personality and Social Psychology Bulletin*, 8, 573-78.

Amabile, Teresa M. (1996), *Creativity in Context*. New York: Westview Press.

Barsalou, Lawrence W. (1999), "Perceptual Symbol Systems," *Behavioral and Brain Sciences*, 22: 577-660.

Barsalou, Lawrence W. (2008), "Grounded Cognition," *Annual Review of Psychology*, 59: 617-645

Bongers, Karin C.A. and Ap Dijksterhuis (2009), "Consciousness As a Trouble Shooting Device? The Role of Consciousness in Goal-pursuit," In *Oxford Handbook of Human Action*, ed. Ezequiel Morsella, John A. Bargh, and Peter M. Gollwitzer, New York: Oxford University Press, 589-604.

Bos, Maarten W., Ap Dijksterhuis, and Rick B. van Baaren (2008), "On the Goal-dependency of Unconscious Thought," *Journal of Experimental Social Psychology*, 44, 1114-20.

Burroughs, James R. and David G. Mick (2004), "Exploring Antecedents and Consequences of Consumer Creativity in a Problem Solving Context," *Journal of Consumer Research*, 31 (2), 402-411.

Burroughs, James R, David G. Mick, and Page C. Moreau (2008), "Toward a Psychology of Consumer Creativity," in C. Haugtvedt, P. M. Herr, & F. K. Kardes (Eds.), *Handbook of consumer psychology*, 1011-1038. New York: Taylor & Francis Group.

Coles, Jeffrey L., Naveen D. Daniel, and Lalitha Naveen (2006), "Managerial Incentives and Risk-taking" *Journal of Financial Economics,* 79, 431–468

Dahl, Darren W. and Page C. Moreau (2002), "The Influence and Value of Analogical Thinking During New Product Ideation," *Journal of Marketing Research*, 39 (February), 47-60.

Dijksterhuis, Ap (2004), "Think Different: The Merits of Unconscious Thought in Preference Development and Decision Making," *Journal of Personality and Social Psychology,* 87 (5), 586–98.

Dijksterhuis, Ap, Maarten W. Bos, Loran F. Nordgren, and Rick B. van Baaren (2006), "On Making the Right Choice: The Deliberation-without-Attention Effect," *Science,* 311 (5763), 1005–7.

Dijksterhuis, Ap and Teun Meurs (2006), "Where Creativity Resides: The Generative Power of Unconscious Thought," *Consciousness and Cognition,* 15 (1), 135–46.

Dijksterhuis, Ap and Loran F. Nordgren (2006), "A Theory of Unconscious Thought," *Perspectives on Psychological Science,* 1 (2), 95–109.

Eisenberger, Robert and Judy Cameron (1996), "Detrimental Effects of Reward," *American Psychologist*, 51 (11), 1153-66.

Eysenck, Michael W. and M. Christine Eysenck (1982), "Effects of Incentive on Cued Recall," *Quarterly Journal of Experimental Psychology*, 34(A), 489-498.

Kiefer, Markus and Manfred Spitzer (2000), "Time Course of Conscious and Unconscious Semantic Brain Activation," *Neuroreport,* 11 (11), 2401-17.

Moreau, C. Page and Darren W. Dahl (2005), "Designing the Solution: The Impact of Constraints on Consumer Creativity," *Journal of Consumer Research*, 32 (June), 13-22.

Moskowitz, Gordon B., Peizhong Li, and Elizabeth R. Kirk (2004), "The Implicit Volition Model: On the Preconscious Regulation of Temporarily Adopted Goals," in *Advances in Experimental Social Psychology,* Vol. 36, ed. Mark P. Zanna, San Diego, CA: Academic Press, 317-413.

Price, Linda L. and Ridgway, Nancy M. (1982), "Use Innovativeness, Vicarious Exploration and Purchase Exploration: Three Facets of Consumer Varied Behavior," in *AMA Educator's Conference Proceedings*, Bruce Walker, ed., 56-60.

Runco, Mark A. and Ivonne Chand (1995), "Cognition and Creativity," *Educational Psychology Review*, 7 (3), 243-67.

Tetlock, Philip E. (1983), "Accountability and Complexity of Thought," *Journal of Personality and Social Psychology*, 45 (July), 74-83.

Wegner, Daniel M. and Laura Smart (1997), "Deep Cognitive Activation: A New Approach to the Unconscious," *Journal of Consulting and Clinical Psychology,* 65, 984–95.

Zhong, Chen-Bo, Ap Dijksterhuis, and Adam D. Galinsky (2008), "The Merits of Unconscious Thought in Creativity," *Psychological Science*, 19 (9), 912-18.

The Waxing and Waning of Desire

Chairs: Kathleen Vohs, University of Minnesota, USA
Wilhelm Hofmann, University of Chicago, USA

Paper #1: How Best To Think about the Future: Which Outcome Elaboration Strategies Help Control Desire?

Gergana Nenkov, Boston College, USA
Kelly Haws, Texas A&M University, USA
Min Jung Kim, Texas A&M University, USA

Paper #2: Not All Health Claims Are Created Equal: Dissociating the Dynamics of Guilt and Desire Invoked by Food Indulgences

Suresh Ramanathan, Texas A&M, USA
Nina Belei, Maastricht University, The Netherlands
Kelly Geyskens, Maastricht University, The Netherlands
Caroline Goukens, Maastricht University, The Netherlands
Jos Lemmink, Maastricht University, The Netherlands

Paper #3: Engaging in Self-Control Intensifies Desires and Feelings

Kathleen Vohs, University of Minnesota, USA
Roy Baumeister, Florida State University, USA
Nicole Mead, Tilburg University, The Netherlands
Suresh Ramanathan, Texas A&M, USA
Brandon Schmeichel, Texas A&M University, USA

Paper #4: Everyday Temptations: An Experience Sampling Study on How People Control Their Desires

Wilhelm Hofmann, University of Chicago, USA
Kathleen Vohs, University of Minnesota, USA
Roy Baumeister, Florida State University, USA

SESSION OVERVIEW

At its core, marketing is about managing consumers' desires. Indeed, managing desires could be said to be the crux of the human condition. Hence this session brings together four papers that detail how consumers manage (or fail to manage) their desires. Some of the approaches, such as Nenkov et al's and Ramanathan et al's work, are centered on the cognitive aspect of controlling desire. Our first paper, Nenkov, Haws, and Kim, instructed participants to use different mental processes to imagine what will happen if they do or do not control their desires. Their findings about which processes are best to use, for whom, and when offers self-regulators two new cognitive tools to increase the odds that they will reach their goals. The second paper by Ramanathan et al will discuss the way that consumers react when they see health claims on food items. The mere mention of a hedonic attribute, such as fat content (even statements that a food is "low fat") makes foods more appealing, whereas functional attributes, such as a food's antioxidant content, makes them less appealing. Vohs and Hofmann's papers speak to the motivation and emotional components of desire. Vohs's work shows that one central reason that prior self-control leads to later self-control failure (the ego-depletion effect) is because people experience their desires as more potent – depleted people more than others feel their emotions more strongly, feel overtaken by powerful urges to eat, and so on. Hofmann took the idea of desire to the streets and collected data on more than 7000 naturally-occurring desires. His work demonstrates people's everyday attempts to control their desires, and how they are met with varying success. In summary, each paper takes a unique and novel tack on the study of consumer desires, bridging cognitive, emotional, and motivational approaches.

This symposium is a model of "building connections," and therefore embodies the theme of 2011 ACR because the research spans various aspects of the self (cognitive, emotional, motivational, and behavioral), multiple methodological approaches, and sample characteristics. Researchers will discuss lab-based experiments as well as large-scale field studies. Data were gathered from multiple countries around the globe, which means that diverse populations are represented. Actual behavior was measured, in addition to thoughts, evaluations, and feelings. Specific groups might find this work of particular interest: scholars of self-regulation, goal achievement, motivation, and the self, along with scientists interested in judgment and decision making, eating, and addiction. In short, the findings being presented represent a wide range of approaches, and thusly will forge connections among scholars of diverse backgrounds.

How Best To Think about the Future: Which Outcome Elaboration Strategies Help Control Desire?

EXTENDED ABSTRACT

Thinking about the potential consequences of decisions is a promising strategy for controlling currently tempting desires in order to reach long-term goals (Nenkov et al. 2008; Haws et al. 2011). Because there are various ways in which one might elaborate on potential future outcomes it is important to understand which future outcome elaborations most effectively to control the desire one is facing in the present moment. In this research, we tested which outcome elaboration approaches will be most likely to help self-control. We propose that fluency between individual propensities and elaboration strategies as well as between various components of the elaboration itself will facilitate goal-directed behavior.

In our research, we first manipulate the valence of outcome elaboration and examine how these outcome elaboration approaches match with individual tendencies to elaborate on potential outcomes (EPO; Nenkov et al. 2008). Then, we turn our focus to jointly manipulating the valence and the level of abstraction of outcome elaboration and showing that there is a natural match between negative and concrete and positive and abstract outcome elaboration approaches, which enhances their effectiveness in promoting desire control. Overall, we suggest that natural matches occur that lead to enhanced desire control based on outcome elaboration.

Prior research shows that some people tend to elaborate on potential future consequences more (i.e., high EPO) than others (i.e., low EPO) and this natural tendency has been linked with an increased incidence of exerting self-control (Nenkov et al. 2008). Therefore, some understanding of the types of elaboration commonly used by those higher in EPO would be beneficial in determining the most effective outcome elaboration strategies. For example, when considering an indulgent opportunity, a decision maker could focus on the benefits (or potential positives) to be gained from yielding to desire or the costs (or potential negatives) that might be incurred. We suggest that higher EPO consumers are much more likely to focus on the potential negatives of indulgence, and that this type of outcome elaboration comes easily to them. On the contrary, lower EPO consumers fail to elaborate at all.

To test these prediction, we focus study 1 participants (n = 187) on thinking about either the positive or negative potential outcomes of yielding to desire in a domain of their choice (i.e., money or time management). Separately, we assess their individual propensity to elaborate on potential future outcomes (EPO; Nenkov et al. 2008).

Our results show that consumers higher in EPO are overall less likely to choose a vice option following outcome elaboration than their lower EPO counterparts and that negative outcome elaboration enhanced their self-control even further. Process evidence suggests that for high EPO individuals, the negatively biased outcome elaboration task was "not complex", whereas for low EPO participants, negative elaboration was more "complex" than was positive elaboration. As such, we have some initial evidence that the fluency experienced by EPO consumers when elaborating on negative potential outcomes drives their greater self-control success.

Next, we wished to further explore the role of valence in consequence elaboration and how valence might impact the nature of the consequences considered. Based on past literature (Trope, Liberman, and Wakslak 2007), we propose that there is a match between negative outcome elaboration and concrete construal level and positive outcome and abstract construal level. To test this contention, in study 2, we directed participants to elaborate on potential outcomes by focusing on either the positive or negative consequences of failing to control desires. Participants (n=103) provided potential outcomes consistent with a domain of their choice (i.e., money or time management). We then coded the consequences participants listed as: referring to why vs. how, being abstract or concrete, or referring to the short-term or long-term temporal distance. Results revealed that negative outcomes, as compared to positive ones, were more focused on how consequences can be achieved, more long-term oriented, and overall more concrete (i.e., more specific and detailed, low-level, referring to means to an end, process, planning, and details). As such, there seems to be a natural tendency for negative consequence elaboration to be more concrete.

Study 3 pinpointed the role of construal level. Participants (n=145) were given one of four instructions for potential outcome elaboration related to the self-control domain of their choice. These instructions represented a 2 (valence: positive or negative) X 2 (construal level: concrete or abstract) design. Unlike studies 1 and 2, we asked study 3 participants to consider the positive consequences of exercising self-control, rather than of yielding to desire. Our results revealed that elaborating on the negative and concrete outcomes of yielding to desire most benefitted participants' intention to control their desires. Yet, elaborating on the positive outcomes of exercising self-control also promoted effective self-control when the consequences considered were abstract rather than concrete. Process evidence suggests that the natural match between negative/concrete and positive/abstract outcome elaboration approaches explains the results.

Overall, our research provides new insights into how considering the consequences of yielding to desire can impact self-control effectiveness. Our results suggest that when it comes to outcome elaboration, one size does not fit all, and customizing elaboration on potential outcomes approach will aid goal attainment.

REFERENCES

Haws, Kelly L., William O. Bearden, and Gergana Y. Nenkov (forthcoming), "Consumer Spending Self-Control Effectiveness and Outcome Elaboration Prompts," *Journal of the Academy of Marketing Science*.

Nenkov, Gergana Y., J. Jeffrey Inman, and John Hulland (2008) "Considering the Future: The Conceptualization and Measurement of Elaboration on Potential Outcomes," Journal of Consumer Research, 35 (1), 126-141.

Trope, Yaacov, Nira Liberman, and Cheryl Wakslak (2007), "Construal Levels and Psychological Distance: Effects on Representation, Prediction, Evaluation, and Behavior," *Journal of Consumer Psychology*, 17(2), 83-95.

Not All Health Claims Are Created Equal: Dissociating the Dynamics of Guilt and Desire Invoked by Food Indulgences

EXTENDED ABSTRACT

Healthier alternatives of unhealthy foods are increasingly prominent in today's supermarket shelves. Typically, such foods feature claims stressing either the presence of food attributes that are perceived to benefit health (e.g., antioxidants, vitamins) or the absence of attributes perceived to be unfavorable for health (e.g., fat, sugar). It is assumed that such 'better-for-you' options of unhealthy food should reduce feelings of guilt associated with eating the food, arguably because the presence of health claims make their consumption easier to justify, thereby providing consumers with an implicit license to eat.

In contrast, the literature on the effects of hedonic (e.g., fun, tasty) versus functional (e.g., safe, nourishing) attributes on stimuli perception, preference, and choice predicts that consumers should eat less of unhealthy food carrying a health claim because they (unwittingly) subscribe to the unhealthy = tasty intuition. We propose a more nuanced framework suggesting that it is the nature of the attributes highlighted in a claim that determines how much of the food is consumed.

Experiment 1 showed that seemingly similar health claims attached to unhealthy food result in very different consumption patterns, despite the fact that they are all perceived as equally tasty. Claims emphasizing a functional food attribute (e.g., antioxidants) induce a significant decrease in consumption compared to a control condition, whereas claims about a hedonic food attribute (e.g., low-fat) result in a significant increase in consumption. These opposing consumption patterns, which were triggered by ostensibly similar health claims, suggest that different mechanisms are at work for health claims for attributes that highlight the hedonic qualities of the food (e.g., fat = tasty) versus claims that highlight health-related functional attributes (e.g., antioxidants=beneficial for health; cholesterol=detrimental for health).

Experiment 2 examined whether health claims featuring hedonic versus functional food attributes evoke different levels of health goal accessibility. We suggest that claims stressing functional food attributes versus hedonic attributes lead to greater accessibility of the health goal. In addition, we expected indulgence goals to be highly accessible regardless of the presence or absence of health claims and independent of the attributes emphasized in claims. Using a lexical decision task, we tested whether different claims led to different response latencies for words relating to health and indulgence. The results showed that hedonic attributes led to slower response times towards health words when compared to functional attributes, while response latencies towards indulgence words were no different across conditions.

In Experiment 3, we provide a more fine-grained analysis of the processes underlying different types of health claims by investigating the emotional consequences of conflicting goals triggered by functional versus hedonic food attributes. In particular, we dissociate the feelings of anticipated desire and guilt upon exposure to a picture of a tempting food carrying a health claim featuring either a functional or a hedonic food attribute. We recorded participants' moment-to-moment reactions regarding desire and guilt. Results reveal that the goals activated by food attributes differing in their hedonic versus functional nature evoke very different trajectories of desire and guilt. While both types of claims provide similarly high levels of desire as they are attached to indulgences, the time course of guilt is very different in nature. Specifically, health claims featuring hedonic attributes evoke an immediate ramp up in desire for the food while guilt is at a low level. Notably, there is a gradual increase in guilt over time, suggesting that people are experiencing an ironic rebound of suppressed guilt. This finding runs counter to an ease of justification argument, which would imply reduced guilt over time. In contrast, functional attributes cause a reduced immediate desire towards temptations, suggesting an immediate devaluation of the product, coupled with a rapid ramp-up in guilt.

Together, our findings reveal that seemingly similar health claims may activate very different levels of health goal accessibility, leading to different dynamics of perceived desire and guilt and hence eventually to opposite consumption patterns of the unhealthy food they are attached to. Our findings have broad relevance to the food industry, and suggest that the nature of attributes emphasized in the health claim can have significant effects on consumption.

Engaging in Self-Control Intensifies Desires and Feelings

EXTENDED ABSTRACT

Following effortful acts of choice or self-control, people enter into a state that has been called ego depletion, which is defined by a reduced capacity to engage in further executive activities. Behavioral conflicts can be analyzed as motivations between impulse and restraint. Viewed as such, ego depletion represents a weakening of restraint. The assumption is that the impulse itself is unchanged by depletion, although this has not been tested.

The present investigation took a new approach to understanding the relations among depletion, impulse, and restraint. The core hypothesis was that ego depletion would intensify the subjective experience of feelings and desires. That is, we questioned the standard assumption that depletion weakens restraints but leaves feelings and desires unaffected. The behavioral changes that ensue during the depleted state may therefore come from not only a weakening of inner controls and restraints but also from an intensification of feelings and desires. Essentially, evaluative reactions would be intensified by depletion.

Experiment 1 tested the hypothesis that depletion would intensify emotional reactions to specific stimuli. Ego depletion was manipulated with the Stroop procedure. Some participants used their self-control to override the automatically activated information of the known meaning of the word in order to give an answer as to the color of the ink in which the word is printed. Other participants were given a nondepleting version of this task in which columns of Xs were shown and their ink color names given. The dependent measure included both positive and negative emotional responses. We presented participants with pictures known to elicit pleasant and unpleasant reactions and asked them to rate how they felt while looking at each one. The prediction was that ego depletion caused by the incongruent Stroop task would intensify both positive and negative feelings. Results supported the hypothesis: after doing the more difficult and depleting Stroop task, participants reported stronger feelings in response to emotionally evocative pictures, as compared to participants who had done the easy version of the Stroop task and not depleted their resources.

Experiment 2's self-regulatory depletion manipulation was to have participants read aloud a relatively dry, boring passage with lively verbal inflection and accompanying hand gestures. Partici-

pants in the nondepletion condition read aloud the text without specific instructions to be emotional. The outcome measure involved evaluations of stimuli for which most participants would have few or no pre-existing associations. Specifically, participants were asked to rate Chinese characters. Because no one in our sample could speak or read Chinese, these figures had no meaning to them. They could therefore only react to the aesthetic impact of the character as if it were something akin to abstract art or a figure to have tattooed on oneself. Classic work by Zajonc showed that viewers can and do have positive and negative emotional feelings about Chinese characters. Our prediction was that these feelings would be stronger in depleted than in non-depleted participants. The results supported this hypothesis, in that depletion caused people to react relatively strongly to Chinese characters. Participants reported how these characters made them feel, how attractive they were, and how much they liked each of the characters. Overall, depleted participants gave more extreme ratings than non-depleted ones.

In experiment 3, the depletion manipulation asked participants to write an essay without using the letters A or N, whereas participants no-depletion condition were asked to write an essay without using the letters X and Z. Our dependent measures were ratings and consumption of cookies in a taste-testing task. To assess the motivation to consume more cookies, participants rated their desire to have another cookie after finishing each cookie. Participants were left alone to eat and rate the cookies. The results showed that, in line with predictions, depleted participants had stronger desire than nondepleted participants to keep eating more cookies. Thus, depletion intensified the desire to eat another cookie. Consistent with previous research, participants in the depletion condition ate more cookies overall than participants in the no-depletion condition. Even more important, analyses indicated that participants' motivation to eat more cookies mediated the effect of depletion condition on number of cookies consumed.

Experiment 4 tracked subjective feelings over time. First, participants watched a videotape that contained irrelevant words onscreen. Participants in the depletion manipulation were told to "avoid looking at or reading any words that may appear on the screen," while those in the control condition were given no instructions regarding the words on the screen. After the depletion manipulation, participants were given a wrapped gift. They were allowed to open it, but were asked to wait. They used a joystick to report their momentary level of desire to open the gift. The results showed that mean desire to open the package was higher for depleted than non-depleted persons. Thus, intensification of the urge was an enduring consequence of depletion, rather than a fleeting or one-time-only experience. The peak level of desire expressed during the entire period by each depleted participants was higher than the peak level of desire reached by nondepleted participants, on average. Depleted participants were also marginally quicker than nondepleted ones to reach their peak level of desire.

In summary, we reported a series of studies that used multiple different methods and measures to test the hypothesis that depletion intensifies feelings. The depletion tasks involved cognition and emotion, attention and behavior, and inhibiting and enhancing responses. The intensified reactions included emotions and attitudes, good and bad feelings, and approach and avoidance behaviors. In short, depletion enhances feelings and evaluations of stimuli, which contributes to its effect on worsening self-regulation subsequently.

Everyday Temptations: An Experience Sampling Study on How People Control Their Desires

EXTENDED ABSTRACT

In recent years, research on human self-control has flourished. Self-control can be defined as the ability to override or change one's inner responses, as well as to interrupt undesired behavioral tendencies (such as impulses) and refrain from acting on them. However, most research has been conducted in laboratory settings even though suitable methods such as the daily construction method and experience sampling have been proposed. Given the paucity of knowledge of how people control their desires in naturalistic settings, our study sought to provide an in-depth analysis of everyday self-control through the use of experience sampling methodology. Specifically, we were driven by the following main questions: What kind of urges and desires do people experience over the course of their daily lives? To what extent do desires conflict with important long-term goals, and how often and how successfully do people resist them? Further, to what extent do people's successes and failures trigger self-conscious emotions such as guilt, pride, and regret? And do these self-conscious emotions in response to lapses aid subsequent self-control as predicted by feedback models or hinder subsequent self-control as suggested by findings on the spiraling effects of emotional distress?

To study desire and self-control in vivo, we conducted an experience sampling study on a heterogeneous sample of 205 adults in Western Europe. Participants were prompted at random with 7 signals per day over the course of a week. They indicated if they had current or recent desires and, specified the content of the desire from a list of 15 main and more than 70 subcategories. Moreover, participants provided information on the details and their possible self-control attempts: how strongly the desire was experienced, whether the desire conflicted with an important goal, whether and how they tried to resist the desire, whether they executed the desire-relevant behavior or not. In addition, participants reported their current levels of guilt, regret, and pride and reported on various circumstantial variables such as level of alcohol intoxication.

Participants reported more than 7,000 desire episodes (75% of all occasions that they were beeped). Approximately one-third of desires conflicted moderately to highly with other goals. Multilevel analyses showed that degree of conflict predicted the likelihood with which participants attempted to resist the present desire, and that resistance had a strong negative effect on enactment. Specifically, 83% of all resistance attempts were successful, leaving a nontrivial amount (17%) of self-control failures among resisted desires. Desire strength, desire-goal conflict, and successful resistance varied across domains, with sexual desires, spending impulses, and sports inclinations most likely to be successfully resisted, and desires for media use and work least likely to be successfully resisted. Self-control success was further moderated by situational factors such as alcohol consumption, ego depletion due to previous resistance attempts on the same day, and whether other people in the immediate environment already engaged in the desire-related behavior of interest.

Regarding self-conscious emotions, as expected, guilt experiences were strongest when desires were resisted but enacted (i.e., self-control failure) and pride experiences were strongest when desires were resisted and not enacted (i.e., self-control success). Feelings of regret, in contrast, were most pronounced when unproblematic (i.e., unresisted) desires were not enacted. To address the question of how previous self-conscious emotions may aid or hinder subsequent self-control, we regressed each person's conflict, resistance, and enactment reports on his or her previous feelings of guilt, regret, and pride within the same specific type of desire (e.g., sweets, beer, watching TV) and included as a moderator whether the preceding occasion counted as a lapse or not (in the case of guilt and regret), or as self-control success (in the case of pride). We found that the intensity of guilt reactions to lapses had an indirect effect on subsequent enactment via increased feelings of conflict, and a greater likelihood of resisting the problematic desire. For regret, there was only an indirect effect on subsequent conflict experiences. Pride emerged as the most potent self-conscious emotion in that pride in response to self-control success predicted less subsequent enactment. As in the case of guilt, this effect was mediated via increased conflict experiences and a greater likelihood of resistance.

In sum, these data provide rich insights into people's regular struggles and successes in overcoming temptation. Moreover, we suggest mechanisms (increasing experience of conflict, increased resistance) by which self-conscious emotions may aid subsequent self-control.

Health, Wealth, and Consumer Welfare

Chair: Min Zhao, University of Toronto, Canada

Paper #1: Enhanced Choice: A Method to Motivate Behavior Change

Punam Keller, Dartmouth College, USA
Bari Harlam, CVS/Caremark
George Loewenstein, Carnegie Mellon University, USA
Kevin Volpp, University of Pennsylvania, USA

Paper #2: The Fewer, the Better: Number of Goals and Savings Behavior

Dilip Soman, University of Toronto, Canada
Min Zhao, University of Toronto, Canada

Paper #3: On Assets and Debt in the Psychology of Perceived Wealth

Abigail Sussman, Princeton University, USA
Eldar Shafir, Princeton University, USA

SESSION OVERVIEW

The fact that consumers need to save more and engage in healthier behaviors is beyond dispute. The key question is – what specific prescriptions can be offered based on the literature that consumers could use to change behavior and improve savings. To motivate consumers to change behavior, different strategies have been suggested such as introducing the opt-out policies while using the better choice as the default. Other programs such as saving a proportion of payroll in the saving account automatically have also been employed to increase consumer saving. This session tries to propose new approaches that help consumer act toward better welfare related with their health and wealth, investigate the psychological rationales behind it, and understand consumers' perceived wealth and debt and their subsequent financial behavior.

The first paper by *Keller and colleagues* examines people's decision in healthcare context (e.g., flu shot or automatic prescription refill) and introduces a new choice strategy: Enhanced Active Choice which is a forced-choice structure without default (e.g., choosing between getting a flu shot to reduce the risk of getting the flu vs. not getting a flu shot and increasing the risk of getting the flu). Results from four studies demonstrate that Enhanced Active Choice motivates behavior change by advantaging and increasing loss aversion for one option. Moving from the general choice policy in the healthcare domain to more specific behavior change in the financial domain, the second paper by *Soman and Zhao* examines how number of savings goal impacts consumers' savings intention. Contrary to common belief, they demonstrate that a single savings goal leads to greater savings and savings intention than multiple goals due to the implementation intention evoked by the single goal. Further, they show that this effect is attenuated when the saving is easier to implement or when multiple goals involve little competition among themselves. Although the specific studies in *Keller and colleagues* are related with healthcare decisions and the studies in *Soman and Zhao* are related with savings behaviour, the general principles of Enhanced Active Choice or using fewer number of reasons to prompt an implemental mindset can both be widely applied in healthcare, saving, donations or other domain related with consumer welfare. Finally, *Sussman and Shafir* take a different perspective and explore the psychology of perceived wealth. Their findings show that keeping positive net worth constant, people feel and are seen as wealthier when they have lower debt (despite fewer assets) because debt stands out in a positive net worth scenario. In contrast, those with nega-

tive worth feel and are seen as wealthier with greater assets (despite greater debt), because the possession of assets attracts more attention as it stands out in a negative wealth contexts. These findings have important implications on people's subsequent spending and borrowing behavior, which ultimately impacts their welfare.

The papers in this session proposal are all in advanced stages of completion. Taken together, the session is designed to provide an integrative overview of new research aimed at enhancing our understanding of consumer decision making and psychology related with their health, wealth and welfare in general. The likely audience for this session will be consumer researchers in general and specifically those who are interested in consumer's financial decision-making, consumer welfare and public policy. Thus we expect to draw the interest of a wide range of researchers. John Lynch, an expert in consumers' decision making, will lead discussions to simulate future research directions at the end of the session.

Enhanced Choice: A Method to Motivate Behavior Change

EXTENDED ABSTRACT

Enrollment in tax-favored savings plans is 50% higher when employees are automatically enrolled compared to when they opt-in (Madrian and Shea 2001). Opt-out' policies that automatically assign people to carefully selected default choices are effective for a number of overlapping reasons. *Loss aversion* encourages people to stick with the default because moving away from the default typically involves losses and gains, and losses receive disproportionate weight (Johnson and Goldstein 2003). The effect of loss aversion is further exacerbated by *present-bias* – the inordinate weight people place on costs and benefits that are immediate (O'Donoghue and Rabin 1999). *Procrastination* also works in favor of opt-out policies, again because deviating from the default often involves positive action, which people procrastinate in taking. Finally, opt-out policies exert such a strong influence on behavior in part because people assume that defaults have been selected for a reason – i.e., that defaults constitute implicit recommendations of specific courses of action (McKenzie, Liersch, and Finkelstein 2006).

Limitations of Opt-out

Yet, for all their advantages, opt-out policies have diverse and severe limitations, especially in some settings. First and foremost, because opt-out policies yield decisions through the inaction of the decision maker, they are less likely to engender the kind of committed follow-up that is often useful when it comes to implementing the decision. Family members of an elderly person facing the option of going on life support may be more likely to honor an affirmative decision by that person to eschew heroic measures than they would be to honor a decision that arose simply because the person failed to affirmatively state that they wanted such measures (Spital 1993).

Second, opt-out 'choices' in many situations are less likely to reflect decision makers' true preferences than will more active choices (Payne, Bettman, and Johnson 1993). For example, there is growing evidence that the shared optimum inherent in an automatic 401(k) enrollment plan may be inappropriate (Carroll et al. 2009) or unsustainable (Lusardi and Mitchell 2007) for some people.

Third, in some situations, passive choices are more likely to result in waste or inefficiency. If a person's failure to affirmatively state that they don't want to recycle is taken as an intention to re-cycle, the recycling truck may end up making a lot of wasted trips to pick up recyclables that never materialize.

Fourth, opt-out choices are often legally or ethically unacceptable. For instance, in a retirement saving context, we might want employees to sign up for "auto escalation" to boost their contributions by a percentage point or so a year or sign up for a supplementary retirement account (Thaler and Benartzi 2004), but it is illegal to auto-enroll employees in auto escalation plans.

Fifth, opt-out policies can be counterproductive if those who implement them view them as a substitute for other interventions, such as educational programs that give people the information they need to make an informed choice.

Finally, employers may not adopt automatic enrollment because they don't want to assume the burden of responsibility for planning for their employees. They may fear, to some extent rightfully, that some employees may interpret defaults as implicit advice (McKenzie, Liersch, and Finkelstein 2006) and may be upset with their employer during market downturns.

Active Choice: Avoiding the Problems Associated with Opt-Out

Three studies, two on organ donation (Spital 1993, 1995) and one on retirement planning (Carroll et al. 2009) attempt to achieve the same basic goal as opt-out – of ensuring that people who would benefit from an intervention, receive it – without the disadvantages of opt-out. Instead of waiting for people to opt-in, Spital (1993, 1995) found support in public opinion surveys for the idea of forcing people to choose whether they want to or don't want to donate their organs. Sixty three percent of a random sample of 1000 adults in the United States said they would support mandatory choice (Spital 1993).

In an observational study, Carroll and colleagues (2009) measured the impact on savings plan enrollment in a firm that required all new employees to explicitly choose between enrolling and not enrolling in a 401(k) plan. The language (I want to enroll vs. I don't want to enroll) was deliberately designed to not advantage any one option (Carroll et al. 2009). The result was a 28% increase in enrollment in the "Active Decision" condition compared to when employees opted-in.

Building on the research by Carroll et al. (2009) and Spital (1993; 1995) we advance the concept of forced choice by testing four important enhancements. Taking advantage of the opportunities afforded by a controlled study, we control for additional enrollment materials such as one-on-one coaching from human resources and other enrollment prompts such as reminders.

Second, we provide conceptual and empirical evidence for the cognitive processes that make Active Choice effective. We predict greater regret aversion for the new opportunity expressed as a forced choice than as a default.

Third, we examine a modified approach that we call 'Enhanced Active Choice' that advantages the option preferred by the communicator by highlighting losses incumbent in the non-preferred alternative. For example, Enhanced Active Choice might reframe the alternatives as a choice between: "I want to enroll in a 401(k) plan and take advantage of the employer match" versus "I don't want to enroll in a 401(k) plan and don't want to take advantage of the employer match. We believe dislike for the non-preferred alternative will be more marked when the costs of non-compliance are highlighted in the choice format.

In sum, our main hypotheses are (H1) that Active Choice ('unenhanced' or basic and 'enhanced') will result in more compliance than opt-in non-enrollment defaults, and (H2) that Enhanced Active

Choice will result in more compliance than basic Active Choice. We test these hypotheses in four studies involving three different decision tasks: intention to get a flu shot (study 1), desire to get a flu shot reminder (study 2), and enrollment and disenrollment in a prescription drug refill program (studies 3 and 4).

The Fewer the Better: Number of Goals and Savings Behavior

EXTENDED ABSTRACT

Goals play an important role in different aspects of consumer life such as risk-taking behavior (Atkinson 1957) or spending and savings behavior (Shefrin and Thaler 1988; Soman and Cheema 2004). Prior research suggests that multiple goals lead to greater performance (Locke and Latham 1990), or that the greater the number of means to pursue a goal, the more likely is one to pursue on that goal (Kruglanski et al. 2002). Drawing on research on implementation mindset (Gollwitzer 1999), we make the opposite prediction and argue that presenting a single savings goal (e.g., saving for children's education) leads to higher saving achievement than presenting multiple savings goals (e.g., saving for children's education, retirement and future housing).

Researchers on implementation intention have studied different stages that individuals go through when they make goal-related decisions (Gollwitzer 1999; Gollwitzer and Bayer 1999): an initial stage with a deliberative mindset, in which individuals are uncertain about their goals and seek to define a desired outcome by considering the tradeoffs between the goals; and a subsequent stage with an implemental mindset in which individuals have already established the goal they wish to pursue and are considering when, where, and how to attain the goal. This stream of research has demonstrated that forming implementation intentions leads to more successful goal attainment than merely forming a goal.

While implemental mindsets can be induced in different ways such as instructing people to think about the how (vs. the why) or simply asking people to consider which of a number of alternative products they would prefer(Xu and Wyer 2007, 2008), we propose that presenting consumers with a single goal can also help evoke an implementation intention compared with multiple goals because multiple goals evoke tradeoffs consideration among goals which hinders people from translating the savings goals into action. However, when people only have one goal, they no longer need to make goal trade-offs and are more likely to move onto the second stage of the goal pursuance -- a position to think about implementing the goal. As a result, their commitment with the task at hand (i.e., saving) will be stronger and their savings intention will be higher. Further, based on prior research that implementation intention has its greatest benefits in complex and difficult situations (Gollwitzer 1999; Gollwitzer and Brandstatter 1997), we also expect that the advantage of a single savings goal over multiple savings goal on consumer saving will be attenuated when the goal is easy to implement.

We conducted four studies to test our hypotheses. In study 1 (n=83) which was conducted in a small town in India with local farmers and workers in a financial literacy program, we either told participants to save more to finance their children's education or to save more to finance their children's, any healthcare needs they might have, and to provide a nest-egg for when they retire. Participants in the control condition were given no specific goals at all. The results showed that single goal led to higher savings rate over the next 6 months than multiple goals, followed by no specific goal at all.

In study 2 (n=194), participants in an executive skills were introduced to a hypothetical savings program that required them to deposit a minimum of $300 each month for 10 years to be invested in bonds and government securities. Participants in the difficult-to-save conditions were told that they have a monthly discretionary amount of $400 after paying for the essential monthly expenses, whereas participants in the easy-to-save conditions were told to have a monthly discretionary amount of $1200. Further, in the single goal conditions, participants were reminded that they should start thinking about providing for their children's future education. In the multiple-goal conditions, more goals were reminded (i.e., children's future education, housing expenses, retirement savings and other slush funds for emergencies). The results showed that when it was difficult to save, single goal led to higher savings intention than multiple goals; however, when it was easy to save, the advantage of single goal was attenuated. We also measured participants' implementation mindset, and found its mediation role in the aforementioned results.

In study 3 (n=156), rather than measuring participants' implementation mindset, we manipulated their mindset based on the same scenario as in study 2. We again found that single goal led to greater savings intention than multiple goals when participants didn't receive any mindset manipulation or when they received a goal intention manipulation. However, when participants received implementation intention manipulation, multiple goals led to equally high savings intention as single goal. This further confirmed implementation intention as the underlying process for the advantage of single goal over multiple goals.

Because our key premise is that multiple goals evoke trade-off consideration among the goals and thus hinder people from moving into an implemental mindset, we believe that if the competition among the multiple goals and thus the trade-off is removed, the effect of single goal over multiple goals will be attenuated. In study 4 (n=274) where we used non-competing goals (i.e., saving for future wellbeing such as peace of mind, flexibility, and independence), we indeed found that a single goal (i.e., saving for future wellbeing such as peace of mind) no longer led to higher savings intention than multiple goals, further confirming that the disadvantage of multiple goals was due to the hurtle to the implemental mindset.

Our work adds to research on financial decision making by demonstrating a new way to increase savings behaviour/intention -- limiting the number of savings goals to evoke an implementation mindset. Our findings have important implications to the goal literature, literature on attitude change (e.g., number of argument; Petty and Cacioppo 1984), and to policy-makers in encouraging consumer saving.

On Assets and Debt in the Psychology of Perceived Wealth

EXTENDED ABSTRACT

Perceptions of wealth are central to economic behavior and feelings of well-being. To date, research on wealth perception has mostly focused on relative wealth, namely, how well off people are when compared to those around them (e.g. Frank 1999, 2007), and on conspicuous consumption, whereby people purchase visible status items to signal wealth (e.g. Heffetz 2010; Veblen 1899).

While these perspectives are important, they focus on features that, at best, act as correlates of wealth. People are influenced by the perceived wealth of others, but that, of course, does not fully correspond their actual wealth. Nor do the social motivations to impress others through financial extravagances. While important, these perspectives do not provide insight into a person's sentiments about her actual wealth. In contrast, the present studies look at wealth perception as it is influenced by factors directly related to wealth, namely, people's assets and debt. We explore how these factors shape perceptions of wealth, both one's own and others', as well as the willingness to engage in important financial transactions, including borrowing, lending, and spending, that emanate from such perceived wealth.

We first examine how full knowledge of total assets and debt enters into the perception of wealth. We find that keeping total net worth constant, people with positive net worth are seen as wealthier when they have lower debt (despite, consequently, having lower assets). In contrast, keeping total net worth constant, those with negative net worth are considered wealthier when they have greater assets (and, consequently, greater debt). Across a series of studies, we find that, when judging the wealth of people with equal positive net worth, approximately three-quarters of participants view those with lower debt and lower assets to be in a better financial position than those with higher debt and correspondingly higher assets. In contrast, when judging the wealth of people with equal negative net worth, approximately three-quarters of participants viewed those with higher debt and higher assets as in better financial position than those with lower debt and correspondingly lower assets.

We show this pattern to be robust to possible interpretations that appeal to liquidity constraints or to computational demands, and we find that it applies to participants' judgments both about themselves and about others. We also extend the findings to contexts where they yield counter-normative judgments, in which the perceptions described above persist when net worth differs by approximately 20% (e.g., where a person of $10,000 net worth but lower debt is perceived as wealthier than a person of $12,000 net worth but greater debt).

In follow-up studies, we extend these findings to several financial decisions, including reported willingness to borrow, lend, and spend. Specifically, we demonstrate that people with the preferred wealth distributions are more likely to take on additional debt, and that others are more likely to evaluate them as in a better position to borrow money. Furthermore, those with preferred wealth profiles (although equal or lower actual wealth) are willing to spend more to purchase luxury items.

To explain these results, we test the hypothesis of an attentional shift when subjects confront positive versus negative net worth scenarios. We first show a positive correlation between asset balances and perceived wealth for those with equal negative net worth ($r = .73, p = .017$), and an asymmetric negative correlation between asset balances and perceived wealth for those with equal positive net worth ($r = -.91, p < .001$). We then provide more direct evidence that in the positive net worth scenario, debt (rather than assets) draws subjects' attention, by coding participants' initial reactions to financial profiles. The burden of holding debt stands out as a salient negative relative to one's overall positive state, disproportionately affecting perception. Conversely, in negative net worth scenarios, the possession of assets attracts more attention as it stands out against one's overall negative state.

We discuss how the findings go beyond a prospect theoretic account, and we explore how they can be used to explain why some individuals are debt averse, avoiding financially wise low interest loans, while others are debt seeking, taking on economically questionable high interest loans. Finally, we consider several policy implications, with an emphasis on the consequences for borrowing among the poor.

Interestingly, the same general impulse for financial wealth and stability can trigger opposing behaviors: a striving for greater assets despite larger debt in some circumstances, and for lower debt, even if it means lower assets, in others. Such impulses, furthermore, may not always agree with what might be best financially. For example, it is likely that those with negative net worth who are eager to borrow (and may feel wealthier as a result) will only have access to high interest loans, thus exacerbating their already precarious finances. On the other hand, those with positive net worth who could benefit from taking on low interest debt, such as student loans, may be reluctant to make a profitable investment in their education, because of its negative impact on their perceived wealth.

Impressions of financial stability, assets, and debt have been shown to impact not only financial behavior, but also overall health and well-being (Miron-Shatz 2009; Nelson, Lust, Story, and Ehlinger 2008). Better insight into the perceptions and impulses that yield financial behaviors may enrich our understanding of the relevant psychology, and contribute to behaviorally informed financial design and policy.

REFERENCES

Atkinson, John W. (1957), "Motivational Determinants of Risk-taking Behaviour," *Psychological Review*, 64(6), 359-372.

Carroll, Gabriel, James Choi, David Laibson, Brigitte Madrian, and Andrew Metrick (2009), "Optimal Defaults and Active Decisions," *Quarterly Journal of Economics, 124*, 1639–1676.

Gollwitzer, Peter (1999), "Implementation Intentions: Strong Effects of Simple Plans," *American Psychologist,* 54, 493-503.

Gollwitzer, Peter and Ute Bayer (1999), "Deliberative versus Implemental Mindsets in the Control of Action, in *Dual-process Theories in Social Psychology,* ed. Shelly Chaiken and Yaakov Trope, New York: Guilford, 403-422.

Gollwitzer, Peter and Veronika Brandstaetter (1997), "Implementation Intentions and Effective Goal Pursuit," *Journal of Personality and Social Psychology, 73*(1)*,* 186-199.

Frank, Robert H. (1999). *Luxury Fever: Money and Happiness in an Era of Excess*, Princeton, NJ: Princeton University Press.

Frank, Robert H. (2007). *Falling Behind: How Rising Inequality Harms the Middle Class*, Berkeley, CA: University of California Press.

Heffetz, Ori (2010), "A Test of Conspicuous Consumption: Visibility and Income Elasticities," *The Review of Economics and Statistics, Forthcoming. Available at SSRN: http://ssrn.com/abstract=1004543*

Johnson, Eric and Daniel Goldstein (2003), "Do Defaults Save Lives?" *Science, 302*, 1338–1339.

Lusardi, Annamaria and Olivia Mitchell (2007), "Baby Boomers Retirement Security: The Role of Planning, Financial Literacy and Housing Wealth," *Journal of Monetary Economics, 54*, 205-224.

Kruglanski, Arie, James Shah, Antonio Pierro, and Lucia Mannetti (2002), "When Similarity Breeds Content: Need for Closure and the Allure of Homogeneous and Self-resembling Groups," *Journal of Personality and Social Psychology*, 83, 648-62.

Locke, Edwin and Gary Latham (1990), *A Theory of Goal Setting and Task Performance,* Englewood Cliffs, NJ: Prentice-Hall.

Madrian, Brigitte and Dennis Shea (2001), "The Power of Suggestion: Inertia In 401(K) Participation and Savings Behavior," *Quarterly Journal of Economics, 116*, 1149-1187.

McKenzie, Craig, Michael Liersch, and Stacy Finkelstein (2006), "Recommendations Implicit in Policy Defaults," *Psychological Science, 17*, 414-420.

Miron-Shatz, Talya (2009), "Am I Going to Be Happy And Financially Stable?: How American Women Feel When They Think About Financial Security," *Judgment and Decision Making,* 102-112.

Nelson, Melissa, Katherine Lust, Mary Story, and Ed Ehlinger (2008), "Credit Card Debt, Stress and Key Health Risk Behaviors among College Students," *American Journal of Health Promotion,* 400-407.

O'Donoghue, Ted and Matthew Rabin (1999), "Doing It Now or Later," *The American Economic Review, 89,* 103-124.

Payne John, Jim Bettman and Eric Johnson (1993), *The Adaptive Decision Maker*. New York, NY: Cambridge University Press.

Petty, Richard and John Cacioppo (1984), "The Effects of Involvement on Responses to Argument Quantity and Quality: Central and Peripheral Routes to Persuasion," *Journal of Personality and Social Psychology*, 46, 69-81.

Shefrin, Hersh and Richard Thaler, "The Behavioral Life-Cycle Hypothesis," *Economic Inquiry*, 26, 609-43.

Soman, Dilip and Amar Cheema (2004), "When Goals are Counter-Productive: The Effects of Violating a Behavioral Goal on Performance," *Journal of Consumer Research*, 31(1), 52-62.

Spital, Aaron (1993), "A Consent for Organ Donation: Time for Change." *Clinical Transplant, 7,* 525-528.

Spital, Aaron (1995), "Mandated Choice: A Plan to Increase Public Commitment to Organ Donation," *Journal of American Medical Association, 273*, 504-506.

Thaler, Richard and Shlomo Benartzi (2004), "Save More Tomorrow: Using Behavioral Economics to Increase Employee Savings," *Journal of Political Economy, 112*, 164-187.

Veblen, Thorstein (1899), *The Theory of the Leisure Class.* Reprint 1965, MacMillan, New York.

Xu, Jing and Robert Wyer (2007), "The Effect of Mind-Sets on Consumer Decision Strategies," *Journal of Consumer Research*, 34, 556-66.

Xu, Jing and Robert Wyer (2008), "The Comparative Mind-set: From Animal Comparisons to Increased Purchase Intentions," *Psychological Science*, 19, 859-64.

The Best Attended Session at ACR: New Research on Optimism

Chairs: Simona Botti, London Business School, UK
Stefano Puntoni, Erasmus University Rotterdam, The Netherlands

Paper #1: The Effect of Large Incentives on Optimistic Responding: Evidence That Optimism Is Real

Joseph P. Simmons, University of Pennsylvania, USA
Cade Massey, Yale University, USA

Paper #2: When the Personal Becomes Interpersonal: Public Posturing in Unrealistic Optimism

Steven Sweldens, INSEAD, France
Stefano Puntoni, Erasmus University Rotterdam, The Netherlands
Justin Kruger, New York University, USA
Maarten Vissers, Fortis Bank, The Netherlands

Paper #3: Too Optimistic about What the Future Holds?: How Greater Confidence Can Lead to Fewer Purchases

Francesca Gino, Harvard Business School, USA
Uriel Haran, Carnegie Mellon University, USA
Don Moore, UC Berkeley, USA

Paper #4: When Thinking Positive Gets the Better of Us: The Role of Optimism in Uninformed Consumer Choice

Selin Malkoc, Washington University in St. Louis, USA
Ayelet Gneezy, UC San Diego, USA
Simona Botti, London Business School, UK

SESSION OVERVIEW

Optimism is an important concept in research areas as diverse as subjective wellbeing, decision making, personality, and social comparisons. Each of these areas defines optimism in slightly different ways but all agree that, despite the forces working against them, hope and wishful thinking color much of human experience. In the consumer context, individuals' tendency to be optimistic about the nature of current and future events plays a crucial role in a wide range of substantively important phenomena. As the papers in this session show, optimism can influence decisions that have serious, and sometimes long-term, consequences in domains such as health, food, gambling and ethics. The thread linking the four papers in this special session proposal is a focus on the prevalence of optimism and on its potentially negative consequences for consumers' welfare. The aim of the session is to provide a picture of current theorizing on optimism within consumer research. The session is based on 15 completed studies, across a variety of methods, research areas, and substantive settings.

The first two papers focus on the robustness and prevalence of optimism and posit that optimistic responses may emerge as a consequence of either truly held optimism or other intrapersonal or interpersonal factors. Although both papers find evidence consistent with a significant truly held optimism, the picture they portray is rather different—something that we expect to trigger a lively debate during the session. Simmons and Massey show that even in the presence of real and large accuracy incentives people remain optimistic in their predictions about future events, suggesting that optimistic responses tend to be indeed truly believed. Sweldens and colleagues investigate the role of public posturing in comparative optimism in the health domain, and conclude that a large upward bias exists in researchers' beliefs about the prevalence and magnitude of comparative optimism for negative life events. The last two papers examine the consequences of optimism, investigating contexts where optimism leads to suboptimal outcomes for consumers. Gino and colleagues hy-

pothesize that confident decision makers are more likely to cheat by overstating their current performances because they believe that they will indeed improve them in the future. Thus, managers' optimism about their ability to eventually address weaknesses in their offering leads to dishonest marketing practices that are harmful to consumers. Malkoc and colleagues investigate situations where consumers have little information about choice options, such as unfamiliar food or accommodation types, and must draw inferences about their attributes. In these cases, optimism may be misleading and even detrimental, as consumers give unwarranted positive evaluations and seek for more risk than they should.

Perhaps ironically given the topic, we expect this session to provide a lively debate and to be of interest to a substantial proportion of the ACR community. In particular, we expect the session to appeal to researchers in the decision-making area studying how individuals make predictions about the future, as well as to researchers with a substantive interest in consumer welfare. We believe that the proposal fully expresses the spirit of "building connections" that is the theme of this year's ACR. While all four papers address issues related to optimism, each provides distinct conceptual and substantive contributions in research areas that are often deemed as separate islands within the literature. Indeed, the four papers draw a bridge between organizational research on ethics, economics research on judgment under uncertainty, social psychological research on comparative judgments, and decision making research in marketing.

The Effect of Large Incentives on Optimistic Responding: Evidence That Optimism Is Real

EXTENDED ABSTRACT

Does wanting an event to happen increase the likelihood of believing that it will? Although demonstrations of optimistic biases in forecasts of task completion (Buehler, Griffin, & Ross, 1994), task performance (Camerer & Lovallo, 1999), health outcomes (Weinstein, 1980), political outcomes (Krizan, Miller, & Johar, 2010), and sporting outcomes (Massey, Simmons, & Armor, 2011) seem to support this notion, researchers have questioned whether optimistic responses really reflect true beliefs.

Because optimistic responding is typically a low-cost endeavor (i.e., incentives for making accurate predictions are usually absent or trivial), scholars have argued that people may prefer to respond optimistically even when they do not believe it. For example, a sports fan may predict that his favorite team will win an upcoming game not because he genuinely believes this but out of a low-cost desire to remain loyal to his team. Thus, optimistic responding may reflect cheap talk rather than true beliefs (cf. Armor & Sackett, 2006). Our investigation tests this hypothesis. Specifically, we investigated whether optimistic responding persists in the face of large incentives to be accurate.

In a web survey, we asked 770 NFL football fans from across the United States to predict the winner of a single game. Roughly half (the *fans*) were asked to predict a game involving their favorite team and the other half (the *non-fans*) were asked to predict a game involving two teams that they were relatively neutral about. We also manipulated incentives. Participants were promised either a small incentive ($5) or a large incentive ($50) for making an accurate prediction. If optimism is extreme cheap talk (i.e., if it is worth less than

$5), then optimism should be absent from both conditions. If optimism involves a more expensive form of cheap talk, then optimistic responding should occur within the $5 condition only (i.e., only the $50 incentive should eliminate optimism).

Oddsmakers in Las Vegas offer a point spread for each NFL game. The spread incorporates all known information in order to offer the best prediction of the game's point differential, and thus serves as an excellent normative standard against which to judge predictions (Simmons, Nelson, Galak, & Frederick, in press). Most important for our purposes, the point spread defines the most likely winner (the *superior team*) and the most likely loser (the *inferior team*). Within our fan condition, participants were marginally significantly more likely to be fans of superior teams (54.5%) than fans of inferior teams, $\chi^2(1) = 3.36$, $p = .07$. Thus, on aggregate, fans *should* exhibit optimism, because they (and everyone else) should predict that superior teams will win games. Thus, it is important to distinguish between fans of superior teams (who should predict their favorite teams to win) and fans of inferior teams (who should not). Accordingly, our analysis partitions participants into three groups: fans of superior teams ($n = 222$), (2) non-fans ($n = 363$), and (3) fans of inferior teams ($n = 185$). Optimism is manifest if fans of superior teams are more likely than fans of inferior teams to predict superior teams to win the games.

Consistent with the claim that optimistic responding reflects true beliefs, optimism was evident in both the $5 and $50 conditions. Indeed, within the $50 condition, fans of superior teams (94.6%) predicted that the superior team would win more often than did non-fans (75.8%) and fans of inferior teams (47.3%), indicating rampant optimism even when the stakes were considerable. (There were no significant effects of incentives on optimistic responding).

Thus, optimistic responding was evident even when $50 was on the line. Although this is consistent with the claim that optimistic responding reflects true beliefs rather than cheap talk, it is possible that $50 is not a large enough incentive to motivate people to make predictions that they believe. To help resolve this issue, we analyzed the predictions of "true believers," whose responses to four follow-up questions strongly implied that they believed the predictions that they made. Specifically, our sample of "true believers" (1) indicated that their predicted winner had a greater than 50% chance of winning the game; (2) indicated, on a 7-point scale, that they would be at least slightly more surprised if their predicted winner lost; (3) rated their accuracy motivation a 7 (extremely motivated) on a 7-point scale; and (4) indicated genuinely believing that their predicted winner would win the game.

If optimism is just cheap talk, then "true believers" should not respond optimistically. But they did. Indeed, even among the heavily incentivized "true believers", fans of superior teams (93.2%) predicted that the superior team would win more often than did non-fans (81.9%) and fans of inferior teams (62.2%). Thus, optimism was evident even among those who seemed to believe their predictions.

The fact that optimistic responding persisted among those who (1) were paid $50 for an accurate prediction, and (2) gave every indication that they believed their predictions, strongly supports the claim that optimism is more than just cheap talk. Though one can never definitively *prove* that an optimistic response is truly believed, we believe the onus is now on optimism's non-believers to show otherwise.

When the Personal Becomes Interpersonal: Public Posturing in Unrealistic Optimism

EXTENDED ABSTRACT

People tend to report that negative events are less likely—and positive events more likely—to happen to them than to others. Unrealistic optimism is one of the most robust empirical findings in the literature on judgment and decision making, so much so that it is widely regarded as a truism. The extant literature has identified numerous motivational and cognitive factors that contribute to this phenomenon. However, an additional cause of unrealistic optimism may be that participants in such studies are motivated to present themselves in a flattering light. After all, developing a drinking problem, being fired, and contracting venereal disease are not merely undesirable, they are also socially stigmatizing. To admit that one is likely to become an alcoholic is to say that one cannot be trusted to resist temptation; to admit that one is likely to be fired may imply that that one is not competent enough to hold down a job; and to admit that one is likely to contract venereal disease may imply that one is sexually irresponsible, dirty, or worse. Just as people tend to underreport their engagement in socially undesirable activities—such as alcohol abuse and unprotected sex (Tourangeau and Yan 2007; cf., also, Fisher 1993)—so, too, might people deny their likelihood of experiencing events that imply participation in such activities. In other words, one reason people may demonstrate an optimistic bias is simply that they lie.

The insight that socially desirable responding, self-presentational concerns, and public posturing more generally might play a role in unrealistically optimistic predictions is hardly new (e.g., Helweg-Larsen, Sadeghian, and Webb 2002; Tyler and Rosier 2009), and it is one of the reasons why research in this area is almost always conducted under conditions of anonymity. In particular, Tyler and Rosier (2009) argue that respondents can sometimes report optimistic responses because of a desire to present oneself as having a positive outlook on life. Given that such a self-image could be conveyed by responding optimistically to questions concerning virtually any prediction about the future, this account presents a troubling alternative explanation for many findings in the optimism literature. As highlighted in the examples above, however, there is another reason why people might intentionally misrepresent their beliefs about the future: the social stigma associated with specific life events. We therefore propose that optimistic responding is often the result of respondents' effort to avoid the social disapproval associated with admitting the possibility of certain life events. Our studies tested a series of predictions stemming from this theorizing.

First, if the motive to avoid event-specific social stigmas inflates unrealistically optimistic responding, then the magnitude of unrealistic optimism should vary as a function of the social sensitivity of the event in question. Thus, unrealistic optimism should be greater for socially stigmatizing events (e.g., becoming an alcoholic) than for less socially sensitive events (e.g., developing cancer). We provide support for this idea in five separate studies, spanning a variety of methods: meta-analytic, correlational, and experimental. For example, in a replication of Weinstein's (1980) seminal study, we find a strong correlation between an event's social sensitivity and the magnitude of unrealistic optimism, even controlling for a number of additional event characteristics (Study 1). Similarly, presenting a medical condition (burnout syndrome) as affecting fragile individuals leads to a large reduction in optimistic responding compared to when the same condition is described as affecting committed individuals (Study 2).

Second, the influence of event social sensitivity on unrealistically optimistic predictions should depend on individual and situational factors that are known to influence socially desirable responding. In line with this prediction, the responses of individuals with high levels of concern over impression management exhibited a stronger relationship between event sensitivity and unrealistically optimistic predications (Study 3). In Study 4 we manipulated instead the extent to which participants felt that they could be held accountable for their responses. We varied whether participants' judgments were solicited with no mention of confidentiality, with the usual assurances of confidentiality, or with an "enhanced" confidentiality condition in which the anonymity of participants' responses was emphasized. We find that the relationship between event social sensitivity and likelihood estimates varies as a function of the confidentiality condition. It is noteworthy that it was not the condition in which participants were given no promise of confidentiality where we observed a difference compared with the standard confidentiality condition, but rather the condition in which we took special steps to emphasize that confidentiality (beyond what is typically done in the literature).

Finally, building on these results, we propose that past work on unrealistic optimism may exaggerate the level of optimism truly held by research participants but that this exaggeration should be limited to predictions involving socially stigmatizing events. We test this hypothesis by using event social sensitivity as a predictor in Study 5, a meta-analysis of recent unrealistic optimism literature including 27 independent studies, 8826 participants, and 102 unique events. We find that social sensitivity is a significant predictor of unrealistic optimism over and beyond other variables investigated in prior research. Remarkably, in the case of events high in social sensitivity, we find an effect size for unrealistic optimism that is about twice as large as that for events low in social sensitivity.

Too Optimistic about What the Future Holds? How Greater Confidence Can Lead to Fewer Purchases

EXTENDED ABSTRACT

Recent years have witnessed various cases of corporate scandals, in addition to a long list of unethical behaviors by companies, managers, employees and consumers. Partly because of this pervasiveness of dishonesty in organizations and society more broadly, scholars have started investigating what may explain unethical behavior. Prior research in behavioral ethics has largely conceptualized ethical decisions as a function of individual and contextual factors. For example, prior work has examined the effect of individual traits such as age and gender (e.g., Muncy and Vitell, 1992), and contextual factors such as peer beliefs (e.g., Tyson, 1992), codes of ethics (e.g., Trevino and Youngblood, 1990), culture (e.g., Donaldson and Dunfee, 1994) and relative benefits and sanctions (e.g., Trevino and Youngblood, 1990). Yet, to date, research has overlooked a potentially important factor: the level of confidence and optimism the person facing an ethical dilemma is experiencing. In this paper, we demonstrate that feelings of confidence significantly influence both unethical behavior and judgments of ethicality. We propose that feelings of confidence can lead decision makers to cross ethical boundaries by overstating their performance, by deceiving potential consumers, or by offering them products that are of low quality or have safety issues.

The story we mirror in our studies goes as follows: A decision maker (e.g., a manager) believes she is experiencing just a bad round or she is not finding all the time needed to test a product to offer to a customer. The same decision maker also believes that she will be able to catch up during the next round – or when more time is available to properly test a product which is ready for the market. The more overconfident the decision maker is, the more she is likely to experience these feelings and to have this type of beliefs about her ability to catch up in the future. In turn, these strong beliefs license her to be deceitful when explaining the feature of the product to a consumer, or to cheat by overstating performance.

Across two studies we find evidence consistent with these main hypotheses. Confident decision makers are more likely to cheat by overstating their performance, believing they'll catch up in the future, compared to people in a control condition or who are not very confident in their own abilities. In Study 1, decision makers can lie about their performance in a given round, and know that there will be other rounds subsequently. When they experience a sense of heightened confidence, they are more likely to over-report their performance believing that they will be able to catch up. Our results show that in fact they do not. Similarly, decision makers experiencing confidence are more likely to lie about features of a product so that it looks good in the eyes of potential customers compared to people in a control condition. These main finding was demonstrated in a second study in which decision makers are paid based on how consumers react to their products. In this case, a heightened sense of confidence leads decision makers to be more likely to hide problems the product has and lie about the effectiveness and quality of the product.

In this research, we also explore the effects of feeling (too) confident on judgments of ethicality. Specifically, a third study demonstrates that feelings of confidence are also related to the acceptability of different ethical behaviors in the consumer domain. Specifically, after a procedure used to induce overconfidence in half of the participants, all participants answered Vitell and Muncy's (2005) Consumer Ethics Scale, which includes four different categories of ethical behavior. The categories are: Actively benefiting from illegal activity (e.g., Changing price tags on merchandise in a retail store, or Drinking a can of soda in a supermarket without paying for it); Passively benefiting at the expense of others (e.g., Getting too much change and not saying anything, or Not saying anything when the server miscalculates the bill in your favor); Actively benefiting from questionable behavior (e.g., Breaking a bottle of salad dressing in a supermarket and doing nothing about it, or Using an expired coupon for merchandise), and No harm/no foul (e.g., Tasting grapes in a supermarket and not buying any, and Spending over an hour trying on different dresses and not purchasing any). The results of this third study show that participants who felt confident rated the various unethical behaviors as less acceptable than individuals in the control condition, suggesting that confidence may also heightened moral leniency.

Together, the results of these studies provide a rich understanding of the influence of confidence on dishonest and deceitful behavior toward others. By contributing to both research on consumer behavior and behavioral ethics, this research allows us to extend existing models of unethical decision making by focusing on the level of confidence and optimism of the wrongdoer.

When Thinking Positive Gets the Better of Us: The Role of Optimism in Uninformed Consumer Choice

EXTENDED ABSTRACT

One of the authors was recently enjoying a plate of smoked salmon at an airport restaurant. The menu indicated that the salmon would be accompanied by toasted bread and a small bowl of an unfamiliar dish called Smetana. The Smetana turned out to look (and taste) very similar to whipped butter, but in the absence of more diagnostic information, she continued to spread it on the toasted bread without the slightest pang of guilt. Reality hit only when, after pointing at the empty Smetana bowl and asking for another one, the waiter brought what he described as "more butter." The butter was, of course, left untouched.

This paper investigates similar situations in which consumers' have limited diagnostic information about choice options and thus casts an optimistic glow on the evaluation of that option. Research has shown that individuals tend to be optimistic when assessing the likelihood of a desirable (but not undesirable) event, a bias known as the wishful thinking or desirability bias. Individuals are also unrealistically optimistic in their relative comparisons, believing that negative (positive) events are less (more) likely to happen to them than others. In this paper we build on research on positivity offset to investigate a different type of optimism related to consumers' evaluation of a decision outcome rather than to its likelihood assessment. Positivity offset is defined as the individuals' tendency to show a positive motivational approach at very low levels of evaluative activation. As a result of positivity offset, individuals may exhibit relatively positive rather than neutral expectations for unknown future events and may form positive impressions of unknown others. We therefore predict that when there is little or no diagnostic information about an option, consumers exhibit a general optimistic tendency by evaluating that option more positively than it would be warranted and thus seeking for more risk than they would have otherwise.

We tested this prediction in six studies. The first study replicated the circumstance described initially. Participants read a scenario in which they imagined being in a foreign country and tasting a local specialty. The specialty was shown in a picture illustrating a familiar bowl of whipped butter, but it was described either with less diagnostic ("Smetana") or more diagnostic ("Smetana, a whipped-butter-like spread" or "a whipped-butter spread") information. Participants were assigned to one of the three information conditions and asked to evaluate the dish. Results show that, relative to those in the two more diagnostic conditions, participants in the less diagnostic ("Smetana") condition thought that the spread was healthier, less fatty, and tastier, and reported the intention to eat more of it. Controlling for motivated reasoning (worry about weight and liking of the spread) did not alter the conclusions.

In the second study we aimed to directly rule out motivated reasoning as an alternative explanation and collect further evidence for our optimistic glow hypothesis. Participants imagined being in Turkey and having to decide whether or not to stay in an accommodation. The accommodation was illustrated in a picture showing a classic US Motel. As in the previous study, however, the accommodation was given either a non-diagnostic ("Pansiyon") or a more diagnostic ("Motel" or "Pansiyon (Motel-like)") description. To control for the motivated reasoning explanation, participants were asked to imagine either being tired, and as such motivated to stay in the accommodation, or not. Consistent with study 1, results show that participants were more likely to stay in the accommodation in the less diagnostic "Pansiyon" condition than in the other two, more diagnostic, conditions, regardless of whether or not they had a motivation to do so.

Next three studies we added more information about the evaluation target than simply an image and a short description. In studies 3 and 4, participants were told to imagine buying a bookcase from an online retailer. Participants were provided with customers' ratings of the retailer that were on average favorable (unfavorable) in the positive (negative) information condition, and with no ratings in the no-information condition. Participants were then asked whether or not they would buy the bookcase. The two studies differed in the manipulation of the mean and variance of the reported customers'

ratings. Results of both studies shows that, regardless of the rating variance, participants in the no-information condition were as likely to buy the bookcase as those in the positive information condition and more likely than those in the negative information condition. Study five replicated these findings with a different product category. In particular, participants imagined choosing a hiking trail and were provided with reviews from previous hikers. Once again, we found that participants in the no-review condition were as likely to buy the bookcase as those in the positive review condition and more likely than those in the negative review condition.

Last study moved to a real choice and consumption situation. Participants were told that the study was about tasting and evaluating Bolivian chocolates. The participants were either given no information, positive information (a vignette about the good reputation of Bolivian chocolate) or negative information (a vignette about the bad reputation of the Bolivian chocolate). In addition to tasting and evaluating the chocolate, participants were also given an option to snack on this chocolate during the 30-min session. The results showed that those who were given no information about Bolivian chocolates found it to be as tasty, high quality, and enjoyable as those who were given positive information and significantly more than those who were given negative information. More importantly, this pattern was replicated with the actual consumption of the chocolates during the study.

Overall, this set of studies supports our hypothesis that consumer are optimistic when evaluating options about which they are relatively uninformed. Participants seemed to give a "credit slack" to options about which they had less (or no) diagnostic information, with could lead to potentially harmful consequences in the cases of relatively unhealthy or unsafe alternatives, such as fatty food, shady accommodations, and untrustworthy retailers.

REFERENCES

Armor, D. & Sackett, A. M. (2006), "Accuracy, Error, and Bias in Predictions for Real versus Hypothetical Events," *Journal of Personality and Social Psychology*, 91, 83-600.

Buehler, R., Griffin, D., & Ross, M. (1994), "Exploring the Planning Fallacy: Why People Underestimate their Task Completion Times," *Journal of Personality and Social Psychology*, 67, 366-381.

Camerer, C. & Lovallo, D. (1999), "Overconfidence and Excess Entry: An Experimental Approach," *American Economic Review*, 89 (1), 306-318.

Donaldson, T. & Dunfee, T. W. (1994), "Toward a Unified Conception of Business Ethics: Integrative Social Contracts Theory," *Academy of Management Review*, 19, 252-284.

Fisher, R. J. (1993), "Social Desirability Bias and the Validity of Indirect Questioning," *Journal of Consumer Research*, 20 (2), 303-315.

Helweg-Larsen, M., Sadeghian, P., & Webb, M. S. (2002), "The Stigma of Being Pessimistically Biased," *Journal of Social and Clinical Psychology*, 21 (1), 92-107.

Krizan, Z., Miller, J. C., & Johar, O. (2010). Wishful thinking in the 2008 U.S. presidential election. Psychological Science, 21, 140-146.

Massey, C., Simmons, J. P., & Armor, D. A. (2011), "Hope Over Experience: Desirability and the Persistence of Optimism," *Psychological Science*, 22 (2), 274-281.

Muncy, J. & Vitell, S. (1992), "Consumer Ethics: An Investigation of the Ethical Beliefs of the Final Consumer," *Journal of Business Research*, 24, 297-311.

Vitell, S. J. & Muncy, J. (2005). The Muncy-Vitell Consumer Ethics Scale: A Modification and Application. Journal of Business Ethics, 62, (3), 267-275.

Simmons, J. P., Nelson, L. D., Galak, J., & Frederick, S. (in press), "Intuitive Biases in Choice vs. Estimation: Implications for the Wisdom of Crowds," *Journal of Consumer Research*.

Trevino, L. K and Youngblood, S. A. (1990), "Bad Apples in Bad Barrels: A Causal Analysis of Ethical Decision Making Behavior," *Journal of Applied Psychology*, 75, 378-385.

Tourangeau, R., & Yan, T. (2007), "Sensitive Questions in Surveys," *Psychological Bulletin*, 133 (5), 859-883.

Tyler, J. M., & Rosier, J. G. (2009), "Examining Self-Presentation as a Motivational Explanation for Comparative Optimism," *Journal of Personality and Social Psychology*, 97 (4), 716-727.

Tyson, T. (1992), "Does Believing that Everyone Else is Less Ethical Have an Impact on Work Behavior?," *Journal of Business Ethics*, 11, 707-717.

Vancouver, J. B., Thompson, C. M., Tischner, E. C., & Putka, D. J. (2002), "Two Studies Examining the Negative Effect of Self-Efficacy on Performance," *Journal of Applied Psychology*, 87, 506-516.

Weinstein, N. D. (1980), "Unrealistic Optimism about Future Life Events," *Journal of Personality and Social Psychology*, 39 (5), 806-820.

Decision Difficulty 2.0

Chairs: Jonah Berger, University of Pennsylvania, USA
Aner Sela, University of Florida, USA

Paper #1: Creating the Illusion of Choice through Selective Information Search and Retrieval

Rom Schrift, University of Pennsylvania, USA
Ran Kivetz, Columbia University, USA
Oded Netzer, Columbia University, USA

Paper #2: Getting Mired in Simple Decisions: The Role of Shrinking Attribute Weight Variance

Aner Sela, University of Florida, USA
Jonah Berger, University of Pennsylvania, USA

Paper #3: Winning through Conflict: When Goal-Conflict Increases Motivation

Jordan Etkin, University of Maryland, USA
Anastasiya Pocheptsova, University of Maryland, USA
Uzma Kahn, Stanford University, USA

Paper #4: The Obligation to Choose

Sheena Iyengar, Columbia University, USA

SESSION OVERVIEW

Conflict is one of the most definitive characteristics of choice. Without it, choice would merely involve the identification of the "best" or dominant option. But in most cases choice is not this easy. Making tradeoffs between alternatives, for example, or considering multiple options often leads to excessive decision difficulty. Indeed, much work has demonstrated that choice conflict often has negative, paralyzing effects, including increased difficulty, choice deferral, procrastination, increased anticipated regret, and decreased satisfaction with the chosen option (Dhar and Simonson 2003; Iyengar and Lepper 2000; Schwartz 2004; Tversky and Shafir 1992).

But while decision difficulty can sometimes have negative consequences, new insights suggest that experiences of conflict and difficulty serve additional purposes, and have further consequences and antecedents than previously considered. While situational factors often generate difficulty, might consumers sometimes make their own choices more difficult? Either to service a goal of making a diligent decision or through struggling to make the right choice? And while difficulty is usually seen as bad, might it be beneficial in some instances?

The current session addresses these and related questions as it offers cutting-edge insights into the causes and consequences of decision difficulty in consumer choice. The first paper (Schrift, Kivetz, and Netzer) demonstrates that consumers' desire to make diligent decisions leads them search for or recall option information in a way that artificially increases choice difficulty, creating an illusion of effortful deliberation. The second paper (Sela and Berger) shows that making tradeoffs between options leads people to lose sight of which product attributes are important, making choice more difficult and decreasing satisfaction with the chosen option. While the first two papers focus on downsides of decision difficulty, the third (Etkin, Pocheptsova, and Kahn) illustrates that difficulty can actually sometimes be beneficial. When choosing between conflicting goals, difficulty can provide a signal of value, making the goals seem more important and increasing consumers' motivation to achieve them. Finally, Sheena Iyengar, one of the foremost scholars in choice difficulty, will discuss some of her recent work on individuality, choice, and freedom, and the consequences of the obligation to choose.

Taken together, the talks illuminate the informative, motivating, and even reassuring nature of choice difficulty. Given the fundamental nature of decision difficulty in consumer behavior, and the variety of topics these talks cover, the session should be of interest to a broad set of audiences. Not only should it appeal to researchers working on judgment and decision making, choice, cognition, and inference making, but also to those who study the self-concept, goals, and motivation more broadly.

Creating the Illusion of Choice by Selective Information Search and Retrieval

EXTENDED ABSTRACT

Voluminous research in behavioral decision theory and social cognition argues that consumers simplify their decisions in order to make easy, confident, and justifiable choices. Such demonstrations of effort and conflict reduction behaviors can be seen in different streams of literature such as pre-decisional distortion of information (e.g., Russo, Medvec, and Meloy 1996, 1998), motivated reasoning and judgment (e.g. Kunda, 1990; Kruglanski 1990), and confirmation bias (Lord, Ross, and Lepper, 1979). Specifically, decision makers were found to reduce the effort in choice not only by selectively searching and attending external information (e.g. Mills, 1965; Mills & Jellison, 1968) but also by selectively accessing and retrieving information from memory. As Kunda (1990) stated: "…they (people) search memory for those beliefs and rules that could support their desired conclusion."

While simplifying processes in decision-making are important and ubiquitous, recent findings demonstrate that, in some situations, consumers also complicate their decisions (Schrift, Netzer, and Kivetz 2011) and strive for compatibility between the effort they anticipate and the effort they experience. Building on this research, we demonstrate that when consumers make important choices they are motivated to engage in a deliberate decision process that adequately vets the chosen alternative. Consequently, if the decision feels too easy and one alternative seem like the obvious choice, consumers artificially construct a more effortful decision process by (i) distorting the information they recall about the available alternatives, (ii) selectively interpreting ambiguous information in a manner that intensifies the conflict in choice and prolongs the decision process, and (iii) conducting an intensive search for information prior to choice. Such tactics enable consumers to feel that a diligent process of choice was performed and essentially help them create an illusion of choice.

In a series of studies we demonstrate consumers' complicating behavior. First, we show that when faced with an important yet obvious choice, participants retrieve information from memory in a manner that intensifies the conflict in choice. Specifically, respondents distort their memory and recall the inferior alternative as more attractive, thus bolstering its evaluation. Conversely, respondents distort their memory and denigrate the leading alternative in the set by recalling its aspects more negatively. Thereby, consumers construct a more effortful choice. Interestingly, such biases in memory search and selective retrieval are temporal and occur only in the pre-decisional phase. Once the decision is made and the need for conflict disappears, consumers' memory "improves" and the distortions attenuate. We demonstrate such complicating behavior in decisions involving job candidates and dating partners.

Advances in Consumer Research
Volume 39, ©2011

The second manner in which consumers are found to make their decision more complex is by interpreting exiting information in a manner that intensifies the choice conflict. In particular, when confronted with important yet relatively easy decisions between two models of cars, participants interpret the relatively ambiguous car review as more positive when it pertained to the inferior option but as more negative when it pertained to the superior option. Interestingly, this behavior was observed only when participants made the choice for themselves but not when they were helping a friend with his choice. This result helps rule out several alternative explanations and supports an effort compatibility principle as an underlying mechanism.

Next, we explore a third way by which consumers artificially create a more effortful choice, namely, by conducting an extensive search for information. Specifically, when respondents face an easy (as opposed to difficult) choice of a roommate or advisor they generate more questions about the potential candidates and acquired greater amount of information from the environment prior to reaching their decision. Finally, we show that such conflict enhancement behavior is more pronounced among consumers who are intrinsically motivated to work hard and associate effort with positive outcomes (i.e., subscribe to a "protestant ethic").

Getting Mired in Simple Decisions: The Role of Shrinking Attribute Weight Variance

EXTENDED ABSTRACT

Why do seemingly simple choices sometime suck people in and end up being much more difficult than they seemed at the outset? We suggest one reason is that making tradeoffs leads people to lose sight of which product attributes are really important. When choosing a flight, for example, most people would agree a priori that price and number of connections are more important than beverages or in-flight movie selection. But while these differences in importance may seem clear in the abstract, we argue that the act of making choices often muddies the distinction. In particular, we suggest that making tradeoffs between options reduces the variance in perceived attribute importance (i.e., difference in importance ratings of the various attributes) and makes unimportant attributes seem more important. This convergence of attribute importance, in turn, often makes choice more difficult.

We suggest this effect is driven by the focus that considering tradeoffs engenders. When considering differences in attribute levels across options, people focus on comparisons between levels *within* an attribute (e.g., how much better one movie selection is than another) and pay less attention to comparisons *between* the attributes (e.g., whether movie selection is as important as price). Consequently, attribute hierarchy becomes less salient. Further, the fact that there are tradeoffs (i.e., things to forego) within each attribute leads them all to seem equally important (rather than equally unimportant). Moreover, because tradeoff-making increases perceived attribute importance, it tends to have a particularly pronounced effect for attributes that start out seeming relatively unimportant than for attributes that seem important to begin with.

We test this possibility in three experiments. In Experiment 1, we examined how making attribute tradeoffs impacts the variance in attribute importance, and in particular, the importance of relatively unimportant attributes. In the attributes-first condition, participants indicated how important each of six attributes (e.g., flight duration, number of stops, and baggage fee) would be for them when buying a flight ticket (1 = extremely unimportant; 7 = extremely important). In the evaluation-first condition, participants were shown choice options before rating the attributes. They were asked to imagine buy-

ing a domestic flight and to consider four options described on the same six attributes as in the rating task (e.g., a longer flight departing from a convenient airport but with a long overall duration versus a shorter flight from a less convenient airport).

Results demonstrate that making trade-offs led people to lose sight of which attributes are more important. The variance of attribute importances decreased significantly when participants considered the options before rating the attributes ($M = 1.62$), compared to when they first rated the attributes before seeing the options ($M = 2.34$; $p < .01$). Further, this variance shrinkage was driven by an increase in the average importance of the least important attributes (those rated as less important in a pre-test), with no change in the average perceived importance of the most important attribute (ns). Decreased attribute importance variance, in turn, increased choice difficulty, decreased the extent to which participants felt that one option fitted them better than others, and decreased choice satisfaction and certainty ($\alpha = .85$); $M = 4.84$ vs. $M = 5.51$; $p < .01$).

In Experiment 2, we further tested whether this effect is driven by changed perceptions of unimportant attributes. We did this by manipulating the importance of the attributes that contained the trade-offs. Participants were all shown two flight options described by eight attributes. In the unimportant trade-offs condition only the unimportant attributes (e.g., beverages and in-flight entertainment) contained tradeoffs, while in the important trade-offs condition only the important attributes (e.g., price and number of connections) contained tradeoffs. Participants then rated all the attributes on the same 7-point scales used in the prior study.

Results demonstrate that making trade-offs decreased the variance in attribute important weights when the trade-offs were on unimportant attributes ($F(1,41) = 3.96$, $p < .05$). While the importance given to more important attributes did not change across conditions ($F < .40$, $p > .50$), unimportant attributes were seen as more important when trade-offs needed to be made on those attributes ($F(1,41) = 9.38$, $p < .005$).

Experiment 3 directly tests the proposed mechanism by examining whether the effects are moderated by focus of attention within individual attributes. Participants were shown four flight options, one in each column, described by four attributes, one in each row, but we varied how the information was displayed using a manipulation shown to influence whether people process the information by options or by attributes (Wen and Lurie 2010). In the by-attributes focus condition, a horizontal box was drawn around all levels within each attribute, highlighting the values of the same attribute across options. In the by-options conditions, a vertical box was drawn around all the attributes within each option, highlighting the values of different attributes within a given option. In the control condition no boxes were used. As predicted, focusing people on comparisons within an attribute (by-attribute condition) led them to lose sight of which options were important, shrinking attribute variance and increasing the perceived importance of the unimportant attributes.

Taken together, these studies demonstrate that tradeoff making can lead people to lose sight of their priorities. Focusing on within-attribute differences causes people to see unimportant attributes as relatively more important, undermining between-attribute differences. This, in turn, can make choice more difficult and frustrating, leading people to get stuck in decisions that initially seemed rather easy.

Winning through Conflict: When Goal-Conflict Increases Motivation

EXTENDED ABSTRACT

One important decision that people make every day is how to balance the pursuit of multiple goals. The decision becomes difficult when striving towards one goal prevents pursuit of other goals in the individual's goal system (Fishbach and Ferguson 2007; Kruglanski et al. 2002). For instance, a person may wish to get a promotion at work, but also to spend more time with family; one may want to loose weight and enjoy tasty foods, or save money for college and travel the world.

Reconciling the pursuit of multiple conflicting goals is psychologically aversive and induces decision difficulty. A consistent finding in prior literature suggests that goal conflict has a negative effect on goal pursuit, decreasing the likelihood that individuals will strive to achieve the conflicting goals. For example, among a group of smokers that wished to quit smoking, those that perceived their goal to quit smoking as conflicting with their other goals were less successful in quitting relative to those who perceived less conflict (McKeeman and Karoly 1991).

In contrast to past research, we propose that goal conflict can have a positive impact on motivation. Our proposition is based on the finding that subjective experiences of difficulty serve as input into judgment, even when judgment is unrelated to the source of experienced feelings of difficulty (Schwarz 2004). Though subjective difficulty often decreases subsequent evaluations (Novemsky et al. 2007), recent research suggests that it may also have positive effects, such as making products seem more unique (Pocheptsova, Labroo, and Dhar 2010) and instrumental to goal attainment (Labroo and Kim 2009), and increasing the perceived importance of decisions (Sela and Berger 2011). Building on this literature, we propose that subjective experience of difficulty associated with negotiating conflict among one's goals will influence evaluation of those goals. Just as people expect important decisions to be more difficult than less important decisions (Chaiken and Maheswaran 1994; Sela and Berger 2011), we believe they will expect to experience more conflict when thinking about more versus less important goals. Thus, when people experience goal conflict and associated feelings of difficulty in pursuing multiple goals, they may interpret these feelings of difficulty as a signal of goal importance.

The proposed effect of inter-goal conflict on goal importance has a number of downstream implications for goal-pursuit. The importance of one's goals is a key driver of commitment and motivation to pursue the goals; as people are more likely to strive towards more important goals (Kruglanski et al. 2002). Thus, if the subjective difficulty associated with goal conflict increases the perceived importance of one's goals, goal conflict may also increase motivation. Contrary to the previous work that has found inter-goal conflict to have a detrimental effect on goal-pursuit, we propose that people will be more motivated to pursue their goals when they feel the goals are in conflict with each other relative to when they are not.

Across a series of three studies we find consistent support for our proposition. Our first study tested the impact of goal conflict on perceptions of goal importance. Participants read a scenario where they were going on a ski trip with friends and also had an upcoming quiz in class. In the low conflict condition the quiz was three weeks before the ski trip, but in the high conflict condition, the quiz was immediately after the ski trip. Among several unrelated measures, participants rated importance of "academic success" and "spending time with friends". As we expected, participants rated both goals (to

do well in school and socialize with friends) as more important when conflict was high versus low ($p < .05$).

In study 2, we tested the second part of our proposition: the effect of goal conflict on motivation. Participants were asked to list two goals that they were currently pursuing. Half of participants were asked to list two examples of how those goals were in conflict with each other (high conflict condition); the remaining half were not asked for any examples (low conflict condition). After some filler tasks, we measured how conflicted participants felt and their motivation to pursue both goals. As we expected, participants in high conflict condition were more motivated to pursue their goals ($F(1, 25) = 5.98, p < .05$).

Finally, Study 3 replicated the positive impact of goal conflict on motivation and showed that enhanced perceptions of goal importance mediated this effect. We activated a performance goal and a hedonic goal for all participants by asking them to endorse a series of statements related to each goal (e.g., "I want to achieve success", "I want to relax and enjoy life"). Goal conflict was manipulated by asking participants to either list two (high conflict condition) or eight (low conflict condition) examples of how these goals conflicted. Listing eight examples is expected to be more difficult, thus creating the perception that the performance and hedonic goals were in less conflict relative to the two examples condition (Schwarz et al. 1991). Next, all participants indicated their willingness to pay for several goal-related products (e.g., highlighters, movie tickets) and completed a series of measures assessing their motivation to pursue the conflicting goals and perceptions of goal importance. Results showed that participants were willing to pay more for the goal-related products when they perceived more conflict among their goals ($F(1, 68) = 3.72, p < .06$). Consistent with previous results, goal conflict increased perceptions of goal importance ($F(1, 67) = 5.56, p < .05$) and motivation $F(1, 68) = 4.16, p < .05$). Finally, the positive effect of goal conflict on motivation was mediated by perceived importance of both goals.

Taken together these studies demonstrate that inter-goal conflict may have a positive impact on goal-pursuit. Contrary to previous work, we find that experiencing conflict among one's goals can actually increase motivation to pursue those goals. In particular, experiencing conflict among one's goals enhances the perceived importance of those goals, which in turn increases motivation to pursue them.

The Obligation to Choose

EXTENDED ABSTRACT

In his book *Powers of Freedom*, sociologist Nikolas Rose (1999) writes:

> Modern individuals are not merely 'free to choose,' but *obliged* to be free, to understand and enact their lives in terms of choice. They must interpret their past and dream their future as outcomes of choices made or choices still to make. Their choices are, in their turn, seen as realizations of the attributes of the choosing person—expressions of personality—and reflect back upon the person who has made them. (p. 87)

This talk considers the obligation to choose from a psychological perspective, exploring its origins and its consequences for consumers today.

Academics and practitioners alike have historically assumed that our choices are based upon our preferences, and that these preferences are derived directly from our self-interests, which are apparent to one and all. However, decades of research have now demonstrated repeatedly and compellingly, across a variety of different choosing domains, that just as our choices are based on our preferences, our preferences are derived from our choices and the decision context (Bettman, Luce, & Payne 1998). People regularly make choices that deviate from their stated preferences (e.g. Nisbett & Wilson, 1977), and moreover, they exhibit inconsistency in the strength and duration of their stated preferences (e.g. Hsee & Hastie, 2006; Tversky, Slovic, & Kahneman 1990).

Prior research has identified both cognitive and affective factors that contribute to the instability of preferences. In addition to these previously identified causes, there is another factor at play. The act of choosing for the modern day individual is associated not only with function and value but just as significantly with identity (e.g. Berger & Heath, 2007; Simonson & Nowlis 2000). When making a choice, the average individual is not just asking him or herself, "What do I want?" but rather, "What kind of individual am I, and given who I am, what *should* I want, and given what I *should* want, what do I choose?" If choosing is seen as the means by which individuals realize themselves, the burden of choice grows considerable and unavoidable.

When constructing and expressing identity, modern individuals, particularly those immersed in more individualistic cultures, feel the pressure to establish themselves as distinct from others, yet not so different that they become outcasts (Brewer, 2003). In studies that investigate people's preferences for items ranging from the common to the unique, people believe themselves to be more unique than everyone else, but in fact they either conform to the unique items (Kim & Markus, 1999) or they choose less preferred options only in order to avoid the label of "copycat" (Ariely & Levav, 2000). Thus, the modern individual can feel obliged to sacrifice personal preference in service of maintaining the appearance of a unique and independent identity.

This problem of the obligation to choose is especially acute in a world of ever-increasing choice. On top of the social burdens of choosing, the presence of more choice imposes a cognitive burden; people have to identify the attributes of the many options and engage in the task of comparing and contrasting all of them. There is over a decade of research documenting the negative consequences of offering people more choice: people delay making the choice, even if it is to their detriment (Iyengar, Huberman, & Jiang, 2004); they make worse choices (Iyengar & Kamenica, 2010; Thaler & Sunstein, 2008, p. 159-174); they exhibit less confidence in their preferences (Chernev, 2003); and they are less satisfied with the outcomes (Iyengar & Lepper, 2000; Schwartz et al., 2004).

Furthermore, this obligation to choose does not simply lead us to larger choice sets in familiar domains but to an expansion of the range of domains in which we expect choice to be available. Individuals believe they are obligated to never say "no" to choice, even when choosing is likely to be physically and emotionally costly. Choices that were heretofore unimaginable now often make up the typical person's choosing experience over a lifespan. For example, in recent studies that compare individuals who made life and death choices for loved ones with individuals for whom someone else made the choice, the choosers are revealed as suffering more for having made the choice than the non-choosers for having been relieved of the choice (Botti, Orfali, & Iyengar, 2009).

We have come to believe that every choice is important and that we must make all our own choices, perhaps because this preserves the illusion of control. But if we want to use choice as a tool to set ourselves free and to shape our futures, then we must rethink the assumption that choosing is always an act of freedom.

Hidden in the Darkness: The Role of Dark versus Bright Sensory Cues in Consumer Decision Making

Chair: Kuangjie Zhang (INSEAD)

Paper #1: Dim or Bright? The Influence of Illuminance on Creativity

Chen Wang, University of British Columbia, Canada
Ravi Mehta, University of British Columbia, Canada
Rui (Juliet) Zhu, University of British Columbia, Canada
Jennifer Argo, University of Alberta, Canada

Paper #2: Vices Lurking in the Dark: The Impact of Background Color on Indulgent Consumption

Kuangjie Zhang, INSEAD, France
Monica Wadhwa, INSEAD, Singapore

Paper #3: The Impact of Emotion on Color Preference: Evidence of Affective Fit

Chan Jean Lee, UC Berkeley, USA
Eduardo Andrade, UC Berkeley, USA

SESSION OVERVIEW

Consumers are exposed to a variety of incidental sensory cues in their every day life. An increasing body of research on sensory marketing shows that such incidental sensory cues can have far reaching impact on consumer decision making. For example, both ambient and product related sensory cues including touch (Peck 2009), scent (Morrin 2009), music (Zhu and Meyers-Levy 2005) and ceiling-height (Zhu and Meyers-Levy 2005) have been shown to impact consumers' product evaluations and preferences. Despite this growing body of research on sensory cues in marketing, relatively little is understood about how product-specific and ambient cues related to brightness interact with consumers' decision making. In an attempt to address this gap, in this session, we bring together an integrated set of three papers that elucidate the interactive relationship between dark versus bright sensory cues and consumer decision making. More specifically, this session explores two aspects of this interactive relationship. While the first two papers examine how dark versus bright sensory cues impact consumer preferences and consumer creativity, the third paper complements the first two papers by examining how consumers' affective states influence the preference for dark versus bright sensory cues.

Session Overview. The session will begin with a focus on the impact of dark versus bright ambient cues on consumer creativity. Chen Wang will present her work with Ravi Mehta, Rui (Juliet) Zhu, and Jennifer Argo. They suggest that dim (versus bright) ambience reduce individuals' inhibition, which leads to greater relational processing and subsequently results in heighted consumer creativity. Kuangjie Zhang will then present his work with Monica Wadhwa that builds on the first paper by examining the impact of dark versus bright product related cues on hedonic consumption. Specifically, they argue that consumers are influenced by the metaphoric relationship between darkness and product nature. Their findings demonstrate that when products are displayed with a dark versus bright background, it leads to greater wanting for indulgent products. Finally, Chan Jean Lee will present her work with Eduardo Andrade that complements the first two papers by examining the other side of this interactive relationship between dark versus bright sensory cues and consumer behavior. Specially, they investigate whether being in a certain affective state influences consumers' choices for bright versus muted colors. Their findings show that when in a happy state, consumers prefer products with bright colors. However, when in an

unhappy state, consumers show an enhanced preference for muted colors. They suggest that this relationship is governed by the matching of one's current emotional state with the emotional tone of the color.

To increase audience participation and provide insights about the three papers, the session will involve the participation of Darren W. Dahl as a discussant. Dahl has expertise in the area of creativity, new product development, and emotions in consumption contexts. Dahl, thus, has a unique perspective for synthesizing these papers and leading a discussion about an appropriate research agenda for continued work in this area. Each presenter will limit his/her talk to 15-20 minutes, to allow ample time for Dahl to speak and to engage the audience in a discussion of research ideas.

We believe that the features of this proposal suit the evaluation criteria for ACR 2011 symposium proposals. Notably, the session includes papers that are likely to have a broad appeal, yet maintain a coherent theme. We feel that this session brings together three papers that provide cutting edge insights into the incidental, seeming irrelevant sensory cues that drive consumer behavior and decision-making. In addition to attracting researchers interested in the domains of consumer perception and sensory marketing, we expect further interest from those who work within the application areas represented.

Dim or Bright? The Influence of Illuminance on Creativity

EXTENDED ABSTRACT

Creativity prevails in the consumption domain. Although a large body of extant research has been directed in exploring factors that influence consumer's creative performance in terms of the creative process itself (Dahl and Moreau 2007; Moreau and Dahl 2005), few attempts have been made to investigate how the external environmental factors affect consumer's creativity. Thus, the current research seeks to fill this gap by studying the effect of an important environmental variable, namely, ambient illuminance, on consumers' creative performance.

The central thesis of this research is that dim ambience reduces individual's inhibition, subsequently resulting in greater relational processing, thus leading to enhanced creativity. Prior research has provided relevant support for our theorizing. Specifically, research on environmental illuminance has shown that darkness promotes aggressive behavior (Page and Moss 1976) and dishonesty (Zhong et al. 2010) by reducing individual's inhibition. Moreover, according to Viskontas et al. (2004), inhibitory mechanisms allow one to selectively attend to relevant stimuli while suppress irrelevant features to the focal problem. Therefore, people with decreased inhibition may engage in remote association and relational processing, which are crucial elements to enhance creativity (Smith 1995).

Study 1 demonstrates the basic main effect of ambient illuminance on creativity. We predict that dim (versus bright) ambience leads to relational processing and subsequently results in heightened creativity. The ambient illuminance was manipulated by the number of lights in the room. Specifically, in the dim condition, the room was lit by 2 fluorescent light tubes mounted to the ceiling, with the total luminance of 150 lux. By contrast, in the bright condition, the room was lit by 20 fluorescent light tubes, with the total luminance of 1500 lux. To measure creativity, we used the Remote Associates

Advances in Consumer Research
Volume 39, ©2011

Test (RAT; Mednick 1962), a task commonly used to test creative thinking. In this task, participants were asked to generate the missing target word, based on the given stimulus words that were related to the unreported target word. To assess the underlying cognitive process, we adopted the recall task from Battig and Montague (1969). In this task, participants were given a list of 36 items belonging to six categories and were asked to examine them carefully for future task. After extensive filler questions to clear memory, participants engaged in a free recall task and subsequently a cued recall task with the category names given. As predicted, those in the dim condition generated more correct answers on RAT than those in the bright condition. More importantly, the adjusted ratio of clustering (ARC; Hunt and Einstein 1981), indicating the degree of relational processing, mediates the relationship between illuminance and creativity performance.

Study 2 built on the study 1 by assessing the effect of dim versus bright illuminance on two dimensions of creativity, namely, originality and appropriateness (Burroughs et al. 2008; Moreau and Dahl 2005). We hypothesize that dim ambience leads to higher originality, whereas bright ambience enhances appropriateness. We argue that if dimness, compared to brightness, engages individuals to make unusual conceptual connections and thus promotes relational processing, it should enhance originality of the ideas. By contrast, if bright (versus dim) illuminance makes people focus on specific details of the problem and thus hinders relational processing, it should enhance appropriateness of the ideas (Dahl and Moreau 2002). In this study, the ambience manipulation remained the same as that in study 1. The main task was the shoe polish problem-solving task (Burroughs and Mick 2004), in which participants were asked to generate as many solutions as possible to polish shoes given a constrained situation. After the experiment, twelve judges were hired to evaluate the originality and the appropriateness of the generated ideas on 7-point scales. As predicted, we found that those in the dim room generated more novel but less appropriate solutions, whereas those in the bright room produced more appropriate but less novel ideas.

Study 3 seeks to replicate the effect in a different domain of ad evaluation. We hypothesize that those in the dim room, who mostly engage in relational processing, would show more favorable evaluation towards the ad containing remotely related visuals. By contrast, those in the bright room, who primarily engage in item-specific processing, would have higher evaluation towards the ad with closely associated visuals. We employed a 2 (illuminance: dim vs. bright) x 2 (ad type: remotely related vs. closely related) between subject design. The ambience manipulation remained the same as the previous studies. In the focal task, participants were asked to evaluate the ad on three items (i.e., make sense, easy to understand, creative) on 7-point scales. A 2x2 ANOVA revealed a significant interaction between illuminance and ad type. Specifically, the pattern was consistent with our hypothesis such that those in the dim room favored the remotely-related ad, whereas those in the bright room preferred the closely-related ad.

Study 4 extends previous results by testing the multi-mediation of disinhibition and relational processing. In the same lab setting, participants' creativity performance was assessed by using Brick Task (Friedman and Förster 2000), in which they were to asked to generate as many usages as possible for a brick. To measure the underlying process, we included items that assess inhibition level, and used the recall task to generate ARC as that in study 1 to assess relational processing level. By following the *Multiple-Step Multiple Mediator Model* (Preacher and Hayes 2008), we demonstrated the multi-mediation effect, such that dim ambience reduced people's in-

hibition, leading to greater relational processing, thus subsequently enhancing creativity.

Taken together, this research advances our understanding of the impact of illuminance, an important ambience variable, on consumer's creativity. Our findings have important implications on environmental planning and product design.

Vices Lurking in the Dark: The Impact of Background Color on Indulgent Consumption

EXTENDED ABSTRACT

Consumers are influenced by the metaphoric relationship between color and product nature. Prior research suggests that brightness is often associated with goodness and purity, whereas darkness is often associated with evil and sin (Meier, Robinson, and Clore 2004; Sherman and Clore 2009). For example, in the Bible, Jesus is the "light of the world," whereas Satan is the "prince of darkness." However, just as the allure of Satan's temptations is hard to resist for humans, darkness may as well be associated with sinful pleasure and indulgence. In other words, darkness conceals two components, the sinful component and the pleasurable component. Indeed, a pretest revealed that while people consider black color more sinful than white color, they also consider black color more pleasurable and fun. Similarly, indulgent or vice consumption has been characterized as both pleasurable and guilt-evoking in consumer research (Khan and Dhar 2006; Kivetz and Simonson 2002). Drawing upon an integration of these perspectives, we hypothesize that dark background as compared to bright background is likely to enhance consumers' wanting for indulgent products. However, when indulgent consumption is incongruent with consumers' overriding goal (Fishbach, Friedman, and Kruglanski 2003), dark background would make the sinful component more salient than the pleasurable component, thus reducing consumers' wanting for indulgent products.

We tested our hypotheses in a series of three studies. Study 1 tested our main hypothesis by examining consumer choices. Participants were randomly assigned to one of the two conditions (picture background: bright vs. dark). To manipulate the picture background, we used gray scale as the relevant chromatic dimension. In all studies, bright is manifested in the color white (100% gray scale), and dark is manifested in the color black (0% gray scale). All participants first evaluated an indulgent food item (i.e., a beef and cheese burger) and a healthy food item (i.e., an organic green salad with chicken). After evaluating the food items, participants proceeded to a choice question, which asked them to choose one of the two food items they would like to have for dinner. As predicted, a logit analysis revealed that dark background color led to more indulgent food choices over healthy food choices among participants. Next, we computed the wanting index by subtracting wanting score for the salad from wanting score for the burger. We examined if the differences in wanting mediated the effect of background color on food choice. Following the bootstrapping procedure (Preacher and Hayes 2008), the indirect effect of background color on choice (through wanting) was significant, whereas the direct effect of background color on food choice became not significant. Thus, wanting for vice over virtue mediated the effect of background color on food choice.

In study 2, we tested our conceptualization that this dark versus bright background effect is eliminated or even reversed when indulgent consumption is incongruent with an overriding goal. Specifically, we argue that when people are primed with a health goal, dark background would make the indulgent products more sinful than pleasurable, thus reducing the wanting for indulgent consumption. The study consisted of a 2 (goal prime: health goal vs. control) ×

2 (background color: dark vs. bright) between-subjects design. We manipulated the goal priming by asking participants to first complete a scrambled sentence task (e.g., Chartrand and Bargh 1996). In the health goal prime condition, participants were given 20 sets of five words each and asked to make sentences using four of the five words. Ten out of the 20 sentences included a word (italicized in the samples below) intended to prime a health goal (e.g., it ate she usually *healthy*, *exercise* week they every hang). In the control condition, participants performed 20 sets of five words with neutral information (e.g., you held pencil building the, she building opened door the). After the goal priming task, participants moved on to a purportedly unrelated study in which they were asked to evaluate several food items. Specifically, they were asked to report how much they wanted and how much they were willing to pay for a sequence of three indulgent food items (a beef burger, a cookie, and a meat combo sandwich). Half of the respondents were shown the pictures with dark background, whereas the other half were shown the pictures with bright background. We computed a composite wanting score and the total willingness to pay for all the three items. A significant interaction between background color and goal prime emerged. In the control condition, dark background color led to greater wanting and higher willingness to pay for the indulgent food items, as compared to bright background color. In contrast, when participants were primed with a health goal, the result reversed such that dark background color led to reduced wanting and lower willingness to pay for the indulgent food items.

Finally, we generalize our findings by moving away from the food consumption context in study 3. Specially, we examined whether the dark versus bright background color of a potential co-worker's picture also affects people's co-worker selection choice (Dhar and Wertenbroch 2000). Participants were asked to imagine that they were assigned to a project. Half of them were told that the project requires one to be proficient on social skills, whereas the other half were told that the project requires one to be proficient on technical skills. Next, participants received the pictures of two candidates (one with dark background color and the other with bright background color), and they were asked to decide whom to work with. The matching between the background color and each specific candidate picture was balanced. Interestingly, a logit analysis revealed that participants were more likely to choose a co-worker whose photo background is dark (vs. bright) for a project that requires one to be proficient on social skills (vs. technical skills).

Together, these results suggest that dark background color, as opposed to bright background color, enhance consumers' wanting for indulgent consumption, and this effect is moderated by the salience of consumers' health goal. Our findings have wide implications for product packaging and advertisement design.

The Impact of Emotion on Color Preference: Evidence of Affective Fit

EXTENDED ABSTRACT

Judgments about colors are frequent in the market place. Consumers often buy products in the colors that they find most pleasing at the time of purchase and, knowing that, firms often rely on colors to appeal emotionally and aesthetically to consumers. Colors are associated with and inducers of specific emotional states: more saturated and lighter colors are perceived to be happier, more exciting, and purer (i.e., most often, positive emotions), whereas more muted and darker colors tend to be more strongly associated with sadness, distress or disgust (i.e., most often, negative emotions). However, in spite of the robust evidence of color's impact on emotion, the literature is surprisingly silent about the inverse relationship—that is, the impact of a viewer's emotion on his/her color preference. The current research investigates how an individual's emotional state influences his or her preferences for colors that have either congruent or incongruent emotional tones. Based on the literature on emotion and aesthetics, three conflicting hypotheses have been identified: emotion-*judgment* congruence (sad (vs. control/happy) people will show decreased preference for colors in general, independent of the emotional tone of the color), emotion-*target* congruence (sad (vs. control/happy) people will show increased preference for sad colors); and emotion-target incongruence (sad (vs. control/happy) people will show increased preference for happy colors).

Across four experiments emotions were induced through videos and color preferences were measured once before and again after the emotion inducing experience to control for massive individual differences characteristic of color preference. Thus, *preference change* due to emotion induction served as the main dependent variable. We asked participants to evaluate multiple colors (20 ~ 24 colors), which allowed us to focus on general emotional tones across colors, independent of specific color characteristics.

In the first two experiments, we induced either sadness or happiness and observed how people's preference for sad (vs. happy) colored square (Exp1) and colored t-shirts (Exp2) changed. Sadness increased preference for sad colors whereas happiness increased preference for happy colors, despite the use of different color stimuli (24 colors from HSL vs. 20 colors from retailers), different context (color squares vs. color t-shirts), and different evaluator's initial impression (people initially liked the color squares in general vs. people initially disliked the colored t-shirts in general).

The increase in preference for sad colors among sad participants represents an empirically unique and theoretically challenging phenomenon. Why would sad people prefer colors that make them even sadder? We identify three potential accounts: fluency (i.e., congruent (vs. incongruent) emotional tone of the color is more easily processed, thus liked), role fulfillment theory (i.e., the emotional tone of the color fulfilling people's "expectations" more (vs. less) effectively is preferred), and attitudinal commitment (i.e., colors of which meaning is coherent with their internally justified meaning and committed attitude toward the situation are preferred). Contrary to fluency (a pure perceptual process) or the role fulfillment hypothesis (an expectation-confirmation process), the attitudinal commitment account, which is proposed here, implies that the strength of one's attitudinal commitment and the strength of a color stimulus's attitudinal signal should impact emotion-target congruence effects. Specifically, emotional experiences that reflect personal beliefs, attitudes, and meaning to which one is highly committed (i.e., experiences that are high in attitudinal commitment—e.g., sadness) are more likely to produce emotion-target congruence effects than emotional reactions which inherit little personal view or value to which an individual could be attached (i.e., experiences that are low in attitudinal commitment—e.g., visceral disgust). Likewise, colored objects that provide stronger signals of one's own attitude, taste, and values (e.g., t-shirt) are more likely to produce the emotion-target congruence effects than colored objects that are unrelated to one's values and attitudes and are often chosen based on instrumental reasons (e.g., post-its). Experiments 3 and 4 provided evidence consistent with the attitudinal commitment account and inconsistent with fluency or role fulfillment accounts. That is, people like emotion-congruent colors when they find their emotion reflects a committed (vs. not-committed) attitude toward the situation (experiment 3) and when the colored object signals (vs. not does signal) one's committed attitude (experiment 4).

People like emotion-incongruent colors when their negative emotion does not reflect their committed attitude.

Our findings shed light into some conflicting findings in the emotion and aesthetics literature. Whereas there has been evidence showing that people in negative moods like emotion-incongruent aesthetic stimuli to lift their spirits (e.g., comedy, cheerful songs, game show), there has also been evidence that people in negative emotions increase preference for mood-congruent aesthetic stimuli. Consistent with our theorizing, the emotion-target congruence effect was often observed when people personally experienced loneliness, sadness, or regret (i.e., when the negative emotion contains a committed attitude and meaning toward a situation). On the other hand, emotion-target incongruence effect was observed when negative emotion was induced through bogus lab performance feedback or physical annoyance (i.e., when negative emotion has less committed values and meaning).

Finally, our findings imply where aesthetic pleasure comes from. In spite of the importance of aesthetic pleasure in people's daily life and psychological well-being, it mostly remains mysterious for scientists due to its complexity and subjectivity. In particular, the popularity of dramas, tear-jerker stories, and gloomy music challenge attempts to theorize about aesthetic pleasure based on hedonistic principles. Our findings show that aesthetic judgment is not only a matter of context and inherent taste, but also a function of the relationship between the emotional tone the stimulus conveys and the feeling one has at the time of the evaluation. Future studies are needed to explore the important relationships among emotion, emotional tone of aesthetic stimuli, and aesthetic pleasure.

Experiencing the Senses: The Interplay of Sensory Perception and Cognition

Chairs: Aradhna Krishna, University of Michigan, USA
Ryan Elder, Brigham Young University, USA

Paper #1: The "Visual Depiction Effect" in Advertising: Facilitating Embodied Mental Simulation through Product Orientation

Ryan Elder, Brigham Young University, USA
Aradhna Krishna, University of Michigan, USA

Paper #2: Something Smells Fishy: Suspicion Enhances Identification of Fishy Smells, and Fishy Smells Arouse Suspicion

Spike Lee, University of Michigan, USA
Norbert Schwarz, University of Michigan, USA

Paper #3: Guilt-Free by Association: How Images of Other Consumers Influence Subsequent Taste Perceptions

Morgan Poor, Indiana University, USA
Shanker Krishnan, Indiana University, USA
Adam Duhachek, Indiana University, USA

Paper #4: In Search of a Surrogate for Touch: The Effect of Haptic Imagery on Perceived Ownership

Joann Peck, University of Wisconsin-Madison, USA
Victor Barger, University of Wisconsin-Madison, USA
Andrea Webb, University of Wisconsin-Madison, USA

SESSION OVERVIEW

Inputs and interactions among multiple sensory modalities and the cognitions they afford affect what we imagine, what we experience, and how we process new information. The goal of this symposium is to introduce to marketing current research exploring the interplay of cognition and sensory perception, and to inspire further research within this promising area. The four presentations will address the complex interactions of cognition and sensory perception as it applies to consumer behavior—the impact of perceptual simulation on sensory experience, metaphorical transfer of meaning from smell, the impact of visual inputs on taste perception, and the consequences of imagined haptic experience. As such, the special session is designed to provide a relatively broad overview of research connecting cognition and sensory perception, so that it has a larger scope for generating directions for future research.

The first paper by Elder and Krishna explores the impact of visual product depictions on facilitating mental simulation, and ultimately affecting behavioral intentions. Across four studies they show that visually depicting a product that facilitates more (vs. less) mental simulation results in heightened purchase intentions. Also, occupying the perceptual resources required for mental simulation attenuates the impact of visual product depiction on purchase intentions. These mental simulations are also hypothesized to occur at a more automatic level, with differential consequences from deliberate forms of imagery.

The second paper by Lee and Schwarz explores that cognitions, by way of metaphorical transfers of meanings, can affect sensory perceptions. Specifically, the authors show that participants are more accurate at identifying a smell when a related metaphorical concept is activated. Across five experiments, the authors reveal a bidirectional effect of a fishy smell on conceptual activation of "fishy" or devious behavior and "fishy" behavior on the recognition of a fishy smell.

The third paper by Poor, Krishnan, and Duhachek examines the consequences of visual images on taste perception. The authors show that visual images for unhealthy foods lead to more positive taste

perceptions, whereas visual images for healthy foods lead to more negative taste perceptions. Interestingly, by depicting a person consuming the food, these effects can be reversed. The authors propose that observing consumption leads to a differential goal set, leading to altered expectations for the consumption experience.

The fourth paper by Peck, Barger, and Webb addresses the consequences of imagined touch on perceived ownership. The authors show that imagining touch can have the same effect on perceived ownership as physical touch. They additionally propose a cognitive resources explanation and test it using haptic interference. The impact of imagined touch has differential consequences depending on an individual's preference for touch information.

The underlying constructs across each of the four papers present a cohesive representation of the interaction of cognition and sensory perception. The symposium will prove beneficial not only to researchers interested in sensory perception, but also to those interested in better understanding perceptual processes and their impact on cognitive processes, imagery, and processing.

Mental Simulation from Product Depiction: When Visual Stimuli Facilitate Sensory Experience

EXTENDED ABSTRACT

We utilize the theory of grounded cognition (Barsalou 2008) to explicate the effects of mental simulations on consumer behavior. One component of grounded cognition is that our initial perceptions of an object are simulated upon subsequent encounters with not only the object itself, but also representations of that object, such as verbal and visual depictions. For example, when we use a mug, the brain encodes and integrates all of the different sensory perceptions related to the mug (e.g., how it looks, how it feels to grasp it, etc.). When we later produce knowledge of a mug, we mentally simulate prior perceptions associated with the mug, leading to neural activation of many of the same sensory regions of the brain active during perception (Goldberg et al., 2006; Simmons et al., 2005).

These simulations also include motor activity and the connection between vision and motor response. As supported by the literature, visual perceptions lead to simulations of the actions they afford (Tucker and Ellis 1998; Symes et al. 2007). For example, an object that appears to be graspable leads to mental simulations of grasping the object. We propose that the amount of mental simulation that this perception-action link affords should lead to differential consequences on behavioral intentions. With the present research, we propose that visually depicting a product which facilitates more (vs. less) mental simulation will result in higher (vs. lower) purchase intentions.

Studies 1a and 1b were designed to provide support for our initial hypothesis. The stimuli used in the studies were images of bowls of yogurt and hamburgers. The visual depictions were manipulated by flipping the image of over a vertical axis, such that the spoon (yogurt) or hand (hamburger) was oriented toward the right or the left. Participants saw one of the two images of the stimulus, and then proceeded to the questionnaire. The specific measure of interest is how likely the participant would be to purchase the item depicted. We also capture the participants' handedness.

Prior to analysis, we coded the data to reflect whether the visual depiction of the stimuli matched or mismatched the participant's handedness. This was done in all subsequent studies. As hypothesized, when the visual orientation matched the participant's dominant hand, purchase intentions were significantly higher than the mismatch condition.

With study 2 we seek to further explore the underlying process. As we propose that it is mental simulation underlying the results, restricting the ability to mentally simulate should attenuate the effects. Recent research shows that blocking the ability to perceive has consequences on conceptual knowledge (Oberman, Winkielman, and Ramachandran 2007). As our studies examine motor simulation, we have participants engage the senses used for such simulation. We operationalize this by having participants hold an object in their hand while viewing an advertisement. We posit that this simulation blocking will attenuate the effect of visual product orientation on purchase intentions.

The design for study 2 is a 2 (orientation: match, mismatch) x 4 (simulation block: dominant, non-dominant, both hands, none) between subjects design. In the simulation block conditions, participants either held a clamp in their dominant hand, non-dominant, or did not hold a clamp while viewing the advertisements. Participants viewed four advertisements, including the target advertisement which showed a cake with the fork either on the left or right.

Our analysis revealed a significant interaction. Follow-up contrasts reveal that within the no simulation block condition, the match condition leads to significantly higher purchase intentions than the mismatch condition, replicating the findings from the prior studies. Additionally, when the non-dominant hand is blocked, the pattern of results replicates the no-simulation block condition. Within the both hand simulation block condition, there is no significant difference between orientation conditions. However, within the dominant simulation block condition, the results are reversed. Thus, when participants' actual perceptual experiences are blocked, mental simulation is impeded with consequences on behavioral intentions.

Study 3 was designed to test whether the effects of visual product depiction on mental simulation obtained in our earlier studies are more automatic than other forms of imagery. We anticipate that instructions to fully imagine interacting with the stimulus should attenuate the effect of visual product depiction on purchase intentions, as given instructions to imagine, individuals can mentally pick up and rotate the object, and the initial orientation of the object should be of less importance.

Study 3 uses a 2 (product orientation: match, mismatch) x 2 (imagine instructions: yes or no) between subjects design. In the imagine instructions condition, participants were told to imagine using the product depicted (hammer). We get a significant interaction between orientation and imagery instructions. Follow up contrasts reveal that when participants are not given instructions to imagine using the hammer, the match condition leads to significantly higher purchase intentions than the mismatch condition. When participants are instructed to imagine, there is no significant difference in purchase intentions.

We posit that the process underlying our results is mental simulation. Should it be mental simulation underlying the results, a positive experience should become more positive, and a negative stimulus should become more negative, as the simulated experience is aversive. Thus, the prediction for study 4 is that the initial positive effect of the visual depiction on purchase intentions will be reversed for a negatively valenced stimulus.

In order to test our hypotheses, we created create two sets of stimuli: one positively valenced (Asiago Cheese and Tomato Soup), and one negatively valenced (Cottage Cheese and Tomato Soup). The manipulation of visual depiction used in study 4 is made by sim-

ply altering which side of the bowl the spoon is on. This study is thus a 2 (orientation: match, mismatch) x 2 (valence: positive, negative) between subjects design.

Analysis of study 4 shows that within the positively valenced condition, the match condition leads to significantly higher purchase intentions than the mismatch condition. However, within the negatively valenced condition, the results are reversed. The findings from study 4 are supportive of a simulation account such that the visual depiction facilitates mental simulation, which in turn drives behavioral intentions.

Something Smells Fishy:
Suspicion Enhances Identification of
Fishy Smells, and Fishy Smells Arouse Suspicion

EXTENDED ABSTRACT

Across languages, suspicion can be expressed metaphorically as dislikeable odors (Soriano & Valenzuela, 2008). In English, the specific odor is fishy; if something smells fishy, it creates "doubt or suspicion" (Merriam-Webster, 2010). Extending grounded social-cognition research beyond its current focus on visual and tactile perception and on conceptual metaphors presumed to be universal (e.g., Affectionate=Warm; Moral=Pure; Important=Heavy; Powerful=High), we explore the grounding of suspicion in smell as instantiated in the English language.

Does social suspicion affect smell identification? In Experiment 1, participants were asked to close their eyes, sequentially open five test tubes wrapped in aluminum foil, sniff the content, and identify each smell. After giving instructions about this task, for half of the participants ($n = 40$), the experimenter hurriedly took away a form underneath the response sheet as if it was something participants were not supposed to see, and she remarked, "we're not trying to hide anything here." For the other half, she did not act or make the remark ($n = 40$). Next, all participants completed the smell identification task by identifying the smell of five consumer products ("autumn apple" fragrance oil, onion flakes, "creamy caramel" fragrance oil, "orange nectar" fragrance oil, and fish oil). Responses that included the item's name or any one of its ingredients were coded as *identified*. As predicted, participants induced to feel suspicious showed higher accuracy in identifying fish oil; suspicion did not affect accuracy in identifying any other smell. This pattern suggested a metaphor-specific effect of social suspicion on smell identification.

What is the psychological process that underlies this metaphor-based influence? Using an experimental causal-chain design (Spencer, Zanna, & Fong, 2005), Experiments 2-4 tested each step of our hypothesized causal chain: "Feeling suspicious → Accessibility of suspicion concepts → Accessibility of fish concepts → Identification of fishy smell."

In Experiment 2, participants were induced to feel suspicious ($n = 25$) or not induced ($n = 24$), and did a word-completion task. Of the 20 items, 10 could be completed with suspicion-related words (e.g., *doubt, dubious, suspicious*). As expected, participants induced to feel suspicious wrote more suspicion-related words; thus, a feeling of suspicion increased the accessibility of suspicion concepts.

In Experiment 3, participants were primed with suspicion concepts in a scrambled-sentence task (based on the suspicion-related items in the word-completion task of Experiment 2; $n = 57$) or primed with unrelated concepts ($n = 59$). Next, they did a word-completion task with 20 items, 10 of which could be completed with fish-related words (e.g., *fishing, gills, fin, tuna*). As expected, participants primed with suspicion concepts wrote more fish-related words; thus, suspicion concepts increased the accessibility of fish concepts.

In Experiment 4, participants were primed with fish concepts in a scrambled-sentence task (based on the fish-related items in the word-completion task of Experiment 3; $n = 19$) or primed with unrelated concepts ($n = 15$). Next, they completed the smell identification task used in Experiment 1. As expected, participants primed with fish concepts showed higher accuracy in identifying fish oil. There was no effect on any other smell. Thus, priming fish-related concepts specifically enhanced identification of fish oil.

Results from Experiments 2-4 suggest that the metaphor-specific effect of social suspicion on smell identification is mediated by a process of metaphoric concept association. Recognizing the unconscious nature of this process, we tested for the reversed causal effect in Experiment 5: Does incidental exposure to a fishy smell increase social suspicion? Participants were individually approached by an experimenter in a campus hallway and asked to complete an "investment decision task" (the trust game) together with another "participant" (a confederate). The participant and the confederate were each given 20 quarters. The participant first decided how much to give the confederate; any amount given would be quadrupled in value (e.g., $0.25 would become $1.00). The confederate could then decide to give any amount (all, some, or none) back to the participant. With trust, participants should give more money based on the expectation that the confederate would return a reasonable proportion of the investment; with suspicion, participants should give less money. Depending on condition, another confederate sprayed a segment of the hallway with one of three substances (fish oil, fart spray, water) while the experimenter recruited the participant (thus keeping recruitment unaffected by the smell). As predicted, participants who smelled something fishy (fish oil) invested less money than those who smelled another aversive odor (fart spray) or no odor (water). The last two conditions did not differ, indicating that the impact of a fishy smell is due to their metaphorical meaning, not mere negative affect. Thus, incidental exposure to a fishy smell increased social suspicion and undermined trust, as reflected in less cooperation in an economic trust game.

In sum, five experiments support the grounding of suspicion in smell. We find bidirectional effects, as social suspicion increases accuracy in identifying a fishy smell and exposure to a fishy smell increases social suspicion. Because the grounding is based on a metaphor, effects are specific to the metaphor and limited to a fishy smell. Our data further support the assumption that metaphor-based influences are mediated by nonconscious concept associations. These results extend grounded social-cognition research beyond the visual and tactile domains and shed light on the underlying mechanism. They also raise new questions about the operation of grounded concepts with identical structure (suspicion grounded in smell) but different cultural-linguistic instantiations (e.g., "fishy" in English).

Seeing is Believing: Exploring the Conditions Under Which Food Images Influence Taste Perceptions

EXTENDED ABSTRACT

Appetizing food images are rampant in marketing. The influence that such images have on taste perception, however, is still not well understood. In the current research, we posit that food images do influence taste perceptions, but that this relationship is moderated by the type of food featured in the ad and the image context.

When a product is consumed, its actual sensory attributes are compared and contrasted with any preexisting expectations. A mismatch between the expected and actual attributes of the product produces either positive or negative "disconfirmation" (Cardello & Sawyer, 1992). According to assimilation theory, when disconfirma-

tion occurs, perceived product performance will assimilate (become similar) to the level of expectation (Hovland, Harvey, & Sherif, 1957). In the domain of food, this means expected sensory qualities would combine with experienced sensory qualities, causing actual evaluations to more closely resemble the expected evaluation.

Previous research by Raghunathan and colleagues (2006) demonstrated that consumers hold an implicit belief that foods characterized as healthy are less tasty than foods characterized as unhealthy and that this intuition can color consumers' inferred and actual taste evaluations. Building on this research, we propose that an image of a healthy (unhealthy) food will activate negative (positive) expectations about the tastiness of the featured food and that these expectations will combine with the actual taste experience, causing taste evaluations to more closely resemble the expected evaluation than if the same item were evaluated without image exposure. More formally:

Hypothesis 1a: Exposure to an image of an unhealthy (healthy) food will enhance (reduce) taste perceptions during subsequent consumption of that food, relative to no image exposure.

Hypothesis 1b: The number of positive minus negative sensory thoughts produced during consumption will mediate this effect.

Second, we propose that this pattern of results can be reversed when the context of the image viewed includes a person actually consuming the featured food (consummatory image). To explain this effect, we turn to the literature on goal contagion and argue that a consummatory image may prime automatic goal activation and pursuit (Aarts, Gollwitzer, & Hassin, 2004). When an individual sees an image of someone eating a healthy food, they may infer that the person is pursuing a healthy eating goal, and consequently adopt and pursue that goal themselves. In contrast, consuming unhealthy foods is a behavior often associated with the goal of seeking indulgence, which may involve mixed feelings. Thus, seeing an image of someone indulging in an unhealthy food, particularly when the person is shown eating alone, may act as a negative goal-related cue, which we argue will de-activate an indulgence goal or in other words, activate a healthy eating goal.

As such, we expect that exposure to consummatory images may automatically activate a healthy eating goal and that this temporary motivational state may color consumers' expectations about the subsequent taste experience (Markman, Brendl, & Kim, 2007). More specifically, we expect that seeing an image of someone eating a healthy (unhealthy) food will activate a healthy eating goal and that this will positively (negatively) influence expectations about the taste of goal (in)consistent food, such that when the food is then eaten, the consumer evaluates it as tasting better (worse) than if they had only seen an image of the food alone. More formally:

Hypothesis 2a: Exposure to a consummatory image of an unhealthy (healthy) food will reduce (enhance) taste perceptions during subsequent consumption of that food, relative to a pure food image.

Hypothesis 2b: The number of positive minus negative sensory thoughts produced during consumption will mediate this effect.

In experiment one, we test H1a and H1b employing a 2 (image exposure: yes, no) x 2 (food type: healthy, unhealthy) between-subjects design. Subjects were told that they would be helping pretest stimuli for a future study on food advertising. Subjects in the image exposure conditions were shown five different food images of either apples (healthy) or chocolate (unhealthy) and asked to indicate the pleasantness of each image on a nine-point scale (unpleasant-pleasant). Next, subjects tasted a sample of the same food item featured in the images, listed any thoughts they had while tasting it, and rated its taste on four nine point scales anchored by bad/good quality, flavorless/flavorful, not at all /very delicious, bad/good taste). Subjects in the no image exposure- healthy/ unhealthy conditions only completed the respective taste tests. As expected, the results showed that subjects that saw images of chocolate rated the chocolate sample better than those that only tasted the sample. In contrast, those that saw images of apples rated the apple sample worse than those that only tasted the apple. These effects were mediated by the net positive sensory thoughts produced during consumption.

In experiment two, we test H2a and H2b using a 2 (image context: food alone, food consumed) x 2 (food type: healthy, unhealthy) between-subjects design. The procedure mirrored that of experiment one, except that all subjects were exposed to a series of eighteen food images prior to the taste test. Image context was manipulated by using images that either featured only the target food item or the target food item actually being consumed. As expected, the results showed that subjects exposed to images of just chocolate rated the chocolate sample better than those that saw images of chocolate being consumed. In contrast, subjects that saw images of apples being consumed rated the apple sample better than those that saw images of just apples. These effects were again mediated by the net positive sensory thoughts produced during consumption.

Taken together, our findings show that exposure to food images primes expectations, which influence subsequent taste perceptions. More importantly, we show that the direction of this effect depends on the type of food featured and the context of the image. We are currently running additional studies, which demonstrate the generalizability of these findings and identify important boundary conditions. These findings also have important implications for marketers of both healthy and unhealthy food products, as well as consumers trying to adhere to a healthier diet.

In Search of a Surrogate for Touch:
The Effect of Haptic Imagery on Perceived Ownership

EXTENDED ABSTRACT

Previous research has shown that consumers value objects more highly if they own them, a finding commonly known as the endowment effect (Thaler, 1980). This effect is not limited to legal ownership; psychological ownership, characterized by the feeling that something "is mine," also produces the endowment effect. One antecedent of psychological ownership is the ability of an individual to control an object by touching it. Peck and Shu (2009) show that when individuals are given the opportunity to touch an object (versus not), they report a greater sense of perceived ownership and value the object more highly.

If touch is not available, could imagining touch act as a surrogate? According to MacInnis and Price (1987), imaging is a resource demanding process in which sensory information is represented in working memory. Bone and Ellen (1992) conjecture that imagery "may involve sight, taste, smell and tactile sensations" (p. 93). Although research on imagery and the tactile system is limited (Klatasky, Lederman & Matula, 1993), there is some evidence for the interdependence of touch and imagery (Katz, 1925).

Since imaging requires cognitive resources and the effects of imagery are mediated by resource availability (Bone & Ellen, 1992; Unnava, Agarwal & Haugtvedt, 1996), blocking out perceptual distractions during imaging may enhance its effects. In some instances, consumer behavior researchers have instructed participants to close their eyes when imaging (e.g., Bone & Ellen, 1992; Keller & McGill, 1994 (Experiment 1); Petrova & Cialdini, 2005 (Study 3)), although this was not the focus of these studies. We hypothesize and find that closing one's eyes while imagining touching an object leads to greater psychological ownership than imagining touching an object when one's eyes are open.

An experimental study was designed to examine the effect of touch imagery on perceived ownership. The design was a 4 (imagery/touch: imagery eyes closed, imagery eyes open, no touch no imagery, touch with no imagery) x 2 (product: Koosh ball, blanket), with the first factor manipulated between subjects and the second factor varied within subjects. Three hundred and twenty-six individuals participated in the study.

Our first hypothesis predicted that when participants imagined touching the product with their eyes closed, perceived ownership would be greater than when participants imagined touching with their eyes open. We found a main effect of touch/imagery for perceived ownership. Both the touch condition and the touch imagery with eyes closed condition resulted in a significantly greater sense of ownership than the touch imagery with eyes open condition and the no touch-no imagery condition.

We next conducted a second study in order to examine the process in more detail. We hypothesized that when a person closes her eyes to imagine, she is focusing her cognitive resources, which results in similar effects to actual touch. In the second study, we had participants imagine touching a product (as in Study 1) but we manipulated whether haptic interference was present and also whether the interference "fit" with the imagined object. The design of this study was a 2 (vision: eyes open, eyes closed) x 3 (haptic stimulus: none, congruent, incongruent) with both factors manipulated between subjects. Three hundred and eighty-seven individuals participated. In addition to replicating our first study, we found that when a person imagines touch with eyes closed, the presence or absence of haptic stimuli does not significantly impact haptic imaging unless the stimulus is incongruent with the product being imagined.

The third study delves deeper into both the process and the individual difference in Need for Touch (Peck and Childers, 2003). Consumers may base their product evaluations not on the product information with which they are presented, but rather on the fluency with which that information can be processed (Lee and Labroo, 2004). Since individuals high in NFT are more proficient at processing haptic information, we hypothesize that they do not need to close their eyes to effectively imagine touch, whereas individuals low in NFT do. As a result, it should be easier to interfere with the haptic imaging of a person lower in NFT. We find the predicted results in this experiment. To further elaborate on the process, we also measure the vividness of the haptic images.

We are currently conducting a study that extends the previous studies by investigating perceived control as an antecedent of perceived ownership. In the previous studies, we hypothesized that touch and haptic imaging both led to an increase in perceived ownership due to the ability to control the object. In this study, we directly measure perceived control as further evidence of the process. We also limit the time for imagining touch to provide further support for our cognitive resources explanation. Data collection is underway and the results will be available for presentation at ACR.

Innovative Community Exchange Systems: Grassroots Social Experiments in Sustainability

Chairs: Julie Ozanne, Virginia Tech, USA
Lucie Ozanne, University of Canterbury, New Zealand

Paper #1: Building Community Efficacy and Welfare through Time Bank Exchanges

Lucie Ozanne, University of Canterbury, New Zealand
Julie Ozanne, Virginia Tech, USA

Paper #2: Hybrid Pro-Social Exchange Systems: The Case of Freecycle

Zeynep Arsel, Concordia University, Canada
Susan Dobscha, Bentley College, USA

Paper #3: "The Indefinite Future": Ideas, Ideals, and Idealized Ideology in the Global Eco-Village

Robert Kozinets, York University, Canada
Frank-Martin Belz, Technische Universität München, Germany

SESSION OVERVIEW

Significant existing research documents the negative impact of consumption on the environment (see, for example, Kilbourne and Beckmann 1998). Less attention is given to exploring the burgeoning local experiments by individual consumers and communities who seek to live more sustainably (Prothero et al. 2011). We bring together three empirical studies of local community-based initiatives that offer alternative models of exchange based on life affirming values of sharing (Belk 2010), capacity building, and wise stewardship over the earth's limited resources.

Specifically, across the three papers, we examine the ongoing social construction and negotiation of new norms and values within three local community engagement projects: a community time bank, an online item exchange community, and ecovillages. To varying degrees, each of these experiments was inspired and is connected to international social movements; yet the exchange systems are inescapably enacted within local environs that are shaped in minor and major ways. These exchange systems are relatively new so we are able to see the actual development and formation of new social norms and community practices to affirm these values. We examine how these experiments in sustainability both expand and limit the capacities of communities to transformation. We seek to move toward a better understanding of collective efficacy and to inform the development of an applied theory of community change. These experiments provide useful insights to the challenges facing us as we move haltingly toward a more sustainable post-consumer culture (Mick 2006).

Lucie Ozanne and Julie Ozanne examine the development of a time bank community. Time banks are based on a form of community exchange that assumes everyone's time is equal in value. As such, time becomes a unit of value in which participants give and receive help in exchange for time credits. While consumers import norms and social expectations from market-mediated and family-mediated exchange, the time bank requires different norms to release its potential to enact social change.

Zeynep Arsel and Susan Dobscha examine an internet-mediated item exchange community that is international in reach but operates at a local grass roots level. This Freecycle community is often considered to be a gift economy in which people post free goods that are then presented as gifts (Giesler 2006). The authors explore contradictions between the top-down policies of an organization guided by a specific ethos and the bottom-up contestation of the local participants

engaged in meaning making. The potential of this community is at times thwarted by these organizational policies.

Rob Kozinets and Frank-Martin Belz provide perhaps the most dramatic example in their examination of intentional and sustainable communities called ecovillages. Not surprisingly, this lived experience has a more profound influence impacting members' connection to their food, the land, and one another.

Jean-Sébastien Marcoux, who is trained as an anthropologist and has published provocative work on the contrary nature of gift giving (Marcoux 2009), is well suited to comment on the contradictions found within these experiments. In conclusion, this session should be of particular interest to scholars concerned with issues such as sustainability, community building, community resilience and efficacy, sharing, gift giving, generosity, and altruism.

Building Community Efficacy through Time Bank Exchanges

EXTENDED ABSTRACT

A time bank is a locally-based exchange system in which labor flows through non-reciprocal exchange (Seyfang 2004). Community members "deposit" an hour of labor by giving services to another time bank member and, in return, can "withdraw" an hour of service from different members (Williams 2004). The time bank in this study began in 2005 with just a handful of members and now claims over 300 members, which represents about 13% of the local town. To date, over thirty thousand hours have been exchanged and currently an average of four hundred hours is traded each month. While original members were all individuals, memberships now includes organizations ranging from the local school, radio station, medical center, community garden, and childcare facility.

Part-time field work spanned approximately eighteen months and included participant observation of both the internal administration of the time bank and external community events as well as actively trading in the time bank. Besides field notes, the data collected included focus group interviews, over twenty formal interviews, and time bank communications, trades, and publicity. Data collection is completed and the data analysis is well underway.

Time bank trades are facilitated through an online trading system, which documents the breadth and diversity of the skills that exist in the community. Thus, the community becomes aware of the latent and often untapped potential of its members, which positively impacts the community identity as resourceful. Similarly, even individuals who may feel like they have no 'marketable' skills become aware of capacities they possess that are valued by others and can be traded (e.g., companionship, canning preserves, dog walking). The time bank breaks down barriers and allows neighbors to request and offer help through indirect exchanges. Through time bank exchanges, traders become more deeply integrated into the local community. Early in the field work, traders struggled to transport social norms derived from marketplace and more familial exchange. More recently, the time bank is emerging as a community resource guided by a different logic.

While traditionally relational and reciprocal exchange is highly valued (Dwyer, Schur, and Oh 1987), the weak ties of non-reciprocal exchange allow the community to tap into the significant distributed expertise of the community (Sampson 2002). Increasingly the time bank is seen as a way to mobilize the power of this network increasing collective efficacy and contributing to the quality of community life. Time bankers rally to engage in community projects, such as working on the summer street festival, facilitating the weekly farmers' market, participating in the annual clothes swap, and volunteering at the local visitor information center finding that even physically demanding tasks are more pleasant when shared (Belk 2010). Time bank members initiated a scheme to "tag bust" and clean-up graffiti. The time bank creatively responded to cuts in government funding by training time bankers to run physical fitness courses and adult education classes--participants then paid in time credits. The time bank is used to socialize the youngest community members on being civic minded and altruistic. For instance, the local school encourages their student body "to learn about the benefits of community and giving" through beach clean-ups and other community enhancing projects.

Rather than suffering from the classic economic free rider problem, community time wealth accrues and needs to be redistributed. Time bank members regularly gift their time credits to members who are in need of support or toward community projects. A community treasure chest of time credits enables the time bank to direct community effort to priority initiatives, such as volunteer assistance with reading recovery programs, art and drama projects, and working bees at the school. As one older informant states: "I go into the school each week and work with a few children who need a bit of extra help with reading. All my grandchildren live in the North Island, so it is lovely to have this contact with these delightful beings."

Perhaps the most dramatic example of the time bank's potential for collective efficacy and community resiliency was evidenced in the aftermath of the first New Zealand earthquake; the time bank helped people rally when the civic services became over whelmed. For instance, the health center turned to the time bank to activate members to phone elderly patients to check on their safety. When the volunteer fire brigade was besieged with calls to dismantle unsafe chimneys and structures, the time bank assisted. Members also manned the information center providing a retreat and social valve for residents to vent their anxieties. Direct support was provided to residents, whose homes were severely damaged, providing them with shelter and support. The time bank acted as a conduit of information regarding tunnel and road closures and local infrastructure and support. Perhaps most importantly, community members were given the opportunity to act constructively helping others during a crisis that often left people feeling helpless and alone.

Hybrid Pro-Social Exchange Systems:
The Case of Freecycle

EXTENDED ABSTRACT

Freecycling is an organization that facilitates non-reciprocal exchange of goods within local communities with the goal of reducing waste (Freecycle website). This exchange is pro-social since the participants who offer their possessions to others do so at a personal cost and without immediate gain (Penner et al. 2011). It is often characterized as a gift system given no financial exchange occurs; instead, the exchange is governed by a principle of generalized reciprocity across members (Nelson and Rademacher 2009). Initiated informally by a group of friends in Tucson, AZ who realized that their trash might be another's treasure (company documents), members now number over 8 million users across 85 countries. The institutional mission is to promote gifting among its members, divert goods with existing use value from landfills, and reduce the overall impact of consumption on the environment.

Freecyling provides free goods to consumers for a diverse range of reasons. The majority of the participants are similarly minded, socially cooperating, free laboring individuals who redistribute goods in a creative and novel way. In fact Nelson, Rademacher, and Paek (2007) found that members of a local Freecycle community had a distinctly less materialistic relationship with consumer culture and higher levels of civic involvement and politicized consumption than non-Freecyclers. Whereas the assumption is that Freecyclers are acting upon some greater moral imperative when they gift these items, previous research suggests that participants who joined Freecycle could actually fit into one of four categories of motivation: self-interest, decluttering, environmental concerns, and helping others (Nelson, Rademacher, and Paek 2007).

We have conducted a multi-method analysis utilizing blog mining, archival search, and interviews with 22 regular participants of Freecycling. Both authors also are active participants of the community since 2007 and exchanged goods through their local Freecycle chapters. Our data analysis revealed several interesting tensions between the goals of the institution (the owners of the Freecycle brand) and its community members (participants in local chapters). Specifically, these tensions arise from institutional norms being imposed upon the participants rather than from the patterns of consumption that emerged from freecycling. While others find improved community cohesion as a result of these pro-social communities (Ozanne and Ozanne 2010), our research suggests a more complicated picture.

Our work extends theories on exchange following Belk's (2010) article on sharing. Belk outlines a typology of marketplace exchanges that correspond to three divergent cultural patterns with their own rituals and behaviors: sharing, gift giving, and commodity trade. The case of Freecycling exhibits characteristics of all three prototypes in contrast to the organization's frame of "gifting." Furthermore, within each exchange, tensions and paradoxes arise from the institutional misalignment of norms and expectations. For example, while the mission of Freecycle is to offer and request goods free, participants are discouraged from providing information related to personal predicaments (a counterindication of sharing) and from expecting reciprocity (counterindication of gifting). We suggest that this complex and paradoxical practice of impersonal "sharing out" (Belk 2004; Widlock 2004) provides a fruitful context to further extend theories of exchange.

We find four main tensions arising from the mismatch between the institutionally imposed norms and community participation. These tensions suggest the hybrid and ambiguous status of this exchange system vis-a-vis Belk's typology. The first tension arises around the issue of materialism. While the aim of Freecycle is to reduce overconsumption, some informants are materialistic in their motives and actually hoard goods. In some ways, Freecycle allows them moral license to acquire too much. Still, we argue that this hybrid exchange system allows people to engage in variety seeking and collecting while minimizing their ecological impact when compared to buying "new" goods. The second tension arises when nontraditional items are commodified. For example, pets and personal services are considered inappropriate from the institution's perspective, whereas local participants disagree and frequently defy this rule. The third tension arises on the need for personalization and communal bonding. Freecycle's policy is to remove personal stories from listings to discourage pity exchanges and increase market efficiency. Yet, participants express a strong need for divestment rituals and the transfer of symbolic meaning of goods through storytelling. We argue that this tension creates an impediment to community, an asset that Freecycle's policies undermine or at least undervalue. The last tension arises on the non-profit nature of the system. While no official policy exists on reselling goods, participants express conflicting views about the appropriateness of this practice. This divergence highlights the varying motives consumers have for participation in contrast to the institutionalized mission.

Finally, we argue that the institutional framing of Freecycling as a "gift economy" is oversimplified since it ignores the hybridized form of exchange. Similar to Eckhardt and Bardhi's work (2010) that found that not all consumers who used car-sharing services were motivated by environmental concerns, we suggest that a gift-based positioning does not fully capture the experiences participants have while engaging in the redistribution of goods. We further argue that institutionalized emphasis on efficiency and impersonalization impairs the community building potential that some participants value.

"The Indefinite Future":
Ideas, Ideals, and Idealized Ideology in the Global Eco-Village

EXTENDED ABSTRACT

Intentional communities have a long and checkered history as wellsprings of social experimentation and innovative new cultural forms (Brown 2002; Sargisson and Sargent 2004). In contemporary parlance, intentional communities include not only such specific and relatively temporary (anti) consumption-related happenings as the Burning Man project (e.g., Kozinets 2002) and the Rainbow Family Gathering (Niman 1997), but also more lasting manifestations such as ecovillages, cohousing communities, residential land trusts, communes, student co-ops, urban housing cooperatives, intentional living, alternative communities, and cooperative living. Each of these is considered to be a quasi-experimental "project" where people strive to live out a common vision in their everyday lives. Oftentimes, this vision is one that combines the environmental with the communitarian and which seeks to question in a collective setting the base of values underlying contemporary consumer culture and simultaneously to explore what could or should replace it (Dawson 2010).

In this cross-cultural, longitudinally-oriented, multi-sited research, we seek to deepen our knowledge of the ideologies of consumption that support and underlie participation in one particular and ecologically-oriented form of intentional community: eco-villages. The commonly accepted and value-laden definition of ecovillages is that they are "human-scale, full-featured settlements in which human activities are harmlessly integrated into the natural world in a way that is supportive of healthy human development and can be successfully continued into the indefinite future" (Gilman 1991, quoted in Dawson 2006, p. 13).

Eco-villages are a fascinating place for consumer researchers to ponder the transition of consumer culture and contemporary society into a more eco-friendly and sustainable form for a variety of reasons. First, they come in many shapes and sizes, and thus attract consumers from the most ecologically radical to those with merely a firm commitment and interest in sustainable living. Second, they are part of an organized and successful international intentional community movement. Third, the global network of eco-villages is not only transnational but transcultural, having been partially founded on an alliance between sustainability-based communities and networks of traditional communities in developing countries. And fourth, eco-villages are explicitly ideological enterprises concerning themselves with the alteration of the economic values underpinning contemporary consumer culture, particularly, the linkage of economic growth and personal and social well being.

We begin with an overview of the core notions of intentional community. We develop our understanding of ecovillages as a concept and a movement. We then introduce our research that was conducted at three different eco-villages, speaking three different languages, in three different countries (Germany, Scotland, and French Canada). We undertook an ethnographic exploration of eco-village life and conducted (and are in the process of conducting) over one dozen interviews, as well as using participant-observational techniques. Data collection and analysis at two sites has been completed, with a second wave possible before the October presentation. Initial data collection in the third site is planned for June, and full analysis will be completed by October. As of February, we have more than enough data collected and analyzed to present, even without the third site.

As with the other presentations in this session, the members of eco-villages are concerned with sharing, capacity building, and the wise use of the planet's limited resources. However, the levels and depths of commitment, and the range of ideological engagement is more pronounced and perhaps profound. At the Findhorn ecovillage in Scotland that we studied, the ecological footprint per person is a bit over half of the UK average, which is the lowest footprint recorded for any settlement in the industrial world.

Perhaps even more interesting than the achievement of low energy usage is the means for its accomplishment. Most of the energy-saving activities also are credited with increasing the well being of eco-village members. For example, the decision by eco-villages to grow a significant amount of their own food creates a social situation where community members must work together cooperatively. Similarly, living together necessitates new social forms of engagement. The net effect, as with other types of intentional community both temporary and permanent, is that economic activity becomes local and thus ideologically linked to the immediately social. This powerful relocation of production is a common theme of the eco-village experience, along with a series of other reconnections—reconnecting people with their food, reconnecting people with their land, reconnecting people with indigenous people and practices, and reconnecting people with other people with whom they live. Add to this an educational and experiential ethos, and you have a potent potential for social change.

What is the net effect with our encounter with the distant boundaries of living as an ecovillage embedded consumer and consumer researcher? It is nothing short of informing our understanding of connection, disconnection, and reconnection. There are answers to our questions about new transitional forms of living that can lead the way to a more ecologically sustainable post-consumer culture.

REFERENCES
Belk, Russell (2010), "Sharing," *Journal of Consumer Research*, 36 (5), 715-34.
Bardhi, Fleura and Giana Eckhardt (2009), "Market Mediated Collaborative Consumption in the Context of Car Sharing," *Association for Consumer Research Conference*, Pittsburgh, PA.
Brown, Susan Love, ed. (2002), *Intentional Community: An Anthropological Perspective*, Albany: SUNY Press.
Dwyer, Robert F., Paul H. Schurr, and S. Oh (1987), "Developing Buyer Seller Relationships," *Journal of Marketing*, 51 (2), 11-27.
Gilman, Robert (1991), "The Ecovillage Challenge," *In Context*, 29, 10.

Kozinets, Robert V. (2002), "Can Consumers Escape the Market? Emancipatory Illuminations from Burning Man," *Journal of Consumer Research*, 29, 20-38.

Marcoux, Jean-Sébastien (2009), "Escaping the Gift Economy," *Journal of Consumer Research*, 36 (4), 671-85.

Penner, Louis A., John F. Dovidio, Jane A. Piliavin, and David A. Schroeder (2011), "Prosocial Behavior: Multilevel Perspectives," *Annual Review of Psychology.* 56 (1), 365-92.

Nelson, M. R., M. A. Rademacher, and H. Paek (2007), "Downshifting Consumer = Upshifting citizen? An Examination of a Local Freecycle Community," *The Annals of the American Academy of Political and Social Science*, 611 (1), 141-56.

Sargisson, Lucy and Lyman Tower Sargent (2004), *Living in Utopia: New Zealand's Intentional Communities*, Aldershot, England: Ashgate.

Seyfang, G. (2004), "Working Outside the Box: Community Currencies, Time Banks and Social Inclusion," *Journal of Social Policy*, 33, 49-71.

Widlock, Thomas (2004), "Sharing by Default: Outline of an Anthropology of Virtue," *Anthropological Theory*, 4 (1), 53–70.

Williams, C.C. (2004), "Informal Volunteering: Some Lessons from the United Kingdom," *Journal of Policy and Analysis and Management*, 23 (3), 613-16.

Individual vs. Collective Autonomy: How Culture Shapes Judgments and Behaviors

Chairs: Carlos Torelli, University of Minnesota, USA
Pankaj Aggarwal, University of Toronto, Canada

Paper #1: Sins of Omission and Sins of Commission: Differences in Brand-Switching Intentions Due to Culturally Different Theories of Agency

Sharon Ng, Nanyang Technological University, Singapore
Hakkyun Kim, Concordia University, Canada
Akshay R. Rao, University of Minnesota, USA

Paper #2: The Effects of Brand Translations and Their Cultural Symbolisms on Brand Evaluation among Young Chinese Consumers

Hean Tat Keh, The University of Queensland, Australia
Carlos Torelli, University of Minnesota, USA
Jessie Hao, Guang Dong University of Foreign Studies, China
Chi-yue Chiu, Nanyang Technological University, Singapore

Paper #3: Can Collectivism Promote Bribery?

Nina Mazar, University of Toronto, Canada
Pankaj Aggarwal, University of Toronto, Canada

SESSION OVERVIEW

With the emergence of China and India as drivers of global growth there has been a corresponding increase among Western companies to market effectively to consumers in these countries (Ecker, 2008; Tse, 2010). Global marketers often guide their market decisions by contrasting the more collectivist orientation of Easterners with Westerners' individualist orientations (Shavitt, Lee & Torelli, 2008). Building on the notion that Easterners and Westerners differ in their conceptions of individual versus collective autonomy (Menon et al., 1999), this symposium sheds light on how these culturally-patterned conceptions of autonomy shape people's judgments and behaviors. In doing so, we uncover the psychological mechanisms underlying people's tendencies to: a) switch brands when facing unsatisfactory product experiences, b) favor brands that symbolize individual autonomy, and c) rely on bribery as a business tool for gaining competitive advantage.

The first paper by Ng, Kim & Rao examines how Westerners' (Easterners') emphasis on individual (collective) autonomy affects their attributions and degree of counterfactual thinking, and their subsequent brand-switching intentions. In three studies, the authors demonstrate that for East Asians (Westerners), brand-switching intentions were higher (lower) when encountering an unsatisfactory product experience attributed to an exercise of individual versus collective autonomy (i.e., an individual vs. a group choice). In contrast, East Asians (Westerners) exhibited lower (higher) brand-switching intentions when the unsatisfactory product experience was attributed to the *failure* to exercise individual versus collective autonomy. Furthermore, the effect of unsatisfactory product experiences due to an exercise (or lack thereof) of a culturally-nurtured conception of autonomy on brand switching was mediated by the experience of counterfactual thinking and regret.

The second paper by Keh, Torelli, Hao & Chiu investigates how younger, educated Chinese consumers evaluate different types of translations (semantic, phonetic, and phonosemantic) of Western brand names, as a function of their symbolism of individual autonomy values as well as consumers' own cultural value priorities. Results from two studies demonstrate that young Chinese consumers are more likely to infer individual autonomy values from phonetic or phonosemantic brand name translations than from semantic transla-

tions, particularly for products with high and very high levels of value-expressiveness. In addition, semantic and phonosemantic translations create the favorable impression that the marketer is sensitive to Chinese culture. As phonosemantic translations benefit from both kinds of effects, they are the most favorably evaluated. Findings also reveal that phonetic translations are evaluated more positively than semantic translations, indicating that the effect of value inference is stronger than that of marketer cultural sensitivity. This is corroborated by findings showing that consumers who endorse autonomy values attribute higher levels of value congruence to the phonetic and phonosemantic brand name translations and hence like them better.

The final paper by Mazar and Aggarwal investigates the extent to which a lowered sense of personal responsibility fostered by a collective conception of autonomy influences the likelihood to bribe when entering a foreign market. In a business to business context, three studies find a significant effect of the degree of collectivism versus individualism present in a national culture on the propensity to offer bribes abroad. Furthermore, the effect is mediated by the lowered sense of personal responsibility. Together, the results suggest that the collective conception of autonomy nurtured in collectivist cultures promotes the propensity to offer a bribe in a business exchange through lower perceptions of personal responsibility for one's actions.

This session discusses very important issues in cross-cultural consumer behavior and presents the completed work from three papers. In keeping with the theme of ACR 2011, this session 'connects' research on culturally-patterned conceptions of individual versus collective autonomy to inform marketing researchers about the psychological mechanisms underlying cultural patterns of judgments and behaviors in the global marketplace. We anticipate this session will attract not only those interested in global, specific marketing issues (e.g., branding, advertising), but those interested more generally in cross-cultural consumer behavior. We will save 20-25 minutes for Ana Valenzuela, an expert in cross-cultural psychology, to discuss the presentations and to receive questions from the audience. Dr. Valenzuela will spend a few minutes integrating the implications of the three streams of research to bridge connections between the current projects and will provide a roadmap for future research. She will then moderate questions and comments from the audience.

"Sins of Omission and Sins of Commission: Differences in Brand-Switching Intentions Due to Culturally Different Theories of Agency"

EXTENDED ABSTRACT

People naturally make mistakes. When events unfold in an unsavory fashion, humans experience regret and mentally picture how those events could have unfolded differently, if they had either by acted differently, or if they had not acted in a manner that led to the unsavory outcome. Such counterfactual thinking can lead to a modification of the individual's future behavior (Roese 1994).

Recent advances in psychology have documented cross-cultural differences in the construal of agency (Menon, Morris, Chiu, and Hong 1999; Morris, Menon, and Ames 2001). In Western cultures, individualism is emphasized, while in Eastern cultures collectivism is emphasized. This difference in emphasis of individual versus group action has an impact on the degree of counterfactual thinking that individuals might experience. That is, Westerners might experience counterfactual thinking to a greater degree due to their individual behavior, while Easterners might experience counterfactual thinking to a greater degree due to their group's collective behavior. Such differences in counterfactual thinking have implications for perceptions of regret and the intention to change behavior in the future. We examine this issue in a consumption context by varying cultural orientation, action or inaction as the cause of a regret-inducing purchase, and whether the individual or group was the agent making the original purchase decision; our dependent variable is people's brand- switching intentions as a result of the regret-inducing purchase experiences.

In study 1, we examined our core premise that Eastern and Western cultures differ in the extent to which individuals or groups are perceived to engage in action. To this end, a 2 (Cultural prime: Chinese vs. US prime) (Decision Unit: Individual vs. Group) between-subjects experiment was conducted. In order to manipulate different cultural orientations, we employed cultural priming (Chen, Ng, and Rao 2005; Ng and Houston 2006). In addition, we varied the decision context (a decision to adopt a new medicine) by stipulating that the decision was to be made either individually or collectively among a group of medical patients. An ANOVA run on consumers' propensity to act (i.e., choose the new medicine) revealed a significant two-way interaction ($F(1, 55) = 6.54, p < .05$), indicating a greater expectation for the individual to act in the US culture and greater expectation for the group to act in the Chinese culture. These results corroborate the idea that people's implicit theories of individual versus group agency vary across culture.

In study 2, we tested our main hypotheses by examining the degree of counterfactual thinking and brand-switching intentions. For this purpose, we employed a 2 (Cultural prime: Chinese vs. US prime) 2 (Frame: Action vs. Inaction) 2 (Decision Unit: Individual vs. Group) design, in the context of a computer purchase for a personal or family business. First, the ANOVA run on the number of counterfactual thoughts revealed a significant three-way interaction ($F(1, 275) = 27.13, p < .01$). Further analyses involving contrasts showed that Chinese-primed participants generated more counterfactual thoughts when the negative event occurred as a consequence of the individual's (vs. the group's) action ($F(1, 275) = 4.26, p < .05$). Conversely, US-primed participants generated more counterfactual thoughts when the negative event occurred due to actions of the group (vs. the individual; $F(1, 275) = 15.76, p < .01$). Similarly, participants in the Chinese prime condition generated more counterfactual thoughts when the group (vs. individual) failed to act ($F(1, 275) = 5.21, p < .05$), whereas the opposite was true for US-primed ones ($F(1, 275) = 3.28, p < .09$). These results indicate that individuals' propensity to experience counterfactual thinking due to an action or inaction changes when the domain of decision-making shifts from the individual to the group.

The same analysis on brand-switching intentions also revealed a similar set of findings ($F(1, 275) = 17.31, p < .01$). Specifically, brand-switching intentions were higher among Chinese-primed participants when the sub-par outcome occurred due to the individual's (vs. group's) actions ($F(1, 275) = 3.58, p < .05$), while failure due to group inaction led to greater brand-switching intentions than failure due to individual inaction. In contrast, US-primed participants exhibited the opposite pattern. Moreover, meditational analysis using the bootstrapping method confirmed the indirect effect of counterfactual thinking on brand-switching intentions.

Study 3 replicated the finding of study 2, using a different consumption context (i.e., investment brokerage firm). Similar to study 2, participants were asked to imagine that they encountered unsatis- factory investment outcomes due to poor advice from their brokerage firm that had encouraged action (to sell their stocks) or had encouraged inaction (to not sell their stocks). The participants assigned to the group decision-making condition were asked to imagine that they were members of a finance team that invests in the stock market. In this study, we measured feelings of regret (as a proxy for counterfactual thinking) and brand-switching intention (switching to another investment brokerage firm). As expected, the 2 (Cultural prime) 2 (Frame) – 2 (Decision Unit) ANOVA revealed significant three-way interactions on both feelings of regret ($F(1, 201) = 28.83, p < .01$) and switching intentions ($F(1, 201) = 31.83, p < .01$). Further, it was found that feelings of regret mediated participants' switching intentions.

Taken together, the results provide converging evidence concerning cultural differences in counterfactual thoughts and brand-switching behavior due to differences in the expectations of group versus individual action and inaction. Theoretically, this research contributes to the emerging discipline of cross-cultural psychology and its application to consumer behavior. In particular, one novel advance includes identifying the role of the agent (the individual or group) who engages in an action (or stays passive), in the manifestation of regret. In addition, from a practical perspective, our research is likely to be of value to organizations contemplating entry into growing Eastern markets (e.g., China and India), where brand-switching intentions are shaped and formed differently than in the West, and where decisions are frequently made by groups rather than by individuals.

The Effects of Brand Translations and Their Cultural Symbolisms on Brand Evaluation among Young Chinese Consumers

EXTENDED ABSTRACT

A good brand name reduces the burden on marketing communications to build awareness and link brand associations, and plays a crucial role in influencing product evaluation and purchase decisions (Keller, Heckler, and Houston 1998). Consequently, for global brands, failure to provide proper brand name translation in the local language may lead to disastrous results (Zhang and Schmitt 2001). Due to language and cultural differences, brand name translation from Western languages into Chinese tends to be a difficult task (Zhang and Schmitt 2004). While many Western languages are phonographic, which uses either letters or syllables to represent the sound components of the spoken language, Chinese is a logographic language that is visually represented by 50,000 characters (Schmitt, Pan, and Tavassoli 1994).

There are three common ways of translating brand names into Chinese: by sound (phonetic translation), by meaning (semantic translation), and by sound plus meaning (phonosemantic translation). The present research examines how younger, educated Chinese consumers evaluate these three different types of translations of Western brand names as a function of their symbolism of individual autonomy values as well as consumers' own cultural value priorities.

Specifically, we contend that different methods of brand name translations may elicit different cultural meanings, particularly among the younger, educated Chinese consumers who are highly familiar with both Chinese and Western cultures (Zhang 2010). Among these consumers, phonetic translations will directly remind of the brand's Western origin and the dominant individual autonomy values in the West, whereas semantic translations that are decoded with reference to the Chinese language will call out associations with the conservatism values in Chinese culture (Schwartz 1992). Finally, a phonosemantic translation contains both semantic references in the Chinese language and phonetic references in the Western language, and would elicit both conservatism values as well as individual autonomy values, respectively. These effects will be further moderated by the value-expressiveness of the product. In a collectivist society such as China, consumers are highly attentive to the symbolic meanings embodied in a brand, particularly for value-expressive products (Tse 1996). Hence, we propose that the pattern of association between brand translation and symbolic meanings will be more pronounced for products with higher (versus lower) levels of value-expressiveness.

Brand name translation should then impact brand evaluation in two different ways. First, a phonetic or a phonosemantic translation may activate favorably evaluated autonomous values that are highly regarded by young Chinese consumers, born following the institution of the one-child policy (Zhang 2009). Second, a semantic or a phonosemantic translation may create the impression that the marketer is sensitive to and respects Chinese culture, and hence increases Chinese consumers' positive attitude towards the brand translation (Koslow, Shamdasani, and Touchstone 1994). Taken together, these two mechanisms suggest that symbolic meanings inferred from brand translation and inferred marketer cultural sensitivity may have independent, additive effects on brand evaluation.

More importantly, these two effects occur simultaneously in contrasting fashion for phonetic and semantic brand translations. Although semantic brand translation benefits from greater perceptions that the marketer is sensitive to Chinese culture, it suffers from weaker associations with the favorably-evaluated autonomy values. As younger, educated Chinese consumers may find autonomy values to be particularly self-relevant, we anticipate that this drawback of semantic translations would outweigh its benefit of favorable perceptions of marketer cultural sensitivity. Although both phonetic and phonosemantic translations are favorably associated with autonomy values, only phonosemantic translation benefits from greater levels of marketer cultural sensitivity. We then predict that, in descending order, younger, educated Chinese consumers' favorability of the three forms of brand name translation are phonosemantic, phonetic, and semantic. As phonetic and phonosemantic translations (compared to semantic ones) are more strongly associated with autonomy values at higher (vs. lower) levels of value expressiveness, by extension the positive effects of these associations on brand evaluations should also be stronger for higher levels of value expressiveness.

Finally, consumers' preference for brand translation is related to their own psychological characteristics. Because consumers prefer brands that are congruent with the personality traits that constitute their self-schemas (i.e., self-congruity, Aaker 1999), those who endorse autonomy values should show a stronger preference for phonetic or phonosemantic brand name translations (relative to semantic translations) than should others who endorse conservatism values.

In study 1, young Chinese students at a large public university in Beijing (China) participated in a 3 (Value-Expressiveness of the product: low, high, or very high) × 3 (Translation: phonetic, phonosemantic, or semantic) within-subjects design. Participants indicated the human values embodied or symbolized by each brand translation and evaluated them. Later, they also rated the importance of individual autonomy and conservatism values for themselves. Results showed that participants perceived phonetic and phonosemantic translations to embody greater autonomy values than they did semantic translations, particularly for products with high and very-high levels of value-expressiveness. In addition, phonosemantic translations were evaluated more favorably than phonetic and semantic ones. Phonetic translations were also evaluated more favorably than

semantic ones for high (marginally) and very high levels of value-expressiveness. Furthermore, the self-importance of autonomy values positively predicted evaluation of phonetic translations, but only for high and very high levels of value-expressiveness.

Study 2 examined consumers' evaluations of brand name translations (phonetic, semantic or phonosemantic) of the same product brand upon making salient either the value-expressive function (high value-expressiveness) or the utilitarian function (low value-expressiveness) of the product. Participants perceived phonetic and phonosemantic translations to embody greater autonomy values than they did semantic translations, particularly when the value expressive function of the product was made salient. These associations translated into favorable brand evaluations among participants for whom autonomy values are self-relevant. In addition, relative to phonetic translations, phonosemantic translations induced perceptions that the marketer is sensitive to Chinese culture, which mediated the difference in brand evaluation between these two types of translations. In summary, our research highlights the importance of considering consumers' inferences about brand symbolism in terms of individual autonomy values when translating Western names into Chinese language, and particularly so for value-expressive products targeting younger, educated Chinese consumers.

Can Collectivism Promote Bribery?

EXTENDED ABSTRACT

Bribery is considered a morally repugnant business practice with remarkable consensus transcending national boundaries (Husted, Dozier, McMahon, & Kattan, 1996). Yet, over $1 trillion or 3% of the world Gross Domestic Product (GDP) are paid annually in bribes, stymieing economic growth and threatening democratic and moral values (The World Bank, 2004). Furthermore, cross-national data such as Transparency International's (2010) Bribe Payers Index (BPI), which rates countries on the perceived willingness of their companies to bribe abroad, suggest substantial variability across national cultures in the propensity to initiate bribes (Riaño & Hodess, 2008). What is not sufficiently considered, however, is whether and how national culture might shape individuals' propensity to initiate bribes.

A decision to offer a bribe typically involves a conflict of interest; a dilemma between behaving in accordance with one's moral standards and benefiting from bribing such as winning a contract. Standard theories of moral agency suggest that individuals can selectively disengage internal moral control to permit detrimental conduct without violating their moral standards by, for example, reinterpreting one's actions or the negative consequences of one's actions, vilifying the target of one's actions, and, most strongly, by obscuring personal causal agency through diffusion of responsibility (Bandura, Barbaranelli, Caprara, & Pastorelli, 1996; Mazar, Amir, & Ariely, 2008). The easier it is for individuals to employ any of these mechanisms, the more likely they are to engage in immoral behavior, such as initiating a bribe.

One prominent dimension of national culture is the degree of collectivism or the extent to which individuals see themselves as interdependent and part of a larger group or society (Hofstede, 1980). According to previous research, individuals in collectivist cultures tend to hold relatively more favorable attitudes toward sharing of responsibilities (Hui, 1988), see others as providing a 'cushion' for their risky actions (Hsee & Weber, 1999), make situational rather than dispositional attributions, and have a weaker sense that they themselves determine who they are (Triandis, 2001). Consequently, we hypothesized that individuals in collectivist cultures would find it easier to disengage regulatory self-sanctions from detrimental conduct through diffusion or displacement of responsibility, and show a higher propensity to bribe abroad than individuals in individualist cultures. Further, we suggest that this effect would be mediated by collectivists' lower perceived responsibility for their actions. We tested this premise in three studies.

In the first study, we tested the correlation between a country's degree of collectivism and the propensity of its companies to offer bribes abroad while controlling for national wealth. Regression results show that the degree of collectivism was positively related to the propensity to bribe and that even after controlling for wealth it explained over half of the residual variability in the model.

Going beyond correlational data, Study 2 examined the existence and nature of a causal relationship between collectivism and bribery. In this study, participants were primed with collectivism or individualism in an experimental laboratory set-up. Results confirmed our hypothesis with participants in the collectivist condition being more willing to offer a bribe than those in the individualist condition. Importantly, participants in the collectivist condition held themselves significantly less accountable for their actions than those in the individualist condition, and this difference in perceived responsibility fully mediated the effect of the prime on participants' decision to offer a bribe.

The third study tested for the alternative account that participants' lower perceived responsibility for their actions was due to a post hoc rationalization consequent to the decision to bribe. Our results show that even in the absence of a decision to bribe, participants primed with a collectivist mindset held themselves significantly less accountable for their actions than those primed with an individualist mindset – suggesting that the effect is not due to a post-hoc rationalization of a decision to bribe.

Our research shows that the degree of collectivism influences people's willingness to offer a bribe, and that the effect is driven by people's reduced perceived responsibility for their own actions. By drawing attention to cultural orientation and the relevance of internal control mechanisms, this paper highlights the importance of understanding the psychological processes underlying cross-national differences, which would be crucial in designing a richer set of policies to curb the supply-side of corruption and its staggering costs.

REFERENCES

Aaker, Jennifer L. (1999), "The Malleable Self: The Role of Self-Expression in Persuasion," *Journal of Marketing Research*, 36 (1), 45-57.

Bandura, A., Barbaranelli, C., Caprara, G., & Pastorelli, C. (1996). Mechanisms of moral disengagement in the exercise of moral agency. *Journal of Personality and Social Psychology, 71*(2), 364-374.

Chen, Haipeng, Sharon Ng, and Akshay R. Rao (2005), "Cultural Differences in Consumer Impatience," Journal of Marketing Research, 42 (3), 291-301.

Hofstede, G. (1980). *Culture's consequences: International differences in work-related values*. London: Sage.

Hsee, C. K., & Weber, E.U. (1999). Cross-national differences in risk preference and lay predictions. *Journal of Behavioral Decision Making*. 12(2), 165-179.

Hui, C. H. (1988). Measurement of individualism-collectivism. *Journal of Research in Personality, 22*(1), 17-36.

Husted, B. W., Dozier, J. B., McMahon, J. T., & Kattan, M. W. (1996). The impact of cross-national carriers of business ethics on attitudes about questionable prac- tices and form of moral reasoning. *Journal of International Business Studies*, 27, 391-411.

Keller, Kevin Lane, Susan E. Heckler, and Michael J. Houston (1998), "The Effects of Brand Name Suggestiveness on Advertising Recall," *Journal of Marketing*, 62 (1), 48-57.

Koslow, Scott, Prem N. Shamdasani, and Ellen E. Touchstone (1994), "Exploring Language Effects in Ethnic Advertising: A Sociolinguistic Perspective," *Journal of Consumer Research*, 20 (4), 575-85.

Mazar, N., Amir, O., & Ariely, D. (2008). The dishonesty of honest people: A theory of self-concept maintenance. *Journal of Marketing Research, 45*(6), 633-644.

Menon, Tanya, Michael W. Morris, Chi-Yue Chiu, and Ying-yi Hong (1999), "Culture and the Construal of Agency: Attribution to Individual Versus Group Dispositions," Journal of Personality and Social Psychology, 76 (5), 701-17.

Morris, Michael W., Tanya Menon, and Daniel R. Ames (2001), "Culturally Conferred Conceptions of Agency: A Key to Social Perception of Persons, Groups, and Other Actors," Personality and Social Psychology Review, 5 (2), 169-82.

Ng, Sharon and Michael J. Houston (2006), "Exemplars or Beliefs? The Impact of Self-View on the Nature and Relative Influence of Brand Associations.," *Journal of Consumer Research*, 32 (4), 519-29.

Riaño, J. & Hodess, R. (2008). *Bribe payers index 2008*. Berlin: Transparency International.

Roese, Neal J. (1994), "The Functional Basis of Counterfactual Thinking," Journal of Personality and Social Psychology, 66 (5), 805-18.

Schmitt, Bernd H., Yigang Pan, and Nader T. Tavassoli (1994), "Language and Consumer Memory: The Impact of Linguistic Differences between Chinese and English," *Journal of Consumer Research*, 21 (3), 419-31.

Schwartz, Shalom H. (1992), "Universals in the Content and Structure of Values: Theoretical Advances and Empirical Tests in 20 Countries," in *Advances in Experimental Social Psychology*, Vol. 25, M. Zanna, Ed., New York: Academic Press, 1-65.

The World Bank (2004). *The costs of corruption* (http://go.worldbank.org/VAT2-EY5A00, April 8, 2004, accessed: July 19, 2010).

Transparency International (2010). *Corruption perception index 2010*. Berlin: Transparency International.

Triandis, H. (2001). Individualism-collectivism and personality. *Journal of Personality, 69*(6), 907-924.

Tse, David (1996), "Understanding Chinese People as Consumers: Past Findings and Future Propositions," in *The Handbook of Chinese Psychology*, Michael Bond, ed. Hong Kong: Oxford University Press, 352-63.

Zhang, Jing (2009), "The Effect of Advertising Appeals in Activating Self-Construals: A Case of Bicultural Chinese Generation X Consumers," *Journal of Advertising*, 38 (1), 63-82.

--- (2010), "The Persuasiveness of Individualistic and Collectivistic Advertising Appeals among Chinese Generation X Consumers," *Journal of Advertising*, 39 (3), 69-80.

Zhang, Shi and Bernd H. Schmitt (2001), "Creating Local Brands in Multilingual International Markets," *Journal of Marketing Research*, 38 (3), 313-25.

Consequences of Choosing: When Does Choosing Leave Consumers Worse Off?

Chairs: Joseph Redden, University of Minnesota, USA
Simona Botti, London Business School, UK

Paper #1: Forced to Do What I Want: When Imposing Selfishness Increases Well-Being

Jonathan Berman, University of Pennsylvania, USA
Deborah Small, University of Pennsylvania, USA

Paper #2: The Chooser's Curse: The Ability to Choose Increases Satiation

Joseph Redden, University of Minnesota, USA

Paper #3: Turning the Page: The Impact of Choice Closure on Satisfaction

Yangjie Gu, London Business School, UK
Simona Botti, London Business School, UK
David Faro, London Business School, UK

Paper #4: Focus! Creative Success Is Enjoyed Through Restricted Choice

Anne Laure Sellier, New York University, USA
Darren Dahl, University of British Columbia, Canada

SESSION OVERVIEW

Choice is widely viewed as a good thing for consumers because they know what they prefer. However, recent research has highlighted the negative consequences of choosing on consumer satisfaction (e.g., see Iyengar and Lepper, 2000). In fact, a recent meta-analysis found that the net effect on satisfaction of having more choice is unclear (Scheibehenne et al., 2010). Sometimes people benefit from a larger assortment, yet other times they find choosing from so many options to be overly costly.

The proposed symposium has four papers that all explore factors influencing the effect of choice on consumer satisfaction,, following Chernev, Bockenholt and Goodman's (2010) call for more research on moderating factors of choice overload effects. The first paper shows that choosing lowers satisfaction when it requires making a trade-off between a selfish and prosocial option. The second paper demonstrates the importance of repeated choices, as choosing increased the rate of satiation. The third paper identifies closure as a way to mitigate the negative effects of choosing from a large selection. The fourth paper establishes the role of expertise, but in sharp contrast to prior research (eg., Mogilner, Rudnick and Iyengar, 2008), as providing a large assortment in a creative task made people more satisfied with the assortment, but less satisfied with the creative process, as well as less creative.

The four papers all contribute to a common theme – identify when choosing will negatively affect satisfaction. We expect our session will generate widespread interest as it spans a range of research interests, and invoke a fruitful discussion on how these ideas can connect to the general topic of consumer well-being.

Forced to Do What I Want: When Imposing Selfishness Increases Well-Being

EXTENDED ABSTRACT

The present research investigates how choice freedom affects individual well-being when choosing between a selfish and a prosocial option. Recent research has identified situations in which externally imposed options, as opposed to free choice, increases individual well-being (Botti and Iyengar, 2004; Botti, Orfali and Iyengar, 2009). While much of this research has focused on choices where

the outcomes affect the self exclusively, we instead examine choices where there is a direct trade-off between a self-benefitting option and an option that improves the welfare of others. Although classic economic theory assumes agents are strictly self-interested, there is much evidence, both from the real world as well as from tightly-controlled laboratory experiments, suggesting that people sometimes make significant self-sacrifices to help others less fortunate than themselves (Camerer and Thaler, 1995).

When faced with such trade-offs, regardless of the ultimate decision, we expect that many individuals face intrapersonal conflict. We expect that imposing a selfish option removes the experience of intrapersonal conflict. As a result, individuals can enjoy the pleasure of self-benefitting outcomes without experiencing self reproach for forgoing helping others. The studies presented here test our hypothesis that people are less happy and satisfied with outcomes when faced with a choice between a selfish and prosocial option than those who have a selfish outcome externally imposed.

In our first study participants were placed into one of three conditions. Participants in the *choice* condition were given the option to either receive a windfall sum of $3.00 or donate this money to UNICEF. Participants in the *imposed selfishness* condition received a windfall sum of $3.00, while those in the *imposed prosocial* condition donated $3.00 to UNICEF. Our main DVs include an 11 item measure of present state happiness and positive affect ($\alpha = .91$) and a two item measure of satisfaction with outcome ($\alpha = .81$). An ANOVA revealed an overall effect of condition on happiness ($F(2, 104) = 5.4, p = .006$) and satisfaction with the outcome ($F(2, 104) = 7.8, p < .001$). Specifically, participants who were forced to receive $3.00 were significantly happier ($M = 4.5$) than those who were given a choice ($M = 3.9$; $t(74) = 2.5, p = .01$) and those who were forced to donate ($M = 3.5$; $t(59) = 3.1, p = .003$). Analysis on our choice satisfaction measure revealed the same pattern of results (all p's $<.002$). Participants in the free choice condition did not significantly differ in happiness ($t(75) = 1.1, p = ns$) or choice satisfaction ($t(75) = 0.94, p = ns$) from those in the imposed donation condition.

One possible explanation stems from the finding that comparisons between options reduce the value of each option (Brenner, Rottenstreich and Sood, 1999). In our first study, participants in the choice condition, by design, considered both selfish and prosocial options, while those in the imposed conditions were unaware of the alternative option. It is possible that participants in the choice condition felt worse about their decision because their attention was drawn to the relative disadvantage of each option, thereby reducing the perceived value of each option.

To control for option information, we conducted a second study in which each participant was made aware of all the possible outcomes. In particular, they were told that some participants will receive $3.00 in cash while others will donate $3.00 to UNICEF. If our previous findings were solely a result of informational differences between conditions, then we should find no effects in this study where all participants have identical information. However, if the presence of choice between a selfish and prosocial option induces intrapersonal conflict, then we should find similar results as our first study.

The results of our second study support the intrapersonal conflict hypothesis. An ANOVA revealed an overall effect of condition on happiness ($F(2, 213) = 4.0, p = .02$) and satisfaction with the outcome ($F(2, 213) = 9.1$, $p < .001$)). Specifically, participants who were forced to receive $3.00 were significantly happier (M = 4.1) than those who were given a choice (M = 3.6; $t(143) = 2.3$, $p = .02$) and those who were forced to donate (M = 3.6; $t(143) = 2.6$, $p = .009$). Analysis on our choice satisfaction measure revealed the same pattern of results (all p's <.001). Participants in the free choice condition did not significantly differ in happiness ($t(75) = .41$, $p = $ ns) or choice satisfaction ($t(75) = 0.72$, $p = $ ns) from those in the imposed donation condition.

Together these studies demonstrate evidence that imposing a selfish option on an individual can lead to greater positive affect and post outcome satisfaction than letting people choose between a selfish and prosocial option. When a selfish option is imposed, individuals can enjoy the pleasure from that option without feeling intrapersonal conflict. One open question is why imposed prosocial behavior fails to raise happiness, as it likewise reduces the conflict between selfishness and prosocial behavior. It is possible that when forced, individuals do not feel causal and responsible for the good deed and this feeling of ownership of the behavior is what produces happiness. Yet choosing prosocial behavior is no better for happiness because of the inherent conflict of the choice. Future research will seek to resolve these open questions.

The Chooser's Curse: The Ability to Choose Increases Satiation

EXTENDED ABSTRACT

There are only four places to have lunch near my office. I am regularly reminded of this painful fact every day around noon when I decide where to eat lunch. Although I pick whichever option sounds the best that day, the problem is that I am quite satiated with all of them. I often wonder if this daily act of deliberating and choosing heightens my satiation. In other words, would I be better off if someone simply told me where to eat lunch each day? Similarly, would I get less bored with my music if I used a shuffle feature rather than selecting each song myself? Generally speaking, do people get more satiated when they choose, or when others choose for them?

Common sense dictates that letting people choose should increase enjoyment. In fact, a core tenet of economics is that consumers maximize utility, and what they prefer can be determined from what they choose (called revealed preference). Therefore, in a repeated consumption setting, people know when their satiation is growing with an item and switch to a more preferred alternative. Only the consumer would be privy to their moment-to-moment preferences; hence, selections from any other source should be more satiating.

The present research posits that repeated choosing instead increases satiation because it makes the repetition more salient. Recent research has identified perceived repetition as an important antecedent of satiation (Redden, 2008). Kahn and Wansink (2004) similarly found that people expected to enjoy M&M candies more (and indeed ate more) when the variety of colors were easier to visually perceive. People also recovered faster from satiation when reminded of the variety of other things they had also recently consumed (Galak, Redden, and Kruger, 2009). These findings all indicate that satiation depends on the extent to which people notice the variety and repetition of what they consume.

This research proposes that choosing affects perceptions of repetition by acting as a recurring reminder that one is repeatedly having more of the same thing. Given the aforementioned work identifying perceptions of repetition as a key driver of satiation, highlighting the fact that an experience is increasingly repetitive will make it subsequently more satiating. Alternatively, if a sequence is not chosen but

instead exogenously determined (e.g., random), the repetitive nature of the consumption would be less salient. This leads to the prediction that an individual will satiate more with a sequence they choose versus a randomly selected sequence. That is, the enjoyment for people allowed to choose will decline faster with repeated consumption, and eventually be less than for those not allowed to choose. Of course, this is not saying that choosing will increase satiation in all cases (e.g., a food allergen or a hated song).

Five empirical studies confirm these predictions. All of the studies have a similar setup: some participants choose their own sequence while others receive a random sequence, and all participants rate their enjoyment at periodic intervals. Study 1 shows that participants who chose which song to hear on each trial satiated faster than those for whom each song was randomly selected. Study 2 establishes the general nature of this effect by extending it to art, and showing that it does not depend on the number of available options, or whether those options vary on each trial. Study 3 provides mediation evidence that choosing triggers thoughts of repetition that subsequently lead to more satiation. Studies 4 and 5 give further support to the proposed process by showing that cuing judgments of repetition makes a random sequence as satiating as a chosen one, and the satiating effect of choosing disappears if all of the choices are made before consumption begins. Overall, the studies provide consistent evidence that letting a person choose their own consumption sequence satiates them faster because it highlights the repetitive nature of the experience.

This research adds a new negative effect to the choice literature, and highlights repeated consumption as an important moderator. This research also deepens our theoretical understanding of the processes underlying satiation. Choosing increases satiation because it encourages thoughts of repetition. This proposed process highlights the critical role of self-reflective thoughts in determining how satiated one feels, and establishes choosing as a novel antecedent. By exploring choosing and satiation, this work joins two literature streams not typically considered together, and demonstrates their interplay. Widespread choice in consumers' everyday lives may help explain the ubiquity of satiation, and repeated choosing may be necessary to see the full effects of choosing on satisfaction.

Turning the Page: The Impact of Choice Closure on Satisfaction

EXTENDED ABSTRACT

When moving from a difficult period to another stage of life people sometimes use metaphors such as "*turning* the page", "*closing* the door", or "*turning* the back". These metaphors combine the physical act of closing with the psychological state of ending a challenging time, reflecting people's intent to make a new start. In this paper we suggest that such metaphors can play an important role in the domain of choices. We show that the physical act of closing embodied in these metaphors can psychologically bring a difficult decision process to an end and allow people to focus on their experience with the decision outcome. We refer to this process as *choice closure.*

We investigate a specific case of difficult decisions—choices made from extensive sets (Iyengar and Lepper, 2000). Research has shown that an increase in the number of options to compare during the decision process enhances regret and decreases the attractiveness of the chosen option relative to the forgone options in the postdecisional phase (Brenner, Rottenstreich, and Sood, 1999; Cameron, Wertenbroch, and Zeelenberg, 2003; Hsee and Leclerc, 1998; Inbar, Botti, and Hanko, forthcoming). By metaphorically and thus psychologically ending the decision process, choice closure can inhibit further comparisons between the chosen and the forgone options and therefore improve satisfaction with the final outcome. This hypothesis was tested in four studies.

Studies 1 and 2 tested the predicted effect of choice closure on satisfaction by comparing choices from larger versus smaller sets. In both studies participants chose a chocolate from an assortment of either 24 (large set) or 6 (small set) chocolates. In study 1 choice closure was manipulated by asking participants to taste the chosen chocolate in front of the original assortment (no-closure) or after turning their backs to it (closure). In study 2 choice closure was manipulated by asking participants to taste the chocolate in front of a tray containing the assortment either before (no-closure) or after covering it with a transparent lid (closure). We predicted that the action of turning one's back to the choice set or covering the tray would facilitate choice closure. As hypothesized, in both studies participants in the closure condition were more satisfied than those in the no-closure condition when choosing from the larger set, but this difference was not significant in the small-set condition. As a result of this increase in satisfaction, choice closure mitigated the choice overload effect. Whereas in the no-closure condition participants choosing from the smaller set were more satisfied than those choosing from the larger set, in the closure condition this difference was not significant.

The next two studies tested the hypothesized process underlying choice closure. In study 3, we experimentally removed the link between the physical act of closing and the psychological process of choice closure by providing an external reason for closing. This study was a 2 (choice closure: closure vs. no-closure) x 2 (reason: reason vs. no reason) between-subjects design. All participants were asked to choose one biscuit to taste from among a large assortment of 24 biscuits described in a menu. Closure was manipulated by having the menu open or closed during the tasting task, whereas reason was manipulated either by providing no reason for keeping the menu open or closed or by providing a reason that was unrelated to the decision task. In the no-reason condition, the menu was kept open (no-closure) or participants were asked to close it (closure condition) after making their choice. In the reason condition participants were told that the menu had to be kept open because the experimenter had to read some information that was written inside it (no-closure) or that they had to close menu because the experimenter had to read some information that was written on its back cover (closure). Results from studies 1 and 2 were replicated in the no-reason condition: participants who physically closed the menu after making their choice indicated greater satisfaction with the selected biscuit than participants who left the menu open. As expected, however, in the reason conditions this difference in satisfaction was not significant. Also consistent with our explanation, participants who closed the menu in the no-reason condition were more satisfied than those who closed the menu in the reason condition, but there was no difference in satisfaction between participants who kept the menu open across the two reason conditions.

Study 4 directly manipulated the proposed process by varying the focus on the foregone options. This study was a 2 (choice closure: closure vs. no-closure) x 3 (focus: control vs. alternatives-focus vs. outcome-focus) between-subjects design. The procedure in the control condition was similar to the no-reason condition in study 3: participants chose a tea from a 24-tea menu and either left the menu open or closed it before drinking their selected tea. In the alternatives-focus condition, after making a choice, participants took part in a "memory enhancement technique" task that involved recalling information about the chosen and forgone options. In the outcome-focus condition participants performed a "meditation technique" that

involved focusing on a single object — the chosen tea. The results in the control condition replicated our prior studies: participants in the closure condition were more satisfied with the tea selected from a large assortment than those in the no-closure condition. Consistent with our hypothesized process, the memory enhancement technique reduced participants' satisfaction in the closure condition (but had no effect on those in the no-closure condition). In contrast, the mediation technique enhanced the satisfaction of the participants in the no-closure condition (but had no effect on the participants in the closure condition).

To summarize, this paper argues that the physical action of closing triggers the psychological process of choice closure due to which consumers stop comparing the chosen and the forgone options, make peace with their decision, and start focusing on the assessment of the decision outcome. Our studies show that when choices are difficult, choice closure has a positive effect on satisfaction.

Focus! Creative Success Is Enjoyed Through Restricted Choice

EXTENDED ABSTRACT

Does increasing choice in the number of creative inputs offered to consumers (e.g., more choice in ingredients for cooking) affect their creativity? We draw on the choice literature (e.g., Iyengar & Lepper, 2000; Schwartz, 2004) to provide understanding for the counterintuitive effects we identify. We find that increasing the choice of creative inputs for consumers experienced in a creative task can hurt objective creative outcomes. Consumers that have experience and knowledge in a creative pursuit are shown to be objectively less creative with more input choice, while inexperienced consumers are relatively unaffected by differences in input choice. Based on creativity research (e.g., Henderson, 2004; Russ, 1993), we argue that it is the difficulty experienced consumers have to focus when choosing among extensive creative input options that likely results in reduced task enjoyment, which has negative implications for the consumers' creativity. In contrast, regardless of their experience level, we find that consumers perceive *themselves* as being more creative, the more choice they have. Two studies document these effects.

We first conducted an experiment on knitting, a 2 (Choice: moderate vs. extensive) x 2 (Knitting level: experienced vs. inexperienced) between-subjects design facilitated by a yarn store, where knitters received instructions. 76 knitters (74 women, mean age = 29.82 years) participated in return for a \$20 gift certificate. Based on a pretest, we categorized participants who could (not) knit cables as (in)experienced. Participants were required to knit a scarf for a three-year old girl over a week, and to choose 12 balls of yarn from a display of either a moderate (6) or relatively extensive (12) color selection. Participants were provided with needles, were told to be creative and utilize only the materials provided, however they liked.

A week later, participants returned their scarf, reported how creative they thought their scarf was (1 = not at all/7 = very creative), assessed how pleasant the creative process had been (not at all/very enjoyable, very boring/very much fun). Then, two experts in creative knitting evaluated the creativity of the scarves on a 10-point scale ("not creative at all" (1)/"extremely creative" (10)). Focusing on the latter averaged measure, a 2x2 ANOVA only revealed a main effect of Choice, such that knitters with extensive rather than moderate choice reported that their scarf was *more* creative ($M_{moderate}$ = 4.55 vs. $M_{extensive}$ = 5.09, F(1, 72) = 4.19, $p < .05$, r^2 = .05). We averaged the knitting experts' creativity ratings (r = .66, $p < .01$) to form an objective creativity index. A 2x2 ANOVA showed a significant two-way interaction ($F(1, 72) = 7.75$, $p < .007$, $r^2 = .10$). As expected, we found a choice overload effect: scarves knit by experienced knitters under moderate rather than extensive choice were more creative ($M_{moderate} = 7.67$ vs. $M_{extensive} = 5.56$, $t(72) = 3.80$, $p < .001$, $r^2 = .17$). There was no difference for inexperienced knitters $t<1$. Further, the average of the two measures of knitters' enjoyment during the process ($r = .29$, $p < .02$) mediated the experts' ratings.

A second study tests whether restricting choice also enhances creators' ability to focus on promising creative paths, which drives the enjoyment and subsequent creativity results we observed in the knitting study. 59 experienced crafters (13 men, age = 21.2 years) created a Christmas tree ornament after choosing from a moderate or an extensive choice of shapes they could use as creative components. Orthogonally to this choice manipulation, creators were required to either rehearse a two- or an eight-digit number as they were creating their ornament (Gilbert & Osborne, 1989). We predicted that participants rehearsing a two-digit number - an effortless task - would enjoy the creative process more when provided with a moderate rather than an extensive choice of shapes, which should transcend into more creative ornaments. In contrast, participants rehearsing an eight-digit number should generally find it relatively difficult to focus during the creative task. If restricting choice should make them generally enjoy the process more, this enjoyment should no longer translate into more creative outcomes when their ability to focus is simultaneously compromised. After collecting the ornaments from crafters, 10 peers evaluated the creativity of the ornaments (e.g., Dahl, Chattopadhyay, and Gorn, 1999) on 7-point scales ("not at all"/"extremely creative"). After averaging peers' "creative" item (Cronbach-a = .89), we ran a Choice x Rehearsed digit ANOVA using this creativity index as the dependent variable. It only revealed a significant two-way interaction, $F(1, 55) = 9.22$, $p < .02$, $r^2 = .14$), such that the ornaments of participants with limited choice rehearsing two digits were rated as significantly more creative compared to the ornaments of all other participants, all p's < .05. As predicted enjoyment of the creative task mediated these effects, but only when crafters were not cognitively busy. This research documents a new type of choice overload effect, one durably affecting post-choice creativity. Also, while prior research found that more choice benefits (e.g., Chernev, 2003) or does not affect experienced consumers (e.g., Mogilner, Rudnick, and Iyengar, 2008), we find that more choice can hurt experienced consumers.

Interpretations and Responses to Identity Threats

Chairs: Boyoun (Grace) Chae, University of British Columbia, Canada
Rui (Juliet) Zhu, University of British Columbia, Canada

Paper #1: We Hate Your Products: The Effects of Social Identity Threat on Out-group Product Evaluation

Boyoun (Grace) Chae, University of British Columbia, Canada
Darren Dahl, University of British Columbia, Canada
Rui (Juliet) Zhu, University of British Columbia, Canada

Paper #2: Choosing Identity: The Effects of Publicly Versus Privately Communicated Threats on Consumer Preferences

Madelynn Mathews, University of Calgary, Canada
Katherine White, University of Calgary, Canada
Jennifer Argo, University of Alberta, Canada

Paper #3: Observing Flattery: A Social Comparison Perspective

Elaine Chan, Tilburg University, The Netherlands
Jaideep Sengupta, HKUST, Hong Kong

Paper #4: Are They Who They Claim? Intentionality and Authenticity in Identity Signaling with Brands

Rosellina Ferraro, University of Maryland, USA
Amna Kirmani, University of Maryland, USA
Ted Matherly, University of Maryland, USA

SESSION OVERVIEW

It is well-accepted that consumers choose specific brands to express and reinforce their identity (Kline, Kline and Kernan 1993). A large amount of research has shown that such identity-related consumptions satisfy consumers' association and communication goals (Escalas and Bettman 2005; Cayla and Eckhardt 2008). However, recent literature has started to document how consumers strategically change their consumption behaviors in order to protect their identity or to restore their threatened identity (Gao, Wheeler and Shive 2009; White and Argo 2009). This session adds to this latter research by introducing four papers that demonstrate how consumers interpret and react to identity threats in various consumption contexts.

The first paper (Chae et al.) examines how consumers interpret a national brand failure as a social identity threat and use out-group product evaluation to restore that threatened identity. The authors find that a national brand failure can threaten consumers' social identity when such information comes from an out-group member. Thus, as a way to restore their threatened social identity, consumers derogate out-group products. The second paper (Mathews et al.) demonstrates another means consumers engage in to restore their threatened social identity. The authors document that when a particular aspect of social identity is threatened, consumers favor identity-related products when the threat is communicated publicly versus privately. Desire for self-consistency appears to drive this identity restoration behavior. The third paper (Chan and Sengupta) adds to this literature by demonstrating a novel way to induce identity threat. Specifically, when a consumer observes others being flattered, s/he is likely to experience social comparison and thus feel threatened. Interestingly, as a result, s/he will endorse the salesperson's recommendations to a greater extent as a way to reduce the threat. The last paper (Ferraro et al.) examines the identity threat from a different, yet interesting angle. Specifically, they demonstrate that conspicuous brand usage can lead to negative perception of the brand users' identity.

In sum, these papers add to our knowledge in the identity threat literature by documenting a series of important variables that can induce such threats (e.g., national brand failure, flattery), and demonstrating coping behaviors consumers engage in to protect and restore

their identity. We expect that this special session will be well-attended and will stimulate much thoughts and interests to this important research domain.

We Hate Your Products: The Effects of Social Identity Threat on Out-group Product Evaluation

EXTENDED ABSTRACT

How does Toyota Motor Corp.'s massive recall in 2009 and 2010 change the Japanese' consumption behavior? Does this recall change their attitudes toward domestic versus foreign products? In this research, we examine how consumers respond to a national brand failure. Specifically, we focus on how a national brand failure can threaten consumers' social identity, and consequently affect their evaluation of in-group versus out-group products.

Social identity theory (SIT: Tajfel and Turner 1986) postulates that individuals strive for a positive social identity. The individual's need for positive social identity leads people to create, maintain, or enhance any valued distinctiveness of the in-group. The attempt to achieve positive group distinctiveness can lead to favorable evaluation of one's own group (Brewer 1999) or derogation of out-group values (Rabbie, Benoist, Oosterbaan, and Visser 1974; Worchel, Andreoli, and Folger 1977). Of particular relevance to this research, extant literature has shown that when an out-group is perceived to threaten the group identity, people will react to the threatening out-group with hostility (Li and Brewer 2004)

Based on the SIT, we propose that a national brand failure can threaten in-group members' social identity, which consequently leads to derogation of out-group products as a means to restore the impaired identity. Importantly, we theorize that the source of such information will moderate the effect. When the national brand failure information is coming from an out-group member, it will be perceived as a threat, and thus leads to out-group product derogation. However, when such information is coming from an in-group member, it will not be perceived as a threat and will thus attenuate the above effect. A series of three studies were conducted to provide systematic support to our theorizing.

Study 1 tested our hypotheses using a failure of Samsung electronics, the largest company in South Korea. All participants were South Koreans. The study was a 3 (Brand information: Brand failure from in-group source, Brand failure from out-group source and Neutral information) X 2 (Product country of origin: Korea vs. the USA) between subject design. Participants were first asked to evaluate a short essay, which contained the Samsung brand failure information or the neutral information. The brand failure information was described to be written either by a Korean (i.e., in-group source) or an American (i.e., out-group source). People in the control condition received information about Samsung's new fridge launch with no identification of the information source. Next, participants worked on a seemingly unrelated task where they evaluated a MP3 player that was either "Made in Korea" or "Made in the USA". Participants rated the products on three 9-point scales: "good/ bad", "unfavorable/ favorable" and "dislike/ like" (White and Dahl 2006). Data analysis revealed a significant 2-way interaction. When Koreans received the Samsung failure information from an out-group member, they formed more unfavorable evaluations towards the American product than those who received the neutral information. However, when Koreans received the Samsung failure information from an in-group member, their attitude toward the American product did not differ from that of the control group.

Study 2 replicated the out-group derogation using the context of Toyota's recall. In this study, we further demonstrated that the out-group derogation was robust even when a third party provided the brand failure information. The study was a 2(Brand Information: Brand failure vs. Neutral information) X 2 (Product country of origin: Japan vs. the U.S.A) between subject design. A procedure similar to that of Study 1 was implemented. In the brand failure condition, the writer of the article was a Canadian (i.e., a third party). The results replicated those observed in study1, such that the Japanese participants evaluated American electronics more negatively when they were presented with the brand failure versus neutral information.

Study 3 aims to provide further evidence to the underlying process. If identity threat is the underlying mechanism, then offering in-group members an opportunity to affirm their identity should attenuate the effects observed earlier (Steele 1988; Derks, van Laar, and Ellemers 2009). Study 3 was designed to test this hypothesis via a 2 (affirmation: group affirmation vs. no affirmation) X 2 (product country of origin: Made in Canada vs. Made in the USA) between subject design. All participants were Canadians in this study. We first introduced a threat manipulation by having all participants read a report about a national brand (i.e., Tim Horton) failure, written by an American. The second task involved the affirmation manipulation. In the *group* affirmation condition, participants were asked to recall the 2010 Vancouver Olympics Winter Games, which is likely to induce national pride and thus affirm Canadians' positive identity. In the *no* affirmation condition, participants were asked to recall a movie they watched or a book that they read recently. The focal task involved asking participants to evaluate an organic cereal that was either "Made in Canada" or "Made in the U.S.A". As expected, we replicated earlier findings only in the on affirmation condition, such that participants formed more negative product evaluations when it was made in the USA versus Canada. However, importantly, this effect disappeared in the group affirmation condition.

The current research offers several contributions. First, it demonstrates that a national brand failure can lead to social identity threat. Second, it extends the SIT literature by showing that the out-group derogation can be directed toward any out-group. Finally, it illustrates that group affirmation mitigate the out-group derogation induced by social identity threat.

Choosing Identity: The Effects of Publicly Versus Privately Communicated Threats on Consumer Preferences

EXTENDED ABSTRACT

Advertisers often link products to different social identities (i.e. gender, occupation, nationality). Consider a recent tagline that highlights male gender-identity: "Maximum Taste, No Sugar, and Maybe Scorpion Venom. Pepsi Max, the First Diet Cola for Men." Marketing practitioners often assume that linking the brand with an aspect of social identity leads target consumers to evaluate the brand more favorably. Recent research, however, suggests that the effectiveness of identity-linking strategies may depend on contextual factors. For instance, White and Argo (2009) find that when consumers experience a threat to an aspect of their social identity (e.g., they receive negative information about their gender identity), they sometimes avoid products associated with that identity. The present research provides evidence for the reverse effect, whereby consumers evaluate identity-linked products *more favorably* when a social identity has been threatened.

Following social identity theory (Tajfel and Turner 1979), we view social identity as encompassing one's identity derived from the groups to which the person belongs or is affiliated with. Previous research largely finds that products linked with important social identities tend to be evaluated favorably (Kleine, Kleine, and Kernan 1993). However, when an aspect of identity becomes temporarily threatened consumers sometimes respond by avoiding identity-linked products (White and Argo 2009). While these authors found the dissociative effect is mitigated for individuals who strongly value and identify with the threatened group (i.e., those high in collective self-esteem derived from that specific group), this research did not find instances of an *associative effect*, whereby a *social identity threat* induces consumers to *increase* preference for products linked to that social identity.

One instance wherein an associative effect may emerge is when the threat is communicated publicly as compared to privately. Given that people are both motivated to compensate for short comings under threat (Pyszcynski, Greenberg, and LaPrelle 1985) and to maintain self-consistency when information about the self is made public (Schlenker 1975; Tedeschi et al. 1971), receiving a *public threat* to an aspect of one's own social identity, should lead to a desire to maintain self-consistency. In the context of a publicly communicated identity threat, avoiding a product that is linked with that aspect of one's own identity would convey an inconsistent self, whereas maintaining or enhancing one's evaluations of the product would convey a more consistent self. The present research predicts and finds that consumers will be more likely to favor identity-linked products under threat when the communication is public rather than private. We anticipate that this will be pronounced among consumers high in self-consistency motives.

In study 1, participants (*n*=242) took part in a 2(Threat: no threat vs. social identity threat) x 2(Communication: public vs. private) between-subjects design. The social identity that was threatened was university student identity. Participants took part in small groups and were first exposed to a research article that either reported that their own university performed similarly to (no threat) or worse than (social identity threat) other universities in its class (White, Argo, and Sengupta 2011). Communication was manipulated by either having the experimenter read the article aloud to the participants or by having participants read it silently to themselves. Participants completed some filler items and manipulation check items. Our dependent measure was each participant's choice of either an identity-linked (clipboard displaying the university logo) or neutral (plain clipboard) at the end of the study. Binary logistic regression with threat, communication, and their interaction term as independent variables and product choice as the dependent variable revealed only a significant interaction between threat and communication (β =.80, Wald = 6.70, $p < .02$). Under conditions of identity threat, participants were more likely to chose the university clipboard when the communication was public (79%) rather than private (59%, $p < .05$). In the no threat condition, participants did not differ in their selections of the university clipboard when the communication was public (48.1%) versus private (60.6%; $p < .18$).

In study 2, participants (*n*=186) took part in a 2(Threat: no threat vs. social identity threat) x 2(Communication: public vs. private) x Self-Consistency Motives between-subjects design. Threat and communication were manipulated as in Study 1. Participants responded to 4 self-consistency motive-items (e.g., "To be consistent with who I am," "To demonstrate that I have stable preferences"). Participants also completed 4 self-enhancement motive-items (e.g., "To look like I made good selections," "To be associated with desirable products") to rule this out as a potential explanation. They then made a series of hypothetical choices (matched for dollar value) between university-linked vs. neutral items (university bookstore or restaurant gift certificate; university t-shirt or movie passes; university hat vs. local hockey team hat). Neutral items were coded as 0 and university items were coded as 1, and the identity preference score was calculated by summing across all items. Regression analysis with threat, communication, and the continuous mean-centered self-consistency scale and all interactions as independent variables predicting the preference index revealed the anticipated 3-way interaction ($p < .05$). When under threat, those low in self-consistency did not differ in preferences in response to public vs. private communication ($p < .18$). However, when under threat, those high in consistency preferred the university products when the communication was public as opposed to private ($p < .02$). As predicted, self-enhancement motives did not moderate the effects.

When a social identity threat is communicated publicly, compared to privately, participants show greater preference for identity-linked products. We extend work that finds evidence of consumers engaging in self-enhancing self-presentational strategies in public settings (Ratner and Kahn 2002; White and Dahl 2006), to show that motives for self-consistency can also motivate consumer behavior in public contexts. Indeed, classic consumer research suggests that while consumers are often motivated to present themselves in a positive light, sometimes self-consistency motives will drive product preferences (Sirgy 1982). Finally, we contribute to literature showing associative responses to products when identity is viewed positively (Cialdini et al. 1976), to demonstrate when associative responses to identity-linked products when that particular identity is viewed in a negative light.

Observing Flattery: A Social Comparison Perspective

EXTENDED ABSTRACT

Prior research on flattery has shown that in contrast to the targets of flattery, who frequently respond positively, objective outsiders react negatively to the flatterer – in part because they are able to subject the flattering message to objective scrutiny and thus detect any underlying ulterior motive (Campbell and Kirmani 2000). What, however, if the flattery is palpably sincere – e.g., you witness a salesperson complimenting a stylishly-dressed customer on her dress sense after the customer has already made her purchases? In such cases, the use of flattery may represent a win-win persuasion tactic: a positive response from the target, without any negative reaction from observers (Vonk 2002). The current inquiry, however, draws on dual attitudes theory (Wilson, Lindsey and Schooler 2000) to posit that even when others receive compliments that observers perceive to be sincere, they still develop an automatic negative reaction (the implicit attitude) towards the flatterer because of the envy caused by social comparison. Further, this negative implicit attitude co-exists with the more neutral evaluation (the explicit attitude) that arises because of a belief in the flattery being sincere.

Apart from documenting the dual attitudes induced in observers by flattery, we add to the flattery literature in two other ways. First, we illuminate the social comparison process that induces the implicit attitude by identifying theoretically-derived boundary conditions. Second, we examine the behavioral consequences of observing sincere flattery, finding that flattery which is directed at others can function as a surprisingly effective persuasive message for observers, inducing them to act in a manner that would be desired by the flatterer – because of the observer's wish to reduce felt envy. We predict that this is particularly likely to occur after a delay, because the motivation to reduce envy can persist even after the negative reaction to the source of flattery is forgotten (cf. Kumkale and Albarracin 2004).

Five experiments tested these hypotheses. Experiment 1 used a 3 (flattery: after-purchase vs. before-purchase vs. control) x 2 (attitudes measure: implicit vs. explicit) between-subjects design to examine the thesis that observing sincere flattery induces two distinct attitudes. Participants imagined that they were shopping in a clothing store and had overheard a conversation between a stylishly-dressed shopper and a salesperson. The conversation, which contained compliments on that shopper's fashion sense, was described as occurring either before or after that shopper had made a purchase (the latter condition should increase perceptions of sincerity; cf. Campbell and Kirmani 2000). Those in the control group imagined overhearing a neutral conversation that did not contain any compliments. Participants' evaluations of the salesperson were then collected under either time-constrained (5 seconds per item; implicit measure) or unconstrained conditions (unlimited time; explicit measure). As predicted, for after-purchase (i.e., sincere) flattery, the implicit attitude was lower than the explicit attitude, but no such difference existed in the before-purchase (insincere flattery) and control conditions. Further, planned comparisons revealed that the implicit attitudes resulting from observing flattery were lower than the control group's evaluations – in both before- and after-purchase flattery conditions (thus, perceived sincerity did not enhance implicit attitudes). In contrast, explicit attitudes were lower in the before-purchase condition compared to the other two conditions.

Experiment 2a used a 2 (peer vs. non-peer) x 2 (measures of store attitudes: explicit vs. implicit) design to identify a boundary condition (based on social comparison theory) for the discrepancy between implicit and explicit attitudes. Participants were exposed to a store message containing very positive comments, which had purportedly been given to another consumer; this consumer either belonged to the same university as the participant (peer condition) or a foreign one (non-peer). Implicit or explicit store evaluations were then obtained. In the peer condition, as before, the implicit attitude was lower than the explicit attitude. However, people are less likely to be envious of dissimilar others – accordingly, no difference was found for implicit vs. explicit attitudes in the non-peer condition. This pattern of results was replicated in Experiment 2B, using within-subjects measures of implicit and explicit attitudes.

Experiment 3 used a 3 (Enhancement: self-enhancement vs. other-enhancement vs. control) x 2 (Measures: explicit vs. implicit) design to identify another boundary condition relating to social comparison. In the self-enhancement (vs. other-enhancement) condition, participants wrote about an attribute on which they rated themselves well (vs. better than others), before being exposed to the same flattery manipulation and dependent variables as in Experiment 2A. Those in the control condition proceeded directly to the flattery manipulation. In the control and self-enhancement conditions, the implicit attitude was lower than the explicit attitudes, as before. However, such a discrepancy was not observed in the other-enhancement condition (implicit attitudes improved), supporting the premise that when participants have less reason to be envious of others, the negative effects of observing flattery are diminished.

Finally, Experiment 4 examined the behavioral consequences of observing flattery. This study used a 2 (Flattery: after purchase vs. control) x 2 (Measures: explicit vs. implicit) x 2 (Timing of behavioral measure: immediate vs. delayed) design. The procedure was the same as in Experiment 1, except that after attitude measurement, participants were also asked to report their likelihood of buying a pair of expensive, stylish jeans from the store, either immediately or after a 30-minutes delay. The attitudes results again showed that the implicit attitude was lower than the explicit attitude in the flattery condition, with no difference observed in the control. Of more interest, while there was no difference between flattery vs. control in immediate intentions to buy the stylish jeans, this changed after a delay – observing flattery increased purchase intentions compared to the control. Finally, in this and in other studies, measures of envy provided process support for our theorizing: greater envy was reported in the flattery conditions vs. the control.

Taken together, results from our studies provide new insights into how observers react to flattery, in terms of the outcome (dual attitudes), the underlying process (relating to social comparison) as well as counterintuitive behavioral consequences.

Are They Who They Claim? Intentionality and Authenticity in Identity Signaling with Brands

EXTENDED ABSTRACT

Research on identity signaling largely assumes that observers will interpret the brand identity signal as intended. In this paper, we examine whether this is a valid assumption. Drawing a parallel between identity signaling and impression management, we suggest that identity signaling is inferred when observers think that a consumer's brand usage is motivated by a desire to gain social approval. We propose that identity signaling motives are likely to be salient when the signaler uses the brand in a conspicuous manner, i.e., intentionally draws attention to brand usage. The driver who revs up his Mustang's engine as he roars by is likely to be seen as behaving more conspicuously than the one who drives quietly. Such conspicuous behaviors will make observers suspicious about the motives underlying the behavior, leading to an inference of identity signaling.

We suggest that under some conditions, this inference of extrinsically motivated behavior will trigger perceptions that the consumer is not authentic, which we define as the degree to which the signaler is perceived as behaving in a manner consistent with her true self. Suspicion that the signaler is motivated by impression management will raise questions about the signaler's authenticity and reduce the perception that the target possesses the trait he is attempting to signal through the brand. This process is consistent with research that shows that suspicion of ulterior motives leads to inferences that the target is insincere (Campbell and Kirmani 2000; Vonk 2002). In our context, if a consumer is seen as intentionally using a brand (e.g., Apple iPad) to create an impression, she will be perceived as behaving in a manner that is unlike her true self. The observer would infer that if the consumer is using the iPad to show off, it is doubtful that she inherently enjoys it. This means that she is unlikely to possess the traits of a typical iPad user, i.e., innovativeness.

In three studies, we demonstrate that conspicuous brand usage will lead to perceptions of inauthenticity and dampen brand-relevant trait perceptions. Study 1 was a two-level, one-factor (Conspicuousness: low, high) between-subjects design. Participants engaged in a face-to-face interview with an interviewer who introduced himself as "James." James asked them to describe a special vacation they remembered. During the interview, James did or did not engage in conspicuous behavior related to BMW. In both conditions, James placed a set of car keys in front of him, with the BMW key logo visible. In the high conspicuousness condition, he also name-dropped the BMW brand. After the interview, participants were asked some questions about the interviewer, including his perceived competence (brand-irrelevant trait), wealth (brand-relevant trait), and authenticity (authentic, genuine, sincere), all on seven-point scales. Consistent with the hypothesis, the interviewer was perceived as more authentic and wealthier in the low conspicuous condition compared to the high conspicuous condition (Wealthy: $M_{low} = 5.42$, $M_{high} = 5.00$; authentic: $M_{low} = 4.85$, $M_{high} = 4.20$). However, perceived competence, the brand-irrelevant trait, did not vary across conditions ($M_{low} = 5.87$, $M_{high} = 5.79$).

Study 2 examined whether the negative effects of identity signaling were moderated by self-brand connection, which is the "extent to which consumers have incorporated brands into their self-concept" (Escalas and Bettman 2003). We hypothesized that when observers' self-brand connection was high (i.e., the brand was highly meaningful to them), they would react more positively to a target who was using the brand appropriately (i.e., low conspicuous). However, they would react more negatively to a target using the brand for extrinsic reasons (high conspicuous). The study involved one manipulated between-subjects variable (Conspicuousness: low, high) and one measured variable (Self-brand connection). Participants saw a video of a woman using an iPad in a coffee shop. In the low conspicuous condition, she holds the iPad in her hands. In the high conspicuous condition, she puts the iPad on a black stand so that the iPad is standing up on the table. In addition, she glances around the room as though to make sure others are watching. Self-brand connection was measured using the seven-item scale in Escalas and Bettman (2003). The brand relevant trait was innovativeness (combination of innovative and creative) and the brand irrelevant traits were sophisticated, stylish, classy, affluent, rich, and athletic. Extrinsic motivation was measured by three items (Elaine was trying to show off, gain approval, and impress others). Regression analysis showed significant effects of Conspicuousness on extrinsic motivation, authenticity, and perceived innovativeness. The target was perceived as more extrinsically motivated, less authentic, and less innovative when she was conspicuously using the iPad than when she was not. In addition, higher self-brand connection resulted in higher perceived authenticity and innovativeness. However, the interaction effect was not significant.

In study 3, we examined whether the negative effects of conspicuousness were moderated by perspective taking. Perspective taking involves applying aspects of the self to the target person (Davis et al 1983) and thus lessens the negative inferences made of the target. Because we see ourselves as authentic, we are more likely to see others whose perspective we take as authentic. Using the same video stimuli to manipulate conspicuousness as in study 2, the study also varied perspective taking (low, high). The results replicated the effects of study 2 when perspective taking was low; when perspective taking was high, however, conspicuous behavior did not hurt perceptions of the target. Thus, putting oneself in the other's shoes made them seem authentic and innovative even when they were using the iPad conspicuously.

Overall, these results show that conspicuous *use* of brands, as opposed to conspicuous brands, may result in an inference of identity signaling. Unless the observer is able to take the perspective of the signaler, identity signaling will result in negative perceptions of the signaler's authenticity and possession of brand-relevant traits.

When Doing Good Makes It Okay To Be Bad? New Directions in Licensing Research

Chair: Uzma Khan, Stanford University, USA

Paper #1: The Strategic Pursuit of Moral Credentials
Anna Merritt, Stanford University, USA
Daniel Effron, Stanford University, USA
Steven Fein, Williams College, USA
Ken Savitsky, Williams College, USA
Daniel Tuller, Stanford University, USA
Benoît Monin, Stanford University, USA

Paper #2: Interpersonal Implications of Self-Licensing
Evan Polman, Cornell University, USA
Uzma Khan, Stanford University, USA

Paper #3: Frugal Materialists: Licensing and Experiential versus Materialistic Pursuits
Rachel Ruttan, Cornell University, USA

Paper #4: Hurting the Body...and the Soul: Physical Pain Can Mitigate Moral Pain
Niro Sivanathan, London Business School, UK
Chen-Bo Zhong, University of Toronto, Canada

SESSION OVERVIEW

Prior research has demonstrated that virtuous acts, or simply feeling virtuous, can allow people to subsequently transgress and behave in less-than-virtuous ways—a phenomenon commonly referred to as the *licensing effect* (for review see Merritt, Effron & Monin, 2010). The licensing effect has been demonstrated in a wide array of domains including, consumer choice, moral behavior, political correctness and prosocial behavior (Monin & Miller, 2001; Khan & Dhar, 2006; Sachdeva, Iliev & Medin, 2009; Mazar & Zhong, 2010). For example, participants who first imagined doing something altruistic were more likely to indulge in frivolous purchases later on (Khan & Dhar, 2006) and those who initial had an opportunity to support Barack Obama were more likely to say that a particular job was better suited for Whites (Effron, Cameron, & Monin, 2009). Interestingly, the effect does not require actual behavior and mere intentions of good behavior are enough to subsequently license bad behavior.

While the last decade has witnessed a burgeoning interest in licensing research, so far most studies have focused on demonstrating the main effect. The current session takes the research forward and examines antecedents, consequences and social implications of self-licensing. In the spirit of the conference theme of "building connection" the session includes four complementary papers (all in advanced stages) that each approach the subject from a unique angle and illuminates a new aspect of self-licensing.

The first paper by Merritt el. al. demonstrates that when people anticipate acting in a way that could seem immoral, they attempt to establish their moral values ahead of time—in other words, they strategically earn moral credentials. Authors argue that the strategic pursuit of moral credentials is intended to encourage favorable attributions for the upcoming morally ambiguous behavior. The research represents an important extension to existing work on moral licensing, which has shown that people are more likely to act in morally ambiguous ways when they have previously established their morality (Merritt et al., 2010; Miller & Effron, 2010). The present research demonstrates that people sometimes pursue moral credentials strategically when they are tempted to act in morally questionable ways.

The second paper by Polman and Khan explores interpersonal implications of self-licensing behavior and feelings. Authors show

that people who believe they are virtuous lower the standards and demands of virtue for themselves, yet raise the demands for others. For example, individuals who imagined performing community service were less likely to make a donation later on but raised their expectations from others to donate. The findings suggest that good deeds can not only license less-than-virtuous behavior for the self but ironically can induce moral hypocrisy whereby people raise their demands from others.

The third paper by Ruttan examines how the nature of an initial purchase can moderate the licensing effects in subsequent purchase behavior. The authors distinguish between experiential and material purchases and show that an experiential purchase can license greater indulgence subsequently relative to an initial material purchase. For example, Ruttan finds that in a choice between a luxury and a necessity item, individuals who previously purchased an item from a set of experiential products were more likely to choose the luxury item compared to individuals who had initially purchased from a set of material products. The author explains that more positive self-attributions associated with experiential purchases license further indulgence.

The fourth paper by Zhong and Sivanathan builds on neurological and social psychology research to predict and show that physical pain can mitigate moral pain. This finding has important implications for the phenomenon of self-licensing as physical pain may compensate for less virtuous behavior and choices, which one would otherwise avoid. Consistent with this implication, participants who held a cold ice-pack while watching a series of photos of malnourished and diseased children were less willing to make a donation compared to those who held an ice-pack at room temperature. The research illustrates the role of embodied cognition in licensing effects.

Together, the papers in the session extend our understanding of the licensing effect beyond the existing literature. Given the fundamental relevance of the topic to consumer, social and political research we expect it to appeal to academics and practitioners across diverse research areas. Thus, the session is likely to foster a fruitful and interdisciplinary dialogue in the spirit of the conference theme of building connection.

The Strategic Pursuit of Moral Credentials

EXTENDED ABSTRACT

Past research on moral credentials (Monin & Miller, 2001; Effron, Cameron, & Monin, 2010) has shown that people who have had an opportunity to establish their moral values feel licensed to engage in morally ambiguous behavior. But do people attempt to credential *themselves* when they expect to need a moral license? The present research examines whether people will *strategically pursue* moral credentials in anticipation of acting in morally dubious ways. In particular, we argue that people seek to establish their morality in a preemptive attempt to ensure that their future behavior does not appear immoral to others or to themselves – in other words, to manage the attributional ambiguity that may characterize their future behavior (Berglas & Jones, 1978; Dutton & Lennox, 1974; Norton, Vandello, & Darley, 2004; Snyder, Kleck, Strenta, & Mentzer, 1979). One may seek moral credentials not only when one's intentions are truly nefarious, but also when one worries that one's intentions could *appear* so. In either case, we propose that individuals who wish to or expect to act in morally ambiguous ways will seek the "attributional cover"

Advances in Consumer Research
Volume 39, ©2011

(Kelley, 1973) of moral credentials. In three studies, we investigated this claim by examining how participants responded to the threat of appearing racist.

In Study 1, participants evaluated candidates for a hypothetical job. In a key condition, hiring the more qualified candidate would mean choosing a White applicant over a slightly less qualified Black applicant, a choice that might appear to reflect racial bias. As predicted, participants in this condition, relative to those in control conditions, were more likely to label others' behavior as racist prior to stating their hiring decision, in an attempt to demonstrate racial sensitivity.

Study 2 replicated the results from Study 1 and ruled out a possible alternative explanation: merely seeing racial inequality (in the candidates' qualifications) could prime racism, which could in turn lead participants to see more racism in the behaviors they evaluated. As in Study 1, participants in one condition saw a White applicant competing with a slightly less qualified Black applicant. We added a new a condition in which the White candidate was overwhelmingly and unambiguously more qualified than the Black candidate, meaning participants could pass over a Black job candidate with relatively little worry of looking racially biased. As predicted, participants only sought nonracist credentials when the difference between the candidates was smaller, and choosing the White applicant put them at risk of feeling or appearing racist.

Study 3 replicated the strategic moral credentials effect using a more direct manipulation of the threat of appearing racist and a dependent measure with more consequential implications. Participants expected to take a psychological test (the race IAT) that was described as either diagnostic or non-diagnostic of racial bias. Before taking the test, they indicated how likely they would be to hire a Black job applicant relative to other non-minority applicants. As predicted, participants who expected to take the diagnostic test, and who were presumably more worried about revealing racial bias, ranked the Black applicant higher than participants in the non-diagnostic condition or a baseline condition.

These studies suggest that individuals pursue moral credentials in order to manage the moral ambiguity surrounding their future behavior and provide attributional cover from recriminations. This research represents an important extension to work on moral licensing, which has shown that people are more likely to act in morally ambiguous ways when they have previously established their morality (Merritt et al., 2010; Miller & Effron, 2010). The present research demonstrates that people sometimes pursue moral credentials strategically when they are tempted to act in morally questionable ways. For example, someone who wishes to tell a joke that plays on stereotypes about Blacks may first note that "some of my best friends are Black," or a manager wishing to promote a male employee over an equally-qualified female employee may conspicuously suggest that his company expand its maternity leave benefits. Sometimes, pursuing credentials may allow people to act comfortably on legitimate motives (e.g., to give critical feedback to a student who happens to be a member of a minority group, or hire the most qualified candidate, regardless of race or gender); other times, it may license people to act on more nefarious (e.g., prejudicial) motives.

Although all of our studies targeted participants' concerns over appearing racially biased, we believe that people will seek moral credentials in other domains in which they fear that their future behavior may appear selfish, unfair, or otherwise immoral. People may even seek credentials in non-moral domains when they wish to engage in potentially discrediting behavior, as when someone establishes his sophistication by conspicuously expressing his love of Shakespeare and fine wine before mentioning his subscription to a celebrity gos-

sip magazine. Future research should investigate the strategic credentials effect in a range of moral and non-moral contexts.

Interpersonal Implications of Self-Licensing

EXTENDED ABSTRACT

Recent research has shown that past good deeds can liberate people to engage in less-than- virtuous behaviors that they would otherwise avoid (Khan & Dhar, 2006; Monin & Miller, 2001). While the relation between feeling virtuous and engaging in less-than-virtuous behavior is well-known, most of the literature on such licensing effects has focused on self-licensing and has generally ignored how feeling virtuous influences people's judgments of others and their behavior.

In this paper, we propose that people who believe that they are virtuous will lower the standards and demands of virtue for themselves, yet raise the bar for others. Our prediction is based on research showing that people manage and tailor judgments of themselves and others in a way that maintains a positive self-image (Jordan & Monin, 2008). For example, people predict that they would donate, cooperate in the prisoner's dilemma game, and volunteer to charitable causes — however, most people's actual behaviors fall short of their predictions (Epley and Dunning, 2000). These mistaken beliefs about self-behavior could lead to extreme, harsh, and erroneous judgments of others' behavior. Direct evidence suggests that people spontaneously think of themselves when they judge others (Balcetis & Dunning, 2005). If people are manipulated to experience a high moral self-worth, then they may predict themselves behaving in ethical ways, and subsequently apply these high standards of their predicted self-behavior to their judgments of others. As a consequence, judgments of others may suffer under the weight of these inflated, overly charitable predictions about the self. In short, we predict that while feelings of virtue will license one's own transgressions, they will have the opposite effect on judgments of others' behavior. Three studies support our prediction and the proposed mechanism.

In Study 1, participants were asked to recall either 2 or 10 recent examples of their moral behavior. Based on the logic that it is more difficult to recall 10 examples of recent moral behavior than 2 examples (cf. Schwarz et al., 1991), we predicted that the experienced difficulty associated with recalling 10 examples would undermine participants' feelings of virtue. Next, participants responded to three moral transgressions (*viz.* speeding, tax dodging, stealing) by rating how acceptable it would be if others engaged in the described behavior, or alternatively, if they themselves engaged in the described behavior. We found that participants in the virtue condition rated their own combined transgressions (M = 4.87) as more acceptable than participants in the control condition (M = 4.03, $p < .05$). In addition, participants in the virtue condition rated others' combined transgressions (M = 2.37) as less acceptable than participants in the control condition (M = 2.93, $p < .10$). Taken together, this indicates that feeling virtuous concurrently lowers the standards and demands of moral behavior that individuals have for themselves, yet raises the bar for others.

Study 2 replicated the main findings using consequential decisions and real monetary outcomes. In particular, feelings of virtue were manipulated by prompting participants to imagine that they have decided to spend a few hours doing community service. A control condition was also included in which participants were not prompted to imagine that they were doing community service. This manipulation has been used successfully in past research (Khan & Dhar, 2006) and has been shown to affect feelings of virtue but not other constructs, such as mood. Next, participants completed a packet of surveys unrelated to the present study, until at the end they were asked how much they would like to donate to research on cancer — any amount from zero cents to twenty cents. Alternatively, participants were asked how much they think others should donate. We found that participants in the virtue condition donated less money (M = 3.52) than participants in the control condition (M = 5.98, $p < .05$). Moreover, participants in the virtue condition urged others to donate more money (M = 12.92) than participants in the control condition (M = 9.05, $p < .05$).

We proposed that feelings of virtue lead to overly generous predictions of moral self-behavior, which in turn lead to relaxed standards for the self and higher standards for others. Study 3 tests this mechanism by providing mediation evidence. We manipulated feelings of virtue by asking participants to write a story about themselves that included ten words such as *caring*, *generous*, and *fair*. In contrast, in a control condition participants wrote a story including words such as *book*, *keys*, and *house*. Next, participants responded to four scenarios from Allison et al. (1989) that measure self-predictions of moral behavior (e.g., "Think about Judy, who must choose between studying for an exam and driving a friend who has been called home for an emergency to the airport. If you were in Judy's position, what are the chances, from 0 to 100%, that you would drive your friend to the airport?"). Finally, participants responded to moral dilemmas describing less-than-virtuous behavior (*viz.* eating dog meat, lying on a resume), and rated how wrong it would be if others engaged in the unethical behavior, or alternatively, if they themselves engaged in the unethical behavior. We carried out two bootstrapping procedures to determine (1) whether self-predictions of moral behavior mediates the relation between feelings of virtue and judgments of the self, and (2) whether self-predictions of moral behavior mediates the relation between feelings of virtue and judgments of others. Results of the bootstrap analyses confirmed that self-predictions of moral behavior did act as a mediator in both cases (the indirect effect was estimated between -.678 and -.039 for self-judgments, and between .022 and .324 for social judgments.

In sum, the results further our understanding of the licensing effects that operate in the domain of self and how they can affect interpersonal judgment. Across three studies we observed a moral license for pursuing less-than-virtuous behavior among participants induced to experience feelings of virtue. However, the reverse occurred among judgments of others; participants induced to experience feelings of virtue evaluated others' morally dubious behaviors more negatively compared to control participants.

Frugal Materialists: Licensing and Experiential versus Materialistic Pursuits

EXTENDED ABSTRACT

Past research on licensing effects has demonstrated that preferences for an indulgent or vice item will be higher if people's prior decisions have helped to boost their relevant self-concepts (e.g., Khan & Dhar, 2006). Although past work has conceptualized vice items in terms of their relative luxuriousness, we proposed that similarly virtuous or indulgent choices will have differential effects on subsequent choice depending on their classification as experiential or material purchases (Van Boven & Gilovich, 2003; Van Boven, 2005).

Experiential purchase are different from material ones since the experiences are open to positive reinterpretation, are less prone to disadvantageous comparisons, and are more likely to cultivate successful social relationships (see Van Boven, 2005 for review). Thus, experiential purchases may have more positive self-attributions than material purchases. Building on this notion we predicted and found that the more positive evaluations associated with experiential than with material purchases (Van Boven, Campbell, & Gilovich, 2010) will subsequently provide a moral license among individuals to select an indulgent item. Four studies provide support for our proposition.

In Study 1, 152 participants were asked to recall either a material or an experiential purchase. Participants recalled purchases that were at least $50 to ensure that the purchase was of sufficient importance to generate continued thought (cf., Carter & Gilovich, 2010). Participants also indicated the cost of the item and independent raters indicated whether participants' items were relative luxuries or necessities by rating each purchase on a nine-point scale (1 = *utilitarian*, 9 = *hedonic*) (Khan & Dhar, 2006). Following the recall task, participants indicated their willingness to pay for various experiential and material indulgent items. The results revealed that, when controlling for cost and indulgence of purchases, participants in the experiential purchase condition were willing to pay significantly more for both experiential and material items than were participants in the material purchase condition. Moreover, participants in the material purchase condition were significantly less willing to pay for future material items than for experiential items. Thus, material consumers may feel the need to 'cleanse' following consumption (Sachdeva, Iliev, & Medin, 2009).

In Study 2, we asked participants to select among an array of material purchases (electronic gadgets) or experiential purchases (vacations), and then, after a choice was made, we examined preference for a luxury item or a necessity. Consistent with the results of Study 1, participants in the material condition were significantly less likely to choose the luxury item than were participants in the experiential condition. Taken together, these results suggest that the type of purchase consumers make can influence their preferences for vice and virtue options.

In Studies 3 and 4, we examined potential mechanisms through which experiential and material purchases differentially impact subsequent choices. First, following research demonstrating that people tend to hold negative stereotypes of materialistic people, perceiving them to be more selfish and extrinsically motivated than are experiential people (Van Boven et al., 2010), we examined whether changes in self-concepts mediate the impact of material and experiential purchases on subsequent choices. The results indicated that the more positive self-attributions associated with the purchase of experiential items mediated the effect of purchase type on subsequent preference for vice or virtue items. Finally, in Study 4, we examined whether the tangible nature of material purchases makes them a more salient source of guilt than are non-tangible experiential purchases. Interestingly, results revealed that, by taking away participants' ability to view a recently selected material good, participants experienced less guilt and were less likely to purchase virtuous items in a subsequent task. The results of Study 4 suggest that material purchases "leave a trace", which may contribute to people's tendency to cleanse following material purchases.

As concerns are raised about modern society's materialistic pursuit of happiness and well-being (Fromm, 1976), it is important to understand how consumers respond to material versus experiential purchases over time. The results of the current studies provide consistent evidence that materialistic consumers experience self-image threats that may cause them to make more virtuous choices in the future. These results have important implications both for consumer welfare and for marketing practitioners. For example, marketers of more indulgent material products may highlight the experiential aspects of a product in order to boost consumers' relevant self-concepts and continue purchasing into the future.

Hurting the Body...and the Soul: Physical Pain Can Mitigate Moral Pain

EXTENDED ABSTRACT

Pain and death are part of life. To reject them is to reject life itself - Havelock Ellis

The unpleasant sensation associated with tissue damage, experienced as physical pain and the distressing experience of social estrangement, experienced as social pain, are both ubiquitous elements of human life (Wall, 1999). Our daily lives are not only met with physical bumps and bruises, but also "broken hearts", "bruised egos" and "hurt feelings". Despite the latter form of pain not resulting from bodily harm, the terms used to express them, function metonymically to describe physical pain. This metaphorical overlap has peaked the interest of researchers, in recent time, to question if both forms of *pain* are truly comparable, or simply a muddling of linguistic license (Eisenberger, Lieberman, & Williams, 2003; DeWall & Baumeister, 2006, DeWall et. al., 2010).

This work, collectively, has found the similarity between physical and social pain in fact extends beyond the linguistic overlap to share a common underlying operational system (Betti, Zappasodi, Rossini, Aglioti, & Tecchio, 2009; Eisenberger et al., 2003; DeWall & Baumeister, 2006; Dewall et. al., 2010; Lieberman et. al., 2004; Price, 2000; Rainville et. al., 1999). Specifically, these studies find that the anterior cingulated cortex (ACC) is implicated in sensing and computing the unpleasant components of both physical (Lieberman et. al., 2004; Rainville et. al., 1999) and social pain (Eisenberger et. al., 2003). Based on this work, we examine the dynamic between physical pain and social suffering. Drawing upon previous work on misattribution of arousal, we suggest that social pain may be lessened if people could misattribute the source of pain to physical causes.

A well-established line of work has found that the influence of arousal would be reduced if people could misattribute arousal to alternative sources. Dienstbier and Hunter (1971), for example, have shown that if individuals could explain away their somatic reactions to their contemplation of cheating, they were more likely to cheat. Likewise, Nisbett and Schachter (1966) found that people were better able to tolerate laboratory-induced electric shocks when provided the opportunity to misattribute pain associated arousal symptoms (e.g., palpitation, tremor) to a placebo they took before the experiment. In line with this logic, if physical pain is an integral part of social suffering such that social agony is accompanied by somatic reactions that resemble physical pain, we expect people to be better able to deal with social suffering if they could misattribute their pain to physical sources.

We test this prediction in three experiments. In the first experiment we had participants hold an icepack versus the same pack at room temperature while watching a series of photos of malnourished and diseased children. Afterwards participants were approached by the experimenter and asked whether they would be willing to donate part of the money they earned from participating in the study, to a charity. We found that participants who held the cold ice-pack while exposed to photos of suffering children were less willing to donate. Thus, experiencing physical pain not only "toughened" people when dealing with social agony but also made them less disposed to stimuli that induce sympathy.

In the second experiment, participants were shown a similar set of photographs as in Experiment 2, except that in one of the conditions each of those photos was immediately preceded by a photograph of thorny plants, designed to remind people of physical pain (Bar & Neta, 2006). In the other condition (the control condition), the proceeding photographs were soft-edged plants. Participants were then approached by the experimenter and asked for a charitable donation. We found that even the subtle reminder of physical pain through images of thorny plants, reduced donations to and unrelated charity.

Finally, the third experiment extended the effect to social pain. Participants held an icepack versus the same pack at room temperature while they engaged in an online cyber-ball game designed to create the experience of social exclusion and rejection (Williams, Cheung, & Choi (2000). In this game, participants engaged in a virtual ball-tossing exercise where they tossed a ball around with three other participants who were supposedly connected online. In actuality, a computer program controlled the throws of the other players (Williams et al., 2000). Participants received the ball twice in the beginning, but were excluded from the remaining 30 throws. We found that participants who held an cold icepack during the cyberball game reported feeling *less* excluded and rejected from others compared to those held a similar pack at room temperature. This suggests the physical discomfort of holding the cold icepack had reduced the pain from being socially rejected.

Across three studies we consistently found that physical pain helps people withstand their social suffering, and in turn can reduce their motivation to help those in need. These set of findings hold important implications to the practice of self-harm. For instance, inflicting physical pain on the self is a common part of religious ceremonies. Catholicism, Hinduism, and the Muslim religion, all have rituals that involve whipping, piercing, and other physically painful acts. Even though the impetus for inflicting physical pain vary in this context, the common underlying belief tends to be the link between physical pain and purity; physical pain can purify the soul and bring one closer to deity. Paradoxically, our findings suggest the opposite: Experiencing physical pain made it easier to navigate the social pain of seeing others suffer, and in turn reduced our willingness to help others. Taken together, this suggests that sticks and stones, not only break your bones, as indicated by the old proverb, but may also numb your pain of compassion.

When Opposites (May Not) Attract: Insights from Next-Generation Priming Influences on Consumer Behavior

Chairs: Heather M. Johnson, University of Maryland, USA
Kate E. Min, Duke University, USA

Paper #1: The Competing Goal Strikes Back: Volitional Fulfillment of Nonconscious Goals Enables Opposing Goals to Rebound

Robin Tanner, University of Wisconsin-Madison, USA
Juliano Laran, University of Miami, USA
Kate E. Min, Duke University, USA
Tanya Chartrand, Duke University, USA

Paper #2: In Pursuit of Luxury: Anterior Cingulate Cortex Activation in Response to Luxury Brands Depends on Goal-Congruent Cues

Adam Craig, University of South Carolina, USA
Heather M. Johnson, University of Maryland, USA
Stacy Wood, North Carolina State University, USA
Yuliya Komarova, Fordham University, USA

Paper #3: Are There Situations in Which Consumers Want to be Primed?

Amy Dalton, HKUST, Hong Kong
Juliano Laran, University of Miami, USA

Paper #4: Save or Spend?: When Priming of Related Constructs Can Activate Opposing Behaviors

Promothesh Chatterjee, University of Kansas, USA
Randall Rose, University of South Carolina, USA
Jayati Sinha, University of Iowa, USA

SESSION OVERVIEW

General orientation and objectives. The idea of temporary concept activation or "priming" has gained tremendous interest in consumer decision-making and consumer behavior, with recent demonstrations that consumers' adaptive functioning may actually be explained by nonconscious processes (Chartrand, Huber, Shiv, & Tanner, 2008). With it now becoming clear that consumer behavior can be automatically determined to some degree, it is important to move past the demonstration phase of automaticity research, and to to build richer and more complete theories of automatic behavior in the consumption context. In this session, our purpose is to provide next generation insights into automatic behavioral effects with a particular focus on understanding why subtly different but related primes lead to different behavioral outcomes. In particular, the four papers in this session address the following second generation research questions:

Paper 1. What are the downstream consequences for behavior of nonconscious goal fulfillment?

Paper 2. What are the neurological processes underlying the effect of the thrift and prestige primes which many marketing researchers have used?

Paper 3. Are consumers more likely to be influenced by environmental cues in certain circumstances?

Paper 4. Why do very similar priming constructs sometimes lead to very different results?

Potential audience. We expect this session to be of interest to researchers interested in the influences of primes on consumer behavior; the automatic and nonconscious psychological underpinnings of consumer behavior; and the downstream implications of said influences and processes for marketers.

Issues to be covered. These papers collectively emphasize the presumed usefulness of priming as a tool for encouraging indulgence, with the aim of the session being to highlight the circumstances in which one might actually find reversals (e.g., less consumption/indulgence) as well as the psychological and neurological underpinnings of these effects. Across the papers and paradigms, the priming stimuli and measures are related to spending/saving or indulgence/restraint-type constructs, speaking to consumers' proclivity to indulge and influence factors affecting this (automatic) tendency. Data has been collected for the studies described in papers 1 through 4. Drafts of papers 1 and 2 are available upon request.

The Competing Goal Strikes Back: Volitional Fulfillment of Nonconscious Goals Enables Opposing Goals to Rebound

EXTENDED ABSTRACT

A considerable body of research has demonstrated that environmental cues can trigger goals that are then pursued without conscious awareness (see Moskowitz, Li, & Kirk, 2004, for a review). Nonconscious goal pursuit (NCGP) research has for the most part focused on delineating the process by which single goals are selected, pursued, and fulfilled. More recently, there have been calls for researchers to answer 'second generation questions' (Bargh, 2006) such as how multiple goals interact with each other and how they interact with conscious decisions. We contribute to answering these questions by investigating how the NCGP process plays out over time for goals which chronically conflict, as understanding how individuals resolve opposing motivations is central to our understanding of the dynamics of self-regulation (Koo & Fishbach, 2009). For example, consider an individual driving to the grocery who is exposed to an environmental cue suggesting indulgence (e.g., a billboard showing a luxury ice-cream brand). Such incidental cue exposure may lead the individual to automatically pursue a goal to indulge, perhaps leading him to buy an unplanned candy bar (Chartrand, Huber, Shiv, & Tanner, 2008) In this research, our particular interest is in how the NCGP process plays out downstream from this goal-fulfilling purchase.

We explore two questions: First, can the fulfillment of a nonconsciously activated goal (hereafter the focal goal) lead a competing goal (a goal to eat healthy in the above example) to rebound and influence subsequent behavior? Second, do the volitional circumstances underlying such goal fulfillment matter? In particular, for automatically pursued goals, is any opportunity for goal-consistent behavior sufficient to fulfill the goal (i.e., passive receipt of a goal-fulfilling means, such as a candy), or does the individual need to make a volitional decision to undertake goal-consistent behavior (i.e., decision to obtain a goal-fulfilling means)? To explore these questions we utilize a sequential task paradigm in which individuals are given the opportunity to pursue a primed focal goal before being given an opportunity to pursue either the focal goal or a chronically opposing goal.

In experiment 1, we examined how the automatic pursuit and fulfillment of an *indulgence* goal influenced the subsequent pursuit of an opposing *health* goal (goals that are in chronic opposition for most individuals, Finkelstein & Fishbach 2010). We found that when no goal was primed, eating a chocolate led to an increased desire for indulgent foods. However, when an indulge goal was first primed, eating the chocolate led to an increased desire for healthy foods. Thus, fulfillment of the primed indulge goal appeared to cause the opposing health goal to rebound. However, since all participants who ate the chocolate did so of their own choice, it is not clear whether the indulge goal was fulfilled by the mere, physical consumption of the chocolate itself or by the volitional act of choosing to consume it.

Experiment 2 was designed both to replicate the results of the first experiment using a different opposing goal pair (thrift vs. luxury), and also to disentangle the volitional act of *actively choosing* a goal-fulfilling means from its *mere receipt*. When a thrift goal was primed and followed by one's own decision to be thrifty (i.e., choosing Hanes socks), the thrift goal appeared to be fulfilled, leading to extremely high preference for the relatively more luxurious option (i.e., allocating great amounts of money to a luxury store). However, when the thrift goal (vs. neutral) was primed and was followed by unsolicited receipt of a thrifty option (i.e., being awarded Hanes socks), then the thrift goal did not appear to be satisfied, and continued to influence preference (i.e., allocating great amounts of money to an economical store). Thus, these results suggest that the nonconscious goal system is not entirely passive and suggests that fulfillment of nonconscious goals actually requires volitional intent to behave in a goal consistent way.

We find that the fulfillment of automatically pursued goals enables opposing goals to rebound and influence behavior. Importantly, it reveals that the effects of environmental primes can be substantially more complex than the single goal and behavior cases that have been previously studied. While speculative, this complexity suggests the possibility that the unconscious goal system is capable of adaptively managing multiple goals. Further, it is interesting to see that there needs to be some volition for the opposing goal to rebound after initial goal fulfillment. Simply giving participants a means to satisfy a primed goal did not generate rebound, which suggests that the primed goal is not fulfilled without people actively deciding on goal-fulfilling means. These results are fascinating as they suggest an interaction between nonconsciously primed goals and consciously made decisions. Future research should explore the level of consciousness necessary for a decision to pursue a goal be regarded as enough for goal fulfillment, how much movement toward focal goal fulfillment is necessary (i.e., make a goal-consistent decision, perform a goal-consistent behavior, perform a large amount of goal-consistent behavior) for a competing goal to rebound, and whether there are situations in which merely being given an opportunity to pursue a goal is enough to fulfill a primed goal or at least decrease its activation level, which was not the case in experiment 2. The investigation of these issues could not only provide information on how unconscious goal pursuit operates, or how conscious goal pursuit directs behavior, but also helps us understand how both interact and allow us to aid individuals in the management of their multiple goals.

In Pursuit of Luxury: Anterior Cingulate Cortex Activation in Response to Luxury Brands Depends on Goal-Congruent Cues

EXTENDED ABSTRACT

The acquisition of beautiful, costly, or prestigious goods is an age-old human consumption behavior that finds its modern expression in luxury brands. Given the strong appeal of luxury brands even in inauspicious personal or societal economic environments, two questions emerge: (a) Is there a neuropsychological component to luxury brand appeal and, (b) if so, how might environmental cues modulate neuropsychological goal value associated with indul-gence? Goal value is the extent to which a choice option may serve as a means towards goal attainment (Hare et al. 2008). We hypothesize that there is a neuropsychological response to luxury brands that is congruent with desire or motivation (and different from more prosaic brands), but that this response depends on the presence of consumption-related cues that modulate luxury goal value. For consumers who wish to reduce their consumption of expensive luxuries, such results would provide good news. Though luxury brands "feel" good, exposure to messages of frugality reduces the value to which a brand may facilitate a goal, and, thus perhaps the temptation.

While indulgence goals may seem more prevalent in the marketplace, current consumption contexts also promote well-established goals to save. To examine neural encoding of the value by which brands may facilitate individuals' goals, we compare luxury brands to other well-regarded and familiar brands that are positioned in terms of practicality.

Research on consumer attitudes toward luxury is often limited by methods prone to socially desirable responding, self-generated validity, or the inability to articulate complex cognitive/emotional responses operating automatically. The use of fMRI methodology allows us to circumvent these issues and more directly assess neural processes underlying response to brands across conditions. Based on two recent fMRI studies that offer important insight into a neuroeconomic perspective of luxury valuation, we designed an fMRI protocol to examine activation in areas of the brain known to play a role in goal valuation (Hare et al. 2008, Plassmann et al. 2008). Research finds that rostral anterior cingulate cortex (rACC) activation is correlated with computations of amount of reward associated with an option under consideration (i.e. goal value; Litt, Plassmann, Shiv, & Rangel, 2011). Broadly speaking, automatic goal value computation would allow recognition of the means to a desirable end state and a signal to other systems regarding the degree to which an option should be approached (Ferguson & Bargh, 2004). As a basis for our research, these findings suggest a) the probable existence of a neurophysiological component to the appeal of luxury brands, b) that this valuation is likely to be goal-oriented, and c) that the rACC encodes context dependent goal valuation activation.

We propose that goal valuation effects depend on congruency between the cued goal (indulgence vs. frugality) and the brand. Secondly, we do not expect increased goal-activation for practical brand images when they are preceded by cues related to frugality, as utilitarian goals do not invoke the same degree of associated reward value. For goal and automaticity researchers, it will be interesting to see that this pattern of results is consistent with goal-means valuation rather than mere schema activation, as this distinction represents an important debate in current priming research.

To test these hypotheses, we scanned 24 participants while they viewed four cue-brand conditions in a 2 x 2 within-subjects design that crossed the consumption goal cued (indulgence or frugality) and the brand logos presented (luxury or practicality). Thus, in condition 1, three indulgence-oriented words preceded three luxury brand logos (IL); in condition 2, three frugality-oriented words preceded three practical brand logos (FP); in condition 3, three indulgence-oriented words preceded three practical brand logos (IP); and, in condition 4, three frugality-oriented words preceded three luxury brand logos (FL). Cue words were carefully chosen to avoid pejoratively nuanced consumption goals (e.g., spoiled, cheap). Brand logos were pretested to ensure familiarity and that both luxury and practical brands were equally well-regarded.

Imaging analyses indicated that, as predicted, congruency between an indulgence cue and luxury brand resulted in increased rACC activity compared to conditions where a luxury brand was preceded by a frugality cue. We did not observe this increase in activation when a practical brand was preceded by a frugality cue. This suggests that enhanced goal-activation for luxury logos that are preceded by indulgence-oriented cues are stronger for the goal of indulgence and is not simply a mere-congruency effect. Importantly, temptations towards indulgence may be modulated by the presence of frugality cues: frugality cues preceding luxury brands reduced the goal value for luxury brands.

The contributions of this research are two-fold. First, building on recent research on relative goal value, our study shows that the appeal of luxury brands is associated with neurological responses contingent on the presence of consumption related cues—the mere presence of a luxury cue affects the valuation of luxury brand representations. This study is the first to demonstrate that goal valuation occurs automatically within a passive viewing context. Automatic valuation would be a necessary precursor to the selection of luxury goods when an indulgence goal has been activated. Second, and viewed in the light of recent research on passive goal guidance (Laran & Janiszewski, 2009), our study raises important questions regarding the nature of nonconscious goal intensity. Traditional priming studies activate goals in an on/off manner (Bosmans & Baumgartner, 2005) and goal means (brands, etc.) are generally limited to dichotomous choices. However, our study and other recent neuroeconomic studies (Hare et al. and Plassmann et al.) utilize and measure a range of and observe differences in valuation, thus suggesting that nonconsciously activated goals and subsequent behaviors are dependent on goal intensities that must reach a threshold before the goal pursuit is initiated. Thus the question remains whether goal value intensity signals may facilitate intensification of active goals and suppression of other goals to passive operation.

Are There Situations in Which Consumers Want to be Primed?

EXTENDED ABSTRACT

We propose that sometimes people "want to be primed" – that is, without explicit awareness or intent, people become more receptive to environmental influence. People become more receptive to environmental influence when the source of influence is well-liked (and less receptive when the source is disliked). Moreover, people become more receptive to environmental influence when facing difficult decisions because external cues can help make decisions. Importantly, we propose that people's receptiveness to external influence can have unintended consequences for unrelated behavioral decisions. The effect of wanting to be primed is not the same as losing self-control. Rather, we find that wanting to be primed increases indulgence when environmental cues prime "spending" but decreases indulgence when cues prime "saving." Wanting to be primed is also different from experiencing cognitive load. Indeed, we find that wanting to be primed can reverse effects in situations where cognitive load would exacerbate them. We test our hypotheses through a combination of field and laboratory studies.

To begin, we tested whether people are more receptive to priming effects when they encounter marketing stimuli that they like. In the main atrium of a university campus, where student groups and vendors set up table displays, we displayed 7 cardboard boxes (keyboard, laptop, and monitor boxes) that depicted either Dell or Apple brand logos. The experimenter stood approximately 3 meters away, to avoid being linked to the display. Passing students were offered candy in exchange for answering two short questions. First, participants imagined an upcoming shopping trip where they must decide whether to spend a lot or try and save money. Participants reported their willingness-to-spend. The second question asked participants' liking of the brand Apple (Dell).

Pretesting suggested that Apple is associated with expensiveness and Dell with value. Therefore, exposure to Apple should prime spending and Dell should prime saving, producing different effects on willingness-to-spend. We predicted and found that brand liking moderates these effects: greater liking of Apple (Dell) increased (decreased) willingness-to-spend. Moreover, whereas liking a brand caused brand-consistent behavior, disliking a brand provoked brand-inconsistent behavior. These findings support the hypothesis that people are more (less) receptive to influence by stimuli they like (dislike).

Study 2 tested the hypothesis that people want to be primed when facing difficult decisions, and addressed an alternative explanation based on cognitive load. Cognitive load was addressed in two ways: First, by examining expected rather than actual task difficulty (which should minimize difficulty's effect on load); Second, by examining a situation where cognitive load and wanting to be primed predict different behaviors. Research suggests that people automatically react against unwanted sources of persuasion, including insincere flattery (Chan and Sengupta 2010). If cognitive load underlies the effect of difficulty, then difficulty should have no effect or even strengthen these automatic effects. However, if wanting to be primed underlies the effect of difficulty, then difficulty should reverse these effects. That is, if difficulty makes people more receptive to environmental influence, sources of persuasion would no longer be unwanted.

Study 2 used a 2 (difficult vs. easy decision) X 2 (expensive vs. inexpensive store) between-subjects design. Participants completed a shopping task followed by a decision-making task. Before the shopping task, participants were informed that the upcoming decision-making task was difficult (easy). This was our sole manipulation of difficulty. In the shopping task, participants evaluated a mailbox flyer containing insincere flattery – statements obviously intended to persuade readers to visit a new "designer" ("discount") department store. In the decision-making task, participants imagined needing a new apartment and choosing between one that is superior but expensive and another that is inferior but better value. The dependent measure was apartment preference.

We predicted that participants expecting a difficult (vs. easy) upcoming task would be more receptive to environmental influence. Thus, whereas participants in the easy decision condition would automatically react against the flyer's insincere flattery, participants in the difficult decision condition would not. Supporting this hypothesis, the inexpensive (vs. expensive) store flyer reduced preference for the inexpensive apartment among participants anticipating an easy decision. Conversely, the inexpensive (vs. expensive) store flyer enhanced preference for the inexpensive apartment among participants anticipating a difficult decision. These results support the hypothesis that when decisions are difficult (easy), people are more (less) receptive to environmental influence.

Study 3 examined the interaction between liking, difficulty, and brand. We reasoned that when people face difficult decisions, they want to be primed regardless of how much they like particular brands. Thus, we predicted a 3-way interaction in which liking moderates priming effects in easy decision contexts (replicating study 1's results), but not difficult contexts. We conducted the study in a mall in the days leading up to Christmas and Valentine's Day. Mall patrons shopping for gifts were offered candy in exchange for answering two questions. First, participants generated a number from 1 to 10 to express how difficult Christmas (Valentine's Day) shopping has been for them. Next, participants thought about a future shopping trip, after the holiday, and indicated their willingness-to-spend on that trip (the DV from study 1). To dissociate our proposed effect from a depletion effect, whereby difficult decisions may uniformly increase willingness-to-spend, we alternated between stopping people walking by expensive and inexpensive stores. If greater shopping difficulty makes people want to be primed, the particular store participants were standing in front of would moderate willingness-to-spend.

Three key findings were obtained. First, as in study 1, liking the brand caused a priming effect and disliking it reversed the effect. Second, in line with study 2, brand's effect strengthened as perceived decision difficulty increased. Third, we obtained the predicted 3-way interaction between liking, difficulty, and brand. Only when shopping was considered easy did participants show (reverse) priming effects in response to brands they (dis)like. When shopping was considered difficult, people behaved in line with the brands' associations. Thus, decision difficulty is an important boundary condition for the effect of liking.

Collectively, these studies support the hypothesis that sometimes people are more receptive to priming effects; in particular, people want to be primed when they encounter marketing stimuli that they like and decision contexts that are difficult.

Save or Spend?: When Priming of Related Constructs Can Activate Opposing Behaviors

EXTENDED ABSTRACT

In this research we examine two related constructs (cash and credit) that when activated encourage opposing behaviors. At a functional level both serve as a medium of exchange, but we argue that credit cards and cash are forms of money that are likely to have affectively and semantically different mental representations, consequently these forms of money are likely to have different downstream behavioral implications. For example, priming potential donors with cash concepts may lead to the kind of self-sufficiency orientation (neither willing to take help nor willing to give help) that has been noted in prior research (Vohs, Mead, & Goode, 2006), but priming a different form of money such as credit cards may elicit a very different orientation. Why would this be the case?

Mere exposure to credit card brands has been shown to substantially increase spending (Feinberg, 1986). Later studies have validated the notion that credit cards do facilitate spending relative to cash (Prelec & Simester, 2001; Soman, 2001). Consumers' prior experiences of instant gratification of desire when paying with a credit card may invoke a buy-now-pay-later mentality that is strongly associated with rewards (Mendoza & Pracejus, 1997; Shimp & Moody 2000). Prior neurological studies suggest that many rewards are processed similarly in the brain (Montague, King-Casas, & Cohen, 2006). An activated generalized reward system can give rise to non-specific effects. For example, exposure to sexy cues leads to more impatience in intertemporal choice between monetary rewards (Van den Bergh, Dewitte, & Warlop, 2008). Similarly, we suggest that with repeated credit card purchase experiences ending in immediate gratification of desires, this may result in a general accessibility of benefit considerations relative to cost considerations when exposed to credit primes.

On the other hand, when paying with cash, people are acutely aware of the pain of payment (Prelec & Loewenstein, 1998) because of the vivid memory trace (Soman, 2001). Theorists generally regard social pain, monetary-loss pain, and physical pain as overlapping pain systems (Knutson et al., 2007; Rick, Cryder, & Loewenstein, 2008). Overlapping pain systems suggest a heightened sensitivity to

costs. Thus, with repeated transactions, strong associations are developed between cash as a payment mechanism and various costs or losses that are affectively negative concepts.

Because there are likely to be clear differences in the associative networks surrounding credit card and cash payments, we hypothesize that attention to dramatically different informational inputs can be induced by priming cash versus credit concepts (Bargh, 2006; Fitzsimons, Chartrand, & Fitzsimons, 2008). This activation of different associations in memory biases the processing of subsequently encountered stimuli depending on its consistency with the implications of the activated concept (Bodenhausen, 1988; Darley & Gross, 1983). Evidence that is consistent with the activated concept may receive more attention and rehearsal, and may therefore be much more likely to be incorporated into the decision maker's mental representation of the scenario compared to inconsistent information. Using these ideas in the present context, we propose that different downstream outcomes between credit card payments and cash payments arise at least in part due to the attention to *benefits* highlighted by *credit card* primes versus the attention to *costs* highlighted by *cash* primes. Costs of helping behavior could be financial as in the case of monetary contributions, or in terms of commitments of time and effort. Benefits of helping behavior could include social benefits or self-enhancement benefits.

A pretest identified the words that participants associate with credit cards and cash. Across all studies, participants initially engaged in a scrambled-sentence task, in which they constructed grammatically correct sentences using four words from a list of five scrambled words (adapted from Bargh & Chartrand, 2000).

In study 1, participants were randomly assigned to either a cash or credit card (or control) condition using a sentence unscrambling task as described. Following a short unrelated questionnaire, the participants were told that the University Student Welfare was looking for some volunteers and that any amount of time that participants can volunteer per month would be helpful. We found that participants volunteered significantly more time when primed with *credit card* ($M_{credit card}$ = 6.46 hours) than when primed with *cash* (M_{cash}=2.34 hours) (with participants in the control condition volunteering M = 4.03 hours). We replicated the same study with money donated as the dependent variable and found similar results.

In study 2, we explored whether participants primed with different money concepts focus differentially on either the *benefit* or *cost* aspects of the donation option and therefore, identify cost or benefit related words at different rates when participating in a word-completion task. Similar to previous studies, participants completed a scrambled sentence task meant to activate cash vs. credit card concepts. The participants were then given information about a particular charity, and the pros and cons of volunteering were listed in a paragraph. Subsequently, the participants completed a word completion task and time was measured (counterbalanced). The word completion task entailed completing 25 words which were left incomplete (9 were neutral words and rest equally split between the two conditions). As expected, participants in the *credit card* condition identified more words related to *benefits* compared to those in the cash condition (M = 1.92 vs. 1.02, p < .05). In contrast, those in the *cash* condition identified more target words related to *costs* than those in the credit card condition (M = 2.67 vs. 1.49, p<.05). In addition, we replicated the main effect findings from the previous study. In sum, our findings demonstrate that while *cash* and *credit* are both concepts related to money, they lead to opposing effects in terms of donation behavior. Further, we find evidence that this effect is at least partially due to differential activation of *benefit* versus *cost* aspects of donations.

When Looks Matter: Dynamics of Exposure and Attention in Self-Control Dilemmas

Chair: Suresh Ramanathan, Texas A&M, USA

Paper #1: Gaze Patterns Reveal Preference Editing During Self-Control Choices

Siegfried Dewitte, K.U. Leuven, Belgium
Suresh Ramanathan, Texas A&M, USA
Sabrina Bruyneel, K.U. Leuven, Belgium
Ralf van der Lans, HKUST, Hong Kong

Paper #2: Effects of Focus of Attention on Desire and Resistance Towards Temptations

Suresh Ramanathan, Texas A&M, USA
Wilhelm Hofmann, University of Chicago, USA

Paper #3: Self-Inferred Norms Reduce Desire and Consumption Through Changing Product Perceptions

Aiste Grubliauskiene, K.U. Leuven, Belgium
Siegfried Dewitte, K.U. Leuven, Belgium
Luk Warlop, K.U. Leuven, Belgium

SESSION OVERVIEW

The psychological underpinnings of self-control and failures thereof have been a topic of rich debate in the literature. Much has been written about how and why people make unhealthy or unwise choices. Some researchers have explained such choices as a result of lapses in executive function due to limited resources (Baumeister, Vohs and Tice 2007), while others have argued that lower-order affective reactions towards stimuli or automatic positive attitudes towards them may drive such reactions (Hofmann, Friese and Strack 2009; Shiv and Fedorikhin 1999). What is as yet under-researched is the nature of cognitive and affective processes set into motion immediately upon exposure to a vice or virtue and how these attentional processes unfold over time. The three papers in this session provide valuable insights on how our preferences and emotions change dynamically upon exposure to tempting options.

The first paper by Dewitte and colleagues focuses on the dynamics of gaze patterns when people are making choices from pure (virtue-virtue or vice-vice) or mixed (virtue-vice) choice sets with equally attractive options. Using eye-tracking, they show that contrary to established research showing that people fixate on the option finally chosen, self-control decisions involving choices between virtues and vices elicit greater gaze fixations on the option not chosen. They suggest that people's attentional processes are actively involved in trying to distorting the value of the option that is not chosen when both options are equally attractive, a phenomenon they call preference editing. The second paper by Ramanathan and Hofmann focuses on the dynamics of felt desire and resistance towards temptations and shows that the root to indulgence decisions by impulsive individuals lies in the recurrence and stickiness of desires rather than weakening resistance, and that trying to change attention away from temptations towards healthier options may backfire if such individuals' reward circuitry has already been activated. Finally, the third paper by Rutkauskaite, Dewitte and Warlop provides insights into how people's desires towards temptations and consumption can be reduced by changing their innate preferences via pre-exposure to temptations in a non-consummatory setting. They argue that implicit or tacit norms for behavior in a given setting are more effective than explicit or stated norms, not just in the short-term in terms of reducing consumption but also altering the preferences for temptations in the long-term.

Together, these papers bring deep psychological insights about self-control hitherto unexplored in the literature. In particular, they provide a window to the role of exposure and attention in self-control dilemmas, showing how people's innate preferences can be changed either towards virtues or vices by self-initiated processes (Dewitte et al, Rutskaukaite et al), and how external attempts to change these preferences via attentional retraining (Ramanathan and Hofmann) or via explicit norms (Rutskaukaite et al) may have counter-productive effects. Using cutting-edge techniques such as eye-tracking and new analytical methods such as recurrence analysis that were originally developed in the hard sciences, the papers in this session represent the essence of the conference theme, "building connections." Within a coherent theme, the three papers represent diverse conceptual and methodological interests and have a broad appeal to audience from marketers to policy makers. All papers are in an advanced stage of completion. We expect this session to be of interest to researchers in the domains of affect regulation and self-control, as well as cognitive learning. Researchers in decision neuroscience may find the session interesting because of the potential it holds for continued exploration of basic neural mechanisms involved in self-control decisions. Scholars interested in studying the design of public policy interventions aimed at reducing indulgence and increasing healthy behavior may also find the prescriptive recommendations emerging from this session to be of interest. We thus expect an inter-disciplinary appeal from this session integrating unique methodological and theoretical contributions with pragmatic and prescriptive recommendations.

A session on exposure and attention would be incomplete without a discussion leader of the stature of Rik Pieters from Tilburg University. Rik is an expert in attentional processes and is one of the most respected researchers in the field. He will share his views on the papers and attempt to build connections among them for the benefit of the large audience that we expect this session to attract!

Gaze patterns reveal preference editing duringself-control choices

EXTENDED ABSTRACT

In this paper we address the question as to whether choosing between a fruit dessert (virtue) and a high-calorie dessert (vice) relies on the same decision process as choosing between two fruit desserts or two high-calorie desserts. In general, we question whether self-control choices rely on the value computation processes that have been documented in the decision literature (e.g. Busemeyer and Townsend 1993). We propose an alternative process that we coin 'preference editing', where the valuation of the choice options is distorted rather than computed during the decision process. We use eye-tracking methodology to document preference editing during self-control choice.

Decision models (e.g. Busemeyer and Townsend 1993) assume that decision makers stochastically sample evidence about the options in the choice set, feeding into a relative decision value, which reflects the relative advantage that one of the options has at a certain moment. Decision makers continue sampling until the relative decision value passes a decision threshold, at which point a choice is made. Krajbich, Armel, and Rangel (2010) linked this type of decision model to eye-movements. Notice that this value computation process does not affect the initial value of the options. We assume that this model has difficulties dealing with self-control choices because of the mixed nature of vice options. The alternative process, preference editing, assumes that during self-control choices, the decision maker distorts the valuation of the options as a way to cope with the decision problem (Dewitte, Bruyneel, and Geyskens 2009). This distortion process implies the value of one of the options will have become more negative than that of the other option.

To gauge the process of preference editing, we tracked people's gaze during a sequence of binary choices (cf. Krajbich, Armel, and Rangel 2010), either in mixed choice situations (vice – virtue) or in pure choice situations (vice – vice or virtue – virtue). To control for stimulus effects, each choice option served as an option in both the mixed and one of the pure choice situations. The choice options within a pair were matched on attractiveness, following the results of a pretest. Based on our preference editing model, we put forward two specific predictions about the gaze pattern during self-control choice.

The first pattern is the match between choice and the last fixation (do consumers choose what they look at last or not?). Krajbich et al.'s (2010) validated decision model predicts that the last fixation will not be on the selected option in cases where the item the decision maker looks at last is valued less than the other item. If there is no such value difference between the two options, the last fixation will be on the selected option. Our preference editing account implies that the value of the two (initially equally attractive) options will diverge during the choice process. So our first prediction states that preference editing would be revealed in people's gaze pattern when a lower proportion of last fixations would be on the chosen option in the mixed condition compared to the pure condition.

Preference editing also implies that different gaze patterns lead to the selection of the vice and the virtue, which is not the case for value computation models, when the two options were matched on attractiveness. While choosing between (equally attractive) fruit and high-calorie desserts, choosers' preference editing can go in two directions. Choosers may either downplay the health feature of the option set, which makes the virtue less and the vice more valued. Alternatively they may downplay the taste dimension of the choice set, which would make the virtue relatively more valued than the vice, leading to a relative value gap in favor of the virtue. Comparing these two preference editing paths suggests that the path towards the virtue requires longer editing than the path towards the vice. If the impact of taste is reduced (path towards choosing the virtue), the value of BOTH options is reduced in absolute terms because the virtue also scores positively on the taste dimension. In contrast, reducing the impact of health (path towards choosing the vice) works faster because it reduces the net value of the virtue while increasing the net value of the vice. This leads to our second prediction. Choosing a virtue from a virtue-vice pair will take more fixations than choosing a vice. In contrast, choosing the same virtues from virtue – virtue pairs will not take more fixations than choosing the same vices from vice – vice pairs.

We recorded 62 participants' eye-movements while they were choosing one product from 10 product pairs. Half of participants got 10 product pairs of the mixed type (vice-virtue) and the other half received a product pair series of the pure type (either virtue-virtue or vice-vice, also between subjects). Consistent with our account that self-control requires more preference editing than non-self-control choices, we found that the last fixation (the one while choosing) was less often on the selected option in self-control choice situations (67%) than in the two pure choice situations (81%, $p < .05$), although all pairs were matched on attractiveness. Also consistent with preference editing, we found that in the mixed condition, choosing the virtue required more fixations than choosing the vice ($r = .39$,

$p < .05$), but that the number of fixations did not differ between the two pure conditions (F < 1).

Our data strongly suggest that self-control choices do not trigger the standard value computation processes but rather distort valuation of the options. This implies that engaging in self-control choices may have effects on subsequent decisions as it implies preference editing (e.g. Dewitte et al. 2009). Our findings also raise the question as to what would happens in self-control situations where the two options are not matched on attractiveness. Would the value computation process suffice in this case or do these situations still require preference editing? Future research should also address the question which decision situations require preference editing and which can be solved with value computation.

Effects of Focus of Attention on Desire and Resistance Towards Temptations

EXTENDED ABSTRACT

Picture yourself at the local grocery store. As you enter, you may see a display of fruits on sale. Your eyes are drawn to the display for a while. Continuing on, you see a rich chocolate cake in the bakery section, inviting you with its sheer decadence. You look away, trying to focus on the healthier fruits instead. Yet, your eyes keep returning to the cake, drawn by its luscious, creamy, dark brown appearance. You "succumb" to the temptation and buy a large wedge of the cake.

This is a common enough story that occurs in almost everyone's life. The idea that we "succumb" to temptations has a nice Puritanical ring to it – temptations are "bad" and must be avoided. If people acted impulsively, it must be because they were weak in self-control (i.e., lacked resources or were otherwise unable to resist the temptation) or had a weak activation of "higher-order" goals such as eating healthy or saving expenses. Drawing on dual-process theories of the mind (Hofmann, Friese, & Strack, 2009; Metcalfe & Mischel, 1999; Strack & Deutsch, 2004) and the elaborated intrusion theory of desire (Kavanagh, et al. 2005), we propose instead in this paper that indulgence may be the result of a pattern of recurrent desires that lead to and are in turn driven by attentional adhesion to the tempting stimulus. We suggest that people who experience desire may get "trapped" in that state for longer periods of time. We also propose that the recurrence and stickiness in desires is affected by pre-exposure to rewards, but that the timing of pre-exposure can change the patterns of desire experienced by people.

The literature on problem behaviors commonly advocates the retraining of attention away from temptation or towards healthy or more prudent choices (Schoenmakers, Wiers, Jones, Bruce, & Jansen, 2007). We suggest that there are boundary conditions to the efficacy of these methods, and indeed, such methods may fail spectacularly under some circumstances for some people, manifesting in even stronger and more persistent desires towards temptations. Specifically, impulsive people whose reward system is already active may respond to attentional retraining with more recurrent desires towards subsequently presented temptations, potentially causing greater indulgence.

Experiment 1 examines the psychological processes underlying such attentional biases. In particular, we were interested in the dynamics of desire and avoidance towards the temptation in an attempt to determine whether indulgence is caused by strengthened desire or weakened avoidance. We changed the design of the dot probe task such that the dot probe would appear more frequently (90% of the trails) either at the location of the dessert picture or the fruit picture, thus manipulating attention in one direction. Subsequently, we measured desire-avoidance reactions towards a tempting chocolate snack on a 2-D grid by moving a mouse cursor continuously for 60 seconds. Participants indicated whether they felt little or a lot of desire and avoidance towards the snack right at the moment on two orthogonal dimensions. Using a new technique from dynamical psychology called Recurrence Analysis, we examined the trajectories followed by the time series for desires and avoidance, specifically looking for the extent to which the trajectories visited the same region in state space over time. Results confirmed that impulsive individuals who were manipulated to attend to desserts showed higher recurrence of desires and remained longer in a state of desire but not non-impulsive individuals, suggesting only impulsive individuals kept revisiting the same hedonic goal and were trapped in that goal state for a longer period of time. This phenomenon of trapped states is described in dynamical system theory as a "fixed point attractor" wherein individuals keep returning to a given state or goal despite occasional fluctuation (Carver 2005, Vallacher and Nowak 1999).

In experiment 2, we further explore how training attention engagement towards either towards temptation or healthy options can impact subsequent behavior when reward-seeking systems are activated at different time points. We followed the same procedure as in experiment 1 except that participants were additionally asked to sample a small piece of chocolate before or after the dot probe task. Sampling even a small bite of chocolate can cause activation of the reward-seeking system (Wadhwa et al. 2008). Results showed that impulsive individuals experienced higher recurrence of desire towards temptation when manipulated to attend to desserts if sampling before. More interestingly, impulsives experienced even higher recurrence of desire when they attended to healthy options first and then sampled a temptation. This data pattern suggests that reactance against goals inconsistent with their chronic goals may arise as a consequence of forced attention engagement on healthy options among impulsive individuals, hence training to focus on virtue can be a bad strategy to reinforce healthy behavior.

In summary, our research demonstrates that indulgent behavior exhibited by impulsive individuals is an immediate consequence of an engagement bias towards temptation that results in greater desires rather than weaker self-control. However, strengthened desire is not only limited to an elevated level of desire, but also extends to a more frequent recurrence of desire state and a longer trap time in that state. Forcing attention away from the temptation may backfire, resulting in higher recurrence of desire and consequently greater indulgence in impulsive individuals.

Self-Inferred Norms Reduce Desire and Consumption through Changing Product Perceptions

EXTENDED ABSTRACT

Self-control has traditionally been seen as the struggle between desire and will-power (Hoch and Loewenstein 1991). While both components are important for explaining self-control, prior research aimed at improving self-control has predominantly focused on the willpower component, while taking the desire component as a given. Still, changing consumers' preferences and their resulting desires may prove more successful for improving consumers' self-control in the long run. Preferences are more stable than the ability to exert willpower. Imagine that you truly prefer apples over ice cream. You will take an apple not only now, but you will probably also choose apples over ice cream next time around. In contrast, if you follow your friends' explicit recommendation and deliberately choose an apple against your own taste preference, you will probably not choose apples again on future occasions. Hence, changing preferences is a

potentially more reliable tool to help consumers to deal with temptations. The current paper examines non-consummatory pre-exposure to temptation as a technique to sustainably change preference.

The potential benefits of exposure to a temptation have been subject to debate. On the one hand, pre-exposure to temptation effectively reduces desire when the control conflicts during pre-exposure and post-exposure are similar (Dewitte et al. 2009; Geyskens et al. 2008). On the other hand, physical presence often increases craving for and consumption of the tempting product (Mischel et al. 1972; Wansink 1996). We propose that the nature of normative control, which can be explicit or tacit, will moderate the effect of pre-exposure on temptation on subsequent self-control ability. Explicit consumption norms, such as those communicated by parents or marketing actions, may discourage the succumbing to temptation in the short run, as long as the norm is still activated. But their effects may wane when the accessibility of the norm fades. Tacit norms, inferred from the prevalent circumstances (e.g. known rules of conduct during a formal reception) might prevent succumbing also in the longer run. Self-inferred norms urge people to actively cope with the behavioral conflict induced by the temptation. People do not need such coping strategies when explicit norms are present, which allow reliance on social force. We claim that ignoring the tempting nature of the temptation is one important way to reduce desire for a vice product and hence to deal effectively with temptation. We tested three implications of this claim. First we test whether, compared to an explicit norm, a tacit norm more effectively reduces the relative attractiveness of the vice product. Second, using multidimensional scaling, we test whether activation of tacit norms diminishes the importance of the most tempting dimension of a temptation in a perceptual map. Third, we tested whether activation of the tacit norm has more residual impact on consumption after a delay than the activation of the explicit norm. Our data are the first to show that self-inferred norms effectively change product perceptions, and through it, reduce desire and consumption of the temptation.

In two experiments, we exposed participants to a temptation in two successive phases. We manipulated the norm (explicit or tacit) during pre-exposure in the first phase, and the delay (present or absent) between two phases. We also added a control condition without pre-exposure to temptation. In the pre-exposure phase, participants engaged in a knowledge task. In the experimental condition, they matched candy flavors with wrapper colors. The context of the task strongly suggested that they should not consume. They were either told to not eat candies (explicit norm) or were told nothing (tacit norm). In the control condition, participants engaged in a similar knowledge task not involving candy (Geyskens et al. 2008). The second phase started either immediately or after a 15 minute delay. Participants were asked to taste and evaluate a different vice product. In Study 1 we measured the amount of candy consumed during the second phase (as a measure of self-control) and the change of preference ranking for the candy used in the second phase. In Study 2, we measured perceptions of drinks varying in sweetness and freshness and measured the importance of the sweetness dimension in the participants' revealed perceptual map.

In Study 1, we replicated the effect of pre-exposure to temptation (Geyskens et al 2008). Participants consumed less in the four experimental conditions than in the control condition ($F (1, 97) = 16.39$, $p < .01$). Planned contrasts showed that delay increased consumption in the explicit norm condition ($F (1, 71) = 4.84$, $p < .05$) but not in the tacit norm condition ($F < 1$). Also the findings for preference rankings were in line with predictions. The type of norm affected preferences ($F (2, 97) = 6.35$, $p < .05$): Compared to the control condition ($M = 1.52$) and to the explicit norm condition ($M =$

1.00), the preference for the tempting product was lower in the tacit norm condition (M = 0.11). The former two did not differ (F (1, 97) <1). In Study 2, we found that the sweetness dimension, representing the tempting nature of the temptation in phase 1, was properly reflected in the multidimensional map of a set of 6 drinks varying on sweetness and freshness. Individual difference scaling (INDSCAL) analysis revealed that the sweetness dimension weights were significantly lower with the tacit norm (M = .98) compared to the explicit norm (M = 1.07, F (1, 57) = 4.48, p < .05) and to the control condition (M = 1.13, F (1, 57) = 7.37, p < .01), while the latter two did not differ (F<1). With a tacit norm, sweetness effectively becomes a less salient dimension in the product perceptions after exposure to a sweet temptation, whereas this is not the case with the explicit norm.

Two studies show that explicit norms enhance self-regulation in the short run, but tacit norms reduce preferences for the temptation and enhance self-regulation in the long run. The most interesting finding was that people who experience a tacit norm alter their perception of the most tempting dimension of a vice product, by diminishing its importance. From a social marketing perspective, nudging consumers to infer their own norms may be more effective for longer-lasting self-control enhancement than directly imposing the norm.

REFERENCES

Baumeister, Roy F, Kathleen D. Vohs and Diane M. Tice (2007), "The Strength Model of Self-Control," *Current Directions in Psychological Science, 16*, 351–355.

Busemeyer, Jerome R., and Townsend, J.T. (1993) "Decision field theory: A dynamic-cognitive approach to decision making in an uncertain environment". *Psychological Review, 100*, 432-459.

Dewitte, Siegfried, Sabrina Bruyneel, and Kelly Geyskens (2009), "Self-Regulation Enhances Self-Regulation in Subsequent Consumer Decisions Involving Similar Response Conflicts," *Journal of Consumer Research*, 36 (3), 394 – 405.

Carver, Charles S. (2005), "Impulse and Constraint: Perspectives from Personality Psychology, Convergence with Theory in Other Areas, and Potential for Integration. *Personality and Social Psychology Review, 9(4)*, 312-333.

Geyskens, Kelly, Siegfried Dewitte, Mario Pandelaere, and Luk Warlop (2008), "Tempt Me Just a Little Bit More: The Effect of Prior Food Temptation Actionability on Goal Activation and Consumption," *Journal of Consumer Research*, 35 (4), 600-610.

Hoch, Stephen J. and George F. Loewenstein (1991), "Time Inconsistent Preferences and Consumer Self-Control," *Journal of Consumer Research*, 17 (4), 492-507.

Hofmann, Wilhelm., Malte Friese and Fritz Strack (2009). Impulse and Self-Control from a Dual-Systems Perspective," *Perspectives on Psychological Science, 4(2)*, 162-176.

Kavanagh, David J., Jackie Andrade and Jon May (2005), "Imaginary Relish and Exquisite Torture: The Elaborated Intrusion Theory of Desire," *Psychological Review, 112(2)*, 446-467.

Krajbich, Ian, Carrie Armel and Antonio Rangel (2010), "Visual Fxations and the Computation and Comparison of Value in Simple Choice," *Nature Neuroscience, 13*, 1292-1297.

Metcalfe, Janet and Walter Mischel (1999), "A Hot/Cool-System Analysis of Delay of Gratification: Dynamics of Willpower," *Psychological Review, 106(1)*, 3-19.

Mischel, Walter, Ebbe B. Ebbesen, and Antonette R. Zeiss (1972), "Cognitive and Attentional Mechanisms in Delay of Gratification," *Journal of Personality and Social Psychology*, 21 (2), 204 – 218.

Schoenmakers, Tim, Reinout W. Wiers, Barry T. Jones, Gillian Bruce, and Anita T.M. Jansen (2007), "Attentional Re-training Decreases Attentional Bias in Heavy Drinkers Without Generalization," *Addiction, 102(3)*, 399-405.

Shiv, Baba and Alexander Fedorikhin (1999), "Heart and Mind in Conflict: The Interplay of Affect and Cognition in Consumer Decision Making," Journal of Consumer Research, 26(3), 278-292.

Strack, Fritz and Roland Deutsch (2004), "Reflective and Impulsive Determinants of Social Behavior," *Personality and Social Psychology Review, 8(3)*, 220-247.

Vallacher, Robin R. and Andrzej Nowak (1999), "The Dynamics of Self-Regulation" In R. S. Wyer, Jr. (Ed.), Perspectives on Behavioral Self-Regulation: Advances in Social Cognition, Vol. 12 (pp. 241-259). Mahwah, NJ: Lawrence Erlbaum Associates.

Wadhwa, Monica, Baba Shiv and Stephen M. Nowlis (2008), "A Bite to Whet the Reward Appetite: The Influence of Sampling on Reward-Seeking Behaviors," *Journal of Marketing Research, 45(4)*, 403-413.

Wansink, Brian (1996), "Can Package Size Accelerate Usage Volume?" *Journal of Marketing*, 60 (3), 1 – 14.

Contextual Cues and Consumption

Chair: Jordan Etkin, University of Maryland, USA

Paper #1: Mixed Signals: The Impact of Partitioning on Consumption

Jordan Etkin, University of Maryland, USA
Rebecca K. Ratner, University of Maryland, USA

Paper #2: Unrelated Variety: When Greater Dissimilarity Can Increase Satiation

Jannine Lasaleta, University of Minnesota, USA
Joseph Redden, University of Minnesota, USA

Paper #3: Partitioned Grocery Carts: How Assortment Allocation Cues Can Increase Fruit and Vegetable Purchases

Brian Wansink, Cornell University, USA
Dilip Soman, University of Toronto, Canada
Kenneth Herbst, Wake Forest University, USA
Collin Payne, New Mexico State University, USA

Paper #4: The Effect of Goal Specificity on Continued Consumer Goal Pursuit

Stephen Nowlis, Washington University in St. Louis, USA
Maura Scott, University of Kentucky, USA

SESSION OVERVIEW

Contextual cues exert a powerful influence on consumer behavior. These types of cues may be physical, such as the way a grocery aisle is organized or the way that items are grouped. They may also be psychological, such as the way information is presented or framed. Of particular interest to marketers and consumer behavior researches alike is the influence of contextual cues on consumption. Contextual cues may increase consumption, such as when they increase perceptions of variety in the set or decrease satiation, but they may also decrease consumption, by serving as stopping rules or enhancing motivation to pursue goals of self-restraint. In addition to influencing the amount consumed, contextual cues may also change what is consumed. Consumption choices tend to be sensitive to the way that items are grouped, a phenomenon known as partition dependence; consequently, changing the way that items are grouped may alter the composition of consumers' consumption choices. In this session, we explore the impact of contextual cues on consumption across a variety of situations. Our findings bring to light new ways that contextual cues may be strategically used to influence consumption.

The first paper (Etkin and Ratner) focuses on the role of partitioning (i.e., breaking a single large quantity into multiple smaller quantities) in influencing consumption; in particular, they show that the exact same partitions can both increase and decrease consumption, depending on actual and perceived variety among items and on the magnitude of transaction costs associated with partitions. The second paper (Lasaleta and Redden) explores the role of framing on satiation. Contrary to what has been shown in previous work, these authors find that framing items as more similar can actually increase perceptions of variety, increasing consumption by reducing satiation. In the third paper, Wansink, Soman, Herbst, and Payne test the impact of contextual cues on real consumption behavior in a field study. These authors examine the impact of partitioning a grocery cart including one section specifically for fruits and vegetables on actual purchases of fruits and vegetables. Their findings show that simple contextual cues such as these partitioned grocery carts can have a real impact on consumption by altering the content of consumers' shopping carts. Lastly, Nowlis and Scott explore how the framing of numerical goals impacts consumption. When pursuing a goal to restrain consumption, these au-

thors show that range goals (e.g., consume 20-30% of the M&Ms) decrease consumption relative to number goals (e.g., consume 30 M&Ms). Further, participants with range goals reported feeling better about themselves and being more motivated to pursue their relevant goals relative to participants with number goals.

We expect that this session will be of interest to a wide audience: specifically, researchers interested in contextual cues, consumption, self-restraint, and motivation. These four papers all feature research that makes novel theoretical contributions to existing work on the impact of contextual cues on consumer behavior and are of substantive relevance for decreasing overconsumption and improving consumer health and welfare. Several studies have been conducted for each of the papers described below and several are available as working papers.

Mixed Signals: The Impact of Partitioning on Consumption

EXTENDED ABSTRACT

Previous research has made opposing predictions about how partitioning (i.e., breaking a single large quantity into multiple smaller quantities) will affect consumption. On one hand, some work has shown that partitions increase consumption (Kahn and Wansink 2004), suggesting that people might consume more from several smaller bowls of candy than from a single large bowl of candy. On the other hand, other work has shown that partitions decrease consumption (Cheema and Soman 2008; Rolls et al. 2004; Wansink 2004; Wansink, Geier, and Rozin 2011), suggesting that people might consume less from several small bowls of candy than they would from a single large bowl. What might explain these divergent findings?

We propose that partitions serve multiple roles in influencing consumption: they act both as decision points to continued consumption and as signals of variety. Partitions serve as decision points by defining the appropriate amount to consume and by drawing attention and inducing costs to keep consuming (Cheema and Soman 2008; Coelho Do Vale et al. 2008; Geier et al. 2006; Wansink et al. 2004). In their role as decision points, partitions exert a negative effect on consumption. However, partitions can also serve as signals of variety by highlighting the variety in a set of items (Kahn and Wansink 2004; Mogilner et al. 2008). In their role as signals of variety, partitions exert a positive effect on consumption (if the partitions indicate more variety than was perceived in the absence of partitions).

In the present research we identify two factors that determine how partitioning will influence consumption: the degree of variety within the set (i.e., whether items are identical or varied) and the magnitude of transaction costs coupled with the partitions. When dividing a large set of varied items, partitions can act both as decision points and as signals of variety. However, because there is no actual variety among a set of identical items, partitions primarily serve the role of decision points when separating identical items. Thus, we expect partitioning to have a more positive impact on (i.e., increasing) consumption when items are varied versus identical. Further, we expect the magnitude of transaction costs to go between partitions to exert a negative effect on consumption. Because this negative effect should be partially offset in the varied condition due to the positive influence on consumption of partitions as signals of variety, we predict the magnitude of transaction costs to go between partitions will have a less negative impact on consumption of varied versus identical items.

Across three studies we find consistent support for our predictions. Study 1 provides a demonstration of how the effects of partitioning differ depending on the degree of variety in a set of items (identical vs. varied jellybeans) and the magnitude of transaction costs to go between partitions on consumption of a real snack. We gave participants in this study a snack of 60 jellybeans and varied whether those jellybeans were all the same flavor (identical condition) or 12 different flavors (varied condition), whether the jellybeans were partitioned (into 12 groupings) or unpartitioned, and whether partitions were primarily psychological (i.e., divided into different, adjacent small jars) or coupled with transaction costs to go between partitions (i.e., each jar was individually wrapped in saran wrap, requiring participants to unwrap each one separately). As we expected, dividing the candies with mere partitions had a more positive effect on consumption when items were varied ($F(1, 243) = 6.31, p < .05$) than identical ($F(1, 243) = 2.18, p > .1$), and the presence of a more substantial transaction cost to go between partitions (i.e., saran wrap) had a more negative effect on consumption when items were identical ($F(1, 243) = 3.89, p < .05$) than varied ($F < 1$).

In study 2 we sought to replicate the differential effects of partitioning on the consumption of varied versus identical items while holding the items themselves constant. We gave participants a "virtual" snack of 60 plain M&Ms that were either partitioned (i.e., depicted on a computer screen and separated by grid lines) or unpartitioned (i.e., no grid lines). To manipulate perceptions of variety, in the identical condition we reminded participants that M&Ms are all chocolate, whereas in the varied condition we reminded participants that though M&Ms are all chocolate, they come in many different colors. Consistent with the results of study 1, partitioning had a more negative effect on consumption when participants were instructed to think of the M&Ms as identical ($F(1, 204) = 10.64, p < .01$) than varied ($F < 1$).

Finally, in study 3 we explored the role of magnitude of transaction costs to go between partitions in influencing consumption. Participants were given a virtual snack of either varied or identical jellybeans, which were either partitioned or unpartitioned. Unlike in the previous two studies, here all partitions were coupled with transaction costs to go between partitions. In particular, we covered the partitions with virtual "lids", similar to the saran wrap used in study 1, and we required participants to remove these virtual lids before they could select the jellybeans within the partitions. We manipulated the magnitude of the transaction cost by varying the time it took participants to remove the virtual lids. In the small cost condition, the lids took one second to be removed; in the large cost condition, the lids took three seconds to be removed. As we expected, the magnitude of the transaction cost to go between partitions had a more negative effect on consumption of identical versus varied items. Specifically, consumption linearly decreased as the magnitude of the transaction cost increased when the jellybeans were identical ($F(1, 169) = 13.90, p < .01$), but no such trend was apparent when the jellybeans were varied ($F < 1$).

Previous research makes conflicting predictions regarding the impact of partitioning on consumption. In the present work, we offer a way to reconcile some of these opposing findings by identifying the degree of variety in a set of items and magnitude of transaction cost as two factors that determine the direction of influence of partitions. Our framework contributes to the literature on partitioning by offering a more comprehensive view of partitions as occupying multiple roles in influencing consumption behavior.

Unrelated Variety: When Greater Dissimilarity Can Increase Satiation

EXTENDED ABSTRACT

People satiate with repeated consumption, creating a "hedonic treadmill" whereby they no longer enjoy their favorites and must find new sources of enjoyment. One way to slow down satiation is greater variety. For example, Rolls et al. (1984) found that participants ate 40% more yogurt when the flavor was varied, presumably because they satiated less.

Accordingly, the prevailing belief is that greater variety slows satiation. Variety here depends on the extent to which items in the assortment share attributes (Hoch, Bradlow and Wansink 1999; Kahn and Wansink 2004; Tversky 1977). That is, variety increases as stimuli are less similar to each other, and greater dissimilarity reduces satiation. We challenge this view by showing that consumers satiate faster if two stimuli are so dissimilar that they are placed into different categories.

Categorization research shows that satiation depends on how people categorize the episodes. For instance, consumers satiated slower on jellybeans when they were subcategorized by flavor versus a single general category (Redden 2008). Subcategorization focuses people on the variety among the items they are consuming. However, we propose that when the items seem too dissimilar, people no longer consider them to be a source of variety for each other. Thus, increasing dissimilarity can reduce perceptions of variety and accelerate satiation.

Imagine dinner at a restaurant where one is bombarded by a myriad of sounds, aromas, conversations, and décor. Even so, satiation with the large chicken entrée still seems to creep in. It seems that, although immersed in variety, people consider only particular stimuli (i.e., the meal itself) as a potential source of variety. People seem to place stimuli into different subcategories, with satiation being affected only by "relevant" stimuli in the same subcategory.

Given this role of categorization, we propose a non-monotonic relationship between similarity and satiation. When similarity is high, we predict increases in similarity will increase satiation. This follows from past work on variety and satiation (e.g., Rolls et al. 1984). However, when similarity is low, we predict increasing similarity will decrease satiation because it encourages people to appreciate the full variety in the overall experience. Three studies confirm these predictions.

Study 1 asked participants (n=84) to rate their enjoyment while eating seven chocolate candies. Participants were told they would be periodically asked to also eat small crackers. In the related condition, participants were told that the crackers were another snack food; in the unrelated condition, they were told the crackers were fillers between candy ratings. Participants satiated faster in the unrelated condition than the related condition. Framing the filler crackers as another snack food (i.e., more similar) actually decreased satiation.

Study 2 replicated these results for participants (n=150) listening to a classical music piece twelve times. Here, participants were told that between clips they would hear nature sounds. Participants in the related condition were told, "from time to time, you will also hear some nature sounds that are much like music. Research has found that nature sounds follow patterns and rhythms often found in classical music." Those in the unrelated condition were told, "from time to time, you will also hear some nature sounds to fill time in between the music." Results show ratings of enjoyment declined slower in the related condition than the unrelated condition. Process evidence indicates that perceptions of variety mediate this effect – the variety offered by nature sounds helped reduce satiation more when participants thought of them as similar and related to the classical music.

Study 3 further tests our theoretical framework by demonstrating the U-shape relationship between similarity and satiation. Participants (n=304) rated a classical music piece twelve times, with an intervening sound clip after every third play. The study followed a 2 (intervening sound clip: pop song, nature sounds) x 2 (similarity: alike, dislike) design. The pop song (U2's "With or Without You") was chosen to be mildly similar to the classical music; the nature sounds to be highly dissimilar. After hearing both clips one time, similarity was manipulated by asking participants to write how the two clips were alike (alike condition), or dislike each other (dislike condition). Results indicate an interaction between the intervening sound clip and similarity. With unrelated nature sounds, participants satiated less when focused on how these were like the classical music. Participants apparently did not view the nature sounds as a form of variety unless explicitly encouraged to consider how they are related. In contrast, for the somewhat similar pop song, participants satiated more when asked to focus on how it was like the classical music. Participants presumably already saw the pop song as offering variety in the music so pointing out the similarities increased their satiation.

In conclusion, the prevailing notion in the literature is that variety reduces satiation, and variety largely depends on the similarity of the stimuli. We propose instead that perceived variety depends on how stimuli are categorized. When seen as largely unrelated (e.g., classic music and nature sounds), increasing perceived similarity helps consumers appreciate both of these stimuli as offering variety. This may explain why people often fail to appreciate the variety around them (Galak, Redden, and Kruger 2009). It also suggests a reason why time often is not enough to recover from satiation – people see the variety of intervening experiences as unrelated to what is currently being consumed.

Partitioned Grocery Carts: How Assortment Allocation Cues Can Increase Fruit and Vegetable Purchases

EXTENDED ABSTRACT

Given increasing concerns over the growing obesity problem in the United States, large efforts have been initiated to encourage the purchase of healthier foods (Kessler 2009; Nestle 2002). Unfortunately, many attempts to encourage healthier shopping behavior – such as in-store education programs and soft drink taxes – have often been unsuccessful because they were ignored by consumers or ran counter to the incentives of supermarkets (Brownell and Frieden 2009). After these unsuccessful attempts, the question needs to be reframed: How can distracted shoppers be prompted to develop healthier shopping habits that can be profitable to grocery stores?

Two research questions are addressed: 1) How does partitioning influence purchase and assortment allocations when grocery shopping? 2) What shoppers are most influenced by partitioning? Because the use of partitioned carts could provide an inexpensive intervention which would not restrict or penalize choice, the answer to these questions would be of interest to a wide range of stakeholders:

• **Supermarkets**. Using modified shopping carts could shift the distribution of sales to higher-margin foods (such as perishable produce), and it may do so without decreasing total food sales.

• **Consumers**. A simple "half-cart" rule-of-thumb could subtly emphasize the tradeoffs between healthy and less healthy foods while grocery shopping.

• **Public Policy Officials**. Partitioned carts could be championed and more quickly accepted by supermarkets than common policy proposals that focus on nutrition information, taxation, or subsidies.

After providing an overview of decision making under nutritional uncertainty, the notion of social norms and mental accounting categorization is reviewed and related to this overlooked context of grocery shopping and grocery carts. In this context, the potentially moderating influences of the size of a shopper's family, their experience as a grocery shopper, and the extent to which they are distracted are then discussed. Study 1 examines whether shoppers purchased fruit and vegetables in proportion to the size of a cart's partition, and Study 2 examines who is most influenced by partitions.

Together, these results show that partitioning a shopping cart with colored inserts or a simple strip of yellow duct tape caused healthy choices to become salient, and it led customers to spend more money on fruit and vegetables while shopping. In Study 1, shoppers with partitioned carts purchased a combined total of 51% more fruit and vegetables than did those in the control condition ($17.54 vs. $11.61), and in Study 2, shoppers with partitioned carts purchased a combined total of 76% more ($18.81 vs. $11.61). The mere presence of these visual benchmarks increased choice set consideration and promoted purchase without any corresponding decrease of total sales per shopper.

Healthy foods are profitable foods for grocery stores to sell. There are often higher profit margins for these foods, and there are higher spoilage costs for not quickly selling them if they are perishable. Yet, the impact of partitioning is not only relevant to produce or to fruit and vegetables purchases. These were simply the operationalizations in the two studies. A retailer could just as easily use partitioning to suggest another categorization scheme, such as store brands versus national brands, or natural foods versus processed foods. Similarly, consumers could use a similar process with fat versus non-fat foods or low sodium and high sodium foods.

The Effect of Goal Specificity on Continued Consumer Goal Pursuit

EXTENDED ABSTRACT

This research focuses on the effect of goal specificity on the interest in continued goal pursuit. For example, consumers might set a specific goal to lose 2 pounds; or, consumers might set a less specific goal to lose 1 to 3 pounds. Thus, when setting a goal, consumers may consider: should my goal be a single number (i.e., a number goal) or a range (i.e., a range goal)? We examine if one type of goal is superior to the other in terms of increasing motivation to continue pursuing the goal. For example, would a consumer be more likely to stick to a weight loss goal if the goal was a specific number or if the goal could fall within a range of outcomes?

Individuals pursuing relatively more difficult and specific goals (e.g., a number goal) tend to experience greater performance levels, but lower success rates, compared to people pursuing easier and non-quantitative goals (e.g., work at a moderate pace). This phenomenon has been termed the "performance-success dilemma" (Locke and Latham 1990) since it may be easier to succeed with an unspecific goal ("just do your best") yet this can lead to lower overall performance. Prior research shows that as goals increase in specificity, performance variance decreases, when controlling for difficulty (Locke et al. 1989).

Goals can serve as reference points that influence a consumer's willingness to initiate goal pursuit and to continue to pursue the goal over time (Heath, Larrick and Wu 1999). We propose that range goals are different from number goals in important ways that influence the motivation to continue. Range goals contain two reference points (e.g., lose 5 - 15 pounds), whereas a number goal contains only one reference point (e.g., lose 10 pounds). This two reference point structure of the range goal can result in 1) greater success relative to the number goal, even when the performance level is the same and 2) perceptions that the range goal is more challenging than the number goal. We propose that a range goal offers both attainability at the low end of the range and challenge at the high end of the range; whereas a number goal will be perceived to be challenging but less attainable. We propose that consumers with range goals will be more interested in continued goal pursuit over time (vs. consumers with a number goal).

Study 1 was a 2 (goal type: number, range) x 3 (timing: T1, T2, T3) mixed design experiment. Participants were 53 females in a 10-week weight loss program, $M_{AGE} = 47$ and $M_{BMI} = 31.01$ (BMI 30+ is obese). Participants attended weekly group sessions to weigh-in and learn about healthy lifestyle practices. Although actual weight loss was not significantly different between the number goal and range goal conditions, success rates were higher for participants with range goals (vs. number goals), ($F = 8.90$; $p < .005$). People with range goals also enjoyed the process ($F = 11.22$; $p < .005$) and felt good about themselves ($F = 4.81$; $p < .05$) to a greater degree than those with number goals. We measured interest in continued goal pursuit using re-enrollment behavior at the end of the 10-week program. Participants with range goals re-enrolled at a higher rate than those with number goals ($M_R = 79.6\%$ vs. $M_N = 49.9\%$; $F = 4.44$, $p < .05$).

Study 2 was a 2 (goal type: number, range) between subjects experiment, with 110 undergraduates. Participants tried to consume as few M&Ms as possible while there were 100 M&Ms were in front of them for 40 minutes. As in study 1, consumers with range goals experienced a higher success rate than those with number goals ($M = 58.62\%$ vs. $M = 32.69\%$; $F = 7.80$, $p < .01$). Furthermore, people with range goals felt better about themselves ($M = 3.77$ vs. $M = 2.79$; $F = 6.99$, $p < .01$).

To examine the underlying process, Study 3 assigned participants to an anagram task with a low number (solve 2), high number (solve 8), or range (solve 2 – 8) goal. We found that consumers with low number goals found the goal more attainable but less challenging, people with high number goals found the goal more challenging

but less attainable, and people with range goals perceived high levels of both attainability and challenge. People with range goals experienced significantly higher motivation (vs. low number and high number). The low and high number conditions led to lower motivation for different reasons. Although the low number goals led to high success rates, they lacked challenge; although the high number goals were challenging, they led to lower success rates.

In Study 4 consumers participated in a shopping task. Their goal was to save money by purchasing grocery items at the lowest price. Using their grocery list and coupon book, participants attempted to complete their shopping in four minutes. After answering a few practice questions, participants were asked to set a low number, high number, or range goal for the number of points they would earn (by saving money) in the game. As in study 3, the low number goals were more attainable but less challenging, the high number goals were less attainable but more challenging, and the range goals were both attainable and challenging. Consumers with range goals were more motivated relative to those with low or high number goals.

Study 5 examines how to improve motivation among people with a number goal. Consumers tend to think of themselves, and their performance on a task, as better than the average person in their reference group (Alicke et al. 1995). Thus, when consumers are asked to explicitly compare their performance against the performance of abstract reference group members, they tend to be happier with their own performance. Since number goals are challenging, but are less attainable (lower success rates), in Study 5, we manipulate feelings of success (independent of performance). We predict that motivation will increase for a number goal when consumers compare their performance to a peer group. Study 5 was a 2 (range, number) x 2 (control, average student) between subjects experiment. Our findings demonstrated an interaction for motivation; consumers in the number conditions experienced more motivation when they considered their performance relative to the average student; individuals in the range conditions showed no differences, presumably because they already feel good due to attaining a challenging goal.

On Sunshine, Snow, and Sex: Environmental Effects in Consumer Preference

Chairs: Nicholas Reinholtz, Columbia University, USA
Vladas Griskevicius, University of Minnesota, USA

Paper #1: Sunny Days, Risky Ways: Exposure to Sunlight Increases Risk Taking

Nicholas Reinholtz, Columbia University, USA
Leonard Lee, Columbia University, USA
Michel Pham, Columbia University, USA

Paper #2: Warm it Up with Love: The Effect of Physical Coldness on Liking of Romance Movies

Jiewen Hong, HKUST, Hong Kong
Yacheng Sun, University of Colorado, USA

Paper #3: More than Just "Sex Sells": The Economics of Attraction Motives in Complex Social Consumption Contexts

Adam Craig, University of South Carolina, USA
Stacy Wood, North Carolina State University, USA
Jennifer Vendemia, University of South Carolina, USA

Paper #4: The Influence of Environmental Sex Ratio on Financial Earnings

Kristina Durante, University of Texas at San Antonio, USA
Vladas Griskevicius, University of Minnesota, USA
Jeffry Simpson, University of Minnesota, USA
Stephanie Cantu, University of Minnesota, USA

SESSION OVERVIEW

A substantial body of consumer research has demonstrated the power of one's immediate environment on his or her judgments and decisions. Environmental cues have been shown to affect awareness of available choices, shape decision goals, and even alter how consumers process information. However, research on environmental effects has only recently begun to consider elements of the natural environment, such as sunlight and temperature, as sources of influence in decision processes. These variables, although often overlooked, are omnipresent in the lives of consumers and thus it is important to understand what effects they may have.

In this proposed session, we will be looking at cutting-edge research about environmental effects on consumer behavior. The first two papers focus on environmental factors related to weather, examining how light and temperature influence financial decisions and consumer preferences. The final two papers focus on social factors in the environment, examining how the ratio of men to women in the environment influences consumer behavior. Three of the papers combine both experimental studies and archival data, while the fourth paper uses experimental fMRI techniques to provide deeper insights into environmental effects.

In the first paper, **Reinholtz, Lee, and Pham** examine whether exposure to sunlight will increase an individual's tendency to take risks. The authors conduct a laboratory study in which they manipulate a participant's direct exposure to sunlight. Participants in the sunlight condition show an increased preference for risk. Further, the authors find evidence for their hypothesis in real world behavior, looking at both individuals parking cars illegally and baseball players stealing bases.

In the next paper, **Hong and Sun** examine another weather related environmental effect: the influence of physical temperature on a consumer's movie selection. The authors find that cold temperatures lead consumers to show a greater preference for romance movies. The authors further show that this result is driven by an association of romance movies with psychological warmth. Finally, the authors

show evidence of this effect in the real world, using data from an online movie rental business and local weather data.

The third paper moves away from cold, but continues with the theme of romance. **Craig, Wood, and Vendimia** look at how sex ratios in the immediate environment affect an individual's desire to signal status. The authors show that the presence of same-sex individuals (and thus a competitive environmental sex ratio) increase preference for status signaling compared to situations in which there are only members of the opposite sex. The authors supplement this work with a neuroimaging study that shows increased activation in a region of the brain associated with reward.

In the final paper, **Durante, Griskevicius, Simpson, and Cantu** examine the effect of environmental sex ratio (the ratio of men to women in a given location) on career choices and financial goals. The authors show that metropolitan areas with a scarcity of marriageable men tend to produce women who are more oriented towards financial success. Further, the authors show that experimentally manipulating information on local sex ratio can influence both men's and women's desires to invest in career rather than starting a family.

The papers in this session show how various aspects of the environment influence consumer's behavior in surprising ways. The papers build connections by not only examining diverse aspects of the environment, but also by using a diverse set of methodologies inside and outside the laboratory, including fMRI. This session should appeal to a wide range of audiences, including those interested in embodied cognition, conspicuous consumption, risk, neuroimaging, and evolutionary approaches.

Sunny Days, Risky Ways: Exposure to Sunlight Increases Risk Taking

EXTENDED ABSTRACT

The sun influences human life in many obvious ways. In this paper, we investigate a less obvious way in which the sun may impact human experience. Specifically, we look at the link between sunlight exposure and risk taking. Some evidence hints that exposure to sunlight may increase an individual's tendency to take risks. For example, stocks are more likely to experience positive returns on days in which there is no cloud cover over the market's host city (Saunders 1993; Hirshleifer and Shumway 2003). We extend this research by looking at other operationalizations of risk taking behavior. We use both lab and field studies to support the hypothesis that exposure to sunlight increases an individual's tendency to take risks.

In our first study, we employ a sunlight manipulation in the laboratory. We conducted the study on a sunny day and when participants entered the lab, we either had the curtains drawn (so there was no sun exposure) or the curtains up (so the sun could shine into the lab). After completing a filler task to allow for acclimation to the room conditions, participants completed the Balloon Analogue Risk Task (Lejuez et al. 2002). The BART is a standard measure of risk taking in which participants inflate a virtual balloon to the greatest level possible before it explodes. The more the participants inflate the balloon, the more they are paid for the task. However, participants earn no money if the balloon explodes (probability of explosion is an increasing function of the total number of pumps). Using the BART, we found that participants inflated the balloons to a greater level in the sunlight condition (with the shades up). In other

Advances in Consumer Research
Volume 39, ©2011

words, we found that sunlight exposure increased the participant's preference for risk. We also found that prior exposure to sunlight (how long participants had been in the sun that day) was also positively correlated with risk-seeking.

In our second study, we collected data at a parking lot in Singapore. Twice-a-day for two weeks, we recorded information on every car parked in the lot. Crucially, because of Singapore's parking payment system, we were able to record the time at which the driver parked the car, whether the car's legal parking period had expired, and the extent to which the car was or was not in violation. We supplemented this primary data with climate measurements from a local weather station. Using logistic regression, we found that the level of solar radiation (sunlight) at the time of parking was a positive predictor of whether the car was in violation. In other words, the sunnier it was outside when an individual parked, the more likely they were to leave their car in violation. Further, we found that higher levels of sunlight at the time of parking were correlated with more severe parking violations.

In our third study, we analyzed 40 years of historical data from Major League Baseball games. In this data, we look at attempted stolen bases as the primary measure of risk taking. We find that stolen base attempts were more likely during day games than during night games. Importantly, we find this effect attenuates for games played in indoor stadiums. Further, we find that baserunners tend to be more successful at stealing bases during night games, suggesting that the increase attempt rate for day games is not motivated by a greater likelihood of success. As a final test of our hypothesis, we merged 15 years of weather data with the baseball data set. For games played in outdoor stadiums, we find that higher levels of solar radiation are positively correlated with more stolen base attempts. Interestingly we also find a positive effect of day-time solar-radiation levels on risk taking in night games. One possible explanation for this finding is that cumulative exposure to sunlight, and not just current exposure, can lead to increased risk taking. This would be consistent with our findings in Studies 1 and 2.

In sum, across three different operationalizations, we find that exposure to sunlight is linked to increased levels of risk seeking. We find positive effects on risk taking for both current level of sun exposure and cumulative level of sun exposure. Possible mechanisms for this effect include an "affective" path and a more direct path. Although the affective path is plausible, research is mixed on the link between positive affect and risk taking. The direct path is intriguing because it implicates a more innate biological basis. It is possible that the tendency to take greater risks while the sun is shining evolved as an adaptive behavior. Current work is focusing on identifying evidence in support of one of these paths versus the other.

REFERENCES

Hirshleifer, David A. and Tyler Shumway (2003), "Good Day Sunshine: Stock Returns and the Weather," *Journal of Finance*, *58* (3), 1009–1032.

Lejuez, C. W., Jennifer P. Read, Christopher W. Kahle, Jerry B. Richards, Susan E. Ramsey, Gregory L. Stuart, David R. Strong, and Richard A. Brown (2002), "Evaluation of a Behavioral Measure of Risk Taking: The Balloon Analogue Risk Task (BART)," *Journal of Experimental Psychology: Applied*, *8* (2), 75–84.

Saunders, Edward M. Jr. (1993), "Stock Prices and Wall Street Weather," *American Economic Review*, *83*, 1337–1345.

Warm It Up With Love: The Effect of Physical Coldness on Liking of Romance Movies

EXTENDED ABSTRACT

Are romance movies more desirable when people are cold? Building on research on embodied cognition (Barsalou 2008; Niedenthal et al. 2005), we hypothesize that physical coldness (vs. warmth) activates a desire for psychological warmth, which in turn leads to increased liking for romance movies. We tested our hypothesis in three laboratory experiments and one analysis of online movie rentals.

Study 1 tests our basic hypothesis that physical coldness leads to increased liking for romance movies. We manipulated physical coldness by giving participants a warm or a cold drink. Participants were first told that they would be taking part in a drink evaluation study. Those in the warm condition were given a cup of hot tea and those in the cold condition were given a cup of iced tea. Participants were told to finish the drink slowly while completing another study on movie preference, which was our main dependent measure. For the movie preference task, we selected four genres (romance, action, comedy, and thriller) and three movies from each genre based on the categorization used by the Internet Movie Database (IMDb. com). Participants were given the information of the movies while drinking the tea. For each movie, participants were first presented with the title, a synopsis, a fictitious viewer rating (ranging from 8.5 to 8.8 out of 10), and the genre of the movie. They were then asked to indicate how much they would like to watch the movie and how good they think the movie would be. The order of the movies presented was randomized. Thus, a 2 (physical temperature: cold vs. warm) × 4 (genre: romance vs. action vs. comedy vs. thriller) × 3 (replicate within genre) mixed design was employed, with physical temperature as a between-subject factor, and genre and replicate as within-subject factors. Consistent with our predictions, we found that physical coldness led to increased liking for romance movies, but not for other genres.

Study 2 was designed to examine the mechanism underlying the effect observed in study 1 that physical coldness increases people's liking of romance movies. We argued that the reason that physical coldness increases liking for romance movies is that physical coldness activates a desire for psychological warmth and romance movies are associated with psychological warmth. To provide evidence for this conjecture, we measured the extent to which people associated romance movies with psychological warmth. Although people in general associate romance movies with psychological warmth, there should be individual differences in terms of the extent of this association. We expected that people's perceived association between romance movies and psychological warmth would moderate the effect. Specifically, for participants who associate romance movies with psychological warmth, physical coldness would lead to increased liking for romance movies; conversely, for those who do not associate romance movies with psychological warmth, the effect of physical coldness on liking of romance movies should be attenuated. The results supported our predictions.

Study 3 was designed to examine people's lay belief about the relationship between physical warmth and psychological warmth. That is, whether they believe psychological warmth can compensate for physical coldness. To examine this issue, we manipulated the salience of people's physical temperature by varying the order of the movie preference task and the measure of physical coldness. Thus, a 2 (physical temperature: cold vs. warm) × 2 (salience of physical temperature: salient vs. nonsalient) × 3 (replicate) mixed design was used. We found that when participants' physical temperature was measured after the movie preference task, as we did in studies 1 and 2, we replicated our earlier findings that physical coldness increases liking of romance movies; however, when participants' physical temperature was made salient by measuring it before the movie preference task, there was no effect of physical coldness on their preference for romance movies. These results seem to suggest that, at an explicit level, participants did not believe that psychological warmth can (or should) compensate for physical coldness and thus corrected for this influence.

Finally, in study 4, to demonstrate the external validity of the observed effect, we tested our hypothesis using detailed rental records from an online movie rental company in the U.S. The data span a period of nearly three years, from August 2002 to May 2005. In this study, since we could not manipulate physical temperature, we used weather temperature as a proxy for physical coldness (warmth). After controlling for customers' idiosyncratic preference for romantic movies, the availability and quality of the movies in stock, and any seasonal effect that is unrelated to temperature, we still found a significant negative relationship between weather temperature and consumption preference for romance movies; and such relationship was not observed for other major genres (action, comedy, drama, and thriller).

In sum, in three laboratory studies and one study using online movie rental data, we provide support for the hypothesis that physical coldness increases liking of romance movies, but not for other major genres. The current research adds to the growing literature on embodied cognition by showing that physical coldness activates a goal of seeking psychological warmth. Our data also seem to suggest that the association between physical warmth and psychological warmth might operate at a subconscious level and that people do not believe that psychological warmth can (or should) compensate for physical coldness at an explicit level. The current research also adds to past research on seasonality in the movie industry (Eliashberg, Elberse, and Leenders 2006; Radas and Shugan 1998) and offers practical implications for optimizing the release time for romance movies.

REFERENCES

Barsalou, Lawrence W. (2008), "Grounded Cognition," *Annual Review of Psychology, 59* (1), 617–645.

Eliashberg, Jehoshua, Anita Elberse, and Mark Leenders (2006), "The Motion Picture Industry: Critical Issues in Practice, Current Research, and New Research Directions," *Marketing Science, 25* (6), 638–661.

Niedenthal, Paula M., Lawrence W. Barsalou, Piotr Winkielman, Silvia Krauth-Gruber, and François Ric (2005), "Embodiment in Attitudes, Social Perception, and Emotion," *Personality and Social Psychology Bulletin, 9* (3), 184–211.

Radas, Sonja & Steven M. Shugan (1998), "Seasonal Marketing and Timing Introductions," *Journal of Marketing Research, 35* (3), 296–315.

More than Just "Sex Sells": The Economics of Attraction Motives in Complex Social Consumption Contexts

EXTENDED ABSTRACT

Marketers often use provocative tactics to capture consumers' interest in brands, products, and messages. Ads often depict an attractive model in a sexually suggestive pose or setting even when the image has little to do with the product message. Recent research demonstrates that incidental exposure to sexual stimuli lead male consumers to choose smaller, more immediate rewards (Van den Bergh, Dewitte, and Warlop 2008) and to spend more of their resources to signal social status or uniqueness (Griskevicius et al. 2007). Many marketers might look at these effects and see them as evidence of the old business adage, "sex sells."

Recent research in consumer behavior has additionally shown that the presence of other people, even those unrelated to the consumer, activate relational goals that influence status signaling behavior (Argo et al. 2005). Here, we examine the role of a particular type of "mere presence" effect: sex ratio, or the ratio of males to females in an environment. While basic reward sensitive perspectives demonstrate that viewing attractive individuals of the opposite sex increases status signaling (Griskevicius et al. 2007) and risk taking (Ariely and Loewenstein 2006; Van den Bergh et al. 2008) through motivation for reward, both advertisements and retail environments contain more complex social groups. Specifically, it is unclear how same-sex presences may impact status and reward seeking behavior.

Derived from biological research, research on sex ratios may accurately predict the effect of a varied social environment (or advertising context) on an individual's status signaling behavior (Baumeister and Vohs 2004). Sex ratio research predicts that as the competition level increases (i.e., number of same-sex individuals relative to opposite-sex individuals increases), behaviors designed to signal status should increase. Thus, we propose a reward perspective that incorporates sex ratio and provides two behavioral studies and one neuroimaging study that support a sex ratio sensitive reward model. Across two behavioral studies that utilize priming paradigms, we demonstrate that competitive sex ratios a) increase status signaling above sex ratios that lack competition and b) depend on the attractiveness of same-sex competition.

In Study 1, we primed sex ratio using a sequence of images that depict attractive opposite and same sex faces. The study had four conditions: a Control condition with no faces and three Sex Ratio conditions that varied the ratio of same-sex individuals from zero (No Competition), to a few (Low Competition), to many (High Competition). Status signaling (operationalized as willingness to pay for status products; Griskevicius et al. 2007) was then measured for a series of status-related items in an ostensibly unrelated task. Findings showed that Low and High Competitive sex ratios result in increased status signaling relative to both No Competition sex ratios and neutral control. Thus, mere exposure to mixed-sex groups led people to be more willing to pay for status products when the sex ratio contained same-sex individuals.

Study 2 extended the findings from the first study. Using a similar paradigm as the first study, Study 2 manipulated the attractiveness of same-sex competition photos, thus varying competition not only through quantitative ratio but qualitative competitiveness. Results conceptually replicate Study 1, showing that mere exposure to competitive sex ratios led people to want to signal status. In addition, we show that the presence of attractive competitors produced to the strongest desire to signal status.

Study 3 utilized a novel functional magnetic resonance imaging (fMRI) paradigm to explore neural changes in response to sex ratios. A sex ratio model suggests that the desirability of the opposite sex increases when competition is present. Thus, we examined the brain's response to sets of images that contain either competition or no competition. Within the Nucleus Accumbens (NAcc), an area of the brain that encodes desirability (Aharon et al. 2001), we observe an increase in neural activation for pictures of attractive opposite sex faces when they have been viewed in the presence of attractive same sex faces. Thus, we find that exposure to competitive sex ratios increase reward value in the nucleus accumbens.

Our contribution is twofold: first, we find that the age old advertising maxim that "sex sells" is not as simple as conventional wisdom holds. Instead, our data suggest that the response to sexual cues is likely a complex strategic response that nonconsciously incorporates environmental conditions. Second, this study is an important step in understanding the effects of heterogeneous social groups on consumer decision making. Just as significant individuals motivate behavior (Fitzsimons and Bargh 2003), so do the psychophysical properties of a group. Overall, our results have useful implications for marketers designing advertisements depicting attractive models or retail spaces which facilitate customer—employee interaction.

REFERENCES

Aharon, Itzhak, Nancy Etcoff, Dan Ariely, Christopher F. Chabris, Ethan O'Connor, and Hans C. Breiter (2001), "Beautiful Faces Have Variable Reward Value: FMRI and Behavioral Evidence," *Neuron*, *32* (3), 537–51.

Ariely, Dan and George Loewenstein (2006), "The Heat of the Moment: The Effect of Sexual Arousal on Sexual Decision Making," *Journal of Behavioral Decision Making*, *19* (2), 87–98.

Argo, Jennifer J., Darren W. Dahl, and Rajesh V. Manchanda (2005), "The Influence of a Mere Social Presence in a Retail Context," *Journal of Consumer Research*, *32* (2), 207–12.

Baumeister, Roy F. and Kathleen D. Vohs (2004), "Sexual Economics: Sex as Female Resource for Social Exchange in Heterosexual Interactions," *Personality & Social Psychology Review (Lawrence Erlbaum Associates)*, *8* (4), 339–63.

Fitzsimons, Gráinne M. and John A. Bargh (2003), "Thinking of You: Nonconscious Pursuit of Interpersonal Goals Associated with Relationship Partners," *Journal of Personality and Social Psychology*, *84* (1), 148–63.

Griskevicius, Vladas, Joshua M. Tybur, Jill M. Sundie, Robert B. Cialdini, Geoffrey F. Miller, and Douglas T. Kenrick (2007), "Blatant Benevolence and Conspicuous Consumption: When Romantic Motives Elicit Strategic Costly Signals," *Journal of Personality and Social Psychology*, *93* (1), 85–102.

Van Den Bergh, Bram, Siegfried Dewitte, and Luk Warlop (2008), "Bikinis Instigate Generalized Impatience in Intertemporal Choice," *Journal of Consumer Research*, *35* (1), 85–97.

The Influence of Environmental Sex Ratio on Financial Earnings

EXTENDED ABSTRACT

The ratio of males to females in the environment is known to be an important factor in determining animal behavior (Guttentag and Secord 1983). Changes in sex ratio influence behavior via the economic logic of evolutionary biology. Because it is more difficult for the plentiful sex to attract mates, the plentiful sex has to work harder for evolutionary success. The most commonly observed pattern in animal behavior is that when the opposite sex becomes scarce, individuals increase intrasexual competition.

Sex ratios also vary in human populations. For example, whereas Las Vegas, Nevada, has 1.16 men per every woman, Birmingham, Alabama, has 0.88 men per every woman (Kruger, 2009). Sex ratios can also vary between nations. Multiple Asian countries have recently become strongly male-biased. In the most striking case, China will soon have a surplus of over 40 million men, producing an adult sex ratio of over 1.2 men for every woman (Hesketh 2009).

Correlational research at the population level has begun to examine how sex ratio relates to various human behaviors. Paralleling findings in animal behavior, a scarcity of the opposite sex in human population is associated with increased competition among the plentiful sex. For example, male aggression and violence increase as populations become more male-biased (Barber 2003). Similarly, female aggression increases as populations become more female-biased (Campbell 1995). The plentiful sex appeals to amplify competition when there is a scarcity of the opposite sex.

Drawing on emerging theory in evolutionary psychology, we hypothesized that sex ratio might have a considerable effect on financial aspirations. For example, a scarcity of marriageable men might motivate women to allocate more time and effort into earning immediate monetary rewards. Although the reasons why women choose to devote a great deal of time and effort toward earning money is likely to be complex, we contend that an often overlooked factor in women's desire for monetary rewards is the ratio of adult men to women in the local population.

Study 1 looked at U.S. population data to examine the link between sex ratio and women choosing high-paying careers. We looked at sex ratio in the top 10 largest metropolitan areas in the U.S. and the percentage of women in the top 10 highest-paying careers. Findings showed that a scarcity of marriageable men was strongly related to more women entering high-paying careers. This finding, based on real-world data, suggests that the availability of mates could have important implications for whether women pursue monetary rewards.

Because earning a high salary may come at the expense of investing time into family, Study 2 tested the prediction that experimental manipulations of perceived sex ratio should influence how women prioritize earning money vs. starting a family. Women viewed photo arrays of men and women that were ostensibly indicative of the local population. The arrays were either male-skewed, female-skewed, or equal sex ratio (control). Participants then indicated their desire to pursue high-paying careers versus starting a family. Consistent with predictions, experimentally manipulated female-biased sex ratios led women to increase their desire for earning a lot of money rather than having a family.

Study 3 sought to conceptually replicate the experimental findings for women using a different sex ratio manipulation and test whether sex ratio influences men's career aspirations. Participants read news articles describing the local population as either male-biased or female-biased. Participants then indicated their desire to pursue high-paying careers versus starting a family. Findings showed that when there was a scarcity of men, women once again prioritized earning money relative to investing in family. Findings also revealed a parallel pattern for men: When women were scarce, men were more interested in pursuing high-paying careers.

Study 3 also examined a key individual difference, which provided insight into which individuals were driving the effects. We examined how sex ratio influenced desire for high-paying careers for people who differed in attractiveness, meaning that they were differentially able to compete for mates. Findings showed that a scarcity of women led men to aspire to high-paying careers when those men were more attractive. Conversely, a scarcity of men led women to aspire to high-paying careers when those women were less attractive. This pattern suggests that women who can secure a mate more easily might be less inclined to pursue a high-paying career. However, increased competition appears to motivate less attractive women to allocate greater effort to careers that offer more financial rewards.

Our findings highlight people's sensitivity to a particular feature of the social environment—the ratio of adult men to women. Just as sex ratio has important effects on animal behavior, we find that it also has theoretically consistent and important effects on humans. We find that a scarcity of the opposite-sex leads both men and women to invest in high-paying careers. For women in particular, this suggests that whether a woman chooses a briefcase or a baby—whether she invests heavily into a career or into family—appears to be related to the local mating ecology and the availability of mates.

REFERENCES

Barber, Nigel (2003), "The Sex Ratio and Female Marital Opportunity as Historical Predictors of Violent Crime in England, Scotland, and the United States," *Cross-Cultural Research, 37,* 373–391.

Campbell, Anne (1995), "A Few Good Men: Evolutionary Psychology and Female Adolescent Aggression," *Ethology and Sociobiology, 16,* 99–123.

Guttentag, Marcia and Paul F. Secord (1983), *Too Many Women? The Sex Ratio Question,* Beverly Hills, CA: Sage.

Kruger, Daniel J. (2009), "Male Scarcity is Differentially Related to Male Marital Likelihood Across the Life Course," *Evolutionary Psychology, 7,* 280–287.

Hesketh, Therese and Wei Xing Zhu (2006), "Abnormal Sex Ratio in Human Populations: Causes and Consequences," *Proceedings of the National Academy of Sciences, 103,* 271–275

Things That Make Us Overeat

Chairs: Klaus Wertenbroch, INSEAD, France
Anne Klesse, University of Maastricht, The Netherlands

Paper #1: Health Claims, Overeating, and Flavor Intensity: Behavioral and FMRI Insights into the Paradox of Low-Fat Food and High-Fat People

Hilke Plassmann, INSEAD, France
Pierre Chandon, INSEAD, France
Monica Wadhwa, INSEAD, Singapore
Nicolas Linder, University of Bonn, Germany
Bernd Weber, University of Bonn, Germany

Paper #2: The Variety Paradox: Variety Sounds Good, But it Ruins Your Diet

Anne Klesse, University of Maastricht, The Netherlands
Caroline Goukens, Maastricht University, The Netherlands
Kelly Geyskens, Maastricht University, The Netherlands
Klaus Wertenbroch, INSEAD, France
Ko de Ruyter, University of Maastricht, The Netherlands

Paper #3: Complementary Food Consumption with Imagined Consumption

Young Eun Huh, Carnegie Mellon University, USA
Joachim Vosgerau, Carnegie Mellon University, USA
Carey Morewedge, Carnegie Mellon University, USA

Paper #4: Effect of Character Weight and Health Knowledge on Children's Eating

Margaret C. Campbell, University of Colorado, USA
Kenneth C. Manning, Colorado State University, USA
Bridget Leonard, University of Colorado at Boulder, USA
Hannah Manning, Rocky Mountain High School, USA

SESSION OVERVIEW

Obesity is on the rise. At last count, 68% of US adults were classified as overweight and 34% as obese, more than twice as many as 30 years ago (Flegal et al. 2010). Since it is unlikely that the genetic make-up of the US population has changed drastically during the last decades, the rapid increase in obesity is rather due to environmental and behavioral changes (Stroebe et al 2008). Accordingly, extant research has frequently investigated influences in the eating and food environment (Wansink 2004) and demonstrated that consumers are sometimes aware of these influences on their consumption and develop strategies to guard against them. For instance, consumers know that package size affects the amount they consume and try to protect themselves from these influences by buying smaller packages (Wansink and Park 2001; Wertenbroch 1998).

This session adds to and advances existing research in this field by presenting four paradoxical effects in the domain of food consumption that consumers might not expect or, even worse, that result from consumers' strategies to protect themselves from self-control inhibitors. The first paper by **Plassmann, Chandon, Wadhwa, Linder, and Weber** uses behavioral and fMRI studies to show that individuals perceive products labeled as "light" to be less intense in taste than products labeled "regular" and, hence, consume more of them to reach the desired flavor satisfaction. This effect is driven by an increase in wanting and helps to explain the paradoxical effect that consumers overeat "healthy" products although they expect to like them less. In the second paper, **Klesse, Goukens, Geyskens, Wertenbroch, and de Ruyter** demonstrate that dieters actively engage in variety-seeking behavior because they believe it helps them

to lose weight not knowing that this strategy often backfires. This research demonstrates that eating a variety of food items compared to eating the same food decreases individuals' monitoring capacity and makes them underestimate how much they have consumed. Moreover, they demonstrate that variety affects subsequent seemingly unrelated decisions by increasing desire for high-calorie food items. In the third paper, **Huh, Vosgerau, and Morewedge** demonstrate that complementary food consumption (foods consumed together like crackers and cheese) occurs even when the consumption of one food is only imagined. This research demonstrates that simply imagining the consumption of one food increases wanting of a complementary food. In the fourth paper, **Campbell, Manning, Leonard, and Manning** consider the effect of overweight cartoon characters on children's consumption. Specifically, they show that overweight cartoon characters make the concept of eating more salient, thus increasing children's consumption of low-nutrient food. This paper is the first to show that perceived weight of others, even fictitious characters, influences children's eating behavior.

Taken together, the papers (all in advanced stages) reveal four unobtrusive factors that foster increased calorie intake. In doing so, this session demonstrates that risks can be inconspicuous, might arise from consumers' strategies to lose weight, and affect consumers of all ages. As this session integrates diverse paradoxical eating phenomena, we believe it contributes to "building connections" by encouraging communication between researchers from different research areas: it is expected to appeal to a broad audience, especially those interested in self-control and factors that influence our consumption behavior outside of awareness.

Health Claims, Overeating, and Flavor Intensity: Behavioral and FMRI Insights into the Paradox of Low-Fat Food and High-Fat People

EXTENDED ABSTRACT

As the popularity of healthier menus increases, so does the weight of many Americans. How can we explain the American food paradox of simultaneous increase in obesity and in the popularity of healthier food choices? One explanation is that people eat more when foods are positioned as healthy, for example when they have a "low-fat" label (Chandon and Wansink 2007). However, other studies (Raghunathan, Naylor, and Hoyer 2006) have shown that people expect healthy food to taste less good. How can we reconcile these two findings and explain why people eat more when they expect the food to taste less good?

Existing research on the psychology of food consumption suggest that this paradox may be explained by calorie compensation. Stated simply, people may eat more when the food is perceived as healthy because they expect that it contains fewer calories and hence that they can eat more of it without gaining weight (Wansink and Chandon 2006). Self-control failures and goal balancing may also explain the paradox to the extent that foods positioned as healthy causes lapses in self control (Scott et al. 2008) and that the availability of healthy foods may actually increase people's motivation to consume indulgent, tasty food (Finkelstein and Fishbach 2010).

This research provides and tests another explanation of the American food paradox. Our hypothesis is that people expect food positioned as healthy to have a less intense flavor, and consume

Advances in Consumer Research
Volume 39, ©2011

more of it to achieve the desired levels of flavor satisfaction and satiation. This mechanism was not identified before because of the well-known difficulty for people to distinguish between the intensity and valence of flavor, especially for commercially successful foods which have mild levels of intensity and pleasant flavors (Bartoshuk et al. 2006). In other words, when people say that they expect healthy food to taste less good, what they actually mean is that they expect its flavor to be less intense. We test these predictions in three studies.

In a first study, 69 participants were asked to add milk to a chocolate or vanilla powder that was either labeled "light" or "regular". We found that people added less milk when the powder was labeled "light" (M = 101 ml, SEM = 2.9) than when it was labeled "regular" (M = 109 ml, SEM = 3.0; F(1,68) = 8.52, p = .006) yet these participants expected that they would have to drink more of the prepared drink to feel full and satiated for three hours when it was labeled "light" (M = 158 ml, SEM = 14.0) as compared to when it labeled regular (M = 129 ml, SEM = 9.3; F(1,68) = 3.19, p = .08). In addition, this effect was stronger among people with a high score on the reward responsiveness personality scale (Carver and White 1994), F(1,68) = 3.77, p = .05, suggesting that the effect is driven by an increased "wanting" for light products.

These findings suggest that participant expected the "light" powder to provide a less intense flavor, which would have to be compensated by higher quantity. These results are inconsistent with a hedonic motivation explanation since people would not drink more of a drink that they expect to taste less good. They cannot also be explained by calorie compensation, which would have led people to compensate for the lower calories of the powder by pouring more, not less, milk. Further, while self control and goal balancing theories predict the presence of healthy food to trigger consumption of indulgent food, an enhanced wanting for light and therefore healthy drink that is expected to taste less good cannot be explained by these theories.

To get a better understanding of the role played by expectations of flavor intensity in driving the results of study 1, we conducted an fMRI study to investigate the effect of nutrition and composition claims on flavor perception and its neuropsychological bases. Unlike in study 1, we compared three different types of claims that were pretested to have different effects on taste expectations: "organic" (seen as a promise of healthy food & better taste), "light" (healthy but low taste), and "regular" (control condition). We found that people expected to enjoy chocolate and vanilla drinks more when they were labeled "organic" (M = 6.1) versus "regular" (M = 5.6) versus "light" (M = 5.2). People also expected the taste to be significantly less intense when the foods were labeled "light" (M = 5.1) versus "regular" (M = 5.9) or "organic' (M = 6.1), although the difference between "regular" and "organic" was not statistically significant.

Analyses of the brain activity while people were consuming identical foods with the three different labels showed more activity in the brain areas that respond to flavor pleasantness (i.e. the orbitofrontal cortex) in the "organic" versus "regular" label condition, but more activity in the brain areas that respond to flavor intensity (i.e. the ventral striatum, amygdala) in the "light" versus "regular" label condition. This results support earlier findings about the unreliability of self-reported measures of flavor intensity, which did not adequately represent brain activity, and demonstrate the value of measuring brain activity to understand the effects of food claims.

Overall, our results suggest that people expect lower flavor intensity of light products, and thus eat more to achieve the same level of reward as with regular food. This may explain the paradoxical phenomenon that people overeat light products even though they expect to like them less. In an ongoing study, we are trying to understand further the process behind the effects of health and nutrition claims manipulating people reward seeking drive ("wanting") and measured subsequent consumption behavior through pharmacological interventions.

The Variety Paradox: Variety Sounds Good but It Ruins Your Diet

EXTENDED ABSTRACT

Americans are obsessed with dieting. They try different diets and spend more than 30 billion dollar fighting fat (Freedman 2010). Many dieting programs offer a variety of diet food, suggesting that eating a variety of food is healthy and helps lose weight. In line with these claims, we find that individuals who are on a diet are more likely to integrate variety in their choice (Study 1) and believe that eating a variety of different food helps them to lose weight (Study 2). Yet research on the variety effect shows that variety increases consumption (Raynor and Epstein 2009; Rolls et al. 1981).

The primary purpose of our research is to explain the discrepancy between individuals' beliefs that variety is good on the one hand and the consequences of these beliefs on the other. Why do individuals think integrating variety into their choice is good for them if in fact it increases consumption? We present two studies that examine consumer beliefs and then conduct an experiment to explain the discrepancy.

Study 1 investigates whether consumers who want to lose weight and those that don't differ in their likelihood to switch away from a food previously eaten and try out something new. Sixty-five students either tasted a small piece of chocolate cake or chocolate waffle. Afterwards, participants went into an adjacent room one by one where an experimenter offered them the choice between a piece of cake or waffle (identical to those in the taste test). We measured variety seeking as switching away from the product eaten during the taste test. Comparing dieters and non-dieters on their likelihood to switch away from the product eaten first, shows that dieters are significantly (p =.02) more likely to integrate variety in their choices than non-dieters.

Study 2 assesses whether dieters believe that integrating variety into their choices helps them lose weight. Fifty-eight female students who wanted to lose weight were asked to carefully watch their food patterns during one week. They subsequently provided feedback about their experience. They responded to the item 'during this week, I integrated more variety in my choice than normal' and rated their dieting behavior during the week on a scale from 1 to 10 (10 = very good). A regression analysis of dieting behavior ratings on variety choice ratings as the predictor variable showed that individuals believe that integrating variety into their consumption choices is beneficial for losing weight (B = .40, p = .027).

Study 3 investigates whether eating a variety of different food items compared to eating only one type of food has an influence on how well individuals know how much they consumed. The study also examines whether the two conditions differ in the amount of calories consumers choose in a subsequent seemingly unrelated decision. Forty-six participants either ate different cookies or the same type of cookie while watching a documentary. Afterwards, participants had to indicate how many cookies they ate. Participants then left the room one by one. In an adjacent room, a researcher told them that they could pick a Santa Claus gift choosing between tangerines, almond biscuits, and chocolate.

First, we checked the accuracy of participants' assessments of how much they had consumed. The results revealed a significant difference (p = .046) between the two conditions: participants in the no-variety condition slightly overestimated how many cookies they ate (M = .25), whereas those in the variety condition underestimated their cookie consumption (M = - 1.0). Although controlling for the absolute number of cookies consumed (quantity) slightly reduces the effect (p = .05), quantity (p = .93) cannot explain the difference in accuracy. Second, we investigated whether the two conditions differed in the amount of calories participants chose in the subsequent decision. Participants in the variety condition chose items higher in calories (159 kcal) than those in the no-variety condition (80 kcal) (p = .06). A regression analysis of number of different cookies eaten on calories chosen reveals a significant positive relationship (p = .01). Participants were more likely to select a Santa Claus gift rich in calories if they integrated more variety in their consumption of cookies.[1]

Our studies show that people who diet seek more variety and believe variety to be beneficial for them in reaching their goal to lose weight. Further, we demonstrate that integrating variety into one's food choices makes individuals underestimate how much they ate. This might provide an explanation for why consumers mistakenly believe variety to be good for them. We believe that the underestimation of how much they ate is due to the way individuals keep track of the items consumed. Specifically, we think individuals who eat two cookies track the amount of cookies consumed as an aggregate quantity while individuals who eat one vanilla cookie and one chocolate cookie might track the amounts separately, failing to add up the partitioned amounts to an aggregate number. In a follow-up experiment, we will test whether this way of 'bookkeeping' is responsible for underestimating the amount of cookies consumed.

Complementary food consumption with imagined consumption

EXTENDED ABSTRACT

A key aspect of micro-economic theories of consumer behavior is the interdependence in consumption, in particular the complementarity relations between products. Complements are goods which are customarily consumed together, for example, bread and jam or cheese and crackers. An increase in the consumption of one item causes an increase in the consumption of its complements (Bucklin, Russell, and Srinivasan 1998). Whereas prior research on product complementarity has focused on the impact of consumption/price of one item on the consumption/price of its complements, the current research examines the effect of imagined consumption of an item on subsequent actual consumption of its complements.

Research on mental imagery suggests that the processes of mental imagery are similar to the processes involved in the perception of actual stimuli. Mental imagery of an experience has been found to engage similar physiological (e.g., Huber and Krist, 2004) and neurological processes (Kosslyn, Ganis, and Thompson 2001), and to similarly affect behavioral responses (e.g., Wohldmann, Healy, and Bourne 2007) as the actual consumption experience. More recently, Morewedge, Huh, and Vosgerau (2010) demonstrated that imagined consumption of a food engenders habituation to the food as does the actual consumption. If imagined consumption can act as a substitute for the sensory experience of consuming a food, imagining consuming a food should, like actual consumption of the food, increase the subsequent consumption of its complements. Across three studies we test this proposition.

Study 1 examined whether imagined consumption of a food (grapes) increases subsequent consumption of foods complemen-

tary to the food imagined (cheese) with a 2 (imagined consumption: grapes vs. cheese) x 2 (amount of imagined consumption: small vs. large) between-subjects design. Half of participants imagined eating either 3 or 30 grapes and the other half imagined eating either 3 or 30 cheddar cheese cubes. After the imagined consumption, all participants were given a bowl containing 40g of cheddar cheese cubes and ate cheese cubes ad libitum. We found that participants who imagined eating 30 grapes ate significantly more cheese cubes than did participants who imagined eating 3 grapes. The opposite was found for, participants who imagined eating cheese cubes. Participants who imagined eating 30 cheese cubes ate significantly less cheese cubes than those who imagined eating 3 cheese cubes (Morewedge et al. 2010). These results provide initial evidence that complementary food consumption occurs even when one of the foods is imagined being consumed.

Study 2 tests whether complementarity is necessary to increase the subsequent food consumption with a 2 (imagined consumption experience: eating crackers vs. eating M&M's) x 2 (amount of imagined consumption: small vs. large) between-subjects design. Before participants actually consumed cheese as in study 1, half of participants imagined eating either 3 or 30 crackers (complementary food) and the half of participants imagined eating either 3 or 30 M&M's (non-complementary food). Participants who imagined eating 30 crackers subsequent consumed more cheese than those who imagined eating 3 crackers. However, there was no difference in cheese intake between those who imagined eating 30 M&M's and those who imagined eating 3 M&M's. The results suggest that imagining eating foods does not increase the subsequent consumption if the imagined food and the consumed food are not complements.

Two psychological processes appear to regulate food intake (Berridge 2007). One process is food liking or palatability (i.e., the pleasure derived from eating a given food), and the other is food wanting or appetite (i.e., motivation to obtain a food). We conducted study 3 to examine which process is responsible for the effect of imagined consumption of complements. Half of participants imagined eating 3 grapes and the other half imagined eating 30 grapes. After the imagined consumption of grapes, all participants indicated how pleasurable it would be to eat the cheese right then (liking) and how much they would be willing to pay for one pound of cheese (wanting). We found that participants who imagined eating 30 grapes indicated significantly higher WTP than did participants who imagined eating 3 grapes. However, liking did not differ significantly between the two conditions. The findings suggest that imagined consumption increases subsequent consumption of its complementary food by increasing wanting, but not liking, of foods complementary to the food imagined. This is consistent with the findings by Morewedge et al. (2010) that imagined food consumption engenders habituation to a food (decrease in wanting) but does not affect liking of the food.

In summary, we found that complementary food consumption occurs even when one of the foods is imagined rather than actually consumed. People who imagined eating a large amount of food (e.g., cracker) subsequently consumed more of its complementary food (e.g., cheese) than those who either imagined eating a small amount of the food or imagined eating non-complementary foods. The present investigation attests to the importance of top-down processes that regulate food consumption.

---

[1] Experiment 3 provides further evidence that dieters integrate more variety in their choice: Comparing dieters and non-dieters (variety condition) shows that dieters eat more different cookies (p =.06).

Effect of Character Weight and
Health Knowledge on Children's Eating

EXTENDED ABSTRACT

Just as overweight and obesity is increasing for adults, so it is for children. Since 1980, while the adult obesity rate has doubled, the childhood obesity rate has tripled with rates now near 17% (CDC). Increasingly, overweight and obese children are being diagnosed with obesity-related diseases that were previously the domain of adults, such as Type 2 diabetes.

While recent research has focused on environmental factors that influence adults' consumption, little research examines such influences on children. Research has shown that perceived weight of others influences how much indulgent food adults eat (McFerran et al 2009, Campbell & Mohr 2011), but there has been no research that examines such effects on children. In fact, while there is a significant body of research on priming effects on adults' behavior, little research examines whether such effects occur for children as well.

The primary purpose of this research is to examine whether the weight of cartoon characters influences children's consumption of low nutrient, high calorie food (e.g., cookies). This is an important topic because while children are regularly exposed to overweight characters in entertainment and marketing, there is little evidence as to how this impacts their behavior.

Research on adults suggests that exposure to someone overweight activates an overweight stereotype that includes the ideas that overweight people over-eat indulgent foods and that they are not committed to taking care of their health. It is the activation of these parts of the stereotype that is believed to lead adults exposed to someone overweight to eat more (Campbell & Mohr 2011). This raises two questions: 1) do children hold an overweight stereotype that includes overeating and low health commitment, and 2) does exposure to an "overweight" character activate an overweight stereotype in children. The limited research on the content of children's overweight stereotypes suggests that there are developmental differences in stereotype specificity; young children merely hold general negative attitudes, with increasing specificity with age (Penny & Haddock 2007). Thus, it is unclear whether children's overweight stereotypes are specific enough to include the link between eating and becoming overweight. If this link does not exist, the body weight of characters is unlikely to influence their consumption. Second, it is unclear whether a cartoon character will serve to activate a human stereotype.

We propose that the link between eating indulgent foods, weight and health are taught to many children at a very young age. Parents and other authority figures frequently tell children to eat or not to eat certain foods and to limit consumption of indulgent foods. Thus, we propose that even young children will have a stereotype that links overweight and eating. Because children consistently see non-human characters in "human" situations, we also propose that overweight characters will activate children's overweight stereotypes and increase food consumption.

Importantly, there is evidence that in adults, increasing the accessibility of health goals or the stereotype-behavior link can reduce the effects of the prime (Campbell & Mohr 2011). Yet, with children, evidence from the development literature indicates that young children may not be able to use knowledge as a cognitive defense because of difficulty in retrieving stored information (Brucks, Armstrong, & Goldberg 1988). We propose that there will be developmental differences in children's ability to make use of their health knowledge to reduce the effects of the stereotype prime on eating.

We present three studies that, together, examine the influence of perceived weight of cartoon characters on the quantity of indulgent food eaten for children in three stages of consumer socialization: the reflective stage (ages 11 – 16), the analytical stage (ages 7 – 11), and the perceptual stage (ages 3 – 7; Roedder John 1999). Additionally, the third study will examine whether young children have the cognitive ability to make use of health knowledge to reduce the effects of the stereotype prime.

Study 1 examines the prime to behavior link for children aged 12 to 13 (n=60), and finds that children take more candies when exposed to an overweight character than when exposed to a normal weight character (M=3.7 vs M=1.5, p = .04). Considering that children's environments are much more complex than simply one prime character, study 2 examines the prime effect on behavior when the prime is a combination of an overweight and a normal weight character for children aged 13 to 14 (n=75). Results show that children take fewer candies when exposed to a normal weight character alone (Mnormal=1.7) than either an overweight character alone (Moverweight=3.2; p < .01) or the overweight and normal weight characters together (Mcombination=3.2; p < .01). Taken together, Studies 1 and 2 demonstrate the robustness of the prime to behavior link for children in the reflective stage of development.

Study 3 will examine the prime to behavior link for children in the analytical stage (age 9 – 10, n=100 – 150), and in the perceptual stage (age 6 – 7, n=100 – 150), and test whether the children have the cognitive ability to make use of health knowledge to reduce the effects of the stereotype prime. Data for this study will be collected in March and April (we have agreement from a school). We hypothesize that both groups of children will show the prime to behavior link, but that only the older group of children will have the cognitive ability to use their health knowledge to reduce the effects of the stereotype prime.

Overall, this set of studies contributes to the literatures on stereotype priming and children's development by examining the prime to behavior links of an overweight prime on children across three stages of development. We find a robust prime effect of an overweight character (alone and with a normal-weight character), and examine the potential of health knowledge activation to reduce these prime effects.

REFERENCES

Bartoshuk, Linda M, Valerie B Duffy, John E Hayes, Howard R Moskowitz, and Derek J Snyder (2006), "Psychophysics of sweet and fat perception in obesity: problems, solutions and new perspectives," *Philosophical Transactions of the Royal Society B: Biological Sciences*, 361 (1471), 1137-48.

Brucks, Merrie, Gary M. Armstrong, and Marvin E. Goldberg (1988), "Children's Use of Cognitive Defenses against Television Advertising: A Cognitive Response Approach," *Journal of Consumer Research*, 14 (March), 471–482.

Bucklin, Randolph E., Gary J. Russell, and V. Srinivasan (1998), "A Relationship between Price Elasticities and Brand Switching Probabilities," *Journal of Marketing Research*, 35, 99-113.

Campbell, Margaret C., and Gina S. Mohr (forthcoming), "Seeing is Eating: How and When Activation of a Negative Stereotype Increases Stereotype-Conducive Behavior," in *Journal of Consumer Research*.

Carver, Charles S. and Teri L. White (1994), "Behavioral Inhibition, Behavioral Activation, and Affective Responses to Impending Reward and Punishment: The BIS/BAS Scales," *Journal of Personality and Social Psychology*, 67 (2), 319-33.

Centers for Disease Control and Prevention, "Obesity, Halting the Epidemic by Making Health Easier: At a Glance 2010"

Chandon, Pierre and Brian Wansink (2007), "The Biasing Health Halos of Fast-Food Restaurant Health Claims: Lower Calorie Estimates and Higher Side-Dish Consumption Intentions," *Journal of Consumer Research*, 34 (3), 301-14.

Finkelstein, Stacey R. and Ayelet Fishbach (2010), "When Healthy Food Makes You Hungry," *Journal of Consumer Research*, 37 (3), 357-67.

Flegal, Katherine M., Margaret D. Carroll, Cynthia L. Ogden, and Lester R. Curtin (2010),"Prevalence and Trends in Obesity Among US Adults, 1999-2008," *Journal of the American Medical Association*, 235-41.

Freedman, Marjorie R., King, Janet, and Eileen T. Kennedy (2001), "Popular Diets: A Scientific Review," *Obesity Research* 9, 1-40.

Huber, Susanne and Horst Krist (2004), "When is the Ball Going to Hit the Ground? Duration Estimates, Eye Movements, and Mental Imagery of Object Motion," *Journal of Experimental Psychology: Human Perception and Performance*, 30 (3), 431-444.

Kosslyn, Stephen M., Giorgio Ganis, and William L. Thomson (2001) "Neural Foundations of Imagery, "*Nature Reviews Neuroscience*, 2, 635-642.

Morewedge, Carey K., Young Eun Huh, and Joachim Vosgerau (2010) "Thought for food: Imagined Consumption Reduces Actual Consumption," *Science*, 330, 1530-1533.

Penny, Helen, and Geoffrey Haddock (2007), "Children's Stereotypes of Overweight Children," *British Journal of Developmental Psychology*, 25, 409-418.

Raghunathan, Rajagopal, Rebecca Walker Naylor, and Wayne D. Hoyer (2006), "The Unhealthy = Tasty Intuition and Its Effects on Taste Inferences, Enjoyment, and Choice of Food Products," *Journal of Marketing*, 70 (4), 170-84.

Raynor, Hollie A. and Leonard H. Epstein (2001), "Dietary Variety, Energy Regulation, and Obesity," *Psychological Bulletin*, 127, 1-17.

Roedder John, Deborah (1999), "Consumer Socialization of Children: A Retrospective Look at Twenty-Five Years of Research," *Journal of Consumer Research*, 26 (December), 183-213.

Rolls, Barbara J; Edward. A. Rowe; Edmund T. Rolls; Breda Kingston, Angela Megson, and Rachel Gunary (1981), "Variety in a Meal Enhances Food Intake in Man," *Physiology & Behavior*, 26, 215-221.

Scott, Maura L., Stephen M. Nowlis, Naomi Mandel, and Andrea C. Morales (2008), "The Effects of Reduced Food Size and Package Size on the Consumption Behavior of Restrained and Unrestrained Eaters," *Journal of Consumer Research*, 35 (3), 309-23.

Stroebe, Wolfgang, Wendy Mensink, Henk Aarts, Henk Schut, and Arie W. Kruglanski (2008), "Why Dieters Fail: Testing the Goal Conflict Model of Eating," *Journal of Experimental Social Psychology*, 44 (1), 26-36.

Wansink, Brian (2004), "Environmental Factors that Increase the Food Intake and Consumption Volume of Unknowing Consumers," *Annual Review of Nutrition*, 24, 455-79.

Wansink, Brian and Pierre Chandon (2006), "Can 'Low-Fat' Nutrition Labels Lead to Obesity?," *Journal of Marketing Research*, 43 (4), 605-17.

Wansink, Brian and SeaBum Park (2001), "At the Movies: How External Cues and Perceived Taste Impact Consumption Volume," *Food Quality and Preference*, 12:1 (January), 69-74.

Wertenbroch, Klaus (1998), "Consumption Self-Control by Rationing Purchase Quantities of Virtue and Vice," *Marketing Science*, 17 (4), 317-337

Wohldmann, Erica, Alice F. Healy and Lyle E. Journe (2007) "Pushing the limits of imagination: Mental practice for learning sequences," *Journal of Experimental Psychology: Learning, Memory, and Cognition*, 33, 254-261.

Price Psychology: Advances On Context Effects In Pricing Research

Chair: Nina Mazar, University of Toronto, Canada

Paper #1: The Effects of Price Primacy on Decision-Making and Perceptions of Product Value

Uma Karmarkar, Stanford University, USA
Baba Shiv, Stanford University, USA
Brian Knutson, Stanford University, USA

Paper #2: Starting Prices and Consumer Response to Customization

Marco Bertini, London Business School, UK
Luc Wathieu, Georgetown University, USA

Paper #3: Stable Context-Dependent Preferences? The Origin of Market Price-Dependent Valuations

Nina Mazar, University of Toronto, Canada
Botond Koszegi, UC Berkeley, USA
Dan Ariely, Duke University, USA

Paper #4: The Moderating Effect of Construal Level on Price Judgments

Marcus Cunha Jr., University of Washington, USA
Julian Saint Clair, University of Washington, USA
Jeffrey Shulman, University of Washington, USA

SESSION OVERVIEW

Recent findings in consumer behavior, psychology, and economics have questioned one of the key tenets of neoclassical utility theory: That preferences are stable and independent of the external environment that consumers face. Today, the general, well-accepted assumption instead is that preferences are influenced by contextual factors. One of the most important domains for the study of such influences in marketing and consumer behavior has been pricing. In fact, a vast amount of research has provided evidence for contextual price influences on people's internal notion of value as manifested in price judgments, willingness-to-pay, and product-choices (e.g., Adaval & Monroe, 2002; Alba, Mela, Shimp, Urbany, 1999; Aradhna, Wagner, Yoon, & Adaval, 2006; Janiszewski & Lichtenstein, 1999; Monroe, 2003; Niedrich, Weathers, Hill, & Bell, 2009; Simonson & Drolet, 2004). This symposium builds upon the existing body of research on reference pricing and takes an in-depth look at the underlying mechanisms via which exposure to prices influences consumers' judgments and behaviors. As such, this session offers important new insights into the power of prices and their affects on the consumer mind.

The first paper by Karmarkar, Shiv, and Knutson presents functional magnetic resonance imaging (fMRI) as well as behavioral data showing that early attention to price leads consumers to think about value, focusing the evaluation process on whether a product is *worth* the given price. That is, rather than categorizing items as liked or disliked, consumers tend to shift to a process that is more consistent with a threshold mechanism, in which a product qualifies for purchase if its value is judged to be high enough. The second paper by Bertini and Wathieu focuses on the presence or absence of a starting price for products that require a certain degree of customization (e.g., a laptop computer). Across three experiments they find that a starting price acts to split a total expense into a component related to the benefits desired by most consumers and a component related to idiosyncratic preferences. This perceptual split helps consumers to more actively realize that the product has an element of personalization, which increases their engagement in the customization-process, leading to decreased price sensitivity, higher quality perception, and

improved likelihood of purchases. The third paper by Mazar, Koszegi, and Ariely presents evidence that a target products' distribution of selling prices in the market affects individuals' expressed reservation prices for that product, and focuses on investigating the source of such context-dependency. The results from this paper rule out a rational reaction to information and favor the possibility of an error in the expression of preferences rather than the existence of true differing preferences across markets or contexts. These findings have important implications not only for consumer welfare and policy but also marketing strategy. The final paper by Cunha Jr., Saint Clair, and Shulman examines the extent to which consumer price perception and judgments of a target product are affected by the distribution of prices of non-target products when considering a product set. It identifies construal level as an important factor that influences context-dependent price judgments. Whereas consumers using low-level, concrete construal attend to specific features of the price distribution of the non-target products (e.g. the range or frequency) and their judgments contrast away from these features, consumers using high-level, abstract construal attend to global features of that price distribution (e.g. the mean) and their judgments assimilate toward these features.

In keeping with the conference theme "Building Connections," the four papers in this session bring together a variety of theoretical (reference dependence, expectation disconfirmation, range-frequency theory, construal level-theory) and methodological approaches (neuroscientific methods and experimental design) to investigate the power of prices. We believe this session will inspire interest and foster discussion on important questions such as: What are the underlying psychological mechanisms by which prices affect consumers' judgment and decision making? How can prices affect the type of information processing? What are possible mediators of those effects? and To what extent are consumer welfare and marketer demand impacted in a positive or negative way?

This symposium is likely to appeal to researchers interested in price perception, preference and choice, judgment and decision-making, situation/context effects, and inference making. The findings have important implications for marketers as well as individual consumers and policy. Note: The findings of all four papers have been written up, i.e. in manuscripts that are either prepared or under review, or near publication.

The Effects of Price Primacy on Decision Making and Perceptions of Product Value

EXTENDED ABSTRACT

When consumers first attend to a product, they are engaged affectively, causing them to categorize the item as positive or negative. Research by Knutson et al. (2007) provides evidence that individuals' evaluations and subsequent purchase decisions are predicted most strongly by this initial liking (or disliking) reaction. In contrast, price is a difficult piece of information for consumers to evaluate independently (Hsee et al. 2003, 2005). It would be reasonable then, to assume that price plays a fixed role in the computation of value and should be factored into a decision the same way at any time. However, it is also possible that encountering price early on sets a context for processing subsequent information, thus shaping product perceptions and choice behavior. Price can signal an item's value or worth, to the point that price knowledge can bias perceptions of product quality at both the behavioral and neural level (e.g. Rao and Monroe 1989; Shiv et al. 2005, Plassmann et al. 2008). Thus we posit that price primacy leads consumers to think about value, focusing the evaluation process on whether a product is *worth* the given price. Rather than categorizing items as liked or disliked, this process would be more consistent with a threshold mechanism, in which a product qualifies for purchase if its value is judged to be high enough.

To investigate this hypothesis, seventeen individuals (9 females) made shopping decisions in an incentive compatible fMRI task adapted from Knutson et al. (2007). Across trials, a price was presented either before or after a photo of a product and participants then indicated whether they wanted to buy it (yes/no). Two of these choices were randomly selected to have real world consequences at the end of the experiment. Following the scanner task, participants listed their reservation price for each product. A value score, conceptually similar to consumer surplus, was calculated by subtracting the offered price from the individual's reservation price to determine how (in)expensive participants found each item to be. Participants also rated how much they liked each product - regardless of purchase - on a scale from 1 (Do Not Like) to 7 (Like Very Much).

Neural data were analyzed from the time during the decision process before participants indicated their choice, but when both price and product information was available to them. We focused these analyses on how price primacy influenced the neural coding of value (i.e. the integration of price and product information) and reward (i.e. liking for the product). Across trials, perceptions of value significantly correlated with brain activity in the medial prefrontal cortex (MPFC). This is consistent with previous research showing that activity in MPFC and nearby brain areas appears to be involved in integrating information such as product attributes or choice set composition, thus responding to the current worth or value of a decision target (e.g. Knutson et al. 2003, 2007; Hare et al. 2008).

Comparing product versus price primacy trials revealed qualitative differences in MPFC activity during the evaluation process. In product-first trials, MPFC activation increased for items that were subsequently purchased and decreased for items that were subsequently rejected. In price-first trials, MPFC activation also showed some increase for items that were chosen for purchase. However, for items that were not purchased, activity in these areas did not decrease, but remained at baseline. These results suggest that in product-first contexts, wanted items have a positive value but unwanted items seem to be actively rejected with an explicit assignment of a negative value. The process is quite different in price-first contexts; here, unwanted items seem to be passively excluded from consideration, or ignored, consistent with our hypothesis of a threshold-type mechanism.

Liking of the product was correlated with activity in the Nucleus Accumbens (NAcc), a brain region associated with anticipated reward (e.g. Knutson et al. 2001, 2007; Erk et al 2002, but see Hare et al. 2008). NAcc activity patterns were similar across price and product primacy trials. Similarly, no differences were found in the behavioral liking ratings for purchased products between trial types (p = .35). Such findings allow us to rule out the possibility that price primacy simply reduces engagement or liking by diminishing the reward value of the subsequently viewed product.

Together these results are consistent with our proposed framework in which price primacy specifically influences the determination of a product's value, shifting the process from a question of "do I like it?" to one of "is it worth it?" In the latter case, products deemed "not worth it" are merely insufficiently positive, as opposed to actively negative in value.

Such an account also makes the interesting behavioral prediction that price primacy could specifically enhance consideration of utilitarian or practical items, because their worth is easily accessible in terms of need or functionality. Furthermore, our data suggest that price primacy should not have an impact on hedonic or frivolous purchasing. These are products whose worth can be described in terms of how strongly rewarding they are found to be, and the results from the shopping task showed that early exposure to price did not diminish liking or the reward response for desired products.

These predictions were tested in second study; a between-subjects behavioral experiment comparing purchasing rates across category (hedonic/utilitarian) and primacy (product/price; N = 122). Participants were asked to indicate their intent to purchase either four hedonic or four utilitarian products, under price or product primacy conditions. As in the fMRI task, participant decisions were incentive compatible. There was a significant interaction of category by primacy (F(1,118) = 4.04; p <.05) such that price primacy significantly increased purchase rates for utilitarian products (F(1,118) = 8.211; p<.01) but did not change rates for hedonic products (F<<1). The results of this experiment confirm the behavioral predictions made by the neural data.

Starting Prices and Consumer Response to Customization

EXTENDED ABSTRACT

Consumers often make decisions about products that require a certain degree of customization. From the perspective of a firm, providing customization is costly but it can lead to greater value creation and surplus extraction if a sufficient number of consumers are responsive to, and prepared to pay for, this benefit.

The way customizable products are priced in a market tends to follow a certain pattern. Instead of posting only the price a consumer is asked to pay for the good she ultimately chooses, sellers often advertise a low starting price for the base or entry model and make adjustments to this figure as additional features are chosen based on individual preferences. An airline, for example, may offer flights on a particular route at prices "starting from" a certain figure. As the traveler then makes decisions on departure day and time, departure and arrival airports, number of stops, and class of service, the actual—typically higher—fare is revealed. Similarly, manufacturers of laptop computers promote base models at starting prices and then take potential buyers through an intricate customization process that leads to the final purchase price.

Debates and regulations on "bait-and-switch" (the practice that lures consumers into a shop on the basis of a low price without actually offering any viable alternative at that price) assume that starting prices are deceptive tensile claims. The argument is that consumers are initially attracted by a low price point and, for reasons such as insufficient adjustment, switching costs, and escalation of commitment, become insensitive to or willing to accept the added expense. There is support for this view in practice, as evidenced by the acts of several customer protection agencies questioning the fairness of starting prices and trying to limit or abolish their use.

Beyond the interpretation of starting prices as pure marketing gimmick, the existing literature suggests that they might be detrimental to firms. Based on theories of reference dependence and expectation disconfirmation, one could indeed argue that consumers lured by a starting price experience will experience the incremental expense leading to the final price as a source of strong disutility that could jeopardize the transaction or damage the consumption experience.

The goal of our research is to propose and test a new understanding of the role of starting prices in the context of customization. Our explanation portrays the practice in a positive light, linking the presence of a starting price to consumer engagement in customization. Consistent with recent research describing how price can stimulate engagement and lead to new perceptions of value, we propose that a starting price acts to split a total expense into a component related to the benefits desired by most consumers and a component related to the benefits desired as a result of idiosyncratic preferences. This perceptual split helps potential buyers to more actively realize that the good has an element of personalization, which impacts demand in a positive manner to the extent that customization is beneficial and deserving of attention.

We tested our theory across three experiments in which starting prices were present or absent and in which the benefits of customization were perceived to be high or low. The general prediction was that variations in the perceived value of customization would carry over to product judgments only when a starting price was posted (to support consumer engagement in the process).

The first experiment crossed price presentation with the amount of control (low vs. high) participants exerted over the choice of customized features. Research has shown that the value of customization diminishes in the absence of self-determination. For the same desired offering, we found that adding a starting price improved likelihood of purchase and decreased price sensitivity when participants selected the customizable features, but not when the same set of features were selected by the seller.

The second experiment crossed price presentation with one of two primed judgment criteria (utilitarian vs. hedonic). Customization is expected to be beneficial when consumers seek self-expression. We reasoned self-expression is consistent with the desire to fulfill a hedonic goal, not a utilitarian goal. Similar to experiment 1, we observed a significant difference in perceived product quality across these two judgment criteria only when a starting price was introduced.

Finally, the third experiment crossed price presentation (four levels) with category expertise (low vs. high). Category expertise was measured because consumers are less likely to view customization as beneficial when they are uncertain of their own preferences (i.e., in the case of novices). The change to four price presentation levels allowed us to provide evidence for the psychological mechanism we propose. Specifically, three of these conditions included a starting price that represented a small, medium, or large portion of the final price. If consumers associate the difference between a final price and a starting price with the amount of customization present in a product, then variations in the latter should lead to changes in product perceptions. The results corroborate our theory. For expert participants, we found that perceptions of customization and product valuation were inversely related to the size of the starting price. There was no effect of price presentation for novices.

Stable Context-Dependent Preferences?
The Origin of Market Price-Dependent Valuations

EXTENDED ABSTRACT

Today, the general, well-accepted assumption is that preferences are not stable and independent of the external environment that decisions makers face but instead influenced by contextual variables. One of the most important domains for the study of such influences has been pricing. For example, anchoring individuals on an arbitrary selling price derived from their social security number subsequently affected valuations (Ariely, Loewenstein, & Prelec, 2003). However, in a typical purchase situation, whenever consumers intend to buy a familiar product, they have accumulated various experiences with the product's available market prices or at least have some expectation about the distribution of this product's selling prices at various retailers. And it is less known to what extend the knowledge of the distribution of given market prices influences consumers' internal valuations. For example, in Richard Thaler's (1985) "beer on the beach" example, which traditionally has been interpreted in terms of transaction utility, respondents provided their hypothetical willingness-to-pay for a bottle of cold beer delivered to them on the beach by a friend. Participants were told that the friend would get the beer, in one condition, from a local store and, in the other condition, from a fancy hotel. The results showed that participants' willingness-to-pay was significantly higher in the latter condition. We view these results as consistent with the idea that expectations of the distribution of market prices for a product influences consumers' valuations: Because respondents expected beer prices to be higher in the "hotel-market" than in the "local stores-market", they responded by raising their reservation price.

In the market place a product is often offered for various different prices across retailers, in particular, with various steep discounts. And even if the price-range stays the same, the distribution of these prices (i.e. their frequency) varies across time and markets, and consumers often have some experience, knowledge, or expectation of this distribution. The existing reference price literature (e.g., Aradhna, Wagner, Yoon, & Adaval, 2006; Simonson & Drolet, 2004) has not demonstrated if and how varying distributions (i.e. frequencies) of the same market prices for a product would affect individuals' internal valuations of that product, but predictions based on previously accumulated findings support the notion that the distribution should have an effect (Monroe, 2003). In particular, research on categorical price judgments based on Parducci's (1965) rang-frequency theory suggests that individuals do seem to shift their purchase decisions in response to distributional attributes such as range, modality, or skewing (e.g., Alba, Mela, Shimp, Urbany, 1999; Janiszewski & Lichtenstein, 1999). While these studies focused on price judgments rather than on valuations (maximum willingness-to-pay) and studied the influence of the price distribution of competing products in the market rather than of the target product itself in the market, along similar lines, we hypothesized that even if the range of a product's selling prices was the same, a left-skewed distribution would elicit lower reservation prices for a familiar product in comparison to a right-skewed distribution.

Our interest, however, goes beyond merely identifying another contextual factor. Instead we wanted to focus on investigating the origin of such context-dependency. That is, while the previously demonstrated anchoring effects with non-informative, irrelevant single prices (see e.g., Adaval & Wyer, 2010; Nunes & Boatwright, 2004 for incidental effects) are clearly mistakes in individuals' expressions of preferences, it is less clear whether such market-dependent valuations are necessarily mistakes and to what extent they might be stable within the same markets. At least three possible causes for such a context-dependency come to mind: 1) rational reactions to information, 2) true changes in valuations (i.e. individuals have real, that is stable, context-dependent preferences), or 3) biased (i.e. erroneous) expressions of true context-*in*dependent valuations. If reservation prices depend on the prices buyers expect to face in the market, demand will in general depend on supply, with important implications for marketers' pricing strategies and for pricing models. Therefore, understanding the source for this dependency is crucial to determine not only marketing strategy but also welfare and policy implications.

We address these questions with three studies. First, we present two experiments with a visual description of a product's market price-distribution in which we found that participants' willingness-to-pay in consequential purchasing tasks were dramatically lower when the price distribution was skewed to the left than when it was skewed to the right. More important, in these experiments we investigated possible underlying reasons for the price distribution-dependence of preferences. Our results rule out a rational reaction to information and favor the possibility of an error in the expression of one's preferences rather than the existence of true differing preferences across markets or contexts. Next, Experiment 3 replicated the findings in a setting that more closely resembled a market situation: a multi-period market simulation in which participants merely experienced the distribution of selling prices in the market. Our findings suggest that despite having stable valuations of products, consumers are rarely willing to pay that valuation when encountering lower prices unless they are prompted to think carefully about the value that the product provides to them (Experiment 2) or when they are being "reminded" that the distribution of selling prices should not matter (Experiment 1). This means that consumers might sometimes end up making sub-optimal purchase decisions and not purchase the product for a price at which they would still receive a positive net utility from it. We speculate that this systematic behavioral pattern (bias) arises from consumers being distracted by the wrong goal: instead of focusing on the utility that the product itself offers, they are shortsightedly focusing on optimizing the pleasure of getting a good deal.

Together, our results suggest that a market with its price distribution is an inherently powerful contextual variable that determines expressed preferences in purchasing decisions even for products for which consumers should have a relatively good idea of the consumption utility that it provides and in the absence of a clear, explicit anchor.

The Moderating Effect of Construal Level on Price Judgments

EXTENDED ABSTRACT

When judging multiple products, consumers' price perceptions are often influenced by the characteristics of the price distribution and price judgments are well accounted for by range-frequency theory (Parducci 1965). This theory posits that consumers focus on specific elements of the consideration set, such as the most and least expensive products (i.e., range) or the density of the distribution (i.e., frequency), and that judgments contrast away from the direction of change to these elements such that a price increase for the most expensive product makes the other products seems less expensive (Cunha and Shulman 2011; Niedrich, Sharma, and Wedell 2001). The present research demonstrates that the level of abstractness with which consumers construe product prices (i.e., construal level) moderates this standard contrast effect.

Construal level theory (CLT; for a review see Trope and Liberman 2010) contends that consumers construe stimuli on a continuum of abstractness ranging from low-level, concrete construal to high-level, abstract construal. CLT research shows that consumers processing at low construal focus on subordinate, specific features and process contrastively. In contrast, consumers processing at high construal focus on superordinate, global features and process inclusively. For example, when asked to group a multitude of items into categories, participants processing at low construal formed a large number of specified categories (e.g. snacks, sodas) while those processing at high construal formed fewer, broader categories (e.g. food, beverages; Liberman, Sagristano, and Trope 2002). Additionally, when asked to rate the similarity between social groups (e.g. men and women, self and others), participants processing at low construal perceived less similarity while participants processing at high construal perceived more similarity (Forster 2009; Forster, Liberman, and Kuschel 2008). These findings are said to result from differential attentional focus (specific vs. global features) and processing style (contrastive vs. inclusive).

The tendency for consumers processing at low construal to focus on specific features and process contrastively is consistent with the predictions of range-frequency theory wherein consumers use specific features of the distribution as standards of comparison. However, the tendency for consumers using high construal to focus on global features of the stimuli distribution and process inclusively is at odds with range-frequency theory. What feature of a consideration set might serve as a "global feature"? Prior research has proposed the mean of a consideration set as a potential referent relative to which consumers might make judgments (Monroe 2003). Considering that the mean of a set serves as a summary measure, which captures the typicality of the elements of the set, it is plausible to conceptualize it as a global feature of a consideration set. As such, it can be predicted that consumers' processing at low construal will show results consistent with range-frequency theory in which price judgments of target products contrast away from shifts in specific elements of the context (e.g. the range). Alternatively, price judgments by consumers processing at high construal will instead assimilate toward shifts in global features (e.g. the mean).

We test this prediction in two experiments. In experiment 1 we activate low (high) construal by priming negative (positive) affect (see Gasper and Clore 2002; Labroo and Patrick 2009), while in experiment 2 we use a classification (inference) learning task (Markman and Ross 2003). After the construal manipulations, participants were randomly assigned to price-context conditions in which they saw the prices of a number of gourmet cheeses and rated them on expensiveness. A subset of these prices were target prices that remained constant across context conditions while the remaining prices were manipulated to shift the range, frequency, and mean of the set.

Across both experiments we obtain results consistent with our predictions. The construal manipulations worked as expected ($ps <$ .01) and the interactions between construal and price-context were significant (E1: $p < .05$; E2: $p < .01$). Specifically, participants in low construal judged target prices as less expensive when the range and frequency were shifted upward but not when the mean was shifted upward; a contrast response. In comparison, participants in high construal judged targets as more expensive when the mean was shifted upward but not when the range or frequency were shifted upward; an assimilation response.

In sum, this research identifies construal level as an important factor that influences contextual price judgments. Whereas consumers using low-level, concrete construal attend to specific features of the context (e.g. the range or frequency) and their judgments contrast away from these features, consumers using high-level, abstract construal attend to global features of the context (e.g. the mean) and their judgments assimilate toward these features. This latter finding is at odds with extant research on contextual judgments, which supports range-frequency theory. For practice, the implication is that marketers may alter their perceived price position by activating high or low construal using a simple affective prime. For theory, the implication is that construal level may affect contextual judgments and information integration in general, extending beyond judgments of price alone.

REFERENCES

Adaval, R. & Wyer, R. S. (2010). Conscious and Nonconscious Influences of a Price Anchor: Effects on Willingness to Pay for Related and Unrelated Products. *Journal of Marketing Research*, in press.

Alba, J. W., Mela, C. F., Shimp, T. A., & Urbany, J. E. (1999). The Effect of Discount Frequency Cue and Depth on Consumer Price Judgments. *Journal of Consumer Re*search, 26 (September), 99-114.

Aradhna, K., Wagner, M., Yoon, C., & Adaval, R. (2006). Effects of Extreme-Priced Products on Consumer Reservation Prices. *Journal of Consumer Psychology, 16 (2)* 179-193.

Ariely, D., Loewenstein, G., & Prelec, D. (2003). Coherent Arbitrariness: Stable Demand Curves without Stable Preferences. *Quarterly Journal of Economics,* 118(1), 73-105.

Cunha, Marcus, Jr. and Jeffrey D. Shulman (2011), "Assimilation and Contrast in Price Evaluations," *Journal of Consumer Research*, 37 (February), 822-35.

Erk, Susanne, Manfred Spitzer, Arthur P. Wunderlich, Lars Galley, Henrik Walter. (2002) "Cultural Objects Modulate Reward Circuitry." *Neuroreport* 13(18):2499-503.

Forster, J. (2009), "Relations between Perceptual and Conceptual Scope: How Global Versus Local Processing Fits a Focus on Similarity Versus Dissimilarity," *Journal of Experimental Psychology-General*, 138 (February), 88-111.

Forster, Jens., Nira Liberman, and Stefanie Kuschel (2008), "The Effect of Global Versus Local Processing Styles on Assimilation Versus Contrast in Social Judgment," *Journal of Personality and Social Psychology*, 94 (April), 579-99.

Gasper, Karen and Gerald L. Clore (2002), "Attending to the Big Picture: Mood and Global Versus Local Processing of Visual Information," *Psychological Science*, 13 (Jan), 34-40.

Hare, Todd A., John O'Doherty, Colin F. Camerer, Wolfram Schultz and Antonio Rangel. (2008) "Dissociating the Role of the Orbitofrontal Cortex and the Striatum in the Computation of Goal Values and Prediction Errors." *Journal of Neuroscience* 28(22): 5623-5630.

Hsee, Christopher K., Yuval Rottenstreich and Zhixing Xiao (2005) "When Is More Better?: On the Relationship Between Magnitude and Subjective Value." *Current Trends in Psychological Science* 14:234-37.

Hsee, Christopher K., Fang Yu, Jiao Zhang, and Yan Zhang (2003), "Medium Maximization," *Journal of Consumer Research*, 30(1), 1–14.

Janiszewski, C. & Lichtenstein, D. R. (1999). A Range Theory Account of Price Perception. *Journal of Consumer Research*, 25(March), 353-368

Knutson, Brian, Charles M. Adams, Grace W. Fong, and Daniel Hommer. (2001) "Anticipation of Increasing Monetary Reward Selectively Recruits Nucleus Accumbens." *Journal of Neuroscience* 21, RC159.

Knutson, Brian, Grace W. Fong, Shannon M. Bennett, Charles M. Adams and Daniel Hommer. (2003) "A Region of Mesial Prefrontal Cortex Tracks Monetarily Rewarding Outcomes: Characterization with Rapid Event-Related fMRI." *NeuroImage* 18(2):263-72.

Knutson, Brian, Scott Rick, G. Elliott Wimmer, Drazen Prelec, and George Loewenstein. (2007) "Neural Predictors of Purchases." *Neuron* 53(1):147-56.

Labroo, Aparna A. and Vanessa M. Patrick (2009), "Psychological Distancing: Why Happiness Helps You See the Big Picture," *Journal of Consumer Research*, 35 (Feb), 800-09.

Liberman, Nira, Mivhael D. Sagristano, and Yaacov Trope (2002), "The Effect of Temporal Distance on Level of Mental Construal," *Journal of Experimental Social Psychology*, 38 (November), 523-34.

Markman, Arthur B. and Brian H. Ross (2003), "Category Use and Category Learning," *Psychological Bulletin*, 129 (July), 592-613.

Monroe, K. B. (2003). *Pricing: Making Profitable Decisions*. Boston, Massachusetts: McGraw-Hill/Irwin.

Niedrich, Ronald W., Subhash Sharma, and Douglas H. Wedell (2001), "Reference Price and Price Perceptions: A Comparison of Alternative Models," *Journal of Consumer Research*, 28 (December), 339-54.

Nunes, J. C., & Boatwright, P. (2004). Incidental prices and their effect on willingness to pay. *Journal of Marketing Research*, 41(1) 457-466.

Parducci, A. (1965). Category judgment: A range-frequency model. Psychological Review, 72, 407-418.

Plassmann, Hilke, John O'Doherty, Baba Shiv and Antonio Rangel. (2008) "Marketing Actions Can Modulate Neural Representations of Experienced Pleasantness." *Proceedings of the National Academy of Sciences.* 105(3): 1050-4.

Rao Akshay R., and Kent B. Monroe. (1989) "The Effect of Price, Brand Name, and Store Name on Buyers' Perceptions of Product Quality." *J Marketing Res.* 26(3):351-357.

Shiv, Baba, Ziv Carmon, and Dan Ariely. (2005) "Placebo Effects of Marketing Actions: Consumers Get What They Pay For." *Journal of Marketing Research*, 42 (4): 383-93.

Simonson, I., & Drolet, A. (2004). Anchoring effects on consumers willingness-to-pay and willingness-to-accept. *Journal of Consumer Research,* 31(4) 681-690.

Thaler, R. H. (1985). Mental accounting and consumer choice. *Marketing Science,* 4(3) 199-214.

Trope, Yaacov and Nira Liberman (2010), "Construal-Level Theory of Psychological Distance," *Psychological Review*, 117 (Apr), 440-63.

The Effect of Individual and Contextual Factors on Food Consumption

Chair: Nitika Garg, University of New South Wales, Australia

Paper #1: Does Liking or Wanting Determine Inter-stimulus Intervals in Food Intake?
> Carey Morewedge, Carnegie Mellon University, USA
> Baba Shiv, Stanford University, USA
> Emily Garbinsky, Stanford University, USA

Paper #2: Attenuating Sadness' Effect on Consumption: Helplessness, Choice, and Self-Awareness
> Nitika Garg, University of New South Wales, Australia
> J. Jeffrey Inman, University of Pittsburgh, USA

Paper #3: I Am How Much I Eat: How Self-Monitoring Influences Food Consumption Across Genders
> Brian Wansink, Cornell University, USA
> Kevin Kniffin, Cornell University, USA
> Collin Payne, New Mexico State University, USA
> Junyong Kim, Purdue University Calumet, USA
> Se-Bum Park, KAIST Business School, Korea

SESSION OVERVIEW

Summary of Papers vis-a-vis Session Theme

Social cognition and marketing researchers have been examining how various factors such as (incidental) emotion and packaging, influence consumer decision making and perceptions (e.g., Isen et al. 1978; Pham and Raghunathan 1999; Keltner, Ellsworth, and Edwards 1993; Lerner and Keltner 2000, 2001; MacInnis and Price 1987; Wansink 1996). While individual and contextual factors have been found to affect various aspects of decision making, their influence on food consumption is not well understood. For instance, the effect of product familiarity and liking, the impact of incidental affect (consumer's mood or emotion), role of choice and self-monitoring on consumption behaviors such as the amount of a food product consumed, are research issues that have not been examined in detail in the existing literature. These are some of the questions that motivate this special session.

The research presented in this session focuses on food consumption and builds on previous literature in that area (Wansink 1994, 1996; Shiv and Fedorikhin 1999). It further builds connections with other research areas such as incidental affect (Isen 2001; Keltner, Ellsworth, and Edwards 1993; Lerner and Keltner 2000, 2001; Tiedens and Linton 2001), choice (Iyengar and Lepper 2000; Langer and Rodin 1976), self-monitoring (Snyder 1987), and product familiarity and liking (Berridge and Robinson 2003; Finlayson, King, and Blundell 2007). Specifically, the objective of the session is to present a set of studies that draw on different theoretical bases and methodological approaches to highlight various facets of food consumption and thus, present a more holistic view of this area of research. Notably, all three papers in the session highlight the impact of individual and contextual variables (product familiarity and liking, incidental affect, self-monitoring) on *actual food consumption* rather than related dependent variables such as preference or intention. Further, the papers in the proposed session combine both the marketing as well as the social cognition literature to present a broad spectrum of research with new insights into consumption behavior.

In the first paper, Carey Morewedge (CMU), Baba Shiv (Stanford University) and Emily Garbinsky (Stanford University) focus on whether product satiety influences the interval (measured in number of days) that individuals desire between consumption episodes for both, novel and familiar food products. Further, they examine the role that product liking plays in this relationship. Results reveal a significant relationship between product satiety and the inter-stimulus interval, such that individuals who consumed more of a food product the previous day (high satiety) desired a longer delay in their delivery of the product than those in the low satiety condition. Notably, a mediation analysis revealed that the relationship between the amount of food consumed and the desired delay was mediated by individuals' decrease in product liking. However, the mediating role of product liking disappears for a familiar product. That is, although high satiety leads to increased desire for longer delays in delivery, this relationship is not mediated by product liking in the case of a familiar product. Thus, these findings replicate and extend existing findings regarding satiation and highlight the role of individual factors such as product familiarity and liking in food consumption.

The second paper focuses on attenuating the relationship between sadness and food consumption. The paper is co-authored by Nitika Garg (University of New South Wales) and Jeff Inman (University of Pittsburgh). Sadness' core appraisal theme of loss and helplessness has been known to evoke an implicit goal of reward replacement which leads sad (vs. neutral and happy) individuals to consume more of a tasty, fatty food product (e.g., M&Ms). In a series of three experiments with real food consumption, the authors suggest that sadness' influence on consumption can be attenuated by providing individuals an opportunity to choose (even if the choice is trivial) which counteracts appraisals of helplessness and enhances a sense of individual control. Notably, this holds only when the choice is relevant for 'self' (vs. 'others'). Finally, the paper tests the moderating effect of self-awareness on the sadness-consumption relationship. Overall, the studies provide theoretical moderators and mediators of the sadness-consumption relationship and reveal the underlying mechanism that might explain this relationship.

In the third paper, Brian Wansink (Cornell University) and co-authors examine how self-monitoring of one's consumption in the presence of others has a significant effect on the amount of food consumed. In an externally valid field study, the authors found that in dating couples at a movie theatre, the effect of self-monitoring on consumption varied across genders. Specifically, while women monitored how much popcorn they ate and ate less, men monitored what they ate and ate more. Follow up studies in a lab setting suggest that both ate in accordance with what they thought was appropriate for their gender. Their results suggest that increased self-monitoring in social setting affects males and females differentially because of the differences in social norms that they perceive to be applied to them.

This session brings together several leading scholars (e.g. Shiv, Wansink, and Inman) who have been very active in the field of consumption and consumer decision making. Further, the proposed session offers a variety of implications useful to *academics, consumers, managers, nutritional researchers* as well as to *public policy professionals* and highlights the impact of individual and contextual factors on consumption behavior, in particular. By employing a diverse range of theoretical constructs and exploring various moderators and mediators of food consumption, the papers in the session try to 'build and broaden' the connections across a number of research domains, thus advancing our theoretical understanding of consumption in general.

Advances in Consumer Research
Volume 39, ©2011

Audience Likely to Attend

Given the growing concern with over-consumption in the US and across the world, this session focuses on an important topic in consumer behavior (i.e., an examination of the effect of contextual factors on various dimensions of consumption). Participation of researchers using a combination of theoretical and methodological orientations to shed light on different aspects of food consumption (choice, nature of consumption, extent of consumption, delay in consumption), and its susceptibility to a host of individual and contextual factors such as self-monitoring, product familiarity, and affect, will help to provide a more complete picture of how consumer behavior and decision making is influenced by such factors and should appeal to a broad array of conference attendees.

Session Time Allocation

We firmly believe that interaction between the audience and the speakers is an essential ingredient to generate an insightful discussion. Thus, each speaker will be limited by the session chair to a 20 minutes presentation. The discussion leader, Baba Shiv, will then engage the audience in a discussion and interesting directions for future research in this area. It will be the aim of the session to generate a meaningful discussion on this important topic. Thus, we will try and leave as much time as possible for audience questions.

Does Liking or Wanting Determine Inter-stimulus Intervals in Food Intake?

EXTENDED ABSTRACT

The extent to which an individual likes and wants various items affects the choices that they make. While liking and wanting are similar constructs, they have typically been distinguished in the following manner: liking refers to the amount of pleasure that is derived from a stimulus while wanting refers to a desire to obtain that stimulus (Finlayson, King, & Blundell, 2007b). For this reason, liking is considered to be a hedonic or affective component while wanting has been classified in terms of motivation (Finlayson, King, & Blundell, 2007a).

Numerous studies have been conducted to show that these two constructs are indeed separable. Examples include the finding that wanting an addictive substance is not necessarily coupled with enjoyment of that substance (Robinson & Berridge, 1993) and that thwarting participants from winning a particular prize results in increased wanting of that prize (higher willingness to pay) but decreased liking (greater likelihood of switching prizes after they finally obtain it) (Litt, Khan, & Shiv, 2009). Additionally, liking and wanting have been linked to different neural substrates (Berridge, 1996) since the manipulation of dopamine has been shown to change motivated behavior (wanting) but not taste liking (Berridge & Robinson, 2003).

Knowing that liking and wanting have separate influences on behavior, the goal of this research is to investigate which construct (liking or wanting) influences the inter-stimulus interval with regard to food intake (which we define as the amount of time that passes before individuals choose to once again consume a particular food that they recently ate).

Study Method. The effects of liking and wanting were investigated for both novel and familiar food items. In Study 1, which examined a novel stimulus, participants were either assigned to the low satiety condition (where they were asked to eat 5 Nut Thins) or the high satiety condition (where they were asked to eat 15 Nut Thins). All participants were asked to provide ratings after eating each cracker regarding how much they liked the Nut Thins and the extent to which they wanted to continue eating them. The dependent

variable was the number of days that each participant indicated that they would like to have a free box of Nut Thins delivered to their home. This was measured in a follow up survey that was completed the next day.

In Study 2, which examined a familiar stimulus, all procedures were identical to Study 1 with the exception that participants who were assigned to the low satiety condition were asked to eat 5 Pringles while participants that were assigned to the high satiety condition were asked to eat 15 Pringles. Once again, all participants were asked to provide ratings after eating each chip regarding how much they liked the Pringles and the extent to which they wanted to continue eating them. The dependent variable was the number of days that each participant indicated that they would like to have a free can of Pringles delivered to their home. This was measured in a follow up survey that was completed the next day.

Results. Study 1 results showed a significant relationship between satiety condition and desired delay of free boxes such that participants who consumed more Nut Thins the previous day indicated a longer delay in their delivery of free boxes, $\beta = 11.482$, $t(29) = 2.236$, $p = 0.034$. More importantly, the data also fulfilled the criteria for a mediation model (Baron & Kenny, 1986). First, satiety condition (low or high) had a significant effect on the decrement in liking ($\beta = 1.182$, $p = 0.011$). That is, participants in the high satiety condition who consumed more Nut Thins experienced a greater decrease in liking. Second, the decrement in liking significantly impacted the desired delay ($\beta = 5.218$, $p = 0.006$). Finally, when desired delay was regressed on both satiety condition and decrease in liking, the coefficient for desired delay was no longer significant ($\beta = 1.530$, $p = 0.884$).

Study 2 results once again showed a significant relationship between satiety condition and desired delivery of free boxes such that participants who consumed more Pringles the previous day desired a longer delay in their delivery of free boxes, $\beta = 0.739$, $t(33) = 2.092$, $p = 0.044$. However, the data no longer fulfilled the criteria for a mediation model.

Ongoing Work and Extensions. In follow-up investigations, we are exploring the effect of placing participants under low or high cognitive load while performing the liking and wanting rating tasks for novel stimuli. It is hypothesized that the decrement in liking will mediate the desired delay of free boxes for participants placed under low load but not for those under high load. Additionally, in future studies, we plan to obtain behavioral measures of liking and wanting in addition to measures of actual (instead of merely predicted) future consumption.

Conclusions. The results provide insight into the extent to which liking and wanting influence readiness to repeat consumption experiences. Specifically, the findings suggest that the decrease in liking that accompanies increased food consumption is an important predictor for length of time until repeated consumption when the food is novel, but when consumption involves a more familiar food, this decrease in liking is no longer relevant. Not only do the results highlight the importance of first impressions in the domain of food intake, but they also suggest that different processes may be operating during the decision of when to eat a recently consumed food depending on whether that food was novel or familiar.

Attenuating Sadness' Effect on Consumption: Helplessness, Choice, and Self-Awareness

EXTENDED ABSTRACT

Research on incidental emotion – emotion consumers imbue from their environment in isolation to the task at hand – has documented the pervasive tendency of emotions to carry over from one situation to another, coloring behavior in unrelated tasks (for reviews, see Forgas 1995; Isen 1993; Keltner and Lerner 2010; Loewenstein and Lerner 2003; Schwarz 2000). In the domain of consumption, emotions have been shown to influence in-store shopping (Woodruffe 1997) and in-home food choice (Wansink, Cheney, and Chan 2003). With the nation increasingly concerned with overeating and obesity, understanding how incidental affect influences food intake along with its mediators and moderators is an important topic.

One of the most curious carryover examples of emotion effects involves sadness and consumption. Its effects depart from what one would predict based on emotional valence. The standard prediction of a valence-based model would be that any negative emotion, including sadness, should trigger generalized negative valuation. That is, a negative state should lead one to perceive the world in negative ways. While disgust fits that predicted pattern, sadness does not. Sadness actually triggers positive valuation of new products, as measured by willingness to pay (Lerner et al. 2004).

Additionally, this carryover effect drives consumption behavior across diverse domains such as consumption and willingness to pay. In the domain of eating, for example, sadness (relative to happiness) leads to increased consumption of tasty, fattening food products, such as buttered popcorn and M&M candies (Garg, Wansink, and Inman 2007). Sadness' effect on consumption can be understood by examining its core relational theme of loss and helplessness (Lazarus, 1991) which might trigger implicit goals of reward replacement (Raghunathan and Pham 1999) and changing one's circumstances (Lerner et al. 2004). Notably, sadness is associated not with simple loss (e.g., loss of a replaceable possession) but rather with a sense of irrevocable loss (e.g., loss of a loved one). Recent research has argued that it is this combination of loss and helplessness associated with sadness that leads to compensatory tendencies (Garg and Lerner 2011).

In the present research, we hypothesize that given these underlying themes of loss and helplessness associated with sadness (Frijda, Kuipers, & ter Schure 1989; Lazarus 1991), sadness' effect on consumption can be attenuated by increasing decision makers' sense of individual control and decreasing their sense of helplessness. We focus on helplessness because it connects to the issue of control, which has proven important in guiding emotion effects, based on past investigations using the appraisal tendency framework (Garg et al. 2005; Lerner & Keltner 2000), and because it is part of sadness' core relational theme (Lazarus 1991). In the process, we replicate and extend the existing research in the sadness-consumption domain. Specifically, we conduct a series of three studies to examine whether offering a choice of a product can attenuate sadness' influence on consumption of hedonic food (in grams) and whether the focus of decision making (for self or for others) matters in the choice context. Further, we explore the role of self-awareness in the sadness-consumption relationship. Prior research (Cryder, Lerner, Gross, and Dahl 2008) has found self-focus to be a mediator of sadness' effect on willingness to pay where the more self-focused a sad individual was, the more he/she was willing to pay for an object. On the other hand, existing research also shows that self-awareness reduces intake of fatty food products (Sentyrz and Bushman 1998). These alternative views regarding the moderating effect of self-awareness on sadness' effect are tested.

Study 1 examines whether explicit choice of a hedonic (vs. a non-hedonic) good attenuates sadness' effect on hedonic food consumption. We expect that a choice will be more powerful than simple endowment because it will afford some semblance of control to individuals and might therefore alleviate the helplessness associated

with sadness. To test this hypothesis, we compare participants endowed with a hedonic gift to those who are specifically asked to choose between a hedonic gift and a non-hedonic one. A 3 (emotion: sad, happy, neutral) x 2 (choice of a gift, no-choice) between-subjects design was implemented to test the hypotheses of the study. Results find that only when sad individuals are afforded an opportunity to make a choice, does it succeed in overriding the effect on consumption (> 50% drop in amount consumed). Also as predicted, neutral and happy individuals display no drop in consumption and are similar across choice versus no-choice conditions.

Study 2 has a twofold purpose: to validate our findings from Study 1 by replicating the results and, more importantly, to clarify whether the locus of choice - for self or others – influence its efficacy in attenuating sadness' effect. Study 2 used a 2 (emotion: sad, happy) x 3 (choice for self, choice for others, no-choice) between-subjects design to examine this question. Results reveal that the effect of sadness is attenuated only when choice affects self.

The final study aims to examine whether self-awareness moderates sadness' effect. Prior research has found that participants in the high self-awareness condition (where they could see themselves in a mirror) curtail their consumption of fatty food products (Sentyrz and Bushman 1998). However, existing research also shows that sadness increases self-focus and this increased self-focus increases individuals' willingness to pay more to acquire a new object (Cryder et al. 2008). We argue that while self-awareness will attenuate consumption for individuals in other emotion conditions (e.g., neutral), it will actually amplify consumption for sad individuals. Study 3 will test this hypothesis with a 3 (emotion: sad, happy, neutral) x 2 (self-awareness: low, high) between-subjects design.

The empirical examination is well underway. Studies 1 and 2 are complete and Study 3 will be fielded in the spring of 2011. Overall, the current research aims to provide critical insight into the theoretical moderators and mediators underlying the sadness-consumption relationship. This will have important implications for the strategies employed to attenuate emotion effects and for improving our understanding of managing unbidden consumption and its negative consequences.

I am How Much I Eat:
How Self-Monitoring Influences
Food Consumption Across Genders

EXTENDED ABSTRACT

What causes us to attenuate or extenuate our consumption of food when we are with others? Past studies have identified multiple factors such as the number of companions (De Castro 1990, 1994), the attractiveness of these companions (Mori, Chaiken, & Pliner 1987), and even the serving sizes we are given (Wansink 1996; Wertenbroch 1998). Although these studies have studied each of these factors in isolation, their findings suggest that there may be systematic interactions between these factors.

This research investigates how gender-specific self-perceptions influence how closely one monitors what they eat when on a date, and how this subsequently influences how much of a food they choose to consume. Although past work has indicated that females perceive it more feminine to constrain their consumption, there is little corresponding consumption-related evidence as to what males perceive as masculine.

We often act in ways that we hope others perceive as socially desirable. This impression management motivation can cause us to monitor and modify the amount of food we eat in public, particularly in dating situations. In this research, we present a field study in a movie theatre and two lab studies that examines whether both men and women eat in accordance with what they think is appropriate for their gender. In general, it will be examined whether increased self-monitoring in social settings differentially affects the way males and females react to larger serving size because of the differences in social norms that they perceive to be applied to them. It also influences perceptions of other males/females who ate more/less than average. Heavy male eaters were seen by males as being more masculine (being able to bench press more weight and so on), but were seen much less attractive to females.

Situational cues, such as package size, have been shown to have a powerful and unknowing influence on consumption. Interestingly, females on dates tend to exhibit a high level of self-monitoring, and render these cues as ineffective. However, males' eating behaviors are associated with their self-images to a lesser degree. The eating behavior of males, however, is associated with their self-image to a lesser degree. While more males described themselves as hearty eaters than females (Study 2), neither their self-representation strategy (Study 1), nor others' evaluation of them (Study 3) were significantly influenced by food intake. As the result, food consumption volume by males is not surprisingly more susceptible to the effect of serving size.

Malleable Memory and Consumption Decisions

Chairs: Meng Zhu, Johns Hopkins University,USA
Carey Morewedge, Carnegie Mellon University, USA

Paper #1: Feels Far or Near? How Subjective Perception of When One Last Consumed Influences Satiation

Jeff Galak, Carnegie Mellon University, USA
Ellie Kyung, Dartmouth College, USA
Joseph Redden, University of Minnesota, USA
Yang Yang, Carnegie Mellon University, USA

Paper #2: Atypical Pasts Spur Future Consumption

Meng Zhu, Johns Hopkins University, USA
Carey Morewedge, Carnegie Mellon University, USA

Paper #3: If It Feels Right...Do It: Cultural Congruence as a Consumption Cue

James Mourey, University of Michigan, USA
Daphna Oyserman, University of Michigan, USA

Paper #4: Persuasive Advertising with Sophisticated but Impressionable Consumers

Dominique Lauga, UC San Diego, USA

SESSION OVERVIEW

Memory draws on content that one has experienced in the past, but memory for experiences—the taste of a cookie, an advertisement that we saw, or pleasant honeymoon memories—appear to be largely constructed at the time of recollection. Not only is memory influenced by various contextual factors such as the place or mood in which a past experience is recalled, people's memory of events is often inconsistent with their actual experiences (Fredrickson & Kahneman, 1993; Mitchell, Thompson, Peterson, & Cronk, 1997; Morewedge, Gilbert & Wilson 2005; Sutton, 1992; Wurtz, Kruger, Scollon, & Diener 2003). Thus, the malleability of memory provides a fruitful ground for consumer research.

This symposium takes a close look at the relationship between malleable memory and consumption decisions. In an attempt to gain better understanding of the interplay between memory construction and consumption, the papers examine how subtle contextual cues influence the actual content and the retrieval process of consumer memory, and how the constructed recollection of past product and service experiences subsequently influences current and future consumption decisions.

Galak, Kyung, Redden and Yang study the influence of subjective perception of time since the last remembered consumption of a good on satiation toward that good. They show that consumers consume less and derive less pleasure from consumption when they merely have the subjective sense of having consumed more recently (manipulated by using a scale anchored by "Now" and "One Day ago" vs. "Now" and "One Month Ago"). **Zhu and Morewedge** demonstrate that consumers tend to recall extremely positive rather than neutral and negative consumption experiences and this atypical recollection increases future consumption. Consumers appear to overweight the desirability of consumer goods and services on such atypically positive memories. Furthermore, they show that this effect is driven by motivated reasoning and it disappears when people know they will not have to repeat the consumption experience in the future. **Oyserman and Mourey** examine the impact of cultural cues on the ease of retrieval and the resultant feeling of fluency on consumption. They show that people make meaning through culture such that culturally-congruent (vs. culturally–incongruent) cues "feel right", and the resulting feelings of fluency encourages consumers to

"keep going" (vs. "stop and reconsider") in consumption and purchase contexts. Finally, **Lauga** examines how marketing cues can influence memory formation and subsequently influence consumption. Employing a modeling approach, she demonstrates that consumers base their purchasing decisions upon their recollections of product quality (which can be swayed by advertising). The results suggest that engaging in persuasive advertising might be optimal even with sophisticated consumers.

Taken together, the four papers (all in advanced stages) in this session elucidate the relationship between memory construction and consumption decisions, noting when, why and how the content and retrieval of past consumption experiences impact enjoyment and quantity of current consumption as well as the intention of future consumption.

In keeping with the conference theme "Building Connections," the papers in this session bring together a variety of theoretical approaches, including both experimental and modeling methods. As the session integrates diverse research, it is expected to appeal to a broad audience, including those interested in memory, satiation, fluency, motivated reasoning, experienced utility, consumption behaviors, and judgments and decision making. Talks will be kept brief to allow ample time for audience interaction.

Feels Far or Near? How Subjective Perception of When One Last Consumed Influences Satiation

EXTENDED ABSTRACT

Repeated consumption usually leads to a decrease in enjoyment and in motivation to consume, a phenomenon known as "satiation" (Coombs and Avrunin 1977). This process is ubiquitous and manifests in almost every consumption domain from food (Rolls, Rolls, and Rowe 1983) to massage(Nelson and Meyvis 2008). Recent work has increasingly shown that, satiation results from psychological process (McSweeney and Swindell 1999) as well as from physiological signals (O'Donohue and Geer 1985). In particular, satiation can be constructed based on whether people recall their past consumption (Higgs 2002, 2008; Rozin et al. 1998), the ease of retrieval of past consumption, and the subjective sense of how much they have consumed (Redden and Galak).

In the current research, we explore another critical antecedent to satiation – the subjective perception of when one last consumed. Across three experiments, holding constant the objective time of when a particular stimulus was consumed, we find that people feel more satiated and consume less when they merely have the subjective sense of having consumed more recently.

In Experiment 1, participants were randomly assigned to three conditions and answered questions regarding their eating behavior. Participants in the *Long Ago* and *Not Long Ago* conditions were asked to indicate when they last had anything to eat by drawing an arrow on a scale. In order to manipulate the subjective feeling of when participants last ate, the scale anchors differed by condition. For the *Long Ago* condition, the right end of the scale was anchored with "Now" and the left side was anchored with "One Day Ago". For the *Not Long Ago* condition, the right end of the scale was anchored with "Now" and the left side was anchored with "One Month Ago". In both of these conditions, participants were asked to draw the arrow starting from the right side of the scale and ending in the position that reflects when they last ate. Participants in the *Control* condition were not presented with the scale. We found a significant effect of this manipulation on desire to eat and on hunger. Specifically, participants in the *Not Long Ago* condition wanted to eat significantly less and felt less hungry than those in the *Long Ago* condition and *Control* condition.

In Experiment 2, we replicate the findings from Experiment 1, demonstrate the effect for a non-food stimulus (music), and, most importantly, measure actual enjoyment following the manipulation. The experiment consisted of two parts, both administered in a single one-hour lab session. During the first part of the experiment, participants listened to a 30-second clip of a favorite song 12 times in a row. Then, 35 minutes after the completion of their listening experience, participants in the *Long Ago (Not Long Ago)* condition indicated when they last heard their favorite song on a 101- unmarked slider scale anchored with "1 Hour Ago" ("1 Week Ago") and "Now". As predicted, and consistent with Experiment 1, we found participants felt more satiated and enjoyed their favorite song substantially less when they felt like the first part of the experiment occurred more recently (*Not Long Ago* condition) as compared to either the *Control* or the *Long Ago* conditions.

Finally, to examine whether changing people's subjective perception of when they last ate influences their actual food purchase behavior, we conducted a field experiment with a local branch of the restaurant, Panera Bread (Experiment 3). Customers were intercepted prior to entering the restaurant and were asked to indicate when they last had anything to eat on a scale similar to the one used in Experiment 1. Next, participants were asked to indicate their subjective sense of when they last ate on a 9-point scale anchored with "Feels like it happened a while ago" and "Feels like it happened recently". Participants were then allowed to enter the restaurant and make their purchase decision. Most critically, we obtained itemized register receipts for each participant and were thus able to determine the amount of food purchased (in calories) and, presumably, consumed for each participant. As predicted, the participants in the *Not Long Ago* condition purchased food with lower caloric value than those in the *Long Ago* and *Control* conditions. Importantly, the subjective sense of when participants last ate mediated the relationship between the independent variable and the number of calories consumed.

In sum, the results of three experiments suggest that the subjective perception of when one last consumed has a significant impact on satiation. People consume less and derive less pleasure from consumption when they merely have the subjective sense of having consumed more recently.

Atypical Pasts Spur Future Consumption

EXTENDED ABSTRACT

We examine whether consumers are influenced by atypical consumption experiences and whether this biased recollection from memory influences their future consumption. Based on a substantial body of research suggesting that people tend to recall atypical events that are both memorable and unrepresentative of their class (Frederick & Kahneman 1993; Morewedge, Gilbert & Wilson 2005; Tversky & Kahneman 1973), we expect that consumers are more likely to recall extreme rather than neutral consumption instances. In particular, we predict that consumers tend to naturally recall extremely positive rather than negative product and service experiences (even in unpleasant consumption domains). We argue this is the case because (1) consumers have presumably chosen to purchase goods from certain vendor rather than another, (2) consumers often engage in motivated reasoning which leads them to confirm what

they already believe while ignoring contrary evidence supporting its alternatives or negative (Kunda 1990). Further, based on evidence showing that remembered experience (but neither on-line nor anticipated experience) directly predicts the desire to repeat the experience (Wurtz, Kruger, Scollon, & Diener 2003), we predict that the biased recollection of extremely positive consumption experiences increases consumers' willingness to pay for goods and their purchase intention. In three experiments, we demonstrate the proposed phenomenon and the mediating role of pleasantness of recalled experience. We also find evidence that motivated reasoning underlies this selective accessibility effect.

Experiment 1A investigates whether consumers naturally recall extremely positive rather than neutral or negative consumption experiences. 90 students first described an airline flight, the best airline flight or three airline flights that they took that they clearly remember, and then reported the pleasantness of the experience. We found that students who recalled any air travel experience recalled an experience as good as participants who were explicitly asked to recall the best experience, whereas both recalled a significantly better experience than participants asked to recall three airline flights. Further, we found that while the first two instances described by participants who recalled three experiences were equally pleasant, the last instance was relatively less pleasant.

Experiment 1B tests whether this biased recollection influences participants' future consumption. 106 CMU undergraduates were asked to recall either one, the best or the worst airline flight they had that they clearly remember (in a fourth condition, they didn't answer any recall question); and then indicate if they had to travel to Chicago in two weeks (1) whether they would prefer to fly or to drive and (2) what the most they would be willing to pay for a flight from Pittsburgh is. We found that participants having recalled no memory, a flight, or the best flight they could remember were willing to pay more for a flight from Pittsburgh to Chicago, and exhibited a stronger preference for flying from Pittsburgh to Chicago, as compared to participants who recalled the worst flight they could remember. There were no differences, however, in WTP and preference between the three former conditions. A separate pretest indicates that air travel is a consumption domain that CMU undergraduate students consider as pleasant. Taken together, these findings of Experiment 1 suggest that consumers tend to recall extremely positive experiments in consumption domains they find pleasant, and that this biased recollection of atypical memories spurs future consumption.

The objectives of Experiment 2 are to (1) test whether consumers naturally recall extremely pleasant experiences in negative domains and (2) test whether the effect of memory recalled on future consumption is mediated by pleasantness of recalled experience. A separate pre-test indicated that cellular customer service is a consumption domain that consumers consider as unpleasant. 158 respondents were randomly assigned to either the recall any, recall worst or recall best condition, in which they described one experience, the worst experience, or the best experience they had in the last five years with the cellphone customer service department respectively. Next all participants reported the pleasantness of the experience recalled and finally indicated the likelihood that they will switch to another provider or renew with their current provider when their contract expires. We found that participants in the recall any condition recalled an experience as good as participants in the recall best condition whereas both recalled a significantly better experience than participants in the recall worst condition. Participants who recalled any experience were as likely to stick with their current provider as participants who were explicitly asked to recall the best experience, whereas both were significantly more likely to stick with their provider than participants recalling the worst customer service experience. The data also fulfilled the criteria for a mediation model, suggesting that the effect of memory recalled on the likelihood to switch vs. renew is mediated by pleasantness of the recalled experience.

Experiment 3 examines whether the observed selective accessibility effect is driven by motivated reasoning. If indeed consumers are motivated to remember extremely positive rather than neutral and negative experiences, they should only be motivated to do so when they have to repeat this experience again in the future. To test this idea, we asked 152 Pittsburgh pedestrians to complete a commercial evaluation study. Half of the participants were asked to evaluate two sets of beer commercials (*beer commercial next condition*) and the other half were asked to first evaluate one set of beer commercials and then evaluate one set of soda commercials (*soda commercial next condition*). All participants first viewed and rated the pleasantness of five beer commercials, including one pleasant, one unpleasant and three average commercials (based on pleasantness ratings obtained from a separate pretest). After evaluating the first set of beer commercials, participants were asked to recall and briefly describe one of the beer commercials they just watched. After describing the commercial, participants evaluated the second set of commercials (either beer or soda). As predicted, we found that participants in the beer commercial next condition were more likely to recall the best beer commercial from the first set rather than the worst or average commercials, as compared to participants in the soda commercial next condition.

If It Feels Right…Do It: Cultural Congruence as a Consumption Cue

EXTENDED ABSTRACT

On the 4th of July, do Americans put more food on a patriotic plate? Does a green border subtly encourage people to do more of a task? Can subtle exposure to traditional wedding photos make you more willing to buy an unrelated consumer product? In short, can cultural meanings deeply rooted in memory influence consumption when cued?

Culture is a meaning-making framework; the characteristic way humans perceive their environment (Triandis, 1972). In this sense, culture provides a blueprint or outline for how one is to behave and what one can expect of others across a variety of situations. What is culturally appropriate seems right, while what is culturally inappropriate seems off or wrong (Triandis, 2007). Because all of human life occurs within culture, and cultural knowledge is deeply rooted in memory, what feels right or wrong 'goes without saying'. While social scientists have long studied culture, the implications of this feeling of fluency, the telltale marker that culture is at work, has not yet been studied directly. Instead, researchers have either focused on describing a particular culture or on comparing and distinguishing between cultures, particularly contrasting East and West and describing the content and consequences of cultural 'syndromes' such as individualism and collectivism (for a review, Oyserman, Coon, & Kemmelmeier, 2002).

Rather than focusing on a specific culture or on specific differences between cultures, the current studies focus on the consequences of the feeling of fluency that being immersed in a culture provides. Within situations that are culturally appropriate, people from that culture can feel at ease, they know what to expect and how the situation will unfold. These feelings of ease can spill over into unrelated judgments, including, as we show here, consumer judgments. We build from two major tenants of behavioral decision

research and social cognition research: first, that preferences are constructed in the process of making a choice (Bettman, Luce, & Payne, 1998; Novemsky, Dhar, Schwarz, & Simonson, 2007) and second, that metacognitive judgment, the feelings that emerge while thinking, are a major source of constructed preferences (Schwarz & Clore, 1996; Schwarz, 2004). These prior studies have focused on feelings of ease or difficulty that come to mind in the process of choosing or judging. For example, they show that difficult to read print font (Song & Schwarz, 2008b) or being required to give many examples (as reviewed by Schwarz, 2004) both cue feelings of difficulty that spill over into the judgment task. Building on this prior work, in three studies we provide evidence that subtle cultural cues influence consumption such that cues congruent with deeply-rooted cultural memory "feel right," create a sense of fluency, and encourage more consumption while culturally-incongruent cues "feel wrong," create a sense of disfluency, and discourage consumption.

In our first set of studies, we had participants complete an anagram descrambling task that was framed in either a red, green, or black (control) border. After completing a series of the puzzles, participants were asked how much they would like to continue playing the game. We hypothesized that the colors green and red, well-established cultural cues for going and stopping, respectively, would wield a subtle influence on the decision to do more puzzles or not. As predicted, participants in the green condition were significantly more likely to want to do more puzzles, while those in the red condition were less likely to want to do more puzzles compared to the control group. To assess the generalizability of this initial finding, we developed a second study in which participants in a virtual restaurant buffet were asked to choose food to put on their plate and to indicate the serving size of each food they desired. Participants were randomly assigned to a green- or red-bordered plate. As predicted, participants with the green-bordered plate put significantly more food on their plate (with respect to serving size) compared to participants with the red-bordered plate.

In our second set of studies, we wanted to demonstrate that the effect of cultural congruence was not limited only to color. For this study, we conducted two separate experiments at picnics providing participants with plates decorated in holiday-congruent or holiday-incongruent themes. The experiments took place on the 4th of July and Labor Day, two patriotic American holidays. At both picnics, participants were randomly assigned into experimental (holiday-themed) and control (no-theme, white control) plate conditions. The themed plates were holiday-congruent on the 4th of July (American flag, stars and stripes) and holiday-incongruent on Labor Day (Halloween-themed pumpkins, black cats). Participants were randomly given a plate, went through the food line, and selected their food. After their selection, participants were stopped, ostensibly to chat but really to discreetly weigh their plate on a digital scale (in ounces). As predicted, cultural congruence mattered: participants put significantly more food on a holiday-congruent plate and less food on a holiday-incongruent plate compared to control.

In our third study, we wanted to demonstrate that the effects of cultural congruence could spill over from the immediate situation into an irrelevant subsequent task. The stimuli for this study consisted of wedding photographs with culturally congruent or incongruent themes. Specifically, participants were asked to rate the quality of wedding photographs for an online wedding planning site. Participants were randomly assigned to a "traditional wedding" condition – in which the photos featured a bride in a white dress, a groom in a tuxedo, a formal tiered wedding cake, and a traditional wedding party – or to a "nontraditional wedding" condition – in which the photos featured a bride in a green dress, a groom in a purple tuxedo, a wedding cake that was neither tiered nor formal, and no wedding party. Following the rating task, participants completed an ostensibly unrelated consumption task in which they decided to purchase a fleece blanket or not. As predicted, participants who rated traditional wedding photos prior to the consumption task were significantly more likely to buy the fleece than participants who rated the nontraditional photos.

In sum, across three studies we show that culture congruence influences consumption in a variety of contexts via subtle feelings of fluency/disfluency. Theoretical and managerial implications are also discussed, including applications for brand cultures.

Persuasive Advertising with Sophisticated but Impressionable Consumers

EXTENDED ABSTRACT

The goals of advertising campaigns are diverse; they vary from creating awareness for a new product to affecting repeated purchases. To achieve these goals, firms decide not only how much to advertise but also how to advertise their products. Firms may select the content of their advertisements to convey information about their product quality directly to consumers. Firms may also choose uninformative advertisements. One explanation behind uninformative advertising is to signal product quality to consumer by "burning money." The message contents of advertisements are, in that case, irrelevant and their only effect is to reveal information indirectly to consumers. However, the content of uninformative advertisements might have a direct effect on consumers in itself, through persuasion for example. A vast literature documents and uses cognitive psychology to analyze persuasion in advertising. Firms may therefore select uninformative advertising because of its direct effect on consumers through the persuasive elements of its message. This strategic decision may also convey information to consumers indirectly and signal the product quality. The focus of this paper is to address the following questions about persuasive advertising. When consumers understand how persuasion works, will persuasive advertising ever be optimal for a firm? If the answer to the previous question is yes, will persuasive advertising always be associated with high-quality products? Finally, when firms can select persuasive or informative advertising, does one type of advertising dominate the other one?

I propose a model in which consumers are uncertain about the quality of a product sold by a monopolist. At the time of purchase, consumers do not know the exact product quality but try to assess it using their beliefs about quality. These beliefs could be, for instance, the recollections that consumers have of the product, which are generated by all past interactions between consumers and the product, including past personal experiences, word-of-mouth, official consumer reports, and of course advertisements. Some consumers having positive recollections and some consumers having negative recollections generate different beliefs about quality. The likelihood of having a positive recollection is an increasing function of quality thus recollections reveal some information about product quality. Furthermore, the firm may engage in persuasive advertising to increase the number of positive recollections. Specifically, in this paper, persuasive advertising is assumed to change the distribution of prior beliefs that consumers have about product quality. After being exposed to an advertisement, consumers might be more likely to remember the positive aspects of their last experience with the product than they would have remembered without the advertisement. In addition, consumers are sophisticated as they are fully aware that the firm can choose to engage in persuasive advertising, which increases the likelihood of positive recollections. They know whether they have seen persuasive advertisements and that they might be affected by them. However, they do not know if a positive recollection is the consequence of persuasive advertising or true experience as, of course, they do not know the recollection they would have had without persuasive advertising.

This paper shows that consumers cannot fully undo the effects of advertising, and engaging in persuasive advertising might be optimal even with sophisticated consumers. In addition, I show that persuasive advertising is not necessarily a signal of high quality. Under some market conditions, the fact that consumers fully understand the effects of advertising allows firms to signal a high quality by choosing a high price and by not engaging in advertising. If a firm chooses not to engage in persuasive advertising, consumers with positive signals know that their signals come only from the intrinsic product quality and were not artificially improved by a marketing campaign. As consumers with negative signals do not buy, the product quality has to be high enough to generate substantial positive signals and make choosing a high price profitable. As a result, choosing a high price and not engaging in advertising can help signal a high-quality product.

Depending on market conditions and the degree of advertising persuasion, persuasive advertising can signal an intermediate-quality range, a high-quality range, or even a low-quality range. Similarly, persuasive advertising is not naturally associated with high prices. Two factors drive the relationship between persuasive advertising and prices. First, firms use both price and advertising to signal their quality. Therefore, when advertising does not signal high quality, it is not associated with high prices. Second, keeping everything else constant, exposure to persuasive advertising lowers the expectation of product quality, which reflects the consumers' willingness to pay. Indeed, a positive signal with persuasive advertising does not carry as much good news as a positive signal without persuasive advertising. The latter signal was generated only through the intrinsic product quality while the former could be spurious and could have been negative without persuasive advertising.

Finally, I introduce informative advertising to study how firms use different types of advertising strategically. Informative advertising is based on a claim that is a hard/verifiable piece of information about the product. The monopolist chooses now between persuasive advertising, informative advertising, or no advertising. I show that the option of engaging in persuasive advertising might block the full unraveling of information in equilibrium. Some firms, instead of releasing some information in informative advertisements, choose persuasive advertising. Moreover, high-quality products are not always promoted with the same type of advertising. Specifically, persuasive advertising could signal a higher or lower quality product than a product promoted with informative advertising.

REFERENCES

Bettman, James, Mary Frances Luce and John Payne (1998), "Constructive Consumer Dhoice Processes," *Journal of Consumer Research*, 25, 187–217.

Coombs, Clyde H. and George S. Avrunin (1977), " Single-Peaked Functions and the Theory of Preference," *Psychological Review*, 84 (2), 216-30.

Fredrickson Fredrickson, Barbara L& Daniel Kahneman (1993), "Duration neglect in retrospective evaluations of affective episodes," *Journal of Personality and Social Psychology*, 65 (1), 45–55.

Higgs, Suzanne (2002) "Memory for Recent Eating and Its Influence on Subsequent Food Intake," *Appetite*, 39 (2), 159-66.

Higgs, Suzanne (2008) "Cognitive Influences on Food Intake: The Effects of Manipulating Memory for Recent Eating," *Physiology & behavior*, 94 (5), 734-39.

Kunda, Ziva (1990) "The Case for Motivated Reasoning," *Psychological Bulletin*, 108 (3), 480-498.

McSweeney, Frances K. and Saraantha Swindell (1999), "General-Process Theories of Motivation Revisited: The Role of Habituation," *Psychological Bulletin*, 125 (4), 437-57.

Mitchell, T. R., Thompson, L., Peterson, E., & Cronk, R. (1997), "Temporal adjustments in the evaluation of events: The 'rosy view'," *Journal of Experimental Social Psychology*, 33 (4), 421–448.

Morewedge, Carey K., Daniel T. Gilbert and Timothy D. Wilson (2005), "The Least Likely of Times: How Remembering the Past Biases Forecasts of the Future," *Psychological Science*, 16 (8), 626-630.

Nelson, Leif D. and Tom Meyvis (2008), "Interrupted Consumption: Disrupting Adaptation to Hedonic Experiences," *Journal of Marketing Research*, 45 (6), 654-64.

Novemsky, Nathan, Ravi Dhar, Norbert Schwarz and Itamar Simonson (2007), "Preference fluency in choice," *Journal of Marketing Research*, 44(3), 347-356.

O'Donohue, William T. and James H. Geer (1985) "The Habituation of Sexual Arousal," *Archives of Sexual behavior*, 14 (3), 233-46.

Oyserman, Daphna, Heather M., Coon and Markus Kemmelmeier (2002) "Rethinking Individualism and Collectivism: Evaluation of Theoretical Assumptions and Meta-analyses," *Psychological Bulletin*, 128, 3-72.

Redden, Joseph P. and Jeff Galak, "The Subjective Sense of Feeling Satiated: The Role of Metacognitions in the Construction of Satiation."

Rolls, Edmund T., Barbara J. Rolls, and Eeward A. Rowe (1983), "Sensory-Specific and Motivation-Specific Satiety for the Sight and Taste of Food and Water in Man," *Physiology & behavior*, 30 (2), 185-92.

Rozin, Paul, Sara Dow, Morris Moscovitch and Suparna Rajaram (1998), "What Causes Humans to Begin and End a Meal? A Role for Memory for What Has Been Eaten, as Evidenced by a Study of Multiple Meal Eating in Amnesic Patients," *Psychological Science*, 9 (5), 392.

Schwarz, Norbert (2004), "Meta-cognitive experiences in consumer judgment and decision making," *Journal of Consumer Psychology*, 14 (4), 332–48.

Schwarz, Norbert and Gerald L., Clore (1996), "Feelings and phenomenal experiences," In E. Tory Higgins and Arie W. Kruglanski (Eds.), *Social psychology: Handbook of basic principles* (pp. 433-465). New York: Guilford Press.

Song, Hyunjin and Norbert Schwarz (2008), "Fluency and the detection of misleading questions: Low processing fluency attenuates the Moses illusion," *Social Cognition*, 26 (6), 791-799.

Song, Hyunjin and Norbert Schwarz (2008), "If it's hard to read, it's hard to do: Processing fluency affects effort prediction and motivation," *Psychological Science*, 19, 986-988.

Sutton, R.I. (1992), "Feelings about a Disneyland visit: Photographs and reconstruction of bygone emotions," *Journal of Management Inquiry*, 1, 278–287.

Triandis, Harry.C. (2007), "Culture and psychology: A history of their relationship," In S. Kitayama and D. Cohen (Eds.), *Handbook of Cultural Psychology* (pp. 59-76).

Triandis, Harry.C. (1972), "The analysis of subjective culture," New York: Wiley.

Tversky, Amos and Daniel Kahneman (1973), "Availability: A heuristic for judgment frequency and probability," *Cognitive Psychology*, 5 (2), 207–232.

Wurtz, Derrick, Justin Kruger, Christie Napa Scollon and Ed Diener (2003), "What to do on spring break? The role of predicted, on-line, and remembered experience in future choice," *Psychological Science*, 14 (5), 520–524.

Zauberman, Gal, Rebecca K. Ratner and B. Kyu Kim (2009), "Memories as Assets: Strategic Memory Protection in Choice over Time," Journal of Consumer Research, 35 (February), 715-728.

Surprising Influences on Consumer Well-Being

Chair: Zoe Chance, Harvard Business School, USA

Paper #1: How the Meaning(s) of Happiness Impacts Choice

Cassie Mogilner, University of Pennsylvania, USA
Jennifer Aaker, Stanford University, USA
Sep Kamvar, Stanford University, USA

Paper #2: Balancing Ideal Affects In the Pursuit of Happiness

Anne Laure Sellier, New York University, USA
Gita Johar, Columbia University, USA
Jennifer Aaker, Stanford University, USA

Paper #3: Fate or Fight?

Christopher Hsee, University of Chicago, USA
Shirley Zhang, University of Chicago, USA

Paper #4: Prosperity through Philanthropy

Zoe Chance, Harvard Business School, USA
Michael I. Norton, Harvard Business School, USA

SESSION REVIEW

The four papers in this session uncover new and surprising factors that influence consumer well-being, from ironic effects of competition and resource depletion to culture- and age-specific definitions of happiness. Our first two papers break happiness down into joyful excitement and serene contentment. These authors find that although two people may report being equally happy, their experiences—and their ensuing choices—may be quite different. Paper 1 investigates the relationship between age, or future-thinking, and happiness type; Paper 2 takes a cross-cultural perspective, exploring surprising differences between what events European- and Asian-Americans should focus on if they want to be happier. Our final two papers explore the psychological consequences of resource-allocation. Paper 3 identifies ironic situations in which getting stuck with an inferior outcome leaves people more satisfied than competing for a superior one. Paper 4 finds that re-allocating one's own resources to other people can improve perceived financial well-being. The effects studied in these papers are not "known," and largely unexpected.

Audience and Level of Completeness

Since each paper in the session breaks meaningful new ground, we expect to generate significant interest. We expect the symposium to connect a broad ACR audience including researchers interested in happiness, economics, aging, cross-cultural comparisons, prosocial behavior, and decision making. All four papers are completed or close to completion.

Session Plan

Our goal for the session is to spark high-level thinking about the psychological drivers and marketing outcomes of consumer well-being. We plan to do this by (1) giving presenters sufficient time to clearly present their findings, and (2) encouraging audience interaction with the presenters.

Summary

In sum, while all this research addresses the topic of consumer well-being, each paper provides unique answer to the fundamental question, "What does it mean, and what does it take, to be happy?" We believe that by integrating a discussion of psychological perspectives (Papers 1 and 2), situational variables (Paper 3), and behavioral triggers (Paper 4), we will not only appeal to a broad cross-section of ACR members, but also make important theoretical and practical contributions. By integrating the commonalities in the research questions

and interests among these papers, while highlighting their distinctive contributions, we hope to provide a springboard for future research.

How the Meaning(s) of Happiness Impacts Choice

EXTENDED ABSTRACT

Over the past decade, the concept of happiness has enjoyed much resonance among researchers across disciplines. Psychologists, economists, and political scientists have made tremendous strides in determining the best measures of happiness, ways to increase happiness, and why happiness is important (Diener and Chan 2011; Diener and Seligman 2002; Dunn, Aknin, and Norton 2008; Easterlin 2003; Healy, Malhotra, and Mo 2010; Isen and Labroo 2003; Kahneman et al. 2004, 2006; Lyubomirsky, Sheldon, and Schkade 2005; Mogilner 2010; Van Boven and Gilovich 2003).

This growing interest in happiness has also impacted business where researchers have begun to explore how to design organizations to increase employees' happiness (Hsieh 2010; Lyubomirsky, King, and Diener 2005), and how to create brands that cultivate consumers' happiness (Isen, Labroo, and Durlach 2004; Mogilner and Aaker 2009). For instance, in the face of the struggling economy, advertisers have looked to connect with consumers on a more simple and fundamental level by promising happiness. Examples are numerous: Nesquick claims, "You can't buy happiness, but you can drink it." Dunkin Donuts promoted a new breakfast sandwich as "The happiest sandwich on Earth," etc. Through particularly engaging efforts, marketers have also designed interactive campaigns to generate happiness. One example is Coca-Cola's recent "Open Happiness" campaign, which recognizes life's simple pleasures and encourages consumers to take a small break from the day to connect and share happiness with others.

Despite the growing interest in happiness, an empirical understanding of what "happiness" means is still limited. Indeed, the possibility that happiness may take on distinct forms remains largely unexplored. Even more scarce is research examining the impact of happiness on choice. Does the promise of happiness drive consumer choice? Or does it depend on what happiness means to that particular consumer?

Attempting to address these questions, we conducted three studies that show there are indeed distinct types of happiness—one more aligned with excitement; the other more aligned with peacefulness and calm. Furthermore, we show that the meaning of happiness is not stable, and we identify temporal focus (how present vs. future focused an individual is) to be one factor that influences which meaning individuals tend to adopt. Of central interest, we show how one's particular definition of happiness plays out to influence which option consumers are likely to choose.

Existing research has demonstrated the young people are chronically more focused on the future than older people (Carstensen, Isaacowitz, and Charles 1999; Mogilner, Kamvar, and Aaker 2011). In experiment 1, we influenced a sample of young adults (18-24 years old) to shift their focus to the present moment so as to test for the effect of temporal focus on individuals' definitions of happiness and choice between an exciting or calming option. The results revealed participants in the control condition to define happiness more in terms of feeling excited than feeling calm, whereas those who were led to shift their focus to the present moment defined happiness more as feeling calm than excited. Furthermore, participants' choices between non-caffeinated teas indicated as either calming (i.e., chamomile) or exciting (i.e., peppermint) reflected how they defined happiness.

The previous experiment showed that young people could be influenced to define happiness like older people by increasing their focus on the present moment. The goal of experiment 2 was to examine whether older people could be influenced to define happiness like young people by increasing their focus on the future. Thus, a sample of older participants (50-71 years old) was first presented with a sentence unscramble priming task that exposed them to either future-focused words or neutral words. We then manipulated the extent to which participants felt excited and calm and measured how happy they felt. Specifically, participants were made to feel excited or calm by listening to either an exciting or calming version of the song, "Such Great Heights," and they rated how happy they felt while listening to each song. Participants listened to both songs, the order of which was counterbalanced between participants. The results revealed that those in the control condition felt happier when feeling calm than when feeling peaceful, whereas those in the future-focused condition felt happier when they felt excited than when they felt calm. Participants were then asked to choose which song they'd like to receive an MP3 of, and their choice of MP3 reflected their associated levels of happiness. These results imply that our finding young adults to define happiness in terms of excitement (rather than calm) in experiment 1 may be the result of their tendency to think about the future. Therefore, older adults who are influenced to shift their focus away from the present and towards the future are more likely to experience a "young" form of happiness and to choose products accordingly.

In the final experiment we relied on age to determine participants' temporal focus, and we used the same procedures as in the previous experiment. The results revealed that younger adults felt happier when they felt excited than when they felt peaceful, whereas older adults felt happier when they felt peaceful than when they felt excited. Furthermore, participants' experiences of happiness mediated their decisions between receiving an MP3 of the calming song and exciting song.

Together, these findings show that the meaning of happiness can shift both moment-to-moment and over the life course, and that one's definition of happiness predictably impacts choice.

Balancing Ideal Affects In the Pursuit of Happiness

EXTENDED ABSTRACT

The ability to understand how people can durably increase their happiness has received considerable attention in the literature (e.g., Seligman 2005). In particular, techniques such as writing about happy events were showed to have long-lasting effects on self-reported happiness.

What *type* of happy events people should focus on remains unclear. Affect Valuation Theory (Tsai 2006; Tsai et al. 2007) suggests that the desirability of different positive affect states varies across cultures. Americans seem to desire experiencing high-arousal positive (HAP) emotions (e.g., excitement), while Asians seem to prefer low-arousal positive (LAP) emotions (e.g., peacefulness). Theoretically, then, focusing on one's culturally defined ideal affect should lead to greater happiness (e.g., Lewin 1935). We question this intuition. While invariably focusing on a single type of ideal affect will positively influence happiness by moving one's actual state closer to their ideal state, it is possible that the increments in happiness will be less the longer people focus on the same ideal state, because only one

dimension of their affective spectrum is evolving (Tsai et al. 2007). For this reason, people focusing on their culturally defined ideal affect (HAP or LAP emotions) may benefit from switching their focus to the alternative ideal affect.

We tested this prediction in an experiment in which European- and Asian-Americans kept a journal of good experiences. Participants focused on either exciting good things, peaceful good things, or good things (control). We predicted that European-Americans would be happier after focusing on peaceful emotions, while Asian-Americans would be happier after focusing on exciting emotions. In addition, we predicted that the closer our participants would actually be to their culturally defined ideal affect in the beginning of the study, the more they would benefit from focusing on the alternative ideal affect.

Ninety-three European- and Asian-American students (age = 20.4 years, 71 women) participated in our study in exchange for $15. In a first session, participants reported whether they were European- or Asian-American, the extent to which they had felt a number of positive emotions (e.g., elated, enthusiastic) during the past week and indicated their current mood. All participants were then instructed to keep a journal every night for a week. Instructions for the exercise varied in that participants were asked to write about three (a) exciting things, (b) peaceful things or (c) things that went really well on that day, and why they went well. A week later, participants returned their completed journal, and reported the same measures as in the first session, and a seven-item scale assessing general life happiness (e.g., "My life could be more cheerful than it is now," "These are the best years in my life," a = .67), before being debriefed, thanked and paid.

After averaging the items measuring general life happiness, An Ethnicity x Exercise ANOVA on this index revealed a significant two-way interaction, $F(1, 87) = 5.81$, $p < .004$. Euro-Americans$_{peaceful}$ reported being happier than Euro-Americans$_{exciting}$ (M = 2.98 vs. M = 2.37 respectively, $t(87) = 2.06$, $p < .04$). Conversely, we found that Asian-Americans$_{exciting}$ were happier than Asian-Americans$_{peaceful}$ (M = 2.59 vs. M = 2.08 respectively, $t(87) = 1.97$, $p = .05$).

Focusing on participants' positive emotions and mood, a series of factor analyses revealed two recurrent factors at the end of both sessions: an HAP and an LAP emotions factor. After averaging the items for the HAP and the LAP emotions separately for each session, we computed the difference in each of these scores to create an HAP and an LAP index. An Ethnicity x Exercise ANOVA on the HAP index revealed a significant two-way interaction, $F(1, 86) = 3.56$, $p < .04$, such that Asian-Americans$_{exciting}$ reported a more positive difference in high arousal over the week, compared to Asian-Americans$_{peaceful}$ (M = 0.32 vs. M = -0.38 respectively, $t(86) = 2.21$, $p < .03$).

An Ethnicity x Exercise ANOVA using the LAP index as the dependent variable also revealed a significant two-way interaction, $F(1, 86) = 3.04$, $p = .05$, such that Euro-Americans$_{exciting}$ experienced a more positive difference in LAP emotions than Asian-Americans$_{exciting}$ (M = 0.54 vs. M = -0.21 respectively, $t(86) = 2.28$, $p < .03$), and than Euro-Americans$_{control}$ (M = -0.14, $t(86) = 2.17$, $p < .04$).

Next, we centered the high- and low arousal data at the end of the first session by transforming them into deviation scores (Aiken & West 1991). Life Happiness was regressed on high arousal, low arousal, type of happiness exercise for European-Americans and type of happiness exercise for Asian-Americans (both effects coded 1 for exciting exercise and -1 for peaceful exercise), the interaction of each type of exercise with high arousal, and the interaction of each type of exercise with low arousal. There were four significant effects: (1) an effect of high arousal, such that the greater the high arousal in the beginning of the study, the greater the eventual life happiness index, b = .55, $t(83) = 4.84$, $p < .001$. There was a negative effect of type of exercise for European-Americans, such that those who worked on the peaceful exercise had a more positive life happiness index compared to those who worked on the exciting exercise, b = -.27, t(83) = 1.97, p =.05. Third, the reverse occurred for Asian-Americans, b = .28, t(83) = 2.29, p <.03. Finally, supportive of our prediction, there was a significant interaction effect between type of exercise for European-Americans and their HAP score in the beginning of the study. It was such that the greater European-Americans' HAP score initially, the greater difference in life happiness they experienced when they did the peaceful exercise rather than the exciting exercise, b = -.45, t(83) = 2.30, p < .03.

Our findings reveal that people may have a "happiness capital" associated with each type of ideal affect they focus on as a result of their culture. As people's actual affect gets closer to their ideal affect, this capital gets exhausted, and it becomes increasingly beneficial to switch to the alternative ideal affect.

Fate or Fight?

EXTENDED ABSTRACT

This research compares people's hedonic experiences in two resource allocation systems: binding assignment and free competition. In the binding assignment system, superior and inferior resources are unequally and irrevocably assigned to different individuals so that some can enjoy the superior resource without risks of losing it whereas others can only access the inferior resource. In the free competition system, each individual can compete equally for the superior resource but the winner may lose it if he/she does not stay competitive.

We seek to make two contributions here. One is methodological: to introduce an experimental procedure that mimics the two systems and allows researchers to compare people's hedonic experiences in the two systems while holding objective outcomes constant. The other is empirical: to explore whether binding assignment can be hedonically better than free competition.

The Method

Our method consists of two between-participant conditions: fate (simulating binding assignment) and fight (simulating free competition). In the fate condition, two participants are run at a time. They are seated in isolated cubicles separated by a divider, each facing a computer. The "resources" are a video and a book. The video is pretested to be more enjoyable than the book, so the video is the superior resource and the book the inferior resource. The experiment lasts a fixed period (e.g., 8 minutes), during which only one participant can watch the video and the other cannot. Who can watch the video is randomly determined at the outset and cannot be changed. The book is available to both participants, with one copy on everyone's table. Either participant can read it at any time. Participants are not allowed to do anything else.

The fight condition is similar to the fate condition except that the participants can compete equally for the video. At the beginning of the experiment, half of the video image is displayed on one participant's screen and the complementary half on the other's. Any time during the experiment, either participant can drag more of the video image toward his/her screen (and thereby away from the other's screen) by pressing a dedicated key on the computer. If the other participant does not press his/her key in response, the first participant can watch the video fully on his/her screen without having to press the key further. If both participants press their keys simultaneously, the video will move toward the participant who presses his/her key at a faster rate. As in the fate condition, each participant also has the

book and can read it at any time. Participants report their feelings during the experiment.

Note that the method is zero-sum in terms of objective outcome, in the sense that relative to fate, fight neither increases nor decreases the duration or the image size of the video. Nevertheless, fight is not zero-sum in terms of hedonic experience. This is what we discuss next.

The main finding

We have conducted several experiments using this paradigm and the main finding is:

> The fate participants – even the disadvantaged fate participants, who cannot watch the video, are happier than the fight participants.

This finding is counter-normative. Normatively the disadvantaged fate participants are in an absolutely worse situation than the fight participants, because the former have no opportunities to watch the video and the latter do. The worst scenario for the fight participants is to stop fighting for the video and read the book instead, which is no worse than the situation of the disadvantaged fate participants. Yet they are happier.

Explanation

In the fate condition, both the advantaged and the disadvantaged members can enjoy what they have with peace of mind: The advantaged members can enjoy the video without disruptions, real or imagined. The disadvantaged members, because they have no hope of accessing the video, accept their fate, ignore the video and just enjoy the book. On the other hand, participants in the fight condition lack such peace. They are not able to enjoy the video because their rivals are competing with them; nor are they willing to enjoy the book, because the video is tantalizing them. Our finding echoes recent research showing that the opportunity to ameliorate one's state can undermine one's ability to adapt to the state (e.g., Gilbert & Ebert, 2002; Smith et al., 2009).

Boundary Conditions

The reason why even the disadvantaged fate participants were happier than fight participants is that they were able to ignore the superior resource (the video) and enjoy the inferior resource (the book). This suggests two pre-conditions for the fate-better-than-fight effects: (a) that the disadvantaged and the advantaged members are isolated from each other so that the disadvantaged members cannot easily compare with the advantaged members and thereby can ignore the video they are enjoying, and (b) that the disadvantaged members can amuse themselves with the book. These two pre-conditions in turn suggest two moderators: (a) whether comparison between the disadvantaged and advantaged fate participants is inhibited or facilitated, and (b) whether the book is available or unavailable.

Consistent with the theory, we found evidence for two moderators:

> The fate-better-than-fight effects are stronger when comparison between the members is inhibited than when it is facilitated.

> The fate-better-than-fight effects are stronger when the inferior resource (the book) is available than when it is unavailable.

General Discussion

The current research suggests that an unequal assignment system may make people happier than does a free competition system if the advantaged and the disadvantaged are segregated and the disadvantaged are given some alternative, albeit inferior, resource to enjoy.

However, the current research assumes that free competition is zero-sum in objective outcomes. Obviously, most free competition systems in the real world are not zero-sum; they may increase productivity and profit. The purpose of the current research is not to trivialize such positive outcomes, but instead to call attention to people's hedonic experiences during the process. We recommend that when assessing the overall worthiness of a system, one should consider not only the outcome produced, but also the experience evoked.

Prosperity through Philanthropy

EXTENDED ABSTRACT

Affluence is associated with luxury, wasteful consumption, and generosity. These behaviors might appear to result from an excess of resources, however scholars have noted that conspicuous consumption is high among the poor as well as the rich. A particular topic of debate among economists has been the U-shaped curve of charitable giving, that is, that the poor and the wealthy give a greater proportion of their income than does the middle class. Why do the poor give more? Part of the difference in behavior can be explained by religion, retirement status, identification with the needy, and dependence on social ties. We propose, and our experimental findings suggest, an additional explanation: the poor may give more because charity provides the psychological benefit of feeling wealthy. We propose that philanthropy may have an unintentional self-signaling effect—when we observe ourselves making charitable donations, we infer we must be prosperous. Therefore, in addition to the observed increase in happiness from charitable giving (e.g. Dunn, Aknin & Norton, 2008), givers also benefit from an increase in perceived financial well-being.

In Study 1, we documented the main effect of donations on subjective wealth. Seventy-three members of an online panel were compensated probabilistically for their participation (according to typical practice in this subject pool) with a 1/25 chance of winning a $25 Amazon.com certificate. All participants saw a picture of a very sick child from the Make-A-Child-Smile web site and read a brief biography written by the child's mother. In the Donation condition, they were asked to make a binding pledge of $5 of their $25 subject payment, so that if they were selected to receive payment, we sent a $20 certificate to the participant, and $5 to the child's family. In the Control condition, no donation was requested. All participants then responded to our Subjective Wealth Scale, comprised of statements such as "I'm well-off financially," and "Compared to the people I spend time with, I'm satisfied with my standard of living." Those who had chosen to donate reported higher subjective wealth levels (M=5.3) than those in the control condition (M=3.2). Furthermore, when we collapsed the Donation condition across both donors and non-donors, the difference remained significant ($M_{Donation}$=5.0).

There is ample evidence that recognition is a strong motivator for charitable giving, implying that when we give to charity, we are purchasing wealth and status. In the U.S., only 1% of all donations are anonymous; and when donations are publicized by tier ("Silver," "Gold," etc.), most gifts are at the lower bound of each one. We suggest that donors observe and are influenced by their own status-signaling behavior, even though the signal reveals no new information.

Gift-giving produces some of the same psychological effects as charitable donations (Dunn, Aknin & Norton, 2008), and signaling motives are strongest in romantic contexts (Griskevicius et al, 2007; Souzou & Seymour, 2005; Saad & Gill, 2003); therefore, we tested our wealth-signaling hypothesis in the domain of Valentine's day spending. Because women care more about wealth and status, men have a stronger motive to signal wealth—and this will happen during courtship, when women have incomplete information about their partners' financial status. We predicted that spending money on a Valentine would generally make givers feel wealthier, and also that this effect would be greatest among single men. We asked 99 members of an online subject pool, who had celebrated Valentine's Day with a partner, to describe their Valentine's Day, and how much money they had spent on their partner. In a conceptual replication of Study 1, we found that spending more on a Valentine was associated with increased subjective wealth (β=.22), and that this relationship was strongest for single men (β=.56). Those men had also spent the most on their Valentines ($M_{single men}$=$80 vs M_{total}=$40).

Finally, we explored the effect of increases in subjective wealth due to giving on product preferences. Although luxury and premium brands are associated with power and status, theorists (e.g. Bordieu, 1984) have proposed that lower-status groups embrace these behaviors because they want to emulate high-status groups; and in fact, many brands have increased their logo size during the current recession (e.g. Volkswagon, Polo). A recent empirical analysis (Han, Nunes, Dreze, 2010) found that branding was more conspicuous on lower-priced status goods, even within the same brand. We therefore tested the hypothesis that giving money, by increasing donors' perceptions of wealth and power, would decrease their need for status-signaling premium-branded products.

Two hundred ninety-one undergraduate students completed this laboratory study. Each received a sealed envelope containing $1 and was randomly assigned to one of three conditions: Give (select a DonorsChoose classroom project, and give the money to this cause), Lose (return the money to the experimenter), and Keep (pocket the money). Givers, therefore, were no wealthier than Losers, but, like the marginally better-off Keepers, had received a signal of wealth and status. Following this manipulation, all participants completed the Subjective Wealth Scale, and finally, they made a series of hypothetical product choices among 20 pairs of similar products. These products were items that participants in the study (i.e. young, unemployed, and living in a dorm) might purchase regularly. We gathered price information and photos of various pharmacy and grocery store products from drugstore.com and peapod.com, matching one store brand and one premium product in each category (e.g. StopNShop Kapop! vs Orville Redenbacher's microwave popcorn). Replicating Studies 1 and 2, Givers felt wealthier than Losers (3.9 vs 3.3), in fact, as wealthy as the Keepers (3.8). Consistent with previous literature, Losers reported stronger preferences for higher-priced branded products than Keepers did (50% vs 42%), despite feeling poorer. And consistent with our hypothesis, Givers' product preferences aligned with Keepers (only 39% premium brand choices) rather than Losers.

In sum, our current research shows that while decreasing objective wealth, giving money away can increase subjective wealth. We have gathered evidence in support of our self-signaling hypothesis, that we interpret charitable donations as signals of wealth and power, even when the donations are our own.

Servicescapes: Spaces of Representation and Dispute in Ethnic Consumer Identity Construction

Chairs: Ela Veresiu, Witten/Herdecke University, Germany
Luca M. Visconti, ESCP Europe, France
Markus Giesler, York University, Canada

Paper #1: Ethnic Entrepreneurship: Creating an Identity-Enhancing Assemblage of Public and Private Servicescapes in the Global City

Ela Veresiu, Witten/Herdecke University, Germany
Markus Giesler, York University, Canada

Paper #2: How Marketplace Performances Produce Interdependent Status Games and Reconfigurations of Identity Resources: The Case of Rural Migrant Service Workers

Tuba Üstüner, Colorado State University, USA
Craig Thompson,, USA

Paper #3: Culturally and Linguistically Appropriated Servicescapes: The Making of Ethnicity in the Context of Healthcare Services

Luca M. Visconti, ESCP Europe, France
Federica de Cordova, Università degli studi di Verona, Italy

SESSION OVERVIEW

Careful attention to time-space intersections is a fundamental feature of consumer research (Arnould and Thompson 2005; Peñaloza, Toulouse and Visconti forthcoming). The relevance of physical space is particularly striking when considering the powerful role of commercial spaces in shaping (and constraining) consumer identity projects (e.g., Borghini et al. 2009, Maclaran and Brown 2005). Over the past decade servicescapes (Booms and Bitner 1981)—the role of physical surroundings in consumption settings—has become an increasingly important area of consumer research. Among others, Borghini et al. (2009) have recently documented the identity enhancing and empowering potential of themed commercial spaces on retail consumers.

Studies investigating the role of the marketplace in ethnic consumer identity construction, however, have clearly prioritized *time* over *space* (Askegaard, Arnould, and Kjeldgaard 2005; Oswald 1999; Peñaloza 1994; Üstüner and Holt 2007). To date space has been mostly objectified in terms of the crystallized notions of *country of origin* and *country of destination* (Visconti 2010). This constitutes a paradoxical omission since migration should structurally stimulate reflexivity upon the movement between and within spaces. Consequently, the spaces in which migrant consumers operate require much more theoretical attention than has currently been devoted.

What happens when ethnic migrant consumers, commonly portrayed as inherently disempowered relative to the cultural majority, interact with various servicescapes both as providers and consumers of services? The goal of this session is to investigate the role of commercial and non-commercial, private and public servicescapes in the making and negotiating of ethnicity. Collectively, the three completed empirical studies demonstrate that the servicescape is not ideologically neutral nor is it epiphenomenal to the construction, contestation, and sharing of ethnic structures. Additionally, the authors show that the migrants' access, utility, and experience in consuming and producing services are highly affected by various servicescape structures.

In detail, Veresiu and Giesler first highlight the role of global cities' public and private servicescapes in enabling partial and inconsistent identity-enhancing tactics for ethnic migrant consumers,

which they define as ethnic entrepreneurship. Next, Üstüner and Thompson cast a new theoretical light on the institutional shaping of servicescape relationships by investigating the role of commercial space in mediating sociocultural differences between urban customers and migrant, rural laborers. Finally, Visconti and de Cordova document the strategic role of space in public services. Relying upon the theoretical pillars of cultural psychology, they display four forms of servicescapes in the sphere of healthcare.

Overall, this session should appeal to a broad audience, including scholars (and managers) in the field of acculturation studies, service marketing, experience management, and space/place attachment. We anticipate our discussant Lisa Peñaloza will encourage audience participation and provide important directions for future research, drawing from her pioneering studies on consumer acculturation and the contemporary marketplace. Consistent with the ACR 2011 theme, this session builds bridges on four levels: (1) contributions stem from various theoretical domains, including consumer research, cultural psychology, sociology, and anthropology; (2) the separate research streams of servicescapes and migrant identity construction are brought together; (3) the ambits of public and private servicescapes are contrasted; and, (4) managerial practices and academic reflections are conceptually integrated.

Ethnic Entrepreneurship: Creating an Identity-Enhancing Assemblage of Public and Private Servicescapes in the Global City

EXTENDED ABSTRACT

Consumer acculturation—the adaptation to an unfamiliar consumer cultural environment by ethnic minorities—is of great and growing interest to consumer researchers (Askegaard, Arnould, and Kjeldgaard 2005; Oswald 1999; Peñaloza 1994; Üstüner and Holt 2007). Previous studies have documented migrant consumers' negotiation of competing identity positions and cultural value systems in both North American and non-North American contexts. While this work is groundbreaking, it has devoted surprisingly little theoretical attention to the strategic role of market-mediated physical space in ethnic consumer identity construction. How do migrant consumers leverage their surroundings in order to construct their identities? What is the role of spaces in allowing migrant consumers to acquire agency?

To interrogate these important yet equally under researched questions, we focus on a well-defined commercial space: the servicescape. Booms and Bitner (1981) developed the concept in order to emphasize the impact of the physical environment in which the service process unfolds. Over the years, consumer research has expanded the theoretical boundaries of servicescapes by investigating retail atmospherics, themed environments, brandscapes, cybermarketscapes, retroscapes, as well as public-, private- and gendered-servicescapes (e.g., Brown and Sherry 2003; Sherry 1998; Visconti et al. 2010). Yet it is surprising to find that the role of ethnicity in servicescape structures has remained largely unexplored.

In this paper, we bring these two disparate research streams together by means of a detailed ethnographic investigation of migrant individuals of Roma ethnicity in a particular space, the global city. Sociologist Saskia Sassen (2006) has argued that global cities play a profound role in enabling migrant consumers to create a tenuous visibility and establish a meaningful presence. We build upon her theoretical insights by investigating the role of public and private servicescapes on migrant consumer identity construction. More specifically, we develop the construct of ethnic entrepreneurship as an underrepresented mode of producerly-consumption through which an array of servicescapes found in global cities is transformed into an assemblage of deliberative relationships and resources allowing migrant individuals to leverage their ethnicity and expand their economic and social possibilities.

To illustrate ethnic entrepreneurship, we conducted a multi-sited ethnographic and netnographic (Kozinets 2002) investigation of Roma individuals in Toronto, Berlin and Pisa. The study intentionally spans three cities for the purpose of interpretive triangulation. Couched in participant observation and historical research, 70 in-depth, semi-structured interviews were completed with Roma individuals, local citizens and city officials. Roma informants were solicited through non-profit organizations and personal recommendations. During our conversations with the Roma, everyday living activities were discussed (e.g., housing, working, education, healthcare, food, clothing, and entertainment). In order to better understand the overall sociocultural and political environment of the respective cities, we also interviewed national citizens, which were solicited from anti-Roma websites and online discussion forums, as well as public officials across the social services, immigration, child welfare, education, and public shelter sectors. The data set was completed in the winter of 2010 and subsequently analyzed using a hermeneutical approach (Thompson 1997).

Our findings reveal how ethnic identity construction is mediated through the global city's public and private servicescapes. For example, we found that our informants strategically use and creatively combine all available servicescapes in the global city's network in order to reinforce their identity and the core values of their ethnicity. All of the Roma informants demonstrated an extraordinary capacity to develop and utilize personal networks not only in their narratives, but also by attempting to recruit us (in the role of researchers) to translate documents, to assist in employment search, to recommend new hospitals for long-term care, etc. We discuss these findings in detail and compare the limitations of servicescapes in a small town (Pisa) versus a global city (Toronto).

The contributions of this research are threefold. First, it advances consumer acculturation research by exploring the lucrative role of a particular space, global city servicescapes, in ethnic consumer identity construction. Second, it contributes to the research on servicescapes by analyzing the relationship between ethnicity and both public and private servicescapes. Third, this study contributes to the sociology of globalized spaces literature by interrogating ethnic entrepreneurship as the migrant consumer's contribution to reinforcing and advancing the global city theoretical construct.

How Marketplace Performances Produce Interdependent Status Games and Reconfigurations of Identity Resources: The Case of Rural Migrant Service Workers

EXTENDED ABSTRACT

This study investigates how socio-cultural differences between consumers and service workers are mediated by the institutionalized power relationships and asymmetrical interdependencies that operate in a servicescape context. These socio-cultural dimensions of servicescape interactions and institutional identities have fallen in a theo-retical blind spot that exists between the respective analytic orientations of the service relationship (Arnould 2005; Berry 2002; Vargo and Lusch 2008) and sociology of servicework paradigms (Hochschild 1983, 2003; Sherman 2007). This oversight is particularly glaring because, in the global service economy, these occupations are increasingly being filled by workers matriculating from deeply impoverished rural areas (Sassen 2006). Indeed, one of the most significant trends impacting global economic development is a massive population shift from rural to metropolitan areas (Meng 2005). Numerous studies of developing economies have documented that rural inhabitants have considerably less access to educational resources and, a higher proportion of households headed by individuals with little or no formal education, than their socio-economic counterparts in urban areas (Ferreira and Walton 2006).

These socio-economic shifts also create a structural mismatch between the socio-cultural backgrounds these service workers bring to the urban glamour zones and the aptitudes needed to effectively perform aesthetic labor (Witz, Warhurst, and Nickson 2003). Although many forms of service work fall on the low end of the income and occupational status scales, they are by no means a province for unskilled or deskilled workers. Many of these service jobs are highly interactive, requiring specific forms of cultural knowledge, practical skill, and interpersonal acumen that generate symbolic and aesthetic value for a metropolitan and well-educated clientele.

Our analysis highlights the commercially-mediated power relations that create a new class of aesthetic laborers and also bind customers' and workers' identities in a network of asymmetrical interdependencies known as figurations (Elias 1978). Our research context is the hairdressing industry in metropolitan regions of Turkey. Much like their North American and European counterparts, Turkish hair salons tend to foster long-term relationships between hairdressers and customers. These relationships also represent an intersection between the rural, socio-economic periphery of the globalizing economy and its consumer-oriented socio-economic center points (Sassen 2006).

To gain insights into the relational dynamics of this servicescape context, we interviewed 9 hair salon-owners, 11 staff at varying stages in their careers, and 11 middle or upper-middle class women who patronize such salons. The interviews were conducted in Turkish and ranged from 1 ½ hour to 2 ½ hours in length. All interviews were audio recorded and transcribed verbatim (and translated into English). Each interview began with general questions about the participants' background, personal interests and life goals, and then proceeded with queries about their specific experiences as salon workers or customers. In keeping with the conversation with a purpose of depth interviewing (McCracken 1988), participants largely set the flow of the interview, with the first author asking follow-up questions and probing for more descriptive details. In making sense of the interview data, we used an iterative, part-to-whole process of hermeneutic analysis (Thompson 1997). Initially, we first independently analyzed the entire set of transcripts and formed provisional understandings of emergent thematic commonalities.

Our analysis reveals that these servicescape figurations play out through an intricate system of interpersonal strategies and alliances. Salon owners become the de facto enforcers of customers' institutionalized authority through their actions in creating an appropriate salon aesthetic and socially conditioning (through sometimes heavy handed methods) their employees in the prevailing middle class norms. Owing to the fact that the salon is, indeed, a path for attaining economic and cultural resources, rural migrant and urban underclass men accept these modes of governance and internalize them as forms of self-improvement and in turn gradually become distanced from their rural or squatter social networks and cultural heritages. As these men build their professional reputations as hairdressers, they also begin to believe, and not without some practical justification, that they can wield subtle forms of influence over their middle class clientele. For customers and hairdressers, the structural realities of class stratification, become less relevant to their interactions than their respective perceptions of who is being placed in a position of greater dependency over the course of the relationship.

Accordingly, customers and hairdressers' servicescape interactions are oriented toward managing and recalibrating the asymmetrical interdependencies which bind them together. In many cases, these relational practices are conventional aspects of the servicescape script. These standardized conventions enable customers to experience their class-based advantages as self-evident entitlements which can go without saying and that need no justification. For example, customers' expectations of empathy and indeed anticipatory emotional responsiveness become one of the de facto means through which they implement their class privileges over hairdressers and other salon workers.

In contradistinction to the repressive portrayals of emotional (and aesthetic) labor advanced by the sociology of servicework paradigm, we show that hairdressers (and their young apprentices) view servicescape figurations as an empowering means to pursue their own consumer-oriented identity projects, rather than as an alienating disciplinary regime. Seen in this light, the Turkish hairdressers are strategically deploying the cultural and economic resources gained through their subordinated position in these servicescape figurations to circumvent other pressing socio-cultural limits on their consumer identities.

Our analysis also brings into sharper relief how confluences of class and gender positions are manifested and negotiated in the institutional positions, interaction norms, and shifting power relations of a servicescape. On the hairdressers' side, their reconfigured identity positions demonstrate that patriarchal advantages are not equally distributed across class strata (or even geographic region as social actors move from rural to urban settings). As these working class/squatter men seek to gain higher class standing by entering the metropolitan hairdressing profession, they also abdicate some traditional forms of patriarchal authority. In effect, they are trading a subcultural species of gender capital, having currency in a socio-economically marginalized social sphere, for forms of capital (e.g., economic, social, and cultural) (Bourdieu 1990; Holt 1998) which provide more utility in metropolitan and middle class status systems.

Culturally and Linguistically Appropriated Servicescapes: The Making of Ethnicity in the Context of Healthcare Services

EXTENDED ABSTRACT

"Shoppers are not anonymous, historyless individuals when they walk in the door, and stores are not monolithic spaces that affect all who enter in uniform and predictable ways (…). In the confrontation between historically situated people and socially constructed spaces, people are repeatedly reconstructed as particular people *in that place*." (Chin 1998: 612).

Since the pioneering work of Tuan (1974) and the foundation of the servicescape concept (Booms and Bitner 1981), space in the marketplace has represented a key part of our mundane experience as both shoppers and consumers. Scholars in the field have variously defined servicescape. Tighter elaborations set the boundaries of servicescape to the built-environment and the physical components of the context in which the seller and the customer interact (Booms

and Bitner 191; Bitner 1992). Within such tangible space, the service allows for sociality but the focus remains on the "language of the objects" (Bitner 1992: 62), including ambient conditions, spatial layout, and material artifacts.

Recent positions extensively interpret the servicescape, for example by highlighting its social dimension (Tombs and McColl-Kennedy 2003). More radically, Sherry (1998: 6) draws from Relph's (1976) idea that spaces may include intentions, attitudes, purposes, and experiences. Venkatesh (1998) further expands this notion to comprise the imaginary of the cyberspace. Again, Chin (1998) argues that servicescape implies also the planning and design of physical space, and thus the intentional, purposeful making of the service model as fulfilled by its spatiality.

Our research adheres to this comprehensive formulation of servicescape. In fact, our inquiry combines the tangible and the immaterial, the functional and the symbolic components of healthcare servicescapes. In particular, we focus on the ways in which migrants are transported, accompanied, served, and assisted by healthcare services in Italy. Within these services, the aim is to investigate the role of space in the representation, making, contestation, negotiation, rejection, and socialization of ethnicity. This project is grounded on the evidence that health inequalities against ethnic minorities are perpetrated (Ibrahim 2003; Rosenbaum and Montoya 2007), due to intentional and unintentional mistakes committed along the process of service design and supply.

Empirically and methodologically, our interpretations emerge from a meta-analysis (Hunter and Schmidt 2004) of the projects we have conducted, or supervised, during the last ten years in Lombardy, Italy. One of the researchers holds a Ph.D. in marketing, and has analyzed particularly the logics, intentions, and implications of the servicescape design. The other researcher has a Ph.D. in cultural psychology and has taken part to the elaboration and testing of alternative forms of servicescape for migrant patients. Data are generated from quite an extended set of methods, including ethnography, action research, observation, participant observation, researcher introspection, questionnaire collection, group discussion, short and depth interviews with patients, doctors, and medical staff in various service settings (first aid, pediatrics, psychiatry, proximity health-services, maternity wards, etc.) and contexts (within the service, at school, at home, etc.).

Our analysis shows four main forms of servicescape, which we label: i) undifferentiated; ii) assisted; iii) ad hoc, and iv) transcultural. *Undifferentiated* servicescapes put forward a biomedical approach, which assumes that the constructs of body, health, and illness are not cultural specific. The homogenizing frame of these services, which is erroneously proposed as universalism, is detectable from physical and ideological components of the servicescape: monolingual banners and flyers, Westernized space design, presence of traditional medical personnel, and willingness to treat all customers the same regardless of their ethnic/national origin. *Assisted* servicescapes acknowledge the higher barriers that ethnic patients usually have to access and properly consume the service. Here, the built-environment reveals an attempt to facilitate ethnic customers by means of multilingual communications and the presence of professional facilitators (i.e., linguistic and cultural mediators). Third, *ad hoc* servicescapes are meant to meet the exclusive and distinctive needs of ethnic patients, and thus result in the complete revision of the physical, social, and conceptual dimensions of the servicescape. Communications are often in the languages of the customers, environments are more welcoming and informal, treatments can be alternative and conscious of cultural traditions, and the service design is frequently ethno-specific (Nathan 2001). At the same time, socialization is enclavized since customers of the service are solely immigrants. Finally, *transcultural* servicescapes constitute the most sophisticated example of "medical pluralism" (Goldstein 2004). In this case, the areas of the servicescape mostly put under revision are the social and the immaterial ones. Socialization does not show ethnic divides but admits forms of social exchange receptive of cultural differences since the medical personnel here contests ethnocentric, univocal modes of relation. Also, the service design is totally reframed in order to leverage cultural commonalities across ethnicities. The built environment often presents adaptations: Psychiatric services have abandoned the semiotic separation between the physician and the patient (usually imposed by the doctor's desk) in favor of a circular display of chairs where the patient, his/her relatives, and the various members of the medical team are equally titled to generate and negotiate interpretations.

Our findings demonstrate that healthcare servicescapes not only may differently incorporate ethnic customers (the four forms aforementioned) but also—and more intriguingly—contribute to eternize or contest ethnic structures. According to the physical, social, and ideological traits of the servicescape, ethnicity acquires completely different valences, ranging from transparency (undifferentiated services) to inconvenience (assisted services), and from otherness (ad hoc services) to open confrontation (transcultural services). As Proshanksy (1978: 150 quoted in Rosenbaum and Montoya 2007: 208) contends, "there is no physical setting that is not also a social, cultural, and psychological setting", and—we argue—also a political and ideological one.

REFERENCES

Arnould, Eric (2005), "Animating the Big Middle*," Journal of Retailing*, 81 (2), 89-96.

Arnould, Eric J. and Craig Thompson (2005), "Consumer Culture Theory (CCT): Twenty Years of Research," *Journal of Consumer Research*, 31: 868-82.

Askegaard, Søren, Eric J. Arnould, and Dannie Kjeldgaard (2005), "Postassimilationist Ethnic Consumer Research: Qualifications and Extensions," *Journal of Consumer Research*, 32 (June): 160-70.

Berry, Leonard L. (2002), "Relationship Marketing of Services— Perspectives from 1983 to 2000," *Journal of Relationship Marketing*, 1 (1), 59-78.

Bitner, Mary Jo (1992), "Servicescapes: The Impact of Physical Surroundings on Customers and Employees," *Journal of Marketing,* 56 (April): 57-71.

Booms, Bernard H., and Mary J. Bitner (1981), "Marketing Services by Managing the Environment," *Cornell Hotel and Restaurant Administration Quarterly*, 23 (May): 35-9.

Borghini, Stefania, Nina Diamond, Robert V. Kozinets, Mary Ann McGrath, Albert Muñiz Jr., and John F. Sherry Jr. (2009), "Why are Themed Brandstores so Powerful? Retail Brand Ideology at *American Girl Place," Journal of Retailing,* 85 (3), 363-75.

Bourdieu, Pierre (1990), *Language and Symbolic Power*, ed. John B. Thompson, Cambridge, MA; Harvard University Press.

Brown, Stephen and John F. Sherry Jr. (2003), *Time, Space, and the Market: Retroscapes Rising*, New York: M. E. Sharpe.

Chin, Elizabeth (1998), "Social Inequality and the Context of Consumption. Local Groceries and Downtown Stores," in *Servicescapes: The Concept of Space in Contemporary Markets*, ed. John F. Sherry Jr., Chicago, IL: NTC Business Books, 591-617.

Elias, Norbert (1978), *What is Sociology?*, New York: Columbia University Press.

Ferreira, Francisco H. G, and Michael Walton (2006), *World development report 2006: equity and development*, Washington: The World Bank.

Goldstein, Michael S. (2004), "The Persistence and Resurgence of Medical Pluralism," *Journal of Health Politics, Policy and Law*, 29 (4-5): 925-45.

Hochschild, Arlie Russell (1983), *The Managed Heart: Commercialization of Human Feeling*, Berkeley, CA: University of California Press.

--- (2003), *The Commercialization of Intimate Life*, Berkeley, CA: University of California Press.

Holt, Douglas B. (1998), "Does Cultural Capital Structure American Consumption?," *Journal of Consumer Research*, 25 (1), 1-25.

Hunter, John E., and Frank L. Schmidt (2004), *Methods of Meta-Analysis: Correcting Error and Bias in Research Findings*, Thousand Oaks, CA: Sage.

Ibrahim, Said A. (2003), "Eliminating Health Inequalities," *American Journal of Public Health*, 93 (10): 1618.

Kozinets, Robert V. (2002), "The Field Behind the Screen: Using Netnography for Marketing Research in Online Communities," Journal of Marketing Research, 39 (1), 61-73.

Maclaran, Pauline and Stephen Brown (2005), "The Center Cannot Hold: Consuming the Utopian Marketplace," *Journal of Consumer Research*, 32 (2), 311-23.

McCracken, Grant (1988), *The Long Interview*, Newbury Park: Sage Publications.

Meng, Erika (2004), "Global Economy, in Global Trends Influencing CIMMYT's Future," In *Global Trends Influencing CIMMYT's Future,* eds. The Global Trends Task Force in Support of Strategic Planning at CIMMYT (International Maize and Wheat Improvement Center). Mexico City, Mexico: CIMMYT, 18-21.

Nathan, Tobie (2001), *Les Empêcheurs pas Seuls au Monde*, Paris: Le Seuil.

Oswald, Laura R. (1999), "Cultural Swapping: Consumption and the Ethnogenesis of Middle-class Haitian Immigrants," *Journal of Consumer Research*, 25 (March): 303-18.

Peñaloza, Lisa (1994), "Atraversando Frontieras/Border Crossing: A Critical Ethnographic Exploration of the Consumer Acculturation of Mexican Immigrants," *Journal of Consumer Research*, 21 (1): 32-54.

Peñaloza, Lisa, Nil Toulouse, and Luca M. Visconti (ed.), *Marketing Management: A Cultural Perspective*, London: Routledge, forthcoming.

Proshanksy, Harold M. (1978), "The City and Self-identity," *Environmental Behavior*, 10 (2): 147–69.

Relph, Edward, (1976), *Place and Placelessness*, London: Pion Ltd.

Rosenbaum, Mark S., and Detra Y. Montoya (2007), "Am I Welcome Here? Exploring How Ethnic Consumers Assess Their Place Identity," *Journal of Business Research*, 60: 206-14.

Sassen, Saskia (2006), *Territory, Authority, Rights: From Medieval to Global Assemblages*, Princeton, NJ: Princeton University Press.

Sherman, Rachel. 2007. *Class acts: Service and inequality in luxury hotels.* Berkeley: University of California Press.

Sherry, John F., Jr. (1998) (ed.), *Servicescapes*, Chicago, IL: NTC Business Books.

Thompson, Craig J. (1997) "Interpreting Consumers: A Hermeneutical Framework for Deriving Marketing Insights from the Texts of Consumers' Consumption Stories," *Journal of Marketing Research*, 24 (4), 438-455.

Tombs, Alastair, and Janet R. McColl-Kennedy (2003), "Social-servicecape Conceptual Model," *Marketing Theory*, 3 (4): 447–75.

Tuan, Yi-Fu (1977), *Space and Place: the Perspective of Experience*, London: University of Minnesota Press.

Üstüner, Tuba and Douglas B. Holt (2007), "Dominated Consumer Acculturation: The Social Construction of Poor Migrant Women's Identity Projects in a Turkish Squatter," *Journal of Consumer Research*, 34:1, 41-56.

Vargo, Stephen L. and Robert F. Lusch (2004), "Evolving to a New Dominant Logic for Marketing," *Journal of Marketing*, 68 (1), 1–17.

Venkatesh, Alladi (1998), "Cyberculture: Consumers and Cybermarketscapes," in *Servicescapes: The Concept of Space in Contemporary Markets*, ed. John F. Sherry Jr., Chicago, IL: NTC Business Books, 343-75.

Visconti, Luca M. (2010), "Cityscapes and Migration: Encapsulating Acculturation in the Urban Collective Space," in Advances in Consumer Research Volume 38, eds. Darren W. Dahl, Gita V. Johar, and Stijn M.J. van Osselaer, Duluth, MN: Association for Consumer Research, forthcoming.

Visconti, Luca M., John F. Sherry Jr., Stefania Borghini and Laurel Anderson (2010), "Street Art, Sweet Art? Reclaiming the "Public" in Public Place," *Journal of Consumer Research,* 37 (October), 511-529.

Witz, Anne, Chris Warhurst, and Dennis Nickson (2003), "The Labour of Aesthetics and the Aesthetics of Organization," *Organization*, 10 (1), 33-54.

Consumption Begins with the Eyes:
Building Connections between Vision and Consumption

Session Chair: Ann Kronrod, MIT, USA

Paper #1: Where Do You Draw the Line? Perceptual and Mental Boundaries

Spike Lee, University of Michigan, USA
Norbert Schwarz, University of Michigan, USA

Paper #2: Look at Me Now: Automatic Change Detection as a Moderator of Processing Fluency

Stewart A. Shapiro, University of Delaware, USA
Jesper Nielsen, University of Arizona, USA

Paper #3: The Glance Effect in Decision Making

Ann Kronrod, MIT, USA
Joshua Ackerman, MIT, USA

Paper #4: The Road to Fantasized Consumption is Paved with Visual Roadblocks

Heather Barry Kappes, New York University, USA
Adam Alter, New York University, USA

SESSION OVERVIEW

Objective and general orientation: The session encourages the motto for ACR2011 conference, "building connections", highlighting the multiple connections between vision and thought. Exploring the effects of what we see on what and how we think, four papers manipulate visual experiences and examine diverse outcomes at different stages of mental processing. Lee and Schwarz demonstrate that visual lines serve as mental boundaries, affect basic categorization, and have downstream consequences for social cognition. Shapiro and Nielsen are interested in the effect of a changing visual object (e.g. a moving logo) on processing fluency, resulting in higher effectiveness of the ad. Kronrod and Ackerman examine the effect of giving a glance at a familiar object on decisions made about that object. Finally, Kappes and Alter investigate the influence of visual disfluency (difficulty in perceiving written information) on fantasies about various consumption experiences.

Likely Audience and issues to be covered: The session highlights the impact of visual stimuli common in daily life (lines, familiar objects, moving logos, fussy fonts) on different stages of thought, from basic categorization and attitude formation to decision-making and fantasized consumption. We expect it to attract a diverse audience, whose fields of interest range from visual perception to grounded cognition, categorization, attitudes, fluency, decision making, fantasy and mental simulation.

Rationale and contribution to consumer research: Whether watching TV at home, browsing through the internet or scanning through products lined up on a store shelf, consumers are engaged in a process where what they see affects what they think. This session digs deeper into the effects of visual stimuli on thought, by asking questions about more advanced stages of thought, such as fantasy, albeit without neglecting the processes that lay at the base of those effects, such as categorization.

The chair will open the session with a brief overview of the tight connection between the papers and highlight the gradual thematic progression of the session from paper 1 to paper 4. Since the session is about visual effects, part of the stimuli used in the papers presented will be displayed in the room for higher vividness and involvement of the audience.

Where Do You Draw the Line?
Perceptual and Mental Boundaries

EXTENDED ABSTRACT

Concepts are organized together if they share taxonomic membership (e.g., carrot and eggplant) or thematic relationship (e.g., rabbit and carrot; Markman & Hutchinson, 1984). Both are based on concept features. But can *irrelevant* features bias categorization? In everyday parlance, "drawing a line" is used as a metaphoric expression for marking a boundary. We test whether increasing the accessibility of graphical lines is sufficient to activate the metaphoric meaning of mental boundary. Study 1 addresses basic categorization effects and subsequent studies explore downstream consequences for thinking about others (Study 2), oneself (Study 3), and one's past and present (Study 4). In all studies, students were approached on campus for voluntary participation. Questionnaires were printed on horizontally-oriented, letter-size paper.

Study 1: Taxonomic-Thematic Categorization

In two allegedly unrelated projects, participants first estimated lengths of four lines, one at the middle of each page. The lines were either horizontal ($n = 66$) or vertical ($n = 67$). Next, participants were given a triad of concepts and asked to "circle the two that are most closely related." The triad was carefully positioned with (a) the top concept above and the bottom concepts below where the horizontal lines appeared earlier and (b) the top concept right through and the bottom concepts on different sides of where the vertical lines appeared earlier.

The central concept (carrot) could be categorized taxonomically with one concept (eggplant-carrot) or thematically with another (rabbit-carrot); the latter two could not be categorized together (eggplant-rabbit). If visual lines activate mental boundaries, participants should "draw a line" between concepts on different sides. Concepts on the same side should be more likely to be categorized together; concepts crossing the mental boundary should be less likely to be categorized together.

As predicted, the two bottom concepts (eggplant and carrot) were more likely to be categorized together after seeing horizontal than vertical lines (54 vs. 26), but the top and bottom-right concepts (rabbit and carrot) were more likely to be categorized together after seeing vertical than horizontal lines (41 vs. 12), $\chi^2(1, N = 133) = 25.66, p < .001$. Apparently, visual lines steered basic categorization.

Study 2: Social Perception

Does the line effect extend to social perception? Participants listed features or traits of students in different schools. Six underlined spaces appeared on the left under the label "LAW", six on the right under "BUSINESS." The number of listed features that were different between law and business was divided by the total number of features, yielding the percentage score as dependent variable. There was a 5-inch vertical line between the two lists ($n = 21$), a 5-inch horizontal line above both lists ($n = 26$), or no line at all ($n = 23$).

As expected, participants listed more different features between law and business students if there was a line between the two lists ($M = 79\%$, $SD = 22\%$) than if the line was above them ($M = 64\%$, $SD = 26\%$; $t(67) = 2.01, p = .05$) or if there was no line at all ($M = 64\%$, SD

= 28%; $t(67) = 1.99$, $p = .05$). The last two conditions did not differ, $t(67) = 0.04$, $p = .97$. This pattern suggests that a visual line draws a mental boundary between two concepts only if it separates them in physical space.

An alternative account is that there is something unique about vertical lines. Mere presence of vertical lines may have activated a "categorization goal." Study 3 addressed this concern and further tested if the line effect would generalize to perception of self-other differences.

Study 3: Self-Other Perception

Participants listed features or traits of "yourself" (on the left) and "a student that can represent UM" (on the right). There were two vertical lines between the two lists ($n = 49$) or encompassing both lists ($n = 50$), or two horizontal lines encompassing both lists ($n = 44$).

Participants listed more different features between self and other if the two lists were separated by lines in the middle ($M = 78\%$, $SD = 24\%$) than if they were encompassed by two vertical lines ($M = 57\%$, $SD = 30\%$; $t(140) = 3.70$, $p < .001$) or two horizontal lines ($M = 58\%$, $SD = 29\%$; $t(140) = 3.48$, $p = .001$). The last two conditions did not differ, $t(140) = 0.10$, $p = .93$, suggesting that simply seeing vertical lines is not enough. The lines have to separate the concepts in physical space in order to separate them in mental space.

Study 4: Past and Present

On a one-page questionnaire, participants wrote down "a negative event that happened during the last two years" on the left and judged their life satisfaction on the right—"Taking all things together, how satisfied are you with your life as a whole these days?" and "How happy do you feel about how your life is going?" ($0 = not\ at\ all$, $10 = very\ much$). The two items were highly correlated ($r = .91$, $p < .001$) and averaged. A 6.5-inch line appeared either vertically between the two sides ($n = 25$) or horizontally underneath both parts ($n = 26$).

Participants were more satisfied with their life if there was a line between their past event and present judgment ($M = 8.00$, $SD = 1.31$) than if the line appeared underneath both parts ($M = 7.06$, $SD = 1.80$), $t(49) = 2.13$, $p = .04$.

Conclusions

Visual lines serve as perceptual inputs to cue categorization. It produces downstream consequences for subsequent categorization (Study 1), thoughts about social others (Study 2), oneself (Study 3), and one's past and present (Study 4). These findings combine insights from embodiment and metaphor perspectives to show how lines carve up perceptual and mental space. Follow-up work is testing how incidental exposure to carefully oriented lines may instantiate category boundaries (Bless & Schwarz, in press). Process issues and potential moderators (or as the professional jargon goes, "boundary" conditions) will be discussed.

REFERENCES

Bless, H., & Schwarz, N. (2010). Mental construal and the emergence of assimilation and contrast effects: The inclusion/exclusion model. In M.P. Zanna (Ed,), *Advances in Experimental Social Psychology, 42*, 319-373.

Markman, E. M., & Hutchinson, J. E. (1984). Children's sensitivity to constraints on word meaning: Taxonomic versus thematic relations. *Cognitive Psychology, 16*, 1–27.

Look at Me Now: Automatic Change Detection as a Moderator of Processing Fluency

EXTENDED ABSTRACT

Scholars have assembled an impressive body of work demonstrating how stimulus characteristics can direct attentive processing from one area of the visual field to another. Within advertising, researchers have demonstrated how specifics of ad design can direct attentive processing to important elements within a visual display (e.g. brand logos within an ad or ads within a newspaper or website), thus increasing the ad's effectiveness. Among factors known to attractive attentive processing, primarily through abrupt onsets that disrupt the visual field (Treisman 1986; Treisman and Gormican 1988), are size, contrast, and color. More recent research has demonstrated that shifts in attentive processing from one ad element to another can be initiated via preattentive processing. For example, Nielsen, Shapiro, and Mason (2010) demonstrated that preattentive processing can detect the emotionality of non-focal ad elements, and due to the sensitive nature of emotional stimuli, such detection subsequently directs attentive processing to the emotional stimulus.

The current research further examines how preattentive, or automatic, processing may affect the allocation of processing resources in ways that improve ad effectiveness through increased processing fluency. Specifically, we build on research pertaining to change blindness and change detection and demonstrate that changes in the perceptual relationship between a target stimulus (e.g. a brand logo) and other contextual elements (other elements within the ad) can be detected automatically. As a consequence of implicitly detecting a change, greater processing resources are directed to the changing stimulus without the participant's awareness. Specifically, between exposures, we subtly change relative placement of a stimulus (e.g. brand logo) within a visual scene (e.g. an advertisement) and demonstrate that participants automatically detect these changes and unknowingly increase the processing resources allocated to the changing stimulus. This in turn facilitates the amount of processing fluency that the logo enjoys. Across three experiments we demonstrate how this increased allocation of processing resources improves ad effectiveness through the metacognitive experience of perceptual fluency (as evidenced by improved response times, higher preference for the brand, and increased likelihood of brand choice).

Experiment 1 first explores the effect of automatic change detection on advertising effectiveness by demonstrating increased valuation of brand logos whose perceptual relationship with other contextual elements within an advertisement vary between exposures. Specifically, we compare the evaluation of logos that move location within an ad (changing its perceptual relationship to other ad elements) from one ad exposure to the next to the evaluation of brand logos that remain in the same location across exposures. We further manipulate awareness of the relative location and demonstrate that, consistent with prior research into the effect of metacognitive experiences on judgments, when participants are aware of a potential influence on their judgments, the positive effect of fluency is negated.

Experiment 2 achieves three goals. First, we directly measure fluency and demonstrate that fluency, as measured by faster response times, is enhanced by changing the logo's perceptual relationship with other contextual elements between exposures. Further, we demonstrate that the increased fluency is the result of automatic detection (i.e. without intention or awareness; Crabb and Dark 2003) of the location changes of the logos which directs processing resources to the changed element (ad logo) without the participant's awareness. Further, analyses on explicit logo recognition revealed no effect of change detection on logo recognition.

Experiment 3 directly contrasts our proposed resource allocation account with the alternative account that fluency may be the result of increased neural activity generated from the changing image that, in turn, increased stimulation from exposure (Janiszewski and Meyvis 2001) I in a fully crossed forced choice experiment participants are more likely to select moving over non-moving logos and importantly, logo movement had no effect on the evaluation of the advertisement within which the logos were embedded, suggesting that the increased preference for the logos is not the result of a general stimulation account, but instead is driven by an increased evaluation of only the moving logo. Thus, these results favor the resource allocation account over an increased stimulation account.

REFERENCES

Crabb, Brian T and Veronica J. Dark (2003), "Perceptual implicit memory relies on intentional, load-sensitive processing at encoding," *Memory and Cognition*, 31(7), 997-1008.

Janiszewski, Chris and Tom Meyvis (2001), "Effects of Brand Logo Complexity, Repetition, and Spacing on Processing Fluency and Judgment," *Journal of Consumer Research*, 27 (June), 18-32.

Nielsen, Jesper H., Stewart Shapiro, and Charlotte Mason (2010), "Emotion and Semantic Onsets: Exploring Orienting Attention Responses in Advertising," *Journal of Marketing Research*, 46(7), December, 1138-1150.

Treisman, Anne (1986), "Features and Objects in Visual Processing," *Scientific American*, 255 (November), 114-25.

Treisman, Anne and Stephen Gormican (1988), "Feature Analysis in Early Vision: Evidence from Search Assymentries," *Psychological Review*, 95 (1), 15-48

The Glance Effect in Decision Making

EXTENDED ABSTRACT

People often give a short glance at an object (e.g. one's pet) when they think about it or make decisions related to it (e.g. whether to buy a new food bowl). Allegedly, when the object of a decision is familiar and well known, there is no need to look at it in order to make decisions because the relevant information already exists in the mind. Moreover, in many cases the decision about a familiar object has nothing to do with the object's looks. Thus, a glance at one's pet would not contribute information to the decision about whether it needs a new bowl. We suggest, however, that although there are no pertinent cues in the object's external appearance or spatial location, giving the object a glance while making a decision about it can influence decision making. This may occur because a glance at the object raises the accessibility of (non-visual) information about the object that is stored in the mind (e.g. Uchida, Kepecs and Mainen 2006). We expect this Glance Effect to affect a variety of metacognitive and decision processes, including the quality of the decision, depth of thought and post decisional attitudes, such as confidence in the decision and satisfaction with it. We explore the Glance Effect in three experiments, described below.

In study 1, we show the predominance of the Glance Effect phenomenon. Forty university employees were interviewed regarding their building facilities and various objects within these buildings. Notably, the questions had nothing to do with the objects' looks (e.g. "Are there many people allergic to carpet dust here?"). After each question, the experimenter asked the participants to rate on a 7-pt scale their confidence in their reply. While the participants were giving their replies, the experimenter made record of their glances and also wrote down their replies. Out of 120 replies, 101 (84%) were accompanied with a glance at the object, while 19 (16%) were not. Further, glances at objects produced higher confidence in subsequent decisions than decisions made without glancing.

In study 2, 152 participants answered a series of decision questions about familiar objects (e.g. "should cats be named after national heroes?"), with answers ranging from "definitely yes" to "definitely not" on a 7-pt. scale. Half of the sample saw a picture of the object (e.g. a cat) along with the question. Decision time and post decisional attitudes (perceived accuracy and correctness of the answers, as well as the difficulty to make a decision and confidence in the decision) were recorded for each item. . We find that a glance at a picture of the object elevates both one's confidence in the decision and perceived accuracy, and reduces perceived difficulty of making the decision, compared to the no glance condition. However, decisions with glances did not take significantly longer time than decisions without an image, implying no additional processing effort.

Study 3 addresses the effect of object familiarity on the role of the glance. We predict that glances will be more deliberative when objects are unfamiliar and thus information comes only from the image (Glimcher and Dorris 2004). In this experiment, we also make an initial measurement of decision quality. In a 2 (yes/no previous information) by 2 (yes/no image at decision stage) design, 240 participants were presented with 3 decision questions about unfamiliar objects (e.g. "Would you recommend planting *Acokanthera Schimperi* around a public playground?"). Response options ranged from "definitely yes" to "definitely no" on a 7-pt scale, with "I have no clue" as an additional option. Half of the sample received the question with a picture of the object and the other half saw no image. Also, prior to making a decision, half of the sample learned information about the object and the other half received no information prior to making the decision. For instance, participants learned that *Acokanthera Schimperi* is an extremely poisonous plant used to prepare poison arrows in Ethiopia. Data collection is ongoing. For the group who has prior knowledge when making the decision, we expect the image to enhance confidence in the decision, while not changing the decision itself. As a replication of the result in Study 1, we also expect no effect of glancing on decision time among these participants, as the Glance Effect does not require extra processing. However, for the group who has no previous information about the object, we expect decision time while viewing an image to increase due to the time it takes to learn the image. Further, we expect no significant difference in confidence between glance and no glance condition among these participants,) as the visual information they will receive by glancing at the objects is unrelated to the questions and therefore cannot help make a decision.

To conclude, glances can significantly affect metacognitive decision experiences such as confidence, post-decision attitudes, and they may improve decision quality as well. Understanding the role of visual information search in individuals' judgments and decisions, even judgments and decisions that are logically unconnected to this visual information, is thus important for future decision research and application. For example, marketers and consumers both may benefit from exposure to objects related to current decisions, as these decisions might involve greater deliberation, more positive attitudes, and less decision-making difficulty.

REFERENCES:

Glimcher, Paul W. and Dorris, Michael (2004). Neuronal Studies of Decision Making in the Visual-Saccadic System. In Gazzaniga, M S (Ed.) Cognitive Neuroscience 3rd Ed., pp. 1215-1228 . Summer-Institute-in-Cognitive-Neuroscience.

Uchida N, Kepecs A, Mainen ZF (2006). Seeing at a glance, smelling in a whiff: rapid forms of perceptual decision making. Nature Reviews: Neuroscience, 7(6), 485-491

The Road to Fantasized Consumption is Paved with Visual Roadblocks

EXTENDED ABSTRACT

The consumer decision-making process begins when potential consumers imagine themselves using a product. Robust findings indicate that people choose options that they imagine will maximize their prospects of enjoyment, reward, and happiness. Thus, positive fantasies about products or experiences are often the first step toward consumption. However, little research to date has examined when people generate such positive fantasies.

We conducted a series of studies on this topic, focusing on the effect of one prominent variable: visual processing fluency, or the metacognitive experience of ease or difficulty associated with perceiving written information (cf. Alter & Oppenheimer, 2009). Experiencing disfluency—encountering visuoperceptual or other cognitive roadblocks—leads people to think more deeply and more abstractly than does experiencing fluency (Alter et al., 2007; Alter & Oppenheimer, 2008). Accordingly, we posited that disfluency should aid in generating fantasies that depict richly imagined hypothetical scenarios which transport people out of the mundane constraints of daily life. That is, disfluency should lead people to generate fantasies that are more positive and less constrained by reality.

To test these ideas, we manipulated the fluency of descriptions of various hypothetical scenarios, and asked participants to fantasize themselves in the scenarios. In multiple studies employing different paradigms, student participants who generated fantasies about scenarios such as eating a favorite candy bar, touring a dream home, and taking a vacation reported that their fantasies were more positive when these scenarios were presented in disfluent fonts than in fluent fonts. When participants were asked to write down the contents of their fantasies, and naïve raters coded the degree to which these fantasies were constrained by reality (e.g., conceding that the dream home was presently unaffordable), participants in the disfluent prompt condition were also found to have generated fantasies that were less constrained by reality than participants in the fluent condition.

Additional studies applied these ideas outside the lab. Dieters were given a fluent or disfluent prompt to fantasize about a hypothetical future after completing a weight loss program. Fantasies were seemingly less constrained by reality in response to the disfluent prompt: Participants reported thinking that it would be easier to lose their desired amount of weight after fantasizing in this condition than in the fluent fantasy prompt condition. In a second naturalistic application, raters examined whether blogs that described fantasies differed in content depending on whether the blogs were formatted fluently or disfluently. The blog descriptions were rated by separate groups of participants for positivity and for fluency (ease of reading). The fantasies were perceived to be more positive the less fluent they were, suggesting that visual disfluency prompts positive fantasies even in daily life.

The present findings differ from a plethora of existing research showing that—with some exceptions—people evaluate fluent stimuli more positively than disfluent stimuli. However, whereas these earlier findings examine the direct relationship between fluency and evaluation, we examine how fluency affects evaluation indirectly by shaping the cognitive approach that people adopt when perceiving and processing the target stimuli. That is, fluency changes the way people process information, which in turn alters their preferences indirectly. Accordingly, disfluency not only guides judgment directly by making a product feel more appealing, instrumental, or special; it also influences evaluation indirectly by stimulating unconstrained positive consumption fantasies.

These findings have clear implications for consumer behavior, as they highlight a relatively simple way to enhance enjoyment in fantasy, and to in turn increase the likelihood that a fantasized product or experience is selected amongst others. Since consumption begins when purchasers imagine the benefits of a new acquisition, advertisements and promotional material that are somewhat visually disfluent should promote consumption by compelling richer, more enjoyable fantasies. Paradoxically, then, the same cognitive roadblocks that follow metacognitive difficulty also encourage people along the road to positive fantasies.

REFERENCES

Alter, Adam L., and Daniel M. Oppenheimer (2008), "Easy on the Mind, Easy on the Wallet: The Roles of Familiarity and Processing Fluency in Valuation Judgments," *Psychonomic Bulletin & Review,* 15 (October), 985-90.

Alter, Adam L., and Daniel M. Oppenheimer (2009), "Uniting the Tribes of Fluency to Form a Metacognitive Nation," *Personality and Social Psychology Review,* 13 (August), 219-35.

Alter, Adam L., Daniel M. Oppenheimer, Nicholas Eplcy, and Rebecca N. Eyre (2007), "Overcoming Intuition: Metacognitive Difficulty Activates Analytic Reasoning," *Journal of Experimental Psychology: General,* 136 (November), 569-76.

From the Mind to the Feet: The Influence of Shopper Activities on Unplanned Purchases
Chair: Yanliu Huang, Drexel University, USA

Paper #1: Shopping Goals and Unplanned Buying Across Cultures and Countries

George Knox, Tilburg University, The Netherlands
Daniel Corsten, Instituto de Empresa Business School, Spain
David Bell, University of Pennsylvania, USA

Paper #2: Lost Your License to Spend?: The Moderating Role of Savings on the Licensing Effect of Virtuous Shopping Basket Composition on Impulsive Spending

Didem Kurt, University of Pittsburgh, USA
Karen Stilley, Saint Vincent College, USA

Paper #3: The Effect of In-Store Travel Distance on Unplanned Purchase with Applications to Store Layout and Mobile Shopping Apps

Yanliu Huang, Drexel University, USA
Sam Hui, New York University, USA
J. Jeffrey Inman, University of Pittsburgh, USA
Jacob Suher, TNS Sorensen, USA

SESSION OVERVIEW

The fact that approximately half of shoppers' purchases are unplanned to some extent and are subject to the influence of in-store factors (Inman and Winer 1998; POPAI 1995) makes in-store marketing increasingly important. The augmented significance of in-store marketing strategies makes it critical to understand the factors encouraging unplanned purchases in the store. Despite the importance of this topic, surprisingly few marketing researchers have investigated how decisions are made in the store and the relevant factors that influence unplanned buying. Most of this research focuses on the effect of contextual factors such as the existence of store display and the hedonicity of product category (Inman, Winer, and Ferraro 2009). Regarding the influence of internal factors (i.e., customer characteristics) on unplanned purchases, prior research mainly looks at relatively *static* customer traits that are fixed across shopping trips such as gender, income level, and household size (Kollat and Willett 1967). Very little research has captured the effects exerted on unplanned purchases by relatively *dynamic* shopper activities specific to each shopping trip such as shoppers' overall shopping trip goal, distance they travel in the store, composition of their shopping basket (vice vs. virtuous), and the amount of accumulated savings from their previous purchases. Furthermore, most prior studies on the influence of customer factors on unplanned buying ignore the active role played by shoppers to plan their shopping trips in order to make better in-store decisions.

The purpose of this session is to report the findings of recent research to address the gap as discussed above. Specifically, this session adds to our understanding of the influence of dynamic customer activities on unplanned buying as well as how customers actively plan their buying behavior by engaging in high-level cognitive activities such as goal setting and health self-concept management. The three papers touch on different aspects of such activities: how culture drives goal setting to plan purchases prior to entering retail stores; how consumers' accumulated saving and shopping basket composition interplay to affect their health self-concept and their following unplanned spending; and how consumers' in-store travel distance influences unplanned buying and how to design effective marketing strategy to increase unplanned purchases via increasing shoppers' path length.

The opening paper by Knox, Corsten, and Bell relies on longitudinal survey panel data collected from the United States, China, Western Europe, and Brazil to investigate cultural drivers of shoppers' tendency to plan purchases prior to entering retail stores. They specifically look at how cultures influence consumers' "pre-shopping" mental activities such as the formation of the overall trip goal and store-specific shopping objectives to generate unplanned buying. They find that unplanned purchases are the highest in the United States where the "individualism" characterizes the culture. Furthermore, individualistic cultures seem to encourage the tendency to think abstractly about shopping goals before entering the store, which, in turn, facilitates unplanned buying in the store.

In two experiments and a grocery field study, Kurt and Stilley show that the composition of the current shopping basket (i.e., virtue vs. vice) licenses subsequent impulsive spending in the in-store shopping setting, but that this effect is moderated by accumulated savings on already purchased items. Particularly, a virtuous basket composition leads to higher subsequent impulsive spending due to increased health self-concept as compared to a vice basket composition. However, when shoppers save money on earlier purchases, the licensing effect disappears as a result of a decrease in the health self-concept premium for the virtue condition.

Finally, Huang, Hui, Inman, and Suher collect grocery shoppers' in-store trip length in a field study through Radio Frequency Identification tracking. By using an instrumental variables approach, they estimate the causal effect of in-store path length on unplanned spending and find that the elasticity of unplanned spending on in-store travel distance is around 1.44. That is, increasing path length by 10% for each shopper (an average of around 140 feet) will increase unplanned spending by about 14.4%, or $2.27 per shopper. They also conduct two sets of policy experiments to investigate the effectiveness of two shopper marketing strategies, product category relocation and location-based mobile apps, in increasing in-store travel distance and unplanned spending. Their results suggest that adding an additional "planned" category into a consumer's shopping list by strategically promoting this category makes them travel longer in the store and leads to as much as 28% increase in the overall amount spent on unplanned purchases. However, relocating product categories only has a limited effect (around 5%) on increasing unplanned buying.

This session aims at enhancing our understanding of how shoppers' dynamic activities specific to each shopping trip influence their unplanned buying in the store. The papers also demonstrate how customers actively engage in mental activities such as goal setting and self concept management both before and during their shopping trips. In addition, each paper offers its unique perspective regarding the methods we can use to study the effects of these dynamic customer activities in an in-store shopping setting. The focus of this session is part of a larger literature on consumers' pre-purchase information processing and in-store decision making. This is consistent with many ACR members' research interests.

Shopping Goals and Unplanned Buying Across Cultures and Countries

EXTENDED ABSTRACT

It is difficult to overstate the importance of "unplanned buying" to retailers as they rely on incremental purchases to implicitly take share from competitors and also to stimulate additional consumption. Unplanned buying is reportedly widespread—"Supermarkets are places of high impulse buying ... – fully 60 to 70 percent of purchases there were unplanned, grocery industry studies have shown us" (p. 171 *The Science of Shopping by* Paco Underhill)—and generated when consumers are exposed to in-store marketing activity. Unplanned buying also increases in the absence of "time pressure" (e.g., Park, Iyer, and Smith 1989), consumer and category factors (Inman, Winer, and Ferraro 2009), and consumer planning and exposure to marketing on the "path-to-purchase" before entering a retail store (Bell, Corsten, Knox 2011).

In this study, we investigate how "pre-shopping" factors—the overall trip goal, store-specific shopping objectives, and prior marketing exposures that the shopper brings to the store interact with cultural factors to generate unplanned buying at the individual shopper level. Our study, unlike most prior academic studies, relies on rich survey panel data in which the same shopper is observed taking several trips. Moreover, we utilize detailed panel data collected from shoppers in the United States, Western Europe (Germany and Spain), Asia (China), and Latin America (Brazil). Shoppers were also interviewed in the home on standard measures of propensity to favor brands (over private labels), attitudes towards shopping, and methods of information gathering.

To test our hypotheses, we estimate a series of fixed effects Poisson and Tobit models in a quasi-experimental design. Specifically, the *same* shopper in a given country is observed invoking different goals, shopping in different stores, and buying under different circumstances. Across countries, shoppers are matched to allow testing of key dimensions of the cultural differentiation framework laid out in Hofstede (2001). Following the procedure in Erdem, Swait, and Valenzuela (2006), we directly integrate the cultural factors into our models of unplanned buying. We introduce a number of measures of observed heterogeneity across shoppers (e.g., demographics) to control for differences in their overall propensity to make unplanned category purchase decisions.

We have four new substantive findings. First, among the countries considered, we find that unplanned buying is the highest in the United States and that the average extent of unplanned buying within a country varies across countries in a manner consistent with Hofstede (2001). Specifically, the average rate of unplanned buying is positively related to "Individualism" in a culture and it is negatively related to "Uncertainty Avoidance". Second, at the individual level, unplanned buying not only increases with the abstractness of the overall shopping trip goal established before the shopper enters the store (Bell, Corsten, Knox 2011) but also further increases within individualistic cultures. Using an instrumental variables approach we find that the tendency to think abstractly about shopping goals is highest in individualistic cultures, i.e., there is a level effect of culture on goal abstraction, holding income and other factors constant. Third, we identify cultural determinants of store and trip-specific shopping goals. This is important because while *any* reason for choosing a store by definition has a positive effect on store traffic, not all store choice reasons have a positive effect on unplanned buying. The tendency to visit a specific store because of proximity to *other* stores, for example, is indicative of a predetermined goal for that store and therefore leads to less unplanned buying there. Finally, we identify a number of culturally-based moderators of unplanned buying. Prior research shows, for example, that consumers react to crowding by buying more variety to assert freedom (Levav and Zhu 2009) and that they do more unplanned buying in crowded stores (Bell, Corsten, and Knox 2011). Everything else held constant, this effect is amplified in Brazil and China where consumption is argu-

ably more socially construed, i.e., where consumers use brands to signal status and to indicate group membership.

We conclude the study by identifying a number of descriptive differences in routine shopping behavior across cultures, including attitudes to the shopping process and the cost benefit trade-offs made by consumers. The rich panel data for shopping trips and comprehensive in-home interview data collected by our research partner (a global CPG firm) provides a basis for a number of conjectures we intend to explore in future work. Overall, our findings illustrate that country-level variation in a remarkably ubiquitous and routine consumer behavior, i.e., unplanned buying while grocery shopping in supermarkets, is quite well predicted by cultural differences. Since cultural factors are enduring and systemic, our findings have important implications for researchers, managers, and policy makers.

Lost Your License to Spend? The Moderating Role of Savings on the Licensing Effect of Virtuous Shopping Basket Composition on Impulsive Spending

EXTENDED ABSTRACT

According to the licensing effect (Khan and Dhar 2006), committing a prior virtuous act increases one's preference for a hedonic item (versus utilitarian) as the virtuous act enhances consumers' self-concepts and mitigates the negative self-attributions resulting from the choice of the more hedonic option. While the extant literature on the licensing effect largely focuses on the impact of consumers' previous actions and choices on their relative preference for a hedonic compared to utilitarian item of the same value, this paper examines the licensing effect of virtuous acts on shoppers' wealth management, namely impulsive spending.

Impulsive spending contradicts with the goal of not spending money unnecessarily and thus, leads to negative self-attributions (Mukhopadhyay and Johar 2009). Related research suggests that although consumers often try to avoid purchases that will cause them to exceed their mental budgets (Heath and Soll 1996), they look for ways to justify excess spending above their budgets (Cheema and Soman 2006). Consistent with this view, licensing effect on impulsive spending is expected to manifest itself during a shopping trip where consumers make a series of purchase decisions. That is, given the self-indulgent nature of impulsive purchases, consumers tend to seek reasons that can help them reduce the negative self-attributions associated with impulsive spending. In this research, we propose that the composition of the current shopping basket (i.e., virtue vs. vice) will license impulsive spending in the in-store shopping setting, but that this effect will be moderated by accumulated savings on already purchased items.

Recently, studies have shown that, in a single-shot choice setting, a price discount on a hedonic item increases purchase likelihood because the discount mitigates guilt associated with purchasing the hedonic item (Mishra and Mishra 2010; Khan and Dhar 2010). Extending this work, we contend that greater savings on prior purchases can reduce positive self-attributions associated with a virtuous shopping basket. Therefore, we propose that, in a sequential choice setting, promotional savings will attenuate the licensing effect of a virtuous shopping basket composition and that this will occur because of a reduction in the health self-concept premium associated with purchasing virtuous items.

The first study consists of two phases: (1) initial choices (i.e., planned purchases amounting $4) and (2) subsequent choice (i.e., impulsive spending). Participants, who were unaware of the second phase and endowed with $4, were asked to choose one product in each of the two categories that they were shown. Those assigned to the vice shopping basket condition chose a brand of potato chips and a brand of cookies to purchase while those in the virtuous shopping basket condition chose a brand of pretzels and a type of grapes. In all conditions, the price of the initial choices summed to $4.00, however some items were portrayed to be on sale using the following manipulation. In addition to showing participants the current price of each item, we reported the last week's price in a separate column next to the current price column. One item in the second category was noted to be on sale (with a label emphasis – *ON SALE!*) with the original price being $3.50 marked down to the sale price of $2.50 The other option within this category was sold at its regular price of $2.50. Accordingly, a participant who chose the sale item would perceive that they had saved $1.00, but total spending of all participants was actually equal to $4.00 prior to the impulsive spending task. After making their initial choices, participants were then asked to indicate their willingness to pay for Snickers bars. Consistent with the licensing effect, we find that, in the no savings condition, the virtuous shopping basket composition licenses increased impulsive spending on Snickers bars. In contrast, when participants saved money on their prior choices, the licensing effect of the virtuous basket disappears as there is no significant difference in impulsive spending between vice and virtue conditions.

The second study builds on the first study in several ways. First, we demonstrate that the licensing effect of virtuous basket composition extends to impulsive spending on a relatively *virtuous* item (Soyjoy Nutrition Bar) and that, as in Study 1, this effect does not manifest in the savings condition. Second, to better reflect the real shopping experience, we increased the number of product categories in the initial choice phase and altered the composition of the shopping baskets (e.g., 3 virtue items plus 1 vice item rather than 2 virtue items). Third, we find that virtuous basket composition leads to higher health self-concept than a vice basket composition but that savings attenuate this difference. Finally and most importantly, we show that health self-concept mediates the moderating role of savings on the effect of virtuous shopping basket composition on subsequent impulsive spending.

Furthermore, to test our thesis in a real shopping setting, we leveraged data from the field study conducted by Stilley, Inman and Wakefield (2010). In this study, 400 customers were intercepted as they entered two different grocery stores located in a southwestern city. Before they entered the store, respondents were asked to estimate how much they intended to spend in total. Since respondents kept track of their purchases in order using a hand-held scanner, we were able to measure the composition of their shopping basket and the amount of accumulated savings before they make impulsive purchases (i.e., items bought after respondents exceeded their mental budgets). We again find that lower hedonicity rating of the shopping basket is associated with higher subsequent impulsive spending only when accumulated savings are low, providing external validity for our results.

Using both simulated and real shopping data, this paper documents the moderated licensing effect of virtuous prior shopping on subsequent impulsive spending. In particular, participants who earlier purchased more utilitarian (vs. hedonic) products are later willing to spend more on impulsive purchases but only when they did not realize any savings on their prior purchases.

The Effect of In-Store Travel Distance on Unplanned Purchase with Applications to Store Layout and Mobile Shopping Apps

EXTENDED ABSTRACT

Retailers have traditionally located frequently purchased products (e.g., milk) in strategic locations that encourage shoppers to cover a longer distance in the store. In this case, consumers will be exposed to more products and in-store stimuli along the way, thus become more likely to make unplanned purchases. In addition, recent advances in location-based mobile marketing have made it possible to integrate shoppers' location with their loyalty card information and offer targeted promotions to increase distance traveled.

The effectiveness of in-store shopper marketing strategies aimed at increasing in-store travel distance is contingent on whether there is a *direct* effect of longer in-store trip distance on unplanned purchasing, and if so, the magnitude of this effect. Rather surprisingly, the academic research literature has largely been silent on this important practical issue. While Granbois (1968) and Inman, Winer and Ferraro (2009) include a metric related to trip length (e.g., number of aisles shopped) and show that it is positively correlated with the likelihood of unplanned purchases, to the best of our knowledge there has been no study that explicitly estimates the direct relationship between in-store trip length and unplanned spending. Part of the reason for this gap in research is that before the recent development of radio frequency identification (RFID) tracking, in-store trip length was difficult and costly to obtain. Further, even if in-store trip length can be measured reliably and cost-effectively, a direct interpretation of the regression coefficient of in-store path length on the amount of unplanned purchases is still misleading because in-store path length is endogenous.

The endogeneity of in-store path length is caused by omitted in-store and out-of-store variables, simultaneity/reversed causality, and measurement error. First, some omitted in-store and out-of-store variables can cause changes in both unplanned purchases and in-store path lengths. Suppose that a shopper is attracted by the display of an unplanned item and purchases that product. Then both in-store path length and the amount of unplanned purchases increase, but there is no direct causal relationship between the two, resulting in a spurious correlation. Second, since both in-store path length and the amount of unplanned purchases arc generated during the same shopping trip, it is difficult to empirically tease apart the direction of causality between them. For instance, it is possible that a shopper decides to buy an unplanned product first, then incurs the additional distance to purchase that product. Third, the difficulty of accurately measuring in-store trip length may lead to a noisy measure.

To combat the aforementioned endogeneity issues, we construct an instrumental variable based on the length of a "reference path," which is determined by the store layout, a shopper's planned purchases, and an assumption about her search strategy. Specifically, we consider two possible strategies, an infinitely forward-looking traveling-salesman strategy (TSP) or a one-step-look-ahead strategy (a "greedy" algorithm). We show that the length of this reference path is strongly correlated with the length of the actual in-store path. Importantly, since the reference path is determined *before* the shopper starts her grocery trip, this instrumental variable temporally precedes the dependent variable (amount spent on unplanned purchases).

Our field study was conducted in a medium-sized grocery store located in a northwestern U.S. city. We collected data from 300 shoppers by offering each of them a $5 store gift card as participation compensation. Each participant first completed an entrance survey. The questions therein included: (1) whether they had a shopping list today; (2) their total shopping budget; (3) whether they were shopping alone; and (4) their familiarity with the store in terms of the product locations. Finally, on a list of all product categories in the store, they checked all the products they planned to purchase during the current shopping trip. This forms the "planned" set of products for each respondent. After finishing the entrance survey, the experimenter helped participants to put on a PathTracker® belt. The RFID (Radio Frequency Identification) tag on the PathTracker® belt emits a radio frequency signal every five seconds, which is then picked up by the antennas at the perimeter of the store, allowing us to track the (x,y) coordinate of the shopper in the store at any time. We compute the total in-store path length for each shopper using their shopping path obtained from the RFID tracking. After completing their shopping trip and checking out, participants completed an exit survey in which they answered several demographic questions, including their gender, age, household size, household income, and whether they have children. The store provided the transaction history for this specific shopping trip for all of the participants. By comparing each shopper's total purchases to the planned categories stated in the entrance survey, we compute the amount of money that each shopper spent on unplanned purchases.

With our empirical data collected through the field study and having constructed a valid instrument, we estimate the causal effect of in-store path length on unplanned spending using two-stage least squares. We estimate that the elasticity of unplanned spending on in-store travel distance is around 1.44, which is 53% higher than the corresponding OLS estimate that does not account for endogeneity. To put this into perspective, for our dataset, increasing path length by 10% for each shopper (an average of around 140 feet) will increase unplanned spending by about 14.4%, or $2.27 per shopper, which is 53% higher than the (uncorrected) OLS estimate.

Having estimated the effect of in-store travel distance on unplanned purchases, we then use our econometric framework to conduct two sets of policy experiments to explore the potential effectiveness of (a) location-based mobile apps to deliver in-store targeted promotions and (b) product placement strategies in increasing unplanned purchases via increasing shoppers' path length. We find that by strategically promoting an additional product category (hence adding an additional "planned" category into a consumer's shopping list), the overall amount of unplanned purchase can be increased by as much as 28%. In contrast, we find that relocating product categories only has a limited effect (around 5%) on increasing unplanned purchases.

REFERENCES

Bell, David R., Daniel Corsten, and George Knox (2011), "From Point-of-Purchase to Path-to-Purchase: How Pre-Shopping Factors Drive Unplanned Buying," *Journal of Marketing,* 75(1), 31-45.

Erdem, Tulin, Joffre Swait, and Ana Valenzuela (2006), "Brands as signals: A cross-country validation study*," Journal of Marketing*, 70 (1), 34-49.

Hofstede, Geert (2001), *Culture's Consequences: comparing values, behaviors, institutions, and organizations across nations* (2nd ed.). Thousand Oaks, CA: SAGE Publications.

Granbois, Donald H. (1968), "Improving the Study of Customer In-Store Behavior," *Journal of Marketing*, 32 (4), 28-33.

Inman, J. Jeffrey, Russell S. Winer, and Rosellina Ferrrao (2009), "The Interplay Between Category Characteristics, Customer Characteristics and Customer Activities on In-Store Decision Making, *Journal of Marketing*, 73 (September), 19-29.

Inman, J. Jeffrey and Russell S. Winer (1998), "Where the Rubber Meets the Road: A Model of In-Store Consumer Decision-Making," *Marketing Science Institute Report* 98-122.

Kollat, David T. and Ronald P. Willett (1967), "Customer Impulse Purchasing Behavior," *Journal of Marketing Research*, 4 (May), 21–31.

Levav, Jonathan and Rui (Juliet) Zhu (2009), "Seeking Freedom Through Variety," *Journal of Consumer Research*, 36 (December), 600-10.

Park, C. Whan, Easwar S. Iyer, and Daniel C. Smith (1989), "The Effects of Situational Factors on In-Store Grocery Shopping Behavior: The Role of Store Environment and Time Available for Shopping," *Journal of Consumer Research*, 15 (4), 422–33.

Point of Purchase Advertising Institute (POPAI) (1995), *The 1995 POPAI Consumer Buying Habits Study*, Englewood, NJ: Point-of-Purchase Advertising Institute.

Cheema, Amar and Dilip Soman (2006), "Malleable Mental Accounting: The Effect of Flexibility on the Justification of Attractive Spending and Consumption Decisions," *Journal of Consumer Psychology*, 16 (1), 33-44.

Heath, Chip and Jack B. Soll (1996), "Mental Budgeting and Consumer Decisions," *Journal of Consumer Research*, 23 (June), 40-52.

Khan, Uzma and Ravi Dhar (2006), "Licensing Effect in Consumer Choice," *Journal of Marketing Research*, 43 (May), 259-266.

--- and --- (2010), "Price Framing Effects on Purchase of Hedonic and Utilitarian Bundles," *Journal of Marketing Research*, 47 (December), 1090-1099.

Mishra, Arul and Himanshu Mishra (2011), "The Influence of Price Discount versus Bonus Pack on the Preference for Virtue and Vice Foods," *Journal of Marketing Research*, 48 (February),196-206.

Stilley, Karen M., J. Jeffrey Inman, and Kirk L. Wakefield (2010), "Spending on the Fly: Mental Budgets, Promotions, and Spending Behavior," *Journal of Marketing*, 74 (May), 34-47.

Context Effects on Processing Positive and Negative Stimuli in fMRI Data
Chair: Nader Tavassoli, London Business School, UK

Paper #1: I Can Almost Taste It Now: Tracking the Neural Effects of Anticipatory Delays on Consumption

Uma Karmarker, Stanford University, USA
Hilke Plassmann, INSEAD, France
Baba Shiv, Stanford University, USA
Antonio Rangel, California Institute of Technology, USA

Paper #2: Neural Mechanisms Underlying Individual Variability in Susceptibility to Framing Effects

Vinod Venkatraman, Duke University, USA
David Smith, San Jose State University
Scott Huettel, Duke University, USA

Paper #3: Context Influences on Neural Bases of Judgments about Brand and Social Relationships

Carolyn Yoon, University of Michigan, USA
Angela H. Gutchess, Brandeis University
James R. Bettman, Duke University, USA

Paper #4: Goal-Directed Versus Habitual Responding at Different Times of Day

Gemma Calvert, Neurosense Ltd., UK
Adrian Owen, University of Western Ontario, Canada
Nader T. Tavassoli, London Business School, London, UK

SESSION OVERVIEW

In decision-making or consumption, the valence of incoming information can determine its eventual effects. Losses looming larger than gains would be the canonical example of these types of differences. While that effect is quantitative, it is also possible for information to be processed in a qualitatively different manner depending on its positive or negative nature. Thus it becomes important to ask if the mechanisms engaged by incoming information do or do not depend on its valence. The 4 papers in this session examine the processing of positive versus negative inputs in different contexts. By using functional magnetic resonance imaging, these studies provide insight into the neural as well as behavioral effects of valenced information in contexts that serve to activate different processing areas of the brain. This makes the convergent methodology especially valuable, as it allows us to compare the impact of valence and the involvement of convergent and divergent brain areas across settings.

From a methodological aspect, all 4 papers in this session rely on the fMRI technique to gain insight into underlying cognitive processes. In recent years, neuroimaging techniques such as functional magnetic resonance imaging (fMRI) have provided a unique opportunity for assessing the relationship between patterns of cortical and subcortical activation in different brain areas and different aspects of cognitive processing in healthy individuals. FMRI measures the increase in oxygenated blood flow that is tightly correlated with neural (synaptic) activity. Thus fMRI images can contrast brain activity across tasks varying on specific variables of interest, potentially revealing differences in underlying mechanisms. As such, this session also provides a forum for one of the most exciting new research methodologies in consumer research.

I Can Almost Taste It Now: Tracking the Neural Effects of Anticipatory Delays on Positive and Negative Consumption

EXTENDED ABSTRACT

The question that we address in this research is how a period of anticipation might shape the neural coding of the consumption experience. More specifically, how does the brain react to positive or negative consumption experiences that occur after a brief versus a long delay?

Several studies have suggested that in many cases the anticipation of a positive or negative consumption experience can change the value that is experienced at consumption (e.g., Loewenstein, *The Economic Journal*, 1987; Nowlis et al., *JCR*, 2004). For example, Nowlis et al. (2004) show that uncertain anticipatory periods can intensify both hedonic and aversive taste experiences.

Data from neuroscientific research presents a more complicated picture. For example, in the realm of taste, anticipation evokes its own pattern of neural activity but this can include activations of some of the same neural circuitry involved in processing rewarding experiences (O'Doherty et al., *Neuron*, 2002). Thus it is possible this reward could "carry over" to the consumption experience. In addition, a period of negative anticipation or "dread" before a known experience such as an electrical shock activates many of the same brain areas that are involved in processing physical pain (Berns et al., *Science*, 2006). However, Berns et al. (2006) also found that delays before receiving a shock did not alter the eventual experience of pain. Thus, it remains unclear how anticipation can actively change the consumption experience itself and whether this is different for experiences with different valences.

A related and unexplored issue is whether the duration of the anticipatory period prior to consumption affects the consumption experience. For instance, will increasing the duration enhance or attenuate any effects on the consumption experience? To address these questions, we examined the effects of a short or long anticipation time on a positive or negative consumption experience at the neural level using functional magnetic resonance imaging (fMRI). On any particular trial, participants received a brief cue that indicated the valence of a liquid they would receive (unpleasant salty tea or pleasant sweet juice), as well as the number of seconds they would have to wait from the onset of the cue for the liquid to arrive. This anticipation period lasted either 2 (short) or 6 (long) seconds. They were further instructed to hold the liquid in their mouths until directed to swallow, and received a neutral rinse solution at the end of every trial. Thus data was collected from 17 participants who received four trial types, comprising a 2 (negative vs. positive) by 2 (2 vs. 6s) within-subject design.

We examined the first four seconds during which participants were actually tasting the sample liquid. Our focal analysis contrasted neural activity during this taste experience when duration of the anticipatory period had been long, compared to short. Activity in affective and valuation related brain areas was stronger when the participants had only had a short time to expect the onset of the taste. Specifically activity in the bilateral insula, caudate nucleus, anterior cingulate cortex and medial prefrontal cortex were all more active when taste was preceded by a short rather than a long cue. Interestingly, the overall pattern found was similar for both pleasant and unpleasant liquids.

Advances in Consumer Research
Volume 39, ©2011

These results suggest that the emotional or value processing of taste attenuates as the duration of anticipation gets longer. Further careful analysis is required to draw conclusions from these initial results. However, one tantalizing possibility may be that since there is overlap between neural areas involved in the anticipation and experience of taste, a long anticipatory delay allows sufficient time for the brain to react to the expected pleasant or unpleasantness of the upcoming experience. Thus by the time the stimulus itself arrives, the affective neural response has habituated.

On the surface, this appears to disagree with behavioral work such as Nowlis et al. (2004.) However, it should be noted that in those experiments, participants were unaware of when they would be receiving their outcome, thus it came as a surprise. In addition, the anticipatory period was much longer. In our experiment, the durations were defined and were within a timescale that could easily be estimated by the participant. However, given this conflict, future studies need to explore whether the impact of a post-choice delay in the consumption experience is affected by whether the delay is certain or uncertain.

A main contribution of this study lies in suggesting that the length of an anticipatory delay may decrease the intensity of the experience itself. For familiar positive outcomes, this suggests that it is better not to provide consumers information about a pleasant experience too far in advance. However, for aversive experiences it may have a silver lining, allowing people to prepare for negative events.

Neural Mechanisms Underlying Individual Variability in Susceptibility to Framing Effects

EXTENDED ABSTRACT

Context often biases decision preferences. For instance, presenting the same product attribute as a positive (i.e. 75% fat-free) or a negative frame (i.e. 25% fat) has been shown to impact customer attitudes and buying preferences. While this basic "framing effect" has been well-characterized, little is known about its underlying individual variability or about its extensions across contexts.

In a large-sample fMRI experiment (N=58), participants engaged in a risky choice task that manipulated decision frames. On each trial, participants were shown a starting amount before choosing between a "sure" and "gamble" option. The sure option was framed such that the participant could keep (gain frame) or lose (loss frame) a fixed proportion of the starting amount. The gamble option did not differ according to frame and was represented by a pie chart reflecting the probability of winning the entire starting amount. On each trial, subjects either played for themselves or for a pre-selected charity of their choice. We used four fixed starting amounts ($10, $20, $30, $40) and three different probabilities of winning (25%, 50% and 75%). The expected-value relationship between the two options varied across trials.

We observed increased gambling in loss frames (Mloss = 45%) compared to gain frames (Mgain = 28%), an effect that was greater when participants played for their chosen charity compared to themselves (t(57) = 2.79, p < 0.05). We found that distinct brain regions contributed to framing decisions involving charity and self. Strikingly, individual's relative susceptibility to self and charity framing effects was correlated with activation in ventromedial prefrontal (vmPFC). This suggests that individual differences in relative decision biases for self and charity framing effects could be rooted in value computations within vmPFC.

Contextual Influences on Neural Bases for Brand and Social Relationship Judgments"

EXTENDED ABSTRACT

Consumers' relationships to brands, particularly ones they identify closely with, have many of the same qualities as interpersonal relationships (e.g., Fournier, *JCR,* 1998). Accordingly, judgments of one's relationships with brands and with people may be subserved by the same neural system. There are, however, likely to be meaningful differences as well. Yoon et al. (*JCR,* 2006) compared personality judgments of the self to those of other persons and brands, and found reliable dissociations in patterns of neural activations underlying the judgments. Comparisons of neural responses for personality judgments about brands versus persons indicated significantly greater activation in the left inferior prefrontal cortex (LIPC). In addition, they found significantly greater activations of the medial prefrontal cortex (MPFC) for person personality judgments. They further found that although personality judgments about the self relative to other persons differentially engaged the MPFC regions, this activation pattern did not extend to judgments about brands that are self-relevant compared to brands that are not self-relevant. However, these findings do not necessarily preclude the possibility that the MPFC and reward-related regions are activated during processing of brands that invoke a strong sense of the self. In order to investigate this, we conducted two fMRI studies that examined the neural bases for judgments about positive facets of relationships with brands or people who are close (rather than distant).

Study 1 was a 2 (target: person vs. brand) x 2 (closeness to self: close vs. distant) block design in which participants made judgments about their relationships with people and brands varying in closeness to the self. The behavioral session took place approximately two weeks prior to the fMRI session. It was intended to identify six names for each of the "close" and "distant" target persons as well as six names of each of the "close" and "distant" brands for each participant. Because participants differed on which brands and persons were regarded as close versus distant, the four sets of target stimuli for inclusion in the fMRI sessions were unique to each individual.

Fifteen volunteers were recruited for the behavioral session in which participants were given a list of 85 brand names and were asked to write down the first product or service name that came to mind next to each brand. They were then instructed to keep these branded products in mind as they rated them for familiarity, attitudes, and the degree to which they identified with each of them. This was followed by ratings for 90 well-known people on familiarity, attitudes, and degree of identification. Next, the participants wrote down up to 12 names of people (with both first and last names) with whom they currently had a close relationship (e.g., mother, best friend). Finally, these 'close' persons were also rated on the same three scales.

Fourteen (7 females) of the 15 volunteers completing the behavioral session participated in the fMRI session. They were selected on the basis of our being able to identify an individual-specific set of 6 close brands, 6 distant brands, 6 close persons, and 6 distant persons. Across participants, the close and distant sets of brands were rated equivalently in terms of familiarity, but varied in the extent to which the respondents identified with them. Likewise, close and distant persons were rated similarly in terms of familiarity and attitudes, but varied in the extent to which the respondents identified with them. The brands and persons were then each divided randomly into three lists for each participant in the fMRI session. Each list thus contained two targets for each of the four treatment conditions.

Participants were scanned during three functional runs while making judgments about whether or not the word appearing with the name of a person or brand described a facet of their relationship with the target. Within each block, four trials included the same one brand (or one person) and were concurrently presented with a sequence of four different relationship words. A target (e.g, close or distant brand) was presented on the screen along with a fixation cross for 500 msec. A relationship word then appeared below the fixation cross for 4500 msec, during which time the participant made the relationship judgment. Participants indicated whether or not the word described their relationship with the given brand or person by pressing the key under their index finger for 'yes', or middle finger for 'no'. They were asked to make each judgment as quickly, yet accurately, as possible. The total fMRI session lasted about 45 minutes.

Consistent with prior findings by Yoon et al. (2006), we found that MPFC was implicated in judgments for relationship with people and LIPC for relationships with brands. Moreover, the enhanced engagement of the reward-related regions to self-relevant information was found for close person relationship judgments only, as evidenced by a significant interaction of Close minus Distant Persons, in contrast to Close minus Distant Brands. However, we did not find any support for the notion that the reward-related regions are differentially engaged during judgments about relationships with close (vs. distant) brands.

The results of Study 1, in fact, suggested that our ability to detect neural responses to judgments about relationships with brands were compromised. While the activations in reward-related regions for relationship judgments about close people were robust, they completely swamped any neural signal changes for brand relationship judgments. Based on these findings, we hypothesized that neural measures are highly sensitive to context and limiting the study task to brand relationship judgments may be necessary to observe differences in neural activations in reward-related regions. This idea was tested in a follow-up study.

In study 2, 18 (9 female) individuals participated in the behavioral and fMRI sessions that closely followed the procedures in Study 1. The target stimuli however comprised only close and distant brands. As expected, study 2 results indicated enhanced activations in the MPFC as well as the OFC for close versus distant brands.

The two studies, taken together, serve to highlight the importance of accounting for the experimental context in assessing and interpreting neural findings. Theoretical and methodological implications are discussed.

Goal-Directed Versus Habitual Responding at Different Times of Day

EXTENDED ABSTRACT

Contemporary theories of instrumental learning suggest a dual-process model: a simple, though less flexible, stimulus-response system and a more cognitive goal-directed system (Dickinson & Balleine, *Animal Learning & Behavior,* 1994). The critical distinction between the two is that the goal-directed system maintains an active representation of an outcome, or goal, such that a change in the expected outcome (or a change in a person's motivational state) should change behaviour. There is accumulating evidence that the caudate nucleus plays a role in this process, whereas its sub-cortical neighbour, the putamen, sub-serves cognitive functions more limited to stimulus-response, or habit, learning (Grahn, Parkinson, & Owen, *Progress in Neurobiology,* 2008). Measures of anatomical and functional connectivity demonstrate a clear link between the caudate and regions of the frontal lobe known to be responsible for 'executive' functions that require the generation and monitoring of appropriate strategies, and evaluation of potential outcomes for successful performance (e.g., the globus pallidus acts as the hub for connections between caudate and frontal cortex; Doyon et al., *European Journal of Neuroscience,* 1996).

Of particular interest to this paper, is that caudate nucleus is highly innervated by dopamine neurons and that there is significant increase in the concentration of dopamine in the caudate nucleus during sleep (we measure and confirm this via related levels of cortisol in participants' saliva samples). We hypothesise that this should engage individuals in more goal-directed behaviour in the morning. In particular, it has been demonstrated that the caudate is highly involved in learning and memory, particularly regarding feedback processing (Packard, & Knowlton, *Annual Review of Neuroscience,* 2002). We therefore hypothesized that consumers would respond differently at different times of day to marketing messages that challenge versus reinforce established preferences for products or services.

Participants were immersed in an fMRI scanner throughout. During Stage 1, participants indicated their preferred brand (among 6) within 6 product categories (e.g., chocolate bars, yogurts, laundry detergents). Participants were exposed to all possible pairings within a category, providing a preference rank order.

During Stage 2, participants repeated the task, but first read a statement relating to one of the brands shown before choosing. The statements were based on known key drivers behind consumer choice in each category from TNS market research data. There were 4 statement types designed to either reinforce their brand preference or to reverse their revealed preference. Statement types 1 and 2, below, encourage switching, by devaluing the preferred brand relative to the alternative, whereas statement types 3 and 4 reinforce the previously preferred brand.

1. A positive statement about the previously non-preferred brand (e.g., if the preferred brand is compared to Cadbury's Dairy Milk: "Cadbury's Dairy Milk stimulates the brain's pleasure centres better than any other chocolate bar")

2. A negative statement about the previously preferred brand (e.g., if Mars was the preferred brand: "In blind taste tests, Mars is consistently rated as the lowest on flavour and richness against its key competitors").

3. A positive statement about the previously preferred brand (e.g., if Mars was the preferred brand: "Mars outsells every other chocolate bar on the market").

4. A negative statement about the previously non-preferred brand (e.g., if the preferred brand is compared to Twix: "Twix has the highest number of calories and additives of any chocolate bar").

The more participants engaged the goal-directed (habitual) system to make choices during stage 2, the more (less) sensitive they should be to information that devalues their preferred brand and the more they should reverse their choices from stage 1.

The data were then divided into AM vs. PM testing periods to find out whether consumers are more likely to switch (when prompted by an appropriate statement) in the morning or evening. The choice data showed that negative statements about a preferred brand and positive statements about a less-preferred brand significantly increased the tendency to select the previously less preferred brand to a greater degree in the morning than in the evening. The fMRI images show that these switching statements engaged goal-directed brain areas (caudate nucleus, globus pallidus and frontal cortex) more in the morning more than the evening.

In contrast, the habit system was more influential in the afternoon than in the morning. Positive statements about the preferred brand and negative statements about a less-preferred brand resulted in significantly higher preference consistency in the evening than the morning. The fMRI images show that reinforcing preferences resulted in greater activation in habit learning brain areas, such as the putamen.

The results show that the same information is processed differently based on the readiness of specific brain areas. Goal-directed brain areas were more active in the morning, resulting in a greater response to marketing communications that challenged revealed preferences. In contrast, habit forming brain areas were more active in the evening, resulting in a greater response to marketing messages that reinforced preferences. These results are similar to behavioural data that showed variety-seeking in terms of switching away from a leading brand was more common in the morning than in the afternoon (Roehm & Roehm, *Marketing Letters,* 2004). The authors speculated that variety seeking provided stimulation, and that the diurnal arousal-peak in the afternoon resulted in a lower utility for such stimulation. Our results suggest a different picture, namely that consumers are more habitual in their behaviour late in the day because of increased activity in the brains habitual learning areas versus goal-directed learning areas. As such, this finding builds on the result that older adults perform resource-demanding tasks—such as a message's argument strength—better in the morning than in the afternoon or evening (Yoon, Lee & Danziger, *Psychology & Marketing,* 2007).

New Insights Into The Endowment Effect And Loss Aversion

Chairs: Scott Rick, University of Michigan, USA
Katherine Burson, University of Michigan, USA

Paper #1: Expectations as Endowments: Evidence on Reference-Dependent Preferences from Exchange and Valuation Experiments
Keith Ericson, Harvard University, USA
Andreas Fuster, Harvard University, USA

Paper #2: The Intermediate Alternative Effect: Considering a Small Tradeoff Increases Subsequent Willingness to Make Large Tradeoffs
Gabriele Paolacci, Ca' Foscari University of Venice, Italy
Katherine Burson, University of Michigan, USA
Scott Rick, University of Michigan, USA

Paper #3: Attachment Without Possession: Resolving the WTA/WTP Disparity
Arul Mishra, University of Utah, USA
Himanshu Mishra, University of Utah, USA
Tamara Masters, University of Utah, USA

Paper #4: Cognitive Aging and Decision Making
Ye Li, Columbia University
Martine Baldassi, Columbia University
Eric Johnson, Columbia University
Elke Weber, Columbia University

SESSION OVERVIEW

The endowment effect, introduced by Thaler (1980), follows from two fundamental findings of Tversky and Kahneman (1981): (i) reference-dependent preferences that (ii) reveal loss aversion, a heightened sensitivity to losses relative to gains. Though much is now understood about reference-dependent preferences and loss aversion, many important questions remain for marketers. For example, although it is clear that preferences are often reference-dependent, it is less clear how reference points develop and change over time. Moreover, although many researchers have identified behavior consistent with loss aversion, we know little about the explanatory power of loss aversion (versus competing accounts) across contexts, and the cognitive underpinnings of loss aversion. The objective of this session is to discuss emerging research into the nature of ownership and loss.

The four papers included in this session are all in late stages of completion (one working paper and three papers in advanced rounds of review). The first two papers focus on the source and malleability of reference points, and the latter two papers focus on the explanatory power and nature of loss aversion. Ericson will begin by presenting experiments that tease apart competing explanations for reference point formation (ownership versus recent expectations). He finds that recent expectations about owned goods (e.g., expecting not to receive them) attenuates the endowment effect, suggesting that reference points are not strictly determined by actual ownership. Then Paolacci will present experiments demonstrating that the endowment effect can be reduced by forcing owners to consider trading for "intermediate alternatives." His studies reveal that participants who trade their endowment for an intermediate alternative actually shift their reference point to that intermediate. Even participants who reject a trade to an intermediate option are affected by considering it—their reference point is weakened.

Moving the focus to loss aversion, Mishra will then present experiments that physiologically manipulate perceived ownership to examine whether the endowment effect is best explained by loss aversion or by ownership-induced attachment. She argues for a more nuanced view of the underlying process—endowed participants are strongly influenced by attachment whereas non-endowed participants are influenced by reference-dependence and loss aversion. Finally, Johnson will present research demonstrating that loss aversion is neither a simple constant, nor simply a function of individuals or attributes. Using a large-scale field experiment where individual measures of loss aversion for several attributes of a product are developed, he shows that much of the variance in loss aversion can be explained by the consumer's knowledge of the attribute and the attribute's importance to the consumer.

We expect these papers will provoke productive discussions about the nature of loss aversion, ownership, and reference points. This session will appeal to a wide range of consumer behavior scholars and especially those interested in the endowment effect, loss aversion, spending behavior, behavioral economics, and decision-making.

Expectations as Endowments: Evidence on Reference-Dependent Preferences from Exchange and Valuation Experiments

EXTENDED ABSTRACT

Evidence from a variety of settings indicates that people are loss averse: they dislike losses much more than they enjoy equal-sized gains. Yet little is known about the determination of the reference points relative to which gains and losses are defined. Kahneman and Tversky's (1979) highly influential prospect theory, where loss aversion was first introduced, left the reference point imprecise. It has often been taken to be the status quo (Samuelson and Zeckhauser 1988), meaning that individuals are reluctant to give up things they currently possess. An alternative view, advocated by Kőszegi and Rabin (2006, 2007, 2009), is that reference points are determined by recent expectations about outcomes, which need not correspond to the status quo. Since the status quo often determines expectations, much existing evidence is consistent with either alternative. However, the implications of loss aversion frequently differ depending on the assumed reference points. This study provides new experimental evidence that reference points are determined, at least in part, by expectations: people appear loss averse around their expected outcomes.

We present two experiments in which we manipulate expectations separately from endowments. Our first experiment tests whether expectations affect exchange behavior. We endow all subjects with the same item (a mug), and randomize the probability that they will be allowed to exchange that item for an alternative (a pen). We find that subjects who are more likely to expect to keep their endowed item (because they have a low probability of being allowed to exchange) are more likely to choose to keep their item if given the opportunity to exchange. This finding is predicted if individuals have expectation-based reference points, but not by theories that identify the reference point with the status quo or by theories in which preferences do not depend on reference points. It suggests that the expectation of continued ownership, rather than current formal ownership per se, induces a reluctance to part with possessions (a phenomenon Thaler [1980] called the "endowment effect"). As a consequence,

Advances in Consumer Research
Volume 39, ©2011

loss aversion need not impede transactions that individuals expect to occur.

Our second experiment measures the effect of expectations on subjects' monetary valuation of an item. Subjects are not initially endowed with any item, but learn that they will receive a mug for free with either high (80%) or low (10%) probability. All subjects also know that with probability 10%, they instead have a choice between the mug and money. We elicit their mug/money choices for varying amounts of money, which gives a measure of their willingness-to-accept (WTA) for the mug. To increase the precision of our estimated treatment effect, we also elicit WTA for an unrelated item, a pen. This allows us to proxy for idiosyncratic factors that affect valuation of university merchandise. We estimate that subjects who were randomly assigned to have a high expectation of leaving with the mug value the mug about 20-30% higher than subjects who were less likely to leave with the mug, an effect that is both statistically and economically significant.

Moreover, we also conduct a variation of our second experiment to untangle whether expectations matter because people experience gains and losses with respect to a reference point, or because likely ownership of an item increases individuals' estimates of its consumption utility. According to the former theory, expectations should only affect the valuation of the mug currently in a person's reference point. The latter theory, which we refer to as "motivated taste change", instead predicts that expecting to own one mug should also increase the valuation of a second, identical mug. We do not find any evidence that motivated taste change is the source of our results: subjects' expectations of getting one mug do not affect their valuation of a second mug conditional on getting the first mug.

The Intermediate Alternative Effect: Considering a Small Tradeoff Increases Subsequent Willingness to Make Large Tradeoffs

EXTENDED ABSTRACT

Countless studies have demonstrated that ownership of a good makes decision-makers reluctant to trade that good for an alternative. This "endowment effect" (Thaler 1980) is most often interpreted as a manifestation of reference-dependent preferences that exhibit loss aversion—the tendency for losses to have greater hedonic impact than comparable gains (e.g., Tversky and Kahneman 1981). We introduce a straightforward method to reduce the common reluctance to trade an endowment for a "target alternative." We propose that the process of deciding whether or not to trade the endowment for an "intermediate alternative" (an option that possesses some characteristics of the endowment and some characteristics of the target alternative) subsequently reduces the extent to which trading for the target alternative is viewed as a loss, which in turn stimulates trading. We hypothesize that this "intermediate alternative effect" operates by weakening the extent to which one's endowment is treated as a reference point. In addition, if the intermediate is actually adopted, the reference point shifts in the direction of the target alternative.

The notion that considering (even rejecting) an intermediate alternative can weaken one's reference point is consistent with work demonstrating that individuals with extensive trading experience, such as professional sports card dealers (List 2003) and real-estate investors (Genesove and Mayer 2001), are less affected by loss aversion. Facing an opportunity to trade one's endowment for an intermediate alternative might instill a "trading mindset," reducing the extent to which one's endowment represents one's reference point (cf. Knetsch and Wong 2009). This should, in turn, make the prospect of trading one's endowment feel like less of a loss.

Moreover, when people actually trade for the intermediate alternative, their reference point should shift toward the target, which should in turn increase the attractiveness of the target. This intuition builds on prior work demonstrating that similarity between alternatives reduces the reluctance to trade (Chapman 1998). Thus, people who refuse to "leap" from their endowment to a distant target alternative might instead "walk" to it.

Study 1 tested our basic behavioral hypothesis that people who consider trading their endowment for an intermediate alternative will subsequently be more likely to trade for a distant (target) alternative than people who do not initially consider the intermediate alternative. In a hypothetical concert scenario, participants were endowed with a set of four seats in a theater and were asked whether they would trade that set for an alternative set. The endowment was a set of side-by-side seats in the back of the theater, and the "target" was a set of completely separated seats in the front row, or vice versa. In the Baseline condition, participants were asked whether they wanted to trade their endowment for the target. In the Intermediate condition, participants decided whether they wanted to trade their endowment for an intermediate alternative (a set of partially separated seats in the middle of the theater) before deciding whether they wanted to trade for the target. As predicted, participants were significantly more likely to trade for the target in the Intermediate condition than the Baseline condition (47% vs. 30%).

Study 2 used real choices and examined whether trading for the intermediate shifts one's reference point or merely weakens it. The endowment was two bags of attractive M&M's (custom-printed with the school's logo), and the target was four bags of unattractive M&M's (custom-printed with a spider picture), or vice versa. There were three conditions: Baseline, Intermediate, and Parallel. The Baseline condition was the same as in Study 1. In the Intermediate condition, participants first decided whether they wanted to trade their endowment for an intermediate alternative (one attractive bag and two unattractive bags). In the Parallel condition, participants first decided whether they wanted to trade their endowment for a "parallel" alternative that differed only slightly from the endowment (differing only in the extent to which the picture was outlined vs. filled with color). Overall, consistent with Study 1, trading was significantly greater in the Intermediate condition than the Baseline condition (47% vs. 25%), with the Parallel condition falling in between (35%). When we focused only on participants who adopted either the intermediate or the parallel alternative, we found that intermediate-adopters were significantly more likely than parallel-adopters to subsequently trade for the target (63% vs. 33%). Because adopting the parallel alternative can only weaken one's reference point, but not shift it in the direction of the target, this significant difference suggests that adopting the intermediate alternative does not merely weaken the reference point, but shifts it as well.

Study 3 provided a more sensitive test of the reference point dynamics underlying the intermediate alternative effect. It was a concert scenario similar to Study 1, and there were three conditions: Baseline, Intermediate, and No Endowment. In the Baseline condition, participants were endowed with a set of side-by-side seats that were moderately far from the stage. They were then asked to imagine that they had to move to a set of side-by-side seats in the back row (even further back than the endowed set), and were asked how satisfied they would be with those seats. In the Intermediate condition, participants were first asked whether they wanted to move to a set of partially separated seats in the middle of the theater, and were then asked how satisfied they would be with the back-row seats. In the No Endowment condition, participants were simply asked how satisfied they would be with the back-row seats. Intermediate-adopters were significantly less satisfied with the back-row seats than Baseline participants, suggesting their reference point had shifted toward the stage. Baseline participants were significantly less satisfied with the back-row seats than No Endowment participants, but there was no significant difference between intermediate-rejectors and No Endowment participants, suggesting that rejecting the intermediate weakened participants' reference point.

Taken together, the results suggest that intermediate alternatives mitigate the endowment effect. Intermediate alternatives help by weakening and, if adopted, shifting the owner's reference point. Marketers and policy makers are advised to help people walk toward the desired outcome rather than trying to force them to leap.

Attachment Without Possession: Resolving the WTA/WTP Disparity

EXTENDED ABSTRACT

The notion of what we possess becoming an extension of ourselves is acutely realized by many of us when a scratch on our car gives us immense pain. William James aptly said "between what a man calls me and what he simply calls mine the line is difficult to draw. .... A man's Self is the sum total of all that he can call his" It is intuitive to predict over-valuing what we own. We acquire things to define who we are and over time through this need to define ourselves we start perceiving what we own to be a part of us or extensions of ourselves.

An intriguing question is, how would we value an object which feels like an extension of ourselves but we don't own it. More specifically, in this work we explored if an object is made to feel like part of one's body how would it influence valuation across two conditions: 1) when one owns the object and 2) when one doesn't own it. By answering these questions, we try to disentangle the mechanism responsible for the commonly observed WTA/WTP disparity (also known as the Endowment Effect, Thaler 1980). Two main theories have been used to explain the WTA/WTP disparity. The loss aversion account suggests that selling prices tend to be higher than buying prices because people use reference points to assess any change in their current state. For a seller whose current reference point is ownership of the object, removing the object from the endowment creates a loss. Since losses are aversive, this leads to the seller demanding a higher selling price compared to a buyer for whom obtaining an object (to an endowment without it) appears like a gain (Kahneman, Knetsch, and Thaler 1991). The mere ownership account suggests that people are reluctant to relinquish the objects they own simply because they associate those goods with themselves and become attached to them (Beggan 1992). This leads sellers to demand more than what a buyer is willing to pay for an object.

However, in studies of WTA/WTP disparity these two explanations tend to be confounded. For instance, when we consider a seller he always owns the object and also loses it in a trade. So his higher WTA could be driven by ownership as well as loss aversion. To understand which factor is playing a critical role, we need to have a seller who is less attached to it and losing it in trade. On the buyers' side, in past work we have a buyer who is always not attached to the object but considers acquiring it. So to assess the role of attachment we need to compare a buyer who is not attached to an object to a buyer who is attached to the object. This has been a challenge in controlled settings, since how can one make a buyer attached to an object that he does not own and a seller who is less attached to an object he is going to lose?

To achieve this (i.e., a buyer who is attached to the object yet does not own it), we utilized neuroscience literature on the malleabil-

ity of human perception which suggests that the representation of our body is reconstructed moment to moment based on sensory information (Damasio 1994). An important element in interpreting our embodiment is vision – e.g., how we learn to recognize ourselves in a mirror (Ramachandran and Rogers-Ramachandran 2008). The sense of sight is so strong, that when visual input conflicts with cues from other senses, vision tends to dominate. This dominance has been used to relieve phantom limb pain for amputees. Ramachandran and Blakeslee (1998) placed a mirror between an amputee's missing and existing limb. Moving the existing limb by lateral inversion in the mirror made it appear as if the missing limb was moving and eased the pain. Similar visual manipulations by synchronized tapping of a rubber hand and participants' hand have resulted in participants experiencing the sensation that the rubber hand is part of their body (Ramachandran and Blakeslee 1998, Botvinick and Cohen 1998).

Across two studies, we used the tapping manipulation to give a visual illusion that a coffee mug had become a part of the participant's body. The experimenter with her right hand tapped the mug and with her left hand synchronously tapped the participant's hand which was inside a black box. Participants who reported experiencing a sensation of the mug feeling like a part of their body formed the experimental group while those reporting no feelings formed the control group. Subsequently participants were shown the same mug and randomly assigned to the role of buyers (sellers) and their WTP (WTA) was elicited.

In study 1, WTA/WTP disparity emerged across buyers and sellers in experimental and control groups. However, compared to control group sellers, the sellers in the experimental group (who felt a sensation when the mug was tapped) indicated a significantly higher selling price (WTA). However, there was no difference in buying price (WTP) for the control versus experimental group. Study 2 replicated the findings of study 1 and also found that the experimental-group sellers generated more positive attributes for the mug than control-group sellers. Buyers in both the control and experimental group generated equal number of positive and negative attributes indicating a balanced view.

The loss aversion account would not predict any change in the difference between WTA and WTP across control and experimental groups since the tapping manipulation doesn't alter buyers and sellers reference points. The ownership account would predict an increase in both WTP and WTA from control to experimental conditions as a result of the tapping manipulation (we document change in only WTA). Our pattern of results is inconsistent with both of these accounts and hints towards a more nuanced view in which possession strongly influences sellers' WTA while reference point influences buyers' WTP.

Cognitive Moderators of Loss Aversion

EXTENDED ABSTRACT

Loss aversion suggests that losses have a greater impact upon choice than the equivalent sized gain. Despite extensive use in consumer theory, we know less about the cognitive mechanisms underlying the effects, and their implications. This raises a number of questions: Are there systematic individual or attribute differences? To what extent does cognition or affect moderate these effects?

Answering these questions has both practical and theoretical importance. In this paper, we will examine potential moderators of loss aversion, with our goal being to provide a set of facts that characterize the nature of loss aversion across attributes, individuals, and their characteristics to inform future theory.

To accomplish our goal, we extend existing methods three ways: (1) We develop methods for measuring loss aversion within individuals and use those measures to assess loss aversion for several attributes. This represents a substantial new way to view loss aversion, acknowledging that it may not be a stable individual difference variable. (2) We examine how loss aversion varies across people and attributes, rather than focusing solely on variation across people. (3) We look at moderators of loss aversion, using multi-level models to tease apart these effects. Multi-level models are useful because some potential moderators are a function of relatively stable personal characteristics (like income or age) that change slowly while other potential moderators may vary across attributes such as a consumer's rating of importance.

With few exceptions, loss aversion is assessed between respondents, comparing the average price given by two groups for a single good or attribute, making it impossible to examine individual or attribute differences. To extend this prior work, we developed a method for not only assessing loss aversion between respondents, but within a respondent applied across several attributes. To accomplish this, we asked a series of questions about the size and nature of the coefficient of loss aversion for various attributes and consumer characteristics. Specifically, respondents either gave their choice or selling price for a set of 4 car attributes: Fuel Consumption (in liters per 100 km) Comfort (leather seats, power adjustment, etc.), Safety (airbags, etc.) and Information Systems (the kind of navigation systems). These were selected to vary independently on the proposed moderators, and are important to car purchasing. After almost an hour, respondents were asked the other question, to minimize influence on one set of answers to the other.

We used a survey of 360 people conducted by personal interviews by a professional market research company. All substantive experimental factors were varied within subjects. They included our main concern: A 2 (selling vs. choosing) by 4 (attribute) factorial that elicited indifference prices.

Data was analyzed by comparing three models. The first model provides a test of one simple characterization of loss aversion, that loss aversion is a constant within an individual. Our second model allows for loss aversion to be trait-specific. Finally our third model examines if the variation in loss aversion that we see is a result of specific attribute differences in loss aversion within respondent. This third model provides the best fit for the data, suggesting that merely analyzing loss aversion as a constant or on an attribute level is not as meaningful as an analysis including variation within the individual. Additional models introduce controls and potential moderators.

In addition to the models discussed above, two overall moderators of loss aversion were discovered during analysis: expertise and age. Participants who knew more about a given attribute (fuel consumption) showed less loss aversion. Younger participants also showed less loss aversion than their older counterparts.

In conclusion, we demonstrate a method for measuring loss aversion at the individual level. This method could be of use in the analysis individual and attribute differences in loss aversion in consumer behavior in other settings. Further, we have explored the nature of loss aversion in one purchase domain, one that features substantial expenditures by actual consumers. Our basic result suggests that loss aversion is widespread in this setting. In addition, there is significant heterogeneity, and loss aversion is not simply a constant, a characteristic of an attribute or an individual. This is important,

since it suggests that choice models that employ loss aversion should model this heterogeneity. Finally, we find that a substantial amount of loss aversion can be explained by the decision maker's knowledge of the attribute, the attributes' importance to the decision-maker and finally, the individual's age. This result also has implications for the application of loss aversion, suggesting who will be the most loss averse. In particular, it emphasizes the role of specific product knowledge and suggests that some individuals, particularly those who are older or less educated, may be more likely to be loss averse.

REFERENCES

Beggan, James K. (1992), "On the Social Nature of Nonsocial Perception: The Mere Ownership Effect," *Journal of Personality and Social Psychology*, 62, 229–37.

Botvinick, Matthew and Jonathan Cohen (1998), "Rubber Hands Feel Touch That Eyes See," *Nature*, 391, 756.

Chapman, Gretchen B. (1998), "Similarity and Reluctance to Trade," *Journal of Behavioral Decision Making*, 11 (1), 47-58.

Damasio, Antonio R. (1994), *Descartes' Error: Emotion, Reason, and the Human Brain*. New York: G.P.Putnam.

Genesove, David and Christopher Mayer (2001), "Loss Aversion and Seller Behavior: Evidence from the Housing Market," *Quarterly Journal of Economics*, 116 (4), 1233-60.

Kahneman, Daniel, Jack L. Knetsch, and Richard Thaler (1990), "Experimental Tests of the Endowment Effect and the Coase Theorem," *Journal of Political Economy*, 98 (December), 1325–48.

Kahneman, Daniel and Amos Tversky (1979), "Prospect Theory: An Analysis of Decision Under Risk," *Econometrica*, 47 (2), 263-91.

Knetsch, Jack L. and Wei-Kang Wong (2009), "The Endowment Effect and the Reference State: Evidence and Manipulations," *Journal of Economic Behavior and Organization*, 71 (2), 407-13.

Kőszegi, Botond and Matthew Rabin (2006), "A Model of Reference-Dependent Preferences," *Quarterly Journal of Economics*, 121 (4), 1133-66.

Kőszegi, Botond and Matthew Rabin (2007), "Reference-Dependent Risk Attitudes," *American Economic Review*, 97 (4), 1047-73.

Kőszegi, Botond and Matthew Rabin (2009), "Reference-Dependent Consumption Plans," *American Economic Review*, 99 (3), 909-36.

List, John A. (2003), "Does Market Experience Eliminate Market Anomalies?" *Quarterly Journal of Economics*, 118 (1), 41-71.

Ramachandran, Vilayanur S and Sandra Blakeslee (1998), *Phantoms in the Brain: Human Nature and the Architecture of the Mind*. Fourth Estate.

Ramachandran, Vilayanur S. and Diane Rogers-Ramachandran (2008) "Touching Illusions," *Scientific American Special Edition*, 18 (2).

Samuelson, William and Richard Zeckhauser (1988), "Status Quo Bias in Decision Making," *Journal of Risk and Uncertainty*, 1 (1), 7-59.

Thaler, Richard (1980), "Toward a Positive Theory of Consumer Choice," *Journal of Economic Behavior and Organization*, 1 (1), 39–60.

Tversky, Amos and Daniel Kahneman (1981), "The Framing of Decisions and the Psychology of Choice," *Science*, 211 (4481), 453-8.

Spending Hurts? Examining the Antecedents and Consequences of the Pain of Paying

Chair: Nicole Robitaille, University of Toronto, Canada

Paper #1: Is Paying Painful?: Neuropsychological Underpinnings of Abstract and Somatosensory Costs During Consumer Decision Making

> Hilke Plassmann, INSEAD, France
> Nina Mazar, University of Toronto, Canada
> Antonio Rangel, California Institute of Technology, USA

Paper #2: The Origin of the Pain of Paying

> Nina Mazar, University of Toronto, Canada
> Hilke Plassmann, INSEAD, France
> Nicole Robitaille, University of Toronto, Canada
> Axel Linder, University of Tübingen, Germany

Paper #3: Habitually Consistent, Contextually Inconsistent: Dispositional and Contextual Determinants of Financial Decisions

> Manoj Thomas, Cornell University, USA
> Joowon Park, Cornell University, USA

SESSION OVERVIEW

Recent research in behavioral economics has illustrated the critical role hedonics plays in an individual's consumption decisions. For example, Prelec and Loewenstein (1998) suggested that that when making purchase decisions, people experience competition between the anticipated pleasure derived from acquiring and consuming the product and the anticipated losses incurred not only from the money given up in the transaction (product price) and the hassle of executing the payment (transaction cost) but also from the *pain of paying*, the disutility derived from parting with money. It is the outcome of this hedonic competition that results in a consumer's decision of whether or not to purchase. Interestingly, however, our understanding of the pain of paying concept is still rather vague.

The objective of the current session is to provide further evidence for the existence of pain of paying and to examine both its antecedents and consequences. With three paper presentations followed by a comprehensive discussion we seek to help foster a better understanding of the of pain of paying, including what it is, how it is experienced, what is driving it, and how it influences consumers decisions.

In the first paper, Plassmann, Mazar and Rangel used neuroimaging to examine how the human brain processes different types of costs during purchase decisions. Building upon previous research, Plassmann et al. investigated whether the neural representation of costs differ between abstract costs (e.g. paying money) and somatosensory costs (e.g. tolerating electric shocks). Although they found that purchase decisions involving money and shocks were similar on a behavioral level, they found significant differences at a neural level. More specifically, the authors found that making decisions involving somatosensory costs recruited brain areas involved in pain processing, while making decisions involving monetary prices did not. Simply put, the pain of paying (i.e. paying with money) is not experienced the same as the paying with physical pain.

In the second paper in this session, Mazar and colleagues examined with behavioral experiments whether the pain of paying is experienced as a physical pain, psychological pain, or whether it is not experienced as a pain at all. In two studies, they found that making psychological pain more salient decreased consumers' willingness to pay for hedonic as well as utilitarian products, and these differences were not driven by individual's liking of the products, their mood, or their arousal levels. Making physical pain more salient did not dif-

fer from the control group. The authors are currently running a third study, which will be completed by the time of the ACR conference. This new study, which more directly manipulates participants' experience of pain of paying while purchasing (through placebo pills), examines whether making people more/less sensitive to their pain decreases/increases their willingness-to-pay.

The first two papers complement each other and together show that the pain of paying is more closely related to psychological pain than physical pain. The third paper in this session extends this work and examines the impact that individual differences in pain of paying have on consumers' financial decisions. In their paper, Thomas and Park demonstrated that people who experience greater pain of paying are more predisposed to prepay their loans. In addition, they demonstrated the *domain specificity* of pain of paying, showing that these prepayment preferences only occur when the decisions are framed in terms of monetary gains; when gains are framed as non-monetary, pain of paying no longer has an effect on individuals preference to prepay. Together the studies in this paper suggest that financial decisions are influenced by the interaction of individuals' innate sensitivity to pain of paying and the framing of decisions.

As our purchase decisions involve a hedonic trade-off between gains and losses, a clear fundamental understanding of pain of paying and its effects is important. In keeping with the conference theme "Building Connections," the three papers in this session significantly contribute to this understanding by taking a number of different methods (e.g., neuroscience methods, behavioral experiments) and approaches (e.g., priming, decision framing) to help to define what the pain of paying is, its underlying processes, and how individual differences in pain of paying influence decisions. This session focuses on a very current topic as the pain of paying plays a crucial role in individuals' overspending and undersaving. As such, we believe this session will appeal to a wide audience at ACR. We also have a discussant, Scott Rick, with great experience and knowledge in the domain of pain of paying; he has published fMRI research looking at the neural predictors of purchases (Knutson et al., 2007) and has developed a scale to measure individual differences in pain of paying (Rick et al., 2008). His comments are sure to add further insight to the presented findings and initiate a thought-provoking and constructive debate with the audience of this session. Note: The findings of all three papers have been written up, i.e. in manuscripts that are either prepared or under review.

Is Paying Painful? Neuropsychological Underpinnings of Abstract and Somatosensory Costs During Consumer Decision Making

EXTENDED ABSTRACT

A seminal account proposed for the hedonics underlying consumption decisions distinguishes between two opposing factors: rewarding factors like the pleasure derived from consumption and aversive factors like the costs of the consumption often referred to as "pain of paying" (Prelec and Loewenstein, 1998). Previous research in neuroeconomics has investigated how decision utility computations are represented in the brain (Plassmann et al., 2007) and whether these representations differ for different modalities such as primary or secondary rewards (Chib et al., 2009). However, despite its importance for consumer decision-making, little is known about how the human brain computes aversive factors during purchasing, namely the costs associated with the item for purchase. This is the central question of this paper. In particular, we investigated whether the representation of costs in the brain differ between abstract costs (e.g. paying money) or somatosensory costs (e.g. tolerating electric shocks) that are matched in economic value.

Consumer behavior theories have suggested that consumers consider abstract monetary prices as a potential loss that triggers a negative affective response that resembles the emotional or psychological components of pain processing (so-called "pain of paying", see (Prelec and Loewenstein, 1998, Rick et al., 2008). A recent neuroimaging study found that when subjects decide to buy, areas of the brain that are known to represent the sensation of physical (but not psychological) pain - the Insula – are less activated as compared to when subjects decide *not* to buy (Knutson et al., 2007). These results suggested that the act of paying does physically "hurt" when prices are perceived as too high, i.e. it triggers a physical pain sensation. However, these results were based on inverse inferences about the Insula as their study did not allow for comparing the act of paying with the experience of physical pain. Given that the Insula is a highly interconnected brain area that has also been found to be involved in various other mental processes important for consumer decision-making, the current findings are inconclusive. Our paper addresses these shortcomings and provides a direct test of the physical pain of paying hypothesis.

We investigated the neural basis of cost computations by scanning hungry subjects' brains (N=21, aged 18-35, mean 23.65 years) while making 280 purchasing decisions for liked food items. Subjects could either pay in monetary units ($0-$1.50) or in subjectively equivalent physical pain units (electric shocks). Several days before the fMRI experiment, we performed a calibration of each individual's subjective pain tolerance levels in which we matched their pain tolerance to monetary values using a BDM auction mechanism (Becker, DeGroot, and Marschak, 1964). Because of the characteristics of this auction, we can assume that in that pre-screening study individuals bid their 'true' utility for the right to avoid receiving an electric shock of different intensities (Wertenbroch and Skierra, 2002). During a second pre-scanning task, subjects underwent another BDM task, this time to sample subjects' willingness-to-pay (WTP) for the 40 different food items. The fMRI task consisted of two different, within-subject trial types: Trials in which subjects could decide to buy 40 food items at four different monetary prices ($0, $0.50, $1.00, $1.50) (= 160 '$ trials') and trials in which they could decide to buy the same 40 food items for tolerating pain (electric shock) at three different pain intensities (=120 'V trials') that were matched with the three different non-zero monetary prices.

For the behavioral data analysis of the main study, we created dummy variables for WTP and purchasing prices in money and physical pain trials and entered them into a mixed effects logistic regression analysis. The model was significant (Wald $\chi^2(2)$=1222.23, DF=22, p<.000) and had significant regression coefficients for each predictor ($\beta_{wtp\_\$}$ = 3.31, p<.000; β_{wtp_v} = 3.68, p<.000; $\beta_{price\_\$}$ = -2.69, p<.000; β_{price_v} =-2.52, p<.000). We tested differences in the regression coefficients between WTP and price predictors in each trial (money or shock) type and found significant differences for WTP and price in both, money and voltage trials (both p<.000). We also tested differences in the regression coefficients between money and voltage trials for WTP and price predictors and found no significant differences between trial type (price$_v$ vs. price$_\$$: p<.216; wtp$_v$ vs. wtp$_\$$: p<.09). For the fMRI data analysis we estimated a hierarchical mixed effect GLM to investigate differences and overlaps for brain areas that correlated with the size of monetary and physical pain costs. We found that the Insula, a region involved in physical

pain processing, correlated positively with the size of physical pain prices, but not with the size of monetary prices (p<.005, uncorr.). A conjunction analysis revealed that no overlapping areas can be found (p<.005, uncorr.).

Taken together, these results show that while people's brains react differently to "monetary" and "physical pain" their behavior does not. Our fMRI results suggest that paying with money might trigger very different processes than those involved with more "physical" forms of costs. We suggest that the act of paying recruits systems involved in psychological rather than physical pain processing. These results call into question the current findings in the neuroscientific literature: That is, our findings call into question that for everyday consumption decisions paying triggers a similar sensation as suffering physical pain. Our results have important implications for disadvantageous decision-making such as overspending and transformative consumer research.

The Origin of the Pain of Paying

EXTENDED ABSTRACT

In our daily lives we are continuously faced with the decision of whether or not to buy different goods and services. As research from behavioral economics suggests, when purchasing a product, people experience hedonic competition between the anticipated pleasure derived from acquiring and consuming the product and the anticipated losses incurred not only from the money given up in the transaction (product price) and the hassle of executing the payment (transaction cost) but also from *pain of paying,* the disutility derived parting with money (Prelec & Loewenstein, 1998). It is the trade off between these anticipated gains and losses that determines the decision of whether or not to purchase. Interestingly, however, our understanding of the pain of paying construct is still inconclusive.

Early findings from judgment and decision making, in support of the pain of paying, demonstrated that people like to prepay for purchases and decouple spending from consumption (Prelec & Lowenstien, 1998). Recent findings from neuroeconomics (Knutson et al., 2007) went further and showed that a decision to purchase activated not only brain areas involved in reward processing (Nucleus Accumbens) but also deactivated brain areas (in particular (the anterior Insula) that have been linked not only to physical pain but also to arousal (i.e. disgust and anxiety). The current research extends these previous findings and seeks to provide a better understanding of what the pain of paying is: how is it experienced and what is driving it.

One of the biggest unknowns that the current paper is focusing on is whether the pain of paying is in fact experienced as a physical pain, psychological pain, or whether it is not experienced as a pain at all. To address this question, as a first step we examined whether making pain more salient would influence consumer's willingness-to-pay for products, and if so, which types of pain would have an influence. In Study 1 participants were primed, using a scrambled sentence task, with either psychological pain related words (e.g., *sorrow, grief, heartbreak*), physical pain related words (e.g., *aching, sore, cramps*), or neutral words (e.g., *pen, ball, carpet*). Participants were then given the opportunity to purchase a box of Godiva chocolates for real with their own money. They provided their willingness-to-pay (WTP) using a choice-based Becker-DeGroot-Marschak (BDM) auction (Becker, DeGroot & Marschak, 1964); a pre-test confirmed that only participants that understood the BDM auction-procedure proceeded to this task. Finally, participants completed liking, mood, and arousal measures. Our findings indicate that participants primed with psychological pain-related words were willing to pay significantly less for the chocolates as compared to participants primed with neutral words or with physical pain-related words (there was no significant difference between the latter two conditions), and these differences were not driven by how much participants liked the chocolates, their mood, or their arousal (those measures were not statistically different across conditions).

Study 2 extended these results by looking at how making pain more salient would influence consumer's willingness-to-pay for a non-hedonic product with a clear and known face value: a $20 Amazon.com gift card. Similar to the first study participants were primed with either psychological pain-related words, physical pain-related words, or neutral words. They then provided their WTP for the Amazon.com gift card through a choice-based BDM auction (a pre-test confirmed that only participants that understood the BDM auction-procedure proceeded to this task). Finally, they completed liking, mood, and arousal measures. Again, we found that participants primed with psychological pain-related words were willing to pay significantly less as compared to participants primed with neutral words or with physical pain-related words, and these differences were neither driven by how much participants liked the gift card nor by participants' mood or arousal.

Study 1 and Study 2 provide support for the idea that the pain of paying might be experienced as a pain that is similar to psychological rather than physical pain. However, the support is indirect, as we did not directly manipulate participants' experience of pain while purchasing (if it exists). Instead our primes simply made pain-related concepts more salient. Furthermore, if there exists a pain of paying, making people less sensitive to it, should increase WTP. We are currently running a third study to address these two points. In particular, in Study 3, participants are given a placebo pill disguised as either a drug that decreases sensitivity to pain (either physical or psychological), a drug that increases sensitivity to pain (either physical or psychological), or a vitamin supplement (control). That is, we have five-between subjects-conditions. After taking the "medication", participants are given a series of tasks; including a purchasing task as well as a number of manipulation checks. We predict that participants who believe they have consumed a psychological pain-relieving drug will be willing to pay significantly more than participants in the other conditions, while participants given a psychological pain-enhancing drug will be willing to pay significantly less. We predict no differences in willingness-to-pay between the control and physical pain drug conditions. We expect this study to be completed by the time of the ACR conference.

Habitually Consistent, Contextually Inconsistent: Dispositional and Contextual Determinants of Financial Decisions

EXTENDED ABSTRACT

The changes in the financial services industry have expanded access to loans for the vast majority of consumers. The easy availability of loans has helped consumers to improve their quality of life and has catalyzed economic growth. However, this easy availability of loans also presents some challenges; it requires consumers to be more careful in managing their loan repayments. Not all consumers seem to be good at this. Some consumers fall into a debt trap and spend a large proportion of their income paying interest on their loans. One way consumers can reduce their interest burden is by using their disposable income to prepay (i.e., paying ahead of schedule) their loans. The present research was conceived to understand the factors that predict consumers' loan prepayment behaviors. Specifically, in this research we try to address the question: how do

consumers decide whether to use their disposable income (e.g., a bonus) to prepay a loan or to use it for other purposes?

In this paper, we present two seemingly contradictory hypotheses that offer insights into how people decide whether or not to reduce their debts by prepaying their loans. The first hypothesis, the *dispositional orientation* hypothesis, posits that financial decisions are influenced by the pain of payment experienced by people. Money activates distinct cognitive and emotional responses in tightwads and spendthrifts. Tightwads relish saving money; so they are always willing to forego their current consumption to save money by prepaying their loans. Spendthrifts do not relish saving as much; they would rather have disposable cash in hand than prepay their loans. It is this difference in habitual response towards money (rather than economic valuations of financial gains) that causes the individual difference in financial management.

The second hypothesis, the *domain specificity* hypothesis, posits that the effects of dispositional orientation are restricted to monetary framing of options. Dispositional responses to money are less likely to manifest when financial gains are presented in (economically equivalent) non-monetary units. The notion that individuals differ in the way they spend and save money is not new; the subjective utility model, which is the bedrock of homo economicus' decision making, assumes that people map financial gains onto stable utility functions and people have different utility functions. However, the subjective utility model and the pain of payment model differ on one important aspect – domain specificity. Subjective utility model implies domain invariance of financial gains; that is, equivalent representations of gains should evoke the same responses from decision makers. In contrast, the pain of payment model proposes that tightwads and spendthrifts will differ in their decisions when a financial gain is presented in a monetary frame (dollars), but not when the same gain is presented in a non-monetary frame (e.g., number of installments).

Study 1 was designed to test the dispositional orientation and domain specificity hypotheses. One hundred and ninety-six adults (average age 35.3) participated in this study. A majority (77%) reported having taken a loan and 47% reported having prepaid their loans. Participants were asked to imagine that they had an outstanding loan of $8,000 from a bank that requires a monthly payment of $159 for 120 months. They were asked to consider six different loan prepayment options and for each option they had to indicate whether they would avail the option to prepay the loan, or continue with the current loan payment plan. The framing of the prepayment was manipulated; participants were randomly assigned either to monetary framing condition or non-monetary framing condition. In the monetary framing condition, prepaying the loan allowed the participant to reduce her monthly payment amount. In the non-monetary framing condition, each prepayment plan allowed them to reduce the number of monthly installments. Then to test the effect of their dispositional orientation to money, their pain of payment was measured using Rick et al.'s (2008) scale. The results revealed a predicted two-way interaction between pain of payment and monetary framing, $p < .05$. Participants with higher pain of payment were more likely to prepay the loan, but only in the monetary frame. Furthermore, follow-up process measures revealed that participants with higher pain of payment were more likely to construe loan prepayment as "saving money in the long run" than as "spending money in the short run" and this construal mediated the effect of pain of payment only in the monetary framing condition.

The pain of payment model posits that unlike tightwads, spendthrifts do not have an innate predisposition to save money. They consider money as a medium (or an instrument) to gain satisfaction. Consequently, they are more likely to compare the satisfaction from savings with the satisfaction from spending money. This conceptualization suggests that spendthrifts' loan prepayment decisions will be contingent on the salience of alternative options. Juxtaposing and contrasting the loan prepayment option with a regretful spending option could increase the attractiveness of the former option. We investigated this issue in **study 2**. The basic setup was similar to the study 1; we manipulated monetary vs. non-monetary framing of gains from prepayment and measured pain of payment. Additionally, we introduced a third factor: an alternative avenue to spend the money. Half the participants were told that they could either use the bonus money to prepay the loan or deposit it in a savings account. The other half were told that they could either use the money to prepay the loan or use it to go on a vacation. There was a significant three-way interaction of pain of payment, gain frame, and alternative ($p < .05$). Analysis of simple slopes revealed that pain of payment was a significant predictor of amount prepaid only when the gain was presented in the monetary frame and the alternative was depositing money in the savings account ($p < .05$). Further analysis found that spendthrifts found it much easier to justify keeping money in the savings account only when the gain was presented in the monetary frame. Together, these findings characterize the complex interplay of innate dispositions towards money and framing of options in financial decisions.

REFERENCES

Becker, Gary S., Morris H. DeGroot, and Jacob Marschak (1964), "Measuring Utility by a Single-Response Sequential Method," *Behavioral Science*, 9, 226-232.

Chib, Vikram S., Antonio Rangel, Shinsuke Shimojo, John P. O'Doherty (2009), "Evidence for a Common Representation of Decision Values for Dissimilar Goods in Human Ventromedial Prefrontal Cortex," *Journal of Neuroscience,* 29, 12315-12320.

Knutson, Brian, Scott Rick, Elliott Wimmer, Drazen Prelec, George Loewenstein (2007), "Neural Predictors of Purchases," *Neuron,* 53, 147-156.

Plassmann, Hilke, John O'Doherty, Antonio Rangel (2007), "Orbitofrontal Cortex Encodes Willingness to Pay in Everyday Economic Transactions," *Journal of Neuroscience,* 27, 9984-9988.

Prelec Drazen, George Loewenstein (1998), "The Red and the Black: Mental Accounting of Savings and Debt," *Marketing Science*, 17, 4-28.

Rick Scott I., Cynthia E. Cryder, George Loewenstein (2008), "Tightwads and Spendthrifts," *Journal of Consumer Research*, 34, 767-782.

Wertenbroch, Klaus and Bernd Skiera (2002), "Measuring Consumers' Willingness to Pay at the Point of Purchase," *Journal of Marketing Research*, 39, 228-241.

The Dark Side of Social Groups: How Social Reference Groups Inhibit Consumption

Chairs: Breagin Riley, Syracuse University, USA
Renee Gosline, MIT, USA

Paper #1: Resisting Normative Influences in the Context of Product Placements
Cristel Russell, University of Auckland, New Zealand
Valeria Noguti, University of Technology Sydney, Australia

Paper #2: A Negative Judgment Gives Satisfaction Provided it Smacks of Jealousy: Why Negative Feedback from Strong and Anonymous Ties Inhibits Decision Making
Renee R. Gosline, MIT, USA
Jeff K. Lee, Harvard Business School, USA
Breagin K. Riley, Syracuse University, USA

Paper #3: Masking Behavior: Examining the Influence of Social Networks on Men's Consumption Practices
Linda Tuncay Zayer, Loyola University Chicago, USA

Paper #4: How Consumers Rhetorically Align the Interests of Multiple Social Networks
Markus Giesler, York University, Canada
Robin Canniford, University of Melbourne, Australia

SESSION OVERVIEW

Decision making is often a social process, as we are generally influenced by others' opinions while making choices, like what to order at a restaurant (Ariely and Levav 2000), how to navigate a career (Levin and Cross 2004), and which new products to purchase (Van den Bulte and Joshi 2007). Beyond traditional investigations of how individuals' attitudes and behaviors are impacted by reference group members' attitudes and behaviors, however, lies a dynamic and growing domain of social influence. The prevalence and popularity of online social networks (e.g., facebook) have enabled peers, friends, acquaintances, and even strangers to make more than 500 billion product- and service-related impressions on one another (Forrester 2010).

Ample research focuses on how social reference groups encourage others to consume. For example, Van den Bulte and Joshi (2007) focused on the diffusion of innovations, leveraging the sociological idea that some consumers are more likely than others to convince people to purchase products. Relatedly, many firms are trying to leverage these reference groups to aid marketing efforts. For example, many firms are integrating their websites with various facebook features to provide shoppers with information regarding how many people, as well as whom specifically in their social networks, "like" the consumption item.

Unfortunately, the current research on social networks presents a rosy picture which focuses on how social reference groups encourage and facilitate consumption, but ignores the reality that, in many ways, social groups are prohibitive, effectively restricting (Wooten 2006) or reducing certain consumption behaviors (Grayson and Ambler 1999). In this special session, we follow in the path of the "dark side" scholars and *extend the research on how social reference groups impact consumption by focusing on how such groups inhibit consumption.*

Specifically, the four papers proposed for this session leverage various methodological and philosophical approaches to examine situations where the attitudes of peers, friends, and social network members cause individuals to reconsider consuming an item. The first paper uses social-psychological experimentation to examine how consumers' perceptions of the influence of TV series on peers,

affect consumers' own intentions to buy products placed within those series. The second paper employs experimental and quasi-experimental techniques to investigate situations where relying on advice from strong social network ties, which are proposed to be more trustworthy than weak ties (Granovetter 1973), is actually less helpful when making consumption decisions. The third paper employs qualitative methods, including text analysis, to examine how consumers use masking behaviors to avoid conflicts within one social network, while freely and openly discussing and consuming within another. The fourth paper draws upon sociological theory and uses in-depth interviews to examine how consumers (re)construct consumption narratives in an effort to both respectfully resolve between-network disagreements, and consume without dissonance.

Combined, the four papers in this session examine how social reference groups inhibit consumption. These papers make several important contributions. Theoretically, these papers extend and refine literatures concerned with understanding how social reference groups affect behaviors. Scholars concerned with topics that emphasize the importance of social groups in the consumption process, including *identity construction*, *advice acceptance*, and *the use of product ratings and reviews,* will find this session especially interesting, as the research presented sheds light on sources of and responses to reference-group-related tensions.

Practically, these papers suggest that firms should exercise caution and employ strategy when leveraging social networks, rather than immediately sharing the opinions of various social groups. Practitioners concerned with leveraging social reference groups as a way of transmitting information about peer approval or social capital will find the discussion of how groups inhibit individual consumption compelling, as it might help explain the poor results from various marketing campaigns. Lastly, this session demonstrates how theoretical advancements can occur when scholars from various backgrounds share interests in related consumption phenomena. Our authors leverage experimental social psychology, sociology, economic sociology, marketing, and anthropology to present clear examples of how social reference groups inhibit consumption.

Resisting Normative Influences in the Context of Product Placement

EXTENDED ABSTRACT

In this research we investigate how perceptions of the influence of TV series on peers impact the effects of product placements. Because people frequently interact around TV, co-viewing programs or even developing communities of consumption around them (Kozinets 2001; Schau et al. 2009), product placement effects are likely to be affected by viewers' perceptions of how others are influenced by TV series. We define these perceptions as *peer-connectedness*, in parallel to Russell et al's (2004) studies on audience connectedness.

We focus here on conditions that favor a reduction in consumers' desire to purchase placed products as a function of peer-connectedness. Peer-connectedness is proposed (and shown) to reduce consumers' desire to purchase products that appear in TV series, contingent upon some conditions, based on individual differences or contextual variables.

One of the individual difference moderators in this research is psychological reactance. Reactance (Brehm 1966) is a motivational

Advances in Consumer Research
Volume 39, ©2011

state due to a threat to behavioral or attitudinal freedom. People engage in opposite behavior to restore the freedom and/or adopt or avoid positions on the issue (Wright and Brehm 1982). Building on Brehm's (1966) work, other researchers proposed that people naturally vary in the degree to which they pursue these opposite behaviors and developed measures for this psychological reactance trait (Hong 1992; Hong and Page 1989). The reactance trait has been shown to be an important predictor of attitudes and behavior. For instance, individuals who score high on reactance move against expert product recommendations (Fitzsimons and Lehmann 2004), and reject goals associated with relationship partners, pursuing opposite goals instead (Chartrand et al. 2007).

The second set of moderating factors in our research are situational tendencies to conform. Conformity operates largely out of awareness. Although people consider interpersonal influences the least important factor in their decisions, these usually have one of the largest impacts (Nolan et al. 2008). Moreover, imitation studies have shown that people unconsciously imitate others as the perception of others' behaviors automatically generates behavioral outputs (Dijksterhuis and Bargh 2001) and that even brief encounters with others can increase one's tendency to subsequently choose the same brand these others buy (Ferraro et al. 2009). In this research, we employ a scrambled sentence task to non-consciously prime conformity and non-conformity (Epley and Gilovich 1999) and assess its impact on responses to product placement in TV series, depending on different levels of perceived peer-connectedness to the series.

Peer-connectedness was manipulated by explicitly communicating the percentage of peers who are connected to the series (study 1) or implicitly, through a news article focused on Generation Y (the participants' peer group) that presented a relevant peer as either highly connected or not connected to the series (study 2). Product placements were digitally inserted in visuals of the series. In study 2, conformity and non-conformity were primed experimentally in a first, unrelated part of the experiment, following Epley and Gilovich's scrambled task procedure (1999) designed to generate either high or low tendency to conform. Purchase intentions for a series of brands, including the focal brands, were measured. The psychological reactance scale (Hong 1992; Hong and Page 1989) was included in a separate section. Prior consumption of focal brands and demographic information were controlled for.

The analyses reveal a three-way interaction between peer-connectedness, conformity, and reactance. Whereas there were no significant differences in purchase intentions across conditions for participants high in reactance, there was a cross-over interaction between conformity priming and peer-connectedness amongst low reactance participants. Low reactance participants were less likely to follow a peer when primed for non-conformity and more likely to follow a peer when primed for conformity. When these participants were told that the peer was highly connected to a TV series, non-conformity priming reduced intentions to buy the products placed in the series to which that peer was highly connected. However, those low reactance participants who were told that their peer was not connected to the series were more likely to want to buy the placed products when primed for non-conformity.

Together, the series of experiments identifies conditions that trigger behavioral tendencies that go counter to the direction of the perceived influence of TV series on peers. Given that detrimental consumption practices such as smoking, doing drugs, or heavy drinking (Pechmann and Wang 2010; Russell et al. 2009) are often displayed in entertainment programs, the finding that peer-connectedness information can reduce the impact of undesirable consump-

tion images (such as smoking) suggests that it could serve as a tool to lessen the influence of TV programs on their vulnerable audiences.

REFERENCES

Balasubramanian, Siva K., James A. Karrh, and Hemant Patwardhan (2006), "Audience Response to Product Placements - an Integrative Framework and Future Research Agenda," *Journal of Advertising*, 35 (3), 115-41.

Chartrand, Tanya L., Amy N. Dalton, and Gavan J. Fitzsimons (2007), "Nonconscious Relationship Reactance: When Significant Others Prime Opposing Goals," *Journal of Experimental Social Psychology*, 43 (5), 719-26.

Dijksterhuis, Ap and John A. Bargh (2001), "The Perception-Behavior Expressway: Automatic Effects of Social Perception on Social Behavior," *Advances in experimental social psychology*, 33, 1-40.

Epley, Nicholas and Thomas Gilovich (1999), "Just Going Along: Nonconscious Priming and Conformity to Social Pressure," *Journal of Experimental Social Psychology*, 35 (6), 578-89.

Ferraro, Rosellina, James R. Bettman, and Tanya L. Chartrand (2009), "The Power of Strangers: The Effect of Incidental Consumer Brand Encounters on Brand Choice," *Journal of Consumer Research*, 35 (5), 729-41.

Fitzsimons, Gavan J. and Donald R. Lehmann (2004), "Reactance to Recommendations: When Unsolicited Advice Yields Contrary Responses," *Marketing Science*, 23 (1), 82-94.

Hong, Sung-Mook (1992), "Hong's Psychological Reactance Scale: A Further Factor Analytic Validation," *Psychological Reports*, 70 (2), 512-14.

Hong, Sung-Mook and Sandra Page (1989), "A Psychological Reactance Scale: Development, Factor Structure and Reliability," *Psychological Reports*, 64 (3), 1323-26.

Kozinets, Robert V. (2001), "Utopian Enterprise: Articulating the Meanings of Star Trek's Culture of Consumption," *Journal of Consumer Research*, 28 (1), 67-88.

Nolan, Jessica M., P. Wesley Schultz, Robert B. Cialdini, Noah J. Goldstein, and Vladas Griskevicius (2008), "Normative Social Influence Is Underdetected," *Personality and Social Psychology Bulletin*, 34 (7), 913-23.

Pechmann, Cornelia and Liangyan Wang (2010), "Effects of Indirectly and Directly Competing Reference Group Messages and Persuasion Knowledge: Implications for Educational Placements," *Journal of Marketing Research*, 47 (1), 134-45.

Russell, Cristel Antonia, Dale W. Russell, and Joel W. Grube (2009), "Nature and Impact of Alcohol Messages in a Youth-Oriented Television Series," *Journal of Advertising*, 38 (3), 97-111.

Schau, Hope Jensen, Albert M. Muniz, and Eric J. Arnould (2009), "How Brand Community Practices Create Value," *Journal of Marketing*, 73, 30-51.

Yang, Moonhee and David R. Roskos-Ewoldsen (2007), "The Effectiveness of Brand Placements in the Movies: Levels of Placements, Explicit and Implicit Memory, and Brand-Choice Behavior," *Journal of Communication*, 57 (3), 469-89.

A Negative Judgment Gives Satisfaction Provided it Smacks of Jealousy: Why Negative Feedback from Strong and Anonymous Ties Inhibits Decision Making

EXTENDED ABSTRACT

A lot of evidence supports the idea that people often seek advice from people across their social networks: friends and loved ones, acquaintances, and strangers. For example, Grannovetter (1978) acknowledges that generally speaking, close friends and loved ones give good advice because they are trustworthy and desire for us to have positive outcomes. Although prior research does not provide a full explication of how advice of varying valences is accepted across the spectrum of social network ties, it does provide insight into what consumers do with received advice. Specifically, it suggests that advice received from people with whom we share close relationships is helpful to the extent that the advice-giver is perceived as trustworthy and that trustworthiness increases with tie strength. This idea leads to our first hypothesis: usefulness of feedback increases with tie strength. This means that feedback from strangers is least useful while feedback from strong ties is most useful.

Research on social structure raises some doubt about the expected positive relationship between helpfulness and tie strength. Simmel (1908), for example, identified the potentially benevolent role of the stranger, who is "not bound by roots to the particular constituents and partisan dispositions of the group," and possesses a "distinctly objective attitude [of both] indifference and involvement" (1908, 145). These prescient words aptly characterize the modern impact of input from strangers on online websites and message boards, as well as offline interactions in restaurants and hair salons. It may be that when strangers offer input, it is deemed honest and trustworthy due to the stranger's objectivity. This leads to our second hypothesis: feedback from both strangers and strong ties is more useful than feedback from weak ties.

Nevertheless, weak ties, which are typically portrayed as untrustworthy, can be quite helpful, not due to benevolence but because they occupy "gaps" or structural holes between social network clusters (Burt 1992). Granoveter (1978; 1983) suggests that weak ties are helpful because they provide not only unique information relative to friends and loved ones, but also more reliable information relative to strangers. Granovetter also suggests that weak ties are sometimes seen as being most in competition with us. This competition takes place within the context of a "field" or social setting wherein individuals compete for social capital or the valued social relations between people (Bourdieu 1984). The quest to maximize social capital is a competition that is of great relevance, particularly when people estimate social reactions to their decisions: Making poor decisions is risky because doing so may lead to a decrease in social capital. We argue that competition for social capital is strongest between weak ties (Burt 1992; Marsden 1987). Strong ties tend to be permanent relationships which are less reliant on social capital, while anonymous relationships do not technically exist and thus do not depend on social capital. As a result, advice from weak ties, though not benevolent, is most helpful specifically because it provides social-capital related feedback. Thus, our third hypothesis is that feedback from weak ties will be more useful than that from strong or anonymous ties.

We test these three hypotheses in a series of studies. Study 1 is designed to test the three hypotheses and employs a 3 (social network tie: anonymous, weak, strong) x 2 (valence: negative, positive) design with "change in purchase intention" as the dependent measure. Results show that positive feedback from weak ties increases purchase intent significantly more than positive feedback from anonymous and strong ties. Negative feedback from weak ties decreases purchase intent significantly less than negative feedback from anonymous and strong ties. Based on these results, hypotheses one and two are rejected in favor of hypothesis three: weak ties are more helpful when making decisions than anonymous and strong ties.

Study 2 is designed to test perceived trustworthiness and perceived helpfulness of feedback as a function of social network tie

and valence. This study has a 3 (social network tie: anonymous, weak, strong) x 2 (valence: negative, positive) design with perceived trustworthiness and perceived helpfulness of the feedback as dependent measures. Results show that, regardless of valence, feedback from weak ties is perceived as less trustworthy but more helpful than feedback from anonymous and strong ties. Based on these results, perceived trustworthiness is eliminated as a potential mediator for the usefulness of feedback.

Study 3 examines social capital as a moderator of the relationship found in studies 1 and 2. Study 3 employs a 3 (social network tie: anonymous, weak, strong) x 2 (valence: negative, positive) x 2 (social capital signal: low, high) design. Results show that the helpfulness of feedback from weak ties is significantly higher when the social capital signal is stronger than when it is weaker. This suggests that weak ties are more helpful than anonymous and strong ties when making decisions because they provide valuable social capital-related information.

Together, these three studies show that feedback received from trusted sources (anonymous and strong ties) is not particularly helpful when making decisions.

This research makes two significant contributions. It advances the social networks literature by demonstrating that weak ties can be more helpful than anonymous and strong ties when making decisions, not through trust but through social-capital-related signaling. It also advances the advice acceptance literature by testing a theoretical model of consumer responses to acceptance of advice within social networks, and showing that the concepts of "trustworthy" and "helpful" are not interchangeable.

REFERENCES

Bourdieu, Pierre (1984), Distinction: A Social Critique of the Judgment of Taste. London: Routledge.

Burt, Ronald S. (1992), Structural Holes: The Social Structure of Competition. Cambridge, MA: Harvard University Press.

Granovetter, Mark (1973), "The strength of weak ties," *American Journal of Sociology*, 78 (6) 1360–1380.

Granovetter, Mark (1983), "The strength of weak ties: A network theory revisited," *Sociological Theory*, 1, 201-233.

Marsden, Peter V. (1987), "Core Discussion Networks of Americans," *American Sociological Review*, 52: 122-131.

Rogers, Everett (1995), Diffusion of Innovations," 4th ed. New York: Free Press.

Simmel, Georg (1971), "The Stranger." In Donald N. Levine (ed.), On Individuality and Social Forms. 144-149. Chicago, IL: The University of Chicago Press.

Masking Behavior: Examining the Influence of Social Networks on Men's Consumption Practices

EXTENDED ABSTRACT

Recent research has explored men's shopping behavior and consumption practices (Otnes and McGrath 2001; Holt and Thompson 2004; Tuncay and Otnes 2008). However, while past research has demonstrated the influence of peers and other reference groups in consumer behavior (e.g. Bearden and Etzel 1982; Childres and Rao 1992; Escalas and Bettman 2003), research on how men's behaviors in the marketplace may be constrained or facilitated by their social networks has not been fully explored. For instance, Zayer and Neier (2011) discuss how men have "secret affairs" with certain brands of grooming products or fashion goods because they fear being ostracized by peers. Similarly, Tuncay (2005, 231) found that men often engage in "masking" behavior, or "actions individuals take to hide or deemphasize the consumption behavior they display to others." Goffman (1956) sheds light on the potential motivations behind this masking behavior in his discussion of the presentation of self. He notes how misrepresentation, or a "discrepancy between fostered appearance and reality," can occur when the performer is not "authorized to give the performance." (1956, p. 59). That is, men may engage in masking behavior with regard to certain consumer goods because they feel they are not "authorized" to give a performance which may be perceived as outside of the boundaries of traditional heterosexual and masculine behavior. In fact, recent scholars have identified some men as culturally vulnerable in terms of their identities when they consume fashion and grooming products (Tuncay and Otnes, 2008). This is attributed to the fact that shopping in general is still deemed by society as a feminine pursuit (Miller, 1998). Indeed, past research (Belk et al., 1982, p. 4) has shown that individuals make inferences with regard to other's consumption patterns and that this phenomenon can lead to "prejudicial stereotyping."

But what roles do social networks play in this masking behavior? This research explores how men's social networks simultaneously constrain and sometimes facilitate consumption of fashion and grooming products. To explore this research question, a qualitative study was conducted with fifteen men in their 20s and 30s. Most of the informants were college-educated, working professionals and lived in urban settings. This research utilizes three qualitative methods: collage construction, in-depth interviews, and shopping with consumers. These methods have been used effectively in past consumer research. For example, Belk et al. (2003) uses collages in the exploration of consumer desire. Moreover, the shopping with consumers technique is paired with in-depth interviews in the exploration of ambivalence experienced by women during wedding dress shopping (Otnes, Lowrey, and Shrum 1997). Using these methods, over 180 pages of textual data were generated from the transcripts and field notes.

Findings suggest that men feel constrained in the performances they give with regard to masculinity and consumption, particularly in the presence of other men. Alternatively, men may be "freed" to experiment with new forms of consumption due to the influence of female others. For example, some men discussed shopping for clothes, using anti-wrinkle creams and getting pedicures and manicures at the urging of female significant others or female friends. However, they were hesitant to share that information with male others due to the potential stigma of femininity or "gayness" that was associated with those consumption practices. These findings suggest that social networks play a powerful role in men's consumption practices. Even as gender roles are shifting in today's society, traditional gender ideologies still persist and may cause tension among male consumers of fashion and grooming products because they are concerned with what others may think, particularly male others. On the other hand, female others may open up consumption possibilities for men as they urge their male partners or friends to try out new products and services.

REFERENCES

Bearden, William O. and Michael J. Etzel (1982) "Reference Group Influence on Product and Brand Purchase Decisions," *Journal of Consumer Research*, 9 (September), 183-194.Belk, R.W., Bahn, K.D. and Mayer, R.N. (1982), "Developmental recognition of consumption symbolism," *Journal of Consumer Research*, 9 (1), 4-17.

Belk, Russell W., Güliz Ger and Søren Askegaard (2003), "The Fire of Desire: A Multi-Sited Inquiry into Consumer Passion," *Journal of Consumer Research*, 30 (December), 326-351.

Childers, Terry and Akshay Rao (1992), "The Influence of Familial and Peer-Based Reference Groups on Consumer Decisions," *Journal of Consumer Research*, 19 (2), 198-211.

Escalas, Jennifer Edson and James R. Bettman (2003) "You Are What You Eat: The Influence of Reference Groups on Consumers' Connections to Brands," *Journal of Consumer Psychology*, 13 (3), 339-348.

Goffman, Erving (1956), *The Presentation of the Self in Everyday Life*, New York: Doubleday.

Holt, Douglas B. and Craig J. Thompson (2004), "Man-of-Action Heroes: The Pursuit of Heroic Masculinity in Everyday Consumption," *Journal of Consumer Research,* 31 (September), 425-40.

Otnes, Cele and Mary Ann McGrath (2001), "Perceptions and Realities of Male Shopping Behavior," *Journal of Retailing*, 77, 111-37.

Otnes, Cele C., Tina M. Lowrey, and L.J. Shrum (1997), "Toward an Understanding of Consumer Ambivalence," *Journal of Consumer Research*, 24(1), 80-93.

Tuncay, Linda (2005), "How male consumers construct and negotiate their identities in the marketplace: three essays," Dissertation at the University of Illinois at Urbana-Champaign, Urbana, IL.

Tuncay, Linda and Otnes, Cele C. (2008), "The use of persuasion management strategies by identity-vulnerable consumers: the case of urban heterosexual male shoppers," *Journal of Retailing*, Vol. 84 (4), 487-499.

Zayer, Linda Tuncay and Stacy Neier (2011), "An exploration of men's brand relationships," *Qualitative Market Research: An International Journal*, 14 (1), 83-104.

How Consumers Rhetorically Align the Interests of Multiple Social Networks

EXTENDED ABSTRACT

The idea that consumption is "embedded" in networks of social relations is of great and growing importance to marketing theory and practice (e.g., Iacobucci 1996; Fischer, Otnes, and Tuncay 2009; Epp and Price 2008). This research proposes that consumers' individual preferences and decisions are profoundly influenced by the specific norms and beliefs that structure their immediate social environment. For instance, it is likely to assume that a woman will not use cosmetic Botox when such a move stands in sharp symbolic contrast to the ways in which an important social network (e.g., her family) defines the process of bodily aging. However, consumers are never part of only one social network. For example, although the woman's family may categorically reject Botox, her Botox-using girlfriends may perceive her family's Botox rejection as a disempowering traditionalism. Little theoretical attention has been devoted to the question of how consumers navigate these competing network interests.

In this presentation, we draw from actor-network theory in sociology (e.g., Latour 1992; Callon 1986) to develop a common process model of rhetorical alignment that explains how consumers bring the competing interests of multiple social networks together. Actor-network theory proposes that the acceptance of a certain practice (e.g., Botox consumption) presumes a network of interested actors - actors who perceive this practice as indispensible for attaining their own interests. We demonstrate how consumers draw from cultural value systems to create self-narratives that effectively translate strategic definitions of one social network (e.g., the community of Botox users) into the interests and identities of the other social network (e.g., the family), combating recurring accusations of betrayal and expanding the overall agentic horizon.

To illustrate the process of rhetorical alignment, we investigate the consumption of cosmetic Botox on two mutually constituted levels. First, we review the larger network of cultural norms and beliefs that motivates multiple (dis-) authenticating interpretations of cosmetic Botox and similar anti-aging solutions in a given social network. We find that these interpretations are steeped in a well-documented ideology of embodied aging (e.g., Hurd 2010; Bludau 2010) that produces multiple, competing interpretations about what constitutes a gracefully aging self and how to best accomplish it. After that, we analyze the gracefully aging self-narratives our sample of middle-class Baby Boomer women created to strategically align their Botox consumption with the goals and interests of their Botox-critical families. The latter analysis is based on in-depth interviews with 32 middle-class Baby Boomer women from Toronto (Canada).

The contributions of this presentation are threefold. First, it introduces actor-network theory to the study of networked consumption to demonstrate how consumers consolidate the exigencies of multiple social networks. Second, it demonstrates changes in the co-constitutive relationship between a given social network and the market-mediated interests of individual members. Finally, this presentation contributes to the discussion about the role of sovereignty in social networks. From a conventional theoretical standpoint, consumers are forced to resolve the tensions among multiple social networks by taking a side (e.g., with my family priorities) or by concealing an incompatible choice. However, we demonstrate how consumers create tenuous agentic space by creating self-narratives that combine seemingly competing network interests in culturally reso-

nant ways. At the same time, however, we also provide important theoretical boundary conditions, such as the existence of a culturally shared protocol of norms (here, the cultural identity model of aging gracefully).

REFERENCES

Bludau, Juergen (2010), *Aging, But Never Old: The Realities, Myths, and Misrepresentations of the Anti-Aging Movement.* Santa Barbara: Praeger.

Callon, Michel (1986) "Some Elements of a Sociology of Translation: Domestication of the Scallops and the Fishermen of St Brieuc Bay," in *Power, Action and Belief: A New Sociology of Knowledge*, ed. John Law, London: Routledge and Kegan Paul.

Epp, Amber M. and Linda L. Price (2008), "Family Identity: A Framework of Identity Interplay in Consumption Practices," *Journal of Consumer Research*, 35 (June), 50-70.

Fischer, Eileen, Cele C. Otnes, and Linda Tuncay (2007), "Pursuing Parenthood: Integrating Cultural and Cognitive Perspectives on Persistent Goal Striving," *Journal of Consumer Research*, 34 (December), 425-40.

Hurd Clarke, L. (2010), *Facing age: Women growing older in anti-aging culture.* Toronto: Rowan and Littlefield.

Iacobucci, Dawn (1996), *Networks in Marketing.* Thousand Oaks: Sage Publications.

Latour, Bruno (1983), "Give Me a Laboratory and I will Raise the World," in *Science Observed*, ed. K. D. Knorr-Cetina and M. J. Mulkay, Beverly Hills, CA: Sage.

Getting There: The Perception of Goal Progress and its Effects on Goal Pursuit

Chair: Elaine Chan, Tilburg University, The Netherlands

Paper #1: So Near and Yet So Far: The Mental Representation of Goal Progress

Szu-chi Huang, University of Texas at Austin, USA
Ying Zhang, University of Texas at Austin, USA
Susan Broniarczyk, University of Texas at Austin, USA

Paper #2: Goal Monitoring: Does One Step Forward Seem Larger Than One Step Back?

Margaret C. Campbell, University of Colorado, USA
Caleb Warren, Bocconi University, Italy

Paper #3: The Dual Effects of Optimism on Post-Purchase Goal Pursuit

Elaine Chan, Tilburg University, The Netherlands
Anirban Mukhopadhyay, HKUST, Hong Kong
Jaideep Sengupta, HKUST, Hong Kong

Paper #4: Pleasure, Pain, and Focus on Initial vs. End States as Determinants of Motivation in Goal Pursuit

Juliano Laran, University of Miami, USA
Keith Wilcox, Babson College, USA

SESSION OVERVIEW

Session Objective: The extant goals literature converges on the idea that making goal progress influences subsequent goal-pursuit actions. However, there is relatively little research devoted to understanding the antecedents that drive perceptions of goal progress. The purpose of this special session is to present current research that examines such antecedents from a variety of perspectives, and also illuminates the mechanisms by which perceptions of progress drive subsequent goal-directed behavior. In doing so, this session hopes to spark interest in a new direction for research on goals and goal-related action.

Overview: Much work in the goals arena has suggested that the perception of making goal progress has an effect on subsequent goal-directed behavior. Thus, taking a step towards goal fulfillment has been found to produce subsequent behavior that is either consistent with the goal or is disengaged from it, depending on contextual factors (Fishbach and Dhar 2005). There is, however, relatively scant research that takes a step back to examine what actually determines individuals' perceptions of progress. The papers in this session offer new insights into the goals literature by proposing a range of perspectives regarding this issue (including both situational and personality-related factors); at the same time, the papers also extend work on how and when progress perceptions influence subsequent behavior.

Papers: In the first paper, Huang, Zhang and Broniarczyk demonstrate that the interpretation of progress is contingent on whether individuals are at the initial or the advanced stage of goal pursuit. Across four studies, they show that at the initial stage of goal pursuit, individuals exaggerate their progress level, which in turn motivates them to strive for the goal. On the other hand, individuals downplay their progress level when nearing goal attainment. This discrepancy then induces greater effort in the goal pursuit. In the second paper, Campbell and Warren propose that individuals infer different perceptions of goal progress from an initial behavior, depending on whether the behavior is framed as goal consistent or inconsistent. Among other findings, they show that even for behavior that has objectively the same magnitude (e.g., saving vs. spending $30), consumers overweigh the positive influence of goal-consistent behavior versus the negative influence of goal-inconsistent behavior when assessing

progress; in turn, this has a negative impact on goal attainment. In the third paper, Chan, Mukhopadhyay and Sengupta examine the interactive influence of optimism and mental simulation (focusing on outcome vs. process) on perceptions of goal pursuit, and its consequences on subsequent behavior. They examine this question in the context of anticipatory purchasing – defined as the purchase of products that the buyers are unable to use at the time of purchase, but would like to in the future (e.g., clothes that are currently a size too tight). Across five studies, they show that for optimists, deciding to make an anticipatory purchase heightens goal commitment under an outcome-focus, while inducing perceptions of goal progress under a process-focus: subsequent behavior is goal-consistent in the former case and goal-inconsistent in the latter. On the other hand, for pessimists, the anticipatory purchase decision actually leads to a reduction in commitment under outcome-focus (leading to goal-inconsistent later behavior), while it does not change perceptions of goal progress or commitment under a process focus. Finally, Laran examines the moderating influence of goal valence on the relationship between progress perceptions and subsequent behavior. Given an "approach pleasure" goal, a perceived lack of progress motivates goal-directed behavior when individuals focus on the end state (vs. the initial state). However, given an "avoid pain" goal, the pattern is reversed: lack of progress motivates behavior when individuals focus on initial state (vs. the end state).

Contribution: The topic of goal pursuit is both important and relevant to consumer research. Each of the four papers in this session presents novel and interesting results. Together these provide new examination of the antecedents of goal progress, as well as enhancing our understanding of consequences for goal-directed behavior. All four papers include multiple completed studies; none of the four has been presented at ACR previously. Elaine Chan (Tilburg University) will serve as the session chair. All speakers have agreed to serve and present their respective papers if this special session is accepted.

Likely audience: We believe that this session addresses an important yet under-researched aspect of goals research, and has the potential to be well attended by researchers interested in motivation, goals, and self-control. We hope that a discussion of this emerging area will spark lively and productive debate.

So Near and Yet So Far: The Mental Representation of Goal Progress

EXTENDED ABSTRACT

In the course of goal pursuit, people actively monitor their levels of progress on goal attainment, and these assessments have a profound influence on their subsequent motivation (Carver & Scheier, 1998; Louro, Pieters, & Zeelenberg, 2007). However, what determines people's assessment of their progress? Is it always the case that people try to form accurate mental representations of their progress level on a goal? In the present research, we explore the possibility that the mental representation of progress level, rather than being a faithful reflection of one's actual level of progress, can function as a self-regulatory mechanism that helps ensure the attainment of important goals.

We adopt the dynamics of self-regulation (Fishbach, Dhar, & Zhang, 2006; Koo & Fishbach, 2008) as the theoretical framework, and propose a self-regulatory analysis of people's mental representation of goal progress. We propose that when individuals have just started pursuing a goal and have accumulated limited progress, they are primarily concerned about the attainability of the goal. Therefore, they are likely to exaggerate their progress level in their mental representation to signal a higher chance of eventual goal attainment, which helps to elicit greater motivation. However, when people have made substantial progress and are approaching the end point of the pursuit, the attainment of the goal is relatively secured and they are more concerned about reducing the remaining discrepancy. At this stage, individuals are likely to downplay their progress to create greater perceived discrepancy between their current and the ideal state, which in turn helps elicit greater effort in the pursuit.

We further propose that, because this alteration of mental representation is an instrumental mechanism to boost effort and to ensure successful goal attainment, it should occur only when efforts are necessary and effective in helping to secure the attainment of important goals. In other situations, such as when the goal is unimportant or when efforts are ineffective in helping goal attainment, such changes in mental representations should not occur.

Four studies were conducted to test present predictions. Participants in Study 1 completed a color recognition task and were offered either a low- or a high-value reward for successful completion. We manipulated their perceived stage in the pursuit by convincing participants that they either had just started the task, or were approaching the end point. We found that when participants just started the task, those aiming for high- (vs. low-) value reward exaggerated their progress in the task; conversely, when participants were approaching the end point, those aiming for high- (vs. low-) value reward downplayed their progress. Such alternation of mental representation of progress led to greater subsequent motivation in the pursuit, which was measured by greater amount of time participants spent in memorizing colors to complete the task for the reward.

In Study 2, participants completed a word identification task and were offered a limited-edition school-symbol magnet as a reward for reaching 21,500 points by the end of the task; we measured participants' willingness-to-pay for the reward as a proxy for their perceived goal value. We also manipulated their perceived stage in the pursuit by providing feedback on their current points; after answering 15 word-identification questions, participants in the initial-stage conditions received 3,157 points, whereas those in the advanced-stage conditions received 11,813 points. We measured participants' mental representation of progress and their subsequent motivation in earning more points for the reward, and found consistent patterns as in Study 1.

In Study 3, participants worked on a pitch differentiation task and were offered $20 bonus reward for reaching 23,900 points in the task. We informed participants either that pitch identification is an innate ability and cannot be improved through practice, or that it can be improved through effort. We also manipulated their perceived stage in the pursuit by providing feedback on their accumulated points (7,966 points in initial-stage conditions vs. 15,932 points in advanced-stage conditions). We found that participants only altered their mental representation of progress level when they believed that they could improve their pitch identification skills through practice, and such alteration of mental representation of progress again led to greater subsequent effort in the task.

In Study 4, we tested the hypothesis in a field study with a t-shirt donation campaign. Students were invited to donate their used t-shirts to a charitable cause, and we manipulated the importance of the goal by changing the cause for the campaign. In addition, we manipulated the stage in the pursuit by showing participants different visual stimuli: people were shown a picture of either two (initial stage) or 10 (advanced stage) full boxes of used t-shirts, presumably

the donations we have taken so far for the campaign. We measured participants' mental representations of progress by asking them to estimate the number of t-shirts in these boxes, and we recorded the number of t-shirts they donated as the indicator of their motivation to help attain this collective goal. We found that when the cause of donation was highly important (vs. less important), people exaggerated the number of used t-shirts in the picture to signal higher goal attainability when there were only two full boxes, but downplayed the number of used t-shirts when they saw 10 boxes of t-shirts. This alternation of mental representation again led to greater motivation, i.e., more t-shirts people donated to help ensure the attainment of the goal they deemed more important.

Goal Monitoring: Does One Step Forward Seem Larger Than One Step Back?

EXTENDED ABSTRACT

Consumers often pursue continuing goals, like saving for retirement or maintaining a healthy weight, where attainment depends on a number of behaviors and decisions made over time. Although the literature suggests that accurately monitoring progress towards such goals is essential for goal attainment (Baumeister and Heatherton 1996; Carver and Scheier 1982), surprisingly little research investigates whether consumers are typically accurate in monitoring goal progress. Accurate monitoring requires that consumers perceive the impact of their behaviors on goal progress in an unbiased manner. At a minimum, accuracy requires that the influence of a behavior be perceived similarly irrespective of whether that behavior moves the consumer closer to or further from goal attainment. For example, a consumer with a savings goal should perceive a $30 departure from a budget as carrying the same psychological weight regardless of whether it represents extra savings or extra spending.

The focal question of our research is whether consumers accurately weight the influence of goal-consistent behaviors, like saving $30 or resisting a scoop of ice cream, relative to goal-inconsistent behaviors, like spending $30 or eating a scoop of ice cream, on perceived goal progress. Research suggests that consumers' perceptions of progress could be biased in either direction (Baumeister et al. 2001; Ahluwalia 2002). However, because (1) consumers selectively distort information in order to maintain a positive impression of themselves (Dunning 1999, 2007; Taylor and Brown 1988), and (2) goal-consistent behaviors reflect positively on one's self whereas goal-inconsistent behavior threaten one's self-view (Prelec and Bodner 2003), we hypothesize that consumers overweight the influence of goal-consistent relative to goal-inconsistent behaviors when assessing their progress.

Our first study asked members of an online survey panel to think of a personal goal, one behavior that moved them closer to the goal, and one behavior that moved them further from the goal. Consistent with our hypothesis, respondents were more likely to recall a goal-consistent behavior than a goal-consistent behavior (89% vs. 64%); furthermore, respondents who listed both behaviors rated the goal-consistent behavior as having a larger impact than the goal-inconsistent behavior ($M = 6.7$ vs. 4.8; scale from 1-9).

Studies 2 and 3 used hypothetical scenarios to explicitly control for the magnitude of the goal-consistent and goal-inconsistent behaviors that participants evaluated. In study 2, undergraduate participants rated running one more mile as having a larger influence than running one less mile on progress towards an exercise goal ($M = 2.3$ vs. 1.4; scale from 0-4). Similarly, in study 3, undergraduate participants believed that saving an additional $30 helped their progress towards a savings goal more than spending an additional $30 hurt it ($M$ = 4.2 vs. 3.3; scale from 1-7).

In study 4, we measured perceived goal progress indirectly by having participants estimate the calories in desserts. Because weight loss depends on the number of calories consumed, the calories in a food provide an objective measure of the impact of eating (or not eating) a food on progress towards a weight-loss goal. Consistent with the hypothesis that consumers underweight the impact of goal-inconsistent behaviors relative to goal-consistent behaviors, participants perceived desserts (i.e., a piece of cake or five ounces of ice cream) that they imagined eating as having fewer calories than desserts that they imagined foregoing (M_{cake} = 386 vs. 475; $M_{ice\ cream}$ = 197 vs. 262).

Our final two studies explored whether the tendency to overweight the impact of goal-consistent behaviors relative to goal-inconsistent behaviors is related to goal attainment. Consumers who perceive goal-consistent behaviors as having a larger influence than equivalent goal-inconsistent behaviors may think that they are making adequate goal progress even when they are not. Consequently, an optimistic goal monitoring bias may cause consumers to prematurely release their goals (Fishbach and Dhar 2004; Zhang, Fishbach, and Kruglanski 2007), thus discouraging goal attainment.

Study 5 investigates whether consumers who are typically less successful at attaining long-term goals reliant upon self-regulation are more likely to show an optimistic bias in goal monitoring than consumers who are more successful at attaining such goals. As in previous studies, undergraduate participants who imagined studying one or two additional nights thought their behavior would help their performance on an upcoming exam more than participants who imagined studying one or two fewer nights thought their behavior would hurt. Importantly, however, this tendency was less prevalent amongst participants with high self-control than participants with low self-control ($M_{high\text{-}control\ (+1SD)}$ = 4.7 vs. 4.5; $M_{low\text{-}control\ (\text{-}1SD)}$ = 4.9 vs. 3.6).

Online panel respondents in study 6 played a multi-round word game in which they won or lost points during each round. We manipulated the difficulty of the first two rounds such that most participants lost 100 points in one round and gained 100 points in another. As in previous studies, participants thought that gaining 100 points helped their progress towards a high score goal more than losing 100 points hurt it (M = 6.9 vs. 6.3; scale from 1-9). Furthermore, participants who showed a larger optimistic bias in the first two rounds performed worse in subsequent rounds than participants who showed a smaller optimistic bias ($M_{high\text{-}bias(+1SD)}$ = 43.1, $M_{low\text{-}bias(\text{-}1SD)}$ = 148.5; possible score range: -800 to 800).

In six studies, we show that consumers tend to overweight the impact of goal-consistent behaviors relative to goal-inconsistent behaviors. Furthermore, two studies suggest that this tendency is negatively associated with successful goal attainment. Because consumers believe that goal-consistent behaviors have a larger influence than objectively equivalent goal-inconsistent behaviors, they may believe that they are moving closer to their goals even when they are objectively not progressing. We hope that drawing attention to this bias provides a first step towards helping consumers accurately monitor their progress and, ultimately, improve their chances of reaching their goals.

The Dual Effects of Optimism on Post-Purchase Goal Pursuit

EXTENDED ABSTRACT

Consumers often purchase products that they are unable to use at the time, in anticipation that they may be able to do so later. For instance, people may buy clothing that is currently too small, in the hope of fitting into them later. In this research, we investigate how such anticipatory purchase decisions (to buy or not) affect consumers' likelihood of engaging in subsequent behavior that is consistent with the purchase (e.g., dieting or exercising after purchasing jeans that are too small). Drawing upon the optimism, mental simulation and goals literatures, we show that the type of mental simulation (outcome- vs. process-focus) that consumers use when making their anticipatory purchase decision can lead optimists and pessimists to make differing inferences regarding commitment vs. progress towards the goal. These inferences then dictate the nature of subsequent purchase-consistent decisions.

We propose that when consumers focus on the intervening process required to make the product usable (e.g., exercising to fit into a pair of smaller-sized jeans), the purchase decision itself acts as a signal of progress towards the goal. For optimists, the sense of accomplishment triggered by the purchase decision provides a justification to stop pursuing the focal goal (Fishbach and Dhar 2005). In contrast, pessimists, because of the unfavorable expectations they chronically hold, do not view the purchase decision as progress. Consequently, we predict that optimists reduce goal-congruent actions (e.g., exercising) after the anticipatory purchase, while pessimists are not affected by this illusory progress. Further, we predict that a different pattern should emerge under an outcome focus. Here, thinking about the final outcome (e.g., looking good) during the initial purchase increases the salience of the underlying goal (e.g., a fitness goal). Such increased goal salience leads optimists and pessimists to engage in different coping strategies: optimists become more committed to the goal and therefore more likely to pursue it, while pessimists tend to react in a non-adaptive manner by disengagement – i.e., the very salience of the goal makes them ironically less likely to pursue it (Scheier et al. 1986). Accordingly, under an outcome focus, making an anticipatory purchase should induce optimists (pessimists) to increase (decrease) goal-congruent actions.

We tested these hypotheses in five experiments. Experiment 1 used a 2 (focus: outcome vs. process) x 2 (optimism: optimists vs. pessimists) x 2 (decision: buy vs. no buy) between-subjects design. Participants first took part in a survey, which included a question about the size of jeans that they could just fit in. After a filler task, they completed a different survey about buying jeans. We manipulated thought focus by asking participants to make their decisions by visualizing either the end benefits of wearing the jeans (outcome-focus) or the process they would have to go through in order to be able to fit into the jeans (process-focus). Next, they read the description of the jeans, which were always one size smaller than their current sizes. They then reported their likelihood of purchasing the jeans, which served as the measure of anticipatory purchasing. Afterwards, participants moved on to an ostensibly unrelated study, in which they reported their likelihood of trying out fitness equipment. Lastly, they filled out a standard optimism scale (Scheier and Carver 1985). As hypothesized, under process-focus, optimists displayed a reduced likelihood of trying the exercise equipment after buying (vs. not buying) the jeans, while pessimists were unaffected by their purchase decision. Under outcome-focus, on the other hand, optimists were more likely to try the equipment as a consequence of buying (vs. not buying) the jeans, while the predicted ironic effect was obtained for pessimists: buying (vs. not buying) the jeans actually reduced the likelihood of trying the exercise equipment. This pattern of results was replicated in another study (Experiment 2) which manipulated purchase decision rather than treating it as a measured variable. Experiment 3 provided further support for our posited mechanism by measuring both goal commitment and goal progress, and obtaining findings consistent with predictions. Under a process-focus, optimists inferred greater goal progress when they decided to make (vs. not make) the anticipatory purchase, while pessimists remained unaffected. Given an outcome-focus, in contrast, deciding to make (vs. not make) the anticipatory purchase increased goal commitment for optimists, while decreasing it for pessimists.

Having obtained converging evidence for our overall framework, the next two experiments sought to provide more detailed insights into the mechanism under outcome-focus, especially that underlying the ironic effects of anticipatory purchase for pessimists. We have argued that it is the very salience of the focal goal which causes pessimists to disengage from it (leading to an ironic effect on subsequent behavior). If true, it should be possible to attenuate pessimists' decommitment by lowering the salience of the focal goal. In support of this prediction, Experiment 4 and 5 both showed that it was possible to attenuate and even reverse the ironic effect for pessimists (i.e., make them more likely to engage in goal-consistent behavior) by reducing the salience of the focal goal.

Taken together, results from these five studies, which included manipulated and measured purchase decision, chronic and situational inductions of optimism, as well as different purchase contexts, provide a nuanced perspective of how and why optimism affects goal-related action subsequent to making an anticipatory purchase decision. In doing so, this research offers new insights into the substantive domain of anticipatory purchasing, and builds theoretical knowledge in two important areas of consumer research: the literature on goals, and that on optimism.

Pleasure, Pain, and Focus on Initial vs.
End States as Determinants of Motivation in Goal Pursuit

EXTENDED ABSTRACT

Research on goal pursuit has focused on two factors that determine individuals' motivation to reach their goals. One of these factors is the amount of goal pursuit an individual has engaged in (Fishbach and Dhar 2005; Kivetz, Urminsky, and Zheng 2006; Laran and Janiszewski 2009). A second factor is whether the pursuit process is focused on what has been accomplished or on what still needs to be accomplished (Zhang and Huang 2010). We explore an important determinant of people's motivation in goal pursuit, goal valence, which may interact with factors previously explored in the literature and expand previous findings. We propose that any goal pursuit process is focused on approaching pleasure or avoiding pain, as stated by the hedonic principle (Elliot and Harackiewicz 1996; Forster, Higgins, and Idson 1998), and that this goal valence will moderate the extent to which goal focus and goal progress influence motivation. When people approach pleasure (e.g., save $600 to be able to go on a cruise vacation), the goal pursuit process is motivating. Therefore, the more people look backward and focus on how much goal pursuit they have engaged in, the more motivated they are to reach the goal. When they look forward, the more there needs to be done the more motivated people are to reach the final, pleasurable end state that characterizes approaching pleasure. When people avoid pain (e.g., save $600 to pay off a debt), avoiding the initial state is motivating. Therefore, the more people look backward and focus on how close they are to the initial, painful state, the more motivated they are to reach the goal.

When they look forward, the less there needs to be done the more motivated people are to reach the final end state and avoid the initial, painful state.

The first study examine people's motivation to save $1000 to pay off a debt (avoid pain) vs. to go on a vacation (approach pleasure). The design was a 2 (goal valence: approach pleasure vs. avoid pain) by 2 (focus: backward vs. forward) by 2 (progress: smaller vs. greater) between-subjects design. We showed participants a line featuring the amount of money they had saved so far. We manipulated backward vs. forward focus by showing the quantities in a $0 to $1000 (focus on what had been saved) or a $1000 to $0 (focus on what needed to be saved) order. In the smaller (greater) progress condition, participants were told they had saved $600 ($700) so far. An ANOVA on how much effort participants were willing to put into saving money revealed an interaction of the goal valence, focus, and progress factors ($F(1, 228) = 42.84$, $p < .01$). When approaching pleasure, in the backward focus condition, participants were willing to put less effort into saving money in the smaller progress ($M = 6.00$) than in the greater progress condition ($M = 7.46$; $F(1, 228) = 8.32$, $p < .01$). In the forward focus condition, participants were willing to put more effort into saving money in the smaller progress ($M = 7.71$) than in the greater progress condition ($M = 5.91$; $F(1, 228) = 11.92$, $p < .01$). When avoiding pain, however, in the backward focus condition, participants were willing to put more effort into saving money in the smaller progress ($M = 7.22$) than in the greater progress condition ($M = 5.19$; $F(1, 228) = 11.89$, $p < .01$). In the forward focus condition, participants were willing to put less effort into saving money in the smaller progress ($M = 5.40$) than in the greater progress condition ($M = 7.61$; $F(1, 228) = 11.15$, $p < .01$).

In the first study, participants were told that they were paying off a debt and that they would go on vacation only if they were able to pay off the debt. In order to make this avoid-pain goal into an approach-pleasure goal, the second study told participants that they had already made a decision to go on vacation and now were paying off the debt they acquired. This would make the goal to pay off a debt not painful to start with, since it was accompanied by the decision to go on vacation. The goal amount was now $2000, and we measured how much participants were willing to save. An ANOVA on the saving measure revealed an interaction of the goal valence, focus, and progress factors ($F(1, 291) = 20.81$, $p < .01$). When approaching pleasure, in the backward focus condition, participants were willing to save less money in the smaller progress ($M = \$437.97$) than in the greater progress condition ($M = \$546.69$; $F(1, 291) = 7.79$, $p < .01$). In the forward focus condition, participants were willing to save more money in the smaller progress ($M = \$550.63$) than in the greater progress condition ($M = \$462.55$; $F(1, 291) = 4.89$, $p < .05$). When avoiding pain, however, in the backward focus condition, participants were willing to save more money in the smaller progress ($M = \$563.95$) than in the greater progress condition ($M = \$481.73$; $F(1, 291) = 4.80$, $p < .05$). In the forward focus condition, participants were willing to save less money in the smaller progress ($M = \$469.51$) than in the greater progress condition ($M = \$545.24$; $F(1, 291) = 3.73$, $p = .05$).

A third study demonstrated similar results within a coffee rewards program. Across three studies, we demonstrate that, in addition to goal progress and direction of focus, whether the goal is to approach pleasure or to avoid pain needs to be examined when people research motivation. We show that goal valence can completely reverse effects previously found in goal pursuit, and that having people focus on the painful or pleasurable aspects of a goal can be an important tool in motivating consumers.

REFERENCES

Ahluwalia, Rohini (2002), "How Prevalent Is the Negativity Effect in Consumer Environments?" *Journal of Consumer Research*, 29 (September), 270-9.

Baumeister, Roy F. and Todd F. Heatherton, Todd F. (1996), "Self-Regulation Failure: An Overview," *Psychological Inquiry*, 7 (1), 1-15.

Baumeister, Roy F., Ellen Bratslavsky, Catrin Finkenauer, and Kathleen D. Vohs (2001), "Bad Is Stronger Than Good," *Review of General Psychology*, 5 (December), 323-70.

Carver, Charles S. and Michael F. Scheier (1982), "Control Theory: A Useful Conceptual Framework for Personality-Social, Clinical, and Health Psychology," *Psychological Bulletin*, 92 (June), 111-35.

--- (1998), *On the Self-Regulation of Behavior*, New York, NY: Cambridge Univesity Press.

Carver, Charles S., John W. Lawrence, and Michael F. Scheier (1996), "A Control-Process Perspective on the Origins of Affect," *Striving and Feeling: Interactions Among Goals, Affect, and Self-Regulation*, ed Leonard L. Martin and Abraham Tesser, Hillsdale, NJ, England: Lawrence Erlbaum, 11-52.

Dunning, David (2007), "Self-Image Motives and Consumer Behavior: How Sacrosanct Self-Beliefs Sway Preferences in the Marketplace," *Journal of Consumer Psychology*, 17 (4), 237-49.

--- (1999), "A Newer Look: Motivated Social Cognition and the Schematic Representation of Social Concepts," *Psychological Inquiry*, 10 (1), 1-11.

Elliot, Andrew J. and Judith M. Harackiewicz (1996), "Approach and Avoidance Achievement Goals and Intrinsic Motivation: A Mediational Analysis," *Journal of Personality and Social Psychology*, 70 (3), 461-75.

Fishbach, Ayelet and Ravi Dhar (2005), "Goals as Excuses or Guides: The Liberating Effect of Perceived Goal Progress on Choice," *Journal of Consumer Research,* 32 (December), 370-377.

Fishbach, Ayelet, Ravi Dhar, and Ying Zhang (2006), "Subgoals as Substitutes or Complements: The Role of Goal Accessibility," *Journal of Personality and Social Psychology*, 91 (2), 232-42.

Forster, Jens, E. Tory Higgins, and Lorraine Chen Idson (1998), "Approach and Avoidance Strength During Goal Attainment: Regulatory Focus and the "Goal Looms Larger" Effect," Journal *of Personality and Social Psychology*, 75 (5), 1115-31.

Kivetz, Ran, Oleg Urminsky, and Yuhuang Zheng (2006), "The Goal-Gradient Hypothesis Resurrected: Purchase Acceleration, Illusionary Goal Progress, and Customer Retention," *Journal of Marketing Research*, 43 (1), 39-58.

Koo, Minjung and Ayelet Fishbach (2008), "Dynamics of Self-Regulation: How (Un)accomplished Goal Actions Affect Motivation," *Journal of Personality and Social Psychology*, 94 (2), 183-95.

Laran, Juliano and Chris Janiszewski (2009), "Behavioral Consistency and Inconsistency in th Resolution of Goal Conflict," *Journal of Consumer Research*, 35 (6), 967-84.

Louro, Maria J., Rik Pieters, and Marcel Zeelenberg (2007), "Dynamics of Multiple-Goal Pursuit," *Journal of Personality and Social Psychology*, 93 (2), 174-93.

Prelec, Drezen and Ronit Bodner (2003), "Self-Signaling and Self-Control," *Time and Decision: Economic and Psychological Perspectives on Intertemporal Choice*, ed George Loewenstein, Daniel Read, and Roy Baumeister, New York, NY: Sage, 277-98.

Scheier, Michael F. and Charles S. Carver (1985), "Optimism, Coping and Health: Assessment and Implications of Generalized Outcome Expectancies," *Health Psychology*, 4 (3), 219-47.

Scheier, Michael. F., Jagdish K. Weintraub, and Charles S. Carver (1986), "Coping with Stress: Divergent Strategies of Optimists and Pessimists," *Journal of Personality and Social Psychology*, 51 (6), 1257-64.

Taylor, Shelley E. and Jonathon D. Brown (1988), "Illusion and Well-Being: A Social Psychological Perspective on Mental Health," *Psychological Bulletin*, 103 (March), 193-210.

Zhang, Ying, Ayelet Fishbach, and Arie W. Kruglanski (2007), "The Dilution Model: How Additional Goals Undermine the Perceived Instrumentality of a Shared Path," *Journal of Personality and Social Psychology*, 92(April), 389-401.

The Good, the Bad, and the Ugly: Pro-Social, Selfish, and Unethical Behavior

Chairs: Rosellina Ferraro, University of Maryland, USA
Ajay Abraham, University of Maryland, USA

Paper #1: The "Cellph"-ish Effects of "Self"-phone Usage
Anastasiya Pocheptsova, University of Maryland, USA
Rosellina Ferraro, University of Maryland, USA
Ajay Abraham, University of Maryland, USA

Paper #2: The Dark Side of Rapport: Selfish Behavior in Negotiations
Sandy Jap, Emory University, USA
Diana Robertson, University of Pennsylvania, USA
Ryan Hamilton, Emory University, USA

Paper #3: The Heat of Economic Hardship: Empathy Gaps for Financial Deprivation Induce Moral Hypocrisy
Eesha Sharma, New York University, USA
Nina Mazar, University of Toronto, Canada
Adam Alter, New York Univeristy, USA
Dan Ariely, Duke Univeristy, USA

Paper #4: Predicting Consumers' Selfishness versus Predicting a Consumer's Selfishness: Asymmetries in Forecasts for Individuals versus Collectives
Clayton R. Critcher, UC Berkeley, USA
David Dunning, Cornell University, USA

SESSION OVERVIEW

A charitable organization is soliciting volunteers to help with distributing food to homeless people on the weekends. Would the likelihood of volunteering change if potential volunteers suddenly happened to receive a phone call or a text message before making their decision? Would the likelihood of volunteering differ if potential volunteers were asked to think about how likely others were to volunteer vs. how likely another individual was to volunteer? A buyer and a seller are negotiating over a piece of prime real estate. Would a high level of rapport lead one of them to lie to the other? Is one of them more likely to lie if she just lost money in a lottery?

These scenarios highlight everyday situations in which people make decisions about behaving in a self-centered and potentially antisocial manner. Each paper in the session investigates either the antecedents of selfish behavior or the impact of selfish behavior on subsequent judgments and decisions. Previous research suggests that a focus on the self can have negative outcomes (Baumeister, Smart, and Boden 1996). Additionally, moral systems have been conceptualized as mechanisms to "regulate selfishness and make cooperative social life possible" (Haidt and Kesebir 2010), implicating ethicality as an antecedent of selfish behavior. While the four papers approach the notion of selfish behavior in diverse ways, each one hinges on the implication of the self as a building block for their framework.

In the first paper, Pocheptsova, Ferraro, and Abraham show that usage of mobile phones, which function as psychological and physical extensions of the self, leads to an increased self-focus which, in turn, increases selfish behavior. They show that participants placed greater value on their time after using a mobile phone and were less likely to volunteer for a charity. Next, Jap, Robertson, and Hamilton question the notion that increased rapport should lead to more pro-social behavior in negotiations. They examine the context where conflict between negotiators' core needs means that a successful deal can only be reached when one or both parties acts unethically or "misbehaves," for example, by lying to the negotiation partner. They show that the desire to build or maintain rapport can lead buyers

and sellers to engage in unethical behavior by lying in impasse settings to achieve the desired selfish outcome. In the third paper, Alter, Mazar, and Ariely show that in hot states, specifically, when considering one's financial standing as weak relative to others, people are motivated to rectify this deficiency even if they are required to engage in morally questionable conduct. However, when individuals do not feel financially worse off (i.e., are in a cold state) they fail to appreciate this drive. Participants judged immoral acts committed out of financial deprivation more harshly than when they too experienced a similar state of financial deprivation. Finally, Critcher and Dunning conclude the session by proposing that thinking about an individual's selfish behavior versus a collective of individuals' selfish behavior results in different judgments. When focusing on individuals, estimates are influenced by consideration of an internal moral conscience, whereas when focusing on collectives, estimates are influenced by a consideration of social prohibitions. The authors show that an individual consumer's behavior is perceived as more pro-social than collective consumers' behavior, and further show the relative importance of the moral conscience and social prohibitions.

This session is likely to appeal to consumer researchers who are interested in selfish behavior and consumer judgments, in general, and more specifically in self-product connections, negotiations, and moral behavior. The research has both theoretical and practical implications. Although the positive effects of self-extending possessions have been documented (Belk 1988), Pocheptsova et al. demonstrate the unintended negative consequences of the same phenomenon, suggesting direct implications for the marketing of mobile phone products as well as their use as an advertising medium. Jap et al. also demonstrate a negative consequence of selfishness. Whereas previous research has shown that rapport has positive effects, the authors find evidence of antisocial behavior as a result of individual's selfish desire to secure a deal. Alter et al. add to these findings by demonstrating unethical behavior as a consequence of an otherwise unacceptable excuse (financial deprivation), highlighting an avenue for future research that focuses on the self-relevance of such excuses. Lastly, the paper by Critcher and Dunning raises questions regarding the estimates elicited by consumer researchers in surveys about others' behavior, and whether there are fundamental differences in how individuals respond to logically equivalent questions. Additionally, the research suggests that charitable advertisements that use reference statistics focused on individuals could lead to more pro-social behavior.

Taken together, the papers in the session highlight a number of domains where consumers behave selfishly, which have implications for social welfare. Understanding the mechanisms underlying such behavior can help consumer researchers find better ways to encourage consumers to behave more pro-socially.

The "Cellph"-ish Effects of "Self"-phone Usage

EXTENDED ABSTRACT

Mobile phones have become ubiquitous in our lives (Clark and Pasquale 1996). Consequently, human-computer interaction research has focused on the potentially detrimental effects of using digital devices on human cognition and behavior (Bianchi and Phillips 2005). In a similar vein, we address how the usage of mobile phones can have unintended negative consequences on social behavior.

Past research has demonstrated the self-expressive and identity-signaling roles that possessions, products, and brands play in consumers' lives (Aaker 1999; Belk 1988). They serve as means for differentiating from others and provide reinforcement for one's identity (Escalas and Bettman 2005). Belk (1988) suggests that our possessions are part of an extended self, and that the energy we invest in objects increases their potential for self-extension. Given how much time people spend on mobile phones, they are likely to be a strong component of people's extended selves. Further, because people hold mobile phones in their hands and because mobile phones serve as the interface for communication with others, essentially operating as mouths and ears, mobile phones also can be considered as physical extensions of the self. We expect that because mobile phones are both a psychological and physical extension of the self, their use increases activation and focus on the self. This increased focus on the self causes people to pay more attention to their self-interest, and to pursue outcomes that are aligned with their self-interest, at the expense of outcomes that might be beneficial to others. In other words, people engage in more selfish behavior. To test this proposition, we ran two experiments utilizing different measures of selfish behavior – the value participants place on their time and pro-social intentions.

Participants in the first experiment were randomly assigned to either a mobile phone condition or a toy condition. Participants were asked either to spend two minutes using the mobile phone as they normally would (except for making phone calls) or using the toy to create multiple shapes. Using the toy to make multiple shapes should provide an experience similar to doing multiple activities, such as texting, playing games, etc., on a mobile phone. In this experiment, we measured the value placed on one's time in two ways. First, participants were asked to indicate whether they preferred to receive two songs downloads now or to wait and receive more song downloads in the future. The results indicate that participants in the mobile phone condition were more impatient, expressing greater preference to download two songs now rather than wait and receive more song downloads. Second, participants were asked to indicate how much they would need to be paid to complete an additional 30-minute study, with a higher dollar amount indicating more value of their time. The results support the prediction, with participants in the mobile phone condition expecting to be paid significantly more to do another study ($M = \$19.80$) than participants in the toy condition ($M = \$12.98, F(1, 44) = 6.72, p < .05$).

In experiment 1, the toy did not possess any communication capabilities so it is possible that the observed differences across conditions were not due to increased self-focus, but due to activating associations with instant gratification, which may have resulted in placing greater value on own time. Experiment 2 was designed to rule out this alternative explanation. Participants were randomly assigned to either a mobile phone condition or a Facebook condition. We chose Facebook because it allows for instant communication, which, like mobile phones, could increase the need for instant gratification. Facebook, like mobile phones, is a part of students' identities, but unlike mobile phones, is not a physical extension of the self and thus should lead to a lower focus on the self relative to mobile phones. Participants were instructed to spend three minutes using either their mobile phones or their Facebook accounts on a computer Web browser. Then, they were presented with a short description of a local charity and asked how likely they would be to volunteer for the charity, and more specifically, how likely they would be to volunteer for three-hours one Saturday a month. Participants in the mobile phone condition were less willing to volunteer in general ($M = 3.27$) or for one Saturday a month ($M = 3.53$) than participants in the toy condition were to volunteer in general ($M = 3.65, F(1, 191)$ = 4.07, $p < .05$) or for one Saturday a month ($M = 3.96, F(1, 191) = 3.95, p < .05$).

In summary, we propose that the usage of mobile phones leads to a greater focus on the self, which in turn, results in more selfish behavior. In experiment 1, we found that the usage of mobile phones affected how much people valued their time. Experiment 2 replicated these results with a different measure of self-focus and using a Facebook condition to rule out instant gratification as an alternative explanation. Taken together, these two experiments offer convergent evidence for our propositions. An implication of these findings is the need for deeper introspection on the use of devices such as mobile phones for both marketers and consumers if an unintended consequence of their usage is to make people behave in fundamentally more selfish ways.

The Dark Side of Rapport:
Selfish Behavior in Negotiations

EXTENDED ABSTRACT

A considerable body of research has extolled the virtues of establishing rapport in negotiations. In conventional wisdom, negotiations have come to be seen less as a zero-sum exchange in which one side's gains can only come at the expense of the other side, and more as congenial affairs in which everyone can win. Experts on negotiation have even gone so far as to claim that the relationship among the negotiators is just as important as the substance of the negotiation (Fisher and Shapiro, 2005). Empirical work has largely supported this view. Negotiators who are high in rapport tend to be more likely to reach an agreement and more satisfied with the outcome. Although rapport generally has been found to have positive effects in standard negotiation settings, we investigate the effects of rapport in a context that has received less attention: impasse settings, where conflict between negotiators' core needs means that a successful deal can only be reached when one or both parties acts unethically or "misbehaves," for example, by lying to the negotiation partner. In a series of three experiments, we find that negotiators who have a high level of rapport are more likely to behave unethically than negotiators who have a low level of rapport.

The conventional view is that increased rapport, such as that facilitated through face-to-face communication leads to a higher incidence of ethical behavior (Naquin and Paulson, 2003). Valley, Moag and Bazerman (1998) found that individuals negotiating face-to-face are more likely to tell the truth than those negotiating either by telephone or in writing, in part because people believe that it is more costly to the relationship to lie face-to-face. Face-to-face encounters seem to prime social norms of honesty and a positive relational atmosphere (DePaulo, Kashy, Kirkendol, Wyer, and Epstein, 1996; Naquin and Paulson, 2003).

In contrast to the conventional view, we propose that in some circumstances rapport can lead to an increase in selfish behavior through deceiving the negotiation partner. At the core of our argument is the notion that sometimes negotiating involves giving the negotiation partner bad news—information that is contrary to the partner's preferences and could jeopardize coming to a successful deal. This negative information represents a psychological conflict for a negotiator who is trying to build or maintain a high level of rapport. Building rapport often involves seeking out areas of agreement, while sharing information that the partner does not like can result in conflict. Thus, we predict that when a negotiation involves core requirements that are in conflict, a negotiator seeking to build or maintain rapport may be more likely to deceive their partner than to disappoint them with the truth—acting selfishly by lying rather than facing an unpleasant situation.

All three experiments used the Bullard Houses case, a widely used ethics case developed by Northwestern University's Dispute Resolution Research Center in the Kellogg School of Management. The case involves interactions between one buyer agent and one seller agent negotiating over a piece of prime real estate. This case was selected for these experiments because it leads to a negotiation impasse in which it is easy to misbehave ethically in more than one way and its usage across the three experiments contributes to comparability across varying manipulations and populations. Participants were assigned to dyads, with each member of the pair assigned to either the role of the buyer agent or the seller agent and given information pertinent to their role. In short, the seller's agent is required to know how the buyer will use the property, while the buyer's agent is directed not to reveal the use of the land or the buyer's identity in order to protect the firm's goals and interests. In this way, the case is intentionally constructed so as to create an impasse based on conflicting core priorities between buyer and seller agents.

In our first experiment, rapport was manipulated through the medium in which negotiations were conducted. Building on research showing that face-to-face interactions tend to foster higher levels of empathy, positive affect, mutual attentiveness and coordination, we had some pairs of participants negotiate face-to-face (high rapport) and others negotiate from separate rooms using an instant messaging program (low rapport). We found greater incidence of selfish and unethical behavior in the high rapport condition than in the low rapport condition, including 1) a greater likelihood of reaching a deal (which could only be reached if one or both parties behaved unethically; 84.6% vs. 42.9%; $X2(1) = 6.85$, $p < .01$) and 2) a content analysis of the transcripts of the negotiations, which revealed a greater incidence of misleading statements, overpromising, lying and dissembling among high rapport participants ($F(1,50) = 25.97$, $p < .001$).

Because there are more differences between face-to-face and computer-mediated negotiations than just rapport, our second experiment manipulated rapport while holding constant the medium in which negotiations were conducted. All participants in the second study conducted negotiations via instant messaging (low rapport), but some of the participants engaged in a five minute rapport-building exercise before beginning (high rapport). These participants discussed positive aspects of their student experience and shared personal information about themselves, including name, hometown and major. As in the first experiment, participants in the high rapport condition were more likely to behave selfishly and unethically, including being more likely to reach a deal (97.0% vs. 79.5%; $X2(1) = 4.41$, $p < .05$) and a self-report measure of whether they had made false statements in order to conceal their true purpose (3.5 vs. 2.6; $t = -2.12$, $p < .05$).

In the third experiment, we find that the negative effects—but not the positive effects—of high rapport are reduced when negotiators are given a simple reminder before negotiations begin that one's actions can have long-term repercussions for one's reputation. Taken together, this research supports the idea that, despite its several advantages, in certain situations rapport has a dark side, of which negotiators must be wary.

The Hot-Cold Empathy Gap: Financial Deprivation Licenses Immorality

EXTENDED ABSTRACT

Morality is considered to have evolved as a mechanism of survival, restricting excessive self-interested behavior and fostering human cooperation (Shermer 2004). The basic idea behind this assumption is that individuals strive to live in accordance with their moral standards and refrain from transgressions through motivated self-regulatory mechanisms that help them to exercise moral agency. Yet, recent theories in social cognition and morality suggest that individuals selectively disengage these mechanisms so they can engage in brief instances of questionable conduct without violating their moral standards. In particular, self-sanctions can be disengaged by reinterpreting one's actions or minimizing the negative consequences of one's actions, vilifying the target of one's actions, and, most strongly, by obscuring personal causal agency through diffusion or displacement of responsibility (Bandura, Barbaranelli, Caprara, & Pastorelli, 1996; Mazar, Amir, & Ariely, 2008). Thus, the easier it is for individuals to employ any of these mechanisms and deactivate moral control, the more likely they are to engage in immoral behavior, such as cheating, without changing their moral standards. Such processes can lead to moral hypocrisy, where people impose strict moral standards while behaving less morally (Lammers, Stapel, & Galinsky, 2010). However, researchers have yet to examine whether such moral hypocrisy is conscious and deliberate or instead represents a subconscious failure to recognize the role of transient states.

Prior research has shown that not only are individuals' preferences and behaviors state-dependent but also they misjudge and mispredict their own as well as others' preferences and behaviors across affective states. This bias has been coined the "hot-cold empathy gap" (Loewenstein, 1999). Traditionally, the "hot-cold empathy gap" has been used to explain mispredictions of how drive states caused by bodily needs such as hunger, thirst, anxiety, and exhaustion affect judgment and decision making. What is less known is to what extent this also applies to non-bodily driven states. For example, one of the most important drivers in our western, developed world is money, which enables people to acquire tangible as well as intangible commodities (social influence, adoration, happiness, etc; Lea & Webley, 2006). One of the crucial distinctions between money and more bodily drive states is that one's absolute financial standing seems to matter less than one's standing relative to other people (Shafir, Diamond, Tversky, 1997). Thus, if money is indeed such a strong motivator, we posit that feeling financially worse off than others should motivate people to rectify this deficiency even if they are required to engage in morally questionable conduct. Furthermore, we hypothesize that when individuals do not feel financially worse off (i.e., when they are in a cold state) they fail to appreciate this drive and therefore judge immoral acts committed out of financial deprivation more harshly than when they too experience a similar state of financial deprivation (i.e., when they are in a hot state).

We tested our predictions in a series of four studies. In Study 1 we administered a survey in which individuals were asked whether they agreed with the statements that (1) one's financial situation is not an acceptable excuse for dishonesty, (2) all people, regardless of their financial standing, should be held equally accountable for dishonest behavior, (3) people who are financially deprived do not deserve more leeway when they behave dishonestly, and (4) when assessing the extent to which people are honest or dishonest, one should take into account how financially deprived they are. Participants held the general belief that financial standing should not matter. Interestingly, however, Study 2 and 3 show that being financially worse off than one's peers objectively (by losing instead of winning money in a lottery) or subjectively (by asking people to write down two vs. 10 reasons why they are financially better or worse off than their peers), increased lying to earn more money in a subsequent cheating task with real consequences. Finally, in Study 4, people, who were made to feel financially worse of than their peers (i.e., people who wrote two reasons for why they felt deprived; "hot" state), were more lenient in their sentencing of deprived but not non-deprived offenders, while people, who were not made to feel financially worse off than their peers (i.e., people who wrote six reasons for why they felt deprived; "cold" state), did not differentiate between those offenders.

Predicting Consumers' Selfishness versus Predicting a Consumer's Selfishness: Asymmetries in Forecasts for Individuals versus Collectives

EXTENDED ABSTRACT

Marketers, policymakers, and consumers alike have cause to forecast others' morally-relevant behaviors. For example, the government may consider what percentage of consumers will submit fraudulent warranty claims. Alternatively, a charity may forecast the likelihood that a consumer will donate to charity.

These examples differ most obviously in the behavior they focus on, but they differ in another key, but heretofore unappreciated, sense. The first example focuses the forecaster on consumers in general, while the second question focuses the forecaster on an individual (though non-individuated) consumer. Both consumer behavior and JDM researchers have treated forecasts of non-individuated individuals and collectives interchangeably. But might such forecasts systematically differ?

In five studies, participants estimated what percentage of consumers would engage in a morally-relevant behavior (collective condition), or they indicated the percent likelihood that a randomly selected individual from the population would display that behavior (individual condition). These two questions are normatively equivalent; for example, from a room with 30% women, the probability than any specific person is female is also 30%. Studies 1 and 2 demonstrated that people forecast that individuals will behave more prosocially than will collectives. Studies 3 through 5 provided correlational and experimental support for why a difference emerged.

In Study 1, all participants forecasted whether others would comply with a request. We framed compliance as being helpful (compliance = pro-social condition) or as failing to stand up for what is right (compliance = anti-social condition). Participants estimated—for an individual or for a collective—whether people would comply. The predicted 2 (framing: compliance = prosocial or compliance = antisocial) X 2 (target: individual or collective) interaction emerged, $F(1, 120) = 4.14, p = .04$. Regardless of whether it meant complying or resisting compliance, individuals—more so than collectives—were predicted to behave pro-socially. Because the same behavior was framed as pro-social or anti-social, alternative explanations appealing to specific features of compliance—as opposed to its pro-sociality—are made less plausible.

In Study 2, participants estimated others' (or an other's) likelihood of engaging in a range of pro-social and anti-social behaviors (identified as highly representative of these categories through pretesting) in the next month. Conceptually replicating Study 1, a 2(behavior: pro-social or anti-social) X 2(target: individual or collective) interaction emerged, $F(1, 305) = 5.44, p = .02$. A (non-individuated) consumer was forecasted to behave more pro-socially than were consumers as a whole.

Might these differences emerge for an artifactual reason--reflecting a difference between forecasts made in continuous terms ("How likely is this consumer to....) versus discrete terms ("What percentage of consumers will...."). Study 3 addressed this concern

by eliciting all judgments in a discrete form, asking "Thinking of a randomly selected Cornellian, how many times in the next year will he or she…" versus "Thinking of all Cornell students, how many times will the average student…" The same 2(behavior: pro-social or anti-social) X 2(target: individual or collective) interaction emerged, $F(1, 218) = 11.89, p = .001$.

Why might these differences emerge? Miller (1999) suggested that consumers subscribe to a descriptive "norm of self-interest," believing others to be generally motivated by selfishness. We identified two sources of constraint on consumers' selfishness. First, consumers have an internal moral conscience that pushes them to do the right thing. Second, there are social prohibitions on anti-social behavior that constrain it. Might forecasts of individuals versus collectives differ because each target type (individual or collective) focuses the forecaster on a different consideration? One hint from past research comes from findings that suggested that people were more sensitive to internal experiences when considering an individual than a group (Hsee & Weber, 1997). Also, Flynn and Lake (2008) found that people underestimated the impact of social pressure when considering an individual's behavior.

Participants in Study 3 rated, for each behavior, how much there would be internal pressure from one's moral conscience, and how much there would be social pressure, to do the right thing. And indeed, hierarchical linear modeling showed that forecasts for individuals were influenced by how much it was assumed an internal moral conscience would lead one to behave pro-socially, whereas social forces were neglected. Forecasts for collectives showed the reverse pattern.

Studies 4 and 5 confirmed this mechanistic account experimentally. In Study 4, participants saw the same set of selfless behaviors that had been slightly modified to speak to one's moral conscience more or less. For example, in the high appeal to moral conscience condition, participants forecasted donation rates to Doctors Without Borders. In the low appeal to moral conscience condition, participants forecasted donation rates to the Chamber of Commerce. Consistent with our account, when selfless behaviors had a strong appeal to a person's moral conscience, individuals were judged as more likely to do them than were collectives, $t(234) = 3.72, p < .001$. The asymmetry was eliminated when the behaviors had low appeal to moral conscience, $t(234) = 1.25, p > .24$.

In Study 5, participants learned about a dictator game that was played either publicly (high social pressure) or anonymously (low social pressure). Participants forecasted whether dictators would behave very anti-socially, giving only one penny to the other player. A 2(public pressure: high or low) X 2 (target: individual or collective) interaction emerged, $F(1, 86) = 4.58, p = .04$. Under high social pressure, both individuals and collectives were seen as equally unlikely to be stingy, $t < 1$. But under low social pressure, collectives were forecasted to be more anti-social, $t(86) = 2.40, p = .02$. Removing the social constraints on bad behavior only influenced forecasts of collectives.

Psychologically, forecasting a consumer's behavior differs from forecasting consumers' behavior. Given this distinction has not been previously appreciated, we hope that these findings may help make sense of when and why there may be disagreements about forecasts of consumers' (or a consumer's) behavior. With an understanding of how these forecasts tend to differ, future research may uncover when forecasts of one type or the other lead to more accurate predictions of the future.

Receiving Feedback during Goal-Pursuit: When Good Hurts and Bad Helps

Chair: Jordan Etkin, University of Maryland, USA

Paper #1: Can Losing Lead to Winning?

Jonah Berger, University of Pennsylvania, USA

Devin Pope, University of Chicago, USA

Paper #2: Squeezing Wine from Sour Grapes: How Consolation Goods Impact Motivation to Buy an Envied Product

Cait Lamberton, University of Pittsburgh, USA

Kirk Kristofferson, University of British Columbia, Canada

Darren Dahl, University of British Columbia, Canada

Paper #3: Feeling Good at the Right Time

Nadav Klein, University of Chicago, USA

Ayelet Fishbach, University of Chicago, USA

Paper #4: Conquering Conflict: Multifinal Means in Multiple-Goal Pursuit

Jordan Etkin, University of Maryland, USA

Francine Espinoza, European School of Management and Technology, Germany

Anastasiya Pocheptsova, University of Maryland, USA

SESSION OVERVIEW

Many of consumers' choices are goal-driven. For example, consumers may go to the gym because they value being healthy and have dinner with friends or family because they wish to maintain strong interpersonal relationships. Successful goal pursuit requires consumers not only to initiate, but to sustain motivation to pursue their desired goal(s) (Kruglanski et al. 2002). One factor that has been shown to affect motivation is feedback received during the course of goal-pursuit (Fishbach and Dhar 2004). Not surprisingly, previous research finds that receiving positive feedback regarding the success or potential success of one's goal directed efforts enhances motivation, while receiving negative feedback diminishes motivation. In this session we explore situations where feedback on goal pursuit affects motivation in unexpected ways. In particular, we look at situations where positive feedback hurts motivation and negative feedback helps motivation.

The first two papers focus on unexpected positive consequences of receiving negative feedback during goal pursuit. The paper by Berger and Pope shows that loosing by a little relative to one's competition can increase the effort invested in pursuing a goal. These authors argue that one's competition can serve as a reference point for goal pursuit; increasing motivation when slightly behind the competition. Indeed, basketball teams that were slightly behind at halftime were actually more likely to win than teams slightly ahead at halftime. The paper by Lamberton, Kristofferson, and Dahl shows that failing to obtain an envied product does not always decrease motivation to obtain it. In fact, when a low-value consolation prize is offered in place of a desired product, initial failure to obtain the envied good can actually increase purchase motivation.

The next two papers focus on unexpected negative consequences of receiving positive feedback during goal pursuit. The paper by Klein and Fishbach demonstrates that receiving premature positive news regarding the success of goal pursuit (i.e. being offered a job) decreases valuation of the outcome. Finally, Etkin, Espinoza and Pocheptsova show that though positive mood is generally thought to signal that goal pursuit is going well, it can also have a detrimental impact on subsequent motivation in multiple-goal pursuit by decreasing perceptions of means multifinality.

The four papers in this session propose to make a novel contribution to existing research on goal-pursuit by examining the impact of receiving feedback on subsequent motivation. We expect this session to be of interest to researchers working in the areas of motivation and consumer goals, as well as to those interested in the impact of contextual cues (such as framing) on consumer behavior. Each of the papers described below has multiple completed studies, and several are available as working papers.

Can Losing Lead to Winning?

EXTENDED ABSTRACT

Intuition suggests that being ahead in everything from bonus competitions to sales contests should increase the likelihood of winning. In sports, for example, teams which are ahead early in the game win over two thirds of the time and teams that are further ahead tend to win more. But could being slightly behind actually increase success? Could losing lead to winning?

We suggest this possibility based on research on goals and motivation. Although finishing part of a project or scoring a touchdown requires the same amount of effort whether a person or team is ahead or behind, goals can act as reference points (Heath, Larrick, and Wu 1999). Consequently, position relative to a goal can influence motivation in a manner consistent with Prospect Theory's key tenets (Kahneman and Tversky 1979). Loss aversion suggests that compared to people who are above their goal by a similar amount, people who are below or behind their goal will work harder because they see their performance as a loss. Further, due to diminishing sensitivity, people who are slightly below their goals should work harder than those for whom the goal is further away (Heath, Larrick, and Wu 1999; Kivetz, Urminsky, and Zheng 2006). These ideas have important implications for competition. Because winning involves doing better than adversaries, an opponent's performance should serve as a salient reference point. Consequently, whether people code their current performance as a gain or loss should depend on whether they are ahead or behind at that particular moment. As a result, being slightly behind may actually increase motivation and success.

We test how losing by a little affects motivation and performance in both the laboratory and the field. First, we analyze over 18,000 NBA basketball games (Study 1) and 45,000 collegiate basketball games (Study 2) to examine how being slightly behind at halftime affects whether teams win or lose. Building on these findings, we then use controlled experiments to directly test the causal impact of being slightly behind on individual effort (Study 3) and the role of self-efficacy in these effects (Study 4).

Study 1 consists of all NBA games played between the 1993 and 2009 seasons. Importantly, rather than just looking at overall winning percentages based on halftime score, we use a regression discontinuity design to estimate the *causal* impact of being slightly behind. Not surprisingly, the further teams are ahead, the more likely they are to win. Every two-points better a team is doing relative to its opponent at halftime is associated with a 6-8% increase in the probability of winning. There is a strong discontinuity, however, around zero. Rather than having a winning percentage that is 6-8% less than teams ahead by a point (as the model would predict), teams that are behind by one point are actually *more* likely than their opponents to win (triumphing in 58.2% relative to 57.1% of games). This is particularly noteworthy given that they are worse than their opponents

Advances in Consumer Research
Volume 39, ©2011

(looking at season winning percentage) and mechanically, have to score two more points than their opponent to emerge victorious. Regression specifications confirm that being slightly behind significantly increases a team's chance of winning. Overall, teams that are losing at halftime win 5.8 to 8.0% more often than expected (p's < .05). Ancillary analyses illustrate that these effects are robust to numerous controls (e.g., season winning percentage and home team) and are not due to differences in coaching. Study 2 finds similar results in NCAA games. Further, consistent with the notion that these effects are driven by motivation, minute-by-minute scoring data shows that being behind at halftime has the greatest impact immediately following when teams are behind.

Study 3 examines how competitive feedback influences effort. Participants engaged in a short competition task (pressing the 'a' and 'b' keys as quickly as possible) divided into two 30-sec periods. Between periods, participants were either told nothing or given competitive feedback: They were either told they were far behind, slightly behind, tied, or slightly ahead of another participant with whom they were competing. These conditions allow us to test whether being slightly behind increases effort, relative to being tied, being slightly ahead, or even not receiving any feedback at all. Further, they allow us to test whether the motivating effects of being behind hold even for being far behind and whether being slightly ahead induces complacency. As expected, being behind opponents led people to exert more effort, but only when they were slightly behind. Participants informed that they were slightly behind exerted more effort than participants in any of the other conditions, all $ts > 1.96$, $ps < .05$. All other conditions were equivalent, all $ts < 1.0$, $ps > .35$, indicating that being far behind did not increase effort and being slightly ahead did not decrease effort. Study 4 used a similar paradigm and shows that the motivating effects of being slightly behind are stronger among people who believe they can achieve their goal (i.e., have higher self-efficacy).

Taken together, the findings demonstrate that losing can sometimes lead to winning. Being slightly behind boosts winning among NBA and NCAA teams and experimental results show these motivating effects occur among individuals and underscore our proposed mechanism. In conclusion, encouraging people to see themselves as behind others, albeit slightly, should increase motivation and effort, and ultimately success.

Squeezing Wine from Sour Grapes: How Consolation Goods Impact Motivation to Buy an Envied Product

EXTENDED ABSTRACT

On one hand, the marketers of highly-demanded items benefit from consumer motivation: Open the doors, and rabid devotees will strip your shelves of every item in your inventory. On the other hand, recent work (Van de Ven, Zeelenberg and Pieters, 2010) suggests that individuals who walk away empty-handed may be demotivated to purchase the envied product, switching to a competitor's product or abandoning the purchase altogether. Which consumers are most likely to lose motivation to purchase an envied good in such situations? More importantly, what can marketers do to preserve, and even enhance, consumers' motivation to purchase an envied good?

Our research suggests that first, self-esteem plays a substantial role in determining the motivational effects of envy on willingness-to-pay for an initially desired product. Second, providing opportunities to obtain either high or low value consolation items alternately undermine or preserve consumers' motivation to purchase the envied good. Specifically, the possibility of obtaining a high-value consolation good facilitates the generation of positive counterfactuals

(Kahneman & Miller, 1986). These positive counterfactuals exacerbate sour grapes effects, lowering motivation to purchase the desired item. However, if individuals generate negative counterfactuals or are provided a low-value consolation opportunity in these situations, their motivation to obtain the desired good appears to be preserved or even enhanced.

Study 1 followed a 2 (winner present, winner absent) x continuously-measured self-esteem between subjects design. In a first phase of data collection, participants provided their own self-esteem level (Rosenberg, 1979) as well as their comfort in engaging in upward social comparison (Gibbons and Buunk 1999). Vancouver Canucks tickets were selected to be used as the envied good. Approximately two weeks later, participants attended a lab session. In the "winner" condition sessions, they were told that one session participant would win front row tickets to a Canucks game. The winning ticket was placed under a Confederate's seat. In the no-winner condition, participants completed all measures, still accompanied by the confederate, but no prize was discussed or awarded. Embedded in a battery of unrelated tasks, participants provided their perceptions of the confederate as well as their willingness to pay for Canucks' tickets. This willingness-to-pay measure constitutes our measure of motivation to purchase the envied good.

Higher self-esteem individuals were chronically less comfortable than their lower self-esteem colleagues with upward social comparison. This tendency appeared to lead them to provide lower ratings of a winning than a non-winning confederate. By contrast, lower self-esteem individuals showed no negative effects on the perception of the winning confederate. They did, however, show significantly lower motivation to purchase the Canucks' tickets in the winner as opposed to no winner sessions. Among these individuals, we thus see a "sour grapes" effect with regard to the envied good – seeing someone else win the tickets lowered their motivation to purchase them.

Assuming that some consumers will experience either chronic or situationally low self-esteem, how can marketers fight the sour grapes effect? In Study 2, we attempted to see if providing a consolation opportunity might reduce or even reverse these effects on participants' motivation to pursue the envied good. The envied good in this study was a Wii gaming system. To focus on product-related effects, self-esteem was first lowered by providing false feedback on GRE-type quiz performance. Procedures were then like those in study 1, including both winner and no winner sessions. However, here participants received no consolation opportunity, a high-value consolation opportunity (the chance to win a PS3 gaming system on a subsequent occasion), or a low-value consolation opportunity (the chance to win an inexpensive Catchphrase game.) In the no consolation condition, the prior sour grapes effect was replicated. Interestingly, when individuals were given a high-value consolation opportunity, motivation to buy the Wii was decreased even *more* than it had been when no consolation opportunity was offered. By contrast, providing a less-valuable consolation opportunity completely reversed the sour grapes effect. That is, a low-value consolation opportunity *heightened* participants' motivation to purchase the Wii system.

We argue that the exacerbation of the sour grapes effect in the high-value consolation case is akin to the "silver medal" effect. When offered a chance to win a relatively high-value consolation prize, participants could easily generate positive counterfactuals, experiencing strong negative affect related to the originally envied product. By contrast, positive counterfactuals are not readily activated by a low-value consolation.

To directly test this explanation, study 3 followed a 2 (positive counterfactual generation v negative counterfactual generation) x 3 (no consolation, high-value consolation good, low-value consolation) design. Participants recruited using Amazon's MTurk system (M(age) =, income =, x% male) were first placed in a low self-esteem mindset by writing a short essay about a failure experience in their life (White & Lehman, 2005). Subsequently, they read a scenario where a neighbor had won a 3D Plasma television, while they had either won nothing, won only a subsequent opportunity to win either a smaller, 2D flat-screen TV (high-value consolation) or won a chance to win a traditional CRT television (low-value consolation). They were then asked to generate either positive or negative counterfactuals regarding their situation (White & Lehman, 2005). As predicted, in the no consolation condition as well as in the high-value consolation, positive counterfactuals conditions, the sour grapes effect was replicated. However, having participants generate negative counterfactuals reversed the sour grapes effect for high-value consolation participants, such that their motivation to purchase the envied TV was significantly greater than in the no consolation prize condition.

Taken together, results from these studies support the theory that consideration of a high-value consolation opportunity can decrease motivation because the good substitute makes positive counterfactuals highly accessible. Interestingly, this offers a means by which marketers may squeeze wine from sour grapes. First, if relatively valuable consolation opportunities are available, they may be able to cue negative counterfactuals in the shopping environment. Second, marketers may both save money and enhance motivation, by providing only a token item to offset the potentially negative consequences of envy.

Feeling Good at the Right Time

EXTENDED ABSTRACT

It has long been established that people are happy when they find out they attained their goals. Research has not addressed, however, whether people hold expectations about the timing of when they would learn that they attained their goals. For example, a job applicant may expect to learn the results of the application via an official offer letter to be sent, say, a week after the final interview. But sometimes attainment news arrives sooner than expected. An HR representative may contact the job applicant with positive news before the official offer letter is sent. How do people experience premature good news? Different lines of research appear to support divergent predictions.

On the one hand, if emotion is viewed solely as a reaction to surprise (e.g. Carver & Scheier, 1990; Orthony, Clore, & Collins, 1988; see also Wilson & Gilbert, 2008), one might expect that premature news would lead to heightened positive emotion. This is because premature news is surprising not only due to its content but also due to its timing. Our research, however, predicts the opposite. We hypothesize that when news arrives prematurely, people hold back positive emotion. Specifically, we predict that compared to those who receive timely news, people who receive premature news would be less happy both when they receive premature news, and when they eventually receive timely news.

We motivate our predictions with self-regulatory theory. Specifically, people typically experience positive emotion following goal attainment and prior to disengaging from the goal (Higgins, 1987; Forster, Liberman, & Higgins, 2005). But when people perceive good news to be premature, they may not want to disengage too early. Accordingly, we hypothesize that holding back positive emotion would lead to sustained engagement in the goal.

We further hypothesize that holding back positive emotion has consequences in terms of goal value. Previous research has shown

that affective cues influence goal value (Aarts, Custers, & Holland, 2007; Ferguson, 2008). Since premature news leads to the holding back of positive emotion, it consequently should lead to the devaluation of the goal.

We present three studies to support our hypotheses. In study 1, participants applied to a mock summer internship. In one condition, they received the results of their applications via hardcopy letter. In another condition, participants received the results via an unofficial computer message before receiving the official letter. We find that compared to those who received only the official letter, participants who received the premature computer message were less happy both when they received the computer message (an aversion to feeling happy too early) and when they eventually received the official letter (when they were no longer surprised).

In study 2, we replicate our finding that premature news leads to the holding back of positive emotion, as well as establish the link between emotion and goal value. Specifically, participants played a game of rock-paper-scissors in which they were told they had to win two out of three rounds. Premature news was manipulated by obligating participants in one condition to play three rounds even when they won the first two rounds. Participants in the second condition stopped playing after winning the first two rounds. The results showed that participants who had to play a third round despite winning the first two rounds were less happy after the second round than participants who won the first two rounds and stopped playing. Importantly, participants who were obligated to play three rounds and held back their happiness were also willing to accept less money for the prize they got for winning, a Twix bar.

Study 3 was conducted to replicate our previous findings and establish the link between emotion and goal engagement. Participants played a game in which they had to guess which of three face-down cards was the joker. Premature news was manipulated by letting participants in one condition flip the cards they did not pick, thus informing them that they either won or lost before revealing the identity of the card they picked. In a second condition, participants were not given the opportunity to prematurely flip any card. The results showed that participants who knew ahead of time that they won were less happy than participants who learned of their victory in an official manner. Replicating our goal devaluation finding, mediation analysis showed that participants who held back their happiness also rated winning the game as less important than participants who did not hold back their happiness, with the intensity of positive emotion as the mediator. Finally, as an operationalization of goal engagement, we gave all participants the opportunity to read a passage related to the game for as long as they liked and measured the time they spent doing so. As predicted, participants who held back their happiness also spent more time reading than participants who did not hold back their happiness. Mediation analysis indicated that holding back positive emotion mediated the effect of premature news on longer reading times.

As a whole, the present research shows that people are sensitive not only to the content of attainment information, but also to its timing. In addition, the present research reveals an ironic effect of premature news, namely that premature news leads people to maintain engagement in a goal but to end up valuing it less.

Conquering Conflict: Multifinal Means in Multiple-Goal Pursuit

EXTENDED ABSTRACT

People often have multiple goals that they wish to pursue at the same time. For example, a person may strive to be successful professionally, spend time with family, and be healthy. Multiple-goal pursuit is inherently a complex phenomenon, requiring individuals to spread their limited pool of mental, emotional, and physical resources across several different goals (Kruglanski et al. 2002). Such multiple-goal pursuit can create the sense that one's goals are in conflict, which is a psychologically aversive state that has detrimental consequences for motivation (Emmons and King 1988; Riediger and Freund 2004).

How can people overcome inter-goal conflict and stay motivated to pursue their multiple goals? One way to attenuate the negative impact of inter-goal conflict on multiple-goal pursuit is by using means to goal attainment that are instrumental to the pursuit of not one but multiple goals at the same time. Choosing such "multifinal" means in the course of goal pursuit allows individuals to jointly pursue their multiple conflicting goals, making multifinal means (relative to unifinal means) more highly valued (Chun and Kruglanski 2005; Kruglanski et al. 2002).

Previous research on single-goal pursuit has found that positive mood signals effectiveness of goal-directed behavior and increases motivation to pursue the active goal (Louro, Pieters, and Zeelenberg 2007). We propose that in the context of multiple goals, positive affect will also influence consumers' ability to perceive means as multifinal, which will in turn negatively affect multiple-goal pursuit. Positive affect has been found to result in recognition of more, and more different, aspects or features of items (Isen et al. 1985; Isen et al. 1987), giving rise to a greater recognition of differences and increasing the complexity and richness of a set (Kahn and Isen 1993). Applying these findings to the context of multiple goals, we argue that positive mood would increase perceptions of inter-goal conflict. Further, such an increase in perception of goal-conflict would lead to increased difficulty in perceiving any single means as instrumental to several conflicting goals. Therefore, we predict that positive mood will make it more difficult to perceive multifinality among means to goal attainment, leading to lower motivation to pursue multiple goals.

Across several studies, we find support for our propositions. In study 1, we tested our basic proposition that positive mood increases perceptions of inter-goal conflict. Mood was manipulated by varying the outcome of an Ultimatum Game (positive mood = accept offer, negative mood = reject offer). Next, all participants were primed with three goals (a performance goal, a pleasure goal, and a self-improvement goal) and then reported their perceptions of conflict among the goals. To measure inter-goal conflict, we timed participants as they listed as many means as they could think of related to the three goals. Consistent with previous research that suggests inter-goal conflict has a detrimental impact on motivation, we

reasoned that participants who experienced heightened inter-goal conflict (in the positive mood condition) would have more difficulty completing the means listing task relative to participants who experienced less goal conflict (i.e. negative mood). Consistent with this logic, it took participants in a positive mood more time (in seconds) to list an equivalent number of means as it did participants in a negative mood ($M_{positive}$=125.5 vs. $M_{negative}$=97.02).

Study 2 directly investigated the effect of positive mood on perceptions of means multifinality. Mood was manipulated by showing participants one of two video clips pretested to induce positive vs. negative mood. Next, instead of priming goals, we asked participants to list five important goals they were currently interested in pursuing. Finally, we asked participants to list (up to 10) means to achieve their goals and rate the extent to which the listed means served multiple goals. As we expected, participants in a positive mood perceived the means they listed as less multifinal than participants in a negative mood ($M_{positive}$=4.9 vs. $M_{negative}$=5.76).

Study 2 showed that positive mood makes perceiving means multifinality more difficult. As a result, we reason that positive mood should also decrease effort invested in using available means to goal attainment. However, this effect should be attenuated if individuals are made aware of means multifinality. Consistent with previous research that suggests positive mood is beneficial for goal pursuit (Custers and Aarts 2005; Fishbach and Labroo 2007), we expect positive mood to increase motivation in multiple-goal pursuit when available means to goal attainment are explicitly described as multifinal. In study 3 we test this reasoning by giving participants a means to multiple-goal attainment and measure the energy devoted to its use. After watching the sad versus happy videos, participants were primed with three goals (the same goals as used in study 1), and then were presented with an anagram task that was described as either unifinal (helping to achieve the first primed goal) or multifinal (helping to achieve all three primed goals). Motivation to pursue the primed goals was measured via the time participants persisted in the anagram task. We find that participants in a positive (vs. negative) mood persisted less in the task when it was presented as being unifinal ($M_{positive}$=133.88 vs. $M_{negative}$=196.15), but they persisted more than participants in a negative mood when the task was described as multifinal ($M_{positive}$=191.54 vs. $M_{negative}$=159.96), supporting our prediction.

Taken together, our findings support our proposition that positive mood leads to greater perceptions of inter-goal conflict and affects the perceptions of and use of multifinal means. Our findings contribute to the literatures on mood and motivation by expanding our understanding of the interplay between emotions, means, and goal-pursuit in the context of multiple goals.

The Engaged Consumer: Creating, Disseminating, and Negotiating Value in the Realm of Social Media

Session Chair: Daiane Scaraboto, York University, Canada

Paper #1: "You Guys Have Been Along Long Enough To Know":
The Collective Development of Consumer Co-Creation

Daiane Scaraboto, York University, Canada
Robert Kozinets, York University, Canada

Paper #2: Value-Creation in Brand-Related User-Generated Content on YouTube

Andrew Smith, York University, Canada
Eileen Fischer, York University, Canada
Chen Yongjian, York University, Canada

Paper #3: "Hey, What's in it for Us?": How to Initiate and Maintain Participation and Collaboration with Creative Consumer Crowds

Andrea Hemetsberger, University of Innsbruck, Austria
Robert Kozinets, York University, Canada

SESSION OVERVIEW

The dissemination of communication technologies and, in particular, the transformations brought up with a social Web, confirm that our consumer culture has become deeply intertwined with an information economy. In this context, generating massive amounts of content, participating, sharing, and collaborating are some key practices daily enacted by a large number of networked individuals. Observing these changes and the new patterns of interaction among individuals, and between communally embedded individuals and companies, scholars in different fields have proposed new frameworks to understand the relationships and activities developed in this participatory, networked environment.

While an existing body of literature has problematized the relationships between marketers and communities (Kozinets 2001; Muniz and O'Guinn 2001; Schouten and McAlexander 1995), consumer researchers are only beginning to explore the dynamics between consumers and marketers who collaborate using the new social media. In this "many-to-many" model of communication, individuals who merely received content now become involved, frequently assuming a central role in the production and dissemination of value (Jenkins 2006). These new dynamics of collaboration in participatory cultures have blurred the boundaries between consumers and producers of entertainment and media content (Schau and Russell 2004), brand communications (Kozinets, de Valck, Wojnicki, and Wilner 2010), brand meaning (Muniz and Schau 2007), and overall value (Schau, Muniz, and Arnould 2009; Cova, Kozinets, and Shankar 2007). As Jenkins (2006, 3) observes, "rather than talking about [media] producers and consumers as occupying separate roles, we might now see them as participants who interact with each other according to a new set of rules that none of us fully understand."

While acknowledging that participants may have different degrees of status and influence, participatory cultures have been celebrated as avenues for consumer empowerment (Jenkins 2006). Lessig (2008, 111), for example, observes that, "in a culture in which it [participation] is common, its citizens develop a kind of knowledge that empowers as much as it informs or entertains." It is important to note, however, that in this collective, many-to-many approach, aspects other than creativity and agency have been moved unstable. As observed by Lauwaert (2009, 9), in participatory developments "not only money is fed back into the circuit of capital that moves from production to commodity to consumption and back to production, but also the voluntary, unpaid labor of devoted fans."

These reflections resonate with a recent stream of research on marketing, consumer culture, and related fields that explore the possibilities, outcomes, and implications for consumers of a co-creation economy. The exploitation of consumer (or fan) labour evoked by Lauwaert (2009) has been analytically developed by consumer researchers (Cova and Dalli 2009; Bonsu and Darmody 2008; Zwick, Bonsu, and Darmody 2008) and scholars in other disciplines (Foster 2009; Arvidsson 2008, 2005; Lazzarato 1996). Consumer culture scholars have also explored the infinitely co-creative potentialities of consumers and the benefits they extract from their creative acts (Schau et al. 2009; Kozinets, Hemetsberger, and Schau 2008; Kozinets 2001; McAlexander, Schoutern, and Koening 2002).

Building on the scholarly work described above, and observing current developments in consumer culture, this session focuses on the phenomenon of value (co)creation by consumers. Our studies, and the discussion we hope to generate during the session, represent an attempt at understanding how the shifting relations between consumers and marketers have been transformed by the current focus on more public, more community-based, more socially networked, more collective forms of interaction. Assembling connections between media studies and consumer research, and emphasizing a cultural/anthropological approach, this session will offer a refreshing perspective on the topic of collaborative value creation, which has been of interest to consumer researchers for a long time (Kozinets 1999; Schouten and McAlexander 1995; McCracken 1989).

The presentations included in this session will focus on the value creating practices of consumers involved in generating content for social media, and the online interactions of consumers as they acquire knowledge and skills to negotiate the allocation of collectively created value. In all cases, the authors have collected data, developed analyses of their datasets, and crafted preliminary manuscripts to report their findings. This session is aimed at provoking lively discussion among participants that will contribute to the refinement and further development of the papers included here, and of other scholarly research on the topic. With that in mind, presentations will be kept shorter than 20 minutes, leaving enough time for discussion and questions from the audience. The session will be mediated by colleague Hope J. Schau, a scholar renowned for her work on consumer culture, brand communities, new media, and value creation in the marketplace. Likely participants in this session are colleagues interested in marketer-consumer collaboration, value creation, social media, consumption communities, and internet-based research.

"You Guys Have Been Along Long Enough To Know": The Collective Development of Consumer Co-Creation

EXTENDED ABSTRACT

Although his meaning transfer model has been widely critiqued for its static qualities, McCracken's (1989) descriptions of culture-in-action leave no doubt as to the infinitely co-creative potentialities of consumers and their communities. Schouten and McAlexander (1995) recognized the creative activity of consumer "subcultures" and their importance to the marketing function of contemporary business. Kozinets (1996) described and argued for the importance of the intensely productive and communal activities emerging online, and explicitly theorized the marketing implications of the "creative activity" of online communities and its influence on word-of-mouth and promotions (Kozinets 1999).

Almost a decade later, Prahalad and Ramaswamy (2004, 5) proclaimed that "[c]onsumers now seek to exercise their influence in every part of the business system. Armed with new tools and dissatisfied with available choices, consumers want to interact with firms and thereby co-create value." This proposition that the consumer has become a desirable co-creator of value is also central to another widely-lauded contribution, the service-dominant logic approach/brand proposed by Vargo and Lusch (2004).

These reflections have initiated a stream of research on consumer culture, marketing, and related fields that explore the possibilities, outcomes, and implications of a co-creation between businesses and communally-situated consumers. Within this literature, two oppositional perspectives emerged. First, a critical perspective conceptualizes co-creation and the new business practices proposed by its advocates as a reconfiguration of marketers' exploitation and control of consumers. From this standpoint, "the co-creation economy is about experimenting with new possibilities for value creation that are based on the expropriation of free cultural, technological, social, and affective labor of the consumer masses."(Zwick, Bonsu, and Darmody 2008, 166). Similarly, it has been proposed that when marketers foster experimentation, creativity, and interaction among consumers, they are merely investing in elements that will result in the alienation of consumers and the expropriation of their free labour by the company (Arvidsson 2005; Foster 2009). A more positive view of the phenomenon points to the (mostly non-economic) rewards and benefits available for consumers who engage in co-creation processes. Scholars subscribing to this perspective understand co-creation as an agentic and expressive act, not a deterministic response (Etgar 2008). They have investigated, for example, the personal and social benefits obtained by consumers who engage in value-creation within brand communities (Kozinets 2001, 2007; Kozinets, Hemetsberger, and Schau 2008; McAlexander, Schoutern, and Koening 2002; Schau et al. 2009) and the psychological implications of consumer participation in co-creation (Bendapudi and Leone 2003).

What is lacking, from both perspectives, is a consumer-centric understanding of what community members themselves think about the allocation of value when participating in co-creation projects with companies. Inspired by cognitive studies of consumer knowledge development (Ahluwalia and Burnkrant 2004; Campbell and Kirmani 2000; Friestad and Wright 1994, 1995), culturally situated investigations of consumer attitudes toward corporations (Giesler 2008, Arsel and Thompson 2004, Kozinets 2002), consumer thinking about their rights and responsibilities (Henry 2010), and on the development of "moral economies" in fan communities (Jenkins, Ford, and Green, forthcoming), we investigate the collective development of co-creation expertise by consumers who congregate using social media. By looking at how consumers develop co-creation expertise and build a repertory of strategies to negotiate co-created value with marketers we hope to advance our understanding of how marketers and consumers should share economic and non-economic benefits of co-creation.

To be clear, our focus is not on the development of co-creation knowledge at the individual level, nor at the widely shared, cultural level. Rather, we argue that an intermediary level of co-creation intelligence development can be identified in collectives that evolve around conversations in social media. Social media have increased consumers' ability to share, cooperate with one another, and engage in collective action with very little interference from companies. Therefore, the opportunities available for consumers to learn about collaborating with marketers have also multiplied. In order to explore this new environment for understanding consumers' perspectives on co-creation, we conducted a qualitative study of the geocaching community.

Geocaching is a "global treasure-hunt" for enthusiasts who combine online communities and GPS technologies to play hide-and-seek with various "caches" in locations around the world. Geocaching was initiated in 2000 by a group of GPS enthusiasts and soon grew into a hobby practiced by an estimated 2 million people. From its inception, geocaching has motivated heavy reliance on collaboration and sharing to the refinement, development, and maintenance of the game. Currently, geocaching is a fascinating hybrid of interwoven commercial and gift economies. The main website concentrating information essential to the game is a commercial enterprise to which hundreds of volunteer players willingly contribute, and thousands of others subscribe (at an optional paid membership). Several open-source developments unfold within this website and in peripheral non-commercial websites. Geocaching is a consumer community context in which we can study the lived complexity of the commercial intertwining with the communal, and where collaboration between consumers and companies can be traced beyond the creative stage, in multiple online sites.

As suggested in Kozinets (2010), we combined netnography with traditional, in-person ethnographic techniques to investigate the online and offline activities of individuals who play geocaching. The dataset used in this paper focuses on the online aspects of the activity, and includes hundreds of pages of online data representing geocachers' interactions on different social media (e.g. online forums, blogs, Twitter) which were collected over a three-year period of participant observation online.

Preliminary results suggest that in observing, posing questions, sharing stories, and discussing critical episodes online, community members learn to differentiate between three types of co-creation projects, each of which is accompanied by a specific frame for economic and non-economic value negotiation: volunteer +community projects; company+community projects; and volunteer +company projects. Consumers draw from community-specific values and broader, external logics (e.g. work/play, market logics, web 2.0 culture) to determine adequate frames to each type of collaboration. Observing that consumers collectively gauge their expectations and demands in relation to value that is created in different collaboration modes, our study complements current understandings of consumers as co-creators of value.

Value-Creation in Brand-Related User-Generated Content on YouTube

EXTENDED ABSTRACT

The production of online, brand-related, user-generated content (UGC), is one way consumers can potentially co-create value. UGC is published content that demonstrates a degree of creative effort, which may draw on marketers' offerings, and is "created outside of professional routines and practices" (OECD 2007; Kaplan and Haenlein 2010, 61). It takes on many forms, including product reviews, social network site posts, blogs, advertisements, and contributions to collaborative projects. It may be created independently by online users, or facilitated or sponsored by firms (Berthon, Pitt & Campbell 2008; Christodoulides 2009). While research on the benefits or perils of brand-related UGC is nascent (Burmann 2010), some scholars have investigated the value that specific forms of online UGC might create for firms. For example, Chevalier and Mayzlin (2006) find that increases in positively valenced user reviews on Amazon.com and Barnesandnoble.com predicts increases in book sales, and that extremely negative reviews have a greater impact on sales than do extremely positive ones. Studying forums hosted on company websites, Chiou and Cheng (2003) find that favourableness and frequency of brand-related UGC can influence consumer brand perceptions, with negatively valenced messages having a greater impact on low-image brands. While these studies focus on UGC more narrowly, there is also community-level research (e.g. Kozinets, Hemetsberger, and Schau 2008; Füller, Matzler and Hoppe 2008) that conceptualizes UGC as part of collective consumer innovation processes that create value for firms. Collectively, these studies provide important substantiation of the value of online UGC for firms.

Complementing research that examines the value created for firms, some research also suggests that UGC creates value for other consumers; brand community research (e.g. Kozinets 2001; Muñiz and Schau 2005) is the most prominent in this regard. For example, in a recent meta-analytic study of brand communities, Schau, Muñiz and Arnould (2009) conceptualize the practices and processes through which brand communities create value. They identify twelve value-creating practices, grouped across four thematic areas: social networking, impression management, community engagement, and brand use. Online UGC is a component of a number of the practices identified.

While it has been extremely fruitful to explore value creation in brand communities, not all brand-related UGC is created within brand communities. Indeed, the majority of consumers are probably not impassioned brand advocates or brand community members. It is thus important that we develop a better understanding of the potential value to consumers of UGC that is not generated within a brand community. Our research takes up this challenge. It examines the applicability of recent brand community research on value creation (in particular Schau, Muñiz and Arnould's (2009)) but also looks for additional types of potential value-creating elements in online brand-related UGC generated in a context that does not require or presuppose a brand community: YouTube.

YouTube is a content community (Kaplan and Haenlein 2010) and popular social media site (Burgess and Green 2009) that draws approximately 490 million unique visitors per month (Elliot 2011). More than other popular user-driven social media channels (e.g. Facebook and Twitter), YouTube hosts consistently rich UGC and more permanent and accessible records of responses to posted content. This makes it an appropriate context for exploring how value may be created in brand-related UGC, such as consumer-created videos, and the value that other consumers, such as those responding to the videos, derive from that UGC or fail to derive from that UGC. While some have argued that the practice of viewing, but not responding to UGC, itself offers value to other users by supporting contributors and the overall community (e.g. Jenkins 2006), this study will focus only on those who do publicly respond online. The data for this study consists of approximately 50 UGC 'haul' and 'outfit-of-the-day' videos, and all accompanying comments for those videos, sampled around two brands – Lululemon and American Apparel – that were posted to YouTube between June, 2010 and January, 2011.The posts were selected at random from Google search results for: 'brand' on 'site:YouTube.com'. The two brands were sampled because they generate enough interest from consumers to be featured in UGC in this content community, and are in the same category: clothing manufacturing and retailing. The number of comments per video start at zero and run into the thousands, although most range from the tens to the low hundreds.

While YouTube is not a 'brand-community', it is conceivable – since only a small percentage of social network participants create content (Burgess and Green 2009) – that brand-related video postings and comments will be dominated by motivated Lululemon or American Apparel brand community members or brand 'haters'; this does not bear out in the data set, and the focal brands are often fea-

tured, with equal emphasis, alongside a constellation of other brands. Analysis of the data set suggests that some of the value-creating practices found in brand communities, such as 'evangelizing', are mirrored in content elements of UGC found on Youtube; other community practices are not. Moreover, the UGC of these less brand-involved consumers involves elements that may not feature in UGC created within brand communities. For example, one type of content we frequently observed was "multi-brand integration," in which consumers suggest appropriate pairings of multiple brands, none of which appears focal or central to the ensemble. Analysis also seeks to establish the connection between these potentially value-creating elements of UGC and what types of value 'vocal' consumers indicate they are deriving. This research seeks to contribute to the discussion on the socially engaged consumer by broadening our knowledge of the elements of UGC that may create value, and on the types of value consumers appear to derive from UGC when they are not embedded in brand communities.

"Hey, what's in it for us?": How to Initiate and Maintain Participation and Collaboration with Creative Consumer Crowds

EXTENDED ABSTRACT
You guys have been along long enough to know": The collective development of consumer co-creation knowledge in social media

Social media have fundamentally altered our view of the consumer – from the 'passive recipient' to the 'active agent'. Literature on how to monetize social media's potential to activate consumers has exploded in recent years (Florida, 2004; Surowiecki, 2005; Tapscott & Williams, 2006) yet, the insights are mainly of tactical nature; its strategic implications are still under-theorized. But how should we initiate and maintain online cooperation with consumers? A classic answer would be to use all available channels to get access to online communities and social networks via promotional initiatives. Yet, typical exploitation strategies that aim to integrate consumer-users into marketing efforts of business organizations have also provoked susceptibility and conflict in social online media. A recent cross-cultural investigation into Facebook users' reactions to advertising attempts indicate that the respondents do not find Facebook ads informative or funny and have a low threshold level for irritation. A large majority would definitively or possibly leave Facebook if commercials on Facebook became more dynamic or mixed with friends' content (Kornum, Christensen, and Hemetsberger, under review). Similarly, Kozinets, de Valck, Wojnicki, and Wilner (2010) problematized the tensions that arise in consumer communities when community bloggers are asked to act as both, a continuing community member, as well as a marketing agent, in order to establish a trustful, credible and persuasive word-of-mouth campaign. Their findings suggest that messages need to be consistent with the goals, context and history of the blog and the bloggers, acknowledge and discharge commercial-communal tensions, and fit with the community's norms and objectives. Based on ample empirical evidence, researchers concordantly suggest that consumers should actually be treated as equivalent partners in a co-creative process of joint engagement in various value-creating practices (Merz et al., 2010; Schau, Muniz, and Arnould 2010; Kozinets, Hemetsberger, and Schau 2008). Consumers are creative, innovative participants and networked collaborators in a web of collective intelligence and partners for commercial endeavors in various ways. They are approached by companies as creative force (Tapscott and Williams 2006; Vargo and Lusch 2004; Lévy 1997), as innovators (Füller et al., 2007; von Hippel 2005; Prahalad and Ramaswamy 2004), and as marketers, engaging in word-of mouth (Kozinets et al. 2010). In the context of creative consumer crowds, where companies' interests are less informative-persuasive but more work-oriented, tensions among company intent and consumer interests take on a different quality and rather revolve around issues of accessing resources, and ownership (Giesler and Humphreys 2007).

In this special session we would like to present a framework that addresses these issues. Our framework proposes two main forms of interaction – participation and collaboration – and discusses feasible patterns of interaction. We distinguish primarily telo- from communo-ludic oriented communities and suggest appropriate participation and collaboration strategies of two-way interaction among communities and business organizations, based on two exploratory cases of participative and collaborative practices. Depending on the communal orientation, we see both models of community activation characterized by a 5-stage process. Participation processes are characterized by: (1) motivating: the allocation of resources to the consumer community, (2) asking: launching the idea and elicitation of consumer responses, (3) measuring: the evaluation of the outcome of these processes, (4) answering: providing meaningful responses to the creative contributors of the consumer community, and (5) responding: giving back to the community. Collaboration processes encompass: (1) education: both internal and external knowledge sharing, (2) sharing: provision of appropriate resources and a type of "social contract" governing intellectual capital sharing, (3) coordination: systems and processes to streamline the active consumer participation process, (4) evaluation: a communally-directed, producer-controlled, or hybrid-cooperative model of judging output, and (5) implementation: some sort of meaningful "closure" to the process and the sharing of results or collective outcome.

Our discussion carves out important strategic and tactical implications for each of the five stages, and details their differential expression for participation and collaboration business strategies. Different forms of activation demand different input and processes on the company's side, depending on the communo-ludic or telo-specific orientation of the contributor(s). For example, although the notion of sharing is important in both types of communal interaction, the boundedness, directionality, and hierarchical control of resources can be markedly different in the pursuit of participation versus collaboration strategies. Second, whereas communo-ludic oriented contributors need a lot of communal space and exchanges, relatively little resources and know-how, telo-specific orientation is characterized by knowledge sharing and creation and access to resources. These notions have important implications for marketing theory and practice. Creative consumer crowds are equipped with different power based on their amount of social and intellectual capital. Companies who are willing to cooperate will need to legitimate their leading role through careful development of participative and collaborative practices.

REFERENCES

Arvidsson, Adam (2005), "Brands: A critical perspective", *Journal of Consumer Culture* 5(2), 235-58.

--- (2008), "The ethical economy of consumer coproduction," *Journal of Macromarketing, 28* (4), 326-338.

Bonsu, Sammy K., and Aron Darmody (2008), "Co-creating second life: Market-consumer co-operation in contemporary economy," *Journal of Macromarketing, 28 (4),* 355-368.

Cova, Bernard, and Dalli, Daniele (2009), "Working consumers: the next step in marketing theory?" *Marketing Theory, 9* (3), 315-339.

Cova, Bernard, Robert V. Kozinets, and Avi Shankar (2007), *Consumer Tribes.* Oxford and Burlington, MA: Butterworth-Heinemann, 194-211.

Foster, R. J. (2009), "The Work of the New Economy: Consumers, Brands, and Value Creation," *Cultural Anthropology, 22* (4), 707-731.

Jenkins, Henry (2006). *Convergence Culture: Where Old and New Media Collide.* New York University Press.

Kozinets, Robert V. (2001), "Utopian Enterprise: Articulating the Meanings of Star Trek's Culture of Consumption," *Journal of Consumer Research,* 28 (June), 67-88.

--- (1999), "E-Tribalized Marketing? The Strategic Implications of Virtual Communities of Consumption," *European Management Journal,* 17 (3), 252-264.

Kozinets, Robert V., Kristine de Valck, A. J. Wojnicki, and Sarah Wilner (2010), "Networked Narratives: Understanding Word-of-Mouth Marketing in Online Communities," *Journal of Marketing, 74* (2), 71-89

Kozinets, Robert V., Andrea Hemetsberger and Hope Jensen Schau (2008), "The Wisdom of Consumer Crowds: Collective Innovation in the Age of Networked Marketing, *Journal of Macromarketing* 28, (4) 339 – 354.

Lauwaert, M. (2009). *The place of play: Toys and digital cultures.* Amsterdam: Amsterdam University Press.

Lazzarato, M. (1996). "Immaterial Labor" in *Radical thought in Italy: A potential politics.* Virno, P. and Hardt, M. (editors). University of Minnesota Press.

Lessig, Lawrence (2008). *Remix: Making Art and Commerce Thrive in the Hybrid Economy.* The Penguin Press.

McAlexander, James H., Schouten, John W. and Koening, Harold F. (2002), "Building Brand Community," *Journal of Marketing,* 66 (January), 38–54.

McCracken, Grant (1989), *Culture and Consumption,* Indianapolis, IN: Indiana University Press.

Muñiz, Albert M. and Hope J. Schau (2007), "Vigilante marketing and consumer-created communications," *Journal of Advertising, 36* (3), 35-50.

Muñiz, Albert M. and O'Guinn, T. C. (2001), "Brand Community," *Journal of Consumer Research,* 27 (March), 412-32.

Schau, Hope J., Muñiz, A. M. and Arnould, E. J. (2009), "How Brand Community Practices Create Value," *Journal of Marketing, 73* (5), 30-51.

Schau, Hope J. and Cristel A. Russell (2004), "Special Session Summary Consuming Television: Connectedness and Community in Broadcast Media", in *Advances in Consumer Research Volume 31,* 544-547.

Schouten, John and McAlexander, J. (1995), "Subcultures of Consumption: An Ethnography of the New Bikers," *Journal of Consumer Research, 22* (June), 43-61.

Zwick, Detlev, Sammy K. Bonsu, and Aron Darmody (2008), "Putting consumers to work: Co-creation and new marketing govern-mentality," *Journal of Consumer Culture* 8 (2), 163-96.

Consumer Gambling: Building Disciplinary Connections for a Better Understanding

Chair: June Cotte, University of Western Ontario, Canada

Paper #1: The Impact of Ambient Adjustments on the Temporal Monitoring of At-Risk Gamblers

Theodore Noseworthy, University of Western Ontario, Canada

Karen Finlay, University of Guelph, Canada

June Cotte, University of Western Ontario, Canada

Paper #2: Measuring the Effects of Pictorial and Text Messages on Memory and Gambling Intentions Within a Casino Environment

Alyssa Z. Rodrigo, University of Guelph, Canada

Karen Finlay, University of Guelph, Canada

Harvey Marmurek, University of Guelph, Canada

Paper #3: Shopping + Gambling = Shambling: The Online Context of Penny Auctions

Michael Giebelhausen, Cornell University, USA

Stacey Robinson, East Carolina University, USA

June Cotte, University of Western Ontario, Canada

Paper #4: Together We Stand, Divided We Fall: Categorization and the Process of Legitimation

Ashlee Humphreys, Northwestern University, USA

Kathryn LaTour, University of Nevada, Las Vegas, USA

SESSION OVERVIEW

Gambling is a massive industry, garnering billions of dollars in consumption across the world; global gambling revenue rose from $82.2 billion in 2005 to approximately $125 billion by the end of the decade (Associated Press 2006). As gambling grows, it also changes as it moves into the online world (Cotte and Latour 2009). Most recently, many auction shopping sites have integrated gambling elements into their design (Geibelhausen, Robinson and Cotte, 2011). This session brings together four sets of researchers who have investigated the topic of gambling from a variety of different perspectives, and with diverse methods. We are building connections between addiction psychologists, consumer psychologists, and sociologists. We are also bridging the experimental tradition to the CCT tradition to jointly investigate an important substantive consumption issue. Finally, our session discussion leader is a public health and sport marketing theorist, with more of an outsider, public-health perspective on gambling behavior. All four research teams have already collected their data and are either in early phases of analysis and interpretation (Giebelhausen, Robinson and Cotte; Humphreys and Latour) or have completed the analysis and will be submitting papers for publication soon (Noseworthy, Finlay and Cotte; Rodrigo, Finlay, and Marmurek).

The structure of the session is designed deliberately to move from the *inside out*. That is, we begin with two presentations that study problem gamblers from a psychological perspective, demonstrating how context and priming can reduce at-risk problematic gambling behavior. The data for the first two papers was gathered using a simulated casino laboratory. In the first, Noseworthy, Finlay and Cotte use music to affect dissociation; they demonstrate that the ambient context can reduce dissociation and gambling for at-risk gamblers, without affecting recreational gamblers' behavior. In the second, Rodrigo, Finlay, and Marmurek show that priming gamblers with different imagery in the casino environment can also influence their gambling behavior. After these two papers, we build a connection to the consumer world outside the laboratory, with a discussion of a new substantive gambling phenomenon. Dubbed "shambling"

by Giebelhausen, Robinson and Cotte, these authors present field data gathered online and in-person concerning penny auction sites, which are rapidly multiplying online, and which combine elements of shopping and gambling. Finally, we move to the *outside* view, concluding with Humphreys and Latour's examination of the legitimation process of online gambling; these authors use both archival and consumer survey data.

We believe the session is likely to make an important contribution to consumer research in several ways. Obviously, this is a substantively focused session, and we hope to encourage more research on what is rapidly becoming an important experiential consumption practice. But beyond this, the methodological collision of at least five major methodologies for data collection (experiments, netnography, ZMET interviews, surveys, and archival data) also demonstrates the strengths of building connections between multiple perspectives on a difficult issue. Finally, we contribute to the transformative consumer research tradition, with a clear focus on potential public policy remedies and interventions designed around consumer welfare. The potential audience for this session would also be diverse. Groups as varied as consumer psychologists interested in dissociation and temporal estimates and sociologists interested in societal processes of legitimation should all find something appealing here.

The 75 minute session would be organized as follows. Each paper will be presented in 12-15 minutes, leaving at least 15 minutes for Stephen McDaniel to offer his unique perspective and to engage the audience in active discussion of the topic. There are many ways to approach the study of gambling, and we hope to challenge audience members to get involved with the discussion and add their own unique perspectives to the session.

The Impact of Ambient Adjustments on the Temporal Monitoring of At-Risk Gamblers

EXTENDED ABSTRACT

Time and temporal issues have a long history when it comes to casino gambling. There is a common belief that casino designers actively discourage the use of temporal cues. And indeed, many casinos have neither window nor clock to infer duration of play. For many gamblers, it may be important to accurately keep track of time spent gambling, but that can be hampered if they enter a dissociative state. Dissociation is "the lack of normal integration of thoughts, feelings, and experiences" (Bernstein and Putnam 1986; 728) and involves an *aberrant perception of time* (American Psychiatric Association 1994).

Dissociative experiences occur when attention is deeply absorbed or focused, and when there is a loss of awareness or a lack of monitoring of internal states and external activities (Eisen and Lynn 2001). It also occurs during periods of fatigue, stress, or intense absorption (Csikszentmihalyi 1997). Hence, dissociation is relatively common; it equally afflicts males and females; it tends to decline with age, while being unaffected by socioeconomic status, education, religion, or place of birth (Ross, Joshi, and Currie 1991). Nevertheless, there are individuals who suffer a predisposition to dissociate. These individuals not only have difficulty self-regulating destructive patterns in their behaviour, but are also highly susceptible to external ambiguity, such that cues in the environment around them affect their psycho-emotional state (Nordin and Nylander 2007). But despite growing evidence linking dissociation and addiction, there has been little effort to explain why there is such an overwhelming occurrence of dissociation in casino gamblers. That is, if the predisposition itself is not relegated to the gambling context, why then is dissociative behavior so prominent in casinos?

The typical casino environment is designed to coerce arousal during consumption (Jefferson and Nicki 2003). Aroused states have a tendency to lead one to focus on fewer temporal cues (Mantel and Kellaris 2003). However, music in the context can overcome this by offering a syntactual structure that individuals can anchor on to infer duration (Noseworthy and Finlay 2009). It could be that individuals who are predisposed to dissociation may be quite susceptible to the common casino environment. Thus, music could be used to combat a maladaptive response to gambling.

Two-hundred participants ($n = 100$ *low-risk/non-problem gamblers*; $n = 100$ *high-risk/problem gamblers*) were recruited from a prescreened sample of identified gamblers who varied in their propensity to engage in problematic gambling behavior. Each volunteer was paid $25 for their participation, and was assigned to one of two experimental conditions in a 2 (environmental stimuli: control vs. music) x 2 (gambler type: low-risk/non-problem gamblers vs. high-risk/problem gamblers) x 4 (disruption points: diss1 vs. diss2 vs. diss3 vs. diss4) mixed factorial design. Gambling disruption served as the within-subjects factor and environmental stimuli and gambler type served as between-subjects factors. Participants were randomly interrupted from play at four different intervals: 6-minutes, 10-minutes, 4-minutes, and 12-minutes. Environmental factors were varied such that in the control condition, participants gambled with no auditory interference. That is, they gambled as they would in a typical casino. The music condition differed in that a music track—developed by a media-production company—played in the background along with the ambient casino sound.

Participants were tested in a slot machine laboratory and level of dissociation was assessed on a five-point scale (never, rarely, occasionally, frequently, all the time) through five items: (1) *Did you lose track of time?*, (2) *Did you ever feel like a different person?*, (3) *Did you feel like you were in a dream?*, (4) *Did you feel like you were watching yourself gamble?*, and (5) *Did you experience memory blackout?* (Jacobs 1988). Participants responded to the same five items after each time they were disrupted from play. They were also instructed to respond in terms of the incidence of play that occurred since they were last interrupted, or in the case of the first stoppage, since their play began. Similarly, after each interruption, participants were asked to estimate the elapsed time since their last interruption.

Overall, dissociation significantly predicted participants' placement in the problematic gambling index ($\beta\beta = .31$, $t(94) = 3.19$, $p < .005$), as well as a significant proportion of variance in the index ($R^2_{adj} = .09$, $F(1, 95) = 10.17$, $p < .005$). There was a three-way interaction between disruption, gambler type, and environmental stimuli ($F(3, 94) = 4.38$, $p < 01$). Dissociation decreased as a function of disruption in play. That is, dissociation dropped from disruption point #1 to disruption point #2 ($M_{p1} = 2.00$ vs. $M_{p2} = 1.84$; $p < 001$), from point #2 to point #3 ($M_{p2} = 1.84$ vs. $M_{p3} = 1.71$; $p < 005$), and then leveled off from #3 to #4 ($M_{p3} = 1.71$ vs. $M_{p4} = 1.75$; $p > 05$). At disruption point #1, there was a significant interaction between environmental stimuli and gambler type ($F(1, 96) = 28.00$, $p < 001$). The level of dissociation in *low-risk/non-problem gamblers* (LR-NPGs) did not significantly vary with the introduction of music into the ambient environment ($M = 1.52$ vs. $M_c = 1.72$; $F < 2$). Conversely, the level of dissociation in *high-risk/problem gamblers* (HR-PGs) varied significantly with the introduction of music into the ambient environment ($M = 2.78$ vs. $M_c = 1.94$; $F(1, 96) = 36.30$, $p < 001$). A similar phenomenon occurred at disruption point #2; the level of dissocia-

tion in LR-NPGs did not significantly vary with the introduction of music into the ambient environment ($M = 1.42$ vs. $M_c = 1.60$; $F < 1.5$), but dissociation in HR-PGs did vary with the introduction of music ($M = 2.60$ vs. $M_c = 1.68$; $F(1, 96) = 33.78$, $p < 001$). The same pattern happened at disruption points #3 and #4.

High risk problem gamblers displayed understated estimates of elapsed duration (disruption point #1 = $t(1, 25) = -2.75$, $p < .05$; #2 = $t(1, 25) = -2.50$, $p < .05$; #3 = $t(1, 25) = -1.93$, $p = .06$; #4 = $t(1, 25) = -1.65$, $p = .10$). As expected, the effect became more muted as the disruption points progressed, indicating distraction helped mitigate dissociation. Importantly, HR-PGs did not display understated estimates when music was introduced in the ambient environment (*p*'s ranging .21-.45 linearly across the four disruption points). This was consistent with the LR-NPGs.

The results of this study help explain the overwhelming occurrence of dissociation in casino gamblers. Although the predisposition itself is not relegated to the gambling context, dissociative behavior is so prominent in casinos partly because of the environment itself; this knowledge can be used to help at-risk gamblers. Many casino operators openly advocate mitigating problem gambling, but are reluctant to influence the recreational gambler. We show that subtle changes in the casino ambient environment can have dramatic consequences.

Measuring The Effects of Pictorial and Text Messages on Memory and Gambling Intentions Within a Casino Environment

EXTENDED ABSTRACT

Problem gambling is prevalent in today's society with the increase of available opportunities for people to gamble. Marketers and policy makers are searching for innovative ways to convey harm reduction messages to gamblers inside and outside the casino environment. This study investigated the effects of pictorial and text messaging about the risks of excessive gambling within casinos. It followed a 2 x 2 x 2 between-subjects design. The first factor was whether participants were exposed to information that primed gambling-related concepts (the consequences of excessive amounts of time and money spent) versus an unrelated at-risk concept (environmental sustainability) prior to completing subsequent experimental procedures. In an ostensibly unrelated task, respondents were asked to evaluate a brochure that had been developed to help first-year university students to adapt to life on their own. In the gambling-related condition, the brochure contained information about time and money management. In the condition unrelated to gambling, the brochure contained information about environment sustainability and tips for going green. Following exposure to brochure information, all respondents answered four questions about the effectiveness of the brochure's message and appearance.

The second factor was the presence of a pictorial versus a text message on a television screen to the right of the slot machine at which each individual was playing in a gambling setting. Text messages were in the form of three sentences (e.g., "Do you know how much money you have spent?") which appeared individually for 30-second intervals on a TV screen for 30 minutes while respondents played slot machines in the setting. Pictorial messages were three different pictures (e.g., an individual with empty pockets turned inside-out) which similarly each appeared for 30-second intervals on a TV screen for a total of 30 minutes.

The third factor was type of memory measure for the text or pictorial message following 30 minutes of play on the slot machines. Measures were either implicit (word association, stem completion) or explicit (unaided recall, recognition). For the word association test, respondents were given a set of ten pictures and asked to write the first word that came to mind when they viewed the picture. Seven of the pictures were unrelated stimuli (e.g., a pile of crayons, a sunflower) and three of the pictures were pictorial message stimuli that had been displayed in the lab (man with empty pockets turned inside-out, set of 16 clocks set at different times). For the stem completion test, participants were given a set of ten word stems and asked to complete the stem with the word that came most easily to mind. Similarly, words relating to the primed target were included (CL_ _ _ clock; BR_ _ _ broke). The explicit recall test first asked respondents to write down anything that came to mind about the slots lab experience, after which they were asked to list everything they remember seeing in the lab. For the explicit recognition test, respondents were given a set of six questions asking them to indicate if they remembered seeing any of the messages that appeared in the slot lab ('yes' or 'no' answer).

Participants (n=201, screened to be age 19 or older, who had bet money on a slot machine in last 6 months) were greeted at the lab, instructed to complete the priming task, and asked to play slot machines for 30 minutes during which either pictorial or text messaging was present in the gambling lab. All individuals began the play task with 8000 credits, an amount found to sustain 30-minutes of play time in past studies. They were instructed that they could play for as long as they liked but were free to stop at any point in time. They were also informed that the researcher might have to ask them to stop playing if another participant arrived. This was done for all participants after 30 minutes. Individuals were either reimbursed with a course credit if they were sourced from a university participant pool or with a ballot to win a $50 cash prize (odds of 1 in 20 chances to win). Subsequent analyses confirmed that results did not vary by remuneration type. Following slot play, all participants were asked to leave the slot lab and complete the computer-assisted questionnaire. Memory measures were taken first, then all participants completed the at-risk gambling intentions scale (ARGIS) composed of five questions measuring perceived intention to gamble beyond levels of money and time spent while in the slot lab. Responses were indicated on a 7-point scale anchored by 1 "don't agree at all" to 7 "strongly agree" to questions such as, "I would gamble/play more money that I intended", "I would have trouble quitting without placing one more bet". Demographic and gambling severity information was also collected.

A random-groups ANOVA showed no effects of priming on implicit measures and a reverse effect than that anticipated for explicit recall measures. Recall was higher with no prime than with a prime. It was concluded that the processing of an earlier prime may be lost or distracting in the complex context of a gambling environment. Text messages were directionally more effective when indexed by implicit memory tests while picture messages were significantly more effective when indexed by explicit memory tests. This latter effect is consistent with the picture superiority effect (Weldon and Roediger, 1987). At-risk concepts presented pictorially in this study were better remembered explicitly than were concepts presented textually. The measure of ARGIS was lower when messages were presented pictorially and no prime was included. It appears that under conditions where participants were able to process pictorial messages in the lab (no distracting prime related to at-risk gambling concepts), recall of at-risk messages was higher, corresponding to an intent to gamble within planned levels of time and money. Results inform effective communication of harm reduction messages for marketers and policy makers. Pictorial messages which reinforce the risks of gambling should be used inside the casino, in bathrooms or even on slot machines themselves.

Shopping + Gambling = Shambling: The Online Context of Penny Auctions

EXTENDED ABSTRACT

An emerging form of e-commerce, penny auctions, has garnered recent attention from consumers, investors, and regulators. However, consumer researchers have yet to explore this new phenomenon which has been likened to a combination of bingo, online shopping and slot machine addiction. In penny auctions, consumers participate in a game where the winner is awarded the opportunity to purchase a product for pennies on the dollar. Losers, and there is no limit to the number of people that can lose in a single auction, may spend large sums and walk away empty handed. The primary distinction between penny auctions and traditional online auctions is that consumers must pay a fee each time they place a bid. Because of the collective losers' bidding fees, a product sold at a 90% discount is equivalent to a traditional retail transaction featuring a 910% mark-up (e.g., the price starts at zero, it costs $1 to place a bid, the price of the product goes up one penny for each bid placed . If an item worth $100 is sold at a 90% discount ($10), this means that there were 1000 bids placed during the course of the auction. Ignoring shipping fees, the penny action collects $1010 in total revenue and the winner must pay an additional $10 for the product. Assuming the penny auction website purchased the product at retail, which is often the case, effective markup is 910%).

While penny auctions have been equated to discount shopping and games of skill, they have also labeled by some critics as an addictive form of gambling. In this research, we provide an introduction to penny auctions, and a first step towards delineating the gambling element of this new consumption genre. We explore the meaning and experience of this game-based shopping using data gathered with Zaltman Metaphor Elicitation (ZMET) interviews. Finally, we outline some of the policy implications of our work, and situate our recommendations for consumer welfare squarely in the transformative consumer research tradition.

Since 2005, penny auctions have grown from a single auction website to more than 150 websites with millions of bidders (The Economist, 2009; Pennells, 2008). There is debate regarding the proper classification of penny auctions (Pennells, 2008; Gimein, 2009). Are they a new form of online gambling or simply a harmless variety of online shopping? A review of the penny auction's genealogy suggests the former. Penny auctions are modeled after the dollar auction game invented by game theory pioneer Martin Shubik, which relies upon the concept of escalation of commitment (Shubik, 1971; Thaler, 2009). Once the consumer has bid on an item, they have a difficult time walking away – they feel invested in the game. The combination of escalation of commitment and absurdly low prices for popular products (e.g., Apple iPad that retails for $699 selling for $18.07; Louis Vuitton and Gucci handbags advertised at 90% off) yields an environment that has been referred to as evil, dangerous and addictive (Gimein, 2009; Luscombe, 2010; Thaler, 2009). While such words would hardly be used to describe an average consumer shopping experience, they could very well be used to describe a gambling experience (Cotte 1997).

We interviewed penny auction shoppers using depth interviews with visual images, and ultimately collages, that participants create (Zaltman 1997; Zaltman and Coulter 1995). This method assumes that much of this content is non-conscious and based in images, not words (Zaltman 1997, Zaltman and Coulter 1995). The interview technique we used helps interviewers delve into the metaphors that participants use to represent the meanings of penny auctions, either explicitly to others, or implicitly to themselves (Coulter and Zaltman 2000; Lakoff and Johnson 1980). We add to this data a more netnographic approach (Kozinets 2002), using online forum and discussion data.

Our analysis of the data sourced from online forums and our ZMET interviews suggests that many participants are resistant to the idea that penny auctions are equivalent to gambling. One key delimiter appears to be the presence or absence of a "buy-it-now" option. In some auctions, this option allows losers to apply their spent bids towards the purchase of the product they were pursuing. The argument is that you are no worse off and potentially far better off, if you use a penny auction website to acquire a product you were planning on purchasing anyway. Of course this argument presumes that individuals are bidding on items that they can afford to buy. However, much of the attraction of penny auctions is that they provide a chance to acquire things one otherwise could not afford. Presumably, this line of reasoning also assumes that individuals' interest in items is driven by something other than the price. A review of the online discussion board reveals numerous stories of consumers who found themselves bidding on items they did not particularly want. A closer examination reveals further evidence of addictive behavior including extensive credit card debt, negative impacts on work and family life, and an inability to stop despite repeated attempts.

There are a number of policy implications associated with this work. One obvious implication is that if penny auctions are a form of online gambling disguised as entertainment shopping, attention must be paid to regulate the industry to protect consumers. We plan to present our data and conclusions during the session.

Together We Stand, Divided We Fall:
Categorization and the Process of Legitimation

EXTENDED ABSTRACT

There are a variety of ways in which any particular consumption practice can be categorized by consumers. Is smoking marijuana more like drinking alcohol or is it more like using cocaine? Is texting while driving more like drunk driving or more like not wearing a seatbelt? Certainly, the ways in which consumption practices are socio-culturally grouped has important implications for their legitimacy. Previous research has evaluated the role of categorization in the emergence of new products (Rosa et al 1999), the evaluation of products (Meyers-Levy and Tybout 1989), and product extensions (Park et al 1991). How does categorization—the ways in which certain consumption practices are grouped together on a socio-cultural level—affect the legitimation process?

Casino gambling has gone through almost a century of becoming a legitimate recreational experience in the United States. Casino gambling began as part of the saloon experience and became associated with western expansion. The Puritan-based culture attempted to control or ban gambling based on moral grounds from the onset (Schwarz 2006). Gambling was legalized in Nevada on March 19, 1931 and the first official casino, the Northern Club on Fremont Street, opened in Las Vegas, which would come to be known as "Sin City." Casino gambling became associated with illegal gambling circuits and legalized casinos were a place mobsters could launder their money (Manning and Samuelson 2008). The original large Strip casinos were managed or at least funded under mob figures Bugsy Siegel and Meyer Lansky. In the 1950s it was the government (namely the Committee to Investigate Organized Crime in Interstate Commerce) that opposed casino gambling and tried to clean up the

mob influence. Casino gambling is now allowed in all but two U.S. states. The tavern-style casinos of the past have been replaced by mega-resort casinos which are luxurious, regulated, and funded by Wall Street. From 1992-2003, the U.S. casino industry saw its revenue more than double, from $10.2 billion to over $27 billion, and consumers spent more money in casinos than they spent on movies or amusement parks (Roush 1993; American Gaming Association 2004). Smith (1996) observed the increasing access to casino gambling and argued that the "…mythic archetype of a rugged individualist gambler" based on the wild west images of card players and urban images of pool hustlers was crumbling, and that the understood meaning of gambling was evolving into that of a safe, harmless, recreational activity.

Lotteries are a popular type of gambling most often run by governments and local states. Questions regarding legitimization of this type of gambling have not needed to be addressed like casinos because of the association with governmental entities. The first English lottery was approved by King James I in 1612 and that granted the Virginia Company of London the right to raise money to found its original settlement in the United States. Lotteries played a significant role in the financing of building and improving the colonies. However, like casinos, lotteries went through their own set of scandals. The Louisiana State Lottery (1868-1892) became the most notorious state lottery because it was a breeding ground of corruption. In 1890 Congress banned the U.S. postal service from carrying lottery tickets and in 1892 upheld a law to put a complete halt to all lotteries in the U.S. Lotteries were illegal in the United States until after World War II. It was not until the 1960's that the first modern day lotteries began to emerge as a way to raise revenue for the state governments. The first modern state lottery was established in New Hampshire in 1964 and currently there are lotteries in 42 states.

While the activity of legalized casino gambling is increasingly accepted in the United States, gambling itself remains tainted by its history. Therefore any new entity that offers consumers a gambling experience is likely required to go through its own legitimization process. We posit that the manner in which this new type of gambling is categorized will affect how it becomes legitimized. Specifically, we suggest that the expansion of lotteries and games into the online environment will be more quickly legitimated because of their relationship to state institutions, which are themselves legitimate, whereas the online casino gambling will be more slowly legitimated because of their categorization with land casinos. We also predict that legalization of online casinos is necessary for legitimization to occur, and that online gambling offered by operators of current land casinos will benefit from faster legitimation as compared to new online casino entities that have not established themselves.

Media analysis. To better understand the introduction and classification of online casino gambling, we conducted a media analysis of newspaper articles about online gambling published between 1980 and 2010. Data was collected on three topics: lottery, casinos, and online gambling. This resulted in 5,445 newspaper articles for analysis. The articles were analyzed by first selecting a subsample of 545 articles for qualitative analysis. Following qualitative analysis, an automated content analysis was conducted using a custom dictionary and two standard dictionaries to assess changes in themes concerning legitimation and categorization of gambling practices over time.

Survey. During December 2010 legalization of online gambling was being considered in the United States. At that time we conducted a national survey of 471 gamblers (246 that gamble online, 225 that only gamble in land casinos). Elsbach (1994) developed a 12-item survey to measure organizational legitimacy based on media analysis and depth interviews. We adapted Elsbach's scale (1994) to investigate how legalization would affect consumers' perceptions of legitimization as well as future online gambling behavior.

Our findings help us better understand the legitimation process for once illegitimate consumption practices. For "sin" industries like gambling, even when legitimization occurs, any new development or extension of them brings up underlying cultural tensions and forces this new extension to go through the legitimization process all over again. We find, however, that this depends on the ways in which the consumption practice is aligned with past and future practices.

The Underwater Consumer: The Psychology of Personal Debt

Chairs: Robert Meyer, University of Pennsylvania, USA
Eric Johnson, Columbia University, USA

Paper #1: Heads in the Sand and Safe Harbors: Biases in Information Gathering about Future Financial Risks
Robert Meyer, University of Pennsylvania, USA

Paper #2: Time Preferences, Mortgage Choice and Strategic Default
Eric Johnson, Columbia University, USA
Stephen Atlas, Columbia University, USA
John Payne, Duke University, USA

Paper #3: Cognitive Abilities and Household Financial Decision Making
Sumit Agarwal, Federal Reserve Bank of Chicago, USA
Bhashkar Mazumder, Federal Reserve Bank of Chicago, USA

Paper #4: There is Light at the End of the Tunnel: Helping Consumers Avoid Financial Decision Making Biases by Inducing Broad Bracketing
Krishna Savani, Columbia University, USA
Elke Weber, Columbia University, USA
Eric Johnson, Columbia University, USA

SESSION OVERVIESW

The goal of this Special Session is to report the findings of recent research aimed at understanding of a major contemporary problem in consumer finance: the causes and consequences of consumer debt. Since onset of the global economic recession in 2008-2009 levels of household debt in the United States has reached epidemic proportions, reaching $2.4 trillion--an equivalent of $7,800 per-person (American Bankruptcy Institute, 2011). Yet, as pervasive as the problem has become, economists and consumer researchers have only begun to gain a deep understanding of the psychological processes that underlie why consumers come to fall into debt, how their ongoing financial decision making is affected by it, and, most critically, what remedial steps might be taken to correct it.

The objective of this session is to present an array of recent research findings aimed at gaining such an understanding. The session will be structured around four papers that address a different related question about the antecedents and consequences of consumer debt:

1. *Origins*: What are the psychological mechanisms that cause consumers to make choices that expose them to large downstream financial risks?

2. *Processes and Consequences:* How does the presence of debt affect the quality of on-going financial decisions made by consumers, and what are the processes that lead to radical remedial actions, such as walking away from a mortgage?

3. *Individual differences*: As widespread as problems of consumer debt may be, there is also widespread variability in its severity among consumers with equivalent financial means. What cognitive trait factors might explain why some consumers are prone to recurrent problems of debt while others seem to be just as robustly skilled at avoiding it?;

4. *Remedies:* How can knowledge about (1) through (3) be used to "nudge" consumers toward better coping with

financial problems in the short run, and allow them to be better financial decision makers going forward?

To illustrate, the opening paper of the session, "Heads in the Sand and Safe Harbors: Biases in Information Gathering about Future Financial Risks" explores theoretically and empirically a question that is often asked in the wake of major financial mistakes: why was information that would have altered consumers to coming risk not sought or attended to? The second two papers, "Time Preferences, Mortgage Choice and Strategic Default", and "Cognitive Abilities and Consumer Household Decision Making", then turn to the study of how cognitive traits lead individuals to financial decision making errors, including poor mortgage choices and poor management of credit-card debt. Finally, "There is Light at the end of the Tunnel: Helping Consumers Avoid Financial Decision Making Biases by Inducing Broad Bracketing", proposes an approach to correcting financial myopia biases by encouraging consumers to think of the sequential, repetitive, and pervasive nature of financial decisions.

While the immediate goal of the session is to present a set of recent research findings on the study of the causes and consequences of consumer debt, it also has the longer-term goal of bringing attention to an emerging research area that has large public policy implications. It is a problem whose solutions will require the joint effort of scholars with a diversity of theoretical and methodological orientations, hence one of the secondary goals of the session is to illustrate the benefits of the accumulated knowledge that can arise from such intellectual interbreeding.

Heads in the Sand and Safe Harbors: Biases in Information Gathering about Future Financial Risks.
Robert J. Meyer, the University of Pennsylvania

EXTENDED ABSTRACT

It is often argued that the root of many poor financial decisions lies in the failure of consumers to adequately gather and interpret information that would have otherwise allowed them to avoid damaging financial events. An archetype is the Walter Madoff investment scandal, where private investors, banks, and even federal investigators appeared to turn a blind eye to evidence pointing to the scheme's underlying Ponzi structure. Yet, a limitation of such critiques that they are all done with the benefit of hindsight; it is far from clear that, given the wide variation in conflicting signals investors often receive about the risks posed by their investments, bad financial outcomes are not simple evidence that risky choices do not always pay off than a systematic bias in the gathering and interpreting of information.

The purpose of this research is to extend an emerging body of work that suggests that financial information search is often biased toward the seeking of good news and the avoidance of bad (e.g., Karlsson, Loewenstein and Seppi 2009). We examine the particular case of investments in high-risk instruments that yield a strong positive payoff in the short run but risk catastrophic collapse in the longer run. Our central hypothesis is the longer investors stay in a fund and realize abnormally high rates of return the less likely they are to seek out and/or attend to information that would call for abandonment of the fund for safer, but lower returning, alternatives. Such a bias is predicted based on two information-censoring mechanisms that have been documented in other areas of learning: confirmation biases, in

Advances in Consumer Research
Volume 39, ©2011

177

which individuals are prone to seek out information that confirms rather than disconfirms beliefs when making inferential judgments (Wason 1968), and knowledge protection biases, in which new information tends to get underweighted if would act to disrupt an existing knowledge structure (Cuhna, Janiszewski, and Laran 2008).

This general hypothesis is tested using data from a controlled laboratory experiment in which participants are given a monetary endowment that is initially invested in a risky "money machine" that provides a high rate of return for a finite investment period (20 periods). At the start participants are told that there is a possibility that the machine is infected with a virus that could wipe out the principal and all accumulated interest before the 20-period investment horizon expires. At any point they have the option to transfer all of the money they earned to a safe fund that poses no risk but that provides a low rate of return. These switching decisions are revocable, such that a participant can re-invest in the risky fund at a later point if desired. To help make the stay or switch decision, at each point in time in the simulation participants can, for a small price, purchase a research reports that provides a noisy signals of the likelihood that invested funds have a short-term risk of liquidation. At the end of the task participants are compensated based on their cumulative earnings over the 20-period investment horizon.

We first show that the optimal policy for purchasing information and making stay/switch decisions is a threshold rule mirroring that arises in two-armed bandit problems in sequential statistics (e.g., Robbins 1952). Specifically, given priors about the virus probability there exists a critical threshold sample risk probabilities τ^h and τ^l such that the participant should continue purchasing research reports until either the sample proportion of healthy reports is either less than the lower bound τ^l (in which case the machine is deemed safe and he or she should stay with the risky fund until the end) or τ^l (in which case it is deemed unsafe and the risky fund should be abandoned. The critical values of τ^h and τ^l are a time-varying function of the reliability of each sample report, the prior, the cost of information and insurance, and the participant's utility function over outcomes (or their degree of risk aversion).

Drawing on prior behavioral work on confirmation biases in learning we hypothesize that information search behavior will display an optimistic knowledge protection bias marked by two features:

1. A "head in the sand" effect in which information gathering among those who remain in the risky fund will decrease as the terminal period becomes proximate to a greater degree that that prescribed by a rational information-purchase model; and

2. An imagined-regret bias in which positive reports about the riskiness of the fund that are gathered after it is abandoned for the safe fund will trigger an excessive rate of re-investment in the high-risk instrument.

These hypotheses are tested using data from 148 participants enrolled in a Northeastern University, which provide support for the predicted information-search biases. As predicted, participants who stayed invested in the risky fund become less likely to purchase research reports that provide information about its risk status as the task proceeded. Likewise, as predicted participants exhibited a excessively high rate of return to the risky investment after having first abandoned it for a the safer fund. The data also revealed an unexpected "safe harbor" effect, where marginal rates of information gathering *increased* after participants had shifted their investments to the safe fund. That is, participants acted as if they held asymmetric beliefs about the value of the research reports depending on the direction of its action implications: when they were invested in the risk fund they were reluctant to gather information that might have instructed them to seek the safer fund, but while invested in the safe fund they were more inclined to purchase reports that might have instructed them to re-invest in the riskier alternative.

REFERENCES

Cunha, Marcus, Chris Janiszewski, and Juliano Laran, "Protection of Prior Learning in Complex Consumer Learning Environments." *Journal of Consumer Research*: April 2008.

Karlsson, Niklas, Georrge Loewenstein, and Duane Seppi (2009): "The Ostrich Effect: Selective Attention to Information", *Journal of Risk and Uncertainty* 38, 2009; 95-115.

Robbins, H., (1952), "Some Aspects of the Sequential Design of Experiments*", Bulletin of the American Mathemtaical* Society, 58, 529-532.

Wason, Peter C. (1968), "Reasoning about a rule", *Quarterly Journal of Experimental Psychology* (Psychology Press) 20 (3): 273–28.

Time Preferences, Mortgage Choice and Strategic Default

EXTENDED ABSTRACT

A decade ago, the subprime mortgage industry appeared to offer a promising alternative to homeowners who could not qualify for traditional mortgage financing. That promising alternative has turned out to be a nightmare, both for the lenders and homeowners. After the housing market peaked, an increasing number of American homeowners found that the underlying value of their home was less than the amount they owed on their mortgage. These homeowners had negative home equity, a situation alternatively known as having an "underwater" home.

Both the design of financial products and public policy interventions must recognize that consumers are heterogeneous. This paper investigates how individual differences in time preferences (individual differences in tastes for outcomes across time) along with other factors affect mortgage choices that lead to and follow negative home equity such as the decision to "walk away" from a mortgage that is "underwater." We focus on two related questions: First, who is more likely to have a mortgage that is larger than their current house value? Second, who is more likely to strategically default, i.e. to abandon the mortgage and move away? We are interested in mortgage choice and potential abandonment both because they are of substantial practical interest, and also because they are prototypical of many consumer choices that involve a stream of consequences across time.

In our inquiry, first, we review a traditional economic analysis of mortgage choice (Campbell and Cocco, 2003). Although that model does allow for some individual differences in tastes, we suggest some more behaviorally informed parameters of time preferences and risk taking will allow us to capture greater consumer heterogeneity in tastes, abilities, and knowledge. A quasi-hyperbolic discount function suggests that more present bias will cause decision-makers to overweight earlier consequences relative to those that may occur later (Angeletos et al. 2001; Benhabib et al. 2009; Laibson 1997). In particular, we expect present-biased respondents to tend to overweigh immediate (vs. future) consequences such as increased later payments and the risk of housing equity loss.

When abandoning an underwater mortgage, most of the costs (particularly the non-economic costs) are immediate and without an accompanying immediate gain. Finding a rental unit, moving, potential changes of schools and loss of neighbors, might be offset by longer-term savings, because the rent may be lower than current mortgage payments. However, this choice represents more of an intertemporal tradeoff. We therefore expect individuals with more present bias to overweight these costs and be *less* likely to walk away. Thus present-biased individuals may face a form of economic double jeopardy: They are more likely to arrange a riskier mortgage, and are less likely to walk away from the consequences. In contrast, the delayed consequences of mortgage abandonment pit a near-term unattractive option (i.e. continued payment with no buildup of equity) against the longer-term benefits of potentially having positive home equity. In this case we expect people who are impatient to be *more* likely to abandon their current mortgage.

Our survey of 244 US homeowners who have mortgages (roughly half of whom were underwater) allows us to evaluate these specific hypotheses about how individual differences in values, abilities, and knowledge may be related to mortgage choices and the intentions to strategically default. The homeowners answered questions about themselves (including debt literacy, and cognitive reasoning), their home, their financial stake in the home, and about financial conditions that would prompt walking away from their mortgage. Notably, we elicit individual-level quasi-hyperbolic discounting and prospect theory parameter estimates as the first application of the adaptive method developed by Toubia et al. (2010). We then use this data in a set of regression analyses of the relationships between consumer differences in values, ability, and knowledge, home equity status and preceding mortgage decisions. We also relate consumer heterogeneity to willingness to walk away from their mortgage, and consider models that simultaneously estimate both mortgage choices. Finally, we discuss the implications of our results for the study of household financial decision-making.

In mortgage choice we find that the two separate components of time preference work in similar directions. We find that consumers who weigh immediate outcomes more heavily (more present biased), are more likely to be "underwater" with their mortgages. Similarly, those who discount the future more are also more likely to be underwater. Importantly, consumers with stronger present bias are also more likely to have initially borrowed more, a second mortgage and an adjustable interest rate. These findings do not appear to be driven by the "reverse" effect of underwater status on time preferences, nor by changes in the stringency of mortgage standards.

The importance of modeling these two components of time preferences separately is illustrated by our analysis of walking away from a mortgage. Here present bias and discount rates work, as predicted, in opposite directions. Because the costs of abandoning a mortgage are mostly in the near term, present-biased households are more likely to continue paying a mortgage, even with negative equity. In contrast, more general (i.e. exponential) time discounting was associated with a greater willingness to walk away. The findings are robust to the inclusion of several preference controls including probability weighting, sensitivity to value changes, loss aversion, debt literacy, cognitive reasoning, and demographic factors.

The present findings might appear to endorse the view that time preferences have an almost trait-like status. However, we see the discounting parameters as convenient summaries of more complex cognitive processes. That is, they reflect constructed as well as revealed values. Such a constructive process view suggests possible interventions, particularly combined with the observation that present bias has different roles in mortgage choice and in walking away. Finally, our analysis of mortgage choice and abandonment suggests principles that can be applied to many consumer decisions that, in

economics, are the province of life cycle models. These include balancing savings and retirement across the lifetime, the choice to rent or to own, and the decision to insure against longevity risk through annuities.

REFERENCES

Angeletos, G. M., D. Laibson, A. Repetto, J. Tobacman, and S. Weinberg (2001), "The hyperbolic consumption model: Calibration, simulation, and empirical evaluation," Journal of Economic Perspectives, 15 (3), 47-68.

Benhabib, J., A. Bisin, and A. Schotter (2009), "Present-bias, quasi-hyperbolic discounting, and fixed costs," Games and Economic Behavior, 69 (2), 205-23.

Campbell, J. Y. and J. F. Cocco (2003), "Household risk management and optimal mortgage choice," Quarterly Journal of Economics, 118 (4), 1449-94.

Laibson, D. (1997), "Golden eggs and hyperbolic discounting," Quarterly Journal of Economics, 112 (2), 443-77.

Toubia, O., E. J. Johnson, T. Evgeniou, and P. Delquié (2010), "Estimation of risk and time preferences: response error, heterogeneity, adaptive questionnaires, and experimental evidence from mortgagers." Working Paper.

Cognitive Abilities and Household Financial Decision Making.

EXTENDED ABSTRACT

We analyze the effects of cognitive abilities on two examples of consumer financial decisions where suboptimal behavior is well defined. The first example refers to consumers who transfer the entire balance from an existing credit card account to a new account, but use the new card for convenience transactions, resulting in higher interest charges. The second example refers to consumers who face higher APRs because they inaccurately estimate their property value on a home equity loan or line of credit application. We match individuals from the US military for whom we have detailed test scores from the Armed Services Vocational Aptitude Battery test (ASVAB), to administrative datasets of retail credit from a large financial institution. We show that our matched samples are reasonably representative of the universes from which they are drawn. We find that consumers with higher overall composite test scores, and specifically those with higher math scores, are substantially less likely to make a financial mistake later in life. These mistakes are generally not associated with the non-mathematical component scores.

We also conduct some complementary analyses using two other data sources. We use the National Longitudinal Survey of Youth (NLSY) to show that higher ASVAB math scores are associated with lower subjective discount rates. Finally, we use the Health and Retirement Survey (HRS) to demonstrate that particular forms of cognitive ability matter for specific types of suboptimal behavior. We find that the mathematical component of the test is what matters most for financial decision making and financial wealth.. In contrast, non-mathematical aptitudes appear to matter for non-financial forms of suboptimal behavior (e.g. failure to take medicine). The HRS results also demonstrate the large ramifications of low math ability on long-term economic success.

There is Light at the end of the Tunnel: Helping Consumers Avoid Financial Decision Making Biases by Inducing Broad Bracketing

EXTENDED ABSTRACT

Narrow choice bracketing is a pervasive problem in consumer decision making: people often consider decisions in isolation rather than simultaneously assessing the consequences of a series of decisions. One of the reasons postulated for narrow bracketing is *cognitive inertia*—people's tendency to "deal with problems as they are presented to them" (Read et al., 1999, p. 188). Cognitive inertia implies that consumers fail to realize that each individual choice is one of a much larger series of choices. In the present research, we developed a manipulation to encourage consumers to broadly bracket their decisions by making them realize that choices are sequential, repetitive, and pervasive.

To induced broad bracketing, we showed participants a 6-minute video in which an actor performed various everyday actions in an apartment (e.g., eating candy, opening mail, listening to a music CD, etc.). In the *choice bracketing condition*, participants were asked to press a button whenever the actor made a choice, whereas in the *control condition*, they were asked to a non-choice judgment, such as to press a button whenever the actor touched an object with his hands. Participants in both condition identified 39 actions on average.

Study 1 examined how the choice bracketing manipulation influenced financial decision making in the domain of risk aversion. After the manipulation, participants were asked to make 20 choices between pairs of high-risk and low-risk gambles of equal expected value (e.g., 20% chance of winning $10.00 vs. 80% chance of winning $2.50). Whereas participants in the control condition were risk averse, choosing risky gambles in only 25% of the trials, participants in the choice bracketing condition were risk neutral, choosing risky gambles on 49% of the trials, consistent with the idea that participants in the choice condition were broadly bracketing their decisions and thus were more tolerant of risk.

In Study 2, following the manipulation, participants were asked to choose between pairs of gambles with ambiguous and unambiguous probabilities of winning (e.g., 40% chance of winning $20 vs. 30-50% chance of winning $21). The ambiguous gambles offered a 5% premium over the unambiguous gambles, with probability of winning in a 20% range about that of the unambiguous option. We found that participants in the choice bracketing condition were significantly less ambiguity averse, choosing the ambiguous gambles in 60% of the trials, compared to those in the control condition, who chose ambiguous gambles in 45% of the trials.

In Study 3, participants were asked to make 36 choices between pairs of immediate vs. delayed payoffs in which we varied the hyperbolic discount rate that the delayed option offered over the immediate option. We hypothesized that participants in the choice bracketing condition would be less impulsive overall and would be more sensitive to the temporal discount rate. We found a condition X discount rate interaction, such that at lower discount rates, where impatience is less costly, participants in both conditions were equally impatient, but at higher discount rates, where impatience is more costly, participants in the choice bracketing condition were significantly more patient than those in the control condition.

Study 4 explicitly tested whether the choice manipulation induced broader bracketing. Previous research has found that people are less loss averse when they have to make many decisions simultaneously rather than one decision at a time (Gneezy & Potters, 1997; Thaler, Tversky, Kahneman, & Schwartz, 1997). While participants in the control condition would be expected show this difference, if the choice condition spontaneously puts participants in a broad bracketing mindset, then we would hypothesize that those making individual decisions would be just as loss aversion as those making simultaneous decisions.

To test this hypothesis, we used a 2 (choice bracketing vs. control) X 2 (individual vs. simultaneous decisions) design. In each of 9 trials, participants could invest a portion of 100 cents in a lottery. They had a 67% chance of losing their investment and a 33% chance of gaining multiplying their investment by 3.5 times. This lottery has a positive expected return of 16.67%. In the *individual decisions condition*, participants decided how much to invest in one lottery at a time and saw the result of each lottery immediately after their decision. In the *simultaneous decisions condition*, participants had to decide how much to invest in 3 lotteries at a time, and were thus compelled to broadly bracket their decisions.

We found that while control participants invested a larger amount in the individual decisions condition than in the simultaneous decisions condition, those in the choice bracketing condition invested the same amount irrespective of whether they were asked to make decisions individually or simultaneously. In other words, the choice manipulation made participants in the individual decisions condition just like those in the simultaneous decisions condition.

Finally, Study 5 replicated and extended the finding of Study 4 using a different lottery structure. We also found that whereas the outcome on one trial (i.e., whether participants won or lost the lottery) influenced participants' decision on the next trial in the control condition, there was no such effect in the choice bracketing condition, again consistent with the broad bracketing mechanism—if people are considering many decisions simultaneously, then they should not be affected by the ups and downs of individual outcomes.

These converging findings suggest realizing that choices are sequential, repetitive, and pervasive can improve consumers' cognitive myopia in financial decision making—after seeing an actor in a video make a large number of choices, participants appear to no longer "deal with problems as they are presented to them," but instead re-construe presented problems with a portfolio mindset rather than an individual-decisions mindset. Notably, our manipulation induced broad bracketing by changing consumers' construal of their decisions instead of changing the structure of the choice task. Future research can attempt to develop educational interventions to mitigate the dark side of consumers' financial decision making in important real life decisions.

REFERENCES

Gneezy, Uri, and Jan Potters (1997), "An experiment on risk taking and evaluation periods," *Quarterly Journal of Economics,* CXII, 631-645.

Read, Daniel, George Loewenstein, and Matthew Rabin (1999), "Choice bracketing," *Journal of Risk and Uncertainty, 19,* 171-197.

Thaler, Richard, Amos Tversky, Daniel Kahneman, and Alan Schwartz (1997), "The effect of myopia and loss aversion on risk taking: An experimental test," *Quarterly Journal of Economics,* CXII, 647-666.

The When, Why and How of Default Effects:
Exploring Mechanism, Moderators and the Effective Use of Defaults

Chair: Jennifer Danilowitz, Yale University, USA

Paper #1: Partitioning Default Effects

Daniel Goldstein, London Business School, UK
Isaac Dinner, IE Business School, Spain
Eric Johnson, Columbia University, USA
Kaiya Liu, University of South Dakota, USA

Paper #2: In Defaults We Trust

Michael J. Liersch, New York University, USA
Craig R. M. McKenzie, UC San Diego, USA

Paper #3: When Shopping Carts Come Pre-Loaded: Default Effects in Assortments

Jennifer Danilowitz, Yale University, USA
Ravi Dhar, Yale University, USA
Stephen Hoch, University of Pennsylvania, USA

SESSION OVERVIEW

It is well accepted that default options are one of the most powerful tools in the choice architect's repertoire. Defaults have been shown to alter consumer decisions in a wide range of important domains, from organ donation (Johnson and Goldstein, 2003) to financial planning (Choi, Laibson, Madrian and Metrick 2003). Policy makers are advocating "Optimal Defaults" as a pillar of behavioral change, and marketing practitioners are increasingly utilizing defaults through tactics like starter carts and automatic re-purchasing plans. In the midst of this widespread adoption of defaults, it is vital that the theoretical community continue to develop a more thorough understanding of why and in what circumstances these effects pertain. However, while much research has shown the effect to be robust and influential across substantive policy domains, we know relatively less about the underlying processes and moderating factors which may influence how default choices impact preferences. This complicated and likely multiply determined effect demands continued attention and cooperation between scholars if we are to develop a clear understanding of how it operates The present session seeks to deepen our understanding of this important effect, specifically by working to disentangle some of the proposed processes that may give rise to default effects.

Goldstein, Dinner, Johnson and Liu (*paper 1*) divide explanations for default effects into three categories: (i) effort, (ii) implied endorsement, and (iii) reference dependence. Three studies replicate the default effect and examine the mediating power of these proposed mechanisms in depth. Focusing on the third explanation the authors utilize an aspect listing methodology to demonstrate that Query Theory can account for reference dependent preferences in defaults.

Liersch and McKenzie (*paper 2*) broaden our understanding of implicit recommendations as a mechanism of default effects. In doing so, they provide evidence for a novel moderator of defaults; trust. Two studies demonstrate that when people do not trust the source of the default, they are less likely to adhere to the default option. In fact, an unrelated mis-trust manipulation from a prior study caused people to exhibit a *reverse* of the default effect.

Danilowitz, Hoch and Dhar (*paper 3*) extend the impact of defaults to choices made from an assortment. A major difference between a single choice and assortment choice is shoppers can select both default and non-default options. Using an online shopping paradigm, three studies demonstrate that the presence of defaults

increases overall amount purchased. They show popularity and variety of the default options are important moderating variables and provide initial evidence of an alternate mechanism for default effects in an assortment.

Extant research has effectively demonstrated the breadth of the default effect in a variety of domains. Together these three papers contribute to a new and deeper understanding of how default effects work to generate such profound behavioral changes. The three papers are closely focused on a single cohesive topic, but use novel perspectives and methodologies to further our understanding of the subject matter. The discussion will be detailed and diverse, capitalizing on the expertise of the authors in this subject area yet allowing for their varied approaches to the topic. This unique combination will foster an exciting and lively discussion of great interest to a wide audience.

Session Plan: Our goal for the session is to inspire a deeper level of thinking about the psychological workings of defaults. We will achieve this through the sharing of detailed new findings followed by an expert-led general discussion period. Each presenter will have 15 to 18 minutes to share their results, including clarifying questions. Dr. Jonathan Levav, a well recognized expert in defaults, assortment and choice will serve as a discussant. Following the three presentations, Dr. Levav will spend 10 minutes commenting on the papers, and then facilitate an open discussion between the panel members and audience.

Building Connections: This session will appeal to a broad cross section of ACR attendees, ranging from traditional choice theorists to process focused psychologists. In addition, these findings are of practical significance to industry practitioners and policy makers interested in utilizing default options to alter consumption behavior. In sum, these papers provide both deep theoretical and actionable practical insights into the powerful default effect. As a result, this session is the ideal cohesive and compelling platform for building connections between academic sub-disciplines, industry and policy makers.

Partitioning Default Effects

EXTENDED ABSTRACT

Many active decisions have a default option that is chosen more often than expected if it were not labeled the default. No-action defaults often affect consequential life decisions such as choices of auto insurance (E. J. Johnson, et al., 1993) and retirement savings (Madrian & Shea, 2001) which affects how billions of dollar are spent, and policy matters such as organ donation, which affects thousands of lives (Abadie & Gay, 2006; E. J. Johnson & Goldstein, 2003).

Why do default effects occur? Past research (E. J. Johnson & Goldstein, 2003; McKenzie, Liersch, & Finkelstein, 2006) has suggested that defaults may be chosen for three reasons. The first is effort: choosing the default option requires no physical action and can free one from laborious calculation. The second is implied endorsement: decision-makers may infer a default has been pre-selected due to its merit or the desires of those presenting the choice. Finally, defaults may result from reference dependence: the default option may represent a reference point which colors the evaluation of other options as gains or losses. This paper provides novel empirical evidence that reference dependence can change the evaluation of options in a way that leads to default effects, and examines how various factors relate to the likelihood of choosing the default. We generate these hypotheses in the theoretical framework of Query Theory (E. J. Johnson, Haubl, & Keinan, 2007; E. U. Weber, et al., 2007).

Isolating specific causes of the default effect is important for generating interventions to change the frequency of default-based choice. For example, if effort causes a default to be chosen more frequently, making execution of the choice easier should reduce default effects. Thus, when a policy maker or marketer presents a decision maker with a choice they should consider the effects of various defaults as well as understand their cause.

The experiments in this work examine participant's choices between either a cheap, but inefficient Incandescent Light Bulb, or an efficient, but expensive Compact Fluorescent Light Bulb (CFL), a choice which on aggregate can affect roughly $600 million in annual US energy costs (EnergyStar, 2010). The first experiment examines the relative effects of these three explanations on the choice of a default option. The second experiment extends these results by introducing an external measure of effort. In the third experiment we manipulate the queries shown to participants in order to test for a relationship between query consideration and choice. Effort is measured by self- reports in Experiment 1 and by reaction times in Experiment 2. Implied endorsement is measured, as in McKenzie, Liersch and Finkelstein (2006), by using the decision-makers' perceptions. The effect of reference dependence on the evaluation of the options is measured using an aspect listing protocol, a method that has been used to study the endowment effect (E. J. Johnson, Haubl, & Keinan, 2007), attribute labeling (D. J. Hardisty, Johnson, & Weber, 2010) and intertemporal choice (Weber, et al., 2007)

We explore the ability of one specific memory-based view, Query Theory, to account for reference dependent preferences in defaults. Query Theory suggests that when individuals are making a decision they: (1) identify different arguments in decision making by making unique queries, such as generating reasons for or against owning a particular object, and (2) execute these queries sequentially. Further, because of output interference (Anderson, Bjork, & Bjork, 1994; Roediger, 1973), the order of executing these queries determines what is recalled, and consequently preferred. Specifically, the first query results in the retrieval of a greater number of reasons and therefore has more impact than the second query. If Query Theory produces reference dependent preferences in default choices, then we would predict that the existence of a default option will make queries in favor of that option be listed earlier and more often.

Then, according to Query Theory there is support following two hypotheses:

(1) Order hypothesis: Participants are more likely to retrieve positive aspects of the default object and negative aspects of the non-default object before considering negative aspects of the default and positive aspects of the non-default.

(2) Content hypothesis: Participants are more likely to retrieve positive aspects of the default object and negative aspects of the non-default object than to retrieve negative aspects of the default and positive aspects of the non-default.

Following Hypotheses (1), a corollary would be that manipulating the order in which queries are requested will also affect the decision in a ways that can mediate a default effect. Further, we expect these differences in retrieval to both predict choice and to mediate the effects of defaults.

Across all experiments we keep a common scenario in which the participant must choose between Compact Fluorescent Light bulbs (CFL) or Incandescent Light bulbs. The scenario describes renovations done at the participant's home where one of the bulb types has been installed, and thus becomes the de facto default. A contractor then offers the participant the opportunity to switch from the default bulb for no additional cost. Light bulbs are chosen as the focus of this study because of the associated energy savings from reduced electrical consumption. The participants are split into two groups with the default bulb depending on the condition. All three experiments have a minimum of 2 between-participants conditions where the default bulb is either an Incandescent or a CFL.

To investigate the query theory hypothesis, participants record thoughts (i.e., considered aspects of the choice) while making the decision. In Experiment 1 aspects are listed concurrently to determine how thoughts differ during the decision making process. In Experiment 2 aspects are listed retrospectively, which allows for measurement of choice decision time without the contaminating effort of aspect listing. Experiment 3 uses a 2×2 design varying the type of default bulb and aspect listing order, which means first listing aspects for the default and then listing aspects against the default, or the reverse. Following the light bulb scenario, participants completed a questionnaire to assess implied endorsement as well as demographics.

In Defaults We Trust

EXTENDED ABSTRACT

Research has shown that people tend to adhere to choice defaults (e.g., Johnson & Goldstein, 2003). For example, employees are more likely to participate in a retirement plan when Human Resources Departments set the default as "participate", rather than "not participate" (a "default effect"; Madrian & Shea, 2001). Although default effects are probably multiply determined, recent findings have shown that defaults are at least sometimes perceived to be the recommended course of action -- an implicit recommendation -- which helps explain default effects (McKenzie, Liersch, & Finkelstein, 2006). This implies that trust may play a role in default effects: If people do not trust the source of the default, they may be less likely to exhibit default effects.

To evaluate this hypothesis, we conducted an initial experiment involving over 400 participants. In Experiment 1, participants were first asked to imagine the existence of a new company – ImaginationCo – that provided innovative and exciting new products and services. They were then told that in an attempt to reach new customers, ImaginationCo partnered with an established company who owned a large consumer database (which included their information). Finally, participants were informed that the established company sent them a survey asking for decisions about their potential relationship with ImaginationCo. (To make results more generalizable, participants were randomized to one of eight established companies: HP; Dell; Wal-Mart; Target; McDonald's; In-N-Out; The Wall Street Journal; or The National Enquirer.)

The survey involved a series of choices about whether to receive coupons and special offers from ImaginationCo, and whether to give ImaginationCo personal information such as home address and email. In one condition, the default was "do", while in another condition the default was "do not", send me information about, or give my personal information to, ImaginationCo. After completing the survey, participants answered a variety of demographic questions (e.g., gender; age). Embedded in these questions was a question about trust in the established company – i.e., "To what extent do you agree with the following statement?: [Wal-Mart] has a lot of integrity and elicits a high degree of trust." Participants answered this question on a scale of 0-7, where "0" was "strongly disagree" and "7" was "strongly agree".

Results of Experiment 1 showed the typical default effect. Importantly, a regression analysis indicated that there was a significant positive linear relationship between the size of the default effect and trust level in the established company – i.e., as the default effect decreased, so did levels of trust. For example, when trust in the established company was high (participants with trust ratings of 5-7), default effects were substantial: The average participant in the "do" default condition chose to receive or give information to ImaginationCo over 50% of the time, while those in the "do not" default condition chose to receive or give information a little more than one third of the time. However, there was no default effect when trust was low (participants with trust ratings of 0-2).

A second experiment examined whether participants who were deceived in a prior unrelated study were less likely to adhere to default effects when completing the questionnaire from Experiment 1. The reasons for this study were twofold. First, whereas Experiment 1 showed a correlation between default effects and trust, Experiment 2 aimed to establish causality between trust violations (in this case, via incidental deception) and diminished default effects. Second, understanding how different types of trust violations impact default effects is of importance. For example, deception has been shown to be particularly damaging to trust, in some cases making trust irreparable (Schweitzer et al., 2006). Thus, exploring how deception affects people's willingness to adhere to defaults provides a meaningful test of Experiment 1 findings.

Experiment 2 was identical to Experiment 1 with one critical exception. Whereas the level of trust was not independently manipulated in Experiment 1, it was independently manipulated via incidental deception in Experiment 2 to establish a causal arrow from trust violations to diminished default effects. In particular, before participants completed the "ImaginationCo" questionnaire from Experiment 1, all participated in an initial "eye tracking" study. In the eye tracking study, participants were told that their eye movements were being tracked while looking at a picture. However, eye movements were not being tracked. Critically, for one group of participants (n=22), they were told of this deception (the "deception" group) immediately after the eye tracking study. However, for another group (n=22), they were not told (the "no deception" group). Both groups of participants then completed the "ImaginationCo" questionnaire from Experiment 1.

Results of Experiment 2 showed that when making a choice to "receive" information, the "no deception" group exhibited substantial default effects, while the default effect was *reversed* for the "deception" group. For decisions related to "giving" personal information to ImaginationCo – which may have already induced skepticism (Brown & Krishna, 2004) – there was no significant default effect for those who had, or had not been deceived. Results suggest that trust causally impacts people's willingness to stay with the default option.

In sum, findings from Experiment 1 support the notion that defaults act as implicit recommendations: To the extent that people do not trust the source of the default, people are less likely to take the recommended course of action (i.e., they are less likely to stay with the default). In fact, in Experiment 2, while default effects were robust for non-deceived participants, deceived participants exhibited a default effect *reversal*, suggesting the possibility that implicit advice may not simply be ignored, but rejected, when trust is violated. Such reputational influences on default effects should be considered when establishing defaults. Defaults have not only proven effective in business contexts (Johnson et al., 2002), but also in areas such as retirement savings (Madrian & Shea, 2001) and organ donation (Johnson & Goldstein, 2003), where the positive social impact of default effects is potentially large. However, if trust in defaults' sources is

compromised – as can be the case in political and corporate environments – people may discontinue adhering to default options, thereby limiting their influence.

When Shopping Carts come Pre-Loaded: Default Effects in Assortments

EXTENDED ABSTRACT

Most research that has examined the effect of a default option to date has focused on binary choices, when one of two options is designated the default. The common finding is that an option is more likely to be selected when it is the default vs. when it is not. For example Johnson and Goldstein (2003) show that in a choice between being an organ donor or not, most people will choose be a donor if that is the default. However, if not donating is the default, most people will instead choose to not donate. Unlike binary choices that force consumers to choose a single option, in many real world situations consumers can choose multiple options from a choice set. For example, when shopping for groceries one is not forced to choose a single item – either milk or eggs. Instead, shoppers can select both milk *and* eggs. When the choice situation allows a consumer to select more than one option, it is unclear how setting some of the items as defaults will impact the overall number of products purchased. A major difference between a single choice and assortment choice is that shoppers can include both default and non-default options in their final selections.

Building on Yaniv and Schul (1997) we propose that when defaults are present in an assortment people employ two distinct criteria to select items for purchase. When they consider adding new products to the purchase set, people compare it against a higher, inclusion threshold. If they are instead evaluating a default option, they will compare the product against a lower exclusion threshold, to determine if they should remove the item. We test the overall effect and our explanation by presenting assortments where default options vary across purchase conditions. In each experiment participants were presented with a specific online shopping goal, such as buying food for a party or stocking a new home office, and then they were asked to select as many items as they wished to purchase from an assortment of 16 products. In the default conditions, some or all the items were pre-checked for purchase (depending upon the experiment) and the respondent could uncheck them. In the no-default control conditions, respondents were simply shown a list of the assortment and asked to select as many as they wished to purchase.

In Study 1 we investigate the basic default effect within a large assortment. Ninety-eight adult participants (34 male, $M_{age} = 38 \ SD = 13.4$) were recruited from an online panel and randomly assigned to one of two conditions: all defaults vs. no defaults. Participants were told to imagine they were hosting a gathering, and were shopping for party snacks that could be delivered by a local retailer. They were then shown a 16 item assortment of drinks, desserts, fried foods and healthy snacks. In the all default condition all 16 items were pre-checked for purchase when the assortment appeared on the screen, while in the no default condition none of the items were pre-checked. Respondents in the all default condition purchased more total items than people in the no default option condition ($F \ (1, 97) = 26.78$, $p<.001$). This finding was replicated in a second, office supply shopping scenario ($F \ (1, 97) = 19.33, p<.001$).

As stated previously, we posit that shoppers select more items in the default condition because they use a higher threshold to add new products than they do to retain default products. Two studies test our explanation by varying whether the default items are among the most or least attractive options in the assortment. We expect that designating unattractive options as default will result in a larger final purchase. This occurs because when the defaults are unattractive respondents compare them against the lower threshold, and retain some of those less appealing options they would not have added. Everyone then adds the attractive options, which exceed the higher "add" threshold. Study 2 tests this hypothesis using the same scenario and assortments described above, with either the four most or four least popular items from study 1 pre-checked as the defaults, and a no-default control condition. Two important results emerged. First, when the four most attractive items were the default, people purchased a similar amount as the no default condition; $M = 5.7$ vs $M = 5.4$, n.s.. This is consistent with the hypothesis that the most popular default options generally exceed the "add" threshold, and so were chosen whether they were defaults or not. Second, participants in the least popular condition purchase more of their unpopular default items, and more items overall, $M = 6.4$, $F(1, 124) = 4.07$, $p<.05$. This supports our hypothesis that when the less popular items are defaults, participants use the lower, "remove" criterion, and retain those items in their purchase set, and then evaluate other, higher valued options against the "add" threshold.

A final study shows that the arrangement default options can prime a specific mindset, such as variety seeking, which in turn lowers the "add" and "remove" thresholds for products that increase variety. Because the 16 item assortment consists of four sub-categories (e.g. desserts, fried foods) a set of four default options can be constructed that is either high in variety (one from each of the different sub-categories) or low in variety (all four from one sub-category). We predict that in a variety seeking mindset the evaluation thresholds will be lowered for options which add to variety. Therefore variety seekers will both retain more of the default options, and choose more non-default options, resulting in a larger purchase. Study 3 tests this hypothesis by presenting one product from each of the four sub-categories as pre-checked in the high-variety condition, while pre-checking four products from one sub-category in the low-variety condition. As predicted, when participants see the high-variety defaults they adopt a variety seeking mindset ($M_{High} = 3.2$ $M_{Low} = 2.9$ $F(1,191) = p <.01$), subsequently purchase more items overall,($F(1,320) = 1178$ $p < .001$), and their final choices are drawn from a more sub-categories, 2.9 vs. 2.5.

The current research extends our understanding of the powerful default effect into consumer choice from assortments, and offers support for a novel and straightforward dual threshold mechanism for default effects.

Control Freaks: Exploring When and Why
Consumers Seek Control through Consumption

Chair: Keisha Cutright, University of Pennsylvania, USA

Paper #1: When Shopper Marketing Backfires

Leonard Lee, Columbia University, USA

Ziv Carmon, INSEAD, Singapore

Ravi Dhar, Yale University, USA

Ayelet Fishbach, Univeristy of Chicago, USA

Paper #2: Powerlessness and Consumption: The Shaping of Who and What We Value

Derek Rucker, Northwestern University, USA

David Dubois, Northwestern University, USA

Adam Galinsky, Northwestern University, USA

Paper #3: Seeking Variety to Overcome Social Exclusion

Jonathan Levav, Stanford University, USA

Dirk Smeesters, Erasmus University Rotterdam, The Netherlands

Paper #4: The Beauty of Boundaries: When and Why We Seek Structure in Consumption

Keisha Cutright, University of Pennsylvania, USA

SESSION OVERVIEW

Objective: The belief that we have control over outcomes in our lives is considered to be a primary motivator of behavior—the reason we keep fighting towards our goals and the reason we aren't paralyzed by fears of what the future holds (e.g., Kelley, 1971; Miller, 1979). However, events often arise that threaten this sense of control, from terrorist attacks and natural disasters to the temptations and relationships of daily life. This session explores how consumption plays a critical role in one's ability to restore a sense of control in the face of such threats. More specifically, this session identifies situations that trigger an individual's need for control and explores how a variety of behaviors serve this need. Consistent with the conference theme of "building connections," our session takes a set of intriguing, yet previously isolated behaviors and demonstrates how they each serve a common goal.

General orientation: The focus of the session is on what instigates an individual's need for control and the resulting impact on consumption behavior. We begin by exploring the control that individuals assert over the self and its impulses. We then expand our view of control to explore the control that individuals seek to assert over others. Finally, we broaden our lens even further to investigate the control that individuals seek to assert over the environment. After the 15 minute presentations, we will discuss the implications of the research for developing integrative theories of control that illuminate the role of consumption.

Likely audience: The true appeal of this session is that while the papers are tightly connected around individuals' basic motivation to control their lives, each paper is different enough to generate interest from a broad audience. The session's papers will attract researchers interested in topics such as personal control, power, compensatory consumption, goal striving, self-regulation, nonconscious influences, shopper-marketing, variety-seeking and aesthetics.

Issues and topics: The Lee et al. paper begins the session by exploring how shopper marketing often induces consumers to assert greater control over their lives, particularly as it relates to controlling their impulses to spend money on vices. The second paper, Rucker et al., broadens our investigation of control beyond individuals'

impulses and investigates how we assert control over others (i.e., power) through our purchases. The authors explore how feeling powerless drives behavior differently depending on product status and the purchase recipient. The third and fourth papers focus on the tools that individuals use to assert a feeling of control over their environments more generally. Levav and Smeesters demonstrate that when feelings of isolation instigate a desire for control, individuals assert control over the environment by seeking variety in their product choices. Cutright's research demonstrates that when feelings of control are threatened, individuals seek environments with greater order and structure.

Contribution: This session's major contribution is in providing a broad view of the ways that consumers' desire for control can be instigated and resolved. By doing so, this session connects consumption behaviors that might have otherwise continued to be viewed as isolated, unrelated behaviors (e.g., avoiding vices, seeking variety, preferring boundaries, choosing status products). In doing so, this session "builds connections" that will generate a more complete understanding of when and why a desire for control drives consumption behavior.

State of completion: The papers included in this session are at advanced stages of completion, but have not yet been accepted at any journals. The authors are eager to receive feedback.

When Shopper Marketing Backfires

EXTENDED ABSTRACT

Retailers often try to entice shoppers to spend with a variety of shopper marketing tools. From conspicuous product samples and promotional coupons, to subtle sounds and scents in the retail environment, prior research has shown that these marketing devices can induce shoppers to loosen their purse strings. In this work, we investigate when such shopping prompts might backfire. We propose that shopping prompts can have two conflicting outcomes: while they can stimulate the desire for instant gratification and induce greater spending, they can also lead shoppers to exercise greater self-control in order to counter these temptations to spend. The net impact of shopping prompts thus depends on the relative magnitudes of these two effects.

To test the possibility that shoppers prompted to shop might ironically exercise greater restraint in their spending, we conducted two field experiments, one in a crowded campus supermarket in the U.S., and the other in a convenience store in Asia.

A total of 200 regular shoppers participated in **Experiment 1**. Upon entering the store, half of these shoppers were first offered a regular shopping basket from the store, whereas the other half of the shoppers was not offered a shopping basket. The results revealed that shoppers who were offered a basket spent significantly less than those who were not offered a basket ($p = .03$). Importantly, both shoppers who accepted the basket and those who did not accept the basket spent less than shoppers who were not offered a basket.

In **Experiment 2**, we used a different method to prompt shopping in the store. A total of 230 regular shoppers participated in this experiment and were randomly assigned to one of two conditions: half of them received a $1-off coupon and a promotional flyer, whereas the other half received a coupon but not a flyer. The pro-

185

Advances in Consumer Research
Volume 39, ©2011

moted items (displayed on the flyer with color pictures) were mostly hedonic vices (e.g., branded sweet drinks, chocolates, and snacks).

This experiment produced three main findings: (1) shoppers who received a promotional flyer spent less than those who did not (p = .03); (2) analyzing the type of products shoppers purchased (based on shoppers' shopping receipts), we found that shoppers who received a flyer bought a larger proportion of utilitarian virtue products (vs. hedonic vice products), compared to those who did not receive a flyer (p = .04); and, (3) there was no difference in shoppers' rated attractiveness of the promotional items across conditions, or the number of promotional items they actually purchased in the store.

Experiments 1 and 2 indicate that shoppers who are prompted to shop may ironically spend less than those who are not similarly prompted to shop. The differential impact of shopping prompts on the purchase of vice versus virtue products further suggests the validity of our proposed self-control account.

We tested directly whether priming shopping can activate the higher-order goal of prudent shopping in **Experiment 3**. Participants (N=39) were randomly assigned to either a *shopping-prime* condition or a *control* condition. They were shown a series of 15 photographs and instructed to evaluate the technical qualities (composition and lighting) of each photograph. Participants in the *shopping-prime* condition were shown 10 photographs depicting shopping activities plus five other filler photographs, while participants in the *control* condition were shown 10 photographs depicting people engaging in activities unrelated to shopping (e.g., jogging, talking on a phone) and the same five filler photographs. Next, in a purportedly unrelated task, they were asked to rate the importance of a number of different goals to them when they shop, including the target goal ("being careful not to overspend.") Consistent with our self-control account, participants in the *shopping-prime* condition rated the target goal significantly higher than control participants (p = .03).

Our proposed explanation for the possible failure of shopping prompts to achieve their objective involves the activation of higher-order goals by these prompts, and thus increased shopper motivation to exercise restraint in spending. However, such restraint may not apply to all types of products. In particular, some products are relative vices (e.g., cigarettes, ice cream) that provide immediate rewards but long-term costs, while others are relative virtues (e.g., vitamins, apples) that might be associated with some immediate costs but provide significant rewards in the long run. Prior research has shown that relative vices tend to be associated with greater feelings of guilt and whose consumption are often deliberately constrained and rationed, whereas relative virtues are less likely to be targets of consumption self-control (Wertenbroch 1998). Hence, if tempting shopping prompts can induce shoppers to exercise greater self-control, we expect this tendency to be more pronounced if these shopping prompts are targeted at vices rather than at virtues. If this hypothesis holds, it will also help rule out alternative accounts such as shopper reactance to marketing persuasion—since these alternate accounts should apply to all types of products.

To test whether tempting participants to shop would result in reduced purchase of vice (vs. virtue) products, in **Experiment 4**, 64 participants were randomly assigned to one of four conditions in a 2 (Shopping Prime: Yes vs. No) X 2 (Type of Products: Vice vs. Virtue) between-subjects design. They were first asked to complete the same photograph-evaluation task as in experiment 3. Thereafter, they were invited to shop in a mock store set up in the lab. Half of these participants were shown an assortment of vice products (chocolates, candies, etc.) whereas the other half were shown an assortment of virtue products (hand sanitizer, pens). Consistent with our hypothesis, participants who were primed to shop spent less when they were exposed to vice products, compared to those who were exposed to virtue products or those who were not primed to shop (interaction effect: p = .05).

Overall, our research lends support to the notion that, in order to maximize marketing effectiveness, it is critical for marketers and retailers to consider not only the characteristics of shopper marketing, but also how these marketing tools interact with shopper motivation and the immediate shopping environment to affect shopper response.

Powerlessness and Consumption: The Shaping of Who and What we Value

EXTENDED ABSTRACT

Power—the perceived or actual control one has over resources or people— is a fundamental force behind human behavior (Magee and Galinsky 2008). However, only recently has power been brought into marketing to understand consumer behavior. It has been argued that because states of powerlessness are aversive consumers seek to alleviate them by altering the way they consume (Rucker and Galinsky 2008). In particular, it has been proposed that low power increases consumers' desire for high-status products and for conspicuous consumption. For instance, Rucker and Galinsky (2008) found that low-power individuals, compared to high-power and baseline participants, were willing to pay more for status-related objects.

In addition to the finding that powerlessness shapes what consumers value (i.e., status products), recent findings (Rucker, Dubois and Galinsky 2011) have shown that powerlessness can shape who consumers value. Specifically, Rucker and colleagues (2011) found that low-power participants placed a greater value on others and thus spent more on purchases for them. In contrast, high-power participants placed a greater value on the self and spent more on themselves. Of note, in this research the authors did not manipulate product status, but rather used products that did not have associations to status (e.g., everyday chocolates).

At first blush, the two papers may potentially seem at odds. That is, the original work by Rucker and Galinsky (2008) found that low-power increased consumers' spending, presumably on items they intended to acquire for themselves, whereas Rucker and colleagues (2011) suggested low-power increased spending on gifts for others and not for purchases for oneself.

We propose that the effects of powerlessness on who and what consumers value play out in a dynamic fashion depending on the product status and the purchase recipient when both are explicitly brought to the forefront of consumers' attention. First, in the case of products that lack an association with status, we suggest that compensatory motives will not be met by acquiring the product. As a consequence, the value of the recipient should be the focal factor in how power affects consumers' behavior. As such, we would expect that the findings of Rucker et al. (2011) would perfectly replicate among objects unrelated to status.

Second, in the case of high-status products, we predict that the specific value of status to high and low power participants will be salient, and that this may dominate the relative value of self versus others fostered by power. When the product is for oneself, we hypothesize that low-power participants will value a status object more for the self than high-power participants, consistent with Rucker and Galinsky (2008). In contrast, when products are associated with high status but purchases are directed at others, we do not expect differences. This is because given the product status would make the needs of low-power participants salient, a focus on their own needs may prevent them from spending more on others or thinking about the relative value of others.

These ideas are tested across two experiments, using different power manipulations and dependent measures. Experiment 1 uses high-status products and crosses power with product recipient. Experiment 2 focuses on both high and low status products crossed with power and product recipient.

Experiment 1. Participants were randomly assigned to a role of high power (i.e., a boss) or low power (i.e., an employee) for a later task in the experiment. Subsequently, as part of an ostensibly unrelated task, they were offered the opportunity to purchase Godiva chocolates (pre-tested to be perceived as high status, $p < .01$) for themselves or another person. Results were conceptually consistent with Rucker and Galinsky (2008) when the purchase was for themselves: low-power participants spent more than both baseline and high-power participants, $ps < .05$, which did not differ from one another, $p > .7$. In contrast, when the intended recipient was another person, there were no observed differences in the amount individuals spent, $p > .4$. This latter outcome is consistent with the idea that when a product is associated with status, but for another person, low-power participants don't value it more than high-power participants because the high level of status of the product leads them to focus on their own goals rather than on the value of others.

Experiment 2. Participants were randomly assigned to a 3 (Power: low, high, baseline) × 2 (Purchase Recipient: self, other) × 2 (Product Status: low, high) × 2 (Category: Chocolate, Restaurant) between-participants design. They received an ad copy for either chocolates or a restaurant and asked how much they would be willing to pay for a bag of chocolates or a dinner at the restaurant (stimuli adapted from Rucker, et al., 2011). The ad copy was used to manipulate power, product status and intended recipient. To manipulate power, the ad either began with, "Remember a Time You Felt Powerless?" or "Remember a Time You Felt Powerful?" In the baseline condition, the ad did not mention anything. To manipulate status, the ad featured a picture for a product pre-tested to be either low or high in status. The low-status product featured Hershey's Kisses (a pizza parlor), whereas the high-status product featured Godiva Gems (a fine French restaurant). To manipulate the intended recipient, the ad copy ended with "A Perfect Gift to Give Yourself" or, "A Perfect Gift to Give Others."

As product category did not interact with our other variables of interest, we collapsed across this dimension. A significant 3-way interaction between power, product status, and intended recipient emerged, $p = .01$. Among status products, we replicated experiment 1's findings. Among non-status products, results confirmed our hypotheses and replicated Rucker et al. (2011). When the intended recipient was oneself, high-power participants were willing to pay more than low-power participants, $p < .05$. This pattern reversed when the intended recipient was another person, with low-power participants willing to pay more than high-power participants, $p < .01$.

Overall, the present findings replicate and provide new insights into how powerlessness drives consumption.

Seeking Variety to Overcome Social Exclusion

EXTENDED ABSTRACT

With the growing popularity of online social networks and wireless technologies, personal social communication has decreased and Americans are feeling increasing social isolation. Social isolation thwarts various basic human needs (Kipling 2007); in this research we focus on the need to assert control and mastery over one's environment. We study the effect of social exclusion on decision-making and hypothesize that people who are made to feel socially isolated attempt to assert mastery and control over their environment through their choices. Previous research demonstrates that in Western cultures people seek variety as a form of self-expression and to assert themselves in their environment (Kim and Drolet 2003, Levav and Zhu 2009). Thus, we examine how social isolation leads to variety seeking choices, and how these are moderated and mediated by desire for control and locus of control across five studies.

In **study 1**, participants were asked to complete a personality scale and then given one of three (randomly assigned) types of bogus feedback about their results (see Twenge et al. 2001). In the exclusion condition they were told that they would end up lonely in life; in the inclusion condition they were told that they would end up having good social relationships in life; and in the misfortune condition they were told they would end up having some sort of physical misfortune later in life. The latter condition was added to control for the effect of negative affect on choice. Finally, we also included a control condition where people did not complete the personality questionnaire. Having received the feedback, participants were asked to complete an ostensibly unrelated study in which they could choose any five candy bars out of a bowl containing eight different candy bars. Participants in the loneliness condition sought significantly more variety than those in the inclusion, misfortune, or control conditions. The latter three conditions did not differ from each other.

In **study 2,** we manipulated social exclusion using a task in which participants were asked to play a three-player Internet ball-tossing game called Cyberball. Depicted on the screen were three "Cyberball" icons, intended to represent three other ostensible players, and an animated hand at the bottom of the screen, intended to represent the participant. Participants had no information about the (fictional) other players and were told that they would never meet them. We operationalized exclusion versus inclusion by manipulating the number of ball tosses to the participant. In the exclusion condition, the participant only received two tosses at the beginning of the game. In the inclusion condition, the participant received the ball as often as the other players. In the control condition, participants did not play the Cyberball game. Following the game, participants completed a desire for control scale, followed by a choice task similar to study 1. We found that participants in the exclusion condition picked a greater variety of flavors than those in the inclusion or control conditions. The inclusion and control conditions did not differ from each other. More importantly, we found that desire for control fully mediated the effect of the exclusion manipulation on participants' variety-seeking.

In **study 3**, we replicated the Cyberball manipulation, but followed the game with a filler task that included Rotter's locus of control scale. Next, participants proceeded to a choice task similar to the previous studies. We replicated the results of study 2, but found a greater effect for participants for participants who were high in locus of control (i.e., those who had an external locus of control). Thus, participants who tended to believe in their ability to exert control over their environment were more likely to seek variety in the face of social exclusion.

In **study 4**, we tested whether we could eliminate our effect by manipulating people's theories about the meaning of the choices they make. We used the same feedback manipulation as in study 1, followed by a short essay based on Millard's theory of reasoned action in which people read that choice is a vehicle for self-mastery or choice is not a vehicle for self-mastery. We find that our social exclusion manipulation only led to variety seeking for participants who read the self-mastery essay but not for those who read the opposite.

Finally, in **study 5** we tested whether an intervening opportunity to exert control eliminates socially excluded participants' need to seek variety. Participants completed the same bogus feedback task as in study 1, and then played a round of the dictator game in which they were either the recipient or the dictator (or a control condition where no game was played). This was followed by a candy choice as in study 1. We found that participants who were led to believe that their future would be lonely and who played the role of dictator—thus exerting control—no longer sought variety in the subsequent candy choice task. In contrast, their counterparts who played the role of recipients did seek variety, just like control participants who were led to believe in a lonely future but did not play the dictator game.

The Beauty of Boundaries: When and Why We Seek Structure in Consumption

EXTENDED ABSTRACT

To avoid feeling as if the outcomes in their lives are randomly determined, individuals often choose to believe instead that they have personal control over their lives. In other words, they believe that they can intentionally produce desired outcomes and prevent undesired ones (Skinner, Chapman, and Baltes 1988). But, how do people respond when their perceptions of control are threatened? How do they avoid the anxiety-provoking fear of a random world?

This research demonstrates that one way that people respond to threats to their personal control is by seeking order and structure in their consumption environments and choices, or "structured consumption." I suggest that one intriguing way that individuals achieve a sense of "structured consumption" is by seeking boundaries in their physical environment. I posit that boundaries, by their very nature, dictate where things belong and consequently represent the establishment of order and structure in the environment. Such boundaries can include the tangible aspects of products, such as the frame surrounding a painting. However, boundaries can also be intangible, such as when a distinct place is identified for a given object and is differentiated from that of others without the presence of a physical border. As an example, organized environments (i.e., space that is organized such that everything is in its place) reflect the presence of strong intangible boundaries. I posit that when feelings of control are low, individuals desire the sense of order and structure that such boundaries provide.

Several experiments were conducted to test this hypothesis. In **study 1**, I manipulated feelings of control by giving people high control or no control over a series of loud noises using a classic noise manipulation (Glass, Singer & Friedman 1969). Participants then chose between a postcard with a clear boundary around it versus one that contained the same content, but without the boundary. The results indicated that those in the low control condition were more likely to choose the bounded postcard than those in the high control condition.

In **study 2**, I illustrated how this preference is mediated by individuals' desire for structure. Individuals were assigned to a writing exercise that manipulated their feelings of control (without impacting mood or esteem.) They were assigned to a low control, high con-

trol or neutral condition. In the low control condition, participants wrote about a positive outcome in their lives when they were not in control. In the high control condition, they wrote about a positive outcome when they were in control (Kay et al. 2008). In the neutral condition, participants wrote about a movie that they saw and enjoyed. They were then asked mediating questions about their desire for structure. Finally, they were asked to choose between a bounded and an unbounded logo across 10 different pairs of logos (in addition to fillers). Individuals in the low control condition were more likely to choose the logos with boundaries than those in the high control condition. The neutral and high control conditions did not differ from one another. Importantly, the relationship between control and logo preferences was mediated by individuals' enhanced motivation for structure when feelings of control were low.

In **study 3**, I demonstrated how this desire extends beyond tangible boundaries to the more intangible boundaries that appear in retail settings using a 2 (control: low vs. high) x 2 (convenience store design: organized vs. disorganized) between-subjects design. Participants were first assigned to a low or high control condition (see study 2). They were then assigned to shop in either an organized store (i.e., strong boundaries) or disorganized store (i.e., weak boundaries) in the lab. The dependent variable was the number of items participants chose in the store. When individuals were in the low control (but not high control) condition they were more likely to buy items from the store if they were in the organized (vs. the disorganized) store. Moreover, individuals were more likely to buy items in the organized store if they were in the low control condition than if they were in the high control condition. This pattern of results was mediated by individuals' enhanced appreciation for boundaries when in the low control (vs. the high control) condition.

Finally, in **study 4**, I explored why boundaries are valuable as a means of structure. I focus primarily on the functional benefits offered by boundaries. I posit that when individuals are low in control they are more likely to feel overloaded by the number of things that could happen to them, and thus feel overwhelmed by the number of things to which they need to pay attention in their environment (i.e., attentional overload). Boundaries, by containing objects in a given space, should help alleviate such feelings of overload by allowing individuals to focus more easily on the aspects of the environment. In this study, I manipulated feelings of control (see study 2) and then measured individuals' feelings of attentional overload. Next, I measured individuals' preferences for a painting with a clear boundary around it versus the same painting without the boundary. Results indicated that individuals in the low control condition were more likely to choose the painting with the boundary around it. This was driven by the increased feelings of attentional overload among the low control participants.

Together, these four studies illustrate a novel means by which individuals respond to personal control threats. Seeking order and structure through boundaries may not only allow individuals to avoid fears that the world is random, but may also lend confidence to the idea that they can reassert control over the more structured environment.

Of Time, Temperature, Taste, and Touch: Integrating Perspectives on Grounded Cognition

Chairs: Aparna Labroo, University of Toronto, Canada
Charles Y. Z. Zhang, University of Michigan, USA

Paper #1: Past to the Left, Future to the Right: How Does Thinking about Time Affect Choice

Charles Y. Z. Zhang, University of Michigan, USA
Norbert Schwarz, University of Michigan, USA

Paper #2: Warm or Cool Color?: Exploring the Effects of Color on Donation Behavior

Ravi Mehta, University of British Columbia, Canada
Boyoun (Grace) Chae, University of British Columbia, Canada
Rui (Juliet) Zhu, University of British Columbia, Canada
Dilip Soman, University of Toronto, Canada

Paper #3: Eat Sweet, See Deceit: Does Gustatory Sweetness Underlie Affective Experience from Smile Perception?

Haotian Zhou, University of Chicago, USA
Aparna Labroo, University of Toronto, Canada

Paper #4: Washing Away Your Luck: Physical Cleansing Affects Risk-Taking Behavior

Alison Jing Xu, University of Toronto, Canada
Rami Zwick, UC Riverside, USA
Norbert Schwarz, University of Michigan, USA

SESSION OVERVIEW

In recent years, a large number of findings have emerged on the topic of grounded cognition. For example, we now know that moral dirtiness is experienced as a need to physically cleanse (Zhong and Liljenquist 2006), that touching a warm cup increases warmth perception in the personality of others (Williams and Bargh 2008), that fishy taste can increase suspicion (Lee and Schwarz 2011), that the sensation of approaching an object in space or time can make an outcome appear more positive (Labroo and Nielsen 2010), and that one can literally wash away post decisional dissonance (Lee and Schwarz 2010b). This multitude of findings offers some commonalities but also highlight several differences. For instance, in contrast to several decades of research on priming that at best provided limited or mixed evidence pertaining to cross modal effects, with most findings suggesting that accessible knowledge is applied within activated cognitive structures and only if the information is considered diagnostic, these findings on grounded cognition present robust evidence of cross modal knowledge transfer effects. On the other hand, a systematic understanding of when and why these effects arise and how they relate to each other is lacking.

The current session brings together four papers each exploring one of four different ways in which cognition may be grounded. Across four papers, we discuss (a) how thought can be interpreted as suggesting that abstract domains may be grounded in metaphorical thinking, (b) how incidental sensory experiences influence judgment, (c) when physical experience may be necessary at least in part for affective experience during social perception, and (d) psychological existentialism and how the physical world can leave behind metaphoric residues. Each of them can influence consumer decision making.

The first paper by Zhang and Schwarz investigates issues pertaining how thought about abstract domains such as time is metaphorically grounded in more concrete domains such as space. Thus, thinking about time (e.g., future vs. past) increases attention to the corresponding direction in the dimension of space (right vs. left). The second paper by Mehta et al. then investigates how thought is grounded in sensory experience, and how incidental sensory experiences can influence judgment and behavior in unrelated domains. In particular, physical experience of warm/cool serves as an intermediate between two different dimensions of cognition that are grounded in it, namely color and interpersonal warmth. As a result, seeing the warm color may activate the consequential judgment and behavior of being helpful through inducing the actual feeling of warmth, resulting in donating of time rather than money. The third paper by Zhou and Labroo implicates the role of the physicality in affective experience arising from social perception. The data suggest that an experience of gustatory sweetness might constitute at least part of the affective response to others' smile--satiating people with sweet foods appears to make them unable to experience affective response to genuine smiles of others. The final paper by Xu et al. brings together ideas of existentialism and sympathetic magic to suggest that as the world often leaves residues of sweat, dust, and contaminants, many other acts leave virtual residues. Thus, luck is sticky, and washing hands after experiencing good/bad luck wipes off the residuals of previous luck.

Introductory remarks will introduce these conceptually distinct classes of grounding effects and each speaker will link to the conceptual framework to explore similarities and differences between each set of findings. In addition, the last 10 minutes of the session will be devoted to tying the papers together and encouraging questions from and discussions with the audience in order to develop a more enriched understanding of grounded effects. In line with the theme of ACR of "building connections," the primary goal of this session is to develop conceptual frameworks and provide structure to understanding grounded cognition effects. The session participants will illuminate different ways in which grounded effects occur and connect the findings more generally to past cognitive perspectives. The session will raise questions about the state of the area of grounded cognition and highlight avenues for future research.

We expect this session will be of interest to a broad audience at ACR. Not only is this a topic of emerging interest, but future theoretical developments in this area are likely to tie back to and draw from past research on priming, mimicry, metaphor, and feelings and sensations. A more integrated understanding of issues pertaining to grounded cognition is also likely to develop knowledge in these basic areas this research draws from.

Past to the Left, Future to the Right:
How Does Thinking about Time Affect Choice

EXTENDED ABSTRACT

As research in embodied cognition indicates, abstract concepts, such as time, are understood and structured through metaphorical mappings from more concrete and experiential domains, such as space (Clark, 1973; Lakoff and Johnson, 1980). Across languages people use spatial metaphors to talk about time. For example, in English, we say that a technology is "ahead of its time", or that a project is "far behind schedule". Using spatial metaphors to describe time enforces associations between the two domains and imports relational structures from space to time. In fact, recent evidence suggests that people do not only talk about time in spatial terms, but they also use their spatial knowledge to think about time. Boroditsky and colleagues (Boroditsky 2000, 2001; Boroditsky, Fuhrman, and Mc-

Cormick, 2010; Fuhrman and Boroditsky 2010; Santiago et al. 2007) showed that people are able to use information made available by spatial primes to think about time. They further showed that metaphorical mappings between time and space are directional, with the directionality being language specific. For example, English speakers project the past to the left side in space and the future to the right, while Hebrew and Arabic speakers do the opposite. Such directional relations have cognitive and behavioral consequences. For example, people respond to a time related stimulus (e.g., a picture that represents the past) faster when the response format is consistent with their time representation (e.g., hitting a key on the left); they also order cards that represent current, past, and future events accordingly.

The current research provides a first experimental test of whether the directional relation between time and space affects consumer choice. Specifically, we test whether English speakers are more likely to choose items displayed on the left when making a choice pertaining to the past, but displayed on the right when a choice pertaining to the future. We propose and show that when making a choice pertaining to future or past time points, people initially attend to alternatives in the corresponding areas of their visual field, which advantages choice alternatives displayed in the respective area. Finally, this research also speaks directly to a theoretical question about the inferential structure of the spatial-temporal metaphor: whether there is a continuous relation between space and time along the whole mental "time line" or just a dichotomous left-right relation. These issues are addressed in three studies.

In study 1, participants were asked to think about either their last vacation trip, or their next vacation trip. Then, they were shown four pictures of natural sceneries, all printed in color and presented horizontally, covering the width of a letter-size page presented in landscape format. The order of pictures was counterbalanced and participants were asked to choose the picture that best captures how they feel about their past/future vacation trip. By coding the picture locations as 1, 2, 3, and 4 (from left to right), ordinal regression shows that, on average, the pictures chosen to describe a past vacation are .55 units to the left of pictures chosen to describe a future vacation, independent of the actual content of the pictures. This result also suggests that the reconstruction of past events and the imagination of future ones may be disproportionately influenced by cues that appear in different areas of the visual field.

Study 2 replicates study 1 in a product choice context. Participants were asked to report the approximate date of their last/next vacation. Then, they were shown four photo albums with detailed information, arranged horizontally in color print on letter-sized paper in landscape format. Participants were asked to choose an album for keeping photos from that past/future trip. Linear regression shows a significant positive relationship between the temporal distance of the reported vacation and the position of the picture chosen. The further the trip is in the past (future), the more participants chose albums displayed on the left (right), independent of the specific features of the albums shown. This result not only demonstrates an influence of the spatial-temporal metaphor on product choice, but also reveals a continuous mapping between time and space, suggesting that the spatial-temporal metaphor works not only on a directional level, but also on a quantitative level.

Study 3 sheds light on how spatial-temporal associations translate into choice. Participants were presented with a list of 10 positive adjectives, arranged horizontally on letter-sized paper in landscape format in counterbalanced order. They were asked to choose the three words from this list that are most vs. least descriptive of what they were like 5 years ago vs. will be like 5 years into the future; this results in a 2 (most vs. least descriptive) x 2 (past vs. fu-

ture) between-subjects design. Replicating studies 1 and 2, the same words were more likely to be selected as descriptive of one's past self when displayed on the left, but as descriptive of one's future self when displayed on the right. However, when the task was to select words that are not descriptive, this directional influence reversed. This reversal suggests that attention plays a critical role in this process: When thinking about the past (future), participants first attend to the left (right). All words they see are desirable for describing the self, resulting in their acceptance when the task is to select descriptive words, but in their rejection when the task is to select non-descriptive words.

In combination, these studies provide first evidence for metaphorical mapping effects in the visual display of choice alternatives. People think about time in analogy to space and treat time as moving in the direction of writing. In an English language context, this directs attention to the left for the past, but to the right for the future, giving choice alternatives displayed in the respective space an advantage.

Warm Or Cool Color? Exploring the Effects of Color on Donation Behavior

EXTENDED ABSTRACT

Color is a fundamental aspect of human perception. Every visual stimulus processed by the human perceptual system contains color information (Elliot and Maier 2008). Thus, it is no surprise that extensive research has been done to examine the effects of color on human cognition and behavior, such as test performance (Soldat et al.1997), creativity (Mehta and Zhu 2009), mate preference (Elliot et al. 2010), and consumer buying processes (Bellizzi et al. 1983). A large portion of this line of research has focused on the differential impacts of warm versus cool colors (e.g., Elliot et al. 2010; Mehta and Zhu 2009). Warm and cool colors are distinguished based on their wavelength (Bellizzi et al. 1983). Longer wavelength colors (e.g., red and yellow) are known as warm colors whereas short wavelength colors (e.g. blue and green) are known as cool colors.

We extend this line of research by examining the effects of warm versus cool colors on prosocial behavior, particularly donation behavior. Building on recent research on embodied cognition, we hypothesize that warm (vs. cool) colors are likely to induce differential feelings of ambient temperature (i.e., warmer vs. cooler), activate warmth (vs. competence) concepts, and subsequently enhance donations in terms of time (vs. money). Theories on embodied cognition suggest that cognitive thoughts are grounded in the same neural systems that govern sensation, perception and action (Barsalou 1999; Connell 2007). Thus, sensory data, such as visual information and physical sensations, is stored together in memory with associated mental concepts or experiences. Once the sensory data is experienced, other related components, such as other physical sensations and the corresponding concepts are likely to be activated as well.

Along this line of arguments, we hypothesize that warm versus cool colors can make people actually feel warmer versus cooler. In daily life, warm colors are usually associated with situations that involve warmer temperatures, such as the sun, fireplace, and tropical areas. Similarly, cool colors are usually associated with situations that involve cooler temperatures, such as ocean and forest. Embodied cognition suggests that sensations that share similar affect states are usually stored together in memory (Barsalou 2008; Connell 2007). Thus, it is possible that exposure to warm (cool) colors would induce warmer (cooler) feelings of ambient temperature.

Next, we posit that these warmer (cooler) physical sensations are likely to activate warmth (competence) related concepts. This is again consistent with theories on embodied cognition which suggests that embodiments, such as physical sensations, are stored together with corresponding semantic concepts in memory, and thus the experience of embodiment can activate the corresponding concept and vice versa (Barsalou et al. 2003). Warmth and competence are the two fundamental dimensions in social judgments through the lens of stereotypes (Aaker et al. 2010; Fiske et al. 2002). For example, rich people are often seen as high in competence whereas the elderly are usually perceived as high in warmth (Fiske et al. 2002). Because abstract concepts are metaphorically based on concrete physical experiences, the feeling of warmer ambient temperature when one is exposed to warm colors might activate warmth-related concepts, such as being a warm and friendly person. Similarly, the feeling of cooler temperature when one is exposed to a cool color will may activate cool concepts, such as being confident and competent (Scherbaum and Shepherd 1987).

Finally, we posit that these alternative concepts (warmth vs. competence) will affect donation behavior differently. If a helping behavior demands more personal warmth or closeness (e.g., spending time with others; Nock and Kingston 1988), the exposure of warm color would enhance such behaviors. However, if a helping behavior demands more competence (e.g., giving money to others; Tang 1992), the exposure of cool color might enhance such behaviors. A series of four studies provide support to our theorizing.

Study 1 demonstrated that a warm (vs. cool or neutral) color led to greater helping behavior when it primarily involves time commitment. Participants completed a computer based study, where the screen background color was used to manipulate color. The color was either warm (yellow) or cool (light blue). The focal task involved having participant imagined three scenarios where they had to help a friend, an acquaintance and a stranger in need and their likelihood to help was measured. Data revealed that those in the warm color condition were more likely to offer help than those in the other conditions. Study 2 demonstrated that when the helping context specifically involved money donation, cool color helped.

Study 3 tested the underlying processes for the above observed effects. The study employed a 2 (color: warm vs. cool) X 2 (nature of donation: money vs. time) between subjects design. Participants were presented with an ad for an NGO seeking help either with volunteering time or donating money. We replicated findings from previous studies, and more importantly demonstrated the process mechanism. Specifically, initial evidence suggests that warm (cool) colors make people feel warmer (cooler) which then activates warmth (competence) perceptions, and consequently prompts people to donate more of their time (money).

The final study was a field experiment. We manipulated color through survey papers. We randomly stopped participants outside of a mall and asked them to indicate their intention to donate to an organization either in terms of money or time. Results replicated our lab study.

Eat Sweet, See Deceit: Does Gustatory Sweetness Underlie Smile Perception

EXTENDED ABSTRACT

The ability to recognize genuineness in the facial expressions of another individual is an important aspect of everyday social and consumer functioning, but might this ability be impacted by a person's chronic desire for or momentary consumption of sugar? In the current research we suggest that the gustatory experience of sweetness can satiate a person's desire for sweetness and as a consequence raise the threshold level of what is considered sweet. We further suggest that the detection of sweetness in another person's emotional expressions such as a genuine smile relies on simulating the action which may include muscles involved in the gustatory experience of sweetness. Thus, once a person has been satiated with sweet foods, the person will be less able to detect genuine sweetness in others emotional expressions, because being satiated with sweetness raises the threshold level of what is considered sweet.

Recent research suggests the detection of a genuine smile from fake may rely on the somatosensory simulation of smiles that enables perceivers to experience the meaning of the smile as genuine or non-genuine. The idea is that different facial musculature is involved in expression of different types of emotion, and genuine versus non-genuine smiles involve the activation of different groups of muscles (Frank, Ekman, & Friesen, 1993; Miles & Johnston, 2007). A genuine smile has smoother and more regular facial movements compared to non-genuine smile (Hess & Kleck, 1994). Moreover, simulation of these facial expressions helps perceivers understand how that smile feels and to distinguish a genuine smile from a non-genuine one based on the affective experience produced by simulating it. For example, mimicry helps people distinguish genuine smiles from non genuine ones (Niedenthal et al. 2009). Surakka and Hietanen (1998) additionally found that objectively genuine smiles induced higher pleasurable experience in perceivers than non-genuine smiles. Moreover, restricting a person's ability to mimic the emotional expressions of others by injecting Botox (vs. Restylene) reduces the pleasurable experiences associated with seeing smiling others (Havas et al. 2010). But might the gustatory experience of sweetness also numb these sweet sensations and reduce pleasure associated with genuine smiles, leading people to see such smiles as fake? Two studies investigated this issue.

In Study 1, individual differences of participants in preference for sweetened over non-sweetened options were assessed first in a multi-part survey. Later, participants viewed 20 clips of smiles with 10 portraying objectively genuine smile (a.k.a. Duchenne smile) and 10 portraying objectively non-genuine smile (a.k.a. non-Duchenne smile); and indicated the pleasantness of the affective feeling elicited by each smile. We hypothesized that people with a stronger sweetness preference would rate others' smiles as less pleasant because the sweet sensation produced by simulated smiles is likely to be below their preferred level of sweetness. However, such a relationship, if exists, should hold only when perceivers actually simulate the smiles they see. Given that automatic simulation of smile was greatly attenuated when viewing Non-Duchenne smiles compared to Duchenne ones (Surakka & Hietanen, 1998), we also predicted that the negative relationship between preference for sweetness and pleasant feeling generated by viewing smile would be stronger for Duchenne smiles than Non-Duchenne smile. The results are in supportive of our predictions: for Duchenne smile, a significant negative correlation between sweet preference and pleasant feeling elicited by the smiles emerged; whereas for non-Duchenne smiles, this negative correlation was almost non-existent.

Study 2 was conducted to investigate whether participants' judgment of smile would be affected if their sweet sense were fatigued by ingesting high-sugar content food. Participants were randomly assigned to one of four experimental conditions. Those in a sweet or a salty condition were asked to eat high-sugar content and high-sodium content snack respectively under the guise of a food tasting task. Those in the sweet thoughts (positive affect) or the neutral affect condition completed an essay task, where they were asked to write about a past episode where they felt lucky or how to use their cellphones to send text message, respectively. After the experimental manipulations, participants in all four groups watched the same 20 videos used in Study 1 and classified each smile as either fake or genuine. The idea is that if sweet sensation is at least part of the affective experience generated by the simulation of other's smile, then it should be possible to attenuate the intensity of affective experience by first adapting the sweet sense. Assuming that affective experience engendered by simulated smile indeed forms the basis for understanding smile (Maringer et al., in press), we predicted that the adaptation of sweet sense would make participants more likely to judge a smile as non-genuine. We also expected the increased likelihood of interpreting a smile as non-genuine after sweet adaptation to be smaller in the in the cases of Non-Duchenne smiles than Duchenne ones because the former tended be simulated to a lesser degree than latter. The results support our hypothesis. Specifically, higher proportion of Duchenne smiles were judged as fake in the sweet-snack condition compared to the other three conditions; whereas the proportion of non-Duchenne smiles judged as fake did not differ across the conditions.

Overall, our studies support the idea that sweet sensation might constitute at least part of the affective experience generated by the simulation of perceived smiles and hence play a role in the understanding of others' smiles. It seems that when people describe a smile as sweet, they do taste a tinge of sweetness.

Washing Away Your Luck: Physical Cleansing Affects Risk-Taking Behavior

EXTENDED ABSTRACT

Anecdotes suggest that people attempt to improve their luck by touching lucky persons or objects (Radford & Radford, 1961) and attempt to maintain or change their luck through strategic cleansing behaviors. For example, British fishermen used to abstain from washing during a period of good catches for fear of washing their luck away (Radford & Radford, 1961). Similarly, gamblers and athletes keep wearing the same unwashed socks or shirts during a winning streak, but welcome clean cloths after a losing streak (Gmelch, 1974; Vyse, 1997). These practices suggest a belief that good or bad luck is an essence attached to the self or to objects, which can be transferred (Wohl & Enzle, 2002) as well as washed away.

The belief that one may "wash away" one's luck suggests that the psychological impact of washing extends beyond the metaphorical link between physical and moral purity identified in recent embodiment research. For example, washing one's hands alleviates the upsetting consequences of one's own and others' unethical behavior (Zhong & Liljenquist, 2006) and attenuates the impact of disgust on moral judgment (Schnall, Benton, & Harvey, 2008). Conversely, engaging in a moral transgression elicits a desire to clean the "dirty" body part (Lee & Schwarz, 2010a; Zhong & Liljenquist, 2006). Going beyond the moral domain, Lee and Schwarz (2010b) found that washing one's hands can eliminate post-decisional dissonance effects in a free-choice paradigm, leading them to suggest that washing can more generally "wipe one's slate clean" by metaphorically removing traces of the past. However, that cognitive dissonance is an aversive arousal state (Zanna & Cooper, 1976) and shares this characteristic with people's responses to moral transgressions (Haidt, 2001). In both cases, the promises of a metaphorical cleansing may match the person's desire to alleviate a negative state. If so, the clean-slate effect (Lee & Schwarz, 2010b) may be limited to things people want to "wash their hands of" – experiences that are negative, though not necessarily immoral. As the above superstitious behaviors indicate, bad luck is one of the negative experiences that prompt washing. In contrast, good luck is something that motivates the avoidance of washing, presumably in an effort to preserve one's good luck. It is

not clear whether incidental physical cleansings only clean the slates we want to clean, removing only undesired traces of the past, or they also remove even traces we'd rather preserve. Two experiments were conducted to address these questions.

In experiment 1, participants were first asked to recall either an incident in which they had good luck financially or an incident in which they had a bad luck financially. Then, in an ostensibly unrelated product evaluation, all participants evaluated an antiseptic wipe – half examined the wipe without actually using it, whereas the others tested it by cleansing their hands. Finally, participants worked on a managerial decision task with choice between a riskless option (i.e., To reject a product improvement recommendation and stay with current level of profitability) and a risky option (i.e., To adopt the product improvement recommendation, which has 75% chance of succeeding and increasing the profit and 25% chance of failing and decreasing the profit). We found that without a hand-cleaning, participants who recalled past good luck were more likely to choose the risky option than those who recalled past bad luck. Thus, accessible memories of past luck influenced current risk taking. More important, the influence of past luck was significantly attenuated by hand cleaning: Participants who recalled past bad luck were more likely to choose the risky option when they had cleaned their hands than when they had not; conversely, participants who recalled past good luck were less likely to choose the risky option when they had cleaned their hands than when they had not. Therefore, good and bad luck can be "washed away".

Experiment 2 tests the robustness of the observed effects by providing participants with a salient current episode of good or bad luck, namely a winning or losing streak in a real gamble. Specifically, participants received an initial endowment of $100 HKD, which they could use to gamble. At the end of the first round of gambling, participants were self-selected into three categories: good luck (i.e., who had a winning streak), bad luck (i.e., who had a losing streak), and mixed luck (i.e., who had both winning and losing bets). Next, in an ostensibly unrelated product evaluation study, all participants evaluated organic hand soap; half examined the soap without actually using it, whereas the other half tested the soap by washing their hands. Finally, participants participated in a second round of gambling. They received an additional endowment of $50 and could bet any amount from $0 to $50. If they bet $X and won, they earned an additional $X, otherwise they lost the money they had bet. The amount of their bet serves as the dependent variable. The results showed that participants who had good luck in the initial round of gambling bet more money in the second round than participants who had bad luck. More importantly, participants who had bad luck in the first round bet more money in the second round if they had washed their hands. In contrast, those who had good luck in the first round later bet less money if they had washed their hands. Because losses loom larger than gains (Kahneman & Tversky, 1979), participants with mixed luck would resemble participants who experienced bad luck, and they bet more after washing than not washing their hands.

In sum, our studies show that people perceive good and bad luck as an essence that can not only be transferred by touching lucky people or objects (Wohl & Enzle, 2002), but also removed with soaps and wipes. Second, our findings bear on an issue that has received little attention in embodiment research: is the influence of metaphors limited to conditions where the metaphor is consistent with the person's goals and desires? The answer is that accessible applicable metaphors exert their influence independent of the person's motivation.

REFERENCES

Aaker, Jennifer, Kathleen D. Vohs, and Cassie Mogilner (2010), "Nonprofits Are Seen as Warm and For-Profits as Competent: Firm Stereotypes Matter," *Journal of Consumer Research*, 37 (August), 224-37.

Barsalou, Lawrence W. (1999), "Perceptual Symbol Systems," *Behavioral and Brain Sciences*, 22 (August), 577-660.

--- (2008), "Grounded Cognition," *Annual Review of Psychology*, 59, 617-45.

Barsalou, Lawrence W., Paula M. Niedenthal, Aron K. Barbey and Jennifer A. Ruppert (2003), "Social Embodiment," in *The Psychology of Learning and Motivation*, 43, ed. Brian H. Ross, San Diego, CA: Academic Press, 43-92.

Boroditsky, Lera (2000), "Metaphoric Structuring: Time through spatial metaphors," *Cognition*, 75(1), 1-28.

--- (2001) Does language shape thought? English and Mandarin speakers' conceptions of time. Cognitive Psychology, 43(1), 1-22.

Connell Louise (2007), "Representing Object Color In Language Comprehension," *Cognition*, 102, 476–85.

Fiske, Susan T., Amy J. C. Cuddy, Peter Glick, and Jun Xu (2002), "A Model of (Often Mixed) Stereotype Content: Competence and Warmth Respectively Follow from Perceived Status and Competition," *Journal of Personality and Social Psychology*, 82 (June), 878–902.

Fong, Mary (2000), "'Luck Talk' in celebrating the Chinese New Year," Journal of Pragmatics, 32, 219-37.

Fuhrman, Orly and Lera Boroditsky (2010). "Cross-Cultural Differences in Mental Representations of Time: Evidence from an Implicit Non-Linguistic Task," *Cognitive Science*, 34(8), 1430-51.

Gmelch, George (1974), "Baseball magic," in *Conformity and Conflict*, ed. James Spradley & David W. McCurdy, Boston, MA: Little, Brown, 346-52.

Haidt, Jonathan (2001), "The emotional dog and its rational tail: A social intuitionist approach to moral judgment," *Psychological Review*, 108, 814-34.

Havas, David A., Arthur M. Glenburg, Carol A. Gutowski, Mark J. Lucarelli, and Richard J. Davidson (2010), "Cosmetic Use of Botulinum Toxin-A Affects Processing of Emotional Language," *Psychological Science*.

Kramer, Thomas and Lauren Block (2008), "Conscious and Nonconscious Components of Superstitious Beliefs in Judgment and Decision Making," *Journal of Consumer Research*, 34, 783-93.

Lakoff, George and Mark Johnson (1980), *Metaphors We Live by*, Chicago, IL: University of Chicago Press.

--- (1999), *Philosophy in the flesh: the embodied mind and its challenge to western thought.* New York, NY: Basic Books.

Lee, Spike. W. S. and Norbert Schwarz (2010a). "Of dirty hands and dirty mouths: Embodiment of the moral purity metaphor is specific to the motor modality involved in moral transgression," *Psychological Science*, 21, 1423-25.

--- (2010b), "Washing away postdecisional dissonance," *Science*, 328, 709.

Mehta, Ravi and Rui (Juliet) Zhu (2009), "Blue or Red? Exploring the Effect of Color on Cognitive Task Performances," *Science*, 323, 1226-9.

Nock, Steven L. and Paul William Kingston (1988), "Time with Children: The Impact of Couples' Work-Time Source," *Social Forces*, 67 (September), 59-85.

Radford, Edward and Mona Radford (1961). *Encyclopedia of superstitions – A history of superstition*, New York, NY: Barnes & Noble.

Santiago, Julio, Juan Lupiáñez, Elvira Pérez, and Maria Funes (2007), "Time (also) flies from left to right," *Psychonomic Bulletin & Review*, 14(3), 512-16.

Scherbaum, Carol J. and Donald H. Shepherd (1987), "Dressing for Success: Effects of Color and Layering on Perceptions of Women in Business," *Sex Roles*, 16 (7), 391-99.

Schnall, Simone., Jennifer Benton, and Sophie Harvey (2008), "With a clean conscience: Cleanliness reduces the severity of moral judgments," *Psychological Science*, 19, 1219-22.

Tang, Thomas Li-Ping (1992), "The Meaning of Money Revisited," *Journal of Organizational Behavior*, 3, 197-202.

Vyse, Stuart A. (1997), *Believing in magic: The psychology of superstition, New York: Oxford University Press.*

Williams, Lawrence E. and Bargh, J. A. (2008), "Experiencing physical warmth promotes interpersonal warmth," *Science*, 322, 606-7

Wohl, Michael J. A. and Michael E. Enzle (2002), "The deployment of personal luck: Sympathetic magic and illusory control in games of pure chance," *Personality and Social Psychology Bulletin*, 28, 1388-1397.

Zanna, Mark P. and Joel Cooper (1976). "Dissonance and the attribution process," in *New directions in attribution research*, Vol. 1, ed. John H. Harvey, William J. Ickes, and Robert. F. Kidd, Hillsdale, NJ: Erlbaum, 199-217.

Zhong, Chenbo and Katherine Liljenquist (2006), "Washing away your sins: Threatened morality and physical cleansing," *Science*, 313, 1451-2.

Conservation through Consumption

Chair: Lisa Cavanaugh, University of Southern California, USA

Paper #1: Greed or Green? The Impact of the Color Green on Conservation of Monetary and Natural Resources

Nina Mazar, University of Toronto, Canada
Eugene Caruso, University of Chicago, USA
Chen-Bo Zhong, University of Toronto, Canada

Paper #2: Incidental Resource Cues and Conservation in Consumption

Meng Zhu, Johns Hopkins University, USA
Ajay Kalra, Rice University, USA

Paper #3: Moral Compensation and the Environment: Affecting Individuals' Moral Intentions through How They See Themselves as Moral

Jennifer Jordan, University of Groningen, The Netherlands
Francesca Gino, Harvard Business School, USA
Ann Tenbrunsel, University of Notre Dame, USA
Marijke Leliveld, University of Groningen, The Netherlands

Paper #4: When You Don't Care Enough to Give the Very Best: When Gifting Leads to Less (vs. More) Green Choices

Lisa Cavanaugh, University of Southern California, USA
Francesca Gino, Harvard Business School, USA
Gavan Fitzsimons, Duke University, USA

SESSION OVERVIEW

Environmental conservation is a major concern for countries, marketers, and consumers. Virtually every choice that consumers make has an environmental impact, which degrades or improves the state of the environment and its natural resources. Consumers are increasingly aware of their impact on the environment. In response, marketers have offered a growing array of products and services for facilitating more green consumption behavior. While making environmentally friendly choices may be guided by deeply held values (e.g., moral identity; Aquino and Reed 2002, Leonard-Barton 1981) or logic (e.g., cost-effectiveness; Hahn 2000), this session takes a different approach. More recently, researchers have attempted to gain a better understanding of more transitory factors and psychological mechanisms that influence conservation behavior (e.g., Goldstein, Cialdini, and Griskevicius 2008). Building upon these ideas, we focus on how both momentary situations and self-perceptions significantly influence consumers' decisions to engage in more or less green behavior. Since situations and self-perceptions are highly malleable, this session offers important insight into affecting larger scale conservation through everyday choices made by consumers. Our aim is to investigate and foster discussion around an important question: when and why will consumers choose to conserve through their consumption choices? This symposium argues that greener consumption is more multiply determined than many have assumed to date and focuses on two key factors: incidental cues and momentary self-perceptions.

The first two papers examine how incidental cues influence conservation. The second two papers focus on how momentary self-perceptions shape green behaviors. Together we present evidence and develop frameworks which explore when and why consumers engage in green behaviors. Mazar, Caruso, and Zhong demonstrate that environments which prime the color green elicit different consumption behaviors depending on the context in which relevant associations are activated. Zhu and Kalra show that incidental cues to non-excessiveness of one resource influences consumers usage of a different resource. Jordan, Gino, Tenbrunsel, and Leliveld demonstrate how augmenting consumers' self-image and moral reference points influences their choices of conservation and ethical behaviors. Finally, Cavanaugh, Gino, and Fitzsimons identify when and why consumers choose to give green and ethically superior gifts to others.

In keeping with the conference theme "Building Connections," the papers in this session bring together a variety of theoretical approaches and investigate different mechanisms for impacting green behavior, which are likely to inspire interest and debate. For instance, under what circumstances does priming versus shifting motivation account for conservation behavior? How do self-perceptions interact with environmental factors to influence conservation? How broadly do these effects hold across different types of conservation-related consumption behaviors?

This symposium is likely to appeal to researchers interested in social cognition, social influence, moral psychology, relationships, and transformative consumer research. The research presented contributes to our understanding of when and why consumers behave the way they do in the domains of resource usage, ethical gift-giving, and socially conscious consumption behaviors more generally. These findings have important implications for marketers, individual consumers, and society. Note: Each speaker has agreed to serve (presenters noted with single asterisk) if the proposed session is accepted. All of the research described below has been written up, i.e. in manuscripts that are either prepared, under review, or near publication.

Greed or Green? The Impact of the Color Green on Conservation of Monetary and Natural Resources.

EXTENDED ABSTRACT

Green signifies life and nature and has become synonymous with the movement to raise awareness and concern for the environment (Mazar & Zhong, 2010). In fact, manufacturers even use green packaging just to create the impression that their products are environmentally friendly (Chandler & Schwarz, 2010). Incidentally, green is also the color of paper money in the U.S., and is associated with greed and envy. Thus, the same color can be associated with both conscientious and selfish behaviors.

The present research explores whether priming the color green can elicit different behaviors depending on the context in which the prime-relevant associations are activated. A large literature on priming has reported that social behaviors can be elicited by subtle contextual cues. For example, exposure to pictures of exclusive restaurants can improve manners in a subsequent eating task (Aarts & Dijksterhuis, 2003). These results are often interpreted as due to contextual cues activating associated norms and goals that lead to consistent behaviors. For instance, because the Apple brand tends to be associated with originality, briefly exposing consumers to the Apple logo increases their creativity on a subsequent idea generation task (Fitzsimons, Chartrand, & Fitzsimons, 2008).

More recently, researchers have attempted to gain a better understanding of the mechanisms by which these effects operate (e.g., Bargh, 2006). Factors that influence the effect of primes include personal characteristics of the people exposed to the prime (e.g., novices vs. experts; Mandel & Johnson, 2002; see also Wheeler & Berger, 2007) as well as the features of the judgment target (e.g., level of ambiguity; Higgins, 1996) or the situation (e.g., desirability of the behavior; Macrae & Johnston, 1998). Building upon these ideas, we suggest that the same prime can activate different behaviors depending on the context. Specifically, exposure to green color in the context of environmental decisions might make the eco friendliness association salient and prime environmentally friendly, conscientious behavior, whereas exposure to green color in the context of financial decisions might make the money and greed association salient and produce behaviors that aim to promote self interest. We test this prediction in three studies.

In Study 1, 146 visitors to a museum engaged in a hypothetical dictator game in which they were given $20 to divide with another anonymous participant. Some of the participants completed this questionnaire in a room with a green floor and green walls, whereas others completed it in an adjacent room with a black floor and off-white walls. Participants who made their allocation decision in the green room kept more of the money for themselves (M=$12.26, SD=4.16) than participants who made their allocation decision in the non-green room (M=10.29, SD=3.46), t(144)=3.11, p=.002.

In Study 2, 72 students seated in individual cubicle desks in a lab participated in a product test study, in which they were asked to mix their own powder-drink by adding water to it and then rate the attractiveness of the color of the drink and how quickly the powder dissolved. Participants were given a measuring cup and were instructed to go to a water station and take as much water as they felt they needed for the task. Participants were randomly assigned to one of two color conditions. Those in the green prime condition had a green placemat on their desk and a green screensaver on the computer screen, whereas participants in the control condition had a white placemat and a white screensaver.

Participants primed with the green color took significantly less water (M=265.3 ml, SD=123.5 ml) than those in the control condition (M=355.7 ml, SD=179.5 ml), t(66)=2.49, p=.015. The color prime did not affect how appealing the color of the drink looked nor how fast participants thought the powder dissolved.

In Study 3, 144 participants seated in a lab engaged in a hypothetical variant of a public goods game in which they were asked to imagine they were part of a 100-person community that was going through a challenging period. Participants were randomly assigned to one of two color conditions (green vs. control-black) and one of two context conditions (money vs. water) in a between-participants design. We manipulated the color of the screensaver and mousepad to be either both green (green condition) or both black (control condition). Those in the money condition read about a challenging economic period that limited "the amount of money available, for example, to cover utility bills," whereas participants in the water condition read about a challenging draught period that limited "the amount of water available, for example, to take showers." Participants then had to face a social dilemma, in which they were asked to indicate how much money [water] they would take for themselves, leaving less resources available for the public good.

Consistent with our prediction, we found a significant color X context interaction on the amount of resources taken, F(1, 140)=4.48, p=.036. In the money condition, participants primed with green (M=61.49, SD=32.21) took more money than participants in the control condition (M=54.58, SD=27.08); in the water condition, participants primed with green (M=52.30, SD=24.74) took less water than participants in the control condition (M = 65.21, SD = 27.68).

Across three studies we show that, compared to a neutral color, green can increase selfishness in the context of money but decrease it in the context of natural resources. These results shed further light on the processes by which nonconscious primes can elicit different patterns of behavior within the same group of people depending on which of its associations are relevant in a particular context.

Incidental Resource Cues and Conservation in Consumption

EXTENDED ABSTRACT

Conservation and environmental issues is a textbook case of a "wicked problem" as the problems are complex and ambiguous (Rittel and Webber 1973). In many consumption contexts, waste arises primarily from consumers' over-acquisition of the amount of resources required. While a rich body of research has explored factors that influence the level of consumption and provided important insights for understanding how much people consume (e.g., Folkes, Martin and Gupta 1993; Wansink 1996), prior research has not distinguished between how much is acquired versus how much is consumed and the difference between the two. We conceptualize waste in consumption as the difference between the amount of resources acquired and the amount of resources required for a consumption situation. We propose that waste in consumption has two instantiations, pure loss of resources (which occurs when the amount of resources acquired is greater than the amount of resources consumed) and inefficiency in usage (which occurs when the amount of resources consumed is greater than the amount of resources required). Conservation can be achieved by reducing both pure loss and inefficiency.

The focus of this research is to examine the impact of resource availability on conservation in consumption. We conceptualize abundance to be an excessive supply of resources whereas non-abundance is sufficient but non-excessive supply of resources. Non-abundance differs from scarcity in the sense that scarcity refers to insufficient supply of resources. We focus on situations where the supply is always sufficient but simply differs in terms of excessiveness. We anticipate that perceiving resources as non-abundant can curtail acquisition, thereby temporally prompting conservation behaviors. Evidence for our theorization can be found in the biological literature, which shows that species lower consumption rates when resources appear to become scarcer (Hanson and Leggett 1986). Additionally, the sociology literature suggests that in late-modern and industrialized society, abundance became more taken-for-granted supplanting non-abundance, which has lead to highlighted consumerism and attendant over-acquisition (Côté 1993). Broadly building upon evidence suggesting that environmental cues in a prior context can influence decision-making in subsequent unrelated contexts by affecting mental representation and accessibility of different knowledge structure (Bargh et al., 1996; Dijksterhuis, Chartrand and Aarts 2007; Förster, Liberman and Friedman 2007; Kay et al. 2004), we posit that incidental cues indicating one particular resource as non-abundant can reduce the cognitive accessibility of the general construct of abundance and trigger the tendency to conserve. Further, this conservation tendency can persist into subsequent consumption even when different resources are utilized.

Experiment 1A shows that incidental cues highlighting non-excessiveness of a resource (a pencil stub) can reduce pure loss of an unrelated resource (lead participants to acquire and waste less water in a later sampling task). Experiment 1B extends the main effect to inefficiency in usage, showing that simply taking away vs. leaving a drink bottle on participant's desk in a drink sampling reduced the amount of paper participants used in a later wrapping task.

Experiment 2 tests whether cues indicating non-abundance can reduce the accessibility of cognitive representation of the general construct of abundance. To do so, we first exposed participants to either non-abundance or abundance cues in a sampling task. We then measured the accessibility of cognitive representations of the notion of abundance employing a lexical decision task that requires participants to determine whether certain letter strings are words or not. Consistent with our theorization, we found that participants who were exposed to the non-abundance cue responded slower to abundance related words than participants initially exposed to the abundance cue, and that there was no significant difference in the response times for neutral words across conditions.

Experiment 3 tests whether the perception of abundance vs. non-abundance is sufficient to prompt conservation in subsequent consumption. We show that providing the same amount of resource (1/3 cup of cooking oil) in a larger vs. smaller container led participants to perceive the resource as less abundance and subsequently motivated them to taking an extra action to conserve energy (turn off lights when leaving an empty room). Importantly, we find that when the cooking oil was provided in the bigger vs. smaller cup, participants still indicated that they had sufficient amount of resources. These findings suggest that the deviation from abundance (i.e., non-abundance, denoting the sufficient but non-excessive supply of resources) rather than scarcity (i.e., denoting insufficient supply) is adequate to prompt conservation behaviors.

In the last experiment, we discriminate against different theoretical accounts that could be responsible for the carry-over effect of incidental resource cues on conservation. We find that giving participants a chance to conserve in a social domain that is unrelated to consumption before taking resources for subsequent consumption attenuated the influence on non-abundance cues on conservation. These results suggest that the underlying mechanism is motivational, as once the motivation is satisfied, participants no-longer engaged in conserving behaviors. However, the non-motivational accounts of priming conservation-related concepts and traits predict the opposite pattern, as engaging in a conservation action would have made conservation-related concepts and traits even more accessible and salient. Our findings are consistent with recent literature on "green licensing" showing that purchasing green products can produce unintended effects licensing people to act unethically in subsequent tasks (Mazar and Zhong 2010).

This research offers several theoretical contributions. While extant consumer behavior literature has primarily focused on consumption, our theoretical approach also incorporates resource acquisition. While the level of specificity examined in the existing literature on supply and usage is domain specific, our research demonstrates that cues suggesting non-excessiveness of a particular resource not only influence perceptions of the cue-specific resource but also impact the cognitive accessibility of the general notion of abundance and therefore trigger conservation behaviors regarding an unrelated resource. Our findings also offer implications for marketing practitioners. From a firm's standpoint, costs can be curtailed if employees waste fewer resources. Additionally, it is in the firms' best interest that consumers waste less when (1) consumers pay a fixed price and then make consumption quantity decisions, (2) consumers have the option to use firm resources that they do not have to pay for.

Moral Compensation and the Environment: Affecting Individuals' Moral Intentions Through How They See Themselves as Moral

EXTENDED ABSTRACT

To maintain a positive moral self-image, individuals engage in compensation: current moral behavior licenses future immoral behavior and current immoral behavior stimulates future moral behavior (Jordan et al., 2011; Monin & Miller, 2001; Zhong & Liljenquist, 2006). In the current investigation, we examine the relationship between behaviors that stimulate changes to one's moral self-image (Jordan et al., 2011) and his or her ethical intentions and actions. We argue that moral compensatory effects are a function of changes to one's moral self-image. In other words, it is not the mere priming of a moral or immoral frame via one's behavior that leads to compensatory effects. But rather, such behavior must be sufficient enough to impact one's moral self-image in order to lead to compensatory effects. Recalls or priming that only lead to small changes to the moral self (i.e., are not severe) are unlikely to have an impact on one's self-image (Baumeister, 1999).

We examine this question via two studies. In Study 1, we have individuals recall either few or many (im)moral behaviors that they take in regards to the environment. In Study 2, we provide individuals with either minor or extreme feedback about the states of their moral selves. We then examine their intent to engage, as well as their actual engagement in, in various moral or immoral behaviors.

Study 1. We used a field-based experimental study to investigate the relationship between the valence and magnitude of one's moral recalls and subsequent intentions to behave ethically.

Participants, Design, and Procedures

Through a partnership with a CO2 offsetting NGO, we surveyed 186 individuals who had offset their flight emissions. These participants first recalled their past (im)moral behavior, after which they were asked about their support for programs encouraging CO^2 emission offsetting, constituting our dependent variable. We manipulated moral self-image via a 2 x 2 between-participants design: the valence of participants' recalled behavior (moral/immoral behaviors) and the magnitude of their recalled behavior (either asked to recall two or eight environment-related activities). To measure ethical intentions, individuals were then asked to indicate how likely they would be to (1) support regulations for mandatory CO^2 offsetting premiums, (2) how willing they would be to pay a mandatory premium for CO^2 offsetting, and (3) how much they support corporate initiatives to offset CO^2 emissions even if it meant them having to pay higher prices ($\alpha = .81$).

Results

Replicating the moral compensation effects, we found a main effect of recall, $F(1, 185) = 4.87$, $p = .03$. Individuals who recalled environmental conservation activities reported lesser intentions to engage in activities to offset their CO^2 emissions ($M = 6.36$, $SD = 0.91$) than did those who recalled environmental destruction activities ($M = 6.55$, $SD = 0.52$). In support of moral self hypothesis, results also demonstrated an interaction between the valence of recall and the magnitude of recall, $F(1, 185) = 8.06$, $p = .005$. Those who recalled eight moral items (i.e., those that elicited a more positive moral self-image) were significantly less likely to support programs to offset CO^2 emissions than were those who recalled eight immoral items (i.e., those that elicited a more negative moral self-image), $t(185) = 3.31$, $p = .001$. However, there was no difference between individuals who recalled two moral versus two immoral items, $t(185) = 0.49, p = .63$.

Study 2. Study 2 extends the results of Study 1 by more obtrusively manipulating the state of individuals' moral selves via providing them with explicit moral-self feedback. Also, in contrast to Study 1, we examine the effects on both immoral behavior and environmentally-related moral behavior.

Participants were 106 students. We manipulated moral self-image by providing individuals with feedback on the states of their moral selves. Participants believed that they were participating in two separate studies. They were first asked to write about the activities they do to help the environment. We then told them that this was actually a validated measure of people's moral selves. Participants then received one of five types of feedback: they were (1) highly above, (2) slightly above, (3) slightly below, or (4) highly below average in morality. A control condition received no feedback. They then began Study 2, which they were told was about transferring paper-and-pencil measures to the computer. They had to complete 15 math problems in their heads and had an opportunity to cheat on each. We measured how many times, out of the 15, they looked at the answers (Jordan et al., 2011; von Hippel et al., 2005). At the end of the study, we gave them a coupon, which they could cash in for a drink at the university's café (valued at €1.40) or could place in a box, and €2 would be donated to the environmental charity, Greenpeace, on their behalves.

Results

As predicted by the moral compensation hypothesis, there was an effect of moral feedback, such that individuals who received feedback that they were highly moral (M = 6.31, SD = 7.62), cheated on significantly more problems than those receiving feedback that they were highly immoral (M = 1.94, SD = 2.61), $t(18.28) = -2.18$, $p = .$ 04; however, consistent with the moral self hypothesis, there was no difference for those receiving feedback that they were slightly moral vs. immoral, $t(35.78) = .09$, $p = .93$. In addition, extremity of moral feedback affected individuals generosity towards the environment, $X^2(1,106) = 13.63$, $p = .02$, with 3 out of 16 individuals in the extremely moral condition versus 9 out of 17 in the extremely immoral condition donating it to Greenpeace. In contrast, these values for the slightly above and below conditions were equivalent (7/19 for the slightly above; 10/19 for the slightly below).

These findings provide support for our prediction that moral compensation operates through changes to individuals' moral self-image: one's moral or immoral self-recalls must be substantial enough to impact how much he or she sees him or herself as a moral person. Current experiments are examining actual changes to individuals' moral selves and how these changes explain these compensatory findings.

When You Don't Care Enough to Give the Very Best: When Gifting Leads to Less (vs. More) Green Choices

EXTENDED ABSTRACT

Consumers often need to decide what gifts to give to valued others. They often face choices between environmentally or ethically inferior vs. superior versions of the same gift. Do you buy a box of chocolates or Fair Trade chocolates; a bottle of wine or biodynamic wine; a cotton or organic cotton shirt; a bouquet of tulips or Rainforest Alliance Certified tulips for those you love? Retailers and media outlets increasingly emphasize opportunities to give green gifts, but we know relatively little about when and why consumers choose to give environmentally and ethically superior vs. inferior gifts. Common wisdom would suggest that consumers spend more or buy superior goods for people they care most about. However, we find that the signal value of green gifts changes across different types of relationships and gender, challenging common assumptions regarding when consumers choose to give green.

While most people claim they care about environmental conservation and view themselves as ethical individuals, it is likely that, in the past, they have chosen to purchase environmentally unfriendly or unethically produced products (e.g., products produced through child labor or environmental degradation). We know that ethicality can influence the likelihood consumers purchase products *for themselves* (Luchs, Naylor, Irwin, and Raghunathan 2009; Sen and Bhattacharya 2001; Stahilevitz and Meyers 1998). However, we

know relatively little about when and why consumers are motivated purchase green products *for others*. Research on gift-giving (Belk, 1979; Otnes and Beltramini, 1996; Vesterlund, 2006) suggests that individuals' motives for offering gifts and factors that influence gift-giving vary markedly; they include duty, self-interest, love, reciprocity, compliance with social norms, and concern for others (Goodwin, Mick and DeMoss 1990; Smith, and Spiggle, 1990; Sherry, 1983; Wolfinbarger, 1990). Notably, gifts offer an important form of symbolic communication (Sherry, 1983) and impose an identity on both the giver and the receiver (Schwartz, 1967). In sum, gift exchanges hold tremendous signal value. To date, very little is known about what drives consumers' demand for green products when given as gifts. The present research addresses this gap and asks the following question: when and why do consumers choose more vs. less green gifts for others? We investigate this question across different types of gifts and different types of relationships (i.e., romantic vs. platonic).

In study one, we examine choices of products gifted to a significant other (romantic partner) for a major holiday. The study employed a 2 (media exposure: yes vs. no) x 2 (respondent's gender: male vs. female) between-subject factorial design. The media exposure manipulation consisted of a 4-minute video from NBC's Today Show about opportunities to buy green gifts (media exposure condition) or not (no media condition) prior to making their choices. Greenness of gifts was operationalized through the use of standard vs. fair trade brands of chocolate and greeting cards. Participants examined actual products and chose one of the two products to gift to their romantic partner; 5% of the participants (randomly chosen) received the actual product of their choice. We found that the percentage of females choosing green gifts was significantly *lower* than their male counterparts. Here the green option may simply be seen as an added benefit rather than having ethicality or signaling implications. Thus, in study two we manipulate the explicitness of ethicality information.

In study two, participants were asked to choose one of two bottles of wine as a gift for their significant other for a special occasion. Study 2 consisted of a 2 media exposure (yes vs. no) x 2 (respondent's gender: male vs. female) x 2 information about ethicality (explicit vs. implicit) between-subject design. Consistent with study 1, females chose fewer green gifts for romantic others, regardless of whether the ethicality information was implicit or explicit. Since females are typically thought to be more responsive to ethical and conservation appeals, these findings are noteworthy. Under what circumstances *do* females give green gifts? In particular, to what extent does the type of relationship matter?

In studies three and four, participants chose between two bouquets of flowers for a close female friend, and we varied the durability of the ethical cue. That is, whereas the marker of ethicality on packaging (e.g., a box containing chocolate or a bottle containing wine) is fleeting, gifts with enduring markers of ethicality may offer a different and more enduring signal. In study four, flowers were accompanied by branded vases, and in study five, participants made choices of durable goods (e.g., a shirt) for a friend. Respondent's gender (male vs. female) was measured; durability of ethical cue (not durable vs. durable) and knowledge of options (recipient knows vs. recipient does not know) were manipulated between subjects. We found that females were more likely to choose the green gift options, particularly for female friends, but only when the ethical information was durable. Study six replicates and extends these findings by systematically varying the gift-recipient (romantic partner vs. friend) within a single study and providing additional process evidence.

Previous work suggests that consumers buy lower quality green products for themselves as a "costly signal" associated with status (Griskevicius, Tybur, and Bram Van den Bergh 2010). In our studies, we investigate choices for others and hold quality constant and also offer higher quality green products. Our results show when and why consumers choose green goods for others as a way to signal distinct forms of relational value and desired impressions of the self rather than to consume in ways consistent with expressed values (i.e., pro-environmental attitudes or moral identity) or status. Across studies we find that the probability of choosing a green or environmentally friendly gift depends largely on the giver's perception of its distinct signal value to the recipient in the context of the relationship. Consumers, particularly women, are especially sensitive to the signal value of gifts and more strategic about when they choose to give ethically and environmentally superior gifts. Our findings suggest that gift-giving is not simply about the joy of giving, nor about the joy of buying green or ethically superior gifts for the sake of *being* green but rather the signaling benefit of *being seen* as green or ethical *but only* by select groups of others. The distinct asymmetries between genders in choices of gifts and distinct signaling motivations for green behaviors offer a rich area for future research.

New Theoretical, Managerial, and Societal Perspectives on the Consumer

Chair: Ahir Gopaldas, York University, Canada

Paper #1: The Consumer Role: Core Characteristics and Personal Boundaries

Jodie Whelan, University of Western Ontario, USA
Miranda Goode, University of Western Ontario, Canada
June Cotte, University of Western Ontario, Canada

Paper #2: A Less-Than-Immaculate Conception: Investigating the Relationship between Product Developers and their Imagined Consumer

Sarah Wilner, Wilfred Laurier University, Canada

Paper #3: The Construction of the Individual Consumer-Citizen and the Commodification of Risk

Can Uslay, Chapman University, USA
Gokcen Coskuner-Balli, Chapman University, USA
Dhruv Bhatli, University of Paris, France

Paper #4: Consumer Culture Theories of the Consumer and Developing New Conceptualizations

Ahir Gopaldas, York University, Canada

SEESION OVERVIEW

Objectives. The consumer in all his or her theoretical and practical manifestations ought to be a primary focus of consumer research. However, many consumer researchers are educated in only one or two dominant conceptions of the consumer (e.g., consumer as information processor, meaning maker, or utility maximizer). Much too quickly, these conceptions become taken-for-granted implicit assumptions, fostering myopic theoretical refinements rather than revolutionary theoretical breakthroughs. The objective of this special session is to awaken consumer researchers to multiple old and new ways of thinking about the consumer. Specifically, the objective of the papers is to foreground and evaluate conceptions of the consumer from role-theoretic (paper 1), managerial (paper 2), societal (paper 3), and meta-theoretical (paper 4) perspectives.

One might say that the creators of this special session snatch Consumer from his everyday job as a minion at Marketing Imaginary Limited and seat him on a curious but caring therapeutic couch. They dig deep into the unconscious of consumer experience (paper 1), consumer management (paper 2), consumer society (paper 3), and consumer research (paper 4). They analyze his job function (paper 1), ask what his managers think of him (paper 2), wonder what society expects of him (paper 3), and of course, dig up his past and imagine his possible futures (paper 4).

1. Jodie Whelan, Miranda Goode, and June Cotte filter consumer research to distill the core characteristics of the consumer role; they pinpoint *materialism*, *self-focus*, *empowerment*, and *hopefulness*. They then collect visual data to discern how individual persons actually enact the consumer role and discover five variations: the *blended* consumer, the *romantic* consumer, the *unidimensional* consumer, the *self-aware* consumer, and the defensive consumer. What these authors do for the consumer concept in consumer research is as important as what Kohli and Jaworski (1990) did for the marketing concept (a.k.a., market orientation) in marketing research – they bring a foundational and fundamental but curiously under-theorized concept to life.

2. Sarah Wilner goes where few consumer researchers have gone before – into the depths of Fortune 500 marketing departments – to explore how managers relate to their imagined consumers. Over time, the author discovers that marketer-consumer relationships range from the personal (*consumer as friend*) to the professional (*consumer as client*) and from the intimate (*relating via empathy*) to the clinical (*relating via data*). What is not revealed in this abstract is the incredible behind-the-scenes work it requires to gather such data. Beyond professional networking and international travel, this research necessitates gaining the trust of not lay consumers but highly-skilled consumer research practitioners. Illuminating both the inner workings of marketer minds and the departmental politics of product development, this paper drops us right into the *real* intersection of consumer research and marketing strategy.

3. Can Uslay, Gokcen Coskuner-Balli, and Dhruv Bhatli spotlight a curious trend in contemporary society. As institutions become more concerned with safety (under the rubric of risk management), citizens are increasingly engaging in risky consumer behavior. To solve this puzzle, this paper takes us on an exciting journey from Kennedy to Reagan, from gambling to marijuana, and from global risks to individual anxieties. When the dust settles, we discern the connection between the construction of the individualist consumer citizen and the commoditization of risk. This paper attempts the sort of macro-social analysis that too few consumer researchers dare. How are societies changing? More importantly for us, how are consumers changing? And, what are the links among these changes in societies and consumers?

4. Ahir Gopaldas first surveys how consumer culture theorists have variously conceptualized the consumer (e.g., consumer as meaning maker, self concept, relationship partner, community member, structured agent, etc.). He then identifies the unique implications of each conceptualization for collecting qualitative data, building grounded theory, and constructing marketing strategy. While other papers in this session offer new perspectives on the consumer using exciting data, this paper cashes out the empirical, theoretical, and managerial payoffs of the perspectives that already exist. Finally, and most importantly, he discusses how junior scholars can develop new conceptualizations of the consumer to answer recurring calls for 'new perspectives' in marketing theory and practice.

Questions for Discussion. In 2007, John Deighton clarified what ought to be the *core content* of consumer research: *not* general theories of human behavior that can be applied to consumption, *but* consumption-specific constructs and relationships that are our expertise exclusively. In 2010, Deborah MacInnis and Valerie Folkes took stock of the content debate in consumer research from a sociology of science perspective and offered the following conclusion: "con-

199

Advances in Consumer Research
Volume 39, ©2011

sumer behavior is distinguished from other fields [of human behavior] by its focus on a consumer role" (899). Also in 2010, the JCR editorial team invited consumer researchers to produce 'integrative summaries' and 'new perspectives' because "both types of papers are important means by which a field moves forward." Accordingly, the discussants are invited to evaluate one session-wide question and four paper-specific questions. Do the papers in this session begin to realize the increasingly unanimous vision for truly consumer-specific research? In other words, do the papers in this session re-shape the boundaries of consumer research in a visionary or dangerous direction?

1. Does exploring the phenomenological (de)activation of the consumer role within and beyond consumption contexts sharpen or blur the boundaries of consumer research?

2. Consumer psychology and consumer culture theory have thrived for decades on laboratory experiments and consumer ethnographies. Should we care how managers think of and relate to consumers?

3. Most consumer researchers don't read history, let alone futures studies. Should we continue assuming consumer behavior is a hard (trans-historical) science or start observing how 'consumer' is a fragile concept evolving with society?

4. Will positioning conceptualizations of the consumer – numerous, contested, and ever-changing as they are – at the heart of consumer research provide the discipline an enduring and anchoring theoretical puzzle or foster a Tower of Babel?

Building Connections. Consumer research has a responsibility to the broader social science community: it must lead the academic conversation on the meanings and functions of the consumer concept. This special session takes this scholarly duty to advance theories of the consumer rather seriously. However, the authors of these papers also collectively aim to make important connections across disciplinary, methodological, and social boundaries. First, although the papers are mostly crafted in the tradition of consumer culture theory, they extensively converse with other disciplines: consumer psychology (paper 1, 4), marketing strategy (paper 2, 4), and the sociology of consumption (paper 3, 4). Second, the session also connects methodological solutions to conceptual problems in a novel or at least non-routine way. By strategically employing image-based projective techniques (paper 1), extended ethnographic engagements (paper 2), multi-sited netnographic research (paper 3), and meta-theoretical analysis (paper 4), the session celebrates the diversity of methods in the qualitative marketing research toolkit (Belk 2006). Finally, this special session also hopes to build social connections in a quite literal way: the authors and discussants collectively represent 3 countries, 7 universities, and scholars at multiple stages of their career – from PhD candidates to JCR editors.

The Consumer Role: Core Characteristics and Personal Boundaries

EXTENDED ABSTRACT

Despite the centrality of the consumer role in today's society, a rich description of the role is surprisingly underdeveloped. Describing the consumer role is extremely important, because as Folkes (2002) points out, "when situational cues lead people to perceive themselves as customers, they then interpret the world differently than when they do not perceive themselves as customers, and that influences their behavior" (1). In other words, a clear definition of the consumer role will provide us with the foundation needed to further investigate the consequences of being a consumer—both within and beyond the consumer context. Using role theory and boundary theory, we first provide a detailed conceptualization of the consumer role and second, use image-based qualitative interviews to explore how individuals embody the consumer role in their daily lives.

Core Characteristics of the Consumer Role. Like actors playing specific roles, people behave in ways that are different and predictable depending on the context and the role they occupy. Broadly speaking, roles are defined as a "certain persona—replete with specific goals, values, beliefs, norms, interaction styles, and time horizons" (Ashforth, Kreiner, and Fugate 2000, 475). To simplify, we define the consumer role as the core set of characteristics that guide behavior during the pursuit and acquisition of marketplace goods and services.

To identify the core characteristics of the consumer role, we rely on a thorough literature review of the history of consumerism and research on compulsive buyers. From this, we identify four core characteristics of the consumer role: materialism, self-focus, empowerment, and hopefulness. First (and not surprisingly), the consumer role is linked to materialism. Materialism is the value an individual places on the acquisition and possession of material goods, especially for their symbolic purposes (Richins and Dawson 1992). Not only does the Veblenesque account of the rise of consumerism highlight the symbolic importance of consumer goods (Veblen 1899/1953), but compulsive buyers also tend to be highly materialistic (O'Guinn and Faber 1989). In addition, if the consumer role is materialistic, it must also be self-focused as materialism is a self-focused value (Burroughs and Rindfleisch 2002). Empowerment is another core characteristic. Stearns (2001) proposes that the consumer revolution occurred because women were desperate to regain control over their lives, a feeling that is often echoed by compulsive buyers (Faber 2000; Krueger 1988; O'Guinn and Faber 1989). Lastly, Campbell's (1987) account of the consumer role as being driven by hope, daydreaming, and disillusionment is supported by the consistent finding that compulsive shoppers have a high propensity to fantasize and are quickly disenchanted with their purchases (Faber 2000; Krueger 1988; O'Guinn and Faber 1989). Thus, we propose that the consumer role is materialistic, self-focused, hopeful, and empowering.

It is important to note that traditional role theory regards roles as shared, social conceptions that "are clearly defined and agreed upon by society" (Solomon et al. 1985, 101). Recently, however, research explores how an individual's own understanding of a social role results in a role that, to some degree, is unique to the individual (Neale and Griffin 2006). To explore how the consumer role varies across individuals, we turn to boundary theory and image-based qualitative interviews.

Consumer Role Boundaries. Individuals create boundaries to maintain or modify social roles (Nippert-Eng 1996). Depending on the strength of their boundaries, roles may be classified along an integration-segmentation continuum: integrated roles have weak and flexible boundaries and segmented roles have strong and inflexible boundaries (Ashforth et al. 2000; Clark 2000; Nippert-Eng 1996). To better understand individual variations in consumer role boundaries and their subsequent impact on the enactment of the consumer role, we conducted nine depth interviews using visual images selected by our participants (Zaltman 1997; Zaltman and Coulter 1995). Our analysis revealed five variations of the consumer role, which we characterize along the integration-segmentation continuum as the blended consumer, the romantic consumer, the unidimensional consumer, the self-aware consumer, and the defensive consumer.

For the blended consumer, consumer role boundaries are largely non-existent. The consumer role is highly integrated and almost inseparable from other life domains. The consumer role is not the dominant role but is subsumed under another more salient role. The romantic consumer is also highly integrated but still somewhat separable. This consumer embraces the consumer role precisely because of the characteristics identified above, with little or no concern for the potentially negative consequences of being a consumer (e.g., overspending). Boundaries are virtually nonexistent, and transitioning into the consumer role occurs frequently and often unintentionally. The unidimensional consumer also embraces the consumer role, but to a lesser degree. Though this individual is materialistic, self-focused, hopeful and empowered when in the consumer role, at least one of these characteristics is clearly dominant. The self-aware consumer is mindful of both the pros and cons of being a consumer and erects some boundaries to maintain control of when and why the consumer role is entered. Lastly, the defensive consumer erects strong boundaries and is extremely weary of being under the influence of the consumer role.

In exploring the consumer role along the integration-segmentation continuum, several interesting insights emerge. First, the more segmented the consumer role, the less likely the individual is to experience both advantages and disadvantages of the consumer role. Further, maintaining extreme segmentation seems exhausting given how pervasive the consumer role is in today's society. Lastly, the more segmented the consumer role, the more mindful transitioning into the consumer role is likely to be.

Implications. Our research provides a rich conceptual description of the consumer role, while also demonstrating that this role is highly influenced by the idiosyncratic nature of consumer role boundaries. Counter to boundary theory's penchant to examine role integration/segmentation in the context of two roles (e.g., work and family), we also show that roles and their boundaries can be studied independent of other roles. Finally, our research provides the conceptual foundation necessary to explore further why people seek out the consumer role, how individuals can manage their consumer role transitions, and how the consumer role can impact behavior and relationships in non-consumer contexts.

A Less-Than-Immaculate Conception: Investigating the Relationship Between Product Developers and Their Imagined Consumer

EXTENDED ABSTRACT

Consumer researchers have examined consumers' relationships with brands, products and organizations (e.g. Fournier 1998; Muniz and O'Guinn 2001; Bhattacharya and Sen 2003) but remain largely indifferent to the perspective of the managers who produce the objects and symbols with which consumers interact (for exceptions see Cayla and Eckhardt 2006; Desroches and Marcoux 2007). This is fundamentally problematic because, "for a relationship to truly exist…the partners must collectively affect, define and redefine the relationship" (Fournier 1998:344).

Accordingly, this paper examines managers' relationships with their imagined consumers (Cayla and Eckhardt 2006) in the context of product development. Product development is a rich context for examining the relationships producers construe with consumers, because it is during this process that managers actively explore and address the fundamental nature of consumers' motivations, desires and behaviors. The study was initiated by examining the myriad of tools, artifacts and processes that are employed to construct or otherwise reify consumers in the course of product development. This foundation in turns, informs the study's focal question: What is the nature of the relationship between members of product development teams and the consumers they develop for?

Method. The author conducted a multisited ethnographic study of five Fortune 500 firms' strategic business units over 18 months. Data from focal firms was collected via semi-structured interviews with key informants; participant-observation of product development activities and collection of archival information from the firms as well as media reports. Additional interviews with informants in nine other consumer goods and consulting firms were conducted to enhance the validity of findings. Sampled firms represent multiple industries and product categories including: consumer packaged goods; consumer durables; high-tech equipment and medical services.

Findings. Relationships between members of product development teams and their consumers vary along two primary continua: a role orientation ranging from personal (e.g. consumer as friend) to professional (e.g. consumer as client) and an interaction dimension ranging from the intimate (e.g. empathy or shared experience) to the clinical (e.g. data dominates). Importantly, the nature of each manager's relationship with a given target reveals a mental model reflecting both personality traits and life experiences. Thus, managerial relationships with consumers can vary considerably, even among members of the same product development team. Conversely, managers may be motivated to revise initial schemas about consumers in the course of collective sensemaking (cf. Weick et al. 2005).

To illustrate, managers with a strong professional role orientation as well as a sense of empathy for their consumer subjects might construe the targeted consumer as a potential victim, deserving of protection or advocacy. This is the case with Katherine[1], who works in research and development for 'Better Living'[2], maker of personal care products. She explains, "I kind of see myself as a soldier for the consumer. There are definitely marketers and other people inside the company for whom it's more about chasing the money than the longer term solution…I'm more worried about the long-term consumer behavior than quarter-to-quarter" (personal interview, August 2009).

Producer-consumer relationships are subject to the vicissitudes of insight gleaned from consumer intelligence and as such are an integral factor linking consumer research and product development. For example, at 'Crunchies', a packaged food company, retail transaction data indicated that mothers of teenage boys were key buyers of the company's bestselling snack. Given stereotypes of mothers as the nuclear family's primary provider of nourishment and caretaker of health, producers assumed that the mothers would be concerned with these issues when making purchase decisions and product development efforts focused on increasing the snacks' nutritional profile. However, subsequent ethnographic research revealed that many mothers were more interested in increasing their son's social capital than salubrity. These mothers aspired to create a context in which their teen was seen by peers to have the "right stuff" (including snack foods), and for their home to become the preferred place for her son's friends to gather. The discovery of this insight instantly converted the development team's interpretation of the buyer segment from hard-to-please "Shopper Moms" to impressively cool "Kick Ass Moms."[3] This reframing of the consumer not only shifted

---

[1] Informants have been given pseudonyms to provide anonymity.

[2] Organizational identities have also been masked to preserve confidentiality and comply with non-disclosure agreements.

[3] Verbatim segment names provided by informants.

the focus of product development activity from nutrition to season-ing with adolescent appeal, it fundamentally changed the nature of the producer-consumer relationship. Once characterized by limited mutual affect and buyer-dominant power (see Hinde 1995:6), the re-lationship became one in which the customer not only ceded power but was also vulnerable, for both her son's popularity and her legacy as a mother were at stake. Interestingly, while the company had hired a brand consultancy to create an elaborate consumer archetype com-plete with a lifestyle "mood board," the director of brand innovation (and author of the "Kick Ass Mom" epithet) denied using personas as a reference or representational tool. In interviews, not one mem-ber of the team could remember the archetype's name. They did, however, all know his mom's.

Implications. Recognizing that producers, like consumers, seek and value relationships with their dyadic counterpart illumi-nates aspects of the logic by which consumer research is specified, interpreted and ultimately applied. However, there remain at least two significant challenges to the creation of meaningful producer-consumer relationships. The first is evinced in the remainder of Katherine's statement above, which continues: "The thing about our marketing department is that they focus max three years out and so from a brand perspective…it's still more quarter-to-quarter focus. That's how their bonuses are structured." Katherine's cynicism to-wards marketers on the development team reveals the inescapable tension produced by conflicting consumer orientations among mem-bers or functional areas. While copious research has examined the implications of cross-functional cooperation/conflict on new product performance, it has neither considered product developers' envisag-ing of consumers nor the resulting relationships a source of contesta-tion. This finding suggests that surfacing managers' tacit relation-ships with consumers may aid in reducing resource-draining conflict. This might, for example, take the form of an instrument akin to the Myers-Briggs Type Indicator which could be employed to diagnose managers' predispositions and expose them to potential sources of divergence.

A second fundamental challenge is organizational turbulence. If "temporality distinguishes the relationship from the isolated transac-tion," (Fournier 1998:346; see also Hinde 1995:2), given the volatil-ity of current organizational design, producers will be fated to mere transactional interactions despite their stated desire for close and sus-tained consumer relationships. All of the focal firms in the sample have engaged in relentless reorganization since the inception of the research project, with managers laid off or repeatedly re-assigned from key consumer research and interpretive roles. Without conti-nuity of interaction and experience with valued consumer segment, individual managers may be unable to foster empathy for their con-sumer subjects, a condition Fournier et al. (1998) argue fosters a marketplace marked by consumer alienation and dissent. Senior ex-ecutives, removed from day-to-day operations, understandably may not experience the same quality or intensity of consumer relationship experienced by their managers. It is imperative, therefore, that deci-sion makers motivated to reorganize in the name of revised strategic goals be sensitized to the ramifications of frequent relational disloca-tion among managers and their consumers.

The Construction of the Individualist Consumer-Citizen and the Commodification of Risk

EXTENDED ABSTRACT

There is a paradox in post-industrialized societies. On one hand, societies are characterized by an increasing concern with the man-agement of risk (Beck 1992). On the other hand, there is an increas-ing consumer involvement in risky activities (e.g. extreme sports, home birth, gambling, consumption of diet pills, marijuana, and junk food).

The socio-cultural conditions that gave rise to this paradox are closely linked to the construction of the individualist, self-interested citizen in free market economies (Cohen 2003). The consumerism movement initiated by Kennedy in the sixties came of age at the end of the seventies in all but emerging or closed markets. In the US, especially after the election of Reagan, neoliberal discourses with decreased government intervention gained prominence (Aaker and Day 1982). Being subject to the uncertainties of capitalism itself and facing the difficulties of calculating risks, the state transferred its re-sponsibilities to its citizens, other market institutions (Neary and Tay-lor 2006), and communities of reflexive doubt (Giddens 1991). Sci-entific and technocratic expert communities, like the state, delegated ultimate responsibility of risk management to consumers (Thompson 2005). Furthermore, the state became increasingly involved in the commoditization of risk, as exemplified in the increasing production and marketing of gambling by the state (Young 2010).

In this cultural setting, we explore how consumers conceptual-ize, experience and justify their involvement with risky consump-tion practices. Towards this objective, we conducted a netnographic analysis to observe consumer interactions on various online con-sumer platforms (communities, discussion forums, blogs and social networks) focusing on consumption practices such as online gam-bling, marijuana consumption and drug use for weight loss and body enhancement. The data collected are mainly electronic messages ex-changed by online users and were later coded and interpreted.

Implications. The contributions of this research are threefold. First, our analysis aims to assess consumers' conceptualization of various types of risks. Young (2010) suggests that there is a dialecti-cal relationship between global and undifferentiated risk (associated with anxiety) and individual differentiated risk (associated with plea-sure). Global risks are "unbounded, external and affect all society" whereas individual risks "appear as personal choice, are bounded and internal" (265). We build on his thesis by exploring the rela-tion between global and individual risk. For example, consuming junk food is a pleasure-based consumption activity that poses in-dividual consequences on an immediate term. However, it can also be transformed into a more global anxiety with the increasing rates of obesity and national health problems. Furthermore, we examine how anxiety-based risks are experienced at the individual level and elaborate on the multiplicity of discourses and practices these indus-trial risks create. For instance, consumers might share the anxiety of global warming but neither experience nor act upon it in a uniform fashion.

Second, our netnographic study illuminates the nature of con-sumer decision-making experiences as consumers face a multipli-cation of expert communities. We investigate whether consumers find the increasing individualism and commodification of risk as liberatory or overwhelming. Consumers' risk taking propensities are underlied by two forces: simplification and complification (Howard and Sheth 1969). Consumers reduce the complexity of decisions by using heuristics or shortcuts and satisficing criteria. On the other hand, the countervailing force of complification necessitates the con-sideration of additional options and involves risk. Our study suggests that in most developed consumer markets the need for complifica-tion is on the rise. Based on their risk-taking propensity, consumers are taking additional risk and expressing their individuality. In many cases, this creates great opportunities for marketers to recognize and respond to these individual desires with new and customized offer-ings (e.g. insurance policies for extreme sports and bank loans for plastic surgery). In other cases, the outcome is tension between simplifying regulation efforts that reduce the risk-taking propensity of the population to a normative uniform/risk-averse function (e.g., do not gamble online).

Third, we demonstrate how various groups construct notions of risk and safety and how they define the boundaries of individualism and free choice. Risk and safety are legitimated and promoted in accord with the economic and political interests of the involved agents –consumers, marketers and the state. The recent discussion on the legalization of marijuana is a case in place documenting the multifaceted process of 'normalization'.

Consumer Culture Theories of the Consumer and Developing New Conceptualizations

EXTENDED ABSTRACT

This article has three objectives. First, it surveys how consumer culture theorists have variously conceptualized the consumer in consumer culture theory. Examples include the consumer as *meaning maker* (e.g., Levy 1959), *feeling being* (e.g., Hirschman and Holbrook 1982), *self concept* (e.g., Belk 1988), *metaphorical processor* (e.g., Zaltman 1995), *relationship partner* (e.g., Fournier 1988), *community member* (e.g., Muniz and O'Guinn 2001), *structured agent* (e.g., Crockett and Wallendorf 2004), *network actor* (Epp and Price 199, and *multiphrenic self* (e.g., Bahl and Milne 2010)).

Second, the article identifies the unique implications of each conceptualization for collecting qualitative data, building grounded theory, and constructing marketing strategy. For example, the conceptualization of the consumer as a *multiphrenic self* suggests motivating consumption in one of two ways. Marketers can promote a product as a self-serving solution to a particular kind of self shared by many consumers (i.e., an archetypal self). Alternatively, marketers can promote a product to the meta-self as a solution to common goal conflicts among selves. The conception also hints that new markets may be created by inventing new archetypes (e.g., *GQ* men and *Harley* bikers). To demotivate consumption, advocates could help consumers identify their multiple selves and heal their dysfunctional selves. Thereafter, consumers must learn strategies for resolving conflicts among selves (e.g., coalition), such that a few versatile consumables can serve the interests of multiple selves.

Third, and most importantly, the article discusses how theorists, especially junior scholars, can develop new conceptualizations of the consumer to answer recurring calls for 'new perspectives' in consumer and marketing research. The value of articles that explicitly or implicitly offer new conceptualizations of consumption (Belk 1988; Fournier 1998; Muniz Jr. and O'Guinn 2001) is evidenced in their relatively high citation counts, disproportionate numbers of awards, and frequent appearance in doctoral course syllabi. Owing to the importance of new conceptualizations, this article addresses the question: *how do theorists develop new conceptions?*

New conceptions develop in three main acts: ideation, construction, and publication. In the first act of ideation, the initial inspiration for new conceptions may arise from intellectual 'kindling' as diverse as cognitive dissonance, eclectic reading, empirical research, new technologies, other fields of research, lay theories, personal experience, projective exercises, theory-data tensions, or thought experiments (Langley 1999; Weick 1989; Zaltman, LeMasters, and Heffring 1982). An idea is often expressed in tropes such as analogies and metaphors (Lakoff and Johnson 1980; Morgan 1980, 1986; Weick 1989). For example, Muniz Jr. and O'Guinn (2001) began a vigorous stream of marketing literature with the simple notion that

groups of people who consume the same brand and derive benefits from shared experiences are analogous to communities.

Second, no matter how their initial idea is kindled, theorists 'discipline' their imagination (cf. Weick 1989) with theoretical materials from other disciplines to support their conceptions. Thus far, conceptual innovators in consumer research have drawn heavily on the social sciences such as anthropology, economics, psychology, and sociology and a bit less extensively on the natural sciences such as neuroscience and humanities such as literary criticism. Theorists can also discipline their imagination using empirical materials, but theory is always necessary. The theoretical approach is exemplified by Belk (1988). The author draws on multiple streams of philosophy, psychology, sociology, and anthropology to evidence the idea that consumption is often like an extension of one's self concept. The mixed theory-data approach is exemplified by Fournier (1998). The author tacks back and forth between relationship psychology and informants' longitudinal engagements with brands to explicate the idea that consumption is like an interpersonal relationship. (For a longer discussion of theory construction as disciplined imagination via problem statements, thought trials, and selection criteria, see Weick (1989).)

Third, following ideation and construction, conceptions face the arduous task of warranting publication. 'A' journals such as JCR require that authors demonstrate how their conception makes a distinct contribution to the field. Authors can choose to highlight how their new conceptualization reveals (i) new aspects of the consumer, (ii) new consumption activities, or (iii) new motivating forces. For example, Bahl and Milne (2010) inject new insight into the role of the self in consumer behavior (cf. Ahuvia 2005; Belk 1988; Sirgy 1982) on all three dimensions. (i) Consumers do not have one self concept, but multiple selves and a meta-self. (ii) Consumer choice is not as simple as negotiating whether a product matches one's identity, but having a conversation among multiple selves – a conversation that may end in various outcomes ranging from domination to coalition. (iii) Consuming is motivated by not only the need to sustain one's selves but also by the need to achieve harmony among them.

REFERENCES

Aaker, David A. and George S. Day (1982), *Consumerism: Search for the Consumer Interest*, New York, NY: The Free Press.

Ahuvia, Aaron C. (2005), "Beyond the Extended Self: Loved Objects and Consumers' Identity Narratives," *Journal of Consumer Research*, 32 (1), 171-84.

Ashforth, Blake E., Glen E. Kreiner, and Mel Fugate (2000), "All in a Day's Work: Boundaries and Micro Role Transitions," *The Academy of Management Review*, 25 (3), 472-91.

Bahl, Shalini and George R. Milne (2010), "Talking to Ourselves: A Dialogical Exploration of Consumption Experiences," *Journal of Consumer Research*, 37 (1), 176-95.

Beck, Ulrich (1992) *Risk Society: Towards a New Modernity*, London: Sage.

Belk, Russell W. (1988), "Possessions and the Extended Self," *Journal of Consumer Research*, 15 (2), 139.

Belk, Russell W. (2006), *Handbook of Qualitative Research Methods in Marketing*, Northampton, MA: Edward Elgar.

Bhattacharya, C. and Sankar Sen (2003), "Consumer-Company Identification: A Framework for Understanding Consumers' Relationships with Companies," *Journal of Marketing*, 67: 76-88.

Burroughs, James E. and Aric Rindfleisch (2002), "Materialism and Well-Being: A Conflicting Values Perspective," *Journal of Consumer Research*, 29 (December), 348-70.

Campbell, Colin (1987), *The Romantic Ethic and the Spirit of Modern Consumerism*, New York: Basil Blackwell Inc.

Cayla, Julien and Giana M. Eckhardt (2008), "Asian Brands and the Shaping of a Transnational Imagined Community," *Journal of Consumer Research*, 35(2):216-230.

Clark, Sue Campbell (2000), "Work/Family Border Theory: A New Theory of Work/Family Balance," *Human Relations*, 53 (6), 747-70.

Cohen, Lizabeth (2003), *A Consumers' Republic: The Politics of Consumption in Postwar America*, New York: Vintage Books.

Deighton, John (2007), "From the Editor: The Territory of Consumer Research: Walking the Fences," *Journal of Consumer Research*, 34 (3), 279-82.

Deighton, John, Debbie MacInnis, Ann McGill, and Baba Shiv (2010), "Editorial: Broadening the Scope of Consumer Research," *Journal of Consumer Research*, 36 (6), v-vii.

Desroches, Pascale and Jean-Sebastien Marcoux (2007), "Constructing the Market Through the Colour Spectrum," *Proceedings of the European Association of Consumer Research*. Volume 8, eds. Borghini, McGrath and Otnes. Duluth, MN: Association for Consumer Research.

Faber, Ronald J. (2000), "A Systematic Investigation into Compulsive Buying," in *I Shop, Therefore I Am: Compulsive Buying and the Search for the Self*, ed. April Lane Benson, Northvale, New Jersey: Jason Aronson Inc., 27-53.

Folkes, Valerie S. (2002), "Presidential Address: Is Consumer Behavior Different?," in Advances in Consumer Research, Vol. 29, ed. Susan M. Broniarczyk and Kent Nakamoto, Valdosta, GA: Association for Consumer Research, 1-4.

Fournier, Dobscha, Susan and David Glen Mick (1998), "Preventing the Premature Death of Relationship Marketing," *Harvard Business Review*, January-February.

Fournier, Susan (1998), "Consumers and Their Brands: Developing Relationship Theory in Consumer Research," *Journal of Consumer Research*, 24 (4), 343-53.

Fournier, Susan (1998), "Consumers and Their Brands: Developing Relationship Theory in Consumer Research," *Journal of Consumer Research*, 24: 343-373.

Giddens, Anthony (1991) *Modernity and Self-Identity: Self and Society in the Late Modern Age,* Cambridge: Polity.

Henry, Paul C. (2010) "How Mainstream Consumers Think about Consumer Rights and Responsibilities," *Journal of Consumer Research*, 37 (December), 670-87.

Hinde, Robert (1995), "A Suggested Structure For a Science of Relationships," *Personal Relationships*, 2:1-15.

Howard, John A. and Jagdish N. Sheth (1969), *The Theory of Buyer Behavior*, New York: John Wiley & Sons, Inc.

Kohli, Ajay K. and Bernard J. Jaworski (1990), "Market Orientation: The Construct, Research Propositions, and Managerial Implications," *Journal of Marketing*, 54 (April), 1–18.

Krueger, David W. (1988), "On Compulsive Shopping and Spending: A Psychodynamic Inquiry," *American Journal of Psychotherapy*, 42 (October), 574-84.

Lakoff, George and Mark Johnson (1980), *Metaphors We Live By*, Chicago: University of Chicago Press.

Langley, Ann (1999), "Strategies for Theorizing from Process Data," *Academy of Management Review*, 24 (4), 691-710.

MacInnis, Deborah J. and Valerie S. Folkes (2010), "The Disciplinary Status of Consumer Behavior: A Sociology of Science Perspective on Key Controversies," *Journal of Consumer Research*, 36 (6), 899-914.

Morgan, Gareth (1980), "Paradigms, Metaphors, and Puzzle Solving in Organization Theory," *Administrative Science Quarterly*, 25 (4), 605-22.

Morgan, Gareth (1986), *Images of Organization*, Beverly Hills: Sage Publications.

Muniz Jr., Albert M. and Thomas C. O'Guinn (2001), "Brand Community," *Journal of Consumer Research*, 27 (4), 412-32.

Muñiz, Jr., Alfred and O'Guinn, Thomas (2001) "Brand Community," *Journal of Consumer Research,* 27: 412–32.

Neale, Matthew and Mark A. Griffin (2006), "A Model of Self-Held Work Roles and Role Transitions," *Human Performance*, 19 (1), 23-41.

Neary, Mike and Taylor, Graham (2006) 'From the Law of Insurance to the Law of the Lottery:An Exploration of the Changing Composition of the British State', in J. F. Cosgrave (Ed.), *The Sociology of Risk and Gambling Reader*, pp. 339–354. New York: Routledge.

Nippert-Eng, Christena (1996), "Calendars and Keys: The Classification Of "Home" And "Work"," *Sociological Forum*, 11 (3), 563-82.

O'Guinn, Thomas C. and Ronald J. Faber (1989), "Compulsive Buying: A Phenomenological Exploration," *Journal of Consumer Research*, 16 (September), 147-57.

Richins, Marsha L. and Scott Dawson (1992), "A Consumer Values Orientation for Materialism and Its Measurement: Scale Development and Validation," *Journal of Consumer Research*, 19 (December), 303-16.

Sirgy, M. Joseph (1982), "Self-Concept in Consumer Behavior: A Critical Review," *Journal of Consumer Research*, 9 (3), 287.

Solomon, Michael R., Carol Surprenant, John A. Czepiel, and Evelyn G. Gutman (1985), "A Role Theory Perspective on Dyadic Interactions: The Service Encounter," *The Journal of Marketing*, 49 (Winter), 99-111.

Stearns, Peter N. (2001), Consumerism in World History, London: Routledge.

Thompson, Craig J. (2005), "Consumer Risk Perceptions in a Community of Reflexive Doubt," *Journal of Consumer Research*, 32 (September), 235–48.

Veblen, Thorstein (1899/1953), *The Theory of the Leisure Class: The Challenging Analysis of Social Conduct That Ironically Probes Misused Wealth and Conspicuous Consumption*, New York: Mentor.

Weick, Karl E. (1989), "Theory Construction as Disciplined Imagination," *Academy of Management Review*, 14 (4), 516-31.

Weick, Karl, Sutcliffe, Kathleen and David Obstfeld (2005), "Organizing and the Process of Sensemaking," *Organization Science*, 16(4):409-421.

Young, Martin (2010), "Gambling, Capitalism and the State: Towards a New Dialectic of the Risk Society," *Journal of Consumer Culture*, 10, 254-73.

Zaltman, Gerald (1997), "Rethinking Market Research: Putting People Back In," *Journal of Marketing Research*, 34 (November), 424-37.

Zaltman, Gerald and Robin Higie Coulter (1995), "Seeing the Voice of the Customer: Metaphor-Based Advertising Research," *Journal of Advertising Research* (July/August), 35-51.

Zaltman, Gerald, Karen LeMasters, and Michael Heffring (1982), *Theory Construction in Marketing: Some Thoughts on Thinking*, New York: Wiley.

Scarcity and Survival in the Marketplace

Chair: Julio Sevilla, University of Miami, USA

Paper #1: Beggars Will Be Choosers: Financial Deprivation Induces Responsiveness to Scarcity

Eesha Sharma, New York University, USA
Adam Alter, New York University, USA

Paper #2: The Less there is, the More I Want: The Effect of Scarcity on Satiation

Julio Sevilla, University of Miami, USA
Joseph Redden, University of Minnesota, USA
Shenghui Zhao, University of Miami, USA

Paper #3: Survival Mindset and Food Choices

Juliano Laran, University of Miami, USA
Anthony Salerno, University of Miami, USA
Shweta Oza, University of Miami, USA

Paper #4: There's Only One Left, Do I Want It?: The Effects of Brand and Display Characteristics on Purchase Intentions for Scarce Products

Iana Castro, San Diego State University, USA
Stephen Nowlis, Washington University in St. Louis, USA
Andrea Morales, Arizona State University, USA

SESSION OVERVIEW

One popular strategy companies use is to manage consumers' perceptions of the availability of a product (Verhallen 1982; Inman, Peter and Raghubir 1997). Because people think that scarce products are more valuable, such tactic will likely increase sales. Nevertheless, the topic of scarcity has been under-researched in the marketing literature. It is imperative for marketers to learn more about when and with whom this practice will be more effective, in which other ways it could influence people's behavior, and when it could potentially backfire and hurt a firm's performance.

This special session proposal brings together four papers that study scarcity in the marketplace from four intriguing and unexplored angles. All of these papers are in advanced stages and have 3-5 completed studies. The session aims to provide a broader understanding of the phenomenon of scarcity and highlights recent developments on this topic area across different domains including social comparison, hedonic consumption, nutrition and retailing. The session demonstrates that scarcity is a complex weapon of influence (Cialdini 2001) that affects not only how much people value an object but also the way in which they feel about themselves, their enjoyment of a consumption experience, and the type of nutritional decisions they make. Moreover, this session shows that the effects of scarcity on product evaluations will vary depending on the brand and store environment.

The first paper, by Sharma and Alter, demonstrates that people will seek, select, and consume scarce items as a mechanism to cope with the negative affect associated with upward social comparison. They show that financially deprived individuals pay more attention and prefer scarce products due to their motivation to seek opportunities to restore their sense of parity relative to others. This research extends our knowledge of scarcity by showing that, ironically, the less resources people have, the higher their desire to acquire scarce rather than abundant products will be.

The second paper, by Sevilla, Redden and Zhao, shows that people will not only be more likely to prefer scarce products more when they are financially deprived, but they will also satiate from them at a slower rate when they get the opportunity to consume them. The authors show that people satiate slower during repeated consumption

of a product when it is presented to them as scarce. This effect is not explained by higher initial liking of seemingly scarce stimuli due to scarcity-quality inferences, instead, it is explained by an urge to take advantage of an apparently rare consumption opportunity, which prevents people from paying attention to the amount being consumed.

The first two papers of the session show that while people will pay more attention to scarce products when they are financially deprived, they will pay less attention to the amount consumed if they think a stimulus is scarce. This may suggest that through evolution, humans may have discovered that scarce resources are instrumental to the survival of their species, and consequently, have learned to pursue them more during hostile times, and to become less sensitive to satiation from them when they have the rare opportunity to consume them. The third paper, by Laran, Salerno and Oza, examines scarcity from a survival and consumption standpoint. They show that people will be more likely to seek highly caloric and filling foods when they are primed with survival. They explain that this behavior is due to the adoption of a mindset that leads people to maximize the use of their resources. The authors rule out alternative explanations related to a desire to seek indulgence. They also show an attenuation of the effect in cases when people's financial standing is improved and a reversal when subjects are primed with long as opposed to short term survival. This research provides an intriguing alternative explanation for people's preference to consume the highly caloric and filling "comfort foods" during difficult times.

While the first three papers of the session look at scarcity from a more intrinsic and visceral perspective, the fourth paper, by Castro, Nowlis and Morales, takes a more rational approach. The authors offer a model of how scarcity operates in the retail environment and explain the situations in which this cue increases and decreases purchase intentions. The authors show that making a product appear to be scarce has a positive effect on unfamiliar brands and a negative effect on familiar brands. This is because scarcity cues on unfamiliar brands indicate that a product is highly demanded, thus, desirable. On the other hand, scarcity cues on familiar brands serve as mental contaminants and lead to lower purchase intentions. This paper represents a different approach to the study of scarcity, as it shows that consumers do not only have affective reactions to this type of market cues, but also have come to understand them as rational indicators of how products and brands operate in the marketplace.

We hope that this session will contribute to our understanding of how consumers interpret scarcity cues in the marketplace. Hopefully, the session will point out to new research avenues and approaches to the study of this relevant marketing cue. We hope to generate an interesting discussion among members of our likely audience, which should be integrated by researchers on Retailing, Environmental cues for quality perceptions, Branding, Hedonic Consumption, Social Psychology, and all marketers in general, including practitioners. We consider that the topic of scarcity may be instrumental to build connections among people from different areas in Marketing as it is relevant to most of them, and can be studied from a wide variety of perspectives.

Beggars Will Be Choosers: Financial Deprivation Induces Responsiveness to Scarcity

EXTENDED ABSTRACT

People routinely compare themselves with others on a range of dimensions that are salient, subjectively relevant, and difficult to evaluate objectively (Festinger 1954; Suls and Miller 1977). However, these social comparisons can be distressing when they highlight shortcomings. Specifically, comparison to a superior standard can produce negative affect and arousal, which people are motivated to resolve (Brickman and Bulman 1977; Tesser 1988). These motivations, in turn, influence how people gather, process, and remember information (e.g., Balcetis and Dunning 2006; Festinger 1957; Heider 1958; Kunda 1990). Accordingly, we combine the literatures on upward social comparison and motivation to identify a novel mechanism by which consumers might cope with the unpleasantness associated with upward social comparison. We focus on consumers' sense of financial wellbeing, and how feelings of financial deprivation can influence their responsiveness (i.e., attention, preference, choice, and consumption) to stimuli in their environment.

Financial wellbeing is ripe for social comparison, as wealth is important to most people and difficult to evaluate in the absence of comparison standards (Hsee et el. 2009). We define *financial deprivation* as a state in which consumers feel financially inferior to a salient comparison standard—either another person or their own financial position earlier in time. We suggest that financially deprived consumers are motivated to ameliorate the unpleasant arousal associated with deprivation by responding more sensitively to stimuli that have the potential to restore their sense of parity relative to others. We propose that scarce stimuli serve such a function, in contrast to stimuli that are abundantly available to others.

The existing literature provides a range of evidence that scarcity increases the desirability of goods (Fromkin 1970; Inman, Peter, and Raghubir 1997; Lessne and Notarantino 1988; Lynn 1989, 1991, 1992; Rucker and Galinsky 2008; Simonson 1992; Verhallen 1982). We extend this literature by proposing that consumers' sense of financial deprivation will interact with their responsiveness to scarcity. Specifically, we suggest that consumers will attempt to repair their sense of deprivation by attending to and possessing goods that most people cannot possess. Though non-scarce items might mitigate unpleasant affect and arousal as well, we suggest that only scarce items imply gains relative to a financially superior other person (since, in theory, scarce items are less likely to be available to that other person). Accordingly, we expect scarce items to be less desirable to financially deprived people when those items are limited due to prior consumption by (rather than supply restrictions to) the general population.

Five studies examine the influence of financial deprivation on consumer responsiveness to scarcity. Results demonstrate that: (1) financial deprivation induces sensitivity to scarce but not abundant stimuli; (2) sensitivity to scarcity explains the selection of goods that are limited versus plentiful; (3) the motivation to ameliorate feelings of deprivation prompts responsiveness to scarcity; and (4) these effects attenuate when consumers attribute their feelings to an external source.

In study 1, participants performed a discrimination task in which they determined the relative frequency of black and white gumballs in an array. However, half of the participants were instructed to identify which color was *more* frequent in the array; the other half identified which was *less* frequent. Participants also completed several questions regarding their financial wellbeing. People who felt less financially comfortable tended to discriminate between the black and white gumball colors with greater accuracy, but significantly more so when the task was a framed as a scarcity (rather than abundance) detection exercise. The interaction between participant performance and task framing (scarcity vs. abundance detection) provides preliminary evidence that people are more sensitive to scarcity cues when they feel financially deprived.

Study 2 employed a similar design, but assessed responsiveness to scarcity with a behavioral consumption measure. Participants were given a cup containing 15 M&M's of one color and 5 M&M's of another color. As expected, participants who were relatively more financially deprived tended to consume a higher percentage of the scarce rather than abundant M&M's.

In study 3, we manipulated financial deprivation by asking participants to write about a time when they felt either financially worse (deprived condition) or better (flush condition) than their peers. Participants then completed a timed discrimination task in which they estimated the relative frequency of two different characters from the *"Where's Waldo?"* book series. As predicted, participants who wrote about feeling deprived (vs. flush) did better at detecting scarce *"Where's Waldo?"* characters. This study provides causal evidence of a relationship between deprivation and sensitivity to scarcity.

In study 4, we employed a design similar to study 2 but compared deprived participants to a neutral control group consisting of participants who wrote about feeling financially matched with their peers. Participants then made several choices between various scarce and abundant goods available during "Restaurant Week." In line with the previous studies, participants who wrote about feeling deprived (versus participants in a control condition) performed with greater accuracy on a discrimination task (from study 1). Mediation analysis revealed that participants' sensitivity to scarcity (i.e., their ability to detect scarce stimuli) explained their selection of scarce rather than abundant goods.

In study 5, we found that deprived participants only preferred scarce items when they were unable to attribute the unpleasant arousal associated with deprivation to an external source. Specifically, deprived participants preferred scarce (rather than abundant) candy except when they were led to attribute their feelings to a clip of whale songs (Van Boven et al. 2010) that they had heard earlier in the experiment. This study provides evidence that deprived participants' preference for scarcity is indeed driven by a motivational component, and cannot be explained by mere priming.

This work suggests that feeling financially deprived has systematic effects on consumer attention, preference, and choice. There are many real world implications of this work, particularly given the tendency for most people to feel financially deprived at least in some contexts. The effects we illustrate speak to these implications, while addressing factors such as mood and cognitive ability. We find that beggars will be choosers—choosers who prefer what's scarce.

The Less There Is, The More I Want: The Effect of Scarcity on Satiation

EXTENDED ABSTRACT

Satiation occurs when people find a stimulus less pleasant as they consume more of it (Coombs and Avrunin 1977). Although satiation partially depends on the objective amount consumed, recent research has shown that its occurrence can be delayed (Rozin 1998, Nelson and Meyvis 2008; Redden 2008; Nelson, Meyvis and Galak (2009), accelerated (Morewedge, Huh and Vosgerau 2010), or even partly reversed (Galak, Redden and Kruger 2009) by psychological factors.

Past research on the psychological determinants of satiation has looked at aspects such as memory (Rozin 1998; Galak, Redden and Kruger 2009), imagination (Morewedge, Huh and Vosgerau 2010), categorization (Redden 2008) and consumption rate (Nelson and Meyvis 2008; Nelson, Meyvis and Galak 2009). However, no paper has investigated how different beliefs about the properties of a product affect the speed at which people satiate from it. In this research we show that merely telling people that a product is scarce will make them satiate from it at a slower pace.

Past research also has shown that scarce products are highly desirable (Verhallen 1982; Verhallen 1994; Inman, Peter and Raghubir 1997). In this paper, we manipulate people's beliefs about how scarce a product is, and observe a slower satiation rate associated to its consumption. We also show that the increased enjoyment is not due to an improvement in perceived taste associated with beliefs about higher quality of the stimulus, as ratings of initial liking are the same for stimuli that are believed to be either scarce or common. Instead, we find that attention to the quantity consumed mediates the effect. This is because when people encounter a situation where they have access to a scarce product, they will feel an urge to take advantage of this rare opportunity, and this leads them to consume it in larger amounts.

This phenomenon may have an evolutionary foundation. Covasa and Ritter (1999) have shown that rats develop the ability to become less sensitive to the consumption of oleate, an important compound present in fat. Since lipids are scarce nutrients that this species does not have frequent access to, in the rare occasions they do, they will consume it in abundant amounts, given the uncertainty about when the next time they will have access to it will be.

This reduced sensitivity to oleate in rats is similar to a human loss of the ability to keep track of consumption of a presumably scarce product. In this case, the insensitivity to satiation to a stimulus believed to be scarce is not physiological but psychological in nature, as the elements tested in our studies cannot be identified by the human body as being vital for survival as is the case of oleate in rats. Three studies provide support to our hypothesis that making people believe that a product is scarce will decrease the satiation rate during consumption.

Study 1 provides evidence for the effect in a consumption setting. We asked participants to consume chocolate and provide sequential ratings of their enjoyment of the experience in a between-subjects design. Half of the participants were told that the chocolate they were eating was made from cocoa grains that grew only in a few places of the world during a limited time every year, which led them to believe it was scarce. The other half were told that it grew in many parts of the world throughout the year, which indicated that it was widely available. It is important to mention that this scarcity manipulation did not make participants believe that one stimulus was of higher quality than the other, as they only differed in terms of their natural availability. This was reflected in our results, which showed that participants provided equal initial enjoyment ratings for the chocolate in both conditions. However, participants in the scarce condition subsequently satiated from the chocolate at a slower pace. A mediation analysis showed that the differences in the slopes of satiation between conditions, was explained by attention to the quantity being consumed.

Study 2 replicated the results of the first study and demonstrated the generalizability of the effect using Hawaiian landscapes pictures as stimuli. In a between-subjects setting similar to the one used in Study 1, it was shown that participants satiated slower from looking at the pictures when they were told that these belonged to landscapes that could be captured only during a limited time every year due to environmental factors.

Study 3 provides further support for attention to quantity as the underlying mechanism behind the effect. In a design similar to Study 1, it was shown that the difference in enjoyment of the chocolate between the scarce and the common conditions disappeared when participants were asked how many pieces of candy they had eaten at the end of every consumption episode.

This research contributes towards the understanding of the psychological nature of satiation by looking at a new dimension of the consumption experience. It is demonstrated that erroneous beliefs about the nature of a stimulus can affect the rate at which people satiate from it. This paper also introduces an additional benefit of promoting scarcity in the marketplace, as it is shown that people satiate at a slower pace from products that are claimed to be scarce, regardless of the veracity of these claims.

Survival Mindset and Food Choices

EXTENDED ABSTRACT

As the war on obesity wages on, consumer researchers remain motivated to learn more about the reasons why people continue to make poor food choices. Past research on food choice has shown that people's poor food choices can result from their own misconceptions related to food (Chandon and Wansink 2007), cognitive resources (Shiv and Fedorikhin 1999), emotional state (Ramanathan and Williams 2007), and food choices made from prior meals in the day (Khare and Inman 2006).

We propose an alternative explanation to people's unhealthy food choices. Certain people engage in a survival mindset and instinctively eat filling and high-calorie food, often without consideration of the overall healthiness or even tastiness of the food. We define survival mindset as a sense of adversity and resource deprivation that one must withstand by making the best use of one's resources in order to live longer (Hill and Stamey 1990). The concept of survival is a lingering concern as unemployment rates continue to hover around 10% within the United States (U.S. Bureau of Labor Statistics 2010). However, this sense of resource deprivation need not be economic in nature; it can refer to food, water, shelter, and other basic resources that humans require to function. This mindset, when activated, leads consumers to choose food items perceived to be more filling or higher-calorie to compensate for the sense of resource deprivation and to aid sustainability.

Across four studies, we use an array of priming procedures to activate a survival mindset, and provide evidence for the processes that lead from a survival mindset to consumers' food choices. Study 1 shows that a survival mindset leads to choices of food items perceived to be more filling (i.e., keep people fed longer). Study 2 differentiates a survival mindset from a willingness to indulge by showing that a survival mindset leads to choices of food items that are high in calories, while a willingness to indulge leads to choices of food items that are tasty. Study 3 shows that a survival mindset can lead to choices of food items that are tasty and unhealthy, but that increasing the perception of the amount of resources available attenuates the effect of a survival mindset on these choices, compared to people in a pleasure-seeking mindset. Study 4 shows that a survival mindset leads to choices of filling food items when this mindset is associated with perceptions of short duration (i.e., survival in the short term), but that it can lead to choices of healthy food items when it is associated with perceptions of long duration (i.e., survival in the long term).

Study 1 primed people with the concept of survival and found that these people are more likely to select filling food compared to people who are not primed. We either asked participants to write about what is important for survival (survival condition) or not (control condition). After the writing task, participants chose between a (less filling) grilled chicken caesar salad and a (more filling) turkey and cheese sandwich. Participants primed with survival are more likely to select the sandwich than the control group participants. Additionally, neither group differed in anxiety or mortality salience, ruling them out as alternative explanations (Greenberg, Solomon, and Pyszczynski 1997).

Study 2 primed survival versus pleasure and observed people's preferences for a foot-long sub, depending on whether the sub was framed as being high-calorie versus tasty. Participants completed a scrambled word task containing either survival words (i.e., deficiency, outlast) or pleasure words (i.e., indulgence, pleasantness). We show that people primed with the concept of survival favor the sub more when framed as high-calorie, while the pleasure primed participants favor the sub when framed as tasty. Study 2 shows that the survival prime is distinct from a pleasure prime and that people primed with survival are not choosing high calorie foods out of taste and indulgence (Raghunathan, Naylor, and Hoyer 2006).

Study 3 shows money is a moderating variable that has the potential to alleviate perceived resource deprivation and attenuate the effect of the survival prime on food choice. We used a lexical decision task to prime people with either survival or pleasure and then ask them to choose between cupcakes and a garden salad. Additionally, some participants were given one dollar under the guise of a thank you gift. Participants primed with survival selected cupcakes without money and the healthier garden salad with money. Pleasure primed participants primarily selected cupcakes regardless of receiving money or not. The results show how to assist survival-primed consumers to make healthier food decisions.

Study 4 used a procedure similar to study 1 and introduced the concept of survival duration as a moderating variable between the survival prime and food choice. We manipulated duration by having participants think about how long or short various events last and show that this carries over into how long survival is thought to last. Participants primed with the belief of short-term survival (short duration) were more likely to choose the (unhealthier) sandwich. By contrast, participants primed with the belief of long-term survival (long duration) were more likely to choose the (healthier) salad. Mediation evidence is provided, where survival short-duration participants select food according to what's filling, while the survival long-duration participants select food according to what's healthier.

Our research demonstrates people's reasons for some of their food choices. This research is unique in that no study that we know of has specifically examined how a survival mindset influences people's food choices. Oftentimes, the most filling and high-calorie foods are seen as being a sort of hedonistic "comfort food." However, our theory supports the notion that in certain circumstances, people might view these foods as purposeful and utilitarian rather than hedonistic in function. Furthermore, we find promising results in our later studies, suggesting ways in which we can attenuate the effect of the survival mindset on food choice and help consumers to make healthier food choices.

There's Only One Left, Do I Want It? : The Effects of Brand and Display Characteristics on Purchase Intentions for Scarce Products

EXTENDED ABSTRACT

Retail executives know that the presentation of their products matters. The general belief is that pristine aisles with fully stocked shelves and perfectly organized product displays can increase purchase intentions, whereas cluttered aisles with empty shelves and messy displays lower them. Although retailers currently strive to keep shelves and displays fully stocked and organized in the belief that this will maximize sales, it may be the case that this, in fact, is not the best way to increase revenues. In this paper, we examine whether, and under what conditions, the organization, appearance, and number of products on retail shelf displays will impact purchase intentions for those products.

By looking at a product display, consumers are exposed to the type of product, whether the brand is familiar or unfamiliar, how many products are available, the appearance of the product display, and the prices associated with the product. While each of these cues provides independent information about the products being displayed, we study the interactive effects of these cues on consumer inferences and purchase intentions. For example, imagine a consumer at a supermarket who is considering buying a product from a disorganized display with only one product left on the shelf. Will the scarce product availability and appearance of the display interact in a way that systematically influences the consumer's preference for the product? Prior research in the scarcity literature suggests that scarcity attributed to market conditions (i.e., popularity) should increase the desirability of a product (Verhallen 1982; Verhallen and Robben 1994). However, most of this research has not focused on how the availability of the product interacts with other important cues in the retail environment to affect purchase intentions, nor how cues in the retail environment influence perceptions of scarcity. Our research thus looks at how cues in the retail environment, such as the appearance of the shelf or the familiarity of the brands on the shelf, interact with the availability of the product to influence purchase intentions. In the proposed scenario, the fact that the display is disorganized and there is only one product left may suggest that others are buying the product; therefore, consumers may infer that the scarcity is due to popularity and preference for the product may increase. However, if consumers are familiar with the brand, then they will use other information about the product to make their decision, thereby reducing the effect of such cues on purchase intentions.

Prior research on shelf displays has focused on topics such as assortment and assortment reductions, amount of category space, number of stock keeping units, amount of space allocated to a product, shelf locations, the effectiveness of product displays, and stockouts (e.g., Chandon, Hutchinson, Bradlow and Young 2009; Turley and Milliman 2000; Fitzsimons 2000). However, little research has addressed the interaction of retail cues such as the appearance of the shelf display and the availability of the product on consumer preference.

Our research offers three important contributions. First, we examine how specific cues in the retail environment, such as the messiness of the shelf display, interact with the availability of the product (i.e., the number of products available on display) to influence perceptions of product popularity and purchase intentions. Second, we examine how the availability of the product interacts with characteristics of the product itself, such as its familiarity and whether or not it is a food product, to influence purchase intentions. Third, we show how other characteristics of the product, such as its price, moderate these effects and how these effects translate into the impressions of the store that sells them. In so doing, we are able to develop a comprehensive theoretical model of how scarcity operates in the retail environment, identifying when it increases purchase intentions, when it decreases purchase intentions, as well as the underlying mechanisms driving these two divergent outcomes.

Across a series of five studies, we find when consumers infer that products are scarce due to popularity, consumers are more likely to buy these products because of quality perceptions, but only when they are unfamiliar nonfood brands. We also find that scarce products are less likely to be purchased when they are familiar food brands because of contamination effects. In addition, we find that the price of the product is an important moderator of these effects.

Adding and Subtracting: Decision Making During Accumulation and Decumulation of Retirement Savings

Chair: Kirstin Appelt, Columbia University, USA

Paper #1: Making the Future Self More Vivid to Increase Retirement Saving

Hal Ersner-Hershfield, Northwestern University, USA
Dan Goldstein, Yahoo! Research and London Business School, UK

Paper #2: Live to or Die by: Framing Effects on Life Expectations and Life Annuity Choice

Namika Sagara, Duke University, USA
John Payne, Duke University, USA
Suzanne Shu, UCLA, USA
Kirstin Appelt, Columbia University, USA
Eric Johnson, Columbia University, USA

Paper #3: Options, Not Returns: Overcoming the Annuity Paradox

Kirstin Appelt, Columbia University, USA
Eric Johnson, Columbia University, USA

SESSION OVERVIEW

Within the next decade, 31 million Americans will retire (Reno and Lavery 2009). On average, they will spend 20 years in retirement (National Commission on Fiscal Responsibility and Reform 2010). At the same time, the retirement landscape is changing as defined-benefit retirement plans (the employer pays a specified monthly benefit for the duration of retirement) are replaced by defined-contribution retirement plans (the employer contributes a specified amount to the employee's retirement account, but the employee is responsible for managing the account himself) (Brown, 2000). As a result, consumers are increasingly in charge of funding their own retirement and deciding how to manage their resources, at a time when their retirement is lasting longer than ever before.

Retirement decision making has two crucial phases: the accumulation of wealth approaching retirement *and* the decumulation of wealth during retirement. Evidence suggests both that many Americans do not save enough for retirement (EBRI 2010; NIA 2007; Thaler and Benartzi 2004) and that almost half of Americans are concerned that they will not be able to maintain a reasonable standard of living during retirement (Society of Actuaries 2010). However, although consumers face challenges during both accumulation and decumulation, most research has focused on the accumulation phase. This session gathers leaders in the area of consumer finance to address *both* phases of retirement decision making.

This session connects these two phases by tracing retirement decision making from accumulation through decumulation. First, Ersner-Hershfield and Goldstein discuss insufficient saving for retirement during the working years. They offer a new avenue for increasing retirement savings: Data from three studies indicate that increasing the vividness of the future self can motivate the current self to save more money for retirement.

Next, Sagara et al. focus on the importance of life expectancy for accumulation and decumulation decisions. To determine how much to save for retirement and how to spend during retirement, consumers need to estimate how long they will live. Most economic models, such as the life-cycle model (Skinner 2007), assume that consumers have rational expectations of their own life expectancy. Sagara and colleagues suggest that this may not be the case and that, instead, life expectancy is a constructed estimate that depends cru-

cially on question framing. Data from three studies show that consumers give longer life expectancies when asked about living to a certain age (vs. dying by a certain age), and that framing affects decumulation preferences.

The third paper investigates decumulation decisions in an uncertain world. Retirees have a finite amount of retirement savings, but they do not know how they will live and how long those savings must last. They are therefore faced with a large degree of longevity risk—the risk that they will outlive their assets. Annuities, which provide guaranteed lifetime income, offer a solution to longevity risk, yet few Americans purchase them. Appelt and Johnson investigate the "annuity puzzle" (Yaari 1965) from two perspectives: potential annuity features that may overcome consumers' reluctance to annuitize and individual differences that may affect annuitization. Data from two studies suggest that consumers prefer annuities that guarantee a specified number of payments (period certain annuities) or liquidity in case of emergencies (annuities with cash-back options) and that time and risk preferences moderate these effects.

Taken together, these three papers connect the accumulation and decumulation phases of retirement wealth. Because this is a developing area, we have asked John Lynch to lead the discussion. As an expert in the field of consumer finance, John will be instrumental in encouraging the building of connections. John will discuss the connections between accumulation and decumulation, with an emphasis on the contributions of the three papers to that discussion. John will also discuss how behavioral consumer finance generally and retirement decision making specifically can serve as nodes connecting different research areas as well as research and public policy. We have allotted 15 minutes for the discussion.

The recent economic crises indicate both the importance of consumer finance and the importance of behavioral factors within consumer finance. Furthermore, in the last two years, the government has shown significant interest in behavioral consumer finance with the establishment of the Consumer Financial Protection Bureau, a series of Senate committee hearings on retirement decision making, and a series of meetings about behavioral consumer finance issues in Washington, D.C. This session, which highlights new research from behavioral consumer finance, specifically retirement decision making, is well-timed and potentially influential. Given the relevance of the findings to research and public policy, we expect a broad audience, including researchers interested in consumer finance, preference construction, intertemporal choice, and framing; individuals interested in retirement issues; and policy makers.

Making the Future Self More Vivid to Increase Retirement Saving

EXTENDED ABSTRACT

The number of years that the average American will spend in retirement is at an all-time high (Lee 2001), as life expectancy at age 65 has increased to 18 years (Arias 2007). Most Americans risk outliving their retirement savings. Furthermore, despite a recent small increase in saving rates, retirement experts estimate that 43% Americans will still be unable to maintain pre-retirement standards of living in retirement (due in part to the recent reduction in home values) (Bernheim et al. 2000; Munnell, Webb, and Golub-Sass 2009). In short, people are living longer but saving less.

Under-saving is sometimes attributed to "myopia" or excessive discounting of the future. The inability to vividly imagine one's wants and desires at a distant age could account for some of the empirically observed discounting phenomena. As expressed by Parfit (1971), the failure to give adequate weight to the future might be "caused by some failure of imagination, or some false belief. It is claimed, for example, that when we imagine pains in the further future, we imagine them less vividly, or believe confusedly that they will somehow be less real, or less painful" (p. 161). Loewenstein (1996) has noted that a more vivid impression of ourselves engaging in some action in the future might intensify the emotions that are linked to thinking about that scenario. These intensified emotions might, in turn, allow an individual to be better informed regarding the future consequences of a current decision. For example, pulmonologists tend to smoke less than other doctors, in part because seeing blackened and withered lungs on a daily basis increases the negative emotions that are associated with smoking (Loewenstein 1996).

Thus, to the extent that people can feel more connected to a vividly imagined future self, they should be motivated to save money in a long-term domain. Accordingly, we conducted three experiments to examine the association between a vivid perception of one's self in the future and the propensity to save more for retirement. In Studies 1 and 2, a novel technology, immersive virtual reality (VR), was developed to make one's perception of one's future self more realistic. In study 1, a control group of college undergraduates (n = 25) entered an immersive VR environment and saw a digital representation of their current selves in a virtual mirror, while the experimental group of college undergraduates (n = 25) saw an age-morphed version of their future selves in the virtual mirror. Upon exiting the VR environment, all participants were given a hypothetical money allocation task, among other tasks. The experimental condition participants were significantly more likely to allocate money toward a hypothetical retirement savings account (M = $178.10) than control participants (M = $73.90).

In study 2, we sought to rule out two alternative explanations for our findings from study 1. First, because the monetary allocation task occurred directly after the virtual reality paradigm, it is possible that participants in the experimental condition felt pressure to allocate more to the long-term account. Thus, in study 2, we separated the virtual reality portion of the study from the decision-making portion, and provided a cover story that masked our research purposes. Secondly, it is possible that experimental condition participants in study 1 were merely primed with the concept of aging, and this prime prompted them to save more for retirement (i.e., Bargh and Chartrand 1999). As such, in study 2, we exposed participants to either their own aged avatar or another research participant's aged avatar, and did so after a lengthy experimental delay. Results indicated that participants in the future self condition demonstrated significantly more patience on financial decision-making tasks (M = .30) than did participants in the future other condition (M = -.27).

Although these findings are encouraging, there are several unresolved issues. First, this approach to virtual reality is expensive and time-consuming for participants, and most companies or banks will not be able to utilize immersive virtual reality to convince their employees or customers to adopt a longer-term perspective when making decisions about retirement savings. Secondly, experimental condition participants in Studies 1 and 2 were simply shown a neutral image of their future selves. Loewenstein's (1996) work suggests that in order to make a true connection to the future self, the future emotional consequences of current decisions must be made clear. Indeed, previous research has demonstrated that exposure to virtual cause-and-effect actions can change actual behavior. For example,

compared to a control group, when participants were shown a virtual version of themselves gaining weight, they were more likely to go to the gym (Fox and Bailenson 2008). Accordingly, study 3 used a more accessible format to address the cause-and-effect nature of retirement decision-making.

Namely, we used a web-based study design in which all participants were shown a slider bar that they could move to make allocations from a hypothetical paycheck to a hypothetical retirement account. As they moved the slider bar toward future consumption, their annual take-home pay decreased (indicated in today's dollars), but their annual retirement income increased (again, indicated in today's dollars). In the current self condition, however, participants were shown the monetary amounts as well as an image of their current self, which changed emotional expression as a function of the allocations that they chose to make (sadder as more money was allocated toward future consumption, happier as more money was allocated toward present consumption). In the future self condition, participants were shown the monetary amounts as well as an image of their future self, which changed emotional expression as a function of the allocations that they chose to make (happier as more money was allocated future consumption, sadder as more money was allocated toward present consumption). Again, results indicated that participants in the future self condition allocated a significantly higher percentage of pay toward retirement (M = 6.76%) than did participants in the current self condition (M = 5.20%). Results will be discussed in the context of Parfit's (1971) and Loewenstein's (1996) work.

Live to or Die by: Framing Effects on Life Expectations and Life Annuity Choice

EXTENDED ABSTRACT

How long do you expect to live? Answering this question is essential to making informed judgments and choices about savings, decumulation of retirement wealth, health, and many other decisions. Yaari (1965), for instance, begins his classic article on life-annuity choice by saying that "one need hardly be reminded that a consumer who makes plans for the future, must, in one way or another, take account of the fact that he does not know how long he will live (p.137)." Most lifetime consumption models assume that individuals take into account their probability of living to different ages when planning how to decumulate their assets during retirement. The importance of getting these estimates correct has become greater in recent years as employers have shifted from offering defined benefit plans, which provided income regardless of how long an individual lived, to offering defined contribution plans, under which the individual is solely responsible for ensuring that he does not run out of savings during his lifetime.

We address the issue of life expectancy and its effects on decumulation decisions through three large-scale studies. Our research questions include understanding how individuals' judgments about their life expectation probabilities may change according to how the question is framed, how these judgments are affected by the knowledge individuals have about themselves, and how these judgments affect preferences for life annuity products. We predict that beliefs about how long one might live are, like preferences, often constructed responses that will reflect seemingly irrelevant task factors (and biases) as well as valid knowledge (truth) and random error. As a result, simple changes in how questions are worded can produce substantial biases in both judgments and preferences.

In three online studies (total n = 2,172), two different frames were used to elicit individuals' probabilities for life expectancy for ages 65, 75, 85 and 95. Specifically, in one condition, respondents were asked to provide probabilities of *living to* a certain age or older, while in the other condition, they were asked to provide probabilities of *dying by* a certain age or younger. Note that the answers to these two approaches should perfectly mirror each other if framing has no effect. Following this subjective probability task, respondents in study 2 were asked to either indicate their purchase probability for a single life annuity or their allocation of retirement assets between the annuity and a self-management option. In study 3, respondents used a type-aloud protocol to report their thoughts as they considered the probability of living to [dying by] 85 years old or older [younger]. Respondents in study 3 later coded each of their own previously-listed thoughts as emphasizing life, death, or neither, and being positive, negative, or neither.

The results from all three studies consistently indicate that question framing strongly affects both judgments and preferences. For comparison purposes, all probabilities were converted to "live to" numbers (i.e., responses to "die by" questions were subtracted from 100%). An analysis of each respondent's data to determine the elevation and slope of each probability line per respondent allowed measurement of how framing and individual differences affect the line. The coefficient for framing was significant and large for both elevation and slope, while age, health, and gender also had significant effects. Respondents asked the question framed as a "live to" prediction provided higher probabilities across all age ranges than those asked the question framed as "die by". For example, in study 1, individuals in the live-to frame thought they had about a 55% chance of being alive at age 85, whereas individuals in the die-by frame thought they had about a 32% chance. There was also a ten-year gap in median expected age of death (85 years for the live-to frame and 75 years for the die-by frame).

Does the effect of framing on probability judgments for life expectancy also affect preference for annuities? The answer is yes. Likelihood of annuity purchase was significantly affected by average predicted life expectancy as well as by framing, and self-reported health. Allocation to annuities showed weaker effects, but was still significantly affected by life expectations, health, and age. Individual difference measures for numeracy, confidence in investment ability, and importance of making money last also had significant effects on preference.

Study 3 tested whether Query Theory (Johnson, Häubl, and Keinan 2007), which suggests that framing affects responses by changing the order in which individuals consider thoughts about the various choice options, explains the effect of frame on life expectancy. We found that the framing effect for age 85 was significantly partially mediated by the relative number of thoughts in favor of being alive at age 85. As predicted, individuals had more thoughts in favor of being alive at age 85 when presented with the live-to frame (vs. the die-by frame) and this partially mediated the effect of frame on the subjective probability of being alive at age 85.

The results of these studies demonstrate that both judgments and preferences about important future events, such as how to decumulate retirement assets, are sensitive to framing effects. Although there have been many framing studies (see Keren 2011 for an overview), the vast majority have involved evaluations of objects or preferences between options. In contrast, these studies ask how framing affects a prediction question. Consistent with explanations for other framing effects, different ways of posing the same question appear to direct attentional resources to different attributes, which results in different responses (Keren 2011). In fact, our mediation analysis suggests that respondents had more positive thoughts about being alive at 85 years old in the "live-to" condition than in the "die-by" condition, and this in turn, predicted subjective probabilities of being

alive at age 85. Individual differences in age and health, which could be considered private information, also affected these predictions. Thus, it seems that judgments of an important future event, for which individuals should have both private and public information, may be "constructed" in the sense that judgments are subject to predictable biases, such as how the event is framed.

Options, Not Returns: Overcoming the Annuity Paradox

EXTENDED ABSTRACT

When they retire, consumers are faced with decisions about managing their saving and spending, ideally providing themselves a comfortable standard of living for as long as they live. Using a limited amount of retirement savings, they must fund a retirement of unknown but potentially long duration. This presents consumers with the very real possibility that they will outlive their savings, an outcome called "longevity risk" by economists.

A life annuity is an "insurance product that allows an individual to convert a lump-sum of wealth into a stream of income that is guaranteed to last for as long as an individual (and if desired, his or her spouse) lives" (Brown 2011). Thus, an annuity is a potentially attractive solution for dealing with longevity risk. Not only does an annuity offer guaranteed lifetime income, it also typically provides a higher income than otherwise possible because the assets of those who die early subsidize the payments to those who die late (Brown 2000). Despite the economic attractiveness of annuities, few Americans choose to annuitize any of their retirement savings, a phenomenon termed the "annuity puzzle" (Yaari 1965).

In contrast to the standard life-cycle model used to analyze retirement savings and spending in economics (Skinner 2007), we suggest a behavioral model that posits relatively narrow framing, loss aversion, and quasi-hyperbolic discounting. The model suggests that annuities are unattractive for at least two reasons: First, decision-makers are loss averse and risk averse to the possibility of "losing" their retirement savings to the annuity company should they die early. Second, they discount, perhaps too much, the income stream provided by the annuity. Thus, loss aversion, risk aversion, and discounting are barriers to buying annuities. We examine the implications of this model using two strategies. First, we ask whether features designed to overcome these barriers to annuitization will be attractive to consumers. Specifically, we contrast the appeal of a standard economic feature (a higher rate of return) and two behavioral features (a guaranteed minimum term and available liquidity). Second, we ask whether individual differences in time and risk preferences, numerical ability (i.e., numeracy), and financial literacy explain annuity preferences and moderate the effects of annuity features on preference.

We conducted two web-based studies (total *n* = 1,416) using community samples of Americans aged 45 to 70 who had faced or would soon be facing retirement decisions. Participants read information about advantages and disadvantages of two options for decumulating retirement wealth: annuities and self-managed accounts. They were then presented with a general annuity followed by a series of four annuities with different features in a fractional factorial design: (1) return: low (5%) or high (7%); (2) period certain: a guaranteed minimum term of 15 years (i.e., if the annuitant dies within 15 years of purchasing the annuity, the annuitant's heirs would receive the remaining years of payments) or no guaranteed minimum term; and (3) available liquidity: a cash-back option (i.e., the annuitant or the annuitant's heirs can withdraw the balance of the annuity as a lump sum at any time) or no cash-back option. For each annuity, participants were asked how likely they would be to purchase the annuity. In study 2, participants also completed measures of time and risk preferences as well as numeracy and financial literacy, allowing for tests of individual differences.

In study 1, consistent with the annuity puzzle, participants reported being unlikely to purchase the base annuity—an annuity offering a 5% return and no period certain or cash-back option. However this differed significantly as the features of the annuity changed: Participants were significantly more likely to purchase annuities offering either a guaranteed minimum term or a cash-back option. Interestingly, participants were insensitive to the rate of return on the annuity, equivalent to $2,000 a year on a $100,000 annuity. In other words, participants were attracted to annuities with behavioral features designed to minimize risk aversion and loss aversion, but not to an annuity offering a standard economic incentive.

In study 2, we replicated the findings from study 1 and additionally tested the impact of individual differences in preferences and abilities. For a general annuity, as predicted, participants who were present-biased were less likely to annuitize. Participants who were risk averse were marginally more likely to annuitize, which is to be expected since annuities reduce the risk of longevity. Neither numeracy nor financial literacy predicted annuity preference. Numeracy did, however, moderate the effect of rate of return such that highly numerate participants preferred the high-return annuity to the low-return annuity more than those who were low in numeracy.

Impatience moderated the effect of the period certain feature and the cash-back feature such that impatient participants preferred these options marginally more than patient participants. Risk aversion moderated the effect of the period certain feature such that risk-averse participants preferred the period certain feature more risk-seeking participants. In other words, the attractiveness of the economic incentive was moderated by numerical ability whereas the attractiveness of the behavioral features was moderated by time and/or risk preferences. Notably, financial literacy did not predict preference for annuitization or any annuity features.

These results support a more behavioral model of retirement decision making. As hypothesized by Brown (2000) and Hu and Scott (2007), retirees may be insensitive to standard economic incentives for increasing annuitization. Participants did not show a preference for an increased rate of return. Instead, they were drawn to annuities offering a guaranteed minimum term or available liquidity. This pattern of results suggests that retirees are most concerned with ensuring that, should they die early, their money does not remain with the insurance company and with having access to their money. Additionally, we find that likelihood of annuitization is driven by time and risk preferences rather than financial literacy or numeracy. These results suggest that financial education may not be sufficient to solve the annuity puzzle. Instead, to encourage annuitization, it may be better to appeal to consumers' time and risk preferences by designing annuity products that address these preferences.

When Gifts Go Unappreciated
Chair: Mary Steffel, University of Florida, USA

Paper #1: How Surprisingly Little Thoughts Count in Gift-Giving: On Receiver's Motivated Appreciation for Giver's Thoughts

Yan Zhang, National University of Singapore, Singapore
Nicholas Epley, University of Chicago, USA

Paper #2: Social Comparison in Decisions for Others: Considering Multiple Gift Recipients Leads to Unique but Less-Liked Gifts

Mary Steffel, University of Florida, USA
Robyn LeBoeuf, University of Florida, USA

Paper #3: When Do Gifts Help Charitable Giving and When Do They Hurt?

George E. Newman, Yale University, USA
Y. Jeremy Shen, Yale University, USA

SESSION OVERVIEW

Consumers invest considerable time and money annually on selecting gifts for others: The average American spends 15 hours gift shopping and more than $800 on gifts during the holidays alone, according to Consumer Reports. Despite the considerable investment made by givers, these gifts often fail to have the intended effect on recipients. According to Waldfogel (1993), gifts produce about 10% less satisfaction than would have been produced if the recipients had spent the same amount on themselves. The objective of this symposium is to explore the how discrepancies between giver and recipient perspectives can lead givers to invest time and resources into gifts that fail to have the intended effect on recipients.

First, Yan Zhang and Nicholas Epley will demonstrate that although gift givers believe that investing more thought into gifts will increase recipient appreciation, thoughts count for very little unless gift receivers are motivated or otherwise triggered to consider a gift giver's thoughts, such as when a friend's gift has relatively little objective value, or is considered to be objectively undesirable. Next, Mary Steffel and Robyn LeBoeuf will show that, when givers select gifts for multiple recipients, they strive to personalize gifts so as to convey an understanding of recipients' unique identities. Yet this leads them to pass up gifts that would be better liked in favor of unique gifts, even when recipients will never compare gifts. George Newman and Y. Jeremy Shen will then show that, contrary to the common-sense notion that offering a thank-you gift might encourage reciprocity, in the context of charitable giving, people are actually less likely to donate when they are given a thank-you gift for donation. Finally, for the last 15 minutes of the session, Susan Broniarczyk will provide comments on the talks and discuss broader themes and future research directions.

Together, these studies contribute to consumer theory by illuminating how psychological factors such as attention, motivation, comparisons, and incentives lead gift givers to invest time and resources into gifts that fail to have the intended effect on recipient liking and reciprocation. They further suggest practical advice to givers for better anticipating when to give a gift, what gift to give, and how to present it in such a way as to elicit the intended response. This research is of broad interest to researchers in consumer psychology in general and to researchers in gift giving, prosocial behavior, and judgment and decision making in particular.

How Surprisingly Little Thoughts Count in Gift-Giving: On Receiver's Motivated Appreciation for Giver's Thoughts

EXTENDED ABSTRACT

Gift-giving is a social exchange that includes both the objective value of a gift as well as the symbolic meaning of the exchange itself. The objective value of a gift is sometimes considered to be of secondary importance in people's evaluations of a gift, as when people claim, "it's the thought that counts," suggesting that a thoughtful gift will be appreciated more than a thoughtless gift. Based on this belief, gift givers spend a lot of time and effort to choose or design gifts, expecting that their time and effort will be appreciated when the gift is delivered.

However, because it often takes motivation and attentional resources to consider another person's thoughts, we predicted that thoughts would count for very little in evaluating gift exchanges unless gift receivers were motivated or otherwise triggered to consider a gift giver's thoughts. The tendency to focus on one self's feeling suggests that how appreciative receivers feel toward a giver would be largely determined by how they feel about the gift, but not so much by factors that are not pertain to the gift itself, such as giver's thoughts and intensions, suggesting that thoughts would count very little for receivers.

People only consider others' thought in certain situations. For instance, when others' behavior is inconsistent with one's expectations or social norms, people tend to make sense of such behaviors by appealing to underlying intentions, goals, or thoughts. In the context of gift giving and receiving, we suggest that gift receivers are motivated to think about givers' intentions and reasons of choosing a specific gift when they receive gifts that are undesirable, or of very little objective value. People usually expect to receive desirable gifts or gifts of some value to them. A gift that is undesirable or of very little objective value violates this expectation. If there is no objective value in another person's act of kindness, then a receiver would try to explain this seemingly meaningless act of kindness by justifying the symbolic meanings of this act. Receivers then shift their attention to givers' thoughts and underlying reasons of their gift choices. As a result, a receiver's gratitude would be largely influenced by the amount of apparent thought another person put into the act. Gift givers, on the other hand, are directly aware of the amount of thought they put into their gift, and therefore predict that their thoughts will "count" more than they actually do.

Four studies confirmed this prediction. In the first study, participants recalled either a past gift-giving or a gift-receiving experience. They were also instructed to recall either a liked or a disliked gift. As predicted, receivers' appreciation for desirable gifts was not correlated with how much thought they believed givers invested. For undesirable gifts, however, receivers' appreciation was highly correlated with how much thought they believed givers invested. Givers, on the contrary, predicted that their thought would be appreciated if receivers liked the gift, and that their thought would be dismissed if receivers disliked the gift. Response time results show that receivers took longer to answer the appreciation questions for undesirable gifts than for desirable gifts, suggesting that thinking about giver's thoughts takes extra effort from receivers. We replicated these results in a second study with Mother's Day gifts.

We further suggest that this inconsistency between givers and receivers would only happen between acquaintances but not strangers. For gifts given by strangers, receivers do not need to make sense of receiving an undesirable gift, so they would not consider giver's thoughts even when a gift is bad. Consistent with our predictions, a third study that involved real gift exchange returned results similar to the first two recall studies among acquaintances, but not among strangers.

The fourth experiment found that although thought counts very little in most cases, investing thoughts into a gift made givers feel more socially connected with receivers, which may help maintain and develop the relationship between givers and receivers.

This research has important implications in how to manage gift-exchanges. When choosing gifts, most people want their thoughts to be appreciated. However, our research shows that people receive extra credit for their thoughts only when they had chosen gifts disliked by receivers. Since a desirable gift is highly appreciated regardless of whether givers invest thoughts or not, maybe the most important thing for gift givers is to choose the right gift rather than investing enough thought. It is the thought that counts, this research suggests, but only when giving loved ones bad gifts.

Social Comparison in Decisions for Others:
Considering Multiple Gift Recipients Leads to Personalized but Less-Liked Gifts

EXTENDED ABSTRACT

Gift giving is a challenge, and sometimes, this challenge is compounded by having to choose gifts for multiple recipients. Having multiple recipients in mind not only means that more gifts are needed, but it may change what givers focus on when making gift selections. We hypothesize that, when people select gifts for multiple recipients, they focus on what differentiates the recipients instead of on what each would like best, leading givers to select unique gifts over gifts that would be better liked.

There are at least two reasons why such an effect might arise. First, givers may actually perceive recipients differently when they are presented together versus separately (e.g., Hsee 1996). Alternatively, givers may want to personalize gifts in order to convey an understanding of recipients' unique identities (e.g., Belk 1996; Schwartz 1967), and this personalization motive may be highlighted in the multiple-recipient context. Although it may be important to differentiate gifts when recipients are likely to compare gifts, if recipients are unlikely to do so, then it makes less sense for givers to pass up gifts that would be better liked in favor of unique gifts.

Studies 1-3 explore whether givers who are purchasing items for multiple recipients favor unique gifts over better liked gifts. In each study, givers selected a gift for one recipient or two unacquainted recipients from a list of options in which one gift would clearly be better liked by both recipients. For example, in one study, participants selected a birthday card for one or two recipients: the target recipient and another recipient who was shown laughing (suggesting that he had a better sense of humor). Although most givers in the one-recipient condition (70%) gave the target recipient the card that was rated funniest in a pre-test, in the two-recipient condition, only a minority gave him this card (26%), $\chi^2(1) = 9.03$, $p = .003$. This happened despite the fact that givers who gave one of the other cards predicted that the target recipient would enjoy that card less than did givers who gave the funny card, $t(45) = 2.38$, $p = .02$, $d = .68$.

Study 4 examined a perceptual account for the current effects. Givers either chose a gift for one friend, chose a gift for two friends,

or considered both friends but only choose a gift for one. One of the available gifts was clearly the most appropriate gift. Some givers *gave* an item and others *predicted* which item the recipient(s) would choose. A contrast analysis indicated that givers were less likely to *give* the target recipient the better gift when they selected gifts for both her and another recipient (42%) than when they considered the target recipient alone (86%) or considered both recipients but selected a gift for the target recipient only (82%), $z = 3.88$, $p < .001$. Givers *predicted* that the target recipient would choose the better gift for herself regardless of condition, $\chi^2(2, N = 168) = .42$. Thus, merely considering two people together does not alter perceptions of recipients' tastes and does not drive the tendency to differentiate gifts.

Studies 5 and 6 examined whether givers differentiate gifts to convey their understanding of recipients' identities. In Study 5, participants chose between the movies *Up!* and *Star Trek* for a recipient who had a main interest in animation and a secondary interest in science fiction. Participants chose which movie would convey a better understanding of the recipient. Half of each sample considered this choice in isolation, and the other half considered this choice in the context of having already chosen to give *Up!* to another friend. Fewer thought that *Up!* conveyed a better understanding of the target when they were also giving *Up!* to another recipient (52%) than when they were getting it only for the target recipient (97%), $\chi^2(1, N = 61) = 17.39$, $p < .001$.

In study 6, givers imagined selecting gifts for two close friends, for whom they would put considerable thought into their gift choices, or for two casual acquaintances. Both recipients preferred animated movies, but the target recipient had a secondary interest in science fiction. That target recipient was less likely to receive the better gift (the animated movie) in the close-friends condition (31%) than in the casual-acquaintances condition (47%), $\chi^2(1, N = 157) = 3.97$, $p < .05$, indicating that givers were less likely to diversify their gift choices for casual acquaintances. Thus, the more motivated givers are to put thought into their selections, the more likely they are pass up better liked gifts for unique gifts.

Finally, study 7 explored whether focusing givers' attention on recipient liking, by asking them to first predict which items recipients would choose for themselves, might encourage givers to select gifts that maximize recipient liking. Indeed, givers who first predicted which items recipients would choose for themselves were more willing to give two recipients the same gift than those in the control condition, who were more likely to diversify their gift selections. (Seventy-six percent gave the target recipient the better gift in the predict-liking condition and 54% did so in the control condition, $\chi^2(1, N = 73) = 3.93$, $p < .05$.)

In sum, the social context in which a gift is selected influences gift choices. When people select gifts for multiple recipients, they focus on what differentiates recipients rather than what each recipient would like best. This leads givers to pass up gifts that they believe would be better liked for unique gifts. This tendency is rooted in the motivation to convey an understanding of recipients' unique identities and is ameliorated by encouraging givers to consider which items recipients would choose for themselves.

REFERENCES

Belk, Russell W. (1996), "The Perfect Gift," in *Gift Giving: A Research Anthology,* ed. Cele Otnes and Richard F. Beltramini, Bowling Green, OH: Bowling Green State University Popular Press.

Hsee, Christopher K. (1996), "The Evaluability Hypothesis: An Explanation for Preference Reversals Between Joint and Separate Evaluations of Alternatives," *Organizational Behavior and Human Decision Processes, 67, 3,* 247-257.

Schwartz, Barry (1967), "The Social Psychology of the Gift," *The American Journal of Sociology, 73, 1,* 1-11.

When Do Gifts Help Charitable Giving and When Do They Hurt?

EXTENDED ABSTRACT

Donations are one of the largest sources of revenue for most nonprofits and charities and, as a result, a great deal of research in psychology, economics, and marketing has explored what factors encourage charitable giving. This paper focuses on the effectiveness of offering small 'thank-you' gifts, such as a pen, coffee mug, or tote bag, as means of soliciting charitable donations and specifically, the factors that are likely to increase or decrease the effectiveness of such offers.

Motivated by previous work on differences between social and monetary markets (e.g., Heyman and Ariely 2004), I hypothesize that consumers may evaluate the same offer very differently depending on whether they are primed with altruistic versus market motivations. Specifically, when an offer is framed as a "donation," altruistic goals are primed and therefore, benefits to the self (such as a tote bag given as a thank-you gift) are likely to decrease charitable giving due to crowding out of altruistic motivations. In contrast, when the identical offer is framed as a purchase (e.g., a tote bag that is offered for sale), a market motivation is primed, and therefore, highlighting the potential charitable benefits should increase donations because the charitable benefit is now seen as an additional benefit of the market purchase. In other words, altruistic motivations may be "tainted" by incentives, while market motivation may only be enhanced through additional incentives (including charitable ones). These predictions were tested in a series of studies.

As an initial test of people's lay beliefs, adults were asked to predict whether a thank-you gift (a pen bearing a PBS logo) would encourage people to donate more, less, or the same amount to public broadcasting compared to a donation request that did not offer a thank-you gift. The majority of participants (68%) predicted that thank-you gifts would *increase* donation amounts. Analogously, participants predicted that the group who was offered a thank-you gift would donate significantly more money than the group who was not.

In Study 2, a new group of adult participants were presented with the same materials as in Study 1. However, the presence or absence of a thank-you gift was manipulated between-subjects. In stark contrast to Study 1, participants who were simply asked for a donation (without any offer of a thank-you gift) were willing to donate significantly more than participants who were offered a thank-you gift. Moreover, the total amount of money donated was also higher in the no-gift condition than in the gift condition. Thus, despite people's predictions, the offer of a thank-you gift actually decreased donations both in terms of the average amount per individual as well as the total amount donated.

Study 3 replicated this effect using actual donations, rather than hypothetical ones. In this experiment, participants were asked to donate a percentage of their winning from a lottery to the Save-the-Children foundation. Replicating the previous experiment, participants who were offered a thank-you gift donated significantly less compared to participants who were simply asked for a donation.

Study 4 examined the mechanism that thank-you gifts reduce donation amounts because the external incentive undermines or "crowds out" participants' altruistic motivations (e.g., Deci 1975; Lepper and Greene 1980). To test this explanation, the same gift (a cloth shopping bag bearing the organization's logo) was framed as either something that could be used in a personally beneficial way (for shopping) or in a manner that benefited others (to increase awareness of the cause). As in previous studies, participants in the no-gift condition were willing to donate significantly more than participants in the benefit-to-self condition. However, consistent with the crowding out hypothesis, participants in the benefit-to-others condition also donated significantly more than participants in the benefit-to-self condition. Donation amounts in the no-gift condition and the benefit-to-others conditions were not statistically different. Thus, merely reframing the gift as consistent with altruistic goals attenuated the negative effect of thank-you gifts on donation amounts.

Study 5 sought to test the predicted interaction effect by framing the offer as either a "donation" or a "purchase." In two donation conditions, participants were asked how much they would be willing to donate to Smithsonian Folkways recordings, a non-profit aimed at helping musicians in underprivileged countries. Half of the participants were asked how much they would be willing to donate, while the other half were asked for a donation that included an electronic mp3 album as a thank-you gift. Consistent with the previous findings, participants donated more when simply asked for a donation compared to when they were also offered a gift. In two additional conditions, participants were asked how much they would be willing to pay for an electronic mp3 album (the same as offered in the thank-you gift condition). Half of the participants were merely asked how much they would be willing to pay for the album, while the other half were told that all of the proceeds would go to benefit the Smithsonian non-profit. In these conditions, the pattern of results reversed such that participants were willing to pay more for the album when it offered a charitable benefit compared to when no benefit was highlighted. Thus, the mere framing of an offer as either a donation or a purchase seemed to moderate whether the gift increased or decreased donations.

In sum, although people have the strong prediction that the offer of thank-you gifts should increase donations, such offers actually reduce charitable donations both in terms of the average amount donated per individual as well as the total amount donated. This effect is consistent with the hypothesis that the offer of external incentives undermines or "crowds out" altruistic motivations. However, if the same offer is presented as a "purchase," additional incentives (including charitable ones) increase willingness to pay since a market, rather than altruistic goal has been activated.

REFERENCES

Deci, Edward L., (1975), *Intrinsic Motivation*. New York: Plenum Press.

Heyman, James, and Dan Ariely, (2004), "Effort for Payment: A Tale of Two Markets," *Psychological Science, 15, 11,* 787-793.

Lepper, Mark R., and Greene, David, (1980), *The Hidden Costs of Reward.* New York: Lawrence Erlbaum Associates.

When the Choice is Not Your Own: Choosing for and Receiving Products Selected by Others

Chair: Linyun Yang, University of North Carolina, Charlotte, USA

Paper #1: You've Got a (Bad) Friend in Me: Self-Construal and Choosing for Others

Sarah Moore, University of Alberta, Canada
Eugenia Wu, Cornell University, USA
Gavan Fitzsimons, Duke University, USA

Paper #2: Strategic Self-Presentation in Joint Consumption: Stereotypes as Social Tools

Linyun Yang, University of North Carolina, Charlotte, USA
Tanya Chartrand, Duke University, USA
Gavan Fitzsimons, Duke University, USA

Paper #3: Is it Riskier to Receive than to Give?: The Effect of Social Closeness on Gift Recipients' Responses to Identity-Inconsistent Gifts

Morgan Ward, Southern Methodist University, USA
Susan Broniarczyk, University of Texas at Austin, USA

Paper #4: I Didn't Think I Would Like What You Chose for Me: Relationship Norms and Satisfaction with Consumer- versus Provider-Chosen Outcomes

Pankaj Aggarwal, University of Toronto, Canada
Simona Botti, London Business School, UK
Ann McGill, University of Chicago, USA

SESSION OVERVIEW

Though the majority of prior research has focused on how consumers select and evaluate products for their own personal use (Bettman, Luce, and Payne 1998), there are many situations in which consumers choose for others or have products chosen for them. In these "social consumption" situations, the chooser must balance his needs and preferences with those of others. For instance, when selecting wine for the table, a diner must decide whether to choose something he personally likes or something that everyone will likely enjoy. In addition, the products chosen or received in social situations hold special meaning for consumers. First, they indicate whether the chooser is considerate of and willing to accommodate others. Second, chosen products communicate the giver's perceptions of the recipient's desires, preferences, and needs. For example, when a close friend gives an individual a book of brain teasers, she may infer that this friend thinks she enjoys being cognitively challenged. The objective of this special session is to explore these dynamics from both the perspective of the chooser and recipient.

The first two papers focus on how consumers select products to share with others and demonstrate that consumers adopt a variety of approaches when making such choices. Moore, Wu, and Fitzsimons examine how interdependent and independent individuals differ when choosing products to share with others. While interdependents consistently incorporate the preferences of others, independents generally behave selfishly when choosing—but only when they can do so without the risk of social censure. For instance, independents select a more expensive bottle of their preferred wine when choosing for a group, but are less likely to do so when dining with just one person. Yang, Chartrand, and Fitzsimon's paper examines how low and high self-monitors use stereotypes to inform their product choices in shared consumption situations. They find that, relative to low self-monitors, high self-monitors are more likely to recognize that choosing something liked by the consumption partner may not always ensure a positive interpersonal experience. For instance, when

choosing an item to consume with an attractive woman, men who are high, rather than low, self-monitors are more likely to recognize that selecting something feminine, though likely to be enjoyed by the woman, may compromise the choosers' romantic attractiveness.

The next two papers take the perspective of the recipient and examine consumers' inferences regarding whether the chooser has their best interests in mind. Ward and Broniarczyk examine how consumers interpret identity-inconsistent gifts. When consumers receive an identity-inconsistent gift from a close friend, they give their friend the benefit of the doubt and assume that the gift reflects their own identity in a way they cannot see. However, when consumers receive an identity-inconsistent gift from a distant friend, they assume that the giver is more concerned with personal convenience and saving money than with giving, and respond by distancing themselves from the giver. Aggarwal, Botti, and McGill's paper demonstrates that these dynamics also exist in customer-provider relationships. In a communal relationship, customers expect the provider's choices on their behalf to align with their own selections. However, in an exchange relationship, customers perceive the provider's choices as self-serving and in conflict with their own choices, and expect to be dissatisfied with the provider's choice. Ironically, these low expectations lead consumers to be pleasantly surprised and more satisfied with the provider's choice compared to their own choice in an exchange, but not in a communal, relationship.

These papers each demonstrate that products chosen for others hold special meaning to consumers and are important to building social ties. In other words, choosing for and receiving products from others serve as a way for consumers and firms to literally "build connections" with each other. Furthermore, the papers illustrate the important tradeoffs that people make to choose items that will fulfill their own needs and simultaneously satisfy those of the other person. By taking the perspectives of both the chooser and the recipient, by examining different chooser-receiver relationships, and by identifying unique moderators of choosing and receiving, these papers build multiple connections between the experiences of the chooser and recipient. We believe this session provides a comprehensive picture of the dynamics of social consumption and will appeal to a broad audience, including those interested in gift-giving, perspective-taking, self-construal, and relationship dynamics.

You've Got a (Bad) Friend in Me: Self-Construal and Strategic Selfishness

EXTENDED ABSTRACT

What does it mean to "choose like a good friend"? As social beings, we spend our lives in the company of others—a fact that frequently compels us to choose collectively on behalf of ourselves and those others. Do we make reservations for 6 at a bistro or a steakhouse? Watch a kung-fu flick or a comedy? Go bowling or grab a drink? Making choices can be tough enough when we're choosing for ourselves (Schwartz 2004), but the difficulties are compounded when we must consider the preferences of others in addition to our own. In this research, we examine how individuals balance self and other preferences when choosing collectively.

The importance of satisfying relationships to our physical and psychological well-being (Eisenberger, Lieberman, and Williams 2003) suggests that it might be wise to balance others' preferences with our own in making collective decisions. In trying to ensure that everybody is happy, we stand a better chance of ensuring group harmony and strengthening our social relationships. Extant research suggests, however, that not everyone is naturally disposed to make more other-oriented choices. Specifically, those with independent self-construals have been shown to emphasize self-preferences in decision-making, while those with interdependent self-construals naturally balance self and other preferences (Cross, Bacon, and Morris 2000). For interdependents, then, "choosing like a good friend" comes easily. Thus, we suggest that in choosing for self and others, interdependents should make "friend-friendly" choices regardless of the choice situation. For independents, however, their emphasis on self preferences can be inconsistent with maintaining strong relationships and "choosing like a good friend." We argue that rather than dependably forgoing their relationships or their personal preferences, independents skillfully balance self and other in social consumption situations: they generally behave selfishly—but only when they can do so without the risk of social censure, in contexts where their selfishness can be hidden from the group. When the social situation suggests that selfish choices cannot be made without discovery, however, we suggest that independents strategically attempt to disguise their self-centered natures and make more "friend-friendly" choices.

Unlike prior research, then, which shows that interdependents are more situationally sensitive than independents (e.g., Lewis, Goto and Kong 2008; Haberstroh, Oyserman, Schwarz, Kühnen and Ji 2002), we suggest that in social consumption situations, independents behave strategically in context-sensitive ways, while interdependents are contextually insensitive. We build on this literature to examine how individuals balance their fundamental need for fulfilling relationships with their personal self-interests, and examine how individuals use the social context around them to manage their interpersonal relationships. Specifically, we suggest that interdependents reliably make choices that take the preferences of others into account along with their own—regardless of the social and choice context around them. On the other hand, we expect independents to use situational cues to strategically determine how to choose in order to preserve their social relationships while still satisfying their own preferences.

We examine the influence of self-construal on social consumption using a common collective decision: choice of wine for the table at a restaurant. Across four studies, participants were told that they were out to dinner with friends and that they had $110 to spend on one bottle of red and one bottle of white wine for the evening. Individuals then chose a bottle of red and white wine off a real wine list. We measured wine preferences (how often participants drank red versus white wine) and self-construal (Singelis 1994) as independent variables, and measured the prices and perceived quality of the red and white wines chosen as dependent variables. We expect interdependents to make balanced choices and to choose equally expensive bottles of red and white wine, regardless of their own wine preferences. Independents, on the other hand, should selfishly choose better (more expensive) wines of the type they prefer—unless this choice puts them at risk of social censure.

In study 1, we compared choosing for others in a dyadic versus a group setting. We expected that interdependents would display context insensitivity and make balanced choices regardless of the social setting, but that independents would display context sensitivity and make balanced choices only in the dyadic setting, where selfishness is harder to conceal and the risk of social censure due to selfishness is greater. As expected, personal wine preference did not influence interdependents' choices in the dyad or group conditions, nor did it influence independents' choices in the dyad condition. However, in-

dicating their context sensitivity, independents in the group condition behaved selfishly and chose more expensive red (white) wine as their preference for red (white) wine increased.

In studies 2a and 2b, we replicated and extended our group condition findings from study 1. In study 2a, we found that independents continued to choose selfishly in a group situation and that they were aware of doing so: independents rated the chosen wine bottle of their own preference as being of higher quality and more enjoyable than the other bottle, while interdependents showed no such effects. In study 2b, we replicated this finding by priming instead of measuring self-construal, and by using an actual choice measure of wine preference.

In study 3, we explored how group characteristics affect independents' choices. Specifically, we manipulated whether the group was comprised of wine experts or novices. Given that wine novices have a lower level of wine knowledge, we expected that independents would choose especially selfishly when choosing for novices because the likelihood of having their selfishness detected is low. In contrast, we expected that independents would choose less obviously selfishly when choosing for a group of wine experts. All participants were primed to be independent before choosing wine. As expected, independents chose more expensive bottles of the wine they preferred when choosing for novices, and rated this wine as being of higher quality and more enjoyable. When choosing for experts, however, independents chose equally priced bottles of red and white wine regardless of their individual preferences, though they continued to rate the bottle they preferred as being of higher quality and more enjoyable. Thus, independents again displayed context sensitivity and made less obviously selfish choices when choosing on behalf of self and experts.

Taken together, this work suggests that independents are "strategically selfish" in social consumption situations: they generally behave selfishly, but take pains to hide their selfishness when there is a risk of exposure. Thus, in contrast to prior work, we show that independents, rather than interdependents, are context sensitive in social consumption situations where they must balance their own preferences with others'. Importantly, these results are not driven by biased assumptions about others' preferences (Davis, Hoch and Ragsdale, 1986)—independents who liked red wine did not choose more expensive red wines because they assumed everyone at the table would be drinking red wine, just like them. We measured and manipulated individuals' expectations about group preferences in our studies to rule out this alternative explanation. In short, then, when selecting someone to make a decision for your group, choose interdependent individuals—or you might end up drinking a bargain blend while they enjoy an award winning vintage.

REFERENCES

Cross, Susan E., Pamela L. Bacon, and Michael L. Morris (2000), "The Relational-Interdependent Self-Construal and Relationships," *Journal of Personality and Social Psychology*, 78 (4), 791-808.

Davis, Harry L., Stephen J. Hoch, and E. K. Easton Ragsdale (1986), "An Anchoring and Adjustment Model of Spousal Predictions", *Journal of Consumer Research*, 13(1), 25-37.

Eisenberger, Naomi I., Matthew D. Lieberman, and Kipling D. Williams (2003), "Does Rejection Hurt? An fMRI Study of Social Exclusion," *Science*, 302(5643), 290-92.

Haberstroh, Susanne, Daphna Oyserman, Norbert Schwarz, Ulrich Kuhen, and Lin-jun Ji (2002), "Is the interdependent self more sensitive to question context than the independent self? Self-construal and the observation of conversational norms", *Journal of Experimental Social Psychology,* 38(3), 323–29.

Lewis, Richard S., Sharon G. Goto, and Lauren L. Kong (2008), "Culture and context: East Asian American and European American differences in P3 event-related potentials and self-construal", *Personality and Social Psychology Bulletin,* 34(5), 623–34.

Schwartz, Barry (2004). *The paradox of choice.* New York: HarperCollins.

Singelis, Theodore M. (1994), "The Measurement of Independent and Interdependent Self-Construals," *Personality and Social Psychology Bulletin,* 20(5), 580-91.

Strategic Self-Presentation in Joint Consumption: Stereotypes as Social Tools

EXTENDED ABSTRACT

Consumers often engage in shared consumption in order to become acquainted with and learn more about each other. For example, new friends may go see a movie together to socialize, or a salesperson may take a new client to dinner to learn about the client's needs. Given the importance of making a good impression in the early stages of a relationship, the products consumers choose for joint consumption are quite important and have the potential to make or break a budding relationship (Raghunathan and Corfman 2006; Ramanathan and Mcgill 2007). When consumers are just beginning to get to know each other, they have very little information regarding their consumption partner's preferences and expectations for the interaction. How might they go about making their product choices? We propose that consumers use stereotypes as a resource to help inform their choices. Because stereotypes are socially shared and provide information about social groups based on easily identified qualities (e.g., race, gender), they may prove useful in inferring the preferences and anticipating the behavior of one's consumption partner (Kunda and Thagard 1996).

However, consumers understand that simply choosing something liked by the consumption partner may not be enough to ensure a positive interpersonal experience because chosen products may communicate a number of things about themselves to others, especially if chosen products are consistent with stereotypes. In order to ensure that selected items will be favorably received, we find that consumers also consider the type of relationship they wish to pursue during the interaction and also the expectations their consumption partner might have. We find that some consumers are more adept at considering these factors than others. High self-monitors, compared to low self-monitors, have richer, more easily accessible knowledge structures regarding other people and the appropriateness of certain behaviors in specific social situations (Snyder and Cantor 1980). In turn, they use this information as a guide for monitoring their own self-presentations. Thus, high self-monitors relative to low-self monitors should be more willing and able to select products that convey impressions that facilitate positive consumption experiences.

In studies 1 and 2, we examine how male consumers' product choices may be constrained by the need to uphold the role of a masculine man when trying to pursue a romantic relationship with a female consumption partner and how these constraints shape the impressions male consumers wish to present. In study 1, we examine the social implications of expressing gender role consistent or inconsistent product preferences for males and find that males are penalized romantically (but not platonically) if they express gender role violating (i.e., feminine) product preferences.

In study 2, we explore the implications of these findings for choosing products for shared consumption. We examine how males choose products when consuming with a female, depending on whether these males are high or low self-monitors and also whether they are motivated to pursue a romantic relationship. Both low and high self-monitors relied on gender stereotypes and assumed their consumption partner would enjoy reviewing feminine TV shows and magazines (e.g., *Sex and City* and *Elle Décor*). However, they ultimately chose different products to share with their female consumption partner. When not motivated to foster a romantic relationship, high self-monitors were more likely than low self-monitors to fully accommodate their female consumption partner and select stereotypically feminine items. However, when motivated to pursue a romantic relationship, it was low self-monitors that were more likely to select feminine items while high self-monitors were more likely to select gender neutral items (e.g., *Weeds* and *Condé Nast Traveler*). This suggests that only high self-monitors realized that selecting feminine items could compromise their romantic attractiveness.

In study 3, we examine another important determinant of impression management efforts: the audience's expectations. More specifically, we study the types of impressions male consumers wish to present when selecting products to consume with a feminist consumption partner. In this study, we find that male participants used the stereotype associated with feminists to infer that she may expect him to be sexist; thus, they adjusted their joint consumption choices in an attempt to compensate for these negative expectations.

Both low and high self-monitors recognized that selecting stereotypically feminine items would likely be construed as a sign of prejudice in this study. However, only high self-monitors recognized that selecting a gender neutral item may also hold the same risks, because the feminist may interpret the selection as a compromise between the male's masculine preferences and her presumably feminine preferences. Thus, high self-monitors were more likely than low self-monitors to select masculine items in order to avoid indicating that they were applying gender stereotypes to their consumption partner. On the other hand, low self-monitors were more likely than high self-monitors to select gender neutral items because they were less likely to realize that selecting gender neutral items could be negatively received by a feminist consumption partner.

Taken together, these studies suggest that when choosing products to share with people they are unfamiliar with, consumers rely on stereotypes to help infer the preferences and anticipate the responses of their consumption partner. However, consumers differ in their willingness and ability to select products that will be favorably received. In contrast to low self-monitors, high self-monitors recognize that simply choosing something liked by the consumption partner may not be enough ensure a positive interpersonal experience, because chosen products communicate a number of things about themselves to others, especially if these products are consistent with stereotypes.

REFERENCES

Kunda, Z. and P. Thagard (1996), "Forming impressions from stereotypes, traits, and behaviors: A parallel-constraint-satisfaction theory," Psychological Review, 103 (2), 284-308.

Raghunathan, Rajagopal and Kim Corfman (2006), "Is Happiness Shared Doubled and Sadness Shared Halved? Social Influence on Enjoyment of Hedonic Experiences," *Journal of Marketing Research,* 43 (3), 386-94.

Ramanathan, Suresh and Ann L. Mcgill (2007), "Consuming with Others: Social Influences on Moment-to-Moment and Retrospective Evaluations of an Experience," *Journal of Consumer Research*, 34 (4), 506-24.

Snyder, Mark and Nancy Cantor (1980), "Thinking About Ourselves and Others - Self-Monitoring and Social Knowledge," *Journal of Personality and Social Psychology*, 39 (2), 222-34.

Is it Riskier to Receive than to Give?: The Effect of Social Closeness on Gift Recipients' Responses to Identity-Inconsistent Gifts

EXTENDED ABSTRACT

Behavioral scientists have long viewed personal identity as a dynamic construct, inextricably linked to the feedback one receives from both his/her social relationships and environment. People's identities are built from the outside in, as the relationships an individual holds dear shape his/her understanding of who s/he is through how s/he is seen by others (Cooley 1902; Swann et al 2000). While an individual's identity is somewhat flexible, most people are motivated to sustain a consistent and coherent sense of self and prefer to surround themselves with people who verify their self-concepts. Consequently, individuals avoid or distance themselves from relationship partners who do not affirm important identities (Swann 2005).

One important social interaction that shapes an individual's perception of him/herself and supports important social ties is the exchange of gifts (Ruth, Brunel, and Otnes 1999). When a recipient receives a gift, s/he has a porthole into how the giver perceives him/her as a gift is supposed to embody the giver's interpretation of the recipient's desires, preferences and needs and by extension, his/her identity (Belk 1999; Sherry 1983). Given that individuals' identities are responsive to interactions with their relationship partners (Josephs, Bosson, and Jacobs 2003) and that they deeply value verifying feedback from those closest to them, receiving a gift that is inconsistent with one's existing self-concept may cause the gift recipient to feel some dissonance. We predict that in response to receiving such a gift, the recipient may reduce his/her dissonance by 1) revising, expanding or changing his/her existing self-identity in order to accommodate the chosen gift or 2) withdrawing from the relationship partner in order to avoid receiving non-verifying feedback. In a two experiments, we find that depending on the social closeness between the giver and recipient and how identity-consistent the gift is, recipients exhibit each of these responses.

In study 1, using a 2 (gift: identity-inconsistent vs. identity-consistent) x 2 (social closeness of recipient: close vs. distant) experimental design, we instructed participants to recall receiving an identity-inconsistent (vs. consistent) gift from a close (vs. distant) friend. After writing about the gift, they answered questions about whether the gift had made them see themselves in a new way or changed their identity and how it had affected their friendship with the giver. As predicted, close (vs. distant) recipients were more likely to indicate that the identity-inconsistent (vs. consistent) gift had changed the way they saw themselves. Conversely, distant (vs. close) recipients were more likely to indicate that the identity-inconsistent (vs. consistent) gift had caused them to feel more socially distant to the giver.

In order to understand why recipients had different responses to identity-inconsistent gifts given by close (vs. distant) friends, we conducted a follow-up study in which we manipulated rather than measured the identity-inconsistency of the gift. In study 2, a 2 (gift: identity-consistent vs. identity-inconsistent) x 2 (social closeness of

recipient: close vs. distant) experimental design, participants read a scenario about receiving an identity-consistent (vs. inconsistent) gift from a close (vs. distant) friend. In identity-consistent gift scenarios, recipients either received a CD of their favorite group's new album or a DVD of their favorite movie; in identity-inconsistent scenarios they received either a puzzle or slippers. After reading the scenario, participants answered questions about how self-reflective the gifts were.

The data reveal an identity-consistence x social closeness interaction on the self-reflectiveness of the gift such that givers felt that the identity-inconsistent (vs. consistent) gifts were more (vs. less) self-reflective when they were given by close (vs. distant) friends. In other words, recipients' judgments of the self-reflectiveness of the identity-consistent (vs. inconsistent) gift is qualified by their relationship with the recipient.

Respondents were also asked to answer the open-ended question: "Why do you think your close (vs. distant) friend chose this gift for you?" Respondents in the close friend condition indicated that they thought that their friend had chosen this gift because s/he had seen something in the gift that matched his/her identity in a way that the recipient had not seen in him/herself:

- There must have been something about the puzzle that made her think of me.

- He wanted me to explore my creative side. The puzzle would probably have some deeper meaning once finished.

On the other hand, those receiving the identity-inconsistent gift from a distant friend were not as likely to attribute such powerful insights to the gift giver and simply thought the giver did not know him/her very well and was more concerned with saving time or money than choosing something appropriate:

- She probably tried to choose something that wasn't too expensive yet too cheap.

- He didn't spend long buying it.

- He hasn't seen me in so long and doesn't know my interests that well so he went for something really safe like slippers when he should have went on his gut feeling.

The data from these two studies corroborate the prediction that close recipients are likely to change or expand the way they see themselves in order to incorporate identity-inconsistent gifts from their close friends. Furthermore, the open-ended responses indicate that they do so because they think that their close friends see something in the gift that matches a part of their identity that they are not aware of. Conversely, individuals who thought their distant (vs. close) friends had chosen an identity-inconsistent gift subsequently felt more emotionally distant from the giver.

I Didn't Think I Would l Like What You Chose for Me: Relationship Norms and Satisfaction with Consumer- versus Provider-Chosen Outcomes

EXTENDED ABSTRACT

Prior research demonstrates that personally-made, as compared to externally-made, choices lead to greater task enjoyment and more positive affect (Brehm 1966; Langer 1975). More recent research, however, has found that cultural norms regulating interpersonal exchanges may moderate these beneficial effects of self-choice (Iyengar and Lepper 1999). The present research examines the manner in which relationship norms underlying customer-provider interactions moderate expected and actual satisfaction with a self-chosen relative to a provider-chosen outcome.

Two types of customer-provider relationships are examined: communal and exchange (Clark and Mills 1993). Communal relationships are based on a mutual concern for the partner's well-being; exchange relationships are based on the principle of *quid pro quo*. Communal and exchange relationship norms carry expectations not only about the partner's behavior but also about the partner's intentions, as they provide guidelines about the motivation underlying the interaction: a desire to satisfy the other's needs versus a desire to get something back (Clark and Mills 1993). In a communal relationship, customers are more likely to expect the provider to make choices that are in line with the choices that they themselves would make. On the other hand, in an exchange relationship, customers are more likely to perceive the provider's self-serving choices as conflicting with their own. As a result, we hypothesize customers to expect lower satisfaction with a provider- than with a self-made choice in exchange relationships but little or no difference in communal relationships. These initial expectations may exert an ironic effect when actual satisfaction is considered. Drawing on prior research on expectation confirmation and disconfirmation (Oliver 1980), we suggest that exchange customers will be positively surprised by a valued outcome chosen by the provider resulting in actual satisfaction being higher than expected satisfaction. Conversely, communal customers' expectation would be simply met by the same outcome, resulting in actual and expected satisfaction being no different. Thus, we hypothesize that the moderating effect of relationship norms would reverse when actual rather than expected satisfaction is assessed.

Four studies test these hypotheses. The first two studies examine the moderating role of relationship norms on expected satisfaction. The next two studies examine the reverse moderating effect on actual satisfaction.

In study 1, we rely on the relative salience of communal and exchange norms underlying the existing relationship between undergraduate Management students and their university. The self-choice (university-choice) context involved four Strategy courses. Regression results supported our hypothesis. At one standard deviation below the mean of the Net communality score (corresponding to a more exchange orientation), expected satisfaction in the university-choice condition was significantly lower than in the self-choice condition. However, at one standard deviation above the mean of the Net communality score (corresponding to a more communal orientation), expected satisfaction was no different across the self- and the university-choice conditions. Study 2 was conducted to replicate the effect by manipulating relationship norms and by taking more direct measure of perceived intentions underlying the two relationships. Scenarios describing interactions between a customer and a bookstore were used to prime communal or exchange relationship norms. The self-choice (bookstore-choice) context involved four books as part of a promotional give-away. As predicted, exchange participants' expected satisfaction was lower in the bookstore-choice than in the self-choice condition, whereas communal participants' ex-

pected satisfaction did not differ across the two choice conditions. A follow-up study confirmed that participants in the bookstore-choice condition were more likely to perceive the bookstore to be motivated by the customer's best interest in the communal condition but by its own best interest in the exchange condition.

The next two studies investigated the reverse moderating effect of relationship norms by examining their influence on actual rather than expected satisfaction. Study 3 was a field study involving two actual bookstores – one positioned as a communal bookstore and the other as exchange. The self-choice (bookstore-choice) context involved four books as part of an actual promotional give-away. As we hypothesized, customers of the exchange bookstore were *more* satisfied with the bookstore-chosen book than with the self-chosen book; there were no differences in satisfaction between bookstore- and self-choice customers of the communal bookstore. A post-test showed that, different from actual satisfaction, expected satisfaction follows the same pattern of results as studies 1 and 2. Study 4 examined the effect of relationship norms on actual satisfaction in a laboratory setting. Relationship norms were primed in an interpersonal context; the self-choice (company-choice) condition involved four new healthy juice options being tested by a beverage company. Measures of expected and actual satisfaction were taken. Consistent with our hypothesis, exchange participants reported a significantly higher net satisfaction change in the company-choice condition than in the self-choice condition, indicating greater actual satisfaction than expected satisfaction. However, communal participants experienced a similar net satisfaction change irrespective of whether they were in the company-choice or in the self-choice condition, indicating no difference between actual and expected satisfaction.

This paper shows that satisfaction is not necessarily greater with a self-chosen outcome, and that providers should consider the potential limitation of personal freedom when deciding to bear the costs of granting more choice opportunities to their customers. In general, if individual well-being is to be maximized, perhaps the focus should be less on who makes the final choice, and more on the type of relationship that binds those who experience the decision outcome with those who decide for them.

REFERENCES

Brehm, Jack W. (1966), *A Theory of Psychological Reactance*. New York: Academic Press.

Clark, Margaret S. and Judson Mills (1993), "The Difference Between Communal and Exchange Relationships: What It Is and Is Not," *Personality and Social Psychology Bulletin*, 19(6), 684-691.

Iyengar, Sheena S. and Mark R. Lepper (1999), "Rethinking the Value of Choice: A Cultural Perspective on Intrinsic Motivation," *Journal of Personality and Social Psychology*, 76 (3), 349-366.

Langer, Ellen J. (1975), "The Illusion of Control," *Journal of Personality and Social Psychology*, 32 (2), 311-28.

Oliver, Richard L. (1980), "A Cognitive Model of the Antecedents and Consequences of Satisfaction Decisions," *Journal of Marketing Research*, 17 (4), 460-469.

Counterfeit Connections: Linking Lies, Luxury, and Louis Vuitton

Chairs: James Mourey, University of Michigan, USA
Carolyn Yoon, University of Michigan, USA

Paper #1: Laud the Fraud, Just Not in Public: Counterintuitive Benefits of Counterfeit

T. Andrew Poehlman, Southern Methodist University, USA
James Mourey, University of Michigan, USA
Lawrence Williams, University of Colorado, USA
Carolyn Yoon, University of Michigan, USA

Paper #2: "I Know Enough to Buy the Fake": Intelligence, Knowledge and the Valuation of Luxury Brands

Claudia Townsend, University of Miami, USA
Sanjay Sood, UCLA, USA
Dan Ariely, Duke University, USA

Paper #3: Far Away or So Close: The Influence of Counterfeits on Genuine Brand Preference

Keith Wilcox, Babson College, USA
Juliano Laran, University of Miami, USA
Sankar Sen, Baruch College, USA

Paper #4: Collateral Damage Effects of Non-Deceptive Counterfeits on Legitimate Brands

Aaron Ahuvia, University of Michigan, Dearborn, USA
Stefano Pace, Bocconi University, Italy
Giacomo Gistri, University of Macerata, Italy
Simona Romani, L.U.I.S.S. University, Italy
Lucio Masserini, University of Florence, Italy

SESSION OVERVIEW

Objective: Counterfeit goods represent a $600-650 billion global market, and mere mention of the word "counterfeit" connotes negativity, fraudulence, and inferior quality. Countries and companies have taken significant and costly actions to deter counterfeiting for reasons ranging from lost revenue to the tarnishing of a brand. But what if counterfeit had some positive effects on companies, consumers, or brands? What if "smarter" consumers actually preferred counterfeit products more than "less intelligent" shoppers? What if an abundance of counterfeit actually *boosted* the price of a genuine product? In the spirit of "creating connections," the objective of this session is to link together several unexpected discoveries regarding counterfeit to provide a robust understanding of when counterfeit is, in fact, detrimental and when it actually might *benefit* consumers and companies producing the genuine product.

General Orientation: The present session connects several surprising findings regarding how counterfeit helps or hinders companies and consumers. The four papers included in the session address: 1) the counterintuitive benefits of counterfeit, 2) the role of consumer intelligence in perceptions of signaling and quality of counterfeit, 3) the extent to which construal level and self-goals influence preference for counterfeit or genuine products, and 4) the collateral damage effects of counterfeit on brands *other* than the brand being counterfeited. Each paper integrates with the others to collectively illustrate the "connection" among counterfeit's many components. Each presentation will last for 15-20 minutes and, afterwards, a discussion will take place regarding how the connection of these findings could motivate future research on the topic of counterfeit. Included in our group of authors is a diverse group of researchers, which should generate a lively and productive discussion.

Likely Audience: The appeal of this session is that it considers the topic of counterfeit from a variety of perspectives: consumer

intelligence, market implications beyond the counterfeited brand, counterintuitive benefits, construal theory, consumer goals, public policy, and luxury/non-luxury goods. Given the diversity of approaches taken to explore the core topic of counterfeit, the issues addressed in this session should generate broad audience appeal. Thus in the spirit of the conference theme, our goal is to *connect* researchers with diverse backgrounds to have a lively, informative discussion on the subject of counterfeit.

Issues and Topics: The Poehlman et al. paper sets the stage for the session by exploring the counterintuitive benefits that counterfeit can have in the marketplace. Whereas prior research has emphasized the negative consequences of counterfeit, this paper demonstrates that perceived prevalence of counterfeit can boost the market price consumers would pay for genuine products in the marketplace. While high levels of counterfeit boost high-end brands, low perceived levels of counterfeit boost low-end brands. In either case, companies must be perceived as being active in their anti-counterfeit efforts resulting in the ironic implication that, in some cases, companies may privately need to condone and even encourage counterfeiting while publicly seeming to fight counterfeiting. Next, the Townsend et al. paper explores the tradeoff between signaling and quality with respect to counterfeit, specifically considering the role of consumer intelligence. The authors contend that "smart" consumers are more aware of the signaling power of luxury brands and of the unsubstantiated markup of some luxury products to convey "quality." As such, smarter consumers are more likely than less intelligent consumers to prefer counterfeit products to benefit from the signaling, self-presentation aspects of counterfeit while avoiding the feeling that they are paying more for quality that does not justify the premium price. The third paper, Wilcox et al., investigates how construing products at an abstract or concrete level can actually increase or decrease preference for a genuine product. Specifically, construing products concretely leads to a comparison of differences, thereby encouraging preference for a genuine product; construing products abstractly leads to thoughts of similarity, encouraging preference for a counterfeit. A self-expression goal trumps the effect, however, as consumers with the goal to self-express prefer the genuine brand regardless of processing style. Finally, the fourth paper moves beyond prior work to show how counterfeit negatively impacts brands *other than* the brand being counterfeited. Specifically, the work demonstrates the "collateral damage" a counterfeit excises on other, genuine brands that may have otherwise been purchased in the absence of the counterfeit product. The results suggest the striking finding that 90% of lost sales come from other, genuine brands and not the brand actually being counterfeited. Collectively, the papers offer four distinct perspectives on counterfeit but connect together to illustrate that counterfeit has some unexpected, surprising consequences that warrant further exploration.

Contribution: To date, surprisingly little research has addressed the topic of counterfeit and almost no research, to our knowledge, has considered the potentially beneficial effects of counterfeit. Thus, this session's major contribution is to bring counterfeit research to the forefront of consumer research, connecting both the negative and positive implications counterfeit has for consumers and companies. We also highlight the role of consumer psychology in counterfeit, linking prior work from the company's perspective with novel work from the consumer's perspective. By bridging these various perspectives on the topic of counterfeiting, we seek to encourage future research on the subject that continues to link different methodologies and theoretical accounts.

Connecting Questions: Some questions to be included in the follow-up discussion are: To the extent that counterfeiting is inevitable, is it feasible for companies and consumers to benefit from counterfeit strategies? How can a company's strategy link to the findings presented here regarding the consumer psychology of counterfeit? Regarding consumer education, when might "intelligent" consumers still prefer the genuine brand? And when might "less intelligent" consumers prefer counterfeit? Is it possible to link consumer intelligence to how consumers construe products (i.e., abstractly or concretely)? When might non-counterfeited brands benefit from the presence of counterfeit (linking the first and last papers)? And perhaps the biggest "connecting" question of all is: how do we integrate the findings that counterfeit may have beneficial consequences with its known detrimental effects?

Status of Papers: All the papers included in this special session are completed or near completion.

Laud the Fraud, Just Not In Public: Counterintuitive Benefits of Counterfeit

EXTENDED ABSTRACT

For luxury brands, combating counterfeit is a top priority: in one year alone, Louis Vuitton conducted over 6,000 raids, participated in over 13,000 legal proceedings, and led to the arrest of nearly 1,000 individuals. Coach, the luxury brand famous for its handbags, even provides a step-by-step process for reporting counterfeit in its effort to curb the practice. Many companies explicitly advertise their "zero tolerance" policy with respect to counterfeit citing the lost revenues and additional costs stemming from counterfeit. Yet, surprisingly, some counterfeited brands are publicly silent on their views towards counterfeit. Nike, for example, takes a relatively quiet approach to combating counterfeit, despite footwear being the most counterfeited product category. This stark contrast in dealing with counterfeit raises some interesting questions including whether it is in a company's best interest to be perceived as taking an active or passive role in fighting counterfeit or if, in some instances, counterfeiting can even *help* a company producing the genuine brand.

The present research explores how perceptions of counterfeiting prevalence, luxury and non-luxury brand status, and company responses to counterfeit interact and affect genuine products and consumer behavior. In four studies, we demonstrate that counterfeit can both positively and negatively influence perceptions of a genuine product's market price, that the perceived status of a brand moderates the effect, and, ironically, that a company's vigilance with respect to fighting counterfeit is an essential component necessary to obtain benefits from high levels of counterfeit.

In our first study, we wanted to test our hypothesis that the perceived prevalence of counterfeit could influence perceptions of genuine brand product prices. We randomly assigned participants into one of three conditions: high-counterfeit, low-counterfeit, and control. We presented participants with a Louis Vuitton bag and asked them, relative to a counterfeit bag, how much more expensive they thought a real Louis Vuitton bag would be. On average, participants in the high counterfeit condition perceived a greater percentage difference (383%) compared to the control group (235%), while participants in the low counterfeit condition perceived a much smaller markup (183%) than the other two groups. The data from this initial provided evidence that perception of the prevalence of counterfeit does, in fact, affect perceptions of real market prices for products. This finding supported our hypothesis that prevalent counterfeiting of a brand implies that brand is popular and valuable, which subsequently influences perceived market price of the genuine product.

In our second study, we wanted to replicate the initial finding from study one, as well as explore whether counterfeiting could have potentially beneficial effects in the marketplace in a non-luxury product domain. To test the hypothesis that the perception of high levels of counterfeit might lead consumers to increase their estimated value of a real, non-counterfeit product in the marketplace, we randomly assigned participants to high- and low-counterfeit conditions, or to a control condition. We then asked participants questions regarding perceptions of a product's real market price, counterfeit price, and cost to produce. The product used for the study was a pair of Nike brand shoes, which, aside from being a relevant product for the population (college undergrads), also represents one of the most counterfeited product categories (footwear). As predicted, when participants thought that counterfeit was pervasive, the perceived market price of a real pair of Nike shoes was significantly higher than the control group's estimated real market price. When participants thought that counterfeiting was less common, the market price of real Nike shoes was significantly lower than the control group's estimated price. The results replicate the finding from the initial study.

In our third study, we explored whether the effect found in study two generalized to all brands, even lower-status brands, or if high perceived prevalence of counterfeiting actually hurt low-end brands. We hypothesized that the "greater counterfeit means popular product" effect would not be true for low-end brands. Instead, we expected to see the opposite: high perceptions of counterfeiting for a low-status brand should hurt the real market price of the product, as cheaper substitutes are readily available. The target brand for this study was Crocs footwear, and the design was identical to that of the second study. As predicted, when participants thought counterfeit was pervasive, the perceived market price of a real pair of Crocs was significantly lower than the control group's estimated real market price. When participants thought counterfeiting was less common, the market price real Crocs shoes was significantly higher than the control group's estimated price. Thus the indirect benefit of counterfeiting on the market price of genuine products is contingent on brand status, with premium brands benefitting from more counterfeit and lower brands benefitting from less.

Our fourth study addressed the role of company vigilance in response to counterfeit. We hypothesized that, even though counterfeit may have peripheral benefits, companies must be perceived as actively combating counterfeiting or else the effects will be eliminated. To test our hypothesis, we presented participants with Nike shoes, manipulated the level of counterfeit (low vs. high) and Nike's explicit vigilance towards fighting counterfeit (active vs. passive). As anticipated, perceptions of a company's role in fighting counterfeit made a difference: benefits only accrue if the company is actively fighting counterfeit. This produces the ironic results that companies should outwardly fight counterfeit but inwardly hope their products are counterfeited to boost brand popularity and the real market price of genuine goods.

Across four studies we provide evidence for counterfeit's sometimes-counterintuitive effect of boosting the perceived market price of genuine (i.e., non-counterfeit) products. We demonstrate that when counterfeiting is perceived as being prevalent, the perceived market price of genuine, high-end products gets a boost, whereas when counterfeiting is perceived as being less common, the perceived market price of genuine, low-end products gets a boost. We also show that the effects only hold when consumers perceive that a company is making an effort to combat counterfeiting. Theoretical and managerial implications are discussed.

"I Know Enough to Buy the Fake": Intelligence, Knowledge and the Valuation of Luxury Brands

EXTENDED ABSTRACT

One of the reasons consumers purchase publicly consumed luxury branded products is the ability of these products to signal membership in an aspirational group or to suggest something about the user's social status or wealth (Bearden and Etzel 1982, Childers and Rao 1992). At the same time, luxury brands justify their high prices by offering remarkable product quality (Garfein 1989, Quelch 1987) and product quality is also a significant reason consumers purchase luxury brands (Gentry et al 2001). Despite the interest in the topic of what values consumers ascribe to a luxury brand, less understood is how such valuations may differ systematically across individuals. In the present research we examine how general intelligence (as measured by the cognitive reflection task (Frederick 2005) and the Mill Hill Vocabulary test (Raven 1981)) as well as brand knowledge affects the propensity to value luxury brands for their high quality and/or ability to signal to others. In the process of exploring this issue we uncover surprising findings as to how these individual differences influence willingness to pay for counterfeit products.

In our first study we examine the relationship between intelligence and valuation of luxury brands for their signaling abilities. Both luxury products and brands as well as more mundane publicly displayed products have been shown to be particularly useful when attempting to reveal association with a reference group (Bearden and Etzel 1982). But not all product categories are equally adept at offering a venue for self-presentation to others. By nature goods that are used or consumed in front of others are more capable of fulfilling this purpose (Childers and Rao 1992; Shavitt, Lowrey, and Han 1992). To properly use a luxury brand for self-presentation purposes, one must be aware both that others are making inferences based on one's possessions, and also understand for which product categories this is likely to be most relevant. It seems likely that more intelligent consumers are more likely to understand that viewers will judge them by their products and also that this is only possible when the good is publicly displayed. We, therefore, hypothesized that more intelligent individuals value luxury brands more for their signaling abilities than do less intelligent individuals and, because more intelligent people are likely better able to decipher when these abilities are relevant, their valuation of luxury brands is more product-category specific. We tested this by asking respondents to choose between one option that was inconspicuously branded with a luxury brand but less well designed and one that was better designed but carried an unknown brand name. Product aesthetics is a public attribute that, like brand, viewers use to make inferences about people. Therefore, when brand is not outwardly evident, a choice driven by signaling ought to favor the highly aesthetic option, not the luxury branded option. However, such an effect should only be present for the publicly consumed product categories; with privately consumed product categories where signaling to others is much more difficult, the motive to signal ought not come into play. Indeed we found that in public product categories (jeans, jacket, purse) more intelligent individuals are more likely to select the more aesthetic option over the luxury branded option than less intelligent individuals. However, this difference disappeared in private categories (cosmetics, deodorant, nightgown). This is consistent with our hypothesis and revealed a greater understanding among the more intelligent population of when luxury brands are able to signal to others.

In our second study we examined how both intelligence and brand knowledge relates to valuation of luxury brands for their high quality. Consumers do not buy luxury brands only for the conspicuousness of the brand name and ability to signal, but also because of the superior quality that these products presumably offer (Gentry et al. 2001, Nia and Zaichkowsky 2000, O'Cass and Frost 2002, Quelch 1987). And yet, a luxury brand implies premium pricing that suggests that, although quality may be high, someone searching based on a value-per-dollar basis ought not to purchase a luxury branded product (Patrick and Hagtvedt 2009). Indeed, some have gone so far as to define luxury brands as those for which functionality to price ratio is low but which have a high ratio of high intangible benefits to price (Nueno and Quelch 1998). Our hypothesis follows that more intelligent individuals would be less likely than less intelligent individuals to value luxury brands because of the implied higher quality. While the quality of a luxury brand may be high, the evidence suggests that it is not high enough to justify the cost if an intelligent valuation is undertaken. We also offered a hypothesis about the influence of brand knowledge on propensity to value luxury brands for their quality. Because luxury brands are marketed as the utmost in quality, any past experience most likely leads to a decrease in perceptions of quality. Therefore, we also hypothesized that consumers with more brand knowledge value luxury brands less for their quality than those with less knowledge.

To test these two hypotheses we asked respondents their willingness to pay for counterfeits given the price of the relevant luxury branded good. A counterfeit good offers the same self-presentation abilities but without the presumed quality. Indeed, consumers value counterfeits more when seeking self-presentation to project a specific image and value counterfeits less when motivated by intrinsic product aspects such as quality or reliability (Wilcox, Kim, and Sen 2009). Thus, an examination of how valuation of counterfeits varies with intelligence would uncover differences in perceptions of quality as motivation for purchase of luxury brands. Subsequently, we expected more intelligent individuals and more knowledgeable individuals to value counterfeit versions of products more than would less intelligent individuals and less knowledgeable individuals, respectively. Indeed, our results confirmed our hypotheses revealing the ironic results that across both publicly and privately consumed product categories, respondents with greater intelligence or greater brand knowledge consistently valued the counterfeit products more than did less intelligent or less knowledgeable consumers.

Implications with respect to luxury brands, counterfeits, as well as consumer metacognitions are discussed.

Far Away or So Close: The Influence of Counterfeits on Genuine Brand Preference

EXTENDED ABSTRACT

Imagine that you are considering buying a new Louis Vuitton watch. As you contemplate the purchase, you notice a similar looking counterfeit Louis Vuitton watch being sold on the street. Would the presence of the counterfeit version affect your decision to buy the genuine version? The widespread presence of anti-counterfeiting efforts suggests that it will. In fact, many estimates of the economic impact of counterfeiting are predicated on the assumption that sales of counterfeit products replace the sales of genuine items. For instance, it is estimated that the luxury brand industry incurs as much as $12 billion each year in lost sales due to the purchase of counterfeit products (International Chamber of Commerce 2004). Thus, it is generally assumed that counterfeit brands reduce the demand for genuine luxury brands.

Previous research, however, offers mixed conclusions regarding the influence of counterfeits on the demand for genuine brands. Wilcox, Kim and Sen (2009) demonstrate that in many cases the presence of the counterfeit reduces consumers' desire to purchase genuine luxury brands. Commuri (2009) finds that while counterfeits can make consumers of genuine products abandon luxury brands, they may also lead them to view themselves as champions of the brand. Nia and Zaichkowsky (2000) argue that in certain contexts counterfeits can enhance demand for the real brands. Thus, while it is apparent that counterfeits can influence consumers' desire for genuine brands, it is unclear whether counterfeits have a positive or negative effect on genuine brand preference.

This current research demonstrates that the availability of counterfeit brands can decrease or increase desire for genuine luxury brands. We propose that the influence of counterfeit brands on consumers' preference for genuine luxury brands depends on consumers' processing mindset. Processing at a local, concrete level leads consumers to identify dissimilarities (Förster, Liberman, and Kuschel 2008) between the products and contrast the genuine brand with the counterfeit version. As a result, the presence of a counterfeit version increases desire for the genuine version. Processing at a global, abstract level leads consumers to identify similarities between the products and assimilate the genuine brand with the counterfeit version. As a result, the presence of the counterfeit reduces desire for the genuine version. We show that the assimilation process that reduces desire for genuine brands can be interrupted by consumers' goals. When consumers have active self-expression goals (i.e., purchase brands to express their values), which are inconsistent with counterfeit consumption, the counterfeit increases consumers' desire for the genuine version even when they process at an abstract level.

This conceptualization is investigated in three studies. In the first study, we manipulated processing style by having participants write about all of the things they consider when they think of why (abstract mindset) versus how (concrete mindset) they intend to improve their health. Then, as part of an unrelated study, they were asked to indicate their likelihood of purchasing a genuine Louis Vuitton watch when a counterfeit version was or was not available.

As expected, participants who adopted a concrete mindset were more likely to purchase the genuine watch when a counterfeit version was available compared to when one was not available. Participants who adopted an abstract mindset were less likely to purchase the genuine watch when a counterfeit version was available.

The second study replicates the results of the first study using temporal construal (immediate versus distant future) to manipulate processing style. We show that when the purchase is being made in the immediate future (concrete mindset) the counterfeit increases consumers' desire for the genuine version; when the purchase is being made in the distant future (abstract mindset), the counterfeit decreases consumers' desire for the genuine version.

Additionally, we demonstrate that priming a self-expression goal, by having participants evaluate an advertisement for an unrelated product promoting self-expression, interrupts the assimilation process when people process at an abstract level. Specially, we show that a self-expression goal increases consumers' desire for a genuine brand when a counterfeit is available, even under an abstract mindset.

The third study demonstrates that the effects observed in previous studies are due to assimilation and contrast. Specifically, we show that perceptions regarding the similarity between the genuine and the counterfeit brand mediate the influence of the counterfeit on consumers' preference for the genuine brand. Additionally, we measured the strength of self-expression goal activation in this study to demonstrate that the results in the second study were due to an active self-expression goal and not a reaction to a primed concept.

These findings suggest that goals can override processing style and have a positive effect on genuine brand preference. Thus, managers may want to consider appealing to self-expression motives through their marketing communications because doing so may increase sales, particularly in markets where counterfeits are available.

Collateral Damage Effects of Non-Deceptive Counterfeits on Legitimate Brands

EXTENDED ABSTRACT

"Non-deceptive" counterfeits are products known to be counterfeit by the end users who purchase them (Grossman and Shapiro 1988; Eisend and Schuchert-Güler 2006; Gistri et al. 2009). There is much debate around the effects of non-deceptive counterfeits on the original brands they copy. One common area of dispute is the extent to which non-deceptive counterfeit goods serve as direct substitute purchases for authentic luxury brands (Eisend and Schuchert-Güler 2006, Nia and Zaichkowsky 2000, Wee, Tan and Cheok 1995). For example, had counterfeit Gucci handbags not been available, how many consumers would have purchased an authentic Gucci handbag in their stead? (Nia and Zaichkowsky 2000, Silverstein and Fiske 2003, Van Kempen 2003)

The debate is often framed so that a direct substitution effect indicates that counterfeits are a problem; whereas the lack of a direct substitution effect shows that counterfeits are relatively benign, a victimless crime. The current research seeks to reframe this debate by introducing the notion of "collateral damage effects." Collateral damage effects occur when the purchase of a brand X fake substitutes for the purchase of a brand Y original. Take for example, a consumer who purchases a fake Gucci purse for $100. Had fakes not been available, might the consumer have spent $250 on an authentic entry-level luxury brand (like Coach in the US or Hogan in Europe)? If so, the legitimate brand suffered from unfair competition. It was penalized for following trademark law, by losing sales to a competitor operating outside the law.

Collateral damage effects come in three types: trade up, parallel, and trade down effects. Were counterfeits somehow eliminated, in a trade up effect the erstwhile counterfeit consumer would now purchase a brand which cost more than the counterfeit, in a parallel effect the consumer would purchase a brand priced the same as the counterfeit, and in a trade down effect the consumer would now purchase a brand which cost less than the counterfeit. Which of these effects occurs depends on the preferences and budget of the consumer. In our initial exploratory study we use a student sample at an Italian public university. This population often sees counterfeits as "fun" and does not always try to hide the product's counterfeit status. Therefore, the purchase of a fake does not necessarily indicate a strong desire to own a prestige brand. Furthermore, these students are often under strict budget constraints. Hence, we hypothesize that for this population, if the fakes were not available we would primarily see parallel or trade down collateral effects.

An experimental study using a within-subjects design was used to our hypothesis. The sample consisted of more than 350 female undergraduate students living in two medium-size cities of Italy. While Italy is best known for its production of legitimate luxury brands, it is also Europe's largest producer of counterfeits (OECD 2007). Subjects were required to express their purchase intention and choice among five levels of women's handbags: (1) budget products at € 30, (2) quality non-luxury brands at € 80, (3) counterfeit high-end designer luxury brands at € 80, (4) authentic entry-level luxury brands at € 200, and (5) authentic high-end designer luxury brands at € 550. After expressing their purchase intention and choice for that consideration set, subjects repeated their purchase intention and choice for a new consideration set identical to the previous set, except with the choice of counterfeit brands removed.

To test H1 we analyzed the transition matrix, which shows how the choice of individual subjects changed from consideration set 1 (with counterfeits) to consideration set 2 (without counterfeits). Out of the 350 subjects, 48 choose counterfeit products when that choice was available. After the counterfeit option was removed from the choice set, only 3 of the 48 counterfeit choosers then chose an authentic luxury brand at € 550. The log-linear model employed fit well, supporting the hypothesis. A further examination of the data show that the 48 subjects who initially chose counterfeits, mainly selected products at same price level (€80) as the counterfeit brands

(25 subjects made this choice). The remaining 20 subjects were evenly distributed between the 10 who chose a lower priced budget brand (€30) and the 10 who stretched their budget upward to choose an entry-level luxury brand (€200).

These results suggest the importance of collateral damage effects generally as a major form of economic loss from counterfeit luxury goods, as more than 90% of the sales lost to counterfeits in this simulation came from brands other than those being counterfeited. Measured in number of items sold, counterfeits in this experiment took their biggest bite out of non-luxury brands at the same price level as the counterfeits. In addition, because the prices on luxury and entry level luxury brands are quite high, even a smaller number of lost sales in these two categories can be as significant as a much larger number of lost sales to less expensive brands.

Don't Throw Out the (Process) Baby With the (Representational) Bathwater: Boundary Conditions on Embodiment

Chairs: Ana Valenzuela, Baruch College, USA
Jesse Chandler, Princeton University, USA

Paper #1: When Hugs Mean Human: Antecedents and Consequences of Embodied Anthropomorphism
Rhonda Hadi, Baruch College, CUNY, USA
Ana Valenzuela, Baruch College, CUNY, USA

Paper #2: I Can Feel It!: Haptic Sensations on Prosocial Behaviors
Chen Wang, University of British Columbia, Canada
Rui (Juliet) Zhu, University of British Columbia, Canada

Paper #3: When You Can't Judge a Book by its Cover: Metacognitive Inferences about Embodied Cues
Jesse Chandler, Princeton University, USA
David Reinhard, University of Michigan, USA
Norbert Schwarz, University of Michigan, USA

SESSION OVERVIEW

Recently, there has been increased interest in the how embodied cues affect consumer behavior. Embodied perspectives challenge old assumptions about how knowledge is represented by demonstrating that even abstract concepts are not amodal but rather distributed across sensory systems (Barsalou, 2008). As a result, sensory cues (e.g. temperature) can lead to the activation of metaphorically related concepts (e.g. social affiliation; Williams & Bargh, 2008). However, recent embodied perspectives include additional assumptions about how embodied concepts affect choice and behavior, often assuming that their influence is automatic, without specifically testing these effects (e.g. Williams, Huang and Bargh 2009; Zhong and DeVoe 2009).

Thus embodied accounts conflate the automatic *activation* of concepts with the automatic *application* of accessible concepts to downstream choice and behavior, leaving little room for processes that are crucial to the impact of other accessible information, including bodily feedback or semantic primes (Schwarz & Clore, 2007). The three papers in this session explore the intersection between target and consumer characteristics in determining boundary conditions for embodiment effects. Despite their reliance on diverse theoretical frameworks, the papers share the common focus of moving research on embodiment from its current emphasis on existence proofs to a more nuanced understanding of how and when context determines whether embodied cues are relevant to consumers' evaluations and behavior.

In the first paper, Hadi and Valenzuela show that if an individual performs physical actions that signal humanness, anthropomorphic beliefs and emotional attachment will follow. However, they identify that the product needs to be imbued with anthropomorphic traits in order for the process to occur. In the second paper, Wang and Zhu find across five experiments, that haptic sensations of roughness can enhance prosocial behavior, but only among people who are not familiar with the target (Study 2) or among those with low trait levels of empathy (Study 3). In the third paper, Chandler, Reinhard and Schwarz show that consumers refrain from relying on embodied cues when they are aware that they may lack sufficient knowledge needed to form a judgment.

Together, these three papers highlight that the conditions under which embodied cues might influence consumer behavior

are narrower than the current literature might otherwise suggest. People need to know enough about a target for accessible information to be applicable (Hadi and Valenzuela's paper) and to feel capable of making a judgment (Chandler, Reinhard and Schwarz's paper) yet at the same time the information conveyed by the cues cannot be redundant with otherwise accessible information (Wang and Zhu's paper). In the process, they emphasize the importance of connections between psychology and consumer research, that is, explanations of human behavior must not only be computationally and anatomically plausible but also explain behaviors and decisions that matter.

Our discussant, Robert Wyer, will highlight the importance of building temporal connections between research programs conducted in different eras: newer embodied approaches have found evidence supporting novel predictions that challenge some of the core assumptions of older theories of human behavior but at the same time, the empirical findings generated by older theories remain true and must be parsimoniously explained. He will discuss how process models developed in the older semantic priming literature can serve as a useful starting point for the development of embodied approaches. This will transition into an interactive discussion that should appeal not only to researchers in embodiment but also researchers grounded in more traditional approaches to cognitive psychology and consumer behavior.

SESSION FORM

The format of the session will encourage discussion and participation for the audience. Paper presentations will last 20 minutes each and the role of the traditional "discussant" will be different. After the three papers are presented, the "discussant" will limit his remarks about the topic to about 5 minutes before opening up the floor for general discussion. The "discussant" will conclude the session by integrating presentations and discussion.

When Hugs Mean Human: Antecedents and Consequences of Embodied Anthropomorphism

EXTENDED ABSTRACT

It is not uncommon for individuals to physically interact with products in a human-like manner. Children hug their teddy bears. A gambler may kiss a pair of dice, hoping for a lucky roll. One may lovingly stroke the steering wheel of a beloved car. Such examples represent affectionate physical actions towards non-human objects. Although it is often assumed that these actions are consequences of anthropomorphic thought, a growing literature emphasizes the bidirectional relationship between movements and concepts. Across three studies we demonstrate that embodied affiliative cues increase positive feelings toward objects. Importantly, we also demonstrate that these effects only occur when people make the gesture toward a target that is imbued with attributes that imply agency.

Anthropomorphism is the attribution of humanlike properties, characteristics or mental states to nonhuman agents and objects (Guthrie 1993, for a recent review see Epley, Waytz & Caccioppo, 2007). Marketers capitalize on anthropomorphic tendencies by portraying brands as having human traits and personalities (Aaker

Advances in Consumer Research
Volume 39, ©2011

1997). Likewise, consumers treat objects with anthropomorphic features as if they are alive and experience interpersonal emotions in reaction to those interactions (e.g., Schultz, Kleine & Kerman, 1989). Recent research suggests that these tendencies are relevant to consumer choice: the presence of anthropomorphic traits may lead to reduced replacement intentions on behalf of the consumer (Chandler and Schwarz 2010) and consumers feel more intimate with an anthropomorphized brand (Guese & Haelg 2009).

Embodied gestures of affiliation may lead to more positive attitudes towards objects. Experimental research has shown that bodily sensations are closely linked to feelings and thoughts, leading the mere experience of a bodily sensation can have an impact on an individual's thinking or feeling (Barasalou 2008). For example, unobtrusively making a facial expression that resembles a smile can lead people to form more positive evaluations of cartoons (Strack et al. 1988). Likewise, more recent research has also demonstrated that approach movements lead to more favorable (or less unfavorable) evaluations of objects (Labroo & Nielsen 2010).

In the present research, we demonstrate that affiliative gestures may lead to affiliative tendencies, but only if the target of evaluation has features that signal "humanness."

Study 1 provides initial evidence of an embodied anthropomorphism effect. The study was a field study and the design was a 2 (interaction: hug vs. no hug) X 2 (packaging: face vs. no face) between subjects design. Respondents (N=80) were stopped and asked to either examine and hug, or simply examine a product (a cell phone or dryer sheets), before evaluating it. The results produced a significant Face x Hug interaction on purchase intention ("I would buy this product"; $F(1,69) = 3.71$, $p<.05$). Simple effects analysis revealed that the physical interaction (hug) only translated into increased purchase intention for products with an anthropomorphic trait (human face).

Study 2 replicated Study 1 with a different product category (a book with or without a face on the cover), and investigated the role of anthropomorphic tendencies as a potential mediator. To the extent that affiliative gestures increase the accessibility of social concepts, they should also increase the likelihood that ambiguously anthropomorphic objects are treated as "human". The experimental was again a 2 (interaction: hug vs. no hug) X 2 (cover: face vs. no face) between subjects design. a. Results indicated a significant book cover x hug interaction on evaluation ($p< 0.03$) and purchase intention ($p< 0.06$). Further, results support a significant book cover x hug interaction on anthropomorphism ("this book has a mind of it's own") ($p< 0.06$). Anthropomorphic tendencies correlated ($r = 0.42$) with emotional attachment ("I feel connected to this book"). Additional analysis suggests that the relationship between physical interaction and evaluation is mediated by anthropomorphism.

Study 3 (N=87, all females) differentiated the consequences of human-like activity from those of mere bodily approach, as documented by Labroo & Nielsen (2010). The study took the form of a 3(interaction: hug vs. pull vs. hold) X 2 (cover: face vs. no face) design. The product category used was again dryer sheets. We identified significant three-way interactions on product evaluation ($p< 0.07$), purchase intention ($p< 0.02$) and emotional attachment ($p< 0.01$). The effect of hugging on evaluation, purchase intention and emotional attachment was only significant when the fabric softener package exhibited a human face. The direction of the effect for pulling the product was also significant but in the opposite direction (better evaluations and higher purchase intentions when pulling the package with <u>no face</u>). There

was no effect of human-like traits in the package when consumers just held the product.

Our findings expand our understanding of embodiment to suggest that affiliative physical actions will increase the likelihood that an ambiguously anthropomorphic object will be treated in human-like terms. Compatible with this particular gesture, this leads to more positive evaluations and increased purchase intentions. Importantly, embodied cues do not exert such an influence when they are inapplicable to the target of judgment. Thus, our research also introduces a boundary condition for such embodied effects. Future research should study whether anthropomorphic cues always increase positivity would rather depend on the valence of the human-like physical interaction.

I Can Feel It! Haptic Sensations on Prosocial Behaviors

EXTENDED ABSTRACT

The haptic sensation is an important yet the least studied sense in consumer behavior. Current research on haptic cues primarily focuses on the presence versus absence of haptic information (Peck and Childers 2003), without investigating the impact of specific haptic attributes such as texture, while touch is always present. Additionally, the dependent measures are mostly of product evaluation (Krishna and Morrin 2008), rather than actual behaviors. Finally, research on haptic cues is organized around the phenomenon itself rather than according to the processes that govern their use. In five studies we advance our understanding of the haptic sensation by studying the impact of one specific haptic attribute (i.e., rough versus smooth texture) on people's prosocial behaviors.

According to embodied cognitive perspective (Barsalou 2008), mental action is largely grounded in a physical substrate. Thus, sensory data, such as physical sensations and motor movements, is stored together in memory with associated mental concepts or experiences. When sensations are experienced they activate corresponding conceptual experiences. Following this logic, haptic roughness might trigger memories or concepts related to rough time or hardship. Prior research has shown that similar psychological experiences induced through other means enhance empathy (Batson et al. 1996; Banissy and Ward 2007). Thus, if haptic cues of roughness active associations of personal difficulty, people might experience heightened empathy towards the needy others, and subsequently engage in more helping behaviors.

The influence of haptic cues should further be determined by whether people are familiar with the target. People experience more empathy towards familiar others than unfamiliar others (Small and Simonsohn 2008). Thus, when individuals are familiar with the target, the feelings of empathy caused by haptic sensation are likely to have little benefit beyond the already high level of empathy. However, when empathetic concerns are low, additional haptic sensations or roughness are likely to increase helping behavior.

In Study 1, we demonstrate the basic effect of haptic roughness versus smoothness on willingness to help. To manipulate the haptic sensation, we used a moisturizing hand wash in the smooth condition, and a scrub hand wash in the rough condition, under the cover story of product evaluation. The dependent variable was participants' willingness to donate to two fictitious non-profit organizations. Consistent with our hypothesis, those in the rough condition showed higher willingness to donate than those in the smooth condition.

In Study 2, we tested whether haptic cues influenced familiar targets. We again manipulated the haptic sensation by using the two different hand washes. The dependent variable was again willingness to donate, but towards familiar charities (e.g., Aids.org) and unfamiliar charities (i.e., Schizophrenia Foundation) respectively. A 2x2 ANOVA revealed a significant interaction between the haptic sensation and familiarity. Specifically, for the unfamiliar charities, those in the rough condition showed higher willingness to donate than those in the smooth condition. However, for familiar charities, there was no such difference.

In Study 3, we demonstrated that empathy mediates the influence of haptic sensation and familiarity on helping behavior. Participants completed the experiment with a confederate. To induce familiarity, the dyad was asked to self disclose personal information to each other (adapted from Sedikides et al. 1999). Those in the unfamiliar condition did not perform this task. The haptic manipulation was the same as before. The participant then had an opportunity to help the confederate perform a problem-solving task. We measured whether the participant offered help or not. Finally, the participant's situational empathy level was assessed. Replicating Study 2, there was a significant interaction between familiarity and haptic sensation. Specifically, towards an unfamiliar confederate, the participant was more likely to help in the rough (vs. smooth) condition. In contrast, towards a familiar confederate, the participant was equally likely to help regardless of the haptic sensations. Extending this finding, empathy mediates this interaction effect.

In Study 4, we provided further support for the mediating role of empathy by measuring individuals' dispositional empathy level. We found that the interaction effect of familiarity and haptic sensation was only evidence among low-empathizers.

In Study 5, we tested whether our lab findings can be replicated in the field. We created a street fundraising event involving pedestrians as participants. The study had a 2 (haptic sensation) X 2 (familiarity) between subjects design. To manipulate the haptic sensation, we attached either a projection sheet or a piece of sandpaper on a clipboard that a participant had to hold while completing the survey. In the survey, participants were asked to indicate the amount of money they would like to donate to a familiar or unfamiliar charity. Results replicated those observed in Study 2.

Through a series of five experiments, conducted in both lab and field contexts, we find support to our theorizing, such that haptic sensations of roughness can enhance prosocial behavior, but only when the target is unfamiliar. Findings from this research provide important theoretical and practical implications.

When you Can't Judge a Book by its Cover: Metacognitive Inferences about Embodied Cues

EXTENDED ABSTRACT

Perceptual experiences can influence thoughts and feelings in ways predicted by conceptual metaphor theory (for a review, see Landau, Meier and Kiefer 2010). For example, physical weight can influence perceptions of importance (Jostmann, Lakens and Schubert 2009). Researchers often assume that the underlying associative processes exert the strongest influence when people know little about the target (Landau et al. 2010). If so, the impact of perceptual cues on metaphorically related judgments should be *attenuated* when more diagnostic information is available, paralleling observations in other domains (Chen and Chaiken 1999).

However, other research indicates that people refrain from relying on heuristic cues when they are aware that they may lack the knowledge needed to form a judgment (Leyens, Yzerbit, and Schadron 1992). For example, category based stereotyping is higher when people have some individuating information about the target than when they have none (Leyens et al. 1992, see also Croizet and Fiske 2000). From this perspective, perceptual cues may exert *more* influence on metaphorically related judgments when they pertain to a target about which the perceiver has at least some information. We tested this possibility by exposing participants to an incidental perceptual cue and examining the effect of this cue on related perceptual experiences (Study 1) and metaphorically related concepts (Studies 2 and 3) under conditions of high and low information. Across all three studies we find that perceptual cues have no effect when people do not have sufficient information to make a decision.

In Study 1, participants estimated the weight of a CD depicting either light or heavy visual cues. Both CDs were fictitious albums. In the heavy condition the CD cover depicted a picture of weightlifting dumbbells and was titled "With a heavy heart, I say goodbye." In the light condition, the CD cover depicted a picture of a kite floating in the sky and was titled "Float." Crucially, half of the participants were handed the CD to make the rating while the other half had the CD placed in front of them and were instructed to make their estimate without touching the CD. Weight cues influenced participants' judgments when they held the CD, leading people to perceive the CD depicting the heavy image as heavier than the CD depicting the light image. Visual weight cues did not exert an influence when they did not hold the CD.

Study 2 examined whether the influence of perceptual cues on metaphorically related judgments also depended on having sufficient knowledge to form a judgment. Participants were asked to form "impressions of a book." The book was unfamiliar (Eva Hornung's *Dogboy*) and the hardcover copy weighed either 439g or 675g, due to a concealed weight. Participants were asked to examine the book cover before answering questions; half were handed the book face up, displaying the front cover (author and title), whereas the other half were handed the book face down, displaying the back cover with a synopsis and reviews. Participants reported their interest in reading the book, how much they would pay for it and the likelihood that it would be named among the most influential books by The New York Times. The book's weight influenced participants' judgments on all three dependent variables when they saw its informative back cover, but not when they saw its uninformative front cover.

Study 3 replicates this finding using a naturalistic manipulation of whether participants had sufficient knowledge. Participants were presented with a hardcover copy of a potentially familiar book (*The Catcher in the Rye*) that was either of normal weight (404 grams) or included a concealed weight (605 grams). Participants rated its influence on American literature and indicated whether they had read the book. Consistent with our hypothesis, participants who had read *Catcher in the Rye* considered it more influential when holding the heavy rather than light copy. In contrast, participants who had not read it were unaffected by its weight.

Across all three studies, people who knew something about the target – either because they could hold it (Study 1) or received some pertinent information (Study 2) or had read it (Study 3) --*were* influenced by the book's physical weight, whereas those who knew nothing about the book *were not*. This observation has important theoretical implications. First, it extends the notion of *judgeability* from the social (Leyens et al. 1992) to the nonsocial domain. Context effects on judgment require that one forms a judgment to begin with – and having insufficient information may discourage one from doing so. Hence, bodily sensations may only be incorporated into metaphorically related judgments when other information justifies evaluations of the target.

Second, recent embodiment research emphasized purely associative accounts (e.g. Williams, Huang and Bargh 2009; Zhong and Leonardelli 2008) that leave little room for the inferential processes underlying the impact of other subjective experiences on judgment and choice, including bodily feedback (Schwarz and Clore 2007). The present studies challenge this assumption and suggest that metacognitive assessments influence the use and disuse of sensory information in metaphorically related evaluations.

Finally, our findings highlight that additional knowledge does not always protect against the influence of incidental sensory information of merely metaphorical relevance – instead, it may increase one's susceptibility.

Harming, Stealing, Lying, and Cheating: Exploring the Antecedents and Consequences of Unethical Consumption Behavior

Chairs: Rebecca Walker Naylor, The Ohio State University
Peter McGraw, University of Colorado, Boulder

Paper #1: That's Not How I Remember It: Willfully Ignorant Memory for Ethical Product Attribute Information

Rebecca Naylor, The Ohio State University, USA
Julie R. Irwin, The University of Texas at Austin, USA
Kristine Ehrich, University of San Diego, USA

Paper #2: "I Couldn't Help It": The Role of Perceived Personal Control and Social Norms in Unethical Consumer Behavior

Jennifer Jordan, University of Groningen, The Netherlands
Bob Fennis, University of Groningen, The Netherlands

Paper #3: Money in the Present or Time in the Future?: How Switching Focus Makes People Honest

Francesca Gino, Harvard Business School, USA
Cassie Mogilner, University of Pennsylvania, USA

Paper #4: Feeling Moral about Money: How Moral Emotions Influence Consumer Spending Decisions

Hyun Young Park, New York University, USA
Tom Meyvis, New York University, USA

SESSION OVERVIEW

Consumers arguably want to be seen as (and to see themselves) as moral actors. Yet, consumers engage in unethical behaviors, including buying products that harm the environment, stealing, lying, and cheating. The over-arching theme for this session is to explore both the antecedents and consequences of these types of unethical behaviors on the part of consumers.

In the first paper, Naylor, Irwin, and Ehrich propose that willfully ignorant memory plays an important role in why consumers buy products with poor performance on ethical attributes (e.g., products that harm the environment). They show that, in order to protect themselves from emotionally-laden tradeoffs between ethical attributes and other desirable product attributes (e.g., price and quality), consumers misremember negative ethical attribute information at a greater rate than they do positive ethical attribute information. In the second paper, Jordan and Fennis examine a variety of unethical behaviors, including plagiarizing, cheating, stealing, buying stolen goods, and lying. They show that consumers are particularly likely to engage in these behaviors when they feel a lack of personal control and are exposed to information indicating that engaging in these unethical behaviors is the norm. In the third paper, Gino and Mogilner explore how a difference in short-term versus long-term focus influences the decision to behave unethically. They show that priming money leads individuals to focus on the present, thereby increasing the likelihood of cheating on a task, while priming time leads them to focus on the future, thereby decreasing the likelihood of cheating. Thus, the first three papers focus primarily on exploring why consumers engage in unethical behaviors. The fourth paper focuses instead on the consequences of unethical behaviors. Specifically, Park and Meyvis examine the impact of the specific emotions that stem from moral violations on subsequent spending decisions (e.g., donating to charities, spending on the self vs. others, etc.).

In keeping with the conference theme of building connections, each author agrees to link the antecedents of unethical behavior to its consequences (and, in the case of Park and Meyvis, the converse). Moreover, there are several common themes across pairs of papers

in the session in addition to the broader theme of understanding the antecedents and consequences of unethical behaviors. Specifically, both papers 1 and 3 explore the short-term rewards of unethical behavior; participants in paper 1 employ willfully ignorant memory because it allows them to avoid the negative emotions that come with ethical attribute tradeoffs in the short-run, while participants in paper 3 who are primed with money focus on the benefits to ethically questionable behavior in the present, not the potential long-term costs of the behavior. Papers 2 and 3 both suggest ways in which consumers can be encouraged to engage in more ethical behavior, through the use of social norms in paper 2 and by priming time (vs. money) in paper 3. Papers 3 and 4 both contribute to our understanding of the psychological meanings of money, and papers 1 and 4 both address the emotional impact of morally questionable behavior. Presenters will point out these connections during the session. Three of the papers have at least three studies completed. The authors of Paper 2 anticipate having at least one additional study completed by the time the paper would be presented.

We anticipate a wide audience for this session because it will not only contribute to the literature on moral decision making and (un)ethical consumer behavior, but will also have broad appeal to a diverse group of conference attendees, including researchers with an interest in ethical behavior, decision making, memory, social norms, the psychological effects of money, and affect.

That's Not How I Remember It: Willfully Ignorant Memory for Ethical Product Attribute Information

EXTENDED ABSTRACT

Many consumers report that they care about ethical issues and are willing to pay more for ethically produced goods (Trudel and Cotte 2008). However, products with positive ethical attributes (i.e., sustainable products) are, in many product categories, not market leaders (Porges 2007), and products that have poor performance on ethical attributes continue to sell well. For example, despite the damage to the environment from logging old-growth rainforests, consumers continue to buy cabinets, furniture, and other products made from rainforest wood (Rainforest Relief 2011). Further illustrating the problem, although a recent survey by GfK Roper Consulting found that 62% of Americans believe that environmental pollution poses a serious risk (Neff 2010), a recent Mintel study found that only 36% of Americans regularly buy green products (Mintel 2009). Taken together, findings like these indicate that, in the domain of ethically produced goods, there appears to be a gap between consumers' explicitly stated attitudes and their purchasing behavior (Devinney, Auger, and Eckhardt 2010).

Past research has addressed the causes of this gap by asking why consumers might be reluctant to buy sustainable products. Ehrich and Irwin (2005) showed that consumers, particularly those who care about the ethical issue in question, do not seek ethical attribute information at the rate they would have used the information if it were readily available. This willful ignorance is driven by a desire to avoid the negative emotions that stem from discovering that an otherwise desirable product performs poorly on an ethical attribute. Avoiding the information is a self-protection mechanism. Our primary research question expands the notion of willful ignorance: We explore what happens if consumers are not allowed to remain willfully ignorant, that is, when they are not allowed to ignore ethical attributes. The primary purpose of our studies, therefore, is to test whether consumers who know that a product is unethical will engage in subsequent types of self-protection mechanisms to deal with this negative information.

We propose that consumers will engage in what we call *willfully ignorant memory*, incorrectly recalling poor performance on an ethical attribute (i.e., that furniture is made from non-sustainable rainforest wood) at a higher rate than they do positive performance on an ethical attribute (i.e., that furniture is made from sustainable tree farm wood). Because ethical attributes are linked to protected values (Baron and Spranca 1997), particularly for consumers who care deeply about these issues, it is easier to forget that a product performs poorly on an ethical attribute than to have to make difficult and emotion-laden tradeoffs between ethical attributes and other product attributes that the consumer finds desirable. We test our hypotheses across three studies involving hypothetical brands of desks (adapted from the stimuli used by Ehrich and Irwin 2005). The desks differed on three attributes: wood source, quality/workmanship, and price, where wood source is the ethical attribute. All three studies share a similar basic procedure; after being given an opportunity to store the information about the six desks in memory, participants were then asked to recall all of the information they could about the desks (i.e., to retrieve this information from memory) after a distracter task or tasks. In Study 1 we show that consumers are more likely to misremember (either recalling the information incorrectly or failing to recall any information about the attribute) that a desk is made from rainforest wood than that it is made from tree farm wood. Further, this pattern of forgetting is unique to ethical attributes (vs. attributes without ethical implications) and is especially likely to occur for those who care about the ethical issue in question (i.e., protection of the rainforests). Study 2 expands this basic methodology by testing memory at both storage and retrieval; in this study we demonstrate that willfully ignorant memory occurs both when ethical attribute information is stored in memory and when it is retrieved from memory. Finally, in Study 3, we use a mood manipulation immediately before retrieval to demonstrate that a consumer's mood interacts with how much they care about the ethical issue to influence willfully ignorant memory: participants who care a great deal about the ethical issue in question who are in a negative (vs. neutral) mood are more likely to misremember poor (vs. positive) performance on an ethical attribute.

Theoretically, our results show a new and strikingly non-normative reaction to ethical attributes: the people who care the most about the underlying ethical issue are less likely to accurately remember ethical attribute information. These results add to our growing knowledge of how consumers react to ethical attributes and our understanding of why purchases may show a discrepancy between ethical attitudes and behaviors. The malleability of memory protects consumers from having to make difficult decisions and, perhaps, even to persuade themselves that they are more moral decision makers than they actually are. If memories are not accurate, then consumers are not likely to remember that they have not purchased highly ethical items in the past and may not accurately remember the ethical attributes of their current possessions.

"I Couldn't Help It": The Role of Perceived Personal Control and Social Norms in Unethical Consumer Behavior"

EXTENDED ABSTRACT

Recent research (Fennis and Aarts 2010) demonstrates that a lack of personal control, conceptualized as the experience of reduced self-agency or authorship, leads individuals to become more susceptible to various forms of (proximate) social influence. The current investigation extends this research into to the domain of moral judgment and behavior by examining how consumers lacking personal control are influenced by social norms in their environment and how this influence affects their tendency to engage in (un)ethical judgment and behavior. We predict that a lack of perceived control will lead to unethical behavior, but not unconditionally. Instead, we argue that impaired perceived control promotes unethical behavior only when such unethical behavior is considered a descriptive norm in the consumer's environment (i.e., the behavior is perceived to be supported by a majority of like-minded consumers). Paradoxically, we also propose that experiencing impaired personal control does not produce a reduction in unethical behavior when supported by ethical descriptive norms. This is because of the proposed mechanism of the control to unethical behavior relationship: social responsibility. As others have demonstrated (e.g., Festinger 1956; Cialdini 2001), individuals are most likely to look to their social environment for cues on how to think and act when the appropriate behavior is ambiguous (ethical situations are normally ones where the correct behavior is ambiguous, Jordan 2009). First, we propose that consumers who lack perceived control are more likely to look to the social world for cues on how to think and act (Fennis and Aarts 2010), and that such an outward search reduces their feelings of self-responsibility for the resulting behavior when they can find social norms that support such behavior. And second, we propose that such a search will only affect an increased engagement in unethical behavior (but not ethical behavior) because it provides a license to act immorally (consumers are more likely to engage in immoral behavior if they do not feel personally responsible for it, Jones 1991); consumers need no license to engage in moral behavior. Hence, there appears to be a clear asymmetry in the impact of social contexts on unethical behavior. In sum, we propose that perceived personal control will be the driving force behind the impact of normative social cues on (un)ethical consumer judgment and behavior.

Using a 2 (perceived personal control: low, high) x 3 (immoral social norm, moral social norm, no norm) between-participants design, we examine the personal control to unethical behavior relationship in a context of immoral versus moral social norms communicated in a series of target behaviors. Participants were sixty students at a university in The Netherlands. They believed that they were participating in two separate studies: Study 1 examined personal situations and Study 2 examined the types of activities that students participated in. We manipulated the experience of personal control by adapting a procedure previously developed by Whitson and Galinsky (2008), which first asked participants to recall a situation where they either *were in complete control* or *completely lacked control*. Then, in "Study 2," we asked them to report how much they planned to engage in a variety of activities in the next six months (1 = *not at all*; 7 = *definitely*). Five of these activities were unethical in nature (plagiarize, cheat, steal small items, buy an item you know is stolen, and lie to get out of an obligation) and five were ethically-neutral (go on a foreign holiday, dine at a new restaurant, write a hand-written letter, attend a concert, and make an unusual recipe). Both the unethical and neutral activities were selected because of their mundane, albeit not quotidian nature. We also told them that the computer allowed them to see other people's responses in real-time. Thus, to manipulate social norms, we manipulated whether a majority of their fellow participants reported engaging or not engaging in these behaviors via a pie chart for each target behavior. Participants in the *no norm* condition did not see this information.

Consistent with predictions, we found that for the unethical behaviors, perceived personal control and social norms interacted, $F(2, 54) = 5.06$, $p = .010$, such that a lack of personal control affected unethical behavior - but only when the individual received information that such unethical behavior was normative. Specifically, in comparison to those primed with a sense of personal control, individuals primed with a lack of personal control were more likely to engage in unethical behavior if they were exposed to the norm that a high number of like-others engaged in the behavior, $t(54) = 3.01$, $p = .002$. Individuals were not more (or less) likely to engage in these behaviors when exposed to moral norms of non-engagement, $t(54) = 0.936$, $p = .35$, nor when normative information was presented, $t(54) = -1.20$, $p = .23$. In addition, there was a marginal main effect of control, $F(1,54) = 3.02$, $p = .088$, such that lacking perceived control (M = 2.52, SD = 0.80) led to slightly more engagement in unethical behavior than did possessing perceived control (M = 2.14, SD = 0.86). However, there was no main effect of social norms, $F(2, 54) = .07$, $p = .93$. Also in line with our reasoning, perceived control and social norms did not interact to affect neutral behaviors, $F(2, 54) = .839$, $p = .45$. Although there was a main effect of social norms, $F(2, 54) = 4.79$, $p = .01$, such that social norms of engagement did increase people's reported participation in these neutral behaviors (M = 4.73, SD = 1.17), relative to social norms of non-engagement (M = 3.76, SD = 1.22), or the condition where no information on social norms was provided (M = 3.95, SD = 1.08).

From cheating to stealing, unethical behavior is problematic for suppliers, such as retail outlets, web-shops, manufacturers, and (commercial and non-commercial) service providers. This investigation demonstrates that one such influence on unethical behavior is a lack of personal control paired with immoral social norms. Current research is examining the proposed mechanism of this relationship, perceived responsibility.

Money in the Present or Time in the Future? How Switching Focus Makes People Honest

EXTENDED ABSTRACT

The accounting scandals and the collapse of billion-dollar companies at the beginning of the 21st century have forever changed the business landscape. These cases of corporate corruption add to a long list of instances of unethical behavior within organizations across a variety of settings (e.g., Frank et al., 2003): employees violate company rules, workers sabotage their peers, consumers shoplift, students cheat on exams, citizens evade taxes, and managers overstate performance to shareholders. Such unethical behaviors are costly to organizations and economic systems more broadly. Dishonest behavior is not limited to such prominent examples of one person or organization causing harm to many individuals. Although less well publicized, the small transgressions of large numbers of people have just as large an impact on our daily lives. For instance, an estimated $16 billion is losses to the US retail industry are due to the purchase, use, and then return of worn clothing (Speights & Hilinski, 2005). These losses are not caused by the behavior of just a few people regularly revolving their entire wardrobes, but by that of many individuals who are returning just one shirt or sweater.

In fact, an increasing amount of empirical evidence in social psychology, as well as in the marketing and organizational behavior literatures demonstrates that dishonesty often results not from the actions of a few people who cheat a lot, but from the actions of a lot of people who cheat a little (Mazar, Amir, & Ariely, 2008; Gino, Ayal, & Ariely, 2009). When given the opportunity to act dishonestly, many individuals do cross ethical boundaries, if only "by a little bit," rather than to the maximum extent (Ayal & Gino, 2011; Gino et al., 2009; Mazar et al., 2008).

Unethical behavior, in its various forms, is often tempting because it offers short-term benefits (i.e., monetary rewards), but it is also likely to harm an individuals' moral self-concept and to engender long-term costs (e.g., tainted reputation or lower social acceptance). For instance, a salesperson who cares about morality may be tempted to lie to a consumer interested in purchasing a product because these behaviors are associated with higher financial rewards. These short-term benefits, however, may risk long-term harm to her reputation and trustworthiness, to established relationships, and to long-term profitability. Thus, the decision to behave unethically commonly requires people to weigh two opposing forces: the desire to maximize self-interest and the desire to maintain a positive moral self-image and future relationships. To resolve the internal conflict between the short- and long-term benefits of dishonest acts, individuals must exert self-control (Mead, Baumeister, Gino, Schweitzer, & Ariely, 2009). That is, self-control is the psychological capacity that enables people to enact behaviors that are consistent with their long-term goals (e.g., of being an ethical person) and refrain from engaging in behaviors that are driven by short-term, selfish motives.

In this paper, we explore how this difference in short-term versus long-term focus influences the decision to behave unethically. We suggest that priming money leads individual to focus on the present, while priming time leads them to focus on the future. Because of this shift in focus from present to the future, priming individuals with time rather than money can encourage ethical behavior.

We find evidence consistent with these predictions in three studies. In a first study, participants engaged in two-unrelated tasks. They first completed a scrambled-words task that exposed them to time-related, money-related, or neutral words (Mogilner & Aaker, 2009). In particular, participants received a list of word sets, each of which contained four words, and they were instructed to use three of the words in each set to create a sentence. Participants had three minutes to create as many sentences as possible. Upon completion of this first task, participants completed an ostensibly unrelated task: a problem-solving task under time pressure. Participants had five minutes to find the correct solution to various math problems. We gave participants the opportunity to cheat on this task by over-reporting their performance and thus earn undeserved money. The results of the study show that compared to the control condition (i.e., neutral prime), participants in the money-prime conditions were *more* likely to cheat by over-reporting performance while participants in the time-prime conditions were *less* likely to cheat.

We replicated the same findings in a second study that employed only one between subjects manipulation with two conditions: money prime versus time prime. In this second study, we used the same manipulation as in study 1 but a different task to measure our main dependent variable. The new task was a computer-based mental-arithmetic task in which participants had to calculate the answers to 20 different problems, presented individually (adapted from von Hippel, Lakin, & Shakarchi, 2005). The experimenter informed participants that the computer had a programming glitch: As they were working on each problem, the correct answer would appear on the screen unless they stopped it from being displayed by pressing the space bar right after the problem appeared. The experimenter also informed participants that although no one would be able to tell whether they had pressed the space bar or not, they should try to solve the problems on their own (thus being honest). In actuality, this was a feature of the program and not a glitch, and the number of space-bar presses was recorded. We used the number of times participants did not press the space bar to prevent the answer from appearing as our measure of cheating. The results of this second study showed that participants cheated more frequently in the money-prime condition as compared to the time-prime condition.

Finally, we conducted a third study in which we examined the potential psychological mechanism explaining the result observed in our first two studies. The findings of this third study demonstrated that time primes, compared to money primes, discourage unethical behavior since they trigger a future rather than a present focus.

Taken together, our findings offer a potentially powerful tool to discourage dishonesty in organizations and society more broadly: inducing people to switch focus from the present to the future can encourage ethical behavior.

Feeling Moral about Money: How Moral Emotions Influence Consumer Spending Decisions

EXTENDED ABSTRACT

Much of the money we spend is money we have earned or received in some legitimate fashion. However, in some instances, we may receive money that does not make us feel all that good. Even in the absence of any illegal activity, we may feel somewhat guilty about money (e.g., when we feel we did not deserve to be paid that much) or feel angry about money (e.g., when we feel we should have been paid more than what we received). This research examines how moral emotions such as guilt and anger may change how we spend the money associated with these emotions. As such, we extend prior research that has shown that the valence of emotions attached to money can influence consumer choice (Levav and McGraw 2009) by identifying the unique consequences of different types of negative moral emotions.

We examine two groups of moral emotions: a triad of "self-focused" emotions that includes guilt, shame and embarrassment, and a triad of "other-focused" emotions that includes contempt, anger, and disgust. We examine the effect of these emotions on various spending categories including spending on self vs. others, donations to charity, savings, hedonic vs. utilitarian products, vices vs. virtues, and necessities vs. luxuries. According to the prior research on moral emotions and appraisal tendency, self-focused emotions are experienced when the *self* is responsible, whereas other-focused emotions are experienced when the *other* is responsible in a controllable situation (Tangney, Stuewig, and Mashek 2007; Lerner and Keltner, 2000). While self-focused emotions lead to behaviors that try to repair the negative consequence caused by the self, other-focused emotions result in the blaming of others and punitive behaviors. Based on these findings, we hypothesize that when people earn tainted money by committing moral violations, they will be more likely to engage in moral repair processes such as spending more on others than on themselves, and donating more to charity than those who earn untainted money. On the other hand, when people receive an unfair sum of money due to another's moral infringement, they will engage in punitive processes such as spending less on others than on themselves and donating less to charity.

We also hypothesize that emotions have differential effects on spending decisions depending on whether they are moral or non-moral. Prior research suggests that guilt leads to utilitarian or virtu-

ous choice over hedonic or vicious choice to help prevent anticipated guilt or launder experienced guilt (Kahn, Dhar, and Wertenbroch, 2005). However, these findings examine non-moral guilt arising from self-control failures. We expect that guilt, shame, and embarrassment resulting from moral transgressions would not be laundered through virtuous or utilitarian spending decisions that are related to the self alone, but would be laundered only through decisions relating to the others such as donations to charity. However, we expect that these moral emotions would lead to hedonic avoidance (similar to non-moral guilt) because hedonic products exacerbate these negative moral emotions.

Finally, we confirm that moral emotions influence spending decisions only when they are associated with the money being spent and not when they are associated only with the situation in which the money was received. In line with the Emotional Accounting literature, we expect that money is labeled by moral feelings, and the moral emotion label determines how the money is spent.

In a first scenario-based study, participants who obtained a partial refund by lying about damage to the product prior to purchase felt more guilt, shame and embarrassment about the refund, and spent it more on others, donated more to charity, spent less on themselves, and spent less on hedonic products than those who received a partial refund under legitimate terms. On the other hand, participants who received a partial refund though they were entitled to a full refund felt more anger, contempt and disgust about the refund, and spent the refund less on others, donated less to charities, and spent more on themselves than those who obtained a legitimate partial refund. In a second scenario study, we observe that shame, embarrassment and guilt has a greater impact on people's spending decisions (spending on self vs. other, charitable donations, hedonic purchases) when those feelings result from a moral violation than when they result from a failure to exert self-control. Furthermore, in a third scenario study, we demonstrate that these moral feelings affect spending decisions only when they are associated with the money being spent, not when people feel the same moral emotions for a different reason.

The results of the scenario studies were replicated in studies with actual money. In Study 4, one group of participants received money as a reward for their participation in the Implicit Attitude Test that tested their prejudice against disabled people, whereas another group of participants were promised to receive the money when they faced an unwanted truth, that is, when their test results showed that they had a strong prejudice against the disabled. Compared to those who received the money as a reward for their participation, those who received money because they held a strong prejudice against the disabled experienced a greater level of self-focused emotions, and engaged in the moral-repair spending decisions as in the scenario studies. However, this effect disappeared when the participants received a negative test result, but were given the money as a reward for their participation. In Study 5, participants who received an unfair sum of money in a Dictator Game felt a greater level of anger, contempt, and disgust, which led to less spending on others vs. themselves, and less charitable donations. Again, this effect disappeared when participants received the money as a reward for their participation although they were treated unfairly during the game.

These results support our hypotheses that emotions have different influences on consumer spending decisions depending on (1) whether their source is related to moral transgressions or not, (2) whether the moral violation was committed by the self or by another, and (3) whether moral emotions are felt about the money or about the situation.

REFERENCES:

Baron, Jonathan and Mark Spranca (1997), "Protected Values," *Organizational Behavior and Human Decision Processes*, 70 (April), 1-16.

Ehrich, Kristine R. and Julie R. Irwin, (2005), "Willful Ignorance in the Request for Product Attribute Information," *Journal of Marketing Research*, 42 (August) 266-77.

Gino, F., Ayal, S., & Ariely, D. (2009), "Contagion and Differentiation in Unethical Behavior: The Effect of One Bad Apple on the Barrel," *Psychological Science*, 20(3), 393-398..

Lerner, J. S., & Keltner, D. (2000), "Beyond Valence: Toward a Model of Emotion-specific Influences on Judgment and Choice," *Cognition and Emotion,* 14(4), 473-493.

Levav, J. and McGraw, P. (2009), "Emotional Accounting: How Feelings about Money Influence Consumer Choice," *Journal of Marketing Research,* 46 (February), 66-80.

Mazar, N., Amir, O., & Ariely, D. (2008), "The dishonesty of Honest People: A Theory of Self-Concept Maintenance," *Journal of Marketing Research*, 45, 633–644.

Mogilner, C., & Aaker, J. (2009), "'The Time vs. money Effect': Shifting Product Attitudes and Decisions through Personal Connection," *Journal of Consumer Research*, 36, 277-291.

Tangney, J. P., Stuewig, J., & Mashek, D. J. (2007), "*Moral Emotions and Moral Behavior,*" *Annual Review of Psychology*, 58, 345-372.

Antecedents, Consequences, and Variants of Indecisiveness

Chairs: Gulden Ulkumen, University of Southern California, USA
Selin Malkoc, Washington University in St. Louis, USA

Paper #1: The Effect of Category Width and Comparison Orientation on Choice Conflict
> Gulden Ulkumen, University of Southern California, USA
> Selin Malkoc, Washington University in St. Louis, USA

Paper #2: Negative Not Positive Emotion Increases Variety-Seeking among Indecisive Consumers
> Hyewook Jeong, UCLA, USA
> Aimee Drolet, UCLA, USA

Paper #3: Three Faces of Indecisiveness
> Craig Fox, UCLA, USA
> Emily Barkley-Levenson, UCLA, USA

SESSION OVERVIEW

A fundamental question in consumer research is: Why do consumers often struggle to make decisions? This session takes a fresh look at the antecedents, consequences, and variants of indecisive behavior.

The first paper, by Ulkumen and Malkoc, examines situational determinants of choice conflict, as measured by response latency, as well as by self-reported choice difficulty and confidence. In order to form preferences over options, a decision maker must first distinguish among them. In this paper the authors show that a contextual manipulation designed to make the options appear more similar leads to greater difficulty making a decision. Further, the authors find that exposure to broad (vs. narrow) categories leads to greater sensitivity to an instruction to focus on similarities or differences when making a subsequent choice. In particular, participants primed to categorize broadly have greater difficulty making decisions when prompted to focus on similarities among options than when prompted to focus on differences. There is no such effect among participants primed to categorize narrowly. Taken together this research suggests that an important cause of indecision is difficulty distinguishing among options, which is strongly affected by the structure of previously encountered categories.

The second paper, by Jeong and Drolet, examines how indecisive consumers cope with their difficulty making a choice. They find that participants who are chronically indecisive tend to seek more variety. They find a similar effect among consumers who are indecisive due to situational factors (an increased number of choice options. Indecisive consumers seek more variety in order to cope with the negative emotions they experience when choosing. They show that negative emotion further increases variety-seeking among indecisive consumers. These findings provide a striking counterpoint to previous research showing that positive emotions lead to greater variety seeking. The increasing effect of positive emotion on variety-seeking does not hold for indecisive consumers who seek variety for different reasons (i.e., to cope with negative emotion) than decisive consumers.

The third paper by Fox, Barkley-Levenson, and Wieland examines the multi-dimensional character of chronic indecisiveness. In particular, they find that traditional measures of indecisiveness reflect a preference to avoid making tradeoffs or consider opportunity costs when choosing. This can give rise to impulsive behaviors for items that are considered one-at-a-time, or decision conflict when items are considered simultaneously. Moreover, these authors find that this common form of decision difficulty is one of three variants of chronic indecisiveness. The other two are a tendency to seek exhaustive information in the pursuit of the optimal choice, and a

tendency to be unprepared when the decision moment arrives to procrastination or poor organization.

Taken together, these three papers provide important new insights into the nature of indecisiveness. They suggest that there are distinct reasons why different kinds of consumers (e.g., neurotic/impulsive indecisives) may have difficulty making decisions (e.g., they have a hard time distinguishing among options and worry about making a bad decision), and they may pursue distinct coping strategies (e.g., seeking variety to avoid experiencing these negative emotions). Thus, in order to predict various manifestations of indecisive behavior, one must take into account: (1) the consumer's chronic tendencies toward different variants of indecisiveness; (2) the cognitive and motivational context of the choice elicitation; and (3) the affective consequences of various coping strategies available to consumers.

Audience. We expect this session to draw a large and diverse audience including researchers interested the general areas of decision-making and choice and researchers who are interested in the specific areas of choice difficulty, conflict and indecisiveness.

Strengths. All three papers in the session are in advanced stages; they are either under review or close to being submitted for review. They investigate a related phenomenon (indecisiveness) using a variety of different empirical approaches.

Fit and contribution. All three papers in this session deal with indecisiveness and choice conflict. Collectively they address the interaction of dispositions and situations in determining the conflict that consumers experience while choosing, and ways in which they cope with this conflict.

Session format. We will have three papers, with 15 minutes of presentation time each plus 5 minutes of Q & A time allocated to each paper. This will ensure that we have 15 minutes of discussion at the end of the session. Our discussant, Eric Johnson is a leading authority in consumer choice.

The Effect of Category Width and Comparison Orientation on Choice Conflict

EXTENDED ABSTRACT

In this research, we demonstrate the effects of categorization on decision conflict. Specifically, we show that being exposed to broad or narrow categorizations in a previous, unrelated task influences the conflict consumers experience in a subsequent choice task.

Previous research shows that various aspects of external categories can influence important decision outcomes in the same decision context, such as choice, decision difficulty and decision time. One aspect of categorization that has been shown to influence information processing is category width (CW), (Ülkümen, Chakravarti, and Morwitz 2010). Incidental exposure to narrow versus broad categorizations instigates a more multidimensional processing orientation in subsequent, unrelated decisions. In contrast, participants exposed to broad categories base their attitudes on fewer pieces of salient information, and therefore become more susceptible to context effects.

In this paper, we extend previous research by examining the effects of CW on choice conflict. When choosing between two products, consumers feel more conflicted to the extent that they focus on the similarities between them. If consumers previously exposed to broad categorizations adopt the comparison orientation made salient by the environment, then they should focus on *either* similarities *or* differences between products. In contrast, if consumers previously exposed to narrow categorizations employ both salient and non-salient orientations, then we would expect them to consider *both* similarities *and* differences. Thus, we hypothesize that broad categorizers will take a longer time to decide, experience more choice conflict, and feel less confident about their choice when they are primed with similarities than differences. In contrast, for narrow categorizers, choice time, conflict and confidence are should not be influenced by comparison orientation. We test our predictions in four lab studies.

EMPIRICAL STUDIES

Study 1 had a 2 (CW: broad, narrow) x 2 (Focus: similarity, difference) between subjects design. Participants first completed the CW manipulation, where they responded to questions about themselves that differ in the number of response categories. For some participants, the response options constituted many, narrow categories (narrow condition), while for others, the response options comprised a few, broad categories (broad condition). Next, participants were primed with a comparison orientation by listing either similarities or differences between a pair of pictures (Markman and Gentner 1996). Participants then viewed pictures of two wristwatches and made a choice between them. Response time was recorded unobtrusively. The results suggest that in the Broad CW condition, participants took longer to make a choice when they focused on the similarities as opposed to the differences between the two watches. In contrast, in the Narrow CW condition, the focus manipulation did not influence participants' choice time.

The aim of study 2 was to examine whether the difference in choice time observed in the previous study is due to experienced conflict. Participants first completed the same CW manipulation as in study 1. Next, they were shown pictures of two wristwatches, and they were intruded to list either their similarities or differences, and to make a choice between them. We find that the conflict experienced during choice, and the decision confidence were influenced not only by the comparison orientation, but also by the width of previously encountered categories. In the Broad CW condition, participants took longer to choose, were less confident in their decision, and felt more conflicted when they focused on the similarities between two watches, than when they focused on their differences. However, these variables were not influenced by the focus manipulation in the Narrow CW condition. Moreover, conflict index mediated the interactive effect of similarity and CW on confidence.

In study 3 participants completed a different manipulation of CW (Shopping Task, Ülkümen et al 2010). After making a choice between several backpacks, participants were told their selection was out of stock and were offered an alternative backpack, which was either objectively similar to or different from their selection. We measured participants' attitudes toward the new backpack, and their consideration of similarities and/or differences while choosing. We find that the focus manipulation influenced attitudes only in the Broad CW condition, such that participants liked the new offering more when they focused on its similarity to the original backpack, than when they focused on its difference. Moreover, in the Broad CW condition participants considered relatively more differences (similarities) when they were presented with the different (similar) backpack. The focus manipulation did not influence participants' consideration of similarities and differences in the Narrow CW condition.

Participants first completed the same CW manipulation as in the first two studies. Next, they were shown a furniture catalog and told to make a choice between two target chairs. We manipulated similarity perceptions by varying the context. Viewing the two chairs in the context of other similar (different) chairs should direct participants' attention to the differences (similarities) between the two target chairs. Participants reported their decision confidence and conflict, willingness to pay for the two chairs, and their relative consideration of similarities and differences. The results on decision conflict and confidence replicated results from previous studies. Participants considered differences (similarities) more when the context primed them to focus on differences (similarities), but only in the Broad CW condition. We also found that in the Broad CW condition, the price difference between the two chairs was larger in the difference (vs. similarity) focus condition. As expected, the focus manipulation did not influence the price difference in the Narrow CW condition.

DISCUSSION

In four studies we show that the experienced choice conflict is significantly influenced not only by comparison orientation, but also by the width of categories consumers are exposed to prior to choice. Using multiple manipulations of similarity orientation, we demonstrate that consumers exposed to broad categorizations experience more choice conflict when a similarity (vs. difference) orientation is made salient. In contrast, consumers exposed to narrow categorizers consider both similarities and differences between products regardless of the salient comparison orientation.

Negative Not Positive Emotion Increases Variety-Seeking among Indecisive Consumers

EXTENDED ABSTRACT

Past research has generally found an increasing effect of positive emotion on consumers' tendency to variety-seek. The present research finds that this relationship between positive emotion and variety-seeking does not hold for indecisive consumers. Among these consumers, the opposite is true; negative emotion increases indecisive consumers' tendency to choose mixed assortments of products. The findings of this research imply that current views on when and why consumers seek variety should be revisited and revised accordingly.

One way indecisive consumers might cope with the negative emotions associate with choice is by avoiding choosing one option, which might be the "wrong" option is by choosing a mix of options. Ironically, varied choice-making involves more choice-making, thereby prolonging the negative emotion indecisive consumers seek to avoid.

The assumption that indecisive consumers are more likely to use a variety-seeking strategy and do so to cope with the negative emotions associated with choice has not heretofore been tested. To do so, we conducted three pilot experiments. Pilot 1 found that more indecisive consumers have a higher preference for variety packs compared to less indecisive consumers. In Pilot 2, consumers were asked to make a series of choices over time. Results show that indecisive consumers were more likely to change their choices versus repeat them. In summary, these two pilot experiments support the supposition that indecisive versus decisive consumers are more likely to vary their choice making. Pilot 3 shows that indecisive consumers seek variety to cope with the negative emotions associated with choice and do so successfully. In this experiment, indecisiveness was again associated with increased variety-seeking. Indecisive consumers who chose a mixture of options felt less negative emotion post-choice. Interestingly, among decisive consumers, variety-seeking was not associated with increased positive emotion post-choice.

The above findings suggest that 1) indecisive consumers variety-seek for different reasons than decisive consumers and 2) causes of increased variety-seeking among decisive consumers, such as positive emotion, might not cause increased variety-seeking among indecisive consumers. Indeed, three experiments demonstrate that positive emotion decreases indecisive consumers' increased tendency to seek variety whereas negative emotion further increases this tendency. These experiments test the effect of positive versus negative (vs. neutral) emotion on indecisive consumers whereby indecisiveness is due to disposition (i.e. chronic indecisiveness) or due to situation; situational indecisiveness is created by "over-loading" consumers by providing them with too many choice options.

The present research explains these results by suggesting that indecisive consumers, having learned that variety-seeking is a successful strategy for coping with the negative emotions they associate with choice, generalize this lesson. They then use the strategy of variety-seeking to cope with negative emotion caused by other conditions other than indecision.

The findings of the present research imply that current views on when and why consumers seek variety should be revisited and revised accordingly.

Three Faces of Indecisiveness

EXTENDED ABSTRACT

What are the causes and consequences of indecisive behavior? To answer these questions it is helpful to understand the dimensions of chronic indecision. We recruited several samples totaling more than two thousand adult participants and asked them to rate the frequency with which they exhibit a number of different behaviors. In addition we asked participants to complete a number of related individual difference scales. Finally, we asked participants to make a number of hypothetical choices as well as consumer choices with incentive-compatible consequences.

Factor analysis of our decision behavior inventory revealed three major dimensions of indecisiveness: (1) Neurotic/Impulsive indecisiveness (e.g., "When I'm hungry I stand in front of the refrigerator for a while trying to figure out what I want"; "I try on more than one outfit in the morning before I pick one I like"); (2) Perfectionistic/Compulsive indecisiveness (e.g., "When I make a big electronics purchase I spend days or weeks thoroughly researching the options before choosing"; "I like to sleep on things before making a big decision"); (3) Unprepared indecisiveness (e.g., "When I receive an invitation for a future event such as a party or wedding, I respond yes or no right away" [reverse scored]; "I know what movie or movies I want to rent before I go to the store or online"[reverse scored]).

Type 1 behaviors correlate most strongly with traditional measures of indecisiveness (notably, Frost & Shows, 1993 and the decisiveness subscale of Need for Cognitive Closure, Webster & Kruglanski, 1994). Type 1 indecisiveness also correlates highly with several subscales of the Melbourne Decision Making Questionnaire (MDMQ, Mann et al., 1997) including hypervigilance, procrastination, and buck-passing. It is is highly correlated with the decision difficulty subscale of the maximizing scale (Nenkov et al., 2008). Type 1 behavior is positively correlated with avoidant indecisiveness ("I try to put off making decisions") and aversive indecisiveness ("I become anxious when making a decision") (Spunt et al. 2009); however, when both are included in a multiple regression, only aversive indecisiveness significantly predicts type 1. Surprisingly, type I indecisiveness is *positively* correlated with urgency measures of impulsivity (Whiteside & Lyman, 2001; e.g. "I have trouble controlling my impulses"), and these individuals also report impulsive shopping behaviors (e.g., ""When I go shopping for food I end up buying things I hadn't planned to buy because they look good"). In sum, type 1 indecisive individuals dislike making decisions and are

distressed by them, and thus will avoid deciding by procrastinating or deferring to others, and they avoid making tradeoffs. The impulsive behaviors exhibited by such consumers suggests that they do not tend to consider the opportunity costs of their choices.

Type 2 indecisiveness is strongly associated with the decision difficulty subscale of the maximizing scale. However, it is not correlated with any measures that reflect distress or anxiety during decision-making, such as the MDMQ hypervigilance subscale or the aversive subscale of Frost & Shows (1993). Instead, type 2 indecision exhibits a strong positive correlation with the MDMQ vigilance subscale, which captures the tendency to collect information and evaluate alternatives carefully before making a choice. Similarly, this factor is *negatively* correlated with one form of impulsivity— lack of premeditation (Whiteside & Lyman, 2001). Furthermore, type 2 indecisiveness is positively correlated with the high standards subscale of the maximizing scale, suggesting that type 2 indecisives seek exhaustive information due to a desire to select the best possible option. In sum, type 2 individuals appear indecisive because they take a great deal of time to think and research before deciding, but the decision process itself does not necessarily distress them.

Type 3 indecisiveness is not associated with having difficulty making decisions (no significant correlations with the decision difficulty subscale of maximizing or with the hypervigilance subscale of MDMQ). This factor is, however, associated with the nonplanning subscale of the Barratt Impulsivity Scale (Patton et al., 1995), suggesting that individuals high in this dimension to not plan ahead. Likewise, type 4 indecisiveness correlates strongly with the avoidant subscale of the Frost & Shows (1993), and is negatively correlated with the MDMQ vigilance scale. Overall, individuals high in type 3 indecisiveness seem to be disorganized but not distressed decision-makers, often unprepared when the decision moment arrives. Although they delay the decision-making process, type 3 indecisives do not necessarily experience difficulty when they making choices.

Subsequent studies revealed several behavioral regularities that distinguish different forms of indecisiveness. Individuals higher in Type 1 (neurotic/impulsive) indecisiveness are more susceptible to both attraction and compromise effects in choices among various consumer products, suggesting greater reliance on reason-based choice heuristics to avoid making difficult tradeoffs. In a task in which participants were presented with pairs of products available on Amazon. com, Type 1 indecisives read fewer pairs of user reviews before indicating their preferred option; they had a greater tendency to reverse their initial decisions in a task in which they chose between pairs of items that they would hypothetically save from a sinking ship. In addition they reported a greater number of items in their Amazon. com shopping carts that they had not yet purchased. All of these tendencies are consistent with the "impulsive" characterization of this dimension. Individuals higher in Type 2 (perfectionistic/compulsive) indecisiveness consumed more information before making a decision between pairs of Amazon.com products, and reported a greater number of items on their Amazon wish list. These tendencies are consistent with the notion of a compulsive search for ideal options, even if they cannot immediately be afforded (and thus remain on the wish list). Individuals high in Type 3 (unprepared) indecisiveness reported waiting longer before getting engaged to be married. Moreover, after controlling for age, gender, and education, they earn substantially less money. This is consistent with the notion that the capacity to plan ahead for decisions is associated with positive life outcomes.

The present research suggests that the dominant view of indecisiveness as a unidimensional construct must be revised, and that distinct clusters of behavior that may be deemed "indecisive" have distinct antecedents and consequences.

Connecting the Physical, Conceptual, and Emotional:
Understanding Multi-sensory Experiences in Embodied Cognition

Chairs: Anastasiya Pocheptsova, University of Maryland, USA
Dilip Soman, University of Toronto, Canada

Paper #1: Brighten Up: Emotional Expressions and Perception of Color Brightness

Hyunjin Song, Yale University, USA
Andrew Vonash, Florida State University, USA
Brian Meier, Gettysburg College, USA
John Bargh, Yale University, USA

Paper #2: Does a Heavy Heart Create a Heavy Body? The Connection between Conceptual, Physical and Emotional Heaviness

Xue Zheng, National University of Singapore, Singapore
Jayanth Narayan, National University of Singapore, Singapore
Dilip Soman, University of Toronto, Canada

Paper #3: Lethargic Mind: How Perceived Fat Consumption Affects Mind's Agility

Anastasiya Pocheptsova, University of Maryland, USA
Aparna Labroo, University of Toronto, Canada

Paper #4: My Hands Are Tied – My Lips Are Sealed: Prevented Embodiment Limits Communicational Cooperativeness

Ann Kronrod, MIT, USA
Joshua Ackerman, MIT, USA

SESSION OVERVIEW

Research on embodied cognition proposes an intriguing counterintuitive notion that bodily states can cause cognitive states (Barsalou 2008). This is happening because bodily sensations are interlinked with a number of perceptual, motor and introspective states that have been acquired through experience (Barsalou 2008, Niedenthal, 2007). Therefore, an activation of such bodily states can have an impact on one's thinking and vice versa. For example, feeling of physical warmth has been shown to impact one's perception of interpersonal warmth (Williams and Bargh, 2008) and sensation of effort affects one's judgment of goal relevance (Labroo and Kim 2009).

In this session, we build upon the existing literature on embodied cognition in two ways. First, the papers in the session strive to build a bridge between embodied cognition literature and consumer research by proposing novel domains where bidirectional link between body and mind would affect consumer behavior. For example, Song and co-authors show how emotional expressions affect consumers' perception of the brightness of the products and suggest ways for marketers to use such metaphorical connection in strategic ways. Further, Zheng and colleagues show that negative affect can impact's one perception of fullness during food consumption and therefore leads consumers to eat less.

Second, more importantly, the session pushes the boundaries of embodied cognition research by examining multi-sensory experiences underlying embodiment effects. A number of papers in the session strive to integrate several modalities (including cognitive, motivational and affective processes) and therefore going beyond just reversing the link between cognition and bodily sensations shown in previous literature. For example, Pocheptsova and Labroo examine the relationship between bodily sensations, introspection and perception in the domain of cognitive performance. They show that consuming fat-rich food, remembering past consumption as well as perceiving the food to have high fat-content are interlinked

with a feeling of mental sluggishness. In similar vein, Zheng and colleagues, show that negative emotion, physical fullness and concept of heaviness are interlinked in cognition and activation of one of these modalities leads to activation of another. Finally, Kronrod and Ackerman conclude the session by showing how preventing one from embodiment of cognitions can negatively affect behavior and communication. This approach to studying embodied cognition highlights the importance of multiple modalities in cognition.

Taken together the papers in this session provide a better understanding of how multiple modalities may combine to result in embodiment effects. The papers are also closely tied together, paper 1 links affect to perception showing that smiling faces are perceived as brighter, paper 2 links affect to consumption showing that that negative feelings can make a person feel heavy, paper 3 links consumption to cognition showing that heaviness from fat but not protein consumption can result in mental exhaustion, and paper 4 links gesture to speech showing that tying hands can result in tongue tied. In introductory comments, the session chair will highlight the different modalities the papers span, and session participants will attempt to build connections between their findings and modalities considered by other session participants. The goal is to develop a better understanding of the relationship between affective experience, perception, consumption, and cognition, and to question the role that embodiment plays in these cross modal effects.

We expect that this session will be of interest to a wide audience: specifically, researchers interested in gaining the theoretical understanding of embodied cognition, as well as researchers interested in learning how research on embodied cognition can provide better insight in understanding consumer behavior. All four papers in the session feature research that makes substantial theoretical contributions to the existing embodied cognition literature while being grounded in phenomena that are marketing relevant. We hope that the session will generate fruitful discussion on the topic of integration of consumer research and embodied cognition literature.

Brighten Up: Emotional Expressions and Perception of Color Brightness

EXTENDED ABSTRACT

From cosmetics, paints, and clothing to housings, furniture, and stationeries, color is one of the most important features in products. And marketing messages regarding these various products are often accompanied by message deliverers with certain emotional expressions. While the impact of colors on consumer judgment and the impact of emotional expressions on consumer judgment had been investigated rather separately (e.g., Deng, Hui, & Hutchinson, 2010; Yeung & Wyer, 2004), many metaphoric expressions suggest that these two domains are closely integrated. For instance, the metaphoric mapping of 'brightness' and 'smiling' seems to be a universal cross-cultural phenomenon manifested in the expression 'bright smile' in many languages, including English, German, Italian, Korean, Chinese and Russian. The present research examined whether a face with emotional expression in fact influence the perception of brightness in color even when an actual perceptual difference in brightness does not exist

The most relevant work stems from metaphoric association between valence or morality and brightness (e.g., 'a bright day'). For instance, people respond faster to positive or moral words printed in white than in black, and faster to negative or immoral words printed in black than in white (Meier, Robinson, & Clore, 2004; Sherman & Clore, 2009). Furthermore, priming with positive words causes people to perceive gray patches as brighter (Meier, Robinson, Crawford, & Ahlvers, 2007). In the present research, we conducted four experiments to examine whether positive versus negative emotional expressions also influence the perception of brightness in color.

In Study 1, 171 people (120 females) participated in an online study and were presented with a set of two schematic faces side by side, one smiling and one frowning, in one of three colors (gray, yellow or red). Each face consisted of a circle with two eyes and a mouth, and the only difference between the smiling and the frowning face was the angle of the mouth. Participants were told that there is a subtle difference in stimuli color and were asked to detect which one was brighter. In Study 2, 113 people (73 female) followed the same procedure as Study 1 except that the question was phrased in terms of 'lighter' instead of 'brighter' and participants only saw one of two colors, yellow and red. In both studies, regardless of the colors and wording of questions, the majority of people chose the smiling face as brighter (lighter) than the frowning face (In all cases, more than 65% people chose the smiling face, $p<.05$).

In Study 3, 74 people (45 females) participated in an online study and were randomly presented with either the smiling or frowning gray face used in Study 1. Participants observed the stimuli at their own pace and indicated the brightness of the stimuli on a 9-point gray shades scale on the next page. Each shade of the scale differed 5 points in luminance, where 9 was the darkest (luminance = 150), 1 was the brightest (luminance = 110), and 7 was the correct shade (luminance = 140). Finally participants reported their mood on a 9-point scale (-4 = very negative to +4 = very positive) so we could ensure that the effects were not related to mood. In Study 4, 123 people (63 females) followed the same procedure as Study 3 except that the stimuli were realistic faces. We adopted the smiling and frowning gray scale images of a male model called J. J. in Ekman and Friesen's (1976) classic facial expression pictures modified by Horstmann and Bauland (2006). The stimuli differed from each other only in terms of elements to depict facial expressions. To equate facial luminance, we painted the two faces with the same pink color (hue = 9, saturation = 210, luminance = 203). The pink scale had 9 shades with a 5-point luminance difference in each shade, 9 was the darkest (luminance = 188), 1 was the brightest (luminance = 228), and 6 was the correct answer (luminance = 203). The results showed that participants perceived the smiling face as brighter (Study 3: $M = 4.68$, $SD = 1.69$; Study 4: $M = 4.76$, $SD = 1.76$) than the frowning face (Study 3: $M = 5.51$, $SD = 1.69$; Study 4: $M = 5.36$, $SD = 1.62$), $t(72) = -2.07$, $p = .043$, $d=.49$ (Study 3); $t(121) = -1.97$, $p = .05$, $d=.35$ (Study 4).

In sum, these four studies demonstrated that people perceive smiling faces as brighter or lighter than frowning faces. Our research reveals a novel link between emotional expressions and lightness perception, and these results likely have important implications for consumer behaviors. For instance, advertising campaigns for certain products that emphasize their brightening functions (e.g., cosmetics and bleach) may be more effective when they are accompanied by smiling models. On the other hand, in advertisements of products whose darkness is valued such as black attires, mascara, hair dye, and tanning products, smiles may not always be an effective strategy.

Does a Heavy Heart Create a Heavy Body?
The Connection between Conceptual, Physical and Emotional Heaviness

EXTENDED ABSTRACT

The Oxford English dictionary defines heaviness as the state or quality of being heavy to describe "weightiness and ponderousness" as well as "dejectedness of mind; sadness, grief." Thus, heaviness as a concept has meanings in the domains of weight (physical heaviness), state of mind (emotional heaviness) and, more generally, as a property of concepts.

Past research has shown that negative emotions have destructive physical consequences. Epidemiologically, negative emotions lead to a variety of diseases such as diabetes (Carnethon, Kinder, Fair, Stafford, & Fortmann, 2003) and hypertension (Everson, Goldberg, Kaplan, Julkunen, & Salonen, 1998;). However, there is little theory and empirical research on the physiological consequences of emotion.

Although the embodied emotion literature has shown that there is a linkage between emotion concepts and bodily experience, previous studies mostly focus on bodily experience as an antecedent of emotion concepts. For example, Niedenthal (2007) found that the bodily expression of emotion influence the way in which emotional information is processed. These studies manipulate bodily reactions (e.g. researchers affixed golf tees to the inside of participants' eyebrows to manipulate negative affect) to study the effect of bodily expressions on emotional information processing.

Metaphors using physiology related concepts such as "heavy hearted" and "feeling sad and heavy" depict the feeling of sad or grief in our daily life. Zhong and Leonardelli (2008) suggest that the linguistic coupling between body related words and cognition-related concepts such as feeling cold and social rejection may reflect people's predisposition to describe concepts based upon their bodily experience. Therefore, the linguistic association between sadness and heaviness may reflect sad people's bodily experience of feeling heavy.

Embodiment theories suggest that cognition not only relies on abstract and modal mental representations but also on amodal perceptual content from various sensors-motor regions in the brain that process bodily information (Barsalou, 1999; Gallese & Lakoff, 2005), which implies the linkage between emotion concepts and bodily experience. Specifically, when abstract concepts are activated, perceptual simulation occurs (Schubert, 2005). When people recall, think, read or talk about the abstract concepts, it will re-enact people's similar states based on stored sensory, motor, and introspective states that accompanied with the experience of those concepts (Barsalou, Niedenthal, Barbey, & Ruppert, 2003). For example, the activation of elderly stereotype leads to behavioral changes consistent with the concept: people actually walk slower (Bargh, Chen, & Burrows, 1996). The activation of specific emotion concepts of pride and disappointment is accompanied by changes in posture: people increase their posture height while generating of pride words (Oosterwijk, Rottevee, Fischer, & Hess, 2009). Therefore, activation of an abstract concept triggers bodily experience.

Given that negative emotion such as sadness or grief are coupled with heaviness in our daily languages and the activation of an abstract concept induces related bodily experience, we propose that conceptual heaviness and emotional heaviness will lead to physical heaviness. In the current study, we manipulated the activation of an abstract concept; heaviness, and investigate embodiment effect as consequences.

In the first study, we investigated whether conceptual heaviness will induce people's feeling of heaviness and influence their eating behavior. Sixty-six undergraduates participated in the study. They first played a word game in which they were required to identify words in a word-grid. These words were either related to heavy (e.g.; heavy, ton, steel, sink) or words related to light (e.g., light, cloud, balloon, float). Then they proceed to a marketing product evaluation task in which they were asked to eat a sandwich and evaluate how full they felt. They were also offered a tray of mini muffins and asked to help themselves to as many as they liked. We found that individuals who were primed with heavy related words felt fuller (*M*=6.38, *SD*=1.48) compared to those who were primed with light related words (*M*=4.06, *SD*=1.7), *F(1,65)*=29.49, *p*<.01. They also took less muffins (*M*=1.03, *SD*=.91) than individuals in light condition (*M*=1.91, *SD*=1.2), *F(1,65)*=11.6, *p*<.01.

In the second study, we examined whether emotional heaviness will induce people's physical feeling of heaviness. Sixty-nine students participated in the study. They first watched either a five-minute long film clip from a movie. The clip was either sad, happy, or neutral. Then they evaluate an average student's weight and their own weight using multiple measures (e.g., how many bricks equal your weight, how much will a spring compress if you stand on it, how thick does ice on a lake have to be to not crack under your weight). We found that individuals who were primed with emotional heaviness perceived others as being heavier, *F (2,68)=8.72,p<.01*. They also perceive themselves as being heavier, *F(2,68)=5.47,p<.01*. An in the third study, we show that physical heaviness can induce a feeling of emotional heaviness.

These findings that conceptual heaviness and emotional heaviness are associated with physical heaviness are a novel extension of the embodied emotion literature. In addition, negative emotion does not only cause mental health problems but also physiological consequence- feeling of physical heaviness.

Lethargic Mind: How Perceived Fat Consumption Affects Mind's Agility

EXTENDED ABSTRACT

Fat storage is usually an indicator of (lack of) physical fitness, but can ingesting fatty foods decline one's cognitive performance? Further, does merely remembering eating fat-rich food impair one's ability to do cognitive tasks? Building on the literature of embodied cognition, we explore how the feeling of physical sluggishness that occurs after the consumption of fat-rich (but not protein rich) foods translates into similar feeling of mental sluggishness that manifests itself in one's impaired ability to perform various cognitive tasks.

The notion that cognition includes not only abstract mental representations but also a perceptual simulation has recently received increased interest in psychology and consumer behavior literature (see Barsalou 2008 for review). Such bidirectional connection between mind and body has been shown in a number of domains, including emotion (Niedenthal 2007), social isolation (Zhong and Leonardelli 2008), interpersonal perceptions (Williams and Bargh 2008) and even brand evaluations (Labroo and Nielsen 2010). Current paper expands on our understanding of embodied cognition by integrating three different modalities: bodily sensations, introspection and action. We test our proposition of multimodality of cognition in a novel domain: cognitive performance. To our knowledge, we are the first to show how actual and simulated consumption of fat-rich foods affects one's cognitive performance.

We test our hypotheses in a series of three studies. In Study 1 (n = 63) we aim at establishing the direct link between fat-rich food consumption and mental sluggishness. We propose that consumption of fat-rich foods would create a sensation of physical sluggishness, which in turn will manifest itself in mental slowness. In this study we

asked participants to complete two ostensibly unrelated tasks. The first task was a taste study, during which half of participants were asked to sample eight plain crackers and another half were asked to sample the same crackers generously covered with a butter spread. After completing the taste study, participants were asked to solve a word puzzle and find as many words as they could within five minutes. We found that participants who just consumed butter found fewer words than participants who consumed just crackers. We did not observe any differences in mood between two conditions, and the difference in taste did not explain our results, when used as a covariate in the analysis.

Study 2 (n = 80) followed a similar design: participants completed a taste study and an unrelated cognitive task. However, in this study all the participants consumed exactly the same food: crackers covered with cream cheese. We used this design to rule out direct effect of consumption of fat-rich foods on mental performance. To manipulate participants' *perception* that they have just consumed a fatty food, for half of the participants we described the cream cheese as full fat (by providing them a nutrition label with high calories and fat content), whereas for another half we described the same cream cheese as being fat-free (low calories and zero fat). After completing the tasting study, participants were asked to solve 10 SAT math problems in allotted time of five minutes. Consistent with the results of Study 1, we found that participants who believed they consumed fat-rich cream cheese solved fewer math problems than did participants who believed they consumed a fat-free cream cheese. Importantly, we did not find a difference in a number of math problems attempted between the two conditions, suggesting that perceived consumption of fat does not affect one's motivation to solve problems, but rather influences one's ability to solve them. Furthermore, consistent with our theorizing, we find that participants who believed that they have consumed a full fat cream cheese rated themselves as being more tired than did the participants who believed they consumed a fat-free cream cheese.

Finally, in Study 3 (n = 53) we asked the participants to list breakfast foods they had consumed earlier in the day. Half of participants was asked to list fat-rich breakfast foods, for example, bacon and eggs, whereas another half was asked to list protein-rich breakfast foods, for example, bacon and eggs, and to describe the sensations consumption of those fat-rich or protein-rich foods entailed. This design was used to examine whether mere mental simulation of fat-rich food consumption has similar effect on cognitive performance. After completing the first part of the study, participants were asked to complete an unrelated anagrams study. In this study participants were asked to solve nine anagrams. Unlike the design of Studies 1 and 2, we did not limit the amount of time participants spent on the cognitive test and instead measured actual time spent. Consistent with our earlier results, participants that were just reminded of the fat-rich food they have consumed solved fewer anagrams than did the participants who were reminded about protein-rich foods. We did not find any difference in the time spent on anagrams between the conditions, again ruling out the potential role of motivation in explaining our results.

Using three different manipulations of fat-rich food consumption (from actual consumption to the memory of one) and across three different cognitive domains we find that consumers are less successful in cognitive tasks after consuming fat-rich foods. Further, our studies clearly show that mental sluggishness is not a result of actual physiological changes in the body or one's motivation to perform cognitive tasks. Taken together these results provide converging evidence for the connection between physical sluggishness associated with fat-rich food consumption and mental agility.

My Hands Are Tied – My Lips Are Sealed: Prevented Embodiment Limits Communicational Cooperativeness

EXTENDED ABSTRACT

According to Grice's Cooperativeness Principle (1975), to achieve a successful conversation partners make all efforts to understand and to be understood. This requires making inferences about each other in order for the speaker to adjust her/his language and for the addressee to retrieve the intended meaning of the speaker. However, interlocutors do not always make those inferences easily. One possible situation, in which inference is difficult to make, involves *prevented embodiment*. Research on embodiment reveals that bodily simulations of external social or mental states influence comprehension and perception (e.g. Wells & Petty 1980, Spivey, Tyler, Richardson, & Young, 2000). For example, Glenberg & Kaschak (2002) found that participants were faster at judging the sensibility of a sentence when its meaning (forward-backward) was compatible with the hand movement required for the response. Richardson, Spivey, Barsalou, & McRae (2003) find that the sentence-movement compatibility effect occurs even when the sentences refer to abstract actions that involve directional communication, such as "You told Liz the story" vs. "Liz told you the story".

However, to our knowledge no previous research has specifically examined how actively *preventing* the natural expression of embodiment can affect behavior and communication. In this work, we test whether limitation of embodiment would distort one partner's ability to make inferences about the other party, causing limited communicational cooperation. As comprehension is claimed to be dependent on and aided by embodiment (e.g. Lakoff & Johnson, 1999, Barsalou, 1999; Glenberg & Robertson, 2000), it makes sense that inference, which is part of comprehension, is also grounded in bodily states. But what happens when embodiment is prevented, due to situational (e.g. holding a box) or medical (e.g. broken arm) reasons? Does prevention of embodiment affect our communicational cooperativeness?

We test this effect in two hypotheses: H1: Prevented embodiment reduces cooperative communication among both parties in a conversation, resulting in: a) Lower ability of addressees to process language, which requires making effortful inferences about the speaker's intended meaning. This will occur, for instance, in comprehension of natural language vs. fixed expressions, and in non-conventional vs. conventional request phrasing; b) Lower ability of speakers to make inference about the hearer, resulting in lower ability of speakers to adjust their language to the hearer.

We examine these hypotheses in two language comprehension and one language production experiments, which manipulate prevented embodiment and measure cooperativeness in communication. Studies 1 (N=22) and 2 (N=40) test H1a. We find that comprehension of sentences containing the verb "stand" and non-conventionally phrased requests for actions that are typically performed in a standing position occurs more slowly when done in a sitting posture (which prevents the embodiment of the sense of "stand"), compared with a standing posture. However, idioms and expressions with the word "stand" and conventional requests, both requiring less inferential effort and therefore less cooperativeness, were not processed more slowly in sitting posture.

Study 3 examines H1b. Participants (N=80), half of them with their hands held in a pocket behind their backs (to prevent hand movement), were recorded while giving oral instructions for simple household tasks that require the hands, such as washing the dishes. The instructions were to be given either to imaginary human assistants, or to an imaginary helper robot, assuming that people intuitively should use different communication style with a robot vs. humans (e.g. more detailed instructions, less polite communication) intuitively attributing lesser knowledge and feelings to the robot vs. humans. The recorded instructions were then coded and analyzed. Consistent with predictions, participants with full ability to embody gave instructions to the robot, which were more detailed than their instructions to the human. These participants were less confident in the robot's understanding and tried harder to maintain coherence of their instructions to the robot than to the human. However, participants who were prevented from embodying did not manage to adjust their language to the addressees' needs. Namely, they were similarly detailed, confident and coherent with both the robot and the human.

These findings suggest that prevention of embodiment can impair various aspects of communication, including mental processes that require combination of information from multiple sources and inference making. While communication cooperativeness, as examined in this work, is important in interpersonal communication, it is also highly important in marketing communication and advertising, as well as in retail behavior and in negotiations. We intend to further inquire into the effect of prevented embodiment on general interpersonal cooperativeness, e.g. in games, within negotiation and business contexts.

All in the Family: Intra-Family Coalitional Influences on Consumption

Chairs: Linda Price, University of Arizona, USA
Hope Schau, University of Arizona, USA

Paper #1: Connected Coalitions: Preserving Brand Loyalty Across Distances

> Amber Epp, University of Wisconsin-Madison, USA
> Hope Schau, University of Arizona, USA
> Linda Price, University of Arizona, USA

Paper #2: The Ambivalent Role of Adult Siblings in Family Decisions about Elder Care

> Aimee Huff, University of Western Ontario, Canada
> June Cotte, University of Western Ontario, Canada

Paper #3: Helping or Hindering?: The Ambivalent Role of Siblings as Socialization Agents within Family Consumption

> Ben Kerrane, Bradford University, UK
> Margaret Hogg, Lancaster University, UK

Paper #4: Intergenerational Transfer of Consumption Practices within Families

> Paul Connell, SUNY Stony Brook, USA
> Hope Schau, University of Arizona, USA
> Linda Price, University of Arizona, USA

SESSION OVERVIEW

Prior research documents the significance of family and kinship networks in brand loyalties (Cotte and Wood 2004; Fournier 1998; Hoyer 1984; Moore, Wilkie, and Lutz 2002), consumer socialization (Carlson and Grossbart 1988; John 1999; Moschis 1985, 1987), decision-making (Commuri and Gentry 2000) and intergenerational transfers (Curasi et al 2003 and 2004; Ekerdt and Sergeant 2006; Lastovicka and Fernandez 2005). However, very little research has investigated coalitional or collective consumption processes within kinship networks (Epp and Price 2008). Epp and Price (2008, p.55) argue that we might better understand consumption processes "by examining how particular brands are embedded in family and relational identity enactments." By family and relational identity enactments, they refer to the interplay among the rituals, narratives, social dramas, intergenerational transfers and everyday interactions that make up family life. They theorize that brand loyalties, consumer decision-making, consumer socialization, and intergenerational transfers often implicate multiple identity bundles in dynamic interplay within a family's social interactions and consumption practices. Specifically, they emphasize that family identity (i.e., "who we are as a family") is contingent on shared interactions among relational bundles within the family that engage in both complementary and competing consumption practices. For example, individuals, various coalitions (father/sons; mother/daughters; siblings; couple, etc), and the collective family instantiate and negotiate identity through consumption and other practices. Empirical research supports that the level of synergy and discord among individual, relational and collective identity goals is consequential for object meaning and consumption activities (Epp and Price 2010; 2011). Moreover, research shows that siblings play an important role in shaping coalitional and family consumption practices (Cotte and Wood 2004). Despite this, few studies explicitly focuses on coalitional influence. This session contributes to the emerging literature on family identity by investigating how coalitional and collective dynamics inform brand loyalty, decision-making, consumer socialization and intergenerational transfers.

This session tightly coalesces around uncovering how coalitional identities and practices interplay with family life: Epp et al uncover the role of coalitions in how family life is practiced across distances and through technologies with implications for brand loyalty. Huff and Cotte examine coalition dynamics evidenced in navigating emotionally stressful decisions about elder care for parents. Kerrane and Hogg investigate the dynamic and often volatile role of sibling relationships in consumer socialization. Connell et al demonstrate how synergy and discord among identity projects within a family impacts the intergenerational transfer of consumption practices. All four papers share an emphasis on sibling and other coalitional relationships within families. All papers touch on member roles and member identities as they intersect with the family collective identity. In addition to theoretical cohesion, the papers share a methodological focus, using depth interviews with multiple family members to reveal family consumption. Although further iterations of data analysis are possible, each of the presentations is based on completed data collection and writing is expected to be completed by the time of the conference.

We anticipate our session will have broad appeal drawing researchers interested in social and collective identity, family brand loyalties and decision making, consumption practices, consumer socialization and intergenerational transfer. In particular, although all four papers bring different perspectives all four papers engage practice theory and social identity theory with family as the focal site for investigation. As longitudinal investigations are still relatively rare and collective depth interviews are an emergent data collection method, this session will also engage the interest of interpretive researchers more generally.

Connected Coalitions: Preserving Brand Loyalty across Distances

EXTENDED ABSTRACT

Today's consumers operate in a dynamic, global environment in which family life is practiced across distances and through technologies in ways unimaginable in the past. Our study investigates the implications for marketers of "doing family" through technologies. Researchers tend to focus on culturally loaded and normatively shaped activities families consider sacred such as dinner or holiday traditions (e.g. Epp and Price 2008; Gibbs 2006; Wallendorf and Arnould 1991). It is not uncommon for brands to become caught up in our meaningful family practices (Brady 2007; Warde 2005). Given that families are quite mindful of enacting traditions, we anticipate that families would strive to hold on to these when confronted with separation.

We collected longitudinal data from 23 families experiencing a physical separation (e.g. college, commutes, divorce, military) to address this question: what conditions shape brand loyalties during separation? Phase 1 included in-depth, family interviews to identify a range of practices and embedded brands central to defining the family and its coalitions (e.g. siblings, parent-child). Phase 2 included participant diaries to track the evolution of these practices. Phase 3 consisted of follow-up family interviews, using the diary entries to attend to changes in practices, brands, and technology use.

Paradoxically, very few families performed sacred activities while separated. Although the challenge to preserve centrally-held practices resonates, the ability to hold on to these traditions in a tech-mediated form requires tremendous creativity, mindfulness, and commitment. In contrast, everyday, coalitional activities were carried across distances more easily by the available modalities. Simple traditions that may involve only subsets of the family such as sisters sharing their favorite snack (Potter Family), mother-daughter shopping outings (Duncan Family), or brothers playing their guitars together (Thomas Family) can be important for constituting relational identities (Epp and Price 2008, 2010, 2011). These activities typically are considered profane, defined as "ordinary and part of everyday life" (Belk et al. 1989, p. 6). Simple coalitional activities establish a "shared world" among family members, are playful and naturally emergent, idiosyncratic, and may be less intentional or conscious. Among the families we interviewed, simple practices often were not recognized as important until they were missed during separation.

Several factors account for the ease of transferability of everyday coalitional practices as opposed to sacred family traditions. First, sacred activities tend to have strict minimum requirements (e.g. particular members, brands, contexts, materials, and meanings). Further, the time dependent, rigid structure and emotionality of sacred traditions are difficult to simulate with existing technologies. For example, the Foster family provided a detailed account of family dinner, but when their son Michael left for college, dinner conversation tapered, parents often read at the table, their daughter texted friends while eating, and many associated restaurants/brands were abandoned until Michael returned home. Unlike sacred family activities, coalitional activities tend to require fewer elements necessary for their performance, so contextual factors are easier to replicate. Given this, many families adapt these activities across distances relatively effortlessly (e.g. couple co-views their favorite TV shows by calling during the commercials—Moore-Mason Family). Technologies have made us more asynchronous, so time-independent, coalitional activities are better able to survive in this harsh environment. Lily Potter explains how this emerges organically among sisters: "we would open a can of condensed milk and eat it right out. So, when I do that by myself, I might text her…'I just opened a can of condensed milk!'" These nods to a once face-to-face activity accentuate the absence of another person; they prompt a previously shared world and attempt to recapture a piece of it.

Second, even in families who are motivated to maintain elaborate activities, shortcomings or differences in preferred technologies can derail their efforts. For instance, when asked what could save family dinner, the Fosters responded: "We could put a computer screen on the table and Skype you [Michael] in while we have dinner; that would be too weird though" (Jed, Father). Partly, this is a problem of mixed modalities. Although Michael is open to Skype, his parents characterize themselves as low-tech ("I hate email…I don't like to text, cell…it's just a huge intrusion" Jed, Father). Each family exists within its own technology ecology. The communication patterns both prior to and during a separation determine how, if at all, each modality is used to preserve activities and embedded brands. In comparison with elaborate activities, simple coalitional activities are likely to survive the mixed modalities dilemma. No matter which technologies comprise the family's ecology, members readily found a combination that worked. For example, co-viewing a favorite TV show could be facilitated by phone (as above), via text, or using Skype, among other modalities. Providing families with templates for how elaborate activities could be translated from face-to-face to technology-mediated could help families who have trouble envisioning such shifts and/or who view this as foreign or strange, given its absence from cultural templates for "doing family."

Third, the very structure of technology has prompted a shift from uniting families to connecting coalitions. Technology frequently favors dyads (or small coalitions), rather than facilitating family-level interactions, and this has a profound impact on the activities/brands that survive separation. Turkle (2010) echoes this point as she quotes Winston Churchill, "We shape our buildings and then they shape us" (p. 19). The technologies that dominate today can be isolating for distant families. Even when the intent is to involve a missing member—such as when Lily texts her sister to include her in the Potter family's movie night, but mom views this as excluding because texts are dyadic—technologies can fall short.

Our study suggests that firms should focus on embedding their brands in simple, coalitional activities rather than strive to find sanctuary in elaborate family traditions. Coalitions improvise these practices while separated, but companies could prompt this transformation. Minor improvements to technology, ads that depict "sharing the day," or basic templates may serve as a catalyst for families who are willing, but do not see the bridge that allows them to preserve simple activities. Managers also could provide mechanisms for translating the sacred. To do so, companies must deconstruct elaborate traditions into their various components and generate imaginative ways to repackage and transfer the sentiment. We have diverse examples in our data: sending picture texts of a life-sized cutout of a distant sister doing fun things with her family (Potter); calling to include a son in prayer time before dinner (Marino), posting videos of the family at the dog park on YouTube to include the husband (Powell), or sending postcards marked with stories of the family's travels to an absent son (Norris). These simple, yet meaningful actions initiated valued connections among coalitions. Firms could easily generate models for how brands could carry these meanings and be involved in the pieces of sacred that move across distances.

The Ambivalent Role of Adult Siblings in Family Decisions about Elder Care

EXTENDED ABSTRACT

This paper explores the experiences of adult siblings making choices about elder care for their parents, with a particular focus on the ways in which adult siblings can generate ambivalence in consumption. Decisions about elder care are rarely made by a single family member, and usually involve the family's adult children. As a result, adult siblings find themselves having to negotiate with each other and rely on each other for emotional support, because this context is typically marked by stress and tension within the family. Further, family transitions, such as the need for long-term elder care, can threaten family identity, thereby complicating consumption behavior.

Prior research has shown that family identity shapes consumption enactments within the family (Epp and Price 2008, 2010, 2011), and that siblings can play an important role in shaping each other's consumption practices (Cotte and Wood 2004). We extend this research by studying adult siblings who are faced with an important family decision yet who are no longer contained within the same household, and we pay particular attention to the ways that stressful consumption decisions are approached. Specifically, we are concerned with understanding how siblings, as a relational group within the family, reconcile discrepancies between their individual preferences and those of the group, how the consumption process is influenced by siblings, and how the family's collective sense of itself shapes and is shaped by elder care consumption for senior family members.

Using depth interviews, we uncover the ambivalent role that adult siblings play in shaping the consumption experiences of individuals. We then link these individual experiences to the role of consumption in family transitions, and the ways in which family identity both guides and challenges choice and use of elder care. We find that individuals hold unique sets of preferences (e.g., interpretation of what is best for the parent), involvement (e.g., willingness to participate in the decision process), and resources (e.g., time, money) in regard to their parents' need for elder care. When siblings combine their unique perspectives to make a family decision, discrepancies amplify the stress for each individual and for the family as a whole. Interestingly, however, the existence of siblings also seems to facilitate coping with the stress. Siblings, then, play an ambivalent role by both generating and tempering the stress associated with choosing long-term commercial elder care for a parent. The ultimate choice is further shaped by the underlying family dynamics, family identity, and the interplay between siblings. We compare and contrast the experiences of adult siblings with only children in this context, and find further support for our model; when an adult child has no siblings, decision making appears to be less complicated but the ongoing consumption appears to be more emotionally burdensome.

This research contributes to our understanding of family decision-making, the dynamic and sometimes volatile nature of sibling relationships in the family consumption process, and the ways in which family identity can both challenge and facilitate consumption. Our unit of analysis is the relational group of adult siblings, which is a novel perspective in consumer research.

Helping or Hindering? The Ambivalent Role of Siblings as Socialization Agents within Family Consumption

EXTENDED ABSTRACT

Sibling relationships have been largely overlooked within existing consumer research into the role of the family within consumer socialization (Cotte and Wood, 2004). The family has been represented as the most important consumption unit (Commuri and Gentry 2000) because it plays a significant role in the consumer socialization of children (John, 1999). So far, research attention has largely focussed on the role of parents in socializing their children into being consumers. Current research has explored the socialization styles of parents (Carlson and Grossbart, 1988) or the communication patterns that parents adopt (Carlson, Walsh, Laczniak and Grossbart, 1994) in facilitating the acquisition of consumption knowledge for children. In contrast the role that siblings may play in teaching one another consumption skills has been relatively neglected (Cotte and Wood, 2004). In this paper we specifically explore the role that siblings play within the context of consumer socialization. We focus on understanding sibling relationships ('sibship') and how such relationships, as one component of the family environment, shape the consumer socialization of children.

A series of in-depth interviews were conducted with six families in our exploratory study, capturing the stories of twenty-nine family informants. Following calls for family research that capture the dynamics of family life (Hamilton and Catterall 2006; Tinson and Nancarrow 2005) interviews were conducted with both children and their parents. Consent was sought from parents and guardians to approach their children in order to then seek the children's consent to be involved in the data collection process (Mandell 1991). Methods by which valid consent can be obtained from children were adhered to (Mason 2004). The interviews were conducted in the family home, usually in the kitchen at the dining table. Each family was visited between three and five times and interviews were conducted over a period ranging from four to twelve months. The interviews with family members were conducted in three stages and explored themes such as family history, intra-family relationships and how family members got their own way.

Our exploratory study highlights that sibling relationships were far from static, and were often ambivalent and volatile in nature. Our family stories show how the siblings discussed consumption issues with each other. Siblings were often children's first point of contact when considering consumption issues and choices. This is significant as the children studied suggested that they would rather lose face with their siblings, who appeared to vet selected brands and products, before they ran the risk of losing face with their peers. In this case, the family provided a safe and private environment in which to seek and update their consumer knowledge about products and brands. Consumption choices, and in particular brand selection, were often shaped by siblings who were important filters, as well as sources, for market-place information.

However, given the ambivalent nature of sibling relationships each child did not have equal access to this consumption advice or approval process. We identify both supportive/co-operative and hostile/aggressive dimensions of sibling relationships. Such relationship types had implications in terms of the consumption and consumer socialization of the children studied. Where relationships were supportive siblings would lend each other help in influencing their parents to buy them products, with siblings openly discussing consumption issues and brand choices with one another. Where relationships were hostile and aggressive such information and advice sharing was not apparent, but rather siblings would deliberately withhold their opinions or consumption help, or offer incorrect opinions in the hope that this would subsequently tarnish their brother's/sister's image and reputation with their peers. As such although siblings had the potential to be important socialization agents for children, unlike the socializing actions of parents the children studied did not always have good and constructive consumer socialization intentions in mind.

Intergenerational Transfer of Consumption Practices within Families

EXTENDED ABSTRACT

Our research examines intergenerational transfers of consumption practices (ITCP). We recognize ITCPs as socially embedded in the consumption practices of families which contain multiple and sometimes conflicting identity projects across units of analysis (the individual, intra-family coalitions and the family collective). Through in-depth interviews with sixteen members of five families, we examine this complex interplay of identity projects in a given ITCP and demonstrate how identity interplay affects synergy and discord within the transfers.

Our investigation departs from prior research in three key ways. First, we examine consumption practices rather than special objects and brand preferences. Consumption practices are central to creating, sustaining and passing forward individual and collective identity (Gregson, Metcalfe and Crewe 2007; Warde 2005). However, prior research has focused on the transfer of special objects, heirlooms (Belk 1988; Curasi, Price, and Arnould 2004; Price, Arnould, and Curasi 2000), brand preferences (Cotte and Wood 2004; Fournier 1998; Hoyer 1984; Moore, Wilkie, and Lutz 2002), and wealth (Brandford 2009) without much consideration of the practices that surround them and within which objects and brand preferences are implicitly embedded. The foregrounding of objects and brand preferences is useful in understanding how their meanings are transferred across family generations, but it obscures the intergenerational enactment of practices that is often at the heart of these exchanges.

Second, we study intergenerational transfers within families, while previous research has focused on dyads and often on just one half of the dyad (e.g., daughters in mother-daughter dyads by Moore et al 2002). ITCPs are situated within consumer collectives, such as families with identity projects at individual, coalitional and collective levels (Brewer and Gardner 1996; Epp and Price 2008) with varying degrees of synergy and discord (Epp and Price 2008; 2010; 2011). Families' ITCP may be contested as identity projects interplay. For example, a successful transfer of a consumption practice such as soccer or baseball between a father and son may stifle another son's individual identity project as he is pulled into this coalitional practice. Similarly, the embracing of soccer or baseball as a family identity may serve to exclude particular members or coalitions within the family. Hence, by examining ITCP within families, not dyads, we uncover how varying degrees of synergy and discord surrounding consumption practices affect intergenerational transfer.

Third, because we focus on consumption practices rather than objects, and networks rather than dyads, we uncover the dynamics

underlying thwarted intergenerational transfers. Prior research has noted how consumers strategize and sometimes fail to transfer their special possessions to the next generation (Belk, Sherry and Wallendorf 1988; Belk, Wallendorf and Sherry 1989; Curasi, Price and Arnould 2004; Price, Arnould and Curasi 2000). Explanations for failed transfers of special possessions generally center on a failure of one generation to communicate object meanings to the next generation through stories and use. However, we show how the interplay of identity projects may lead to thwarted intergenerational transfers. Prior research occasionally describes, how the dynamics of coalitional consumption practices (such as multiple generations of males hunting or fishing together) positively impact the transfer of special objects (such as guns and fishing rods) (c.f., Price et al 2000). However, existing research does not uncover how coalitional consumption practices may negatively affect other family members who resist or are excluded. Thus, we explore both synergistic and discordant elements of consumption practices, how these implicate identity projects, how they are negotiated between and among family members, and how they influence ITCP (Epp and Price 2011).

Finding Meaning in Numbers: How Consumers Contextualize Numeric Information

Chairs: Stephen A. Atlas, Columbia University, USA
Oleg Urminsky, University of Chicago, USA

Paper #1: The Effects of Scale Expansion on Preference, Prediction, and Judgment

Richard P. Larrick, Duke University, USA
Katherine Burson, University of Michigan, USA
Min Kay, Duke University, USA

Paper #2: Psychology-Compatible Elicitations: The Uncertainty Effect as a Case Study

Uri Simonsohn, University of Pennsylvania, USA

Paper #3: Making Sense of the Nonsense: When Are Consumers Sensitive to Magnitude Variation in Unfamiliar Numerical Information?

Luxi Shen, University of Chicago, USA
Oleg Urminsky, University of Chicago, USA

Paper #4: Buying Daily Pleasure with Daily Payments: Narrow Framing Favors Scope Insensitive Accounts

Stephen A. Atlas, Columbia University, USA
Daniel Bartels, Columbia University, USA

SESSION OVERVIEW

The consumer research literature holds many examples where perception of magnitude influences consumer choice. Expanding a ratio scale to include more discrete units (such as from feet to inches or years to days) has been shown to encourage more discrimination along the scale (Burson, Larrick and Lynch, 2009). This can lead to choice errors when consumers over-use uninformative numerical information (such as in the money illusion effect of Shafir, Diamond and Tversky, 1997), and problems also arise when consumers fail to extract knowledge from informative numbers. This special session aims to contribute to the literature by exploring new frameworks for understanding how consumers extract meaning from numbers, when they are sensitive to changes in magnitude, and the implications for consumer choice. Contextual and task cues shift how we process numeric information and can lead to very different outcomes from otherwise equivalent information.

The first paper, by Larrick, Burson, and Kay explores when scale expansion, such as from dollars to cents or years to days, alters consumer judgment. They find that scale expansion effects are robust to incentives and independent of accountability, and that only experts weigh cues consistently across units.

The second paper, by Simonsohn, explores how the context and task cues provided by elicitation methods can influence intuitive psychological processes responsible for numeric perception and insight. He demonstrates that the psychological processes responsible for the otherwise-robust Uncertainty Effect are attenuated when respondents report willingness to pay on a list containing multiple prices (multiple-price-list elicitation). He argues that failure to elicit preferences through methods that are "psychologically compatible" with the psychological processes of interest can cause artifactual interactions with manipulations. In this case, psychologically incompatible elicitation can interfere with consumers' intuitive thought processes involved in deriving meaning from numbers and perceiving scale.

The third paper, by Shen and Urminsky, explores how consumers evaluate information in unfamiliar units. They suggest that consumers' relative attention to units and numbers determines magnitude sensitivity, and hence posit and find that unit salience has a critical role in reliance on numeric inference. They find that in the absence of a unit salience cue, consumers are highly sensitive to magnitudes with unknown units, even in single evaluation for consequential decisions with ample decision time. However, when the decision process prompts unit salience, the effect of magnitude is eliminated.

The fourth paper, by Atlas and Bartels, explores how reframing a price as a series of recurring payments (e.g. "Pennies-a-Day", Gourville, 1998) affects how consumers value a transaction's benefits. They argue that a proposed payment schedule encourages consumers to imagine commensurate benefits; hence dividing a single price into a series of recurring payments increases willingness to purchase when a transaction's benefits are more scope-insensitive than its costs. In other words, narrow framing favors scope-insensitive accounts.

Together, these four strongly interconnected papers provide new perspectives on how consumers understand and derive meaning (e.g. sense of scale) from numbers and contextual cues. Each paper will advance the field's understanding of when people are sensitive to changes in magnitude. One other common theme across each of these studies is that our results persist with high involvement, such as when subjects make incentive-compatible choices and important decisions. These perspectives yield insight into consumer choice across a wide range of settings, and carry theoretical as well as practical implications for consumer research. In particular, this proposed session builds connections between numerosity, scope insensitivity, and mental accounting in the consumer choice domain. Data collection in all papers is complete and all participants have agreed to present, should the session be accepted. The use of numeric stimuli in decision making research is ubiquitous, and we expect that the novel approaches to numeric decision making presented in this session will interest a broad range of consumer researchers. The session should be of particular interest to those interested in mental accounting and financial decision making. These topics have attracted considerable attention and interest in recent years and we anticipate that the results presented in this special session will stimulate future research. The chairs will facilitate audience discussion drawing further connections between these perspectives as well as between scale in mental accounting and other areas of consumer research.

The Effects of Scale Expansion on Preference, Prediction, and Judgment

EXTENDED ABSTRACT

Consumers often encounter quantified product information. For example, consumers might receive quantitative information about costs, energy consumption, or ratings of reliability. Each of these pieces of information is open to alternative expressions: Costs might be summarized in dollars or cents; energy consumption might be expressed per month or per year; and ratings of reliability might be on a 5-point or 100-point scale. In each case, identical ratio information is conveyed after being multiplied by an arbitrary factor. Although the informational content is held constant, scale change alters preference and judgment. Scale size matters.

A number of studies in marketing and in cognitive psychology have shown changes in scale size affect perceptions of risk (Pacini & Epstein, 1999; Stone, Yates, & Parker, 1997; Yamigishi, 1997) and changes in currency denomination affect purchase behavior (Wertenbroch, Soman, & Chattopadhyay, 2007). For example, Yamigishi

(1997) has shown that people judge ratios expressed with small numerators and denominators (6/100) as less risky than smaller ratios expressed with large numerators and denominators (57/1000). These effects have been explained in terms of decision makers focusing on the "numerosity" (Pelham, Sumatra, & Myaskovsky, 1995) of numerators, and giving little attention to the less salient denominator (Reyna & Brainerd, 2008; Stone et al., 1997). Burson, Larrick, and Lynch (2009) proposed that many previous scale change effects could be captured under a general principle of discriminability. For any ratio scale, multiplying the scale by an arbitrary factor greater than 1 increases the perceived difference between different alternatives. By increasing the perceived difference, or discriminability, on that attribute, expanded scales shift preference to an alternative favored on that scale. Burson et al. (2009) demonstrated that enhanced discriminability produced preference reversals in multi-attribute choice. In one study, two cell phone plans were expressed in terms of price per month and number of disconnected calls per 1,000 calls. Option A cost \$32 per month and had 42 dropped calls per 1,000 calls; Option B cost \$27 per month and had 65 dropped calls per 1,000 calls. The small difference in price and large difference in dropped calls led the majority of subjects to favor Option B. However, when the same information was presented as price per year (\$384 and \$324) and dropped calls per 100 calls (4.2 and 6.5), the large difference in price and small difference in dropped calls led the majority of subjects to favor Option A.

This talk will present three new studies testing moderators of scale expansion effects: Accountability, incentives, and expertise.

Accountability. We tested the effect of accountability in an employee evaluation task. Subjects were asked to rate sales people based on two attributes: Number of sales (expressed per week or per year) and number of customer complains (expressed per customer or per 100 customers). When one attribute was expanded (e.g., sales per year) the other attribute was contracted (e.g., complaints per customer). Scale expansion was crossed with an accountability manipulation in which subjects had to explain their choice. Based on previous research, we constructed competing hypotheses: Accountability would reduce scale-induced preference reversals by making subjects think harder about the information, thereby undoing the effect of arbitrary changes in scale; and accountability would increase scale-induced preference reversals because subjects would use the magnitude of (arbitrary) differences to justify their choices. Contrary to expectations, we found no interaction between scale expansion and accountability. As in previous studies, scale expansion produced a significant preference reversal; accountability had an additional main effect, shifting preference to the employee who had the most sales. This study suggests that accountability has a largely orthogonal effect to the effect of scale expansion.

Incentives and expertise. We tested the effect of incentives and expertise in a performance prediction tasks. Subjects were presented with data for 20 Major League Baseball pitchers. The names of the pitchers were masked. Subjects were given each pitcher's rate of striking out a batter and giving up home runs to a batter. Strikeouts predict better pitcher success and home runs predict worse pitcher success (as measured by a well-known statistic called "earned run average"). All subjects were paid for the accuracy of their predictions. When the rate for one statistic was expanded (e.g., home runs per 100 innings), the rate for the other statistic was contracted (e.g., strike outs per batter), creating two conditions. For each subject, we regressed his or her predictions for the 20 pitchers on the two cues to derive a weight for cue use. We found a significant effect of expansion: A cue received more weight when it was expanded than when it was contracted. Incentives do not seem to be sufficient

to eliminate the effect. We also measured expertise in baseball using both subjective measures (self-ratings of knowledge and confidence) and objective measures (a quiz about baseball statistics such as "OPS"). We found that expertise significantly moderated the effect of scale expansion. Those with low and intermediate levels of knowledge were susceptible to scale effects. However, those most expert weighted the two cues consistently regardless of how the statistics were scaled.

Psychology-Compatible Elicitations: The Uncertainty Effect as a Case Study

EXTENDED ABSTRACT

A significant portion of consumer research has examined the impact on elicited preferences and judgments of employing alternative elicitation modes or frames. When studying unrelated phenomena, however, consumer researchers typically choose how to elicit variables of interest based primarily on convenience, be it of obtaining more data from a given number of participants, of arriving at easier-to-analyze variables, or of employing measures that are easier to explain to participants.

While it may be inevitable to in one way or another influence preferences through their elicitation, the notion of "psychology-compatible" put forward in this paper involves *elicitations that do not interfere with the psychological processes of interest to a study.*

Psychological-compatibility is violated when elicitation mechanisms have asymmetric effects across conditions; when rather than having a main effect, such as anchoring all valuations up or down, the artifactual consequences of the mechanism interacts with what the experiment seeks to manipulate.

This paper provides a concrete demonstration of the consequences of violating psychological-compatibility using the Uncertainty Effect, the valuation of a lottery below its worst outcome, as a case study. It shows that the otherwise robust finding disappears when preferences are elicited through a commonly employed mechanism, the multiple-price-list, as it reduces respondents' reliance on the psychological processes likely to be behind the Uncertainty Effect.

Multiple-price-list elicitations present participants with a table with dollar amounts listed in ascending order, and requires respondents to indicate for each price if they would be willing to pay it or not (e.g., would you pay \$1 for this mug yes/no, would you pay \$1.50 for this mug yes/no, etc.) They have been used for eliciting willingness-to-pay at least since the seminal paper on the endowment effect by Kahneman, Knetsch and Thaler (1990). In addition to valuations, such lists are also often employed to elicit time and risk preferences.

One appealing feature of the multi-price-list is that it lends itself to an intuitive incentive compatible design, where one of the yes/no decisions can be chosen at random to count for real payoffs.

For the purposes of the current paper, however, the central feature of the multiple-price-list elicitation is the format in which it presents prices. Prior research has shown that presenting numerical stimuli side-by-side induces people to think more analytically and less intuitively, even on subsequent and unrelated questions (Hsee & Rottenstreich, 2004; Hsee, Rottenstreich, & Xiao, 2005; Zeelenberg, 1999), and to be more sensitive to differences in magnitude or scope among options (Hsee, 1996; Hsee, et al., 1999).

These findings imply that the format in which prices are presented in the multiple-price-list is likely to increase participants' overall reliance on System 2, attenuating the impact of their System 1 reactions to the stimuli being evaluated.

In addition, by providing a list of possible answers, the multiple-price-list may induce subjects to use the range of values to construct a reasonable answer (Parducci, 1965; Schwarz, Hippler, Deutsch, & Strack, 1985; Sudman, Badburn, & Schwarz, 1996). For instance, subjects may implicitly (or explicitly) place the low and high prize on the table and select a number in between as their valuation of the lottery, effectively eliminating stochastically dominated answers from the consideration set. The multiple-price-list, then, may also act as a decision aid that bolsters the impact of System 2 on decisions.

Considering that the Uncertainty Effect is a revolutionarily important phenomenon probably caused by a System 1 process, people's intuitive negative reaction to risk (Simonsohn, 2010; Loewenstein, Weber, Hsee & Welch, 2001) and that the multiple-price-list is a commonly used elicitation technique conjectured here to attenuate the influence of System 1, the present research employs the Uncertainty Effect and multiple-price-list elicitations as a case study for introducing the notion of psychological-compatibility.

This paper presents the results from four between-subject experiments eliciting valuations for binary lotteries or for their worst outcome. Studies 1 and 2 replicate the Uncertainty Effect employing open-ended elicitations of willingness-to-pay (e.g., "what is the most you would pay?"), Studies 2, 3 & 4 do not replicate it using multiple-price-list elicitations.

If, as hypothesized, this discrepant set of results is explained by the side-by-side presentation of prices in the multiple-price-list, then the Uncertainty Effect should again be replicated if one were to modify it and present prices one at a time rather than simultaneously. Studies 3 & 4 do so and do indeed again replicate the Uncertainty Effect. Furthermore, consistent with the notion that the multiple-price-list eliminates the Uncertainty Effect by affecting the System 1 reaction to *uncertainty*, only the valuation of lotteries shifts across elicitation methods.

Making Sense of the Nonsense:
When Are Consumers Sensitive to Magnitude
Variation in Unfamiliar Numerical Information?

EXTENDED ABSTRACT

A broad range of consumer decisions involve judging numerical information in conjunction with a unit of measurement, which may not be familiar to consumers. Suppose, for example, that you are traveling in a foreign country where people use units of measurement that you are not familiar with. You may need to evaluate a container with volume 128X, a distance of 3,000Y, or a product priced at Z50. How do consumers judge numerical information in unfamiliar units?

Two main streams of research provide inconsistent predictions. The literature on numerosity and the money illusion (e.g., Shafir, Diamond and Tversky 1997; Wertenbroch, Soman and Chattopadhyay 2007) found that consumers judge unfamiliar information by its face value and therefore over-use numerical information which may not be informative, demonstrating magnitude sensitivity. In contrast, research on evaluability (e.g., Hsee, Loewenstein, Blount, & Bazerman, 1999; Hsee & Rottenstreich, 1994; Hsee & Zhang, 2010; Kahneman & Knetsch 1992) found that consumers fail to make inferences from numerical information with unfamiliar or hard-to-evaluate units when judging a single stimulus. In these studies, they do not use numeric information even when it may be informative, showing magnitude insensitivity.

We in this research provide an account of when it is that consumers do and do not utilize absolute magnitude information that is displayed in unfamiliar units, in order to reconcile these inconsistent findings. We propose that whether the numerical information is incorporated into judgments depends on the degree of mental salience of the specified units. In particular, when the unfamiliar unit is salient, the

consumer recognizes that the information is useless and disregards the absolute magnitude in her evaluation. However, when the unfamiliar unit is not salient and instead the number is salient, she proceeds as if the number per se is meaningful and tries to make sense of the absolute magnitude and incorporate it into her evaluation. Therefore, the unit salience determines consumers' magnitude sensitivity.

We tested our predictions in a series of three studies involving different contexts (judgments of length, price and monetary value), and involving both hypothetical scenarios and real bidding behavior. We manipulated the salience of unite by enlarging or shrinking the relative font size of the unit (between-subjects) and demonstrated that this subtle manipulation can reverse consumers' magnitude sensitivity. At the same time, we ruled out a list of five alternative explanations.

In the first study, participants evaluated the price of a hotel room in Rio. The room rate was displayed in an ad containing the numerical component of the price and a currency symbol, R. We manipulated both the numeric magnitude and the relative font size in a 2x2 between-subjects design. Half of the participants saw a label with an unfamiliar (fictional) currency symbol in relatively small font (unit salient), while the other participants saw a label with the currency symbol in a relatively large font (unit non-salient). Likewise, half of the participants saw a large-magnitude price (344) and half saw a small-magnitude price (138). We found that in the unit-non-salient condition, evaluations of the price were magnitude-sensitive but participants in the unit-salient condition were insensitive to price variation. This magnitude-sensitivity reversal occurs only for unfamiliar units. In a parallel study with an identical design except that a familiar currency symbol, $, was adopted, the reversal in magnitude sensitivity disappeared and, as expected, participants in both unit-salient and unite-non-salient conditions were price-sensitive.

In an incentive-compatible replication, participants were told that they would be bidding on an amount of a foreign currency, with the currency symbol denoted by X, and that they would find out the country of origin after bidding. In a 2x2 between-subjects factorial design, participants bid on either X6.83 or X0.69 (representing $1 in either Chinese Yuan or UK pounds, respectively). In the stimuli, either the currency symbol, X, was written in a relatively large font (unit salient) or in a relatively small font (unit non-salient); the remaining information was in a small (normal) font. The BDM procedure was adopted to encourage accurate judgments. We found that when the currency was salient, there was no significant difference in bids for the two amounts. However, when the currency was not salient, participants were magnitude sensitive and bid nearly $5 more for the larger-magnitude stimulus (X6.83) than for the small-magnitude stimulus (X0.69).

We replicate these findings in a third study, where participants made estimates based on unfamiliar units of length in which the font size and numeric magnitudes varied. We replicate the reversal of magnitude-sensitivity based on the font size when comparing moderately low and high numbers (3 vs. 12). Magnitude sensitivity for low unit-salience did not extend to a third pair of conditions, however, in which we used dramatically higher numbers in order to prompt an evaluation of the units.

We ruled out five alternative accounts of our findings across all studies. First, we found that the effect is not due to lack of attention. In the hotel study, for example, we asked participants to recall the information they saw. Data from the participants who failed to recall were excluded, though including their data did not qualitatively change the result. In addition, we found whether controlling response time or not, in the foreign currency study, did not moderate the effect, which rules out the explanation from system 1 intuitive thinking. Third, via the comparison between unfamiliar and familiar currency, we found that fluency does not play a role in the effect. Forth, emphasizing on either the outcome by bidding with real money or the process by reasoning aloud did not affect the effect, suggesting that lack of involvement also does not explain our finding. Lastly, we tried a third magnitude, a value out of a range that consumers could make sense of in a certain context, and found that they stopped showing magnitude-sensitivity. This indicates that the salience does not lead to an anchoring (on the salient component) and insufficient adjustment process.

Buying Daily Pleasure with Daily Payments: Narrow Framing Favors Scope Insensitive Accounts

EXTENDED ABSTRACT

How do consumers evaluate purchases with tangible and intangible consequences distributed across time? For many decisions, consumers are faced with the difficult task of weighing a stream of intangible benefits (e.g., the increased productivity provided by a new laptop over the five years they own it) against a stream of more tangible costs (e.g., monthly installments, if the laptop is financed). Our interest in is decisions involving somewhat affectively-loaded intangible benefits, like a choice about whether leasing a flashy new car is worth hundreds of dollars each month or whether to acquiesce to an emotional plea to contribute 37 cents per day to help starving children. We propose that periodic pricing, such as per-day-framing (e.g., 37 cents a day), encourages consumers to evaluate the intangible benefits commensurate with periodic payments (e.g., the utility experienced by the thought of helping a starving child each day), while aggregate framing (e.g., $135 a year) encourages consumers to evaluate an aggregate benefit (e.g., the utility experienced by a year's worth of helping). In other words, per-day-framing encourages people to evaluate the imagined per-day benefits of purchasing.

Gourville (1998) introduced "Pennies-a-Day", which suggests that separating a cost into a series of small payments (e.g. 37 cents a day) can increase the attractiveness of a purchase opportunity because consumers assimilate the cost with the category of small, ongoing, trivial expenses retrieved from memory, such as a cup of coffee. However, we find evidence that per-day pricing can increase purchase intentions even when costs are large (i.e. outside the domain of trivial expenses), and that per-day pricing enhances consumers' perceptions of per-day benefits, which presents an alternate account of the Pennies-a-Day effect. We propose that narrowly bracketing daily prices changes consumers' representation of the transaction's intangible benefits. Consequently, the valuation of the intangible consequences influence whether narrow framing promotes purchase. Specifically, we explore the critical role of scope sensitivity over the domain of gains and losses proposed by a transaction.

Evaluations are scope insensitive when they respond to the presence of a stimulus but not changes in its magnitude (Hsee, Rottenstreich and Xiao, 2005). For example, individuals react more negatively to the news that they will lose $100 than they would if they already lost $1,900 and will now lose an additional $100. As figure 1 illustrates, narrow framing favors scope insensitive accounts, whereby the first units confer large marginal value. Importantly, McGraw, Shafir and Todorov (2010) find that monetary outcomes are often more scope sensitive than non-monetary outcomes, which may help to explain why the domain of charitable donations comprises much of the extant Pennies-a-Day literature. More generally, an effective temporal reframing strategy exists if the transaction's cost-tied-benefits are more scope insensitive than the transaction's costs. In these cases, consumers prefer more payment events to fewer payment events.

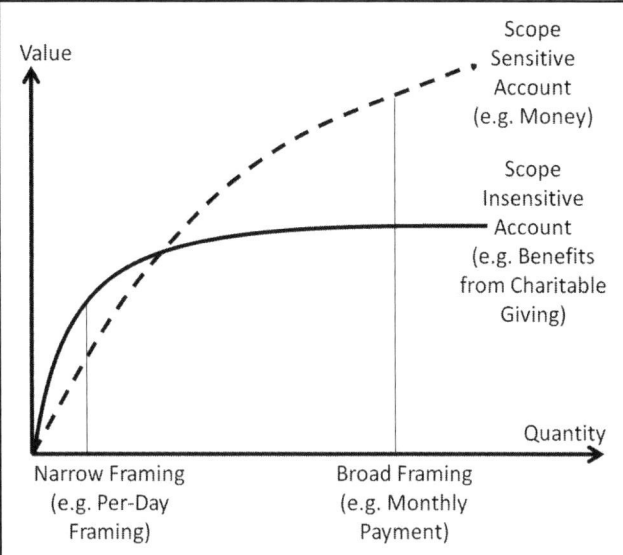

Figure 1. Broad framing favors scope sensitive accounts, while narrow framing favors scope insensitive accounts

In one study, we found that per-day pricing can increase donations outside of the 'trivial' cost domain. Consumers are more willing to pay for a luxury automobile when the price on a daily basis than on a monthly basis (6.9 vs. 5.0 on a 0-11 scale, p=0.03). This result is consistent with the "Pennies-a-Day" framework in that consumers are willing to spend more in the context of a recurring expense. However, the daily cost far exceeds $5, the previously accepted upper bound on trivial expenses (Gourville, 2003). This suggests that another process, beyond assimilation with trivial, recurring expenses, drives the Pennies-a-Day effect.

A second study explores the benefits associated with making daily payments. We find that Pennies-a-Day pricing increases a transaction's perceived benefits, and that purchase likelihood is mediated more strongly by perceived benefits than by cost triviality. In one study we asked subjects to rate their likelihood of donating a daily amount or equivalent yearly amount to a charity. In each case, the actual donation would be automatically deducted from their monthly paychecks, rendering the donation requests otherwise equivalent. We found that subjects were more willing to donate to the cause under the daily frame, and they not only expected the payment to be less costly but also expected the donation to bring them more daily pleasure. Subjects' perceptions of the daily pleasure they would obtain from the donation, as well as perceived costs, each partially mediated the effect of pricing frame on willingness to donate, and together these two factors account for 51% of the variance in willingness to donate. Additionally, we find that the projected daily pleasure accounts for willingness to purchase more strongly than evaluations of whether the cost is trivial. This result suggests that narrow, per-day framing can encourage purchase by enhancing perceived benefits tied to the purchase event.

Our framework has implications for how consumers construct value across a wide variety of situations: we propose that framing a transaction's tangible cost narrowly (e.g. per-day pricing) encourages consumers to represent intangible benefits narrowly. This can exaggerate the advantages of the transaction when its benefits are more scope-insensitive than its costs. Ongoing studies test for an expected reversal when a transaction's costs are more scope insensitive than its benefits.

The Price is Right? Effects of Internal and External Reference Prices on Consumer Judgments

Chair: Shelle Santana, New York University, USA

Paper #1: When Recall Disrupts Memory: Evidence for Implicit Reference Prices

Manoj Thomas, Cornell University, USA
Ellie Kyung, Dartmouth College, USA

Paper #2: When Partitioning Prices, Firms Better Deliver!

Ajay Abraham, University of Maryland, USA
Rebecca Hamilton, University of Maryland, USA
Joydeep Srivastava, University of Maryland, USA

Paper #3: Buying What You Can Get For Free: How Self-Presentation Motives Influence Payment Decisions in Pay-What-You-Want Contexts

Shelle Santana, New York University, USA
Vicki Morwitz, New York University, USA

SESSION OVERVIEW:

Product pricing is one of the most important decisions that a firm can make, yet consumers often respond to pricing information in surprising ways. For example, consumers are highly influenced by reference prices, which are sometimes provided by the firm or the context, but are often constructed by consumers as a way to help process price information. The same reference price can in some situations increase the consumer's likelihood of purchase, but in other situations may decrease it. The goal of this proposed session is to expand our current understanding of how consumers integrate and respond to internal and external reference prices. Each paper in the session investigates this research objective from a unique theoretical perspective, offering a broader view of the different ways reference prices impact consumers' consumption experiences.

The first paper by Thomas and Kyung focuses on cognitive processes that influence the recall of internal reference prices. Specifically, the authors compare the effectiveness of explicit and implicit memory-based processes consumers use when they form price magnitude judgments. Results from two experiments show that consumers' make more accurate price judgments when they use implicit memory of reference prices to form price judgments (i.e., they judge price magnitudes without trying to first recall past prices) versus when they use explicit memory (i.e., they first try to recall past prices). This research demonstrates that, ironically, in certain instances, consumers can make more accurate price judgments by *not* recalling the prices.

The second paper by Abraham, Hamilton, and Srivastava examines how partitioned pricing can form an external reference price for a product component. This external reference price in turn shapes consumers' expectations of service delivery and their subsequent attitudinal responses to service failures. The authors posit that the increased salience of a partitioned component increases consumers' performance expectations for that component. Thus, when a service failure related to that component occurs, consumers are significantly more dissatisfied when firms use partitioned pricing than when they do not. Results from four studies support their predictions and shed new light on how reference prices highlighted by partitioned pricing affect consumers' consumption experiences.

The third paper by Santana and Morwitz explores how social factors can influence how consumers form internal reference prices and how they react to external ones in pay-what-you-want (PWYW) pricing contexts. Under a PWYW pricing strategy, the seller is purely

a price taker, and the consumer can pay any price they choose for a product—including zero. While the most rational response of the buyer is to pay nothing, very few consumers actually do. The authors propose and demonstrate that self presentation motives significantly influence willingness-to-pay (WTP) in PWYW contexts. Results from three studies show that individuals with high self presentation motives demonstrate a higher WTP, are more sensitive to reference prices, and express more aversion toward the PWYW experience.

Audience: The potential ACR audience for this session is quite broad. Apart from providing new theoretical insights for researchers interested in behavioral pricing, the session will attract a cross-section of ACR conference attendees who are interested in diverse areas of research such as memory and judgment, numerical cognition, customer satisfaction, and self presentation and impression management.

Level of Completeness: For all three papers, the theorizing has been completed and multiple studies have already been conducted. Since all three papers are close to completion, we expect this to be an interesting and high quality session.

Discussion Leader: The proposed session addresses important questions relating to how consumers form and use reference prices. For example, is it necessary for consumers to use explicit memory-based reference prices in determining price magnitude judgments? Does partitioned pricing pose unknown risks to the firm by inadvertently activating higher expectations for the partitioned component? Finally, what factors lead consumers to buy products that can be obtained for free? The discussion following the session is expected to focus on how these papers provide insights into answering these questions and thereby contribute to a broader and richer understanding of how consumers respond to a range of pricing scenarios they encounter in the marketplace.

Aradhna Krishna will be the discussion leader for this session. Aradhna is a recognized leader in the field of behavioral pricing research, and thus has a unique perspective for discussing these papers and leading a discussion about an appropriate research agenda for continued work in this area.

Plan for the Session: Our goal for the session is to give each presenter sufficient time to clearly present his or her findings, to encourage audience interaction with the presenters, and to facilitate a discussion about future research. We plan to allocate the session time in the following manner. Each paper will be presented for 15 minutes, followed by 5 minutes of question and answer. We will leave 15 minutes at the end of the session for a general audience discussion lead by Aradhna Krishna.

Summary: In sum, while each of the papers examines the formation and impact of reference prices, each provides different conceptual and methodological contributions. We believe that by examining a range of cognitive, attitudinal, and social factors that impact how reference prices are formed and used, we will not only appeal to a broad cross-section of ACR members, but also make an important contribution to theory. By highlighting the synergy in our research questions, we hope to provide significant insight and lay the foundation for future research on reference prices.

When Recall Disrupts Memory:
Evidence for Implicit Reference Prices

EXTENDED ABSTRACT

Consumers often evaluate offer prices by comparing them with previous prices they have encountered for the same product. Several econometric studies have shown that consumers, during their weekly trips to grocery stores, make purchase decisions by comparing the offer prices of products with prices observed on their previous trips. The memory-based comparison standard used in such price evaluations is referred to as reference price. The results from these studies suggest that consumers actually use brand- and pack-specific reference prices for such memory-based comparisons. That is, while evaluating the price of a 12 oz. pack of Starkist brand tuna, consumers use the previous week's price of the 12 oz. pack of Starkist brand tuna as the reference price. Such a conceptualization raises the inevitable question: how can consumers possibly remember the prices of hundreds of brands and products? Do they actually recall and compare the prices of so many brands and products on their weekly shopping trips? Several researchers have suggested that consumers' do not recall the prices from their memory for reference prices for such comparisons; rather, their price comparisons are based on implicit memory (Adaval and Monroe 2002; Monroe and Lee 1999; Thomas and Menon 2007; Thomas and Morwitz 2009). Implicit memory refers to the ability to use memory-based information without consciously remembering the information. Monroe and Lee (1999) characterized implicit price knowledge as the ability to "know the price without recalling it." The purpose of the present research is to study the roles of explicit and implicit memory in price comparison process.

In this research we address a hitherto unaddressed question: Does attempting to recall the reference price increase or decrease the accuracy of memory-based price comparisons? Common sense suggests that attempting to recall the reference price should not reduce the accuracy of memory-based price comparisons. That is, while judging whether an offer price is higher or lower than a reference price, consumers who try to explicitly recall the reference price should be at least as accurate as those who do not try to recall the reference price. In this paper, we suggest that this naïve view of memory may not be always correct. We posit, and empirically demonstrate, that actually trying to recall the reference price can reduce the accuracy of memory-based price comparisons.

We suggest that a reference price can be stored in memory using two distinct types of representations: 1) an analog representation on an internal number line that is not accessible to consciousness but can used in implicit memory tasks, and 2) symbolic representations that can be consciously recalled. Since a reference price can be available in implicit memory as an analog representation even when it is cannot be recalled, this literature suggests that people can make memory-based comparisons even when they are unable to explicitly recall the reference price. We posit that while comparing the prices of many products (as in a grocery store situation), recall attempts can disrupt implicit memory processes. More specifically, when people attempt to recall a reference price, they will be less accurate in judging whether the target price is lower or higher than the reference price. In contrast, when they make magnitude judgments without attempting to recall the reference price, they will be able to effectively rely on their implicit memory to judge whether the target price is lower or higher. We will refer to this effect as the Recall Induced Disruption of Implicit Memory, or simply the *memory disruption effect*.

Two experiments offer evidence for the memory disruption effect. In Experiment 1, participants were asked to respond to a simu-lated shopping task wherein they had to consider whether or not to include 20 different everyday grocery items in their shopping carts. After the shopping task, they were presented with a surprise memory test. They saw the 20 items again; but this time the products had new prices that could have been higher, lower, or the same as before. Their task was to identify whether the new prices are lower, higher, or the same as before. They also had the option of submitting a "don't know" response indicating that they did not know whether the magnitude of the new price is lower or higher. Half the participants (assigned to the explicit memory condition) were told that they have to try and recall the previous price before judging the magnitude of the new prices. The other half did not have to explicitly recall the previous prices before making the magnitude judgments. We examined the effect of explicit recall on judgment accuracy. As predicted, explicit recall reduced the accuracy of relative magnitude judgments. Participants in the implicit memory condition were more accurate than those in implicit memory condition, 46% vs. 38%, p < .05. Further, explicit recall did not increase incorrect judgments (p > .60), but it increased the proportion of "don't know" responses, 28% vs. 20% p < .05.

Experiment 2 replicated and extended these results in two ways. First, instead of presenting participants with a surprise recall task (incidental encoding condition), they were warned that there would be a memory test after the shopping task (intentional encoding condition). Second, we did not randomize the order of presentation to test whether the effect is caused by recall-induced interference. The effects reported previously were replicated in the intentional encoding condition as well. Additionally, although we observed the standard primacy and recency effects of order on accuracy, explicit (vs. implicit) recall did not interact with these effects. These results suggest that the memory disruption effect is not caused by recall-induced interference.

The memory disruption effect offers a more nuanced conceptualization of memory-based reference prices. Although several studies on memory have demonstrated that remembering can cause forgetting, to our knowledge none of the extant research has examined whether remembering can affect performance in a subsequent numerical judgment task. This is the first paper to demonstrate that in a numerical comparison task, trying to recall a number from memory can disrupt subsequent numerical judgments.

REFERENCES

Adaval, Rashmi and Kent B. Monroe (2002), "Automatic Construction and Use of Contextual Information for Product and Price Evaluations," *Journal of Consumer Research*, 28 (March), 572-87.

Monroe, Kent B. and Angela Y. Lee (1999), "Remembering versus Knowing: Issues in Buyers' Processing of Price Information," *Journal of the Academy of Marketing Science*, 27 (2), 207-25.

Thomas, Manoj and Geeta Menon (2007), "When Internal Reference Prices and Price Expectations Diverge: The Role of Confidence," *Journal of Marketing Research*, 44 (3), 401-9.

Thomas, Manoj and Vicki G. Morwitz (2009), "The Ease-of-Computation Effect: The Interplay of Metacognitive Experiences and Naïve Theories in Judgments of Price Differences," *Journal of Marketing Research*, 46 (1), 81-91.

When Partitioning Prices, Firms Better Deliver!

EXTENDED ABSTRACT

Firms using a partitioned pricing strategy divide the price of a product or service into two or more mandatory components (Morwitz, Greenleaf and Johnson 1998). For example, an online book seller may list separate prices for a book and for shipping the book, even though the buyer must purchase both components together. Research has shown that price partitioning increases the salience of partitioned components (Bertini and Wathieu 2008; Chakravarti et al 2002) and that the nature of the components partitioned from the base price can significantly influence consumers' reactions to a firm's offers even when consumers know that the total price is the same (Hamilton and Srivastava 2008).

Because prices play a role in forming consumers' expectations about goods and services (Mitra and Fay 2010), we propose that the greater salience of the prices of partitioned components may increase consumers' expectations about the performance of these components. Expectations are consumers' pre-purchase beliefs about the performance of the product or service (Oliver and Winer 1987). If expectations serve as a referent for comparison, higher expectations may decrease satisfaction because performance less favorable than consumers' high expectations can create expectancy disconfirmation (Oliver 1980; Yi 1990).

Thus, partitioning prices may have negative consequences for firms, such as lower satisfaction with the partitioned component and even the overall transaction, when partitioned components fail to meet consumers' performance expectations. We propose that expectancy disconfirmation will mediate this effect. To test our predictions, we ran a series of four studies.

Our first two studies show that when a specific component is partitioned out of the base price, customers' expectations for that component significantly increase. In study 1, participants evaluated airline tickets for which the price of in-flight entertainment was either partitioned or included in the total price. Expectations for in-flight entertainment increased when this component was partitioned even though expectations for other components such as baggage service did not differ across conditions. We replicated this effect in study 2 for a hotel stay in which parking was either partitioned or included in the total price.

In study 3, we extended our examination to the potential downstream effects of partitioned pricing by manipulating the service experience of the customer. Participants were given price information about an airline flight in which in-flight entertainment was either partitioned or included in the total price. After responding to items measuring their expectations for the flight and their expectations for the in-flight entertainment, participants were exposed to the service delivery manipulation. In the control condition, participants read that the in-flight entertainment system worked as expected. In the mild failure condition, they read that the in-flight entertainment service shut down for about 10 minutes during the flight.

Although satisfaction with the in-flight entertainment service did not differ across the partitioned and non-partitioned conditions when there was no failure, satisfaction was significantly lower in the partitioned versus the non-partitioned conditions when there was a mild failure. We observed the same pattern of results for satisfaction with the flight, suggesting that dissatisfaction with the partitioned component bleeds over to the overall service experience. To examine the underlying process in more detail, we tested whether the difference between the expected quality of the in-flight entertainment service and its experienced quality mediated the effect. Indeed, this difference, which we label expectancy disconfirmation, mediated the

effect of the interaction between service failure and partitioning on satisfaction.

In study 4, we replicated the results of study 3 in the context of attending a sports event. Participants imagined that they purchased a ticket for a football game that came with parking at the stadium on the day of the game. The price of parking was either partitioned or included in the total price. In addition to the control condition and a mild service failure condition, we included a delight condition, in which the service experience was better than expected, and a non-use condition, in which the participants imagined that they did not use the partitioned component. Overall satisfaction and satisfaction with parking did not differ significantly across the partitioned versus non-partitioned conditions in the no failure condition or in the delight condition. However, when the price was partitioned, satisfaction was significantly lower in the mild failure condition and marginally lower in the non-use condition than when the price was not partitioned. Again, expectancy disconfirmation mediated the effects.

In summary, price partitioning seems to increase consumers' expectations for partitioned components. Although there are no differences in satisfaction when firms meet or exceed expectations, we see that when partitioned components fail to meet consumers' expectations, consumers are significantly more dissatisfied when firms use partitioned pricing than when they do not. Notably, even when consumers do not encounter a service failure, they may be more dissatisfied under partitioned pricing when they do not consume the partitioned component. Given these potential negative consequences, we advocate caution in the use of price partitioning. When firms partition prices, they seem to be held more accountable for a positive service experience.

REFERENCES

Bertini, Marco and Luc Wathieu (2008), "Attention Arousal through Price Partitioning," *Marketing Science*, 27 (2), 236–46.
Chakravarti, Dipankar, Rajan Krish, Pallab Paul, and Joydeep Srivastava (2002), "Partitioned Presentation of Multicomponent Bundle Prices: Evaluation, Choice, and Underlying Processing Effects," *Journal of Consumer Psychology*, 12 (3), 215–29.
Hamilton, Rebecca W. and Joydeep Srivastava (2008), "When 2+2 is not the Same as 1+3: Variations in Price Sensitivity Across Components of Partitioned Prices," *Journal of Marketing Research*, 45 (4), 450–61.
Mitra, Debanjan and Scott Fay (2010), "Managing Service Expectations in Online Markets: a Signaling Theory of E-tailer Pricing and Empirical Tests," *Journal of Retailing*, 86 (2), 184–99.
Morwitz, Vicki G., Eric Greenleaf, and Eric Johnson (1998), "Divide and Prosper: Consumers' Reactions to Partitioned Prices," *Journal of Marketing Research*, 35 (4), 453–63.
Oliver, Richard L. (1980), "A Cognitive Model of the Antecedents and Consequences of Satisfaction Decisions," *Journal of Marketing Research*, 17 (4), 460–69.
Oliver, Richard L. and *Russell* S. Winer, (1987), "A Framework for the Formation and Structure of Consumer Expectations: Review and Propositions," *Journal of Economic Psychology*, 8 (4), 469–99.
Yi, Youjae (1990), "A Critical Review of Consumer Satisfaction," in *Review of Marketing 1990*, Valarie A. Zeithaml, ed. Chicago: American Marketing Association, 68–123.

Buying What You Can Get For Free: How Self Presentation Motives Influence Payment Decisions in Pay-What-You-Want Contexts

EXTENDED ABSTRACT

When setting a price, firms can choose from a number of different strategies ranging from maximum seller control to maximum buyer control. Most firms choose the former, where the seller has maximum control and the buyer is purely a price taker—they must pay the seller's posted price to secure their desired good. However, some firms employ a Pay-What-You-Want (PWYW) pricing strategy where the buyer has maximum control and the seller is purely a price taker. In these instances, the seller must provide the good to the buyer at any price the buyer sets—including zero.

Standard economic theory holds that the most rational response by the buyer in a PWYW scenario is to pay nothing; yet, research shows that consumers rarely do (Gneezy, Gneezy, Nelson, and Brown 2010; Kim, Natter, and Spann 2009). Researchers offer a number of different explanations for this seemingly irrational behavior, including social exchange norms (Elster 1989), fairness and reciprocity (Bolton and Ockenfels 2000), and altruism (Maner and Gailliot 2007), to name a few. We add to this stream by proposing and demonstrating that consumers' self presentation motives significantly influence willingness-to-pay (WTP) in PWYW contexts.

Self presentation has been defined as the use of behavior to communicate information about oneself to others (Baumeister 1982). In a PWYW context, we posit that consumers pay more than zero because their payment acts as a means to project a favorable image of themselves to others. Therefore, we predict that the percentage of participants who pay for their product will be significantly greater than zero, and that relative to individuals with low self presentation concerns, those with high self presentation concerns will: 1) have higher WTP, 2) be more sensitive to reference prices in the environment, and 3) have a more aversive experience. The two studies we have conducted to date support these predictions.

In Study 1, participants were offered the opportunity to PWYW for a breakfast combo consisting of coffee or tea and their choice of a bagel, danish, or donut. Self presentation was manipulated by whether payment was made publicly or privately (Baumester 1982). A suggested retail price for the combo was either provided or not. We measured participants' willingness to pay, how motivated they were to impress others when they generated their payment price, and how motivated they were to spend an appropriate amount. Participants also evaluated how much they enjoyed the PWYW process, what emotions they felt, and whether they would prefer to PWYW or pay a regular posted price in the future.

As predicted, the number of subjects who paid more than zero was significantly greater than zero—in fact all subjects submitted a non-zero payment amount. Participants in the public condition had a significantly higher WTP and a motivation to impress others than their private payment counterparts. Furthermore, the motivation to impress others mediated the effect of visibility on WTP, whereas the effect of a spend accuracy motive did not. Relative to participants in the private condition, those in the public condition enjoyed PWYW less, had lower positive emotions, and had a greater preference to pay a regular posted price vs. PWYW in the future.

Study 2 tests whether our predictions hold for individuals with chronic self presentation concerns, and further examines how reference price magnitude moderates WTP and consumers' emotional reaction to PWYW. Since individuals with high self presentation concerns tend to be more attuned to social norms and cues in their environment and actively manage their behavior to please others,

we expected high self monitoring individuals to be more sensitive to reference price information. In this study, self presentation was a measured individual difference variable based on Snyder's (1974) 25-item Self Monitoring Scale. Reference price magnitude was manipulated by having the retailer provide a very low or a very high suggested price for the breakfast combo. No reference price information was provided in the control condition. We expected high self monitors to pay significantly less (more) than low self monitors when provided with a very low (high) reference price. Furthermore, we expected a more aversive subjective experience of PWYW for high self monitors.

The results supported our predictions. First, when a very low (high) reference price was provided, high self monitors paid significantly less (more) than low self monitors. In deciding on what to pay, high self monitors were more motivated by impressing others, and low self monitors were more motivated by spending the right amount of money. High self monitors reported a more aversive subjective experience, as well as higher levels of negative emotions such as anger, guilt, sadness, shame, frustration, and worry. Interestingly, the interplay between external references and self monitoring appears to influence post-purchase behavior as well. When no or low reference prices are provided, high self monitors reported being more likely to avoid the vendor in the future, but when a high reference price is provided, they are less likely to avoid the vendor in the future.

We are currently running a third study to test overt pressure as a boundary condition of self presentation motives in PWYW. Baumeister (1982) argues that if one is primarily concerned with one's public image, then conformity should decrease as overt pressure increases, since in these conditions yielding and conforming is bad for one's public image. In study 3 we manipulate overt pressure based on learning what close others pay in these settings (paying zero or very low prices). So far, preliminary results support our predictions. This study and an extension will be completed in the next few months.

In sum we show that self presentation concerns explain why consumers pay more than zero in PWYW pricing, how they react to firm provided reference prices, and how they react to social pressure. This research demonstrates the powerful effects of social forces in economic transactions, and why a buyer might prefer the economic disadvantage of traditional pricing structures over the economic advantages of PWYW.

REFERENCES

Baumeister, Roy F. (1982), "A Self-Presentational View of Social Phenomena," *Psychological Bulletin,* 91 (1), 3-26.

Bolton, Gary E. and Axel Ockenfels (2000), "ERC: A Theory of Equity, Reciprocity, and Competition," *American Economic Review*, 90 (1), 166-93.

Elster, Jon (1989), "Social Norms and Economic Theory," *The Journal of Economic Perspectives*, 3 (4), 99-117.

Gneezy, Ayelet, Uri Gneezy, Leif D. Nelson, and Amber Brown (2010), "Shared Social Responsibility: A Field Experiment in Pay-What-You-Want Pricing and Charitable Giving," *Science*, 329 (July), 325-327.

Kim, Ju-Young, Martin Natter, Martin Spann (2009), "Pay-What-You-Want—A New Participative Pricing Mechanism," *Journal of Marketing*, 73 (1), 44-58.

Maner, Jon K. and Matthew T. Gailliot (2007), "Altruism and Egoism: Prosocial Motivations for Helping Depend on Relationship Context," *European Journal of Social Psychology*, 37 (2), 347-58.

Making Decisions by Making Sense of Time
Chair: Kyu Kim, University of Southern California, USA

SESSION OVERVIEW

Recently there has been growing interest in individuals' subjective sense of future time such as time perspective, time perception, or perceived temporal distance in the areas of consumer research and psychology. But still, not much is known about what influences subjective sense of time has on consumers' judgment and decision making. The proposed symposium touches on three aspects of future time judgment–time horizon perspective, perceived temporal scarcity of life, and time compartmentalization– and discusses whether and how it impacts consumer preference in various domains including preference for private vs. public consumption and intertemporal preference.

The first presentation (Sellier and Morwitz) focuses on consumers' perception of the amount of time ahead of them as being limited versus expansive, and demonstrates that such time horizon perspective influences their preference to consume alone or together. The second presentation (Kim, Zauberman, and Bettman) addresses the relationship between perceived temporal scarcity of life and subjective prospective temporal judgment, and demonstrates that consumers whose temporal scarcity of life were heightened became more impatient for delayed monetary outcomes because waiting time until the receipt of delayed rewards is subjectively expanded. The third presentation (Soman and Tu) shows that consumers compartmentalize future time using ongoing duration markers–events that occur in the same period as the present are perceived to be closer and viewed with more of an implemental mindset– and that the time compartmentalization influences preference and choices in various consumer settings.

All of these presentations demonstrate that subjective sense of future time plays a key role in driving consumers' judgment and decision making in various domains. Considering the growing interest in subjective time perception and in time-related decisions in consumer research, we expect that this symposium will attract a broad audience who are interested in time perception research or those who are interested in consumers' judgment and decision making in various domains in general.

We believe that this session will stimulate an interesting and in-depth discussion between presenters and audience, and among presenters about different aspects of subjective sense of time and their relationship to consumer decision making. To ensure enough interaction between presenters and audience, we limited the number of presentations to three but invited a discussant, Kristin Diehl, who will lead a quality discussion during the session. We believe this session will be more interactive than any other sessions at ACR.

These presentations are in a completed stage or close to completion, and are not presented in ACR conferences previously.

I Want to be Alone: The Role of Time Horizon Perspective on the Valuation of Social Presence

EXTENDED ABSTRACT

Consumers generally seek the presence of others they like when engaging in consumption activities, except in certain socially undesirable or embarrassing situations (e.g., Dahl, Manchanda and Argo 2001; Loveland, Smeesters and Mandel 2008). We ask: Do consumers ever seek to be alone, outside of socially undesirable contexts? Using Socioemotional Selectivity Theory (SST, Carstensen 1992), we develop hypotheses about the moderating impact of one factor, namely time horizon perspective (i.e., consumers' perception of the amount of time ahead of them as being limited versus expansive) on the extent to which social presence is valued. We find that consumers have a relative preference to be alone versus with someone they like when they perceive the time ahead of them as expansive rather than limited. We further show that this effect depends on whether the person or the nature of the activity, are more associated with love/caring or with knowledge/achievement.

While research has shown that time perspective influences consumers' evaluation of ads (e.g., Williams and Drolet 2005), SST and consumer research have not yet addressed the question of whether consumers' time perspective can affect overall how they value social presence. We propose that a limited time horizon should enhance the value of social presence, because consumers primarily focus on interacting with others for emotional support. In contrast, an expansive time horizon involves banking information that does not directly require the presence of others to pursue achievement-related goals. We therefore predict that consumers perceiving time as expansive versus limited should value social presence less when engaging in consumption activities.

A first pilot study tests this general hypothesis: on the street, 52 people were asked to respond to two ostensibly unrelated surveys. The first survey manipulated participants' time horizon perspective. Participants either wrote about five life projects for which they perceived they had either "limited time" or "all the time in the world" to achieve. Participants in a third - control - condition wrote about activities they liked to engage in. Next, all participants filled out an "enjoyment survey," which asked them to rate, for each of 23 activities, whether they would prefer to engage in them alone or with someone they like. The list included a broad range of activities, selected from research on well-being (Kahneman, Krueger, Schkade, Schwartz, and Stone 2004). On average across activities, participants with a limited time perception preferred to be with someone they like more than did those with an expansive time perspective. Participants in the control condition fell in-between. A cluster analysis of the activities revealed similar results for each cluster.

SST predicts that emotion-related goals or achievement-related goals receive priority depending on whether time is perceived as limited or expansive respectively. One question, then, is whether the type of person consumers envision engaging in consumption activities with moderates the main effect of time horizon we found. To examine this possibility, we ran a 2 (Time horizon: limited vs.

Advances in Consumer Research
Volume 39, ©2011

expansive) x 2 (Presence: congruent with emotion- vs. achievement-related goals) full-factorial design. 75 students filled out either the same Limited or Expansive time survey as before. They then were asked to read the description of either the classmate who was consistent with a love/caring or an achievement goal (consistent with a limited time or an expansive time perspective) and to picture that person in their mind, and reported the extent they would prefer to engage in the same 23 activities as before, alone versus with the person they had in mind. A 2x2 ANOVA revealed a significant two-way interaction. Participants who had thought of a love/caring related classmate wanted to be alone significantly more when time was expansive rather than limited. In contrast, participants who had thought of an achievement-related classmate equally valued social presence regardless of whether time was expansive or limited. Again, the pattern of results was the same for each cluster in a cluster analysis.

A final study examined whether the impact of time perspective on valuation of being with others changes when the consumption activity itself varies in how it relates to love and caring rather than achievement. This study was a 2 (Time horizon: limited vs. expansive) x 2 (Movie: about-love vs. about-achievement) between-subjects design. We manipulated participants' time horizon as before, before participants read one of four synopses of a soon to be released movie. Based on a pretest, two of the movies were primarily about love, while the other two were primarily about achievement. After reading these synopses, 105 participants indicated the extent to which they would prefer seeing the movie alone versus with someone they like. Because our results were identical for the two pairs of movies, we report the combined results. A 2x2 ANOVA only revealed a significant two-way interaction. Participants who had read the description of the movies about-love/caring reported wanting to be alone significantly more when time was perceived as expansive versus limited. In contrast, participants who had read the description of the movies about-achievement equally valued social presence regardless of time horizon.

While social interaction is core to our survival, we find that when consumers sense that they have a large amount of time ahead of them, they become relative loners. Our findings also suggest that additional insights may be gained from manipulating the type of other consumer presence in mere presence research.

The Impact of Perceived Temporal Scarcity of Life on Temporal Distance Judgments

EXTENDED ABSTRACT

Although theoretically future time might be infinite, the individual's own lifespan is often the most salient and natural context within which temporal duration is judged. We argue that the individual's perceived lifespan is in turn influenced by reminders of mortality (and hence scarcity of life). Thus, the extent of an individual's own perceived temporal space (i.e., the scarcity of that individual's perceived lifespan) provides the context that influences judgments of perceived temporal distance to specific future events.

When individuals are reminded of their death, it heightens their perceived temporal scarcity of life (e.g., how much time is perceived to be left in life). Their perceptions of remaining lifetime are a highly salient context for other temporal judgments for them. As a result, perceived distance to a future point in time will be inversely influenced by how much time is perceived to be left in life, just as magnitude judgment of a target stimulus is inversely related to the perceived magnitude of a context stimulus in human perception and judgment (Sherman, Ahlm, & Berman, 1978).

In study 1 we manipulated temporal scarcity of life by reminding participants of their death. To manipulate temporal scarcity of life, participants in the death condition were presented with a word-search puzzle on a computer screen, in which death-related words were embedded among other letters (King et al., 2009). For those in the control condition, a similar word-search puzzle but with neutral words was presented. Once participants found the target words, they were directed to the next screen, where their perceived temporal distance was measured. Specifically, participants were asked to think about a day in one month and then to indicate how long or short they considered the duration to be from today to a day in one month by moving a slide bar on a 150 mm continuous line scale with endpoints labeled as very short and very long. Confirming our prediction, participants who were reminded of their death perceived the same 1-month duration to be subjectively longer than those in the control condition. This effect was not driven by changes in construal level, anxiety, or emotional reactions.

In study 2 we manipulated temporal scarcity of life not by reminders of death but by simply manipulating how much time is perceived to be left in life. For this purpose, we utilized the findings of a recent neurobiological study reporting that basic human cognitive functions peak at age 39 and sharply decline thereafter (Bartzokis et al., 2009). This information should heighten the perceived temporal scarcity of life among young individuals ('There is only about 20 years before my brain breaks down!') compared to a condition providing information about one's total life expectancy, which is longer. One noteworthy feature of this manipulation is that mortality is more likely to be associated with the life expectancy condition, which is predicted to trigger less temporal scarcity in this case. Results indicated that participants in the high-scarcity condition perceived the same temporal distance on an objective scale (e.g., 3 months) to be subjectively longer than those in the low-scarcity condition.

In study 3 we manipulated temporal scarcity of life by manipulating how much time is perceived to be left in life but further tested the behavioral implications of this finding we examine the effects of perceived temporal scarcity of life for intertemporal decisions, namely the degree of impatience for delayed monetary rewards. While college students generally reveal a greater degree of impatience in intertemporal decisions than older adults (Green, Fry, & Myerson, 1994; Read & Read, 2004), we predict that impatience among college students may be further elevated by heightening their perceived temporal scarcity of life. Results in time perception replicated study 1 and 2–participants in the high-scarcity condition perceived the same temporal distance to be subjectively longer than those in the low-scarcity condition. Importantly, for impatience, as revealed in a delay-discounting task, we found that participants in the high-scarcity condition requested more money if they had to wait for three months to receive rewards than those who in the low-scarcity condition. Such changes in perceived temporal distance or impatience level were not driven by affective responses to our manipulations.

Taken together, the present research demonstrates a novel aspect of the relationship between perceived psychological space and perceived temporal distance: when psychological space associated with perceived lifespan is subjectively contracted, temporal distance judged within this space is perceived to be relatively expanded.

Looking Ahead: Duration Markers and Their Effects on Choice

EXTENDED ABSTRACT

Consumers often need to make decisions involving outcomes that are to happen in the future. In the intertemporal choice literature, one decision that has been studied extensively is the choice between a smaller and sooner (SS), and a later and larger (LL) reward (Soman et al. 2005). A second type of decision has to do with commencing effort towards a task that is due sometime in the future (O'Donoghue and Rabin 1999). Most of the literature in this area has treated future time as a continuous variable, and very little research has attempted to study how consumers encode future time (but, see Bettman et al. 2009). The standard view of intertemporal decisions is that the key driver driving the decision should be the duration between the present and the future outcome (e.g., Ainslie and Haslam 1992).

In this research, we propose that consumers do not always encode future time as linear, but rather as categories. People routinely compartmentalize time periods into pre-determined units like days, months and years. In addition, there are many other "markers" of time that people often use in an ongoing manner - students tend to compartmentalize their time by terms, farmers by harvesting seasons, etc. (Ahn, Liu and Soman 2009; Zauberman et al. 2010). We propose that these "markers" result in a categorization process (Tversky 1985), whereby events that are to happen before the next marker loom larger than events that are to happen right after the marker. As Harry Potter noted when thinking about his Triwizard task; "February twenty fourth looked a lot closer from this side of Christmas." [from Rowling, J.K, *The Goblet of Fire*]

Consumers are consequently more likely to start expending efforts on a task that (holding actual duration constant) will occur before the marker, than for one that will happen after a marker. Likewise, the choice for an SS option decreases when the LL option is before a marker – when the LL option is beyond a marker, it seems all the more distant and not as likely to be chosen.

We conducted a series of seven field and laboratory studies to demonstrate this basic effect. In a field study, for example, farmers in India were presented with a savings plan that would earn a 20% match from the government if they deposited Rs. 5000 within six months and asked if they would open an account. Those for whom the deadline occurred in December of the same year (offer made in June) were 30% likely to open an account then, whereas those for whom the deadline was in January (offer made in July) the following year were only 8% likely. Similarly, MBA students who had consulting work due in 10 days were more likely to start working on it now if they were recruited 25 days (vs. 5 days) before a relevant marker - the formal dinner.

We propose two explanations that might underlie the effects of categorization on decision-making. First, building on the well-established notion that perceived duration drives decision making (e.g. Bettman et al. 2009), we suggest that events that occur in the same category as the present are perceived to be closer in time than those that are beyond the marker. Second, it is likely that events in the present category are viewed with more of an implemental mindset (Gollwitzer 1999) as compared to events that are to happen after the marker. We tested these two competing explanations in a further series of five studies. In one study, we manipulated markers semantically by asking participants to imagine that they would go on a weekend trip after (vs. before) a certain date. We found support for both explanations; participants in the "before" condition were more willing to start packing immediately, chose a bottle of insect repellent (rather than deferring choice) and perceived the departure date as closer. In the next study, we asked participants to think about a forthcoming event for themselves, or for someone else. Since people can only experience the implementation tendency for self, we reasoned that duration perception may vary with marker only in the "self" condition, and found supporting evidence. In a third study, we examined the effects of markers on task commitment. Participants were told that they had promised a friend to help move, but now faced a conflict. We showed participants a calendar in which the present and the move date were either in the same color-coded zone, or in different zones, and found that participants were more committed to help when the event was in the same zone. In other studies, we also found a) greater impatience for consumption that was to occur before the marker and b) a discontinuity in behavior around the marker.

Our findings suggest that consumers tend to categorize future time and use category membership to determine temporal proximity. As a result, duration markers have a surprisingly large effect on decision making. We also suggest that duration markers can be used as a self-regulation device in a "choice architecture" sense to spur individuals to action by suitably presenting duration markers that suggest that the target event will occur in this period. Our findings contribute to the literature on intertemporal choice by showing that duration markers serve as categorization criteria of "now" and "later", and thus shed light on the most fundamental process in intertemporal choice.

New Directions in Mindset Priming

Chairs: Margaret Gorlin, Yale University, USA
Zixi Jiang, Peking University, China

Paper #1: Of the Bold and the Beautiful: Feeling Beautiful Leads to Bolder Choices

Zixi Jiang, Peking University, China
Margaret Gorlin, Yale University, USA
Jing Xu, Peking University, China
Ravi Dhar, Yale University, USA

Paper #2: Can Religion and Money Substitute for Each Other?

Kathleen Vohs, University of Minnesota, USA
Ezgi Akpinar, Erasmus University Rotterdam, The Netherlands

Paper #3: The Influence of Mating Mindsets on Brand Extension Evaluation

Alokparna (Sonia) Monga, University of South Carolina, USA
Zeynep Gürhan-Canli, Koc University, Turkey

Paper #4: Don't Get Framed Again: How a Divergent Thought Mindset Mitigates Framing Effects

Robin Tanner, University of Wisconsin-Madison, USA
Kate E. Min, Duke University, USA
Tanya Chartrand, Duke University, USA

SESSION OVERVIEW

It is now well-established in the literature that many decisions are strongly influenced by non-conscious processing (Chartrand et al. 2008; Dijksterhuis et al. 2005). Subtle situational cues or primes can put decision makers into various mindsets and have carryover effects on subsequent decisions and judgments. What is relatively less understood is how these primes can activate not only certain goals and associations, but also different processing styles and different levels of certainty about preferences. The current set of papers, although from diverse domains, all look at the effect of priming different mindsets and processing styles on decisions, and also explore the effect of varying levels of certainty on one's choices and judgment.

Tanner, Min, and Chartrand demonstrate that inducing a divergent mindset can debias problem framing effects. People primed with a divergent mindset become more creative, and as a result, process the problem differently and become less susceptible to framing effects. Monga and Zeynep Gürhan-Canli also investigate how creativity changes one's processing style, but they apply it to a different domain: brand extensions. They show that male participants primed with a "mating," or relationship, mindset experience higher levels of creativity and evaluate more extreme brand extensions more positively. The other two projects in this session show that inducing a certain mindset can impact not only one's processing style, but also confidence in one's decisions. Jiang, Gorlin, Xu, and Dhar explore the influence of a physical attractiveness mindset on choice and find that people made of feel more attractive become more certain about their preferences, leading them to make bolder choices. Finally, Vohs and Akpinar demonstrate that religious primes increases tolerance for uncertainty and reduce desire for money, whereas money primes reduce the need to rely on religious coping.

All of the projects in this session focus on new dependent variables that have not been investigated through mindset priming: from perceptions of brand extensions to susceptibility to framing effects to bold versus timid choices. In line with this year's theme of "Building Connections," we would like to urge session participants to think about way to combine these non-conscious mindsets with different

dependent variables, through the confidence and creativity mechanisms, in order to generate novel predictions.

Audience and Level of Completeness

We expect this symposium to attract a wide ACR audience including researchers interested in priming mindsets, decision automaticity and non-conscious effects, decision making, and practical implications of these effects for marketing. These four papers all feature novel connections between mindset primes and decisions, which both make a theoretical contribution and have appeal to marketing practitioners. All of the projects are completed (all of the data has been collected) or close to completion and several are available as working papers upon request.

Session Plan

Our goal for the session is to build connections among the presented mindset primes and the effects that they can have on decision-making. We plan to do this by (1) giving all presenters sufficient time to clearly present their findings, (2) encouraging audience interaction with the presenters, and (3) facilitating an interactive discussion about future research directions and marketing implications. We plan to allocate the session time in the following manner: each presenter will be allotted 15 minutes for their presentation, including a few minutes for questions and answers at the end of each presentation. We will also reserve some time for a general audience discussion lead by the session chairs. In the general discussion, we will encourage the session participants to think about the confidence and creativity mechanisms, and in light of this, to consider novel ways to combine the mindsets presented in these projects with choice and judgment dependent variables to generate new research ideas.

Of the Bold and the Beautiful: Feeling Beautiful Leads to Bolder Choices

EXTENDED ABSTRACT

Beauty has been universally prized throughout history. It has been associated with a host of positive attributes: for example, beautiful people are perceived to have more favorable personality traits, to be more socially competent, more intelligent, and are believed to have more successful life outcomes (Dion et al. 1972; Eagly et al. 1991). Despite this ingrained unconscious belief in society that "beautiful is good," the question of whether people's perceptions of their own physical attractiveness impact their decision making has been relatively unexplored. We propose that through activating the non-conscious belief that beauty is related to positive qualities, inducing a feeling of greater physical attractiveness can make people more confident, and this confidence will change their processing style, leading to different decisions. We sought to investigate the effects of beauty in the domain of choice. Previous literature in choice theory suggests that people tend to gravitate to compromise options and options that are average on all dimensions when they are experiencing choice difficulty and cannot effectively resolve tradeoffs (Dhar and Simonson 2003; Simonson and Tversky 1992). Thus, choosing compromise and all-average options represents the decision-makers inability to express a firm preference and take a stand.

Combining the literature on choice with our prediction that priming people with a beauty mindset will boost their confidence, we propose that physical beauty can alter the choices that people

Advances in Consumer Research
Volume 39, ©2011

make. Making people feel more physically attractive can provide them with the confidence to resolve tradeoffs and thus lead them to make bolder, more self-expressive choices. Drawing on Maimaran and Simonson (in press), who propose that choosing an extreme over a compromise option or an enriched over an impoverished option are both instances of "bold" or self-assertive choice, we argue that people who feel more beautiful will be more likely to choose enriched over impoverished options and extreme over compromise options than control participants.

Our predictions were tested in a series of three studies. In study 1 we investigated the effect of one's own perceived physical attractiveness on choice of an impoverished versus an enriched option. First, we induced a feeling of physical beauty through a mindset prime. Participants in the beauty condition listed three objects or situations that make them feel physically attractive and then wrote a short paragraph about two of those items. Control participants listed three things they did in the past week and similarly elaborated on two. Participants primed with beauty perceived themselves as more physically attractive (on a 1-9 scale) than control participants, M = 6.36 vs. 5.03, p < 0.01, indicating that the manipulation was successful. . Participants then chose between two impoverished/enriched scenarios, a vacation and a roommate scenario (adapted with changes from Shafir, 1993). Participants in the beauty condition were more likely than control participants to choose the enriched over the impoverished option both in the vacation scenario (69.7% vs. 40.6%, p < .05) and in the roommate scenario (51.5% vs. 25.0%, p < .05), supporting our prediction that those primed with beauty would make bolder choices.

In study 2 we sought to replicate our findings using another method of priming and to extend them to the compromise effect. Female participants were assigned to either the beauty or control condition. In the beauty condition, women were made to feel more attractive by looking at unattractive faces, under the cover story of judging familiarity, whereas those in the control condition evaluated city scenes. Previous research has found that women perceive themselves as more attractive after looking at people who are less attractive than they are (Cash et al. 1983). Following the prime, participants chose among three options in two scenarios: a class and a roommate scenario. Participants exposed to unattractive faces both rated themselves as more attractive on a 1 to 9 scale than control participants (M = 6.44 vs. M = 5.39 p < .01; and, as predicted, were less likely to choose the compromise option both in the class (13.9% vs. 43.8%, p < .01) and in the roommate (27.8% vs. 65.6%, p < .01) scenarios.

In study 3, we replicated the results of Study 2 and tested the mechanism behind the effect. Students, assigned to either the beauty or control condition, completed the same priming manipulation as in Study 1 and then made choices in the same compromise scenarios used in Study 2. Participants rated their self-efficacy on an 8-item generalized self-efficacy scale (Bandura, 1982). Participants primed with beauty reported higher self-efficacy on a 1 to 7 scale than control participants (M = 5.99 vs. M = 4.84, p < .01), indicating greater confidence in the ability to achieve their goals, and were less likely to choose the compromise option in both the class (19.4% vs. 41.7%, p < .05) and roommate (44.8% vs. 63.3%, p < .05) scenarios. Perceived self-efficacy mediated the effect of beauty prime on choice. When class choice was regressed on both beauty prime and self-efficacy, the effect of beauty became insignificant (Wald = 1.45, β = -.56, SE = .47, p > .1), while the effect of self-efficacy remained significant (Wald = 5.72, β = -.46, SE = .19, p < .05). The mean indirect effect from the bootstrap analysis was negative and significant (a* b = -.53), with a 95% confidence interval excluding zero (-1.08 to

-.07), indicating that participants who felt more physically attractive made more extreme choices because of their increased confidence in their abilities.

In conclusion, we demonstrate that making people feel more beautiful increases their confidence and consequently increases their ability to resolve tradeoff difficulties and leads to greater choice of self-assertive options.

Can Religion and Money Substitute for Each Other?

EXTENDED ABSTRACT

What avenues do consumers have to establish and maintain a sense of control over life's ups and downs? We proffer that religion and money are two psychological resources that people might call upon to offset feelings of uncertainty. The present research tested whether mentally activating religion or money concepts can substitute for each other when people consider coping with negative events.

Consumers sometimes try to cope with negative events through religious coping, which can emotionally offset some of the negative consequences of such events. Research has suggested that there is a psychological mechanism translating uncertainty into religious extremism (Hogg, Adelman and Blagg 2009). We tested the notion that even just activating the idea of religious concepts would give people the feeling that they can cope with uncertain events.

There is also evidence to suggest that money can aid coping with uncertain situations in life. The most basic functions of money - saving and borrowing - allow people to prepare for an uncertain future (Lonergan 2010). Having money appears to protect people from unfortunate and uncertain situations in life, mainly through providing control over outcomes (Johnson and Krueger 2006). The psychological effects of money include enhancing the belief that one can achieve his or her own goals (Zhou, Vohs and Baumeister 2009). These findings suggest that mere reminders of money could elicit the sense that one can cope with uncertain and negative situations.

The commonality between the psychological effects of money and religion suggests that money and religion might be interchangeable, in their ability to help people cope with negative and uncertain life events. When facing uncertain negative events, religious primes should increase consumers' tolerance for uncertainty, which would in turn reduce their desire for money. Money primes should reduce consumers' need to rely on religious coping. We present four studies in which we provide novel evidence for the substitution effect of religion and money.

In Study 1, we demonstrated that religious priming (versus neutral priming) led to less desire for money. Half of the participants were primed with religious concepts using the scrambled-sentence paradigm, while the others completed a neutral version. Next, participants read a list of eleven pleasant things (e.g., TV, sunshine, spring, chocolate, beach) and asked if they were willing to permanently forgo those items in exchange for 1 million Euros. As predicted, participants primed with religious concepts were less willing to exchange pleasant things for money as compared to participants primed with neutral concepts.

Study 2 tested the mediating role of tolerance for uncertainty between religious priming and desire for money. First, all participants were asked to imagine a negative event that had occurred in their life and write down their reactions towards it. Next, participants completed a word-search puzzle task, which was used to prime religious or neutral concepts. After the priming task, participants thought back to the negative life event, and rated their tolerance for uncertainty. Participants completed a scale that assessed the degree to which participants could put up with the uncertainty due to the negative life event. Finally, participants listed 10 things that they valued in life (besides money) and then indicated whether they would agree permanently giving up each item in exchange for 1 million Euros. The results confirmed our predictions showing that mentally activating religious concepts, as opposed to neutral concepts, led to more tolerance for uncertainty regarding negative events, and which in turn weakened the desire for money. The meditational analyses were significant.

In Study 3, we manipulated the salience of money by having half of the participants count coins and Euro bills and the other half count glass beads. Then, all participants remembered a negative event that had occurred in their life and wrote down their reactions towards it. Thinking on the negative event they had described, participants completed a scale that assesses the degree to which various types of religious coping are involved in dealing with negative events. In line with the substitution hypothesis, participants who were reminded of money were less likely to rely on religious coping compared to participants under neutral conditions.

In Study 4, participants first recalled a negative event over which they did or did not have control. Next, they were randomly assigned either to money primed condition or neutral condition, which was activated by showing images of money versus seashells on the screen background used. Thinking on the negative event they had described, participants completed religious coping scale. Our results showed us money priming decreased the likelihood of relying on religious coping in the face of negative events when participants perceived that they had control over the situation, while this effect was not observed the event was perceived as uncontrollable. Individuals were more likely to rely on religious coping when they perceived not having control (compared to when they had control).

Our results imply exercising caution for religious or marketing organizations whose efforts are affected by the relationship between religion and consumption. Indeed, one of the most powerful anti-consumer movements is rooted in religious ideologies — namely, fundamental Islam's tenets encouraging modesty and protecting oneself from materialism (Kozinets and Handelman 2004). This research at the intersection of religion and money is a step in further understanding the role of religion on consumers and their consumption.

The Influence of Mating Mindsets on Brand Extension Evaluation

EXTENDED ABSTRACT

Prior research on brand extensions has focused on identifying a variety of factors that influence brand extension evaluations among consumers (Aaker and Keller 1990). One key factor is the degree to which consumers are able to see a connection between the parent brand and the extension. When consumers perceive some kind of fit between the parent brand and the extension (e.g., Gillette shampoo), the brand extension is evaluated favorably. However, when consumers perceive less fit (e.g., Gillette floor cleaner), the brand extension is evaluated negatively (Aaker and Keller 1990). Missing, however, from this research is a consideration of how transient mindsets might influence brand extension evaluations. In our research, we focus on a specific type of mindset—the mating mindset, which has generated some attention recently (Griskevicius et al. 2006).

Emerging research demonstrates that individuals in a mating mindset show boosts in creativity (Griskevicius et al. 2006). For instance, male participants, when primed with thoughts about short-term mating relationships (that is, a mating mindset), generated stories that were more creative, imaginative and original. In contrast, female participants did not show this effect. We draw upon this research to propose that male consumers in a mating mindset would be able to find novel ways to connect the brand to the extension, leading to more favorable brand extension fit perceptions and evaluations. This effect would not emerge for female consumers.

Study 1 tested our hypothesis in a 2 (mindset: mating, non-mating) x 2 (gender: male, female) between subjects design with Kodak filing cabinet and McDonald's chocolate bar as brand extension stimuli. Participants in the mating [vs. non-mating] mindset condition were asked to imagine and write about meeting someone desirable and spending a wonderful day and a dinner with this person [vs. imagine getting ready to go to a concert with a same-sex friend]. Participants responded to the brand extension using standard scales of brand extension evaluation (e.g., the brand extension is 1= poor and 7 = excellent), brand extension fit (e.g., the brand extension is 1=inconsistent with the brand and 7 = consistent with the brand) and open-ended thoughts. Our results demonstrate that male consumers in a mating mindset give more favorable responses, compared to those in a non-mating mindset. Female consumers, however, are not affected by the mindset. Male consumers in the mating mindset generate more relational thoughts (connecting the parent brand to the extension) than those in a non-mating mindset. Importantly, our results are not driven by positive mood, positive arousal, negative arousal and total thoughts.

Next, we examine how consumers respond to brand extensions from different types of parent brands, prestige versus functional brands (Park, Milberg, and Lawson 1991). Prior research has shown that prestige brand concepts (e.g., Rolex) are more abstract and hedonic than functional brand concepts (e.g., Timex), allowing prestige brands to extend more easily into distant product categories (e.g., neck ties, scarves) (Hagtvedt and Patrick 2009; Park, Milberg, and Lawson 1991). We predict that for the functional brand, male consumers in a mating mindset, due to boosts in creativity, will be able to find novel ways to link the parent brand and the extension. Thus, brand extension responses will be more favorable for male consumers than female consumers. No gender differences would be expected to emerge for extensions of prestige brands, where relational thoughts are accessible to both male and female consumers allowing both groups of consumers to connect the brand and the extension.

Study 2 tested our hypothesis in a 2 (brand: functional, prestige) x 2 (gender: male, female) x 2 (mindset: mating, non-mating) between subjects design. Honda sunglasses and BMW sunglasses were the brand extension stimuli for the functional and prestige brands respectively. Our findings confirm that for functional brands, male consumers in a mating mindset provide more favorable brand extension responses (and more relational thoughts) than female consumers. For the prestige brands, brand extension responses (and relational thoughts) of female consumers rise to the level of male consumers, in effect closing the gap between male and female consumers.

Finally, we explore the process in greater depth by examining the role of creativity. Prior research shows that when consumers want to express their creativity, they tend to perform better on creativity tasks (Fitzsimons et al. 2008). If creativity is indeed driving our effects for male consumers, we suggest that the exercise of expressing creativity in an alternative manner would satisfy the male consumers need to express creativity, thus reducing the need to express creativity while evaluating brand extensions in a subsequent task. Consequently, brand extension responses in a mating mindset will be more favorable when an alternative creativity task is absent than when it is present. In contrast, for female consumers in a mating mindset, who do not show boosts in creativity, the presence of an alternative creativity task will not affect their brand extension responses.

Study 3 tested our hypothesis with a 2 (alternative creativity task: present, absent) x 2 (gender: male, female) between subjects design. A mating mindset was induced in all participants. In the alternative creativity task present condition, participants were asked to respond to seven problems from then Remote Associates Test (RAT; Mednick 1962) taken from Bowden and Jung-Beeman (2003). In the absent condition, participants did not complete the RAT task. As predicted, we found that male consumers gave more favorable brand extension responses when an alternative creativity task is absent than when it is present. In contrast, for female consumers, the presence (vs. absence) of an alternative creativity task did not affect their brand extension responses.

Don't Get Framed Again: How a Divergent Thought Mindset Mitigates Framing Effects

EXTENDED ABSTRACT

It is now widely accepted that individuals make different choices when faced with alternative descriptions of the same decision problem (Tversky & Kahneman, 1981). How a choice is framed appears to influence decisions of any type, including many that have fundamental consequences for the welfare of the chooser. The most prominent example of a framing effect is the now classic "Asian Disease" decision scenario (Tversky & Kahneman, 1981) in which participants are asked to choose between two programs for dealing with the outbreak of a disease which has infected 600 people. In the gain frame condition participants are told Program A would save 200 individuals with Program B having a 1/3 chance of saving all 600 lives and a 2/3 chance of saving none. In the loss frame condition, however, participants are told 400 individuals would die in Program A with Program B having a 1/3 chance of no deaths and a 2/3 chance of 600 deaths. Although both conditions present probabilistically identical choices, individuals presented with the gain frame strongly prefer the "sure" Program A option to save 200 people while those faced with the loss frame strongly prefer the "risky" Program B choice.

With such framing effects appearing to be so pervasive and research on attenuating these framing effects generally serving to demonstrate how robust they are, an important question is how can they be overcome? The present research addresses this question by taking a novel mindset approach. Specifically, we examine the effect of divergent thought mindset on how people respond to a classic decision framing problem. Depending on the particular problem, creative thinking requires differing degrees of divergent and convergent thought (Guilford, 1959). Convergent thinking can be thought of as "connecting the dots," and involves recognizing similarities between adjacent pieces of information, preserving the already known, and reapplying set techniques (Cropley, 2006). Our particular focus is on divergent thinking, which is associated with "thinking outside the box," and involves shifting perspective, seeing new possibilities, a deviation from the usual approach, and associating ideas from remote fields (Cropley, 2006). It is this broad emphasis on deviating from the usual approach which suggests the possibility that divergent thinking may help mitigate framing effects. We argue that framing effects can be conceptualized in terms of automatic associations between contextual cues and how a given decision scenario is mentally represented and processed. In the Asian disease problem, for ex-

ample, the gain and loss frames lead individuals to invoke different attitudes toward risk (Tversky & Kahneman, 1981). As such, given divergent thought's emphasis on deviating from the usual approach, an intriguing possibility is whether individuals induced to think in a divergent fashion might be less susceptible to framing effects.

In two experiments we examined the effect of a divergent thinking mindset on individuals' susceptibility to the Asian disease framing effect. In experiment 1, we utilized a general creative mindset prime manipulation (Sassenberg & Moskowitz, 2005) and asked participants to describe three situations in which they engaged in creative behavior. Responses were coded in terms of whether they best represented convergent or divergent thought. Next, participants were presented with either the gain or loss framed version of the Asian disease problem described earlier, and indicated their relative preference between the two programs on a 6-point scale anchored from "I strongly favor program A" (1) to "I strongly favor program B" (6). Participants in both the convergent thought condition (Mgain = 2.7 vs. Mloss = 4.9, F(1, 100) = 9.21, p < .01) and control condition (Mgain = 2.9 vs. Mloss = 4.1, F(1, 100) = 12.21, p < .01) were subject to the usual framing effect, that is, they indicated stronger preferences for the certain option (i.e., program A) when the alternatives were presented in terms of gains than losses. In the divergent thought condition, however, we observed no such framing effect (Mgain = 3.5 vs. Mloss = 3.7, F < 1, p = ns).

In experiment 2, our goal was to replicate the debiasing effect of divergent thought using an experimenter-provided prime. In the divergent thought condition, participants read a brief scenario about a student engaging in creative free-style rapping who had to "think outside the box" to come up with his rhymes. In the control condition participants read a scenario describing an individual engaged in mundane activities. We again found that participants in the control condition were subject to the standard framing effect and indicated a stronger preference for the certain option (i.e., program A) when the alternatives were presented in terms of gains (M = 2.7) rather than losses (M = 4.6). However, in the divergent thought condition this difference in preference across frames was substantially reduced (Mgain = 3.1, Mloss = 3.8). They were largely immune to the effect of the frames, as they were essentially indifferent between program A and program B regardless of whether they were faced with the gain or loss frame.

In sum, we found that a divergent thought mindset, whether invoked by participant-generated (experiment 1) or by experimenter-generated (experiment 2) primes, significantly armed participants from falling prey to the framing effect typically observed in the classic Asian disease problem. While existing research on attenuation of biases has tended to focus on thinking harder (e.g., LeBoeuf & Shafir, 2003), our data suggest that a subtle cue that leads individuals to automatically think in a divergent fashion is potentially more effective than a deliberate increase in conscious effort.

In future studies, we aim to better isolate the process underlying the debiasing effect, and to explore whether it extends to other heuristics and biases. On the process front, we plan to utilize time constraints (and/or cognitive load) to understand whether the debiasing process requires cognitive resources, or whether it operates purely at the heuristic level. As far as other biases are concerned, we speculate that the availability heuristic (Tversky & Kahneman, 1973), representativeness heuristic (Kahneman & Tversky, 1972), and planning fallacy (Kahneman & Tversky, 1979) might all rely to some degree on automatic associations. As such, we intend to explore if a divergent thought mindset ameliorates these biases.

It Shrinks, Stretches, Contracts, and Expands:
Exploring the Remarkable Malleability of Time
Chair: Melanie Rudd, Stanford University, USA

Paper #1: Awe Expands People's Perception of Time, Alters Decision Making, and Enhances Well-Being

Melanie Rudd, Stanford University, USA
Kathleen D. Vohs, University of Minnesota, USA
Jennifer Aaker, Stanford University, USA

Paper #2: Giving Time Gives You More Time

Zoë Chance, Harvard Business School, USA
Cassie Mogilner, University of Pennsylvania, USA
Michael I. Norton, Harvard Business School, USA

Paper #3: Proximity to a Goal and Time Slack

Ji Hoon Jhang, University of Colorado at Boulder, USA
John Lynch, University of Colorado, USA

Paper #4: The Impact of Auditory Tempo on Prospective Temporal Distance Judgments and Consumer Preference

Kyu Kim, University of Southern California, USA
Gal Zauberman, University of Pennsylvania, USA

SESSION OVERVIEW

Unlike objective time (i.e., standard clock time), subjective time is a highly malleable medium. For instance, time can sometimes seem to be contracted or limited, and at other times expanded or plentiful. However, in today's society, the perception of time as contracted or limited seems to be an increasingly dominant perception (e.g., Carroll 2008; Fay 1992; Robinson 1990; Robinson and Godbey 1997). Indeed, for many consumers, time has become a precious resource and the ultimate scarcity (e.g., Becker 1965; Juster and Stafford 1991; Leclerc, Schmitt, and Dube 1995). In response to this consumer trend, a great deal of time perception research has focused on identifying the factors that lead to a contracted or limited perception of time (e.g., Bailey and Areni 2006; Conti 2001; Kellaris and Kent 1992) and exploring the physical, mental, and behavioral consequences of increased time pressure and time urgency (e.g., Nationwide Mutual Insurance Company 2008; Roxburgh, 2004; Yan et al. 2003). But in a world where time is so often constricted, a better understanding of how time can be stretched is also of great importance. Specifically, what factors are capable of expanding the perception of time? And what consequences might this expanding of time have for consumer behavior and well-being? Furthermore, as much of the extant research that looks at differences in time perception has focused on relatively unchangeable factors (such as age, gender, and culture; Block, Hancock, and Zakay 2000; Block, Zakay, and Hancock 1998; Hill, Block, and Buggie 2000; McCormack et al. 1999), can we identify time-expanding factors that can be deliberately altered (so that people can expand their—or others'—perceptions of time)?

With four papers (all in the final stages of completion), this session addresses these questions, and related issues, by integrating various research perspectives in order to identify factors that lead to and the consequences that result from perceptions of expanded time. **Rudd, Vohs, and Aaker** approach these questions from an emotion perspective and identify one distinct positive emotion—awe—that makes time seem more plentiful and consumers feel less impatient. Their results also highlight potential consequences of expanding time perception, as they find that this altering of time enables awe to influence subjective well-being, preferences for experiential (versus

material) goods, and one's willingness to donate time. **Jhang and Lynch** also identify a way to expand time, as they investigate how proximity to certain goals influences perceptions of spare time (now and in the future) and explore how this affects one's desire to delay attractive interruptions. **Chance, Mogilner, and Norton** focus their attention on consumer behaviors, and illuminate a surprising way by which people can feel they have more time: by giving time to others. Compared to wasting time, spending time on oneself, and even gaining time, spending time on another (whether they are well known or not) was found to counteract perceived time famine. Finally, **Kim and Zauberman** look at how perceived durations can be expanded. Specifically, they examine how one type of sensory perception—auditory tempo—influences prospective temporal distance and the downstream consequences this has for willingness-to-pay and intertemporal choice. Taken together, these different lines of research provide diverse insights on the study of time perception yet still maintain a coherent theme.

As all four papers share a common focus on deepening our theoretical understanding of factors that influence consumers' perceptions of time, this session is likely to be of substantial interest to those active in time perception research. However, we also expect this session to have broader appeal. For instance, as each of our papers explores time perception from a different domain, this session should also appeal to those who study emotions, goals, consumer actions, sensory perceptions, and decision-making more broadly. In addition to creating connections between diverse research areas (by demonstrating time perception's applicability to many research domains), this session should also build connections between academia and industry. Specifically, this session focuses not only on advancing our theoretical understanding of time perception, but also on identifying time-expanding factors that could be potentially manipulated by marketers (in order to achieve or avoid the downstream consequences of time expansion identified in our research, such as greater willingness-to-pay and preferences for experiential alternatives). We hope that attracting a diverse audience will help facilitate a lively and fruitful discussion, and believe that the presentations on the antecedents and consequences of expanded time perception will elicit active idea generation for future research on time perception.

REFERENCES

Bailey, Nicole and Charles S. Areni (2006), "When A Few Minutes Sounds Like A Lifetime: Does Atmospheric Music Contract Perceived Time?" *Journal of Retailing*, 82 (3), 189-202.

Becker, Gary S. (1965), "A Theory of the Allocation of Time," *The Economic Journal*, 75 (September), 493-517.

Block, Richard A., Peter A. Hancock, and Dan Zakay (2000), "Sex Differences in Duration Judgments: A Meta-Analytic Review," *Memory and Cognition*, 28 (8), 1333–1346.

Block, Richard A., Dan Zakay, and Peter A. Hancock (1998), "Human Aging and Duration Judgments: A Meta-Analytic Review," *Psychology and Aging*, 13 (4), 584–596.

Carroll, Joseph (2008), "Time Pressures, Stress Common for Americans," http://www.gallup.com/poll/103456/Time-Pressures-Stress-Common-Americans.aspx.

Conti, Regina (2001), "Time Flies: Investigating the Connection between Intrinsic Motivation and the Experience of Time," *Journal of Personality,* 69 (1), 1–26.

Advances in Consumer Research
Volume 39, ©2011

Fay, W. Bradford (1992), "The Great Time Famine," *Marketing Research*, 4 (3), 50-51.

Hill, Oliver W., Richard A. Block, Stephen E. Buggie (2000), "Culture and Beliefs about Time: Comparisons among Black Americans, Black African and White Americans," *Journal of Psychology*, 134 (4), 443-461.

Juster, F. Thomas and Frank P. Stafford (1991), "The Allocation of Time: Empirical Findings, Behavioral Models, and Problems of Measurement," *Journal of Economic Literature*, 29 (2), 471-522.

Kellaris, James J. and Robert J. Kent (1992), "The Influence of Music on Consumers' Temporal Perceptions: Does Time Fly When You're Having Fun?" *Journal of Consumer Psychology*, 1 (4), 365-376.

McCormack, Teresa, Gordon D. A. Brown, Elizabeth A. Maylor, Richard J. Darby, and Dina Green (1999), "Developmental changes in Time Estimation: Comparing Childhood and Old Age," *Developmental Psychology*, 35 (4), 1143–1155.

Nationwide Mutual Insurance Company (2008), "Driving While Distracted Public Relations Research," http://www.nationwide.com/pdf/dwd-2008-survey-results.pdf.

Robinson, John P. (1990), "The Time Squeeze," *American Demographics*, 12 (2), 30-33.

Leclerc, France, Bernd H. Schmitt, and Laurette Dubé (1995), "Waiting Time and Decision Making: Is Time Like Money?" *Journal of Consumer Research*, 22 (1), 110-119.

Robinson, John P. and Geoffrey Godbey (1997), *Time for Life: The Surprising Ways Americans Use Their Time*, University Park: Pennsylvania State University Press.

Roxburgh, Susan (2004), "'There Just Aren't Enough Hours in the Day': The Mental Health Consequences of Time Pressure," *Journal of Health and Social Behavior*, 45 (2), 115-131.

Yan, Lijing L., Kiang Liu, Karen A. Matthews, Martha L. Daviglus, T. Freeman Ferguson, and Catarina I. Kiefe (2003), "Psychosocial Factors and Risk of Hypertension," *Journal of the American Medical Association*, 290 (16), 2138–2148.

Awe Expands People's Perception of Time, Alters Decision Making, and Enhances Well-Being

EXTENDED ABSTRACT

Time is a scarce consumer commodity (Leclerc, Schmitt, & Dube, 1995). In fact, feeling one has too much to do and too little time is known as "time famine" (Perlow, 1999) and produces undesirable consequences including fatigue, stress, and even postponing a doctor's visit when ill (Lehto, 1998; Vuckovic, 1999). Although science cannot expand the amount of time in each day, could it shift consumers' perceptions of how much time is available? Three experiments examined whether experiencing awe can expand time perceptions and, in turn, impact consumer decision-making and well-being.

Can awe, defined as the feeling that arises when one encounters a stimulus so strikingly vast (in time, scope, complexity, ability, or power) it provokes a need to update one's mental schemas (Keltner & Haidt, 2003), increase perceived time availability? Prior research and theory suggest so. Experiences involving awe, such as optimal athletic performances (Ravizza, 1977) and spiritual events (Fredrickson & Anderson, 1999) often involve a sense of timelessness. The phenomenology of awe, therefore, suggests it might expand time perceptions. Two psychological theories are also relevant. The first is the extended-now theory (Vohs & Schmeichel, 2003), which demonstrates focusing on the present moment elongates time perceptions. Awe captivates people's attention on what is unfolding

before them, which the extended-now theory predicts would expand time perceptions. The second is Socioemotional Selectivity Theory, which shows people seek to acquire knowledge when time feels expansive (Carstensen, Isaacowitz, & Charles, 1999). Awe's triggers within people a desire to create new knowledge structures (Keltner & Haidt, 2003), which therefore may be a signal that awe leads the mind to perceive time as expansive.

Awe's predicted ability to expand time perceptions was also hypothesized to have several consequences. First, perceived time availability is thought to affect certain prosocial decisions. For instance, time scarcity hinders the tendency to help someone in distress (Darley & Batson, 1973) and is a common barrier to volunteering (Hall et al., 2009). Therefore, awe, by creating the perception of plentiful time, might increase one's willingness to spend time helping others. Second, time perception can influence people's decisions about how to live life. For instance, insufficient time is an oft-cited reason for not engaging in leisure experiences (Mannell & Zuzanek, 1991). Time perception may also influence decisions to acquire experiences versus material goods (Van Boven & Gilovich, 2003), as one inherent quality of experiential goods is they require the experiencer devote time to savor the attendant feelings and sensations (Quoidbach et al., 2010). Thus, by inducing a sense of ample time availability, awe might enhance preferences for experiences. Third, time perception is often an indicator of well-being. For instance, people who report feeling "always" rushed have lower life satisfaction than do others (Robinson & Godbey, 1997) and feeling one has little time available has been linked to depressive symptoms (Roxburgh, 2004). Thus, awe, through expanding time perceptions, might boost momentary life satisfaction.

Experiment 1 tested whether feeling awe expands time perceptions. To demonstrate that awe's temporal consequences are not characteristic of all positive emotions, awe was contrasted with happiness. Because awe is often elicited during events that one might associate with minimal time pressure (such as exposure to nature; Shiota, Keltner, & Mossman, 2007), it is possible that perceiving time as expansive is merely a prerequisite for experiencing awe, and not a consequence thereof. To address this alternative account, all participants were initially primed to perceive time as constricted, using a sentence unscramble task (Srull & Wyer, 1979). Next, participants watched either a one minute awe-eliciting or happiness-eliciting commercial for an LCD television. Participants subsequently reported their agreement on a perceived-time-availability index ("I have lots of time in which I can get things done," "time is slipping away" (reverse-scored), "time is expanded," and "time is boundless") and current emotions. Manipulation checks confirmed awe (versus happiness) condition participants experienced more awe and less happiness. An ANOVA then revealed awe (versus happiness) condition participants perceived greater time availability. Furthermore, across both conditions, stronger feelings of awe were correlated with greater perceived time availability.

Experiment 2 tested whether awe, via influencing time perceptions, affects willingness to volunteer time. In this experiment, momentary impatience was the measure of time perception, as it is associated with perceiving time as insufficient (Glass, Snyder, & Hollis, 1974; Lang & Markowitz, 1986). To elicit emotions, participants wrote about a personal experience, with those in the awe [happiness] condition writing about an experience that made them feel awe [happiness]. Participants then reported their feelings of impatience, willingness to donate time, willingness to donate money, and current emotions. Manipulation checks confirmed awe (versus happiness) condition participants experienced more awe and less happiness. An ANOVA then revealed awe (versus happiness) condition participants reported reduced impatience and a greater willingness to volunteer time. Finally, a mediation analysis determined awe's influence on time donation was driven by its influence on time perception: Awe (versus happiness) reduced impatience, which in turn increased willingness to donate time. Importantly, the awe and happiness conditions did not differ in willingness to donate money (a non-temporal form of prosociality), ruling out the alternative explanation that awe simply increases all prosociality.

Experiment 3 tested whether awe influences well-being and consumption decisions via expanding time. To elicit emotions (awe versus neutral), participants read stories depicting prototypical elicitors of the target emotion (Griskevicius, Shiota, & Neufeld, 2010). Participants subsequently reported their feelings of impatience, momentary life satisfaction, hypothetical choices between experiential versus material goods, and current emotions. A manipulation check confirmed awe (versus neutral) condition participants experienced more awe. ANOVAs then revealed awe (versus neutral) condition participants reported reduced impatience, greater life satisfaction, and preferred more experiential (versus material) goods. Mediation analyses determined awe's influence on life satisfaction and experiential (versus material) choices was driven by its influence on time perception: Awe (versus neutral feelings) reduced impatience, which in turn increased life satisfaction and preferences for experiential goods.

In sum, awe increased willingness to volunteer time, preferences for experiential goods, and life satisfaction, all through expanding perceptions of time. Thus, awe-eliciting experiences might offer an effective solution to the feelings of time starvation that plague consumers in modern society.

REFERENCES

Carstensen, Laura L., Derek M. Isaacowitz, and Susan T. Charles (1999), "Taking Time Seriously: A Theory of Socioemotional Selectivity," *American Psychologist*, 54 (March), 165-181.
Darley, John M. and C. Daniel Batson (1973), "From Jerusalem to Jericho: A Study of Situational and Dispositional Variables in Helping Behavior," *Journal of Personality and Social Psychology*, 27 (1), 100-108.
Frederickson, Laura M. and Dorothy H. Anderson (1999), "A Qualitative Exploration of the Wilderness Experience as a Source of Spiritual Inspiration," *Journal of Environmental Psychology*, 19 (1), 21 39.
Glass, David C., Melvin L. Snyder, and Jack F. Hollis (1974), "Time Urgency and the Type A Coronary-Prone Behavior Pattern," *Journal of Applied Social Psychology*, 4 (2), 125-140.
Griskevicius, Vladas, Michelle N. Shiota, and Samantha L. Neufeld (2010), "Influence of Different Positive Emotions on Persuasion Processing: A Functional Evolutionary Approach," *Emotion*, 10 (2), 190-206.
Hall, Michael, David Lasby, Steven Ayer, and William David Gibbons (2009), *Caring Canadians, Involved Canadians: Highlights from the Canada 2007 Survey of Giving, Volunteering and Participating*, Ottawa, ON: Statistics Canada.
Keltner, Dacher and Jonathan Haidt (2003), "Approaching Awe, a Moral, Spiritual, and Aesthetic Emotion," *Cognition and Emotion*, 17 (2), 297-314.
Lang, Dorothy and Martin Markowitz (1986), "Coping, Individual Differences, and Strain: A Longitudinal Study of Short-Term Role Overload," *Journal of Occupational Behavior*, 7 (3), 195-206.
Leclerc, France, Bernd H. Schmitt, and Laurette Dubé (1995), "Waiting Time and Decision Making: Is Time like Money?" *Journal of Consumer Research*, 22 (1), 110-119.
Lehto, Anna-Maija (1998), "Time Pressure as a Stress Factor," *Society and Leisure*, 21 (2), 491-511.
Mannell, Roger C. and Jiri Zuzanek (1991), "The Nature and Variability of Leisure Constraints in Daily Life: The Case of the Physically Active Leisure of Older Adults," *Leisure Sciences*, 13 (4), 337-351.
Perlow, Leslie A. (1999), "The Time Famine: Toward a Sociology of Work Time," *Administrative Science Quarterly*, 44 (1), 57–81.
Quoidbach, Jordi, Elizabeth W. Dunn, K. V. Petrides, Moïra Mikolajczak, (2010), "Money Giveth, Money Taketh Away: The Dual Effect of Wealth on Happiness," *Psychological Science*, 21 (6), 759-763.
Ravizza, Kenneth (1977), "Peak Experiences in Sport," *Journal of Humanistic Psychology*, 17 (4), 35-40.
Robinson, John P. and Geoffrey Godbey (1997), *Time for Life: The Surprising Ways Americans Use Their Time*, University Park: Pennsylvania State University Press.
Roxburgh, Susan (2004), "'There Just Aren't Enough Hours in the Day': The Mental Health Consequences of Time Pressure," *Journal of Health and Social Behavior*, 45 (2), 115-131.
Shiota, Michelle N., Dacher Keltner and Amanda Mossman (2007), "The Nature of Awe: Elicitors, Appraisals, and Effects on Self-concept," *Cognition and Emotion*, 21 (5), 944-963.
Srull, Thomas K. and Robert S. Wyer (1979), "The Role of Category Accessibility in the Interpretation of Information about Persons: Some Determinants and Implications," *Journal of Personality and Social Psychology*, 37 (October), 1660-1672.
Van Boven, Leaf and Thomas Gilovich (2003), "To Do or To Have? That Is the Question," *Journal of Personality and Social Psychology*, 85 (December), 1193-1202.
Vohs, Kathleen D. and Brandon J. Schmeichel (2003), "Self-regulation and the Extended Now: Controlling the Self Alters the Subjective Experience of Time," *Journal of Personality and Social Psychology*, 85 (2), 217-230.
Vuckovic, Nancy (1999), "Fast Relief: Buying Time with Medications," *Medical Anthropology Quarterly*, 13 (March), 51–68.

Giving Time Gives You More Time

EXTENDED ABSTRACT

Many of us feel we are victims of a "time famine" (Perlow 1999), having too much to do and not enough time to do it. For example, parents are spending both more time working and more time with their children, yet still feel they are falling short (Bianchi, Robinson, and Milkie 2007)…if only there were a few more hours in a day. Given that our time is objectively constrained by a 24 hour day, and ultimately mortality, one important question is whether there are ways to feel like we have more time. We examine one way in which doing more can result in feeling less busy. In a series of experiments, we find that giving time to another person counteracts the time famine, making time feel more expansive and the future full of possibilities.

Volunteering time can benefit givers in multiple ways, from reducing depression (Musick and Wilson 2003), to improving physical health (Thoits and Hewitt 2001), to delaying death (Oman, Thoresen, and McMahon 1999). Giving support to others lessens anxiety over one's own troubles (Krause 1986) and giving a massage can lower stress even more than receiving one (Field et al. 1998). In short, volunteering can make people healthier and happier. But no studies have yet explored the effect of giving time on time perceptions. One might expect that since adding obligations reduces the time available for other things, any additional activities, including volunteering, would amplify time-related stress. We anticipate the reverse outcome for two reasons: if giving time is meaningful, it could encourage a long-term perspective; also, precisely because donating time is indicative of a surplus of time and energy, one might infer such a surplus even when volunteering is obligatory.

In our first study, participants spent five minutes either giving time or wasting time, and then answered a series of time perception questions. Those in the giving time condition selected one of four gravely ill children, read a short biography written by the child's mother, then wrote a letter to that child—which we subsequently mailed. Those in the wasting time condition counted the "e"s in a long passage of nonsense text. Our dependent variable was endorsement of the time-focused statements from Carstensen and Lang's (1996) Future Time Perspective scale (e.g. "Most of my life lies ahead of me"). Consistent with our hypothesis, we found that individuals who had given time felt they had more time than did those who had wasted it.

Study 2 was conducted in two parts. In the morning, participants completed an online, between-subjects questionnaire which included instructions to either spend time doing something for themselves or for any other person at some point during the day. We gave no further directions regarding how this time should be spent. In the evening, participants completed a follow-up survey asking how they had spent their time, how much time they had spent, and how they felt about it, as well as measuring future outlook. We found that regardless of the amount of time spent, those who given time to another person felt that they had more time in general than those who spent time on themselves. They also reported the experience was less relaxing and enjoyable, but more meaningful and loving. These findings suggest that experiences which reduce time-related anxiety do not necessarily need to feel relaxing or fun. Additionally, those who gave time to someone else were more inclined to say it didn't feel like much time at all. This result dovetails with our finding that they also reported that the future feels longer—if you have plenty of time ahead of you, then an hour isn't much at all.

In a follow-up study, we asked participants to remember a previous instance in which they had spent time doing something for someone else or for themselves. As our dependent variable, we used a resource slack measure (Zauberman and Lynch 2005) of perceived free time. We found that, consistent with our previous results, those who remembered investing an hour or two felt they had more free time if they recalled time spent on another. However, those who remembered investing months or years (e.g. going to college or caring for a sick relative) reported having more free time after remembering something they had done for themselves. We confirm in this experiment that spending time on others can increase the amount of time you feel you have available, but that this effect is limited to small amounts of leisure time, rather than major volunteer commitments which constrain other important obligations and pursuits.

In our next study, we tested the boundaries of our effect by comparing giving time to getting time, and we explored a behavioral consequence of subjective time abundance. In this experiment, participants either gave ten minutes (editing a high school student's senior essay) or received 10 minutes (leaving the lab early). We then asked how much time they might want to devote to participating in future studies, and we followed up by measuring actual time spent.

Those in the giving time condition reported having more spare time, intended to participate in more future surveys, and were marginally more likely to actually spend more time on surveys a week later. In a follow-up study, we showed the cyclical nature of the volunteering/busy-ness relationship. We first asked participants to complete a writing exercise that primed being busy or not being busy. Next, we offered them the opportunity to leave early or to spend fifteen minutes editing an essay, as in the previous experiment. Those who had been primed with being busy were less likely to give time to help someone else.

In sum, we find that spending time on another person can make one's life feel less busy, and that feeling less busy increases the likelihood of helping out. The converse is true as well: when feeling the pressure of a time famine, we are less likely to engage in socially supportive activities that could alleviate this stress.

REFERENCES

Bianchi, Suzanne M., John P. Robinson, and Melissa A. Milkie (2006), *Changing Rhythms of American Family Life*, New York: Russell Sage Foundation.

Carstensen, Laura L. and Frieder R. Lang (1996), "Future Time Perspective Scale," unpublished manuscript, Stanford University.

Field, Tiffany M., Maria Hernandez-Reif, Olga Quintino, Saul Schanberg, and Cynthia Kuhn (1998), "Elder Retired Volunteers Benefit from Giving Massage Therapy to Infants," *Journal of Applied Gerontology,* 17 (2), 230–240.

Krause, Neal (1986), "Social Support, Stress, and Well-Being among Older Adults," *Journal of Gerontology,* 41 (4), 512-519.

Musick, Marc A. and John Wilson (2003), "Volunteering and Depression: The Role of Psychological and Social Resources in Different Age Groups," *Social Science & Medicine*, 56 (2), 259–269.

Oman, Doug, Carl E. Thoresen, and Kay McMahon (1999), "Volunteerism and Mortality among the Community Dwelling Elderly," *Journal of Health Psychology,* 4 (3), 301–316.

Perlow, Leslie A. (1999), "The Time Famine: Toward a Sociology of Work Time," *Administrative Science Quarterly*, 44 (1), 57–81.

Thoits, Peggy A. and Lyndi N. Hewitt (2001), "Volunteer Work and Well-Being," *Journal of Health and Social Behavior,* 42 (June), 115–131.

Zauberman, Gal and John G. Lynch (2005), "Resource Slack and Propensity to Discount Delayed Investment of Time versus Money," *Journal of Experimental Psychology: General*, 134 (1), 23-37.

Proximity to a Goal and Time Slack

EXTENDED ABSTRACT

Zauberman and Lynch (2005) showed that people tend to say "Yes" to attractive opportunities in the distant future that they would say "No" to if the same activity had to be performed today or tomorrow. The present research seeks to understand what drives an individual's different perceptions of time slack ("spare time") in the near and distant future.

People believe that today they are exceptionally busy but that they will be less busy in the more distant future. Zauberman and Lynch (2005) speculated that this illusion that one will be less busy in the future than today might arise because people have formed goals for the use of their time in the very near but not the more distant future. We conjecture that people are more likely to have goals for their time for the present than for the future (Lynch, Netemeyer, Spiller, and Zammit 2010). Since goals are known to become reference points (Heath, Larrick, and Wu 1999), we suggest that people's propensity to delay investments of some resource (i.e., time) to reap a reward reflects their expected pain from not attaining the proximate goal if they accept an offer requiring the same resource. Our conjecture that goals for time use now versus in the future play a role in propensity to delay time investments additionally leads us to seek to understand how proximity to a goal influences perceptions of time slack ("spare time").

We hypothesize that we can reverse the Zauberman and Lynch (2005) finding of lesser perceived time slack for now than for some point in the future when people have a salient goal of using their time at that point in the future, but no salient goal for use of time in the very short run. In Study 1, travelers (n=75) were approached at airports when they were waiting at the gates for their flights. They reported their perceived time slack for three different points of time (i.e., now vs. that evening vs. a week later). In addition, they reported the current time, their departure time, and their arrival time. Consistent with our hypothesis, the result showed that participants perceived greater time slack for now and for the next week than for that evening. More importantly, when we used the remaining time to departure as a grouping variable or covariate, we found that temporal proximity to a goal (i.e., boarding/departure) differently influences an individual's perceptions of time slack over time. When one's flight is not scheduled to depart for an hour or more, one perceives that one has more spare time "now" than tonight: the goal of boarding is not active and the goal of evening activities is active. But when boarding time approaches, boarding becomes the focal and proximate goal, and one perceives that one has little spare time "now."

In Study 2a and 2b, we next test the premise that goal proximity affects willingness to be interrupted for some other attractive task requiring the use of the same resource (i.e., time) and whether one would prefer to be interrupted now or later. Each individual participant's goal was to win two out of four Nintendo Wii games in 10 minutes. We manipulated proximity to a goal by interrupting participants at different points of their goal progress in the first game (either at about 20-30% or 60-70% of the first game). Then, they were asked if they wanted to perform the interrupting task (i.e., another Wii game) now or in the middle of the second game. We also manipulated the attractiveness of the second game. Unsurprisingly, participants were more likely to prefer to be interrupted now versus later when the later task was attractive rather than unattractive. But, our key finding was that people were more willing to be interrupted when they had made less rather than more progress in the first game, suggesting that goal proximity-based perceptions of time slack affected their preference to delay interruption.

In sum, this paper extends the time perception literature by demonstrating that perceptions of "spare time" now and in the future are related to proximity to a goal requiring use of that time. Furthermore, goal proximity affects the strength of motivation to pursue a focal task and desire to delay "attractive interruptions" that require time as a resource.

REFERENCES

Heath, Chip, Richard P. Larrick, and George Wu (1999), "Goals as Reference Points," *Cognitive Psychology*, 38 (1), 79-109.
Lynch, John G., Richard G. Netemeyer, Stephen A. Spiller and Alessandra Zammit (2010), "A Generalizable Scale of Propensity to Plan: The Long and the Short of Planning for Time and for Money," *Journal of Consumer Research*, 37 (1), 108-128.
Zauberman, Gal and John G. Lynch (2005), "Resource Slack and Propensity to Discount Delayed Investment of Time versus Money," *Journal of Experimental Psychology: General*, 134 (1), 23-37.

The Impact of Auditory Tempo on Prospective Temporal Distance Judgments and Consumer Preference

EXTENDED ABSTRACT

Existing research on interval timing in the second-to-minute range has found that external tempo (i.e., repetitive stimulation by auditory or visual stimuli) influences individuals' judgments of elapsed time by changing their internal tempo, or the speed of their internal clocks. For instance, listening to fast pulses or being presented repeatedly with fast visual flickers has been shown to induce overestimation in judgment of elapsed time. In this article we demonstrate that auditory tempo, such as sine pulses or beats of music, influences judgment of future time—that is, perceived prospective temporal distance—and various time-related judgments.

Although perception of prospective temporal distance and elapsed time are not identical, there are theoretical reasons to expect that they are related. Even if we assume that prospective temporal distance is a purely abstract construct, not governed by the same process governing the perception of elapsed time (such as an internal clock), judgment of abstract information is influenced by individual experiences in related and more concrete domains (Lakoff and Johnson 1999; Landua, Meier, and Keefer 2010). When individuals judge prospective temporal distance—which is abstract information to process—their perceptions of current or elapsed time would constitute the most relevant temporal inputs that can be used to form their perception of future time. Thus, auditory tempo, which influences judgment of elapsed time, may also influence judgment of prospective temporal distance.

In Study 1, we first examined whether individuals' estimates of elapsed time are significantly associated with their prospective temporal distance. Specifically, participants judged the elapsed duration of 12 randomly presented tones lasting 2 to 30 seconds and another 12 prospective durations ranging from 10 to 60 days using a physically-unbounded psychophysical line scale. Results showed that these two types of time perceptions are significantly correlated. Such association between elapsed time perception and prospective temporal distance judgment implies that a common psychological process may be involved in both processes and that auditory tempo may influence judgment of prospective temporal distance by serving as a perceptual input for judgment of prospective temporal distance. To directly test this prediction (in Study 2 and 3) we used different speeds of sine pulse, which have been used in the elapsed time perception literature, or different beats of the same music—the tempo of the same music piece was changed either to be faster (98 beats per minute) or slower (55 beats per minute) than the original tempo (76.5 beats per minute) without changing the music's pitch—to manipulate the speed of tempo and tested whether fast tempo influences perceived length of prospective duration. Results showed that participants who listened to fast pulses judged the same prospective durations to be longer than those who listened to slow pulses.

A similar effect was observed not only for prospective temporal distance judgment but also for time estimation for various future events (Study 4). Specifically, participants who listened to the faster music estimated everyday activities such as preparing for a final exam, booting their computers, or writing an email to take longer compared to those who listened to a slower version of the same music. But, auditory tempo did not influence calorie judgment of foods, ruling out an alternative explanation that what is influenced by tempo may be judgment of number rather than judgment of duration (Study 4).

In Studies 5, 6, and 7, we tested the impact of auditory tempo on various time-related judgments such as willingness-to-pay for products with a duration attribute (Study 5), and intertemporal preferences for a product (Study 6) or for monetary outcomes (Study 7). Results confirmed that different tempos of music significantly influenced time-related judgments as predicted. Specifically, participants who listened to fast tempo music were willing to pay more for the same vacation package and revealed greater impatience for products and money when making intertemporal tradeoff decisions.

Taken together, the current research demonstrates an intriguing relationship between tempo and prospective temporal distance judgment, and its implication for consumer preference. It further suggests that elapsed time judgment and prospective temporal distance judgment are highly related (i.e., one serves as perceptual input for the other), shedding a new light on the nature of prospective temporal distance judgment.

REFERENCES

Lakoff, George and mark Johnson (1999), *Philosophy in the Flesh: The Embodied Mind and Its Challenge to Western Thought,* New York: Basic Books.

Landau, Mark J., Brian P. Meier, and Lucas A. Keefer (2010), "A Metaphor-Enriched Social Cognition," *Psychological Bulletin,* 136 (6), 1045-1067.

The Value of Money

Session Chair: Stephen A. Spiller, UCLA, USA

SESSION OVERVIEW

Money is a remarkable technology fulfilling three primary functions: a medium of exchange, a unit of account, and a store of value. It is an integral part of most consumer interactions and pervades every aspect of our consumer lives. Other media of exchange, such as gift cards and reward points, fulfill similar functions and are nearly as ubiquitous. The value we place on money determines the extent to which we strive to accumulate it and our reluctance to part with it when making purchases. Normatively, money's value is determined by the utility gained by using the marginal dollar. In this session, we consider a variety of important non-normative influences on the perceived value of money and media of exchange. In doing so, we help to answer how money is psychologically imbued with value.

First, Wiltermuth and Gino show that organizing incentives such as time and money into categories increases motivation to work for those incentives. Such categories may be arbitrary, and the effect is robust to gain and loss frames; merely separating them into categories increases their value. Second, Spiller and Ariely examine how the set of possible purchases influences the value of a resource. Normatively, only the best use of a resource should affect its value. Instead, other possible but irrelevant uses affect the value placed on a resource as well. Third, DeVoe, Pfeffer, and Lee find that the accumulation of money increases the importance individuals place on money. By earning money through labor, the symbolic value of money is associated with one's self-esteem and sense of competence, thereby increasing its importance. Finally, Vohs, Lasaleta, and Sedikides show that feelings of nostalgia weaken the desire for money. Nostalgia provides a sense of social support, weakening the reliance on money to provide such support in its place, and thus decreasing its value.

Each paper advances our understanding of a truly fundamental question in consumer behavior: how do consumers value money and other media of exchange? Overall, the session provides a coherent set of distinct drivers of money's perceived value with a wide variety of implications for marketing and consumer behavior. These papers will likely appeal to researchers interested in a variety of fields including gift cards, incentives, labor, materialism, the social and cognitive roles of money, and retro brand appeals.

"I'll Have One of Each": How Separating Rewards into (Meaningless) Categories Increases Motivation

EXTENDED ABSTRACT

Researchers have long sought to understand how to foster motivation more effectively. Much of this research has highlighted rational mechanisms that increase or make salient the benefits the worker obtains by applying effort. For instance, Adam Grant's (2007, 2008) work has shown that highlighting the pro-social impact of people's work increases their motivation. Hackman and Oldham (1976) have similarly shown that task identity, task significance, and positive feedback all influence motivation. In the present research, we propose that even factors that should not rationally affect motivation may do so. Specifically, we hypothesize that categorizing rewards can increase motivation, even when those categories are arbitrary.

We put forth this hypothesis because we believe people clump rewards into categories and are more sensitive to increases in the number of categories of rewards than they are to increasing the magnitude of rewards within a category. Thus, our work draws inspiration from Thaler's (1999) work on mental accounting.

We tested our hypothesis across three experiments. In Study 1, 157 undergraduate students (53% female; M_{age} = 21.0) at a large, private university on the West Coast first completed an anagram unscrambling task (Cameron and Miller, 2010). Unbeknownst to the participants, the third and ninth anagrams were nearly impossible to solve. In one condition, successfully unscrambling anagrams ostensibly earned participants $2 per anagram solved. In another condition, successfully unscrambling anagrams allowed them to skip four minutes of a boring task. In a third condition, successfully unscrambling anagrams earned participants $1 and allowed them to skip two minutes of the boring task. Thus, these participants earned half the money and saved half the time that did participants in each of the other two conditions. The dependent variable was the amount of time participants persisted in the task. As predicted, participants in the two categories of benefit condition persisted longer (M = 9.1 minutes, SD = 3.1) than did those in the monetary benefit (M = 7.0, SD = 2.6) or time benefit conditions (M = 6.9, SD = 3.7), $ps < .05$.

Studies 2 and 3 examined the hypothesis that separating incentives into categories can increase motivation, even when those categories are meaningless. Across these studies, we instructed participants that they would be transcribing a number of sections of type-written text to help us to prepare for a future study, in which we would study how handwriting can affect the perceptions people have of others. We manipulated whether a collection of items purchased from a local dollar store were portrayed as belonging to a single category or to two categories. In the categorization condition, participants were told that Category 1 was in the Purple Storage Container and Category 2 was in the Clear Storage Container. These participants were told that they could take home one of the items from either category if they transcribed for ten minutes and that they could take home an item from the other category if they transcribed for twenty minutes. In the no-categorization condition, participants were told that they could take home one item if they transcribed for ten minutes and two items if they transcribed for twenty minutes. Participants were told that may spend as much time or as little time transcribing these sections as they liked. Participants were then told to take a look at the rewards that they could win. The rewards were not sorted into specific categories; rather, there was a mix of statio-

Advances in Consumer Research
Volume 39, ©2011

nery, hardware, and food items in each container. The likelihood of participants transcribing sections of text for a full twenty minutes served as the primary dependent variable.

Study 2 participants in the categorization condition were more likely to transcribe for the full twenty minutes (34.4%) than were participants in the no-categorization condition (9.7%), $p = .03$. They also reported that they were more motivated to obtain the second reward (M = 4.22, SD = 2.21) than did participants in the no-categorization condition (M = 3.07, SD = 1.95), $p = .03$. Bootstrapping analysis revealed a significant indirect effect.

Study 3 replicated the categorization effect using a loss frame. In this case, participants selected their prizes at the beginning and were asked to return one if they did not work twenty minutes and return two if they did not work for ten minutes. Motivation to obtain the second item again mediated the effect.

We conclude from our results that that separating incentives into categories can increase motivation, even when the basis for the categorization is meaningless.

Irrelevant Outside Options
Influence the Value of Money

EXTENDED ABSTRACT

How do consumers represent the value of money? We propose that holding constant the value of a resource's best use, liking for the category of possible and accessible uses is an important (but normatively irrelevant) determinant of the perceived value of money.

Economically, money is as valuable as the goods it buys. Understanding other non-normative influences on the value of money informs our understanding of consumers' propensities to spend, save, and earn money. Because money is associated with a large, heterogeneous group of products, the associations between money and its best uses are weak (Weber and Johnson 2006). As a result, other inputs associated with a resource that are not its best uses, and that are therefore irrelevant, may be likely to affect its perceived value as well. In four studies, we demonstrate that accessible but irrelevant items in the category of possible purchases affect how consumers value media of exchange. In Studies 1 and 2 we examine the perceived value of artificial media of exchange, and in Studies 3 and 4 we examine the perceived value of gift cards.

Measured set composition. In Study 1, we ask: Do resource uses other than the most valuable use affect the value of the resource? Undergraduate students (total $N=42$; usable $N=34$) learned how each of several certificates could be used to purchase one product from associated subsets of 1, 2, or 3 products. For example, one certificate could be exchanged for one product from the set: notepad, packet of pens, roll of tape. Each certificate should be worth as much as its most valuable use. Participants reported how much they would be willing to pay for each certificate and then reported how much they would be willing to pay for each product. Regressing certificate willingness to pay (WTP) on (a) set size, (b) maximum product WTP across its subset of products, (c) average product WTP across its subset of products, and (d) certificate fixed effects revealed that participants were willing to pay more for certificates associated with larger sets ($p<.0001$), marginally more for certificates associated with sets with higher maximum product WTPs ($p<.09$), and more for certificates associated with sets with higher average product WTPs ($p<.05$). Holding constant the value of the most valuable product, other less valuable products affected certificate WTP.

Manipulated set composition. In Study 2 (total $N=83$; usable $N=71$), we replicate Study 1 and manipulate the value of products. In addition to replicating Study 1's results, we find that controlling

for maximum WTP and set size, manipulating a set of products to replace a high-valued product with a low-valued product decreases WTP ($p<.0001$). Controlling for the value of the best use of a medium of exchange, experimentally decreasing the value of irrelevant options decreases the perceived value of the medium.

Category attractiveness. In Study 3, we ask: Does the effect of category attractiveness hold when considering media of exchange with which consumers have considerable experience and which are associated with broader sets of goods? Undergraduate students ($N=100$) reported WTP for five gift cards associated with real stores, the ultimate uses of those gift cards, WTP for those ultimate uses, and liking for those stores. Controlling for WTP for the ultimate use of the gift card (the normative determinant of gift card WTP), liking for the set of products offered at the store was an important determinant of card WTP (between-subject: $p<.05$; within-subject: $p<.0001$). Consumers value real-world media of exchange according to how much they like the category of products it could be used to buy, not just the actual product it will be used to buy.

Subcategory accessibility. In Study 4 ($N = 147$), we ask: Can merely increasing the accessibility in memory of an unattractive subcategory of uses (without changing the set of possible uses) decrease the perceived value of a resource? We find that it does. Our manipulation was subcategory accessibility of different ways one could spend a Barnes & Noble gift card: one third of participants generated books and textbooks they could buy (typical subcategory), one third of participants generated music and movies they could buy (atypical subcategory), and one third of participants did not generate any purchases. Making typical subcategories more accessible should have little effect on what a participant thinks about: they are already accessible. Making atypical subcategories more accessible should change what the participant thinks about: they are not already accessible. Value (our DV) was operationalized as the number of times a Barnes & Noble gift card was chosen out of ten pairwise choices against other gift cards. At the end of the study, participants reported whether they would rather use the Barnes & Noble gift card on books and textbooks or on music and movies (Category Preference).

Accessibility interacted with Category Preferences to influence Gift Card Value ($F(2, 135) = 7.88$, $p = .0006$). Individuals who preferred movies and music chose the gift card more often when music and movies were made accessible ($M=4.94$) than when nothing was made accessible ($M=3.47$) or when books were made accessible ($M=2.80$). Individuals who preferred books and textbooks chose the gift card more often when books were made accessible ($M=6.44$) or when nothing was made accessible ($M=6.12$) than when music and movies were made accessible ($M=4.66$). Most importantly, increasing the accessibility of less accessible, less valuable uses (i.e., making music and movies accessible for individuals who would prefer to buy books and textbooks) decreased the value of the gift card (M's = 6.12 vs. 4.66, $p < .02$).

Liking for the category of possible accessible purchases, not just the marginal purchase, determines the perceived value of a medium. Reducing the fungibility of money may perversely increase its perceived value if eliminating unattractive uses increases liking for the category as a whole. Given that limited-use resources with attractive categories of uses are perceived as more valuable, consumers will be less likely to spend them, more likely to save them, and more likely to exert effort to earn them.

Money Makes Money More Important

EXTENDED ABSTRACT

The strange part is, the more I made, the more I got preoccupied with money. When suddenly I didn't have to think about money as much, I found myself starting to think increasingly about it. Money corrupts the mind.

–Daniel Vasella, CEO of Novartis

Although individual differences are undoubtedly important in affecting inter-individual variations in the importance people place on money, the importance of money may also be endogenously affected by *how* and *how much* money people receive. To the extent that there is variability in money's importance, the standard prediction is that more money should make money *less* important, following the principle of diminishing marginal utility. However, we argue that more money can cause people to place *greater* importance on money when it is earned from labor, because the symbolic value of money implicates one's self-esteem and is a signal of competence.

We initially tested this hypothesis by contrasting two different forms of income (labor income per hours worked versus investment income) using a nationally representative longitudinal survey that permitted us to see how changes in income affected changes in the importance people place on money. At two time periods five years apart, respondents rated the subjective importance of money (i.e., How important is having a lot of money?) on a 1 (*not at all important*) to 10 (*extremely important*) scale. We ran a first-differenced regression that removed constant individual differences and included measures of changes in the number of hours worked per week, changes in the number of household children, changes in total outstanding loans on all the property respondents owned, and changes in the total number of discretionary possessions. Consistent with the hypothesis that money that is earned from labor provides symbolic information about self-esteem and competence, changes in the amount of labor income earned per hour were positively associated with changes in the importance of money, $\beta = .04$, $t(3067) = 2.39$, $p = .017$. However, changes in investment income were negatively associated with changes in the importance of money, $\beta = -.04$, $t(3067) = 2.10$, $p = .036$.

Next, we used experiments to further explore the causal association between how and how much money is received and the subsequent importance placed on money. We wanted to see if we could experimentally manipulate "income" on a small scale and obtain similar causal effects on the importance of money by developing an experimental treatment which would clearly distinguish "earned" income with its implications for the self from income that had no relevance to people's feelings of self-esteem or competence. Towards this end, we utilized a laboratory setting where participants could be randomly assigned to experimental treatments. Specifically, some participants received unexpected additional money as part of the experiment. In a condition analogous to labor income, participants were told that they had received this unanticipated money as a consequence of their work performance—information that should directly cause them to view the money as being associated with self-esteem and competence. If the critical factor is whether or not money reflects the performance of an individual and his or her work, we thought that if people received money because of random chance, that money would not have the same implications for the self and would, therefore, not engender additional symbolic value in terms of money's importance (or at least not to the same extent). We examined participants post-manipulation ratings on the value importance of money subscale (Mitchell and Mickel 1999) that has been used

in prior research. Specifically, participants rated their agreement to four statements ("I value money very highly", "Money is important", "I daydream about being rich", and "I believe the more money you have, the happier you are") on a 1(*strongly disagree*) to 7(*strongly agree*) scale.

Participants who received $10 randomly did not differ in the importance of money ($M = 5.07$, $SD = 1.32$) from their counterparts who had received $1 randomly ($M = 5.17$, $SD = 1.16$), $F(1, 28) = .83$, *ns*. However, participants who received $10 because of the performance of their labor did rate the value importance of money as significantly higher ($M = 5.50$, $SD = .84$) than participants who received $1 ($M = 4.71$, $SD = .88$), $F(1, 37) = 8.20$, $p = .007$. In a follow-up experiment, we replicated the findings of this previous study on the importance of money subscale using a different experimental task with a similar amount by source of money interaction, $F(1, 89) = 4.92$, $p = .029$. Additionally, we found that the amount by source interaction was mediated by the more proximal construct of participant's perceived competency ($z = 1.81$, $p = .07$) than by the more global construct of self-esteem ($z = .48$, $p = .63$).

By demonstrating that the amount as well as the source of income is a critical variable in how important money is to individuals, the present findings extend and elaborate on a decision making literature that attests to the fact that people do not experience all dollars as the same. Additionally, the fact that the acquisition of money from people's labor caused people to value money more supports theoretical perspectives emphasizing the symbolic value of money as distinct from instrumental or individual difference accounts explaining its importance. Money is not just a medium of exchange or a store of value, but can have drug-like properties—the more you have, the more you want. Thus, money can become even more important than its economic value alone would dictate when it is a signal of one's competency at work.

Nostalgia Weakens the Desire for Money

EXTENDED ABSTRACT

Nostalgia is commonplace in marketing, and nostalgic themes have been particularly pervasive during recent times of economic crisis. In 2009, PepsiCo launched nostalgic versions of their popular sodas, Pepsi-Cola and Mountain Dew. The so-called throwback beverages, based on original formulas and packaging, were meant to evoke sentiments of the 1960s and 1970s (Elliot 2009). Similarly, General Mills introduced retro packaging for their Big 5 cereals (Trix, Lucky Charms, Cheerios, Cinnamon Toast Crunch, and Honey Nut Cheerios) to induce a wistfulness of the past.

Despite nostalgia's pervasiveness in marketing, little is known about how nostalgia might affect spending in general – beyond spending for nostalgic products themselves. In this article, we test how nostalgia motivates consumption. We tested whether nostalgia's ability to give people a sense of social support would decrease the desire of money. In this research, we bridge two literatures: one demonstrating that nostalgia increases perceptions of social support (Wildschut et al. 2006) and another suggesting that social support and money are oppositional forces (Heyman and Ariely 2004).

We reasoned that, when people perceive they are backed by ample social support, they will find money less desirable than it would be otherwise. This reasoning comes from the idea that both money and social support enable people to get what they need from society, such as shelter, security, nourishment, and companionship (Fiske 1994; Heyman and Ariely 2004). Once a person has enough of either money or social support, she will feel that her needs are met and therefore crave the other less. That is, if consumers believe that they can satisfy their wants and needs through social support, then their motivation for money will weaken. Four experiments tested whether the psychological state of nostalgia, due to its ability to foster a sense of social connectedness, would weaken the desire for money.

Experiment 1 induced nostalgia using copy on print advertisements. In the nostalgia condition, participants viewed advertisements that focused on nostalgic memories from one's past, whereas in the control condition participants viewed advertisements that focused on making new memories. Our operationalization of desire for money was the behavior of giving away money in a pooled investment game (Fehr and Gachter 2000). Participants had the opportunity to contribute their money to a common pool. We found that participants in the nostalgia condition gave up more of their money to the common pool than participants in the control condition.

Experiment 2 tested desire for money using the dictator game (Guth et al. 1982). This involves a one-shot exchange, in which a participant decides unilaterally how much money (if any) to give to another player with the rest of the money remaining with the participant. First, however, we used an autobiographical narrative task to differentially elicit feelings of nostalgia. Some participants wrote about a time they felt nostalgic (defined as) "a sentimental longing for a personally experienced past." Participants in the control condition were instructed to write about an ordinary event from their past. Then participants played the dictator game, in which they were always assigned to be the dictator. As predicted, participants in the nostalgic event condition gave significantly more money to the responder than those in the ordinary event condition.

Experiment 3 measured desire for money using a perceptual task – size of coins drawn. Bruner and Goodman (1947) interpreted the fact that poor children drew larger coins than wealthier children as greater motivation to have money. Participants in the nostalgia condition wrote about a nostalgic event, whereas participants in the control condition wrote about the route they took home from high school. Then ps drew on a piece of paper the size of a 50-cent piece and $1 coin. We measured the diameter of the coins, and as predicted nostalgic participants, compared to those in the control condition, drew smaller coins. We took this to signal a weaker desire for money.

Experiment 4 measured willingness to pay as the indicator of desire for money. This study returned to the advertising copy method of eliciting nostalgia (or not) in our participants. After viewing an advertisement that cued perusal childhood memories (nostalgia condition) or an advertisement that cued the idea of making new memories (control condition), they perused pictures of 24 products and were instructed to indicate their willingness to pay for each. As expected, willingness to pay among participants in the nostalgic memory condition was higher than in the control condition.

The present research tested the hypothesis that nostalgia reduces the desire for money. Prior research hinted at the idea that money and social connectedness are opposing motivational forces. Our research used this insight to test whether nostalgia would lead people to behave as if they had little motivation toward money. Four experiments supported this claim, by showing that in interpersonal and intrapersonal contexts, including spending money on products or giving it to others, people in a nostalgic mood desire money less than they would otherwise.

REFERENCES

Bruner, Jerome S. and Cecile C. Goodman (1947), "Value and Need as Organizing Factors in Perception", *Journal of Abnormal and Social Psychology*, 42 (1), 33-44.

Cameron, Jessica S., and Dale T. Miller (in press), "Unethical behavior in loss versus gain frames," in D. De Cremer (Ed.), *Psychological perspectives on ethical behavior,* Charlotte, NC: Information Age.

Elliot, Stewart (2009), "Warm and Fuzzy Makes a Comeback," *The New York Times*, http://www.ft.com/cms/s/0/17ba137c-a171-11df-9656-00144feabdc0.html.

Fehr, Ernst and Simon Gächter (2000), "Fairness and Retaliation: The Economics of Reciprocity," *Journal of Economic Perspectives*, 14 (Summer), 159-81.

Fiske, Alan P. (1992), "The Four Elementary Forms of Sociality: Framework for a Unified Theory of Social Relations," *Psychological Review*, 99 (October), 689–723.

Grant, Adam M. (2007), "Relational job design and the motivation to make a prosocial difference," *Academy of Management Review, 32(2)*, 393 – 417.

Grant, Adam M. (2008), "The significance of task significance: Job performance effects, relational mechanisms, and boundary conditions," *Journal of Applied Psychology, 93*(1), 108-124.

Güth, Werner, Rolf Schmittberger, and Bernd Schwarze (1982), "An Experimental Analysis of Ultimatum Bargaining," *Journal of Economic Behavior & Organization*, 3 (4), 367-88.

Hackman, J. R. & Oldham, G. R. (1976). "Motivation through the design of work: test of a theory," *Organizational Behavior and Human Decision Processes, 16* (2), 250 – 279.

Heyman, James and Dan Ariely (2004), "Effort for Payment: A Tale of Two Markets," *Psychological Science*, 15 (11), 787-93.

Hsee, Christopher K., Yu, Fang, Zhang, Jiao, & Zhang, Yan (2003), "Medium Maximization," *Journal of Consumer Research, 30*, 1-14.

Mitchell, Terence R., Amy E. Mickel, (1999), "The meaning of money: An individual-difference perspective," *Academy of Management Review* 24 (3) 568-578.

Thaler, Richard (1999), "Mental accounting matters," *Journal of Behavioral Decision Making, 12,* 183-206.

Weber, Elke U. and Eric J. Johnson (2006), "Constructing Preferences from Memory," in *The Construction of Preference*, ed. Sarah Lichtenstein and Paul Slovic, New York: Cambridge University Press, 397-410.

Wildschut, Tim, Constantine Sedikides, Jamie Arndt, and Clay Routledge (2006), "Nostalgia: Content, Triggers, Functions," *Journal of Personality and Social Psychology*, 91 (5), 975-93.

Collecting the Collectives: Brand Communities, Subcultures of Consumption, and Tribes

Chairs: Tandy Chalmers Thomas, Queen's University, Canada
Hope Schau, University of Arizona, USA
Linda Price, University of Arizona, USA

Paper #1: Consumption Community Dimensions
Tandy Chalmers Thomas, Queen's University, Canada
Hope Schau, University of Arizona, USA
Linda Price, University of Arizona, USA

Paper #2: Refining and Extending the Concept of Brand Community
Albert Muñiz, DePaul University, USA
Yun Mi Antorini, University of Aarhus, Denmark

Paper #3: Renewing Subcultural Ideology: Reclaiming Surf's Soul
Michael B. Beverland, University of Bath, UK
Francis J. Farrelly, RMIT University, Australia

Paper #4: Consumption Communities
Robin Canniford, University of Melbourne, Australia
Avi Shankar, University of Bath, UK

SESSION OVERVIEW

The purpose of this session is to deepen our understanding of consumption oriented communities, specifically bridging the conceptual gaps between various kinds of communities. Consumption oriented communities refer to groups of consumers who self-select into a group that shares a common commitment to a product class, brand, consumption activity, or consumer-based ideology. Over the past twenty years, consumer researchers have explored a variety of such collectives ranging from extreme sports groups (Celsi, Rose, and Leigh 1993), to temporary anti-brand festivals (Kozinets 2002), to in-line skating tribes (Cova and Cova 2002), to brand cults (Belk and Tumbat 2005), to brand communities (Muñiz and O'Guinn 2001), and consumption subcultures (Schouten and McAlexander 1995). In fact, over 100 different consumption communities have been discussed in marketing and consumer research journals. The prevalence of this work is not surprising giving the theoretical and practical import of consumption communities. Achrol and Kotler (1999), for example, proclaimed that the combination of consumer collectives and strategic marketing efforts "represent the most dramatic scenario of change for marketing in the next millennium" with effective management of consumer communities being a popular topic for marketing managers (Fournier and Lee 2009; Fournier, Sele, and Schoegel 2005).

Despite the prevalence of research on consumption communities, our knowledge of these communities is hindered by a lack of consistency in how these communities are conceptualized and how different kinds of communities relate to each other. To date, most research in marketing and consumer behavior has focused on one particular type of group, either a brand community (or multiple brand communities) (e.g., Schau, Muñiz, and Arnould 2009) or a consumption subculture (e.g., Beverland, Farrelly, and Quester 2010), or a consumer tribe (e.g., Otnes and Maclaran 2007). The theoretical and definitional linkages between these groups remain unknown. The purpose of this session is examine the commonalities and differences between different consumption communities to bridge the knowledge bases associated with each kind of consumption community.

Each of the papers in this session converge on this single issue: a lack of meaningful definitions and distinctions that hinders our understanding of contemporary consumption collectives. Each pa-

per also offers fruitful insights into these communities and proposes solutions to this problem. First, Thomas et al. present a conceptual paper where they discuss structural dimensions common to all consumption communities, postulating that communities, regardless of whether they are brand communities, subcultures of consumption, or tribes, vary according to these dimensions. They propose that using this cluster-based conceptualization highlights opportunities for new and important research. Next, Muñiz and Yun tackle the theoretical quandaries surrounding brand communities. Specifically articulating the need for researchers to be judicious in their application of the brand community concept, calling for theoretical rigor that encapsulates both emic and etic understandings of the dynamism and complexities of these collectives. Beverland and Farrelly follow, exploring the intricacies of subcultures of consumption. In this work, they present the processes through which consumption subcultures evolve, focusing on the often underexplored relationship between these communities and mainstream society. Specifically, they illuminate the conceptual shortcomings of traditional subculture theory by articulating how consumption subcultures prevail in the marketplace. The session concludes with Canniford and Shankar who clarify the definitions of the three most common forms of consumption communities (brand communities, subcultures of consumption, and consumer tribes) and discuss the marketing implications derived from a better understanding of the distinctions between these communities.

We expect this session to appeal to a broad range of consumer researchers, especially those interested in consumer culture theory, subcultures of consumption, brand communities, consumer tribes, social networks, and consumer-brand relationships.

Consumption Community Dimensions

EXTENDED ABSTRACT

Consumption oriented collectives are groups of consumers who self-select into a group that shares a commitment to a product class, brand, consumption activity, or consumer-based ideology. Consumer research has explored a variety of these collectives including, but not limited to, consumer tribes (Cova and Cova 2002), subcultures of consumption (Schouten and McAlexander 1995), brand communities (Muñiz and O'Guinn 2001), brand cults (Belk and Tumbat 2005), and microcultures (Thompson and Troester 2002).

Examining the body of literature on consumption collectives as a whole, however, reveals significant ambiguity about what constitutes each type of collective and how they are similar or different. As such, researchers have struggled to both integrate work across collectivity types as well as determine how to best understand collectives that do not fall neatly into the predefined categories. To avoid this ambiguity, many researchers have simply ignored the differences between collectives, treating each collectivity as theoretical equivalents, stating that "there is no sharp theoretical distinction to be drawn between [various consumption collectives]" (Thompson and Troester 2002 p. 533). We contend, however, that the differences between collectives are theoretically meaningful and have important implications for consumer researchers and marketing practitioners. Specifically, we postulate that conceptualizing collectives as clusters of characteristics attenuates much of the theoretical ambiguity aris-

Advances in Consumer Research
Volume 39, ©2011

ing from trying to disentangle seemingly similar collectivity definitions. To this end, we analyzed approximately 100 papers focusing on consumption collectives published in consumer and marketing journals, identifying eight primary dimensions (described next) on which collectivities vary: duration, appeal, access, dispersion, focus, orientation towards the marketplace, structure of resource flows, and heterogeneity. Importantly, these dimensions represent continuous and interrelated spectrums.

The first dimension, time, or temporal duration, refers to the manner in which collectives differ in how long they exist. On the one hand, some collectives are temporary and form for a constrained period of time (e.g., Flash Mobs (Barnes 2006; Thorley 2009); Burning Man Festival (Kozinets 2002)). On the other hand, other collectivities are characterized by a prolonged lifespan (e.g., Apple Newton Community (Muñiz and Schau 2005)).

The second dimension, appeal, refers to the degree to which collectives are attractive to consumers. Collectives with limited appeal tend to only attract a small group of consumers. This sometimes results from the collectivity being oppositional to mainstream cultural ideologies and behaviors (Copes and Williams 2007), such as the voluntary simplicity community (Cherrier 2009). In contrast, other collectives are broadly appealing and tend to espouse values and behaviors aligned with mainstream society (e.g., the Tom Petty and the Heartbreakers brand community (Schau and Muñiz 2007)). Importantly, appeal refers to consumers' perceptions of a collectivity at a single point of time: as collectivities evolve, so does their appeal.

The third dimension, access, refers to the ease with which consumers can join a collective. This is influenced by two factors: (1) barriers to entry related to the minimum requirements for membership (i.e., obstacles consumers face in gaining entry to the collective (Von Hippel 2005)) and (2) the degree to which the collective encourages and facilities membership growth. The next dimension, dispersion, refers to the degree to which collectivities are localized (in person), dispraised (online), or hybrid (both on and offline) (Wind, Mahajan, and Gunther 2002). For example, river rafting communities (Arnould and Price 1993) typify a localized community, online communities typify dispersed groups (e.g., Mathwick, Wiertz, and Ruyter 2008), while the Hummer brand community is an example of a hybrid community (Luedicke, Thompson, and Giesler 2010).

Collectivities also differ in their focus: the degree to which they are centered on a brand, activity, or ideology. For example, the Saab community is brand focused (Muñiz and O'Guinn 2001), the surfing community is activity focused (Canniford and Shankar 2007), while the Burning Man community is predominately ideologically focused (Kozinets 2002).

The sixth dimension, orientation towards the marketplace, refers to the degree to which the marketplace plays a collaborative role in the collective. Synergistic collectives, such as the Harley-Davidson community (Schouten and McAlexander 1995), work collaboratively with the marketplace to achieve common goals. Oppositional communities, such as the Community Supported Agriculture community (Thompson and Coskuner-Balli 2007) are countercultural in nature and oppose mainstream marketplace tendencies. Collectives also differ in how the flow of resources is structured. Fournier and Lee (2009), for example, discuss different community structures (webs, hubs, pools) representing where resources are stored, dispersed, and received.

Finally, collectives differ in terms of heterogeneity. Specifically, they vary in the extent to which they exhibit diversity in how members orient towards the collective, especially with reference to the roles played within the collective, the meanings derived from membership, and the resources created within the collective (Fourni-

er et al. 2005; Thomas, Schau, and Price 2010). Communities can, therefore, be described as clusters of these eight dimensions, occupying a particular cultural space defined in relation to other communities. For example, the running community described by Thomas et al. (2010) would be characterized as an enduring, hybrid, activity focused community that is easy to join with broad appeal. It is also highly heterogeneous with diffuse resource flows and a synergistic relationship with the marketplace.

To date, consumption collective research has only explicitly articulated the focus dimension. Assessing the theoretical implications of all the dimensions, as well as clusters of dimensions, illuminates areas for future research and aids our understanding of communities. To illustrate this, we classified each community discussed in extant marketing and consumer research along the proposed dimensions, focusing on how the community was conceptualized by the researchers in terms of the dimensions, and indentified under-researched areas that have important implications for consumer research. Overall, this classification helps reduce some of the theoretical ambiguities associated with consumption collectives stemming from the parallel development of multiple streams of related research.

Refining and Extending the Concept of Brand Community

EXTENDED ABSTRACT

Since Muñiz and O'Guinn (2001) first articulated the term, brand community has been the subject of a lot of good research. It is much easier now to account for brand-centered consumer collectives and the value they produce. Still, ten years later, there remains a need for conceptual clarity. The term 'brand community' is over-applied, occasionally to the brink of irrelevance. If everything is a brand community, then nothing is a brand community.

To illuminate the theoretical quandaries surrounding consumption collectives, brand centered and otherwise, and to divine conceptual remedies, we draw upon seven years of research on the Adult Fan of LEGO (or AFOL) brand community. The AFOL brand community can be traced back to 1985 when a few adult North American LEGO enthusiasts formed the first LEGO Train club. Between 1985 and the present, what began as a small scale offline group of loosely connected North American LEGO enthusiasts developed into a global community. The LEGO Group estimates that there are currently at least 40,000 active AFOLs around the world (the LEGO Group 2009). These users interact in a variety of face-to-face and online venues (Bender 2010; Chrisman, Hanes, and Weisman 2009).

Between 2003 and 2010, we engaged in a multi-site, ethnographic research program to examine community development in the Adult Fans of LEGO community. We employed two ethnographic methods, participant observation and depth interviews. We observed AFOLs in face-to-face and online contexts. We participated in eight conventions in North America, Denmark and Germany. We observed AFOLs at smaller and local events such as visits to the LEGO factory and the LEGOLAND Park in Billund, Denmark, monthly LEGO user group meetings and locally arranged LEGO shopping trips. We closely followed several LEGO online forums, studying hundreds of conversation threads, and collecting profiles uploaded by members of the LEGO User Group Network (Lugnet.com). We conducted 25 depth interviews with members of the community.

What we see in the AFOL community helps us understand the differences between the multiple forms of consumer collectives (tribes, communities, and subcultures). First, researchers need to address the emic versus the etic issue involved in applying the label brand community. Researchers need to balance the etic perspective, applying labels based on evidence of agreed-upon requisite markers, with the emic perspective, that is, what the community feels they are and why they feel that way. Some groups prefer to be labeled as a tribe or a subculture, possibly owing to the politics involved; being a subculture is more subversive and positions one against the mainstream. Other groups prefer the term and form community. Sometimes, a group may prefer an inaccurate term.

The LEGO data demonstrate that AFOLs are a community rather than a subculture or a tribe. The AFOLs brand community easily possesses the three markers of brand community (Muñiz and O'Guinn 2001). What we see in AFOLs is a community that is quite self-aware. They understand the significance of the form their collective assumes. Many members have pondered their collective and discussed it with other members, in both face to face and online settings. The discussions are often related to topics such as concerns about recruitment of new members, the overall wellbeing of the community, and legitimization. Although most visible in cases of boundary drawing, we assert that self-awareness is an essential part of communities' processes of coming to terms with who they are and what their community is about.

Second, researchers must understand the dynamism in these collectives over time. Communities change and evolve. For example, as a community matures and attracts new members, it evolves. Neighborhoods and cliques can develop that have their own expression of affiliation and therefore also shape the nature of the overall collective. Although extant work does not preclude this possibility, it also does not address it very explicitly, either.

In the AFOL community, we see three distinct and shifting development stages: a founding and early growth stage, a growth stage, and a midlife stage in which the community undergo changes in structure and organization. We see these developments being initiated by a series of crises that among other things have to do with growth in the number of members, new and different demands for community leadership and an increasing specialization in regards to brand usage. At the same time, we see how AFOLs eagerly embrace new information technologies and how these platforms offer new opportunities to interact and thus organize the community. We believe that insights into the way communities, tribes, and subcultures change and evolve can provide us with a much deeper understanding of what is distinct about each of the groups, but also how they may in fact be related. In further cultivating this perspective we believe that the work of organizational theorists (Greiner 1998/1972; Martin 2002; Schein 1992) is an invaluable source of inspiration.

Finally, conceptual clarity and depth must be achieved. It is essential that we develop a typology that not only includes communities, tribes, and subcultures, but also forms of affiliation that are less involved or committed, that reflect different development stages, and that account for the changes and dynamics that the different types of affiliations undergo. We further assert that it is necessary to develop a typology for the different forms of brand community, tribes, and subcultures. Fournier and Lee (2009) offer interesting ideas on different brand community forms, but their conceptualizations present some difficulties. Their categories are neither exhaustive nor exclusive. Based on their definitions, Apple could be said to exhibit characteristics of both pools (shared goals and values) and hubs (admiration for an individual via the centrality of Steve Jobs). Moreover, it is not clear from their descriptions whether or not all three of their forms possess the three key markers derived by Muñiz and O'Guinn (2001) from the sociology of community. Thus, it is unclear if these three forms are even brand communities. Still the notion of the source of the unity for the collective is valuable and should be included in any such typology.

Renewing Subcultural Ideology: Reclaiming Surf's Soul

EXTENDED ABSTRACT

Can a subculture's ideology endure in the face of mainstreaming? Subcultures often undergo an "identity crisis" when they are mainstreamed (Schouten, Martin, and McAlexander 2007; Thompson and Coskuner-Balli 2007), or when consumption practices associated with a subculture become popularized through commercial activities. Although mainstreaming results in increased interest in the subculture, tension also arises when members feel the subculture's authenticity is undermined (Thompson and Coskuner-Balli 2007; Schouten, Martin, and McAlexander 2007). In more extreme situations, the subculture's power to provide the context for self-authentication and authoritative performances is severely diminished as the subculture is no longer seen as an operant resource (Arnould, Price, and Malshe 2006).

To date, research on how subcultures respond to mainstreaming has focused on exit (whereby original members leave the subculture), or loyalty (whereby original members stay within the subculture) (Goulding and Saren 2007; Schouten, Martin, and McAlexander 2007; Thompson and Coskuner-Balli 2007), resulting in tension, fragmentation (Thompson and Coskuner-Balli 2007), and in some cases decline (Fox 1987). However, others have also implicitly identified an alternate response where the enduring power of many counter-cultural images or subcultures can be explained by cultural entrepreneurship, or the ability of the subculture to rework mainstreaming threats into an evolving narrative that continues to work for the majority of members (Heath and Potter (2005)) (see Belk and Costa (1998), Kates (2002), and Kozinets (2001) for specific examples of "reworking"). Building on the seminal framework of Hirschman (1970), we highlight that the benefits to subcultural endurance of "voice with loyalty" strategies demand greater attention in research on subcultural processes (Holt and Thompson 2004; Humphreys 2010).

Based on four years of ethnographic research in the Australian surf culture, we examine the means by which surfers ensure the endurance of the core ideology lying at the heart of their subculture. The ideological conflict at the heart of Australian surfing involved tensions between "soul surfers" (defined by their intrinsic love of surfing for its own sake) and "competitive surfers" (the latter of which were seen as the bearers of mainstreaming). Mainstreaming manifested itself within the community in three ways: breaching key performance norms, de-ritualization of subcultural performance, and the loss of object-indexicality. The tension arising from these three outcomes not only challenges the dominant ideology of soul surfers but also has a significant negative impact for all surfers as increased aggression on the beach and in the water leads to a collective "race-to-the bottom" (Heath and Potter 2005) whereby everyone's ability to achieve self-authentication is reduced.

We identified managing dialectical conflict between opposing ideologies as being central to Subcultural endurance and renewal in the face of mainstreaming. For an ideological dominance to endure, soul surfers needed to find creative solutions to the following dialectical conflict: freedom vs. anarchy; rebellion vs. conformity; and authenticity vs. fashion. To navigate these dialectical conflicts, soul surfers deployed four voice related tactics at the intra-, outer-, and inter-cultural levels to achieve three critical subcultural outcomes (threat identification, narrative updating, and attracting new recruits). These voice tactics were: creating new symbolic community boundaries (through emphasizing iconicity and indexicality), rewriting the motives of key subcultural actors (such as successful competitive surfers), and de- and re-mythologizing cultural artifacts (such as clothing and surf boards).

Our research highlights that subcultures are decidedly more resilient in the face of commercial co-optation or mainstreaming than is often depicted in the literature. To date, much of the literature has described the relationship between subculture and commerce in terms of conquest, "selling out", and/or dilution, typically focusing on how subcultures have declined in terms of their wider cultural impact and as resources for members' life projects, or how they have been reconstituted into new cultural realities through exit. In contrast, we contend voice is central to ideological endurance in subcultures because consumers' emotional bonds remain only as long as they can keep a narrative going.

Consumption Communities

EXTENDED ABSTRACT

An unwelcome consequence of the resurgence of the concept of community in marketing and consumer research studies is the plethora of accompanying terms to describe these different forms and types of community. In this work, we clarify three of the most common community concepts to identify the difference between subcultures of consumption, brand communities, and consumer tribes. In doing so, we focus on consumer tribes and articulate the distinctive characteristics of tribes, discussing the marketing implications arising from these characteristics.

Sub-cultures of Consumption. Early theories of subculture described communities that developed strong interpersonal bonds, ritualized modes of expression, and beliefs that precluded other social affiliations in order to subvert dominant institutions such as family, schooling, and class politics (Goulding et al. 2002). Research in marketing contributed to this perspective by describing the "shared commitment to a particular product class, brand or consumption activity" that often features within subcultural communities (Celsi et al. 1993; Schouten and McAlexander 1995 p. 43). Further research, however, has explained that unlike sociological studies of subculture, consumption communities rarely display political resistance, robust social structures, or firm gender hierarchies (Martin et al. 2006). Moreover, consumers enjoy membership of a plethora of fragmented groups in which identity is constructed and discarded at will (Firat and Venkatesh 1995). Characterized as self-selecting micro-communities, these groups construct multiple trajectories of identity held together by temporary experiences and consumption activities (Belk and Costa 1998; Kates 2002; Kozinets 2001; Schouten and McAlexander 1995).

Brand Communities. A popular means to describe such micro-communities focused on brands is 'brand community,' a set of social relationships that are structured around the use of a focal brand (Muñiz and O'Guinn 2001). Shifting the emphasis away from consumers' reactions to alienating social structures, studies of brand community suggest that the shared use of products and services structures interpersonal connections amongst likeminded individuals, as well as distinction from non-users of focal brands (Muñiz and O'Guinn 2001; McAlexander and Schouten 1998; Schau et al. 2009). In particular, brand communities generate shared rituals and ways of thinking and traditions, as well as a sense of moral responsibility towards other members, and religious zeal towards the focal brand (Muñiz and O'Guinn 2001; Muñiz and Schau 2005). These characteristics enhance the co-creation of value by consumers and firms by upholding brand values, maintaining appeal, increasing members' affiliation and commitment to the brand and offering managers dialogue with loyal consumers (Brown et al. 2003; Fournier et al. 2001; McAlexander et al. 2002; Schau et al. 2009).

Consumer Tribes. Despite the theoretical usefulness and descriptive power of brand community and consumption subcultures, recent research has found that many consumption communities do not locate their socialization around singular brands or activities. Rather, consumer tribes exist when members identify with one another, have shared experiences and emotions, and engage in collective social action all of which can be facilitated through a variety of brands, products, activities, and services (Cova and Cova, 2002). What our research contributes to is to explain how these tribes form and how this interplays with marketing actions.

Consumer tribes differ from subcultures of consumption and brand communities in a number of important ways (Cova 1997; Cova and Cova 2002; Cova et al. 2007). First, tribes are multiple. Unlike subcultures of consumption and brand communities, tribes rarely dominate consumers' lives. Rather, they represent temporary escape from the stresses and pressures of the working week (Goulding et al. 2002) and membership of one kind of tribe does not preclude membership from other tribes or communities. On the contrary, tribal theory stresses the occurrence of flows between different identities under different circumstances (Bennett 1999).

Second, tribes are playful. Tied to multiplicity of membership and fluidity of identity, tribal consumption is often devoid of the long-term moral responsibility or religious zeal felt by members of a brand community (Muñiz and O'Guinn 2001; Muñiz and Schau 2005), or the respect afforded to social hierarchies and core products or activities exhibited in subcultures of consumption (Schouten and McAlexander 1995). Instead, value is placed on the possibility to invigorate passion and generate social links through deconstructing and reassembling marketplace resources (Cova et al. 2007).

Third, tribes are transient. Connected to these features of multiple identity and play, tribes emerge, and disappear as combinations of people and resources alter. This generates unpredictable and emergent processes of consumption that may be critical and liberatory at one moment, yet at the next moment mean little beyond sensory intensity and pleasure (Goulding et al., 2009). This playful acceptance of rapidly changing and contradictory meanings engenders a balance of power between consumers and producers that oscillates between manipulation and emancipation (Cova et al., 2007).

Fourth, tribes are entrepreneurial. Stemming from the possibilities for play, and an empowered and emancipated attitude to the market, are new paths for entrepreneurial ventures (Cova et al. 2007). Rather than relying on ready-made consumption resources, tribes regularly produce and customize market offerings (Kozinets 2001; 2007). These practices of bricolage alter the power balance between marketers and consumers, as tribal members take the lead in dictating procedures of co-production (Shankar et al. 2006).

Tribes offer a useful means to describe communal experiences of consumption that differ from consumption subcultures and brand communities. Tribes are not enduring subversions of dominant institutions as subcultures often are, nor do they seek iconic brands as loci for consumption experiences like brand communities. On the contrary, within tribes, the social links established between consumers–or consumer-to-consumer linking value– are more important than whatever is being consumed (Cova 1997). Moreover, unlike both subcultures and brand communities, community membership is fragmented and transient. These defining characteristics mean that the approaches to leveraging subcultures or brand community are inappropriate (e.g., Algesheimer et al. 2005; Holt 2004; McAlexander et al., 2002; Schau et al. 2009).

Compounding this problem is a tendency for tribal thinkers to favor theoretical descriptions of the commonalities and ordering structures of tribes over methods of leveraging tribes. Some authors have conceived of tribes as *marketing-proof*, capable of eluding attempts to manage or control them (Cova et al. 2007; Kozinets 2002). Others suggest that tribes are too fragmented, messy and illogical to manage effectively. Instead, managers are advised to acknowledge and respect the autonomy and integrity of a tribe (Cova and Cova 2001). Our task therefore is to investigate and explain how consumers form tribes in a manner that can be understood and replicated. In order to achieve this, we use communities of practice (Wenger 1998; 2000) as a theoretical means to understand how consumers build tribal communities and learn to be tribal.

The Face as a Picture of the Mind

Chairs: Oleg Urminsky, University of Chicago, USA
Hal E. Hershfield, New York University, USA

Paper #1: A Picture is Worth a Thousand Inferences: Appearance-Based First Impressions Predict Leader Selection and Mate Choice

Christopher Olivola, Warwick Business School, UK
Paul Eastwick, Texas A&M University, USA
Eli Finkel, Northwestern University, USA
Dan Ariely, Duke University, USA
Alexander Todorov, Princeton University, USA

Paper #2: Familiarity Hijack: Imperceptible Celebrity Facial Cues Influence Trust and Preference

Robin Tanner, University of Wisconsin-Madison, USA
Ahreum Maeng, University of Wisconsin-Madison, USA

Paper #3: Looking Into Future's Mirror: How Representations of the Aged Self Impact Impatience

Oleg Urminsky, University of Chicago, USA
Daniel Bartels, Columbia University, USA

SESSION OVERVIEW

As Cicero observed long ago, the face is a picture of the mind. In this symposium, we explore how facial perceptions can impact decisions related to voting, dating, sales, and personal finance. Talks will focus on both real images of faces and those that have been altered using morphing technology. The session presents novel findings using facial manipulating and judgment, an emerging research method for studying holistic decision making.

How people perceive, judge, and evaluate faces has been a central construct in basic social psychology, yet has received relatively little attention in consumer behavior. Building on methods that use novel facial morphing technology, the proposed session will contribute to a better understanding of how consumers use information about facial images to inform their decisions. The papers investigate how different aspects of facial images can affect voting decisions, mating choice, purchasing intentions, and long-term financial decision-making. This session will unify the findings of the individual papers into a broader framework for investigating the impact on consumer choice on how consumers perceive and are affected by images of the face. In contrast with much of the decision making research on these topics which focuses on deliberate processing of information, facial stimuli present an ideal context in which to systematically study the role of spontaneous holistic thinking.

In the first paper, **Olivola, Eastwick, Finkel, Ariely and Todorov** use experimental methods combined with naturalistic data from real elections, a major online dating site, and speed dating events, to show how appearance-based social inferences impact two important decision-making domains: political choice (voting) and mate choice (dating). Olivola and colleagues show how different aspects of facial appearance impact decision-making as a function of both context and the perceiver's context. In the domain of voting, the more a political candidate looked like a Republican (i.e., the greater portion of naive raters who guessed that the candidate was actually a Republican) the larger that person's vote share in conservative states, regardless of whether the candidate as actually a Republican or not. In terms of dating behavior, using data from an online data set as well as a speed-dating experiment, Olivola and colleagues demonstrate that appearing fun and outgoing afforded benefits to both male and female daters, while appearing smart and serious was positively related to dating success for males, but hurt females.

Next, **Tanner and Maeng** investigate the effect of morphing unfamiliar faces with those of well known public figures. Across four studies, using a variety of measures, participants show a clear preference for the morphed faces, despite a complete lack of conscious recognition of the public figures in question. This effect is shown to reverse in a set of studies conducted before and after the Tiger Woods scandal, in which unfamiliar faces were imperceptibly morphed with Woods.

In the third paper, **Urminsky and Bartels** explore the role that facial cues play in inferences and judgments concerning the self. Participants were shown photos of themselves that had either merely been aged (low change) or had been aged and also morphed with a generic demographic match (high change). When participants were prompted to first focus on their present selves, subsequently seeing high-change representations of their future selves increased willingness to pay to expedite future benefits.

Finally, discussant **Hershfield,** who has done recent work on the role of facial perception and emotion in intertemporal choice, will offer a broad discussion of the contributions of the individual papers. In contrast with a traditional discussant role, Hershfield will also describe and contrast the different facial morphing methods that have been used to impact consumer behavior. Specifically, he will present a brief primer on the ways that facial morphing technology can be used in consumer research, and will discuss the relative benefits and disadvantages of various morphing techniques (e.g., using avatars (digital representations of people) versus photographs) and software packages.

Given the relevance of the proposed topic to central issues in consumer research, this session is likely to have a significant effect on future research in a number of areas and contribute to a multidisciplinary approach to studying facial perception and its relationship to decision-making. The goal of this session is to both present intriguing new research which employs these methods as well as to provide practical in-context information to scholars who wish to employ facial perception and facial morphing in their research. Thus, we anticipate broad interest in this session among consumer researchers. The papers employ a variety of approaches (lab and field studies, as well as the use of cutting edge technology), and the session will offer a broad perspective on the ways in which the image of the face can play a role in consumer behavior. Data collection in all papers is complete and all participants have agreed to present, should the session be accepted.

A Picture is Worth a Thousand Inferences: Appearance-Based First Impressions Predict Leader Selection and Mate Choice

EXTENDED ABSTRACT

Of all the things that people might want to carefully market, perhaps the most important is themselves. We often form opinions about the characteristics of other people from single, static samples of their appearance –the very first thing we see when, or even before, we meet them. These appearance-based first impressions of a person's characteristics can have an important impact on subsequent judgments and decisions concerning that person. Furthermore, recent research has shown that these inferences occur spontaneously and rapidly, making them difficult to recognize or control. This talk explores the impact of appearance-based social inferences in two important decision-making domains: political choice (voting) and mate choice (dating).

In the first part of the talk, we briefly review evidence that politicians who happen to possess faces that make them look competent enjoy greater electoral success, and describe recent modeling efforts to extract the physiognomic features that govern facial competence using multi-dimensional computerized facial stimuli. We then present the results of a new study that further illustrates the surprisingly powerful influence of candidate appearances on elections. Participants in this study were shown photos of actual U.S. political candidates running for Senator or Governor. In particular, they were shown pairs of headshots representing the two rival candidates and asked to guess which one was the Republican (or Democrat). We find that the more a candidate looks like a Republican (i.e., the greater the proportion of participants who guessed that he/she was the Republican) the larger that person's vote share in conservative states, regardless of his/her actual affiliation. In contrast, we found no such relationship in liberal states, suggesting that voting in those states is less influenced by candidate appearances. The relationship between looking conservative and electoral success in right-leaning states holds when we control for incumbency status or candidate age differences, and even when we only consider elections involving Caucasian male candidates. Furthermore, we find that the looking conservative (vs. liberal) is unrelated to looking attractive, competent, or trustworthy, suggesting that the apparent effect of facial conservatism/liberalism is unrelated to inferences of more basic personality traits. These results are particularly surprising when we consider the fact that candidate photos and their political party affiliations are provided on the voting ballots.

In the second part of the talk, we turn to the domain of mate choice (dating). We describe a pair of studies examining the impact of first impressions on online matchmaking and speed dating success. Using two naturalistic data sets of real daters interacting through a major online dating site and at speed dating events, we examined the relationship between appearance-based personality trait inferences and romantic success (as measured by emails received and successful matches). Judges were shown photos obtained from the dating site or taken at the speed dating events and, using only these photos, rated daters along various personality dimensions. We find that these photo-based personality trait inferences significantly predict dater success in both the domains of Internet matchmaking and speed dating. Appearing fun and outgoing was positively related to success for both male and female daters (i.e., they we contacted by more online dating users and selected by more speed daters). In contrast, while appearing smart and serious was positively related to success for male daters, this relationship was reversed for female daters, so that women whose profile photos made them look more smart-serious attracted fewer male online dating site users. Most of these relationships remain significant when we control for attractiveness, ruling out the possibility that our results can be entirely explained as halo-effects of beauty. Furthermore, even after controlling for self-reported demographics and relationship preferences provided by daters in online profiles and speed dating questionnaires, personality trait inferences still significantly predict dater success. This suggests that photo-based first impressions can impact a decision to contact a potential mate, even when relevant information about the person is readily available. Finally, our unique data sets also allow us to measure the predictive impact of appearances in terms of other tangible dimensions. For example, we find that for male users, each standard deviation increase in how fun-outgoing one looks is equivalent to growing 7.57 inches (19.04 cm), receiving a $32,399 raise, or to a 1.5 standard deviation increase in physical attractive-

ness. Whereas for female users, each standard deviation increase in how smart-serious one looks is equivalent to gaining 46.5 pounds (21.3 kg), receiving a $27,404 salary cut, or to a standard deviation decrease in physical attractiveness.

In sum, these results suggest that, in spite of the old adage warning us not to "judge a book by its cover," people form opinions about the characteristics of others from single, static samples of their appearance and that these impressions, in turn, can even impact who they choose as leaders and lovers.

Familiarity Hijack: Imperceptible Celebrity Facial Cues Influence Trust and Preference

EXTENDED ABSTRACT

Social psychologists have long observed that individuals have a preference for people similar to themselves (Shanteau and Nagy, 1979; Park and Schaller, 2005). More recently, researchers interested in facial similarity have used new graphical technology to morph individual's own faces into the faces of others. For example, Bailenson et al. (2009) created composite images by morphing the faces of politicians with the faces of experimental participants in a ratio of 65% politician, 35% participant. This ratio is significant as the authors demonstrate that it produces composite faces within which individuals could not perceive their own image, instead believing they were viewing unaltered pictures of the politicians in question. However, attitudes toward the composites reflected a different story, with participants consistently demonstrating stronger liking for the images containing 35% of their own face, despite reporting no conscious awareness of recognizing face in the composite images.

This finding raises several interesting theoretical questions. In particular, it is not clear if liking for the composite faces was driven by similarity (as the authors argued) or familiarity since the two are essentially confounded when morphing an individual's own face into a composite image. Furthermore, familiarity could itself encompass multiple possible mechanisms, including full implicit recognition (i.e. sufficient to report trait assessments of the minority face in the morph) or implicit recognition sufficient only to retrieve a high level valence judgment of him or her. The current work explores these issues by examining the effects of morphing the faces of public figures into unfamiliar faces. Since the faces of public figures are familiar but not similar to the average individual, they provide us with a potential method of teasing apart the previously confounded effects of similarity and familiarity.

In Study 1 (N=109) participants rated the trustworthiness (a key component of source credibility) of two faces on a -5 to +5 scale. Face one (henceforth "Tiger morph") consisted of a male neutral male face morphed with 35% of the face of Tiger Woods. Face 2 ("Control morph") was the same neutral face morphed with 35% of the face of a stock model of similar age and attractiveness to Tiger Woods. Both composite images were pretested and found to be equally attractive. However, participants rated the Tiger morph as being significantly more trustworthy (M = 1.75) than the control morph (M=0.95; t(107)=-2.2, p < .03). This result pertained despite 100% of subsequently debriefed participants expressing no recognition of Tiger in the composite image. As such, these data support a familiarity explanation as underlying the effect of facial morphing on preference, but are inconsistent with a pure similarity explanation.

Study 2 was a replicate of study 1 designed to explore whether the positive trust result accrued from participants being able to report specific trait information about Tiger (which implicit recognition might enable), or whether it was simply due to participants accessing general positive perceptions of Tiger. The study was identical to study 1 except that a 1-10 scale was used, and participants were additionally asked to report their perceptions of the athletic ability of the individual pictured. Consistent with study 1, participants rated the Tiger morph (M = 5.33) as more trustworthy than the control morph (M = 4.0, t(31) = -1.9, p < .07). However, they perceived no difference between the athletic ability of the Tiger morph (M = 2.1) and the control morph (M = 2.4, p > 0.3). As such these data support the more general valence explanation as driving the positive effect on trust, and are inconsistent with an explanation based on full implicit recognition of the individual in question.

Study 3 (N=319) enabled us to further explore whether implicit perceptions of the the general valence of the celebrity in question drove our results to date. Participants rated their likelihood to buy (1-10 scale) from one of two salesman. Face one ("control morph") was a neutral salesman image morphed with 35% of the same control face used in studies 1 and 2, while face two ("Tiger morph") consisted of the salesman face morphed with 35% of the face of Tiger Woods. Rather serendipitously, data was collected in two tranches, both before - and at the peak of - the Tiger Woods scandal. Thus study 3 was a 2 Familiarity (Tiger vs. control) X 2 Timing (pre-scandal vs. post scandal) design. Results indicated no main effect of familiarity or timing but a significant interaction between the two (F = 13.2, p<.001). While pre-scandal participants indicated they were more likely to buy from the Tiger morph (MTiger = 1.5, Mcontrol = 1.0) this pattern reversed post-scandal (MTiger = -.1, Mcontrol = 1.0). These results thus further support the idea that implicit recognition (of Tiger) took place to a degree sufficient for an overall valence judgment to be reported to consciousness.

One problem with studies 1 to 3 was that in each task participants were instructed to make the relevant judgments based only on the face pictured. This leaves open the possibility that the morphing manipulations may have had little effect without our explicit direction to focus on the faces, which would clearly reduce the marketing implications of the findings. To address this issue, in study 4 (N=104) participants were simply asked to view an ad for the charity Doctors without Borders, and then to rate how likely they would be to donate to the charity (1-10 scale). The ad consisted of a logo, a supposed picture of the CEO Nicolas De Torrente, and a statement from him requesting a donation. In fact, in the morph condition the pictured face consisted of the actual face of De Torrente morphed with 35% of the face of Tom Hanks, while in the control condition that face pictured was genuinely De Torrente. Despite not being instructed to pay attention to the facial component of the ad, participants reported a greater likelihood of donation (M=3.7) in the Tom Hanks condition than in the control condition (M=2.8; t(102) = 2.3, p < .03).

Looking Into Future's Mirror:
How Representations of the Aged Self Impact Impatience

EXTENDED ABSTRACT

A great deal of research has attempted to explain people's intertemporal choices, often by investigating how people think about the future in general, as well as their future needs and the future consequences of their actions. Recent research has suggested an equally important role of the way that people think of their future selves, specifically the degree to which a person feels connected to their future self (e.g. Parfit 1984, Ersner-Hershfield, Wimmer, & Knutson, 2009, Bartels and Urminsky 2010). In Bartels and Urminsky (2010), for example, participants who were manipulated (via informational or metacognitive cues) to believe that the defining elements of their personal identity would remain more stable over time were then more willing to forego near-term consumption for long-term benefits.

In this paper, we argue that visualization plays a key role in how people feel about their relationship to the future self. In particular, we propose that imagining one's future self or seeing a representation of the future self will affect how people feel about their future selves. Given the automaticity with which people process facial information, we propose that thinking of one's future self as having a more dissimilar face will correspond to a reduced motivation to provide benefits for the future self. In particular, we argue that it is the contrast between the current self and a dissimilar future facial representation of the self that reduces this motivation.

In the first phase of Study 1, we photographed participants' faces and created two representations of their aged face. The first picture merely used aging software to create a picture representing what the participant might look like when they were older. The second picture first morphed the participants' face with a generic gender and race matched face, and then applied the aging software with the same parameters. Final corrections and adjustments for hair color were conducted for both in Photoshop. These pictures were then extensively pre-tested with a separate group of participants (at a separate location, unfamiliar with the first set of participants) to assure equivalence in estimated age, attractiveness and other factors across the two photos for each participant.

In the second phase, conducted a few weeks later, participants were invited to return to the lab. They were asked to enter their current email address and then were shown one of the two pictures at random, either their merely-aged face (meant to represent minimal change) or their morphed-aged face (representing significant change while aging). Our hypothesis was that participants would spontaneously conflate visual facial change with change to personal identity and, based on prior connectedness research, would be more impatient when viewing the high-change picture. We find that participants viewing the high-change picture (vs. the low change picture) were willing to pay more in order to expedite a $100 gift certificate that they would otherwise receive in a year.

We find that participants in the merely-aged condition were more patient, and were not willing to pay as much to expedite the gift certificate, compared to participants in the morphed-aged condition. This effect cannot be accounted for by the perceived attractiveness or competence of the future self.

In Study 2, we use a similar methodology to replicate the effect with a new sample several months later. In addition, we manipulate the degree of current self vs. future contrast by asking participants in the present-salient condition to type in their current email address (as in Study 1, emphasizing the present self) before being asked to consider a picture of their future self. In the future-salient condition, participants did not enter their current email and were asked to direct their attention to picture of their future self. We find that participants in the present-salient condition replicate the effects of Study 1, and are willing to pay less when shown a more dissimilar picture of their future self. However, in the future-salient condition, the effect was reversed, such that participants were actually willing to pay more to expedite the future benefit when viewing the merely-aged face, consistent with viewing the more similar future self as sharing the same pool of resources.

Combining across the two studies, we find that participants who focus on the future picture are willing to spend *more* to speed up the gift certificate when looking at the more similar face ($42 vs. $27). In contrast, when participants' attention is first directed to their current self before looking at the future self picture, they are willing to spend less to expedite the gift certificate when the picture is more similar ($17 vs. $24, interaction p<.05).

Competitive Papers—Full

A Longitudinal Study of Consumers' Need for Uniqueness on Development of Networks

Seung Hwan (Mark) Lee, University of Western Ontario, Canada
Gail Leizerovici, University of Western Ontario, Canada

ABSTRACT

Based on a longitudinal field study of a college dormitory network, we find that the three components of consumer's need for uniqueness (CNFU) each play a distinct role in the development of a consumer's social network. Results suggest the rate of individual's network growth (perceptual and actual) depends on individual's CNFU.

Research suggests consumers with high need for uniqueness may be both successful and unsuccessful in maintaining and attaining social relationships (Lynn & Harris, 1997; Snyder & Fromkin, 1980; Tian, Bearden, & Hunter, 2001). Unique individuals exhibit an exclusive appeal that elicits positive social evaluations (e.g. a person displaying a creative style of fashion such as a seven button suit). On the other hand, unique individuals may encounter social disapproval if they choose to be too extreme with their consumption choices (e.g., a person displaying an odd form of fashion such as an orange spandex suit). Despite these presumptions, there has been no direct attempt to explicitly investigate the social benefits and costs of being unique on the development of individuals' social network. While scholars have speculated on the social consequences of being unique (e.g., Snyder & Fromkin, 1980; Tian et al., 2001), we do not know the impact which unique consumers have on their friendship selection processes. In response, we explore an emerging social network (longitudinally) to investigate the effects of consumers' need for uniqueness (CNFU) on individuals' social network development.

There are reasons to suggest that being unique in a network can have positive and negative consequences to individuals' social network development. For instance, being too unique can result in social sanctions (Ruvio, 2008). Consumers sometimes use products that deviate from social norm (Tian et al., 2001); breaking rules or challenging existing rules at the risk of social disapproval results in negative evaluations such as the perception of poor style (Tian et al., 2001). Thus, individuals may encounter negative social reactions and social disapproval which in turn constrains one's social network development (i.e., make less friends). Conversely, scholars have suggested that the desire for uniqueness is influenced by the individual's need for social assimilation and social approval (Ruvio, 2008). Here, uniqueness is sought only to the point where it precludes individuals from social isolation or strong disapproval (Snyder & Fromkin, 1980). In such cases, consumers may use distinctiveness as an opportunity to elicit positive social evaluations through making creative choices that enhance their personal style. That is, individuals distinguish themselves in the hopes of obtaining greater social rewards (Santee & Maslach, 1982). Thus, being unique is beneficial to one's social network development (i.e., make more friends).

Given that the literature has identified that being unique has both positive and negative consequences for the consumer, our present research investigates the social benefits and costs of CNFU on individuals' social network development. Regrettably, research in this domain has a limited understanding of how CNFU influences networks. While previous research has implied numerous social outcomes for unique individuals (Ruvio, 2008; Tian et al., 2001), not much is known about how relationships are formed and maintained over time. For this reason, the current study is designed to explore the effects of CNFU on the dynamic transformation of individuals'

social network. Specifically, we ask the following questions: how does CNFU positively or negatively affect the dynamic growth of individuals' social network? How does CNFU influence consumers' choice of friendships and their ability to attract friendships in an emerging social network? These research questions provide a guiding framework for our study.

Findings from our longitudinal network research contribute to the extant literature in two distinct ways. Theoretically, we show that the extent to which individuals actively widen or condense their social network is dependent on whether they are creative with their identity or avoid peers that have similar identities. Further, the extent to which unique consumers are able to attract friendships is dependent on whether their unique display is within the confines of group norms. Furthermore, we find differences in how CNFU affects individual's perception of their social network vs. their actual network (as rated by others). These findings add to the current stock of knowledge and validate the important role of CNFU in consumer networks. Methodologically, this is one of the first longitudinal studies in consumer behavior to track the developmental patterns of an emerging social network. Using the latest social network method, the current research introduces an actor-based modelling technique (Snijde, van de Bunt, & Steglich, 2010; Snijders, Steglich, Schwinberger, & Huisman, 2007) to observe the unique effects of CNFU on individuals' social network development.

CONCEPTUAL FRAMEWORK

There is plethora of evidence to suggest that consumers have a desire to differentiate themselves from others or to "counterconform" (Berger & Heath, 2007; Snyder & Fromkin, 1980; Tian et al., 2001). Counterconformity is an individual's motivation to maintain a sense of distinctiveness; people constantly define themselves on various self-related dimensions in order to develop their exclusive social identities (Tian et al., 2001). Furthermore, when people see themselves as highly similar to others, they become motivated to seek a unique personal identity within their social environment (Berger & Heath; 2007; Snyder & Fromkin, 1980). For example, individuals who were led to believe that they were similar to others subsequently attached greater importance to being independent, placed a higher value on rare items, generated more unusual uses for an object, and conformed less with others on judgment tasks (Duval & Wicklund, 1972; Fromkin, 1970).

According to uniqueness theory, consumers are known to purchase products that serve as expressive symbols of uniqueness (Snyder & Fromkin, 1980; Tian et al., 1977). Individuals are motivated to acquire unique possession for the purpose of determining and shaping their self-image, as well as using these possessions to establish individuality within their social networks (Lynn & Harris, 1997; McAlister & Pessemier, 1982). Acquiring unique possessions ultimately provides the opportunity to signal and communicate a desired identity to others (Berger & Heath, 2007). Given that consumers are known to counterconform, this also reflects the underlying motivation behind consumers' need for uniqueness (CNFU), the trait of interest in our longitudinal study.

Consumers' Need for Uniqueness (CNFU)

Conceptually, CNFU is "the trait of pursuing differences relative to others through the acquisition, utilization, and disposition of consumers goods for the purpose of developing and enhancing one's self-image and social image" (Tian et al., 2001). Thus, CNFU is a personality trait that is related to uniqueness theory, where the underlying self presentation goal entails choosing options that have carefully considered social consequences (Worchel, Lee, & Adewole, 1975; Tian et al., 2001).

Extant literature has identified that consumers vary in the manner which they exhibit counterconforming behaviors (Ruvio, Shohan, & Brencic, 2008; Tian et al., 2001). In particular, CNFU has demonstrated that consumers can express their counterconformity via three distinct behaviours: creative counterconforming behavior, unpopular counterconforming behavior, and avoidance of similarity behavior (Ruvio et al., 2008; Tian et al., 2001). CNFU is regarded as the higher order construct that encompasses these three distinct counterconforming dimensions. Given that there are conceptual differences among the three dimensions, we predict each type of counterconforming behavior will play a distinct role in individuals' social network development.

Creative choice counterconformity (CC) refers to an individual's ability to acquire and use products that reflect a personal style which is socially accepted and valued by others (Snyder & Fromkin, 1977; Tian et al., 2001). Individuals with a high need for CC strive to establish a unique identity without risking their social reputation or image (Snyder & Fromkin, 1980). While creative choices involve some risk (Kron, 1983), these acts are made strategically in order to obtain positive social evaluations and approval from their network of friends (Santee & Maslach, 1992; Snyder & Fromkin, 1977). An example of this might be the choice to purchase and use a socially accepted electronic product, such as an iPad, in a manner that is creatively different from the norm. Thus, CC reflects individual's ability to create a personal style that is viewed as socially acceptable. It is expected CC will have a positive effect on individuals' social network development (i.e., make more friends) over time.

In contrast, consumers may make "unpopular" choices that are considered unacceptable and thus display a behavior that risks social disapproval. Unpopular choice counterconformity (UC) refers to an individual's selection of products or brands that reflect norm-breaking consumption behavior (Tian et al., 2001). Individuals with high need for UC face the risk of social disapproval because their choices may be considered taboo and socially unacceptable (Tian & Bearden, 1992). For example, an individual's choice to refrain from spending, or "downshift" (see Schor, 1998) may appear to counterconform with popular consumer culture. Such behavior may be judged as socially norm-breaking, such as when a "downshifter" decides to live off only the basic necessities. While it is possible that these choices may gain social approval over time (Heckert, 1989), violating social customs may initially draw negative social reactions from others (Santee & Maslach, 1982). In consequence, this form of behavior is likely to lower a person's social image and reputation in his or her social circles (Tian et al., 2001). Thus, UC reflects the individual's desire to challenge social norms via their engagement in unpopular decisions. It is expected UC will have a negative effect on individuals' social network development (i.e., make less friends) over time.

Finally, avoidance of similarity (AS) refers to an individual's desire to discontinue the use of or have the loss of interest in products which are mainstream in the market (Tian et al., 2001). Avoiding similarity prompts individuals to suspend the use of their current possessions and resist purchasing widely adopted products in order to avoid appearing similar to others (Ruvio, 2008). Individuals with high need for AS seek innovative trends to resist conformity (Thompson & Haytko, 1977). For example, they avoid similarity by pursuing a "minority choice" that establishes their dissimilarity from others (Tian & Bearden, 1992). This perspective embodies a rejection of popular mainstream products to subsequently enforce the individual's uniqueness via their dissimilarity. For example, an individual high in AS may choose to only purchase and wear vintage clothes. In this manner, this individual is avoiding and resisting mainstream trends and products in lieu of lesser known ones. Thus, AS is driven by an individual's motivation to avoid similar others by engaging in consumption that is deemed to be dissimilar. Further, in the pursuit of avoiding similar others, such individuals may be perceived negatively. Appearing dissimilar may result in subsequent negative judgments as such extreme consumption displays contradict socially approved signalling behaviors (i.e. see Colarelli & Dettmann, 2003). As a result, it is expected AS will negatively affect individuals' social network development over time.

METHODOLOGY

To test the influence of the three types of counterconformity, we conducted a longitudinal field study. This field study uses social network analysis to track the changing and dynamic patterns in an emerging social network. Social network analysis (SNA) has emerged as a key technique in modern research to develop a better understanding of the structures of relationships and their effects on behavior (Wasserman & Faust, 1994). Network analysis investigates the quantitative structural properties of networks which typically cannot be extracted from a study of individual or dyadic relationships (Webster & Morrison, 2004). The network data collected allows researchers to trace the connections between individuals (linkages and ties), which cannot be realized through a traditional sample survey method. Other marketing studies on CNFU that have attempted to capture relational data using traditional sample survey methods and the use of retrospective data suffer from inaccuracy in describing properties of the networks and the connections between individuals (c.f. Reingen & Kernan, 1986; Iacobucci & Hopkins, 1992). With SNA, this method allows the gathering of information from all members included within a network. This ultimately provides a significant advantage to understanding how CNFU influences social network development. Moreover, this study introduces a stochastic actor-based model to observe the change in network dynamics over time (Snijders et al., 2010). The following study captures these relational changes and simultaneously assesses the effects on CNFU on these network changes.

PARTICIPANTS AND PROCEDURE

The data were collected from 71 first year college dormitory students from a single floor at a large North American university. Participants filled out questionnaires at two different time-periods. At both time periods, a paper-and-pen questionnaire was administered for every student living on the floor. Time 1 (T1) data was collected approximately 5-6 weeks after the start of the academic school year to allow participants to have some perception of their social network. Time 2 (T2) data was collected 5-6 weeks after the start of their second semester (early February). At T1, 76 of 83 students (response rate of 92%) provided usable data for analysis. At T2, 71 of 83 students (response rate of 86%) provided usable data for analysis. However, to ensure parallel comparison between the two time-periods, we included only those that have responded in both time-period. Thus, five participants were dropped from the T1 data. Figure 1 is a graphical display of the social network over time.

Friendship Nomination. In both time periods, participants were asked to indicate their social relationships with every other student on their floor. Students were provided an alphabetical listing of all of the occupants and were asked to rate their level of friendship (1 – do not or barely know; 2 – acquaintance; 3 – friend; 4 – close friend) with every other student on the floor.

Figure 1:
Diagrams of Network Change over Time: College Dormitory Network

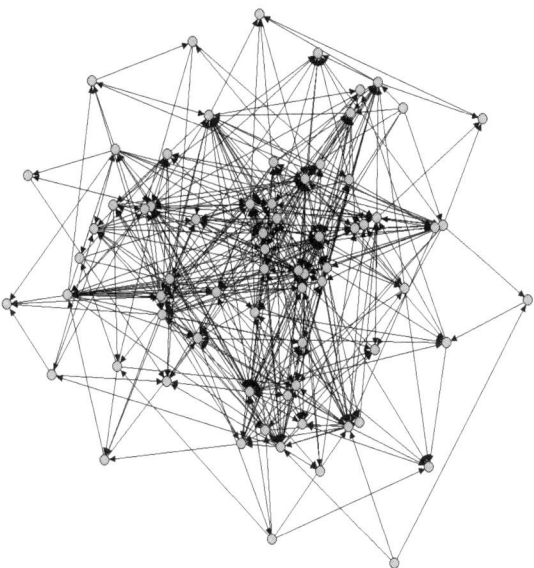

Time 1

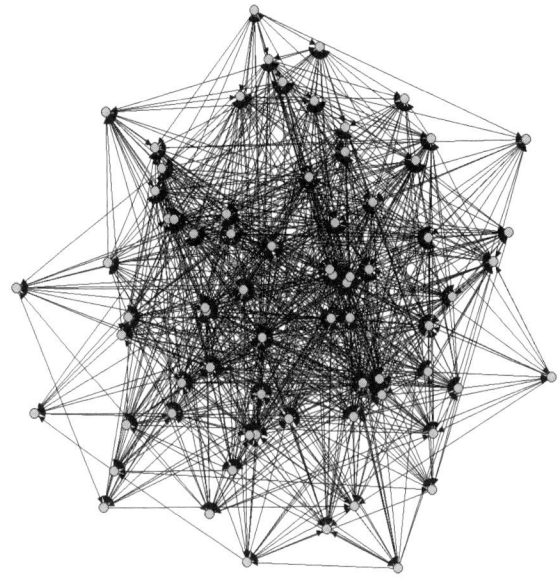

Time 2

The data then was arranged into an NxN binary matrix (Wasserman & Faust, 1994). Each cell (Xij) in this matrix corresponded to i's relation to j as reported by i. Then, the network matrix was used to calculate individual's out-degree ties (the total number of people the focal person nominated as friends or close friends) and their in-degree ties (the total number of people that nominated the focal person as a friend or a close friend). Out-degree is considered to be a measure of the individual's perception of popularity and in-degree is considered to be a measure of the individual's popularity (as rated by others) in a social network (Freeman, 1979; Lee, Cotte, & Noseworthy, 2010). Given that this was a longitudinal study, we were able to track the change in development of out-degree ties and in-degree ties over time. Providing a list of participants to respondents (i.e. the roster method) helped us overcome potential recall biases and is considered to be a more reliable method of network data collection than asking respondents to come up with names on their own (Wasserman & Faust, 1994).

Consumers' Need for Uniqueness. Consumers' need for uniqueness was measured using a short-form 12-item scale adapted from Ruvio et al. (2008). A parsimonious measure of CNFU was used in favor of the original 31-item scale (see Tian et al., 2001) to minimize respondent fatigue. The 12-item CNFU index was scored on a 7-point Likert-type scale ranging from 1 to 7 with descriptive anchors "Strongly disagree" and "Strongly agree". Sample items on the scale included, "I often combine possessions in such a way that I create a personal image that cannot be duplicated" (Creative Choice), "When it comes to the products I buy and the situations in which I use them, I have broken customs and rules" (Unpopular Choice), and "I often try to avoid products or brands that I know are bought by the general population" (Avoidance of Similarity). Each component of CNFU included 4 items which was averaged to create a single factor for each dimension (for a total of three factors). An exploratory factor analysis confirmed that each of the dimensions loaded on its respective factors (.73 and above) with sufficient internal reliability (Cronbach alpha over .80). The CNFU index was assessed only at T1. CNFU was not measured again at T2 because conceptually, it is a stable trait that does not change substantially over time (Tian &

McKenzie, 2001). Methodologically, it was done to minimize survey length and respondent fatigue as each participant was asked to rate their friendship status with every other person on their floor.

DATA ANALYSIS

To analyze the effects of CNFU on individuals' social network development, a stochastic actor-oriented model of network dynamics was assessed using the SIENA 3.14 (Simulation Investigation for Empirical Network Analysis) software (Snijders et al., 2007). SIENA is part of the StOCNET program collection (Boer, Huisman, Snijders, & Zeggelink, 2007) that is used to carry out statistical estimation of dynamic actor-driven models. The actor-oriented model follows a Markov process where it is assumed that the properties of the next state depend on the properties of the previous state (Meyn & Tweedie, 1993). That is, the events of two time periods observed in this study were not assumed to be independent events. The actor-oriented model is useful for modeling network dynamics that can represent a wide variety of influences on network change, especially for representing theories about how actors alter their social ties over time (Snijders et al., 2010). This method is considered appropriate for observing the rate of change in networks and for observing the effects of personal characteristics on individuals' friendship selections over time. This technique has been successfully applied in other areas of research; scholars have investigated the effects of the big five personality traits, smoking, and delinquency behaviors on social network development (Burk, Steglich, & Snijders, 2007; Mercken et al., 2010; Selfhout et al., 2010). A technical and more detailed explanation of the processes and assumptions of this method can be found elsewhere (see Huisman & Snijders, 2003; Snijders et al., 2010).

The actor-oriented model, when elaborated upon for application use, contains parameters that are estimated from the observed data by a statistical procedure (Snijders et al., 2010). For instance, the effects of CNFU on the development of network ties are assessed by examining the parameter estimates of three selection effects: *ego effect, alter effect, and the similarity effect* (Burk et al., 2007). These selection effects are derived from a sociological understanding of relationships, where actual or perceived similarity (homophily) among friends is a result of the influence that an individual has (alter) has on the focal individual (ego) (Kandel, 1978). In the context of our research, a positive (negative) ego effect implies that CNFU is positively (negatively) associated with an individual's ability to build social ties, and thus, is likely to increase (decrease) the number of friendship nominations made over time. A positive (negative) alter effect implies that CNFU is positively (negatively) associated with being attractive as a friend, and thus, is likely to result in an individual receiving more (fewer) friendship nominations over time. Lastly, a positive (negative) similarity effect implies that individuals prefer friendships with others that have similar (dissimilar) levels of CNFU (i.e., homophilous selection). Since the CNFU construct consists of multiple dimensions (creative counterconformity, unpopular counterconformity, and avoidance of similarity), these three selection effects were estimated for each of the three dimensions.

Moreover, additional effects were included in the final analysis as covariates. The analysis included three network effect covariates that naturally occur in developing networks (Mercken et al., 2010; Snijders et al., 2010). We included *density effect, reciprocity effect, and transitivity effect*. Density effect is the tendency for people to selectively nominate friends. A significant negative estimate implies that individuals do not nominate friends at random. Reciprocity ef-

fect is the tendency of individuals to reciprocate relationships. A significant positive estimate implies people tend to select those whom they share a dyadic relationship with. Finally, transitivity effect is the tendency for people to form triadic relationships over time. A significant positive estimate implies people tend to select friendships with those who are friends of friends. The inclusion of these covariates was necessary to ensure that the effects of CNFU were not confounded by these factors (Snijders et al., 2010; Wasserman & Faust, 1994).

The SIENA output provides parameter values for the selection effects and the network effects. Overall, a total of 12 parameters were simultaneously entered into a model: ego, alter, and similarity effects of each of the three CNFU dimensions plus the three covariates (density, reciprocity, and transitivity effects). The dependent variable is the change (or the lack thereof) in friendship ties from time 1 to time 2 (absent → present or present → absent). Table 1 summarizes and provides a description of each of the effects examined in this study. In addition to the studied effects, interaction terms were also created (CC x UC), (UC x AS), (CC x AS), (CC x UC x AS) and modeled separately in another analysis. However, none of the interaction terms revealed any significant results, and thus were omitted from the report.

Table 1
Description of Network and Selection Effects

Parameters	Descriptions
Network Effects:	
Density	General tendency to choose friend at random
Reciprocity	Tendency to reciprocate friendships
Transitivity	Tendency to prefer triadic closure (become friends of friends' friend)
Selection Effects:	
CC Ego	The rate CC determines social activity (friendship nomination)
CC Alter	The rate CC determines popularity (nominated by others as a friend)
CC Similarity	Preference for choosing a friend with similar CC (homophily)
UC Ego	The rate UC determines social activity (friendship nomination)
UC Alter	The rate UC determines popularity (nominated by others as a friend)
UC Similarity	Preference for choosing a friend with similar UC (homophily)
AS Ego	The rate AS determines social activity (friendship nomination)
AS Alter	The rate AS determines popularity (nominated by others as a friend)
AS Similarity	Preference for choosing a friend with similar AS (homophily)

RESULTS

Means, standard deviations, and correlations among the relevant variables at T1 and T2 are reported in Table 2. The final sample (N=71) included 37 females and 34 males. Overall, the total number of ties in the network equaled to 472 ties in T1 and 1194 ties in T2. The average out-degree and in-degree ties in T1 were 6.65. The average out-degree and in-degree ties in T2 were 16.82. Table 3 illustrates the aggregated results of the parameters modeling the selection effects (ego, alter, and similarity), as well as the network effects (density, reciprocity, and transitivity). As expected, all three of the network effects were significant predictors of network development. The density parameter was significantly negative ($B = -1.63$, $SE = .05$, $t = -30.67$, $p < .001$), indicating that people did not tend

to nominate friends at random (making friendship was a selective procedure). The reciprocity effect was significantly positive ($B = .67$, $SE = .08$, $t = 8.17$, $p < .001$), indicating people preferred to have reciprocal friendships. Lastly, the transitivity effect was significantly positive ($B = .06$, $SE = .00$; $t = 17.54$, $p < .001$), indicating people's preference to form triadic relationships over time. These results are consistent with previous longitudinal network studies in other disciplines (e.g., Burk et al., 2007; Mercken et al., 2010), further underlining the necessity to control for such network mechanisms when observing dynamic networks.

Table 2
Overall Means, Standard Deviations, and Correlations

	M (SD)	1	2	3	4	5	6	7
1. Out-Deg T1	6.65 (5.12)	1						
2. In-Deg T1	6.65 (4.68)	.45**	1					
3. Out-Deg T2	16.82 (8.67)	.57**	.13	1				
4. In-Deg T2	16.82 (5.70)	.28*	.55**	.24*	1			
5. CC	3.62 (1.26)	.12	.01	-.08	-.02	1		
6. UC	3.36 (1.20)	-.09	-.00	-.11	-.09	.45**	1	
7. AS	4.53 (1.14)	.03	-.03	-.12	.05	.59**	.37**	1

Significance levels: *** $p < .001$, ** $p < .01$, * $p < .05$

Table 3:
SIENA Estimation Results

Parameters	Estimates	Std. Error	*t*-value
Network Effects:			
Density	-1.63	.05	-30.67***
Reciprocity	.67	.08	8.17***
Transitivity	.06	17	17.24***
Selection Effects:			
CC Ego	.07	.03	2.39*
CC Alter	-.03	.03	-.96
CC Similarity	.30	.16	1.87+
UC Ego	.06	.03	2.10*
UC Alter	-.05	.02	-2.00*
UC Similarity	.11	.16	.70
AS Ego	-.14	.03	-4.16***
AS Alter	.04	.03	1.49
AS Similarity	-.15	.19	-.78

*Note: CC = Creative Counterconformity; UC = Unpopular Counterconformity; AS = Avoidance of Similarity. Unstandardized estimates are shown. Significance of mean parameters is calculated by dividing the parameter estimates by their standard errors.

*Significance levels: *** p < .001; ** p < .01; * p < .05, + p < .1

More importantly, the findings from the three selection effects for each dimension of CNFU provide interesting insights on the role of CNFU in emerging networks. When examining the CC param-eters, the results reveal a significant positive estimate for the CC ego effect ($B = .07$, $SE = .03$, $t = 2.39$, $p < .05$) and the CC similarity effect ($B = .30$, $SE = .16$, $t = 1.87$, $p < .1$). The results show CC is positively associated with the rate of growth in outgoing ties and the rate in which individuals select similar others over time. When examining the UC parameters, the results show a significant positive estimate for the UC ego parameter ($B = .06$, $SE = .03$, $t = 2.10$, $p < .05$), but a significant negative estimate for the UC alter parameter ($B = -.05$, $SE = .02$, $t = -2.00$, $p < .05$). The results show UC is positively associated with the rate of growth in outgoing ties over time. Conversely, UC is negatively associated with the rate of growth in incoming ties over time. Finally, regarding the AS parameters, the results show a significant negative estimate for the AS ego parameter ($B = -.14$, $SE = .03$, $t = -4.16$, $p < .001$). In contrast to the other two dimensions, AS is negatively associated with the rate of growth in outgoing ties over time. All other effects are not significant.

GENERAL DISCUSSION

The findings clearly demonstrate that the three dimensions of CNFU each play a unique role in the development of a social network. Over time, the results suggest unique individuals have a desire to widen their personal network, but not if they have a need to avoid similar others. The results also suggest the individuals' rate of network growth diminishes if they violate social norms.

People with a higher need for CC increased their number of friendship nominations (ego effect) and tended to make friendships with those who were similar to them (similarity effect). This pattern of observed events is further supported by the *optimal distinctiveness theory* (Brewer, 1991). According to this theory, people are motivated by two competing needs: the desire to be unique (capacity to freely express his/her unique identity) and the desire to be social (capacity to socially acclimatize with their peers). Brewer argues that people's desire for uniqueness is constrained and influenced by their desire for social assimilation. That is, individuals experience social dissonance if there is an imbalance between differentiation and assimilation (Brewer, 1991).

CC individuals tend to establish their unique identity by making creative choices that are socially applauded by others (Tian et al., 2001), thereby deriving a fine balance between uniqueness and social acceptance goals. These individuals look for an optimal level of distinctiveness as the goal is to both maximize their level of differentiation and their social utility (Brewer, 1991). However in order to achieve this feat, CC individuals must actively build a personal network to increase others' exposure to their uniqueness. By enlarging their social network, CC individuals increase their opportunities to display their creative choices, fulfilling this particular social need, while also fulfilling their need for differentiation. Moreover, since CC individuals are concerned with their social identity (as much as their unique identity), they are more likely to seek individuals who will appreciate their creative efforts. Thus, CC individuals will choose to develop friendships with similar others to be able to experience their peers' support and encouragement.

Although, and counter-intuitively, the data shows CC individuals did not necessarily attract more friends over time. We know that CC individuals want to creatively differentiate themselves in the hopes of obtaining positive social rewards such as gaining more friendships and/or popularity (Santee & Maslach, 1982). However, our research shows that this does not necessarily translate into being perceived as more attractive friendship partners by others. In other words, while CC individuals believe that they develop more social ties over time, others in the social network do not have the same sentiments. Thus, the fact that CC individuals perceive that they obtain more friends than they actually do suggests an inherently erroneous overestimation of their network size. This is an important finding because it clearly delineates that what CC individuals perceive is altogether different from their reality. Thus, it is possible that these individuals are overestimating the benefit that they achieve from being creatively unique.

Next, UC was positively associated with the rate of growth in outgoing ties over time (ego effect), but was negatively associated with the rate of growth in incoming ties over time (alter effect). Similar to CC individuals, UC individuals seek to widen their social network in order to increase their exposure to others. Unfortunately, it appears that these unique displays come at a social cost. UC individuals make extreme consumption choices that are often reprimanded for deviating from the social norms and customs (Tian et al., 2001). As a consequence, they become less attractive as friendship partners because of the inherent symbolism attached to such unique consumption choices (Snyder & Fromkin, 1980; Tian et al., 1977). In addition, research has shown that people who assert their unpopular choices tend to have a lack of concern for others (Tepper & Hoyle, 1996). This lack of concern which UC individuals display in front of others may translate into loss of friendships, as they may have greater difficulty in fostering social relationships. Therefore, the inability to distinguish themselves in a socially appropriate manner, as well as their general lack of regard for others appear to be considerable factors to their lower and less popular selection rates over time.

Finally, AS was strongly negatively associated with the rate of growth in outgoing ties (ego effect). This result stands in stark contrast to the other two dimensions that imply unique individuals tend to increase their social network over time. This particular finding also indicates that people with a higher need for AS do not have the same desire to display their unique identity to others in their network. AS individuals define their unique identity by avoiding similar others (Ruvio et al., 2008). That is, instead of finding creative (such as CC) or extreme (such as UC) ways to diverge from the norm, AS individuals would avoid others to reduce the risk of having their identity copied (Tian et al., 2001). Prior research suggests that people diverge in their consumption choices to ensure that others will make desired identity inferences about them (Berger & Heath, 2007). That is, a large part of maintaining the unique self is by deciding whom to communicate this unique identity to. Given this motivation, AS individuals will actively seek to reduce their social network in order to maximize their unique appeal as well as to protect their unique identity from becoming mainstream. When personal networks get larger, the impact of one's uniqueness becomes marginalized, particularly in cases where there are others who possess similar identities. Therefore, AS individuals will actively seek to reduce their network to enforce and maintain their distinct identities.

Collectively, these results illustrate an interesting narrative. First, it appears that unique individuals who strive to be creative (CC) or unpopular (UC) with their choices widen their social network in an effort to further promote their unique characteristics. In contrast, unique individuals who strive to avoid similar others (AS) are more cautious of maintaining their unique appeal, and in turn reduce the size of their network in order to protect their identity from becoming common and diluted. This suggests individuals' desire to attain or maintain social ties is dependent on one's specific uniqueness motivation. Second, it appears that CC individuals tended to bond together over time. Since CC individuals are more conscious of the social outcomes of their unique identity, these individuals are more likely to stick together to support each other's unique identity. Finally, consistent with previous research, UC individuals experienced a negative social outcome (i.e., were regarded less attractive as friends) despite the perception that they had built a larger network.

Individuals high in CNFU tend to make choices that mirror their underlying counterconforming motivations. Such choices can extend beyond the relationships developed with others, to consumption decisions made to reflect their individual preferences. For example, these individuals may prefer distinct product designs and attributes that are not likely to be possessed by others (Snyder & Fromkin, 1980). In response, marketers have tried to generate ad messages that portray uniqueness appeals and product scarcity appeals as a means of attracting those who desire to be dissimilar from others (Lynn & Harris, 1997; Snyder, 1992). Given this real effort and trend, the findings from this research stand to contribute to the body of work used by today's marketing practitioners.

Our findings suggest that unique individuals (for example, CC / UC) have a desire to actively build their personal network with specific motivations in mind. While some individuals may strive to find other creatively likeminded friends (CC), others may strive to stick to a rather small network of individuals who exhibit dissimilar preferences (AS). As a result, marketers are advised that highlighting the social benefits of a unique product can act as a tool for enhancing a particular individual's social appeal. In particular, our results show that CC and UC individuals appear to have a clear desire to build their social network. However, these groups of individuals also seem be unsuccessful in doing so. Furthermore, our findings suggest that unique individuals are less attractive as social partners if they are in violation of social norms (UC). Hence, too much extremity in product designs, for example, which is incongruent with social norms, may create challenges for counterconforming consumers looking to maintain their social relationships. To circumvent this issue, marketers could emphasize the "optimal distinctiveness" (Brewer, 1991) of their extreme product offerings. This provides clarity regarding the product's capacity to provide social differentiation, while simultaneously balancing the importance of and providing social assimilation.

This study has several limitations. First, the current study is limited to the confines of the artificial boundary of the network as the data contains only the friendships that were developed within the same floor. Although these floor friends represent an important part of one's social environment, it is possible that the results may be confounded by the friendships that were formed outside of this network (e.g., other floors, other dorms, etc.). Second, the SIENA model is limited to assessing dichotomous network ties (0 for absence, 1 for presence); thus, the network data fails to capture the effect of CNFU on the strength of relationship ties. Third, SIENA analysis makes the assumption that all network members are equally available as potential friends. However, this study may contain biased parameters as people who are roommates or live in the same wing of the floor may have a higher likelihood of forming friendships. Finally, the longitudinal data was collected within a short period of five months. It is possible that examining only two data points in five months may be too restrictive, and more data in successive waves may be necessary to capture the broader extent of peoples' social network development.

Despite these shortcomings, this study offers important advantages. Logistically, the impact of potential antecedents to network development is best observed in a group of individuals brought together into the same setting at the same time. In the past, CNFU has primarily been studied at the individual level. This research contributes by providing a more macro-level view of the influence that CNFU has on individuals' social networks. Further, this study is among the first longitudinal studies in consumer behavior to track the developmental patterns of a social network. Aside from its theoretical advances, the present study provides a methodological contribution to the marketing field by presenting actor-based modeling techniques to observe the growth and development of networks. The use of an actor-oriented model provides significant advantages over other traditional methods as it is a useful statistical technique for modeling dependencies beyond dyadic relationships (Steglich et al., 2010).

In conclusion, given the lack of research in this area, we recommend exploring other individual characteristics or traits as well as moderators that may differentially influence the development of consumer networks. Further, more research in the area of CNFU is encouraged to uncover its impact on individuals' network outcomes. Finally, the actor-oriented model presented here may be applied to other areas in marketing to address a variety of network-related questions. Thus, it would be fruitful for researchers to utilize this modeling technique to further extend our discipline's knowledge of consumer networks.

REFERENCES

Berger, Jonah and Chip Heath (2007), "Where Consumers Diverge from Others: Identity Signaling and Product Domains," *Journal of Consumer Research*, 34 (2), 121-34.

Boer, Peter, Mark Huisman, Tom A. Snijders, Christian Steglich, Lotte Wichers, and Evelien Zeggelink (2007), "Stocnet: An Open Software System for the Advance Statistical Analysis of Social Networks," Groningen: ICS / Science Plus.

Brewer, Marilyn B. (1991), "The Social Self: On Being the Same and Different at the Same Time," *Personality and Social Psychology Bulletin*, 17 (5), 475-82.

Burk, William J., Christian Steglich, and Tom A. Snijders (2007), "Beyond Dyadic Interdependence: Actor-Oriented Models for Co-Evolving Social Networks and Individual Behaviors," *International Journal of Behavioral Development*, 31 (4), 397-404.

Colarelli, Stephen M. and Joseph R. Dettmann (2003), "Intuitive Evolutionary Perspectives in Marketing Practices," *Psychology and Marketing*, 20 (9), 837-65.

Duval, Shelley and Robert A. Wicklund (1972), *A Theory of Objective Self Awareness*, New York, NY: Academic Press.

Freeman, Linton C. (1979), "Centrality in Social Networks: Conceptual Clarification," *Social Networks*, 1 (3), 215-39.

Fromkin, Howard L. (1970), "Effects of Experimentally Aroused Feelings of Undistinctiveness Upon Valuation of Scarce and Novel Experiences," *Journal of Personality and Social Psychology*, 16 (3), 521-29.

Heckert, Druann M. (1989), "The Relativity of Positive Deviance: The Case of French Impressionists," *Deviant Behavior*, 10 (2), 131-44.

Huisman, Mark and Tom A. Snijders (2003), "Statistical Analysis of Longitudinal Network Data with Changing Composition," *Sociological Methods & Research*, 32 (2), 253-87.

Iacobucci, Dawn and Nigel Hopkins (1992), "Modeling Dyadic Interactions and Networks in Marketing," *Journal of Marketing Research*, 29 (1), 5-17.

Kendel, Denise B. (1978), "Homophily, Selection and Socialization in Adolescent Friendships," *American Journal of Sociology*, 84 (2), 427-36.

Kron, Joan (1983), *Home-Psych: The Social Psychology of Home and Decoration*, New York, NY: Potter.

Lee, Seung Hwan (Mark), June Cotte, and Theodore J. Noseworthy (2010), "The Role of Network Centrality in the Flow of Consumer Influence," *Journal of Consumer Psychology*, 20 (1), 66-77.

Lynn, Michael and Judy Harris (1997), "The Desire for Unique Consumer Products: A New Individual Differences Scale," *Psychology & Marketing*, 14 (6), 601-16.

McAlister, Leigh and Edgar Pessemier (1982), "Variety Seeking Behavior: An Interdisciplinary Review," *Journal of Consumer Research*, 9 (3), 311-22.

Mercken, Liesbeth, Tom A. Snijders, Christian Steglich, and Hein de Vries (2010), "Dynamics of Adolescent Friendship Networks and Smoking Behavior," *Social Networks*, 32 (1), 72-81.

Meyn, Sean P. and Richard Tweedie (1993), *Markov Chains and Stochastic Stability*, New York, NY: Springer.

Reingen, Peter H., Brian L. Foster, Jacqueline J. Brown, and Stephen B. Seidman (1984), "Brand Congruence in Interpersonal Relations: A Social Network Analysis," *Journal of Consumer Research*, 11 (3), 771-83.

Ruvio, Ayalla (2008), "Unique Like Everybody Else? The Dual Role of Consumers' Need for Uniqueness," *Psychology & Marketing*, 25 (5), 444-64.

Ruvio, Ayalla, Aviv Shoham, and Maja M. Brencic (2008), "Consumers' Need for Uniqueness: Short-Form Scale Development and Cross-Cultural Validation," *International Marketing Review*, 25 (1), 33-53.

Santee, Richard T. and Christina Maslach (1982), "To Agree or Not to Agree: Personal Dissent and Amid Social Pressure to Conform," *Journal of Personality and Social Psychology*, 42 (4), 690-700.

Schor, Juliet B. (1998), *The Overspent American: Upscaling, Downshifting and the New Consumer*, New York, NY: Basic Books.

Selfhout, Maarten, William J. Burk, Susan Branje, Jaap Denissen, Marcel van Aken, and Wim Meeus (2010), "Emerging Late Adolescent Friendship Networks and Big Five Personality Traits: A Social Network Approach," *Journal of Personality*, 78 (2), 509-38.

Snijders, Tom A., Christian Steglich, Michael Schwinberger, and Mark Huisman (2007), *Manual for Siena Version 3.1*: University of Groningen: ICS / Department of Sociology; University of Oxford: Department of Statistics.

Snijders, Tom A., Gerhard G. van de Bunt, and Christian E.G. Steglich (2010), "Introduction to Stochastic Actor-Based Models for Network Dynamics," *Social Networks*, 32 (1), 44-60.

Snyder, C. Rick and Howard L. Fromkin (1977), "Abnormality as a Positive Characteristic: The Development and Validation of a Scale Measuring Need for Uniqueness," *Journal of Abnormal Psychology*, 86 (5), 518-27.

--- (1980), *Uniqueness: Human Pursuit of Difference*, New York, NY: Plenum.

Tepper, Kelly and Rick H. Hoyle (1996), "Latent Variable Models of Need for Uniqueness," *Multivariate Behavioral Research*, 31 (4), 467-94.

Thompson, Craig J. and Diana L. Haytko (1997), "Speaking of Fashion: Consumers' Uses of Fashion Discourses and the Appropriation of Countervailing Cultural Meanings," *Journal of Consumer Research*, 24 (1), 15-42.

Tian, Kelly T., William O. Bearden, and Gary L. Hunter (2001), "Consumers' Need for Uniqueness: Scale Development and Validation," *Journal of Consumer Research*, 28 (1), 50-66.

Tian, Kelly T. and Karyn McKenzie (2001), "The Long-Term Predictive Validity of the Consumers' Need for Uniqueness Scale," *Journal of Consumer Psychology*, 10 (3), 171-93.

Webster, Cynthia M. and Pamela D. Morrison (2004), "Network Analysis in Marketing," *Australian Marketing Journal*, 12 (2), 8-18.

Worchel, Stephen, Jerry Lee, and Akanbi Adewole (1975), "Effects of Supply and Demand on Ratings of Object Value," *Journal of Personality and Social Psychology*, 32 (5), 906-14.

Discourses of Technology Consumption:
Ambivalence, Fear, and Liminality

Margo Buchanan-Oliver, University of Auckland, New Zealand
Angela Cruz, University of Auckland, New Zealand

ABSTRACT

Why are consumer narratives of technology consumption fraught with ambivalence (Mick and Fournier 1998), identity tensions (Schau and Gilly 2003), anxiety (Meuter et al. 2003; Mick and Fournier 1998), and even fear (Clarke 2002; Helman 1988; Virilio 1997)? What is it about technology consumption, an arguably everyday experience in the context of increasingly ubiquitous digital, biomedical, information and communication technologies in today's "technology-intensive" markets (John, Weiss, and Dutta 1999, 78), that evokes such primal reactions in consumers? In the seemingly banal act of consuming technology, what exactly comes under threat?

To explore these questions, we turn to the emerging discourse of posthumanism as articulated by Campbell, O'Driscoll, and Saren (2005), Giesler (2004), Giesler and Venkatesh (2005), Schroeder and Dobers (2007), and Venkatesh, Karababa, and Ger (2002). Significantly, posthumanist discourses challenge the underlying assumptions of the predominant information processing paradigm, which frames the majority of research on technology consumption (e.g. Bettman 1979; Bettman, Luce, and Payne 1998) and focus on how consumers mentally process the functional benefits of technology products. Within this paradigm, the following metaphors of consumers and their technologies remain unquestioned: firstly, technology is a positive enabler, secondly, the consumer is a disembodied consciousness, and thirdly, technology is extrinsic to human identity.

In challenging these prevailing metaphors, the emerging posthuman paradigm instead acknowledges multiple and complex framing views around technology consumption which are already widespread in popular imagination and other academic disciplines. In particular, the concept of liminality provides a potent deconstruction of these metaphors. Liminality refers to a hybrid condition characterised by ambiguity, indeterminacy, contradiction, incoherence, and blurring of boundaries. Within popular culture, the genre of science fiction sees classic literary texts (e.g., Gibson's (1986) 'Neuromancer', Asimov's (1967) 'I, Robot', Huxley's (1955) 'Brave New World') and popular films (e.g.,'The Terminator', 'Blade Runner', and 'The Matrix') representing a liminal vision of human-machine interactions alongside their psychological and socio-cultural repercussions. These rich discourses are similarly well-entrenched in academic disciplines ranging from media and communications studies (Turkle 1984, 1997) to cognitive neuropsychology (Clark 2003), to cultural studies and critical theory (Balsamo 1996; Shilling 2005; Stone 1996).

These liminal visions, however, are fraught with pervasive anxieties and tensions. Virilio (1997, 20), for instance, in his account of the social destruction wrought by information technology and global media, vividly articulates a fear of technology in depicting

the catastrophic figure of an individual who has lost the capacity for immediate intervention … and who abandons himself for want of anything better, to the capabilities of captors, sensors and other remote control scanners that turn him into a being controlled by the machine.

In a similar vein, Woodward (1994) writes that "most of us fear the future prospect of frailty as a cyborg, ""hooked up" … to a machine." Even though such texts often draw on spectacular imagery to underline the implications of technology consumption, they have

significant impact on consumers' lives as they infuse and inform the wider circuits of meaning (McCracken 1986) which shape the way consumers imagine and interact with their technologies.

While previous studies have examined visual representations of posthumanism as represented by the figure of the cyborg (Campbell et al. 2005; Schroeder and Dobers 2007; Venkatesh et al. 2002), our approach is more theoretical. We present the concept of liminality as a recurrent theme within interdisciplinary theoretical discourses of technology consumption and explore its key thematics in terms of four liminal tensions: bodies/machines, human/nonhuman, past/future, and here/not-here. We consider the implications of this concept for extending the paradigm of posthuman consumer research and uncovering fundamental ambivalences, tensions, and fears concerning technology consumption. We argue that marketers and advertisers need to reflect on such concerns in their communication of technology products in order to pierce the heart of what technology means to consumers and achieve deep resonance with their target audience.

METHODOLOGY

We carried out a wider project seeking to explicate the range and complexity of theoretical discourses which shape narratives and practices of technology consumption. In doing so, we followed an interdisciplinary approach to theory development. We sourced key interdisciplinary conceptual works lensing technology consumption using keyword searches in ACR proceedings and ABI/Inform, and further expanded our list of source texts through reference list and Google Scholar searches. Applying a discourse analysis methodology situated within hermeneutic interpretivism (Crotty 1998), main concepts and key themes were induced from each source text and categorised into broader themes. A "hermeneutical back and forth between part and whole" (Spiggle 1994, 495) was facilitated through constant comparison between the literature sources and the emerging theoretical framework. This enabled the development of provisional categories for subsequent exploration, thereby aiding the induction of broader, underlying themes from these sources.

We found the concept of liminality to be a recurrent central theme in the academic literature examined. We further found two main discursive strands of body-machine liminality and space-time liminality, within which key liminal tensions between bodies/machines, human/nonhuman, past/future, and here/not-here are articulated. Drawing on exemplary source texts, we discuss these findings in the following section.

FINDINGS: LIMINALITY IN TECHNOLOGY
CONSUMPTION

The Concept of Liminality

Liminality refers to a hybrid condition characterised by ambiguity, indeterminacy, contradiction, incoherence, and blurring of boundaries. Originally theorised by Turner (1967) as a key characteristic of the second stage of ritual involving a passage between two states, liminality refers to "a state of transition between two or more boundaries" (Campbell et al. 2005, 346). In anthropological conceptions (Turner 1967), the liminal moment is seen as a temporary state in between, which is eventually resolved through a boundary crossing or role transition.

Advances in Consumer Research
Volume 39, ©2011

However, liminality can also describe an underlying condition which pervades all aspects of consumers' reality, being and experience, in that all dichotomies, boundaries and 'states' of being are partial and transitional. A liminal view of consumer experience asserts that consumer meanings, identities, and experience are transitional and dynamic rather than absolute and natural. This perspective asserts the essential unsustainability of traditional dichotomies such as human/machine, mind/body and real/virtual, which are revealed to be artificial constructions.

The theme of liminality plays a key role in Haraway's (1991) seminal 'Cyborg Manifesto', in which the figure of the cyborg is used to underline and celebrate the hybridity, contingency, partiality, and incoherence of embodied subjectivity. A figure which is both human and machine, both flesh and metal, both spiritual and material, and ambiguous in gender, the cyborg for Haraway (1991) embodies liminality in its juxtaposition of contradictory opposites and in its potential to break down traditional dichotomies between human and animal, organism and machine, physical and non-physical. In this vein, Venkatesh et al. (2002, 446) also write that the emerging posthuman paradigm "views the intersection of human and machine as a postmodern possibility in contrast to the received view under modernist thinking which considers these two entities as distinctly separate."

Thus we can already see the radical potential and concurrent threat posed by a liminal worldview, in its dissolution of modernist boundaries and its insistence in partiality. Furthermore, as liminal states of being do not fit in easily with regular narratives or extant categories, they tend to be conceived as polluted, taboo, and associated with impurity, alterity, exclusion, danger and Otherness (Clarke 2002). Hence, what boundaries are thus contaminated when we consider technology consumption through a liminal perspective? To answer this, we develop two key discursive strands which further explicate and expand this concept: body-machine liminality and space-time liminality.

Body-Machine Liminality

Body-machine liminality refers to a blurring of boundaries between bodies and machines, making it increasingly difficult to delineate differences between human bodies and their nonhuman machines. While body-machine liminality is articulated in a wide range of representational and embodied practices including anthropomorphism in advertisements (Dobers and Schroeder 2001) and the cosmetic modification of the human body (Balsamo 1996, Featherstone 2000, Schouten 1991), we focus our discussion on two key liminal tensions between bodies/machines and human/nonhuman.

Bodies/machines. Ideas of the body and the machine metaphorically inform and shape one another. As metaphorical associations between bodies and machines are repeatedly re-iterated in linguistic discourse, audiovisual representation and embodied practice, resemblances between bodies and machines in appearance or behaviour are underlined (Schroeder and Dobers 2007).

On one hand, the appearance and performance of the machine is often understood to be like the appearance and performance of the human body. This metaphorical association serves to transfer our understanding of the familiar domain of the human body to help us understand potentially abstract domains of technological functioning. Schroeder and Dobers (2007) for instance, cite the example of a print advertisement which uses commonplace understandings of the human digestive system to represent data storage in computers. While there may be a tendency for this trope to be used to communicate functional benefits, the converse notion that machines break down and are as imperfect and vulnerable as the human body is under-

standably absent in aspirational marketing communications which position technological offerings as infallible.

At the same time as our understanding of technology is informed by our understanding of the human body, the increased adoption of these technologies into the everyday means that the opposite also happens: our understanding of machines come to structure the ways in which we understand ourselves (McLuhan 1967; Turkle 1984, 1997). The human body is increasingly seen as a machine – an assemblage of multiple parts and systems whose parts can be replaced when broken and whose performance can be optimised.

Human/nonhuman. Additionally, the metaphor of technology as a tool, suggesting that which is external to and distinct from the body, is rendered less compelling than the metaphor of technology as prosthesis, suggesting something which, in addition to extending human capability, is incorporated into the self and inevitably comes to constitute one's sense of who one is. Zylinska (2002, 3) points out this "inherently prosthetic nature of human identity" in which humans extend themselves with technologies that either literally or figuratively become incorporated as part of the self. Similarly, Balsamo (1996) theorises that there are 'degrees of cyborgism' rather than a reductive human-machine dichotomy. Indeed, Haraway's (1991, 150) statement that "we are all chimeras, theorized and fabricated hybrids of machine and organism" has become increasingly relevant in light of commonplace technologies such as pacemakers and hearing aids.

However, we must emphasize that prostheticism is not limited to biomedical technologies, but also applies to everyday prosthetic devices such as cell phones and laptops. Clark (2003) insists that prostheticism characterises humans' everyday interaction with technology, casting humans as 'natural-born cyborgs' in our unique and inherent capacity to think and feel through our best technologies. He argues that the inherent plasticity of the human brain is such that human subjectivity is necessarily diffused over a fluid and interactive network of biological and non-biological components. In this view, there is no reason for the 'biological skin-bag' to be privileged as the site of human subjectivity (Clark 2003). Indeed, it is when technologies become transparent in use that we feel they are part of us and inseparable from our bodies, such that "technologies can alter, augment, and extend our sense of presence and our potential for action" (Clark 2003, 125).

This everyday fusion between the body and technology is dramatically visualised in images of cyborgs, in which non-biological material literally pierces, merges with, or enters the 'biological skin-bag' (Clark 2003). However, because this image of the cyborg violates extant categories and destabilises what it means to be human, it commonly invokes notions of Otherness, the abject and the unnatural, carrying with it mythic resonances of Frankenstein's monster and evoking anxieties and fears around pollution, contamination, recombination and miscegenation (Helman 1988). The increasingly pervasive notion of technology-as-prothesis, as represented by the image of the cyborg, can therefore potentially provoke ambivalent identifications and fearful reactions in consumers – a sense in which technology consumption renders us both human and nonhuman.

Space-Time Liminality

Technology consumption also confounds the experience of presence. This is explored in the discursive strand of space-time liminality, which underlines how technology enables various modes of 'space-shifting' and 'time-shifting'. Here, technology consumers experience being both 'elsewhere' and 'elsewhen', confounding modernist conceptions of space and time as fixed and linear. Indeed, a consideration of the spatiotemporal dynamics of technology consumption uncovers its inherent paradoxes, as explored in the liminal tensions of past/future and here/not-here.

Past/future. Technology facilitates 'time travel' by allowing consumers to experience times apart from and in addition to the present, thereby challenging conceptions of time as linear and unidirectional. Technology often facilitates a Janus-faced time perspective, characterised by a simultaneous gaze to the future and the past. On one hand, technology is strongly associated with and represented using futuristic images, with technology being seen to propel us into the future and draw futuristic conceptions of progress into our everyday realities (Davis 2004). On the other hand, technology also preserves memories and history. In particular, through the proliferation of recording technologies (Manuel 1993) such as video cameras, consumers can readily preserve particular moments in time and to access their pasts in an 'untarnished' way.

Over and above this, technology is implicated in shaping a dynamic relationship to time which resists simplistic categorisations of past, present, and future. Consider, for instance, how the act of using a camera involves a Janus-faced gaze to both past and future: in the act of taking a picture, there is a translation of the present moment into a documented past for consumption in the future. In this way, the past is always present in the future, and vice versa.

Here/not-here. Technology also confounds the conception and experience of space. As technology enables us to extend our subjectivities beyond our immediate physical surroundings, the location of the individual subject with respect to the biological body becomes increasingly complicated (Stone 1996) and the subjective experience of space is transformed.

Consider, for instance, the experience of telepresence, which simply refers to being in two places at once. Steuer (1992, 76, cited in Hoffman and Novak 1996) defines telepresence as the "mediated perception of an environment", a subjective state in which the consumer perceives both his or her immediate physical environment as well as a computer-mediated environment. Here, telepresence refers to the experience of being drawn into the space of the screen as exemplified in an immersive video gaming experience (Darley 2000). With an emphasis on the social, Minsky (1980) defines telepresence as social presence in the absence of physical presence. This conception of telepresence can be divided into real-time telepresence, involving the simultaneous co-presence of communicating parties through technologies such as the telephone or instant messaging, and virtual telepresence, for instance in personal websites (Schau and Gilly 2003) which do not require real-time feedback.

Consider also the ways in which technology facilitates the division of once-coherent spaces into separate fragments, enabling consumers to set up personal boundaries within shared spaces. As an example, the act of putting on a pair of earphones allows one to set up an individual zone within the shared space of a living room or a bus, or enables one to set up a zone of privacy within a public space (Van Dorst 2005). In addition, technology facilitates the intersections of and leakages between once-separate spheres, such as the public and private spheres (Buchecker 2005; McDougal 2005). Take for instance, the use of a cell phone in a restaurant. Here, the user enters a private space within a public space, but at the same time other patrons have a glimpse of this space through the one-sided conversation. Thus there is a sense of intrusion on both ends – the private intrudes into the public as someone's conversation interrupts a meal, while the public intrudes into the private, with other people listening in on one's conversations.

In these ways, subjectivity is seen to be spread out across and between spaces in a way that resists modernist conceptions of space

and confound simple dichotomies between the "real" and the "virtual". In this vein, Druckery (1996, 12) asserts that computer-mediated environments "collapse the border between material and immaterial, the real and the possible" such that dichotomies and boundaries between the 'real world' and 'virtual world' are rendered less relevant. In short, everyday instances of technology consumption can be conceptualised as liminal states, enabling consumers to straddle the boundaries between here/not-here across multiple, intersecting, and permeable spaces.

IMPLICATIONS AND FURTHER RESEARCH

Our discussion of liminality, while confined to theory, carries implications for consumers' lives. In the context of increasingly ubiquitous digital, biomedical, information and communication technologies, these interdisciplinary discourses represent wider culturally constituted meanings which impact the consumer experience of technology consumption through various circuits of meaning (McCracken 1986). As we have observed, posthuman representations already pervade advertising texts (Campbell et al. 2005; Schroeder and Dobers 2007; Venkatesh et al. 2002) and popular fiction (Asimov 1967; Gibson 1986; Huxley 1955). This underlines their potential to constitute shared cultural meanings which are used by groups

> to make collective sense of their environments and orient their members' experiences and lives… [framing] consumers' horizons of conceivable actions, feeling, and thought, making certain patterns of behaviour and sense-making interpretations more likely than others
>
> (Arnould and Thompson 2005, 869).

Through the concept of liminality as explicated in this paper, we build on the emerging paradigm of posthuman consumer culture (Campbell et al. 2005; Giesler 2004; Giesler and Venkatesh 2005; Schroeder and Dobers 2007; Venkatesh et al. 2002). We shift our attention from the visual representation of posthumanism to explicating the key dimensions of liminality as a theoretical concept. To demonstrate how a liminal frame provides a different way of understanding technology consumption, we now consider how it might extend or re-interpret extant consumer research.

As we have seen in our discussion of space-time liminality, the posthuman paradigm in explaining consumers' constructions of online identities eschews a simple dichotomy between the online self and the physical self (Schau and Gilly 2003). Indeed, this dichotomy is symptomatic of an assumed Cartesian dualism, which separates the mind from the body and privileges the rational over the embodied and holistic aspects of technology consumption (Shilling 2005). Rather, the concept of liminality emphasizes the subjective experience of presence across multiple, intersecting, and permeable spaces, in which the physical location of the body is not privileged.

In addition, our discussion of liminality further expands Mick and Fournier's (1998) paradoxes of technology, in which consumer ambivalence with respect to technology was explained through eight polar opposites which characterise technology products. We present four additional paradoxes as articulated in the key liminal tensions between bodies/machines, human/nonhuman, past/future, and here/not-here. Furthermore, over and above the idea of technology-as-tool, the concept of liminality emphasises the metaphor of technology-as-prosthesis – that which comes to be incorporated into our very selves and is constitutive of human identity and subjectivity. In doing so, this perspective reveals a deeper ambivalence which goes beyond the advantages and disadvantages of technology, and concerns its implications for how we use technology to constitute and conceive of ourselves as human.

Similarly, while Kozinets (2008) maps out various oppositional identity positions which consumers interpellate into their narratives, the underlying metaphor of technology as a tool remains unquestioned. In order to probe the deep-seated reasons for why someone interpellates a particular ideology of technology into their identity narrative, we need to consider the fundamental assumptions which underlie these identity narratives. Might Kozinets' (2008) 'Green Luddite' position, for instance, be interpreted as a selected coping strategy in response to the liminal erosion of a clearly delineated human subject?

Thus, having shown that liminality is a key concept in theoretical discourses of technology consumption, and briefly demonstrated its potential for framing consumer research, further research questions can be considered. From a theoretical perspective, are there other key concepts in interdisciplinary discourses which would similarly be useful? From an emic standpoint, to what extent do discourses of liminality pervade consumer narratives? If consumers are aware of the key paradoxes within popular cultural texts and within the broader theoretical discourses of liminality, exploring the extent to which these are articulated in their narratives and appropriated into their identity projects may reveal deeper-running complexities and tensions in consumers' views of technology. We argue that marketers and advertisers need to reflect on such complexities and tensions in their communication of technology products in order to pierce the heart of what a constantly morphing technology means to consumers, thereby assisting them to achieve deep resonance with their target audience.

CONCLUSION

In order to probe the deep-seated reasons for why consumers experience technology in particular ways (Schau and Gilly 2003), feel the way they do about technology (Mick and Fournier 1998), or interpellate particular ideologies of technology into their identity narratives (Kozinets 2008), we need to consider the fundamental assumptions which frame these experiences, feelings, and narratives. The concept of liminality, and the posthuman paradigm more broadly, provides a way to articulate how fundamental assumptions are destabilised and negotiated in consumer narratives of technology consumption. Furthermore, our discussion of key liminal tensions enables us as theorists to identify exactly what comes under threat, and why such deep-seated consumer anxieties and fears are evoked, in seemingly banal narratives of technology consumption – the hitherto unquestioned meanings of being human, having a body, and inhabiting a particular space and time. By being aware of these fundamental anxieties and fears, marketers and advertisers will be better able to communicate technology products in ways that deeply resonate with their target audiences.

REFERENCES

Arnould, Eric J. and Craig J. Thompson (2005), "Consumer Culture Theory (CCT): Twenty Years of Research," *Journal of Consumer Research*, 31 (March), 868-82.

Asimov, Isaac (1967), *I, Robot*, London: Dennis Dobson.

Balsamo, Anne Marie (1996), *Technologies of the Gendered Body: Reading Cyborg Women*, Durham: Duke University Press.

Bettman, James R. (1979), *An Information Processing Theory of Consumer Choice*, MA: Addison-Wesley.

Bettman, James R., Mary Frances Luce, and John W. Payne (1998), "Constructive Consumer Choice Processes," *Journal of Consumer Research*, 25 (December), 187-217.

Buchecker, Matthias (2005), "Public Place as a Resource of Social Interaction," in *Spatiality, Spaces and Technology*, ed. P. Turner and E. Davenport, Dordrecht: Kluwer, 79-96.

Campbell, Norah, Aidan O'Driscoll, and Mike Saren (2005), "Cyborg Consciousness: A Visual Cultural Approach to the Technologised Body," in *European Advances in Consumer Research*, Vol. 7, ed. Karin M. Ekstrom and Helene Brembeck, Goteborg, Sweden: Association for Consumer Research, 344-51.

Clark, Andy (2003), *Natural-Born Cyborgs: Minds, Technologies, and the Future of Human Intelligence*, New York: Oxford University Press.

Clarke, Julie (2002), "The Human/Not Human in the Work of Orlan and Stelarc," in *The Cyborg Experiments: The Extensions of the Body in the Media Age*, ed. Joanna Zylinska, New York: Continuum, 33-55.

Crotty, Michael (1998), *The Foundations of Social Research*, St Leonards, NSW: Allen & Unwin.

Darley, Andrew (2000), *Visual Digital Culture: Surface Play and Spectacle in New Media Genres*, London and New York: Routledge.

Davis, Erik (2004), "The Emergence of Virtual Commodities," in *Advances in Consumer Research*, Vol. 31, ed. Barbara E. Kahn and Mary Frances Luce, Valdosta, GA: Association for Consumer Research, 400-02.

Dobers, Peter and Jonathan E. Schroeder (2001), "Representing IT: Embodying the Electronic Economy," in *16:e Nordiska Foretagsekonomiska Amnesknoferensen*, Uppsala.

Druckery, Timothy (1996), "Introduction," in *Electronic Culture: Technology and Visual Representation*, ed. Timothy Druckery, New York: Aperture Foundation, 12-25.

Featherstone, Mike (2000), "Body Modification: An Introduction," in *Body Modification*, ed. Mike Featherstone, London: Sage Publication, 1-14.

Gibson, William (1986), *Neuromancer*, London: Grafton.

Giesler, Markus (2004), "Consuming Cyborgs: Researching Posthuman Consumer Culture," in *Advances in Consumer Research*, Vol. 31, ed. Barbara E. Kahn and Mary Frances Luce, Valdosta, GA: Association for Consumer Research, 400-02.

Giesler, Markus and Alladi Venkatesh (2005), "Reframing the Embodied Consumer as Cyborg: A Posthumanist Epistemology of Consumption," in *Advances in Consumer Research*, Vol. 32, ed. Geeta Menon and Akshay R. Rao, Duluth, MN: Association for Consumer Research, 661-69.

Haraway, Donna J. (1991), "A Cyborg Manifesto: Science, Technology, and Socialist-Feminism in the Late Twentieth Century," in *Simians, Cyborgs, and Women: The Reinvention of Nature*, New York: Routledge.

Helman, Cecil (1988), "Dr Frankenstein and the Industrial Body: Reflections on 'Spare Part' Surgery," *Anthropology Today*, 4 (3), 14-16.

Hoffman, Donna L. and Thomas P. Novak (1996), "Marketing in Hypermedia Computer-Mediated Environments: Conceptual Foundations," *Journal of Marketing*, 60 (3), 50-68.

Huxley, Aldous (1955), *Brave New World: A Novel*, Harmondsworth: Penguin.

John, George, Allen M. Weiss, and Shantanu Dutta (1999), "Marketing in Technology-Intensive Markets: Toward a Conceptual Framework," *Journal of Marketing*, 63 (4), 78-91.

Kozinets, Robert V. (2008), "Technology/Ideology: How Ideological Fields Influence Consumers' Technology Narratives," *Journal of Consumer Research*, 34 (April), 865-81.

Manuel, Peter Lamarche (1993), *Cassette Culture: Popular Music and Technology in North India*, Chicago: University of Chicago Press.

McCracken, Grant (1986), "Culture and Consumption: A Theoretical Account of the Structure and Movement of the Cultural Meaning of Consumer Goods," *Journal of Consumer Research*, 13 (June), 71-82.

McDougal, Lorna (2005), "The Intersection of Real and Virtual Workspace," in *Spatiality, Spaces and Technology*, ed. P. Turner and E. Davenport, Dordrecht: Kluwer, 67-78.

McLuhan, Marshall (1967), *Understanding Media: The Extensions of Man*, London: Sphere Books.

Meuter, Matthew L., Mary Jo Bitner, Amy L. Ostrom, and Stephen W. Brown (2005), "Choosing among Alternative Service Delivery Modes: An Investigation of Customer Trial of Self-Service Technologies," *Journal of Marketing*, 69 (April), 61-83.

Mick, David Glen and Susan Fournier (1998), "Paradoxes of Technology: Consumer Cognizance, Emotions, and Coping Strategies," *Journal of Consumer Research*, 25 (September), 123-43.

Minsky, Marvin (1980), "Telepresence," *Omni* (June), 45-51.

Schau, Hope Jensen and Mary C. Gilly (2003), "We Are What We Post? Self-Presentation in Personal Web Space," *Journal of Consumer Research*, 30 (3), 385-404.

Schouten, John W. (1991), "Selves in Transition: Symbolic Consumption in Personal Rites of Passage and Identity Reconstruction," *Journal of Consumer Research*, 17 (March), 412-25.

Schroeder, Jonathan E. and Peter Dobers (2007), "Imagining Identity: Technology and the Body in Marketing Communications," in *Advances in Consumer Research*, Vol. 34, ed. Gavan Fitzsimons and Vicki Morwitz, Duluth, MN: Association for Consumer Research, 155-57.

Shilling, Chris (2005), *The Body in Culture, Technology and Society*, London: Sage.

Spiggle, Susan (1994), "Analysis and Interpretation of Qualitative Data in Consumer Research," *Journal of Consumer Research*, 21 (December), 491-503.

Stone, Allecquere Rosanne (1996), *The War of Desire and Technology at the Close of the Mechanical Age*, Cambridge: MIT Press.

Turkle, Sherry (1984), *The Second Self: Computers and the Human Spirit*, New York: Simon and Schuster.

Turkle, Sherry (1997), *Life on the Screen: Identity in the Age of the Internet*, New York: Simon & Schuster.

Turner, Victor (1967), *The Forest of Symbols: Aspects of Ndembu Ritual*, Ithaca, New York: Cornell University Press.

Van Dorst, Machiel (2005), "Privacy Zoning: The Different Layers of Public Space," in *Spatiality, Spaces and Technology*, ed. P. Turner and E. Davenport, Dordrecht: Kluwer, 97-116.

Venkatesh, Alladi, Eminegul Karababa, and Guliz Ger (2002), "The Emergence of the Posthuman Consumer and the Fusion of the Virtual and the Real: A Critical Analysis of Sony's Ad for Memory Stick," in *Advances in Consumer Research*, Vol. 29, ed. Susan M. Broniarczyk and Kent Nakamoto, Valdosta, GA: Association for Consumer Research, 446-52.

Virilio, Paul (1997), *Open Sky*, London and New York: Verso.

Woodward, Kathleen (1994), "From Virtual Cyborgs to Biological Time Bombs: Technocriticism and the Material Body," in *Culture on the Brink: Ideologies of Technology*, ed. Gretchen Bender and Timothy Druckery, Seattle: Bay Press, 47-64.

Zylinska, Joanna (2002), "Extending McLuhan into the New Media Age: An Introduction," in *The Cyborg Experiments: The Extensions of the Body in the Media Age*, ed. Joanna Zylinska, New York: Continuum, 1-12.

"Free" Gifts and Irrational Preferences:
An Exploration for Effects of Promotional Enticements on Financial Decision Making

Nese Nasif, University of Texas, Pan American, USA
Michael S. Minor, University of Texas, Pan American, USA

*"This is the foundation of all: we are not to imagine or suppose,
but to discover, what nature does or may be made to do."*

-Francis Bacon (1561-1626)

1. INTRODUCTION

Behavioral economics emerged as a way to better explain, as compared to traditional economic theory, what psychological factors affect consumer decisions. Traditional finance theory assumes that investors act rationally, in that they consistently perform utility-optimizing behaviors. Choices are made through continuous and dependable cost-benefit analysis, often without direct realization of the underlying thought processes, and repeated consumption does not result in any violations of transitivity. Moreover, consumers have complete preferences (i.e. consumers *have* preferences for any set of products that are compared) which are revealed through their consumption choices of certain products at certain prices. However, researchers in other fields and contemporary economists have published criticisms to the traditional theory, citing a great deal of irrationality in observed behavior. They argue that such behavior is not new, but rather, traditional utility theory has been unable to reconcile seemingly irrational consumption decisions in economic agents.

Traditionally, economic models dismissed variation in emotional responses within market transactions, particularly those resulting from extrinsic influences, as having a significant impact on consumption preferences. That is, emotions are taken as given in an economic model, optimization of utility is revealed through consumption choices, and the rational every-consumer would not make consumption choices that left her worse off in resources and/or unhappier than a different consumption alternative. However, a great deal of observations of consumption behavior that deviates from classical utility theory necessitated new models and theoretical frameworks upon which to explain such deviations. Caplin and Leahy (2001) applied anxiety as a cost to investors' portfolio decisions. The authors found that holders of seemingly under-priced, risky securities were not considering the cost of anxiety associated with holding them. Indeed, "stock ownership entails psychic costs [because the investor] has to live with the anxiety that accompanies the holding of a risky portfolio" (p. 69). The anxiety-costs viewpoint can also help to reconcile other seemingly irrational decisions, like why people put off investing in a retirement account early in their careers when the future returns should be the highest.

Psychology has long accepted cognitive limitations in decision-making and has increasingly merged with the economics disciplines, such as finance, in order to document and attempt to explain seemingly irrational consumption. For example, both disciplines now accept the concept of "optimism bias", where otherwise risk-averse people consume financial products with provisions that are relatively risky in terms of their incomes, because they are optimistic about their future financial positions to an irrational degree (see, e.g., Ariely 2009; Lovallo & Kahneman 2003; Weinstein, 1980). Zweig (2007) illustrates this point by highlighting the fact that, although credit cards are considered to be a competitive industry, few card companies drop their yearly interest rates below 20 percent. This occurs, in part, because nearly half of all credit card users believe they will pay their credit balance in full each month. In reality, 75 percent rollover credit card balances and pay interest charges. Thus, many consumers tend to disregard the interest rate when initially obtaining a credit card, because they do not foresee ever having to use it.

Gintis (2009) argues the illogicality of economics, sociology, anthropology, and social psychology all separately attempting to explain human decisions and organization. He contends that researchers in each field continue to produce incompatible results based on varying and conflicting assumptions. Collaboration between psychology and economics, particularly, has advanced scholarly research in neurofinance. Economists, psychologists, and related business scholars have produced studies applying game theory, modified models of utility, and various decision-making experiments to consumption behaviors. Moreover, books such as *The Winner's Curse* (Thaler 1994), *Predictably Irrational* (Ariely 2008), *Buyology* (Lindstrom 2008), *Nudge* (Thaler & Sunstein 2009), *Priceless* (Poundstone 2010), among several others, have become global best-sellers, making a once enigmatic topic more accessible to the general, educated public.

Merchants exploited our irrational consumption compulsions long before scholars attempted to publish observations of such behavior. Many people fall prey to "deals", without actually thinking about the fact that they are consuming irrationally. For instance, retailers commonly use "anchor pricing" in order to encourage consumption of an item that would otherwise be considered too expensive to the consumer. Ninety dollars may seem like an exorbitant price to pay for a purse, but placed "on sale" for that amount and placed next to comparable purses that cost hundreds of dollars more, one's sentiments may change to consider the ninety-dollar purse as being reasonably priced, or even a bargain (Poundstone 2010).

In practice, businesses have profited from our irrational preferences for "free" items for quite some time. In 2000, Amazon.com offered free shipping on orders of $100 or more, and in 2003 it lowered the free shipping threshold to $25. Sales increased dramatically. Rather than paying $3.99 shipping, for instance, on a $16 book, consumers would add on a second, otherwise not demanded, book for a total of $32 in order to qualify for the "free" shipping. Thus, the consumers are increasing their purchasing volume and monetary spending, but in exchange, gaining an otherwise superfluous item and the ephemeral utility received from "free" shipping.

This paper explores the phenomenon of seemingly low-value products working as incentives to induce individuals into becoming consumers of various financial products. Choosing banking services and opening credit cards have the potential to significantly affect financial outcomes, such as credit scores, interest accumulation, and debt volume, and so we would expect consumers to place a high value on their selections of such financial products. However, in reality, we observe consumers filling out credit card applications in exchange for seemingly low-value products, such as t-shirts or one-time retail discounts, and opening checking accounts in order to receive, for example, a $50 gift card. Moreover, the prevalence of free gifts given away in exchange for the completion of a credit card application or the opening of a banking account seems to indicate that this must be a profitable practice for financial companies. If these consumption behaviors are rational, than we could assume that only the individuals who value a particular free gift object at the same level or above the value of the costs of consuming the new financial account would choose to consume the financial product tied to the free gift. Otherwise, these consumption patterns seem to violate the assumption of transitive preferences in most consumers.

Heyman and Ariely (2004) propose that the apparent irrationality occurring in the market transaction where a free item is involved should be viewed within a different context than one for positively priced products. The authors propose that consumers apply "market norms" in making decisions about products which carry a positive price. Alternatively, people

Advances in Consumer Research
Volume 39, ©2011

respond to free products through "social norms". Dan Ariely, along with various co-authors throughout the past decade, has conducted several experiments documenting the change in human behavior that occurs when positively priced products are adjusted to zero price. For instance, Ariely et al. (2006) offered to sell students a certain candy for 1¢, which resulted in an average purchase of four pieces. However, when the price of the candy became free, more students consumed the candy, but few took more than one piece. The authors propose that when a price was attached to the candy, it was a "market norm" to exchange money to the extent that the benefits of the candy exceeded the monetary cost. Alternatively, when offered for free, "social norms" guided consumption choices.

In a similar series of experiments, Shampanier et al. (2007) offered a popular, mass-market type of chocolate for 1¢ and a more luxurious brand of chocolate for various positive prices in different trials (e.g. 26¢ in one of the experiments). Next, they lowered the price of each by the same constant of 1¢, which made the former chocolate free and the more luxurious chocolate 1¢ cheaper. Subjects were also permitteded to select no chocolate for consumption at any stage of the experiments. The net benefit between the two products remained unchanged, since they each decreased in price by the same amount. Economic theory would suggest that a few participants who consumed nothing could now afford to buy the low-end chocolate at its cheaper price, and the decrease in price of the higher-end chocolate may have reached the reservation prices of some people who originally chose the low-end candy. Thus, we would expect to see a marginal increase in the quantity demanded of each product. Rather, the authors found that the zero-priced chocolate experienced a sizable "overreaction" in increased demand. In particular, a majority of those who originally purchased the high-end chocolate had decided that, even with no net change in benefits between the two products, they now preferred to consume the zero-priced chocolate. Such a change in behavior, particularly in those who originally chose to consume the high-end chocolate at its higher prices violates the transitivity condition of rational preferences.

In economic theory, rational consumers will exhibit transitive preferences through their consumption choices. As shown in Figure 1, this means that if a consumer values Product A at a higher amount than Product B and values Product B at a higher amount than Product C, then it must be the case that this same consumer will value Product A at a higher amount than Product C.

Figure 1: Transitive Preferences

$$A > B \text{ and } B > C \Rightarrow A > C$$

In order to test this rationale in the context of free gifts and two different types of retail financial products, the following hypotheses were proposed:

Hypothesis 1a: *On average, individuals will value, on their own, the products which financial companies use as free gifts at a lower value than the value they place on the costs of opening an additional credit card account.*

Hypothesis 1b: *On average, individuals will value, on their own, the products which financial companies use as free gifts at a lower value than the value they place on the costs of opening a new checking account.*

Hypothesis 2a: *On average, an individual who is not actively seeking an additional credit card will choose to complete a credit card application in exchange for certain types of free gifts.*

Hypothesis 2b: *On average, an individual who is not actively seeking a new bank checking account will choose to open a checking account in exchange for certain types of free gifts.*

Hypothesis 3a: *On average, individuals, who would not otherwise be induced to do so, will complete an application for a new credit card in exchange for certain types of free gifts, even though the costs of completing the application are higher than the individual values*

of the free gifts. That is, we will observe a violation of transitivity in consumption preferences when a particular free gift is tied to the consumption of a new additional credit card.

Hypothesis 3b: *On average, individuals, who would not otherwise be induced to do so, will open a new bank checking account in exchange for certain types of free gifts, even though the costs of opening the account are higher than the individual values of the free gifts. That is, we will observe a violation of transitivity in consumption preferences when a particular free gift is tied to the consumption of a new checking account.*

The next section describes the methodology of the experiment. Section 3 provides a discussion of the results, section 4 will conclude, and section 5 includes a discussion of potential caveats of the current experiment and suggestions for future research and follow-up to this study.

2. METHODOLOGY

2.1 Survey

In order to test the hypotheses of preferences, without biasing the survey-taker towards a particular response, three different survey instruments were created. One survey, hereafter referred to as the "gift value" survey, asked responders to write the maximum dollar amount they would pay to obtain various products. The products were included on this list because, as of this writing, they are current or past free gifts actually offered by local and national banks and credit card companies as incentives to consume new checking accounts and credit cards. A second survey, hereafter referred to as the "finance value" survey, asked responders to write separately the minimum values of the compensation needed in order for them to fill out the application for a credit card or open a new checking account. The third and final survey, hereafter referred to as the "free gift" survey, asked responders to choose which, if any, free gifts would incite them to fill out a credit card application and which, if any, free gifts would incite them to open a checking account. The free gifts were identical to the products whose values were assessed by separate survey takers in the "gift value" survey.

Each survey was randomly distributed to a single individual, with any one person taking only one of the three types of surveys. There were several reasons for this experimental design. Although it would be ideal to test transitivity of preferences in each individual, asking each observation to value the gifts and their financial data/time/effort/etc. separately runs the risk of inducing transitivity of preferences on the "free gift" questions, since the participants would be consciously engaging in an analytical thought process that may not otherwise occur when these choices are presented in actual markets. That is, in reality, the responder may not stop to consider the valuations of bundled products separately when choosing whether or not to be incited to consume one product in exchange for the receipt of the free gift product. Having responders consider the value of everything separately, before considering the choice of signing on to a financial product paired with a free gift, may illuminate the rational or irrational behavior that would, otherwise, occur subconsciously in reality.

The downside of having each individual complete only one of the three separate surveys is that a much larger sampling is necessary in order to ensure that the distribution of individuals, in terms of their backgrounds characteristics are similarly distributed across all three surveys.

2.2 Data

In total, 214 surveys were collected, mostly from an undergraduate student population. From these surveys, 195 provided usable data. The "finance value" surveys was the only one of the three survey types that had surveys excluded from the analysis. Nineteen

surveys were excluded from the analysis, either because (1) at least 50 percent of the experimental questions went unanswered or (2) the answers were extraordinary outliers[1].

3. Findings

The "gift value" survey had 78 respondents. Figure 2 illustrates the comparison of consumer-reported values with market values and Table 1 reports the descriptive statistics for each product. On average, survey respondents valued the gifts at less than their market retail value. In most of the cases, the mode of the survey respondents' valuations more closely matched with the manufacturer's suggested retail prices (MSRP) as compared to the aggregated average of all respondents. This makes sense, since we would expect a random sampling of the population to carry varying reservation prices for the same item. For example, we would expect a Dallas Cowboys supporter to value that team's fan apparel more than someone who supports another team or is disinterested in American football. Similarly, we would expect somebody who would not, otherwise, consume McDonald's food to value a $5 McDonald's gift card at a value less than $5. Thus, in order to produce more conservative results, the mode and the MSRP will be considered, in addition to survey-reported averages, in this analysis.

---

[1] For example, stating that one would fill out any arbitrary, otherwise undemanded, credit card application for no compensation resulted in the exclusion of that survey. The survey asked for responses under the assumption that the responder was not currently demanding a new credit card. Thus, there has to be some cost to fill out the application that is greater than zero, or else we would have to assume that the responder had a current demand for a new credit card. A few surveys put absurd dollar figures, including necessitating a million dollars or more in order to fill out a credit card application. It seems unlikely that the opportunity costs of time, effort, revelation of personal information, and effects on one's financial status due to filling out a credit card application would amount to such a high value. The surveys excluded for the first reason would have biased negatively the costs of consuming an additional credit card or checking account, and the surveys excluded for the latter reason would have biased positively the costs of consuming an additional credit card or checking account.

Figure 2: Log-Value of Free Gift Products

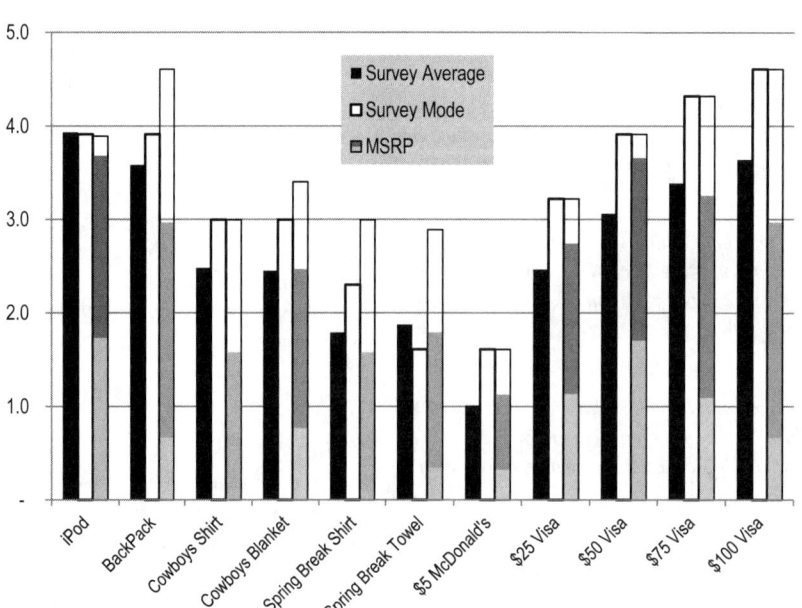

Table 1: Individual Values of "Free Gift" Products

Product (as stated on actual survey)	Survey Respondents, N = 78 (log-value in parenthesis)				MSRP
	Average	Standard Deviation	Mode		
2-GB Apple iPod Shuffle (choice of color)	$50.98 (3.93)	$2.07 (0.73)	$50		$49.00
SwissGear Backpack with laptop compartment (Black)	$35.88 (2.43)	$2.43 (0.89)	$50		$100.00
entry to win one of five Apple iPads (nationwide drawing)	$4.78 (1.57)	$3.63 (1.29)	$1		n/a
10,000 frequent flyer miles in your preferred loyalty program (assume free round-trip flight = 25,000 miles)	$38.49 (3.65)	$8.58 (2.15)	$100		n/a
Dallas Cowboys official logo shirt	$11.96 (2.48)	$4.16 (1.43)	$20		$19.99
Dallas Cowboys official logo blanket	$11.61 (2.45)	$4.04 (1.40)	$20		$29.99
coupon for 20% off of your full purchase at your favorite retailer	$4.10 (1.41)	$3.82 (1.34)	$5		n/a
$100 off of $1,000 of your credit card balance in 3 months from first use	$16.29 (2.79)	$5.35 (1.68)	$20		< $100
entry into winning one of four 2011 Toyota Tacoma compact pick-up trucks (nationwide drawing)	$8.60 (2.15)	$4.22 (1.44)	$10		n/a
2011 Spring Break t-shirt	$5.99 (1.79)	$2.53 (0.93)	$9		$19.99
2011 Spring Break beach blanket	$6.51 (1.87)	$2.64 (0.97)	$8		$17.99
$5 gift card to McDonald's	$2.75 (1.01)	$2.02 (0.70)	$5		$5
$25 Visa Gift Card	$11.76 (2.46)	$3.20 (1.16)	$25		$25 (plus loading fee)
$50 Visa Gift Card	$21.34 (3.06)	$3.71 (1.31)	$50		$50 (plus loading fee)
$75 Visa Gift Card	$29.47 (3.38)	$4.26 (1.45)	$75		$75 (plus loading fee)
$100 Visa Gift Card	$38.08 (3.64)	$4.60 (1.53)	$100		$100 (plus loading fee)

The "finance value" survey had 45 surveys. Table 3 reports the average, standard deviation, median, and mode of survey responses on how much each survey participant valued the costs of applying for a new credit card or opening a new checking account. The median and mode estimates for both products fell at $100, while the survey averages for credit cards and checking accounts fell at $115 and $144, respectively. Figure 3 illustrates the comparisons. Thus, in order to provide the most conservative estimates possible, the mode and the median will be considered, in addition to survey-reported averages, in this analysis.

Table 2: Individual Values of the Costs of Opening Financial Accounts

Product	Survey Respondents, N = 45 (log-value in parenthesis)			
	Average	Standard Deviation	Mode	Median
Personal Credit Card	$115.00 (4.74)	$3.72 (1.31)	$100	$100
Individual Checking Account	$144.11 (4.97)	$2.89 (1.06)	$100	$100

Figure 3: Log-Value of Financial Products

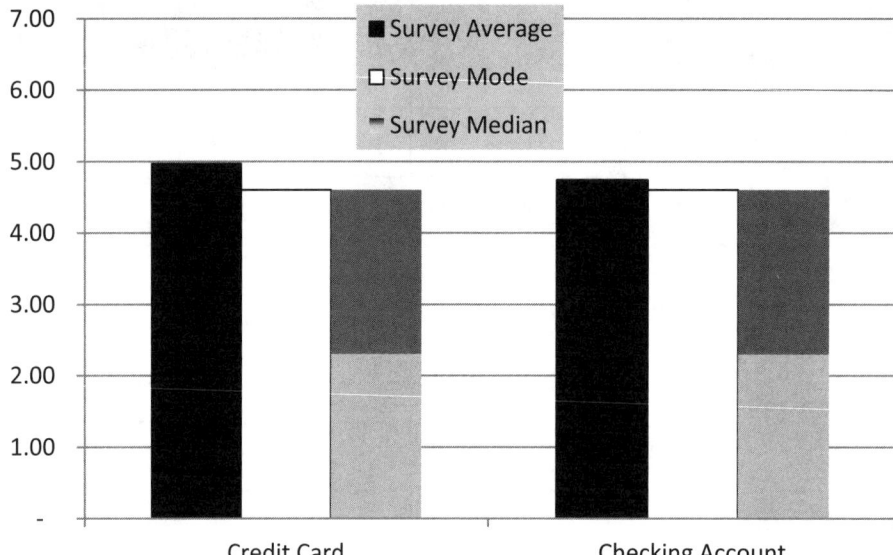

The "finance value" survey had a lower number of observations than the other two surveys, because, as mentioned above, some of the data gathered were unusable for the analysis due to respondent error. The end of this section provides a brief discussion of possible impediments for survey-takers in being able to respond accurately or at all to the experimental questions on this survey.

Finally, the "free gift" survey constructed a scenario where survey takers were asked to assume that each was not actively seeking a new credit card or checking account, although the respondent may be induced to consume the financial product with a large enough incentive (the consumer's reservation price). With that in mind, the respondents were asked to indicate which free gift products would induce each of them to fill out a credit card application and/or open a new checking account. There were 72 respondents to this survey, of which 58 percent stated that they would fill out a credit card application in exchange for a choice of at least one of the free gifts listed on

the survey. Another 17 percent stated that they would fill out a credit card application for a free gift but not for any of the ones listed on the survey. Only 25 percent stated that they would not be induced to fill out a credit card application for any type of free gift. With regards to a bank checking account, 72 percent of the survey respondents claimed that they would open a new checking account in exchange for one of the free gifts listed on the survey, 6 percent stated that they would open a new checking account for a free gift other than what was listed on the survey, and only 22 percent stated that they would not be incited by a free gift to open a new checking account. The details for this survey are summarized in Table 3.

Table 3: Preferences for "Free Gift" Products

Credit Card, N = 72		Checking Account, N = 72	
Free Gift	Percentage of respondents that would consume the financial product in exchange for the gift (frequency in parenthesis)	Free Gift	Percentage of respondents that would consume the financial product in exchange for the gift (frequency in parenthesis)
10,000 frequent flyer miles in your preferred loyalty program (assume free round-trip flight = 25,000 miles)	31% (22)	$25 Visa Gift Card	10% (7)
choice of Dallas Cowboys official logo shirt or blanket	22% (16)	$50 Visa Gift Card	19% (14)
coupon for 20% off of your full purchase at your favorite retailer	25% (18)	$75 Visa Gift Card	29% (21)
$100 off of $1,000 of your credit card balance in 3 months from first use	26% (19)	$100 Visa Gift Card	68% (49)
entry into winning one of four 2011 Toyota Tacoma compact pick-up trucks (nationwide drawing)	22% (16)	2-GB Apple iPod Shuffle (choice of color)	31% (22)
2011 Spring Break t-shirt or beach blanket	10% (7)	SwissGear Backpack with laptop compartment (Black)	18% (13)
$5 gift card to McDonald's	4% (3)	entry to win one of five Apple iPads (nationwide drawing)	14% (10)
induced by at least one of the above free gifts	59% (42)	induced by at least one of the above free gifts	72% (52)
could be induced by a free gift but not any of the above free gifts	17% (12)	could be induced by a free gift but not any of the above free gifts	6% (4)
could not be induced by any free gift	25% (18)	could not be induced by any free gift	22% (16)

3.1 Discussion of Results

Much of economic theory rests on the assumption that consumers are rational agents, meaning that their preferences exhibit completeness and transitivity. Completeness essentially means that consumers have preferences for consumption choices, and transitivity ensures that preferences maintain their order. Thus, consumers should be willing to consume a financial product that they would otherwise find too costly to consume, which has a free gift attached to its consumption, only if the free gift compensates fully for the cost of consuming the financial product.

However, this experiment has shown that respondents' preferences often violated transitivity when a "free" gift was attached to the financial product. Products that would otherwise have a lower value on their own seem to increase in value to the consumer when they are presented as free gifts, rather than as products to be consumed separately from the financial product. Otherwise, a consumer that had no demand for the financial product without the free gift should not choose to consume the financial product.

None of the free gifts were valued at an amount equal to or higher than the respondents valued the costs of filling out a credit card application or opening a new checking account. This finding provides support for both Hypothesis 1a and Hypothesis 1b. If, instead, we consider the mode and the MSRP values of the $100 Visa gift card along with the mode and median values of the opening a checking account, then the costs of opening the accounts equal the benefit value of the free gift. However, even considering this most conservative scenario, the consumer would be merely indifferent between consuming and not consuming the financial product with the $100 gift card

Of the 72 respondents to the "free gift" survey, 59 percent stated that they would consume a new credit card, which they would not otherwise demand, for one of the listed free gifts. Similarly, 72 percent stated that they would consume a new checking account that they would not otherwise demand for one of the listed gifts. Adding in the respondents that stated that they could be induced by a free gift not listed on the survey, these figures rise to 76 percent and 78 percent, respectively. These findings support both Hypothesis 2a and Hypothesis 2b.

The finding that the average respondent values, median, and MSRP values of the free gift products are lower, often to a large degree, than the costs of consuming a financial product that was not currently demanded would lead us to believe that consumers would not be enticed to consume the financial products in exchange for the lower-valued free gifts. However, we found that a substantial proportion of respondents made the decision to consume an additional, otherwise undemanded, credit card or checking account in exchange for a free gift on the list. This fact violates the transitivity assumption of rational preferences and lends support to Hypothesis 3a and Hypothesis 3b.

4. CONCLUSION

Thaler and Sunstein (2009) note, "often people have a problem in mapping products into money" (p. 95), particularly when the direct benefits of a product in exchange for its costs are obscured in intricate pricing schemes and purchase stipulations. Such is often the case when financial products are concerned. The bundled nature of many financial products, combined with the heuristic reactions to a "free" label, may inhibit consumers from appropriately maximizing their utilities from these products. Indeed, when consuming a credit card, its main function may be to allow the delay of payments for purchases for a certain length of time, but many credit cards are accompanied by, for example, car rental insurance, rewards programs, and a spectrum of liability protections and interest rate terms. Similarly, access to ATMs and branches, paper checks, direct deposit services, and deals on associated banking products, such as mortgage loans and savings accounts, are coupled with the consumption of a checking account. Thus, the "price" at which one pays for the main function of each of these financial products actually includes the purchase of several other related services that consumers have come to expect from credit cards and checking accounts. When financial companies set a price on the main product of delayed payment, in the case of a credit card, and safe storage and distribution of money, in the case of a checking account, at zero price, consumers appear to ignore the potential opportunity costs of consuming the zero price product. As Ariely (2008) observes,

> When choosing between two products, then, we often overreact to the free one. We might opt for a FREE! checking account (with no benefits attached) rather than one that costs five dollars a month. But if the five-dollar checking account includes free traveler's checks, online billing, etc., and the FREE! one doesn't, we may end up spending more for this package of services with the FREE! account than with the five-dollar account. (p. 60)

The apparent irrationality in the consumption of retail financial products, such as credit cards and checking accounts, is exacerbated by the observations that a great deal of consumers are willing (eager?) to consume otherwise undemanded financial products in exchange for "free" items that they would otherwise assess at a value lower than what they consider to be the opportunity cost of consuming the financial product.

5. POTENTIAL CAVEATS AND SUGGESTIONS FOR FUTURE RESEARCH

As the social sciences continue to explore and attempt to model consumer behavior that seems to violate economic rationality, it is important to design experiments that more closely resemble realistic environments and contexts, than what was presented in this study, under which consumer choices occur. It would be interesting to see if different outcomes would occur under an experiment which recorded *revealed* rather than *stated* preferences.

Additionally, the purpose of this study was to verify that potential violations of transitivity exist when consumers are exposed to the bundling of free gifts with the consumption of particular financial products. It was found that a considerable amount of irrational consumption behavior exists in these markets, at least according to the standard economic definition of rational preferences which presumes transitive preferences. However, it is yet to be researched what sort of traits in a consumer, if any, are correlated with different degrees of irrationality in this context. This experiment collected some superficial demographic data on age, sex, ethnicity, education, and income.

However, it may be likely that such characteristics as, for example, risk aversion, perceptions and familiarity of particular financial products, and other consumption-related attributes are significant predictors of the variation in consumer irrationality. Successors to this study should consider closer scrutiny of each observation case.

Specific terms of financial product were not described in detail on the surveys. In a realistic setting for the consumption of these products, consumers are presented with a great deal of provisions on interest rates, fees, and information disclosure, to name a few. This leads to the difficulty for consumers to decipher the true value of such products and map them to comparable monetary values. Future research may want to control for variables associated with common stipulations that accompany credit card and checking account products.

Any future research should also consider the environment in which the financial product is marketed to consumers. For example, at major sports venues, credit card companies regularly erect booths where a t-shirt or other fan paraphernalia related to the home team is offered as the free gift in exchange for the completion of the credit card application form. This is because the card companies are aware that the value of their free gift increases or decreases within the context of the setting. (This is also why we often observe, for example, the sudden increase in the price of umbrellas by convenience stores in big cities when it's raining.) Consumers have been found to demand Dallas Cowboys fan gear at the team's football stadium during a game or a spring break t-shirt promoted by an attractive seller on the beach at South Padre Island at higher values than if they were offered these things while conducting other tasks in unrelated settings. There should also be an attempt to control for the anchoring effect created by price differences. For example, a respondent may have been willing to undertake the process of opening a checking account in exchange for a $50 gift card. However, when listed as a possible free gift next to $75 and $100 gift cards, the respondent may place less value on the $50 gift card than she would have by itself, and respond that it would take at least a $75 gift card to induce her to open the checking account.

Another caveat of the current exploration was the assumption that participants of the survey had full knowledge of the attributes of the financial and other products that they were asked to value. For instance, it may have been the case that some respondents had not ever experienced the process of opening a checking account, which would make them unable to fully associate the opportunity costs involved in that task. Similarly, certain respondents may not have been aware that the brand on the free gift product of the backpack was relatively high-end and generally associated with superior quality.

Additionally, it would be valuable to be able to study rationality of consumption within each observation case. As this study was conducted through surveys, the respondents were separated into three groups of which each took a survey on a different component of variables involved in transitivity. The alternative, where each respondent would have filled out each of the three surveys carried the risk that a significant number of respondents would have identified the research premise. This would have distorted the results if the realization of the research premise induced the respondents to provide responses that appeared rational, even if that would not be their true behavior under realistic consumption scenarios where consumers do not generally stop to consider if each purchase decision maintains transitivity. Indeed, Shampanier et al. (2007) conducted a follow-up to their candy experiments in which, this time, participants were guided through each trade-off involved in their consumption decisions, including during price changes. When participants were required to analyze the costs and benefits of each choice, the authors found that "when people have access to available cognitive inputs" the "zero-price effect" vanishes and consumers make decisions according to their "true" or "rational" economic preferences (p. 754).

REFERENCES

Ariely, D. (2008). *Predictably irrational: The hidden forces that shape our decisions.* New York, NY: Harper Collins.

Ariely, D. (2009). "The curious paradox of 'optimism bias'." *Business Week*, August 24, 48.

Ariely, D., U. Gneezy, & E. Haruvy (2006). "Social norms and the price of the zeros." Working paper.

Caplin, A. & J. Leahy (2001). "Psychological expected utility theory and anticipatory feelings." *Quarterly Journal of Economics, 116*(1), 55-79.

Gintis, H. (2009). *The bounds of reason: Game theory and the unification of the behavioral sciences.* Princeton, NJ: Princeton University Press.

Heyman, J., & D. Ariely (2004). "Effort for payment: A tale of two markets." *Psychological Science, 15*(11), 787-793.

Lindstrom, M. (2008). *Buyology: Truth and lies about why we buy.* New York, NY: Doubleday.

Lovallo, D. & D. Kahneman (2003). "Delusions of success: How optimism undermines executives' decisions." *Harvard Business Review*, July, 56–63.

Poundstone, W. (2010). *Priceless: The myth of fair value (and how to take advantage of it).* New York, NY: Hill & Wang.

Thaler, R.H. (1994). *The winner's curse: Paradoxes and anomalies of economic life.* Princeton, NJ: Princeton University Press.

Thaler, R.H. & C.R. Sunstein (2009). *Nudge: Improving decisions about health, wealth, and happiness.* New York, NY: Penguin Group.

Weinstein, N. D. (1980). "Unrealistic optimism about future life events." *Journal of Personality and Social Psychology, 39*(5), 806–820.

Zweig, J. (2007). *Your money and your brain: How the new science of neuroeconomics can make you rich.* New York, NY: Simon & Schuster.

Is the Crucifix Sacred? Exploring the Catholic Consumption of sacred vessels in Building Connection with the *Sacred*

Leighanne Higgins, University of Strathclyde, UK
Kathy Hamilton, University of Strathclyde, UK

ABSTRACT

This paper aims to contribute further towards sacred consumption theories offered within consumer culture. So far, research has often pointed to instances of transcendence been found through the consumption of objects and possessions (Belk, 1988; Belk et al, 1989), white water rafting (Arnould & Price, 1993) and salsa dancing (Hamilton and Hewer, 2009). Additionally, a 'celebrity sacralization process' (Hamilton & Hewer, 2011) has been witnessed in the consumption of celebrity icons such as Barry Manilow (O'Guinn, 1991), Tom Petty and the Heartbreakers (Schau & Muniz, 2007) and Kylie Minogue (Hamilton & Hewer, 2011). In turn proving the stance taken by Belk, Wallendorf & Sherry (1989, 2) of religion being one but "not the only context in which the concept of the sacred is "operant" to be correct.

This said, relatively little research has been conducted looking at the consumption of the sacred from a religious perspective, for example within well-established religions such as Catholicism. As such the voice of the religious consumer is very much unrecognized within Consumer Culture Theory to date. This study contributes to this gap with the key aim of investigating the role of sacred vessels (religiously linked objects and services, such as crucifixes and Mass) for Catholic consumers.

THE IMPORTANCE OF RELIGION WITHIN CONSUMER CULTURE

Weber's (1930) 'Protestant Work Ethic' suggested that Puritan ethics of focus on working towards personal wealth and success, led to capitalism, secularization and "disenchantment" within society. Since Weber's concept, well-established religions and their followers have been under attack continuously, from works such as that by Gabriel Vahanian and his 'Death in God' movement of the '60's, to the numerous studies such as the 2001, 'American Religious Identification Survey' which highlighted a 9 percent decline in the number of people identifying themselves with religion. Nonetheless, in recent years there has been a resurgence in the number of people interested and consuming spirituality, in particular New-age holistic spiritualities of life (Heelas, 2008, 6), which are the consumption of spiritual experiences found "in our most valued lived experiences on what it is to be alive", but similarly are spiritualities which are "consumed, for the sake of enhancing hedonistic experiences". Heelas (2008, 6) even suggests that the popularity of the consumption of such holistic spiritualities of life might in time, "provide a worthy successor to Christianity in western settings". In short, proclaiming the situation for well-established religions such as Catholicism to be very bleak.

However, little reference, if any, is ever made to research such as the 'Beliefnet Poll' conducted in 2005, which demonstrated that 90% of Americans refer to themselves as believers. Or, the UK-wide study conducted by the charity 'Tearfund' in 2008, which found that despite perceptions of declining faith levels, 12.8 million adults in the UK go to church at least once a year. Furthermore, from the Catholic perspective, and on a global scale, the 2010 edition of the Pontifical Yearbook pointed towards an increase in the worldwide population of Catholics, with a figure of 1.166 billion, concluding that around 1 in 6 people worldwide are Catholic. Thus, there is research illustrating that the consumption of well estab-lished religions such as Catholicism is still very active and a large practice, yet as such within Consumer Culture Theory often overlooked.

CONSUMER CULTURE & SACRED CONSUMPTION

The growing abandonment of Durkheim's sacred and profane dichotomy within consumer culture, led by pioneering researchers in the field (Belk et al, 1989) and their theory of a growing sacralization of the secular and secularization of the sacred has led to the aforementioned growing acceptance of the sacred being "operant" (Belk, 1989, 8) in domains out with religion. Over the last 20 years a growing interest in consumer culture around the area of sacred consumption has occurred, resulting in shopping malls now being viewed by many as "cathedrals of consumption" (Ritzer, 2005, 7) and consumption subcultures such as that of the new bikers (Schouten & McAlexander, 1995, 50), providing "magical and otherworldly" experiences. Nevertheless, to date in consumer culture the emphasis has been upon the sacralization of the secular domains, with very little focus upon the consumption of spiritual and religious goods in order to bring about transcendental experience (Rinallo, 2009). This study will aim to contribute towards such a gap through its focus upon religiously linked objects and services, and as such a major concept used within this study has been Eliade's (1958, 9) "cryptic and clear hierophanies".

A basic description of hierophany is a manifestation of the sacred to man (Eliade, 1958). For Eliade (1958, 8) however, "some hierophanies are not clear, are indeed cryptic, in that they only reveal the sacred meaning embodied or symbolized in part, or, as it were, in code, while others (more truly *manifestations*) display the sacred in all its modalities as a whole". As such, for a Catholic consumer, a clear manifestation would be attributed to a holy site such as Lourdes, whilst an unclear or "cryptic" manifestation would be the connection build with God during the consumption of salsa dancing (Hamilton & Hewer, 2009) or other secularly deemed activities. Arnould & Price (2004, 53) echo Eliade's concept of "cryptic hierophanies", in their belief of "salvific moments" being one of three ways by which the sacred can be "identified". These moments relate to the, "unscripted eruptions of the sacred in otherwise mundane contexts" such as at "sporting events". As aforementioned, a critique in sacred consumption theory to date has been their predominant focus upon the sacralization of the secular, and through the adoption of Eliade's (1958) concept of "cryptic and clear hierophanies", we further add to this critique. As we suggest that to date, the consumption of the "cryptic hierophany" has been the focus, with very little, to no research conducted upon the consumption of "clear hierophanies", and as such this study focuses upon the "clear hierophanies", such as religiously linked objects and services, like, Mass and the crucifix, often consumed by the Catholic consumer.

In 2001, Iacobucci critiqued consumer behavior for it's lack of emphasis upon the, ""S'acred", stating that she wished to, "begin a tradition" of research that focused upon, "the subset or a narrower instantiation of the 's'acred, specifically involving an individual's experience with religion, spirituality, worship, and God" (2001, 110-111). Hence, so far within this paper, we have only referred to the un-capitalized sacred, and our reasoning for this is due to the study's grounding within platonic thinking. Iacobucci's (2001) aforementioned differentiation between the 'small' sacred and the 'capital' Sacred, is platonic thinking at it's finest. As Plato believed that tangible things were mere forms of an Absolute, and thus Plato like Iacobucci (2001), and ourselves believe there is a difference between the form of the sacred and the Absolute Idea of the Sacred. A predominant research focus upon cryptic hierophanies, has resulted in Iacobucci's (2001) estimation that to date a metaphorical level of sacred has been researched as opposed to the Absolute level of the Sacred. We agree with this opinion and as such we will differentiate throughout this paper between the sacred and the *Sacred*, with the former relating to the sacred at a metaphorical level and the latter relating to the Absolute form of the *Sacred.*

THE RELIGION-CONSUMPTION DICHOTOMY

Focus within consumer culture has been as aforementioned on breaking down the dichotomy of the sacred and the profane, but an even greater dichotomy exists between religion and consumption, and the belief that the two of them cannot integrate. We believe this dichotomy has came about due to the generally "negative associations" (Heelas, 2008, 83) held regarding consumption. Wattanasuwan (2005, 183) discusses that we are all "enslaved" to consumption and likewise Ekstrom & Brembeck (2001, 1-2) state, "consumption (and consumerism) is gradually trickling into all areas of human life". Thus, the general negative feeling shared towards consumption by many, has led to the belief that religion and consumption cannot be mixed positively. As such, we suggest this may be the reason for a lack of focus upon the religious consumer within consumer culture to date.

However, some papers have rallied to join Iacobucci's (2001, 110-111) call for beginning "a tradition" of research focusing on an, "individual's experience with religion, spirituality, worship, and God". And in doing so have managed to demonstrate that there is no need for such a dichotomy, as religion and consumption can be and are mixed together, and positivity reigns from such mélange. Touzani & Hirschman (2008: 379) in their representation of the Muslim consumer found that, "religious patterns can be and are appropriated into consumption styles without undermining Islam itself". Similarly, Sandikci & Ger (2010, 33) found in their work that, "Islam is neither a threat nor a panacea for consumerism and capitalism", whilst Higgins & Hamilton (2011) found though their work on the consumption of sacred pilgrimage sites, like Lourdes, that the religious pilgrims accepted the near proximity of the commercialized side of Lourdes as a "modern day penance" to their pilgrimage. Furthermore, the use of the word consumption can be dated back to biblical times, as the New Testament mentions that on Pentecost, a day of huge significance within Christianity, the Apostles were consumed by the fire of the Holy Spirit and as such became one with God. So, consumption has been around as long as religion, and likewise has been mixed together over the centuries, thus proving that there is a need for more research focused on breaking down the religion-consumption dichotomy. As such, this study will further add to this growing "tradition", by offering the voice of the Catholic consumer, and investigating the ways in which Catholic consumers consume "clearer hierophanies" such as Mass and crucifixes, as a method for building connection with God.

METHOD

It is often said that 'a chain is only as strong as it's weakest link' and due to this we thought it best to deal with what could possibly be viewed as a weakness in this study – one of the researcher's Catholic beliefs. This study was in conjunction with a wider study, investigating the affects of the current financial crisis upon the consumption of Catholic Mass in Scotland. This phenomenon was recognized within the home parish of the main researcher, and as such we adopted a single case study. Although some may argue that this is too close a position for the researcher, previous research within the area, raised awareness of the reservations many religious consumers feel at being interviewed about faith. As such through familiarity within the parish, the researcher was able to overcome the access and trust issues that can often arise in single case studies (Dutton & Dukerich, 1991). Furthermore, it was our belief, that the shared religion resulted in a high level of 'verstehen' (Wax; 1967) being encapsulated within the researcher, which was believed to only further strengthen the research, as it resonated with Schouten & McAlexander (1995:44) and their finding that deeper integration with the subculture of new bikers enabled, "access to informants near the core of the subculture" to improve greatly. Thus, as a member of the Catholic faith, the presence of 'verstehen' within the researcher enabled gaining of a better understanding of respondents.

The case study parish has the motto of "serving the community" and approximately 1200 regular Sunday mass attendees. We conducted one to one interviews with twenty-one of these regular attendees; half of the sample was generated through a response sheet distributed throughout the parish. The other half was generated through a snowballing method. All respondents were Catholic, and as shown in table one, they ranged in age, gender and occupation.

Table One: Profile of Respondents

Respondent's Name	*Gender*	*Age*	*Occupation*
Chloe	Female	50-64	Retired nurse
Craig	Male	25-34	Secondary School Teacher
Faye	Female	35-49	Unemployed
Fr. Grant	Male	50-64	Priest
Fr. Jack	Male	35-49	Parish Priest
James	Male	35-49	Ironmonger
Kevin	Male	35-49	Works in Prisons
Lisa	Female	50-64	Classroom assistant (Primary school)
Maria	Female	16-24	Works in benefits dept
Moira	Female	50-64	Seamstress

Miriam	Female	50-64	Retired Primary Teacher
Paul	Male	50-64	Retired/ Now a part-time Lolly-Pop Man
Penny	Female	50-64	Sales Assistant
Philip	Male	50-64	Retired
Rachael	Female	35-49	Nursing background/ works in health sector (NHS)
Renee	Female	65+	Retired Primary Headmistress
Ryan	Male	35-49	College Lecturer
Sally	Female	35-49	Interpreter for deaf
Sister Catherine	Female	50-64	Nun
Sister Julie	Female	35-49	Nun
Tom	Male	50-64	IT Technician

The parish priest of the single case study assisted by allowing the interviews to be conducted in a social room within the parish, providing a context where both the interviewer and the respondent felt comfortable (Thomson & Hayto, 1997). On average the interviews lasted 90 minutes. Interview discussion centered-around the aforementioned idea of Mass consumption during the current financial crisis, with peripheral discussions around coping and the sacred consumption practices adopted by Catholic consumers. This latter theme emerged from preliminary interviews whereby the theme of sacredness emerged as important and relevant to consumer culture. The interviews were audio-recorded and transcribed. A hermeneutic logic was then followed to analyze the data, following both intra-textual (Thompson, 1997) and inter-textual cycles (Thompson, 1996), whereby similar patterns and major points of difference were collated across all transcriptions.

FINDINGS

Although many themes emerged throughout the study, the key theme from the research to be discussed within this paper is that of *the consumption of sacred vessels*. However, prior to discussing this key theme, it is important to understand our findings from this research on the Catholic consumer's perceptions of the *Sacred*.

Sacred Perceptions

"It means to me the accumulated wisdom of 2000 years, where people have tried to live out their relationship with God and it becomes shared in that sort of body of teaching or way of spirituality"

(Fr Jack).

In order to understand the Catholic consumer's perception of the *Sacred*, it is important to firstly, understand respondents definition of Catholicism. The preceding definition from Fr. Jack, the parish priest of the single case study, is apt as it demonstrates a shared viewpoint amongst all participants in this study – that Catholicism is a way of life. But more than that, the reference of Catholicism being about ones 'relationship with God' indicates towards individuality being present within Catholicism, resonating with the all-embracing, universal meaning of the word. Highlighting that Catholicism can mean different things to each individual Catholic, but that at its core they will each share a set of beliefs unifying them together as one distinct religious institution. This shared unity amongst Catholic consumers was revealed in many ways throughout the study, one such way being the shared perception of the *Sacred*.

All respondents agreed that the *Sacred*, *"can be open to interpretation"* (James) and that connection with the *Sacred*, *"can come in the most strange sort of ways"* (Philip). This said, all respondents shared descriptors of the *Sacred* as being: "out of this world", "everlasting and immortally beautiful", "irreplaceable", "holy". Similarly, the respondents all shared the belief in the *Sacred* being an "intangible presence", often difficult to explain and understand.

Lisa: *"I mean people use the term 'out of this world' and it is like that in a way, it is beyond the reach yet striving to reach it"*.

Fiona: *"sacred means for me, a set apartness from the daily grind of the world, it is something that is above all of that - it is something that is not of this world ".*

Craig: *"I personally would not say that the most sacred thing to me is something that I could physically hold or touch"*.

Ryan: *" I think it is a personal relationship with God. Yeah, I suppose a sacred space or a sacred time is a time when you would feel very much one-to-one with God so yeah, I think it is your relationship with God"*

This shared belief in the intangible quality of the *Sacred*, resonates with Belk et al's (1989, 9) offering of "intangibles" as one of six potential sacred consumption domains. However, within Consumer Culture Theory to date, there appear issues regarding terminology, and as such our findings show that for the Catholic consumer it is the actual absolute *Sacred* which is intangible, and connection with this intangible *Sacred* is built through the consumption of religiously linked objects and services such as Mass, and the crucifix. As such, respondent's shared belief in this intangible *Sacred*, led onto deep discussion into what many would believe to be a rhetoric question – is the crucifix sacred? We found that for the Catholic consumer, the crucifix – the actual tangible, crucifix positioned within chapels, and homes, and worn upon necks worldwide – is not *Sacred*, leading onto the key theme and contribution from this study – *the consumption of sacred vessels*.

The consumption of sacred vessels

"…Give them something to look at and they will understand it, but they don't understand that presence and I don't either, but I

know it is there, and I couldn't logically try to give you an explanation, but there is something there, but we give ourselves something to fixate on" (James).

This response successfully introduces the idea of sacred vessels, as it indicates a common belief amongst Catholic consumers, that the *Sacred* sought after by mankind is untouchable and incomprehensible whilst we are living. Studies to date, on the resurgence of spiritualities of life (Hellas, 2008), and within consumer culture, have shown that, "humans are spiritual seekers, even in a consumer society that so many critics say leads to apathy and meaninglessness" (Scott & Maclaren, 2009, 60), indicating that man has an awareness of the presence of an Absolute, which for the Catholic consumer is God. But, our research suggests, in order to connect with this presence we give ourselves tangible resources to help us fixate and understand the *Sacred*. Continuously respondents illustrated that the crucifix, religious statues of Our Lady, and other saints, although special and deserving of respect, were but, "reminders", "figureheads", "connectors", "vessels" which all help the religious consumer to communicate and connect with the absolute *Sacred*, with God.

Chloe: *" I love to light candles and pray at Our Ladies alter – but I don't look at that as being a golden calf, as Sacred, it is just a vessel in which to pray through, a vessel to get through to God".*

Maria: *"At the end of the day the crucifix is only a wooden cross, it is more what that sort of stands for that I would class to be Sacred rather than the object or the cross itself".*

Miriam: *"Objects cannot actually themselves be Sacred but they can focus, they can be an visual representation of something ".*

James: *"You could remove the statue and the presence would still be there, the statue is only a figurehead".*

This vessel idea was further supported through the examples of respondent's consumption of religious jewelry such as, the wearing of medals and crucifixes upon their necks.

James: *"I wear a crucifix – and I don't know if I would say that it was that Sacred - but it is so, so special to me. And I get up every morning and I make sure it is on the right way, it's never off my body - it's always there... but it just makes me feel as though there is somebody with me"*

Tom: *"I wear medals round my neck and I have always worn symbols around my neck, but they are not Sacred, they are just a reminder, they are a help to me, if I forget things and all of a sudden I hear them jangle, it is a sort of wake up call".*

The wearing of such jewelry symbolizes the Catholic consumers connection with God, resonating with Fernandez & Veer's (2004, 55) work on the symbolism of jewelry during Hindu wedding rituals. And as such this research contributes further to symbolic consumption theories (McCracken, 1988).

To date, within symbolic consumption the emphasis has been upon the 'self-concept' whereby consumers "employ consumption not only to create and sustain the self but also to locate us in society" (Wattanasuwan, 2005, 179), and as such, "material possessions serve as symbolic mediators between the self and others" (Wattanasuwan, 2005, 182). Symbolic consumption, however, has been researched at more conspicuous levels (Schouten, 1991), with the aim of con-

sumption being the consumer's attempts to create the identity they wish to communicate with others. Popular New- Age spiritualities of life resonate very much with what has been looked at within symbolic consumption to date, as these spiritualities offer consumers the chance of self-spirituality, with the focus of these new-age spiritualities being "locked"(Heelas, 2008, 7) within the self. However, this study points to a different dimension of symbolic consumption. For the sacred consumption of candles, and the wearing of religious jewelry are all consumed at an individual and private level, aiding the Catholic consumer to build further their connection with the *Sacred*. But this symbolic consumption practice is not about creating an identity for others to see, but is about the personal connection build with the *Sacred*.

Furthermore, the symbolic consumption of Mass differs from that mentioned above and within symbolic consumption theories to date, as it is a shared consumption practice.

Ryan: *"I thoroughly enjoy mass, I love the way that it crosses so many boundaries; time, history, geography, people who have died, people who are still to come, we pray for the people here now and we pray for the whole church. I think it's a deep leveller, knowing that for 12 hours before us and 12 hours after us people will still be celebrating mass throughout the world and I think that's just a beautiful concept".*

Philip: *"I live almost six thousand miles away from my mother, and that she still goes to mass, that she will be having a different but a similar experience to me because we are part of something big".*

The idea of being part *"of something bigger than myself"* echoed amongst respondents and as such it came to the forefront that Mass is a symbolic consumption practice adopted by Catholic consumers as a way of developing and building their personal relationship with God. Further than this however, through the shared symbolic consumption of Mass, the Catholic consumer focuses not upon the self, but upon the fact that through their faith, they belong and are part of something "much bigger" than the self, and through this selflessness, the Catholic consumer is able to build connection with the entire Catholic community as well as with the *Sacred*. Belk et al (1989, 31) suggest that consumption of the sacred is rooted in consumers' needs for self-differentiation through their consumption of something out with the ordinary, in turn providing, "meaning in life and a mechanism for experiencing stability, joy, and occasionally ecstasy through connection". However our findings demonstrate the antithesis, as we demonstrate that consumption of sacred vessels enable connection with the absolute idea of the *Sacred* but also enable collectivism with the entire body of Catholicism. As such our research resonates more with Belk's (2010, 725) discussion on the idea of "sharing-in" whereby "others are included within the aggregate self". For through the shared consumption of Mass respondents felt barriers of race, age, and social-class break down between them. However, at a deeper level, the preceding usage of the word 'community' and the sharing-in amongst respondents whilst consuming Mass, enables a symbolic consumption practice that narrows the boundaries between: life and earth, the past, present and future, geographical separations, in short it symbolizes the connection build with the entire body of Catholicism as it has been for the last 2000 years, and as it will continue to be in the future.

Plato stated, "the truth of the matter, is after all, only known to God" (Plato Republic, 1954: 282). We likewise conclude that due to it's discombobulate nature, complete understanding of the

Sacred is an improbable if not impossible feat, and as such it is incorrect to state that research to date in consumer culture has focused upon the *Sacred* in it's entirety. This said, we suggest that what has been researched to date in consumer culture has in fact been the '*consumption of sacred vessels*' not the consumption of the absolute form of the *Sacred*. Thus in short, Arnould & Price's (1993) respondents consumed the sacred vessel of white water rafts as a method for building connection with their *Sacred*; likewise Hamilton & Hewer's (2009) "salseros" consumed the salsa dance floor as a sacred vessel for connecting with their *Sacred*. And in the religious context our Catholic consumers consume the crucifixes in their churches, homes, and around their necks as sacred vessels for building connection with their absolute *Sacred*. As such the material world provides a platform enabling man to connect with the *Sacred*, and likewise for the Catholic consumer the shared symbolic consumption of Mass is a sacred vessel enabling connection to be build with God, but likewise to build connection with the entire body of Catholicism.

Continuously, throughout the analysis process, we debated whether, in fact *sacred vessels of consumption* was the correct terminology. Primarily the usage of the word *vessel* was debated, especially in light of the recent work from Fernandez & Lastovicka (2011) on fetishes, which demonstrates the idea of 'conduits' with the more powerful. However, the shared usage of the word 'vessel' amongst respondents made us turn to the bible for answers, leading us to the biblical sense of the word of vessel as meaning something believed to hold or embody a particular quality and the sacred vessels discussed in this research behold a particular quality, which enables connection with the absolute *Sacred*. A priest once mentioned to us that the sign of the cross made before a prayer is the dialing of a telephone call between man and God. Likewise, for the respondents in this research the statues, the crucifix, the Mass, are not bridges or portals, for this almost gives the impression of them being immaterial and moving. Instead using the telephone metaphor, the statues, crucifix, Mass are all material telephones, which enable the dialing/ connection between man and the absolute *Sacred* to occur. Hence we remain with the term vessel, as opposed to bridge, portal or conduit to communicate the often, material nature of these metaphorical sacred vessels. Secondly, our reasons for this particular terminology stemmed from the spirituality of life movement (Heelas, 2008), which differentiates between spirituality and transcendence theism (religion), suggesting that the former is about man creating and giving meaning to life, whereas the latter is relating to the idea of being given the meaning of life from a higher being such as, God. As such we questioned if perhaps the "cryptic hierophanies" studied within consumer culture to date such as Schouten & McAlexander's (1995) new bikers, had in fact been the consumption of spirituality as opposed to sacred consumption? However, this seemed a somewhat arrogant viewpoint, and as such it did not sit well with the researchers. For who has the right to claim that the connection build with the *Sacred* through spiritualities of life, differs from those build through Catholicism or any other well-established religion? Thus we suggest that the *Sacred* is *Sacred*, and mans approximation of the *Sacred* cannot be changed, due to our inability to understand the *Sacred* in it's entirety. In turn suggesting that the *Sacred* connection built by white water rafters, salseros, celebrity aficionados, new-age life spiritualists, Catholics and a plethora of other consumers who practice sacred consumption habits is the same *Sacred*, and does not change. It is the *sacred vessels* for building connection with the *Sacred* that changes, not the over-arching Absolute itself. In saying this we recognized from our study, that the aforementioned terminological issue has

it's routes in the idea of transcendence, and as such we suggest that future research lies in furthering consumer culture's terminology, particularly in the area of transcendence.

CONCLUSIONS

This study has added to Iacobucci's (2001, 110-111) call for a "tradition" of research within consumer culture that researches "an individual's experience with religion, spirituality, worship, and God", and as such, we have shown that it is possible for consumption and religion to come together in useful ways. Hence, illustrating that the dichotomy existing between religion and consumption within consumer culture and society as a whole, should be eliminated. Our primary focus for this paper has been upon the Catholic consumption of sacred vessels to build connection with the *Sacred*. Thus, regarding theoretical contributions, we have further contributed to sacred consumption theory, but also an emergent contribution for this study has been within the area of symbolic consumption.

On deciding the title for this paper we questioned the appropriateness of the use of the question, "is the crucifix sacred?" But upon reflection we realized that without such discussion this paper and as such its realizations would never have been born. As the crucifix is key to understanding our findings and contributions to sacred consumption theory, for if the most significant symbol for one of the widest established religions is not regarded as *Sacred*, it is fair to concur that the majority of sacred consumption studies to date, if not all, have not focused upon the absolute idea of the *Sacred*. As such, we conclude that in Consumer Culture Theory to date, the *Sacred* in itself has not been studied, but in fact '*sacred vessels*' enabling connection with the absolute idea of the *Sacred* have been the predominant focus. And as such, we suggest the deconstruction of sacred consumption theory to date to incorporate such a finding.

Regarding symbolic consumption our work has contributed by showing that the consumption of sacred vessels such as religious jewelry and candles are symbolic consumption practices, which for the Catholic consumer are consumed at the individual, and private level, not at the conspicuous level but with the aim of drawing closer and building connection with the *Sacred*. Likewise, our findings have demonstrated that the consumption of Mass is not an individually symbolic consumption practice, but a shared one. Focusing upon building personal connection with God, but likewise about building connection with the body of Catholicism in its entirety. Thus, we have shown symbolic consumption practices from the Catholic consumer, which go against the norms of conspicuous symbolic consumption, which have been the forerunners within symbolic consumption theory to date. Additionally, this research points towards the complete antithesis of self-differentiation within sacred consumption as we demonstrate that the consumption of sacred vessels builds communication with God/ the absolute *Sacred*, but simultaneously builds connection and communality with the entire body of Catholicism.

Ger (2005:79) questioned, "How does sacred religion appropriate the profane consumption...how does the spiritual interplay with the material?" We reference St. Paul in answering this query, "the world, life and death, the present and the future are all your servants; but you belong to Christ and Christ belongs to God" (3:16-23). Thus, God gave man the material world to serve their needs, in short it is a playground for man to interact upon, and as such draw closer to Him. The findings from this study agree with St. Paul, as they demonstrate that material goods provide an interactional platform with the *Sacred*, for through consumption of the material world consumers are able to build connection and draw closer to the *Sacred*. Our research therefore, adds further to research such as Touzani & Hirschman (2008) and Sandikci & Ger (2010) which have proven that the dichotomy existing between religion and consumption is a false one, as consumption does not demean religion, but often has a "symbiotic relationship" with it.

Throughout this study we have discovered that within consumer culture there appear issues regarding terminology. Through our adoption of Plato and Iacobucci's (2001) differentiation between the metaphorical form of the sacred and the absolute idea of the *Sacred*, we have introduced a body of theory addressing such terminological issues, with our *consumption of sacred vessels* concept. Nonetheless, confusion remains within consumer culture whereby words such as sacred, spiritual, and especially transcendent are all used inter-changeably. And as such, we suggest that instead of continuous focus upon secularizations, sacralizations, or even upon the consumption of religiously/spiritually linked goods, which help build connection with the *Sacred*, we need to start questioning and focusing upon terminology. And in doing so we shall be able to further diminish the religion-consumption dichotomy present within consumer culture and society today. We believe a predominant conundrum exists in consumer culture's usage of the word transcendence, and as such we suggest that future research begins with questioning transcendence terminology, by asking and answering: "What is transcendence and in what ways do the transcendental feelings experienced during differing consumption practices resonate or differ?

REFERENCES

Arnould, E.J., Price, L.L. (1993), 'River Magic: Extraordinary Experience and the Extended Service Encounter', *Journal of Consumer Research*, 20 (June), 24-44.

Arnould, E.J. (2004). 'Beyond the Sacred-Profane Dichotomy in Consumer Research', *Special Session Summary for Advances in Consumer Research*, Vol. 31 (1), pp. 52-54.

Belk, R.W. (1988). 'Possessions and the extended self', *Journal of Consumer Research*, Vol.15 (1), pp.139-168.

Belk, R.W., Wallendorf, M., and Sherry, J.F. (1989), 'The sacred and the profane in consumer behavior: theodicy on the Odyssey', *Journal of Consumer Research*, Vol. 16, June, pp. 1-37.

Belk, R.W. (2010), 'Sharing', *Journal of Consumer Research*, 36 (Feb), 715-734.

Dutton, J. E., & Dukerich, J. M. (1991). 'Keeping an eye on the mirror: The role of image and identity in organizational adaptation'. *Academy of Management Journal*, vol. 34, pp.517–554.

Ekstrom, K.M, Brembeck, H. (eds) (2004). Elusive Consumption, Oxford: Berg, pp.1-7.

Eliade, M. (1958). Cited in Belk, R.W., Wallendorf, M., and Sherry, J.F. (1989), 'The sacred and the profane in consumer behavior: theodicy on the Odyssey', *Journal of Consumer Research*, Vol. 16, June, pp. 1-37.

Fernandez, K.V., Lastovicka, J.L. (2011). "Making Magic: Fatishes in Contemporary Consumption", *Journal of Consumer Research*, Vol. 38, pp. 1-23.

Fernandez, K.V., Veer, E. (2004). "The Gold that Binds: The Ritualistic Use of Jewelry in A Hindu Wedding", *Advances in Consumer Research*, Vol. 31, pp.55.

Fox, A. (1945). *Plato for Pleasure*, Westhouse Publications, UK, pp. 170.

Ger, G. (2005). 'Religion and Consumption: The Profane Sacred', *Advances in Consumer Research: Special Session Summary,* vol.32, pp.79-81.

Hamilton, K., Hewer, P. (2009), 'Salsa Magic: An Exploratory Netnographic Analysis of the Salsa Experience', in *Advances in Consumer Research* Vol. 36, ed. Ann L. McGill and Sharon Shavitt, Duluth MN: Association for Consumer Research, 502-508.

Heelas, P. (2008). *Spiritualities of Life: New Age Romanticism & Consumptive Capitalism*, Blackwell Publishing, pp. 283.

Hewer, P.A., Hamilton, K.L. (2011 Forthcoming) *On Consuming Celebrities: The Case of the Kylie E-Community. Advances in Consumer Research*, vol. 28.

Higgins, L., & Hamilton, K.L. (2011 Forthcoming) *Sacred Places: An Exploratory Investigation of Consuming Pilgrimage.* Advances in Consumer Research, vol. 28.

Iacobucci, D. (2001). 'Commonalities between research methods for consumer science and biblical scholarship', *Marketing Theory*, vol.1 (1), 109-133.

McCracken, G. (1988). *Culture & Consumption: New Approaches to the Symbolic Character of Consumer Goods and Activities*, Bloomington: Indiana University Press.

O'Guinn, T. C. (1991), "Touching Greatness: The Central Midwest Barry Manilow Fan Club," in *Highways and Buyways: Naturalistic Research from the Consumer Behavior Odyssey,* Special Volumes, Association for Consumer Research, 102-111.

Radice, B., Baldick R. (eds). (1954). *Plato: The Republic*, Penguin Classics, pp. 405.

Ritzer, George (2005), *Revolutionizing the Means of Consumption: Enchanting a Disenchanted World*, US: Pine Forge Press, pp.258.

Sandikci, O., Ger, G. (2010). "Veiling in Style: How Does a Stigmatized Practice Become Fashionable?", *Journal of Consumer Research*, Vol. 37, pp. 15-35.

Schau, H.J., Muniz, A.M. Jnr. (2005). 'Temperance and Religiosity in a Non-Marginal, Non–Stigmatized Brand Community, Cited in Cova, B., Kozinets, R., Shankar, A. (2007). *Consumer tribes*, Butterworth Heinemann, Elsevier, 1st edition, pp. 339.

Schouten, J.W. (1991). "Selves in Transition: Symbolic Consumption in Personal Rites of Passage and Identity Reconstruction", *Journal of Consumer Research*, Vol. 17, pp. 412- 425.

Schouten, J.W., McAlexander, J.H. (1995). 'Subcultures of Consumption: An Ethnography of the New Bikers', *Journal of Consumer Research*, vol.22 (June 1995), pp. 43-61.

Scott, L., Maclaran, P. (2009), '"Roll your own" Religion: Consumer Culture and the Spiritual Vernacular', in *Advances in Consumer Research*, Vol. 36, ed. Ann L. McGill and Sharon Shavitt, Duluth, MN: Association for Consumer Research, 60-63.

Thompson, C.J. (1996).'Caring Consumers: Gendered Consumption Meanings and the Juggling Lifestyle'. *Journal of Consumer Research*, vol.22 pp.338-407.

Thompson, C.J. (1997). 'Interpreting Consumers: A Hermeneutical Framework for Deriving Marketing Insights from the Texts of Consumers' Consumption Stories'. *Journal of Marketing Research*, vol. 34 pp. 438-455.

Thompson, C.J., Hayto, D.L. (1997). 'Speaking of Fashion: Consumers Uses of Fashion Discourses and the Appropriation of Countervailing Cultural Meanings'. *Journal of Consumer Research*, vol. 24 pp. 15-42.

Touzani, M., Hirschman, E.C. (2009). 'Cultural Syncretism and Ramadan Observance: Consumer Research Visits Islam', *Advances in Consumer Research,* Vol. 35, pp: 374-380.

Wattanasuwan, K. (2005). "The Self & Symbolic Consumption", *The Journal of American Academy of Business*, March, pp. 179-184.

Wax, M. L. (1967). 'On Misunderstanding Verstehen: A Reply to Abel'. *Journal of Sociology & Social Research.* Vol: 51. Pg: 323-333.

Weber, M. (1985) [1904-5]. *The Protestant Ethic and the Spirit of Capitalism*, London.

A Luxury Perspective on Brands - Characteristics, Value, and the Eye of the Beholder

Renu Emile, AUT School of Business, Auckland, New Zealand
Margaret Craig-Lees, AUT School of Business, Auckland, New Zealand

INTRODUCTION

This paper is part of a wider study that investigates whether and how consumers use products or brands to construct, support or communicate aspects of their self to others. A facet of the study is to ascertain if consumers identify luxury brands. If so, what brands do they speak of? How do they use them in relation to their self? The self is, to a degree, a nebulous concept and difficult to operationalize. Reed (2002) lists six paradigms and also presents a cogent argument for the notion that 'the self, social relationships, and social identity' paradigm should dominate consumer research. The self is "a reflective mirror born out of social interaction with the individual's social milieu, as an object that arises out of social interaction; an outgrowth of people's reactions of appropriate behaviour; as an enacted role for a particular audience; as a universe of potential different identities that may guide behaviour" (Reed 2002: 250-251).

Reed's use of the term social identity accords with that of Tajfel and Turner (1979, 1986). The self, social relationships, and social identity paradigm does not negate the notion that the self comprises of at least two interacting facets - the persona (the self as denoted by characteristics and abilities) and the social self (the self as denoted by roles and status). It recognises that these are interrelated and their formation is a function of social interaction. The consumption of product/brand choice is a social activity - irrespective of a public/private consumption situation, primarily because the meanings associated with product/brand choice are socially constructed.

CHARACTERISTICS OF THE LUXURY BRAND: THE BRAND MANAGER PERSPECTIVE

Characterising the luxury brand is tricky as luxury is an elusive concept. Phau and Prendergast (2000) note the subjectivity of the term and the consequential difficulty in the differentiation from the ordinary. In other words, the perception of what is or not a luxury brand is context driven and people dependent, and it may be hard indeed to categorise products or brands as luxury or non-luxury. Vigneron and Johnson (2004) contend that even though a brand may be perceived as luxurious, not all luxury brands are deemed equally luxurious. For example, while both a Cadillac and a Rolls-Royce may be perceived as luxury cars, the Rolls-Royce could be considered to be more luxurious than the Cadillac. This being said, the notion of the 'luxury' brand is widely recognised. The decision to position a brand as a luxury brand is of course the province of the brand manager. Once such a decision is made, then specific actions are required in order to create and maintain this position.

Kapferer (1998) lists product aesthetics, quality, uniqueness, sensuality as key attributes that need to be combined with exclusivity - in terms of distribution and permission (i.e., who should be associated with and/or allowed to use). Central to the luxury brand position is a strong brand identity. According to Keller (2009), a luxury position requires actions that will result in a premium image such as a selective (exclusive) channel strategy, premium pricing strategy with strong quality cues and few discounts and mark downs, the use of high status persons as endorsers, attention to logos, symbols, packaging and consistent linking to prestigious communication mediums and events linked to the brand. Similarly, Fionda and Moore (2009), based on interviews with managers of luxury brands found that they advocate attention to quality, and craftsmanship, design signature/

uniqueness, premium price, exclusivity of editions, range and distribution, consistent linking to prestigious communication mediums and the creation of events linked to the brand. Undoubtedly, the intention is for the consumer to see the brand as special in some way at both the personal and public level; the latter of course using the brand as a 'Veblen' good, a means to displaying wealth and status.

CONSUMERS AND LUXURY BRANDS

To date, the handful of studies that investigate consumers' perceptions of luxury brands and/or products examine brands preselected by the researcher and assess responses to predetermined scales (Dubious and Paternault 1995; Dubois, Czellar and Laurent 2005; Christodoulides, Michaelidou and Li 2009; Husic and Cicic 2009; Vickers and Renand 2003; Vigneron and Johnson 2004). To facilitate the identification of luxury brands, Vigneron and Johnson developed a brand luxury index (BLI). The BLI items comprise of attributes - non-personal such as conspicuousness, uniqueness and quality, and personal such as hedonism and extended self - to form an overall index of luxury. The scale was developed using data collected from a student sample in Australia. Christodoulides et al. (2009) tested the scale in the context of Taiwanese students and report concerns with dimensionality and contextual issues. They conclude that more research is necessary to determine the viability of the scale.

Even so, extant studies that examine consumer perceptions of luxury brands suggest that consumers are able to identify characteristics of products or brands they associate with the concept of luxury. For example, the participants in the Dubious and Paternault (1995) study associate luxury goods with the attribute of rarity and by definition exclusivity. Dubois, Czellar and Laurent (2005) found that their 'elitist' segment, i.e., those consumers who acknowledge the luxury concept also identified rarity and exclusivity as luxury attributes. The exclusivity factor is linked to the notion that only people of refinement and good taste appreciate luxury goods. Vickers and Renand (2003) examined how consumers use luxury goods and their findings support the notions of exclusivity, refinement and status, in particular the public conferring of status. Husic and Cicic (2009) also found that the key role of the luxury brand is the communication of prestige and status.

Wiedman, Hennigs and Siebels (2007) developed a framework to study luxury value perception - a framework that could be used across cultures. Similar to Vigneron and Johnson, they suggest that when determining the value of the 'luxury' element, what should be measured is value in relation to price, quality, usability, uniqueness, self-identity, hedonic, materialistic, conspicuousness and prestige. These constructs form the nexus of their proposed conceptual framework.

METHODOLOGY

This study concerns with examining how young adult consumers use brands in the context of managing aspects of their self. One facet of the task is to ascertain if they identify luxury brands. If they do, how they do so. The underlying premise is that if brands are deemed to be luxury, the attributes should be clearly articulated to consumers, and so consumers should have understanding of the explicit and implicit meanings in their decision to use the brand. This study explores the degree of consciousness accorded to the notion of luxury in relation to products or brands by specifically addressing the following questions: Do consumers display a conscious awareness of the luxury element in the products/brands they choose to display aspects of the 'self'? If so, what brands do they speak of? How do they talk about the concept in general and in relation to their self?

The study focuses on young adults between the ages of 18 and 21 and uses a set of interpretive procedures (Denzin and Lincoln, 2000). The study requires data that is essentially individual interpretations and inferences of phenomena, so is positioned within the interpretivist paradigm and adopts a phenomenological oriented approach to data collection (Husserl 1970; Schutz, 1970; Thompson, Locander and Pollio 1989). Participants were instructed to photograph those products or brands that indicated an aspect of their self such as their personality, characteristics, abilities, attitudes, roles and status. The auto-photography approach allows participants to speak for themselves and reduces researcher bias (e.g., Kjeldgaard 2004; Noland 2006; Ziller 1990). Once the cameras were returned and photographs developed, each participant was interviewed for about an hour.

The transcribed interviews were analyzed as per guidelines suggested by Potter and Wetherell (1987), Wetherell and Potter (1988),

Owen (1984) and Carabine (2001). Essentially this meant identifying themes, words and phrases for variability and consistency across interviews. To reduce subjective bias, the transcribed interviews were also analyzed by two independent analyzers. Differences were sorted by mutual discussion and agreement.

FINDINGS & DISCUSSION

The final sample comprised of twenty eight participants. 12 (42 %) were of European ethnicity, 7 (25%) of Maori, 5 (18%) of Indian, 3 (15%) of Chinese, and 1 (3%) of Middle East ethnicity. Participants identified brands across fifteen product categories. These were - shoes, bags, clothes, Mp3 players, mobile phones, cars, computers, cosmetics, food and drink, electronic equipment, sunglasses, perfume, wallet and watches, alcohol and wine, and miscellaneous. Of the fifteen product categories, eight accord with those identified by Fionda and Moore (2009) as luxury i.e., fashion (couture, ready-to-wear and accessories), perfumes and cosmetics, wines and spirits and watches and jewellery (See Table 1).

Table 1: Product categories and brands identified

Products	Brands Identified
Shoes	Witchery, New Balance, Vans, Nike, Converse, Puma, Adidas
Bags	*Lacoste, Louis Vuitton,* Adidas, Rip Curl, Billabong
Clothes	Ksubi, Levis, Diesel, Quick Silver, Billabong, Laura Parker, Witchery, Abercrombie and Fitch, Workshop, Dickies, Horley, Supre, True Religion Jeans, *Ralph Lauren,* Kathmandu, Mossimo,
Cosmetics & Hair products	Elizabeth Arden, Thin Lizzy, Neutrogena, Mac, Revlon, Maybelline, Fantasy cream, Smash Box, Cetaphil
Sunglasses	*Gucci,* Le Specs, *Ray-Ban, Dolce & Gabbana,* Wayfarer
Perfumes	*Lancome, Christian Dior,* Elizabeth Arden, Marc Jacobs (Daisy), *Van Cleef & Arpels, Yves Saint Laurent (YSL), Chanel,* Kylie Minogue, Jo Malone, *Oscar de La Renta*
Wallets and Watches	Ripcurl, Glassons, Guess, Adidas, *Omega,* Baby-G
Alcohol/Wine	Lindauer, Malibu, Barbados Rum, Speights, Tui, 42 Below, Smirnoff Vodka, Villa Maria

Whilst most of the brands selected in the product categories identified in Table 1 are high-end global brands, a few are high-end regional brands, e.g., Billabong and Rip Curl. Thirteen of the high-end, global brands selected (italicised in Table 1) feature on a luxury brands list (Luxury Brands List, 2010). However, participants also speak of some others that do not figure on the luxury brands list. These include Ksubi, Laura Parker, Workshop, True Religion Jeans, Kathmandu, Elizabeth Arden (See Exhibit 1 for sample extracts).

Christodoulides, Michaelidou and Li (2009) suggest that luxury products or brands can be categorised in terms of a hierarchy. At the bottom of the hierarchy is accessible luxury which in terms of socio-economic dimensions refers to luxury products that are attainable by the middle socio-economic class. The mid-level hierarchy relates to product purchases by the professional socio-economic class, while the top of the hierarchy is associated with an elite socio economic class. Though the participants own some high-end luxury brands, the product forms selected, to an extent, accord with the life stage and

the socio-economic status of the sample. Christian Dior and YSL perfume and/or sunglasses are more accessible to this group than the haute couture linked to this brand. High-end clothing brands that from the way participants talk about them, are considered luxury.

It is evident that participants have an acute awareness of what selected brands communicate, and use them to clarify who they are to themselves and to communicate some aspects of their self to others. Though not specifically directed to identify brands that could be deemed 'luxury', participants talk about their selections in terms of conspicuousness, exclusivity, quality, refined taste, and status. See, for example, words highlighted in bold in sample extracts - Exhibit 1. By speaking of brands in terms of highlighted characteristics, participants reflect the elements associated with luxury brands in the literature (e.g., Dubious and Paternault, 1995; Dubois et al., 2005; Kapferer, 1998; Phau and Prendergast 2000; Vickers and Renand, 2003; Vigneron and Johnson 2004; Wiedman et al. 2007).

Exhibit 1: Sample Extracts

> *This is an Australian brand called Ksubi…umm…they are quite expensive… it is quite expensive, quite upmarket…the designers…they design for people who want to be different (Quote One - Photograph of Ksubi shorts - Jessica)*
>
> *Because Elizabeth Arden is one of those brands that everybody knows and it is quite esteemed and it is quite high up. It is almost exclusive I suppose (Quote Two - Photograph of Elizabeth Arden Perfume - Sarah)*
>
> *This is an Omega watch. It is a well known brand as well…It is a Swiss watch, and Swiss watch is best so it shows me the right time and it says it is a luxury accessory as well…As I told you before I like expensive things and when I can afford them I buy them (Quote Three - Photograph of Omega - Paul)*
>
> *The reason I took so much pictures of Ralph Lauren is because when people look at Ralph Lauren they see 'he's a high achiever, he is successful' and that 'he is talented and he looks good'…It means they are successful… they are rich (Quote Four - Photograph of Ralph Lauren T-Shirts - Craig)*
>
> *Absolutely, I mean you know a Laura Parker dress has a definite brand standard and social advantages would include like a higher social circle recognising that maybe them going 'hey she looks cool, I could hang out with her' (Quote Five - Photograph of Laura Parker Ball Dress - Melissa)*
>
> *The Yves St Laurent perfume (Baby Doll) is special to me because my mum brought it for me, but I love it, it smells really good and all my friends, every time I wear it, are like "you smell really good". It's just perfume I suppose… it appeals to mostly girls my age (Quote Six - Photograph of Yves St. Laurent perfume - Laura)*

Cornell (2002) notes that luxury is difficult to define but that it involves a strong element of human involvement; that luxury goods represent value to both the individual and their reference groups. The extracts in Exhibit 1 demonstrate that participants are cognizant of the social benefits that luxury goods afford. They are well aware that the message communicated is that they are persons of taste and refinement, successful, and that they are members of an elite group. They are able to clearly articulate what the brands represent to themselves and what they think the brands communicate to others. They value the hedonic and sensory benefits of the brands they identify; whether the sensory pleasure is enhanced by the brand image is not clear, however, there is a distinct link between perceptions of quality and the brand. The central value of the perfume in Quote Six, for example, is the smell and the value accorded by Laura's reference group.

Whilst the brands that the participants link to the attributes that research suggests are associated with luxury brands are global and feature on accredited lists as luxury brands, some do not. The Elizabeth Arden, Kathmandu, Ksubi, Workshop, and True Religion Jeans though high-end brands, their status as luxury brands is debatable. Even so, participants talk about them in terms of luxury attributes suggesting that what is a luxury brand is also contingent on the consumer's frame of reference. This means that future research should take into account variance across groups - in particular socio-economic factors that determine the elite hierarchies. Such research would not only contribute to a better understanding of the relativity of the term 'luxury', but would also provide insightful findings for both academics and practitioners alike.

The study also suggests a strong link between brand management - particularly positioning and communication in the creation of brand value - and thus the directions as to how the brand can be used and what it means. It may well be that the brands spoken of in terms of luxury do give unambiguous information to young adult consumers, and therefore, evoke luxury related associations more readily in comparison to other brands. The implications for practitioners lie in matching up their brand offerings with the potential and needs of various target markets.

CONCLUSION

This paper provides evidence for the notion that luxury as a concept is context dependent and is a function of demographic factors such as age, life stage and income. It identifies a range of fashion brands that young adult consumers speak of in terms of luxury connotations in the literature. Even though some may not be formally classified as luxury either in the scholarly literature or in industry rankings, young adult consumers perceive luxury value in the choices they make. They use the brands to communicate that they are persons of taste and social class. In other words, luxury lies in the eyes of the beholder. Last and importantly, the study emphasizes the connection between brand management, especially communication and positioning, and perceptions of luxury as one of vital significance for branding practitioners.

REFERENCES

Bryman, Alan and Bell Emma (2007), *Business Research Methods,* Oxford: Oxford University Press, Oxford.

Carabine, Jean (2001), "Unmarried motherhood 1830-1990: A genealogical analysis", in *Discourse as data: A guide for analysis,* eds. Margaret Wetherell, Stephanie Taylor and Simeon J. Yates, Sage, London, 267-310.

Christodoulides, George, Michaelidou, Nina and Li, Ching Hsing (2009), "Measuring perceived brand luxury: An evaluation of the BLI scale", *The Journal of Brand Management,* 16 (5-6), 395-405.

Cornell, Andres (2002), "Cult of luxury: The new opiate of the masses", *Australian Financial Review,* 27 April, 47.

Denzin, Norman K., and Lincoln, Yvonna S. (2000), "The discipline and practice of qualitative research", in *Handbook of qualitative research,* eds. Norman K. Denzin and Yvonna S. Lincoln, Sage, London, 1-57.

Dubois, Bernard, Czellar, Sandor and Laurent, Gilles (2005), "Consumer segments based on attitudes toward luxury: Empirical evidence from twenty countries", *Marketing Letters,* 16 (2), 115-128.

Dubois, Bernard, and Paternault, Claire. (1995), "Observations: Understanding the World of International Luxury Brands: The "Dream Formula"", *Journal of Advertising Research,* 35 (4), 69-76.

Fionda, Antoinette M., and Moore, Christopher M. (2009), "The anatomy of the luxury fashion brand", *Brand Management,* 16 (5/6), 347-363.

Husic, Melika and Cicic, Muris (2009), "Luxury consumption factors", *Journal of Fashion Marketing and Management,* 13 (2), 231-245.

Husserl, Edmund (1970), *Logical investigation,* Atlantic Highlands, NJ.: Humanities Press.

Kapferer, Jean-Noel (1998), "Managing Luxury Brands", *Journal of Brand Management,* 4 (4), 251-260.

Keller, Kevin L. (2009), "Managing the growth tradeoff: Challenges and opportunities in luxury branding", *Brand Management,* 16 (5/6), 290-301.

Kjeldgaard, Dannie (2004), *Consumption and the global youth segment: Peripheral positions, central immersion,* Odense, Denmark: University Press of Southern Denmark. "Luxury brands list", http://www.myluxury.info/luxury-brands-list (accessed February 15, 2010).

Noland, Carey M. (2006), "Auto-photography as a research practice: Identity and self-esteem research", *Journal of Research Practice,* 2 (1), M1.

Owen, William F. (1984). "Interpretive themes in relational communication", *Quarterly Journal of Speech,* 70, 274-287.

Patton, Michael Q. (2002), *Qualitative research and evaluation methods,* London: Sage.

Phau, Ian and Prendergast, Gerald (2002), "Consuming luxury brands: The relevance of the 'Rarity Principle'", *Brand Management,* 8 (2), 122-138.

Potter, Jonathan and Wetherell, Margaret (1987), *Discourse and Social Psychology: Beyond attitudes and Behaviour,* London: Sage.

Reed, Americus (2002). "Social identity as a useful perspective for self-concept-based consumer research", *Psychology and Marketing,* 9 (3), 235-266.

Schutz, Alfred (1970), *On phenomenology and social relations,* Chicago: University of Chicago Press.

Tajfel, Henri and Turner, John C. (1979), *An Integrative Theory of Intergroup Conflict,* Monterey, CA : Brooks/Cole.

Tajfel, Henri and Turner, John C. (1986), *The Social Identity Theory of Intergroup Behavior,* Chicago: Nelson.

Thompson, Craig J., Locander, William B. and Pollio, Howard R., (1989), " Putting consumer experience back into consumer research: The philosophy and method of existential-phenomenology", *Journal of Consumer Research,* 16, 133-146.

Vickers, Jonathan S. and Renand, Franck (2003), "The Marketing of Luxury Goods: An exploratory study - three conceptual dimensions", *The Marketing Review,* 3 (4), 459-478.

Vigneron, Franck and Johnson, Lester W., (2004), "Measuring perceptions of brand luxury", *The Journal of Brand Management,* 11 (6), 484-506.

Wetherell, Margaret and Potter, Jonathan, (1988), "Discourse analysis and the identification of interpretive repertoires", in *Analysing Everyday Explanation: A Casebook of Methods*, ed. Charles Antaki, Sage, London, 168-183.

Wiedman, Klaus-Peter, Hennigs, Nadine and Siebels, Astrid (2007), "Measuring consumers' luxury value perception: a Cross-Cultural Framework", *Academy of Marketing Review,* 7, 1 -18.

Ziller, Robert C. (1990), *Photographing the self: Methods for observing personal orientations,* Newbury Park, CA.: Sage.

On the Use of Multi-Unit Auctions in Measuring Consumers' Willingness to Pay for Products

Faical Akaichi, University of Arkansas, USA
Rodolfo M. Nayga, University of Arkansas, USA
Jose M. Gil, CREDA, Polytechnic University of Catalonia, Spain

INTRODUCTION

Experimental auctions have become a popular tool to assess consumers' willingness to pay (WTP) for food products. Their popularity partly stems from their incentive compatibility property where people have the weakly dominant strategy of revealing their true valuation for a good. In experimental auctions, people are put in an active market environment with real economic consequences. Experimental auctions also provide quite a relatively easy way to assess heterogeneity in valuations across people. According to Lusk and Shogren (2007), over 100 academic studies have utilized experimental auctions to examine consumers' valuation of different products. Some of these studies focused on the valuation of food safety and health attributes (e.g., Fox et al., 2002; Dickinson and Bailey, 2002; Shaw et al., 2006) or on willingness to pay for new food products (e.g., Kassardjian et al., 2005; Rousu et al., 2005; Alfnes, 2007). Many other studies have also been carried out to test methodological aspects of auctions such as the comparison between WTP and willingness-to-accept (WTA) (Knetch et al., 2001; Shogren et al., 2001b), the learning effect (List and Shogren, 1999), the endowment effect (Lusk et al., 2004a; Corrigan and Rousu, 2006), the optimum mechanism of auctions (Rustrom, 1998; List and Lucking-Reiley, 2000; Lusk et al., 2004c), and risk preferences (McClelland et al., 1993). In these studies, however, participants were asked to report their WTP only for a single unit of the auctioned product[1].

In real market, however, consumers may be interested in buying multiple units. In fact, while the use of single-unit auctions is useful in assessing consumers' valuation of a single unit of a product, consumers can be interested as well in purchasing not just one but multiple units of a product. Also, due to increasing time constraints, many consumers are becoming increasingly concerned about optimizing shopping efficiency by purchasing multiple units of products (e.g. soda, beer, water, juice etc.) to save several trips to the store. This tendency in consumer behavior has provided an incentive to producers and retailers of food products to adjust their marketing strategies to benefit from these changes in consumer preferences. Considerable effort, for instance, has been devoted to the packaging and the promotion of products that consumers are used to buying in multiple units. In fact, producers and retailers are increasingly marketing food products in bundles of multiple-units (e.g. six-pack: 6 identical units in the same bundle). Also, they are increasingly using multi-unit price promotions such as "buy two and pay one", "buy X units and save $Y" etc. There is however scant literature on assessment of consumer behavior in a multi-unit shopping scenario

The use of single-unit auction to examine consumers' WTP for multiple units of a product is inadequate unless we assume that consumer preferences for subsequent units are similar to the first one (e.g. WTP is independent of the quantity purchased). However it is well known that for a normal good consumer demand is decreasing in price and hence, we would expect a lower WTP for each additional unit purchased beyond the first unit. Also, the assumption that consumers' WTP is in-

dependent of the auctioned quantity is unrealistic since it leads to zero price elasticities. Finally, the effects of various factors determining consumers' WTP can be different for different quantities of the purchased product. For example, it is possible that some of the factors that are statistically significant in determining WTP for a single unit may become statistically insignificant for multiple units of purchase.

A modified format of single-unit auction was used by Rousu et al (2008) to measure consumers' WTP for multiple units of the same product with the objective of examining the effect of selling complements and substitutes on consumers' WTP. The modified format involves auctioning different quantities of a product in several rounds. For example, they auctioned one unit in the first round, a bundle of two units in the second round and a bundle of three units in the third round. Then they randomly choose a round to be the binding round. Although this modified format can be a good method to assess consumer behavior in multi-unit shopping scenario, the unfairness of its pricing rule can discourage certain participants from bidding their true valuations. Since a different quantity is auctioned in each round and only one round is chosen as binding, participants who are willing to pay a positive price for large quantity will have a higher probability to win than others. In other words, suppose that we use the second price auction in which the participant with the highest bid wins the auctioned product and pays an amount equal to the second highest bid. Now, suppose that two subjects are participating in a second price auction of three rounds. In the first round one unit is auctioned, two units are auctioned in the second round and three units are auctioned in the third round. Suppose that participant 1 is willing to buy just one unit and bids a value of 10 in the first round and zero in both the second and third rounds. Participant 2 is willing to buy the three units and bids a value of 8 in the first round, a value of 12 in the second round and a value of 14 in the third round. Hence, participant 2 is willing to pay 8 for the first unit, 4 for the second unit and 2 for the third unit. Now if the binding round is the first one, the winner is participant 1. But if the binding round is the second or the third round, participant 2 is declared the winner although s/he reports a lower value for the first unit. That is participant 2 has a chance to win in the three rounds but participant 1 can win only if the first round is selected. Therefore, due the unfairness of this pricing rule, participant 1 cannot win any unit if the binding round is the second or the third round even though his or her WTP for the first unit is the highest. The feeling of unfairness can discourage participant 1 from bidding his or her true value.

Fortunately, auction theory provides an auction mechanism that allows us to measure consumers' WTP for multiple units and avoid the unfairness of the pricing rule of the modified format of single-unit auction. This auction mechanism is called multi-unit auction. Multi-unit auctions can be described as an auction where multiple identical units are auctioned and participants are asked to report their WTP for each unit. Among multi-unit auction formats, the most common mechanisms used in the empirical literature are the uniform-price and the multi-unit Vickrey auctions. The uniform-price auction mechanism has been used frequently in Treasury bill and Federal Communications Commission (FCC) auctions due to its straightforward implementation and, therefore, understandable pricing rule. All winners pay the same price which is equal to the highest rejected bid. In the multi-unit Vickrey auction, which is a generalization of the second price auction (Vickrey), the winner pays an amount corresponding to the sum of the bids (excluding his or her own bids) that are displaced by his or her successful bids (Krishna,

---

* Faical Akaichi (Corresponding author) and Rodolfo M. Nayga, Jr. are with the Department of Agricultural Economics and Agribusiness, University of Arkansas. Email: fakaichi@uark.edu (479-575-2321) and rnayga@uark.edu (479-575-2299). José M. Gil is with CREDA-UPC-IRTA. Email: chema.gil@upc.edu (+34-9355-21210).

[2] While the participant can be asked to report his/her WTP for different products, at the end of the auction only one product is randomly drawn to be sold to the winner.

Advances in Consumer Research
Volume 39, ©2011

2002). In spite of its demand-revealing property, the Vickrey auction, however, is not popularly used in real auctions due to the complexity of its pricing rule that makes it difficult to understand and implement in the real world. Since the main objective of this paper is to show the usefulness of multi-unit auction in assessing consumer behavior in multi-unit shopping scenario, we use the uniform price auction due to the simplicity of its pricing rule.

So how does the uniform price auction eliminate the unfairness of the pricing rule of the modified format of the single-unit auction? In the uniform price auction, each participant reports a separate bid for each auctioned unit in the same round. That is if three units are auctioned, each participant has to report his/her WTP for the first unit, his/her WTP for the second unit and his/her WTP for the third unit. The bids are then sorted and if for example the number of auctioned units is three, the three highest bidders are declared winners and they pay for each unit won an amount equal to the fourth highest bid. Let's revisit the last simple example provided above involving two bidders. Recall that participant 1 bids 10 for the first unit and zero for the second and the third unit (i.e. 10, 0, 0) and participant 2 bids 8 for the first unit, 4 for the second unit and 2 for the third unit (i.e. 8, 4, 2). Sorting the bids we obtain (10, 8, 4, 2, 0, 0). Following the pricing rule of the uniform price auction, participant 1 wins a unit with his/her bid 10 and pays a price equal to 2 and participant 2 wins two units with his/her bids 8 and 4 and also pays a price equal to 2 for each unit. We can see that the pricing rule of uniform price auction is fair since the determination of the winner depends only on his/her bids and not on the binding round like in the modified single-unit auction. As a result, both participants win based on their bids and not on the probability of a round being chosen as the binding round.

Using the uniform price auction in a laboratory experiment, we will show how the multi-unit auction allows us to obtain: 1) consumers' WTP for multiple units of the same product; 2) demand curve; 3) price elasticity; and the factors influencing consumers' WTP for different quantities of a food product. Also, using a multi-unit auction, we will be able to test two hypotheses:

Hypothesis 1   *Consumers' WTP is decreasing in the number of units.*

Hypothesis 2   *The direction and/or the magnitude of the effect of factors determining consumers' WTP can be different for each additional unit auctioned beyond the first unit.*

EXPERIMENTAL DESIGN

Forty undergraduate students took place in the study. To increase the number of observations we carried out the uniform price auction in five rounds. Hence, a total of 200 observations were obtained from the experiment. We did not post the clearing price after each round to avoid the problem of bid affiliation (Corrigan and Rousu, 2006). In each round, participants were asked to report their WTP for small packages (40 grams each) of organic chips. This product type and package size are popularly sold in vending machines in schools[2]. Participants were randomly assigned between two treatments. In the first treatment, participants were grouped in groups of 10 subjects. In the second treatment participants were grouped in groups of 2 subjects. This distribution of participants allows the assessment of the effect of varying the number bidders on consumers' WTP. However, since the objective of the paper is to show the usefulness of multi-unit auctions, the results on the effect of varying the number of bidders are not dis-

cussed in this paper.

The experiment was performed in a room equipped with ten computers. We used the z-tree software (Fischbacher, 2007) to collect bids and to determine the winner and the clearing price. Participants also had to complete a questionnaire on various aspects related to organic products, in general, and organic chips, in particular. The responses were used to characterize the participants and to analyze the main determinants of consumers' WTP for organic chips. The information collected via the questionnaire showed that all participants are regular or occasional consumers of conventional chips. 62.5% of participants characterized themselves as regular or occasional purchasers of organic food and only 17.5% of participants revealed being occasional consumers of organic chips.

The experiment was performed in three steps. In step 1, each subject sat in a table separated from the rest to minimize any possible interactions and allow anonymous bidding. After taking a seat, each participant received an envelope which contained 10€ as compensation for their participation, his or her identification number (to maintain anonymity) and a questionnaire. We then asked participants to complete the questionnaire. In step 2, once the questionnaire was completed, the actual experiment began. One of the main determinants of success in experimental auctions is a good understanding by the participants of the operating procedures used in the auction mechanism. To achieve this goal, we gave each participant a printed material that included an explanation of how the specific auction works and some examples to illustrate the auction. After reading and discussing the instructions, participants were given the opportunity to ask questions to dissipate any doubts about the process. Finally, to permit a better understanding of the auction mechanism and a good familiarity with the software, we carried out a training session, auctioning four identical units of organic chips and informed participants that no actual economic exchange will take place at the end of the training session. In this session, we asked participants to bid the amount they are willing to pay for each item of organic chips. Once all participants reported their bids through the computer, the software determined the identification number of the winner(s) and the price he/she (they) has (have) to pay.

In step 3, once the participants became familiar with the procedure, we announced the start of the real auction of organic chips. Each participant had to submit, again through the computer, how much he or she was willing-to-pay for each unit of organic chips. We made clear that we were asking for the marginal WTP. That is the WTP for the first unit, then the second unit, then the third unit and finally the fourth unit and not the WTP for one unit, two units, three units and four units. The marginal WTP is necessary to estimate the demand function and, hence, the price elasticity. Once all participants finished reporting their bids, the software determined the winner(s) and the clearing price. The same process was repeated four more times (i.e., with four additional rounds of bidding). At the end of the fifth round, one round was chosen randomly to determine the binding round. The winner(s) in the binding round was (were) appointed as the winner(s) of the auction. Once the results were announced, the experiment ended by handing the product to the winner(s) who had to pay the corresponding market-clearing price.

RESULTS

To illustrate the usefulness of multi-unit auctions in assessing consumer behavior in a multi-unit shopping setting of food products, we report in this section the results of the construction of the demand curve, estimation of price elasticity and consumer surplus as well as the determination of the factors that influence consumers' WTP for multiple units of organic chips.

3.1 Demand Curve and consumer surplus

Based on our first hypothesis, our first task was to check if

---

[2] For simplicity, we will use in the rest of the paper the term unit instead of package.

WTP values decrease as the number of units increases. The demand curve exhibited in Figure 1, clearly shows that the means of the WTP for organic chips is decreasing as the number of units being auctioned increases. In fact, results from uniform price auction indicate that the average WTP per unit decreases from 0.86€ when the quantity of organic chips is equal to one unit to 0.53€ when the quantity of organic chips is equal to four units. This result confirms the inadequacy of using the original format of single-unit auctions and the appropriateness of multi-unit auctions in assessing consumers' WTP for multiple units of food products. Also, this finding reflects the importance of switching from a strategy of constant or flat prices to a price-discount strategy to increase sales. In fact, since consumers' WTP is decreasing in the number of units, a price discount - that makes the market price decreasing as the number of units increases - may motivate buyers to buy more units.

Figure 1: WTP for organic chips

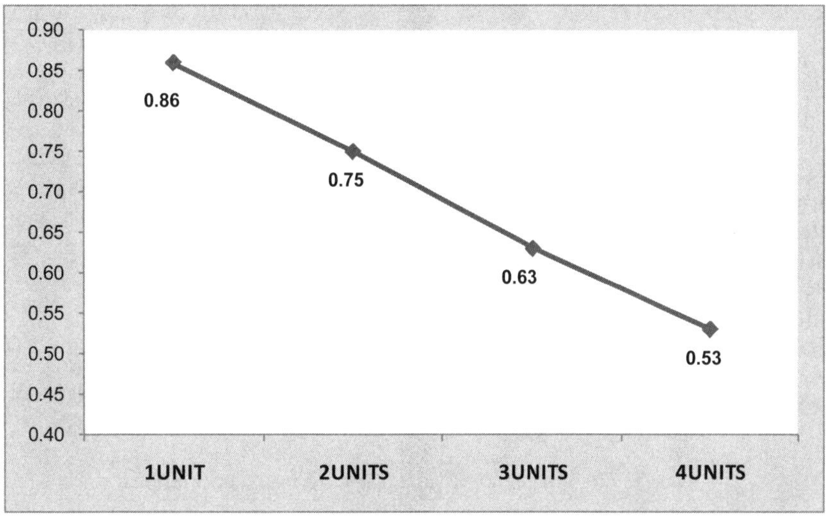

As previously discussed, an advantage of the use of multi-unit auctions is that it allows us to obtain the demand curve, and hence, the calculation of consumer surplus. This information is very useful when we want to investigate consumer welfare effects of the introduction of new products, new food policies/programs, etc. In Figure 2, consumer surplus is shown by the area under the demand curve and above the real market premium price. For illustration purposes, we assume that the real market premium price based on current market estimates is 0.70€[3]. We can see that participants can benefit from purchasing two units of the auctioned organic chips in the market since their average WTP for these units is higher than the market price (i.e., the consumer surplus is positive).

_____

[3] There was an attempt by a retailer of high quality foods in Barcelona to introduce its own brand of organic chips (small size package) with a market price of 0.70€/unit.

Figure 2: Consumers surplus in the case of organic chips

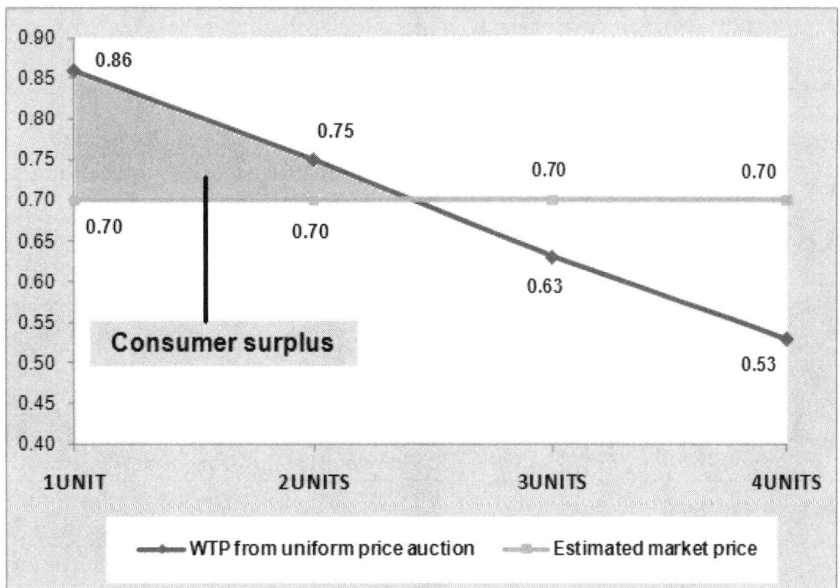

Consumer surplus information can also help the seller decide the optimal bundle size for the product if s/he decides to sell his/her product in bundles of multiple units. In our case, the producer of the auctioned organic chips can, at most, introduce into the market bundles of two units since our results showed that there are buyers who are willing to purchase two units at a premium price of 0.70€/unit. However, if the producer wants to introduce bundle of more than 2 units, results in figure 2 show the necessity of discounting the market price (e.g. 0.53€/unit) to attract buyers. We can see that obtaining this kind of information would not be possible if we used single-unit auctions to determine consumers' WTP.

3.2 Inverse Price Elasticity

One of the prominent advantages of the use of multi-unit auction is that it allows the derivation of price elasticity which can then be used, among others, in evaluating consumer demand and welfare implications of policy interventions (e.g., product taxes, price ceilings, price floors). In a real shopping setting, consumer faces a fixed market price and has to determine the quantity s/he is willing to buy at that price. In multi-unit auctions, however, participants are offered a determined quantity of a product and s/he has to report his/her WTP for that quantity. Hence what we measure are inverse elasticities rather than elasticities. In other worlds, the inverse elasticity measures the responsiveness of marginal WTP (i.e. the WTP for each additional auctioned unit) to changes in the quantity. To estimate the inverse elasticity of the organic chips, we specify a model that relates the marginal WTP to the auctioned quantity of organic chips. We choose a log-log specification mainly for two reasons: (1) it allows us to interpret the coefficient associated with the quantity as elasticity; and (2) because our data showed that marginal consumers' WTP is decreasing with quantity. The model estimated for the organic chips was:

$$\ln WTP_{ij} = \alpha + \beta \ln Q_j + \delta X_i + \varepsilon_{ij}$$

where WTP_i is participant i's marginal WTP for the quantity j of organic chips, Q_j is the quantity of organic chips that varies from one to four units (i.e. j = 1,2,3,4). The quantity is independent of i since all participants were asked to bid for the same quantity. β is the corresponding coefficient of the quality and represents also the inverse elasticity. X_i is a vector of other explanatory variables and δ s are the corresponding coefficients. ε_{ij} is the random error term. The description of the variables used in the estimation of this model and the model presented in the next section is exhibited in Table 1. Since there are four observations for each participant (i.e. marginal WTP value for each unit), we estimated the demand equation using a random effect model to account for unobserved heterogeneity. Finally, the zero values of marginal WTP were replaced by a very small number (0.0001€) since the natural log of zero is undefined.

Table 1: The independent variables used in the estimations

Label of independent Variables	Name	Description
Log (the quantity of organic chips)	LN(QUANTITY)	Variable that takes the value 1, 2, 3 or 4 if the auctioned quantity is equal to 1, 2, 3 or 4 units.
First round	ROUND1	Dummy variable that takes the value 1 if the round is the first one; and 0 otherwise
Second round	ROUND2	Dummy variable that takes the value 1 if the round is the second one; and 0 otherwise
Third round	ROUND3	Dummy variable that takes the value 1 if the round is the third one; and 0 otherwise
Fourth round	ROUND4	Dummy variable that takes the value 1 if the round is the fourth one; and 0 otherwise
Fifth round	ROUND5	Dummy variable that takes the value 1 if the round is the fifth one; and 0 otherwise
Treatment	TREATMENT10	Dummy variable that takes the value 1 if the participant is grouped in a group of 10 subjects; and 0 otherwise
Price of conventional chips	PRICE	Continue variable: the price at which participant used to buying small size package of conventional chips
Log(Price of conventional chips)	LN(PRICE)	Continue variable: log (the price at which participant used to buying small size package of conventional chips)
Consumption frequency of conventional chips	REG_CONS	Dummy variable that takes the value 1 if the participant is regular consumer of conventional chips; and 0 otherwise
Consumption frequency of conventional chips	OCC_CONS	Dummy variable that takes the value 1 if the participant is occasional consumer of conventional chips; and 0 otherwise
Consumption frequency of organic foods	REGBUY_OF	Dummy variable that takes the value 1 if the participant is regular buyer of organic foods; and 0 otherwise
Consumption frequency of organic foods	NOCONS_OF	Dummy variable that takes the value 1 if the participant is not consumer of organic foods; and 0 otherwise
Taste of organic foods	TASTE	Dummy variable that takes the value 1 if the participant agrees with the statement that organic foods are tastier than conventional foods; and 0 otherwise

Aspect of organic foods	ASPECT	Dummy variable that takes the value 1 if the participant agrees with the statement that organic foods have a worse aspect comparing to conventional foods; and 0 otherwise
Availability of organic foods	UNAVAILABLE	Dummy variable that takes the value 1 if the participant agrees with the statement that organic foods are unavailable in the most frequented supermarkets; and 0 otherwise
Environment	ENVIRONMENT	Dummy variable that takes the value 1 if the participant agrees with the statement that organic farming improve the sustainability of the environment; and 0 otherwise
Gender	GENDER	Dummy variable that takes the value 1 if the participant is male; and 0 otherwise
Household	HOUSEHOLD	Dummy variable that takes the value 1 if the participant lives in household of more than two members; and 0 otherwise
Income	INCOME	Dummy variable that takes the value 1 if the household's income is more than 2500€/month; and 0 otherwise

The results of the estimation of the random effect model are displayed in Table 2. The coefficient of the log of the variable quantity represents the inverse elasticity which is equal to -2.78. This value indicates that an increase of 10% in the quantity of organic chips would decrease consumers' WTP by 27.8%. Since consumers' WTP is highly elastic to an increase in the quantity, producers and retailers of organic chips should consider the introduction of multi-unit price promotions if they want to fit consumer preferences.

Table 2: Results from the estimation of random effect model: Logarithmic specification

EXPLICATIVE VARIABLES	ESTIMATED COEFFICIENT
CONSTANT	2.753
LN(QUANTITY)	**-2.782***
TREATMENT 10	-1.130*
OCC_CONS	-0.636
LN(PRICE)	1.259
UNAVAILABLE	-1.077
TASTE	-1.110*
ENVIRONMENT	2.480***
GENDER	-1.154**
HOUSEHOLD	-1.432**
INCOME	0.414
Observations	200
R²: Within	0.35
Between	0.30
Overall	0.33

*** (**) (*) Statistically significant at 1% (5%) and (10%) level

3.3 Determining factors of consumers' WTP for multiple units of organic chips

The objective of this section is to show the usefulness of multi-unit auctions in assessing the determinants of consumers' WTP for multiple units. To tackle this objective we test hypothesis 2 which stated that the determining factors of consumers' WTP can be different from one unit to another. Hence, it is inadequate to use single-unit auctions, in its original format, to determine the key factors of consumers' WTP for a single unit and then assume that the consumers' WTP for any additional unit will be influenced by the same determinants of the first unit. To test hypothesis 2, we estimated a random effect Tobit model[4] for each auctioned unit. We estimated separate

models to assess the factors influencing the WTP of each auctioned unit. We specified the four models as follows:

$$y_{irj} = \begin{cases} y^*_{irj} & if \quad y^*_{irj} > 0 \\ 0 & if \quad y^*_{irj} \leq 0 \end{cases}$$

$$y^*_{irj} = x_{irj}\beta_j + u_{ij} + \varepsilon_{irj} \qquad \forall i = 1,...N; \ r = 1,...,5; \ and \ j = 1,...,4$$

where i indexes cross-section units such that $i = 1, 2, ..., N$ (N is the number of participants); r indexes the number of rounds (time series units) such that $r = 1, 2, 3, 4, 5$; and j indexes the units auctioned in the experiment ; The matrix X_{irj} contains data on the observable explanatory variables. Y_{irj} is the price consumer i is willing to pay for the jth unit of organic chip in the rth round. $\beta_j = (\beta_{j,1}...\beta_{j,k_j}) \in R^{k_j}$ are

---

[4] We used a random effect Tobit model: 1) to account for the panel nature of our data (five observations from each participant); and 2) participants' WTP are censored at zero.

vectors of parameters to estimate. The effects of relevant unobservable variables and time-invariant factors are captured by the vector u_{ij} and the stochastic disturbances of the model for the six auctioned units are captured by the vector ε_{irj}. Table 1 shows the description of the variables used in the estimation of the four models.

Results from the estimation of the four random effect Tobit models are displayed in Table 3. Among all variables, only the variable ENVIRONMENT is a key determinant of the WTP for all the units. In fact, participants who think that organic farming improves the sustainability of the environment are willing to pay a higher price for all units. In general, our results show that the WTP for the first unit and the second unit of organic chips is affected by the same factors. For example the higher is the price that participant is used to paying for conventional chips, the higher is his/her WTP for the first two units of organic chips. Also, participants who revealed being non consumers of organic foods (NOCONS_OF) reported a significant higher price premium for the first two units of

organic chips, perhaps, because they wanted to try the new product. If we look at the determinants of the WTP for the third and the fourth unit, we can see that three of the significant factors (PRICE, NOCONS_OF and ASPECT) for the first and the second units are no longer statistically significant. Also, the results show that in comparison with female participants, male participants were willing to pay less for the two last units of organic chips. However, this variable is not significant for the first two units. Finally, we found that regular buyers of organic foods have significant higher WTP only for the fourth unit. Therefore, our results confirm the hypothesis that the effect of various variables on the WTP can be different between the first unit and subsequent units. Hence, assuming constant effects of variables across the different units can lead to misleading inferences. In conclusion, our findings showed the necessity of assessing the determinants of consumers' WTP for each auctioned unit and, hence, the adequacy of using multi-unit auctions in measuring the WTP for multiple units of a food product.

Table 3: Results from the estimation of a Tobit model for each unit

VARIABLES	UNIT1	UNIT2	UNIT3	UNIT4
CONSTANT	0.102	0.177	-0.064	-0.613
ROUND2	0.000	0.000	-0.041	0.026
ROUND3	-0.053	-0.074	-0.032	-0.006
ROUND4	-0.086	-0.048	0.029	0.106
ROUND5	-0.012	-0.037	0.012	0.107
TREATMENT10	-0.138	**-0.162****	-0.258	-0.243
REG_CONS	0.061	0.077	0.137	0.090
PRICE	**0.725****	**0.609****	0.469	0.610
REGBUY_OF	-0.111	-0.073	0.337	**0.612****
NOCONS_OF	**0.274*****	**0.167***	0.083	-0.081
TASTE	0.059	-0.008	-0.133	-0.140
ASPECT	**0.320*****	**0.195****	0.141	-0.173
ENVIRONMENT	**0.440*****	**0.347*****	**0.560*****	**0.856****
GENDER	0.048	0.020	**-0.369*****	**-0.539*****
HOUSEHOLD	**-0.376*****	**-0.356*****	**-0.291***	-0.205
INCOME	0.060	0.073	0.025	0.278
Log likelihood	-37.50	-43.70	-96.17	-75.84
Wald chi2	57.32	42.61	18.24	16.93
Prob > chi2	0.00	0.00	0.25	0.32

*** (**) (*) **Statistically significant at 1% (5%) and (10%) level**

CONCLUSIONS

Due to its demand revealing properties, experimental auctions have gained recognition among applied economists and marketers interested in valuing new products and product attributes. Numerous studies have used experimental auctions to elicit consumers' WTP for food products. However, these studies used single-unit experimental auctions in which the participants were asked to report their WTP for a single unit of the auctioned product. The results from these single unit auctions are useful only in cases where consumers are content to purchase only one unit of the product being valued or when the objective of the study is to assess consumers' WTP for a single unit of a food product. However, due to increasing opportunity cost of time and other reasons, consumers nowadays tend to purchase multiple units of the same products per shopping trip. In these

cases, using single-unit auction to study consumers' WTP for a new product can produce limited results. In this paper, we introduced the use of multi-unit auctions in the assessment of consumers' WTP for food products and showed how the implementation of this method permits the user to obtain useful parameters to analyze consumer behavior and consumers' WTP in a multi-unit setting. With multi-unit auctions, one can estimate the demand curve, consumer surplus, the inverse price elasticity, and the determinants of consumers' WTP for various units of a product.

While we showed in this study the promise of the use of multi-unit auctions to assess consumers' WTP for food products, it is important to note that in contrast to single-unit experimental auctions, multi-unit auctions could involve significantly more complicated tasks related to the determination of winners and calculation of the clearing price especially in cases when both the number of bidders and number of units are high. Since the main objective of this paper was to show the usefulness of the implementation of multi-unit auction in assessing consumer behavior in a shopping setting of multiple units, we only used the uniform price auction due to its simple pricing rule. However, other mechanisms such as multi-unit Vickrey auction and the Ausubel auction - that have a more complicated pricing rule but better theoretical characteristics – can be an interesting alternative to be used in future empirical researches. In addition, multi-unit auctions could be prone to other methodological issues such as demand reduction effects and these should be evaluated and taken into account in the future. Nevertheless, we hope that our study will motivate others to use multi-unit auctions in determining consumers' valuation of multiple units of food products with and without important policy related issues.

REFERENCES

Alfnes, Frode (2007), "Willingness to pay versus expected consumption value in Vickrey auctions for new experience goods," *American Journal of Agricultural Economics,* 89, 921-931.

Corrigan, Jay R. and Matthew C. Rousu (2006), "Posted prices and bid affiliation: evidence from experimental auctions," *American Journal of Agricultural Economics*, 88,1078–1090.

Dickinson, David L. and Dee Von, Bailey (2002), "Meat Traceability: Are U. S. consumers willing to pay for it? " *Journal of agricultural and resource economics*, 27, 348-364.

Fischbacher, Urs (2007), "z-Tree: Zurich Toolbox for Ready-made Economic Experiments," *Experimental Economics*, 10, 171-78.

Fox, John A., Dermot J. Hayes. and Jason F. Shogren (2002), "Consumer Preferences for Food Irradiation: How Favorable and Unfavorable Descriptions Affect Preferences for Irradiated Pork in Experimental Auction," *Journal of Risk and Uncertainty*, 24, 75-95.

Kassardjian, Elsa, Joanna, Gamble, Anne, Gunson. and Sara R. Jaeger (2005), "A new approach to elecit consumers' willingness to purchase genetically modified food apples," *British Food Journal*, 107, 541-555.

Knetsch, Jack L., Fang-Fang, Tang. and Richard H. Thaler (2001), "The endowment effect and repeated market trials: is the Vickrey auction demand revealing?" *Experimental economics*, 4, 257-269.

Krishna, Vijay (2002), *Auction Theory*. Academic Press San Diago, California, USA.

List, John A. and Jason F. Shogren (1999), "Price information and bidding behavior in repeated second-price auctions," *American journal of Agricultural Economics*, 81, 942-949.

List, John A. and David, Lucking-Reiley (2000), "Demand Reduction in Multi-Unit Auctions: Evidence from a Sports card Field Experiment," *American Economic Review*, 90, 961–972.

Lusk, Jayson L. and Jason F. Shogren (2007), *"Experimental Auctions: Methods and Applications in Economic and Marketing Research.* Cambridge University Press, Cambridge, UK.

Lusk, Jayson L., Ty, Feldkamp. and Ted C. Schroeder (2004a), "Experimental Auction Procedure: Impact on valuation of Quality Differentiated Good," *American Journal of Agricultural Economics*, 86, 389-405.

Lusk, Jayson L. and Darren, Hudson (2004c), "Willingness-to-Pay Estimates and Agribusiness Decision Making," *Review of Agricultural Economics*, 26, 152-169.

McClelland, Gary H., William D. Schulze. and Dar L, Coursey (1993), "Insurance for low-Probability hazards: A biomodal response to unlikely events," *Journal of Risk and Uncertainty*, 25, 318-321.

Rousu, Matthew C., Daniel C. Monchuk, Jason F. Shogren. and Katherine M. Kosa (2005), "Consumer Willingness to pay for "second generation" genetically engineered products and the role of marketing information," *Journal of Agricultural and Applied Economics*, 37, 647-657.

Rousu, Matthew C., Robert H. Beach. and Jay R. Corrigan (2008), "The Effects of Selling Complements and Substitutes on Consumer Willingness to Pay: Evidence from a Laboratory Experiment," *Canadian Journal of Agricultural Economics*, 56, 179-194.

Rustrom, Elisabet E, (1998), "Home-Grown Values and Incentive Compatible Auction Design," *International Journal of Game Theory*, 27, 427–441.

Shaw, Douglass W., Rodolfo M. Nayga. and Andres, Silva (2006), "Health benefits and uncertainty: an experimental analysis of the effect of risk presentation on auction bids for a healthful product," *Economics Bulletin*, 4, 1-8.

Shogren, Jason F., Sungwon, Cho, Cannon, Koo, John, List, Changown, Park, Pablo, Polo. and Robert, Wilhelmi (2001b), "Auction mechanism and the measurement of WTP and WTA," *Resource and Energy Economics*, 23, 97-109.

Dynamic Ideologies: The Case of Slow Food

Miranda Mirosa, University of Otago, New Zealand
Ben Wooliscroft, University of Otago, New Zealand
Rob Lawson, University of Otago, New Zealand

INTRODUCTION

There is a need for more discussion amongst consumer researchers about what ideology actually is and how it may be used in a consumer context. The concept of ideology remains incomplete on a number of grounds. Most importantly, little consideration has been given to the dynamism of ideologies (Kozinets 2008) even though ideologies do change, as extended goals shift over time. In this article, we investigate the interaction between consumer movements and dynamic ideologies. The Slow Food (SF) movement, a contemporary movement concerned with food quality, taste, environmental/cultural sustainability and social justice (Sassatelli and Davolio 2010) is used as a case study of dynamic ideology. Given that the SF Movement has undergone significant changes in recent years, shifting from a focus on gastronomy (good food), to the environment (clean food), to social justice (fair food) issues (Parkins and Graig 2006), it is an appropriate case study for studying how movement ideologies change overtime.

It is natural to turn to the new social movement literature on movement ideologies for guidance, given that well established and rich theories of movement ideologies are here. Unlike the classical reductionism of Marxism which relied on analyzing social movements in terms of production, new social movement theorists have turned to the spheres of culture, politics and ideologies and often include consumerist elements into analyzes rending their frameworks useful for analyzing contemporary consumer movements such as SF (Cherrier and Murray 2002; Kozinets 2002; Kozinets and Handelman 2004). We use the work of Italian theorist Melucci (1943-2001), one of the key new social movement theorists (Buechler, 1995). Melucci's work (as opposed to work by other key new social movement theorists such as Touraine, Castells and Habermas) takes the dynamic nature of ideology into consideration and is the theoretical basis for this paper.

DEFINING IDEOLOGY

Ideology is most commonly used in political discourse however other types of ideologies exist including social, ethical, environmental and epistemological ideologies. Geuss (1981) suggests that the definitions of the term ideology fall into three categories—descriptive, pejorative and positive. The descriptive definitions of ideology are self-explanatory and discuss ideology in a neutral sense. In this context, ideologies are close to the concept of worldview. The pejorative definitions refer critically or negatively to the relationship between power and maintaining dominance. If the motivation is unconscious, then this is considered self-deception. Here ideology represents ideas which are fundamentally flawed. The positive definitions consider ideology in a more favorable light and it is in this sense that ideology is defined in this article; specifically, an adapted version of Melucci's definition (1996, p. 349). "Ideology is a set of symbolic frames which collective actors use to represent their own actions to themselves and to others within a system of social relationships in the pursuit of interests judged to be desirable."

IDEOLOGY WITHIN THE CONSUMER RESEARCH LITERATURE

Whilst the concept of ideology has been theorized extensively in other social sciences, consumer researchers have not fully considered the various meanings of ideology. The most relevant work is in the literature on consumer movements, especially consumer resistance.

Penaloza and Price (1993) have delineated this area of research which explores the meaning of behaviors such as boycotting (Kozinets and Handelman 1998). However, within consumer resistance literature, ideology has been pushed aside and no mention is made of how consumers' ideologies determine the acts of resistance. The one notable exception is Kozinets and Handelman 2004 who use Touraine's 1981 "identity, opposition and totality" theory to investigate how members of anti-advertising, anti-Nike and anti-GE movements construct ideologies. Their study is important because it highlights that the new social movement paradigm has the potential to be an appropriate framework for the study of ideology in a consumer context.

The socio-historic patterning of consumption research program is also relevant. This literature considers institutional and social structures such as class, gender, ethnicity, community, family and other formal groups and how they influence consumption (Arnould and Thompson 2005). Literature on how consumers' belief structures (or their ideologies) influence consumption includes studies on occupation and values (Rosenberg 1980) and class and conformity (Kohn 1989). More recently, Kozinet's study 2008 looks at how ideological fields influence consumers' technology narratives. Kozinets highlights how researchers have failed to consider the dynamic nature of ideology and have the tendency to "treat particular ideologies as totalized and static categories" (Kozinets 2008, 878). Also of significance is the work of Kilbourne (1995, 1998) who worked alongside others (Kilbourne, Beckmann, and Thelen 2002) on the subject of the dominant social paradigm (DSP). Although it is not explicitly implied in the marketing literature, the notion of a DSP appears to be very similar to the notion of dominant ideology as described by Marx and Engels in their 1845 work *The German Ideology* (translated by Lawrence and Wishart 1970). The DSP seems to function as an ideology that seeks to legitimize and justify dominant social process. The fundamental difference between DSP and ideology lies in the definition of ideology. While DSP literature relies on a more critical Marxist definition of ideology, here we employ a positive definition of the concept and discuss ideology as a representation of set of ideas of those individuals and groups that are in fact counter to the ideas of their dominant culture.

MELUCCI'S FRAMEWORK OF IDEOLOGY

Like Touraine 1981, Melucci (1996) suggests that the three analytical elements that make up the form of an ideology of a movement are: identity (members are able to articulate a self-identity which determines the limits of collective identity and the legitimacy of the movement), opposition (there is identification by movement members of an adversary); and totality (members are able to articulate shared objectives). Developing Touraine's (1981) trichotomy, Melucci (1996) adds a time dimension to this model by proposing the three constituent elements of the ideology take on changed cultural contents and roles as the movement develops from a formative phase into a consolidative phase.

The formative phase occurs during the nascent state of the movement. It is a "moment of the fusion of the various components of a movement into a new form of solidarity in which the expressive dimensions and emotional identification with collective goals prevail" (Melucci 1996, 350). During this phase, ideology legitimizes the movement's goals and identity by referring back to the past. It is also used to overcome the "inadequacy of practice" (Melucci 1996,

Advances in Consumer Research
Volume 39, ©2011

350). For example, when a movement does not yet have the capacity for action, leaders may use their movement's ideology to produce symbols.

During the consolidation phase, "the mobilized social group, the adversary, and the collective goals are redefined in a more pertinent manner; ideology becomes a more complex and detailed symbolic system" (Melucci 1996, 352). Two aspects of ideology become important. Integration of the movement as a whole is accomplished by a repeated proposal for values and norms; the control of deviant behavior; and the stabilization of certain rituals. Secondly, ideology fulfills a strategic function. This can take place by widening the margins within which the movement acts in the political system or by expanding the movement's base by encouraging groups which were previously outside the conflict to become involved.

BACKGROUND TO THE SF MOVEMENT

The conceptualization of the SF Movement includes a multiplicity of different organizations, interest groups and individuals. The initiator and main driver of the movement since it officially become an international organization in 1989 is the official SF organization which has attracted over 100,000 subscribed members who belong to 1000 local chapters in over 150 countries (SF.Editore, 2011). Each of the organization's nine national associations (in Italy, France, Germany, Netherlands, Switzerland, UK, Japan, USA and Australia) hosts a range of events. The organization's ideology is nicely summed up by the current marketing slogan that they use: "Good, Clean and Fair". This ideology has evolved since SF began. As the president of the SF Movement Carlo Petrini explains: "[Its] a result of our twenty-year journey.... While respecting our original search for pleasure and taste, it includes the ever more urgent ecological and social issues emerging around the world" (SF.Editoire 2009, online).

METHODOLOGY

Historical method (adopted from Shafer 1974) provides the best research design method for capturing a dynamic evolutionary concept such as change (Kumcu 1987). The data was collected at both the organizational level (a mix of secondary data found in SF archives, documents and publications and primary data obtained by attending a SF organization Meeting of International Councilors in Switzerland in 2008) and at the individual activist level (primary data collected in semi-structured interviews conducted with members from either the SF organization or the wider SF Movement). In interviews, respondents were asked a series of questions pertaining to their own personal life histories (e.g. their own current beliefs and experiences of ideological change). They were also asked to serve as an expert informer on various aspects of the SF Movement. This critical approach to data collection provides a human and subjective account of change and allows insights into aspects of ideology (such as movement identity) that are not otherwise apparent from organizational texts. Interview respondents were selected to achieve diversity and to ensure a rich and more realistic historical data. Thus, different types of SF members (official members of the SF organization as well as unofficial members of the wider SF Movement) were interviewed. Respondents were also selected to have a variety of nationalities in order to acknowledge this aspect of the SF Movement. As with the analysis of the organizational texts, the main aim for the data collection in the interview stage was depth. Thus, when a new respondent's stories added no extra relevant information, the interview process was considered complete The researchers obtained access to impressive wide range of people for this research, including founding leaders of the international SF organization based in Italy as well as grassroots members from seven other countries (see Table 1). In total, 23 respondents were interviewed.

Table 1 An overview of the respondents interviewed.

Pseudonym *	Involvement **	Nationality ***	General interest
Glenn	M	A/N	An academic who founded and leads a SF convivium
Rosa	M	I/N	Owns an Italian cooking school. Founded a SF convivium
Jim	M	E	SF convivium leader. Was owner of a local restaurant
Carmel	M	I	Manager for a SF office at the International headquarters
Agosto	M	I	Academic at the University of Gastronomic Sciences
Raul	M	I	Holds a senior position in the SF Italy organisation
Santo	M	I	Holds a senior position in the SF Italy organisation
Piero	M	I	On the international SF board and is manager of a SF office
Elisa	M	A/S	Director of a geographical area at SF international headquarters
Fiorella	M	I	Works at the SF Study Centre
Pam	S	N	Works for national organic association. A Green Party member
Jane	S	N	Political studies student who organises a campus eco-group
Sam	S	N	Academic teaching global politics of food

John	S	N	Community social justice advocate and an environmentalist
Bianca	S	N	Chairperson of a local farmers' market
Vincent	S	I/N	Owns and manages a fresh pasta making factory
Tibold	S	G	PhD student studying wine
Gilbert	S	E/N	Retired café owner and psychiatric nurse. A home gardener
Ray	S	N	Academic whose research area includes wine and food tourism
Doug	S	E/N	Culinary-tourism academic. Experience in hospitality industry
Ruby	S	N	High school French teacher. A Green Party member
Rob	S	N	High school art teacher who runs adult cooking classes
Kaye	S	N	National spokesperson for a multinational fast food company

* To ensure the promised confidentiality, each respondent has been given a fictional name;
**M=Member S=Supporter;
***A=Australian, N= New Zealander, I=Italian, E=English, G=German S=Spanish.

Given the interpretive stance of the research, the historical materials were contextualized within Melucci's theoretical framework as the primary means to reveal the reality of the historical framework used to structure the analysis. Chronological periodization of this information presents the history of the SF Movement and the changing elements and ideological roles scattered throughout the narrative which are then brought together at the end of the findings section in a summary table.

FINDINGS: THE HISTORY OF THE SF MOVEMENT AND INSIGHTS INTO SF IDEOLOGY

1980 –Mid-1990s. The roots of SF can be traced back to a specific place, person and time. The environment is Bra (a small town in northwest Italy) and the person is Carlo Petrini "the main animator of the town" (Carmel), who along with a number of other friends who were "passionate about local food and local music would organize folk festivals to celebrate traditions and histories" (Raul). Petrini and his friends from Bra became interested in wine and in 1980 "they came up with the idea of founding a club—something like the then trendy gastronomical academies, but with the specific goal of spreading the culture of good food even among ordinary people" (Petrini and Padovani 2006, 12). This club was the nucleus of what would later become Arci Gola—the forerunner of the SF organization. At this time, the Socialist and Communist parties in Italy supported a nationwide network called Arci which organized an array of cultural events. Based on a common interest in food and wine and spurred on by Petrini, an oeno-gastronomic group, Arci Gola started in 1983. Initially the group's main goal was to support local producers by increasing the value and demand for local cuisine and products by creating a market for high quality food and wine products. As the group developed, it also began to advocate the right to material and convivial pleasure for everyone and that the flavor of the food was a serious matter.

In 1986, the Arci Gola group—annoyed by the fact that Mc-Donald's was opening a store at Rome's famous Piazza di Spagna—protested against an invasion of American fast food by handing out bowls of free pasta in front of the fast food restaurant (SF.Editore 2002). In 1987, Arci Gola published its first journal and soon began producing articles and books. On the cover of its first journal, a common snail is introduced as the organization's official logo (chosen because it moves slowly and calmly eats its way through life, SF.Editore 2001). Notable in these early works is "[A]n un-

compromising and tough language that stakes out its opposition to businessmen, bureaucrats and the local church in a single J'accuse" (Petrini and Padovani 2006, 28). The use of war and military terms such as lieutenant, defensive maneuver, self-destruction and enemy (c.f. Petrini and Padovani 2006, 4, 70, 71, 81) provides a case in point. Thanks to the success of these media, the ideas promoted by the group gained wide attention. Later that year, Petrini organized a conference called *At the Table with the Italian Communist Party*, and in his opening speech "he exalted the culture of honesty and authenticity at the table, what he called the slow food approach of eating well and slowly and he spoke out against the effects of fast-food and against the constant rush to make a profit" (Petrini and Padovani 2006, 58).

In 1989, a manifesto of the slow food approach was written and presented in Paris at the inauguration of the international SF Movement. The spirit of the manifesto is summarized nicely by Porta (cited in Petrini and Padovani 2006, 73): "The Slow Food manifesto [1987] is after all the dream of holding the old kitchen stove in our arms, our chest against its knobs, in a slow embrace". At this event, participants celebrated the bicentennial of the French Revolution and the pioneer chefs that became the celebrities during the Revolution. SF was not only applauding the renowned chefs, but the fact that good quality cuisine was available to the masses. This idea is a central tenet of the SF concept and to this day SF fights to liberate the traditional Italian taverns from the threat of a fast food culture.

After the official launch, SF leaders started expanding the conceptual makeup of SF and the range of activities they conducted. In 1990 they launched the SF Editore Publishing House which was initially the main tool used by the organization to build their profile. Reading early SF publications, one is struck by many examples of SF using symbols, cultural models and language from their country's political past. Many terms with strong communist connotations, such as comrades and fraternity, were regularly used by leaders of the organization when addressing or discussing their membership. For example, in the original SF manifesto, Porta writes, "Comrades, enough with these sloppy grilled chops" (1987, cited in Petrini and Padovani 2006, 7). The next pivotal moment in the development of the organization was the SF World Congress which was held in 1990. A significant outcome of this meeting was a statute outlining the main tasks of the organization including the improvement of food culture, the defense of food heritage including culinary practices and the promotion and distribution of quality products. After the congress, "the value of the term *Slow* as a global marketing tool became clear [and] we realized that we had to consolidate our image and build a truly international movement" (Petrini and Padovani 2006, 136). This meant re-positioning the political standpoint of the organization away from the organization's Leftist origins and towards a stance where "we're not aligned with governments" (Elisa) so that the SF organization "could ask for support from left, right, center or whatever" (Peiro) and thus SF increased the political domain within which the organization was able to operate.

In 1992 the first national SF association outside Italy was opened in Germany and one year later, SF opened a national office in Switzerland. Following the success of SF in these two countries, the decision was made at the 1994 SF Italy National Congress to invest in the development of SF internationally. SF also decided to adopt the objective of improving local products, not just in Italy but in the other countries where SF had a presence. This was a significant change, as up until that date, SF's goals were often seen by its members to be largely about promoting the Italian way of life and Italian products both nationally and abroad.

Mid-1990s–Mid-2000s. Along with this new emphasis on improving the quality of local food, SF started branching out into other areas. Raul explains, "So for the first 10 years [the goal] was to promote the food quality... but we started to see there was a great danger of extinction in not only the products but also their producers". In 1996, SF put forward the idea of creating an "Ark" built on the biblical metaphor of Noah's Ark which would save traditional and rare food species from the big flood of industrial foods. The following quote from Petrini (1996, cited in Petrini and Padovani 2006, 93) illustrates how the organization's leaders used symbols, cultural models and language from the bible to help bring this concept to fruition: "Since the flood was imminent... our ark could be the only salvation. The incoming storms threatened to inflict genocide... we had to build an ark... once the flood was over, we would come down from the ark, back to earth, like Noah". The launching of this event was indicative of the changing direction of SF ideology, "Looking back you could say that that moment [1996] was the first great change... it was the moment when we started talking about biodiversity and biodiversity means talking about the environment (Raul).

By the mid-1990s, both the Italian Arci Gola SF organization and the International SF organization had grown significantly and the organization's leaders decided to consolidate their efforts. This merging was important as it symbolized SF's strategic decision to leave behind the strong Italian identity that had characterized the organization up until this time. Given this change in focus, movement leaders espoused new principles that promoted the direction they envisioned for the international movement. Amongst these were the principles of diversity and unity as SF's president Petrini explains, "The importance of the former, the strength of the latter. What we are: different. And what we have to be: united" (Petrini 2003, 10).

Also in the mid-1990s, SF leaders started developing the organization's focus on biodiversity into a more widespread and complex notion of general food environmentalism. This thinking was formalized in 1999 when the organization introduced SF as an eco-gastronomic organization, as explained by Petrini (Petrini and Padovani 2006, 118), "An environmentalist who is not a gastronomist is sad; a gastronomist who is not an environmentalist is silly. We changed our point of view with the idea of defending good food in a healthy environment. This move ratified our transformation into an eco-gastronomic movement". With this new positioning as an eco-gastronomic organization, SF moved away from opposing the culinary aspects of fast food and new adversaries were defined, as Glenn explains, "Its opponents have been much more delineated as

the global trans-national food corporations and agricultural mono-cropping... and in that sense that is now more explicitly identified as what SF is against".

A noteworthy event in 2000 was the founding of the SF USA national association with headquarters in New York City. The growth of SF USA was exponential in the following years adding a new flavor to the organization. In 2001, two new SF websites appeared. As the SF ideology spread around the world facilitated by the creation of an international website, the organisation kept its feet firmly planted in the ground by engaging in two fresh conflicts: (1) The campaign against hygienic norms that the organization leaders believed would jeopardize the production of raw milk cheeses; and (2) the No GMO Wine campaign which was launched against the Europe's commercialization of transgenic vines. Notably, at this time there was "a really conscious effort to build particular types of relationships around eco-green activism in food" (Sam). For example, SF became involved in an alliance of associations (including NGOs such as Greenpeace, farmers associations, organizations of distributors and corporations) by sharing a manifesto saying no to GMO.

Mid-2000s–2010. The year 2004 was a big year in the history of the SF with the high point being a world meeting of food communities; Terra Madre event. This event signified the SF organization's increased awareness of ethical issues surrounding agricultural and gastronomy. Evidence of SF leaders referring to the past to help defend this new focus for their movement can be seen in the ceremonies' closing speech, where one leader made direct reference to a social movement which had come before SF, "the feelings of Terra Madre [were similar] to those that arose during the assembly of Sem Terra, the movement that gave strength and a voice to Brazilian farmers" (SF.Editore 2006, online). This new facet to SF ideology would later be more clearly articulated as fair food, "Thanks to Terra Madre, where we started working with the farmers especially in the South of the world, we understood... the real concept of 'fair' in food today" (Raul). There is evidence SF members used ideology at this event to create symbolic gestures that represent their high hopes for the future in this domain. Petrini explains, "When the Middle Eastern meeting was held, people were a bit stiff to start with, but after a few minutes Israel, Palestine, Iraq and Lebanon understood they were all part of the same family and symbolically dipped bread in salt. The great fraternal gesture of dipping bread in salt!" (SF.Editore 2006, online). The Terra Madre event really consolidated the SF ideology which at present is based on three basic principles: good, clean and fair.

Also in 2004, SF officially opened the world's first University of Gastronomic Sciences in Italy. The university aims to transform gastronomy into a multidisciplinary science and mirroring an important step in the development of the SF ideology. The SF organization has since adopted the term neo-gastronomy to explain their commitment to this multifaceted approach to food which includes giving consideration to a range of production, consumption, sustainability, quality and social justice issues. In 2007, at the fifth International SF Congress, the top priority was increasing the organisation's membership numbers and it was decided that the SF organisation would change their statutes to allow them to become "more flexible, especially in developing countries" (Elisa). As well as aiming to include more members in their movement, SF actively worked to attract the support of a number of groups and organisations that were previously outside their domain. For example, SF and Fair-trade Italia "united to support a three-year project entitled 'Sustainable agriculture, biodiversity protection and fair trade, together against poverty' co-financed by the European Union" (SF.Editoire 2008, online).

In 2008, the third Terra Madre was held and for the first time event organizers invited participants to bring their instruments. Santo explains the logic behind this addition to the event: "Only our actual lives tend to separate food from music… with Terra Madre we want to defend and promote food communities, music, common interests". This was significant in that it revealed the far reaching extent of the SF organization's ambitions, "We don't want to only preserve the knowledge of food and the knowledge of culture, but also the knowledge about our cultural traditions" (Raul). SF's shared organizational culture was particularly obvious at this event; with many gestural codes (such as using a peasant's horn from the Peruvian Andes to call event participants to a meeting) and cultural rituals (such as wearing traditional costumes throughout the event).

2010 saw local Terra Madre regional meetings held in the Balkans, Brazil, Georgia, Azerbaijan, Kazakhstan and Argentina, indicative of the direction that SF is currently taking. Looking forward, the "future of Slow Food is really difficult to predict" (Agosto) and it seems likely that there will be the continual extension of the SF ideology into other domains with the expansion of the scope of activities by the organization. The SF leaders are, however, quick to point out that "the main focus must remain on food" (Piero). Evidence of the changing content and form of SF ideology has been scattered throughout the above narrative and is now synthesized in Table 2.

DISCUSSION

The top section of Table 2 shows that three elements of ideology (identity, opposition, and totality) are present throughout the history of SF and that the content of these elements of ideology have changed considerably over the years. The bottom section of Table 2 shows examples of how ideology has served different functions throughout the evolution of the SF Movement. While Melucci's model of ideological change predicts that movements pass through just two phases of ideological development throughout the movement lifecycle (a formative and consolidative phase), our study revealed not two but three distinct periods of ideological change. These periods are as follows: (1) 1980s to ~1995, Recreational-gastronomy; (2) ~1995 to ~2005, Ecological- gastronomy; and (3) ~2005 to ~2010, Neo-gastronomy. Furthermore, the SF data revealed that each time the ideology changed, it appears to have passed through a new formative phase of development before becoming consolidated.

Much of the literature on lifecycles in marketing suggests that the lifecycle of a product (or in this case an ideology) may be more complex than the framework proposed by Melucci. Melucci's framework appears stuck in the metaphor of the product lifecycle of 30 or so years ago in marketing (e.g. birth, growth, maturation, death) and the two phases (formative and consolidative) do not capture the richness of the true diffusion process over time. For example, Dhalla and Yuspeh 1976 say that it is possible to restart this cycle again and again. Applying this theory to the context of ideology could inform and strengthen Melucci's framework of ideological development.

Table 2 A historical summary of the elements and role of the SF Movement's ideology

	Elements of Ideology		
	SF self-identity	SF adversaries	SF shared objectives
1980s to ~1995	Italian focused More characteristics of a club or an association (e.g. exclusive, hierarchal structure	Bad food/wine Speed (fast life), fast food Openly oppositional	Recreational or Oeno-gastronomy: Promote '*good*' food (quality gastronomy) and the right to pleasure Celebrate slow and conviviality support small producers and improve food culture
~1995 to ~2005	More internationally focused More characteristics of an organization	Industrial foods and standardization Mono-cropping, GMOs and hygienic norms	Eco-gastronomy: Promote '*clean*' food - 'good' food in a healthy environment Defend biodiversity
~2005 to ~2010	Very internationally focused (local identity in a global world) More movement characteristics (e.g. inclusive, emphasizes networks)	(as above) + fighting against 'cultural' globalization Less oppositional (promoting message "for not against")	Neo-gastronomy: Promote '*fair*' food - social dimension of food Virtuous globalization Extension into new domains

Role of ideology					
Formative	Consolidative	Formative	Consolidative	Formative	Consolidative
1980s to ~1995		~1995 to ~2005		~2005 to ~2010	
Referring to past (ex. Military language and Communist connotations) Producing symbols (ex. French Revolution)	Putting forward proposal for values, norms (ex. SF's Manifesto) Widening the margins of the political system (ex. Moving away from Leftist origins)	Referring to past and producing symbols (ex. Noah's Ark)	Proposal for values, norms (ex. Diversity and unity) Networking (ex. No-GMO alliance)	Referring to past (ex. Sem Terra Movement) Producing symbols (ex. Dipping bread in salt gesture)	Creating rituals (ex. Ways of dressing at Terra Madre event) Networking (ex. SF and Fair- trade Italia Project)

Figure 1 suggests an extended model of ideological change in a consumer movement. The points A, B, and C show the moments where the ideology is re-launched. The problem with applying product life-cycle theory to SF is that it is impossible to predict how the product (in this case SF ideology) will finally be adopted. Furthermore, the product life cycle model has traditionally been used to explain sales and repeat sales, which are arguably quite different from the case at hand. Given these limitations, the proposed model is useful as a metaphor but not as strong predictive model.

Although our findings suggest that the ideology changes over and over again, Melucci's framework still provides significant insights into what happens to an innovation, such as an ideology, as it diffuses over time and thus it complements the diffusion of innovation models (as ex-plained by Rogers 1976). For example, over time "the mobilized social group, the adversary, and the collective goals are redefined in a more pertinent manner [and] ideology becomes a more complex and detailed symbolic system" (Melucci 1996, 352). Furthermore, the framework recognises that it is not only the innovation itself changing as it diffuses over time, but that the purpose for which it is used is also changing. Further research which investigates using product life cycle and diffusion of innovation models to help explain ideological change is warranted. Of particular interest are questions such as 'are the concepts of early adopt-ers and laggards still relevant?' and if so, 'when new ideological stages emerge, is there a period of tension between early adopters and those still consuming previous ideological underpinnings?'.

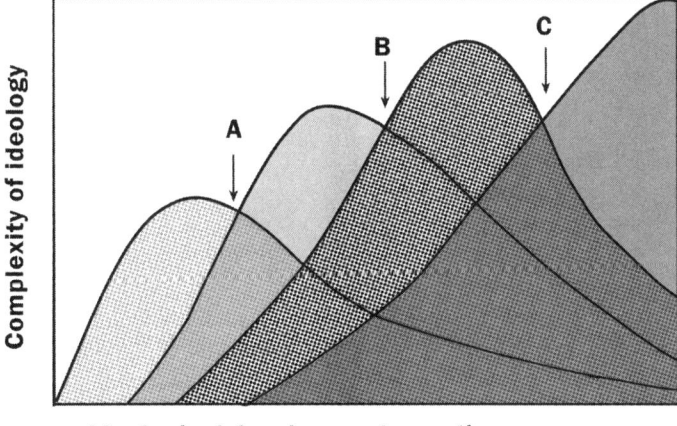

Ideological development over time

Figure 1. Ideological development of a consumer movement over time.

CONCLUSION

There are two major contributions that this article makes toward understanding interactions between consumer movements and ideology. Firstly, the research proposes that Melucci's framework as it stands is useful to consumer behavior researchers for understanding ideological change in the context of contemporary consumer activist movements, in particular for conceptualizing the form of an ideology and as such it provides an appropriate definition for the concept of ideology that can be used in the consumer movement context. This will allow consum-er behaviour researchers to differentiate ideology from (and compare ideology to) other similar concepts and theories they are more familiar with such as values, ideas and the dominant social paradigm. Melucci's framework is also useful in that it helps to operationalize ideology by providing a process with which to identify and categorise ideological change.

Secondly, this article highlights that lifecycle literature in market-ing has the potential to add strength and vigor to Melucci's framework. Melucci's framework as it stands has only two simple stages and does not go far enough to capture the dynamics of ideological change, which appears to be re-formed over and over again as the movement develops. To this end, a new model of ideological development is proposed that builds on Melucci's (1996) framework, and provides a comprehensive tool for the analysis of movement ideology.

REFERENCES

Arnould, E., and C. Thompson (2005), "Consumer Culture Theory (CCT): Twenty Years of Research," *Journal of Consumer Research,* 31 (4), 868-882.

Buechler, S. M. (1995), "New Social Movement Theories," *The Sociological Quarterly* 36 (3), 441-464.

Cherrier, H., and J. Murray (2002), "Drifting Away from Excessive Consumption: A New Social Movement Based on Identity Construction," *Advances in Consumer Research,* 29, 245-248.

Dhalla, NK., and S. Yuspeh (1976), "Forget the product life cycle concept," *Harvard Business Review,* 54 (1), 102-112.

Geuss, R. (1981), *The Idea of a Critical Theory: Habermas and the Frankfurt School,* Cambridge, UK: Cambridge University Press.

Kilbourne, W. (1995), "Green Advertising: Salvation or Oxymoron?" *Journal of Advertising,* 24 (2), 7-19.

Kilbourne, W. (1998), "Green marketing: a theoretical perspective," *Journal of Marketing Management,* 14 (6), 641–655.

Kilbourne, W., Beckmann, S., and E. Thelen (2002), "The role of the dominant social paradigm in environmental attitudes: a multinational examination," *Journal of Business Research,* 55 (3), 193-204.

Kohn, M. L. (1989), *Class and Conformity: A Study in Values,* Chicago, IL: University of Chicago Press.

Kozinets, R. V. (2002), "Can Consumers Escape the Market? Emancipatory Illuminations from Burning Man," *Journal of Consumer Research,* 29 (1), 20-38.

Kozinets, R. V. (2008), "Technology/Ideology: How Ideological Fields Influence Consumers' Technology Narratives," *Journal of Consumer Research,* 34 (6), 865-881.

Kozinets, R. V., and J. Handelman (1998), "Ensouling Consumption: A Netnographic Exploration of the Meaning of Boycotting Behavior," *Advances in Consumer Research,* 25 (1), 475-480.

Kozinets, R. V., and J. Handelman (2004), "Adversaries of Consumption: Consumer Movements, Activism, and Ideology," *Journal of Consumer Research,* 31, 691-794.

Kumcu, E. (1987), "Historical method: Toward a relevant analysis of marketing systems," in *Philosophical and Radical Thought in Marketing,* eds. F. Firat, N. Dholakia and R. Bagozzi, Toronto: Lexington Books, 117-133.

Lawrence, and Wishart (Eds.). (1970), *Karl Marx and Frederick Engels: Collected Works,* New York and London: International Publishers Co Inc.

Melucci, A. (1996). *Challenging Codes: Collective Action in the Information Age,* Cambridge, UK: University Press.

Parkins, W., and G.Graig (2006), *Slow Living,* Oxford, UK: Berg Publishers.

Penaloza, L., and L. Price (1993), "Consumer Resistance: A Conceptual Overview," *Advances in Consumer Research,* 20 (1), 123-128.

Petrini, C. (2003), "The Slow Dreamers. *Slow: The International Herald of Taste,* (45), 10-13.

Petrini, C., and G. Padovani (2006), *Slow Food Revolution: A New Culture for Eating and Living* (Francesco and Santovetti, Trans.), New York, NY:Rizzoli International.

Rogers, E. M. (1976), "New Product Adoption and Diffusion. *Journal of Consumer Research,* 2(4), 290-301.

Sassatelli, R., and F. Davolio (2010), "Consumption, Pleasure and Politics," *Journal of Consumer Culture,* 10 (2), 202-232.

SF.Editoire. (2008, 19th June), "Slow Food at the Organic World Congress, Italia," http://press.slowfood.com/press/eng/leggi.lasso?cod=3E6E345B0f1d42A10DXNX14DB842&ln=en

SF.Editoire. (2009, September), "Slow Food International Homepage," http://www.slowfood.com/

SF.Editore. (2002, 24th February), "Food in the Slow Lane, SF Press Area," http://press.slowfood.com/press/eng/leggi.lasso?cod=161&ln=en

SF.Editore. (2006, 30th October), "Terra Madre's Closing Assembly, Italia," http://press.slowfood.com/press/eng/leggi.lasso?cod=552698291925e27E51nnTSmAEEA5&ln=en

SF.Editore. (2011), "Slow Food International, About Us, 28 Januray," http://www.slowfood.com/international/1/about-us

SF.Nation. (2009), "Slow Food Nation 08 Homepage," http://slowfoodnation.org/2008-event/the-main-event/

Shafer, R. J. (1974), *A Guide to Historical Method,* Homewood, IL: Dorsey Press.

Touraine, A. (1981), *The Voice and the Eye: An Analysis of Social Movements.* Cambridge, UK: Cambridge University Press.

Challenging the Culture-Free Hypothesis of Cognitive Age among Older Consumers: Evidence from a Cross-National Survey

Florian Kohlbacher, German Institute for Japanese Studies (DIJ) Tokyo, Japan
Lynn Sudbury Riley, Liverpool John Moores University, UK
Ágnes Hofmeister, Corvinus University of Budapest, Hungary

INTRODUCTION

The current ageing of the world's population is probably the most profound demographic change in the history of humankind. It is a pervasive and truly global phenomenon, without precedent or parallel, largely irreversible, and with the young populations of the past unlikely to occur again. Indeed, at the world level, the number of older persons will exceed the number of children by 2047, which has already occurred in many developed regions. The profundity of this demographic change will impact on economic growth, labor markets, pensions, health care, housing, migration, politics, and of course consumption (United Nations 2007). If the second half of the 20th century focused on the young, the 21st century will have to focus on the mature.

Despite the growing importance of the 50+ population and its perception as an attractive market segment, older consumers are still routinely neglected by many marketing and advertising practitioners (Niemelä-Nyrhinen 2007; Simcock and Sudbury 2006; Uncles and Lee 2006) and what is known about their consumer behavior still lags far behind what is known about other important segments (Williams et al. 2010; Yoon et al. 2005). This is particularly true of research conducted outside the USA, where there is a marked lack of a coherent body of knowledge pertaining to senior consumers which can guide international marketing decisions.

Self-perceived or cognitive age has emerged as a key variable in studying older people and their consumer behavior (Psychology & Marketing 2001; Wilkes 1992). The relatively sparse number of studies that have investigated this type of age identity in cross-national settings have concluded that cognitive age is "culture-free" (cf. also Barak 2009; Van Auken and Barry 2009; Van Auken, Barry, and Bagozzi 2006). Using data from an empirical study in four different countries, we challenge this view of cognitive age as culture free and thus aim to make a contribution to knowledge on older consumers on an international scale.

SELF-PERCEIVED AGE

Chronological age is a constant in daily life, in age related research, and in marketing. The use of chronological age as an objective measure that shapes the lives of individuals can be illustrated by the age restrictions imposed by the government. For example, chronological age dictates the point at which an individual can drive, vote, drink alcohol, marry, and claim a state pension. In research, chronological age is the most commonly used yardstick when studying the ageing process (Cunningham and Brookbank 1988). In marketing, chronological age is the most frequently used of all demographic variables to describe consumer behavior research and to segment consumer markets (Barak and Schiffman 1981).

Despite these numerous uses, the limitations of chronological age have long been acknowledged (Adams 1971; Heron and Chown 1967). Whilst chronological age may be a useful clue to performance during early life (Jarvik 1975), ageing does not perfectly coincide with chronological age (Bell 1972) so homogeneity in individual lifestyles and conditions among age groups cannot be assumed. Indeed, the number of years lived is a poor indicator of a person's attitudes and consumer behavior (Chua, Cote, and Leong 1990; Van Auken, Barry, and Anderson 1993).

Given the limitations of chronological age, the implications of the cliché that a person is as young, or as old, as they feel may be more useful in understanding the behavior of older people. Research shows that the age a person perceives themselves to be, or identifies with, constrains them to recognize changes in themselves and to perceive that attitudes toward them have changed (Peters 1971). Thus, the age a person identifies with gives an insight into the behaviors that the individual thinks society expects from them (Guptill 1969). Likewise, an individual's self-perceived age gives a better understanding of their likely consumer behavior than can chronological age alone (Barak and Schiffman 1981; Cleaver and Muller 2002; Schiffman and Sherman 1991; Stephens 1991). For this reason, self-perceived age has been used in research investigating older consumers and values (Kohlbacher and Chéron 2010; Sudbury and Simcock 2009b), attitudes toward senior sales promotions (Moschis and Mathur 2006; Sudbury and Simcock 2010; Tepper 1994), brand purchasing (Uncles and Lee 2006), innovative purchasing (Sherman, Schiffman, and Dillon 1988; Stephens 1991), information seeking (Barak and Rahtz 1990), interest in fashion (Wilkes 1992), complaining behavior (Dolinsky et al. 1998), media usage (Barak and Gould 1985; Johnson 1993), internet use (Eastman and Iyer 2005; McMellon, Schiffman, and Sherman 1997) and in segmentation studies (Sudbury and Simcock 2009a).

There are many different ways of measuring self-perceived age, and these methods fall into two major groups. The first, and oldest, is age identity (Cavan et al. 1949), concerning the age category (young, middle-aged, old) in which people perceive themselves to be, and is used extensively in gerontology studies. A second type of measure grew in response to the recognition that ageing is multidimensional (Birren 1968), comprising biological, psychological, and sociological dimensions, none of which can be understood without reference to the others (Riley 1985). The cognitive age scale (Barak and Schiffman 1981) is one such multidimensional scale, which incorporates the different dimensions of aging by asking people how old they think they look (biological), how old they feel (psychological and biological), and how old they rate their behavior and interests (social). This typology has its roots in the consensus reached by philosophers concerning the existential stances with regard to the human condition, which are knowing, feeling, and acting (Bengtson, Reedy, and Gordon 1985). The cognitive age scale has become the most popular measure of self-perceived age in marketing research pertaining to seniors. The superiority of the cognitive age scale over other available instruments is due to its ease of administration and understanding by respondents (Stephens 1991), its validity (Van Auken and Barry 1995), and its multidimensionality. As a matter of fact, ease of administration and understanding are crucial issues in scale employment with samples of older people (Flynn Reinecke 1993).

The overwhelming finding from studies of age identity is that the vast majority of older adults do not identify with the age categories 'elderly' or 'old', preferring instead to consider themselves 'middle aged'. This finding holds true even for people past retirement age (when, arguably, they are deemed old by society), and it is not until people are well into their seventies that more and more begin to admit to an old age status (Blau 1956). Those studies that have utilized the multidimensional scales to measure the self-perceived age of older people (for example Barak 1998; Barak and Gould 1985; Clark, Long, and Schiffman 1999; Goldsmith and Heiens 1992; Johnson

1995, 1996; Kastenbaum et al. 1972; Mathur, Sherman, and Schiffman 1998; Sudbury 2004) have found a strong degree of consistency, in that:

- There is little agreement between self-perceived age and chronological age, although the two correlate.
- There is a strong bias towards a more youthful self-perceived age in comparison to chronological age.
- The look age dimension is closest to actual age than any of the other self-perceived age dimensions.

Whilst the majority of studies into self-perceived age, at least from a marketing perspective, have been conducted in the US, the relatively sparse and recent research conducted outside America tentatively suggests that self-perceived age is a universal concept that can be measured globally, in different languages, and in a reliable and valid manner (Barak 2009). Indeed, the cross-cultural research by Barak and associates suggests that the cognitive age scale is reliable and can be used in diverse cultures and that there is a universal nature of the way human beings - irrespective of culture - perceive and feel about cognitive age (Barak et al. 2001; Barak et al. 2003; Mathur et al. 2001). As a result, researchers have suggested that cognitive age is "culture free" (cf. also Barak 2009; Van Auken and Barry 2009; Van Auken et al. 2006).

Nevertheless, in a recent review of the literature Barak (2009: 8) concluded that that cross-cultural global age research is still in an early pioneering stage and that follow up and replication studies are needed. Indeed, validity is a dynamic process that results from the accumulation of evidence over time (Wells 1975) and the aggregation of results (Peter 1981), with Epstein (1980: 796) arguing that "there is no more fundamental requirement in science than that the replicability of findings be established". In fact, replications play a valuable role in ensuring the integrity of a discipline's empirical results and they are considered to be important for the advancement of science and for discovering empirical generalizations (Easley, Madden, and Dunn 2000; Hubbard and Armstrong 1994; Hubbard and Lindsay 2002). This is particularly important when researching consumers by age group as period and cohort effects play a crucial role in addition to age effects (Cole et al. 2008; Fukuda 2010; Palmore 1978; Rentz, Reynolds, and Stout 1983); this means that e.g. findings about older consumers 10 or 20 years ago may no longer hold true today. Given that the few cross-national studies on cognitive age have been conducted at least 10 years ago, our paper makes an important contribution to the literature by checking whether the culture-free assumption of cognitive age also holds true for the current cohorts of older consumers.

In time, it may be possible to acknowledge the phenomenon as a useful marketing tool that is truly global. On this basis, the present study contributes to the small but growing body of knowledge pertaining to self-perceived age outside the USA, and for these reasons four countries which have little or no previous research in this field have been selected.

METHODOLOGY

The study comprised part of a major piece of international research into older consumers across several culturally disparate nations, and utilized questionnaires. The lower age parameter of 50 was selected on the basis that this is the starting point for many age-related services offered to older consumers (for example, SAGA, Age UK, Seniorsurfers.net). Besides, previous research has called for including middle-aged respondents in order to better understand aging mechanisms and their impact on consumer behavior (e.g. Cole et al. 2008). The two self-perceived age instruments, both age identity and cognitive age, were used. Additionally, respondents completed a battery of socio-demographic questions.

The four nations selected are Japan, Germany, UK, and Hungary. Japan is ranked number one in every international league table that considers population ageing, with 28% of its population already age 60 or over and a median age of 43 years (United Nations 2007). Despite the fact that it is the country most severely affected by the megatrend that is population ageing only two previous studies have considered self-perceived age from a marketing perspective, and both found Japan's older population to feel about 8 years younger than their actual age (Kohlbacher and Chéron 2010; Van Auken et al. 2006).

Germany is ranked 3rd in the league tables produced by the United Nations (2007) with 25.3% of its population already 60 or above. Despite this, there has never been a marketing study into the self-perceived ages of German's senior consumers, although a previous gerontological study suggests that Germany's older population feel about 12 years younger than their chronological age (Smith and Baltes 1999). Data from the German Aging Survey in 1996, however, found their age identity about 6.5 years younger than their chronological age (Westerhof and Barrett 2005; Westerhof, Barrett, and Steverink 2003).

The UK is ranked 17th from a total of 192 countries with 22% of its population already 60 or over. The three previous studies conducted in Britain (Sudbury 2004; Sudbury and Simcock 2009b; Szmigin and Carrigan 2000) suggest older British consumers feel about 10 years younger than their actual age. Finally, Hungary is ranked 19th in the league tables and has more than 21% of its population already aged 60 or above. Despite this, and the fact that Hungary is an important market that has made a major transition from communism to a market that has attracted much inward investment, no previous study has been conducted into the self-perceived ages of its older consumers. Overall, our sample thus consists of the following four countries in three regions: 1) Japan, the most aged society in the world, and – in our sample – the representative of Asia, 2) Germany and 3) Hungary as the representatives from continental Europe, one being the largest and oldest of the Western economies on the Continent and the other an a recent member of the European Union with a communist past, 4) the UK as a representative of the Anglo-Saxon European culture.

The questionnaire was translated and back translated by teams in Japan, Germany, and Hungary before being piloted across all four countries. Several changes were made on the basis of the pilot study. Three lists were purchased, one German (n = 6000), one British (n = 5000), and one Japanese (n = 1044) that contained randomly selected names and addresses of people aged 50+, and a questionnaire and pre-paid envelope was posted to them all. Piloting in Hungary demonstrated the difficulties of self-completion among many older Hungarian adults, thus the distribution strategy was adapted in that country, where a team of trained researchers administered the questionnaire face-to-face to 200 adults aged 50+.

A total of 1368 usable questionnaires were received. After removing cases with missing values for the scales used in this paper, 1293 questionnaires remained in the data set. Table 1 details the final sample by age and country.

Table 1: Total Sample by Chronological Age and Country

Country	N	Response Rate (%)	Mean Age	Std. Deviation
UK	456	3.5	66.24	8.21
Germany	211	9.1	63.50	8.41
Japan	426	40.1	64.11	8.56
Hungary	200	N/A	58.66	5.63
Total	**1293**		**63.92**	**8.39**

The reliability of the cognitive age scale was found to be acceptable (Cronbach's alphas ranged from .88 for the UK sample to .91 for the Hungarian and Japanese samples). A confirmatory factor analysis (CFA) using AMOS 18 led to composite reliabilities ranging from .88 for the UK to .91 for Hungary and Japan and average variances extracted ranging from .65 in the UK to .72 in Japan. While we are able to establish partial measurement invariance, the model fit for scalar invariance was only marginally satisfactory, but judged sufficient given the exploratory nature of this research.

Cognitive age was found to be highly correlated with chronological age (ranging from r=.6 in Hungary to r=.81 in Japan, p<.01) and with age identity (ranging from rho=.46 in Germany to rho=.68 in Hungary, p<.01).

FINDINGS

Table 2 details the age identities of the sample by country, where it can be seen that the vast majority of older adults, regardless of their nationality, consider themselves to be middle aged. Conversely, few people still feel young, although these differ slightly between nationalities, with only 2.4% of Germans feeling young, compared to almost 8% of older UK adults. This is despite the fact that the UK sample is older than the German sample by almost 3 years. Nevertheless, particularly noteworthy are the differences in those who admit to an old identity. In the UK and Germany less than 15% of older adults admit to feeling old, in comparison to one quarter of Hungarians and more than 30% of Japanese respondents. Indeed, a Chi-square test for independence indicated that there is a significant association between nationality and age identity (χ^2= 57.315, df = 6, p < .001), with fewer than expected British and Germans, and greater than expected numbers of Japanese and Hungarians, admitting to an old age identity.

Table 2: Age Identity by Country

Country	Age Identity		
	Young (%)	Middle-Aged (%)	Old/Elderly (%)
UK	7.89	77.41	14.69
Germany	2.37	85.31	12.32
Japan	7.04	62.21	30.75
Hungary	5.50	69.00	25.50

χ^2=57.315, df = 6, p < .001

Consistent with previous research, our multi-national sample found little agreement between cognitive and chronological age, although a strong and positive correlation was found between the two (r = 0.71, n = 1293, p <.01). Indeed, across the sample as a whole only 125 (9.7%) respondents had cognitive ages that were greater than their actual age. In contrast, the vast majority (87.2%) perceived themselves to be younger than their actual age. There were, however, comparisons between the nations. Table 3 classifies the differences in actual and cognitive age by country, where it can be seen that greater numbers of Hungarians (28.5%) felt older than their age, while only 3.8% of Germans felt older. Indeed, at least 87% of seniors from the UK, Japan and Germany felt younger than their actual age, while this figure drops to 66.5% for older Hungarians.

Table 3: Cognitive Age Compared to Actual Age, by Country

Country	Cognitive age older than actual age (%)	Cognitive age same as actual age (%)	Cognitive age younger than actual age (%)
UK	5.04	1.75	93.20
Germany	3.79	2.84	93.36
Japan	8.69	3.99	87.32
Hungary	28.50	5.00	66.50

Table 4 details the mean chronological and cognitive ages by country, as well as the youth bias (defined as the difference between chronological and cognitive age) where it is clear that there is a bias towards a more youthful self-perceived age. In all four samples paired-samples t-tests demonstrated that chronological and cognitive age are significantly different.

Table 4: Mean Chronological and Cognitive Age by Country

Country	Mean Chronological Age	Mean Cognitive Age	Youth Bias
UK	66.24	56.00	10.24
Germany	63.50	54.42	9.08
Japan	64.11	57.61	6.51
Hungary	58.66	54.99	3.67
Total	63.92	56.11	7.81

Noticeably, however, the youth bias ranges from less than 4 years for Hungarians to over 10 years for UK seniors. One-way ANOVA showed these differences to be significant (Welch (3, 1289) = 55.596, p < .001). Post-hoc comparisons revealed Hungary to have a significantly lower youth bias than any other country, while the UK has a significantly greater youth bias than Japan. Conversely, no significant differences emerged between Germany and the UK.

Finally, table 5 shows the percentages of seniors by nation who feel younger than their actual age by cognitive age dimension, whilst table 6 provides the mean cognitive age dimensions by country.

Table 5: Youthful Self-perceived Age by Dimensions of Cognitive Age (per cent)

Country	Feel age	Look age	Do age	Interests age
UK	86.84	80.92	89.91	89.25
Germany	85.31	81.52	85.78	86.26
Japan	75.35	78.40	81.22	81.46
Hungary	56.00	59.50	65.50	71.50

Consistent with previous research, for the sample as a whole look age is the dimension closest to chronological age. Once again, however, there are contrasts between the nations, as the difference between look age and the other dimensions are greater in the UK and Germany in comparison to Japan and Hungary. In these latter countries, there is little difference between look age and other dimensions, and indeed in Hungary the mean look age is actually marginally higher than feel age.

Table 6: Mean Actual and Cognitive Age Dimensions

Country	Actual age	Feel age	Look age	Do age	Interests age
UK	66.24	55.09	60.29	54.17	54.45
Germany	63.50	54.95	57.13	53.10	52.49
Japan	64.11	58.36	59.32	57.51	55.23
Hungary	58.66	56.25	56.15	54.55	53.00
Total	**63.92**	**56.32**	**58.81**	**55.15**	**54.16**

DISCUSSION

This research has found the 'young at heart' philosophy to be true for older consumers in all four nations under study. The vast majority of seniors feel middle-aged, and are not yet ready to admit they feel old. Moreover, many of the patterns to emerge have some similarities to American research in that there is little agreement between cognitive and chronological age, with a strong youth bias. Likewise, the expectation that the look age dimension would be closest to actual age than any of the other self-perceived age dimensions emerged in all the samples with the exception of Hungary.

However, despite some similarities to previous research and across countries, the significant differences found between the nations in this study are its most important contribution to knowledge. We thus successfully challenged the view of cognitive age as "culture-free". Clearly, Japanese and Hungarian seniors are more likely to admit to being old than are their British and German counterparts, and this pattern was repeated in the cognitive age results.

Wahl and Kruse (2003) argue that research into older adults should be designed and interpreted with a consideration of the social and cultural contexts in which these adults live.

The tendency for older people to report younger self-perceived ages has been viewed as a form of denial in the United States, where it has long been noted that youth is valued over old age (Guy, Rittenburg, and Hawes 1994). Such an ideology is not limited to American culture: British writing provides overwhelming support for the contention that in the UK old age is associated with negative characteristics; indeed in contrast to some other European countries Britain still has age discrimination built into the fabric of its society, and ageing is often portrayed in negative ways in the media (Joseph Rowntree Foundation 2004; Williams et al. 2010). In a similar vein, Catterall and Maclaran (2001) argue that the underpinning assumptions inherent in the concept of cognitive age reflect a Western preoccupation with youthfulness. However, given that the youth bias also exists in non-western nations, this view is challenged.

While the UK sample demonstrates similarities to American studies which typically report an age bias of between 8 and 12 years (Barak 1998; Sherman, Schiffman, and Mathur 2001), a number of studies conducted outside the US show the bias to be less pronounced. Chua, Cote and Leong (1990) conducted their cognitive age study in Singapore and found that English-speaking respondents were more likely to feel younger than their actual age in comparison to Chinese-speaking respondents. This difference was interpreted as a result of differing cultures, and as such was one of the first known studies to speculate that cultural forces may impact self-perceived age. However, given the much larger body of knowledge that suggests otherwise, this consideration appears to have been forgotten, neglected, or ignored in much subsequent research. Moreover, Chua, Cote and Leong (1990) interpreted their differences as a result of age being more respected in Eastern as opposed to Western cultures. However, it is not just Eastern cultures that have been found to have a less pronounced youth bias, as older Finnish adults have also been found to have a greater acceptance of their actual age in comparison to older Americans (Uotinen 1998). Thus, particularly in view of the significance of the European Union, it would seem that more research is needed across European nations before seniors markets are targeted with a pan-European marketing strategy. A recent meta-analysis, using data from 598 studies conducted over 30 years, into cultural value dimensions found that cultural values were more strongly related to older adults in comparison to younger people (Taras, Kirkman, and Steel 2010). Clearly, then, the life-experiences of individual nations needs to be considered.

The nations selected here are very different with regards to the life-experiences of older adults. Older Germans have experienced re-unification (and before that the separation), migration of younger adults from Eastern to Western Germany which has affected older people's social networks and integration, war guilt and a lack of focus on war veterans that is in stark contrast to the UK and US, and different social welfare arrangements which produce continuity of income in old age (Wahl and Kruse 2003). Language is an important part of culture, and interestingly the Hungarian language belongs to the Finno-Ugric family and is one of the few languages spoken within the European Union that are not of Indo-European origin. Moreover, older Hungarians have lived through the collapse of communism and the transition to a market economy, and a large study into the formulation of a consumer society and on the development of local identities in Central Europe found that a special type of consumer society came into being into these countries, with Hungary being one of them (Wessely 2000). From a consumer values perspective, the socialist system in Hungary which emphasized altruism and concern for the community has been replaced with more materialistic values, but there are still major generational differences (Hofmeister Toth and Neulinger 2009). Finally, older Japanese seniors have – just like their German counterparts – experienced the post-war efforts to rebuild their country and finding a new national identity. American occupation during the post-war years and the subsequent globalization have led to an acculturation process that has had a strong impact on Japanese values, thinking and consumer behavior (cf. also Francks 2009).

In sum, this research has answered a recent call for replication studies to be undertaken in the field of cross-cultural global age research, which is still in an early pioneering stage (Barak 2009). The study also adds to the small but growing amount of empirical evidence pertaining to seniors outside the US. Results lend support for the claim that the concept of cognitive age is reliable and can be used in diverse cultures, and that there is a universal way that human beings perceive and feel about self-perceived age (Barak 2009; Barak

et al. 2001). However, the latter holds only true as far as the general tendency to feel younger than one's actual age is concerned, but not to the degree and magnitude of the youth bias. Indeed, our findings seem to challenge the assumption of cognitive age as culture free. This is actually not all too surprising given the disparate cultures and life-experiences that these seniors have experienced. Some previous studies have also found some indications that culture may play at least some role in the perception of age (Chua et al. 1990; Mathur et al. 2001; Uotinen 1998), but the prevailing view in the cross-national literature on cognitive age saw it as culture free and universal. This view will now have to be changed.

LIMITATIONS AND NEED FOR FURTHER RESEARCH

We cannot know for sure if culture is the (sole) explanation for the differences we have found across the four countries surveyed. Other factors on the individual or sample level may be confounding our results. Indeed, previous research has identified various antecedents and correlates of cognitive age (Barak and Stern 1986; Mathur and Moschis 2005; Ong, Lu, and Abessi 2009) and further research will necessary to disentangle cultural effects from those of other correlates. Besides, subjective age might also be a social phenomenon and in that case the usefulness and applicability of the cognitive age concept could change along with changing social attitudes such as the one towards aging for example (cf. e.g. Catterall and Maclaran 2001). Thus, it is impossible to explain why the young-at-heart bias differs across the nations studied here, but these results do set a clear research agenda, in that further research into the underlying antecedents of cognitive age, particularly across nations outside America (and especially across the European Union) is needed.

It is hoped that the different sampling methods which were needed due to cultural differences did not impact the results, but we note that Hungary, where the administration of the questionnaires was different, has emerged as significantly different to the other nations from a self-perceived age perspective. Future research will have to address data equivalence and measurement issues in greater detail (Barak 2009; Hult et al. 2008; Reynolds, Simintiras, and Diamantopoulos 2003; Singh 1995). Further research needs to delve into the antecedents of the concept of self-perceived age, and consider different life experiences and cultures as potential antecedents. Finally, employing cohort analysis on longitudinal or repeated cross-sectional data may help to shed further light on older consumers (Cole et al. 2008; Fukuda 2010; Rentz et al. 1983).

MANAGERIAL IMPLICATIONS

This study has important implications for marketing practice. In advertising, for example, the use of "cognitive-age congruent" models or spokespersons should prove fertile as a consumer's self-perceived age interacts with the perceived age of the model or spokesperson seen in an ad, and can subsequently influence the response to the advertising message (Chang 2008; Van Auken and Barry 2009). This may also explain why older people are often underrepresented in advertising, a fact that also holds true for TV commercials in the UK (Simcock and Sudbury 2006), Germany (Kessler, Schwender, and Bowen 2010), and Japan (Prieler et al. 2009). Research has also shown the importance of understanding motivational differences that underlie the effects of aging on attitudes toward and recall of advertisements (Drolet, Williams, and Lau-Gesk 2007) and heeding to the cognitive age of the target group will likely be an additional, crucial factor.

From an international marketing perspective, the study lends support to the usefulness of self-perceived age as a way of segmenting and targeting senior consumers across the globe. In the same way as a youth segment represents an example of a universal global common segment (Kjeldgaard and Askegaard 2006), there is growing evidence that a 'young at heart' senior global market exists (Barak 2009) and this study lends further support to that. That is not to suggest that older adults can be treated as an undifferentiated monolith. Indeed, the differences between the nations suggest that local differences still need to be considered in advertising and positioning strategies. Nevertheless, it provides a starting point for marketers wishing to target this growing and important global phenomenon that is the senior market.

REFERENCES

Adams, David L. (1971), "Correlates of Satisfaction among the Elderly," *The Gerontologist*, 11 (4-II), 64-68.

Barak, Benny (1998), "Inner-Ages of Middle-Aged Prime-Lifers," *International Journal of Aging and Human Development*, 46 (3), 189-228.

--- (2009), "Age Identity: A Cross-Cultural Global Approach," *International Journal of Behavioral Development*, 33 (1), 2-11.

Barak, Benny and Steven Gould (1985), "Alternative Age Measures: A Research Agenda," in *Advances in Consumer Research*, Vol. 12, ed. Elizabeth C. Hirschman and Moris B. Holbrook, Provo, UT: Association for Consumer Research, 53-58.

Barak, Benny, Anil Mathur, Keun Lee, and Yong Zhang (2001), "Perceptions of Age-Identity: A Cross-Cultural Inner-Age Exploration," *Psychology & Marketing*, 18 (10), 1003-29.

Barak, Benny, Anil Mathur, Yong Zhang, Keun Lee, and Emmanuel Erondu (2003), "Inner-Age Satisfaction in Africa and Asia: A Cross-Cultural Exploration," *Asia Pacific Journal of Marketing and Logistics*, 15 (1/2), 3-26.

Barak, Benny and Don R. Rahtz (1990), "Cognitive Age: Demographic and Psychographic Dimensions," *Journal of Ambulatory Care Marketing*, 3 (2), 51-65.

Barak, Benny and Leon G. Schiffman (1981), "Cognitive Age: A Nonchronological Variable," in *Advances in Consumer Research*, Vol. 8, ed. Kent B. Monroe, Ann Arbor, MI: Association for Consumer Research, 602-06.

Barak, Benny and Barbara Stern (1986), "Subjective Age Correlates: A Research Note," *The Gerontologist*, 26 (5), 571-78.

Bell, Benjamin (1972), "Significance of Functional Age for Interdisciplinary and Longitudinal Research," *Aging and Human Development*, 3 (2), 145-47.

Bengtson, Vern L., Margaret N. Reedy, and Chad Gordon (1985), "Aging and Self-Perceptions: Personality Processes and Social Contexts," in *Handbook of the Psychology of Aging*, Vol. 2, ed. James E. Birren and K. Warner Schaie, NY: Van Nostran Reinhold Company, 544-93.

Birren, James E. (1968), "Principles of Research on Aging," in *Middle Age and Aging: A Reader in Social Psychology*, ed. Bernice L. Neugarten, Chicago: University of Chicago Press, 545-51.

Blau, Zena Smith (1956), "Changes in Status and Age Identification," *American Sociological Review*, 21 (2), 198-203.

Catterall, Miriam and Pauline Maclaran (2001), "Body Talk: Questioning the Assumptions in Cognitive Age," *Psychology & Marketing*, 18 (10), 1117-33.

Cavan, Ruth S., Ernest W. Burgess, Robert J. Havinghurst, and Herbert HGoldhamer (1949), *Personal Adjustment in Old Age*, Chicago: Science Research Associates.

Chang, Chingching (2008), "Chronological Age Versus Cognitive Age for Younger Consumers," *Journal of Advertising*, 37 (3), 19-32.

Chua, Caroline, Joseph A. Cote, and Siew Meng Leong (1990), "The Antecedents of Cognitive Age," in *Advances in Consumer Research*, Vol. 17, ed. Marvin E. Goldberg, Gerald Gorn and Richard W. Pollay, Provo, UT: Association for Consumer Research, 880-85.

Clark, Sylvia D., Mary M. Long, and Leon G. Schiffman (1999), "The Mind-Body Connection: The Relationship among Physical Activity Level, Life Satisfaction, and Cognitive Age among Mature Females," *Journal of Social Behavior and Personality*, 14 (2), 221-40.

Cleaver, Megan and Thomas E. Muller (2002), "I Want to Pretend I'm Eleven Years Younger: Subjective Age and Seniors' Motives for Vacation Travel," *Social Indicators Research*, 60 (1-3), 227-41.

Cole, Catherine, Gilles Laurent, Aimee Drolet, Jane Ebert, Angela Gutchess, Raphaëlle Lambert-Pandraud, Etienne Mullet, Michael I. Norton, and Ellen Peters (2008), "Decision Making and Brand Choice by Older Consumers," *Marketing Letters*, 19 (3-4), 355-65.

Cunningham, Walter R. and John W. Brookbank (1988), *Gerontology: The Psychology, Biology, and Sociology of Aging*, London: Harper & Row.

Dolinsky, Arthur L., Stephen J. Gould, Dennis J. Scotti, and Robert N. Stinerock (1998), "The Role of Psychographic Characteristics as Determinants of Complaint Behavior by Elderly Consumers of Physician Health Care Services," *Journal of Hospital Marketing*, 12 (2), 27-51.

Drolet, Aimee, Pattie Williams, and Loraine Lau-Gesk (2007), "Age-Related Differences in Responses to Affective Vs. Rational Ads for Hedonic Vs. Utalitarian Products," *Marketing Letters*, 18 (4), 211-21.

Easley, Richard W., Charles S. Madden, and Mark G. Dunn (2000), "Conducting Marketing Science: The Role of Replication in the Research Process," *Journal of Business Research*, 48 (1), 83-92.

Eastman, Jacqueline K. and Rajesh Iyer (2005), "The Impact of Cognitive Age on Internet Use of the Elderly: An Introduction to the Public Policy Implications," *International Journal of Consumer Studies*, 29 (2), 125-36.

Epstein, Seymour (1980), "The Stability of Behavior: Implications for Psychological Research," *American Psychologist*, 35 (9), 790-806.

Flynn Reinecke, Leisa (1993), "Do Standard Scales Work in Older Samples?," *Marketing Letters*, 4 (2), 127-37.

Francks, Penelope (2009), *The Japanese Consumer: An Alternative Economic History of Modern Japan*, Cambridge: Cambridge University Press.

Fukuda, Kosei (2010), "A Cohort Analysis of Household Vehicle Expenditure in the U.S. And Japan: A Possibility of Generational Marketing," *Marketing Letters*, 21 (1), 53-64.

Goldsmith, Ronald E. and Richard A. Heiens (1992), "Subjective Age: A Test of Five Hypotheses," *The Gerontologist*, 32 (3), 312-17.

Guptill, Carleton S. (1969), "A Measure of Age Identification," *The Gerontologist*, 9 (2), 96-102.

Guy, Bonnie S., Terri L. Rittenburg, and Douglas K. Hawes (1994), "Dimensions and Characteristics of Time Perceptions and Perspectives among Older Consumers," *Psychology & Marketing*, 11 (1), 35-56.

Heron, Alastair and Sheila Chown (1967), *Age and Function*, London: J.&A. Churchill, Ltd.

Hofmeister Toth, Agnes and Agnes Neulinger (2009), "Changing Consumption Patterns in Hungary," in *8th International Congress on Marketing Trends*, Paris.

Hubbard, Raymond and J. Scott Armstrong (1994), "Replications and Extensions in Marketing: Rarely Published but Quite Contrary," *International Journal of Research in Marketing*, 11 (3), 233-48.

Hubbard, Raymond and R. Murray Lindsay (2002), "How the Emphasis on 'Original' Empirical Marketing Research Impedes Knowledge Development," *Marketing Theory*, 2 (4), 381-402.

Hult, G. Tomas M., David J. Ketchen Jr., David A. Griffith, Carol A. Finnegan, Tracy Gonzalez-Padron, Nukhet Harmancioglu, Ying Huang, M. Berk Talay, and S. Tamer Cavusgil (2008), "Data Equivalence in Cross-Cultural International Business Research: Assessment and Guidelines," *International Journal of Business Studies*, 39 (6), 1027-44.

Jarvik, Lissy F. (1975), "Thoughts on the Psychobiology of Aging," *American Psychologist*, 30 (5), 576-83.

Johnson, Edna B. (1995), "Cognitive Age: A Key to Understanding Consumer Alientation in the Mature Market," *The Mid-Atlantic Journal of Business*, 31 (3), 259-70.

--- (1996), "Cognitive Age: Understanding Consumer Alienation in the Mature Market," *Review of Business*, 17 (3), 35-40.

Johnson, Rose L. (1993), "Age and Social Activity as Correlates of Television Orientation: A Replication and Extension," in *Advances in Consumer Research*, Vol. 20, ed. Leigh McAlister and Michael L. Rothschild, Provo, UT: Association for Consumer Research, 257-61.

Joseph Rowntree Foundation (2004), "From Welfare to Well-Being - Planning for an Ageing Society," York: Joseph Rowntree Foundation: avaialable from http://www.jrf.org.uk/publications/welfare-well-being-planning-ageing-society-summary-conclusions-joseph-rowntree-foundati.

Kastenbaum, Robert, Valerie Derbin, Paul Sabatini, and Steven Artt (1972), "The Ages of Me: Toward Personal and Interpersonal Definitions of Functional Aging," *Aging and Human Development*, 3 (2), 197-211.

Kessler, Eva-Marie, Clemens Schwender, and Catherine E. Bowen (2010), "The Portrayal of Older People's Social Participation on German Prime-Time Tv Advertisements," *Journal of Gerontology: Social Sciences*, 65B (1), 97-106.

Kjeldgaard, Dannie and Sørren Askegaard (2006), "The Glocalization of Youth Culture: The Global Youth Segment as Structures of Common Difference," *Journal of Consumer Research*, 33 (2), 231-47.

Kohlbacher, Florian and Emmanuel J. Chéron (2010), "Segmenting the Silver Market Using Cognitive Age and the List of Values: Empirical Evidence from Japan," in *European Advances in Consumer Research (EACR) Conference*, London.

Mathur, Anil, Benny Barak, Yong Zhang, and Keun S. Lee (2001), "A Cross-Cultural Procedure to Assess Reliability and Measurement Invariance," *Journal of Applied Measurement*, 2 (3), 241-55.

Mathur, Anil and George P. Moschis (2005), "Antecedents of Cognitive Age: A Replication and Extension," *Psychology & Marketing*, 22 (12), 969-94.

Mathur, Anil, Elaine Sherman, and Leon G. Schiffman (1998), "Opportunities for Marketing Travel Services to New-Age Elderly," *The Journal of Services Marketing*, 12 (4), 265-77.

McMellon, Charles A., Leon G. Schiffman, and Elaine Sherman (1997), "Consuming Cyberseniors: Some Personal and Situational Characteristics That Influence Their on-Line Behavior," in *Advances in Consumer Research*, Vol. 24, ed. Merrie Brucks and Deborah J. MacInnis, Provo, UT: Association for Consumer Research, 517-21.

Moschis, George P. and Anil Mathur (2006), "Older Consumer Responses to Marketing Stimuli: The Power of Subjective Age," *Journal of Advertising Research*, 46 (3), 339-46.

Niemelä-Nyrhinen, Jenni (2007), "Baby Boom Consumers and Technology: Shooting Down Stereotypes," *Journal of Consumer Marketing*, 24 (5), 305-12.

Ong, Fon Sim, Yap-Ying Lu, and Masoud Abessi (2009), "The Correlates of Cognitive Ageing and Adoption of Defensive-Ageing Strategies among Older Adults," *Asia Pacific Journal of Marketing and Logistics*, 21 (2), 294-305.

Palmore, Erdman (1978), "When Can Age, Period, and Cohort Be Separated?," *Social Forces*, 57 (1), 282-95.

Peter, J. Paul (1981), "Construct Validity: A Review of Basic Issues and Marketing Practices," *Journal of Marketing Research*, 18 (2), 133-45.

Peters, George R. (1971), "Self-Perceptions of the Aged, Age Identification, and Aging," *The Gerontologist*, 11 (4-II), 69-73.

Prieler, Michael, Florian Kohlbacher, Shigeru Hagiwara, and Akie Arima (2009), "How Older People Are Represented in Japanese Tv Commercials: A Content Analysis," *Keio Communication Review*, 31, 5-21.

Psychology & Marketing (2001), "Special Issue on Cognitive Age and Consumption," *Psychology & Marketing*, 18 (10), 999-1133.

Rentz, Joseph O., Fred D. Reynolds, and Roy G. Stout (1983), "Analyzing Changing Consumption Patterns with Cohort Analysis," *Journal of Marketing Research*, 20 (1), 12-20.

Reynolds, N.L., A.C. Simintiras, and A. Diamantopoulos (2003), "Theoretical Justification of Sampling Choices in International Marketing Resesarch: Key Issues and Guidelines for Researchers," *Journal of International Business Studies*, 34 (1), 80-89.

Riley, Matilda White (1985), "Age Strata in Social Systems," in *Handbook of Aging and the Social Sciences*, ed. Robert H. Binstock and Ethel Shanas, NY: Van Nostrand Reinhold Company, 369-411.

Schiffman, Leon G. and Elaine Sherman (1991), "Value Orientations of New-Age Elderly: The Coming of an Ageless Market," *Journal of Business Research*, 22 (2), 187-94.

Sherman, Elaine, Leon G. Schiffman, and William R. Dillon (1988), "Age/Gender Segments and Quality of Life Differences," in *American Marketing Association (AMA) Winter Educators' Conference*, Chicago.

Sherman, Elaine, Leon G. Schiffman, and Anil Mathur (2001), "The Influence of Gender on the New-Age Elderly's Consumption Orientation," *Psychology & Marketing*, 18 (10), 1073-89.

Simcock, Peter and Lynn Sudbury (2006), "The Invisible Majority? Older Models in Uk Television Advertising," *International Journal of Advertising*, 25 (1), 87-106.

Singh, Jagdip (1995), "Measurement Issues in Cross-National Research," *Journal of International Business Studies*, 26 (3), 597-619.

Smith, Jacqui and Paul B. Baltes (1999), "Trends and Profiles of Psychological Functioning in Very Old Age," in *The Berlin Aging Study: Aging from 70 to 100*, ed. Paul B. Baltes and Karl Ulrich Mayer, New York: Cambridge University Press, 197-226.

Stephens, Nancy (1991), "Cognitive Age: A Useful Concept for Advertising?," *Journal of Advertising*, 20 (4), 37-48.

Sudbury, Lynn (2004), "Subjective Age Perceptions in the Uk: An Empirical Study," *Quality in Ageing - Policy, practice and research*, 5 (1), 4-13.

Sudbury, Lynn and Peter Simcock (2009a), "A Multivariate Segmentation Model of Older Consumers," *Journal of Consumer Marketing*, 26 (4), 251-62.

--- (2009b), "Understanding Older Consumers through Cognitive Age and the List of Values: A U.K.-Based Perspective," *Psychology & Marketing*, 26 (1), 22-38.

--- (2010), "To Use or Not to Use? Age Based Sales Promotions and the Older Consumer," in *American Marketing Association (AMA) Summer Educators' Conference*, Boston.

Szmigin, Isabelle and Marylyn Carrigan (2000), "The Older Consumer as Innovator: Does Cognitive Age Hold the Key?," *Journal of Marketing Management*, 16 (5), 505-27.

Taras, Vas, Bradley L. Kirkman, and Piers Steel (2010), "Examining the Impact of Culture's Consequences: A Three-Decade, Multilevel, Meta-Analytical Review of Hofstede's Cultural Value Dimensions," *Journal of Applied Psychology*, 95 (3), 405-39.

Tepper, Kelly (1994), "The Role of Labeling Processes in Elderly Consumers' Responses to Age Segmentation Cues," *Journal of Consumer Research*, 20 (4), 503-19.

Uncles, Mark and David Lee (2006), "Brand Purchasing by Older Consumers: An Investigation Using the Juster Scale and the Dirichlet Model," *Marketing Letters*, 17 (1), 17-29.

United Nations (2007), "World Population Ageing 2007," New York: UN Department of Economic Affairs, Population Division.

Uotinen, Virpi (1998), "Age Identification: A Comparison between Finnish and North-American Cultures," 46 (2).

Van Auken, Stuart and Thomas E. Barry (1995), "An Assessment of the Trait Validity of Cognitive Age Measures," *Journal of Consumer Psychology*, 4 (2), 107-32.

--- (2009), "Assessing the Nomological Validity of a Cognitive Age Segmentation of Japanese Seniors," *Asia Pacific Journal of Marketing and Logistics*, 21 (3), 315-28.

Van Auken, Stuart, Thomas E. Barry, and Robert L. Anderson (1993), "Towards the Internal Validation of Cognitive Age Measures in Advertising Research," *Journal of Advertising Research*, 33 (3), 82-84.

Van Auken, Stuart, Thomas E. Barry, and Richard P. Bagozzi (2006), "A Cross-Country Construct Validation of Cognitive Age," *Journal of the Academy of Marketing Science*, 34 (3), 439-55.

Wahl, Hans-Werner and Andreas Kruse (2003), "Psychological Gerontology in Germany: Recent Findings and Social Implications," *Ageing & Society*, 23 (2), 131-63.

Wells, William D. (1975), "Psychographics: A Critical Review," *Journal of Marketing Research*, 12 (2), 196-213.

Wessely, Anna (2000), "Utazó Emberek, Utazó Tárgyak [Travelling People, Travelling Objects]," *Replika*, 39 (March), 95-106.

Westerhof, Gerben J. and Anne E. Barrett (2005), "Age Identity and Subjective Well-Weing: A Comparision of the United States and Germany," *Journal of Gerontology: Social Sciences*, 60B (3), 129-36.

Westerhof, Gerben J., Anne E. Barrett, and Nardi Steverink (2003), "Forever Young? A Comparison of Age Identities in the United States and Germany," *Research on Aging*, 25 (4), 366-83.

Wilkes, Robert E. (1992), "A Structural Modeling Approach to the Measurement and Meaning of Cognitive Age," *Journal of Consumer Research*, 19 (2), 292-301.

Williams, Angie, Virpi Ylänne, Paul Mark Wadleigh, and Chin-Hui Chen (2010), "Portrayals of Older Adults in Uk Magazine Advertisements: Relevance of Target Audience," *Communications*, 35 (1), 1-27.

Yoon, Carolyn, Gilles Laurent, Helene H. Fung, Richard Gonzales, Angela H. Gutchess, Trey Hedden, Raphaëlle Lambert-Pandraud, Mara Mather, Denise C. Park, Ellen Peters, and Ian Skurnik (2005), "Cognition, Persuasion and Decision Making in Older Consumers," *Marketing Letters*, 16 (3), 429-41.

Measuring Consumers' Emotional Reactions to Company Crises: Scale Development and Implications

Lynette McDonald, University of Queensland, Australia
A. Ian Glendon, Griffith University, Australia
Beverley Sparks, Griffith University, Australia

INTRODUCTION

Crises negatively impact an organization's financial stability, its relationship with its publics, its image and reputation, as well as its ability to function, and to deliver its products and services (Jin and Cameron 2007). Between 2003 and 2006 almost half of U. S.-based multinationals were affected by major crises that caused catastrophic business impacts (PricewaterhouseCoopers 2006). In 2010, global insurance claims for man-made crises were $5 billion (Swiss Re 2010).

Crises trigger emotions in impacted consumers. These emotions guide the interpretation of an unfolding crisis, shaping attitudes towards the organization (Jin, Pang, and Cameron 2007). Emotions influence stakeholders' future organizational interactions, powerfully influencing post-crisis behavior (Coombs and Holladay 2005) such as product boycotts (Choi and Lin 2009). Yet crisis emotions' influence on behavioral tendencies is little investigated (Coombs and Holladay 2005). A strong need exists to explore the variety of crisis-generated emotions (Choi and Lin 2009) to understand emotions and to develop effective crisis management strategies.

The recently increasing momentum of crisis emotion research suggests the need for psychometrically-validated scales that reflect consumers' experienced crisis emotions. However, no studies that reported significant effects for emotional response to organizational crises used scales that had been tested, not just for reliability and predictive validity, but for content validity, unidimensionality, and convergent and discriminant validity as specified by Churchill (1979), Gerbing and Anderson (1988), and Hair et al. (2009). Measures should incorporate the diversity of most frequently experienced emotions in a particular context, and use readily understood words (Richins 1997), ideally using laypersons' own emotion lexicon (Carpenter and Halberstadt 1996). Across three studies we develop an instrument to measure crisis emotions as a tool for managers and scholars to identify consumers' crisis emotional responses and intensity, predict behavioral outcomes, guide crisis communication strategies, and indicate degree of crisis management success.

CRISIS AND EMOTIONS

Organizational crises trigger consumer emotions which drive behavioral intentions towards a firm and its product. Crisis studies using Weiner's (1986) attribution theory (WAT) or Coombs and Holladay's (2002) Situational Crisis Communication Theory (SCCT) based on WAT, identified that crisis cause attributions determine emotions, with emotions driving behavioral intentions. That is, crisis emotions immediately precede behaviors. Anger directly predicts negative purchase intentions (Coombs and Holladay 2007; Jorgensen 1996), negative word-of-mouth (WOM) behavior (Coombs and Holladay 2007), boycott (Choi and Lin 2009), punitiveness, and indirectly leads to reduced investment intentions (Jorgensen 1996). Fear leads to venting intentions or avoidance, while sadness results in a preference for emotional support and positive thinking as coping strategies (Jin 2009).

Limitations of Existing Crisis Emotion Measures

Consumer emotions are context specific (Richins 1997). Those resulting from service failures (e.g., Folkes 1984) differ from those relating to consumption (e.g., Laros and Steenkamp 2005). As scales should include context-specific emotion words (Carpenter and Halber-

stadt 1996; Richins 1997), crisis emotion scales would benefit from words acquired from consumers' own crisis language. Researchers using modified scales or scale parts still must follow standard scale development and refinement procedures (Ortinau 2011). Scales should be conceptually defined, have content validity, use multiple indicators, be unidimensional, and have convergent, discriminant, and nomological validity (Hair et al. 2009).

Of 11 studies reporting significant effects for emotional response to various organizational crises, none used emotion scales that fulfilled all criteria. Using exploratory factor analysis, Kim and Cameron (2011) adapted emotion scales originally created for public health advertising, to identify four scales (anger, sadness, fear, surprise). Six studies applying multiple-item emotion scales (Coombs and Holladay 2007, 2008, 2009; Jin and Cameron 2007; Jorgensen 1996; Lee 2004) only report reliability scores. Jorgensen's (1996) 4-item scale tests negative affect, rather than any specific emotion, and includes reversed-scored items (e.g., angry, sympathetic). Coombs and Holladay's (2008, 2009) 3-item anger scale uses Jorgensen's (1996) items. Coombs and Holladay's (2007) 3-item anger scale lists only two items and cannot be assessed for content validity. Jin and Cameron's (2007) two 3-item scales do not measure emotion but affect in the form of emotion valence and arousal. Lee's (2004) sympathy scale includes frustration. The 4 remaining crisis emotion scales (Choi and Lin 2009; Coombs and Holladay 2005; Jin 2009; Jorgensen 1994) use 1-item measures. These are psychometrically less reliable than multiple-item measures; highly reliable measures are crucial to statistical analyses to minimize error variance effects (Loo 2001). In sum, no identified studies reported fully-tested crisis emotion scales. We develop and validate multiple-item self-report crisis emotion scales to enable managers and researchers to more comprehensively examine consumers' varied crisis emotions.

CRISIS EMOTION SCALE DEVELOPMENT AND TESTING

Following well-established scale development procedures (Bearden, Netemeyer, and Mobley 1999; Churchill 1979; Gerbing and Anderson 1988), we started with construct specification and domain, allowing an understanding of the theory on which the construct is embedded (Peter 1981). Item generation followed in study 1, trait validation in study 2, and evaluation of convergent, discriminant, and nomological validity in study 3.

Construct Specification and Domain

The emotion concept has no single agreed definition (Izard 1993). Attribution-appraisal theorists (Frijda 1986; Weiner 1986) consider that emotion comprises discrete states generated by cognitive appraisals leading to specific affect, action tendencies and physiological reactions (Scherer 2000). Thus, one distinguishing feature of primary emotions is "action readiness" (Frijda 1986). However, dispute remains about the number of distinct primary emotions (Laros and Steenkamp 2005). Shaver et al. (1987) and Nyer (1997) contended that six primary emotion categories exist: anger, fear, joy, love, sadness, and surprise.

Different emotions call for varied coping strategies, generating distinct behaviors (Nyer 1997; Scherer 2000). Anger functions to regain control, focusing on obstruction removal (Frijda 1986). Fear acts to protect (Frijda 1986) and motivate escape from danger (Izard 1993). Joy signals readiness for friendly interaction (Izard 1993). Sadness communicates trouble to self and others (Izard 1993), allowing recuperation and disengagement (Frijda 1986). Surprise's function is reorientation (Frijda 1986) and may be either undesirable (shock) or desirable (pleasant surprise) (Ortony, Clore, and Collins 1988). Love creates a desire for continued interaction (Epstein 1984).

Study 1: Item Generation

The second step in scale development is item generation and pool editing (Churchill 1979). As a researcher's meaning for a measure may not accord with respondents' imputed meaning (Gerbing and Anderson 1988), focus groups were conducted to establish consumers' emotion words in an organizational crisis context. The objective was to produce a commonly employed word set, with the most frequently recurring words considered to be valid indicators of importance (Havlena, Holbrook, and Lehmann 1989). Focus group size was congruent with Lunt's (1996) recommendation of six to 10. The 52 participants from a major Australian city, recruited predomi-

nantly via media publicity, were allocated among eight groups. Ages ranged from 19 to 79 years ($M = 43$, $SD = 14$), 58% were males, and 61% had college education or higher. Most had low (48%) to average (35%) incomes assessed according to government-sourced information. Almost all participants had been personally impacted by organizational crises. Crises varied from an airline fleet grounding, three product recalls (two following extortion threats, one following salmonella poisoning), two separate legionella outbreaks, and a two-week shutdown of a city's natural gas supply. As the intention was to later test emotions in a nomological net, discussion of attitudes and behaviors was invited. Videotape transcriptions and whiteboard discussion summaries were content analyzed using an iterative approach. Shaver et al.'s (1987) list of 135 emotion words was used to categorize the 80+ emotion words elicited. Anger category words dominated emotion content (42.6%), followed by fear (20.9%), sadness (20.5%), joy (9.1%), surprise (3.6%), and love (3.3%) (see table 1). The most frequently occurring words in each category were used for scale development (Havlena et al. 1989).

TABLE 1
STUDY 1: MOST COMMONLY-USED EMOTIONS WORDS

Emotion	Emotion words
Anger	angry, annoyed, contempt, disgusted, frustrated, outraged, dislike
Fear	fear, worried, uneasy, apprehensive, scared, concerned, distressed
Sad	disappointed, sympathetic, hopeless, insecure, sorry, unhappy
Joy	relieved, satisfied, enjoyment, contented, glad
Surprise	surprised, shocked, amazed
Love	liking, compassion

Study 2: Scale Dimensionality and Internal Consistency

Study 2 assessed the six emotion scales' internal consistency, dimensionality, and criterion validity (Gerbing and Anderson 1988). As crisis emotions are generated via cognitive appraisal, airline crash vignettes similar to Jorgensen (1996) and Lee's (2004) were created with differing causes to generate differing attributions, eliciting a variety of emotions in a between-subjects factorial design.

Undergraduate students ($N = 316$, 65% female, $M_{age} = 23$ years, $SD = 6$) from an Australian east coast university were randomly assigned to one treatment. Participants were asked to imagine themselves or their families were recent airline customers, then read a mocked-up front-page newspaper story on the crash cause, complete with a large photograph. The self-paced questionnaire asked participants about their feelings towards the company and towards flying with the company using 7-point scales with not at all/very much end points. Adjectival forms of the table 1 words were used where pos-

sible, congruent with other emotion scales.

As there was a minimum of 300 cases (Tabachnik and Fidell 2001), an exploratory factor analysis (EFA) investigated scale item loadings (Churchill 1979; Gerbing and Anderson 1988) using principal axis factoring (PAF) with oblique rotation in SPSS. The correlation matrix indicated neither extreme multicollinearity nor singularity (Hair et al. 2009). Items with low construct loadings (< .4 were deleted and those with high loadings were retained (Churchill 1979). Love did not appear as a separate factor and was excluded from further analysis. As complex items loaded on more than one factor, an oblique rotation was conducted. This yielded a five-factor solution explaining 62.2% of the variance, with only one complex item which, being correlated at .55 with joy, was retained. Sadness was renamed sympathy to reflect its content. Standardized factor loadings and inter-item correlations in table 2 provide evidence of construct validity.

TABLE 2
STUDY 2 EFA: STANDARDIZED SCALE FACTOR LOADINGS

	Factor loading/Item-total correlation				
	Fear	Joy	Sympathy	Surprise	Anger
Emotions towards service use					
Insecure	.89*				
Worried	.88/.81				
Scared	.83/.82				
Fearful	.81/.83				
Uneasy	.78/.80				
Apprehensive	.75/.69				
Concerned	.73/.79				
Distressed	.69/.70				
Unhappy	.62*				
Satisfied		.74/.57			
Glad		.68/.69			
Liking		.68*			
Contented		.65/.66			
Enjoyment	-.32	.55/.58			
Emotion towards the company					
Relieved		.54/.54			
Contented		.52/.54			
Sympathetic			.80/.66		
Sorry			.68/.55		
Compassion			.50/.47		
Shocked				.60/.53	
Amazed				.58/.46	
Surprised				.52/.49	
Annoyed					.62/.68
Outraged					.61/.74
Disgusted					.60/.67
Dislike					.58/.60
Contempt					.56/.52
Unhappy					.56*
Frustrated					.56/.60
Angry					.48/.63
Hopelessness					.46*
% of total variance explained	33.26	10.80	7.17	6.11	4.11

* removed due to being classified as belonging to a different emotion category
NB: Factor loadings < .4 omitted

Study 3: Scale Confirmation

Study 3 refined each emotion scale to increase its internal consistency, maximize reliability, and enhance validity (Churchill 1979; Gerbing and Anderson 1988). Scales were assessed for construct and discriminant validity via confirmatory factor analyses (CFA) (Gerbing and Anderson 1988) to check construct validity, unidimensionality, and to determine factor score weightings. The goal was to retain items that formed a reliable and valid measure of crisis emotions. Extra items were added to the shorter sympathy and surprise scales to enhance reliability. As the relationship between emotions, attitude and behaviors had been established (Jin 2009; Lee 2004), nomological validity was examined by testing the relationship between the theoretically related measures or constructs (Bearden et al. 1999) of attitude and behaviors in a nomological net. The 6-item attitude scale

(α = .81) by Milliman, Fugate, and Afzalurrahim (1991, in Bruner II and Hensel 1998) was selected for its face validity when applied to company crises. Fifteen items from behavioral intention scales by Zeithhaml, Berry, and Parasuraman (1996) and Singh (1988 in Bruner, James, and Hensel 2001) were selected, as they closely resembled participants' reported behaviors in study 1. All measures were tested using the same procedures and samples as previously described for the emotion measures, evaluating their construct and discriminant validity.

Study 3 followed the same procedures as study 2, generating emotions through a cognitive appraisal process. A randomly-selected general population sample from a recently updated State electoral roll for a major Australian city received a mailed questionnaire. With voting legally compulsory in Australia, this was the best publicly-available sample source as 93% of citizens aged 18+ appear on electoral rolls (Australian Electoral Commission Annual Report 2006-2007). The rolls are commonly used for population surveys. Of 4500 questionnaires posted, 942 responses were received (907 usable responses, 21% response rate), within the 20% to 25% range typically produced by random samples generated through publicly-available sources (Hunsaker et al. 2002). Respondents were aged from 18 to 95 years (M = 46, SD = 16), and 60% were female. Government-sourced data indicated that respondents' demographic profile (age, gender, education, income) closely matched the local population, although respondents were slightly more educated, and females and the 45 to 54 age group were slightly over-represented. Following Byrne's (2001) recommendation, the sample was split in two for EFA (n = 453) and CFA (n = 454).

Exploratory factor analysis (EFA). The study 2 EFA procedures were repeated. No correlations approached 1, indicating neither extreme multicollinearity nor singularity (Hair et al. 2009), although several same-scale items correlated at .8, suggesting convergent validity (Yavus and Babakus 1995). Items with construct loadings below the .4 level at which a variable is normally retained were the joy words felt towards the company of "relieved" and "contented" and the anger word, "frustrated." These were removed from analysis. The emotion scales were tested by requesting a 5-factor solution, which explained 71.7% of the variance, and as part of a nomological net with attitudes and behaviors as a 9-factor solution to determine whether they were correlated with measures of these theoretically-related constructs. Item-total correlation, advocated in constructing unidimensional scales (Gerbing and Anderson 1988), indicated that, except for same-scale items, no emotion items inter-correlated at .7 or above. The emotion scale items were not highly correlated with attitude or behaviors and neither solution had complex items, indicating good discriminant validity.

The EFA resulted in a 6-item anger scale (angry, annoyed, contempt, disgusted, outraged, dislike), a 4-item sympathy scale (sympathetic, compassion, empathy, sorry), a 4-item joy scale (glad, enjoyment, contented, satisfied), a 5-item surprise scale (surprised, astounded, astonished, amazed, shocked), and a 7-item fear scale (concerned, worried, apprehensive, uneasy, scared, distressed, fearful). All attitude items were retained, and behavior had three factors (loyalty, complaining, disloyalty).

Confirmatory factor analysis (CFA). Using the other half-sample, a CFA using AMOS with maximum likelihood estimation provided construct and discriminant validity tests (Anderson and Gerbing 1988), testing the model fit and the scales' content validity. Scales were first separately analysed using 1-factor congeneric models representing the regression of each set of observed variables (scale items) on its respective latent variable (Byrne 2001). Items with correlated error terms indicated redundancy (Byrne 2001) and were removed to improve fit indices and internal reliability, with scales reduced to four items for parsimony. Each scale was tested and revised to obtain reasonable fit statistics (see table 3) which ranged from excellent to satisfactory. For the Normed Fit Index (NFI), Comparative Fit Index (CFI), and Adjusted Goodness of Fit (AGFI), values over .90 are satisfactory, over .95 indicate a good fit (Kaplan 2000), and 1.00 indicates that the data fit the model perfectly (Byrne, 2001). Root Mean Square Error of Approximation (RMSEA) values between .05 and .08 are satisfactory, below .05 indicate a good fit (Kaplan 2000), while zero indicates an exact fit (Byrne 2001).

TABLE 3
STUDY 3: 1-FACTOR CONGENERIC MODELS' FIT

	Anger	Fear	Joy	Surprise	Sympathy
χ^2 (df)	0.20 (2)	1.65 (2)	0.70 (1)	0.85 (2)	2.80 (2)
NFI	1.00	1.00	1.00	1.00	.99
CFI	1.00	1.00	1.00	1.00	1.00
AGFI	1.00	.98	.99	.97	.99
SRMR	.01	.02	.01	.04	.06
RMSEA	.00	.04	.00	.00	.06
Alpha	.89	.93	.83	.80	.85
AVE	68%	77%	57%	46%	58%
N items	4	4	4	4	4

After finalizing a suitable CFA structure, factor score weightings were calculated on the entire original sample (Byrne 2001). Scale reliability was tested using Cronbach alpha and by calculating average variance extracted (AVE), which reflects the overall amount of variance in the indicators accounted for by the latent construct, which should exceed 50% (Hair et al. 2009). This occurred for all scales except surprise, which was 46%. The anger, sympathy and surprise scales (see Appendix for items) measured feelings towards the company. The fear scale measured feelings towards product or service use. The joy scale measured feelings towards product or service use, and towards the company in crisis. The final latent variable model showed acceptable fit statistics, χ^2 (160) = 468.50, p < .001, CFI = .94, NFI = .92, AGFI = .88, RMSEA = .07, SRMR = .18, with factor loadings as per figure 1. This model's reliability using AVE calculations was 68%. The fit statistics indicated this model to be preferred to a higher order construct model for positive and negative emotion.

FIGURE 1
STUDY 3: STANDARDIZED ESTIMATES SHOWING DISCRIMINANT VALIDITY OF THE EMOTION SCALES

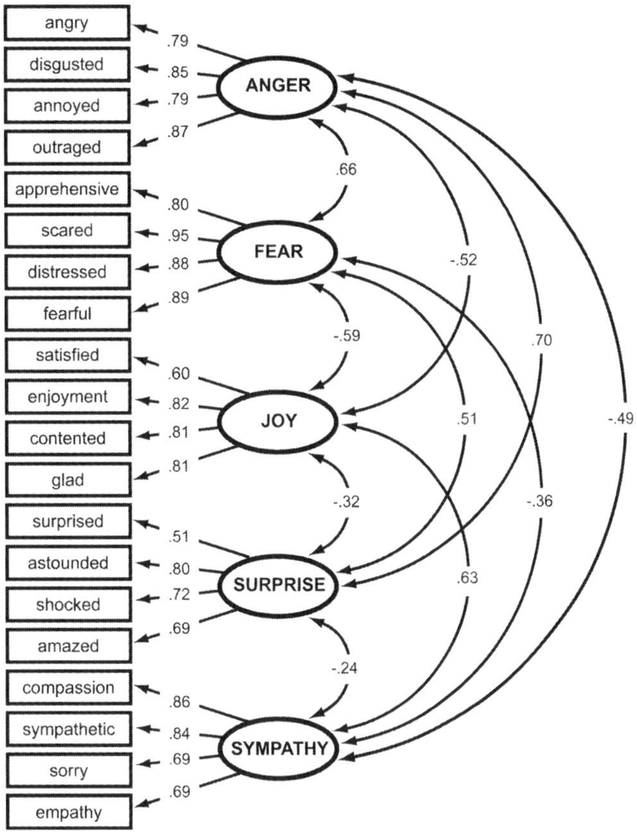

Predictive validity with other constructs. The final stage involved demonstrating that the emotion scales had nomological validity against attitudes and behaviors of loyalty, disloyalty, and complaining using standard regression analyses. First the attitude and behavior scales' fit indices were examined, resulting in five 4-item scales. All emotions significantly predicted attitude, $F(5, 837) = 151.48, p < .001$. All emotions except sympathy significantly predicted disloyalty, $F(5, 838) = 235.04, p < .001$. Joy, fear, and sympathy significantly predicted loyalty, $F(5, 838) = 153.43, p < .001$. Anger and fear significantly predicted complaining, $F(5, 838) = 74.31, p < .001$.

DISCUSSION

Research on the burgeoning field of emotional reactions to crises is hindered by the absence of scales using words that incorporate consumers' own crisis emotion lexicon and which are psychometrically robust. To extend research in this field, we developed and tested crisis emotion scales, demonstrating their convergent and discriminant validity, internal reliability, and predictive validity. Testing resulted in three negative emotion scales (anger, fear, surprise) and two positive emotion scales (joy, sympathy) suitable for examining emotions felt towards a company and its products or services. The scales, albeit in early testing stages, may stimulate further research aimed at understanding consumer crisis emotions–positive and negative–in particular, the relationship between emotions and attitude and behaviors. This is important in view of concrete evidence of consumers' negative reactions to crises, evidenced in the marketplace in product boycotts and reduced market share. Further, the creation of a joy measure facilitates tests of this positive crisis emotion, which currently attracts little research attention.

Although an airline crash is considered a severe crisis (Lee, 2004), anger, fear, surprise, sadness, and sympathy felt towards organizations has also been identified in studies examining response to less severe scenarios. These include Kim and Cameron's (2011) product defect scenarios involving burns, and Coombs and Holladay's (2005) 10-scenario study, which included rumor, organizational misdeed and human-error product recalls. This indicates that our scales may apply to less severe, less emotionally-intense crises. Further research is required to examine the stability of the scale across different crisis types and settings.

The study also extends the limited existing research on crisis emotion effects on attitude and behaviors, finding that emotions impacted consumers' attitudes and differentially impacted their reported behaviors. Anger predicted complaining, disloyalty and attitude. Fear predicted disloyalty, complaining and attitude, and negatively predicted loyalty. Joy predicted loyalty and attitude, and negatively predicted disloyalty. Sympathy predicted attitude and loyalty. Surprise predicted disloyalty and negatively predicted attitude. These differing emotion reactions emphasize the need for managers to identify which emotions are likely to arise when a crisis erupts in order to implement intervention measures to minimize damage to the brand and company reputation, and to attenuate loss of customers, sales, and market share.

These short easily administered self-report emotion measures provide managers with a toolkit to assess current consumer emotions–and their strength–in order to predict likely attitudinal and behavioral consequences of an organizational crisis and to be able to tailor responses. If the dominant emotion is fear, then crisis statements should provide information about specific actions to take (e.g., product return), followed by information to help consumers cope with the crisis (e.g., seek advice from the organization's website) or focus on possible positive outcomes. Surprise (akin to shock) may require both forms of action. If anger is uppermost, crisis communication should incorporate image repair information (e.g., highlighting organizational safety). Finding positive emotions signals that the company does not need to expend major resources dealing with the crisis. These scales may also assist in gauging the success of interventions, including emotion-tailored crisis communication, and assessing the effectiveness of crisis management strategies.

As the scales were developed using an Australian sample and tested using airline crash scenarios, further scale validation using different respondent samples and different crisis types is warranted to examine the scales' robustness and the scope of their application. Investigating emotional responses to actual crises with real implications for consumers is important to capture the dynamic processes occurring during crises.

APPENDIX
CRISIS EMOTION SCALES

1. Emotions towards the company

For *each* word below, please circle the number that best describes the feelings that you have about X. When I think about X, I feel...

(a) angry[1]	(b) surprised[2]	(c) sympathetic[3]	(d) contented[4]
(e) annoyed[1]	(f) shocked[2]	(g) sorry[3]	(h) enjoyment[4]
(i) disgusted[1]	(j) amazed[2]	(k) compassion[3]	(l) glad[4]
(m) outraged[1]	(n) astounded[2]	(o) empathy[3]	(p) satisfied[4]

[1]Anger scale, [2]Surprise scale, [3]Sympathy scale, [4]Joy scale.

2. Emotions towards using the service/product

For *each* word below, please circle the number that best describes the feelings that you have towards using *X's* product/service. Towards using product/service I feel...

(a) contented[4]	(b) scared[5]
(c) enjoyment[4]	(d) apprehensive[5]
(e) glad[4]	(f) fearful[5]
(g) satisfied[4]	(h) distressed[5]

[4]Joy scale, [5]Fear scale.

NOTE: Responses are based on a 7-point Likert-type scale, anchored by *not at all* (1) and *very much* (7).

REFERENCES

Anderson, James C. and Gerbing, David W. (1988), "Structural Equation Modeling in Practice: A Review and Recommended Two-Step Approach," *Psychological Bulletin*, 103 (3), 411–423.

Australian Electoral Commission. *Australian Electoral Commission Annual Report 2006-2007 Outcome 1 – An effective electoral roll*, Canberra.

Bearden, William O., Richard G. Netemeyer, and Mary F. Mobley (1999), *Handbook of Marketing Scales*, Newbury Park, CA: Sage.

Bruner II, Gordon C. and Paul J. Hensel (1998), *Marketing scales handbook: A compilation of multi-item measures*, Vol. II, Chicago, Illinois: American Marketing Association.

Bruner II, Gordon C., Karen E. James, and Paul J. Hensel (2001), *Marketing scales handbook: A compilation of multi-item measures*, Vol. III, Chicago, Illinois: American Marketing Association.

Byrne, Barbara M. (2001), *Structural Equation Modeling With AMOS: Basic Concepts, Applications And Programming*, Mahwah, NJ: Erlbaum.

Carpenter, Sandra L. and Amy G. Halberstadt (1996), "What makes people angry? Laypersons' and psychologists' categorizations of anger in the family," *Cognition and Emotion*, 10, 627-656.

Choi, Yoonhyeung, and Ying-Hsuan Lin (2009), "Consumer Responses to Mattel Product Recalls Posted Online Bulletin Boards: Exploring Two Types of Emotion," *Journal of Public Relations Research*, 21 (2), 198–207.

Churchill, Gilbert A. (1979), "A Paradigm For Developing Better Measures Of Marketing Constructs," *Journal of Marketing Research*, 16, 64–73.

Coombs W. Timothy and Sherry J. Holladay (2002), "Helping Crisis Managers Protect Reputational Assets," *Management Communication Quarterly*, 16 (2), 165–186.

--- (2005), "An Exploratory Study of Stakeholder Emotions: Affect and Crises," in *The Effect of Affect in Organizational Settings: Research on Emotion in Organizations*, ed. Neal Ashkanasy, Wilfred J. Zerbe, and Charmine E. J. Härtel, Oxford, Elsevier, 263–280.

--- (2007), "The Negative Communication Dynamic. Exploring the Impact of Stakeholder Affect on Behavioral Intentions," *Journal of Communication Management*, 11 (4), 300–312.

--- (2008), "Comparing Apology to Equivalent Crisis Response Strategies: Clarifying Apology's Role and Value in Crisis Communication," *Public Relations Review*, 34 (3), 252–257.

--- (2009), "Further Explorations of Post-Crisis Communication: Effects of Media and Response Strategies on Perceptions and Intentions," *Public Relations Review*, 35 (1), 1–6.

Epstein, Seymour (1984), "Controversial Issues in Emotion Theory," *Review of Personality and Social Psychology*, 5, 64–88.

Folkes, Valerie S. (1984), "Consumer Reactions to Product Failure: An Attributional Approach," *Journal of Consumer Research*, 10 (4), 398–409.Frijda, Nico H. (1986), *The Emotions*, New York: Cambridge University Press.

Gerbing, David W. and James C. Anderson (1988), "An Updated Paradigm for Scale Development Incorporating Unidimensionality and its Assessment," *Journal of Marketing Research*, 25, 186–192.

Hair, Joseph F., William C. Black, Barry J. Babin, and Rolph E. Anderson (2009), *Multivariate Data Analysis* (7th ed.), Upper Saddle River, NJ: Prentice-Hall.

Havlena, William J., Morris B. Holbrook, and Donald R. Lehmann (1989), "Assessing the Validity of Emotional Typologies," *Psychology and Marketing*, 6 (2), 97–112.Hunsaker, Frank G., Dominic A. Cioffi, Peter C. Amadio, James G. Wright, and Beth Caughlin (2002), "The American College of Orthopedic Surgeons Outcomes Instruments: Normative Values from the General Population," *Journal of Bone and Joint Surgery*, 84 (2), 208–215.

Izard, Carroll E. (1993), "Organizational and Motivational Functions of Discrete Emotions," ed. Michael Lewis and Jeannette M. Haviland, *Handbook of Emotion*, New York: The Guilford Press, 631-641.

Jin, Yan (2009), "The Effects of Public's Cognitive Appraisal of Emotions in Crises on Crisis Coping and Strategy Assessment," *Public Relations Review*, 35 (3), 310–313.

Jin, Yan, and Cameron, G.T. (2007), "The Effects of Threat Type and Duration on Public Relations Practitioner's Cognitive, Affective, and Conative Responses in Crisis Situations," *Journal of Public Relations Research*, 19 (3), 255–281.

Jin, Yan, Augustine Pang, and Glenn T. Cameron (2007), "Integrated Crisis Mapping: Towards a Publics-Based, Emotion-Driven Conceptualization in Crisis Communication," *Sphera Publica*, 7, 81–96.

Jorgensen, Brian K. (1996), "Components of Consumer Reaction to Company-Related Mishaps: A Structural Equation Model Approach," *Advances in Consumer Research*, Vol. 23, eds. Kim P. Corfman and John G. Lynch Jr., Association for Consumer Research, Association for Consumer Research, 346–51.

Kaplan, David (2000), *Structural Equation Modeling: Foundations and Extensions*, Thousand Oaks, CA: Sage.

Kim, Hyo J. and Cameron, Glen T. (2011), "Emotions Matter in Crisis: The Role of Anger and Sadness in the Publics' Response to Crisis News Framing and Corporate Crisis Response," *Communication Research*, 1, 1-30.

Laros, Fleur. J., and Jan-Benedict E. Steenkamp, (2005), "Emotions in Consumer Behavior: A Hierarchical Approach," *Journal of Business Research*, 58, 1437–1445.

Lee, Betty K. (2004), "Audience-Oriented Approach to Crisis Communication: A Study Of Hong Kong Consumers' Evaluation of an Organizational Crisis," *Communication Research*, 31 (5), 600–618.

Loo, Robert (2001), "A Caveat on Using Single-item versus Multiple-item Scales," *Journal of Managerial Psychology*, 17 (1), 68-75.Lunt, Peter (1996), "Rethinking the Focus Group in Media and Communications Research," *Journal of Communication*, 46 (2), 79–98.

Nyer, Prashanth U. (1997), "A Study of the Relationships Between Cognitive Appraisals and Consumption Emotions," *Journal of the Academy of Marketing Science*, 25 (4), 296–304.

Ortinau, David J. (2011), "Writing and Publishing Important Scientific Articles: A Reviewer's Perspective," *Journal of Business Research*, 64, 150–156.

Ortony, Andrew, Gerard L. Clore, and Allan Collins (1988), *The Cognitive Structure of Emotions*, Cambridge, UK: Cambridge University Press.

Peter, J. Paul (1981), "Construct Validity: A Review of Basic Issues and Marketing Practices," *Journal of Marketing Research*, 18 (2), 133–145.

PricewaterhouseCoopers (2006). *Barometer Surveys: Management Barometer*. Retrieved from http://www.barometersurveys.com/production/barsurv.nsf/vwAllNewsByDocID/865270A1E53CD90285257249004B4175

Richins, Marsha L. (1997), "Measuring Emotions in the Consumption Experience," *Journal of Consumer Research,* 24 (2), 127–146.

Scherer, Klaus R. (2000), "Emotion," in ed. Hewstone Miles and W. Stroebe, *Introduction To Social Psychology: A European Perspective,* Oxford, UK: Blackwell, 151-191.

Shaver, Phillip, Judith Schwartz, Donald Kirson, and Cary O'Connor (1987), "Emotion Knowledge: Further Exploration of a Prototype Approach," *Journal of Personality and Social Psychology,* 52 (6), 1061–1086.

Swiss Re. *Media information: Preliminary estimates from Swiss Re sigma 2010.* Retrieved from http://www.swissre.com/media/media_information /Preliminary_2010_catastrophes_estimates_from_sigma.html

Tabachnik, Barbara G., and Linda S. Fidell (2001), *Using Multivariate Statistics* (4th ed.), Boston: Allyn and Bacon.

Weiner, Bernard (1986), *An Attributional Theory Of Motivation And Emotion,* New York: Springer.

Yavas, Ugur, and Emir Babakus (1995), "Purchasing Involvement in Saudi Arabia: Measure Development and Validation," *Journal of International Consumer Marketing,* 8 (1), 23–30.

Using Self-Perceived Age and the List of Values to Study Older Consumer in 4 Nations

Florian Kohlbacher, German Institute for Japanese Studies (DIJ) Tokyo, Japan
Lynn Sudbury, Liverpool John Moores University, UK
Agnes Hofmeister, Corvinus University of Budapest, Hungary

ABSTRACT

This study is the first one to look into the relationship between personal values and self-perceived age for older consumers in the UK, Germany, Hungary and Japan. Apart from overall cross-national differences, interesting differences in value rankings by self-perceived age groups emerged within countries as well.

Population ageing has emerged as a powerful megatrend affecting a large number of countries around the world. Indeed, the United Nations (2007) suggests that this megatrend is probably the most profound demographic change in the history of humankind. It is a pervasive and truly global phenomenon, without precedent or parallel, largely irreversible, and with the young populations of the past unlikely to occur again. Globally, the number of older persons will exceed the number of children by 2047, which has already occurred in many developed regions. The profundity of this demographic change will impact on economic growth, labour markets, pensions, health care, housing, migration, politics, and of course consumption. It is surprising, therefore, that older consumers are still relatively neglected by both marketing academics and practitioners alike (Niemelä-Nyrhinen, 2007; Simcock and Sudbury, 2006). This situation is particularly true for countries outside the United States of America, where what is known about the consumer behaviour of seniors still lags far behind what is known about other important segments (Kohlbacher and Chéron, 2010; Williams et al., 2010).

Similarly, as Kahle and Kennedy (1988) point out, business has too often neglected the importance of values, despite the prominence given to them by philosophers and social scientists, and the fact that values have been shown to influence a range of consumer behaviours. An understanding of the impact of age and values on the consumer behaviour of a particular cohort can therefore be a powerful tool for market planning, product development, demand forecasting and innovation (Muller, Kahle and Chéron, 1992). With this in mind, this paper aims to make a contribution to knowledge by analysing and comparing the values of older consumers across four nations outside North America.

Theoretical background and previous research

Cognitive age: The significance of a persons' age in wider society is apparent in many walks of life. One's chronological age dictates, for example, the point at which one can legally drive an automobile, marry, consume alcohol, vote, and enlist in the military. Although chronological age is still widely used in both marketing research and segmentation practice, its limitations as an indicator of values, attitudes and behavior have long been known (Adams, 1971; Chua, Cote and Leong, 1990), and are acknowledged in everyday parlance -'he's got an old head on young shoulders', 'she's still very young at heart'- and it may well be that the adage that one is as young or as old as one feels provides more useful insights into the behavior of older people.

Measurement methods for ascertaining how old a person feels, i.e., a person's self-perceived age, fall into two major groups. The first, and oldest, is age identity (Cavan *et al.*, 1949), concerning the age category (young, middle-aged, old) in which people perceive themselves to be. A second type of measure grew in response to the recognition that ageing is multidimensional (Birren, 1968), comprising biological, psychological, and sociological dimensions, none of which can be understood without reference to the others (Riley, 1985). The cognitive age scale (Barak and Schiffman, 1981) is one

such multidimensional scale, which incorporates the different dimensions of aging by asking people how old they think they look (biological), how old they feel (psychological and biological), and how old they rate their behavior and interests (social). Cognitive age has been shown to be useful in order to better understand consumer behavior in later life across a variety of marketing studies from Internet usage and senior innovators to use of senior promotions and segmentation (Eastman and Iyer 2005; Moschis and Mathur 2006; Sherman, Schiffman, and Dillon 1988; Sudbury and Simcock 2010), and is now well established in the marketing literature.

Personal Values: Research pertaining to personal values agrees that they are an integral influence upon human behaviour, with their impact being recognised across social science disciplines (Vinson et al., 1977; Clawson and Vinson, 1978). Whilst there is some debate on how values are created, evolve, and impact human behaviour, and indeed there is a lack of agreement on a 'formal' definition of values, many researchers adopt Rokeach's (1968) contention that values are "enduring beliefs that a specific mode of conduct or end-state of existence is personally or socially preferable to an opposite or converse mode of conduct or end state" (p. 550). Thus, values appear to be ideal states for which an individual strives.

Values not only have hierarchical primacy over attitudes (Homer and Kahle, 1988; Kahle, Liu and Watkins, 1992), but influence a variety of consumer behaviours, including reactions to products (Batra, Homer and Kahle, 2001; Kahle, 1986), media preferences (Beatty et al., 1985), positioning (Kennedy, Best and Kahle, 1988), advertising, packaging, personal selling, and retailing (Beatty, Homer and Kahle, 1988). Moreover, age differences in the importance placed on different values have been identified (Kahle, Beatty and Homer, 1986; Kahle, Poulos and Sukhdial, 1988), with a recent American study (Gurel-Atay et al. 2010) finding older Americans to have significantly different rankings of values than other age groups. Conversely, the same study found no differences between the several younger age groupings, suggesting that value systems do indeed change at different life stages. Indeed, the literature devoted to older consumers clearly suggests that older people have different values to younger people (Wolfe 1988; Yovovich 1983), and suggests that the older generation may value trustworthiness and being responsible and sensible above other values (De Jonquieres, 1993), while several authors cite security, safety, social connectedness and spirituality as key (Dychtwald and Flower, 1989; Schewe, 1990, 1991; Wolfe 1994).

While a body of research suggests that the most important values are handed down from generation to generation (Kahle, Liu and Watkins, 1992; Kahle, Poulous, and Sukdial, 1988), one explanation for generational differences was proffered by Crosby, Gill and Lee (1984) who suggested that economic conditions, historical and political events, and the specific deprivations experienced by different cohorts may be the antecedents for age differences. Clearly, this argument gives rise to the need for a cross national investigation into the differing values of adults of the same generation who have experienced very different economic conditions and historical and political events. On this basis, the current study aims to fill a significant gap in the literature by studying the value bases of an important cohort of older consumers, drawn from four nations that have experienced very different political and economic conditions during the life-times of these older adults.

Cognitive Age and Personal Values: There are only a few previous studies into older adults and values, and none of these are multi-national. The first, an Australian study (Cleaver and Muller 2002), found 'fun and enjoyment' to be associated with feeling younger than one's actual age, while those who felt older valued 'security'. However, only one previous study (Sudbury and Simcock 2009) has used cognitive age to study the values of older consumers. Conducted in the UK, these authors found that significant differences did emerge between cognitive age and value rankings. A major gap in current knowledge is a cross-national comparison of older consumers and values, in order to provide marketing practitioners with some insight into this important area of consumer behavior, which can help guide their international marketing strategies.

METHODOLOGY

The study comprised part of a major piece of international research into older consumers across several culturally disparate nations, and utilized questionnaires. The lower age parameter of 50 was selected on the basis that this is the starting point for many age-related services offered to older consumers (for example, SAGA, Age UK, Seniorsurfers.net). Besides, previous research has called for including middle-aged respondents in order to better understand aging mechanisms and their impact on consumer behavior (e.g. Cole et al. 2008). Barak and Schiffman's (1981) cognitive age scale was used. As for personal values, the LOV scale developed by Kahle (1983) was employed and requested respondents to read all eight statements shown in Table 2 carefully before giving their answer on a scale of importance from 1 to9. Additionally, respondents completed a battery of socio-demographic questions.

The four nations selected are Japan, Germany, UK, and Hungary. Japan is ranked number one in every international league table that considers population ageing, with 28% of its population already age 60 or over and a median age of 43 years (United Nations 2007). Older Japanese adults have experienced US occupation of post-war Japan (1945-1952), and then the remarkable post-war economic recovery which continued through the 1970s and 1980s which eventually made Japan the world's second-largest economy, before succumbing to the Asian economic crisis in 1998. Germany is ranked 3rd in the league tables produced by the United Nations (2007) with 25.3% of its population already 60 or above. Irrespective of whether these people lived in East or West Germany before reunification, all have experienced dramatic political and economic upheavals. The UK is ranked 17th from a total of 192 countries with 22% of its population already 60 or over. Despite its membership of the European Union, its close relations with the Untied States reflects a common language and ideals, and it is therefor possible that the values of older UK adults are influenced to a greater extent by America than its European neighbors. Finally, Hungary is ranked 19th in the league tables and has more than 21% of its population already aged 60 or above. Older Hungarians have lived through forty-seven years of military presence, many have experienced economic hardship, and all have experienced the transition to a market economy. Overall, our sample thus consists of the following four countries in three regions: 1) Japan, the most aged society in the world, and – in our sample – the representative of Asia, 2) Germany and 3) Hungary as the representatives from continental Europe, one being the largest and oldest of the Western economies on the Continent and the other an a recent member of the European Union with a communist past, 4) the UK as a representative of the Anglo-Saxon European culture.

The questionnaire was translated and back translated by teams in Japan, Germany, and Hungary before being piloted across all four countries. Several changes were made on the basis of the pilot study. Three lists were purchased, one German (n = 6000), one British (n = 5000), and one Japanese (n = 1044) that contained randomly selected names and addresses of people aged 50+, and a questionnaire and pre-paid envelope was posted to them all. Piloting in Hungary demonstrated the difficulties of self-completion among many older Hungarian adults, thus the distribution strategy was adapted in that country, where a team of trained researchers administered the questionnaire face-to-face to 200 adults aged 50+. A total of 1368 usable questionnaires were received.

Results
Table 1 details the final sample by age and country.

Table 1: Total Sample by Chronological Age and Country

Country	N	Mean Age	Std. Deviation
UK	502	66.6	8.57
Germany	227	63.3	8.42
Japan	439	64.31	8.66
Hungary	200	58.66	5.64
Total	**1368**	**64.16**	**8.60**

The reliability of the cognitive age scale was found to be acceptable (Cronbach's alphas were .88 for the UK sample, .89 for the German sample, and .91 for both the Japanese and the Hungarian samples).

LOV Scale by Score and Rank: Mean scores (measured from 1 = not at all important to 9 = very important) and values by rank (1 = most valued, 8 = least valued) for each nation appear in Table 2.

Table 2: List of Values Average Scores and Rank in the 4 Countries

Value	UK		Germany		Japan		Hungary	
	Mean	Rank	Mean	Rank	Mean	Rank	Mean	Rank
Self-Respect	8.26	1	8.08	1	6.54	6	8.44	4
Security	7.93	2	7.77	3	7.86	2	8.76	1
Accomplishment	7.82	3	7.50	5	7.17	5	7.68	6
Warm Relationships	7.78	4	7.63	4	7.95	1	8.48	3
Fun and Enjoyment	7.59	5	8.02	2	7.63	3	6.21	8
Self-Fulfillment	7.46	6	6.71	8	7.48	4	7.74	5
Being Well Respected	7.43	7	6.97	7	6.40	7	7.65	7
Sense of Belonging	7.35	8	7.18	6	4.98	8	8.22	2

The sample of UK older respondents ranked "self-respect" followed by "security" as their highest values. In Germany, "self-respect" was the top score, too, with "Fun and enjoyment" being second. The Japanese respondents gave a top mean score to "Warm relationships with others", followed by "security". In Hungary, "security" was highest and "Sense of belonging" was the second highest. The least important values were: "Sense of belonging"in the UK and Japan,, "Self-fulfillment" in Germany, and "Fun and enjoyment" in Hungary.

LOV by Cognitive Age Decade: The LOV scores are further investigated in relation to four cognitive age groups. The four groups were formed along cognitive age decades (cognitive age in e.g. the 50s), comprising of cognitive ages lower than 50 (<50s), cognitive ages in the 50s, 60s, and finally cognitive ages equal to 70 or greater (>=70s). The ranking/ mean scores of values for our respondents slightly fluctuates with cognitive age. In Germany for example, "Security" and "Fun and enjoyment" switch ranks in higher cognitive age, thus as the cognitive age of older Germans increases, security appears to become more important and "Fun and Enjoyment becomes less important. Similarly, the lower the cognitive age, the greater the importance placed on "Being Well Respected". In Japan, "Fun and enjoyment" is more important for those with a younger cognitive age, but becomes less important for older cohorts, who then place more importance on "Warm relationships with others". Cognitively younger UK adults value "Fun and Enjoyment" to a greater extent than do their cognitively older counterparts, while a sense of belonging becomes more important the older one feels. Finally, in Hungary cognitive age appears to affect the importance placed on "security", which has a positive relationship with cognitive age, while a "sense of belonging" becomes less important.

A Kruskal Wallis nonparametric test was calculated to check if there was an overall significant statistical rank difference between cognitive age groups for each value. A significant difference was found for "Warm relationships" in Germany (Chi-square = 10.109; df = 3; p = .018), "Self-fulfillment" in the UK (Chi-square = 7.577; df = 3; p = .056) – even though only on the 10% level – in Germany (Chi-square = 9.902; df = 3; p = .019), and Japan (Chi-square = 9.725; df = 3; p = .021), "Being well respected" in Germany (Chi-square = 7.753; df = 3; p = .051) and Japan (Chi-square = 8.587; df = 3; p = .035), "Fun and enjoyment" in the UK (Chi-square = 8.919; df = 3; p = .030) and Germany (Chi-square = 8.508; df = 3; p = .037), "Security" in the UK (Chi-square = 6.367; df = 3; p = .095), and finally "Self-respect" in Germany (Chi-square = 8.998; df = 3; p = .029).

Bivariate Kendall's tau b correlations between cognitive age groups and "Self-fulfillment", Being well respected" and "Fun and enjoyment" were computed and found negative and significant (Respectively: -.106, -.085, and -.036) in the UK. In Germany, significances were only found for "Self-fulfillment" (tau-b=-.127) and "Fun and enjoyment" (tau-b= -.150), while in Japan all three were significant (tau-bs: -.113, -.110, and -.083). This confirms the lower importance of the above three personal values with higher cognitive age. In Hungary, a significance was only found for security (tau-b = .131), with a positive relationship between cognitive age and this value.

DISCUSSION

In terms of cognitive age, the results for the mature markets in our sample countries reveal an average difference between actual age and cognitive age of 7 years in the UK and Germany and 5.5 years in Japan and 6.5 years in Hungary. I.e. in all countries studied, respondents felt younger than their actual biological by at least 5 years. Although a difference of 5-7 years is substantial, it is smaller than the difference of 10.3 years found by Szmigin and Carrigan (2000) and that of 10.3 and 9.7 years found by Sudbury and Simcock (2009) in the UK, or of 8.4 years found by Van Auken et al. (2006) for their Japanese sample. This is also lower than a difference of 11.97 years found in France by Guiot (2001) and of 10.2 years in Australia (Cleaver and Muller 2002). This may be due to the recent tendency for the youth bias – i.e. the difference between chronological age and cognitive age – to become smaller as the images of age and aging change. E.g. age 60 used to be perceived as old until recently, but with rising life expectancy and longevity it is nowadays not perceived as old, but rather middle-aged. It is as the saying goes, "50 is the new 40" or even the "new 30", i.e. people considered 'old' in previous generations are much younger now in outlook and appearance as well as attitude. Thus, there is no more need to adjust ones cognitive age downward so strongly as it used to be the case. Also, as life spans increase, the old '3 decades plus 10' i.e. 70 is the expected life span, is changing – so perhaps old is now measured on how long people expect to live. This is only speculation, but other researchers seem to back up this assumption. Catterall and Maclaran e.g. (2001) have argued that subjective age might also be a social phenomenon and that thus the usefulness and applicability of the cognitive age concept could change along with changing social attitudes such as the one towards aging. Indeed, the meaning of individual age categories is dependent on the given culture and social environment in which they are used (Maddox and Campbell 1985). Thus, it is to be expected that the meanings of distinct categories will differ between cultures, but a degree of consensus would be found among people in the same culture, with only minor variation from one person to another (Fry 1988).

In the Asian context, Chua et al. (1990) advanced the hypothesis that those identifying with the Chinese culture in Singapore have a higher cognitive age than those identifying with the English culture. In Malaysia, Ong et al. (2009) found the differences between chronological and cognitive age to be 10.8 years for a convenience sample of people aged 40 and older. Although preliminary, the results for the Japanese context tend to confirm a slightly lower age difference than in Europe. Overall, the results with respect to the applicability of the cognitive age concept and scale to both Western and non-Western context seem to confirm the findings from previous research (cf. e.g. Barak 2009). In a similar vein, the cross-cultural research by Barak and associates suggests that the cognitive age scale is reliable and can be used in diverse cultures and that there is a universal nature of the way human beings – irrespective of culture – perceive and feel about cognitive age (Barak et al. 2001; Barak et al. 2003; Mathur et al. 2001). However, these studies also found that the cognitive age scale exhibits only partial measurement invariance across the three countries, which implies that culture may play at least some role in the perception of age (Mathur et al. 2001). This is partly supported by Uotinen's (1998) study which showed differences between residents of Finland and those in the northeastern United States in terms of cognitive age, with the former expressing a greater acceptance of their present age status. Nevertheless, despite some cultural differences in subjective age perceptions, the empirical evidence collected so far in various countries rather indicates that cognitive age is a universal characteristic, irrespective of the cultural background. Our study seems to confirm this for the overall tendency to feel younger than one's biological age, but there are still differences in terms of the magnitude of the difference between actual age and cognitive age.

Cognitive Age and LOV Differences: Any cross-cultural comparison of our data is difficult since perfect equivalence of meaning and measurement is not guaranteed. However, preliminary data analysis suggests at least partial measurement invariance for our samples. A tentative interpretation of the ranking similarities and differences between older respondents in the four countries seems to point to a strong importance of "Security" but to a substantial ranking difference of the importance of "Self-respect", ranked first by British and German respondents, but sixth by Japanese and fourth by Hungarian respondents. In addition, Japanese respondents give top ranking to "Warm relationships with others" while it comes third for Hungarians and fourth for both British and German respondents. This finding suggests the overall importance of this value for older consumers. "Fun and enjoyment" seems to be fairly important to Germans and Japanese (ranked second and third respectively), but not so important for British (ranked fifth) and rather unimportant for Hungarians (ranked last). Finally, while British, German and Japanese older consumers do not perceive "Sense of belonging" as particularly important (ranked eighth, sixth, eighth, respectively), it is the second most important value for Hungarians. Cultural and historical effects may be at play here, but further research is necessary to establish whether this is really the case or not.

Even though probably quite problematic to compare due to time differences and the nature of the study, it may be interesting to mention some results on older US consumers from the study by Kahle et al. (1988) to which Sudbury and Simcock (2009) also compared their results. Kahle et al. (1988) found that the three most important values to those US consumers aged 60 and older in 1976 were ""Security", "Self-respect" and "Warm relationships", while in 1986 the order was "Warm relationships", "Security", and "Self-respect" (Kahle et al. 1988). They also found substantial changes between their data from 1976 and 1986 and then further changes in 2007 in a follow-up study (Gurel-Atay et al. 2010). Indeed, comparing rank-order cor-

relations between 1976 and 2007 revealed that only Americans age 60 and older showed a significantly different ranking of values than those in 2007 in terms of the relative importance of the nine values (Gurel-Atay et al. 2010: 60). This means that values changes mainly occurred among older cohorts. In 2007, the most important values to consumers age 60 and older were "Self-respect", "Self-fulfillment", and "Warm relationships" (Gurel-Atay et al. 2010).

An additional study by Muller et al. (1992) compared LOV data for younger and older baby boomers from the US and Canada at three points in time (1976, 1986 and 1989). Results tended to show not only cross-sectional differences at the same period but also sequential shift over time. Overall, the following cultural differences were found: "Warm relationships" and "Self-fulfillment" were found to be more important for Americans than for Canadians, who valued "Security" more than Americans. In relation to age group, a drop in importance of "Fun and enjoyment" was noted between the younger and the older group in Canada but not in the US. However, the importance of "Self-respect" and "Sense of accomplishment" tended to increase with age for both groups. These results confirm that age has an impact on value importance but that additional underlying cultural factors and time are also influencing the value system of consumers.

CONCLUSION AND PRACTICAL IMPLICATIONS

Findings showed that mature consumers in the UK, Germany, Japan and Hungary feel on average 5-7 years younger than their actual age. This is in line with research from other countries, lending support to the assumption of cognitive age as a self-concept being – at least to a certain extent – culture free or universal. Specifically, it seems that the phenomenon of older people having age identities different from their chronological age as well as the direction of the differences (and the factors influencing it) may be universal, while the detailed characteristics of cognitive age and the magnitude of the age difference may be influenced by individual, social as well as cultural factors.

Our results indicate that Sudbury and Simcock's (2009) approach of combining cognitive age and personal values to better understand older consumers is a viable one and also applicable to other countries such as Germany, Japan, and Hungary. Using subjective age measures and personal values will help to change the traditional way of viewing the mature market as a monolith and to open the path for breaking it up into different segments. Companies following this approach should become able to better cater to the needs of older consumers, thus increasing business opportunities while at the same time contributing to the well-being of the fastest growing age group in the world.

Indeed, this study has important implications for marketing practice. In advertising, for example, the use of "cognitive-age congruent" models or spokespersons should prove fertile as a consumer's self-perceived age interacts with the perceived age of the model or spokesperson seen in an ad, and can subsequently influence the response to the advertising message (Chang 2008; Van Auken and Barry 2009). This may also explain why older people are often underrepresented in advertising, a fact that also holds true for TV commercials in the UK (Simcock and Sudbury 2006), Germany (Kessler, Schwender, and Bowen 2010), and Japan (Prieler et al. 2009). Research has also shown the importance of understanding motivational differences that underlie the effects of aging on attitudes toward and recall of advertisements (Drolet, Williams, and Lau-Gesk 2007) and heeding to the cognitive age as well as the values of the target group will likely be an additional, crucial factor.

From an international marketing perspective, the study lends support to the usefulness of self-perceived age together with personal values as a way of segmenting and targeting senior consumers across the globe. In the same way as a youth segment represents an example of a universal global common segment (Kjeldgaard and Askegaard 2006), there is growing evidence that a 'young at heart' senior global market exists (Barak 2009) and this study lends further support to that. That is not to suggest that older adults can be treated as an undifferentiated monolith. Indeed, the differences between the nations suggest that local differences still need to be considered in advertising and positioning strategies. Nevertheless, it provides a starting point for marketers wishing to target this growing and important global phenomenon that is the senior market.

REFERENCES

Barak, Benny (2009), "Age Identity: A Cross-Cultural Global Approach," *International Journal of Behavioral Development*, 33 (1), 2-11.

Barak, Benny and Steven Gould (1985), "Alternative Age Measures: A Research Agenda," in *Advances in Consumer Research*, Vol. 12, ed. Elizabeth C. Hirschman and Moris B. Holbrook, Provo, UT: Association for Consumer Research, 53-58.

Barak, Benny, Anil Mathur, Keun Lee, and Yong Zhang (2001), "Perceptions of Age-Identity: A Cross-Cultural Inner-Age Exploration," *Psychology & Marketing*, 18 (10), 1003-29.

Barak, Benny, Anil Mathur, Yong Zhang, Keun Lee, and Emmanuel Erondu (2003), "Inner-Age Satisfaction in Africa and Asia: A Cross-Cultural Exploration," *Asia Pacific Journal of Marketing and Logistics*, 15 (1/2), 3-26.

Barak, Benny and Don R. Rahtz (1999), "Perceived Youth: Appraisal and Characterization," *International Journal of Aging and Human Development*, 49 (3), 231-57.

Barak, Benny and Leon G. Schiffman (1981), "Cognitive Age: A Nonchronological Variable," in *Advances in Consumer Research*, Vol. 8, ed. Kent B. Monroe, Ann Arbor, MI: Association for Consumer Research, 602-06.

Beatty, Sharon E., Lynn B. Kahle, Pamela M. Homer, and Shekhar Misra (1985), "Alternative Measurement Approaches to Consumer Values: The List of Values and the Rokeach Value Survey," *Psychology & Marketing*, 2 (3), 181-200.

Burroughs, James E. and Aric Rindfleisch (2002), "Materialism and Well-Being: A Conflicting Values Perspective," *Journal of Consumer Research*, 29 (3), 348-70.

Catterall, Miriam and Pauline Maclaran (2001), "Body Talk: Questioning the Assumptions in Cognitive Age," *Psychology & Marketing*, 18 (10), 1117-33.

Chang, Chingching (2008), "Chronological Age Versus Cognitive Age for Younger Consumers," *Journal of Advertising*, 37 (3), 19-32.

Chua, Caroline, Joseph A. Cote, and Siew Meng Leong (1990), "The Antecedents of Cognitive Age," in *Advances in Consumer Research*, Vol. 17, ed. Marvin E. Goldberg, Gerald Gorn and Richard W. Pollay, Provo, UT: Association for Consumer Research, 880-85.

Cleaver, Megan and Thomas E. Muller (2002), "I Want to Pretend I'm Eleven Years Younger: Subjective Age and Seniors' Motives for Vacation Travel," *Social Indicators Research*, 60 (1-3), 227-41.

Cole, Catherine, Gilles Laurent, Aimee Drolet, Jane Ebert, Angela Gutchess, Raphaëlle Lambert-Pandraud, Etienne Mullet, Michael I. Norton, and Ellen Peters (2008), "Decision Making and Brand Choice by Older Consumers," *Marketing Letters*, 19 (3-4), 355-65.

Drolet, Aimee, Pattie Williams, and Loraine Lau-Gesk (2007), "Age-Related Differences in Responses to Affective Vs. Rational Ads for Hedonic Vs. Utilitarian Products," *Marketing Letters*, 18 (4), 211-21.

Eastman, Jacquline K. and Rajesh Iyer (2005), "The Impact of Cognitive Age on Internet Use of the Elderly: An Introduction to the Public Policy Implications," *International Journal of Consumer Studies*, 29 (2), 125-36.

Fry, Christine L. (1988), "Theories of Age and Culture," in *Emergent Theories of Aging*, ed. James E. Birren and Vern L. Bengtson, New York, NY: Springer, 447-81.

Guiot, Denis (2001), "Antecedents of Subjective Age Biases among Senior Women," *Psychology & Marketing*, 18 (10), 1049-71.

Gurel-Atay, Eda, Guang-Xin Xie, Johnny Chen, and Lynn Richard Kahle (2010), "Changes in Social Values in the United States: 1976-2007," *Journal of Advertising Research*, 50 (1), 57-67.

Gwinner, Kevin P. and Nancy Stephens (2001), "Testing the Implied Mediational Role of Cognitive Age," *Psychology & Marketing*, 18 (10), 1031-48.

Henderson, Kenneth V., Ronald E. Goldsmith, and Leisa R. Flynn (1995), "Demographic Characteristics of Subjective Age," *The Journal of Social Psychology*, 135 (4), 447-57.

Homer, Pamela M. and Lynn B. Kahle (1988), "A Structural Equation Test of the Value-Attitude-Behavior Hierarchy," *Journal of Personality and Social Psychology*, 54 (4), 638-46.

Kahle, Lynn B., ed. (1983), *Social Values and Social Change: Adaptation to Life in America*, New York: Praeger Publishers.

Kahle, Lynn B., Sharon E. Beatty, and Pamela M. Homer (1986), "Alternative Measurement Approaches to Consumer Values: The List of Values (Lov) and Values and Life Style (Vals)," *Journal of Consumer Research*, 13 (3), 405-09.

Kahle, Lynn B. and Patricia Kennedy (1988), "Using the List of Values (Lov) to Understand Consumers," *The Journal of Services Marketing*, 2 (4), 49-56.

Kahle, Lynn B., Basil Poulos, and Ajay Sukhdial (1988), "Changes in Social Values in the United States During the Past Decade," *Journal of Advertising Research*, 28 (1), 35-41.

Kahle, Lynn B., Gregory Rose, and Aviv Shoham (1999), "Findings of Lov Throughout the World, and Other Evidence of Cross-National Consymer Psychographics: Introduction," *Journal of Euromarketing*, 8 (1/2), 1-13.

Kamakura, Wagner A. and Thomas P. Novak (1992), "Value-System Segmentation: Exploring the Meaning of Lov," *Journal of Consumer Research*, 19 (1), 119-32.

Kessler, Eva-Marie, Clemens Schwender, and Catherine E. Bowen (2010), "The Portrayal of Older People's Social Participation on German Prime-Time Tv Advertisements," *Journal of Gerontology: Social Sciences*, 65B (1), 97-106.

Kjeldgaard, Dannie and Sørren Askegaard (2006), "The Glocalization of Youth Culture: The Global Youth Segment as Structures of Common Difference," *Journal of Consumer Research*, 33 (2), 231-47.

Kohlbacher, Florian and Emmanuel J. Chéron (2010), "Segmenting the Silver Market Using Cognitive Age and the List of Values: Empirical Evidence from Japan," in *European Advances in Consumer Research (EACR) Conference*, London.

Lee, Julie Anne, Geoffrey N. Soutar, and Jordan Louviere (2007), "Measuring Values Using Best-Worst Scaling: The Lov Example," *Psychology & Marketing*, 24 (12), 1043-58.

Maddox, George L. and Richard T. Campbell (1985), "Scope, Concepts, and Methods in the Study of Aging," in *Handbook of Aging and the Social Sciences*, ed. Robert H. Binstock and Ethel Shanas, New York: Van Nostrand Reinhold Company, 3-31.

Maslow, Abraham H. (1954), *Motivation and Personality*, New York: Harper.

Mathur, Anil, Benny Barak, Yong Zhang, and Keun S. Lee (2001), "A Cross-Cultural Procedure to Assess Reliability and Measurement Invariance," *Journal of Applied Measurement*, 2 (3), 241-55.

Mathur, Anil and George P. Moschis (2005), "Antecedents of Cognitive Age: A Replication and Extension," *Psychology & Marketing*, 22 (12), 969-94.

Moschis, George P. (2003), "Marketing to Older Adults: An Updated Overview of Present Knowledge and Practice," *Journal of Consumer Marketing*, 20 (6), 516-25.

Moschis, George P. and Anil Mathur (2006), "Older Consumer Responses to Marketing Stimuli: The Power of Subjective Age," *Journal of Advertising Research*, 46 (3), 339-46.

Muller, Thomas E., Lynn B. Kahle, and Emmanuel J. Chéron (1992), "Value Trends and Demand Forecasts for Canada's Aging Baby Boomers," *Canadian Journal of Administrative Sciences / Revue Canadienne des Sciences de l'Administration*, 9 (4), 294-304.

Novak, Thomas P. and Bruce MacEvoy (1990), "On Comparing Alternative Segmentation Schemes: The List of Values (Lov) and Values and Life Styles (Vals)," *Journal of Consumer Research*, 17 (1), 105-09.

Ong, Fon Sim, Yap-Ying Lu, and Masoud Abessi (2009), "The Correlates of Cognitive Ageing and Adoption of Defensive-Ageing Strategies among Older Adults," *Asia Pacific Journal of Marketing and Logistics*, 21 (2), 294-305.

Prieler, Michael, Florian Kohlbacher, Shigeru Hagiwara, and Akie Arima (2009), "How Older People Are Represented in Japanese Tv Commercials: A Content Analysis," *Keio Communication Review*, 31, 5-21.

Rokeach, Milton (1973), *The Nature of Human Values*, New York: The Free Press.

Schiffman, Leon G. and Elaine Sherman (1991), "Value Orientations of New-Age Elderly: The Coming of an Ageless Market," *Journal of Business Research*, 22 (2), 187-94.

Schiffman, Leon G., Elaine Sherman, and Mary M. Long (2003), "Toward a Better Understanding of the Interplay of Personal Values and the Internet," *Psychology & Marketing*, 20 (2), 169-86.

Schwartz, Shalom H. (1992), "Universals in the Content and Structure of Values: Theoretical Advances and Empirical Tests in 20 Countries," in *Advances in Experimental Social Psychology*, Vol. 25, ed. Mark Zanna, New York: Academic Press, 1-65.

Sherman, Elaine, Leon G. Schiffman, and Anil Mathur (2001), "The Influence of Gender on the New-Age Elderly's Consumption Orientation," *Psychology & Marketing*, 18 (10), 1073-89.

Sherman, Elaine, Leon G. Schiffman, and William R. Dillon (1988), "Age/Gender Segments and Quality of Life Differences," in *American Marketing Association (AMA) Winter Educators' Conference*, Chicago.

Simcock, Peter and Lynn Sudbury (2006), "The Invisible Majority? Older Models in UK Television Advertising," *International Journal of Advertising*, 25 (1), 87-106.

Sirgy, M. Joseph (1982), "Self-Concept in Consumer Behavior: A Critical Review," *Journal of Consumer Research*, 9 (3), 287-300.

Smith, Jacqui and Paul B. Baltes (1999), "Trends and Profiles of Psychological Functioning in Very Old Age," in *The Berlin Aging Study: Aging from 70 to 100*, ed. Paul B. Baltes and Karl Ulrich Mayer, New York: Cambridge University Press, 197-226.

Sudbury, Lynn (2004), "Subjective Age Perceptions in the Uk: An Empirical Study," *Quality in Ageing - Policy, practice and research*, 5 (1), 4-13.

Sudbury, Lynn and Peter Simcock (2009), "Understanding Older Consumers through Cognitive Age and the List of Values: A U.K.-Based Perspective," *Psychology & Marketing*, 26 (1), 22-38.

--- (2010), "To Use or Not to Use? Age Based Sales Promotions and the Older Consumer," in *American Marketing Association (AMA) Summer Educators' Conference*, Boston.

Szmigin, Isabelle and Marylyn Carrigan (2000), "The Older Consumer as Innovator: Does Cognitive Age Hold the Key?," *Journal of Marketing Management*, 16 (5), 505-27.

--- (2001), "Time, Consumption, and the Older Consumer: An Interpretive Study of the Cognitively Young," *Psychology & Marketing*, 18 (10),0 1091-116.

United Nations (2007), "World Population Ageing 2007," New York: UN Department of Economic Affairs, Population Division.

Uotinen, Virpi (1998), "Age Identification: A Comparison between Finnish and North-American Cultures," 46 (2).

Van Auken, Stuart and Thomas E. Barry (1995), "An Assessment of the Trait Validity of Cognitive Age Measures," *Journal of Consumer Psychology*, 4 (2), 107-32.

--- (2009), "Assessing the Nomological Validity of a Cognitive Age Segmentation of Japanese Seniors," *Asia Pacific Journal of Marketing and Logistics*, 21 (3), 315-28.

Van Auken, Stuart, Thomas E. Barry, and Richard P. Bagozzi (2006), "A Cross-Country Construct Validation of Cognitive Age," *Journal of the Academy of Marketing Science*, 34 (3), 439-55.

Westerhof, Gerben J. and Anne E. Barrett (2005), "Age Identity and Subjective Well-Weing: A Comparision of the United States and Germany," *Journal of Gerontology: Social Sciences*, 60B (3), 129-36.

Westerhof, Gerben J., Anne E. Barrett, and Nardi Steverink (2003), "Forever Young? A Comparison of Age Identities in the United States and Germany," *Research on Aging*, 25 (4), 366-83.

Wilkes, Robert E. (1992), "A Structural Modeling Approach to the Measurement and Meaning of Cognitive Age," *Journal of Consumer Research*, 19 (2), 292-301.

Seeking the Opinions of Others Online:
Evidence of Evaluation Overshoot

Brent Coker, University of Melbourne, Australia

The internet has evolved into a social tool whereby people share their life experiences with the world. This sharing of information provides opportunities to seek the opinions of others about products to aid purchase decision making. Product review sites, blog comments, star rating systems, and discussion forums are some of the sources commonly referenced before actual purchase.

Consumers sharing information about their experiences with brands is of course not new. Past research identified early on that purchase decisions may be influenced by conversations with friends or family, or from reading consumer reports (e.g., Dichter 1966). What is new however is the amount of information available from people who are unknown to the purchaser. Most product reviews have been written by strangers, which may dilute the credibility of the review to some extent. Traditional word-of-mouth is more likely to be between trusted sources such as friends and family, or endorsed third party organizations (Brown and Reingen 1987). However, with online sources there is more chance of reviews being inaccurate as a result of contamination such as dishonesty or rumor (Dellarocas 2003). For example, in early 2009, a cosmetic surgery company was ordered to pay $300,000 in penalties and costs for writing false positive customer reviews about the quality of their service (Miller 2009). In another example, false rumors about Kryptonite bicycle locks cost the company significantly from a false instructional movie posted on uTube explaining how easy the locks were to pick. Actual estimates of how authentic most product reviews are online are difficult to determine, though exploratory studies in some product categories suggest a significant number of positive product reviews are false (Shay and Pinch 2005).

In order to form a balanced judgment, and mitigate the chances of forming a positive evaluation form false positive review, consumers are motivated to process both negative and positive information about a brand. Reading positive reviews about a hotel on tripadvisor.com for example is often accompanied by reading negative reviews in order to identify what could go wrong, no matter how rosy the positive reviews may be. Thus, the development of a brand judgment from review information may involve online processing of both negative and positive information. In fact, it is rare to find a product that has attracted entirely positive or negative reviews; there are always some consumers who appear to have had a better, or worse, experience with a product or service than the majority. Reviews on a five-star rating system for example typically resemble a negative skewed distribution for popular products, and a positive skew for unpopular products.

Although the effects of negative WOM vis-à-vis positive negative WOM have been explored (Richins 1983), there is little understanding of how consumers form attitudes and judgments when exposed to both positive and negative information. It is important for Marketers to understand how consumer judgments are formed in this context given the internet is now a main source of information for product evaluations (Anderson et al. 2010) .Before the emergence of the internet, WOM networks were much smaller, characterized by single valenced information (Brown and Reingen 1987). Since the emergence of the internet as a social channel, consumers have more opportunity to evaluate a product using both positive and negative information than in the past.

Against this background, this study is the first to understand how consumers form brand judgments when word-of-mouth (WOM) information is mixed in valence. An individual's attitude towards the brand will take shape in a positive or negative direction as information of each valence is processed. (Blanc et al. 2008; Blanc and Tapiero 2001; Feldman and Lynch 1988; Schwarz and Bless 1992; Wilson and Hodges 1992; Wilson et al. 2000). Using asymmetric affective perseverance theory to explain judgments in these conditions, we document in two experiments evidence of judgment overshoot whereby the participants make overly positive judgments towards a product after processing mixed valenced information. The findings of this research contribute to the literature in several ways. First, this study is the first to investigate how consumers form judgments when exposed to mixed WOM information about a product Second, this is the first study to find evidence of judgment overshoot in the context of product attitude formation. Third, this study is the first to apply asymmetric affective perseverance theory to explain consumer behavior. In Sum, the goal of this research is to understand how judgments towards products and services are formed when information given about a product or service is a mixture of both positive and negative.

Asymmetric Affective Perseverance

Conventional wisdom suggests that the order in which oppositely valenced information is presented will have no bearing on final judgment. For example, a negative review about a hotel after reading a positive review should result in the same end judgment as when the same reviews were read in the opposite order. Asymmetric Affective Perseverance holds however that the order in which oppositely valenced information is processed does impact end judgments. Specifically, a shift from positive evaluation to negative evaluation is more difficult than a shift from negative to positive, consumers are less successful at adjusting their attitudes in a positive to negative direction than they are at adjusting their attitudes in a negative to positive direction. This results in a more positive attitude when information is presented from positive to negative, than when presented from negative to positive order. Related theories have also posited that invalidated information may continue to contaminate future judgments (Bekerian and Bowers 1983; Greenwald and Banaji 1995; Lindsay and Johnson 1989).

The phenomenon of asymmetric affective perseverance is attributed to people's relative difficulty in shifting their attitude in a positive to negative direction, than in a negative to positive direction. Anecdotally, a person given bad news when in a positive state of mind will find it the shift in ill often experience disbelief, deferral, and dismissal before a relatively negative affective state sinks in (Lubinsky 1994). In contrast, the shift from relative despair to happiness is often instantaneous, and has a stronger effect on imagined outcomes than negative factors. In general, human beings prefer to remain optimistic and are more willing and hopeful towards adopting a positive outlook than remaining in a relative state of negativity (Greenwald 1980).

People tend to prefer the positive side of things rather than the negative side (Greenwald 1980; Taylor 1988). This bias towards positivity is rooted in self serving attributions. Much research has documented evidence of people being over positive in their self evaluation. Tests have shown that people generally believe that they are better than they actually are on a number of factors (Alicke and Govorun 2005). For example, people's evaluation of other people, places, and things which they are associated with is often positively skewed (Pelham, Mirenberg, and Jones 2002). People believe they have improved more than their counterparts on a task (Wilson and Ross 2001), and tend to describe themselves in ways that cast them in a more positive light (Dunning and Cohen 1992).

Wilson et al (2000), argued that oftentimes a person's attitude does not get completely replaced when it is overridden by a new attitude, and might continue to influence judgments even though the valence of judgment is opposite. To demonstrate, Wilson et al. showed participants photos of a sex offender, alongside the prosecutor responsible for convicting the sex offender. Participants also listened to taped descriptions describing each person. The aim was to evoke a strong negative attitude towards the sex offender, and a positive attitude towards the prosecutor. In the experimental condition, the photos were shown the wrong way around –the photo of the prosecutor was actually the sex offender. Participants' attitudes towards the sex offender were then measured and compared against the control group. The results found that attitudes towards the sex offender were significantly more positive in the experimental group than in the control group, suggesting the positive attitude that was evoked when it was thought the prosecutor was the good guy continued to contaminate judgments when replaced.

Wilson et al's (2000) experiment demonstrated contamination of positive attitude on negative attitude. Golding, Fowler, Long, and Latta (1990) on the other hand tested the contaminating effect of negative information on positive information, and found no effect. Participants were given facts about a person, with the experimental group receiving some negative facts. The group given negative facts were then told the negative facts were untrue. When measured, their attitudes were no different from the control group who were given no negative information. This seeming ability for people to better control the contaminating effects of negative information have been reported in other studies. For example, efforts to understand how inadmissible evidence given during a trial have contaminated judgments generally not found that negative information was easily discounted when jurors were told the information was inadmissible (Pickel 1995; Schul and Manzury 1990; Sommers and Kassin 2001).

Other literature documents evidence of asymmetric effect of affective contamination. Petty and Wegener (1994) found that rating the desirability of vacations in desirable holiday destinations lowered evaluations of taking a vacation in non-holiday destination city. After participants were made aware of the manipulation, their desires towards visiting the non-holiday destination cities were still less than the control group who were not told about the desirable holiday destinations. This experiment suggested the participants under-corrected their evaluations, and were unsuccessful at completely correcting for the mental contamination from the holiday destination priming. Effects of imperfect memory replacement have been reported in at least two other studies (Bekerian and Bowers 1983; Lindsay and Johnson 1989)

One explanation for asymmetry in attitude adjustment might be because negative attitudes are easier to retrieve than positive attitudes, and therefore are held more salient and therefore more easily updated than positive attitudes. Eiser et al (2003) for example demonstrated asymmetry in the acquisition of positive and negative evaluations, suggesting positive experiences tended to predominate over negative ones. People might be more reluctant to change their attitude from good to bad than they would be to change their attitude from bad to good, because shifting from positive to negative results in a loss of mental positivity.

Experiment 1

The purpose of Experiment 1 was to assess attitudes towards a product after the information shaping the attitude was invalidated. Specifically, the design of experiment one simulated the scenario of processing information about a product online that turned out later on

to be untrue. Such a situation might occur for instance if a consumer reads a review about a product online, reads a rumor, or reads some information about a brand on a social networking which they later find to be false. Consistent with the theory of asymmetric affective perseverance, we should be positive attitude contaminating judgments towards the brand after positive information is invalidated, and negative information having a non-contaminating effect.

Participants, Design, and Procedure. By email, 229 undergraduate students were invited to participate, of which 128 accepted. Respondents were randomly assigned into a control or experimental group. Both groups were told about two new apparel fashion brands who sold a wide range of formal and casual clothing for men and women that were soon to start selling in the local market. Both brands, Rokit and Rokout, were described by six neutral facts each to illicit ambivalent and equal attitudes between each brand.

Although the aim was to illicit neutral attitudes, it was understood that respondents would likely form at least mild attitudes even if the information given was neutral (Bargh et al. 1996; Fazio 1995). The aim was to minimize attitude strength. After evaluating each brand from the information given, respondents were asked to rate their attitudes towards each brand on three items (-3 = bad, negative, undesirable; +3 = good, positive, desirable). Intentions to purchase each brand were also measured on four items measuring likelihood (seven-points: 1= very low, 7 = very high), probability (seven-points: 1= very low, 7 = very high), willingness (seven-points: 1= very low, 7 = very high), and agreement with the statement "I would consider purchasing Rokit/Rokout clothing" (seven-points: 1= strongly disagree, 7 = strongly agree).

The experimental group was told that talk of these two brands coming to the local market had stirred considerable discussion on social networking sites such as Facebook, MySpace, Bebo, and Twitter. Then, a summary of topics discussed about each brand was listed. The Rokit brand had six negative topics, designed to evoke a negative attitude towards the brand. The Rokout brands also had six topics, but were all positive, designed to evoke positive attitudes towards the brand. Then, respondents were told that expert investigators were hired to scrutinize the facts about each brand and determine if they were true. The investigators discovered the facts were all untrue, except for the original neutral facts. The aim was to motivate respondents to re-evaluate each brand, discounting the false information they had heard. Once again, attitudes and intentions to purchase were measured, and respondents were asked to choose which brand they preferred. The experiment was conducted on a web survey.

Results. Before the manipulation, mean attitude for the Rokit brand in the control group was 0.56 (SD = 1.10), and mean attitude for the Rokout brand in the control group was 0.56 (SD = 1.28). Mean attitude for the Rokit brand in the experimental group was 0.87 (SD = 1.01), and mean attitude for the Rokout brand in the experimental group was 0.91 (SD = .88). These preliminary tests suggested perceptions of the brands were similar, providing a good base for comparison.

After manipulation, a paired samples t-test suggested the manipulations were successful. Attitudes towards the Rokit brand were significantly lower (M = -1.63; SD = 1.47) $t(55)$ = 12.66, p < .0001, and attitudes towards the Rokout brand were significantly higher (M = 1.96; SD = .86) $t(55)$ = 8.50, p < .0001 than before the negative and positive rumors were given. Furthermore, likelihood of purchase was lower after reading the negative rumors about the Rokit brand (M = 2.72; SD = 1.58), $t(55)$ = 8.27, p < .0001, and higher after reading the positive rumors about the Rokout brand (M = 5.31; SD = 1.09), $t(55)$ = -7.95, p < .0001. When asked to choose a brand, 93% chose the positively evaluated Rokout brand.

The experiment predicted that consumers' should be successful at reverting attitudes towards a brand back to the same state of indifference when negative information is discredited. In contrast, positive information should continue to contaminate judgments after invalidated. After respondents were told the positive facts about Rokout were rumors and were untrue, attitudes remained significantly higher in the experimental group ($M = 1.05$; $SD = .99$) than in the control group ($M = 0.56$; $SD = 1.28$), $F(1, 127) = 5.48$, $p < .05$. Furthermore, likelihood of purchase continued to be higher in the experimental group ($M = 4.57$; $SD = 1.09$) than in the control group ($M = 4.09$; $SD = 1.36$), $F(1, 127) = 4.75$, $p < .05$.

Contrasted against the positive rumor manipulation, after par-

ticipants were told the negative information was untrue there was no difference in attitude towards the Rokit brand in the experimental group ($M = 0.58$; $SD = 1.15$) than in the control group ($M = 0.56$; $SD = 1.10$), $F(1, 127) = .02$, NS. Likelihood of purchase was also not significantly different in the experimental group ($M = 4.23$; $SD = 1.18$) compared to the control group ($M = 3.91$; $SD = 1.36$), $F(1, 127) = 1.94$, NS.

Twenty percent of participants who originally chose the Rockit brand (before the manipulation) ended up choosing the Rockout brand after they were told the rumored facts were false. Two percent who originally chose the Rokout brand ended up choosing the Rokit brand.

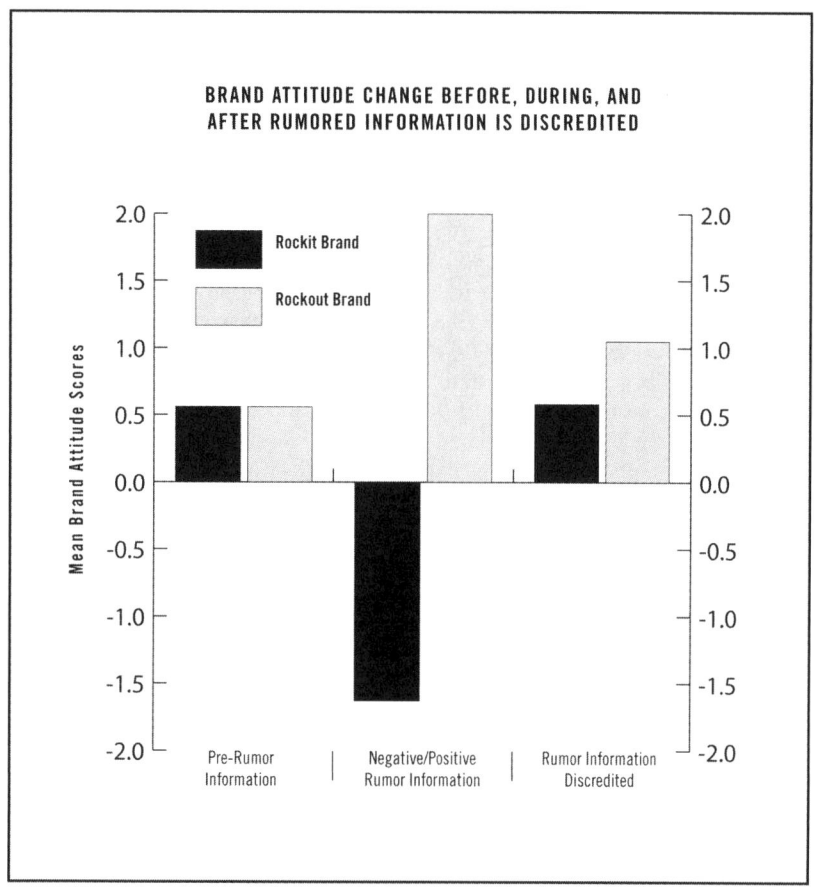

Figure 1: Attitudes towards Rokit and Rokout apparel brands as a function of rumored information manipulations.

Experiment 1 Discussion

The results in experiment 1 found evidence of an enduring effect of positive attitude after invalidating positive information. The results suggested that participants were relatively successful at removing encoded negative information, but are unsuccessful at re-adjusting their attitude back to a state of relative indifference when removing encoded positive information. Those who were exposed to the discredited negative information had similar mild attitudes as those who were not exposed to any misinformation. In contrast, those who were exposed to discredited positive misinformation had significantly higher attitudes towards the brand than those who were not exposed. The results add evidence to the prediction that re-encoding of attitudes occurs asymmetrically, with negative to positive re-encoding being more complete than positive to negative re-encoding.

Experiment 2

The aim of experiment three was to test asymmetrical affec-

tive perseverance in the context of reading product reviews. Specifically, the contaminating effect of positive attitude on evaluation was tested in a hotel review exercise whereby positive and negative hotel reviews were presented in opposite order. To assess how time moderates affective perseverance, an additional variable of "length of time between reviews" was included. The aim was to assess how time trend information given about positive-to-negative or negative-to-positive ordered reviews might moderate asymmetrical affective adjustment. Earlier negative reviews followed by more recent positive reviews should be perceived as improvement and less likelihood of having a bad experience than if reviews are ordered from earlier positive reviews to more recent negative reviews. When time trend information is absent, such as when reviews about a hotel are taken from the same holiday weekend, we should observe a more positive skew in hotel rating when reviews are ordered from positive to negative because of positive contamination. In contrast, if trend information over time is available for reviews ordered from positive to negative, then we should not observe a positively skewed evaluation of the hotel from positive contamination, because the reviews should suggest a decline in quality over time.

Participants, Design, and Procedure. Two-hundred and eighty undergraduate and graduate students were invited to participate by email. One hundred and thirty one responded. Participants were randomly split into four groups. All participants were asked to imagine they were planning a trip to Los Angeles with two of their closest friends. They were then shown five mixed reviews of a hotel taken from tripadvisor.com, and asked to imagine they were considering this hotel to book for their holiday. For consistency, all reviews contained references to staff service quality, room comfort, and hotel cleanliness. Actual location in LA and price information were not given. In addition to comments, each review had a graphic one, two, three, four, or five star rating from the reviewer. Two groups had the reviews ordered in descending order from five star to one star—positive to negative, and the other two groups had the reviews ascending from one star to five star—negative to positive. Two groups were told the reviews were taken in order over the previous year. The other two groups were told the reviews were taken from last weekend. This resulted in a 2 (review trend/no review trend) x 2 (positive-to-negative order/negative to positive order review) between subjects design.

Respondents were shown the reviews one-by-one, and given adequate time to read and consider each review. Then, respondents were asked to rate their attitudes towards booking the hotel on three items (-3 = bad, negative, undesirable; +3 = good, positive, desirable). Intentions to book the hotel were also measured on four items measuring likelihood (seven-points: 1= very low, 7 = very high), probability (seven-points: 1= very low, 7 = very high), willingness (seven-points: 1= very low, 7 = very high), and agreement with the statement "I would consider booking this hotel for our trip to LA" (seven-points: 1= strongly disagree, 7 = strongly agree).

Results. In the no trend information groups, attitudes towards booking the hotel when the reviews were ordered in a positive to negative order were higher (M = 4.06; SD = 0.98) than when the same hotel reviews were ordered in a negative to positive order (M = 3.55; SD = 1.14), $F(1, 55)$ = 3.19, p = .08. The difference was marginally significant. Intentions to book the hotel when the reviews were ordered in a positive to negative order were also higher (M = 3.55; SD = 1.29) than when the same hotel reviews were ordered in a negative to positive order (M = 2.83; SD = 1.39), $F(1, 55)$ = 4.00, p = .05. These results suggested positive contamination, consistent with the findings in study one.

When trend information was available, we expected to observe no positive contamination. Attitudes towards booking the hotel when the reviews were ordered in a positive to negative order were lower (M = 4.04; SD = 1.26) than when the same hotel reviews were ordered in a negative to positive order (M = 4.79; SD = 1.26), $F(1, 74)$ = 6.69, p < .05. Intentions to book the hotel when the reviews were ordered in a positive to negative order were also lower (M = 4.29; SD = 1.55) than when the same hotel reviews were ordered in a negative to positive order (M = 5.30; SD = 1.24), $F(1, 74)$ = 10.07, p < .01. However, this result does not disprove our assumption that trend information when reviews were ordered from positive to negative would attenuate positive contamination, leading participants to believe that the hotel was decreasing in quality over time. It does not eliminate the possibility that participants actually thought reviews ordered from negative to positive meant the hotel was improving over time, which would also explain the significant difference in attitudes towards booking when trend information was available. A test for interaction between trend information and order of review valance clarified what was happening.

The interaction was significant $F(1, 127)$ = 9.14, p < .01. Unexpectedly, the results suggested attitudes towards booking the hotel when reviews were ordered from positive to negative were the same whether trend information was given or not. In contrast, attitudes towards booking the hotel with trend information was significantly higher when reviews were ordered negative to positive than when no trend information was given (figure 3).

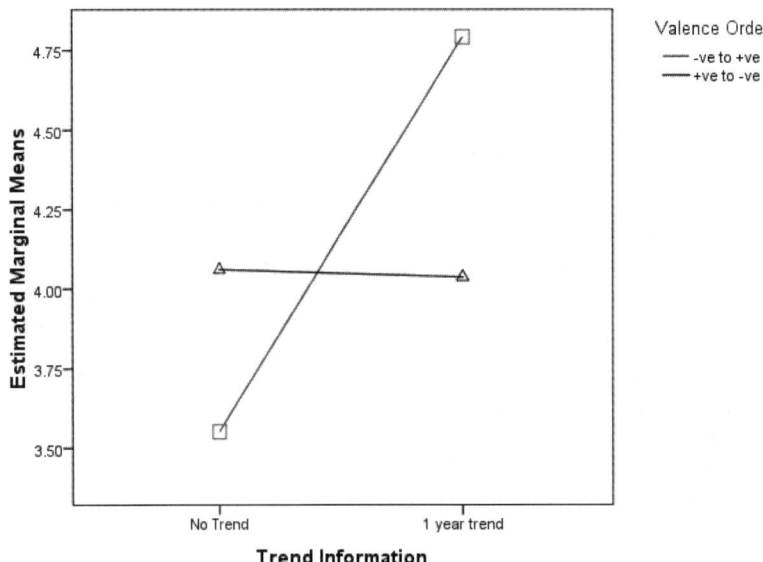

Interaction Between Trend Information and Rank Order of Review Postivity on Attitude towards Booking Hotel

Figure 2: Interaction between trend information and rank order of reviews

Discussion. The results were consistent with those found in study one. When the reviews were ranked from positive first to negative last, participants rated the hotel more favorably than when the reviews were ranked from negative to positive. This suggests participants were less successful at adjusting their attitudes from a positive to negative valence, than they were adjusting their attitudes from a negative to positive valance as attitudes were updated when reading the reviews. In other words, the positive reviews read earlier on appeared to have continued to contaminate judgments even after reading negative reviews.

The surprising result was that evaluations towards the hotel were the same between trend and no trend groups, when reviews were ordered from positive to negative. This suggested that participants did not perceive reviews ordered from negative to positive over time as evidence that the establishment was worsening in quality, and would therefore lead to greater chance of having a bad experience. One reason for this result may be due to design—just five reviews might not have been enough for participants to believe the trend over time was consistent, and therefore would not have reached the conclusion of worsening quality over time. In contrast however, there was a significant difference in trend for those presented with the reviews in a negative to positive order; they rated the hotel significantly higher when given trend information. Presumably, participants believed this was evidence the hotel was improving over time, a good sign they would enjoy a quality stay. This might have been an easier conclusion to reach with only five reviews than the other conclusion in the other group of worsening quality, and appears consistent with past research that people have a bias to prefer the positive side of things and hope for the best rather than focus on the negative side (Greenwald 1980; Taylor 1988).

General Discussion

This research documented evidence of asymmetrical affective perseverance when consumers form attitudes towards brands from information that is of opposite valence. Two experiments provide converging evidence that consumers may overshoot their judgments towards brands when positive information is found to be untrue, or is invalidated. In the first experiment, evidence of positive contamination was demonstrated after positive information was invalidated. Despite the information being discounted, participants continued to have significantly higher attitudes and intentions to purchase the brand than those who were not exposed to the manipulation. This research sheds light on the continued influence effect which suggests that discredited information on judgments is contingent on how the misinformation is replaced (Johnson and Seifert 1994, 1998), by showing that positive attitudes towards a brand are replaced less easily, and often incompletely, compared to negative attitudes.

The implications of this research for marketers are interesting. Consumers increasingly base their decisions to purchase from online review systems, and online communities are full of queries for advice on products and services to aid decision making. But although consumers have more information to aid their decision making than ever before, there is also more chance of hearing a wider gamut of evaluation, making evaluation more difficult as negative information must be weighed against the positive. The results of this research are encouraging to marketers by suggesting that consumers do not forget a good deed easily—good service given early on has at least some positive flow on to future judgments, even if the more recent information is comparatively negative. On the other hand, the results suggest consumers are relatively forgiving, being relatively successful at controlling previously encoded negative information from contaminating judgments when the information is replaced by more recent, or more accurate positive information. There is certainly power to the positivity of brands.

There are certain limitations to the findings of this research, which offer direction for future investigation in this area. In both studies, hypothetical brands were introduced. Thus, the asymmetrical replacement affect demonstrated in this research was not tested on existing brands. It was assumed that attitudes are context sensitive constructions, which easily change as new information is encoded. Attitudes were constructed on the spot, rather than formed slowly over time. Accordingly, one could argue that some negative attitudes could be more enduring, and therefore more difficult to replace. For example, research into aversive racism has found that people may hold strong implicit attitudes towards other people which are very difficult to change (Gaertner and McLaughlin 1983).

REFERENCES

Alicke, Mark D and Olesya Govorun (2005), "The Better-Than-Average Effect," in *The Self in Social Judgment. Studies in Self and Identity*, ed. Mark D. Alicke, David A. Dunning and Joachim I. Krueger, London: Psychology Press, 85-106.

Anderson, Eric T., Nathan M. Fong, Duncan I. Simester, and Catherine E. Tucker (2010), "How Sales Taxes Affect Customer and Firm Behavior: The Role of Search on the Internet," *Journal of Marketing*, 47 (2), 229-39.

Bargh, John A, Shelly Chaiken, Paula Raymond, and Charles Hymes (1996), "The Automatic Evaluation Effect: Unconditional Automatic Attitude Activation with a Pronunciation Task," *Journal of Experimental Social Psychology*, 32 (1), 185-210.

Bekerian, D. A and J. M Bowers (1983), "Eyewitness Testimony: Were We Misled?," *Journal of Experimental Psychology: Learning, Memory, and Cognition*, 9 (1), 139-45.

Blanc, Nathalie, Panayiota Kendeou, Paul van den Broek, and Denis Brouillet (2008), "Updating Situation Models During Reading of News Reports: Evidence from Empirical Data and Simulations," *Discourse Processes*, 45 (2), 103-21.

Blanc, Nathalie and Isabelle Tapiero (2001), "Updating Spatial Situation Models: Effects of Prior Knowledge and Task," *Discourse Processes*, 31 (3), 241-62.

Brown, Jacqueline Johnson and Peter H. Reingen (1987), "Social Ties and Word-of-Mouth Referral Behavior*," *Journal of Consumer Research*, 14 (3), 350-62.

Dellarocas, Chrysanthos (2003), "The Digitization of Word of Mouth: Promise and Challenges of Online Feedback Mechanisms," *Management Science*, 49 (10), 1407-24.

Dichter, Ernest (1966), "How Word of Mouth Advertising Works," *Harvard Business Review*, 44 (November-December), 147-57.

Dunning, D and G L Cohen (1992), "Egocentric Definitions of Traits and Abilities in Social Judgment," *Journal of Personality and Social Psychology*, 63, 341-55.

Eiser, J. Richard, Russell Fazio, Tom Stafford, and Tony J Prescott (2003), "Connectionist Simulation of Attitude Learning: Asymmetries in the Acquisition of Positive and Negative Evaluations," *Personality and Social Psychology Bulletin*, 29 (10), 1221-35.

Fazio, Russell H (1995), "Attitudes as Object-Evaluation Associations: Determinants, Consequences, and Correlates of Attitude Accessibility," in *Attitude Strength*, Mahwah, NJ: Erlbaum, 247-82.

Feldman, Jack M and John G Lynch (1988), "Self-Generated Validity and Other Effects of Measurement on Belief, Attitude, Intention, and Behavior," *Journal of Applied Psychology*, 73 (3), 421-35.

Gaertner, Samuel. L and John. P McLaughlin (1983), "Racial Stereotypes: Associations and Ascriptions of Positive and Negative Characteristics," *Social Psychology Quarterly*, 46 (1), 23-30.

Golding, Jonathan M, Alan L Ellis, Jerry Hauselt, and Sandra A Sego (1990), "Instructions to Disregard Potentially Useful Information: The Effects of Pragmatics on Evaluative Judgments and Recall," *Journal of Memory and Language*, 29, 212-27.

Greenwald, A. G. (1980), "The Totalitarian Ego: Fabrication and Revision of Personal History," *American Psychologist*, 603-18.

Greenwald, Anthony G and Mahzarin R Banaji (1995), "Implicit Social Cognition: Attitudes, Self-Esteem, and Stereotypes," *Psychological Review*, 102 (1), 4-27.

Johnson, Hollyn M and Colleen M Seifert (1994), "Sources of the Continued Influence Effect: When Misinformation in Memory Affects Later Inferences," *Journal of Experimental Psychology: Learning, Memory, and Cognition*, 20 (6), 1420-36.

--- (1998), "Updating Accounts Following a Correction of Misinformation," *Journal of Experimental Psychology: Learning, Memory, and Cognition*, 24 (6), 1483-94.

Lindsay, D. Stephen and Marcia K Johnson (1989), "The Eyewitness Suggestibility Effect and Memory for Source," *Memory & Cognition*, 17 (3), 349-58.

Lubinsky, Mark S. (1994), "Bearing Bad News: Dealing with the Mimics of Denial," *Journal of Genetic Counseling*, 3 (1), 5-12.

Miller, Claire C (2009), "Company Settles Case of Reviews It Faked," *The New York Times*.

Pelham, B W, M C Mirenberg, and J T Jones (2002), "Why Susie Sells Seashells by the Seashore: Implicit Egoism and Major Life Decisions," *Journal of Personality and Social Psychology*, 82, 469-87.

Petty, Richard E and Duane T Wegener (1994), "Flexible Correction Processes in Social Judgment: Correcting for Context-Induced Contrast," *Journal of Experimental Social Psychology*, 29 (2), 137-65.

Pickel, Kerri L (1995), "Inducing Jurors to Disregard Inadmissible Evidence: A Legal Explanation Does Not Help.," *Law and Human Behavior*, 19 (4), 407-24.

Richins, Marsha L. (1983), "Negative Word-of-Mouth by Dissatisfied Consumers: A Pilot Study," *Journal of Marketing*, 47 (1), 68-78.

Schul, Yaacov and Frieda Manzury (1990), "The Effects of Type of Encoding and Strength of Discounting Appeal on the Success of Ignoring an Invalid Testimony," *European Journal of Social Psychology*, 20 (4), 337-49.

Schwarz, Norbert and Herbert Bless (1992), "Constructing Reality and Its Alternatives: An Inclusion/Exclusion Model of Assimilation and Contrast Effects in Social Judgment.," in *The Construction of Social Judgments*, ed. Leonard L Martin and Abraham Tesser, Hillsdale, NJ: Lawrence Erlbaum Associates, 217-45.

Shay, David and Trevor John Pinch (2005), "Six Degrees of Reputation: The Use and Abuse of Online Review and Recommendation Systems," Available at SSRN: http://ssrn.com/abstract=857505.

Sommers, Samuel R and Saul M Kassin (2001), "On the Many Impacts of Inadmissible Testimony: Selective Compliance, Need for Cognition, and the Overcorrection Bias," *Personality and Social Psychology Bulletin*, 27 (10), 1368-77.

Taylor, Shelley E.1; Brown, Jonathon D. (1988), "Illusion and Well-Being: A Social Psychological Perspective on Mental Health," *Psychological Bulletin*, 103 (2), 193-210.

Wilson, A E and M Ross (2001), "From Chump to Champ: People's Appraisals of Their Earlier and Present Selves," *Journal of Personality and Social Psychology*, 80, 572-84.

Wilson, Timothy D and Sara D Hodges (1992), "Attitudes as Temporary Constructions," in *The Construction of Social Judgments*, ed. Leonard L Martin and Abraham Tesser, Hillsdale, NJ: Lawrence Erlbaum Associates, 37-65.

Wilson, Timothy D, Samula Lindsey, and Tonya Y Schooler (2000), "A Model of Dual Attitudes," *Psychological Review*, 107 (1), 101-26.

MANIPULATIONS

Experiment 1

Rokit Apparel Company Neutral Facts

- Rokit was founded by Peter Thompson in 2002
- Rokit's offices are located in Holmby Hills in Los Angeles
- Rokit currently has 40 employees
- Annual revenue of Rokit clothing is 16 million
- Rokit has plans to expand and open new stores in Arazona and New Mexico
- the corporate colors of Rokit are blue and yellow

Rokout Apparel Company Neutral Facts

- Rokout was founded by John Watson in 2002
- Rokout's offices are located in Palos Verdes in Los Angeles
- Rockout currently has 39 employees
- Annual revenue of Rokout clothing is 15 million
- Rokout has plans to expand and open new stores in Oregon and Washington
- The corporate colors of Rokout are red and black

Rokit Apparel Company Negative Facts

- Rokit were recently fined by local authorities for false advertising
- Rokit were recently under investigation for exploiting foreign workers in their factories
- Two factories owned by Rokit continue to pump industrial run off into nearby rivers without regard for the local ecosystem
- Rokit is known for being a difficult place to work, underpaying employees and offering few benefits to employment
- Rokit is known for taking immediate legal action against retailers who do not pay on time
- Rokit factories are known for producing higher than average carbon emissions

Rokout Apparel Company Positive Facts

- Rokout performs routine checks on the working environment and conditions in their factories
- Rokout uses biodegradable packaging to package all their apparel before shipping.
- Rokout donates 1% of all revenue made on apparel sales to support cancer research
- Rokout cares about small clothing stores who sell their apparel, and offers generous payment terms and does not take court action against non-payment until all other options have been explored
- Rokout offers generous working conditions to employees including subsidized medical insurance and paid annual leave
- Rokout has invested in research to reduce carbon emissions from their factories

Experiment 2

The asymmetric effect moderated by temporal distance
2 (review valence order) x 2 (long/short timeframe) between subjects design
[Temporal manipulation –Short timeframe]:
The following reviews were all submitted to a well known online Hotel Review website. The Reviews are all from the second weekend in February 2010.
[Temporal manipulation – Long timeframe]:
The following reviews were all submitted to a well known online Hotel Review website. The Reviews, in order they were taken, span January 2009 through to January 2010.

Imagine you are planning a trip to Los Angeles with two of your closest friends. In planning your trip, you consider the following hotel which is within your budget. Please read the reviews from people who have stayed in this hotel, and answer the questions that follow.

[For consistency, all reviews contained references to: staff service quality, room comfort, and cleanliness.]

HOTEL A

REVIEW ONE

Staff on the front desk gave us the key to our room, and were rude. Upon arriving at the front door we wanted to leave, the carpets were filthy, plaster was peeling off the walls and when we opened the door we could have cried. The room was terrible. The furniture looked extremely dated and the shower area was disgusting. The bed was hard and uncomfortable. Went down to the front desk and asked if we could change rooms, the new room was even worse. With this in mind we checked out and booked into a different hotel across the road. In all honesty this was the worst hotel that we have ever stayed in (albeit very short)

★ ☆ ☆ ☆ ☆

REVIEW TWO

The air-con is in the corner alcove so air circulation to the bedding area is next to nonexistent. Bed is crammed in there so you can barely get out of it on 1 side and the TV credenza at the foot of the bed also blocks egress. The Kitchen and living area were great with lots of space. The carpet baseboard was coming off in 1 corner. Bathroom had previous guest's hair in the tub and on the floor, but room service were able to remedy that when we called down to the desk. Sink made a horrible noise when you turned the water on. You cannot have the closet and the bathroom door open at the same time as they block each other. Some plaster issues in the bath. Staff were reasonably courteous, but could have been better.

★ ★ ☆ ☆ ☆

REVIEW Three

This hotel is merely ok to me. The rooms are kinda smallish, but they are pretty nice. They have nice LCD type TV's, and a nice little kitchen. They are pretty small, however, for this kinda hotel. It is average overall, but staff were quite helpful recommending some nice restaurants down the street.

★ ★ ★ ☆ ☆

REVIEW FOUR

Room was fine, bed very comfy! Bathroom is on the small side, but was fine for a hotel bathroom. We had no problems with the staff. Breakfast was *very* busy, food was great, but it was difficult to get a seat. We took our breakfasts back to our room. Room servcie were on time, and did quite a good job cleaning up. Good experience overall.

★ ★ ★ ★ ☆

REVIEW FIVE

I have to say from start to finish this has been one of the better stays I have experienced at a hotel. The staff at the hotel was probably the most polite and attentive people I have come across. Whenever we needed something, they were all very engaged and very helpful. The room itself was better than I expected. With very clean and nicely done bedrooms, separate bathroom, and rather big kitchen area - complete with most everything you would need. The free breakfast buffet each morning was awesome and was changed up daily. I can't say enough how impressed I was with everything. All in All... this is the place to stay when going to L.A.

★ ★ ★ ★ ★

The Processing of Threat Appeals in the Prevention of Obesity: Weighing the Weight Issue

Birgit Wauters, Vrije Universiteit Brussel, Belgium
Malaika Brengman, Vrije Universiteit Brussel, Belgium
Wim Janssens, Universiteit Hasselt, Belgium

OBESITY AND USING THREAT APPEALS TO PREVENT OBESITY

According to the estimations of the World Health Organization a quarter of the worldwide population is overweight and 6.13% have a BMI higher than 30, indicating obesity. While mass media campaigns have an important responsibility in raising awareness about obesity and other unhealthy behaviors (Lewis, Watson, and Tay 2007; Miles, Rapoport, Wardle, Afuape, and Duman 2001), the effectiveness of such campaigns is not always clear (Brengman, Wauters, Macharis, and Mairesse 2010) and therefore questioned by some researchers (Berry 2006; Hillsdon, Thorogood, White, and Foster 2002). One frequently used message tactic in campaigns promoting health behavior change is a threat or fear appeal (Wong and Cappella 2009). By describing the negative consequences of certain riskful actions, e.g., lung cancer for smokers, social marketers try to convince the receiver of the message to adopt the change in behavior or lifestyle that the message prescribes (Witte 1992). While numerous academics have proposed different theories to explain the process through which threat appeals motivate behavioral change (Janis 1967; Leventhal 1971; Rogers 1975), the underlying theoretical framework for our study is the 'Extended Parallel Process Model' (EPPM) presented by Witte (1992), as it integrates various previous theories in order to explain when and why threat appeals are effective and why they sometimes fail. According to the EPPM, which integrates Leventhal's (1971) 'Parallel Process Model' and Rogers' (1975) 'Protection Motivation Theory', two parallel message appraisals occur when someone is exposed to a threat appeal message: (1) 'threat appraisal' and (2) 'efficacy appraisal'. 'Threat appraisal' involves the assessment of (i) the 'severity' of the threat (i.e., how severe are the negative consequences) and (ii) 'susceptibility' to the threat (i.e., how vulnerable am I to this threat). Someone has to perceive the threat as severe and to be at risk in order for the threat appeal to produce the necessary fear to motivate action. 'Efficacy appraisal' or coping appraisal involves the assessment of (i) 'response efficacy' (i.e., the belief that the recommended behavior is actually effective to avert the threat) and (ii) 'self-efficacy' (i.e., the belief to be able to perform the recommended behavior). According to the EPPM (Witte 1992), threat appeals can have three different effects based on these two message appraisals: a null effect, an intended effect (i.e., 'danger control') or an unintended effect (i.e., 'fear control'). When perceived threat is low, threat appeals are assumed to have no effect on behavioral change. In this case people are not motivated to perform the recommended behavior because they do not feel the health risk is serious or personally relevant. If the message fails to evoke at least some moderate threat, Witte (1992) argues that it will not motivate people to consider the 'efficacy appraisal'. On the other hand, when perceived threat is high, the ultimate response to the threat appeal will depend on the 'assessment of efficacy'. In case perceived efficacy is high, people will engage in 'danger control' (i.e., attempting to control the threat by performing the recommended behavior as intended by the sender of the message). If the perceived efficacy is low, however, people may try to manage their fear by engaging in an unintended maladaptive response: 'fear control' (i.e., alleviating the fear by denial of the threat). Hence, as fear causes a negative emotional state, the person experiencing this emotion wants to neutralize this feeling by either coping with the risk and following the recommended behavior (i.e., cognitive reaction / danger control) or by reacting defensively and denying the potential problem (i.e., emotional reaction / fear control) (Tanner, James, Hunt,

and Eppright 1991). The proposed danger has to be experienced as relevant and the recommended behavior will only reduce the threat if it is seen as effective (Das, de Wit, and Stroebe 2003). Thus far not many studies have been conducted with the threat of overweight and obesity as a specific topic. In a study about the effects of threatening communication towards mothers on their health beliefs and the weight of their obese children, Kirscht et al. (1975) investigated the role of different levels of threat on the weight of obese children. Results showed that the threatening communication had a positive effect on the weight status of the children: the most threatening communication caused the most weight loss, followed by the low level threat appeal and the control group.

RESEARCH OBJECTIVE

This article investigates the processing of threat appeal messages against obesity, and more specifically the possible differences in processing between people who think they experience overweight or obesity and persons who do not think they are overweight or obese. The hypotheses will be based on the threat appeal framework of Witte. A meta-analysis indicates that the stronger the evoked fear, the more persuasive the threat appeal is (Witte and Allen 2000). Therefore we claim that a threat appeal which evokes fear will have a positive relation with behavioral intention.

Hypothesis 1: *Evoked fear has a positive effect on behavioral intention.*

Finding the problem of overweight and obesity severe, one of the elements of the threat appraisal, will probably result in feeling fear and wanting to overcome the overweight issue.

Hypothesis 2a: *Perceived severity has a positive effect on evoked fear.*

Hypothesis 2b: *Perceived severity has a positive effect on behavioral intention.*

Since 'perceived susceptibility' is conceptualized as 'an individual's beliefs about his or her chances of experiencing a threat' (Witte 1992, 332), people who find themselves highly susceptible to overweight or obesity are expected to indicate feeling emotions of 'fear'. They probably will also be motivated to do something about their problem and will most likely have the intention to change their current lifestyle and behavior.

Hypothesis 3a: *Perceived susceptibility has a positive effect on evoked fear.*

Hypothesis 3b: *Perceived susceptibility has a positive effect on behavioral intention.*

Having a threat appeal message with strong arguments and a good recommended response to avert the threat (in our case: talk to your GP about overweight or obesity) will enhance the 'response efficacy'. If the recommendation is seen by the respondent as effective, this will have a positive effect on the behavioral intention. The perceived response efficacy of the message will, on the other hand, have a negative impact on the evoked fear. If the respondent positively evaluates the response efficacy, he or she will feel less fear.

Hypothesis 4a: *Response efficacy has a negative effect on evoked fear.*

Hypothesis 4b: *Response efficacy has a positive effect on behavioral intention.*

'Self efficacy' refers to the perceived ability of a person to act on the recommendation. In this study self-efficacy captures a person's perceived ability to keep his or her weight under control. If one finds him/herself easily capable of keeping his/her weight under control and not sliding off to overweight or obesity, the threat appeal will most likely not evoke any emotions of fear. The effect of self efficacy on behavioral intention and evoked fear is expected to be negative in this context.

Hypothesis 5a: *Self efficacy has a negative effect on evoked fear.*

Hypothesis 5b: *Self efficacy has a negative effect on behavioral intention.*

If the receiver finds the message of personal relevance, he or she will process the information carefully (Ajzen, Brown, and Rosenthal 1996). In this case the person can make a thorough judgment of the quality and effectiveness of the threat appeal. A more thorough, systematic and further elaboration of the message content is made, if people are highly involved with the message topic (Petty and Cacioppo 1986). When the threat of being obese or overweight does not attract the receiver's attention, he or she will not be motivated to process the message in depth and hence, this will influence the effectiveness of the appeal negatively. When people report not feeling overweight or obese, the threat message will be less relevant since they already perceive to successfully keep control of their health and weight. Pritchard, King, and Czajka-Narins (1997) stated in a study on body mass indices and self perception that someone's perception of his or her weight is more important than the actual BMI category regarding his or her reception of health programs. If someone feels overweight or obese, this person will be more likely to respond to health programs, regardless of actually belonging to the overweight or obese BMI categories. Therefore we hypothesize that respondents with feelings of overweight will be more motivated to process the threat appeal and thus will have stronger relations between the elements of the coping and threat appraisals and behavioral intention.

Hypothesis 6:   *People perceiving themselves as obese or overweight will display stronger relations between perceived severity, susceptibility, response efficacy and self efficacy and behavioral intention than respondents who do not think they are overweight or obese.*

METHODOLOGY

The respondents were asked to participate in the study and were given a paper and pencil-based questionnaire consisting of two parts; the first part had to be filled in before the respondents were confronted with the threat appeal message and gauged for the participants' health behavior. After exposure to the appeal they were asked to fill in the second part containing questions about the threat appeal, such as the level of 'evoked fear', 'self efficacy' and 'response efficacy', 'severity', 'behavioral intention' and 'susceptibility'. Their perceived weight status and body mass index (BMI) was also asked in the questionnaire. 169 participants were found, 87 females and 82 males, with a mean age of 27 years (min. 17, max. 60, SD= 10). Two threat appeals with different levels of fear were developed with respect to the issue of obesity and its consequences. The high threat message presented severe consequences of being overweight, e.g., high blood pressure, a stroke and cancer. The stimulus with the low level of threat had as consequences among others: skin problems, high cholesterol and back problems. The illustration in the advertisement for the low threat was: a white background with 6 rulers indicating a fictive percentage of the mentioned consequences and next to the rulers the different consequences cited in the text was labeled. The high threat had a black background with a noose made of a measuring cord, stipulating that one with obesity is condemned to be hanged by the threat.

The choice was made not to work with the BMI due to several reasons. First of all, the respondents were asked to fill in their own weight and height what could lead to a wrongful estimation of these parameters (Kuczmarski, Kuczmarski, and Najjar 2001). A second restraint against using the BMI is that it does not take into consideration the amount of body fat (Kuczmarski and Flegal 2000), nor does it take into account the skeletal size, amount of body water, muscle mass and gender. Kuczmarski and Flegal (2000) gave the example of a very athletic and muscled person who may be heavy but does not have excessive body fat. Seeing that relative weight and the body mass index do not quantify total body adiposity (Gray and Fujioka 1991) it cannot be concluded that everybody who is overweight also has too much fat nor can we say that people who are not obese will not have obese levels of body fat (Frankenfield 2001). Furthermore, studies have indicated that ethnic differences also play an important role in percentage of fat and BMI (Bell, Adair, and Popkin 2002; Deurenberg, Deurenberg-Yap, and Guricci 2002). Another reason for not using the BMI is that its categories are static, meaning that a person weighing 63,7kg and measuring 1,60m has a BMI of 24,88 is labeled as having a normal weight and somebody with a weight of 64kg and the same height is labeled overweight, although those two persons differ only 300grams in weight. Add to this the differences of cut offs between health organizations and the changes of these cut offs during the years (Kuczlarski and Flegal 2000). When applying the cut offs of the *Third National Health and Nutrition Examination Survey* data, the USA counts 61.7 million overweight people. When using the BMI categories of the WHO this number increases with more than 20 million, leading towards 97.1 million overweight citizens in the United States (Kuczmarski and Flegal 2000). The current weight status is also very important in regard to own perceptions of normal and overweight classification. Crawford and Campbell (1999) found differences between the health authorities' definitions of ideal and overweight and the people's definitions. On top of this, lay definitions also varied across sex, ages and current weight status. Men and women, who were not overweight by the BMI classification but considered themselves to be overweight, engaged in actions towards weight loss and prevention to gain weight. These own perceptions of weight status are very important seeing that it is unlikely that somebody who does not believe having a weight problem will be susceptible for weight control promotion (Crawford and Campbell 1999; Pritchard et al. 1997). Given above mentioned reasons we expect that the respondents' own opinion about their body and weight/height ratio will be more suitable for this study. These findings are supported by the study of Rahman and Berenson (2010). They examined whether low-income multiethnic women of a reproductive age perceive their weight correctly. The investigated population included both overweight and normal weight women. Rahman et al (2010) concluded that weight misperception, perceiving oneself as overweight but not being overweight according to authorities' measurement and the other way around, is common for women with overweight as well as for women without overweight. An important recommendation is thus to take the person's own perception into account which is done in this study. The hypothesis that there might be discrepancies between being categorized in a certain BMI-category and a person's own judgment about being overweight or not was tested. A cross tabulation was conducted between (no) perceived overweight and the BMI categories and found significant differences between the 2 variables (χ^2= 65,184 df=4, p<.000). 10.3% of the respondents who were categorized in the overweight category according to the WHO did not perceive themselves as being overweight Also 25% of the respondents who fell under the cut-off of the overweight limit (BMI $\leq$ 24.9) consider themselves at risk of being overweight. These findings along with the reasons mentioned below, have led to working with the personal indication of being overweight.

MODEL CONSTRUCTS

The amount of fear evoked by the threat appeal, hereunder labeled as '*evoked fear*' (translated into Dutch from Madden, Allen, and Twibble 1988) was measured with 3-items (α =.79; "The advertisement is fearful, repulsing and upsetting/distrubing"). All variables were measured on a five-point Likert type scale. '*Severity*' (3-items, α =.82; "How important do you find the problem of overweight and obesity", "How important do you find the possible consequences of overweight or obesity", "To what degree do you find overweight and obesity to be a societal problem"); '*susceptibility*' (3-items, α =.86; "The chance that one day I will suffer from overweight or obesity is very large", "I find it hard not to get overweight", "I often diet to keep my weight under control"); '*response efficacy*' (2-items, α =.74; "Somebody who suffers from overweight or obesity, can easily overcome this", "Keeping your weight under control is easy") and '*self efficacy*' (1-item; "If I would suffer from overweight or obesity, I would be able to easily overcome this"). The respondents'

behavioral intention was the dependent variable by Cronin et al., 2000 but translated (2-items, α=.86; "After seeing the advertisement, I will devote more attention to keep my weight under control"; "After seeing the advertisement, I will, if necessary, consult my family doctor to keep my weight under control"). The respondents were divided based on a median split between persons who think that they suffer from overweight or obesity, labeled as *(no) perceived overweight* ("I think I'm suffering from overweight or obesity").

RESULTS

Student's t-tests were conducted on perceived susceptibility and severity, response and self efficacy, evoked fear and behavioral intention for two groups of respondents based on their own perception of their weight status. The results (see table 1) reveal significant differences in the '*perceived susceptibility*' experienced by the two groups. Respondents who indicated that they think to suffer from overweight perceived themselves more susceptible (3.38 vs. 1.76, p <.001). The '*severity*' of obesity is not perceived differently by the two groups (p=.818). Also the '*amount of fear*' generated by the threat appeals led to no significant differences (p=.539). Respondents with no perceived overweight have a significant higher '*response efficacy*' (2.31 vs. 1.96, p=.009) and '*self efficacy*' (2.71 vs. 2.07, p <.001) than the respondents who feel overweight or obese. A significant difference in '*behavioral intention*' between people with no perceived overweight and those with overweight issues is also found. The results show that respondents who perceive themselves as overweight will have a significantly higher intention to change their behavior than people with no perceived overweight (2.66 vs. 1.90, p <.001).

	Perceiving no overweight [n=99]		Perceiving overweight [n=70]		
	M	SD	M	SD	p-value [c]
Perceived Susceptibility	1,76	0,778	3,38	0,953	<.001
Perceived Severity	3,96	0,734	3,93	0,818	.818
Response Efficacy	2,31	0,930	1,96	0,797	.009
Self Efficacy	2,71	1,052	2,07	0,89	<.001
Evoked Fear	2,77	1,015	2,87	1,039	.539
Behavioural Intention	1,90	0,884	2,66	0,923	<.001

Table 1: Two Tailed Student's t-test

To discover how the respondents processed the threat appeal message Partial Least Squares (PLS) path analysis, a variance-based technique, was used (statistical software application: SmartPLS 2.0 by Ringle et al. 2005). This method was preferred because of the small amount of respondents in each group. Chin and Newsted (1999) claim PLS to be a good estimator of path models when sample sizes are small. The recommended rule of thumb by Chin (1998) prescribes that the overall sample size should be at least 10 times the number of receiving causal arrows of the dependent variable with the largest number those incoming arrows. In our study, this dependent variable is '*behavioral intention*' which receives 5 incoming arrows; meaning that we need at least 50 cases to fulfill Chins (1998) rule of thumb. Given our number of participants, respectively 99 in the group of no perceived overweight and 70 in the group of people with perceived overweight, this sample size can be seen as sufficient "for obtaining stable estimates" (Chin 1998, 311).

Before looking at results, an evaluation of the quality criteria needs to be done. Hereby the used measures are tested on their reliability and validity (see table 2). The communalities reflecting the average percentage of variance explained by a row factor for this row factor, need to exceed the value of .5 according to Höck and Ringel (2006, 15) and this is accomplished in this model. The next measures of quality are the composite reliability and Cronbachs alpha (α). The composite reliability values are acceptable for both models as they all exceed .60 (Höck and Ringel 2006). The Cronbach alpha values are deemed good when $\alpha \geq$.80, acceptable when $\alpha \geq$.70 and for exploratory purposes when $\alpha \geq$.60 (Chin, 1998). The scale reliability for behavioral intention on both models is below .70 (α= .67 for no perceived overweight and α= .64 for perceived overweight). Given an acceptable value for the composite reliability and the known underestimation of reliability by Cronbachs alpha (Chin 1998) these scales will also be considered as acceptable. The R^2 explains the overall effect size. In the model for people with perceived overweight, 28% of their behavioral intention and 20% of their evoked fear is explained by the model. The percentages for people with no perceived overweight are somewhat lower; namely 22% for behavioral intention and 19% for evoked fear. All four R^2 values can be considered as ranging between moderate and low (Chin, 1998). Nevertheless, sufficient criteria for quality are met by both models, indicating these models as good and their results adequate for interpretation.

The next step is testing and interpreting the structural model, as displayed in table 3. The average variance extracted (AVE) reflecting the average communality for each latent factor and indicating convergent validity, needs to exceed the value of .5 according to Höck and Ringel (2006, 15). The two models fulfill this criterion. When looking at the two groups separately, the results reveal different processing patterns for people perceiving themselves as having overweight than for those who do not. Similar for both groups are the impacts of perceived severity on evoked fear (β= .326, p <.001 for no perceived overweight, β= .396, p= .003 for perceived overweight) and the significant relations between evoked fear and behavioral intention (β= .207, p= .042 for no perceived overweight, β= .324, p= .008 for perceived overweight). For respondents with perceived overweight, the perceived severity generated through the threat leads to feelings of fear and this evoked fear is the only motivation by which the respondents with perceived overweight process the threat appeal leading towards an intention to change their current behavior. No significant relations could be revealed either between the efficacy variables and behavioral intention or between the threat appraisal variables and behavioral intention for people with perceived overweight.

For people who do not find themselves overweight or obesity, a different way of processing is found. Here, significant relations are found

for perceived severity (β= .251, p= .005), response efficacy (β= .443, p< .001), self efficacy (β= -.268, p= .015), and evoked fear (β= .207, p= .042) and behavioral intention, and also between the threat appraisal and evoked fear. Besides the afore mentioned similar relationships revealed among both groups, perceived severity also has a positive significant impact on evoked fear among respondents who perceive themselves as not overweight. Feeling vulnerable to the threat of overweight; '*perceived susceptibility*', will also lead to feelings of fear and shock (β= .179, p= .037). For people with no perceived overweight, response efficacy has the strongest impact on behavioral intention, followed by self efficacy. Taking a closer look, this last relation between self efficacy and behavioral intention is a negative one, what could be odd at first sight. However, looking at the content of the variables, the negative relation is explainable when following the reasoning of the respondents: '*I could easily overcome overweight or obesity, if I would suffer from it*' (self efficacy). '*But I do not think I'm overweight or obese*' (perceiving no overweight). '*So I will not pay extra attention to keep my weight under control*' (behavioral intention). The strongest influence on evoking fear comes from the supposed severity of obesity or overweight. In the overall model only one relation, namely between response efficacy and behavioral intention, is significant (β= .443 for no perceived overweight, β= -.019 for perceived overweight, *t-value*= 2.278 and p= .026). For people with no perceived overweight the evaluation of the response efficacy in the threat appeal had a significant higher impact on behavioral intention than for people with perceived overweight.

Perceived overweight (* p<.05 ** p<.01 ***p<.001)

	1	2	3	4	5	6
Perceived Severity	0,786				0,203	0,396**
Perceived Susceptibility		0,683			0,1	0,027
Response Efficacy			0,524		-0,019	-0,168
Self Efficacy				1	-0,107	0,131
Behavioral Intention					0,726	0,324**
Evoked Fear						0,637

No perceived overweight (* p<.05 ** p<.01 ***p<.001)

	1	2	3	4	5	6
Perceived Severity	0,694				0,251**	0,326***
Perceived Susceptibility		0,616			-0,034	0,179**
Response Efficacy			0,794		0,443***	-0,039
Self Efficacy				1	-0,268**	-0,111
Behavioral Intention					0,751	0,207**
Evoked Fear						0,761

Table 3: The root square average variance extraction is given on diagonals, weights and p-values.

DISCUSSION

In this study we investigated the processing of threat appeal message against obesity. We were specifically interested in two different groups, namely people who feel overweight or obese and people who indicate that they do not perceive themselves as overweight. By making this distinction we get a better view on how people for whom the health message is intended, process this appeal, since those are the people who we want to inform about the negative consequences of having too much

weight. However, the inclusion in the investigation of the other group: those who have no perceived overweight, is of equal importance. Seeing that the number of people with overweight grows every year (Wyatt et al. 2006), healthcare practitioners need to inform not only people who are already perceived themselves as overweight, but also those who may become and feel overweight in the future. Confronting them with the consequences of overweight like high blood pressure, diabetes, strokes and worse will hopefully help them keeping their weight under control. As the saying goes: '*prevention is better than cure*' (in this case it may be easier as well). The results of the Students t-tests tell us that there are significant group differences for perceived susceptibility, the two variables of the coping appraisal and behavioral intention. As for the last variable the respondents who perceive to be overweight intended significantly more to keep their weight under control in the future than those without perceived overweight. These results are in line with previous research, as Kirscht et al. (1975) also found a positive effect on the effective weight status of children after the exposure to threatening communication. The respondents with perceived overweight also felt themselves to be significantly more susceptible to the threats of obesity displayed in the message. This may seem logical, but a high perceived susceptibility is nonetheless an important factor in the threat appeal framework. If a person does not think he or she is in danger of the threat, the person will not be motivated to perform a mental assessment of efficacy and ultimately will not perform the recommended behavior (Witte 1992). The significant discrepancies in our sample between being categorized in a BMI-category and a person's own judgment about being overweight or not, have led us to work with the respondents' indication of being overweight. Previous literature (Crawford and Campbell 1999; Deurenberg et al. 2002) has also indicated that weight misperception is common due to several reasons. The recommendation of using the respondents' perception instead of the BMI-categories is thus taking into account in this study. Concerning the dimensions of the efficacy appraisal, there were significant differences between the two groups: people with no perceived overweight indicate a higher response and self efficacy than the members of the other group.

The people with no perceived overweight thus find the recommendation to avert obesity significantly better and also find themselves more capable of doing something about these weight issues. For people with perceived overweight, having mean scores which are too low on the efficacy appraisal traits, may have negative consequences. Witte (1992) indicates that after assessing the threat, people confronted with a threatening message will assess their and the recommendations' efficacy. If those are insufficient, this will lead to a controlling of the fear instead of the danger of the threat. Therefore it is necessary to create a decent amount of response and self efficacy (in our case: mean scores respectively 1.96 and 2.07 on a 5 point Likert scale going for '*Strongly disagree*' until, '*Strongly agree*') to avert a fear control reaction. Given the lower mean scores but the fact that the behavioral intention of the respondents with perceived overweight is tolerable, we may conclude that the threat appeal message will lead towards a controlling of the threat of overweight and obesity as opposed to the denial of the warning among this group of respondents.

The processing patterns were exposed with Partial Least Squares path modeling. The results indicated differences in processing between the two groups, but not in the way that we predicted. For people who perceive themselves to be overweight, significant relations were found between perceived severity and evoked fear (confirming hypothesis 2a) and evoked fear and behavioral intention (confirming hypothesis 1). The respondents for whom the threat appeal should be relevant experience emotions of fear due to the perceived severity of the threat. The results also confirm the theory of Witte (1992) who restored the value of the emotion of fear back into the health messages after it got on a sidetrack due to the Protection Motivation Theory of Rogers (Tanner, 2006). For people with perceived overweight, the relation between evoked fear and behavioral intention was the only significant one by which they processed the appeal (disconfirming hypotheses 2b, 3b, 4b and 5b) and therefore we must underline the importance of evoking fear emotions linked to the magnitude of the threat appeal (Boster and Mongeau (1984); Sutton (1982), Witte and Allen (2000)). Hypotheses 4a and 5a claiming a negative effect of response and self efficacy on evoked fear cannot be confirmed. This may be due to the fact that those

two constructs are aspects of the efficacy appraisal and thus may be less influencing personal feelings and more cognitive processes, like behavioral intention. As for the full model only the relation between response efficacy and behavioral intention was significant. It was expected that people with perceived overweight would display stronger relations than the respondents who did not think they were overweight or obese. Nevertheless, the only significant relation pointed toward a higher impact of response efficacy on behavioral intention for people with no perceived overweight, although it was thought that this message and its content would be less relevant for the latter and thus would be processed less carefully by people with perceived overweight (Ajzen et al. 1996). As mentioned above, it is not only interesting to know how people with perceived overweight process such threat appeals, also the processing pattern of people without overweight can be very interesting for healthcare workers. Here, three significant relations were discovered, namely one between perceived severity and behavioral intention (confirming hypothesis 2b), one negative relation between self efficacy and behavioral intention (confirming hypothesis 5b) and the strongest one between response efficacy and behavioral intention (confirming hypothesis 4b). Only perceived susceptibility did not seem to have any effect on behavioral intention (disconfirming hypothesis 3b). For a person with no perceived overweight his or her perceived vulnerability did have a significant relation with evoked fear, through which behavioral intention can be reached (confirming hypothesis 3a). Although the relation between perceived susceptibility and behavioral intention is not direct, as it is mediated by evoked fear, all 5 components of Witte's theory (1992) have significant relations with the intention of a person to keep his/her weight under control in the future. This study thus underlines the importance of having threat appraisals and efficacy appraisals in a threat appeal in order to, on the one hand evoke fear and on the other hand have a direct impact on the behavioral intention of the receiver.

CONCLUSION

The two different processing patterns in which evoked fear is central for people with perceived overweight and on the other hand perception of severity and the coping appraisals are important for people who do not feel overweight is a new finding in threat appeal research. If the aim of the health messages is to prevent people getting overweight or worse there should be a focus on the coping and threat appraisals rather than on fear only as these are the significant factors by which those respondents assess an appeal. If the goal is to diminish the number of overweight people the focal point should be on evoking the right amount of fear.

BIBLIOGRAPHY

Ajzen, Icek., Thomas C. Brown, and Lori H. Rosenthal (1996), "Information Bias in Contingent Valuation: Effects of Personal Relevance, Quality of Information, and Motivational Orientatio,". *Journal of Environmental Economics and Management, 30,* 43-57.

Altabe, Madeline. (1998), "Ethnicity and Body Image: Quantitative and Qualitative Analysis," *International Journal of Eating Disorders, 23 (2),* 153–159.

Bell, A. Colin, Linda. S. Adair and Barry M. Popkin. (2002), "Ethnic Differences in the Association between Body Mass Index and Hypertension," *American Journal of Epidemiology,* 155 (4), 346-353.

Berry, Tanya R. (2006), "Who's Even Interested in the Exercise Message? Attentional Bias for Exercise and Sedentary-lifestyle Related Words," *Journal of Sport and Exercise Psychology,* 28, 4-17.

Boster, Franklin J. and Paul A. Mongeau (1984), "Fear-arousing Persuasive Messages," in *Communication yearbook,* ed. R.N. Bostrom, Beverly Hills, CA: Sage Publications, 330-375.

Brengman, Malaika, Birgit Wauters, Cathy Macharis, C. and Olivier Mairesse. (2010), "Functional Effectiveness of Threat Appeals in Exercise Promotion Messages," *Psicologica,* 31 (3), 577-604.

Cash, Thomas F. and Patricia E. Henry. (1995), "Women's Body Images: The Results of a National Survey in the U.S.A," *Sex Roles,* 33 (1-2), 19-28.

Chin, Wynne W and Peter R. Newsted (1999), "Structural Equation Modeling Analysis with Small Samples using Partial Least Squares," in *Statistical strategies for small sample research,* ed. Rick H. Hoyle, Thousand Oaks, CA: Sage Publications, 307-342.

Chin, Wynne W. (1998), "The Partial Least Squares Approach to Structural Equation Modeling," in *Modern methods for business research,* ed. Georges A. Marcoulides, Mahwah, 295-358.

Crawford, David and Karen Campbell (1999), "Lay Definitions of ideal Weight and Overweight," *International journal of obesity,* 23, 738-745.

Cronin, Joseph J.J., Margaret K. Brady and G. Thomas M. Hult (2000), "Assessing the Effects of Quality, Value and Customer Satisfaction on Consumer Behavioral Intentions in Service Environment," *Journal of Retailing,* 76 (2), 193-218.

Das, Enny H.H.J., John B.F. de Wit and Wolfgang Stroebe (2003), "Fear Appeals Motivate Acceptance of Action Recommendations: Evidence for a Positive Bias in the Processing of Persuasive Messages," *Personality and social psychology bulletin,* 29 (5), 630-664.

Deurenberg Paul, Mabel Deurenberg-Yap and Syafri Guricci (2002), "Asians are Different from Caucasians and from each other in their Body Mass Index/Body Fat per cent Relationship," *Obesity Reviews,* 3 (3), 141-146.

Frankenfield, David. C., William A. Rowe, Robert N. Cooney, J. Stanley Smith and Dolores Becker (2001), "Limits of Body Mass Index to Detect Obesity and Predict Body Composition," *Nutrition,* 17 (1), 26-30.

Floyd, Donna .L., Steven Prentice-Dunn, and Ronald Rogers (2000), "A Meta-Analysis of Research on Protection Motivation Theory," *Journal of Applied Social Psychology,* 30 (2), 407-429.

Gray David S. and Ken Fujiokaa (1991), "Use of Relative Weight and Body Mass Index for the Determination of Adiposity," *Journal of Clinical Epidemiology,* 44 (6), 545-550.

Henley, Nadine and Robert J. Donovan (2002), "Identifying Appropriate Motivations to Encourage People to Adopt Healthy Nutrition and Physical Activity Behaviors," *Journal of Research for Consumers,* 4, s.n.

Hillsdon, Melvyn, Margaret Thorogood, Ian White and Charlie Foster (2002), "Advising People to take More Exercise is Ineffective: a Randomized Controlled Trial of Physical Activity Promotion in Primary Care," *International Journal of Epidemiology,* 31, 808-815.

Höck, Michael and Christiane M. Ringle (2006), "Strategic Networks in the Software Industry: an Empirical Analysis of the Value Continuum," IFSAM VIIIth World Congress Berlin 2006.

Janis, Irving L. (1967), "Effects of Fear Arousal on Attitude Change: Recent Developments in Theory and Experimental Research," in *Advances in experimental social psychology,* ed. Leonard Berkowitz, New York: Academic Press, 166-225.

Kirscht, J.P., Becker, M.H., Haefner, D.P. and Maiman, L.A. (1975), "Effects of Threatening Communications and Mothers' Health Beliefs on Weight Change in Obese Children," *Journal of Behavioral Medicine,* 1 (2), 147-157.

Kuczmarski, Robert J. and Katherine M. Flegal (2000), "Criteria for Definition of Overweight in Transition: Background and Recommendations for the United States," *American Journal Clinical Nutrition,* 72, 1074-1081.

Kuczmarski Marie Fanelli, Robert J. Kuczmarski and Mattew Najjar (2001), "Effects of Age on Validity of Self-Reported Height, Weight, and Body Mass Index: Findings from the Third National Health and Nutrition Examination Survey, 1988-1994," *Journal of the American Dietetic Association,* 101 (1), 28-34 quiz 35-6.

Leventhal, Howard (1971), "Fear appeals and Persuasion: the Differentiation of a Motivational Construct," *American Journal of Public Health,* 61 (6), 1208-1224.

Lewis, Ioni, Barry Watson and Richard Tay (2007), "Examining the Effectiveness of Physical Threats in Road Safety Advertising: the Role of the Third-Person Effect, Gender and Age," *Transportation Research Part F,* 10, 48-60.

Madden, Thomas J., Chris T. Allen and Jacquelyn L. Twibble (1988), "Attitude toward the Ad: an Assessment of Derse Measurement Indices under Different Processing Sets," *Journal of Marketing Research,* 25 (August) 242-252.

Miles, Anne, Lorna Rapoport, Jane Wardle, Taiwo Afuape and M. Duman (2001), "Using the Mass-Media to Target Obesity: an Analysis of the Characteristics and Reported Behaviour Change of Participants in the BBC's `Fighting Fat, Fighting Fit' Campaign," *Health Education Research,* 16 (3), 357-372.

Petty, Richard E. and John T. Cacioppo (1986), *Communication and persuasion: Central and peripheral routes to attitude change,* New York: Springer-Verlag.

Pritchard, Mary E., Sondra L. King and Dorice M. Czajka-Narins (1997), "Adolescent Body Mass Indices and Self-Perception," *Adolescence,* 32.

Ringle, Christian M., Sven Wende and Will Alexander (2005), SmartPLS Release: 2.0 (beta). Hamburg, Germany.

Rogers, Ronald W. (1975), "A Protection Motivation Theory of Fear Appeals and Attitude Change," *Journal of Psychology,* 91, 93-114.

Sutton, Stephen R. (1982), "Fear Arousing Communications: A Critical Examination of Theory and Research," in: *Social psychology and behavioral medicine,* ed. J. Richard Eiser, New York: Wiley, 303-338.

Tanner, John F.J. (2006), "Read this or Die: a Cognitive Approach to an Appeal to Emotions," *International Journal of Advertising,* 25 (3), 414-416.

Tanner, John F.J., James B. Hunt and David R. Eppright (1991), "The Protection Motivation Model: A Normative Model of Fear Appeals," *Journal of Marketing,* 55, 36-45.

Wadden, Thomas A. and Albert J. Stunkard (1985), "Social and Psychological Consequences of Obesity," *Annals of Internal Medicine,* 103 (6 Part 2), 1062-1067.

Wardle, Jane and Lucy Cooke (2005), "The Impact of Obesity on Psychological Well-Being," *Childhood Obesity,* 19 (3), 421-440.

WHO. (2006a), "Obesity and Overweight," http://www.who.int/mediacentre/factsheets/fs311/en/index.html

WHO. (2010), "BMIclassification," http://apps.who.int/bmi/index.jsp?introPage=intro_3.html

Witte, Kim. (1992), "Putting the Fear back into Fear Appeals. The Extended Parallel Process Model," *Communication Monographs,* 59, 329-349.

Witte, Kim, and Mike Allen (2000), "A Meta Analysis of Fear Appeals: Implications for Effective Public Health Campaigns," *Health Education and Behavior,* 27, 591-615.

Wong, Norman C.H. and Joseph N. Cappella (2009), "Antismoking Threat and Efficacy Appeals: Effects on Smoking Cessation Intentions for Smokers with Low and High Readiness to Quit," *Journal of Applied Communication Research,* 37 (1), 1-20.

Wyatt, Sharon B., Karen P. Winters and Patricia M. Dubbert (2006), "Overweight and Obesity: Prevalence, Consequences, and Causes of a Growing Public Health Problem," *The American Journal of the Medical Sciences,* 331 (4), 166-1.

Images of Identity in Consumer Research:
A Study of the Worship, Experimentation, Community and Domination of Signs

Lauren Gurrieri, Griffith Univesity, Australia
Helene Cherrier, Griffith Univesity, Australia

ABSTRACT

This paper seeks to understand how consumers negotiate contested symbolic meanings 'permanently' marked on the body. It offers four images of identity – assumed, trialled, tribal and trapped. In doing so, the research aims to provide a metaphorical understanding of identity work in consumer research.

The Discursive Construction of the Consuming Subject

In contemporary consumer culture, consumption is considered a key site from which one discursively constructs their identity, whereby 'we are what we consume' (Bauman 2007). Accordingly, Arnould and Thompson (2005) identify consumer identity projects as a research program of consumer culture theory. This focus on consumption is the consequence of the fragmented consumer of postmodernity, whose sense of self is no longer conceived as a unified construction driven by well-defined, purposeful and rational needs, instead comprising fragmented patterns of consumption and engagement in multiple experiences (Benwell and Stokoe 2006). As identity is constantly changing and emergent, it is through consumption and its symbolic meanings, as constituted through enduring socio-historic discourses, that consumers are able to construct identities (Thompson and Hirschman 1995).

Two views of this postmodern condition exist (Goulding, Shankar and Elliott 2002). First, a more pessimistic view of society as dystopian and alienating, conceives fragmented consumers fraught with identity confusion and struggling with sign domination (e.g. Baudrillard 1981; Jameson 1984). In the absence of overarching narratives, the self is placed in a position of vulnerability and dominant discourses create normalising or disciplinary effects, with various social and historical forces affecting identity work and constraining individuals in ways that attempt to inscribe what can be said and who can be what. Second, a more liberatory account presents subjects embracing fragmentation as a force that frees them from conformity. In the place of traditional institutions, consumption becomes a means of constructing and expressing multiple identities (e.g. Firat and Venkatesh 1995). Under this perspective, the self becomes a symbolic project and consumers express accounts of who they are from available symbolic materials, which also provide a means of participating in social life (Elliott and Wattanasuwan 1998; Featherstone 1991).

In addition to these two conceptualisations, consumer identity construction can be read as a dialogical or dialectical process emerging from a tension between 'sign experimentation' and 'sign domination' (Murray 2002), namely interplay between agency and structure. In this perspective, mass consumption, social categories and normative discourses influence consumption patterns yet still allow for a form of creative identity play. For example, Holt and Thompson's (2004, 439) study of masculinity in America conceives social categories as a frame of reference that "encourage and constrain particular kinds of consumer creativity". Similarly, Murray (2002) shows consumers' construction of style resulting from a tension between sign experimentation and sign domination. On the one hand consumers draw on the meanings of signs to construct symbolic statements about themselves and on the other they respond to normalising and disciplinary discourses ascribing what can be said and what can be worn.

Whilst understanding the dialectical interplay between agency and structure has been a preoccupation in studies on non-permanent consumption behaviour, very few studies have discussed the agency/

structure interplay in permanent forms of body alteration such as body sculpting, piercing, scarification and tattoo. For example, Askergaard, Gertsen and Langer's (2002) study on plastic surgery adopts an agentic approach to an individual's reflexive construction of identity. Similarly, Sanders' (1985) study on tattoo consumption accepts the agentic power of deviant consumers who manoeuvre the risks of consuming marginal products. In contrast to this view of consumption as an expressive movement taking place in open discursive systems, Patterson and Schroeder (2010) consider tattoo consumption resulting from a dialectical interplay between agency/sign experimentation and structure/sign domination. For the authors, the skin "reflects the dynamic relationship between inside and outside, self and society, between personal identity projects and marketplace cultures. It represents the meeting place of structure and agency; a primary site for the inscription of ideology and a text upon which individuals write their own stories" (Patterson and Schroeder 2010, 254). Under this perspective, identity becomes something worked on by multiple actors, bridging the individual and the social (Patterson and Schroeder 2010). For embodied identity statements such as tattoos, the interpretations that take place between actors can be diverse, contested and complex. Patterson and Schroeder (2010) note that tattooing brings with it a set of competing and contested understandings between the individual and group, deviant and mainstream, public and private, personal and social and subject and object. It is this instability and ambiguity of both the skin and tattooing which make them rich sites for examinations of consumer identity construction as a dialogical process between agency and structure.

Taking a dialectical and multifaceted view of identity construction, this paper seeks to understand how consumers navigate across contested symbolic meanings 'permanently' marked on the body, shifting the focus from meaning to action. In contrast to Patterson and Schroeder's (2010) study on tattoo consumption amongst heavily tattooed women we consider one particular tattoo, the Southern Cross tattoo, which symbolises heavily contested meanings in Australia. Our objectives are threefold. First, we contribute to the consumer culture theory debate on the agency/structure dialectic in the consumption of permanent bodily modification. Second, we offer insights on what consumers do with the multiplicity of symbolic meanings available to them, shifting the focus from meaning to action. Finally, we propose four images of consumer identity – assumed, trialled, tribal and trapped – to provide a metaphorical understanding of identity work in consumer research.

Methodological Overview

Discourse analysis was conducted on texts derived from a combination of data collection procedures. Firstly, netnographic data on the Southern Cross tattoo was collected from weblogs, online tattoo discussion forums and news reports to provide a genealogical understanding of the symbol. Secondly, interviews of 60 to 120 minutes in length were conducted with five Australian informants based in Melbourne, Sydney and Brisbane who have the Southern Cross tattoo. Finally, memos and reflections written at various stages of the empirical process were documented and collected to facilitate reflexivity. The analysis sought to identify the ways identity was constructed and worked upon. Informed by grounded analysis procedures (Locke 2001), the interview data was coded using a three-stage process of open coding, identification of mid-level themes, and then broader conceptual categories. During this process we frequently returned to the literature to make sense of emerging themes and to sharpen our interpretations as guided by constructionist sensitivities and assumptions about language. Collaborative readings of the data were also undertaken by the authors in order to bring multiple perspectives to the data, its coding and subsequent interpretations.

The Southern Cross Symbol and its Contested Meanings

The Southern Cross is a symbol fundamental to the Australian cultural psyche, providing an observable way for people to be recognised as belonging to the Australian 'tribe' (Maffesoli 1996). The Crux constellation is dominated by a cross-shaped asterism of four bright stars, commonly known as the Southern Cross. The Southern Cross has great significance in many cultures of the Southern Hemisphere where it is visible at any time of the year, unlike in the Northern Hemisphere where it is only occasionally seen by those south of latitude 30 degrees. For thousands of years, the Southern Cross has been an object of reverence around the world, such as for Christians who claim it was last visible from Jerusalem at the time of the crucifixion of Jesus Christ. Over time, the Southern Cross has become most closely associated with the Australian identity.

The Southern Cross is an important element of Aboriginal Dreamtime, the Cross conceived as a stingray being pursued throughout the southern sky by a shark (the pointers). The Crux itself is mythologised as a possum sitting in a tree that represents the sky deity Mirrabooka, a clever man immortalised into the night sky by Biami, the creator, to assist in watching over people on earth. Since the colonial era, the Southern Cross has been used as a national symbol in Australia, residing on various state and territory flags as well as the national flag, where the four stars are said to represent the moral virtues of justice, prudence, temperance and fortitude. A stylised Southern Cross dominates the 'Eureka flag', first used in Victoria in 1854 as the battle flag of the Eureka Stockade – a key event in the development of Australian democracy where goldfield workers protested against Government sanctioned mining licenses. The Eureka flag has since continued as a symbol of protest, egalitarianism, liberty and revolution, particularly pertaining to class as reflected in its adoption by numerous trade unions. The Eureka flag has been proposed by the republican movement as an alternative national flag, as first suggested by the iconic poet Banjo Patterson in his poem 'Our Own Flag'. Finally, the Southern Cross is referenced in the lyrics of the Australian national anthem, the title of the victory song of the Australian national cricket team whilst numerous institutions such as hospitals, universities and railway stations also bear the name 'Southern Cross', illustrating its deep cultural embedment.

In recent times, two phenomena have resulted in the Southern Cross symbol taking on different and highly contested sets of meanings. Firstly, a growing trend towards 'marketplace patriotism' has emerged, whereby Australian symbols – overwhelmingly the Southern Cross – are emblazoned on every product imaginable. Consuming patriotism also extends to embodied practices, such as body modification. This can be observed in the ever-increasing number of Australians, including Australian athletes at the Sydney Olympics in 2000, showing the emblem of the Southern Cross tattooed on their skin. Secondly, a nationalist, xenophobic 'Aussie Pride' movement that developed out of the racially motivated Cronulla riots have latched on to the Southern Cross symbol as emblematic of their 'cause'. This is most clearly apparent in the 'Southern Cross Soldiers', a group who band together around the belief that "there is only one ethnicity in Australia: Australian" (SCS website, 2010). The Southern Cross Soldiers are the largest organised group aligned to the 'Aussie pride' movement with chapters throughout Australia. Members are tattooed with the Southern Cross as a way of alleging their membership to the group, which adopts a US 'gangsta' style through the appropriation of cultural expressions, such as rap music. As a consequence, the Southern Cross has taken on connotations of racial

vilification, leading some to brand it the 'Aussie Swazie'.

Whilst we may think of national symbols as sacred, non-contested, coherent, untouchable and ever present, the case of the Southern Cross illustrates the deep contestation of its meanings within contemporary Australian society, partially the consequence of these various appropriations. What does this mean for people who have chosen to 'permanently' etch their skin with the symbol of the Southern Cross as a part of their own personal narrative? We explore this question in the ensuing sections, which provide insights into how consuming subjects engage with contested symbolic meanings in the process of identity construction. We begin by outlining the findings from the research study, which demonstrate that four discourses were drawn on in processes of identity construction for those engaging with the embodied experience of consuming the Southern Cross symbol as a tattoo, namely worship, experimentation, community and domination.

Discourses of Worship

Our informants drew on discourses of worship in talk about tattooing their skin with the Southern Cross. By imprinting their skin with the symbol, our informants performed an act of devotion that adoringly acknowledged their love for their country: Australia. They spoke about how they considered the Southern Cross to be a quintessentially Australian symbol, and by laying claim to it in this way the informants were able to demonstrate their avowal. Demi, a nurse aged 36, considers herself a "*proud Australian*" and inked her allegiance as an act of praise to the country in which she has lived her entire life:

> There was no question of anything else. I wanted the Southern Cross and that was it. It shows I'm an Aussie ¼ The Southern Cross, it's unique. There's no explanation needed. You just know.

The strong emotions that were raised in speaking about her tattoo gave Demi goose bumps. She believed her tattoo provided her with "*proof of my patriotism*", using her body as a text to "*mark my territory*" and "*show how this means so much to me*". As Demi mentions in the excerpt above, the symbol is "*unique*" and does not need an explanation, it "*shows I'm an Aussie.*" Demi and all of our informants did not consider expressing their commitment to 'being Australian' through any other symbol. They considered the Southern Cross to be the most highly recognisable symbol associated with Australia, thus best enabling them to communicate their national pride and "*prove*" (Demi) their heritage. Moreover, other national symbols, such as the flag, were "*tainted*" (Jack) by their association with Britain. In contrast, the Southern Cross was a sacred symbol (Belk, Wallendorf and Sherry 1989). Our informants celebrate their deep connection to their country using the Southern Cross as a value-expressive symbol to being "*an Aussie*" (Demi) and a "*proud Australian*" (Leon). For example, below Josh explains how the symbol is a sacred artefact that provides "social cohesion and societal integration" (Belk et al. 1989, 31):

> It's over my heart and they say things like you're wearing your country over your heart that was why I got it there. It's something that belongs to all of us whether you're born here or not. If you choose to live here then I believe you choose to live under the Southern Cross, you choose to live our way – and then you're entitled to have a tattoo of the Southern Cross.

For Josh, a construction worker aged 44, his Southern Cross tattoo signified his adherence to the '*Australian way of life*', it was a mark that demonstrated he was committed to his country and maintaining its cultural traditions. Tattooing the Southern Cross is clearly not for the mass but is reserved to the "*entitled*" individuals who belong to Australia. Josh and all of our informants constructed their experience of being tattooed as affirming their devotion and being emblematic of a spiritual pledge taken for their country. The informants uncritically spoke about the Southern Cross as something greater than themselves. This was strongly reflective and nostalgic, with informants constructing their tattoo as a "*tribute*" (Josh) or mark of respect to cultural heroes who have passed on but are forever remembered for the ways they shaped the nation. As Leon, an electrician aged 19, reflects:

> I'm proud of our ancestry, it makes us who we are and what we will be. I've got a grandfather that served in World War II, two of my uncles who served over in Timor and Afghanistan and so I'm proud of people who serve our country and make it a safe place to be. That makes me proud of who I am and where I've come from and what my country's done. Yeah, what our country is and what it stands for and what it's got to offer. When I was young I marched in the Anzac Day marches and wore his medals, I've just grown up with a pride knowing he served the country and served so that I can be here today. Yes, just made me proud at the end of the day, not just me but for everyone that's here now.

Leon describes his Southern Cross tattoo as a psychic bridge to "*our ancestry*" and his "*grandfather*." Wearing the Southern Cross denotes the bearer's status of being Australian and descending from Australians. For many of our informants, this patriotic worship had far reaching consequences for their other consumption choices. For Josh, who was suffering from terminal cancer, various sacrifices were personally made in order to ensure he was duly "*living under the Southern Cross*", always placing the country before himself:

> I've got absolutely no desire to travel anywhere in the world until I've seen all of Australia and that's never going to happen. There's just too much to see here. So I'm never going to leave our shores because there's nothing else I want to see first ¼ I was a farmer for about 16 years. I lost thousands and thousands of dollars worth of crops with hail storms and what have you. When I did have a good crop so did every other bugger and you couldn't sell it. The idea of importing food into Australia is just absolute bullshit. I hate going into a supermarket in the middle of winter and finding cherries for sale. I mean you can't, it's just not right. We should not be importing food. We can produce everything that we need here. That's what I believe anyway. So I only buy what we produce.

When pressed about what the Southern Cross symbol personally meant to them, most of the informants felt they were unable to answer. They considered the decision to get the tattoo not to be a rational, conscious one. Rather, the informants spoke of a kind of divine imperative or epiphany that drove them to ink their skins. As Leon noted, "*I don't think it's something I wanted to do, it's something I needed to do*". They constructed the Southern Cross as a sacred symbol, something extraordinary that was not to be tampered with but treated with respect and awe. This sacralisation of the Southern Cross further fuelled its construction as a symbol of reverence. For the informants, the tattoo provided them with an enduring expression of worship, its materiality functioning as a kind of sacrament. For Leon, undertaking the rite of tattooing the cross conferred upon him permanent sanctity. It provided a transcendent experience, and he was proud to be able to display the scars that signified the physical agony he made the sacrifice for:

> It's going to stay with me forever. It's not something that will just go away, it's pretty much there for good. It's something I chose for everyone to see at all times. It's a clear way of doing it. I wanted to express that I am proud of being Australian, whether it be the bearing of the cross or showing I went through the pain.

For other informants, the tattoo became so intimately connected with their being they came to regard it as a natural part of their body. As Demi noted, the tattoo became "*an identity: it's a mark, a stamp, a birthmark*". This naturally occurring state was reinforced through references to the cosmic connection of the symbol, namely the Southern Cross in the sky, the seemingly eternal nature of which was constructed as reflecting their permanent undertaking of tattooing. For Jack, a retail worker aged 26, both the constellation and his tattoo provided "*a constant reminder of who I am and what it is to be Australian*". As many of the informants noted, both were "*always there*". In this way, the Southern Cross symbol came to be emblematic of a kind of everlasting life, something to be worshipped and sacralised.

Discourses of Experimentation

In talk about their tattoo, the informants also drew on discourses of experimentation. The act of inking their skin enabled them to construct a narrative about who they were and facilitated a way of communicating their identity work to those around them. For Demi, her tattoo represented the trying of personal circumstances she had weathered and overcome to be the person she is today:

> I think tattoos are an individual thing, because you choose what you want to have so it's a personal thing. There's always a story behind it. The taxi driver the other day had a black rose on his arm with the names of his parents who had passed, his brother and his cousin who are passed and that was his family memorial. He'll continue to get names added. That was him whereas for me this is the Southern Cross ¼ your past and your history shapes who you are today, those mistakes and errors and outbursts and whatever in your past that has made you who you are ¼ about my ex-husband and about what he has done, that's made me who I am ¼ it changed my life to move on and now I've got the confidence to show who I am.

Our informants felt that the act of imprinting their skin enabled them to draw on meanings of the symbol and rework them as part of their identity. For example, Jack tattooed his shoulder with the Southern Cross as a rite of passage to mark the end of his youth. For him, the meanings of rebellion associated with the symbol resonated with his personal narrative and he considered the tattoo to function as forever telling that story:

> I guess it would be along the lines of the Eureka Flag, being the rebel thing to do. It's probably become the younger generations' Eureka Flag. It's just something to do to rebel against modern society and everything else. It's probably just to be different, in a way and not be stereotyped into one dimension type of stuff. Because probably at the time it was a rebellious thing that my parents weren't huge tattoo fans. Then because I moved out of home for more independence it was another step towards that ¼ Just the choice to live how I want to live and do what I want to live. Just the freedom aspect to it. It's just a part of me and it's something that I have to show who I am.

The process of being tattooed with the Southern Cross allowed our informants to both appropriate its cultural meanings and construct their own personalised meanings. In this way, the informants engaged in acts of bricolage (De Certeau 1984), adopting and adapting symbolic resources to build their own stories. For Kate, a photographer in her mid 20s, her Southern Cross tattoo was a means of creatively expressing her personal myth – something fundamental about her life (Velliquette, Murray and Evers 2006). For Kate, the tattoo functioned as a way of remembering her home, family and friends when she was living overseas. In this way, the tattoo embodied her myth and enabled her to meaningfully interpret her life experiences:

> I went to England and I was going to live there for two years and work and be away from home. I'm very attached to my family; we're very, very close. I lived at home for quite a while and it was very hard moving out for the first time. I guess being an only child and being close to my parents, it was hard. So being over in England it was just being away from everything that I've known. No friends, family, no nothing. I didn't know anybody in England ¼ there was nothing home about it over there. I wanted something that I could have with me wherever I was, I'd know I was home.

Yet, some informants struggled with the symbol being "*public property*" (Jack), perceiving its collective appropriation as hampering the interpretation of their embodied self-narrative. In response, some sought to modify the symbol as an act of self-expression. Leon personalised the symbol by placing it amongst others he believed collectively elaborated his identity. In doing so, he attempted to take control of its meanings, moving it from the public sphere to the private. Interestingly, Leon chose to augment his Southern Cross tattoo with other shared symbols commonly associated with the Australian national identity, signalling he still felt bound to observe an existing identity script.

Discourses of Community

For some informants, the Southern Cross tattoo provided a sense of belonging, functioning as an identity marker that signalled a shared consciousness with others. The informants divulged how strangers would approach them upon seeing the symbol, interested to hear their story, compare tattoos or communicate feelings of camaraderie. In this way the informants drew on discourses of community, constructing the tattoo as creating a dialogue with others that conferred social benefits. For Josh, his tattoo became a "uniform", an identity badge that linked him to others connected to the symbol:

> I like the way when you're at the beach and you haven't got a shirt on people notice it. Obviously they may have different opinions and different ideas as to why someone might get it. But to me it's like they realise that I'm Australian ¼ It's good to know that I'm a part of all of that. Like I belong. It's a little stamp of being here, like part of Australia I guess. It's just knowing that you're part of a team.

Having branded themselves with the Southern Cross, the informants claimed they felt more connected to the legends, traditions and values commonly associated with being an Australian. In doing so, many of the informants came to perform an identity that slipped into typecasting of what a 'typical' Australian was considered to be. For instance, Jack emphasised how his '*ockerisms*' or Australian clichés reinforced his belonging to the community accessible through his tattoo:

> Out of what I've been told from my group of friends, I'm more Australian than anyone else. Just the way I act and a few of my sayings ¼ like the 'no worries' and 'she'll be right mate', pretty much your stock standard Australian sayings will just come out naturally to me ¼ I guess it [the tattoo] may have appeared to have an effect on me to my friends and outsiders.

The communality of the tattoo also provided some informants with an understanding of the types of people to whom they felt akin.

Leon noted his tattoo provided him entry to a group called 'Aussie Patriotism Ink', an online community who bond over patriotic symbols tattooed on the skin. Leon considered the people within the group to be likeminded in ways beyond the mere act of inking the skin:

> It's just a group of people like myself ¼ A lot of the blokes on the site I know are tradesmen. A lot of them go camping, love the outdoors, love sports, go 4WD and whatnot. Most of them are Caucasian, Australian, Christian ... I suppose you say they fit.

In a subcultural sense (Hebdige 1981), Leon shared how members of the group sought out a minority style interpreted in accordance with subversive values that were critical of dominant societal standards. Members embraced casual tradesperson attire such as 'wifebeater' singlets, stubby shorts and thongs and espoused nationalistic, xenophobic values that ran counter to the prevailing climate of political correctness:

> When you try to express your love for your country and you see so many people that aren't Australian it can be frustrating. There was more Australians living here than there is now and it's more frustrating than anything seeing a country that you love and having so many other people moving into it ¼ you do want it for yourself. When I'm going camping I rarely see someone who is Asian or Indian ¼ I don't think they share the same sort of beliefs and enjoy the same activities that we do.

Leon noted how having a Southern Cross tattoo brought together and identified members of the group empowering them to feel "*more Australian*", however this also spilled over into understandings of who they were unlike and othered and excluded:

Discourses of Domination

Finally, informants drew on discourses of domination in talk about themselves and their tattoo. Some informants claimed they felt stereotyped as a result of their Southern Cross tattoo. For Kate, who was "*ashamed*" of her working class background and experienced considerable obstacles in coming out as gay, being classed as a 'bogan' or racist was a highly fraught identity struggle:

> Even though to me it means something else, no one else knows that. So everyone thinks you're that demographic. I know a few people who have it and they're the typical tradies. I'm still centred around that fear - V8 supercars, Bathurst, football, tradie - because to me they're all the people who have it. They're all the people I've come across who have it or really just bogan people. That's kind of the category I've been lumped in now. That's what I see now that I've been pigeonholed ¼ it's horrible.

For Kate, this stereotyping resulted in feelings of social exclusion, whereby the symbol came to dominate her identity and shape perceptions of what others thought of her. Describing it being "*like a gang tattoo*", Kate felt branded as a deviant and outcast by the symbol. This created a sense of cultural anxiety, with Kate feeling the need to constantly reconstruct her identity to others to mitigate the undermining power of the Southern Cross upon her identity work. She claimed that the tattoo even attracted physical violence, to the extent that she was often concerned for her physical safety in public spaces. In this way, Kate ascribed considerable agency to the tattoo, constructing it as overpowering all other visible symbolic cues on her body that could be read to interpret her identity:

I just don't feel the same with it. I always feel that sense of somebody looking at me, somebody judging me. It feels like it's going to consume you and then you're going to become that, you have to become that symbol that everybody thinks you are ¼ it attracts a lot of anger and hate, others pick people out for having it. I feel that. If you go to a pub or a bar you don't know if you're going to be standing there and someone's going to come up and have a go at you.

In an attempt to counter these feelings of categorisation, the informants employed various coping strategies and made particular sacrifices. Jack was always concerned about being approached by the "*wrong type of people*" because of his tattoo. For this reason, he kept his tattoo covered and hidden the vast majority of the time, only revealing it when in front of people he trusted such as family and friends. For Leon, who feels he has been unfairly treated and labelled as unintelligent as a result of his tattoo, his coping strategy was to "*remember the reasons why I got it*" in an attempt to reassert control over the symbol's interpretation. Yet for Kate, it has reached the point where she feels she must dispose of the symbol by getting the tattoo covered up to disidentify herself from what she considers to be its negatively connoted meanings:

A lot of people, when I tell them I'm getting it covered over, a lot of my closer friends are like 'oh it's a part of who you are and we all know you for it'. It's like yeah but it's kind of not me anymore, I don't want it. If I could scratch it off I would. If I could just get rid of it today I would. If I had the money right now I'd be gone down there and get her to do a design and get

it right and get it done ¼ I don't want to get angry over it. It's something that's meant to make me feel good, it's not meant to make me feel unhappy.

Kate tried growing her hair longer, wearing scarves and high collared shirts to cover the tattoo on her neck, but felt that its meanings still haunted her. By letting go of the symbol and its visibility entirely, Kate believes she can gain a sense of control over her identity construction, enabling her to "*be myself again*". For her, this comes at the cost of needing to defend her identity and letting go of part of her personal history:

Images of Identity: A Consumer Research Agenda

We contend that the discourses outlined provide a useful lens for examining how identity has been constructed in consumer research. Extant research emphasises the interplay between agentic and structural forces in identity construction, whereby tensions arise in dialectical interactions between individuals acting in self-interest and social structures that seek to control their actions (e.g. Holt 2002). To Murray's (2002) framework on the juxtaposition between sign experimentation and sign domination we add two forces that play critical roles in identity work, namely sign worship and sign community. Further, we propose that each sign discourse relates to an 'image' of identity. Image refers to the "overall idea or conceptualisation, capturing how researchers relate to — and shape — a phenomenon" (Alvesson 2010, 194). We offer four images of identity – assumed, trialled, tribal and trapped – to provide a metaphorical understanding of conceptualisations of identity work in consumer research. These are outlined in Table 1 below.

Discourses	Images of identity	Key characteristics of identity work	Examples
Worship	Assumed	• Uncritical appropriation of symbolic meanings • Identity construction is driven by a spiritual-like quest to be associated with something 'greater than oneself'	Muniz and Schau (2005) O'Guinn and Belk (1989)
Experimentation	Trialled	• Bricolage of symbolic meanings • Identity construction is motivated by the desire for self-expression	Arnould and Price (1993) Murray (2002)
Community	Tribal	• Sharing of symbolic meanings • Identity construction is directed by being situated in a specific social space	Kozinets (2001) Schouten and McAlexander (1995)
Domination	Trapped	• Inscription of symbolic meanings • Identity construction is regulated and controlled by social structures	Holt (1998) Murray (2002)

Table 1: Sign Discourses and Images Of Identities

In providing these images of identity, we seek to extend Arnould and Thompson's (2005) framework of consumer culture theory, which identifies identity projects as a key research agenda for consumer researchers. By specifying four areas of research pertaining to consumer identity, we aim to provide a platform from which future researchers can navigate the diverse work that is currently undertaken in the field of identity. It is important to note that studies may simultaneously address multiple images of identity, which har-

bour slippage and overlap. Consequently, this framework does not purport to offer static 'categories' of identity, but rather function for the purpose of analytic explanation. Finally, as discursive approaches to identity represent a growing area of interest in marketing research (e.g. Ellis and Ybema 2010), this research seeks to offer a starting point for future investigations of the role that discourses play in constructing and legitimising relations, meanings and identities in the field of consumer research.

REFERENCES

Alvesson, M. (2010), "Self-doubters, strugglers, storytellers, surfers and others: Images of self-identities in organization studies," *Human Relations,* 63, 193-217.

Arnould, E. J. and Thompson, C. J. (2005), "Consumer culture theory (CCT): Twenty years of research," *Journal of Consumer Research,* 31, 868-882.

--- and Price, L. (1993), "River magic: Extraordinary experience and the extended service encounter," *Journal of Consumer Research,* 20 (June), 24-45.

Askegaard, S., Gertsen, M. C. and Langer, R. (2002), "The body consumed: Reflexivity and cosmetic surgery," *Psychology & Marketing,* 19(10), 793-812.

Baudrillard, J. (1981), *Simulacra and simulation,* Ann Arbor: University of Michigan Press.

Bauman, Z. (2007), *Consuming life,* Boston: Polity Press.

Belk, R. W., Wallendrof, M. & Sherry, J. F. (1989), "The sacred and the profane in consumer research: Theodicy on the odyssey," *Journal of Consumer Research,* 16 (June), 1-38

Benwell, B. & Stokoe, E. (2006), *Discourse and identity,* Edinburgh: Edinburgh University Press.

de Certeau, M. (1984), *The practice of everyday life,* Berkeley: University of California Press.

Elliott, R. & Wattanasuwan, K. (1998), "Brands as symbolic resources for construction of identity," *International Journal of Advertising,* 17, 131-144.

Ellis, N. & Ybema, S. (2010). "Marketing identities: Shifting circles of identification in inter-organizational relationships", *Organization Studies,* 31, 279-305.

Featherstone, M. (1991), *Consumer culture and postmodernism,* London: Sage.

Firat, A. F. & Venkatesh, A. (1995), "Liberatory postmodernism and the reenchantment of consumption," *Journal of Consumer Research,* 22, 239-267.

Goulding, C., Shankar, A. and Elliott, R. (2002), Working weeks, rave weekends: Identity fragmentation and the emergence of new communities, *Comsumption, Markets and Culture,* 5(4), 261-284.

Hebdige, D. (1981), *Subculture: The meaning of style,* London: Metheun.

Holt, D. B. (2002), "Why do brands cause trouble? A dialectical theory of consumer culture and branding," *Journal of Consumer Research,* 29 (June), 70–90.

--- (*1998*), "Does *cultural capital* structure American consumption?,"' *Journal of Consumer Research,* 25, 1-25.

--- and Thompson, C.J (2004), "Man-of-action heroes: The pursuit of heroic masculinity in everyday consumption," *Journal of Consumer Research,* 31 (September), 425–40.

Jameson, F. (1984), "Postmodernism, or the cultural logic of late capitalism," *New Left Review,* 53-92.

Kozinets, R. V. (2001), "Utopian Enterprise: Articulating the meanings of Star Trek's culture of consumption", *Journal of Consumer Research,* 28(1), 67-88.

Locke, K. (2001), *Grounded theory in management research,* London: Sage Publications.

Maffesoli, M. (1996), *The time of the tribes: The decline of individualism in mass society,* London: Thousand Oaks.

Muniz A.M. Jr. and Schau, H.J (2005), "Religiosity in the abandoned Apple Newton brand community," *Journal of Consumer Research,* 31 (March), 737-47.

Murray, J.B. (2002), "The politics of consumption: A re-inquiry on Thompson and Haytko's (1997) 'Speaking of Fashion'", *Journal of Consumer Research,* 29(3), 427-440.

O'Guinn, T.C. and Belk, R.W (1989), "Heaven on earth: Consumption at Heritage Village, USA," *Journal of Consumer Research,* 16(2), 227-238.

Patterson, M. and Schroeder, J.E. (2010), "Borderlands: Skin, tattoos, and consumer culture theory," *Marketing Theory,* 10(3), 253-267.

Sanders, C. R. (1985), "Tattoo consumption: Risk and regret in the purchase of a socially marginal service", in *Advances in Consumer Research,* 12, Elizabeth C. Hirschman and Moris B. Holbrook (Eds.), Provo, UT: Association for Consumer Research, 17-22.

Schouten, J.W. and McAlexander, J.H (1995), "Subcultures of consumption: An ethnography of the new bikers," *Journal of Consumer Research,* 22, 43-61.

Thompson, CJ. (1996), "Caring consumers: Gendered consumption meanings and the juggling lifestyle," *Journal of Consumer Research,* 22 (March), 388–407.

--- & Hirschman, E. C. (1995), "Understanding the socialized body - a poststructuralist analysis of consumers self-conceptions, body images, and self-care practices," *Journal of Consumer Research,* 22, 139-153.

Velliquette, A.M., Murray, J.B and Evers, D.J. (2011), "Inscribing the personal myth: The role of tattoos in identification", in Russell W. Belk (ed.) *Research in Consumer Behavior, Volume 10,* Emerald Group Publishing Ltd, 35-70.

Ybema, S., Keenoy, T., Oswick, C., Beverungen, A., Ellis, N. and Sabelis, I. (2009), "Articulating identities", *Human Relations,* 62, 299-322.

How Best to Get their Own Way? Children's Influence Strategies within Families

Ben Kerrane, Bradford University, UK
Margaret Hogg, Lancaster University, UK

ABSTRACT

How do children decide how best to try and get their own way? Despite extensive studies of children's influence strategies there has been little research into understanding *why* children utilise given influence strategies i.e. *"the underlying motivations of strategy usage"* (Palan and Wilkes 1997, p.167). The motivations that drive the choice of different influence strategies result from a combination of personal goals and environmental factors. The family environment provides children with some of their most important experiences about how best to compete for limited resources (e.g. time, attention, money). Choices about the allocation of income across family members' preferences are central to children's consumer socialization. In order to throw more light on the motivations for children's choice of particular strategies in their family environment (Cotte and Wood 2004), we investigate the family environments in which the influence strategies are played out; and how far the family environment has a moderating effect on the types of influence strategies that children use.

Our contribution is thus twofold. Firstly we seek to better understand the family environments in which children reside; and secondly, to identify the implications that the different family environments may have in relation to each child's choice of influence strategies within their family setting. Our study responds to Cotte and Wood's (2004) and Flurry's (2007) call for research that explores further the purchase influence of children in families, specifically by exploring how the family environment affects the influence strategies that children employ.

Child Influence Strategies: The Research Context

Research over the past forty years has established that *"purchase decisions within the family are not always the outcome of individual choice, but rather, family members influence each other"* (Hamilton and Catterall 2006, p.1032). Examinations of children's influence strategies began with a study of cereal choices which identified that both the child's assertiveness and the mother's child-centeredness were central to mother's susceptibility to their child's requests (Berey and Pollay 1968). In another cereal choice supermarket setting, children were more successful if they told their mothers to buy their preferred cereal, or if they demanded their choice, rather than if they simply asked their mother for it, or requested the item (Atkin 1978).

Another study specifically asked adolescents to write a series of essays entitled "How I get my way with my mother … father … best friend". Fifteen influence strategies were identified, sub divided by whether the strategies used were direct or indirect (Cowan, Drinkard and MacGavin 1984). Direct strategies included the use of more overt behaviours (asking, begging and pleading, telling or asserting, reasoning, demanding or arguing, stating importance, bargaining and persistence), whereas indirect strategies are believed to occur when *"the influencer acts as if the person on the receiving end is not aware of the influence"* (Johnson 1976, p. 100). Indirect influence strategies included the use of negative affect (such as the use of crying, sadness and anger), positive affect (including the use of sweetness and innocence), verbal manipulation (often involving telling lies), eliciting reciprocity, using an advocate, evasion and laissez-faire (taking independent action, regardless) (Cowan *et al.* 1984). Adolescents directed more influence strategies towards their mothers than their fathers, and of those strategies directed towards mothers most involved the use of negative affect.

Examining explicitly the mother-child dyad, twelve child influence strategies were identified by Cowan and Avants (1988) which included: ask, bargain, show positive feelings, do as I please, show negative affect, persistence, beg and plead, perform good deeds, reason, cry and get angry. What is significant from this study is that strategies were related to the level of parental resistance that the children expected to encounter: high (anticipating non-compliance strategies e.g. beg and plead, cry) or low (autonomous strategies e.g. tell), and whether or not an equal power relationship existed between the parent and child (egalitarian strategies e.g. bargain and reason).

A study of the power strategies of popular and rejected black South African children identified four dimensions of influence strategies: direct and indirect influence strategies (as identified by Cowan *et al.* 1984), and bilateral and unilateral strategies (Bonn 1995). Falbo and Peplau (1980) had earlier identified the concept of bilateral and unilateral dimensions within influence strategies in their study of intimate relationships. Whereas bilateral strategies require the cooperation and responsiveness of the target (e.g. bargaining), unilateral strategies do not. Bonn (1995), through interviews with children involving hypothetical situations, identified a range of strategies, including persuasion, bargaining and compromise (bilateral, direct strategies); suggesting, ingratiating, and deception (bilateral, indirect strategies); sadness, crying and anger (unilateral, indirect strategies); and asking, threatening and coercion (unilateral, direct influence strategies). Rejected children often used unilateral influence strategies, frequently involving the use of aggression (Bonn 1995).

More recent work on adolescents and their parents identified four classes of influence strategies[1]: bargaining, persuasion, emotional, and request strategies (Palan and Wilkes 1997). In a diary study which applied Palan and Wilkes' (1997) influence strategy framework focussing on children's impact on innovative decision-making, children were subsequently found to employ persuasion strategies most often, followed by request and bargaining strategies (Götze, Prange and Uhrovska 2009). In only a few cases were children found to utilise emotion based strategies (Götze *et al.* 2009).

Lee and Collins (2000) and Lee and Beatty (2002), through videotaped recordings of family interactions during a simulated decision-making situation, recognised the potential for coalitions to form within families. Five main influence strategy types were identified: experience strategies (using experience and knowledge as a source of information to influence the outcome of a decision), legitimate strategies (which emphasise positional power and stereotypes), emotion strategies, bargaining strategies and coalition strategies (Lee and Collins 2000). Seven dimensions of children's direct influence strategies, ask nicely, bargain, show affection, just ask, beg and plead, show anger and con, have also been identified (Williams and Burns 2000). More recently the child influence strategies of justifying and highlighting the benefits of purchases, forming coalitions, compromising and remaining persistent, have also been documented (Thompson, Laing and McKee 2007).

Ultimately although we do have a solid understanding of the repertoire of influence strategies that children are believed to use, we do not have an adequate understanding as to *why* children utilise given influence strategies – or indeed whether every child has access to every type

---

[1] It should be noted that Palan and Wilkes (1997) identified seven influence strategies, although the latter three (expert, legitimate and directive) were strategies solely utilised by parents in response to their adolescent's use of an influence strategy.

Advances in Consumer Research
Volume 39, ©2011

of influence strategy identified.

In addition to child influence strategies, a number of studies have also assessed children's influence on family decision processes i.e. their level of ability, and the type of situations in which children employ their influence strategies. The influence of children has been found to vary along the stages of decision-making. Results across studies were consistent in that children's influence was reported to be highest in the problem recognition stage, and significantly lower in the decision-making stage (Szybillo and Sosanie 1977; Belch *et al.* 1985; Lee and Beatty 2002). Recent research, however, particularly in studies involving innovative or technically complex products, suggests that children have much greater influence than previously acknowledged across *each* stage of the buying decision process (Götze *et al.* 2009; Wang, Holloway, Beatty and Hill 2007). Similarly children are believed to exert more influence for products they will use themselves (Beatty and Talpade 1994; Belch *et al.* 1985; Darley and Lim 1986; Shoham and Dalakas 2003).

Demographic factors are also suggested to affect the child's level of influence. Older children are suggested to exert more influence than younger children in family decisions (Jenkins 1979; John 1999), and past research indicated that female children were more influential than were male children in family decision-making (Atkin 1978; Moschis and Mitchell 1986). Recently, however, the moderating effect of a child's gender in relation to influence on decision-making has been called into question (Flurry 2007; Wang et al 2007). A child's birth position has also been related to their ability to influence family decisions, with first born children exerting greatest purchase decision influence (Churchill and Moschis 1979; Flurry 2007). Children who earn income have also been found to have more influence in purchase decisions than those children who do not (Moschis and Mitchell 1986; Flurry 2007).

Other family related factors are also suggested to affect a child's involvement in family decision-making. Children are suggested to have greater influence: in larger families which contain lots of children (Jenkins 1979; Ahuja and Stinson 1993), although debate does surround the link between child influence potential and family size (Ward, Wackman and Wartella 1977); as the number of years their parents have been married increases (Jenkins 1979); when both parents have an income of their own (Foxman, Tansuhaj and Ekström 1989; Hall, Shaw, Johnson and Oppenheim 1995), with parents in dual income families characterised as being busier and feeling guiltier and softer when it comes to their children's requests (Beatty and Talpade 1994; Geuens, Mast and De Pelsmacker 2002); in higher income families (Ekström 2007; Jenkins 1979), although one study did find that children in poor families exert considerable influence on family consumption, to the extent that consumption is often organised around their needs (Hamilton and Catterall 2006); as the education of their parents increases (Ahuja and Stinson 1993); as the family's social class increases (Atkin 1978; Moschis and Mitchell 1986), although Lee and Beatty (2002) question this relationship; and in relation to family type, with children of single parent or stem families suggested to exert considerable influence over family decisions (Ahuja and Stinson 1993; Bates and Gentry 1994; Hall *et al.* 1995; Mangleburg and Grewal 1999).

In terms of the family environment, *family communication pattern* (Carlson, Walsh, Laczniak and Grossbart 1994) and *parental socialization style* (Carlson and Grossbart 1988) have been linked to child influence. Five general parental socialization styles have been identified, *authoritarian, rigid controlling, neglecting, authoritative* and *permissive* (Carlson and Grossbart 1988), which we argue directly relates to both the extent of a child's influence in family purchase decisions and the types of influence strategy that they can employ.

For example, a child of authoritarian parents, who expect unquestioned obedience and who discourage parent-child communication (Johnson, McPhail and Yau 1994), is not expected to influence family decisions (Hall *et al* 1995; Ward and Wackman 1972). Authoritarian parents are also likely to view, for example, the use of persuasion or bargaining tactics in a negative light (Johnson *et al* 1994).

Family communication pattern, *"the frequency, type and quality of communication that takes place amongst family members"* (Carlson *et al.* 1994, p.29), also affects a child's influence in family purchase decisions. Four family communication patterns are identified; *laissez-faire, protective, pluralistic* and *consensual* (see Carlson *et al.* 1994 for a review). Children within families characterised as having a laissez-faire family communication pattern, involving limited parent-child communication of any kind (Moschis and Moore 1979; John 1999), are less likely to participate in shaping the family decision-making process, whereas children within pluralistic families are more likely to.

Children appear to make informed choices about which influence strategy they will employ (Williams and Burns 2000). Their decisions are informed by the historical success or failure of utilizing such strategies in previous decision-making situations (Bao *et al.* 2007; Götze *et al.* 2009; Thompson *et al.* 2007). However, relatively little is known about children's choice processes. This study explores how far the family environment has a moderating effect on the types of influence strategies that children choose to use, throwing light on the underlying motivations which children have in relation to strategy employment. Within consumer research, the family environment has been characterised as being a homogenous environment for each child. This assumption about the homogeneous nature of the family environment underpins current work on family communication pattern and parental socialization style studies. However Cotte and Wood (2004) called for further investigation of the "shared" nature of the family environment. This study therefore seeks to explore how children's varying experiences of their family environment facilitates or hinders children's choices of different influence strategies.

Methodology

Phenomenological interviews (Thompson, Locander and Pollio 1989) were conducted with six families living in the North West of England. Following calls for family research which captures the dynamics of family purchase decision-making (Hamilton and Catterall 2006; Tinson and Nancarrow 2005) interviews were conducted with both children and their parents. As many family members as possible were included in the data collection process. In line with other interpretivist studies (see for instance Thompson and Troester 2002) purposive sampling (Miles and Huberman 1984) was used to identify and recruit a range of family types and not just nuclear family forms.

In view of changing family configurations, we explored child influence strategies across a range of family forms (Thompson *et al.* 2007), including a lesbian headed family with both adopted and biological children; a family headed by a cohabiting couple; a family headed by a single mother; and a blended family.[2] All these family forms represent types identified by Harrison and Gentry (2007a, 2007b) as receiving inadequate research attention. Two nuclear families were also recruited from different socio-economic groups. An emphasis on studying consumers in-depth necessitated a smaller sample size to be used to allow thick descriptions to emerge (Carrigan and Szmigin 2006) which is common for interpretivist consumer research.

---

[2] A blended family has been described by Belch and Willis (2001) as a step family; however, Schultz et al. (1991) state that blended families have to be complex stepfamilies in which both spouses were parents before the current marriage

The families were recruited partly through personal contacts; partly through placing online appeals for participants in family newspapers and publications; and partly by contacting relevant family organisations in the North West region. The interviews were largely conducted in the family home, usually in the kitchen at the dining table, although one interview was conducted at one respondent's place of work. Each family was visited between three and five times and interviews were conducted over a period ranging from four to twelve months. Respondents were first asked for their consent to participate in the research process, assured of anonymity, told about the purpose of the research and then asked for permission to record the conversations.

Consent was sought from parents and guardians to approach their children in order to then seek the children's consent to be involved in the data collection process (Mandell 1991). Methods by which valid consent can be obtained from children were adhered to (Mason 2004). Recognising that children are potentially vulnerable research participants (Morrow and Richards 1996) the children were interviewed within the family home where an adult was always present, although not necessarily within earshot.

Interviews were tape recorded in full, lasted between 60 and 130 minutes, and were transcribed verbatim. The interviews with family members were conducted over three stages and explored themes such as family history and how family members got their own way. In stage one an interview was conducted with the parents/guardians, although two points are worth highlighting at this stage. In two of the families the fathers chose not to participate in any part of the data collection, and fathers generally had much less involvement than mothers in the interview process as a whole (although every attempt was made to capture their voices, principally by utilizing a male researcher to seek their views). Following this initial interview, stage two involved interviews with the children. Given that children, particularly younger children, may feel uncomfortable in a one-on-one interview situation (Mayall 2001) the children were given the option to have another sibling present during their interview.

Indeed in the second stage of the interviewing process the membership of the interviews was very fluid. Some children preferred to be interviewed individually, whereas in other families the children freely left and returned to the interview as other siblings joined and departed. Accordingly with some of the families one longer style visit was conducted with the children (comprising several shorter interviews with single and multiple children, often with overlapping attendance), whereas in other families the children preferred to have a much more contained interview. A semi participatory researcher role was adopted with the children (Mandell, 1991). Following this stage of interviewing, a final family group interview was conducted at stage three with as many family members as possible present. As with Hamilton and Catterall (2006) a financial incentive was offered to the families to thank them for their participation.

The interpretation of the interview texts was undertaken using a hermeneutical process (Thompson 1991; Thompson, Locander and Pollio 1990) which involved moving iteratively, back and forth between interview texts (within and across family cases) and the literature. Emerging themes in the data drove subsequent reading in the literature (Thompson 1996). Following hermeneutical principles (at the methodological level) a constant shift when reading between individual transcripts and the entire data set enabled a greater emergent understanding to develop in which elements of the part gave further meaning to the whole. Each family case was analysed on an idiographic basis which allowed for categorization of data from which larger conceptual classes emerged. These concepts were then compared across family cases, following Spiggle's (1994) initial steps for qualitative data analysis.

Findings

Across all six family cases, the family stories highlight the significant differences which exist *within* the families studied, and of the different treatment of family members by other family members. Each child did not have the same level of access to influence strategies, particularly in relation to his or her ability to form a coalition with other family members. Similarly the level of resistance to an influence strategy also varied depending on the child's characteristics and unique position within their family's environment. Our presentation, in a similar vein to Thompson (2005), highlights two family cases which illuminate the global themes found across all the families in this study. The family stories of the Baldwin and Jones families are introduced because these family stories emphasise the significant differences in children's experiences within the family environment, and highlight how these different family environments affect the influence strategies which the children employ.

The Baldwin Family Story

Carole and Ray Baldwin have been married for two years, having met following the death of Carole's first husband, Greg, and the unrelated breakdown of Ray's marriage to his first wife, Paula. Both Carole and Ray have children from their previous marriages, and so the Baldwin family is considered to be a blended family (Belch and Willis, 2001). Carole has four children from her first marriage: three grown up non-resident children, George, Kathy and Marie; and one resident child, Jessica (14), who lives with Carole and Ray in their new family home. Ray also has two non-resident children, Jamie and Anthony, who live with their mother. Ray tries to see his sons whenever he can. Carole and Ray have also had a biological child together, Nina (5).

The relationship that Carole and Ray have with Nina and Jessica is markedly different for each child. Whereas Nina is considered to be a good child, Jessica is not, with sibling comparison within families suggested to be common (Schachter and Stone 1985). Whilst Ray spends a great deal of time with Nina he spends little time with Jessica, with stepfathers often finding greater satisfaction in rearing their biological vs. step-children (Thoits 1992). Indeed, it is common for stepfathers to spend little time, and adopt a disengaged parenting style, with their step-children (Coleman, Ganong and Fine 2000). As a result Ray and Jessica do not have a strong relationship, and despite Ray's marriage to Carole, Ray has no intention of adopting Jessica as his own child:

> *Carole:* I said to [interviewer's name] before, that's why we ignore her [Jessica] (..) all of the time that she [Jessica] was sat there rabbitting on, Nina was sat there (.) and, and, she just wrote that [passing Ray a piece of paper that Nina had written on]
> *Ray:* I need a hug?
> *Carole:* That's what she's [Nina] like (..) it's like good child [Nina], bad child [Jessica]
> *Ray:* It's not bad child, it's pain in the arse child
> *Jessica:* But I got good grades
> *Ray:* I'm very pleased that you got good grades (.) but that's for your science, not for your maths
> *Jessica:* Yeah, but if I get another sticker I get a credit card, and then after that (.) after that, if I do good, I get a certificate
> *Ray:* If you do well, not if you do good
> *Jessica:* And then I do a certificate
> *Ray:* So you're not doing very well at English, then, are you?

Jessica is very aware that her parents treat her step-sister in a much more positive manner. Whereas Carole and Ray describe Jessica respectively as *"crafty"* and *"stupid"*, Nina is described by Carole as *"innocent and sweet"*, much to Jessica's annoyance:

> *Interviewer:* Do you think that Nina gets more [things] than you?
> *Jessica:* I guess so (.) but then she gets little stuff. But they make me pay for my own things now; I have to pay money towards them
> *Interviewer:* Do you think your Mum and Ray give in more to Nina than you?
> *Jessica:* Yes! She's their little angel (..) I get treated like a right skivvy

The different treatment of the girls affects both the manner in which they attempt to influence the decisions of their parents and their success in doing so. Whereas Carole and Ray believe that Nina doesn't ask for things, and is happy with what she has, Jessica suggests otherwise. As the following extract suggests, which describes how the girls asked for Christmas presents, Carole believes that Nina hasn't directly asked for any presents:

> *Carole:* This one [Nina] doesn't ask (.) you haven't asked for anything yet
> *Jessica:* Yes she has (..) she's asked for, she's about circled all the Argos catalogue
> *Carole:* She's ticked things; she's ticked things (.) she's not actually asked
> *Jessica:* Yeah, but Ray said I can have
> *Carole:* At her age
> *Jessica:* She was asking for things before the Christmas disco
> *Carole:* At her age, they just watch the telly and everything that comes up it's I want one of them, I want one of them, I want one of them, without particularly realising what it is (..) so I don't think you've actually decided properly, have you, what you want? You're quite happy with anything (.) aren't you?
> *Nina:* I'm happy with anything

In the individual interview with Nina she commented *"I want lots and lots of stuff"* and she is aware that she doesn't have to try too hard to get what she wants. Nina directs emotion based strategies towards her parents, and utilizes her affection to get the things that she wants, most often from her father, as Carole and Ray comment:

> *Carole:* Ray and Nina have a very close bond (.) more so than Ray and Jessica. Nina's very tactile with Ray, Nina, she's always hugging him and she doesn't ask for anything back, but I think she's building foundations for a big whammy when she's older (…) she gets up in the morning and she'll come down, and the first thing she'll do is, she'll come and get hold of him, she'll come downstairs, and she'll grab his leg and just squeeze him
> *Ray:* She can get away with murder!

Accordingly Nina doesn't have to try too hard to influence her parents, particularly Ray. As a result she utilizes a limited range of influence strategies, largely using unilateral, positive effect, influence strategies. Jessica, on the other hand, coupled with her perceived parental rejection, tries much harder to influence the decisions her parents make. Carole feels that Jessica's persistence has hampered her ability to get things from her parents, and it is suggested that the over employment of child influence strategies may lead to parents becoming immune to their influence (Ekström 2007):

> *Carole:* What Jessica tends to do, she's like a dripping tap (..) and she drip, drip, drip, drips until you get that fed up of it she ends up with nothing (.) and she's not sussed this out yet. If she doesn't mither, and she just (..) all she's got to do is mention it the once … the minute he walks through the door it's, Ray? With her there's a tone (..) it's a definite, you just hear it

Faced with this high level of parental resistance, Jessica does not direct bilateral influence strategies towards her parents as she lacks their support. Accordingly she uses unilateral influence strategies (Bonn 1995), which often involve the use of negative affect (Cowan *et al.* 1984) and violence. What is interesting to note within this family, however, is that Jessica tries to bolster her own influence potential and success. Recognising the power that Nina holds over her mother and step-father, and the expected parental resistance should Jessica act alone in her strategy employment, Jessica forms temporary coalitions with her step-sister in order to utilize Nina's influence potential. This would seem to support the notion that children consider the expected level of parental resistance in their strategy selection (Cowan and Avants 1988). One such occasion involved the purchase of an iToy. Jessica wanted this toy which connected to her PlayStation, but she couldn't afford it by herself. Realising this, and accepting that her mother and step-father were unlikely to purchase it for her, she approached Nina and asked her to contribute some of the money that she had received from Christmas towards the cost of the iToy. Together they could afford the toy, but Jessica was equally aware that she still needed to persuade her parents, as the gatekeepers of her consumption, that this was a sound decision made by both girls:

> *Jessica:* I knew Mum wouldn't let me have it (..) so I teamed up with Nina, they'd give her anything. I don't think Nina even wanted it
> *Interviewer:* But she still paid for some of it?
> *Jessica:* Yeah, but she's not bothered with it

Carole was concerned about this purchase, and what she considered to be the *"bullying"* that she felt had gone on between Jessica and Nina. Jessica, faced with the conditions of her position within her family's ecology, feels that she has little choice but to collude with Nina in order to get the things that she wants. Such coalitions are often very short lived, with Jessica ending the coalition once she has what she wants. The ability to form a coalition has also been linked to the ability to 'sell' a proposition (Thomson *et al.* 2007); although we suggest that this alone is not enough. The cause needs to be just, *and* the child needs to hold positive relationships with other family members, particularly their siblings, to be able to form a coalition. It is also unlikely that Jessica could form a coalition with her parents, as Lee and Collins (2000) and Lee and Beatty (2002) suggest is possible for some children.

The Jones Family Story

Debbie Smith and Paul Jones have been living together for just under twenty years. They have four children together who live in the family home: Michael (14), Anna (12), Adam (9), and Tina (7). Again, the children in the Jones family are not treated in a similar way by either their parents or their fellow siblings. Whereas Paul sees Michael as his mother's *"golden boy"*, his siblings do not share the same favourable position as Michael in their parents' eyes:

> *Interviewer:* Who do you give in to the most?
> *Debbie:* Paul would probably say my 'golden boy', as he calls him, Michael. I don't know what it is, perhaps it's because he's

my first born, but I suppose he does get away with doing more things. I think partly it's because I feel sorry for him, there's no one around here for him to hang around with, and he's doing well at school and with his drama and with his music (..) he's just a good boy, dead reliable and dependable

In the eyes of his mother at least, Michael's birth position (Lee and Collins 2000) grants him certain privileges in his family. However, this preferential parental treatment is not viewed favourably by his siblings, who are often antagonised by this, as Michael's sister, Anna, comments:

Anna; Michael just gets (.) he gets whatever he wants, just one word with Mum and he's got it. She'll get him anything (…) I don't get anything like he does

Anna in particular feels that there is a great deal of comparison between herself and Michael, with Michael seemingly able to monopolise their mother's time, with Debbie taking an active interest in Michael's leisure pursuits. Michael is a promising young actor, and Debbie pays for him to attend drama classes and often drives him to rehearsals:

Anna; It's always Michael does this, Michael can do that, why don't you be more like Michael? Michael's the one who's doing the best, he can act, he can sing, he's clever at school (..) he's all Mum ever talks about, the rest of us don't get a look in

Such is the tension between Michael and the rest of his siblings, who also view his ability to successfully influence their parents in a detrimental light, that Michael is often excluded and ostracised by his siblings. Although many of the products that Michael owns are relatively expensive and high-tech, purchased through his earnings as a young actor, his siblings do not show a great deal of interest in them. When Anna, however, won an Apple iPod in a supermarket prize draw Adam and Tina were immediately fascinated with it, and wanted one just like Anna's, even though Michael had bought himself one months before:

Michael; Anna's was better (.) better because it was hers, and she's the cool one, so it was just better

Although Michael can, and does, form a coalition with his mother, as the following quote suggests, he would struggle to gain this level of support from other family members (particularly his siblings):

Debbie; He'll [Michael] come round, and he'll put his arms around you (.) and he'll just say you know what I'd really like? … And then it's up to me to break the news to Paul (..) he wants what? My God! Does he realise how many hours I've got to put in to get that? And then I'll say, well I'll give you my family allowance, and we'll cut down on food, and we'll got to ALDI instead of ASDA [supermarkets].

Debbie also suggests that she tries harder to get Michael the things that he wants in relation to her other children, and as a result Michael simply has to use unilateral influence strategies. Faced with minimal parental resistance Michael uses autonomous influence strategies, including telling and asking (Cowan and Avants 1988) to influence his mother, and subsequently his father. The other children, however, employ a range of influence strategies. Anna, deemed to be a boisterous child by her parents, often makes deals with them, or uses laissez-faire influence strategies. Over the Christmas period

Anna also did not ask for any presents, with not asking proving to be a very effective influence strategy for Anna to use. Recognising her non-demands, Debbie and Paul bought her a range of presents, including an expensive video camera. Such an influence strategy, of not asking, has not been fully recognised within existing child influence strategy frameworks:

Paul; Anna did well out of it [Christmas]. She didn't ask for anything, but she had to have something. We ended up buying her a video camera (.) so she did well

Tina, supporting Kipnis's (1976, p.46) assertion that children can only *"beg, ask, plead or whine in order to influence their parents"*, demands items, cries, or plays on their emotions to get what she wants. Adam frequently asks his parents for things.

We also have further empirical evidence from the Jones family story to suggest that the repertoire of influence strategies available to children may be somewhat restricted, dependant on their place within the family environment. As Michael is viewed as being *"dull and boring"* by Tina, and indeed his siblings as a whole, he does not have access to their support. Consequently Michael has little choice but to employ unilateral influence strategies, or form a coalition with his mother. Anna, on the other hand, is well liked by her younger brother and sister, and Anna effectively exploits this. Recognising the high level of parental resistance to her influence strategies, and aware that her mother thinks that Anna *"wants every single week, every single week … it's all year round with Anna"*, Anna encourages Adam and Tina to ask their parents for things on her behalf, or she forms a coalition with them:

Debbie; She's [Anna] quite clever now, she gets the others to put a word in for her so she gets what she wants
Interviewer; So they come to you and say Anna wants this?
Debbie; Adam and Tina, usually (.) she's quite clever, she knows if she really, really wants something that it's no good just asking all the time because I'd get sick of it (.) so what she does is she makes other people ask for the things she wants, you know … she ends up getting things even though she herself hasn't asked for them … to her it might look like she's not asking for much, but she has, even if she's not come out and asked me for things.

DISCUSSION

Michael Jones, unlike his siblings, faces minimal parental resistance to his influence strategies, and he is able to garner considerable support from his mother, and subsequently his father. Mothers have been found to work best with sons in coalitions, particularly when the son is the eldest child (Lee and Collins 2000). Nina Baldwin can also easily influence the decisions of her parents, and both Nina and Michael therefore need to utilize only a limited range of autonomous influence strategies (e.g. tell, ask, positive affect).

Birth order, we suggest, is therefore related to a child's influence strategy choice and the subsequent parental resistance to its employment. First born children within the families studied were found to have a greater influence in the decision-making process. Although birth order has been related to a child's success in employing influence strategies (Cotte and Wood 2004; Dunn and Plomin 1990; Lee and Collins 2000), we suggest that disruption in the family can affect this.

Whilst existing literature suggests that it should be Nina Baldwin who is compared with Jessica, with older children often used as a benchmark for younger children (Buhrmester and Furman 1990; Harris 1995), this is not the case in the Baldwin family. Similarly

Jessica should hold more influence in the decision-making process because of her age (John 1999), but her position within the family has been disturbed because of the changes to her family form. As the Baldwin family has changed, so too has the power distribution amongst the resident children. Jessica's position within her family has been displaced, and Nina (the biological child of both couples) is treated as if she were the first born child who is suggested to hold greater influence. In effect Nina is the first born child of this new coupling, and it appears as if a new, "second" family has been created composed of Carol, Ray and Nina.

A child's ability to influence the decisions made by their parents relates to how that child is situated within the family ecology, and how they are viewed by their parents (as figure 1 suggests). Michael

Jones and Nina Baldwin are viewed in a favourable light by their parents, and need only use *autonomous* influence strategies to get what they want. They also face limited parental resistance. Anna Jones and Jessica Baldwin, for example, are not held in such high regard by their parents. Consequently both girls need to adopt much more aggressive and *confrontational* influence strategies, and need to fight for what they want because of the high level of parental resistance. Accordingly, as shown across each family, a child does not have automatic access to each influence strategy identified earlier; Anna and Jessica, for example, can not form coalitions with their parents, and they would struggle to effectively utilize the influence strategy of positive affect.

Figure 1: Influence Strategy Matrix

	Lone Influence	**Strategy Type** Group Influence		
Child's Position in Family	Favourable	*Autonomous* e.g. Emotion; Positive Affect; Ask e.g. Michael; Nina	*Cooperative* e.g. Deals; Bargaining; Positive coalitions e.g. Michael and Debbie; Nina and Ray or Carole	Little Resistance
	Unfavourable	*Confrontational* e.g. Demand; Show aggression; Laissez-faire e.g. Jessica; Anna	*Collaborative* e.g. Coalitions (which involve coercion) e.g. Jessica and Nina	Strong Resistance

With regards to coalition formation, however, both Jessica and Anna recognise their low standing in their parent's eyes. It has been suggested that "weaker" family members can unite to counter the influence or resistance of a "stronger" family member (Pearson 1989), and so in an effort to boost their own influence potential (and to stand a greater chance of getting the things that they want) the girls utilize a sophisticated series of coalition formation strategies.

Although Jessica and Anna could never form a direct coalition with their parents, they both have the potential to begin by forming a coalition with their siblings in order to exert indirect influence on their parents. In the first stage of strategy deployment Jessica and Anna recruit other siblings to work with them to facilitate their influence strategies. Once this sibling-based coalition is formed then the group as a whole attempts to influence the decisions of their parents in the second stage of this coalition-based strategy. Jessica Baldwin often utilizes this strategy, first influencing Nina to work alongside her, and then both Nina and Jessica work together in a coalition to influence their parents. Alone Jessica could never influence her parents in this way, but she cloaks her influence strategy with the presence of her step-sister. Such a strategy has been termed *collaborative*, as although co-operation is needed to form the coalition, such co-operation may not always be granted by a child's free volition. Carole Baldwin, for example, believes that often Jessica bullies Nina into working together in this way (with Carole feeling that many of the things that the two girls ask for together are only really wanted by Jessica), and an element of parental resistance is encountered because of this.

What is interesting to highlight is that whilst individually Jessica Baldwin would utilize confrontational influence strategy types (demanding; showing aggression), when she works in coalition with

Nina the strategy types are much less aggressive. We, therefore, have early findings which suggest that coalition formation can affect the types of influence strategy which the group as a whole employs. It is almost as if Nina's presence, and her success in influencing her parents, dilutes the normally aggressive strategies which Jessica alone employs.

One other form of influence strategy type, termed *cooperative*, was evident which involved the use of less coercion in employing collaborative influence strategies. In such coalitions (such as that of Michael Jones and Debbie Smith; or Nina and Carole or Ray Baldwin) the members freely agreed to work in collaboration with one another to influence others. Due to the coalition membership (which often includes a parent) little parental resistance was encountered.

The familial environments which exist within each family story suggest that it is probably rare for any one family to be composed of a single universal family environment, except possibly in the case of only children. We found little empirical support for the idea of a universal parental socialization style and family communication pattern within a family, although this seems to have been an assumption which has underpinned earlier studies (Carlson and Grossbart 1988; Carlson et al. 1994). Rather, different socialization tendencies exist within the same family. Children therefore appear to have different levels of access to the range of influence strategies identified, principally in relation to their ability to form coalitions with siblings and/or their parents to influence family purchase decisions. A child's family environment does therefore, we suggest, effect the types of influence strategy which they choose to employ.

As Flurry (2007) and Palan and Wilkes (1997) point out, considerable gaps exist in both our understanding of the influence strategies which children use and in terms of understanding the choices they make when choosing which influence strategy to employ. Our paper has attempted to fill some of these gaps by suggesting that the family environment can restrict a child's choice of influence strategy. Ultimately children experience their family in different ways, and this has implications for the types of strategy which they choose to use and those that they have access to.

Opportunities exist to explore the influence strategies of children across a greater range of family types, and also to explore in further depth whether children direct different types of influence strategies towards different family members (e.g. siblings, grandparents, step-parents). Similarly opportunities exist to explore multiple family consumption sites (e.g. can children switch strategy use in different family settings, or homes), and families of different cultures, to investigate whether such factors also influence the choice processes involved in selecting which influence strategy to employ.

REFERENCES

Ahuja, R. D. and Stinson, K. M. (1993) Female-Headed Single Parent Families: An Exploratory Study of Children's influence in Family Decision Making. *Advances in Consumer Research.* Vol. 20, pp. 467-474.

Atkin, C. (1978) Observation of Parent-Child Interaction in Supermarket Decision-Making. *Journal of Marketing.* Vol. 42, pp. 41-45.

Bao, Y., Fern, E. F. and Sheng, S. (2007) Parental Style and Adolescent Influence in Family Consumption Decisions: An Integrative Approach. *Journal of Business Research.* Vol. 60, pp. 672-680.

Bates, M. J., and Gentry, J. W. (1994) Keeping the Family Together : How we Survived the Divorce. *Advances in Consumer Research.* Vol 21, pp 30 – 34.

Beatty, S. E. and Talpade, S. (1994) Adolescent Influence in Family Decision Making: A Replication With Extension. *Journal of Consumer Research.* Vol. 21 (2) pp. 332-341.

Belch, G. E., Belch, M. A. and Ceresino, G. (1985) Parental and Teenage Child Influences in Family Decision Making. *Journal of Business Research.* Vol 13, pp 163-176.

Belch, M. A. and Willis, L. A. (2001) Family decision at the turn of the century: Has the changing structure of households impacted the family decision-making process? *Journal of Consumer Behaviour.* Vol. 2 (2) pp 111 – 124.

Berey, L. A., and Pollay, R. W. (1968) The Influencing Role of the Child in Family Decision Making. *Journal of Marketing Research.* Vol 70 (2) pp 70 – 72.

Bonn, M. (1995) Power strategies used in conflict resolution by popular and rejected black South African children. *Early Child Development and Care.* Vol. 114, pp 39 – 54.

Carlson, L., and Grossbart, S. (1988) Parent Style and Consumer Socialisation of Children. *Journal of Consumer Research.* Vol. 15 pp 77 – 94.

Carlson, L., Walsh, A., Laczniak, R. N. and Grossbart, S. (1994) Family Communication Patterns and Marketplace Motivations, Attitudes, and Behaviours of Children and Mothers. *The Journal of Consumer Affairs.* Vol. 28 (1) pp 25-53.

Carrigan, M. and Szmigin, I. (2006) 'Mothers of invention': Maternal Empowerment and Convenience Consumption. *European Journal of Marketing.* Vol. 40 (9/10) pp 1122-1142.

Churchill, G. A. and Moschis, G. P. (1979) Television and Interpersonal Influences on Adolescent Consumer Learning. *Journal of Consumer Research.* Vol. 6, pp. 23-35.

Coleman, M., Ganong, L. and Fine, M. (2000) Reinvestigating Marriage: Another Decade of Progress. *Journal of Marriage and the Family.* Vol. 62, pp 1288-1307.

Cotte, J. and Wood, S. L. (2004) Families and Innovative Consumer Behaviour: A Triadic Analysis of Sibling and Parental Influence. *Journal of Consumer Research.* Vol. 31, pp 78 – 86.

Cowan, G. and Avants, S. K. (1988) Children's Influence Strategies: Structure, Sex Differences, and Bilateral Mother-Child Influence. *Child Development.* Vol. 59, pp 1303-1313.

Cowan, G., Drinkard, J. and MacGavin, L. (1984) The Effect of Target, Age, and Gender on use of Power Strategies. *Journal of Personality and Social Psychology.* Vol. 47, pp 1391-1398.

Darley, W. F. and Lim, J. S. (1986) Family Decision Making in Leisure-Time Activities : An Exploratory Analysis of the Impact of Locus of Control, Child Age Influence Factor and Parental Type of Perceived Child Influence. *Advances in Consumer Research.* Vol. 13, pp 370 – 374.

Ekström, K. (2007) Parental Consumer Learning or 'Keeping Up With Children'. *Journal of Consumer Behaviour.* Vol. 6, pp. 203-217.

Falbo, T. and Peplau, L. A. (1980) Power Strategies in Intimate Relationships. *Journal of Personality and Social Psychology.* Vol 38 (4), pp 618 – 628.

Flurry, L. A. (2007) Children's Influence in Family Decision-Making: Examining the Impact of The Changing American Family. *Journal of Business Research.* Vol. 60, pp. 322-330.

Foxman, E. R., Tansuhaj, P. S., and Ekström, K. M. (1989) Family Members' Perceptions of Adolescents' Influence in Family Decision Making. *Journal of Consumer Research.* Vol 15, pp 482 – 491.

Geuens, M., Mast, G. and De Pelsmacker, P. (2002) Children's influence on family purchase behaviour:The role of family structure. *Asia Pacific Advances in Consumer Research.* Vol 5, pp 130 – 135.

Götze, E., Prange, C. and Uhrovska, I. (2009) Children's Impact on Innovative Decision Making: A Diary Study. *European Journal of Marketing.* Vol. 43 (1/2) pp. 264-295.

Hall, J., Shaw, M., Johnson, M. and Oppenheim, P. (1995) Influence of Children on Family Consumer Decision Making. *European Advances in Consumer Research.* Vol. 2, pp 45 – 53.

Hamilton, K. and Catterall, M. (2006) Consuming Love in Poor Families: Children's Influence on Consumption Decisions. *Journal of Marketing Management.* Vol. 22 (9-10), pp. 1031-1052.

Harrison, R. and Gentry, J. (2007a) Single Fathers and Household Production and Consumption: Their Story, and their Children's. *European Advances in Consumer Research,* proceedings forthcoming.

Harrison, R. and Gentry, J. (2007b) The Vulnerability of Single Fathers Adjusting to their New Parental Role. *European Advances in Consumer Research,* proceedings forthcoming.

Jenkins, R. L. (1979) The influence of Children in Family Decision Making: Parents' Perceptions. *Advances in Consumer Research.* Vol. 6, pp. 413-418.

John, D. R. (1999) Consumer Socialisation of Children: A Retrospective Look at Twenty-Five Years of Research. *Journal of Consumer Research.* Vol. 26 pp 183 – 213.

Johnson, M., McPhail, J., and Yau, O. (1994) Conflict in Family Purchase Decision Making: A Proposal for an Investigation of the factors influencing the choice of conflict resolution strategies by children. *Asia Pacific Advances in Consumer Research*. Vol. 1, pp. 229-236.

Johnson, P. (1976) Women and Power: Toward a Theory of Effectiveness. *Journal of Social Issues*. Vol. 32, pp 99-110.

Lee, C. K. C. and Beatty, S. E. (2002) Family Structure and Influence in Family Decision Making. *The Journal of Consumer Marketing*. Vol 19 (1) pp 24 – 39.

Lee, C. K. C. and Collins, B. A. (2000) Family Decision Making and Coalition Patterns. *European Journal of Marketing*. Vol. 34 (9) pp 1181 – 1198.

Mandell, N. (1991) 'The Least Adult Role in Studying Children' In F. Waksler (Ed.) *Studying the Social Worlds of Children: Sociological Readings* (pp 38-59). London: Falmer Press.

Mangleburg, T. and Grewal, D. (1999) Family Type, Family Authority Relations, and Adolescents. Purchase Influence. *Advances in Consumer Research*. Vol. 26, pp 379-384.

Mason, J. (2004) 'The Legal Context' In S. Fraser, V. Lewis, S. Ding, M. Kellett and C. Robinson (Eds) *Doing Research with Children and Young People* (pp 43-58). London: Sage.

Mayall, B. (1994) *Children's Childhoods: Observed and Experienced*. London: Falmer Press.

Miles, M. B. and Huberman, A. M. (1984) *Qualitative Data Analysis: A Sourcebook of New Methods*. Beverly Hills: Sage.

Morrow, V. and Richards, M. (1996) The ethics of social research with children: An Overview. *Children and Society*. Vol. 10, pp 90 – 105.

Moschis, G. P. and Mitchell, L. G. (1986) Television Advertising and Interpersonal Influences on Teenager's Participation in Family Consumer Decisions. *Advances in Consumer Research*. Vol. 13, pp 181 – 186.

Palan, K. M. and Wilkes, R. E. (1997) Adolescent-Parent Interaction in Family Decision Making. *Journal of Consumer Research*. Vol. 24, pp 159 – 169.

Schachter, F. F. and Stone, R. K. (1985) Difficult Sibling, Easy Sibling: Temperament and the Within-Family Environment. *Child Development*. Vol. 56, pp 1335-1344.

Shoham, A. and Dalakas, V. (2003) Family Consumer Decision-Making in Israel: The Role of Teens and Parents. *The Journal of Consumer Marketing*. Vol. 20 (2/3) pp. 238-251.

Spiggle, S. (1994) Analysis and Interpretation of Qualitative Data in Consumer Research. *Journal of Consumer Research*. Vol. 21, pp 491-503.

Szybillo, G. J. and Sosanie, A. (1977) Family Decision Making: Husband, Wife and Children. *Advances in Consumer Research*. Vol. 4, pp 46-49.

Thoits, P. A. (1992) Identity Structures and Psychological Well-Being: Gender and Marital Status Comparisons. *Social Psychology Quarterly*. Vol. 55, pp 236-256.

Thompson, C. J. (1996) Caring Consumers: Gendered Consumption Meanings and the Juggling Lifestyle. *Journal of Consumer Research*. Vol. 22, pp 388-407.

Thompson, C. J. (2005) Consumer Risk Perceptions in a Community of Reflexive Doubt. *Journal of Consumer Research*. Vol. 32, pp 235-248.

Thompson, C. J. and Troester, M. (2002) Consumer Value System in the Age of Postmodern Fragmentation: The Case of the Natural Health Microculture. *Journal of Consumer Research*. Vol. 28 (4) pp 550-571.

Thompson, C. J., Locander, W. B. and Pollio, H. R. (1989) Putting Consumer Experience Back into Consumer Research: The Philosophy and Method of Existential-Phenomenology. *Journal of Consumer Research*. Vol. 16, pp 133 – 146.

Thompson, E. S., Laing, A. W. and McKee, L. (2007) Family Purchase Decision Making: Exploring Child Influence Behaviour. *Journal of Consumer Behaviour*. Vol. 6, pp. 182-202.

Tinson, J. and Nancarrow, C. (2005) The Influence of Children on Purchases: The Development of Measures for Gender Role Orientation and Shopping Savvy. *International Journal of Market Research*. Vol. 47 (1) pp. 5-27.

Wang, S., Holloway, B. B., Beatty, S. E. and Hill, W. W. (2007) Adolescent Influence in Family Purchase Decisions: An Update and Cross-National Extension. *Journal of Business Research*. Vol. 60, pp. 1117-1124.

Ward, S., and Wackman, D. (1972) Children's Purchase Influence Attempts and Parental Yielding. *Journal of Marketing Research*. Vol. 9, pp 316-319.

Ward, S., Wackman, D. B. and Wartella, E. (1977) The Development of Consumer Information-Processing Skills: Integrative Cognitive Development and Family Interaction Theories. *Advances in Consumer Research*. Vol. 4, pp 166-171.

Williams, L. A. and Burns, A. C. (2000) Exploring the Dimensionality of Children's Direct Influence Attempts. *Advances in Consumer Research*. Vol. 27, pp 64 – 71.

Consuming Buddhism: The Pursuit Of Happiness

Siwarit Pongsakornrungsilp, Walailuk University, Thailand

Theeranuch Pusaksrikit, The University of the Thai Chamber of Commerce, Thailand

INTRODUCTION

Buddhism has been an important part of Thai religion and culture for hundreds of years. In the past few years the emerging trend in Thailand has been the renewal of interest in Buddhism, particularly among younger generations. People now experience Buddhism through new media including YouTube, Facebook, and Twitter. Materials such as CDs, DVDs, and MP3s are full of Buddha's teachings. In addition, there is evidence showing that a dozen Dhamma pocket books have been listed in the 100 top selling pocket books (Se-Ed, 2011). It becomes very common to see many Thai people attending sessions of Dhamma talks, watching Dhamma TV programs, or listening to Dhamma songs. Moreover, on New Year's Eve, instead of going out for partying, thousands of people choose to come to temples for chanting and praying. During New Year celebrations, many of them take temple tours to pay respect to the images of Buddha at various well-known temples. The increase in sales of certain types of religious consumption reaches millions of Thai Buddhists. This indicates that Thai Buddhists are getting religion in many other ways. Religious consumption is very much a part of Thai society whether people consume through print media, electronic media, music, films, clothing, and other sacred objects.

Religious consumption is an activity that covers various parts of life, including the marketplace (Daniels, 2005), identity formation/maintenance (Wattanasuwan and Elliott, 1999), and entertainment (Romanowski, 1996). While religious consumption is a general phenomenon, it is a distinct feature for some more than others. As consumers' economic power increases, choices in material religious consumption grow significantly (Park and Baker, 2007). Along with the increase in consumption of material religious products, there is the growing recognition of practicing religion.

In consumer research, many scholars (e.g., Pongsakornrungsilp, Pusaksrikit, and Schroeder, 2010; Skousgaard, 2006; Veer and Shankar, 2011; Wattnasuwan and Elliott, 1999) have employed spirituality and religion to understand consumer behavior. For example, Wattanasuwan and Elliott (1999) studied the identity consumption among teenage Buddhists in Thailand in order to understanding how these teenagers who are dominated by Western consumer culture construct their selves through Buddhism.

Although religious consumption is not a recent phenomenon, it is important to understand how religious consumption associates and transforms consumer experience in spirituality. Buddhists consume their religion following the principle of Buddhism. Thus, this paper aims to study through the lens of Buddhist people about why and how Buddhists acquire and consume Buddhism in Thailand.

Furthermore, this study provides an additional perspective of Buddhism consumption by demonstrating that Buddhism is not entirely related to the abandonment of self or no-self as mentioned in many works (e.g. Wattanasuwan and Elliott, 1999). In fact, many studies state that consumers who have the strong belief in spirituality tend to attach themselves with materialism. This study demonstrates the different stages of consuming Buddhism whereby the self and material attachments do gradually dilute when Buddhists have pursued the Buddhism practices such as performing meritorious deeds, praying, and meditation. It is worth noting that only at the nirvana stage, one is no self or emptiness (Buddhadasa Bhikkhu, 2009). In the next section, we employ the concept of spirituality to demonstrate consumer insights related their religious belief.

Thai Buddhist Consumers and Buddhism Consumption

Buddhism plays a key role in Thai people's lives as it is the major religion in Thailand. Approximately 94 per cent of Thais are Buddhists (National Statistical Office, 2010). Buddhism is seen by Thai people as a way of living, a national identity, and the characteristics of being Thai (Wattanasuwan and Elliott, 1999). 'Wat' or temple has become the center of mind for Thai Buddhists. It is mentioned by the Office of National Buddhism (2009) that there are 35,773 temples in Thailand. Moreover, Buddhist temples are the center of Thai communities in foreign countries. For many Thais, experiencing or connecting with Buddhism often occurs through consuming the sacred material objects or religious goods. These sacred objects are highly personal and accessible to a large number of consumers (Park and Baker, 2007). The distribution of popular religious goods has been an integral part of Buddhist culture in Thailand since the 19th century. With the development of production and technology, more religious products are now available than ever before.

However, it is accepted that consuming religious material objects does not make you a good Buddhists (Punyanantaphikku, 2007). Doing so is seen as having only a superficial adherence to the tenets of Buddhism (Wattanasuwan and Elliott, 1999). In fact, Buddhist consumption is not a concept most Thai Buddhists are engaged in, even though most of them declare to be Buddhists themselves. According to Puntasen (2005), there are two main reasons for this occurrence. First, most Thais who claim to be Buddhists do not really understand the core concept of Buddha's teaching due to the dominance of capitalism worldview. Looking outside this economic worldview becomes much more difficult as most economic teaching and training emphasize an appreciation of economic mechanisms. Second, the main objective of Buddhism consumption is not to gain pleasure from material possession, but to maintain physical and mental well-being by being involved in the principle of right thought, action, and livelihood (Zadek, 1993). This principle serves as the fundamental tool to relieve individuals and society from suffering (see also Pongsakornrungsilp et al., 2010).

Consumption is said to be one of the main marketing activities. It is simply defined as the acquisition, usage, and disposition of goods and services to satisfy demand or desire (Kotler and Kwller, 2009). The fundamental concepts in the consumer behavior process are want, choice, consumption, and satisfaction, which describe the basic process of people's lives. Buddhism consumption, however, defines consumption differently. Buddhism consumption is defined as the acquisition, usage and disposition of goods and services to satisfy the desire for true well-being (Payutto, 1994). It considers whether or not physical and mental well-being is adversely affected by that consumption. This consideration is often overlooked by producers and marketers. The main purpose of Buddhism consumption is to form a basis for the further development of human capability (Payutto, 1994).

The key characteristics of Buddhism consumption are that the desires are controlled by moderation and the objective of well-being (Payutto, 1994). Buddhism consumption, therefore, holds on to the middle path. Too little consumption will lead to deficiencies that can be harmful to physical and mental well-being. Too much accumulation of material wealth will bring more pain as a result of cravings (Puntasen, 2005). Today's society encourages consumption that can lead to delusion, intoxication, and health and mental problems. Buddhists recognize that certain demands can be satisfied through mindful consumption (Sheth, Sethia, and Srinivas, 2011). Additionally, refraining from consuming can play a role in satisfying spiritual needs. In this study, Buddhism consumption which is so central to millions of Thais will be understood more holistically by including not only what one believes, but how one exercises such belief. Hence, the questions are raised in relation to how and why Buddhism is consumed, and how religious consumption is associated with Buddhist belief.

SPIRITUALITY

Spirituality is a distinct element that influences people's way of life. It involves either religious or non-religious beliefs and behavior, which people can obtain individually and collectively through acquiring skills, practices, artifacts, or qualifications during their spiritual journey within a social group (Skousgaard, 2006). Spirituality concept is sometimes constructed in a close link with materialist view (Reindfleish, 2005). Gould (2006) identifies this view as spiritual materialism, in which it occurs when consumers consume spirituality in the same way as they consume products. He then illustrates material-spiritual orientation and divides it into four levels: (1) completely materialistically orientated without a spiritual connection, (2) asceticism, (3) spiritualized self-transformation, and (4) spiritualized self-liberation (Gould, 2006, p. 66).

Spirituality and religion are shared constructs that have idiosyncratic characteristics (Miller and Thoresen, 2003). While many empirical studies treat both constructs quite the same, Miller and Thoresen (2003) suggest the way to differentiate these constructs is by viewing religion as a social phenomenon and viewing spirituality on an individual level.

Research regarding the influence of spirituality and religion has been thoroughly studied in the field of psychology. The findings support the notion that individuals who are highly spiritual or religious have fewer physical and mental health problems, recover from illness quickly and experience less stress (Duffy, 2006). In addition, it also shows that highly spiritual individuals can develop a worldview that promotes well-being and an optimistic view on life. This is because spirituality can help transform a negative into a positive perspective. In Pongsakornrungsilp et al.'s (2010) study on co-creation brand through myth-making and spirituality, they found that spiritual experience is the authentic experience that interact, share and co-create power to benefit people's minds and their belief in order to form the consumption process and the meaning of the brands. However, the limited research on spirituality, religion, and consumption restricts the understanding of the dynamics of spirituality in the marketplace (Skousgaard, 2006). It is possible that spirituality can help explain the dynamics between individuals and religious consumption.

METHODS

We employed two main methods for this study. First, we proposed to understand how consumers consume Buddhism from one of the most

visited online Buddhism communities in the world, Palungjit.com. There were around 339,110 members in February 2011 (Palungjit.com, 2011). We conducted the empirical netnographic study by observing, participating, and co-creating (as insiders) the culture of a group within Palungjit.com. This group is co-created by different members who have different backgrounds. In this forum, members have different intentions to collaborate in the collective network such as searching for amulets, donating their resources, and discussing their meditation experience and other Buddhism practices. There have been 3,226 regular members with 42,243 posts and 1,610,796 views since May 2010. We also used personal messaging (PM) to follow up additional data from prominent informants.

Additionally, we also employed ethnographic method to collect data by participating in different Buddhism practices such as attending a meditation retreat, listening to Dhamma talks, and performing meritorious deeds. We conducted participant and non-participant observation during the practices. As mentioned by Kozinets (2010), netnographic study should not require only one data collection technique, but researchers also need additional study to insure that they can get the relevant data. One of the authors also attended a 5-day meditation retreat in the participation observation method, and also interviewed other attendants during February, 2011. Both netnography and ethnography allow authors to understand how and why Buddhists commit to Buddhism practices.

RESULTS

This study provides additional insights of Wattanasuwan and Elliott's (1999) Buddhism consumption. Their data were collected from Thai Buddhists who live in the urban community, especially in Bangkok, where Western culture has dominated consumer culture. Buddhist teenagers domesticate through postmodern activities such as music, films, and western-branded products (Wattanasuwan and Elliott, 1999). These teenagers view Buddhism as the extraordinary way to escape from their complicated lives. On the other hand, this study considers various groups of Buddhists who engage in Buddhist rituals and experience consumer culture in a different manner.

This study found that Thai Buddhists consume Buddhism in various ways with different purposes. Most Thai Buddhists have experienced Buddhism since childhood and gradually adopt additional practices when they grow up (e.g., performing meritorious deeds, praying, and practicing meditation). Learning from family and schools, many Thai Buddhists acculturate Buddhism practices into their everyday lives. Many of them observe five *sila* or precepts and consume some practices as parts of Thai culture. The findings show that many Thai Buddhists go through different stages of Buddhism consumption. Moreover, this study also found the dematerialization among Buddhism practices. As demonstrated in Figure 1, materialism and spirituality are degraded from lower to higher levels.

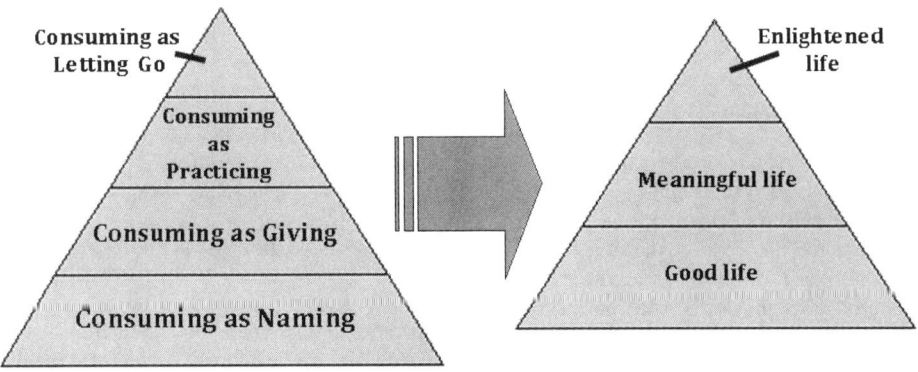

Figure 1: Buddhism Consumption and Purposes

Consuming as Naming

The first stage of consuming Buddhism is related to accepting oneself as a Buddhist. In general, many Thais become Buddhists following their Buddhist parents. There is no need to participate in any affirmation rituals. This stage is a fundamental level of becoming Buddhist. However, many Buddhists do not acculturate Buddhism in their everyday life, despite the fact that they live in the Buddhist environment. The following posts are examples of consuming as naming:

Dara: "I declare myself as Buddhist, but I never really engage in any kinds of Buddhist practices. I only follow the religion my parents respect."

Ed: "Being a Buddhist is something I've become since I was little. I learned about Buddhism in school, so I know about the historical part but I hardly practice Buddhism."

Like Dara and Ed, many Buddhists do not engage in Buddhist practices, even though they know the importance of Buddhism since their childhood. They understand what is 'good' or 'bad' and 'right' or 'wrong', but they do not embody with Buddhism practices and path. They consume Buddhism merely as a small part of their cultural identity. This is because they consider Buddhism as the morality rather than the religion (Buddhadasa Bhikkhu, 2009). Quite often many Buddhists who touch on a superficial part of Buddhism will consider Buddhism as the sacred religion when they face problems or suffer from their desires. Therefore, spirituality is employed to persuade these Buddhists to engage in Buddhism.

Consuming as Giving

The second stage refers to consuming as giving. Giving away material objects and performing meritorious deeds are very typical types of Buddhism consumption. Many Buddhists engage in this type of consumption since their childhood and continue doing so in their adulthood. However, the concept of giving for Buddhists is defined in various levels. Besides giving away things to people in needs, some Buddhists also view donating their blood, organs, or even their dead bodies as the beginning of eliminating their selfhood. Many also attempt to give the knowledge of Buddha's teaching or Dhamma in the forms of CD, DVD, books, and leaflets to others as they believe giving Dhamma is the best of giving.

Giving is a very important foundation of consuming Buddhism. By performing these giving activities, many Buddhists intend to accumulate 'Boon' or merit that they believe the merit can provide them with good fortune and strengthen them to overcome any obstacles. This spirituality of consumption is one of the main life goals which most Buddhists want to achieve. In addition, many Buddhists believe that the next life and the samsaric circle (birth – death – rebirth) depend on the obtained merit (Payutto, 1994). They expect to gain more merit so that they can have their life after death in heaven. This study found that the more Buddhists engage in giving activities, the more they connect with their religion.

Charlie: "I've given monks foods since I was a little... Accumulating merit would bring good things into my life. So I believe you have to make merits as often as you can."

Patty: "My mum always asks me to join her deeds at the temple. When I was sick or unhappy, I would go to make merits by giving food, money or products to monks. It makes me feel better."

Dorn: "Every week, I go to the temple to give alms. I dedicate the merit to the venerable monks who produced the amulets. Doing this would give them supernatural power which can increase my luck and fortune."

This study shows that Buddhists consider practicing the rituals of giving as the ordinary experience that they participate in their daily life. We found from participating in this practice that most Buddhists feel delightful to participate, socialize, and share in order to make merits. As mentioned by Dorn, spirituality is one of the aspects that some Buddhists would like to gain from engaging in giving. This demonstrates the *intrinsic-active-self oriented value* (Holbrook, 2006) which consumers obtain from Buddhism practices. At this stage, accumulating merits may help these givers/donors learn to give and distribute their wealth to others. For many Buddhists this action, however, does not lessen their desire to occupy material objects. This is because many of them give with the purpose of reciprocity. It is not that they want to receive things back from receivers, but their hope is to gain spirituality in this life or the next life. The second stage represents the accumulation of merits through the means of giving to gain the better life in return. Additionally, these Buddhists still have the desire to consume material objects to satisfy their needs and wants.

Consuming as Practicing

Moving to the third stage, a few Buddhists begin to realize that gaining wealth or becoming rich is not their ultimate life goal. They try to search for other ways to bring them the feeling of true happiness. As mentioned by Jit, she and her husband acquire various material objects, but they feel that this material acquisition cannot provide them the real happiness.

Jit: "My husband and I came from poor family background. We work extremely hard until we now have everything; a big house, a luxurious car, a lot of money to spend. Although I have all those things I want, I still don't feel happy. There is something still missing in my life..."

At this stage, praying and meditating become common practices among some Buddhists in order to make them feel calm and peaceful. They regularly listen to Dhamma talks or read Dhamma books. These Buddhists have more opportunities to learn Dhamma and accumulate knowledge of Buddhism in order to obtain a peaceful mind. They view that performing good deeds or accumulating merit by donating is only a small part of consuming Buddhism. As found in our data, consumers believe that practicing spirituality can create happiness. However, some Buddhists are much more attached with materiality and spirituality. They define the meaning of practices as a symbolic meaning of spirituality and materiality. Some perceive that practicing can give them greater merit than giving. They therefore expect to gain a high level of merits from their practice.

Montri: "I always pray to Lord Buddha every night before going to bed. I chant different Buddha praises. During my pray, I am in peace. I believe that praying would give me more merit than giving alms."

Ton: "Praying is like working. We work to gain some capital (merit). I believe that this capital can have a huge effect to my life. Like doing business, you need enough capital to run your business. So, merit is the capital for you to run your life."

Some Buddhists also choose to commit to meditation retreat as the basic way to obtain an intensive meditation. Practicing religion by participating in meditation retreat currently becomes extremely appealing to both young and adult Buddhists. These meditation retreat courses are held in various places throughout the country. Many of them are fully booked. Some places even have to book a year in advance. Retreat participants have to live with limited consumption following Buddhist's eight precepts. They have to refrain from: killing; stealing; unchaste behavior; lying; using alcohol and drugs; eating after noon; listening to music and entertainments, wearing jewelry and makeup; and using high and luxurious seats and beds.

Pen: "My interest in Dhamma comes from a best-seller pocket book "Khemtid Chevit" (Life Compass). This book creates the interest in Dhamma among young generation. As my interest grows, I then search to read a few more Dhamma books by other authors and start to attend meditation retreats. I used to ask my friends to come along, but they didn't want to. I then realize that it really depends on their past Karma."

Consuming Buddhism is the way to understand the causes of sufferings and find the way to eliminate those sufferings permanently so that they can lead the way to liberate from the samsaric cycle. Some Buddhists, however, merely expect to obtain the peaceful mind from attending meditation retreats. They thus can temporarily escape from their problem. Very few of them continually practice meditation seriously after finishing the retreats. This is an inauthentic Buddhism practice which is not the real objective of attending meditation retreat. In other words, it is similar to what found in brand community study (Muñiz and O'Guinn, 2001) that some community members have used brand in the wrong way.

Buddhists consider their practices in two meanings: peace and spirituality. To obtain the spirituality from the practice, these practitioners tend to focus on materiality of their consumption or what Sheth et al. (2011) use the term as acquisitive consumption. On the other hand, practitioners who search for peace emphasize gaining experience and knowledge of symbolic meaning. This knowledge would activate them to search for an additional level of Buddhism practice. These Buddhists still have demands in consumption, but some of them obtain more mindful mindset than another (see also Sheth et al., 2011).

Consuming as Letting Go
By accumulating and gaining knowledge from performing Buddhist rituals, a few Buddhists are interested in finding the real happiness of Buddhism – Nirvana – liberating from samsaric cycle (birth-death-rebirth) or laws of Karma (see also Wattansuwan and Elliott, 1999). Some Buddhists follow the next stage of Buddha's teaching that the key to provide the real happiness is being mindful in every thought and action. To achieve this stage, contemplating their mind is considered as the way they gain pure and strong mind.

Terk: "The core concept of Buddhism is not the learning process from the outside – that are resources such as books, CDs, or masters – but we should learn from the inside or learning to know ourselves."
Noi: "Mindfulness is the process of mind-aware practice. We have to contemplate our mind until we obtain consciousness and awareness in every moment. This process takes time, and we have to work hard. Then, we will enlighten the laws of karma."

Both Terk and Noi demonstrate an interesting issue about the liberation of samsaric cycle or Nirvana which consumes time and requires practices. However, samsaric cycle or laws of karma is not just about birth-death-rebirth, but it also relates to the awareness of nature around the self. Practicing mindfulness is the way for Buddhists to gain a strong mindset which influences them to concern the nature, and also avoid them to harm others including human beings, animals, and environment.

Dang: "Buddha has taught us to realize or be aware of nature how we can accept or live with the real situation even we don't want to. We have to concern this point during the contemplating session."
Kathy: "Buddhism is about peace and nature. Practicing mindfulness can help us understand this issue. It gradually brings us back to reach the nature. I may not attend the nirvana in this life, but I will never give up."

As mentioned above, although the highest goal of Buddhism consumption is obtaining nirvana, many Buddhists do only expect to gain a peaceful mind. In fact, practicing mindfulness is the process of accumulating mindset which supports consumers to live with nature and community (Sheth et al., 2011). Then, Buddhists who are in this stage still require goods and services as other consumers do, but their consumption would concern to themselves, environment, and community without any cravings. Moreover, Buddhism does not instruct them to abandon everything, but it shows how people can consume or behave with less harmful to environment and other consumers. This is in line with the Buddhist way that consuming Buddhism is the co-creation process of wisdom and insights for understanding "What is truly what?" Selfhood and material attachments are causes of sufferings, and engaging in Buddhist path is the only way to be free from sufferings and samsaric cycle (Buddhadasa Bhikkhu, 2009).

DISCUSSION AND CONCLUSION

This study gives an insight into what the motivations for Buddhism consumption are and contributes the prevalence of religious consumption experienced by non-Christian believers. We have extended Gould's (2006) spiritual materiality in Buddhism by demonstrating the empirical data. The findings show four stages of Buddhism consumption to achieve three main life goals. The first stage refers consuming Buddhism as naming themselves to be Buddhists. This level is the most common for most Buddhists. However, many of them do not practice Buddhism but refer themselves as Buddhists following their parents and ancestors. The second stage refers to consuming as giving. Many Buddhists believe that by giving away from small things to donating their lives, or even giving Buddha's teaching to others will lead them to the good life. Sacrificing their material and non-material objects in order to gain tranquility and spirituality is the first level of obtaining happiness in world view. The third stage refers to consuming as practicing. The main activities for Buddhists to practice are reading Dhamma books, listening to Dhamma talks, chanting, meditating, and attending meditation retreat. It is through these practices that Buddhists can find the way to search for true happiness. These practices will lead them to gain *the meaningful life*. The final stage refers to consuming as letting go. This is the hardest stage for Buddhists as they learn to think and to behave mindfully in every moment and action in order to letting go of their desire and their selfhood. It is through this consumption that Buddhists can find the way to search for true happiness. By maintaining this practice, they hope to reach *the enlightened life*. This life emphasizes the search for happiness from persistence and mindfulness.

This study has highlighted that there are different levels of Buddhism consumption, and each level can pursue through different strategies. The findings from this study provide an additional perspective to the controversial issue in consumer culture (e.g. Kilbourne, 1989). The level of consumption does not influence the level of happiness. Instead it is much more important for people to accept the real situation during the consumption process. In all stages of Buddhism consumption, the materiality has gradually degraded from Buddhists who participate in performing meritorious deeds to attending meditation retreats. For example, the second stage, consumers are much more attachment with materiality, whereby consumers co-create spirituality as a symbolic meaning through the objects. They attach their self by viewing that the more they give, the more they get merit. This shows the interconnection between spirituality and materiality. Thus, consumers tend to display 'self' in their consumption. Even in the third and fourth stages where some Buddhists intensively focus on practicing and contemplating, Buddhists still require consumption, but their cravings (e.g., prestige, beauty, scent, luxury, and so on) are lower than other Buddhists who are in a lower stage. In other words, Buddhism is not a threat to consumer culture. Buddhism is the way of learning, understanding, and accepting the nature and situation, and it also helps us understanding causes of problems or sufferings in order to search the ways to get rid of them (Payutto, 1994). Therefore, it is arguable that self is not generally prohibited in the Buddhism but reducing the level of selfness can decrease sufferings.

This study shows that religious consumption is an important issue and Buddhism as a spiritual source has much to offer. Consuming Buddhism has formed a nurturing ground for people to discover a method of personal transformation. This study shows that consumption alone may not give people's lives satisfactory meanings. Consuming Buddhism can make them aware of how they should live to gain an ultimate life goal.

Although a collective process in this study can provide an additional perspective on Buddhism consumption, we focus only on an individual process that consumers engage in Buddhism activities. Future research may explore the collective process of Buddhism consumption. Moreover, additional consumption in each stage which provides unique meanings related to materiality, spirituality, and beliefs toward Buddhism need to be explored. Future research should also examine the similarities and differences between preferences in people's selection of religious consumption. In addition, it is interesting to understand non-consumption practice, which may be evidenced by studying how Buddhist monks consume. A sense of monk's religious identity in an era of materialism may take the different form of restraining one's purchases from goods. The knowledge of monk's consumption may help to gain the understanding in creating sustainable consumption. Furthermore, supply side factors that influence religious consumption such as the availability and marketing of religious items also deserve scholarly attention. Further research inquiry into these issues will extend our understanding of religious consumption.

REFERENCES

Buddhadasa Bhikkhu, (2009), *Handbook for Mankind*, Bangkok: Department of Religious Affairs, Ministry of Culture.

Daniels, P. (2005), "Economic systems and the Buddhist worldview: The twenty first century nexus," *The Journal of Socio-Economics*, 34, 245-268.

Duffy, R. D. (2006), "Spirituality, Religion, and Career Development: Current Status and Future Directions," *The Career Development Quarterly*, 55, 52-63.

Gould, J. S. (2006), "Cooptation Through Conflation: Spiritual Materialism is Not the Same as Spirituality," *Consumption, Markets and Culture*, Vol. 9 (1), 63-78.

Holbrook, M. B. (2006), "Consumption Experience, Customer Value, and Subjective Personal Introspection: An Illustrative Photographic Essay," *Journal of Business Research*, 59 (6), 714-725.

Kilbourne, W. (1989), "The Critical Theory of Herbert Marcuse and its relationship to consumption", *American Marketing Association Proceeding*, 172-175.

Kotler, P. and Keller, K. L. (2009), *Marketing Management*, 13th edition, Upper Saddle River, New Jersey: Pearson Prentice Hall.

Miller, W. R. and Thoresen, C. E. (2003), "Spirituality, religion, and health: An emerging research field," *American Psychologist*, 58, 24-35.

Muñiz, A. M., Jr. and O'Guinn, T. C. (2001), "Brand Community," *Journal of Consumer Research*, 27 (1), 412-32.

National Statistical Office (2010), A Number of Buddhists in Thailand. On WWW at http://www.nso.go.th. Accessed on 22.12.10.

Office of National Buddhism (2009), A Number of Buddhism Temples in Thailand. On WWW at http://www.onab.go.th. Accessed on 10.01.11.

Palungjit.com (2011), An Online Buddhism Community, On WWW at http://www.palungjit.com. Accessed on 16.01.11.

Park, J. Z. and Baker, J. (2007), "What would Jesus buy: American consumption of religious and spiritual material goods," *Journal for the Scientific Study of Religion*, 46 (4), 501-517.

Payutto, P. A. (1994), *Buddhist Economic: A Middle Way for the Market Place*, trans. Dhammavijaya and Bruce Evans, 2nd edition, Bangkok: Buddhadhamma Foundation.

Pongsakornrungsilp, S., Pusaksrikit, T., and Schroeder, J.E. (2010), "Co-Creation through Fear, Faith and Desire," *European Advances in Consumer Research*, Vol. 9.

Puntasen, A. (2005), *Buddhist Economics, Evolution Theories, and Its Application to Other Economic Subject,* Bangkok: Amarin Publisher.

Punyanantaphikku (2007), No Amulet in Buddhism, *Dhammaleela*, 79, June 2007.

Romanowski, W. D. (1996), *Pop Culture Wars: Religion & the Role of Entertainment in American Life*, Downers Grove, Illinois, InterVarsity Press.

Se-Ed (2011), "The 100 Best Seller Books," On WWW at http://www.se-ed.com/eshop/BestSeller/100BestSeller.aspx. Accessed on 12.01.11.

Sheth, J. N., Sethia, N. K. and Srinivas, S. (2011), "Mindful Consumption: a Customer-Centric Approach to Sustainability," *Journal of Academy Marketing Science*, 39, 22-39.

Skousgaard, H. (2006), "A Taxonomy of Spiritual Motivations for Consumption," *Advances in Consumer Research*, Vol. 33, 294-296.

Wattanasuwan, K. and Elliott, R. (1999),"The Buddhist self and symbolic consumption: The consumption experience of the teenage Dhammakaya Buddhists in Thailand," *Advances in Consumer Research*, 26, 150-155.

Zadek, S. (1993), "The practice of Buddhist economics?: Another view," *American Journal of Economics & Sociology*, 52 (4), 433-445.

Brands as Resources in Intergenerational Cultural Transfer

Sandy Bulmer, Massey University, New Zealand
Margo Buchanan-Oliver, University of Auckland, New Zealand

ABSTRACT

Brands are part of the backdrop in which everyday family life unfolds. Household product names, games and entertainment systems, advertising jingles, distinctive packaging, branded service experiences, and commercials with familiar narratives and imagery form the reality of many young lives. Children experience brands as an integral part of their lives, much of it influenced by their families. The ways that parents choose and use brands, as trust mechanisms, heuristic frames, and symbols acting as "vessels of meaning and sentiment" (Holt 2006a, p.357), surely affects their children. Certainly, parents train their daughters and sons which brands to buy, and this type of intergenerational influence on brand equity is reported in the literature (see, for example Moore et al. 2002). Yet, despite understanding that brands play an important role in consumer culture, relatively little research has been done to investigate the ways that parents use brands as resources in their parenting.

Previous research generally has studied the socialization of children as consumers and investigated brands in terms of purchase and usage preferences passed on through families. However, consumer culture theory (Arnould and Thompson 2005) suggests that consumers not only consume brands in the traditional sense, they also use and experience them through advertisements and other marketing communications, termed 'mediated experiences' (Elliott and Wattanasuwan 1998). Brand commercials are used by consumers for purposes other than the persuasive and mostly commercial ones intended by brand owners (Arnould and Thompson 2005; Elliott and Wattanasuwan 1998; O'Donohoe 1994; Ritson and Elliott 1999). This paper explores the conceptualization of brands as resources used by parents in the intergenerational transfer of culture. The qualitative study reported analyses interviews with women and narrative accounts of their life histories to extend understanding of the role of brands in the intergenerational transfer of culture. Such an exploration is needed to extend our understanding of the ways brands impact on children over and above purchase and usage preferences imparted by parents.

THEORETICAL BACKGROUND

Brands as Resources

Consumer goods and brands play important roles within a cultural setting. There is a well developed literature on the symbolic role of consumer goods and the use of brands as resources in adult society (Arnould and Thompson 2005; Belk 1988; Bourdieu 1994; Csikszentmihalyi and Rochberg-Halton 1981; Elliott and Wattanasuwan 1998). Brands, partly through their advertisements, have a role to play in the expression of self-identity and in fostering community (Cova 1997; Firat and Dholakia 1998; Muñiz and O'Guinn 2005; Schouten and McAlexander 1995). Certainly, there is ample evidence to suggest that advertising is discussed amongst adults in everyday settings, and studies have reported the social uses of advertising amongst teenagers (Ritson and Elliott 1999). However, the literature does not yet provide much insight into parent/child conversations around brands and their advertisements.

There is a two way link between culture and brands—each impacts on the other. McCracken's (1986) seminal work in cultural anthropology advanced a theoretical account of the structure and movement of cultural meaning, suggesting advertising plays a role in providing representation of the culturally constituted world. More recently, Thompson and Tian (2008) have reported that brands, through their commercial activities, are involved in leveraging culturally rooted identities that provide narrative resources for identity projects. Their study showed that the socio-cultural context affects the way that traditions and particular constructions of the past are mythologized by advertisers and other marketing agents. Brand experiences are also thought to permit and support social connections and the building of community. For example, Cova (1997) has argued for the wider, macro-societal and communal 'linking value' of products and services (and by default the brands that symbolically represent and emblematize them). Marketers are in no doubt that brands and culture are inextricably intertwined (Holt 2006b) and yet this intersection has not been fully explored in order to conceptualize other dimensions to the relationship between culture and brands.

Cultural Transfer

Socialization during infancy and childhood is understood to be the most intense period of cultural learning (Giddens 2001) when families teach their children the information, codes, skills, attitudes, conceptions, beliefs, systems and values that constitute cultural knowledge. According to Bourdieu's (1986) concept of cultural capital, a process of domestic education is responsible for the level of cultural knowledge acquired by children, although Bourdieu "does not report how exactly cultural knowledge is transmitted within the families" (Becker 2010, p.19). Some parental activities that impact on children's cultural knowledge have been identified by education researchers, such as telling stories and reading books to children, playing cards and board games with them, doing jigsaw puzzles, visiting zoos, libraries and museums (Becker 2010). Cultural messages are reportedly embedded in daily parent-child interactions (Dunn and Brown 1991) where cultural knowledge is repeated and re-affirmed, but little is known about exactly how this occurs.

As they mature, children are impacted by other socializing influences in the social environment, particularly schools, peer groups and mass media. Media and cultural studies researchers have shown clear links between television, children and cultural identity—for example, Barker (1997) suggests that television programs become a site for discussion (about relationships and cultural taboos) amongst children and a point of contact between children and adults. Researchers have particularly focused on the globalizing forces of mass media impacting on the world of the child, as young people develop an increasingly cosmopolitan identity (Barker 1999). Much less has been written about the impact of advertising and brand stories on incidental conversations and opportunistic teaching occasions that contribute to cultural transfer and ultimately play a part in parents' attempts to acculturate and socialize their children.

CULTURAL KNOWLEDGE

Cultural knowledge takes many different forms and impacts on all processes of life. At one level culture is concerned with refined and sophisticated society and the visible, overt creative expressions of literature, art, music and architecture. Cultural knowledge in these spheres is necessarily predicated on more fundamental socio-cultural knowledge that is essential for the most basic and mundane operations of society. Within a culture there are ideas which define the things that are "considered important, worthwhile and desirable" (Giddens 2001, p.22). These values are enshrined in the cultural norms of behavior, both of which are actively learned rather than inherited or passively acquired. Social roles, social identities and self-identity are negotiated by individuals as they interact with others in society and use cultural knowledge as a framework to guide their social interactions. Thus, cultural knowledge is required for both micro and macro aspects of life as individuals negotiate and link their personal and public worlds.

Having a shared sense of the past and a common interpretation of history is one dimension of cultural knowledge. Halbwachs (1992) proposed that social groups actively construct and sustain a sense of unity and cohesion by reproducing collective and cultural memories. Collective forgetting and remembering involves reconstructing histories that serve to unite society and emphasize defining moments of the past, thus creating a 'usable past' (Brooks 1915). Advertisers evoke the shared past using archival materials and recreations of easily recognized scenes, relying on the audience's imagination to complete the story. The way that an individual evaluates the past impacts on how they evaluate the way they are and the way they were. Personal nostalgia (Stern 1992), the content of an individual's memories, what they remember about their personal past and their point of view/perspective on the past, has implications for how the past affects the present (Wilson and Ross 2003) and colors the transmission of cultural knowledge to younger generations.

Cultural knowledge enables familiarity with myths, symbols, codes and meanings that confer insider status within a cultural group. There are many place based myths that are considered foundational in a culture. Desire for attachment to place is evident in the powerful myth New Zealanders tell the outside world, of a kind of unspoiled Garden of Eden at the bottom of the world. The propagators of this myth consider it a great blessing to live in harmony with the wild and sacred natural world of New Zealand (Bell 1996). Scenic representations, buildings, signage, statues and symbolic artifacts link members of society. Thus, distinctive, quintessential cultural knowledge is passed on so that new generations are acculturated and socialized into their own society.

Another specialized form of cultural knowledge is persuasion knowledge (Friestad and Wright 1994, 1995). Part of being socialized into a culture means learning how to negotiate everyday life in places of commerce, to make sense of the media and communications technology, and to how cope with commercial/persuasive messages. The behaviors and skills required are based on particular cultural knowledge that very young children start to learn while accompanying family members as they shop. The literature points to programs in schools that aim to develop what is termed media literacy, knowledge and skills needed to function in contemporary media culture (Potter 2011). Parents also actively teach their children about advertising and marketing, passing on cultural knowledge about how consumers are influenced by commercial messages, how to identify and resist persuasion attempts, and how to perform the role of a wise consumer.

METHOD

The findings reported in our paper are drawn from a study of brands and national identity. Themes of intergenerational national identity transfer were identified in this study. However, other unexpected connections between brands and intergenerational cultural transfer (unrelated to national identity) emerged, and these are discussed in the following section. In summary, the study employed narrative analysis, and utilized a two part interview method using life history and narrative techniques in conjunction with the use of a selection of actual television brand advertisements. Interviews were conducted with middle aged women in a major New Zealand city. Snowball sampling was used to recruit friendship pair participants—ten pairs of friends (twenty individual informants) participated in

the study. The interviews were digitally audio-taped and transcribed, using pseudonyms to preserve participant anonymity. Subsequent thematic analysis and coding was facilitated using NVivo8 qualitative data management software. The entire study utilized a discourse analysis methodology.

Autobiographical narratives, in the form of life histories illustrating national identity, were elicited from each individual participant. These depth interview sessions were designed to focus on issues in terms of the implications and experiences of individual consumers, so that important findings would flow from detailed analyses of particular life histories (Firkin 2004). In the second part of the fieldwork protocol, interviews were conducted with friendship pairs, as reported in studies by Banister and Hogg (2004). Two people, who had related consumption characteristics and similar world views, were interviewed together, providing "an effective means through which to ensure a more natural setting within which to negotiate identity talk" (Banister and Hogg 2004, p.857). During the interviews participants were shown six well known television brand communications. This was used to set the scene for discussing experiences of brands and identity. As the discussion evolved, conversation moved on from the selected brands' advertisements to other occasions of consuming brand narratives and the subsequent experiences of identity. It was during this time that intergenerational themes were revealed.

FINDINGS AND DISCUSSION

Beliefs, Values and Norms

Generally talking to their children about advertising was a theme common amongst the participants. However, it was not just the overarching *concept* of advertising that people talked about; parents used specific, branded stories as a resource in passing on cultural knowledge to their children. Sensitive issues (possibly including relationships, puberty and death) could be introduced (by parent or child) into a discussion as a result of shared ad viewing. Participant comments relating to the U by Kotex *Beaver* tampon ad indicated this. During the interviews both Tess and Belinda noted their relief at not having to answer questions arising from the U by Kotex commercial but were aware of the potential for such parent child discussions.

I have seen the beaver one once. (Tess)
You had to explain it to your [seven year old] *daughter? (laughter) (Sharon)*
No, God no! (Tess)
... you'd take an interest in it, like the beaver ad because it relates to you because you know your daughter [a teenager] *didn't pick up on that* [vulgar terminology]. *(Belinda)*
Lana, who had young school-aged children, commented in general:
... if there was something that had a bit of an adult theme about it and I wanted to give the kids a kind of bare level thing on it I might say, "Oh yes well," you know, kind of disguise the adult theme in something that's a bit more appropriate for them. (Lana)

While the brand itself (U by Kotex) might not have been discussed, the interviews clearly illustrated the ways that the narratives embedded in brand advertisements act as resources for parents as they interact with their children and transfer cultural knowledge of taboos, socially appropriate language and sexual mores onto the next generation. This occurrence almost certainly was not intended or explicitly considered by the brand owners and their advertising agents, highlighting the polysemy in advertising (Phillips 1997; Puntoni,

Schroeder, and Ritson 2010).

Other types of cultural beliefs and stereotypes were also passed on by parents in this study. Brand advertising provided the script for parents to illustrate strongly held beliefs about being culturally distinct, to a new generation—for example, children were told about the much talked about trans-Tasman (Australia-New Zealand) rivalry, as illustrated in the Mitre 10 *Sandpit* ad.

> Yeah, yeah, saying they're gonna build a wall and they ask the Aussie guy and he says, "Oh you're dreaming mate," when they asked if he would come over and help. (Georgina)
> Spoke to my kids about that. Oh they were laughing, thought it was hilarious. (Helen)
> Yeah? (Researcher)
> Yeah, they thought it was really funny. (Helen)
> "No surprises there!"(Georgina)

The children in the example above were already aware of the practice of making Australians the butt of local New Zealand humor which highlights Australian cultural stereotypes: laziness, stupidity, brashness and boorishness. Both their mothers reinforced this stereotypical belief when the opportunity presented itself, thanks to the Mitre 10 home handyman brand narrative. Furthermore, due to the mothers' singular commentary and discussion about the advertisement they culturally heightened the issue in their children's consciousness and affirmed the cultural lensing the brand advertisement provided. Similarly, Marcia highlighted that she made a point of talking to her children about ads which exemplified beliefs about Australians. A recent trip to Australia with her children had provided much brand advertising material to feed conversations comparing Australians and New Zealanders.

> Do you ever talk about ads with your kids? (Researcher)
> Oh only the Australian stupid dickhead ones, eh? They're so bad. You know, they think they've got a sense of humor but they don't match us at all, have you noticed that? They're bloody shocking. You know they're Australian even if they don't have an accent you think, "That was made in Australia." (Marcia)
> After denigrating Australian people for a while, Marcia continued;
> And their ads are the same, they're really, they're very immature and just stupid. You sort of look at them and think, "What?" You know, yeah. (Marcia)
> So you talked to your kids about those when you were there? (Researcher)
> And when we're here because if we see them here we know they're Australian because of the tone, yeah. (Marcia)

Social Memories

The findings in this study clearly demonstrate the facility of brands to embed collective memories and a shared sense of the past in their narratives. The women in this study used the social memories and the usable past provided by brand stories as conversational resources for use in object lessons re-creating the past. In the following text units, Belinda refers to a famous local soda brand advertisement. The brand narrative tells of a group of carefree children who are enjoying a small community swimming pool during the summer vacation. Cinematographically, it evokes the feel of the 1970s and the advertisement is edited to simulate a nostalgic documentary.

> I saw that on TV and my daughter was with me and I said, "That was what it was like when we were kids." And she just went,

> (gagging noise made). (Belinda)
> So there, you do. You do talk to people. You talk to your kids. (Researcher)
> Yeah, I did say, "Oh that's exactly what it was like when we were kids," and I said, "Me and Meredith used to do that," and I told, she knows Meredith. And I told her and she goes, "Uh. Oh yeah." (Belinda)
> She looked really bored? (Researcher)
> She looked like I was saying we went to school on a horse and cart basically. Like when we were kids we used to get all about the war and I used to think, "Oh God, here he goes." So, yeah. (Belinda)
> So why did you mention it to your daughter? (Researcher)
> I think I did say something to her because I just sometimes think that we're just too PC nowadays. Everything has to, you know, the kids are just so molly coddled, now they can't walk the streets, they can't, everything. You know, it's just not the same for safety or, I'm not saying that there was safety in those days 'cause we still had people that were a bit peculiar, if not very peculiar, but you didn't worry about it like you do now, do you? (Belinda)

Belinda used the famous brand soda advertisement to illustrate the simple pleasures of her girlhood, a "golden age" where earlier generations of children were independent, never bored and did not have to worry about contemporary issues such as 24/7 parental supervision, sun protection and swimming pool safety protocols.

> But they'd be thinking, "Where's the lifeguard? Where's the sun screen? Where's the parents?" (Belinda)
> "And can I plug my iPod in somewhere?" (Ann)
> *Yeah. (Belinda)*
> *"And where can I put my* [hair] *straightener for afterwards?" (Ann)*
> *Yeah. Yeah. "And where's the shower block 'cause I don't want to get chlorine in my hair?" You know, it's, they couldn't relate to that at all, no. (Belinda)*

As Ann later mentioned:

> I think we're just trying to make that generational point that this is how life used to be and everybody was happy with it, you know? (Ann)

It was important to the women in the study to teach their children about the past, because collective reaffirmations of identity help individuals within a society to maintain a sense of self-identity and connectedness to others. The patterns of leisure, dress and family life that represent a culture at a certain time were evocatively captured in the commercial brand narrative. These brand nostalgic stories provided an opportunity for parents to teach their children how identities continue to evolve as individuals, as socially constructed concepts of the family and as a culture. These consumers of such historical constructions used them to locate themselves within a long term context by comparing then and now, who we were and who we are now.

Ways of Talking About Place

Findings from this study clearly showed that parents used brand advertising to socialize their children into the accepted ways of talking about the land and important symbolic places valued by society.

> Now you already said the kids ... Did you say you talked about the scenery with them? (Researcher)
>
> Yeah, like when I saw that Air New Zealand ad for the first time.

(Donna)

So what did you say …? (Researcher)
I just said to them that, "Look how beautiful our country is, you know. That's what our country looks like out of Auckland." (Donna)

In general, the findings showed that brand ads provided commonly available representations of places in the heart (such as holiday homes) and, as such, constitute a widely available conversational resource, as noted by Virginia and Waverley.

[My husband] *might have said "You know that ad? Well that's like the bach* [holiday home] *that we used to go to and we'd, like that, we used to do that too." We'd often use ads as a point of reference when talking about a story, of recreating a story from our childhood or something because everyone knows ads. (Virginia)*
I do the same. (Waverley)

The study provided evidence that brand commercials for products and services ranging from airlines, banks and paint to cheese employed the cultural codes and conventions for representing, visualizing and telling stories about place. This meant that even if families were unable to visit such places, brands put resources at their disposal to facilitate the intergenerational flow of cultural knowledge relating to place, as the previous text units show.

Persuasion Knowledge

The findings of this study showed that at the most basic level, ads provided an opportunity to educate children about the ways of the world. For example, the techniques used in making ads were sometimes a point of discussion between parents and children.

So what would you say if it was your kids and they, if you were having a discussion, what would be the nature of the discussion that you'd have with them? (Researcher)
Just, "How do you think they worked out, how do you think they've done that?" Like the latest Gorilla [she then realizes her mistake—she does not mean the Gorilla ad]*, Cadbury ad has got, they're playing, they're doing a song with their eyebrows, they're raising their eyebrows up and stuff so it's all computer generated. (Georgina)*

In this case above, the brand provided resources and the parents of pre-teens used shared viewing occasions as an opportunity to develop knowledge about how ads are made. This form of cultural knowledge is part of what Friestad and Wright (1994, 1995) termed persuasion knowledge—culturally relevant knowledge about advertisers' goals and tactics. Georgina used Cadbury resources and the Socratic Method to stimulate critical thinking and illuminate particular ideas that she deemed important for her children to know.

While older children may learn to be media savvy through personal interactions with peer groups and at school, parents still play a part in intergenerational cultural transfer and developing persuasion knowledge. Waverley and Virginia revealed that their teenage daughters, who are friends, have had parental discussions and compared notes about ads.

Do you talk with your daughter about it? (Researcher)
Imogen knows the tunes to all the ads and I say, "My God, you know that song off by heart," but we don't really have a conversation about it. (Waverley)

You haven't talked about how they're trying to get you to do something because of the ad? (Virginia)
Oh yeah, we do talk about things like that. (Waverley)
Yeah, yeah, yeah I knew Waverley would. (Virginia)
Yeah, I'm from the perspective of how they're manipulating your mind, we often talk about things like that. (Waverley)
Yeah, 'cause I knew you would. That's because, yeah, because Waverley, sorry Imogen and Jody have talked about that ad so our children have talked about stuff about what it's doing or its suggestiveness. Yeah. (Virginia)
From a persuasiveness marketing angle. We do talk about things like that. (Waverley)

In the previous example a more critical, media studies approach has been used by the mothers in discussing the influence and social impact of ads. Again, the mothers responded to specific brand communications, using them as a launching pad for discussions with their children about commercial motivations, persuasion and how to be an informed consumer, all based on essential cultural knowledge.

CONCLUSIONS

The findings provide support for Elliott and Wattanasuwan's (1998, p.135) claims that mediated experiences of brands can provide resources that, "*interlaced with lived experience,*" are used in imagining the self within a particular socio-cultural and historical context. The intergenerational processes facilitated by brands are an extension of Ritson and Elliott's (1999) concept of the social uses aspect of advertising. With respect to brand narratives, these findings confirm Thompson and Tian's (2008) claim that commercial activities offer views of the past and provide narrative resources for cultural identity projects.

Evidence from this study provides insights into the intergenerational transfer of cultural knowledge. The mothers who participated in our study provided unexpected narratives which demonstrated the process of domestic education referred to by Bourdieu (1986). Usage of television brand advertising for teaching and learning during unscheduled occasions was for them, an unremarkable, everyday type of parenting experience. However, evidence of this has not been reported previously in the consumer research and marketing literature.

Particular forms of cultural knowledge, embedded in brand narratives, were utilized during the ongoing process of socialization. Beliefs, values and norms relating to taboos, socially appropriate language and sexual mores were recognized by the adults as being available in brand ads for use in acculturation. Culturally based stereotypes were provided by advertisements and acted as a resource for affirming cultural beliefs and reinforcing appropriate responses to culturally referenced humor. Collective memories and a shared sense of the past was made available in nostalgic advertisements, assisting parents to reaffirm the connections between society, parents and their children and to maintain a sense of self-identity in relation to others. Cultural knowledge relating to accepted ways of talking about the land and important symbolic places was utilized by parents in response to certain brand narratives. Finally, cultural knowledge pertaining to the role of wise consumer was leveraged by parents as a result of shared consumption of particular brand narratives

This study enlarges what is known about what consumers do with brand advertisements. Even though society may have a slight sense that brands *should* not be part of the cultural landscape (Bengtsson and Ostberg 2006), the evidence is clear that, in the New Zealand setting at least, brands are significant cultural markers. A key message for brand owners from this study is that consumers can derive value from brands in ways that were previously unknown, that is, as resources in intergenerational cultural transfer. The findings underscore the important role and significance of brand marcoms as a widely accessible cultural resource used by parents in socializing their children.

We are suggesting that brand experiences and brand resources such as advertisements, play a broader socially contributive role in establishing and reinforcing elements of culture at the macro level within society in general and within families at the micro level. Brand commercials could function as one of the ties that bind generations together, enabling intergenerational knowledge transfer and memorial reconstruction at the national, the familial and individual levels. Brand advertisements are, by their ubiquity and their emotionally and symbolically infused brand narratives, pervasive meaning vessels which encapsulate cultural attitudes and values, deploying myths, popular memory and culturally relevant icons, and act as creators of nostalgic reverie. The nature of advertising scheduling on television generates serendipitous occasions for young and old to consume together, creating opportunities for cultural teaching and learning. In essence, the transfer of cultural knowledge that contributes to the socialization of children into a culture might be facilitated by brands.

REFERENCES

Arnould, Eric J and Craig J Thompson (2005), "Consumer Culture Theory (CCT): Twenty Years of Research," *Journal of Consumer Research*, 31 (4), 868-82.

Banister, Emma N and Margaret K Hogg (2004), "Negative Symbolic Consumption and Consumers' Drive for Self-Esteem: The Case of the Fashion Industry," *European Journal of Marketing*, 38 (7), 850-68.

Barker, Chris (1997), *Global Television: An Introduction*, Malden, MA: Blackwell Publishers.

Barker, Chris (1999), *Television, Globalization and Cultural Identities*, Buckingham: Open University Press.

Becker, Birgit (2010), "The Transfer of Cultural Knowledge in the Early Childhood: Social and Ethnic Disparities and the Mediating Role of Familial Activities," *European Sociological Review*, 26 (1), 17–29.

Belk, Russell W (1988), "Possessions and the Extended Self," *Journal of Consumer Research*, 15 (2), 139-68.

Bell, Claudia (1996), *Inventing New Zealand: Everyday Myths of Pakeha Identity*, Auckland: Penguin Books.

Bengtsson, Anders and Jacob Ostberg (2006), "Researching the Cultures of Brands," in *Handbook of Qualitative Research Methods in Marketing*, ed. Russell W Belk, Cheltenham: Edward Elgar Publishing Ltd, 83-93.

Bourdieu, Pierre (1986), "The Forms of Capital," in *Handbook of Theory and Research for the Sociology of Education*, ed. John G Richardson, New York: Greenwood Press, 241-58.

Bourdieu, Pierre (1994), *Distinction: A Social Critique of the Judgement of Taste*, London: Routledge.

Brooks, Van Wyck (1915), *America's Coming-of-Age*, Whitefish, MT: Kessinger Publishing.

Cova, Bernard (1997), "Community and Consumption: Towards a Definition of the "Linking Value" of Products or Services," *European Journal of Marketing*, 31 (3/4), 297-316.

Csikszentmihalyi, Mihaly and Eugene Rochberg-Halton (1981), *The Meaning of Things—Domestic Symbols and the Self*, Cambridge: Cambridge University Press.

Dunn, Judith F and Jane Brown (1991), "Becoming American or English? Talking About the Social World in England and the U.S.," in *Cross Cultural Approaches to Parenting*, ed. Marc H Bornstein, Hillsdale, NJ: Lawrence Erlbaum Associates, 155-72.

Elliott, Richard H and Kritsadarat Wattanasuwan (1998), "Brands as Symbolic Resources for the Construction of Identity," *International Journal of Advertising*, 17 (2), 134-44.

Firat, A Fuat and Nikhilesh Dholakia (1998), *Consuming People: From Political Economy to Theaters of Consumption*, London: Routledge.

Firkin, Patrick (2004), "'New Zealand Experience(s)': Biographical Narratives of Professional Migrants on Working in New Zealand," Auckland: Labour Market Dynamics Research Programme Massey University, Research report series 2004/2.

Friestad, Marian and Peter Wright (1994), "The Persuasion Knowledge Model: How People Cope with Persuasion Attempts," *Journal of Consumer Research*, 21 (1), 1-31.

Friestad, Marian and Peter Wright (1995), "Persuasion Knowledge: Lay People's and Researchers' Beliefs About the Psychology of Advertising," *Journal of Consumer Research*, 22 (1), 62-74.

Giddens, Anthony (2001), *Sociology*, Cambridge: Polity Press.

Halbwachs, Maurice (1992), *On Collective Memory*, Chicago, IL: University of Chicago Press.

Holt, Douglas B (2006a), "Jack Daniel's America: Iconic Brands as Ideological Parasites and Proselytizers," *Journal of Consumer Culture*, 6 (3), 355-77.

Holt, Douglas B (2006b), "Toward a Sociology of Branding," *Journal of Consumer Culture*, 6 (3), 299-302.

Leiss, William, Stephen Kline, and Sut Jhally (1986), *Social Communication in Advertising: Persons, Products & Images of Well-Being*, Toronto: Methuen.

Moore, Elizabeth S, William L Wilkie, and Richard J Lutz (2002), "Passing the Torch: Intergenerational Influences as a Source of Brand Equity," *Journal of Marketing*, 66 (2), 17-37.

Muñiz, Albert M and Thomas C O'Guinn (2005), "Marketing Communications in a World of Consumption and Brand Communities," in *Marketing Communication: New Approaches, Technologies, and Styles*, ed. Allan Kimmel, Oxford: Oxford University Press, 63-85.

O'Donohoe, Stephanie (1994), "Advertising Uses and Gratifications," *European Journal of Marketing*, 28 (8/9), 52-75.

Phillips, Barbara J (1997), "Thinking into It: Consumer Interpretation of Complex Advertising Images," *Journal of Advertising*, 26 (2), 77-87.

Potter, W James (2011), *Media Literacy*, Thousand Oaks, CA: Sage Publications.

Puntoni, Stefano, Jonathan E Schroeder, and Mark Ritson (2010), "Meaning Matters: Polysemy in Advertising," *Journal of Advertising*, 39 (2), 51-64.

Ritson, Mark and Richard H Elliott (1999), "The Social Uses of Advertising: An Ethnographic Study of Adolescent Advertising Audiences," *Journal of Consumer Research*, 26 (3), 260-77.

Schouten, John W and James H McAlexander (1995), "Subcultures of Consumption: An Ethnography of the New Bikers," *Journal of Consumer Research*, 22 (1), 43-61.

Stern, Barbara B (1992), "Historical and Personal Nostalgia in Advertising Text: The Fin De Siècle Effect " *Journal of Advertising*, 21 (4), 11-22.

Thompson, Craig and Kelly Tian (2008), "Reconstructing the South: How Commercial Myths Compete for Identity Value through the Ideological Shaping of Popular Memories and Countermemories," *Journal of Consumer Research*, 34 (5), 519-613.

Wilson, Anne E and Michael Ross (2003), "The Identity Function of Autobiographical Memory: Time Is on Our Side," *Memory*, 11 (2), 137-49.

Movement, Knowledge and Consumption within Elderly Care Environments

Tim Stone, University of Aberdeen, Scotland
Paul Hewer, University of Strathclyde, Scotland
Douglas Brownlie, University of Stirling, Scotland

INTRODUCTION

Everyday life within care homes has been the focus of much media interest within Europe and the United States of America over recent years. This interest has taken the form of reports that focus on the lack of a dignified existence (Parkinson 2010), the financial implications of care for the elderly (Morris; 2004; Duffy 2003; Carvel and Meikle 2002), profit over care (Duhigg 2007), maladministration (BBC 2007), inaccurate reporting of problems (Copple 2008), the stress associated with relocating groups of elderly people from one care home to another (Grant 2004; Portlock 2003; Sapsted 2002), nutritional standards (BBC 2009) government legislation (Butler 2003; Cunningham 2002), physical, mental and/or racial abuse of elderly people in care homes (Fackelmann 2007; Smith 2007; Gonzales 2004; Marsh 2003) and the spread of infection (BBC 2009). In the light of these mass media representations the notion emerges whereby these accounts have focussed on a range of problematic issues associated with elderly consumers who live in such institutions. However, as Thompson (1998) suggests, this problem centred approach can be critiqued for not explicitly considering the living arrangements of elderly consumers (Kim et al. 2003; Gibler et al. 1998; Gibler et al. 1997) as meaningful human situations in their own right. Moreover, elderly consumers' voices are often muted within gerontological studies of consumption within care environment (Stone 2009; Wilson 1997; Wilson 1991).

Theoretical Positioning

Consumer research examines how identities are carefully forged through co-constituted, co-produced market generated materials (Arnould & Thompson 2005). Within the tradition of consumer culture theory (henceforth, CCT), consumers, more often than not, are seen to adopt a pro-active role in constructing desirable and expressive identities. In the light of such scholarly revelations, researchers' have directed their attention toward and throughout marketplace cultures in order to reflect upon how "consumer culture is instantiated in a particular cultural milieu and the implications of this process for people experiencing it...through the pursuit of common consumption interests" (ibid: 871 in line with Epp and Price 2010; Schau, Gilly & Wolfinbarger 2009; Kates 2002; Kozinets 2002; Kozinets 2001; Thompson and Tambyah 1999; Belk and Costa 1998; Thompson 1996; Holt 1995; Schouten and McAlexander 1995).

Tim Ingold (forthcoming), reflecting upon contemporary thought within social anthropology, art and architecture, calls for a "profound understanding of the lived world and for enquiries into what the possibilities for human life might be." Ingold forwards a vision of culture as a textured meshwork of interwoven threads. This Ingoldian characterisation of context is based on fundamental understandings of the role of movement and bodily knowledge in bringing the meshwork of culture back to life. Our study is positioned in such a way as to cast new rays of light upon Ingold's theory by investigating accounts of movement and bodily knowledge within institutional spaces where bodily movement and subsequent knowledge is subject to careful calculation and strategization. Principally, our work investigates how elderly consumers in care produce affectual meaning. With the discipline of consumer research in mind, this study has implications for the way in which CCT is utilised as a theoretical point of reflection, challenging us to reconsider the terms we use within gerontological studies of consumption.

Within discussions of CCT it has become relatively commonplace to draw upon the symbolic, interpretive anthropology of Geertz (1973),

and/or the deconstructionalist philosophy of Bourdieu (1990), and/or pioneering consumer research (Belk, Wallendorf, and Sherry 1989; Belk 1988; Belk 1987; Holbrook 1987; McCracken 1986; Mick 1986 Hirschman and Holbrook 1982) to explore various aspects of consumption within the dominant social paradigm of market capitalism. Such scholarly endeavour either explicitly or implicitly acknowledges that studies of "consumer culture" tend to fall in line with an anthropological tradition that views "culture" as "a system of inherited conceptions expressed in symbolic forms by means of which [wo]men communicate, perpetuate, and develop their knowledge about and attitudes toward life" (Geertz 1973: 89). Following on from this, culture, not forgetting the promptings of genetic predisposition (Ingold forthcoming), can be seen to play an important role in continually enabling a coherent, intelligible, public system of symbols (Erickson & Murphy 2008) to emerge, develop, structure and transform shared everyday experiences and belief systems throughout the life course.

Such a proposition might enable a question to appear in the reader's mind: How do people inherit symbolic cultural conceptions? Geertz (1973) suggests that when human beings are very young; a gap exists between emerging bodily knowledge and meaningful day-to-day functioning. Commenting on this gap, Ingold (forthcoming) forwards the proposition that such a lacuna is filled by essential guidelines for a certain way to live that is passed from one generation to the next. From this perspective, culture is acquired through observation learning and replication rather than being innate. "Equipped with these representations, freshly encultured individuals can go forth into the world where they will encounter diverse environmental conditions, causing their knowledge to be 'expressed' in one way or another, in the subtle variations and idiosyncrasies of observed behaviour" (ibid.). Reflecting upon such a proposition, the notion emerges whereby culture can be either be thought of as a subtle "system of inherited conceptions" (Geertz 1973) or an acquired diverse "blueprint of activity" (McCracken 1986) or a "framed horizon of conceivable action, feeling and thought" (Arnould and Thompson 2005) that organises a wide range of individual and shared symbolic experiences and knowledge generation practices (Martin et al. 2006; Bengtsson et al. 2005; Goulding and Shankar 2004; Maxwell 2003; Fung 2002; Goulding et al. 2002; Kates 2002; Kozinets 2001; Schouten and McAlexander 1995).

However, current thought within anthropology, suggests that such a conceptualisation of culture that is based on an assumed, coherent and static cultural boundary is problematic (Ingold forthcoming; Kottak 2008; Rapport and Overing 2007). Such cultural models are based on the premise that, over time, involvement within the world is converted into an internal schema which becomes manifest in outward appearance and behaviour. Moreover, from such a perspective, people become closed off from the outer world of interactions with their surroundings. By virtue, cultural actors are framed in such a way that suggests that communal meaningful activities come into being within inverted, closed and static boundaries (Ingold 2008). Rather as Ingold (1998: 330 his italics) stresses, "what we do *not* find are neatly bounded and mutually exclusive bodies of thought and custom, perfectly shared by all who subscribe to them, and in which their lives and works are fully encapsulated". Along similar lines, Rapport and Overing (2007: 298) state, "[t]here is no longer traditional, bounded cultural worlds in which to live – pure, integrated, cohesive, place rooted – from which to depart and which to return, for all is situated and all is moving". From this we argue that cultural life "does not begin here or end there, or connect a point of origin with a final destination, but rather it keeps on going, finding a way through the myriad of things that form, persist and break up its currents. Life, in short, is a movement of opening, not of closure" (Ingold forthcoming).

With such a perspective in mind, human-beings do not propel themselves across a carefully constructed "blueprint of human activity" (McCracken, 1986) nor should they be thought of as being enclosed within "framed horizons of conceivable action, feeling and thought" (Arnould and Thompson 2005). Rather, we argue, along with Ingold (forthcoming; 2008), that there is significant value in trying to recover that original openness to the world to probe the complexities and nuances of context and environment in the deepest possible sense. Such an epistemological and ontological perspective embraces the notion that human-beings issue forth through a world-in-formation along a tangled mesh of continuous and never-ending interweaving lines of genetics, life experiences, growth and movement. Or, to stick more closely to Ingold's (ibid.) lines of argument, this world-in-formation can be thought of as a dynamic, transformative, relational meshwork of continued flux (or becoming), never the same from one moment to the next.

From this perspective, human beings become meaningful as a consequence of their "patterns of activity and movement signatures" (ibid.) that can be found inscribed into particular identities, relationships, people, communities, things and so on (Rapport and Overing 2007). "As walking, talking and gesticulating creatures, human beings generate lines [of movement] wherever they go" (Ingold 2007: 1). With such nomothetic practices in mind, every person can be thought of as being instantiated in the world as an unfolding, tangled mesh of movement along ways of life (Ingold forthcoming). Thus movement becomes a critical vista for enabling the world (or the meshwork) to endlessly renew itself (ibid.; Ingold 2007); movement thus becomes a fundamental precursor for all socio-cultural experience within and throughout the meshwork of life.

Developing the emerging discussion still further, the authors argue that meshwork movement is responsible for the becoming, growth and reproduction of inter-place cultural knowledge. For example, the development of a knowledge system within science is attributed to "the work that goes into moving its diverse components – including practitioners, their know-how and skills, technical devices and standards of evaluation – from one local site of knowledge production to another" (Turnbull 1993: 30 in Ingold 2000: 229). Ingold (2000: 227) further suggests that knowledge "comes from a history of previous flights, of take-offs and landings, and of incidents and encounters en-route. In other words it is forged in movement, in the passage from place-to-place and the changing horizons along the way". Thus far from being copied, ready-made, into the mind in advance of its encounter with the world, knowledge is perpetually becoming within the open field of relations established through the immersion of the actor-in-the-world. Knowledge, in this view, is not transmitted as a complex structure but is the ever emergent product of a complex process of movement; put simply, "movement is itself the inhabitant's way of knowing" (Ingold forthcoming).

Part of CCT's allure resides in the call to encourage consumer researchers to reflect upon the contextual, productive, symbolic and experiential aspects of consumption and how these interact with lifestyle goals, and personal & social circumstances (Arnould and Thompson 2005). However, in an attempt to open up gerontological cultural discourse within consumer research, this paper will place emphasis on meshwork "movement" and "knowledge" in order to better understand how elderly consumers construct their lives within care home environments.

METHODOLOGY

A major factor in selecting qualitative, unstructured, in-depth interviews is because the outlined approach enables the researchers to engage with the elderly in such a way that enables them to reflect upon the flux of their experiences. Viewed in this way, in-depth interviews enable deep understandings of the nature of what it *feels* to be a consumer within in a care home to emerge. Furthermore, such a methodological approach also enables the researcher to gain in-depth first person understandings of how participants define their own lives (Aberg et al. 2005). In this case, the researchers invited participants to give relatively unrestricted account of their lives within their respective care homes. By virtue, each participant was invited to talk about some of the things in their room with the goal of obtaining first person descriptions of these things.

The identification of suitable care homes that could enable the initialization of the fieldwork depended on practical considerations such as the type of care home and the number of people who were fit enough to be interviewed. Following on from this, letters were written to several care homes within the United Kingdom containing information about the nature of the research project, enquiring whether it would be possible to conduct interviews with elderly people within that particular institution. By virtue, the managers of St. Augustine's and Cedar View (names changed) provided the lead researcher with access to their respective institutions and suggested potential participants. As such, it was necessary to work around the routines of daily living, such as meal times, visiting professional carers (such as physiotherapists, vicars, chiropodists etc.) or social activities (such as trips to the theatre, tea dances, visiting friends etc.), in an attempt to ensure that any interview would not disrupt the social and/or care needs of the potential participants. In light of this, sixteen potentially suitable participants were approached and informed of the research objectives in the hope that they would agree to participate. Of this group, eight participants happily gave their consent to be interviewed at a mutually agreeable time. These are identified within the following table:

Case.	Name.	Care Home	Brief Description of the Care Home
1.	Violet.	St. Augustine's.	St. Augustine's (name changed) is located within Stirlingshire (Scotland) and is nestled in a quiet, leafy residential street in an affluent area with picture postcard views of the surrounding countryside. The original building was a large house that has been extended so that it can meet the needs of 22 residents.
2.	Lottie.	St. Augustine's.	
3.	Doreen.	St. Augustine's.	
4.	Harry.	St. Augustine's.	
5.	Rita.	St. Augustine's.	
6.	George.	Cedar View.	*Cedar View* (name changed) is located within Norfolk (England) and is in close proximity to the Norfolk Boards, the East of England coastline and the historic city of Norwich. The building has been constructed in such a way that reflects modern (but sensitive) design principles. The building can comfortably accommodate 44 residents.
7.	Anne.	Cedar View.	
8.	Bill	Cedar View.	

Findings

We examine, with no framed apriori expectations, the lives and movements of elderly people within care environments through discussion of a small selection of vignettes around the central theme of movement.

Movement: *George and his Correspondence*

George suggested that he had attempted to personalise his room with moveable items of furniture and correspondence aids in such a way as to feel more flexible, organised and comfortable:

> **George**: *"I put this extra furniture in and this large wooden hostess style trolley that can be used as a portable table is wonderful because it's on casters and I can swing it round and use it as a table."*

To this end, the wonderful, multifunctional, flexible nature of the objects within George's room (such as a hostess trolley that can be used as a table and a word processor that can be used as a typewriter) seemed to compensate, at least to some extent, for his lack of mobility:

> **George**: *"Of course, now I've got my word processor so that I can write letters because I couldn't write letters because I've got arthritis in both hands. When I'm writing anything in the diary I have to be very careful so that I can read it [laughing]. I haven't used it as a word processor for years. I just use it as a typewriter."*

As the preceding text reveals, George did not primarily navigate his life-world with his legs and feet (he was wheelchair bound), but rather with his arms, hands and fingers. Set within this context, George indicated that he often experienced problems moving his arthritic hands and fingers to the extent that he had been forced to adopt a more careful, considered and restricted approach to daily living within Cedar View. Such kinaesthetic knowledge (Ingold forthcoming) could be seen to affect his attempts to use his word processor/typewriter to correspond with friends and family and to make entries into his diary. With such an interpretation in mind, Ingold (ibid.) suggests that it seemed as if George's life-world, at least to some extent, had been kept intact by the presumably painful tuning of relatively small horizontal and vertical movements of his arthritic hands over the keyboard in order to maintain his social ties. Such a finding appears to suggest that George's frail arms, hands and fingers were crucial elements in enabling him to carry out such manual operations (ibid.). At the time of the interview, such fragile lines of movement could be seen to revive and enhance his sense of well being and improve the quality of his life. However, the text seems to suggest, George was finding it harder to control his hands, especially when he attempted to write legibly in his diary. Whilst such a task was still feasible at the time of the interview, the proposition emerges whereby this manual activity could cease if the pain in George's hands becomes too great. Furthermore, by extension, it would also seem reasonable to propose that a time will come when George is also unable to use his word-processor and independently maintain his social connections.

Perhaps with similar thoughts in mind, George subsequently suggested that such activities appeared to be consuming more (and more) of his time and energy. Such a process, in more general terms, seemed to create restrictions in the nature and scope of bodily movements that were available to him in the latter phase of his life. The implications of this would seem to suggest that lines of movement, slowly but surely, lose agency in old age and that such potentially reviving undercurrents (Kirkby 2009) are only capable of improving feelings of well-being when the body (or in the case of Bill, mostly his arms, hands and fingers) are capable of movement and relatively free from pain.

Movement: *Lottie and the Need for Physiotherapy*

Lottie's vignette begins by revealing lines of movement that have come into being as a result of a period of serious illness and the subsequent extended need for medical care within a hospital. Such a figural experience seemed to leave a lasting impression on Lottie's diminishing sense of independence and overall quality of life. Moving to the time of the interview, it seemed as if Lottie had come to terms with her life within St. Augustine's House as the following text suggests:

> **Lottie**: *"I am here and here I stay [sad laughter]. You find yourself in a position that you just have to do as things will do with you. I hope I can stay here because I have been here a long time now. I've been here four years and it feels like home."*

Within this period of time, Lottie suggested that she had come to reluctantly accept that she was no longer in a position where she could physically respond to the flux of a world in-formation (Ingold forthcoming). Such a relatively passive world-view seemed to be based on the notion that Lottie was no longer capable of physically responding to or resisting any dynamic changes in relation to the conditions of being-in-the-world (ibid.). As such, Lottie was crucially dependent on the carers within St. Augustine's House to meet such basic needs as getting out of bed, going to the toilet, getting dressed, being taken to the dining room, being taken to her room, sitting in her chair, getting undressed, taking medication, going to bed etc. Such extensive physical limitations, for example, had a negative impact on Lottie's sense of communal identity (Bauman 2004) as she could no longer visit friends in other rooms without the occasional assistance of a carer.

Furthermore, Lottie also noted that many of her friends within St. Augustine's House had become immersed within the ebb and flow of the untimely and inescapable eddies of death. Having encountered such, dark, depressing and unsettling experiences, it would seem reasonable to suggest that Lottie's sense of being embedded within an institutional community had been eroded on several occasions. No doubt, repeatedly experiencing such an unpleasant and upsetting phenomena as bereavement would seem to suggest that, at the very least, lines of social interaction (Ingold 2007) can subside over a relatively short period of time. This could also be attributed to the rather depressing notion that as fellow residents become frailer they become less capable of extended periods of physical activity and/or verbal communication the longer they stay within the care home. Or, to use Lottie's words:

> **Lottie**: *"They are well when they come in and they get frailer as they go on. They don't get stronger. They go downhill. There was a man up above called George something. He has gone downhill very much this last while."*

Set within such a physically degenerative context, Lottie revealed that, despite being in her nineties, she tried to ensure that she could continue to move such limbs as her arms and legs by visiting the physiotherapist on a regular basis. However, such bio-mechanical movements seemed to exact an uncomfortable toll, in the sense that Lottie's muscles were sore for a least a day or so after visiting the health professional. Knowledge of life, in this context, seemed to be derived through feeling muscular pain. Whilst reflecting upon such experiences, Lottie stated such movements produce the knowledge that she *"would be no use at doing exercises."* Subsequently, Lottie stated that she was more than happy to sit and enjoy the peace and quiet as these aspects provided her with warmth, comfort and an improved sense of well-being. Movement, for Lottie, as Ingold (forthcoming) suggests, may not be independent or regular but a pattern is nevertheless established through the unfolding of her everyday lived experiences.

Movement: *Bill's Experiences of Feeling Cold*

Bill discussed the various procedures that had been put in place within Cedar View to facilitate care:

> **Bill**: *"Everything is wired up here. If I want something, I just pull this cord which operates a buzzer down there. They come up and turn it off in here and see what the trouble is."*

When asked if he used the Tele-care System regularly, Bill seemed to suggest that he was comforted by the knowledge that he could easily use this device (there was a very long cord that hung within easy reach of his bed). This was a particularly important aid to living as such a device not only enhanced Bill's safety, it presumably also functioned in such a way as to maintain his dignity and, perhaps to a lesser extent, his sense of independence. Such benefits could be seen to be important to Bill as he could not sit up without the assistance of a carer. However, despite such physical limitations, he claimed that he rarely used the Tele-care System. Whenever he felt the need to call for help, via focussed and emplaced hand movements, more often than not, he tended to use the device when he was in his innermost peaceful sanctum – his bed:

> **Bill**: *"I actually used it earlier this or was it yesterday morning? I can't tell which. They came in and said, "What's the matter?" "Cor," I said, "I think I am getting cold. Of course everyone here sleeps with their windows and doors shut. I can't sleep with the window shut. I must have it open."*

Following on from this, Bill indicated the carers quickly responded to the call for help by placing more blankets on his bed. Subsequently, he drifted back into a restful sleep. Reflecting upon such an experience would seem to suggest that temperate experience, movement, bodily knowledge (Ingold 2010) and sleep are the very roots of being. As such, and with Bill's experiences of care in mind, bodily knowledge comes into being through the very air that Bill breathes and feels (ibid.) when he is in bed and, as a consequence, depending on the temperature, he either experiences a good or a bad night's sleep. In the latter case, as illustrated within the interview text, Bill woke up, realised he was cold and uncomfortable and felt the need to reach for, grasp and pull the help cord. This would seem to suggest that both Bill's and his carer's movements and bodily knowledge are generated within collective fields of practice (Valtonen & Veijola 2010; Ingold 2000 in line with Turnbull 1989). Such collective practice, in an institutional sense, implies that Bill's bodily knowledge is generated by motional thought along particular temperate pathways (Ingold forthcoming) that lead to the natural, non-institutionalised world at large. From Bill's perspective, such institutionalised practices suggest that falling asleep and being asleep are highly meaningful collectively enacted bodily experiences (Valtonen and Veijola, 2010) that tend to occur when both Bill's body and mind recognise that his room and bed are to his liking and that help is, quite literally, to hand at any time during the night.

In addition to the insights revealed within the previous three sections, it also emerged that several participants found it very difficult to move from one place to another without the aid of a wheelchair. Such a crucial aid to living enables residents' to maintain a certain amount of physical and social independence. Indeed, as Ingold (forthcoming) comments, "locomotion is the start point for perceptual activity." For those elderly people who find it difficult to manoeuvre themselves throughout the home it was not un-common to find such people in either electric or manual wheelchairs. Such manoeuvrable, relatively high-tech objects could, perhaps, be seen as a source of empowerment and facilitate communal links within the home. However, whilst such a scenario would seem to be welcomed by most, it should be noted that such things require the user to have good eyesight – something that is not the norm within a care home. As Violet commented, "*I don't go into the sitting room so much because they are all elderly and I don't see so well anymore. I would hate to run into someone's feet.*"

REFLECTIONS

By way of a contribution to CCT we argue that elderly people in care homes do not find themselves in a position whereby they are at liberty to "make and re-make their identities over the courses of their lifetimes & choose to what degree the new identities are consistent with the old" (Schau et al. 2009: 256). Such a proposition would seem to add a note of caution and nuance to the CCT tradition and its consideration of the way consumers' use symbolic resources to enact personal and collective identities (Arnould and Thompson 2005). To this end, we offer a bespoke set of terms to the CCT community (see Glossary of Terms) to appreciate how the burden of identity work is negotiated in such institutions as care homes for the elderly.

As previously intimated, our findings suggest that elderly consumers in care environments are engaged in relations of deep dependency which leave their imprint within multiple and diverse trails of becoming (Ingold forthcoming) that embrace relatively frail social and material movements (such as those within a wheelchair) and personalised (and institutionalised) bodily knowledge. For example, and reflecting upon the empirical part of this paper, the reader could think of *George* and the primary need to navigate point-to-point lived experiences with frail arms, hands and fingers; or *Lottie* and her reliance on carers to get out of bed, go to the toilet, get dressed and undressed; or *Bill's* reliance on carers to sit him up in bed or to provide him with warmth whilst sleeping as illustrative experiential examples that reveal how the elderly engage with their surroundings in order to dwell within and understand care environments.

In order to navigate these fragile lines of immersed dwelling and becoming (ibid.) consumer researchers need to appreciate how the elderly within care environments bring (meshwork) form into being (ibid.) through the continued movements and interactions that are also associated with friends and family, professional carers, material artefacts and the institution as a whole. By virtue, physical and emotional pain, fear, sadness, debilitation, depression, restriction, un-happiness and, perhaps most importantly, loss of independence emerge and have significant agency within such environments. Moreover, let's not forget that such deep, dark and distressing feelings are negotiated and processed without the luxury of choice or independent access to market mechanisms.

Therefore, we argue, elderly care environments are incredibly demanding social, individual and material spaces within which consumption (of care services) is alive, active and constantly becoming. It involves levels of penetration, inscription, dependency and movement where simple notions of exchange and use, symbolic display and service delivery are insufficient to capture the emotional investments involved as a matter of routine. As Bauman (2004) suggests, in a society of consumers, such elderly people are 'flawed consumers' but consumers nonetheless, who, through no fault of their own, find themselves dwelling in unyielding currents, without the continued close support of their local community, friends and immediate family, within institutions that, more often than not, only strive to meet residents' basic care needs...if they are lucky. Such fragile and elderly consumers, to put in bluntly, would not survive on their own (ibid.). Within such restricted contexts, the notion of loving care remains just that, a notion that is rarely articulated within institutional care strategies.

APPENDIX ONE:
INGOLDIAN GLOSSARY OF TERMS

Please note; the following terms are all derived from Ingold (forthcoming) unless otherwise stated.

Becoming – "In a world of becoming even the ordinary, the mundane or the intuitive gives cause for astonishment – the kind of astonishment that comes from treasuring every moment, as if, in that moment, we are encountering the world for the first time, sensing its pulse, marvelling at its beauty, and wondering how such a world is possible."

Being-in-the-world – "A condition of being alive to the world, characterised by a heightened sensitivity and responsiveness, in perception and action, to an environment that is always in flux, never the same from one moment to the next."

Bodily knowledge – "Far from being copied, ready-made, into the mind in advance of its encounter with the world, knowledge is perpetually under construction within the field of relations established through the immersion of the actor-perceiver in a certain context. Knowledge, in this view, is not transmitted as a complex structure but is the ever emergent product of a complex process. It is not so much replicated as reproduced."

Ingoldian anthropology – "A sustained and disciplined inquiry into the essence of the conditions and potentials of human life that is located [at the nexus between] art, architecture and anthropology."

Life – "The essence of life is that it does not begin here or end there, or connect to a point of origin with a final destination, but rather it keeps on going, finding a way through the myriad of things that form, persist and break up its currents. Life, in short, is a movement of opening not of closure."

Lines- "Individual or group, we are composed of lines...or rather, bundles of lines...There are lines of life, lines of writing... lines of luck or misfortune, lines of flight, lines of becoming and so on" (Ingold, forthcoming. In line with Deleuze and Guattari, 2004: 215 – 223).

Meshwork – "The world we inhabit. What is commonly known as the 'web of life' is precisely that: not a network of connected points but a meshwork of interwoven lines."

Movement – "Different beings, whether or not they qualify as persons, have characteristic patterns of movement – which reveal them for what they are" (Ingold, 2000: 98).

ACKNOWLEDGEMENT

The authors of this work would like to take this opportunity to sincerely thank Professor Tim Ingold (University of Aberdeen, Scotland.) for providing the lead author with an advance copy of his new, unique and thought provoking book entitled *Being Alive. Essays on Movement, Knowledge and Description*.

REFERENCES

Aberg, Anna, Birgitta Sidenvall, Mike Hepworth, Karen O'Reilly & Hans Lithell (2005), On loss of activity and independence, adaptation improves life satisfaction in old age – a qualitative study of patients' perceptions, *Quality of Life Research*, Vol. 14, pp. 1111 – 1125.

Arnould, Eric and Craig Thompson, (2005), Consumer Culture Theory (CCT): Twenty Years of Research, *Journal of Consumer Research*, Vol. 31, March, pp. 868-882.

Bauman, Zygmunt (2004), *Wasted Lives: Modernity and its Outcasts*, Polity.

BBC News (2009), Infections warning for care homes, available at http://news.bbc.co.uk/1/hi/health/8266443.stm, accessed on 1st October 2009 at 15.33hrs.

BBC News (2009), Nutrition 'concern' in care homes, available at http://news.bbc.co.uk/1/hi/scotland/8261416.stm, accessed on 1st October 2009 at 15.31hrs.

BBC News (2007), MP reports council on care homes, available at http://bbc.co.uk, accessed on 15th August 2008 at 14.13hrs.

Belk, Russell (1988), Possessions and the Extended Self, *Journal of Consumer Research,* Vol. 15, September, pp. 139-168.

Belk, Russell (1987), Presidential Address: Happy Thought, Advances *in Consumer Research*, Vol. 14, ed. Melanie Wallendorf and Paul Anderson, Provo, UT: Association for Consumer Research, 1–4.

Belk, Russell and Janeen Arnold Costa (1998), The Mountain Man Myth: A Contemporary Consuming Fantasy, *Journal of Consumer Research*, Vol. 25, December, pp. 218–40.

Belk, Russell, Melanie Wallendorf and John Sherry (1989), The Sacred and the Profane in Consumer Behavior: Theodicy on the Odyssey, *Journal of Consumer Research*, Vol. 16, June, pp. 1–39.

Bengtsson, Anders, Jacob Ostberg & and Dannie Kjeldgaard (2005), Prisoners in paradise: Subcultural Resistance to the Marketization of Tattooing, *Consumption, Markets and Culture*, Vol. 8, No. 3, pp. 261-274.

Bourdieu, Pierre. (1990), *The logic of practice*, Oxford: Polity Press.

Butler, Carl (2003), Red Tape is Killing off our Care Homes: Shocking New Figures Show 700 Beds Lost in a Year, *Daily Post (Liverpool)*, 20th February, p. 11.

Carvel, John and James Meikle (2002), Care homes are in crisis, pensioners' leaders warn, *The Guardian*, June 1st.

Copple, Bert (2008), Report points to understatement of U.S. nursing home care problems, available at http://michiganhomecare.wordpress.com, accessed on 15th August 2008 at 14.19hrs.

Cunningham, June (2002*),* Where the heartache is, *The Herald*, November 11th, 14.

Deleuze, Giles and Felix Guattari (2004), *A thousand plateaus: capitalism and schizophrenia*, trans. B. Massumi. London: Continuum [originally published as *Mille Plateaux*, vol. 2 of *Capitalisme et Schizophrénie*, Paris: Minuit, 1980].

Duffy, Judith (2003), OAP's Facing Care Crisis, *Daily Record*, March 13th, p. 2.

Duhigg, Charles (2007), At Many Homes, More Profit and Less Nursing, available at http://nytimes.com, accessed on 15th August 2008 at 14.21hrs.

Epp, Amber and Linda Price (2010), The Storied Life of Singularised Objects: Forces of Agency and Network Transformation, *Journal of Consumer Research*, Vol. 36, February, pp. 820 – 837.

Fackelmann, Karen (2007), Blacks receive unequal nursing-home care, report finds, available at http://www.usatoday.com, accessed on 15th August 2008 at 14.35hrs.

Fung, Anthony (2002), Women's Magazines: Construction of Identities and Cultural Consumption in Hong Kong, *Consumption, Markets and Culture*, Vol. 5, No. 4, pp. 321-336.

Geertz, Clifford (1973), *The Interpretation of Culture*, Fontana Press.

Gibler, K. M., Lumpkin, J. R. and George Moschis (1998), Making the decision to move into retirement housing, *Journal of Consumer Marketing*, Vol. 15, No. 1, pp. 44- 54.

Gibler, Karen, James Lumpkin and Moschis, G.P. (1997), Mature Consumer Awareness and Attitudes Toward Retirement Housing and Long-Term Care Alternatives, The *Journal of Consumer Affairs*, Vol. 31, No. 1, pp. 113-138.

Gonzales, Victor (2004), Abuse in the Nursing Home, available at http://www.cbsnews.com, accessed on 15th August 2008 at 14.31hrs.

Goulding, Christina, Avi Shankar & Richard Elliott (2002), Working Weeks, Rave Weekends: Identity Fragmentation and the Emergence of New Communities, *Consumption, Markets and Culture*, Vol. 5, No. 4, pp. 261-284.

Grant, Graham (2004), Agony of vulnerable OAP's thrown out of their homes, *Daily Mail*, p. 8.

Hirschman, Elizabeth and Morris Holbrook (1982), "Hedonic Consumption: Emerging Concepts, Methods, and Propositions, *Journal of Marketing*, Vol. 46, Summer, pp. 92–101.

Holbrook, Morris (1987), What Is Consumer Research? *Journal of Consumer Research*, Vol. 14, June, pp. 128–32.

Holt, Douglas (1995), How Consumers Consume: A Typology of Consumption Practices, *Journal of Consumer Research*, Vol. 22, June, pp. 1–16.

Ingold, Tim, (Forthcoming), *Being Alive. Essays on Movement, Knowledge and Description*, Great Briton: Routledge.

Ingold, Tim (2010), Footprints through the weather-world: walking, breathing, knowing, *Journal of the Royal Anthropological Institute*, pp. 121 – 139.

Ingold, Tim (2007), *Lines. A Brief History*, Great Briton: Routledge.

Ingold, Tim (2000), *The Perception of the Environment. Essays in Livelihood, dwelling and skill*, Great Briton: Routledge.

Ingold, Tim (1998), Evolution of society, in Fabian, A.C. (Ed.), Evolution: society, science and the universe, Cambridge: Cambridge University Press, pp. 79 – 99.

Kates, Stephen (2002), The Protean Quality of Subcultural Consumption: An Ethnographic Account of Gay Consumers, *Journal of Consumer Research*, Vol. 29, December, pp. 383-399.

Kim, Sung-Hyuk, Hong Bumm Kim and Woo Gon Kim (2003), Impacts of senior citizens' lifestyle on their choices of elderly housing, *Journal of Consumer Marketing*, Vol. 20, No. 3, pp. 210-226.

Kirkby, Peter Wynn (2010), Lost in 'Space': An Anthropological Approach to Movement, in Kirkby, Peter Wynn (Ed.), *Boundless Worlds: An Anthropological Approach to Movement*, United States: Berghahn Books

Kottak, Conrad (2008), *Anthropology. Exploring Human Diversity*, McGraw Hill Higher Education.

Kozinets, Robert (2001), Utopian Enterprise: Articulating the Meanings of Star Trek's Culture of Consumption, *Journal of Consumer Research*, Vol. 28, June, pp. 67-88.

Marsh, Breezy (2003), 'Zombie' drugs shame our care homes, *Daily Record*, March 14th, p. 23.

Martin, Diane, John Schouten and James McAlexander (2006), Claiming the Throttle: Multiple Femininities in a Hyper-Masculine Subculture, *Consumption, Markets and Culture*, Vol. 9, No. 3, pp. 171-205.

Maxwell, Heather (2003), Divas of the Wassoulou Sound: Transformations in the Matrix of Cultural Production, Globalization, and Identity, *Consumption, Markets and Culture*, Vol. 6, No. 1, pp. 43-63.

McCracken, Grant (1986), Culture and Consumption: A Theoretical Account of the Structure and Movement of the Cultural Meaning of Consumer Goods, *Journal of Consumer Research*, Vol. 13, June, pp. 71–84.

Mick, David (1986), Consumer Research and Semiotics: Exploring the Morphology of Signs, Symbols, and Significance, *Journal of Consumer Research*, Vol. 13, September, pp. 196–213.

Morris, Nigel (2004), Politics: Howard promises to protect savings of old people in care, *The Independent*, September 15th.

Parkinson, Michael (2010), Michael Parkinson: The dignity every mother deserves, http://www.telegraph.co.uk/health/6997417/Michael-Parkinson, accessed on 15/02/10 at 10.17hrs.

Portlock, Simon (2003), Call for inquest after five deaths; Former patients die after being saved from Leamington care home, *Coventry Evening Telegraph*, March 13th, p. 5.

Rapport, Nigel & Joanna Overing (2007), *Social and Cultural Anthropology. The Key Concepts*, New York and London: Routledge.

Sapstead, Diane (2002), Downing St. accused of ignoring plight of tragic Alice, *The Daily Telegraph*, July 3rd, p. 20.

Schau, Hope Jenson, Mary Gilly & Mary Wolfinger (2009), Consumer Identity Renaissance: The Resurgence of Identity-Inspired Consumption in Retirement, *Journal of Consumer Research*, Vol. 36, August, pp. 255 – 276.

Schouten, John and James McAlexander (1995), Subcultures of Consumption: Ethnography of the New Bikers, *Journal of Consumer Research*, Vol. 22, June, pp. 43-61.

Smith, David (2007), Cops investigate elder abuse report at care home, available at http://www.examiner.com, accessed on 15th August 2008 at 14.30hrs.

Stone, Tim (2009), Understanding consumption within a care home: an interpretation of George's experiences of life and death, *Journal of Consumer Behaviour*, Vol. 8, September, pp. 166 – 178.

Stone, Tim (2009), Reflections upon the use of existential-phenomenological methods to study elderly consumers in care homes, *The Marketing Review*, Vol. 9, No. 3, pp. 213 – 230.

Thompson, Craig (1998), Living the texts of everyday life: A hermeneutic perspective on the relationship between consumer stories and life-world structures, in Stern, B. B. (Ed.), *Representing Consumers: Voices, Views and Vision*, Routledge: London.

Thompson, Craig (1996), Caring Consumers: Gendered Consumption Meanings and the Juggling Lifestyle, *Journal of Consumer Research*, Vol. 22, March, pp. 388–407.

Thompson, Craig and Siok Tambyah (1999), Trying to Be Cosmopolitan, *Journal of Consumer Research*, Vol. 26, December, pp. 214–41.

Turnbull, David (1993), Local knowledge and comparative scientific traditions, *Knowledge and Policy*, Vol. 6, pp. 29 – 54.

Turnbull, David (1989), Maps are territories: science is an atlas, Geelong: Deakin University Press.

Valtonen, Anu. and Soile Veijola (2011), Sleep in Tourism, *Annals of Tourism Research*, Vol. 38, Issue 1, pp. 175 – 192.

Wallendorf, Melanie and Eric Arnould (1988), My favourite things: A cross-cultural enquiry into object attachment, possessiveness, and social linkage, *Journal of Consumer Research*, Vol. 14, March, pp. 531-547.

Wenger, Etienne (1998), *Communities of Practice: Learning, Meaning & Identity*, Cambridge (UK): Cambridge University Press.

Wilson, Gail (1997), A post-modern approach to structured dependency theory, *Journal of Social Policy*, Vol. 26, No. 3, pp. 341-350.

Wilson, Gail (1991), Models of ageing and their relation to policy formation and service provision, *Policy and Politics*, Vol. 19, No. 1, pp. 37-47.

'Land of History and Romance': Consuming Nostalgia through the British Italian Cookbook

Elizabeth Parsons, Keele University, UK
Benedetta Cappellini, University of London, UK

INTRODUCTION

In this paper we explore the role of nostalgia in the production and consumption of British Italian cookbooks. We provide an interpretive analysis of British Italian cookbooks from across the 51 year period 1954-2005 exploring the ways in which their authors evoke past times, people and places in their promotion of Italian cuisine. Undeniably food as an ultimately sensual product which we engage with on an intimate level 'may be particularly effective in transporting consumers back in time' (Baker, Karrer and Veeck 2005, 402). Through examining the nostalgic rendering of Italian food culture in British Italian cookbooks, we explore some of the ways in which these books might transport the consumer back in time.

Although there is a growing interest in understanding food consumption, the majority of consumer studies dedicate their attention to looking at people's practices and discourses (Marshall 2005). What we know much less about is how such everyday food consumption practices, and the market mythologies attached to them, are *reconstructed* in texts such as cookbooks. Although there is a growing interest amongst consumer researchers in looking at 'symbolic meanings, cultural ideals, and inducements encoded in popular culture texts' (Arnould and Thompson 2005, 875), little has been said about culinary representations. Despite some recent exceptions (Brownlie, Hewer and Horne 2005; Schneider and Davis 2010) the written world of food remains an understudied topic of investigation in the consumer research community. In addition consumer researchers have long been interested in the role of nostalgia in the consumption process (Baker and Kennedy 1994; Havlena and Holak 1996; Holbrook and Schindler 2003). However, as yet little work has explored the role of nostalgia in relation to the written word. This focus on the written text is particularly apposite because it embraces both the author and reader in the production and consumption of nostalgic discourse. Such a focus then blurs the boundaries between production and consumption given the dialetic relationship between author and reader. Within this relationship nostalgic discourses are co-produced, reinterpreted and mobilized by both parties for specific ends (which we explore in the course of the paper).

With the above absences in mind in this paper we explore the British-Italian cookbook as consumption text but also on a wider level as a cultural artefact. Cookbooks offer us insights into the axis of political, cultural and social context of their making. They have been seen by a range of scholars as important historical – cultural resources, examined as cultural artefacts to be studied in relation to their cultural and social contexts (McDonagh and Prothero 2005). Considered not simply a collection of food recipes, they have been studied as a privileged source in representing 'unusual cultural tales' and 'revealing artefacts of culture in the making' (Appadurai 1988, 22). Most recently, consumer researchers have identified cookbooks 'as constructed social forms which are amenable to textual analysis' (Brownlie et al. 2005, 7). We similarly explore British Italian cookbooks through this lens using a socio-historical approach. The paper begins with a review of relevant literature and outline of the interpretive approach to textual analysis pursued. This is followed by a socio-historical analysis of cookbooks as cultural artefacts. In closing we observe our contributions to existing theorisation of nostalgia and culinary representations within consumer research.

CULINARY CULTURE, CONSUMPTION AND NOSTALGIA

In this paper we use two specific strands of literature to aid us in our project of exploring representations of Italian culinary culture. The first is work within consumer research which explores the role of nostalgia in structuring consumer meanings and experiences. The second includes work from cultural geographers which explores the evocation of place through what might be termed 'nostalgic food cultures'.

Consumer researchers have long found the idea of nostalgia useful in understanding consumer motivations and behaviours (Baker and Kennedy 1994; Havlena and Holak 1996; Holbrook and Schindler 2003). The nostalgia concept is useful here in that it not only encompasses memories and imaginings of the past, but idealised versions of these memories with their negative elements largely stripped away (Goulding 1999). A second vital component of nostalgia is that it generally acts as a counterpoint to a less attractive, and most often undesirable, present. Another element of nostalgia, according to Davis (1979), includes a longing for past experiences. However, as we are at pains to illustrate in this paper, nostalgic consumption does not have to rely on individual experience, rather what we have seen in recent years is an increased and deliberate commodification of nostalgic experience (Brown 2001), in product design (Weaving 2008), retail environments (Maclaran and Brown 2005) and historical theme parks and leisure environments (Goulding 1999) and of course (cook)books. The impetus behind this marketing drive, and the attendant consumption of these products, is undoubtedly increasing consumer anxiety in the face of a fragmented global postmodern consumer culture wherein consumers struggle for stable reference points for their sense of identification and belonging (Strauth and Turner 1988). In Western affluent contexts the market reaction is a plundering of the past in attempts to reclaim, and repackage for sale to the consumer, a sense of place, belonging and authenticity. However, while we observe that there has certainly been a recent resurgence of market interest in past times, and this is where our socio-historical approach becomes significant, our analysis shows nostalgic consumption has much earlier roots and is likely to be part of a more deep seated human condition (Davis 1979).

Baker and Kennedy (1994) delineate three levels of nostalgia: real, simulated and collective; they argue that each level has a different degree of attendant emotional intensity. While we observe that these levels are perhaps a little discrete they do usefully identify the nuances in individual experience (real), the role of the media and other objects in simulating nostalgia (simulated) and the role of collectivities in nostalgic experience (collective) such as culture, generation or nation. Our analysis identifies elements of all three of these levels of nostalgia. Often cookbook narratives rely on the author's individual experiences, but equally, and simultaneously they evoke collective nostalgia surrounding Italian landscape, people and food cultures, in addition these cookbooks in themselves might be seen as simulating (and indeed stimulating) nostalgic experiences in the consumer.

In their interpretive exploration of nostalgia as a driver of consumption Holbrook and Schindler (2003), similarly identify the collective dimension of nostalgia. They attribute this collective dimension of nostalgia in the UK and US to the Baby Boomer generation. However, in this paper they relate nostalgia very closely to individual consumer experience drawing on earlier work in this respect (Holbrook and Hirschman 1982). In our examination of British Italian cookbooks while we do explore the experiences of the authors in framing nostalgia we also emphasise the commodification of nostalgia on a more general and collective level. The stories and images of Italy that emerge from our reading do not necessarily always rely on the reader/consumers past experiences for their meaning.

Both consumer researchers (Brownlie et al. 2005; Hewer and Brownlie 2007) and others (Appadurai 1988; Cinotto 2005) have explored the ways in which cookbooks represent and reproduce national cultures and identities. Geographers have also been interested in nostalgia and its links to food in helping them to understand the ways in which places are imagined and become meaningful. Duruz's (2005) evocative interweaving of participants food stories, everyday practices and memories to explore the themes of identity, place, ethnicity and belonging in London and Sydney really emphasises the strength of links between imagined food cultures and a sense of place. She finds in these stories a 'nostalgia for 'traditional' country cooking and the 'past', she also observes the 'catalogues of the effort these women make towards maintaining their culinary heritage' (2005, 67). As such we should also recognise the significance of cookbooks in maintaining culinary heritage. This is particularly the case for cookbooks at the beginning of the period we study where there is no doubt that the authors were keen to both promote and preserve a particular version of Italian culinary heritage. As such the stories that we will be exploring below are attempts at preserving a slice of Italian history as much as they are instructions in Italian cooking.

However, we want to acknowledge the potential pitfalls and misrepresentations of talking about a definitive Italian food culture. In our globalised world it can be argued that all cuisines are necessarily 'hybrid' (Cook, Crang and Thorpe 2000; Duruz 2005). As Cook et al. observe: 'ingredients, knowledges, technologies and practices – culinary and otherwise – cannot have any straightforward 'origins'' instead they identify the 'messy boundary crossings of ingredients, cuisines, people and their histories' (2000, 113). It is in this spirit that we explore the narratives within British Italian cookbooks as hybrid and contested.

METHODOLOGY

This paper emerges from a wider study looking at the representation and consumption of Italian food in the UK. In this paper we provide an interpretive reading of continuities and discontinuities of discourses surrounding nostalgia as they emerged in representations of Italian food in cookbooks. Our approach follows previous interpretive consumer studies providing a critical reading of media discourses in popular magazines (Martens and Scott 2005; Schneider and Davis 2010) and cookbooks (Brownlie et al. 2005). As Brewis and Jack (2005, 51) point out providing a critical reading implies that we do not assert that what we understand from the cookbooks is what authors intended to communicate, or even what consumers would see in these texts. Our interpretive reading would offer 'a think piece, a broad-brush polemic' (Brewis and Jack 2005, 51) and as such it provides one understanding of how discourses about nostalgia have been reconstructed in the examined cookbooks. Our reading focused on Italian culinary culture, the authors' travel stories and anecdotes about Italy as well as recipes, products, cooking and shopping practices. In the current paper we have focused on the nostalgic representation of Italy and its culinary culture and the way consumers are encouraged to reconstruct a nostalgic food experience in their homes.

A multicultural team iterated the analysis and as such a 'triangulation across co-authors led to new insights and resolved differences in interpretation' (Askegaard, Arnould and Kjeldgaard 2005, 163). The triangulation across authors does not simply increase the validity of our analysis, but most importantly enriches our interpretive reading by combining two understandings of the examined discourses. One author is Italian, and thus familiar with Italian food culture, Italian ingredients, dishes, domestic consumption practices, and mealtime conventions; and one author is English and thus familiar with similar elements of British food culture. Data analysis and interpretation followed the general form used in interpretive research and hence a continuous interaction between data and theoretical frameworks has been privileged as a crucial part of the hermeneutical process (Spiggle, 1994; Thompson, 1997).

Following previous research looking at food discourses in a socio-historical perspective (Martens and Scott 2005; Schneider and Davis 2010) our sample has been selected using a chronological criteria. 8 cookbooks have been selected from 1954 to 1974, 22 cookbooks from 1975 to 1995 and 14 cookbooks from 1996 to 2005. The first period is relatively has underrepresented because of the scarcity of published cookbooks, rather the second period is overrepresented because of the explosion of cookbooks published in the late seventies (see Cinotto, 2005). Another sampling criterion was based on the popularity of the writer. Celebrity chefs, such as Elizabeth Davis (1954), Jamie Oliver (2005) were selected together with less popular cookbooks recommended by these celebrities. This criterion was applied because, as scholars have shown (Brownlie et al. 2005), celebrity chefs have had a significant impact on British food culture.

ANALYSIS: THREE PERIODS OF NOSTALGIA

From our analysis we have identified three distinct periods wherein discourses around nostalgia have been reconstructed in different ways (see table 1). Each of these periods is not a discrete stage with a clear beginning and end, rather periods overlap and continuities and discontinuities with the previous and subsequent phases are evident. Given this, it is still possible to identify a broad set of features which characterise each period as distinct.

Table 1 Changing Representations of Nostalgia in British Italian Cookbooks 1954-2005

	1954-1970 **An Exotic and Rich Culinary Heritage**	**1971-1986** **A Romanticised, Pre-modern Past**	**1990-2005** **The Simple and Authentic Life**
Intended readership	Affluent housewife	Working mother	Male or female cook
Discourses of Nostalgia	Real nostalgia: escaping post-war food rationalisation	Simulated nostalgia: escaping the juggling lifestyle	Collective nostalgia: escaping a collective and frenetic lifestyle
Consuming Nostalgia	Shopping and cooking exotic products	Cooking convenient dishes	Following culinary gurus's shopping recommendations

1954- 1970 An Exotic and Rich Culinary Heritage

This period is characterised by the production of books written by women with a direct link to Italy. These authors frequently refer to their own past travel experiences in evoking a very personalized nostalgic view of Italy's glorious culinary past. Some of these authors were British middleclass female authors with a taste for travel such as Elizabeth Davis (1954) and others were middle class Italian immigrant women such as Taglienti (1956). The autobiographical notes, which appear in the introduction as well as in the presentation of the recipes, illustrate the writer's privileged consumption experiences, such as dinner with diplomats and Italian aristocrats or adventurous lunches at village festivals.

The intended readership consists of housewives who need to be "educated" and guided in their new consumption experiences of dealing with exotic Italian products.

> There is, I know, a school of writers who seem to believe that English housewives are weak in the head and must not be exposed to the truth about the cooking of other countries; must not shocked by the idea of making a yeast dough, cleaning an ink-fish, adding nutritive value to a soup with olive oil [...] (David 1963, 25n6).

While cookbooks of this period are addressed to a female readership, it is not the case that women from all walks of life are targeted. Indeed authors seem to address women who share similar privileged and nostalgic consumption experiences, or at least those who aspire to share in such privilege (and the associated cultural capital) through the acquisition of knowledge of foreign cuisines.

> Do you remember your first meal on the Rome Express after you left Modena? Or your first fettuccini at Alfredo's in Rome? Or the café granita at Doney's in Florence? If your tongue still quivers at the thought of the succulent scaloppine con olive, the pasta golden and its sugo di formaggio e burro, the icy block coffee crystals melting on your tongue on a hot day, this book will fill you with nostalgia as well as nourishments. If, on the other hand, you are as yet unacquainted with these joys of Italian cooking, it will introduce you to many new gastronomic delights (Taglienti, 1956, 1)

This complicity between reader and writer rooted in the cultural capital of the privileged leisured class is illustrated in recalling nostalgic memories of exclusive cafes in Florence, luxurious train rides but also ingredients and dishes. The author entreats the reader to recreate her own sense of nostalgia through buying familiar products and transforming them into dishes which are familiar from their pasts. Also the author invites readers who have not experienced this culinary past to invent these memories in their kitchen, through consuming new products and transforming them into evocative dishes.

The nostalgic tone of this period seems particularly acute in some cookbooks, like Elizabeth Davis's (1950) *Mediterranean Food* wherein the author's adventures in the South of Europe are compared with 'icy and hungry weeks' in London (David 1950, X). As she describes, recalling food experiences from the past is an enjoyable way to escape the present. In a passage that is particularly evocative of Murcott's (1995, 225) observation that cookbooks are a 'representation of imaginary experiences remote from everyday life'; David's descriptions of the food as 'richly flavoured' and 'brightly coloured' must have contrasted sharply with the food available in the rather drab post war years of early 1950s England:

> But even if people could not very often make the dishes here described, it was stimulating to think about them; to escape from the deadly boredom of queuing and frustration of buying the weekly rations: to read about real food cooked with wine and olive oil, eggs and butter and cream, and dishes richly flavoured with onions, garlic, herbs, and brightly coloured Southern vegetables [...] I took refuge from reality writing down memories of the food I had cooked and eaten during my Mediterranean years. (David 1950, X)

In describing the disappointing present in England these cookbooks seem to talk to a leisured class who is encouraged to take refuge in their past through exotic products and challenging consumption practices. Also these books seem to deliberately play upon aspiration through the mobilization of nostalgic discourse. Readers who have not had these privileged travel experiences are encouraged to imagine and recreate them through learning new food consumption skills and practices at home.

1971-1986 A Romanticised, Pre-modern Past

At the end of the Seventies and during the Eighties the numbers of cookbooks really took off (Cinotto 2005). Cookbooks written by writers with no evident links with Italian culture started to appear. Although there are still cookbooks written by Italian immigrants (Hazan, 1980) or British travellers, many publications are written by authors not claiming any travel experiences in Italy or childhood memories about Italian food. Also cookbooks written by supermarket chains, like Sainsbury's (Reynolds 1981), appeared. The increased numbers of publications generate a heterogeneous representation in terms of advised ingredients, recipes and cooking techniques. In fact there are cookbooks only for vegetarians, for single people, for fast cooking, for low fat cooking, but also for cooking only one dish like pasta or pizza. This fragmentation of Italian food representations seems to reflect a more general trend involving the fragmentation and increasing incoherence of food discourses during this period, in particular those surrounding food choice which commentators have termed gastronomy (Fischler 1993).

While cookbooks from this period re-present Italian food in contradictory terms regarding shopping and cooking advice, they are very homogenous in presenting a nostalgic idea of Italy and its gastronomic culture. The author's biographic notes about Italy and its food gradually disappear but descriptions of villages and small communities immersed in a fairyland become very popular.

> To buy food at the market you have to get up early, because by eight o'clock the best has already gone. Peasants from villages near and far will not miss coming to town on market day. They used to either walk from miles away, or come in donkey and horse carts, but motorcycles and cars are now the more usual transport. But the market atmosphere remains unchanged. (Birch 1985, 17)

This new nostalgic tone is used to describe an Italian society immersed in a past without time and space coordinates. The same tone is also adopted in illustrating Italian food. Italian cuisine is described as 'authentic', a term used to underline how the food is a product of a society bypassed by modernity and thus uncorrupted by modern life. As this author points out 'a typical Italian meal is still very much as it was in the eighteenth century' (Barker 1979, 6).

Another new element of this nostalgic representation is the emphasis on the Italian family, especially Italian women as mothers. Introduced as the centre of Italian society, the family is also depicted as the centre of gastronomic activity. As Marcella Hazan observes 'eating in Italy is essentially a family art, practised for and by the family' (1980, 4). The everyday work surrounding family meals is depicted solely as the preserve of women (in particular mothers). Represented as housewives devoted to their husbands and children, women are usually illustrated in the act of serving a meal, cooking or preparing food.

> *For although the legal position of women in Italy has improved greatly over the last two decades, it is still rare, though known, for babbo to turn his hand to cooking- never the washing up of course!- and in the family it is still basically mamma who runs the show. She forms her children's taste in food so firmly that it remains with them all their lives.* (Spike-Huges and Charmain1986, 7)

The emphasis on Italian mothers as housewives "enjoying" feeding their family, is particularly relevant if we consider that cookbooks of this period are not aimed at upper and middle class housewives, but at working women who, as studies suggest, juggle their domestic practices with restricted budgets and inflexible time schedules (Thompson 1996). In fact cookbooks "talking" to working mothers emphasise the convenience of Italian recipes which can be prepared quickly and easily with locally available products.

> *The above traditional technique still stands and works wonderfully with imported Italian rice. If we have time we prefer the traditional, grand method. If we do not have the time, there are still ways to make risotto in the modern kitchen. There are two ways to go, depending on the cook ware as well as the rice in the market.* (Romagnoli and Romagnoli, 1980:135)

We notice a contradiction in the representation of Italian food in this period. On the one hand Italy and its culinary culture are represented through the apparently "relaxed" lifestyle of Italian mothers who not having a job outside the home, have time to leisurely shop in local markets and generally enjoy the work of feeding their family. On the other hand the recipes and consumption practices are addressed to British working women and therefore highlight the economy, both in terms of time and effort, of Italian cooking. We interpret this contradiction as a simulated nostalgia (Baker and Kennedy 1994) where consumers are not required to revisit their own past in order to reconstruct their nostalgia, they can access their simulated nostalgic experience through mass produced items, and convenient recipes saving time and effort in their kitchens. In other words British readers could aspire to live in this "once upon a time" dreamland, with very little effort. Mothers in full time employment with juggling lifestyles can, in part, buy into the figure of the time rich Italian mother who unproblematically places family first by consuming convenient Italian recipes.

1990-2005 The Simple and Authentic Life

In this period the production of cookbooks increases further and the representation of Italian culinary culture becomes even more fragmented than in the previous period (Cinotto 2005). While there is a very heterogeneous representations of recipes, advice and recommendations, images and ideas of Italy as a country are resonant with the representation of the previous period. Descriptions of a harmonic country which remains untouched by modernity are frequently illustrated through images of children wearing traditional dresses, crowded little markets, and devoted housewives preparing family meals.

> *Despite the advent of industrialization and mass-marketing, traditional foods are still central to the cultural identity of each re-*

> *gion. This is partly due to the way in which recipes are learned: orally passed from generation to generation, and rarely written down in cookbooks, they survive in families for years with little or no changes made to them.* (Capalbo 2001, 6)

Italy is depicted as a country firmly rooted in tradition, a place where globalisation has yet to impact on people's food habits, where recipes are orally passed from generation to generation. In some cases these descriptions are explicitly political in tone, the below extract depicts Italian culinary culture as actively resistant to the forces of globalisation:

> *The Common market may eventually impose American uniformity on Europe, in generations to come the food may become uniformly tasteless [...] If the forces of mediocrity are gathering, Italy will be the last centre of resistance.* (Barrett 1993, VII)

In this period references to Italian mothers and British working mothers seem to disappear. This is probably due to fact that many male culinary gurus (Cinotto 2005), such as TV chefs like Jamie Oliver and famous restaurateurs like Antonio Carluccio, dominate the production of cookbooks. Although their representations of Italian food vary, their intended audience is very similar. As the restaurateur Aldo Zilli emphasises, his intended audience consists of 'working people', regardless of their gender, social class or household composition.

> *My main aim is to give you an insight into Italian cooking, showing you how easy it is to create delicious dishes. Forget the fuss! Simplicity is the key....some of them (recipes) are so quick and easy that they are great for working people who do not have much time to cook.* (Zilli 1998, VIII)

Stressing the idea that Italian food is a convenient option, in terms of saving time and effort, the intended audience becomes defined in terms of lifestyle. There are explicit references to people who cannot afford to spend time (and effort) in the kitchen, but that would like to cook their own meals.

As with the authors from the fifties, celebrities emphasise their Italian origins or their travels in Italy as a guarantee of their competence in reproducing an "authentic" Italian food experience. This is especially the case with Jamie Oliver who's book: Jamie's Italy (2005) is a description of his gastronomic tour of the country. This book is noteworthy as in many respects it epitomises the way in which Italy and its gastronomic culture are currently represented in the UK. In the book Jamie celebrates the pre-modern, slow pace of Italian life, which he describes in these terms:

> *I've witnessed so many young people and teenagers in Italy living a 'modern-day-life' which we would have seen in Britain seventy years ago- yes, they have mobile phones and computers but they're not seen as an essential part of everyday life and not as many people have them as here.* (2005, XI)

This nostalgic representation of Italy, as a country still in the past and unaffected by modernity, does not require a particular understanding. Indeed Italian cooking know-how is presented as thoroughly embodied by the culinary subject. Italian cooking skills are tacit in nature, absorbed in the course of everyday life in the family kitchen. As such Italian cooking is presented as accessible to all, as Oliver observes:

> *The truth is, when I'm in Italy I feel Italian—even with my very basic grasp of the language I manage to get by, and you know*

why? Because, like all Italians, I love my family for better or for worse and because food has been something I've grown up around. (Oliver 2005, X)

This accessibility of old world Italian culture is extended to British consumers and offered as an antidote to British living, lost as it has been to the forces of modernity and globalisation. Here Italian culture is presented as offering readers an opportunity to revisit a nostalgic past, a past grounded in authenticity, where readers might escape from the anxieties of contemporary British life.

The "authentic" and nostalgic Italian experience is reconstructed with elements of continuity and discontinuities in relation to the cookbooks of the 1980s. As in previous cookbooks, in this period the nostalgic past is reconstructed through the concept of convenience. However, here convenience becomes even more specific, for example the required time is measured in minutes, and the required work is evaluated in more detail by the author. Saving time probably receives greatest emphasis, calculated for the entire process, from the preparation to the cooking. In addition the level of required cooking skills is also identified in many books, and there are suggestions as to how to reduce the amount of time and effort required (for example by using electronic devices such as food processors and microwaves).

CONCLUSION

In this paper we have identified three different phases of nostalgic representation of Italy and its food. From this analysis we have three key observations to make about nostalgia and its role in the consumption experience. First we acknowledge the commodification of nostalgia, and second (drawing from Baker and Kennedy's 1994 earlier work) we observe that its form and intensity varies according to socio-historical context, finally we suggest that nostalgic food cultures and their representations are central to consumers' sense of identity and belonging.

Each of the periods analysed encompasses different modes of nostalgia, but all of them present nostalgia as a consumption experience that consumers can access through the shopping, cooking and display of Italian food. As such, our study highlights the commodification of nostalgia, which is portrayed as an "object" that can be consumed by following the author's shopping recommendations and cooking advice.

Our socio-historical approach to the analysis of these texts has also underlined the role of nostalgic consumption in escaping an undesirable present (Davis 1979). In each period the features of this undesirable present and its socio-economic underpinnings differs. The promotion of an exotic and rich food culture in the fifties is an antidote to a post-war country with a strict rationing of such foods. The promotion of a pre-modern, traditional food culture in the eighties is in response to the time poor "juggling lifestyle" required by the increased presence of women in the workplace during this period. In the most recent phase a simple and authentic food culture is emphasised in response to an increasingly fragmented, post-modern, inauthentic lifestyle.

In addition we see Baker and Kennedy's (1994) three levels of nostalgia (*real, simulated and collective*) reflected in each of these three periods with different emphases in each. In the first period the emphasis is on '*real*' nostalgic experience. Here authors rely on their own past experience and the text emerges as an intimate dialogue between the female author and imputed middle class female reader through remembered holidays and travels to Italy. This form of nostalgia represents a personal past which is shared with people who have had (or have aspired to have) the same experiences. Nostalgia is reconstructed through products and dishes from an individual past,

and as such the reader is invited to discover specific products in local shops and delicatessens, as well as "learn" new cooking skills. In the second period nostalgia is not a class based experience any longer, but rather a '*simulated*' experience wherein women can imagine (aspire to) a vaguely "better" reality, wherein life is suspended in a "once upon a time" atmosphere. Consumers are not required to revisit their own past in order to reconstruct their nostalgia, they can access their simulated nostalgic experience through mass produced items, and convenient recipes saving time and effort in the kitchen. In the last period nostalgia seems to have been democratized. It is not an experience reserved for women, but it is a '*collective*' dialogue wherein also men are admitted as authors and readers. Because it is not gender and class bound any longer, nostalgia is represented as a collective experience an escape from the current lifestyle available to everybody. However it is also an individual experience as cookbooks represent the celebrity gurus "own" version of nostalgia, which consumers can access through consumption. As in the first period nostalgia is consumable through shopping more than through other consumption practices. Indeed consumers are invited to recreate their nostalgic experience by rehearsing their cultural capital in their shopping trips to delicatessens and markets.

Finally, we'd like to make some comments about the consumption of these texts, in particular their context of consumption. In a contemporary Western consumer context where home cooking and dining and the traditional rituals, knowledges and practices associated with them are in decline, it is perhaps not surprising that the values of tradition, family and home are recurrent in the British Italian cookbooks we analysed. In fact evidence suggests that narratives of the kitchen table, the smells and sounds of home cooked food and the central role of the maternal figure are typical in remembrances of home across a range of cultural contexts (Duruz 2001). Cutting across all three periods we see nostalgia operating to invoke a sense of authenticity and belonging through consumption. In an increasingly globalised context where boundaries become increasingly blurred 'the discomforts of fragmentation, disruption and "placelessness" have produced nostalgic longings for a secure world and for secure positionings within it' (Duruz 2001, 22). Our socio-historical analysis of cookbooks has identified the centrality of food, food cultures and the representation of these as important antidotes to feelings of placelessness and alienation.

REFERENCES

Appadurai, Arun (1988), "How to Make a National Cuisine: Cookbooks in Contemporary India," *Comparative Studies in Society and History*, 1, 3-24 .

Arnould, Eric J. and Craig J. Thompson (2005) "Consumer Culture Theory (CCT): Twenty Years of Research", *Journal of Consumer Research*, 31 (4), 868-882.

Askegaard, Soren, Eric J. Arnould and Dannie Kjeldgaard (2005) "Postassimilationist Ethnic Consumer Research: Qualifications and Extensions," *Journal of Consumer Research*, 32 (1), 160-170.

Baker, Stacey M. and Patricia F. Kennedy (1994), "Death by Nostalgia: A Diagnosis of Context Specific Cases," *Advances in Consumer Research*, 21, Sage, Provo, UT, 380-387.

Baker, Stacey M., Holli C. Karrer and Ann Veeck (2005), "My Favourite Recipes: Recreating Emotions and Memories Through Cooking," *Advances in Consumer Research*, 32, Sage, Provo, UT, 402-403.

Barker, Alex (1979) *Italian Cooking*, London: McDonald Educational.

Barrett, Judith (1993) *Food from an Italian Garden*, London: Michael Joseph.

Birch, Laura (1985) *Traditional Italian Food*, London, Fontana Paperbacks.

Brewis, Jo and Gavin Jack (2005), "Pushing Speed? The Marketing of Fast and Convenience Food," *Consumption, Markets and Culture*, 8 (March), 49-67.

Brown, Stephen (2001) *Marketing — The Retro Revolution*, London: Sage.

Brownlie, Douglas, Paul Hewer and Suzanne Horne (2005), "Culinary Tourism: An Exploratory Reading of Contemporary Representations of Cooking," *Consumption, Markets and Culture*, 1, 7-26.

Capalbo, Carla (2001) *Perfect Pasta and Pizza. Fabulous Food the Italian Way*, London: Lorenz Books.

Cinotto, Simone (2005) "Italian Cookbooks: rappresentazioni dell'altro culinario," *Slow*, IX, 49 (February), 48-53 .

Cook, Ian, Phil Crang and Mark Thorpe (2000), "Regions to be Cheerful: Culinary Authenticity and Its Geographies," in *Cultural Turns/Geographical Turns: Perspectives on Cultural Geography* Eds. I. Cook, D Crouch, S. Naylor and J.R. Ryan (Prentice-Hall: Englewood Cliffs, NJ), 109-139.

David, Elizabeth (1950) *Mediterranean Food*, London: John Lehmann.

David, Elizabeth (1963) [1954] Drawings by Renato Guttuso, *Italian food*, London, Mcdonald.

Davis, Fred (1979), *Yearning for Yesterday: A Sociology of Nostalgia*, New York: The Free Press.

Duruz, Jean (2001), "Home Cooking, Nostalgia, and the Purchase of Tradition", *TDSR*, 12 (2), 21-32.

Duruz, Jean (2005), "Eating at the Borders: Culinary Journeys," *Environment and Planning D: Society and Space*, 23, 51-69.

Fischler, Claude (1993), "Food Habits, Social Change and the Nature/Culture Dilemma," *Social Science Information*, 19, 937-53.

Goulding, Christina (1999), "Heritage, Nostalgia and the "Grey" Consumer," *Journal of Marketing Practice: Applied Marketing Science*, 5 (6/7/8), 177-199.

Havlena, William J. Susan L. Holak (1996), "Exploring Nostalgia Imagery Through the Use of Consumer Collages," *Advances in Consumer Research*, 23, 35-42.

Hazan, Marcella (1980) *The Classic Italian Cookbook*, London: Pepermarc.

Hewer, Paul and Douglas Brownlie (2007), "Consumer Culture Matters: Insights from Contemporary Representations of Cooking," *Advances in Consumer Research*, 34, 175-179.

Holbrook, Morris B. and Elizabeth, C. Hirschman (1982), "The Experiential Aspects of Consumption: Consumer Fantasies, Feelings, and Fun," *Journal of Consumer Research*, 9 (September), 132–140.

Holbrook, Morris B. and Robert Schindler (2003), "Nostalgic Bonding: Exploring the Role of Nostalgia in the Consumption Experience," *Journal of Consumer Behaviour*, 3 (2), 107-127.

McDonagh Pierre, and Andrea Prothero (2005), "Food, Markets and Culture: The Representation of Food in Everyday Life'" *Consumption, Markets, and Culture* 8, (1), 1–5.

Maclaran, Pauline and Stephen Brown (2005), 'The Center Cannot Hold: Consuming the Utopian Marketplace', *Journal of Consumer Research*, 32 (2), 311-323.

Marshall, David (2005), "Food as Ritual, Routine or Convention," *Consumption, Markets and Culture*, 8 (1), 69-85.

Martens, Lydia and Sue Scott, (2005), "'The Unbearable Lightness of Cleaning': Representation of Domestic Practice and Products in Good Housekeeping Magazine (UK):1951-2001," *Consumption, Markets and Culture*, 8 (4), 379-401.

Murcott, Anne (1995), "Raw, Cooked and Proper Meals at Home" in Marshall D. (ed). *Food Choice and the Consumer*, Blackie Academic and Professional: London, 219-236.

Oliver, Jamie (2005) *Jamie's Italy*, London: Penguin.

Reynolds, Mary (1981*) The Sainsbury's Book of Italian Cooking*, Cathay Books: London.

Romagnoli Margaret and Franco Romagnoli (1980) *The new Italian cooking*, London: An   Atlantic monthly press book.

Schneider Tanja, Davis Teresa (2010) "Advertising Food in Australia: Between Antinomies and Gastro-anomy," *Consumption, Markets and Culture*, 13 (1), 31-41.

Spiggle, Susan (1994) "Analysis and interpretation of qualitative data in consumer research" *Journal of Consumer Research*, 21(3), 491-503.

Spike-Huges Anne and Charmain, Robert. (1986) *The Pocket Guide to Italian Food and Wine*, London: Xanadu.

Strauth, Georg and Turner, Bryan S. (1988), 'Nostalgia, Postmodernism and the Critique of Mass Culture', *Theory, Culture and Society*, 5, 509-26.

Taglienti, Maria Luisa. (1956) *The Italian Cookbook*, London: William Kimber.

Thompson Craig J. (1996), "Caring Consumers: Gendered Consumption Meanings and the Juggling Lifestyle," *Journal of Consumer Research*, 22 (4), 388-407.

Thompson, Craig J. (1997) "Interpreting consumers: A hermeneutical framework for deriving marketing insights from the texts of consumer's consumption stories", *Journal of Marketing Research*, 34(4), 438-455.

Weaving, Andrew (2008) *Living Retro*, Ryland: Peters & Small Ltd

Zilli, Aldo (1998) *Aldos' Italian Food for Friends*, London: Metro.

Beyond Enemy Lines: Sociality in Consumer Activism

Leah Carter Schneider, York University, Canada
Robert Kozinets, York University, Canada

INTRODUCTION

Consumers and market entities clash in the marketplace over competing values, goals, and practices (Kozinets and Handleman 2004). Drawing on battle myths and discourses, consumers give meaning to and narrate market conflicts (Giesler 2008). In particular, the identification and characterization of an enemy is a fundamental component of consumer activists' ideology (Kozinets and Handleman 2004). Specific firms (e.g., Thompson, Rindfleisch, and Arsel 2006; Friedman 1991; Friedman 1996), hegemonic market discourses and movements (e.g., Thompson and Coskuner-Balli 2007; Kozinets 2002a), and "unenlightened" consumers (e.g., Kozinets and Handleman 2004; Luedicke, Thompson, and Giesler 2010) alike have been cast as adversarial foes in various market conflicts. Consumer activists, contrastingly, characterize themselves as heroic, wise rebels (Giesler 2008; Kozinets and Handleman 2004). Extant research on counter-market activities and movements appears to focus primarily on describing and exploring activism in dyadic terms between adversary and activist in market conflicts, including organized boycotts, doppelganger image creations, and escapist retreats (e.g., Kozinets 2002a; Giesler 2008; Kozinets and Handleman 2004; Holt 2002; Thompson et al. 2006; Friedman 1991; Friedman 1996).

Although marketplace conflicts center on adversarial relationships between a focal consumer hero and corporate/market antagonist, "supporting" relationships can arise or transform in ways that contribute to the enactment of activist initiatives and the development of market interactions. Relationships outside of the hero-ad-versary dyad, such as alliances between unlikely partners or friends who rally together with the hero to fight a common enemy, may be necessary for desired goal achievement and create a lasting effect on long-term market interactions. We therefore propose that consumer activism is more complex than consumers fighting against market foes, and by extension, more socially dynamic than linear models of consumer resistance (e.g., Giesler 2008) have suggested.

In this paper, we explore consumer activism to extend theoretical and practical understanding of the underlying complexity of market relationships that underpin resistance activities. Integrating consumer resistance, consumer community, and business alliance literatures, we address questions regarding the interplay between consumer relationships and activism: how and why consumer campaigns, a specific site of consumer activism, create a space for influencing market-based relationships, the role of alliances during campaigns, and how consumer community relationships are internally transformed as a result of campaigning.

CONSUMER RESISTANCE AND ACTIVISM

Consumer resistance colors marketplace dynamics. Rather than passively accepting hegemonic producer domination, consumers exert their individual and collective power by opposing market structures and discourses through innovative, nonconformist activities (Holt 2002). In order to begin to understand the importance of relationships in activism, we first address what is meant by activism. From past research, it appears that the actualization of consumer resistance varies in the marketplace (Figure 1).

FIGURE 1: CONSUMER RESISTANCE FRAMEWORK

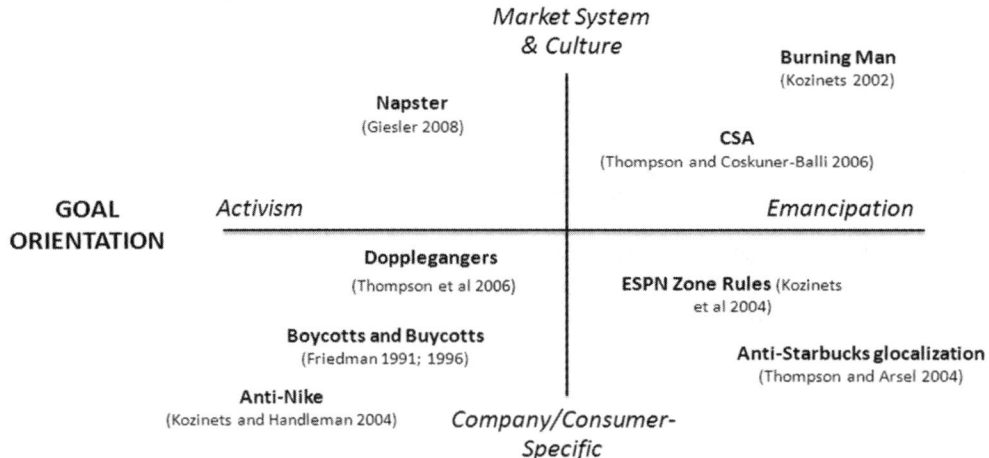

First, the goal orientation of resistance activities can range from goals centered on resistance *within* the market system that seek changes to the system, companies, or practices, to goals of emancipation *from* a market entity or system's rules, constraints, or hegemony. Some consumer projects have attempted to bring about desired changes to specific practices, policies, decisions, or behaviors to market-based entities. On the opposing side of the goal orientation dimension, consumer resistance efforts focus on breaking free from market rules, constraints, or hegemonic discourses. By so doing, these movements and activities create new systems of exchange and values that run counter to the dominant market system (e.g., counter-cultural movements, hypercommunities, and so on; Thompson and Coskuner-Balli 2007; Kozinets 2002a).

The second dimension organizes consumer resistance according to an identified adversary against whom consumers fight. Some resistance efforts primarily focus on micro-level resistance against a specific opponent, such as Starbucks, Wal-Mart, and Nike corporations (Thompson et al. 2006). Resistance activities can also challenge macro-level adversaries that include the capitalist market system (Giesler 2008) and dominant exchange discourses or norms (Kozinets 2002a; Thompson and Coskuner-Balli 2007). Rather than focusing resistance efforts on a specific company, these movements or behaviors attempt to resist an established and pervasive structure or discourse (e.g., the Napster rebellion against the market's music system).

Activism, from this resistance mapping, appears to be a subset of market resistance movements and behaviors. Consumer activists attempt to change an external entity (organization, business, and so on) or marketing norms, practices, and policies (Kozinets and Handleman 2004) in order to protect consumers from amoral, destructive, or undesirable corporate/marketer actions (Trentmann 2001). Consumer campaigns represent an organized, communal effort of activism. Campaigns are visible and vocal manifestations of a breach between consumers and producers, and can include campaigns that arise within pre-existing communities and communities that arise with particular campaign causes. As campaigns are a type of consumer resistance, it is likely that they arise in markets and exchange relationships marked by transitions and instability. In campaigning, activists group together and engage in deliberate activities oriented to achieve specific goals, often one primary goal, during a condensed time frame. Because campaigns are primarily goal driven, leveraging or forming new relationships may be necessary and beneficial tactics for consumers to pursue in order to attain desired goals.

CONSUMER SOCIALITY & ALLIANCES

Consumer activism is a social endeavor that is facilitated by communities formed by like-minded consumers (Muñiz and O'Guinn 2001). Consumer communities, though gathering spaces both online and offline for consumers who exhibit similar interests, values, goals, tastes, lifestyles, skills, and consumption preferences (Muñiz and O'Guinn 2001; Schouten and McAlexander 2002; Kozinets, Hemetsberger, and Schau 2008; Muñiz and Schau 2005), are not homogenous. Rather, collectives vary in purpose, participation, relationships, and core practices of the community (Kozinets, Hemetsberger, and Schau 2008; Schau, Muñiz, Arnould 2009). Kozinets, Hemetsberger, and Schau (2008) distinguished different consumer collectives, classifying them according to their goal orientation (i.e., telo-specific and communo-ludic) and contributor distribution (i.e., high and low), with activist communities engaged in campaigning exhibiting telo-specific qualities. Boundaries between community types are considered fluid, allowing for the possibility that communities may shift between one "type" to another over time due to new goals or contributor distribution, though the transformation process over time has been little discussed in the existing literature.

Changes in the environment and market uncertainty experienced in a consumer community may provide a catalyst for mobilizing a community to action, thereby transforming a community's goals in ways that simultaneously facilitates the formation of new alliances and propels a community from its previous orientation. In an organizational context, firms respond to external threats, such as likely losses, by altering internal and external practices, structures, and goals (Chattopadhyay, Glick, and Huber 2001) and exploring opportunities for alliances with other companies to control or mitigate market uncertainty (e.g., Thompson 1967; Pfeffer and Salancik 1978). Alliances between businesses can generate various benefits such as resource pooling (Das and Teng 2000), risk sharing (Ohmae 1989), and competency development (Hamel, Doz, and Prahalad

1989). The concept of alliances and the potential benefits derived from business-to-business alliances may be extended to explain and analyze relationships between consumer groups and other market entities that emerge in response to market instability.

Consumer communities, like organizations, must navigate problematic market changes utilizing a myriad of tactics and resources in order to survive and thrive in the marketplace. Organizing and enacting a consumer campaign represents a site of destabilized market conditions in which consumers' communal actions address a breakdown between consumers and producers. The act of campaigning may transform consumer communities in systematic ways, and incorporate the strategic use of consumer-generated alliances in order to actualize campaign and community goals. Breaking out of the hero-enemy myopia that has previously characterized consumer resistance research may therefore bring to light previously neglected phenomena occurring at the intersection of consumer relationships and activism.

METHOD

We investigated the social relationships associated with the three consumer-generated campaigns that emerged in pre-existing communities: "Save Polaroid," "Nuts for Jericho," and "Save Chuck." Each campaign arose as a result of the core production company either discontinuing or threatening to discontinue production of the community's central product. We selected these sites as prime candidates for exploring the sociality of consumer activism, as these communities negotiated past and present goals, relationships, and market tensions, and thus were more suitable for the purpose of this study than campaigns that did not originate in a pre-existing community.

To begin unpacking the complex system of relationships in consumer activism, we first conducted an historical analysis of fan campaigns. By so doing, we identified previous activities and relationships noted in the accounts as formed during the consumer campaigns, which in turn guided protocol formation. In order to capture a more inclusive picture of the social relationships impacted by the campaigns, we then conducted ten in-depth interviews with campaign leaders/organizers. Following McCracken (1988), the primary author elicited a "grand tour" overview of each informant's experience and probed for further detail about relationship formation and transformation using emergent prompts and pre-determined questions. The interviews lasted approximately 90 minutes each, with interview times ranging from 45 minutes to 150 minutes, and were transcribed verbatim by the author.

We triangulated the interview data with netnographic data (Kozinets 2002b; Kozinets 2010) obtained through group message boards, media articles, and websites devoted to the activist campaigns. The primary gathering place for the consumer communities and organizing space for campaigns occurs online. By investigating the consumer-generated content and conversations on the websites, we were able to examine the members' negotiation of relationships and initiative enactment throughout the campaigns.

Following the hermeneutic method of data analysis (Thompson 1997), we analyzed each interview separately, noting themes that both arose within the data and aligned with themes pre-determined from the literature. We then compared interviews and related themes in order to identify commonalities across the interviews within each campaign, and then across all three campaigns. It is significant to note that the initial impetus for data collection was to probe consumer campaigns from a strategy perspective. However, through the data collection process and analysis over subsequent rounds, a resounding theme of sociality appeared as a central component coloring much of the leaders' discussion of their experiences with the campaign. The focus on internal and external sociality is therefore an emergent theme from the data.

FINDINGS

From the data set, three interrelated themes emerged that explored the complexity of consumer campaign relationships. As the consumer communities faced potentially community-threatening discontinuation of their core products, the communities experienced a shift in goals, identities, and focus that created transitory, liminal spaces for altering relationships within and external to the community. The fluidity of relationships experienced during the campaign periods not only facilitated the coordination of the strategic campaign efforts, but also impacted community relationships in the short and long term.

Communal Liminality

Consumer campaigns appear to be sites of communal liminality in which a consumer collective underwent transformations as they encountered and negotiated market threats. The campaigns represented liminal playspaces for the campaigners in which they could create new actions beyond their traditional methods and resources. Occurring during times of market unrest and change, the campaigns were organized in response to external threats, with the communities fighting to save their products and by extension, ensure their survival as vibrant, living communities. By organizing goal-oriented campaigns, the communities experienced a state of transition and flux, attempting to negotiate not only their community membership, but also their new identity as rallied troops armed for battle and the corresponding activities.

Before the discontinuations and subsequent campaigning, members identified the communities as predominantly fan collectives. Members gathered at their leisure to share consumption experiences, stories, opinions, knowledge, critiques, innovative ideas with one another. Community activities, such as the Polaroid Nerd-Outs (day gatherings of Polaroid users to go on Polaroid-taking excursions), enhanced the anti-digital and consumerism group identity of the Polaroid community. Both "Jericho" and "Chuck" communities were considered to be "fanatic" communities prior to their respective campaigns: actively debating storyline developments, dissecting plot twists, and judging episode quality as the respective seasons progressed. Informants noted that the core of active members were a relatively small group of contributors, although the communities were frequented by numerous lurkers who did not actively join in the community (Kozinets 1999).

Product discontinuation threatened the core reason for the groups' existing. Informants responded by leading the community to shift the primary orientation of the community. In place of central interactions and activities that focused on the consumption experiences with the products, members adopted an overarching, task-oriented goal to rescue their beloved products. Succinctly stated by Christian, "Here's the goal. The goal is to get the show back." Additional campaign goals, such as spreading the word about the campaign, recruiting new members, and so on, supported the overarching, primary motivational goal of rescuing the products in question. The primary goals served as the rallying cry and unifying point for the consumers to exert a common, shared effort during the campaign periods that effectively mobilized communities to new, Telo-specific orientations.

As the campaigners enacted the campaigns, the identities of the overall communities also shifted. Previously loose collectives of individuals, informants described the communities no longer as just fan communities, but as troops, armies, and soldiers ready for the ensuing conflict. As Steve noted, "it was like a war we were in, and we were taking on CBS trying to bring the show back." As armies of devoted, action-ready combatants, the communities and their leaders were positioned to enter into battle as a unified collective, focusing

efforts and energies on rescuing the beloved products, though some individuals resisted the change in orientation.

However, the shift between states was not seamlessly accomplished. Steve described that in the "Jericho" community, "some pockets were still talking about the episodes, which was fine. Most of the rest of us were busy caught up in saving the show. During the show, fans…everybody was great in talking about the episodes. During the campaign, obviously people were fighting to save the show. Everybody was together and everything else to save it." It therefore appears that shifting orientations is not without difficulty, as some consumers may resist the change. As a result, the communities experienced relative hybrid states of both fan and activist orientations that most likely further contributes to the feeling of instability and liminality.

Fluidity of Relationships & External Relationships

The relatively short time frame for coordinated action, as well as the specific and singularly focused goals of the campaigns, positioned community members to fluidly engage in or dissolve relationships both externally and internally. We define the construct of relationship fluidity as the mobility of individuals or organizations to form/reform relationship constellations or characterizations. Capitalizing on the changeable nature of relationships opened the door for campaigning consumers to incorporate desirable allies into their folds – allies who could provide resources such as bargaining power with the networks, distribution and communication channels, and so on. Relationship fluidity also created an opportunity for communities to adjust course and manage emergent issues throughout the campaigns when faced with external opposition or change. Consequently, relationship fluidity played a key role in the management and negotiation of communal instability during the campaign periods.

The formation of short-term alliances generated needed resources for the enactment of novel consumer initiatives. Potential market allies were targeted by community members as those market entities whose sentiments and sympathies aligned with the product or community, or those who would benefit from participating in the campaign. Alliances were explored both with previously affiliated market players and third-party companies. Zoey, in conceptualizing the "Finale and a Footlong" initiative of having consumers purchase Subway sandwiches on the day of the "Chuck" season finale, described: "it turned out to be a very easy way that…shows this advertiser, 'We noticed. We noticed your product, and we're going to buy it, because you were on the show.' I was hoping that Subway would see it and they might want to be further involved." As a result, Greg related that "we heard that the VP of marketing at Subway had called Ben Silverman, who was the head of NBC at the time, and talked to him about Chuck. And that's all the info we got at that point. And then we heard more and more from our sources that NBC was talking with Subway and that actually, Subway had initiated the conversation because of the fan campaign." Based on the spike in sales and immensely positive public relations, Subway entered the conflict as an ally to the consumers. By so doing, Subway was able to provide the communities with vicarious bargaining power in negotiations with the network, offering themselves as a more visible and involved sponsor in the show, and providing an added monetary incentive for NBC to renew "Chuck."

Alliances were also formed with third-party companies that provided capabilities and resources unavailable to the individual consumer or community. During the "Nuts for Jericho" campaign, campaign leaders suggested using an online nut company as a way to revolutionize the campaign:"Most campaigns, people send their individual purchase in. This vendor agreed to pull funds. So you could put in however much you could afford, and at the end of the day, he would tally it and he shipped every couple of days." (Gina) Congregating the orders served to motivate fans to continue their efforts, as the daily and weekly tallies of nuts delivered were published on the nut distributor's website, through his personal videos of delivering the nuts to the network, and on the community's discussion boards. The formation and utilization of an external, third-party ally in this case therefore served a strategic purpose in providing additional pools of resources previously unneeded by the community. However, once the need was fulfilled, the momentary alliance between the third-party producer and the community dissolved, leaving good memories and a ton of nuts at CBS' studios. Thus, in this case, forming alliances represented a fluid resource that was rooted in the transitory nature of the campaign and the goals needing to be achieved at that point in time.

Relationship fluidity not only contributed needed resources to the campaigns for strategic purposes, but also allowed for the communities to adjust to the changing external environment by characterizing new players as potential allies or foes, as seeming fit by the circumstances. For example, for the Polaroid community, as it became evident that Polaroid was no longer going to be producing instant film, community members sought alternative avenues for production so that they could achieve their goal of saving instant film. Fuji film was targeted by leaders for community appeals, as a producer of instant film, though the products would not work directly with Polaroid cameras. Although petitions and letters were sent to the company, the members were disappointed in the non-realization of their potential ally. "We never really got any response from anyone at Fuji. And it's only through like third hand that [we learned] they were not interested… we were sad that they kind of ignored us and our request that they make something the looked like Polaroids and could work with Polaroid cameras." (Dean) The possibility of forming an alliance with Fuji, diffused by the lack of cooperation and interest on the part of the company, resulted in dissolving the hopes and abandoning the ally characterization of the company. The Polaroid community moved on to identifying other possible allies in the market and extending their efforts to encourage an alliance.

Therefore, it appears that the communities exhibited movement in their characterization of and allegiance with market players. Relationship fluidity provided communities with the ability to identify and engage in short-term alliances with external companies that increased pool of needed resources for specific campaign initiatives. The characterization and supplication for involvement seems to be influenced by the goal orientation, external conditions, and novelty of desired initiatives.

Community Transformation

Community relationship transformations. During and after the campaigns, internal community relationships also underwent significant transformations. Consumer-community, consumer-consumer, consumer-brand, and consumer-market relationships were affected as consumers engaged in their activist efforts. First, community leaders sought to revolutionize member overall focused on "rallying the troops," (Marcus) sending out calls to arms to transform lurkers into active members, recruit new members, and motivate members into action. "The activities we designed were really to get people out of their seats, away from their computers, and into the real world to take action." (Dean) Current members worked to recruit new members to the community, as Sam noted in the "Save Polaroid" plan: "Phase 1 was create a lot of noise. Get people interested in what's going on. The choir kind of already knew, but it brought new members into the choir." New recruits cited exposure to the campaigns through the

media and active networking by members as primary causes for their participation. In addition to the stream of new members, community leadership structures emerged and transformed during the campaign periods. In order to coordinate and direct widespread action, leadership groups were formed within the larger community in order to act as gatekeepers, motivators, and strategists for the campaigns:

"But we had a very tight-knit group of maybe 20 people. These are all people we had all communicated with each other on the boards. We knew each other at least in cyberspace. And Sarah [main leader] basically pulled everybody together, and, you know, we held meetings on Skype. Kind of strategy meetings, saying, okay, what are we going to do this next week, and how are we going to do it, and what's the most effective thing to do." (Christian)

New leaders also rose up in the ranks of the community by their active campaigning, innovative ideas for campaign initiatives, visibility through frequent communications, or by the expertise offered from prior campaign activities. Thus, the combination of the influx of new participants and the restructuration of the community leadership contributed to the redistribution of contributors from a small nucleus of contributors to a more diverse set of active participants, with distinctive leadership groups propelling the campaign forward. The overall orientation of the communities therefore shifted in response to the active mobilization of the communities through the campaign process.

Market player transformation. The campaigning communities shifted their focus from primarily enjoying the products as consumers to seeking and incorporation of market logics within the community, thus evolving the consumer-market relationship. Campaign leaders educated themselves to the behind-the-scene business structure that contributed to the production of the products, key decisions makers, and ways of "speaking" to the companies in ways that would be impactful. When organizing the "Finale and a Footlong" initiative for the "Save Chuck" campaign, Greg discussed the importance of communicating to the network in a way that would garner legitimate attention:

"This was a very similar idea, except that I wanted it to be a little more cohesive with the marketing strategy, and for the show itself, because they care if we send them a bunch of nerd candy? I'm like..yeah. It's cute and it's funny. But what are they going to do with it? So instead of sending them candy and nuts, which sounds like Valentine's Day, but instead of sending them a product, if we can coordinate and show an actual purchase to a key sponsor or advertiser, I think a happy advertiser is always going to be welcome at a network."

Moving beyond buzz-worthy gimmicks, such as sending large quantities of products that represent the show, Chuck's leaders leveraged experiences from previous consumer campaigns and knowledge of the television advertising system to elevate their campaign to fight using the logic that would appeal to the network as a business. "It's based upon ratings and whether or not it's going to be profitable. Because at the end of the day, NBC, Warner Brothers, and other advertisers like Subway are businesses. They need to sell a product and make a profit. And you know, by doing this, we were playing the game." (Mindy) The leaders used their understanding of the market system for their particular as a way to strategically tailor their initiatives to have the greatest impact on a business level.

"Save Polaroid" members considered the competitive landscape and product line alignment of potential producers in a bid to find an appropriate producer-product fit for instant film, "that a company like Fuji and a company like Ilford who had a strong focus on analog film might be interested in buying some of the film from Polaroid and really moving forward, adding one more product to their list of products and sort of shoring up their analog base." (Dean) Campaigning consumers did not campaigning simply based on the platform of passionate fan support, as had been touted in prior campaigns. Rather, the informants entered into the market dialogue by employing research, market analyses, and business knowledge as tools for strategy development and campaign initiatives. Thus, the act of campaigning appears to create a catalyst for members to adopt a more market-oriented sensibility that incorporated business knowledge within the community. Individual members led the way for the community, strengthening and leveraging market-oriented relationships based on the adoption and application of market logics.

Long-term community relationship transformations. The respective battles fought during the campaigns continued to affect consumer-brand and consumer-consumer relationships within the communities. Some informants were unable to go back to the "good 'ole days," continuing to act in a mobilized state as a result of feeling an increased and vested interest in the community-brand relationship. These stalwart campaigns continued to discuss new ways to promote the product, garner new community members, and so on, long after the immediate threats had been resolved. "I knew from what Jericho had done, you know, their failure really. I mean, they got the show back, but then it failed. And I knew from their failure that our work had just begun. That we had to do something bigger. We had to motivate the fan base even more." (Mark) Ardent members acknowledged that they felt an increased burden of responsibility for the success of their products in later incarnations, and that they would be held accountable for both failures and successes by both other members and producers. The relationship between some community members and the product was strengthened through this increased responsibility and residual sense that the consumers were partly responsible for their successful campaigns in bringing back the desired products.

The relationships within the communities between individual consumers after the campaigns were tested and in some cases, dissolved. Some members, exhausted from the intense campaigning period or disillusioned with other community members, effectively "resigned" their status within the communities. It appears that without the guiding and unifying goal to save the product, conversations descended into bickering and argumentation as individuals fought over the direction of the community, leading some consumers exiting the main community and forming exclusive segments. Gina, who assumed a new role in the overall "Jericho" community as an emissary and middleman, mentioned that "there's some people that still won't talk to each other. And there's probably some people in my other group that I don't talk to. There's not too many people in the Jericho group I don't talk to, because it just seems so silly." Acting as a go-between, Gina had to forge new connections between the divergent groups in order to continue sharing information in the overall group. The vacuum of post-campaign directive goals and attitudes appears to have contributed to the destabilization of previously strengthened relationships, and altered the structure of community networks. Campaigning thus appears to have exerted more than a momentary transformative power on internal relationships. Organizing and fighting to save a product seems to have shifted communities in ways that led to new relationships forming or changing over time within the community.

DISCUSSION

Beyond the front lines of consumer hero and market foe lies a complex system of relationships that arise and shift in relation to the response of rising to resist market decisions. Based on the transformations of communities to new orientations and the liminal space in which consumers function as both consumers and activists aiming to achieve particular goals, fluid alliances provided access to needed skills and capabilities of useful market players, represented a method for dealing with the ever-changing external environment, and transformed a community both during and after the campaign period.

Consumer campaigns, like other forms of consumer resistance (e.g., Thompson et al 2006; Giesler 2008), are of strategic importance for companies. Not only can unaffiliated companies develop alternative streams of revenue when collaborating with consumer communities during campaign periods, but also targeted companies can improve consumer relations by actively working with communities to facilitate the mobilization and reorientation of consumer groups into viable promotion and production collaborators. Activists, as part of their goals, work to recruit members through word-of-mouth marketing, testimonials, product trial offers, and so on. As emissaries and ambassadors of the products, companies can benefit from the mobilization and involvement of activists in the marketplace. Further, because consumers utilize the campaigns as opportunities to learn more about and engage with the market on a business level, companies have the chance to cultivate co-creative relationships with market savvy individuals after campaign periods. Thus, we recommend that companies expand their perspective of consumer campaigners: though some many seem to be fanatic extremists, they have the potential to greatly contribute to the future of the product.

Our contributions to consumer literature are five fold. First, contrary to Giesler's (2008) linear, dramatic model of consumer resistance, we find that activism is more fluid and multidimensional in terms of the social structures and actors involved in consumer-generated campaigns. Relationship fluidity appears to be a necessary and useful construct when discussing consumer activism, and by extension, the strategic use of and characterizations of external partnerships. Second, we also note the strategic importance of emergent campaign goals in enabling and guiding relationship formations in activism. New goals fostered the transformation from community orientations, provided a standard under which consumers could gather, and acted as a key criterion for engaging in external alliances. Third, we extend beyond Muniz and Schau's (2005; 2007) findings to suggest that through activism, consumer communities are motivated to engage with market discourses and practices to become strategically minded consumer organizations who are further integrated into the market system. Fourth, we contribute a conceptualization of consumer resistance behaviors that identifies the nuanced differences of consumer resistance as exhibited in the marketplace. Finally, we address longitudinal community transformations, a hitherto neglected area of consumer research, and suggest that the transformations resulting from consumer activism create both short-term adjustments, and long-term shifts in community activities, foci, and networks.

We suggest that corporations take a broader perspective when confronting consumer campaigns. Not only can unaffiliated companies develop alternative streams of revenue when collaborating with consumer communities during campaign periods, but also targeted companies can improve consumer relations by actively working with communities to facilitate the mobilization and reorientation of consumer groups into viable promotion and production collaborators.

REFERENCES

Chattopadhyay, Prithviraj, William H. Glick, and George P. Huber (2001), "Organizational Actions in Response to Threats and Opportunities," *Academy of Management Journal*, 44 (5), 937-955.

Das, T.K. and Bing-Sheng (2000), "A Resource-Based Theory of Strategic Alliances," *Journal of Management*, 26 (1), 31-61.

Eisenhardt, Kathleen M. and Claudia Bird Schoonhoven (1996), "Resource-based View of Strategic Alliance Formation: Strategic and Social Effects in Entrepreneurial Firms," *Organization Science*, 7 (2), 136-150.

Friedman, Monroe (1991), "Consumer boycotts: A conceptual framework and research agenda," *Journal of Social Issues,* 47, 149-168.

--- (1996), "A Positive Approach to Organized Consumer Action: The 'Buycott' as an Alternative to Boycott," *Journal of Consumer Policy,* 19, 439-451.

Giesler, Markus (2008), "Conflict and Compromise: Drama in Marketplace Evolution," *Journal of Consumer Research*, 34 (April), 739-753.

Hamel, Gary, Yves L. Doz, and C.K. Prahalad (1989), "Collaborate with Your Competitors – and Win," *Harvard Business Review*, 67 (January/February), 133-139.

Holt, Douglas B. (2002), "Why Do Brands Cause Trouble: A Dialectical Theory of Consumer Culture and Branding," *Journal of Consumer Research*, 29 (June), 70-90.

Kozinets, Robert V. (1999), "E-Tribalized Marketing? The Strategic Implications of Virtual Communities of Consumption," *European Management Journal,* 17 (3), 252-264.

--- (2002a), "Can Consumers Escape the Market?: Emancipatory Illuminations from Burning Man," *Journal of Consumer Research*, 29 (June), 20-38.

--- (2002b), "The Field behind the Screen: Using Netnography for Marketing Research in Online Communities," *Journal of Marketing Research*, 39 (February), 61-72.

--- (2010), *Netnography: Doing Ethnographic Research Online.* Thousand Oaks: Sage.

Kozinets, Robert and Jay Handleman (2004), "Adversaries of consumption: consumer movements, activism and ideology", *Journal of Consumer Research*, 31(December), 691-704.

Kozinets, Robert, Andrea Hemestberger, and Hope Jensen Schau (2008), "The Wisdom of Consumer Crowds: Collective Innovation in the Age of Networked Marketing," *Journal of Macromarketing*, 28, 339-354.

Luedicke, Marius K., Craig J. Thompson, and Markus Giesler (2010), "Consumer Identity Work as Moral Protagonism: How Myth and Ideology Animate a Brand-Mediated Moral Conflict," *Journal of Consumer Research*, 36 (6), 1016-1032.

McAlexander, James H., John W. Schouten and Harold F. Koenig (2002), "Building Brand Community," *Journal of Marketing*, 66 (1), 38-54.

McCracken, Grant (1988), *The Long Interview*. Newbury Park: Sage Publications.

Muñiz, Albert M. Jr., and Thomas C. O'Guinn (2001), "Brand Community," *Journal of Consumer Research*, 27 (March), 412–32.

Muñiz, Albert M. Jr. and Hope Jensen Schau (2005), "Religiosity in the Abandoned Apple Newton Brand," *Journal of Consumer Research*, 31 (4), 737-747.

Muñiz, Albert M. Jr. and Hope Jensen Schau (2007), "Vigilante Marketing and Consumer-Created Communications," *Journal of Advertising*, 36 (3), 187-202.

Ohmae, Kenichi (1989), "The Global Logic of Strategic Alliances," *Harvard Business Review*, 67 (March/April), 145-154.

Pfeffer, Jeffrey and Gerald Salancik (1978), *The External Control of Organizations: A Resource Dependence Perspective.* New York: Harper and Row.

Schau, Hope Jensen, Albert M. Muñiz Jr., and Eric J. Arnould (2009), "How Brand Community Practices Create Value," *Journal of Marketing*, 73 (3), 30-51.

Schouten, John W. and James McAlexander (1995), "Subculture of Consumption: An Ethnography of the New Bikers," *Journal of Consumer Research*, 22 (March), 43-51.

Thompson, Craig J. (1997), "Interpreting Consumers: A Hermeneutical Framework for Deriving Marketing Insights from the Texts of Consumers' Consumption Stories," *Journal of Marketing Research*, 34 (November), 438-455.

Thompson, Craig J. and Gokcen Coskuner-Balli (2007), "Countervailing Market Responses to Corporate Co-optation and the Ideological Recruitment of Consumption Communities," *Journal of Consumer Research*, 34 (February), 595-612.

Thompson, Craig J., Aric Rindfleisch, and Zeynep Arsel (2006), "Emotional Branding and the Value of the Doppleganger Brand Image," *Journal of Marketing*, 70 (January), 50-64.

Thompson, James D. (1967), *Organizations in Action.* New York: McGraw-Hill.

Trentmann, Frank (2001), "Bread, Milk, and Democracy: Consumption and Citizenship in Twentieth-Century Britain," in *The Politics of Consumption*, ed. Martin Daunton and Matthew Hilton, New York: Berg, 129-164.

Learning to Resist: The Challenges Faced by Beginner Voluntary Simplifiers

Paul Ballantine, University of Canterbury, New Zealand
Paula Arbouw, University of Canterbury, New Zealand
Lucie Ozanne, University of Canterbury, New Zealand

INTRODUCTION

As a form of resistance against the dominant marketing system, anti-consumption has existed since the start of consumerism (Kozinets and Handelman 2004), with anti-consumption being defined as a "resistance to, distaste of, or even resentment or rejection of, consumption more generally" (Zavestoski 2002a, 121). This definition suggests that the concepts of anti-consumption and consumer resistance are inextricably linked, and this paper seeks to explore how these concepts can be used to understand the challenges faced by beginner voluntary simplifiers (a category of anti-consumers) when they try to remove themselves from (or resist) the market.

The idea of voluntary simplicity was first introduced by Gregg (1936), who took his inspiration from the great spiritual leaders of history who he believed practiced the lifestyle. When describing the term, Gregg (1936) identifies concepts such as 'singleness of purpose', 'sincerity and honesty within', and the 'avoidance of exterior clutter', as being the central tenets of voluntary simplification. More recently, Etzioni (1998, 620) defines voluntary simplicity as "the choice out of free will ... to limit expenditures on consumer goods and services, and to cultivate non-materialistic sources of satisfaction and meaning". This definition also emphasizes the voluntary nature of the lifestyle, in that it should not occur through either coercion by authorities or as a means of budgeting through tough economic times (Leonard-Barton 1981). To date, the literature on voluntary simplicity has largely focused on either defining or operationalising the term (e.g., Etzioni 1998; Iyer and Muncy 2009; Leonard-Barton 1981), exploring the motivations behind the lifestyle (e.g., Shaw and Newholm 2002; Zavestoski 2002b), or examining the practices of experienced voluntary simplifiers (e.g., Craig-Lees and Hill 2002; Huneke 2005).

To counter the problem that much of the extant literature focuses on those people who have fully adopted the voluntary simplifier lifestyle, McDonald et al. (2006) recognize the importance of a large consumer segment that displays voluntary simplifier behavior, but are not committed or fully converted to the voluntary simplifier lifestyle, terming these people beginner voluntary simplifiers. Within the beginner voluntary simplifier segment, they distinguish between three types of simplifiers: *apprentice simplifiers*, who are voluntary simplifiers in the making; *partial simplifiers*, people that settle for lifestyles with some beginner simplifier features; and *accidental simplifiers*, people that simplify involuntarily because of economic reasons and are often not concerned with the ethical or environmental aspects of consumption.

The focus of this study is on those people who exhibit many of the characteristics of apprentice simplifiers (i.e., they have decided to adopt the voluntary simplifier lifestyle, but are in the early stages of doing so), but for the purpose of this paper, they will still be referred to as beginner voluntary simplifiers. Although not explicitly focusing on this group, Ballantine and Creery (2010) explore the disposition activities of voluntary simplifiers, noting the difficulty associated with the early stages of adopting the lifestyle, and its role in identity construction. The authors also suggest a vague endpoint to the journey of becoming a voluntary simplifier, with some of their participants professing a desire to live 'off the grid', and others indicating that they will always have some reliance on the market for what they need. In this respect, the journey of becoming a voluntary simplifier can be viewed as a liminal transition (Noble and Walker 1997; Turner 1969), where an individual separates themselves from an existing role (i.e., a mainstream consumer) and undergoes a transitional process (the liminal period) before fully incorporating their new role as a voluntary simplifier into their daily lives.

Such a perspective is consistent with the idea that consumption and anti-consumption, and the attitudes individuals hold about their choices, can act as a form of identity creation and expression (Zavestoski 2002b). For example, attitudes about consumption can be linked to the undesired self, which serves as a reference point for judging overall life satisfaction (Hogg, Banister, and Stephenson 2009). Moreover, consumption is no longer always related to a positive self-concept, with anti-consumption increasingly becoming important in this area (Zavestoski 2002b). Furthermore, anti-consumption can be practiced in several ways, and does not necessarily have to mean non-consumption; it ranges from resistance to the rejection of consumption, and has varying degrees of visibility (Hogg et al. 2009). However, irrespective of what form of anti-consumption behavior occurs, the literature suggests that these behaviors are context dependent, and that the behaviors, challenges and attitudes associated with anti-consumption are highly affected by social, cultural and market influences (Zavestoski 2002b). In many instances, anti-consumption behaviors go against social norms, and therefore, can be stressful (Iyer and Muncy 2009), with Cherrier and Murray (2007) also noting the emotional costs associated with resisting consumption.

Although Bekin, Carrigan, and Szmigin (2005) note that market resistance is a reason why people adopt the voluntary simplifier lifestyle, the literature suggests that not everyone is able to successfully adopt the lifestyle and escape the consumer society. Arnould (2007) argues that the whole idea of anti-consumption reinforces social classes, because only the wealthy can afford to resist the market by adopting voluntary simplicity lifestyles. Similarly, Taylor-Gooby (1998) suggests that voluntary simplicity is a luxury for rich and secure minorities, arguing that the 'greening' of capitalism should be a worldwide project. For both Arnould (2007) and Taylor-Gooby (1998), the notion of being able to escape the market is a romanticized idea, with Arnould providing the example of an African community that is deprived of consumption to support his point-of-view. To counter this, some authors (e.g., McDonald et al. 2006) have highlighted how voluntary simplicity does not necessarily have to be practiced away from the market. Even though voluntary simplifiers can stay within the market, Taylor-Gooby (1998) would criticize them for doing so, arguing that they often keep much of their wealth, and that their approach is too silent; ignoring the possibility of a more activist approach.

Taken together, the literature indicates that market resistance is a reason why many people adopt the voluntary simplifier lifestyle, that consumer resistance is often a difficult act to undertake, and that little is known about individuals early in their transition into becoming a voluntary simplifier, so it is of interest to explore the challenges beginner voluntary simplifiers experience when they try to remove themselves from the market. Thus, a key contribution of this paper is to address the following research question: what challenges do beginner voluntary simplifiers face when trying to resist the market from which they are trying to escape?

Given the above focus, this study will not explore the reasons for adopting the lifestyle, nor will it examine the activities undertaken while adopting the lifestyle; the focus is instead on the challenges en-

Advances in Consumer Research
Volume 39, ©2011

countered when adopting the lifestyle, and the reasons it may be difficult to do so. This study also explores resistance to the market as a whole, as opposed to resistance to a specific brand (e.g., Lee, Motion, and Conroy 2009) or specific marketplace behavior (e.g., Close and Zinkhan 2009), which has often been the focus of the literature to date.

METHODOLOGY

This study was interested in the challenges faced by beginner voluntary simplifiers as they adopt their new lifestyle. Since these experiences are subjective, and full of emotional and symbolic content (e.g., Holbrook and Hirschman 1982), rich exploratory qualitative data was gathered from participants. Moreover, given the purpose of this study was to understand the experiences of participants in their own words, an interpretivist methodological approach (e.g., Lincoln and Guba 1985) was taken.

Fourteen beginner voluntary simplifiers were interviewed for this study using a series of in-depth semi-structured interviews. Each interview was approximately one hour in length. The participants ranged in age from 22 to 58, and they were all in the early stages of adopting the voluntary simplifier lifestyle (i.e., they had made the decision to adopt the lifestyle within the previous six month period). Six participants were male and eight were female. To recruit participants, both purposive and snowball sampling were used. Purposive sampling allowed participants to be selected on the basis of specific criteria (i.e., they were beginner voluntary simplifiers), and also allowed diversity to be built into the sample (Lincoln and Guba 1985). These participants were contacted through a sustainability network based in Christchurch, New Zealand. The members of this network were interested in learning about and practicing behaviors consistent with voluntary simplifier behavior. Snowball sampling then meant that those people interested in participating in this study could act as a link, where they identified other potential participants (Miles and Huberman 1994) with similar values, but who were not members of the sustainability network. Based upon a series of questions asked during the recruitment process, the participants in this study perceived themselves as wanting to achieve a lifestyle consistent with the definition of voluntary simplicity provided by Etzioni (1998).

The interviews had a phenomenological focus (i.e., they were from the perspective of the participants). Although an interview guide was followed, the interviews had the nature of a conversation, allowing the researcher to follow the interviewees lead and adjust the course of the interview to the topics that emerged. This approach allowed participants to provide thick descriptions, where they were able to articulate their experiences as they perceived them. To analyze the challenges faced by participants when adopting the voluntary simplifier lifestyle, a within case analysis (Miles and Huberman 1994) was used to gain insight, and was undertaken in the form of coding and sorting, which Tesch (1990) describes as decontextualising as the data are separated from their original cases. The data were then recontextualised through the identification of themes present across cases. The themes were constructed from reoccurring statements or concepts described by the participants (Miles and Huberman 1994). Given the potential for multiple interpretations of the data, two independent judges were used to authenticate the findings.

ANALYSIS AND RESULTS

Six main themes emerged from the interviews, which allow us to understand the challenges faced by beginner voluntary simplifiers as they adopt their new lifestyle and try to resist the pressures of the market. These themes were: habitual consumption, nongenerosity, planning and organizing, substituting experiences, money as an enabler, and balancing social activities and reducing consumption.

Habitual Consumption

All participants found adopting the lifestyle most difficult at the start, but easier later on, as they were able to break their habits and change their mindset. Many also felt frustrated and deprived while doing so. Kayla (aged 22) typified many participants when she reflected "I was tired and working heaps and kind of over it, and I think that was mainly because I was needing to change my ways, my routines, and changing all of that is quite hard. It takes a lot of energy and thought, and you are constantly nagging with yourself".

After a period of adjustment, participants frequently noticed that they did not miss the things they had previously been used to. Moreover, participants often formed new habits which they were happy about. Andrea (aged 27), for example, created the habit of bringing her own lunch to work rather than buying it, stating "It's really good getting into that habit and it's not that hard. Once I got a routine, for example the lunches, it kind of got easier. So originally I had to change my bad habits, but once I had a routine and I could stick to that it got easier I think".

Of all behavior, habits are often the hardest to break because they are ingrained and automatic (Verplanken and Wood 2006), so it was not surprising that participants experienced some difficulty while trying to alter their habitual consumption behavior. It was also evident that after a period of adjustment, behaviors consistent with the voluntary simplifier lifestyle became the norm. However, the short-term difficulty associated with changing habitual consumption behavior could act as a barrier for any individual undertaking the lifestyle.

Nongenerosity

Another challenge faced by participants was nongenerosity, or the unwillingness to share or give possessions to others (Belk 1984). This often manifested itself in not spending money on others, but also included the reduced giving of material items like gifts, as participants felt they needed to look after their own needs first. For Thomas (aged 31), needing to be careful with money in social situations was a negative experience, but he suggested that self-awareness was a way of overcoming this, saying "It does make you a little bit more stingy, which has the potential for impacting either your quality of life or your social interaction ... but simply being aware of that reflex seems to do enough to counterbalance it".

Other participants found that being more frugal did not have to result in nongenerosity as they made personal gifts, supporting the idea that a positive outcome of frugality is increased creativity, especially when using and re-using resources (e.g., Lastovicka et al. 1999).

Planning and Organizing

Reducing consumption often required a substantial effort to plan and organize. Homemade lunches, supermarket shopping, homemade gifts, and alternative social activities were common areas where advanced planning was needed. Many participants, when adopting the lifestyle, found planning and organizing difficult due to the time and effort involved. For example, Harry (aged 31) observed "I had to be more organized which I wasn't used to and was very difficult. I wasn't used to planning and thinking ahead. I normally buy as I go".

Participants also realized that consumption was a form of buying time. For example, when buying fast food, the extra money spent was seen as payment for the time saved. Voluntary simplicity can be viewed as the luxury consumption of time (Arnould 2007), and when first adopting the lifestyle, participants reflected that they needed to find a balance between time and money.

Substituting Experiences

Participants found that reducing their consumption via substitution did not have a major effect on their well-being, although the process of finding alternative solutions for their previous consumption behavior was often challenging. The substitution of previous consumption behaviors by voluntary simplifiers is discussed in the literature (e.g., Bekin et al. 2005), and participants in this study found alternatives such as watching movies at home instead of going out, or in the instance of Daniel (aged 44): "I bought fake maple syrup instead of real maple syrup … In a lot of cases I ended up compromising on quantity or cost…".

As exemplified by this quote, the participants came across the dilemma of whether to reduce their consumption in terms of quality or quantity. Another participant decided to buy more expensive beer, because he found he gained the same satisfaction from consuming less. Ahuvia (2008) recognizes a tension in anti-consumption known as the *Rolex Dilemma*, which indicates that anti-consumption requires people to choose between items that are better quality and will last longer versus items that are cheaper but of poorer quality, and this trade-off was found to affect all participants.

Money as an Enabler

When adopting the lifestyle, participants encountered the realization that money was acting as an enabler for activities that made them happy. With this, they often struggled to balance their reducing consumption while still participating in the activities they loved. However, reducing consumption could sometimes go too far, with Dylan (aged 23) stating "There is obviously under consumption, so you've got to find a range which is comfortable for you. Spending that much and getting all the emotional, physical, mental and spiritual fulfillment that you need … Money isn't really going to get you happiness … It's not an end in itself, it is a means to an end, so if you get what you want without spending any money you are fine".

Thus, while participants recognized the role of money in facilitating consumption, they also realized that money was often only a means to an end. Moreover, many activities undertaken by participants had little monetary cost (e.g., going for walks, picnics),

while others did require a level of financial commitment (e.g., outdoor sports such as kayaking and rock climbing, or activities such as dance lessons). With these activities often being linked to a sense of well-being, participants reported that their expectations about what activities they could still participate in as part of the voluntary simplicity lifestyle played a role in how they maintained their quality of life, while still decreasing their consumption in a manner consistent with the lifestyle they had adopted.

Balancing Social Activities and Reducing Consumption

Another challenge for participants was balancing social activities while reducing consumption, as much of their social interaction was based around consumption activities like going out for coffee, movies, or drinks. Thus, they often struggled to find a balance between reducing their consumption and maintaining their social network as the following reflection by Monique (aged 31) suggests: "Sometimes I found it a bit socially isolating as well for the reason that I want to go to a café and be around other people and want to go out with friends".

To address these issues, participants tried to find social activities that were either based on cheaper/reduced consumption (e.g., buying coffee instead of lunch), or free consumption. Free activities included going for walks, picnics and home gatherings, which are considered by Etzioni (1998) as typical downshifter behaviors. However, some participants found it easier to stop participating in social activities, which led them to feeling unhappy and deprived, as the interaction of their social group was facilitated by material or service consumption. Monique (aged 31) exemplified this problem, stating "It was demoralizing. I stopped participating in social activities because the interaction of my social group is based on material or service consumption. I felt rude going around to peoples' houses without bringing anything for example, because it's something I have always done. You take something".

Proposed Conceptual Model

Figure 1 highlights how these six themes can be used to depict the journey of becoming a voluntary simplifier.

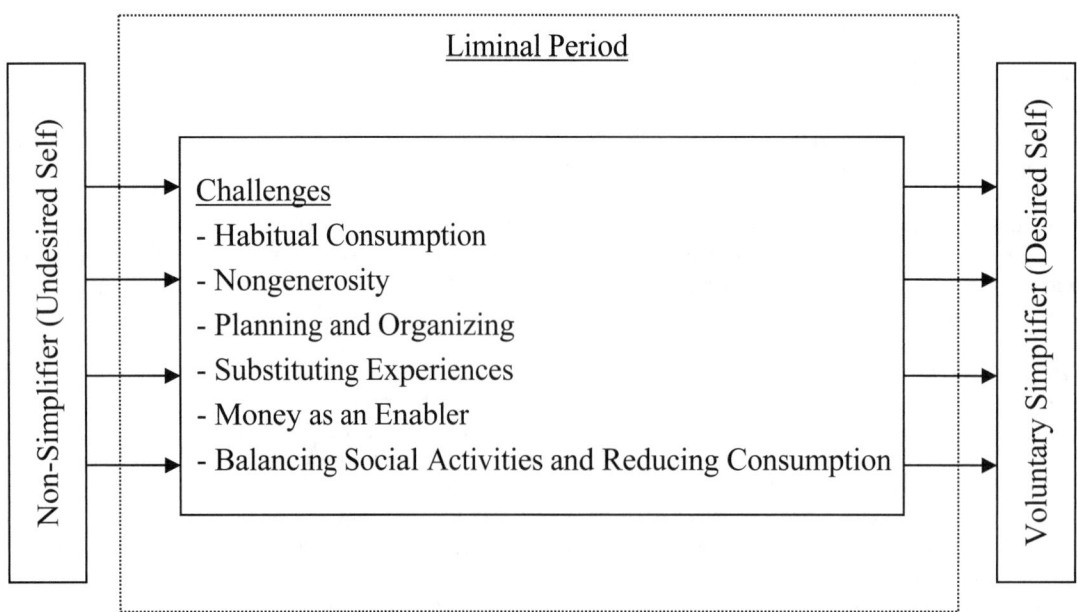

FIGURE 1: CHALLENGES FACED WHILE BECOMING A VOLUNTARY SIMPLIFIER

At the start of the journey, a non-simplifier (i.e., a mainstream consumer) may experience a sense of an undesired self, which leads them to consider adopting a lifestyle of lessened consumption, such as that provided by voluntary simplification. After making the decision to change their marketplace behavior, an individual enters a liminal period (Noble and Walker 1997; Turner 1969), where they start the transition towards becoming their desired extension of self (Belk 1988); that of becoming a voluntary simplifier, and the anti-consumption practices which are inherent with that lifestyle. Between these two states, this study has highlighted the challenges an individual may encounter during the transition period, where they are a beginner voluntary simplifier trying to resist the market.

DISCUSSION

While choosing to embrace the anti-consumption ethos of the lifestyle, the participants in this study faced many challenges in the journey of becoming a voluntary simplifier. Perhaps the most challenging aspect of adopting the lifestyle for participants was reducing consumption while still maintaining social ties that were often centered around consumption. In this regard, even though the participants in this study held values around lessened consumption, their social network made it difficult for them to resist their previous market behaviors. This perspective is echoed in the liminality literature, in that the detachment from prior relationships and social roles, which is part of the liminal period, is often an uncomfortable experience for those people who are in between their previous role and the one they wish to assume (Noble and Walker 1997). Many participants were also found to reflect upon the challenges they experienced by incorporating the dimension of financial cost in their discourse. For all participants, this was often reflective of their expectations about voluntary simplification, in that by choosing an anti-consumption lifestyle, their lessened focus on consumption was considered together with the financial costs associated with their previous consumption practices, thus making money a surrogate measure of their progress.

The literature suggests that beyond basic levels of consumption, one can increase their well-being more with social interaction than with further consumption (Cummins 2000). However, if one's social interaction is based on consumption activities, and the values of a social group are not open to alternative consumption, then consumption acts as an enabler for social interaction and long-term well-being. A common motivation for voluntary simplification is social influence (McDonald et al. 2006), and if beginner voluntary simplifiers experience social resistance (e.g., social norms that support consumption), then the transition to adopting the lifestyle is made more difficult.

There are many ways anti-consumption attitudes may manifest themselves, and the voluntary simplifier lifestyle is but one of these. Synonymous with this lifestyle is the idea of consumer resistance, although in the case of voluntary simplifiers, the focus of their resistance is the entire market, and the consumption values and practices of that market. Building upon the conceptual model introduced earlier, while anti-consumption is a dominant discourse for beginner voluntary simplifiers, their resistance to the marketplace can be seen as changing in focus, depending on where they are in the journey of adopting their new lifestyle. Moreover, while voluntary simplifiers are often perceived as a distinct social group, this study suggests their resistance of the market exists at the individual level, and the challenges faced when adopting the lifestyle are often idiosyncratic to each person. In this respect, this paper highlights the transitory nature of resistance; while anti-consumption may be a prevailing discourse for beginner voluntary simplifiers, how they resist the market (and the challenges they have doing so) is continually evolving.

CONCLUSION

The study suggests that beginner voluntary simplifiers encounter several challenges while in the early stages of adopting their new lifestyle. In his 2002 paper, Kozinets asked whether it is possible to evade the market, finding that if it is possible, it is most likely to be temporary and local. Extending this, Cherrier (2009) suggests that whether anti-consumption is a resistance to dominant powers or one's own domination, it depends on a sense of identity grounded in social positions, empowerment, and a vision of society. Overall, this study highlights that while beginner voluntary simplifiers hold a strong anti-consumption ethic, the way this manifests itself is influenced by both themselves and their existing social network. In this respect, the true challenge for beginner voluntary simplifiers is how to resist the influence of the market in which their daily activities and social ties are so firmly imbedded.

REFERENCES

Ahuvia, Aaron (2008), "If Money Doesn't Make Us Happy, Why Do We Act as if it Does?" *Journal of Economic Psychology*, 29 (4), 491-507.

Arnould, Eric J. (2007), "Should Consumer Citizens Escape the Market?" *The ANNALS of the American Academy of Political and Social Science*, 611 (1), 96-111.

Ballantine, Paul W. and Sam Creery (2010), "The Consumption and Disposition Behaviour of Voluntary Simplifiers," *Journal of Consumer Behaviour*, 9 (1), 45-56.

Bekin, Caroline, Marylyn Carrigan, and Isabelle Szmigin (2005), "Defying Marketing Sovereignty: Voluntary Simplicity at New Consumption Communities," *Qualitative Market Research*, 8 (4), 413-29.

Belk, Russell W. (1984), "Three Scales to Measure Constructs Related to Materialism: Reliability, Validity, and Relationships to Measures of Happiness," in *Advances in Consumer Research*, Vol. 11, ed. Thomas C. Kinnear, Provo, UT: Association for Consumer Research, 291-97.

--- (1988), "Possessions and the Extended Self," *Journal of Consumer Research*, 15 (September), 139-68.

Cherrier, Helene (2009), "Anti-Consumption Discourses and Consumer-Resistant Identities," *Journal of Business Research*, 62 (2), 181-90.

Cherrier, Helene and Jeff B. Murray (2007), "Reflexive Dispossession and the Self: Constructing a Processual Theory of Identity," *Consumption, Markets and Culture*, 10 (1), 1-29.

Close, Angeline G. and George M. Zinkhan (2009), "Market Resistance and Valentine's Day Events," *Journal of Business Research*, 62 (2), 200-07.

Craig-Lees, Margaret and Constance Hill (2002), "Understanding Voluntary Simplifiers," *Psychology & Marketing*, 19 (2), 187-210.

Cummins, Robert A. (2000), "Personal Income and Subjective Well-Being: A Review," *Journal of Happiness Studies*, 1 (2), 133-58.

Etzioni, Amitai (1998), "Voluntary Simplicity: Characterization, Select Psychological Implications, and Societal Consequences," *Journal of Economic Psychology*, 19 (5), 619-43.

Gregg, Richard B. (1936), *The Value of Voluntary Simplicity*, Wallingford, PA: Pendle Hill.

Hogg, Margaret K., Emma N. Banister, and Christopher A. Stephenson (2009), "Mapping Symbolic (Anti-) Consumption," *Journal of Business Research*, 62 (2), 148-59.

Holbrook, Morris B. and Elizabeth C. Hirschman (1982), "The Experiential Aspects of Consumption: Consumer Fantasies, Feelings, and Fun," *Journal of Consumer Research*, 9 (September), 132-40.

Huneke, Mary E. (2005), "The Face of the Un-Consumer: An Empirical Examination of the Practice of Voluntary Simplicity in the United States," *Psychology & Marketing*, 22 (7) 527-50.

Iyer, Rajesh and James A. Muncy (2009), "Purpose and Object of Anti-Consumption," *Journal of Business Research*, 62 (2), 160-68.

Kozinets, Robert V. (2002), "Can Consumers Escape the Market? Emancipatory Illuminations from Burning Man," *Journal of Consumer Research*, 29 (June), 20-38.

Kozinets, Robert V. and Jay M. Handelman (2004), "Adversaries of Consumption: Consumer Movements, Activism, and Ideology," *Journal of Consumer Research*, 31 (December), 691-704.

Lastovicka, John L., Lance A. Bettencourt, Renée S. Hughner, and Ronald J. Kuntze (1999), "Lifestyle of the Tight and Frugal: Theory and Measurement," *Journal of Consumer Research*, 26 (June), 85-98.

Lee, Michael S.W., Judith Motion, and Denise Conroy (2009), "Anti-Consumption and Brand Avoidance," *Journal of Business Research*, 62 (2), 169-80.

Leonard-Barton, Dorothy (1981), "Voluntary Simplicity Lifestyles and Energy Conservation," *Journal of Consumer Research*, 8 (December), 243-52.

Lincoln, Yvonna S. and Egon G. Guba (1985), *Naturalistic Inquiry*, Beverly Hills, CA: Sage.

McDonald, Seonaidh, Caroline J. Oates, C. William Young, and Kumju Hwang (2006), "Toward Sustainable Consumption: Researching Voluntary Simplifiers," *Psychology & Marketing*, 23 (6), 515-34.

Miles, Matthew B. and A. Michael Huberman (1994), *Qualitative Data Analysis: An Expanded Sourcebook*, Thousand Oaks, CA: Sage.

Noble, Charles H. and Beth A. Walker (1997), "Exploring the Relationships Among Liminal Transitions, Symbolic Consumption, and the Extended Self," *Psychology & Marketing*, 14 (1), 29-47.

Shaw, Deidre and Terry Newholm (2002), "Voluntary Simplicity and the Ethics of Consumption," *Psychology & Marketing*, 19 (2), 167-85.

Taylor-Gooby, Peter F. (1998), "Comments on Amitai Etzioni: Voluntary Simplicity: Characterization, Select Psychological Implications, and Societal Consequences," *Journal of Economic Psychology*, 19 (5), 645-50.

Tesch, Renata (1990), *Qualitative Research: Analysis Types and Software Tools*, New York: Falmer Press.

Turner, Victor W. (1969), *The Ritual Process: Structure and Anti-Structure*, New York: Aldine De Gruyter.

Verplanken, Bas and Wendy Wood (2006), "Interventions to Break and Create Consumer Habits," *Journal of Public Policy & Marketing*, 25 (1), 90-103.

Zavestoski, Stephen (2002a), "Guest Editorial: Anticonsumption Attitudes," *Psychology & Marketing*, 19 (2), 121-26.

--- (2002b), "The Social-Psychological Bases of Anticonsumption Attitudes," *Psychology & Marketing*, 19 (2), 149-65.

Competitive Papers—Extended Abstracts

What Happens When Consumers Acculturate to Multiple Cultural Contexts?

Bernardo Figueiredo, University of New South Wales, Australia
Julien Cayla, Australian School of Business University of New South Wales, Australia

EXTENDED ABSTRACT

Movement is a key process in global consumer culture. Globalization and advances in technology, communication and transportation have intensified the circulation of goods, services, and people (Appadurai 1990; Ger and Belk 1996; Sherry 1998). Flows of information and ideas "from one culture enter another culture, and create individuals who exhibit elements of multiple cultures" (Craig and Douglas 2006,330). As a consequence, exposure to multiple cultural contexts (through media, through extensive travelling, or by living in large multicultural cities) is an everyday reality for millions of consumers (Klugman 2009).

Despite this, the consumer acculturation literature, i.e. the body of literature concerned with the behavior of consumers and other marketplace actors in their movement from one cultural context to another, has not yet examined the case of very mobile consumers, professionals who frequently shift locations and cultural contexts, people we call circulating consumers. The goal of this article is to bridge this gap by examining this process of circulation as "more than simply the movement of people, ideas, and commodities from one culture to another", but also as "a cultural process with its own forms of abstraction, evaluation, and constraints" (Lee and LiPuma 2002,6).

The consumer acculturation literature has made important contributions to understanding consumer behavior of migrants. Studies from the assimilationist phase have shown that ethnic groups have particular patterns of consumption and that understanding them is important for organizations as they try to develop advertising and sales promotions targeting these communities (Deshpande, Hoyer, and Donthu 1986; O'Guinn and Faber 1985).

Later, works from the post-assimilationist phase (Askegaard, Arnould, and Kjeldgaard 2005; Oswald 1999; Penaloza 1994; Thompson and Tambyah 1999; Üstüner and Holt 2007) challenged the idea of assimilation - i.e. the idea that immigrants are eventually assimilated into the mainstream culture, and advanced the theory on consumer acculturation in three main ways: 1) They have demonstrated that consumer acculturation processes are complex phenomena that involve processes of movement, adaptation and translation, diverse agents from home and host cultures, diverse identity outcomes and elements from the marketplace (Askegaard et al. 2005; Oswald 1999; Penaloza 1994); 2) They have shown how marketers, retailers, middleman, products, services, brands shape and are shaped by consumers' efforts to acculturate (Peñaloza 2000); 3) They have explained how cultural and social structures (e.g.: social class positions, ideological compatibility, consumer culture) can lead to differing patterns of consumer acculturation (Üstüner and Holt 2007).

However, the consumer acculturation literature has tended to focus on movement from one place to another. As noticed by Üstüner and Holt (2007,41) acculturation has been treated as "what happens when peoples socialized in one (minority) culture migrate and so come into continuous first-hand contact with a new (dominant) culture". They have not addressed cases of consumers having to adapt and acculturate more than once. Nor has it considered the cumulative effect of acculturation on consumers' subsequent experiences.

Given that to multiple cultural contexts – or multi-acculturation - has become a much more common phenomenon, especially among employees of multinational corporations (Black, Mendenhall, and Oddou 1991; Nowicka 2006; Sklair 2001), the need to address this gap becomes crucial. In short, the purpose of this paper is to examine how consumers acculturate to multiple cultural contexts. More specifically, what is particular to consumer multi-acculturation? How is it different from single acculturation processes? How does it help us to expand current understanding about consumer behavior?

We interviewed 38 expatriates, from 20 different countries of origins, ranging from 25-55 years old, 19 having a partner and 19 single or divorced. They were all professionals with a tertiary degrees, diverse occupations and diverse geographic mobility paths. Informants were asked to describe their life trajectories and explain their motivations for living in different countries (McCracken 1988). The identification of major life themes and life projects (Mick and Buhl 1992) together with iterative processes of comparison, dimensionalization, and integration (Spiggle 1994) created the necessary conditions to compare and contrast consumers` histories of living in different countries and find the most relevant categories which allowed researchers to group findings by themes

We contribute to the expansion of consumer acculturation literature in three different ways. First, by looking at circulating consumers, we identify a specific type of consumer behavior characterized by very pronounced cultural reflexivity. This reflexivity is expressed through four different aspects: 1) Awareness that one's own cultural identity may vary and that it can even be multiple; 2) Awareness that different cultural identities are perceived differently by different people or in different contexts; 3) Realization that cultural identities may be learned; 4) Indexicality based on first-hand experiences.

Second, we show that multiple acculturation affects consumers notions' of time. It is suggested that reflexive time of multi-acculturated consumes can be represented by a spiral shape, as it cyclical and progressive at the same time. We detail the effects of such notions on consumption practices.

Finally, our research advances the understanding of what it means to live in a global and multicultural marketplace, especially as it deals with consumers' adaptation to multiple cultural contexts. Through our circulating consumers we show that multi-acculturation (i.e. multiple processes of acculturation) may lead to metacculturation (i.e. a higher order of acculturation characterized by high cultural reflexivity). We also show that consumer metacculturation (Askegaard, Kjeldgaard, and Arnould 2010) is a level of acculturation with its own dynamics. Metacculturated consumers are aware of different aspects of their cultural identities and they will try to monitor and manage these aspects in order produce diverse identity outcomes. The consumption of cultures (Firat 1995) becomes a way of managing the self.

REFERENCES

Appadurai, Arjun (1990), "Disjuncture and Difference in the Global Cultural Economy," *Public culture*, 2 (2), 295-310.

Askegaard, Soren, Eric Arnould, and Dannie Kjeldgaard (2005), "Postassimilationist Ethnic Consumer Research: Qualifications and Extensions," *Journal of Consumer Research*, 32 (1), 160-70.

Askegaard, Soren, Dannie Kjeldgaard, and Eric Arnould (forthcoming), "'Metacculturation': Cultural Identity Politics in Greenlandic Food Discourses," 1-47.

Askegaard, Soren, Dannie Kjeldgaard, and Eric J. Arnould (2010), "Metacculturation: Cultural Identity Politics in Greenlandic Food Discourses," in *Advances in Consumer Research*, Vol. 38, ed. Darren W. Dahl, Gita V. Johar and Stijn M.J. Van Osselaer, Duluth, MN Association for Consumer Research.

Askegaard, Soren, Dannie Kjeldgaard, and Eric. J. Arnould (2009), "Reflexive Culture's Consequences," in *Beyond Hofstede: Cultural Frameworks for Marketing and Management*, ed. Cheryl Nakata, London: Palgrave Macmillian, 101-22.

Black, J.Stewart, Mark Mendenhall, and Gary Oddou (1991), "Toward a Comprehensive Model of International Adjustment: An Integration of Multiple Theoretical Perspectives," *The Academy of Management Review*, 16 (2), 291-317.

Craig, Samuel and Susan Douglas (2006), "Beyond National Culture: Implications of Cultural Dynamics for Consumer Research," *International Marketing Review*, 23 (3), 322-42.

Deshpande, Rohit, Wayne Hoyer, and Naveen Donthu (1986), "The Intensity of Ethnic Affiliation: A Study of the Sociology of Hispanic Consumption," *Journal of Consumer Research*, 13 (September), 214-20.

Elliott, Richard and Andrea Davies (2006), "Using Oral History Methods in Consumer Research," in *Handbook of Qualitative Research Methods in Marketing*, ed. Russel W. Belk, Cheltenham: Edward Elgar Pub, 244-54.

Firat, A Fuat (1995), "Consumer Culture or Culture Consumed," in *Marketing in a Multicultural World. Ethnicity, Nationalism, and Cultural Identity*, ed. Janeen A. Costa and Gary J. Bamossy, London: Sage Publications, 105-25.

Geertz, Clifford (1973), *The Interpretation of Cultures*, New York: Basic Books.

Ger, Guliz and Russel W. Belk (1996), "I'd Like to Buy the World a Coke: Consumptionscapes of the "Less Affluent World","" *Journal of Consumer Policy*, 19 (3), 271-304.

Giddens, Anthony (1991), *Modernity and Self-Identity: Self and Society in the Late Modern Age*, Stanford, CA: Stanford Univ Pr.

Grayson, Kent and David Shulman (2000), "Indexicality and the Verification Function of Irreplaceable Possessions: A Semiotic Analysis," *Journal of Consumer Research*, 27 (1), 17-30.

Hayashi, Shuji (1988), *Culture and Management in Japan*, Tokyo: University of Tokyo Press

Klugman, Jeni (2009), "Overcoming Barriers: Human Mobility and Development," in *Human Development Report 2009*, New York United Nations development programme, 229.

Lee, Benjamin and Edward LiPuma (2002), "Cultures of Circulation: The Imaginations of Modernity," *Public culture*, 14 (1), 191-213.

McCracken, Grant. D. (1988), *The Long Interview*, Thousand Oaks, CA: Sage Publications.

Mick, David G. and Claus Buhl (1992), "A Meaning-Based Model of Advertising Experiences," *Journal of Consumer Research*, 19 (3), 317-38.

Nowicka, Magdalena (2006), *Transnational Professionals and Their Cosmopolitan Universes*, Frankfurt: Campus.

O'Guinn, Thomas and Ronald Faber (1985), "New Perspectives on Acculturation: The Relationship of General and Role Specific Acculturation with Hispanics' Consumer Attitudes," *Advances in Consumer Research*, 12, 113-17.

Oswald, Laura R. (1999), "Culture Swapping: Consumption and the Ethnogenesis of Middle-Class Haitian Immigrants," *Journal of Consumer Research*, 25 (4), 303-18.

Penaloza, Lisa (1994), "Atravesando Fronteras/Border Crossings: A Critical Ethnographic Exploration of the Consumer Acculturation of Mexican Immigrants," *Journal of Consumer Research*, 21 (1), 32-54.

Peñaloza, Lisa (2000), "The Commodification of the American West: Marketers' Production of Cultural Meanings at the Trade Show," *The Journal of Marketing*, 64 (4), 82-109.

Sherry, John F. (1998), "The Soul of the Company Store: Nike Town Chicago and the Emplaced Brandscape," in *Servicescapes: The Concept of Place in Contemporary Markets*, ed. John F Sherry, Lincolnwood NTC Businessbooks, 109-46.

Sklair, Leslie (2001), *The Transnational Capitalist Class*, Somerset, NJ Blackwell Publishers.

Spiggle, Susan (1994), "Analysis and Interpretation of Qualitative Data in Consumer Research," *Journal of Consumer Research*, 21 (3), 491-503.

Stayman, Douglas M. and Rohit Deshpande (1989), "Situational Ethnicity and Consumer Behavior," *The Journal of Consumer Research*, 16 (3), 361-71.

Thompson, Craig J. and Siok K. Tambyah (1999), "Trying to Be Cosmopolitan," *Journal of Consumer Research*, 26 (3), 214-41.

Üstüner, T. and D. Holt (2007), "Dominated Consumer Acculturation: The Social Construction of Poor Migrant Women's Consumer Identity Projects in a Turkish Squatter," *Journal of Consumer Research*, 34, 41–56.

Psychological and Neurophysiological Investigations of Close Consumer-Brand Relationships

Martin Reimann, University of Southern California, USA
Raquel Castaño, Tecnológico de Monterrey, México
Judith Zaichkowsky, Copenhagen Business School, Denmark
Antoine Bechara, University of Southern California, USA

EXTENDED ABSTRACT

Consumer researchers have become increasingly interested in the concept of consumer-brand relationships. Myriad consumer-brand relationship constructs have been offered in the extant literature, including brand attachment (Thomson, MacInnis, and Park 2005), brand commitment (Wang 2002; Warrington and Shim 2000), brand connectedness (Winterich 2007), brand devotion (Pichler and Hemetsberger 2007), and brand love (Ahuvia 2005; Albert, Merunka, and Valette-Florence 2008; Carroll and Ahuvia 2006; Fournier 1998). Research on these concepts has improved our understanding of the consequences of close consumer-brand relationships for various consumer behaviors, such as loyalty and positive word-of-mouth.

Little research, however, has focused on the underlying mechanisms that may explain consumer behaviors related to close brands. In particular, the motivational-emotional aspects associated with close brand relationships have not been fully explored. In general, why do people desire to enter and maintain relationships? And what is the emotional significance of such close relationships? Such questions are at the heart of the social-psychological self-expansion theory (Aron and Aron 1986), which has been applied extensively to human relationships (e.g., Aron, Aron, and Smollan 1992; Aron et al. 1991; Aron et al. 2000; Aron, Paris, and Aron 1995), but not yet to brand relationships. In brief, self-expansion theory suggests that in early stages, close relationships are motivated by rapid self-expansion—the acquisition of resources, perspectives, and identities that enhance one's ability to accomplish goals—whereas in later stages, close relationships are associated with the inclusion of others in the self, i.e., people tend to consider the close other as part of themselves.

Conceptualization

Recently, Reimann and Aron (2009) suggested that these ideas may not only be relevant to interpersonal relationships, but also to consumers' close relationships with brands. It is well known that in addition to close relationships with persons, people also form a similar type of relationship with objects (Belk 1988). More than not, these objects are specific brands, which consumers relate to and use to identify their "selves" (Ahuvia 2005). Similar to loved others, brands can create a "warm feeling" among consumers, form a pleasurable experience of being cared for, and ultimately bond consumer in a close connection (Fournier 1998). Brands can give consumers "ideal selves" to aspire to, as the presentation of self through possessions allows consumers to differ from what may be their "real selves" (Goffman 1959). Given this resemblance, it seems feasible to apply theories on close interpersonal relationships to consumer-brand relationship. As mentioned above, the specific appeal of self-expansion theory for brand research lies in its motivational-emotional account. Additionally, it emphasizes the dynamic character of close relationships and allows for predictions on changes in motivations and emotions as the relationship matures. Thus, self-expansion theory promises a richer understanding of brand relationships at various points of the brand lifecycle and, thus, the development of relevant practical implications for brand image management.

In an effort to test self-expansion theory in the context of brand relationships, the contribution of this paper is to determine (1) whether rapid self-expansion and inclusion in self are greater for close versus neutral brands and (2) whether levels of self-expansion and inclusion of close brands change over time. Using a multi-method approach, the present research adds both to knowledge of psychological and neurophysiological responses to brands as well as brain areas associated with close brand relationships.

Methods

The present research builds on self-expansion theory and applies the framework's key elements—rapid self-expansion and inclusion in the self—to consumers' close relationships with brands. To test self-expansion theory empirically in the context of consumer-brand relationships, a variety of psychological and neurophysiological methodologies, including self-reports, skin conductance recording, and functional magnetic resonance imaging, are drawn upon. Specifically, consumers' skin conductance responses (SCR), which measure the arousal dimension of emotion (Boucsein 1992), have the potential to shed new light on how consumers expand their "selves." A process tracing methodology, the recording of SCR helps provide novel insights on otherwise hidden processes in consumer judgments (Figner and Murphy 2010). For example, Damasio et al. (2000) were able to detect subtle differences in self-generated emotions by recording SCR, which would otherwise be hard to obtain. Additionally, by utilizing functional magnetic resonance imaging (fMRI), the analysis of neurophysiological mechanisms in the brain at the point in time when they take place, not in retrospective, becomes feasible (Shiv 2007; Shiv et al. 2005) because fMRI is not subject to cognitive processes overlapping actual emotional processes (Reimann et al. 2010). Participants do not have to remember how they relate to a brand as they do when they provide self-reports, so the fMRI process helps clarify how consumers include brands in their "selves."

Major Findings

In three experiments, this research provides novel insights into branding by studying the psychological and neurophysiological mechanisms of how consumers relate to their beloved brands. Building on self-expansion theory, the authors propose that self-expansion for a brand, operationalized in terms of emotional arousal, decreases over the brand relationship span, while inclusion of the brand in the self increases over time. In experiment 1, results indicate greater self-reported emotional arousal and inclusion for close versus neutral brands, as well as a decrease in emotional arousal and an increase in inclusion of close brands over time. Experiment 2 measures skin conductance responses to reveal increased emotional arousal, corroborating the results based on self-reported data. In experiment 3, a functional magnetic resonance imaging study reveals an association between long-term close consumer-brand relationships and activation of the insula, a brain area previously found to be a crucial mechanism in diverse, yet related psychological phenomena such as urging, addiction, loss aversion, and interpersonal love.

REFERENCES

Ahuvia, Aaron C. (2005), "Beyond the Extended Self: Loved Objects and Consumers' Identity Narratives," *Journal of Consumer Research*, 32 (1), 171-84.

Albert, Noël, Dwight Merunka, and Pierre Valette-Florence (2008), "When Consumers Love Their Brands: Exploring the Concept and Its Dimensions," *Journal of Business Research*, 61 (1), 1062-75.

Aron, Arthur, Etaine N. Aron, Michael Tudor, and Greg Nelson (1991), "Close Relationships as Including Other in the Self," *Journal of Personality and Social Psychology*, 60 (2), 241-53.

Aron, Arthur and Elaine N. Aron (1986), *Love and the Expansion of Self: Understanding Attraction and Satisfaction*, New York, New York: Hemisphere.

Aron, Arthur, Elaine N. Aron, and Danny Smollan (1992), "Inclusion of Other in the Self Scale and the Structure of Interpersonal Closeness," *Journal of Personality and Social Psychology*, 63 (4), 596-612.

Aron, Arthur, Christina C. Norman, and Elaine N. Aron (1998), "The Self-Expansion Model and Motivation," *Representative Research in Social Psychology*, 22, 1-13.

Aron, Arthur, Christina C. Norman, Elaine N. Aron, Colin McKenna, and Richard E. Heyman (2000), "Couples' Shared Participation in Novel and Arousing Activities and Experienced Relationship Quality," *Journal of Personality and Social Psychology*, 78 (2), 273-84.

Aron, Arthur, Meg Paris, and Elaine N. Aron (1995), "Falling in Love: Prospective Studies of Self-Concept Change," *Journal of Personality and Social Psychology*, 69 (6), 1102-12.

Bartels, Andreas and Semir Zeki (2000), "The Neural Basis of Romantic Love," *NeuroReport*, 11 (17), 3829-34.

--- (2004), "The Neural Correlates of Maternal and Romantic Love," *Neuroimage*, 21 (3), 1155-66.

Beauregard, Mario, Jérôme Courtemanche, Vincent Paquette, and Évelyne Landry St-Pierre (2009), "The Neural Basis of Unconditional Love," *Psychiatry Research: Neuroimaging*, 172 (2), 93-98.

Bechara, Antoine (2005), "Decision Making, Impulse Control and Loss of Willpower to Resist Drugs: A Neurocognitive Perspective," *nature neuroscience*, 8 (11), 1458-63.

Bechara, Antoine and Antonio R. Damasio (2005), "The Somatic Marker Hypothesis: A Neural Theory of Economic Decision," *Games and Economic Behavior*, 52 (2), 336-72.

Bechara, Antoine, Hanna Damasio, Daniel Tranel, and Antonio R. Damasio (1997), "Deciding Advantageously before Knowing the Advantageous Strategy," *Science*, 275 (5304), 1293-95.

Belk, Russell W. (1988), "Possessions and the Extended Self," *Journal of Consumer Research*, 15 (2), 139-68.

Boucsein, Wolfram (1992), *Electrodermal Activity*, New York, NY: Plenum Press.

Britton, Jennifer C., Stephan F. Taylor, Keith D. Sudheimer, and Israel Liberzon (2006), "Facial Expressions and Complex Iaps Pictures: Common and Differential Networks," *Neuroimage*, 31 (2), 906-19.

Carroll, Barbara A. and Aaron C. Ahuvia (2006), "Some Antecedents and Outcomes of Brand Love," *Marketing Letters*, 17 (2), 79-89.

Carver, Charles S. and Michael F. Scheier (1990), "Origins and Functions of Positive and Negative Affect: A Control-Process View," *Psychological Review*, 97 (1), 19-35.

Chikama, Masanori, Nikolaus R. McFarland, David G. Amaral, and Suzanne N. Haber (1997), "Insular Cortical Projections to Functional Regions of the Striatum Correlate with Cortical Cytoarchitectonic Organization in the Primate," *Journal of Neuroscience*, 17 (24), 9686.

Clarke, Stephanie and Judit Miklossy (1990), "Occipital Cortex in Man: Organization of Callosal Connections, Related Myelo and Cytoarchitecture, and Putative Boundaries of Functional Visual Areas," *Journal of Comparative Neurology*, 298 (2), 188-214.

Craig, A.D. (Bud) (2002), "How Do You Feel? Interoception: The Sense of the Physiological Condition of the Body," *Nature Reviews Neuroscience*, 3 (8), 655-66.

Damasio, Antonio R., Thomas J. Grabowski, Antoine Bechara, Hanna Damasio, Laura L. B. Ponto, Jarvizi Parvizi, and Richard D. Hichwa (2000), "Subcortical and Cortical Brain Activity During the Feeling of Self-Generated Emotions," *nature neuroscience*, 3 (10), 1049-56.

Dawson, Michael E., Anne M. Schell, and Diane L. Filion (2007), "The Electrodermal System," in *Handbook of Psychophysiology*, Vol. 3, ed. JT Cacioppo, LG Tassinary and GG Berntson, Cambridge: Cambridge University Press, 158-81.

Escalas, Jennifer E. and James R. Bettman (2005), "Self-Construal, Reference Groups, and Brand Meaning," *Journal of Consumer Research*, 32 (3), 378-89.

Everitt, Barry J. and Trevor W. Robbins (2005), "Neural Systems of Reinforcement for Drug Addiction: From Actions to Habits to Compulsion," *nature neuroscience*, 8 (11), 1481-89.

Fellows, Lesley K. (2004), "The Cognitive Neuroscience of Human Decision Making: A Review and Conceptual Framework," *Behavioral and Cognitive Neuroscience Reviews*, 3 (3), 159-72.

Figner, Bernd and Ryan O. Murphy (2010), "Using Skin Conductance in Judgment and Decision Making Research," in *A Handbook of Process Tracing Methods for Decision Research: A Critical Review and User's Guide*, ed. Michael Schulte-Mecklenbeck, Anton Kuehberger and Rob Ranyard, New York, NY: Psychology Press, 163-84.

Fournier, Susan (1998), "Consumers and Their Brands: Developing Relationship Theory in Consumer Research," *Journal of Consumer Research*, 24 (4), 343-53.

Goffman, Erving (1959), *The Presentation of Self in Everyday Life*, New York, NY: Anchor-Doubleday.

Grubb, Edward L. and Harrison L. Grathwohl (1967), "Consumer Self-Concept, Symbolism and Market Behavior: A Theoretical Approach," *Journal of Marketing*, 31 (4), 22-27.

Kirmani, Amna (2009), "The Self and the Brand," *Journal of Consumer Psychology*, 19 (3), 271-75.

Knutson, Brian, Scott Rick, G. Elliott Wimmer, Drazen Prelec, and George Loewenstein (2007), "Neural Predictors of Purchases," *Neuron*, 53 (1), 147-56.

Levy, Sidney J. (1959), "Symbols for Sale," *Harvard Business Review*, 37 (4), 117-24.

Malhotra, Naresh K. (1988), "Self Concept and Product Choice: An Integrated Perspective," *Journal of Economic Psychology*, 9 (1), 1-28.

McClernon, F. Joseph, F. Berry Hiott, Scott A. Huettel, and Jed E. Rose (2005), "Abstinence-Induced Changes in Self-Report Craving Correlate with Event-Related Fmri Responses to Smoking Cues," *Neuropsychopharmacology*, 30 (10), 1940-47.

Mesulam, M.-Marsel and Elliot J. Mufson (1982a), "Insula of the Old World Monkey Iii: Efferent Cortical Output and Comments on Function," *Journal of Comparative Neurology*, 212 (1), 38-52.

--- (1982b), "Insula of the Old World Monkey: Architectonics in the Insulo-Orbito-Temporal Component of the Paralimbic Brain," *Journal of Comparative Neurology*, 212 (1), 1-22.

Myrick, Hugh, Raymond F. Anton, Li Xingbao, Scott Henderson, David Drobes, Konstantin Voronin, and Mark S. George (2004), "Differential Brain Activity in Alcoholics and Social Drinkers to Alcohol Cues: Relationship to Craving," *Neuropsychopharmacology*, 29 (2), 393-402.

Naqvi, Nasir H. and Antoine Bechara (2009), "The Hidden Island of Addiction: The Insula," *Trends in neurosciences*, 32 (1), 56-67.

--- (2010), "The Insula and Drug Addiction: An Interoceptive View of Pleasure, Urges, and Decision-Making," *Brain Structure and Function*, 214 (5-6), 1-16.

Nunnally, Jum C. (1978), *Psychometric Theory*, New York, NY: McGraw-Hill.

Phan, K. Luan, Tor D. Wager, Stephan F. Taylor, and Israel Liberzon (2004), "Functional Neuroimaging Studies of Human Emotions," *CNS spectrums*, 9 (4), 258-66.

Phan, K. Luan, Tor D. Wager, Stephan F. Taylor, and Israel Liberzon (2002), "Functional Neuroanatomy of Emotion: A Meta-Analysis of Emotion Activation Studies in Pet and Fmri," *Neuroimage*, 16 (2), 331-48.

Pichler, Elisabeth A. and Andrea Hemetsberger (2007), ""Hopelessly Devoted to You": Towards an Extended Conceptualization of Consumer Devotion," *Advances in Consumer Research*, 34 (1), 194-99.

Poels, Karolien and Siegfried Dewitte (2006), "How to Capture the Heart? Reviewing 20 Years of Emotion Measurement in Advertising," *Journal of Advertising Research*, 46 (1), 18-37.

Reimann, Martin and A Aron (2009), "Self-Expansion Motivation and Inclusion of Close Brands in Self: Towards a Theory of Brand Relationships," in *Handbook of Brand Relationships*, ed. Joseph Priester, Deborah MacInnis, and Choong W. Park, New York, NY: M.E. Sharpe, 65-81.

Reimann, Martin, Judith Zaichkowsky, Carolin Neuhaus, Thomas Bender, and Bernd Weber (2010), "Aesthetic Package Design: A Behavioral, Neural, and Psychological Investigation," *Journal of Consumer Psychology*, 20 (4), 431-41.

Richins, Marsha L. and Peter H. Bloch (1986), "After the New Wears Off: The Temporal Context of Product Involvement," *Journal of Consumer Research*, 13 (2), 280-85.

Russell, James A., Anna Weiss, and Gerald A. Mendelsohn (1989), "Affect Grid: A Single-Item Scale of Pleasure and Arousal," *Journal of Personality and Social Psychology*, 57 (3), 493-502.

Shimp, Terence A. and Thomas J. Madden (1988), "Consumer-Object Relations: A Conceptual Framework Based Analogously on Sternberg's Triangular Theory of Love," *Advances in Consumer Research*, 15 (1), 163-68.

Shiv, Baba (2007), "Emotions, Decisions, and the Brain," *Journal of Consumer Psychology*, 17 (3), 174-78.

Shiv, Baba, Antoine Bechara, Irwin Levin, Joseph Alba, James Bettman, Laurette Dube, Alice Isen, Barbara Mellers, Ale Smidts, Susan Grant, and A. McGraw (2005), "Decision Neuroscience," *Marketing Letters*, 16 (3/4), 375-86.

Shiv, Baba and Joel Huber (2000), "The Impact of Anticipating Satisfaction on Consumer Choice," *Journal of Consumer Research*, 27 (2), 202-16.

Sirgy, M. Joseph (1982), "Self-Concept in Consumer Behavior: A Critical Review," *Journal of Consumer Research*, 9 (3), 287-300.

Strong, Greg and Arthur Aron (2006), "The Effect of Shared Participation in Novel and Challenging Activities on Experienced Relationship Quality: Is It Mediated by High Positive Affect?," in *Intrapersonal Processes in Interpersonal Relationships*, ed. Kathleen D. Vohs and Eli J. Finkel, New York, NY: Guilford, 342-59.

Talairach, Jean and Pierre Tournoux (1988), *Co-Planar Stereotaxic Atlas of the Human Brain*, New York, NY: Thieme

Thomson, Matthew, Deborah J. MacInnis, and C. Whan Park (2005), "The Ties That Bind: Measuring the Strength of Consumers' Emotional Attachments to Brands," *Journal of Consumer Psychology*, 15 (1), 77-91.

Tucker, Paula and Arthur Aron (1993), "Passionate Love and Marital Satisfaction at Key Transition Points in the Family Life Cycle," *Journal of Social and Clinical Psychology*, 12 (2), 135-47.

Wang, Guangping (2002), "Attitudinal Correlates of Brand Commitment," *Journal of Relationship Marketing*, 1 (2), 57-75.

Warrington, Patti and Soyeon Shim (2000), "An Empirical Investigation of the Relationship between Product Involvement and Brand Commitment," *Psychology and Marketing*, 17 (9), 761-82.

Winterich, Karen P. (2007), "Self-Other Connectedness in Consumer Affect, Judgments, and Action," Dissertation, University of Pittsburgh, Joseph M. Katz Graduate School of Business, Pittsburgh, PA.

Complaining When You Are To Blame:
The Role of Impression Management on the Impact of Complaining on Product Attitudes

Lea Dunn, University of British Columbia, Canada
Darren Dahl, University of British Columbia, Canada

EXTENDED ABSTRACT

Complaining in consumer research has commonly been defined as "a means of making one's feelings known when unfair seller practices are encountered [and] when disappointment with a product arises" (Fornell and Westbrook 1979, p.105). Complaining research has historically only examined the impact of consumer complaining in situations in which the product is to blame for the product failure. Researchers in this area have found that complaining (versus not complaining) typically leads to increased product satisfaction. It is hypothesized that the cathartic release of negative emotion brought on by complaining allows consumers to feel better about the situation than if they had held onto the negative comments by not complaining (Bearden and Oliver 1985; Nyer 2000). Companies, therefore, are encouraged to elicit complaints from consumers to create a beneficial company-consumer relationship (Prim and Pras 1999).

According to attribution theory (Weiner 1985; Folkes 1988), however, complaining behavior and outcomes can be determined by whether the consumer attributes the blame to external sources (i.e., the product) or internal sources (i.e., the consumer). Most research, if not all, (dis)satisfaction and complaining research has focused on only the external attribution side, ignoring those consumers with internal attributions of blame. The current paper focuses on the under-represented side of internal attributions and how internal attributions of blame impact the outcomes of complaint behavior. Specifically, we propose that for consumers with internal attributions of blame, complaining is actually detrimental to the product satisfaction and evaluations.

In study 1, we manipulated whether the participant believed the failure was their fault or the products and whether they complained or not. We predicted that consumers who attributed the failure to the product itself would rate the product more favorably after complaining than before complaining. On the other hand, consumers who attributed the failure to their use of the product would rate the product less favorably after complaining than before complaining. We tested these predictions by running a 2(attribution: fault v. no fault) x 2(complaint: no complain v. complain) factorial design. Participants were told that they would assemble, use, and evaluate a "new product". Specifically, they asked to assemble a food processor and make a smoothie to test how well the product worked. Unbeknownst to the participants, the product and ingredients were insufficient to create the expected final product. In the fault condition, participants were told that no other participant was having trouble with the product and therefore, the participant themselves must be to blame for the product failure. In the no fault condition, participants were told that the product was having problems and they were not to blame for the product failure. After using the product, the complaint condition was manipulated by either having the participants complain (complain condition) or not complain (no complain condition). The main dependent variables were product and brand evaluations as well as purchase intentions. The results revealed that, as predicted, consumers who were to blame for the product failure rated the product lower after complaining while the consumers who blamed the product rated the product higher after complaining.

In study 2, we tested the hypothesis that impression management was the underlying mechanism for the previous study's results. In this study, we examined impression management in two ways.

First, we manipulated social presence, an indicator of impression management. Second, we took a measurement of an individual difference of impression management, self-monitoring. In a 2(social presence: friend present v. no friend present) x 2(impression management: high self-monitoring v. low self-monitoring) design, participants read a scenario wherein they failed several times to assemble a home entertainment system correctly. Social presence was manipulated by either having friends present during the assembly and evaluation of the product or simply present during the assembly of the product. Regression analysis revealed main effects for social presence and self-monitoring as well as an interaction of the two. High self-monitors rated the product less favorably in the presence of others than when alone, while low self-monitors rated the product more favorably in the presence of others than when alone. These results provide support for the idea that consumers with internal attributions of blame are using complaining to impression manage by shifting the blame from themselves to the product, thus lower their product satisfaction ratings.

Finally, in study 3 we found that having the consumer take accountability for the complaint mitigate the effects shown in the previous studies. Specifically, we manipulate accountability through both the accountability to the company (signed their name v. didn't sign their name) and to the social audience (friend present v. no friend present). In this study, participants read a scenario that they failed to use a website to correctly order a product. To manipulate the social audience, a friend was either present or not present during the whole experience. Accountability to the company was manipulated by having the participants either sign their complaint or not sign their complaint. Results found that when asked to take accountability for their complaint in the presence of others, participants rated the product higher when they complained than those consumers that that did not take accountability for their actions or when the participants were not in the presence of others. Thus, taking accountability for their complaint led consumers to be more honest in their attributions of blame by not shifting the blame for the failure from themselves to the product.

Taken together, these studies demonstrate that there is an important distinction between external and internal attributions of blame when it comes to the outcomes of complaining. In particular, asking consumers with internal attributions of blame to complain may actually be detrimental to subsequent product evaluations. This pattern of results is due to consumers attempting to maintain an impression of competence by shifting the blame from themselves to the product. Finally, these results can be alleviated by having consumers take accountability for the veracity of their complaint. These results represent the first empirical evidence of the impact of complaining on consumers with internal attributions of blame and have several important implications for companies consumer complaint policies.

REFERENCES

Aiken, Leona S., and Stephen G. West (1991), *Multiple Regression: Testing and interpreting interactions*. Thousand Oaks: Sage.

Bearden, William O. and Jesse E. Teel (1983). "Selected Determinants of Consumer Satisfaction and Complaint Reports," *Journal of Marketing Research*, 20(Feb), 21-8.

--- and J. Barry Mason (1984), "An investigation of influences on consumer complaint reports," *Advances in Consumer Research*, 11(1), 490-495.

--- and Richard L. Oliver (1985), "The role of public and private complaining in satisfaction with problem resolution, " *Journal of Consumer Affairs*, 19, 222-240.

Bennett, Roger (1997), "Anger, Catharsis, and Purchasing Behavior Following Aggressive Customer Complaints," Journal *of Consumer Marketing*, 14(2), 156-177.

Dahl, Darren W., Rajesh V. Manchanda, and Jennifer J. Argo. (2001), "Embarrassment in consumer purchase: The roles of social presence and purchase familiarity," *Journal of Consumer Research*, 28(3), 473-481.

Day, Ralph L. (1980), "Research Perspectives on Consumer Complaining Behavior," in Theoretical Developments in Marketing, C. W. Lamb and P. M. Dunne, eds. Chicago: American Marketing Association, 211-15.

--- and E. Laird Landon (1976), "Collecting Comprehensive Complaint Data by Survey Research," in *Advances in Consumer Research,* 3, B.B. Anderson (Ed)., Atlanta: Association for Consumer Research, 263-268.

Dewitt, T. and Michael K. Brady (2003), "Rethinking Service Recovery Strategies: The Effect of Rapport on Consumer Responses to Service Failure," *Journal of Service Research*, 6(2), 193-207.

Diener, Edward, Scott C. Fraser, Arthur K. Beaman, and Roger T. Kelem (1976). "Effects of deindividuation variables on stealing among Halloween trick-or-treaters," *Journal of Personality and Social Psychology*, 33(2), 178-183.

Dipboye, Robert L. (1977), "A critical review of Korman's self-consistency theory of work motivation and occupational choice," *Organizational Behavior and Human Performing*, 18, 108-126.

Festinger, Leon, Albert Pepitone, and Theodore M. Newcomb (1952). "Some consequences of de-individuation in a group," *Journal of Abnormal and Social Psychology,* 47, 382-389.

Folkes, Valerie S. (1984a), "An Attributional Approach to Post-Purchase Conflict Between Buyers and Sellers," in *Advances in Consumer Research*, 11, 500-503.

--- (1984b), "Consumer Reactions to Product Failure: An Attributional Approach," *Journal of Consumer Research*, 10(March), 398-408.

--- (1988), "Recent attribution research in consumer behavior: A review and new directions," *Journal of Consumer Research*, 14, 548-565.

Fornell, Claes and Robert A. Westbrook (1979), "An Exploratory Study of Assertiveness, Aggressiveness, and Consumer Complaining Behavior," in Advances in Consumer Research, Vol. 6, W. L. Wilkie, ed. Miami: Association for Consumer Research, 105-10.

Goffman, Erving (1959). *The presentation of the self in everyday life.* Gardencity, NY: Doubleday.

Hocutt, Mary Ann, Goutam Chakraborty, and John C. Mowen (1997), "The Impact of Perceived Justice on Consumer Satisfaction and Intention to Complain in a Service Recovery," in *Advances in Consumer Research*, 24(4), 457-463.

Leary, Mark R. (1995). *Self-presentation: Impression management and interpersonal behavior.* Boulder: Westview.

Kettle, Keri, and Gerald Häubl (2011), "The signature effect: How signing one's name influences consumption-related behavior," *Journal of Consumer Research*, 44.

Kowalski, Robin M. (1996), "Complaints and Complaining: Functions, Antecedents, and Consequences," *Psychological Bulletin*, 119(2), 179-196.

---(2002), "Whining, griping, and complaining: Positivity in the negativity," *Journal of Clinical Psychology*, 58(9), 1023-1035.

Lennox, Richard D., and Raymond N. Wolfe(1984). "Revision of the self-monitoring scale," *Journal of Personality and Social Psychology*, 46, 1349-1364.

Lu, Ruiling and Linda Bol. (2007), "A comparison of anonymous versus identifiable e-Peer review on college student writing performance and the extent of critical feedback," *Journal of Interactive Online Learning*, 6(2), 100-115.

Nyer, Prashanth U. (2000), "Investigating into whether complaining can cause increased consumer satisfaction," *Journal of Consumer Marketing,* 17(1), 9-19.

Oliver, Richard and Wayne S. Desarbo (1988), "Response determinants in satisfaction judgments," *Journal of Consumer Research*, 14, 495-507.

Pierce, Jon L., Tatiana Kostova, and Kurt T. Dirks (2001), "Towards a theory of psychological ownership in organizations," *Academy of Management Review*, 26, 298-310.

Prim, Isabella and Bernard Pras (1999), "Friendly Complaining Behaviors: Toward a Relational Approach," *Journal of Market-Focused Management,* 3(3-4), 333-352.

Ramanthan, Suresh, and Ann L. McGill (2007). "Consuming with others: Social influence on moment-to-moment and retrospective evaluations of an experience," *Journal of Consumer Research,* 34, 506-524.

Richins, Marsha L. (1980), "Consumer Perceptions of Costs and Benefits Associated With Complaining," in Refining Concepts and Measures of Consumer Satisfaction and Complaining Behavior, Keith Hunt and Ralph L. Day (Eds.), Bloomington: Indiana University, 50-3.

--- (1983). "An Analysis of Consumer Interaction Styles in the Marketplace," *Journal of Consumer Research*, 10(1), 73-82.

--- (1985), "The role of product importance in complain initiation," in *Proceedings of the Conference of Consumer Satisfaction, Dissatisfaction, and Complaining Behavior*, R.L. Day and H.K. Hunt (Eds.), Bloomington, IN: Indiana University Press, 50-53.

Snyder, Mark (1974), "The self-monitoring of expressive behavior," *Journal of Personality and Social Psychology*, 30, 526-537.

Weiner, Bernard. (1985), "'Spontaneous' causal thinking," *Psychological Bulletin*, 97(1), 74-84.

Resources Running Out:
How Arbitrary Resource Fragmentation Decreases Consumer Spending

Bert Weemaes, K.U. Leuven, Belgium
Siegfried Dewitte, K.U. Leuven, Belgium
Luk Warlop, K.U. Leuven, Belgium

EXTENDED ABSTRACT

In recent years, consumers' liquid assets have become increasingly fragmented. The money that consumers can use to pay for a purchase tends to be distributed across a multitude of carriers of value including cash, bank accounts, electronic purse smart cards, stored value cards and certificates, prepaid cell phone credit, online wallets, and so on. Given this evolution, the primary objective of this research was to explore if and when such incidental budget divisions influence consumers' decisions.

This manuscript suggests that people are particularly averse to seeing a resource, like the money in their wallet, the funds on their electronic purse, or their PayPal account, run out. Using a variety of operationalizations, five studies show that when decision situations are structured such that a decision to spend would result in a resource running out, consumers' propensity to spend decreases. The first study demonstrates the effect by showing that cueing an incidental resource amount reduces the propensity to spend, but only when the cued amount would largely run out when it would be used to pay the item under consideration. Further studies show that the effect continues to occur when consumers are well aware that they have access to more resources, for example when they are also carrying a debit card that allows them to pay purchases directly from their bank account (study 2) or when they are carrying more cash money (study 3). The effect is also observed when the boundaries that separate a resource from the remainder of a consumer's resource pool are manifestly arbitrary (study 4), and when spending merely creates the illusion of a resource running out (study 5). The effect is shown to be independent of perceived total wealth and of the accessible account effect (Morewedge, Holtzman, and Epley 2007) in study 2, of source effects (Shefrin and Thaler 1988) in study 3, and of perceived resource availability in study 4.

We offer an explanation based on the idea that different cognitive perspectives lead to different valuations (Ariely, Huber, and Wertenbroch 2005; Carmon and Ariely 2000; Heath, Larrick, and Wu 1999; Novemsky and Kahneman 2005). Specifically, we suggest that seeing a resource run out causes a shift in the cognitive perspective that is used to evaluate transactions. Imagining a specific resource running out makes the loss of resources associated with spending money very salient. We propose that this leads consumers to evaluate the money that would be given up in the transaction in the loss domain, which consequently reduces the propensity to spend.

We provide evidence for the process (loss frame activation) through three different routes. The first approach focuses on demonstrating the mediating role of anticipated pain of paying (Prelec and Loewenstein 1998; Rick, Cryder, and Loewenstein 2008) as phenomenological reflection of loss aversion for money. Consistent with the prediction that anticipated pain of paying mediates the effect, all five studies show that the effect of seeing a resource running out on the propensity to spend is moderated by Rick et al.'s (2008) spendthrift-tightwads scale. The effect was strongest for spendthrifts and weakest among tightwads, who already feel pain of paying spontaneously. In addition, anticipated pain of paying is shown to statistically mediate the effect of seeing a resource running out on consumers' spending intentions in studies 2 and 3. The process that underlies our explanation is more directly tested in studies 4 and 5 which provide evidence of shifts in cognitive perspective as measured by written protocols (study 4), and by proportionality judgments (study 5).

From a consumer welfare perspective, our results are particularly relevant to consumers who identify themselves as chronic over-spenders (i.e. spendthrifts). These consumers may benefit from compartmentalizing their funds into relatively small parts. Ironically, consumers who want to reduce their spending may benefit from carrying a larger array of payment modes. Merely carrying different payment modes that typically contain small amounts, like cash and electronic purse smart cards rather than relying only on credit or debit cards, may help to reduce spending. Our research also has implications for marketers who promote the use of stored value cards to facilitate or encourage spending (e.g. cell phone carriers, public transit authorities, retail chains; Raghubir and Srivastava 2008). Our research implies that such cards may sometimes backfire by discouraging consumers from spending when spending would imply that the card would (largely) run out.

REFERENCES

Aiken, Leona S. and Stephen G. West (1991), *Multiple Regression: Testing and Interpreting Interactions*: Thousand Oaks, CA: Sage.

Ariely, Dan, Joel Huber, and Klaus Wertenbroch (2005), "When Do Losses Loom Larger Than Gains?," *Journal of Marketing Research*, 42 (2), 134-38.

Barnett, Vic and Lewis Toby (1994), *Outliers in Statistical Data*, New York, NY: Wiley.

Carmon, Ziv and Dan Ariely (2000), "Focusing on the Forgone: How Value Can Appear So Different to Buyers and Sellers," *Journal of Consumer Research*, 27 (3), 360-70.

Heath, Chip, Richard P. Larrick, and George Wu (1999), "Goals as Reference Points," *Cognitive Psychology*, 38 (1), 79-109.

Hoch, Stephen J. and George Loewenstein (1991), "Time-Inconsistent Preferences and Consumer Self-Control," *Journal of Consumer Research*, 17 (4), 492-507.

Hsee, Christopher K., Fang Yu, Jiao Zhang, and Yan Zhang (2003), "Medium Maximization," *Journal of Consumer Research*, 30 (1), 1-14.

Kahneman, Daniel and Amos Tversky (1979), "Prospect Theory: An Analysis of Decision under Risk," *Econometrica*, 47 (2), 263-91.

Morgan-Lopez, Antonio A. and David P. MacKinnon (2006), "Demonstration and Evaluation of a Method for Assessing Mediated Moderation," *Behavior Research Methods*, 38 (1), 77-87.

Novemsky, Nathan and Daniel Kahneman (2005), "The Boundaries of Loss Aversion," *Journal of Marketing Research*, 42 (2), 119-28.

Prelec, Drazen and George Loewenstein (1998), "The Red and the Black: Mental Accounting of Savings and Debt," *Marketing Science*, 17 (1), 4-28.

Raghubir, Priya and Joydeep Srivastava (2008), "Monopoly Money: The Effect of Payment Coupling and Form on Spending Behavior," *Journal of Experimental Psychology: Applied*, 14 (3), 213-25.

Rick, Scott I., Cynthia E. Cryder, and George Loewenstein (2008), "Tightwads and Spendthrifts," *Journal of Consumer Research*, 34 (6), 767-82.

Rick, Scott I. and George Loewenstein (2008), "Intangibility in Intertemporal Choice," *Philosophical Transactions of the Royal Society B-Biological Sciences*, 363 (1511), 3813-24.

Tversky, Amos and Daniel Kahneman (1992), "Advances in Prospect Theory: Cumulative Representation of Uncertainty," *Journal of Risk and Uncertainty*, 5 (4), 297-323.

Zauberman, Gal and John G. Lynch, Jr. (2005), "Resource Slack and Propensity to Discount Delayed Investments of Time Versus Money," *Journal of Experimental Psychology: General*, 134 (1), 23-37.

Moderating Shelf-Based Scarcity

Jeffrey Parker, Columbia University, USA
Don Lehmann, Columbia University, USA

EXTENDED ABSTRACT

Shelf-based scarcity is said to occur when one product on a shelf is less stocked (more depleted) than its competitor(s). Recent research has documented the strong impact that shelf-based scarcity can have on consumer preferences. Specifically, van Herpen, Pieters, and Zeelenberg (2009) showed that consumers tend to infer that scarcer products are more popular and of higher quality, and that they prefer scarcer products significantly more than abundant products. Building on these findings, Parker and Lehmann (forthcoming) identified the process through which shelf-based scarcity impacts choice. These authors found that, while both popularity and quality inferences are made based on shelf-based scarcity, it is popularity inferences that are the primary driver of shelf-based scarcity effects.

The results of these papers suggest that shelf-based scarcity is a robust phenomenon. For example, shelf-based scarcity is found to have a significant and positive impact on choices made from a wide variety of product categories (e.g., from wine to motor oil to clothing to household cleaners), and Parker and Lehmann (forthcoming) demonstrate that shelf-based scarcity effects occur even when consumers are making real choices (i.e., choosing products which they will pay for and keep) from branded products in well-known product categories. Further, consumers are still found to prefer scarcer products even when they are given explicit popularity and quality information about the available alternatives.

These papers also made the first inroads into identifying the boundary conditions of shelf-based scarcity effects. First, van Herpen, Pieters, and Zeelenberg (2009) found that consumers tend to not prefer scarcer alternatives when they are shopping in an identity-relevant category (e.g., clothing) and the store is frequented by local customers (i.e., people they are likely to encounter). Adopting a different focus, Parker and Lehmann examined the impact of shelf-based scarcity in the presence of other ubiquitous retail cues (including the aforementioned popularity and quality information), and found that shelf-based scarcity effects are overwhelmed when a price promotion is available in the product category. Additionally, these authors determined that consumers with strong prior preferences were largely unaffected by shelf-based scarcity (i.e., they did not prefer scarcer products more). While some very important boundary conditions of shelf-based scarcity effects have been identified by the aforementioned work, there is still much to learn about this phenomenon.

This project picks up where these papers left off and more deeply investigates the conditions under which shelf-based scarcity does not have a positive (and may have a negative) impact on preferences. First, we conceptually replicate the van Herpen, Pieters, and Zeelenberg (2009) findings regarding identity-relevant goods in a subtler manner. Specifically, we ask participants to choose from two winter jackets (an identity-relevant product category), one of which is scarcer than the other. The jackets are manipulated to differ either in a conspicuous manner (i.e., in a way which others could identify) or in an inconspicuous manner (i.e., in a way that others would not notice). Measuring the participants' need for uniqueness (Fromkin and Snyder 1980), we find that high need-for-uniqueness participants prefer the scarcer jacket significantly less than low need-for-uniqueness participants, but only when the jackets differ conspicuously (i.e., could be used to signal one's identity).

Next, we turn our attention to a crucial link in the process underlying shelf-based scarcity effects that was identified by Parker and Lehmann (forthcoming); the link between shelf-based scarcity and popularity inferences. The literature to this point seems to suggest that this link is universally strong and positive. However, if true, this would suggest that shelf-based scarcity effects could only be attenuated by either making popularity a negative characteristic or by introducing an overwhelming cue (e.g., a price promotion) into the choice context.

We argue that consumers will not always believe that scarcer alternatives a more popular and present two studies supporting our contention. First, building on the shelf-location effects literature (see, e.g., Valenzuela and Raghubir 2009), we posit that shelf-based scarcity effects will be moderated by the location of the scarcer product. Specifically, we hypothesize and demonstrate that the relative advantage of being a scarcer alternative is reduced when the scarcer alternative is located on the bottom (vs. an upper) shelf. We show that, because consumers do not expect scarcer products to be on bottom shelves, scarcer products are neither (i) believed to be relatively more popular nor (ii) more preferred when they are located on the bottom (vs. an upper) shelf.

Second, we investigate whether consumers' persuasion knowledge (Friestad and Wright 1994) impacts their responses to shelf-based scarcity by manipulating the salience of retailers' persuasion motives and tactics. If consumers believe that retailers are attempting to manipulate their choices, they are likely to discount cues which the retailer is able to manipulate (e.g., shelf-based scarcity). This is exactly what we find. When retailers' persuasion motives and tactics are made salient there is no longer a strong and positive impact of shelf-based scarcity on choice.

Taken together, these studies add to our understanding of how and when shelf-based scarcity impacts consumers' preferences. Both the theoretical and managerial implications are discussed.

REFERENCES

Friestad, Marian, and Peter Wright (1994), "The Persuasion Knowledge Model: How People Cope with Persuasion Attempts," *Journal of Consumer Research*, 21(1), 1-31.

Fromkin, Howard L., and C.R. Snyder (1980), "The Search for Uniqueness and Valuation in Scarcity," In K. J. Gergen, M. S. Greenberg, & R. H. Willis (Eds.), *Social exchange: Advances in theory and research*, New York: Plenum Press.

Parker, Jeffrey R., and Donald R. Lehmann (forthcoming), "When Shelf-Based Scarcity Impacts Consumer Preferences," *Journal of Retailing*.

Meier, Brian P and Michael D. Robinson (2004), "Why the Sunny Side is Up: Associations between Affect and Vertical Position," *Psychological Science,* 15, (April), 243-247.

Morales, Andrea C. (2005), "Giving Firms an 'E' for Effort: Consumer Responses to High-Effort Firms," *Journal of Consumer Research*, 31(4), 806-812.

Muller, Dominique, Charles M. Judd, and Vincent Y. Yzerbyt (2005), "When Moderation is Mediated and Mediation is Moderated," *Journal of Personality and Social Psychology*, 89(6), 852-863.

Schubert, Thomas (2005), "Your highness: Vertical Positions as Perceptual Symbols of Power," *Journal of Personality and Social Psychology*, 89(1), 1-21.

Snyder, C. R., and Harold L. Fromkin (1977), "Abnormality as a Positive Characteristic: The Development and Validation of a Scale Measuring Need for Uniqueness," *Journal of Abnormal Psychology, 86 (October)*, 518-27.

Tian, Kelly Tepper, William O. Bearden, and Gary L. Hunter (2001), "Consumers' Need for Uniqueness: Scale Development and Validation," *Journal of Consumer Research*, 28(1), pp. 50-66.

Valenzuela, Ana, and Priya Raghubir (2009), "Position-based Beliefs: The Center-stage Effect," *Journal of Consumer Psychology*, 19(2), 185-96.

Valenzuela, Ana, and Priya Raghubir (2010), "Are Consumers Aware of Top-Bottom but not of Left-Right Inferences? Implications for Shelf Space Positions," *working paper*, Baruch College.

van Herpen, Erica, Rik Pieters, and Marcel Zeelenberg (2009), "When Demand Accelerates Demand: Trailing the Bandwagon," *Journal of Consumer Psychology,* 19, 302-312.

The Instrumental and Detrimental Role of Materialism in the Development of Networks

Seung Hwan (Mark) Lee, University of Western Ontario, Canada

EXTENDED ABSTRACT

Materialism is the dispositional view towards consumption of objects and possessions as an important part of achieving higher goals, such as self-definition and self-enhancement (Chaplin and John 2007). For example, Richins and Dawson (1992, p. 304) state that "it is the pursuit of happiness through acquisition rather than through other means (such as personal relationships, experiences, or achievements) that distinguishes materialism." In other words, materialism is the importance that people place on consumption relative to other values, such as relationships, as a means by which to achieve certain goals (Richins and Dawson 1992).

Research has shown that there are positive and negative consequences of materialism (Burroughs and Rindfleisch 2002; Chaplin and John 2007; Dittmar, Long, and Bond 2007; Fitzmaurice 2008; Van Boven and Gilovich 2003). Overall, research in marketing, for the most part, has depicted materialism as a destructive trait; Hirschman (1991) refers to materialism as one of the "dark sides" of consumer behavior. For example, materialism has been associated with negative personal outcomes, such as social ineptitude (Richins 1987) and narcissistic behavior (Cohen and Cohen 1996), which can hinder an individual's motivation and ability to effectively form social relationships and networks. If materialism is, in fact, negative and destructive, why are we witnessing the rising levels of materialism among consumers (Goldberg et al. 2003; Chaplin and John 2010)?

Perhaps there is a brighter side to materialism. Past researchers have shown that materialistic behavior is associated with positive personal outcomes, such as attaining a higher standard living (Richins and Rudmin 1994) and attaining desirable characteristics (e.g., cultured, sophisticated) (Christopher and Schlenker 2004). This debate about the nature of materialism leads to the main research question: Is materialism *instrumental* or *detrimental* to an individual's social network development?

Findings from a longitudinal field study from an emerging social network (Study 1) reveal that materialism is instrumental to an individual's social network development (i.e., more materialistic people made more social connections over time). However, a caveat is that this benefit is perceptual, not actual. That is, there appears to be a discrepancy between consumers' perceptual social network versus their actual social network, a phenomenon coined here as the *perceptual network fallacy*. Materialistic individuals overestimated the number of friends they had in their social network in two separate time-periods (early and later stages of network development). This finding is important to consumers because materialistic individuals are accustomed to acquiring material goods in response to their belief that possessions will enhance their social standing (i.e., they will become more popular/central in a network). However, the findings of this research suggest that this belief is merely perceptual.

Moreover, in support of this theory, the findings from Study 2 reveal that conversing about product possessions is what primes materialistic individuals to overestimate their friendship desirability. While previous research has noted the negative impact of discussing possessions with others (Van Boven et al. 2010), the current research goes one step further to show that this effect is even stronger for materialistic individuals. In support, the data show that materialistic individuals were rated less desirable by others when they were first given the opportunity to converse about product possessions. Interestingly, the data also show that materialistic individuals rated themselves higher on friendship desirability. Thus, materialistic individuals perceive that conversing about product possessions enhances their self-value, although this was clearly not the case. Materialistic individuals continue to purchase and talk about products that elevate their social image because they mistakenly perceive that doing so will benefit them socially (Bagwell and Bernheim 1996). Unfortunately, they are oblivious to the detrimental effects, a condition that explains why the magnitude of perceptual network fallacy grows over time. As networks mature, materialistic individuals gain more opportunities to talk about their product possessions with others. As a result, such conversations continue to contribute to the growing gap between these individuals' out-degree and in-degree ties over time, thus magnifying their erroneous perception of their position within the network.

In conclusion, this research provides another lesson to consumers regarding the dangers of materialistic consumption. Growing levels of materialism among teenagers have raised concerns among parents and educators alike (Chaplin and John 2010; Goldberg et al. 2003). Adolescents purchase certain objects (e.g., cell phones, MP3 players, brand-name clothing) because they perceive that material possessions will help them gain a desirable status (e.g., popularity) in their social network. However, it must be recognized that these are erroneous perceptions. Indeed, materialistic individuals do not gain more friends over time. They only believe that they will. Therefore, consumers could be warned that their efforts to use material consumption in order to gain favorable network positions may not be successful.

REFERENCES

Bagwell, Laurie and Douglas Bernheim (1996), "Veblen Effects in a Theory of Conspicuous Consumption," *American Economic Review*, 86 (3), 349-73.

Banerjee, Robin and Helga Dittmar (2008), "Individual Differences in Children's Materialsim: The Role of Peer Relations," *Personality and Social Psychology Bulletin*, 34 (1), 17-31.

Belk, Russell W. (1985), "Materialism: Trait Aspects of Living in a Material World," *Journal of Consumer Research*, 12 (3), 265-80.

--- (1988), "Possessions and the Extended Self," *Journal of Consumer Research*, 15 (2), 139-68.

Brewer, Marilyn B. (1991), "The Social Self: On Being the Same and Different at the Same Time," *Personality and Social Psychology Bulletin*, 17 (5), 475-82.

Browne, Beverly A. and Dennis O. Kaldenberg (1997), "Conceptualizing Self-Monitoring: Links to Materialism and Product Involvement," *Journal of Consumer Marketing*, 14 (1), 31-44.

Burroughs, James E. and Aric Rindfleisch (2002), "Materialism and Well-Being: A Conflicting Values Perspective," *Journal of Consumer Research*, 29 (3), 348-70.

Casciaro, Tiziana (1998), "Seeing Things Clearly: Social Structure, Personality, and Accuracy in Social Network Perception," *Social Networks*, 20 (4), 331-51.

Chaplin, Lan N. and Deborah R. John (2007), "Growing up in a Material World: Age Differences in Materialism in Children and Adolescents," *Journal of Consumer Research*, 34 (4), 480-93.

--- (2010), "Interpersonal Influences on Adolescent Materialism: A New Look at the Role of Parents and Peers," *Journal of Consumer Psychology*, 20 (2), 176-84.

Chatman, Jennifer A. and Sandra E. Spataro (2005), "Using Self-Categorization Theory to Understand Relational Demography-Based Variations in People's Responsiveness to Organizational Culture," *Academy of management Journal*, 48 (2), 321-31.

Christopher, Andrew N., Terell P. Lasane, Jordan D. Troisi, and Lora E. Park (2007), "Materialism, Defensive, and Assertive Self-Presentational Tactics, and Life Satisfaction," *Journal of Social and Clinical Psychology*, 26 (10), 1145-62.

Christopher, Andrew N. and Barry R. Schlenker (2004), "Materialism and Affect: The Role of Self-Presentational Concerns," *Journal of Social and Clinical Psychology*, 23 (2), 260-72.

Cohen, Patricia and Jacob Cohen (1996), *Life Values and Adolescent Mental Health*, Mahwah, NJ: Erlbaum.

Csikszentmihalyi, Mihaly and Eugene Rochberg-Halton (1981), *The Meaning of Things: Domestic Symbols and the Self*, New York, NY: Cambridge University Press.

Deci, Edward L. and Richard M. Ryan (1985), *Intrinsic Motivation and Self-Determination in Human Behavior*, New York, NY: Plenum.

Dittmar, Helga, Karen Long, and Rod Bond (2007), "When a Better Self Is Only a Button Click Away: Associations between Materialistic Values, Emotional and Identity-Related Buying Motives, and Compulsive Buying Tendency Online," *Journal of Social and Clinical Psychology*, 26 (3), 334-61.

Dittmar, Helga and Lucy Pepper (1994), "To Have Is to Be: Materialism and Person Perception in Working-Class and Middle-Class British Adolescents," *Journal of Economic Psychology*, 15 (2), 233-51.

Fitzmaurice, Julie (2008), "Splurge Purchases and Materialism," *Journal of Consumer Marketing*, 25 (6), 332-38.

Fitzmaurice, Julie and Charles Comegys (2006), "Materialism and Social Consumption," *Journal of Marketing Theory and Practice*, 14 (4), 287-99.

Freeman, Linton C. (1979), "Centrality in Social Networks: Conceptual Clarification," *Social Networks*, 1 (3), 215-39.

Goldberg, Marvin E., Gerald J. Gorn, Laura A. Perrachio, and Gary Bamossy (2003), "Understanding Materialism among Youth," *Journal of Consumer Psychology*, 13 (3), 278-88.

Hirschman, Elizabeth C. (1991), "Exploring the Dark Side of Consumer Behavior: Metaphor and Ideology in Prostitution and Pornography," in *Gender & Consumer Behavior*, Vol. 1, ed. Janeen A. Costa, Salt Lake City, UT: Association for Consumer Research, 303-14.

Holt, Douglas B. (1995), "How Consumers Consume: A Typology of Consumption Practices," *Journal of Consumer Research*, 22 (1), 1-16.

Kasser, Tim (2002), "Sketches for a Self-Determination Theory of Values," in *Handbook of Self-Determination Research*, ed. Edward L. Deci and Richard M. Ryan, Rcohester, NY: University of Rochester Press, 123-40.

Kasser, Tim and Aaron Ahuvia (2002), "Materialistic Values and Well-Being in Business Students," *European Journal of Social Psychology*, 32 (1), 137-46.

Kasser, Tim and Richard M. Ryan (1993), "A Dark Side of the American Dream: Correlates of Financial Success as a Central Life Aspiration," *Journal of Personality and Social Psychology*, 65 (2), 410-22.

--- (2001), "Be Careful What You Wish For: Optimal Functioning and the Relative Attainment of Intrinsic and Extrinsic Goals," in *Life Goals and Well-Being: Towards a Positive Psychology of Human Striving*, ed. Peter Schmuck and Ken M. Sheldon, Goettingen, Germany: Hogrefe & Huber, 116-31.

Lee, Seung Hwan (Mark), June Cotte, and Theodore J. Noseworthy (2010), "The Role of Network Centrality in the Flow of Consumer Influence," *Journal of Consumer Psychology*, 20 (1), 66-77.

McCracken, Grant D. (1988), *Culture and Consumption: New Approaches to the Symbolic Character of Consumer Goods and Activities*, Bloomington, IN: Indiana University Press.

Pollay, Richard W. (1986), "The Distorted Mirror: Reflections on the Unintended Consequences of Advertising," *Journal of Marketing*, 50 (2), 18-36.

Richins, Marsha L. (1987), "Media, Materialism, and Human Happiness," in *Advances in Consumer Research*, Vol. 14, ed. Melanie Wallendorf and Paul Anderson, Provo, UT: Association for Consumer Research, 352-56.

--- (1994), "Special Possessions and the Expression of Material Values," *Journal of Consumer Research*, 21 (3), 522-33.

Richins, Marsha L. and Scott Dawson (1992), "A Consumer Values Orientation for Materialism and Its Measurements: Scale Development and Validation," *Journal of Consumer Research*, 19 (3), 303-16.

Richins, Marsha L. and Floyd W. Rudmin (1994), "Materialism and Economic Psychology," *Journal of Economic Psychology*, 15 (2), 217-31.

Schroeder, Jonathan E. and Sanjiv S. Dugal (1995), "Psychological Correlates of the Materialism Construct," *Journal of Social Behavior and Personality*, 10 (1), 243-53.

Solomon, Michael R. (1983), "The Role of Products as Social Stimuli: A Symoblic Interactionism Perspective," *Journal of Consumer Research*, 10 (3), 319-29.

Srivastava, Abhishek, Edwin Locke, and Kathryn Bartol (2001), "Money and Subjective Well-Being: It's Not the Money, It's the Motives," *Journal of Personality and Social Psychology*, 80 (6), 959-71.

Tian, Kelly T., William O. Bearden, and Gary L. Hunter (2001), "Consumers' Need for Uniqueness: Scale Development and Validation," *Journal of Consumer Research*, 28 (1), 50-66.

Van Boven, Leaf, Margaret C. Campbell, and Thomas Gilovich (2010), "Stigmatizing Materialism: On Stereotyping and Impressions of Materailistic and Experiential Pursuits," *Personality and Social Psychology Bulletin*, 36 (4), 551-63.

Van Boven, Leaf and Thomas Gilovich (2003), "To Do or to Have: That Is the Question," *Journal of Personality and Social Psychology*, 85 (6), 1193-202.

Wasserman, Stanley and Katherine Faust (1994), *Social Network Analysis: Methods and Applications*, Cambridge, MA: Cambridge University Press.

Effects of Family Structure on Compulsive Buying: A Life Course Perspective

Andrew Baker, Georgia State University, USA
George Moschis, Georgia State University, USA
Edward Rigdon, Georgia State University, USA
Anil Mathur, Hofstra University, USA

EXTENDED ABSTRACT

Compulsive buying has been a topic of great interest to researchers and policy makers for decades because it is believed to affect the well-being of millions of U.S. consumers. It can be viewed as form of maladaptive behavior, as it correlates strongly with other forms of compulsive behaviors, such as alcoholism and eating disorders (Faber et al. 1995), which are considered maladaptive phenomena (e.g., Simmons et al. 2002). Although it is recognized that compulsive behavior is rooted (at least partly) in early-life experiences (e.g., Rindfleisch et al.1997), little is known about the processes that link early-life experiences to this form of consumer behavior (Rindfleisch et al. 1997).

The life course paradigm offers a viable framework for studying childhood-adulthood links because it suggests that behavior is embedded with circumstances one has experienced at earlier stages in life. It has been used to study similar phenomena of maladaptive behavior such as binge eating and drinking (e.g., Simmons et al. 2002). This paper uses the life course framework as a blueprint for organizing, integrating, and developing a theory-driven model to explain compulsive buying. A model of compulsive buying that has appeared in leading scientific journals (Rindfleisch et al. 1997) is also tested and compared to the life course model, using a sample and measures similar to those used by its builders. The results suggest that previous efforts to study this consumption phenomenon could be better understood in the context of the broader multi-theoretical life course paradigm.

The life course paradigm suggests that biological and psychological changes during an individual's life and social demands across the life course that are defined by typical life events and social roles create physical, social, and emotional demands and circumstances to which one must adapt. This adaptation entails the processes of socialization, stress and coping, and development and growth or decline. These processes are the underlying change mechanisms of the three most widely-accepted life-course perspectives: normative (socialization), stress, and human capital, respectively (Moschis 2007).

Previous research finds that young consumers from disrupted homes have higher compulsive buying tendencies than those from intact homes (e.g., Rindfleisch et al. 1997), viewing stress as the mechanism or process that links family disruption to compulsive buying. In contrast, the life course paradigm suggests a number of causal mechanisms relating family structure to the child's problem behavior in general and compulsive buying in particular. According to this paradigm, compulsive buying tendencies may be the result of not only stressful experiences of disruptive family events (as suggested by the stress perspective); they may also be attributed to negative consequences these family events have on the child's socialization experiences (as suggested by the normative perspective) and his or her psychological development (as suggested by the human capital perspective). Because the various disciplinary approaches to life course research are complementary, the life course paradigm provides a framework for integrating diverse theoretical perspectives

into a multi-theoretical model, which is consistent with recent efforts of life course researchers to develop models that include variables derived from diverse theories (e.g., Mortimer and Shanahan 2003). Thus, based on the power of the life course paradigm to integrate multiple theoretical perspectives, we draw from each of the three theoretical perspectives to provide an integrated model to explain compulsive buying.

The results generally support the life course model, helping us see the contributions of each perspective to our understanding of compulsive buying tendencies. They highlight the mechanisms that may link family disruptions to compulsive buying, beyond those suggested by previous research that has assume stress as an explanation. Specifically, our data suggest that family disruption events experienced in formative years leads to the depletion of socioeconomic resources that interfere with socialization practices and deter human capital development due to ineffective parent-child communications. The youth's experience of stressors from living in disrupted family settings and their experience of socioeconomic deprivation appear to be responsible for the social processes—interactions with peers and parents who stress conformity rather than self-direction and attempt to exercise a greater control over their child's activities, which are fostered in such family settings. These processes appear to put the child at risk of developing compulsive buying tendencies.

Although earlier research has suggested the possibility of mechanisms (other than stress) for the development of compulsive consumer behaviors, such as family socialization practices (e.g., Rindfleisch et al. 1997), research along these suggested directions has been hampered due to a lack of theoretical frameworks. The present study shows how earlier research on compulsive buying can be examined within the broader life course paradigm.

REFERENCES

Faber, Ronald J., Gary A. Christenson, Martina De Zwann, and James Mitchell (1995), "Two Forms of Compulsive Consumption: Comorbidity of Compulsive Buying and Binge Eating," *Journal of Consumer Research*, 22 (4), 296-304.

Mortimer, Jeylan T. and Michael J. Shanahan, (2003), *Handbook of the Life Course*. New York: Kluwer/Plenum.

Moschis, George P.(2007), "Life Course Perspectives on Consumer Behavior," *Journal of the Academy of Marketing Science,* Vol. 35 (2), (June), 295-397.

Simmons, Ronald, Eric Stewart, Leslie C. Gordon, Rand D. Conger, and Glen H. Elder, Jr. (2002), "A Test of Life-Course Explanations for Stability and Change in Antisocial Behavior from Adolescence toYoung Adulthood," *Criminology*, 40(2), 4001-433.

Rindfleisch, Aric and James E. Burroughs, and Frank Denton (1997), "Family Structure, Materialism and Compulsive Consumption," *Journal of Consumer Research,* 23 (March), 312-25.

"When Knowing is Better than Expecting"
Resolving Different Types of Ambivalence by (Biased) Information Processing and Spreading Word-Of-Mouth

Nico Heuvinck, Ghent University & University College Ghent, Belgium
Iris Vermeir, Ghent University, Belgium
Maggie Geuens, Ghent University & Vlerick Leuven Gent Management School, Belgium

EXTENDED ABSTRACT

When consumers simultaneously evaluate an attitude object as positive and negative, they are said to experience attitudinal ambivalence (Kaplan 1972). As ambivalence is generally experienced as aversive and unpleasant (Newby-Clark et al. 2002; Nordgren et al. 2006; van Harreveld et al. 2009a), it is assumed to induce ambivalent people to thoroughly scrutinize any information that enables them to resolve their ambivalence (Jonas et al., 1997; Nordgren et al. 2006; van Harreveld et al. 2009b). However, ambivalence can also be resolved through biased information processing (Nordgren et al. 2006; van Harreveld et al. 2009b). Clark et al. (2008), for example, found that ambivalent individuals increase processing of proattitudinal information and avoid processing of counterattitudinal information. The direction of the bias is thus in line with the initial valence of the attitude (Nordgren et al. 2006; van Harreveld et al. 2009b).

This paper builds on and refines these findings in two major ways. First, we distinguish between two different types of subjective ambivalence: *manifest ambivalence* (knowing conflicting information) versus *univalent ambivalence* (expecting conflicting information). Second, next to information processing, we also investigate word-of-mouth (WOM) as a potential coping mechanism. The objective of this paper is then to investigate different types of subjective ambivalence, and information processing and spreading WOM as ways to deal with this ambivalence.

In Study 1, we manipulated univalence, univalent ambivalence, and manifest ambivalence by varying the amount of positive and negative features respondents received about an MP3-player (cf. Priester et al. 2007), and by varying the opinion of one's best friend. Ambivalence was measured by capturing the degree to which respondents' reactions toward this MP3-player are conflicted, mixed, and indecisive. The extent of information processing was measured by means of a thought-listing procedure (cf. Nordgren et al. 2006). Thoughts were coded on valence and total number of arguments listed. Results show that manifest and univalent ambivalent individuals experience the same level of subjective ambivalence and generate the same number of thoughts, but the valence of their thoughts significantly differs. Univalent respondents seem to focus more on positive thoughts than univalent ambivalent respondents who in turn generate more positive thoughts compared to manifest ambivalent individuals. Hence, the type of ambivalence induces a different information processing.

Study 2 addresses whether people in the univalent ambivalent condition attempt and/or succeed in resolving their ambivalence through generating especially positive thoughts and individuals in the manifest ambivalent condition through mainly negative thoughts. This study is similar to Study 1, except for two modifications. First, we now also measured ambivalence aversion (by means of the items irritation, frustration and discontentment, cf. Nordgren et al. 2006). Second, a repeated measure of subjective ambivalence was obtained at the end of the questionnaire. Study 2 replicates the findings of Study 1. In addition, manifest ambivalent respondents report more intense negative emotions than participants in the univalent ambivalent and univalent condition. This higher ambivalence aversion seems to motivate manifest ambivalent consumers to process information that can resolve their conflict. Results confirm that for manifest ambivalent respondents the biased (negative) information processing helps to reduce the discomfort of ambivalence. That is, ratings of subsequent ambivalence were lower than ratings of initial ambivalence. For univalent and univalent ambivalent people, there was no difference between initial and subsequent ambivalence.

WOM has been shown to be one of the most employed strategies for reducing cognitive dissonance (Festinger, 1957). By spreading WOM to others, consumers try to convince themselves of their opinion by convincing others of the same opinion. Therefore, we believe that WOM can also be an effective coping mechanism to reduce subjective ambivalence. To the best of our knowledge, this has only been discussed in the cognitive dissonance literature (e.g. Festinger, 1957) and the service literature (e.g. von Wangenheim, 2005) to cope with evaluative incongruence, but has not yet been investigated in relation with ambivalence.

Study 3 was similar to Study 1 except for one modification. Measures of positive and negative WOM replaced the thought-listing task. Positive WOM captured the degree to which respondents would recommend/ tell others to buy the MP3-player whereas negative WOM covered the extent to which respondents would warn/tell others not to buy it. Results indicate that, although they experience the same extent of ambivalence, manifest ambivalent people spread more negative and less positive WOM than univalent ambivalent and univalent people. This could be due to the awareness of these conflicting (negative) features and/or to the fact that negative features weigh more heavily in the evaluation of an attitude object than positive ones (Ito et al., 1998).

Study 4 investigates whether spreading negative WOM could also account as an effective coping mechanism to resolve the agony of ambivalence for manifest ambivalent individuals. Study 4 was similar to Study 2, except for one modification. That is, instead of a thought-listing task, WOM was assessed using an open-ended question, the answers of which were coded for valence and number of arguments. This study replicated the effects found in Study 3. That is, manifest ambivalent people spread more negative and less positive WOM compared to univalent ambivalent individuals as well as univalent attitude holders. Similar to Study 2, we show that manifest ambivalence is experienced as more aversive than univalent ambivalence and univalence. In addition, manifest ambivalent attitude holders generate more negative WOM (motivated by the aversion) which reduced their feelings of ambivalence.

Taken together, our findings show the relevance of distinguishing between the types of ambivalence (univalent versus manifest ambivalence). They also shed light on the difference of the underlying structure of feelings of ambivalence and how people cope with these different types of ambivalence in terms of information processing and WOM as a means to reduce the aversion caused by the type of ambivalence. It seems that both biased (negative) information processing and negative WOM helps manifest ambivalent people to resolve their subjective ambivalence level. A possible explanation for this finding may reside in the fact that manifest ambivalence is experienced as more aversive compared to univalent ambivalence.

REFERENCES

Clark, J.K., Wegener, D.T., and L.R. Fabrigar (2008), "Attitudinal ambivalence and message-based persuasion: motivated processing of proattitudinal information and avoidance of counterattitudinal information," *Personality and Social Psychology Bulletin, 34*, 565-577.

Festinger, L. (1957), *A theory of cognitive dissonance*, Evanston, IL: Row, Peterson.

Ito, T.A., Larsen, J.T., Smith, N.K., and J.T. Cacioppo (1998), "Negative information weighs more heavily on the brain: the negativity bias in evaluative categorizations," *Journal of Personality and Social Psychology, 75*, 887-900.

Jonas, K., Diehl, M., and P. Brömer (1997), "Effects of attitudinal ambivalence on information processing and attitude-intention consistency," *Journal of Experimental Social Psychology, 33*, 190-210.

Kaplan, K.J. (1972), "On the ambivalence-indifference problem in attitude theory and measurement: a suggested modification of the semantic differential technique," *Psychological Bulletin, 77*, 361-372.

Newby-Clark, I.R., McGregor, I., and M.P. Zanna (2002), "Thinking and caring about cognitive inconsistency: when and for whom does attitudinal ambivalence feel uncomfortable?," *Journal of Personality and Social Psychology, 82*, 157-166.

Nordgren, L.F., van Harreveld, F., and J. van der Pligt (2006), "Ambivalence, discomfort and motivated information processing," *Journal of Experimental Social Psychology, 42*, 252-258.

Priester, J.R., Petty, R.E., and K. Park (2007), "Whence univalent ambivalence? From the anticipation of conflicting reactions.," *Journal of Consumer Research, 34*, 11-21.

van Harreveld, F., Rutjens, B.T., Rotteveel, M.R., Nordgren, L.F., and J. van der Pligt (2009a), "Ambivalence and decisional conflict as a cause of psychological discomfort: feeling tense before jumping off the fence," *Journal of Experimental Social Psychology, 45*, 167-173.

van Harreveld, F., van der Pligt, J., and Y.N. de Liver (2009b), "The agony of ambivalence and ways to resolve it: introducing the MAID model," *Personality and Social Psychology Review, 13*, 45-61.

von Wangenheim, F. (2005), "Postswitching negative word-of-mouth," *Journal of Service Research, 8*, 67-78.

"The Good, the Bad and the Certain"
When Ambivalent Attitudes Affect Intention Differently

Nico Heuvinck, Ghent University & University College Ghent, Belgium
Maggie Geuens, Ghent University & Vlerick Leuven Gent Management School, Belgium
Iris Vermeir, Ghent University, Belgium

EXTENDED ABSTRACT

When consumers simultaneously evaluate an attitude object as positive and negative, they are said to experience attitudinal ambivalence (Kaplan 1972; Priester and Petty 1996). Although attitudinal ambivalence is usually treated as a general construct (Kaplan 1972), the underlying structure of the feelings of ambivalence may lead to very different consumer responses. Building on Priester et al. (2007), we distinguish two different types of subjective ambivalence: *manifest ambivalence* (knowing conflicting information) versus *univalent ambivalence* (anticipating/expecting conflicting information). The objective of this paper is to investigate the impact of these different types of subjective ambivalence on attitude certainty (conceptualized by attitude clarity and attitude correctness) and attitude-intention correspondence.

Ambivalence is generally associated with uncertainty as the conflict between positive and negative reactions attenuates the certainty of holding an attitude (e.g. Jonas et al. 1997; Petrocelli et al. 2007; Petty et al. 2006; Tormala and Rucker 2007). However, we suggest that attitude certainty associated with an ambivalent attitude will be influenced by the type of conflicting reactions that underlie subjective ambivalence. When conflicting reactions are anticipated (i.e., univalent ambivalence), people will be less certain of their ambivalent attitude compared to when conflicting reactions are known (i.e., manifest ambivalence) or rather absent (i.e., univalence).

In Study 1, we manipulated attitudinal ambivalence (univalence, univalent ambivalence, and manifest ambivalence) by varying the amount of positive and negative features respondents received about an MP3-player (cf. Priester et al. 2007), and by varying the opinion of one's best friend. Respondents indicated their attitudes, attitude certainty (Clarkson et al. 2008; Petrocelli et al. 2007; Tormala and Petty 2002), type of conflicting reactions, and subjective ambivalence toward the MP3-player (Priester et al. 2007). The results show that although manifest and univalent ambivalent individuals experience the same level of subjective ambivalence, univalent ambivalent attitudes are held with less certainty compared to manifest ambivalent and univalent attitudes. Hence, the type of ambivalence, fed by different conflicting reactions, indeed induces different levels of attitude certainty.

According to Petrocelli et al. (2007), attitude certainty is composed of (1) attitude correctness and (2) attitude clarity. Attitude correctness refers to the extent to which one feels confident that his/her attitude is correct, valid, or justified. Individuals with high attitude correctness not only believe that their attitude is correct, but also think that other people should have the same attitude. Attitude clarity is the extent to which people know what their true attitude toward a topic is and to what extent this attitude is clear to them. We argue that univalent ambivalent people are less likely to know their true attitude (cf. attitude clarity) toward a focal product because they anticipate, but are not really aware of any conflicting information. In contrast, manifest ambivalent individuals are well aware of conflicting information. Therefore, we believe that they perceive their attitude to be clearer compared to univalent ambivalent individuals. In contrast, concerning attitude correctness, we do not expect any differences between manifest and univalent ambivalent individuals. Univalent ambivalent individuals can be as convinced as manifest ambivalent individuals that their attitude is correct/valid given the available information.

Study 2 was identical to Study 1, except for one modification; at the end of the questionnaire, we assessed attitude clarity and attitude correctness (cf. Petrocelli et al. 2007). Besides replicating the findings of Study 1, Study 2 shows that univalent ambivalent respondents indeed feel that their attitude toward the MP3-player is less clear as compared to manifest ambivalent and univalent participants. Also in line with expectations, univalent ambivalent individuals feel equally confident as manifest ambivalent and univalent individuals that their attitude is correct, valid or justified. Hence, it seems that the lower attitude certainty experienced by univalent ambivalence (versus manifest ambivalence and univalence), is driven by a difference in attitude clarity rather than a difference in attitude correctness.

Several studies have shown that attitudinal ambivalence results in lower attitude-behavior consistency (e.g. Armitage and Conner 2000; Conner et al. 2002; Costarelli and Colloca 2004; Thompson et al. 1995). In contrast, Jonas et al. (2007) and Sengupta and Johar (2002) found that ambivalent attitudes lead to higher attitude-behavior consistency. We argue that the type of conflicting reactions underlying attitudinal ambivalence could help explain these different results. People are spontaneously motivated to make sense of inconsistencies in order to arrive at an integrated evaluation (Srull and Wyer 1989). Accordingly, exposure to inconsistencies stimulates information processing, increasing the strength and the predictive ability of the attitude (Jonas et al. 1997; Petty et al. 1995). Since manifest ambivalent people are confronted with positive and negative information, they will probably consider both in an effort to create an integrated judgment that is predictive of behavior (i.e., a strong attitude). Univalent ambivalent people are aware of only positive items and merely *anticipate* on negative information. As an outcome, judgments can be expected to be less integrated and hence less predictive of behavior. Moreover, attitudes held with high, rather than low, certainty yield greater attitude-behavior consistency (e.g. Rucker and Petty 2004, Tormala et al. 2006; Tormala and Petty, 2004a, 2004b; Tormala and Rucker 2007). The results of Study 1 and 2 show that manifest ambivalent people indicate higher attitude certainty compared to univalent ambivalent people. Hence, manifest ambivalent people can be expected to also display higher attitude-intention correspondence.

Study 3 was similar to Study 2, except for one modification. At the end of the questionnaire we assessed respondents' intention to buy the MP3-player (cf. Costarelli and Colloca 2007; Jonas et al. 1996). Study 3 replicated the results of Studies 1 and 2. Moreover, we show that attitudes are more predictive of behavioral intentions in the manifest ambivalent and univalent condition compared to the univalent ambivalent condition which is not mediated by attitude certainty.

Taken together, the findings of our three studies shed light on the difference of the underlying structure of feelings of ambivalence and how the type of attitudinal ambivalence (manifest versus univalent) influences attitude certainty (conceptualized as attitude clarity and attitude correctness) and attitude-intention consistency. These findings have important implications for both theorists as practitioners.

REFERENCES

Armitage, C.J. and M. Conner (2000), "Attitudinal ambivalence: a test of three key hypotheses," *Personality and Social Psychology Bulletin,* 26, 1421-32.

Clarkson, J.J., Z.L. Tormala, and D.D. Rucker (2008), "A new look at the consequences of attitude certainty: The amplification hypothesis," *Journal of Personality and Social Psychology,* 95, 810-25.

Conner, M., P. Sparks, R. Povey, R. James, R. Sheperd, and C.J. Armitage (2002), "Moderator effects of attitudinal ambivalence on attitude-behavior relationships," *European Journal of Social Psychology,* 32, 705-18.

Costarelli, S. and P. Colloca (2007), "The moderation of ambivalence on attitude-intention relations as mediated by attitude importance," *European Journal of Social Psychology,* 37, 923-33.

Jonas, K., M. Diehl, and P. Brömer (1997), "Effects of attitudinal ambivalence on information processing and attitude-intention consistency," *Journal of Experimental Social Psychology,* 33, 190-210.

Kaplan, K.J. (1972), "On the ambivalence-indifference problem in attitude theory and measurement: a suggested modification of the semantic differential technique," *Psychological Bulletin,* 77, 361-72.

Petrocelli, J.V., Z.L. Tormala, and D.D. Rucker (2007), "Unpacking attitude certainty: Attitude clarity and attitude correctness," *Journal of Personality and Social Psychology*, 92, 30-41.

Petty, R.E., C.P. Haugtvedt, and S.M. Smith (1995), "Elaboration as a determinant of attitude strength: creating attitudes that are persistent, resistant, and predictive of behavior," In R.E. Petty & J.A. Krosnick (Eds.), *Attitude strength: antecedents and consequences,* Mahwah, NJ: Lawrence Erlbaum, 93-130.

Petty, R.E., Z.L. Tormala, P. Briñol, and W.B.G. Jarvis (2006), "Implicit ambivalence form attitude change: An exploration of the PAST model", *Journal of Personality and Social Psychology*, 90, 21-41.

Priester, J.R. and R.E. Petty (1996), "The gradual threshold model of ambivalence: relating the positive and negative bases of attitudes to subjective ambivalence," *Journal of Personality and Social Psychology,* 71, 431-49.

Priester, J.R., R.E. Petty, and K. Park (2007), "Whence univalent ambivalence? From the anticipation of conflicting reactions," *Journal of Consumer Research,* 34, 11-21.

Rucker, D.D. and R.E. Petty (2004), "When resistance is futile: consequences of failed counterargung for attitude certainty," *Journal of Personality and Social Psychology,* 86, 219-35.

Sengupta, J. and G.V. Johar (2002), "Effects of inconsistent attribute information on the predictive value of product attitudes: toward a resolution of opposing perspectives," *Journal of Consumer Research,* 29, 39-56.

Srull, T.K. and R.S. Wyer (1989), "Person memory and judgment," *Psychological Review,* 96, 58-83.

Thompson, M.M., M.P. Zanna, and D.W. Griffin (1995), "Let's not be indifferent about (attitudinal) ambivalence," In R.E. Petty & J.A. Krosnick (Eds.), *Attitude strength: antecedents and consequences,* Mahwah, NJ: Lawrence Erlbaum, 361-86.

Tormala, Z.L., J.J. Clarkson, and R.E. Petty (2006), "Resisting persuasion by the skin of one's teeth: the hidden success of resisted persuasive messages," *Journal of Personality and Social Psychology,* 91, 423-35.

Tormala, Z.L. and R.E. Petty (2002), "What doesn't kill me makes me stronger: The effects of resisting persuasion on attitude certainty," *Journal of Personality and Social Psychology,* 83, 1298-1313.

Tormala, Z.L. and R.E. Petty (2004a), "Resistance to persuasion and attitude certainty: the moderating role of elaboration," *Personality and Social Psychology Bulletin,* 30, 1446-57.

Tormala, Z.L. and R.E. Petty (2004b), "Source credibility and attitude certainty: a metacognitive analysis of resistance to persuasion," *Journal of Consumer Psychology,* 14, 427-42.

Tormala, Z.L. and D.D. Rucker (2007), "Attitude certainty: a review of past findings and emerging perspectives," *Social and Personality Psychology Compass,* 1, 469-92.

The Sacred and the Profane in Islamic Consumption

Aliakbar Jafari, University of Strathclyde, UK
Ahmet Suerdem, Istanbul Bilgi University, Turkey

EXTENDED ABSTRACT

The majority of existing literature on consumption in Islamic societies is based on the premises of reductionist conventional theories that make general assumptions about Islamic ideation with little attention and relevance to Moslems' daily life practices. Such conventional theories – that come from two camps outside and inside of the Moslem world – make superficial analogies between the West and Islam. The former is epitomized in Weber's (1958, 1965) trivial analysis of Islam, economy and society in which whilst protestant ethic is driven by value-based rationality, Moslems' value systems are based on militant (*jihad*) instrumental-rationality (short term self-interest and pillaging) and emotional (martyrdom) motivations. Therefore, neither capital accumulation is possible nor worldly pleasures are pursued. As a result, Moslems essentially wash their hands off the worldly blessings. Generated from within the Moslem world, the latter stream of theories also adopts a reductionist approach. Consumption in this perspective is largely analyzed within the rigid framework of *Halal* (lawful) and *Haram* (unlawful), the *Mustahabb* (favored) and *Makruh* (disliked). Such dichotomous categorizations – which legitimize some deeds and demonize others (Soroush, 2000) – prevail in the Islamic discourse as Moslem scholars barely transgress these rigid boundaries to study consumption from other possible angles (e.g., social, cultural, aesthetic). Typically, trenched in an 'ideologized Islam' (Soroush, 2000), consumption culture is viewed (see, for example, Khan 1984; Kahf 1996; Kalantari 2008; Ormanlar 1999; Razzaghi 1996) as the essence of Western capitalism (and, of course, its subsequent Modernity) which seeks to impose its value systems (socio-cultural and economic) on Islamic societies.

Both of these perspectives have encouraged narrow binary oppositions of 'Islam versus the West', 'the Occident versus the Orient', and 'Modernity versus religion'. Whilst the first stream has adopted an 'Orientalist' (Said 1978) approach to define Western Modernity in relation to an anti-Modern Islam, the second perspective has, in a self-Orientalist manner, responded to the superficial assumptions of the first camp in a superficial way. The above-mentioned Moslem scholars have failed to analyze the ever-changing conditions of contemporary life in Moslem societies and overlooked the context-dependency of consumption (Hasan 2005) and the historical trajectories that have traditionally shaped foundations of the private and public lives of Moslems (Jafari 2009). Therefore, there is a need to transgress these clichéd assumptions that are not capable of explaining Moslems' complicated and often paradoxical everyday life consumption practices in contemporary society.

On the other hand, due to the cultural turn's emphasis on identity issues, the culture of consumption in contemporary Moslem societies has been predominantly analyzed from the lens of Consumer Culture Theory (Arnould and Thompson 2005). The existing studies of consumption culture in Islamic societies have examined this subject mainly with reference to the global expansion of consumer culture and multiple discourses associated with globalization (Pink 2009; Sandikci and Ger 2002), issues of resistance or ideological/political identity formation and negotiation (Kiliçbay and Binark 2002; Jafari and Goulding 2008; Fischer 2008), and formation of modern identities in new national and international geographies (Wong 2007; Üstüner and Holt 2007; Sandikci and Ger 2010). These studies have all extended our knowledge of consumption practices within the Moslem world. For instance, they have proposed 'multiple roots to modernity' (Sandikci and Ger 2002); hence, contesting the clichéd perceptions of a hegemonic Western Modernity. They have also opposed the puritan views which portray consumption culture in Islamic societies "as a threat, harmful to religion as it privileges hedonism, pleasure, individualism and an excessive lifestyle" (Wong 2007, 451).

Whilst we acknowledge that the expansion of consumption culture in Moslem societies is associated with pervasive globalization (Kiliçbay and Binark 2002; Sandikci and Ger 2010) and that Moslems practice multiple modernities and Islams (Wong 2007), we argue, as the core of our theoretical contribution, that the popularization of material consumption in the Moslem world is largely stimulated by the embeddedness of this culture within the everyday practices of Islam. We draw on Soroush (2000) and contend that Islam is both secular and plural and it is these characteristics that pave the way for Moslems' multiple interpretations of Islam as a source of constituting their lives.

In our argument, we are not apologetic. We do not seek to defend Islam as a Modern religion juxtaposed with the West. On the contrary, we emphasize that such binary oppositions are political/ideological concepts that are often augmented by biased media in populistic ways. Therefore, we contest the portrayal of Islam as a rigid ideological system and demonstrate that in their everyday life consumption activities (the profane), Moslems constantly (re) interpret religious guidelines of Islam (the sacred) as cultural codes rather than rigid doxas. With reference to Haddorff's (2000) typology of the market-religion interactions, we discuss that in Islam's view, there is a close symbiotic relationship between the sacred and the profane to the extent that abandoning either one to the benefit of the other is reproached (Naraghi 2009/1771-1829). Transgressing the boundaries between the two, peoples' cultural understanding of Islam (Soroush 2000) plays a crucial role in constituting localized cultural forms of Islam. For instance, popular religious activities such as rituals and feasts are all socio-cultural sites where the boundaries between the sacred and profane are transgressed as cultural sense making activities. In such situations, not only are the 'sacred' and the 'profane' symbiotically present (Belk et al., 1989; Wuthnow, 1994a, 1994b, 1996; Muñiz and Schau, 2005), but also the Halal (lawful) and Haram (unlawful), the Mustahabb (favored) and Makruh (disliked), and the Islamic and un-Islamic may all be juxtaposed to shape Moslems' mundane consumption practices.

Therefore, we propose the term 'authorized selection' to denote the fact that with reference to religion, individuals authorize themselves to selectively interpret Islam and justify their own choices (lifestyles and consumption practices). Based on the premises of this paper, we humbly invite our fellow scholars to forsake the clichéd binary oppositions (e.g., the West vs. Islam) and apologetic approaches and embark on fresh investigation of very exciting and paradoxical consumption practices that prevail not only in the Moslem world but also in the population of other creeds.

REFERENCES

Arnould, Eric J. and Thompson, Craig J. (2005), "Consumer Culture Theory: Twenty Years of Research," *Journal of Consumer Research*, 31 (4), 868-83.

Badran, Margot (2008), *Feminism in Islam: Secular and Religious Convergences*. Oxford: Oneworld Press.

Bauman, Zigmunt (2000), *Liquid Modernity*. Cambridge: Polity.

Belk, Russell W., Melanie Wallendorf, and John F. Sherry (1989), "The Sacred and the Profane in Consumer Behavior: Theodicy on the Odyssey," *Journal of Consumer Research*, 16(1), 1-38.

Bocock, Robert (1993), *Consumption*. London: Routledge.

Durkheim, Emile (1984/1893), *The Division of Labor in Society*. W. D. Halls (Trans.). New York: Basic Books.

Durkheim, Emile (1915/1912), *The Elementary Forms of Religious Life*. J. W. Swain (Trans.). New York: Free Press.

Eickelman, Dale F. (2000), "Islam and the Language of Modernity," *Daedalus,* 129(1), 119-36.

Featherstone, Mike (1998), *Consumer culture and postmodernism.* London: Sage.

Fırat, A. Fuat and Alladi Venkatesh (1995), "Liberatory Postmodernism and the Reenchantment of Consumption," *Journal of Consumer Research*, 22(3), 239-67.

Fischer, Johan (2008), *Proper Islamic Consumption: Shopping among the Malays in Modern Malaysia*. Copenhagen: NIAS Press.

Haddorff, David. W. (2000) "Religion and the Market: Opposition, Absorption, or Ambiguity?" *Review of Social Economy* 58 (4), 483–504.

Hasan, Zubair (2005), "Treatment of Consumption in Islamic Economics: An Appraisal," *Islamic Economics*, 18(2), 293-46.

Jafari, Aliakbar (2009), "Misconceptions of Culture in Cross-cultural Business and Management Studies," *International Journal of Management Concepts and Philosophy*, 3(4), 349-61.

--- (2010) "A Historical Review of the (Re)Formation of Markets in the Context of Islamic Capitalism (7th -13th Centuries)", paper presented at the 1ˢᵗ Interdisciplinary Market Studies Workshop, Stockholm School of Economics, June.

--- and Christina Goulding (2008), "We Are Not Terrorists! UK Based Iranians, Consumption, and the 'Torn Self'," Consumption, Markets, and Culture, 11(2), 73-93.

Kahf, Monzar (1992a), 'The Theory of Consumption,' in ed. Seyyed Tahir, Aidit Ghazaly and Syed Omar Syed Agil. *Readings in Microeconomics in Islamic Perspective*. Malaysia: Longman, 61-68.

--- (1992b) 'A Contribution to the Theory of Consumer Behavior in Islamic Society,' in ed. Seyyed Tahir, Aidit Ghazaly and Syed Omar Syed Agil. *Readings in Microeconomics in Islamic Perspective*. Malaysia: Longman, 90-103.

--- (1996) The Demand Side or Consumer Behavior. In *Principles of Islamic Economics*, Kuala Lampur: International Islamic University Malaysia.

Kalantari, Ahmad (2008), *Eslam va Olgooye Masraf*. Qom: Boostan.

Khan, M. Fahim (1984), "Macro Consumption Function in an Islamic Framework," *Journal of Research in Islamic Economics,* 1(2), 1–24.

--- (1995), *Essays in Islamic Economics*. Islamic Foundation UK.

Kiliçbay, Baris and Mutlu Binark (2002), "Consumer Culture, Islam and the Politics of Lifestyle," *European Journal of Communication*, 17(4), 495-511.

Majlesi, Bagher (2000/1601-1698), *Baharolanvar Vol. 73*. Tehran: Compani.

Marty, Martin (1995), 'Materialism and Spirituality in American Religion' in ed. Robert Wuthnow. *Rethinking Materialism: Perspectives on the Spiritual Dimension of Economic Behavior*. Grand Rapids, MI: Eerdmans Publishing Company, 237-253.

Marx, K. and F. Engles (1967/1848), *The Communist Manifesto*. London: Penguin.

Mernissi, Fatemeh (1987), *Beyond the Veil: Male-Female Dynamics in Modern Moslem Society*. Bloomington: Indiana University Press.

Moidfar, Said (2000), Jame'eh Shenasi-e Masael Ejtemaei Ma'aser dar Iran. Tehran: Sarzamin-e-Ma.

Motahari, Morteza (2000), Mas'aleye Hejab. Tehran: Sadra.

Muñiz, Albert M. and Hope J. Schau, (2005) "Religiosity in the Abandoned Apple Newton Brand Community," *Journal of Consumer Research*, 31(4), 737–47.

Naraghi, Ahmad (2009/1771-1829), *Me'rajossaadah*. Tehran: Eslamiyeh Publications.

Ormanlar, C. (1999), 'Giyim Kuşam Modaları,' in ed. Oya Baydar and Derya Ozkan. 75. *Yılında Değişen İnsan: Cumhuriyet Modaları*. Istanbul: Tarih Vakfi, 42–91.

Pink, Johanna (2009), *Moslem Societies in the Age of Mass Consumption*. Newcastle: Cambridge Scholars Publishing.

Rahman, Fazlur (1980), *Major Themes of the Koran*. The University of Chicago Press.

Razzaghi, Ebrahim (1996), *Olgooye Masraf va Tahajome Farhangi*. Tehran: Chap-Pakhsh.

Sadri, Mahmoud (2001), "Sacral Defense of Secularism: The Political Theologies of Soroush, Shabestari, and Kadivar," *International Journal of Politics, Culture and Society*, 15(2), 257-70.

Said, Edward (1978), *Orientalism*. New York: Random House.

Sandikci, Ozlem and Guliz Ger (2002), "In-Between Modernities and Postmodernities: Theorising Turkish Consumptionscape," in *Advances in Consumer Research*, Vol. 29, ed. Susan M. Broniarczyk and Kent Nakamoto, Valdosta, GA: Association for Consumer Research, 465-470.

--- (2007) "Constructing and Representing the Islamic Consumer in Turkey," *Fashion Theory*, 11 (2-3), 189-210.

--- (2010) "Veiling in Style: How Does a Stigmatized Practice Become Fashionable," *Journal of Consumer Research*, 37 (1), 15-36.

Schmidt, Leigh E. (1995), *Consumer Rites: The Buying and Selling of American Holidays*. Princeton: Princeton University Press.

Schor, Juliet (1999), "The New Politics of Consumption," *Boston Review*, 24(3-4), 4-9.

Soroush, Abdulkarim (2000), *Reason, Freedom, and Democracy in Islam*. Ed. Mahmoud Sadri and Ahmad Sadri. Oxford: Oxford University Press.

--- (2004) Islam and the Concept of Secularity. Lecture delivered at CUA School of Law, the USA. May 10 2004. Available: http://digitalmedia.cua.edu/events/event_dsp.cfm?event=582.

Thompson, Craig J. (1999), "A New Puritanism?" *Boston Review*, 24(3-4), 23-24.

Üstüner, Tuba and Holt, Douglas B. (2007), "Dominated Consumer Acculturation: The Social Construction of Poor Migrant Women's Consumer Identity Projects in a Turkish Squatter," *Journal of Consumer Research*, 34(1), 41-56.

Varul, Matthias Z. (2008), "After Heroism: Religion versus Consumerism. Preliminaries for an Investigation of Protestantism and Islam under Consumer Culture," *Islam and Christian–Muslim Relations*, 19 (2), 237–255.

Weber, Max (1958/1904-1905), *The Protestant Ethic and the Spirit of Capitalism*. T. Parsons (Trans.). New York: Scribner.

--- (1965), *The Sociology of Religion*. E. Fischoff (Trans.). London: Methuen.

Wong, Loong (2007), "Market Cultures, the Middle Classes and Islam: Consuming the Market?," *Consumption, Markets and Culture,* 10(4), 451-80.

Wuthnow, Robert (1994a), 'Religion and Economic Life,' in ed. Neil J. Smelser and Richard Swedberg. *Handbook of Economic Sociology*. Princeton: Princeton University Press, 620–46.

--- (1994b), *God and Mammon in America*. New York: The Free Press.

--- (1994c), *Producing the Sacred: An Essay on Public*. Champaign: University of Illinois Press.

--- (1996) *Poor Richard's Principle: Recovering the American Dream through the Moral Dimension of Work, Business, and Money*. Princeton: Princeton University Press.

I Want It Now! Query Theory Explains Discounting Anomalies for Gains and Losses

Kirstin Appelt, Columbia University, USA
David Hardisty, Columbia University, USA
Elke Weber, Columbia University, USA

EXTENDED ABSTRACT

Imagine a consumer expecting to receive $100 now, but being given the option to receive $110 in 3 months instead. Now imagine the consumer expects to receive $110 in three months, but is given the option to receive $100 now. Although in both scenarios consumers often prefer the sooner amount despite it being smaller, they tend to prefer it more strongly in the first scenario than in the second scenario. Initial expectations influence consumer preferences such that they are more impatient when faced with a delay (when the default is to receive a smaller, sooner gain, but there is an option to receive a larger, later gain instead) than with an acceleration (when the default is to receive a larger, later gain, but there is an option to receive a smaller, sooner gain instead). This is the classic "direction effect": people discount delayed gains more than accelerated gains (Loewenstein 1988). For losses, however, this direction effect is reversed and people discount delayed losses *less* than accelerated losses (Benzion, Rapoport, and Yagil 1989; Shelley 1993).

We use Query Theory as a process account to explain the effect of direction (delay vs. acceleration) on intertemporal choice. Query Theory suggests that decision makers construct their preferences by asking internal queries about the available choice options (e.g., $100 now or $110 later; Johnson, Haubl, and Keinan 2007; Weber et al. 2007). Query Theory posits that queries are asked sequentially and that arguments for the default choice option are generated first. In other words, when presented with a delay scenario, people first query their episodic knowledge base for arguments in favor of the default (i.e., "What argues for choosing $100 now?"), before considering arguments in favor of the alternative (i.e., "What argues for choosing $110 later?"). Due to output interference, retrieval for later queries is less successful and, thus, the balance of support tends to favor the default option (Johnson et al. 2007). Weber et al. (2007) successfully used Query Theory to explain the direction effect within gains, but it has not yet been applied to discounting of losses.

The present research was designed to replicate the sign (gains vs. losses) by direction (delay vs. acceleration) interaction using a between-subjects design and to confirm and extend Query Theory to the discounting of losses.

Method

In a 2 (sign: gain vs. loss) x 2 (direction: delay vs. acceleration) between-subjects design, U.S. residents (N = 607) were randomly assigned to read one of four hypothetical decision scenarios: delayed gain, accelerated gain, delayed loss, or accelerated loss. Participants used a type-aloud protocol to record their thoughts before making their decisions (Johnson et al. 2007; Weber et al. 2007). Participants subsequently coded their own previously recorded thoughts as favoring receiving [paying] now, favoring receiving [paying] later, or favoring neither.

Results

Replicating the sign effect, participants discounted gains more than losses. Replicating the sign by direction interaction, participants discounted delayed gains *more* than accelerated gains, but delayed losses *less* than accelerated losses.

As predicted by Query Theory, across sign, thoughts favoring receiving/paying now (i.e., now thoughts) clustered earlier in the delay conditions (when now was the default) than in the acceleration conditions (when later was the default), the proportion of now thoughts was greater in the delay conditions than in the acceleration conditions, and the effect of direction (delay vs. acceleration) on the proportion of now thoughts was fully mediated by thought clustering. In other words, when the default was to receive [pay] now, thoughts favoring receiving [paying] now were clustered earlier, which led to a greater proportion of these thoughts.

As predicted, a greater prominence of now thoughts (i.e., earlier and more now thoughts) translated to *greater* discounting of gains and to *lower* discounting of losses. In fact, the prominence of now thoughts significantly mediated the relationship between direction and discounting for gains *and* for losses. As predicted by Query Theory, now thoughts were more prominent for delayed outcomes than accelerated outcomes and this led to increased discounting of gains and reduced discounting of losses.

Discussion

Using a between-subject design, our study replicated the sign effect and the sign by direction interaction effect (i.e., the direction effect for gains and the reverse direction effect for losses). More importantly, we provide a process-level causal account for the sign by direction interaction. Confirming a Query Theory process account, the overall prominence of now thoughts mediated the effect of direction on discounting for gains *and* losses.

Because our study is the first to compare the processes underlying discounting of gains and losses, our results can uniquely inform interventions to help consumers make intertemporal choices they are less likely to regret, whether it's the dieter who succumbs to the dessert tray (Metcalfe and Mischel 1999), the worker who retires with insufficient savings (Thaler and Benartzi 2004), or the community that overfishes their lake (Hendrickx, Poortinga, and van der Kooij 2001). Because the intertemporal choice literature studies mostly gain decisions, a naïve choice architect might assume that acceleration frames are a panacea to reduce discounting. Our study confirms that the story is more nuanced. For gains, impatience (i.e., the desire to have the gain now) increases discounting. To decrease the discounting of gains, we need to *decrease* impatience. For losses, however, impatience (i.e., the desire to get the loss over with now) translates to lower discounting. Therefore, to decrease discounting of losses we need to *increase* impatience. Whether with changes to how decisions are presented (e.g., with different default options or with different framings) or how options are considered (i.e., training people to consider the alternative option before the default option), giving consumers the tools to change the prominence of their impatient "act now" thoughts when faced with intertemporal decisions will arm them against making decisions they will later regret.

REFERENCES

Baron, Reuben M. and David A. Kenny (1986), "The moderator-mediator variable distinction in social psychological research: Conceptual, strategic, and statistical considerations," *Journal of Personality and Social Psychology,* 51 (December), 1173-82.

Benhabib, Jess, Alberto Bisin, and Andrew Schotter (2010), "Present-bias, quasi-hyperbolic discounting, and fixed costs," *Games and Economic Behavior,* 69 (July), 205-23.

Benzion, Uri, Amnon Rapoport, and Joseph Yagil (1989), "Discount rates inferred from decisions: An experimental study," *Management Science,* 35 (March), 270-84.

Figner, Bernd, Weber, Elke U., Steffener, J., Krosch, Amy, Wager, Tor D. and Johnson, Eric J. (2010), *"Framing the future first: Brain mechanisms that increase patience in intertemporal choice,"* Manuscript submitted for publication.

Franklin, Benjamin. (1748). *Advice to a young tradesman.*

Hardisty, David J., Orlove, Ben, Krantz, David H., Small, Arthur and Milch, Kerry F. (2010), *"It's about time: An integrative approach to effective policy,"* Manuscript in preparation.

Hendrickx, Laurie, Wouter Poortinga, and Renate van der Kooij (2001), "Temporal factors in resource dilemmas," *Acta Psychologica,* 108 (September), 137-54.

Johnson, Eric J., Gerald Haubl, and Anat Keinan (2007), "Aspects of endowment: A Query Theory of value construction," *Journal of Experimental Social Psychology: Learning, Memory and Cognition,* 33 (May), 461-74.

Kahneman, Daniel, Jack L. Knetsch, and Richard H. Thaler (1991), "Anomalies: The endowment effect, loss aversion, and status quo bias," *Journal of Economic Perspectives,* 5 (Winter), 193-206.

Laibson, David. (1997), "Golden eggs and hyperbolic discounting," *The Quarterly Journal of Economics,* 112 (May), 443-77.

Lichtenstein, Sarah, and Paul Slovic (2006), *The construction of preference.* New York, NY: Cambridge University Press.

Loewenstein, George. F. (1988), "Frames of mind in intertemporal choice," *Management Science,* 34 (February), 200-14.

Mazur, James E. (1987), "An adjusting procedure for studying delayed reinforcement," in *Quantitative Analyses of Behavior,* vol. 5, *Effect of delay and intervening events on value,* ed. Michael L. Commons, James E. Mazur, John A. Nevin and Howard Rachlin, Hillsdale, NJ: Erlbaum, 55-73.

Metcalfe, Janet and Walter Mischel (1999), "A hot/cool-system analysis of delay of gratification: Dynamics of willpower," *Psychological Review,* 106 (January), 3-19.

Novemsky, Nathan and Daniel Kahneman (2005), "The boundaries of loss aversion," *Journal of Marketing Research,* 42 (May), 119-28.

Samuelson, Paul A. (1937), "A note on the measurement of utility," *The Review of Economic Studies,* 4 (February), 155-61.

Shelley, Marjorie K. (1993), "Outcome signs, questions frames and discount rates," *Management Science,* 39 (July), 806-15.

Shrout, Patrick E. and Niall Bolger (2002), "Mediation in experimental and nonexperimental studies: New procedures and recommendations," *Psychological Methods,* 7 (December), 422-45.

Thaler, Richard H. (1981), "Some empirical evidence on dynamic inconsistency," *Economics Letters,* 8 (August), 201-07.

Thaler, Richard H. and Shlomo Benartzi (2004), "Save More Tomorrow™: Using behavioral economics to increase employee saving," *Journal of Political Economy,* 112 (February), S164-87.

Thaler, Richard H. and Cass R. Sunstein (2008), *Nudge: Improving decisions about health, wealth, and happiness.* New Haven, CT: Yale University Press.

Tversky, Amos and Daniel Kahneman (1991), "Loss aversion in riskless choice: A reference-dependent model," *The Quarterly Journal of Economics,* 106 (November), 1039-61.

Weber, Bethany J. and Gretchen B. Chapman (2005), "The combined effects of risk and time on choice: Does uncertainty eliminate the immediacy effect? Does delay eliminate the certainty effect?" *Organizational Behavior and Human Decision Processes,* 96 (March), 104-18.

Weber, Elke U., Appelt, Kirstin C., Treuer, Galen, Goll, Apollonia, Filbin, Robert W. and Crookes, Raymond. (2010), *"Smoking or non-smoking? Query Theory explains public reactions to changes in status quo,"* Manuscript in preparation.

Weber, Elke U., Christopher K. Hsee and Joanna Sokolowska (1998), "What folklore tells us about risk and risk taking: Cross-cultural comparisons of American, German, and Chinese proverbs," *Organizational Behavior and Human Decision Processes,* 75(August), 170-86.

Weber, Elke U. and Eric J. Johnson (2009), "Mindful judgment and decision making," *Annual Review of Psychology,* 60 (January), 53-85.

Weber, Elke U. and Johnson, Eric J. (forthcoming). Knowing what we want by arguing with ourselves. *Behavior and Brain Sciences._*

Weber, Elke. U., Eric J. Johnson, Kerry F. Milch, Hannah H. Chang, Jeff C. Brodscholl, and Dan G. Goldstein (2007), "Asymmetric discounting in intertemporal choice: A Query Theory account," *Psychological Science,* 18 (June), 516-23.

Zauberman, Gal and John G. Lynch Jr. (2005), "Resource slack and propensity to discount delayed investments of time versus money," *Journal of Experimental Psychology: General,* 134 (February), 23-37.

When Loyalty and Habit Collide

Leona Tam, Old Dominion University, USA
Liu-Thompkins Yuping, Old Dominion University, USA

EXTENDED ABSTRACT

When shoppers repeatedly buy from a business, it is often driven by two very distinct forces: loyalty and habit. The former refers to a deeply held, enduring commitment to rebuy from a business, and may encompass beliefs of product superiority, positive and accessible brand reactions, and a strong intention to continue buying from the business (Oliver 1999). As a key concept in relationship marketing, loyalty has been studied extensively in the marketing discipline. In contrast, the other driver of repeat purchase, habit, has received scant attention from marketing researchers. Most research on habit has arisen from behavioral, social, and health psychology. In these disciplines, habit is defined as a behavioral disposition in which past responses are triggered directly by associated contextual cues (Beatty and Kahle 1988). One important characteristic of habit is that contexts (e.g., time, location, etc.) function outside of awareness to cue performance of repeated responses or preference towards such responses.

Because of the parallel development of loyalty and habit research in different disciplines, few existing studies have examined loyalty and habit simultaneously, although both of these two forces can exert an influence on a shopper's repeat buying decisions. One particularly important question missing from the literature is how loyalty and habit may interact with each other. In other words, when both loyalty and habit are present, what is the combined outcome of these forces? Do the two effects add up and reinforce each other, or is the mechanism more complicated? These are the questions we would like to answer in this paper.

Specifically, we examine the interplay between loyal and habitual forces in determining shoppers' reaction to marketing actions. Although models of brand switching have long incorporated inertia into the study of brand loyalty (e.g., Jeuland 1979), it is largely a reflection of shoppers' tendency to make the same brand choice across transactions without considering the theoretical origin of such inertia. Our paper represents one of the few efforts at integrating the habit literature into loyalty research, thereby offering a theoretical ground for the diverse responses repeat shoppers may exhibit toward marketing actions. Furthermore, by examining the interaction between loyalty and habit, this paper will represent an initial step toward recognizing and understanding the complex ways in which these two forces can affect shopper behavior. This will be a valuable addition to loyalty research and will deepen our understanding of the psychology behind shoppers' repeat purchase behavior.

Considering loyalty and habit together could generate one of two possible and equally plausible effects on consumer responses. On one hand, loyalty and habit could have an additive effect, that is, positive consumer response to marketing actions such as sales promotion could be stronger when both loyalty and habit are present. This is because attitudinal loyalty and habit can lead to similar purchase behaviors, despite the different ways in which they work. For instance, both attitudinally loyal consumers and habitual consumers may repeatedly purchase a brand, and that brand may claim a high share of wallet for both groups of consumers. Furthermore, as a consumer's loyalty evolves from the early more effortful cognitive and affective stages to more behaviorally oriented conative and action stages, the consumer's purchase behavior will become increasingly driven by habitual forces that are characterized by action inertia and high resistance to change (Oliver 1999). Given these close ties between attitudinal loyalty and habit, it is reasonable to expect that the two can reinforce each other or at least complement each other's effects. Reflecting this view, the marketing science literature has often considered both idiosyncratic loyalty and inertia as additive forces in predicting consumers' brand choice (e.g., Jeuland 1979; Roy, Chintagunta, and Haldar 1996). This literature shows that including an inertia effect in a brand choice model outperforms a model that only considers long-term loyalty effects (Jeuland 1979).

On the other hand, loyalty and habit could interfere with each other, that is, the positive effect of loyalty on consumer responses could be diminished when habit is strong. Studies of the habit-goal interface suggest this possibility. These studies show that habitual behavior is triggered via contextual cues in an automatic and effortless fashion (Wood and Neal 2007). Therefore, when a situation does not encourage or allow effortful processing, habitual responses are more likely to result than more conscious and effortful goal fulfillment. This explains the loyalty-habit interference because behavior as a result of loyalty rises through a chain of cognitive, affective, and conative processes (Oliver 1999). Feeling loyal does not necessarily translate into loyal behavior, but rather it requires an effortful implementation of loyalty intention into actual behavior. As a result, it is likely to be dominated by responses from habitual forces when such efforts are not made.

We conducted three studies to explore these two possible interaction patterns between loyalty and habit. Our results showed consistent interference between loyalty and habit over a variety of consumer responses, including reaction to brand-related marketing offers, resistance to alternatives in a stock-out situation, and tendency to engage in word-of-mouth. A fourth study is currently being conducted to examine the mechanism underlying such interference.

REFERENCES

Aiken, Leona S. and Stephen G. West (1991), Multiple Regression: Testing and Interpreting Interactions. Thousand Oaks, CA: Sage Publications.

Beatty, Sharon E. and Lynn R. Kahle (1988), "Alternative Hierarchies of the Attitude-Behavior Relationship: The Impact of Brand Commitment and Habit," *Journal of the Academy of Marketing Science*, 16 (2), 1-10.

Bem, Daryl J. (1967), "Self-Perception: An Alternative Interpretation of Cogitive Dissonance Phenomena," *Psychological Review*, 74 (2), 183-200.

Chaudhuri, Arjun and Morris B. Holbrook (2001), "The Chain of Effects from Brand Trust and Brand Affect to Brand Performance: The Role of Brand Loyalty," *Journal of Marketing*, 65 (2), 81-93.

Cheema, Amar and Andrew M. Kaikati (2010), "The Effect of Need for Uniqueness on Word of Mouth," *Journal of Marketing Research*, 47 (June), 553-63.

Faziox, Russell H., Paul M. Herr, and Timothy J. Olney (1984), "Attitude Accessibility Following a Self-Perception Process," *Journal of Personality and Social Psychology*, 47 (2), 277-86.

Forehand, Mark and Andrew Perkins (2005), "Implicit Assimilation and Explicit Contrast: A Set/Reset Model of Response to Celebrity Voice-Overs," *Journal of Consumer Research*, 32 (December), 435-41

Gibson, Bryan (2008), "Evaluative Conditioning Change Attiutudes towards Mature Brands? New Evidence from the Implicit Association Test," *Journal of Consumer Research*, 35 (June), 178-88.

Greenwald, Anthany G., Debbie E. McGhee, and Jordan L. K. Schwartz (1998), "Measuring Individual Differences in Implicit Cognition: The Implicit Association Test," *Journal of Personality and Social Psychology,* 74 (6), 1464-80.

Greenwald, Anthony G., T. Andrew Poehiman, Eric Luis Uhlrnann, and Mahzarin Banaji (2009), "Understanding and Using the Implicit Association Test: III. Meta-Analysis of Predict Validity," *Journal of Personality and Social Psychology*, 97 (1), 17-41.

Jeuland, Abel P. (1979), "Brand Choice Inertia as One Aspect of the Notion of Brand Loyalty," *Management Science*, 25 (7), 671-82.

Ji Song, Mindy and Wendy Wood (2007), "Purchase and consumption habits: Not necessarily what you intend," *Journal of Consumer Psychology*, 17 (4), 261-76.

Oliver, Richard L. (1999), "Whence Consumer Loyalty?," *Journal of Marketing*, 63, 33-44.

Rego, Lopo L., Matthew T. Billett, and Neil A. Morgan (2009), "Consumer-based brand equity and firm risk," *Journal of Marketing*, 73 (November), 47-60.

Reichheld, Frederick F. (2003), "The One Number You Need to Grow," *Harvard Business Review*, 81 (December), 46-54.

Roehm, Michelle, Ellen Bolman Pullins, and Harper A. Roehm, Jr. (2002), "Designing Loyalty-Building Programs for Packaged Goods Brands," *Journal of Marketing Research*, 39 (2), 202-13.

Roy, Rishin, Pradeep K. Chintagunta, and Sudeep Haldar (1996), "A Framework for Investigating Habits, "the Hand of the Past," and Heterogeneity in Dynamic Brand Choice," *Marketing Science*, 15 (3), 280-99.

Verplanken, Bas and Sheina Orbell (2003), "Reflections on Past Behavior: A Self-Report Index of Habit Strength," *Journal of Applied Social Psychology*, 33 (6), 1313-30.

Wood, Wendy and David T. Neal (2007), "A New Look at Habits and the Habit-Goal Interface," *Psychological Review*, 114 (4), 843-63.

Wood, Wendy, Leona Tam, and Melissa Guerrero Witt (2005), "Changing circumstances, disrupting habits," *Journal of Personality and Social Psychology*, 88 (6), 918-33.

Yi, Youjae and Hoseong Jeon (2003), "Effects of loyalty programs on value perception, program loyalty, and brand loyalty," *Journal of the Academy of Marketing Science*, 31 (3), 229-40.

Zaichkowsky, Judith Lynne (1994), "The Personal Involvement Inventory: Reduction, Revision, and Application to Advertising," *Journal of Advertising*, 23 (December), 59-70.

Say "I Don't," not "I Can't":
How Verbal Frames Provide Psychological Empowerment

Vanessa Patrick, University of Houston, USA
Henrik Hagtvedt, Boston College, USA

EXTENDED ABSTRACT

In this research, we propose that the language used to communicate self-regulatory efforts serves as a feedback mechanism that signals to oneself either a sense of empowerment or a lack thereof, thus influencing goal achievement. Specifically, with five studies we demonstrate that using the word "don't" (vs. "can't") has a favorable influence on feelings of empowerment and perceived effectiveness of the refusal strategy, as well as on actual behavior.

A stream of research in the judgment and decision-making literature has focused on the influence of different types of framing that are logically equivalent (e.g., ½ vs. 50%; 3% fat versus 97% fat-free). More recently, research in linguistics and persuasion has focused on the influence of words that are not entirely equivalent but nonetheless quite similar and often used interchangeably (e.g., think vs. feel; anytime between vs. only between).

The focus of the current research falls into this latter category of verbal framing. We investigate how the decision not to veer away from one's goal may be framed in terms of a determined (don't) versus deprived (can't) refusal. We theorize that utilizing a determined (don't) versus deprived (can't) verbal framing signals the level of empowerment and control one has in achieving one's self-regulatory goal, resulting in a differential influence on the likelihood that we will engage in goal-directed behavior. Saying "I don't do X" connotes a firmly entrenched attitude rather than a temporary situation, and it emphasizes the personal will that drives the refusal. Thus, using the word "don't" serves as a self-affirmation of one's personal willpower and control in the relevant self-regulatory goal pursuit, leading to a favorable influence on feelings of empowerment, as well as on actual behavior. Saying "I can't do X" emphasizes an external cause, resulting in less feelings of empowerment and thus also hindering the self-regulatory goal pursuit in question.

In Study 1, 47 undergraduates participated in an experiment based on a dieting scenario. Participants were told that they had come up with a strategy "about how to respond when you see a food item that you want to eat, but is not good for your weight loss goal." Every time they saw a tempting food item, they would tell themselves either "I don't eat X" or "I can't eat X," depending on the experimental condition. An ANOVA with perceived effectiveness as the DV revealed the expected main effect ($M_{don't}$ = 4.91 vs. $M_{can't}$ = 3.50, $F(1, 44)$ = 8.36, $p < .01$). A similar ANOVA on perceived empowerment also revealed the expected main effect ($M_{don't}$ = 5.91 vs. $M_{can't}$ = 4.79, $F(1, 45)$ = 6.73, $p < .05$). Mediation analysis supported full mediation by the empowerment index of the influence of verbal framing on the effectiveness index.

In studies 2a and 2b, we replicate these results and also demonstrate a boundary condition: the results are reversed when an external cause for the goal pursuit is made salient. This is consistent with Deci and Ryan's (1987, 1025) characterization of autonomy and empowerment as that which is "an inner endorsement of one's actions, the sense that they emanate from oneself and are one's own." Thus, when the cause or motivation for refusal is externally driven or derived, a deprived (can't) framing, which better emphasizes and aligns with the external cause, is more effective.

In Study 2a, 179 adults first read a scenario in which they imagined that they had decided to work out at the gym on a regular basis. They were given the "don't" or "can't" framing, and those in the internal (external) condition were told to imagine that they did this for their own (a friend's) sake. A two-way ANOVA with perceived effectiveness as the DV revealed the expected framing x focus interaction ($M_{don't, internal}$ = 5.98 vs. $M_{don't, external}$ = 4.60 vs. $M_{can't, internal}$ = 4.79 vs. $M_{can't, external}$ = 5.81, $F(1, 174)$ = 16.59, $p < .001$). Further, mediation analysis supported full mediation by the empowerment index of the influence of verbal framing on the effectiveness index in the internal focus condition.

In Study 2b, 120 undergraduates read a scenario in which they imagined that they had a goal to lose weight. A two-way ANOVA with perceived effectiveness as the DV revealed a main effect of focus ($M_{internal}$ = 3.30 vs. $M_{external}$ = 4.88, $F(1, 116)$ = 20.66, $p < .001$) and the expected framing x focus interaction ($M_{don't, internal}$ = 4.09 vs. $M_{don't, external}$ = 4.08 vs. $M_{can't, internal}$ = 2.52 vs. $M_{can't, external}$ = 5.63, $F(1, 116)$ = 20.74, $p < .001$). Further, mediation analysis supported full mediation by the empowerment index of the influence of verbal framing on the effectiveness index in the internal focus condition.

Study 3 provided further support for empowerment as the process mechanism underlying the effectiveness of the "don't" strategy by using a priming task to induce an increased (vs. decreased) reliance on empowerment via the priming of autonomous (vs. controlled) motivation. A two-way ANOVA with perceived effectiveness as the DV revealed a main effect of verbal frame ($M_{don't}$ = 5.25 vs. $M_{can't}$ = 4.27, $F(1, 79)$ = 4.49, $p < .05$) and the hypothesized interaction ($M_{don't, autonomous}$ = 5.74 vs. $M_{can't, autonomous}$ = 3.76, $M_{don't, controlled}$ = 4.65 vs. $M_{can't, controlled}$ = 4.63, $F(1, 79)$ = 4.20, $p < .05$).

In Study 4, 30 working women participated in an intervention exercise in which they adopted a new strategy for healthy living and reported how the strategy was working for them every day for a 10-day period. Participants were assigned to either a "don't" or a "can't" framing condition, or a non-specific control condition. Results revealed that 8 (of 10) participants in the "don't" condition persisted the full ten days, whereas only 1 (of 10) participant in the "can't" condition and 3 (of 10) participants in the control condition did so. An ANOVA with number of days of persistence as the DV revealed the expected main effect ($M_{don't}$ = 9.20 vs. $M_{can't}$ = 2.90 vs. $M_{control}$ = 5.20, $F(2, 27)$ = 11.82, $p < .001$).

REFERENCES

Bandura, Albert (1997), *Self-efficacy: The Exercise of Control*, New York: Freeman.

Bargh, John A. (1992), "Does Subliminality Matter to Social Psychology? Being Aware of the Stimulus versus Aware of its Influence," in *Perception Without Awareness*, ed. R.F. Bornstein and T. Pittman, New York: Guilford Press, 236-55.

Bargh, John A. and Kimberly Barndollar (1996), "Automaticity in Action: The Unconscious as Repository of Chronic Goals and Motives," in *The Psychology of Action*, ed. Peter M. Gollwitzer and John A. Bargh, New York: Guilford, 457-71.

Baron, Reuben M. and David A. Kenny (1986), "The Moderator-Mediator Variable Distinction in Social Psychological Research: Conceptual, Strategic, and Statistical Considerations," *Journal of Personality and Social Psychology*, 51, 1173-82.

Baumeister, Roy F., Kathleen D. Vohs, and Dianne M. Tice (2007), "The Strength Model of Self-Control," *Current Directions in Psychological Science*, 16 (6), 351-55.

Carver, Charles S. and Michael F. Scheier (1998), *On the Self-regulation of Behavior*, New York: Cambridge University Press.

Cheema, Amar and Vanessa M. Patrick (2008), "Anytime Versus Only: Mindsets Moderate the Effect of Expansive Versus Restrictive Frames on Promotion Evaluation," *Journal of Marketing Research*, 45 (August), 462-72.

Deci, Edward L. and Richard M. Ryan (1980), "The Empirical Exploration of Intrinsically Motivated Processes," in *Advances in Experimental Social Psychology*, Vol. 13, ed. L. Berkowitz, New York: Academic Press, 39-80.

--- (1987), "The Support of Autonomy and the Control of Behavior," *Journal of Personality and Social Psychology*, 53(6), 1024-37.

--- (2000), "The "What" and "Why" of Goal Pursuits: Human Needs and the Self-Determination of Behavior," *Psychological Inquiry*, 11(4), 227-68.

--- (2002), *Handbook of self-determination research*. Rochester, NY:University of Rochester Press.

Diener, Edward and Robert Biswas-Diener (2005), "Psychological Empowerment and Subjective Well-Being", in *Measuring Empowerment: Cross-disciplinary Perspectives*, ed. Deepa Narayan, Washington, DC: World Bank, 125-140.

Dweck, Carol S. (1999), *Self-theories: Their Role in Motivation, Personality and Development,* Philadelphia: Psychology Press.

Gollwitzer, Peter M. (1999), "Implementation Intentions: Strong Effects of Simple Plans," *American Psychologist*, 54 (7), 493-503.

Gollwitzer, Peter M. and Ute C. Bayer (1999), "Deliberative Versus Implemental Mindsets in the Control of Action," in *Dual-process Theories in Social Psychology*, ed. Shelly Chaiken and Yaacov Trope, New York: Guilford, 403-22.

Gollwitzer, Peter M. and Gordon B. Moskowitz (1996), "Goal Effects on Action and Cognition," in *Social Psychology: Handbook of Basic Principles*, ed. E. Tory Higgins and Arie W. Kruglanski, New York: Guilford Press, 361-99.

Haws, Kelly L. and Cait Poynor (2008), "Seize the Day! Encouraging Indulgence for the Hyperopic Consumer," *Journal of Consumer Research*, 35 (December), 680-91.

Higgins, E. Tory (1989), "Self-Discrepancy Theory: What Patterns of Self Beliefs Cause People to Suffer?" in *Advances in Experimental Social Psychology*, Vol. 22, ed. L. Berkowitz, New York: Academic Press, 93-136.

--- (1997), "Beyond Pleasure and Pain," *American Psychologist*, 52 (December), 1280-1300.

Hodgins, Holley S., Ariel B. Brown, and Barbara Carver (2007), "Autonomy and Control Motivation and Self-Esteem," *Self and Identity*, 6, 189-208.

Hoegg, JoAndrea and Joseph W. Alba (2007b), "Linguistic Framing of Sensory Experience: There is some Accounting for Taste," in *Psycholinguistic Phenomena in Marketing Communications, ed. Tina Lowrey, Mahwah, NJ: Lawrence Erlbaum Associates.*

Kuhl, Julius and Jurgen Beckmann (1994), *Volition and personality: Action versus state orientation,* Göttingen, Germany: Hogrefe.

Levesque, Chantal and Luc G. Pelletier (2003), "On the Investigation of Primed and Chronic Autonomous and Heteronomous Motivational Orientations," *Personality and Social Psychology Bulletin*, 29 (12), 1570-84.

Mayer, Nicole D. and Zakary L. Tormala (2010), ""Think" Versus "Feel" Framing Effects in Persuasion," *Personality and Social Psychology Bulletin*, 36(4), 443-54.

Niederhoffer, Kate G. and James W. Pennebaker (2002), "Linguistic Style Matching in Social Interaction," *Journal of Language and Social Psychology*, 21 (4), 337-60.

Poynor, Cait and Kelly L. Haws (2008), "Lines in the Sand: The Role of Motivated Categorization in the Pursuit of Self-Control Goals," *Journal of Consumer Research*, 35 (February), 772-87.

Rothman Alexander J., Peter Salovey, Carol Antone, Keough Kelli, and Martin C. Drake (1993), "The Influence of Message Framing on Intentions to Perform Health Behaviors," *Journal of Experimental Social Psychology,* 29 (5), 408–33.

Rotter, Julian B. (1990), "Internal Versus External Control of Reinforcement: A Case History of a Variable," *American Psychologist*, 45, 489-93.

Schifter Deborah E. and Icek Ajzen (1985), "Intention, Perceived Control, and Weight Loss: An Application of the Theory of Planned Behavior," *Journal of Personality and Social Psychology*, 49 (3), 843-51.

Shiv, Baba, Julie A. Edell Britton, and John W. Payne (2004), "Does Elaboration Increase or Decrease the Effectiveness of Negatively versus Positively Framed *Messages?" Journal of Consumer Research*, 31 (1), 199-208.

Sitzmann Traci and Katherine Ely (2010), "Sometimes You Need a Reminder: The Effects of Prompting Self-Regulation on Regulatory Processes, Learning, and Attrition," *Journal of Applied Psychology*, 95 (1), 132-44.

Taylor, Shelley E., Lien. B. Pham, Inna D. Rivkin, and David A. Armor (1998), "Harnessing the Imagination: Mental Simulation, Self-Regulation, and Coping," *American Psychologist*, 53 (4), 429-39.

Wicklund, Robert A. and Peter M. Gollwitzer (1982), *Symbolic Self-Completion,* Hillsdale, N.J.: Lawrence Erlbaum.

Benign Marketing Violations: How and When Humorous Marketing Hurts Brands

Caleb Warren, Bocconi University, Italy
Peter McGraw, University of Colorado, USA

EXTENDED ABSTRACT

Humor is generally enjoyed by consumers and assumed to benefit marketers (Beard 2005; Eisend 2009). Although humor is pervasive in marketing, we highlight a potential risk of pursuing humor: humor attempts risk harming brand attitudes. In accordance with the benign violation theory (BVT; McGraw and Warren 2010; Veatch 1998), we propose that humor occurs when a violation is simultaneously interpreted as benign. If a violation is necessary for humor, the presence of a violation may arouse negative affect, which can have a substantial negative effect on brand attitudes. Thus, one reason for the equivocal relationship between humor and brand attitude observed in the literature (Eisend 2009; Weinberger and Gulas 1992) may be that researchers typically do not measure the negative reactions that frequently accompany humor.

Studies 1a and 1b explored the relationship between perceived humor, negative affective reactions, and brand attitude in two samples of print advertisements. Study 1a used 60 print advertisements assembled using three searches on Google Images. Specifically, we took 20 ads identified using each of the following searches: "funny print advertisement," "offensive print advertisement," and "print advertisement." Study 1b used 36 advertisements created by asking marketing students to craft a humorous headline for a fictional online retailer. Participants rated each advertisement on perceived humor, negative affective reactions, or brand attitude. In both studies, negative affect predicted brand attitude better than perceived humor. Regression analyses revealed a strong negative effect of negative affect on brand attitude ($\beta_{Study1a}$=-.64; $\beta_{Study1b}$=-.53) and a positive but weaker effect of perceived humor ($\beta_{Study1a}$=.26; $\beta_{Study1b}$=.07).

Study 2 tested our predictions across the marketing mix. We contrasted product, distribution, pricing, and promotion tactics depicting benign violations with similar tactics not depicting violations. For example, we compared reactions to a store that institutes a pricing policy that blatantly discriminates against wealthier, monolingual English speakers (i.e., a sign reads: Orange Juice $5; Jugo de Naranja $4) with reactions to a store that charges all customers the same price (the sign reads: Orange Juice $5; Jugo de Naranja $5). Most consumers consider blatant price discrimination unfair (i.e., a violation). However, the discrimination may simultaneously seem benign both because it can be justified by an alternative norm (the monolingual English speakers can probably afford to pay the extra dollar) and because the discrimination is psychologically distant (it is geographically far away and victimizes other people). Participants rated perceived humor, negative affective reactions, and brand attitude in response to one of four marketing tactics (product, distribution, price, promotion). Consistent with the BVT, humor perceptions were greater in response to marketing tactics depicting a benign violation than those not involving a violation. However, benign violations also elicited more negative affect and led to lower brand attitudes. The observed differences were similar for the product, distribution, pricing, and promotion tactics. Regression analyses revealed a strong negative effect of negative affect on brand attitude (β =-.56). The effect of perceived humor was not significant (β =-.11).

Study 3 tested if the relationship between humor and brand attitude depends on whether the absence of humor refers to marketing tactics that do not involve violations (i.e., strictly benign tactics) or to tactics that involve violations that do not seem benign (i.e., malign violations). Although both may lack humor, strictly benign tactics should elicit little negative affect compared to malign violations. Consequently, although humorous benign violations likely hurt brand attitudes relative to purely benign tactics (see study 2), humorous marketing may help brand attitudes relative to tactics depicting malign violations.

Study 3 tested this hypothesis by adding a third condition to the aforementioned pricing stimuli. We added a malign violation condition in which the store charges poorer, monolingual Spanish speakers $5 and wealthier English speakers $4 (i.e., the sign at the store reads: Orange Juice $4; Jugo de Naranja $5). The price discrimination here cannot be justified by an alternative fairness norm so should be seen as less benign than discriminating against wealthier English speakers. As in study 2, comparing a benign pricing tactic to a benign violation revealed a negative relationship between humor and brand attitude. Conversely, comparing a malign violation to one involving a benign violation revealed a positive relationship between humor and brand attitude. The discrepant relationship between perceived humor and brand attitude can be explained by negative affective reactions. Regression analyses revealed a strong negative effect of negative affect on brand attitude (β =-.60), but no detectable effect of perceived humor (β =.03).

In study 4 we explored whether the effect of humor on brand attitude depends on the type of violation used to create humor. Different violations may be equally effective in creating humor, but elicit different emotional and behavioral reactions (Rozin et al. 1999). For example, humor created through purity violations, which tend to elicit disgust and withdrawal (Chapman et al. 2009; Lerner, Small, and Loewenstein 2004), may hurt brands more than humor created through harm violations, which tend to elicit anger and approach (Carver and Harmon-Jones 2009). Participants viewed one of three advertisements for a fictional cola: a control ad not depicting a violation, a humorous ad depicting a purity violation, or a humorous ad depicting a harm violation. Although participants found the two ads depicting a violation equally humorous, they reported lower brand attitudes and less interest in drinking cola when humor was created by depicting a purity violation rather than a harm violation.

Benign violations evoke humor. Arousing humor through marketing tactics, however, is risky because successful and unsuccessful attempts alike may elicit negative affective reactions, and these negative reactions have a powerful effect on brand attitude. Consequently, the relationship between humor and brand attitude depends on the specific benign violation used to create humor and whether this method enhances or reduces negative affective reactions. Collectively, our studies suggest that (1) marketers attempting to use humor should be careful of the strategy they use, and (2) researchers attempting to understand the consequences of humor need to measure negative affective reactions in addition to perceptions of humor.

REFERENCES

Alden, Dana L., Ashesh Mukherjee, and Wayne D. Hoyer (2000), "The Effects of Incongruity, Surprise and Positive Moderators of Perceived Humor in Television Advertising," *Journal of Advertising*, 29 (Summer), 1-15.

Apter, Michael J. (1982), *The Experience of Motivation: The Theory of Psychological Reversals*. London: Academic Press.

Baumeister, Roy F., Ellen Bratslavsky, Catrin Finkenauer, and Kathleen D. Vohs (2001), "Bad Is Stronger Than Good," *Review of General Psychology*, 5, 323-70.

Beard, Fred K. (2005), "One Hundred Year of Humor in American Advertising," *Journal of Macromarketing*, 25 (June), 54-65.

--- (2008), "Advertising and Audience Offense: The Role of Intentional Humor," *Journal of Marketing Communications*, 14 (February), 1-17.

Brooker, George (1981), "A Comparison of the Persuasive Effects of Mild Humor and Mild Fear Appeals," *Journal of Advertising*, 10, 29-40.

Brown, Mark R., Roop K. Bhadury and Nigel K. Pope (2010), "The Impact of Comedic Violence on Viral Advertising Effectiveness," *Journal of Advertising*, 39 (Spring), 49-65.

Caccioppo, John T. and Gary G. Berntson (1994), "Relationship Between Attitudes and Evaluative Space," *Psychological Bulletin*, 1994 (May), 401-23.

Carver, C. S. and E. Harmon-Jones (2009), "Anger Is an Approach-Related Affect: Evidence and Implications," *Psychological Bulletin*, 135 (March), 183-204.

Chattopadhyay, A. and K. Basu (1990), "Humor in Advertising - the Moderating Role of Prior Brand Evaluation," *Journal of Marketing Research*, 27 (November), 466-76.

Eisend, Martin (2009), "A Meta-Analysis of Humor in Advertising," *Journal of the Academy of Marketing Science*, 37 (Summer), 191-203.

Freud, Sigmund (1928), "Humor," *International Journal of Psychoanalysis*, 9, 1-6.

Gelb, Betsy D. and Charles M. Picket (1983), "Attitude-Toward-the-Ad: Links to Humor and to Advertising," *Journal of Advertising*, 12, 34-42.

--- and George M. Zinkhan (1986), "Humor and Advertising Effectiveness After Repeated Exposures to a Radio Commercial," *Journal of Advertising*, 15, 15-34.

Gruner, Charles (1997), *The Game of Humor: A Comprehensive Theory of Why We Laugh*, New Brunswick, NJ: Transaction Publishers.

Hemenover, Scott H. and Ulrich Schimmack (2007), "That's Disgusting!..., but Very Amusing: Mixed Feelings of Amusement and Disgust," *Cognition & Emotion*, 21, 1102-13.

Koestler, Arthur (1964), *The Act of Creation*, New York: Macmillan.

La Fave, Lawrence, Jay Haddad and William A. Maesen (1976), "Superiority, Enhanced Self-Esteem, and Perceived Incongruity Humor Theory," in *Humor and Laughter: Theory, Research, and Applications,* ed. Anthony J. Chapman, and Hugh C. Foot, New York: Wiley, 63-91.

Lee, Yih Hwai and Charlotte Mason (1999), "Responses to Information Incongruency in Advertising: The Role of Expectancy, Relevancy, and Humor," *Journal of Consumer Research*, 26 (September), 156-69.

Lerner, Jennifer S., Deborah A. Small, and George Loewenstein (2004), "Heart Strings and Purse Strings - Carryover Effects of Emotions on Economic Decisions," *Psychological Science*, 15 (May), 337-41.

Martin, Rod A. (2007), *The Psychology of Humor: An Integrative Approach*, Burlington, MA: Elsevier Academic Press.

McGraw, A. Peter and Caleb Warren (2010), "Benign Violations: Making Immoral Behavior Funny," *Psychological Science*, 21 (August), 1141-49.

Preacher, Kristopher J. and Andrew F. Hayes (2008), "Asymptotic and Resampling Strategies for Assessing and Comparing Indirect Effects in Multiple Mediator Models," *Behavior Research Methods,* 40, 879-91

Priester, Joseph R. and Richard E. Petty (1996), "The Gradual Threshold Model of Ambivalence: Relating the Positive and Negative Bases of Attitudes to Subjective Ambivalence," *Journal of Personality and Social Psychology*, 71 (September), 431-449.

Ramachandran, V. S. (1998), "The Neurology and Evolution of Humor, Laughter, and Smiling: The False Alarm Theory," *Medical Hypotheses*, 51, 351-54.

Rozin, Paul, L. Lowery, S. Imada, and Jonathan Haidt (1999), "The CAD Triad Hypothesis: A Mapping between Three Moral Emotions (Contempt, Anger, Disgust) and Three Moral Codes (Community, Autonomy, Divinity)," *Journal of Personality and Social Psychology*, 76 (April), 574-86.

Veatch, T. C. (1998), "A Theory of Humor," *Humor-International Journal of Humor Research*, 11 (May), 161-215.

Weinberger, Marc G. and Charles S. Gulas (1992), "The Impact of Humor in Advertising - a Review," *Journal of Advertising*, 21 (December), 35-59.

Wyer, Robert S. and James E. Collins (1992), "A Theory of Humor Elicitation," *Psychological Review*, 99 (October), 663-88.

The Role of Regulatory Fit on the Inclination to Forgive or Seek Revenge Against Sellers Following a Product Failure in the Marketplace

Rajat Roy, Curtin University, Australia

Subimal Chatterjee, SUNY Binghamton, USA

EXTENDED ABSTRACT

In recent times, several companies have found themselves facing the wrath of the marketplace following the failures of their products. For example, Toyota had to recall more than 8 million vehicles worldwide following incidences of sudden unintended acceleration and faulty brakes in their different automobile models that added to an estimated $3 billion loss for the automaker. In the aftermath of product failures, the injured party may wish to forgive the transgressor (if the latter shows repentance), or punish the transgressor (if the victim is encouraged to seek revenge). Santelli, Struthers and Eaton (2009) have found that apologies are more effective when there is a fit or match between the frame of the transgressor's message (emphasizing a gain versus minimizing a loss) and the victim's regulatory orientation (promotion versus prevention focus), relative to when there is a misfit between the two. Our research extends the Santelli et al. (2009) research in understanding how regulatory fit can affect a consumer's desire to forgive (or seek revenge) following a market transgression.

In Study 1 (the forgiveness study), we randomly assigned one hundred eighty five undergraduate students (93 females) from a university in Western Australia to one of the six cells of a 2 (regulatory focus: promotion or prevention focus) by 3 (frame: neutral, promotion-framed apology, prevention-framed apology) between subjects design. We primed promotion (prevention) focus by asking participants to write down their current hopes and aspirations (duties and obligations), and how these may have changed over time. After they had completed their essays, all participants read about a product failure scenario (their car breaks down all of a sudden, and they have missed a very important meeting), and depending upon their experimental conditions, read a promotion-framed apology, prevention-framed apology, or a neutral message from the CEO of the company that made the car. The promotion-framed message contained phrases like "I am hopeful that our relationship with our customers can move forward after this," and "I will strive to do whatever it takes to gain back your trust." The prevention-framed message contained phrases like "I feel it is my duty to repair our relationship with our customers," and "I am obligated to do whatever it takes to not lose your trust."

The two main dependent variables used for this study were "tendency to forgive" (TTF) and "future intentions" (FI). We measured TTF using two 9-point items anchored on "strongly agree" (scale value = 9) and "strongly disagree" (scale value = 1). They were (1) "After listening to the CEO, I am more inclined to forgive the company for my troubles," and (2) "After listening to the CEO, I will forgive the company for my troubles." We measured FI with four 9-point strongly agree / strongly disagree items. They were (1) "I am likely to do business with this company in future," (2) "I am likely to recommend this company to my friends," (3) "I am likely to trust this company in the future," and (4) "I am likely to be satisfied with the future car models of this company." We found that promotion-primed participants were more inclined to forgive the transgressor following a promotion-framed apology ($M = 5.78$) than a prevention-framed apology ($M = 3.82$), and prevention-primed participants were more inclined to forgive the transgressor following a prevention-framed apology ($M = 5.83$) than a promotion-framed apology ($M = 3.61$). Similarly, the promotion-primed participants

were more likely to do future business with the transgressor company following a promotion-framed apology ($M = 4.98$) than a prevention-framed apology ($M = 3.14$), and prevention-primed participants were more likely to do future business with the transgressor company following a prevention-framed apology ($M = 4.69$) than a promotion-framed apology ($M = 2.48$).

In Study 2 (the revenge study), we randomly assigned one hundred eighty three undergraduate students (89 females) from a university in Western Australia to one of the six cells of a 2 (regulatory focus: promotion or prevention focus) by 3 (frame: neutral, promotion-framed revenge, prevention-framed revenge) between subjects design. Similar to Study 1, we primed promotion (prevention) focus by asking participants to write down their current hopes and aspirations (duties and obligations), following which all participants proceeded to the next part of the study, wherein they read the same car failure scenario from the first study. However, this time instead of the CEO-seeking-apology scenario, participants read that a lawyer, on television, was inviting victims to join a lawsuit against the company. Depending upon their experimental conditions, the participants read a promotion-framed revenge message, prevention-framed revenge message, or a neutral message. The promotion-framed message contained phrases like "I am sad to note that the company did not do everything possible to ensure your trust," and "join in the lawsuit and help those who have suffered by the actions of this company get what is due to them." The prevention-framed message contained phrases like "I am sad to note that the company did not do what it was obligated to do," and "join in the lawsuit so that those who have suffered do not lose what they are due by the actions of the company."

The two main dependent variables used for this study were "desire to seek revenge" (DSR) and "future intentions" (FI). We measured DSR using a two 9-point items anchored on "strongly agree" (scale value = 9) and "strongly disagree" (scale value = 1). They were (1) "I want to take revenge on the company for my troubles," and (2) "I want to punish this company." We measured FI with three 9-point strongly agree / strongly disagree items. They were (1) "I will not do business with this company in future," (2) "I will not recommend this company to my friends," and (3) "I will not trust this company in the future." We found that the prevention-primed participants were more inclined to seek revenge following a prevention-framed message ($M = 6.39$) than a promotion-framed message ($M = 4.60$), but promotion-primed participants were only directionally more inclined to seek revenge on the transgressor following a promotion-framed revenge message ($M = 5.61$) than a prevention-framed message ($M = 5.05$). Similarly, promotion-primed participants reported more negative future intentions towards the transgressor company following a promotion-framed message ($M = 8.01$) than a prevention-framed message ($M = 5.59$), whereas prevention-primed participants were more inclined to avoid the transgressor following a prevention-framed message ($M = 8.25$) than a promotion-framed message ($M = 5.91$).

REFERENCES

Santelli, Alexander G., Ward C. Struthers and Judy Eaton (2009), "Fit to Forgive: Exploring the Interaction between Regulatory Focus, Repentance, and Forgiveness," *Journal of Personality and Social Psychology,* 96, 2, 381–94.

Coping with Mixed Emotions: Exploring the Temporal Arousal of Positive Emotion Relative to Negative Emotion

Loraine Lau-Gesk, University of California, Irvine, USA
Thomas Kramer, University of South Carolina, USA
Sayantani Mukherjee, California State University, Long Beach, USA

EXTENDED ABSTRACT

People often rely on their past experiences as guide for their future decisions. Positive experiences are repeated, negative ones avoided. However, rarely are our memories purely positive or purely negative, but instead they are filled with both ups and downs. Rather than feeling pure happiness from a successful negotiation (Thompson, Valley, and Kramer 1995), financial windfall (Levav and McGraw 2009), or visit to "the happiest place on earth" (e.g., Disneyland; Sutton 1992), people often endure mixed emotions from such experiences presumed so clearly positive. Despite their ubiquity, complex experiences comprised of both positive and negative emotions have been studied much less than their single-valenced emotion counterparts, with existing mixed emotions research mostly focused on demonstrating that positive and negative emotions may arise simultaneously or sequentially within the duration of a given experience (Otnes, Lowrey, and Shrum 1997), identifying how and when they may be triggered (Kahneman 1992) and linking them to feelings of discomfort (Priester and Petty 1993; Thompson, Zanna, and Griffin 1995).

More recent research shows that people typically react negatively to mixed emotions unless they acquire the necessary skills to cope with or overcome the discomfort associated with them. For example, those more prone to accepting duality due to their own experiences with conflict accumulated over a lifetime appear better equipped to cope with and thereby respond more favorably to mixed emotions than those with far fewer experiences with facing conflict. The elderly (vs. young), East Asians (vs. westerners) and biculturals (vs. monoculturals) represent such individuals likely associated with higher duality acceptance and thus lower feelings of discomfort with mixed emotions (Kramer, Lau-Gesk, and Chiu 2009; Williams and Aaker 2002).

Beyond examining individual differences, the literature is largely silent about moderators of the relationship between judgment and mixed emotions. Moreover, specific coping processes underlying more favorable reactions to mixed emotions have yet to be pinpointed. Thus, the present research aims to achieve three main objectives. First, it identifies properties that underlie recalled sequential mixed emotional experiences that may bolster or hinder successful coping. Specifically, we explore the temporal arousal of positive emotion relative to negative emotion, and how this property may facilitate coping processes. Varying the temporal arousal of positive, relative to negative, emotion leads us to our second objective of examining sequential patterns of mixed emotional experiences that range in valence and intensity. Most investigations of sequential mixed emotions have focused on two emotion events (i.e., one negative and one positive) and therefore two experiential patterns (negative to positive; positive to negative). In contrast, we focus on far more complex and previously unexamined mixed emotion sequences because of our focus on temporal arousal of positive, relative to negative, emotion. Third, this research pinpoints the specific coping processes involved that lead to more favorable reactions to mixed emotions that arise sequentially.

Specifically, we examine consumers' overall evaluations of mixed emotional experiences varying in temporal arousal of positive versus negative emotion. We argue that relatively close (vs. distant) temporal arousal of positive emotion relative to negative emotion provides cognitive resources necessary to cope with mixed emotions and hence lower the discomfort otherwise associated with it. This in turn leads them to evaluate mixed emotional experiences favorably.

Four studies across a variety of contexts test our main thesis that greater cognitive resources become available to construe mixed experiences in a favorable light with close (vs. distant) temporal arousal of positive emotion relative to negative emotion. In particular, we rely on far more complex sequential mixed emotional experiences than previously investigated, ones that are comprised of multiple emotional events of either valence that vary in emotion intensity levels so that temporal arousal manipulations occur in the middle of the entire experience rather than at the beginning, end or both. This allows us to isolate any effects that may arise from temporal arousal. Indeed, prior studies have used at most three sequential events that vary on valence only (e.g., good and bad events: Linville and Fischer 1991; negative, neutral, and positive events: Lau-Gesk 2005). Specifically, we examine the effect of temporal arousal of the most intense positive emotion relative to the most intense negative emotion, given their robust influence on overall evaluations (Fredrickson and Kahneman 1993).

Study 1 relies on arcade patrons who experience sequentially close (vs. distant) temporal arousal of positive emotion relative to negative emotion, while playing a videogame. Study 2 manipulates temporal arousal of positive emotion relative to negative emotion, through a movie night experience. Results of these two studies show that consumers evaluate sequential mixed emotional experiences more favorably when the temporal arousal of positive emotion is close (vs. distant) to negative emotion. The next two studies examine reappraisal likelihood as the driver of the temporal arousal effect on evaluations of mixed emotional experiences. Study 3 manipulates reappraisal likelihood by imposing cognitive load on half of the study participants and finds differences in evaluations of a mixed romantic relationship experience due to close (vs. distant) temporal arousal of positive emotion relative to negative emotion, eliminated in these conditions. As further support for our theory, we measure reappraisal likelihood in study 4 and show that cognitive load will not moderate the effect of temporal arousal of positive, relative to negative, emotion on evaluation of a mixed emotional experience in a jelly belly sampling context, for those participants high in reappraisal tendencies because of their chronic use of reappraisal as their coping strategy. A suppression coping strategy is ruled out as well (Gross and John 2003).

REFERENCES

Andrade, E. B. (2005). Behavioral consequences of affect: Combining evaluative and regulatory mechanisms. *Journal of Consumer Research, 32*, 355-362.

Baron, Reuben M. and David A. Kenny (1986), "The Moderator-Mediator Distinction in Social Psychological Research: Conceptual, Strategic, and Statistical Considerations," *Journal of Personality and Social Psychology*, 51 (6), 1173-82.

Cacioppo, John T., Wendi L.Gardner, and Gary G. Berntson (1997), "Beyond Bipolar Conceptualizations and Measures: The Case of Attitudes and Evaluative Space," *Personality and Social Psychology Review*, 1(1), 3-25.

Folkman, Susan and Judith T. Moskowitz (2000), "Positive Affect and the Other Side of Coping," *American Psychologist*, 55 (6), 647-54.

Fredrickson, Barbara L. and Daniel Kahneman (1993), "Duration Neglect in Retrospective Evaluations of Affective Episodes," *Journal of Personality and Social Psychology*, 65 (1), 45-55.

Fredrickson, Barbara L. and Robert W. Levenson (1998), "Positive Emotions Speed Recovery from the Cardiovascular Sequelae of Negative Emotions," *Cognition and Emotion*, 12 (2), 191-220.

Fredrickson, Barbara L. and Marcial F. Losada (2005), "Positive Affect and the Complex Dynamics of Human Flourishing," *American Psychologist*, 60, 678-686.

Grant, Adam M. and Sabine Sonnentag (2010), "Doing Good Buffers against Feeling Bad: Prosocial Impact Compensates for Negative Task and Self-Evaluations," *Organizational Behavior and Human Decision Processes*, 111, 13-22.

Gross, James J. and Oliver P. John (2003), "Individual Differences in Two Emotion Regulation Processes: Implications for Affect, Relationships, and Well-being," *Journal of Personality and Social Psychology*, 85 (2), 348–62.

Kahneman, Daniel (1992), "Reference Points, Anchors, Norms, and Mixed Feelings," *Organizational Behavior and Human Decision Processes*, 51, 296-312.

Kramer, Thomas, Loraine Lau-Gesk and Chi-yue Chiu (2009), "The Interactive Effects of Duality Expertise and Coping Frames on Responses to Ambivalent Messages," *Journal of Consumer Psychology*, 19 (4), 661-72.

Larsen, Jeff T., Peter A. McGraw, and John T. Cacioppo (2001), "Can People Feel Happy and Sad at the Same Time," *Journal of Personality and Social Psychology*, 81 (October), 684-96.

Lau-Gesk, Loraine (2005), "Understanding Consumer Evaluations of Mixed Affective Experiences," *Journal of Consumer Research*, 32 (1), 23-8.

Lau-Gesk, Loraine and Joan Meyers-Levy (2009), "Emotional Persuasion: When the Valence versus the Resource Demands of Emotions Influence Consumers' Attitudes," *Journal of Consumer Research*, 36 (December), 585-99.

Linville, Patricia W. and Gregory W. Fischer (1991), "Preferences for Separating or Combining Events," *Journal of Personality and Social Psychology*, 60 (January), 5–23.

Luce, Mary F., JohnW. Payne, and James R. Bettman (2000), "Coping with Unfavorable Attribute Values in Choice. *Organizational Behavior and Human Decision Processes, 81*, 274-299.

Montgomery, Nicole Votolato and H. Rao Unnava (2009), "Temporal Sequence Effects: A Memory Framework," *Journal of Consumer Research*, 36 (June), 83-92.

Nowlis, Stephen M., Barbara E. Kahn, and Ravi Dhar (2002), "Coping with Ambivalence: The Effect of Removing a Neutral Option on Consumer Attitude and Preference Judgments," *Journal of Consumer Research*, 29 (December), 319–34.

Otnes, Cele, Tina Lowrey, and L. J. Shrum (1997), "Toward an Understanding of Consumer Ambivalence," *Journal of Consumer Research*, 24 (June), 80–93.

Priester, Joseph R. and Richard E. Petty (1996), "The Gradual Threshold Model of Ambivalence: Relating the Positive and Negative Bases of Attitudes to Subjective Ambivalence," *Journal of Personality and Social Psychology*, 71 (March), 431–49.

Ramanathan, Suresh and Patti Williams (2007), "Immediate and Delayed Emotional Consequences of Indulgence: The Moderating Influence of Personality Type on Mixed Emotions," *Journal of Consumer Research*, 34 (August), 212-23.

Schwarz, Norbert, Daniel Kahneman, and Jin Xu (2009)," Global and Episodic Reports of Hedonic Experience. In R. Belli, D. Alwin, & F. Stafford (Eds.) *Using Calendar and Diary Methods in Life Events Research*, pp.157-174, Newbury Park, CA: Sage.

Thompson, Megan M., Mark P. Zanna, and Dale W. Griffin (1995), "Let's Not Be Indifferent about (Attitudinal) Ambivalence," in *Attitude Strength: Antecedents and Consequences*, ed. Richard E. Petty and Jon A. Krosnick, Mahwah, NJ: Erlbaum, 361–86.

Vohs, Kathleen D. and Ronald J. Faber (2007), "Spent Resources: Self-Regulatory Resource Availability Affects Impulse Buying," *Journal of Consumer Research*, 33 (4), 537-547.

Williams, Patti and Jennifer Aaker (2002), "Can Mixed Emotions Peacefully Co-exist?" *Journal of Consumer Research*, 28 (March), 636-49.

The Pantomime of Persuasion:
Fit Between Sales-Agent Nonverbal Communication and Influence Strategies

Bob Fennis, University of Groningen, The Netherlands
Marielle Stel, University of Tilburg, The Netherlands

EXTENDED ABSTRACT

We are all frequently approached and sometimes harassed by volunteers, fundraisers, and sales-representatives attempting to get us to say "yes" to their offer. These agents have at their disposal a wide variety of influence strategies aimed at increasing the odds of compliance. Studies have focused on what agents have to say to foster persuasion, but have largely ignored the interplay with nonverbal communication in this process (e.g., Burger 1999; McFarland, Challagalla, & Shervani 2006). Furthermore, the influence of fit (and misfit) between nonverbal communication and influence strategies on the consumers' compliance has not yet received empirical investigation. The present research aims to fill this void by examining the impact of influence strategies when embedded in nonverbal behavior that either fits or misfits the key orientation of the strategy. We propose that nonverbal communication can "boost" the persuasive impact of influence strategies to the extent that it fits the strategy's orientation, and conversely, that a misfit between nonverbal behavior and type of strategy may render it ineffective in fostering compliance.

Previous research on social influence has focused primarily on identifying and testing verbalized scripts that agents may use to induce compliance and persuasion on the part of the recipient (Cialdini & Goldstein 2004). For instance, research on personal selling has identified a host of persuasive techniques that sales representatives use to convince prospective buyers, such as information exchange, the use of recommendations, requests, promises, or ingratiation (McFarland et al., 2006). In addition, studies have focused on several well-defined influence techniques employing heuristic decision making to induce compliance. Well-known examples include the "Door-In-The-Face" technique (DITF; Cialdini et al. 1975), in which the target request is presented as a concession to an unreasonably large initial request, and the "Disrupt-Then-Reframe" technique (DTR; Davis & Knowles 1999; Fennis, Das, & Pruyn 2004, 2006; Kardes, Fennis, Hirt, Tormala, & Bullington, 2007), where an otherwise conventional sales script is interrupted by a subtle, odd element in (i.e., the "disruption", for example stating the price of an offer in pennies before stating it in dollars) followed by a persuasive phrase that concludes the script (i.e., the "reframe", e.g., "it's a bargain!").

Interestingly, Knowles and Linn (2004) have recently argued that the DITF and DTR might operate differently because they rely on different orientations. More specifically, these authors have proposed that some influence strategies may work because they increase an approach orientation, while others are effective because they mobilize an avoidance orientation. More specifically, what they term "alpha strategies" persuade people by activating approach forces, increasing people's motivation toward a goal by making the offer or request more attractive. One of the ways to activate such an approach orientation is to engage a norm of reciprocity in which granting a small favor or concession prompts recipients to reciprocate and return the favor (Knowles & Linn, 2004). As demonstrated by Cialdini et al. (1975), the DITF hinges on the principle of reciprocity (e.g., Cialdini et al., 1975; Fennis, Janssen & Vohs, 2009; Gouldner, 1960): a large request by the agent is typically declined after which the agent presents the smaller request as a clear concession, thus provoking a counter-concession on the part of the recipient (i.e., compliance).

"Omega strategies", on the other hand, attempt to persuade people by minimizing avoidance forces, reducing people's motivation to move away from a goal. One way of minimizing avoidance forces is to reduce the extent of recipient counterargumentation in response to a persuasion attempt (Knowles & Linn, 2004). As shown by Fennis et al. (2004), this process also underlies the impact of the DTR technique where the disruption interferes with the consumer's counterargumentation thus increasing the persuasive impact of the reframe.

There is reason to assume that nonverbal communication may play a role of significance in these settings —by itself and in interplay with these verbal influence strategies. For instance, a study of McGinley, LeFevre, and McGinley (1975) showed that agents with open body positions were evaluated more positively and were more persuasive than agents with closed body positions. In addition, Cesario and Higgins (2008) investigated the influence of fit between the recipient's orientation and the influence agent's nonverbal style. They distinguished between an eager and a vigilant nonverbal style. An eager nonverbal style is approach oriented and involves animated, broad opening movements, hand movements openly projected outward, forward-leaning body positions, fast body movements, and fast speech rate. A vigilant nonverbal style is avoidance oriented and involves gestures showing precision, motions that represent slowing down, backward-leaning positions, slower body movements, and slower speech (Cesario & Higgins, 2008). They showed that when recipients in a promotion focus —who perceive goals as hopes and aspirations and prefer eager, advancement strategies (Higgins, 1998)— viewed a message delivered in an eager nonverbal style, they developed more positive attitudes and also behaved more in accordance with the recommendation than when there was a misfit between nonverbal style and regulatory orientation. Likewise, when recipients in a prevention focus —who perceive goals as duties and obligations and prefer vigilant, cautious strategies (Higgins, 1998)— viewed a message delivered in a vigilant nonverbal style, they too showed more persuasion and advocacy congruent behavior. The experience of regulatory fit underlies these effects, such that a fit between the recipient's focus and the orientation indicated by the nonverbal style can augment persuasion and compliance, whereas a misfit can do the opposite and decrease persuasion and compliance (Cesario & Higgins, 2008).

Importantly, the experience of fit can arise from the interplay between message characteristics and recipient's orientation or it may reside in different features of the persuasive appeal itself (see for example Evans & Petty, 2003; Koenig, Cesario, Molden, Kosloff & Higgins, 2009). Hence, we extend previous research by examining the impact of fit and misfit within one and the same persuasive appeal and assess the effectiveness of (mis)fit of the type of verbal influence strategy and nonverbal style on consumers' behavioral compliance with a sales request.

More specifically, we argue that the impact of alpha (approach) and omega (avoidance) influence strategies will be moderated by the type of nonverbal style. We propose that the effectiveness of these influence strategies will be boosted in situations of fit and attenuated in situations of misfit with the type of nonverbal style. Hence, alpha influence strategies will receive a boost when they are delivered with an eager non-verbal style. Similarly, the impact of omega influence strategies will be increased when delivered with a vigilant nonverbal style. In contrast, the impact of alpha (omega) strategies will be reduced when delivered in a vigilant (eager) nonverbal style influence.

Advances in Consumer Research
Volume 39, ©2011

REFERENCES

Baker, S. M. & Petty, R.E. (1994). Majority and minority influence: Source position imbalance as a determinant of message scrutiny. *Journal of Personality and Social Psychology, 67,* 5-19.

Burger, J. M. (1999). The Foot-In-The-Door Compliance Procedure: A Multiple-Process Analysis and Review. *Personality and Social Psychology Review, 3,* 303-325.

Cesario, J., & Higgins, E. T. (2008). Making message recipients "feel right": How nonverbal cues can increase persuasion. *Psychological Science, 19,* 415-420.

Cialdini, R. B. (2009). *Influence: Science and practice* (5th ed.). Boston, MA: Allyn & Bacon.

Cialdini, R. B., & Goldstein, N. J. (2004). Social Influence: Compliance and Conformity. *Annual Review of Psychology, 55,* 591-621.

Cialdini, R. B., Vincent, J. E., Lewis, S. K. Catalan, J., Wheeler, D., & Darby, B.L. (1975). Reciprocal Concessions Procedure for Inducing Compliance: The Door-In-The-Face Technique. *Journal of Personality and Social Psychology, 31,* 206-215.

Davis, B. P., & Knowles, E. S. (1999). A Disrupt-Then-Reframe Technique of Social Influence. *Journal of Personality and Social Psychology, 76,* 192-199.

Evans, L. M., & Petty, R. E. (2003). Self-guide framing and persuasion: Responsibly increasing message processing to ideal levels. *Personality and Social Psychology Bulletin, 29,* 313-324.

Fennis, B. M., Das, E. H. H. J., & Pruyn, A. T. H. (2004). If You Can't Dazzle Them With Brilliance, Baffle Them With Nonsense: Extending the Impact of the Disrupt-Then-Reframe Technique of Social Influence. *Journal of Consumer Psychology, 14,* 280-290.

Fennis, B. M., Das, E. H. H. J., & Pruyn, A. T. H. (2006). Interpersonal Communication and Compliance: The Disrupt-Then-Reframe Technique in Dyadic Influence Settings. *Communication Research, 33,* 136-151.

Fennis, B.M., Janssen, L., & Vohs, K.D. (2009). Acts of benevolence: A limited-resource account of compliance with charitable requests. *Journal of Consumer Research, 35,* 906-924

Gouldner, A. W. (1960). The norm of reciprocity: A preliminary statement. *American Sociological Review, 25,* 165-170.

Higgins, E.T. (1998). Promotion and prevention: Regulatory focus as a motivational principle. In M.P. Zanna (Ed.), Advances in experimental social psychology (Vol. 30, pp. 1–46). New York: Academic Press.

Kardes, F. R., Fennis, B. M. Hirt, E. R., Tormala, Z. L. & Bullington, B. (2007). The role of the need for cognitive closure in the effectiveness of the disrupt-then-reframe influence technique. *Journal of Consumer Research. 34,* 377-385.

Karmarkar, U.R. & Tormala, Z. L. (2010). Believe me, I have no idea what I'm talking about: The effects of source certainty on consumer involvement and persuasion. *Journal of Consumer Research, 36,* 1033-1049.

Knowles, E. and Linn, J. (2004). Approach-avoidance model of persuasion: Alpha and omega strategies for change. In E. Knowles & J. Linn (Eds.). *Resistance and persuasion* (pp. 259-282). Mahwah, NJ: Erlbaum.

Koenig, A. M., Cesario, J., Molden, D. C., Kosloff, S., & Higgins, E. T. (2009). Incidental experiences of regulatory fit and the processing of persuasive appeals. *Personality and Social Psychology Bulletin, 35,* 1342-1355.

Lee, A. Y., & Aaker, J. L. (2004). Bringing the frame into focus: The influence of regulatory fit on processing fluency and persuasion. *Journal of Personality and Social Psychology, 86,* 205-218.

McFarland, R. G., Challagalla, G. N., & Shervani, T. A. (2006). Influence tactics for effective adaptive selling. *Journal of Marketing, 70,* 103-117.

McGinley, H. LeFevre, R. & McGinley, P. (1975). The influence of a communicator's body position on opinion change in others. *Journal of Personality and Social Psychology, 31,* 686-690.

They Say High, I Say Low: The Effect of Power on Consumer Response to Social Influence

Mehdi Mourali, University of Calgary, Canada
Zhiyong Yang, University of Texas at Arlington, USA

EXTENDED ABSTRACT

Consumers regularly experience feelings of being both powerful and powerless. These feelings may be triggered by awareness of socioeconomic status (Henry 2005), bargaining position (Dwyer 1984), or situational contexts. For instance, facing a critical product or service failure such as a canceled flight or a botched medical procedure may induce a psychological state of feeling powerless (Gelbrich 2010), whereas being able to influence an important company decision may evoke a sense of empowerment (Fuchs et al. 2010). In this paper, we examine how consumers' sense of power affects the way they respond to conformity pressure when evaluating a new product.

Prior research (Briñol et al. 2007; Galinsky et al. 2008) suggests that powerful consumers' evaluations should be impervious to others' opinions because powerful consumers either pay no attention to these opinions, or dismiss them entirely when judging a product's attractiveness. We propose an alternative mechanism inspired by research on identity signaling (Berger and Heath 2007). Unlike previous research, which emphasizes powerful individuals' reliance on internal states versus external information, the proposed approach focuses on the social process of communicating one's power and independence to others. The signaling hypothesis suggests that high power consumers often diverge from others' opinions to communicate their independence and power to others, even if doing so contradicts their privately-held attitudes.

We tested the signaling hypothesis in two experimental studies. Study 1 consisted of a 3 (power: control vs. low vs. high) × 3 (peer feedback: control vs. positive vs. negative) between-subjects design. Participants' sense of power was manipulated using a mindset priming technique adapted from Galinsky et al. (2003). Those assigned to the high power condition were instructed to write about a time when they had power over another person, whereas those in the low power condition were instructed to write about a time when someone else had power over them. Respondents in the control group were asked to write about their day yesterday. Next, participants took part in a second, ostensibly unrelated, task, in which they evaluated the attractiveness of a new product. After reading the product description, participants were presented with a feedback sheet and were asked to rate how much they liked the product and how useful they found it (1 = not at all; 11 = extremely). The feedback sheet contained 36 lines, such that many participants could provide their ratings on the same page. In the peer influence conditions, the feedback sheet already contained evaluations from 10 other participants, who apparently (from a respondent's view) completed the product evaluation at an earlier time. One group was given an evaluation sheet containing 10 positive feedbacks, with an average attractiveness rating of 9.9/11. Another group received a sheet containing 10 negative feedbacks, with an average attractiveness rating of 2.15/11. A control group received a blank feedback sheet.

The results indicate that, in the absence of any peer influence (i.e., baseline condition), powerful consumers' attitudes did not differ from the attitudes of those in the low power and control groups. However, in the presence of peer influence, powerless consumers tended to conform to the expressed opinions of others whereas powerful consumers deliberately sought to deviate from the opinion expressed by the majority. Their concern with signaling independence was such that their evaluations diverged even from their own privately-held attitudes, as measured in the baseline condition.

Study 1 provides clear evidence that high power can lead to anti-conformity, as predicted by the signaling hypothesis. Nevertheless, the psychological mechanism underlying the observed effects remains unclear. We do not know whether powerful consumers diverge from others' opinions because they want to signal their power and individuality or because high power simply increases consumers' need to differentiate from other people. Study 2 was conducted to test the psychological process. It featured a 2 (power: high vs. low) × 3 (feedback: negative vs. positive vs. none) × 3 (opportunity to express uniqueness: signal vs. express but not signal vs. control) between-subjects design. In line with the signaling hypothesis, we found that providing powerful consumers with an opportunity to signal their individuality prior to the focal task helps fulfill their signaling goal and results in greater conformity during the later evaluation task. However, providing powerful consumers with an opportunity to express uniqueness but not to signal it does not reduce their tendency to express counter normative attitudes.

REFERENCES

Anderson, Cameron and Jennifer L. Berdahl (2002), "The Experience of Power: Examining the Effects of Power on Approach and Inhibition Tendencies," *Journal of Personality and Social Psychology*, 83(December), 1362-77.

Bargh, John A., Michelle Green, and Gráinne Fitzsimons (2008), "The Selfish Goal: Unintended Consequences of Intended Goal Pursuits," *Social Cognition*, 26 (5), 534-54.

Bargh, John A., Paula Raymond, John B. Pryor, and Fritz Strack (1995), "The Attractiveness of the Underling: An Automatic Power Sex Association and its Consequences for Sexual Harassment," *Journal of Personality and Social Psychology*, 68 (May), 768-81.

Bearden, William O. and Michael J. Etzel (1982), "Reference Group Influence on Product and Brand Purchase Decisions," *Journal of Consumer Research*, 9 (September), 183-94.

Berger, Jonah and Chip Heath (2007), "Where Consumers Diverge from Others: Identity Signaling and Product Domains," *Journal of Consumer Research*, 34 (August), 121-34.

Briñol, Pablo, Richard E. Petty, Carmen Valle, Derek D. Rucker, and Alberto Becerra (2007), "The Effects of Message Recipients' Power before and after Persuasion: A Self-Validating Analysis," *Journal of Personality and Social Psychology*, 93 (December), 1040-53.

Burnkrant, Robert E. and Alain Cousineau (1975), "Informational and Normative Social Influence in Buyer Behavior," *Journal of Consumer Research*, 2 (December), 206-15.

Chen, Serena, Annette Y. Lee-Chai, and John A. Bargh (2001), "Relationship Orientation as a Moderator of the Effects of Social Power," *Journal of Personality and Social Psychology*, 80 (February), 173-187.

Cialdini, Robert B. and Noah Goldstein (2004), "Social Influence: Compliance and Conformity," *Annual Review of Psychology*, 55 (February), 591-621.

Dwyer, F. Robert (1984), "Are Two Better than One? Bargaining Behavior and Outcomes in an Asymmetrical Power Relationship," *Journal of Consumer Research*, 11 (September), 680-83.

Fiske, Susan T. (1993), "Controlling Other People: The Impact of Power on Stereotyping," *American Psychologist*, 48(June), 621-28.

Fiske, Susan T. and Eric Dépret (1996), "Control, Interdependence, and Power: Understanding Social Cognition in Its Context," *European Review of Social Psychology, 7* (1) 31-61.

Förster, Jens, Nira Liberman, and E. Tory Higgins (2005), "Accessibility from Active and Fulfilled Goals," *Journal of Experimental Social Psychology*, 41 (3), 220-39.

French, John R. P., Jr., and Bertram Raven (1959), "The Bases of Social Power," in *Studies in Social Power*, ed. Dorwin Cartwright, Ann Arbor, MI: Institute for Social Research, 150-67.

Fuchs, Christoph, Emanuela Prandelli, and Martin Schreier (2010), "The Psychological Effects of Empowerment Strategies on Consumers' Product Demand," *Journal of Marketing*, 74 (January), 65-79.

Galinsky, Adam D., Deborah H. Gruenfeld, and Joe C. Magee (2003), "From Power to Action," *Journal of Personality and Social Psychology*, 85 (September), 453-66.

Galinsky, Adam D., Deborah H. Gruenfeld, Joe C. Magee, Jennifer Whitson, and Katie Liljenquist (2008), "Power Reduces the Press of the Situation: Implications for Creativity, Conformity, and Dissonance," *Journal of Personality and Social Psychology*, 95 (6), 1450-66.

Gelbrich, Katja (2010), "Anger, Frustration, and Helplessness after Service Failure: Coping Strategies and Effective Informational Support," *Journal of the Academy of Marketing Science*, 38 (5), 567-85.

Goldstein, Noah J., Robert B. Cialdini, and Vladas Griskevicius (2008), "A Room with a Viewpoint: Using Social Norms to Motivate Environmental Conservation in Hotels," *Journal of Consumer Research*, 35 (October), 472-82.

Guinote, Ana (2007), "Power Affects Basic Cognition: Increased Attentional Inhibition and Flexibility," *Journal of Experimental Social Psychology*, 43 (July), 685-97.

--- (2008), "Power and Affordances: When the Situation Has More Power over Powerful than Powerless Individuals," *Journal of Personality and Social Psychology, 95* (August), 237-52.

Guinote, Ana, Charles M. Judd, and Markus Brauer (2002), "Effects of Power on Perceived and Objective Group Variability: Evidence That More Powerful Groups Are More Variable," *Journal of Personality and Social Psychology*, 82 (5), 708-21.

Hecht, Marvin A. and Marianne LaFrance (1998), "License or Obligation to Smile: The Effect of Power and Sex on Amount and Type of Smiling," *Personality and Social Psychology Bulletin*, 24 (12), 1332-42.

Henry, Paul C. (2005), "Social Class, Market Situation, and Consumers' Metaphors of (Dis)Empowerment," *Journal of Consumer Research*, 31 (March), 766–78.

Hollander, Edwin P. (1958), "Conformity Status and Idiosyncrasy Credits," *Psychological Review*, 65, 117-27.

Jetten, Jolanda, Matthew Hornsey, and Immaculada Adavres-Yorno (2006), "When Group Members Admit to Being Conformist: The Role of Relative Intragroup Status in Conformity Self-Reports," *Personality and Social Psychology Bulletin*, 32 (February), 162-73.

Keltner, Dacher, Deborah H. Gruenfeld, and Cameron Anderson (2003), "Power, Approach, and Inhibition," *Psychological Review*, 110 (April), 265-84.

Liberman, Nira, Jens Förster, and E. Tory Higgins (2007), "Completed vs. Interrupted Priming: Reduced Accessibility from Post-Fulfillment Inhibition," *Journal of Experimental Social Psychology*, 43 (2), 258-64.

Maimaran, Michal and S. Christian Wheeler (2008), "Circles, Squares, and Choice: The Effect of Shapes Arrays on Uniqueness and Variety Seeking," *Journal of Marketing Research,* 45 (December), 731-40.

Mangleburg, Tamara F., Patricia M. Doney, and Terry Bristol (2004), "Shopping with Friends, and Teen's Susceptibility to Peer Influence," *Journal of Retailing, 80* (2), 101-116.

Monin, Benoît and Dale T. Miller (2001), "Moral Credentials and the Expression of Prejudice," *Journal of Personality and Social Psychology*, 81 (1), 33-43.

Montgomery, Robert L. (1971), "Status, Conformity, and Resistance to Compliance in Natural Groups," *Journal of Social Psychology*, 84 (2), 179-206.

Mourali, Mehdi and Frank Pons (2009), "Power and Choice: Do Powerful Consumers Prefer Bold Options?", in *Advances in Consumer Research* Volume 37, eds. Margaret C. Campbell, Jeff Inman, and Rik Pieters, Duluth, MN : Association for Consumer Research.

Nail, Paul R. (1986), "Toward an Integration of Some Models and Theories of Social Response," *Psychological Bulleting*, 100 (2), 190-206.

Nail, Paul R., Geoff McDonald, and David A. Levy (2000), "Proposal of a Four-Dimensional Model of Social Response," *Psychological Bulletin*, 126 (3), 454-70.

Smith, Pamela K. and John A. Bargh (2008), "Nonconscious Effects of Power on Basic Approach ad Avoidance Tendencies," *Social Cognition*, 26 (1), 1-24.

Thibaut, John W. and Harold H. Kelley (1959), *The Social Psychology of Groups*. New York: Wiley.

Weick, Mario and Ana Guinote (2008), "When Subjective Experiences Matter: Power Increases Reliance on the Ease of Retrieval," *Journal of Personality and Social Psychology*, 94(June), 956-70.

Willis, Richard H. (1963), "Two Dimensions of Conformity-Nonconformity," *Sociometry*, 26 (4), 499-513.

Willis, Richard H. (1965), "Conformity, Independence, and Anticonformity," *Human Relations*, 18 (4), 373-88.

Seeing Things in a Different Light: Agent vs. Consumer Responses to Persuasion Attempts

Wenxia Guo, University of Manitoba, Canada
Kelley Main, University of Manitoba, Canada

EXTENDED ABSTRACT

Since the Persuasion Knowledge Model (PKM; Friedtad and Wright 1994) was first introduced, numerous investigations have explored how consumers see an agent's behavior in a different light based on their persuasion knowledge (see for e.g. Campbell and Kirmani 2000). However, there is another set of circumstances in which persuasion attempts might be seen in a different light, when the target of a persuasion attempt has experience as both consumer and agent.

The PKM allows for the situation where individuals have the dual role of agent and consumer (Friestad and Wright 1994), however to date no literature has examined this question. The focus instead has been on consumer reactions (e.g. Sharma and Levy 1995). Utilizing theories of role conflict and salience in addition to the literature on processing motivations, we propose that for dual role consumers, the salience of their role as an agent will lead them to respond to persuasion attempts based more on accuracy motivated processing (Vonk 1999). In contrast, a consumer with no experience as sales agent will respond to a persuasion attempt in line with defense motivated processing (Fisher 1993). These different processing motivations influence whether or not consumers and agents will respond to different cues in the persuasion attempt. We are particularly interested in those cues that are related to ulterior motives: accessibility and acknowledgement.

Ulterior Motive Accessibility

The nature of sales with performance-contingent rewards (Mallin and Pullins 2009) leads to an enduring perception that ulterior motives are guiding the behavior of sales agents. Research has revealed that the accessibility of ulterior motives has a significant impact on consumer responses to persuasion attempts (Campbell and Kirmani 2000). We expect that the accessibility of ulterior motives will moderate agent and consumer responses to the persuasion attempt. In particular, for agents, their accuracy motivation will allow for an adjustment of their perceptions of the other sales agent in the face of information suggesting they are more or less likely to be influenced by ulterior motives. In contrast, consumers who are more likely to process information according to defense motivations will be insensitive to information relating to ulterior motives.

Study 1

This was a 2 (ulterior motive accessibility: high vs. low) × 2 (role: consumer vs. agent) between-subjects design (N=86). Consumer role was a measured variable wherein participants identified whether they had previous working experience in sales. All participants were asked to imagine an interaction with a salesperson where they were going to buy a pair of sunglasses. Half of the participants were told that the store eliminated the commission based reward policies (low ulterior motive accessibility) and the other half were told that the store used commission based reward policies (high ulterior motive accessibility). The persuasion attempt consisted of the salesperson flattering consumers on the sunglasses that they were trying on: "that's a great pair of sunglasses. I think they look good on you".

As expected, results indicated that that agents had significantly higher trustworthiness toward the other salesperson with low as compared to high ulterior motive accessibility ($F(1,82) = 16.21$, $p < 0.001$). In contrast, consumers' trustworthiness toward the salesper-son were not influenced by the accessibility of the ulterior motives ($F(1,82)=0.13$, $p=0.53$).

Ulterior Motive Acknowledgement

Wood and Eagly (1981) found that participants were more likely to trust those individuals who offered information against their own self-interest. Accordingly, we argue that when a sales agent offers information that argues against his/her self-interest during the persuasion attempt or acknowledges the presence of ulterior motives, consumers will be less defensive. This tactic has been referred to as "stealing thunder" and was first studied in the context of trial experts' assertions (Williams et al. 1993). In the current context, the acknowledgement of possible ulterior motives through the use of the stealing thunder tactic should serve to lessen consumer's defensive reactions to persuasion attempts. However, this tactic is unlikely to have an effect for accuracy motivated agents as they tend to evaluate overall information.

Study 2

This was a 2 (ulterior motive acknowledgement: no vs. yes) × 2 (role: consumer vs. agent) between-subjects design (N=72). As in Study 1, participants self-identified whether they had prior sales experience. The ulterior motive acknowledgement manipulation occurred during the persuasion attempt. The no acknowledgement of ulterior motive condition involved the persuasion attempt from the sales agent making the same flattering statement as in Study 1. Those in ulterior motive acknowledged condition were told "You may think that I am just trying to make a sale, but that's a great pair of sunglasses..."

In line with propositions, results showed that for consumers, acknowledging ulterior motives led to higher trustworthiness than not acknowledging ulterior motives ($F(1,68)=4.34$, $p<0.05$). However, agent trustworthiness were not influenced by ulterior motive acknowledgement ($F(1,68)=1.89$, $p>0.1$). Further, results of a similar study conducted with salesclerks at their place of employment (M = 6.5 years of experience) further confirmed accuracy motivated processing of the acknowledgement of ulterior motives.

Study 3

In the final study, we manipulate accuracy motivations to demonstrate how this may change consumer vs. agent responses. This was a 2 (ulterior motive acknowledgement: yes vs. no) × 2 (role: consumer vs. agent) × 2 (motivation priming: accuracy vs. control) between-subjects design (N=139). All manipulations were the same as in Study 2 with the addition of the accuracy motivation manipulation. Results demonstrated that priming consumer participants with accuracy motivation attenuated the effect of ulterior motive acknowledgement ($F(1,65)=1.03$, $p=0.3$). However, priming agent participants' with accuracy motivation, trustworthiness did not change ($F(1,65)=0.53$, $p=0.47$).

General Discussion

Through manipulating the accessibility and acknowledgement of ulterior motives, this research demonstrates that when responding to persuasion attempts from salespeople, a single role consumer tends to be defense motivated, whereas an individual with dual roles as both a consumer and an agent is accuracy motivated. The present study contributes to the literature by: (1) comparing different responses of single vs. dual role consumers thereby extending PKM, (2) introducing role salience as the reason for these differing responses, and (3) demonstrating the impact of different persuasion tactics (i.e. stealing thunder).

REFERENCES

Arpan, Laura and Donnalyn Pompper (2003), "Stormy Weather: Testing "Stealing Thunder" as a Crisis Communication Strategy to Improve Communication Flow between Organizations and Journalists," *Public Relations Review*, 29, 291-308.

Babin, Barry J., James S. Boles, and Williams R. Darden (1995), "Salesperson Stereotypes, Consumer Emotions, and their Impact on Information Processing," *Journal of the Academy of Marketing Science*, 32(2), 94-105.

Bhattacharya, C.B. and Sankar. Sen (2003), "Consumer-Company Identification: A Framework for Understanding Consumers' Relationships with Companies," *Journal of Marketing*, 67(2), 76-88.

Brehm, J. W. (1966). *A Theory of Psychological Reactance*. New York: Academic Press.

Burke, Ronald J. (1980), "The Self: Measurement Requirements from an Interactionist Perspective," *Social Psychology Quarterly*, 43(1), 18-30.

Burke, R. J. and Greenglass, E. R. (1987). *International Review of Industrial and Organizational Psychology*, In C.L. Coopr & I.T.Robertson (Eds. pp273-320). New York: Wiley.

Campbell, Margaret C., and Kirmani Amna (2000), "Consumers' Use of Persuasion Knowledge: The Effects of Accessibility and Cognitive Capacity on Perceptions of an Influence Agent," *Journal of Consumer Research*, 27, 69-83.

Chen, Serena and Chaiken Shelly (1999). The heuristic-systematic model in its broader context. *In Dual-Process Theories in Social Psychology* (pp. 73-96). S. Chaiken & Y. Trope Eds., New York: Guilford Press.

Clee, Mona A. and Robert A. Wicklund (1980), "Consumer Behavior and Psychological Reactance," *Journal of Consumer Research*, 6(4), 389-405.

Darke, Peter R., and Robin B. Ritchie (2007), "The defensive consumer: Advertising deception, defensive processing, and distrust," *Journal of Marketing Research*, (February), 114-127.

DePaulo, Peter J. (1988), "Research on Deception in Marketing Communications: Its Relevance to the Study of Nonverbal Behavior," *Journal of Noveral Behavior*, 12(4), 253-273.

Easley, Richard W., William O. Bearden, and Jesse E. Teel (1995), "Testing predictions derived from inoculation theory and the effectiveness of self-disclosure communications strategies," *Journal of Business Research*, 34, 93-105.

Edwards, Jeffrey R. and Nancy P. Rothbard (2000), "Mechanisms Linking Work and Family: Clarifying the Relationship between Work and Family Constructs," *The Academy of Management Review*, 25(1), 178-199.

Fisher, Robert J. (1993), "Social Desirability Bias and the Validity of Indirect Questioning," *Journal of Consumer Research*, 20(2), 303-315.

Fitzsimons, Gavan J. and Donald R. Lehmann (2004), "Reactance to Recommendations: When Unsolicited Advice Yields Contrary Responses", *Marketing Science*, 23, 1, 82-94.

Friestad, Marian.R. and Peter Wright (1994), "The persuasion knowledge model: How people cope with persuasion attempts," *Journal of Consumer Research*, 21, 1-31.

Hartman, Katherine B. (2006), "Television and Movie Representations of Salespeople: Beyond Willy Loman," *The Journal of Personal Selling & Sales Management*, 26(3), 283-292.

Kalra, Ajay, Mengze Shi, and Kannan Srinivasan (2003), "Salesforce Compensation Scheme and Consumer Inferences," *Management Science*, 49(5), 655-672.

Kivetz, Ran (2005), "Promotion Reactance: The Role of Effort-Reward Congruity," *Journal of Consumer Research*, 31(March), 725-736.

Mallin, Michael L. and Ellen B. Pullins (2009), "The Moderating Effect of Control Systems on the Relationship between Commission and Salesperson Intrinsic Motivation in a Customer Oriented Environment," *Industrial Marketing Management*, 38, 769-777.

Main, Kelley.J., Darren W. Dahl, & Peter R. Darke (2007), "Deliberative and automatic bases of suspicion: empirical evidence of the sinister attribution error," *Journal of Consumer Psychology*, 17(1), 59-69.

Marks, Stephen. R. (1977), "Multiple roles and role strain: Some notes on human energy, time and commitment," *American Sociological Review*, 39, 567-578.

Mohr, Alexander and Jonas F. Puck (2007), "Role Conflict, General Manager Job Satisfaction and Stress and the Performance of IJVS," *European Management Journal*, 25(1), 25-35.

Sharma, Arun and Michael Levy (1995), "Categorization of Customers by Retail Salespeople," *Journal of Retailing*, 71(1), 71-81.

Vonk, Roos (1999), "Effects of outcome dependency on correspondence bias," *Personality and Social Psychology Bulletin*, 25(3), 382-389.

Wei, Mei-Ling, Eileen Fischer, and Kelley J. Main (2008), "An Examination of the Effects of Activating Persuasion Knowledge on Consumer Response to Brands Engaging in Covert Marketing," *Journal of Public Policy & Marketing*, 27(1), 34-44.

Werbel, James and Michael H. Walter (2002), "Changing Views of Work and Family Roles: A Symbiotic Perspective," *Human Resource Management Review*, 12, 293-298.

Williams, Kipling.D., Martin J. Bourgeois, and Robert T. Croyle (1993), "The in criminal and civil trials," *Law and Human Behavior*, 17, 597-609.

Wood, Wendy and Alice H. Eagly (1981), "Stages in analysis of persuasive messages: The role of causal attributions and message comprehension," *Journal of Personality and Social Psychology*, 40, 246-259.

Buying the Girlfriend Experience:
An Exploration of Men's Experiences with Escort Workers

Aimee Huff, University of Western Ontario, Canada

EXTENDED ABSTRACT

Cuddling and talking – we shared interests, but most importantly, she made me feel like there was no other place she would rather be in that moment in time. (Lub, Montreal)

The informant who posted this comment is not referring to his wife or girlfriend, but to an encounter with a female sex worker – an escort – with whom he shared a particular type of commercial sex encounter known as the girlfriend experience (GFE). As the focus of this paper, the GFE differs from other types of commercial sex encounters in that it involves more than the exchange of money for sex; in order to derive the true value of the GFE, the male customer must not only pay the sex worker, but must also provide her with sexual pleasure and emotional intimacy. The result is that the encounter feels, to him, more like a romantic encounter with a girlfriend than straight-up sex. For an hour or two, or perhaps an entire evening, the customer indulges in his fantasies of a romantic encounter with a legitimate girlfriend and seeks to be perceived as a nice guy by the escort. This context provides the basis for an examination of the ways in which consumers engage in a form of consumption that has been largely overlooked by consumer researchers, and how consumers experience the blurring of boundaries between purely transactional service encounters and those that entail a deeper connection between provider and consumer. In addition to shedding light on this consumption context in the form of description, I seek to illuminate some aspects of GFE consumption that are theoretically interesting (beyond the context itself) to consumer researchers.

The purpose of this paper is to explore the experiences of male customers of escorts who provide GFE. In doing so, I offer a deeper understanding of the consumption of covert pleasure, consumer fantasies, and the ways in which consumers co-create value in the consumption experience. While different forms of prostitution exist, I am explicitly concerned with indoor prostitution, which encompasses call-girls, escort services, and massage parlor workers. The motivation for this focus is two-fold. First, there is substantially less research on indoor prostitution, in comparison with street prostitution. Second, and more important for this consumer research, "indoor [commercial sex] interactions are typically longer, multifaceted, and more reciprocal" than interactions between street prostitutes and their customers (Weitzer 2009, 220). Therefore, the experiences of male customers of indoor prostitutes are more likely to be characteristic of a romantic, intimate encounter with a partner (Malarek 2009; Sanders 2008), and therefore be of greater curiosity to consumer researchers interested in the blurring of boundaries between commercial transactions and social relationships. Further, I take a rather narrow perspective on sex work. I am explicitly concerned with consumption of prostitution services in a context where use of such services is legal, and I choose to focus on a context where sex workers are more likely to be employed of their own free will (Weitzer 2009).

Using a combination of netnography and depth interviews, I seek to understand how customers (i.e., johns) experience and reflect on GFE. Findings are organized around three central consumption themes: covert pleasure, co-creation of value, and consumer fantasies.

GFE is defined by covert pleasure – a combination of emotional and physical intimacy in a context where consumption is socially contentious and often kept secret. The emotional intimacy compo-

nent is essential to the GFE, and is closely intertwined with the requisite physical intimacy. These two hedonic and highly emotional aspects comprise the pleasure in GFE (Holbrook and Hirschman 1982), and this pleasure is of a covert nature (Frank 2002; Malarek 2009): johns are highly concerned with keeping their dirty little secrets from family and friends, in part due to the socially contentious nature of prostitution usage, and in part due to the physical risks associated with their hobby. The pleasure of GFE is a flow experience, wherein the john's total immersion in the high-risk context provides a cathartic and highly satisfying end state, which he seeks to experience again (Celsi, Rose, and Leigh 1993).

This context also provides an interesting perspective on value co-creation. Deriving value – in the form of pleasure – from the GFE requires the john to give more than money. He is compelled to give a short-term commitment of emotional and physical intimacy, and he becomes accountable for his own level of pleasure in the consumption experience. That is, he derives pleasure from ensuring that the escort has a pleasurable experience, and from adequately performing his role in the GFE such that he can form a temporary emotional connection with her. The escort and the john have roles that require and enable them to create value together (Payne, Storbacka, and Frow 2008), and the john becomes essential as a co-producer of the service (Vargo and Lusch 2004).

Immersion in the fantasy of the girlfriend is critical to the GFE. As he works to perform and co-create value from the experience, the john engages in a temporary escape from reality wherein the norms of everyday life are suspended (Goulding et al. 2009). The fantasy revolves around a romanticized notion of what a girlfriend is, not the reality (Belk and Costa 1998). The more adept the john becomes at immersing himself in the fantasy and performing his role in the GFE, the more value he derives from the experience and the better he performs in subsequent GFEs (Holbrook et al. 1984).

In this study, I seek to establish some preliminary connections between a rather novel research context and three existing streams of consumer research. These connections provide the basis for further developments in our understanding of experiential consumption, the ways that consumers engage in play and fantasy to derive pleasure, how consumers manage and experience consumption in a secretive context, and the ways that consumers can play an active role in value co-creation.

REFERENCES

Arnould, Eric J. (2006), "Service-Dominant Logic and Consumer Culture Theory: Natural Allies in an Emerging Paradigm," in *Research in Consumer Behavior: Consumer Culture Theory*, ed. Russell W. Belk and John F. Jr. Sherry, San Diego: Elsevier.

Belk, Russell W. and Janeen Arnold Costa (1998), "The Mountain Man Myth: A Contemporary Consuming Fantasy," *Journal of Consumer Research*, 25 (December), 218-40.

Bernstein, Elizabeth (2007), "Buying and Selling The "Girlfriend Experience": The Social and Subjective Contours of Market Intimacy," in *Love and Globalization: Transformations of Intimacy in the Contemporary World*, ed. Mark B. Padilla, Jennifer S. Hirsch, Miguel Munoz-Laboy, Robert E. Sember and Richard G. Parker, Nashville, TN: Vanderbilt University Press.

Celsi, Richard L., Randall L. Rose, and Thomas W. Leigh (1993), "An Exploration of High-Risk Leisure Consumption through Skydiving," *Journal of Consumer Research*, 20 (June), 1-23.

Fitchett, James A. (2004), "The Fantasies, Orders and Roles of Sadistic Consumption: Game Shows and the Service Encounter," *Consumption, Markets & Culture*, 7 (4), 285-306.

Frank, Katherine (2002), *G-Strings and Sympathy: Strip Club Regulars and Male Desire*, Durham: Duke University Press.

Goulding, Christina (2003), "Issues in Representing the Postmodern Consumer," *Qualitative Market Research - An International Journal*, 6 (3), 152-59.

Goulding, Christina, Avi Shankar, Richard Elliott, and Robin Canniford (2009), "The Marketplace Management of Illicit Pleasure," *Journal of Consumer Research*, 35 (February), 759-71.

Holbrook, Morris B., Robert W. Chestnut, Terence A. Oliva, and Eric A. Greenleaf (1984), "Play as a Consumption Experience: The Roles of Emotions, Performance, and Personality in the Enjoyment of Games," *Journal of Consumer Research*, 11 (September), 728-39.

Holbrook, Morris B. and Elizabeth C. Hirschman (1982), "The Experiential Aspects of Consumption: Consumer Fantasies, Feelings, and Fun," *Journal of Consumer Research*, 9 (September), 132-40.

Holt, Thomas J. and Kristie R. Blevins (2007), "Examining Sex Work from the Client's Perspective: Assessing Johns Using on-Line Data," *Deviant Behavior*, 28, 333-54.

Holzman, Harold R. and Sharon Pines (1990), "Buying Sex: The Phenomenology of Being a John," in *Deviant Behavior*, ed. Clifton D. Bryant, New York: Hemisphere Publishing Corp.

Kozinets, Robert V. (2010), *Netnography: Doing Ethnographic Research Online*, Thousand Oaks, CA: SAGE.

Le Bel, Jordan L. and Laurette Dube (1998), "Understanding Pleasures: Source, Experience, and Remembrances," in *Advances in Consumer Research*, Vol. 25, ed. Joseph W. Alba and J. Wesley Hutchinson, Provo, UT: Association for Consumer Research.

Lever, Janet and Deanne Dolnick (2000), "Clients and Call Girls: Seeking Sex and Intimacy," in *Sex for Sale*, ed. Ronald J. Weitzer, New York: Routledge.

Lowman, John and Chris Atchison (2009), "Men Who Buy Sex: A Survey in the Greater Vancouver Regional District," *Canadian Review of Sociology*, 43 (3), 281-96.

Macleod, Jan, Melissa Farley, Lynn Anderson, and Jacqueline Golding (2008), "Challenging Men's Demand for Prostitution in Scotland," Glasgow: Women's Support Project.

Malarek, Victor (2009), *The Johns: Sex for Sale and the Men Who Buy It*, Toronto: Key Porter Books.

McLaren, Leah (2010), "The Secret Life of a Bay Street Hooker," in *Toronto Life* Vol. December, Toronto: St. Joseph Media Corp.

Monto, Martin A. (2000), "Why Men Seek out Prostitutes," in *Sex for Sale*, ed. Ronald J. Weitzer, New York: Routledge.

--- (2004), "Female Prostitution, Customers, and Violence," *Violence Against Women*, 10 (2), 160-88.

Payne, Adrian F., Kaj Storbacka, and Pennie Frow (2008), "Managing the Co-Creation of Value," *Journal of the Academy of Marketing Science*, 36, 83-96.

Sanders, Teela (2008), "Male Sexual Scripts: Intimacy, Sexuality and Pleasure in the Purchase of Commercial Sex," *Sociology*, 42 (3), 400-17.

Sawyer, Steven, Michael E. Metz, Jeffrey D. Hinds, and Robert A Brucker, Jr. (2001), "Attitudes Towards Prostitution among Males: A "Consumers' Report"," *Current Psychology*, 20 (4), 363-76.

Vargo, Stephen L. and Robert F. Lusch (2004), "Evolving to a New Dominant Logic for Marketing," *Journal of Marketing*, 68 (January), 1-17.

--- (2008), "Service-Dominant Logic: Continuing the Evolution," *Journal of the Academy of Marketing Science*, 36, 1-10.

Vargo, Stephen L., Paul P. Maglio, and Melissa Archpru Akaka (2008), "On Value and Value Co-Creation: A Service Systems and Service Logic Perspective," *European Managment Journal*, 26, 145-52.

Weitzer, Ronald (2005), "New Directions in Research on Prostitution," *Crime, Law & Social Change*, 43, 211-35.

--- (2009), "Sociology of Sex Work," *Annual Review of Sociology*, 35, 213-34.

Weitzer, Ronald J. (2000), "Why We Need More Research on Sex Work," in *Sex for Sale*, ed. Ronald J. Weitzer, New York: Routledge.

Zelizer, Vivianna (2005), *The Purchase of Intimacy*, Princeton, NJ: Princeton University Press.

The Effect of Nostalgic Consumption on the Activation of the Interdependent Self and Prosocial Behavior

Jia (Elke) Liu, University of Groningen, The Netherlands
Dirk Smeesters, Erasmus University Rotterdam, The Netherlands

EXTENDED ABSTRACT

Coke and Pepsi have recently introduced "throwback" versions of their soft drinks. The packages and advertising are expected to increase people's preferences for the product in times of anxiety and loneliness (Loveland, Smeesters, and Mandel 2010), because the warm feelings associated with the past generate positive affect and foster social connectedness (Wildschut et al. 2006; Wildschut et al. 2010). This sentimental longing for a period of the past is called nostalgia. Despite its ubiquity, little is known about whether nostalgia can affect overt interpersonal behavior and the process by which that might happen. In the present paper, we want to further advance knowledge about nostalgia in various ways. Specifically, we examine whether nostalgia affects people's view and construal of the self, and the interpersonal behavioral consequences of this shift in self-construal. We test our idea in the context of consumption cues. Whereas past research often activated nostalgia by explicitly asking participants to reflect on a nostalgic event, we want to examine whether emotions of nostalgia can also be triggered by seemingly neutral consumption experiences (i.e., watching a video clip, eating a cookie).

Although negative emotions might be part of nostalgic recollections (e.g., disappointments, losses), nostalgia is a predominantly positive emotion (Wildschut et al. 2006), which involves a strong social component. Most nostalgic recollections contain memories of interactions with close others, such as family members, friends, and partners (Wildschut et al. 2006). The social component of nostalgia is also reflected in the connection between loneliness and feelings of nostalgia (Zhou et al. 2008), because nostalgia can be a source of social connectedness and increase people's perceived interpersonal competence (Wildschut et al. 2010). These findings suggest that nostalgia highlights the association between the self and close others. However, the question remains whether nostalgia also affects one's self-view in relation to others in general.

One of the defining elements in the perception and construal of the self is the interconnectedness with other people. An interdependent self-construal defines the self in relation to others, whereas an independent self-construal perceives the self as a bounded and independent entity with unique personal traits (Markus and Kitayama 1991). Interdependent self-construal reflects the self as socially embedded and emphasizes the connectedness to others. This seems to be consistent with nostalgic themes. Indeed, although people can differ in their chronic inclinations towards interdependent versus independent self-construals, both types of self-construal can coexist within the individual and may be activated in different contexts (Brewer and Gardner, 1996; Gardner, Gabriel, & Lee 1999). Interdependent self-construal is associated with a stronger preference for closeness with others, emotionally, psychologically, and physically (Aron, Aron, and Smollan 1992; Holland et al. 2004). This increased preference for closeness to others is not only limited to significant others, but also to unknown others. This preference for interpersonal closeness is further translated into an other-focused and prosocial orientation. Indeed, interdependent self-construal increases people's inclination to engage in volunteering and probability to donate to charity (Ashton-James et al. 2007).

In three studies, we examined whether a nostalgic experience activates an interdependent self and affects interpersonal behavior. Whereas in past studies nostalgia was activated by either a nega-tive experience (e.g., loneliness) or explicitly asking participants to reflect on a nostalgic event, in the present studies we tested whether seemingly neutral consumption cues related to the past can also activate nostalgia. Specifically, we asked participants to watch a video clip or consume a product that reminds them of the past.

In experiment 1, we asked participants to fill out the Twenty-Statement Test (Kuhn and McPartland, 1954) to assess their self-construal (Gardner et al. 1999; Mandel 2003), after they watched a video clip either from a nostalgic television show or from a non-nostalgic television show. The results indicated that participants who watched a nostalgic video (M = 6.35, SD = 2.34) reported more interdependent self-construals compared to participants who watched a non-nostalgic video (M = 3.80, SD = 2.07, F(1, 38) = 13.71, p < .01). These results provide initial support for the hypothesis that nostalgia increases the interdependence of people's self–construals.

Experiment 2 replicated and corroborated the findings of experiment 1 using a behavioral measure (physical proximity to others) and a different nostalgic manipulation. Specifically, we found that after consuming a nostalgic cookie (M = 1.54, SD = 1.02) (vs. a non-nostalgic cookie, M = 2.19, SD = 1.03, F(1, 59) = 6.77, p < .05), participants sat closer to an unknown person.

The last experiment showed that consumption of nostalgic cookies (vs. consumption of non-nostalgic cookies) rendered participants more helpful. Participants in the nostalgic condition were more likely to help an unknown other to pick up pens from the floor (71%) compared with those in the non-nostalgic condition (37%, $\chi^2(1, N = 48) = 5.15, p < .05$). This effect is mediated by an enhanced interdependent self-construal.

Our findings extend research on nostalgia and nostalgic consumption in several ways. First of all, our studies showed that a nostalgic experience can alter how the self is defined and construed. That is, nostalgia promotes an interdependent self-construal. This construal may have potential implications for cognitive, motivation, and other behavioral correlates. Second, our findings indicate that nostalgia not only makes people feel close to significant others, but also fosters a general preference for interpersonal closeness, even to unknown others. Third, whereas past research activated nostalgic feelings by manipulating negative experiences or explicitly asking people to recall a nostalgic experience (Wildschut et al. 2006, 2010; Zhou et al. 2008), we successfully manipulated nostalgic feelings by presenting participants with ordinary consumption cues related to the past (a video in Experiment 1 and a cookie in Experiments 2-3), things that people encounter frequently in daily life. This seems to suggest that any experience or object that reminds people of the past can induce nostalgia.

REFERENCES

Aron, Arthur, Elaine N. Aron, and Danny Smollan (1992), "Inclusion of Other in the Self Scale and the Structure of Interpersonal Closeness," *Journal of Personality and Social Psychology, 63*, 596–612.

Ashton–James, Claire E., Rick B. van Baaren, Tanya L. Chartrand, Jean Decety, and Johan Karremans (2007), "Mimicry and Me: The Impact of Mimicry on Self-Construal," *Social Cognition, 25*, 518-35.

Advances in Consumer Research
Volume 39, ©2011

Baron, Ruben M. and David A. Kenny (1986), "The Moderator–Mediator Variable Distinction in Social Psychological Research: Conceptual, Strategic, and Statistical Considerations," *Journal of Personality and Social Psychology*, 51 (December), 1173–82.

Brewer, Marilynn B. and Wendi Gardner (1996), "Who Is This 'We'? Levels of Collective Identity and Self Representations," Journal of Personality and Social Psychology, 71 (1), 83–93.

Elliott, Stuart (2009), "Warm and Fuzzy Makes a Comeback," *New York Times*, April 6.

Gardner, Wendi L., Shira Gabriel, and Angela Y. Lee (1999), ""I" Value Freedom, but "We" Value Relationships: Self-Construal Priming Mirrors Cultural Differences in Judgment," *Psychological Science, 10,* 321–26.

Holbrook, Morris B. (1993), "Nostalgia and Consumption Preferences: Some Emerging Patterns of Consumer Tastes," *Journal of Consumer Research*, 20 (September), 245–56.

Holbrook, Morris B. and Robert M. Schindler (2003), "Nostalgic Bonding: Exploring the Role of Nostalgia in the Consumption Experience,"*Journal of Consumer Behavior*, 3 (2), 107–27.

Holland, Rob W., U Roeder, U., Rick B. van Baaren, Aafje Brandt, and Bettine Hannover, (2004), "Don't Stand So Close to Me: Self–Construal and Interpersonal Closeness," *Psychological Science, 15*, 237–42.

Kuhn, Manford H. and Thomas S. McPartland (1954), "An Empirical Investigation of Self-Attitudes,"*American Psychological Review*, 19 (1), 68–76.

Loveland, Katherine E., Dirk Smeesters, and Naomi Mandel (2010), "Still Preoccupied with 1995: The Need to Belong and Preference for Nostalgic Products," *Journal of Consumer Research*, 37 (October), 393-407.

Macrae, C. Neil and Lucy Johnston (1998), "Help, I Need Somebody: Automatic Action and Inaction," *Social Cognition, 16*, 400–17.

Mandel, Naomi (2003), "Shifting Selves and Decision Making: The Effects of Self-Construal Priming on Consumer RiskTaking," Journal of Consumer Research, 30 (June), 30–40.

Markus, Hazel and Shinobu Kitayama (1991), "Culture and the Self: Implications for Cognition, Emotion and Motivation," Psychological Review, 98 (April), 224–53.

Preacher, Kristopher J. and Andrew F. Hayes (2004), "SPSS and SAS Procedures for Estimating Indirect Effects in Simple Mediation Models," Behavior Research Methods, Instruments, and Computers, 36 (4), 717–31.

Routledge, Clay, Jamie Arndt, Constantine Sedikides, and Tim Wildschut (2006), "A Blast from the Past: The Terror Management Function of Nostalgia," Journal of Experimental Social Psychology, 44 (January), 131–40.

van Baaren, Rick B., William W. Maddux, Tanya L. Chartrand, Cris De Bouter, and Ad van Knippenberg (2003), "It Takes Two to Mimic: Behavioral Consequences of Self–Construals," *Journal of Personality and Social Psychology. 84*, 1093–1102.

Watson, David, Clark Lee A., and Tellegen Auke (1988), "Development and Validation of Brief Measures of Positive and Negative Affect: The PANAS Scales," *Journal of Personality and Social Psychology*, 54 (6), 1063–70.

Wildschut, Tim, Constantine Sedikides, Jamie Arndt, and Clay Routledge (2006), "Nostalgia: Content: Trigger, Functions," Journal of Personality and Social Psychology, 91 (5), 975–93.

Wildschut, Tim, Constantine Sedikides, Clay Routledge, Jamie Arndt, & Filippo Cordaro, (2010), Nostalgia as a Repository of Social Connectedness: The Role of Attachment-Related Avoidance," *Journal of Personality and Social Psychology*, 98 (4), 573-86.

Zhou, Xinyue, Constantine Sedikides, Tim Wildschut, and DingGuo Gao (2008), "Counteracting Loneliness: On the Restorative Function of Nostalgia," Psychological Science, 19 (10),1023–29

On Simple Names and Complex Diseases:
Processing Fluency, not Representativeness, Influences Evaluation of Medications

Simone Dohle, ETH Zurich, Switzerland
Michael Siegrist, ETH Zurich, Switzerland

EXTENDED ABSTRACT

Today's patients play an active role in decisions about which medications to take. This fact is also reflected in the growing market of over-the-counter (OTC) drugs that are available to consumers without a prescription from a health care professional. Since OTC drugs are sold in pharmacies, groceries, or convenience stores, the assumption can be made that recommendations from physicians and other health professionals are one, but not the sole, determinant of a patient's choice of OTC drug purchases. Compared to prescription medications, the decision to buy OTC drugs will also be influenced by factors such as advertisement, recommendations from family and friends, habits, appearance, and the name of a product. In addition, the possibility exists that consumers might apply heuristics, or rules of thumb, when evaluating and choosing health products and medications.

One important heuristic that could play a major role in the evaluation of medications is the representativeness heuristic (Gilovich, Griffin, and Kahneman 2002). Representativeness predicts that consumer evaluations should be more positive for a medication with a complex name, because people believe that complex names more strongly resemble the cause of a disease than do simple names. In contrast, fluency theory suggests that complex names imply hazardousness and thus will negatively influence consumer evaluations (Reber, Schwarz, and Winkielman 2004; Schwarz 2004; Schwarz and Song 2008). Two experiments were conducted to test these conflicting predictions that can be derived from representativeness heuristic and fluency theory.

In experiment 1, participants ($N = 22$) judged ten fictitious medications: five had an easy-to-pronounce name, five had a difficult-to-pronounce name. The medications were presented in two different random orders. Judgments about the medications were made about hazardousness, effectiveness, side effects, and willingness to buy. The easy-to-pronounce medications were perceived as safer than those with the difficult-to-pronounce names. Participants also expected that medications with an easy name had fewer side effects compared with medications with a difficult name. As well, willingness to buy was higher for medications with easy-to-pronounce names than for medications with hard-to-pronounce names. Furthermore, mediation analysis showed that hazardousness fully mediated the relationship between ease of pronunciation and willingness to buy. However, we found no effect of name on the medication's perceived effectiveness; easy-to-pronounce names were perceived as similar in effectiveness to difficult-to-pronounce names. Taken together, experiment 1 revealed a clear support for the fluency hypothesis. We cannot rule out, however, that participants assumed that all of the presented medications were used for the treatment of a rather simple illness. According to this, only simple, easy-to-pronounce names would be representative of the illness, and representativeness could still account for the effect. Thus, a limitation of the first study is that we did not control for the complexity of the disease.

Experiment 2 employed a 2 (simple vs. complex name) □ 2 (simple vs. complex illness) within-subject design. In the first part of the experiment, participants ($N = 28$) were asked to imagine that they were suffering from headaches and that different medications could be considered to treat the headache. Subsequently, respondents judged four medication names on the same dependent variables as used in experiment 1 (hazardousness, effectiveness, side effects,

and willingness to buy). Two medication names had an easy-to-pronounce name; two had a difficult-to-pronounce name. In the second part, participants were asked to imagine that they were diagnosed with pancreatic cancer and that different medications could be considered to treat the cancer. Then, two easy- and two difficult-to-pronounce names were presented and participants judged the medication names on the four dependent variables. We controlled for presentation order effects. We also employed a yoked design; the order of the medication names was rotated such that for every medication name encountered by a participant in the simple-illness condition, there was a participant who had encountered the same medication name in the complex-illness condition. Again, experiment 2 provided clear support for the fluency hypothesis: Participants were more inclined to buy medications with simple, easy-to-pronounce names because they perceived these medications to be less harmful. The effect of simple vs. complex names was not qualified by type of illness, which would be expected according to the representativeness heuristic.

Our results have important implications for both health promotion and brand naming. From our research, it can be assumed that consumers believe that a medication with a complex name is more harmful and will lead to more side effects, and thus, they will be less likely to buy the product. This is of particular importance given the evident worldwide trend towards making more drugs available for self-medication. Thus, decisions at the point of purchase of OTC drugs may be influenced by factors other than recommendations from health professionals, and our results suggest that the name of the medication may be an important driver of a consumer's purchasing decisions. This effect might be particularly strong for product innovations, because these products are less likely to be influenced by habits. However, the complexity of a drug's name is not typically part of pharmaceutical brand management strategies (Robins 2006; Schuiling and Moss 2004). Managers should be aware of the fact that a drug's name may raise specific expectations. A medication with side effects and a high potential for misuse should not be branded with a simple name because this may further bolster consumers in their belief that the drug is innocuous. On the other hand, if a consistent and accurate intake of medications is important for therapeutic success, a simple medication name may support compliance with the treatment regimen.

Our research suggests that a medication name is powerful driver of consumers' evaluations and preferences. Whether it is a rather harmless headache or a life threatening disease, a complex drug name raises different expectations compared to a simple drug name. Consideration of these effects is important for assisting patients in the best possible way and for preventing wrong expectations. This, of course, also implies a huge responsibility for all brand managers and health professionals.

REFERENCES

Alter, Adam L. and Daniel M. Oppenheimer (2006), "Predicting Short-Term Stock Fluctuations by Using Processing Fluency," *Proceedings of the National Academy of Sciences of the United States of America*, 103 (24), 9369-72.

Blackwell, Barry, Saul S. Bloomfield, and C. Ralph Buncher (1972), "Demonstration to Medical Students of Placebo Responses and Non-Drug Factors," *The Lancet*, 229 (7763), 1279-82.

Bolton, Lisa E., Americus Reed II, Kevin G. Volpp, and Katrina Armstrong (2008), "How Does Drug and Supplement Marketing Affect a Healthy Lifestyle?," *Journal of Consumer Research*, 34 (5), 713-26.

Botti, Simona, Kristina Orfali, and Sheena S. Iyengar (2009), "Tragic Choices: Autonomy and Emotional Responses to Medical Decisions," *Journal of Consumer Research*, 36 (3), 337-52.

Chaiken, Shelly (1987), "The Heuristic Model of Persuasion," in *Social Influence: The Ontario Symposium*, ed. Mark P. Zanna, James M. Olson and C. Peter Herman, Hillsdale, NJ: Erlbaum, 3-39.

Food and Drug Administration (2010), "Regulation of Nonprescription Products," http://www.fda.gov/aboutfda/centersoffices/cder/ucm093452.htm.

Gilovich, Thomas, Dale W. Griffin, and Daniel Kahneman (2002), *Heuristics and Biases: The Psychology of Intuitive Judgement*, Cambridge, U.K.; New York: Cambridge University Press.

Gilovich, Thomas and Kenneth Savitsky (2002), "Like Goes with Like: The Role of Representativeness in Erroneous and Pseudo-Scientific Beliefs," in *Heuristics and Biases: The Psychology of Intuitive Judgement*, ed. Thomas Gilovich, Dale W. Griffin and Daniel Kahneman, Cambridge, U.K.; New York: Cambridge University Press, 617–24.

Judd, Charles M., David A. Kenny, and Gary H. McClelland (2001), "Estimating and Testing Mediation and Moderation in within-Subject Designs," *Psychological Methods*, 6 (2), 115-34.

Kanayama, Gen, Amanda J. Gruber, Harrison G. Pope, John J. Borowiecki, and James I. Hudson (2001), "Over-the-Counter Drug Use in Gymnasiums: An Underrecognized Substance Abuse Problem?," *Psychotherapy and Psychosomatics*, 70 (3), 137-40.

Levine, Deborah A. (2007), "'Pharming': The Abuse of Prescription and over-the-Counter Drugs in Teens," *Current opinion in pediatrics* (19), 270–74.

Pratkanis, Anthony R. (1995), "How to Sell a Pseudoscience," *Skeptical Inquirer*, 19, 19–25.

Reber, Ralf, Norbert Schwarz, and Piotr Winkielman (2004), "Processing Fluency and Aesthetic Pleasure: Is Beauty in the Perceiver's Processing Experience?," *Personality and Social Psychology Review*, 8 (4), 364-82.

Robins, Rebecca (2006), "Brand Matters: The Lingua Franca of Pharmaceutical Brand Names," in *Pharmaceutical Branding Strategies: Thought Leader Perspectives on Brand Building*, ed. Steven Seget: Business Insights.

Schuiling, Isabelle and Giles Moss (2004), "How Different Are Branding Strategies in the Pharmaceutical Industry and the Fast-Moving Consumer Goods Sector?," *Brand Managment*, 11 (5), 366–80.

Schwarz, Norbert (2004), "Metacognitive Experiences in Consumer Judgment and Decision Making," *Journal of Consumer Psychology*, 14 (4), 332-48.

Schwarz, Norbert and Hyunjin Song (2008), "When Thinking Is Difficult: Metacognitive Experiences as Information," in *The Social Psychology of Consumer Behavior*, ed. Michaela Wänke, New York: Psychology Press.

Shapiro, Arthur K. (1960), "A Contribution to a History of the Placebo Effect," *Behavioural Science*, 109-135 (5), 109-35.

Shimp, Terence A. and Robert F. Dyer (1979), "Pain-Pill-Pleasure Model and Illicit Drug Consumption," *Journal of Consumer Research*, 6 (1), 36-46.

Shiv, Baba, Ziv Carmon, and Dan Ariely (2005), "Placebo Effects of Marketing Actions: Consumers May Get What They Pay For," *Journal of Marketing Research*, 42 (4), 383-93.

Song, Hyunjin and Norbert Schwarz (2009), "If It's Difficult to Pronounce, It Must Be Risky," *Psychological Science*, 20 (2), 135-38.

Thompson, W. Grant (2000), "Placebos: A Review of the Placebo Response," *American Journal of Gastroenterology*, 95 (7), 1637-43.

Arousal Congruency and Consumer Choice

Fabrizio Di Muro, University of Winnipeg, Canada
Kyle B. Murray, University of Alberta, Canada

EXTENDED ABSTRACT

In this paper we examine how consumers' choices are affected by the interplay between their level of arousal and the valence of their current affective state We are particularly interested in the extent to which the arousal dimension of a consumer's mood affects the choices that s/he will make. We predict that such preferences will be consistent with theories of mood regulation (Larsen 2000; Salovey, Hsee, & Mayer 2001; Thayer, Newman and McClain 1994) – that is, the choices that consumers make will reflect a desire to maintain positive moods and mitigate negative moods. Extending the current literature, we propose that in addition to regulating the valence of their moods – i.e., the extent to which their affective state is positive or negative – consumers will also make choices that allow them to manage their level of arousal. We define arousal as the *subjective experience* of energy mobilization, which can be conceptualized as an affective dimension ranging from sleepy to frantic excitement (Mehrabian and Russell 1974). This is in contrast to objective or physiological arousal, which is defined as the release of energy collected in the tissues (Duffy 1962; Cacioppo, Bernston and Crites 1996) and has been measured using pulse rate (Pham 1996) and systolic blood pressure (Sanbonmatsu and Kardes 1988).

We predict that consumers in a positive mood will tend to prefer products that are *congruent* with both the level of arousal and the valence of their current affective state. For example, people who are feeling relaxed (i.e., a pleasant low-arousal mood) will tend to choose relaxing products and experiences (e.g., lying on the beach or drinking tea); while those who are feeling excited (i.e., a pleasant high-arousal mood) will tend to choose exciting products and experiences (e.g., going surfing or consuming an energy drink). In contrast, we predict that consumers in a negative mood will tend to prefer products that are *incongruent* with both the level of arousal and the valence of their current affective state. For example, people who are depressed (i.e., an unpleasant low-arousal mood) will tend to choose exciting products and experiences (e.g., going surfing or consuming an energy drink); while those who are feeling frustrated (i.e., an unpleasant high-arousal mood) will tend to choose relaxing products and experiences (lying on the beach or drinking tea).

Similar to previous research (Pham 1998; Pham, Cohen, Pracejus & Hughes 2001; Schwarz and Clore 1988), we propose that consumers use the affect they are experiencing as information about their likes and dislikes. However, we propose that it is not only a consumer's current mood that provides preference information; but that affect produced in response to evaluating the congruency between one's current mood and the products or experiences being considered for consumption also influences consumer preferences. For example, imagine a relaxed consumer standing in front of a convenience store cooler, making the decision to purchase either an ice tea or an energy drink. We predict that while considering these two products, she will experience positive affect toward the ice tea (i.e., a product associated with relaxation), which is congruent with her current state of relaxation, but negative affect toward the energy drink (i.e., a product associated with excitement) that is incongruent with her current mood. We contend that it is this product specific affect (PSA) that will inform preferences rather than the consumer's general mood state. More formally, we propose a moderated mediation model (see figure 2 in the paper); which predicts that the interactive effect of arousal and valence on consumer choice is mediated by PSA.

Overall, this paper contributes to the extant literature by demonstrating that consumers make choices that are driven by a desire to regulate *both* the arousal and the valence of their affective states. Moreover, we detail the psychological mechanism through which the interaction of these two dimensions of mood affect consumer choice. In doing so, this research reveals a systematic link between variations in consumers' moods and preferences that can account for dramatic differences in choice shares.

In this paper, we find that consumers' preferences for products and experiences vary with both the level of arousal and the valence of their current mood in a manner that is consistent with mood regulation (Larsen 2000; Salovey, Hsee, & Mayer 2001; Thayer, Newman and McClain 1994). Although prior research has documented similar effects with valence alone, our results demonstrate that arousal also plays a critical role. In addition, as predicted, the choices that consumers make are driven by the product-specific affect they experience, which varies systematically as a function of both the valence *and* arousal dimensions of their current mood. The four experiments reported in this paper provide strong evidence in support of the moderated mediation model of the effect of mood on consumer choice.

The first study used color to manipulate the level of arousal consumers were feeling and examined the impact of arousal on consumer choice when mood valence was positive. The results revealed that consumers made decisions that were congruent with their level of arousal. The second study replicated these findings with a different choice set, and extended the results of the first study by illustrating that PSA mediates the relationship between arousal and consumer choice. To test the full moderated mediation model (figure 2), studies 3a and 3b used scent and sound to manipulate both arousal and valence. These two studies found strong support for the model – that is, the effect of the interaction between level of arousal and mood valence on consumer choice was mediated by PSA.

REFERENCES

Baron, R.M. and D.M. Kenny (1986), "The Moderator-Mediator Variable Distinction in Social Psychological Research: Conceptual, Strategic, and Statistical Considerations," *Journal of Personality and Social Psychology*, 51(6), 1173 – 82.

Gorn, G., Chattopadhyay, A., Sengupta, J. and S. Tripathi (2004), "Waiting for the Web: How Color Affects Time Perception", *Journal of Marketing Research,* (May) 215 – 25.

Husain, G., Thompson, W.F. and E.G. Schellenberg (2002). "Effects of Music Tempo and Mode on Arousal, Mood, and Spatial Abilities," *Music Perception*, 20(2), 151 – 171.

Isen, A (1987), Positive Affect, Cognitive Processes and Social Behavior. In: Berkowitz, L., ed, Advances in Experimental Psychology. Academic Press, NY, 203 – 51.

Larsen, R. (2000), "Toward a Science of Mood Regulation," *Psychological Inquiry*, 11(3), 129 – 41.

Manucia, G., Baumann, D., and Cialdini, R. (1984), "Mood Influence on Helping: Direct Effects of Side Effects?" *Journal of Personality and Social Psychology*, 46, 357 – 64.

Mehrabian A. and J. Russell (1974), *An Approach to Environmental Psychology*, Cambridge, MA: MIT Press.

Pham (1998), "Representativeness, Relevance, and the Use of Feelings in Decision Making," *Journal of Consumer Research*, 25 (September), 144 – 159.

Preacher, K. D. Rucker and A. Hayes (2007), "Adressing Moderated Mediation Hypotheses," *Mulitvariate Behavioral Research* 42 (June) 185 – 227.

Russell, J.A. (1980), "A Circumplex Model of Affect," *Journal of Personality and Social Pscyhology*, 36, 1152 – 1168.

Schwarz, N. and Clore, G.L. (1983), "Mood, Misattribution, and Judgments of Well-Being," *Journal of Personality and Social Psychology*, 45, 513 – 523.

Thayer, R.E., Newman, J.R., and T. M. McClain (1994), "Self-regulation fo mood: Strategies for changing a bad mood, raising energy and reducing tension," *Journal of Personality and Social Psychology,* 67, 910 – 925.

Salting the Sidewalk In Case the Snowstorm Hits:
Consumption as a Buffer against the Potential for Threat

Soo Kim, Kellogg School of Management, USA
Derek Rucker, Northwestern University, USA

EXTENDED ABSTRACT

Consumers are known to engage in compensatory consumption—the act of purchasing or physically consuming goods to address a threat to the self (Rucker and Galinsky forthcoming). However, we, as consumers, do not seem to react solely to the negativity of the threat after it has been experienced. We are proactive and take actions to mitigate the possibility of potential threat. Based on this idea, the present work focuses on the idea of consumption in response to anticipated threat and its implications for understanding how consumers respond to various forms of threat.

Building on past research that suggests the possibility that people can buffer the self prior to receiving a threat through self-affirmations (e.g., Dalton 2008; Steele, Spencer, and Lynch 1993), we propose that consumers use consumption to buffer themselves against anticipated threat. More importantly, although anticipated and experienced threat can produce compensatory consumption, we propose that anticipated threat and experienced threat are psychologically distinct constructs with differential consequences.

Building on Mandel and Smeesters' (2008) account that threatened consumers increase general consumption because it provides them with the opportunity to be distracted from their self-awareness, we propose that, when consuming products in the heat of threat, consumers will be more likely to increase their overall consumption of both threat-related and threat-unrelated products. However, when consumers are consuming in response to the anticipation of threat the need to distract themselves from the threat may not be as strong as when they are in the heat of threat, as there is no actual experience of threat present. For these consumers, the best consumption strategy may be to consume only products that are presumed to provide protection specifically against the anticipated threat.

To test our hypotheses, we present a pretest and two experiments designed to test whether anticipated threat leads consumers to consume in a manner that will buffer themselves against potential threat and to examine how consumption in response to anticipated threat differs from consumption in response to experienced threat.

Pretest

A pretest was conducted to distinguish anticipated threat from experienced threat. Participants in both the anticipated threat condition and the control condition were asked to first read a brief introduction to a test of their "Perceptual Intelligence" and then were asked on the next screen to indicate either how they currently felt (current feeling of threat) or how scoring low on the test would make them feel (anticipated feeling of threat) on a 7-point scale ranging from "Not Threatened" to "Threatened." Participants in an experienced threat condition reported how much threat they experienced after receiving a bad result from the "Perceptual Intelligence" test. As predicted, the results indicated that consumers do not experience actual threat when they are merely introduced to a potentially threatening test of intelligence. However, consumers seemed to anticipate the potential of threat from the possibility of receiving a disappointing result.

Experiment 1

Experiment 1 tested whether consumers use threat-specific products to buffer themselves against a potential threat to their intelligence, despite no experienced threat.

Participants in the anticipated threat condition were first introduced to a "Virtual Perception Game" that was supposedly designed to assess their "Perceptual Intelligence." However, before they actually played the game or received results they were asked to complete a second, unrelated experiment while the computer program loaded the "Virtual Perception Game." In this "second" experiment, participants' task was to evaluate the cover of a recent music album and they were asked to indicate how long they would like to listen to the music before evaluating the album cover. Participants were randomly presented either threat-related music (i.e., "Music and the Mind") or threat-unrelated music ("Music and Relaxation") and asked how long they would like to listen to it in minutes. Participants in the experienced threat condition, on the other hand, first completed the "Virtual Perception Game" and received disappointing feedback designed to elicit threat. Then they moved on to the "second" study, in which they either indicated how long they would like to listen to the threat-related music or the threat-unrelated music.

As predicted, our findings from the current study and the pretest show that consumers strategically use products to buffer themselves from anticipated threat. Furthermore, we demonstrate that when consumers are engaging in hypothetical consumption (i.e., desired listening time), they strategically value threat-related products more than threat-unrelated products both when actually experiencing threat or merely in the anticipation of threat.

Experiment 2

Experiment 2 investigated how consumers' consumption in response to anticipated threat and experienced threat differ. As noted, for anticipated threat, consumers should only show greater consumption of products that may buffer them specifically against the anticipated threat. However, we predicted that when experiencing actual threat, given an opportunity to distract themselves through actual consumption, consumers would increase consumption more generally as a means to distract themselves.

The overall procedure was similar to Experiment 1. However, unlike Experiment 1 we measured how long participants actually listened to an unfamiliar piece of music that was framed as either threat-related (i.e., enhancing cognitive abilities) or threat-unrelated (i.e., relaxing).

As predicted, we found that when provided with the opportunity to actually consume the product (e.g., actually listen to music), consumers consuming in response to anticipated threat only consumed more (i.e., listened to the music longer) when the product was framed as threat-related, whereas consumers experiencing threat consumed both threat-related and threat-unrelated products more.

Our findings indicate that consumers consume products not only to cope with the experience of threat but that they also strategically consume threat-specific products to protect themselves against anticipated threat. In addition, we find that anticipated threat consumption and experienced threat consumption differ in an important aspect: When consumers consume in response to anticipated threat they only increase consumption of threat-related products, as a buffering strategy. However, once they experience threat they consume both threat-related and threat-unrelated products. It seems that we, as consumers, not only salt the sidewalk in anticipation of the snowstorm but also know exactly what kind of salt to use, at least until the snowstorm hits.

REFERENCES

Cryder, C. E., J. S. Lerner, J. J. Gross, and R. E. Dahl (2008), "Misery Is Not Miserly: Sad and Self-Focused Individuals Spend More," *Psychological Science*, 19 (Jun), 525-30.

Dalton, Amy N. (2008). "Look on the Bright Side: Self-Expressive Consumption and Consumer Self-Worth," unpublished dissertation, Department of Business Administration, Duke University, Durham, NC 90120.

Gao, Leilei, S. Christian Wheeler, and Baba Shiv (2009), "The "Shaken Self": Product Choices as a Means of Restoring Self-View Confidence," *Journal of Consumer Research*, 36 (Jun), 29-38.

Heine, S. J., T. Proulx, and K. D. Vohs (2006), "The Meaning Maintenance Model: On the Coherence of Social Motivations," *Personality and Social Psychology Review*, 10, 88-110.

Levav, Jonathan and Rui Zhu (2009), "Seeking Freedom through Variety," *Journal of Consumer Research*, 36, 600-10.

Loewenstein, G. (1996), "Out of Control: Visceral Influences on Behavior," *Organizational Behavior and Human Decision Processes*, 65 (Mar), 272-92.

Mandel, Naomi and Dirk Smeesters (2008), "The Sweet Escape: Effects of Mortality Salience on Consumption Quantities for High- and Low-Self-Esteem Consumers," *Journal of Consumer Research*, 35, 309-23.

Mead, Nicole L., Roy F. Baumeister, Tyler F. Stillman, Catherine D. Rawn, and Kathleen D. Vohs (2011), "Social Exclusion Causes People to Spend and Consume Strategically in the Service of Affiliation," *Journal of Consumer Research*, 37, 902-19.

Rucker, Derek D. and Adam D. Galinsky (2008), "Desire to Acquire: Powerlessness and Compensatory Consumption," *Journal of Consumer Research*, 35 (Aug), 257-67.

Rucker, Derek D. and Adam D. Galinsky (forthcoming), "Compensatory Consumption," In Russell Belk and Ayalla Ruvio (Editors), *Identity and Consumption,* Routledge.

Steele, C. M. and T. J. Liu (1983), "Dissonance Processes as Self-Affirmation," *Journal of Personality and Social Psychology*, 45, 5-19.

Steele, C. M., S. J. Spencer, and M. Lynch (1993), "Self-Image Resilience and Dissonance - the Role of Affirmational Resources," *Journal of Personality and Social Psychology*, 64 (Jun), 885-96.

Tice, D. M., E. Bratslavsky, and R. F. Baumeister (2001), "Emotional Distress Regulation Takes Precedence over Impulse Control: If You Feel Bad, Do It!," *Journal of Personality and Social Psychology*, 80 (Jan), 53-67.

Increasing Attention at What Cost?
Consumer Reactions to Context Sensitive Advertising

Claudiu Dimofte, San Diego State University, USA
Ronald Goodstein, Georgetown University, USA
Ajay Kalra, Rice University, USA

EXTENDED ABSTRACT

This research investigates consumers' reactions to "context sensitive advertising," a strategy used by advertisers across multiple channels to increase consumer attention and improve consumer attitudes. Although advertisers believe in the efficacy of context sensitive ads, there is little empirical evidence to support their beliefs. Furthermore, the academic literature is ambivalent about the role of ad-context congruity on memory and persuasion. We propose and support that while context sensitive advertising may indeed enhance consumers' ad processing, it may do so at the risk of eliciting negative attitudinal reactions. Specifically, we establish a positive main effect of context sensitivity on attention and recall. Attitudes and persuasion, however, are dependent upon how well the context matches the product being advertised. Two competing theoretical accounts for these reactions are tested and the effects are shown to be due to consumers' superior motivation to process context sensitive advertisements as opposed to an ease of processing rationale.

Enhancing consumers' levels of ad processing is vital for companies that aim to make enduring impressions on their target customers. To do so, firms often employ tactics that encourage consumers to process a stimulus in greater detail than they might otherwise. These tactics commonly fall under the rubric of "attention-getting devices" (e.g., Broniarczyk and Gershoff 2003; Gardner 1983). One such tactic that consumers are seeing more often in advertising settings is a practice referred to as "contextual advertising" (e.g., Ciaramita, Murdock, and Plachouras 2008) or "context-sensitive advertising" (e.g., Hristova and O'Hare 2001; hereafter CSA). In general, CSA refers to the practice of placing ads within a contextual environment in which the text and images (i.e., theme) of both tend to be mutually relevant (e.g., Ciaramita et al. 2008). For instance, since 1989 Anheuser Busch has used its "Bud Bowl" series of ads during the NFL season. These TV ads are shown during professional football games and feature animated beer cans playing a championship game where either Bud or Bud Light wins in a dramatic fashion. More recently, news reports on the just completed electoral season were peppered with political campaign-style ads for Toyota Corolla, which supposedly "approved this message." The premise behind CSA is that consumers are more likely to pay attention to the ad if its thematic focus matches the context in which it appears (Lee and Mason 1999).

CSA is increasingly being utilized across a variety media channels including television, print, and the Internet (e.g., Bronner and Neijens 2006; Kenny and Marshall 2000). For example, part of Google's phenomenal success in banner advertising placement (based on a product called AdSense that competes with Yahoo!'s Content Match and Quigo's AdSonar) has been attributed to including context sensitive algorithms in its ad placement system (e.g., Feng, Bhargava, and Pennock 2007), an implicit acknowledgment that even in the web domain control over the consumer-marketer dyad rests with the former and innovative ways to change that are highly valued. Further, several communications companies that create syndicated news stories also offer to place tailored advertisements from firms selling products related to the story. In one illustrative case, a story about dentistry was distributed to TV stations along with an ad from Procter & Gamble for their Crest toothpaste, to be placed immediately after news stations ran that story (Saunders 2001). In Japan, one of the four major broadcasting networks has been recently testing "context-linked ads" that are placed in the middle of various TV dramas and feature actors and storylines straight out of those shows, making it difficult for consumers to separate promotion from entertainment (Chozick 2006). CSA thus refers to two distinct strategies. The first is the well known approach of matching the product category with the editorial context (e.g., the toothpaste ad with the dentistry story). The second is adjusting the ad theme to match the editorial context (e.g., the Budweiser ad featuring animated, football-playing beer cans). As the application of CSA across media outlets continues to expand (e.g., Lee and Jun 2007), consumers' reactions to these tactics seems warranted. .

Our research predicts consumers' cognitive and attitudinal reactions to CSA based on extant theories in the field. We propose that while CSA may enhance consumers' processing, its effect on their attitudes may not always favor the advertised brand. Specifically, we hypothesize that while a high degree of congruity between the ad's theme and its context may indeed increase attention, consumers' attitudes will depend upon the match between the ad's theme and the product category being advertised. This second aspect of congruity has largely been overlooked by those investigating the effects of CSA.

From a more general perspective, the study of context effects in advertising is not new to consumer researchers. For instance, prior research has examined how consumers' involvement with and liking of an ad's context affects message effectiveness (e.g., Dahlén 2005; Pavelchak, Antil, and Munch 1988; Shapiro, MacInnis, and Park 2002) and how context-induced moods affect processing (e.g., Aylesworth and MacKenzie 1998). Context effects have also been studied in terms of how fit between context and advertising might influence message effectiveness (e.g., Dahlén et al. 2008; Russell, Norman, and Heckler 2004). Russell et al. (2004), for example, explore the idea of connectedness (in a television realm) in terms of relatedness between program plot and product placements within that program. Similarly, Moorman, Neijens, and Smit (2002) investigate the effects of congruity between the product advertised and its context. More recent research investigates how one commercial in a larger pod of ads might serve as the context for subsequent ads in that set (Lee and Labroo 2004). Our re-inquiry extends prior research by investigating two levels of fit that remain simultaneously unexplored by analyzing the combined effects of congruity between an advertisement's theme and its media context on the one hand and between the ad's theme and the product being advertised on the other. Across multiple studies, we find that while consumers may pay more attention to CSA, their resulting attitudes depend on the fit between the context and the product being advertised.

Exploring Counterfeit Purchase Behavior – Towards a Unified Conceptual Framework

Piyush Sharma, The Hong Kong Polytechnic University, Hong Kong
Ricky Y. K. Chan, The Hong Kong Polytechnic University, Hong Kong

EXTENDED ABSTRACT

Introduction

Prior research on counterfeit purchase behavior shows mixed findings, possibly because it focuses on the 'direct' and 'independent' effects of attitudes, ethical judgments, and subjective norms, and ignores the role of important constructs such as counterfeit proneness and product evaluations. This paper addresses these gaps with a unified conceptual framework with counterfeit proneness as a focal construct and product evaluation as a key mediator of the process of counterfeit purchase behavior. Using a study with 610 ethnic Chinese shoppers in Hong Kong across four product categories it shows that counterfeit proneness influences the attitudes, ethical judgments, and subjective norms about buying a counterfeit product, which in turn affect the evaluation of a counterfeit product and purchase intentions.

Conceptual Framework

In this paper, we combine the economical, ethical, and socio-psychological perspectives of counterfeit purchase behavior to put forth many hypotheses. First, we propose that counterfeit proneness has a positive effect on the attitude, subjective norms, and ethical judgments about buying a counterfeit product. Next, we posit that the subjective norms and ethical judgments have a positive effect on the attitude towards buying that counterfeit product. Next, we argue that the attitude, subjective norms, and ethical judgments about buying a counterfeit product have a positive effect on the evaluation of that counterfeit product. Finally, we suggest that the evaluation of a counterfeit product has a positive effect on the purchase intentions towards it.

Methodology

We used a field-survey design with a structured questionnaire to collect data from 610 ethnic Chinese shoppers in Hong Kong to test all our hypotheses, across four product categories (luxury watches, anti-virus software, movie DVD, and backpack). We chose these four products based on their varying scores on involvement, consumption context, and purchase motivation. For example, luxury watches scored high on involvement level, public consumption, and hedonic purchase motivation; anti-virus software high on involvement level, private consumption, and utilitarian purchase motivation; movie DVD low on involvement level, and high on private consumption and hedonic purchase motivation; and finally backpack low on involvement level, and high on public consumption and utilitarian purchase motivation.

Data Analysis and Results

We first tested the measurement model using confirmatory factor analysis on all the scales with AMOS 6.0 (Anderson and Gerbing 1988; Byrne 2004), and found a good fit ($\chi2$ = 447.11, p < .001; df = 175, $\chi2$/df = 2.55; CFI = .96, RMSEA = .036, and SRMR = .045). All the fit parameters are better than the cut-off values (RMSEA < .06, SRMR < .08, CFI > .95) advised by Hu and Bentler (1999) and (1 < $\chi2$/df < 3) proposed by Wheaton et al. (1977). The construct reliabilities (.84 to .93) as well as the average variance extracted (AVE) of all the constructs (.54 to .66) are quite high, hence all the constructs appear to be reliable (Bagozzi and Yi 1988). All the parameter estimates (λ) are significantly different from zero at the 5% level, showing convergent validity; and none of the confidence intervals of the correlation coefficients for each pair of scales includes 1.0, which shows discriminant validity (Anderson and Gerbing 1988).

Next, we tested the overall structural model using the pooled data from all the four product categories. The model provided a good fit to the data ($\chi2$ = 495.75, p < .001, df = 181, $\chi2$/df = 2.74; CFI = .95, RMSEA = .044, SRMR = .059). All the path coefficients were significant and in the expected directions. However, we only found evidence for partial mediation by product evaluation in the influence of subjective norms and attitude, and fully mediation in the influence of ethical judgments on purchase intentions. We also found significant differences in the strength of all the hypothesized relationships between past users and non-users of counterfeit products, as well as across the four product categories.

Discussion

Our findings have several important conceptual and managerial implications. First, we introduce a new conceptual framework that integrates diverse theoretical perspectives to explain mixed and sometimes divergent findings reported in prior research. Our findings show that it is not just individual attitudes, subjective norms, or ethical beliefs, but a combination of all these factors that influences consumers' evaluation and purchase intentions for counterfeit products. We even validate these findings across four different product categories.

Our findings support prior research with ethnic Chinese consumers that show favorable attitudes towards counterfeit products despite strong socio-normative influences due to the collectivistic nature of Chinese societies (Lee and Workman 2009; Wan et al. 2009). Hence, companies planning to market genuine brands to ethnic Chinese consumers should look the ethical or socio-normative aspects of counterfeit purchase in their communication, because these may have minimal impact on their attitudes towards counterfeit products.

Limitations and Future Research

Hong Kong, the setting for this research, is well known for widespread availability and frequent usage of counterfeit goods. Hence, future research in other parts of the world would be useful in order to compare our findings in those markets. We also restricted our sample to ethnic Chinese consumers to ensure high internal validity by controlling the influence of cultural factors, hence it would be useful to explore the influence of culture on counterfeit purchase behavior by including cultural factors such as individualism, uncertainty avoidance etc. Finally, future research may include other variables such as innovativeness, risk taking, and change seeking, to explore their influence on counterfeit purchase behavior and consumption.

Socializing Through Cultural Consumption

Babak Taheri, University of Strathclyde Business School, UK
Aliakbar Jafari, University of Strathclyde Business School, UK

EXTENDED ABSTRACT

Museums are "social constructs, and powerful ones at that, and they need to assume their place in the mainstream of contemporary life, not sit eccentrically on the margins" (Fleming 2005, 1). Throughout history, societies have endeavored to protect their museums as evidence of their dynamism. Yet, despite their crucial role in (re)generation of cultures and civilizations, currently museums are not shielded against the storms of the recent global economic recession. In the UK, for example, in response to state budget cuts, publicly-funded museums (which have traditionally been free to enter) have been reviewing their policies to save money. Under unprecedented pressure, museums are urged to prove their societal worth to avoid possible risks of closure, severe staff redundancy, or the introduction of entrance fees. Although such pressures had already been highlighted by a number of arts enthusiasts (e.g., Fleming, 2005; Hooper-Greenhill 2007; Caru and Cova 2005), the impacts of the current economic downturn seem to go beyond simply economic rehabilitation through budget cuts, and imply significant socio-cultural considerations.

The reactive strategic plans (e.g., introducing entrance fees in order to self-fund museums) signal important policy implications for cultural (re)production and consumption in society. Amongst many critics of the British government's hasty spending review, Mark Serwotka – General Secretary of the British Public and Commercial Services Union – has expressed serious concerns over the impact of budget cuts on society: "It is essential [that] our cultural life is protected and the universal access provided by free admission is maintained to prevent the arts returning to being a privilege only the wealthy can enjoy" (Jury, 2010). Serwotka's statement reminds us of Bourdieu's (1984) analysis of social stratification through consumption of culture that marks distinct social boundaries. If broadly established, these polarizing social distinctions may eventually widen the gap between the less-privileged strata of society and those who have the luxury of re-energizing themselves by 'high' culture.

Drawing upon the importance of museums to contemporary life, in this paper we address the key theme of the conference and seek to communicate our findings primarily with cultural authorities and also with our fellow scholars. Our study, we believe, can remind cultural authorities of the multifaceted role of museums in human society. Also, we modestly believe that our findings refine theory. We use Falk and Dierking's (1997) three salient contexts affecting visitors' experiences of museums (physical, personal, and social) as our departure point in the literature review. We echo the recent calls (Falk and Dierking 1997, 2000; Hein 1998; Hooper-Greenhill 2007; Matarasso 1997; vom Lehn 2006; vom Lehn and Heath 2005; vom Lehn et al. 2001, 2007) for further research into the role of social context in museum visitors' experience. We argue that the social context has not received sufficient attention is the studies of cultural consumers' visiting experience. Addressing this research gap, we then embark to study the social context in more depth. Yet, whilst prior research (Diamond 1986; Blud 1990a and b; Hilke and Balling 1985; vom Lehn et al. 2007) has analyzed the role of social context mainly in terms of fostering learning through social interaction in the physical context of the museum, we demonstrates that people derive high levels of satisfaction from socializing in the museum and extend the social context to the world beyond the museum walls.

Our analysis of interpretive in-depth interviews with seventeen female and male individuals (aged between 25 and 58, educated and from middle-class backgrounds) in Glasgow (the UK) reveals that our informants' socializing experience is confined in neither the learning process (i.e., finding about the contents of the museum) nor the context of the visited sites. Upon their visits to cultural sites (e.g., museums and art galleries), these individuals socialize with others (e.g., family members, friends, and strangers) around the contents of the museum. Our informants draw upon different types of catalysts (e.g., nostalgic feelings, photography, exhibits, etc.) to establish new or strengthen their existing human relations in the social context of the cultural site. Yet, for them, this is not the end of the story. Our findings further reveal that these people not only socialize with others during their visits to the museum, but also continue to socialize with others outside of the museum context. They extend the social context of the museum to the outside world beyond the physical environment of the museum. They take their experience with them to create more conversations and social ties outside the museum. In some cases their individual forms of cultural consumption turn into 'collective forms of consumption' (Cova 1997) through socializing with others. All these instances demonstrate the great potential of museums as 'cultural institutions' in whose context people "can create, share, and connect with each other around content" (Simon 2010, ii).

Based on our findings, therefore, we emphasize the societal dimension of museums as socio-cultural institutions that foster social bonds among different members of contemporary society. In our study, we do not propose that these social ties exclusively rely on conversations around the museums' contents; such socializing practices may occur in other contexts such as Disneyland, theme parks, and theatres and music concerts as well. Yet, we emphasize that in everyday life situations, museums are dynamically present in people's socio-cultural spheres. They constitute an important part of people's socializing agendas. Therefore, we invite our fellow scholars to take this subject further by investigating how these social contexts operate for different people with varying socio-cultural and economic backgrounds. Also, it would be interesting to conduct longitudinal research in order to understand how enduring the museum-embedded social ties are and if they pave the way for the emergence of new social ties and networks. We also sincerely invite policymakers and cultural authorities to rethink their policies and protect museums as significant social contexts that glue human beings together in the age of fragmentation of human relations.

REFERENCES

Alderson, Arthur, Azamat Junisbai and Isaac Heacock (2007), "Social status and cultural consumption in the United States", *Poetics*, 35 (2/3), 191-212.

Baloglu, Seyhmus (2001), "Image Variations of Turkey by Familiarity Index: Informational and Experiential Dimensions", Tourism Management, 22 (2), 127-33.

Black, Graham (2009), *The Engaging Museum: Developing Museums for Visitor Involvement*, London: Routledge.

Blud, Linda M. (1990a), "Social Interaction and Learning Among Family Groups Visiting a Museum", *Museum Management and Curatorship*, 9 (1), 43-51.

--- (1990b) "Sons and Daughters: Observations on the Way Families Interact during a Museum Visit", *Museum Management and Curatorship*, 9 (3), 257-264.

Bourdieu, Pierre (1984), *Distinction: A Social Critique of the Judgment of Taste*. Cambridge, MA: Harvard University Press.

Caru, Antonella and Bernard Cova (2005), "The Impact of Service Elements on the Artistic Experience: The Case of Classical Music Concerts", *International Journal of Arts Management*, 7 (2), 39-54.

Cova, Bernard (1997), "Community and consumption: towards a definition of the linking value of products or services", *European Journal of Marketing*, 31(3/4), 297-316.

Doering, Zahava (1999), "Strangers, guests or clients? Visitor experiences in museums", *Curator*, 42 (2), 74-87.

Edmonds, Ernest, Lizzie Muller and Matthew Connell (2006), "On Creative Engagement", *Visual Communication*, 5(3), 307-322.

Falk, John H. and Lynn D. Dierking (1997), *The Museum Experience*. Washington D.C.: Whalesback.

Fienberg, Joyce and Gaea Leinhardt (2002), "Looking through the Glass: Reflections of Identity in Conversations at a History Museum", in *Learning Conversations in Museums* ed. G. Leinhardt, K. Crowley and K. Knutson: Mahwah: Lawrence Erlbaum Associates, 167-211.

Fleming, David (2005) Managing change in museums. The museum and change international conference, 8-10 November, Prague, Czech Republic.

Glaser, Barney G. and Strauss, Anselm L. (1967), *The Discovery of Grounded Theory: Strategies for Qualitative Research*, London: Weidenfeld and Nikolson.

Goulding, Christina (1999), "Heritage, nostalgia, and the 'grey' consumer", *Journal of Marketing Practice: Applied Marketing Science*, 5 (6/7/8), 177-199.

--- (2000), "The Museum Environment and the Visitor Experience," *European Journal of Marketing*, 34(3/4), 261-278.

--- (2001), "Romancing the past: Heritage visiting and the nostalgic consumer", *Psychology & Marketing*, 18 (6), 565-92.

Higgins, E. Tory and Abigail Scholer (2009), "Engaging the consumer: The science and art of the value creation process", *Journal of Consumer Psychology*, 19 (2), 100-14.

Hilke, D.D. & Balling, J. (1985), *The Family as a Learning System: An Observational Study of Families in Museums*, Washington DC: Smithsonian Institution Press.

Hirschman, Elizabeth C. (1986). Humanistic inquiry in marketing research: Philosophy, method, and criteria. *Journal of Marketing Research*, 23, 237-249.

--- (1994) Consumers and Their Animal Companions. *Journal of Consumer Research*, 20 (4), pp. 616-32.

Hollway, Wendy and Tony Jefferson (1997) Eliciting Narrative Through the In-Depth Interview. *Qualitative Inquiry* 3 (1): 53-70.

Holt, Douglas B. (1998), "Does Cultural Capital Structure American Consumption?," *Journal of Consumer Research*, 23(June), 1-25.

Hooper-Greenhill, Eilean (2007), *Museums and Education: Purpose, Pedagogy, Performance (Museum Meanings)*, UK: Routledge.

Jury, Louise (2010), British Museum reduces opening hours as budget cuts begin to bite. Available from: http://www.thisislondon.co.uk/standard/article-23883635-british-museum-reduces-opening-hours-as-budget-cuts-begin-to-bite.do

Leinhardt, Gaea and Mike Gregg (2002), "Burning Buses, Burning Crosses: Student Teachers See Civil Rights," in *Learning Conversations in Museums*, ed. G. Leinhardt, K. Crowley and K. Knutson: Mahwah: Lawrence Erlbaum Associates, 139-66.

Malone, Thomas W. (1981), "Toward a Theory of Intrinsically Motivating Instruction", *Cognitive Science*, 5(4), 333-69.

McLean, Kathleen (1999), "Museum Exhibitions and the Dynamics of Dialogue", *Daedalus*, 128 (3), 83-107.

Mencarelli, Re´mi, Se´verine Marteaux, and Mathilde Pulh (2010), "Museums, consumers, and on-site experiences", *Marketing Intelligence and Planning*, 28 (3), 330-48.

Moscardo, Gianna (1996), "Mindful Visitors, Heritage and Tourism", Annals of Tourism Research, 23 (2), 376-97.

Pattakos, Alex (2010), "Discovering the deeper meaning of Tourism", In: Wurzburger, R., Aageson, T., Pattakos, A. and Pratt, S. (eds.) *Discovering the deeper meaning of tourism Creative Tourism: A Global Conversation*. Santa Fe,Sunstone Press.

Pershey, Edward (1985), "Life and Times in Silk City, an Exhibit in Paterson New Jersey", *Technology and Culture*, 26 (3), 623-28.

Piscitelli, Bob and Kim Weier (2002), "Learning with, through and About Art: The Role of Social Interactions," in *Perspectives on Object-Centered Learning in Museums*, ed. S. Paris. UK: Routledge, 121-151.

Simon, Nina (2010), *The Participatory Museum*. CA, Santa Cruz: Museum 20.

Stebbins, Robert (2009), *Leisure and Consumption: Common Ground/Separate Worlds*, New York: Palgrave.

vom Lehn, Dirk (2006), "Embodying Experience: A Video-Based Examination of Visitors' Conduct and Interaction in Museums," *European Journal of Marketing*, 40(11/12), 1340-359.

--- Dirk, Jon Hindmarsh, Paul Luff, and Christian Heath (2007), Engaging constable: revealing art with new technology. In Conference on Human Factors in Computing Systems (CHI). San Jose: ACM. 1485-1494.

Welsh, Peter H. (2005), "Re-Configuring Museums", *Museum Management and Curatorship*, 20 (2), 103–130.

Coping with My Loneliness: The Effects of Social Exclusion on Consumer Choice of Unique Products

Ying Ding, Peking University, China
Jing Xu, Peking University, China
Echo Wen Wan, University of Hong Kong, Hong Kong

EXTENDED ABSTRACT

The experience of being rejected, excluded, or isolated is quite pervasive in people's social life. Prior literature contends that social exclusion can impair individual's psychological as well as physiological well-beings (Williams 2007), and that people have the motivation to reduce the negative experiences of social exclusion. However, diverging findings has been reported on the behavioral consequences following the experience of social exclusion (Williams 2007). On the one hand, results from some research indicated that social exclusion can lead to prosocial behaviors as an attempt to rebuild social connections (DeWall, Maner and Rouby 2009; Maner et al. 2007). However, other studies suggested a link between social exclusion and antisocial behaviors such as aggression and decreased motivation to help (Twenge et al. 2001; Twenge et al. 2007).

In the current research, we identify dual coping mechanisms toward social exclusion in the domain of consumer choice. Based on the literature of social exclusion (Williams 2007) and need for uniqueness theory (Snyder and Fromkin 1980), we propose that consumers' response to social exclusion depends on how they interpret the experience of being excluded and that consumers may strategically choose to differentiate or assimilate to others as a means to cope with deprivation of social relationships. Two factors are considered which may influence the perception of whether or not it is desirable to regain social acceptance. To begin with, prior work has linked self-affirmation with greater perceived control and personal resources (Schmeichel and Vohs 2009). We expect that excluded individuals with self-affirmation or greater resources are less likely to perceive rebuilding social connection as a way to cope with the exclusion, as they can easily resort to other ways of remedy. For instance, Zhou, Vohs and Baumeister (2009) demonstrated that handling money can reduce distress over social exclusion. Hence, it is plausible that excluded individuals with self-affirmation have a more readily accessible need for uniqueness and in turn tend to choose more unique products. Accordingly, we propose that following the experience of social exclusion, consumers with self affirmation (or rich resource) are more likely to choose distinctive products, as compared to those without self-affirmation (poor resource).

The second factor is individual's belief about whether things can be changed or fixed. Previous literature differentiated two types of implicit theories people hold about the world around us. Entity theory contends that everything is fixed and can not be changed, whereas incremental theory emphasizes on malleable traits and can be changed (Dweck and Leggett 1988). Hence, following the experience of social exclusion, individuals who hold a belief in incremental theory would consider regaining social acceptance is infeasible and be motivated to seek conformity through choosing less unique options. Conversely, excluded individuals who believe in entity theory would consider rebuilding social relationship to be infeasible. They will be more likely to regard themselves as unique individuals and tend to choose unique options to express their distinctiveness.

Across three experiments, we tested the propositions by using different manipulations of social exclusion and got consistent results. Specifically, experiment 1 documented the moderating role of self-affirmation. We employed a 2 (social exclusion: exclusion vs. inclusion) x 2 (self-affirmation: yes vs. no) between-subjects factorial design and we manipulated social exclusion by Cyberball task. Fol-

lowing the social exclusion and self-affirmation manipulation, participants made a choice between two vacation spots, with one of the options preferred by majority (common option) based on previous survey and another one preferred by minority (unique option). Possessions are extensions of self and prior literatures indicate that distinctive products preferred by a minority of people can signal one's individuality whereas those preferred by majority others convey a sense of belongingness (Ames and Iyengar 2005; Tian, Bearden and Hunter 2001). The results implied that socially excluded participants were more likely to choose the unique option after self-affirmation compared to those without self-affirmation. Based on the mediated moderation analysis, we found the moderation effect of self-affirmation and social exclusion on the choice of unique products was mediated by individuals' need for uniqueness. Furthermore, we showed in experiment 1 that the negative feeling of being socially excluded can be reduced significantly after product choice.

We tested how resource influences the effect of social exclusion on product choice in experiment 2 that employed a 2 (social exclusion: exclusion vs. inclusion) x 2 (resource availability: poor resource vs. rich resource) between-subjects design. After recalling an experience of being socially excluded or included, participants received the scenarios which used to manipulate resource perception. Then participants made choices to donate for one of two endangered animals, one supported by majority (common option) and the other supported by minority (unique option). The results revealed that excluded participants with rich resource chose more unique option than those with poor resource.

In experiment 3, we incorporated a marketing relevant manipulation of social exclusion and tested whether social exclusion interacts with the belief in changeability in affecting product choice. This experiment followed a 2 (social exclusion: exclusion vs. inclusion) x 2 (changeability: entity theory vs. incremental theory) between-subjects design. We found that, following the experience of social exclusion, participants who believe in entity theory would be more likely to choose the unique option than those who believe in incremental theory. In addition, our results indicated that the interaction effect of social exclusion and changeability on the choice of unique products was mediated by consumers' need for uniqueness.

To summarize, our findings suggest that consumers' response to social exclusion depends on the interpretation of whether it is desirable to regaining social connection (self-affirmation and resource) and whether they believe it is possible to change the state of being socially excluded (changeability). As a result, excluded consumers may tend to choose more unique or common products as a strategy to cope with social exclusion.

REFERENCES

Ames, Daniel R. and Sheena S. Iyengar (2005), "Appraising the Unusual: Framing Effects and Moderators of Uniqueness Seeking and Social Projection," *Journal of Experimental Social Psychology*, 41(3), 271-82.

Baumeister Roy F., Leary Mark R. (1995), "The Need to Belong: Desire for Interpersonal Attachments as a Fundamental Human Motivation," *Psychological Bulletin*, 117 (May), 497–529.

---, C. Nathan DeWall, Natalie J. Ciarocco, and Jean M. Twenge (2005), "Social Exclusion Impairs Self-Regulation," *Journal of Personality and Social Psychology*, 88(4), 589–604.

Belk, Russell W. (1987), "A Child's Christmas in America: Santa Claus as Deity, Consumption as Religion," *Journal of American Culture*, 10 (Spring), 87-100.

Chiu, Chi-yue, Hong, Ying-y, and Dweck, Carol S. (1997), "Lay Dispositionism and Implicit Theories of Personality," *Journal of Personality and Social Psychology*, 73 (July), 19-30.

Cohen, Geoffrey L., Aronson, Joshua and Steele, Claude M. (2000), "When Beliefs Yield to Evidence: Reducing Biased Evaluation by Affirming the Self," *Personality and Social Psychology Bulletin*, 26(9), 1151–164.

DeWall, Nathan C., Maner, Jon. K. and Rouby, Aaron D. (2009), "Social Exclusion and Early-Stage Interpersonal Perception: Selective Attention to Signs of Acceptance," *Journal of Personality and Social Psychology*, 96 (April), 729-41.

Downey Geraldine and Feldman, Scott I. (1996), "Implications of Rejection Sensitivity for Intimate Relationships," *Journal of Personality and Social Psychology*, 70 (June), 1327–343.

Dweck, Carol S. and Leggett, Ellen. L (1988), "A social-Cognitive Approach to Motivation and Personality," *Psychological Review*, 95 (April), 256-73.

Eisenberger Naomi I., Lieberman Matthew D., Williams Kipling D. (2003), "Does Rejection Hurt? An fMRI Study of Social Exclusion," *Science*, 302 (October), 290–92.

Gardner, Wendi L., Pickett, Cynthia L. and Brewer, Marilynn. B. (2000), "Social Exclusion and Selective Memory: How the Need to Belong Influences Memory for Social Events," *Personality and Social Psychology Bulletin*, 26 (April), 486–96.

Maner, Jon. K., DeWall, Nathan C., Baumeister, Roy F. and Schaller, Mark (2007). "Does Social Exclusion Motivate Interpersonal Reconnection? Resolving the "Porcupine Problem"," *Journal of Personality and Social Psychology*, 92 (January), 42–55.

MacDonald Geoff, Leary Mark R. (2005), "Why Does Social Exclusion Hurt? The Relationship between Social and Physical Pain," *Psychological Bulletin*, 131 (March), 202–23.

Maslow, Abraham H. (1943), "A Theory of Human Motivation," *Psychological Review*, 50(4), 370-96.

Mead, Nicolel L., Baumeister, Roy F., Stillman, Tyler F., Rawn, Catherine D., and Vohs, Kathleen D. (2010), "Social Exclusion Causes People to Spend and Consume Strategically in the Service of Affiliation," *Journal of Consumer Research*, 37 (Feb), 902-19.

Muller, Dominique, Judd Charles M., and Yzerbyt, Vincent Y. (2005), "When Moderation is Mediated and Mediation is Moderated," *Journal of Personality and Social Psychology*, 89 (December), 852-63.

Schmeichel, Brandon J. and Vohs, Kathleen (2009), "Self-Affirmation and Self-Control: Affirming Core Values Counteracts Ego Depletion," *Journal of Personality and Social Psychology*, 96(4), 770–82.

Snyder, C. R. and Howard L. Fromkin (1980), Uniqueness: The Human Pursuit of Difference. New York, NY: Plenum.

--- and --- (1970), "Abnormality as a positive characteristic: The development and validation of a scale measuring need for uniqueness," *Journal of Abnormal Psychology*, 86(5), 518-27.

Sobel, Michael E. (1982), "Asymptotic Confidence Intervals for Indirect Effects in Structural Equation Models," in *Sociological Methodology*, ed. Samuel Leinhardt, San Francisco: Jossey- Bass, 290–312.

Steele, Claude M. (1988). The Psychology of Self-Affirmation: Sustaining the Integrity of the Self. In L. Berkowitz (Ed.), *Advances in experimental social psychology* (Vol. 21, pp. 261–302). New York: Academic Press.

Thomaes, Sander, Albert Reijntjes, Bram Orobio de Castro, and Brad J. Bushman (2009), "Reality Bites-or Does It? Realistic Self-Views Buffer Negative Mood Following Social Threat," *Psychological Science*, 20 (9), 1079-080.

Tian, Kelly T., Bearden, William O, and Hunter, Gary L. (2001), "Consumers Need for Uniqueness: Scale Development and Validation," *Journal of Consumer Research*, 28 (June), 50–66.

Twenge, Jean M., Baumeister, Roy F., Tice, Dianne M. and Stucke, Tanja S. (2001), "If You Can't Join Them, Beat Them: Effects of Social Exclusion on Aggressive Behavior," *Journal of Personality and Social Psychology*, 81 (December), 1058–069.

Twenge, Jean M., Baumeister, Roy F., Dewall, Nathan C., Ciarocco Natalie J. And Bartels, Michael J. (2007), "Social Exclusion Decreases Prosocial Behavior," *Journal of Personality and Social Psychology*, 92 (January), 55-66.

Warburton, Wayne A., Kipling D. Williams and David. R. Cairns (2006). "When Ostracism Leads to Aggression: The Moderating Effects of Control Deprivation," *Journal of Experimental Social Psychology*, 42 (2), 213–20.

Williams, Kipling D. (2007), "Ostracism," *Annual Review of Psychology*, 58, 425–52.

Williams, Kipling D., Cheung Christopher K.T. and Choi Wilma (2000). "CyberOstracism: Effects of Being Ignored Over the Internet," *Journal of Personality and Social Psychology*, 79 (November), 748–62.

Zhou, Xin Y., Vohs, Kathleen D. and Baumeister, Roy F. (2009), "The Symbolic Power of Money: Reminders of Money Alter Social Distress and Physical Pain," *Psychological Science*, 20 (June), 700-06.

Surveillance 2.0: Meso Legitimation of Sharing in Healthcare through Social Media

Handan Vicdan, Eastern Kentucky University, USA

EXTENDED ABSTRACT

This research aims to introduce a new marketing system established through social media in healthcare, and how it serve as an enabler of sharing private health data and mutual surveillance among healthcare actors. Through netnographic inquiry of this system called PatientsLikeMe (PLM), I explore how PLM legitimizes the sharing of private health information in the current healthcare market where privacy dominates relations among healthcare actors. PLM is a community organization that gathers patients with diverse health problems (e.g., MS, ALS, Mood, Parkinson, HIV, organ transplant) and other healthcare actors (e.g., pharmaceuticals, caregivers, physicians/researchers). It enables healthcare actors to engage in clinical research in its platform, hence facilitating the acceleration of medical research and generation of medical knowledge by patients. Findings reveal the community (meso) mediated dynamics of surveillance in healthcare through this social media platform.

PLM enables sharing and mutual surveillance in healthcare through intensifying connectedness among diverse healthcare actors and the resulting mobility and flow of health data through this community platform. Sophisticated surveillance tools in PLM enable patients to continuously monitor and watch their and others' disease conditions and treatments, hence intensify sharing and connectedness in healthcare, not only among patients and between patients and physicians, but also among healthcare providers. Constant real-time surveillance of and by healthcare actors in PLM through tracking tools leads to increased disease literacy and support, and connectedness among healthcare actors both inside and outside of the community. Patient ability to create a centralized record of her/his health data also increases connectedness among healthcare providers with increased flow of health data. Transition of data flow among healthcare providers is also less flawed when patients create a centralized record of their conditions in PLM, which also reduces diagnosis and treatment errors. By enabling intra, inter and outer communal sharing and learning, PLM increases patient connectedness to other patients worldwide, their families and caregivers, and their physicians both inside and outside of the community. Multiple ways of learning in the community help patient improve on self-presentation and disease literacy, and as a result, influence relations both inside the community (e.g., increased empathy and tolerance in patient-to-patient connectedness, and increased self-awareness of one's health condition through constant monitoring) and outside of the community (interpretation and presentation of what is learned in the community through surveillance tools to other parties outside of the community).

PLM also intensifies patient-to-physician connectedness. Increased disease literacy and enhanced understanding of the disease by patients and physicians in the community also influence their outside community relations. Physicians/researchers can track specific patients and improve on their treatment methods. Patients can better present their conditions to physicians and engage in proactive dialogues with their physicians. Patients, equipped with more theoretical and experiential knowledge about their diseases, increasingly demand validation of any type of claim made or information presented by other patients and physicians in the community with alternative sources of knowledge and scientific evidence. In addition, research conducted in PLM community serves as a form of validation and a useful check for traditional clinical trials. Patients and physicians can employ a more personalized medicine through constant monitoring of disease progression and the resulting centralized records, which also serves as a form of validation and analysis in physician-patient encounter outside of the community. Physicians, researchers and pharmaceutical firms can also recruit patients from PLM for their own research. Hence, patients are enabled to have increased access to clinical trials both in and outside of PLM, which also intensifies patient-pharmaceutical connectedness. Patient-to-state connectedness is also enabled by PLM. The state cannot interfere with the practice of sharing private health data, since PLM is not a healthcare provider but an opt-in service. Connectedness between patients and the state reflects the acknowledgement of patient license gained through social networking. Patients can directly report drug side effects to FDA, which also serves as a form of validation for the state and influences state intervention in healthcare market regulation (improved state supervision of pharmaceutical industry to eliminate subversion and exploitation by pharmaceutical companies)

PLM also strives to establish 'sharing' as a right versus privacy (a right not to share) for the discovery of new medical knowledge, hence initiates a shift in focus from proprietorship to partnership in sharing of private health data. Patients exhibit increasing willingness to embrace the responsibilization of sharing and getting involved in creating, organizing and distributing medical knowledge in collaboration with other healthcare actors, which will accelerate the medical research process and discovery of new treatments. Discrimination and delayed research process as a result of practices of privacy in healthcare, and the disguised practices of state institutions (e.g., patient non-awareness of her/his inherent rights in data sharing) to protect patient right to privacy seem to be some of the causes of patient turn to alternative sources of knowledge and support.

Consequently, findings articulate how PLM as a social networking platform in the healthcare market is beginning to initiate a shift from state intervention to community intervention in organizing sharing, generation, and distribution of private patient data, and from privacy to sharing as a form of organizing roles and relations in the current healthcare system. The processes of organization, sharing, generation of and access to private health information are also beginning to be controlled by institutions like PLM. Contemporary medicine had long served as a disciplinary entity to maximize our lifespan and normalize our bodies, hence prevent us from death. State institutions and healthcare providers utilized 'security' and 'fear' as discourses of power in this process (Epstein 2006), particularly as a means to protect patient privacy and increase mortality salience among patients. With the increased use of Internet for acquisition, analysis, aggregation, dissemination, deployment and sharing of private health data and information, healthcare industry and the state established policies (HIPAA) to protect patient privacy. These policies strictly set boundaries on the flow of patient health records to third parties (e.g., insurance companies, employers), increase consumer sensitivity and fear about privacy, and serve as a barrier to research and discovery (Brown 2008). Macro institutions' excessive reliance on secrecy and desire to have control over patient health information (Weitzner et al. 2008) are now beginning to be challenged by a meso level institution (PLM), the foundation of which is based on sharing private health data.

REFERENCES

Adams, Anne (1999), "Users' Perception of Privacy in Multimedia Communication," Proceedings of CHI '99, Pittsburgh, PA.

Appadurai, Arjun (1991), "Global Ethnoscapes: Notes and Queries for a Transnational

Anthropology", in R. G. Fox (ed.), *Recapturing Anthropology: Working in the Present*, pp. 191-210. Santa Fe, NM: Sch. Am. Res. Press.

Arnst, Catherine (2008), "Health 2.0: Patients as Partners," *BusinessWeek*, (December 4).

Bauman, Zygmunt (1996), "From Pilgrim to Tourist – or a Short History of Identity," in S. Hall and P. du Gay (ed.), *Questions of Cultural Identity*, pp 18-36. London: Sage.

Belk, Russell W. (2007), "Why Not Share Rather Than Own?" *The Annals of the American Academy of Political and Social Science*, 611(1), 126-140.

--- (2010), "Sharing" *Journal of Consumer Research*, 36 (Feb), 715-734.

Benn, Stanley I. (1971), "Privacy, Freedom and Respect for Persons," in R. J. Pennock and J. W. Chapman (ed.), *Privacy*, pp.1-26. New York: Atherton Press.

Bleicher, Paul (2006), "Web 2.0 Revolution: Power to People," *Applied Clinical Trials*, 34-36.

Brown, Bob (2008), "Research and the Privacy Rule: The Chill is on," *Journal of Health Care Compliance*, 35-36.

Cova, Bernard, and Stefano Pace (2006), "Brand Community of Convenience Products: New Forms of Customer Empowerment – The Case 'My Nutella the Community'," *European Journal of Marketing*, 40 (9/10), 1087-1105.

Culnan, Mary J. (1993), "How Did They Get My Name?: An Exploratory Investigation of Consumer Attitudes toward Secondary Information Use," *MIS Quarterly*, 17(3), 341-363.

Denzin, Norman K., and Yvonna S. Lincoln (2000), "Introduction: The Discipline and Practice of Qualitative Research," in Denzin, N.K., Lincoln, Y.S. (Eds), *Handbook of Qualitative Research*, pp.1-28. Sage, London.

Elliott, R., and N. Jankel-Elliot (2003), "Using Ethnography in Strategic Consumer Research," *Qualitative Marketing Research*, 6 (4), 215-223.

Epstein, Charlotte (2006), *Guilty Bodies, Productive Bodies, Destructive Bodies: Crossing The Biometric Borders.* Paper Presented at International Studies Association Conference.

Eysenbach, Gunther, John Powell, Marina Englesakis, Carlos Rizo, and Anita Stern (2004), "Health-related Virtual Communities and Electronic Support Groups: Systematic Review of the Effects of Online Peer-to-peer Interactions," *BMJ*, 328, 1166-1170.

Foucault, Michel (1975), *The Birth of the Clinic: An Archeology of Medical Perception.* NY: Vintage.

--- (1977), *Discipline and Punish: The Birth of the Prison*, NY: Vintage.

--- (1990), *The History of Sexuality.* New York: Vintage Books.

Galanxhi, Holtjona, and Fiona Fui-Hoon Nah (2006), Privacy Issues in the Era of Ubiquitous Commerce," *Electronic Markets*, 16 (3), 222-232.

Gavison, Ruth (1980), "Privacy and the Limits of the Law," *Yale Law Journal*, 89 (3), 421-471.

Glaser, Barney G. and Anselm L. Strauss (1967), *The Discovery of Grounded Theory: Strategies for Qualitative Research*, Aldine Publishing Co, Chicago, IL.

Goodwin, Cathy (1991), "Privacy: Recognition of a Consumer Right," *Journal of Public Policy & Marketing*, 10 (1), 149-166.

Hardey, Michael (2001), "E-health: The Internet and the Transformation of Patients into Consumers and Producers of Health Knowledge," *Information, Communication & Society*, 4 (3), 388-405.

Hummel, Johannes, and Ulrike Lechner (2001), "Communities: The Role of Technology," Proceedings of the 9th European Conference on Information Systems.

Jadad Alejandro R., Murray W. Enkin, Sholom Glouberman, Philip Groff, and Anita Stern (2006), "Are Virtual Communities Good for Our Health?" *BMJ*, 332, 925-926.

--- (1999), "Promoting Partnerships: Challenges for the Internet Age," *BMJ*, 319, 761-64.

Kozinets, Robert V. (2002), "The Field Behind the Screen: Using Netnography for Marketing Research in Online Communications," *Journal of Marketing Research*, 39 (1), 61-72.

---, John F. Sherry, Diana Storm, Adam Duhachek, Krittinee Nuttavuthisit, and Benet Deberry-Spence (2004), "Ludic Agency and Retail Spectacle," *Journal of Consumer Research*, 31 (3), 658-72.

--- (2006), "Netnography 2.0," in Russell W. Belk (ed.), *Handbook of Qualitative Research in Marketing*, 129-142, Cheltenham, UK: Edward Elgar.

--- (2010), *Netnography: Doing Ethnographic Research in the Age of the Internet.* Sage Publications, Thousand Oaks: CA.

Lessig, Lawrance (1999), *Code and Other Laws of Cyberspace.* New York: Basic Books.

Miller, Peter, and Nikolas Rose (2008), *Governing the Present: Administering Economic, Social and Personal Life.* Polity Press: UK.

Peñaloza, Lisa, and Alladi Venkatesh (2006), "Further Evolving the New Dominant Logic of Marketing: From Services to the Social Construction of Markets," *Marketing Theory*, 6 (3), 299-316.

Rabinow, Paul (1996), *Artificiality and Enlightenment: From Sociobiology to Biosociality: Essays on the Anthropology of Reason.* Princeton University Press: NJ.

Rose, Nikolas (2007), *The Politics of Life Itself: Biomedicine, Power, and Subjectivity in the Twenty-First Century.* Princeton University Press: NJ.

Shamir, Ronen (2008), "The Age of Responsibilization: On Market-embedded Morality," *Economy and Society*, 37 (1), 1-19.

Tyson, Ted R. (2000), "The Internet: Tomorrow's Portal to Non-Traditional Health Care Services," *Journal of Ambulatory Care Management*, 23 (2), 1-6.

Vargo, Stephen L., and Robert F. Lusch (2004), "Evolving to a New Dominant Logic for Marketing", *Journal of Marketing*, 68 (January), 1-17.

Weitzner, Daniel J., Harold Abelson, Tim Berners-Lee, Joan Feigenbaum, James Hendler, and Gerald Jay Sussman (2008), "Information Accountability," *Communications of the ACM*, 51 (6), 82-87.

Westin, Alan F. (1967), *Privacy and Freedom.* Athenaeum: NY.

Zikmund, W., and B. Babin (2006), "*Exploring Marketing Research* (9th ed.). South-Western.

Zwick, Detlev, Samuel Bonsu, and Aron Darmody (2008), "Putting Consumers to Work: 'Co-creation' and New Marketing Govern-mentality," *Journal of Consumer Culture*, 8 (2), 163-196.

Product or Cause? The Impacts of Product Type and Cause Framing in Cause-Related Marketing Advertising

Chun-Tuan Chang, National Sun Yat-sen University
Yu-Kang Lee, National Sun Yat-sen University
Ting-Ting Chen, National Taiwan University

EXTENDED ABSTRACT

Because of increasing public concern over social and environmental matters, many companies have begun to affiliate their products with a range of popular causes related to social and ecological issues. Partnership between product and cause is referred to as cause-related marketing (CRM) (Varadarajan and Menon, 1988). One influential variable that has been identified to determine the success of CRM is its advertising (Chang, 2008 and 2011; Lafferty and Edmondson, 2009). This article contributes to this evolving stream of research by comparing the two execution styles (i.e., product-oriented vs. cause-focused) in promoting CRM campaigns. This research will demonstrate that these two execution styles might not be equally persuasive in all conditions, and could be moderated by two variables: product type and cause framing.

The findings from two experiments raise concerns about the effectiveness of visuals, as well as questions when different visuals (cause or product photo as dominance) are persuasive. The results suggest that selection of cause/product as visual can be an effective tool for influencing consumer behavior, notably in product purchase behaviors. Different from Lafferty and Edmondson (2009) in which the examined cause was low in importance and familiarity (i.e., the Conservancy's efforts to protect the Northern Rocky Mountain Grizzlies' habitat). In current research, World Vision in Study 1 was considered as a non-profit with high credibility and familiarity (Chang, 2008). Using a fictitious non-profit (i.e., Medical Research Charities Association), cause importance was considered as a covariate in Study 2. Extending recent developments in execution style of CRM advertising literature, the present research identifies boundary conditions associated with the roles of product type and cause framing in consumer evaluations of CRM ads. In doing so, the study is capable of providing insight into the important, but previously unanswered questions of "Under what conditions do cause-focused ads facilitate consumer attitudes and purchase intentions? Conversely, when does a cause-focused ad backfire?" The findings presented here establish that the influence of execution style on consumer response is relatively complex and contingent on product type and cause framing. In terms of the relative effects of different product types, this study shows systematic effects on consumer responses by comparing hedonic and utilitarian products/values. Five observations are noteworthy.

First, the beneficial effects of using a cause as a visual focus occur when a hedonic product is promoted or when a product is perceived hedonic. Emotion contagion can be used to explain such a phenomenon. People think with their hearts for hedonic consumption, which arouses emotions including pleasure and guilt. Consistent to charity donation literature (e.g., Chang and Lee, 2009; Small and Verrochi, 2009), visuals of a cause may cause vividness and stimulate sympathy and, thus, more positive attitudes and purchase intentions. The congruence between emotion from hedonic product purchase and emotion evoked by a cause image facilitates people to purchase the promoted with a cause. From a practical point of view, the findings here should be considered encouraging companies who wish to employ cause photos in initiating CRM ads.

Second, a product photo as a visual emphasis is more effective when a utilitarian product is promoted or when a product is perceived utilitarian. Using a product as focal visuals provides precise benefits/attributes. This matches well with the rationality of utilitarian consumption. The finding echoes Lafferty and Edmondson (2009) that the photo of a utilitarian product (i.e., granola bars) had a greater effect on purchase intentions than the cause photo.

Third, investigating impacts of value framing is an important marketing issue because both self-benefit and other-benefit appeals are commonly used as good-faith attempts to communicate why the cause should be supported. However, they may not be equivalent with respect to their ability to enhance CRM effectiveness. An other-benefit appeal facilitates the effects of a cause-focused ad on hedonic product advertising, while a self-benefit appeal enhances the effects of product-oriented ad on utilitarian product promotion. This lends qualified support to the phenomenon of value congruity (Brunel and Nelson, 2000; Chang, Lee, and Chen, 2009) in charity promotion contexts. Altering the frame of a persuasive message is a relatively straightforward task. An appropriately framed message could be incorporated into CRM campaigns to increase its effectiveness.

Fourth, it appears that cause framing could play a similar role as what execution style does in CRM advertising since both influences are contingent on product type. One major difference between cause framing and execution style is the format of presentation: the former is verbal portrayal and the latter is visual display. When comparing each interaction with product type, the experiment results indicate a stronger influence of execution style. The results echo an old saying "a picture is worth a thousand words." Actually, image display is widely used in a charitable communication to boost vividness effects (Chang and Lee, 2009; Perrine and Heather, 2000; Thornton, Kirchner, and Jacobs, 1991). The use of visuals requires more expenses than verbal description, as more talent, artistic skills and digital enhancement are needed for developing impressive images. Meanwhile, good visuals improve advertising persuasion and increase product sales.

Finally, the main effect of product type is consistently found in Study 1 and 2. The results demonstrate the previously observed effects of product type on CRM by comparing utilitarian and hedonic products (Chang, 2008; Strahilevitz, 1999; Strahilevitz and Myers, 1998). The advantage of perceived hedonic value resides in its ability to elicit more favorable consumer attitudes toward the company and toward the sponsoring firm. The current investigation provides guidance for practitioners to frame the nature of the product in CRM campaigns. Perceived hedonic value is an important element in CRM. Transforming a product with perceived utilitarian value into one with clear hedonic value can be an important re-positioning strategy for a company using CRM to successfully promote the product.

To marketers who intend to promote products with charity incentive, this research provides marketing implications into how consumers respond to differently framed CRM messages based on product features. This research suggests that there are specific optimal ways for information presented in an ad that may optimize the effectiveness of cause-related campaigns. The present research should serve a starting point for entry into this under-researched area.

REFERENCES

Adkins, Sue (2010), "Cause-Related Marketing: Who Cares Wins," Oxford: Butterworth-Heinemann.

Agrawal, Nidhi, Geeta Menon, and Jennifer L. Aaker (2007), "Getting Emotional About Health," *Journal of Marketing Research*, 44(1), 100-113.

Ahtola, Olli T. (1985), "Hedonic and Utilitarian Aspects of Behavior: An Attitudinal Perspective," In *Advances in Consumer Research*, 12, E. C. Hirschman and M. B. Holbrook (eds.), Provo, UT: Association for Consumer Research, 7-10.

Babin, Barry J., William R. Darden, and Mitch Griffin (1994), "Work and/or Fun: Measuring Hedonic and Utilitarian Shopping Value," *Journal of Consumer Research*, 20(4), 644-656.

Batson, Charles Daniel (1991) *The Altruism Question: Toward A Social-Psychological Answer*. Hillsdale, N. J.: Erlbaum.

Baumann, Donald J., Robert B. Cialdini, and Douglas T. Kendrick (1981), "Altruism as Hedonism: Helping and Self-Gratifications as Equivalent Responses," *Journal of Personality and Social Psychology*, 40(6), 1039-1046.

Bendapudi, Neeli, Surendra N. Singh, and Venkat Bendapudi (1996), "Enhancing Helping Behavior: An Integrative Framework for Promotion Planning," *Journal of Marketing*, 60(3), 33-49.

Boulanger, Nolan Christopher (2008), "Cross-Cultural Responses to Cause-Related Marketing Advertising Moderated by Message Framing Effects," master thesis, National Sun Yat-Sen University, (accessed February 28, 2011), [available at http://etd.lib.nsysu.edu.tw/ETD-db/ETD-search-c/view_etd?URN=etd-0813108-115220].

Brunel, Frédéric F. and Michelle R. Nelson (2000), "Explaining Gendered Responses to "Help-Self" and "Help-Others" Charity Ad Appeals: The Mediating Role of World-Views," *Journal of Advertising*, 29(3), 15-28.

Carpenter, Jason M., Marguerite Moore, and Ann E. Fairhurst (2005), "Consumer Shopping Value for Retail Brands," *Journal of Fashion Marketing and Management*, 9(1), 43-53.

Chang, Chun-Tuan (2007), "Interactive Effects of Message Framing, Product Perceived Risk, and Mood: The Case of Travel Healthcare Product Advertising," *Journal of Advertising Research*, 47(1), 51-65.

Chang, Chun-Tuan (2008), "To Donate or not to Donate? Product Characteristics and Framing Effects of Cause-Related Marketing on Consumer Purchase Behavior," *Psychology and Marketing*, 25(12), 1089-1110.

Chang, Chun-Tuan (2011), "Guilt Appeals in Cause-Related Marketing: The Subversive Roles of Product Type and Donation Magnitude," *International Journal of Advertising*, forthcoming.

Chang, Chun-Tuan and Yu-Kang Lee (2009), "Framing Charity Advertising: Influences of Message Framing, Image Valence, and Temporal Framing on Charitable Appeal," *Journal of Applied Social Psychology*, 39(12), 2910-2935.

Chang, Chun-Tuan and Yu-Kang Lee (2010), "Effects of Message Framing, Vividness Congruency, and Statistical Framing on Responses to Charity Advertising," *International Journal of Advertising*, 29(2), 195-220.

Chun-Tuan Chang, Yu-Kang Lee, Kuang-Hao Chen (2009), "The "I" of the Beholder: The Impacts of Gender Differences and Self-Referencing on Charity Advertising," in Advances in Consumer Research Volume 36, eds. Ann L. McGill and Sharon Shavitt, Duluth, MN : Association for Consumer Research, 748-749.

Childers, Jerry L., Susan E. Heckler, and Michael J. Houston (1986), "Memory for the Visual and Verbal Components of Print Advertisements," *Psychology & Marketing*, 3(3), 137-150.

Clow, Kenneth E., Karen E. James, Kristine E. Kranenburg, and Christine T. Berry (2009), "An Examination of the Visual Element Used in Generic Message Advertisements: A Comparison of Goods and Services," *Services Marketing Quarterly*, 30(1), 69-84.

Cobb-Waglgren, Cathy J. and Lois A. Mohr (1998), "Symbols in Service Advertisements," *Journal of Services Marketing*, 12(2), 129-151.

Cunningham, Michael R. (1979), "Weather, Mood, and Helping Behavior: Quasi Experiments With the Sunshine Samaritan," *Journal of Personality and Social Psychology*, 37(11), 1947-1956.

Das, Enny, Kerkhof, Peter, and Kuiper, Joyce (2008), "Improving the Effectiveness of Fundraising Messages: The Impact of Charity Goal Attainment, Message Framing, and Evidence on Persuasion," *Journal of Applied Communication Research,* 36(2), 161-175.

Dhar, Ravi and Klaus Wertenbroch (2000), "Consumer Choice Between Hedonic and Utilitarian Goods," *Journal of Marketing Research*, 37(1), 60-71.

Eagly, Alice H. and Shelly Chaiken (1993), *The Psychology of Attitudes*. New York: Harcourt Brace Jovanovich.

Edell, Julie A. and Richard Staelin (1983), "The Information Processing of Pictures in Print Advertisements," *Journal of Consumer Research*, 10(1), 45-61.

Fisher, Robert J., Mark Vandenbosch, and Kersi D. Anita (2008), "An Empathy-Helping Perspective on Consumers' Responses to Fund-Raising Appeals," *Journal of Consumer Research*, 35(3), 519-531.

Ghingold, Morry (1981), "Guilt Arousing Communications: An Unexplored Variable," In *Advances in consumer research*, Monroe, K., and Arbor, A. eds., MI: Association of Consumer Research, 8(1), 442-448.

Grau, Stacy Landreth, Judith Anne Garretson Folse, and Julie Pirsch (2007), "Cause-Related Marketing: An Exploratory Study of Campaign Donation Structure Issues," *Journal of Nonprofit and Public Sector Marketing*, 18(2), 69-91.

Grau, Stacy Landreth and Judith Anne Garretson Folse (2007), "Cause-Related Marketing (CRM)-The Influence of Donation Proximity and Message-Framing Cues on the Less-Involved Consumer," *Journal of Advertising*, 36(4), 19-33.

Hirschman, Elizabeth, C. (1980), "Innovativeness, Novelty Seeking, and Consumer Creativity," *Journal of Consumer Research*, 7(3), 289-295.

Isen, Alice M. and Paula F. Levin (1972), "The Effect of Feeling Good on Helping: Cookies and Kindness," *Journal of Personality and Social Psychology*, 21(3), 384-388.

Isen, Alice M., Thomas E. Shalker, Margaret Clark, and Lynn Karp (1978), "Affect, Accessibility of Material in Memory and Behavior: A Cognitive Loop?" *Journal of Personality and Social Psychology*, 36(1), 1-12.

Kelly, Bill (1991), "Cause-Related Marketing: Doing Well While Doing Good," *Sales and Marketing Management*, 143(3), 60-65.

Kim, Dan J. and Yujong Hwang (2010), "A Study of Mobile Internet User's Service Quality Perceptions from a User's Utilitarian and Hedonic Value Tendency Perspectives," *Information Systems Frontiers*, forthcoming.

Kim, John, Lim, Jeen-Su, and Bhargava, Mukesh (1998), "The Role of Affect in Attitude Formation: A Classical Conditioning Approach," *Journal of the Academy of Marketing Science*, 26(2), 143-152.

Lafferty, Barbara A. and Ronald E. Goldsmith (2005), "Cause–Brand Alliances: Does the Cause Help the Brand or Does the Brand Help the Cause?" *Journal of Business Research*, 58(4), 423-429.

Lafferty, Barbara A. and Diane R. Edmondson (2009), "Portraying the Cause Instead of the Brand in Cause-Related Marketing Ads: Does it Really Matter?" *Journal of Marketing Theory and Practice*, 17(2), 129-144.

Lavack, Ann M. and Fredric Kropp (2003), "A Cross-Cultural Comparison of Consumer Attitudes toward Cause-Related Marketing," *Social Marketing Quarterly*, 9(2), 3-16.

Levin, Irwin P, Schneider, Sandra L., and Gaeth, Gary J (1998), "All Frames Are Not Created Equal: A Typology and Critical Analysis of Framing Effect," *Organizational Behavior and Health Decision Processes*, 76(2), 149-188.

Maner, Jon K. and Matthew T. Gailliot (2007), "Altruism and Egoism: Prosocial Motivations for Helping Depend on Relationship Context," *European Journal of Social Psychology*, 37(2), 347-358.

Mano, Haim and Richard L. Oliver (1993), "Assessing the Dimensionality and Structure of the Consumption Experience: Evaluation, Feeling, and Satisfaction," *Journal of Consumer Research*, 20(3), 451-466.

Nelson, Michelle R., Fre´de´ric F. Brunel, Magne Supphellen, and Rajesh V. Manchanda (2006), "Effects of Culture, Gender, and Moral Obligations on Responses to Charity Advertising Across Masculine and Feminine Cultures," *Journal of Consumer Psychology*, 16(1), 45-56.

Okada, Erica Mina (2005), "Justification Effects on Consumer Choice of Hedonic and Utilitarian Goods," *Journal of Marketing Research*, 42(1), 43-53.

Olsen, G. Douglas, John W. Pracejus, and Norman R. Brown (2003), "When Profit Equals Price: Consumer Confusion About Donation Amounts in Cause-Related Marketing," *Journal of Public Policy and Marketing*, 22(2), 170-180.

Perrine, Rose M. and Stacie Heather (2000), "Effects of Picture and Even-a-Penny-Will-Help Appeals on Anonymous Donations to Charity," *Psychological Reports,* 86, 551-559.

Polonsky, Michael Jay and Greg Wood (2001), "Can the Overcommercialization of Cause-Related Marketing Harm Society?" *Journal of Macromarketing*, 21(1), 8-22.

Pracejus, John W., G. Douglas Olsen, and Norman R. Brown (2003), "On the Prevalence and Impact of Vague Quantifiers in the Advertising of Cause-Related Marketing (CRM),"*Journal of Advertising,* 32 (4), 19–28.

Rozin, Paul, Carol J. Nemeroff, Marcia Wane, and Amy Sherrod (1989), "Operation of the Sympathetic Magical Law of Contagion in Interpersonal Attitudes among Americans," *Bulletin of the Psychonomic Society*, 27, 367-370.

Sciulli, Lisa M. and Charlene Bebko (2005), "Social Cause Versus Profit Oriented Advertisements: An Analysis of Information Content and Emotional Appeals. *Journal of Promotion Management*, 11(2/3), 17-36.

Shavitt, Sharon (1990), "The Role of Attitude Objects in Attitude Functions," *Journal of Experimental Social Psychology*, 26(2), 124-148.

Simonin, Bernard L. and Julie A. Ruth (1998), "Is a Company Known by the Company it Keeps? Assessing the Spillover Effects of Brand Alliances on Consumer Brand Attitudes," *Journal of Marketing Research*, 35(1), 30-42.

Small, Deborah A. and Nicole M. Verrochi (2009), "The Face of Need: Facial Emotion Expression on Charity Advertisements," *Journal of Marketing Research*, "46(6), 777-787.

Strahilevitz, Michal and John G. Myers (1998), "Donations to Charity as Purchase Incentives: How Well They Work May Depend on What You Are Trying to Sell," *Journal of Consumer Research*, 24(4), 434-446.

Strahilevitz, Michal (1999), "The Effects of Product Type and Donation Magnitude on Willingness to Pay More for a Charity-Linked Brand," *Journal of Consumer Psychology*, 8(3), 215-241.

Subrahmanyan, Saroja (2004), "Effects of Price Premium and Product Type on the Cause-Related Brands: A Singapore Perspective," *Journal of Product and Brand Management*, 13(2), 116-124.

Supphellen, Magne and Michelle R. Nelson (2001), "Developing, Exploring, and Validating a Typology of Private Philanthropic Decision Making," *Journal of Economic Psychology,* 22(5), 573-603.

Tangari, Andrea Heintz, Judith Anne Garretson Folse, Scot Burton, and Jeremy Kees (2010), "The Moderating Influence of Consumers' Temporal Orientation on the Framing of Societal Needs and Corporate Responses in Cause-Related Marketing Campaigns," *Journal of Advertising*, 39(2), 35-50.

Thornton, Bill, Gayle Kirchner, and Jacqueline Jacobs (1991), "Influence of a Photograph on a Charitable Appeal: A Picture May Be Worth a Thousand Words When It Has to Speak for Itself," *Journal of Applied Social Psychology*, 21 (6), 433-445.

Varadarajan, P. Rajan and Anil Menon (1988), "Cause-Related Marketing: A Coalignment of Marketing Strategy and Corporate Philanthropy," *Journal of Marketing*, 52(3), 57-74.

Voss, Kevin E., Eric R. Spangenberg, and Bianca Grohmann (2003), "Measuring the Hedonic and Utilitarian Dimensions of Consumer Attitude," *Journal of Marketing Research*, 40(3), 310-320.

Webb, Deborah J. and Lois A. Mohr (1998), "A Typology of Consumer Responses to Cause-Related Marketing: From Skeptics to Socially Concerned," *Journal of Public Policy & Marketing*, 17(2), 226-238.

White, Katherine and John Peloza (2009), "Self-Benefit Versus Other-Benefit Marketing Appeals: Their Effectiveness in Generating Charitable Support," J*ournal of Marketing*, 73(4), 109-124.

Paying To Be Nice: Consistency and Costly Prosocial Behavior

Ayelet Gneezy, UC San Diego, USA
Alex Imas, UC San Diego, USA
Leif D. Nelson, UC Berkeley, USA
Amber Brown, Disney Research, USA
Michael I. Norton, Harvard Business School, USA

EXTENDED ABSTRACT

Drawing on self-perception theory and research exploring that theory (e.g., Bem 1970, 1972; Goethals and Reckman 1973), we propose that when recent prosocial behavior was personally *costly*, people would interpret that behavior as a signal of their prosocial identity; we predict, and demonstrate, that having drawn that inference, individuals are more likely to subsequently behave prosocially. Prosocial behavior that comes at lower cost, however, offers a more ambiguous signal: prosocial behavior is clearly positive, yet since it came at no cost, it is less likely to be judged as diagnostic of one's prosocial disposition. Under those circumstances the positive act can serve as a license ("my actions have led to a positive outcome...") without a substantial influence on self-perceptions, resulting in a reduction in subsequent prosocial behavior ("... so I am going to be a bit more greedy now."). Field and lab experiments test our hypothesis.

In the Experiment 1, we sought to test the idea that costly forms of altruism would lead to subsequent increases in prosocial behavior, while costless altruism would result in moral licensing. We further expected costly prosocial behavior to send a signal to the self of one's altruistic preferences, leading to an increase in self-reported prosocial identity; in contrast, because costless altruism does not send a strong signal, we expected no change in prosocial identity. To manipulate the cost of altruism, some participants had part of their payment donated to charity (costly altruism); other participants learned that a donation had been given on their behalf, but that it was not deducted from their payment (costless altruism). Control participants were not exposed to the charitable cause. To measure subsequent prosocial behavior, we created a task in which people could either lie to benefit themselves or tell the truth to benefit an unspecified other. Truth telling and reported self-perceptions of prosociality served as our DVs.

The results show that the three treatments differed in the extent to which people reported feeling prosocial, $F(2, 167) = 8.90, p < .001$. Specifically, participants in the Costly treatment reported feeling more prosocial ($M = 3.85, SD = .86$) than those in the Control treatment ($M = 3.27, SD = .82$), $t(109) = 3.59, p < .001$, and those in the Costless treatment ($M = 3.26, SD = .75$), $t(104) = 3.74, p < .001$. Participants in the Control and Costless treatments did not differ in reported prosocial identity, $t(117) = .08, p = .93$. In addition, a comparison of the percentage of participants who told the truth in each treatment revealed a significant difference, $\chi 2 (2) = 18.35, p < .001$. Consistent with our predictions, participants in the Costly Donation treatment were substantially more likely to send a truthful message (71%) than Control participants (52%), $\chi 2 (1) = 4.49, p = .04$, and Costless (30%), $\chi 2 (1) = 18.35, p < .001$. Also, Control participants were more likely to tell the truth than those in the Costless treatment $\chi 2 (1) = 5.82, p = .02$. A mediation analysis confirmed that individuals' truth telling was mediated by their reported self-perceptions of prosociality; the effect of costliness on truth-telling was reduced (from $\beta = .42$ to $\beta = .36, p < .001$) when prosocial identity was included in the equation, and prosocial identity remained a significant predictor of truth-telling ($\beta = .17, p = .02$).

Next, we ran a large field experiment to test our predictions in the wild. We conducted the experiment at a ride in a large American amusement park. Visitors were photographed while on the ride and could purchase their photo. To test the effect of prosocial behavior on subsequent behavior, we randomly assigned participants to one of two treatments that differed with respect to whether the photo was sold with a charitable-giving promotion. On some days the photo was sold such that half of the price was donated to a charity (a major patient-support organization); on others, photos were sold without the charitable element. Participants chose whether to buy the photo, and then walked through a retail area that contained other merchandise. Surveyors intercepted a random sample of photo purchasers at the exit, and asked them three questions: "Did you buy a photo?", "Did you buy any other merchandise?", and in reference to the latter, "Are any of those purchases going to be gifts for others?" Responses to the final question served as our primary dependent measure; buying a gift for someone is a prototypical prosocial behavior (Dunn et al 2008).

Neither photo purchasing ($\beta = -.18, p = .67$) nor the prosocial promotion ($\beta = -.20, p = .62$) influenced subsequent gift buying. However, we observed a marginally significant interaction ($\beta = 1.04, p = .05$). When participants were exposed to the prosocial cue, those who purchased a photo were *more* likely than non-purchasers to buy gifts for others ($\beta = .82, p = .04$), consistent with our costly altruism account. While all participants were exposed to the prosocial cue, only those engaging in a *costly* prosocial behavior demonstrated subsequent increase in prosocial behavior. When participants were *not* exposed to the prosocial cue, photo purchasers and non-purchasers were equally likely to buy gifts for others ($\beta = -.45, p = .43$).

These findings have implications for understanding when and why consistency and licensing may emerge. Furthermore, the current work informs a decades-long dispute across psychology and economics over whether social preferences – selfless behavior toward another – truly exist (Batson et al. 1997; Cialdini et al 1997; Levitt and List 2007). It appears that in part, this debate is rooted in the different orientations toward the study of prosocial behavior, with psychologists generally exploring why people don't help enough and economists exploring why, given a lack of incentives, people help at all (Ariely and Norton 2007; Fehr and Schmidt 1999). By combining both economic and psychological approaches, we show that the two approaches in fact converge: When behavior is costly to the self, that cost serves to make the behavior an informative input in the inference of one's moral disposition, and that changed self-perception also changes one's preferences for future similar behaviors, leading to consistency.

REFERENCES

Andreoni, J. (1989). Giving with impure altruism: Applications to charity and Ricardian equivalence. *The Journal Political Economy, 97*(6), 1447-1458.

Andreoni, J. (1990). Impure altruism and donations to public goods: A theory of warm-glow giving. *The Economic Journal, 100*(401), 464-477.

Aquino, K., & Reed, A. II. (2002). The self-importance of moral identity. *Journal of Personality and Social Psychology,* 83(6), 1423-1440.

Ariely, D., & Norton, M.I. (2007). Psychology and experimental economics: A gap in abstraction. *Current Directions in Psychological Science*, 16(6), 336-339.

Ariely, D., & Norton, M. I. (2008). How actions create—not just reveal—preferences. *Trends in Cognitive Sciences*. 12(1), 13-16.

Aronson, E., & Carlsmith, J. M. (1962). Performance expectancy as a determinant of actual performance. *Journal of Abnormal and Social Psychology, 65*, 178–182.

Baron, R. M., & Kenny, D. A. (1986). The moderator-mediator variable distinction in social psychological research: Conceptual, strategic and statistical considerations. *Journal of Personality and Social Psychology, 51*(6), 1173-1182.

Batson, C. D., Coke, J. S., Jasnoski, M. L., & Hanson, M. (1978). Buying kindness: Effects of an extrinsic incentive for helping on perceived altruism. *Personality and Social Psychology Bulletin, 4*(1), 86-91.

Batson, C., Sager, K., Garst, E., Kang, M., Rubchinsky, K., & Dawson, K. (1997). Is empathy-induced helping due to self-other merging? *Journal of Personality and Social Psychology,* 73(3), 495-509.

Bem, D. J. (1972). Self-perception theory, in L. Berkowitz, ed., Advances in Experimental Social Psychology, Vol. 6, 1-62. New York, NY: Academic Press.

Bem, D. J., & McConnell, H. K. (1970). Testing the self-perception explanation of dissonance phenomena: On the salience of premanipulated attitudes. *Journal of Personality and Social Psychology, 14*, 23–31.

Bénabou, R., & Tirole, J. (2004) Willpower and personal rules. *Journal of Political Economy*, 112(4), 848-886.

Bénabou, R., & Tirole, J. (2010). Identity, morals and taboos: Beliefs as assets. CEPR Discussion Paper no. 6123.

Blume, A., DeJong, D. V., Kim, Y. G., & Sprinkle, G. B. (2001). Evolution of communication with partial common interest. *Games and Economic Behavior,* 37(1), 79-120.

Charness, G. B. & Haruvy, E. (2002). Altruism, fairness, and reciprocity in a gift-exchange experiment: An encompassing approach. *Games and Economic Behavior*, 40, 203-231.

Cialdini, R., Brown, S., Lewis, B., Luce, C. & Neuberg, S. (1997). Reinterpreting the empathy-altruism relationship: When one into one equals oneness. *Journal of Personality and Social Psychology,* 73(3), 481-494.

Cooper, J., & Duncan, B. L. (1971). Cognitive dissonance as a function of self-esteem and logical inconsistency. *Journal of Personality,* 39(2), 289– 302.

Cooper, J., & Fazio, R.H. (1984). A new look at dissonance theory. in L. Berkowitz, ed., Advances in Experimental Social Psychology, Vol. 17, 229-266. New York, NY: Academic Press.

Darley, J.M. & Batson, D. (1973). From Jerusalem to Jericho: A study of situational and dispositional variables in helping behavior. *Journal of Personality and Social Psychology, 27*(1), 100-108.

Dunn, E. W., Aknin, E. B., & Norton, M. I. (2008). Spending money on others promotes happiness. *Science, 319*(21), 1687-1688.

Efron, B., & Tibshirani, R. (1993). *An introduction to the bootstrap.* New York: Chapman & Hall/CRC.

Effron, D., Cameron, J. S., & Monin, B. (2009). Voting for Obama licenses favoring Whites. *Journal of Experimental Social Psychology,* 45(3), 590-593.

Erat, S., & Gneezy, U. (2009). White lies. mimeo.

Falk, A., & Zimmermann, F. (2010). Preferences for Consistency. mimeo.

Fehr, E., & Schmidt, K.M. (1999). A theory of fairness, competition and co-operation. *Quarterly Journal of Economics*, 114(3), 817–868.

Festinger, L. (1957). *A theory of cognitive dissonance.* Stanford, CA: Stanford University Press.

Festinger, L., & Carlsmith, J.M. (1959). Cognitive consequences of forced compliance. *Journal of Abnormal and Social Psychology,* 58(2), 203–210.

Freedman, J. L., & Fraser, S. C. (1966). Compliance without pressure: The foot-in-the-door technique. *Journal of Personality and Social Psychology*, 4, 196-202.

Gneezy, A., Gneezy, U., Nelson, L. D., & Brown, A. (2010). Shared Social Responsibility: A Field Experiment in Pay-What-You-Want Pricing and Charitable Giving. *Science*, 329 (5989), 325-327.

Gneezy, U. (2005). Deception: The role of consequences. *American Economic Review,* 95(1), 384-95.

Goethals, G. R., & Reckman, R. F. (1973). The perception of consistency in attitudes. *Journal of Experimental Social Psychology, 9*, 491–501.

Grant, A. M., Dutton, J. E., & Rosso, B. (2008). Giving commitment: Employee support programs and the prosocial sensemaking process. *Academy of Management Journal,* 51(5), 898-918.

Greenwald, A. G. (1980). The totalitarian ego: Fabrication and revision of personal history. *American Psychologist, 35,* 603–618.

Harbaugh, W. T., Mayr, U., & Burghart, D. R. (2007). Neural responses to taxation and voluntary giving reveal motives for charitable donations. *Science*, 316(5831), 1622-1625.

Heider, F. (1958). *The psychology of interpersonal relations.* New York, NY: John Wiley & Sons.

Khan, U., & Dhar, R. (2006). Licensing effect in consumer choice. *Journal of Marketing Research,* 43(2), 259-266.

Laury, S. K. (2006). Pay one or pay all: Random selection of one choice for payment. mimeo.

Levitt, S.D., & List, J.A. (2007). What do laboratory experiments measuring social preferences reveal about the real world? *Journal of Economic Perspectives*, 21(2), 153-174.

Liu, W., & Aaker, J. (2008). The happiness of giving: The time-ask effect. *Journal of Consumer Research.* 35 (October), 543-557.

Loewenstein, G., Thompson, L., & Bazerman, M. (1989). Social utility and decision making in interpersonal contexts. *Journal of Personality and Social Psychology*, 57(3), 426–441.

Mazar, N., Amir, O., & Ariely, D. (2008). The dishonesty of honest people: A theory of self-concept maintenance. *Journal of Marketing Research*, 45(6), 633-644.

Mazar, N., & Zhong, C. (2009). Do green products make us better people? *Psychological Science*, 21(4), 494-498.

Miller, D.T., & Effron, D.A. (2010). Psychological license: When it is needed and how it functions. In M. P. Zanna and J. M. Olson (Eds.), *Advances in experimental social psychology*, Vol, *43,* pp. 115-155), San Diego, CA: Elsevier.

Moll, J., Krueger, F., Zahn, R., Pardini, M., Oliveira-Souza, R., & Grafman, J. (2006). Human fronto–mesolimbic networks guide decisions about charitable donation. *Proceedings of the National Academy of Sciences*, 103(42), 15623-15628.

Monin, B., & Miller, D.T. (2001). Moral credentials and the expression of prejudice. *Journal of Personality and Social Psychology,* 81(1), 33-43.

Ross, M. (1989). The relation of implicit theories to the construction of personal histories. *Psychological Review,* 96, 341–357.

Sachdeva, S., Iliev, R., & Medin, D.L. (2009). Sinning saints and saintly sinners : the paradox of moral self-regulation. *Psychological Science.* 20(4), 523-528.

Shrout, P. E., & Bolger, N. (2002). Mediation in experimental and nonexperimental studies: New procedures and recommendations. *Psychological Methods,* 7(4), 422-445.

Spence, A.M. (1973). Job market signaling. *Quarterly Journal of Economics,* 87(3), 355-74.

Steele, C. M. (1988). The psychology of self-affirmation: Sustaining the integrity of the self, in L. Berkowitz, ed., Advances in Experimental Social Psychology, Vol. 21, 261–302. San Diego, CA: Academic Press.

Steele, C. M., Spencer, S. J., & Lynch, M. (1993). Dissonance and affirmational resources: Resilience against self-image threats. *Journal of Personality and Social Psychology,* 64(6), 885–896.

Stone, J., & Cooper, J. (2001). A self-standards model of cognitive dissonance. *Journal of Experimental Social Psychology*, 37(3), 228-243.

Thibodeau, R., & Aronson, E. (1992). Taking a closer look: Reasserting the role of the self-concept in dissonance theory. *Personality and Social Psychology Bulletin,* 18(5), 591–602.

The Number-Location Association and Its Marketing Implications

Fengyan Cai, The Chinese University of Hong Kong, Hong Kong
Hao Shen, The Chinese University of Hong Kong, Hong Kong
King-man Hui, The Chinese University of Hong Kong, China

EXTEND ABSTRACT

Extant literature shows that people spontaneously associate numbers with space: a small number is associated with a left location whereas a large number is associated with a right location (Wood and Fischer 2008).

Perceptual symbols system theory suggests that people often behave like as though perceptual associations are literal (Barsalou 1999; Barsalou 2008). People's judgment and decision are consequently biased by the perceptual factors in those associations (Schuber 2005; Nelson and Simmons 2009). For example, because of the association between cardinal direction and vertical position— "North is up", people feel that heading north is going uphill, and hence expect that northbound travel(vs. southbound) will take longer time. Accordingly, we expect that consumers might treat the association between number and location literally. As a result, once the number-location association is activated, consumers' judgment about the quantifiable attributes of a product could be biased by location.

This research will test the effect of location on consumers' judgment from two different perspectives.

Firstly, location can directly bias the consumers' numerical judgment outcome if people incorrectly take location into consideration when making the judgment. In study1 and study2, we presented the stimulus (circles/squares in study1, product image in study2) either on the left side or on the right side of a display, and found that participants estimated that there are more hollow circles or squares (19.87 vs. 16.22, $F(1,78)=5.72$, $p<.05$) and provided a higher market price (36.59 vs. 34.88; $F(1,58)=4.40$, $p<.05$) if the stimulus is shown on the right (vs. left) side.

After the demonstration of the location effect on numerical estimation, study3 and study4 further showed that the effect of location on consumers' judgment depended on whether the judgment is related to numerical judgment. In study3, participants were exposed to two pictures of wine on a wall and were asked to indicate which wine was more expensive and was of a better quality. The order of questions was counterbalanced such that either price question or quality question was asked first. We found that when participants were asked to consider price first, more participants (94% vs. 74%; p for chi-square test <.05) regarded the wine displayed on the right (vs. left) side as more expensive due to the activation of the number-location association. However, if participants were asked to consider the quality first, the location did not influence quality perception (82% vs. 89%; p for chi-square test >.25), as quality is not typically represented in terms of a number. The interaction above is significant ($Wald$=4.73, $Exp(B)$=9.90, $p<.05$). Study4 follow the same logic of study3, and showed that location could also influence consumers' quality judgment as long as the quality judgment is framed as numerical judgment.

Secondly, location can also influence consumers' judgment by facilitating the judgment process. Dehaene, Bossini and Giraux (1993) demonstrated that showing numerical information in its compatible location (large numbers at right locations and small numbers at left locations) can significantly reduce people's response time, and increase accuracy rate. Reduction of response time and high accuracy rate are typical indicators of processing fluency, and processing fluency can increase people's evaluation (Schwarz 2006).

Therefore, we expect that showing numerical information in its compatible location can make people feel fluent, and that the fluency feeling in turn makes consumers evaluate the target in a more favorable way than otherwise. Study5 and Study6 tested this proposition. In study 5, we manipulate the location of a low price slogan in an advertisement. In one condition, the slogan was located on the left side of the store image; in the other condition, the slogan was located on the right side of the store image. Then, participants were requested to indicate their opinion about their patronage intention to the supermarket along a scale from -3(definitely no) to 3(definitely yes). We found that participants' patronage intention was significantly higher when the low price slogan was on the left side (M=2.04) than when it was on the right side (M=0.92, $F(1, 48)$ =21.44, $p<.001$), and this effect is mediated by processing fluency. In study 6, we manipulated the location of discounted price. For half of participants, the discounted price was left to the original price. For the other half of participants, the discounted price was located right to the original price. Similarly, consumers perceived the discount as more attractive when the discounted price was left to the original price (M=-0.18) than when it was on the right to the original price (M=-1, $F(1, 59)$ =6.05, $p<.05$). Taken together, study 5 and study 6 showed that presenting marketing information related to numerical magnitude such as low price slogan and discounted price in its compatible location can make consumers evaluate the marketing information in a more favorable way, and processing fluency plays a mediating role in this effect.

This paper could contribute to extant literature in several ways. First, it may provide new evidence for the number-location association by demonstrating the effect of location on numerical judgment. Second, this paper adds to the research on consumer behavior by proposing an undocumented factor that influences consumers' judgment. Thirdly, this paper explicitly proposes and demonstrates two different ways that location influences consumers' judgment as well as the underlying mechanism for each effect.

REFERENCES

Baron, Reuben M. and David A. Kenny (1986), "The Moderator– Mediator Variable Distinction in Social Psychological Research: Conceptual, Strategic, and Statistical Considerations," *Journal of Personality and Social Psychology*, 51(6), 1173-82.

Barsalou, Lawrence (1999), "Perceptual Symbol Systems," *Behavioral and Brain Sciences*, 22(4), 637-60.

--- (2008), "Grounded Cognition," *Annual Review of Psychology*, 59, 617-45.

Brysbaert, Marc (1995), "Arabic Number Reading: On the Nature of the Numerical Scale and the Origin of Phonological Recoding," *Journal of Experimental Psychology: General*, 124(4), 434–52.

Collins, Allan M. and Elizabeth F. Loftus (1975), "A Spreading-Activation Theory of Semantic Processing," *Psychological Review*, 82, 407-28.

Dehaene, Stanislas, Serge Bossini and Pascal Giraux (1993), "The Mental Representation of Parity and Number Magnitude," *Journal of Experimental Psychology*, 122 (3), 371-96.

Deng, Xiaoyan and Barbara E. Kahn (2009), "Is Your Product on the Right Side? The "Location Effect" on Perceived Product Heaviness and Package Evaluation," *Journal of Marketing Research*, forthcoming

Fias, Wim(2001), "Two Routes for the Processing of Verbal Numbers: Evidence from the SNARC Effect," *Psychological Research*, 65(4), 250-9.

---, Marc Brysbaert, Frank Geypens and Gery D'Ydewalle (1996), "The Importance of Magnitude Information in Numerical Processing: Evidence from the SNARC Effect," *Mathematical Cognition*, 2(1), 95-110.

--- and Martin H. Fischer (2005) "Spatial Representation of Numbers," in *Handbook of Mathematical Cognition*, ed. Campbell JID, New York: Psychology Press, 43-54.

Gevers, Wim and Jan Lammertyn (2005), "The Hunt for SNARC", *Psychological Science*, 47, 10-21.

Hollan, James D. (1975), "Features and Semantic Memory: Set-theoretic or network model," *Psychological review*, 82, 154-5.

Hubbard, Edward M., Manuela Piazza, Philippe Pinel and Stanislas Dehaene (2005), "Interactions between Number and Space in Parietal Cortex," *Nature Reviews Neuroscience*, 6, 435-48.

Hung, Yi-hui, Daisy L. Hung and Ovid J.L. Tzeng(2008), "Flexible Spatial Mapping of Different Notations of Numbers in Chinese Readers," *Cognition*, 106(3), 1441–50.

Huttenlocher, Janellen, Larry V. Hedges, Bryce Corrigan, and L. Elizabeth Crawford (2004), "Spatial Categories and the Estimation of Location," *Cognition*, 93(1), 75-97.

Huttenlocher, Janellen, Larry V. Hedges and Susan Duncan (1991), "Categories and Particulars: Prototype Effects in Estimating Spatial Location," *Psychological Review*, 98(3), 352-76.

Lee, Angela Y. and Jennifer L. Aaker(2004), "Bringing the Frame Into Focus: The Influence of Regulatory Fit on Processing Fluency and Persuasion," *Journal of Personality and Social Psychology*, 86(2), 205-18.

Nelson, Leif D. and Joseph P. Simmons (2009), "On Southbound Ease and Northbound Fees: Literal Consequences of Metaphoric Link between Vertical Position and Cardinal Direction," *Journal of Marketing Research*, forthcoming.

Nuerk, Hans-Christoph, Guilherme Wood and Klaus Willmes (2005), "The Universal SNARC Effect: The Association between Number Magnitude and Space is Amodal," *Experimental Psychology*, 52(3), 187-94.

Schubert, Thomas W.(2005), "Your Highness: Vertical Positions as Perceptual Symbols of Power," *Journal of Personality and Social Psychology*, 89(1), 1-21.

Schwarz, Norbert (2006), "On Judgments of Truth and Beauty," *Daedalus*, 135(2), 136-8.

Smith, Edward E. (1978), "Theories of Semantic Memory", in *Handbook of Learning and Cognitive Process*, ed. William K. Estes, Hillsdale, NJ: Lawrence Erllbaum Associates, 6, 1-56.

Völckner, Franziska and Julian Hofmann (2007), "The Price-Perceived Quality Relationship: A Meta-Analytic Review and Assessment of Its Determinants," *Marketing letters*, 18(3), 181-96.

Whittlesea, Bruce W. A. (1993), "Illusions of Familiarity," *Journal of Experimental Psychology: Learning, Memory, and Cognition*, 19(6), 1235-53.

Williams, Lawrence E., Julie Y. Huang and John A. Bargh (2009), "The Scaffolded Mind: Higher Mental Processes Are Grounded in Early Experience of the Physical World," *European Journal of Social Psychology,* forthcoming.

Wood, Guilherme and Martin H. Fischer (2008), "Numbers, Space, and Action—From Finger Counting to the Number Line and Beyond," *Cortex,* 44(4), 353-8.

Zorzi, Marco, Konstantinos Priftis and Carlo Umiltà (2002), "Brain Damage: Neglect Disrupts the Mental Number Line," *Nature*, 417, 138-9.

Zorzi, Marco, Konstantinos Priftis, Francesca Meneghello, Roberto Marenzi and Carlo Umiltà (2006), "The Spatial Representation of Numerical and Non-numerical Sequence: Evidence from Neglect," *Neuropsychologia*, 44, 1061-7.

Searching in Choice Mode:
Consumer Decision Processes in Product Search with Recommendations

Benedict Dellaert, Erasmus University Rotterdam, The Netherlands
Gerald Haeubl, University of Alberta, Canada

EXTEND ABSTRACT

Consumers increasingly have easy access to vast numbers of products, and they often engage in an extensive search of the set of available alternatives in order to make a purchase. An effective means of assisting consumer search is to provide them with recommendations that sort alternatives in terms of attractiveness. Such assistance may be provided by human advisors (e.g., realtors), but it is increasingly available in the form of recommendations that are generated automatically by information systems. It has been shown that presenting shoppers with a list of alternatives sorted in line with their preferences substantially increases the quality of their purchase decisions (Häubl and Trifts 2000) and enables them to find lower prices and higher quality items in large retail assortments (Diehl, Kornish, and Lynch 2003).

While prior research has investigated how product recommendations affect decision outcomes, little is known about how such decision assistance influences consumer decision *processes* during product search. The present research seeks to fill this gap. This is particularly important because, despite the generally positive consequences of recommendations for consumer welfare, there are also instances in which providing consumers with sorted lists of alternatives may lead to worse decisions (Diehl 2005). A better understanding of consumer decision processes during search with recommendations can shed light on the underlying mechanisms that might undermine the effectiveness of this type of decision assistance.

Our central thesis is that the presence of recommendations transforms the decision processes consumers use during sequential product search relative to searching without such assistance. In particular, we argue that, when engaging in unassisted search (i.e., without recommendations), consumers naturally have a decision orientation that is characterized by forward-looking considerations directed at determining, at each stage of the search, whether or not an *additional* alternative should be inspected (Adam 2001; Bikhchandani and Sharma 1996; Häubl, Dellaert, and Donkers 2010; Weitzman 1979). By contrast, we propose that, when presented with recommendations, consumers adopt a decision orientation in the search process that incorporates considerations more akin to those used in choosing from a predetermined set of alternatives. Such considerations focus on broader comparisons among alternatives *already inspected* in the course of the search. We refer to this phenomenon as searching in "choice mode."

The proposed shift in decision orientation implies that consumer search behavior in the presence of product recommendations is partly governed by influences that are non-normative and that are commonly observed when consumers choose from small predetermined sets of alternatives – i.e., in settings that do not require search (Payne, Bettman, and Johnson 1988; Simonson 1989; Wright 1975). To test this proposition, we examine how recommendations affect the two key decisions that consumers must make at each stage of their search – determining which of the products already inspected is the most attractive one (product comparison decision) and deciding whether to terminate the search or continue it by inspecting an additional product (stopping decision).

Evidence from two experiments provides strong support for such a transformation of search decisions, which manifests itself in two respects. First, searching with recommendations causes consumers to assess a product they encounter not only by comparing it to the best previously found one (as prescribed by normative models of search), but also by making broader comparisons with other inspected alternatives than in unassisted search. Second, recommendations transform how variability in product attractiveness affects stopping decisions such that greater variability causes consumers to search less, which is opposite to what is commonly observed in search without recommendations. These findings provide evidence in support of the proposed shift towards a choice orientation in consumers' search decisions.

REFERENCES

Adam, Klaus (2001), "Learning While Searching for the Best Alternative," *Journal of Economic Theory*, 101 (1), 252-281.

Bikhchandani, Sushil and Sunil Sharma (1996), "Optimal Search with Learning," *Journal of Economic Dynamics and Control*, 20 (1-3), 333-359.

Chakravarti, Amitav, Chris Janiszewski, and Gülden Ülkümen (2006), "The Neglect of Prescreening Information," *Journal of Marketing Research*, 43 (4), 642-653.

Dhar, Ravi (1997), "Consumer Preference for a No-Choice Option," *Journal of Consumer Research*, 24 (2), 215-231.

---- and Itamar Simonson (2003), "The Effect of Forced Choice on Choice," *Journal of Marketing Research*, 40 (2), 146-160.

Diehl, Kristin (2005) "When Two Rights Make A Wrong: Searching Too Much in Ordered Environments," *Journal of Marketing Research*, 42 (3), 313-322.

----, Laura J. Kornish, and John G. Lynch (2003), "Smart Agents: When Lower Search Costs for Quality Information Increase Price Sensitivity," *Journal of Consumer Research*, 30 (1), 56-72.

Fitzsimons, Gavan J. and Donald R. Lehmann (2004), "Reactance to Recommendations: When Unsolicited Advice Yields Contrary Responses," *Marketing Science*, 23 (1), 82-94.

Häubl, Gerald, Benedict G.C. Dellaert, and Bas Donkers (2010), "Tunnel Vision: Local Behavioral Influences on Consumer Decisions in Product Search," *Marketing Science*, 29 (3), 438-455.

---- and Kyle Murray (2003), "Preference Construction and Persistence in Digital Marketplaces: The Role of Electronic Recommendation Agents," *Journal of Consumer Psychology*, 13 (1&2), 75-91.

---- and Valerie Trifts (2000), "Consumer Decision Making in Online Shopping Environments: The Effects of Interactive Decision Aids," *Marketing Science*, 19 (1), 4-21.

Hauser, John R. and Birger Wernerfelt (1990), "An Evaluation Cost Model of Consideration Sets," *Journal of Consumer Research*, 16 (4), 393-408.

Huber, Joel, John W. Payne, and Christopher Puto (1982), "Adding Asymmetrically Dominated Alternatives: Violations of Regularity and the Similarity Hypothesis," *Journal of Consumer Research*, 9 (1), 90-98.

Johnson, Eric J. and John W. Payne (1985), "Effort and Accuracy in Choice," *Management Science*, 31 (4), 395-414.

McFadden, Daniel (1986), "The Choice Theory Approach to Market Research," *Marketing Science*, 5 (4), 275-297.

Murray, Kyle B. and Gerald Häubl (2009), "Personalization without Interrogation: Towards more Effective Interactions between Consumers and Feature-Based Recommendation Agents," *Journal of Interactive Marketing*, 23 (2), 138-146.

Payne, John W., James R. Bettman, and Eric J. Johnson (1988), "Adaptive Strategy Selection in Decision Making," *Journal of Experimental Psychology: Learning, Memory, and Cognition*, 14 (3), 534-552.

Roberts, John H. and James M. Lattin (1991), "Development and Testing of a Model of Consideration Set Composition," *Journal of Marketing Research*, 28 (4), 429-440.

Rosenfield, Donald B., Roy D. Shapiro, and David A. Butler (1983), "Optimal Strategies for Selling an Asset," *Management Science*, 29(9), 1051-1061.

Simonson, Itamar (1989), "Choice Based on Reasons," *Journal of Consumer Research*, 16 (2), 158-174.

Simonson, Itamar and Amos Tversky (1992), "Choice in Context: Trade-Off Contrast and Extremeness Aversion," *Journal of Marketing Research*, 29 (3), 281-295.

Stigler, George J. (1961), "The Economics of Information," *Journal of Political Economy*, 69 (3), 213-225

Swait, Joffre and Wiktor Adamowicz (2001), "The Influence of Task Complexity on Consumer Choice: A Latent Class Model of Decision Strategy Switching," *Journal of Consumer Research*, 28 (1), 135-148.

Tversky, Amos and Itamar Simonson (1993), "Context-Dependent Preferences," *Management Science*, 39 (10), 1179-1189.

Weitzman, Martin (1979), "Optimal Search for the Best Alternative," *Econometrica*, 47 (3), 641-654.

Wright, Peter (1975), "Consumer Choice Strategies: Simplifying vs. Optimizing," *Journal of Marketing Research*, 12 (1), 60-67.

How Goal-Based Labels Drive Choice and Choice Satisfaction

Kristof Geskens, Vlerick Leuven Gent Management School, Belgium
Frank Goedertier, Vlerick Leuven Gent Management School, Belgium
Bert Weijters, Vlerick Leuven Gent Management School, Belgium
Maggie Geuens, Ghent University & Vlerick Leuven Gent Management School, Belgium

EXTENDED ABSTRACT

Increasingly consumers are confronted with an overload of choice. Classic economic theories predict that more choice benefits consumers through better preference matching (Lancaster 1990) and allowing variety seeking (Kahn 1995). Recent research, however, demonstrates that more choice can also lead to confusion, frustration, less satisfaction, and choice paralysis (Iyengar and Lepper 2000; Gourville and Soman 2005; Reutskaja and Hogarth 2009).

To mitigate these negative overchoice effects, previous studies suggest product-based solutions such as creating an alignable assortment (Gourville and Soman 2005) or working with attribute-based categories (Mogilner, Rudnick and Iyengar 2008). In this study we propose a consumer-based solution starting from consumers' ways of processing information. Since the pursuit of goals drives much of consumers' choice behavior (Lawson 1997; Van Osselaer et al. 2005), we advance goal-based labeling as a mechanism to facilitate consumer choice. Goal-based labels (e.g., a "Budget", "Family Trip", or "Professional" camera) may facilitate consumer choice by clearly linking goals with different choice options.

The effect of goal-based labeling on choice is likely to depend on the level of consumer expertise. Because of their extensive category knowledge, experts already have an ideal point (i.e., ideal attribute combination needed to satisfy a goal) in mind (Chernev 2003). Novices, in contrast, lack category knowledge and do not have a readily available ideal point. As a consequence, "translating" a goal into relevant product attributes may be problematic for novices. Goal-based labels can serve as a cue on which novices may rely to facilitate their choice process (Hoeffler and Ariely 1999). Therefore, we expect novices to choose an option with an appropriate goal-based label over an option with a non-meaningful label, even when it is inaccurate (i.e., the choice option does not deliver the benefits needed to satisfy the goal the label suggests). We expect experts to dispose of the cognitive resources to easily process options at a deeper level, which may enable them to make an optimal choice irrespective of the presence of goal-based labels.

Hypothesis 1a   *Goal-based labels will guide the choice alternative selection of novices, but not of experts.*

Hypothesis 1b   *Accurate (vs. inaccurate) goal-based labels increase the likelihood to make an optimal choice for novices, but not for experts.*

Choice satisfaction can be conceptualized as the difference between the perceived costs and perceived benefits of choice (Reutskaja and Hogarth 2009). Because goal-based labels may serve as a cue for choice they can reduce the perceived cost of thinking (Shugan 1980) without reducing the benefits of choice. Since we expect that novices, but not experts, will be guided by goal-based labels, we hypothesize:

Hypothesis 2   *Goal-based labeling has a positive effect on choice satisfaction for novices but not for experts.*

When the number of choice alternatives increases, evaluating and making a well-considered choice becomes more difficult - resulting in lower satisfaction (Iyengar and Lepper 2000, Chernev 2003). Additionally, novices may not know exactly which product attributes enable them to fulfill a specific goal (Brendl, Markman, and Messner 2003), and thus experience uncertainty – which may again result in lower satisfaction. Summarizing, we advance two processes through which goal-based labeling can reduce novices' perceived cognitive costs of choice: (1) a decrease in choice difficulty and (2) a decrease in choice uncertainty. Therefore, we hypothesize:

Hypothesis 3   *The effect of goal-based labeling on choice satisfaction for novice consumers is mediated by perceived choice difficulty.*

Hypothesis 4   *The effect of goal-based labeling on choice satisfaction for novice consumers is mediated by perceived choice uncertainty.*

To test our hypotheses, we conduct an online quasi-experiment with a 2 (expert vs. novice) X 3 (no goal-based labels vs. accurate goal-based labels vs. inaccurate goal-based labels) full-factorial design. We simulate a choice setting using stimuli derived from a sequence of pre-tests. In total, 334 male subjects participated in the main study, grouped into experts ($N = 173$) and novices ($N = 161$). Expertise in the first group was substantially and significantly higher than in the second group, with respective scores on a 20-point scale of $M_1 = 5.89$ (SD = 5.02); $M_2 = 15.28$ (SD = 3.57), t (215) = -15.03, p < .001. Each respondent was randomly assigned to one of three experimental conditions. After being confronted with a scenario prompting a specific goal, each participant was asked to make a choice from the given assortment. Next, respondents had to justify their choice and answer items measuring the mediating and dependent variables.

We first test whether the labeling manipulation affects the proportion of optimal choices. Among novices, the proportion of optimal choices varies significantly across labeling conditions (chi²(2) = 29.9, p < .001), whereas among experts it does not (chi²(2) = .881, p = .644). Among novices, 8.9% of respondents choose the optimal alternative when goal-based labels are absent, whereas in the assortment with accurate goal-based labels significantly more novices make an optimal choice (47.3%; chi²(1)=17.36, p < .001). These findings support H1a.

Next we compare the number of optimal choices for novices versus experts in the accurately and inaccurately labeled conditions. Among novices, in the inaccurately labeled assortment the amount of optimal choices drops to 9.8%, which is significantly lower than in the accurately labeled assortment (where it was 47.3%; chi²(1) = 20.29, p < .001). Among experts the amount of optimal choices does not differ across conditions (chi²(1) = .858, p ─ .354). These result support H1b.

To study the effect of assortment type and expertise on choice uncertainty, choice difficulty and choice satisfaction, we test a path model in which the outcomes (uncertainty, difficulty, and satisfaction) are regressed on assortment type.

In line with H2, the total effect of goal-based labeling on choice satisfaction is positive and significant for novices (B=.59, SE=.18, p=.002), but not for experts (B=.05, SE=.15, p=.361). We find that choice difficulty is not a significant mediator, as its impact on choice satisfaction is not significant (and the impact of goal-based labeling on choice difficulty is only marginally significant). Thus, H3 is not supported.

Among novices (but not among experts) choice uncertainty is significantly and negatively affected by goal-based labeling (B = -1.27; SE = .40; t = -3.19; p = .001). Additionally, choice uncertainty has a significant negative effect on choice satisfaction (B= -.48; SE = .05; t = -9.26; p = .000). Hence, in line with H4, among novices (but not among experts) choice uncertainty mediates the positive effect of goal-based labeling on choice satisfaction. Furthermore, content analysis of participants' reasons for choice shows that novices use goal-based labels to make sense of the attributes of the choice options.

On the basis of the obtained results, we conclude that goal-based labels increase the choice satisfaction of novice consumers, by increasing their perceived choice certainty. A possible explanation for the absence of the hypothesized mediating effect of choice difficulty (H3) is that satisfaction relates to the outcome of the choice, not the process.

REFERENCES

Alba, J.W., and Hutchinson, J.W. (1987). Dimensions of Consumer Expertise. Journal of Consumer Research 13(4), 411-454.

Bergkvist, L., and Rossiter, J. R. (2007). The Predictive Validity of Multiple-Item Versus Single-Item Measures of the Same Constructs. Journal of Marketing Research, 44(May), 175-184.

Bharadwaj, N., Naylor, N.W., and ter Hofstede, F. (2009), "Consumer response to and choice of customized versus standardized systems," *International Journal of Research in Marketing*, 26(3), 216-227.

Brendl, M. C., Markman, A. B., and Messner C. (2003). The Devaluation Effect: Activating a Need Devalues Unrelated Objects. *Journal of Consumer Research*, 29 (4), 463-473.

Castaño, R., Sujan, M., Kacker, M., and Sujan, H. (2008). Managing consumer uncertainty in the adoption of new products: Temporal distance and mental simulation. *Journal of Marketing Research,* 45(3), 320-336.

Chernev, A. (2003). When More is Less and Less is More: The Role of Ideal Point Availability and Assortment in Choice. *Journal of Consumer Research*, 30 (September), 170-183.

Drolet A., Luce M. F., Simonson I (2009). When Does Choice Reveal Preference? Moderators of Heuristic versus Goal-Based Choice. *Journal of Consumer Research*, 36(1), 137-147.

Gourville, J. T., and Soman, D. (2005). Overchoice and Assortment Type: When and Why Variety Backfires. *Marketing Science*, 24 (3), 382-395.

Haynes, G. A. (2009). Testing the boundaries of the choice overload phenomenon: The effect of number of options and time pressure on decision difficulty and satisfaction. *Psychology & Marketing*, 26 (3), 204-212.

Hoeffler, S, and Ariely, D. (1999). Constructing Stable Preferences: A Look Into Dimensions of Experience and Their Impact on Preference Stability. *Journal of Consumer Psychology*, 8 (2), 113-140.

Huffman, C., and Kahn, B. E. (1998). Variety for Sale: Mass Customization or Mass Confusion? *Journal of Retailing*, 74 (4), 491-513.

Iyengar, S. S., and Lepper, M. R. (2000). When Choice is Demotivating: Can One Desire Too Much of a Good Thing? *Journal of Personality & Social Psychology*, 79 (6), 995-1006.

Johnson, E. J., and Russo, J.E. (1984). Product Familiarity and Learning New Information. *Journal of Consumer Research*, 11 (1), 542-550.

Kahn, B. E. (1995). Consumer Variety Seeking among Goods and Services – An Integrative Review. *Journal of Retailing and Consumer Services*, 2 (3), 139-148.

Lancaster, K. (1990). The Economics of Product Variety: A Survey. *Marketing Science*, 9 (3), 189.

Malhotra, N. K. (1982). Information Load and Consumer Decision Making. *Journal of Consumer Research,* 8(4), 419-430

Mitchell, A. A., and Dacin, P. A. (1996). The Assessment of Alternative Measures of Consumer Expertise. *Journal of Consumer Research*, 23 (3), 219-239.

Mogilner, C., Rudnick, T. and Iyengar, S. S. (2008). The Mere Categorization Effect: How the Presence of Categories Increases Choosers' Perceptions of Assortment Variety and Outcome Satisfaction. *Journal of Consumer Research*, 35 (2), 202-215.

Poynor, C., and Wood, S. (2010). Smart Subcategories: How Assortment Formats Influence Consumer Learning and Satisfaction. *Journal of Consumer Research*, 37 (1), 159-175.

Ratneshwar, S., Pechmann, C., and Shocker, A. (1996). Goal-Derived Categories and the Antecedents of Across-Category Consideration. *Journal of Consumer Research*, 23(Dec), 240–250.

Reutskaja, E. and Hogarth, R. M. (2009), Satisfaction in choice as a function of the number of alternatives: When "goods satiate". *Psychology & Marketing,* 26(3), 197-203.

Russo, J. E., and Johnson, E. J. (1980). What Do Customers Know About Familiar Products? *Advances in Consumer Research*, 7 (1), 417-423.

Russo, J. E., and Leclerc, F. (1994). An Eye-Fixation Analysis of Choice Processes for Consumer Nondurables. *Journal of Consumer Research*, 21 (2), 274-290.

Rust, R. T., Thompson, D. V. and Hamilton, R. W. (2006). Defeating Feature Fatigue. *Harvard Business Review*, 84 (2), 98-107.

Scheibehenne, B., Greifeneder, R., and Todd, P. M. (2009). What moderates the too-much-choice effect? *Psychology & Marketing*, 26 (3), 229-253.

Schwartz, B. (2004). The paradox of choice: Why more is less. New York: HarperCollins, Ecco.

Shugan, S. M. (1980). The Cost Of Thinking. *Journal of Consumer Research*, 7 (2), 99-111

Simonson, I. (1999). The Effect of Product Assortment on Buyer Preferences. *Journal of Retailing*, 75 (3), 347-371.

van Osselaer, S., Ramanathan, S., Campbell, M. C., Cohen, J. B., Dale, J. K., Herr, P. M., Janiszewski, C., Kruglanski, A. W., Lee, A. Y., Read, S. J., Russo, J. E., and Tavassoli, N. T. (2005). Choice Based on Goals. *Marketing Letters*, 16 (3/4), 335-346.

A Perceived Control-Based Model of the Effects of Co-Production on Satisfaction

Natália Araujo Pacheco, Universidade Federal do Rio Grande do Sul, Brazil
Renaud Lunardo, Troyes Champagne School of Mangement, France
Cristiane Pizzutti, Universidade Federal do Rio Grande do Sul, Brazil

EXTENDED ABSTRACT

Consumer's participation through co-production is increasingly present in marketing literature. Co-production requires consumer participation in production activities, such as product designing, resource aggregating or other processing activities leading to an output that will be used or consumed (Etgar 2008). From the company perspective, co-production can be an effective marketing tool, as the interaction between customer and firm has been pointed as a source of value creation (Prahalad and Ramaswamy 2004) and competitive effectiveness (Bendapudi and Leone 2003). From the consumer perspective, co-production may be of interest for consumers since it allows them to perceive some control over the process of the desired product or service.

The perceived control concept is related to the perceived ability to significantly alter a situation (Burger 1989; Thompson 1981) and has been showed to exert a crucial role in people's life by exhibiting stress-reducing (Glass and Singer 1972) and motivation-inducing (Skinner, 1995) properties. Having made its first appearance in consumer research not until the 1990s, perceived control has been found out to exert some positive influence on pleasure (Hui and Bateson 1991), mood, involvement (Ward and Barnes 2001), satisfaction (Wathieu et al. 2002) and intention to behave (Mathur 1998). However and quite surprisingly when considering the increase of co-production in consumption activities, a clear need to understand the linkage between the control from the co-creation process and the satisfaction toward the related consumption remains (Lusch and Vargo 2006). More specifically, two questions remain unanswered: first, does co-production lead to higher consumers' satisfaction because it makes them feel more in control? Second, does the perception of control induced by the co-production process always lead to higher satisfaction or, on the contrary, may lead in specific circumstances to lower satisfaction?

This article represents an initial effort to analyze the complex linkages between co-production, perceived control and satisfaction. Understanding how the perception of control influences the process of satisfaction is of interest because of the importance of satisfaction to predict future consumer's choices (Woodruff, Cadotte and Jenkins 1983). Within this perspective, understanding how co-production may contribute to enhance perceived control – and consequently satisfaction – is also of importance.

This research draws on Skinner's (1996) conceptualization of perceived control – an extension of Averill's (1973) model which states that behavioral, cognitive, and decisional control are potential antecedents of perceived control - to explain the effects of co-production on satisfaction. Two experimental studies were developed to investigate whether co-production and other two variables, information and consumer choice, affect perceived control and whether the later has an effect on satisfaction moderated by self-efficacy. The first experiment simulates behavioral and cognitive control, respectively, through co-production and information to examine them as two possible sources of perceived control and satisfaction. The second experiment replicates the first by replacing information by choice. Behavioral and decisional controls are simulated, respectively, through co-production and choice.

Therefore three hypotheses about perceived control's antecedents were tested: consumers who co-produce will perceive greater control when compared to those who do not (hypothesis 1); consumers who gain more information will perceive greater control when compared to those who gain less information (hypothesis 2); and consumers who have choice will perceive greater control when compared to those who have no choice (hypothesis 3). As feeling in control of the environment has been strongly related to satisfaction and performance (Greenberger et al. 1989) the hypothesis about perceived control's impact on satisfaction was also tested: the greater the perceived control, the greater the satisfaction (hypothesis 4). A moderation of self-efficacy on the effect of perceived control on satisfaction should be expected since the increase in perceived control may lead to negative reactions (Burger 1989) specially if co-producers are concerned with their own ability (Ertimur 2008), so a last hypothesis was tested on both experiments: consumers with high self-efficacy will experience greater satisfaction when they perceive higher control than consumers with low self-efficacy (hypothesis 5).

Results of both studies supported the five hypotheses, showing that co-production ($F(1, 93) = 57.48$, $p < .001$ on study 1, and ($F(1, 86) = 110.20$, $p < .001$) on study 2), information ($F(1, 93) = 13.53$, $p < .001$) and choice ($F(1, 86) = 23.34$, $p < .001$) affect perceived control which in turn affects satisfaction ($\beta = .809$, $t(95) = 13.39$, $p < .001$ on study 1, and $\beta = .872$, $t(88) = 16.72$, $p < .001$ on study 2). This last relationship depends on self-efficacy such that consumers with high perceived control and high self-efficacy reported greater satisfaction than those with low self-efficacy. These results suggest that perceived control is a powerful concept in explaining satisfaction consequently to co-production and that self-efficacy is a crucial condition for the positive effect of perceived control on satisfaction. Findings of studies 1 and 2 strongly support Skinner's (1996) model of perceived control and confirm the power of perceived control in explaining the effects of co-production, in addition of information and choice, on consumer' satisfaction.

This research may be of interest to marketing practitioners. As co-production leads to more perceived control, marketers can induce consumers' feelings of empowerment by allowing them to participate in the production process. Giving consumers information about the product or service, or giving them choice also represents for marketers means to induce consumer's perceived control. As emphasized by the wide body of literature dealing with control (Skinner, 1996), such consumer's feeling of control may result in a variety of positive outcome, from emotions to behavioral responses, all them being of great interest for practitioners. However, we found self-efficacy as an important variable for the positive effect of perceived control on satisfaction. Thus it may be argued that co-production must engage consumers in simple process or in processes with which the consumers are familiar in order not to jeopardize the consumer's self-efficacy and in turn its satisfaction.

REFERENCES

Averill, James R. (1973), "Personal Control over Aversive Stimuli and its Relationship to Stress," *Psychological bulletin*, 80 (4), 286–303.

Bendapudi, Neeli and Robert P. Leone (2003), "Psychological Implications of Customer Participation in Co-Production," *Journal of Marketing*, 67 (1), 14–28.

Burger, Jerry M. (1989), "Negative Reactions to Increases in Perceived Personal Control," *Journal of Personality and Social Psychology*, 56 (2), 246–56.

Ertimur, Burcak. (2008), "The Role of Perceived Control in Co-Production", *European Advances in Consumer Research*, v. 8, p. 334–35.

Etgar, Michael (2008), "A Descriptive Model of the Consumer Co-Production Process," *Journal of the Academy of Marketing Science*, 36 (1), 97–108.

Glass, David C. and Jerome E. Singer (1972), *Urban Stress: Experiments on Noise and Social Stressors*, New York: Academic Press.

Greenberger, David, Steven Strasser, Larry Cummings, and Randall Dunhan (1989), "The impact of personal control on performance and satisfaction", *Organizational Behaviour and Human Decision Processes*, 43 (1), 29–51.

Hui, Michael K. and John E.G. Bateson (1991), "Perceived Control and the Effects of Crowding and Consumer Choice on the Service Experience," *Journal of Consumer Research*, 18 (2), 174–84.

Lusch, Robert F. and Stephen L. Vargo. (2006), *The Service-Dominant Logic of Marketing: Dialog, Debate, and Directions*, N.Y: M. S. Sharpe.

Mathur, Anil (1998), "Examining Trying as a Mediator and Control as a Moderator of Intention-Behavior Relationship," *Psychology and Marketing*, 15 (3), 241–59.

Prahalad, C.K. and Venkat Ramaswamy (2004), "Co-Creation Experiences: The Next Practice in Value Creation," *Journal of Interactive Marketing*, 18 (3), 5–14.

Skinner, Ellen A. (1995), *Perceived Control, Motivation, and Coping*, London: Sage Publication.

Skinner, Ellen A. (1996), "A Guide to Constructs of Control," *Journal of Personality and Social Psychology*, 71 (3), 549-71.

Thompson, Suzanne C. (1981), "Will it Hurt Less if I Can Control It? A Complex Answer to a Simple Question," *Psychological Bulletin*, 90 (1), 89–101.

Ward, James C. and James W. Barnes (2001), "Control and Affect: The Influence of Feeling in Control of the Retail environment on Affect, Involvement, Attitude, and Behavior," *Journal of Business Research*, 54 (2), 139–44.

Wathieu, Luc, Lyle Brenner, Ziv Carmon, Amitaya Chattopadhyay, Klaus Wertenbroch, Aimee Drolet, John Gourville, A.V. Muthukrishnan, Nathan Novemsky, Rebecca Ratner, and George Wu (2002), "Consumer Control and Empowerment: A Primer," *Marketing Letters*, 13 (3), 297-305.

Woodruff, Robert B., Ernest R. Cadotte, and Roger L. Jenkins (1983), Modeling Consumer Satisfaction Process Using Experience-Based Norms," *Journal of Marketing Research*, 20 (3), 296–304.

Brands as Product Coordinators: Matching Brands Make Joint Consumption Experiences More Enjoyable

Ryan Rahinel, Unversity of Minnesota, USA
Joseph Redden, Unversity of Minnesota, USA

EXTENDED ABSTRACT

Two product classes are said to be complementary when the utility derived from one good depends on usage of the other good. Such product classes are often jointly consumed as in the case of toothbrushes and toothpaste or tortilla chips and salsa. In the current research, we take the notion of complementarity a level deeper and ask how specific brand combinations within given product classes affect utility during joint consumption (e.g., "Which combination of Tostitos and Old Dutch tortilla chips and salsas would be most enjoyed?"). Previous work suggests that given two brands where one is slightly preferred to the other, one should enjoy as much of the better brand as possible. Contrary to this prediction, we find that consumers experience a bonus in enjoyment from having a single matched brand for both products. We posit that the reason for this "brand matching effect" is that consumers expect a brand to have coordinated its products, through activities like joint product design and testing, to uniquely work well together. The belief that product coordination has taken place is cued when the brands of multiple products match. Four empirical studies support our core prediction that matching brands increases joint consumption.

In the first study, we asked participants to rate the sharpness of pictures said to be created by a printer and ink combination (even though all pictures were actually printed using the same printer and ink cartridge). The design was a 2 (Printer Brand: HP vs. Canon) x 2 (Ink Brand: HP vs. Canon) between-subjects design. Participants rated the pictures as appearing significantly sharper when the printer and ink were labeled as the same brand (vs. different brands) ($p < .03$). A follow-up study in which we did not reveal the brand names but merely told participants that the printer and ink were the same or two different brands replicated this result ($p < .03$).

The second study tested the product coordination explanation against other explanations suggesting general preference for matching on any attribute. We framed labels of tortilla chips and salsa as either brand names (e.g., "Party Time® brand salsa") or general adjectives (e.g., "party time salsa). If our account is correct, then we should observe the brand matching effect in the brand frame case but not in the general adjective frame case. Indeed, tortilla chips and salsa framed as coming from the same brand were enjoyed more than those framed as from different brands ($p < .05$), but there were no differences between the matched and mismatched cases for the adjective frame case ($t < 1$).

The third study sought direct evidence for our product coordination explanation. The design used only the brand frame conditions from Study 2 and asked participants to indicate their perceived coordination (i.e., perceptions of joint research and design) of the two products after the dependent measures. Our core finding that matched brands of tortilla chips and salsa were enjoyed more than mismatched brands was replicated ($p < .02$). In addition, a Sobel test confirmed that perceived coordination mediated the effect of brand matching on rated enjoyment ($p < .03$).

The objective of the fourth study is to provide further process evidence by explicitly manipulating product coordination. We counterbalanced Brand A and Brand B labels that were counterbalanced across the two products. In addition to the brand labels, we also manipulated a line of text participants read before tasting the chips and salsa. In one condition, we told participants that the brand(s) had "coordinated the distribution and coupons for these two products." In the other condition, we told participants that the brand(s) had "coordinated the design of these products and market research on how they tasted together." We expected to replicate the brand matching effect in the former condition but not the latter. In accordance with this prediction, tortilla chips and salsa from the same brand were enjoyed more than those from different brands when participants were told that the brand(s) had coordinated the distributions and coupons for the two products ($p < .04$). This effect was eliminated when we told participants that the brand(s) had coordinated the research and design for the two products ($t < 1$).

The results of these studies contribute to the literature in three important ways. First, we establish brand matching as a way to increase the enjoyment of multiple products consumed jointly without changing what is objectively being consumed. This is in line with previous work, which has shown that the presence of a high quality brand label increases the enjoyment of a single product (Allison and Uhl 1964; Hoegg and Alba 2007). Our finding leads to new insights about how marketers can help consumers enjoy their consumption episodes more without trying to change quality perceptions of the brand. Second, by demonstrating the brand matching effect with unfamiliar brands that have no preexisting associations, our work furthers product coordination as a general role for brands. This contributes to the literature on brand roles, which suggests among other things that brands can serve as a signals of quality and manufacturing competencies (Wernerfelt 1988; Broniarczyk and Alba 1994), figures of attachment (Fournier 1998), and signals of group associations (Belk 1988). Third, by fixing the product categories consumed, our work highlights the role of a product-level fit in consumption enjoyment. This notion of a product-level fit in many ways complements past work on how product extension evaluations are enhanced when they fit with a brand in terms of category-level complementarity (e.g., chips with dip; Aaker and Keller 1990). Our findings demonstrate consumers not only believe that brands that make a specific product can better make products in a complementary category, but also that a brand's complementary extension will work best with existing products from that brand because they were designed and tested together. It is clear that branding is an important question for researchers, made more difficult by the fact that consumers mix brands together quite often. Future research should further our understanding of how brand combinations can ultimately create more enjoyable experiences.

REFERENCES

Aaker, David A. and Kevin Lane Keller (1990), "Consumer Evaluations of Brand Extensions," *Journal of Marketing*, 54 (January), 27-41.

Allison, Ralph I., and Kenneth P. Uhl (1964), "Influence of Beer Brand Identification on Taste Perception," *Journal of Marketing Research*, 1, 36-39.

Alter, Adam L. and Daniel M. Oppenheimer (2008), "Uniting the Tribes of Fluency to Form a Metacognitive Nation," *Personality and Social Psychology Review*, 13 (3), 219-35.

Belk, Russell (1988), "Possessions and the Extended Self," *Journal of Consumer Research*, 15 (September), 139-68.

Berger, Jonah and Chip Heath (2007), "Where Consumers Diverge from Others: Identity-Signaling and Product Domains," *Journal of Consumer Research*, 34 (August), 121-34.

Berlyne, D.E. (1960), *Conflict, Arousal, and Curiosity*. New York: McGraw-Hill.

Boush, David M. and Barbara Loken (1991), "A Process-Tracing Study of Brand Extension Evaluation," *Journal of Marketing Research*, 28 (February), 16-28.

Broniarczyk, Susan M., and Joseph W. Alba (1994), "The Importance of the Brand in Brand Extension," *Journal of Marketing Research*, 31 (May), 214-28.

Cialdini, Robert B., Melanie R. Trost, and Jason T. Newsom (1995), "Preference for Consistency: The Development of a Valid Measure and the Discovery of Surprising Behavioral Implications," *Journal of Personality and Social Psychology*, 69 (2), 318-28.

Fishbach, Ayelet, Rebecca K. Ratner, and Ying Zhang (in press), "Inherently Loyal or Easily Bored?: Nonconscious Activation of Consistency versus Variety-Seeking Behavior," *Journal of Consumer Psychology*.

Fournier, Susan (1998), "Consumers and Their Brands: Developing Relationship Theory in Consumer Research," *Journal of Consumer Research*, 24 (March), 343-73.

Henderson, James M. and Richard E. Quandt (1958), *Mircoecnomic Theory: A Mathematical Approach*. New York: McGraw-Hill.

Hoegg, JoAndrea and Joseph W. Alba (2007), "Taste Perception: More than Meets the Tongue," *Journal of Consumer Research*, 33 (March), 490-98.

Inman, J. Jeffrey (2001), "The Role of Sensory-Specific Satiety in Attribute-Level Variety Seeking," *Journal of Consumer Research*, 28 (June), 105-20.

Lee, Leonard, Shane Frederick, and Dan Ariely (2006), "Try it You'll Like It: The Influence of Expectation, Consumption, and Revelation on Preferences for Beer," *Psychological Science*, 17 (12), 1054-1058.

McAlister, Leigh (1982), "A Dynamic Attribute Satiation Model of Variety-Seeking Behavior," *Journal of Consumer Research*, 9 (September), 141-50.

Park, C. Whan, Sandra Milberg, and Robert Lawson (1991), "Evaluation of Brand Extensions: The Role of Product Feature Similarity and Brand Concept Consistency," *Journal of Consumer Research*, 18 (2), 185-93.

---, Bernard J. Jaworski, and Deborah J. MacInnis (1986), "Strategic Brand Concept-Image Management," *Journal of Marketing*, 50 (October), 135-45.

Plassman, Hilke, John O'Doherty, Baba Shiv, and Antonio Rangel (2008), "Marketing Actions can Modulate Neural Representations of Experienced Pleasantness," *Proceedings of the National Academy of Sciences*, 105 (3), 1050-54.

Schwarz, Norbert (2004), "Metacognitive Experiences in Consumer Judgment and Decision Making," *Journal of Consumer Psychology*, 14 (4), 332-48.

Shine, Byung Chul, Jongwon Park, and Robert S. Wyer Jr. (2007), "Brand Synergy Effects in Multiple Brand Extensions," *Journal of Marketing Research*, 44 (November), 663-70.

Shiv, Baba, Ziv Carmon, and Dan Ariely (2005), "Placebo Effects of Marketing Actions: Consumers May Get What They Pay For," *Journal of Marketing Research*, 42 (November), 383-93.

Wernerfelt, Birger (1988), "Umbrella Branding as a Signal of New Product Quality: An Example of Signaling by Posting a Bond," *RAND Journal of Economics*, 19 (3), 458-66.

The Influence of Status Differentiation on Vertical Brand Extension: Intercultural and Intracultural Comparisons

Xiang Fang, Oklahoma State University, USA
Shengdong Lin, Xiamen University, China

EXTENDED ABSTRACT

Many companies have employed brand extensions as an effective tool to introduce new products. To date, much emphasis has been placed on horizontal brand extensions and research on vertical extensions is rather limited. In this article, our focus is on price-based line extensions in which an existing brand introduces a higher-price version (upward stretch) or a lower-price version (downward stretch). Past research on vertical extensions has examined numerous factors influencing consumers' responses to line stretches such as parent brand image (prestige vs. nonprestige), stretch direction (upward vs. downward), branding strategy (subbrand vs. direct), ownership status (owner vs. nonowner), consumer goal (browsing vs. buying), and extension distance (far vs. close). In this article, we introduced status differentiation as an important factor influencing consumers' responses to line extension.

Status differentiation is defined as "how people differentiate their behaviors or attribute power to others according to perceived status differences" (Matsumoto 2007, p. 414). Individuals may monitor their behavior accordingly when they interact with their superiors, colleagues, or subordinates. Since brands usually contain important symbolic meanings, consumers purchase certain brands to maintain and/or enhance their self-image (congruence between personal image and brand image). We expect that individuals varying on status differentiation may view upward- and downward-stretch differently because the brand's symbolic meanings to individual consumers may change accordingly. Therefore, we argue that status differentiation may moderate the effect of brand image and stretch direction on the prestige perception of the line extensions and the parent brands after extensions. We conducted two studies to test the moderation effect of status differentiation.

Study one employed a 2 (culture: Chinese vs. American) × 2 (stretch direction: upward vs. downward) × 2 (brand image: prestige vs. functional) mixed design with the first two variables as between-subjects factors and brand image as a within-subject factor. One hundred and sixty-night Chinese students and forty-eight American students participated in the study. Status differentiation scores were measured by the 20-item scale developed by Musumoto (2007). We used BMW and Toyota to represent prestige brand and functional brand, respectively. Stretch direction was manipulated by different price tiers. The results showed a significant three-way interaction of culture, brand image, and stretch direction on the prestige perception of the line extensions. Specifically, for a prestige brand BMW, the difference between upward- and downward-extension was greater for Chinese (high status differentiation) than for Americans (low status differentiation). In addition, planned comparisons showed that when BMW extended upward, Chinese participants perceived it as being more prestigious than American participants. However, when BMW extended downward, Chinese perceived it as being much less prestigious than Americans. This pattern failed to emerge for the functional product Toyota. Furthermore, the results revealed that the downward extension of a prestigious brand caused more parent brand dilution for Chinese than for American. We also conducted intracultural comparisons by using the median-split approach on the status differentiation scores for Chinese and American participants, respectively. The similar patterns were observed.

In study two, we attempt to replicate the findings of study one by using the priming technique on status differentiation. To increase the generalizability of our findings, we used two different brands in the watch category, Rolex and Seiko, to represent prestige and functional brands, respectively. The results showed that the difference between upward- and downward-extension was greater for individuals in the high status differentiation condition than for those in the low status differentiation condition. The effect was also transferred to the prestige perception of the parent brand after extension. The patterns were similar to the findings in study one.

Our research makes important contributions to the fields of cross-cultural psychology and consumer research. In cross-cultural psychology, Hong et al.'s (2000) proposed the dynamic constructivist approach suggesting that culture is dynamic and individuals can construct specific cultural meaning systems based on contextual cues. Monga and John (2007) primed analytic thinking in Easterners (chronic holistic thinkers) and holistic thinking in Westerners (chronic analytic thinkers) and found the reverse patterns in the way these cultures influenced brand evaluation. Following this stream of research, we primed status differentiation among Chinese individuals and found that participants indeed shifted their status perceptions according to situational cues although high status differentiation was their chronic tendency. More importantly, the status differentiation beliefs primed temporarily had a significant impact on individuals' responses to line extension.

Our findings also contribute to the growing body of research in cross-cultural consumer behavior (e.g., Aaker 2000; Aaker and Lee 2001; Maheswaran and Shavitt 2000). Most research has focused on the cultural differences along the dimension of individualism/collectivism or independent- and interdependent self construal. We investigate another important concept of status differentiation, which is closely related to power distance (Hofstede 1980). Some research has shown that power distance influences consumers' impulsive purchasing (Zhang et al. 2010) and conspicuous consumption (Rucker and Galinsky 2009). We extend this line of research to the context of brand extensions.

Our research has important managerial implications. In today's highly competitive global environment, it is important for marketers to leverage their brand equity and launch successful brand extensions in foreign markets. Our findings provide some insight into this important strategic decision. Specifically, for a prestige brand entering a culture with high status differentiation, it'd better to use the upward extension due to the enhancement effect. Since the downward extension will hurt the extension evaluation and even the parent brand, companies should avoid it. Instead, companies may use the subbrand strategy or a different brand name to extend downward to prevent the dilution effect.

* This paper was supported by National Natural Science Foundation of China (Project Title: The Influence of Cultural Difference in Categorization Process on Brand Extension Evaluation, NO. 70902040

REFERENCES

Aaker, Jennifer L. (2000), "Accessibility or Diagnosticity? Disentangling the Influence of Culture on Persuasion Processes and Attitudes," *Journal of Consumer Research*, 26 (March), 340–57.

Aaker, Jennifer L. and Angela Lee (2001), "I Seek Pleasures and We Avoid Pains: The Role of Self Regulatory Goals on Information Processing and Persuasion," *Journal of Consumer Research*, 28 (June), 33–49.

Hamilton, Ryan and Alexander Chernev. 2010. The Impact of Product Line Extensions and Consumer Goals on the Formation of Price Image. *Journal of Marketing Research*. 47(1): 51-62.

Hofstede, Geert. (1980), *Culture's Consequences: International Differences in Work-related Values*. Newbury Park, CA: Sage.

Hong, Ying-yi, Michael W. Morris, Chi-yue Chiu, and Veronica Benet-Martı´nez (2000), "Multicultural Minds: A Dynamic Constructivist Approach to Culture and Cognition," *American Psychologist*, 55 (July), 709–20.

Keller, Kevin L. and Aaker, D.A. (1992), "The Effects of Sequential Introduction of Brand Extensions," *Journal of Marketing Research*, 29 (February): 5-50.

Kim, Chung K. and Anne, M. Lavack (1996), "Vertical Brand Extensions: Current Research and Managerial Implications," *Journal of Product and Brand Management*, 5(6): 24-37.

Kim Hung K., Anne M. Lavack, and Margo Smith (2001), "Consumer Evaluation of Vertical Brand Extensions and Core Brands," *Journal of Business Research*, (52): 211-222

Kirmani, Amna, Sanjay Sood, & Sheri Bridges (1999), "The Ownership Effect in Consumer Responses to Brand Line Stretches," *Journal of Marketing*, 63 (1): 81-101.

Lei, Jing, Ko de Ruyter and Martin Wetzels (2008), "Consumer Responses to Vertical Service Line Extensions", *Journal of Retailing*, 84 (September), 268-280.

Maheswaran, Durairaj and Sharon Shavitt (2000), "Issues and New Directions in Global Consumer Psychology," *Journal of Consumer Psychology*, 9(2), 59–66.

Markus, Hazel R. and Shinobu Kitayama (1991), "Culture and the Self: Implications for Cognition, Emotion, and Motivation," *Psychological Review*, 98, 224-253.

Matsumot David (2007), "Individual and Cultural Differences on The Status Differentiation: Status Differentiation Scale," *Journal of Cross- Cultural Psychology*, 38 (4): 413-431.

Monga Alokparna .B and Deborah R. D (2007), "Cultural Differences in Brand Extension Evaluation: The Influence of Analytic Versus Holistic Thinking," *Journal of Consumer Research*, 33(March): 527-536.

Monga, Alokparna Basu and Deborah Roedder John (2010), "What Makes Brands

Elastic? The Influence of Brand Concept and Styles of Thinking on Brand Extension Evaluation," *Journal of Marketing,* 74 (May), 80-92.

Park, C. W., Sandra Milberg, and Robert Lawson (1991), "Evaluation of Brand Extensions: The Role of Product Feature Similarity and Brand Concept Consistency," *Journal of Consumer Research*, 18 (September), 185-193.

Rucker, Derek D and Adam D. Galinsky (2009), "Conspicuous Consumption versus Utilitarian Ideals: How Different Levels of Power Shape Consumer Behavior," *Journal of Experimental Social Psychology*, 45: 549-55.

Shavitt, Sharon, Ashok K. Lalwani, Jing Zhang, and Carlos J. Torelli (2006). "The Horizontal/Vertical Distinction in Cross-Cultural Consumer Research," *Journal of Consumer Psychology*, 16 (4), 325-342.

Sullivan, M.W (1990), "Measuring Spillovers in Umbrella Branded Products," *Journal of Business*, 63(3): 309-29.

Zhang, Yinlong, Karen P. Winterich, and Vikas Mittal (2010),"Power-Distance Belief and Impulsive Buying," *Journal of Marketing Research* (October).

(In)congruity in the Evaluation of Celebrity Co-Brands

Keith Wilcox, Babson College, USA
William Carroll, Saint John's University, USA

EXTENDED ABSTRACT

Celebrity personalities are ubiquitous. Estimates suggests as much as 25% of U.S. advertising involves celebrities in one form or another (Erdogan 1999), and that figure is higher in many other countries (Crutchfield 2010). While the effect of celebrity endorsements on ad and brand evaluation are well documented (Ohanian 1990), the growing phenomenon of celebrity co-branding has receive little attention. When celebrities co-brand a product, they are not simply endorsing it; instead, they partner with a company to co-create a product that shares the identity of both the celebrity and the company. Celebrity co-brands are present in a diverse set of categories. They are perhaps most prevalent in the fashion and accessories industry. For instance, Scarlett Johansson partnered with Reebok to co-design a new line of clothing and footwear called Scarlett 'Hearts' Rbk. Madonna developed a line of sunglasses with Dolce and Gabbana under the brand MDG.

Recently, Monga and Lau-Gesk (2007) examined how consumers evaluate co-brands with two distinct brand personalities versus one personality. They argue that co-brands with dual personalities are considered to be more complex than single personality co-brands. As a result, when the complex self is activated consumers prefer co-brands that combine the benefits associated with two distinct brand personalities (i.e., glamour and trendiness) to those that combine benefits consistent with a single brand personality (i.e., only glamour).

This current research shows that consumers also prefer celebrity co-brands with dual personalities. However, we identify an additional process through which the evaluation of co-brands can be shaped by dual personalities. We propose that the effectiveness of celebrity co-brands depends on whether the personality of the celebrity is congruent or incongruent with the personality of the parent brand. Consumers are more likely to purchase celebrity co-brands when the personality of the celebrity is incongruent with that of the parent (i.e., there is a dual personality) compared to when the celebrity's personality is congruent with that of the parent. Additionally, we demonstrate that the process underlying these findings is a difference in processing motivation. Specifically, we propose that incongruent personalities increase consumers' processing motivation, which results in more favorable evaluations of the co-branded product.

In study 1, we demonstrate that people prefer a co-brand when the celebrity's personality is incongruent with the parent brand (Kayne West and Louis Vuitton) compared to when it is more congruent with the parent brand (George Clooney and Louis Vuitton). We also show that the effect is unique to co-brands and reverses when the celebrity endorses a product by the same parent brand, which is consistent with previous research on celebrity endorsements (Escalas and Bettman 2011; Kahle and Homer 1985). Additionally, we show that the effect of incongruity on consumers' evaluation of a celebrity co-brand is strongest for those that are low in processing motivation (i.e., those that are low in parent brand involvement).

Study 2 replicates the effects observed in the co-brand conditions of study 1 using a single celebrity. Specifically, we manipulated the personality of Daniel Craig such that his personality would be perceived to be more or less congruent with the parent brand (Louis Vuitton). We find that people evaluate the co-brand more favorably when incongruity is high compared to when it is low and that the effect emerges for consumers that are low in brand involvement.

Additionally, we show that our findings are due to incongruity experienced while integrating existing information about the celebrity and parent brand; the effect does not emerge when consumers do not have existing information about the celebrity to integrate with the parent brand.

Study 3 provides direct evidence that processing motivation underlies our results. Specifically, we show that manipulating participants' motivation to process a celebrity co-brand moderates the effect of incongruity on purchase intent. Specifically, we find that when participants' motivation to process the co-brand is relatively high, participants prefer a co-brand that is incongruent compared to one that is congruent. However, reducing participants' motivation to process the co-brand eliminates the effect.

The present work contributes to extant literature that explores the impact of celebrities on consumer behavior. The findings of Study 1 are consistent with previous research that indicates celebrity endorsers are often seen as a peripheral cue for evaluating a product or brand (Petty, Cacioppo, and Schumann 1983). However, we demonstrate that unlike celebrity endorsements, the use of celebrities in co-branding is not based on peripheral processing, instead the image or personality of the celebrity is a central component of the brand. Our results indicate that celebrity co-branding is not simply an extension of celebrity endorsing, but a unique and yet unexamined area of study.

REFERENCES

Aaker, Jennifer .L (1997), "Dimensions of brand personality," *Journal of Marketing Research*, 36, 346–56.

Aaker, David A. and Kevin L. Keller (1990), "Consumer Evaluations of Brand Extensions," *Journal of Marketing*, 54 (January), 27–41.

Artz, Nancy, Alice Tybout and Trudy Kehret-Ward (1993), "The Effect of the Visual Perspective of Distance in Ad Pictures on Ad Liking," *Journal of Consumer Psychology*, 2 (4), 359-79.

Baker, Sara M. and Richard E. Petty (1994), "Majority and Minority Influence: Source-Position Imbalance as a Determinant of Message Scrutiny," *Journal of Personality and Social Psychology*, 67 (1), 5–19.

Choi, Sejung Marina and Nora J. Rifon (2007), "Who Is the Celebrity in Advertising? Understanding Dimensions of Celebrity Images," *The Journal of Popular Culture*, Vol. 40, No. 2, 304-24.

Crutchfield, Dean (2010), "Celebrity Endorsements Still Push Product: Why, in the Era of Social Media, the Rewards Continue to Outweigh the Risks, *Advertising Age*, September 22.

Desai, Kalpesh K. and Kevin L. Keller (2002), "The Effects of Ingredient Branding Strategies on Host Brand Extendibility," *Journal of Marketing*, 66 (January), 73–93.

Dhar, Ravi and Klaus Wertenbroch (2000), "Consumer Choice between Hedonic and Utilitarian Goods," *Journal of Marketing Research*, 37 (February), 60-71.

Erdogan, B. Zafer (1999), "Celebrity Endorsement: A Literature Review," Journal of Marketing Management, 15 (2), 291–314.

Escalas, Jennifer Edson and James R. Bettman (2011), "Connecting with Celebrities: Celebrity Endorsement, Brand Meaning, and Self-Brand Connections" *working paper*.

Friedman, Hershey H., and Linda Friedman (1979), "Endorser Effectiveness by Product Type," Journal of Advertising Research, 19 (October), 63–71.

Goodrum, Charles, and Helen Dalrymple (1990), Advertising in America: The First 200 Years, New York: Harry N. Abrams.

Green, Melanie C. and Timothy C. Brock (2000), "The Role of Transportation in the Persuasiveness of Public Narratives," *Journal of Personality and Social Psychology*, 79 (5), 701-21.

Kahle, Lynn R., and Pamela M. Homer (1985), "Physical Attractiveness of the Celebrity Endorser: A Social Adaptation Perspective," Journal of Consumer Research, 11 (March), 954-961.

Karmarkar, Uma R. and Zakary L. Tormala (2009), "Believe Me, I Have No Idea What I'm Talking About: The Effects of Source Certainty on Consumer Involvement and Persuasion," *Journal of Consumer Research*, 36 (April), 1033-1049.

Kamins, Michael A (1990). "An Investigation into the "Match-up" Hypothesis in Celebrity Advertising: When Beauty May Be Only Skin Deep," *Journal of Advertising* 19 (1),4-13.

Kamins, Michael A., Meribeth J. Brand, Stuart A. Hoeke, and John C. Moe (1989), "Two-Sided Versus One-Sided Celebrity Endorsements: The Impact on Advertising Effectiveness and Credibility," Journal of Advertising, 18 (2), 4–10.

Maheswaran, Durairaj, and Shelly Chaiken (1991), "Promoting Systematic Processing in Low Motivation Settings: Effect of Incongruent Information on Processing and Judgment," *Journal of Personality and Social Psychology*, 61 (1), 13–25.

Maheswaran, Duraiaj, Diane M. Mackie, Shelly Chaiken (1992), "Brand name as a heuristic cue: the effects of task importance and expectancy confirmation on consumer judgments," *Journal of Consumer Psychology*, 1, (4) 317–36.

Marsh, Lisa (2010), "Madonna Launching 'MDG' Sunglasses With Dolce & Gabbana," accessed 1/26/11 [available at http://www.stylelist.com/2010/03/15/madonna-launching-mdg-sunglasses-with-dolce-and-gabbana]

McCracken, Grant (1989), "Who is the Celebrity Endorser? Cultural Foundations of the Endorsement Process." Journal of Consumer Research 16 310 – 21.

Menon, Geeta and Priya Raghubir (2003), "Ease-of-Retrieval as an Automatic Input in Judgments: A Mere-Accessibility Framework?" Journal of Consumer Research, 30 (2), 230-243.

Miles, Jamie (2010), "Kanye West Explains How Louis Vuitton Broke His Heart; Patrick Robinson Discusses Gap's Logo-gate," http://nymag.com/daily/fashion/2010/11/kanye_ace_gala.html

Monga, Alokparna Basu and Loraine Lau-Gesk "Blending Cobrand Personalities:An Examination of the Complex Self" Journal of Marketing Research Vol. XLIV (August 2007), 389–400

Noon, Chris (2006), "Scarlett Johansson To Design Clothes For Reebok," *Forbes.com*, accessed 1/26/11, [available at http://www.forbes.com/2006/07/26/johansson-reebok-sport-cx_cn_0726autofacescan02.html)

Ohanian, Roobina. "Construction and Validation of a Scale to Measure Celebrity Endorsers' Perceived Expertise, Trustworthiness, and Attractiveness." Journal of Advertising 19.3 (1990): 39 – 52.

Park, C. Whan, Sung Y. Jun, and Allan D. Shocker (1996), "Composite Branding Alliances: An Investigation of Extension and Feedback Effects," *Journal of Marketing Research*, 33 (November), 453–66.

Petty, Richard E., John T. Cacioppo, and David Schumann (1983), "Central and Peripheral Routes to Advertising Effectiveness: The Moderating Role of Involvement," Journal of Consumer Research, 10 (September), 135–146.

Rao, Akshay R., Lu Qu and Robert W. Ruekert (1999), "Signaling Unobservable Quality through a Brand Ally," *Journal of Marketing Research*, 36 (2), 258-68.

Simonin, Bernard L. and Julie A. Ruth (1998), "Is a Company Known by the Company It Keeps? Assessing the Spillover Effects of Brand Alliances on Consumer Brand Attitudes," *Journal of Marketing Research*, 35 (February), 30–42.

Tormala, Zakary L. and Victoria L. DeSensi (2008), "The Perceived Informational Basis of Attitudes: Implications for Subjective Ambivalence," *Personality and Social Psychology Bulletin*, 34 (January), 275–87.

West, Patricia M., Joel Huber and Kyeong Sam Min (2004), "Altering Experienced Utiiity: The impact of Story Writing and Self-Referencing on Preferences," *Journal of Consumer Research*, 31, December, 623-30.

Ziegler, Rene, Michael Diehl, and Anja Ruther (2002), "Multiple Source Characteristics and Persuasion: Source Inconsistency as a Determinant of Message Scrutiny," *Personality and Social Psychology Bulletin*, 28 (4), 496–508.

That was Then, This is Now: Focalism in Temporal Comparisons

Steven Chan, New York University, USA
Justin Kruger, New York University, USA

EXTENDED ABSTRACT

Do people really think things were better "back in the good 'ole days?" Nostalgia as a fond longing for the past would suggest that people often think the past is better than the present. In this research, we demonstrate that this nostalgia is in part a temporal focalism bias driven by polls that ask us to compare the present with the past thereby directing greater focus and weighting of the present relative to the past. Reversing the order in such polls, comparing the past with the present, attenuates (and in some cases reverses) the conclusions of the polls.

A focalism effect based on comparing time has not been previously demonstrated. Previous research on focalism has demonstrated that comparing X with Y focuses attention on the features of X more than Y which leads to biases in comparative judgments (Houston and Sherman 1995). A focalism effect related to time is critical to polls and surveys, which often ask the public to compare the present to a reference point in the past. For example, Gallup polls often ask the public to consider whether there is more or less crime now compared with a year ago.

A temporal focalism bias would suggest that the typical question wording, which asks people to compare the present to the past, causes people to focus on conditions of the present more than that of the past. Differential weighting of the focal point leads to biased judgments. Past research on focalism has highlighted this myopic focus on the focal point in comparative judgments (Chambers, Windschid, and Suls 2003). Using the crime question as an example, having a considerable amount of crime today would lead to a judgment that crime today has become worse over time since the state of crime today is weighted more heavily than crime in the past.

In recent years, noted professor and writer Steven Pinker has often presented his idea of the violent-present illusion (2007). Pinker highlights that "contrary to the popular impression that we are living in extraordinarily violent times, rates of violence at all scales have been in decline over the course of history." Pinker presents psychological explanations based on salience, morality, and motivated reasoning. We contend that the present account of temporal focalism is an additional explanation that contributes to the violent-present illusion as well as other temporal comparisons alike.

Across two studies we demonstrate a temporal focalism effect where differential weight is placed on the present (past) when the present (past) is framed as the focal point of a question. In our first study we demonstrate the main effect of temporal focalism. Using questions drawn from and inspired by previous Gallup Poll research, we demonstrate significant differences in judgment when the focal point of comparison is reversed. For example, the question "Do you think that a year ago, there was more or less crime than there is now?" yields a significantly lower nostalgic "violent-present illusion" than the original "Do you think there is more or less crime in the U.S. than there was a year ago?"

Public opinion can even flip: For instance, when participants are polled about how much Congress has accomplished now as compared to before. In each case, whether for crime or Congress, the magnitude of the pervading opinion in people's consideration will be overweighted for the time frame targeted in the question. So because crime is perpetually common whether in the past or the present, and because Congress is always seemingly in a standstill, the direction of temporal comparison will reflect whether more crime (or less action by Congress) is highlighted for the past or the present.

A second study we conducted shows converging evidence with a context that is personally relevant to respondents while also ruling in our differential weighting explanation. Study 2 showed the effect of comparing judged frequency of both common and rare activities performed currently (undergrad) versus in the past (high school). For example, when asked to compare high school to now, participants (undergrad students in this study) were more likely to indicate that they procrastinated (common) more and watched foreign language films (rare) less in high school than now. A second group asked to compare in the reverse order, now to high school, showed a similar overestimation for common and underestimation for rare activities. In addition to the comparative questions, all participants were also asked absolute questions which rated their frequency for each activity both now and in high school (with order counterbalanced across participants). Path analyses revealed that, as hypothesized, absolute ratings for the focal time frame (present or past) were significantly better predictors for the comparative questions than absolute ratings for the non-focal time frame. This supports the differential weighting account.

REFERENCES

Chambers, J. R., P. D. Windschid, and J. Suls (2003), "Egocentrism, Event Frequency, and Comparative Optimism: When What Happens Frequently Is "More Likely to Happen to Me"," *Personality and Social Psychology Bulletin*, 29 (11), 1343-56.

Hoorens, V. (1995), "Self-Favoring Biases, Self-Presentation, and the Self-Other Asymmetry in Social-Comparison," *Journal of Personality*, 63 (4), 793-817.

Houston, D. A. and S. J. Sherman (1995), "Cancellation and Focus - the Role of Shared and Unique Features in the Choice Process," *Journal of Experimental Social Psychology*, 31 (4), 357-78.

Johnson, E. J. and R. J. Meyer (1984), "Compensatory Choice Models of Noncompensatory Processes: The Effect of Varying Context," *Journal of Consumer Research*, 11 (1), 528-41.

Kruger, J. and J. Burrus (2004), "Egocentrism and Focalism in Unrealistic Optimism (and Pessimism)," *Journal of Experimental Social Psychology*, 40 (3), 332-40.

Kunda, Z. (1990), "The Case for Motivated Reasoning," *Psychological Bulletin*, 108 (3), 480-98.

Pinker, S. (2007), "A History of Violence - We're Getting Nicer Every Day," *New Republic*, 236 (12), 18-21.

Schkade, D. A. and D. Kahneman (1998), "Does Living in California Make People Happy? A Focusing Illusion in Judgments of Life Satisfaction," *Psychological Science*, 9 (5), 340-46.

Strack, F., L. L. Martin, and N. Schwarz (1988), "Priming and Communication: Social Determinants of Information Use in Judgments of Life Satisfaction," *European Journal of Social Psychology*, 18 (5), 429-42.

Tversky, A. and D. Kahneman (1974), "Judgment under Uncertainty: Heuristics and Biases," *Science*, 185 (4157), 1124-31.

Wilson, T. D., T. Wheatley, J. M. Meyers, D. T. Gilbert, and D. Axsom (2000), "Focalism: A Source of Durability Bias in Affective Forecasting," *Journal of Personality and Social Psychology*, 78 (5), 821-36.

Windschitl, P. D., J. Kruger, and E. N. Simms (2003), "The Influence of Egocentrism and Focalism on People's Optimism in Competitions: When What Affects Us Equally Affects Me More," *Journal of Personality and Social Psychology*, 85 (3), 389-408.

When Accepted Inequality Deters Responsibility for Helping Others

Karen Winterich, Pennsylvania State University, USA
Yinlong Zhang, University of Texas at San Antonio, USA

EXTENDED ABSTRACT

Though charitable contributions by individuals exceeded $227 billion in 2009, accounting for nearly 75% of total contributions in 2009 (Giving USA 2010), the need for aid is at an all-time high in many areas, including hunger in America (Fraser 2010). As such, understanding motivations for giving, or perhaps more importantly not giving, is critical. Most of the extant literature tends to focus on individual difference factors in explaining the differences in giving with virtually no attention to cultural orientation (Aquino and Reed 2002; Center on Philanthropy 2009; Piliavin and Charng 1990). In this research, we propose that cultural orientation, more specifically, power-distance belief (PDB) may play a critical role in motivations for charitable giving. By comparing giving differences across countries as well as charitable giving differences among individuals, we show that this effect is independent from factors such as income level, education level, or other cultural orientations such as individualism/collectivism. Further, we test the underlying process and also examine a boundary condition for this effect.

According to Oyserman (2006, p. 353), PDB "involves the extent to which a society accepts and views as inevitable or functional human inequality in power, wealth, or prestige." The acceptance of a power disparity suggests that everyone has a rightful place in the social hierarchy, and this social order should be respected and maintained. As such, people maintain an awareness of the disparity and act according to their place in the social hierarchy, and make sure others' social position is well placed. Consumers who are aware of these social orders are more likely to feel the existing social order should be well respected (*Bourdieu 1984*; Miller et al. 1993). In contrast, in low PDB cultures, the norm is to maintain and respect the equality inherent in social interactions (Hofstede 1984, 2001). Individuals in these cultures do not believe that differences in power, wealth, and prestige are inevitable (Oyserman 2006). As such, people may seek out opportunities to achieve equality. In attempting to achieve equality, individuals should be motivated to aid less fortunate others. That is, low PDB consumers, who expect equality, should feel responsible for helping others if these individuals are to obtain equal resources and opportunities.

Given the expectation and acceptance of (in)equality in (high) low PDB cultures and the corresponding feelings of responsibility to aid less fortunate others in order to (maintain social order) achieve equality, we theorize that PDB influences charitable giving. Specifically, high PDB consumers will donate less to charities for less fortunate others than low PDB consumers. We test this hypothesis with cross-country level secondary data on country-level giving and also at an individual level to examine the effect of PDB as a dispositional trait on charitable giving. In both studies, we found a negative correlation between PDB and charitable giving.

We also propose that it is through decreased responsibility for aiding others that PDB influences charitable giving. In other words, we argue that responsibility will mediate the effect of PDB on charitable giving. We test this hypothesis by directly priming PDB and find that participants in high PDB prime tended to donate less than those in low PDB prime, and this difference was mediated by perceived responsibility.

If the perceived responsibility is underlying the PDB effect on charitable giving, then this effect of PDB will be more pronounced if the recipient is perceived based on an exchange norm rather than a communal relationship (Aggarwal and Law 2005). We test this hypothesis by a (Relationship Norms: Communal vs. Exchange) between-subjects design with PDB measured as a continuous variable. We found that when primed with exchange norms, PDB negatively influenced donation likelihood, such that those with higher PDB had a lower donation likelihood, consistent with the results of the first three studies. In contrast, when primed with communal norms, PDB did not influence donation likelihood. Further, the effect of PDB was again mediated by perceived responsibility.

Through a series of five studies we obtained convergent results of PDB on charitable giving. Results from the first two studies (1A and 1B) provide correlational evidence for the relationship between PDB and charitable donations at the country level and the individual level. In study 2, we establish the impact of PDB on charitable donations experimentally by manipulating PDB and examine the underlying role of perceived responsibility. The final study considers relationship norms as a boundary condition for the effect of PDB on charitable donations, demonstrating that high PDB can be influenced to give when primed with communal relationship norms due to the increase in perceived responsibility under communal norms.

With the increasing living standard of consumers from developing countries such as BRIC, it is important to understand the role of cultural orientation in affecting charitable giving from these countries, as these countries have strikingly different cultures from U.S. Our results provide managerial implications for charitable organizations to manage their donation efforts in high and low PDB cultures, as our moderating results suggest ways to enhance consumers' donation intention in high PDB cultures.

Our results also shed light on the theoretical debate on key drivers for charitable giving: both dispositional thesis such as empathy and situational thesis such as responsibly have received empirical support. Our cross-cultural results indicate that both dispositional and situational factors are important in explaining the donation behavior, emphasizing either one too extensively will only lead to misleading conclusions.

REFERENCES

Aaker, Jennifer and Angela Lee (2001), "'I' Seek Pleasures and 'We' Avoid Pains: The Role of Self-Regulatory Goals in Information Processing and Persuasion," Journal of Consumer Research, 28 (June), 33-49.

Aggarwal, Pankaj (2004), "The Effects of Brand Relationship Norms on Consumer Attitudes and Behavior," Journal of Consumer Research, 31 (June), 87–101.

Aggarwal, Pankaj and Sharmistha Law (2005), "Role of Relationship Norms in Processing Brand Information," Journal of Consumer Research, 32 (December), 453–64.

Aquino, Karl and Americus Reed, II (2002), "The Self-Importance of Moral Identity," Journal of Personality and Social Psychology, 83 (6), 1423-40.

Bourdieu, Pierre (1984), Distinction: A Social Critique of the Judgment of Taste. Harvard University Press, Cambridge, MA.

Center on Philanthropy (2010), Understanding Donor Motivations for Giving, New York: CCS.

Charities Aid Foundation (2010), The World Giving Index, Alexandria, VA.

Clark, Margaret S. and Judson Mills (1993), "The Difference between Communal and Exchange Relationships: What It Is and Is Not," Personality and Social Psychology Bulletin, 19 (December), 684–91.

Dunn, Elizabeth,W., Lara B. Aknin, and Michael I. Norton (2008), "Spending Money On Others Promotes Happiness," Science, 319, 1687–88.

Escalas, Jennifer E. and James R. Bettman (2005), "Self-Construal, Reference Groups, and Brand Meaning," Journal of Consumer Research, 32 (December), 378-389.

Frank, Robert H. and Philip J. Cook (1995), The Winner-Take-All Society: Why The Few At the Top Get So Much More Than the Rest of Us, New York: Penguin Books.

Fraser, Ross (2010), Hunger Reaches Record High 1 in 6 Americans at Risk of Hunger, Feeding America, November 15.

Fu, Ping Ping, Rongxian Wu, Yongkang Yang, and June Ye (2008), "Chinese Culture and Leadership," Culture and Leadership Across the World by Jagdeep S. Chhokar, Felix C. Brodbeck, and Robert J. House (Eds.), New York: Taylor & Francis, 877-908.

Gamer, Thesia I. and Janet Wagner (1991), "Economic Dimensions of Household Gift Giving," Journal of Consumer Research 18 (December), 368-79.

Giving USA Foundation (2010), Giving USA 2006, Glenview, IL: Giving USA Foundation.

Griskevicius Vladas, Joshua M. Tybur, Bram Van den Bergh (2010), "Going Green to Be Seen: Status, Reputation, and Conspicuous Conservation," Journal of Personality and Social Psychology, 98 (3), 392-404.

Grunewald, Rob (2003), "Charitable Giving Rates Follow the Economy and Personal Income," FedGazette, November.

Hofstede, Geert (1984), Culture's Consequences: International Differences in Work-Related Values, Beverly Hills, CA: Sage.

Hofstede, Geert (2001), Culture's Consequences: Comparing Values, Behaviors, Institutions, and Organizations across Nations, Thousand Oaks, CA: Sage.

Hofstede, Geert (2011), "Creating Cultural Competence," www.geert-hofstede.com / hofstede_dimensions.php.

Jones, Andrew and John Posnett (1991), "Charitable Donations by UK Households: Evidence From the Family Expenditure Survey," Applied Economics, 23 (February), 343-51.

Miller, Christopher M., Shelby H. McIntyre, and Murali K. Mantrala (1993), "Toward Formalizing Fashion Theory," Journal of Marketing Research, 30 (2), 142-57.

Oyserman, Daphna (2006), "High Power, Low Power, and Equality: Culture beyond Individualism and Collectivism," Journal of Consumer Psychology, 16 (4), 352-56.

Oyserman, Daphna and Spike W. S. Lee (2007), "Priming 'Culture': Culture as Situated Cognition." in Handbook of Cultural Psychology, ed. S. Kitayama and D. Cohen, New York: Guilford Press, 255-79.

Pham, Michel, Joel B. Cohen, John W. Pracejus and G. David Hughes (2001), "Affect Monitoring and the Primacy of Feelings in Judgment," Journal of Consumer Research, 28 (September), 167-88.

Piff, Paul K., Michael W. Kraus, Stephane Cote, Bonnie Hayden Cheng, and Dacher Keltner (2010), "Having Less, Giving More: The Influence of Social Class on Prosocial Behavior," Journal of Personality and Social Psychology, 99 (5), 771-84.

Piliavin, Jane A. and Hong-Wen Charng (1990), "Altruism: A Review of Recent Theory and Research," Annual Review of Sociology, 16, 27–65.

Preacher, Kristopher. J. and Andrew F. Hayes (2004), "SPSS and SAS Procedures for Estimating Indirect Effects in Simple Mediation Models,"false Behavior Research Methods, Instruments & Computers, 36 (4), 717-31.

Schwartz, Shalom (1973), "Normative Explanations of Helping Behavior: A Critique, Proposal, and Empirical Test," Journal of Experimental Social Psychology, 9, 349-64.

Schwartz, Shalom and Amit Ben David (1976), "Responsibility and Helping in an Emergency: Effects of Blame, Ability and Denial of Responsibility," Sociometry, 39 (December), 406-15.

Shen, Hao, Fang Wan, and Robert S. Wyer Jr. (2011), "Cross-Cultural Differences in the Refusal to Accept a Small Gift: The Differential Influence of Reciprocity Norms on Asians and North Americans," Journal of Personality and Social Psychology, 100 (2), 271-81.

Shiota, Michelle N., Dacher Keltner, and Oliver P. John (2006), "Positive Emotion Dispositions Differentially Associated With Big Five Personality and Attachment Style," Journal of Positive Psychology, 1 (2), 61-71.

Singelis, Theodore (1994), "The Measurement of Independent and Interdependent Self-construals," Personality and Social Psychology Bulletin, 20 (5), 580-591.

Srull, Thomas K. and Robert S. Wyer, Jr. (1980), "Category Accessibility and Social Perception: Some Implications for the Study of Person Memory and Interpersonal Judgments," Journal of Personality and Social Psychology, 38 (June), 841-56.

Triandis, Harry C. (1995), Individualism and Collectivism, Boulder, CO: Westview.

United Nations Statistics Division (2006), "Social Indicators," http://unstats.un.org/unsd/demographic/products/socind/inc-eco.htm.

Zhang, Yinlong, Karen Page Winterich, and Vikas Mittal (2010), "Power-Distance Belief and Impulsive Buying," Journal of Marketing Research, 47 (October), 945-54.

Zhao, Xinshu, John G. Lynch, and Qimei Chen (2010), "Reconsidering Baron and Kenny: Myths and Truths about Mediation Analysis," Journal of Consumer Research, 37(August), 197-206.

Reimagining Charity: Kiva's Ideology of Entrepreneurial Charity

Domen Bajde, University of Ljubljana, Slovenia

EXTENDED ABSTRACT

The often encountered physical and cultural distance between givers and recipients of charity and the complex intermingling of social, political, economic and moral dimensions of charity, accentuate the role of imagination and ideology in charitable giving (Godelier 1999). Yet, surprisingly little attention has been afforded to the imaginary and ideological dimensions of charitable giving in consumer research (Bajde 2009). We believe this to be a serious deficit in light of the cultural turmoil surrounding charitable giving recently. The charitable sector has witnessed considerable experimentation with new ideas and practices, in particularly those adopted from the entrepreneurial sphere (Wagner 2002, Moody 2008). In our preliminary study, we focus on a specific example of such experimentation, by exploring the imaginary and ideological contour of Kiva, a charitable nonprofit that combines microfinancing and internet technology to enable individuals to lend (without interest) small amounts of money to impoverished entrepreneurs.

The imaginary of charitable giving subsumes both how individuals imagine (envision) the world and their role in it, as well as the more specific aims, means and consequences of human activities on society and nature (Godelier 1986). Taylor (2002, 106) describes it as "the ways in which people imagine their social existence, how they fit together with others, how things go on between them and their fellows, the expectations that are normally met, and the deeper normative notions and images that underlie these expectations." One of the vital ways in which imaginary conceptions become articulated, is through ideologies, or more explicit systems of interrelated ideas and beliefs, which mediate all aspects of the reality lived and produced by groups and individuals (Geertz 1973). While certain frictions and contradictions within incumbent ideologies are likely, it is when orthodox ideologies are exposed to more radical utopian ideologies (Langdridge 2006) that significant cultural innovation is likely to occur (Holt and Cameron 2010).

The cultural dynamics surrounding Kiva represent fertile ground for the exploration of the imaginary and ideological elements of charitable giving. The imaginary conceptions that make lending through Kiva meaningful to its creators and supporters were surveyed by combining the analysis of consumer narratives (Kozinets 2008) with the analysis of Kiva's brand genealogy (Holt 2004). Consumer narratives pertaining to Kiva were collected on KivaFriends.org, an active forum and community of Kiva lenders. The brand genealogy of Kiva was conducted by analyzing a set of publicly accessible texts originated by Kiva's founders and the media throughout Kiva's six year history. The subsequent sets of data were analyzed through an iterative process of grounded interpretation (Muniz and Schau, 2007). We present our findings by outlining three complementary strands of Kiva's imaginary and ideological underpinnings. Our analysis reveals how these seemingly separate strands form into a unified utopian ideology of *entrepreneurial charity*, which challenges the orthodox view(s) of charitable giving and poverty alleviation.

The first strand encompasses the mythology surrounding Kiva's creators, who join forces with the media to incessantly dramatize and aestheticise the role of entrepreneurialism in Kiva's success. Second, Kiva's supporters partake in the entrepreneurial ideology through building up their Kiva "portfolios" and actively assuming the entrepreneurial role of "angel investors". The traditional "hands off" charitable giving is replaced by inspiring visions of "hands on" entrepreneurial charity (i.e., increased level of control, the use of market mechanisms as safety valves). Lastly, Kiva's ideology of entrepreneurial charity revamps the established conceptions of impoverished beneficiaries of charity by celebrating "the working poor" as entrepreneurs waiting to be unleashed by micro-loans. The patronizing handout of traditional charity is replaced with a dignified "handup" partnership between entrepreneurial investors and borrowers.

We see the contribution of our preliminary study in demonstrating that Kiva represents not only a technological innovation or a viable extension of existent services, but more fundamentally a "cultural innovation" (Holt and Cameron 2010). The cultural innovation of Kiva results in a utopian ideology of entrepreneurial charity that draws upon fresh imaginary conceptions. Our analysis shows how Kiva's triple glorification of entrepreneurialism supports and legitimizes an alternative approach to running a charity, giving to charity and receiving charity. This is achieved by aestheticising and dramatizing the role of entrepreneurialism in ensuring social progress, by invoking the mythic figure of the heroic entrepreneur and by reaffirming a set of entrepreneurial values that morally legitimize Kiva's rejection of orthodox conceptions of poverty and charitable giving.

REFERENCES

Aaker, Jennifer, Chang, Victoria and Jessica Jackley (2010), *Kiva and the Power of a Story* (Case study). Palo Alto: Stanford Business School.

Bajde, Domen (2009), "Rethinking the Social and Cultural Dimensions of Charitable Giving," *Consumption Markets & Culture,* 12 (1): 65-84.

Bornstein, David (2004), *How to Change the World: Social Entrepreneurship and the Power of New Ideas.* New York: Oxford University Press.

Dees, G. J. (2007), "Taking social entrepreneurship seriously," *Society*, 44(3): 24-31.

Dees, G. J., Haas, M. & P. Haas (1998), "The Meaning of "Social Entrepreneurship"," Working Paper, The Kauffman Center for Entrepreneurial Leadership.

Drakopoulou Dodd, Sarah and Alistair R. Anderson (2007), "Mumpsimus and the Mything of the Individualistic Entrepreneur," *International Small Business Journal*, 25(4): 341-360.

Flannery, Matt (2009), "Kiva at Four," *Innovations: Technology, Governance, Globalization*, 4(2): 31-49.

Geertz, Clifford (1973), *The Interpretation of Cultures*. New York: Basic Books.

Godelier, Maurice (1986), *The Mental and the Material*. New York: Verso.

--- (1999), *The Enigma of the Gift*. Polity Press.

Holt, Douglas (2004), *How Brands Become Icons,* Boston: Harvard Business School Press.

Holt, Douglas and Douglas Cameron (2010), *Cultural Strategy: Using Innovative Ideologies to Build Breakthrough Brands*, Ney York: Oxford University Press.

Kozinets, Robert V. (2008), "Technology/Ideology: How Ideological Fields Influence Consumers' Technology Narratives," *The Journal of Consumer Research*, 34(6): 865-881.

Langdridge, Darren (1993), "Ideology and Utopia: Social Psychology and the Social Imaginary of Paul Ricoeur," *Theory & Psychology*, 16(5): 641–659

Moody, Michael (2008), ""Building a Culture": The Construction and Evolution of Venture Philanthropy as a New Organizational Field," *Nonprofit and Voluntary Sector Quarterly*, 37(2): 324-352.

Muñiz, Albert M. Jr. and Hope Jensen Schau (2007), "Vigilante Marketing and Consumer-Created Communications," *Journal of Advertising*, 36, 187-202.

Neck, Heidi, Brush, Candida and Elaine Allen (2009), "The landscape of social entrepreneurship, *Business Horizons*," 52(1): 13-19.

Nicholson, Louise and Anderson, Alistair R. (2005), "News and Nuances of the Entrepreneurial Myth and Metaphor: Linguistic Games in Entrepreneurial Sense-Making and Sense-Giving," *Entrepreneurship: Theory and Practice*, 29 (2): 153-172.

Ogbor, J.O. (2000), "Mythicizing and Reification in Entrepreneurial Discourse: Ideology-Critique of Entrepreneurial Studies," *Journal of Management Studies*, 37(5): 605-635.

Phillips, Adam and Barbara Taylor (2009), *On Kindness*. London: Penguin.

Reis, T. K. and Clohesy, S. J. (2001), "Unleashing new resources and entrepreneurship for the common good: A philanthropic renaissance," *New Directions for Philanthropic Fundraising*, 32: 109–144.

Rieff, David (2002), *A Bed for the Night: Humanitarianism in Crisis*. New York: Simon & Schuster.

Steger, Manfred B. (2008), *The Rise of the Global Imaginary: Political Ideologies from the French Revolution to the Global War on Terror*, New York: Oxford University Press.

Taylor, Charles (2002), "Modern Social Imaginaries", *Public Culture*, 14(1): 91–124

Therborn, Göran (1980), *The Ideology of Power and the Power of Ideology* . London: New Left.

Wagner, Lilya (2002), "The 'new' donor: creation or evolution?" *International Journal of Nonprofit and Voluntary Sector Marketing*, 7(4): 343-352.

Yunus, Muhammad (2006), *Nobel Lecture*. Retrieved on 24 February, 2011 at http://nobelprize.org/nobel_prizes/peace/laureates/2006/yunus-lecture.html

--- (2008), *Creating a World Without Poverty: Social Business and the Future of Capitalism*. Public Affairs.

The Rebound of the Forgone Alternative

Zachary Arens, University of Maryland, USA
Rebecca Hamilton, University of Maryland, USA

EXTENDED ABSTRACT

Consider the case of Robert and Jenny, who are deciding whether to choose Costa Rica or Italy for their upcoming vacation. They find both destinations attractive but because they only have a week off, they have to choose one. After a long discussion, they decide to go to Italy and forgo Costa Rica. Consumers constantly make decisions like this, in which they must forgo alternatives. Thus, it is important to understand what happens to these forgone alternatives. Does forgoing Costa Rica for this vacation make Robert and Jenny more or less likely to visit in the future?

Two theories offer conflicting predictions as to the fate of these forgone alternatives. Cognitive dissonance theory suggests that the consumer's desire for a forgone alternative decreases after a difficult choice because consumers derogate its attractiveness to eliminate cognitive inconsistencies (Brehm 1956; Festinger 1957). In contrast, goal theory suggests that the desire for the forgone alternative should increase over time – consistent with temporal escalation – as long as the goal associated with it remains unfulfilled (Atkinson and Birch 1970; Chartrand et al. 2008).

We resolve this discrepancy by introducing stage of consumption and the substitutability of the chosen and forgone alternatives as key moderators. After making a choice, consumers shift from a deliberative to an implemental mindset (Gollwitzer 1990) and they derogate the forgone alternative to remove doubt and hesitation while pursuing the chosen alternative (Harmon-Jones and Harmon-Jones 2002; Jones and Gerard 1967). After consuming the chosen alternative, though, it is no longer necessary to derogate the forgone alternative. Goal theory suggests that if the goal associated with the forgone alternative is still unfulfilled, its attractiveness should rebound.

Thus, we predict that the attractiveness of the forgone alternative should exhibit a U-shaped pattern, decreasing after choice but increasing after consumption. This rebound effect will be moderated by the degree of substitutability between the chosen and forgone alternatives. When the forgone alternative is perceived to be a weak substitute for the chosen, its goal will be unfulfilled and its value should rebound after consumption. However, when the forgone is perceived to be a strong substitute for the chosen alternative, they share a common goal; therefore, consuming the chosen alternative will satiate the forgone, and its value will not rebound.

Our first study demonstrates the rebound effect by measuring the attractiveness of the forgone alternative at different stages of consumption. Participant rated a set of fun activities and chose between two. This study ruled out regression to the mean as an alternative explanation by controlling for the duration required to complete the chosen activity. The attractiveness of a forgone activity remained low even after a consumption-length delay, but the forgone alternative rebounded after consumption as long as the forgone activity was a weak substitute for the chosen activity. This study also ruled out regret as an alternative explanation.

The second study uses the temporal escalation criterion to demonstrate that the rebound effect is created by a reactivation of the goal associated with the forgone alternative. Participants chose between viewing kangaroo or penguin photographs. After watching the chosen slideshow, the value of the forgone slideshow was greater after a delay than in the absence of a delay, indicating temporal escalation. In contrast, the value of the forgone was unaffected by a delay prior to watching the chosen slideshow.

The third study provides additional evidence that the rebound effect is a goal-driven process by showing that the forgone alternative does not rebound when its goal has been fulfilled. This was accomplished by characterizing both the chosen and forgone alternatives as means or as an end in itself. Participants choose between two animal slideshows. In the means condition, participants believed the purpose of the slideshow was to help them perform better on a verbal test; in the end condition, no connection was made between the slideshow and the test. When characterized as an end, the forgone slideshow became more attractive after watching the chosen slideshow, replicating the rebound effect. However, when characterized as a means, the forgone slideshow become less attractive after watching the chosen slideshow, indicating that the goal has been fulfilled by the chosen slideshow.

Our results reconcile the predictions made by cognitive dissonance and goal theory by demonstrating that stage of consumption and the substitutability between the alternatives moderate the value of the forgone alternative. By revealing the dynamic processes of how consumers value the alternatives that they chose as well as those they forgo, this research offers insights into the interaction between consumers' goals and choices and provides a richer understanding of consumer behavior. Moreover, based on these results, managers might consider systematically reoffering forgone alternatives to customers at the appropriate time. For instance, the Costa Rican tourism board could contact Robert and Jenny next year with a targeted offer that clearly distinguishes Costa Rica from Italy.

REFERENCES

Atkinson, John W. and David Birch (1970), *The Dynamics of Action*, New York: Wiley.

Bargh, John A., Peter M. Gollwitzer, Annette Lee-Chai, Kimberly Barndollar, and Roman Trötschel (2001), "The Automated Will: Nonconscious Activation and Pursuit of Behavioral Goals," *Journal of Personality and Social Psychology*, 81 (December), 1014-27.

Brehm, Jack W. (1956), "Postdecision Changes in the Desirability of Alternatives," *The Journal of Abnormal and Social Psychology*, 52 (May), 384-89.

Brehm, Jack W. and Arthur R. Cohen (1959), "Re-Evaluation of Choice Alternatives as a Function of Their Number and Qualitative Similarity," *Journal of Abnormal and Social Psychology*, 58 (May), 373-78.

Chartrand, Tanya L., Joel Huber, Baba Shiv, and Robin J. Tanner (2008), "Nonconscious Goals and Consumer Choice," *Journal of Consumer Research*, 35 (August), 189-201.

Cohen, Joel B. and Marvin E. Goldberg (1970), "The Dissonance Model in Post-Decision Product Evaluation," *Journal of Marketing Research*, 7 (August), 315-21.

Connolly, Terry and Marcel Zeelenberg (2002), "Regret in Decision Making," *Current Directions in Psychological Science*, 11 (December), 212-16.

Festinger, Leon A. (1957), *A Theory of Cognitive Dissonance*, Stanford, CA: Stanford University Press.

Fishbach, Ayelet, James Y. Shah, and Arie W. Kruglanski (2004), "Emotional Transfer in Goal Systems," *Journal of Experimental Social Psychology*, 40 (November), 723-38.

Gollwitzer, Peter M. (1990), "Action Phases and Mind-Sets," in *Handbook of Motivation and Cognition: Foundations of Social Behavior*, Vol. 2, ed. E. Tory Higgins and Richard M. Sorrentino, New York: The Guilford Press, 53-92.

Harmon-Jones, Eddie and Cindy Harmon-Jones (2002), "Testing the Action-Based Model of Cognitive Dissonance: The Effect of Action Orientation on Postdecision Attitudes," *Personality & Social Psychology Bulletin*, 28 (June), 711-23.

Huffman, Cynthia, S. Ratneshwar, and David Glen Mick (2000), "Consumer Goal Structures and Goal-Determination Processes: An Integrative Framework," in *The Why of Consumption: Contemporary Perspectives on Consumer Motives, Goals and Desires*, ed. S. Ratneshwar, David Glen Mick and Cynthia Huffman, New York: Routledge, 9-35.

Inman, J. Jeffrey and Marcel Zeelenberg (2002), "Regret in Repeat Purchase Versus Switching Decisions: The Attenuating Role of Decision Justifiability," *Journal of Consumer Research*, 29 (June), 116-28.

Jones, Edward E. and Harold B. Gerard (1967), *Foundations of Social Psychology*, New York: Wiley.

Kahn, Barbara E. (1995), "Consumer Variety-Seeking among Goods and Services: An Integrative Review," *Journal of Retailing and Consumer Services*, 2 (July), 139-48.

Kruglanski, Arie W., James Y. Shah, Ayelet Fishbach, Ron Friedman, Woo Young Chun, David Sleeth-Keppler, and Mark P. Zanna (2002), "A Theory of Goal Systems," in *Advances in Experimental Social Psychology*, Vol. 34, ed. Mark P. Zanna, San Diego, CA: Academic Press, 331-78.

Laran, Juliano, Chris Janiszewski, and Marcus Jr. Cunha (2008), "Context-Dependent Effects of Goal Primes," *Journal of Consumer Research*, 35 (December), 653-67.

Losciuto, Leonard A. and Robert Perloff (1967), "Influence of Product Preference on Dissonance Reduction," *Journal of Marketing Research*, 4 (August), 286-90.

Lyubomirsky, Sonja and Lee Ross (1999), "Changes in Attractiveness of Elected, Rejected, and Precluded Alternatives: A Comparison of Happy and Unhappy Individuals," *Journal of Personality and Social Psychology*, 76 (June), 988-1007.

O'Neill, Martin and Adrian Palmer (2004), "Cognitive Dissonance and the Stability of Service Quality Perceptions," *Journal of Services Marketing*, 18 (6), 433-49.

Ratneshwar, S. and Allan D. Shocker (1991), "Substitution in Use and the Role of Usage Context in Product Category Structures," *Journal of Marketing Research*, 28 (August), 281-95.

Sela, Aner and Baba Shiv (2009), "Unraveling Priming: When Does the Same Prime Activate a Goal Versus a Trait?," *Journal of Consumer Research*, 36 (October), 418-33.

Shultz, Thomas R., Elène Léveillé, and Mark R. Lepper (1999), "Free Choice and Cognitive Dissonance Revisited: Choosing 'Lesser Evils' Versus 'Greater Goods'," *Personality & Social Psychology Bulletin*, 25 (January), 40-48.

Steele, Claude M., Steven J. Spencer, and Michael Lynch (1993), "Self-Image Resilience and Dissonance: The Role of Affirmational Resources," *Journal of Personality and Social Psychology*, 64 (June), 885-96.

Tsiros, Michael and Vikas Mittal (2000), "Regret: A Model of Its Antecedents and Consequences in Consumer Decision Making," *Journal of Consumer Research*, 26 (March), 401-17.

van Dijk, Eric and Marcel Zeelenberg (2005), "On the Psychology of 'If Only': Regret and the Comparison between Factual and Counterfactual Outcomes," *Organizational Behavior and Human Decision Processes*, 97 (July), 152-60.

Self-Positivity versus Self-Negativity:
Consumers' Reliance on Base Rate and Case Risk in Perceptions of Health Risk

Dengfeng Yan, HKUST
Jaideep Sengupta, HKUST, Hong Kong

EXTENDED ABSTRACT

Previous literature (Keller, Lipkus, and Rimer 2002; Lin et al. 2003) suggests that consumers' health risk perceptions may be influenced by two types of information. One of these is *base rate*, which reflects the ubiquity of disease in the target population (Lin et al. 2003; Raghubir 2008). Alternately, people may form health risk assessments based on idiosyncratic *case risk information*, which reflects the unique aspects of the target person such as their likelihood of engaging in risky behaviors (e.g., Raghubir and Menon 1998), or possessing certain symptoms of an illness (e.g., Dunning, Heath, and Suls 2004; Menon et al. 2002).

Construal theory literature (e.g., Liberman and Trope 1998; Forster, Friedman and Liberman 2004) suggest that abstract information, compared with concrete information that tends to be relatively more specific and vivid, exerts more impact on representations and judgments of psychologically distant events, while the reverse holds when the focal judgment is about psychologically near events. We argue that this premise contains direct implications for the current research question regarding the relative influence of base rate vs. case risk on health risk assessments. Base rates, by definition, consist of abstracted information about a target category rather than about a specific exemplar of that category (i.e., unconditioned on featural evidence) (e.g., seasonal flu or human flu in the U.S. results in approximately 36,000 deaths each year). On the other hand, case risk provides idiosyncratic, vivid information at a much greater level of specificity. In light of this distinction, and given the preceding arguments arising from construal level theory, it follows that:

Hypothesis	*Consumers' reliance on base rate information for making health risk judgment will be enhanced when the judgment is psychologically distant (versus relatively close). Case risk information (e.g., pathogenic behaviors or syndromes), on the contrary, have a greater influence when the judgment is psychologically close (versus distant).*

This hypothesis has direct implications for previous research on self-positivity bias wherein people tend to underestimate their risk vulnerability as compared to others (for a review, see Menon et al. 2008). Because the base rate (case risk) has a greater influence on judgments regarding others (the self), self-positivity should be most likely to be manifested when the base rate of a health risk is relatively high, while the case risk signals low risk. In such cases, individuals will be prone to judging others more at risk than themselves. In contrast, self-negativity is particularly likely to be manifested when the base rate is relatively low, but the case risk signals high risk – in such cases, individuals will be more prone to judging themselves at risk than others.

Results from four studies provide convergent support for our thesis by using multiple operationalizations of construal levels, different health risks, diverse operationalizations of base rate and case risk information, and several dependent measures. All studies tested our basic proposition by examining respondents' reliance on base rate vs. case risk to form health risk assessments, as a function of psychological distance. Experiment 1-2 focused on the interpersonal dimension of psychological distance. Subsequent studies sought to increase confidence in our construal-based conceptualization by generalizing the obtained effects to other dimensions of psychological distance, and by illuminating the underlying process. Thus, to test the process-related argument that psychological distance has its effect on health risk perception by influencing construal levels, experiment 3 directly manipulated construal type (abstract vs. concrete) prior to the assessment of health risks. Lastly, experiment 4 examined how individuals' self risk perceptions differ across time horizon.

This inquiry adds to the health risk literature in several different ways. First, we present a unifying framework of how individuals' health risk estimates are systematically influenced by base rate and case risk under different conditions. This conceptualization presents a new perspective on how individuals arrive at health risk assessments, and delineates conditions under which the underlying process is more likely to be top-down (enhanced influence of base rate) vs. bottom-up (enhanced influence of case details). Second, while past consumer research on health risk perceptions has reliably documented a self-positivity bias, and also demonstrated ways of attenuating such a bias (Chandran and Menon 2004; Raghubir and Menon 1998), the current inquiry complements these findings by documenting conditions under which a reversal (i.e., a self-negativity effect) is manifested. Such an effect has rarely been obtained before (the exception being research by Lin et al. 2003, who found that pessimistic participants exhibit self-negativity). By predicting and demonstrating the symmetric nature of self-positivity and self-negativity in health risk assessments, the current inquiry is thus able to extend current knowledge in this area.

Third, in addition to documenting the self-negativity effect, the key moderator proposed in our work (construal level) has the potential to integrate several past findings relating to the self-positivity bias in health perceptions. For example, in a seminal article, Raghubir and Menon (1998) found that asking participants to recall three (versus five) risky behaviors significantly increased participants' own vulnerability to HIV. However, perception of others' vulnerability was unaffected by this ease of retrieval manipulation. This finding is consistent with the current conceptualization – the perceived likelihood of engaging in risky behaviors is a form of case-specific information and therefore should be utilized more in the psychologically proximal (i.e., self) condition, as was found in that study. Similarly, and as noted earlier, the finding that the self-positivity bias is reduced by increasing the salience of easy-to-visualize behaviors (such as not bandaging a cut; Menon et al. 2002) also fits with a construal level perspective. Such behaviors are more concrete (visualizability being an aspect of concreteness; Chandran and Menon 2004) and therefore are more likely to influence risk assessments for self vs. others.

REFERENCES

Agrawal, Nidhi and Echo Wen Wan (2009), "Regulating Risk or Risking Regulation? Construal Levels and Depletion Effects in the Processing of Health Messages," *Journal of Consumer Research*, 36 (3), 448-62.

Bar-Hillel, Maya (1980), "The Base-Rate Fallacy in Probability Judgments," *Acta Psychologica*, 44 (3), 211-33.

Advances in Consumer Research
Volume 39, ©2011

Bar-Hillel, Maya and Baruch Fischhoff (1981), "When Do Base Rates Affect Predictions?," *Journal of Personality and Social Psychology*, 41 (4), 671-80.

Chandran, Sucharita and Geeta Menon (2004), "When a Day Means More Than a Year: Effects of Temporal Framing on Judgments of Health Risk," *Journal of Consumer Research*, 31 (2), 375-89.

Freitas, Antonio L., Peter Gollwitzer, and Yaacov Trope (2004), "The Influence of Abstract and Concrete Mindsets Onanticipating and Guiding Others' Self-Regulatory Efforts," *Journal of Experimental Social Psychology*, 40 (6), 739-52.

Keller, R. A., I. M. Lipkus, and B. K. Rimer (2002), "Depressive Realism and Health Risk Accuracy: The Negative Consequences of Positive Mood," *Journal of Consumer Research*, 29 (1), 57-69.

Kim, Kyeongheui, Meng Zhang, and Xiuping Li (2008), "Effects of Temporal and Social Distance on Consumer Evaluations," *Journal of Consumer Research*, 35 (4), 706-13.

Kray, Laura and Richard Gonzalez (1999), "Differential Weighting in Choice Versus Advice: I'll Do This, You Do That," *Journal of Behavioral Decision Making*, 12 (3), 207-17.

Kruger, Justin (1999), "Lake Wobegon Be Gone!! The "Below-Average Effect" and the Egocentric Nature of Comparative Ability Judgments," *Journal of Personality and Social Psychology*, 77 (2), 221-32.

Kunda, Ziva (1990), "The Case for Motivated Reasoning," *Psychological Bulletin*, 108 (3), 480-98.

Kyung, Ellie J., Geeta Menon, and Yaacov Trope (2010), "Reconstruction of Things Past: Why Do Some Memories Feel So Close and Others So Far Away?," *Journal of Experimental Social Psychology*, 46 (1), 217-20.

Leahy, Robert L. (2006), *The Worry Cure: Seven Steps to Stop Worry from Stopping You*, New York: Harmony Press.

Lin, Ying-Ching, Chien-Huang Lin, and Priya Raghubir (2003), "Avoiding Anxiety, Being in Denial, or Simply Stroking Self-Esteem: Why Self-Positivity?," *Journal of Consumer Psychology*, 13 (4), 464-77.

Liviatan, Ido, Yaacov Trope, and Nira Liberman (2008), "Interpersonal Similarity as a Social Distance Dimension: Implications for Perception of Others' Actions," *Journal of Experimental Social Psychology*, 44 (5), 1256-69.

Menon, Geeta, Lauren G. Block, and Suresh Ramanathan (2002), "We're at as Much Risk as We Are Led to Believe: Effects of Message Cues on Judgments of Health," *Journal of Consumer Research*, 28 (4), 533-49.

Menon, Geeta, Ellie J. Kyung, and Nidhi Agrawal (2009), "Biases in Social Comparisons: Optimism or Pessimism," *Organizational Behavior and Human Decision Processes*, 108 (1), 39-52.

Menon, Geeta, Priya Raghubir, and Nidhi Agrawal (2008), "Health Risk Perceptions and Consumer Psychology," in *Handbook of Consumer Psychology*, ed. Curtis Haugtvedt, Paul Herr and Frank Kardes, New York: Lawrence Erlbaum, 981-1010.

Raghubir, Priya (2008), "Is 1/10 N 10/100? The Effect of Denominator Salience on Perceptions of Base Rates of Health Risk," *International Journal of Research in Marketing*, 25 (4), 327-34.

Raghubir, Priya and Geeta Menon (1998), "Aids and Me, Never the Twain Shall Meet: The Effects of Information Accessibility on Judgments of Risk and Advertising Effectiveness," *Journal of Consumer Research*, 25 (1), 52-63.

Trope, Yaacov and Nira Liberman (2010), "Construal-Level Theory of Psychological Distance," *Psychological Review*, 117 (2), 440-63.

Trope, Yaacov, Nira Liberman, and Cheryl Wakslak (2007), "Construal Levels and Psychological Distance: Effects on Representation, Prediction, Evaluation, and Behavior," *Journal of Consumer Psychology*, 17 (2), 83-95.

Vallacher, Robin R. and Daniel M. Wegner (1989), "Levels of Personal Agency: Individual Variation in Action Identification," *Journal of Personality and Social Psychology*, 57 (4), 660-71.

Wakslak, Cheryl J., Yaacov Trope, Nira Liberman, and Rotem Alony (2006), "Seeing the Forest When Entry Is Unlikely: Probability and the Mental Representation of Events.," *Journal of Experimental Psychology: General*, 135 (4), 641-53.

Visual Aesthetics and Product Design: Who, What, and When, They All Matter.

Amitava Chattopadhyay, INSEAD, Singapore
Antonios Stamatogiannakis, IE Business School, Spain
Gerald Gorn, The University of Hong Kong, Hong Kong

EXTENDED ABSTRACT

The visual appeal of a product is important. It can influence whether a product gets noticed as well as whether it is chosen (Hoegg and Alba 2007). Once purchased, a product's aesthetic appeal can continue to provide sensory pleasure over its lifetime (Bloch 1995).

The literature suggests several possible antecedents of visual appeal. Most of them pertain to properties held by the visual stimulus: symmetry (Reber 2002), contrast (Reber and Schwarz 2001), prototypicality (Martindale and Moore 1988), and unity (Veryzer and Hutchinson 1998).

Other authors suggest that aesthetic appreciation is context dependent. For example, the same picture was liked more when it was primed by a matched contour, versus by a mismatched contour (Reber, Winkielman, and Schwarz 1998). Still other research suggests that characteristics of the perceiver affect aesthetic preference. For example, the familiarity that someone has with the stimulus, (Cho and Schwarz, 2010) seems to increase liking. Despite the extensiveness of this research, evidence on how the characteristics of the product, the observer, and the context interact to affect aesthetic judgments remains scarce.

Reber, Schwarz and Winkielman (2004) reviewed research examining the above effects, suggesting that they all increase visual liking because they facilitate processing fluency. They focus on how the individual effects of each of these factors affects aesthetic response, and suggest that they increase aesthetic preference only when they facilitate processing.

This paper adds to the above research and makes three specific contributions. First, it examines aesthetic judgments from an integrative perspective and and using a perceptual fluency account argues that the person (who), the product (what), and the context (when?\) interact to determine visual preference,.

Second, it shows that objective properties of the stimulus (e.g., unity) affect aesthetic preference by facilitating visual processing, by showing that unity has a positive effect on preference when visual, but not verbal, processing resources are constrained. Third, it provides evidence for the substitutability of the sources of perceptual fluency. That is, effects of perceptual fluency on aesthetic judgments are similar regardless whether fluency is caused by the product, the person, or the context.

Object possessing properties such as symmetry, unity, etc. are easier for our visual system to detect and process, and for this reason they are perceived as pleasant (Reber et al. 2004; Ramachandran and Hirstein 1999). This article focuses on unity.

If unity increases aesthetic preference because it facilitates fluent processing, its effects should be most strongly observed when processing is constrained. Under such circumstances the superior ability of the perceptual system to detect and process unity should lead to fluent processing for unified objects but not for non-unified objects. On the other hand, unconstrained processing should be able by itself to lead to processing fluency, even when unity is violated.

In addition, we predict that the effect of unity on aesthetic evaluations will be more positive when visual, but not verbal, processing capacity (Baddeley 1992) is constrained. That is, unity should increase aesthetic preference by making "perceptual" processing fluent (Reber et al. 2004). Finally, we predict that the above effects should be moderated by the observer's inherent ability (Ekstrom et al. 1976)

and preference (Childers, Houston, and Heckler 1985) for visual processing. When these characteristics are low, visual processing should be even more difficult, and thus the role of unity more important.

In two studies we test the prediction that the extent to which unified designs are preferred to non-unified ones depends on the interaction of the load type (visual vs. verbal) with the individual's inherent ability and willingness to process visually. Both studies use a 2 x 2 x 2 factorial design with unity (satisfied vs. not) and product replicate as within participants factors, and load (verbal vs. visual) as a between participants factor.

Load was manipulated by having participants to remember some abstract information (e.g., price and delivery method) about a table (verbal load) versus concrete and visualizable aspects (e.g., shape and number of legs) of a table (visual load). These were pretested to be equal in difficulty. Then participants were asked to choose based on visual attractiveness between the unified and the non-unified versions of two products. Finally, we measured participants' inherent ability (study 1) and preference (study 2) for visual processing.

In the first study we used phone and refrigerator designs, taken from Veryzer and Hutchinson (1998), either satisfying unity or not. A logit analysis revealed the predicted significant load x visual processing ability interaction effect on choice of unified designs. The unified designs were more likely to be chosen by participants low in visual processing ability, when they were under visual, but not verbal load.

In the second study we used the designs of a clock and a vase, either satisfying unity or not. A logit analysis revealed the predicted significant load x visual processing preference interaction effect on choice of unified designs. The unified designs were more likely to be chosen by participants low in visual processing preference, when they were under visual, but not verbal load.

In conclusion, this article takes an integrative approach and suggests that the product, the person, and the context interact to affect visual preference. From a theoretical perspective, we document the specific role played by visual but not verbal processing resources in how unified and non-unified designs are processed and evaluated.. Moreover, we demonstrate the substitutability of the different sources of perceptual fluency; Perceptual fluency increases aesthetic preference regardless whether it stems from the object, the person, or the context. Finally, the results indicate that focusing on how these three factors in isolation affect visual preference, might be incomplete..

From a managerial perspective, designers and managers who wish to offer aesthetically pleasing products should consider the context and the customer characteristics on top of design properties, such as unity. To paraphrase Confucius: "Everything has beauty, but not everyone sees it." At least not always.

REFERENCES

Baddeley, Alan (1992), "Working Memory," *Science,* 255 (5044), 556-59.

Berlyne, Daniel E. (1971), *Aesthetics and Psychobiology.* New York: Appleton-Century-Crofts.

Bloch, Peter H. (1995), "Seeking the Ideal Form: Product Design and Consumer Response," *Journal of Marketing,* 59 (03), 16-29.

Childers, Terry L., Michael J. Houston, and Susan E. Heckler (1985), "Measurement of Individual Differences in Visual Versus Verbal Information Processing," *Journal of Consumer Research,* 12 (2), 125-34.

Cho, Hyejeung, and Norbert Schwarz (2010), "I like those glasses on you, but not in the mirror: Fluency, preference, and virtual mirrors," *Journal of Consumer Psychology,* 20 (4), 471-75.

Ekstrom, Ruth B., John W. French, Harry H. Harman, and Diran Dermen (1976), *Kit of Factor-Referenced Cognitive Tests.* NJ, USA: ETS.

Farah, Martha J. (1988), "Is Visual Imagery Really Visual? Overlooked Evidence from Neuropsychology," *Psychological Review,* 95 (03), 307-17.

Hoegg, JoAndrea and Joseph W. Alba (2007), "A Role for Aesthetics in Consumer Psychology," in *Handbook of Consumer Psychology,* Curt Haugtvedt, Frank Kardes, and Paul M. Herr, eds. Sage, 733-54.

Irwin, Julie R. and Gary H. McClelland (2001), "Misleading Heuristics and Moderated Multiple Regression Models," *Journal of Marketing Research,* 38 (1), 100-109.

Kumar, Minu, and Nitika Garg (2010), "Aesthetic principles and cognitive emotion appraisals: How much of the beauty lies in the eye of the beholder?," *Journal of Consumer Psychology,* 20 (4), 485-94.

Logie, Robert H., Gesualdo M. Zucco, and Alan D. Baddeley (1990), "Interference with visual short-term memory," *Acta Psychologica,* 75 (1), 55-74.

Martindale, Colin and Kathleen Moore (1988), "Priming, Prototypicality, and Preference," *Journal of Experimental Psychology: Human Perception and Performance,* 14 (4), 661-70.

McWhinnie, Harold J. (1968), "A Review of Research on Aesthetic Measure," *Acta Psychologica,* 28, 363-75.

Ramachandran, Vilayanur S. and William Hirstein (1999), "The Science of Art: A Neurological Theory of Aesthetic Experience," *Journal of Consciousness Studies,* 6 (6-7), 15-51.

Reber, Rolf (2002), "Reasons for the Preference for Symmetry," *Behavioral and Brain Sciences,* 25 (3), 415-6.

Reber, Rolf and Norbert Schwarz (2001), "The Hot Fringes of Conciousness: Perceptual Fluency and Affect" *Consciousness and Emotion,* 2, 223-31.

Reber, Rolf, Norbert Schwarz, and Piotr Winkielman (2004), "Processing Fluency and Aesthetic Pleasure: Is Beauty in the Perceiver's Processing Experience?" *Personality & Social Psychology Review,* 8 (4), 364-82.

Reber, Rolf, Piotr Winkielman, and Norbert Schwarz (1998), "Effects of Perceptual Fluency on Affective Judgments" *Psychological Science,* 9 (1), 45-48.

Schwarz, Norbert (2004), "Metacognitive Experiences in Consumer Judgment and Decision Making," *Journal of Consumer Psychology,* 14 (4), 332-48.

Schwarz, Norbert and Gerald L. Clore (1983), "Mood, misattribution, and judgments of well-being: Informative and directive functions of affective states," *Journal of Personality and Social Psychology,* 45 (3), 513-23.

Topolinski, Sascha (2010), "Moving the Eye of the Beholder: Motor Components in Vision Determine Aesthetic Preference" *Psychological Science,* 21 (9), 1220-24.

Veryzer, Robert W. and John Wesley Hutchinson (1998), "The Influence of Unity and Prototypicality on Aesthetic Responses to New Product Designs," *Journal of Consumer Research,* 24 (4), 374-94.

The Impact of Metacognition on Commitment for Attainment versus Maintenance Goals

Antonios Stamatogiannakis, IE Business School, Spain
Haiyang Yang, INSEAD, Singapore
Amitava Chattopadhyay, INSEAD, Singapore

EXTENDED ABSTRACT

Consumers and firms across many domains (e.g., charity, saving, exercising) use goals to regulate behaviour. For example, HSBC offers the "Premier Investor Savings" account, which requires the maintenance of a $25000 minimum balance, but at the same time offers higher interest rates with higher balances.

Depending on the relation between the actual and the desired state of the goal, goals can be classified as either attainment or maintenance goals. Attainment goals are those for which the actual state differs from the desired state (e.g., increase your balance). Maintenance goals are those for which the actual and the desired states match, and need to remain matched (e.g., maintain your balance; Stamatogiannakis, Chattopadhyay, and Chakravarti 2010).

Given the mixed use of these two goal types, it is surprising that we know little on how they compare with each other. Recent research is covering some of this gap. First, people tend to strive for better states when they focus on what they need to do, but they are satisfied with the present state when they consider what they have already done (Koo and Fishbach 2010). Second, modest attainment goals are perceived as easier than objectively easier maintenance goals (Stamatogiannakis et al. 2010). As a result, they are also more attractive (Stamatogiannakis, Chattopadhyay, and Chakravarti 2011). Finally, matching attainment goals with promotion focus and/ or maintenance goals with prevention focus increases outcome evaluations (Brodscholl, Kober, and Higgins 2007).

The current research examines the complex effects of metacognitive experiences (Schwarz 2004) on consumers' commitment to the two types of goals (Kruglaksi et al. 2002). Our findings make several contributions.. First, they show that, as people draw on their subjective experience when making an evaluative judgment (Wänke, Bohner, and Jurkowitsch 1997; Schwarz 2004), perceived goal difficulty, and thereby goal commitment, are affected by how easy or difficult strategies for success are generated. This generation is particularly difficult for maintenance goals (Jiraporn and Desai 2011). Therefore, we predict that a maintenance goal will become more attractive when strategy generation is made easy (e.g., by asking people to generate only one strategy) versus when it is made hard (e.g., by asking people to generate five strategies). Finally, as success strategy generation is relatively easy for attainment goals (Jiraporn and Desai 2011), the attractiveness of these goals will not be affected by the number of strategies that have to be generated, within the range studied in this research (i.e., 1 vs. 5 strategies). We test these predictions in study 1.

After examining the effects of perceived ease of strategies generation, we turn to another metacognitive experience related variable, increased accessibility; Increased accessibility improves processing fluency of related constructs and thus positively impacts preference for such constructs (Schwarz 2004). Specifically, we show that the commitment for the two goal types is dependent on the accessibility of different self-construals. Independent and interdependent orientations coexist within each person (Markus and Kitayama 1991), and they can be primed by contextual cues (Maddux et al. 2010). Independent self-construals emphasize values such as seeking personal achievement, improving individual status, and being distinct and unique (Markus and Kitayama 1991). Thus, they are congruent with attainment goals. Interdependent self-construals, however, emphasize values such as maintaining social relationships, conforming to others, and not standing out (Markus and Kitayama 1991). Thus, they are congruent with maintenance goals. Given that increased accessibility improves processing fluency of related constructs (Schwarz 2004), when independent (interdependent) aspects of self-construals are made more accessible by the situation, people are likely to see attainment (maintenance) goals more favorably. We test these predictions in study 2.

Third, and importantly, the above predictions are tested with goals that are important for the participant, rather than with imaginary goal scenarios.

Experiment one uses a 2 x 3 between participants design. Participants were recruited for two proofreading tasks, lasting three minutes each. After they have completed the first task, some participants were assigned a maintenance goal (i.e., find at least an equal number of mistakes in the second task) and some an attainment goal (i.e., find at least one more mistake in the second task). Further, some participants had to list 1 strategy that would help them achieve their goal, some had to list 5 such strategies, and some did not have to list any strategies. As expected from past research (Stamatogiannakis et al. 2011), attainment goals were more attractive than maintenance goals in the control (0 strategies) condition. In addition, as strategy generation is easy for attainment goals (Jiraporn and Desai 2011) the number of strategies manipulation did not affect attainment goals. However, generating only 1 strategy made maintenance goals more attractive compared to the control condition, and as attractive as attainment goals. However, generating 5 strategies made attractiveness ratings relapse to the control condition levels, and less attractive than attainment goals.

Experiment two uses a 2 x 2 between participants design. Following Gardner, Gabriel, and Lee (1999), we primed independent (interdependent) self-construal by asking participants to read a text and clicking on singular (plural) pronouns such as I and myself (we and ourselves). Then they were asked to think about their favourite charity, and indicate any amount they would like to donate to it. After that, they were asked their willingness to pre-commit to donate exactly the same amount (a maintenance goal), or the same amount plus 1 cent (an attainment goal), a year from now. The priming x goal type interaction was significant. People indicated greater willingness to pre-commit to an attainment (maintenance) goal when primed with an independent (interdependent) self-construal.

To conclude, this paper adds to previous literature comparing attainment with maintenance goals. It demonstrates that at the baseline, and when strategy generation is difficult, attainment goals are more committing than maintenance goals. However, the two goal types are equally committing when strategy generation is easy. Moreover, attainment (maintenance) goals are more committing when an independent (interdependent) self-construal is accessible. Thus, commitment for the two goal types is context dependent, and is affected differently by meta-cognitive experiences.

REFERENCES

Brodscholl, Jeff C., Hedy Kober, and E. Tory Higgins (2007), "Strategies of Self-Regulation In Goal Attainment Versus Goal Maintenance," *European Journal of Social Psychology,* 37 (4), 628-48.

Gardner, Wendi L., Shira Gabriel, and Kristy K. Dean (2004), " The Individual as "Melting Pot": The Flexibility of bicultural self-construals," *Cachiers de Psychologie Cognitive*, 22, 181-201.

Gardner, Wendi L., Shira Gabriel, and Angela Y. Lee (1999), " "I" Value Freedom, but "we" Value Relationships: Self-Construal Priming Mirrors Cultural Differences in Judgment," *Psychological Science*, 10 (4), 321-26.

Jiraporn, Napatsorn and Kalpesh K. Desai (2011), "Maintenance versus Attainment Goals: Influence of Self-Regulation Goal Type on Goal Pursuit Behaviors ", in *Advances in Consumer Research,* Vol. 38, eds. Darren W. Dahl, Gita V. Johar, and Stijn M.J. van Osselaer, Duluth, MN: Association for Consumer Research.

Koo, Minjung and Ayelet Fishbach (2010), "Climbing the Goal Ladder: How Upcoming Actions Increase Level of Aspiration," *Journal of Personality and Social Psychology,* 99 (1), 1-13.

Kruglanski, Arie, James Y. Shah, Ayelet Fishbach, Ron Friedman, Woo Young Chun, and David Sleeth-Keppler (2002), "A Theory of Goal Systems," *Advances in Experimental Social Psychology,* 34, 331-78.

Kühnen, Ulrich, Bettina Hannover, and Benjamin Schubert (2001), "The Semantic-Procedural Interface Model of the Self: The Role of Self-knowledge for Context-dependent versus Context-independent Modes of Thinking," *Journal of Personality and Social Psychology*, 80, 397-409.

Maddux, William, Haiyang Yang, Carl Falk, Hajo Adam, Wendi Adair, Yumi Endo, Ziv Carmon, and Steve Heine (2010), "For whom is Parting from Possessions more Painful: Cultural Differences in the Endowment Effect," *Psychological Science*, 21(12), 1910- 17.

Markus, Hazel Rose, & Shinobu Kitayama (1991), "Culture and the self: Implications for cognition, emotion, and motivation," *Psychological Review*, 98(2), 224-53.

Schwarz, Norbert (2004), "Metacognitive Experiences in Consumer Judgment and Decision Making," *Journal of Consumer Psychology,* 14 (4), 332-48.

Singelis, Ted (1994), "The Measurement of Independent and Interdependent Self-Construals," *Personality and Social Psychology Bulletin,* 20, 580-91.

Stamatogiannakis, Antonios, Amitava Chattopadhyay, and Dipankar Chakravarti (2010), " Maintenance versus Attainment Goals: Why People Think it Is Harder to Maintain their Weight than to Lose a Couple of Kilos ", in *Advances in Consumer Research,* Vol. 37, eds. Margarett C. Campbell, J. Jeffrey Inman, and Rik Pieters, Duluth, MN: Association for Consumer Research.

Stamatogiannakis, Antonios, Amitava Chattopadhyay, and Dipankar Chakravarti (2011), " Attainment versus Maintenance Goals: Differences in Cognitive Processing and Goal Attractiveness ", in *Advances in Consumer Research,* Vol. 38, eds. Darren W. Dahl, Gita V. Johar, and Stijn M.J. van Osselaer, Duluth, MN: Association for Consumer Research.

Trafimow, David, Harry Triandis, and Sharon Goto (1991), "Some Tests of the Distinction between the Private Self and the Collective Self," *Journal of Personality and Social Psychology*, 60 (May), 649–655.

Triandis, Harry C. (1989), "The Self and Behavior in Differing Cultural Contexts," *Psychological Review,* 96, 506-52.

Wänke, Michaela, Gerd Bohner, and Andreas Jurkowitsch (1997), "There Are Many Reasons to Drive a BMW: Does Imagined Ease of Argument Generation Influence Attitudes?," *Journal of Consumer Research,* 24 (2), 170-78.

Small Change: The Subjective Valuation of Coins and Bills

Eric Dolansky, Brock University, Ontario

EXTENDED ABSTRACT

According to the official website of the U.S. Mint, the U.S. treasury would save $500 million per year if individuals used one-dollar coins rather than bills. As a result, on several occasions in the past, the U.S. mint has issued dollar coins, most recently in 2007. None have proven to be very popular (Unser, 2009). So what is preventing Americans from adopting dollar coins?

Individuals tend to exhibit biases when valuing money, despite the explicit denomination of the coin or bill. Mishra, Mishra and Nayakankuppam (2006) found that individuals valued large-denomination bills more highly than an equivalent amount of money presented in smaller bills. Work by Alter and Oppenheimer (2008) indicates that familiarity of the money has an impact on how highly it is valued. A more recent finding ties denomination of money to self-control in spending (Raghubir and Srivistava 2009).

This research aims to extend previous findings by determining if individuals have a bias towards higher valuation of bills as opposed to coins. This topic has been mentioned in the relevant literature (Alter and Oppenheimer 2008; Mishra et al 2006; Raghubir 2006) as worthy of further exploration, however the idea has not been empirically tested. Raghubir and Srivistava (2009) incorporated coins vs. bills as a condition in one of their studies, but it was inconclusive.

In nearly every currency in the world bills are of a higher denomination than coins. This difference in objective valuation could have an impact on subjective valuation, as a representativeness bias (Kahneman and Tversky 1973). As such, coins would tend to be valued less than bills, even when the denominations are the same. It has also been found that people will take an instance and average it to its own category. Thus a coin would be valued to the average value in its category, which would be lower than the average for the bills category (Huttenlocher, Hedges and Bradburn 1990). This leads to the key hypothesis of this paper:

Hypothesis 1   An amount of money presented in paper form (i.e. bill) will be valued higher than an equivalent amount of money presented in coin form.

To test this prediction, study 1 was conducted. Participants ($n - 52$) werc givcn cithcr onc Trinidad and Tobago dollar bill or one Trinidad and Tobago dollar coin and were asked how much of each of nine inexpensive items (e.g. pencils, paper clips) they could buy with that money. Participants were also asked to estimate how many Canadian dollars they could purchase with the money.

Unfamiliar currency was used to eliminate the possibility that familiarity with the money was a cause for any differences found, as in previous research (Alter and Oppenheimer 2008). Participants were told that the exchange rate was approximately 1:1 (the real exchange rate is $6 TT to $1 CDN and would result in too little purchasing power for useful estimates) and were instructed that the purchase amounts they estimated should reflect costs in Canada. Participants were also asked how familiar they were with the currency prior to the experiment. Four participants were removed from the analysis because they were previously familiar with the currency.

Overall H_1 is supported. when all of the estimates are standardized, there is a difference between the objects purchasable with bills (1.34 standard deviations above the mean) than with coins (1.39 standard deviations below the mean, $p = 0.096$). The exchange valuation prediction is more conclusive: participants given coins

estimated they could exchange their $1 TT for $0.798 CDN and those given bills estimated $1.192 ($p = 0.02$), despite being told that both the coins and bills were worth approximately $1 CDN.

Study 2 was planned to refine and extend this effect. Using the same methodology as study one, participants ($n = 82$) were recruited at Niagara Falls, Ontario with the intention of having nationality (i.e. Canadian vs. American) as a found condition. Because Canadian currency contains coins of higher value (up to $2) than American currency does (only up to 25 cents), it was expected that the difference between the values ascribed to coins and bills would be bigger. Specifically:

Hypothesis 2   The effect hypothesized in H1 is moderated by country of origin; the higher the value of coins in a country, the smaller the difference in valuation of coins and bills by those living in it.

The results from study two support this hypothesis. There is a significant interaction between form of money (coins vs. bills) and country of origin for both the total items exhibited an interaction (F = 6.45, $p = 0.013$), as well as the currency exchange question (F = 16.02, $p < 0.001$).

This work provides insight into how individuals value money and implications for research, management, and policy. Policy implications are the most salient here, as it is possible that a shift from bills to coins for a particular denomination (e.g., one dollar in the U.S.) could have an impact on valuation of money overall, as individuals ascribe less purchasing power to the coin than to the bill.

REFERENCES

Alter, Adam L. and Daniel M. Oppenheimer (2008), "Easy on the Mind, Easy on the Wallet: The Roles of Familiarity and Processing Fluency in Valuation Judgments," *Psychonomic Bulletin and Review*, 15 (5), 985-990.

Huttenlocher, Janellen, Larry V. Hedges and Norman M. Bradburn (1990), "Reports of Elapsed Time: Bounding and Rounding Processes in Estimation," *Journal of Experimental Psychology: Learning, Memory and Cognition*, 16 (March), 196-213.

Kahneman, Daniel, and Amos Tversky (1972), "Subjective Probability: A Judgment of Representativeness," *Cognitive Psychology*, 3, 430-454.

Mishra, Himanshu, Arul Mishra and Dhananjay Nayakankuppam (2006), "Money: A Bias for the Whole," *Journal of Consumer Research*, 32 (March), 541-549.

Raghubir, Priya (2006), "An Information Processing Review of the Subjective Value of Money and Prices," *Journal of Business Research*, 59, 1053-1062.

Raghubir, Priya and Joydeep Srivistava (2009), "The Denomination Effect," *Journal of Consumer Research,* 36 (December), 701-713.

Unser, Darrin Lee (2009), "US Dollar Coins Glut, Supply Far Exceeds Demand," http://www.coinnews.net.

The Robin Hood Effect: When High-Level Construals Lead to Immoral Behaviors for the Greater Good

Jessica Rixom, University of Utah, USA
Himanshu Mishra, University of Utah, USA

EXTENDED ABSTRACT

Moral principles (e.g., cheating is wrong, donating is good) can help guide decisions throughout life. Recent research on construal-level theory (CLT; Trope and Liberman 2003) in a moral domain has suggested that these general moral principles act as high-level, abstract constructs. When events are construed at high levels (as opposed to low levels), there is an increased reliance on these moral principles for guidance. For instance, with higher construal levels, immoral acts were judged more harshly and moral acts more virtuously, even when presented with mitigating information (Eyal, Liberman, and Trope 2008). Similarly, it has been shown that people are more cooperative (Sanna et al. 2009) and more willing to help by answering a survey (Agerström and Björklund 2009) when a high-level as opposed to low-level construal is activated. In sum, previous research suggests that when faced with a single moral decision, consumers with high-level relative to low-level construals avoid behaviors that violate moral principles and engage in behaviors that support moral principles.

However, not all moral decisions occur in isolation. Consumers sometimes encounter situations in which violating one moral principle directly enables additional support for another moral principle. While past work on CLT explored events favoring a single moral principle, we investigate situations that pit immoral acts against moral acts. In these situations, we find that people with a high-level construal are willing to violate moral principles in order to increase support for a greater cause, but not solely for personal gain. Specifically, when high-level construals are activated, people are uncooperative in order to help a charity (study 1) and while they will not lie for themselves alone, they will lie to help the less fortunate or to withhold help from wrongdoers who threaten the well-being of others (study 2). We also find that when a low-level construal is activated, people are willing to engage in immoral behaviors for personal gain, with less regard for the overall impact. We term the use of immoral acts by people with a high-level construal for the sake of helping the greater good, the Robin Hood effect.

Study 1 demonstrated the basic effect. Participants were primed with either a high or low-level construal (Freitas, Gollwitzer, and Trope 2004). Then, they played a computer-based fishing cooperation game (Bargh et al. 2001; Sanna et al. 2009), purportedly with someone in another room. Real money was earned for each fish kept. Participants earned money for themselves or a charity, depending on the condition to which they were randomly assigned. In all conditions, the "other participant" earned money for themselves. To promote cooperation, if the fish population dropped too low, then all profits were confiscated. Consistent with previous literature, when earning for themselves, high-level relative to low-level construals were more cooperative (kept fewer fish). However, we find that when earning money for a charity, high-level construals were less cooperative (kept more fish). Said differently, a high-level construal led to uncooperative behavior when doing so meant that the greater good would benefit.

In study 2 we used a dishonesty paradigm adopted from work by Mazar, Amir, and Ariely (2008). Participants solved puzzles and were then primed with a high-level or low-level construal (Freitas et al. 2004). Next, they were asked to indicate how many puzzles they solved correctly so they could be paid for their performance

(a quarter per correct answer, up to $5). The instructions varied by condition. In one payment condition (the benchmark), lying was not possible because the researcher graded the answers. Lying was possible in the other conditions because participants graded their own answers, destroyed the answer sheets, and indicated the number correct on a separate payment form. When the average that participants claimed to solve correctly was significantly lower or higher than the benchmark, lying was inferred.

Consistent with past work, those with high-level (low-level) construals acted morally (immorally) and did not (did) lie for personal gain. In the other two payment conditions, participants read that $5 was set aside and they would earn a quarter for each correct answer with the remaining, unearned money donated to charity. Thus, claiming few (many) correct answers resulted in larger (smaller) donations. The charity either granted wishes to ill children (good charity) or paid legal expenses for companies charged with environmental damage (bad charity). In both conditions, participants with high-level construals lied about the number of correct answers. When the charity was good, participants with high-level construals underreported the number correct. That is, they acted immorally, lied, and hurt themselves financially to ensure larger donations to the good charity. Donations would be made even without lying but they underreported so more would be donated. Conversely, for the bad charity, participants with high-level construals lied by overreporting the number correct. They were immoral, lied, and gained financially in order to reduce the donation to a charity that harms the greater good. When deception was possible, people with low-level construals consistently lied by overreporting the number correct to the same extent, regardless the decision's impact.

The findings add to the research on construal level's impact on decision-making by demonstrating that activating high-level construals do not always lead to adherence to moral principles. Instead, the Robin Hood effect shows that high-level construals can lead to immoral behaviors when violating moral principles benefits the greater good. This work also provides some insight into the day-to-day acts of dishonesty that one may justify in order to help the greater good to more extreme issues such as eco-terrorism in which environmental extremists attempt to advance their notion of a greater good (protect further environmental damage) by committing immoral acts (vandalism) toward companies and individuals.

REFERENCES

Agerström, Jens and Fredrik Björklund (2009), "Moral Concerns Are Greater for Temporally Distant Events and Are Moderated by Value Strength," *Social Cognition*, 27 (April), 261-82.

Bargh, John A., Peter M. Gollwitzer, Annette Lee-Chai, Kimberly Barndollar, and Roman Trötschel (2001), "The Automated Will: Nonconscious Activation and Pursuit of Behavioral Goals," *Journal of Personality and Social Psychology*, 81 (December), 1014-27.

Eyal, Tal, Nira Liberman, and Yaacov Trope (2008), "Judging Near and Distant Virtue and Vice," *Journal of Experimental Social Psychology*, 44 (July), 1204-09.

Federal Bureau of Investigation (2008), "Putting Intel to Work: Against Elf and Alf Terrorists," ed. Federal Bureau of Investigation.

Freitas, Antonio L., Peter Gollwitzer, and Yaacov Trope (2004), "The Influence of Abstract and Concrete Mindsets on Anticipating and Guiding Others' Self-Regulatory Efforts," *Journal of Experimental Social Psychology*, 40 (November), 739-52.

Fujita, Kentaro, Marlone D. Henderson, Juliana Eng, Yaacov Trope, and Nira Liberman (2006a), "Spatial Distance and Mental Construal of Social Events," *Psychological Science*, 17 (April), 278-82.

Fujita, Kentaro, Yaacov Trope, Nira Liberman, and Maya Levin-Sagi (2006b), "Construal Levels and Self-Control," *Journal of Personality and Social Psychology*, 90 (March), 351-67.

Gino, Francesca, Shahar Ayal, and Dan Ariely (2009), "Contagion and Differentiation in Unethical Behavior: The Effect of One Bad Apple on the Barrel," *Psychological Science*, 20 (March), 393-98.

Gino, Francesca and Lamar Pierce (2009), "Dishonesty in the Name of Equity," *Psychological Science*, 20 (September), 1153-60.

Liberman, Nira and Yaacov Trope (1998), "The Role of Feasibility and Desirability Considerations in Near and Distant Future Decisions: A Test of Temporal Construal Theory," *Journal of Personality and Social Psychology*, 75 (July), 5-18.

Liviatan, Ido, Yaacov Trope, and Nira Liberman (2008), "Interpersonal Similarity as a Social Distance Dimension: Implications for Perception of Others' Actions," *Journal of Experimental Social Psychology*, 44 (September), 1256-69.

Mazar, Nina, On Amir, and Dan Ariely (2008), "The Dishonesty of Honest People: A Theory of Self-Concept Maintenance," *Journal of Marketing Research*, 45 (December), 633-44.

Mead, Nicole L., Roy F. Baumeister, Francesca Gino, Maurice E. Schweitzer, and Dan Ariely (2009), "Too Tired to Tell the Truth: Self-Control Resource Depletion and Dishonesty," *Journal of Experimental Social Psychology*, 45 (May), 594-97.

Sanna, Lawrence J., Edward C. Chang, Craig D. Parks, and Lindsay A. Kennedy (2009), "Construing Collective Concerns: Increasing Cooperation by Broadening Construals in Social Dilemmas," *Psychological Science*, 20 (November), 1319-21.

Trope, Yaacov and Nira Liberman (2003), "Temporal Construal," *Psychological Review*, 110 (July), 403-21.

Watson, David, Lee A. Clark, and Auke Tellegen (1988), "Development and Validation of Brief Measures of Positive and Negative Affect: The PANAS Scales," *Journal of Personality and Social Psychology*, 54 (June), 1063-70.

Indulging and Proud of it:
Emotional Responses to Reason-Based Indulgent Consumption

Francine Espinoza, European School of Management and Technology, Germany
Heather M. Johnson, University of Maryland, USA
Yuliya Komarova, Fordham University, USA

EXTENDED ABSTRACT

While consumers may feel mixed emotions following indulgent consumption (e.g., feeling the pleasure of indulgence and frustration for having succumbed to temptation; Ramanathan and Williams 2007), previous research has primarily examined the role of negative emotions emerging from indulgent behavior (e.g., guilt and regret; Kivetz and Simonson 2002). Pride is known to be a powerful specific emotion that affects consumer behavior (Griskevicius, Shiota, and Nowlis 2010; Louro, Pieters, and Zeelenberg 2005; Williams and DeSteno 2008) and yet to date, pride has only been examined as an outcome of avoiding indulgence (Mukhopadhyay and Johar 2007). Given that consumption of luxury products is often marketed as a source of positive emotions (Twitchell 2003), it is important to understand conditions under which consumers may also feel pride after indulging and what downstream consequences such positive emotions can have on evaluations of the luxury product itself.

Although recent research suggests that, contrary to consumers' intuition, indulging with or without a reason does not affect the level of enjoyment (Xu and Schwarz 2009), most researchers agree that enjoyment (basic emotion) and pride (self-conscious emotion) are not the same. Pride is a self-conscious emotion associated with self-achievement; pride emerges after deliberative processing (Roseman et al. 1996, Giner-Sorolla 2001) and from appraisals of one's behavior vis-à-vis a social standard (Lewis 2004; Mascolo and Fischer 1995). Consumers compare the perceptions they hold about themselves (e.g., I am a controlled and frugal individual; I am spontaneous and impulsive) with the situation (e.g., indulging with or without a reason), and pride elicits when these two aspects are congruent (Tracy and Robins 2004). Because having a reason to indulge (I am indulging because I am rewarding myself) is more likely to be congruent with high self-control personality aspects (e.g., I am a controlled and frugal individual, I think through all the alternatives before acting), we predict that high (vs. low) self-control consumers will experience pride when they have a reason to indulge.

In our first study, 135 females were asked to imagine that they bought an expensive dress. They were either given a reason to indulge (reason condition) or not (no reason condition). In the justified condition, participants read that by buying another item they could get a discount on the total purchase, whereas no such information was provided in the unjustified condition. Participants reported the extent to which they felt proud and how satisfied they were with the purchase, each with two items (all r > .71, p < .05) using 7-point scales. We measured self-control using a short self-control scale (Tangney, Baumeister, and Boone 2004). As predicted, regression results revealed a significant interaction between reason and self-control on pride (β = .31, SE = .11, t = 2.87, p < .01) and on satisfaction (β = .21, SE = .10, t = 2.22, p < .03). A spotlight analysis at 1 standard deviation above the mean suggests that high self-control consumers feel more proud (β = .45, SE = .15, t = 2.92, p < .01) and are more satisfied (β = .30, SE = .14, t = 2.18, p < .03) when they have a reason to indulge versus when they do not. A spotlight analysis at 1 standard deviation below the mean suggests that low self-control consumers do not seem to change their emotional response as a function of having a reason to indulge (all p > .1). Mediation analysis further show that when pride was inserted as a criterion in the hierarchical regression predicting satisfaction, pride was significant (β = .23, SE = .08, t = 2.94, p < .01) but the interaction became non-significant (β = .01, SE = .08, t = .17, p > .86, Sobel z = 2.05, p < .05).

Study 2 replicated these results (N = 70, 41.4% male) with a different product (jeans), a different measure of self-control (consumer spending self-control, Haws and Bearden 2010), and while asking participants to recall a reason, which increases the validity of the study given that episodic recall is likely to elicit the same emotions experienced in the actual situation (Xu and Schwarz 2009).

Study 3 (N = 111) used a 3 (no reason vs. consolation vs. reward) between-subjects design. We adapted the manipulations developed by Xu and Schwarz (2009) to distinguish between two types of reason to indulge. Consumers may indulge to console themselves (e.g., after getting a very bad grade in a course) or to reward themselves (e.g., after getting a very good grade). Given that pride is linked to appraisal of success in situations (Higgins et al. 2001; Lewis 2004), we predict that participants will feel proud after indulging more so when they are rewarding themselves than when they are consoling themselves. A regression analysis revealed that reward (β = 1.36, SE = .40, t = 3.41, p < .01) and the interaction between reward and self-control (β = .96, SE = .41, t = 2.33, p < .03) predicted pride. We also found an effect of reward (β = 1.64, SE = .47, t = 3.53, p < .01) and an interaction (β = .94, SE = .48, t = 1.96, p < .05) on satisfaction. Spotlight analyses were consistent with studies 1 and 2, suggesting that high self-control consumers feel more proud (β = 2.32, SE = .50, t = 4.69, p < .01) and more satisfied (β = 2.21, SE = .57, t = 3.85, p < .01) when they indulge to reward themselves as opposed to when they indulge without a reason. Further, pride significantly mediates the effect of reward and the effect of the interaction on satisfaction (Sobel z = 2.28, p < .05).

We contribute to research on affect and self-regulation by exploring conditions under which positive, self-conscious emotions such as pride may emerge after indulgence and influence post-purchase judgments. Our findings also qualify previous research by showing that having a reason to indulge produces different emotional experience and post-consumption judgments when we consider how reasons interact with consumers' level of self-control.

REFERENCES

Auty, Susan and Richard Elliott (1998), "Fashion Involvement, Self-Monitoring and the Meaning of Brands," *Journal of Product & Brand Management*, 7, 109–123.

Canli, Turhan, Zuo Zhao, John E. Desmond, Eunjoo Kang, James Gross, and John D. E. Gabrieli (2001), "An fMRI Study of Personality Influences on Brain Reactivity to Emotional Stimuli," Behavioral Neuroscience, 115 (2), 33–42.

Giner-Sorolla, Roger (2001), "Guilty Pleasures and Grim Necessities: Immediate and Deliberative Affective Attitudes in Dilemmas of Self-control," *Journal of Personality and Social Psychology*, 80, 208-21.

Griskevicius, Vladas, Michelle N. Shiota, and Stephen M. Nowlis (2010), "The Many Shades of Rose-Colored Glasses: An Evolutionary Approach to the Influence of Different Positive Emotions," *Journal of Consumer Research*, 37(2), 238–50.

Haws, Kelly L. and William O. Bearden (2010), "Consumer Spending Self-Control and Consumption Behaviors," *working paper*, Department of Marketing, Texas A&M University, College Station, TX 77843.

Higgins, E. Tory, Ronald S. Friedman, Robert E. Harlow, Lorraine Chen Idson, Ozlem N. Ayduk, and Amy Taylor (2001), "Achievement Orientations from Subjective Histories of Success: Promotion Pride versus Prevention Pride," *European Journal of Social Psychology*, 31, 3-23.

Khan, Uzma and Ravi Dhar (2006), "Licensing Effect In Consumer Choice," *Journal of Marketing Research*, 43 (May), 259-266.

Kivetz, Ran and Itamar Simonson (2002), "Earning the Right to Indulge: Effort as a Determinant of Customer Preferences Toward Frequency Program Rewards," *Journal of Marketing Research*, 39 (2), 155-70.

Lewis, Michael (2004), "Self-Conscious Emotions: Embarrassment, Pride, Shame, and Guilt," In: *Handbook of Emotions*, Michael Lewis and Jeannette M. Haviland-Jones (eds), New York, NY: Guilford Press, 2nd edition.

Louro, Maria J., Rik Pieters, and Marcel Zeelenberg (2005), "Negative Returns on Positive Emotions: The Influence of Pride and Self-Regulatory Goals on Repurchase Decisions," *Journal of Consumer Research*, 31 (March), 833-40.

Mascolo, Michael F. and Kurt W. Fischer (1995), "Developmental Transformations in Appraisals for Pride, Guilt and Shame," In Fischer, K. W. & Tangney, J. P. (Eds.), *Self-Conscious Emotions: Shame, Guilt, Embarrassment and Pride* (pp. 64-113). New York: Guilford.

Mukhopadhyay, Anirban and Gita V. Johar (2007), "Tempted or Not? The Effect of Recent Purchase History on Responses to Affective Advertising," *Journal of Consumer Research*, 33 (March), 445-53.

Muller, Dominique, Charles M. Judd, and Vincent Y. Yzerbyt (2005), "When Moderation Is Mediated and Mediation Is Moderated," *Journal of Personality and Social Psychology*, 89 (6), 852-63.

Nenkov, Gergana, Jeffrey Inman, and John Hulland (2008), "Expectations about the Future: The Conceptualization and Measurement of Elaboration on Potential Outcomes," Journal of Consumer Research, 35 (June), 126-41.

Ramanathan, Suresh and Patti Williams (2007), "Immediate and Delayed Emotional Consequences of Indulgence: The Moderating Influence of Personality Type on Mixed Emotions," *Journal of Consumer Research.* 34 (2), 212–23.

Roseman, Ira J., Ann Aliki Antoniou, and Paul E. Jose (1996), "Appraisal Determinants of Emotions: Constructing a More Accurate and Comprehensive Theory," *Cognition and Emotion*, 10 (3), 241-77.

Schwarz, Norbert and Gerald L. Clore (1983), "Mood, Misattribution, and Judgments of Well-Being: Informative and Directive Functions of Affective States," *Journal of Personality and Social Psychology*, 45 (September), 513–23.

Tangney, June P., Roy F. Baumeister, and Angie Luzio Boone (2004), "High Self-Control Predicts Good Adjustment, Less Pathology, Better Grades, and Interpersonal Success," Journal of Personality, 72, 271-324.

Tracy, Jessica L. and Richard W. Robins (2004), "Putting the Self into Self-Conscious Emotions: A Theoretical Model," *Psychological Inquiry*, 15, 103-25.

Twitchell, James B. (2003). *Living It Up: America's Love Affair with Luxury.* Simon & Schuster Adult Publishing Group.

Williams, Lisa A. and David DeSteno (2008), "Pride and Perseverance: The Motivational Role of Pride," *Journal of Personality and Social Psychology*, 94, 1007-101.

Xu, Jing and Norbert Schwartz (2009), "Do We Really Need a Reason to Indulge?," *Journal of Marketing Research*, 46 (1), 25-36.

Can Imitation by Private-Label Brands Benefit Consumers and National Brands?
A Processing Fluency Perspective

Katie Kelting, University of Arkansas, USA
Adam Duhachek, Indiana University, USA

EXTENDED ABSTRACT

Extremely large assortments are prevalent in today's retail environment, leading to greater choice difficulty among consumers (for a review see Broniarczyk, 2008). While one may predict that the recent surge of private-label brands into the marketplace has seemingly contributed to such an effect, we posit and show the opposite. Specifically, the current research bridges together the assortment, private-label branding, and processing fluency literature to hypothesize how the mere presence of a particular type of private-label brand, specifically *copy-cat private-label brands* (hereafter CCPLBs) or store brands that blatantly imitate the packaging of popular national brands and display the text "compare to [national brand]" directly on their packaging, in a product assortment leads consumers not only to experience greater ease when making a choice from the assortment but also to evaluate their chosen national brand more favorably.

To theoretically support this proposed relationship between CCPLBs in an assortment and choice ease, we examine a specific type of processing fluency called *perceptual processing fluency*, which is defined as the degree of ease with which a target object can be identified on a subsequent encounter and therefore involves the low-level, data driven operations of processing the physical features of the target object (Schwarz, 2004). Being a form of processing fluency, perceptual processing fluency has been shown to affect evaluations. For example, Labroo, Dhar and Lee (2008) showed that when consumers are first primed with a visual identifier for a product (e.g., a dog), they subsequently process a product depicting the visual identifier on its packaging (e.g., a bottle of pet shampoo with a dog on its label) with greater ease and evaluate it more favorably relative to a product not depicting the visual identifier on its packaging (e.g., the same bottle of pet shampoo but without a dog on its label). Therefore, based on these findings and under the assumption that processing a CCPLB and its mimicked national brand is similar to processing the same product twice, we posit that the presence of CCPLBs in an assortment can enhance the perceptual processing fluency of consumers. Specifically, when CCPLBs are present in an assortment, we posit that the high degree of similarity shared between CCPLBs and the national brands that they mimic will not only attract attention as shown by prior research (Sayman, Hoch & Raju., 2002) but also enhance consumers' ability to identify the mimicked national brands in the assortment with greater ease and thus lead consumers to experience greater ease during choice as suggested by perceptual processing fluency theory.

In Study 1, we find support for this hypothesis with a laboratory experiment. In addition to obtaining support for our perceptual processing fluency theoretical perspective, we also examine and statistically eliminate an alternative explanation for the found relationship between CCPLBs in an assortment and choice ease, specifically that the presence of CCPLBs in the assortment may have caused consumers to erroneously see the CCPLBs as additional facings of the national brands in the assortment (e.g., Broniarczyk, Hoyer & McAlister, 1998) or to mentally categorize the various products in the assortment into two groups, such as national versus private-label brands (e.g., Mogliner, Rudnick & Iyengar, 2008). However, to further examine differences between our theoretical perspective and the perspective of this alternative explanation, we examine the moderating role of consumer knowledge and posit how CCPLBs in an assort-

ment may interact with knowledge of a product category to affect the processing fluency of consumers. Specifically, we posit two different effects depending on the theoretical perspective.

First, adopting the perspective alternative explanation which involves CCPLBs causing a perceptual reduction of assortment size/variety, it seems likely that it will be consumers with low (versus high) product category knowledge who will experience greater processing fluency when CCPLBs are present in an assortment due to prior research showing that consumers with low (versus high) knowledge are more prone to visual priming (e.g., Mandel & Johnson, 2002) and to using peripheral cues (e.g., Xu & Wyer, 2010). Therefore, under the assumption that these effects are similar to CCPLBs perceptually reducing the size and/or variety of an assortment, the alternative explanation predicts that it will be consumers with low product category knowledge who will experience greater feelings of ease when they choose a national brand product from an assortment that contains (versus does not contain) CCPLBs.

However, adopting a processing fluency theoretical perspective, we make a different prediction. Specifically, we believe that it will be consumers with high (versus low) product category knowledge who will experience greater processing fluency when CCPLBs are present in an assortment. Support for this notion is provided by considering the definition of consumer knowledge, which suggests that consumers with high (versus low) product category knowledge are more "fluent processors" of national brands in an assortment due to their greater familiarity and expertise (Alba & Hutchinson, 1987). Therefore, when CCPLBs are present (versus absent) in an assortment, we further believe that such brands will activate prior knowledge of the mimicked national brands in the assortment among high knowledge consumers and will help such consumers identify the mimicked national brands in the assortment with greater ease. In addition, due to our adoption of a processing fluency theoretical perspective, we further predict these effects will transfer to their evaluation of a chosen mimicked national brand from the assortment all via a processing fluency mechanism.

In Study 2, we examine and find support for these latter hypotheses via a 2 (assortment type: national brands only versus national brands plus CCPLBs) by 2 (consumer knowledge: low versus high) between-subject laboratory experiment. Specifically, we show that the presence (versus absence) of CCPLBs in an assortment leads high - not low - knowledge consumers to experience greater ease during choice and thus to evaluate their chosen national brand more favorably. Also, via a *LISREL* mediation model, we show that feelings of ease fully mediate the relationship between assortment type and evaluation of the chosen national brand for high knowledge consumers. Thus, the current research theoretically contributes to the processing fluency, private-label branding, and assortment literatures.

REFERENCES

Alba, Joseph. W. & John W. Hutchinson. (1987). Dimensions of consumer expertise. *Journal of Consumer Research*, 13(4), 411-454.

Beverage Industry. (2004). Retailers push private label. Retrieved June 9, 2008 from http://www.bevindustry.com/Archives_Davinci?article=1259

Broniarczyk, Susan M. (2008). *Product Assortment*. In Curtis P. Haugtvedt, Paul M. Herr and Frank R. Kardes (Eds.) Handbook of Consumer Psychology. (pg. 755-799). NY: Psychology Press.

Broniarczyk, Susan M., Wayne D. Howyer and Leigh McAlister. (1998). Consumers' perceptions of the assortment offered in a grocery category: The impact of item reduction. *Journal of Marketing Research*, 35(May), 156-176.

Iacobucci, Dawn (2008), Mediation Analysis, Thousand Oaks, CA: Sage.

Kumar, Nirmalaya and Jan-Benedict E. M. Steenkamp (2007). *Private Label Strategy*. Boston: Harvard Business School Press.

Labroo, Aparna and Angela Lee (2006). Between two brands: A goal fluency account fo brand evaluation. *Journal of Marketing Research*, 43, 374-385.

Labroo, Aparna, Ravi Dhar and Angela Lee (2008). Of frog wines and frowning watches: Semantic priming, perceptual fluency brand evaluation. *Journal of Consumer Research*, 34, 819-831.

Lee, Angela Y. and Aparna Labroo (2004). The effect of conceptual and perceptual fluency on brand evaluation. *Journal of Marketing Research*, 41, 151-165.

Levy, Michael and Barton, A.Weitz (1995). *Retailing Management*, 2nd ed. Chicago: Richard D. Irwin.

Mandel, Naomi and Eric J. Johnson (2002). When web pages influence choice: Effects of visual primes on experts and novices. *Journal of Consumer Research*, 29(2), 235-245.

Mogilner, Cassie, Tamar Rudnick and Sheena S. Iyengar. (2008). The mere categorization effect: How the presence of categories increases choosers' perceptions of assortment variety and outcome satisfaction. *Journal of Consumer Research*, 35(August), 202-215.

Novemsky, Nathan, Ravi Dhar, Norbert Schwarz and Itamar Simonson (2007). Preference fluency in choice. *Journal of Marketing Research*. 44, 347-356.

Pocheptsova, Anastasiya, Aparna A. Labroo, and Ravi Dhar (2010). Making products feel special: Metacognitive difficulty enhances evaluation. *Journal of Marketing Research*, 47(6), 1059-1069.

Sayman, Serdar, Stephen J. Hoch and Jagmohan S. Raju. (2002). Positioning of store brands. *Marketing Science*, 21(4) 378-397.

Schwarz, Nobert. (2004). Metacognitive Experiences in Consumer Judgment and Decision Making. *Journal of Consumer Psychology*, 14(4), 332-348.

Spence, Mark T. and Merrie Brooks (1997). The moderating effect of problem characteristics on experts' and novices' judgments. *Journal of Marketing Research*, 34 (May), 233-247.

Thomas, Manoj and Vicki G. Morowitz (2009). The ease-of-computation effect: The interplay of metacognitive experiences and naïve theories in judgments of price differences. *Journal of Marketing Research*, 46, 81-91.

Tsai, Claire I. and Ann L. McGill (2010). No pain, no gain? How fluency and construal level affect consumer confidence. (forthcoming). *Journal of Consumer Research*.

Warlop, Luk and Joesph W. Alba. (2004). Sincere flattery: Trade-dress imitation and consumer choice. *Journal of Consumer Psychology*, 14(1&2), 21-27.

Xu, A. J., & Wyer, R. S. (2010). Puffery in advertisements: The effects of media context, communication norms and consumer knowledge. *Journal of Consumer Research*, 37, 329-343.

Why Exercise Makes Us Fat:
Compensation between Physical Activity and Food Consumption

Carolina O.C. Werle, Grenoble Ecole de Management, CERAG, France
Brian Wansink, Cornell University, USA
Collin Payne, New Mexico State University, USA

EXTENDED ABSTRACT

When people begin exercise programs they often report gaining weight instead of losing it (Time Magazine, 2009). One of the reasons why individuals may overeat after exercising might be related to calorie underestimation. Another reason may be related to rewarding the self through compensation for the hard time spent while exercising. This paper examines whether compensation through food consumption occurs and investigates a potential solution for these effects: being distracted while exercising.

The purpose of this article is to investigate specifically the relationship between exercising and food consumption – an important issue in the actual context of obesity prevention. Previous research suggests that the presence of a distraction alters the perception of the first action (Fillingim, Roth, & Haley, 1989; Karageorghis & Terry, 1997) and can impact subsequent evaluations, and decisions (Lerouge, 2009; Nowlis & Shiv, 2005; Shiv & Nowlis, 2004). Therefore, the presence or absence of distraction could be one of the keys to better understand the relationship between physical activity and food consumption.

We suggest that the presence of distraction in an initial exertion activity helps consumers to subsequently control themselves during food consumption leading to smaller food intake. Previous research shows that being distracted can be positive, increasing motivation and leading to better choices (Dijksterhuis, Bos, Nordgren, & Van Baaren, 2006; Sanders & Baron, 1975). Additionally, in the context of sequential behaviors (exercise – food intake), previous research suggests that when distracted individuals tend to feel less physical symptoms (like fatigue) associated with physical activity and better mood compared to not being distracted. Therefore, we posit that absence of distraction will result in individuals feeling more exertion (Kivetz & Zheng, 2006), thereby feeling more "licensed" (in search for a reward) and may be more prone to compensate (increasing subsequent food intake).

We further examine how people compensate. It is not clear if people will either compensate exercising in an indiscriminate manner (all types of foods) or in more selective manner over-consuming specific types of food (for instance, hedonic food). Research on hedonic versus utilitarian consumption indicate that hedonic food, specifically, serves as reward (Khan, Dhar, & Wertenbroch, 2005). We thus propose that compensation will be selective and directed to hedonic food (and not a generalized overconsumption). Furthermore, we propose that these effects will be stronger for consumers that are highly conscious of what they eat.

Through two experiments using realistic settings we investigate: 1) whether the presence of a distraction during the physical activity (action 1) influences the subsequent amount of food consumed (action 2); 2) whether the compensation is indiscriminate or selective, and 3) which individuals are more vulnerable to such compensation effects

Study 1 used a one factor, three-level between-subjects design with three conditions: distraction while engaging in physical activity, no distraction, and control – no physical activity). Ninety-five (95) female participants (mean age = 44.52 years old and SD=10.59) were randomly assigned to one of the three conditions. The study was divided in two parts: activity and lunch. Participants in the *no distraction* condition were told that the activity was exercising—walking through a route in the campus—and that this part of the study would take approximately half an hour, and that after that lunch would be served. In the *distraction* condition, participants followed the same walking route, but they did so while performing a fun activity: listening to music. When the participants arrived from their walk, they served themselves lunch out of a buffet composed of pasta with meat, green beans, bread, and a choice of two desserts, apple sauce and chocolate pudding. Portions served were unobtrusively weighed while participants served themselves drinks. When participants finished their lunches, they answered a questionnaire about their lunch experience and were thanked and dismissed.

Results indicate that, in the *no distraction* condition, participants felt more tired (M $_{distraction}$ = 3.48 versus M $_{no\ distraction}$ = 4.79, F(55,1) = 3.85, p=.04) after the physical activity than those in the *distraction* condition. In the same sense, individuals in the *distraction* condition were in a more positive mood after exercising than those in the *no distraction* condition (M $_{distraction}$=7.91 versus M $_{no\ distraction}$ = 7.12, F(55,1) = 7.19, p=.01). Results also indicate that participants in the *no distraction* condition who chose chocolate pudding as a desert served themselves 35% more desert than participants in the *distraction* condition who made the same choice (calories served - chocolate pudding $_{no\ distraction\ condition}$ = 135.30; calories in the chocolate pudding $_{distraction\ condition}$ = 100.10; p=.037). Finally, also as expected, there were no statistical differences across conditions in the total amount of calories served or consumed during the experiment. Together, these results indicate that participants in the *no distraction* condition compensated for exercising but this compensation was selective and exclusively directed to hedonic foods.

In Study 2 we used a different kind of distraction—sightseeing—and we also explored individual differences in compensation effects. We used a one factor, two-level between-subjects design, presence versus absence of distraction during physical activity as the manipulated factor. Fifty-six (56) participants were assigned to one of the two conditions. The instructions and the walking route was the same as in study1, except that in the distraction condition, participants were told that the activity was a campus visit (sightseeing). When the participants arrived from their walk, as a thank-you for their participation, we offered them a sweet snack (M&M's) which was to be poured into zip-loc bags. Results show a significant main effect of the manipulated factor on the amount of M&M's served, such that participants in the *no distraction* condition took more M&Ms (M $_{no\ distraction}$ = 372.3 calorie, SD = 391.9) than those who were in the *distraction* condition sightseeing (M $_{distraction}$ = 166.2 calorie, SD = 222.9; F(1,45) = 5.06, p = .029). These effects were stronger for females and for individuals that are highly conscious of what they eat.

While diet and exercise recommendations seem relatively straightforward, many find it extremely difficult to comply. Our results demonstrate that being distracted during the physical activity can have positive consequences in terms of subsequent food decisions. It avoids compensation that is mainly directed towards hedonic foods.

REFERENCES

Altshuler, J. (1948). A psychiatrist's experiences with music as a therapeutic agent. In M. Schullian & M. Schoen (Eds.), *Music and Medicine* New York: Henry Schulman, Inc.

Anderson, C. B., & Bulik, C. M. (2004). Gender differences in compensatory behaviors, weight and shape salience, and drive for thinness. *Eating Behaviors, 5*, 1-11.

Andrade, E. B. (2005). Behavioral Consequences of Affect: Combining Evaluative and Regulatory Mechanisms. *Journal of Consumer Research, 32*, 355-362.

Baumeister, R. F., Bratslavsky, E., Muraven, M., & Tice, D. M. (1998). Ego depletion: Is the active self a limited resource? *Journal of Personality and Social Psychology, 74*, 1252-1265.

Baumeister, R. F., Sparks, E. A., Stillman, T. F., & Vohs, K. D. (2008). Free will in consumer behavior: Self-control, ego depletion, and choice. *Journal of Consumer Psychology (Elsevier Science), 18*, 4-13.

Berger, B. G., & Motl, R. W. (2000). Exercise and mood: a selective review and synthesis of research employing the Profile of Mood States. *Journal of Applied Sports Psychology, 12*, 69-92.

Bettman, James R., Luce, Mary F., & Payne, John W. (1998). Constructive Consumer Choice Processes. *Journal of consumer research, 25*, 187-217.

Boutcher, S. H., & Trenske, M. (1990). The effects of sensory deprivation and music on perceived exertion and affect during exercise. *Journal of Sport & Exercise Psychology, 12*, 167-176.

Dhar, R., & Simonson, I. (1999). Making Complementary Choices in Consumption Episodes: Highlighting Versus Balancing. *Journal of Marketing Research, 36*, 29-44.

Dijksterhuis, A. (2004). Think Different: The Merits of Unconscious Thought in Preference Development and Decision Making. *Journal of Personality and Social Psychology, 87*, 586-598.

Dijksterhuis, A., Bos, M. W., Nordgren, L. F., & Van Baaren, R. B. (2006). On Making the Right Choice: The Deliberation-Without-Attention Effect. *Science, 311*, 1005-1007.

Edworthy, J., & Waring, H. (2006). The effects of music tempo and loudness level on treadmill exercise. *Ergonomics, 49*, 1597-1610.

Fedoroff, I. D. C., Polivy, J., & Herman, C. P. (1997). The Effect of Pre-exposure to Food Cues on the Eating Behavior of Restrained and Unrestrained Eaters. *Appetite, 28*, 33-47.

Fillingim, R. B., Roth, D. L., & Haley, W. E. (1989). The effects of distraction on the perception of exercise-induced symptoms. *Journal of Psychosomatic Research, 33*, 241-248.

Fishbach, A., & Dhar, R. (2005). Goals as Excuses or Guides: The Liberating Effect of Perceived Goal Progress on Choice. *Journal of Consumer Research, 32*, 370-377.

Fishbach, A., Friedman, R. S., & Kruglanski, A. W. (2003). Leading us not into temptation: Momentary allurements elicit overriding goal activation. *Journal of Personality and Social Psychology, 84*, 296-309.

Garg, N., Wansink, B., & Inman, J. J. (2007). The Influence of Incidental Affect on Consumers' Food Intake. *Journal of Marketing, 71*, 194-206.

Hayakawa, Y., Takada, K., Miki, H., & Tanaka, K. (2000). Effects of music on mood during bench stepping exercise. *Perceptual and Motor Skills, 90*, 307-314.

Herman, C. P., & Polivy, J. (1980). Restrained eating. In A. Stunkard (Ed.), *Obesity* (pp. 208-225). Philadelphia: Saunders.

Huber, J., Goldsmith, K., & Mogilner, C. (2008). Reinforcement versus balance response in sequential choice. *Marketing Letters, 19*, 229-239.

Imbeault, P., Saint-Pierre, S., Almeras, N., & Tremblay, A. (1997). Acute effects of exercise energy intake and feeding behaviour. *British Journal of Nutrition, 77*, 511-521.

Karageorghis, C. I., & Terry, P. C. (1997). The psychophysical effects of music in sport and exercise: A review. *Journal of Sport Behavior, 20*, 54.

Khan, U., & Dhar, R. (2006). Licensing Effect in Consumer Choice. *Journal of Marketing Research, 43*, 259-266.

Khan, U., & Dhar, R. (2007). Where there is a way, is there a will? The effect of future choices on self-control. *Journal of Experimental Psychology: General, 136*, 277-288.

Khan, U., Dhar, R., & Wertenbroch, K. (2005). A behavioral decision theory perspective on hedonic and utilitarian choice. In S. Ratneshwar & D. G. Mick (Eds.), *Inside Consumption: Frontiers of Research on Consumer Motives, Goals and Desires* (pp. 144-165). London: Routledge.

King, N. A. (1999). What processes are involved in the appetite response to moderate increases in exercise-induced energy expenditure? *Proceedings of the Nutrition Society, 58*, 107-113.

King, N. A., Snell, L., Smith, R. D., & Blundell, J. E. (1996). Effects of short-term exercise on appetite responses in unrestrained females. *European Journal of Clinical Nutrition, 50*, 663-667.

Kivetz, R., & Zheng, Y. (2006). Determinants of justification and self-control. *Journal of Experimental Psychology: General, 135*, 572-587.

Kruger, J., Blanck, H. M., & Gillespie, C. (2006). Dietary and physical activity behaviors among adults successful at weight loss maintenance. *International Journal of Behavioral Nutrition and Physical Activity, 3*, 1-10.

Laran, J., & Janiszewski, C. (2009). Behavioral Consistency and Inconsistency in the Resolution of Goal Conflict. *Journal of consumer research, 35*, 967-984.

Lerouge, D. (2009). Evaluating the Benefits of Distraction on Product Evaluations: The Mind-Set Effect. *Journal of Consumer Research, 36*, 367-379.

Lind, E., Welch, A. S., & Ekkekakis, P. (2009). Do 'Mind over Muscle' Strategies Work? *Sports Medicine, 39*, 743-764.

Lluch, A., King, N. A., & Blundell, J. E. (1998). Exercise in dietary restrained women: No effect on energy intake but change in hedonic ratings. *European Journal of Clinical Nutrition, 52*, 300.

Macht, M., & Dettmer, D. (2006). Everyday mood and emotions after eating a chocolate bar or an apple. *Appetite, 46*, 332-336.

Martins, C., Morgan, L. M., Bloom, S. R., & Robertson, M. D. (2007). Effects of exercise on gut peptides, energy intake and appetite. *Journal of Endocrinology, 193*, 251-258.

Milkman, K. L., Rogers, T., & Bazerman, M. H. (2008). Harnessing our inner angels and demons: What we have learned about want/should conflicts and how that knowledge can help us reduce short-sighted decision making. *Perspectives on Psychological Science, 3*, 324-338.

Novemsky, N., & Dhar, R. (2005). Goal Fulfillment and Goal Targets in Sequential Choice. *Journal of Consumer Research, 32*, 396-404.

Novemsky, N., Dhar, R., Schwarz, N., & Simonson, I. (2007). Preference Fluency in Choice. *Journal of Marketing Research, 44*, 347-356.

Nowlis, S. M., & Shiv, B. (2005). The Influence of Consumer Distractions on the Effectiveness of Food-Sampling Programs. *Journal of Marketing Research (JMR), 42*, 157-168.

Pennebaker, J. W., & Lightner, J. M. (1980). Competition of internal and external information in an exercise setting. *Journal of Personality and Social Psychology, 39*, 165-174.

Reger, W. E., Allison, T. A., & Kurucz, R. L. (1986). Exercise, post-exercise metabolic rate and appetite. *Sport Health and Nutrition, 2*, 117-123.

Rejeski, W. J. (1985). Perceived exertion: An active or passive process? *Journal of Sport Psychology, 7*, 371-378.

Ruderman, A. J. (1986). Dietary Restraint: A Theoretical and Empirical Review. *Psychological Bulletin, 99*, 247-262.

Sanders, G. S. (1981). Driven by distraction: An integrative review of social facilitation theory and research. *Journal of Experimental Social Psychology, 17*, 227-251.

Sanders, G. S., & Baron, R. S. (1975). The motivating effects of distraction on task performance. *Journal of Personality and Social Psychology, 32*, 956-963.

Shiv, B., & Fedorikhin, A. (1999). Heart and Mind in Conflict: The Interplay of Affect and Cognition in Consumer Decision Making. *Journal of Consumer Research, 26*, 278-292.

Shiv, B., & Nowlis, S. M. (2004). The Effect of Distractions While Tasting a Food Sample: The Interplay of Informational and Affective Components in Subsequent Choice. *Journal of Consumer Research, 31*, 599-608.

Stubbs, R. J., Sepp, A., Hughes, D. A., Johnstone, A. M., King, N., Horgan, G., et al. (2002). The effect of graded levels of exercise on energy intake and balance in free-living women. *International Journal of Obesity & Related Metabolic Disorders, 26*, 866.

Szmedra, L., & Bacharach, D. (1998). Effect of music on perceived exertion, plasma lactate, norepinephrine and cardiovascular hemodynamics during treadmill running. *International Journal of Sports Medicine, 19*, 32-37.

Terry, P. C., & Karageorghis, C. I. (2006). *Psychophysical effects of music in sport and exercise: An update on theory, research and application.* Paper presented at the Psychology bridging the Tasman: Science, culture and practice, Melbourne.

Time Magazine (2009), "Why Exercise Won't Make You Thin", Health & Science (August 9, 2009), available online at: http://www.time.com/time/health/article/0,8599,1914857-2,00.html

Wansink, B. (2004). Environmental factors that increase the food intake and consumption volume of unknowing consumers. *Annual Review of Nutrition, 24*, 455-479.

All Metaphors in Advertising are not Created Equal: Influences of Product Type and Need for Cognition

Chun-Tuan Chang, National Sun Yat-sen University, Taiwan
Ching-Ting Yen, National Sun Yat-sen University, Taiwan
Ting-Ting Chen, National Taiwan University, Taiwan

EXTENDED ABSTRACT

Metaphors, as one of the rhetorical devices, are the very heart of the modern communication form in advertising. Instead of using literal and direct claim that a product possesses some attribute or benefit, metaphors are attention getting, arousing, affect inducing, and memorable. This article focuses on pictorial metaphors and proposes two types of metaphor: explicit vs. implicit. The difference between explicit and implicit metaphors depends on whether or not the product's likeness is incorporated into the metaphoric picture. An explicit metaphor is clear about the subject, and the viewer can clearly see the product for what it is in the pictorial metaphoric display. In an implicit metaphor, the product is not in the metaphoric illustration and may be depicted in a less prominent place in the ad, such as the bottom corner. The viewer must make an inference as to how the product fits into the theme of the metaphor.

This article contributes to the evolving stream of research by comparing the potential impacts of two metaphors and identifies boundary conditions that influence the effectiveness of metaphor advertising. To be specific, this research demonstrates that the selection of explicit and implicit metaphor could be influenced by two variables: product type and need for cognition (NFC). Although these two variables are identified as influential in metaphor advertising in previous research, they were examined separately and were used to compare with a non-metaphor condition. A 3 (ad type: implicit metaphor vs. explicit metaphor vs. non-metaphor) X 2 (product type: hedonic vs. utilitarian) X 2 (NFC: low vs. high) between-subjects experiment was thus designed wherein individual differences in NFC were measured. Participants were randomly assigned to one of the conditions above. After successful manipulation checks, a series of analysis of variance were conducted to examine proposed hypotheses. The results indicate that focusing on the comparison between two types of metaphor without considering other factors may be overly simplistic. Four observations are noteworthy.

First, that the effects of metaphor type are contingent on individual differences in NFC. This construct delineates the boundary conditions for the metaphor on persuasion. Some metaphor types work better on participants with high NFC. However, these differences did not emerge for participants low in NFC. This is consistent with previous advertising research (e.g., Hautvedt, Petty, and Cacioppo, 1992) which indicated that low-NFC individuals' attitudes in response to a persuasive message are less influenced by the message-relevant cues.

Second, in groups of consumers with high NFC, a strong interaction between product type and metaphor type is observed. This study shows systematic effects on consumer responses by comparing two different product types: hedonic vs. utilitarian. The data from the current research lend support for resource-matching theory. Consumers with high NFC show a more positive attitude and higher purchase intentions in response to an explicit metaphor than an implicit metaphor when a product's utilitarian value is highlighted. Ads using explicit metaphors help high NFC recipients to better structure and more easily organize the message information when the advertised product is utilitarian. The explicit execution of the product image fits into the rational appeal while the pleasure of the metaphoric processing provides sufficient interest to arouse emotion.

Third, an advantage of implicit metaphor on hedonic product promotion is found. Ads using implicit metaphors provide more opportunities for imagination, which fit into the nature of hedonic products. Therefore, ads using implicit metaphors are more likely to arouse favorable attitudes toward the advertised brand and higher purchase intention for hedonic products.

Fourth, metaphor type does not matter to low NFC individuals, and only the superior effects of hedonic over utilitarian product are found. This finding is consistent with past research suggesting that low NFC individuals may be more prone to the influences of symbolic cues and avoid elaborative processing (Martin, Sherrard, and Wentzel, 2005).

The obvious implication of the findings for academic researchers is that moderating variables must be considered in the study of the effectiveness of metaphor in advertising. The experiment reported here offers insight for when different types of metaphor work. The findings substantiate the notion that the perceptual difference between explicit and implicit metaphors is significant for certain individuals but not for others, and product type moderates the effects of metaphor type.

The findings also have important implications for the practice of advertising and marketing communication. Consideration of these two types of metaphor will prove valuable to advertisers that use—or are considering using—metaphors. In terms of message strategy, an ad message should, of course, convey product value. The current investigation provides guidance for practitioners to place the metaphor in the right place in the ad once the product type is determined. In addition to product type, another important contribution of this research is the introduction of NFC into the investigation of metaphor advertising and its potential usefulness as a moderator of metaphor advertising, although cognition has been identified as influential in recent literature (Lagerwerf and Meijers, 2008). Clearly, advertisers who would like to employ metaphors in their ads cannot administer NFC scales to members of their target audience. However, such difficulty does not diminish the importance of understanding of how NFC affects metaphor processing. One can argue that the individual differences in NFC is tantamount to unplanned market segmentation, and that advertisers may improve advertising results through judicious ad placement because audiences with different degrees of NFC may have different media habits. For example, certain technical publications and information/news television programs may attract audience groups with NFC more than *cognitively* undemanding *programs (e.g., gossip magazines or* comedy shows). *Such de facto* market segmentation may offer potential payoffs to advertisers who strive to discover and take advantage of the diversity of audience characteristics.

This research suggests that not all metaphors are created equal, at least in terms of metaphoric type. When seeking the advantages that two types of metaphors (explicit and implicit) provide in obtaining and sustaining attention, advertisers should consider product type and individual differences in NFC. Such knowledge is useful to advertisers who are interested in maximizing the impact of their advertising dollars.

REFERENCES

Haugtvedt, Curt, Richard E. Petty, and John T. Cacioppo (1992), "Need for Cognition and Advertising: Understanding the Role of Personality Variables in Consumer Behavior," *Journal of Consumer Psychology*, 1(3), 239-260.

Lagerwerf, Luuk and Anoe Meijers (2008), "Openness in Metaphorical and Straightforward Advertisements," *Journal of Advertising*, 37(2), 19-30.

Martin, Brett A., Michael J. Sherrard, and Daniel Wentzel (2005), "The Role of Sensation Seeking and Need for Cognition on Web-Site Evaluations: A Resource-Matching Perspective," *Psychology & Marketing*, 22(2), 109-126.

Does Power-Distance Influence Consumers' Preference for Luxury Status Brands?

Youngseon Kim, University of Texas at San Antonio, USA
Yinlong Zhang, University of Texas at San Antonio, USA

EXTENDED ABSTRACT

Consumers' preference for luxury status brands (brands such as Rolex or Louis Vuitton associated with social prestige and status) is a pervasive and growing global phenomenon. Despite that, few theoretical studies have investigated this topic in cross-cultural contexts (Wiedmann, Hennigs, and Siebels 2009). The current research aims to examine the role of cultural orientation, more specifically, power-distance in consumers' preference for luxury status brands.

Two major views of why consumers prefer luxury status brands have been suggested in the literature. One view proposes that consumers whose social status issues are salient tend to use luxury status brands to ascertain their social status (Mandel, Petrova, and Cialdini 2006; Miller, McIntyre, and Mantrala 1993). Luxury status brands, due to their exclusively high social status, can be used for this purpose (e.g., Amaldoss and Jain 2005). This status salience view suggests that any factors to make consumers aware of their social status will lead them to more likely prefer luxury status brands to standard brands. A second view proposes that consumers use luxury status brands to compensate for their lack of social status. For example, Rucker and Galinsky (2008) found that people with low power status tend to engage in compensatory consumption by preferring products associated with social status to products without such an association. The compensatory consumption hypothesis proposes that any factors to make consumers feel that their social status is relatively low can make consumers prefer luxury status brands to standard brands.

Power distance has been defined as the degree of power disparity that people in a culture regard as normal (Hofstede 1980; Oyserman 2006; Triandis 1995). High power-distance cultures facilitate a norm that everyone should have a defined place within the social order. In contrast, in low power-distance cultures, the norm is to maintain and respect the equality inherent in social interactions. Acceptance of power disparity tends to remind cultural members of their social status constantly to act properly (Triandis 1995). This practice may make the status concept salient to them. Consumers with status-salient mindset may prefer luxury status brands to standard brands, for the former brands can help them to ascertain and enhance their social status. Thus, based on the status salience view, consumers with high power-distance would show a stronger preference for luxury status brands (vs. standard brands) than those with low power-distance. If this individual tendency holds, countries with high-power distance (Hofstede 1980, 2001; Oyserman 2006) should show the similar pattern compared to those with low-power distance. So we hypothesize that:

Hypothesis 1a *Countries with high power-distance tend to prefer luxury status brands to standard brands more than those with low power-distance.*

It has been well documented that typical Asian cultures have higher power-distance than the American culture (Hofstede 1980, 2001; Oyserman 2006), accordingly:

Hypothesis 1b *Asian consumers, compared to American consumers, are more likely to prefer luxury status brands to standard brands due to Asians' power-distance being higher than American's power-distance.*

The compensatory consumption view provides a different prediction on the relationship between power-distance and luxury status brands. Based on the very definition of power-distance (Hofstede 1980, 2001; Oyserman 2006; Triandis 1995), when faced with relatively low social status situations, people from high power-distance culture can accommodate these social disparities easily and do not feel the need to compensate for their relatively low social status. In contrast, consumers from low power-distance cultures, when faced with more social disparities, may feel the need to compensate for their low social status through luxury status brand consumption. Accordingly:

Hypothesis 1c *Countries with low power-distance show a stronger preference for luxury status brands compared to standard brands than countries with high power-distance.*

Study 1a was a correlation study based upon the dataset from a 2007 Nielson study in which we included country scores on power-distance, individualism, annual income growth, Gini-Index. Countries with higher-power distance scores showed stronger intention to buy luxury status brands than those with lower-power distance. This result supported hypothesis 1a, not hypothesis 1c. Study 1b was a survey of consumers in which attitude toward luxury status brands and power-distance were measured. The survey was conducted in the U.S. and an Asian country. Asian consumers showed a more favorable attitude toward luxury status brands than their American counterparts. A mediation test showed that the effect of country difference on preference for luxury status brands was partially mediated by power-distance.

Based on the knowledge applicability principle (Aaker 2000; Higgins 1996), the power-distance effect will be evident only if consumers see the status concept is applicable for their decision on luxury status brands. Therefore, the power-distance effect will be stronger for consumers believing in the efficacy of engaging in luxury status brands (buying status belief). Formally:

Hypothesis 2 *The effect of power-distance on consumers' preference for luxury status brands will be significant for consumers who believe that buying luxury status brands can enhance their social status, but not for those who do not hold such a belief.*

If the effect of power-distance on consumers' preference for luxury status brands is due to the salience of social status, the effect should be moderated by factors affecting consumers' need for social status, self-worth. If consumers' need for self-worth is satisfied, they tend not to enhance their social status through luxury status brands, even if they see the efficacy of buying luxury status brands. Therefore:

Hypothesis 3 *When consumers' self-worth is relatively low, the effect of power-distance on consumers' preference for luxury status brands will be more significant for strong than for weak buying status belief; when consumers' self-worth is relatively high, the effect of power-distance on consumers' preference for luxury status brands will not be influenced by buying status belief.*

Study 2 was a 2 (power-distance prime: high vs. low) 2 (buying status belief: strong vs. weak) between-subjects design. The first factor was manipulated, and the second was measured with the scales from Eastman, Goldsmith, and Flynn (1999). Consistent with hypothesis 2, we found that the effect of power-distance on preference for luxury status brands was significant for strong but not for weak buying status belief.

Study 3 was a 2 (power-distance prime: high vs. low) x 2 (buying status belief: strong vs. weak) x 2 (self-worth: relatively high vs. relatively low) between-subjects design. All factors were manipulated. The difference in preferring luxury status brands between high and low power-distance was contingent on buying status belief. However, this was qualified by self-worth. Specifically, the 2-way interaction between power-distance and buying status belief was significant when self-worth was relatively low, but not significant when self-worth was relatively high. Further, we also tested the mediating role of status salience in the effect of power-distance on preference for luxury status brands. The simple mediation test showed that the effect of power-distance on the preference for luxury status brands was mediated by status salience, not by compensatory need for social status.

Our cross-cultural results show that power-distance has a systematic impact on consumers' preference for luxury status brands and support the status salience thesis but not the compensatory consumption thesis.

REFERENCES

Aaker, Jennifer L. (2000), "Accessibility or Diagnosticity? Disentangling the Influence of Culture on Persuasion Processes and Attitudes," *Journal of Consumer Research*, 26 (4), 340-357.

Amaldoss, Wilfred and Sanjay Jain (2005), "Pricing of Conspicuous Goods: A Competitive Analysis of Social Effects," *Journal of Marketing Research*, 44 (February), 30-42.

Eastman, Jacqueline K., Ronald E. Goldsmith, and Leisa Reinecke Flynn (1999), "Status Consumption in Consumer Behavior: Scale Development and Validation," *Journal of Marketing Theory and Practice*, 7 (3), 41-52.

Higgins, E. Tory (1996). "Knowledge Activation: Accessibility, Applicability, and Salience," in *Social Psychology: Handbook of Basic Principles*, ed. E. Tory Higgins and A. Kruglanski, New York, London: Guilford Publications.

Hofstede, Geert (1980), *Culture's Consequences, International Differences in Work-Related Values (Cross Cultural Research and Methodology,* Newbury Park, CA: Sage.

--- (2001), *Culture's Consequences: Comparing Values, Behaviors, Institutions, and Organizations across Nations*, Thousand Oaks, CA: Sage.

Mandel, Naomi, Petia K. Petrova, and Robert B. Cialdini (2006), "Images of Success and the Preference for Luxury Brands," *Journal of Consumer Psychology*, 16 (1), 57-69.

Miller, Christopher M., Shelby H. McIntyre, and Murali K. Mantrala (1993), "Toward Formalizing Fashion Theory," *Journal of Marketing Research*, 30 (2), 142-57.

Nielsen (2008), "April 2008 Consumers and Designer Brands a global Nielson Report," http://tw.nielsen.com/site/documents/GlobalNielsenLuxuryBrandsMay08.pdf.

Oyserman, Daphna (2006), "High Power, Low Power, and Equality: Culture beyond Individualism and Collectivism," *Journal of Consumer Psychology*, 16 (4), 352-56.

Rucker, Derek and Adam D. Galinsky (2008), "Desire to Acquire: Powerlessness and Compensatory Consumption," *Journal of Consumer Research*, 35 (August), 257-67.

Triandis, Harry C. (1995), *Individualism and Collectivism*, Boulder, CO: Westview Press.

Wiedmann, Klaus-Peter, Nadine Hennigs, and Astrid Siebels (2009), "Value-Based Segmentation of Luxury Consumption Behavior," *Psychology & Marketing*, 26 (7), 625-51.

Medium Susceptibility: The Role of Implicit Theories in Consumer Choice

Meng-Hua Hsieh, University of Washington, USA
Shailendra P. Jain, University of Washington, USA

EXTENDED ABSTRACT

Chase Freedom credit cardholders receive five points for every dollar spent in quarterly bonus categories and one point for every dollar spent in other categories. The points presumably motivate consumers to opt to use their credit cards for everyday shopping. Research has examined how certain reward program elements, including effort, medium/points structure, and outcome, influence overall program performance (Bagchi and Li 2011; Hsee et al. 2003; Kivetz and Simonson 2002; van Osselaer, Alba, and Manchanda 2004). A well-documented finding is that consumers demonstrate a tendency to make extra effort to acquire more points even when additional points could not be used to acquire anything of substantial incremental value. This phenomenon is referred to as 'medium maximization effect' (Hsee et al. 2003). However, consumers have different dispositions so they may differ in their reliance on the medium when making decisions. Past research have shown that context effects are moderated by consumer level differences (Mourali, Böckenholt, and Laroche 2007; Zhu and Meyers-Levy 2009). This notion raises the prospect that consumer level differences may also moderate the medium maximization effect.

In our paper, we examine a boundary condition to the medium maximization effect relating to consumers' implicit theories. Indeed, while some studies examining reward programs' effectiveness have explored the impact of consumers' price sensitivity and temporal orientation on the type of rewards chosen (Kim, Shi, and Srinivasan 2001; Kopalle and Neslin 2003), no research to date has explored the effect of the interaction between reward points and consumer characteristics on decisions.

The wide-ranging influence of people's implicit theories on a host of phenomenon has been studied extensively in psychology. Those who subscribe to a belief in fixedness are called entity theorists while those who believe in change are termed incremental theorists (Dweck, Chiu, and Hong 1995a, b; Dweck and Leggett 1988). The role of implicit theories is understudied in marketing literature, with only a handful of exceptions. (Jain, Mathur, and Maheswaran 2009; Yorkston, Nunes, and Matta 2010). Dweck and her colleagues have published a substantial body of work in implicit theory domains like personality, intelligence, morality, and general world order. Our research introduces a novel domain extending implicit theory research and providing evidence that people's ideas of fixedness and malleability are extendible to the economic marketplace as well.

The theoretical premise for this paper's propositions is based on several recent works which demonstrate that entity theorists tend to be more outcome-focused and thus tend to make evaluations on the basis of the outcome. In contrast, incremental theorists focus more on the process and thus rely more on contextual information to make evaluations (Jain et al. 2009; Molden and Dweck 2006; Poon and Koehler 2006). Therefore, we expect that incremental theorists are likely to be more susceptible to a medium than entity theorists because a) incremental theorists are context driven and process focused, and b) medium is the contextual cue and captures the process that is inserted between effort and outcome.

Two experiments show that individuals who believe that the marketplace is changeable (incremental theorists) exhibit a reliance on the medium while those who believe that the marketplace is stable (entity theorists) do not. In study 1, we manipulated the implicit theory of economic marketplace by employing two fictitious scientific articles that argued either in support of the notion of the economic marketplace being fixed or being malleable. The results demonstrate that when a medium was present, incremental theorists chose a higher-effort option that garnered more points but a marginally less advantageous outcome over a lower-effort option that garnered fewer points but a superior outcome. In contrast, entity theorists' likelihood of choosing a higher-effort option was the same regardless of the presence or absence of the medium.

In study 2, the experimental design was a 2 (implicit theory: entity versus incremental) x 2 (medium: no points versus points) x 2 (implicit theory consistency: violation versus confirmation) full factorial design. Participants responded to an implicit theory of the economic marketplace scale. Next, we manipulated implicit theory consistency by exposing participants to scenarios about the test performance of a math person required to take a "year-long required course in English and expository writing" (Plaks, Grant, and Dweck 2005). Participants were subsequently asked to choose between two tasks, for which they would be rewarded with an airline ticket to a desired vacation destination. The results show that under theory confirmation, incremental theorists were more likely to choose a long task in the medium condition as compared to the no-medium condition, while entity theorists' likelihood of choosing a long task was invariant across the medium and no-medium conditions. However, under theory violation, entity theorists appeared to be susceptible to a medium.

The present research is the first to show a consumer level moderator of the medium maximization effect. Furthermore, we introduce a new type of implicit theory to literature – in the domain of the economic marketplace that is relevant to business and policy research. This has important implications for reward program design, marketing communications, and financial decision making.

REFERENCES

Bagchi, Rajesh and Xingbo Li (2011), "Illusionary Progress in Loyalty Programs: Magnitudes, Reward-Distances, and Step-Size Ambiguity," *Journal of Consumer Research*, 37 (5), 888-901.

Chiu, Chi-yue, Ying-yi Hong, and Carol S. Dweck (1997), "Lay Dispositionism and Implicit Theories of Personality," *Journal of Personality and Social Psychology*, 73 (1), 19-30.

Dweck, Carol S., Chi-yue Chiu, and Ying-yi Hong (1995a), "Implicit Theories and Their Role in Judgments and Reactions: a World from Two Perspectives," *Psychological Inquiry*, 6 (4), 267-85.

--- (1995b), "Implicit Theories: Elaboration and Extension of the Model," *Psychological Inquiry*, 6 (4), 322-33.

Dweck, Carol S. and Ellen L. Leggett (1988), "A Social-Cognitive Approach to Motivation and Personality," *Psychological Review*, 95 (2), 256-73.

Hsee, Christopher K., Fang Yu, Jiao Zhang, and Yan Zhang (2003), "Medium Maximization," *Journal of Consumer Research*, 30 (1), 1-14.

Jain, Shailendra P., Pragya Mathur, and Durairaj Maheswaran (2009), "The Influence of Consumers' Lay Theories on Approach/Avoidance Motivation," *Journal of Marketing Research*, 46 (1), 56-65.

Kim, Byung-Do, Mengze Shi, and Kannan Srinivasan (2001), "Reward Programs and Tacit Collusion," *Marketing Science*, 20 (2), 99-120.

Kivetz, Ran and Itamar Simonson (2002), "Earning the Right to Indulge: Effort as a Determinant of Customer Preferences toward Frequency Program Rewards," *Journal of Marketing Research*, 39 (2), 155-70.

Kopalle, Praveen K. and Scott A. Neslin (2003), "The Economic Viability of Frequent Reward Programs in a Strategic Competitive Environment," *Review of Marketing Science*, 1, 1-39.

Levy, Sheri R, Steven J. Stroessner, and Carol S. Dweck (1998), "Stereotype Formation and Endorsement: The Role of Implicit Theories," *Journal of Personality and Social Psychology*, 74 (6), 1421-36.

Liu, Yuping and Rong Yang (2009), "Competing Loyalty Programs: Impact of Market Saturation, Market Share, and Category Expandability," *Journal of Marketing*, 73 (1), 93-108.

Molden, Daniel C. and Carol S. Dweck (2006), "Finding 'Meaning' in Psychology: A Lay Theories Approach to Self-Regulation, Social Perception, and Social Development," *American Psychologist*, 61 (3), 192-203.

Mourali, Mehdi, Ulf Böckenholt, and Michel Laroche (2007), "Compromise and Attraction Effects under Prevention and Promotion Motivations," *Journal of Consumer Research*, 34 (2), 234-47.

Nunes, Joseph C. and Xavier Drèze (2006), "The Endowed Progress Effect: How Artificial Advancement Increases Effort," *Journal of Consumer Research*, 32 (32), 504-12.

Plaks, Jason E., Heidi Grant, and Carol S. Dweck (2005), "Violations of Implicit Theories and the Sense of Prediction and Control: Implications for Motivated Person Perception," *Journal of Personality and Social Psychology*, 88 (2), 245-62.

Plaks, Jason E., Stroessner J. Stroessner, Carol S. Dweck, and Jeffrey W. Sherman (2001), "Person Theories and Attention Allocation: Preferences for Stereotypic versus Counterstereotypic Information," *Journal of Personality and Social Psychology*, 80 (6), 876-93.

Poon, Connie S.K. and Derek J. Koehler (2006), "Lay Personality Knowledge and Dispositionist Thinking: A Knowledge-activation Framework," *Journal of Experimental Social Psychology*, 42 (2), 177-91.

Rydell, Robert J., Kurt Hugenberg, Devin Ray, and Diane M. Mackie (2007), "Implicit Theories about Groups and Stereotyping: The Role of Group Entitativity," *Personality and Social Psychology Bulletin*, 33 (4), 549-58.

van Osselaer, Stijn M. J., Joseph W. Alba, and Puneet Manchanda (2004), "Irrelevant Information and Mediated Intertemporal Choice," *Journal of Consumer Psychology*, 14 (3), 257-70.

Yorkston, Eric A., Joseph C. Nunes, and Shashi Matta (2010), "The Malleable Brand: The Role of Implicit Theories in Evaluating Brand Extensions," *Journal of Marketing*, 74 (1), 80-93.

Zhu, Rui and Joan Meyers-Levy (2009), "The Influence of Self-View on Context Effects: How Display Fixtures Can Affect Product Evaluations," *Journal of Marketing Research*, 46 (1), 37-45.

Doing Privacy: Exploring the Nature of Consumer Privacy and Privacy Management Strategies

Jo En Yap, RMIT University, Australia
Michael B. Beverland, University of Bath, UK
Liliana L. Bove, University of Melbourne, Australia

EXTENDED ABSTRACT

"Privacy invasion is to the information economy what pollution is to the industrial economy – a social cost borne not by those who benefit from pollution, but by the rest of society" (Deighton 2005, 144).

In the context of marketing, the privacy debate is dominated by discussions about consumers' ability to control the collection, dissemination and use of their personal information (i.e., information privacy); and to a lesser degree, consumers' ability to control the type and volume of marketing solicitations into their daily lives (i.e., interaction privacy) (Goodwin, 1991; Jones, 1991; Smith, Milberg and Burke 1996). We believe these approaches, although valuable, are limited for a number of reasons. First, other relevant aspects of privacy found outside the domain of marketing have generally been overlooked. Second, the concepts of information and interaction privacy were conceived in the era of direct and database marketing; and focus primarily on top-down, one-way exchanges from organizations to current and/or prospective customers. Third, instead of reflecting what consumers perceive privacy to be, current meaning(s) of consumer privacy are primarily framed by practitioners, researchers and the media. As such, findings may not fully account for and differentiate between the myriad of technologically advanced privacy related issues experienced by consumers as they navigate through the social-interactive environment of the 21st century (Harper and Singleton 2001; Nguyen and Li 2010; Solove 2002). We believe that a bottom-up approach that produces insights into the ways in which consumers view privacy, and its various forms, would provide a more comprehensive understanding of the concept as it applies in contemporary consumer society. Therefore, the first objective of this study is to explore the nature of consumer privacy.

Furthermore, consumers have largely been portrayed as ignorant and passive players in the marketplace that submissively accept privacy violations and are unable to protect their privacy (Acquisti and Grossklags 2004; Milne 2003; Milne, Rohm, and Bahl 2004; Nehf 2007; Norberg, Horne, and Horne 2007; Sayre and Horne 2000; Spiekermann, Grossklags, and Berendt 2001). This portrayal is in contradiction with current findings of consumers actively exerting their influence and participating in the marketplace; as co-creators of value (Vargo and Lusch 2004) and engaged participants (van Doorn, et al. 2010; Verheof, Reinartz, and Kraft 2010). Therefore, the second objective of this study is to explore the ways in which consumers actively defend or "do" privacy.

To address our research objectives, we conducted image-elicited depth interviews on a theoretical sample of 23 informants; 13 women and 10 men aged between 19 and 60 years of age. Each informant was given a sketchbook and asked to collect and/or draw images that presented their thoughts, feelings and experiences about privacy. They were then asked to explain the significance of each image. Then, informants were given a folder that consisted of around 100 privacy-related images. Informants were asked to select images which resonated with their thoughts and stimulated their emotions; and comment on their selected images. The interviews ranged from one hour to two and a half hours in length, were audio taped and later transcribed. Interviews were analyzed in line with open, axial and selective coding.

Our findings highlight the socio-culturally embedded nature of consumer privacy; where the meaning informants ascribe to privacy–a state of sovereignty over one's personal domain–is shaped by the tension between the greater degree of personalization in all aspects of life and its paradoxical effect, feelings of impersonalization. It was found that three socio-cultural forces largely drive the personalization of life. These forces have been labelled: participation; greater good appeals; and shifting public-private boundaries.

Participation reflects the recognition that disclosure of personally identifiable information is fast becoming a prerequisite to gain access to the market, engage in social networks and live as a member of society. Greater good appeals to security, fairness and community welfare focus on the personal benefits derived from the greater good. Last, shifting public-private boundaries reflect the social trend of living one's life on display, the casualization of relations between people and the insistence of businesses wanting to form relationships with consumers.

As previously alluded, the personalization of life paradoxically engenders feelings of impersonalization. This polar opposite condition of impersonalization is reflected in fuzzy boundaries and the denial of the authentic self. For example, the multiple roles informants play in the course of their daily lives are increasingly difficult to keep separate and the relationship marketing practices of some firms exceed what would normally be considered as the commercial boundary. As such informants acknowledge a need to be more mindful of creating a carefully staged public persona, and thus feel that their sense of authentic self is denied.

This dialectic tension arising from an increased emphasis on the personalization of aspects of life and a greater sense of impersonalization experienced by informants drives consumers desires for privacy and results in consumers actively "doing" privacy through the use of several cognitive and behavioural strategies. These strategies are categorized as: withdraw, defend, attack and reconcile. Withdraw represents avoidance tactics that informants engage in to facilitate the goal of removing one's self from situations that may violate their privacy. Defend represents protective tactics that are largely concerned with proactively enacting and strengthening the barriers of informants' respective personal domains, thus 'minimizing damage'. Attack, represents offensive tactics that informants employ when confronted with a privacy related situation. These tactics are more direct and aggressive in nature. Last, reconcile can take the form where informants either convince themselves that privacy will prevail, or actively negotiate the conditions of disclosure with the requesting party.

In summary, by elucidating the 'what', 'when', 'why' and 'how' of privacy from the consumers' perspective, we offer a more comprehensive understanding of this concept as it applies in contemporary consumer society. Our findings highlight that consumers are active participants in the marketplace and engage in a number of strategies to achieve or maintain sovereignty over their personal domain. In doing so, we contribute to growing literature on customer creativity (Beverland and Farrelly 2010; Epp and Price 2008, 2009; Price 2008; van Doorn et al. 2010; Verheof et al. 2010).

REFERENCES

Acquisti, Alessandro and Jens Grossklags (2004), "Privacy Attitudes and Privacy Behavior: Losses, Gains and Hyperbolic Discounting," in *The Economics of Information Security*, eds. L. Jean Camp and Stephen Lewis, Boston: Kluwer Academic Publishers, 165-78.

Belk, Russell W., Melanie Wallendorf, and John F. Sherry Jr. (1989), "The Sacred and the Profane in Consumer Behavior: Theodicy on the Odyssey," *Journal of Consumer Research*, 16 (1), 1-38.

Beverland, Michael B., and Francis J. Farrelly (2010), "The Quest for Authenticity in Consumption: Consumers' Purposive Choice of Authentic Cues to Shape Experienced Outcomes," *Journal of Consumer Research*, 36 (5), 838-56.

Corbin, Juliet and Anslem, L. Strauss (2008), *Basics of Qualitative Research: Techniques and Procedures for Developing Grounded Theory*, Los Angeles: Sage.

Deighton, John (2005), "Consumer Identity Motives in the Information Age," in *Inside Consumption: Consumer Motives, Goals and Desires*, eds. S. Ratneshwar, David Glen Mick, London: Routledge, Taylor and Francis Group, 233-51.

Epp, Ember M. and Linda L. Price (2008). "Family Identity: A Framework of Identity Interplay in Consumption Practices," *Journal of Consumer Research*, 35 (1), 50-70.

--- and --- (2009). "The Storied Life of Singularized Objects: Forces of Agency and Network Transformation," *Journal of Consumer Research*, 36 (5), 820-37.

Goodwin, Cathy (1991), "Privacy: Recognition of a Consumer Right," *Journal of Public Policy and Marketing*, 10 (1), 149-66.

Harper, Douglas (2002), "Talking About Pictures: A Case for Photo Elicitation," *Visual Studies*, 17 (1), 13-26.

Harper, Jim and Solveig Singleton (2001), "With a Grain of Salt: What Consumer Privacy Surveys Don't Tell Us," Working Paper No. 299930, Social Science Research Network.

Horne, Daniel R., Patricia A. Norberg, and A. Cemal Ekin (2007), "Exploring Consumer Lying in Information-Based Exchanges," *Journal of Consumer Marketing*, 24 (2), 90-9.

Introna, Lucas D. and Athanasia Pouloudi (1999), "Privacy in the Information Age: Stakeholders, Interests and Values", *Journal of Business Ethics*, 22(1), 27-38.

Johnson, Jeffery L. (1989), "Privacy and the Judgment of Others," *The Journal of Value Inquiry*, 23 (2), 157-68.

Jones, Mary Gardiner (1991), "Privacy: A Significant Marketing Issue for the 1990s," *Journal of Public Policy and Marketing*, 10 (1), 133-48.

Lanier, Clinton D. Jr and Amit Saini (2008), "Understanding Consumer Privacy: A Review and Future Directions," Academy of Marketing Science Review, 12 (2), 1-45.

Laufer, Robert S. and Maxine Wolfe (1977), "Privacy as a Concept and a Social Issue: A Multidimensional Developmental Theory," Journal of Social Issues, 33 (3), 22-42.

Lwin, May O., Jochen Wirtz, and Jerome D. Williams (2007), "Consumer Online Privacy Concerns and Responses: A Power-Responsibility Equilibrium Perspective," *Journal of the Academy of Marketing Science*, 35 (4), 572-85.

Milne, George R. (2003), "How Well Do Consumers Protect Themselves from Identity Theft?," *Journal of Consumer Affairs*, 37 (2), 388 – 402.

---, Andrew J. Rohm, and Shalini Bahl (2004), "Consumers' Protection of Online Privacy and Identity," Journal of Consumer Research, 38 (2), 217-32.

Nehf, James P. (2007), "Shopping for Privacy on the Internet," Journal of Consumer Affairs, 41 (2), 351-75.

Nguyen, Thuc-Doan and Eric P.H. Li (2010), "Online Consumer Privacy 2.0," in *Advances in Consumer Research*, Vol. 37, eds., Margaret C. Campbell, Jeff Inman, and Rik Pieters, Duluth, MN: Association for Consumer Research.

Norberg Patricia A., Daniel R. Horne, and David A. Horne (2007), "The Privacy Paradox: Personal Information Disclosure Intentions Versus Behaviors," *Journal of Consumer Affairs*, 41 (1), 100-26.

Parent, W. A. (1983), "Privacy, Morality and the Law," *Philosophy and Public Affairs*, 12 (4), 269-88.

Phelps, Joseph E., Giles D'Souza, and Glen J. Nowak (2001), "Antecedents and Consequences of Consumer Privacy Concerns: An Empirical Investigation," *Journal of Interactive Marketing*, 15 (4), 2-17.

---, Glen J. Nowak, and Elizabeth Ferrell (2000), "Privacy Concerns and Consumer Willingness to Provide Personal Information," *Journal of Public Policy and Marketing*, 27 (1), 27-41.

Price, Linda L. (2008), "Doing Family: The Temporal and Spatial Structuring of Family Consumption," in Advances in Consumer Research, Vol. 35, eds. Angela Y. Lee and Dilip Soman, Duluth, MN : Association for Consumer Research.

Sayre, Shay and David A. Horne (2000), "Trading Secrets for Savings: How Concerned are Consumers about Club Cards as a Privacy Threat?," in *Advances in Consumer Research*, Vol. 27, eds. Stephen J. Hoch and Robert J. Meyer, Provo, UT: Association for Consumer Research, 151-55.

Sheehan, Kim Bartel and Mariea Grubbs Hoy (2000), "Dimensions of Privacy Concern Among Online Consumers," *Journal of Public Policy and Marketing*, 19 (1), 62-73.

Shoeman, Ferdinand D. (1984), "Privacy and Intimate Information," in *Philosophical Dimensions of Privacy*, ed. Ferdinand D. Shoeman, Cambridge: Cambridge University Press, 403-18.

Smith, H. Jeff, Sandra J. Milberg, and Sandra J. Burke (1996), "Information Privacy: Measuring Individuals' Concerns about Organizational Practices," *MIS Quarterly*, 20 (2), 167-96.

Solove, Daniel J. (2002), "Conceptualizing Privacy," *California Law Review*, 90(4), 1087-155.

Spiekermann Sarah, Jens Grossklags and Bettina Berendt (2001), "E-privacy in 2nd Generation E-Commerce: Privacy Preferences vs. Actual Behavior", in *ACM Conference on Electronic Commerce*, Tampa, Florida, October 14-17.

Van Doorn, Jenny, Katherine N. Lemon, Vikas Mittal, Stephan Nass, Doreen Pick, Peter Pirner, and Peter C. Verhoef (2010), "Customer Engagement Behavior: Theoretical Foundations and Research Directions," *Journal of Service Research*, 13 (3) 253-66.

Vargo, Stephen L. and Robert F. Lusch (2004), "Evolving to a New Dominant Logic for Marketing," *Journal of Marketing*, 68 (1), 1-17.

Verheof, Peter C., Werner J. Reinartz, and Manfred Krafft (2010), "Customer Engagement as a New Perspective in Customer Management," *Journal of Service Research*, 13 (3) 247-52.

Viseu, Ana, Andrew Clement, and Jane Aspinall (2004), "Situating Privacy Online: Complex Perceptions and Everyday Practices," *Information, Communication and Society*, 7 (1), 92-114.

Authenticity is in the Eye of the Beholder:
From Changes in Attitudes and Preferences to Placebo Effects

Hang Nguyen, University of Connecticut, USA
Kunter Gunasti, University of Connecticut, USA

EXTENDED ABSTRACT

Products marketed legally and manufactured by the firms owning the production rights of the brand using original ingredients, genuine parts, and raw materials have been referred to as authentic market offerings (Keller 2008). Inauthentic products, on the other hand, are fine copies of the authentic ones (Lai and Zaichkowsky 1999). They may range from compatibles (e.g., IBM compatible battery), imitations (e.g., imitation crab meat), and replicas (e.g., jewelry) to illegal counterfeits. The global market for inauthentic products exceeds $600 billion, eating up revenues of authentic brands and taking away over 750,000 US jobs every year (World Customs Organization 2004; Wilcox, Kim and Sen 2009). Due to extensive application of advanced technology, quality of some inauthentic products has reached the standards of authentic ones (Keller 2008) and for many consumer goods they are almost indistinguishable from originals (Howie 2010). Thus, it is very important to understand how consumers form their perception of product authenticity and how different cues affect consumers' judgments and choices of products.

Past studies on authenticity have focused on various dimensions, definitions, and conceptualizations of the notion (e.g., Beverland and Farrelly 2010; Beverland, Lindgreen, and Vink 2008; Brown, Kozinets and Sherry 2003; Gilmore and Pine 2007; Grayson and Martinec 2004). Recent research has examined consumers' motivations for consuming authentic and inauthentic products (Wilcox et al. 2009; Han, Nunes and Dreze 2010). Although it is widely accepted that consumers value authenticity, there has been no thorough empirical investigation about consumers' authenticity perceptions and to what extent it influences product judgments, purchase decision, and post-consumption behavior.

Consumers may form their perception of product authenticity via intrinsic cues (product exposures/experiences, actual product quality) and/or extrinsic cues (explicit messages, inconspicuous cues) provided by manufacturers and competitors. Using three empirical studies employing different product categories, we investigate the competing effects of authenticity cues on consumer attitudes, willingness to pay, choices, and consumption outcomes. Our studies systematically demonstrate that extrinsic cues play the major role in shaping consumers' authenticity perception, which in turn affects product attitudes, willingness to pay, choices and even consumption outcomes. Study 1 demonstrates that consumers develop lower (higher) attitude favorability and willingness to pay when a product is introduced as an inauthentic (authentic). Study 2 finds that an objectively inferior product with multiple authenticity cues is preferred over a clearly superior compatible counterpart. Finally, study 3 shows that even subtle cues such as packaging can affect perceived authenticity and lead to a placebo effect of product efficacy.

From a theoretical perspective, our research is the first empirical demonstration of the powerful effects of different authenticity cues and the perception of product authenticity on all stages of a consumption process, from product evaluation, purchase intent and decision making to post-consumption behaviors. The effects occur not only for luxury, well-known, but also less-known brands, from conscious to non-conscious levels. We consider this work as an important step toward developing a more comprehensive conceptual framework for consumption of authentic and inauthentic products. From a managerial perspective, our findings have significant implications for marketing managers and public policy makers. We found that even though consumers highly valued authentic products, they were mostly unable to distinguish them. This phenomenon thus creates many difficulties for legitimate manufacturers, especially when manufacturers of imitations may intentionally provide misleading authenticity information for consumers. Firms can evoke consumers' favorable attitudes and responses toward their products by providing authenticity information via extrinsic cues including subtle cues, and they may further elicit post-consumption satisfaction by creating and maintaining the perception of product authenticity.

REFERENCES

Baron, R. M., and Kenny, D. A. (1986), "The moderator-mediator variable distinction in social psychological research: Conceptual, strategic and statistical considerations," *Journal of Personality and Social Psychology,* 51, 1173-1182.

Berger, Jonah and Morgan Ward (2010), "Subtle Signals of Inconspicuous Consumption," *Journal of Consumer Research*, 37 (December).

Beverland, Michael B. (2006), "The 'Real Thing': Branding Authenticity in the Luxury Wine Trade," *Journal of Business Research*, 59 (February), 251–258.

Beverland, Michael B., Adam Lindgreen, and Michiel W. Vink (2008), "Projecting Authenticity through Advertising: Consumer Judgments of Advertisers' Claims," *Journal of Advertising*, 37 (Spring), 5–16.

Beverland, Michael B. and Francis J. Farrelly (2010), "The Quest for Authenticity in Consumption: Consumers' Purposive Choice of Authentic Cues to Shape Experienced Outcomes," *Journal of Consumer Research*, 36 (February), 838-856.

Brown, Stephen, Robert V. Kozinets, and John F. Sherry Jr. (2003), "Teaching Old Brands New Tricks: Retro Branding and the Revival of Brand Meaning," *Journal of Marketing,* 67 (July), 19–33.

Gilmore, James H. and Joseph B. Pine (2007), "Authenticity: What Consumers Really Want," *Harvard Business School Press.*

Grayson K., and Martinec R. (2004), "Consumer Perceptions of Iconicity and Indexicality and Their Influence on Assessments of Authentic Market Offerings," *Journal of Consumer Research*, 31 (September), 296-312.

Gunasti, Kunter and William T. Ross (2010) "How and When Alpha-numeric Brand Names Affect Consumer Preferences," *Journal of Marketing Research*, 47 (December).

Ha, Young-Won and Stephen J. Hoch (1989), "Ambiguity, Processing Strategy, and Advertising Evidence Interactions," *Journal of Consumer Research*, 16 (3), 354-360.

Han, Yong Jee, Joseph C. Nunes and Xavier Dreze (2010), "Signaling Status with Luxury Goods: The Role of Brand Prominence," *Journal of Marketing*, 74 (July), 15-30.

Howie, Michael (2010), "Fake goods are fine, say UK study," http://www.telegraph.co.uk/finance/newsbysector/ retailandconsumer/7969335/Fake-goods-are-fine-says-EU-study.html.

Keller, Kevin L. (2008), "*Strategic Brand Management: Building, Measuring, and Managing Brand Equity,*" 3rd edition, Englewood Cliffs, NJ: Prentice Hall.

Lai, Kay Ka-Yuk and Judith Lynne Zaichkowsky (1999), "Brand Imitation: Do Chinese Have Different Views?" *Asia Pacific Journal of Management*, 16 (2), 179–192.

Peirce, Charles Sanders (1998), *Collected Papers of Charles Sanders Peirce,* ed. Charles Hartshorne, Paul Weiss, and Arthur Blank, 8 vols., Bristol: Thoemmes.

Pearce, Terry (2003), "Leading out loud: inspiring change through authentic communication," *Jossey-Bass, A Wiley Company,* San Francisco.

Richardson, Paul S., Alan S. Dick and Arun K. Jain (1994), "Extrinsic and Intrinsic Cue Effects on Perceptions of Store Brand Quality," *Journal of Marketing*, 58(October), 28-36

Rose, Randall L. and Stacy L. Wood (2005), "Paradox and the Consumption of Authenticity through Reality Television," *Journal of Consumer Research*, 32 (September), 284–296.

Shiv, Baba, Ziv Carmon and Dan Ariely (2005), "Placebo Effects of Marketing Actions: Consumers May Get What They Pay For," *Journal of Marketing Research*, 42 (November), 383-393.

Swaminathan, Vanitha, Karen M. Stilley and Rohini Ahluwalia (2009), "When Brand Personality Matters: The Moderating Role of Attachment Styles," *Journal of Consumer Research,* 35 (April), 985-1002.

Thompson, Craig J., Aric Rindfleisch, and Zeynep Arsel (2006), "Emotional Branding and the Strategic Value of the Doppelganger Brand Image," *Journal of Marketing*, 70 (January), 50–64.

Van, Elizabeth (2006), "The Limits of Authenticity in Vietnamese Consumer Markets," *American Anthropologist*, 108 (2), 286–296

Wilcox, Keith, Hyeong Min Kim, and Sankar Sen (2009), "Why Do Consumers Buy Counterfeit Luxury Brands?," *Journal of Marketing Research*, 46 (April), 247–259.

Woodmansee, Martha (1984), "The Genius and the Copyright: Economic and Legal Conditions of the Emergence of the "Author," *Eighteenth-Century Studies*, 17(4), 425–448.

World Customs Organization (2004), "Counterfeiting Congress Calls for Public-Private Co-operation," news release, (May 26).

Zeithaml, Valarie (1988), "Consumer Perceptions of Price, Quality, and Value: A Means-End Model and Synthesis of Evidence," *Journal of Marketing*, 52 (July), 2-22.

Practice Consumption and Value Creation:
Advancing the Practice Theoretical Ontology of Consumption Community

Benjamin J. Hartmann, Jönköping University, Sweden
Caroline Wiertz, Cass Business School, City University London, UK
Eric Arnould, University of Wyoming, USA

EXTENDED ABSTRACT

How and in what ways do practices create value? Conceptual blind spots persist when it comes to understanding how value creation operates through practices in consumer behavior (Schau, Muniz, and Arnould 2009; Shove and Pantzar 2005; Warde 2005). Specifically, various forms of consumer collectives are considered sites of value creation that matter both to consumers and marketers (Cova 1997; Giesler 2006; Kozinets 1999; Mathwick, Wiertz, and De Ruyter 2008; Muniz and O'Guinn 2001), and this research suggests that it is through practices that they exert their value-creating effects (Schau et al. 2009). Because consumer researchers have equated practices with their performance, practice consumption and its role in value creation remains under-theorized. Addressing this theoretical gap, we conceptualize and empirically analyze the consumption dimension of practices through multi-method research conducted within an online gardening community. Thus, the aim of this project is to move beyond a purely performance-based theoretical ontology of practices and value creation to develop a framework that conceptualizes and integrates a consumption dimension into this theory.

Building on the conception of individuals as 'carriers of practice' (Reckwitz 2002) and practices as 'carriers of value' (Schau et al. 2009), we propose that the source of value lies not only in the performance of practices, but also in their consumption. This is particularly evident in the context of online community, where due to the archival and online setting, all practices that are performed are visible and in fact, consumers often perform them with an audience in mind. Thus, we argue that community practices must not only be performed, but also consumed in order to create value, that is, there are recipients or beneficiaries of practice performance.

Prior research implicitly addresses the consumption of practices, yet leaves it as an under-theorized element. We develop two families of practices based on their transitivity (Hopper and Thompson 1980): 1) socially *intransitive* practices in which the performance of a practice involves a non-human object; and 2) socially *transitive* practices in which the performance of a practice involves another human subject. The social transitivity of practices advances a definition of practice consumption. In order to develop our theorizations on the consumption of (community) practices, we use this conceptualization to revisit and extend the community practice catalogue by Schau et al. (2009) and study it empirically in the context of a commercially owned online gardening community.

As most qualitative research done within the context of online communities builds on netnographic material, such research tends to overemphasize 'on-stage' performances within the community. Thus, studies that explicitly focus on a consumer-centric 'backstage,' and on the subjective experiences of performance and community membership are rare. Consequently, we gathered qualitative empirical material through a community member diary study.

The collection of quantitative measures of practices is one of the key components of this study. The majority of brand and consumption community research in CCT is based on qualitative data. In this study, quantitative data was obtained through an online survey based on Schau et al.'s (2009) catalogue of community practices. We developed scales measuring respondents' subjective perception of how much s/he performs each practice, directly consumes each socially transitive practice, and vicariously consumes each socially intransitive practice.

Our preliminary analysis of qualitative data reveals that community practices do not create value simply through performance but that their consumption matters to consumers in negotiating community membership, community attachment, and value creation. Furthermore, our findings demonstrate that there is a systematic relationship between the performance and consumption of certain community practices, which is embedded in a system of generalized reciprocity (Giesler 2006; Sahlins 1972) and accumulated cultural capital (Bourdieu 1986).

Our preliminary analysis of quantitative data adds precision to the assertion that practices create value in online communities. Our findings support the claim that in most cases, performing a practice is perceived as distinct and different from consuming the practice, and that each creates different types of value. For example, consuming empathizing, which in our context involves getting answers to gardening related questions, leads to heightened perceptions of the usefulness of the online community as an information resource. Performing empathizing, answering a gardening question, on the other hand, does not have an impact on the perceived use value, but leads to heightened perceptions of social recognition. This fine-grained understanding of how practices create value should be useful not only for community management, but is also conducive to further development of a practice theoretical ontology of community. Thus, blurring the distinction between consumption and production (e.g. Firat and Venkatesh 1995) does not efface differences in effects from a practice theoretical angle.

REFERENCES

Bagozzi, Richard P. and Utpal M. Dholahia (2006), "Antecedents and Purchase Consequences of Customer Participation in Small Group Brand Communities," *International Journal of Research in Marketing, 23*(1), 45-61.

Bourdieu, Pierre (1986), "Forms of Capital," in *Handbook of Theory and Research for the Sociology of Education*, ed. John G. Richardson, New York: Greenwood Press, 241-58.

Chin, Wynne W. (1998), "The Partial Least Squares Approach to Structural Equation Modeling," in *Modern Business Research Methods*, ed. G.A. Marcoulides, Mahwah, New Jersey: Lawrence Erlbaum Associates.

Chronis, Athinodoros and Ronald D. Hampton (2008), "Consuming the Authentic Gettysburg: How a Tourist Landscape Becomes an Authentic Experience," *Journal of Consumer Behaviour*, 7 (2), 111-26.

Cova, Bernard (1997), "Community and Consumption," *European Journal of Marketing, 31* (3/4), 297-316.

Falk, Frank R. and Nancy B. Miller (1992), *A Primer for Soft Modeling*, Ohio: The University of Akron Press.

Firat, A. Fuat and Alladi Venkatesh (1995), "Liberatory Postmodernism and the Reenchantment of Consumption," Journal of Consumer Research, 22 (December), 239-267.

Fornell, Claes and David F. Larcker (1981), "Evaluating Structural Equation Models with Unobservable Variables and Measurement Error," *Journal of Marketing Research*, 19 (February), 39-50.

Fornell, Claes and Jaesung Cha (1994), "Partial Least Squares," in *Advanced Methods of Marketing*, ed. Richard Bagozzi, Cambridge, MA: Blackwell, 52-78.

Giddens, Anthony (1984), *The Constitution of Cociety: Outline of a Theory of Structuration*, Cambridge, UK: Polity Press.

Giesler, Markus (2006), "Consumer Gift Systems," *Journal of Consumer Research, 33* (2), 283-90.

Holt, Douglas B. (1995), "How Consumers Consume: A typology of Consumption Practices," *Journal of Consumer Research, 22* (1), 1-16.

Hopper, Paul J. and Sandra A. Thompson (1980), "Transitivity in Grammar and Discourse," *Language, 56* (2), 251-99.

Hulland, John (1999), "Use of Partial Least Squares (PLS) in Strategic Management Research: A Review of Four Recent Studies," *Strategic Management Journal*, 20 (2), 195-204.

Kozinets, Robert V. (1999), "E-tribalized Marketing?: The Strategic Implications of Virtual Communities of Consumption," *European Management Journal, 17* (3), 252-64.

--- (2001), "Utopian Enterprise: Articulating the Meanings of Star Trek's Culture of Consumption," *Journal of Consumer Research, 28* (1), 67-88.

--- (2010), *Netnography: Doing ethnographic research online*, London: Sage.

Latour, Bruno (1996), "On Interobjectivity," *Mind, Culture, and Activity*, 3 (4), 228-45.

MacInnis, Deborah J. and Linda L. Price (1987), "The Role of Imagery in Information Processing: Review and Extensions," *Journal of Consumer Research*, 13 (March), 473-91.

Mathwick, Charla, Caroline Wiertz, and Ko De Ruyter (2008), "Social Capital Production in a Virtual P3 Community," *Journal of Consumer Research, 34* (6), 832-49.

Moran, Ed, Francois Gossieaux, and Jen McClure (2009), "2009 Tribalization of Business Study," http://www.deloitte.com/us/2009tribalizationstudy.

Muniz, Albert M. and Thomas C. O'Guinn (2001), "Brand Community," *Journal of Consumer Research,* 27 (4), 412-32.

Nunnally, Jum C. and Ira H. Bernstein (1994), *Psychometric Theory* (Third Edition): McGraw Hill.

Reckwitz, Andreas (2002), "Toward a Theory of Social Practices," *European Journal of Social Theory*, 5 (2), 243-63.

Rigby, Darrell and Barbara Bilodeau (2009), "Management Tools and Trends 2009," http://www.bain.com/bainweb/PDFs/cms/Public/Management_Tools_2009.pdf.

Sahlins, Marshall (1972), *Stone Age Economics*, Chicago: Aldine-Atherton.

Schatzki, Theodore R. (1996), *Social Practices:A Wittgensteinian Approach to Human Activity and the Social*, Cambridge: Cambridge University Press.

Schau, Hope J., Albert M. Muniz, and Eric J. Arnould (2009), "How Brand Community Practices Create Value," *Journal of Marketing,* 73 (5), 30-51.

Schouten, John W. and James H. McAlexander, J. H. (1995), "Subcultures of Consumption: An Ethnography of the New Bikers," *Journal of Consumer Research,* 22(1), 43-61.

Shove, Elizabeth and Mika Pantzar (2005), "Consumers, Producers and Practices: Understanding the Invention and Reinvention of Nordic Walking," *Journal of Consumer Culture,* 5 (1), 43-64.

Warde, Alan (2005), "Consumption and Theories of Practice," *Journal of Consumer Culture,* 5 (2), 131-53.

Making Space: Revealing Hidden Inconsistencies within the Marketplace

Marcus Phipps, University of Melbourne, Australia
Jan Brace-Govan, Monash University, Australia

EXTENDED ABSTRACT

This paper investigates the private nature of household water consumption. Using three innovative water consumers as indicative examples, the study illustrates how a private marketplace can be challenged and hidden inconsistencies brought into public view. Each consumer sought to remove their household from the public mains supply and in the process challenged central assumptions of the marketplace. When severe drought threatened the adequacy of the city's reservoirs, their countervailing behavior became sought after for inspiration and public discussion.

Marketplaces can seek rejuvenation through opposition (Heath and Potter 2005; Holt 2002; Kozinets 2008; Thompson 2004; Thompson and Coskuner-Balli 2007; Thompson and Haytko 1997; Varman and Belk 2009; Zhao and Belk 2008). Over time, previously rebellious ideologies can become sources for innovation and commercial successes. The subcutural non-commercial sphere of tattooing morphed into a profit-maximizing sphere of the commercial world (Bengtsson, Ostberg, and Kjeldgaard 2005). The rebellious nature of the napster file sharing community was a foreshadow to the commercial success of the Apple iTunes music store (Giesler 2008). The resistance of the voluntary simplicity movement has been refashioned into the contemporary consumption phenomenon of simple living (Gopaldas 2008). Furthermore, contradictions in the marketplace provide opportunities for continued marketplace innovations (Heath and Potter 2005; Kozinets 2008; Thompson 2004; Thompson and Coskuner-Balli 2007).

In particular, public spaces provide an opportunity for countervailing ideologies to contribute to marketplace change (Karababa and Ger 2011; Visconti et al. 2010). However, much marketplace resistance occurs at the private and seemingly invisible household level. The private household level of consumption is underexplored from a consumer culture perspective, yet is such an important part of consumers' identity and subsequent behavior. This paper investigates marketplace resistance from the household level and the processes involved in developing ideological change.

The context of this paper is the urban household water marketplace of Melbourne, Australia. In this marketplace, a severe drought led to a reconceptualisation of the meaning of water consumption, and lifted the previously private nature of water use into public discussion. Three indicative consumers, Neil, Veronica and Andrew, are outlined in the findings to illustrate how private consumer resistance can contribute to wider marketplace change. Each consumer challenged dominant assumptions within the marketplace by developing households' independent of the city's mains water supply.

Challenging the marketplace on a private led to hidden inconsistencies within the marketplace being brought to the surface. Rules and regulations around the installation of rainwater tanks, and the use of graywater, were found to be in conclusion and impossible to follow. The consumers adjusted their behavior to circumnavigate these rules and successfully achieve independence from the mains supply.

A countervailing conceptualisation of what is traditionally considered private in Western societies was provided by the consumers. With a shifted emphasis due to drought, any challenges to the dominant assumption of mains water use were eagerly sought after by the public and the media. The consumer made open their house open to the public and conducted tours to discuss their private consumption behaviors. Inconsistencies in the marketplace were given a stronger public focus, enabling for corrections to be made to the system.

Each innovative consumer's sustainable development were the result of deeply held personal values. The concept of a house as mirror of self (Marcus 1997) resonated with the emergent analysis of the these pioneering individuals. Neil, Veronica, and Andrew used metaphor from their backgrounds in science, medicine and activism respectively to describe their commitment to sustainable development. The study provides an illustration of the processes behind privately held values becoming part of the public discourse.

In contrast to the usual Western norms, these activists were so convinced of the need to move individual water consumption to a conserving, re-using and recycling format that they were prepared to make their private (and family) space public. Previous research would appear to suggest that public behavior is a very important part of marketplace change (Karababa and Ger 2011). Furthermore, marketplace intermediaries were an active part of the shift in social practices. The marketplace become a key facilitator of the uptake of new water consuming behaviors in the provision of water storage tanks, types of hoses and other paraphernalia required to store and re-use water.

This research has important implications around public policy, as public behaviors are more likely to be subject to change then private ones. In particular, private household behaviors have important implications around sustainable consumption. Further research is needed to understand the migration of private behavior into the public discourse and the shifting nature of private/public consumption.

REFERENCE

Australian Bureau of Meteorology (2007), "Melbourne Driest on Record," http://www.bom.gov.au/announcements/media_releases/vic.

Belk, Russell (2010), "Sharing," *Journal of Consumer Research*, 36 (5), 715-34.

Bengtsson, Anders, Jacob Ostberg, and Dannie Kjeldgaard (2005), "Prisoners in Paradise: Subcultural Resistance to the Marketization of Tattooing.," *Consumption, Markets & Culture*, 8 (3), 261-74.

Crockett, David and Melanie Wallendorf (2004), "The Role of Normative Political Ideology in Consumer Behavior," *Journal of Consumer Research*, 31 (3), 511-28.

Duffy, John (1992), *The Sanitarians: A History of American Public Health*, Urbana, Illinois: University of Illinois Press.

Giesler, Markus (2008), "Conflict and Compromise: Drama in Marketplace Evolution," *Journal of Consumer Research*, 34 (6), 739-53.

Gopaldas, Ahir (2008), "Anti-Consumption: Now on Sale," *Advances in Consumer Research*, 35 (1), 730.

Goulding, Christine (2002), *Grounded Theory: A Practical Guide for Management, Business and Market Researchers*, London, England: Sage Publications.

Heath, Joseph and Andrew Potter (2005), *The Rebel Sell: Why the Culture Can't Be Jammed*, Chichester, UK: Capstone.

Hill, Ronald and Mark Stamey (1990), "The Homeless in America: An Examination of Possessions and Consumption Behaviors," *Journal of Consumer Research*, 17 (3), 303-21.

Holt, Douglas (2002), "Why Do Brands Cause Trouble? A Dialectical Theory of Consumer Culture and Branding," *Journal of Consumer Research*, 29 (1), 70-90.

Karababa, Eminegül and Güliz Ger (2011), "Early Modern Ottoman Coffeehouse Culture and the Formation of the Consumer Subject," *Journal of Consumer Research*, 37 (5), 737-60.

Kozinets, Robert (2008), "Technology/Ideology: How Ideological Fields Influence Consumers' Technology Narratives," *Journal of Consumer Research*, 34 (6), 865-81.

Locke, Karen (1996), "Rewriting the Discovery of Grounded Theory after 25 Years?," *Journal of Management Inquiry*, 5 (3), 239-45.

Marcus, Clare (1997), *House as a Mirror of Self: Exploring the Deeper Meaning of Home*, Berkeley, CA: Conari Press.

Melbourne Water (2007), "Weekly Water Update Archives," www.melbournewater.com.au.

Miletic, Daniella (2008), "Hawthorn Home Does Its Bit to Save the Planet," *The Age*, 12 May.

Shove, Elizabeth and Alan Warde (2001), "Inconspicuous Consumption: The Sociology of Consumption, Lifestyles, and the Environment," in *Sociological Theory and the Environment: Classical Foundations, Contemporary Insights*, ed. Riley Dunlap, Frederick Buttel, Peter Dickens and August Gijswijt, Lanham, MD: Rowman & Littlefield Publishers, 230-51.

Thompson, Craig (2004), "Marketplace Mythology and Discourses of Power.," *Journal of Consumer Research*, 31 (1), 162-80.

Thompson, Craig and Gokcen Coskuner-Balli (2007), "Countervailing Market Responses to Corporate Co-Optation and the Ideological Recruitment of Consumption Communities," *Journal of Consumer Research*, 34 (2), 135-52.

Thompson, Craig and Diana Haytko (1997), "Speaking of Fashion: Consumers' Uses of Fashion Discourses and the Appropriation of Countervailing Cultural Meanings," *Journal of Consumer Research*, 24 (1), 15.

Üstüner, Tuba and Douglas Holt (2007), "Dominated Consumer Acculturation: The Social Construction of Poor Migrant Women's Consumer Identity Projects in a Turkish Squatter," *Journal of Consumer Research*, 34 (1), 41-56.

Varman, Rohit and Russell Belk (2009), "Nationalism and Ideology in an Anticonsumption Movement," *Journal of Consumer Research*, 36 (4), 686-700.

Visconti, Luca, John Sherry Jr, Stefania Borghini, and Laurel Anderson (2010), "Street Art, Sweet Art? Reclaiming The "Public" In Public Place," *Journal of Consumer Research*, 37 (3), 511-29.

Wright, Lawrence (1980), *Clean and Decent: The History of the Bath and Loo and of Sundry Habits, Fashions & Accessories of the Toilet, Principally in Great Britain, France & America*, London: Routledge & Kegan.

Zhao, Xin and Russell Belk (2008), "Politicizing Consumer Culture: Advertising's Appropriation of Political Ideology in China's Social Transition," *Journal of Consumer Research*, 35 (2), 231-43.

The Content of a Brand Scandal
Moderating the Effect of Thinking Style on the Scandal's Spillover

Yun Lee, University of Iowa, USA
Nara Youn, Hongik University, Korea
Dhananjay Nayakankuppam, University of Iowa, USA

EXTENDED ABSTRACT

Product-harm crises, or brand scandals, significantly decrease consumer preferences and purchases for the scandalized brands and their families (Ahluwalia, Unnava, and Burnkrant 2000, Dawar and Pillutla 2000) as well as their competing brands (Roehm and Tybout 2006). Given the devastating effects of product-harm crises and the increasing number of product recalls, we investigate how the nature of a brand scandal moderates the effect of thinking style on the scandal's spillover. We propose that whether the nature of a brand scandal is extrinsic or intrinsic to the scandalized brand's quality determines the degree to which analytic vs. holistic thinkers are affected by the negative information. Extrinsic content is a case where the issues pertinent to a brand scandal are more social and values-related in nature (e.g. socially irresponsible brand misconduct, labor abuses, or environmental contamination), whereas in the case of intrinsic content, the issues are primarily related to product defects (e.g. brand scandals that are directly associated with product quality and performance) (Zeithaml 1988, Huber, Vogel, and Meyer 2009, Pullig, Netemeyer, and Biswas 2006). We argue that there are individual differences in how much to care about socially/ethically related issues and their perceived importance, and these individual differences affect the negative impacts of different types of brand scandals. For this, we propose that different types of scandal content as a moderator of the effect of different styles of thinking on scandal spillover.

Nisbett et al. (2001) have argued that there are two different types of thinking styles (i.e., analytic vs. holistic). According to them, holistic thinkers tend to rely on contextual information and relationships between focal issues and environments. On the other hand, analytic thinkers tend to ignore contextual information, but more focus on focal issues by detaching them from the field. Interestingly, in a recent brand scandal study, Monga and John (2008) demonstrated that analytic thinkers are more susceptible to an intrinsic brand scandal case than analytic thinkers. They explain that this is because analytic thinkers less consider contextual explanations which lead them to more revise their beliefs about the scandalized brand. However, the negative impacts of an extrinsic brand scandal case depending on analytic vs. holistic thinking styles are yet to be investigated. We predict that holistic thinkers' cognitive tendencies focusing on contextual information and relationships may lead them to be more susceptible to extrinsic brand scandal cases. In this line of reasoning, the current research addresses this gab by examining whether the negative impact of extrinsic vs. intrinsic brand scandals will vary depending on holistic vs. analytic thinking style. We conducted a pretest to examine whether holistic vs. analytic thinkers are more likely to consider corporate social/ethical responsibilities, and found that holistic thinkers care more about social/values-related issues than analytic thinkers do ($F(1, 60) = 5.71$, $\beta = .35$, $p = .02$). Given these results, we test our predictions across three experiments.

In Experiment 1a, participants were randomly assigned to either analytic or holistic thinking styles. Half of them were asked to complete sentences in a short story using singular pronouns to activate analytic thinking mode, and the other half under holistic thinking mode were asked to do it using plural pronouns (Monga and John 2008; Kühnen et al. 2001). Then they were given a fictitiously created brand scandal news story about McDonalds unethically mis-

leading its customers about the nutritional content of its burgers (i.e., by advertising that they use only "100% pure beef," which has a possibility to be misunderstood as "100% pure protein; Roehm and Tybout, 2006). As expected, the results revealed that holistic thinkers were more susceptible to McDonald's brand scandal on the likelihood of the scandal spillover to a competing brand, Burger King ($F(1,69)=7.39$, $p < .01$, $M_{holistic} = 7.44$, $M_{analytic}=6.46$).

In Experiment 1b, participants were given a picture and randomly asked to describe the scene of the picture to elicit a holistic thinking mode or find objects hidden in picture to elicit an analytic thinking mode (Mong and John 2008). Then they were asked to read a fictitiously created Colgate's intrinsic brand scandal newspaper article (i.e., Antifreeze chemical found in Colgate toothpastes and severe injuries reported). As predicted, replicating the results of Monga and John (2008), one way ANOVA revealed that holistic thinkers were less susceptible to the intrinsic brand scandal spillover than analytic thinkers were.

In Experiment 2, participants were randomly assigned to one of the four conditions composing a 2(thinking styles) × 2(scandal type) between-subjects design. Thinking style manipulation was same as in Experiment 1b. The news story used for intrinsic content is about a product defect of Nike's new shoes that can cause serious ankle and knee injuries. Participants in the extrinsic content condition read a water pollution scandal regarding Nike athletic shoe factories (Roehm and Tybout 2006). A 2(scandal type) × 2(thinking styles) ANOVA yielded a significant interaction ($F(1, 79)=25.86$, $p < .001$). As hypothesized, follow-up contrasts showed that extrinsic scandal was significant for holistic thinkers on the likelihood of the scandal spillover to a competing brand, Adidas ($F(1, 37) = 8.09$, $p=.007$, $M_{extrinsic, analytic} = 3.56$ vs. $M_{extrinsic, holistic} = 4.81$). On the other hand, when the nature of the scandal is intrinsic, the spillover was more likely to occur to analytic (vs. holistic) thinkers ($F(1, 42) = 20.72$, $p<.001$, $M_{intrinsic, analytic} = 4.90$ vs. $M_{intrinsic, holistic} = 3.37$).

Experiment 3 was conducted to increase the robustness of the found effects. Thinking styles manipulation was same as in Experiment 1b. Participants read a fictitiously created Sony's intrinsic (Sony's laptops have battery problems causing severe burns from exploding) vs. extrinsic (Sony's frequent severe violations of environmental protection laws) brand scandal newspaper article. A 2(content: intrinsic vs. extrinsic) × 2(thinking styles: holistic versus analytic) ANOVA yielded a significant content × thinking style interaction. By replicating previous findings, those with analytic tendency revealed a higher likelihood of intrinsic brand scandal spillover, whereas those with holistic tendency showed higher spillover likelihood for extrinsic content.

The findings contribute to a better understanding of how and why consumer attitudes and beliefs can be revised by negative brand publicity depending on thinking styles. Our results also add to a better understanding of how negative brand information can influence consumer beliefs about competing brands. The current research also has managerial implications for marketing managers, suggesting a strategic facilitation of a particular thinking style depending on the contents of brand scandals to mitigate their impacts on consumer attitudes and beliefs.

REFERENCES

Ahluwalia, Rohini, H. Rao Unnava, and Robert E. Burnkrant (2000), "Consumer Response to Negative Publicity: The Moderating Role of Commitment," *Journal of Marketing Research*, 37, 203-214.

Choi, Incheol, Reeshad Dalal, Chu Kim-Prieto, and Hyekyung Park (2003), "Culture and Judgment of Causal Relevance," *Journal of Personality and Social Psychology*, 84 (January), 46–59.

Dawar, N. and Pillutla, M.M. (2000), "Impact of Product-harm Crises on Brand Equity: the Moderating Role of Consumer Expectations," *Journal of Marketing Research*, 37, 215-226.

Huber, Frank, Johannes Vogel, and Frederik Meyer, (2009) "When Brands Get Branded," *Marketing Theory*, 9 (1), 131-136.

Kühnen, Ulrich, Bettina Hannover, and Benjamin Schubert (2001), "The Semantic-Procedural Interface Model of the Self: The Role of Self-Knowledge for Context-Dependent versus Context- Independent Modes of Thinking," *Journal of Personality and Social Psychology*, 80 (3), 397–409.

Monga, Alokparna Basu and Deborah Roedder John (2008), "When Does Negative Brand Publicity Hurt?The Moderating Influence of Analytic versus Holistic Thinking," *Journal of Consumer Psychology*, 18, 320-32.

Nisbett, Richard E., Kaiping Peng, Incheol Choi, and Ara Norenzayan (2001), "Culture and Systems of Thought: Holistic versus Analytic Cognition," *Psychological Review*, 108 (April), 291-310.

Pullig, Chris, Richard G. Netemeyer, and Abhijit Biswas (2006), Attitude Basis, Certainty, and Challenge Alignment: A Case of Negative Brand Publicity," *Journal of the Academy of Marketing Science*, 34 (4), 528-542.

Roehm, Michelle, L. and Alice M. Tybout (2006), "When Will a Brand Scandal Spill Over, and How Should Competitors Respond?," *Journal of Marketing Research*, 43 (August), 366-73.

Zeithaml, Valarie A. (1988), "Consumer Perceptions of Price, Quality, and Value: A Means-End Model and Synthesis of Evidence," *Journal of Marketing*, Vol. 52, No. 3, 2-22.

Rethinking the Schema-Incongruity Effect in Consumer Judgments

Even J. Lanseng, Norwegian School of Management, Norway
Hanne Sivertsen, UC Davis, USA

EXTENDED ABSTRACT

In consumer research the moderate schema-incongruity effect refers to the notion that a product that is moderately incongruent with the schema evoked for it in knowledge is associated with a comparatively positive product evaluation (Mandler 1982). An important result from research on the incongruity effect is that the effect is limited to novices. Based on the argument that experts have elaborate and flexible schema structures that allow them to accommodate a discrepant stimulus, and therefore deter incongruity from being perceived, Perrachio and Tybout (1996) hypothesized and empirically confirmed that the incongruity effect was confined to novices, who have less elaborate and flexible schemata.

Perrachio and Tybout's (1996) hypothesis is nevertheless based on an incomplete argument. It assumes that novices actually possess schemata to employ. Otherwise, there is no basis for incongruity to emerge (i.e. the product has to be incongruent with *something*). However, a well-developed schema structure within a specific domain is what defines the expert, not the novice (Alba and Hutchinson 1987). Experts encode and store information around key functional mechanisms that allow rapid retrieval whenever stored information is relevant. Novices, in contrast, encode and store information around surfaces structures (e.g. physical attributes) that make the retrieval of even their limited relevant knowledge difficult (Chi, Feltovich, and Glaser 1981; Ericsson and Kintsch 1995). Based on this account, the Perrachio and Tybout's (1996) finding would not be predicted. In response, this study discusses that this unexpected finding could be an artifact related to the particular setting (dessert) and operationalization of expertise (gender).

Accordingly, this study predicts the opposite of Perrachio and Tybout's (1996) - that experts, rather than novices, experience incongruity and prefer moderately incongruent stimuli over congruent ones. Novices typically lack a developed schema structure to be used in assessing stimuli, and they will therefore be insensitive to incongruity. Experts typically have well-developed schemata and can therefore perceive incongruity, and respond according to the general prediction of the schema-incongruity theory. Two studies investigated these predictions.

Study 1

The purpose of this study was to observe whether the incongruity effect exists in a stimuli domain where real expertise is allowed for. Wine was deemed an appropriate product category. Several empirical studies suggest that wine experts excel over novices in terms of cognitive and perceptual skills (Hughson and Boakes 2002; Lawless 1984; Lehrer, 1983; Solomon 1990, 1997). A second purpose was to check if the manipulation of congruity versus moderated incongruity worked as planned.

Participants

69 participants were recruited among inhabitants in a small North-Californian university town.

Design and stimuli

The design was a one-factors (Incongruity: Incongruent vs. congruent) between-subject one. Levels of incongruity were manipulated by asking respondents to form expectations about a wine based on a wine label and then let them taste and smell the ostensibly same wine. In the congruent condition the actual wine, which was constant across conditions, was preceded by a label that correctly specified it (Grape: Cabernet Sauvignon, Vintage: 1999, Region: Napa Valley, Barreled: Old oak barrels) whereas in the incongruent condition the same wine was preceded by a label that incorrectly specified it (Grape: Zinfandel, Vintage: 1994, Region: Napa Valley).

To avoid that taste rather than incongruity drives the results, the same physical wine was used in the two conditions. To control that results are not produced by an expectancy bias (i.e. the expected best wine becomes the perceived best wine), participants' expected liking was measured prior to tasting and smelling.

Results

Results from a MANOVA with actual liking and perceive incongruity as dependent measures, the schema-incongruity as a factor and expected liking as a covariate suggested that an incongruity effect was present and that the incongruity manipulation worked as planned.

Study 2

The objective of the second study was to test the prediction that the moderate incongruity effect is limited to experts and to investigate the mediating role of schema-level processing in this regard.

Participants

227 participants were recruited among inhabitants in a small North-Californian university town.

Design and stimuli

The study used a three-factor (Schema incongruity: Incongruent vs. congruent) x (Expertise: Experts vs. novices) x (Information structure: Schema vs. piecemeal) between-subject design. Schema incongruity was manipulated as in Study 1, information structure were manipulated by providing participants with schematic versus piecemeal information, and expertise was a knowledge measure capturing objective wine knowledge through a 20-item quiz-type scale.

Results and discussion

Contrary to previous findings, the results from this study suggest that the moderate incongruity effect is prevalent for experts, but not for novices. The results also supports that the experts' use of established schemata explains this particular moderating effect. Schematic processing of stimuli information mediates the moderating effect of expertise on the incongruity effect. This result strongly suggests that the incongruity effect is a schema-level phenomenon and that this effect should not be expected when piecemeal processing of stimuli information is likely.

General Discussion

An inverted U-shaped relationship between the moderate incongruity effect and expertise may account for the findings in both the Peracchio and Tybout (1996) study and this study. The effect reported in both studies is observed for moderate levels of expertise. For extremely low levels of expertise (i.e. novices) there is no incongruity effect because no schema is developed to assess (in)congruent stimuli. For moderate expertise levels a developed schema to assess (in)congruent stimuli exists and therefore also an accompanying incongruity effect. For extremely high expertise levels the schema structure is so extensively developed that incongruity is resolved without much cognitive effort and with no incongruity effect as a result. In the domain of desserts, most people have developed at least some schema-structure, hence the Peracchio and Tybout (1996) finding that the incongruity effect occurs for novices. In the wine domain few people have developed schema structures that are extensive enough to automatically resolve incongruity, hence the finding that experts can face incongruity and display the incongruity effect. This inverted-U interpretation is supported by a reanalysis of the data across Study 1 and Study 2.

REFERENCES

Alba, Joseph. W. and Wesley J. Hutchinson (1987). Dimensions of Consumer Expertise. *Journal of Consumer Research,* 13 (March), 411-54.

Ballester, Jordi, Hervé Abdi, Jennifer Langlois, Dominique Peyron, and Dominique Valentin (2009), "The Odor of Colors: Can Wine Experts and Novices Distinguish the Odors of White, Red, and Rosé Wines?" *Chemosensory perceptions*, 2 (4), 203-213.

Campbell, Margaret and Ronald C. Goodstein (2001), "The Moderating Effect of Perceived Risk on Consumers' Evaluations of Product Incongruity: Preference for the Norm," *Journal of Consumer Research,* 28 (December), 439-449.

Chi, Michelene T. H., Paul J. Feltovich, and Robert Glaser (1981), "Categorization and Representation of Physics Problems by Experts and Novices," *Cognitive Science,* 5, 121-5.

Cohen, Joel B. and Kunal Basu (1987), "Alternative Models of Categorization: Toward a Contingent Processing Framework," *Journal of Consumer Research,* 13 (March), 455-72.

Ericsson, Anders K., Ralf Th. Krampe, and Clemens Tesch-Romer (1993), "The role of deliberate practice in the acquisition of expert performance," *Psychological Review*, 100 (3): 363-406.

--- and Andreas C. Lehmann (1996), 'Expert and exceptional performance: Evidence on maximal adaptations on task constraints.' *Annual Review of Psychology*, 47: 273-305.

Fiske, Susan T. and Mark A. Pavelchak (1986), "Category-Based versus Piecemeal-Based Affective Responses: Developments in Schema-Triggered Affect," in *The Handbook of Motivations and Cognition: Foundations of Social Behavior*, eds. Richard M. Sorrentino and E. Tory Higgins, New York: Guilford, 167-203.

---, Donald R. Kinder, and W. Michael Larter (1983), "The Novice and the Expert: Knowledge Based Strategies in political Cognition," *Journal of Experimental Social Psychology*, 19 (4), 381-400.

Hughson, Angus L. and Robert A. Boakes (2002), "The knowing nose: The role of knowledge in wine expertise. *Journal of Food Quality and Preference*, 13 (7-8), 463 – 472.

Lawless, Harry T. (1984), "Flavour description of white wine by "expert" and nonexpert wine consumers," *Journal of Food Science* 49, 120–123.

Lehrer, Adrienne (1983), *Wine and Conversation*. Bloomington: Indiana University Press.

Mandler, George P. (1982), "The structure of value: Accounting for Taste," in *Affect and Cognition: The 17th Annual Carnegies Symposium on Cognition,* eds. Margaret S. Clark and Susan T. Fiske, Hillsdale NJ: Lawrence Erlbaum, 3-36.

Maoz, Eyal and Alice M. Tybout (2002), "The Moderating Role of Involvement and Differentiation in the Evaluation of Brand Extensions," Journal of Consumer Psychology, 12 (2), 119-131.

Meyers-Levy, Joan and Alice Tybout (1989), "Schema Congruity as a Basis for Product Evaluation," *Journal of Consumer Research*, 16 (June), 39-54.

---, Therese A. Louie, and Mary T. Curren (1994), "How Does the Congruity of Brand Names Affect Evaluations of Brand Name Extensions?" *Journal of Applied Psychology,* 79 (1), 46-53.

Mitchell, Andrew A. and Peter F. Dacin (1996), "The Assessment of Alternative Measures of Consumer Expertise,"*Journal of Consumer Research,* Vol 23 (December), 219-39.

Mitchell, Deborah J., Barbra E. Kahn, and Susan C. Knasko (1995), "There's something in the air: effects of congruent and incongruent ambient odor on consumer decision making," *Journal of Consumer Research*, 22 (2), 229-238.

--- and Edward E. Smith (1982), "Basic level superiority in picture categorization," *Journal of Verbal Learning and Verbal Behavior*, 21 (1), 1-20.

Parr, Wendy V., David Heatherbell, and K. Geoffrey White (2002), "Demystifying Wine Expertise: Olfactory Threshold, Perceptual Skill and Semantic Memory in Expert and Novice Wine Judges" Chemical Senses, 27 (8), 747-755.

Peracchio, Laura A. and Alice M. Tybout (1996), "The Moderating Role of Prior Knowledge in Schema-Based Product Evaluation," *Journal of Consumer Research, 23* (December), 177-192.

Solomon, Gregg (1990), "Psychology of novice and expert wine talk," *American Journal of Psychology,* 105, 495–517.

--- (1997), "Conceptual change and wine expertise," *The Journal of the Learning Sciences,* 6, pp. 41–60.

Stayman, Douglas M., Dana L. Alden, and Karen H. Smith (1992), "Some Effects of Schematic Processing on Consumer Expectations and Disconfirmation Judgments," *Journal of Consumer Research,* 19 (September), 240–255.

Sujan, Mita (1985). "Consumer knowledge: Effects on Evaluation Strategies Mediating Consumer Judgments," *Journal of Consumer Research,* 12 (June), 31-46.

Sex Matters: The Effect of Brand Gender on Brand Equity

Theo Lieven, University of St. Gallen, Switzerland
Andreas Herrmann, St. Gallen Universität, Switzerland
Jan R. Landwehr, University of St. Gallen, Switzerland
Miriam van Tilburg, University of St. Gallen, Switzerland

EXTENDED ABSTRACT

Brand equity is a key concept in both theoretical and applied studies of marketing (Aaker and Keller 1990; Farquhar 1989; Keller 1993, 2008). This is not surprising, as numerous papers show that a high brand equity contributes decisively to improving consumer satisfaction with and loyalty to the brand and to enabling higher prices for the brand (Aaker 1991, 1996; Park and Srinivasan 1994). Existing research has contributed strongly to the understanding of the determinants of brand equity and identified a brand's personality as one such determinant (Aaker and Biel 1993; Aaker 1997). Like the "big five" model of human personality (Goldberg 1990), brand personality is measured along five dimensions (sincerity, excitement, competence, sophistication, and ruggedness) that apply to consumers' characterization of brands (Aaker 1997). Consumers associate human personality characteristics with brands, because they perceive brands as extensions of their selves (Belk 1988; Gilmore 1919, 2008; Harvey 2005) or because marketers suggest that brands have certain characteristics (Fournier 1998).

Although these personality characteristics certainly impact the perceived attractiveness of a brand, evolutionary psychology papers suggest that the intensity with which an individual expresses his or her gender to other people plays a particularly key role in the perceived attractiveness of this person (Kaplan and Gangestad 2005; Grammer et al. 2003). This is based on the finding that human judgments about the attractiveness of individuals fundamentally represent the result of a process of sexual selection. This selection process favors men who, from the point of view of women, look typically masculine, and women who, from the perspective of men, appear typically feminine. Masculinity and femininity can be linked to very specific physical features, e.g., the waist-to-hip ratio for women and the V-shaped torso for men (Furnham and Radely 1989). According to evolutionary psychological findings, this sexual selection process is so deeply anchored in the decision-making behavior of individuals that one can propose an influence of these principles on the brand choice of consumers (Buss 1994).

Since brands can be equipped with personality characteristics, it should also be possible to equip them with a certain level of masculinity or femininity. An initial paper on this subject (Grohmann 2009) provides insights into the validity of the brand gender construct and the relationship between brand gender and brand perception. However, three key questions have remained unanswered: Whether there is a direct relationship between brand gender perception and brand equity, which features of a brand express its masculinity or femininity, and how these features should be designed to provide an increased expression of an intended brand gender.

The present research is intended to fill these gaps, at least in part. Two studies have been conducted to address these questions. The aim of the first study is to investigate whether the perceived gender of 73 existing brands has an effect on their equity. The inventory developed by Grohmann (2009) serves to detect the gender of a brand. The brand assessment system of a leading market research company can be used as a proxy for brand equity. This analysis provides information on the relative impact of a brand's gender on its equity by showing that a pronounced brand gender is a key driver of brand equity.

The second study aims at investigating the features that characterize masculine and feminine brands. For this purpose, the logos of 73 brands were assessed by individuals with respect to several criteria (e.g., solid versus airy, edged versus curved). These judgments can be connected with the assessments of consumers in study one concerning the perceived brand gender. The results of this study offer concrete information for brand managers concerning which features of a logo should be changed and how, so that the brand conveys the intended degree of masculinity or femininity to consumers. Furthermore, the second study offers theoretical insights regarding the extent to which findings from evolutionary psychology about the significance of individual physical features can be applied to the design of brand logos. Taken together, these two studies serve to show brand managers the repertoire of activities that can be used to intensify perceptions of brand gender and thereby to increase brand equity.

In sum, the findings of the two studies imply that evolutionary based insights about determinants of gender perception in human beings can be applied to brand logo design. This finding stresses the importance of biological shapes and proportions for the design of artifacts in order to achieve an intended perception. In terms of future research, it would be interesting to explore critical boundary conditions and interactions. In this respect, investigating the gender of the product category or of the consumer and their relationship to brand gender would be promising avenues for subsequent research endeavors.

CSR Wins the Cup – How Social Activities Leverage Commercial Sponsorships

Sebastian Uhrich, University of Rostock, Germany
Joerg Koenigstorfer, Pennsylvania State University, USA
Andrea Groeppel-Klein, Saarland University, Germany

EXTENDED ABSTRACT

Sponsors of mega-events are increasingly linking such events to activities in the area corporate social responsibility (IEG 2010). This is because more and more developing countries are hosting mega-events and consumers increasingly expect brands to behave in an ethical manner. CSR-linked sponsorship may positively influence brand perceptions where consumers perceive this engagement to be sincere and the cause worth supporting (Lacey, Close, and Finney 2010; Sen and Bhattacharya 2001). Altruistic motive attribution – a key variable accounting for the success of sponsorships (Rifon et al. 2004) – may mediate this influence and thus leverage the sponsorship. However, it is also possible that the linking of CSR and sponsorship is perceived as thematically incompatible by consumers and causes reactance. It may, for instance, lead to suspicion and skepticism about the reasons why the brand is engaging in social activities (Vlachos et al. 2009), particularly in the case of highly commercialized mega-events such as the Olympic Games, the FIFA World Cup or the Super Bowl.

In this research we examine whether linking the sponsorship of commercial events with CSR activities results in more favorable brand perceptions than commercial sponsorship on its own. We consider the mediating role of altruistic motive attributions for sponsorship and the moderating roles of congruence between sponsors and events, and commitment to CSR. As far as we are aware, this is the first piece of research investigating the effects of a combined CSR/sponsorship strategy from a consumer perspective.

Consumers' perceptions of brands can be influenced positively by social initiatives (Barone, Miyazaki, and Taylor 2000; Ellen, Mohr, and Webb 2000; Sen and Bhattacharya 2001). In a pilot field study looking at the soccer World Cup 2010 in South Africa, we tested the basic proposition that consumers' attitudes to a brand are more positive when they are aware of both the brand's engagement as a sponsor and its parallel social activities, compared to when they are aware of just the sponsorship activities or aware of neither the sponsorship nor the social activities.

A total of 448 individuals participated in the initial field study. Through personal interviews we identified consumers' recognition of the sponsorship activities and CSR, brand attitudes and brand familiarity. We looked at several brands, including both brands belonging to official sponsors of the World Cup and foils. We found that consumers who were aware of both the sponsorship and the CSR activities reported significantly more positive brand attitudes than those who were only aware of the sponsorship activity or aware of neither the sponsorship nor the social CSR activities. The brand *adidas* was the only brand for which this relationship did not hold.

We then provide theoretical background for the effects of linking social activities with sponsorship and investigate the role of potential mediators and moderators. We hypothesized that increases in altruistic motive attributions for the sponsorship mediate the effects of CSR-linked sponsorship communication, and perceived sponsor-event congruence moderates these effects. We base these assumptions on schema and attribution theory, applied to sponsorship-linked marketing (Cornwell et al. 2006; Menon and Kahn 2003).

A total of 127 students participated in a first laboratory experiment applying a one-factorial (content of communication: standard sponsorship *versus* CSR-linked sponsorship; control: CSR) between-subjects design. Sponsor-event congruence was measured via an established scale as a continuous variable. We used press releases about several brands, including the target brand *Sony*, as experimental stimuli. Participants were unaware of the purpose of the study.

ANOVA results show that CSR-linked (*versus* standard sponsorship) sponsorship communication had a positive effect on brand attitude shifts and consumers' CSR perceptions of the brand, whereas brand credibility and the general behavioral tendency to recommend the brand as an employer were not directly affected. However, mediation analyses reveal that CSR-linked sponsorship communication increases attributions of altruistic sponsorship motives, and that this effect mediates the positive effects on all dependent variables. In addition, the results of moderated regressions show that the perception of low congruence of the brand with the sponsored event positively affects the linking of sponsorship information with CSR.

In a second laboratory experiment we investigated whether brands engaging in CSR-linked sponsorship communication can benefit from demonstrating a high level of commitment to social activities, and how these effects are moderated by sponsor-event congruence. As in experiment 1, we used press releases for manipulation purposes. Based on the results of several pretests, we selected *adidas* to represent high-congruence brands and *Coca-Cola* to represent low-congruence brands.

Tests of the indirect effects of CSR commitment on the dependent variables through consumers' attributions of altruistic sponsorship motives show that motive attributions account for the positive effects on perceptions of both the brand and the sponsorship. However, a high level of CSR commitment had negative direct effects on CSR perceptions, brand credibility and sponsorship credibility. Furthermore, a tactical decrease in a brand's commitment to CSR when linked to event sponsorship was more harmful to low-congruence brands than to high-congruence brands.

The results imply that a CSR-linked sponsorship strategy is particularly promising for brands with a low natural congruence to the event, where these brands follow a long-term CSR strategy. For such brands, social engagement adds meaning to the brand. If high-congruence sponsors follow such a strategy, they should ensure that the social engagement is not in conflict with consumers' expectations of the brand's behavior in relation to the event, otherwise the unexpectedness of this information may destroy consumers' consistent and harmonious beliefs about the brand.

CSR-linked sponsorship may become more and more important in the future, particularly as consumers from developing countries represent a growing target group. Through CSR-linked sponsorship, such consumers may feel that they benefit directly from the sponsor's engagement. Moreover, consumers in industrialized countries may attribute good corporate citizenship to brands that follow such a combined strategy.

REFERENCES

Anderson, John R. and Gordon H. Bower (1973), *Human Associative Memory*, Washington, DC: Winston.

Barone, Michael J., Paul W. Miniard, and Jean B. Romeo (2000), "The Influence of Positive Mood on Brand Extension Evaluations," *Journal of Consumer Research*, 26 (4), 386-400.

Batra, Rajeev, Venkatram Ramaswamy, Dana L. Alden, Jan-Benedict E. M. Steenkamp, and S. Ramachander (2000), "Effects of Brand Local and Nonlocal Origin on Consumer Attitudes in Developing Countries," *Journal of Consumer Psychology*, 9 (2), 83-95.

Becker-Olsen, Karen L. Cudmore, and Ronald P. Hill (2006), "The Impact of Sponsor Fit on Brand Equity: The Case of Nonprofit Service Providers," *Journal of Service Research*, 9 (1), 73-83.

Coppetti, Caspar, Daniel Wentzel, Torsten Tomczak, and Sven Henkel (2009), "Improving Incongruent Sponsorships through Articulation of the Sponsorship and Audience Participation," *Journal of Marketing Communications*, 15 (1), 17-34.

Cornwell, T. Bettina (1995), "Sponsorship-linked Marketing Development," *Sport Marketing Quarterly*, 4 (4), 13-24.

Cornwell, T. Bettina (2008), "State of the Art and Science in Sponsorship-linked Marketing," *Journal of Advertising*, 37 (3), 41-55.

Cornwell, T. Bettina, Clinton S. Weeks, and Donald P. Roy (2005), "Sponsorship-linked Marketing: Opening the Black Box," *Journal of Advertising*, 34 (2), 21-42.

Cornwell, T. Bettina, Michael S. Humphreys, Angela M. Maguire, Clinton S. Weeks, and Cassandra L. Tellegen (2006), "Sponsorship-linked Marketing: The Role of Articulation in Memory," *Journal of Consumer Research*, 33 (3), 312-21.

Du, Shuili, C. B. Bhattacharya, and Sankar Sen (2007), "Reaping Relational Rewards from Corporate Social Responsibility: The Role of Competitive Positioning," *International Journal of Research in Marketing*, 24 (3), 224-41.

Ellen, Pam S., Lois A. Mohr, and Deborah J. Webb (2000), "Charitable Programs and the Retailer: Do They Mix?" *Journal of Retailing*, 76 (3), 393-406.

Ellen, Pam S., Deborah J. Webb, and Lois A. Mohr (2006), "Building Corporate Associations: Consumer Attributions for Corporate Socially Responsible Programs," *Journal of the Academy of Marketing Science*, 34 (2), 147-57.

FIFA (2010a), "adidas: Encouraging Learning," http://www.fifa.com/worldcup/news/newsid=1187386/index.html.

FIFA (2010b), "Protection of the Environment," http://de.fifa.com/worldcup/organisation/ticketfund/partners/cocacola.html.

Fleck, Nathalie D. and Pascale Quester (2007), "Birds of a Feather Flock together ... Definition, Role and Measure of Congruence: An Application to Sponsorship," *Psychology & Marketing*, 24 (11), 975-1000.

Gwinner, Kevin and John Eaton (1999), "Building Brand Image through Event Sponsorship: The Role of Image Transfer," *Journal of Advertising*, 28 (4), 47-57.

Hollis (2010), "Football Sponsorship," http://www.hollis-sponsorship.com/features06.asp.

IEG (2010), *Sponsorship Report*, Chicago, IL: IEG.

Kelley, Harold H. and John L. Michela (1980), "Attribution Theory and Research," *Annual Review of Psychology*, 31 (January), 457-501.

Lacey, Russell, Angeline G. Close, and R. Zachary Finney (2010), "The Pivotal Roles of Product Knowledge and Corporate Social Responsibility in Event Sponsorship effectiveness," *Journal of Business Research*, 63 (11), 1222-8.

Lee, Myung-Soo, Dennis M. Sandler, and David Shani (1997), "Attitudinal Constructs towards Sponsorship – Scale Development Using three Global Sporting Events," *International Marketing Review*, 14 (3), 159-69.

MacKenzie, Scott B. and Richard J. Lutz (1989), "An empirical examination of the structural antecedents of attitude toward the ad in an advertising pretesting context," *Journal of Marketing*, 53 (2), 48-65.

Madrigal, Robert M. (2008), "Hot vs. Cold Cognitions and Consumers' Reactions to Sporting Event Outcomes," *Journal of Consumer Psychology*, 18 (4), 304-19.

McDaniel, Stephen R. (1999), "An Investigation of the Match-up Effects in Sport Sponsorship Advertising: The Implications of Consumer Advertising Schemas," *Psychology & Marketing*, 16 (2), 163-84.

Menon, Satya and Barbara E. Kahn (2003), "Corporate Sponsorships of Philanthropic Activities: When do They Impact Perception of Sponsor Brand?" *Journal of Consumer Psychology*, 13 (3), 316-27.

Meyers-Levy, Joan, Therese A. Louie, and Mary T. Curren (1994), "How Does the Congruity of Brand Names Affect Evaluations of Brand Name Extensions?" *Journal of Applied Psychology*, 79 (1), 46-53.

Preacher, Kristopher J. and Andrew F. Hayes (2008), "Asymptotic and Resampling Strategies for Assessing and Comparing Indirect Effects in Multiple Mediator Models," *Behavior Research Methods*, 40 (3), 879-91.

Preacher, Kristopher J., Derek D. Rucker, and Andrew F. Hayes (2007), "Addressing Moderated Mediation Hypotheses: Theory, Methods, and Prescriptions," *Multivariate Behavioral Research*, 42 (1), 185-227.

Quester, Pascale G. and Beverley Thompson (2001), "Advertising and Promotion Leverage on Arts Sponsorship Effectiveness," *Journal of Advertising Research*, 41 (1), 33-47.

Rifon, Nora J., Sejung Marina Choi, Carrie S. Trimble, and Hairong Li (2004), "Congruence Effects in Sponsorship: The Mediating Role of Sponsor Credibility and Consumer Attributions of Sponsor Motive," *Journal of Advertising*, 33 (1), 29-43.

Roy, Donald P. and T. Bettina Cornwell (2003), "Brand Equity's Influence on Responses to Event Sponsorships," *Journal of Product and Brand Management*, 12 (6), 377-93.

Sen, Sankar and C. B. Bhattacharya (2001), "Does Doing Good Always Lead to Doing Better? Consumer Reactions to Corporate Social Responsibility," *Journal of Marketing Research*, 38 (2), 225-43.

Sen, Sankar, C. B. Bhattacharya, and Daniel Korschun (2006), "The Role of Corporate Social Responsibility in Strengthening Multiple Stakeholder Relationships: A Field Experiment," *Journal of the Academy of Marketing Science*, 34 (2), 158-66.

Simmons, Carolyn J. and Karen L. Becker-Olsen (2006), "Achieving Marketing Objectives through Social Sponsorships," *Journal of Marketing*, 70 (4), 154-69.

Speed, Richard and Peter Thompson (2000), "Determinants of Sport Sponsorship Response," *Journal of the Academy of Marketing Science*, 28 (2), 226-38.

van den Brink, Douwe, Gaby Odekerken-Schröder, and Pieter Pauwels (2006), "The Effect of Strategic and Tactical Cause-related Marketing on Consumers' Brand Loyalty," *Journal of Consumer Marketing*, 23 (1), 15-26.

Vlachos, Pavlos A., Argiris Tsamakos, Adam P. Vrechopoulos, and Panagiotis K. Avramidis (2009), "Corporate Social Responsibility: Attributions, Loyalty, and the Mediating Role of Trust," *Journal of the Academy of Marketing Science*, 37 (2), 170-80.

Wakefield, Kirk L., Karen L. Becker-Olsen, and T. Bettina Cornwell (2007), "I Spy a Sponsor. The Effects of Sponsorship Level, Prominence, Relatedness, and Cueing on Recall Accuracy," *Journal of Advertising*, 36 (4), 61-74.

Walker, Matthew, Bob Heere, Milena Parent, and Dan Drane (2010), "Social Responsibility and the Olympic Games: The Mediating Role of Consumer Attributions," *Journal of Business Ethics*, 95 (4), 659-80.

Webb, Deborah J. and Lois A. Mohr (1998), "A Typology of Consumer Responses to Cause-related Marketing: From Skeptics to Socially Concerned?" *Journal of Public Policy and Marketing*, 17 (Fall), 226-38.

Weeks, Clinton S., T. Bettina Cornwell, and Judy C. Drennan (2008), "Leveraging Sponsorships on the Internet: Activation, Congruence, and Articulation," *Psychology & Marketing*, 25 (7), 637-54.

Weiner, Bernard (1989), *Human Motivation*, Hillsdale, NJ: Lawrence Erlbaum Associates.

Zhao, Xinshu, John G. Lynch JR, and Qimei Chen (2010), "Reconsidering Baron and Kenny: Myths and Truths about Mediation Analysis," *Journal of Consumer Research*, 37 (2), 197-206.

Exploring the Influence of Ambient Temperature on Cognitive Task Performance

Luqiong Tong, Tsinghua University, China
Rui (Juliet) Zhu, University of British Columbia, Canada
Yuhuang Zheng, Tsinghua University, China
Ping Zhao, Tsinghua University, China

EXTENDED ABSTRACT

Although both practitioners and academics agree that temperature is important in affecting human cognition and behavior (Goldman, 2001; Hancock *et al.*, 2007), mixed results have been observed in the literature with regards with which or what range of temperature will facilitate cognitive task performances (Ramsey, 1995). While some research suggests that warmer temperatures enhance performance (Chiles, 1958; Pepler and Warner, 1968), some others suggest the opposite (Coleshaw *et al.*, 1983; Thomas *et al.*, 1989). Further, prior research efforts in this domain are limited in a number of dimensions. For example, they have focused on extreme temperatures (i.e., higher than 30 Celsius or lower than 10 Celsius; note that human's comfortable temperature range is between 16 to 29 Celsius, Baker and Cameron 1996), and have included predominately simple tasks, such as word memory and figure matching.

This research aims to address these limitations and therefore advance our understanding on the impact of temperature on task performance. Specifically, we examine how warm versus cool temperature, both within a comfortable range and are commonly experienced, can affect people's performance on simple as well as complex tasks.

Prior research on temperature suggests that heat, which can induce thermal stress, competes for attentional resource and consequently hurts task performance (e.g., Hancock and Warm 1989). Thus, compared to individuals in the cool temperature condition, those in the warm temperature condition should have less attentional resource towards the focal task (Enander 1984, 1986).

A separate line of research has shown that different amounts of attentional resource allocated to the focal task can prompt alternative thinking modes. While abundant attentional resource to the focal task usually results in primarily conscious thinking, limited attentional resource is likely to prompt more unconscious thinking (Dijksterhuis et al. 2006). Thus, we expect that those in the warm (cool) temperature condition, which leads to limited (abundant) attentional resource to the focal task, would be more likely to engage in unconscious (conscious) thinking.

Finally, extant research has documented beneficial effects of unconscious thinking on complex task performance (Dijksterhuis and Nordgren 2006). Specifically, unlike conscious thoughts, which have limited processing capacity, unconscious thoughts don't suffer from the capacity constrain, so unconscious thinking mode can benefit complex tasks. Combing the preceding notions, we hypothesize that warm versus cool temperature would enhance individuals' performance on complex tasks. However, such an effect should be attenuated for simple tasks.

Two laboratory studies were conducted which provided systematic support to our hypothesis. Study 1A and 1B demonstrated the basic effect of temperature on task performances. Specifically, study 1A used 3 (temperature: warm vs. moderate vs. cool) * 2 (task complexity: simple vs. complex) between-subject design. The task used was a classic choice task, which requires participants to select their preferred lottery from four different options (Payne *et al.*, 2008). Options were defined by payoffs for 12 equiprobable events defined by drawing 1 of 4 numbered balls (simple condition) or 1 of 12 numbered balls (complex condition) from a bingo cage. Among the four options, one option had the highest expected value, which represents the correct answer. The study was run with no more than four people per session. The same lab was used, but the temperature was set to warm (25-26 Celsius), moderate (21-22 Celsius), or cool (16-17 Celsius). These temperature conditions followed the comfortable temperature boundaries in Baker & Cameron (1996). Results confirmed our hypothesis, such that when the task was complex, a significantly higher percentage of individuals in the warm temperature condition selected the correct lottery (thus indicating better task performance) than those in the low or moderate temperature condition. However, we did not observe any treatment effect when the task was simple.

Study 1B was a theoretical replication of study1A. By using a different task, we again demonstrated that warm versus cool temperature led to better performance on difficult tasks. Furthermore, additional measures taken in both studies ruled out a number of alternative explanations, such as mood, arousal, and involvement.

Study 2 aimed to shed light to the underlying mechanism. If warm temperature leads to more unconscious thinking and consequently enhances performance on complex tasks, then we should observe equally well performance under the cool temperature if we prompt people to enter the unconscious thinking mode in that condition. Prior research has shown that working memory load manipulation can lead to distraction, and thus reduced attentional resource to the focal task (Lavie, Hirst, and Fockert 2004). So, if we encourage individuals in the cool temperature condition to engage in unconscious thinking by a high load manipulation, they should perform on complex tasks equally well as those in the warm temperature condition. Thus, in this study, we first administered a seemingly unrelated task which varied in memory load in a neutral temperature room. Specifically, participants were asked to remember either a 2-digit number (low load) or an 8-digit number (high load, which would encourage unconscious thinking) throughout the entire study. Then they were escorted to the main lab where temperature was set to warm or cool. The focal task involved the same complex lottery task as in study 1A.

Results supported our theorizing. In particular, for those in the low memory load condition (i.e., people are primarily engaging in conscious thinking before entering the main lab which varied in temperature), we replicated earlier results. That is, warm temperature led to better performance. However, for those who were in the high memory load condition, they performed equally well whether they completed the focal task in warm or cool temperature room, presumably because the high memory load manipulation has prompted them to engage in unconscious thinking, which mitigated the effect of temperature.

Findings from this research make several important contributions. Foremost, they advance our understanding of the impact of ambient temperature on human cognition, esp. task performance. Second, we offer explanation as well empirical evidence with regards to the underlying process that drives these effects. Finally, this research offers practical implications in terms of setting up optimal ambient temperatures in various environments.

REFERENCES

Allan, J. R., T. M. Gibson and R. G. Green (1979), "Effects of Induced Cyclic Changes of Deep Body Temperature on Task Performance", *Aviation, Space and Environmental Medicine*, 50, 585 - 589.

Allen, Margaret A., and Gloria J. Fischer (1978), "Ambient Temperature Effect on Paired Associate Learning", *Ergonomics*, 21, 95-101

Ahn, Hee-Kyung., Nina Mazar, and Dilip Soman (2010), "Being Hot or Being Cold: the Influence of Temperature on Judgement and Choice", in Advances in Consumer Research Volume 37, eds. Margaret C. Campbell, Jeff Inman, and Rik Pieters, Duluth, MN : Association for Consumer Research

Baker, Julie and Michaelle Cameron (1996), "The Effects of the Service Environment on Affect and Consumer Perception of Waiting Time: An Integrative Review and Research Propositions", *Journal of the Academy of Marketing Science*, 24 (4), 338-49.

Cheema, Amar and Vanessa M. Patrick (2011), "Influence of Warm (versus Cool) Temperatures on Consumer Risk-Taking: a Resource Depletion Account", Working paper.

Chiles, W. D. (1958), "Effects of Elevated Temperatures on Performance of a Complex Mental Task", *Ergonomics*, 2, 89-96.

Coleshaw, S. R. K, R. N. M. Van Someren, A. H. Wolff, H. M. Davis, and W. R. Keatinge (1983), "Impaired Memory Registration and Speed of Reasoning Caused by Low Body Temperature", *Journal of Applied Physiology*, 55(1), 27-31

Cunningham, Michael R. (1979), "Weather, Mood, and Helping Behavior: Quasi Experiments with the Sunshine Samaritan", *Journal of Personality and Social Psychology*, 37(11), 1947-1956

De Fockert, Jan. W., Geraint Ree, Christopher D. Frith, and Nilli Lavie (2001), "The Role of Working Memory in Visual Selective Attention", *Science*, 291, 1803–1806

Dijksterhuis, Ap (2004), "Think different: The merits of unconscious thought in preference development and decision making", *Journal of Personality and Social Psychology*, 87, 586–598.

Dijksterhuis, Ap., Maarten W.Bos, Loran F.Nordgren, and Rick B.van Baaren (2006), "On making the right choice: The deliberation-without attention effect", *Science*, 311, 1005–1007.

Dijksterhuis, Ap., and Loran F. Nordgren (2006), "A Theory of Unconscious Thought", *Perspectives on Psychological Science*, 1, 95-109.

Duffy, Elizabeth (1962), *Activation and Behavior*, New York: Wiley

Enander, Ann. E. (1984), "Performance and sensory aspects of work in cold environments: A review", *Ergonomics*, 27, 365–378.

Enander, Ann. E. (1986), "Sensory reactions and performance in moderate cold", Unpublished doctoral dissertation, University of Uppsala, Uppsala, Sweden

Goldman, Ralph. F (2001), "Introduction to Heat-related Problems in Military Operations", In K. B. Pandolf, R. E. Burr, C. B. Wenger, & R. S. Pozos (Eds.), *Medical aspects of harsh environments.* (pp. 3–49). Washington, DC: Borden Institute.

Grether Walter. F. (1973), "Human Performance at Elevated Environmental Temperatures," *Aerospace Medicine*, 44(1), 747-55

Hancock, Peter A. (1982), "Task Categorization and the Limits of Human Performance in Extreme Heat", *Aviation, Space and Environmental Medicine*, 53, 778 - 784.

Hancock, Peter A. (1986), "Sustained Attention under Thermal Stress", *Psychological Bulletin*, 99(2), 263-281

Hancock, Peter A., and I. Vasmatzidis (1998), "Human Occupational and Performance Limits under Stress: the Thermal Environment as a Prototypical Example," *Ergonomic*, 41(8), 1169-1191

Hancock Peter A., and I. Vasmatzidis (2003), "Effects of Heat Stress on Cognitive Performance: The Current State of Knowledge," *International Journal of Hyperthermia*, 19(3), 355-72.

Hancock, Peter. A., Jennifer M. Ross, and James L. Szalma (2007), "A Meta-analysis of Performance Response under Thermal Stressors", *Human Factors*, 49(5), 851-877

Hancock Peter A. and Joel S. Warm (1989), "A Dynamic Model of Stress and Sustained Attention," Human Factors, 31, 5 (October), 519-37

Howarth, E. and M. S. Hoffman (1984), "A Multidimensional Approach to the Relationship between Mood and Weather", *British Journal of Psychology*, 75, 15-23

Ijzerman, Hans and Gun R. Semin (2009), "The Thermometer of Social Relations," *Psychological Science,* 20 (10), 1214-20.

Kahneman, Daniel. (1973), *Attention and effort*, Englewood Cliffs, NJ: Prentice-Hall.

Keller, Matthew C., Barbara L. Fredrickson, Oscar Ybarra, Stephane Cote, Kareem Johnson, Joe Mikels, Anne Conway, and Tor Wager (2005), "A Warm Heat and a Clear Head", *Psychological Science*, 16(9), 724-731

Lavie, Nilli, Aleksandra Hirst, Jan W. de Focket and Essi Viding (2004), "Load Theory of Selective Attention and Cognitive Control", *Journal of Experimental Psychology: General*, 133(3), 339-354

Levav, Jonathan and Rui J. Zhu (2009), "Seeking Freedom through Variety," *Journal of Consumer Research*, 36, 600-610.

National Institute for Occupational Safety and Health (NIOSH) 1980, NIOSH publication no. 81-08, Proceedings of a Workshop on Recommended Heat Stress Standards, F. N. Dukes-Dobos and A. Henschel (eds). (Cincinnati, OH: NIOSH).

Payne, John W., Adriana Samper, James R. Bettman, and Mary Frances Luce (2008), "Boundary Conditions on Unconscious Thought in Complex Decision Making", *Psychological Science*, 19(11), 1118-1123.

Pepler, R. D. and R. E. Warner (1968), "Temperature and Learning: An Experimental Study," Paper No 2089, Transactions of the ASHRAE Annual Meeting, Lake Placid, 1967, 42, 211-19.

Plicher, June J., Eric Nadler and Caroline Bush (2002), "Effects of Hot and Cold Temperature Exposure on Performance: a Meta-Analytic Review", *Ergonomics*, 45(10), 682-698.

Praff, Donald (1968), "Effects of Temperature and Time of Day on Time Judgments", *Journal of Experimental Psychology*, 76(3), 419-422.

Ramsey, Jerry D. (1995), "Task Performance in Heat: A Review", Ergonomics, 38(1), 154-165

Ramsey, Jerry D., Charles L. Burford, Mohamed Youssef Beshir, and Roger C. Jensen (1983), "Effect of Workplace Thermal Conditions on Safe Work Behavior", *Journal of Safety Research*, 14, 105-114

Schaller, Mark and Damian R. Murray (2008), "Pathogens, Personality and Culture: Disease Prevalence Predicts Worldwide Variability in Socio-sexuality, Extraversion, and Openness to Experience," *Journal of Personality and Social Psychology*, 95 (1), 212-21.

Seppänen, Olli, William J. Fisk and Q.H. Lei (2006), "Room Temperature and Productivity in Office Work," Working Paper LBNL-60952

Sternberg, S. (1966), "High-speed Scanning in Human Memory", *Science*, 153, 652–654.

Thomas, John.R., Stephen T. Ahlers, John F. House and John Schrot (1989), "Repeated Exposure to Moderate Cold Impairs Matching-to-sample Performance", *Aviation Space Environment Medicine*, 60(11), 1063-1067.

Watson, David (2000), *Situational and Environmental Influence on Mood*, New York: Guilford.

Williams, Lawrence E. and John A. Bargh (2008), "Experiencing Physical Warmth Promotes Interpersonal Warmth", *Science*, 322, 606-607

Wyon, David. P., M D. Andersen and Gunnar R. Lundqvist(1979), "The Effects of Moderate Heat Stress on Mental Performance", *Scandinavian Journal of Work, Environment & Health*, 5, 352-361.

Zhu, Rui and Joan Meyers-Levy (2009), "The Influence of Self-View on Context Effects: How Display Fixtures Can Affect Product Evaluations," *Journal of Marketing Research*, 46, 37-45.

Enjoy! Hedonic Consumption and Compliance with Assertive Messages

Ann Kronrod, MIT, USA
Amir Grinstein, Ben-Gurion University, Israel
Luc Wathieu, Georgetown University, USA

EXTENDED ABSTRACT

Consumers are often exposed to forceful messages and imperative slogans such as Nike's "Just do it," Sprite's "Obey your thirst," or U.S. Airways' "Fly with US." The frequent use of assertively phrased messages is puzzling, given the mounting research in consumer behavior (e.g., Dillard and Shen 2005; Fitzsimons and Lehman 2004; Lord 1994), communications (e.g., Kellerman and Shea 1996; Quick and Considine 2008; Quick and Stephenson 2007; Wilson and Kunkel 2000), and socio-linguistics (e.g., Levine and Boster 2001; Sanders and Fitch 2001), which suggests that these messages should lower consumer readiness to comply.

To understand the unexpected prevalence of assertive language, we turn to socio-linguistic literature on the language used in compliance-seeking requests. Research has found that people in positive mood tend to use more assertive language in their requests (e.g., Forgas 1997). Correspondingly, people in positive mood expect to be addressed with more direct and assertive language (Bloch 1996; Forgas 1999a, 1999b). This matching pattern appears consistent with language behavior literature which demonstrates that higher compliance occurs when the language of requests fits the receiver's expectations (e.g., Brown and Levinson 1987; Forgas 1998).

Building on this logic, we suggest in this paper that assertive messages are more persuasive than non-assertive messages when they relate to consumption contexts that induce positive mood. In particular, we focus on hedonic consumption, which commonly elicits positive mood (Chaudhuri and Holbrook 2001). We suggest a conceptual model where the effectiveness of assertive messages regarding hedonic products, or products that are framed hedonically, is higher than the effectiveness of non-assertive messages. By contrast, in baseline utilitarian consumption contexts, non-assertive phrasing should yield higher compliance. We explain these effects through the mediation of mood and communication expectations.

Three experimental studies support our hypothesis and its underlying explanation in terms of induced mood and communication expectations. The experiments are preceded by a field data examination of 428 real-life slogans in hedonic and utilitarian product categories. The field data shows that while about 8% of utilitarian product slogans are assertive, a dramatic 24% of hedonic products are assertively phrased. Study 1 tests the conceptual model. We show that compliance depends on the interaction between language (assertive/non-assertive) and communication expectations for assertive/non-assertive language. Such expectations originate from the mood (positive/non-positive) which is induced by different product types (hedonic/utilitarian). Respondents who were thinking about chocolate reported positive mood and higher compliance intentions with an assertive message ("You must try our chocolate!") than with a non-assertive message ("You could try our chocolate"), as well as higher expectations for assertive language. However, respondents who were thinking of opening a bank account did not report positive mood and were more inclined to comply with a non-assertive message ("You could open a bank-account with us"), compared with an assertive one ("You must open a bank account with us!"). Study 2 employs real print ads from business magazines to generalize the findings to contexts involving utilitarian products presented in metaphorically hedonic language and imagery ("hedonic framing"). We find that even when a utilitarian product is merely presented in a hedonic

framing (e.g. consulting services presented as a flight to the moon), an assertive phrasing is more persuasive than a non-assertive one. Study 3 reinforces the notion that assertive language meets communication expectations in hedonic contexts, showing that consumers perceive unknown products advertised using assertive language as more hedonic than the same products promoted with a non-assertive message.

Additional Alternative Explanations

We specifically proposed that hedonic products are likely to prompt a positive mood, which results in the expectation for, and acceptance of, a more direct and assertive communication style. We empirically considered an alternative explanation for the context-dependent effect of message assertiveness, based on the notion that in hedonic product contexts assertiveness could reduce guilt associated with the anticipation of self-indulgence, but this explanation could not account for our findings.

Another alternative explanation may be related to the beneficiary prediction. Specifically, Buller et al. (1992) find that the degree to which the addressee is the beneficiary of a request positively affects compliance with more assertive requests. It is plausible, then, that assertive messages regarding hedonic consumption elicit higher compliance because the consumer is the obvious beneficiary in hedonic consumption contexts. However, this explanation only weakly supports the prediction of the interaction between product type and language, since it mainly predicts that in hedonic consumption contexts *any* request would be effective. More critically, this explanation does not predict why non-assertive phrasing will elicit lower compliance in hedonic product contexts.

Related to the notion of beneficiary, it could be that the assertively phrased messages in hedonic product contexts, such as "You must have this product", are not perceived as commands but rather as advice because the beneficiary in hedonic consumption is more saliently the consumer. This possibility echoes recent findings of Botti and McGill (2011), who relate higher satisfaction with self-made choices in hedonic consumption, compared with utilitarian consumption, to perceptions of hedonic consumption as more self- rather than externally motivated. This explanation is in line with our theorizing of altered communication expectations in hedonic product contexts. However, it suggests an alternative underlying process, where a different phrasing is expected not because the perception of social and communicational rules and borders loosens due to positive mood, but rather because of a different interpretation of the meaning of directive phrases as advice and not as a request. Further, this explanation too does not account for the interaction of language and product type, because it is not clear why assertively phrased advice would be more complied with than non-assertively phrased advice. To account for the possible different interpretations of the word *must* it is possible to use different phrasings in the experimental design. We address this point in Study 2, employing various assertive and non-assertive phrasing variations.

Universality of the Findings

In Study 2, we used English ads, whereas the rest of the studies were in Hebrew. Research suggests English and Hebrew differ in politeness judgment (e.g., Blum-Kulka 1994). Exploring the robustness of the findings across the two languages was important for this work, as it is also important for other works on language behavior.

While additional interesting directions can be proposed, such as that hedonic framing might elicit a promotion focus while a utilitarian framing ad might evoke a prevention focus, the most important conclusion we draw from this work is that assertive messages can be effective, and non-assertive messages can be counter-productive, depending on their meeting consumers' communicational expectations, in ironic application of Burger King's famously assertive slogan *Have it your way!*

REFERENCES

Bloch, Charlotte (1996), "Emotions and Discourse," *Text*, 16(3), 323-41.

Blum-Kulka, Shoshana (1994), —Politeness Revisited: Cross-Cultural Perspectives,‖ *Pragmatics and Cognition*, 2(2), 349-56.

Botti, Simona and Ann L. McGill (2011), —The Locus of Choice: Personal Causality and Satisfaction with Hedonic and Utilitarian Decisions,‖ *Journal of Consumer Research*, 37(6), 1065-78.

Brown, Penelope and Stephen Levinson (1987), *Politeness: Some Universals in Language Use.* Cambridge: Cambridge University Press.

Buller, David B, Beth A. LePoire, Kelly R. Aune, and Sylvie V. Eloy (1992), —Social Perceptions as Mediators of the Effect of Speech Rate Similarity on Compliance,‖ *Human Communication Research,* 19(2), 286-311.

Chaudhuri, Arjunand Morris Holbrook B. (2001), "The Chain of Effects from Brand Trust and Brand Affect to Brand Performance: The Role of Brand Loyalty," *Journal of Marketing*, 65(2), 81-94.

Dillard, James P. and Shen, L. (2005). "On the Nature of Reactance and its Role in Persuasive

Health Communication," *Communication Monographs*, 72(June), 144-68.

Fitzsimons, Gavan J. and Donald Lehmann R. (2004), "Reactance to Recommendations: When Unsolicited Advice Yields Contrary Responses," *Marketing Science*, 23(Winter), 82-95.

Forgas, Joseph P. (1997), "Affect and strategic Communication: The effects of Mood on the Production and Interpretation of Verbal Requests," *Polish Psychological Bulletin*, 28(2), 145-73.

Forgas, Joseph P. (1998), "Asking Nicely? The Effects of Mood on Responding to More or Less Polite Requests," *Personality and Social Psychology Bulletin*, 24, 173-85.

Forgas, Joseph P. (1999a), "On Feeling Good and Being Rude: Affective Influences on Language Use and Request Formulations," *Journal of Personality and Social Psychology*, 76(6), 928-39.

Forgas, Joseph P. (1999b), "Feeling and Speaking: Mood Effects on Verbal Communication Strategies," *Personality and Social Psychology Bulletin*, 25(7), 850-63.

Kellerman, Kathy and Shea, Christine B (1996). Threats, suggestions, hints and promises: Gaining compliance efficiently and politely. *Communication Quarterly*, 44(1), 145-165.

Levine, Timothy and Boster, Franklin (2001), "The Effects of Power and Message Variables on Compliance," *Communication Monographs*, 68 (1), 28-48.

Lord, Kenneth R. (1994),"Motivating Recycling Behavior: A Quasi experimental Investigation of Message and Source Strategies," *Psychology and Marketing*, 11(September), 341-59.

Quick, Brian L. and Jennifer Considine R. (2008), "Examining the Use of Forceful Language When Designing Exercise Persuasive Messages for Adults: A Test of Conceptualizing Reactance Arousal as a Two-Step Process," *Health Communication*, 23(September), 483-91.

Quick, Brian L. and *Michael T. Stephenson* (2007),"Further Evidence That Psychological Reactance Can Be Modeled as a Combination of Anger and Negative Cognitions," *Communication Research*, 34(3), 255-76.

Sanders, Robert E. and Fitch, Kristine L. (2001), "The Actual Practice of Compliance Seeking," *Communication Theory*, 11(3), 263-89.

Wilson, Steven R. and Adrianne Kunkel W. (2000), "Identity Implications of Influence Goals: Similarities in Perceived Face Threats and Facework across Sex and Close Relationships," *Journal of Language and Social Psychology*, 19(2), 195-221.

A Pounding Heart and a Narrower Mind:
How Images of Attractive Women in Mass Media Influence Man's Pro-Social Behavior

Xiuping Li, National University of Singapore, Singapore
Meng Zhang, Chinese University of Hong Kong, Hong Kong

EXTENDED ABSTRACT

Advertisements frequently use physically attractive females to sell products since it is the easiest way to attract consumers' attention and to increase promotional effectiveness (Baker and Churchill 1977). Visual images of attractive females, which are sexually rewarding to heterosexual males (Aharon et al. 2001), have also been found to be able to prime a mating motive. From an evolutionary perspective, a mating motive will make males behave in a way to maximize their opportunity to attract a mate. In the context of consumer behavior, a mating motive is shown to lead male consumers to engage in more conspicuous consumption in order to signal their high status, and lead them be more likely to choose unique or conspicuous options to stand out from others (Griskvicius et al. 2006; Sundies et al. 2011).

How would these attractive women pictures influence people's consumption behavior in domains unrelated to the mating motive? The current research takes a social orientation perspective, and proposes that the mere exposure to such stimuli, as ubiquitously portrayed in mass media, can change male consumers' behavior significantly in subsequent, unrelated tasks. Specifically, as compared to other visual stimuli (e.g., pleasant landscapes, or average-looking women) and non-picture baseline, exposure to the images of attractive women should lead people view themselves as being more socially distant from others. This increased self-other distance, in turn, lead males become less concerned about others' wellbeing in a number of contexts, like belief endorsement, evaluations towards ads and products, volunteering behavior, and donation.

Our hypothesis draws on two streams of literature. First, prior research has shown that "physical attractiveness" is given far more priority than other cues such as "warmth" or "social status" when men are looking for short-term mates compared to when they are looking for long-term mates (Li and Kenrick 2006). Therefore, when a cue of physical attractiveness is present, it might activate the short-term mating motive to a greater extent rather than a long-term one. This short-term mating motive has been suggested to activate a general mind state which focuses on short-term rewards over a long-term one (Li, 2006; Loewenstein 1996; Metcalfe and Mischel 1999). Recent studies by Van den Bergh, Dewitte, and Warlop (2008) have shown support to this prediction by demonstrating that seeing images of attractive females (e.g., a commercial video featuring women in bikinis) leads men to have a greater preference for smaller, more immediate gratification than for larger, more future rewards.

Second, it has been found that temporal distance and social distance are both dimensions of a possible unified concept of psychological distance (Trope and Liberman 2003). Both "present" and "me" are regarded as within an individual's proximal space in relation to "future" and "other". Further, it has been found that the distance perception along the two dimensions can influence how consumers construe events in the similar fashion and sub-additively (Kim, Zhang, and Li 2008). Therefore, if priming of a short-term mating motive can make people focus on the immediate benefits and discount future rewards along the time horizon, the same orientation shift should hold along the social distance horizon. People may become socially myopic as well, and focus more on self benefits/cost and discount benefits/cost occurring to others.

Formally, we propose that the mere exposure to images of attractive women would shift social orientation and increase men's perceived social distance towards others, which in turn, change their behavior in many kinds of consumption contexts. We report the results of six experiments. Participants in all experiments were heterosexual male students between 18 and 24 years of age from a large university. In the experiments, we compared behavior of those participants who had briefly viewed pictures of attractive women, to those who had briefly viewed other pleasant pictures (landscapes, or average-looking women), or non-picture baseline. Specifically, we found that those who viewed attractive women pictures endorsed less belief statements which showed concerns of others (experiment 1), demonstrated a weaker social value orientation in decomposed games (experiment 2), evaluated a product less favorably when an ad emphasized the wellbeing of others (experiment 3), and less likely to choose a green or ethical product more (experiment 4). Interestingly, consistent with our prediction, we found in experiment 5 that seeing pictures of attractive women might not necessarily reduce helping behavior. In fact, exposure to such stimuli could lead participants to be either more or less likely to sign up for volunteering, depending on whether they perceived this kind of help as benefitting themselves or benefitting others. In other words, when they believed that a helping behavior can serve some egoistic motives, exposures to pictures of attractive women could *increase* their interest in volunteering – eliminating the previous results. Experiment 6 then tested the mediating role of perceived social distance directly. The results showed the increased self-other distance mediated the effect of images of attractive women on pro-social behavior. By adding a condition of gender role priming, this experiment also ruled out gender role activation as an alternative explanation. Moreover, the effects cannot be attributed to any differences in affect.

To the best of our knowledge, our research is the first piece of work to explore how mere exposure to attractive women pictures can influence social distance perception and change unrelated consumer behavior accordingly. Important implications can be drawn from our findings. Decision-makers in various fields such as charity organizations that appeal for donations and marketing managers who sell environmentally friendly products might want to reconsider their decisions to place their messages in media that are rich in visual sexual cues (e.g., popular men's magazines, late night TV shows, etc.). According to our results, strategies based on the use of such stimuli may backfire.

REFERENCES

Aharon, Itzhak, Nancy Etcoff, Dan Ariely, Chris F. Chabris, Ethan O'Connor, and Hans C. Breiter (2001), "Beautiful Faces Have Variable Reward Value: FMRI and Behavioral Evidence," *Neuron*, Vol. 32 (November 8th), 537-51.

Aiken, L. S., and West, S. G. (1991), *Multiple Regression: Testing and Interpreting Interactions*. Newbury Park, London: Sage.

Baker, Michael J., and Gilbert A. Churchill. "The Impact of Physically Attractive Models on Advertising Evaluations." *Journal of Marketing Research*, 1977: 538-555.

Batson, C. D., and Shaw, L. L. (1991), "Evidence for Altruism: Toward a Pluralism of Pro-social Motives," *Psychological Inquiry*, 2, 107-122.

Cattarin, J. A., J.K.Thompson, C. Thomas, and R. Williams (2000), "Body Image, Mood and Televised Images of Attractiveness: The Role of Social Comparison," *Journal of Social Clinical Psychology*, 19, 220-239.

Griskevicius, V., N. J. Goldstein, C.R. Mortensen, R. B. Ciadini, and D.T. Kenrick (2006), "Going Along Versus Going Alone: When Fundamental Motives Facilitate Strategic (Non) Conformity," *Journal of Personality and Social Psychology*, 91 (2), 281-294.

Grogan, S. (2008), *Body image: Understanding Body Dissatisfaction in Men, Women and Children*, London: Routledge, Taylor and Francis Group.

Knutson, B., and Cooper, J. C. (2005). Functional magnetic resonance imaging of reward prediction. *Current Opinion in Neurology*, 18, 411-417.

Kahle, Lynn R., and Pamela M. Homer. "Physical Attractiveness of the Celebrity Endorser: A Social Adaptation Perspective." *Journal of Consumer Research (March)*, 1984: 954-961.

Kim, Kyeongheui, Meng Zhang, and Xiuping Li. "Effects of Temporal and Social Distance on Consumer Evaluations." Journal of Consumer Research, 2008: 706-713.

Li, X.P. (2006), "Appetitive Stimuli and Consumption Impulsivity: The Out-of-Domain Effect of Motivationally Appetitive Stimuli", Ph.D Thesis, Rotman School of Management, University of Toronto, Ontario, Canada.

Li, Norman.P. and Kenrick, Douglas.T. (2006), "Sex Similarities and Differences in Preferences for Short-Term Mates: What, Whether, and Why," *Journal of Personality and Social Psychology*, 90 (3), 468-489.

Loewenstein, G., (1996), "Out of Control: Visceral Influences on Behavior," *Organizational Behavior and Human Decision Processes*. 65, 272-92.

Metcalfe, J., and W. Mischel (1999), "A Hot/Cool-System Analysis of Delay of Gratification: Dynamics of Willpower," *Psychological Review*, 106, 3-19.

O'Doherty, J., Deichmann, R., Crtichley, H. D., and Dolan, R.J. (2002), "Neural Responses during Anticipation of a Primary Taste Reward," *Neuron*, 33, 815–826.

Sundie, J.M., D.T. Kenrick, V.Griskevicius, J. M. Tybur, K. D. Vohs, and D. J. Beal (2011), "Peacocks, Porsches, and Thorstein Veblen: Conspicuous Consumptions as a Sexual Signaling System," *Journal of Personality and Social Psychology*, Advance online Publication. doi: 10.1037/ a0021669.

Trope, Y., and N. Liberman (2003), "Temporal Construal," *Psychological Review*. 110, 403-421.

Van den Bergh, B., S. Dewitte, and L. Warlop (2008), "Bikinis Instigate Generalized Impatience in Intertemporal Choice," *Journal of Consumer Research*, 35, 85-97.

Van Lange, P.A.M., (1999), "The Pursuit of Joint Outcomes and Equality in Outcomes: An Integrative Model of Social Value Orientation," *Journal of Personality and Social Psychology*, 77, 337-349.

Van Lange, P. A. M.,W. Otten, E. M. N. De Bruin, J. and A. Joireman (1997), "Development of Prosocial, Individualistic, and Competitive Orientations: Theory and Preliminary Evidence," *Journal of Personality and Social Psychology*. 73, 733-746.

$29 for 70 or 70 for $29: How Presentation Order Affects Perceptions

Rajesh Bagchi, Virginia Tech, USA
Derick Davis, Virginia Tech, USA

EXTENDED ABSTRACT

Typically, firms communicate the price of their goods by advertising the unit price of a single item. However, sometimes pricing, specifically unit pricing, can be presented in different formats. For instance, supermarkets often have $10 for 10 item promotions, wherein each item costs $1, and consumers can buy as many or as few items as they wish. The $10 for 10 item promotion is merely another way of communicating price. But why would a firm decide to communicate price in this manner? Is it advantageous? This research investigates how under certain conditions communicating unit price via multiple item pricing can have positive and negative effects on consumer perceptions of the offering.

One type of product that lends itself nicely to multiple item pricing strategies, is electronic content, such as song and movies. For instance, with Apple's iTunes, a consumer can buy a single song, or a larger amount of content, such as an entire music album. Obviously, few limits exist for how firms offer access to content and files and therefore, different pricing presentation strategies could be easily varied. For instance, Apple's iTunes could change the presentation order by presenting price first, and then number of songs ($29 for 70 songs) or the reverse (70 songs for $29). They could advertise price via larger packages ($29 for 70 songs) or smaller packages ($2.90 for 7 songs). They can also vary how difficult ($29 for 70 songs) or easy ($20 for 50 songs) it is to compute unit prices. How would these varied characteristics affect consumers' perceptions and why? In this research, we investigate the role that three different characteristics of a package (presentation order, package size, and ease of unit price computation) play in consumers' perceptions.

The price information reflects the costs involved, while quantity corresponds to benefits accrued from the exchange. If computations are easier (e.g., $20 for 50), consumers can easily compute unit price ($.40/item). In this case any effect of other package characteristics on perceptions should be attenuated, as unit prices are easily computed and consumers can buy as many or as few items as they wish at the same unit price. But, when unit price computations are harder (e.g., $29 for 70), consumers may not perform calculations necessary and may instead focus on the first piece of information to make inferences.

If price is first, a higher price (e.g., $29) may highlight the costs involved. In contrast, if quantity were first, greater item quantity (e.g., 70 songs) might suggest a larger gain from the exchange. We posit that presentation order may differentially affect consumers' attention and investigate the effects on relevant marketing variables. Furthermore, this "anchoring" effect is likely to be stronger when package size is large as all the numbers are larger.

We predict a three-way interaction of order by package size by computation ease. We expect computation ease to moderate the relationship between order and numerosity on perceptions (e.g., unit price). Formally:

Hypothesis 1 *Calculation Difficulty moderates effects of order and numerosity on perceptions. High Calculation Difficulty: High numerosity: Price-item vs. item-price order will lead to a) higher unit price judgments, b) lower value perceptions, and c) lower trying likelihoods. Low numerosity: Differences attenuated. Low Calculation Difficulty: These differences will be attenuated.*

We report findings from two studies. In study 1, we use an online music context to investigate the effects of the independent variables on unit price judgments. Study 2 uses an online television viewing service to investigate the effects of the independent variables on likelihood of trying the offer and package value perceptions. Both studies are 2 (Order: Price-Item vs. Item-Price) x 2 (Numerosity: High vs. Low) X 2 (Calculation Difficulty: Hard vs. Easy) full factorial between subject designs. Both studies fully support our hypotheses.

Our research thus makes several important theoretical and managerial contributions. We demonstrate how the presentation order of price and quantity information – even when presented simultaneously, as opposed to separately – influences which piece of information is used in judgments via anchoring (Epley and Gilovich 2010; Frederick, Kahneman, and Mochon 2010; Russo 2010; Tversky and Kahneman 1974; Wegener, Petty, Blankenship and Detweiler-Bedell 2010a, 2010b). We find that computation ease influences anchoring, suggesting stronger effects when computations are harder (Thomas and Morwitz 2009). We also show that these effects are most prevalent when packages are large, thus contributing to work on numerosity (Burson, Larrick, and Lynch 2009; Pelham, Sumarta, and Myaskovsky 1994; Wertenbroch, Soman, and Chattopadhyay 2007).

Our findings also have important managerial implications. This research provides insights that can aid in pricing strategies for different objectives, such as decreasing unit price perceptions or increasing trial likelihood. However, our finding that the influence of presentation order is likely to be stronger for larger (vs. smaller) packages is especially relevant for managers.

REFERENCES

Alter, Adam L. and Daniel M. Oppenheimer (2009), "Uniting the Tribes of Fluency to Form a Metacognitive Nation," *Personality and Social Psychology Review,* 13 (August), 219-35.

Bakos, Yannis and Erik Brynjolfsson (1999), "Bundling Information Goods: Pricing, Profits, and Efficiency," *Management Science,* 45 (December), 1613-30.

--- (2000), "Bundling and Competition on the Internet," *Marketing Science,* 19 (1) 66-82.

Burson, Katherine A., Richard P. Larrick, and John G. Lynch, Jr. (2009), "Six of One, Half Dozen of the Other: Expanding and Contracting Numerical Dimensions Produces Preference Reversals," *Psychological Science,* 20 (9), 1074-78.

Epley, Nicholas and Thomas Gilovich (2001), "Putting Adjustment Back in the Anchoring and Adjustment Heuristic: Differential Processing of Self-Generated and Experimenter-Provided Anchors," *Psychological Science,* 12(5), 391-96.

--- (2010), "Anchoring Unbound." *Journal of Consumer Psychology,* 20 (January), 20-24.

Ernst, Ricardo and Panagiotis Kouvelis (1999), "The Effects of Selling Packaged Goods on Inventory Decisions," *Management Science,* 45 (August), 1142-55.

Frederick, Shane, Daniel Kahneman, and Daniel Mochon (2010), "Elaborating a Simpler Theory of Anchoring," *Journal of Consumer Psychology, 20, 17-19.*

Pelham, Brett W., Tin Tin Sumarta, and Laura Myaskovsky (1994), "The Easy Path From Many to Much: The Numerosity Heuristic," *Cognitive Psychology,* 26 (2), 103-33.

Russo, J. Edward (2010), "Understanding the Effect of a Numerical Anchor," *Journal of Consumer Research,* 20, 25-27.

Schwarz, Norbert (2004), "Metacognitive Experiences in Consumer Judgment and Decision Making," *Journal of Consumer Psychology,* 14 (4), 332-48.

Thomas, Manoj and Vicki G. Morwitz (2005), "Penny Wise and Pound Foolish: The Left-Digit Effect in Price Cognition," *Journal of Consumer Research,* 32 (June), 54-64.

--- (2009a), "The Ease-of-Computation Effect: The Interplay of Metacognitive Experiences and Naïve Theories in Judgments of Price Differences," *Journal of Marketing Research,* 46 (February), 81-91.

--- (2009b), "Heuristics in Numerical Cognition: Implications for Pricing," in *Handbook of Pricing Research in Marketing,"* ed. Vithala R. Rao, Cheltenham, UK: Edward Elger, 132-49.

Tversky, Amos and Daniel Kahneman (1974), "Judgment Under Uncertainty: Heuristics and Biases," *Science,* 185 (4157), 1124-31.

Wegener, Duane T., Richard E. Petty, Kevin L. Blankenship, and Brian Detweiler-Bedell (2010a), "Elaboration and Numerical Anchoring: Implications of Attitude Theories for Consumer Judgment and Decision Making," *Journal of Consumer Psychology,* 20, 5-16.

--- (2010b), "Elaboration and Numerical Anchoring: Breadth, Depth, and the role of (Non-) Thoughtful Processes in Anchoring Theories," *Journal of Consumer Psychology,* 20, 28-32.

Wertenbroch, Klaus, Dilip Soman, and Amitava Chattopadhyay (2007), "On the Perceived Value of Money: The Reference Dependence of Currency Numerosity Effects," *Journal of Consumer Research,* 34 (June), 1-10.

Are You Really Paying What You Wish?
Interpersonal Influences on Price Decisions

Sae Rom Lee, Pennsylvania State University, USA
Hans Baumgartner, Pennsylvania State University, USA
Rik Pieters, Tilburg University, The Netherlands

EXTENDED ABSTRACT

Although pay-what-you-wish pricing is increasingly being adopted in the market place, little is known about how consumers make price decisions in the context of these schemes. This is surprising, because such pricing schemes may hold significant cost advantages for consumers and sales and margin implications for firms, who expect to trade-off margin for volume. Because pay-what-you-wish pricing enables the consumer to choose the price paid and this often occurs in social situations, consumers' choice of how much to pay can become a socially embedded decision where the role of other consumers becomes crucial. Yet, no previous research has focused on possible social influences on consumers' price decisions in this context. The current research examines this issue. Two experiments indicate that people do take advantage of pay-what-you-wish pricing opportunities by paying a lower price than the regular suggested price, but in unexpected ways that reflect the social embeddedness of the decision. When people are motivated to make a good impression on certain others, they offer a higher price than what they could pay, primarily due to concerns about what price signals to others about their prestige, unless strong social cues are present indicating that paying a lower price is acceptable.

In the context of pay-what-you-wish pricing, consumers are provided with the unusual chance to choose their own prices. Thus, individuals should be highly motivated to save money on the product purchase by offering a low price. Marketers adopting a pay-what-you-wish pricing scheme often provide a price guideline indicating the regular price of the product. We hypothesize that the price that consumers offer will often be lower than the reference price based on the regular market price, because consumers are motivated to take advantage of the chance to pay less in the pay-what-you-wish shopping context.

However, when individuals are shopping with another person on whom they wish to make a good impression, they will be more concerned about how the other person makes judgments about them based on the price they offer. Individuals then feel pressure to offer a higher price when they desire to be evaluated favorably by another person in the pay-what-you-wish shopping context.

We suggest that the positive effect of impression motivation on price paid is mediated primarily by prestige sensitivity. Consumers will favor high prices due to inferences about the prominence and status that higher prices signal to other people about them. It is also possible that consumers might become less price-conscious when they are motivated to make a good impression. Finding a low price and saving money might no longer be their primary goal to be achieved in the shopping situation when offering a lower price generates social costs of looking cheap or stingy.

If a social signal is present indicating that it is acceptable to offer a lower price, the social pressure to offer a higher price will be diminished. The other person's self-presentational behaviors, verbal communications or personal possessions can signal whether or not the other person expects the focal individual to pay more. For example, how much the other person pays for his or her product can directly signal what the other person thinks is appropriate to do.

In study 1, we tested our predictions in a pay-what-you-wish pricing context. Participants were told that they were at an art museum either with an admired friend or with their best friend, and they were given a chance to pay as much as they wished for a ticket. Participants had to decide how much to pay either before the other person made a decision or after the other person paid a relatively low price. We found that people indeed generally paid a lower price than the regular suggested price. Also, an admired friend (vs. best friend) who stimulated impression motivation increased the price paid by participants, and the positive effect of impression motivation on price paid was mediated primarily by prestige sensitivity and, to a lesser extent, by price-consciousness. In addition, when an admired friend paid a price that was relatively low before participants had to make a decision about how much to pay, this decreased the pressure to pay a higher price.

In study 2, participants imagined that they were either with a date or their best friend when they decided to pay what they wished to pay for an art museum ticket. We used indirect social cues (i.e., lifestyle of the other person inferred from conversation) to signal what is desired by the other person (frugal vs. materialistic values). We also included a control condition in which participants were alone. We again found that participants paid a lower price than the regular price, but a materialistic date (vs. a materialistic best friend or frugal date) increased the price paid. The price paid in the presence of one's best friend or a frugal date was not different from the price paid alone. The positive effect of impression motivation on price paid was mediated by prestige sensitivity.

The results of these two experiments suggest that people are likely to take advantage of pay-what-you-wish pricing opportunities by paying a lower price than the regular suggested price. As predicted, however, when people are concerned about making a favorable impression on another person who is present in the shopping situation, they pay a higher price than what they would have paid if they did not have to impress the other person or if they were alone. Also, the findings suggest that the positive effect of impression motivation on price paid is mediated primarily by prestige sensitivity and, to a lesser extent, by price-consciousness. Further, the findings suggest that if there are social cues indicating that it is appropriate to pay a lower price, the pressure to pay a higher price in the presence of the other person who motivates impression management is attenuated. This research adds to the literature examining interpersonal influences and the role of price in consumption decisions.

REFERENCES

Allen, V. & Levine, J. (1969), Consensus and Conformity. *Journal of Experimental Social Psychology*, 5, 389-399.

Argo, J. J., Dahl, D. W., & Manchanda, R. V. (2005). The Influence of a Mere Social Presence in a Retail Context. *Journal of Consumer Research, 32* (September), 207-212.

Argo, J. J., & Main, K. J. (2008). Stigma by Association in Coupon Redemption: Looking Cheap because of Others. *Journal of Consumer Research, 35* (December), 559-572.

Ariely, D., & Levav, J. (2000). Sequential Choice in Group Settings: Taking the Road Less Traveled and Less Enjoyed. *Journal of Consumer Research, 27* (December), 279-290.

Ashworth, L., Darke, P. R., & Schaller, M. (2005). No One Wants to Look Cheap: Trade-Offs Between Social Disincentives and the Economic and Psychological Incentives to Redeem Coupons. *Journal of Consumer Psychology, 15* (4), 295-306.

Baumeister, R. F., & Leary, M. R. (1995). The Need to Belong: Desire for Interpersonal Attachments as a Fundamental Human Motivation. *Psychological Bulletin, 117* (3), 497-529.

Bearden, W. O., Netemeyer, R. G., & Teel, J. E. (1989). Measurement of Consumer Susceptibility to Interpersonal Influence. *Journal of Consumer Research, 15* (4), 473-481.

Burnkrant, R. E., & Cousineau, A. (1975). Informational and Normative Social Influence in Buyer Behavior. *Journal of Consumer Research, 2* (3), 206-215.

Calder, B. J. & Burnkrant, R. E. (1977). Interpersonal Influence on Consumer Behavior: An Attribution Theory Approach, *Journal of Consumer Research,* 4 (June), 29-38.

Dahl, D. W., Manchanda, R. V., & Argo, J. J. (2001). Embarrassment in Consumer Purchase: The Roles of Social Presence and Purchase Familiarity. *Journal of Consumer Research, 28* (3), 473-481.

Erickson, G. M., & Johansson, J. K. (1985). The Role of Price in Multi-Attribute Product Evaluations. *Journal of Consumer Research, 12* (2), 195-199.

Gneezy, A., Gneezy, U., Nelson, L. D., & Brown, A. (2010). Shared Social Responsibility: A Field Experiment in Pay-what-you-want Pricing and Charitable Giving. *Science, 329*(5989), 325.

Kallgren, C. A., Reno, R. R., & Cialdini, R. B. (2000). A Focus Theory of Normative Conduct: When Norms Do and Do not Affect Behavior. *Personality and Social Psychology Bulletin, 26* (8), 1002-1012.

Kasser, T., & Ryan, R. M. (1996). Further Examining the American Dream: Differential Correlates of Intrinsic and Extrinsic Goals. *Personality and Social Psychology Bulletin, 22,* 280-287.

Kasser, T., & Ryan, R. M. (1993). A Dark Side of the American Dream: Correlates of Financial Success as a Central Life Aspiration. *Journal of Personality and Social Psychology, 65*(2), 410-422.

Kenrick, D. T., Sundie, J. M., Nicastle, L. D., & Stone, G. O. (2001). Can One Ever Be Too Wealthy or Too Chaste? Searching for Nonlinearities in Mate Judgment. *Journal of Personality and Social Psychology, 80* (3), 462-471.

Kim, J. Y., Natter, M., & Spann, M. (2009). Pay What You Want: A New Participative Pricing Mechanism. *Journal of Marketing, 73*(1), 44-58.

Leary, M. R., & Kowalski, R. M. (1990). Impression Management: A Literature Review and Two-Component Model. *Psychological Bulletin, 107* (1), 34-47.

Lichtenstein, D. R., Ridgway, N. M., & Netemeyer, R. G. (1993). Price Perceptions and Consumer Shopping Behavior: A Field Study. *Journal of Marketing Research, 30* (May), 234-245.

Luo, X. (2005). How Does Shopping With Others Influence Impulsive Purchasing? *Journal of Consumer Psychology, 15* (4), 288-294.

McFerran, B., Dahl, D. W., Fitzsimons, G. J., & Morales, A. C. (2010). I'll Have What She's Having: Effects of Social Influence and Body Type on the Food Choices of Others. *Journal of Consumer Research, 36* (April), 915-929.

Mori, D., Chaiken, S., & Pliner, P. (1987). "Eating Lightly" and the Self-Presentation of Femininity. *Journal of Personality and Social Psychology, 53* (4), 693-702.

Preacher, K. J. & Hayes A. F. (2008). Asymtotic and Resampling Strategies for Assessing and Comparing Indirect Effects in Multiple Mediator Models, *Behavior Research Methods*, 40, 879-891.

Preacher, K.J., Rucker, D. R. & Hayes, A. (2007). Addressing Moderated Mediation Hypotheses: Theory, Methods, and Prescriptions, *Multivariate Behavioral Research*, 42, 185-227.

Ratner, R. K., & Kahn, B. E. (2002). The Impact of Private versus Public Consumption on Variety-Seeking Behavior. *Journal of Consumer Research, 29* (September), 246-257.

Riener, G., & Traxler, C. (2010). Norms, moods and free lunch: Longitudinal evidence on payments from a pay-what-you-want restaurant, Bonn, Max Planck Institute for Research on Collective Goods.

Ryan, R. M., Chirkov, V. I., Little, T. D., Sheldon, K. M., Timoshina, E., & Deci, E. L. (1999). The American Dream in Russia: Extrinsic Aspirations and Well-being in Two Cultures. *Personality and Social Psychology Bulletin, 25*(12), 1509.

Schindler, R. M. (1989). The Excitement of Getting a Bargain: Some Hypotheses Concerning the Origins and Effects of Smart-Shopper Feelings. *Advances in Consumer Research, 16,* 447-453.

Schlenker, B. R., & Leary, M. R. (1982). Social Anxiety and Self-Presentation: A Conceptualization and Model. *Psychological Bulletin, 92* (3), 641-669.

Schmuck, P., Kasser, T., & Ryan, R. M. (2000). Intrinsic and Extrinsic Goals: Their Structure and Relationship to Well-being in German and U.S. College Students. *Social Indicators Research, 50* (2), 225-241.

Sengupta, J., Dahl, D. W., & Gorn, G. J. (2002). Misrepresentation in the Consumer Context. *Journal of Consumer Psychology, 12* (2), 69-79.

Singh, D. (1995). Female Judgment of Male Attractiveness and Desirability for Relationships: Role of Waist-to-hip Ratio and Financial Status. *Journal of Personality and Social Psychology, 69* (6), 1089-1101.

Wakefield, K. L., & Inman, J. J. (2003). Situational Price Sensitivity: The Role of Consumption Occasion, Social Context and Income. *Journal of Retailing, 79,* 199-212.

White, K., & Dahl, D. W. (2006). To Be or Not Be? The Influence of Dissociative Reference Groups on Consumer Preferences. *Journal of Consumer Psychology, 16* (4), 404-414.

Wicker, F. W., Lambert, F. B., Richardson, F. C., & Kahler, J. (1984). Categorical Goal Hierarchies and Classification of Human Motives. *Journal of Personality, 52* (3), 285-305.

Inward Looking: The Effect of Lateral Orientation
on Consumer Preference, Perceived Usability and Intent to Purchase

Dante Pirouz, University of Western Ontario, Canada
James M. Leonhardt, UC Irvine, USA
Jesse R. Catlin, UC Irvine, USA

EXTENDED ABSTRACT

If a marketer were to turn to the literature for guidance on how to position a product within an advertisement, s/he would find conflicting results in terms of whether products are preferred facing left or right. Given the sporadic results, s/he may reasonably conclude that facing direction does not matter and thus may orient products within an advertisement based simply on intuition or formatting practicalities. Results from the present research help reconcile these disparate results and helps inform the marketer that spatial orientation is an important component that impacts consumer perceptions. Specifically, the direction a product is facing affects how consumers evaluate products.

In this paper, we limit our focus to the horizontal component of spatial orientation referred to as lateral orientation. Freimuth and Wapner (1979) consider lateral orientation as consisting of two parts: 1) the lateral position of an object along the horizontal midline and 2) the directionality of an object. The directionality of a product refers to the direction a product is perceived to be facing and/or moving. In a first experiment it is shown that spatial orientation has an effect on preference. Precisely which components of a given spatial orientation affect aesthetic appreciation is clarified in a second experiment. In a third experiment we look at whether orientation impacts perceived usability. In a fourth experiment we find test whether orientation affects intent to purchase or usability and the mediator of the effect, using a real advertisement.

Past consumer research on aesthetics has largely focused on the design of the product itself (Bloch 1995; Whitney 1991) and shows that aesthetics affect consumer perceptions of product quality (Garvin 1984; Zeithaml 1988), product differentiation (Dickson and Ginter 1987) and competitive advantage (Holt 1985; Kotler and Rath 1984). Less research has explored the aesthetic ramifications of how a product is oriented within a visual space, which can be referred to as a product's spatial orientation. In consumer research, spatial orientation has been shown to affect visual attention, eye movement (Janiszewski 1998; Rosbergen, Pieters, and Wedel 1997), and even perceptions of weight (Deng and Kahn 2009). An understanding of spatial orientation is important for marketers since it is one of the first aspects of a product processed by the visual system (Flavell and Draguns 1957). For instance, during brief exposures (< 5 s) products are assessed according to their spatial orientation while at longer exposures a more feature (design) based product assessment occurs (Freimuth and Wapner 1979).

Presently, the literature remains conflicted about preferences for right vs. left-facing objects. Some studies have shown a preference for rightward (right facing à) directionality (Christman and Pinger 1997; Freimuth and Wapner 1979; Mead and McLaughlin 1992), while others report instances where rightward directionality becomes insignificant (Christman and Pinger 1997) or even a general preference (Banich, Heller, and Levy 1989) for leftward (left facing ß) directionality. In addition, various studies have reported moderators of directionality preference such as handedness (which is correlated with hemispheric asymmetries) and cultural reading (Braine 1968; Chokron and De Agostini 2000; Christman and Rally 2000; Heath et al. 2005; Nachson 1985).

Support for rightward directionality comes, in part, from an attentional scanning hypothesis (Beaumont 1985; Graffon 1950; Wölfflin 1928). According to this hypothesis, rightward directionality is preferred because it coincides with the direction in which visual attention automatically orients across the visual field. Rightward scanning direction is thought to be the result of visual attention being initiated by the visuospatially oriented right hemisphere (Bradshaw and Nettleton 1983; Bryden 1982; Kosslyn 1987).

In experiment 1 we found lateral orientation to affect preference. Specifically, we found a set of products directed inward to be preferred over the same set of products directed outwards. These findings led us to conclude that preference for directionality was dependent on whether the product was positioned to the right or left of center. Experiment 2 tested for other factors potentially affecting preferred directionality, such as hemispheric processing asymmetries and or reading and writing direction, and found no effect, thus confirming that a preference for right versus left facing direction is dependent on the products lateral position relative to the center of the display. Experiment 3 looked at whether orientation impacts the perception of usability of a product. The results showed that inward facing products were perceived as more usable than outward facing ones. In experiment 4, a real advertisement (taken from a magazine and altered to obscure the brand name and logo) was used to determine whether orientation might impact intent to purchase whether the effect is mediated by processing fluency. Results of this experiment showed that participants who saw the ad with the inward facing product (car) versus the outward facing product had a higher intent to purchase and higher usability rating of the product and that this effect was fully mediated by processing fluency. These effects do not covary with gender or handedness.

In general, the finding that the way in which a product is orientated within a display can have a significant effect on its perceived usability is surprising since nothing about the product itself has changed; rather it is merely displayed in a different lateral orientation. This result supports the view that product evaluations are partially the result of how the stimuli in question are processed and are not the result of the stimuli themselves.; studies by Winkielman et al. (2006) support this view. The biological and psychophysical literature offer possible explanations, and areas for future research, for the occurrence of a preference for inward (versus outward) directionality.

REFERENCES

Alexander, C. (2002), *The Nature of Order. Book 1: The Phenomenon of Life.*, Berkeley, CA: Center for Environmental Structure.

Arnheim, Rudolf (1988), *The Power of the Center: A Study of Composition in the Visual Arts*, Berkeley, CA: University of California Press.

Baker, Michael J. and Gilbert A. Churchill, Jr. (1977), "The Impact of Physically Attractive Models on Advertising Evaluations," *Journal of Marketing Research*, XIV, 538-55.

Banich, M. T., W. Heller, and J. Levy (1989), "Aesthetic Preference and Picture Asymmetries," *Cortex: a Journal Devoted to the Study of the Nervous System and Behavior*, 25 (2), 187-95.

Beaumont, J. G. (1985), "Lateral Organization and Aesthetic Preference: The Importance of Peripheral Visual Asymmetries," *Neuropsychologia*, 23, 103-13.

Bloch, Peter H. (1995), "Seeking the Ideal Form: Product Design and Consumer Response," *The Journal of Marketing*, 59 (3), 16-29.

Bradshaw, J. L. and N. C. Nettleton (1983), *Human Cerebral Asymmetry*, New York, NY: Prentice Hall.

Bradshaw, J.L. and N.C. Nettleton (1981), "The Nature of Hemispheric Specialization in Man," *Behavioral and Brain Sciences*, 4, 51-63.

Braine, L. G. (1968), "Asymmetries of Pattern Perception Observed in Israelis," *Neuropsychologia*, 6 (1), 73-88.

Bryden, M. P. (1982), *Laterality: Functional Asymmetry in the Intact Brain*, New York, NY: Academic Press.

Chokron, S. and M. De Agostini (2000), "Reading Habits Influence Aesthetic Preference," *Cognitive Brain Research*, 10 (1-2), 45-49.

Christman, S. D. and S. Rally (2000), "Directionality Biases in Aesthetic Preference: Effects of Reading Direction," in *27th Annual Meeting of the International Neuropsychological Society*, Denver, CO.

Christman, S. and K. Pinger (1997), "Lateral Biases in Aesthetic Preferences: Pictorial Dimensions and Neural Mechanisms," *Laterality: Asymmetries of Body, Brain, and Cognition*, 2 (2), 155-57.

Deng, Xiaoyan and Barbara Kahn (2009), "Is Your Product on the Right Side? The "Location Effect" on Perceived Product Heaviness and Package Evaluation," *Journal of Marketing Research*, December.

Dhar, Ravi and Klaus Wertenbroch (2000), "Consumer Choice between Hedonic and Utilitarian Goods," *Journal of Marketing Research*, 37 (1).

Dickson, P. R. and J. L. Ginter (1987), "Market Segmentation, Product Differentiation, and Marketing Strategy," *Journal of Marketing*, 51 (2), 1-10.

Flavell, J. H. and J. Draguns (1957), "A Microgenetic Approach to Perception and Thought," *Psychological Bulletin*, 54 (3), 197-217.

Freimuth, M. and S. Wapner (1979), "The Influence of Lateral Organization on the Evaluation of Paintings," *British Journal of Psychology*, 70 (2), 211-18.

Gaffron, Mercedes (1950), "Right and Left in Pictures," *Art Quarterly*, 13, 312-51.

Garvin, D.A. (1984), "What Does Product Quality Really Mean," *Sloan Management Review*, 26 (1), 25-43.

Graffon, M. (1950), "Right and Left in Pictures," *Art Quarterly*, 13 (4), 312-31.

Hatta, T. and A. Kawakami (1997), "Image Generation and Handedness: Is the Hemi-Imagery Method Valid for Studying the Hemisphere Imagery Generation Process?," *Neuropsychologia*, 35 (11), 1499-502.

Heath, R., O. Mahmasanni, A. Rouhana, and N. Nassif (2005), "Comparison of Aesthetic Preferences among Roman and Arabic Script Readers," *Laterality: Asymmetries of Body, Brain, and Cognition*, 10, 399-411.

Hellige, J. B., P. J. Cox, and L. Litvac (1979), "Information Processing in the Cerebral Hemispheres: Selective Hemispheric Activation and Capacity Limitations," *Journal of Experimental Psychology: General*, 108 (2), 251-79.

Hirschman, Elizabeth C. (1986), "The Effect of Verbal and Pictorial Advertising Stimuli on Aesthetics, Utilitarian, and Familiarity Perceptions," *Journal of Advertising*, 15 (2), 27-34.

Holt, Steven (1985), "Design, the Ninth Principle of Excellence: The Product Half of the Business Equation," *Innovation*, 4, 2-4.

Janiszewski, C. (1998), "The Influence of Display Characteristics on Visual Exploratory Search Behavior," *Journal of Consumer Research*, 25 (3), 290-301.

Jonides, J. (1981), "Voluntary Versus Automatic Control over the Mind's Eye's Movement," *Attention and performance IX*.

Jordan, P. W. (1998), "Human Factors for Pleasure in Product Use," *Applied Ergonomics*, 29 (1), 25-33.

Karev, G. B. (1999), "Directionality in Right, Mixed and Left Handers," *Cortex*, 35 (3), 423-31.

Karvonen, Kristiina (2000), "The Beauty of Simplicity," *Proceedings on the 2000 Conference on Universal Usability*.

Kosslyn, S. M. (1987), "Seeing and Imagining in the Cerebral Hemispheres: A Computational Approach," *Psychological Review*, 94 (2), 148-75.

Kotler, Philip and G. Alexander Rath (1984), " Design: A Powerful but Neglected Strategic Tool," *Journal of Business Strategy*, 5 (2), 16.

Kurosu, M. and K. Kashimura (1995), "Apparent Usability Vs. Inherent Usability: Experimental Analysis on the Determinants of the Apparent Usability," in *Conference on Human Factors in Computing Systems*, ACM New York, NY, 292-3.

Lavie, T. and N. Tractinsky (2004), "Assessing Dimensions of Perceived Visual Aesthetics of Web Sites," *International Journal of Human-Computer Studies*, 60 (3), 269-98.

Lindgaard, Gitte and Cahty Dudek (2002), "User Satisfaction, Aesthetics and Usability: Beyond Reductionism," *Proceedings of the IFIP 17th World Computer Congress*.

Mead, A. M. and J. P. McLaughlin (1992), "The Roles of Handedness and Stimulus Asymmetry in Aesthetic Preference," *Brain and Cognition*, 20 (2), 300.

Moscovitch, M. and D. Klein (1980), "Material-Specific Perceptual Interference for Visual Words and Faces: Implications for Models of Capacity Limitations, Attention, and Laterality," *Journal of Experimental Psychology*, 6 (3), 590-604.

Nachson, I. (1985), "Directional Preferences in Perception of Visual Stimuli," *International Journal of Neuroscience*, 25 (3-4), 161-74.

Oldfield, R. C. (1971), "The Assessment and Analysis of Handedness: The Edinburgh Inventory," *Neuropsychologia*, 9 (1), 97-113.

Palmer, S. E. (1991), "On Goodness, Gestalt, Groups, and Garner: Local Symmetry Subgroups as a Theory of Figural Goodness," in *The Perception of Structure: Essays in Honor of Wendell R. Garner*, ed. G. Lockhead and J. Pomerantz, Washington, DC: American Psychological Association.

Palmer, Stephen E., Jonathan S. Gardner, and Thomas D. Wickens (2008), "Aesthetic Issues in Spatial Composition: Effects of Position and Direction on Framing Single Objects," *Spatial Vision*, 21, 421-49.

Palmer, Stephen E. and Kathleen Hemenway (1978), "Orientation and Symmetry: Effects of Multiple, Rotational, and near Symmetries," *Journal of Experimental Psychology: Human Perception and Performance*, 4 (4), 691-702.

Polyak, S.L. (1941), *The Retina*, Chicago: University of Chicago Press.

Prinzmetal, W., J. Leonhardt, and R. Garrett (2008), "Does Gaze Direction Affect Accuracy?," *Visual Cognition*, 16, 567-84.

Rosbergen, Edward, Rik Pieters, and Michel Wedel (1997), "Visual Attention to Advertising: A Segmentâ€ Level Analysis," *Journal of Consumer Research*, 24 (3), 305-14.

Tractinsky, N. (1997), "Aesthetics and Apparent Usability: Empirically Assessing Cultural and Methodological Issues," in *SIGCHI conference on Human Factors in Computing Systems* New York, NY: ACM 115-22.

Tractinsky, N., A. S. Katz, and D. Ikar (2000), "What Is Beautiful Is Usable. Interacting with Computers," *Interacting with computers*, 13 (2), 127-45.

Treisman, Anne M. and Stephen Gormican (1988), "Feature Analysis in Early Vision: Evidence from Search Asymmetries," *Psychological Review*, 95 (1), 15-48.

Tyler, C. W. (1998a), "Painters Centre One Eye in Portraits," *Nature*, 392, 877-8.

Tyler, C.W. (1998b), "Eye Placement Principles in Portraits and Figure Studies of the Past Two Millennia," *SPIE Proc.*, 3299 (431-37).

Vaid, J. and M. Singh (1989), "Asymmetries in the Perception of Facial Affect: Is There an Influence of Reading Habits?," *Neuropsychologia*, 27 (10), 1277-87.

Whitney, D. E. (1991), "Manufacturing by Design," *Design for manufacture: strategies, principles, and techniques*, 37.

Whitney, Daniel E., James L. Nevins, L. De Fazio Thomas, Richard E. Gustavson, Richard W. Metzinger, Jonathan M. Rourke, and Donald S. Seltzer (1988), "The Strategic Approach to Product Design," in *Design and Analysis of Integrated Manufacturing Systems*, ed. W.D. Compton: National Academy Press, 200-24.

Whittlesea, Bruce W. A. (1993), "Illusions of Familiarity," *Journal of Experimental Psychology: Learning, Memory, and Cognition*, 19 (6), 1235-53.

Winkielman, P. and J. T. Cacioppo (2001), "Mind at Ease Puts a Smile on the Face: Psychophysiological Evidence That Processing Facilitation Elicits Positive Affect," *Journal of Personality and Social Psychology*, 81 (6), 989-1000.

Winkielman, P., J. Halberstadt, T. Fazendeiro, and S. Catty (2006), "Prototypes Are Attractive Because They Are Easy on the Mind," *Psychological Science*, 17 (9), 799.

Wölfflin, H. (1928). Uber das Rechts und Links in Bilde. Gedanken zur Kunstgeschichte, pp. 82–90. Schwabe, Basel, Switzerland. (1928), *Uber Das Rechts Und Links in Bilde: Gedanken Zur Kunstgeschichte*, Basel, Switzerland: Schwabe.

Zeithaml, V. A. (1988), "Consumer Perceptions of Price, Quality, and Value: A Means-End Model and Synthesis of Evidence," *Journal of Marketing*, 52 (3), 32-22.

Sticking to it?
How Consumer Goal Progress Affects Goal Perseverance

Aaron Garvey, Pennsylvania State University, USA

EXTENDED ABSTRACT

How does progress toward a goal impact the tendency to pursue that goal? Prior research has identified inconsistent effects of consumer goal progress upon goal perseverance; one stream of research suggests that progress increases the tendency to pursue the focal goal (e.g., Kivetz, Urminsky, and Zheng 2006; Nunes and Dreze 2006), whereas an alternative stream proposes that progress has no such effect (e.g., Fishbach and Dhar 2005; Wilcox, Vallen, Block, and Fitzsimons 2009). The present research introduces a characteristic of goals to help resolve this conflict—cumulative benefits associated with goal progress. The presence of cumulative benefits is proposed to influence perceptions of sunk costs (Arkes and Blumer 1985; Cunha and Caldieraro 2009) associated with goal progress that, in turn, affect goal perseverance.

Cumulative benefits refer to the intrinsic value of goal progress *independent from* the end state. Benefits are cumulative if received as a function of progress prior to achieving the end state (e.g., weight loss), whereas benefits are all-or-nothing if they are only received upon achieving the end state (e.g., completing a marathon). All-or-nothing benefit goals are expected to result in greater perseverance as a function of progress compared to cumulative benefit goals (H1). Differential perceptions of sunk costs as a function of progress are proposed to mediate this effect (H2). In the case of all-or-nothing benefits, higher perceptions of sunk costs due to progress will enhance goal perseverance, whereas the presence of cumulative benefits will mitigate perceptions of sunk costs, thereby also mitigating perseverance.

This research provides several distinct and important contributions. First, the theory and findings shed light on how consumers do, and do not, 'stick' to pursuing goals following progress. Second, this work identifies an underlying process to account for the observed effect of cumulative and all-or-nothing benefits upon goal perseverance, namely differential escalation of perseverance due to perceived sunk costs. Third, this work contributes to resolving disparate findings in the literature regarding goal progress. Fourth, doing so has obvious implications for consumer welfare inasmuch as goal achievement is central to well-being. Finally, the present research has substantive implications for the design and management of consumer loyalty and similar marketing programs.

Three empirical studies were conducted to evaluate the proposed hypotheses.

Study 1

A preliminary study was conducted to determine whether cumulative (vs. all-or-nothing) benefits moderate the influence of goal progress upon goal perseverance. Specifically, progress should increase perseverance more so in the case of all-or-nothing than cumulative benefits.

Method. Participants consisted of 252 university students. A 2(Goal Progress: High/Low)x2(Benefit Type: All-or-Nothing/Cumulative) between subjects design was employed. Participants were placed into a first person scenario in which they were members of a café loyalty card program accumulating 10 stamps toward a free coffee. Subjects were informed of their progress to date (3 or 7 stamps) and the type of benefit associated with progress (free $2.50 coffee for 10 stamps or $.25 discount per stamp). Participants answered four items measuring intent to complete the loyalty card.

Results and discussion. ANOVA of the goal perseverance measure (coefficient α = .91) revealed the predicted two-way interaction of progress and benefit type (F(1,226)=4.69; p<.05). Furthermore, for an all-or-nothing goal, progress increased perseverance (F(1,226)=5.47; p<.05), whereas progress had no effect upon perseverance in the case of a cumulative benefit goal (F(1,226)=.55; p=.46). These results directly support H1, providing evidence for the moderating role of cumulative (versus all-or-nothing) benefits in determining the influence of progress upon perseverance.

Study 2

Study 2 was conducted to evaluate the underlying role of sunk cost perceptions (H2), and to examine "hybrid" goals which provide both all-or-nothing and cumulative benefits. Sunk cost perceptions should drive greater perseverance in the case of an all-or-nothing goal versus a hybrid goal.

Method. Participants consisted of 217 university students. A 2(Goal Progress: High/Low)x2(Benefit Type: All-or-Nothing/Hybrid) between subjects design was employed. The scenario was similar to study 1 except i) participants in the hybrid condition received both the all-or-nothing and cumulative benefits employed in study 1 (effectively doubling total compensation for completing the card) and ii) two items measuring sunk cost perceptions were included.

Results and discussion. ANOVA for goal perseverance (coefficient α = .93) revealed the predicted interaction between progress and benefit type (F(1,195)=4.15; p<.05). For all-or-nothing benefits progress increased perseverance (F(1,195)=11.54; p<.01), whereas in the hybrid condition (all-or-nothing plus cumulative benefits), the effect of progress was not significant (F(1,195)=.18; p=.67). A bootstrap mediation analysis indicated that the indirect effect of goal progress upon perseverance through sunk cost perceptions was significantly stronger in the case of an all-or-nothing versus a hybrid goal (95% CI: .82 to 2.03). These results support H1 and H2.

Study 3

Study 3 examined the effects of all-or-nothing versus cumulative benefits upon goal perseverance during actual goal pursuit with a real outcome.

Method. Participants were 355 university students. A 2(Goal Progress: High/Low)x2(Benefit Type: All-or-Nothing/Cumulative) between subjects design was employed. Participants chose whether to adopt a goal to win a raffle prize that entailed completing 10 tasks to earn tickets. The all-or-nothing (cumulative) condition provided 10 tickets upon successfully completing all 10 tasks (1 ticket per task). At any time participants could abandon the raffle tasks to play a computer game. Participants encountered a difficult, open ended word search puzzle task after completing either 2 (low progress condition) or 8 (high progress condition) simple evaluation tasks. The number of correct words found served as the primary measure for perseverance. Two items measuring sunk costs were recorded.

Results and discussion. ANOVA of goal perseverance revealed the predicted two-way interaction of goal progress and benefit type (F(1,260)=5.56; p<.05). For an all-or-nothing goal, progress increased perseverance (F(1,260)=4.07; p<.05). In contrast, the effect of progress for a cumulative goal was not significant (F(1,260)=1.70; p=.19) A bootstrap mediation analysis indicated that the indirect effect of progress upon perseverance through sunk costs was significantly stronger for an all-or-nothing goal compared to a cumulative goal (95% CI: .07 to 1.63). Supporting H1 and H2, all-or-nothing benefits increased perseverance as a function of progress due to exacerbated sunk costs, whereas cumulative benefits mitigated this effect.

REFERENCES

Ariely, Dan, and Gal Zauberman (2003), "Differential partitioning of extended experiences," *Organizational Behavior and Human Decision Processes*, 91(2), 128-139.

Arkes, Hal R., and Catherine Blumer (1985), "The psychology of sunk cost," *Organizational Behavior and Human Decision Processes*, 35(1), 124-140.

Arkes, Hal R., and Peter Ayton (1999), "The sunk cost and Concorde effects: Are humans less rational than lower animals?" *Psychological Bulletin*, 125(5), 591-600.

Ajzen, Icek (1991), "The theory of planned behavior," *Organizational behavior and human decision processes*, 50(2), 179-211.

Brockner, Joel (1992), "The escalation of commitment to a failing course of action: Toward theoretical progress," *Academy of Management Review*, 17(1), 39-61.

Chartrand, Tanya L., Joel Huber, Baba Shiv, and Robin J. Tanner (2008), "Nonconscious goals and consumer choice," *Journal of Consumer Research*, 35(August), 189-201.

Cunha Jr, Marcus, and Fabio Caldieraro (2009), "Sunk Cost Effects on Purely Behavioral Investments," *Cognitive Science*, 33(1), 105-113.

Dawkins, Richard, and H. Jane Brockman (1980), "Do digger wasps commit the Concorde fallacy?" *Animal Behavior*, 28(1), 892-896.

Dhar, Ravi, and Itamar Simonson (1999), "Making complementary choices in consumption episodes: Highlighting versus balancing," *Journal of Marketing Research*, 36(February), 29-44.

Fishbach, Ayelet, and Ravi Dhar (2005), "Goals as excuses or guides: The liberating effect of perceived goal progress on choice," *Journal of Consumer Research*, 32(December), 370-377.

Fishbach, Ayelet, and Ying Zhang (2009), "The dynamics of self-regulation: When goals commit versus liberate," in Michaela Wanke (Ed.), *Social Psychology of Consumer Behavior*, New York: Psychology Press, 365-386.

Ford, Martin E. (1992), *Motivating humans: Goals, emotions, and personal agency beliefs,* London: Sage.

Garland, Howard, and Stephanie Newport (1991), "Effects of absolute and relative sunk costs on the decision to persist with a course of action," *Organizational Behavior and Human Decision Processes*, 48(1), 55-69.

Gollwitzer, Peter M., and Veronika Brandstätter (1997), "Implementation intentions and effective goal pursuit," *Journal of Personality and Social Psychology*, 73(1), 186-199.

Heath, Chip. (1995), "Escalation and de-escalation of commitment in response to sunk costs: The role of budgeting in mental accounting," *Organizational Behavior and Human Decision Processes*, 62(1), 38-54.

Heath, Chip, Richard P. Larrick, and George Wu (1999) "Goals as reference points," *Cognitive Psychology*, 38(1), 79-109.

Heilizer, Fred (1977), "A review of theory and research on the assumptions of Miller's response competition (conflict) models: Response gradients," *The Journal of General Psychology*, 97(July), 17.

Hull, Clark L. (1932), "The goal gradient hypothesis and maze learning," *Psychological Review*, 39(1), 25-43.

Hull, Clark L. (1938), "The goal-gradient hypothesis applied to some field-force problems in the behavior of young children," *Psychological Review*. 45(4), 271-292.

Kahneman, Daniel and Amos Tversky (1979), "Prospect theory: An analysis of decision under risk," *Econometrica*, 47(2), 263-292.

Kivetz, Ran, Oleg Urminsky, and Yuhuang Zheng (2006), "The goal-gradient hypothesis resurrected: Purchase acceleration, illusionary goal progress, and customer retention," *Journal of Marketing Research*, 43(February), 39-58.

Kruglanski, Arie W., James Y. Shah, Ayelet Fishbach, Ron Friedman, Woo Young Chun, and David Sleeth-Keppler (2002), "A theory of goal systems," in Mark P. Zanna (Ed.), *Advances in experimental social psychology*, New York: Academic Press, 331-378.

Locke, Edwin A., and Gary P. Latham (1990), *A theory of goal setting and task performance,* Englewood Cliffs: Prentice-Hall.

Louro, Maria J., Rik Pieters, and Marcel Zeelenberg (2007), "Dynamics of multiple-goal pursuit," *Journal of Personality and Social Psychology*, 93(2), 174-182.

Miller, Neal E. (1944), "Experimental studies of conflict," in *Personality and the behavior disorders*, Oxford: Ronald Press, 431-465.

Nunes, Joseph C., and Xavier Drèze (2006), "The endowed progress effect: How artificial advancement increases effort," *Journal of Consumer Research*, 32(March), 504-512.

Soman, Dilip (2001), "The mental accounting of sunk time costs: Why time is not like money," *Journal of Behavioral Decision Making*, 14(3), 169-185.

Soman, Dilip, and Amar Cheema (2004), "When goals are counterproductive: the effects of violation of a behavioral goal on subsequent performance," *Journal of Consumer Research*, 31(June), 52-62.

Staw, Barry M. (1976). "Knee-deep in the big muddy: A study of escalating commitment to a chosen course of action." *Organizational Behavior and Human Performance*, 16, 27-44.

Staw, Barry M. (1997), "The Escalation of commitment: an update and appraisal," in Z. Shapira (Ed.), *Organizational decision making,* New York: Cambridge University Press, 191-215.

Thaler, Richard (1980), "Toward a positive theory of consumer choice," *Journal of Economic Behavior and Organization*, 1(March), 39-60.

Wilcox, Keith, Beth Vallen, Lauren Block, and Gavan J. Fitzsimons (2009), "Vicarious goal fulfillment: When the mere presence of a healthy option leads to an ironically indulgent decision," *Journal of Consumer Research*, 36(October), 380-393.

Zhao, Xinshu, Lynch Jr, John G., and Qimei Chen (2010), "Reconsidering Baron and Kenny: Myths and truths about mediation analysis," *Journal of Consumer Research*, 37(August), 197-206.

Marcel Zeelenberg, and Eric Van Dijk (1997), "A reverse sunk cost effect in risky decision making: Sometimes we have too much invested to gamble," *Journal of Economic Psychology*, 18(6), 677-691.

The Nonanalytic Influence of Memory on Product Placement Consequences

Tamara Ansons, University of Michigan, USA
Jason Leboe, University of Manitoba, Canada

EXTENDED ABSTRACT

Despite the enthusiastic use of product placements, researchers have not determined whether or not this form of advertising produces profitable outcomes for featured brands. In a comprehensive review, Balasubramanian, Karrh, and Patwardhan (2006) proposed that outcomes of product placements fall into three broad categories: cognitive, affective and conative/choice effects. Although cognitive outcomes, or memory effects, such as product recognition and recall, have received the most attention from consumer researchers, research that has examined the relationship between the different effects, have revealed an inconsistent association. Most consistent, however, appears to be a negative association between memory effects and evaluation and choice measures (Cowley and Barron 2008; Law and Braun 2000; Matthes, Schemer, and Wirth 2007). To accommodate the complex associations that have been found in previous studies, the current framework emphasizes how the interaction between memory processes and task features give rise to measurable outcomes of product placement.

In past frameworks, memory has been treated as being used more analytically to guide brand preferences. Mainly, if viewers remember a brand being featured during a product placement event, this is thought to instigate a negative response toward the brand through the activation of persuasion knowledge (Campbell and Kirmani 2000; Friestad and Wright 1994). Contrasting this analytic use of memory, we examine how nonanalytic influences, meaning processes that are irrelevant to the current task (Jacoby and Brooks 1984), contribute to consequences observed for brands that are featured during a product placement event. As has been emphasized in other studies (Whittlesea and Price 2001), the nonanalytic influence on subjective judgments is expected to arise out of perceptual fluency that occurs for brands that are presented during a product placement event.

Methodology

Participants were presented with a narrative, which was an adapted excerpt from a novel (Footner 1940). Embedded within the narrative were 20 different brands that varied across a number of different product categories (e.g., bottled water, electronics, clothing). Each of the brands were presented either once or five times within the narrative. Four versions of the passage was created so that, one of two brands from a certain product category appeared during the narrative.

Participants then completed a filler task before completing a recognition task and then a brand choice task. In both the recognition and brand choice task, participants were presented brands that appeared in the narrative and new brands and were asked to judged their recognition for those items (1 = *low* and 4 = *high* on both familiarity and recollection following Higham and Vokey 2004) and their likelihood to select a brand for a close friend (1= *Definitely would not select* to 9 = *Definitely would select*).

Summary of Main Findings

Study 1

Participants' performance on the recognition task indicated that they were better able at recognizing brands that were presented five times in the narrative, compared to brands that were presented once in the narrative. Despite the fact that participants were better able to remember brands that were presented five times, participants reported higher choice ratings for brands that were presented once (5.70 vs. 6.20), $F(1, 90) = 11.83$, $MSE = 0.96$, $p = .001$, and five times (5.70 vs. 6.31), $F(1, 90) = 14.16$, $MSE = 1.18$, $p < .001$, compared to brands that were not presented in the narrative.

Studies 2 and 2a

A possible alternative explanation for the findings observed in study 1 is that participants experienced narrative transportation (Green and Brock 2000), or were highly engaged with the narrative, which lead to a positive response to featured brands (Escalas 2004, 2007). If this were the case, then disrupting the extent to which participants were engaged with the narrative (by presenting the narrative in a random order to some participants) should result in a more negative response to the featured brands. Although participants reported being more engaged in the sequential narrative, compared to the randomly presented narrative, (3.23 vs. 2.71), $t(80) = 3.51$, $p = .001$, choice ratings were only influenced by the prior presentation of the brand, $F(2, 160) = 7.75$, $MSE = 0.59$, $p = .001$. Overall, participants reported higher brand choice ratings for brands that were presented once, compared to brands that were new (6.30 vs. 5.84), $F(1, 81) = 17.28$, $MSE = 0.50$, $p < .001$, and to brands that were presented five times (6.30 vs. 5.99), $F(1, 81) = 6.06$, $MSE = 0.67$, $p = .016$. However, this effect only occurred when the brand's prior presentation in the narrative was not made salient (study 2a).

Study 3

If the presentation of a brand within a narrative activates persuasion knowledge and that information is used analytically when completing the choice task, then altering the activation of persuasion knowledge (by presenting brands blatantly or subtly) should moderate influence of a brand's prior presentation on choice ratings. Although the blatant presentation of the brand resulted in higher persuasion knowledge ratings, compared to when the brand was subtly presented for brands that were presented five times, (5.68 vs. 4.62), $t(121) = -3.02$, $p = .003$, and once, (4.20 vs. 3.29), $t(121) = -2.67$, $p = .009$, analyzing the choice ratings indicated only a main effect of brand presentation number, $F(2, 238) = 3.92$, $MSE = 0.72$, $p = .02$. Overall, participants reported significantly higher choice ratings for brands that were presented five times in the narrative, compared to brands that were new (6.11 vs. 5.81), $F(1, 122) = 6.03$, $MSE = 0.91$, $p = .015$, and compared to brands that were presented once during the narrative (6.11 vs. 5.92), $F(1, 122) = 4.23$, $MSE = 0.52$, $p = .042$.

Concluding Comments

Together, these studies provide evidence in support of the nonanalytic influence of memory. Since choice ratings were not influenced by the level of engagement nor the activation of persuasion knowledge, the nonanalytic influence of memory, and not a more deliberate influence of memory, appeared to influence choice ratings. More broadly, these findings suggest that product placements do result in positive outcomes for featured brand, based on the nonanalytic influence of memory.

REFERENCES

Balasubramanian, Slva K., James A. Karrh, and Hermant Patwardhan (2006), "Audience Response to Product Placements: An Integrative Framework and Future Research Agenda," *Journal of Advertising*, 35 (Fall), 115-41.

Bargh, John (2002), "Losing Consciousness: Automatic Influences on Consumer Judgment, Behavior, and Motivation," *Journal of Consumer Research,* 29 (September), 280-85.

Bornstein, Robert F. (1989), "Exposure and Affect: Overview and Meta-Analysis of Research, 1968-1987," *Psychological Bulletin,* 106 (September), 265-89.

Bornstein, Robert F. and Paul R. D'Agostino (1992), "Stimulus Recognition and the Mere Exposure Effect," *Journal of Personality and Social Psychology,* 63 (4), 545-52.

Campbell, Margaret C. and Amna Kirmani (2000), "Consumers' Use of Persuasion Knowledge: The Effects of Accessibility and Cognitive Capacity on Perceptions of an Influence Agent, *Journal of Consumer Research,* 27 (June), 69-83.

Cowley, Elizabeth and Chris Barron (2008), "When Product Placement Goes Wrong: The Effects of Program Liking and Placement Prominence," *Journal of Advertising,* 37 (March), 89-98.

Escalas, Jennifer E. (2004), "Imagine Yourself in the Product: Mental Simulation, Narrative Transportation, and Persuasion," *Journal of Advertising,* 33 (Summer), 37-48.

--- (2007), "Self-Referencing and Persuasion: Narrative Transportation Versus Analytical Elaboration," *Journal of Consumer Research,* 33 (March), 421-29.

Friese, Malte, Michaela Wänke, and Henning Plessner (2006), "Implicit Consumer Preferences and their Influence on Product Choice," *Psychology and Marketing,* 23 (9), 727-40.

Friestad, Marian and Peter Wright (1994), "The Persuasion Knowledge Model: How People Cope with Persuasion Attempts," *Journal of Consumer Research,* 21 (June), 1-31.

Footner, Hulbert (1940), *Sinfully Rich,* New York, NY and London, UK: Harper.

Green, Melanie C. and Timothy C. Brock (2000), "The Role of Transportation in the Persuasiveness of Public Narratives," *Journal of Personality and Social Psychology,* 79 (5), 701-21.

Higham, Philip A. and John R. Vokey (2004), "Illusory Recollection and Dual Process Models of Recognition Memory," *Quarterly Journal of Experimental Psychology,* 57A (May), 714-744.

Hunt, R. Reed (1995), "The Subtlety of Distinctiveness: What von Restorff Really Did," *Psychonomic Bulletin & Review,* 2 (1), 105-12.

Jacoby, Larry L. and Lee R. Brooks (1984), "Nonanalytic Cognition: Memory, Perception, and Concept Learning," in *The Psychology of Learning and Motivation,* ed. Gordon H. Bower, New York, NY: Academic Press, 1-47.

Jacoby, Larry L., Colleen M. Kelley, Judith Brown, and Jennifer Jasechko (1989), "Becoming Famous Overnight: Limits on the Ability to Avoid Unconscious Influences of the Past," *Journal of Personality and Social Psychology,* 56 (3), 326-38.

Law Sharmistha and Kathryn Braun (2000), "I'll Have what She is Having: Gauging the Impact of Product Placement on Viewers, *Psychology & Marketing,* 17 (12), 1059-75.

Lee, Angela Y. and Aparna A. Labroo (2004), "The Effect of Conceptual and Perceptual Fluency on Brand Evaluation," *Journal of Marketing Research,* 41 (May), 151-65.

Lessiter, Jane, Jonathan Freeman, Edmund Keogh, and Jules D. Davidoff (2001), "A Cross-Media Presence Questionnaire: The ITC Sense of Presence Inventory," *Presence: Teleoperators and Virtual Environments,* 10 (3), 282-97.

Matthes, Jörg, Christian Schemer and Werner Wirth (2007), "More than Meets the Eye: Investigating the Hidden Impact of Brand Placements in Television Magazines," *International Journal of Advertising,* 26 (4), 477-503.

PQ Media (2005), "Product Placement Spending in Media 2005," Retrieved April 25, 2008, from http://www.pqmedia.com/product-placement-spending-in-media.html.

PQ Media (2010), "Global Branded Entertainment Marketing Forecast 2010-2014," Retrieved June 28, 2010, from http://www.pqmedia.com/brandedentertainmentforecast2010.html.

Russell, Cristel A. (2002), "Investigating the Effectiveness of Product Placements in Television Shows: The Role of Modality and Plot Connection Congruence on Brand Memory and Attitude," *Journal of Consumer Research,* 29 (December), 306-18.

Schmidt, Stephen R. (1991), "Can we Have a Distinctive Theory of Memory? *Memory & Cognition,* 19 (6), 523-42.

Schwarz, Norbert, Herbert Bless, Fritz Strack, Gisela Klumpp, Helga Rittenauer-Schatka, and Annette Simons (1991), "Ease of Retrieval as Information: Another Look at the Availability Heuristic," *Journal of Personality and Social Psychology,* 61 (2), 195-202.

van Reijmersdal, Eva A., Peter C. Neijens, and Edith G. Smit (2007), "Effects of Television Brand Placement on Brand Image," *Psychology and Marketing,* 24 (5), 403-20.

von Restorff, Hedwig (1933), Über die Wirkung von Bereichsbildungen im Spurenfeld [On the Effect of Spheres Formations in the Trace Field]. *Psychologische Forschung, 18,* 299-342.

Whittlesea, Bruce W. A. (1997), "Production, Evaluation, and Preservation of Experiences: Constructive Processing in Remembering and Performance Tasks," in *Psychology of Learning and Motivation,* Vol. 37, ed. Douglas L. Medlin, New York, NY: Academic Press, 211-64.

Whittlesea, Bruce W. A. and Jason P. Leboe (2000), "The Heuristic Basis of Remembering and Classification: Fluency, Generation, and Resemblance," *Journal of Experimental Psychology: General,* 129 (1), 84-106.

Whittlesea, Bruce W. A. and John R. Price (2001), "Implicit/Explicit Memory Versus Analytic/Nonanalytic Processing: Rethinking the Mere Exposure Effect," *Memory and Cognition,* 29 (2), 234-46.

Winkielman, Piotr and John T. Cacioppo (2001), "Mind at Ease Puts a Smile on the Face: Psychophysiological Evidence that Processing Facilitation Increases positive affect. *Journal of Personality and Social Psychology,* 81 (6), 989-1000.

Winkielman, Piotr and Norbert Schwarz (2001), "How Pleasant was Your Childhood? Beliefs About Memory Shape Inferences from Experienced Difficulty of Recall," *Psychological Science,* 12 (2), 176-79.

Yang, Moonhee and David R. Roskos-Ewoldsen (2007), "The Effectiveness of Brand Placements in the Movies: Levels of Placements, Explicit and Implicit Memory, and Brand-Choice Behavior," *Journal of Communication,* 57 (3), 469-89.

Zajonc, Robert B. (1968), "Attitudinal Effects of Mere Exposure," *Journal of Personality and Social Psychology Monographs,* 9 (2, Pt 2), 1-27.

Evaluative Conditioning Revisited: An Affective Information Processing Model

Jonathan Hasford, University of Kentucky, USA
David Hardesty, University of Kentucky, USA
Blair Kidwell, University of Kentucky, USA

EXTENDED ABSTRACT

When attempting to influence consumer attitudes toward a particular product, companies often pair brands with naturally appealing images which subsequently transfers the favorable reaction from the image to the brand. This process is known as *evaluative conditioning* and has garnered significant attention by consumer researchers (e.g. Gibson 2008; Stuart, Shimp, and Engle 1987; Sweldens, Van Osselaer, and Janiszewski 2010) since the seminal work of Gorn (1982). Despite nearly three decades of research in evaluative conditioning, one fundamental question remains unanswered; namely, what is the underlying theoretical process that produces evaluative conditioning effects? Despite several proposed models of the evaluative conditioning process, no theoretical approach is capable of fully explaining why the transfer of attitudes from the unconditioned stimulus (i.e. appealing image) to the conditioned stimulus (i.e. brand) occurs (Hofmann et al. 2010). The current research uses an affect-as-information perspective (Schwarz and Clore 1996) to explain evaluative conditioning effects in food choice.

A primary concern within our model is how individuals process emotional information. Specifically, we are interested in understanding how conditioning transfers emotional information via multiple information processing pathways. Whether individuals thoughtfully consider the emotion present or simply rely on affective cues to make evaluations could differentially impact subsequent attitudes that are developed from conditioning. Thus, to further develop the affect-as-information model, we investigate emotional information processing differences and their impact on subsequent evaluations.

Affect-as-Information Perspective

Prior research has suggested that affective transfers may occur during the conditioning process (e.g. De Houwer, Thomas, and Baeyens 2001; Sweldens et al. 2010). We extend this perspective and suggest an affect-as-information model of evaluative conditioning; conditioning occurs based on how individuals process the emotional information present within the unconditioned stimulus. This perspective is based on the role of emotion in initial attitude formation (e.g. Schwarz 1997; Wood 2000) as well as models of attitude formation (Bagozzi, Tybout, Craig, and Sternthal 1979; Fishbein 1967; Schwarz and Clore 1996).

Individuals can process the emotion present in the unconditioned stimulus in one of two ways. Traditional perspectives on the role of affect in information processing suggest that System 1 (implicit, nonconscious) processing typically considers emotion automatically (Evans 2008; Johar, Maheswaran, and Peracchio 2006). However, emotion can also transfer between brand and image consciously, which facilitates explicit information processing (Griskevicius, Shiota, and Neufeld 2010).

The conscious transfer of emotion between stimuli is also dependent on individual characteristics. Individuals differ in their ability to process emotional information (Bless et al. 1996). Individuals who are skilled in using, understanding, and managing emotional information may recognize that emotions elicited from the unconditioned stimulus do not necessarily indicate diagnostic information about the conditioned brand. Conversely, less-skilled others may focus on the emotional cues from the unconditioned stimulus as a primary determinant of subsequent evaluations. This individual difference is critical in understanding the impact of emotional information transferred via conditioning.

The affect-as-information perspective is able to explain several shortcomings of existing evaluative conditioning theories outlined by Hofmann et al. (2010). Contingent aware participants (i.e. those who recognize the pairing of unconditioned and conditioned stimuli) should demonstrate stronger conditioning effects as they more thoughtfully consider the emotion present in the conditioning process. Furthermore, affect-as-information can explain post-conditioning attitudinal changes in the conditioned stimulus when the valence of the unconditioned stimulus changes. Individuals will utilize new information on the unconditioned stimulus and re-evaluate the conditioned stimulus based on the affective change in attitude toward the unconditioned stimulus. Lastly, existing theories of evaluative conditioning lack empirical support for the main propositions of each theory. Study 1 is designed to empirically demonstrate the affect-as-information explanation for evaluative conditioning effects.

Study 1

Eighty-nine participants were assigned to the positive conditioning group, where fictitious brands were paired with attractive images, the negative conditioning group, where fictitious brands were paired with unattractive images, or the control group where all images and brands were randomly presented. After evaluating target healthy and unhealthy fictitious food brands, participants were then given a scenario about attending a football game and asked how likely they were to attend. If the affect-as-information perspective explains evaluative conditioning, then the experienced affect from conditioning trials should not only influence attitudes toward the fictitious brands but towards the likelihood of attending the game as well (Pham 1998).

Participants in the positive-conditioning group had significantly higher ratings for the target brand (M = 5.25) than those in the neutral (control) condition (M = 4.01, p < .05) and those in the negative-conditioning group (M = 2.06, p < .01). Furthermore, in the positive-conditioning group, increased attitudes toward the target brand from conditioning predicted increased likelihood of attending the game ($\beta = .39$, $t = 2.23$, $p < .05$). In the negative-conditioning group, decreased attitudes toward the target brand from conditioning predicted decreased likelihood of attending the game ($\beta = .37$, $t = 2.16$, $p < .05$). Participant attitudes in the control condition were unrelated to likelihood of attending the game. These findings, in conjunction with the refutation of existing evaluative conditioning models by Hoffman et al. (2010), support the affect-as-information perspective underlying evaluative conditioning effects.

Study 2

Having established the superiority of the affect-as-information model for understanding evaluative conditioning effects, we next investigate how individuals differentially process emotional information and suggest that emotional intelligence can limit conditioning's initial transfer of emotion. Eighty-two participants were assigned to the same positive or control conditions from Study 1. Participant emotional intelligence was measured via the Consumer Emotional Intelligence Scale (Kidwell, Hardesty, and Childers 2008). Regression results demonstrated a significant interaction between emotional intelligence and conditioning group ($\beta = -1.61$,

$p < .05$) where higher levels of emotional intelligence decreased the influence of evaluative conditioning on target brand attitudes. These findings suggest that evaluative conditioning tactics do not influence consumers who have high emotional intelligence, while individuals who lack emotional intelligence are susceptible to attitude change from conditioning.

Together, the results of two studies provide new insights into evaluative conditioning research. First, a new theoretical explanation of evaluative conditioning effects is provided via the affect-as-information perspective. Secondly, we show that the ability to thoughtfully understand and utilize emotions (i.e., emotional intelligence) fundamentally changes how individuals process emotion from conditioning trials. We hope this research provides a new dominant perspective in explaining evaluative conditioning effects and furthers interest in this popular domain.

REFERENCES

Baeyens, Frank, Paul Eelen, G. Crombez, and O. Van Den Bergh (1992), "Human Evaluative Conditioning: Acquisition Trials, Presentation Schedule, Evaluative Style and Contingency Awareness," *Behavior Research and Therapy*, 30 (2), 133-42.

Bagozzi, Richard P., Alice M. Tybout, C. Samuel Craig, and Brian Sternthal (1979), "The Construct Validity of the Tripartite Classification of Attitudes," *Journal of Marketing Research*, 16 (February), 88-95.

Bless, Herbert, Gerald L. Clore, Norbert Schwarz, Verena Golisano, Christina Rabe, and Marcus Wolk (1996), "Mood and the Use of Scripts: Does a Happy Mood Really Lead to Mindlessness," *Journal of Personality and Social Psychology*, 71 (4), 665-79.

Cohen, Joel B., Michel Tuan Pham, and Eduardo B. Andrade (2008), "The Nature and Role of Affect in Consumer Behavior," in *Handbook of Consumer Psychology*, Curtis P. Haugtvedt, Paul M. Herr, and Frank R. Kardes (eds.), Taylor and Francis, New York.

Darke, Peter R., Amitava Chattopadhyay, and Laurence Ashworth (2006), "The Importance and Functional Significance of Affective Cues in Consumer Choice," *Journal of Consumer Research*, 33 (December), 322-8.

Davey, Graham C. L. (1994), "Defining the Important Theoretical Questions to Ask About Evaluative Conditioning: A Reply to Martin and Levey (1994)," *Behavior Research and Therapy*, 32 (3), 307-10.

De Houwer, Jan (2007), "A Conceptual and Theoretical Analysis of Evaluative Conditioning," *The Spanish Journal of Psychology*, 10 (2), 230-41.

————, Sarah Thomas, and Frank Baeyens (2001), "Associative Learning of Likes and Dislikes: A Review of 25 Years of Research on Human Evaluative Conditioning," *Psychological Bulletin*, 127 (6), 853-69.

Dempsey, Melanie A. and Andrew A. Mitchell (2010), "The Influence of Implicit Attitudes on Choice When Consumers Are Confronted with Conflicting Attribute Information," *Journal of Consumer Research*, 37 (December), 614-25.

Epstein, Seymour (2010), "Demystifying Intuition: What It Is, What It Does, and How It Does It," *Psychological Inquiry*, 21 (4), 295-312.

Evans, Jonathan St. B. T. (2008), "Dual-Processing Accounts of Reasoning, Judgment, and Social Cognition," *Annual Review of Psychology*, 59 (1), 255-78.

Field, Andy P. (2000), "I Like It, but I Am Not Sure Why: Can Evaluative Conditioning Occur Without Conscious Awareness?" *Consciousness and Cognition*, 9 (1), 13-36.

Fishbein, Martin (1967), "A Consideration of Beliefs and Their Role in Attitude Measurement," in *Reading in Attitude Theory and Measurement*, ed. Martin Fishbein, New York: John Wiley and Sons, Inc.

Germer, Christopher K. (2009), *The Mindful Path to Self-Compassion: Freeing Yourself from Destructive Thoughts and Emotions*, New York: The Guilford Press.

Gibson, Bryan (2008), "Can Evaluative Conditioning Change Attitudes toward Mature Brands? New Evidence from the Implicit Association Test," *Journal of Consumer Research*, 35 (June), 178-88.

Gorn, Gerald J. (1982), "The Effects of Music in Advertising on Choice Behavior: A Classical Conditioning Approach," *Journal of Marketing*, 46 (1), 94-101.

Griskevicius, Vladas, Michelle N. Shiota, and Samantha L. Neufeld (2010), "Influence of Different Positive Emotions on Persuasion Processing: A Functional Evolutionary Approach," *Emotion*, 10 (2), 190-206.

Hofmann, Wilhelm, Jan De Houwer, Marco Perugini, Frank Baeyens, and Geert Crombez (2010), "Evaluative Conditioning in Humans: A Meta-Analysis," *Psychological Bulletin*, 136 (3), 390-421.

Johar, Gita Venkataramani, Durairaj Maheswaran, and Laura A. Peracchio (2006), "MAPping the Frontiers: Theoretical Advances in Consumer Research on Memory, Affect, and Persuasion," *Journal of Consumer Research*, 33 (June), 139-49.

Jones, Christopher R., Russell H. Fazio, and Michael A. Olson (2009), "Implicit Misattribution as a Mechanism Underlying Evaluative Conditioning," *Journal of Personality and Social Psychology*, 96 (5), 933-48.

Kerkhof, Inneke, Debora Vansteenwegen, Frank Baeyens, and Dirk Hermans (2009), "A Picture-Flavor Paradigm for Studying Complex Conditioning Processes in Food Preference Learning," *Appetitie*, 53 (3), 303-8.

Kidwell, Blair, David M. Hardesty, and Terry L. Childers (2008), "Consumer Emotional Intelligence: Conceptualization, Measurement, and the Prediction of Consumer Decision Making," *Journal of Consumer Research*, 35 (June), 154-66.

Lei, Jing, Niraj Dawar, and Jos Lemmink (2008), "Negative Spillover in Brand Portfolios: Exploring the Antecedents of Asymmetric Effects," *Journal of Marketing*, 72 (May) 111-23.

Levey, Archie B. and Irene Martin (1975), "Classical Conditioning of Human 'Evaluative' Responses," *Behavior Research and Therapy*, 13 (4), 205-7.

Lewicki, Pawel, Thomas Hill, and Maria Czyzewska (1992), "Nonconscious Acquisition of Information," *American Psychologist*, 47 (6), 796-801.

Livingstone, Barbara M. and Alison E. Black (2003), "Markers of the Validity of Reported Energy Intake," *Journal of Nutrition*, 133 (3), 895–920.

Nestle, Marion (2003), "Increasing Portion Sizes in American Diets: More Calories, More Obesity," *Journal of the American Dietetic Association*, 103 (1), 39-40.

Petty, Richard E., John T. Cacioppo, and David Schumann (1983), "Central and Peripheral Routes to Advertising Effectiveness: The Moderating Role of Involvement," *Journal of Consumer Research*, 10 (September), 135-46.

Pham, Michel Tuan (1998), "Representativeness, Relevance, and the Use of Feelings in Decision Making," *Journal of Consumer Research*, 25 (2), 144-59.

Raghunathan, Rajagopal, Rebecca Walker Naylor, and Wayne D. Hoyer (2006), "The Unhealthy = Tasty Intuition and Its Effects on Taste Inferences, Enjoyment, and Choice of Food Products," *Journal of Marketing*, 70 (October), 170-84.

Roehm, Michelle L. and Alice M. Tybout (2006), "When Will a Brand Scandal Spill Over, and How Should Competitors Respond?" *Journal of Marketing Research*, 43 (August), 366-73.

Rosenberg, Milton J. and Hovland, Carl I. (1960). Cognitive, Affective and Behavioural Components of Attitude in M.J. Rosenberg, C.I. Hovland, W.J. McGuire, R.P. Abelson & J.W. Brehm (Eds) Attitude Organisation and Change: An Analysis of Consistency Among Attitude Components. New Haven, Ct: Yale University. Cited in Psychology: The Science of Mind and Behaviour (2001).

Schwarz, Norbert (1997), "Moods and Attitude Judgments: A Comment on Fishbein and Middlestadt.," *Journal of Consumer Psychology*, 6 (1), 93-8.

--- and Gerald L. Clore (1996), "Feelings and Phenomenal Experiences," in *Handbook of Social Cognition*, eds. E. Tory Higgins and Arie W. Kruglanski, Hillsdale, NJ: Erlbaum.

--- and --- (2003), "Mood as Information: 20 Years Later," *Psychological Inquiry*, 14 (3), 296-303.

Shapiro, Jenessa R., Joshua M. Ackerman, Steven L. Neuberg, Jon K. Maner, D. Vaughn Becker, and Douglas T. Kenrick (2009), "Following in the Wake of Anger: When Not Discriminating Is Discriminating," *Personality and Social Psychology Bulletin*, 35 (10), 1356-67.

Shimp, Terence A., Eva M. Hyatt, and David J. Snyder (1991), "A Critical Appraisal of Demand Artifacts in Consumer Research," *Journal of Consumer Research*, 18 (3), 273-83.

Slovic, Paul, Melissa L. Finucane, Ellen Peters, and Donald G. MacGregor (2004), "Risk as Analysis and Risk as Feelings: Some Thoughts about Affect, Reason, Risk, and Rationality," *Risk Analysis*, 24 (April), 311-22.

Stuart, Elnora W., Terrence A. Shimp, and Randall W. Engle (1987), "Classical Conditioning of Consumer Attitudes: Four Experiments in an Advertising Context," *Journal of Consumer Research*, 14 (3), 334-49.

Sweldens, Steven, Stijn M. J. van Osselaer, and Chris Janiszewski (2010), "Evaluative Conditioning Procedures and the Resilience of Conditioned Brand Attitudes," *Journal of Consumer Research*, 37 (October), 473-89.

Tice, Dianne M, Ellen Bratslavsky, and Roy F. Baumeister (2001), "Emotional Distress Regulation Takes Precedence Over Impulse Control: If You Feel Bad, Do It!" *Journal of Personality and Social Psychology*, 80 (1), 53-67.

Walther, Eva and Sofia Grigoriadis (2004), "Why Sad People Like Shoes Better: The Influence of Mood on the Evaluative Conditioning of Consumer Attitudes," *Psychology and Marketing*, 21 (10), 755-73.

Watson, David, Lee Anna Clark, and Auke Tellegen (1998), "Development and Validation of Brief Measures of Positive and Negative Affect: The PANAS Scales," *Journal of Personality and Social Psychology*, 54 (6), 1063-70.

Wegener, Duane T. and Richard E. Petty (1996), "Effects of Mood on Persuasion Processes: Enhancing, Reducing, and Biasing Scrutiny of Attitude-Relevant Information," in *Striving and Feeling: Interactions Among Goals, Affect, and Self-Regulation*, eds. L. L. Martin and A. Tesser, Mahwah, NJ: Erlbaum, 329-62.

Wood, Wendy (2000), "Attitude Change: Persuasion and Social Influence," *Annual Review of Psychology*, 51 (1), 539-70.

Zhao, Xinshu, John G. Lynch Jr., and Qimei Chen (2010), "Reconsidering Baron and Kenny: Myths and Truths About Mediation Analysis," *Journal of Consumer Research*, 37 (2), 197-206.

Bolstering versus Counterarguing Mindsets:
Implications for the Effectiveness of Persuasive Messages

Alison Jing Xu, University of Toronto, Canada
Robert S. Wyer, Jr., Chinese University of Hong Kong, Hong Kong

EXTENDED ABSTRACT

People who encounter a persuasive communication might either (a) generate thoughts that bolster the communicator's point of view or (b) attempt to refute the implications of the communication. These dispositions could obviously depend on individuals' prior agreement or disagreement with the point of view being expressed. However, they could also be influenced by a mindset that is activated by the behavior that participants performed before the persuasive communication is encountered (Wyer and Xu 2010). We proposed and found that inducing participants to make supportive elaborations about a series of propositions activated a bolstering mindset that increased the effectiveness of an unrelated advertisement they encountered subsequently. However, inducing participants to refute the implications of a series of propositions activated a counterarguing mindset that decreased the ad's effectiveness. These mindsets had more impact when the cognitive behavior they activated differed from the default behavior that was likely to occur in the absence of these mindsets. However, when a persuasive communication is difficult to refute, a counterarguing mindset that increases participants' awareness of this difficulty could increase their perceptions of the communication's validity and, therefore, could increase its effectiveness rather than decreasing it. Finally, watching a political speech or debate activated different mindsets, depending on participants' a priori attitude toward the politicians involved, and these mindsets influenced the impact of an ad that was presented later. Four experiments tested these possibilities.

Experiment 1 investigated the influence of mindsets on the impact of appealing ads. Participants performed two ostensibly unrelated tasks. Participants in *bolstering mindset* conditions generated thoughts about propositions with which they typically agreed (e.g., "Reading enriches the mind"). In contrast, participants in *counterarguing mindset* conditions generated thoughts about the negations of these propositions (e.g., "Reading is bad for the mind"). In *control* conditions, participants were asked to write three short essays to show their knowledge of neutral topics such as the pyramids of Egypt. After that, all participants were exposed to an ad about a vacation spot and they (1) rated the attractiveness of the vacation spot (2) evaluated the persuasiveness of the ad, and (3) wrote down the thoughts they had about the ad. The results showed that inducing a counterarguing mindset increased the number of negative thoughts that participants generated, and consequently, decreased their evaluations of the vacation spot and the persuasiveness of the ad. However, inducing a bolstering mindset nonsignificantly increased the number of positive thoughts generated, and consequently, increased their evaluations of the vacation spot and persuasiveness of the ad. Mediation analysis showed that the type of thoughts mediated the influence of mindsets on product evaluations.

Experiment 2 explored the influence of mindsets on the impact of an unappealing ad. The results showed that when the ad was unappealing, counterarguing was the default processing strategy. Therefore, inducing a counterarguing mindset had little additional negative effect. However, inducing a bolstering mindset had a significant positive effect on product evaluations.

Experiment 3 showed a boomerang effect of the counterarguing mindset. Bolstering and counterarguing mindsets were induced as in Experiment 1. Then, these and control participants read an appeal

from UNICEF for donations to help disadvantaged children in Africa get an education. Participants then reported their intentions to make a monetary donation and decided how much they would be willing to donate. Because (a) donation appeals usually urge individuals to engage in altruistic behaviors that have socially desirable implications, and (b) the communicators have no intrinsic self-interest in the success of persuasion, we expected that recipients would find it difficult to generate arguments against the appeal's validity. Therefore, inducing a counterarguing mindset would increase participants' perceptions of the appeal's validity and would consequently *increase* its effectiveness rather than decreasing it. Results confirmed these expectations. Participants who adopted a counterarguing mind-set reported higher donation intentions and were willing to donate more money than participants in the bolstering mind-set and control conditions, which did not differ from each other.

Experiment 4 examined whether covertly generate arguments for or against a message without expressing them overtly would be sufficient to activate a general disposition to elaborate or counterargue. Participants were self-categorized as Republicans, Democrats, or Independents, and they were randomly assigned to one of four conditions. In two *speech* conditions, participants first watched either (a) a 10-minute video of Barack Obama's speech on his economic rescue plan in the 2008 presidential campaign or (b) a comparable segment of a speech on economic policy by John McCain. In a third, *debate* condition, participants watched a 10-minute video of the third Presidential debate between John McCain and Barack Obama on their proposed economic plans. In *control* conditions, participants were not exposed to any video. Then, all participants watched a video-taped speech by the president of Toyota that was intended to increase consumers' confidence in Toyota products' safety. After receiving these materials, participants reported their attitudes toward Toyota.

We expected that participants with a strong a priori preference for one of the two candidates would be motivated to generate supportive elaborations of a speech by their preferred candidate but to counterargue the assertions made in a speech by the opposing candidate. On the other hand, both Democrats and Republicans should be highly motivated to support their favorite candidate when watching the presidential debate and, therefore, should acquire a bolstering mind-set in this condition. When participants were politically independent, different effects were expected. These participants were expected to be relatively indifferent to the two candidates and to take their assertions at face value. To this extent, they should elaborate the implications of the speech regardless of who delivers it, and should develop a bolstering mindset. When these participants listened to the presidential debate, however, we expected them to follow the two candidates' attempts to refute one another's positions and, in doing so, to covertly counterargue themselves. Thus, we expected them to acquire a counterarguing mindset. In all cases, activating a bolstering mindset would increase participants' evaluations of Toyota, whereas a counterarguing mindset would decrease their evaluations of Toyota. Because Toyota is a favorable brand, a counteraruing mindset would have a stronger influence than a bolstering mindset does. Results confirmed these expectations.

The present series of studies provide the first demonstration of the effects of a behavioral mindset on the impact of a persuasive communication. In doing so, they extend our general understanding

Advances in Consumer Research
Volume 39, ©2011

of mindsets in three ways. First, mindsets have more impact when the cognitive behavior they activated differed from the default behavior that was likely to occur in the absence of these mindsets. Second, when the behavior induced by a mindset is unsuccessful in attaining the goal to which it is relevant, it can have a boomerang effect. Finally, a mindset can be activated not only by overt behavior but also by unobserved cognitive activity that people engaged in in the previous situation.

REFERENCES

Campbell, Margaret C. and AmnaKirmani (2008), "I Know What You're Doing and Why You're Doing It: The Use of the Persuasion Knowledge Model in Consumer Research," in *The Handbook of Consumer Psychology*, ed. Curtis Haugtvedt, Paul M. Herr, and Frank R. Kardes. Mahwah, NJ: Lawrence Erlbaum Associates.

Chaiken, Shelly (1980), "Heuristic versus Systematic Information Processing in the Use of Source versusMessage Cues in Persuasion," *Journal of Personality and Social Psychology*, 39, 752-766.

Chaiken, S., Wendy Wood, and Alice H. Eagly (1996), "Principles of Persuasion" in *Social psychology: Handbook of basic principles*, ed. E. Tory Higgins and Arie. W.Kruglanski, New York: Guilford Press, 702-42.

Collins, Allan M. and Elizabeth F. Loftus (1975), "A Spreading Activation Theory of Semantic Processing," *Psychological Review*, 82 (6), 407–28.

Dhar, Ravi, Joel Huber, and Uzma Khan (2007), "The Shopping Momentum Effect," *Journal of Marketing Research,* 44(3), 370-78.

Friestad, Marian and Peter Wright (1994), "The Persuasion Knowledge Model: How People Cope with Persuasion Attempts," Journal of Consumer Research, 21 (June), 1-31.

Gollwitzer, Peter M. and Ute Bayer (1999), "Deliberative versus Implemental Mindsets in the Control of Action," in *Dual-process Theories in Social Psychology*, ed. Shelly Chaiken and Yaacov Trope, New York: Guilford Press, 403-22.

Greenwald, Anthony G. (1968), "Cognitive Learning, Cognitive Response to Persuasion, and Attitude Change," in *Psychological Foundations of Attitudes*, ed. Anthony G. Greenwald, Timothy C. Brock, and Thomas M. Ostrom, New York: Academic Press, 148-70.

McGuire, William J. (1964), "Inducing Resistance to Persuasion: Some Contemporary Approaches," in *Advances in Experimental Social Psychology,* 1,ed. Leonard Berkowitz 191 – 229.

Petty, Richard E. and John T. Cacioppo(1986), *Communication and Persuasion: Central and Peripheral Routes to Attitude Change,* New York: Springer-Verlag.

Rucker, Derek D. and Richard E. Petty(2004), "When Resistance is Futile: Consequences of Failed Counterarguing for Attitude Certainty," *Journal of Personality and Social Psychology,* 86(2),219-35.

Schwarz, Norbert and Gerald L. Clore (1983), "Mood, Misattribution, and Judgments of Well-being: Informative and Directive Functions of Affective States,"*Journal of Personality and Social Psychology,* 45 (3), 513 - 523.

Wyer, Robert S. and Alison Jing Xu (2010), "The Role of Behavioral Mind-sets in Goal-Directed Activity: Conceptual Underpinnings and Empirical Evidence," *Journal of Consumer Psychology,* 20(2), 107-25.

Xu, Alison Jing and Robert S. Wyer (2008), "The Comparative Mind-set: From Animal Comparisons to Increased Purchase Intentions," *Psychological Science,* 19 (September), 859-64.

Xu, Alison Jing and Robert S. Wyer (2007), "The Effect of Mind-sets on Consumer Decision Strategies," *Journal of Consumer Research,* 34 (December), 556-66.

Seeing Things from the Other Guy's Point of View: Self-Other Difference in the Context of Endowment

Didem Kurt, University of Pittsburgh, USA
J. Jeffrey Inman, University of Pittsburgh, USA

EXTENDED ABSTRACT

Perspective taking shapes our perception of the world around us and thus, our consumption decisions. However, an accurate understanding of others' perspective cannot be easily achieved (e.g., Van Boven, Dunning, and Loewenstein 2000; Van Boven and Loewenstein 2005). In this paper, we examine the economic magnitude of failed perspective taking by consumers assuming the same role in the context of endowment. Specifically, we investigate whether owners and buyers systematically mispredict the valuation of an object by other owners and buyers, respectively. This is an important question to address since biased predictions may lead people to engage in transactions that are suboptimal (e.g., buyers may overbid for a house). In addition, post-transaction upward external comparisons in trading (e.g., Is the price I paid higher than the price others in a similar situation paid?) have been shown to negatively impact both buyers' and sellers' satisfaction with a transaction (Novemsky and Schweitzer 2004).

We maintain that even being in the shoes of others (e.g., being an owner and estimating valuation of other owners) does not enable people to accurately predict the impact of endowment and lack of ownership on others. We base our prediction on previous research suggesting that people underestimate the extent to which an affective experience influences preferences and choices of others in the same role (e.g., Loewenstein 1996; Faro and Rottenstreich 2006), resulting in a self-other difference in the *value function* of prospect theory. Specifically, we argue that owners fail to appreciate the extent to which endowment affects other owners, whereas buyers fail to realize the extent to which lack of ownership affects other buyers. Accordingly, we predict that owners underestimate the average selling price demanded by other owners, whereas buyers overestimate the average purchase price offered by other buyers. In conjunction, biased estimations by both groups will translate into failed prediction of the endowment effect.

In Study 1, participants ("owners") who were endowed with a coffee mug indicated the lowest price at which they are willing to sell their mugs. They then estimated the average lowest price at which other participants would be willing to sell their mugs ($2 reward was offered to those with close estimations to ensure incentive compatibility). In a separate session, participants ("buyers") who were not endowed with mugs indicated the highest price at which they would be willing to receive the mug instead of that amount of cash. Then, they estimated the average highest price at which other participants would choose to receive the mug instead of cash. As predicted, owners underestimated the average selling price of other owners by 19%. Conversely, buyers overestimated the average buying price of other buyers by 26%. The results also show that there is no significant difference in the estimated average valuations between owners and buyers, suggesting that while estimating other people's valuations, the participants do not anticipate the endowment effect.

Previous research has shown that higher level of perceived general similarity to a target is associated with greater empathy and perspective taking (e.g., Krebs 1975; Batson and Shaw 1991). In Study 2, we investigated whether priming similarities between participants and comparison targets (i.e., average undergraduate student at the same university) might reduce the magnitude of owners' and buyers' prediction errors. Participants assigned to the similarity condition were asked to write down "three ways in which you are similar compared to the average undergraduate student at <school name>." Those in the control condition were not given this task. The average prediction error of owners was reduced by 59% in the similarity condition. Furthermore, similarity priming eliminated overestimation by buyers, whereas overestimation in the control condition is still positive. Accordingly, we find that when estimating others' valuations, participants in the similarity condition anticipate the endowment effect, while participants in the control condition again fail to predict the endowment effect.

In Study 3, to provide further evidence on the proposed underlying mechanism for our findings, we measure participants' perspective taking and empathy (e.g., Davis 1983; Galinsky et al. 2008) and examine their impact on documented estimation errors. We find that greater perspective taking ability is associated with lower estimation errors when participants are high, but not low, in empathy. Overall, the results suggest that owners and buyers with high perspective taking ability and empathy predict others' valuations with the highest accuracy.

Enhanced understanding of the perspective of others in the same role can help consumers avoid suboptimal economic decisions. Our research demonstrates that consumers fail to take an accurate perspective of others even when they are in the shoes of others and that perspective taking can be enhanced by helping individuals consider similarities between themselves and the targets.

REFERENCES

Aiken, Leona S. and Stephen G. West (1991), *Multiple Regression: Testing and Interpreting Interactions*, Sage Publications.

Batson, C. Daniel and Laura L. Shaw (1991), "Evidence for Altruism: Toward a Pluralism of Prosocial Motives," *Psychological Inquiry*, 2 (2), 107-122.

Batson, C. Daniel, Cynthia L. Turk, Laura L. Shaw, and Tricia R. Klein (1995), "Information Function of Empathic Emotion: Learning That We Value the Other's Welfare," *Journal of Personality and Social Psychology*, 68 (2), 300-313.

Carmon, Ziv and Dan Ariely (2000), "Focusing on the Foregone: How Value Can Appear So Different to Buyers and Sellers," *Journal of Consumer Research*, 27 (3), 360-370.

Davis, Mark H. (1983), "Measuring Individual Differences in Empathy: Evidence for a Multidimensional Approach," *Journal of Personality and Social Psychology*, 44 (1), 113-126.

Epley, Nicholas and Eugene M. Caruso (2009), "Perspective Taking: Misstepping Into Others' Shoes," in *Handbook of Imagination and Mental Simulation*, eds. Keith D. Markman, William M. P. Klein, and Julie A. Shur, New York, NY: Psychology Press, 295-309.

Epley, Nicholas, Boaz Keysar, Leaf Van Boven, and Thomas Gilovich (2004), "Perspective Taking as Egocentric Anchoring and Adjustment," *Journal of Personality and Social Psychology*, 87 (3), 327-339.

Faro, David and Yuval Rottenstreich (2006), "Affect, Empathy, and Regressive Mispredictions of Others' Preferences under Risk," *Management Science*, 52 (4), 529-541.

Galinsky, Adam D., Gillian Ku, and Cynthia S. Wang (2005), "Perspective-Taking and Self-Other Overlap: Fostering Social Bonds and Facilitating Social Coordination," *Group Processes and Intergroup Relations*, 8 (2), 109-124.

Galinsky, Adam D., William W. Maddux, Debra Gilin, and Judith B. White (2008), "Why It Pays to Get Inside the Head of Your Opponent: The Differential Effects of Perspective Taking and Empathy in Strategic Interactions," *Psychological Science*, 19 (4), 378-384.

Galinsky, Adam D. and Gordon B. Moskowitz (2000), "Perspective-Taking: Decreasing Stereotype Expression, Stereotype Accessibility, and In-Group Favoritism," *Journal of Personality and Social Psychology*, 78 (4), 708-724.

Hsee, Christopher K. and Yuval Rottenstreich (2004), "Music, Pandas, and Muggers: On the Affective Psychology of Value," *Journal of Experimental Psychology: General*, 133 (1), 23-30.

Kahneman, Daniel, Jack L. Knetsch, and Richard Thaler (1990), "Experimental Tests of the Endowment Effect and the Coase Theorem," *Journal of Political Economy*, 98 (6), 1325-1348.

Krebs, Dennis (1975), "Empathy and Altruism," *Journal of Personality and Social Psychology*, 32 (6), 1134-1146.

Loewenstein, George (1996), "Out of Control: Visceral Influences on Behavior," *Organizational Behavior and Human Decision Processes*, 65 (3), 272-292.

Loewenstein, George and Daniel Adler (1995), "A Bias in the Prediction of Tastes," *The Economic Journal*, 105 (July), 929-937.

Menon, Geeta, Ellie J. Kyung, and Nidhi Agrawal (2009), "Biases in Social Comparisons: Optimism or Pessimism?" *Organizational Behavior and Human Decision Processes*, 108 (1), 39-52.

Morewedge, Carey K., Lisa L. Shu, Daniel T. Gilbert, and Timothy D. Wilson (2009), "Bad Riddance or Good Rubbish? Ownership and Not Loss Aversion Causes the Endowment Effect," *Journal of Experimental Social Psychology*, 45 (4), 947-951.

Novemsky, Nathan and Maurice E. Schweitzer (2004), "What Makes Negotiators Happy? The Differential Effects of Internal and External Social Comparisons on Negotiator Satisfaction," *Organizational Behavior and Human Decision Processes*, 95 (2), 186-197.

Parker, Sharon K. and Carolyn M. Axtell (2001), "Seeing Another Viewpoint: Antecedents and Outcomes of Employee Perspective Taking," *The Academy of Management Journal*, 44 (6), 1085-1100.

Rottenstreich, Yuval and Christopher K. Hsee (2001), "Money, Kisses, and Electric Shocks: On the Affective Psychology of Risk," *Psychological Science*, 12 (3), 185-190.

Van Boven, Leaf, David Dunning, and George Loewenstein (2000), "Egocentric Empathy Gaps Between Owners and Buyers: Misperceptions of the Endowment Effect," *Journal of Personality and Social Psychology*, 79 (1), 66-76.

Van Boven, Leaf and George Loewenstein (2005), "Cross-Situational Projection," in *The Self in Social Judgment*, eds. Mark D. Alicke, David A. Dunning, and Joachim I. Krueger, Psychology Press, 43-64.

Van Boven, Leaf, George Loewenstein, and David Dunning (2003), "Mispredicting the Endowment Effect: Underestimation of Owner's Selling Prices by Buyer's Agents," *Journal of Economic Behavior and Organization*, 51 (3), 351-365.

Van Boven, Leaf, George Loewenstein, and David Dunning (2005), "The Illusion of Courage in Social Predictions: Underestimating the Impact of Fear of Embarrassment on Other People," *Organizational Behavior and Human Decisions Processes*, 96 (2), 130-141.

Connected Consumers: The Influence of Temporal Sense of Community, Socio-Emotional Experience, and Satisfaction on Event Loyalty

Steffen Jahn, Chemnitz University of Technology, Germany
Jan Drengner, Chemnitz University of Technology, Germany
Hansjoerg Gaus, Saarland University, Germany
T. Bettina Cornwell, University of Oregon, USA

EXTENDED ABSTRACT

More than a decade ago, sociologists and marketing researchers identified a rise in postmodern communities held together through shared emotions and consumption practices (Cova 1997). Across contexts, consumption plays a role in bringing people together, and delivering what Cova (1997) calls 'linking value.' Linking value refers to a "product's, or service's contribution to establishing and/or reinforcing bonds between individuals" (Cova and Cova 2002, 603). Live events hold great potential in offering linking value since they are staged anchoring places for consumer collectives.

Existing marketing research, however, has mainly considered live events as a communications platform for brands (Cornwell 2008; McAlexander, Schouten, and Koenig 2002). In spite of events' economic relevance, our understanding of mechanisms that link antecedents with consequences of linking value offered by events is limited. The aim of the present research is to provide a framework that sheds light on the development of linking value and how it may relate to loyalty.

Existing research on this topic either focused on consumer-consumer interaction (CCI) or brand communities. Regarding the nature of CCI processes, Arnould and Price (1993) showed that intimate and extended experiences lead to an evolving feeling of communion that is shaped by direct interaction in small groups around common problems and can be fostered by service staff. Generally, however, CCI researchers have paid relatively little attention to services where CCI is one of the main sources of value creation (Nicholls 2010). Exceptions include small-scale establishments patronized by a group of regular customers, such as taverns or laundromats (Rosenbaum 2006). In the context of larger live events, existing research has not yet answered how CCI may relate to loyalty.

Brand community research, on the other hand, found that brand community engagement increases brand loyalty and that brandfests are able to foster community engagement (Algesheimer, Dholakia, and Herrmann 2005; Bagozzi and Dholakia 2006; Carlson, Suter, and Brown 2008; McAlexander et al. 2002). Brand admirers are thought to identify with other brand admirers, which places emphasis on their social identity. As a consequence, social norms foster loyal behavior (Algesheimer et al. 2005; Dholakia, Bagozzi, and Pearo 2004). Findings from this literature, however, cannot be transferred directly to the general event context. This is because the loyalty object in brand community research is the brand itself. Events in the form of brandfests can increase brand loyalty (Carlson et al. 2008; McAlexander et al. 2002). Consumer-organized events additionally evoke intentions to repeat such events within the same small friendship group (Bagozzi and Dholakia 2006). Importantly, many live events differ from those mentioned. For these events, the baseline event loyalty may be much lower due to the absence of a dominating brand influence. In addition, the normative influence of an in-group might be rather low in many situations.

Extending this work, we argue that events are able to reveal an otherwise latent consumption community (more precisely, events provide the platform on that attendees can jointly uncover and reveal their latent bonds through shared emotions). Need to belong theory maintains that social environments can facilitate intrinsic motivation by supporting people's innate need to belong (Baumeister and Leary 1995; Mead et al. 2011). We contend that the social environment at events can support people's need to belong via a mechanism that transforms shared emotions (the socio-emotional experience) into a temporal sense of community. Satisfying people's need to belong then activates the intrinsic motivation to repatronize this event. Our framework is different from one that highlights social norms and out-group devaluation, such as social identity theory. Rather, it highlights the intrinsic motivation fostered by social interaction in a context of shared interest. The present research contributes to both our understanding of communal consumption phenomena as well as the relevance of such phenomena for individual loyalty. It complements existing research that identified normative pressure as a main mechanism by offering an alternative that is more in line with a consumer value perspective.

To test our conceptual model, we conducted a large-scale survey among 596 visitors of a music festival (28% female, mean age 21.8 years). Results show that attendees' repatronage intentions are influenced not only by overall satisfaction with the event and the socio-emotional experience but also by consumers' temporal sense of community. That is, the linking value that is co-created during events plays a crucial role in attendees' loyalty processes. As expected, consumers' socio-emotional experience is a main driver of temporal sense of community. By means of an alternative model we show that the mechanism of social connectedness on loyalty is direct and not mediated by satisfaction. Thus, satisfying the need to belong adds linking value to an event which increases consumers' intent to patronize again.

Last but not least, our results show that the classic antecedent of loyalty, customer satisfaction, may vary in explanatory power when evaluating collective hedonic experiences such as festivals. Considering a large number of events to be attended because of consumers' need for affiliation and hedonism (Tinsley and Elredge 1995) supports our theory that communal phenomena may individually motivate consumers to be loyal toward the platform for such social interaction. This extends our knowledge in that it is not only norms and intergroup relations that work as mechanisms behind loyalty effects.

REFERENCES

Ahmed, Sara (2004), "Collective Feelings: Or, the Impression Left by Others," *Theory, Culture and Society*, 21 (2), 25–42.

Alon, Anat T. and Frederic F. Brunel (2007), "Dynamics of Community Engagement: The Role of Interpersonal Communicative Genres in Online Community Evolutions," *Consumer Culture Theory* (Research in Consumer Behavior Series Vol. 11), eds. Russell W. Belk and John F. Sherry, Jr., Oxford: Elsevier, 371–400.

Algesheimer, Rene, Utpal M. Dholakia and Andreas Herrmann (2005), "The Social Influence of Brand Community: Evidence from European Car Clubs," *Journal of Marketing*, 69 (3), 19–34.

Arnould, Eric J. and Linda L. Price (1993), "River Magic: Extraordinary Experience and the Extended Service Encounter," *Journal of Consumer Research*, 20 (1), 24–45.

Arnould, Eric J. and Craig J. Thompson (2005), "Consumer Culture Theory (CCT): Twenty Years of Research," *Journal of Consumer Research*, 31 (4), 868–882.

Arthur, Damien (2006), "Authenticity and Consumption in the Australian Hip Hop Culture," *Qualitative Market Research: An International Journal*, 9 (2), 140–156.

Bagozzi, Richard P. and Utpal M. Dholakia (2006), "Antecedents and Purchase Consequences of Customer Participation in Small Group Brand Communities," *International Journal of Research in Marketing,* 23 (1), 45–61.

Baumeister, Roy F. and Mark R. Leary (1995), "The Need to Belong: Desire for Interpersonal Attachments as a Fundamental Human Motivation," *Psychological Bulletin*, 117 (3), 497–529.

Bitner, Mary Jo (1992), "Servicescapes: The Impact of Physical Surroundings on Consumers and Employees," *Journal of Marketing,* 56 (2), 57–71.

Carlson, Brad D., Tracy A. Suter and Tom J. Brown (2008), "Social versus Psychological Brand Community: The Role of Psychological Sense of Brand Community," *Journal of Business Research*, 61 (4), 284–291.

Caro, Laura Martínez and Jose Antonio Martínez García (2007), "Consumer Satisfaction with a Periodic Reoccurring Sport Event and the Moderating Effect of Motivations," *Sport Marketing Quarterly*, 16 (2), 70–81.

Chalip, Laurence (2006), "Towards Social Leverage of Sport Events," *Journal of Sport Tourism*, 11 (2), 109–127.

Cornwell, T. Bettina (2008), "State of the Art and Science in Sponsorship-Linked Marketing," *Journal of Advertising,* 37 (3), 41–55.

Cova, Bernard (1997), "Community and Consumption: Towards a Definition of the "Linking Value" of Product or Services," *European Journal of Marketing*, 31 (3-4), 297–316.

Cova, Bernard and Veronique Cova (2002), "Tribal Marketing: The Tribalisation of Society and its Impact on the Conduct of Marketing," *European Journal of Marketing*, 36 (5-6), 595–620.

Deci, Edward L. and Richard M. Ryan (2000), "The "What" and "Why" of Goal Pursuits: Human Needs and the Self-Determination of Behavior," *Psychological Inquiry*, 11 (4), 227–268.

Deighton, John (1992), "The Consumption of Performance," *Journal of Consumer Research*, 19 (3), 362–372.

Dholakia, Utpal M., Richard P. Bagozzi and Lisa Klein Pearo (2004), "A Social Influence Model of Consumer Participation in Network- and Small-Group-Based Virtual Communities," *International Journal of Research in Marketing*, 21 (3), 241–263.

Fornell, Claes and David F. Larcker (1981), "Evaluating Structural Equation Models with Unobservable Variables and Measurement Error," *Journal of Marketing Research*, 18 (1), 39–50.

Fornell, Claes, Michael D. Johnson, Eugene W. Anderson, Jaesung Cha and Barbara Everitt Bryant (1996), "The American Customer Satisfaction Index: Nature, Purpose, and Findings," *Journal of Marketing*, 60 (1), 7–18.

Garbarino, Ellen and Mark S. Johnson (1999), "The Different Roles of Satisfaction, Trust, and Commitment in Customer Relationships," *Journal of Marketing*, 63 (2), 70–87.

Gursoy, Dogan, Eric R. Spangenberg and Denney G. Rutherford (2006), "The Hedonic and Utilitarian Dimensions of Attendees' Attitudes toward Festivals," *Journal of Hospitality and Tourism Research*, 30 (3), 279–294.

Han, Xiaoyun H., Robert J. Kwortnik Jr. and Chunxiao Wang (2008), "Service Loyalty: An Integrative Model and Examination across Service Contexts," *Journal of Service Research,* 11 (1), 22–42.

Hightower, Roscoe, Michael K. Brady and Thomas L. Baker (2002), "Investigating the Role of the Physical Environment in Hedonic Service Consumption: An Exploratory Study of Sporting Events," *Journal of Business Research*, 55 (9), 697–707.

Holbrook, Morris B. and Elizabeth C. Hirschman (1982), "The Experiential Aspects of Consumption: Consumer Fantasies, Feelings, and Fun," *Journal of Consumer Research*, 9 (2), 132–140.

Holt, Douglas B. (1995), "How Consumers Consume: A Typology of Consumption Practices," *Journal of Consumer Research*, 22 (1), 1–16.

Jöreskog, Karl G. and Dag Sörbom (2004), "LISREL 8.7 for Windows [computer software]," Lincolnwood, IL: Scientific Software International.

Kozinets, Robert V. (2002), "Can Consumers Escape the Market? Emancipatory Illuminations from Burning Man," *Journal of Consumer Research*, 29 (1), 20–38.

Kwortnik, Robert J. and William T. Ross (2007), "The Role of Positive Emotions in Experiential Decisions," *International Journal of Research in Marketing,* 24 (4), 324–335.

Lee, Yong-Ki, Choong-Ki Lee, Seung-Kon Lee and Barry J. Babin (2008), "Festivalscapes and Patrons' Emotions, Satisfaction, and Loyalty," *Journal of Business Research*, 61 (1), 56–64.

Magee, Joe C. and Larissa Z. Tiedens (2006), "Emotional Ties that Bind: The Roles of Valence and Consistency of Group Emotion in Inferences of Cohesiveness and Common Fate," *Personality and Social Psychology Bulletin*, 32 (12), 1703–1715.

McAlexander, James H., John W. Schouten and Harold F. Koenig (2002), "Building Brand Community," *Journal of Marketing*, 66 (1), 38–54.

Mead, Nicole L., Roy F. Baumeister, Tyler, F. Stillman, Catherine D. Rawn and Kathleen D. Vohs (2011), "Social Exclusion Causes People to Spend and Consume Strategically in the Service of Affiliation," *Journal of Consumer Research*, 37 (February), 902–919.

Munuera, Jose L. and Salvador Ruiz (1999), "Trade Fairs as Services: A Look at Visitors' Objectives in Spain," *Journal of Business Research*, 44 (1), 17–24.

Muñiz, Albert M. and Thomas C. O'Guinn (2001), "Brand Community," *Journal of Consumer Research*, 27 (4), 412–432.

Nicholls, Richard (2010), "New Directions for Customer-To-Customer Interaction Research," *Journal of Services Marketing*, 24 (1), 87–97.

Oliver, Richard L. (2010), *Satisfaction: A Behavioral Perspective on the Consumer*, 2nd Edition. Armonk, New York: M. E. Sharpe.

Pons, Frank, Michel Laroche and Mehdi Mourali (2006), "Consumer Reactions to Crowded Retail Settings: Cross Cultural Differences between North America and the Middle East," *Psychology and Marketing*, 23 (7), 555–572.

Porath, Christine, Debby MacInnis and Valerie Folkes (2010), "Witnessing Incivility among Employees: Effects on Consumer Anger and Negative Inferences about Companies," *Journal of Consumer Research*, 37 (2), 292–303.

Ramanathan, Suresh and Ann L. McGill (2007), "Consuming with Others: Social Influences on Moment-To-Moment and Retrospective Evaluations of an Experience," *Journal of Consumer Research*, 34 (4), 506–524.

Rook, Dennis W. (1985), "The Ritual Dimension of Consumer Behavior," *Journal of Consumer Research*, 12 (3), 251–264.

Rosenbaum, Mark S. (2006), "Exploring the Social Supportive Role of third Places in Consumers' Lives," *Journal of Service Research*, 9 (1), 59–72.

Ryan, Richard M. and Edward L. Deci (2000), "Self-Determination Theory and the Facilitation of Intrinsic Motivation, Social Development, and Well-Being," *American Psychologist*, 55 (1), 68–78.

Schau, Hope Jensen, Albert M. Muñiz and Eric J. Arnould (2009), "How Brand Community Practices Create Value," *Journal of Marketing*, 73 (5), 30–51.

Sheldon, Kennon M., Andrew J. Elliott, Youngmee Kimand and Tim Kasser (2001), "What is Satisfying about Satisfying Events? Testing 10 Candidate Psychological Needs," *Journal of Personality and Social Psychology*, 80 (2), 325–339.

Smith, Eliot R., Charles R. Seger and Diane M. Mackie (2007), "Can Emotions be Truly Group Level? Evidence Regarding four Conceptual Criteria," *Journal of Personality and Social Psychology,* 93 (3), 431–446.

Söderlund, Magnus (2006), "Measuring Customer Loyalty with Multi-Item Scales. A Case for Caution," *International Journal of Service Industry Management*, 17 (1), 76–98.

Tajfel, Henri (1982), *Social Identity and Intergroup Relations. European Studies in Social Psychology*. Cambridge: Cambridge University Press.

Tinsley, Howard E. A. and Barbara D. Elredge (1995), "Psychological Benefits of Leisure Participation: A Taxonomy of Leisure Activities Based on their Need-Gratifying Properties," *Journal of Counseling Psychology*, 42 (2), 123–132.

U.S. Census 2010 (resp. 2007 figures): http://factfinder.census. gov/servlet/IBQTable?_bm=yand-geo_id=01000USand-fds_ name=EC0700A1and-_skip=0and-ds_name=EC0771A1and-_ lang=en

Uhrich, Sebastian and Martin Benkenstein (2010), "Sport Stadium Atmosphere: Formative and Reflective Indicators for Operationalizing the Construct," *Journal of Sport Management*, 24 (2), 211–237.

Zeithaml, Valeri A., Leonard L. Berry and A. Parasuraman (1996), "The Behavioral Consequences of Service Quality," *Journal of Marketing*, 60 (2), 31–46.

How "Healthy Eating" Packaging Cues Affect Purchasing and Consumption Behavior

Xiaoyan Deng, The Ohio State University, USA
Barbara Kahn, University of Pennsylvania, USA
Sara Michalski, General Mills, USA

EXTENDED ABSTRACT

Research has consistently shown that consumers oftentimes use external cues to make consumption volume decisions (Chandon and Wansink 2007; Scott, Nowlis, Mandel, and Morales 2008; Vale, Pieters, and Zeelenberg 2008; Wansink and Chandon 2006). According to Brian Wansink (http://mindlesseating.org/faq.php), "Most of us don't overeat because we're hungry. We overeat because of family and friends, packages and plates, names and numbers, labels and lights, colors and candles, shapes and smells, distractions and distances, cupboards and containers." As the obesity crises escalates that currently 34% of adults and 17% of children are obese (Belluck 2010), marketers and researchers have been studying the effects of external cues on consumption rates and how cues can be used to control or prevent overeating.

In this research, we focus on the effects of "healthy eating" packaging cues, more specifically verbal nutrition claims and visual product images featured on the package, on consumers' purchasing and consumption decisions. Across four studies we address several important questions. First, how do packaging cues affect consumers' in-store purchasing and at-home consumption decisions? Second, do verbal and visual cues interact? Third, can packaging cues affect consumers when they are mindless as well as when they are mindful?

Our research reports four important findings. First, in the store, verbal claims can interact with visual cues to affect purchase intentions, but only if the verbal claims are ambiguous. Second, this interaction between ambiguous verbal cues and visual cues only occurs when consumers are mindful. When they are mindless, an independent effect of visual cues is observed. Third, packaging cues influence consumers differently in the store environment from the way they influence consumers at home. Once the package is purchased and taken out of the store, consumers process information more heuristically and there is no interaction between verbal and visual cues even in a mindful state. When making consumption decisions (rather than forming intentions), when consumers are mindful they are influenced only by verbal cues, and when mindless they are only influenced by visual cues. Finally, we find evidence of a boomerang effect that visual cues that indicate "perceived lightness" of a healthy product in store and thus increase purchase and consumption likelihoods for those healthy products which is a socially responsible behavior, backfire in consumption occasions at home by causing consumers to eat more, which is an unhealthy practice.

Our findings contribute to the literature on packaging. Previous research has shown that packaging cues can both influence purchase intentions and later consumption evaluations, when the product experience is ambiguous. For example, Levin and Gaeth (1988) showed that product packaging (identifying ground beef as 75% lean or 25% fat) could affect evaluations towards the product, and even have effects on perceived tastiness of the beef, although the latter effects were somewhat mitigated by tasting the food. We add to this literature by showing that packaging effects can not only frame purchase intentions and consumption evaluations, but can also affect consumption quantities.

Like the previous research, we show that packaging effects are stronger for ambiguous cues (in our case, ambiguous verbal cues).

We however add another moderator: whether the consumer is mindful or not is important in predicting the effects. And unlike most of this previous research, we find boomerang effects rather than consistent evaluations between purchase and consumption occasions. In that regard, our findings are more similar to those described by Vale, Pieters and Zeelenberg (2008) and Wansink and Chandon (2006) who showed that small package formats and low-fat nutrition labels can "backfire" as consumers no longer feel the need to regulate their own behavior. However, our results differ from these more recent studies in that we find these effects not only with nutritional labeling that is evaluated mindfully, but rather also through visual cues that are evaluated mindlessly. Our findings therefore also contribute to the literature on mindless eating by introducing a new marketing cue that influences this type of behavior. We find that when consumers are eating mindlessly, the location of the product image on the package can affect how much consumers eat.

REFERENCES

Bainbridge, Jane (2005), "Health Infusion," *Marketing*, (Dec. 14), 30-31.

Belluck, Pam (2010), "Obesity Rates Hit Plateau in U.S., Data Suggest," *The New York Times*. (accessed December 17, 2010), [available at http://www.nytimes.com/2010/01/14/health/14obese.html].

Chandon, Pierre and Brian Wansink (2007), "The Biasing Health Halos of Fast Food Restaurant Health Claims: Lower Calorie Estimates and Higher Side-Dish Consumption Intentions," *Journal of Consumer Research*, 34:3 (October) 301-314.

Deng, Xiaoyan and Barbara E. Kahn (2009), "Is Your Product on the Right Side? The 'Location Effect' on Perceived Product Heaviness and Package Evaluation*," Journal of Marketing Research*, 46(6).

Dickson, Peter R., and Alan G. Sawyer. (1990). "The Price Knowledge and Search of Supermarket Shoppers," Journal of Marketing 54 (July), 42-53.

Hoch, Stephen J. and Young-Won Ha (1986), "Consumer Learning: Advertising and the Ambiguity of Product Experience," *Journal of Consumer Research*, 13 (September), 221-233.

Holbrook, Morris B., and William L. Moore (1981), "Feature Interactions in Consumer Judgments of Verbal Versus Pictorial Presentations," *Journal of Consumer Research*, 8(June), 103-113.

Lee, Michelle P. and Kwanho Suk (2010), "Disambiguating the Role of Ambiguity in Perceptual Assimilation and Contrast Effects," *Journal of Consumer Research* (February), 890-897.

Levin, I. P., J.D. Jasper, and G. J. Gaeth, (1988) "Framing of attribute information before and after consuming the product," *Journal of Consumer Research*, 15 (3), 374-378.

Meyers-Levy, Joan and Laura A. Peracchio (1994), "How Ambiguous Cropped Objects in Ad Photos Can Affect Product Evaluations," *Journal of Consumer Research 21* (June) 190-204.

Scott, M. L., Nowlis, S. M., Mandel, N., & Morales, A. C. (2008), "The Effects of Reduced Food Size and Package Size on the Consumption Behavior of Restrained and Unrestrained Eaters," *Journal of Consumer Research*, 35(October), 391-405.

Shiv, B. and Fedorikhin, A. (1999), "Heart and Mind in Conflict: Interplay of Affect and Cognition in Consumer Decision Making," *Journal of Consumer Research*, 26 (December), 278-282.

Stapel, Diederik A. (2007), "In the Mind of the Beholder: The Interpretation Comparison Model of Accessibility Effects,"in *Assimilation and Contrast in Social Psychology*, ed. Diederik A. Stapel and Jerry Suls, New York: Psychology Press,143–64.

Vale, R., Pieters, R., & Zeelenberg, M. (2008), "Flying under the Radar: Perverse Package Size Effects on Consumption Self-Regulation.," *Journal of Consumer Research*, 35(October), 380-390.

Wansink, Brian and Jeffrey Sobal (2007), "Mindless Eating: The 200 Daily Food Decisions We Overlook," *Environment and Behavior,* 39:1 (January), 106-23.

Wansink, Brian and Pierre Chandon (2006), "Can "Low Fat" Nutrition Labels Lead to Obesity?," *Journal of Marketing Research*, 43:4 (November), 605-17.

Does a Crowded Store Lead to a Crowded Mind?
Crowding and Mental Construal of Product Features

Ahreum Maeng, University of Wisconsin-Madison, USA
Robin Tanner, University of Wisconsin-Madison, USA

EXTENDED ABSTRACT

Consider the following scenario: You are shopping for a new DVD player at a retailer. You visit the store on a Saturday when the store is crowded and the aisles are full of browsing shoppers. You eventually pick out a DVD player to purchase but decide to think it over at the weekend. You go back early Monday morning when the store is substantially emptier and return to the DVD player aisle to once again compare the players in your consideration set. The question is might the less crowded store environment cause you to mentally construe features of the DVD players differently than on your prior visit, thus potentially causing you to change your choice? The goal of the present research is to investigate this fascinating possibility through the lens of construal-level theory (CLT; Trope and Liberman 2003). Our core theoretical model is that socially crowded environments lead to tense arousal (Worchel and Teddlie, 1976) causing individuals to narrow their conceptual scope (Tucker and Williamson, 1984) which leads them to rely more on lower level construals.

Study 1 used a 2 X 2 design (N = 284) with crowdedness (crowded or uncrowded) and product feature (desirable or feasible) manipulated between subjects. To manipulate crowdedness we utilized a semantic priming approach based on a Cartesian coordinate task (Williams and Bargh, 2008). Specifically, participants viewed a Cartesian plane on which either two (uncrowded condition) or eight (crowded condition) points were plotted. Next, in a supposedly unrelated rating task participants were then asked to rate a DVD player (described over eight attributes) on a 7-point scale (1 to 7). One of the attributes of the DVD player was varied to be either feasibility orientated ("manual is easy to use") or desirability orientated ("player is made of high technology materials"). Results revealed no main effect of either crowdedness or product feature but did reveal an interaction between the two (F(1, 280) = 5.02, $p <$ .03).). Participants in the uncrowded condition rated the DVD player with the desirably feature higher (M = 5.77) then the player with the feasibility feature (M = 5.43). In the crowded condition, however, the player with the feasible feature was rated higher (M $^-$ 5.75) than the one with desirable feature (M = 5.46).

Study 2 (N=131) was designed to generalize the results of study 1 by using both a different crowding manipulation and also a different measure of construal level. To prime the level of crowdedness, participants were asked to complete a picture perception study that required them to record their thoughts on a picture of either a crowded or uncrowded scene. Next, in a supposedly unrelated camping trip study, participants were tasked with sorting 38 camping equipment items into mutually exclusive groups of like items. This measure was borrowed from Liberman et al. (2002) who showed that construal level moderates the number of categories created (with higher level construals leading to fewer discrete categories being perceived). Results revealed that participants did indeed generate more discrete categories after being primed with the picture of a crowded scene (M = 6.0) than did participants primed with the picture of a less crowded scene (M $-$ 5.35, t(129) $-$ -2.491, $p<$.02). Next, to investigate the underlying mechanism, we coded participants' descriptions of how they would feel in the primed scenes in terms of whether they did (coded 1) or did not (coded 0) mention stress or anxiety. Supportive of our theoretical model, this data was used in a mediation analysis

(z= 2.08, p < .04) which revealed that stress/anxiety (i.e., tense arousal) did indeed mediate the effect of the level of crowding on the number of categories that participants generated.

In studies 3a and 3b, rather than relying on primes of crowdedness, we utilized an actual crowding manipulation with participants completing both studies in a small breakout room that was either uncrowded (3 participants at a time) or crowded (16-24 participants at a time). Study 3a utilized the same DVD rating measure as study 1 and the results replicated that study. A 2 (level of crowdedness: crowded vs. uncrowded) x 2 (product feature: feasible vs. desirable) ANOVA revealed no main effects but an interaction between the two ($p <$ .01) with a similar pattern of means to study 1. Study 3b utilized another form of categorization task that required participants to rate on a 1-10 scale whether pairs of typical and atypical exemplars belonged in a relevant category. For example, in the furniture category, chair and sofa were presented as typical exemplars, whereas radio and clock were presented as atypical exemplars. Consistent with prior findings in the CLT literature, we predicted that while crowding would not affect the rated fit of the typical exemplars, the atypical exemplars would be perceived as having greater category fit in an uncrowded environment (where was argue participants rely on higher level construals). Results supported this prediction with main effects of exemplar type and crowding being qualified by the predicted interaction (F(1,170)=3.23, $p <$ 0.07). As expected, participants who were in the crowded room were less inclusive in their categorization of atypical exemplars (M=3.74) than those in the less crowded room (M=4.33; t(170)=-2.85, $p <$ 0.01).

In summary, four studies supported the idea that the crowdedness of the consumer's environment appears to influence the way in which environmental features are mentally construed. Crowding led participants both to prefer a product described with concrete features over one described with abstract features, and also to be less inclusive in categorization tasks. We believe this finding has considerable implications. First, our data suggest that CLT may be defined too narrowly in focusing purely on raw distance per se, and that other factors (such as physical or psychological crowding) may also influence the way we construe our environments. Second, from a pure marketing perspective, one can imagine a plethora of practical implications such as whether high and low traffic stores should use subtly different persuasive appeals.

REFERENCES

Brehm, Jack W. (1966), *A Theory of Psychological Reactance,* Oxford England: Academic Press, 1966.

Bursill, A. E. 1958. "The Restriction of Peripheral Vision During Exposure to Hot and Humid Conditions." The Quarterly Journal of Experimental Psychology 10, 114-129.

Calhoun, John C. (1962), "Population Density and Social Pathology," *Scientific American, 206*(2), 139-150.

Christian, J . J., Flyer, V . & Davis;. D. E . (1960), "Factors in Mass Mortality of a Head of Silka Deer, Cervus Nippon." *Chesapeake Science*, 1, 79-95 .

Desor, J. A. (1972), "Toward a Psychological Theory of Crowding." *Journal of Personality and Social Psychology*, 21(1), 79-83.

Derryberry, Douglas, and Don M. Tucker (1994), "Motivating the Focus of Attention." *In The Heart's Eye: Emotional Influences in Perception and Attention*, 167-196. San Diego, CA US: Academic Press.

Easterbrook, J. A. (1959), "The Effect of Emotion on Cue Utilization and the Organization of Behavior," *Psychological Review*, 66(3), 183-201.

Epstein, Yakov M., and Robert A. Karlin (1975), "Effects of Acute Experimental Crowding," *Journal of Applied Social Psychology*, 5(1), 34-53.

Evans, Gary W. (1979), "Behavioral and Physiological Consequences of Crowding in Humans." *Journal of Applied Social Psychology*, 9(1), 27-46.

Felipe, Nancy J., and Robert Sommer (1966), "Invasions of Personal Space." *Social Problems*, 14(2), 206-214.

Freedman, J., Klevansky, S., & Ehrlich, P. (1971), "The Effect of Crowding on Human Task Performance," *Journal of Applied Social Psychology*, 1(1), 7-25.

Gasper, Karen, and Gerald L. Clore (2002), "Attending to the Big Picture: Mood and Global versus Local Processing of Visual Information." *Psychological Science*, 13(1), 34-40.

Gasper, Karen. (2004). "Do You See What I See? Affect and Visual Information Processing," *Cognition and Emotion*, *18*(3), 405-421.

Glass, David C., and Singer, Jerome E. (1972), *Urban Stress: Experiments on Noise and Social Stressors*. New York: Academic Press.

Griffitt, W., and R. Veitch (1971), "Hot and Crowded: Influences of Population Density and Temperature on Interpersonal Affective Behavior," *Journal* of *Personality and Social Psychology*, 17(1): 92-98.

Hall, Edward. (1959). *The Silent Language*. New York, Doubleday.

Hall, Edward. (1966). *The Hidden Dimension (1st ed.)*. New York, NY US: Doubleday & Co.

Ittelson, W., H. Proshansky, and L. Rivlin (1970) "The Environmental Psychology of the Psychiatric Ward." In H. Proshansky, W. Ittelson, and L. Rivlin (eds.), *Environmental Psychology* (New York: Holt).

Levav, Jonathan, and Rui (Juliet) Zhu (2009), "Seeking Freedom Through Variety." *Journal of Consumer Research*, 36(4), 600-610.

Liberman, N., Sagristano, M., & Trope, Y. (2002), "The Effect of Temporal Distance on Level of Mental Construal," *Journal of Experimental Social Psychology*, 38(6), 523-534.

Luu, Phan, Don M. Tucker, and Douglas Derryberry (1998), "Anxiety and the Motivational Basis of Working Memory," *Cognitive Therapy and Research*, 22(6), 577-594.

Meyers-Levy, J., & Zhu, R. (2007). The Influence of Ceiling Height: The Effect of Priming on the Type of Processing People Use, *Journal of Consumer Research*, *34* (August), 174-186.

Mikulincer, Mario, Peri Kedem, and Dov Paz (1990), "Anxiety and Categorization: I. The Structure and Boundaries of Mental Categories," *Personality and Individual Differences*, 11(8), 805-814.

Reeves, Frank B., and Bruce O. Bergum, (1972), "Perceptual Narrowing as a Function of Peripheral Cue Relevance," *Perceptual and Motor Skills*, 35(3), 719-724.

Schaeffer, Gerald H., and Miles L. Patterson (1980), "Intimacy, Arousal, and Small Group Crowding," *Journal of Personality and Social Psychology*, 38(2), 283-290.

Schmitt, Robert C. (1957), "Density, Elinquency, and Crime in Honolulu," *Sociology & Social Research*, 41, 274-276. Schuessler, Karl (1962), "Components of Variation in City Crime Rates," *Social Problems*, 9, 314-23.

Sommer, R. (1967), "Small Group Ecology," *Psychological Bulletin*, *67*(2), 145-152.

Sommer, R., & Becker, F. (1969), "Territorial Defense and the Good Neighbor," *Journal of Personality and Social Psychology*, *11*(2), 85-92.

Spence, Kenneth W. (1958), "A Theory of Emotionally Based Drive (D) and its Relation to Performance in Simple Learning Situations," *American Psychologist*, 13(4), 131-141.

Stokols, Daniel (1972), "On the Distinction Between Density and Crowding: Some Implications for Future Research," *Psychological Review*, 79(3), 275-277.

Stokols, D., Rall, M., Pinner, B., & Schopler, J. (1973). "Physical, Social, and Personal Determinants of the Perception of Crowding,"*Environment and Behavior*, 5(1), 87-115.

Trope, Yaacov, and Nira Liberman (2003), "Temporal Construal," *Psychological Review*, 110(3), 403-421.

Tucker, Don M., and Peter A. Williamson (1984), "Asymmetric Neural Control Systems in Human Self-Regulation," *Psychological Review*, 91(2), 185-215.

Tyler, Shirley K., and Donald M. Tucker (1982), "Anxiety and Perceptual Structure: Individual Differences in Neuropsychological Function," *Journal of Abnormal Psychology*, 91(3), 210-220.

Weltman, Gershon, Janice E. Smith, and Glen H. Edstrom (1971), "Perceptual Narrowing During Simulated Pressure-Chamber Exposure," *Human Factors*, 13 (2), 99-107.

Williams, Lawrence E. and John A. Bargh (2008), "Keeping One's Distance: The Influence of Spatial Distance Cues on Affect and Evaluation," *Psychological Science*, 19 (3), 302-08.

Worchel, Stephen, and Charles Teddlie (1976), "The Experience of Crowding: A Two-Factor Theory," *Journal of Personality and Social Psychology*, 34(1), 30-40.

Segmenting Customers According to their Multidimensional Contact Sequences – Application of A Multidimensional Sequence Alignment Approach

Sascha Steinmann, University of Siegen, Germany
Gunnar Mau, University of Siegen, Germany
Hanna Schramm-Klein, University of Siegen, Germany
Günter Silberer, University of Goettingen, Germany

EXTENDED ABSTRACT

It is increasingly common for firms to employ online distribution channels alongside its offline distribution channels and marketing channels to rely on these complex combinations as a source of competitive advantage and better serve their customers (Geykens et al. 2002). In such environments, many customers have become multi channel users. They realized contacts between the firm and themselves at different contact points, e.g. store, homepage across the purchase process (Rangaswamy and van Bruggen 2005). These customer contacts are a fundamental element for the attainment of customer knowledge for a supplier. Not only are the kind and number of the customer contacts in a specific process phase relevant to this, but also their functions and importance, not to mention the sequence of these three dimensions during the purchase process.

In general, customer behavior can be viewed as a sequence of interdependent actions over time (Hägerstrand 1970). However, customer behavior in marketing research is mostly treated as a chain of independent activities. Thus, the sequential order and obvious relations of the activities are often neglected. Therefore, Abbott's (1995, p. 94) statement "We assume intercase independence even while our theories focus on interaction" is largely true for marketing research concerning the segmentation of the customers regarding their individual behavior through across the purchase process. Hence, an analysis of the multidimensional sequence of the customer contacts (dimension 1), their functions (dimension 2) and their importance (dimension 3) could provide crucial insights into customer behavior, as well as the needs and preferences of the customers over time. Therefore, this study will demonstrate how multidimensional customer contact sequences can be measured and form the basis for multidimensional customer segmentation. For this, customer contact sequences of $N=304$ customers with a retailer for consumer electronics were surveyed in across the different phases of the purchase process (pre-purchase, purchase, and post-purchase phase).

To gain deeper insights in the differences of customer behavior and powerful clusters, the multidimensional contact sequences were characterized by three dimensions: the customer contact sequence, the sequence of the functions related to the customer contacts, and the sequence of the contact importance. To account for obviously interdependencies between the three dimensions we used a multidimensional sequence alignment approach which identifies elements that can be aligned simultaneously without calculating the costs twice, called "OTMSAM" (Joh et al. 2002). In doing so, the differentiation into four clusters proved to be the best solution (see table 1).

The centroid of the first cluster has realized the lowest number of customer contacts across the purchase process. After two very important contacts with newspaper and TV-advertising in the pre-purchase phase which were used for price comparison and selective information, the desired product was bought in the store. The first contact in the centroid of cluster 2 was realized with the store and was used to obtain general information about the retailer's offers.

TABLE 1
Description of the Clusters by Centroid Sequences

	Multidimensional Centroid Sequences					
Cluster 1 ($n = 115$)						
Contacts	Newspaper advertising		TV-advertising		Store	
Functions[1]	PC	>	GI	>	P	
Importance[2]	6		6		4	
Cluster 2 ($n = 75$)						
Contacts	Store	retailer's homepage		Sales staff		Store
Functions	GI >	SI	>	SI & A	>	P
Importance	5	5		6		6
Cluster 3 ($n = 74$)						
Contacts	TV-advertising	Newspaper advertising	Advertising at the PoS		Sales staff	Store
Functions	GI >	GI >	SI	>	A >	P
Importance	5	5	5		6	6
Cluster 4 ($n = 40$)						
Contacts	Advertising at the PoS	Advertising at the PoS	Sales staff	Store	Store	Sales staff
Functions	GI >	GI >	A >	A >	P >	A
Importance	5	5	4	6	6	6

[1] GI = "general information", SI = "selective information", PC = "price comparison", P = "purchase", A = "advisory"; [2] inquired on a six-step rating scale, 1 corresponds to *entirely unlikely*; 6 corresponds to *very likely*

This contact was followed by a contact with other websites which was used for selective information. These two customer contacts were both realized during the pre-purchase phase and were rated as important contacts. During the purchase phase the product was bought after a consultation of the sales staff. Such contacts were of specific relevance and were therefore rated as very important contacts. The centroid of cluster 3 shows that these customers realized the highest number of contacts in the purchase phase. They sought contact with TV- and newspaper advertising in the pre-purchase phase to obtain general information. These contacts with different kinds of the retailer's advertising were both evaluated as important contacts. During the purchase phase customers' of the third cluster often realized contacts with advertising at the Point-of-Sale which were used for selective information. Such contacts were also rated as important. The following consultation of the sales staff and the purchase of the product in the store were of highest importance to the customers of cluster 3 and evaluated as very important contacts.

The centroid of the fourth cluster shows that these customers realized the highest number of customer contacts across the whole purchase process as well as in the pre-purchase phase. Furthermore, the customer contacts in this multidimensional centroid sequence cover all phases of the purchase process. It is noticeable that all contacts prior to the purchase were realized in the store. After two contacts with different kinds of advertising at the Point-of-Sale for obtaining general information, these customers sought contact with the sales staff followed by two customer contacts in the store for advisory functions. With regard to these findings one may conclude that the opportunity of direct product contacts in the store are of specific relevance to the customers in cluster 4. In the post-purchase phase a contact with the sales staff was used for advisory functions as well. This contact was evaluated as a very important by this customer.

Furthermore, the results of a multinominal logistic regression (Hosmer and Lemeshow 2000) on the cluster level show that cluster membership can be satisfactorily explained and predicted by the sequencing of customer contacts. With regard to the differences in the number of realized contacts as well as of the realized customer contact points, we used the number of the ten most frequently realized transitions (substrings) of two consecutive contacts as independent variables in a first multinominal logistic regression model with the cluster membership as dependent variable. In the second logistic regression model, we control for further variables which could be associated with cluster membership (product related and socio-demographic variables). As model 1 indicates, the sequence information are strongly associated with segment membership and provide a correct classification of 74.6% of the customers. The statistical association between the substrings and cluster membership remains robust, even though significance level of parameters decreases, and correct classification increases slightly (81.4%) when the control variables are included in model 2. Especially, substrings including contacts with the store, contacts with different kinds of the retailer's advertising as well as customer contacts with the sales staff, the price of the product and internet affinity are contributing factors in explaining cluster membership.

REFERENCES

Abbott, Andrew (1995), "Sequence Analysis: New Methods for Old Ideas," *Annual Review of Sociology*, 21 (2), 93-113.

Balasubramian, Sridhar, Rajagopal Raghunathan and Vijay Mahajan (2005), "Consumers in a Multichannel Environment: Product Utility, Process Utility, and Channel Choice," *Journal of Interactive Marketing*, 19 (2), 12 – 30.

Bloch, Peter H., Nancy M. Ridgway and Scott A. Davidson (1994), "The Shopping Mall as Consumer Habitat," *Journal of Retailing*, 70 (1), 23-42.

Dholakia, Ruby R., Miao Zhao and Nikhilesh Dholakia (2005), "Multichannel Retailing: A Case Study of Early Experiences," *Journal of Interactive Marketing*, 19 (2), 63 – 74.

Frambach, Ruud T., Hank C. A. Roest and Trichy V. Krishnan (2007), "The Impact of Consumer Internet Experience on Channel Preference and Usage Intentions Across the Different Stages of the Buying Process," *Journal of Interactive Marketing*, 21 (2), 26–41.

Ganesh, Jaishankar, Kristy E. Reynolds and Michael G. Luckett (2007), "Retail Patronage Behavior and Shopper Typologies: A Replication and Extension Using a Multi-Format, Multi-Method Approach," *Journal of the Academy of Marketing Science*, 35 (3), 369-381.

Geyskens, Inge, Katrijn Gielens, and Dekimpe, Marnik G. (2002), "The Market Valuation of Internet Channel Auditions," *Journal of Marketing*, 66 (2), 102-119.

Hägerstrand, Torsten (1970), "What About People in Regional Science?," *Papers of the Regional Science Association*, 24 (1), 7-21.

Hosmer, David W. And Stanley Lemeshow (2000), Applied Logistic Regression, 2nd Edition, New York: John Wiley and Sons.

Joh, Chang-Hyeon, Theo Arentze, Frank Hofman, and Harry Timmermans (2002), "Activity Pattern Similarity: A Multidimensional Sequence Alignment Method," *Transportation Research B*, 36 (5), 385-483.

Kim, Byung-Do and K. Park (1997), "Studying Patterns of Consumer's Grocery Shopping Trip," *Journal of Retailing*, 73 (4), 501-517.

Kumar, Vipin and Rajkumar Venkatesan (2005), "Who Are the Multichannel Shoppers and How Do They Perform? Correlates of Multichannel Shoppinmg Behavior," *Journal of Interactive Marketing*, 19 (2), 44 – 62.

Larson, Jeffrey S., Eric T. Bradlow and Peter S. Fader (2005), "An exploratory look at supermarket shopping paths," *International Journal of research in Marketing*, 22 (4), 395-414.

Levenshtein, V.I. (1966), "Binary Codes Capable of Correcting Deletions, Insertions, and Reversals," *Soviet Physics Doklady*, 10 (8), 707-710.

Mittal, Vikas, Pankaj Kumar and Michael Tsiros (1999)., "Attribute-Level Performance, Satisfaction, and Behavioral Intentions over Time: A Computation-System Approach," *Journal of Marketing*, 63 (2), 88-101.

Nicholson, Michael, Ian Clarke and Michael Blakemore (2002), "'One Brand Three Ways to Shop': Situational Variables and Multichannel Consumer Behaviour," *International Review of Retail, Distribution and Consumer Research*, 12 (2), 131 – 148.

Payne, John W., James R. Bettman and Eric J. Johnson (1993), *The Adaptive Decision Maker*. Cambridge, UK: Cambridge Press.

Payne, Adrian and Pennie Frow (2004), "The Role of Multichannel Integration in Customer Relationship Management," *Industrial Marketing Management*, 33 (2004), 527-538.

Peterson, Robert A., Sridhar Balasubramanian, and Bart J. Bronnenberg (1997), "Exploring the Implications of the Internet for Consumer Marketing," *Journal of the Academy of Marketing Science*, 25 (4), 329-346.

Rangaswamy, Arvind and Gerrit H. van Bruggen (2005), "Opportunities and Challenges in Multichannel Marketing: An Introduction to the Special Issue," *Journal of Interactive Marketing*, 19 (2), 5 – 11.

Sankoff, David and Joseph B. Kruskal (1983), *Time Warps, String Edits, and Macromolecules: The Theory and Practice of Sequence Comparison*. Mass: Addison-Wesley Reading.

Simons, Luuk P. A. and Harry Bouwman (2004), "Designing a Channel Mix," *International Journal of Internet Marketing and Advertising*, 1 (3), 229 – 250

Sinha, Piyush K. and Dwarika P. Uniyal (2005), "Using Observational Research for Behavioural Segmentation of Shoppers," *Journal of Retailing and Consumer Services*, Vol. 12, 35-48.

Steinmann, Sascha and Günter Silberer (2010), "Clustering Customer Contact Sequences - Results of a Customer Survey in Retailing", *European Retail Research*, 24 (1), 99-122.

Verhoef, Peter C., Scott A. Neslin and Björn Vroomen (2007), "Multichannel Customer Management: Understanding the Research-Shopper Phenomenon," *International Journal of Research in Marketing*, 24 (2007), 129-148.

Venkatesan, Rajkumar, Vipin Kumar and Nalini Ravishankar (2007), "Multichannel Shopping: Causes and Consequences," *Journal of Marketing*, 71 (2), 114-132.

Wallace, David W., Joan L. Giese and Jean L. Johnson (2004), "Customer Retailer Loyalty in the Context of Multiple Channel Strategies," *Journal of Retailing*, 80 (4), 249 – 263.

The Influence of Outcome Alignability on Risky Medical Decisions

Partha Krishnamurthy, University of Houston, USA
Adwait Khare, University of Texas at Arlington, USA

EXTENDED ABSTRACT

People often find themselves having to choose between options that offer certain but moderate outcomes and those that offer uncertain, but potentially excellent outcomes or poor outcomes. There is a rich tradition in decision-making research of studying how people make decisions when options vary in the level of risk associated with the outcomes. Much of this research, however, has been based on options with numerical outcomes.

Although decision-makers often face options with numerically stated outcomes, it is fairly common for decision-makers to confront risk involving non-numerical, qualitative outcome states as well. In medical decision making, for example, health risk information can be conveyed via different information formats such as numeric, verbal, and visual (Lipkus 2007). Consumers, for instance, commonly choose from medicines which provide different levels of qualitative improvement (strong, medium, mild) in pain felt by patients. Similarly, physicians and nurse practitioners routinely use the Wong-Baker FACES Pain Rating Scale which has no numerical aspects to "measure" the level of pain reported by the patients.

Therefore it is important to consider whether the findings from risky contexts involving quantitative outcomes extend to situations with qualitative outcomes. If risk preference is found to be different for qualitative and quantitative outcomes, it can have important implications for strategically presenting risk information. Yet, an analysis of the studies featured in Kühberger's (1998) meta-analysis on risk-preference shows no study on this topic. Thus, our aim is to examine the effect of quantitatively versus quantitatively described, but equivalent, medical outcomes on risk preference.

There is reason to believe that the qualitative–quantitative distinction may be consequential in regards to risk-preference. Our core thesis is as follows. We start with the premise that the evaluation of a risky choice option arises from consideration of both its upside and downside outcome. Therefore, factors that alter one's ability to simultaneously consider both the upside and downside outcome ought to influence the evaluation of the risky option. One such factor relates to how the outcomes are described, qualitative versus quantitative.

Quantitative outcomes lend themselves to numerical calculations and therefore allow for a joint consideration of both the upside and downside outcomes of the risky option. As noted by Kahneman and Tversky (1979), the risky option is evaluated by multiplying each subjectively evaluated numerical outcome with its subjective probability and then adding such products of all the outcomes. Qualitative outcomes, on the other hand, are not amenable to such calculations, and therefore impede consideration of both upside and downside outcome in the risky option. We further argue that when faced with a choice between focusing on the upside versus the downside risk, people will focus on the downside and show greater tendency to avoid the risky outcome. This thesis leads to two predictions. First, qualitative outcomes will induce a focus shift that will be revealed in elevated threat perceptions of the risky option. Second, this focus shift will induce a choice shift against the risky option.

In three studies, we manipulate outcome alignability as high (quantitative outcome information) or low (qualitative outcome information) and demonstrate that (a) risk preference reduces when alignability is lower (study 1), (b) the reduction in risk-preference is mediated by threat perceptions of the risky option (study 3), and (c) the impact of alignability is robust to variations in the operationalization of the equivalence between quantitative and qualitative outcome information (study 2). The findings largely comport with our predictions.

REFERENCES

Dunegan, K. J. (1993). Framing, Cognitive Modes, and Image Theory: Toward an Understanding of a Glass Half Full. *Journal of Applied Psychology*, 78, 491-503.

Gourville, J. T. and Soman, D. (2005). Overchoice and Assortment Type: When and Why Variety Backfires. *Marketing Science*, 24, 382-395.

Hochwarter, W. A., Witt, L. A., Treadway, D. C., & Ferris, G. R. (2006). The Interaction of Social Skill and Organizational Support on Job Performance. *Journal of Applied Psychology*, 91, 482-489.

Highhouse, S. & Yüce, P. (1996). Perspectives, Perceptions, and Risk-Taking Behavior. *Organizational Behavior and Human Decision Processes*, 65, 159-167.

Kühberger, A. (1998). The Influence of Framing on Risky-Decisions: A Meta-Analysis. *Organizational Behavior and Human Decision Processes*, 75, 23-55.

Lipkus, Isaac, M. (2007). Numeric, Verbal, and Visual Formats of Conveying Health Risks: Suggested Best Practices and Future Recommendations. *Medical Decision Making*, 27, 696-713.

Lopes, L. L. (1987). Between Hope and Fear: The Psychology of Risk. *Advances in Experimental Social Psychology*, 20, 255-295.

March, J. G. & Shapira, Z. (1987). Managerial Perspectives on Risk and Risk Taking. *Management Science*, 33, 1404-1418.

Markman, A. B. & Medin, D. L. (1995). Similarity and Alignment in Choice. *Organizational Behavior and Human Decision Processes*, 63, 117-130.

Schneider, S. L. (1992). Framing and Conflict: Aspiration Level Contingency, The Status Quo, and Current Theories of Uncertain Choice. *Journal of Experimental Psychology: Learning, Memory, and Cognition*, 18, 1040-1057.

Stone, D. N. & Schkade, D. A. (1991). Numeric and Linguistic Information Representation in Multiattribute Choice. *Organizational Behavior and Human Decision Processes*, 49, 42-59.

Tversky, A. & Kahneman, D. (1991). Loss Aversion in Riskless Choice: A Reference-Dependent Model. *Quarterly Journal of Economics*, 106, 1039–1061.

Vishwanathan, M. & Narayanan, S. (1994). Comparative Judgments of Numerical and Verbal Attribute Labels. *Journal of Consumer Psychology*, 3, 79-101.

Zhang, S. & Markman, A. B. (1998). Overcoming the Early Entrant Advantage via Differentiation: The Role of Alignable and Nonalignable Differences. *Journal of Marketing Research*, 35, 413-426.

The Effect of Regulatory Focus on the Influence of Injunctive and Descriptive Social Norms

Vladimir Melnyk, Maastricht University, The Netherlands
Erica van Herpen, Wageningen University, The Netherlands
Arnout R. H. Fischer, Wageningen University, The Netherlands
Hans C. M. van Trijp, Wageningen University, The Netherlands

EXTENDED ABSTRACT

Consumers encounter marketing messages using social norms in a variety of situations and contexts where different goals can be dominant. These goals can relate to their hopes and aspirations (i.e., promotion focus) or to their potential losses and duties (i.e., prevention focus) (Avnet and Higgins 2006; Freitas and Higgins 2002). These two focuses prime different routes of motivation for product choice, and may determine the effectiveness of social norms. The influence of norms on actual behavior may depend on its congruence with the consumer's self-regulatory focus.

Social norms can be formulated as descriptive or injunctive norms (Cialdini et al. 1990). Descriptive norms describe the typical behavior of others, and set behavioral standards from which people may not want to deviate (Schultz et al. 2007). Injunctive norms prescribe a behavior, and refer to what people should do in a given situation.

Depending on which regulatory focus is activated at the moment of facing social norms, consumers can be more responsive to either of the norm's formulations. Descriptive norms provide social proof that indicates possible beneficial behaviors (Cialdini 2006; Schultz et al. 2007), and therefore, these norms relate to the achievement of goals. In contrast, injunctive norms provide a request, and following this request is a way to avoid negative consequences (e.g., social disapproval or punishment) (Cialdini et al. 1990). Therefore, injunctive norms relate to prevention focus. The aim of this paper is to investigate the effect of compatibility between injunctive versus descriptive social norms on the one hand, and promotion versus prevention regulatory focus on the other hand to determine which formulation of social norms is the most effective under prevention and promotion focus.

Although social norms can provide a powerful instrument to influence consumers' attitudes, intentions, and product choice, the marketing literature has surprisingly few papers on the topic. Yet, to make optimal use of social norms, it is crucial for marketers to understand under which conditions the effect of social norms can increase the desired behavior or can backfire, and more specifically how to use different social norms in different situations.

Two experiments examine the consequences for attitudes and behavioral intentions of the different norms under prevention and promotion focus. Experiment 1 ($N = 100$) had a 2 (norm formulation: descriptive vs. injunctive) ´ 2 (primed regulatory focus: prevention vs. promotion) between subject design. Formulation of the social norm was manipulated in a fictitious webpage with promoted either a descriptive norm ("Wageningen students buy Fair Trade coffee") or an injunctive norm ("Wageningen students should buy Fair Trade coffee"). To prime regulatory focus participants were asked to write down one or several positive situations that they would like to achieve (vs. negative situations they would like to avoid, for prevention focus condition) within the next few weeks, and describe strategies that they could use to successfully promote this goal (vs. prevent those negative situations, for prevention condition). Experiment 2 ($N = 109$) had a 2 (norm formulation: descriptive vs. injunctive) ´ 2 (ingrained regulatory focus: prevention vs. promotion) between subject design. The manipulation of norm formulation was similar to Experiment 1 except that it was about organic milk. Regulatory focus was incorporated

within the message by providing either prevention- or promotion-related statements. For example, the title of the message ended either with a prevention statement "…to prevent harm to the environment" or with a promotion statement "…for a better environment". Consistent with our expectations results of both experiments show that the effect of descriptive norms is lower when prevention goals are salient than when promotion goals are salient. Unlike descriptive norms, injunctive norms are not affected by regulatory focus.

This study has several managerial implications. In particular it shows that descriptive norms are most successful when a goal approach focus rather than a loss avoidance focus is present. The research also shows that the wording of a normative message can activate a gain or loss avoidance focus. A marketer should therefore carefully design the wording of normative messages, the context in which such a message is received by consumers, as well as the channels of communication. Messages which are focused on problem avoidance may not be very well suited for descriptive norms and should use injunctive norms as a default. Messages using descriptive norms, such as campaigns based on communicating a favorable statistic of the majority of others that perform a behavior, should be conveyed in the context of achieving goals.

This research increases our understanding of the influence of social norms on decision making by showing differential effect of regulatory focus for descriptive and injunctive norms in the promotion of sustainable products, which occurs because different formulations of social norms are compatible to promotion or prevention focus. More specifically, descriptive norms are oriented towards benefits and have a better fit with a promotion than prevention focus, while this is not so for injunctive norms.

REFERENCES

Ajzen, I. (2001). Nature and operation of attitudes. *Annual Review of Psychology, 52,* 27-58.

Avnet, T., & Higgins, E. T. (2006). How regulatory fit affects value in consumer choices and opinions. *Journal of Marketing Research, 43,* 1-10.

Bandura, A. (1977). *Social learning theory.* New York: General Learning Press.

Camacho, C. J., Higgins, E. T., & Luger, L. (2003). Moral value transfer from regulatory fit: What feels right is right and what feels wrong is wrong. *Journal of Personality and Social Psychology, 84,* 498-510.

Cavalli-Sforza, L. L., & Feldman, M. W. (1981). *Cultural transmission and evolution: A quantitative approach.* Princeton, NJ: Princeton.

Cialdini, R. B. (2006). *Influence: The psychology of persuasion.* New York: Collins Business Essentials.

Cialdini, R. B., & Goldstein, N. (2004). Social influence: Compliance and conformity. *Annual Review of Psychology, 55,* 591-621.

Cialdini, R. B., Reno, R. R., & Kallgren, C. A. (1990). A focus theory of normative conduct: Recycling the concept of norms to reduce littering in public places. *Journal of Personality and Social Psychology, 58,* 1015-1026.

Cialdini, R. B., & Trost, M. R. (1998). Social influence: Social norms, conformity, and compliance. In D. T. Gilbert, S. T. Fiske & G. Lindzey (Eds.), *The handbook of social psychology* (pp. 151-192). Boston: McGraw-Hill.

Daryanto, A., de Ruyter, K., Wetzels, M., & Patterson, P. G. (2010). Service firms and customer loyalty programs: a regulatory fit perspective of reward preferences in a health club setting. *Journal of the Academy of Marketing Science, 38*, 604-616.

Deutsch, M., & Gerard, H. B. (1955). A study of normative and informational social influences upon individual judgement. *Journal of Abnormal and Social Psychology, 51*, 629-636.

Freitas, A. L., & Higgins, E. T. (2002). Enjoying goal-directed action: The role of regulatory fit. *Psychological Science, 13*, 1-6.

Higgins, E. T. (1997). Beyond pleasure and pain. *American Psychologist, 52*, 1280-1300.

Higgins, E. T., & Tykocinski, O. (1992). Seff-discrepancies and biographical memory: Personality and cognition at the level of psychological situation. *Personality and Social Psychology Bulletin, 18*, 527-535.

Homburg, C., Wieseke, J., & Kuehnl, C. (2010). Social influence on salespeople's adoption of sales technology: A multilevel analysis. *Journal of the Academy of Marketing Science, 38*, 159-168.

Hornsey, M. J., Majkut, L., Terry, D. J., & McKimmie, B. M. (2003). On being loud and proud: Non-conformity and counter-conformity to group norms. *British Journal of Social Psychology, 42*, 319-335.

Kruglanski, A. W. (2006). The nature of fit and the origins of "feeling right": A goal-systemic perspective. *Journal of Marketing Research, 43*, 11-14.

Lee, A. Y., & Aaker, J. L. (2004). Bringing the frame into focus: The influence of regulatory fit on processing fluency and persuasion. *Journal of Personality and Social Psychology, 86*, 205-218.

Lee, R., Murphy, J., & Neale, L. (2009). The interactions of consumption characteristics on social norms. *Journal of Consumer Marketing, 26*, 277-285.

Lockwood, P., Jordan, C. H., & Kunda, Z. (2002). Motivation by positive or negative role models: Regulatory focus determines who will best inspire us. *Journal of Personality and Social Psychology, 83*, 854-864.

Melnyk, V., Van Herpen, E., & Van Trijp, H. (2009). The influence of social norms in consumer decision making: A meta-analysis. *Advances in Consumer Research, 37*, 463-464.

Nolan, J. M., Schultz, P. W., Cialdini, R. B., Goldstein, N. J., & Griskevicius, V. (2008). Normative social influence is underdetected. *Personality and Social Psychology Bulletin, 34*, 913-923.

Ouellette, J. A., & Wood, W. (1998). Habit and intention in everyday life: The multiple processes by which past behavior predicts future behavior. *Psychological Bulletin, 124*, 54-74.

Reno, R. R., Cialdini, R. B., & Kallgren, C. A. (1993). The transsituational influence of social norms. *Journal of Personality and Social Psychology, 64*, 104-112.

Rhodes, R. E., & Courneya, K. S. (2003). Investigating multiple components of attitude, subjective norm, and perceived control: An examination of the theory of planned behaviour in the exercise domain. *British Journal of Social Psychology, 42*, 129-146.

Rivis, A., & Sheeran, P. (2003). Descriptive norms as an additional predictor in the theory of planned behaviour: A meta-analysis. *Current Psychology, 22*, 218-233.

Safer, D. (1998). *Preferences for luxurious or reliable products: promotion and prevention focus as moderators.* Dissertation Abstracts International: Section B: The Sciences and Engineering, 59, 2488.

Schultz, P. W., Nolan, J. M., Cialdini, R. B., Goldstein, N. J., & Griskevicius, V. (2007). The constructive, destructive and reconstructive power of social norms. *Psychological Science, 18*, 429-434.

Schwenk, G., & Moser, G. (2009). Intention and behavior: A bayesian meta-analysis with focus on the Ajzen-Fishbein model in the field of environmental behavior. *Quality & Quantity, 43*, 743-755.

Terry, D. J., Hogg, M. A., & White, K. M. (2000). Attitude-behavior relations: Social identity and group membership. In D. J. Terry & M. A. Hogg (Eds.), *Attitudes, behavior, and social context: The role of norms and group membership* (pp. 67-94). London: Lawrence Erlbaum.

Veldkamp, A., Van Altvorst, A. C., Eweg, R., Jacobsen, E., Van Kleef, A., Van Latesteijn, H. et al. (2009). Triggering transitions towards sustainable development of the Dutch agricultural sector: TransForum's approach. *Agronomy for Sustainable Development, 29*(1), 87-96.

Walker, S., & Dorsa, E. (2001). Making design work: Sustainability, product design and social equity. *The Journal of Sustainable Product Design, 1*, 41-48.

Young, W., Hwang, K., McDonald, S., & Oates, C. J. (2010). Sustainable consumption: Green Consumer behaviour when purchasing products. *Sustainable Development, 18*, 20-31.

Childlike Anthropomorphic Characteristics in Products

Katarina Hellen, University of Vaasa, Finland
Maria Sääksjärvi, Delft University of Technology, The Netherlands

EXTENDED ABSTRACT

Anthropomorphism, the tendency to see humanlike qualities, such as faces, motivations, and emotions in non-human agents, has been studied in psychology and marketing (Epley, Waytz and Cacioppo 2007; Serpell 2002; Woodside, Sood, and Miller 2008). Previous literature on anthropomorphism has tended to address it as an aggregate concept. In actuality, literature on brand personality indicate that consumers do not perceive brands to just have "a human personality" but that they perceive personalities in more refined ways, for example "rugged", "sophisticated" or "friendly" (Aaker 1997) indicating that people anthropomorphize in a more refined way that previously thought. In this paper, the focus is on anthropomorphism of a specific product – products with childlike characteristics and the purpose was to investigate the nature of childlike anthropomorphic products and consumer reactions to them. Childlike anthropomorphic characteristics are likely to be interesting for marketers as scholars have suggested that humans are deeply programmed to respond positively to children and that this positive reaction extends to adults, animals, and objects to which people attribute childlike features (Morreall 1991; Serpell 2002). These feelings invite people to bond and interact with babies (Langlois et al. 1995; Morreall 1991).

We conducted four studies to examine childlike anthropomorphism. Study 1 was in-depth interviews with consumers (N = 10), five females and five males, conducted to understand their associations with childlike anthropomorphism. After freely discussing the concept of childlike anthropomorphism, the respondents were shown a booklet with 12 childlike anthropomorphic products that they were asked to evaluate. The purpose of Study 2 was to generate dimensions and items for a scale of childlike anthropomorphism in products. To reach this purpose, we used our qualitative study (Study 1) and previous literature. Based on these sources we identified 70 items to that referred to childlike anthropomorphism. We included the items in a questionnaire in a random order. We asked a sample of students (N = 202, 36.8 % females, mean age = 21) to indicate the extent to which the 60 items described their perceptions of well-known products (1 = "not at all", and 7 = "very much so"). 12 products in total were tested, ranging from purses to technical devices such as phones and laptops. The results showed that childlike anthropomorphism in products refers to four distinct dimensions: sweetness, sympathy, simplicity, and smallness.

In Study 3, we reduced the number of scale items by conducting both exploratory and confirmatory analyses. To test the stability of the scale, we employed a new sample of respondents (N = 224, 51.3 % females, mean age = 23). The procedure of study 2 was repeated with one exception; this time, each respondent evaluated only one product. 71 participants evaluated the symbolic product (the pink purse), 77 participants a utilitarian product (e.g., a razor) and 76 a symbolic and utilitarian product (e.g., a camera). Each participant saw a color picture of the product and was asked to rate the product on the 23-item scale. The questionnaire also included Aaker's (1997) brand personality scale. The results showed that childlike anthropomorphism is best represented by a second-order factor model with the four sub-dimensions of sweetness, sympathy, simplicity, and smallness. In Study 4, we focused on the nomological validity of the childlike anthropomorphic product scale by linking it to product evaluation (Oliver 1993) and willingness to attach (Thomson, MacInnis, and Park 2005). On the basis of prior literature on childlike products, we expected childlike anthropomorphism to affect these concepts positively (Lorenz 1943; Morreall 1991; Kinsella 1995; Saunders 1992; Yano 2004). Recognizing human characters in products makes consumers care for their products and feel warmly towards them and thereby it can be expected that childlike anthropomorphic products predict positive product evaluations. Thus, we predict that infant anthropomorphism is positively related to evaluation. Moreover, pioneering work on attachment originate in the realm of parent–infant relationships. According to Bowlby (1980), an attachment is an emotion-laden target-specific bond between a person and a specific object (a person or a physical object). As human infants are associated with strong positive affect and sensitivity to babies has been argued to have evolved in humans to bond and to care for their offspring, it can be expected that childlike anthropomorphism is positively related to willingness to attach to a product. A total of 214 students participated in Study 4 (N = 214, 54.7 % females, mean age = 24). Each respondent evaluated one product. 75 participants evaluated the symbolic product (the pink purse), 73 participants randomly one of the 4 utilitarian products and 66 randomly one of the 11 symbolic and utilitarian products. The questionnaire also included Thomson, MacInnis, and Park's (2005) brand attachment scale. Simple regressions showed that childlike anthropomorphism had a positive impact on product evaluation. We also found a positive relationship between childlike anthropomorphism and willingness to attach. There were clear differences between the genders: women considered the products to be sweeter, whereas men considered the product to simpler and more sympathetic. No differences were found regarding smallness.

Across samples, it was demonstrated that childlike products have four separate dimensions – sweetness, sympathy, simplicity, and smallness. The results show that consumers are attracted to childlike anthropomorphic products, and that they are willing to attach to such products. The results also suggest a gender effect. Both men and women were found to react positively to childlike anthropomorphic characteristics, but they evaluated the dimensions of the scale differently. Across all the three quantitative studies, results show that men perceived childlike characteristics as more sympathetic than did women. This result may be based on that this characteristic in women is a mating cue for men (Baumeister 2010), as men are attracted to women who are perceived as kind and lovable as such qualities are taken as indications that they are good mothers and partners. Further, men are not as sensitive as women to detecting sweetness, who may perceive the childlike products as kind and helpless, triggering feelings of caretaking and protection.

REFERENCES

Aaker, Jennifer L. (1997), "Dimensions of Brand Personality," *Journal of Marketing Research*, 34 (August), 347-356.

Aggarwal, Pankaj and McGill, Ann L. (2007), "Is That Car Smiling at Me? Schema Congruity as a Basis for Evaluating Anthropomophized Products," *Journal of Consumer Research*, 34 (December), 468-79.

Bagozzi, Richard P. and Heatherton Todd F. (1994), "A General Approach to Representing Multifaceted Personality Constructs: Application to State Self-Esteem," *Structural Equation Modeling: A Multidiciplinary Journal*, 1(1), 35-67.

Baumeister, Roy F. (2010), *Is there Anything Good about Men? How Cultures Flourish by Exploiting Men*, New York, Oxford University press.

Bowlby, John (1980), *Attachment and Loss: Vol 3. Loss: Sadness and Depression*, New York, Basic.

Chandler, Jesse and Schwarz, Norbert (2010), "Use does not Wear Ragged the Fabric of Friendship: Thinking of Objects as Alive makes People less Willing to Replace Them," *Journal of Consumer Psychology*, 20 (2), 138-145.

DeVellis, Robert F. (2003), *Scale development*, London: Thousand Oaks: Sage Publications.

Epley, Nicolas, Waytz, Adam, Akalis, Scott and Cacioppo, John T. (2008), "When We Need a Human: Motivational Determinants of Anthropomorphism," *Social Cognition*, 26(2), 143-55.

Epley, Nicholas, Waytz, Adam, and Cacioppo, John T. (2007), "On Seeing Human: A Three-factor Theory of Anthropomorphism," *Psychological Review*, 114 (3), 864-886.

Fournier, Susan (1998), "Consumers and Their Brands: Developing Relationship Theory in Consumer Research," *Journal of Consumer Research*, 24(March), 343-73.

Gorn, Gerald J., Jiang, Yuwei and Johar, Gita V. (2008), "Baby Faces, Trait Inferences, and Company Evaluations in a Public Relations Crisis," *Journal of Consumer Research*, 35(1), 36-49.

Govers, Pascalle C. M. and Schoormans, Jan P. L. (2005), "Product Personality and its Influence on Consumer Preference", *Journal of Consumer Marketing*, 22 (4), 189-197.

Hildebrandt, Kathrine A. (1983), "Effect of Facial Expression Variations on Ratings of Infants'Physical attractiveness," *Developmental Psychology*, 19 (3), 414-17.

Kinsella, Sharon (1995), "Cuties in Japan," in *Women, Media and Consumption in Japan,* ed. Lise Skov and Brian Moeran, Honolulu: University Hawai'i Press, 220-254.

Langlois, Judith H., Ritter, Jean M., Casey, Rita J., and Sawin, Douglas B. (1995), "Infant Attractiveness Predicts Maternal Behaviors and Attitudes," *Developmental Psychology*, 31 (3), 464-472.

Lorenz, Konrad (1943), "Die Angeborenen Formen Möglicher Erfahrung (The Innate Form of Possible Experience)", *Zeitschrift fur Tierpsychologie*, 5, 235-409.

McVeigh, Brian J. (2000), "How Hello Kitty Commodifies the Cute Cool and Camp," *Journal of Material Culture*, 5(2), 225-245.

Morreall, John (1991), "Cuteness," *British Journal of Aesthetics*, 31 (1), 39-47.

Mugge, Ruth, Govers, Pascalle C M. and Schoormans, Jan P L. (2009), "The Development and Testing of a Product Personality Scale, *Design Studies*, 30(3), 287-302.

Mugge, Ruth, Schoormans, Jan P L. and Schifferstein, Hendrik, N J. (2005), "Design Strategies to Postpone Consumers' Product Replacement: The Value of a Strong Person-Product Relationship", *The Design Journal*, 8(2), 38-48.

Nunnally, Jum C. (1978), *Psychometric Theory*, New York, New York: McGraw-Hill.

Oliver, Richard L. (1993), "Cognitive, Affective and Attribute bases of the Satisfaction Response," *Journal of Consumer Research*, 20 (December), 418-430.

Osgood, Charles E., Suci, George S. and Tannenbaum Percy H. (1957), "The Measurement of Meaning, Urbana, IL: University of Illinois Press.

Saunders, John T. (1992), "On "Cuteness"," *Bristish Journal of Aestehetics*, 32 (2), 162-165. Serpell, James A. (2002), "Anthropomorphism and Anthropomorphic Selection—Beyond the "Cute" Response," *Society and Animals*, 10 (4), 437-454.

Sprengelmeyer, R, Perrett, DI, Fagan EC, Cornwell, RE, Lobmaier, JS, Sprengelmeyer, A, Aasheim, HBM, Black, IM, Cameron, LM, Crow, S, Milne, N, Rhodes, EC and Young, AW (2009), "The Cutest Little Baby Face. A Hormonal Link to sensitivity to Cuteness in Infant Faces", *Psychological Science*, 20(2), 149-154.

Sprengelmeyer, Reiner, Perrett, David I. and Young, Andy W. (2010), "Reproductive Hormones Modulate Cuteness Processing", *Psychological Science*, 2(5), 753.

Sundie, Jill M., Kenrick, Douglas T., Griskevicius, Vladas, Tybur, Joshua M., Vohs, Kathleen D., and Daniel J. Beal (2010), "Peacocks, Porsches, and Thorstein Veblen: Conspicuous consumption as a sexual signaling system," *Journal of Personality and Social Psychology*, 1 (November), 1-17.

Thomson, Matthew, MacInnis, Deborah J., and Park, C. Whan (2005), "The Ties that Bind: Measuring the Strength of Consumers' Emotional Attachments to Brands," *Journal of Consumer Psychology*, 15 (1), 77-91.

Waytz, Adam, Cacioppo, John, and Epley, Nicholas (2010), "Who Sees Human? The Stability and Importance of Individual Differences in Anthropomorphism," *Perspectives on Psychological Science*, 5 (May), 219-232.

Woodside, Arch, Sood, Suresh, and Miller, Kenneth E. (2008). "When Consumers and Brands talk: Storytelling Theory and Research in Psychology and Marketing," *Psychology and Marketing*, 25 (2), 97-145.

Yano, Christine R. (2004), "Kitty Litter: Japanese Cute at Home and Abroad," in *Toys, Games, and Media*, ed. Jeffery Goldstein, David Buckingham, and Gilles Brougere, Mahwah, New Jersey: Lawrence Eribaum Associates, 55-71.

Psychological Distance in Hedonic Prediction and Consumption: The Surprising Impact of Distant Events

Jane Ebert, University of Minnesota, USA
Tom Meyvis, New York University, USA

EXTENDED ABSTRACT

Would you prefer a film based on a true story or one that is fictitious, a recently written novel or one written five years ago? For experiential decisions such as these, individuals are often guided by how they expect the experience will make them feel, and their expectations are often wrong: they overestimate the impact of the hedonic experience (Gilbert, Driver-Linn, and Wilson 2002; Kahneman and Snell 1992). Explanations for this bias have focused on predictors' *failure to consider* the context around the focal hedonic experience (Gilbert et al. 2002), such as the effects of experiences occurring subsequent to the focal experience. In contrast, we explore a process where individuals *overconsider* the context around the focal hedonic experience. We focus on psychological distance: a context that encompasses many attributes important in decision-making such as self-relevance, time and likelihood of occurrence, and authenticity (Liberman, Trope, and Stephan 2007).

We propose that psychologically distant events can often have a surprisingly strong emotional impact, equivalent to a similar psychologically near event, because of substantial limitations to the attenuating effect of psychological distance. These limitations result from mechanisms that consumers are not aware of, leading them to overestimate the impact of psychological distance (and underestimate the emotional power of psychologically distant events).

We compare people's predictions and experience of hedonic experiences that are psychologically close or distant, before examining underlying processes and a suboptimal behavioral consequence of the results we obtain. We examine our hypothesis in six studies in which participants either read emotion-inducing newspaper stories or win a prize.

In the story-based studies, psychologically distant experiencers were first told the story was "fictitious" (studies 1A, 2, and 5) or about an event that "happened 10 years ago" (study 1B), while psychologically close experiencers were told the story was "real" (studies 1A, 2, and 5) or about an event that "happened recently" (study 1A). Experiencers then read the story and rated their affective reactions. Predictors read the story and predicted their reactions if they had first been given the information about the story context.

Predictors predict a greater influence of psychological distance on their reactions than experiencers actually experienced. Most often, predictors accurately predict affective reaction to the psychologically close experience and underestimate reaction to the distant experience. In study 3, we replicated this finding with a new experience: winning a prize available immediately (psychologically close) or in 6 weeks (distant).

We examined underlying process in studies 2 and 4. In study 3, we manipulated whether psychological distance information was presented before or after the story, manipulating whether predictors expect it to change experiencers' processing of the story. Predictors overestimate the effect of psychological distance both on experiencers' processing and the direct effect on experiencers' affect. We rule out alternative demand and salience explanations. In study 4, we focus on experiencers. We use the paradigm from study 3, where experiencers who win a prize failed to incorporate psychological distance information. By manipulating whether or not experiencers complete a task after winning the prize, we demonstrate that experiencers who

are no longer absorbed in a hedonic experience are able to incorporate psychological distance information.

In study 5 we demonstrate that these effects can lead to suboptimal decisions. Individuals feel less sad after reading a sad real story than after reading a tragic fictitious story. However, they predict the opposite (that the tragic fictitious story will make them sadder) and so choose to read that story (rather than the less upsetting sad real story).

These results suggest that, when choosing between options that vary on psychological distance attributes, individuals will be influenced by these attributes more than they should, e.g., preferring films based on true stories when, in actual fact, they would be equally happy with fictional films. More generally, this approach connects the affective forecasting literature to work in judgment that examines unwanted or over- correction, such as work on mental contamination (Wilson and Brekke 1994). This approach also builds on prior research that shows that consumers' hedonic experiences are often remarkably insensitive to the context of the experience (e.g., Novemsky and Ratner 2003)—a phenomenon that has recently been attributed to the surprisingly absorbing nature of hedonic experiences (Morewedge et al. 2010). Given the frequency of these effects in judgment, we suspect that this process may prove a common source of systematic error in hedonic prediction.

REFERENCES

Ebert, Jane E.J. (2001), "The Role of Cognitive Resources in the Valuation of near and Far Future Events," *Acta Psychologica*, 108 (September), 155-71.

Ekman, Gösta and Oswald Bratfisch (1965), "Subjective Distance and Emotional Involvement: A Psychological Mechanism.," *Acta Psychologica*, 24, 430-37.

Epley, Nicholas, Boaz Keysar, Leaf Van Boven, and Thomas Gilovich (2004), "Perspective Taking as Egocentric Anchoring and Adjustment," *Journal of Personality and Social Psychology*, 87 (3), 327-39.

Gilbert, D. T. and T. D. Wilson (2007), "Prospection: Experiencing the Future," *Science*, 317 (5843), 1351-54.

Gilbert, Daniel T., Erin Driver-Linn, and Timothy D. Wilson (2002), "The Trouble with Vronsky: Impact Bias in the Forecasting of Future Affective States," in *The Wisdom in Feeling: Psychological Processes in Emotional Intelligence*, ed. Lisa F. Barrett and Peter Salovey, New York: Guilford Press, 114-43.

Gilbert, Daniel T., Elizabeth C. Pinel, Timothy D. Wilson, Stephen J. Blumberg, and Thalia P. Wheatley (1998), "Immune Neglect: A Source of Durability Bias in Affective Forecasting," *Journal of Personality and Social Psychology*, 75 (3), 617-38.

Gilbert, Daniel T., Romin W. Tafarodi, and Patrick S. Malone (1993), "You Can't Not Believe Everything You Read," *Journal of Personality and Social Psychology*, 65 (2), 221-33.

Jensen, A.R. and W.D. Rohwer (1966), "The Stroop Color-Word Test: A Review," *Acta Psychologica*, 25 (1), 36-93.

Johnson, H. Durell (2004), "Hypothetical Situation Realism in Conflict Research: Associations with Adolescent Emotional Responses," *North American Journal of Psychology*, 6 (2), 265-74.

MacInnis, Deborah J., Vanessa M. Patrick, and C. Whan Park (2006), "Looking through the Crystal Ball: Affective Forecasting and Misforecasting in Consumer Behavior," in *Review of Marketing Research*, Vol. 2, ed. Naresh K. Malhotra, Armonk NY: M.E. Sharpe, 43-80.

Morewedge, Carey K., Daniel T. Gilbert, Kristian Ove R. Myrseth, Karim S. Kassam, and Timothy D. Wilson (2010), "Consuming Experience: Why Affective Forecasters Overestimate Comparative Value," *Journal of Experimental Social Psychology*, 46 (6), 986-92.

Nelson, Leif D. and Tom Meyvis (2008), "Interrupted Consumption: Disrupting Adaptation to Hedonic Experiences," *Journal of Marketing Research*, 45 (December), 654-64.

Newcomb, T.M. (1961), *The Acquaintance Process*, New York: Holt, Rinehart and Winston.

Novemsky, Nathan and Rebecca K. Ratner (2003), "The Time Course and Impact of Consumers' Erroneous Beliefs About Hedonic Contrast Effects," *Journal of Consumer Research*, 29 (March), 507-16.

Pham, Michel T. (1998), "Representativeness, Relevance and the Use of Feelings in Decision Making," *Journal of Consumer Research*, 25 (September), 144-59.

Shiv, Baba and Joel Huber (2000), "The Impact of Anticipating Satisfaction on Consumer Choice," *Journal of Consumer Research*, 27 (September), 202-16.

Suh, Eunkook, Ed Diener, and Frank Fujita (1996), "Events and Subjective Well-Being: Only Recent Events Matter," *Journal of Personality and Social Psychology*, 70 (5), 1091-102.

Van Boven, Leaf, Katherine White, and Michaela Huber (2009), "Immediacy Bias in Emotion Perception: Current Emotions Seem More Intense Than Previous Emotions," *Journal of Experimental Psychology: General*, 138 (3), 368-82.

What Not To Wear? Consumer Government in Wardrobe Self-Help

Annu Markkula, Aalto University School of Economics, Finland
Ilona Mikkonen, Aalto University School of Economics, Finland
Handan Vicdan, Eastern Kentucky University, USA

EXTENDED ABSTRACT

In this paper we empirically illustrate consumer government in the context of wardrobe self-help (WHS for short). By providing an empirical example of consumer government in a cultural text, our research contributes to the scholarly work on the government of consumers (Binkley 2006, Du Gay 2004, Moisander and Eriksson 2006, Moisander, Markkula and Eräranta 2010).

Government as a theoretical concept has recently been applied to marketing and consumer research. It has been argued that in the contemporary marketplace where organizations engage in co-creative practices with consumers, consumers are not only being disciplined with orders and rules (Zwick, Bonsu and Darmody 2008) – in addition, or even instead, consumers are being *governed* (Foucault [1979] 2008, 226).

One of the critical aspects of government is facilitating *self-government*; making people to monitor and reshape their own conduct, for example by enticing them on a path of self-improvement (Rose 1999, Zwick et al. 2008). The creation of a self-governing subject can occur through suggesting and offering consumers a range of technologies of the self (see e.g., Philip 2009) or operations that individuals perform on their "own bodies and souls, thoughts, conduct, and way of being" in order to transform themselves (Foucault 1988, 18, Larsson and Sanne 2005, Philip 2009, Rimke 2000).

In this paper, we empirically illustrate these practices in the context of fashion and clothing. Fashion and clothing are a significant part of the world economy (Allwood et al. 2006, 2) and it is widely accepted that this market is dominantly characterized by constant change and emulation of others (Thompson and Haytko 1997, Murray 2002). The past decade, however, has seen a surge of different types of fashion cultural mediators (McCracken 1988) in the form of TV makeover shows and guidebooks. Illustrative of this new trend is the British *What Not To Wear* brand by Susannah Constantine and Trinny Woodall. The brand claims to resist the dominant discourses of the fashion market, which direct consumers towards constant change and emulation of others (Thompson and Haytko 1997). By means of self-help, this new genre claims to liberate consumers to enlightened personal and social success (Gibbins and Taylor 2010).

The data used for this study consists of four books by Constantine and Woodall, which can be considered an exemplifying example of this new cultural mediator genre: What Not to Wear – The Rules (2002); ready 2 dress. How to Have Style Without Following Fashion (2002); What Your Clothes Say about You. How to look different, act different and feel different (2006) and The Body Shape Bible (2007). We analyzed the books using a discourse analytic approach detailed in Holstein and Gubrium (2005) and Moisander and Valtonen (2006). The level of analysis is the discursive practices through which wardrobe self-help establishes the ideal consumer subject. The analysis focuses on the technologies of the self (Philip 2009) that are offered to consumers to work on their conduct.

In the data we identify three specific, intertwined technologies of the self: 1) normalization, 2) confession, and 3) responsibilization. Normalization refers to discursive strategies which make certain practices of dressing the body seem 'normal' and desirable while excluding others, thus creating categories of right and wrong (Koro-Ljungberg, Gemignani, Brodeur and Kmiec 2007). By suggesting a range of actions through which consumers can learn to make the 'right' choices within the limits of the body, they are invited to turn the disciplining gaze upon themselves. Consumers are requested to confess (Besley 2007) to their erroneous, and to categorize and scrutinize themselves according to the guidelines offered by the style gurus. Finally, happiness is strongly associated with the choice of dress, and the individual consumer is made responsible for making the correct choices (Rimke 2000).

Based on the analysis of our empirical data, it can be concluded that the rhetoric used in wardrobe self-help is geared towards shaping and modifying consumer choice of dress by rigorously and carefully defining the limits of acceptability. The rhetoric strongly emphasizes responsibility on the part of the consumer to make right choices, as is customary to self-help literature in general (Redden 2002, Rimke 2002, Hazleden 2003, Blackman 2004, Philip 2009).

Therefore, WSH cannot be perceived as only liberating and empowering. As we have illustrated, WSH can be conceived as government (Zwick et al. 2008). Despite presenting the emulation of models and celebrities as undesirable and challenging the prevailing business strategy of the fashion and clothing sector, which is based on the notion that the cultural value of clothing is perishable (McCracken 1986), WHS still attempts to act upon consumer conduct. The ideal women is nonetheless defined according to the contemporary beauty ideals. This is also an attempt to change consumers bodily (Corrigan 2008, Entwistle 2001, Joy and Venkatesh 1994, Venkatesh, Joy, Sherry and Deschenes 2010), albeit indirectly.

REFERENCES

Allwood, Julian M., Laursen, Søren E., de Rodríguez, Cecilia M. & Bocken, Bocken M. P. (2006) Well dressed? The present and future sustainability of clothing and textiles in the United Kingdom, Cambridge: University of Cambridge Institute for Manufacturing.

Arnould, Eric J. & Thompson, Craig (2005) Consumer culture theory (CCT): Twenty years of research, Journal of Consumer Research 31 (4), 868-882.

Barber, Lynn (2008) The world according to garb, The Guardian, Issue 10 February 2008, http://www.guardian.co.uk/lifeandstyle/2008/feb/10/fashion.features1. Accessed 12 January 2011.

Barnard, Malcolm (2002) Fashion as communication, London: Routledge.

Bernauer, James & Mahon, Michael (2004) Michel Foucault's ethical imagination. In Gutting, G. (Ed.) The cambridge companion to Foucault, 2nd ed., Cambridge: Cambridge University Press, 149-175.

Besley, Tina & Peters, Michael A. (2007) Subjectivity and truth: Foucault, education, and the culture of self, New York: Peter Lang Publishing.

Binkley, Sam (2006) The perilous freedoms of consumption: Toward a theory of the conduct of consumer conduct, Journal for Cultural Research, 10 (4), 343-362.

Black, Sandy (2008) Eco-chic: The fashion paradox, London: Black Dog.

Blackman, Lisa (2004) Self-help, media cultures and the production of female psychopathology, European Journal of Cultural Studies, 7, 219-236.

Advances in Consumer Research
Volume 39, ©2011

Bourdieu, Pierre ([1979] 1984) A social critique of the judgment of taste, London: Routledge and Kegan Paul.

Corrigan, Peter (2008) The dressed society: Clothing, the body and some meanings of the world, London: Sage Publications.

Delhaye, Christine (2006) The development of consumption culture and the individualization of female identity: Fashion discourse in the Netherlands 1880–1920, Journal of Consumer Culture, 6 (1), 87-115.

Denegri-Knott, Janice, Zwick, Detlev & Schroeder, Jonathan E. (2006) Mapping consumer power: An integrative framework for marketing and consumer research, European Journal of Marketing, 40 (9/10), 950-971.

Du Gay, Paul (2004) Devices and dispositions: Promoting consumption, Consumption, Markets and Culture, 7 (2), 99-105.

Entwistle, Joanne (2001) The dressed body. In Entwistle, J. & Wilson, E. (Eds.) Body dressing, Oxford and London: Berg, 33-58.

Foucault, Michel (1982) The subject and power. In Dreyfus, H. L. & Rabinow, P. (Eds.) Michel Foucault: Beyond structuralism and hermeneutics, Hemel Hempstead: Harvestes Wheatsead, 208-226.

Foucault, Michel (1988) The ethic of care for the self as a practice of freedom: An interview. In Bernaur, J. & Rasmussen, D. (Eds.) The final Foucault, Cambridge, MA: The MIT Press, 1-20.

Foucault, Michel ([1979] 2008) The birth of biopolitics. Lectures at the Collège de France 1978-1979: Palgrave Macmillan.

Furedi, Frank (2004) Therapy culture, London: Routledge.

Galvin, Rose (2002) Disturbing notions of chronic illness and individual responsibility: Towards a genealogy of morals, Health, 6 (2), 107-137.

Gibbings, Sheri & Taylor, Jessica (2010) From rags to riches, the policing of fashion and identity: Governmentality and What Not to Wear, vis-à-vis: Explorations In Anthropology, 10 (1), 31-47.

Hall, Stuartt ([1997] 2009) Introduction. In Hall, S. (Ed.) Representation: Cultural representations and signifying practices, London: Sage, 1-12.

Hazleden, Rebecca (2003) Love yourself: The relationship of the self with itself in popular self-help texts, Journal of Sociology, 39, 413-428.

Holstein, James A. & Gubrium, Jaber F. (2005) Interpretive practice and social action. In Denzin, N. K. & Lincoln, Y. S. (Eds.) The SAGE handbook of qualitative research, 3rd ed., London and New York: Sage, 483-505.

Inthorn, Sanna & Boyce, Tammy (2010) It's disgusting how much salt you eat!': Television discourses of obesity, health and morality, International Journal of Cultural Studies, 13 (1), 83-100.

Joy, Annamma & Venkatesh, Alladi (1994) Postmodernism, feminism, and the body: The visible and the invisible in consumer research, International Journal of Research in Marketing, 11 (333-357).

Koro-Ljungberg, Mirka, Gemignani, Marco, Brodeur, Cheri W. & Kmiec, Cheryl (2007) The technologies of normalization and self Qualitative Inquiry, 13 (8), 1075-1094.

Larsson, Jörgen & Sanne, Christer (2005) Self-help books on avoiding time shortage, Time & Society, 14 (23), 213-230.

Lasch, Christopher (1979) The culture of narcissism: American life in an age of diminishing expectations, New York W.W. Norton and Co.

McCracken, Grant (1986) Culture and consumption:A theoretical account of the structure and movement of the cultural meaning of consumer goods, Journal of Consumer Research, 13 (1), 71-84.

McCracken, Grant (1988) Culture and consumption: New approaches to the symbolic character of consumer goods and activities, Bloomington & Indianapolis: Indiana University Press.

McRobbie, Angela (2004) Notes on 'What Not To Wear' and post-feminist symbolic violence, The Sociological Review, 52, 97-109.

Miller, Peter & Rose, Nikolas (1990) Governing economic life, Economy and Society, 19 (1), 1-31.

Miller, Peter & Rose, Nikolas (1997) Mobilizing the consumer: Assembling the subject of consumption, Theory, Culture & Society, 14, 1-36.

Millington, Brad (2009) Wii has never been modern: 'Active' video games and the 'conduct of conduct', New Media & Society, 11 (4), 621-640.

Moisander, Johanna & Eriksson, Päivi (2006) Corporate narratives of information society: Making up the mobile consumer subject, Consumption, Markets & Culture, 9, 257-275.

Moisander, Johanna, Markkula, Annu & Eräranta, Kirsi (2010) Construction of consumer choice in the market: Challenges for environmental policy International Journal of Consumer Studies, (34), 73-79.

Moisander, Johanna & Valtonen, Anu (2006) Qualitative marketing research: A cultural approach, London: Sage Publications.

Murray, Jeff (2002) The politics of consumption: A re-inquiry on Thompson and Haytko's (1997) "Speaking of fashion", Journal of Consumer Research, 29 (3), 427-40.

Oster, Candice & Cheek, Julianne (2008) Governing the contagious body: Genital herpes, contagion and technologies of the self, Health, 12 (2), 215-232.

Philip, Brigid (2009) Analysing the politics of self-help books on depression, Journal of Sociology 45(2), 151-168., 45 (2), 151-168.

Priest, Ann (2005) Uniformity and differentiation in fashion, International Journal of Clothing Science and Technology, 17 (3/4), 253-263.

Redden, Guy (2002) The New Agents: Personal transfiguration and radical privatization in New Age self-help, Journal of Consumer Culture, 2 (1), 33-52.

Rimke, Heidi M. (2000) Governing citizens through self-help literature, Cultural Studies, 14, 61-78.

Rose, Nikolas (1999) Powers of freedom: Reframing political thought, Cambridge: Cambridge University Press.

Schroeder, Jonathan E. (2002) Visual consumption, London: Routledge.

Thompson, Craig J. & Haytko, Diana L. (1997) Speaking of fashion: Consumers' uses of fashion discourses and the appropriation of countervailing cultural meanings, Journal of Consumer Research, 24 (1), 15-42.

Venkatesh, Alladi, Joy, Annamma, Sherry, John F. Jr. & Deschenes, Jonathan (2010) The aesthetics of luxury fashion, body and identify formation, Journal of Consumer Psychology, (forthcoming).

Wright, Katie (2008) Theorizing therapeutic culture: Past influences, future directions, Journal of Sociology, 44 (4), 321-336.

Zwick, Detlev, Bonsu, Samuel K. & Darmody, Aron (2008) Putting consumers to work: 'Co-creation' and new marketing govern-mentality, Journal of Consumer Culture, 8, 163-196.

When Do Metacognitive Experiences Matter?
The Different Roles of Ease of Retrieval

Hélène Deval, Dalhousie University, Canada
Frank R. Kardes, University of Cincinnati, USA
Bruce E. Pfeiffer, University of New Hampshire, USA

EXTENDED ABSTRACT

Although research suggests that judgments are often based on subjective experiences, competing theories of the underlying process coexist in the literature. Schwarz (e.g., 1998, 2004) proposes that metacognitive experiences operate as heuristic cues, suggesting that the effect should be attenuated under high elaboration conditions. In contrast, Petty and colleagues (e.g., 2007, 2009) find stronger effects when people attend to their own thoughts and try to assess their validity (the self-validation hypothesis), suggesting that the effect requires greater elaboration. Since there is empirical evidence for both conceptions, it is possible that the effect depends on differential processing styles at the time of attitude formation that may be related to the specific conditions of the task.

Recall tasks render two distinct sources of information: the recalled content and the subjective experience associated with the recall process (Schwarz 1998). Content and subjective ease of recall can have differential implications for attitude formation. Schwarz and colleagues (e.g., Schwarz et al. 1991; Wänke et al. 1995) conceptualize subjective ease as a heuristic cue, predicting that people are likely to use metacognitive experiences as an input for judgment when adopting a heuristic processing strategy. When adopting a systematic processing strategy, people should rely primarily on the recalled content (Schwarz 1998).

Petty and colleagues (Briñol and Petty 2009; Petty et al. 2007) developed a comprehensive framework for the role of metacognition in judgment based on the self-validation hypothesis. Metacognition refers to second-order thoughts or one's thoughts about thoughts and thought processes. A crucial element of metacognitive thought is the degree of confidence people have about their own thoughts (Petty et al. 2007). The process by which this confidence is assessed is referred to as the self-validation process (Petty, Briñol, and Tormala 2002). Because second-order thought processes require some motivation and ability to go beyond primary cognition (the content of one's thoughts), evaluation of the thought process is more likely to influence judgment when elaborative processing is likely. Conceptually, the self-validation hypothesis suggests that the effect of metacognition is mediated by feelings of confidence or validity associated with a particular argument.

These two empirically supported theories offer competing evidence for the role of metacognitive experiences in attitude formation. To help resolve these competing findings, we investigate the possible differential effect of processing style (memory-based vs. stimulus-based, Hastie and Park 1986) on the use of subjective experience in attitude formation. We expect that the heuristic-cue hypothesis will hold for memory-based processing and the self-validation hypothesis will hold for stimulus-based processing. The following two experiments are designed to test these predictions.

Experiment 1

One hundred and seventy-three undergraduate students were randomly assigned to one of the eight experimental conditions of the 2 (memory-based vs. stimulus-based) X 2 (high vs. low involvement) X 2 (easy vs. difficult) full factorial design. Participants were presented with information about a vacation package. Processing style was manipulated using a processing goal manipulation adapted from Mackie and Asuncion (1990). Involvement was manipulated using an accountability manipulation. Ease or difficulty of processing was manipulated using a reason generation task. After the processing style manipulation and the vacation information, participants were asked to provide either two or eight reasons (easy or difficult) for choosing the package. The primary dependent variable was attitude toward the vacation package.

An ANOVA revealed a three-way interaction supporting our predictions. The ease of processing effect was found in the memory-based condition only under low involvement, supporting the heuristic-cue hypothesis. The ease of processing effect was found in the stimulus-based condition only under high involvement, supporting the self-validation hypothesis.

Experiment 2

Experiment 2 was designed to replicate the findings of experiment 1 using a different stimulus, and different manipulations and operationalizations. Further, since the self-validation hypothesis states that the effect of metacognitive experiences on attitude is mediated by thought confidence, a measure of thought confidence adapted from Briñol et al. 2004 is also captured for analysis.

One hundred and seventy-five undergraduate students were randomly assigned to one of the eight experimental conditions of the 2 (memory-based vs. stimulus-based) X 2 (high vs. low motivation) X 2 (easy vs. difficult) between subjects full factorial design. Participants were presented with information about a 3D HDTV. Processing style was manipulated using a processing goal manipulation adapted from Hastie and Park (1986). Elaboration was operationalized as motivation and manipulated using differing expectations (exciting vs. boring) about an alleged study 2 (Webster 1993). Ease or difficulty of processing was manipulated using a reason generation task. After reading the 3D HDTV information and performing the processing style manipulation, participants were asked to provide either one or ten reasons (easy or difficult) for choosing the TV. Attitude about the TV and thought confidence were measured for analysis.

An ANOVA revealed a three-way interaction supporting our predictions. The ease of processing effect was found in the memory-based condition only under low motivation (elaboration), supporting the heuristic-cue hypotheses. The ease of processing effect was found in the stimulus-based condition only under high motivation (elaboration), supporting the self-validation hypothesis. Further, a mediation analysis (Baron and Kenny 1986) revealed that the effect of ease of retrieval on attitude formation was mediated by thought confidence for stimulus-based judgments, providing additional support for the self-validation hypothesis.

Discussion

Two empirically supported theories offer competing evidence for the role of metacognitive experiences in attitude formation. Across two experiments using different stimuli and a variety of manipulations, we showed that the role of ease of retrieval is contingent on processing style. Subjective ease is used as a heuristic cue when processing is memory-based, while subjective ease impacts attitude formation through confidence as part of the self-validation process when processing is stimulus-based.

It is possible that these differences may be related to the timing of the subjective experience. When judgments are stimulus-based, people evaluate information as they encounter it. In this case, the initial attitude formation precedes the ease of processing effect. In contrast, when judgments are memory-based, people recall relevant pieces of information while forming a judgment. In this case, the ease of processing effect coincides attitude formation.

REFERENCES

Baron, Reuben M. and David A. Kenny (1986), "The Moderator Mediator Variable Distinction in Social Psychological-Research - Conceptual, Strategic, and Statistical Considerations," *Journal of personality and Social psychology*, 51 (6), 1173-82.

Briñol, Pablo and Richard E. Petty (2009), "Persuasion: Insights from the Self-Validation Hypothesis," in *Advances in Experimental Social Psychology*, Vol. 41, ed. Mark P. Zanna, San Diego, CA: Academic Press, 69-118.

Briñol, Pablo, Richard E. Petty, Ismael Gallardo, and Kenneth G. DeMarree (2007), "The Effect of Self-Affirmation in Nonthreatening Persuasion Domains: Timing Affects the Process," *Personality and Social Psychology Bulletin*, 33 (11), 1533-46.

Briñol, Pablo, Richard E. Petty, and Zakary L. Tormala (2004), "Self-Validation of Cognitive Responses to Advertisements," *Journal of consumer research*, 30 (4), 559-73.

Grayson, Carla E. and Norbert Schwarz (1999), "Beliefs influence information processing strategies: Declarative and experiential information in risk assessment," *Social Cognition*, 17 (1), 1-18.

Hastie, Reid and Bernadette Park (1986), "The relationship between memory and judgment depends on whether the judgment task is memory-based or on-line," *Psychological Review*, 93 (3), 258-68.

Kruglanski, Arie W. and Donna M. Webster (1996), "Motivated closing of the mind: ''Seizing'' and ''Freezing''," *Psychological Review*, 103 (2), 263-83.

Mackie, Diane M. and Arlene G. Asuncion (1990), "Online and Memory-Based Modification of Attitudes - Determinants of Message Recall Attitude-Change Correspondence," *Journal of personality and Social psychology*, 59 (1), 5-16.

Petty, Richard E., Pablo Briñol, and Zakary L. Tormala (2002), "Thought Confidence as a Determinant of Persuasion: The Self-Validation Hypothesis," *Journal of Personality & Social Psychology*, 82 (5), 722-41.

Petty, Richard E., Pablo Briñol, Zakary L. Tormala, and Duane T. Wegener (2007b), "The Role of Metacognition in Social Judgment.," in *Social Psychology: Handbook of Basic Principles*, ed. Arie W. Kruglanski and E. Tory Higgins, New York: Guilford, 254-84.

Rothman, Alexander J. and N. Schwarz (1998), "Constructing perceptions of vulnerability: Personal relevance and the use of experiential information in health judgments," *Personality and Social Psychology Bulletin*, 24 (10), 1053-64.

Ruder, Markus and Herbert Bless (2003), "Mood and the reliance on the ease of retrieval heuristic," *Journal of Personality & Social Psychology*, 85 (1), 20-32.

Schwarz, Norbert (1998), "Accessible Content and Accessibility Experiences: The Interplay of Declarative and Experiential Information in Judgment," *Personality and Social Psychology Review*, 2 (2), 87-99.

--- (2004), "Metacognitive experiences in consumer judgment and decision making," *Journal of consumer psychology*, 14 (4), 332-48.

Schwarz, Norbert, Fritz Strack, Herbert Bless, Gisela Klumpp, Helga Rittenauer-Schatka, and Annette Simons (1991), "Ease of Retrieval as Information: Another Look at the Availability Heuristic," *Journal of Personality & Social Psychology*, 61 (2), 195-202.

Tetlock, Philip E. and Jae. I. Kim (1987), "Accountability and Judgment Processes in a Personality Prediction Task," *Journal of personality and Social psychology*, 52 (4), 700-09.

Tormala, Zackary L., Richard E. Petty, and Pablo Briñol (2002), "Ease of Retrieval Effects in Persuasion: A Self-Validation Analysis.," *Personality and Social Psychology Bulletin*, 28 (12), 1700-12.

Wänke, Michaela, Norbert Schwarz, and Herbert Bless (1995), "The Availability Heuristic Revisited - Experienced Ease of Retrieval in Mundane Frequency Estimates," *Acta Psychologica*, 89 (1), 83-90.

Webster, Donna M. (1993), "Motivated Augmentation and Reduction of the Overattribution Bias," *Journal of personality and Social psychology*, 65 (2), 261-71.

Webster, Donna M. and Arie W. Kruglanski (1994), "Individual differences in need for cognitive closure," *Journal of personality and Social psychology*, 67 (6), 1049-62.

"One Size Fits Others":
The Role of Label Ambiguity in Targeting Diverse Consumer Segments

Caglar Irmak, University of South Carolina, USA
David Norton, University of South Carolina, USA
Randall Rose, University of South Carolina, USA

EXTENDED ABSTRACT

Marketers often use product labels to target multiple segments of consumers with a single product. For instance, Calvin Klein's fragrance CK1 is marketed as "unisex," targeting both men and women. APG's Snuggie is labeled as "one size fits all," implying that the same blanket can accommodate a range of adult body types. Such all-inclusive labels point to the "all-fitting" aspect of the product, thereby resulting in the expansion of the potential customer pool. However, we argue in this research that marketers may unintentionally be driving customers away with their omnibus labeling practices because all-inclusive labels communicate to customers that the product is likely to be purchased by not only them but also all sorts of other consumers who may not be like them. We focus on this effect of target market specificity or generality on consumer reactions to such products and develop a counter-intuitive argument that leaving the target market of the product ambiguous may actually benefit marketers.

Previous research has shown that consumers avoid products or behaviors associated with dissociative reference groups, or groups with whom they want to avoid being confused (Berger and Heath 2007, 2008; Simmel 1904/1957; White and Dahl 2006, 2007). Men in a restaurant, for example, avoided steaks labeled as "ladies cut" (White and Dahl 2006), and in product domains perceived to communicate identity, consumers diverged from out-group members' choices more generally (Berger and Heath 2007). Thus, if an all-inclusive product label reminds consumers about other consumer groups with whom they do not want to be associated, it may drive people away from the product.

The value of clear positioning and targeting of brands is so widely accepted that it could be considered a law-like generalization. The merits of these standard marketing activities is not questioned in prominent marketing management texts (e.g., Kotler and Armstrong 2005), However, we argue that leaving the target market ambiguous may help the marketers of products that are targeted to a wide range of consumer segments. We show that the reason people do not like unambiguous information such as all-inclusive product labels is that such information may act as a cue for consumers to consider others in the social space, thus, prompting the inclusion of potentially aversive others. On the other hand, when no social cue is present consumers tend to anchor egocentrically, that is, consider themselves and their preferences as a starting point for evaluating the appropriateness of a product (Naylor, Lamberton and Norton 2011). Therefore, we expect consumers to evaluate products with ambiguous labels more favorably than products with labels that specify an extended target market. We tested our prediction in three studies.

In study 1, we presented participants with a fragrance that is either labeled for both men and women (i.e., unisex) or labeled ambiguously such that the product's gender appropriateness is not specified. We found that consumers evaluate products with ambiguous labels more favorably than products with labels that specify an extended target market.

In the second study, participants were either primed by self or others or were not primed. Then in an ostensibly unrelated task, they were shown three different products (in counterbalanced order: a ball cap, a travel pillow, and a Snuggie) which were either labeled as "one-size-fits-all" or had no such label. Participants were asked

to evaluate the products and indicate their purchase likelihood. The results revealed that ambiguous labeling (vs. one-size-fits-all labeling) led to more positive reactions when participants were primed to think about the self. The control condition showed a similar effect, suggesting that consumers generally anchor on themselves when evaluating products with ambiguous labels. However, in the condition where participants were primed to think of others, there was no significant effect of labeling on consumer reactions, indicating that one-size-fits-all labeling makes people think about others in the target market of the product.

While study 1 findings were in line with our predictions, the results may be explained by consumers' perception that the product labeled "one-size-fits-all" was less customized to them as compared to the product with an ambiguous label. Study 3 was designed to assess this alternative explanation and also test whether the process by which an unambiguous label results in lower product evaluations is due to inclusion of a dissociative group in the target market of the product. Study 3 was therefore a 2 (Customization: non-customized v. customized) x 2 (Label: English only v. English + Spanish), between-participants design. Students were randomly assigned to one of the four conditions above and evaluated a frozen yogurt. In the customization condition, they were able to select from 18 different items to create their own frozen yogurt concoction. In the non-customized condition they were presented with the list of potential menu items, but did not actually select any items. In the English and Spanish condition, menu items were listed in both English and Spanish (e.g., "strawberries/ fresas"). Participants were asked to evaluate their frozen yogurt, indicate their likelihood of purchase and willingness to pay. They were also asked to estimate the size of the target market (expressed in percentage of the US population) for the product. Aversion to Hispanics was measured using a seven-item scale. Results suggest that the inclusion of others in the potential target market lowers the evaluation of a product, but only when the included group is aversive. When consumers are allowed to customize their product, the label effect persists, suggesting that perceived customization level of the product is unlikely to be the underlying process. Further, the estimated market size mediates the relationship between the label and product evaluation, suggesting that those who would choose not to associate with Hispanics are less likely to favor products that target these consumers.

Our findings indicate that marketers may unintentionally be decreasing the attractiveness of their products while attempting to expand their target market. Labels that contain language aimed to attract diverse consumer segments cue consumers to the notion that others may purchase the product as well. When these "others" are seen as an aversive group, consumer reactions are negatively influenced.

REFERENCES

Aiken, Leona S., and Stephen G. West (1991), Multiple Regression: Testing and interpreting interactions. Newbury Park, CA: Sage

Baron, Reuben M. and David A. Kenny (1986), "The Moderator-Mediator Variable Distinction in Social Psychological Research: Conceptual, Strategic, and Statistical Considerations," *Journal of Personality and Social Psychology*, 51 (December), 1173–82.

Berger, Jonah and Chip Heath (2008) "Who Drives Divergence? Identity Signaling, Out-Group

Similarity, and the Abandonment of Cultural Tastes," *Journal of Personality and Social Psychology*, 95(3), 593-607.

--- (2007), "Where Consumers Diverge from Others: Identity-Signaling and Product Domains," *Journal of Consumer Research*, 34(2), 121-134.

Fitzsimons, Gavan J. (2008), "Death to Dichotomizing," *Journal of Consumer Research*, 35(1), 5-8.

Gilovich, Thomas, Victoria H. Medvec, and Kenneth Savitsky (2000), "The spotlight effect in social judgment: An egocentric bias in estimates of the salience of one's own actions and appearance," *Journal of Personality and Social Psychology, 78*, 211-222.

Henry, Philip J., and David O. Sears (2002), "The symbolic racism 2000 scale," *Political Psychology, 23*, 253-283.

Irmak, Caglar, Beth Vallen and Sankar Sen (2010), "You Like What I Like but I Don't Like What You Like: The Role of Uniqueness Motivations in Product Preferences," *Journal of Consumer Research*, 37 (October), 443-455.

Kotler, Philip and Gary Armstrong (2005). Principles of Marketing, Prentice Hall: New Jersey.

Muller, Dominique, Charles M. Judd, and Vincent Y. Yzerbyt (2005), "When moderation is mediated and mediation is moderated," *Journal of Personality and Social Psychology*, 89, 852-863.

Mussweiler, Thomas and Fritz Strack (1999), "Hypothesis-Consistent Testing and Semantic

Priming in the Anchoring Paradigm: A Selective Accessibility Model," *Journal of Experimental Social Psychology,* 35 (March), 136–64.

Naylor, Rebecca Walker, Cait Poynor Lamberton, and David A. Norton (forthcoming 2011), "Seeing Ourselves in Others: Reviewer Ambiguity, Egocentric Anchoring, and Persuasion," *Journal of Marketing Research*.

Norton, Michael I., Jeana H. Frost, and Dan Ariely (2007), "Less is more: When and why familiarity breeds contempt," *Journal of Personality and Social Psychology*, 92, 97–105.

Ruvio, Ayalla, Aviv Shoham, and Maja M. Brencic (2008), "Consumers' need for uniqueness: short-form scale development and cross cultural validation," *International Marketing Review* 25 (1): 33-53.

Simmel, Georg (1904/1957), "Fashion," *American Journal of Sociology*, 62 (6), 541–48.

Tian, Kelly Tepper, William O. Bearden, and Gary L. Hunter, (2001), "Consumers' Need for Uniqueness: Scale Development and Validation," *Journal of Consumer Research*, 28, 50-66.

White, Katherine and Darren W. Dahl (2006), "To Be or *Not* Be? The Influence of Dissociative Reference Groups on Consumer Preferences", *Journal of Consumer Psychology*, 16 (4), 404-414.

--- (2007), "Are All Outgroups Created Equal? Consumer Identity and Dissociative Influence," *Journal of Consumer Research*, 34 (4), 525-536.

The Eyes Have It: Eye Tracking Analysis of Anthropomorphic Car Fronts Using Spatiotemporal Scan Statistics

Christian Purucker, University of St. Gallen, Switzerland
Jan R. Landwehr, University of St. Gallen, Switzerland
David Sprott, Washington State University, USA
Andreas Herrmann, St. Gallen Universität, Switzerland

EXTENDED ABSTRACT

In marketing research, the use of eye tracking methods is widespread and extends across various contexts, such as the effects of TV advertisements on brand perception during fast forwarding (Brasel and Gips 2008), the impact of certain elements in print advertisements on attention-direction (Rosbergen, Pieters, and Wedel 1997), or the positioning of banners in online-advertisements on advertisement perception (Hervet et al. 2010).

Usually, these studies employ eye tracking data analyses that rely heavily on the definition of regions of interest (ROIs; cf. Duchowski 2007). With this method, regions (most commonly rectangular) are marked to encompass certain parts of the stimulus; from these regions, classical eye tracking metrics are calculated (e.g., the total gaze duration). While heavily used by researchers, classical ROI eye tracking metrics are prone to at least four methodological limitations. First, data quality is closely related to the reliability of the ROI definition, and thus highly dependent upon the researcher's ability to define properly the ROI. Areas within the ROI unrelated to the experimental manipulation may add noise to the underlying signal, indeed an ROI may even consist of subregions that behave in opposing ways. This is a serious downside, especially when considering that there is no convention suggesting how tight ROIs need to be defined. Procedures or further descriptions of ROI definitions are usually not provided by most authors in the literature reviewed. Second, the use of classical filter mechanisms in combination with the ROI method may result in misleading data reduction. Third, it can be argued that the definition of ROIs does not reflect physical realities of the human field of view, which suggests a region of decreasing acuity around the fovea (Irwin 1992). Research findings that participants remember objects without a registration of gazes underscore this problem (Kuisma et al. 2010). Finally, ROI analysis can only discover effects previously hypothesized by the experimenter and thus may miss out on a central benefit of eye tracking. In the current research, we develop a new method relying upon spatiotemporal scan statistics that can overcome the limitations of ROI analysis, by offering a convenient way to analyze and visualize eye tracking data.

Spatiotemporal scan statistics automatically identify clusters of points in a point process that differ from the distribution expected under a baseline condition. These statistics, as implemented in the SaTScan software, are widely used in epidemiology to identify disease clusters (Kulldorff et al. 1998). While these statistics are not explicitly limited to epidemiological settings (Kulldorff 1997), applications in other contexts are rare. The use of scan statistics in eye tracking is novel and promising, as it provides a data driven approach to identify deviant gaze clusters. Implementing the scan statistic to eye tracking data assumes that a point process can account for the distribution of data, such as the Bernoulli model. Gaze points observed under a baseline condition are treated as non-cases, while points observed under an experimental variation are treated as cases. For a certain region in space, the probability of a gaze point being a case can thus be calculated. A likelihood ratio test statistic is calculated on the basis of the observed and the expected case to non-case-ratio (Kulldorff 1997). This procedure is applied to the whole study region by moving around a scanning window systematically in space and time. The window varies in size as it moves across the plane, so that for all points all possible window sizes are tested. The statistical significance of the clusters is then evaluated with Monte Carlo simulation (Kulldorff 1997).

The two methods of eye tracking data analysis, the classical ROI-based approach and our technique based on spatiotemporal scan statistics, are compared in an eye tracking experiment focused on perception of car faces. The theoretical grounding of this research is based on findings on anthropomorphic car fronts and literature on schematic faces regarding threat perception that suggest specific differences in the attention-capture of certain features of a car face. In particular, it is expected that car faces resembling threatening faces are avoided by the viewer in the long run.

Participants looked at a series of car faces for 10 seconds each, and rated them afterwards. Twenty-nine students participated in a 2 (headlights or eyes) × 2 (lower air vents or mouth) × 2 (side air vents) within-subjects experiment, whereby each feature existed in a threatening and a non-threatening variant.

Results provide some support for the theoretical expectations of face perception, in that threatening headlights were looked at for shorter periods of time over the whole experiment. Differences between the two eye tracking methods emerged. The ROI technique produced different results depending upon the ROI definition used, and thus clearly illustrates the problems associated with the method. While the scan statistic generally confirmed the key findings of the ROI method, more detailed results were provided by this new method (e.g., with respect to when and where significantly differing gaze clusters emerged). Results also clearly indicate the superiority of the method in terms of visualizing differences in gaze behavior between stimuli.

In summary, while several limitations exist for classical eye tracking analyses that rely on ROIs, these problems do not occur with the data driven approach provided by the scan analysis. In our study, results derived from ROI analysis were partially confirmed by the new method, but clear differences emerged such that greater details could be derived from the scan statistic. Due to the combination of a statistical methodology with a visualization technique, the method is not only attractive to academic eye tracking researchers, but also to marketing practitioners who often rely upon data visualization techniques that do not provide a statistical criterion for hypothesis testing, such as heatmaps. The use of our technique in that field will clearly lead to better practical use of eye tracking data. Finally, our research provides valuable insights for researchers and designers interested in anthropomorphic product design, as the impact of mechanisms of biological preparedness could be demonstrated. In our experiment, threatening and non-threatening car fronts clearly exerted different effects on viewer attention.

REFERENCES

Aggarwal, Pankaj and Ann L. McGill (2007), "Is That Car Smiling at Me? Schema Congruity as a Basis for Evaluating Anthropomorphized Products," *Journal of Consumer Research*, 34 (December), 468-79.

Aribarg, Anocha, Rik Pieters, and Michel Wedel (2010), "Raising the Bar: Bias Adjustment of Recognition Tests in Advertising," *Journal of Marketing Research*, 47 (June), 387-400.

Baraggioli, Francesca and S. Adam Brasel (2008), "Visual Velocity: Content Font Effects and Incidental Online Ad Exposure," in *Advances in Consumer Research*, Vol. 33, eds. Cornelia Pechmann and Linda L. Price, Duluth, MN: Association for Consumer Research, 600-06.

Bojko, Agnieszka (2009), "Informative or Misleading? Heatmaps Deconstructed," in *Human-Computer Interaction*, Vol. 5610, ed. Julie A. Jacko, Berlin: Springer, 30-39.

Brasel, S. Adam and James Gips (2008), "Breaking through Fast-Forwarding: Brand Information and Visual Attention," *Journal of Marketing*, 72 (November), 31-48.

Chandon, Pierre, J. Wesley Hutchinson, Eric T. Bradlow, and Scott H. Young (2009), "Does in-Store Marketing Work? Effects of the Number and Position of Shelf Facings on Brand Attention and Evaluation at the Point of Purchase," *Journal of Marketing*, 73 (November), 1-17.

Duchowski, Andrew T. (2007), *Eye Tracking Methodology. Theory and Practice*, London: Springer.

--- (2002), "A Breadth-First Survey of Eye Tracking Applications," *Behavior Research Methods, Instruments, & Computers*, 34 (November), 455-70.

Feiereisen, Stephanie, Veronica Wong, and Amanda J. Broderick (2008), "Analogies and Mental Simulations in Learning for Really New Products: The Role of Visual Attention," *Journal of Product Innovation Management*, 25 (November), 593-607.

Garcia, Carmen, Vicente Ponsoda, and Herminia Estebaranz (2000), "Scanning Ads: Effects of Involvement and of Position of the Illustration in Printed Advertisements," in *Advances in Consumer Research*, Vol. 27, eds. Stephen J. Hoch and Robert J. Meyer, Provo, UT: Association for Consumer Research, 104-09.

Heller, Ruth, Damian Stanley, Daniel Yekutieli, Nava Rubin, and Yoav Benjamini (2006), "Cluster-Based Analysis of fMRI Data," *NeuroImage*, 33 (September), 599-608.

Hervet, Guillaume, Katherine Guérard, Sébastien Tremblay, and Mohamed S. Chtourou (2010), "Is Banner Blindness Genuine? Eye Tracking Internet Text Advertising," *Applied Cognitive Psychology*, doi: 10.1002/acp.1742.

Irwin, David E. (1992), "Visual Memory within and across Fixations," in *Eye Movements and Visual Cognition. Scene Perception and Reading*, ed. Keith Rayner, New York: Springer, 146-65.

Kuisma, Jarmo, Jaana Simola, Liisa Uusitalo, and Anssi Öörni (2010), «The Effects of Animation and Format on the Perception and Memory of Online Advertising,» *Journal of Interactive Marketing*, 24 (November), 269-82.

Kulldorff, Martin (1997), "A Spatial Scan Statistic," *Communications in Statistics. Theory and Methods*, 26 (March), 1481-96.

Kulldorff, Martin, William F. Athas, Eric J. Feuer, Barry A. Miller, and Charles R. Key (1998), "Evaluating Cluster Alarms: A Space-Time Scan Statistic and Brain Cancer in Los Alamos, New Mexico," *American Journal of Public Health*, 88 (September), 1377-80.

Landwehr, Jan R., Ann L. McGill, and Andreas Herrmann (forthcoming), "It's Got the Look: The Effect of Friendly and Aggressive "Facial" Expressions on Product Liking and Sales," *Journal of Marketing*.

Lohse, Gerald L. (1997), "Consumer Eye Movement Patterns on Yellow Pages Advertising," *Journal of Advertising*, 26 (March), 61-73.

Lundqvist, Daniel, Francisco Esteves, and Arne Öhman (2004), «The Face of Wrath: The Role of Features and Configurations in Conveying Social Threat,» *Cognition and Emotion*, 18 (February), 161-82.

Morris, John S., Arne Öhman, and Raymond J. Dolan (1998), «Conscious and Unconscious Emotional Learning in the Human Amygdala,» *Nature*, 393 (June), 467-70.

Öhman, Arne and Ulf Dimberg (1978), «Facial Expressions as Conditioned Stimuli for Electrodermal Responses: A Case of Preparedness?» *Journal of Personality and Social Psychology*, 36 (November), 1251-58.

Öhman, Arne, Daniel Lundqvist, and Francisco Esteves (2001), «The Face in the Crowd Revisited: A Threat Advantage with Schematic Stimuli,» *Journal of Personality and Social Psychology*, 80 (March), 381-96.

Pieters, Rik and Michel Wedel (2004), "Attention Capture and Transfer in Advertising: Brand, Pictorial, and Text-Size Effects," *Journal of Marketing*, 68 (April), 36-50.

--- (2007), "Goal Control of Attention to Advertising: The Yarbus Implication," *Journal of Consumer Research*, 34 (August), 224-33.

Pieters, Rik, Michel Wedel, and Rajeev Batra (2010), "The Stopping Power of Advertising: Measures and Effects of Visual Complexity," *Journal of Marketing*, 74 (September), 48-60.

Pomplun, Marc, Helge Ritter, and Boris Velichkovsky (1996), "Disambiguating Complex Visual Information: Towards Communication of Personal Views of a Scene," *Perception*, 25 (August), 931-48.

Rinck, Mike and Eni S. Becker (2006), "Spider Fearful Individuals Attend to Threat, Then Quickly Avoid It: Evidence from Eye Movements," *Journal of Abnormal Psychology*, 115 (May), 231-38.

Rosbergen, Edward, Rik Pieters, and Michel Wedel (1997), "Visual Attention to Advertising: A Segment-Level Analysis," *Journal of Consumer Research*, 24 (December), 305-14.

Salvucci, Dario D. and Joseph H. Goldberg (2000), "Identifying Fixations and Saccades in Eye-Tracking Protocols," in *Proceedings of the Eye Tracking Research and Applications Symposium,* ed. Andrew T. Duchowski, New York, NY: ACM, 71-78.

Teixeira, Thales S., Michel Wedel, and Rik Pieters (2010), "Moment-to-Moment Optimal Branding in TV Commercials: Preventing Avoidance by Pulsing," *Marketing Science*, 29 (September-October), 783-804.

Van der Lans, Ralf, Rik Pieters, and Michel Wedel (2008), "Competitive Brand Salience," *Marketing Science*, 27 (September-October), 922-31.

Wedel, Michel and Rik Pieters (2000), "Eye Fixations on Advertisements and Memory for Brands: A Model and Findings," *Marketing Science*, 19 (September-October), 297-312.

Windhager, Sonja, Florian Hutzler, Claus C. Carbon, Elisabeth Oberzaucher, Katrin Schaefer, Truls Thorstensen, Helmut Leder, and Karl Grammer (2010), "Laying Eyes on Headlights: Eye Movements Suggest Facial Features in Cars," *Collegium Antropologicum*, 34 (October), 1075-80.

Zhang, Jie, Michel Wedel, and Rik Pieters (2009), "Sales Effects of Attention to Feature Advertisements: A Bayesian Mediation Analysis," *Journal of Marketing Research*, 46 (October), 669-81.

Appreciating the Local versus Trusting the Global: Shifting Standards in the Evaluation of Product Failures

Eda Sayin, Koc University, Turkey
Nilufer Aydinoglu, Koc University, Turkey
Aysegul Ozsomer, Koc University, Turkey
Zeynep Gurhan-Canli, Koc University, Turkey

EXTENDED ABSTRACT

Consumers have subjective judgment standards, beliefs, and expectations as they evaluate different product groups. Their judgment standards determine the expected performance level of a product, and hence affect evaluations. In this paper, we investigate the effect of shifting standards on consumer evaluations of local and global brands, specifically when there is a product-harm crisis.

A product-harm crisis can be defined as "a well-publicized event where a product is defective or even dangerous" (Dawar and Pillutla, 2000). It has been shown to affect the long-run quality perceptions of a company, and can tarnish a company's reputation, cause market share and revenue loss, and eventually destroy brand equity (Heerde et al., 2007). Corporate response is a crucial determinant of the impact of a product crisis on consumer beliefs that constitute brand equity. A product-harm crisis need not inevitably be detrimental to the company. A company may emerge stronger after a crisis if it responds quickly and effectively to maintain consumer confidence in the brand (Dawar and Pillutla, 2000). Building on shifting standards theory from the social psychology literature, we hypothesize that effective response strategies differ for local and global brands and investigate the most effective strategies for both.

Literature on global and local brands suggests that consumers may prefer global brands to otherwise equivalent local brands since global (as opposed to local) brands are associated with higher levels of quality, prestige and status (Steenkamp et al., 2003). On the other hand, there is evidence documenting a home country bias for local brands based on ethnocentric desires to boost local economies or better customization (Papadoupolos et al., 1990). Local brands have also been associated with feelings of tradition, nationalism and patriotism. Such disparate prior belief structures may result in the shifting of standards with which consumers evaluate global versus local brands. Prior expectations work as a decision heuristic in the interpretation of a product-harm crisis (Darley and Gross, 1983). Selective information processing occurs and consumer expectations provide a buffer for brand equity against the firm's failure to respond effectively and consumers interpret new information in line with their prior beliefs (Dawar, 1998). Using a series of two laboratory experiments, we demonstrate that different consumer perceptions regarding global and local brands lead to different expectations and shifting standards of evaluations for these global and local brands.

Study 1 focuses on the context of single incident product failures to test our underlying contention that consumers may be subject to shifting standards when evaluating global versus local brands. A laboratory experiment demonstrates that consumers have higher expectations of product performance for global brands and that their negative reaction after a product failure would be stronger for global brands compared to local brands. It also shows that consumer evaluations after a product failure would be mediated by consumer expectations and that the mediating effect of the expectations would be moderated by cosmopolitanism (consumer identification with global or local culture). We find that higher expectations for global brands have possible negative effects on brand preference, and that this negative effect is less for individuals with higher cosmopolitanism, compared to those with lower cosmopolitanism.

Study 2 focuses on the context of a major product-harm crisis and explores different consumer reactions toward global and local brands based on how the firms respond to the crisis. How a company responds (whether it takes the responsibility or whether it offers compensation) in case of a product failure is a critical moderator regarding the damage to customer evaluations. Our second study demonstrates that consumers have different evaluations for (global vs. local) brands in terms of taking *responsibility* and *compensating*. When a global company declares no responsibility and does not provide compensation after a product-harm crisis, consumer evaluations are impacted less in comparison to local brands. As consumers have higher quality associations with global brands, they have a tendency to trust global brands and attribute the responsibility to third parties when the global brand declares no responsibility. However, when a global brand declares full responsibility and compensates, it is not as positively evaluated as a local brand, especially by consumers with low cosmopolitanism. When consumers identify themselves with the local culture, they feel more attached to the local brands and the compensation offered by the local brand has more positive effect on evaluations, when compared to global brands.

Accordingly, our combined set of results demonstrate that consumers have different expectations and hence shifting standards when evaluating global versus local brands, specifically when there is a product failure or a more massive product-harm crisis. We further show that their evaluations are affected differently following the specific responses of the firms to the crisis and in line with their level of identification with global or local consumer culture. As such, building on the shifting standards theory from social psychology, our research contributes to the work on product-harm crisis and global and local brand preference within consumer behavior, and have important implications for managers.

REFERENCES

Aaker D. (1991) Managing brand equity. *New York: The Free Press*.

Adaval, R. & Monroe, K. B. (2002) Automatic construction and use of contextual information for product and price evaluations. *Journal of Consumer Research*, Vol. 28, March, 572-588.

Ahluwalia, R., Burnkrant, R. E. & Unnava, H. R. (2000) Consumer response to negative publicity: The moderating role of commitment. *Journal of Marketing Research*, Vol. 37, 203-214.

Balabanis, G., Diamantopoulos, A., Mueller, R. D. & Melewar T. C. (2001) The Impact of nationalism, patriotism and internationalism on consumer ethnocentric tendencies. *Journal of International Business Studies*; 32, 1; 157-175.

Batra, R., Ramaswamy, V., Alden, D. L., Steenkamp J. B. E. M. & Ramachander, S. (2000) Effects of brand local and nonlocal origin on consumer attitudes in developing countries. *Journal of Consumer Psychology*, 9 (2), 83-95.

Biernat, M. & Feugen, K. (2001) Shifting standards and the evaluation of competence:
Complexity in gender-based judgment and decision making. *Journal of Social Issues*, 57, 707-724.

Biernat, Monica & Melvis Manis (1994), Shifting standards and stereotype-based judgments. *Journal of Personality and Social Psychology*, 66 (2), 5-20.

Biernat, M., Manis, M. & Kobrynowicz, D. (1997) Simultaneous assimilation and contrast effects in judgments of self and others. *Journal of Personality and Social Psychology,* 73 (2), 254-269.

Biernat, M., Manis, M. & Nelson, T. (1991) Stereotypes and standards of Judgment. *Journal of Personality and Social Psychology,* 60 (4), 485-499.

Cannon, H. M., Yoon, S. J., McGovan L. & Yaprak, A. (1994) In search of the global consumer. *Annual Meeting of the Academy of International Business.*

Darley, J. M. & Gross, P. H. (1983) A hypothesis-confirming bias in labeling effects. *Journal of Personality and Social Psychology*, 44 (1), 20-33.

Dawar, N. (1998) Product-harm crisis and the signaling ability of brands. *International Studies of Management and Organisation*, 28 (3), 109-119.

Dawar, N., Gurhan-Canli, Z. & Lei, J. (2010). Consumer attribution processes in product-harm crisis: Discounting and sub-typing effects. (working paper)

Dawar, N. & Pillutla M. M. (2000). Impact of product-harm crisis on brand equity: The moderating role of consumer expectations. *Journal of Marketing Research*, Vol.17, 215-226.

Heerde, V. H, Helsen K. & Dekimpe G. D. (2007) The impact of product-harm crisis on marketing effectiveness. *Marketing Science*, Vol. 26, (2), 230-245.

Higgins, T. E., Stangor, C. (1988) A "Change-of-Standard" perspective on the relations among context, judgment and memory. *Journal of Personality and Social Psychology*, 54 (2), 181 -192.

Kapferer, J. N. & Schuiling, I. (2003) How unique are local brands? An empirical comparison of local and international brands in the food industry. (Working Paper) University of Louvain.

Keller, K. L. (1993) Conceptualizing, measuring and managing customer-based brand equity. *Journal of Marketing*, Vol. 57 (1), 1-22.

Kirmani, A. (1990) The effect of perceived advertising costs on brand perceptions. *Journal of Consumer Research*, 17 (September), 160-171.

Leclerc, F., Schmitt, B. H., & Dube, L. (1994) Foreign branding and its effects on product perceptions and attitudes. *Journal of Marketing Research*, 31 (May), 263-70.

McClure, S. M., Li, J., Tomlin, D. Cypert, K. S., Montague, L. M. & Montague, P. R. (2004) Neural correlates of behavioral preference for culturally familiar drinks. *Neuron*, Vol. 44, 379–387.

Milgrom, P. & Roberts, J. (1986) Price and advertising signals of product quality. *Journal of Political Economy*, 94 (August), 796-82 1.

Monroe, K. B. (1973) Buyers' subjective perceptions of price. *Journal of Marketing Research,* Vol. 10, No. 1 (Feb), 70-80.

Muller, D., Judd, C. M. & Yzerbyt V. Y. (2005) When moderation is mediated and mediation is moderated. *Journal of Psychology and Social Psychology*, Vol. 89, No. 6, 852-863.

Rao, A. R. & Monroe, K. B. (1989) The Effect of price, brand name, and store name on buyers' perceptions of product quality: An integrative review. *Journal of Marketing Research*, Vol. 26 (August), 351-357.

Shiv, B., Carmon, Ziv. & Ariely, D. (2005) Placebo effects of marketing actions: Consumers may get what they pay for. *Journal of Marketing Research*, 42, 383-393.

Shimp, T. A. & Sharma, S. (1987) Consumer ethnocentrism: Construction and validation of the CETSCALE. *Journal of Marketing Research*, 24 (August), 280-289.

Siomkos, G. J. & Kurzbard, G. (1994) The hidden crisis in product-harm crisis management. *European Journal of Marketing*, Vol. 28 (2), 30-41.

Smith, N. C, Thomas, R. J. & Quelch, J. A. (1996) A strategic approach to managing product recalls. *Harvard Business Review*, 74, 102-112.

Steenkamp, J. B. E. M., Batra, R. & Alden, D. L. (2003) How perceived brand globalness creates brand value. *Journal of International Business Studies*, 34 (1), 53-65.

Steenkamp, J.B. E. M. & de Jong, M. G. (2010) A global investigation into the constellation of consumer attitudes toward global and local products. Journal of Marketing, 74 (6), 18-40.

Tajfel, H. (1978) Differentiation between social groups: Studies of the social psychology of intergroup relationships. *London: Academic.*

When Do (and Don't) Normative Appeals
Best Influence Consumer Conservation Behaviors?

Katherine White, University of Calgary, Canada
Bonnie Simpson, University of Calgary, Canada

EXTENDED ABSTRACT

This research explores how to most effectively encourage positive conservation behaviors. We do so in the domain of relatively unfamiliar conservation behaviors such as grasscycling and composting. While past research on encouraging conservation behaviors has produced mixed results, one commonly used framework in literature is to examine the effectiveness of different types of appeals in encouraging positive conservation activities. These include self-benefit appeals (based on benefits to oneself), descriptive norm appeals (based on what others are actually doing), and injunctive norm appeals (based on what others think ought to be done).

This research proposes that the effect of appeal type depends on whether the person is encouraged to think about the action in terms of the level of self as an individual (e.g., "why might I grasscycle?") versus the group (e.g., "why might we, as a community, grasscycle?"). In particular, we suggest that matching the type of normative message with a goal-congruent mindset might lead to particularly favorable conservation attitudes, intentions, and behaviors. That is, when the consumer's mindset is at the individual level of the self, benefit appeals might be particularly effective. However, when the consumer's mindset is at the collective level of the self, descriptive norms and injunctive norms might work best.

Three studies were conducted that examined the moderating effect of the individual's mindset (individual level of self vs. collective level of self) on the effectiveness of norm-based appeals in influencing conservation behaviors. The first study examined the effects of the appeals on participants' attitudes towards grasscycling in a laboratory setting. Grasscycling involves leaving ones grass clippings on the lawn so that they can decompose, returning nutrients to the soil, rather than throwing them in the landfill. The second study was conducted in collaboration with a metropolitan city, where marketing communications were manipulated and delivered to households and changes were measured in grasscycling participation. Finally in study 3, we use the public vs. private nature of the setting to manipulate level of self in the context of composting intentions.

In the first study, the nature of the message was manipulated (injunctive norm, descriptive norm, benefit appeal) along with the consumer's mindset (e.g., individual self versus collective self) and these conditions are compared to an information-only control condition. As a preliminary test of the predictions derived from the literature, a 2 (Level of Self: individual vs. collective) x 3 (Message Appeal: normative message vs. injunctive message vs. benefit message) between subjects design was utilized, and a control group that received information only was also included (making for seven experimental conditions). A community sample was randomly assigned to view one of the seven possible messages, and they reported their attitudes towards grasscycling. Results indicated that when a collective level of self was activated, injunctive norms and descriptive norms resulted in more positive attitudes than the benefit appeal. Also as predicted, when the individual level of self was activated, participants reported more positive attitudes to the benefit focused appeal as compared to both the individual self/injunctive norm condition and the information only control condition.

Study 2 tested the effectiveness of six different versions of a marketing message on community residents' actual grasscycling behaviors. A 3 (Appeal Type: descriptive norm, injunctive norm, self-

benefit norm) x 2 (Mindset: individual self vs. group self) experimental design was used, which also included a control condition that received no marketing message, resulting in seven conditions total. A pretest-posttest design was utilized, in which the grasscycling behaviors of households were measured for three weeks before and three weeks after exposure to a version of an advertising appeal. Appeals were delivered in door-hanger form, developed in conjunction with the city. Households ($N = 696$) were selected for participation in the project and randomly assigned to conditions. The dependent measure was the average amount of grass disposed of in the garbage, as put out for weekly garbage collection by each household. This was recorded for 3 weeks at Time 1 (T1 – prior to the marketing intervention) and three weeks at Time 2 (T2 – subsequent to the marketing intervention). Consistent with the hypotheses, when a collective level of self was activated, descriptive norms and injunctive norms resulted in significantly less grass disposal in the garbage at T2 than did the benefit appeal. In addition, when the collective level of self was activated, both the descriptive and the injunctive norm conditions led to more positive actions than the control condition. Also as predicted, the individual/benefit condition led to decreased grass disposal as compared to both the individual self/ injunctive norm condition and the control condition.

In Study 3 an additional conservation behavior, composting, was examined. As well, the setting (public vs. private) was used to manipulate the individual level vs. collective level of the self, and we investigated the potential mediating role of perceived self-efficacy. One hundred and three participants were told their responses to the study would either be public or private. The manipulation of setting was crossed against a manipulation of appeal type (benefit, descriptive norm, injunctive norm), and participants completed measures of composting intentions and perceived efficacy. The results revealed that injunctive appeals were particularly effective in a public setting, while benefit appeals were particularly effective in private. Further, the results were mediated by perceived self-efficacy.

This research highlights the most effective ways to frame messages to encourage changes in consumer conservation behaviors. The combination of the activation of the collective level self with injunctive norm or descriptive norm appeals is particularly effective in influencing conservation behaviors. In addition, the combination of the individual level of self and the communication of benefits positively predicts conservation behaviors. Thus, those wishing to encourage positive conservation behaviors should match their marketing communications, combining the activation of the collective self with injunctive or descriptive norm appeals; or combining the activation of the individual self with benefit appeals.

REFERENCES

Agrawal, Nidhi and Durairaj Maheswaran (2005), "The Effects of Self-Construal and Commitment on Persuasion," *Journal of Consumer Research*, 31 (March), 841-49.
Bonfield, Edward H. (1974), "Attitude, Social Influence, Personal Norm, and Intention Interactions as Related to Brand Purchase Behavior," *Journal of Marketing Research*, 11 (4), 379-89.
Brewer, Marilynn B. and Wendi Gardner (1996), "Who is This 'We'? Levels of Collective Identity and Self-Representations," *Journal of Personality and Social Psychology*, 71 (1), 83-93.

Cialdini, Robert B. (2003), "Crafting Normative Messages to Protect the Environment," *Current Directions in Psychological Science*, 12 (4), 105-09.

Cialdini, Robert B., Carl A. Kallgren, and Raymond R. Reno (1991), "A Focus Theory of Normative Conduct: A Theoretical Refinement and Reevaluation of the Role of Norms in Human Behavior," in *Advances in Experimental Social Psychology*, Vol. 24, ed. Mark Zanna, New York: Academic Press, 201-34.

Cialdini, Robert B. and Noah J. Goldstein (2004), "Social Influence: Compliance and Conformity," *Annual Review of Psychology*, 55 (February), 591-622.

Cobern, Melissa K., Brian E. Porter, Frank C. Leeming, and William O. Dwyer (1995), "The Effect of Commitment on Adoption and Diffusion of Grass Cycling," *Environment and Behavior*, 27 (2), 213-32.

Fisher, Robert J. and David Ackerman (1998), "The Effects of Recognition and Group Need on Volunteerism: A Social Norm Perspective," *Journal of Consumer Research*, 25, 262-75.

Gardner, Wendi L., Shira Gabriel, and Angela Y. Lee (1999), "'I' Value Freedom But "We" Value Relationships: Self-Construal Priming Mirrors Cultural Differences in Judgment," *Psychological Science*, 10, 321-26.

Goldstein, Noah J., Robert B. Cialdini, and Vladas Griskevicius (2008), "A Room With A Viewpoint: Using Social Norms to Motivate Environmental Conservation in Hotels," *Journal of Consumer Research*, 35 (3), 472-82.

Hofstede, Geert (1980), Culture's Consequences: International Differences in Work-Related Values. Beverly Hills, CA: Sage.

Mandel, Naomi (2003), "Shifting Selves and Decision Making: The Effects of Self-Construal Priming on Consumer Risk-Taking," *Journal of Consumer Research*, 30 (1), 30-40.

Menon, Ajay and Anil Menon (1997), "Enviropreneurial Marketing Strategy: The Emergence of Corporate Environmentalism as Market Strategy," *Journal of Marketing*, 61 (January), 51-67.

Mick, David G. (2006), "Meaning and Mattering Through Transformative Consumer Research," in *Advances in Consumer Research*, Vol. 33, ed. Cornelia Pechmann and Linda L. Price, Provo, UT: Association for Consumer Research, 297-300.

Park, Hee Sun, Timothy R. Levine, and William F. Sharkey (1998), "The Theory of Reasoned Action and Self-Construals: Understanding Recycling in Hawai'i," *Communication Studies*, 49 (3), 196-208.

Reno, Raymond R., Robert B. Cialdini, and Carl A. Kallgren (1993), "The Transsituational Influence of Social Norms," *Journal of Personality and Social Psychology*, 64, 104-12.

Schultz, Wesley P. (1999), "Changing Behavior with Normative Feedback Interventions: A Field Experiment on Curbside Recycling," *Basic and Applied Social Psychology*, 21 (1), 25-36.

Schultz, Wesley P., Jessica M. Nolan, Robert B. Cialdini, Noah J. Goldstein, and Vladas Griskevicius (2007), "The Constructive, Destructive, and Reconstructive Power of Social," *Psychological Science*, 18 (5), 429-34.

Tajfel, Henri and John C. Turner (1986), *The Social Identity Theory of Intergroup Behavior*, Chicago, IL: Nelson-Hall.

Trafimow, David, Harry C. Triandis, and Sharon G. Goto (1991), "Some Tests of the Distinction Between the Private Self and The Collective Self," *Journal of Personality and Social Psychology*, 60 (5), 649-55.

Triandis, Harry C. (1989), "The Self and Social Behavior in Differing Cultural Contexts," *Psychological Review*, 96, 506-520.

White, Katherine and Jennifer J. Argo (2010), "When Imitation Doesn't Flatter: The Role of Consumer Distinctiveness in Responses to Mimicry," submitted to *Journal of Consumer Research*.

White, Katherine M., Joanne R. Smith, Deborah J. Terry, Jaimi H. Greenslade, and Blake M. McKimmie (2009), "Social Influence in the Theory of Planned Behavior: The Role of Descriptive, Injunctive, and In-group Norms," *British Journal of Social Psychology*, 48 (1), 135-58.

White, Katherine and John Peloza (2009), "Self-Benefit Versus Other-Benefit Marketing Appeals: Their Effectiveness in Generating Charitable Support," *Journal of Marketing*, 73 (4), 109-24.

Wood, Robert and Albert Bandura (1989), "Impact of Conceptions of Ability on Self-Regulatory Mechanisms and Complex Decision Making," *Journal of Personality and Social Psychology*, 56, 407-15.

Is It Worth the Money?
The Effect of Regulatory Focus on Consumers' Price and Quality Sensitivity

Woo Jin Choi, Texas A&M University, USA
Haipeng (Allan) Chen, Texas A&M University, USA

EXTENDED ABSTRACT

Many consumption decisions involve choosing between a more expensive product with better quality and a cheaper product with inferior quality. Despite the prevalence of such trade-offs, little research has examined consumers' sensitivity to price relative to their sensitivity to quality. In this research, we examine this issue through the theoretical lens of regulatory focus (Higgins 1997).

Regulatory focus theory distinguishes between two basic motivational orientations that individuals employ in the pursuit of their goals: promotion and prevention. One robust finding in this literature is that promotion-oriented people are more sensitive to gains, whereas prevention-oriented people are more sensitive to losses (Avnet and Higgins 2006; Wang and Lee 2006; Aaker and Lee 2001). While quality information can be either promotion or prevention focused (Wang and Lee 2006; Aaker and Lee 2001), to the extent that price is a "give" component to be minimized and quality is a "get" component to be maximized (Monroe 2003; Zeithaml 1988), we propose that *relatively speaking* promotion-oriented consumers will pay more attention to product quality, whereas prevention-oriented consumers will pay more attention to product price. The differential attention paid to price and quality information should, in turn, lead to preferences for products of high quality by promotion-oriented consumers, and preferences for products with low prices by prevention-oriented consumers.

In addition, we further predict that the proposed effect should only exhibit itself under circumstances in which price and quality compete for attention. Under circumstances where price and quality do not compete for attention, we predict that the effect of consumers' regulatory focus on their choices will diminish. For example, consumers may have a high reference point such that they have a sufficiently large budget to afford even the more expensive product, but they have also high quality expectations that cannot be met by either product. In other words, both products represent gains on price and losses on quality. On the other hand, consumers may have a low reference point such that they have a budget that is insufficient to afford even the cheaper product, but they also have low quality expectations that can be satisfied by both products. In other words, both products represent losses on price and gains on quality. Under those circumstances, consumers may be more attentive to the attribute on which both products represent a loss and thus they may pick the product that minimizes the loss, thus mitigating the effect of consumers' regulatory focus on their product choices.

We conducted two pretests and three experiments to test our underlying assumptions and predictions. In the first pretest, we found that participants were more likely to mention "quality" in thinking about what they wanted to get and they were more likely to mention "price" in thinking about what they wanted to avoid in a making a purchase, confirming our assumption that quality is a get component to be maximized and price is a give component to be minimized in a purchase.

In a second pretest, participants were asked to sort a list of 26 words into two groups; In addition to price and quality, the list included 12 promotion-related words and 12 prevention-related words. The results indicate that the word 'quality' is more likely to be grouped with promotion words while the word 'price' is more likely

to be grouped with prevention words, supporting the proposed association between quality (price) and a promotion (prevention) focus.

Experiment 1 then tested the effect of regulatory orientations on consumers' product choices by measuring people's chronic regulatory focus. The results demonstrated that, as predicted, consumers with a chronic promotion (vs. prevention) focus were more likely to choose a more expensive smartphone with better quality over a cheaper smartphone with less quality. We replicated these results in a second experiment by manipulating regulatory focus, using digital cameras as the focal product.

In our final experiment, we tested the proposed boundary condition due to reference point as well as the underlying process of the effect. Consistently with our predictions, we replicated the effect of regulatory focus in the middle reference point condition where the budget and quality expectations were between the two products. However, in the high and low reference point conditions, where price and quality did not compete for consumers' attention, the effect of regulatory orientation was diminished such that participants in the high (low) reference point condition tended to prefer the more expensive (cheaper) product regardless of their regulatory orientations. We also found that attention to quality versus price mediated the effect of regulatory orientation on product preferences.

Our research contributes to the literature in marketing and regulatory focus theory in several important ways. First, by introducing motivation into the equation on price (vs. quality) sensitivity, we contribute to extant research that has modeled price sensitivity as a function of situational factors (e.g., consumption occasion; Wakefield and Inman 2003), strategic variables (e.g., competition; Van Heerde et al. 2008), consumer demographics (e.g., income; Hoch et al. 1995) and other consumer attributes (e.g., brand loyalty; Bell and Lattin 2000).

Second, most research on regulatory focus has centered around the fit between quality-related product attributes and consumers' motivational orientations and typically employs price as a dependent variable to measure the consequences of such a fit (e.g., Avnet and Higgins 2006, 2003; Higgins, Idson, Freitas and Molden 2003). The current research expands upon these studies by considering both price and quality as relevant product features that can simultaneously affect the consequences of the regulatory fit. In doing so, we contribute to regulatory focus theory by introducing price as a critical component into this theoretical framework.

The findings of this research are relevant to marketing practitioners as well. For example, marketers may be able to influence the inclinations of consumers who are deciding between products with different prices and quality. In addition, given the link between culture and regulatory focus (Aaker and Lee 2001; Lee, Aaker and Gardner 2000), our findings can also help companies competing in an increasingly global market to better tailor their marketing campaigns to consumers from different cultural backgrounds.

REFERENCES

Aaker, Jennifer L. and Angela Y. Lee (2001), "'I' Seek Pleasures and 'We' Avoid Pains: The Role of Self-Regulatory Goals in Information Processing and Persuasion," *Journal of Consumer Research*, 28 (June), 33-49.

Advances in Consumer Research
Volume 39, ©2011

Avnet, Tamar and E. Tory Higgins (2006) "How Regulatory Fit Affects Value in Consumer Choices and Opinions," *Journal of Marketing Research,* 43 (February), 1-10.

Bell, David R. and James M. Lattin (2000), "Looking for Loss Aversion in Scanner Panel Data: The Confounding Effect of Price-Response Heterogeneity," *Marketing Science*, 19 (2), 185-200.

Bolton, Lisa E., Luk Warlop, and Joseph W. Alba (2003), "Consumer Perceptions of Price (Un)Fairness," *Journal of Consumer Research*, 29 (March), 474-91.

Chernev, Alexander (2004), "Goal Orientation and Consumer Preference for the Status Quo," *Journal of Consumer Research*, 31 (December), 557-65.

Finnel, Stephanie, Americus Reed II, Karl Aquino (2011), "Promoting Multiple Policies to the Public: The Difficulties of Simultaneously Promoting War and Promoting Foreign Humanitarian Aid," *Forthcoming at Journal of Public Policy and Marketing.*

Gilmore, H. L. (1974), "Product conformance cost," *Quality progress*, 7(5), 16-9.

Hanip, Rosli (2008), "In today's market, Price vs Quality, which is more important ?" http://www.roslihanip.com/business/price-vs-quality

Haws, Kelly L., Utpal M. Dholakia, and William O. Bearden (2010), "An Assessment of Chronic Regulatory Focus Measures," *Journal of Marketing Research*, 47 (October), 967-82.

Heath, Chip, Richard P. Larrick, and George Wu (1999), "Goals as Reference Points," *Cognitive Psychology*, 38 (February), 79-109.

Higgins, E. Tory (1997), "Beyond Pleasure and Pain," *American Psychologist*, 52 (December), 1280-300.

--- (2000), "Making a Good Decision: Value from Fit," *American Psychologist*, 55 (November), 1217-30.

Higgins, E. Tory, Lorraine C. Idson, Antonio L. Freitas, Scott Spiegel, and Daniel C. Molden (2003), "Transfer of Value from Fit," *Journal of Personality and Social Psychology*, 84 (June), 1140-53.

Hoch, Stephen J., Byung-Do Kim, Alan L. Montgomery, and Peter E. Rossi (1995), "Determinants of Store-Level Price Elasticity," *Journal of Marketing Research*, 32 (February), 17-29.

Idson, Lorraine Chen, Nira Liberman, and E. Tory Higgins (2000), "Distinguishing Gains from Nonlosses and Losses from Nongains: A Regulatory Focus Perspective on Hedonic Intensity," *Journal of Experimental Social Psychology*, 36, 252-74.

Kirmani, Amna and Rui Zhu (2007), "Vigilant Against Manipulation: The Effect of Regulatory Focus on the Use of Persuasion Knowledge," *Journal of Marketing Research*, 44 (November), 688-701.

Labroo, Aparna and Angela Y. Lee (2006), "Between Two Brands: A Goal Fluency Account of Brand Evaluation," *Journal of Marketing Research*, 43 (August), 374-85.

Lee, Angela Y., Jennifer L. Aaker, and Wendi L. Gardner (2000), "The Pleasures and Pains of Distinct Self-Construals: The Role of Interdependence in Regulatory Focus," *Journal of Personality and Social Psychology*, 78 (June), 1122-34.

Lockwood, Penelope, Christian H. Jordan, and Ziva Kunda (2002), "Motivation by Positive or Negative Role Models: Regulatory Focus Determines Who Will Best Inspire Us," *Journal of Personality and Social Psychology*, 83 (4), 854-64.

Lynch, John G. and Dan Ariely (2000), "Wine Online: Search Costs and Competition on Price, Quality, and Distribution," *Marketing Science,* 19 (Winter), 83-103.

Monroe, Kent B. (2003), *Pricing: Making Profitable Decisions*, New York: McGraw-Hill/Irwin.

Monroe, Kent B. and Angela Y. Lee (1999), "Remembering versus Knowing: Issues in Buyers' Processing of Price Information," *Journal of the Academy of Marketing Science*, 27 (Spring), 207-25.

Novemsky, Nathan and Daniel Kahneman (2005), "The Boundaries of Loss Aversion," *Journal of Marketing Research*, 42 (May), 119-28.

Petty, Richard E. and John T. Cacioppo (1986), *Communication and Persuasion: Central and Peripheral Routes to Attitude Change*, New York: Springer-Verlag.

Pham, Michel Tuan and Tamar Avnet (2009), "Contingent reliance on the affect heuristic as a function of regulatory focus," *Organizational Behavior and Human Decision Processes*, 108 (March), 268-78.

Preacher, Kristopher J. and Andrew F. Hayes (2004), "SPSS and SAS Procedures for Estimating Indirect Effects in Simple Mediation Models," *Behavior Research Methods, Instruments, and Computers*, 36 (4), 717-31.

Rao, Akshay R. and Kent B. Monroe (1988), "The Moderating Effect of Prior Knowledge on Cue Utilization in Product Evaluations," *Journal of Consumer Research*, 15 (September),253-64.

Rust, Roland T. and Bruce Cooil (1994), "Reliability Measures for Qualitative Data: Theory and Implications," *Journal of Marketing Research,* 31 (February), 1-14.

Van Heerde, Harald, Els Gijsbrechts, and Koen Pauwels (2008), "Winners and Losers in a Major PriceWar," *Journal of Marketing Research*, 45 (October), 499-518.

Wakefield, Kirk L. and J. Jeffrey Inman (2003), "Situational Price Sensitivity: The Role of Consumption Occasion, Social Context and Income," *Journal of Retailing*, 79 (4), 199-212.

Wang, Jing and Angela Y. Lee (2006), "The Role of Regulatory Focus in Preference Construction," *Journal of Marketing Research*, 43 (February), 28-38.

Watson, David, Clark Lee Ann, and Auge Tellegen (1988), "Development and Validation of Brief Measure of Positive and Negative Affect: The PANAS Scales," *Journal of Personality and Social Psychology*, 54 (6), 1063-70.

Zhao, Xinshu, John G. Lynch Jr., and Qimei Chen (2010), "Reconsidering Baron and Kenny: Myths and Truths about Mediation Analysis," *Journal of Consumer Research*, 37 (August), 197-206.

Zeithaml, Valarie A. (1988), "Consumer Perceptions of Price, Quality, and Value: A Means-End Model and Synthesis of Evidence," *Journal of Marketing*, 52 (July), 2-22.

Perception-Specific Average Causal Effects: Implications for Experimental Consumer Research

Walter Herzog, WHU, Germany

EXTENDED ABSTRACT

In experimental consumer research, it seems quite natural to assume that participants' treatment perceptions moderate treatment effects. For example, Cognitive Evaluation Theory (Deci and Ryan 1985; Dholakia 2006) predicts that a loyalty reward *increases* repurchase intentions relative to a "no reward control condition" if consumers interpret the reward as a sign of appreciation. The *same* reward, however, is hypothesized to *decrease* the repurchase intentions of consumers interpreting it as a manipulative trick of the firm. At first glance, these hypotheses can be tested by means of a trivial interaction analysis; treatment assignment (reward versus no reward) and treatment perceptions (appreciative versus manipulative reward interpretation) interact in producing effects on repurchase probability. However, two problems occur on closer inspection.

First, treatment perceptions are unobserved or "latent" in the control condition because the treatment is obviously absent. Second, treatment perceptions are influenced by a multitude of background variables. For example, Cognitive Evaluation Theory predicts that certain prior experiences with the firm (e.g., empathic behavior on the part of the rewarder) shape consumers' interpretation of the reward as "appreciative" or "manipulative," thereby influencing the reward's expected effect on repurchase probability. That is, the background variable's influence on the treatment effect (moderation) is assumed to be mediated by treatment perceptions which are unobserved in the control condition. This proposition is similar (though not technically equivalent) to a "mediated moderation hypothesis" (Muller, Judd, and Yzerbyt 2005) with the important difference that the mediator (classes of treatment perceptions) is categorical and missing for control group subjects.

Although treatment perceptions are important components of many psychological theories, a suitable statistical model has not yet been developed to meet the two mentioned challenges. Based on Rubin's Causal Model (Rubin 1974, 2005) and recent advances in psychometrics (Little and Yau 1998), biometrics (Frangakis and Rubin 2002), and econometrics (Angrist, Imbens, and Rubin 1996), a new method is proposed to estimate *perception-specific average causal effects* (PACE) of a treatment, that is, causal effects of the objectively same treatment for subjects assigning different meanings to the treatment (e.g., "appreciative" versus "manipulative" interpretations of a reward).

Furthermore, the model allows for a direct test of the aforementioned mediated moderation hypothesis with a categorical, partially latent mediator: Background variables (e.g., the rewarder's empathic behaviors) are allowed to influence the treatment effect on the dependent variable *directly* and *indirectly*: First, the background variable can influence the treatment effect directly which is modeled via a simple interaction effect of the background variable and treatment assignment. Second, the background variable can influence the treatment effect indirectly by increasing or decreasing the odds of positive versus negative treatment perceptions which in turn affects the overall treatment effect. If the first route of influence is *not* significant and the second route of influence is significant, the hypothesized treatment perceptions fully mediate the impact of the background variable on the treatment effect. However, if the first route of influence is significant, other mechanisms or other treatment perceptions might be at work in creating the background variable's influence on the treatment effect.

The method is illustrated by means of a prototypical experiment with N=91 student subjects who were assigned to a "loyalty reward condition" (a price reduction for meals at the university's cafeteria) or a control condition (no loyalty reward). In addition to the subjects' appreciative versus manipulative reward perceptions, a number of background variables were measured such as the students' experiences with the cafeteria's employees, that is, their empathic, customer-oriented behaviors. The dependent variable was loyalty intentions. Deci and Ryan's (1985) Cognitive Evaluation Theory suggests that (a) the reward has a PACE>0 for "appreciative perceivers," (b) the reward has a PACE<0 for "manipulative perceivers," and (c) "autonomy-supportive" interpersonal behaviors (empathy) on the part of the reward provider increase the likelihood of appreciative relative to manipulative reward perceptions, thereby improving the reward's overall effect. The latter hypothesis implies that there is no direct effect of empathy on the treatment effect but an indirect effect via specific treatment perceptions. The results are perfectly in line with Deci and Ryan's (1985) predictions: All parameters were significant except for the direct effect of empathy on the treatment effect, that is, full mediated moderation via Deci and Ryan's (1985) postulated reward perceptions is supported. Overall, the results reveal that loyalty rewards are not by definition beneficial or counterproductive—contextual factors shape a reward's "metamessage" and thus *indirectly* its overall effect. This simple illustration shows that the PACE model has the potential to scrutinize so-far untestable assumptions of psychological theories.

Finally, a simulation study was performed to test the robustness of the PACE estimates under varying sample size conditions. The population model matched the estimated model discussed in the former paragraph. Four sample size conditions (N=50, 100, 150, 200) were examined. The analysis suggests that (a) the bias of the PACE estimates is negligible for all sample size conditions and (b) the PACE estimates reach an acceptable power level (80%) for N=100. Overall, the simulation study implies that the PACE model can indeed handle the small sample sizes typically generated in laboratory experiments.

REFERENCES

Angrist, Joshua D., Guido W. Imbens, and Donald B. Rubin (1996), "Identification of Causal Effects Using Instrumental Variables," *Journal of the American Statistical Association*, 91 (June), 444-55.

Angrist, Joshua D. and Joern-Steffen Pischke (2009), *Mostly Harmless Econometrics: An Empiricist's Companion*, Princeton, NJ: Princeton University Press.

Bojanic, David C. and L. Drew Rosen (1994), "Measuring Service Quality in Restaurants: An Application of the SERVQUAL instrument," *Journal of Hospitality & Tourism Research*, 18 (3), 3-14.

Cheung, Mike W.-L. (2007), "Comparison of Approaches to Constructing Confidence Intervals for Mediating Effects Using Structural Equation Models," *Structural Equation Modeling*, 14 (2), 227-46.

Deci, Edward L., Richard Koestner, and Richard M. Ryan (1999), "A Meta-Analytic Review of Experiments Examining the Effects of Extrinsic Rewards on Intrinsic Motivation," *Psychological Bulletin*, 125 (6), 627-68.

Deci, Edward L. and Richard M. Ryan (1985), *Intrinsic Motivation and Self-Determination in Human Behavior*, New York: Plenum.

Dempster, Arthur P., Nan M. Laird, and Donald B. Rubin (1977), "Maximum Likelihood from Incomplete Data via the EM Algorithm," *Journal of the Royal Statistical Society*, 39 (1), 1-38.

Dholakia, Utpal M. (2006), "How Customer Self-Determination Influences Relational Marketing Outcomes: Evidence from Longitudinal Field Studies," *Journal of Marketing Research*, 43 (1), 109-20.

Frangakis, Constantine E. and Donald B. Rubin (2002), "Principal Stratification in Causal Inference," *Biometrics*, 58 (March), 21-29.

Jo, Booil (2002), "Estimation of Intervention Effects with Noncompliance: Alternative Model Specifications," *Journal of Educational and Behavioral Statistics*, 27 (4), 385-409.

Jo, Booil and Bengt O. Muthén (2001), "Modeling of Intervention Effects with Noncompliance: A Latent Variable Modeling Approach for Randomized Trials," in *New Developments and Techniques in Structural Equation Modeling*, ed. George A. Marcoulides and Randall E. Schumacker, Mahwah, NJ: Erlbaum, 57-87.

Little, Roderick J. and Linda H. Y. Yau (1998), "Statistical Techniques for Analyzing Data from Prevention Trials: Treatment of No-Shows Using Rubin's Causal Model," *Psychological Methods*, 3 (2), 147-59.

Muller, Dominique, Charles M. Judd, and Vincent Y. Yzerbyt (2005), "When Moderation Is Mediated and Mediation Is Moderated", *Journal of Personality and Social Psychology*, 89, (6), 852-63.

Muthén, Bengt O. and Kerby Shedden (1999), "Finite Mixture Modeling with Mixture Outcomes Using the EM Algorithm," *Biometrics*, 55 (2), 463-69.

Muthén, Linda K. and Bengt O. Muthén (2010), *Mplus user's guide*, Los Angeles: Muthén & Muthén.

Rubin, Donald B. (1974), "Estimating Causal Effects of Treatments in Randomized and Nonrandomized Studies," *Journal of Educational Psychology*, 66 (5), 688-701.

Rubin, Donald B. (2005), "Causal Inference Using Potential Outcomes: Design, Modeling, Decisions", *Journal of the American Statistical Association*, 100 (March), 322-31.

Consumer Citizenship Behavior:
The Effects of Social Identification on Interpersonal Helping Behavior Among Consumers

Jeff Allen, University of Central Florida, USA
Carolyn Massiah, University of Central Florida, USA
Zachary Johnson, University of Central Florida, USA
Kristin Bowman, University of Central Florida, USA

EXTENDED ABSTRACT

The impact of "citizenship-like" behavior, voluntary interpersonal behavior that benefits the organization, has generated a great deal of interest across disciplines. This research classifies these behaviors as Organizational Citizenship Behaviors (OCBs); that is, the extra role discretionary initiatives of employees engaged in various work behaviors (see Lepine, Erez, and Johnson 2002). This study further expands the concept of citizenship behavior to include interpersonal helping behavior that occurs among consumers in the midst of other consumers. Specifically, the relationship between social identification and helping behavior among consumption community members is investigated. The research demonstrates how this form of consumer behavior creates value for product-based as well as service-based organizations.

Social identification is the perceived belongingness to any social group, formal or informal. According to Social Identity Theory, individuals develop a social self that is attached or connected to the group and its providence (Ashforth and Mael 1989). Members of a social group are more apt to help one another because membership instills a sense of obligation to the group and its individual members (May and Hoffman 1991). It is this sense of responsibility that leads to higher levels of helping behavior (Sturmber, Snyder, and Omato 2005).

The present study differs from current consumer behavior research on interpersonal helping behavior which implies that consumption community members will receive help and non-members will not (Muniz and O'Guinn 2001). Rather than an implied dichotomy, this research presents helping behavioral intentions as falling along a continuum, suggesting that interpersonal helping behavior is not influenced by membership alone. A consumer who perceives a stronger attachment to a community is more likely to engage in helping other members than a consumer with a weaker attachment.

Data for the study was collected at Biketoberfest, a biker rally held in Daytona Beach, Florida that attracts 200,000 plus bikers annually. Self-report surveys were distributed to male bikers during the event. Identification with the biker community and particular subgroup were treated as separate constructs. Respondents (n = 152) were first asked whether they belonged to an organized (e.g., Harley Owners' Group, Racing Club, Antique/Restoration Club) or an informal subgroup (e.g., Iron Butt Gang, Bikers for Jesus, close group of friends) of bikers within the biker community. If a member of more than one subgroup, they were asked to specify club/group most important to them. Respondents were instructed to answer each question twice, once regarding bikers in the subgroup they specified and again for bikers not in their club/group. The helping behavior intentions are of three types: altruistic, product-related, and behavioral scenarios. All items were measured on a 7-point agreement scale ranging from 1="Strongly Disagree" to 7="Strongly Agree."

Item analysis for each scale began by inspecting inter-item correlations for r's < .30 and item-to-total correlations for r's $\geq$ .50. This resulted in deleting several items from the social identification and scenario scales. Reliability for the measures of each construct was assessed using Cronbach's alpha. Alphas ranging from .74 for subgroup identification to .94 for measures of altruistic helping behavior indicate that the scales are internally consistent (Nunnally and Bernstein 1994).

To test the proposed hypotheses, a multivariate multiple regression model using the unweighted least squares technique was employed. Social identification at the community and subgroup levels within the community served as independent variables and the three types of helping intentions were used as simultaneous dependent variables. Initially, a dummy variable was created to capture any difference in helping behavior for informal compared to organized subgroups. However, subgroup formality was nonsignificant in the model and was omitted from further analysis.

Hypothesis #1, that identification with the biker community would have a positive effect on helping other members at the community level, was supported. Estimated paths from community identification to helping behavior at that level were significant (p's < .05) whereas paths to helping behavior at the group level were not. Hypothesis #2, that subgroup identification-helping relations would be stronger for subgroup members than for community members outside of the group, was also supported with one exception. While the path estimates were significant and stronger at the subgroup level, altruistic behavior was significantly related to identification with bikers at the community level as well (i.e., standardized β's = 2.24, p <.001 vs. 1.23, p < .01, in that order).

Our results support a positive relationship between social identification and helping behavior at the larger community level. However, consumption communities are comprised of subgroups in which members of each share an identity. Our findings suggest that when members' identity is salient at the subgroup level, identification-helping relations were stronger for subgroup members than for community members not in their group. Interpersonal proximity and the collective motives arising from the group engender a strong sense of responsibility which makes interpersonal helping more likely between fellow members (Mael and Ashforth 2001; Turner 1984).

Members' subgroup identification was not related to any helping behaviors pertaining to community members outside of their subgroup except for behavior that was altruistic in nature. Interestingly, altruistic behavior may be egoistically motivated, making it difficult to distinguish altruism from self-interest. Underlying reasons of self-interest may motivate this type of behavior, but to a lesser extent than social identification at the community level.

The current research indicates that identification was significantly related to product-based helping behavior with other bikers in the community. This behavior was also evident at the subgroup level. From a marketing standpoint, product-based organizations should develop increasingly bonded relationships with consumers, but have been less clear concerning customers' roles compared to their service-dominant counterparts. This study demonstrates how consumers can voluntarily act on behalf of either a service- or product-based organization to contribute to its success. Together, the findings imply that consumers on their own can act as partial employees to co-create value that benefits the product-oriented organization (Pralahad and Ramaswamy 2000). One way a firm can foster consumer citizenship behavior is by forming communities around its product or service. Through organizationally sponsored community events the bonds that are formed benefit the organization as well as strengthen the consumption community.

REFERENCES

Ashforth, Blake E., and Fred Mael (1989), "Social identity theory and the organization," The *Academy of Management Review*, 14 (1), 20-39.

Bitner, Mary Jo., William T. Faranda, Amy R. Hubbert, and Valarie A. Zeithaml (1997) "Customer contributions and roles in service delivery," *Journal of Service Industry Management*, 8(3), 193-205.

Bettencourt, Lance A. (1997), "Customer Voluntary Performance: Customers As Partners In Service Delivery," *Journal of Retailing*, 73(3), 383-406.

Federouch, A. G. (1990), "A Conceptualization of Market Helpfulness: Theory and Measurement of Consumer Altruism," Doctoral dissertation, University of Pittsburgh.

Groth, Markus (2005), "Customers as Good Soldiers: Examining Citizenship Behaviors in Internet Service Deliveries," Journal of Management, 31(1), 7-27.

Huo Y, Smith H, Tyler T, Lind E. Superordinate identification, subgroup identification, and justice concens: Is spearatism the problem; is assimilation the answer?. *Psychological Science* [serial online]. January 1996;7(1):40-45. Available from: PsycINFO, Ipswich, MA. Accessed January 31, 2011.

Johnson, Michael D., and Fred Selnes (2004), "Customer Portfolio Management: Toward a Dynamic Theory of Exchange Relationships*," Journal of Marketing*, 68(2), 1-17.

Lepine, Jeffrey A., Amir Erez, and Diane E. Johnson (2002), "The Nature and Dimensionality of Organizational Citizenship Behavior: A Critical Review and Meta-Analysis," *Journal of Applied Psychology*, 87 (1), 52-65.

Mael, Fred (1988), "Organizational Identification: Construct Redefinition and a Field Application with Organizational Alumni," doctoral dissertation, Wayne State University.

Mael, Fred and Blake E. Asforth (1992), "Alumni and Their Alma Mater: A Partial Test of the Reformulated Model of Organizational Identification," *Journal of Organizatioanl Behaivor*, 13, 103-23.

Mael, Fred A., and Blake E. Ashforth (2001). "Identification in work, war, sports, and religion: Contrasting the benefits and risks." *Journal for the Theory of Social Behaviour* 31 (2) 197-222. *PsycINFO*. EBSCO. Web. 31 Jan. 2011.

May, Larry and Stacey Hoffman (1991), "Collective Responsibility: Five Decades of Debate in Theoretical and Applied Fields," Rowman and Littlefield.

Muniz, Albert M. and O'Guinn, Tom C. (2001). "Brand Community," *Journal of Consumer Research*, 27 (March): 412-432.

Nunnally, J.C. & Bernstein, I. H. (1994). *Psychometric Theory*, New York: McGraw-Hill.

Podsakoff, Philip M., Scott B. MacKenzie, Julie Beth Paine, and Daniel G. Bachrach (2000) "Organizational Citizenship Behaviors: A Critical Review of the Theoretical and Empirical Literature and Suggestions for Future Research" *Journal of Management*, 26, 513-563.

Prahalad, C.K. and Ramaswamy, Venkatram (2000) "Co-opting Customer Competence," Harvard Business Review, (January-February), 79-87.

Prahalad, C.K. and Venkat Ramaswamy (2004) "Co-creating unique value with customers," Strategy and Leadership, 32(3), 4-9.

Porter, M.E. (1980). Competitive Strategy: Techniques for Analyzing Industries and Competitors. The Free Press.

"Official Bike Week Headquarters." *Officialbikeweek.com*. Web. 24 Jan. 2011. <http://www.officialbikeweek.com/>.

Organ, D. W. (1988), "Organizational citizenship behavior: The good soldier syndrome," Lexington, MA: Lexington Books.

Rosenbaum, Mark S. and Carolyn A Massiah (2007) "When Customers Receive Support From Other Customers: Exploring the Influence of Intercustomer Social Support on Customer Voluntary Performance," Journal of Services Research, 9(3) 257-270.

Schouten, J. W. & McAlexander, J.H. (1995). "Subcultures of consumption: An Ethnography of the New Bikers," Journal of Consumer Research 22 (June), 43-61.

Sturmer, S., M. Snyder, and A.M. Omoto (2005), "Prosocial emotions and helping: The moderating role of group membership," *Journal of Personality and Social Psychology*, 88, 532-546.

Tajfel, Henri. (1969) Cognitive Aspects of Prejudice. *Journal of Social Issues*, 25(4), 79-97.

Tajfel, Henri and John C. Turner (1985), "The Social Identity Theory of Intergroup Behavior" in *Psychology of Intergroup Relations*, ed. Stephen Worchell and William G. Austin, Chicago, IL: Nelson-Hall: 7-24.

Turner, J.C. (1984). Social Identification and psychological Group Formation. In H. Tajfel (ed.), *The Social Dimension: European Developments in Social Psychology*, vol 2. Cambridge, England: Cambridge University Press, 518-538.

Vowel Sounds Shape Level of Mental Construal:
Putting the *ee* in *trees* and the *o* in *forest*

Sam Maglio, New York University, USA
Cristina Rabaglia, New York University, USA
Michael Feder, New York University, USA
Madelaine Krehm, New York University, USA
Yaacov Trope, New York University, USA

EXTENDED ABSTRACT

Mounting research in the tradition of sound symbolism supports the presence of intuitive associations between the sounds contained in words and the objects to which they refer (Hinton, Nichols, and Ohala 1994). One line of work has investigated vowel sounds, ranging from front to back based on the location of the tongue relative to the front of the mouth during articulation. Consider the vowels in the following words, which progress from front to back: bee, bin, bay, bet, ban, cot, home, put, boot (from Klink 2000). All else equal, consumers infer that objects with names including relatively frontal vowel sounds are more sharp, hard, and angular, among others (for a review, see Shrum and Lowrey 2007). Importantly, these inferences translate to behavioral consequences. Yorkston and Menon (2004) found that participants preferred a hypothetical ice cream named Frosh (back vowel) over Frish (front), inferring the former to be especially smooth and thick (features characteristic of back vowels). Taken together, research to date has documented an association between vowel sounds contained in words and the physical properties of the referents.

The present investigation extends beyond what consumers think about an object as a function of vowel sound to how they think about it – that is, the manner in which they represent it and process relevant information. Toward this end, we draw upon the perspective of construal level theory (Trope and Liberman 2010). It posits that a target can be mentally represented either in terms of primary, essential features (high-level construal) or secondary, incidental features (low-level construal). Past research suggests that, when construing a product at a high level of representation, consumers show greater sensitivity to primary over secondary features of that product; lower-level construal reduces or reverses such differentiation.

To explore the relationship between vowel sound and mental construal, we consider a feature common to both: degree of precision. Relative to high level, low-level construal gives rise to greater precision across a host of applications (e.g., Liberman, Sagristano, and Trope 2002). Similarly, the aforementioned characteristics associated with front vowels – sharpness, hardness, angularity – cohere around a sense of greater precision (see Lowrey and Shrum 2007). Thus, front vowels and low-level construal correspond to relatively fine-grained precision relative to the coarser scale of back vowels and high-level construal.

If vowel sound can manipulate construal level, brand names including front vowel sounds might elicit low-level construal of products, whereas back vowels might elicit high-level representation. We test this prediction in three studies, exploring the tradeoff between low- and high-level sources of value and utilizing vowel sound as the construal manipulation. When given a brand name including a back vowel, consumers should prefer products carrying good high-level but poor low-level value versus the opposite; this differentiation should be attenuated or reversed in response to front vowel names.

Study 1 asked participants to evaluate a fictitious ice cream, given a name that included either a front vowel (Frish) or a back vowel (Frosh). Additionally, participants were informed that the ice cream carried either good high-level value but poor low-level value (having a very good taste but being in an inconvenient location) or the opposite (poorer taste, convenient location). Upon indicating their willingness to purchase the ice cream, participants strongly preferred the ice cream named Frosh when defined by the former rather than the latter set of characteristics; this pattern was significantly attenuated for Frish, suggesting that the importance of secondary value (location) in evaluation was enhanced as a result of a front vowel sound.

Studies 2 and 3 provide important replications of this general effect. In Study 2, we tested hand lotions given the name either Kira's (front vowel) or Kora's (back vowel) and used the following characteristics: good absorbability (high-level value) but an ugly gift bag (low-level value) or the opposite (poor absorbability, beautiful gift bag). As in Study 1, the name Kora's resulted in a much stronger differentiation in preference (for high- over low-level value) than did the name Kira's. To show that front vowels do not simply reduce general differentiation, Study 3 tested the names Dari (front vowel) and Daru (back vowel) in the domain of massages. The results indicated that Dari led participants to significantly prefer short-term over long-term pain relief, whereas the opposite pattern of evaluations evinced for the massage named Daru. Thus, we conclude that both back and front vowel sounds are associated with high- and low-levels of construal, respectively.

Across three studies, the vowel sounds included in words affected the level at which consumers represented and evaluated their referents: Front vowels elicited low-level construal while back vowels elicited high-level construal. This held using different operationalizations of high- versus low-level value and different specific vowel sounds (in different pairings) across the studies. Further, we observed a consistent effect of vowel sound independent of location in the word: the only vowel (Study 1), the first of two vowels (Study 2), and the second of two vowels (Study 3).

Given the staggering number of words encountered daily, the implications of the present research are as many as they are ubiquitous. The subtle manipulation of name successfully elicited different levels of mental representation, powerful enough to affect preferences and behavioral intentions. These studies contribute a novel example of a growing body of research documenting the incidental ways in which language influences thought (e.g., Boroditsky 2000), showing that vowel sounds impact not only the what but also the how of mental representation. These results also open the possibility for a volume of future work examining the relationship between sounds and mental processing – particularly for other construal-dependent domains. Finally, our work suggests that in an applied context, people making appeals to popular opinion (e.g., marketers, political candidates) would be well advised to use names (or perhaps even groups of words) that take into account the features that they want their audience to value. In sum, our evidence suggests that very subtle linguistic cues can influence the very nature of mental representation.

REFERENCES

Boroditsky, Lera (2000), "Metaphoric Structuring: Understanding Time through Spatial Metaphors," *Cognition*, 75 (1), 1-28.

Hinton, Leanne, Johanna Nichols, and John J. Ohala, eds. (1994), *Sound Symbolism*, Cambridge: Cambridge University Press.

Klink, Richard R. (2000), "Creating Brand Names with Meaning: The Use of Sound Symbolism," *Marketing Letters*, 11 (1), 5-20.

Liberman, Nira, Michael D. Sagristano, and Yaacov Trope (2002), "The Effect of Temporal Distance on Level of Mental Construal," *Journal of Experimental Social Psychology*, 38 (6), 523-34.

Lowrey, Tina M. and L.J. Shrum (2007), "Phonetic Symbolism and Brand Name Preference," *Journal of Consumer Research*, 34 (October), 406-14.

Shrum, L.J. and Tina M. Lowrey (2007), "Sounds Convey Meaning: The Implications of Phonetic Symbolism for Brand Name Construction," in *Psycholinguistic Phenomena in Marketing Communications*, ed. Tina M. Lowrey and L.J. Shrum, Mahwah, NJ: Erlbaum, 39-58.

Trope, Yaacov and Nira Liberman (2010), "Construal Level Theory of Psychological Distance," *Psychological Review*, 117 (2), 440-63.

Yorkston, Eric and Geeta Menon (2004), "A Sound Idea: Phonetic Effects of Brand Names on Consumer Judgments," *Journal of Consumer Research*, 31 (June), 43-51.

Maintenance Versus Attainment Goals: Preference of Goal Fulfilling Strategies and Influence of Change in Life Circumstances on Goal Pursuit

Napatsorn Jiraporn, State University of New York at Binghamton/Oswego, USA
Kalpesh Kaushik Desai, State University of New York at Binghamton, USA

EXTENDED ABSTRACT

Relapse is common in multiple goal domains such as the failure to maintain smoke cessation behavior and the weight gain among dieters who have successfully lost weight. However, the goal literature has focused mainly on attainment goals in which the desired state exceeds the current state but has neglected the maintenance goals in which the current state is equal to or better than the desired state (Brodscholl, Kober, and Higgins 2006). High record of relapse casts doubt on whether research findings about attainment goals are applicable to maintenance goals. Our research aims to contrast these two goal types.

First, we hypothesize that maintenance goals are characterized by a more ambiguous endpoint of the goal pursuit than attainment goals (H1). This is because maintainers are already in the desired state so the endpoint in terms of when to stop pursuing the goal is less clear. In contrast, attainers have the desired state as a clear endpoint of the pursuit. Second, using mental simulation (Taylor et al 1998) as our theoretical underpinning, we examined how maintainers and attainers evaluate goal fulfilling strategies. Prior research (Thomson, Hamilton, and Petrova 2009) shows that consumers are chronically sensitive to outcomes. However, maintenance goals are less temporally bounded so they should make maintainers focus on the process of using a strategy. Thus, we hypothesize that maintainers will engage in both process-focused and outcome-focused mental simulation. In contrast, attainers, who try to close the gap between the current and the desired state, should engage in more outcome-focused (vs. process-focused) mental simulation (H2) Moreover, because maintainers will consider only strategies that are feasible to use and effective whereas attainers will consider any strategy that seems to deliver satisfactory outcomes, maintainers should consider and use fewer strategies that attainers (H3). Lastly, we examined how the two groups of consumers make trade-off between effort intensity and temporal dispersion of strategy implementation. Specifically, we investigated preference between a temporal dispersed – effortfully less intense strategy (e.g. 15 minutes exercise, 6 times per week) vs. a temporally concentrated – effortfully more intense strategy (e.g. 45 minutes exercise, 2 times per week). We hypothesize that maintainers will prefer the former strategy because it appears to be more feasible to implement whereas attainers will prefer the latter strategy because they are more subject to instrumentality bias, a naïve belief that more intense effort will lead to a better reward (H4).

Study 1 (n = 120) with a 2 (goal type) x 2 (replicates: cholesterol and savings goals) design supported H1, H2, and H3 in both goal domains. The results showed that maintenance goals had a less clear endpoint than attainment goals (($M_{Maintainers}$ = 4.12 vs. $M_{Attainers}$ = 5.28, $F(1, 107)$ = 23.82, p <.01). Maintainers considered fewer number of strategies than attainers ($M_{Maintainers}$ = 3.09 vs. $M_{Attainers}$ = 4.07, $t(59)$ = 3.05, p <.01.). Lastly,-maintainers engaged in both process-focused and outcome-focused thinking ($M_{Process}$ = 5.12 vs. $M_{Outcome}$ = 5.02, $t(32)$ <1. p >.20) while attainers engaged more in outcome-focused thinking ($M_{Process}$ = 4.15 vs. $M_{Outcome}$ = 4.9, $t(27)$ 2.93, p < .01).

Study 2 (n =120) using a 2 (goal type) x 2 strategy type (temporally dispersed – effortfully less intense vs. temporally concentrated – effortfully more intense) design with the latter as a repeated measure successfully replicated all findings from study 1 and tested H4 in both cholesterol and savings domains. Maintainers

preferred a temporally dispersed – effortfully less intense strategy ($M_{Less\ Intense}$ = 5.30 vs. $M_{More\ Intense}$ = 4.54, $t(33)$ = 3.01, p <.05) but inconsistent with H4, attainers viewed both strategies as equally attractive ($M_{Less\ Intense}$ = 5.40 vs. $M_{More\ Intense}$ = 5.42, $t(28)$<1, p >.20).

Study 3 (n =40) measured goal type among actual gym users to replicate findings from studies 1 and 2 and tested H3 in the weight goal domain. Consistent with previous studies, maintainers used fewer strategies than attainers ($M_{Maintainers}$ = 3.25 vs. $M_{Attainers}$ = 4.50, $t(60)$ = 2.23, p <.05), supporting H3. H4 was supported as maintainers preferred a temporally dispersed – effortfully less intense strategy (N= 10 vs. 5, $\chi2\ (1,14)$ = 2.21, p <.05) whereas attainers preferred the temporally concentrated – effortfully more intense strategy (N = 6 vs. 17, $\chi2\ (1,24)$ = 5.26, p <.05) Moreover, attainers showed stronger belief in the instrumentality bias, a belief that more intense effort will give a better reward, than maintainers ($M_{maintainers}$ = 3.70 vs. $M_{attainers}$ = 5.76, t(38) = 5.47, p <.01). Mediation analysis confirmed that instrumentality bias mediates the effort of goal type on strategy choice.

Study 4 (n =54) with a 2 (goal type) x 2 (process-focused vs. outcome focused mental simulation) was conducted among gym users. The mental simulation was manipulated to test whether it is the underlying reason why maintainers considered fewer strategies than attainers. As predicted, we observe no difference in the number of strategies used across process-focused and outcome-focused conditions for maintainers, showing that maintainers naturally engage in both types of thinking ($M_{process}$ = 3.16 vs. $M_{outcome}$ = 2.88, $t(20)$ <1, p>.20). In contrast, attainers who were primed to be process-focused vs. outcome-focused reported fewer strategies ($M_{process}$ = 2.50 vs. $M_{outcome}$ = 4.36, t(32) 3.60, p<.01). Thus, it is likely that mental simulation is the underlying reason why maintainers consider fewer strategies than attainers.

After providing clear evidence that the two goal types differ, we proceeded to examine how life circumstances impact goal adherence of maintainers and attainers. Study 5 (n=109) with a 2 goal type (maintenance vs. attainment) x 2 life circumstance (change vs. stability) between subjects design showed that when going through change in life, attainers and maintainers did not differ in the number of goal-consistent choices selected ($M_{maintainers}$ = 2.08 vs. $M_{attainers}$ = 2.12, $t(48)$ <1, p >.05) indicating that changes in life circumstances did not help or hurt maintainers vs. attainers. However, in the stability condition, maintainers selected fewer number of goal-consistent choices than attainers ($M_{maintainers}$ = 1.30 vs. $M_{attainers}$ = 2.50, $t(49)$ = 3.18, p <.01) indicating that when there is stability in life circumstances, maintainers exhibit lower goal adherence than attainers. Further analysis revealed that maintainers predicted that the goal would be easier and therefore, lessened their self-regulation and showed lower goal adherence.

Results across these five studies robustly established that maintenance goals differ from attainment goals in many important aspects. This research helps managers recognize that consumers striving different goal types are not homogenous and distinct marketing strategies are needed to serve the two consumer groups

REFERENCES

Bagozzi, Richard and Utpal Dholakia (1999), "Goal Setting and Goal Striving in Consumer Behavior," *Journal of Marketing*, 63, 19-32

Baumgartner, Hans and Rik Pieters (2008), "Goal-Directed Consumer Behavior," *Handbook of Consumer Psychology*, eds. Haugtvedt, Curtis P; Herr, Paul M; and Kardes, Frank R., New York, Psychology Press, 367–392

Brodscholl, Jeff, Hedy Kober, and Tory Higgins (2006), "Strategies of Self-Regulation in Goal Attainment Versus Goal Maintenance," *European Journal of Social Psychology*, 37 (4), 628-648

Carstensen, Laura L., Derek M. Isaacowitz, and Susan T. Charles (1999), "Taking Time Seriously: A Theory of Socioemotional Selectivity," *American psychologist*, 54 (3), 165-181

Escalas, J. E. and M. F. Luce (2004), "Understanding the Effects of Process-Focused Versus Outcome-Focused Thought in Response to Advertising," *Journal of Consumer Research*, 31 (2), 274-285

Fishbach, Ayelet and Ravi Dhar (2005), "Goals as Excuses or Guides: The Liberating Effect of Perceived Goal Progress on Choice," *The Journal of Consumer Research*, 32 (3), 370-377

Gourville, John (1998), "Pennies-A-Day: The Effect of Temporal Reframing on Transaction Evaluation," Journal of Consumer Research, 24 (March), 395-408

Labroo, Aparna and Kim, Sara (2009), "The "instrumentality" heuristic: Why metacognitive difficulty is desirable during goal pursuit," *Psychological Science, 20,* 127–134

Phelan, Suzanne, James Hill, Wei Lang, Jullia Dibello, and Rena Wing (2003), "Recovery from Relapse among Successful Weight Maintainers," *The American Journal of Clinical Nutrition*, 78 (6), 1079

Stamatogiannakis, Antonios; Chattopadhyay, Amitava, and Chakravarti, Dipankar (2009), "Maintenance versus Attainment Goals: Why People Think it Is Harder to Maintain their Weight than to Lose a Couple of Kilos," in *Advances in Consumer Research,* 2009

Taylor, Shelley E., Lien B. Pham, Inna D. Rivkin, and David A. Armor (1998), "Harnessing the Imagination: Mental Stimulation, Self-Regulation, and Coping," *American Psychologist*, 53 (4), 429-439

Thompson, Debora V., Rebecca W. Hamilton and Petia K. Petrova (2009), "When Mental Simulation Hinders Behavior: The Effects of Process-Oriented Thinking on Decision Difficulty and Performance," Journal of Consumer Research, 36(4), 562-574

Mackinnon D.P. Warsi, and J.H. Dwyer (1993), "Estimating Mediated Effects in Prevention Studies," Evaluation Review, 17(2) 144-158

Do I Value it Because I Own it or Because I am Averse to Losing Things?
The Effects of Identity, Self-Threat, and Gender on the Endowment Effect

Sara Loughran Dommer, University of Pittsburgh, USA
Vanitha Swaminathan, University of Pittsburgh, USA

EXTENDED ABSTRACT

People typically demand more to relinquish the goods they own than they would be willing to pay to acquire those goods if they did not already own them. This phenomenon is known as the endowment effect.

There are two primary explanations for why the endowment effect occurs. The first is that we have a strong psychological association with objects that we own, potentially due to the ability of our possessions to define and enhance our view of self, which may induce a greater liking for our possessions (Morewedge et al. 2009). In support of this notion, Gawronski, Bodenhausen and Becker (2007) have noted choice of an object results in an association between the object and the self, leading to an increase in evaluation of the chosen object. We call this explanation for the endowment effect the 'self-enhancement account'.

The second explanation for the endowment effect is based on the principle of loss aversion (Kahneman and Tversky 1979; Thaler 1980). Loss aversion refers to the tendency for people to strongly prefer avoiding losses than acquiring gains (Kahnemann and Tversky 1979). Sellers typically think of selling as a loss and buyers typically think of buying as a gain, therefore sellers expect to suffer more than buyers expect to benefit. As a result, sellers demand more compensation than buyers are willing to provide, resulting in higher selling prices than buying prices for an identical good (Kahneman, Knetsch and Thaler 1991). This 'loss aversion account' has traditionally dominated the explanation for why we observe the endowment effect.

Recent research has tried to disentangle the self-enhancement account from the loss aversion account in explaining the endowment effect (Morewedge et al. 2009). We extend this work by identifying two moderating conditions that sort out the self-enhancement versus loss aversion explanations for the endowment effect: self-threat and gender. We suggest that under conditions of self-threat, identity-consistent objects can be used for self-enhancement to alleviate the self-threat, resulting in even greater selling prices for identity-consistent objects. Under a self-threat, when males and females are endowed with an identity-*in*consistent good, however, gender differences emerge. Specifically, the pattern of findings indicates that males are more likely to use goods for self-enhancement, whereas females are more likely to exhibit loss aversion.

In the first study, our results show that the identity-consistent nature of a good moderates loss aversion, but only under a self-threat. When the object is neutral (a plain pen), the gap between selling prices and buying prices is similar under self-threat and no self-threat conditions. In contrast, when the object is identity-consistent (a pen with a university logo), the gap between selling prices and buying prices widens for the self-threat condition relative to the no self-threat condition, indicating that individuals are using these objects to self-enhance.

In a second study, we use a different identity-consistent good and replicate the results from the first study. We also find some evidence that sellers are holding on to their identity-consistent good to lessen some of their anxiety and negative self-views (i.e., to self-enhance). Although there were no significant differences in reported self-views across the buying and selling conditions in the self-threat condition before the endowment effect experiment, following the

endowment effect experiment, sellers reported lower anxiety (i.e., higher views of self) than buyers. This is evidence that the endowment effect results in the identity-consistent condition may be a result of using objects to enhance participant's view of self following a self-threat.

The first two studies provided support for the self-enhancement explanation, but there was limited evidence of the loss aversion explanation. For identity-inconsistent goods, if the loss aversion account is at work, individuals should continue to value the endowed object highly and thus we would expect to see the endowment effect across all conditions. If, however, self-enhancement is at work, then under a self-threat we would expect selling prices to drop as individuals attempt to self-enhance by derogating the out-group. Thus, valuations of an identity-inconsistent good may help us disentangle the self-enhancement and loss aversion account

Under what conditions could an identity-inconsistent good prompt self-enhancement versus loss aversion? Carr and Steele (2010) demonstrate that women are more loss averse than men in the context of decision-making, particularly when faced with a self-threat (e.g., stereotype threat). We hypothesize that in the case of an identity-inconsistent good, males and females will show varying patterns of behavior, due to a differential sensitivity to losses. Specifically, it is expected that females will continue to demonstrate higher selling prices relative to buying prices, which is consistent with a loss-aversion account, whereas males will demonstrate no increase in selling prices relative to buying prices, which is consistent with a self-enhancement account.

In a third study, we find that under self-threat, males lower their selling prices for an identity-inconsistent possession, presumably to show rejection of the out-group, thus eliminating the endowment effect. Females, however, show no such change in selling prices. Thus, following a self-threat loss aversion for an out-group good is eliminated for males but remains unchanged for females. These results indicate that loss aversion may explain the endowment effect for females, particularly when they are endowed with an undesirable good. In contrast, self-enhancement explanation continues to explain the existence of endowment effect for males, because when the nature of the good changes, it causes the endowment effect to disappear.

Our results contribute to the burgeoning stream of research which disentangles the self-enhancement and the loss aversion accounts in explaining the endowment effect (Morewedge et al. 2009). Specifically, we show that under a self-threat, males use objects to help them self-enhance while females fear losing objects (of any identity association).

REFERENCES

Aggarwal, Pankaj and Meng Zhang (2006), "The Moderating Effect of Relationship Norm Salience on Consumers' Loss Aversion," *Journal of Consumer Research*, 33, 413–19.

Ariely, Dan, Joel Huber, and Klaus Wertenbroch (2005), "When Do Losses Loom Larger Than Gains?" *Journal of Marketing Research*, 42, 134–38.

Bartholomew, Kim and Leonard M. Horowitz (1991), "Attachment Styles Among Young Adults: A Test of a Four-Category Model," *Journal of Personality and Social Psychology*, 61, 226–44.

Bartz, Jennifer A. and John E. Lydon (2004), "Close Relationships and the Working-Self Concept: Implicit and Explicit Effects of Priming Attachment on Agency and Communion," *Personality and Social Psychology Bulletin*, 30, 1389–1401.

Becker, Gordon M., Morris H. DeGroot, and Jacob Marschak (1964), "Measuring Utility by a Single-response Sequential Method," *Behavioral Science*, 9, 226–32.

Belk, Russell W. (1988), "Possessions and the Extended Self," *Journal of Consumer Research*, 15, 139–68.

Bonsu, Samuel K. and Russell W. Belk (2003), "Do Not Go Cheaply into That Good Night: Death-Ritual Consumption in Asante, Ghana," *Journal of Consumer Research*, 30, 41–55.

Branscombe, Nyla R., Naomi Ellemers, Russell Spears, and Bertjan Doosje (1999), "The Context and Content of Social Identity Threat," in *Social Identity: Context, Commitment, Content*, ed. Naomi Ellemers, Russell Spears, and Bertjan Doosje, Oxford, England: Blackwell, 35–58.

Branscombe, Nyla R. and Daniel L. Wann (1994), "Collective Self-esteem Consequences of Outgroup Derogation when a Valued Social Identity is on Trial," *European Journal of Social Psychology*, 24, 641–57.

Brown, Jonathon D. and Frances M. Gallagher (1992), "Coming to Terms with Failure: Private Self-Enhancement and Public Self-Effacement," *Journal of Experimental Social Psychology,* 28, 3–22.

Brown, Rupert J. and G. F. Ross (1982), "The Battle for Acceptance: An Exploration into the Dynamics of Intergroup Behavior," in *Social Identity and Intergroup Relations*, ed. Henri Tajfel, Cambridge, England: Cambridge University Press, 155–78.

Carmon, Ziv and Dan Ariely (2000), "Focusing on the Forgone: How Value Can Appear So Different to Buyers and Sellers," *Journal of Consumer Research*, 27, 360–70.

Carmon, Ziv, Klaus Wertenbroch, and Marcel Zeelenberg (2003), "Option Attachment: When Deliberating Makes Choosing Feel like Losing," *Journal of Consumer Research*, 30, 15–29.

Carr, Priyanka B. and Claude M. Steele (2010), "Stereotype Threat Affects Financial Decision Making," *Psychological Science*, 21, 1411-16.

Carvallo, Mauricio and Brett W. Pelham (2006), "When Fiends Become Friends: The Need to Belong and Perceptions of Personal and Group Discrimination," *Journal of Personality and Social Psychology*, 90, 94–108.

Dhar, Ravi and Klaus Wertenbroch (2000), "Consumer Choice between Hedonic and Utilitarian Goods," *Journal of Marketing Research*, 37, 60–71.

Escalas, Jennifer Edson and James R. Bettman (2005), "Self-Construal, Reference Groups, and Brand Meaning," *Journal of Consumer Research,* 32, 378–89.

Gawronski, Bertram, Galen V. Bodenhausen, and Andrew P. Becker (2007), "I Like It, Because I Like Myself: Associative Self-Anchoring and Post-Decisional Change Of Implicit Evaluations," *Journal of Experimental Social Psychology*, 43, 221–32.

Gentry, James W., Patricia F. Kennedy, Katherine Paul, and Ronald Paul Hill (1995), ""Family Transitions During Grief: Discontinuities in Household Consumption Patterns," *Journal of Business Research*, 34, 67–79.

Gibbons, Frederick X. and Meg Gerrard (1991), "Effects of Upward and Downward Social Comparison on Mood States," *Journal of Social and Clinical Psychology*, 8, 14–31.

Haslam, S. Alexander, and Stephen Reicher (2006), "Stressing the Group: Social Identity and the Unfolding Dynamics of Responses to Stress," *Journal of Applied Psychology*, 91, 1037–52.

Haslam, S. Alexander, Anne O'Brien, Jolanda Jetten, Karine Vormedal, and Sally Penna (2005), "Taking the Strain: Social Identity, Social Support, and the Experience of Stress," *British Journal of Social Psychology*, 44, 355–70.

Kahneman, Daniel, Jack L. Knetsch, and Richard H. Thaler (1990), "Experimental Tests of the Endowment Effect and the Coase Theorem," *Journal of Political Economy*, 98, 1325–48.

Kahneman, Daniel, Jack L. Knetsch, and Richard H. Thaler (1991), "The Endowment Effect, Loss Aversion, and Status Quo Bias," *Journal of Economic Perspectives*, 5, 193–206.

Kahneman, Daniel and Amos Tversky (1979), "Prospect Theory: An Analysis of Decision under Risk," *Econometrica*, 47, 263–91.

Kleine, Susan Schultz, Robert E. Kleine III, and Chris T. Allen (1995), "How is a Possession "Me" or "Not Me"? Characterizing Types and an Antecedent of Material Possession Attachment," *Journal of Consumer Research*, 22, 327–43.

Lemyre, Louise and Philip M. Smith (1985), "Intergroup Discrimination and Self-esteem in the Minimal Group Paradigm," *Journal of Personality and Social Psychology*, 49, 660–70.

Lerner, Jennifer S., Deborah A. Small, and George Loewenstein (2004), "Heart Strings and Purse Strings: Carry Over Effects of Emotions on Economic Decisions," *Psychological Science*, 15, 337–41.

Levy, Sidney, L. (1959). "Symbols for Sale," *Harvard Business Review,* 37, 117–24.

Morewedge,Carey K., Lisa L. Shu, Daniel T. Gilbert, and Timothy D. Wilson (2009), Bad Riddance Or Good Rubbish? Ownership and Not Loss Aversion Causes the Endowment Effect," *Journal of Experimental Social Psychology*, 45, 947–51.

Nayakankuppam, Dhananjay and Himanshu Mishra (2005), "The Endowment Effect: Rose-Tinted and Dark-Tinted Glasses," *Journal of Consumer Research*, 32, 390–395.

Oakes, Penelope J. and John C. Turner (1980), "Social Categorization and Intergroup Behavior: Does Minimal Intergroup Discrimination Make Social Identity More Positive?" *European Journal of Social Psychology,* 10, 295–301.

Rindfleisch, Aric, James E. Borroughs and Nancy Wong (2009), "The Safety of Objects: Materialism, Existential Insecurity and Brand Connection," *Journal of Consumer Research*, 36, 1–16.

Shaver, Philip R. and Cindy Hazan (1988), "A Biased Overview of the Study of Love," Journal of Social and Personal Relationships, 5, 473–501.

Swaminathan, Vanitha, Karen Stilley, and Rohini Ahluwalia (2009), "When Brand Personality Matters: The Moderating Role of Attachment Styles," *Journal of Consumer Research*, 35, 985–1002.

Thaler, R. H. (1980). Towards a positive theory of consumer choice. *Journal of Economic Behavior and Organization*, 1, 39–60.

Wills, Thomas A. (1981), "Downward Comparison Principles in Social Psychology," *Psychological Bulletin*, 91, 245–71.

Chocolate Cake Please! Why Do We Indulge More When it Feels More Expensive?

Rajesh Bagchi, Virginia Tech, USA
Lauren Block, Baruch College, USA

EXTENDED ABSTRACT

As unemployment and financial worries increase during this era of global recession, so too do sales of high calorie indulgence items (Miles 2009). Nutritionists call this phenomenon "recession obesity" and attribute it to the low cost of junk food relative to healthier alternatives (Everett and Grogan 2009). We suggest a psychological motivation that drives high calorie indulgences. Specifically, when the imputed costs of payment are higher, such as when making purchases using cash (vs. a credit card) or when pain associated with cash spending is higher, increasing the hedonic benefits of consumption blunts the pain of payment.

A growing literature on the psychological differences in "pain of payment" demonstrates that the use of a credit card leads to more spending compared to cash or checks (Prelec and Simester 2001). A recent explanation argues that the more transparent the outflow, as in cash (versus credit), the greater the pain of payment (Raghubir and Srivastava 2008). In other words, the imputed cost of consumption (defined as the answer to "How much is this pleasure costing me?" Prelec and Loewenstein 1998) is greater for cash than for less vivid forms of payment.

We suggest that the greater the imputed cost of consumption, the greater the likelihood of choosing a more indulgent, high-calorie food. Support can be found in the literature on mood management that demonstrates that when individuals experience negative affect, they seek reparative action, such as through shopping (Tice, Bratslavsky, and Baumeister 2001; Woodruff 2001). Individuals seeking to repair negative moods consume larger amounts of snack foods (Tice et al. 2001) and more hedonic and indulgent foods (Garg, Wansink, and Inman 2007). Because the pain of payment is higher with cash than with other decoupled forms of payments (such as credit), we posit that consumers choose more indulgent foods when purchasing with cash.

In Study 1, we tested if consumers paying in cash indulge more in higher calorie consumption than do those who pay with a card. We recruited 125 customers at a national frozen yogurt franchise retailer. Respondents reported the product purchased and provided responses to several other measures. Indulgence was measured as total calories consumed. As expected, consumers who paid with cash consumed more calories than those who paid with a card (credit or debit; M_{cash} = 439.09 k cal vs. M_{card} = 301.85 k cal; F (1, 122) = 10.85, $p < .002$) and imputed higher costs when paying with cash (M_{cash} = 4.49 vs. M_{card} = 3.84; (F (1, 122) = 6.40, $p < .02$). These costs mediated the effects of method of payment on calorie consumption.

We then replicated these findings in the lab. We recruited 147 undergraduates and first made the payment mechanism (cash or credit) salient, then asked participants to choose products from a menu using that payment method. Consumers who paid with cash selected higher calorie foods relative to those who paid with card (M_{cash} = 500.92 k cal vs. M_{card} = 423.49 k cal; F (1, 144) = 4.60, $p < .04$) and also imputed higher costs (M_{cash} = 3.70 vs. M_{card} = 3.25; F (1, 143) = 3.95, $p < .05$; one participant did not respond).

Because our theorizing is predicated on differences in imputed costs associated with cash vs. credit rather than method of payment per se, in Study 3, we vary earning difficulty. The more difficult it is to earn money, the more painful it is to make a payment, and the higher the imputed cost will be. We recruited 229 undergraduates to select food items for an afternoon snack from a menu. All partici-

pants were told they would be paying with cash earned at their new job. As expected, when difficulty of earning was higher versus lower, consumers selected foods with more calories ($M_{high\ difficulty}$ = 430.77 k cal vs. $M_{low\ difficulty}$ = 348.57 k cal; F (1, 226) = 6.82, $p < .01$). Moreover, participants' perceptions of imputed costs were higher when difficulty of earning money was higher ($M_{high\ difficulty}$ = 4.12 vs. $M_{low\ difficulty}$ = 3.24; F (1, 226) = 24.50, $p < .0001$). Imputed costs also mediated the effect of difficulty of earning on indulgence. We also found that consumers were happier when they consumed more calories in the high imputed costs condition relative to the low imputed costs condition. Thus, the pain of payment is mitigated by an increase in positive affect from consuming the indulgent item. We also test this in Study 4.

Study 4 used a 2 (Imputed Cost: Difficult vs. Easy) x 2 (Food Purchase: Indulgent vs. Not-indulgent) between subjects design, identical to study 3 with the exception that we told half the participants they purchased a slice of a chocolate cake, while the rest learned they purchased a fruit salad.

Participants completed the PANAS scale twice, immediately after the pain of payment manipulation and again after they were informed about food choice. The difference between these two time measurements was regressed on the independent variables. A significant main effect of imputed cost (F (1, 66) = 3.81, $p < .06$) and an interaction of imputed cost by food purchase emerged (F (1, 66) = 4.06, $p < .05$). The purchase of an indulgent dessert increases positive affect when the imputed cost of payment is high versus when the imputed cost is low (F (1, 66) = 7.75, $p < .01$). There is no difference in positive affect for the non-indulgent dessert across levels of imputed cost (F < 1). When imputed cost was high, choosing the chocolate cake led to a directionally higher increase in affect relative to when the fruit salad was chosen (F (1, 66) = 2.27, $p = .13$). These effects were not significant when imputed cost was low.

Together these studies suggest that when imputed costs are high, consumers indulge more. These finding have important implications for consumers, managers, and public policy analysts, but particularly for low-income consumers, who tend to have less access to available credit and for whom earning sustainable wages is more difficult.

REFERENCES

Bublitz, Melissa, Laura A. Peracchio, and Lauren G. Block (2010), "Why Did I Eat That? Perspectives on Food Decision Making and Dietary Restraint," *Journal of Consumer Psychology*, 20, 239-58.

Connolly, Terry, Lisa D. Ordóñatez, and Richard Coughlan (1997), "Regret and Responsibility in the Evaluation of Decision Outcomes," *Organizational Behavior and Human Decision Processes*, 70 (April), 73-85.

Everett, Wendy and Paul S. Grogan (2009), "The Recession is Making us Sick," [http://www.boston.com/bostonglobe/editorial_opinion/oped/articles/2009/07/02/the_recession_is_making_us_sick?mode=PF].

Feinberg, Richard A. (1986), "Credit Cards as Spending Facilitating Stimuli: A Conditioning Interpretation," *Journal of Consumer Research*, 13 (December) 348-56.

Garg, Nikita, Brian Wansink, and J. Jeffrey Inman (2007), "The Influence of Incidental Affect on Consumers' Food Intake," *Journal of Marketing*, 71 (January), 194-206.

Klinger, Eric (1975), "Consequences of Commitment to and Disengagement from Incentives," *Psychological Review*, 82 (1), 1-25.

Mick, David G. and Michelle DeMoss (1990), "Self-Gifts: Phenomenological Insights from Four Contexts," *Journal of Consumer Research*, 17 (December), 322-32.

Miles, Stephanie (2009), "Recession Diet: Comfort Food," (accessed September 2010), [available at http://www.recessionwire.com/2009/07/28/recession-diet-comfort-food/].

Preacher, Kristopher J. and Andrew F. Hayes (2004), "SPSS and SAS Procedures for Estimating Indirect Effects in Simple Mediation Models," *Behavior Research Methods, Instruments, and Computers,* 36 (4), 717-31.

Preacher, Kristopher J. and Andrew F. Hayes (2008), "Asymptotic and Resampling Strategies for Assessing and Comparing Indirect Effects in Multiple Mediator Models," *Behavior Research Methods,* 40 (3), 879-91.

Prelec, Drazen and George Loewenstein (1998), "The Red and the Black: Mental Accounting of Savings and Debt," *Marketing Science*, 17 (1), 4-28.

--- and Duncan Simester (2001), " Always Leave Home Without It: A Further Investigation of the Credit-Card Effect on Willingness to Pay," *Marketing Letters*, 12 (1), 5-12.

Raghubir, Priya and Joydeep Srivastava (2008), "Monopoly Money: The Effect of Payment Coupling and Form on Spending Behavior," *Journal of Experimental Psychology: Applied*, 14 (3), 213-25.

Thomas, Manoj, Kalpesh K. Desai, and Satheeshkumar Seeenivasan (2011), "How Credit Card Payments Increase Unhealthy Food Purchases: Visceral Regulation of Vices," *Journal of Consumer Research*, 38 (June).

Tice, Dianne M., Ellen Bratslavsky, and Roy F. Baumeister (2001), "Emotional Distress Regulation takes Precedence over Impulse Control: If you Feel Bad, Just Do It!" *Journal of Personality and Social Psychology*, 80 (1), 53-67.

Woodruff, Robert B. (1997), "Customer Value: The Next Source for Competitive Advantage," *Journal of the Academy of Marketing Science*, 25 (2), 139-53.

Zhao Xinshu, John G. Lynch, Jr., and Qimei Chen (2010), "Reconstructing Baron and Kenny: Myths and Truths about Mediation Analysis," *Journal of Consumer Research*, 37 (August), 197-206.

Identity Representation in Customization

Kelly Herd, Indiana University, USA
Page Moreau, University of Colorado, USA

EXTENDED ABSTRACT

Identity, what comes to mind when we think of ourselves, includes two major components: a personal identity related to the independent self (i.e., individual traits, characteristics or goals) and a social identity related to the interdependent self (i.e., traits, characteristics and goals that are linked to group membership or personal relationships) (Kirmani 2009; Oyserman 2009). These identities have important implications for the way the self is construed and ultimately represented (e.g., Brewer 1991; Brewer and Gardner 1996; Kleine, Kleine and Allen 1995; Oyserman 2009). Because consumers can have multiple identities that are simultaneously activated and driving behavior (e.g., Oyserman 2009), the current work will separate identity motives (personal and social) and differentially examine their influence on consumers' valuation of customized products and meaning creation. We propose that identity-based motivation, the "readiness to engage in identity-congruent action" (Oyserman 2009, p. 250), is a key factor both prompting consumers to engage in customization activities and influencing how they evaluate the resulting outcomes.

Our first study examines how the activation of an identity motivation enhances the positive influence of design freedom (i.e., the ability to upload images) on consumers' reactions to customized products (i.e., their evaluations at the time of design and satisfaction at delivery).

In this study, two factors were manipulated between-participants: (1) Identity Prime (identity prime vs. no prime) and (2) Design Freedom (low vs. high). All participants go to a live website, designed "skins" (covers for their cell phones or MP3 players) and then received the actual product several weeks later, at which point we capture satisfaction measures.

We find that product evaluations were higher when design freedom was high ($M_{High Design Freedom}$ = 5.6 vs. $M_{Low Design Freedom}$ = 4.8; $F(1, 94) = 6.61$, $p = .01$). This effect was enhanced when participants were exposed to the identity prime, and the interaction was significant ($F(1, 94) = 4.64$, $p < .05$). When participants were primed with identity, the level of design freedom mattered significantly ($M_{Identity Prime, High Design Freedom}$ = 5.8 vs. $M_{Identity Prime, Low Design Freedom}$ = 4.7; $F(1, 47) = 4.14$, $p < .05$). When participants were not exposed to the identity prime, however, the effect was less pronounced ($M_{No Prime, High Design Freedom}$ = 5.5 vs. $M_{No Prime, Low Design Freedom}$ = 5.0; $F(1, 46) = .86$, n/s). We also find that at delivery ten days later, these effects remained.

When identity-primed participants were asked to think about the events in their lives where the device had played an important role, we found great variance in the types of events and experiences that participants described. Thus, in order to better understand the influence of different identity motives on customization, it is important to isolate the effects of these different identity-based motivations (social and personal).

In this study, all participants (N = 87) design customizable coffee mugs and we manipulate two factors were manipulated between-participants: (1) Motivation Primed (social vs. personal identity) and (2) Design Freedom (low vs. high). A two-way ANOVA revealed a significant interaction between the two independent factors ($F(1,84) = 4.6$, $p < .05$). Participants reported higher evaluations of their mugs when allowed high versus low design freedom $M_{High Design Freedom}$ = 5.6 vs. $M_{Low Design Freedom}$ = 5.1). This effect was more pronounced for those primed with personal identity motivations ($M_{Personal, High Design Freedom}$ = 5.7 vs. $M_{Personal, Low Design Freedom}$ = 4.7; $F(1, 42) = 8.4$, $p < .01$) than with

social identity motivations ($M_{Social, High Design Freedom}$ = 5.5 vs. $M_{Social, Low Design Freedom}$ = 5.5; $F(1, 41) = .1$, n/s). The analysis also revealed a significant interaction between the two manipulated factors on satisfaction at pickup ($F(1, 49) = 4.13$, $p < .05$).

Finally, the third study examines how the situational activation of personal identity motivation moderates the effects of a chronic identity motivation (need for uniqueness) to influence consumers' reactions to customized products. As Berger and Heath (2007) indicate, individuals have a "drive to differentiate themselves from others," a need for autonomy influenced both by the individual's relatively stable need for uniqueness (NFU; Tian et al. 2001) and by situational factors leading the person to feel undifferentiated (p. 121).

All participants (N = 67) in this study design a t-shirt using an online website. We manipulate personal identity (salient vs. not salient) and measures chronic need for uniqueness (Tian et al. 2001). We find a main effect of NFU on evaluations (b = .43, t = 2.99, $p < .01$), as well as a main effect of motivation salience (b = 15.9, t = 2.42, $p = .01$). The main effects were qualified by an interaction (b = -.39, t = -2.20, $p < .05$). To better interpret the interaction, we used a spotlight analysis (Fitzsimons 2008) and find that the slope of NFU was significant and positive when personal identity motivation was not made salient (b = .08, t = 2.11, $p < .05$). When the motivation was made salient, however, the slope of NFU was not significantly different than zero (b = -.01, t = -.45, n/s).

From this study, we conclude that simply making personal identity salient at the time of customization can increase product evaluations for consumers with a low chronic identity motivation and allow them to find greater meaning in the products they create.

These studies demonstrate that simply making salient an identity motivation prior to design can significantly influence product evaluations, product satisfaction and the effectiveness of the customization options (i.e., design freedom). Franke and Schreier (2008) suggest that providing consumers with a sufficiently large solution space is essential for customization companies. Our research qualifies this finding, suggesting that customization options offering a high degree of freedom (i.e., image upload) are only effective when certain identity motives are driving customization. Such a finding is important for firms striving to maximize the profitability of customized offerings.

REFERENCES

Berger, Jonah and Chip Heath (2007), "Where Consumers Diverge from Others: Identity Signaling and Product Domains," *Journal of Consumer Research*, 34 (2), 121-34.

Brewer, Marilynn B. (1991), "The Social Self: On Being the Same and Different at the Same Time," *Personality and Social Psychology Bulletin*, 17 (5), 475-82.

Dellaert, Benedict G. C. and Stefan Stremersch (2005), "Marketing Mass-Customized Products: Striking a Balance Between Utility and Complexity," *Journal of Marketing Research*, 42 (2), 219-27.

Fitzsimmons, Gavan J. (2008), "Death to Dichotomizing," *Journal of Consumer Research*, 35 (June), 5–8.

Franke, Nikolaus, Peter Keinz, Christophe Steger (2009), "Testing the Value of Customization: When Do Customers Really Prefer Products Tailored to Their Preferences?" *Journal of Marketing*, 73 (5), 103–121.

Franke, Nikolaus, and Frank Piller (2004), "Value Creation by Toolkits for User Innovation and Design: The Case of the Watch Market," *Journal of Product Innovation Management*, 21 (6), 401–415.

Franke, Nikolaus and Martin Schreier (2008), "Product Uniqueness as a Driver of Customer Utility in Mass Customization," *Marketing Letters*, 19 (1), 93-107.

Franke, Nikolaus, Martin Schreier, and Ulrike Kaiser (2010), "The 'I Designed it Myself' Effect in Mass Customization," *Management Science*, 56 (January), 125–140.

Hirsch, Evan, Matt Egol, and Karla Martin (2005), "The Five Principles of Smart Customization," *Booz Allen Hamilton Publications*, April 19, 2005.

Irwin, Julie R. and Gary H. McClelland (2003), "Negative Consequences of Dichotomizing Continuous Predictor Variables," *Journal of Marketing Research*, 40 (3), 366-71.

Jaruzelski, Barry H. and W. Frank Jones (2007), "Booz Allen Manufacturing Analysts Survey the 2007 Industrial Landscape: Six Issues Will Separate the Winners from the Losers Hamilton Releases 2007 Prognostications," *Manufacturing and Technology News*, 14 (1), p. 6-9.

Kirmani, Amna (2009), "The Self and the Brand," *Journal of Consumer Psychology*, 19 (3), 271-75.

Kleine, Susan Schultz, Robert E. Kleine III, and Chris T. Allen (1995), "How Is a Possession "Me" Or "Not Me"? Characterizing Types and an Antecedent of Material Possession Attachment," *Journal of Consumer Research*, 22 (3), 327-43.

Norton, Michael I., Daniel Mochon, and Dan Ariely (2010), "The 'IKEA' Effect: When Labor Leads to Love," Working Paper.

Oyserman, Daphna (2009), "Identity-based Motivation: Implications for Action-readiness, Procedural-readiness, and Consumer Behavior," *Journal of Consumer Psychology*, 19 (3), 250-60.

Randall, Taylor, Christian Terwiesch, and Karl T. Ulrich (2005), "Principles for User Design of Customized Products," *California Management Review*, 47 (4), 68-85.

Randall, Taylor, Christian Terwiesch, and Karl T. Ulrich (2007), "User Design of Customized Products," *Marketing Science*, 26 (2), 268-80.

Richins, Marsha L. (1994a), "Valuing Things: The Public and Private Meanings of Possessions," *Journal of Consumer Research*, 21 (3), 504-21.

--- (1994b), "Special Possessions and the Expression of Material Values," *Journal of Consumer Research*, 21 (3), 522-33.

Snyder, C. R. and Howard L. Fromkin (1977), "Abnormality as a Positive Characteristic: The Development and Validation of a Scale Measuring Need for Uniqueness," *Journal of Abnormal Psychology*, 86 (5), 518-27.

Tian, Kelly Tepper, William O. Bearden, and Gary L. Hunter (2001), "Consumers' Need for

Uniqueness: Scale Development and Validation," *Journal of Consumer Research*, 28 (1), 50-66.

von Hippel, Eric (2001), "PERSPECTIVE: User Toolkits for Innovation," *Journal of Product Innovation Management*, 18 (4), 247-57.

von Hippel, Eric and Ralph Katz (2002), "Shifting Innovation to Users via Toolkits," *Management Science*, 48 (7), 821-33.

White, Katherine and Jennifer Argo (2010), "When Imitation Doesn't Flatter: The Role of Consumer Distinctiveness in Responses to Mimicry," Working paper.

White, Katherine and Darren W. Dahl (2007), "Are All Out-Groups Created Equal? Consumer Identity and Dissociative Influence," *Journal of Consumer Research*, 34 (4), 525-36.

Talisman Insurance: Does Insurance Coverage Help You Avoid Tempting Fate?

Eric Dolansky, Brock University, Canada
Robert Schindler, Rutgers University, USA
Grant Adams, Rutgers University, USA

EXTENDED ABSTRACT

The feeling that one is "tempting fate" is a common one, and this type of magical thinking could also extend to consumer decisions about insurance. Three studies are presented in which it is shown that individuals estimate a lower probability of a prized possession breaking when it is insured.

In our everyday lives we have all come into contact with magical thinking. Often, everyday instances of magical thinking involve a reluctance to "tempt fate." For example, one might feel that if an umbrella is left at home, there will be a heavy rain. The purchase of property insurance, such as automobile insurance and homeowners insurance, might also be related to magical thinking. While insurance is designed to protect against the financial consequences of a negative event, it might also be viewed as a "talisman" – a means of protecting against the occurrence of the negative event (Tykocinski 2008). The question addressed by this research concerns whether there may be a magical component to the consumer's motivation to buy property insurance.

In a series of experimental studies, Risen and Gilovich (2008) found that when a test scenario's protagonist carried out an action that tempted fate, the protagonist was judged more likely to suffer a negative event than a protagonist who did not tempt fate. Schindler (2009) found that in Japanese price advertisements the number 8, which is considered lucky in Japanese culture, occurred among the rightmost digits of advertised prices far more often than did any other nonzero digit. Kramer and Block (2008) found that positive superstitions pertaining to product attributes (such as color) result in higher satisfaction ratings after product failure.

There is also evidence that the motivation for purchasing property insurance goes beyond the knowledge that one will receive compensation in the event of a financial loss (Tykocinski 2008). An example of what might be involved in this further motivation is provided by Hsee and Kunreuther (2000). They found that, even if the amount of monetary compensation is held constant, the consumer's affection for an object affects his or her desire to have it insured.

Three experimental studies were carried out to test five hypotheses related to talisman insurance. Study 1 was designed to investigate whether the presence of insurance would lead to lower probability estimates of a prized possession breaking (H1) and whether superstitiousness moderates that effect (H2). The scenario presented was one in which respondents imagined that they had just moved to a new city and had left back an heirloom punchbowl. A cousin offered to bring the punchbowl, and whether it was insured differed across conditions. Participants were asked to estimate the likelihood of the bowl breaking en route. A superstitiousness scale was used to create the second condition in the study.

This study showed that while there was no effect of insurance on likelihood estimates of breakage among low-superstitiousness participants (determined by median split), there was a difference in these estimates among high-superstitiousness participants ($p = 0.041$). There was also a significant interaction ($p = 0.02$), supporting H2.

Study 2 used the same design and scenario as Study 1, but rather than examine dispositional superstition, superstitiousness was manipulated using a priming task. It was predicted that the prime would produce effects similar to those based on dispositional super-

stition in Study 1 (H3). A word-completion task was designed with one version having superstition-related words (e.g. "superstition," "luck," "charm") and another version having only neutral words (e.g. "superhero," "duck," "chant").

The results indicated that the primes were successful. Whereas there were no effects of insurance in the non-primed group, there was a significant effect of insurance in the primed group ($p = 0.01$). The interaction found in Study 1 was also replicated here ($p = 0.42$) Furthermore, in both Studies 1 and 2 questions were asked concerning punchbowl mishaps not covered by insurance, such as whether it would be scratched or arrive late. In both studies it was found that the likelihood estimates of these mishaps were largely not affected by the breakage insurance.

Study 3 examined the role of affect toward the object, keeping constant the size of the insurance payment. Within the paradigm of talisman insurance, it seems that greater affect toward an object would lead to more of a sense that moving it would be tempting fate and thus there would a greater perceived likelihood that the object would be lost (H4). A greater probability of loss would lead to insurance having greater value as protector, and there would be higher willingness-to-pay for insurance (H5).

A different moving scenario was used in this study. An antique clock that the participant is told he has high [low] affect for is being moved, and may get lost. Insurance can be bought that will provide $100 in the case of loss. Participants were asked to provide their maximum willingness-to-pay for this insurance. In the second part of the study, participants were told that policies had changed, and that the clock would now be insured [uninsured] regardless of previous willingness-to-pay. They were then asked to estimate the likelihood of the loss of the clock.

The results of Study 3 confirm the finding of Studies 1 and 2 that the presence of insurance lowers the perceived probability of loss. They also support H4 and H5: – affect toward the clock increased the estimated probability that the clock would be lost ($p = 0.006$) and there was a significant correlation between probability of loss and willingness-to-pay for insurance ($p = 0.003$). These results provide evidence that there is a talisman component to insurance and that affect increases the sense that protection is required.

These studies constitute first steps toward understanding how consumers may act on a sense of tempting fate. The findings indicate that individuals do, at least under some circumstances, view insurance as conferring protection that it rationally cannot. More broadly, this investigation illustrates how traditional figures of speech, such as "tempting fate," may correspond to demonstrable psychological phenomena and illustrates how subjecting these traditional concepts to scientific scrutiny can both have practical and theoretical implications.

REFERENCES

Hsee, Christopher K. and Howard C. Kunreuther (2000), "The Affection Effect in Insurance Decisions," *Journal of Risk and Uncertainty* 20:2, 141-159.

Kramer, Thomas and Lauren Block (2008), "Conscious and Nonconscious Components of Superstitious Beliefs in Judgment and Decision Making," *Journal of Consumer Research*, 34 (April), 783-793.

Risen, Jane L. and Thomas Gilovich (2008), "Why People Are Reluctant to Tempt Fate," *Journal of Personality and Social Psychology*, 95 (2), 297-307.

Schindler, Robert M. (2009), "Patterns of Price Endings Used in US and Japanese Price Advertising," *International Marketing Review*, 26 (1), 17-29.

Sloman, Steven A. (1996), "The Empirical Case for Two Systems of Reasoning," *Psychological Bulletin*, 119 (1), 3-22.

Tykocinski, Orit E. (2008), "Insurance, Risk and Magical Thinking," *Personality and Social Psychology Bulletin*, 34, 1346-1356.

Body and Mind: How Mindfulness Enhances Consumers' Responsiveness to Physiological Cues in Food Consumption

Evelien van de Veer, Wageningen University, The Netherlands
Erica van Herpen, Wageningen University, The Netherlands
Hans van Trijp, Wageningen University, The Netherlands

EXTENDED ABSTRACT

External cues in the eating environment regularly override physiological hunger and satiety cues, which has led scholars to characterize eating as *mindless* (Wansink 2004). Whereas it is well known that consumers often fail to attend to physiological cues in their eating behaviour, it is not known whether potential remedies exist to help consumers be more responsive to these cues. The current study demonstrates that *mindfulness,* a state of 'heightened awareness of what is going on at the present moment'(Brown and Ryan 2003) improves consumers' responsiveness to physiological cues. We demonstrate this for mindfulness as a trait as well as for state induced mindfulness, and show that even a short mindfulness training is powerful enough to affect consumers' responsiveness to hunger and satiety cues. Finally, the object of attention matters: Only mindful attention to the body helps consumers to rely on these cues.

The body's feedback system affects not only within-meal consumption but also, and perhaps more importantly, when and how much to eat at a later point in time. This is important because being able to compensate for previous consumption appears to be a critical determinant of maintaining a stable body weight (Cornier et al 2004). Compensation ability is generally impaired when consumers are distracted (Higgs and Woodward, 2006; Mittal et al in press). Consumers may also chronically be more or less responsive to physiological cues. Restrained eating, a form of constant but often unsuccessful dieting, has frequently been associated with a failure to compensate for previous consumption (Herman and Mack 1975) Constant dieting has apparently taught them to ignore bodily sensations (Heatherton, Polivy and Herman 1989). In contrast, people who regularly exercise appear better at compensating for previous consumption (Long, Hart and Morgan 2002). Combining these findings gives an indication that attention, and in particular attention to the body, plays an important role in responsiveness to hunger and satiety cues.

Mindfulness is defined as an 'enhanced attention to what is going on at the present moment' (Brown and Ryan 2003) Mindfulness has been related to beneficial psychological health outcomes, mostly within clinical contexts and longer-term interventions. We propose that mindfulness' ability to foster a mental state of focused attention is relevant for responsiveness to physiological cues. Mindfulness trainings vary in whether they teach individuals to focus attention on bodily sensations, stimuli in the environment or on both simultaneously (Bishop et al. 2004). In the current study we therefore also examine whether the object of mindful attention matters. Can mindful attention per se increase responsiveness to hunger cues, or does it matter where this attention is directed?

In Experiment 1 we assessed the effects of chronic mindfulness assessed by the MAAS (Brown and Ryan, 2003) on compensation for previous food consumption. Participants consumed either a high caloric or a low caloric milkshake. In a second part of the experiment, participants evaluated neutral video fragments with a bowl of M&M's placed next to their screens. The amount of M&Ms consumed constituted the dependent variable. The results show that the interaction between caloric content of the milkshake and dispositional mindfulness significantly predicted consumption amount. More specifically, high mindful participants ate fewer M&Ms when they had previously consumed a high caloric milkshake, than when they had previously consumed a low caloric milkshake. For low mindful participants, the effect of the caloric content of the milkshake did not affect later consumption.

Experiment 2 assessed whether a mental state of mindfulness can be elicited through short audio fragments of mindfulness instructions. Participants listened to a short mindfulness instruction (around four minutes) recorded by a yoga teacher. These instructions focused either on the body or on the environment. In the control condition, participants listened to a recorded story. Results demonstrated that both mindfulness instructions elicited similar levels of state mindfulness, but with foci of attention on the body and environment, respectively.

In Experiment 3, we tested the effects of these same mindfulness manipulations on individuals' capability to compensate for previous consumption. Participants listened to one of the mindfulness instructions conditions. They then consumed either a small Snickers or a large Snickers. In a second part of the experiment, participants evaluated cookies. At the end of the experiment, participants' cookie consumption was assessed. In line with our expectations, there was a significant interaction between portion size and mindfulness. Only in the attention to body condition did portion size have an effect on cookie consumption, such that participants who had been served a large chocolate bar ate fewer cookies than participants who been served a small chocolate bar.

Together, these experiments show that mindfulness improves an consumers' responsiveness to internal cues in food consumption. Furthermore, these results indicate that it matters where this attention is directed, as only mindful attention to the body produced these results. Our findings are in line with findings that have shown that distraction undermines compensation behaviour, namely we have shown that the opposite side of the coin, an enhanced state of attention, can improve compensation behaviour. Our findings add to the mindfulness literature in that, until now, the concept of mindfulness has mostly been applied in clinical contexts. For mindfulness research in general, it may be worthwhile to distinguish between the object of attention in different mindfulness trainings, as our findings suggest these have different effects.

On a practical level, our study shows that consumers can enhance their responsiveness to hunger and satiety cues, an important determinant of a constant body weight. Our findings give consumers more guidance on how responsiveness to hunger and satiety cues can be achieved. Simply focusing on several general and more accessible aspects of the body, such as breathing and posture, can improve eating patterns.

REFERENCES

Alberts, Hugo J., Sandra Mulkens, Maud Smeets and Roy Thewissen (2010), "Coping with food cravings: Investigating the potential of a mindfulness-based intervention," *Appetite*, 55, 160-163.

Bacon, Linda, Judith S. Stern, Marta D. van Loan and Nancy L. Keim (2005), "Size Acceptance and Intuitive Eating Improve Health for Obese Female Chronic Dieters," *Journal of American Dietetic Association*, 105 (6), 929-936.

Bellisle, France, Anne-Marie Dalix and Gerard Slama (2004), "Non food-related environmental stimuli induce increased meal intake in healthy women: Comparison of television viewing versus listening to a recorded story in laboratory settings,"*Appetite,* 43 (2), 175–180.

Bellissimo, Nick, Paul B. Pencharz, Scott G. Thomas, and Harvey G. Anderson (2007), "Effect of television viewing at mealtime on food intake after a glucose preload in boys," *Pediatric Research,* 61(6), 745-749.

Bishop, Scott R., Mark Lau, Shauna Shapiro, Linda Carlson, Nicole D. Anderson, James Carmody et al. (2004). "Mindfulness: A proposed operational definition, "*Clinical Psychology: Science and Practice,* 11, 230-241.

Brown, Kirk W. and Richard M. Ryan (2003), "The benefits of being present: Mindfulness and its role in psychological well-being," *Journal of Personality and Social Psychology,* 84(4), 822-848.

Brown, Kirk W., Richard M. Ryan and J. David Creswell (2007), "Mindfulness: Theoretical foundations and evidence for its salutary effects," *Psychological Inquiry,* 18(4), 211-237.

Blundell, John E., James R. Stubbs, Cheryl Golding, Fiona Croden, Rahul Alam, Stephen Whybrow (2005), "Resistance and susceptibility to weight gain: Individual variability in response to a high-fat diet,"*Physiology & Behavior,* 86, 614-622.

Center for Mindfulness and Justice, http://www. mindfulnessandjustice.org

Cornier, Marc-Andre, Gary K. Grunwald, Susan L. Johnson, and Daniel H. Bessesen (2004), "Effects of short-term overfeeding on hunger, satiety, and energy intake in thin and reduced-obese individuals," *Appetite*, 43, 253-259.

Farb, Norman A., Adam K. Anderson, Helen Mayberg, Jim Bean, Deborah McKeon, Zindel V. Segal (2010), " Attending to the present: mindfulness meditation reveals distinct neural modes of self-reference, " *Social Cognitive and Affective Neuroscience,* 2, 313-322.

Heatherton, Todd F., Janet Polivy, and Peter C. Herman (1989), " Restraint and internal responsiveness: Effects of placebo manipulations of hunger on eating, " *Journal of Abnormal Psychology,* 98, 89-92.

Herman, Peter C. and Deborah A. Mack (1975), "Restrained and unrestrained eating," *Journal of Personality,* 43 (4), 647-660.

Higgs, Suzanne and Morgan Woodward (2009), "Television watching during lunch increases afternoon snack intake of young women," *Appetite,* 52 (1), 39-43.

Holzel, Britta K., James Carmody, Mark Vangel, Christina Congleton, Sita M. Yerramsetti, Tim Gard and Sara W. Lazar (in press), "Mindfulness practice leads to increases in regional brain gray matter density, " *Psychiatry Research: Neuroimaging.*

Jebb, Susan A., Mario Siervo, Gema Fruhbeck, Gail R. Goldberg, Peter R. Murgatroyd and Andrew M. Prentice (2006),"Variability of appetite control mechanisms in response to 9 weeks of progressive overfeeding in humans," *International Journal of Obesity,* 30, 1160-1162.

Jha, Amishi P., Jason Krompunger and Micheal J. Baime (2007), "Mindfulness training modifies subsystems of attention, "*Cognitive Affective and Behavioral Neuroscience,* 7(2), 109-119.

Jha, Amishi P., Elizabeth A. Stanley, Anastasia Kiyonaga, Ling Wong and Lois Gelfand (2010), "Examining the protective effects of mindfulness training on working memory capacity and affective experience, " *Emotion,* 10(1), 54-64.

Kabat-Zinn, Jon. (1990). *Full catastrophic living: Using the wisdom of your body and mind to face stress, pain and illness.* New York: Delta publishing.

May, Jon, Jackie Andrade, Helen Batey, Lisa-Marie Berry and David J. Kavanagh (in press), "Impact of attentional instructions on intrusive thoughts about snack foods, " *Appetite.*

Mittal, Dolly, Richard J. Stevenson, Megan J. Oaten and Laurie A. Miller (in press), "Snacking while watching TV impairs food recall and promotes food intake on a later TV free test meal, " *Applied Cognitive Psychology.*

Long, Samantha.J., Kathryn Hart and Linda M. Morgan (2002), "The ability of habitual exercise to influence appetite and food intake in response to high- and low-energy preloads in man," *British Journal of Nutrition,* 87 (5), 517-523.

Smith, Janna M. and Tanya L. Ditschun (2009), " Controlling satiety: how environmental factors influence food intake, " *Trends in Food Science and Technology*, 20, 271-277.

US army, http://www.army.mil/-news/2010/08/04/43269-mindfulness-helps-soldiers-cope/

Valentine, Elizabeth R., Philip L. Sweet (1999), "Meditation and attention: A comparison of the effects of concentrative and mindfulness meditation on sustained attention, " *Mental Health, Religion and Culture,* 2, 59-70.

Wansink, Brian (2004), "Environmental factors that increase the food intake and consumption volume of unknowing consumers, " *Annual Review of Nutrition,* 24, 455-479.

Wansink, Brian, Collin R. Payne, Pierre Chandon (2007), "Internal and External Cues of Meal Cessation: The French Paradox Redux?" *Obesity,* 15 (12), 2920-2924.

Wansink, Brian (2010), "From mindless eating to mindlessly eating better," *Physiology & Behavior,"* 100, 454-463.

Wenk-Sormaz, Heidi (2005), "Meditation can reduce habitual responding," *Alternative Therapies in Health and Medicine,* 11(2), 42-58.

Stereotype Processing's Effect on the Impact of the Myth/Fact Message Format: The Role of Personal Relevance

Marie Yeh, Kent State University, USA
Robert D. Jewell, Kent State University, USA
Michael Y. Hu, Kent State University, USA

EXTENDED ABSTRACT

This study examines the myth/fact message format within the social marketing context of mental illness (MI). People with mental illness are stereotyped and stigmatized such that many social marketing efforts have been pursued to change widely held misperceptions about them (Hinshaw and Stier 2008). One method used to counter widely held misperceptions for mental illness, as well as a number of other social and health issues, is the myth/fact message format, which frames the message by first stating the myth, the incorrect viewpoint, which is then followed by the counter viewpoint labeled as fact. The use of the myth/fact message in the context of mental illness includes countering negative aspects of the stereotype that surrounds the ailment.

It has been well documented that stereotypes, as well-learned beliefs about the characteristics, attributes and behaviors of members of certain groups, are automatically activated in the presence of a member (or symbolic equivalent) of a stigmatized group; however, those motivated to do so, can intentionally inhibit the automatically retrieval of stereotypes (Devine 1989). This suggests that only those with some kind of motivation will suppress the stereotype. We hypothesized that personal relevance will provide this motivation and that without it, differences in attitudes will not occur due to differences in message format. In addition, we hypothesized that the use of the myth/fact message format, which explicitly expresses a negative aspect of the stereotype, strengthens the association of the negative aspect (Fazio et al 1986; Hunt and Ellis 1999) and consequently, weakens the following fact's ability to discount that negative view. Conversely, utilizing a fact only, rather than the myth/fact approach, should instantiate a new positive belief without reinforcing the negative aspects of the stereotype. But this effect will only be seen in those with personal relevance who have the motivation to suppress the stereotype.

As a commonly used social marketing format, the intent of those who use the myth/fact message is arguably to educate and correct misperceptions. Therefore, we also examined the differential effect of message format on perceived learning. Here we hypothesize the exact opposite effect of personal relevance from what was hypothesized regarding message format's effect on attitudes. As those with personal relevance are familiar with the issue of mental illness, we hypothesize that those with personal relevance will not report differential levels of perceived learning due to message format. However, those without personal relevance would view the myth/fact message format as a heuristic cue for learning and would report higher levels of perceived learning under the myth/fact format than under the fact only condition.

320 students from a large Midwestern university were surveyed in a 2 x 2 x 3 x 2 factorial with one within subject factor (time 1 and time 2) and three between subjects factors, message format (Myth/Fact vs. Fact only) which was manipulated, number of messages (1,3 or 5) which was also manipulated and personal relevance (relevant or not) which was measured. As no differences were found on the number of messages, we collapsed the analysis across number of repetition cells. Attitudes towards mental illness as measured by a scale created for the study and perceived learning about mental illness scale were dependent variables.

Our results demonstrated the differential impact of the myth/fact versus fact only message format on attitudes towards mental illness; specifically, a fact only appeal was more effective in engendering desired behavioral and attitudinal responses. This effect, however, was moderated by personal relevance with MI such that those high in personal relevance reported more unfavorable attitudes under myth/fact than under fact only; those low in personal relevance showed no difference. This finding supports our first set of hypotheses and indicates the role of motivation in suppressing the stereotype. Personal relevance also impacted perceived learning differently than attitudes such that those low in personal relevance reported higher levels of self-reported learning than those high in personal relevance.

We suggest that those for whom the issue of MI is personally relevant were motivated to suppress the stereotype thus overall their attitudes towards mental illness were more favorable. However, those with personal relevance with MI had an existing cognitive schema of non-stereotypical beliefs which was reinforced by the fact only message while the inclusion of the myth reinforced the negative aspects of the stereotype. Personal relevance had the opposite effect on perceived learning reinforcing well-established research findings that find that learning does not lead to attitude change. Findings suggest that while the myth/fact message format may be more effective in enhancing people's perception of learning, its effects on attitudes, the typical focal point on social marketing campaigns targeting misconceptions about stereotyped and stigmatized groups, may be the opposite. Social marketers should carefully consider the goal of a campaign before deciding to use the myth/fact message format.

REFERENCES

Alonso, Jordi et al. (2009), *"Perceived stigma among individuals with common mental disorders,"* Journal of Affective Disorders, 118(1) 180-186.

Altemeyer, Bob (1996), *The Authoritarian Spector.* Cambridge, MA: Harvard University Press.

Belch, George E. (1981), "An Examination of Comparative and Noncomparative Television Commercials: The Effects of Claim Variation and Repetition on Cognitive Response and Message Acceptance," *Journal of Market Research,* 18 (August), 222-49.

Belch, George E. and Michael A. Belch (2009), "Source, Message and Channel Factors," in *Advertising and Promotion: An Integrated Marketing Communication Perspective,* Anonymous New York, NY: McGraw-Hill Irwin, 174-202.

Bither, Stewart W., Dolich, Ira J. and Elaine B. Nell (1971), "The Application of Attitude Immunization Techniques in Marketing," *Journal of Marketing Research,* 8 (February), 56-61.

Devine, Patricia G. (1989), "Stereotypes and Prejudice: Their Automatic and Controlled Components," *Journal of Personality and Social Psychology,* 56 5-18.

Etgar, Michael and Stephen A. Goodwin. (1982), "One-sided Versus Two-sided Comparative Message Appeals for New Brand Introduction," *Journal of Consumer Research*, 8(4) 460-65.

Fazio et al. (1986), "On the Automatic Activation of Attitudes," *Journal of Personality and Social Psychology,* 50 (2) 229-38.

Finkelstein, Joseph, Oleg Lapshin, and Evgeny Wasserman (2008), "Randomized Study of Different Anti-Stigma Media," *Patient Education and Counseling,* 71 204-14.

Gelb, B.D. (2008), "Fine-tuning advertising designed to reduce the stigma of mental illness," *Journal of Current Issues and Research in Advertising*, 30(20) 79-85.

Greenwald, Anthony G. (1968), "Cognitive Learning, Cognitive Response to Persuasion, and Attitude Change," in *Psychological Foundations of Attitudes*; Anthony G. Greenwald, Timothy C. Brock and Thomas M. Ostrom, eds. New York, NY: Academic Press, 147-170.

Hilton, James and William von Hippel (1996), "Stereotypes," *Annual Review of Psychology*, 47 (February), 237-271.

Hinshaw, Stephen P. and Andrea Stier (2008), "Stigma as related to mental disorders," *The Annual Review of Clinical Psychology*, 4 367-93.

Hunt, R. Reed and Henry C. Ellis (1999), *Fundamentals of Cognitive Psychology, 6th Edition*; Boston, MA: McGraw-Hill College.

Kees, Jeremy, Scot Burton, and Andrea H. Tangari (2010), "The Impact of Regulatory Focus, Temporal Orientation and Fit on Consumer Responses to Health-Related Advertising," *Journal of Advertising,* 39 (Spring), 19-34.

McGuire, William J. (1964), "Inducing Resistance to Persuasion: Some Contemporary Approaches," in *Advances in Experimental Social Psychology,* Leonard Berkowitz, ed. New York, NY: Academic Press, 191-229.

Mehta, Nisha et al. (2009), "Public Attitudes towards People with Mental Illness in England and Scotland, 1994-2003," *The British Journal of Psychiatry,* 194 278-84.

Paek, Hye-Jin, Jay Yu, and Beom J. Bae (2009), "Is on-Line Health Promotion Culture Bound?" *Journal of Advertising,* 38 (Spring), 35-47.

Paulhus, Delroy L. (1991), "Measurement and Control of Response Bias," in *Measures of Personality and Social Psychology*, Robinson, John Paul, Philip R. Shaver and Laurence Wrightsman, eds. San Diego, CA: Academic Press, 17-36.

Petty, Richard E. and John T. Cacioppo (1981), *Attitudes and Persuasion: Classic and Contemporary Approaches.* Dubuque, IA: William C. Brown.

--- (1986), "The Elaboration Likelihood Model of Persuasion," in *Advances in Experimental Social Psychology*, Berkowitz, Leonard, ed. Orlando, FL: Academic Press, Inc.

Petty, Richard E., John T. Cacioppo, and Rachel Goldman (1981), "Personal Involvement as a Determinant of Argument-Based Persuasion," *Journal of Personality and Social Psychology,* 41 847-55.

Petty, Richard E., John T. Cacioppo, and David W. Schumann (1983), "Central and Peripheral Routes to Advertising Effectiveness: The Moderating Role of Involvement," *The Journal of Consumer Research,* 10 (September), 135-46.

Petty, Richard E. and Duane T. Wegener (1998), "Attitude Change: Multiple Roles for Persuasion Variables," in *Handbook of Social Psychology,* Anonymous New York, NY: McGraw Hill, 323-390.

Raju, Sekar, Priyali Rajigopal, and Timothy J. Gilbride (2010), "Marketing Healthful Eating to Children: The Effectiveness of Incentives, Pledges, and Competitions," *Journal of Marketing,* 74 (May), 93-106.

Reynolds, William H. (1982), "Development of Reliable and Valid Short Forms of the Marlowe-Crowne Social Desirability Scale," *Journal of Clinical Psychology*, 38(1), 119-125.

Russell, Cristel A., Dale W. Russell, and Joel W. Grube (2009), "Nature and Impact of Alcohol Messages in a Youth-Oriented Television Series," *Journal of Advertising,* 38 (Fall), 97-111.

Swinyard, William R. (1981), "The Interaction between Comparative Advertising and Copy Claim Variation," *Journal of Marketing Research,* 18 (May), 175-86.

Szybillo, George J. and Richard Heslin (1973), "Resistance to Persuasion: Inoculation Theory in a Marketing Context," *Journal of Marketing Research,* 10 (November), 396-403.

Taylor, S. Martin & Michael J. Dear (1981), "Scaling Community Attitudes Toward the Mentally Ill," *Schizophrenia Bulletin*, 7(2), 225-240.

The Effect of Social Threats on Consumer Materialism

Eric Levy, University of Cambridge, UK

EXTENDED ABSTRACT

Why are consumers materialistic? Prior research has identified two paths that lead to materialistic behavior (Kasser 2002): a) exposure to materialistic role models, such as through societal influence, peers, and television (Shrum, Burroughs, and Rindfleisch 2005), and b) events that decrease self-esteem and thereby encourage substitution of love for material objects for real social connections. Although it is known that threats to self-esteem can lead consumers to self-enhance through materialistic purchases, the psychological underpinnings of this effect are not well understood. We propose that such materialistic behavior occurs when the threat to consumers' self-esteem challenges their social (as opposed to private) self-concept. In such circumstances, materialistic pursuits provide a means for repairing one's social self-esteem to the extent that they are likely to impress others.

Four studies utilizing multiple measures of materialism test this proposition. Study 1 tests H1, that social threat will increase preference for materialistic goods significantly more than will performance threat. The study was a 3-group design (threat type: social vs. performance vs. none), and the dependent variable was a chance to win a $100 gift certificate from a more or less materialistic department store (Nordstrom vs. Macy's). A one-way ANOVA found significant differences in materialism (measured by the dollar amount allocated to Nordstrom) between conditions, ($M_{control}$ = $59.96, $M_{performancethreat}$ = $58.96, $M_{socialthreat}$ = $87.08; ($F(2, 69)$ = 4.43, p = .01). Supporting H1, planned contrasts revealed significant differences between the control and social threat conditions ($F(2, 69)$ = 6.54, $p < .01$), and between the social threat and performance threat conditions ($F(2, 69)$ = 6.75, p = .01), but no differences between the control and performance threat conditions ($F(2, 69)$ = .01, p = .93). Study 1 provided preliminary evidence for our key hypothesis that materialism is a result of social threat.

Study 2 examined the underlying psychological process by testing H2, that social self-esteem (but not performance self-esteem) mediates the effect of social threat on materialism. This study employed a 2 (threat type: social vs. performance) x 2 (threat status: threat vs. affirmation) between-subjects experimental design. The Richins (2004) short-form materialism scale (Success Subscale), and the State Self-Esteem Scale (SSES) (Heatherton and Polivy 1991) were the key dependent variables. An ANOVA replicated H1, ($F(1, 180)$ = 3.99, $p < .05$). Planned contrasts revealed that materialism was greater in the social threat than social affirmation condition, ($F(1, 180)$ = 4.08, $p < .05$), but not greater in the performance threat than performance affirmation condition, ($F(1, 180)$ = .65, NS. Consistent with our predictions, social threat resulted in significantly lower social self-esteem for participants than did social affirmation ($F(1, 92)$ = 8.30, $p < .01$), while participants in the social threat and social affirmation conditions did not significantly differ on measures of performance self-esteem ($F(1, 92)$ = .84, NS). Furthermore, using a Baron and Kenny (1986) and Sobel (1982) test, we found support for H2, that social self-esteem (but not performance self-esteem) mediated the effect of social threat on materialistic behavior.

Study 3 provided further insight into how people's social relationships affect materialistic behavior, by testing whether certain relationships can be threat-reducing, and thus decrease materialism following a social threat. The study tests H3, that following a social threat, non-contingent social acceptance will decrease materialistic behavior but contingent social acceptance will not decrease materialistic behavior. Participants rated the desirability of 4 conspicuous luxury items: a BMW 5-series car, a private yacht, a Malibu vacation home, and a luxury house. The study was a 3-group between-subjects design (affirmation type: contingent acceptance vs. non-contingent acceptance vs. none). All participants were exposed to the social threat, and then were randomly assigned to one of the three experimental conditions. H3 was analyzed with a 1-way ANOVA, and significant differences in materialism were found between the groups, ($F(2, 132)$ = 3.68, $p < .05$). As predicted, planned contrasts revealed a significant difference between the control and non-contingent acceptance conditions ($F(2, 132)$ = 4.88; $p < .05$), and between the contingent and non-contingent conditions ($F(2, 132)$ = 5.98, $p < .05$), but no differences between the control and contingent acceptance groups ($F(132)$ = .04, NS).

Our theory holds that materialism is not simply a substitute for social relationships, but rather that people use material goods in an attempt to impress others following a social threat. Thus, Study 4 tests H4, that relative to a no-threat condition, social threat will increase preference for materialistic goods positioned to a social-adjustive attitude function, but not to a utilitarian attitude function. Participants rated the desirability of 3 luxury items: a watch, a briefcase, and a camera, positioned to either a social-adjustive function or utilitarian function. We employed a 2 (threat type: social vs. none) x 2 (attitude function: social-adjustive vs. utilitarian) between-subjects experimental design, and an ANOVA supported H4, ($F(1, 222)$ = 5.04, $p < .05$). Planned contrasts revealed that materialism was greater for social threat than no threat when the luxury goods were positioned to a social-adjustive attitude function ($F(1, 222)$ = 4.15, $p < .05$), but not when the luxury goods were positioned to a utilitarian attitude function ($F(1, 222)$ = 1.32, NS). Consistent with our theory, social threat resulted in significantly lower social self-esteem for participants than did no threat ($F(1, 224)$ = 14.43, $p < .001$).

In sum, four studies provided evidence for our theory. Study 1 showed that social (but not performance) threat led to increased materialism. Study 2 found that social (but not performance) self-esteem mediated this effect, and also replicated the results of study 1. Study 3 established that thinking about a social relationship in which one is accepted non-contingently (i.e., for one's intrinsic self) reduces materialism following a social threat. Finally, study 4 found that materialistic goods positioned toward a social (but not utilitarian) function are preferred more following a social threat, as compared to a no-threat control condition.

REFERENCES

Baron, Reuben M., and David A. Kenny (1986), "The Moderator-Mediator Variable Distinction in Social Psychological Research: Conceptual, Strategic, and Statistical Considerations," *Journal of Personality and Social Psychology*, 51 (December), 1173-82.

Heatherton, Todd F., and Janet Polivy (1991), "Development and Validation of a Scale for Measuring State Self-Esteem," *Journal of Personality and Social Psychology*, 60 (June), 35-52.

Kasser, Tim (2002), *The High Price of Materialism*, Cambridge, MA: MIT Press.

Richins, Marsha L. (2004), "The Material Values Scale: Measurement Properties and Development of a Short Form," *Journal of Consumer Research*, 31 (June), 209-19.

Advances in Consumer Research
Volume 39, ©2011

Shrum, L.J., James E. Burroughs, and Aric Rindfleisch (2005), "Television's Cultivation of Material Values," *Journal of Consumer Research*, 32 (December), 473-79.

Sobel, Michael E. (1982), "Asymptotic confidence intervals for indirect effects in structural equation models," in *Sociological Methodology, ed.* S. Leinhardt,   Washington DC: American Sociological Association, 290-312.

Is Breaking Up Hard to Do? An Investigation of Consumer Response to Sponsor Exit

Julie Ruth, Rutgers University, USA
Yuliya Strizhakova, Rutgers University, USA

EXTENDED ABSTRACT

Most sponsorship research focuses on consumer response to the initiation and maintenance of arrangements between brands and properties they sponsor (Johar and Pham 1999; Pope, Voges, and Brown 2009; Ruth and Simonin 2003, 2006). Less research examines how consumers respond to brands that end sponsorship arrangements. This lack of research is surprising given that sponsor turnover is common and that consumers are exposed to information about the end of sponsor-property relationships.

We investigate consumer responses to a brand's decision to end or "exit" a sponsorship arrangement. Relationship research suggests that *severing a* relationship is a negative act that harms attitudes (Duck and Wood 1995; Fournier 1998; Impett et al. 2010). We expect that consumers will perceive sponsorship exit as a negative act that will transfer negative affect to the departing brand. Research also suggests that pre-existing brand attitudes shape how consumers receive and evaluate new information about a brand (e.g., brand alliances; Simonin and Ruth 1998), and so we incorporate this characteristic into theory building.

Extant sponsorship research shows that consumers are affected by their perceptions of the brand's motives in entering sponsorship relationships (Rifon et al. 2004), and prior brand attitudes can moderate these effects (Javalgi et al. 1994). Based on this and other extant sponsorship research, we propose an interaction effect of prior attitudes toward the brand and sponsor motives on attitudes and purchase intentions toward the departing brand. Likewise, given that numbers are used as heuristics (Goldberg and Hartwick 1990), we develop hypotheses regarding the role of duration of the brand-sponsorship relationship and roster size.

Two studies investigate the effect of the extent to which the brand was well-liked initially, the brand's motives associated with exit, sponsorship relationship duration, and number of brands that remain as co-sponsors upon sponsor exit. Findings suggest that sponsor exit has negative effects on attitudes toward the departing brand, especially among consumers who initially perceive the brand favorably. Sponsor motives, sponsorship duration, and remaining roster size moderate these effects.

REFERENCES

Aaker, David A. and Kevin Lane Keller (1990), "Consumer Evaluations of Brand Extensions," *Journal of Marketing*, 54 (January), 27-41.

Alba, Joseph W. and Howard Marmorstein (1987), "The Effects of Frequency Knowledge on Consumer Decision Making," *Journal of Consumer Research*, 14 (June), 14-25.

Baxter, Leslie A., Michael Mazanec, John Nicholson, Garth Pittman, Kathy Smith, and Lee West (1997), "Everyday Loyalties and Betrayals in Personal Relationships," *Journal of Social and Personal Relationships*, 14(5), 655-678.

Becker-Olsen, Karen L. (2003), "And Now, a Word from our Sponsor: A Look at the Effects of Sponsored Content and Banner Advertising," *Journal of Advertising*, 32 (2), 17-32.

Bergkvist, Lars and John R. Rossiter (2007), "The Predictive Validity of Multiple-Item versus Single-Item Measures of the Same Constructs," *Journal of Marketing Research*, 44 (May), 175-184.

Bousch, David M. and Barbara Loken (1991), "A Process Tracing Study of Brand Extension Evaluation," *Journal of Marketing Research*, 28 (February), 16-28.

Cornwell, T. Bettina, Donald P. Roy, and Edward A. Steinard II (2001), "Exploring Managers Perceptions of the Impact of Sponsorship on Brand Equity," *Journal of Advertising*, 30 (2), 41-51.

Cornwell, T. Bettina (2008), "State of the Art and Science in Sponsorship-Linked Marketing," *Journal of Advertising*, 37 (3), 41-55.

Crimmins, James and Martin Horn (1996), "Sponsorship: From Management Ego Trip to Marketing Success," *Journal of Advertising Research*, 36 (4), 11-21.

Dean, Dwane H. (2002), "Associating the Corporation with a Charitable Event through Sponsorship: Measuring the Effects on Corporate Community Relations," *Journal of Advertising*, 31 (4), 77-87.

Duck, Steve W. and Julia T. Wood (1995), "For Better, for Worse, for Richer, for Poorer: The Rough and Smooth of Relationships," in Steve W. Duck and Wood, J. T. (eds.) *Confronting Relationship Challenges*. Thousand Oaks, CA: Sage, 1-21.

Finkel, Eli J., Caryl E. Rusbult, Madoka Kumashiro, and Peggy A. Hannon (2002), "Dealing with Betrayal in Close Relationships: Does Commitment Promote Forgiveness," *Journal of Personality and Social Psychology*, 82(6), 956-974.

Fournier, Susan (1998), "Consumers and Their Brands: Developing Relationship Theory in Consumer Research," *Journal of Consumer Research*, 24 (March), 343-373.

Goldberg, Marvin E. and Jon Hartwick, (1990), "The Effects of Advertiser Reputation and Extremity of Advertising Claim on Advertising Effectiveness," *Journal of Consumer Research*, 17 (September), 172-79.

IEG (2009), http://www.sponsorship.com/About-IEG/Press-Room/Sponsorship-Spending-To-Rise-2.2-Percent-in-2009.aspx (accessed November 11 2010).

Impett, Emily A., Amie M. Gordon, Aleksandr A. Kogan, Christopher Ovcis, Shelly Gable and Dacher Keltner (2010), "Moving Toward More Perfect Unions: Daily and Long-Term Consequences of Approach and Avoidance Goals in Romantic Relationships," *Journal of Personality and Social Psychology*, 98 (July), 1-16.

Javalgi, Rajshekhar G., Mark B. Traylor, Andrew C. Gross, and Edward Lampman (1994), "Awareness of Sponsorship and Corporate Image: An Empirical Investigation," *Journal of Advertising*, 23 (4), 47-58.

Johar, Gita V. and Michel T. Pham (1999), "Relatedness, Prominence and Constructive Sponsor Identification," *Journal of Marketing Research*, 36 (August), 299-312.

Loken, Barbara and Deborah Roedder John (1993), "Diluting Brand Beliefs: When Do Brand Extensions Have a Negative Impact?" *Journal of Marketing*, 57 (July), 71-84.

Louie, Therese A. and Carl Obermiller (2002), "Consumer Response to a Firm's Endorser (Dis)Association Decisions," *Journal of Advertising*, 31(4), 41-52.

Klayman, Ben (2009), "Bank of America May Not Renew U.S. Olympic Sponsorship," *Reuters*, http://www.reuters.com/article/idUSTRE5527FO20090603 (accessed November 13 2010).

Kuzma, John R., Frank R. Veltri, Ann T. Kuzma, and John J. Miller (2003), "Negative Corporate Sponsor information: The Impact of Consumer Attitudes and Purchase Intentions," *International Sports Journal*, 7(2), 140-147.

Locker Jr., Lawrence, William D. McIntosh, Amy A. Hackney, Janie H. Wilson, and Katherine E. Wiegand (2010), "The Breakup of Romantic Relationships: Situational Predictors of Perception of Recovery," *North American Journal of Psychology*, 12 (3), 565-578.

Madrigal, Robert (2001), "Social Identity Effects in a Beliefs-Attitude-Intentions Hierarchy: Implications for Corporate Sponsorship," *Psychology and Marketing*, 18 (2), 145-65.

Mason, Roger B. and Fabrice Cochetel (2006), "Residual Brand Awareness Following the Termination of a Long-Term Event Sponsorship and the Appointment of a New Sponsor," *Journal of Marketing Communications*, 12 (2), 125-144.

Parker, Heidi M. and Janet S. Fink (2010), "Negative Sponsor Behaviour, Team Response and How This Impacts Fan Attitudes," *International Journal of Sports Marketing and Sponsorship*, April, 200-211.

Petty, Richard E. and John T. Cacioppo (1984), "The Effects of Involvement on Responses to Argument Quality and Quantity: Central and Peripheral Routes to Persuasion," *Journal of Personality and Social Psychology*, 46 (January), 69-81.

PGA Tour (2010), "CA Will Not Renew Sponsorship of World Golf Championships Event." http://www.pgatour.com/2010/tournaments/r473/03/17/ca_news/index.html (accessed November 13 2010).

Pope, Nigel, Kevin E. Voges and Mark Brown (2009), "Winning Ways: Immediate and Long-Term Effects of Sponsorship on Perceptions of Brand Quality and Corporate Image," *Journal of Advertising*, 38 (2), 5-20.

Rees, Paul (2010), "South Africa Sponsor Sasol Will Not Renew Deal for Rugby World Cup," *Guardian*. http://www.guardian.co.uk/sport/2010/jul/20/south-africa-sponsor-sasol-world-cup (accessed November 13 2010).

Rifon, Nora J., S. Marina Choi, Carrie S. Trimble, and Hairong Li (2004), "Congruence Effects in Sponsorship: The Mediating Role of Sponsor Credibility and Consumer Attributions of Sponsor Motive," *Journal of Advertising*, 33 (1), 29-42.

Ruth, Julie A., Cele C. Otnes, and Frédéric F. Brunel (1999), "Gift Receipt and the Reformulation of Interpersonal Relationships," *Journal of Consumer Research*, 25 (4), 385-402.

Ruth, Julie A. and Bernard L. Simonin (2003), "Brought to You by Brand A and Brand B: How Partner Brands Affect Consumers' Perceptions of Joint Sponsorships," *Journal of Advertising*, 32 (3), 19-30.

Ruth, Julie A. and Bernard L. Simonin (2006), "The Power of Numbers: Investigating the Impact of Event Roster Size in Consumer Response to Sponsorship," *Journal of Advertising*, 35 (4), 7-20.

Simonin, Bernard L. and Julie A. Ruth (1998), "Is a Company Known by the Company It Keeps? Assessing the Spillover Effects of Brand Alliances on Consumer Brand Attitudes," *Journal of Marketing Research*, 35 (February), 30-42.

Till, Brian D. and Terence A. Shimp (1998), "Endorsers in Advertising: The Case of Negative Celebrity Information," *Journal of Advertising*, 27(1), 68-82.

Weiner, Bernard (1980), "A Cognitive (Attribution)-Emotion-Action Model of Motivated Behavior: An Analysis of Judgments of Help-Giving," *Journal of Personality and Social Psychology*, 39 (2), 186-200.

If It's Similar, it's More Likely…But Can It Be Worth It?
The Impact of Manipulating Perceived Similarity on Probability Judgments and Outcome Value

Elise Chandon Ince, Virginia Tech University, USA
Hui-Yun Chen, Virginia Tech, USA
Robyn LeBoeuf, University of Florida, USA

EXTENDED ABSTRACT

Sweepstakes have often been used to generate excitement and raise awareness by giving customers opportunities to win the featured prizes. Both the featured prizes and the odds of winning the prizes determine the attractiveness of sweepstakes. Customers, however, usually do not have access to the true odds of winning. Therefore, customers are prone to use other cues to form probability judgments and evaluate the sweepstakes.

According to the probability judgment literature, people develop intuitive probability judgments from extraneous cues such as descriptions of the event (Tversky and Koehler 1994), or the representativeness or availability of exemplars (Kahneman, Slovic, and Tversky 1982). Construal level theory suggests that probability judgments are sensitive to another cue, the perceived proximity to the individual affected by the event. Recently, studies conducted by Wakslak and Trope (2009) manipulated construal level and found that high-level construals, which increase one's subjective distance from an event, lowered subjective probability judgments about the event's likelihood. Put differently, activating concrete construals increases people's perceptions that a target event will occur. We suggest that when an individual affected by an event seems proximal (vs. distant) to the self, that proximity will activate a concrete mindset, and thus, the event in question will seem relatively likely to happen for the self.

Previous research has also shown that limited, scarce resources are deemed more desirable, even when there is no legitimate basis to use scarcity to infer value (Inman, Peter, and Raghubir 1997). If people use an item's perceived scarcity as a heuristic that signals its value, then events that seem unlikely to occur (e.g., "my chances of winning this sweepstakes are low") may also seem to be more valuable, or to have greater impact more generally. Thus, it may be the case that when events happen for distant (vs. proximal) others, the events may seem less likely to occur for the self and thus to seem more valuable, or to more generally have a greater impact.

Therefore, we posit that:

Hypothesis 1	An event happening to a socially close person will be perceived as more likely to happen to the self than an event happening to a socially distant person, which in turn will reduce predictions about the impending event's magnitude.
Hypothesis 2	The relationship between proximity, probability judgments, and perceived magnitude, as defined in H1 will hold true both for positive and negative events.
Hypothesis 3	Questioning the validity of the scarcity heuristic reverses the negative impact of probability judgments on the event's magnitude.

Three studies were conducted to test our predictions. The first study tested H1 and H2. Study 2 replicated the findings, offered a different manipulation of the concept of proximity, and provided further evidence of the mechanism at play. Study 3 provided evidence that the link between perceived probability and predicted magnitude is due to an accessible belief that scarce items are valuable.

Study 1 directly tested the relationships among proximity, probability judgment, and perceived magnitude for two events (getting a flight upgrade and being a victim of credit card fraud). We predicted that greater proximity to a target experiencing one of these events would lead people to perceive the event as more likely to happen for the self, but less valuable or lower in magnitude (e.g., a flight upgrade would seem more likely but less valuable when a close vs. distant other had received an upgrade). Proximity was manipulated by asking participants to focus on how they were similar to or dissimilar to the target individual. As expected, participants who focus on what they had in common with the target individual deemed the event more probable, but predicted that the event's magnitude would be less.

Study 2 replicated these results by manipulating proximity through a different implementation. A feeling of powerlessness was induced to make the target individual appear closer, as feeling powerless reduces the social distance between oneself and others (Rucker, Dubois, and Galinsky 2011). Participants were primed with either high power or low power words and then, on an unrelated task, were told that a radio was giving out concert tickets and that a target individual had already won one. They were then asked to indicate the probability of wining the concert ticket themselves as well as the ticket value. Participants who felt powerless and thus closer to the target individual felt that they were more likely to win, but in return thought that the concert ticket was worth less. We replicated our findings with a negatively valenced event: participants who felt powerless thought that they were more likely to get a flat tire on their way to school (which had just happened to a target individual), but also believed that the price of changing the flat tire would be lower than those who felt powerful. A mediation analysis confirmed that probability judgment mediates the relationship between proximity and outcome value.

We proposed earlier that the scarcity heuristic (i.e. the idea that what is scarce is valuable) explains why people's subjective probabilities that an event will occur and their perception of the event's outcome are negatively correlated. The objective of study 3 was to reverse this relationship. If participants were made aware that scarcity is not always negatively correlated to value, then we should expect opposite results: low probability judgments should not increase, but perhaps even decrease, the perceived outcome value. In study 3, we asked participants to read a short paragraph that was either highlighting that diamonds are scarce, therefore highly valuable, or highlighting that diamonds are relatively common in nature and that their scarcity is a myth put forward by the diamond industry. We found that when participants were primed with the "scarcity is a myth" explanation, proximity still increased probability ratings, but also increased perceived value. In other words, the closer the target individual, the more likely and the more valuable the event.

The current research extends the construal level theory literature and examines the indirect impact of varying psychological distance on perceived event magnitude, with implications for understanding how consumers perceive and anticipate uncertain future events.

REFERENCES

Alter, Adam L. and Daniel M. Oppenheimer (2008), "Effects of Fluency on Psychological Distance and Mental Construal (or Why New York Is a Large City, but New York Is a Civilized Jungle)," *Psychological Science*, 19 (2), 161-67.

Fujita, Kentaro, Marlone Henderson, Juliana Eng, Yaacov Trope, and Nira Liberman (2006), "Spatial Distance and Mental Construal of Social Events," *Psychological Science*, 17(4), 278-82.

Inman, Jeffrey, Anil Peter, and Priya Raghubir (1997), "Framing the Deal: The Role of Restrictions in Accentuating Deal Value," *Journal of Consumer Research*, 24 (1), 68-79.

Kahneman, Daniel, Paul Slovic, and Amos Tversky (1982). *Judgment under uncertainty: Heuristics and biases*: Cambridge Univ Pr.

Lammers, Joris, Diederik Stapel, and Adam Galinsky (2010), "Power Increases Hypocrisy," *Psychological Science*, 21 (5), 737-44.

Liberman, Nira and Jens Förster (2009), "Distancing from Experienced Self: How Global-Versus-Local Perception Affects Estimation of Psychological Distance," *Journal of Personality and Social Psychology*, 97 (2), 203-16.

Liberman, Nira, Michael D. Sagristano, and Yaacov Trope (2002), "The Effect of Temporal Distance on Level of Mental Construal," *Journal of Experimental Social Psychology*, 38 (6), 523-34.

Litt, Ab, Uzma Khan, and Baba Shiv (2010), "Lusting While Loathing," *Psychological Science*, 21 (1), 118-25.

Liviatan, Ido, Yaacov Trope, and Nira Liberman (2008), "Interpersonal Similarity as a Social Distance Dimension: Implications for Perception of Others' Actions," *Journal of Experimental Social Psychology*, 44 (5), 1256-69.

Rucker, Derek, David Dubois, and Adam Galinsky (2011), "Generous Paupers and Stingy Princes: Power Drives Consumer Spending on Self versus Others," *Journal of Consumer Research*, 37(2).

Smith, Pamela and Yaacov Trope (2006), "You Focus on the Forest When You're in Charge of the Trees: Power Priming and Abstract Information Processing," *Journal of Personality and Social Psychology*, 90 (4), 578-96.

Todorov, Alexander, Amir Goren, and Yaacov Trope (2007), "Probability as a Psychological Distance: Construal and Preferences," *Journal of Experimental Social Psychology*, 43 (3), 473-82.

Trope, Yaacov and Nira Liberman (2010), "Construal-Level Theory of Psychological Distance," *Psychological Review*, 117 (2), 440-63.

Tversky, Amos and Derek Koehler (1994), "Support Theory: A Nonextensional Representation of Subjective Probability," *Psychological Review*, 101 (4), 547-67.

Wakslak, Cheryl and Yaacov Trope (2009), "The Effect of Construal Level on Subjective Probability Estimates," *Psychological Science*, 20 (1), 52-58.

Weber, Elke (1994), "From Subjective Probabilities to Decision Weights: The Effect of Asymmetric Loss Functions on the Evaluation of Uncertain Outcomes and Events," *Psychological Bulletin*, 115 (2), 228-42.

Generative Literacy and Consumer Empowerment

Rama Jayanti, Cleveland State University, USA
Sreedhar Madhavaram, Cleveland State University, USA
Michael Wachter, Cleveland State University, USA

EXTENDED ABSTRACT

Responding to the inherent complexities of today's knowledge-intensive economy and the resulting knowledge-intensive consumption, consumer researchers have begun to address consumer literacy (e.g., Wallendorf 2001; Adkins and Ozanne 2005; Ozanne, Adkins, and Sandlin 2005; Viswanathan, Rosa, and Harris 2005). So far, researchers' conceptualization of consumer literacy entwines educational and functional literacy. Equating educational literacy with consumer literacy seems, at the very least, rather limiting given the inherent diversity in products available for consumption in the marketplace and the resulting diversity in complexities related to consumption.

Specifically, while the foundation of educational literacy can be important for consumer literacy research, consumer literacy goes beyond educational literacy. For example, in complex consumption categories involving finance and health related offerings in the marketplace, literacy is highly context specific and knowledge intensive. Consequently, there has been burgeoning interest in functionally rooted financial literacy (e.g., Emund 2010; Huston 2010) and health literacy (e.g., Adkins and Corus 2009: Bone, France, and Aiken 2010) in consumer research. However, despite the seeming importance of the issue of consumer literacy, there is much confusion in the consumer literature regarding the definition/conceptualization and treatment of literacy.

Therefore, we first review the current research on consumer literacy with reference to the conceptualization/ definition and major findings. Second, building on our review, we elaborate on functional versus educational literacy, develop a model of generative literacy, and introduce the notion of a generative cycle of educational and functional literacies for consumer empowerment.

This paper makes several contributions to the consumer literacy research domain. First, our comprehensive and systematic review with reference to the conceptualization/ definition, products focused on, nature of research, and major findings reveals interesting insights into the links between consumer literacy and empowerment, conceptual inconsistencies, public policy issues, and normative strategies for firms. Here, we critically analyze the literature and consciously look for integrative elements and conceptual lacunae in consumer literacy research. Second, building on our review and critical analysis, we (i) propose a 2X2 matrix that helps categorize the differences between low and high levels of educational and functional literacy, reflecting four possibilities that are distinct and present different challenges to researchers and practitioners alike, (ii) summarize the differences between educational and functional literacies, and (iii) develop a figure that illustrates the relationships and moderating factors derived out of the extant literature. Third, we develop and introduce the notion of the generative cycle of educational and functional literacies for consumer empowerment. Herein, we depict dynamic affordances and productive inquiry as linking mechanisms between educational and functional literacies. Overall, our research has several implications for future research as shown in the brief research agenda that follows.

In discussing a research agenda for consumer literacy, we first focus on the context of discovery and, then, the context of justification. As the scope of this research is conceptual, there are several avenues of future research in the context of discovery. First, our integrative and critical review can be subjected to conceptual scrutiny.

Second, the conceptual model of generative literacy that emerged from analysis can be evaluated with reference to parsimony (errors of commission) and comprehensiveness (errors of omission). Furthermore, our conceptualization of generative literacy and the generative cycle of educational and functional literacies for empowerment can also be investigated for conceptual adequacy, consistency, and validity. Third, drawing on the seminal work of Cook and Brown (1999), we introduce the concepts of productive inquiry and dynamic affordances in the context of the generative cycle of educational and functional literacies for empowerment. These two concepts need further development and clarification.

As to the context of justification, our research brings forth concepts such as generative literacy, cognitive predilections, identity management, productive inquiry, dynamic affordances and two new frameworks in the conceptual model of literacy and the generative cycle of educational and functional literacies for empowerment that can be subjected to empirical scrutiny, that in turn, provides several new avenues for future research.

In order to equip the vast majority of people who live on the other side of the social divide with capabilities that they value, transformative consumer research has to take into consideration the generative nature of literacy and strive to balance both educational and functional perspectives for true self and societal empowerment.

REFERENCES

Adkins, Natalie Ross and Canan Corus (2009), "Health Literacy for Improved Health Outcomes: Effective Capital in the Marketplace," *Journal of Consumer Affairs*, 43 (2), 199-222.

--- and Julie L. Ozanne (2005), "The Low Literate Consumer," *Journal of Consumer Research*, 32 (1), 93-105.

--- and --- (2005), "Critical Consumer Education: Empowering the Low-Literate Consumer," *Journal of Macromarketing*, 25 (2), 153-162.

American Heart Association (2011), "Meet the Fats," http://www.heart.org/HEARTORG/GettingHealthy/FatsAndOils/MeettheFats/Meet-the-Fats_UCM_304495_Article.jsp

Bone, Paula Fitzgerald (2008), "Toward a General Model of Consumer Empowerment and Welfare in Financial Markets with an Application to Mortgage Servicers," *Journal of Consumer Affairs*, 42(2), 165-188.

---, Karen Russo France, and Kathryn J. Aiken (2009), "On Break-Up Cliches Guiding Health Literacy," *Journal of Consumer Affairs*, 43 (2), 185-198.

Bormuth, John R. (1975), "The Cloze Procedure: Literacy in the Classroom," in *Help for the Reading Teacher: New Directions in Research*, ed. W.D. Page, Urbana, IL: National Conference on Research in Teaching, 60-90.

Bruine de Bruin, Wandi, Wilbert VanderKlaauw, Julie S. Downs, Baruch Fischoff, Giorgio Topa, and Olivier Armantier (2010), "Expectations of Inflation: The Role of Demographic Variables, Expectation Formation, and Financial Literacy," *Journal of Consumer Affairs*, 44 (2), 381-402.

Conrad, Peter and Valerie Leiter (2004), "Medicalization, Markets and Consumers," *Journal of Health and Social Behavior*, 45, 158-176.

Advances in Consumer Research
Volume 39, ©2011

Cook, Scott D.N. and John Seely Brown (1999), "Bridging Epistemologies: The Generative Dance Between Organizational Knowledge and Organizational Knowing," *Organization Science*, 10 (4), 371-400.

Dewey, John (1910), *How We Think: A Restatement of the Relation of Reflective Thinking to the Education Process*, Lexington, MA: D.C. Heath.

--- (1944), *Democracy and Education*, New York, NY: Free Press. Original published 1916.

Emund, David L. (2010), "Financial Literacy Explicated: The Case for a Clearer Definition in an Increasingly Complex Economy," *Journal of Consumer Affairs*, 44 (2), 276-295.

Evans, Peter (2002), "Collective Capabilities, Culture, and Amartya Sen's *Development as Freedom*", *Studies in Comparative International Development*, 37 (2), 54-60.

Fox, Jonathan, Suzanne Bartholomae, and Lee Jinkook (2005), "Building the Case for Financial Education," *Journal of Consumer Affairs*, 39 (1), 195-214.

Freire, Paolo (1970), *Pedagogy of the Oppressed*, New York, NY: Seabury Press.

Gal, Iddo (2002), "Adult's Statistical Literacy. Meanings, Components, Responsibilities," *International Statistical Review*, 70 (1), 1-25.

Hastings, Justine S. and Lydia Tejeda-Ashton (2008), "Financial Literacy, Information, and Demand Elasticity: Survey and Experimental Evidence from Mexico," Working Paper No. 14538, National Bureau of Economic Research, Cambridge, MA 02138.

Hira, Tahira K., and Cäzilia Loibl (2005), "Understanding the Impact of Employer-Provided Financial Education on Workplace Satisfaction," *Journal of Consumer Affairs*, 39 (1), 173-194.

Hilgert, Marianne A., Jeanne M. Hogarth, and Sondra Beverly (2003), "Household Financial Management: The Connection between Knowledge and Behavior," *Federal Reserve Bulletin*, 89, 309-322.

Howlett, Elizabeth, Jeremy Kees, and Elyria Kemp (2008), "The Role of Self-Regulation, Future Orientation, and Financial Knowledge in Long-Term Financial Decisions," *Journal of Consumer Affairs*, 42 (2), 223-242.

Huston, Sandra J. (2010), "Measuring Financial Literacy," *Journal of Consumer Affairs*, 44 (2), 296-316.

Jae, Haeran and Devon Delvecchio (2004), "Decision Making by Low-Literacy Consumers in the Presence of Point-of-Purchase Information," *Journal of Consumer Affairs*, 38 (2), 342-354.

---, ---, and Deborah Cowles (2008), "Picture–Text Incongruency in Print Advertisements among Low- and High-Literacy Consumers," *Journal of Consumer Affairs*, 42 (3), 439-451.

Jayanti, Rama K. and Jagdip Singh (2010), Pragmatic Learning Theory: "An Inquiry-Action Framework for Distributed Consumer Learning in Online Communities," *Journal of Consumer Research*, 36 (6), 1058-1081.

Kindig, David, Dyanne Affonso, Eric Chudler, Marilyn Gaston, Cathy Meade, Ruth Parker, Victoria Purcell-Gates, Rima Rudd, Irving Rootman, Susan Schrimshaw, and William Smith (2004), *Health Literacy: A Prescription to End Confusion*, Washington, DC: National Academic Press.

Kirsch, Irwin S., and John T. Guthrie (1977), "The Concept and Measurement of Functional Literacy," *Reading Research Quarterly*, 13 (4), 485-507.

---, Ann Jungeblut, Lynn Jenkins, and Andrew Kolstad (1993), *Adult Literacy in America*, Washington, DC: National Center for Education Statistics, U.S. Department of Education.

Kozup, John C., Scot Burton and Elizabeth H. Creyer (2006), "The Provision of Trans Fat Information and its Interaction with Consumer Knowledge," *Journal of Consumer Affairs*, 40 (1), 163-176.

--- and Jeanne M. Hogarth (2008), "Financial Literacy, Public Policy, and Consumers' Self-Protection—More Questions, Fewer Answers," *Journal of Consumer Affairs*, 42 (2) 127-136.

Kutner, Mark, Elizabeth Greenberg, Ying Jin, and Christine Paulsen, (2006). *The Health Literacy of American Adults: Results from the 2003 National Assessment of Adult Literacy*, Washington, DC: National Center for Education Statistics, U.S. Department of Education.

Levy, Marian and Marla B. Royne (2009), "The Impact of Consumers' Health Literacy on Public Health," *Journal of Consumer Affairs*, 43(2), 367-372.

Lusardi, Annamaria and Olivia S. Mitchell (2006), "Financial Literacy and Planning: Implications for Retirement Wellbeing," Working Paper, Pension Research Council, Wharton School, University of Pennsylvania.

---, ---, and Vilsa Curto (2010), "Financial Literacy among the Young," *Journal of Consumer Affairs*, 44 (2), 358-380.

--- and Peter Tufano (2009), "Debt Literacy, Financial Experiences, and Overindebtedness," NBER Working Paper No. 14808.

Lyons, Angela C., Mitchell Rachlis, and Erik Scherpf (2007), "What's in a Score? Differences in Consumers' Credit Knowledge Using OLS and Quantile Regressions," *Journal of Consumer Affairs*, 41 (2), 223-249.

Mandell, Lewis (2005), Financial Literacy: Does it Matter? Washington DC: Jump$tart Coalition, http://www.jumpstartcoalition.org/upload/Mandell%20Paper%20April%20.

McCormack, Lauren, Carla Bann, Jennifer Uhrig, Nancy Berkman, and Rima Rudd (2009), "Health Insurance Literacy of Older Adults," *Journal of Consumer Affairs*, 43 (2), 223-248.

McCray, Alexa T. (2005), "Promoting Health Literacy," *Journal of the American Medical Informatics Association, 12 (2),* 152-163.

Monticone, Chiara (2010), "How Much Does Wealth Matter in the Acquisition of Financial Literacy?," *Journal of Consumer Affairs*, 44 (2), 403-422.

Morrin, Maureen, Susan Broniarczyk, J. Jeffrey Inman, and John Broussard (2008), "Saving for Retirement: The Effects of Fund Assortment Size and Investor Knowledge on Asset Allocation Strategies," *Journal of Consumer Affairs*. 42 (2), 206-222.

Morsy, Zaghloul (editor) (1994), *The Challenge of Illiteracy: From Reflection to Action*, New York, NY: Garland Publishing.

Ozanne, Julie L., Natalie Ross Adkins, and Jennifer A. Sandlin (2005), "Shopping [for] Power: How Adult Literacy Learners Negotiate the Marketplace," Adult Education Quarterly, 55 (4), 251-268.

Perry, Vanessa Gail (2008), "Is Ignorance Bliss? Consumer Accuracy in Judgments about Credit Ratings," *Journal of Consumer Affairs*, 42 (2), 189-205.

Ringold, Debra Jones (2005) "Vulnerability in the Marketplace: Concepts, Caveats, and Possible Solutions," *Journal of Macromarketing*, 25 (2), 202-214.

Sen, Amartya (1999), *Development as Freedom*, New York, NY: Alfred A. Knopf, Inc.

Servon, Lisa J., and Robert Kaestner (2008) "Consumer Financial Literacy and the Impact of Online Banking on the Financial Behavior of Lower-Income Bank Customers," *Journal of Consumer Affairs*, 42 (2), 271-305.

Smith, Rachel and Marla B. Royne (2010), "Consumer Literacy for Credence Services: Helping the Invisible Hand," *Journal of Consumer Affairs*, 44 (3), 598-606.

UNESCO (1975), *Final Report for International Symposium for Literacy*, Persepolis, Iran: Author.

Venezky, Richard L. (1990), "Definitions of Literacy," in *Toward Defining Literacy*, ed. Richard L. Vebezky, Daniel L. Wagner, and Barrie S. Ciliberti, Newark, DE: International Reading Association.

Viswanathan, Madhubalan, and Roland Gau (2005), "Functional Illiteracy and Nutritional Education in the United States: A Research-Based Approach to the Development of Nutritional Education Materials for Functionally Illiterate Consumers," *Journal of Macromarketing*, 25 (2), 187-201.

---, Manoj Hastak, and Roland Gau (2009), "Understanding and Facilitating the Usage of Nutritional Labels by Low-Literate Consumers," *Journal of Public Policy & Marketing*, 28 (2), 135-145.

---, Jose Antonio Rosa, and James Edwin Harris (2005), "Decision Making and Coping of Functionally Illiterate Consumers and Some Implications for Marketing Management," *Journal of Marketing*, 69 (1), 15-31.

---, ---, and Julie A Ruth (2010), "Exchanges in Marketing Systems: The Case of Subsistence Consumer–Merchants in Chennai, India," *Journal of Marketing*, 74 (3), 1-17.

---, Srinivas Sridharan, Roland Gau, and Robin Ritchie (2009), "Designing Marketplace Literacy Education in Resource-Constrained Contexts: Implications for Public Policy and Marketing," *Journal of Public Policy & Marketing*, 28 (1), 85-94.

---, Carlo J. Torelli, Lan Xia, and Roland Gau (2009), "Understanding the influence of literacy on consumer memory: The role of pictorial elements," *Journal of Consumer Psychology*, 19 (3), 389-402.

Wagner, Daniel A. (1993), *Literacy, Culture and Development: Becoming Literate in Morocco*, Cambridge, UK: Cambridge University Press.

Wallendorf, Melanie (2001), "Literally Literacy," *Journal of Consumer Research*, 27 (4), 505-511.

Walsh, Catherine (1991), *Literacy as Praxis: Culture, Language, and Pedagogy,* Stamford, CT: Ablex Publishing Corporation.

Walstad, William B., Ken Rebeck, and Richard A. MacDonald (2010), "The Effects of Financial Education on the Financial Knowledge of High School Students," *Journal of Consumer Affairs*, 44 (2), 336-357.

Willis, Lauren E. (2008), "Against Financial Literacy Education," *Iowa Law Review*, 94: 197-285.

Zarcadoolas, Christina, Andrew F. Pleasant, and David S. Greer (2006), *Advancing Health Literacy: A Framework for Understanding and Action*, Sage.

On Braggarts and Gossips:
Why Consumers Generate Positive But Transmit Negative Word of Mouth

Matteo De Angelis, Luiss University, Italy
Andrea Bonezzi, Northwestern University, USA
Alessandro M. Peluso, Luiss Guido Carli University, Italy
Derek Rucker, Northwestern University, USA
Michele Costabile, Luiss Guido Carli University, Italy

EXTENDED ABSTRACT

Academic research has widely recognized the paramount importance of word of mouth (WOM), the flow of informal communications about products and services that influences 70% of all buying decisions (Balter 2008). Yet a controversy still exists about whether positive or negative WOM prevails in the marketplace, with some studies indicating that negative WOM is more prevalent than positive WOM (e.g., Kamins, Folkes, and Pernes 1997), and others suggesting the opposite is true (e.g., East, Hammond, and Wright 2007). We identify an important moderator that may solve this controversy. We argue that WOM valence varies systematically across two stages over which WOM unfolds. We call these stages *generation* and *transmission*. Consumers *generate* WOM by talking about their own experiences with products, while *transmit* WOM by passing-on information about other people's experiences. We predict that positive WOM tends to be more prevalent than negative WOM in the *generation* stage, whereas negative WOM tends to be more prevalent than positive WOM in the *transmission* stage. What may account for these seemingly contradictory tendencies in generation and transmission? We suggest that consumers engage in WOM to express themselves, particularly to satisfy their basic need to self-enhance (Sedikides 1993; Baumeister 1998). We argue that this need leads consumers to talk about their own positive experiences (thus generating positive WOM) as a direct way to self-enhance (e.g., Shrauger 1975), as well as about negative experiences they heard occurred to others (thus transmitting negative WOM) as an indirect way to self-enhance (e.g., Tesser 1998).

We tested this explanation in three experiments. Experiment 1 tested whether people indeed tend to generate positive WOM but transmit negative WOM. Ninety-three participants were assigned to a 2 (WOM stage: generation vs. transmission) ´ 3 (social setting: talking to a colleague at work, to a person met at a party, or to a stranger on an airplane) between-participants design, and invited to write what they would say to describe product experiences occurred to themselves or to someone else. To assess WOM valence, respondents were asked to rate the valence of each experience on a nine-point scale (1 = very negative, 9 = very positive). Results showed that participants described more positive experiences when they wrote about their own experiences ($M = 6.61$) compared to when they wrote about others' experiences ($M = 4.37$, $F = 15.54$, $p < .01$). This effect of WOM stage was consistent across the three settings, with contrasts that were all significant ($ts \, ^3 \, 2.20$, $ps < .03$).

Experiment 2 tested whether consumers generate positive WOM but transmit negative WOM as a way to self-enhance. We reasoned that people should exhibit this tendency when their need for self-enhancement is relatively high. We then measured self-esteem as a way to appraise the strength of individual self-enhancement motive, with lower self-esteem triggering a stronger need to self-enhance (Shrauger 1975). Two hundred forty participants were assigned to a 2 (WOM stage) ´ 2 (experience valence: positive vs. negative) between-participants design, and invited to read a description of a new brand of laptop computers. WOM stage was manipulated by asking participants to imagine that they had purchased the laptop and used it for about one month (WOM generation), or that they had been told by a third person who had purchased the laptop about her experience (WOM transmission). Experience valence was manipulated by asking them to imagine that the user (them or the third person) felt satisfied (positive experience) or dissatisfied (negative experience) with the product. Participants then completed a three-item measure of likelihood to engage in WOM and a self-esteem scale. The data were examined with a regression analysis, with WOM likelihood as dependent variable, and WOM stage (coded as 0 for generation and 1 for transmission), experience valence (coded as 0 for negative experience and 1 for positive experience), self-esteem, and all interaction terms as independent variables. Results showed a two-way interaction between WOM stage and experience valence ($b = -.74$, $p < .001$) that was consistent with the basic effect found in experiment 1. They also revealed a three-way interaction among WOM stage, experience valence, and self-esteem ($b = .71$, $p < .001$), indicating that self-esteem moderates that basic effect. A spotlight analysis on individuals low versus high in self-esteem ($\pm 1SD$ from the mean) confirmed that only consumers with a low self-esteem tend to generate positive WOM ($M_{Pos} = 5.49$ vs. $M_{Neg} = 4.50$, $t = 4.19$, $p < .001$) but transmit negative WOM ($M_{Neg} = 5.00$ vs. $M_{Pos} = 4.42$, $t = 2.83$, $p < .01$).

Experiment 3 provided convergence on the proposed psychological mechanism. We manipulated, instead of measuring, need to self-enhance through a manipulation of threat to participants' self views. We expected that people in the threat condition generate more positive WOM but transmit more negative WOM than people in the no-threat condition, because threat inherently triggers a stronger need to self-enhance (Tesser 1988). Seventy-one participants were assigned to a 2 (WOM stage) ´ 2 (self-view: threatened vs. non-threatened) between-participants design. They were asked to write a consumption experience that occurred to them (generation) or that they heard occurred to someone else (transmission), and to rate this experience on the same scale as in experiment 1. ANOVA showed a two-way interaction ($F = 9.55$, $p < .017$), with participants under threat describing more positive experiences than participants under no threat ($M_{threat} = 7.61$ vs. $M_{no\text{-}threat} = 6.33$, $t = 1.76$, $p < .03$) in generation, but more negative experiences in transmission ($M_{threat} = 3.82$ vs. $M_{no\text{-}threat} = 5.64$, $t = 2.63$, $p < .01$).

Overall, this research offers a novel perspective on the controversy about prevalence of positive or negative WOM. By distinguishing *generation* from *transmission* we further our understanding of when positive WOM is more likely to be shared than negative WOM and when the opposite is more likely to occur. Furthermore, by showing that people engage in WOM generation and transmission as a way to self-enhance, we offer a parsimonious theoretical account that explains why consumers tend to generate positive but transmit negative WOM.

REFERENCES

Allsop, Dee T., Bryce R. Bassett, and James A. Hoskins (2007), "Word-of-Mouth Research: Principles and Applications," *Journal of Advertising Research*, 47 (4), 398-411.

Balter, Dave (2008), *The World of Mouth Manual: Vol. 2*. Boston, MA: Bzz Pubs.

Baumeister, Roy F. (1998), "The Self," in *The Handbook of Social Psychology*, D.T. Gilbert, S.T. Fiske, and G. Lindzey (Eds.), Hoboken, NJ: John Wiley & Sons, Vol. 1, pp. 680-740.

Berger, Jonah and Chip Heath (2007), "Where Consumers Diverge from Others: Identity Signaling and Product Domains," *Journal of Consumer Research*, 34 (2), 121-34.

Brown, Jonathon D., Rebecca L. Collins, and Greg W. Schmidt (1988), "Self-Esteem and Direct Versus Indirect Forms of Self-Enhancement," *Journal of Personality and Social Psychology*, 55 (3), 445-53.

Brown Jacqueline J. and Peter H. Reingen (1987), "Social Ties and Word-of-Mouth Referral Behavior," *Journal of Consumer Research*, 14 (3), 350-62.

Brown, Ryan P. and Virgin Ziegler-Hill (2004), "Narcissism and the Non-equivalence of Self-Esteem Measures: A Matter of Dominance?," *Journal of Research in Personality*, 38 (6), 585-92.

Bughin, Jacques, Jonathan Doogan, and Ole J. Vetvik (2010), "A New Way to Measure Word-of-Mouth Marketing," *McKinsey Quarterly*, 2, 113-6.

Donavan, D. Todd, John C. Mowen, and Goutam Chakraborty (1999), "Urban Legends: The Word-of-Mouth Communication of Morality through Negative Story Content," *Marketing Letters*, 10 (1), 23-34.

East, Robert, Kathy Hammond, and Malcolm Wright (2007), "The Relative Incidence of Positive and Negative Word of Mouth: A Multi-Category Study," *International Journal of Research in Marketing*, 24 (2), 175-84.

Fiske, Susan T. (2001), "Five Core Social Motives, Plus or Minus Five," *Motivated Social Perception: The Ontario Symposium*, vol. 9, S. Spencer, S. Fein, M. Zanna, and J. Olsen, eds. Psychology Press.

Folkes, Valerie S. (1988), "The Availability Heuristic and Perceived Risk," *Journal of Consumer Research*, 15 (1), 13-23.

Godes, David and Dina Mayzlin (2004), "Using Online Conversations to Study Word-of-Mouth Communication," *Marketing Science*, 23 (4), 545-60.

Helmreich, R. and J. Stapp (1974), "Short Forms of Texas Social Behavior Inventory (TSBI), an Objective Measure of Self-Esteem," *Bulletin of the Psychonomic Society*, 4, 473-75.

Hennig-Thurau, Thorsten, Kevin P. Gwinner, Gianfranco Walsh, and Dwayne D. Gremler (2004), "Electronic Word-of-Mouth Via Consumer-Opinion Platforms: What Motivates Consumers to Articulate Themselves on the Internet?," *Journal of Interactive Marketing*, 18 (1), 38-52.

Herr, Paul M., Frank R. Kardes, and John Kim (1991), "Effects of Word-of-Mouth and Product-Attribute Information on Persuasion: An Accessibility-Diagnosticity Perspective," *Journal of Consumer Research*, 17 (4), 454-62.

Jussim, Lee, HsiuJu Yen, and John R. Aiello (1995), "Self-Consistency, Self-Enhancement, and Accuracy in Reactions to Feedback," *Journal of Experimental Social Psychology*, 31 (4), 322-56.

Kamins, Michael A., Valerie S. Folkes, and Lars Perner (1997), "Consumer Responses to Rumors: Good News, Bad News," *Journal of Consumer Psychology*, 6 (2), 165-87.

Keller, Ed (2007), "Unleashing the Power of Word of Mouth: Creating Brand Advocacy to Drive Growth," *Journal of Advertising Research*, 47 (4), 448-52.

Krueger, Joackim (1998), "Enhancement Bias in Description of Self and Others," *Personality and Social Psychology Bulletin*, 24 (5), 505-16.

Krull, Douglas S. and Jody C. Dill (1998), "Do Smiles Elicit More Inferences than Do Frowns? The Effect of Emotional Valence on the Production of Spontaneous Inferences," *Personality and Social Psychology Bulletin*, 24 (3), 289-300.

Kwan, Virginia S.Y., Oliver P. John, Richard W. Robins, and Lu L. Kuang (2008), "Conceptualizing and Assessing Self-Enhancement Bias: A Componential Approach," *Journal of Personality and Social Psychology*, 94 (6), 1062-77.

Richins, Marsha L. (1983), "Negative Word-of-Mouth by Dissatisfied Consumers: A Pilot Study," *Journal of Marketing*, 47 (1), 68-78.

Richins, Marsha L. (1984), "Word of Mouth Communications as Negative Information", in ATC Kinnear (Ed.), *Advances in Consumer Research,* 11 (pp. 697-702). Ann Arbor, MI: Association for Consumer Research.

Romaniuk, Jenni (2007), "Word of Mouth and the Viewing of Television Programs," *Journal of Advertising Research*, 47 (4), 462-71.

Rozin, Paul and Edward B. Royzman (2001), "Negativity Bias, Negativity Dominance, and Contagion," *Personality and Social Psychology Review*, 5 (4), 296-320.

Samson, Alain (2006), "Understanding the Buzz that Matters: Negative Vs. Positive Word of Mouth," *International Journal of Market Research*, 48 (6), 647-57.

Sedikides, Constantine (1993), "Assessment, Enhancement, and Verification Determinants of the Self-Evaluation Process," *Journal of Personality and Social Psychology*, 65 (2), 317-38.

Shrauger, Sidney J. (1975), "Responses to Evaluation as a Function of Initial Self-Perceptions," *Psychological Bulletin*, 82 (4), 581-96.

Sirgy, M. Joseph (1982), "Self-Concept in Consumer Behavior: A Critical Review," *Journal of Consumer Research*, 9 (3), 287-300.

Swann, William B., John J. Griffin, Steven C. Predmore, and Bebe Gaines (1987), "The Cognitive-Affective Crossfire: When Self-Consistency Confronts Self-Enhancement," *Journal of Personality and Social Psychology*, 52 (5), 881-89.

Taylor, Shelley E. and Jonathon D. Brown (1988), "Illusion and Well-Being: A Social Psychological Perspective on Mental Health," *Psychological Bulletin*, 103 (2), 193-210.

Technical Assistance Research Program (TARP) (1981), *Measuring the Grapevine-Consumer Response and Word-of-Mouth.* Atlanta, GA: Coca-Cola Company.

Tesser, Abraham (1988), "Toward a Self-Evaluation Maintenance Model of Social Behavior," in *Advances in Experimental Social Psychology*, Vol, 21, ed. Leonard Berkowitz, New York: Academic Press, 181-227.

--- and Jennifer Campbell (1982), "Self-Evaluation Maintenance and the Perception of Friends and Strangers," *Journal of Personality*, 50 (3), 261-79.

--- and Del Paulhus (1983), "The Definition of Self: Private and Public Self-Evaluation Management Strategy," *Journal of Personality and Social Psychology*, 44 (4), 672-82.

Weiner, Bernard (1985), "'Spontaneous' Causal Thinking," *Psychological Bulletin,* 97 (1), 74-84.

Westbrook, Robert A. (1987), "Product/Consumption-Based Affective Responses and Postpurchase Processes," *Journal of Marketing Research*, 24 (3), 258-70.

Zuckerman, Miron and Ryan E. O'Loughlin (2006), "Self-Enhancement by Social Comparison: A Prospective Analysis," *Personality and Social Psychology Bulletin*, 32 (6), 751-60.

The Effectiveness of Sponsorship in Legitimacy Formation – The Moderating Role of Pre-Existing Satisfaction

Barbara Caemmerer, ESSCA School of Management, France
Raluca Mogos Descotes, IUT Charlemagne, Nancy University, France

EXTENDED ABSTRACT

Conceptualization

Sponsorship activities have gained great importance in marketing communications as well as academic attention over the last decade (Dalakas and Levin 2005; Roy and Cornwell 2004). Traditionally, there has been the notion that sponsorship activities are carried out in order to reach commercial targets (Cornwell et al. 2006; Jagre, Watson, and Watson 2001). However, with growing awareness of the importance of establishing good relationships with important stakeholder groups (Ferrell and Ferrell 2008), the scope of sponsorship has broadened. For example, Dean (2002) highlights that management objectives concerning sponsorship may be both, economic (such as increased brand awareness and profits) as well as noneconomic (such as goodwill and improved community relations) in nature. Despite this recognition, the majority of studies in this field of research have focused on the assessment of the economic effectiveness of sponsorship activities (Gwinner 1997).

Our study contributes to the extant literature by investigating how event sponsorship impacts on the formation of organisational legitimacy which is broadly defined as the "acceptance of an organization by its environment" (Kostova and Zaheer 1999, 64). From an institutional theory perspective, gaining legitimacy is important as it enhances the likelihood that organisations are able to extract scarce resources from their environment and is thus critical to organisational survival (Meyer and Rowan 1977; Suddaby and Greenwood 2005). However, to our knowledge the effectiveness of sponsorship in the formation of legitimacy has not been explored yet.

We further contribute to knowledge by examining the moderating role of pre-existing attitudes towards the organisation on the link between sponsorship and legitimacy. Most of the sponsorship studies have focused on the balancing effects between attitudes towards the sponsored entity, congruence between the sponsored entity and the sponsor, attitudes towards the sponsorship and the resulting attitudes towards the sponsor (Dalakas and Levin 2005; Dean 2002). The underlying assumption has usually been that positive attitudes towards the sponsored entity will transfer to the sponsor. Therefore, very few studies have controlled for pre-existing attitudes towards the sponsor and their possible impact on the effectiveness of the sponsorship activity. However, there is some evidence to suggest that pre-existing attitudes play a moderating role in sponsorship effectiveness (Basil and Herr 2006).

Finally, we also contribute to the literature by examining the hypothesised model in a public sector context. While there is a growing body of knowledge concerning the sponsorship of regional or local charitable events of private sector organizations to develop community relations and increase goodwill, little is known about the use of sponsorship as a tool to develop relations with important stakeholders by public sector organizations. However, public sector organizations are under huge political pressure to establish and maintain good relations with important publics such as their electorate (McNulty and Ferlie 2004; Sanger 2008). Moreover, public sector organizations increasingly invest resources into the support of local events such as concerts and sports events (Walliser 2006). For these reasons, we believe that it is important from a public administration perspective to investigate the effectiveness of sponsorship activities in a public sector environment.

Method

Using a pre-tested questionnaire, responses from 300 spectators of the finals of the Handball French League Cup tournament in Nantes, which was sponsored by Nantes City Council, were captured assessing the following constructs: 1) Attitudes towards the event (Simmons and Becker-Olsen 2006), 2) perceived sponsor-event congruence (Simmons and Becker-Olsen 2006), 3) attitudes towards public sponsorship (Walliser et al. 2005), 4) legitimacy (Sabadie 2003), and 5) pre-existing satisfaction with Nantes City Council (Sabadie 2003). The procedure yielded 275 usable questionnaires. Hypotheses were tested using partial least squares path modelling (PLSPM) (Chin 1998; Fornell and Bookstein 1982). The moderating effects were tested by performing a median split on the basis of pre-existing satisfaction. This enabled the comparison of two sub-samples.

Major Findings

Our study makes three contributions to the extant literature. First, we assess through which mechanisms events sponsorship impacts on organisational legitimacy (Deephouse and Carter 2005). The estimation of our sponsorship model demonstrates that 1) attitudes towards the sponsored event, 2) positive attitudes towards the sponsorship activity, as well as 3) perceived event-sponsor congruence significantly impact on organisational legitimacy amongst customers. Comparing the three effects, we contribute to the extant literature by showing that attitudes towards the sponsorship activity itself have a stronger impact on organizational legitimacy than attitudes towards the event as well as perceived event-sponsor congruence (Cornwell et al. 2006).

The second main contribution of our study relates to the investigation of the moderating role of pre-existing attitudes towards the sponsor on sponsorship effectiveness (Speed and Thompson 2000). Our results provide insight into an interesting dynamic of the sponsorship model when pre-existing satisfaction with the sponsor is controlled for. First of all, we show that the model has a much stronger explanatory power for the sub-sample with positive pre-existing attitudes than for the sub-sample with negative pre-existing attitudes. Further, we can observe that all but one of the moderated links strengthen with increased pre-existing satisfaction. These findings suggest that customers who hold more positive attitudes towards the sponsor in advance tend to evaluate the sponsorship activities of the organisation more favourably. Therefore, there is some support for the overarching hypothesis of our study that pre-existing attitudes towards the sponsor moderate sponsorship effectiveness with regards to non-economic objectives, here legitimacy formation.

This links into the third area of contribution to the extant literature. In relation to the above discussed results we highlight that, first of all, public management needs to further emphasize the implementation of programs that enhance citizen satisfaction. Such initiatives may include in particular the development of an external service orientation (Parkington and Schneider 1979) through which improved and tailored services can be delivered. If such initiatives are not in place and citizens have negative service experiences and resulting low levels of satisfaction with the public service provider (van Ryzin et al. 2004), sponsorship activities will have less strong an impact on the achievement of non-economic objectives, such as the formation of legitimacy. Focusing on the sponsorship model in particular, it is important to note that public sector bodies should pay attention to the explicit communication of the reasons for the sponsorship activity. Pursuing this perceived event-sponsor match is important (Simmons and Becker-Olsen 2006) as it impacts directly on legitimacy, as well as indirectly through its impact on positive attitudes towards the sponsorship activity.

REFERENCES

Basil, Debra Z. and Paul M. Herr (2006), "Attitudinal Balance and Cause-Related Marketing: An Empirical Application of Balance Theory," *Journal of Consumer Psychology*, 16(4), 391-403.

Chin, Wayne (1998), "The partial least squares approach to structural equation modeling", in Modern Business Research Methods, New Jersey: Lawrence Erlbaum Associates.

Cornwell, Bettina T., Michael S. Humphreys, Angela M. Maguire, Clinton S. Weeks, and Cassandra L. Tellegen (2006), "Sponsorship-Linked Marketing: The Role of Articulation in Memory," *Journal of Consumer Research*, 33, 312-321.

Dalakas, Vassilis and Aron M. Levin (2005), "The Balance Theory Domino: How Sponsorships May Elicit Negative Consumer Attitudes," *Advances in Consumer Research*, 32, 91-97.

Dean, Dwane Hal (2002), "Associating the Corporation with a Charitable Event Through Sponsorship: Measuring the Effects of Corporate Community Relations," *Journal of Advertising,* 31(4), 77-87.

Deephouse, L. David and Suzanne M. Carter (2005), "An examination of differences between organizational legitimacy and organizational reputation," *Journal of Management Studies*, 42(2), 329–360.

Ferrell, O. C. and Linda Ferrell (2008), "A Macromarketing Ethics Framework: Stakeholder Orientation and Distributive Justice," *Journal of Macromarketing*, 28(1), 24-32.

Fornell, Claes, and Fred L. Bookstein (1982), "Two structural equation models: LISREL and PLS applied to consumer exit-voice theory", *Journal of Marketing Research*, 19, 440–453.

Gwinner, Kevin (1997), "A Model of Image Creation and Image Transfer in Event Sponsorship," *International Marketing Review,* 14(3), 145-158.

Jagre, Emma, John J. Watson, and John G. Watson (2001), "Sponsorship and Congruity Theory: A Theoretical Framework for Explaining Consumer Attitude and Recall of Event Sponsorship," *Advances in Consumer Research*, 28, 439-445.

Kostova, Tatiana and Srilata Zaheer (1999), "Organizational Legitimacy under Conditions of Complexity: The Case of the Multinational Enterprise," *Academy of Management Review*, 24(1), 64–81.

McNulty, Terrie and Ewan Ferlie (2004), "Process Transformation: Limitations to Radical Organizational Change within Public Service Organizations," *Organization Studies*, 25 (8), 1389–1412

Meyer, John W. and Brian Rowan (1977), "Institutionalized Organizations: Formal Structure as Myth and Ceremony," *The American Journal of Sociology*, 83 (3), 340 – 363.

Parkington, John J., and Benjamin Schneider (1979), "Some Correlates of Experienced Job Stress: A Boundary Role Study," *Academy of Management Journal*, 22 (2), 270–81.

Roy, Donald P. and Bettina Cornwell (2004), "The Effects of Consumer Knowledge on Responses to Event Sponsorship", *Psychology & Marketing*, 21(3), 185-207.

van Ryzin, Gregg G., Douglas Muzzio, Stephen Immerwahr, Lisa Gulick, and Eve Martinez (2004), "Drivers and Consequences of Citizen Satisfaction: An Application of the American Customer Satisfaction Index Model to New York City," *Public Administration Review*, 64(3), 331 – 341.

Sabadie, William (2003), "Conceptualisation et mesure de la qualité d'un service public", *Recherche et Applications en Marketing*, 18, 1-24.

Sanger, Mary B. (2008), "From Measurement to Management: Breaking through the Barriers to State and Local Performance," *Public Administration Review*, 68 (6), 70–85.

Simmons, Carolyn J. and Karen L. Becker-Olsen (2006), "Achieving marketing objectives through social sponsorships", 70(4), 154-169.

Speed, Richard and Peter Thompson (2000), "Determinants of Sports Sponsorship Response," *Journal of the Academy of Marketing Science*, 28(2), 226-238.

Suddaby, Roy and Royston Greenwood (2005), "Rhetorical Strategies of Legitimacy", *Administrative Science Quarterly*, 50 (1), 35 – 67.

Walliser Bjorn, Kacha Mathieu and Raluca Mogos Descotes (2005), "Legitimizing public authorities as sponsors: an inquiry into the factors related to the perception and the memorization of their sponsorship", *International Review of Public and Non Profit Marketing*, 2(1), 51-58.

Walliser Bjorn (2006), *Le parrainage: sponsoring et mécénat,* Dunod : Paris.

Reversing Ease of Retrieval Effects with Sensory Product Experience

Kelly (Kiyeon) Lee, University of Toronto, Canada
Andrew Mitchell, University of Toronto, Canada

EXTENDED ABSTRACT

Prior research on the ease-of-retrieval effect has shown that ease (vs. difficulty) of retrieval leads to more favorable judgments in the different types of tasks such as recalling instances from the past memory (e.g., Schwarz et al. 1991), listing counterarguments after reading persuasive messages (e.g., Petty, Brinõl, Tormala, and Wegener 2007), and providing reasons for or against choosing one brand over another after reading advertisements (e.g., Wanke, Bohner, and Jurkowitsch 1997).

This research examines whether previous findings of these effects can be extended to product evaluations based on sensory product experience. We believe that these effects with sensory product experience will produce different outcomes compared to prior research because direct product experience will provide a rich base of sensory information as opposed to situations where individuals merely recall instances or read persuasive messages/advertisements. In addition, sensory information obtained from direct product experience is real and is not to be doubted. However, how one interprets this experience will determine how it is evaluated. Examples of product experiences include testing the comfort of a mattress or the sound quality of a stereo (Shapiro and Spence 2002; Wright and Lynch 1995). We expect that the interactive effect of metacognitive experience and sensory information will lead people to magnify the information generated in direct sensory experience situations in spite of having the same subjective feeling of ease or difficulty as in indirect experience situations.

We conducted four experiments to test our expectations. The purpose of experiment 1 is to test our expectations using a soft drink taste test. Participants were told that a company recently developed a new soft drink targeting a young adult group and that the company wanted to know the strengths or weaknesses of this drink. After tasting the drink, participants were asked to generate 10 reasons or 2 reasons why they like or dislike the drink. Even though our participants found it to be more difficult to generate 10 reasons than 2 reasons, they evaluated the drink more positively when listing 10 reasons than 2 reasons in positive-reasons-generation conditions. However, the reverse was true for negative reasons: they evaluated the drink less positively when they listed 10 reasons than 2 reasons in negative-reasons-generation conditions.

The goal of experiment 2 is threefold: First, to generalize our findings of experiment 1, we employed a different product - a hand lotion. Second, we aimed to rule out a motivation account for the findings of experiment 1 by manipulating high vs. low motivation. Previous research has indicated that individuals tend to rely on thought content under high involvement whereas they are more likely to focus on metacognitive experience as a heuristic cue under low involvement (Rothman and Schwarz 1998). Participants in experiment 1 were highly motivated since they were the target market of the drink and their evaluations would be incorporated in the development of the soft drink, which may lead them to rely on thought content, not on metacognitive experience. In experiment 2, we used the same instructions of experiment 1 for the high motivation condition. For the low motivation condition, participants were told that the target market of the hand lotion was older adults and that their opinions would remain anonymous and be used after aggregating them with those of other groups (Maheswaran and Sternthal 1990; Petty, Harkins, and Williams 1980). If we find consistent results un-

der high and low motivation conditions, this indicates that our findings are not due to motivation. Third, we tested whether confidence in thoughts mediates attitude formation drawing on attitude confidence literature on ease-of-retrieval (e.g., Tormala, Falces, Brinõl, and Petty 2007; Tormala, Petty, and Brinõl 2002). We replicated the findings of experiment 1 using the hand lotion: Participants reported greater difficulty in generating 8 reasons than 2 reasons. However, they evaluated the hand lotion more (less) favorably when generating 8 than 2 positive (negative) reasons. Further, we did not find any difference in product evaluations between high and low motivation conditions, which rules out the motivation account. In addition, we found that confidence did not mediate the effects. These findings provide further evidence for the magnified effect of metacognitive difficulty on product evaluations.

Experiment 3 was conducted to rule out another alternative account—a thought-content-effect account. Although we replicated our findings using hand lotion, it may be argued that it is not clear whether participants rely on metacognitive experience or just on thought content (e.g., reasons). To address this issue, we employed a yoked design used by Wänke, Bless, and Biller (1996). The effect of subjective experience should influence only those who generate reasons themselves as demonstrated in experiments 1 and 2. When participants are asked to read reasons generated by others, they make judgments about a test product based on the content of reasons (thoughts) since they do not have subjective experience. We found that individuals (readers) who did not have subjective feeling of ease or difficulty did not show any differences in their attitude toward the hand lotion based on the number of reasons within the same valence, which is different from findings in experiment 2. This indicates that only generators who write their own reasons and feel metacognitive experience (i.e., feeling of ease or difficulty) can show the magnified effect of metacognitive experience on product evaluations.

Taken together, our findings showed that metacognitive difficulty magnifies thought content in the context of direct product experience, which is contrary to previous findings in different contexts. Across experiments 1-3, we obtained the same results in different sensory products (e.g., a soft drink, a hand lotion) and ruled out a motivation account in experiment 2 and a thought-content account in experiment 3.

We believe that this research make several important contributions. First, it contributes to extend our understanding of the role of metacognition in the context of direct product experience by demonstrating that metacognitive difficulty magnifies thought content. Second, it demonstrates the importance of investigating product usage since consumers may have consistent preference by engaging in direct product experience prior to purchase and firms may have better understanding of consumers' preference and demand.

REFERENCES

Bazerman, Max (2001), "Consumer Research for Consumers," *Journal of Consumer Research*, 27, 499-504. (Reprinted in F. Maidment (Ed.) *Powerweb: Introduction to Business*, McGraw-Hill, 2003.)

Fazio, Russell H., Jeaw-mei Chen, Elizabeth C. McDonel, and Steven J. Sherman (1982), "Attitude Accessibility, Attitude-Behavior Consistency and the Strength of the Object-Evaluation Association," *Journal of Experimental Social Psychology*, 18, 339-357.

Fazio, Russell H., Mark P. Zanna, and Joel Cooper (1978), "Direct Experience and Attitude-Behavior Consistency: An Information Processing Analysis," *Personality and Social Psychology Bulletin*, 4, 48–51.

Grayson, Carla E., and Nobert Schwarz (1999), "Beliefs Influence Information Processing Strategies: Declarative and Experiential Information in Risk Assessment," *Social Cognition*, 17, 1–18

Higgins, E. Tory (1989), "Knowledge Accessibility and Activation: Subjectivity and Suffering from Unconscious Sources," in *Unintended Thought*, ed. James S. Uleman and John A. Bargh, New York: Guilford, 75–123.

Kardes, Frank R. (1994), "Consumer Judgment and Decision Process" in *Handbook of Social Cognition*, ed. Robert S. Wyer Jr. and Thomas K. Srull, Hillsdale, NJ: Erlbaum, 323- 417.

Kisielius, Jolita, and Brian Sternthal (1984), "Examining the Vividness Controversy: An Availability-Valence Interpretation, *Journal of Consumer Research*, 12, 418–431.

Maheswaran, Durairaj, and Brian Sternthal (1990), "The Effects of Knowledge, Motivation, and Type of Message on Ad Processing and Product Judgments," *Journal of Consumer Research*, 17, 66-73.

Menon, Geeta, and Priya Raghubir (2003), "Ease of Retrieval as an Automatic Input in Judgments: A Mere-Accessibility Framework?" *Journal of Consumer Research*, 30, 230–243.

Petty, Richard E., Pablo Briñol, Zakary L. Tormala, and Duane T. Wegener (2007), "The Role of Metacognition in Social Judgment," in *Social psychology: Handbook of basic principles* (2nd edition), ed. Arie W. Kruglanski & E. Tory Higgins, New York: Guilford Press, 254-284.

Petty, Richard E., Stephen G. Harkins, and Kipling D. Williams (1980), "The Effects of Group Diffusion of Cognitive Effort on Attitudes: An Information Processing View," *Journal of Personality and Social Psychology*, 38, 81–92.

Rothman, Alexander J., and Nobert Schwarz (1998), "Constructing Perceptions of Vulnerability: Personal Relevance and the Use of Experiential Information in Health Judgments," *Personality and Social Psychology Bulletin*, 24, 1053–1064.

Ruder, Markus, & Herbert Bless (2003), "Mood and the Reliance on the Ease of Retrieval Heuristic," *Journal of Personality and Social Psychology*, 85, 20–32.

Schwarz, Nobert (2004). "Metacognitive Experiences in Consumer Judgment and Decision Making," *Journal of Consumer Psychology*, 14, 332–348.

Schwarz, Nobert, Herbert Bless, Fritz Strack, Gisela Klumpp, Helga Rittenauer-Schatk, and Annette Simons (1991), "Ease of Retrieval as Information: Another Look at the Availability Heuristic," *Journal of Personality and Social Psychology*, 61, 195–202.

Schwarz, Nobert, & Gerald L. Clore (2007), "Feelings and Phenomenal Experiences," in *Social psychology: Handbook of basic principles* (2nd edition), ed. Arie W. Kruglanski & E. Tory Higgins, New York: Guilford Press, 385-407.

Shapiro, Stewart, and Mark T. Spence (2002), "Factors Affecting Encoding, Retrieval, and Alignment of Sensory Attributes in a Memory-Based Brand Choice Task," *Journal of Consumer Research*, 28, 603–617.

Smith, Robert E. (1993), "Integrating Information from Advertising and Trial: Processes and Effects on Consumer Response to Product Information," *Journal of Marketing Research*, 30, 204–219.

Srinivasan, V., William S. Lovejoy, and David Beach (1997), "Integrated Product Design for Marketability and Manufacturing," *Journal of Marketing Research*, 34, 154–163.

Thompson, Debora V., Rebecca W. Hamilton, and Roland T. Rust (2005), "Feature Fatigue: When Product Capabilities Become Too Much of a Good Thing," *Journal of Marketing Research*, 42, 431–442.

Tormala, Zakary L., Carlos Falces, Pablo Brinõl, and Richard E. Petty (2007), "Ease of Retrieval Effects in Social Judgment: The Role of Unrequested Cognitions," *Journal of Personality and Social Psychology*, 93(2), 143–157.

Tormala, Zakary L., Richard E. Petty, and Pablo Briñol (2002), "Ease of Retrieval Effects in Persuasion: A Self-Validation Analysis," *Personality and Social Psychology Bulletin*, 28, 1700–1712.

Tsai, Claire I., and Ann L. McGill (2011), "No pain, No gain? How Construal Level and Fluency Affect Consumer Confidence," *Journal of Consumer Research*, 37, 807–821.

Tybout, Alice M., Brian Sternthal, Prashant Malaviya, Georgios A. Bakamitsos, and Se-Bum Park (2005), "Information Accessibility as a Moderator of Judgments: The Role of Content versus Retrieval Ease," *Journal of Consumer Research*, 32, 76–85.

Wänke, Michaela, Herbert Bless, and Barbara Biller (1996), "Subjective Experience versus Content of Information in the Construction of Attitude Judgments," *Personality and Social Psychology Bulletin*, 22, 1105–1113.

Wänke, Michaela, Gerd Bohner, and Andreas Jurkowitsch (1997), "There Are Many Reasons to Drive a BMW- Does Imagined Ease of Argument Generation Influences Attitudes?" *Journal of Consumer Research*, 24, 70–77.

Wright, Alice A., and John G. Lynch, Jr. (1995). "Communication Effects of Advertising versus Direct Experience When Both Search and Experience Attributes Are Present," *Journal of Consumer Research*, 21, 708–718.

Wyer, Robert S., and Thomas K. Srull (1989), *Memory and Cognition in Its Social Context*, Hillsdale, NJ: Erlbaum.

The Impact of Incidental Ownership of Objects on Subsequent Behavior

Liad Weiss, Columbia University, USA
Gita V. Johar, Columbia University, USA

EXTENDED ABSTRACT

Every single day we acquire new objects – either because we choose them or through some other incidental route such as "hand-me downs" or gifts we never asked for. While it is true that who we are causes us to choose one kind of object over another, is it possible that incidentally acquired objects could cause us to act in ways consistent with those objects? Indeed, the notion that 'we are what we have' is deeply rooted in theories of the "self" (Belk 1988). Previous research has portrayed a motivational process of identity-construction, where people acquire products in order to manage their identity (e.g., Reed 2004). Such research (implicitly) assumes that *wanting* an "identity update" and *choosing* to achieve it via product ownership are necessary conditions for people's identity to be affected by products they own. Extending that research, we demonstrate that these conditions are not necessary, namely that a product can affect people's identity and subsequent behavior even when it was incidentally obtained (e.g., a gift) and the owners have no desire to "update" their identity.

Previous "product-to-behavior" research has shown that product characteristics can affect behavior through brand exposure (via goal activation; e.g., Mazar and Zhong 2010) and product usage (via self-signaling; Gino, Norton, and Ariely 2010). Adding to this literature, we suggest---product ownership---as another route through which product characteristics can affect behavior. We predict that people will behave consistently with product characteristics when they own it (assimilation), but contradictory to them when they interact with the product but do not own it (contrast). Furthermore, we propose a cognitive framework, Egocentric Categorization, to account for these assimilation and contrast effects. Our framework suggests that people may categorize owned and non-owned objects in terms of the category "self" similarly to the way they categorize in-group and out-group members in terms of that category. Further, just like people behave in assimilation to characteristics of 'in-groups' but in contrast to characteristics of 'out-groups,' we suggest that they may behave in assimilation to characteristics of owned objects but in contrast to characteristics of non-owned ones they interact with. Thus, in the ethical behavior domain, for example, when people interact with a product associated with greater (vs. lower) moral characteristics (e.g., reliability, authenticity), they may behave more ethically if they own it but less ethically if they do not.

Our framework predicts that ownership affects behavior through its effect on how people see the self; hence, if people do not "refresh" their self-evaluation after interacting with a product their subsequent behavior cannot reflect product characteristics. People who are low on self-awareness (the state) or private self-consciousness (the trait) tend to reevaluate the self less frequently and their behavior is generally less correlated with their internal states (Gibbons 1990). Therefore, we predict that changes in behavior as a consequence of product ownership are less likely among individuals with lower self-awareness or self-consciousness.

We conducted two laboratory experiments to investigate the aforementioned predictions. We restricted our attention to fidelity in behavior as the dependent variable and used headphones varying in fidelity as the stimulus product category. The headphones differ on fidelity in terms of the extent to which sound is truthfully reproduced and loyal to the original recording. As a cover story, participants in both experiments were asked to help the department of music in selecting gift headphones for invited visitors.

In Experiment 1, the headphones were described as being either high (the "Authentic-Sound" headphones that reproduce the sound exactly as it was recorded) or moderate (the "Better-Sound" headphones that improve the original sound) on fidelity. A separate pretest verified that the high-fidelity headphones were comparable to the moderate-fidelity ones on attractiveness and quality but higher on truthfulness. Two-thirds of the participants were assigned to receive either the set they evaluated ("ownership" condition) or another set ("no-ownership" condition). Another third of the participants (control condition) were informed that they would receive an additional $2 for their input and did not receive any ownership information. Subsequently, after trying on the headphones, evaluating them, entering them into big envelopes and putting them aside, participants' self-awareness was increased by asking them to describe their mirror-image. Finally, in an ostensibly separate study, participants' cheating behavior was surreptitiously documented in a trivia knowledge quiz that incentivized good performance (participation in a $50 lottery) and provided an opportunity to artificially improve one's score by self-reporting their performance.

The results show that, the interaction between ownership and fidelity description on ethical behavior was significant in the predicted direction. In particular, participants in the "ownership" condition acted with *greater* fidelity when the perceived product fidelity was high (vs. moderate). That is, they adjusted their behavior to align with the perceived characteristics of headphones they were randomly assigned *to own*. By contrast, participants in the "no-ownership" condition acted with *lower* fidelity when perceived product fidelity was high (vs. moderate). That is, they contrasted their behavior to the perceived characteristics of the headphones they were randomly assigned *not to own*. It is important to note that, within the control condition, when the ownership construct was not activated, fidelity did not affect cheating behavior. Further analysis showed that owning (vs. not owning) the headphones decreased cheating when the set was described as high on fidelity but did not affect cheating when the set was described as moderate on fidelity. Repeating the same analyses using the amount of cheating as a continuous variable yielded a similar pattern of results.

Experiment 2 complemented the testing of our theoretical framework by varying participants' (measured) self-consciousness level (vs. keeping it high) across conditions while introducing only the high-fidelity headphones in all conditions. They were assigned either to own or not to own these headphones. The same cheating documentation method of experiment 1 revealed that owners (vs. non-owners) of the high-fidelity headphones were less likely to cheat (as found in study 1). Furthermore, consistent with our account that product characteristics affect behavior through an effect on people's self, this difference between owners and non-owners was apparent only among self-conscious individuals.

REFERENCES

Aron, Arthur, Elaine N. Aron, Michael Tudor, and Greg Nelson (1991), "Close Relationships as Including Other in the Self," *Journal of Personality and Social Psychology*, 60 (2), 241-53.

Beggan, James K. (1992), "On the Social Nature of Nonsocial Perception - the Mere Ownership Effect," *Journal of Personality and Social Psychology*, 62 (2), 229-37.

Belk, Russell W. (1988), "Possessions and the Extended Self," *Journal of Consumer Research*, 15 (September), 139-68.

Bem, D. J. (1967), "Self-Perception: An Alternative Interpretation of Cognitive Dissonance Phenomena," *Psychological Review*, 74 (3), 183-&.

Bless, Herbert and Norbert Schwarz (2010), "Mental Construal and the Emergence of Assimilation and Contrast Effects: The Inclusion/Exclusion Model," in *Advances in Experimental Social Psychology*, Vol. 42, San Diego: Elsevier Academic Press Inc, 319-73.

Brewer, Marilynn B. (1991), "The Social Self - on Being the Same and Different at the Same Time," *Personality and Social Psychology Bulletin*, 17 (5), 475-82.

Brewer, Marilynn B. and W. Gardner (1996), "Who Is This ''We''? Levels of Collective Identity and Self Representations," *Journal of Personality and Social Psychology*, 71 (1), 83-93.

Cryder, C. E., J. S. Lerner, J. J. Gross, and R. E. Dahl (2008), "Misery Is Not Miserly: Sad and Self-Focused Individuals Spend More," *Psychological Science*, 19 (6), 525-30.

Cunningham, S. J., D. J. Turk, L. M. Macdonald, and C. N. Macrae (2008), "Yours or Mine? Ownership and Memory," *Consciousness and Cognition*, 17 (1), 312-18.

Dunning, David (2007), "Self-Image Motives and Consumer Behavior: How Sacrosanct Self-Beliefs Sway Preferences in the Marketplace," *Journal of Consumer Psychology*, 17 (4), 237-49.

Duval, T. Shelly and Robert A Wicklund (1972), *A Theory of Objective Self-Awareness*, New York: Academic Press.

Fehr, E. and S. Gachter (2000), "Fairness and Retaliation: The Economics of Reciprocity," *Journal of Economic Perspectives*, 14 (3), 159-81.

Fenigstein, Allan, Michael F. Scheier, and Arnold H. Buss (1975), "Public and Private Self-Consciousness - Assessment and Theory " *Journal of Consulting and Clinical Psychology*, 43 (4), 522-27.

Fitzsimons, Gráinne M., Tanya L. Chartrand, and Gavan J. Fitzsimons (2008), "Automatic Effects of Brand Exposure on Motivated Behavior: How Apple Makes You "Think Different"," *Journal of Consumer Research*, 35 (1), 21-35.

Gibbons, F. X. (1990), "Self-Attention and Behavior: A Review and Theoretical Update," *Advances in Experimental Social Psychology*, 23, 249-303.

Gino, F., M. I. Norton, and Dan Ariely (2010), "The Counterfeit Self: The Deceptive Costs of Faking It," *Psychological Science*, 21 (5), 712-20.

Gordijn, E. H. and D. A. Stapel (2006), "Behavioural Effects of Automatic Interpersonal Versus Intergroup Social Comparison," *British Journal of Social Psychology*, 45, 717-29.

Howard, J. A. (2000), "Social Psychology of Identities," *Annual Review of Sociology*, 26, 367-93.

Hull, J. G. and A. S. Levy (1979), "Organizational Functions of the Self: Alternative to the Duval and Wicklund Model of Self-Awareness," *Journal of Personality and Social Psychology*, 37 (5), 756-68.

James, William (1890), *The Principles of Psychology* Vol. 1, New York: Henry Holt.

Klein, S. B. and J. Loftus (1988), "The Nature of Self-Referent Encoding: The Contributions of Elaborative and Organizational Processes," *Journal of Personality and Social Psychology*, 55 (1), 5-11.

Leary, M. R. and R. M. Kowalski (1990), "Impression Management - a Literature-Review and 2-Component Model " *Psychological Bulletin*, 107 (1), 34-47.

Mazar, N. and C. B. Zhong (2010), "Do Green Products Make Us Better People?," *Psychological Science*, 21 (4), 494-98.

McClelland, David (1951), *Personality*, New York: Holt, Rinehart, & Winston.

Medin, Douglas L., William D. Wattenmaker, and Sarah E. Hampson (1987), "Family Resemblance, Conceptual Cohesiveness, and Category Construction," *Cognitive Psychology*, 19 (2), 242-79.

Pham, Michel Tuan, Caroline Goukens, Donald R. Lehmann, and Jennifer Ames Stuart (2010), "Shaping Customer Satisfaction through Self-Awareness Cues," *Journal of Marketing Research*, 47 (5).

Prelinger, Ernst (1959), "Extension and Structure of the Self," *Journal of Psychology*, 47 (1), 13-23.

Reed, A. (2004), "Activating the Self-Importance of Consumer Selves: Exploring Identity Salience Effects on Judgments," *Journal of Consumer Research*, 31 (2), 286-95.

Sartre, Jean-Paul (1943), *Being and the Nothingness: A Phenomenological Essay on Ontology*, New York: Philosophical Library.

Spears, R., E. Gordijn, A. P. Dijksterhuis, and D. A. Stapel (2004), "Reaction in Action: Intergroup Contrast in Automatic Behavior," *Personality and Social Psychology Bulletin*, 30 (5), 605-16.

Tajfel, Henri, Michael G. Billig, Roberet P. Bundy, and C. Flament (1971), "Social Categorization and Intergroup Behavior," *European Journal of Social Psychology*, 1 (2), 149-77.

Tuan, Y. F. (1980), "The Significance of the Artifact," *Geographical Review*, 70 (4), 462-72.

Wheeler, S. C., K. G. DeMarree, and R. E. Petty (2007), "Understanding the Role of the Self in Prime-to-Behavior Effects: The Active-Self Account," *Personality and Social Psychology Review*, 11 (3), 234-61.

Odd-Ending Price: Justification for the Hedonic Purchase

Jungsil Choi, University of Kansas, USA
Surendra Singh, University of Kansas, USA
Priyam Rangan, University of Kansas, USA

EXTENDED ABSTRACT

In the present paper, we introduce psychological pricing as a means of reducing feelings of guilt associated with the hedonic purchase. We contend that an odd-ending price, which is known to have a discount image (Schindler and Kibarian 2001), will enable a consumer to feel less guilt upon product purchase than an even-ending price.

Odd-ending pricing is a well-researched topic, and several studies have focused on uncovering the mechanism of why and how consumers respond to odd-ending vs. even-ending pricing (Bizer and Schindler, 2005; Manning and Sprott, 2009; Schindler and Kirby, 1997; Thomas and Morwitz, 2005). One of the mechanisms that explain why people perceive an odd-ending price to be cheaper than an even-ending price is the perceived gain effect of odd-ending pricing. Because round numbers are easily accessible in memory, they serve as reference points in price evaluation (Kahneman and Tversky, 1979). Therefore, an odd-ending price gives consumers the impression that they are receiving a discount (i.e., the amount subtracted from the even-ending price; Bader and Weinland 1932; Kreul 1982; Schindler and Kirby 1997).

Another mechanism is related to a consumer's tendency to ignore a price's rightmost digit/s (Bizer and Schindler 2005; Coulter 2001; Manning and Sprott 2009). Because of the habit of reading multiple digit numbers from left to right, people's attention to the rightmost digits is reduced. Price recall tests show that people make more errors when the price of the purchased product is odd-ending rather than even-ending because of the lack of attention paid to the odd-ending price (Schindler and Wiman 1989). This underestimation for the rightmost digits causes consumers to perceive an odd-ending price as being cheaper or as a discount (Quigley and Notarantonio 1992, Schindler and Kibarian 2001).

The present study suggests that utilization of the odd-ending pricing strategy, known to have a discount image, reduces guilt from purchasing a hedonic product, consequently increasing demand for hedonic products. We demonstrate this hypothesis by identifying the mechanism by which an odd-ending price reduces the guilt associated with the hedonic purchase when there is insufficient justification (Study 1) and insufficient motivation to purchase (Study 2). We also show that odd-ending price significantly increases demand for hedonic items, but not for utilitarian items in Study 3.

In Study 1, we used 2 (price difference: odd-ending vs. even-ending) x 2 (justification: volunteering job vs. must-job) between-subjects design. We manipulated justification-available vs. justification-unavailable conditions by having participants imagine two different scenarios about consuming massage services. We find an interaction effect of price × level of justification on feelings of guilt ($p < .05$). Pairwise comparisons show that when level of justification is low, people feel less guilty when the price of massage services is odd-ending compared to even-ending ($p < .05$). However, when a level of justification is high, there is no significant difference in feelings of guilt in terms of price difference ($p = .30$).

There is an interaction effect of price × level of justification on participants' likelihood ($p < .01$). Pairwise comparisons show that people are more likely to consume the hedonic service when the price is odd-ending than even-ending ($p < .05$) when level of justification is low. However, when justification is available, there is no significant difference in the consumption likelihood in terms of price difference ($p > .23$). Moderated mediation analysis shows that feelings of guilt mediate the effect of price-ending on the likelihood of consuming massage services only when level of justification is low (p < .05), but the mediated relationship is not observed when level of justification is high (p > .31).

In Study 2, we used 2 (price: odd-ending vs. even-ending) x 2 (motivation: sufficient motivation vs. insufficient motivation) between-subjects design. We manipulated level of motivation to purchase a product (headphones) by having participants imagine two different scenarios. We included brand familiarity, the purchase relevance, and the degree of knowledge in a product category in all the analyses as covariates. We find similar results of the first study. When people have sufficient motivations to buy headphones, they are not affected by price difference, but they are when they do not have sufficient motivations. Price difference affects feelings of guilt on purchasing the product, overall purchase feelings, and the purchase likelihood only when participants imagined not having sufficient motivations to buy the product.

In Study 3, we demonstrate whether different pricing affects choice of options in terms of option type. For instance, customers add options to their chosen basic model, especially when they buy a car or a new computer. Some options are specific to hedonic pleasure and others to functional utility. We expect that odd-ending pricing will differentially affect purchase decisions when customers choose to buy either hedonic options or utilitarian options. In particular, we hypothesize that an odd-ending price will increase the likelihood of choosing a hedonic option but will not affect the likelihood of choosing a utilitarian option.

As expected, the likelihood of purchasing hedonic options was affected by the type of price. Particularly, wing spoiler was significantly different in terms of price type ($p < .01$). An odd-ending price had a significant impact on the purchase likelihood. We find a marginal difference in the likelihood of purchasing 18" alloy wheel in terms of price type ($p = .07$). However, there was no difference in the likelihood of choosing full nose mask ($p > .4$) and floor mats ($p > .8$). Both full nose mask and floor mats were defined as utilitarian items in the pretest.

This study illustrates when odd-ending pricing strategies become more effective in increasing demand. Theoretically, this study points to another variable that moderates evaluation decisions for hedonic (vs. utilitarian) purchases, by showing the effect of an odd-ending price on purchase intentions. While most previous studies have focused on the efficacy of odd-ending pricing, few studies have revealed why its effect is significant, especially in terms of purchase context. The effect of odd-ending pricing seems to be a subtle but significant stimulus that enables consumers to get past guilt, and make the product purchase.

REFERENCES

Bader, Louis and James D. Weinland (1932), "Do Odd Prices Earn Money?" Journal of Retailing, 8 (January), 102-104.

Baron, Reuben M. and David A. Kenny (1986), "The Moderator-Mediator Variable Distinction in Social Psychological Research: Conceptual, Strategic, and Statistical Considerations," *Journal of Personality and Social Psychology*, 51(6), 1173-1182

Bizer Georgy Y. and Robert M. Schindler (2005), "Direct evidence of ending-digit drop-off in price information processing," *Psychology and Marketing*, 22(10), 771-783

Carslaw, Charles A. P. N. (1988), "Anomalies in Income Numbers: Evidence of Goal Oriented Behavior *The Accounting Review*, 63(2), 321-327

Coulter, Keith S. (2001), "Odd-Ending Price Underestimation: An Experimental Examination of Left-to-Right Processing Effects," *Journal of Product and Brand Management*, 10 (5), 276-292

Giner-Sorolla, Roger (2001), "Guilty Pleasures and Grim Necessities: Affective Attitudes in Dilemmas of Self-Control," *Journal of Personality and Social Psychology*, 80(2), 206-221.

Grewal, D., Krishnan, R., Baker, J., and Borin, N. (1998) "The effect of store name, brand name and price discounts on consumers' evaluations and purchase intentions" *Journal of Retailing*, 74(3), 331-352

Gueguen, Nicolas and Patrick Legoherel (2004), "Numerical Encoding and Odd-Ending Prices: The Effect of a Contrast in Discount Perception," European Journal of Marketing, 38(1/2), 194-208.

Hawkins, Scott A. and Stephen J. Hoch (1992), "Low-Involvement Learning: Memory without Evaluation," *Journal of Consumer Research*, 19(2), 212-225

Johnson, Eric J. and Amos Tversky (1983), "Affect, Generalization, and the Perception of Risk," *Journal of Personality and Social Psychology*, 45(1), 20-31.

Kahneman, Daniel and Amos Tversky (1979), "Prospect Theory: An Analysis of Decision Under Risk, *Econometrica*, 47(2), 263-292.

Khan, Uzma and Ravi Dhar (2006), "Licensing Effect in Consumer Choice," *Journal of Marketing Research,* 43(2), 259–266

Khan, Uzma and Ravi Dhar (forthcoming), "Price Framing Effects on Purchase of Hedonic and Utilitarian Bundles," *Journal of Marketing Research*

Kivetz, Ran and Yuhuang Zheng (2006), "Determinants of Justification and Self-Control," *Journal of Experimental Psychology: General*, 135(4), 572-587.

Kreul, Lee M. (1982), "Magic Numbers: Psychological Aspects of Menu Pricing," *Cornell Hospitality Quarterly*, 23(2), 70-75.

Lee-Wingate, Sooyeon N. and Kim P. Corfman (2004), "A Little Something for Me and Maybe for You, Too: Promotions that Relieve Guilt," *Advances in Consumer Research,* 31, 28

Manning, Kenneth C. (2009), "Price Endings, Left-Digit Effects, and Choice," *Journal of Consumer Research*, 36 (2), 328-335.

Muller, Dominique, Charles M. Judd, and Vincent Y. Yzerbyt (2005). When moderation is mediated and mediation is moderated. *Journal of Personality and Social Psychology*, 89(6), 852-863.

Okada, Erica Mina (2005), "Justification Effects on Consumer Choice of Hedonic and Utilitarian Goods," *Journal of Marketing Research*, 42(1), 45-53.

Ouyang, Y. (2007), "The Effects of Nine-ending Prices on Adolescents' Impulsive Buying Behavior: Personal Traits as Moderating Variables," Master's thesis

Pham, Michael Tuan (1998), "Representativeness, Relevance, and the Use of Feelings in Decision Making," *Journal of Consumer Research*, 25(September), 144-160.

Preacher, Kristopher J. and Andrew F. Hayes (2004), "SPSS and SAS Procedures for Estimating Indirect Effects in Simple Mediation Models," *Behavior Research Methods, Instruments, & Computers*, 36, 717-731.

Preacher, Kristopher J., Derek D. Rucker, and Andrew F. Hayes (2007), "Addressing Moderated Mediation Hypothesis: Theory, Methods, and Prescriptions," *Multivariate Behavioral Research*, 42(1), 185-227.

Prelec, Drazen and George Loewenstein (1998), "The Red and the Black: Mental Accounting of Savings and Debt," *Marketing Science*, 17(1), 4-28.

Robert M. Schindler and Thomas M. Kibarian (2001), "Image Communicated by the Use of 99 Endings in Advertised Prices," *Journal of Advertising*, 30(4), 95-99

Rook, D.W. (1987) "The buying impulse," *Journal of Consumer Research*, 14(2), 189-199

Schindler, Robert M. (2006), "The 99 Price Ending as a Signal of a Low-Price Appeal," *Journal of Retailing*, 82 (1), 71-77

Schindler, Robert M. and Thomas M. Kibarian (1996), "Increased Consumer Sales Response Though Use of 9odd-ending prices," *Journal of Retailing*, 72(2), 187-199

Schindler, Robert M. and Thomas M. Kibarian (2001), "Image Communicated by the Use of 99 Endings in Advertised Prices," *Journal of Advertising*, 30(4), 95-99.

Schindler, Robert M. and Alan R. Wiman (1989), "Effects of Odd Pricing on Price Recall," *Journal of Business Research*, 19(3), 165-177.

Schwartz, Nobert and Gerald L. Clore (1983), "Mood, Misattribution, and Judgments of Well-Being: Informative and Directive Functions of Affective States," *Journal of Personality and Social Psychology*," 45(3), 513-523.

Schwartz, Nobert and Gerald L. Clore (1988), "How Do I Feel About It? Informative Functions of Affective States," in *Affect, cognitive, and Social Behavior*, Klaus Fielder and Joseph Forgas, eds. Toronto: Hogrefe International, 44-62.

Stiving, Mark and Russell S. Winer (1997), "An Empirical Analysis of Price Endings with Scanner Data," *Journal of Consumer Research*, 24(1), 57-67

Strahilevitz, Michal and John G. Myers (1998) "Donations to Charity as Purchase Incentives: How Well They Work May Depend on What You Are Trying to Sell," Journal of Consumer Research, 24 (4), 434-446

Thomas, Jacob K. (1989), "Unusual Patterns in Reported Earnings," *The Accounting Review*, 64(4), 773-787

Thomas, Manoj and Vicki Morwitz (2005), "Penny Wise and Pound Foolish: The Left-Digit Effect in Price Cognition," *Journal of Consumer Research*, 32(1), 54-64

Zheng, Yuhuang and Ran Kivetz (2009), "The Differential Promotion Effectiveness on Hedonic versus Utilitarian Products," *Advances in Consumer Research, 36, 565*

Choosing for a Certain Future: Relying on Hard vs. Soft Attributes When Options Are Temporally Distant

Jiao Zhang, University of Miami, USA

EXTENDED ABSTRACT

Choice and consumption are often temporally separated. For example, people often reserve hotels or rent cars for a future vacation. How does the temporal distance between choice and consumption influence preference and choice? Prior research shows that as the temporal distance increases, affect-based outcomes are discounted more than cognition-based outcomes (e.g., Metcalfe and Mischel 1999); the weight of low-level attributes – peripheral, feasibility attributes – decreases while that of high-level attributes – central, desirability attributes – increases (e.g., Liberman and Trope 1998; Trope and Liberman 2000, 2003).

The present research studies how temporal distance influences the weight of "hard attributes" vs. "soft attributes." An attribute is a hard attribute if it is objective and unequivocal as to which of two options is better on it, and a soft attribute if it is subjective and malleable as to which of the two options is better (Hsee et al. 2003). Examples of hard attributes include the size of a house and the resolution of a digital camera. Examples of soft attributes include the style of a car and the smell of a perfume.

Why should temporal distance influence the weight of hard vs. soft attributes? Research shows that preference uncertainty increases with temporal distance from outcomes (e.g., March 1978; Salisbury and Feinberg 2008; Simonson 1990). Increases in preference uncertainty or perceived risk encourage individuals to choose in a way that appears safe (e.g., Bettman 1973; Dowling and Staelin 1994; Erdem 1998). Individuals tend to believe that basing choices on hard rather than soft attributes is more rational and safer (Hsee et al. 2003). Consequently, we propose that an increase in the temporal distance between choice and consumption would increase preference for options superior on hard versus soft attributes.

Two factors potentially moderate the effect. One is response mode, choice vs. purchase intent. Because individuals tend to feel a weaker need to appear rational when indicating purchase intents than when making choices, we hypothesize that the effect will be found in choice but not in purchase intent. Another is the ease of changing one's choice. Because preference uncertainty has weaker consequences when changing one's choice is easy rather than difficult, we hypothesize that the effect will occur when changing choice is difficult but not when changing choice is easy.

We tested these predictions in three studies. In Study 1, participants were choosing between two stereos differing in sound-richness and sound-powerfulness. Two factors were manipulated between-participants. The first was whether participants would receive the purchased stereo immediately or in three weeks. The second was attribute hardness. In one condition (sound-richness-soft), participants were told that they personally found Model A's sound richer than Model B's, but Model B was more powerful (150 watts) than Model A (50 watts). In another condition (sound-powerfulness-soft), participants were told that they personally found Model B's sound more powerful than Model A's, but Model A had a higher sound-richness rating (150) than Model B (50). In a third condition (both-attributes-hard), participants saw both the sound-richness ratings and the wattages. As predicted, when one of the two attributes was soft, more participants chose the stereo superior on the hard attribute when they would receive the chosen stereo in three weeks rather than immediately. By contrast, when both attributes were hard, temporal distance did not influence choice.

Study 2 tested the role of response mode. The study involved two graphing calculators: one had a better brand (Texas Instruments) and came with a $15 Starbucks gift card; another had a less attractive brand (Hewlett-Packard in one condition and Compaq in another) and came with a $30 Starbucks gift card. The study was a 2 x 2 x 2 between-participants factorial design. The first factor was temporal distance: The purchased calculator and the gift card would be received either in three days or in three weeks. The second factor was the hardness of brand. A pretest showed that Texas Instruments was moderately more attractive than Hewlett-Packard but strongly more attractive than Compaq. We reasoned that the greater the difference in attractiveness between two brands, the harder the difference. The third factor was response mode, choice vs. purchase intent. The results showed a significant three-way interaction. As predicted, in the brand-name-soft condition, an increase in temporal distance increased preference for Hewlett-Packard in the choice condition but increased preference for Texas Instruments in the purchase-intent condition. By contrast, in the brand-name-hard condition, regardless of response mode, an increase in temporal distance slightly increased preference for Texas Instruments.

Study 3 examined the effect of ease of changing choice. Participants were asked to imagine that they wanted to rent a convertible for a weekend vacation in Key West, Florida. They noticed that a well-known car rental company was offering two deals, one featuring a Ford Mustang V6 convertible and the other featuring a Chrysler Sebring convertible. The Mustang convertible came with a $30 gift certificate and the Sebring came with a $50 gift certificate; both certificates were redeemable at any restaurant. In a pretest, participants rated Mustang as being more attractive than Sebring. Notice that the difference in car was relatively soft while that in gift certificate was relatively hard. The study was a 2 x 2 between-participants factorial design. The first factor was the timing of the vacation: next weekend or during a weekend in two months. The second factor was the difficulty of changing one's choice: In the change-easy condition, participants were told that no deposit was required for making a reservation and they could cancel the reservation or switch to the other deal at any time; in the change-difficult condition, participants were told that a $10 deposit was required for making a reservation and that the deposit would not be refunded if they cancelled the reservation or switched to the other deal. As predicted, in the change-difficult condition, preference for Sebring was stronger when the vacation was in the distant rather than near future; in the change-easy condition, preference for Mustang V6 was stronger when the vacation was in the distant rather than near future.

REFERENCES

Campbell, Margaret C. and Ronald C. Goodstein (2001), "The Moderating Effect of Perceived Risk on Consumers' Evaluations of Product Incongruity: Preference for the Norm," *Journal of Consumer Research,* 28 (December), 439-449.

Dowling Grahame R. and Richard Staelin (1994), "A Model of Perceived Risk and Intended Risk-Handing Activity," *Journal of Consumer Research,* 21 (June), 119-133.

Erdem, Tulin (1998), "An Empirical Analysis of Umbrella Branding," *Journal of Marketing Research,* 35 (August), 339-351.

Fredrick, Shane, George F. Loewenstein and Ted O'Donoghue (2002). "Time Discounting and Time Preference: A Critical Review," *Journal of Economic Literature,* 40, 351-401.

Grant, Susan Jung and Alice M. Tybout (2008), "The Effect of Temporal Frame on Information Considered in New Product Evaluation: The Role of Uncertainty," *Journal of Consumer Research,* 34 (April), 897-913.

Kahn, Barbara E. and Robert J. Meyer (1991), "Consumer Multiattribute Judgments under Attribute-Weight Uncertainty," *Journal of Marketing Research,* 17 (March), 508-522.

Kivetz, Ran and Itamar Simonson (2000), "The Effects of Incomplete Information on Consumer Choice," *Journal of Marketing Research,* 37 (November), 427-448.

Liberman, Nira and Yaacov Trope (1998), "The Role of Feasibility and Desirability Considerations in Near and Distant Future Decisions: A Test of Temporal Construal Theory," *Journal of Personality and Social Psychology,* 75 (1), 5-18.

Lynch, John and Gal Zauberman (2006), "When Do You Want It? Time, Decisions, and Public Policy", Journal of Public Policy and Marketing, 25 (1), 67-78.

Malkoc, Selin A., Gal Zauberman and Canan Ulu (2005), "Consuming Now or Later? The Interactive Effect of Timing and Attribute Alignability," *Psychological Science,* 16 (5), 411-7.

March, James G. (1978), "Bounded Rationality, Ambiguity, and the Engineering of Choice," *Bell Journal of Economics,* 9 (Autumn), 587-608.

Markman, Arthur B. and Douglas L. Merdin (1995), "Similarity and Alignment in Choice," *Organizational Behavior and Human Decision Processes,* 63 (2), 117-30.

Meyer, Robert J. (1981), "A Model of Multiattribue Judgments under Uncertainty and Informational Constraint," *Journal of Marketing Research,* 18 (November), 428-441.

Muthukrishnan, A. V., Luc Wathieu and Alison Jing Xu (2009), "Ambiguity Aversion and the Preference for Established Brands," *Management Science,* 55 (December), 1933-1941.

Salisbury, Linda C. and Fred M. Feinberg (2008), "Future Preference Uncertainty and Diversification: The Role of Temporal Stochastic Inflation," *Journal of Consumer Research,* 35 (August), 349-359.

Simonson, Itamar (1990), "The Influence of Purchase Quantity and Timing on Variety-Seeking Behavior," *Journal of Marketing Research,* 27 (May), 150-162.

Slovic, Paul and Douglas MacPhillamy (1974), "Dimensional Commensurability and Cue Utilization in Comparative Judgment," *Organizational Behavior and Human Performance,* 11 (April), 179-94.

Trope, Yaacov and Nira Liberman (2000), "Temporal Construal and Time-Dependent Changes in Preference," *Journal of Personality and Social Psychology,* 79 (6), 876-889.

Trope, Yaacov and Nira Liberman (2003), "Temporal Construal," *Psychological Review,* 110 (3), 403-421.

Wright, Peter and Barton Weitz (1977), "Time Horizon Effects on Product Evaluation Strategies," *Journal of Marketing Research,* XIV (November), 429-433.

Having versus Consuming: How Failing to Estimate Usage Frequency Affects Consumer Preferences for Multi-Feature Products

Joseph Goodman, Washington University in St. Louis, USA
Caglar Irmak, University of South Carolina, USA

EXTENDED ABSTRACT

While the demand for multifunctional products (e.g., smart phones) soars, most consumers do not use the additional features that come with such products (Techview 2009). This conflict between purchase and usage behavior is explained by the complexity of product features. Consumers underestimate learning costs at the time of purchase (Meyer, Zhao, and Han 2008) and fail to take the usability factors into account (Thompson, Hamilton, and Rust 2005) when they purchase multifunctional products.

Consumer research on multifunctional products thus far has focused on consumer reactions to products with novel and complex features (Mukherjee and Hoyer 2001; Thompson et al. 2005). However, in many product markets (e.g., mobile phones, vacation resorts) consumers shop for products with multiple, yet simple, features. When consumers are familiar with a product and its features, they are less likely to underestimate learning costs and usability is unlikely to be a factor in product choice (Kahn and Meyer 1991). Still, even for simple product purchases, for instance, when choosing between pay-per-use and a flat fee for using a swimming pool, consumers often overestimate higher-than-average usage incidents, leading them to overpay for such products (Nunes 2000). Thus, research suggests that consumers are generally poor in accurately predicting their usage rate of products and product features before purchase.

We build on this body of research by testing whether consumers fail to estimate (rather than underestimate) their usage rate of product features. To do so, we let consumers estimate their usage frequency of each feature before choice to determine whether estimation alters their preferences. If consumers fail to estimate usage before choice, usage estimation may lead to a preference reversal, whereby a few-feature product is more likely to be preferred over a product with a greater number of features.

Further, we argue that since usage rate estimation is not likely to fit the mental representation of the product at the time of purchase (Thompson et al. 2005; Trope and Liberman 2010), consumers may need to exert the extra cognitive effort required for estimating usage rate of features before purchase. Consumers with high need for cognition (NFC; Cacioppo, Petty, and Kao 1984) are more likely to think about usage rate of features and try to assess the value of each option when evaluating alternatives in the decision making process as they generally put greater effort to make more accurate decision (Levin, Huneke and Jasper 2000). Accordingly, we predict that when consumers estimate their usage rate of product features before choice they will be more likely to prefer the few-feature product compared to the many-feature product, and this effect of usage estimation on preferences will be stronger (weaker) for those who are low (high) in need for cognition.

In study 1, we demonstrate that consumers prefer a cell phone with a lower (vs. higher) number of functions when they estimate their usage rate of functions before choice compared to control. Further, we show that the effect of usage estimation is moderated by participants' level of NFC such that the effect is stronger for those who are low (high) in need for cognition.

In study 2, we extend the effect to another, low-complexity product domain (i.e., vacation resorts) and show that (1) consumers assess whether a feature is desirable, but do not consider usage frequency, ruling out a heuristic-based explanation of the effect (i.e., "more functions is better), (2) the effect is independent of learning cost, (3) usage estimation reduces the importance of the additional features on the many-feature product and, as a result, makes consumers more likely to prefer the few-feature product.

Finally, in study 3, we provide further evidence for the underlying mechanism of why consumers fail to estimate their usage frequency of feature before choice. We demonstrate that the level of materialistic values (Richins 2004) moderates the effect such that usage rate estimation shifts preferences toward the low-feature product only for those consumers who are low in materialistic values.

Findings from this research have several important contributions. First, in contrast to research showing overestimation of usage as a reason for consumers purchasing multifunctional products (e.g., Meyer et al. 2008), our research demonstrates that the failure to estimate usage rate is an important factor in such consumer decisions. Second, our findings suggest that consumers approach multifunctional product purchase occasions with a mindset of acquiring and spending (cf. Rassuli and Hollander 1986), rather than considering the utilitarian aspects of such products (e.g., how often they are going to use the product features). In line with this contention, we observe the effect only for consumers who are low in NFC (Cacioppo et al. 1984) or low in materialism (Richins 2004). Third, we show that estimation of feature usage rate before choice reduces the importance of features and leads to preference reversals similar to those demonstrated in research on trivial attributes (Brown and Carpenter 2000; Simonson, Carmon, and O'Curry 1994). Finally, in today's economy these findings are especially important as they prescribe to consumers a tool to help avoid overspending and save money.

REFERENCES

Belk, Russell W. (1985), "Materialism: Trait Aspects of Living in the Material World," *Journal of Consumer Research*, 12 (3), 265-80.

Bolton, Ruth N. and Katherine N. Lemon (1999), "A Dynamic Model of Customers' Usage of Services: Usage as an Antecedent and Consequence of Satisfaction," *Journal of Marketing Research*, 36 (May), 171-86.

Brown, Christina L. and Gregory S. Carpenter (2000), "Why Is the Trivial Important? A Reasons-Based Account for the Effects of Trivial Attributes on Choice," *Journal of Consumer Research*, 26 (March), 372–85.

Cacioppo, John T., Richard E. Petty, and Chuan F. Kao (1984), "The Efficient Assessment of Need for Cognition," *Journal of Personality Assessment*, 48 (June), 306-307.

Carpenter, Gregory, Rashi Glazer, and Kent Nakamoto (1994), "Meaningful Brands from Meaningless Differentiation: The Dependence on Irrelevant Attributes," *Journal of Marketing Research*, 31 (August), 339-350.

Deloitte (2010), "Telecommunications Predictions 2010," (accessed July 28, 2010), [available at http://www.deloitte.com/assets/ Dcom-Croatia/Local%20Assets/Documents/2010/-adria_ telecommuncations-predictions-2010.pdf].

Irwin, Julie R. and Gary H. McClelland (2001), "Misleading Heuristics and Moderated Multiple Regression Models," *Journal of Marketing Research*, 38 (February), 100-109.

Johnson, Eric J., Gerald Häubl, and Anat Keinan (2007), "Aspects of Endowment: A Query Theory of Value Construction," *Journal of Experimental Psychology: Learning, Memory, and Cognition,* 33, 461-474.

Kahn, Barbara E. and Robert J. Meyer (1991), "Consumer Multiattribute Judgments under Attribute-Weight Uncertainty," *Journal of Consumer Research*, 17 (March), 508-22.

Khan, Uzma, Ravi Dhar, and Klaus Wertenbroch (2005), "A Behavioral Decision Theory Perspective on Hedonic and Utilitarian Choice," in *Inside Consumption: Frontiers on Research on Consumer Motives, Goals, and Desires*, ed. S. Ratneshwar and David Glen Mick, London: Routledge, 144-65.

Kivetz, Ran and Itamar Simonson (2000), "The Effects of Incomplete Information on Consumer Choice," *Journal of Marketing Research*, 37 (November), 427-48.

Levin, Irwin P., Mary E. Huneke, and J. D. Jasper (2000), "Information Processing at Successive Stages of Decision Making: Need for Cognition and Inclusion–Exclusion Effects," *Organization Behavior and Human Decision Processes*, 82, 2, 171-93.

Meyer, Robert J., Shenghui Zhao, and Jin K. Han (2008), "Biases in Valuation vs. Usage of Innovative Product Features," *Marketing Science*, 27, 6, 1083-96.

Mukherjee, Ashesh and Wayne D. Hoyer (2001), "The Effect of Novel Attributes on Product Evaluation," *Journal of Consumer Research*, 28 (December), 462–72.

Nicolao, Leonardo, Julie R. Irwin, and Joseph K. Goodman (2009), "Happiness for Sale: Do Experiential Purchases Make Consumers Happier than Material Purchases?" *Journal of Consumer Research*, 36 (August), 188-98.

Nowlis, Stephen M. and Itamar Simonson (1996), "The Effect of New Product Features on Brand Choice," *Journal of Marketing Research*, 33 (February), 36–46.

Nunes, Joseph C. (2000), "A Cognitive Model of People's Usage Estimations," Journal of Marketing Research, 37 (November), 397-409.

Richins, Marsha L. (2004), "The Material Values Scale: Measurement Properties and Development of a Short Form," *Journal of Consumer Research*, 31 (June), 209-19.

Richins, Marsha L. and Scott Dawson (1992), "A Consumer Values Orientation for Materialism and Its Measurement: Measure Development and Validation," *Journal of Consumer Research*, 19 (December), 303-16.

Shugan, Steven M. (1980), "The Cost of Thinking," *Journal of Consumer Research*, 7, 2, 99-111.

Simonson, Itamar, Ziv Carmon, and Suzanne O'Curry (1994), "Experimental Evidence on the Negative Effect of Product Features and Sales Promotions on Brand Choice," *Marketing Science*, 13, 1, 23-40.

Techview (2009), "When More is Less: An End, Please, to the Gadget Features Race," *The Economist*, (August 14), [available at http://www.economist.com/node/14248430].

Thompson, Debora Viana, Rebecca W. Hamilton, and Roland T. Rust (2005), "Feature Fatigue: When Product Capabilities Become Too Much of a Good Thing," Journal of Marketing Research, 42 (November), 431-42.

Trope, Yaacov and Nira Liberman (2010), "Construal-Level Theory of Psychological Distance," *Psychological Review,* 117, 2, 440-63.

Van Boven, Leaf and Thomas Gilovich (2003), "To Do or to Have? That Is the Question," *Journal of Personality and Social Psychology*, 85 (6), 1193-1202.

When Humanizing Brands Goes Wrong:
The Detrimental Role of Brand Anthropomorphization amidst Product Wrongdoings

Marina Puzakova, Drexel University, USA
Hyokjin Kwak, Drexel University, USA
Joseph Rocereto, Monmouth University, USA

EXTENDED ABSTRACT

Prior research has established that anthropomorphization of a brand has positive implications for consumers' perceptions and behaviors. For instance, human qualities of emotionality and thought of the M&M brand's characters transfers to the M&M brand, creating a point of differentiation and connection with consumers. What consequences does the marketing tactic of anthropomorphizing a brand have when the brand catches the glare of negative publicity arising from negative brand performance? In September of 2008, independent sources indicated that traces of melamine, a poisonous substance, could be potentially present in M&M's candies. Would consumers' reactions to the incidents of negative media coverage have been different if the M&M brand had been non-anthropomorphized in its marketing promotions?

Our research demonstrates that anthropomorphization of a brand triggers less favorable attitudes toward the brand when consumers are exposed to information regarding negative brand performance. This phenomenon is attributed to the fact that the anthropomorphization of an entity makes individuals see this entity as mindful and intentional, and, thus, to be fully accountable for its actions. In times when people did not attribute intentional capacities strictly to humans, animals and objects alike were subjects for prosecution (Berman 1994; Epley and Waytz 2009). In turn, greater responsibility for an action created greater willingness to punish a target of negative behavior. Prior research in marketing has also established that a firm or a brand's wrongdoings, determined to be intentional, are perceived more negatively than actions categorized as accidental (Folkes 1984; Klein and Dawar 2004). Evidence from previous research indicates that consumers may perceive the locus of responsibility for a failure as external, that is, brand-related, or internal, or context-related (e.g., consumer, external suppliers, retailers); (Laufer and Gillespie 2004). Given negative brand performances, brands that are depicted with anthropomorphic features are more likely to be viewed as committing intentional acts than brands positioned without humanized elements.

Furthermore, our research extends the premise that people apply social beliefs to agents that are being anthropomorphized and interpret the actions of humanized entities in light of this social knowledge. Specifically, we theoretically conceptualize and empirically demonstrate that consumers' implicit theories of personality affect their perceptions of anthropomorphized brands when the brands catch a glare of negative publicity. Researchers in social psychology suggested that a fixed view of personality is associated with a greater emphasis on relying on others' traits in predicting their behavior across various situations (Chiu et al. 1997). By contrast, individuals, who endorse an incremental theory stance, take into account contextual information, do not expect that the same behavior recurs across situations, and are less likely to change their perceptions of transgressors based on a single incident (Dweck and Molden 2008). Precisely, individuals who believe in personality stability view anthropomorphized brands that undergo consumers' backlash from negative performance less favorably than non-anthropomorphized brands. The opposite holds true for consumers who accept the incremental view of personality malleability. That is, consumers who believe in incremental theory, view anthropomorphized brand more favorably than non-anthropomorphized when they deal with negative information about the brand.

We examine hypothesized effects in two experiments. Experiment 1 investigates whether anthropomorphizing a brand creates less favorable perceptions of a brand when consumers learn negative brand information. The results of Experiment 1 demonstrate that a brand represented with humanlike features (e.g., human visual elements of the product, ad copy written in the first, as opposed to in the third person) creates less favorable attitude toward and less trust in the brand. Experiment 2 explores the moderating role of implicit theory of personality. Implicit theory of personality was manipulated by having respondents read an article supporting either entity or incremental theory. The findings of Experiment 2 reveal that anthropomorphized, as opposed to non-anthropomorphized, brands trigger negative reactions from consumers that advocate entity theory stance. They also attribute greater responsibility to the anthropomorphized versus the non-anthropomorphized brand. In contrast, we found that incremental theory proponents have more positive attitude toward the anthropomorphized brand and do not attribute greater brand responsibility for negative brand actions. They are more likely to allow the possibility of inconsistent behaviors, and therefore, are less likely to be negatively affected by the information regarding negative brand performance.

In conclusion, previous research is silent to the question of how the anthropomorphization of a brand affects consumers' perceptions if the brand undergoes public backlash, arising from factual negative information. To our knowledge, this research represents the first theoretical and empirical documentation of the negative effect of brand anthropomorphization on consumers' attitude toward the brand adversely envisaged by mass media.

REFERENCES

Berman, Paul Schiff (1994), "Rats, Pigs, and Statues on Trial: The Creation of Cultural Narratives in the Prosecution of Animals and Inanimate Objects," NYU Law Review, 69, 288-326.

Chiu, Chi Yue, Ying Yi Hong, and Carol S. Dweck (1997), "Lay Dispositionism and Implicit Theories of Personality," Journal of Personality and Social Psychology, 42 (1), 116-31.

Dweck, Carol S. and Daniel C. Molden (2008), "Self-Theories: The Construction of Free Will," in Are We Free? Psychology and Free Will, J. Baer and J.C. Kaufman and R.F. Baumeister, Eds. New York: Oxford University Press.

Epley, Nicholas and Adam Waytz (2009), "Mind Perception," in The Handbook of Social Psychology, S. T. Fiske and D.T. Gilbert and G. Lindzey, Eds. 5th ed. New York: Wiley.

Folkes, Valerie S. (1984), "Consumer Reactions to Product Failure: An Attributional Approach," Journal of Consumer Research, 10 (March), 398-410.

Klein, Jill and Niraj Dawar (2004), "Corporate Social Responsibility and Consumers' Attributions and Brand Evaluations in a Product-Harm Crisis," International Journal of Research in Marketing, 21, 203-17.

Laufer, Daniel and Kate Gillespie (2004), "Differences in Consumer Attributions of Blame between Men and Women: The Role of Perceived Vulnerability and Empathic Concern," Psychology & Marketing, 21 (2), 141-57.

The Globalness Route toward Brand Equity: How Consumer and Brand-Level Factors Change the Route to Success

Bernhard Swoboda, Trier University, Germany
Karin Pennemann, Trier University, Germany
Markus Taube, Mercator School of Management, Germany
Thomas Foscht, University of Graz, Austria

EXTENDED ABSTRACT

The objectives of the present study are to examine (1) how perceived brand globalness (PBG) and perceived brand localness (PBL) serve as halos for brand equity within the service sector (2) mediated by hedonic and functional values and (3) moderated by consumer and brand-level factors.

In the context of consumer products PBG is positively related to consumers' purchase likelihood via quality and prestige (Steenkamp, Batra and Alden 2003). However, results are not consistent (Dimofte, Johansson and Ronkainen 2008) regarding the benefits of global brands. Retailing, for instance, is originally a local business. Thus, retailers are closer to the customer (Evans and Bridson 2005) and see the need for adaptation. Moreover, such local, adapted brands are perceived as higher in affinity and quality (Kapferer 2005).

We propose the indirect impact of PBG and PBL on brand equity mediated via hedonic and functional values (Sweeney and Soutar 2001). Values as a ratio of salient 'give' and 'get' components (Zeithaml 1988) are especially important within the service context (Sweeney and Soutar 2001). Due to their higher accessibility, hedonic (emotional) values especially are preferred (Feldman and Lynch 1988; Verplanken, Hofstee and Janssen 1998). Yet, choosing which route (functional and/or hedonic) toward brand equity is most beneficial depends on brand-level factors such as a brand's country-of-origin and consumer-level factors like consumer identity (Zhang and Khare 2009).

Country-of-origin acts as a halo (Han 1989), which explains how consumers draw inferences from country image specific associations to an object from this country (e.g. products, brands). Quality beliefs (Han 1989) and social status (Batra et al. 2000; Ger and Belk 1996) are inferences drawn from country image and impact consumers in their evaluation of global and local brands.

Furthermore, we apply social identity theory (Tajfel and Turner 1979; Brewer 1991) to explore the moderating role of consumer-level factors. Consumers' identity can be characterized as global or local and therefore evokes preferences for global or local brands due to identification reasons (Zhang and Khare 2009).

We collected consumer data (n=1188) nested in 36 service brands within China as an emerging market. Brands can be grouped according to their origin in Western, Asian and Chinese brands. The hypotheses are tested across three service industries, including fashion retailing, food retailing, and restaurants, assigning equally twelve brands per industry and brand origin to further increase the generalizability of results. We applied classical checks of validity, reliability, and measurement invariance. The model was conceptualized as a moderated mediation and attempted to explain how and when a given effect occurred (Preacher, Rucker and Hayes 2007). First, we estimated the structural model and then conducted the mediation analysis according the suggested procedure by Baron and Kenny (1986) and evaluated other plausible rival models. Finally, we performed two multi-group analyses using brands' country-of-origin and consumer identity as moderators after splitting the sample according the moderators to finalize the moderated mediation.

Results show that PBG and PBL indirectly enhance brand equity and our study shows how. The results emphasize the mediating role of hedonic and functional values, whereby hedonic values, such as socio-emotional value, is a full mediator and functional value, such as quality value, plays a subordinate role as a partial mediator. Which route to success PBG and PBL take depends on brand as well as consumer-level factors.

The brands' country-of-origin is relevant in the way brand equity is built in the consumers' mind. For brands originating from (cultural) peripheral Asian countries, PBG instead of PBL is the primary driver for brand equity via socio-emotional value and quality value in a fully mediated causal chain. Surprisingly, these cultural peripheral brands cannot use their cultural affinity in terms of PBL. Besides, we find evidence that the path to brand equity is based on the functional component quality value, while the direct impact of socio-emotional value disappears. We conclude that cultural peripheral brands like Asian brands are purchased out of cognitive evaluation and without a direct affective appeal. Referring to consumer cultural theory (McCracken 1986) we conclude that brands originating from cultural peripheral countries do not match Chinese identity. This mismatch constrains the building of brand equity.

Brand equity of Western brands is primary driven by PBG fully mediated by socio-emotional value and partially mediated by quality value. Brand equity of Chinese brands is driven by PBL. We conclude that brands with a Western appeal and domestic brands carry cultural values that activate a direct affective impact on brand equity, which is just partially mediated via quality value.

Consumer identity impacts the way brand equity is built in consumers' minds. PBG is the primary driver for brand equity when consumers' identity is global. The mediating role of quality value varies upon the level of consumer identity. For local consumers, emotional appeals seem directly accessible and diagnostic to create brand equity – for global consumers the path to brand equity essentially leads via quality value.

For practitioners our results are useful in several aspects. It is obvious that Western retail brands, like French retail brand Carrefour, try to adapt to the Chinese environment. But it is also obvious that Western brands should not conceal their rather global identity due to the naturally competitive advantage of Asian and Chinese brands especially to deliver local cultural values. The recommended strategy is to leverage brand equity driven by PBG but also cater on the functional basis for specific needs; thus, do not import standardized concepts that ignore specific needs.

REFERENCES

Alden, Dana L., Jan-Benedict E. M. Steenkamp, and Rajeev Batra (2006), "Consumer attitudes toward marketplace globalization: Structure, antecedents and consequences," *International Journal of Research in Marketing*, 23 (September), 227–239.

Batra, Rajeev, Venkatram Ramaswamy, Dana L. Alden, Jan-Benedict E. M. Steenkamp, and S. Ramachander (2000), "Effects of Brand Local and Nonlocal Origin on Consumer Attitudes in Developing Countries," *Journal of Consumer Psychology*, 9 (2), 83–95.

Brewer, Marilynn B. (1991), "The Social Self: On Being the Same and Different at the Same Time," *Personality and Social Psychology Bulletin*, 17 (October), 475–482.

Dimofte, Claudiu V, Johny K. Johansson, and Ilkka A. Ronkainen (2008), "Cognitive and Affective Reactions of U.S. Consumers to Global Brands," *Journal of International Marketing*, 16 (4), 113–135.

Evans, Jody and Kerrie Bridson (2005), "Explaining retail offer adaptation through psychic distance," *International Journal of Retail & Distribution Management*, 33 (1), 69–78.

Ger, Gürliz and Russell W. Belk (1996), "I'd like to buy the world a coke: Consumptionscapes of the less affluent world," *Journal of Consumer Policy*, 19 (3), 271–304.

Han, C. Min. (1989), "Country image: halo or summary construct," *Journal of Marketing Research*, 26 (May), 222–229.

Kapferer, Jean-Noël (2005), "The post-global brand," *Journal of Brand Management*, 12 (June), 319–324.

Preacher, Kristopher J., Derek D. Rucker and Andrew F. Hayes (2007), "Addressing moderated mediation hypotheses: Theory, methods, and prescriptions," *Multivariate Behavioral Research*, 42 (1), 185–227.

Steenkamp, Jan-Benedict E. M, Rajeev Batra and Dana L. Alden (2003), "How perceived brand globalness creates brand value," *Journal of International Business Studies*, 34 (January), 53–65.

Sweeney, Jillian C. and Geoffrey N. Soutar (2001), "Consumer perceived value: The development of a multiple item scale," *Journal of Retailing*, 77 (Summer), 203–220.

Tajfel, Henri and John Turner (1979), "An Integrative Theory of Intergroup Conflict," *in The Social Psychology of Intergroup Relations*, William G. Austin, Stephen Worchel, Monterey:Brooks-Cole, 94–109.

Verplanken, Bas, Godelieve Hofstee, and Heidi J. Janssen (1998), "Accessibility of affective versus cognitive components of attitudes," *European Journal of Social Psychology*, 28 (January/February), 23–35.

Zeithaml, Valerie A. (1988), "Consumer perceptions of price, quality, and value: a means-end model and synthesis of evidence," *The Journal of Marketing*, 52 (July), 2–22.

Zhang, Yinlong and Adwait Khare (2009), "The Impact of Accessible Identities on the Evaluation of Global versus Local Products," Journal of Consumer Research, 36 (October), 524–537.

It is All About Subtlety:
Subtle Efforts to Remedy Subtle Service Failure

Fang Wan, University of Manitoba, Canada
Pingping Qiu, Monash University, Australia
L.J Shrum, University of Texas at Austin, USA

EXTENDED ABSTRACT

Service failure and recovery are complex and dynamic constructs (Bonifield and Cole 2007). However, most existing literature focused on blatant and outrageous service failure (Bonifield and Cole 2007; O'Donohoe and Turley 2007) and the role of strong and outward emotions such as anger in service failure and recovery (Bonifield and Cole 2007; O'Donohoe and Turley 2007). Our research explores an understudied area—the effectiveness of recovery strategies in a subtle service failure situation that involves a passive negative emotion embarrassment. Drawing on research on embarrassment (Grace 2007; Keltner and Buswell 1997) and goal automaticity (Bargh 2002; Leary 1995), we identify that even perfectly friendly and personalized service encounter can fail when it violates contextually activated social goals. More importantly, we propose that in such a situation with a subtle service failure, the effectiveness of various recovery efforts is impacted by subtle cues such as types of recovery strategy, awareness of the recovery efforts and time of service evaluation. Three experiments are reported to demonstrate the impact of these subtle cues in ameliorating the service experience.

In Experiment 1, we identified a service setting with a subtle failure. Specifically, we examined a personalized service scenario in which the server unintentionally discloses the customers' privacy (i.e., reminding the customer of their previous unhealthy food choice in a restaurant) and jeopardize their contextually activated social goals (i.e., impression management goal when dining with a date for the first time plus health goal if the date is a fitness instructor). By conducting a 2 (personalization: high vs. low) by 3 (social goal: dining with a friend, a date, a date as a fitness instructor) between-subjects experiment with restaurant dining scenarios, we identified that even high-personalized service may cause subtle service failure (evoke felt embarrassment and incur negative service evaluation) if this service unintentionally violates the customer's contextually driven social goals. The subtle service failure scenario (high personalization and dining with date as fitness instructor) identified in this study is utilized in the following experiments.

In Experiment 2 we examined whether the server or customer is the recovery initiator will make the service recovery more effective. As research on embarrassment suggests that either the person who feels embarrassed or the others who evokes the embarrassing situation can relieve the felt embarrassment (Miller 1995). We designed strategies with the server (or self) initiating an attempt to mitigate the transgression: "Well, you (or I) may like trying something else today." We further argue that high awareness of server's recovery efforts can exacerbate the attention paid to the previous service failure and can incur more negative attributions about the server, making recovery efforts futile (Kelley 1972; Main et al. 2007). We tested the hypothesis with a 2 (remedy initiator: self vs. server) × 2 (awareness of the remedy effort: high vs. control) between-subjects design, plus a no-remedy control condition. We manipulated awareness of the recovery efforts by measuring responses to the self or the server's recovery attempts either before (high awareness condition) or after (control condition) service experience related measures. ANOVA analyses yielded significant interaction effects $(F(1, 110) = 4.08, p < .05)$, supporting our hypotheses.

Experiment 3 further explores the effectiveness of recovery efforts by examining the different recovery strategies a server can take, as well as the effect of time. Based on service recovery (Hoffman, Kelley, and Rotalsky 1995) and embarrassment literature (Keltner and Buswell 1997), we designed two types of server's recovery strategies, direct (directly correcting the transgression) versus indirect (offering a free coupon—distracting the attention). In addition, according to emotion regulation (Gross et al. 2007) and interpersonal relationship literature (Fletcher and Clark 2002), we argued that distraction (indirect recovery) may help reduce the felt embarrassment and enhance service evaluation in the short run. However, in the long run, the direct recovery (confronting the issue) can be more effective in helping reduce felt embarrassment, and therefore, ameliorate the service experience. In this study, a 2 (recovery method: direct vs. indirect) by 2 (timing of evaluation: immediate vs. delayed) between-subject design was adopted to test the hypothesis. ANOVA findings supported our hypotheses with a significant interaction of the two manipulated factors $(F(1,92) = 7.08, p < .01)$. Two post-hoc experiments further explored why different recovery strategy (direct vs. indirect) created different results when there is a time lag. Results suggested that indirect (vs. direct) recovery suppresses negative emotions in the short run and backfires in the long run.

Taken together, our research examines the subtle service failures and recoveries that involve a passive emotion such as embarrassment. Theoretically, service failure, recovery, and emotions are complex and dynamic processes that may vary dramatically from one situation to another (Bonifield and Cole 2007). We provide nuances of a complex interaction between subtle recovery efforts and consumers' perceptions and subsequent reactions. To service managers, the most important message is that service delivery can be personalized but can not be done at the cost of revealing sensitive information. When embarrassing service encounter is incurred, recovery strategies vary depending on whether a short-term or long-term oriented goal is adopted by service managers. In a short run, indirect strategies such as incentives can be effective. But in a long run, direct strategies are more effective.

REFERENCES

Arora, Neeraj, Xavier Dreze, Anindya Ghose, James Hess, Raghuram Iyengar, Bing Jing, Yogesh Joshi, V. Kumar, Nicholas Lurie, Scott Neslin, S. Sajeesh, Meng Su, Niladri Syam, Jacquelyn Thomas, and Z. Zhang (2008), "Putting One-to-One Marketing to Work: Personalization, Customization, and Choice," *Marketing Letters*, 19 (3), 305-21.

Bargh, John. A. (2002), "Losing Consciousness: Automatic Influences on Consumer Judgment, Behavior and Motivation," *Journal of Consumer Research*, 29, 280-285.

Bearden, William. O. and Michael J. Etzel (1982), "Reference Group Influence on Product and Purchase Brand Decisions," *Journal of Consumer Research*, 9(September), 183-194.

Bonifield, Carolyn and Catherine Cole (2007), "Affective Responses to Service Failure: Anger, Regret, and Retaliatory Versus Conciliatory Responses," *Marketing Letters*, 18 (1), 85-99.

Cialdini, Robert B. (2000), *Influence: Science and Practice* (4th ed.), New York: Harper Collins.

Dahl, Darren W., Heather Honea, and Rajesh V. Manchanda (2005), "Three Rs of Interpersonal Consumer Guilt: Relationships, Reciprocity, Reparation," *Journal of Consumer Psychology,* 15 (4), 307-315.

Edelmann, Robert J. (1981), "Embarrassment: The State of Research," *Current Psychological Reviews,* 1(May-August), 125-138.

Esterlami, Hooman and Peter De Maeyer (2002), "Customer Reactions to Service Provider Overgenerosity," *Journal of Service Research,* 4(February), 205-216.

Fletcher, Garth and Clark (2002), *Blackwell Handbook Of Social Psychology: Interpersonal Processes,* Wiley-Blackwell.

Friestad, Maria and Peter Wright (1994), "The Persuasion Knowledge Model: How People Cope with Persuasion Attempts," *Journal of Consumer Research,* 21(June), 1-31.

Goodwin, Cathy (1993), "A Conceptualization of Motives to Seek Privacy for Non-Deviant Consumption," *Journal of Consumer Psychology,* 1(3), 261-84.

Grace, Debra (2007), "How Embarrassing! An Exploratory Study of Critical Incidents Including Affective Reactions," *Journal of Service Research,* 9 (February), 271-84.

Grandey, Alicia A., Glenda M. Fisk, Anna S. Mattila, Karen J. Jansen, and Lori A. Sideman, (2005), "Is 'service with a smile' enough? Authenticity of Positive Displays During Service Encounters," *Organizational Behavior and Human Decision Processes,* 96(1), 38-55.

Gross, James J. and Robert W. Levenson (1993), "Emotional Suppression: Physiology, Self-Report, and Expressive Behavior," *Journal of Personality & Social Psychology,* 64(June), 970-986.

Gross, James J. and Ross A. Thompson (2007), "Emotion Regulation: Conceptual foundations," in James J. Gross (ed.), *Handbook of Emotion Regulation,* New York: Guilford Press.

Grubb, Edward L. and Barbra L. Stern (1971), "Self-Concept and Significant Others," *Journal of Marketing Research,* 8(August), 382-85.

Harris, Christine R. (2001), "Cardiovascular Responses of Embarrassment and Effects of Emotional Suppression in a Social Setting," Journal of Personality & Social Psychology, 81(November), 886-897.

Hoffman, K. Douglas, Scott W. Kelley, and Holly M. Rotalsky (1995), "Tracking Service Failures and Employee Recovery Efforts," *The Journal of Services Marketing,* 9 (2), 49.

Keltner, Dacher and Brenda N. Buswell (1997), "Embarrassment: Its Distinct Form and Appeasement Functions," *Psychological Bulletin,* 122(November), 250-70.

Kelley, Harold H. (1972), "Attribution in social interaction," in *Attribution: Perceiving the Causes of Behavior,* eds. Edward E. Jones, David E. Kanouse, Harold H. Kelley, Richard E. Nisbett, Stuart Valins, and Bernard Weiner, New Jersey: General Learning Press, 1-26.

Kelley, Scott W., K. Douglas Hoffman, and Mark A. Davis (1993), "A Typology of Retail Failures and Recoveries," *Journal of Retailing,* 69 (4), 429.

Leary, Mark R. (1995), *Self-Presentation: Impression Management and Interpersonal Behavior,* Dubuque, IA: Brown Communications.

Liverant, GI, TA Brown, DH Barlow, L Roemer (2008), "Emotion Regulation in Unipolar Depression: the Effects of Acceptance and Suppression of Subjective Emotional Experience on the Intensity and Duration of Sadness and Negative Affect," Behavior Research and Therapy, 46(Nov), 1201-09.

Main, Kelley J., Darren Dahl, and Peter R. Darke (2007), "Deliberate and Automatic Bases of Suspicion: Empirical Evidence of the Sinister Attribution Error," *Journal of Consumer Psychology,* 17(1), 59-69.

Miller, Rowland S. (1995), "On the Nature of Embarrassability: Shyness, Social Evaluation, and Social Skills," *Journal of Personality,* 63(June), 315-39.

Miller, Rowland S. (1996), *Embarrassment: Poise and Peril in Everyday Life,* New York: Guilford.

Mittal, Banwari and Alfried M. Lassar (1996), "The Role of Personalization in Service Encounters," *Journal of Retailing,* 72 (1), 95-109.

Modigliani, Andre (1968), "Embarrassment and Embarrassability," *Sociometry,* 31(September), 313-26.

O'Donohoe, Stephanie and Darach Turley (2007), "Fatal Errors: Unbridling Emotions in Service Failure Experiences," *Journal of Strategic Marketing,* 15 (1), 17-28.

Parrott, W. Gerrod and Stephanie F. Smith (1991), "Embarrassment: Actual vs. Typical Cases, Classical vs. Prototypical Representations," *Cognition and Emotion,* 5(September-November), 467-88.

Price, Linda L. and Eric J. Arnould (1999), "Commercial Friendship: Service Provider-Client Relationships in Context," *Journal of Marketing,* 63(4), 38-56.

Schlenker, Barry R. (1980), *Impression Management: The Self Concept, Self Identity, and Interpersonal Relations,* Monterey, CA: Brooks/Cole.

White, Tiffany B. (2004), "Consumer Disclosure and Disclosure Avoidance: A Motivational Framework," *Journal of Consumer Psychology,* 14 (1&2), 41-51.

Wirtz, Jochen and Anna S. Mattila (2004), "Consumer Responses to Compensation, Speed of Recovery and Apology after a Service Failure," International Journal of Service Industry Management, 15 (2), 150.

Affect-Rich Experiencers, Affect-Poor Forecasters: Mispredicting The Influence of Outcome Magnitude and Outcome Probability on Experienced Affect

Eva Buechel, University of Miami, USA
Jiao Zhang, University of Miami, USA
Carey Morewedge, Carnegie Mellon University, USA
Joachim Vosgerau, Carnegie Mellon Univeristy, USA

EXTENDED ABSTRACT

Affective forecasters exhibit an impact bias whereby they overestimate their emotional reactions to future events (Gilbert et al. 1998; Wilson & Gilbert, 2003). Despite many demostrations and proposed reasons for this bias, little attention has been paid to how forecasting errors relate to different magnitudes of the outcomes and to the probability with which outcomes occur.

People generally have the intuition that they will experience greater utility from outcomes that are greater in magnitude (Kahneman & Tversky, 1979) and outcomes that are obtained with a smaller probability (Brandstaetter, Kuehberger & Schnerider, 2002; Mellers, et al. 1997). An interesting question is whether people can accurately predict the impact of quantitative specifications of such outcome characteristics on their experienced affect. Hsee and Zhang (2004) have already studied if forecasters in joint evaluation mode can accurately predict the experienced affect of outcomes if they were encountered in isolation. They found that forecasters in joint evaluation mode overpredict the affective difference that magnitude specifications will evoke for experiences in single evaluation mode because the joint evaluation mode renders them more sensitive to magnitude differences.

In the present research we hypothesize that the difference in sensitivity between forecasters and experiencers is not contingent on the discrepancy in presence of other options. While forecasters report an emotional reaction they are not currently feeling, experiencers can feel the emotion vividly (Loewenstein, 1996; Loewenstein, Prelec & Shatto, 1998). This suggests that forecasters are in a more affect-poor state while experiencers are in a more affect-rich state. Previous research has shown that people in a relatively affect-poor state are more sensitive to quantitative specification such as magnitude and probability information (Hsee & Rottenstreich, 2004; Rottenstreich & Hsee, 2001). Therefore we argue that forecasters are generally more sensitive to information about the magnitude of future outcomes and the likelihood with which the outcome will occur than experiencers and thus overestimate the influence of such information on their experienced affect. An implication for this difference in sensitivity is a reversal of the impact bias whereby forecasters may underestimate their affective reaction in certain situations, such as when the outcome is small or the probability of obtaining it is high.

Study 1 tested if forecasters overestimate the importance of magnitude of the outcome on their experienced affect. Participants of a 2 x 2 between subject design participated in a gamble where they rolled a die and won $1 ($20) if they rolled an even number. What participants didn't know is that the die was rigged so that all participants rolled an even number and won $1 ($20). Forecasters predicted how happy they would be about winning $1 ($20) if they rolled an even number. They then rolled an even number and received 1$ ($20). Experiencers rolled an even number, received $1 ($20), and were asked to indicate how happy they were after learning the outcome. Consistent with our proposition, forecasters predicted that they would feel happier about winning $20 than $1, but experiencers showed no difference in happiness about winning $1 or $20. Interestingly, forecasters underpredicted the happiness of winning $1. A follow up study showed that this underprediction also occured for losses of $1.

Study 2 examined if forecasters overestimate the impact of outcome probability on their experienced affect. Participants of a 2 x 2 between subject design played a game in which they could pick a ball from a bag containing 10 balls and win $1 if the ball had a check mark on it. A "draw string bag" was used, making the content of the bag invisible to the participants. In the low (high)-probability condition, participants were told that one (nine) ball(s) had a check mark on it. Unbeknownst to the participants, all 10 balls were winning balls. Forecasters predicted how happy they would be about winning $1 if they drew a winning ball, then drew a winning ball and received $1. Experiencers drew a winning ball, received $1, and were asked to indicate how happy they were after learning the outcome. Forecasters predicted that they would feel happier about winning $1 if their chance of winning was 10% rather than 90%, whereas the experiencers felt equally happy, independent of their chance of winning. Forecasters underestiamteted their happiness about winning $1 with a 90% chance but accurately predicted their happiness about winning with 10% chace. A follow up study showed that this pattern replicated for non-monetary outcomes, such as chocolates.

Study 3 extended the findings of Study 2 to different probability and magnitude specifications. Participants of a 2 x 2 between subject-design played a game in which they could pick one of 10 identical envelopes and win $3 if they drew an envelope containing a winning slip. In the low (high)-probability condition participants were told that two (eight) envelopes contained a winning slip. In reality 5 of the envelopes contained a winning slip of paper and 50% of the participants won $3 (won $0). Forecasters predicted how happy they would be about winning or not winning $3, then drew a winning (losing) envelope and received $3 ($0). Experiencers drew a winning (losing) envelope, received $3 ($0), and were asked to indicate how happy they were after learning the outcome. Forecasters predicted that they would feel happier (unhappier) about winning (not winning) $3 if their chance of winning (not winning) was 20% rather than 90%, whereas the experiencers felt equally happy about winning (not winning), independent of their chance of winning (not winning). Forecasters underpredicted their happiness of winning $3 with a high probability and overpredicted their unhappiness of not winning $3 with a low probability. Process evidence suggests that forecasters are more sensitive to magnitude specifications.

The present research contributes to the existing literature on predicted utility by showing that forecasters are naturally more sensitive to quantitative outcome characteristics than experiencers. Furthermore this research reveals that participants overestimate the impact of outcome magnitude and outcome probability on experienced affect. As a result they exhibit a reversed impact bias whereby they underpredict the affective reactions towards certain outcomes.

REFERENCES

Arkes, H. R., Herren, L.T. & Isen, A. M. (1988).The role of potential loss in the influence of affect on risk-taking behavior. *Organizational Behavior and Human Decision Processes, 42,* 181-193.

Brandstaetter, E., Kuehberger, A., & Schneider, F. (2002). A cognitive-emotional account of the shape of probability weighting function. *Journal of Behavioral Decision Making, 15*, 79-100.

Damasio, A.R. (1994). *Descartes' Error: Emotion, Reason, and the Human Brain*, New York: Gosset/Putnam.

Eastwick, P.W., Finkel, E. J., Krishnamurti, T. & Loewenstein, G. (2007). Mispredicting distress following romantic breakup: Revealing the time course of affective forecasting error. *Journal of Experimental Social Psychology, 44*, 800-807.

Gilbert, D. T., Lieberman, M. D., Morewedge, C. K., & Wilson, T. D. (2004). The peculiar longevity of things not so bad. *Psychological Science, 15*, 14-19.

Gilbert, D.T., Morewedge, C.K., Risen, J.L. & Wilson, T. D. (2004). Looking forward to looking backward: The misprediction of regret. *Psychological Science*, 346-350.

Gilbert, D. T., Pinel, E. C., Wilson, T. D., Blumberg, S. J., & Wheatley, T. (1998). Immune neglect: A source of durability bias in affective forecasting. *Journal of Personality and Social Psychology, 75*, 617-638.

Gilbert, D. T., & Wilson, T. D. (2007). Prospection: Experiencing the future. *Science, 317*, 1351-1354.

Hsee, C. K. (1996). The evaluability hypothesis: An explanation for preference reversals between joint and separate evaluations of alternatives. *Organizational Behavior and Human Decision Processes*, 67, 247-257.

Hsee, C. K. (1998). Less is better: When low-value options are judged more highly than high-value options. *Journal of Behavioral Decision Making, 11*, 107-121.

Hsee, C.K., & Rottenstreich, Y. (2004). Music, pandas, and muggers: On the affective psychology of value. *Journal of Experimental Psychology: General, 126*, 45-53.

Hsee, C. K., Rottenstreich, Y., Xiao, Z. (2005). When is more better? *Current Directions in Psychological Science*, 234-237.

Hsee, C. K., & Zhang, J. (2004). Distinction bias: Misprediction and mischoice due to joint evaluation. *Journal of Personality and Social Psychology. 86*, 680-695.

Hsee, C. K., Zhang, J., Yu, F. & Xi, Y. (2003). Lay rationalism and inconsistency between predicted experience and decision. *Journal of Behavioral Decision Making, 16*, 257-272.

Kahneman, D., & Tversky, A. (1979). Prospect theory: An analysis of decision under risk. *Econometrica, 47*, 263-292.

Loewenstein, G., (1996). Out of control: Visceral influences on behavior. *Organizational behavior and Human Decision Process*, 65, 272-292.

Loewenstein, G. & Lerner, J. (2003). The role of emotion in decision making. In. R.J. Davidson, H.H, Goldsmith & K.R. Scherer (Eds.), *Handbook of affective science.* Oxford, England: Oxford University Press.

Loewenstein, G., Prelec, D., & Shatto, C. (1998). Hot/cold intrapersonal empathy gaps in the under-prediction of curiosity. Unpublished manuscript, Carnegie Mellon University, Pittsburgh, PA.

Markovitz, H. (1952). The utility of wealth. *The Journal of Political Economy*, 60, 151-158

Mellers, B. A., Schwartz, A., Ho, K. & Ritov, I. (1997). Decision affect theory: Emotional reactions to the outcomes of risky options. *Psychological Science. 8.* 423-429.

Morewedge, C. K., Gilbert, D. T., & Wilson, T. D. (2005). The least likely of times: How remembering the past biases forecasts of the future. *Psychological Science, 16,* 626-630.

Morewedge, C.K., Gilbert, D.T, Zhu, M., Myseth, K.O.R, Kassam, K.S., & Wilson, T.D. (2010). Consuming experiences: Why and when affective forecasters overestimate comparative value. Manuscript under review.

Myers, D. G. (2004). Theories of Emotion. *Psychology: Seventh Edition*, New York, NY: Worth Publishers.

Nelson, L.,& Meyvis, T. (2008). Interrupted consumption: Disrupting adaptation to hedonic experiences. Journal of Marketing Research, 45,654-664.

Nygren, T, E., Isen, A. M., Taylor, P. J & Dulin, J. (1996). The Influence of Positive Affect on the Decision Rule in Risk Situations: Focus on Outcome (and Especially Avoidance of Loss) Rather Than Probability. *Organizational Behavior and Human Decision Processes, 66*, 59-72.

Prelec, D., & Loewenstein, G. (1991). Decision making over time and uncertainty: A common approach. Management Science, 37, 770-768.

Robinson, M. D., Clore, G. L. (2001). Simulation, scenarios, and emotional appraisal: Testing the convergence of real and imagined reactions to emotional stimuli. *Personality and Social Psychology Bulletin, 27, 1520-1532*

Rottenstreich, Y., & Hsee, C.K. (2001). Money, kisses, and electric shocks: On the affective psychology of risk. *Psychological Science, 12,* 185-190.

Sieff, E.M., Dawes, R. & Loewenstein, G. (1999). Anticipated versus actual reaction to HIV results. *The American Journal of Psychology*, 122. 297-311.

Slovic, P., Finucane, M., Peters, E. & MacGregor, D.G. (2004). *Risk Analysis,* 24, 1-12.

Slovic, P. & Lichtenstein, S. (1971). Comparison of Bayesian and regression approaches to the study of information processing in judgment. *Organizational Behavior and Human Performance, 6* (6), 649-744.

Wilson, T.D. & Gilbert, D.T. (2003). Affective forecasting. In M. Zanna (Ed.), *Advances in experimental social psychology* (pp.345-411). New York: Elsevier.

Wilson, T. D., & Gilbert, D.T. (2005). Affective forecasting: knowing what to want. *Current Directions in Psychological Science, 14*, 132-134.

Wilson, T. D., Wheatley, T. P., Meyers, J. M., Gilbert, D. T., & Axsom, D. (2000). Focalism: A source of durability bias in affective forecasting. *Journal of Personality and Social Psychology, 78,* 821-836.

Practice What You Preach?

Sunaina Chugani, University of Texas at Austin, USA
Susan Broniarczyk, University of Texas at Austin, USA

EXTENDED ABSTRACT

We take the intriguing position that there is an inherent mechanism built into giving goal-related advice that leads advisors to be less likely to practice what they preach. We posit that when giving advice to pursue (disengage from) a goal, the advisor's expectation that the advice will be acted on allows him to vicariously experience goal progress (regression) through the expected advice-congruent behavior of the recipient. Via goal balancing, this progress (regression) leads the advisor to subsequently disengage from (engage in) the goal (Fishbach and Dhar, 2005) exhibiting advice-inconsistent behavior. When the expectation that advice will be acted on is eliminated (thus taking away the unique vicarious nature of advice-giving), mechanisms such as the desire for consistency, self perception, and goal priming will lead advisors to engage in advice-consistent behavior. Three studies explore these predictions.

Participants in Study 1 advised a friend to either stick to a healthy eating goal or indulge for a special occasion. Advice given was manipulated between subject: to induce participants to give pursue (disengage from) goal advice, scientific evidence was presented stating that individuals should never indulge (indulge occasionally) to increase goal achievement likelihood. After giving advice, participants indicated their preference on an 8-point scale between an unhealthy (1) and healthy snack (8), presented as being a token of thanks while actually serving as a measure of goal-related behavior. As hypothesized, participants who gave advice to stick to the healthy goal preferred the healthy snack less ($M=3.6$) than those who gave disengage advice ($M=4.7$, $F(1,37)=5.15$, $p<0.05$).

Using an academic goal context, Study 2 explored whether giving advice to pursue a goal leads an advisor to experience heightened goal progress. Participants in a goal-related advice condition gave advice to a friend to study for an exam (pursue academic goal) rather than attend a party in neighboring city. This condition was compared to two controls, one in which participants read about their friend's academic goal-related behavior (read about goal pursuit condition; designed to rule out the possibility that progress results from simple goal activation), and the other in which participants gave advice about what microwave to buy (non-goal advice condition; designed to rule out possibility that progress results from giving advice in any domain, regardless of goal-relevance). After completing one of these conditions and in an ostensibly unrelated task, participants reported what percent of the past twenty-four hours they spent pursuing their own academic goal, which served as a measure of perceived academic goal progress.

Results indicate that individuals in the goal-related advice condition reported an inflated sense of academic goal progress ($M=62.67$, $SD=26.71$) relative to the two control conditions together ($M=47.42$, $SD=28.76$; $F(1,82)=5.84$, $p<.05$), the read about goal pursuit condition alone ($M=46.29$, $SD=28.58$, $F(1,82)=5.33$, $p<.05$), and the non-goal advice condition alone ($M=48.75$, $SD=29.53$, $F(1,82)=3.88$, $p=.05$). Thus, participants who gave advice to a friend to pursue the academic goal exhibited more goal progress than individuals who gave non-goal advice and those who simply read about goal pursuit, lending support to our position that advisors experience vicarious goal progress when giving advice to pursue a goal.

Study 3 observed post-advice behavior after turning on and off the vicarious goal progress/regression mechanism by manipulating whether advisors perceived that recipients acted on their advice. This design allowed us to explore the mechanism of vicarious goal progress/regression directly. This study also explored the moderator of goal strength. An advisor will be more attuned to the discrepancy between the current and desired end-state with a goal he is concerned with and invested in (Förster, Liberman, & Friedman, 2007). Therefore, we make the counterintuitive prediction that individuals with high (vs. low) goal strength will be more likely to behave in an advice-inconsistent manner.

First, participants gave advice to a friend about whether to study for an exam (pursue academic goal) or attend a party in a neighboring city over the weekend (disengage from academic goal). Advice given was manipulated between-subject: to induce participants to give pursue (disengage) advice, the test was framed as important (unimportant) and the party as unimportant (important).

After writing down their advice, participants were asked to imagine they called their friend over the weekend to find the friend either acting on given advice or not acting on advice given due to external circumstances. Participants then completed an ostensibly unrelated task where they indicated their preference between watching one of two videos on an 8-point scale: one unrelated to the goal (1 = clips from funny TV shows) and one congruent with the academic goal (8 = how to retain more from studying). Participants watched the videos and answered video questions to complete the cover story. Finally, participants reported the extent to which doing well in school was a priority for them, which served as a measure of academic goal strength.

There was a three-way interaction between advice given, advice acted on, and goal strength on preference between the videos ($F(1,83)=3.83$, $p=0.05$). Spotlight analysis (Irwin & McClelland, 2001) indicated that the interaction between advice given and advice acted on was absent among participants with low academic goal strength ($F(1,83)=0.09$, NS) and present among participants with high academic goal strength ($F(1,83)=10.06$, $p<0.01$). Among those with high goal strength who learned that their advice had been acted on, those who gave advice to pursue the goal were subsequently less likely to prefer the goal-related video than those who gave advice to disengage ($F(1,83)=3.58$, $p=0.06$) replicating the pattern of advice-inconsistent behavior from Study 1. Conversely, those who learned their advice had not been acted on behaved in a pattern of advice-consistent behavior: giving advice to pursue the goal led to a higher preference for the goal-related video than giving advice to disengage ($F(1,83)=7.14$, $p<0.01$).

In sum, this research sheds light on the nascent area of feedback effects of advice-giving on advisors. Three studies provide evidence across two goal domains for the position that advisors experience goal progress/regression when giving goal-related advice to others, leading to advice-inconsistent behavior.

REFERENCES

Aarts, H., & Dijksterhuis, A. (2000). Habits as knowledge structures: Automaticity in goal-directed behavior. *Journal of Personality and Social Psychology, 78*(1), 53-63.

Ackerman, J., Goldstein, N., Shapiro, J., & Bargh, J. (2009). You wear me out: The vicarious depletion of self-control. *Psychological science: a journal of the American Psychological Society/APS, 20*(3), 326.

Bargh, J., Gollwitzer, P., Lee-Chai, A., Barndollar, K., & Trötschel, R. (2001). The automated will: Nonconscious activation and pursuit of behavioral goals. *Journal of Personality and Social Psychology, 81*(6), 1014-1027.

Bem, D. (1967). Self-Perception: An Alternative Interpretation of Cognitive Dissonance Phenomena. *Psychological Review, 74*(3), 183-200.

Carver, C. S., & Scheier, M. F. (1998). *On the self-regulation of behavior*. New York: Cambridge University Press.

Cialdini, R. B., Trost, M. R., & Newsom, J. T. (1995). Preference for consistency: The development of a valid measure and the discovery of surprising behavioral implications. *Journal of Personality and Social Psychology, 69*(2), 318-328.

Custers, R., & Aarts, H. (2005). Beyond priming effects: The role of positive affect and discrepancies in implicit processes of motivation and goal pursuit. *European Review of Social Psychology, 16*(8), 257-300.

Festinger, L. (1957). *A theory of cognitive dissonance*. Stanford: Stanford University Press.

Fishbach, A., & Dhar, R. (2005). Goals as excuses or guides: The liberating effect of perceived goal progress on choice. *Journal of Consumer Research, 32*(3), 370-377.

Fishbach, A., & Zhang, Y. (2009). The Dynamics of Self-Regulation: When Goals Commit Versus Liberate. In M. Wanke (Ed.), *Social Psychology of Consumer Behavior* (pp. 365-386). New York, NY: Psychology Press.

Fitzsimons, G. M., & Finkel, E. J. (2010). Interpersonal Influences on Self-Regulation. *Directions in Psychological Science, 19*(2), 101-105.

Fitzsimons, G. M., & Fishbach, A. (2010). Shifting Closeness: Interpersonal Effects of Personal Goal Progress. *Journal of Consumer Research, 98*(4), 535-549.

Förster, J., Liberman, N., & Friedman, R. S. (2007). Seven principles of goal activation: A systematic approach to distinguishing goal priming from priming non-goal constructs. *Personality and Social Psychology Review, 11*(3), 211-235.

Irwin, J. R., & McClelland, G. H. (2001). Misleading Heuristics for Moderated Multiple Regression Models. *Journal of Marketing Research, 38*, 100-109.

Koo, M., & Fishbach, A. (2008). Dynamics of self-regulation: How (un) accomplished goal actions affect motivation. *Journal of Personality and Social Psychology, 94*(2), 183.

Lockwood, P., & Pinkus, R. (2008). The impact of social comparisons on motivation. In J. Shah & W. L. Gardner (Eds.), *Handbook of motivation science* (pp. 251-264). New York, NY: Guilford Press.

Monin, B., & Miller, D. T. (2001). Moral Credentials and the Expression of Prejudice. *Journal of Personality and Social Psychology, 81*(1), 33-43.

Myrseth, K. O. R., Fishbach, A., & Trope, Y. (2009). Counteractive self-control: When making temptation available makes temptation less tempting. *Psychological Science, 20*(2), 159-163.

Shah, J. (2003). The Motivational Looking Glass: How Significant Others Implicitly Affect Goal Appraisals. *Journal of Personality and Social Psychology, 85*(3), 424-439.

Wilcox, K., Vallen, B., Block, L., & Fitzsimons, G. (2009). Vicarious goal fulfillment: when the mere presence of a healthy option leads to an ironically indulgent decision. *Journal of Consumer Research, 36*(3), 380-393.

Zhang, Y., Huan, S.-C., & Broniarczyk, S. M. (2010). Counteractive construal in consumer goal pursuit. *Journal of Consumer Research, 37*(1), 129-142.

The Big Cost of Small Problems:
Ironic Effects of Malfunction Severity on Consumption Experience

Neil Brigden, University of Alberta, Canada
Gerald Haeubl, University of Alberta, Canada

EXTENDED ABSTRACT

When a product ceases to function properly, the consumer must either take action to remedy the problem or endure the reduced functionality. Naturally, more severe product malfunctions have a greater negative effect on consumption experiences. However, consumers are more motivated to address malfunctions of greater magnitude. This creates the paradox that less severe product malfunctions can result in less favorable consumption experiences than more severe ones because smaller problems are allowed to persist longer. In a series of experiments in which participants faced repair decisions during consumption experiences, we demonstrate this big-cost-of-small-problems effect and examine the underlying mechanism.

We demonstrate that it is indeed possible for minor problems to ironically be more harmful than major ones, even when the cost of repairing the problem is taken into account. We explain this effect by showing that consumers fail to immediately address minor problems because the experienced discomfort fails to reach some threshold that would trigger a response. This effect parallels findings in social psychology where more minor insults have been shown to cause greater distress because they are too small to trigger psychological defenses (Gilbert et al. 2004). Further, we argue that once the decision to not fix the problem is made in the current period, it becomes less likely to be revisited in future periods due to inaction inertia.

Inaction inertia refers to the decreased likelihood of taking an attractive course of action when a similar and superior course of action has been previously foregone (Tykocinski & Pittman 1998; Tykocinski, Pittman & Tuttle 1995). Regardless of what underlies the initial decision to not repair a product, continuing to not repair in subsequent periods, even though the repair continues to be normatively optimal, can be explained by inaction inertia. If a product is worth repairing in a later period, then logically it would have been even better to have repaired the product in an earlier period. An earlier repair would increase the benefit derived as more usage time or usage occasions would still be in the future and thus subject to the improved performance that the repair brings. Thus the initial decision to not repair can be thought of as a missed opportunity, and subsequent opportunities to repair, although potentially still beneficial, will be comparatively inferior.

To test these hypotheses, we conducted a series of experiments where participants were confronted with relatively smaller or larger product malfunctions, made decisions regarding fixing the malfunction, and then reported their enjoyment of the experience. Our evidence shows that smaller malfunctions can indeed lead to inferior consumer outcomes because consumers are less likely to address them.

In experiment 1, participants watched a 10-minute video clip while bursts of audio static (the malfunction) interfered with the consumption experience. The audio static was more frequent in the larger problem condition than in the smaller problem condition. Participants could get rid of the static at any time by pressing a button, but the cost of fixing the problem was that they would hear no audio at all for 1 minute. Participants in the smaller problem condition, despite facing an objectively superior experience reported lower enjoyment ($M=6.72$) than participants in the larger problem condition ($M=7.98$), $t(82)=2.40$, $p<.05$. This difference was driven by the fact that fewer participants in the smaller malfunction condition chose to fix the problem (65% vs. 88%, Fischer's Exact test, p<.05).

In experiments 2a and 2b, we compared situations where participants could fix a problem at any time versus situations where participants had to decide prior to consumption whether to fix the problem. In these experiments, participants played a computer game and the malfunction was in the form of random moves that interfered with the participants' ability to control the game. When participants could fix the problem at any time, the big-cost-of-small-problems effect was replicated. Participants in the smaller malfunction condition reported less enjoyment ($M=5.10$) than those in the larger malfunction condition ($M=6.53$; $t(58)=2.08$, $p<.05$). Again, participants who experienced a smaller malfunction were less likely to fix it compared to those who experienced a larger malfunction (63% vs. 89%, Fischer's Exact test, p<.05). By contrast, when participants had to decide prior to the consumption experience whether to fix the problem, no big-cost-of-small-problems effect occurred. Enjoyment did not differ between the smaller malfunction condition ($M=5.6$) and the larger malfunction condition ($M=5.7$, $t(60)=0.16$, $p>.8$). Fixing rates also did not differ (68% vs. 78%, Fischer's Exact test, p>.1). These results support the hypothesis that consumers can become trapped with smaller problems because they initially put up with them, and then subsequently devalue fixing opportunities because they are inferior to prior fixing opportunities. These results are incompatible with a pure intertemporal-discounting account of the big-cost-of-small-problems effect. Forcing the decision to occur prior to the experience should not eliminate the effect if it was arising merely because of discounting.

In experiment 3, we assigned participants to either experience or forecast enjoyment as if they had chosen to fix or not fix a smaller or larger malfunction using the same game experience as in experiments 2a and 2b. We hypothesized that, if the effect was not due to an affective forecasting error, we should not observe any interactions between experiencing versus forecasting and problem magnitude. As predicted, although forecasts were overly optimistic, they did not differ between problem magnitudes. In addition, the experiencer data provides additional evidence that not fixing the smaller problem in this experience is a non-normative action.

These studies demonstrate that problem magnitude has a dual effect on consumption experience. More severe malfunctions directly reduce consumption enjoyment to a greater degree, but they also indirectly *increase* consumption enjoyment by making it more likely that consumers will address the malfunction. The findings suggest that consumers and marketers might be paying too little attention to minor product malfunctions, allowing them to persist, and suffering disproportionately from them as a result.

REFERENCES

Anderson, Christopher J. (2003), "The Psychology of Doing Nothing: Forms of Decision Avoidance Result From Reason and Emotion," *Psychological Bulletin,* 129, 139-167.

Arkes, Hal R., Yi-Han Kung & Laura Hutzel (2002), "Regret, Valuation, and Inaction Inertia," *Organizational Behavior and Human Decision Processes,* 87, 371-385.

Coelho do Vale, R.M.R.D., Pieters, R., & Zeelenberg, M. (2008). "Flying under the radar: Perverse package format effects on consumption self-regulation," *Journal of Consumer Research*, 35(3), 380-390.

Dunn, Elizabeth W., Jeremy C. Biesanz, Lauren J. Human & Stephanie Finn (2007), "Misunderstanding the Affective Consequences of Everyday Social Interactions: The Hidden Benefits of Putting One's Best Face Forward," *Journal of Personality and Social Psychology, 92,* 990-1005.

Eastwick, Paul W., Eli J. Finkel, Tamar Krishnamurti & George Loewenstein (2008), "Mispredicting distress following romantic breakup: Revealing the time course of the affective forecasting error," *Journal of Experimental Social Psychology, 44,* 800-807.

Gilbert, D. T., Pinel, E. C., Wilson, T. D., Blumberg, S. J. & Wheatley, T. P. (1998), "Immune Neglect: A Source of Durability Bias in Affective Forecasting," *Journal of Personality and Social Psychology, 75,* 617-638.

Gilbert, D. T., Lieberman, M. D., Morewedge, C. K., & Wilson, T. D. (2004), "The peculiar longevity of things not so bad," *Psychological Science, 15,* 14-19.

Herrnstein, R. J., Prelec, D., Lowenstein, G. F., and Vaughan, W. Jr. (1993), "Utility Maximization and Melioration: Internalities in Individual Choice," *Journal of Behavioral Decision Making, 6,* 149-185.

Herrnstein, R. J., and Vaughan. W., Jr (1980). Melioration and behavioral allocation, in Staddon. J. E, R., (ed.). *Limits to Action: The Allocation of Individual Behavior*, pp. 143-76, New York: Academic Press.

Ritov, Ilana & Jonathon Baron (1992), "Status Quo and Omission Biases," *Journal of Risk and Uncertainty*, 5, 49–62.

Thaler, Richard H. and Cass R. Sunstein (2008). "Nudge: Improving Decisions about Health, Wealth and Happiness," Yale University Press. New Haven, CT.

Tykocinski, Orit E. & Thane S. Pittman (1998), "The Consequences of Doing Nothing: Inaction Inertia as Avoidance of Anticipated Counterfactual Regret," *Journal of Personality and Social Psychology,* 75, 607-615.

Tykocinski, Orit E., Thane S. Pittman, & Erin E. Tuttle (1995), "Inaction Inertia: Foregoing Future Benefits as a Result of an Initial Failure to Act," *Journal of Personality and Social Psychology,* 68, 793-803.

Wilson, Tim. D. & Daniel. T. Gilbert (2003). Affective forecasting. In M. Zanna (Ed.), *Advances in experimental social psychology*, Vol. 35 (pp. 345-411). New York: Elsevier.

Wilson, Tim. D., T. P. Wheatley, J. M. Meyers, T. D. Gilbert & D. Axsom (2000), "Focalism: A Source of Durability Bias in Affective Forecasting. *Journal of Personality and Social Psychology, 78,* 821-836.

Zauberman, Gal (2003), "The Intertemporal Dynamics of Consumer Lock-In," *Journal of Consumer Research,* 30, 405-419.

Zauberman, Gal & John G. Lynch, Jr. (2005), "Resource Slack and Propensity to Discount Delayed Investments of Time Versus Money," *Journal of Experimental Psychology: General,* 134, 23-37.

Zeelenberg, Marcel, Bernard A. Nijstad, Marijke van Putten and Eric van Dijk (2006), "Inaction Inertia, Regret, and Valuation: A Closer Look," *Organizational Behavior and Human Decision Processes,* 101, 89-104.

The Effect of Positioning of a Target Brand and a Competitive Brand(s) in an Advertisement on a Consumer's Judgment and on the Selection of the Target Brand

Jungsil Choi, University of Kansas, USA
Myer Duane, University of Kansas, USA

EXTENDED ABSTRACT

This paper examines the effect of the positioning of in relation to a comparison brand or brands in a multi-panel table of a comparative advertisement. At issue is the effectiveness of the advertisement as measured by the consumers' product selection.

The use of a comparison table in the comparative advertisements is effective because audiences get comparable information for each product attribute listed in the table. Consumers tend to compare an object in the right panel with the object in the left panel because they have a tendency to read from left to right. This is especially true for English readers (Eviatar, 1995). Prior studies have shown in a sequential observation of two objects, the later serves as the subject of comparison and the object observed earlier serves as the referent (Bruine and Keren, 2003; Sanbonmatsu, Kardes, and Gibson, 1991; Houston and Sherman, 1995). Therefore, the object placed in the left panel is expected to serve as a referent of comparison and the object placed in the right panel a subject of comparison. When a sponsor's product is positioned in the left panel and a comparison product is positioned in the right panel, the reader is exposed to the superior features of the sponsor's product first, followed by the inferior features of the comparison product. An advertisement arranged such that the sponsor's product is placed in the left panel and the comparison product in the right panel of the comparison table, therefore, would evoke more negative thoughts on a comparison product in the right panel than positive thoughts on a sponsor's product in the left panel.

On the other hand, if the physical positioning of a comparison product and a referent product is reversed, the opposite result is hypothesized. The comparison product, when positioned in the left-hand panel, becomes the referent product with which people compare the features of the product in the right-hand panel. Such an arrangement of a target and a comparison product in a comparison table, therefore, might lead people to have more positive thoughts on a sponsor's product in the right-hand panel than negative thoughts on a comparison product in the left-hand panel.

Jain and Posavac (2004) show that a negative comparative advertisement results in unfavorable attitudes toward an advertised product than a positive comparative advertisement because people are more skeptical of negative comparative messages and tend to judge positive comparative messages to be more believable.

Based on the reading habit from left to right, the comparative advertisement should be perceived as more positive when the sponsor's product is placed in the right-hand panel because it will be perceived as a positive comparative advertisement. In addition, people will perceive higher value and quality when a sponsor's product is placed in the right-hand panel because of the preference for "right" (Valenzuela and Raghubir 2009). Thus, it is hypothesized that physical positioning of the sponsor's product and a comparison product in a comparison table will affect the effectiveness of a comparative advertisement. Specifically, a higher value will be ascribed to the sponsor's product when it is placed in the right-hand panel in a comparison table, and the comparative advertisement and the sponsor's product will be viewed more favorably when the sponsor's product is placed in the right panel and a comparison product is in the left panel.

In Study 1, a different perceived value for the target brand was found depending on its position in the left panel versus the right panel in the comparison table. We found when a target brand was positioned in the right panel as opposed to the left panel the respondents perceived a greater value from the target brand (t (75) = 3.22, $p < .01$). Respondents were found to have a favorable attitude toward a target brand when it was positioned in the right panel as opposed to the left panel (t (75) = 2.06, $p < .05$); however, the positioning of a target brand in the right panel as opposed to the left panel in the comparison table did not result in a significant difference in willingness to buy (t (75) =.41, $p >.68$).

In Study 2 the effects of physical positioning in a one-to-one comparison table were extended to those in a one-to-three comparison table, which is also a very common type of a comparative advertisement. A significant difference in attitudes and the purchase likelihood in terms of physical positioning of a target brand was found. When the target brand is placed in the far right panel as opposed to the far left panel, a significant difference was found in the attitude toward the target brand in terms of its position in the table in the comparison advertisement (F (28) = 11.66; $p < .01$); however, a marginal difference was found in the purchase likelihood in terms of the position of the target brand in the table of the comparison advertisement (F (1, 28) = 3.247; $p < .08$).

In Study 3 it was confirmed that physical positioning affects perception of the valence of comparison advertisements. Planned contrasts show the combination of "right-positioning" + a positive advertisement copy is evaluated as more amicable than the combination of "left-positioning" + a positive advertisement copy (t (106) = 2.11; $p < .04$), the combination of "left-positioning" + a negative advertisement copy (t (106) = 2.12; $p < .04$), and the combination of "right-positioning" + a negative advertisement copy (t (106) = 2.24; $p < .03$). The results confirmed the hypothesis that the combination of "right-positioning" and a positive advertisement copy was considered the most amicable, as it corresponded to a positive comparative advertisement. The similar results were found from attitudes toward the target brand and the purchase likelihood.

These findings have obvious practical implications. Marketing managers and advertisers have not had similar studies concerning the effect of physical positioning of a target and a comparison brand in a table in a comparison advertisement. This paper shows how this minor change results in significant differences in the effectiveness of comparative advertisements.

REFERENCES

Bruine, Wandi de Bruin and Gideon Keren (2003), "Order Effects in sequentially Judged Options Due to the Direction of Comparison," *Organizational Behavior and Human Decision Processes*, 92(1-2), 91-101.

Dehaene, Stanislas, Serge Bossini, and Pascal Giraux (1993), "The Mental Representation of Parity and Number Magnitude," *Journal of Experimental Psychology: General*, 122(3), 371-396.

Deng, Xiaoyan and Barbara E. Kahn (2009), "Is Your Product on the Right Side? The "Location Effect" on Perceived Product Heaviness and Package Evaluation," *Journal of Marketing Research*, 46(6), 725-738.

Eviatar, Zohar. (1995), "Reading Direction and Attention – Effects on Lateralized Ignoring," *Brain and Cognition*, 29(2), 137-150.

Gorn, Gerald J., Amitava Chattopadhyay, Jaideep Sengupta, and Shashank Tripathi (2004), "Waiting for the Web: How Screen Color Affects Time Perception," *Journal of Marketing Research*, 41(2), 215-225.

Gotlieb, JerryB . and Dan Sarel (1991), "Comparative Advertising Effectiveness: The Role of Involvement and Source Credibility," *Journal of Advertising*, 20 (March), 38-45.

Grewal, Dhruv, Sukumar Kavanoor, Edward F. Fern, Carolyn Costley, and James Barnes (1997), "Comparative Versus Noncomparative Advertising: A Meta-Analysis," *Journal of Marketing*, 61(4), 1-15.

Houston, David A. and Sherman Steven J. (1995), "Cancellation and Focus: The Role of Shared and Unique Features in the Choice Process," *Journal of Experimental Social Psychology*, 31(4), 357-378.

Jain, Shailendra Pratap (1993), "Positive Versus Negative Comparative Advertising," *Marketing Letters*, 4(4), 309-320.

Jain, Shailendra Pratap, Nidhi Agrawal, and Durairaj Maheswaran (2006), "When More May Be Less: The Effects of Regulatory Focus on Different Comparative Frames," Journal of Consumer Research, 33(1), 91-98.

Jain, Shailendra Pratap, Bruce Buchanan, and Durairaj Maheswaran (2000), "Comparative Versus Noncomparative Advertising: The Moderating Impact of Prepurchase Attribute Verifiability," *Journal of Consumer Psychology*, 9(4), 201-211.

Jain, Shailendra Pratap, Charles Lindsey, Nidhi Agrawal, and Durairaj Maheswaran (2007), "For Better or For Worse? Valenced Comparative Frames and Regulatory Focus," *Journal of Consumer Research*, 34(1), 57-65.

Jain, Shailendra Pratap, Steven S. Posavac (2004), "Valenced Comparisons," *Journal of Marketing Research*, 41(1), 46-58.

Jackson, Donald W., Jr., Stephen W. Brown, and Robert R. Harmon (1979), "Comparative Magazine Advertisements," *Journal of Advertising Research*, 19 (December), 21-26.

Lin, Hsin-Hui and Yi-Shun Wang (2006), "An Examination of the Determinants of Customer Loyalty in Mobile Commerce Contexts," *Information & Management*, 43, 271-282.

Manel, Susan P. and Frank R. Kardes (1999), "The Role of Direction of Comparison, Attribute-Based Processing, and Attitude-Based Processing in Consumer Preference," *Journal of Consumer Research*, 25(4), 335-352.

Morikawa, Kazunori and Michael K. McBeath (1992), "Lateral Motion Bias Associated with Reading Direction," Vision Research, 32(6), 1137-1141.

Preacher, K. J., and Hayes, A. F. (2004). SPSS and SAS procedures for estimating indirect effects in simple mediation models. *Behavior Research Methods, Instruments, and Computers, 36*, 717-731.

Rayner, Keith, Caren M. Rotello, Andrew J. Stewart, Jessica Keir, and Susan A. Duffy (2001), Integrating Text and Pictorial Information: Eye Movements When Looking at Print Advertisements," *Journal of Experimental Psychology: Applied*, 7(3), 219-226.

Sanbonmatsu, David M., Frank R. Kardes, and Bryan D. Gibson (1991), "The Role of Attribute Knowledge and Overall Evaluations in Comparative Judgment," *Organizational Behavior and Human Decision Processes*, 48(1), 131-146.

Thompson, Debora Viana and Rebecca W. Hamilton (2006), "The Effects of Information Processing Mode on Consumers' Responses to Comparative Advertising," *Journal of Consumer Research*, 32(4), 530-540.

Valenzuela, Ana and Priya Raghubir (2009), "Position-Based Beliefs: The Center-Stage Effect," *Journal of Consumer Psychology*, 19(2), 185-196.

Zhu, Rui and Joan Meyers-Levy (2009), "The Influence of Self-View on Context Effects: How Display Fixtures can Affect Product Evaluations," *Journal of Marketing Research*, 46(1), 37-45.

The Effects of Mindset Abstraction on Memory-Based Consideration Set Formation

Fang-Chi Lu, University of Iowa, USA
Dhananjay Nayakankuppam, University of Iowa, USA

EXTENDED ABSTRACT

"Memory-based consideration set" is suggested to be a set of products consumers recall from memory when facing needs to be fulfilled, and then they make their final choice from this set (Ratneshwar and Shocker, 1991). Consideration set formation is considered as a fundamental stage of pre-choice decision making. Consumers usually engage in a two-stage decision process, screening available brands/products in a product category to form a smaller subset of brands and then making an explicit utility comparison or cost-benefit trade-off before making their final choice decision. Understanding the formation of consideration sets is important from both theoretical and practical perspectives. Consideration of a brand is suggested to mediate the influence of attitude and attitude strength on choice (Priester et al., 2004). Using the scanner data, Hauser and Wernerfelt (1989) found that 70% of the variance accounted for in choice is explained by consideration.

However, consideration sets are dynamic, being influenced by a variety of factors. First, the composition of consideration sets is influenced by personal goals and motives. Ratneshwar and his colleagues (1996) found that across-category consideration was high when there was either goal conflict or goal ambiguity. Chakravarti and Janiszewski (2003) suggested that motivations, to simplify the choice process or to optimize the choice outcome, determine the size and heterogeneity of consideration sets. Second, attitude and attitude strength influence whether a brand is included in a consideration set (Priester et al., 2004). Finally, situational variables, such as usage situation (e.g., Desai and Hoyer, 2000), assortment size (e.g., Heller, Levin, and Goransson, 2002), and advertising (e.g., Mitra and Lynch, 1995) were also suggested to influence the content of consideration sets. In the same vein, the model of constructed choice processes asserts that preferences are construed during the choice process, and subjective construal, experiential information, attribution, goals and satisfaction influence the choice process in a lower-level perceptual, non-conscious way (Griffin, Liu, & Khan, 2004). Taken together, it is implied that influencing the way consumers construe their choice decisions might alter the nature of a consideration set.

More recently, the construal level theory, proposed by Liberman and Trope (2007), suggests that psychological distance of an object systematically changes how the object is mentally construed, which in turn influences people's thoughts and behaviors. According to the theory, low-level construals are concrete, relatively unstructured, contextualized representations that include subordinate and incidental features or event; whereas high-level construals are abstract schematic, decontextualized representations that extract the gist from the available information. Previous research showed that individuals in concrete mindsets are more susceptible to incidental social influence, and have more flexible attitude toward a certain evaluative object (Ledgerwood, Trope, and Chaiken, 2010).

Building upon the construal level theory, we propose that construal levels used for the mental representation of a choice decision influence the search of alternatives in memory and the composition of the formed consideration set. More specifically, we suggest that individuals in concrete mindsets, compared to abstract mindset, are likely to think more concrete, specific details about certain choice decision contexts, and the concrete, fine-grained mental representations activate more associations in memory, thus leading to bigger consideration sets.

Findings from two studies, using alternative manipulations of mindset abstraction and different decision contexts, provided support for our main hypothesis that concrete mindsets induce bigger consideration sets. In Study 1, abstract versus concrete mindset was primed by asking participants to generate either superordinate categories or subordinate exemplars for 20 objects (e.g., actor, book, movie). Next, participants completed a snack product choice task in which a certain snack choice scenario was given, and participants listed the snack items they seriously consider, their final choice and the factors/attributes they used in forming their consideration sets. Extent of hunger was also measured as a covariant. Results of analyses showed that participants who generated subordinate exemplars had bigger consideration set than the ones generating superordinate categories ($M_{concrete}$=7.92, $M_{abstract}$=5.44, $p<0.01$). The procedure of Study 2 is similar to Study 1 except for that the Navon task was used for mindset abstraction priming. Participants were presented with a series of global letters made up of local letters, and they were asked to identify either the global or the local letters. After that, they formed consideration set in a dinner decision context. Consistent with Study 1, participants who identified the local letters generated larger consideration sets than the ones who identified the global letters ($M_{concrete}$=6.96, $M_{abstract}$=5, $p<0.03$).

We propose that this mindset abstraction effect on size of consideration sets is due to the differential extent of associations activated in memory in concrete versus abstract mindsets. We conducted Study 3 to examine this hypothesis. The Navon task was used prime abstract versus concrete mindsets. After the Navon task, participants completed a word association task in which they listed as many associated words as they can for each of the target words presented. The selected target words, varying in the frequency of word occurrence and the size of their association set size, were adopted from previous research (Meyers-Levy, 1989). Findings of Study 3, supporting our hypothesis of the underlying mechanism, revealed a main effect of mindset abstraction. Individuals in concrete mindsets listed more word associations than the ones in concrete mindset, and the main effect was independent of word frequency and word association set size ($M_{concrete}$=9.05, $M_{abstract}$=6.97, $p<0.03$).

The current research shed light on a construal level effect on memory in consideration set formation domain. From a memory perspective, concrete, relative to abstract, mental representations result in many more memory cues. For example, Dural Coding Theory (Pavio, 1986) suggests that concrete words (e.g., tree, party) can be represented visually and verbally, thus have more associations and are better remembered. Going beyond that, we found that individuals' processing mindset (concrete vs. abstract) influence ease of retrieving alternatives from memory, thus affecting the likelihood of certain products being included in the consideration sets.

REFERENCES

Chakravarti, A. and Janiszewski, C. (2003). The Influence of Macro-Level Motives on Consideration Set Composition in Novel Purchase Situations," *Journal of Consumer Research.* 30, 244-258.

Dhar, R. and Simonson, I. (1999). Consumption context effects in choice: Highlighting versus balancing, *Journal of Marketing Research*, 36, 29-44.

Desai, K. K. and Hoyer, W. D. (2000). Descriptive Characteristics of Memory-Based Consideration Sets: Influence of Usage Occasion Frequency and Usage Location Familiarity. *Journal of Consumer research, 27*, 309-323.

Di Pace, E., Longoni, A. M., and Zoccolotti, P. (1991). Semantic processing of unattended parafoveal words, *Acta Psychologica, 77(1)*, 21-34.

Fujita, K., Henderson, M., Eng, J., Trope, Y., and Liberman, N. (2006). Spatial distance and mental construal of social events. *Psychological Science, 17*, 278-282.

Gollwitzer, P. M., and Bayer, U. (1999). Deliberative versus implemental mindsets in the control of actions. In S. Chaiken & Y. Trope (Eds.), *Dual-process theories in social psychology* (pp. 403-422). New York: Guilford Press.

Goukens, C., Siegfried, D., Pandelaere, M., and Warlop, L. (2007). Wanting a Bit(e) of Everything: Extending the Valuation Effect to Variety Seeking. *Journal of Consumer Research, 34*, 386-394.

Griffin, D., Liu, W., and Khan, U. (2005). A new look at constructed choice processes. *Marketing Letter, 16 (3/4)*, 321-333.

Hauser, J. R., & Birger, W. (1989). The competitive implications of relevant-set response analysis. *Journal of Marketing Research, 26(4)*, 391-405.

Heller, D., Levin, I. P., & Goransson, M. (2002). Selection of strategies for narrowing choice options: Antecedents and consequences, *Organizational Behavior and Human Decision Processes, 89(2)*, 1194-1213.

Higgins, T. E. (1997). Beyond pleasure and pain, *American Psychologist, 52*, 1280-1300.

Holden, S. J. S. and Lutz, R. J. (1992). Ask Not What the Brands Can Evoke; Ask What Can Evoke the Brand. *Advances in Consumer Research*, Vol. 19, ed. John F. Sheny and Brian Sterntbal, Provo, UT: Association for Consumer Research, 101-107.

Janiszewski, C (1993). Preattentive mere exposure effects, *Journal of Consumer Research, 20(3)*, 376-392.

Ledgerwood, A., Trope, Y., & Chaiken, S. (2010). Flexibility now, consistency later: Psychological distance and construal shape evaluative responding. *Journal of Personality and Social Psychology, 99(1)*, 32-51.

Liberman, N., Sagristano, M. D., and Trope, Y. (2002). The effect of temporal distance on level of mental construal. *Journal of Experimental Social Psychology, 38*, 523-534.

Liberman, N., Trope, Y., and Stephan, E. (2007). Psychological distance. In A. W. Kruglanski & E. T. Higgins (Eds.), *Social Psychology: Handbook of Basic Principles* (pp. 353-381). New York: Guilford Press.

Luchins, A. S. (1942). Mechanization in problem solving. *Psychological Monographs, 54*, 6.

Meyers-Levy, J. (1989). The influence of brand name's association set size and word frequency on brand memory, *Journal of Consumer Research, 16*, 197-207.

Mitra, A., & Lynch, J. G., Jr. (1995). Toward a reconciliation of market power and information theories of advertising effects on price elasticity, *Journal of Consumer Research, 21*, 644-659.

Navon, D. (1977). Forest before trees: The precedence of global features in visual perception, *Cognitive Psychology, 9*, 353-383.

Nedungadi, P. (1990). Recall and Consumer Consideration Sets: Influencing Choice Without Altering Brand Evaluations. *Journal of Consumer Research, 17 (3)*, 263-76.

Ratneshwar, S., Pechmann, C., & Shocker, A. D. (1996). Goal-derived categories and the antecedents of across-category consideration, *Journal of Consumer Research, 23*, 240-250.

Ratneshwar, S., & Shocker, A. D. (1991). Substitution in use and the role of usage context in product category structures, *Journal of Marketing Research, 28*, 281-295.

Paivio, A. (1986). Mental representations: A dual-coding approach, New York: Oxford University Press.

Priester, J. R., Nayakankuppam, D., Fleming, M. A., & Godek, J. (2004). The A2SC2 model: The influence of attitudes and attitude strength on consideration and choice, *Journal of Consumer Research, 30*, 574-587.

Shapiro, S., Macinnis, D. J., and Heckler, S. E. (1997). The Effect of Incidental Ad Exposure on the Formation of Consideration Sets. *Journal of Consumer Research, 24*, 94-104.

Smith, E. R. (1994). Procedure knowledge and processing strategies in social cognition. In R. S. Wyer & T. K. Srull (Eds.) *Handbook of social cognition* (Vol. 1, pp. 101-151). Hillsdale, NJ: Erlbaum.

Trope, Y., & Liberman, N. (2010). Construal-Level Theory of Psychological Distance. *Psychology Review, 117 (2)*, 440-463.

Wakslak, C., and Trope, Y. (2009). The effect of construal level on subjective probability estimates, *Psychological Science, 20(1)*, 52-58.

McHealthy: How Frequent Dining Programs Increase Healthy Eating Intentions

Elisa Chan, Cornell University, USA
Brian Wansink, Cornell University, USA

EXTENDED ABSTRACT

Fast food restaurants (e.g., McDonald's) are often criticized for cultivating unhealthy eating habits and contributing to obesity in our society (Brownell and Horgen 2003; Nestle 2003). Despite the effort of these restaurants to promote better eating by including more healthy items on the menu, the proportion of obese adults in the United States remains high (e.g. the national prevalence of obesity in adults was 33.8% in 2007-2008, Flegal et al 2010). This phenomenon is referred to as "the American obesity paradox" (Heini and Weinsier 1997) and may partly be explained by the 'health halo' effect which bias calorie estimates and lead to over-consumption (Chandon and Wansink 2007). Apparently, giving consumer more healthy food options does not necessarily translate to them eating more healthily. There is a need to identify ways to promote healthy eating which directly influence consumer's food consumption behavior.

We explore this question in the domain of fast food restaurants and promotional offers. We ask, for example, how having a promotional offer with a long (vs. short) time horizon influences one's healthy eating intention. Drawing on Chandon and colleagues (2000), we acknowledged that the nature of the product seemingly dictate the evaluative emphasis on its promotion. Consequently, we propose that because a long time horizon coincides with the long-term conception of healthy eating, an accumulative, long time horizon promotional offer such as points reward will be more effective in inducing healthy eating intention than an immediate, short time horizon price discount.

Deriving from the theory of goal (Fishbach, Friedman, and Kruglanski 2003), we further propose that this effect of offer will only be evident among individuals whose food consumption decision is dominated by its sensual appreciation (i.e. hedonist). Our reasoning is that hedonist are more likely to have constant struggles between taste and health goals, an accumulative offer (i.e. points reward) makes the health goal temporarily more salient and in turn increases healthy eating intention. Finally, we predict that patrons of a restaurant will be more likely to respond to an offer with long time horizon. They will find a delayed reward offer by a long term promotion more acceptable because of the perceived level of effort.

Results of study 1 supported our hypotheses. To examine the impacts of the independent variable (promotional offer: long time horizon vs. short time horizon) on intention to switch, participants were randomly assigned to either a points reward (i.e. long horizon) or price discount (i.e. short horizon) condition. Points reward and price discount were chosen because they are common. More importantly, they are on the extremes of the time horizon spectrum. On the one hand, point rewards require that people repeatedly make purchases over a period of time to obtain the designated reward which prompts a long term perspective. On the other hand, price discounts provide immediate reward for the purchase which triggers a short term perspective.

As predicted, the two-way interaction between promotional offer x hedonism is significant ($F(1,40) = 5.576$, $p = .02$). A simple main effect analysis revealed that for the high hedonism group, the intention to switch to salad is significant. Specifically, those in the points condition is more prone to make the switch to the healthier salad option than those in the price condition ($M_{points} = 6.08$ vs. $M_{price} = 4.49$, $F(1, 20) = 4.21$, $p = .05$). Moreover, the two-way interaction of promotional offer x patronage is significant ($F(1,40) = 4.554$, p =.04). In particular, patrons are found to be more likely to switch to salad than non-patrons in the points condition. The simple main effects of promotional offer on neither patron nor non-patron were significant ($p's > .05$).

In addition, we believe that two supporting studies in progress will corroborate the results of study 1 and our contention about the temporal orientation elicited by promotional offers and its effect on healthy food choices. First of all, a choice study asks participants to choose between a points reward vs. a price discount for the purchase of a salad. If our hypothesis holds, more people will prefer the points reward in support of our contention that because a healthy food triggers a long term perspective, the promotional offer with the corresponding temporal frame (i.e. points) will more likely be chosen. Secondly, a time frame study aims not only to replicate the results of study 1 but also to provide a temporal orientation measure. If our hypotheses hold, it will provide empirical evidence for our assertion that temporal orientation is the underlying process of the differential impact of the type of promotional offer.

The results of our study show that different types of offer have differential impacts on one's intention to choose a healthy food over an appetitive food. It extends the benefits congruency framework (Chandon, Wansink, and Laurent 2000) to a new dimension. We show that not only do benefits between product and promotion which are congruent in terms of utilitarian or hedonic aspects can improve a target choice; one which is temporally congruent has a similar impact. Our results also contribute to literature on loyalty programs. Extant loyalty programs literature identified effort required, rewards obtained, decisions to join, and likelihood of reaching the reward as the most important issues (Kivetz and Simonson 2003). The current study suggests that the characteristic of the product of which the loyalty program is associated with also play a role.

Interestingly, our results pertain to hedonist – the ones whose actions are often dictated by their sensualities. Moreover, results also reveal that patrons (i.e. existing customers) of a company tend to make the healthy food choice more often when they are given points rewards rather than price discounts. The current study renders a concrete solution to fast food restaurants for their most prominent clientele. Our typical fast food restaurants goers or patrons fit the profile of a hedonist (i.e. those who are more likely to yield to unhealthy yet tasty food). A long time horizon offer is shown to have an influence on healthy eating especially for this group of people. Concisely, we have identified a solution for the loyal-healthy dilemma.

REFERENCES

Brownell, Kelly D. and Katherine Battle Horgen (2003), *Food Fight: The Inside Story of the Food Industry, America's Obesity Crisis, and What We Can Do About It.* New York: McGraw Hill.

Campbell, C. (1987), *The Romantic Ethic and the Spirit of Modern Consumerism*, Basil Blackwell, Oxford.

Carver, Charles S. and Michael F. Scheier (1990), "Origins and Functions of Positive and Negative Affect: A Control-Process View," *Psychological Review*, 97 (January), 19-35.

Chandon, Pierre, Brian Wansink, and Gilles Laurent (2000), "A Benefit Congruency Framework of Sales Promotion Effectiveness," *Journal of Marketing*, 64(October), 65-81.

Chandon, Pierre and Brian Wansink (2007), "The Biasing Health Halos of Fast-Food Restaurant Heath Claims: Lower Calorie Estimates and Higher Side-Dish Consumption Intentions," *Journal of Marketing*, 34(October), 301-314.

Fedorikhin, Alexander and Vanessa M. Patrick (Forthcoming), "Positive Mood and resistance to Temptation: The Interfering Influence of Elevated Arousal," *Journal of Consumer Research*.

Fishbach, Ayelet, Ronald S. Friedman, and Arie W. Kruglanski (2003), "Leading Us Not Unto Temptation: Momentary Allurements Elicit Overriding Goal Activation," *Journal of Personality and Social Psychology*, 84 (2), 296-309.

Flegal, Katherine M., Margaret Carroll, Cynthia L. Ogden, and Lester R. Curtin (2010), "Prevalence and Trends in Obesity Among US Adults, 1999-2008," *The Journal of the American Medical Association*, 303(3), 235-241.

Garg, Nitika, Brian Wansink, and J. Jeffrey Inman (2007), "The Influence of Incidental Affect on Consumers' Food Intake," Journal of Marketing, 71(1), 194-206.

Heini, Adrian F. and Roland L. Weinsier (1997), "Divergent Trends in Obesity and Fat Intake Patterns: The American Paradox," *American Journal of Medicine*, 102(3), 259-264.

Kiley, David (2005), "McDonald's New Campaign is the Appearance of a Good Start," for Bloomsberg Businessweek. Retained from http://www.businessweek.com/the_thread/brandnewday/archives/2005/03/mcdonalds_new_campaign_is_the_appearance_of_a_good_start.html

Kivetz, Ran, and Itamar Simonson (2003), "The Idiosyncratic Fit Heuristic: Effort Advantage as a Determinant of Consumer Response to Loyalty Programs,' *Journal of Marketing Research*, 40(4), 454-467.

Li, Xiuping (2008), "The Effects of Appetitive Stimuli on Out-of-Domain Consumption Impatience,' *Journal of Consumer Research*, 34(5), 649-656.

Nestle, Marion (2003), *Food Polictics: How the Food Industry Influences Nutrition and Health*. Berkeley: University of California Press.

O'Shaughnessy, John and Nicholas J. O'Shaughnessy (2002), "Marketing, the Consumer Society and Hedonism," *European Journal of Marketing*, 35(5/6), 524-547.

Shiv, Baba and Alexander Fedorikhin (1999), "Heart and Mind in Conflict: Interplay of Affect and Cognition in Consumer Decision Making," *Journal of Consumer Research*, 26 (December), 278-282.

Thomas, Manoj, Kalpesh Desai and Satheeshkumar Seenivasan (Forthcoming), "How Credit Card Payments Increase Unhealthy Food Purchases: Visceral Regulation of Vices," *Journal of Consumer Research*.

Tversky, Amos, Sattath, Samuel and Slavic, Paul (1988), "Contingent weighting in judgment and choice," *Psychological Review*, 95, 371-384.

Zimbardo, Philip G. and John N. Boyd (1999), "Putting Time in Perspective: A Valid, Reliable Individual-Differences Metric," *Journal of Personality and Social Psychology, 11* (December),1271-88.

When Creativity Meets Repetition: Frequency Effects Depend on Exposure Duration

Millie Elsen, Tilburg University, The Netherlands
Rik Pieters, Tilburg University, The Netherlands
Michel Wedel, University of Maryland, USA

EXTENDED ABSTRACT

In an increasingly cluttered environment, competition for consumers' limited attention is a key issue. Two strategies that are commonly used by advertisers to maximize attention to their ads are creativity and repetition. Whereas previous research suggests that creative advertising can postpone attention wear-out due to repetition (Pieters, Warlop, and Wedel 2002), it is less clear how combinations of creativity and repetition affect more downstream effects, such as ad and brand evaluation. This research tests the hypothesis that the influence of repetition on evaluations of standard (typical) and creative (atypical) ads critically depends on exposure *duration*. We compare brief and fixed (as when passing billboards by car), long and fixed (as in the case of cinema advertising), and self-paced exposures (as when paging through a magazine). Specifically, we predict that atypical ads do not wear-in at all when exposures are brief and fixed (hypothesis 1), and wear-out faster than typical ads when exposure duration is long and fixed (hypothesis 2), or self-paced (hypothesis 3).

The idea is that comprehension of atypical ads is characterized by a delayed-but-sudden "aha" experience (Topolinski and Reber 2010). For atypical ads to *wear-in*, these ads require at least one exposure that is long enough for this "aha" experience to occur. At such longer exposures, however, processing of atypical ads will lead to more distinctive memory traces and active recognition, and exactly this may accelerate their attitude *wear-out*. We predict the effect of repetition to be critically dependent on the exposure duration, as follows.

When exposures are brief and fixed, atypical ads are liked less than typical ads, because a single glance is insufficient to comprehend them, and this uncertainty is disliked. Subsequent brief exposures do not "add up" to comprehension, hence the negative ad evaluation will not be positively updated. Typical ads, in contrast, which are almost instantly understood ("Ha, it is a car ad"), are immediately evaluated positively. This identification certainty is re-experienced during subsequent brief exposures, which delays wear-out.

When exposures are long and fixed, atypical ads will wear-out faster than typical ads. Because they are unique, atypical ads will leave stronger and more distinctive memory traces, and exactly this may accelerate evaluation wear-out. Upon repeated exposure, atypical ads are more actively recognized as being seen before. This improved memory of atypical ads depresses attitudes, once the novelty of their initial exposure wanes ("Oh, it is that ad again"). In contrast, due to their similarity to other ads in the category, typical ads leave less distinctive memory traces, and generate feelings of familiarity even if they are new. Repeated exposure to typical ads further raises familiarity, and attitudes wear-out less quickly as a result.

When exposure is self-paced, atypical ads should wear-out even more rapidly. Precisely because atypical ads continue to draw attention where other ads wear out, they may be even more readily recognized upon repeated exposure, and evaluations drop even faster. Thus, ironically, the attention-getting qualities of atypical ads may accelerate evaluation wear-out even more.

Three experiments tested these predictions. Experiment 1 tested the idea that many brief exposures to atypical ads are not equivalent to one long exposure. Typical and atypical ads were shown at various exposure durations (from 100 msec to 8 sec) and frequencies (from 1 to 10). As predicted, for atypical ads, comprehension ratings and ad evaluations were very different after many brief exposures as compared to one long exposure, while the differences were much smaller for typical ads. Indeed, many brief exposures to atypical ads did not "add up" to comprehension.

Experiment 2 tested hypothesis 1 and 2. In this experiment, participants evaluated typical and atypical ads that they had seen either zero, one, three or six times in a previous part of the experiment, as well as distracters (which were slightly changed versions of the target ads). Ads were exposed for either 100 msec (brief and fixed) or 10 seconds (long and fixed). As predicted, when exposure duration was brief and fixed, typical ads were immediately evaluated more positively than atypical ads, and additional glances did not improve evaluations of atypical ads, nor deteriorate evaluations of typical ads. Evaluations were driven by differences in comprehension levels between typical and atypical ads, that sustained across the repeated brief exposures. When exposures were long and fixed, atypical ads wore out faster than typical ads, which was predicted to be the result of different bases for recognition (i.e., recollection *vs.* familiarity; Yonelinas 2002). As predicted, participants were well able to discriminate atypical ads from other ads, suggesting that processing of these ads led to distinctive memory traces and active recognition upon repeated exposure. In contrast, false recognition was higher at all frequency levels for typical ads, and this low ability to discriminate suggests that recognition was based on feelings of familiarity, as predicted.

Finally, experiment 3 tested and supported hypothesis 3, that atypical ads also rapidly wear-out under self-paced exposure conditions. However, the accelerated evaluation wear-out of atypical ads was not due to increased attention. Although atypical ads retained attention longer than typical ads at first exposure, subsequently attention quickly dropped, to equal attention levels of typical ads. Rather, atypical ads were more actively recognized than typical ads, as reflected in lower false recognition for these ads at all frequency levels.

Together, the results show that repetition effects crucially depend on the exposure duration. Our predictions and findings are different from two-factor (Berlyne 1970) and related theories, which would predict the opposite, namely that atypical (complex) ads wear-out more slowly than typical (simple) ads, due to positive habituation and later set-in of tedium. Although either one may have positive effects, our results show that combining high creativity and high repetition is less effective. They show that, ironically, exactly because atypical ads attain better memory, the attitudes towards them and their brands wear-out more quickly. On the other hand, typical ads fly under the radar of active recognition, and retain their positive attitudes under repeated exposures as a result. Thus, the "boring" ads appear not so boring after all.

REFERENCES

Anand Punam and Brian Sternthal (1990), "Ease of Message Processing as a Moderator of Repetition Effects in Advertising," *Journal of Marketing Research*, 17, 345-353.

Auble, Pamela M., Jeffery J. Franks, and Salvatore A. Soraci, Jr. (1979), "Effort Toward Comprehension: Elaboration or "Aha!"?" *Memory & Cognition*, 7 (6), 426-434.

Berlyne, Dennis E. (1970), "Novelty, Complexity, and Hedonic Value," *Perception and Psychophysics*, 8 (5A), 279-286.

Cacioppo, John T. and Richard E. Petty (1979), "Effects of Message Repetition and Position on Cognitive Response, Recall, and Persuasion," Journal of Personality and Social Psychology, 37 (1), 97-109.

Cox, Dena and Anthony Cox (1988), "What *Does* Familiarity Breed? Complexity as a Moderator of Repetition Effects in Advertisement Evaluation," *Journal of Consumer Research*, 15 (1), 111-116.

Cox, Dena and Anthony Cox (2002), "Beyond First Impressions: The Effects of Repeated Exposure on Consumer Liking of Visually Complex and Simple Product Designs," *Journal of the Academy of Marketing Science,* 30 (2), 119-130.

Fazio, Russel H., Paul M. Herr, and Martha C. Powell (1992). "On the Development and Strength of Category-brand Associations in Memory: The Case of Mystery Ads," *Journal of Consumer Psychology,* 1, 1-13.

Goodstein, Ronald C. (1993), "Category-based Applications and Extensions in Advertising: Motivating More Extensive Ad Processing," *Journal of Consumer Research*, 20 (1), 87-99.

Graesser, Arthur C., Sallie E. Gordon, and John D. Sawyer (1979), "Recognition Memory for Typical and Atypical Actions in Scripted Activities: Tests of a Script Pointer + Tag Hypothesis," *Journal of Verbal Learning and Verbal Behavior,* 18 (3), 319-332.

Janiszewski, Chris, Hayden Noel, and Alan G. Sawyer (2003), "A Meta-Analysis of the Spacing Effect in Verbal Learning: Implications for Research on Advertising Repetition and Consumer Memory," *Journal of Consumer Research,* 30 (1), 138-149.

Janiszewski, Chris and Tom Meyvis (2001), "Effects of Brand Logo Complexity, Repetition, and Spacing on Processing Fluency and Judgment," *Journal of Consumer Research*, 27 (June), 18-32.

Pieters, Rik, Luc Warlop, and Michel Wedel (2002), "Breaking Through the Clutter: Benefits of Advertisement Originality and Familiarity for Brand Attention and Memory," *Management Science,* 48 (6), 765-781.

Pieters, Rik and Michel Wedel (2011), "AdGist: What Ads Communicate in one Eye Fixation," *Unpublished manuscript,* Tilburg University.

Sasser, Sheila L. and Scott Koslow (2008), "Desperately Seeking Advertising Creativity," *Journal of Advertising*, 37 (4), 5-19.

Smith, Robert E. and Xiaojing Yang (2004), "Toward a General Theory of Creativity in Advertising: Examining the Role of Divergence", *Marketing Theory*, 4 (1/2), 29-55.

Topolinski, Sasha, and Rolf Reber (2010), "Gaining Insight into the "Aha" Experience," *Psychological Science*, 19 (6), 402-405.

Winkielman, Piotr, Jamin Halberstadt, Tedra Fazendeiro, and Steve Catty (2006), "Prototypes are Attractive Because They Are Easy on the Mind," *Psychological Science*, 17 (9), 799-806.

Yonelinas, Andrew P. (2000), "The Nature of Recollection and Familiarity: A Review of 30 Years of Research," *Journal of Memory and Language,* 46, 441-517

Only a Diamond Can Cut a Diamond: The Regulation of Emotions via System Fit.

Daniel Fernandes, Rotterdam School of Management, Erasmus University, The Netherlands
Lawrence Williams, University of Colorado, USA
Christina Kan, University of Colorado at Boulder, USA

EXTENDED ABSTRACT

Negative emotional states can promote a tendency to indulge as an emotion regulation strategy (Macht 1999; Macht, Haupt, and Ellgring 2005). Emotional eating has been regarded as a way to improve negative mood (Thayer 1989, 2001), to mask stress (Polivy and Herman 1999), or to escape from aversive self-awareness (Heatherton and Baumeister 1991). Food brings comfort in the short-term and, therefore, consumers turn to snacks to heal emotional distress (Kaplan and Kaplan 1957).

Two potential mechanisms through which emotions influence indulgent eating have been identified in the literature (see Macht 2008, for a review). On one hand, negative emotions may prompt a deliberate attempt to regulate emotions, leading people to both increase the amount and decrease the quality of food intake (Booth 1994; Kaplan and Kaplan 1957). In this case, the motivational properties of negative emotions may elicit the tendency to emotion regulate by eating sweet and fatty foods (Macht, Haupt, and Ellgring 2005). This suggests that the deliberative effect of negative emotions on behavior occurs via system 2. On the other hand, negative (and sometimes also positive) emotions may enhance the amount and decrease the quality of food intake due to impairment of cognitive control (Boon et al. 2010; Herman and Polivy 1984). According to this hypothesis, intense emotional experiences are cognitively taxing (Heatherton, Striepe and Wittenberg 1998), and can result in an impairment in one's capacity to make healthy food choices. In these cases, the effect of negative emotions on behavior occurs via system 1.

Specific emotions may influence the consumption of unhealthy food by one of these processes. The process behind the effect of sadness on indulgence is posited to be deliberate and conscious (Tice, Bratlavsky and Baumeister 2001). In an attempt to regulate emotions, consumers shift priorities from longer-term goals to shorter-term ones, placing greater value on choices that offer immediate gratification. In contrast to sadness, anxiety may lead to unhealthy food choices as the result of a more automatic process. Elevated levels of arousal can increase cognitive load, interfering with regulatory processes and decreasing resistance to temptation (Fedorikhin and Patrick 2010). Therefore, the elevated level of arousal that typically accompanies anxiety may cause an interference effect, decreasing the cognitive resources available for self-regulation and, consequently, leading people to give in to temptations. This suggestion is consistent with previous research showing that cognitive resources are a necessary requirement for the functioning of self-regulatory processes and that depletion of these resources can lead to decrements in self-regulation and decision-making (Baumeister, Bratlavsky, Muraven, and Tice 1998; Shiv and Fedorihkin 1999). This is also supported by research in emotional eating, which suggests that mental distraction and depletion can interfere with a dieter's resistance to temptation (Herman and Polivy 1993).

In summary, while sadness and anxiety may both enhance the desirability of high fat and carbohydrate 'comfort foods' (Wansink, Cheney, and Chan, 2003), they may do so via distinct processes. While the effect of sadness is routed by System 2 processing, the effect of anxiety is routed by System 1 processing. Accordingly, when trying to aid people with emotional control and reduce their reliance on indulgence as a coping strategy, we predict that the system-level fit between the emotional process and the regulatory strategy will facilitate effective emotion regulation.

Moreover, given that people develop emotion regulation strategies throughout their lives, we predict that age would moderate these effects in the sense that emotional regulation yields an adaptive and constructive learning process. The 'cope by indulgence' emotion regulation strategy should be most pronounced for individuals who do not habitually use reappraisal strategies. One individual difference that predicts the spontaneous use of reappraisal is age; the maturational changes that accompany age are likely to give individuals more perspective on emotional experiences, suggesting that older individuals are more likely to use reappraisal strategies (John and Gross 2004).

Following this reasoning, in the first study, we find that sadness and anxiety increase the selection of unhealthy and indulgent options only among younger participants. Older participants were able to control their reactivity to the sadness and the anxiety manipulations and, therefore, did not enhance the consumption of unhealthy options relative to the healthy ones. In a follow up study, we confirm that older participants are better at regulating their emotions. In subsequent studies, we examine how sadness and anxiety respond to different regulatory strategies. We show that emotion regulation strategies are more effective when they fit with the route of the effects being regulated. Specifically, the effect of sadness is most strongly regulated by explicit emotion regulation goals, while the effect of anxiety is most strongly regulated by implicit emotion regulation goals.

This paper shows that, although sadness and anxiety lead to the same behavioral outcome, that is, unhealthy food choices, interventions designed to mitigate these negative effects can capitalize on the fact that these emotions affect choice via distinct processes (System 2 vs. System 1). A conscious reappraisal goal better regulates the effects of sadness on choice. Conversely, a nonconsciously operating reappraisal goal better regulates the effects of anxiety on choice. Successful emotional control can be attained through implicit and explicit mechanisms that tap into the effects of specific emotions on behavior. This research sheds light on the breadth of the human repertoire of emotion regulation capacities and the extent to which nonconscious processes exert influence on choice.

REFERENCES

Baumeister, Roy F., Ellen Bratlavsky, Mark Muraven and Dianne Tice (1998), "Ego Depletion: Is the Active Self a Limited Resources?" *Journal of Personality and Social Psychology,* 74 (5), 1252-65.

Boon, Bridgette, Wolfgang Stroebe, Henk Schut and Richta IJntema (2010), "Ironic Processes in the Eating Behaviour of Restrained Eaters," *British Journal of Health Psychology*, 7,1-10.

Booth, David A. (1994), *Psychology of nutrition*. London: Taylor and Francis.

Fedorikhin, Alexander and Vanessa M. Patrick (2010), "Positive Mood and Resistance to Temptation: The Interfering Influence of Elevated Arousal," *Journal of Consumer Research,* 37 (December), 698-711.

Heatherton, Todd. F., and Roy F. Baumeister (1991), "Binge eating as escape from self-awareness," *Psychological Bulletin*, 110 (July), 86–108.

Heatherton, Todd F., Meg Striepe and Lauren Wittenberg (1998), "Emotional Distress and Disinhibited Eating: The Role of Self," *Personality and Social Psychology Bulletin*, 24 (3), 301–13.

Herman, C. Peter and Janet Polivy (1984), "A Boundary Model for the Regulation of Eating," *Eating and its Disorders,* 62, 141-56.

--- (1993), "Mental Control of Eating: Excitatory and Inhibitory Food Thoughts," in *Handbook of Mental Control,* Eds D.M.Wegner & J.W.Pennebaker, Englewood Cliffs, NJ: Prentice Hall, 491-505.

John, Oliver P. and James J. Gross (2004), "Healthy and Unhealthy Emotion Regulation: Personality Processes, Individual Differences, and Life Span Development," *Journal of Personality,* 72 (December), 1301-33.

Kaplan, Harold. I., and Kaplan, H. S. (1957). "The psychosomatic concept of obesity," *Journal of Nervous and Mental Disease*, 125, 181–201.

Macht, Michael (1999), "Characteristics of Eating in Anger, Fear, Sadness, and Joy," *Appetite,* 33, 129–39.

--- (2008), "How Emotions Affect Eating: A Five-Way Model," *Appetite,* 50 (Jan.), 1-11.

Macht, Michael, Christine Haupt, and Heiner Ellgring (2005), "The Perceived Function of Eating is Changed during Examination Stress: A Field Study," *Eating Behaviors*, 6, 109–12.

Polivy, Janet and C. Peter Herman (1999), "Distress and eating: Why do dieters overeat?" *International Journal of Eating Disorders,* 26 (September), 153-64.

Shiv, Baba and Alexander Fedorikhin (1999), "Heart and Mind in Conflict: The Interplay of Affect and Cognition in Consumer Decision Making," *Journal of Consumer Research,* 26 (December), 278-92.

Thayer, Robert E. (1989), *The Biopsychology of Mood and Arousal,* New York, NY: Oxford University Press.

--- (2001), *Calm Energy—How People Regulate Mood with Food and Exercise*, New York, NY: Oxford University Press.

Tice, Dianne M., Ellen Bratlavsky and Roy F. Baumeister (2001), "Emotional Distress Regulation Takes Precedence Over Impulse Control: If you Feel Bad, Do It!" *Journal of Personality and Social Psychology,* 80 (1), 56-67.

Wansink, Brian, Matthew M. Cheney and Nina Chan (2003), "Exploring Comfort Food Preferences across Age and Gender," *Physiology and Behavior*, 79 (September), 739–47.

Williams, Lawrence E., John A. Bargh, Christopher C. Nocera and Jeremy R. Gray (2009), "The Unconscious Regulation of Emotion: Nonconscious Reappraisal Goals Modulate Emotional Reactivity," *Emotion*, 9 (December), 847-54.

Maximizing the Effectiveness of Disaster Relief Contribution: The Idea of Fit to Control

Yoshiko DeMotta, Baruch College, USA
Diogo Hildebrand, CUNY Graduate Center, Baruch College, USA
Ana Valenzuela, Baruch College, USA
Sankar Sen, Baruch College, USA

EXTENDED ABSTRACT

Corporations are often willing to help when a major disaster happens. The goals of corporate contributions are to maximize the benefits to the disaster victims and earn a return in terms of consumer attitudes and corporate image (Porter and Kramer 2006). In corporate social responsibility (CSR) programs, consumers perceive a firm's nonmonetary contributions such as goods, services, and employee volunteerism to help communities to be more effortful and evaluate such contributions more positively than their monetary counterparts (Ellen, Webb and Mohr 2000). Due to drawbacks pertaining to nonmonetary contributions, including implementation difficulty and firms' limited capability of providing goods and services, however, firms often decide to donate money to help communities.

Against prior belief, we demonstrate that monetary contributions will generate more positive consumer evaluations of corporate contributions depending on the cause of the disaster. While all disasters negatively affect society, some disasters are perceived as inevitable tragedies of nature (nature-made disasters), while others are perceived as being caused by human practices (human-made disasters). Nature-made hazards include earthquakes, floods, and naturally occurring wildfires, while human-made hazards include terrorist attacks, riots, and arson. In general, nature-made disasters are considered to be less controllable or preventable by their victims and affected communities than human-made ones (Quarantelli 1993). We propose that the controllability perception of the disaster will have differential effects on consumers' emotions and subsequent evaluations of corporate disaster relief effort. Specifically, a seemingly uncontrollable disaster will elicit higher sympathy, and consumers will perceive a firm's effortful, nonmonetary help to be appropriate. On the contrary, a more controllable disaster will elicit lesser degrees of sympathy, and consumers will process the disaster more deliberatively and will desire more utilitarian, monetary help.

We expect that this effect is moderated by desirability of control (DC), a personality disposition that reflects the degree to which people are motivated to control the environment (Burger and Cooper 1979). Although to have control over outcomes appears to be a basic human need (Deci and Ryan 1985), people vary with respect to the strength of this need. Some people are committed to being in charge and determining the outcome of every situation in life, while others have a weaker urge to control their environment (Burger and Cooper 1979). High DC consumers will be motivated to analyze the causal controllability of a disaster and consequently have higher cognitive and affective responses to it. Accordingly, high DC consumers will have stronger emotional responses toward the disaster victims, which will hypothetically affect their fit perception and company evaluations. In other words, they will form a positive attitude toward a firm's effort when the firm appears to take control over the situation by providing resources that match the needs of the victims and affected communities—a condition we label as *fit perception*. On the contrary, low DC consumers are hardly motivated to achieve control over their environment (Burger and Cooper 1979), and thus may not exhibit differential emotions toward victims of the two disasters, nor be particular about how a firm's effort matches the specific needs of the victims.

Hypothesis 1a *Consumers with high desirability of control will evaluate a firm's monetary contribution to a man-made disaster relief effort more positively than its nonmonetary contribution to such disaster.*

Hypothesis 1b *Consumers with high desirability of control will evaluate a firm's nonmonetary contribution to a nature-made disaster relief effort more positively than its monetary contribution to such disaster.*

Hypothesis 1c *Regardless of disaster characteristics, consumers with low desirability of control will equally evaluate a firm's monetary contribution and nonmonetary contribution.*

Hypothesis 2 *Perception of fit will mediate the effect of contribution type and disaster characteristic on company evaluations.*

Three experiments examined our prediction. As expected, the first two studies found that participants evaluated a firm's contribution of money to a human-made disaster more positively than its contribution of service, whereas they evaluated a firm's contribution of service to a nature-made disaster more positively than its monetary contribution. This effect was found only for high DC participants. In addition, the same effect was mediated by greater fit perception between the contribution type and the disaster characteristic. The third study found further support for the role of controllability of a disaster, demonstrating that when a disaster was described as being uncontrollable (controllable), participants evaluated a firm's contribution of services (money) more positively than its contribution of money (services).

Our research aims to provide a better understanding of the process underlying consumer evaluations of a firm's disaster relief effort. Research has shown that in order to optimize the effectiveness of CSR programs, a clear fit between a firm's business and the cause it embraces is crucial (Lafferty, Goldsmith, and Hult 2004; Pracejus and Olsen 2004). Our study contributes to the literature by introducing a new dimension of fit, which may be particularly useful to better understand the effects of CSR programs toward non-recurring causes such as disaster relief effort. Another contribution of our research is in its practical implications. Substantial numbers of firms of all sizes around the world frequently respond to help victims and communities affected by disasters such as the earthquake in Haiti and 9/11 terrorist attacks. However, the effects of such corporate philanthropy are largely unknown. We provide an initial suggestion that corporate contribution can be perceived more favorably when the fit between the controllability of disaster and contribution type is maximized.

REFERENCE

Aiken, Leona S. and Stephen G. West (1991), *Multiple Regression: Testing and Interpreting Interactions*, Newbury Park, CA: Sage.

Bargh, John A. (2002), "Losing Consciousness: Automatic Influences on Consumer Judgment, Behavior, and Motivation," *Journal of Consumer Research,* 29 (2), 280-85.

Bargh, John A. (2006), "What have we been priming all these years? On the development, mechanisms, and ecology of nonconscious social behavior," *European Journal of Social Psychology,* 36 (2), 147-68.

Berkowitz, Leonard (1972), "Social norms, feelings, and other factors affecting helping and altruism," in *Advances in experimental social psychology*, Vol. 6, ed. Leonard Berkowitz, New York: Academic Press, 63-108.

Burger, Jerry M. and Harris M. Cooper (1979), The Desirability of Control, *Motivation and Emotion,* 3 (4), 381-93.

Coke, Jay S., C. Daniel Batson, and Katherine McDavis (1978), "Empathic Mediation of Helping: A Two-Stage Model," *Journal of Personality and Social Psychology*, 36 (7), 752-66.

Deci, Edward L. and Richard M. Ryan (1985), *Intrinsic motivation and self-determination in human behavior*, New York: Plenum.

Ellen, Pam Scholder, Deborah J. Webb, and Lois A. Mohr (2006), "Building Corporate Associations: Consumer Attributions for Corporate Socially Responsible Programs," *Journal of Academy of Marketing Science,* 34 (2), 147-57.

Ellen, Pam Scholder, Lois A. Mohr, and Deborah J. Webb (2000), "Charitable programs and the retailer: Do they mix?" *Journal of Retailing*, 76 (3), 393-406.

Fischhoff, Baruch, Roxana M. Gonzalez, Jennifer S. Lerner, and Deborah A. Small (2005), "Evolving Judgments of Terror Risks: Foresight, Hindsight, and Emotion." *Journal of Experimental Psychology: Applied,* 11 (2), 124-139.

Flippen, Annette R., Harvey A. Hornstein, William E. Siegal, and Eben A. Weitzman (1996), "A Comparison of Similarity and Interdependence as Trigger for In-Group Formation," *Personality and Social Psychology Bulletin*, 22 (September), 882–93.

Higgins, E. Tory, William S. Rholes, and Carl R. Jones (1977), "Category accessibility and impression formation," *Journal of Experimental Social Psychology*, 13 (2), 141-54.

Lafferty, Barbara A., Ronald E. Goldsmith and G. Thomas M. Hult (2004), "The Impact of the Alliance on the Partners: A Look at Cause-Brand Alliances," *Psychology and Marketing*, 21 (7), 509-31.

Lerner, Jennifer S., Deborah A. Small, and George Loewenstein (2004), "Research Report Heart Strings and Purse Strings Carryover Effects of Emotions on Economic Decisions," *Psychological Science,* 15, 337-41.

Lindgreen, Adam, Valerie Swaen, and Wesley J. Johnston (2009), "Corporate social responsibility: an empirical investigation of U.S. organizations," *Journal of Business Ethics*, 85, Supplement 2, 303-23.

Liu, Wendy and Jennifer Aaker (2008), "The Happiness of Giving: The Time-Ask Effect," *Journal of Consumer Research*, 35 (October), 543-57.

Nan, Xiaoli and Kwangjun Heo (2007), "Consumer Responses to Corporate Social Responsibility (CSR) Initiatives," *Journal of Advertising*, 36 (2), 63-74.

Porter, Michael E. and Mark R. Kramer (2006), Strategy & Society: The Link between Competitive Advantage and Corporate Social Responsibility, *Harvard Business Review*, 84 (12), 78-92.

Pracejus, John W. and G. Douglas Olsen (2004), "The Role of Brand/Cause Fit in the Effectiveness of Cause-Related Marketing Campaigns," *Journal of Business Research*, 57 (6), 635-40.

Preacher, Kristopher J. and Andrew F. Hayes (2008), "Asymptotic and resampling strategies for assessing and comparing indirect effects in multiple mediator models," *Behavior Research Methods*, 40 (3), 879-91.

Preacher, Kristopher J., Derek D. Rucker, and Andrew F. Hayes (2007), "Assessing moderated mediation hypotheses: Theory, methods, and prescriptions," *Multivariate Behavioral Research*, 42, 185-227.

Quarantelli, Enrico L. (1993), "Community Crises: An Exploratory Comparison of the Characteristics and Consequences of Disasters and Riots," *Journal of Contingencies and Crisis Management*, 1 (2), 67-78.

Reisenzein, Rainer (1986), "A Structural Equation Analysis of Weiner's Attribution—Affect Model of Helping Behavior," *Journal of Personality and Social Psychology*, 50 (6), 1123-33.

Rottenstreich, Yuval and Christopher K. Hsee (2001), "Money, kisses, and electric shocks: On the affective psychology of risk," *Psychological Science*, 12 (3), 185-90.

Schmidt, Greg and Bernard Weiner (1988), "An Attribution-Affect-Action Theory of Behavior: Replications of Judgments of Help-Giving," *Personality and Social Psychology Bulletin*, 14 (3), 610-21.

Varadarajan, P. Rajan and Anil Menon (1988), "Cause related marketing: a co-alignment of marketing strategy and corporate philanthropy," *Journal of Marketing*, 52 (3), 58-74.

Weiner, Bernard (1980), "A Cognitive (Attribution)-Emotion-Action Model of Motivated Behavior: An Analysis of Judgments of Help Giving," Journal of Personality and Social Psychology, 39 (2), 186–200.

Weiner, Bernard (1985), "An attributional theory of achievement motivation and emotion," *Psychological Review*, 92 (4), 548-73.

Weiner, Bernard, Raymond P. Perry, and Jamie Magnusson (1988), "An attributional analysis of reactions to stigmas," *Journal of Personality and Social Psychology*, 55 (5), 738-48.

Weisz, John. R., Fred M. Rothbaum, and Thomas C. Blackburn (1984), "Standing out and standing in: The psychology of control in America and Japan," *American Psychologist,* 39 (9), 955-69.

Zagefka, Hanna, Masi Noor, Ruper Brown, Georgina R. de Moura, and Tim Hopthrow (forthcoming). "Donating to disaster victims: Responses to natural and humanity caused events." *European Journal of Social Psychology*.

Zhao, Xinshu, John G. Lynch Jr., and Qimei Chen (2010), "Reconsidering Baron and Kenny: Myths and Truths about Mediation Analysis," *Journal of Consumer Research*, 34 (August), 197-206.

Where There is Smoke, There is Fire:
Adolescent Smoking as a Costly Signal of Dispositional Health

Siegfried Dewitte, K.U.Leuven, Belgium

EXTENDED ABSTRACT

After a sharp decline between the sixties and the eighties, adolescent smoking appears to oscillate around a stable percentage of about 20% in 15 year olds. This is the case, despite the anti-smoking campaigns of the last decades. In this paper, I point at a possible reason for this failure to discourage smoking further. I claim that adolescent smoking may serve as a costly signal of dispositional health, towards potential mates. As dispositional health is a highly attractive feature for potential mates, adolescents with good health are very motivated to signal their health (Buss 1989). Costly signaling theory states that agents endowed with a certain (unobserved) quality can inform others about this quality by displaying behavior that entails a cost that is directly related to the quality (e.g. Zahavi and Zahavi 1997). This means that the cost is quality-dependent, reflecting the fact that although the signal is costly to all individuals, it is relatively less costly to those with the quality than to those without the quality. In this circumstances, those devoid of the quality are better off refraining from displaying such behavior because the cost are disproportionably high to them. This differential cost structure renders the signal trustworthy to the audience. The audience knows that only those with the quality can afford the cost that follows from the signal, and hence, can safely infer from the signal that the agent must have the quality.

As society widely agrees on the health damage that smoking entails, smoking is a good candidate as a signal of dispositional health. Healthy adolescents can better afford the immediate physical costs that smoking entails than their less healthy peers. This claim implies three sets of testable predictions.

First, smoking behavior should be related to objective indices of dispositional health (although, obviously, simultaneously harming current health). In study 1, using a health survey methodology, I indeed found that smoking, although associated with short term health costs such as aches and complaints, was more likely in people with an average blood pressure, in people who need less sleep, and in taller people (all controlled for gender). These three are validated indices of long term physical health in the medical and biological literature, and they are relatively unaffected by current health stressors. Consistent with this hypothesis was the evidence that people with a low dispositional health suffered relatively more if they did smoke than people with a high dispositional health, further adding to the suggesting that smoking may serve as a costly signal of dispositional health.

Second, smoking should be perceived as associated with dispositional health, at least when no other indices of health are available. Indeed, a scenario study manipulating a target's smoking status, confirmed this prediction, but only succeed in providing evidence for the process of conveying information. If the information of the dispositional health was conveyed in other ways (by an active life style of the target person), smoking was not perceived as a signal of health (actually, it was associated with *lower* perceived health, which needs an explanation).

An third prediction bears directly on the impact of campaigns. Assuming that the belief that smoking is bad for one's health has not always been widely shared, the application of costly signaling theory to smoking implies that signals may vary due to the context. To test this, I exposed people either to an anti-smoking campaign or to an anti fat-food campaign. Then they saw a person description,

manipulating the target's smoking status. Indeed, the study showed that pre-exposure to a campaign that stresses the health costs of smoking, increased the perception of smoking as a signal of dispositional health.

I close the paper with some recommendations for further studies about the possible costly signaling nature of adolescent smoking, and with recommendations for alternative public policy strategies targeting adolescent smoking and smoking initiation.

REFERENCES

Andrews, J.C., Netemeyer, R.G., Burton, S. et al. (2004). "Understanding adolescent intentions to smoke: An examination of relationships among social influence, prior trial behavior, and antitobacco campaign advertising". *Journal of Marketing, 68,* 110-123.

Batty, G. David, Shipley Martin J., Gunnell David, Huxley Rachel, Kivimaki Mika, Woodward Mark, Lee Crystal Man Ying, Smith George (2009). "Height, wealth, and health: An overview with new data from three longitudinal studies" *Economics and Human Biology, 7,* 137-152.

Buss, D.M. (1989) Sex differences in human mate preferences – evolutionary hypothesis tested in 37 cultures. *Behavioral and Brain Sciences, 12,* 1-14

Currie, Candace. (2001) *www.hbsc.org/downloads/CAS_Fact_Sheet_2.pdf*

CDC (2004). http://tobaccodocuments.org/ftc_rjr/CX000034.html

Erdman, R.A. Passchier J, Kooijman M, Stronks DL. (1993) "The Dutch version of the Nottingham Health Profile: investigations of psychometric aspects" *Psychological Reports 72,* 1027-35.

ESPAD (2011) http://www.espad.org/espad-reports

Farthing, G.W. (2005). Attitudes toward heroic and nonheroic physical risk takers as mates and as friends. *Evolution and Human Behavior, 26,* 171-185.

Gintis H., Smith, E.A., & Bowles, S. (2001). Costly Signaling and Reciprocal altruism. *Journal of Theoretical Biology 213,* 103-119.

Glazer, A., & Konrad, K. A. (1996). A signaling explanation for charity. *American Economic Review, 86,* 1019-1028.

Griskevicius V, Tybur JM, Sundie JM, et al. (2007) "Blatant benevolence and conspicuous consumption: When romantic motives elicit strategic costly signals" *Journal of Personality and Social Psychology, 93,* 85-102

Griskevicius V, Tybur JM, Van den Bergh B (2010) "Going Green to Be Seen: Status, Reputation, and Conspicuous Conservation". *Journal of Personality and Social Psychology,* 98 392-404

Gruber, J. (2001). Youth smoking in the 1990's. Why did it rise and what are the long-term implications? *American Economic Review, 91,* 85-90.

Kirmani, A.; & Rao, A.R. (2000). No pain, no gain: a critical review of the literature on signaling unobservable product quality. *Journal of Marketing 64 (2)*: 66-79

MacFAddyen, L., Hasting, A.; Amos, G. & Marks, E. (2003). "They look like my kind of people" perception of smoking images in youth magazines.

McCool, J.P.; Cameron, L.D., & Petrie, K.J. (2001). Adolescent perceptions of smoking imagery in film. *Social Science & Medicine, 52*, 1577-1587.

Michaelidou N, Dibb Sally and Ali H (2008) "The effect of health, cosmetic and social antismoking information themes on adolescents' beliefs about smoking" *International Journal of Advertising, 27,* 235-250.

Pechmann, Conny, and Reibling E.T. (2008) "An experimental investigation of the joint effects of advertising and peers on adolescents' beliefs and intentions about cigarette consumption" *Journal of Consumer Research, 29,* 5-19.

Pechman, Conny, and Shih, C.F. (1999). "Smoking scenes in movies and antismoking advertisements before movies: Effects on youth". *Journal of Marketing, 63,* 1-13.

Pechmann, C., Zhao, G., Goldberg, M. E., & Reibling E. T. (2003), "What to Convey in Antismoking Advertisements for Adolescents: The Use of Protection Motivation Theory to Identify Effective Message Themes". *Journal of Marketing,* 1-18.

Srull, T.K. and Wyer, R.S (1979) "The role of category accessibility in the interpretation of information about persons – some determinants and implications" *Journal of Personality and Social Psychology, 37,* 1660-1672

UK Cancer Research (2010) http://info.cancerresearchuk.org/cancerstats/types/lung/smoking/#cancer

Youngsted, S.D., and Kripke, D.F. (2004). Long sleep and mortality: rationale for sleep reduction. *Sleep medicine reviews, 8,* 159-174.

Zahavi, A. & Zahavi, A. (1997). *The Handicap Principle: A Missing Piece of Darwin's Puzzle*. New York: Oxford University Press.

Reducing the Pursuit of Material Goods:
The Influence of Positive Affect on Materialism and Conspicuous Consumption

Jin Seok Pyone, Cornell University, USA
Alice M. Isen, Cornell University, USA

EXTENDED ABSTRACT

Much of the previous research has investigated how materialism influences happiness (e.g., Belk 1984; Van Boven and Gilovich 2003). On the other hand, relatively little research has been conducted on the reverse, the influence of positive affect on materialism. In the present research, we examine how mild positive affect that people experience in everyday life influences materialistic and conspicuous consumption behavior.

Based on the affect literature suggesting that positive affect leads to more flexible thinking (Isen 2008) and broadened scope of attention and cognition (Fredrickson and Branigan 2005), we hypothesize that positive affect enables people to think about aspects of their life and their happiness more flexibly (i.e., they can think of various ways of pursuing happiness other than acquiring material goods), and thus they are less likely to rely on material goods as a primary source of happiness or self-worth, while neglecting its other sources.

First, in order to examine a lay theory of materialism, in a pilot study we asked participants to describe materialism in their own words. They defined materialism broadly in two ways: 1) valuing material goods over other, or abstract, values in life (e.g., family or friendship), and 2) engaging in consumption behavior in order to "show off" or signal status. In five studies, we tested the influence of positive affect on materialism as represented in prior research and the lay ideas generated above.

Study 1: What Makes You Happy? Participants were randomly assigned to either a positive or a neutral affect condition. Affect was manipulated using a video clip: a mildly amusing clip (showing a dancing hippo) or a neutral clip (showing moving color bars). After the affect induction task, materialism was measured in a way similar to that used by Chaplin and John (2007). Participants were asked to list things that make them happy using six categories: *Hobbies, Material Things, Achievements, Sports, People, Other*. A ratio index of materialism was obtained by dividing the number of material items by the total number of items, for each participant. The results revealed that people in positive affect reported lower materialism ratios than did those in neutral affect.

Study 2: Money Allocation I - Spending vs. Saving. In Study 2, we measured materialism in the context of impulsive spending behavior. Affect was induced as in Study 1. After the affect induction task, participants were asked to imagine that they received a $500 bonus from the company they had worked for over the last summer, and asked to allocate the $500 between two categories: To Spend and To Save. A 2 (affect: positive vs. neutral) × 2 (category: spending vs. saving) mixed ANOVA, with category as a within-subject factor, revealed a significant interaction between Affect and Category, $F(1, 42) = 7.25$, $p = .01$. People in positive affect allocated less money on spending, and more on saving, than did those in neutral affect, and also they allocated more money to saving than to spending.

Study 3: Money Allocation II -Material vs. Experiential Purchase. In Study 3, following the research by Van Boven and Gilovich (2003), we measured materialism in terms of the type of purchases people pursue (material or experiential). After the affect induction task (as in Study 1), participants were asked what specific things they would like to *buy* or *do* with the $500, and to indicate the amount of money they allotted to each item. A materialism index was created for each subject, by subtracting the amount allocated to experiential purchases (e.g., *going out to dinner with friends, skiing*) from that to material purchases (e.g., *new clothing, handbags*). Results showed that people in positive affect allocated a smaller portion of the money to material purchases (relative to experiential purchases), than did the controls.

Study 4: Conspicuous Consumption I. In Studies 4 and 5, we measured materialism in terms of the underlying motive for buying material goods: the degree to which people want to signal wealth or social status. Participants (all female) were randomly assigned to a 2 (affect) x 2 (signal: high, low) between-subjects design. After the affect induction task, participants were told that they would evaluate a high-end product. Half of the participants saw an image of a Gucci handbag with a salient brand-logo (high signal), and the other half saw a Gucci bag with no logo (low signal). Results revealed that people in neutral (vs. positive) affect perceived the handbag with the salient logo as more attractive, wanted to own it more, and were willing to pay more for it.

Study 5: Conspicuous Consumption II. In Study 5, Conspicuous consumption was measured among male subjects. Participants (all male) read product descriptions about cars from two different brands: a *Low-end* model from BMW and a *Premium* model from Mazda. The BMW model was described so that participants could see that its performance (e.g., engine, fuel efficiency, horsepower, etc) was inferior to that of the Mazda, but as superior as a status symbol. Participants then were asked to make a choice between the two models. The results showed that positive-affect people were more likely to choose the high-end Mazda (performance) over the low-end BMW (status) than were controls.

In sum, results of five studies suggest that under mild positive (vs. neutral) affect, people are less likely to rely on material goods as a primary source of happiness, while neglecting its other sources, and also less likely to engage in conspicuous consumption (i.e., signal status through material goods).

REFERENCES

Belk, Russell W. (1984), "Three Scales to Measure Constructs Related to Materialism: Reliability, Validity, and Relationships to Measures of Happiness," in *Advances in Consumer Research*, Vol. 11, ed. Thomas Kinnear, Provo, UT: Association for Consumer Research, 291–97.

--- (1985), "Materialism: Trait Aspects of Living in the Material World," *Journal of Consumer Research*, 12 (December), 265–80.

Chaplin, Lan Nguyen and Deborah Roedder John (2007), "Growing Up in a Material World: Age Differences in Materialism in Child and Adolescents," *Journal of Consumer Research*, 34 (4), 480-93.

Czikszentmihalyi, Mihaly and Eugene Rochberg-Halton (1981), *The Meaning of Things: Domestic Symbols of the Self*, Cambridge: Cambridge University Press.

Fredrickson, Barbara L. and Christine Branigan (2005), "Positive emotions broaden the scope of attention and thought-action repertoires," *Cognition and Emotion*, 19 (3), 313-32.

Holman, Thomas B. (1981), "The Influence of Community Involvement on Marital Quality," *Journal of Marriage and the Family*, 43 (February), 143–49.

Isen, Alice M. (2008), "Some ways in which positive affect influences problem solving and decision making," in *Handbook of Emotions*, eds. Michael Lewis, Jeannette M. Haviland-Jones, and Lisa Feldman Barrett, NY: Guilford, 548-73.

Isen, Alice M. and Paula F. Levin (1972), "The effects of feeling good on helping: Cookies and kindness," *Journal of Personality and Social Psychology*, 21 (3), 384-88.

Kahneman, Daniel and Angus Deaton (2010), "High income improves evaluation of life but not emotional well-being," *Proceedings of the National Academy of Sciences*, September, 1-5.

Kahneman, Daniel, Alan B. Krueger, David Schkade, Norbert Schwarz, Arthur A. Stone (2006), "Would you be happier if you were richer? A focusing illusion," Science, 312, 1908-910.

Kasser, Tim and Kennon M. Sheldon (2000), "OF WEALTH AND DEATH: Materialism, Mortality Salience, and Consumption Behavior," *Psychological Science*, 11 (4), 348-51.

Nicolao, Leonardo, Julie R. Irwin, and Joseph K. Goodman (2009), "Happiness for Sale: Do Experiential Purchases Make Consumers Happier than Material Purchases?" *Journal of Consumer Research*, 36 (August), 188-198.

Richins, Marsha L. and Scott Dawson (1992), "A Consumer Values Orientation for Materialism and Its Measurement: Scale Development and Validation," *Journal of Consumer Research*, 19 (December), 303–16.

Rucker, Derek D. and Adam D. Galinsky (2008), "Desire to Acquire: Powerlessness and Compensatory Consumption," *Journal of Consumer Research*, 35 (October), 357-267.

Veblen, Thorstein (1899/1994), *The Theory of the Leisure Class*, New York: Dover.

Van Boven, Leaf (2005), "Experientialism, materialism, and the pursuit of happiness," *Review of General Psychology*, 9, 132-42.

Van Boven, Leaf and Thomas Gilovich (2003), "To do or to have? That is the question," *Journal of Personality and Social Psychology*, 85, 1193-202.

Waugh, Christian E. and Barbara L. Fredrickson (2006), "Nice to know you: Positive emotions, self-other overlap, and complex understanding in the formation of a new relationship," *The Journal of Positive Psychology*, 1(2), 93-106.

Seeing Man in Man's Best Friend
The Role of Anthropomorphism on Increasing Prosocial Behavior

Brooke Reavey, Drexel University, USA
Marina Puzakova, Drexel University, USA
Hyokjin Kwak, Drexel University, USA

EXTENDED ABSTRACT

Anthropomorphisms are frequently used in for-profit and non-profit marketing communications. The emerging body of work in consumer behavior is consistent that anthropomorphisms increase consumer likability of the product (Aggarwal and McGill 2007; Holzwarth, Janiszewski, and Neumann 2006; Kim and McGill *in press;* Landwehr, McGill, and Herrmann *in press*). When marketers project human-like intentions, motivations, characteristics, conscious will, soul, spirit and emotions onto nonhuman entities, the entity is anthropomorphized (Aggarwal and McGill 2007; Epley, Waytz, and Cacioppo 2007). Marketers frequently display anthropomorphized entities in varying anthropomorphized levels in their consumer-facing marketing functions. These entities range from the less obvious implicit anthropomorphisms, such as a "smile" in a car grill (Landwehr et al. *in press*) (Aggarwal and McGill 2007) to an explicit anthropomorphism, such as a walking and talking squirrel in a TV commercial. Our study contributes to the growing body of literature on anthropomorphism because we identify implicit and explicit anthropomorphism as the varying degrees of anthropomorphism. We define explicit anthropomorphism as: *imbuing a nonhuman entity with observable and apparent human characteristics.* Examples of explicit anthropomorphism include: talking from the first person, moving like a human (i.e. walking, sitting, etc.), wearing human clothes, and having human features (i.e. eyes, lips, limbs, etc.). We define implicit anthropomorphism as: *imbuing a nonhuman entity with indirect and subtle human characteristics.* Examples of implicit anthropomorphism include: a description in the third person that includes conscientiousness and sentimentality using secondary emotions, having the anthropomorphized entity take on a human shape but continue to maintain its nonhuman form (i.e. feminine shaped perfume bottle, watch hands that look like a smile), or move in a somewhat humanlike manner but maintain mechanistic tendencies. We show that the varied degrees of anthropomorphized stimuli in the appeal affect the respondents' perceptions and intentions on prosocial behavior. Moreover, while many people, but not all, anthropomorphize dogs, the context of our experiment allows us to explore the appropriateness for anthropomorphism as moderated by one's personal beliefs. To our knowledge, this is the first study to theoretically and empirically demonstrate that the varying levels of anthropomorphism stimuli affect consumers differently.

Additionally, prior research shows anthropomorphizing an entity leads to prosocial behavior because endowing an entity with humanlike capabilities (e.g., secondary emotions) leads to empathic care and concern (Waytz, Cacioppo, and Epley 2010a). Both streams of literature, commercial and prosocial behavior, show that anthropomorphizing the entity has a more positive effect on the transaction than non-anthropomorphizing does. However, most literature in the prosocial realm has focused on how negative ads affect donations. Additionally, prior research has focused on the tendency to anthropomorphize rather than rely or test one's personal beliefs on anthropomorphism. Personal beliefs are found to be less likely to change over time (Paluck 2009a, b) than situational variables. Prior research has discovered that consumers who are deeply religious tend to anthropomorphize less, but since religious beliefs tend to be deeply rooted in one's self-concept, we found that personal beliefs about anthropomorphism influence one's level of appropriateness towards the anthropomorphism. To our knowledge this is the first study to theoretically and empirically demonstrate that anthropomorphism leads to positive prosocial behavior. In this regard, we contribute to anthropomorphism theory by detailing the differences between explicit and implicit anthropomorphism and their effects on prosocial behavior.

REFERENCES

Aggarwal, Pankaj and Ann L. McGill (2007), "Is That Car Smiling at Me? Schema Congruity as a Basis for Evaluating Anthropomorphized Products," *Journal of Consumer Research*, 34 (4), 468-79.

Epley, Nicholas, Adam Waytz, Scott Akalis, and John T. Cacioppo (2008), "When We Need a Human: Motivational Determinants of Anthropomorphism," *Social cognition*, 26 (2), 143-55.

Epley, Nicholas, Adam Waytz, and John T. Cacioppo (2007), "On Seeing Human: A Three-Factor Theory of Anthropomorphism," *Psychological Review*, 114 (4), 864-86.

Holzwarth, Martin, Chris Janiszewski, and Marcus M. Neumann (2006), "The Influence of Avatars on Online Consumer Shopping Behavior," *Journal of Marketing*, 70 (4), 19-36.

Kim, Sara and Ann L. McGill (*in press*), "Gaming with Mr. Slot or Gaming the Slot Machine? Power, Anthropomorphism, and Risk Perception," *The Journal of Consumer Research*, update (update), 000.

Landwehr, Jan R., Ann L. McGill, and Andreas Herrmann (*in press*), "It's Got the Look: The Effect of Friendly and Aggressive "Facial" Expressions on Product Liking and Sales," *Journal of Marketing*.

Paluck, Elizabeth Levy (2009a), "Reducing Intergroup Prejudice and Conflict Using the Media: A Field Experiment in Rwanda.," *Journal of Personality & Social Psychology*, 96 (March: 3), 574-87.

Paluck, Elizabeth Levy (2009b), "What Is a Social Norm?," *Journal of Personality and Social Psychology*.

Waytz, Adam, John T. Cacioppo, and Nicholas Epley (2010a), "Who Sees Human? The Stability and Importance of Individual Differences in Anthropomorphism," *Perspectives on Psychological Science*, 5 (3), 219-32.

Waytz, Adam, Nicholas Epley, and John T. Cacioppo (2010b), "Social Cognition Unbound: Insights into Anthropomorphism and Dehumanization," *Current Directions in Psychological Science*, 19, 58-62.

The Effects of Temperature Cues on Food Intake

Barbara Briers, Tilburg University, The Netherlands
Davy Lerouge, Tilburg University, The Netherlands

EXTENDED ABSTRACT

According to the World Health Organization Global InfoBase, today in the United States, almost 67% of the people are overweight and about 34 % are obese. Although food marketing practices and (institution-driven) reductions in physical activity are believed to be the two most important causes of obesity (Keith et al. 2006), emerging literature points to potential harmful effects of artificially manipulating temperature by heating or air-conditioning on food intake because it interferes with our physiological system. For instance, Johnson et al. (2011) reasoned that with increased heating the ambient temperature, less energy is needed to maintain core body temperature resulting in higher rates of obesity. Herman (1993) argued that exposures to lower ambient temperatures by means of air-conditioning can induce a heightened food intake because our physiological systems asks for energy resources to keep the core body temperature sufficiently high.

In sum, emerging literature points to a potential connection between ambient temperature and expanding waistlines, but direct evidence is lacking. Moreover, the relationship between temperature has typically been explained by is physiological processes. We agree that such process can affect food intake when people are exposed to coldness or warmth for longer periods of time, like when troops are stationed in the tropics as opposed in cold areas (Johnson and Kark 1947). Yet, we belief more psychological processes are at work when people are exposed to cold or warm temperatures for a shorter period of time, such as for instance people entering an air-conditioned restaurant and/or receiving an iced drink when seated. Our research aims to test this assumption. More specifically, we put forward that merely activating the concept of coldness is enough to induce people to eat more compared to when activation the concept of warmth. In this research, it is argued that 'temperature primes' – even independent of actual ambient temperature – have the potential to affect eating behaviors.

According to behavior priming literature, cognitively priming environmental cues automatically activates the goals associated with these cues, which in turn solicits corresponding behaviors. The activation and execution of these goals require no conscious awareness or regulation (Bargh et al. 2001; Chartrand and Bargh 1996; Bargh 1990). Given that actual coldness (warmth) embodies the goal of increasing (decreasing) food intake to avoid hypothermia; these findings thus suggest that cognitively priming coldness (warmth) may automatically lead to an increased (decreased) need for food calories. Taken together, the main hypothesis of the current research is that merely activating the coldness concept will lead to higher food intake, compared to merely activating the warmth concept. In three studies we provide evidence for this hypothesis.

In a first study, we want to show first that cold primes lead to desire for energy or calories. To measure desire for calories, we will rely on a basic estimation distortion process to assess the extent to which a person values calories (Tajfel 1957). According to Bruner and Goodman (1947) coins tend to be judged as larger than gray discs of the same size, and children with a lower socioeconomic status overestimate the size of coins more than do children with a higher socioeconomic status. Deprived smokers similarly judge the length of a cigarette as longer than do nondeprived smokers (Brendl, Markman, and Messner 2003). These and other studies demonstrate that objects, such as meals or caloric content, appear larger when val-ued more. Indeed, the results of this study indicated that participants cued with coldness estimated the caloric content of food higher than people cued with warmth.

The second study aimed to provide evidence for this claim by investigation the effect of coldness vs. warmth cues on real consumption amount. Specifically, the results of study 2 illustrated that people cued with coldness ate significantly more compared to those cued with warmth.

If our findings of study 1 and 2 are really driven by coldness cues activating the goal of increasing food intake to avoid hypothermia, then we should also find that that warmth cues should result in an increased desire for more fluids to avoid hyperthermia. This was tested in the study 3. We indeed found that participants cued with coldness wanted significantly more food compared to those cued with warmth, but wanted significantly less fluids.

In sum, our research provides evidence that physiological cues that trigger eating (like temperature) also have the ability to affect food intake in a psychological way: 'temperature primes' – even independent of actual ambient temperature – have the potential to affect eating behaviors. As such, this research opens the debate to what extent short exposures to cold/warm temperatures, such as people entering an air-conditioned restaurant or attending a cocktail party with no air-conditioning, physiologically really are in need for more/less energy to keep up their body temperature. In fact our research indicates that people's reaction to order and/or consume more/less (caloric) food under such circumstances, may also be driven by a psychological need rather than a biological one.

REFERENCES

Bargh, John A. (1990), "Auto-Motives: Preconscious Determinants of Social Interaction," in *Handbook of Motivation and Cognition: Foundations of Social Behavior, Vol. 2.*, ed. E. Tory Higgins and Richard M. Sorrentino, New York, NY US: Guilford Press, 93-130.

Bargh, John A., Peter M. Gollwitzer, Annette Lee-Chai, Kimberly Barndollar, and Roman Trotschel (2001), "The Automated Will: Nonconscious Activation and Pursuit of Behavioral Goals," *Journal of Personality and Social Psychology*, 81 (6), 1014-27.

Brendl, C. Miguel, Arthur B. Markman, and Claude Messner (2003), "The Devaluation Effect: Activating a Need Devalues Unrelated Objects," *Journal of Consumer Research*, 29 (4), 463-73.

Bruner, Jerome S. and Cecile C. Goodman (1947), "Value and Need as Organizing Factors in Perception," *The Journal of Abnormal and Social Psychology*, 42 (1), 33-44.

Chaput, Jean-Philippe, Vicky Drapeau, Paul Poirier, Normand Teasdale, and Angelo Tremblay (2008), "Glycemic Instability and Spontaneous Energy Intake: Association with Knowledge-Based Work," *Psychosomatic Medicine*, 70 (7), 797-804.

Chartrand, Tanya L. and John A. Bargh (1996), "Automatic Activation of Impression Formation and Memorization Goals: Nonconscious Goal Priming Reproduces Effects of Explicit Task Instructions," *Journal of Personality and Social Psychology*, 71 (3), 464-78.

Hansen, Jens Carl, Andrew P. Gilman, and Jon Øyvind Odland (2010), "Is Thermogenesis a Significant Causal Factor in Preventing The "Globesity" Epidemic?," *Medical Hypotheses*, 75 (2), 250-56.

Herman, C. Peter (1993), "Effects of Heat on Appetite," in *Nutritional Needs in Hot Environments: Applications for Military Personnel in Field Operations*, ed. Bernadette M. Marriott, Washington, DC: National Academy Press, 187-214.

Hill, James O. (2006), "Understanding and Addressing the Epidemic of Obesity: An Energy Balance Perspective," *Endocrine Reviews*, 27 (7), 750-61.

Johnson, F., A. Mavroggiani, M. Ucci, A. Vidal-Puig, and J. Wardle (2011), "Could Increased Time Spent in a Thermal Comfort Zone Contribute to Population Increases in Obesity?," *Obesity Reviews*, no-no.

Keith, S. W., D. T. Redden, P. T. Katzmarzyk, M. M. Boggiano, E. C. Hanlon, R. M. Benca, D. Ruden, A. Pietrobelli, J. L. Barger, K. R. Fontaine, C. Wang, L. J. Aronne, S. M. Wright, M. Baskin, N. V. Dhurandhar, M. C. Lijoi, C. M. Grilo, M. DeLuca, A. O. Westfall, and D. B. Allison (2006), "Putative Contributors to the Secular Increase in Obesity: Exploring the Roads Less Traveled," *International Journal of Obesity*, 30 (11), 1585-94.

Logue, Alexandra W. (2004), *The Psychology of Eating and Drinking*, Vol. 3, New York: Brunner-Routledge.

Swinburn, B. and G. Egger (2004), "The Runaway Weight Gain Train: Too Many Accelerators, Not Enough Brakes," *British Medical Journal*, 329 (7468), 736-39.

Tajfel, H. (1957), "Value and the Perceptual Judgment of Magnitude," *Psychological Review*, 64 (3), 192-204.

Wansink, Brian and Pierre Chandon (2006), "Meal Size, Not Body Size, Explains Errors in Estimating the Calorie Content of Meals," *Annals of Internal Medicine*, 145 (5), 326-32.

Watson, D., L. A. Clark, and A. Tellegen (1988), "Development and Validation of Brief Measures of Positive and Negative Affect - the Panas Scales," *Journal of Personality and Social Psychology*, 54 (6), 1063-70.

World Health Organisation (2010), "Fact sheet: obesity and overweight," http://www.who.int/mediacentre/factsheets/fs311/en/index.html.

Young, L. R. and M. Nestle (2002), "The Contribution of Expanding Portion Sizes to the Us Obesity Epidemic," *American Journal of Public Health*, 92 (2), 246-49.

Self in *Selca*, Self-Portrait Photography, as a Model, Photographer, and Consumer

Yoo Jin Kwon, Korea National Open University, Korea
Kyoung-Nan Kwon, Ajou University, Korea

EXTENDED ABSTRACT

Selca is a compound word of self and camera, meaning self-portrait photography in Korea. In this photography, consumers simultaneously play multiple roles: the object of consumption, the creator of the object, and the consumer of the object. To take selca pictures, mostly one stretches one's arm and faces the lens toward oneself. The rapid spread of selca relates to the advent of digital photographing including a diffusion of affordable digital cameras or cell-phones with cameras and the popularity of user-generated contents of Internet social media. This study is to understand how Korean young adults create and view their selca pictures and to conceptualize the meanings of these self-images. The value of our study lies not only in the fact that selca is newly emerging consumption practice but also selca is a context where the complex and dynamic nature of self concepts is manifested.

Consumer researchers with sociological orientation focuses on the Me, self-perception as object and the empirical self (Robert E. Kleine, Kleine, and Kernan 1993). Consumers purchase products in order to highlight or conceal some aspects of self. The consumer-object relationship is well conceptualized by the theory of extended-self (Belk 1988). Belk made the ontological connection of self and possession on the basis of Sartre's (1943) three states of existence (i.e., being, having, and doing). Self-presentation is related to the Me state. At the Me state, people are more sensitive to the self-relevant aspects including how their actions and appearance look to others or evaluation of self.

Data were collected through videotaped, in-depth interviews. Ninety selca enthusiasts were recruited to participate in our interviews. Participant's age ranged nineteen through twenty seven. Descriptive characteristics of the participants, transcripts and observations were analyzed with a constant comparison approach. The interview contents reported in this manuscript, which were initially translated into English, was back-translated by two bi-lingual researchers in this subject area, which was to confirm the accuracy and reliability of the translation.

Our data revealed a few distinctive characteristics of selca. Most characteristics of self-taken photos are related to the fact that the subject of a photograph is the photographer. Our young adult consumers prefer selca to regular photography, because it captures *how they see themselves* rather than *how they look*. Self-centeredness appears to be undeniably a distinct feature of selca: Participants stated that they should be the central feature even in a selca picture with friends. Whether it is a testament shot or a shot with friends or alone, Selca-taking involves a great deal of directing.

Selca involves self who is both the creator and the object of the consumption and selca captures realities and imagery. Our attempt was to untie the complexity of self-images in selca by analyzing how participants accounted for real and unreal aspects of selca and then integrating the ambivalent accounts. Specifically, three themes emerged: (1) construction of self-centered reality, (2) objectified ideality, and (3) extension of self through selca.

Construction of Self-centered Reality. Consumers direct the photographer's effort to setting up environmental conditions within the boundary of reality. Self-centered reality is constructed through different kinds of strategies: selection, learning, and revelation. (1) Selection refers to which part of body or what state of mind participants decide to present. (2) Learning about oneself through selca indicates selca practice as autotelic activities. (3) Revelation refers to that selca captures what other people cannot capture in the person. Two types of self-centered reality also emerged depending on which self consumers choose to present through selca: model self-centered and photographer self-centered reality.

Objectified Ideality. The unreal side of selca embodies the ideality of self-concept. The ideality reflects ideals of beauty and a desirable human character of the society as well as various personal goals. Three strategies emerged as to concretizing the ideality of self: magnifying, negotiation, and multiplying. (1) Magnifying is a way of transforming a reality to an ideality. Many selca techniques are means of exaggerating features that participants want to idealize. (2) Negotiation refers to management of conflicts in taking selca. For example, the two techniques discussed above, high-angle shots and low-angle shots, are incompatible when it comes to a picture of the entire body. (3) Multiplying is to reinforce what is magnified in selca. Many regulars' strategy of possessing many good selca pictures can be understood as a way of multiplying desirable selves. By doing so, the good-looking person in the photos became an existent entity.

Extension of Self through Selca. Consumers juggle between realistic self-awareness and idealized self-images in selca. The discrepancy the participants dealt with is about not only their own selca but also others' selca. Interestingly participants claim that their own selca is true, whereas other people's selca is not true. The dual standard for selca was commonly observed. Participants accept the self-deceptiveness of selca of others to some degree, although they were much more tolerable to their own selca.

Another interesting observation was participants looked back on past selca pictures as actual self at that time. As the memory is reconstructed, a sense of reality at a certain point of time in the past is reconstructed. Gratification people get from good selca pictures is instant, compared to film camera. Therefore, consumers get tempted to take one more picture to get more gratification. The instant gratification spontaneously results in the next action, which creates the iterative process of photographing-viewing-gratification. Consumers embrace the idealized self-image and the realistic ideality whether physical or mental is transformed to the higher appraisal of self (i.e., self-esteem).

We understand selca as a quest for an authentic sense of self. Consumers engage in active and individuated productive consumption, acquiring a sense of authenticity. Through juggling between the reality that individuals define and the objectified positive self images, consumers construct a sense of authentic self. Self-directing and self-deception are features of selca practice as an authenticating act. The popularity of selca in Korea should be understood in its cultural context. In Korea, interdependent self concepts are traditionally dominant and consumers are self-conscious about displaying their effort for self-enhancement. This strong sense of self-consciousness was also observed in the selca practice. At the same time, young generations are exposed to and embrace individualistic self concepts, which are often understood as Western influence. The self-centeredness of selca accords with the individualism of the young generations. By extending self to the hybrid form (e.g., actual and ideal) of self-image, consumers can safely pursue self-enhancement and present self in an acceptable way. Selca embodies how this individualistic self concept is acculturated in a traditionally collectivistic culture by creatively using technological advancements.

REFERENCES

Ahluwalia, Rohini (2008), "How Far Can a Brand Stretch? Understanding the Role of Self-Construal," *Journal of Marketing Research*, 45 (June), 337-50.

Ahuvia, Aaron C. (2005), "Beyond the Extended Self: Loved Objects and Consumers' Identity Narratives," *Journal of Consumer Research*, 32 (1), 171-84.

Arnould, Eric J. and Linda L. Price (2000), "Authenticating Acts and Authoritative Performance: Questing for Self and Community," in *The Why of Consumption: Contemporary Perspectives on Consumer Motives, Goals, and Desires* ed. S. Rarneshwar, David Glen Mick and Cynthia Huffman, London: Routledge, 140-63.

Bahl, Shalini and George R. Milne (2010), "Talking to Ourselves: A Dialogical Exploration of Consumption Experiences," *Journal of Consumer Research*, 37 (June), 176-95.

Begley, Sharon (2008), "Our Imaginary, Hotter Selves," *Newsweek*, February 25, 2008, 49.

Belk, Russell W. (1988), "Possessions and the Extended Self," *Journal of Consumer Research*, 15 (2), 139-68.

Belk, Russell W., Güliz Ger, and Søren Askegaard (2003), "The Fire of Desire: A Multisited Inquiry into Consumer Passion," *Journal of Consumer Research*, 30 (3), 326-51.

Belk, Russell and Joyce Yeh (2011), "Tourist Photographs: Signs of Self," in *Video Library to Accompany Consumer Behavior: Buying, Having, and Being*, ed. Michael R. Solomon: Prentice Hall.

Davies, Julia (2007), "Display, Identity and the Everyday: Self-Presentation through Online Image Sharing," *Discourse: Studies in the Cultural Politics of Education*, 28 (4), 549-64.

Dominick, Joseph R. (1999), "Who Do You Think You Are? Personal Home Pages and Self-Presentation on the World Wide Web," *Journalism and Mass Communication Quarterly*, 76 (4), 646-58.

Gao, Leilei, S. Christian Wheeler, and Baba Shiv (2009), "The "Shaken Self": Product Choices as a Means of Restoring Self-View Confidence," *Journal of Consumer Research*, 36 (1), 29-38.

Glaser, Barney G. and Anselm L Strauss (1967), *The Discovery of Grounded Theory: Strategies for Qualitative Research*, Chicago: Adline Publishing Company.

Goffman, Erving (1959), *The Presentation of Self in Everyday Life* Garden City, NY: Doubleday Anchor Books.

Jain, Shailendra Pratap, Kalpesh Kaushk Desai, and Huifang Mao (2007), "The Influence of Chronic and Situational Self-Construal on Categorization," *Journal of Consumer Research*, 34 (June), 66-76.

James, William (1890), *The Principles of Psychology*, New York: Hold and Company.

Jones, Edward Ellsworth (1990), *Interpersonal Perception*, New York: W.H. Freeman and Co.

Mead, George Herbert (1934), *Mind, Self, and Society*, Chicago: University of Chicago Press.

Myers, David G. (2010), *Social Psychology*, New York: McGraw Hill.

Nuttall, Pete (2009), "Insiders, Regulars and Tourists: Exploring Selves and Music Consumption in Adolescence," *Journal of Consumer Behaviour*, 8 (July-August), 211-24.

Robert E. Kleine, III, Susan Schultz Kleine, and Jerome B. Kernan (1993), "Mundane Consumption and the Self: A Social-Identity Perspective," *Journal of Consumer Psychology*, 2 (3), 209-35.

Rosen, Charles and Henri Zerner (2000), "Scenes from the American Dream," *The New York Review of Books*, August 10, 2000.

Sartre, Jean-Paul (1943), *Being and Nothingness: A Phenomenological Essay on Ontology*, New York: Philosophical Library.

Schneider, David j. (1981), "Tactical Self-Representations: Toward a Broader Conception," in *Impression Management Theory and Social Psychological Research*, New York: Academic Press, 23-40.

Siibak, Andrea (2009), "Constructing the Self through the Photo Selection - Visual Impression Management of Social Networking Websites," *Cyberpsychology: Journal of Psychological Research on Cyberspace*, 3 (1).

Solomon, Michael R. (2009), *Consumer Behavior: Buying, Having, and Being*, New Jersey, US: Pearson Prentice Hall.

Strano, Michele M. (2008), "User Descriptions and Interpretations of Self-Presentation through Facebook Profile Images," *Cyberpsychology: Journal of Psychosocial Research on Cyberspace,*, 2 (2).

Wynn, Eleanor and James E. Katz (1997), "Hyperbole over Cyberspace: Self-Presentation and Social Boundaries in Internet Home Pages and Discourse," *The Information Society*, 13 (4), 297-327.

Lost in Translation:
The Consequences of Culturally Mismatched Thinking Styles on Familiarity Seeking

Minkyung Koo, University of Illinois, USA
Sharon Shavitt, Walter H. Stellner Professor of Marketing, University of Illinois at Urbana-Champaign, USA
Ashok Lalwani, University of Texas at San Antonio, USA
Yifan Dai, University of Illinois, USA
Sydney Chinchanachokchai, University of Illinois, USA

EXTENDED ABSTRACT

Westerners in general hold an analytic world view that emphasizes the independence of individual objects, whereas East Asians tend to adopt a holistic view, emphasizing that the world is composed of interrelated elements (Nisbett et al. 2001). Although research has revealed important antecedents and consequences of cultural differences in thinking styles, little attention has been paid to the consequences of engaging in culturally mismatched thinking styles. This is our focus. Rather than examining the impact of one or another thinking style, we examine the impact of having to perform a task that mismatches (versus matches) one's dominant style.

When a given task calls for processing that is not in line with one's culturally dominant thinking style, self-regulation is required. That is, in order to complete the task successfully, one needs to override the inclination to process information in the usual way and force oneself to process it differently. This inhibition of one's dominant processing style is depleting in that it consumes self-regulatory resources that could have been used in subsequent tasks. Indeed, recent research has shown that these cross-cultural experiences come with self-regulatory costs and consequences: a reduced ability to control one's intentions and a greater likelihood of giving in to temptations (Koo et al. 2010).

The present research builds upon this to examine a broader implication of the impact of engaging in culturally mismatched thinking styles – familiarity seeking. If engaging in a mismatched (versus matched) thinking style leads to reduced self-control and increased indulgence, it may also be expected to lead consumers to make other choices that reflect depletion. Making choices and decisions is known to be depleting and thus to impair subsequent efforts at self-control because decision making and self-control draw upon common resources (Vohs et al. 2008). We thus propose that, in turn, feeling depleted may lead people to be less willing to take on additional effort when making choices. People who experience a mismatch (vs. match) in thinking styles, and who consequently feel depleted may opt instead for old familiar consumption experiences.

Study 1 tested the hypothesis that engaging in culturally mismatched thinking styles lead people to make choices that require less effort, increasing the preference for familiar versus novel options. Participants of Asian and European American ethnicities were recruited to represent holistic and analytic thinkers, respectively. Half of the participants in each cultural background were assigned to an analytic task condition: They were shown a picture in which 11 embedded objects were to be found (Monga and John 2008). The rest of the participants were assigned to the holistic task condition, in which they were shown the same picture but with an instruction to focus on the background. Subsequently, participants were shown a scenario in which they had to make choices regarding an upcoming vacation. Participants were then asked to indicate for the categories of hotel, bar/nightclub, and spa, which option they would be more likely to choose, either a familiar favorite location or a new place.

As predicted, a significant interaction was found between participant ethnicity (Asian vs. European American) and their primed thinking style (analytic vs. holistic) on the mean likelihood of selecting familiar (vs. unfamiliar) choices. European American participants were more likely to favor one of the familiar choices in the holistic than in the analytic thinking condition. In contrast, Asian participants were more likely to favor one of the familiar choices in the analytic than in the holistic thinking condition.

Study 2 further examined the impact of culturally mismatched thinking styles on familiarity-seeking tendency in another domain, namely decision making in a restaurant. Specifically, this study tested whether culturally mismatched experiences would lead consumers to prefer familiar to unfamiliar dishes at a restaurant. In addition, this study examined dominant thinking styles via measured chronic thinking style. The study employed a 2 (measured chronic thinking style: analytic vs. holistic) X 2 (induced thinking style: analytic vs. holistic) between subjects factorial design.

Participants were induced to think either analytically or holistically using the same procedure as in Study 1 (Monga & John, 2008). After the thinking-style manipulation, participants were shown a hypothetical scenario in which they had to make choices in a restaurant. They were then asked to indicate whether they would like to choose one of their familiar favorites or a selection from a new menu for each course: an appetizer, a main dish, and a dessert. Then, participants' chronic thinking styles were measured using the 7 point Analysis-Holism Scale (AHS; Choi et al. 2007).

As expected chi-square tests showed that the percentage of participants who selected an old favorite was significantly greater than those who selected a new choice, especially among those who experienced a culturally mismatched thinking style in the case of the appetizer and the dessert (though not the main dish). Overall, we replicated the significant effects of mismatch on the choice of familiar options at a restaurant. This suggests that the effects observed here are not limited to important and consequential choices, or ones that involve significant risk, such as a hotel. They impact smaller decisions, as well, such as the tendency to order items from a familiar menu rather than from a new set of options.

Taken together, the two studies showed converging evidence that people who engage in a task that mismatches (versus matches) their culturally dominant thinking style are more likely to visit places or select consumer options that they already know well. Our findings have novel implications for the understanding of culture, especially the potential consequences of intercultural interactions in subsequent decision making, and for understanding the impact of depletion on familiarity seeking. Exposure to experiences that require a culturally mismatched thinking style is a commonplace situation. Our research suggests for the first time that, paradoxically, these enriching cross-cultural experiences reduce one's interest in novel (vs. familiar) experiences.

REFERENCES

Bornstein, Robert F. (1989), "Exposure and Affect: Overview and Meta-Analysis of Research," *Pychological Bulletin*, 106 (2), 265-89.

Capaldi, Elizabeth D. (1996), "Conditioned Food Preferences," in *Why We Eat What We Eat: The Psychology of Eating*, ed. Elizabeth D. Capaldi, Washington: American Psychological Association, 53–80.

Choi, Incheol, Minkyung Koo, and Jongan Choi (2007), "Individual Differences in Analytic Versus Holistic Thinking," *Personality and Social Psychology Bulletin*, 33 (5), 691-705.

Ferraro, Rosellina, James R. Bettman, and Tanya L. Chartrand (2009), "The Power of Strangers: The Effect of Incidental Consumer Brand Encounters on Brand Choice," *Journal of Consumer Research*, 35 (5), 729-41.

Frijns, Tom and Catrin Finkenauer (2009), "Longitudinal Associations between Keeping a Secret and Psychosocial Adjustment in Adolescence," *International Journal of Behavioral Development*, 33 (2), 145-54.

Janiszewski, Chris (1993), "Preattentive Mere Exposure Effects," *Journal of Consumer Research*, 20 (3), 376–92.

Ji, Li-Jun, Kaiping Peng, and Richard E. Nisbett (2000), "Culture, Control, and Perception of Relationships in the Environment," *Journal of Personality and Social Psychology*, 78 (5), 943-55.

Ji, Li-Jun, Zhiyong Zhang, and Richard Nisbett (2004), "Is It Culture, or Is It Language? Examination of Language Effects in Cross-Cultural Research on Categorization," *Journal of Personality and Social Psychology*, 87 (1), 57-65.

Kim, Heejung and Hazel Rose Markus (1999), "Deviance or Uniqueness, Harmony or Conformity? A Cultural Analysis," *Journal of Personality and Social Psychology*, 77 (4), 785-800.

Kim, Heejung S. and Aimee Drolet (2003), "Choice and Self-Expression: A Cultural Analysis of Variety-Seeking," *Journal of Personality and Social Psychology*, 85 (2), 373-82.

Koo, Minkyung, Sharon Shavitt, Ashok Lalwani, Yifan Dai, and Sydney Chinchanachokchai (2010), "When one culture meets another culture: The impact of culturally (mis)matched thinking styles on self-regulation," in *Advances in Consumer Research*, Vol. 37, ed. Margaret C. Campbell, Jeffrey Inman, and Rik Pieters, Duluth, MN: Association for Consumer Research.

Lee, Tae-Hee and John Crompton (1992), "Measuring Novelty Seeking in Tourism," *Annals of Tourism Research*, 19 (4), 732-51.

Masuda, Takahiko and Richard E. Nisbett (2001), "Attending Holistically Versus Analytically: Comparing the Context Sensitivity of Japanese and Americans," *Journal of Personality and Social Psychology*, 81 (5), 922-34.

--- (2006), "Culture and Change Blindness.," *Cognitive Science*, 30, 381-99.

Monga, Alokparna Basu and Deborah Roedder John (2007), "Cultural Differences in Brand Extension Evaluation: The Influence of Analytic Versus Holistic Thinking," *Journal of Consumer Research*, 33 (March), 529-36.

--- (2008), "When Does Negative Brand Publicity Hurt? The Moderating Influence of Analytic Versus Holistic Thinking," *Journal of Consumer Psychology*, 18 (4), 320-32.

Moreland, Richard L. and Robert B. Zajonc (1982), "Exposure Effects in Person Perception: Familiarity, Similarity and Attraction," *Journal of Experimental Social Psychology*, 18 (5), 395-415.

Morris, Michael W. and Kaiping Peng (1994), "Culture and Cause: American and Chinese Attributions for Social and Physical Events," *Journal of Personality and Social Psychology*, 67 (6), 949-71.

Ng, Sharon and Michael J. Houston (2006), "Exemplars or Beliefs? The Impact of Self-View on the Nature and Relative Influence of Brand Associations," *Journal of Consumer Research*, 32 (4), 519-29.

Nisbett, Richard E., Kaiping Peng, Incheol Choi, and Ara Norenzayan (2001), "Culture and Systems of Thought: Holistic Versus Analytic Cognition," *Psychological Review*, 108 (2), 291-310.

Peretz, Isabelle, Danielle Gaudreau, and Anne-Marie Bonnel (1998), "Exposure Effects on Music Preference and Recognition," *Memory and Cognition*, 26 (5), 884–902.

Porter, Richard H. and Jan Winberg (1999), "Unique Salience of Maternal Breast Odors for Newborn Infants," *Neuroscience and Biobehavioral Reviews*, 23 (3), 439–49.

Reber, R., P. Winkielman, and N. Schwarz (1998), "Effects of Perceptual Fluency on Affective Judgments," *Psychological Science*, 9 (1), 45-48.

Vohs, Kathleen D., Roy F. Baumeister, Brandon J. Schmeichel, Jean M. Twenge, Noelle M. Nelson, and Dianne M. Tice (2008), "Making Choices Impairs Subsequent Self-Control: A Limited Resource Account of Decision Making, Self-Regulation, and Active Initiative," *Journal of Personality and Social Psychology*, 94 (5), 883-98.

Zajonc, Robert B. and Hazel Markus (1982), "Affective and Cognitive Factors in Preferences," *Journal of Consumer Research*, 9 (2), 123-31.

Zhu, Rui and Joan Meyers Levy (2009), "The Influence of Self View on Context Effects: How Display Fixtures Can Affect Product Evaluations," *Journal of Marketing Research*, 46 (1), 37-45.

How Much to Give and How to Frame It?
Donation Size and Donation Framing in Cause-Related Marketing

Sarah S. Müller, University of Hamburg, Germany
Anne Fries, University of Hamburg, Germany
Karen Gedenk, University of Hamburg, Germany

ABSTRACT

In cause-related marketing (CM) companies promise a donation to a cause every time a consumer makes a purchase. In this research, we analyze the impact of the size and framing of these donation promises on a CM campaign's effects on brand choice and brand image. Framing can be monetary or nonmonetary, or consist of a combination of both types of information. Furthermore, this study considers nonlinear effects of donation size and potential moderating effects of donation frames as well as a financial trade-off for consumers on the impact of donation size on CM success. The authors find that for brand choice, increasing donation size has a positive effect if consumers face no financial trade-off, but the effect is negative if a higher donation comes at higher costs. Donation framing has no substantial impact on brand choice. For brand image, nonmonetary frames are more successful than monetary frames. A large donation may even have a negative effect if the donation frame is monetary. If campaigns use a combination of both frames, the effect of donation size on brand image reveals an inverted U shape.

REFERENCES

Anderson, N. H. (1981), *Foundations of information integration theory*, New York: Erlbaum.

Andreoni, J. (1989), "Giving with impure altruism: Applications to charity and ricardian equivalence," *Journal of Political Economy, 97(6)*, 1447-1458.

Andreoni, J. (1990), "Impure altruism and donations to public goods: A theory of warm-glow giving," *The Economic Journal, 100(401)*, 464-477.

Arora, N., and T. Henderson (2007), "Embedded premium promotion: Why it works and how to make it more effective," *Marketing Science, 26(4)*, 514-531.

Barnes, N. G. (1992), "Determinants of consumer participation in cause-related marketing campaigns," *American Business Review, 10(2)*, 21-24.

Barone, M. J., A. D. Miyazaki, and K. A. Taylor (2000), "The influence of cause-related marketing on consumer choice: Does one good turn deserve another?" *Journal of the Academy of Marketing Science, 28(2)*, 248-262.

Burnett, J. J., and V. R. Wood (1988), A proposed model of the donation decision process. In E. Hirschman, and J. Sheth (Eds.), *Research in Consumer Behavior, 3*, (pp. 1-47). Greenwich, CT: Elsevier JAI.

Dean, D. H. (2003/04), "Consumer perception of corporate donations," *Journal of Advertising, 32(4)*, 91-102.

Eckel, C. C., and P. J. Grossman (2003), "Rebate versus matching: Does how we subsidize charitable contributions matter?" *Journal of Public Economics, 87(3/4)*, 681-701.

Fries, A. J. (2010), "The effects of cause-related marketing campaign characteristics – A literature review," *Marketing - Journal of Research and Management, 6(2)*, 145-157.

Green, D. P., D. Kahneman, and H. Kunreuther (1994), "How the scope and method of public funding affect willingness to pay for public goods," *Public Opinion Quarterly, 58(1)*, 49-67.

Gupta, S., and L. G. Cooper (1992), "The discounting of discounts and promotion thresholds," *Journal of Consumer Research, 19(3)*, 401-411.

Gupta, S., and J. Pirsch (2006), "The company-cause-customer fit decision in cause-related marketing," *Journal of Consumer Marketing, (23)6*, 314-326.

Jaccard, J., R. Turrisi, and C. K. Wan (1990), *Interaction effects in multiple regression*, Thousand Oaks, CA: Sage.

Kahneman, D., and J. L. Knetsch (1992), "Valuing public goods: The purchase of moral satisfaction," *Journal of Environmental Economics and Management, 22(1)*, 57-70.

Kahneman, D., I. Ritov, K. E. Jacowitz, and P. Grant (1993), "Stated willingness to pay for public goods: A psychological perspective," *Psychological Science, 4(5)*, 310-315.

Landreth Grau, S., and J. A. Garretson Folse (2007), "Cause-related marketing (CRM) - The influence of donation proximity and message-framing cues on the less-involved consumer," *Journal of Advertising, 36(4)*, 19-33.

Loipfinger, S. (2008), *Verbrauchertäuschung durch Volvic und UNICEF*. Retrieved September, 28, 2009, from http://www.charitywatch.de/?id=354.

Neslin, S. A. (2002), Sales promotion. In R. Wensley, and B. A. Weitz (Eds.), *Handbook of Marketing* (pp. 310-338), London: Sage.

Olsen, G. D., J. W. Pracejus, and N. R. Brown (2003), "When profit equals price: Consumer confusion about donation amounts in cause-related marketing," *Journal of Public Policy and Marketing, 22(2)*, 170-180.

Ross, J. K., M. A. Stutts, and L. Patterson (1991), "Tactical considerations for the effective use of cause-related marketing," *The Journal of Applied Business Research, 7(2)*, 58-65.

Simonin, B. L., and J. A. Ruth (1998), "Is a company known by the company it keeps? Assessing the spillover effects of brand alliances on consumer brand attitudes," *Journal of Marketing Research, 35(1)*, 30-42.

Strahilevitz, M. (1999), "The effects of product type and donation magnitude on willingness to pay more for a charity-linked brand," *Journal of Consumer Psychology, 8(3)*, 215-241.

Strahilevitz, M. (2003), "The effects of prior impressions of a firm's ethics on the success of a cause-related marketing campaign: Do the good look better while the bad look worse?" *Journal of Nonprofit and Public Sector Marketing, 11(1)*, 77-92.

Strahilevitz, M., and J. G. Myers (1998), "Donations to charity as purchase incentives: How well they work may depend on what you are trying to sell," *Journal of Consumer Research, 24(4)*, 434-446.

Till, B. D., and L. I. Nowak (2000), "Toward effective use of cause-related marketing alliances," *Journal of Product and Brand Management, 9(7)*, 472-484.

van Heerde, H. J., P. S. H. Leeflang, and D. R. Wittink (2001), "Semiparametric analysis to estimate the deal effect curve," *Journal of Marketing Research, 38(2)*, 197-215.

Varadarajan, P. R., and A. Menon (1988), "Cause-related marketing: A coalignment of marketing strategy and corporate philanthropy," *Journal of Marketing*, *52(3)*, 58-74.

Völckner, F., H. Sattler, and G. Kaufmann (2008), "Image feedback effects of brand extensions: Evidence from a longitudinal field study," *Marketing Letters*, *19(2)*, 109-124.

Weisbrod, B. A., and N. D. Dominguez (1986), "Demand for collective goods in private nonprofit markets: Can fundraising expenditures help overcome free-rider behavior?" *Journal of Public Economics*, *30(1)*, 83-95.

Yoo, B., N. Donthu, and S. Lee (2000), "An examination of selected marketing mix elements on brand equity," *Journal of the Academy of Marketing Science*, *28(2)*, 195-211.

Youn, S., and H. Kim (2008), "Antecedents of consumer attitudes toward cause-related marketing," *Journal of Advertising Research*, *48(1)*, 123-137.

Attitudes Shaped by Eye Movements: The Reading Direction Effect

En Li, Central Queensland University, Australia
Donnel Briley, University of Sydney, Australia

EXTENDED ABSTRACT

One of the most established facts in psychology and consumer research is the finding that the mind guides the body (Fazio, Powell, and Williams 1989). For example, the goals consumers have in mind can determine patterns of eye movements (Pieters and Wedel 2007). The present research, however, breaks this traditional perspective by looking at the influence of the body on the mind. Specifically, we posit that eye movements, despite being a subtle bodily process, can play a critical role in shaping consumer attitudes toward moving stimuli.

Consumers frequently encounter alphanumeric stimuli moving horizontally across their fields of vision in the course of everyday life. This research examines whether consumers' habitual reading direction affects their evaluations of such stimuli. Based on visual perception and fluency literature we hypothesize and demonstrate a "reading direction effect," whereby consumers' evaluations of an alphanumeric stimulus are more positive when its movement direction coincides rather than conflicts with their habitual reading direction (study 1). Importantly, we show that this directional effect is driven by motor fluency rather than conceptual fluency (study 2), and its processes involve activation of reading knowledge (i.e., the procedural knowledge used to perform reading activities; study 3).

Predictions

Foundational Prediction. Two modes of eye movement need to be considered to make the foundational prediction: a habitual and a situational mode. On the one hand, evidence from examining human reading behavior suggests that the dominant eye movements in processing alphanumeric characters are made in habitual reading direction (Rayner 1998). Hence, eye movements in such habitual direction are acted more frequently, and possibly, more fluently than eye movements in other directions. On the other hand, when an alphanumeric stimulus moves horizontally across a consumer's field of vision, it evokes eye movements of identical direction (Palmer 1999). If the direction of evoked eye movements coincides (vs. conflicts) with the viewer's habitual reading direction, she might experience a sense of "feeling right" due to heightened motor fluency, as the direction of situational eye movements in this case fits with her habitual eye movement direction. This process might yield enhanced evaluations of the stimulus when the viewer misattributes her fluency experience to the quality of the stimulus itself (Bornstein and D'Agostino 1994).

"Conceptual Fluency" or "Motor Fluency". It is theorized that stimulus movement speed provides a useful criterion for teasing apart conceptual and motor fluency effects. Therefore, if conceptual fluency is the only mechanism driving the reading direction effect, a horizontally moving brand name will always be favored when its movement direction matches the viewer's habitual reading direction, irrespective of its moving speed. However, if the reading direction effect disappears or even becomes reversed when evaluated brands move faster than the threshold speed (i.e., three to four degrees per second; Leigh and Zee 1999), then motor fluency should be an indispensable driving force behind the reading direction effect.

"Always Online" or "Context Sensitive". When people encounter and respond to a moving alphanumeric stimulus, certain knowledge representations stored in memory will be activated and used as they formulate responses to this event. The tendency to be more comfortable engaging in eye movements following rather than opposing habitual reading direction, which derives from such representations, might be chronically accessible and context independent (Higgins, King, and Mavin 1982), or "always online," as a result of such tendency being innate or becoming very well learned via repeated applications across different contexts.

Another possibility is that the context in which a moving stimulus is encountered determines whether the reading direction tendency is accessed. It could be that the knowledge that drives this tendency is not "always online," but becomes activated when a context associated with reading is encountered. That is, the reading direction tendency may only arise when the viewer is in contexts that facilitate reading, but disappear when reading knowledge is less readily available.

Overview of Studies

The results of three studies found support for the reading direction effect, on both pure (brand name; study 1) and mixed alphanumeric stimuli (brand logo; studies 2 and 3). Moreover, it was found that processing fluency mediated the effect in question (studies 1 to 3).

Studies 2 and 3 provided deeper understanding of the reading direction effect. In study 2, the preferences for direction matching only emerged when the stimulus moved at a normal speed. Exposure to a fast moving stimulus, nonetheless, reversed this directional effect. These findings are consistent with the notion that motor, instead of conceptual fluency, is the indispensable driving force of the reading direction effect.

Study 3 pitted "always online" against "context sensitive" model by investigating whether the reading direction effect could arise irrespective of contexts. Participants in this study completed two seemingly unrelated tasks: firstly a reading or pictorial priming task that facilitated or impeded reading knowledge activation, then an evaluation task on a brand logo that moved horizontally. It was demonstrated that the reading direction effect was replicated among reading primed participants, but was removed among pictorial primed participants. These findings suggest that the effect in question should only be sensitive to contexts where reading knowledge is sufficiently accessible.

In summary, consumer attitudes can be shaped by chronic patterns of eye movements, which, despite involving only subtle bodily processes, could nevertheless be quite pervasive in their influence.

REFERENCES

Alter, A. L., and D. M. Oppenheimer (2009), "Uniting the Tribes of Fluency to Form a Metacognitive Nation," *Personality and Social Psychology Review*, 13 (3), 219-35.

Bornstein, F. Robert and Paul R. D'Agostino (1994), "The Attribution and Discounting of Perceptual Fluency: Preliminary Tests of a Perceptual Fluency/Attributional Model of the Mere Exposure Effect," *Social Cognition*, 12 (Summer), 103–28.

Cesario, Joseph and E. Tory Higgins (2008), "Making Message Recipients 'Feel Right': How Nonverbal Cues Can Increase Persuasion," *Psychological Science*, 19 (5), 415-20.

Childers, Terry L., Michael J. Houston, and Susan E. Heckler (1985), "Measurement of Individual Differences in Visual Versus Verbal Information Processing," *Journal of Consumer Research*, 12 (September), 125-34.

Fazio, Russell H., Martha C. Powell, and Carol J. Williams (1989), "The Role of Attitude Accessibility in the Attitude-to-Behavior Process," *Journal of Consumer Research*, 16 (December), 280-88.

Förster, Jens (2004), "How Body Feedback Influences Consumers' Evaluation of Products," *Journal of Consumer Psychology*, 14 (4), 416-26.

Higgins, E. Tory, Gillian A. King, and Gregory H. Mavin (1982), "Individual Construct Accessibility and Subjective Impressions and Recall," *Journal of Personality and Social Psychology*, 43 (1), 35-47.

Janiszewski, Chris and Tom Meyvis (2001), "Effects of Brand Logo Complexity, Repetition, and Spacing on Processing Fluency and Judgment," *Journal of Consumer Research*, 28 (June), 18-32.

Leigh, R. John and David S. Zee (1999), *The Neurology of Eye Movements*, New York: Oxford University Press.

Maass, A., D. Pagani, E. Berta (2007), "How Beautiful is the Goal and How Violent is the Fistfight? Spatial Bias in the Interpretation of Human Behavior," *Social Cognition*, 25 (6), 833-52.

Ouellet, Marc, Julio Santiago, Ziv Israeli, and Shai Gabay (2010), "Is the Future the Right Time?" *Experimental Psychology*, 57 (4), 308-14.

Palmer, Stephen E. (1999), *Vision Science-Photons to Phenomenology*, Cambridge, MA: The MIT Press.

Pieters, Rik and Michel Wedel (2007), "Goal Control of Attention to Advertising: The Yarbus Implication," *Journal of Consumer Research*, 34 (August), 224-33.

Preacher, K. J., D. D. Rucker, and A. F. Hayes (2007), "Addressing Moderated Mediation Hypotheses: Theory, Methods, and Prescriptions," *Multivariate Behavioral Research*, 42, 185-227.

Rayner, Keith (1998), "Eye Movements in Reading and Information Processing: 20 Years of Research," *Psychological Bulletin*, 124 (3), 372-422.

Reber, R., P. Winkielman, and N. Schwarz (1998), "Effects of Perceptual Fluency on Affective Judgments," *Psychological Science*, 9 (1), 45-48.

Shen, Hao, Yuwei Jiang, and Rashmi Adaval (2010), "Contrast and Assimilation Effects of Processing Fluency," *Journal of Consumer Research*, 36 (February), 876-89.

Szego, P. A. and M. D. Rutherford (2008), "Reading-Related Habitual Eye Movements Produce A Directional Anisotropy in the Perception of Speed and Animacy," *Perception*, 37, 1609-11.

Topolinski, Sascha (2010), "Moving the Eye of the Beholder: Motor Components in Vision Determine Aesthetic Preference," *Psychological Science*, 21 (9), 1220-24.

Whittlesea, Bruce W. A. (1993), "Illusions of Familiarity," *Journal of Experimental Psychology: Learning, Memory, and Cognition*, 19 (November), 1235-53.

Yang, Shu-Ju, David A. Gallo, and Sian L. Beilock (2009), "Embodied Memory Judgments: A Case of Motor Fluency," *Journal of Experimental Psychology: Learning, Memory, and Cognition*, 35 (5), 1359-65.

Zhao, Xinshu, John G. Lynch Jr., and Qimei Chen (2010), "Reconsidering Baron and Kenny: Myths and Truths about Mediation Analysis," *Journal of Consumer Research*, 37 (2), 197-206.

Materialism and Consumeristic Philanthropy

Robert Kreuzbauer, Nanyang Technological University, Singapore
Chi-yue Chiu, Nanyang Technological University, Singapore

EXTENDED ABSTRACT

Major charity organizations offer products for donors to communicate their philanthropic intentions and behaviors through consumption. Examples are backpacks, shirts or various accessories from the Red Cross or the Salvation Army with prominent display of the charitable organization's logo on the products. Some charitable organizations even license their logo to for-profit companies and consumers can buy these logos to express their support for charitable causes (Varadarajan and Menon 1988). A notable example is Product (Red), a consumer brand licensed to American Express, Apple, Emporio Armani and other partner companies to raise money for the Global Fund to Fight AIDS, Tuberculosis and Malaria. Each partner company creates a product with the Product (Red) logo and agrees to donate a percentage of the profit to the Global Fund. We posit that consumer support for this kind of *consumeristic philanthropy* arises in part from the need to signal one's status through brand consumption. Because according to previous research (cf. Belk 1988) materialistic consumers, compared to the less materialistic ones, have a greater need for status signaling through consumption, we hypothesize that more materialistic consumers would value consumeristic philanthropy more. However, although materialistic consumers may lack an intrinsic motive to engage in philanthropic behaviors, they may be motivated by the need to signal their status through engaging in such behaviors. Indeed, aside from altruism, charitable giving can be motivated by other motives. For example, individuals may engage in charitable giving because it allows them to project a certain social image to others (Aaker and Akutsu 2009). Thus, although materialistic consumers may not be motivated to give to charity out of intrinsic motivation, they may do so if the charitable giving activity is congruent with their value orientations. We posit that materialistic consumers will find campaigns that couple charitable contributions with appeals to material possessions particularly appealing because they confer opportunities for signaling their status through consumption. As our three studies will show when materialistic consumers are given the opportunity to signal their status through consumeristic philanthropy (i.e. a charitable contribution combined with a material possession or consumer object such as Gap Red), these individuals are even more generous than non-materialistic individuals.

We tested our hypotheses in three studies that used different methods. In study one, we surveyed consumers' levels of materialism, support for consumeristic philanthropy and non-consumeristic philanthropy, and their motivation to signal status through consumption. The results showed that materialism is positively correlated with the motivation to signal status and the support for consumeristic philanthropy. We also show that this positive relationship between materialism and support for consumeristic philanthropy is mediated by the motivation to signal status via consumption.

Studies 2 and 3 use a variant of Haidt's (2007) monetary evaluation task to assess the value consumers attached to status signaling through consumption (study 2) and to consumeristic philanthropy (study 3).

Inspired by this idea, Haidt (2007) designed the monetary evaluation task to assess the "cash values" individuals assigned to moral values. The task consists of two parts. Part 1 assesses the baseline value respondents would assign to a certain action ("How much money would it take to get you to stick a pin into your palm?"). Part 2 assesses the value respondents would assign to the same action when it implicates a certain moral value (e.g., "How much money would it take to get you to stick a pin into the palm of a child you don't know?"). The discrepancy between the two values is used to indicate the value the respondents assign to the moral value under assessment (inflicting harm to innocent people). This assessment technique has been found to be useful for overcoming socially desirable responding and hence useful for capturing socially sensitive responses (e.g., moral values). The current research concerns the value consumers attach to prosocial behaviors. To avoid potential validity threats caused by socially desirable responding, we modified Haidt's monetary evaluation task to assess the values consumers attach to status signaling through consumption (study 2) and the values consumers attach to consumeristic philanthropy (study 3). In both studies, we also measured the participants' levels of materialism. Also study 2 and 3 confirmed our main predictions that levels of materialism will is positively correlated with the values consumers attach to status signaling through consumption and to consumeristic philanthropy.

The current research makes three major contributions. First, it seeks to show that consumeristic philanthropy is mediated by a greater need to signal status through consumption among materialistic consumers. This knowledge is useful because it examines the role of consumer values in the support for charitable sales promotions. In this context the current research studies consumer support for consumeristic philanthropy to materialism which can explain why charitable sales promotions tend to be more successful for conspicuous luxury products (Strahilevitz 1999; Strahilevitz and Myers 1998).

Second, Rindfleisch et al. (2009) commented that materialism research has focused on the nature, antecedents and well-being consequences of materialism. Relatively little is known about the relationship of materialism to other consumer behaviors. The current research fills this gap by examining how materialism and its attendant need to signal status predict consumer support for consumeristic philanthropy.

Finally, the present research may challenge the stereotypic portrayal of materialistic consumers as individuals who care only about acquisition and possession of materialistic goods and who are therefore indifferent to social concerns (Van Hiel et al. 2010). The current research seeks to show that both materialistic and non-materialistic consumers can be motivated to support charitable giving. Our proposition gives rise to the counterintuitive prediction that when given the opportunity to signal their status through consumeristic philanthropy, materialistic consumers may be even more motivated than non-materialistic ones to support charitable activities.

Findings from a survey of 259 American consumers (study 1) support this hypothesis and show that the status signaling mediates the hypothesized relationship. Two experiments (studies 2 and 3) that used a modified monetary evaluation task revealed that more materialistic consumers assign greater value to status signaling through brand consumption and consumeristic philanthropy. These results offer a motivational explanation of consumeristic philanthropy and further clarify the role of materialism in brand consumption.

REFERENCES

Aaker, Jennifer and Toshi Akutsu (2009), "Why Do People Give? The Role of Identity in Giving," *Journal of Consumer Psychology,* 19 (3), 267-70.

Anderson, Jim (2009), "How Is Materialism Destroying Society?" Ezinearticles.com. Available on October 15 at http://ezinearticles.com/?How-is-Materialism-Destroying-Society?&id=3000730

Auerbach, Randy P. Chad M. McWhinnie, Marc Goldfinger, John R. Z. Abela, Xiongzhao Zhu and Shuqiao Yao (2010), "The Cost of Materialism in a Collectivistic Culture: Predicting Risky Behavior Engagement in Chinese Adolescents," *Journal of Clinical and Child Psychology*, 39 (1), 117-27.

Belk, Russell W. (1985), "Materialism: Trait aspects of living in the material world," *Journal of Consumer Rsearch, 12* (December), 265-80.

--- (1988), "Possessions and the Extended Self," Journal of Consumer Research, 15 (September), 139-68.

Burroughs, James E. And Aric Rindfleisch (2002), "Materialism and Well-Being: A Conflicting Values Perspective," *Journal of Consumer Research*, 29 (December), 348-70.

Chaney, Isabella and Nitha Dolli (2001), "Cause-Related Marking in New Zealand," *International Journal of Nonprofit and Voluntary Sector Marketing*, 6 (2), 156-63.

Chaplin, Lan Nguyen and Deborah Roedder John (2005), "The development of self-brand connections in children and adolescents,", *Journal of Consumer Research*, (June), 119-129.

Cui, Yanli, Elizabeth S. Trent, Pauline M. Sullivan, and Grace N. Matiru (2003), "Cause-Related Marketing: How Generation Y Responds," *International Journal of Retail and Distribution Management*, 31 (6), 310-20.

Edwards, Jeffrey R. (1994). Regression analysis as an alternative to difference scores. *Journal of Management, 20* (3), 683-89.

Egri, Carolyn P. and David A. Ralston (2004), "Generation Cohorts and Personal Values: A Comparison of China and the United States," *Organizational Science*, 15 (2), 210-20.

Ellen, Pam S., Lois A. Mohr and Deborah J. Webb (2000), "Charitable Programs and the Retailer: Do They Mix?" *Journal of Retailing*, 76 (3), 393-406.

Escalas, Jennifer Edson and James Bettman (2003), "You Are What You Eat: The Influence of Reference Groups on Consumers' Connections to Brands," *Journal of Consumer Psychology*, 13 (3), 339-48.

Griskevicius, Vladas, Joshua M. Tybur, and Bram Van den Bergh (2010), "Going Green to Be Seen: Status, Reputation, and Conspicuous Conservation," *Journal of Personality and Social Psychology,* 98 (3), 392-404.

Gneezy, Ayelet, Uri Gneezy, Leif D. Nelson, and Amber Brown (2010), "Sharing Social Responsibility: A Field Experiment in Pay-What-You-Want Pricing and Charitable Giving," *Science*, 329 (5938), 325-327.

Grouzet, Frederick M. E., Tim Kasser, Aaron Ahuvia, Jose M. F. Dols, Youngmee Kim, Sing Lau, Richard M. Ryan, Shaun Saunders, Peter Schmuck and Kennon M. Sheldon (2005), "The Structure of Goal Contents Across 15 Cultures," *Journal of Personality and Social Psychology,* 89 (5), 800-16.

Fromm, Eric (1976), *To Have or To Be?* New York: Harper and Row.

Haidt, Jonathan (2007), "The New Synthesis in Moral Psychology," *Science*, 316 (5827), 998-1002.

Han, Young Jee, Joseph C. Nunes and Xavier Dreze (2010), "Signaling Status with Luxury Goods: The Role of Brand Prominence," *Journal of Marketing*, 74 (July), 15-30.

Kasser, Tim (2002), *The High Price of Materialism*. Boston: MIT Press.

Kasser, Tim and Richard M. Ryan (1993), "The Dark Side of the American Dream: Correlates of Intrinsic and Extrinsic Goals," *Journal of Personality and Social Psychology*, 65 (2), 410-22.

Kasser, Tim, Richard M. Ryan, M. Zax and A. J. Sameroff (1995), "The Relations of Maternal and Social Environments to Late Adolescents' Materialistic and Prosocial Values," *Developmental Psychology*, 21 (6), 348-51.

Kropp, Federic, Stephen J. S. Holden, and Anne M. Lavack (2006), "Cause-Related Marketing and Values in Australia," *International Journal of Nonprofit and Voluntary Sector Marketing*, 4 (1), 69-80.

Richins Marsha L (1994a), "Valuing Things: The Public and Private Meanings of Possessions," *Journal of Consumer Researcher*, 21 (December), 504-21.

--- (1994b), "Special Possessions and the Expression of Material Values," *Journal of Consumer Research*, 21 (December), 522-31.

--- (2004), "The Material Values Scale: A Re-inquiry into Its Measurement Properties and the Development of a Short Form," *Journal of Consumer Research*, 31 (June), 209-19.

Richins, Marsha L. and Scott Dawson (1992), "A Consumer Values Orientation for Materialism and Its Measurement: Scale Development and Validation," *Journal of Consumer Research*, 19 (December), 303-16.

Rindfleisch, Aric, and James E. Burroughs (2004), "Terrifying thoughts, terrible materialism? Contemplations on a terror management account of materialism and consumer behavior," *Journal of Consumer Psychology,* 14 (3), 219-224.

Rindfleisch, Aric, James E. Burroughs, & Nancy Wong (2009), "The Safety of Objects: Materialism, Existential Insecurity, and Brand Connection," *Journal of Consumer Research,* 36 (June), 1-16.

Strahilevitz, Michal (1999), "The Effects of Product Type and Donation Magnitude on Willingness to Pay More on a Charity-Linked Brand", *Journal of Consumer Psychology*, 8 (3), 215-41.

Strahilevitz, Michal, and John G. Myers (1998), "Donations to Charity as Purchase Incentives: How Well They Work May Depend on What You Are Trying to Sell," *Journal of Consumer Research*, 24 (1), 434-46.

Tatzel, Miriam (2002), "Money Worlds and Well-Being: An Integration of Money Dispositions, Materialism, and Price-Related Behaviors," *Journal of Economic Psychology*, 23 (February), 103-26.

Van Hiel, Alain, Ilse Cornelis, and Arne Roets (2010), "To Have or To be? A Comparison of Materialism-Based Theories and Self-Determination Theory as Explanatory Frameworks of Prejudice. *Journal of Personality*, 78 (3), 1037-70.

Varadarajan, R. Rajan and Anil Menon (1988), "Cause-Related Marketing: A Coalignment of Marketing Strategy and Corporate Philanthropy," *Journal of Marketing*, 52 (4), 58-74.

Wang, Jeff and Malanie Wallendorf (2006), "Materialism, Status Signaling, and Product Satisfaction," *Journal of Academy of Marketing Science*, 34 (4), 494-505.

Wong, Nancy Y. and Aaron Ahuvia (1998), "Personal Taste and Family Face: Self-Concepts and Luxury Consumption in Confucian and Western Societies," *Psychology and Marketing*, 15 (5), 423-41.

Contrast and Assimilation in Response to a Brand Association Prime: The Case of Cross-Category Brand Alliances

Laura Smarandescu, Iowa State University, USA
Randall Rose, University of South Carolina, USA
Douglas Wedell, University of South Carolina, USA

EXTENDED ABSTRACT

Recent years have witnessed a significant increase in various forms of inter-firm cooperation (e.g., joint ventures, promotional agreements, advertising brand alliances), through which firms pool resources to pursue specific market opportunities. Advertising brand alliances are appealing to firms because they lead to competitive advantages that otherwise would be beyond a company's reach, such as access to new markets and increased demand through leveraging the strengths of two brands (Cooke and Ryan 2000; Eisenhardt and Schoonhoven 1996; Hagedoorn 1993). Little is known about the effect of these alliances on perceptions of brand attributes, or about the inferences made by individuals when primed with these associations. This work focuses on the inference processes used by individuals when they are primed with associations of brands with different memory schemas, belonging to different product categories. Examples of such alliances are between Hewlett Packard and Starbucks, Tide and Oshkosh, Whirlpool and Day Runner, Nike and iPod.

Although research in the area of brand extensions and comparative advertising has previously investigated consumer brand inference, the present work focuses on the inferences that take place when individuals are exposed to an associative prime featuring different brands, with different memory associations (unlike brand extension research), belonging to different product categories (unlike comparative advertising), and in the absence of an explicit comparative claim.

Context plays an important role in a variety of consumer judgments. Context effects have been examined in the areas of consumer choice (Huber, Payne, and Puto 1982; Huber and Puto 1983; Simonson and Tversky 1992), comparative advertising (Manning et al. 2001; Rose et al. 1993), product judgment (Janiszewski, Silk, and Cooke 2003), and product assortment (Chernev 2003). Two types of context effects on people's judgment of a stimulus have been reliably demonstrated in the marketing and social sciences literature: assimilation and contrast. Assimilation is known to occur when judgments of a stimulus are displaced toward a contextual stimulus and refers to a positive relation between the value assigned to the contextual stimulus and the value attributed to the target. On the other hand, contrast occurs when judgments of a stimulus are displaced away from the contextual stimulus, and refers to a negative relation between the values assigned to the contextual stimulus and the target.

Our research shows that each brand partner in a cross-category brand alliance creates a context that is used as an anchor for judgments of the other brand attributes, and we provide evidence that the inference processes that occur are moderated by individual differences in information processing strategy, associated with differences in need for cognition (NFC). As such, allied brand attributes may produce assimilative anchor effects that move perceptions toward the ally's attribute value, or the anchors may serve as standards of comparison that produce contrast and move perceptions away from the ally's attribute value (Wedell, Hicklin, and Smarandescu 2007).

Study 1 was a 2 (alliance present/ absent) x 2 (high/ low NFC, based on a median split) between-subjects design, and examined how priming a brand association influences judgments of non-alignable brand attributes. We found that low and high NFC individuals adopt different inference making strategies when they are primed with a brand alliance. The effects are driven by the more extreme, and thus

salient, user ratings provided for the contextual brand. Data indicate that low NFC individuals used the non-alignable information provided about the contextual brand as an anchor for their judgments of the target brand attributes. On the other hand, high NFC individuals partialed out the non-alignable information given about the contextual brand from their judgment of the target brand on a salient attribute and adjusted their evaluations of this target attribute in a direction opposite to the contextual brand.

Study 2 was a 3 (no alliance control/ low load alliance/ high load alliance) x 2 (high/ low NFC, based on a median split) between-subjects experimental design, and investigated whether the effects of a brand alliance prime on perceptions of a target non-alignable attribute are moderated by individuals' ability (manipulated by cognitive load) and processing motivation (measured by NFC) to process the alliance information. We found that individuals' responses to cross-category brand alliances are sensitive to situational and individual difference factors. Low NFC individuals assimilated their judgments in the direction of the contextual brand irrespective of cognitive load. This result is in line with Martin, Seta, and Crelia (1990) and provides support that assimilation is the default judgment for low NFC. Responses of high NFC individuals were influenced by the amount of cognitive resources they had available at brand alliance encoding. In conditions of limited cognitive ability, high NFC individuals formed unbiased judgments that were not affected by the contextual partner. However, when they had the ability to correct their initial judgment for the *perceived* bias introduced by presence of the alliance partner they over-adjusted their judgment of the target attribute in a direction opposite to the context of the brand ally, a finding supporting Wegener and Petty's (1993) flexible correction model. One key aspect of the flexible correction model is that it assumes that corrections are aimed at removing *perceived* rather than *actual* bias. Hence, high NFC individuals made unbiased judgments under high load, but corrected their judgments for the perceived bias introduced by the contextual brand when they had extra cognitive resources.

Finally, results of study 2 suggest that given enough cognitive resources, high NFC individuals engage in correction at the stage of brand alliance encoding, through a memory updating mechanism and not at the judgment stage. This provides evidence that context effects observed in brand alliances are due to background context and not to the effect of the recent context as observed in classic priming studies.

REFERENCES

Cacioppo, John T., Richard E. Petty, and Chuan F. Kao (1984), "The Efficient Assessment of Need for Cognition," *Journal of Personality Assessment*, 48 (June), 306-307.

Chernev, Alex (2003), "Product Assortment and Individual Decision Processes," *Journal of Personality and Social Psychology*, 85(1), 155-162.

Cooke, Sinead and Paul Ryan (2000), "Global and Transnational Brand Alliances: A Conceptual Investigation of Typologies," *Marketing in a Global Economy Proceedings*, 336-342.

Eisenhardt, Kathleen and Claudia Bird Schoonhoven (1996), "Strategic Alliance Formation in Entrepreneurial Firms: Strategic Needs and Social Opportunities for Cooperation," *Organization Science*, 7.

Gilbert, Daniel T. (2002), "Inferential correction," in *Heuristics and Biases: The Psychology of Intuitive Judgment,* ed. T. Gilovich, D. Griffin, and D. Kahneman, Cambridge, England: Cambridge University Press, 167-184.

Hagedoorn, John (1993), "Understanding the Rationale of Strategic Technology Partnering: Interorganizational Modes of Cooperation and Sectoral Differences," *Strategic Management Journal*, 14, 371-385.

Helson, Harry (1947), "Adaptation-Level as a Frame of Reference for Prediction in Psychophysical Data," *American Journal of Psychology,* 60, 1-29.

---(1964), *Adaptation-Level theory*. New York: Harper and Row.

Herr, Paul M. (1986), "Consequences of Priming: Judgment and Behavior," *Journal of Personality and Social Psychology*, 51 (December), 1106-1115.

---, Steven J. Sherman, S. J., and Russell H. Fazio (1983), "On the Consequences of Priming: Assimilation and Contrast effects," *Journal of Experimental Social Psychology,* 19 (July), 323-340.

Higgins, Tori E., William S. Rholes, and Carl R. Jones (1977), "Category Accessibility and Impression formation," *Journal of Experimental Social Psychology,* 13 (March), 141-154.

Huber, Joel, John W. Payne, and Christopher Puto (1982), "Adding Asymmetrically Dominated Alternatives: Violations of Regularity and Similarity Hypothesis," *Journal of Consumer Research*, 9 (June), 90-99.

--- and Christopher Puto (1983), "Market Boundaries and Product Choice: Illustrating Attraction and Substitution Effects," *Journal of Consumer Research*, 10 (June), 31-45.

Janiszewski, Chris A., Tim Silk, and Allan D.J. Cooke (2003), "Different Scales for Different Frames: The Role of Subjective Scales and Experience in Explaining Attribute Framing Effects," *Journal of Consumer Research*, 30 (December), 311-327.

Manning, Kenneth C., Paul W. Miniard, Michael J. Barone, and Randall L. Rose (2001), "Understanding the Mental Representations Created by Comparative Advertising", *Journal of Advertising*, 30 (2), 27-40.

Martin, Leonard L. (1986), "Set/ Reset: Use and Disuse of Concepts in Impression Formation," *Journal of Personality and Social Psychology*, 51 (September), 493-504.

---, John L. Seta, and Rick A. Crelia (1990), "Assimilation and Contrast as a Function of People's Willingness and Ability to Expend Effort in Forming an Impression," *Journal of Personality and Social Psychology,* 59 (July), 27-37.

Meyers-Levy, Joan and Brian Sternthal (1993), "A Two-Factor Explanation of Assimilation and Contrast Effects," *Journal of Marketing Research*, 30 (August), 359-368.

Miniard, Paul W., Randall L. Rose, Kenneth C. Manning, and Michael J. Barone (1998), "Tracking the Effects of Comparative and Noncomparative Advertising with Relative and Non-relative Measures: A Further Examination of the Framing Correspondence Hypothesis," *Journal of Business Research*, 41(February), 137-143.

Petty, Richard E. and Duane T. Wegener (1993), "Flexible Correction Processes in Social Judgment: Correcting for Context-Induced Contrast," *Journal of Experimental Social Psychology*, 29 (March), 137-165.

Rose, Randall L., Paul W. Miniard, Michael J. Barone, Kenneth C. Manning, and Brian D. Till (1993), "When Persuasion Goes Undetected: The Case of Comparative Advertising," *Journal of Marketing Research*, 30 (August), 315-331.

Simonson, Itamar and Amos Tversky (1992), "Choice in Context: Tradeoff Contrast and Extremeness Aversion," *Journal of Marketing Research*, 29 (August), 281-295.

Stapel, Diederik A. and Piotr Winkielman (1998), "Assimilation and Contrast as a Function of Context-Target Similarity, Distinctiveness, and Dimensional Relevance," *Personality and Social Psychology Bulletin*, 24 (June), 634-646.

Wedell, Douglas. H. (1991), "Distinguishing Among Models of Contextually Induced Preference Reversals," *Journal of Experimental Psychology: Learning, Memory, and Cognition,* 17, 767-778.

Wedell, Douglas H., Suzanne M. Karpick, and Laura Smarandescu (2007), "Contrasting Models of Assimilation and Contrast," in *Assimilation and Contrast in Social Psychology,* eds. D. Stapel and J. Suls, New York: Psychology Press.

---, Parducci, Allan, and Edward R. Geiselmann (1987), "A Formal Analysis of Ratings of Physical Attractiveness: Successive Contrast and Simultaneous Assimilation," *Journal of Experimental Social Psychology*, 23 (May), 230-249.

Wegener, Duane T. and Richard E. Petty (1995), "Flexible Correction Processes in Social Judgment: The Role of Naive Theories in Corrections for Perceived Bias," *Journal of Personality and Social Psychology*, 68 (January), 36-51.

The Impact of Research Design on the Compromise Effect

Nico Neumann, University of New South Wales, Australia
Ashish Sinha, University of New South Wales, Australia
Ulf Böckenholt, Northwestern University, USA

EXTENDED ABSTRACT

The compromise effect, which is a symmetric extremeness aversion context effect (Simonson and Tversky 1992), has been referred to as one of the most relevant and robust behavioral phenomena in marketing (Kivetz, Netzer, and Srinivasan 2004). However, even though the compromise effect has been proven to be sizeable and robust across many scenarios, recent articles have raised concerns: in a critical essay, Simonson (2008) initiates a debate about the external validity of work dealing with constructed preferences, making no exemption for extremeness aversion. He argues that the ease of demonstrating certain preference reversals may have caused many scholars to overstate the role of constructed preferences. Simonson (2008) receives support from Kivetz, Netzer, and Schrift (2008) and Dhar and Novemsky (2008) for many of his arguments.

In this study, we attempt to advance the debate on the meaning of different methodologies for this research area. Using meta-analytic evidence, we examine the impact of research design variables on the results of the compromise effect. We test moderators related to sample and experimental characteristics, such as the influence of attribute-types, choice set comparison types, extension types, the range effect (i.e. distance of options from the middle), sample size and choice tasks (e.g. within- Vs. between-subject designs).

For our analysis, we synthesized 83 cases from 13 studies and modeled the difference between the log-odds ratios (Lipsey and Wilson 2001; Van Houwelingen, Arends, and Stijnen 2002) of the middle option in the experimental condition (middle option share/ others' share) and that in the control condition (share of option that becomes middle option/ other's share) for the absolute and relative shares (two effect sizes from one case). To account for the dependencies of the two effect sizes that stem from the same observation and for the dependency of each case on the corresponding study, we estimated a bivariate multilevel model: the first level consists of the two outcome measures, the second level of the observations, and the third level of the studies that provide the observations. We carried out maximum likelihood estimation for the 3- level model, using the inverse sampling variances as weights.

The results of the meta-analysis confirm that extremeness aversion significantly affects choice behavior and is likely to result in context effects. Across 83 comparisons of choice sets, the introduction of another option leads on average to both absolute and relative share increases of the product that becomes the compromise option when controlling for research design effects. This means that the included studies represent evident violations of the IIA principle, which assumes the relative share of options to stay constant across choice sets. Strategically, the significant increase in relative share demonstrates that the introduction of another product is assumed to take more share away from the other extreme product than from the more similar compromise option.

On average, extremeness aversion also enhances the absolute share of the middle option. However, this effect is more likely for the comparison of two triplets than for the addition of another option to a binary choice set. Nevertheless, we can conclude that there are compromise effects that can violate the regularity axiom, in particular for durable product categories.

In line with previous work (Simonson and Tversky 1992), the present study demonstrates asymmetry in extremeness aversion for price and quality. Relative share changes are likely to be smaller for choice tasks that involve price-quality trade-offs, whereby this impact is moderated by the extension type. For high-extensions, the relative share of the compromise option after the treatment tends to be greater than for low-extensions. Hence, on average, the introduction of a high-quality product takes away more share from the other extreme than the introduction of a low-quality product does. These findings are in agreement with the concept of loss aversion, which was argued to be less strong or not evident for price (Novemsky and Kahneman 2005a, 2005b).

In addition, the results of our model do not suggest a range effect of options on the compromise effect strength. This finding is in agreement with the work of Tsetsos, Usher, and Chater (2010), who find mixed results for the choice of a compromise option as a function of the distance between extreme options in computational simulations.

According to our meta-analysis, there are no significant differences between undergraduates and other sample groups or between within- and between-subject designs for the compromise effect. Sample size appears not to significantly affect the size of the compromise effect either.

Overall, the results suggest that experimental characteristics have a major impact on the obtained extremeness aversion results, while sample characteristics have little impact. We conclude with a discussion of the practical implications of the individual research design effects for future studies. We hope that this work offers a fertile ground and helpful recommendations for further studying extremeness aversion.

REFERENCES

Chernev, Alexander (2004), "Extremeness aversion and attribute-balance effects in choice," *Journal of Consumer Research,* 31(2), 249-263.

Chernev, Alexander (2005), "Context effects without a context: Attribute balance as a reason for choice," *Journal of Consumer Research,* 32(2), 213-223.

Derbaix, Christian (1983), "Perceived risk and risk relievers: An empirical investigation," *Journal of Economic Psychology,* 3(1), 19-38.

Dhar, Ravi, and Nathan Novemsky (2008), "Beyond rationality: The content of preferences," *Journal of Consumer Psychology,* 18(3), 175-178.

Dhar, Ravi, Stephen M. Nowlis, and Steven J. Sherman (2000), "Trying hard or hardly trying: An analysis of context effects in choice," *Journal of Consumer Psychology,* 9(4), 189-200.

Dhar, Ravi, and Itamar Simonson (2003), "The effect of forced choice on choice," *Journal of Marketing Research,* 146-160.

Ferber, Robert (1977), "Research by convenience," *Journal of Consumer Research,* 4(1), 57-58.

Goukens, Caroline, Siegfried Dewitte, and Luk Warlop (2009), "Me, myself, and my choices: The influence of private self-awareness on choice," *Journal of Marketing Research,* 46(5), 682-692.

Ha, Young-Won, Sehoon Park, and Hee-Kyung Ahn (2009), "The Influence of Categorical Attributes on Choice Context Effects," *Journal of Consumer Research,* 36(3), 463-477.

Hardie, Bruce G. S., Eric J. Johnson, and Peter S. Fader (1993), "Modeling loss aversion and reference dependence effects on brand choice," *Marketing Science,* 12(4), 378.

Heath, Timothy B., and Subimal Chatterjee (1995), "Asymmetric decoy effects on lower-quality versus higher-quality brands: Meta-analytic and experimental evidence," *Journal of Consumer Research,* 22(3), 268-284.

Huber, Joel, John W. Payne, and Christopher Puto (1982), "Adding asymmetrically dominated alternatives: Violations of regularity and the similarity hypothesis," *Journal of Consumer Research,* 9(1), 90.

Kivetz, Ran, Oded Netzer, and Rom Schrift (2008), "The synthesis of preference: Bridging behavioral decision research and marketing science," *Journal of Consumer Psychology,* 18(3), 179-186.

Kivetz, Ran, Oded Netzer, and V. Seenu Srinivasan (2004), "Alternative models for capturing the compromise effect," *Journal of Marketing Research,* 41(3), 237-257.

Lehmann, Donald R., and Yigang Pan (1994), "Context effects, new brand entry, and consideration sets," *Journal of Marketing Research,* 31(3), 364-374.

Lipsey, Mark W., and David B. Wilson (2001), *Practical meta-analysis,* Thousand Oaks: Sage Publications.

Luce, R. Duncan (1977), "The choice axiom after twenty years," *Journal of Mathematical Psychology,* 15(3), 215-233.

Mourali, Mehdi, Ulf Böckenholt, and Michel Laroche (2007), "Compromise and attraction effects under prevention and promotion motivations," *Journal of Consumer Research,* 34(2), 234-247.

Novemsky, Nathan, and Daniel Kahneman (2005a), "The boundaries of loss aversion," *Journal of Marketing Research,* 42(2), 119-128.

Novemsky, Nathan, and Daniel Kahneman (2005b), "How do intentions affect loss aversion?," *Journal of Marketing Research,* 42(2), 139-140.

Pocheptsova, Anastasiya, On Amir, Ravi Dhar, and Roy F. Baumeister (2009), "Deciding without resources: Resource depletion and choice in context," *Journal of Marketing Research,* 46(3), 344-355.

Prelec, Drazen, Birger Wernerfelt, and Florian Zettelmeyer (1997), "The role of inference in context effects: Inferring what you want from what is available," *Journal of Consumer Research,* 24(1), 118-126.

Riley, Richard D., John R. Thompson, and Keith R. Abrams (2008), "An alternative model for bivariate random-effects meta-analysis when the within-study correlations are unknown," *Biostatistics,* 9(1), 172.

Sheng, Shibin, Andrew M. Parker, and Kent Nakamoto (2005), "Understanding the mechanism and determinants of compromise effects," *Psychology and Marketing,* 22(7), 591-609.

Simonson, Itamar (1989), "Choice based on reasons: The case of attraction and compromise effects," *Journal of Consumer Research,* 16(2), 158.

Simonson, Itamar (2008), "Will I Like A Medium Pillow? Another Look at Constructed and Inherent Preferences," *Journal of Consumer Psychology,* 18(3), 155–169.

Simonson, Itamar, and Amos Tversky (1992), "Choice in context: Tradeoff contrast and extremeness aversion," *Journal of Marketing Research,* 29(3), 281-295.

Tsetsos, Konstantinos, Marius Usher, and Nick Chater (2010), "Preference reversal in multiattribute choice," *Psychological Review,* 117(4), 1275-1291.

Van Houwelingen, Hans C., Lidia R. Arends, and Theo Stijnen (2002), "Advanced methods in meta-analysis: multivariate approach and meta-regression," *Statistics in Medicine,* 21(4), 589-624.

Wedell, Douglas H. (1991), "Distinguishing among models of contextually induced preference reversals," *Journal of Experimental Psychology: Learning, Memory, and Cognition,* 17(4), 767-778.

This page intentionally left blank.

Film Festival 2011

Marylouise Caldwell and Paul Henry
The University of Sydney.

The ACR Film Festival has now been running for over ten years. This milestone has been achieved in no small measure due to the enormous encouragement and perseverance of the founding co-chairs—Russell Belk and Robert Kozinets. These innovative consumer researchers consistently propelled the growth of audiovisual representation across many years through foundation of the ACR Film Festival, running numerous audiovisual training workshops, publishing several special audiovisual issues in Consumption, Markets, and Culture, publishing articles about how to do video ethnography; as well as production and presentation of a substantial body of their own high quality consumer films. Their personal encouragement also sparked a passionate interest amongst many other researchers in diverse part of the globe. Over this period the Film Festival has attracted entries from every continent, across a broad range of consumer topics, and employing a wide variety of filmic styles.

This global diversity has continued with the 2011 program. Successful entries were drawn from Austria, Canada, Finland, Mexico, New Zealand, and the USA. Two awards were presented. The Judges Choice award went to Joel Hietanen, Joonas Rokka, and Risto Roman from Finland. This was a marvellous piece of filmmaking shot in Helsinki, New York, and London, which explored adherents of the electronic music genre called dubstep. The work really showed the benefits of carefully planning the shoot in advance, the use of insiders as interviewers and guides, and the importance of clearly defining the style and pacing of the film before production begins. The result was an impressive piece of work that held the audience's attention throughout, immersed them in the subculture, and also revealed substantial tensions of theoretical interest. This is the kind of work that demonstrates the fantastic potential of film ethnography in consumer research—the kind of work that we would love to see a lot more of. The second award was for the People's Choice. This was decided by audience vote. The winners were Tracy Harmon and Merlyn Griffiths from the USA. This film explored the reinterpretation of commercial brands for personal expression in ways that were not intended by the marketers. It was a very interesting site of study where informants often situated branded characters in new stories. The Film Festival submissions included a diverse set of other interesting topics that ranged across audience reaction to flash mobs, instilling dietary awareness in preschoolers, religious fervour of sports fans, generational views about respect, dressing up, self actualisation in the workplace, and impact of mobile communications.

This year a workshop session was also held in which participants discussed future opportunities and directions for use of audiovisual formats in consumer research. The session sought to further illuminate Belk and Kozinets' four criteria for assessing consumer ethnography films. These include Topical, Theoretical, Theatrical, and Technical. Participants proposed alternative ways in which these four qualities can be simultaneously advanced in future ACR Film Festivals. In particular, this discussion focussed on ways to reconcile both the theoretical and theatrical ambitions to produce both more rigorous and compelling audiovisual outputs. It has now been clearly demonstrated in numerous wonderful productions that the two qualities can indeed be reconciled. Audiovisual has been shown to be a particularly strong vehicle in fostering visceral responses in audiences and amplifying emotional understandings of informants' social conditions and lived experiences. Really great audiovisual productions strive to tell compelling stories that take the audience along with them in an immersive manner—much like the performative idea of cathartic experience. The additional challenge is to ensure that these stories also have compelling theoretical relevance. There is certainly no conceptual reason why this cannot be achieved in audiovisual presentations. The combination of researcher insights, attention to storytelling, and technical training will ensure this goal is further advanced. In sum, as the technology continues to become even more accessible and user friendly we see tremendous scope for a discipline that studies the socio-emotional determinates of consumer life.

The Customer is Always Right
Kathleen O'Donnell, San Francisco State University, USA

As a kid, Kathy never got the whole "dress up thing." So who would have predicted that 40 years later she would find herself searching for understanding on the playa at Burning Man? Join her as she seeks to uncover the truth about the women of Burning Man, their costumes, and herself in The Costumer is Always Right.

Being Connected: Perceived Customer Value in the Smartphone Age
Monika Koller, WU Vienna, Austria
Alexander Zauner, WU Vienna, Austria
Arne Floh, WU Vienna, Austria
Camillo Foramitti, WU Vienna, Austria

This film explores the role of multidimensional perceived customer value in the field of wireless telecommunications. Consumers' value perceptions derived from their cell phones and wireless services are analyzed along the framework of four value dimensions (functional, economical, emotional, and social) introduced by Sweeney and Soutar in 2001.

Advances in Consumer Research
Volume 39, ©2011

'Pushing the Scene': Tensions and Emergence in an Accelerated Marketplace Culture

Joel Hietanen, Aalto University School of Economics, Finland
Joonas Rokka, Aalto University School of Economics, Finland
Risto Roman, Helsinki University, Finland

We consider how contemporary marketplace cultures emerge and unfold in the accelerated tensions of cultural capital and the proliferation of access through digitalization and the global reach of the internet. Our context is the negotiation between producers/consumers in the emergent and vibrant scene of an electronic music genre called dubstep.

'Post-Materialist Work': Emerging Self-Actualization in the Video Industry

Joel Hietanen, Aalto University School of Economics, Finland
Hannu Uotila, Aalto University School of Economics, Finland

Post-materialist consumption has to date received limited interest in consumer research. This videography investigates how post-materialism is negotiated from the perspective of one's mundane work life in the context of small TV video production companies. Specifically, we uncovered how pursuits of self-actualization and emancipation occur in the practices of professionals.

Impact of an Operatic Flash Mob on Consumer Behavior

Philip Grant, Simon Fraser University, Canada
Anjali Bal, Simon Fraser University, Canada
Leyland Pitt, Simon Fraser University, Canada
Michael Parent, Simon Fraser University, Canada

This film examines the influence of an operatic flash mob on consumer behavior and consumer experience in a public market. Results of a field experiment indicate that the flash mob enhanced consumer arousal, connectedness and positive emotions, as well as consumer-to-consumer interaction.

Brand My Ride: Donks, Bubbles and Boxes: Extended Self-Brand Connections Among Auto Expressionists

Tracy Harmon, University of Dayton, USA
Merlyn Griffiths, University of North Carolina - Greensboro, USA

This film explores the symbolic phenomenon of car branding. We interview consumers who have branded their cars in an effort to present some aspect of themselves to others. We uncover hidden brand connections that are related to various aspects of their extended self-concepts.

Changing Consumer Behavior in Diet and Health: A Video Case Study on Local Matters

Anne Hu, Ohio State University, USA
Curtis Haugtvedt, The Ohio State University, USA

To combat diabetes and obesity in America's youth, Columbus, Ohio non-profit organization Local Matters' aims to change children's behavior and thoughts regarding food through a unique early education program that utilizes sensory and social activities involving food. Parents, teachers, students, and the organization's personnel were interviewed and taped. This short film documents their experiences and provides commentary on the efforts.

Soccer in Mexico: A Sacred Experience?

Claudia Quintanilla, Tecnologico de Monterrey, EGADE Business School, Mexico
Raquel Castaño, Tecnologico de Monterrey, EGADE Business School, Mexico
Maria Eugenia Perez, Tecnologico de Monterrey, EGADE Business School, Mexico

This film explores how devoted fans can turn a soccer game into an experience rich in sacred elements. The differences between "spectators" and "devoted fans" will help us understand the processes underlying distinctions between the sacred and the profane in Mexican fans' soccer experience.

Respect and the Media: A Generational View

Pippa Russell, University of Waikato, New Zealand
Carolyn Costley, University of Waikato, New Zealand
Lorraine Friend, University of Waikato, New Zealand

Respect is an important value for society. It shapes personal, social and business relationships. In our world of technology and social media are the values of respect changing? Do younger and older individuals experience respect differently? This film explores respect and media from the perspectives of Baby Boomers and Generation

Roundtable Summaries

ROUNDTABLE
Sheth Foundation 20th Anniversary Celebration

Chairs:
David Mick, University of Virginia, USA
Richard Lutz, University of Florida, USA

Participants:
Natalie Adkins, Drake University, USA
Russell Belk, York University
Dipayan Biswas, University of South Florida, USA
Larry Feick, University of Pittsburgh, USA
Joel Huber, Duke University, USA
Wes Hutchinson, University of Pennsylvania, USA
Richard Lutz, University of Florida, USA
Brett McFarren, University of Michigan, USA
David Mick, University of Virginia, USA
Chris Puto, University of Saint Thomas, USA
Carlos Torelli, University of Minnesota, USA

It is widely acknowledged that Jagdish Sheth was, and continues to be, one of the true pioneers of the field of consumer research, publishing in 1969 a landmark book with John Howard called *The Theory of Buyer Behavior* (New York: John Wiley & Sons). Based on the success of this book and other achievements in his career, Jag Sheth created the Sheth Foundation in 1991 with his wife, Madhuri.

The mission of the Sheth Foundation is to support the academic scholarship, publications, education, and research of tax-exempt, publicly-supported educational organizations, primarily focusing on the discipline of marketing, by providing support to grant awarding Recipient Organizations. Additionally, the Foundation provides support to other tax-exempt, publicly-supported organizations that are closely related in purpose or function to one or more of the Recipient Organizations and the activities of which carry out the purposes of one or more of the Primary Supported Organizations.

The Madhuri and Jagdish N. Sheth Foundation has had a long and strong affiliation with the Association for Consumer Research. For over a decade the Foundation has been providing support to rising scholars in the context of the ACR/Sheth Foundation Dissertation Grants, on the broad topics of public purpose research and global consumer research. All told, over 25 graduate students have been supported, totaling around $45,000. These students have come from an array of universities, including, for example, University of Illinois, University of Minnesota, Georgia Institute of Technology, University of British Columbia, and Concordia University-Montreal. The Foundation has also served to sponsor and support the Long-Term Contribution Award for articles published in the *Journal of Consumer Research* that are considered—after several years of retrospect—to have been among the most influential over time. Moreover, the Foundation has provided the monies to support the Franco Nicosia award, which is given to the authors of the best competitive paper submission each year at the North American Conference of ACR. Recently, the Foundation also gave a $9,500 matching grant to support Transformative Consumer Research at ACR, which focuses on the intersection of consumer behavior and well-being. In addition, the Foundation for several years paid for the distribution of the *Journal of Consumer Research* to over 100 academic libraries in developing nations worldwide. In total, the Foundation has given over $120,000 for a variety of purposes to support the mission and members of the Association for Consumer Research.

Unfortunately, as the Association for Consumer Research has grown, the range of its members who are aware of the Sheth Foundation's contributions and influence has inevitably shrunk, and among them many may not know about future opportunities for themselves or their doctoral students in seeking support from the Sheth Foundation via ACR. At the same time, there has to date been limited opportunities at ACR conferences for prior recipients of Sheth Foundation support to share their appreciation and to talk about the direct value of the support to their work, in specific projects and in going forward. To address these gaps of communication and solidarity within the context of the partnership between the Sheth Foundation and ACR, this roundtable will bring together past recipients of grants and awards funded by the Foundation and celebrate its role in consumer research. the roundtable will be structured to allow each panel member to discuss (a) the support they received, (b) its role in their career generally, (c) its positive influence on the trajectory of their work, and (d) the practical advice they would give to other ACR members in regard to writing/using grants as well as increasing their chances of making lasting scholarly contributions to the field.

The panel will consist of four seasoned and well-respected consumer researchers who have previously won the ACR/Sheth Long-Term Contribution Award at the *Journal of Consumer Research*. They are: Russ Belk, Joel Huber, Chris Puto, and Wes Hutchinson. These panel members will be especially encouraged, through the moderators and audience participation, to consider why and how they went about their award-winning work in the manner they did, particularly why and how it came to be widely regarded as both important and enduring.

The panel will also consist of four prior recipients of ACR/Sheth Dissertation Grants. They are Natalie Adkins, Dipayan Biswas, Brent McFerran, and Carlos Torelli. These panel members will be especially encouraged, based on their personal experiences, to discuss the process and best practices of writing an award-winning grant proposal for their dissertation. They will also offer advice on using grant monies in the most efficient and effective ways, for improving the potential success of consumer research.

Advances in Consumer Research
Volume 39, ©2011

The roundtable panel will be moderated by the current liaison of ACR to the Sheth Foundation, David Mick, and the previous liaison, Rich Lutz. Attendees of the roundtable will benefit not only from the panel's expertise, but also from the purposefully-selected, cross-fertilizing array of different topical and methodological interests among the panel members (e.g., experimentalists; qualitative researchers; attitudes, perception, and choice research; public policy issues; international marketing). Prior to the conference, the organizers of the roundtable (David Mick and Rich Lutz) will use the ACR's Knowledge Exchange forum to invite forthcoming conference attendees to post the kinds of questions and issues they would most like the panel members to address, in case there are any that the organizers would not have otherwise anticipated.

The session will begin with Rich Lutz giving a concise overview of the history of the Sheth Foundation and its partnership with ACR. Then each of the panel members will have approximately 5 – 7 minutes to talk about the value/meaning of their Sheth Foundation support, including how to maximize writing and using dissertation grants (dissertation grant recipients) or how to maximize the opportunity to make lasting contributions in the field (the long-term contribution award recipients). Rich and David will moderate questions from the audience. Then David will close with a summary and discussion about the future opportunities for maintaining and enhancing the partnership of ACR with the Sheth Foundation, looking also for suggestions from the panel and audience.

Overall, the intended benefits of this session are to (a) celebrate and spread the word about the partnership of ACR with the Sheth Foundation; (b) offer the opportunity for past Foundation support recipients to share their research experiences, accomplishments, and, advice; and (c) discuss how ACR and the Foundation might further enhance their partnership in moving forward.

Nudging our Way to a Better Tomorrow: Bridging the Gap between Consumer Behavior Research and Public Policy

Chair:
Avni Shah, Duke University, USA

Participants:
Jennifer Aaker, Stanford University, USA
Alan Andreasen, Georgetown University, USA
Dan Ariely, Duke University, USA
Paul Bloom, Duke University, USA
Julie Edell Britton, Duke University, USA
Darren Dahl, University of British Columbia, Canada
Gavan Fitzsimons, Duke University, USA
Vladas Griskevicius, University of Minnesota, USA
J. Jeffery Inman, University of Pittsburgh, USA
Punam Keller, Dartmouth College, USA
Angela Lee, Northwestern University, USA
Geeta Menon, New York University, USA
Baba Shiv, Stanford University, USA
Deborah Small, University of Pennsylvania, USA

Purpose

The purpose of this session is to bring together individuals who have contributed to research at the intersection between consumer behavior, marketing, and public policy initiatives. This roundtable discussion will focus on how marketing and consumer behavior researchers have been successful in the past at working with public policy makers to develop methods to influence consumer well-being. Discussion will also focus on ways to encourage researchers to ask research questions that can influence the policy arena and will serve as a forum for individuals to discuss directions for future research.

Rationale

Marketing and consumer research has transformed from an area that received little attention from public policy makers (Greyser, 1973; Wilkie & Gardner, 1974) to becoming a major player in decision-making in government and policy agencies, such as the Federal Trade Commission, the Food and Drug Administration, and Centers for Disease Control and Prevention. Policy makers are attracted to consumer research due to the ability to use multiple methodological approaches to determine what may influence consumer behavior and psychology and subsequently influence problems of interest to the public sector. Furthermore, the popularization of books such as Predictably Irrational and Nudge have elucidated the multitude of ways that consumer behavior research can successfully aid in the effort to improve consumer well being. As the confluence of consumer research and public policy initiatives becomes increasingly apparent, a roundtable session is crucial to showcase how researchers have successfully implemented and executed consumer research in a manner that is both theoretically and experimentally rigorous and yet influential in a spectrum of policy initiatives.

The relationship between public policy makers and consumer research is not a new one. The 1980s marked a major shift in the integration of consumer behavior research into public policy.

One specific example was the use of consumer research methods to investigate the prevalence of deception in advertisements (Maronick, 1990). In the 1990s, consumer research played an important role in providing research in food advertising (FTC 1994), telemarketing sales rules (FTC 1995), and also for the FDA's (1996) regulation for the distribution and sale of cigarettes to minors. More recently, consumer research has influenced food and calorie labeling. After several consumer research groups found that labeling diminished consumption behavior both pre- and post-purchase of an unhealthy high-calorie food item, the U.S. Food and Drug Administration is working to propose guidelines that will require more than 20 chain restaurants to include calorie counts for all menu items, including drinks. Despite the development of academic special interest groups and the important contributions from the *Journal of Public Policy and Marketing*, there is still much improvement to be made.

While, many of these initiatives have resulted in large-scale consumer welfare improvement efforts, there are still critics on both the policy side and the academic side. Academically, only about 3% of articles published in top tier journals concern issues of consumer research and policy (Hill, 2011). A survey conducted at the 1996 AMA/Sheth Doctoral Consortium showed that while two-thirds of doctoral students have an interest in learning about marketing and society, fewer than one in ten had ever taken a single course in this area (Wilkie & Moore, 1997). However, a shift is occurring in academia, with policy issues becoming increasingly popular. Leading researchers are focused on using behavioral techniques to aid in the effort to improve consumer health and welfare issues, retirement planning, fiscal policy, and environmental policy among others.

The timeliness of this roundtable session provides a unique opportunity. As a new generation of consumer researchers emerges, the need to push towards improving policy through research is ever increasing. Scholars who have already played a large role in shaping policy initiatives can productively discuss successful past methodologies. Directing research towards this domain is imperative, and a conference setting is the perfect venue for an integrative and multifaceted discussion amongst some of the preeminent scholars in the field. The researchers in this roundtable session have contributed substantially to public policy initiatives. Thus, they can shed light on how to be successful in this interdisciplinary area and also can provide valuable insight on some of the potential pitfalls, concerns, and questions raised by both reviewers and policy makers.

Our hope is that this roundtable will provide a launchpad for individuals at all stages in their career to brainstorm how consumer behavior research can further influence public policy initiatives. The experience that all of the session participants have should prove invaluable to students, young faculty members, and even those in the later stages of their career for developing ideas that can potentially have a large impact outside of academia.

References

Enforcement Policy Statement on Food Advertising, 59 Fed. Reg. 28388, 28393-94 (June 1, 1994).

Food and Drug Administration. (1996). Regulations restricting the sale and distribution of cigarettes and smokeless tobacco products to protect children and adolescents: final rule. Federal Register 61:41,314-75.

Greyser, Stephen A. (1973). Public policy and the marketing practitioner: Toward bridging the gap," in *Public Policy and Marketing Practices,* Fred C. Allvine, ed. Chicago: American Marketing Association, 219-232.

Hill, Ronald Paul. (2011). "Whither marketing and public policy research? Or has public policy and marketing come of age?" *Journal of Public Policy & Marketing, Spring (in press).*

Maronick, Thomas J. (1990). "Current Research at the Federal Trade Commission" in Patrick Murphy and William Wilkie (eds) Marketing and Advertising Regulation: The Federal Trade Commission in the 1990's. The University of Notre Dame Press.

TSR; Statement of Basis and Purpose and Final Rule, 60 FR 43842, 43854 (Aug. 23, 1995).

Wilkie, William L. & Gardner, David M. (1974). The role of marketing research in public policy decision making. *Journal of Marketing*, 38 (January), 38-47.

Wilkie, William, L. & Elizabeth S. Moore (1997), "Consortium survey on marketing and society issues: Summary and results*," Journal of Macromarketing, 17* (2), 89-9

ROUNDTABLE
Journal of Consumer Research Reviewer Workshop

Chairs:
Darren Dahl, University of British Columbia, Canada
Craig Thompson, University of Wisconsin-Madison, USA

Participants:
Laura Peracchio, University of Wisconsin-Milwaukee, USA
Mary Frances Luce, Duke University, USA
Rebecca Hamilton, University of Maryland, USA
Kent Grayson, Northwestern University, USA
Lauren Block, Baruch College, CUNY, USA
Eileen Fischer, York University, Canada
Gita Johar, Columbia University, USA
Page Moreau, University of Colorado, USA
Bob Meyer, University of Pennsylvania, USA
Dirk Smeesters, Erasmus University, The Netherlands
Ann McGill, University of Chicago, USA

ROUNDTABLE
When Consumers and Companies Do Good: Causes and Consequences

Chairs:
Andrew M. Kaikati, University of Georgia, USA
Michal Strahilevitz, Golden Gate University, USA

Participants:
Sergio Carvalho, University of Manitoba, Canada
Zoe Chance, Harvard School of Business, USA
Paul Connell, Stony Brook University, USA
Fern (Mai Mai) Lin, University of Pennsylvaniat, USA
Peter McGraw, University of Colorado, USA
Rebecca Walker Naylor, The Ohio State University, USA
Christopher Olivola, University College London, UK
Michal Strahilevitz, Golden Gate University, USA
Carlos J. Torelli, University of Minnesota, USA
Jing Wang, University of Iowa, USA

Prosocial behavior is the label for a broad category of actions that are defined by society as generally beneficial to other people and to the ongoing political system (Dovidio et al. 2006). The interest in prosocial behavior has increased in the last 15 years since Bendapudi, Singh, and Bendapudi's (1996) review article noted a dearth of marketing literature in this area. Gaining an understanding of the factors influencing prosocial behavior by consumers is important for charities, such as United Way, that need to compete vigorously for donor dollars. Such an understanding is crucial because individual giving is always the largest single source of donation to charitable organizations (Giving USA Foundation 2007). Furthermore, many companies and consumers are paying attention to the impact of their choices on society at large. Consequently, an increasing number of consumer behavior scholars have begun to look at the causes and consequences of prosocial behavior among consumers and companies.

The goal of this roundtable is to foster an engaging discussion on the antecedents and consequences of prosocial behaviors, by bringing together researchers who are currently approaching different aspects of the topic, from different theoretical perspectives. Consistent with the conference theme of "building connections," we aim to unite researchers under a common goal of providing insights into the study of charitable giving, volunteerism, sustainability, and CSR responses. This roundtable will appeal broadly to those scholars interested in the individual (e.g., personal values; Torelli and Kaikati 2009) and social (e.g., relationships; Small and Simonsohn 2008) factors influencing different types of prosocial behavior as well as the effects of different types of prosocial behavior on consumers' lives. Beyond this, it will also appeal to those interested in research examining the effects on both employees and consumers of prosocial behavior initiated and communicated by organizations (via CSR messages). Our distinguished panel of committed attendees purposely includes scholars from a diverse range of research areas relating to understanding the causes and effects of prosocial behavior. Our panelists are conducting research on many important subjects that fit under the "prosocial" umbrella. These include exploring factors affecting charitable giving and volunteerism, the effects of charitable behavior on consumer welfare and satisfaction, sustainability, how prosocial activities within organizations affect employee morale and job satisfaction, and the many factors influencing consumer responses to corporate social responsibility (including the nature of the product, the nature of the consumer, the communication strategy, and prior CSR activities by the organization). Our panel includes scholars with diverse backgrounds and interests, so that we can learn from each other and foster a community that keeps the big picture in mind, rather than focusing on one narrow research area.

We aim to encourage dialogue before, during, and after the roundtable. This will include identifying key areas of current research, discussing potential synergies between different streams of work, identifying directions for future research, and discussing the challenges of doing research in this area. Due to the huge appeal of this topic to many scholars with diverse perspectives, we hope to not only attract a wide range of scholars from different backgrounds and interests, but also to help foster a community that will continue to be active even after ACR 2011. This roundtable will also draw interest from proponents of Transformative Consumer Research, which has been described as "consumer research in the service of quality of life" (Mick 2006, p. 3). We hope to appeal to a large portion of the TCR community, but will also attract a range of scholars who are not (currently) part of the TCR group. The topics covered will be relevant to those interested in broadening our theoretical understanding of prosocial behavior, those dedicated to doing research with prosocial benefits (TCR), and those focused on managerial implications. Indeed, many on our panel are dedicated to doing research that addresses all three of these goals.

One of the "big picture" questions we will address in our discussion is whether it is prosocial to study prosocial behavior. Indeed, while some have demonstrated the connection between prosocial behavior and happiness (Liu and Aaker 2008, Dunn Aknin and Norton 2008), some are troubled by the idea that nonprofits should focus on keeping their donors and volunteers feeling appreciated and happy, if not downright entertained by their acts of kindness (Strahilevitz 2010). Others worry that research on prosocial behavior is not always taken seriously, particularly in the context of a business school. Given the importance of these topics, we will discuss the potential value of doing research in this area, with a focus on work that is both rigorous in terms of theory, but also potentially helpful in terms of service to society. We will also, as a group, discuss strategies for promoting the value of research on prosocial behavior within a business school setting. Finally, several of the roundtable members will share their experiences and lessons learned from adding a prosocial dimension to their course offerings. This will include sharing experiences on introducing courses centered around CSR and nonprofit principals, and sharing advice on adding prosocial content to existing courses.

Before and after the conference, continued dialogue will be facilitated via a combination of email exchanges (facilitated by the roundtable chairs), postings on the ACR Knowledge Exchange Forum, and postings on the Facebook group "Prosocial Consumer Research." This Facebook group is open to any scholar interested in research in this area. In our pre-ACR dialogue, we will develop a plan for breakout sessions focusing on issues such as consumer responses to CSR, causes and consequences of prosocial behavior by consumers, the prosocial nature of research on prosocial behavior, and the challenges that come with research in this area.

References

American Association of Fundraising Counsel (2007), *Giving USA*. Glenview, IL: American Association of Fundraising Counsel.

Bendapudi, Neeli, Surendra N. Singh, and Venkat Bendapudi (1996), "Enhancing Helping Beahvior: An Integrative Framework for Promotion Planning," *Journal of Marketing*, 60, 33-49.

Dovidio, John F., Jane Allyn Piliavin, David A. Schroeder, and Louis A. Penner (2006), *The Social Psychology of Prosocial Behavior*, Mahwah, NJ: Lawrence Erlbaum Associates.

Dunn, Elizabeth, Lara B Aknin and Michael I. Norton (2008), "Spending Money on Others Promotes Happiness," *Science*, 319, 1687-88.

Liu, Wendy and Jennifer Aaker (2008), "The Happiness of Giving: The Time-Ask Effect," *Journal of Consumer Research*, 543-57.

Mick, David Glen (2006), "Presidential Address: Meaning and Mattering through Transformative Consumer Research," *Advances in Consumer Research*, 33, 1-4.

Small, Deborah and Uri Simonsohn (2008), "Friends of Victims: Personal Experience and Prosocial Behavior," *Journal of Consumer Research,* 35, 532-42.

Strahilevitz, Michal, (2010) "A Model Comparing the Value of Giving to Others to the Value of Having More for Oneself: Implications for Fundraisers Seeking to Maximize Donor Satisfaction," in *The Science of Giving: Experimental Approaches to the Study of Charity*. Oppenheimer, D.M., & Olivola, C.Y. (eds.) (in press). New York: Taylor and Francis.

Torelli, Carlos J. and Andrew M. Kaikati (2009), "Values as Predictors of Judgments and Behaviors: The Role of Abstract and Concrete Mindsets," *Journal of Personality and Social Psychology*, 96 (1), 231-47.

ROUNDTABLE

Giving, Sharing, Consuming: Connecting Consumer Behaviors

Chair:
Prof. Russell Belk York University, Canada

Participants:
Zeynep Arsel, Concordia University, Canada
Domen Bajde, University of Ljubljana, Slovenia
Russell Belk, York University, Toronto, Canada
Jonathan Deschênes (HEC Montréal, Canada
Eileen Fisher, York University, Toronto, Canada
Marine Le Gall-Ely, Université of Bretagne Occidentale, Brest, France
Jean-Sébastien Marcoux, HEC Montréal, Canada
Cele Otnes, University of Illinois, USA
Julie Ozanne, Virginia Tech, USA
Lucie Ozanne, University of Canterbury, New Zealand
Nil Özçağlar-Toulouse, University of Lille, France
Bertrand Urien, Université of Bretagne Occidentale, Brest, France

This roundtable is proposed to continue dialogue engaged in the 2011 gathering in Geneva on connections between giving, sharing and consuming practices and to bring them to a wider audience.

Nowadays, associations, foundations and other NGO's, but also families are supporting numerous social, health and cultural causes. Even if recent humanitarian disasters have confirmed the generosity of individuals, firms and States, they have also highlighted the need for actors involved in charity and humanitarian missions to find new ways to become known, to differentiate themselves and to create a special relationship with donators. The growing concurrence between charities and causes suggests the emergence of a donator who is more attentive to the social as well as economic issues of his or her behavior.

This phenomenon is also accompanied with tensions between giving outside/inside the private sphere (Bajde, 2006, 2009), between giving and sharing (Belk, 2010), between giving/receiving and consuming (Marcoux, 2009; Le Gall-Ely and Urbain, 2011) as well as with the increasing interest for a more sustainable consumption (Bécheur and Toulouse, 2009). In view of the diversity of topics and the rising interest in these fields, it is now time to clearly stipulate the tensions and convergences between each topic.

This roundtable has been proposed to determine what can be done to best address the objectives, first defined in the discussions in the *Observatoire International Don et Consommation*[1] (OIDC) research group created in Geneva (Switzerland) and Brest (France) and bringing together researchers from all over Europe and North-America.

The roundtable will follow on from the 1st colloquium of the OIDC that has taken place in Geneva in June 2011. The current roundtable will focus on the importance of studying the diversity of consumers' behaviors and cultures, what obstacles or issues are specific to giving, sharing and consuming practices researchers, and how research projects can benefit from, and contribute to sharing knowledge with our colleagues based in other parts of the world. To meet this aim, the proposed panel consists of both senior and emerging researchers from all over the world interested in giving, sharing and consuming practices.

Background

Giving and sharing are without doubt topics of growing interest in consumer research, as well as in the fields of anthropology, sociology, psychology, economics and philosophy. A growing number of articles published in the *Journal of Consumer Research* has exposed research regarding these topics in recent years (e.g. Marcoux, 2009; Belk, 2010). Furthermore, the French National Research Agency (ANR) has financed research on these topics and the French Marketing Association (AFM) has provided support to sponsor the latest Price, Free and Gift conference held at Tours University in 2010.

Furthermore, a book published in 2011 (Bergadaà, Le Gall-Ely, and Urien, 2011) is dedicated to essays and research on giving, demonstrating substantial growth in the field. A number of ACR researchers are actively engaged in these research areas (including those named as participants for this roundtable) and further collaboration and dialogue are necessary to better understand how to facilitate developments in the future.

Roundtable Purpose

Rather than focusing on one or two 'experts' in the field, the proposed roundtable will be interactive in nature to encourage a flow of dialogue between attendees. The proposed roundtable will:

1. Encourage active and critical dialogue between persons engaged with giving, sharing and consuming research. Participants will discuss what has and has not been achieved in the past years (in both Europe and North America as well as in other parts of the world).
2. Identify the conceptual, theoretical and methodological tensions and convergences between these topics.
3. Address what specific issues or obstacles consumer researchers face. How can we learn from one another to ensure these obstacles are minimized or removed altogether for researchers in the field? One particular aim is to see how researchers based in different continents could share experiences.

---

[1] http://www.oidc.unige.ch/

Roundtable Structure and Content

The proposed Giving, Sharing and Consuming roundtable will encourage open dialogue from all panel members and attendees. The role of the discussant will be to ensure free-flowing dialogue and to lead the discussion as needed. We propose focusing on three discussion areas to help guide the session and ensure that contributions are made from all participants. The proposed discussion questions are:

1. What has been achieved, in consumer research, to understand the connections between diverse consumers' practices as giving, sharing and consuming in the past?
2. What related research will be forthcoming? (research nearly completed, books to be published…)
3. What avenues for high quality, high impact research collaboration exist among the attendees that can ensure that dialogue continues beyond the roundtable setting?

Contributions and Implications

One of the key contributions of this roundtable will be its assessment of research regarding diverse consumers' practices and their connections. With this roundtable, we hope to expose ACR members to topics besides self-focused consumption and identify the tensions and convergences between the diverse consumers' behavior. Strategies to encourage high impact research on these issues will be discussed at the roundtable, offering participants alike opportunities to continue growing the field of giving, sharing and consuming research. We hope that the roundtable encourages collaborations between researchers by creating networks, facilitating research opportunities by the identification of a research agenda, and promoting further dialogue, and these collaborations will develop across borders.

References

Bajde D. (2006), Other-Centered Behaviour and the Dialectics of Self and Other, *Consumption, Markets and Culture*, 9, 4, 301-316.

Bajde D. (2009), Rethinking the Social and Cultural Dimensions of Charitable Giving, *Consumption, Markets and Culture*, 12, 1, 65–84.

Bécheur A. et Özçağlar-Toulouse N. (2008), *Le commerce équitable : entre utopie et marché*, Paris, Vuibert, 192 p.

Belk R.W. (2009), Sharing, *Journal of Consumer Research*, 36, 5, 715-734.

Bergadaà M., Le Gall-Ely M. et Urien B. (ed.) (2011), *Don et pratiques caritatives*, De Boeck University, Bruxelles.

Deschênes J. et Marcoux J.-S. (2011), Le marketing du don charitable: Une analyse critique et réflexive, chap 5 in Bergadaà M., Le Gall-Ely M. et Urien B. (Eds.), *Don et pratiques caritatives*, de Boeck University, 99-112.

Deschênes, J. (2009), *Exploring the Wish Factory: Ethnographic Insights Into the Charitable Business of Wish Granting*. Thèse de doctorat. Université Concordia.

Fischer E., Gainer B. and Arnold S.J. (1996), Gift Giving and Charitable Donating: How (Dis)similar Are They ? 175-194 in *Gift Giving: A Research Anthology*, C.Otnes and R.Beltramini, Bowling Green, OH, Bowling Green State University Popular Press.

Joy A. (2001), Gift Giving in Hong Kong and the Continuum of Social Ties, *Journal of Consumer Research*, 28, 2, 239-257.

Krebs A., Rieunier S. and Urien B. (2011), Generativity as an explanatory factor in the concept of bequests: stakes and recommendations for cultural institutions, AIMAC conference, july, Anvers, Belgium.

Le Gall-Ely M. et Urbain C. (2011), Don et *care* : histoires de vie, chap 9 in Bergadaà M., Le Gall-Ely M. et Urien B. (ed.), *Don et pratiques caritatives*, De Boeck University, Bruxelles.

Le Gall-Ely M., Gonzalez C. and Urbain C. (2009), Is a Gift always a Gift? An Ethnographic Inquiry into the Diversity of Gift Experiences, *2009 North-American Association for Consumer Research Conference*, Pittsburgh, 22-25th october.

Marcoux J.-S. (2009), Escaping the Gift Economy, *Journal of Consumer Research*, 36, 4, 671-685.

Otnes C. and Beltramini R.F. (1996), *Gift Giving: A Research Anthology*, Bowling Green, OH, Bowling Green State University Popular Press.

Özçağlar-Toulouse N. (2009), What Meaning do Responsible Consumers Give to Their Consumption? An Approach by Narratives, *Recherche et Applications Marketing*, 24 (3), 3-22.

Sherry J.F., McGrath M.-A. and Levy S.J. (1993), The Dark Side of the Gift, *Journal of Business Research*, 28, 225-244.

Sherry J.F. (1983), Gift Giving in Anthropological Perspective, *Journal of Consumer Research*, 10 (2), 157-168.

Urbain C., Le Gall-Ely M. and Gonzalez C. (2010), Generation Y's Representations of who They Are and how They Give, *2010 North-American Association for Consumer Research Conference,* Jacksonville, 7-10th October.

ROUNDTABLE
Embodiment in Consumer Judgment and Decision-Making: Behavioral, Psychological, and Neural Perspectives

Chair:
Martin Reimann, University of Southern California, USA

Participants:
Josh Ackerman, Massachusetts Institute of Technology, Sloan School of Management, USA
Raquel Castano, Tecnologico de Monterrey, EGADE Business School, Canada
Nitika Garg, University of Mississippi, School of Business Administration, USA
Robert Kreuzbauer, Nanyang University, Nayang Business School), Singapore
Aparna A. Labroo, University of Chicago, Booth School of Business, USA
Angela Y. Lee, Northwestern University, Kellogg School of Management, USA
Spike W. S. Lee, University of Michigan, Department of Psychology, USA
Alan J. Malter, University of Illinois at Chicago, College of Business Administration, USA
Maureen Morrin, Rutgers University, Rutgers School of Business, USA
Gergana Y. Nenkov, Boston College, Carroll School of Management, USA
Jesper H. Nielsen, University of Arizona, Eller College of Managemen, USAt
Maria Perez, Tecnologico de Monterrey, EGADE Business School, Mexico
Gratiana Pol, University of Southern California, Marshall School of Business, USA
Martin Reimann, University of Southern California, Department of Psychology, USA
José Antonio Rosa, University of Wyoming, College of Business, USA
Carolyn Yoon, University of Michigan, Stephen M. Ross School of Business, USA
Judith Zaichkowsky, Copenhagen Business School, Marketing Department, Denmark
Chen-Bo Zhong, University of Toronto, Rotman School of Management, Canada

Researchers have long argued whether emotions should be understood as cognitive appraisals (e.g., Frijda, Kuipers, and Ter Schure 1989; Smith and Ellsworth 1985) or perceptions of changes in bodily states (e.g., James 1884; Lange 1885). Specifically, cognitive appraisal theory posits that emotions are elicited by evaluating (appraising) certain objects or events in the environment in terms of their congruence with one's goals (Roseman and Smith 2001). For example, happiness occurs after indulging in a delicious meal because it contributes to one's eating goals. Guilt is elicited in consumers after overeating because it violates goals of staying healthy and slim. On the contrary, bodily perception theory argues that emotions may arise without the intervening process of cognitive appraisal but on the basis of physiological changes in the body (James 1884; Lange 1885) and based on motor action such as muscle flexion/extension or facial expressions (Maxwell and Davidson 2007; Niedenthal 2007). For example, a consumer feels content from eating because of being filled and one feels sad because of crying.

Are emotions cognitive appraisals or bodily perceptions? Both views seem to be partly correct. Recent advances in neuroscience indicate that the brain carries out such cognitive appraisals and bodily perceptions simultaneously, integrating them with cognitive representations such as concepts and beliefs (Bechara 2005; Bechara and Damasio 2005; Reimann and Bechara 2010) and helping modify and guide downstream processing of judgments and decision-making (Bechara et al. 1997).

The central role of bodily perceptions has been shared by the theory of embodied or grounded cognition. This theory typically hold that the body exerts a strong influence on shaping an individual's cognitive representations (Barsalou 2008; Glenberg 1997; Malter 1996). For example, early research wondered why nodding one's head (vs. shaking it) influences the degree to which one agrees with a persuasive message (Wells and Petty 1980) or why standing upright (vs. slumping) increases persistence on an insolvable puzzle task (Riskind and Gotay 1982). More recent research indicated that moving one's eyes helped solve brainteasers (Thomas and Lleras 2007), moving one's hand facilitated solving math problems and increases math performance (Broaders et al. 2007; Goldin-Meadow, Cook, and Mitchell 2009), and firming one's muscles also firms one's willpower and improves self-regulation (Hung and Labroo 2011).

These bodily influences on cognitive representations not only function through actually experiencing physiological and motoric changes but also through merely remembering them and, thus, reexperiencing them (Reimann and Bechara 2010). We extend this notion of bodily influence on cognitive representations and argue that bodily feedback—whether actually experienced or remembered—is also necessary for accurately appraising the goal-congruence of an object or event. For example, standing upright (vs. slumping) lead individuals to evaluate an achievement with greater pride (Stepper and Strack 1993) and, thus, may foster performance-related goals. Individuals who sat on ergonomic chairs (vs. a smaller, forward-tilted chair) appraised the situation as a more powerful leader (Huang et al. 2011), supporting goals of getting ahead in life.

We expect that embodiment theory will contribute significantly to the extant literature as it helps integrate previously competing views of emotion as either cognitive appraisals or perceptions of bodily changes. The notion of embodiment is in line with the Jamesian view of emotion, which argues that a range of bodily states—visceral changes, facial expressions, and muscle action—can cause the brain to interpret emotion (James 1884, 1894). Yet, we additionally argue in the Damasian view, which posits that these bodily states must not necessarily be experienced on the spot but can be merely remembered (Bechara and Damasio 2005; Damasio 1994). This view allows for an integration of both bodily perceptions and cognitive appraisals. It is argued today that cognitive appraisals are a necessary stage between bodily perceptions and downstream processes that trigger behaviors. Although these filtering appraisal processes can be brief and nonconscious, they need to be recognized (Damasio, 2010). We further argue that the mechanisms of embodiment have a profound impact on downstream processes of consumers' judgments and decision-making such as more embodiment leading to more advantageous financial choices (Bechara et al. 1997), resisting the temptation of drugs (Bechara 2005) or calorie-rich foods (Hung and Labroo 2011), and predicting future consequences (Bechara et al. 1994).

Motivation for Organizing the Roundtable Discussion

Despite important previous work on embodiment, several important conceptual and methodological questions remain unanswered. First, how do affect and cognition interact in embodiment? Prior research under the label of 'embodied cognition' postulated that knowledge and thoughts arise from physical interaction with the environment (Glenberg 1997; Glenberg et al. 2003). Are these embodied cognitions purely 'embodied cognitions of affect' in the sense of cognitive appraisal theory?

Second, for which consumer behaviors is embodiment most relevant? Previous work has studied embodiment in a wide variety of consumer behaviors, including product and brand evaluations (Kreuzbauer and Malter 2005), food appraisals (Labroo and Nielsen 2010), donations (Hung and Labroo 2011), and financial decision-making (Bechara et al. 1997; Kuhnen and Knutson 2005). As such, does embodiment apply more broadly as an overarching phenomenon or is it merely domain-specific?

Third, which methodological manipulations work most effectively in the study of embodiment and its role in consumer judgment and decision-making? Published work has applied a broad spectrum of strategies to manipulate embodiment, ranging from muscle action (e.g., arm flexion and extension, movement of head or hand), via facial expressions, to the recording of neurophysiological processes such as heart rate, skin conductance, and brain activity.

Taken together, we propose this roundtable discussion (1) to attain clarity on the aforementioned conceptual and methodological issues, (2) to arrive at an integrative view on the topic of embodiment in consumer judgment and decision-making, and (3) to stimulate the ACR community and discuss ideas and directions for further consumer research on the topic. Additionally, pre-conference discussions are facilitated by participants' e-mail exchanges moderated by the roundtable organizer.

Benefit from Attending the Roundtable Discussion

This roundtable discussion will offer an opportunity for researchers from different backgrounds (i.e., consumer research, marketing, psychology, and neuroscience) to identify mutual interests and develop new collegial relationships. Key benefits of this roundtable discussion will be an exchange of state-of-the-art insights on embodiment between psychology/neuroscience and consumer behavior/marketing scholars and an identification of areas for collaboration to advance the research agenda on this topic.

References

Barsalou, Lawrence W. (2008), "Grounded Cognition," *Annual Review of Psychology*, 59 (1), 617-45.

Bechara, Antoine (2004), "The Role of Emotion in Decision-Making: Evidence from Neurological Patients with Orbitofrontal Damage," *Brain and Cognition*, 55 (1), 30-40.

--- (2005), "Decision Making, Impulse Control and Loss of Willpower to Resist Drugs: A Neurocognitive Perspective," *Nature Neuroscience*, 8 (11), 1458-63.

Bechara, Antoine and Antonio R. Damasio (2005), "The Somatic Marker Hypothesis: A Neural Theory of Economic Decision," *Games and Economic Behavior*, 52 (2), 336-72.

Bechara, Antoine, Antonio R. Damasio, Hanna Damasio, and Steven W. Anderson (1994), "Insensitivity to Future Consequences Following Damage to Human Prefrontal Cortex," *Cognition*, 50, 7-15.

Bechara, Antoine, Hanna Damasio, Daniel Tranel, and Antonio R. Damasio (1997), "Deciding Advantageously before Knowing the Advantageous Strategy," *Science*, 275 (5304), 1293-95.

Broaders, Sara C., Susan Wagner Cook, Zachary Mitchell, and Susan Goldin-Meadow (2007), "Making Children Gesture Brings out Implicit Knowledge and Leads to Learning," *Journal of Experimental Psychology: General*, 136 (4), 539-49.

Damasio, Antonio R. (2010), *Self Comes to Mind: Constructing the Conscious Brain*, New York, New York: Pantheon.

Damasio, Antonio R. (1994), *Descartes' Error: Emotion, Reason, and the Human Brain*, New York, New York: Putnam.

Frijda, Nico H., Peter Kuipers, and Elisabeth Ter Schure (1989), "Relations among Emotion, Appraisal, and Emotional Action Readiness," *Journal of Personality and Social Psychology*, 57 (2), 212-28.

Glenberg, Arthur M. (1997), "What Memory Is For: Creating Meaning in the Service of Action," *Behavioral and Brain Sciences*, 20 (1), 41-50.

Glenberg, Arthur M., David A. Robertson, Michael P. Kaschak, and Alan J. Malter (2003), "Embodied Meaning and Negative Priming," *Behavioral and Brain Sciences*, 26 (05), 644-47.

Goldin-Meadow, Susan, Susan Wagner Cook, and Zachary A. Mitchell (2009), "Gesturing Gives Children New Ideas About Math," *Psychological Science*, 20 (3), 267.

Huang, Li, Adam D. Galinsky, Deborah H. Gruenfeld, and Lucia E. Guillory (2011), "Powerful Postures Versus Powerful Roles," *Psychological Science*, 22 (1), 95102.

Hung, Iris W. and Aparna A. Labroo (2011), "From Firm Muscles to Firm Willpower: Understanding the Role of Embodied Cognition in Self-Regulation," *Journal of Consumer Research*, 37, forthcoming.

James, William (1884), "What Is an Emotion?," *Mind*, 9 (34), 188-205.

--- (1894), "The Physical Basis of Emotion," *Psychological Review*, 1 (5), 516-29.

Kreuzbauer, Robert and Alan J. Malter (2005), "Embodied Cognition and New Product Design: Changing Product Form to Influence Brand Categorization," *Journal of Product Innovation Management*, 22 (2), 165-76.

Kuhnen, Camelia M. and Brian Knutson (2005), "The Neural Basis of Financial Risk Taking," *Neuron*, 47 (5), 763-70.

Labroo, Aparna A. and Jesper H. Nielsen (2010), "Half the Thrill Is in the Chase: Twisted Inferences from Embodied Cognitions and Brand Evaluation," *Journal of Consumer Research*, 37 (1), 143-58.

Lange, Carl Georg (1885), "The Mechanism of the Emotions," in *The Emotions*, ed. E. Dunlap, Baltimore, Maryland: Williams & Wilkins, 33-92.

Malter, Alan J. (1996), "An Introduction to Embodied Cognition: Implications for Consumer Research," in *Advances in Consumer Research*, Vol. 23, eds. Kim P. Corfman and John Lynch, Provo, Utah: Association for Consumer Research, 272-276.

Maxwell, Jeffrey S. and Richard J. Davidson (2007), "Emotion as Motion," *Psychological Science*, 18 (12), 1113-19.

Niedenthal, Paula M. (2007), "Embodying Emotion," *Science*, 316 (5827), 1002-05.

Niedenthal, Paula M., Piotr Winkielman, Laurie Mondillon, and Nicolas Vermeulen (2009), "Embodiment of Emotion Concepts," *Journal of Personality and Social Psychology*, 96 (6), 1120.

Reimann, Martin and Antoine Bechara (2010), "The Somatic Marker Framework as a Neurological Theory of Decision-Making: Review, Conceptual Comparisons, and Future Neuroeconomic Research," *Journal of Economic Psychology*, 31 (5), 767-76.

Riskind, John H. and Carolyn C. Gotay (1982), "Physical Posture: Could It Have Regulatory or Feedback Effects on Motivation and Emotion?," *Motivation and Emotion*, 6 (3), 273-98.

Roseman, Ira J. and Craig A. Smith (2001), "Appraisal Theory: Overview, Assumptions, Varieties, Controversies," in *Appraisal Processes in Emotion: Theory, Methods, Research*, ed. Klaus R. Scherer, Angela Schorr and Tom Johnstone, Oxford, UK: Oxford University Press, 3-19.

Smith, Craig A. and Phoebe C. Ellsworth (1985), "Patterns of Cognitive Appraisal in Emotion," *Journal of Personality and Social Psychology*, 48 (4), 813-38.

Stepper, Sabine and Fritz Strack (1993), "Proprioceptive Determinants of Emotional and Nonemotional Feelings," *Journal of Personality and Social Psychology*, 64 (2), 211-20.

Thomas, Laura E. and Alejandro Lleras (2007), "Moving Eyes and Moving Thought: On the Spatial Compatibility between Eye Movements and Cognition," *Psychonomic Bulletin & Review*, 14 (4), 663.

Wells, Gary L. and Richard E. Petty (1980), "The Effects of Overt Head Movements on Persuasion: Compatibility and Incompatibility of Responses," *Basic and Applied Social Psychology*, 1 (3), 219-30.

ROUNDTABLE
Dorita, this is not Kansas! Is Latin America!

Chair:
Silvia Gonzalez, ITESM Campus, Monterrey, Mexico

Participants:
Enrique Manzur, Universidad de Chile, Chile
Rodrigo Uribe, Universidad de Chile, Chile
Eduardo Torres, Universidad de Chile, Chile
Christian Felzsenztein, Universidad de Chile, Chile
Claudio Aquevque, Universidad de Chile, Chile
Constanza Bianchi, Universidad Adolfo Inañez, Chile
Sandra Milberg, Universidad Adolfo Inañez, Chile
Sergio Olavarrieta, Universidad de Chile, Chile

The first Latin American Conference of the Association for Consumer Research (ACR) was held in Monterrey, Mexico, in 2006. This conference was an important first step for ACR to be present in a new region. The conference was a success in that it promoted exchanges of ideas among researchers from around the world. The ACR LA started with 120 attendees, half of them from Latin American Universities. In 2008, in Sao Paulo, Brazil, was held the second Latin American Conference of the Association for Consumer Research. This time, along with the competitive sessions, methodological workshops, film festival, roundtables and posters, and meet-the-editors sessions, we had the addition of a one-day Transformative Consumer Research pre-conference and a retail expedition. Again, half of the attendees were from Latin American Universities.

In both Conferences, we had participants from all over the world, presenting work relevant to a great variety of countries, and representing a variety of research paradigms and methodologies.

However, we need to ensure that we are in the right track to fulfill its objective of fostering consumer research in the region with the highest ACR standards.

Extraordinary experiences are highly enjoyable (Csikszentmihalyi 1990: 1997). They involve absorbing mental states of being that exceed consumers' day-to-day levels of emotional intensity (Allen, Massiah, Cascio and Johnoson 2008). These type of experiences are crucial in the formation and maintenance of consumer communities (McAlexander and 1998; Schouten and Alexander 1995). Thanks to many supporters, in both Conferences we were able to hold interesting receptions, the off-site reception at the Museum of Contemporary Art in Monterrey, the performance of "The Traveler" a Mexican traditional dances show, a great Samba Night and great Mexican and Brazilian food.. Receptions were very well attended and the dances were spectacular! Now, it is time to question if these enjoyable experiences have had a positive influence in strengthen relationships in the Latin American research community and increased ACR participation that we want to foster in the region. In this roundtable we invite participants to discuss if we are making progress to attract talented Latin American researchers, who do not regularly participate in ACR events. In addition, we want to discuss the organization of the third possible Latin America conference in Chile.

ROUNDTABLE
Fellows Roundtable

Chair:
James Burroughs, University of Virginia, USA

Participants:
Don Lehmann, Columbia University, USA
Brian Sternthal, Northwestern University, USA
John Lynch, University of Colorado, USA
Russell Belk, York University, Canada
Jim Bettman, Duke University, USA
Beth Hirschman, Rutgers University, USA

Roundtable Summaries

Roundtable One
Grant Workshop (Chair: Rucker).
Brief Description: Bring in representatives from major grant making agencies (e.g. NSF, NIH, Templeton) and overview the process of applying for grants.

Roundtable Two
Fellows Session (Chair: Burroughs).
Brief Description: ACR Fellows will share their wisdom and insights related to building a research career. Topics will include building a research program, balancing early career pressures, and mistakes made that might be avoided. Session will be restricted to doctoral students and junior faculty (i.e. Assistant Professors in the first three years).

Roundtable Three
JCR Reviewer Training (Chair: Twist).
Brief Description: Managing Editor Mary-Ann Twist, along with a team of Editors and Associate Editors from the *Journal of Consumer Research* will help to train faculty who are relatively new to journal reviewing on how to perform a quality review. Session will include examples, best practices, and how to avoid submitting problematic reviews.

Roundtable Four
MSI Celebration (Chair: Keller).
Brief Description: A group of faculty closely involved with the Marketing Science Institute will conduct a roundtable to discuss the contributions (and future) of MSI in the marketing and consumer research community. The roundtable will mark the 50th anniversary of the founding of MSI and a celebratory reception will follow the roundtable.

Roundtable Five
Sheth Foundation Resources (Chair: Mick).
Brief Description: A group of former and current recipients of Sheth Foundation grants will discuss how the Foundation has influenced their work, and how to access Sheth Foundation resources for doctoral dissertation research.

Roundtable Six
Embodiment in Consumer Behavior (Chair: Reimann).
Brief Description: A group of researchers interested in the intersection of embodiment (i.e. embodied cognition, embodied emotion) and consumer behavior will meet to discuss and share research ideas and critiques.

Roundtable Seven
Latin America Consumer Research Interest Group (Chair: Gonzalez and Olvarietta).
Brief Description: There have now been two ACR Latin America Conferences. This has produced a vibrant group of scholars both from and interested in consumer research in Latin America. The session hopes to continue to keep the nucleus formed by these conferences thriving by staying connected at the ACR Annual (formerly North American) conference.

Roundtable Eight
Bridging the Gap between Consumer Research and Public Policy (Chair: Shah).
Brief Description: This sessions seeks to bridge the gap between consumer research and shaping public policy, including ways to study marketing from a public policy context, and future research opportunities at the intersection of these two issues.

<u>Roundtable Nine</u>
When Companies and Consumers do Good (Chair: Kaikati).
Brief Description: Consistent with the conference theme of "building connections", this session will unite researchers studying the psychology of charitable giving, volunteerism, sustainability, and CSR responses.

<u>Roundtable Ten</u>
Charity and Gift Giving (Chair: Le Gail-Ely).
Brief Description: Purpose is to continue dialogue initiated by the OIDC (*Observatoire International Don et Consommation*), group of researchers from all over Europe and North-America with an interest in charitable giving and pro-social behaviors, including exploring the tension between pro-social behaviors and traditional self-interested (indulgent) behaviors.

ROUNDTABLE
Grant Writing Roundtable

Chair:
Derek Rucker, Northwestern University, USA

Participants:
John Deighton, Harvard Business School, USA
Deborah Olster, NIH, USA
Brett Pelham, NSF, USA

This roundtable will familiarize faculty and doctoral students with grant writing opportunities and strategies. The discussion will be led by an excellent set of representatives from MSI, the Templeton Foundation, NIH, and NSF. These scholars will be present to discuss the opportunities available from their respective institutions to consumer researchers as well as discuss questions about the grant writing process.

ROUNDTABLE
MSI 50th Anniversary Celebratory Session

Chairs:
Donna Hoffman, UC Riverside, USA
Punam Keller, Dartmouth College, USA

Participants:
John Deighton, Harvard Business School, USA
Don Lehman, Columbia University, USA
Rohit Deshpande, Harvard Business School, USA
John Lynch, University of Colorado, USA
Barbara Kahn, University of Pennsylvania, USA
Page Moreau, University of Colorado, USA
Darren Dahl, University of British Columbia
Kristin Diehl, University of Southern California, USA
Jonah Berger, University of Pennsylvania, USA
Gavan Fitzsimons, Duke University, USA

This unique session will celebrate the Marketing Science Institute's support of consumer research. 2011 marks the year the Marketing Science Institute (MSI) commemorates 50 years of generating and disseminating knowledge that advances the theory, science, and practice of marketing. This celebratory session is designed to stimulate conversations about consumer behavior challenges and opportunities in the years ahead. To achieve these goals, a baker's dozen of the leading CB scholars will highlight their work with MSI in a series of very short, high impact TED-style talks. All of these consumer researchers have strong connections to MSI, with each representing different paradigms, career stages and types of MSI collaborations. The short presentations will emphasize the key aspects of each scholar's MSI research collaboration. In addition to celebrating MSI's contributions over the past 50 years, we hope the session will expose ACR members to the many exciting opportunities MSI offers consumer behavior scholars in support of academic research. Past collaborations with CB scholars have included monetary awards for research and conferences, distribution of research to practitioners, recognition of young scholars, data sets from companies, teaching materials, and idea exchanges.

ROUNDTABLE
Report of the 2011 ACR Long-Term Planning Task Force
(Open to all)

Co-Chairs:
Sharon Shavitt, Walter H. Stellner Professor of Marketing, University of Illinois at Urbana-Champaign, USA
J. Jeffrey Inman, University of Pittsburgh, USA

Participants:
Joel Huber, Duke University, USA
Don Lehmann, Columbia University, USA
John Deighton, Harvard Business School, USA
Linda Price, University of Arizona, USA

Recently an ACR Strategic Task force was created to address the growth, internationalization, and relevance of our field. The task force conducted a member survey and generated recommendations and issues to consider in the future. These outputs plus data on conference submissions will be discussed. We seek input on several recommendations for ACR initiatives to scale up and enhance the field as it rapidly expands, including recommendations for new and existing publication outlets and conference structures.

Working Papers

Bollywood: A 'Consumer Reacculturation Agent'

Amandeep Takhar, University of Bedfordshire, UK

This research investigates the concept of reacculturation, whereby ethnic individuals focus on adopting the customs and traditions of their ethnic minority culture, within an environment that is not their ancestral homeland. The focus within this research is on how third generation, UK born British Sikhs, consume Bollywood films and how the consumption of Bollywood films lead to reacculturation towards their ancestral homeland culture and customs. It is not that research relating to the quest for roots in the construction of one's identity (Nitsch, 1987; Jairath, 1984; Russell, 2007) is new found, but that it previously tended to focus on, individuals experiences as they returned to their ancestral homeland, to get in touch with their roots. However this research focuses on reacculturation that is taking place towards an Eastern (Sikh) culture, within a western (UK) host culture. What's more with the increasing 'crossing of borders' Penaloza, (1994) and diminishing immigrant boundaries it is evident through consumer research within the area of acculturation (Penaloza, 1989, 1994; Oswald, 1999; Askegaard et al., 2005; Ustuner and Holt, 2007), that reacculturation to homeland cultures is becoming a significant factor that influences the consumption processes of individuals from multiple cultural backgrounds. There has been increasing consumer research into the notion of reterritorialization (Askegaard et al., 2005; Ustuner and Holt) whereby migrants "recraft a sense of community and cultural identity in new socio-geographic contexts" (Punathambekar, 2005, p.152); however reacculturation is a term that has been scarcely used by consumer researchers (Wamwara-Mbgua, 2006). I believe the term is particularly appropriate to describe how third generation (i.e. those born in the country to which their family (grandparents and parents) immigrated) immigrants feel a need to reconnect with their roots. To this end I use the 3rd generation of the British Sikh community and their relationship with Bollywood as the research context to generate thoughts in relation to their reacculturation processes.

Significantly Bollywood is recognised as a creative and significant world cinema, the Indian version of Bollywood offers an enormous production output (1000 films/year). It seems the "fascination for all things Bollywood seeped into mainstream Western music, theatre, fashion and television" (Dudrah, 2006, P.17) (e.g. the Westend show Bollywood dreams). According to Prasad (2003) Bombay-based Hindi cinema (Bollywood) has brought "the NRI (Non Resident Indian) decisively into the centre of the picture as a more stable figure of Indian identity" (P.153). Bollywood attempts to convey a "new sense of Indianness" Rajadhyaksha (2003) (p.32), a sense of Indianness that resonates deeply with members of the British Sikh community. There has been little consumer research that examines the impact of this ethnic film medium (Bollywood), especially in terms of how it encourages young British Sikhs to reconnect and reacculturate with the Indian culture. Given the increasing presence of the Bollywood film medium within the UK and the availability of Bollywood films through mainstream chains such as the Odeon, UCI, Vue and Virgin cinemas due to increasing demand from British audiences, it is important to gain insights into the impact of the Bollywood film medium on the third generation of the British Sikh community, in order to understand how Bollywood influences them to reconnect with their ethnic roots and how this may impact their identity projects (Ustuner and Holt, 2007).

The overall research question for this study was how are Bollywood films influencing the third generation of British Sikhs and how is the sense of Indianness conveyed in Bollywood films assisting reacculturation? The study adopts an interpretive research strategy and multi-method research design as advocated by Gill and Johnson, (2002), as a useful means to generate theory-building. It was carried out longitudinally over two and a half years. Stage 1 of the research was conducted through a netnographic approach (Kozinets, 2002), which consisted of online observations of an online film blog known as hindustanlink.com; it involved observations and participant observation of participants (aged 22-35) of the website. Stage 2 focused on the third generation of British Sikhs and involved participant observation, netnography (Kozinets, 2002), in-depth, face to face interviews and autoethnographic accounts. Stage 3 evolved dependent on the emergent constructs from stage 2 and involved online and offline interviews with the third generation of the British Sikh community as well as the participation in the online community of hindustanlink.com. Stage 4, the final stage also involved online interviews with the third generation and participant observation of hindustanlink.com. It adopted a theoretical sampling approach which requires continually comparing and contrasting the data being collected and seeking informants on the basis of the emergent constructs, in line with Cresswell, (2007). Interviews sought to gain in-depth insight into the influence of the Bollywood medium and to encourage informants to explore how the consumption of Bollywood films encouraged them to reacculturate to the Indian culture and traditions. In total the dataset consists of 15 online interviews, 15 face to face interviews, online participant observation, autoethnographic accounts and substantial fieldnotes. The data analysis and interpretation progressed in an iterative and interrelated manner between the online and offline environments, following the analysis and interpretation of qualitative data as recommended by Spiggle (1994) and others (Strauss and Corbin, 1990; Arnould and Wallendorf, 1994).

There were three key themes that emerged in answer to our core research question, 1) the role of Bollywood in the reacculturation and reconnection with the Indian culture, 2) the role of Bollywood films in bringing the family together and 3) the role of Bollywood in enabling third generation British Sikhs to become aware of their diasporic consciousness and in constructing a hybrid East and West Identity.

A prominent theme that is emerging as a result of exposure to Bollywood films is the reacculturation and reconnection with the Indian culture. Young British Sikhs draw on the teachings of Bollywood (Dudrah, 2006; Mehta, 2005) to understand Indian traditions such as how to maintain family honour. Through Bollywood films they also learn about this perfect, once in a lifetime, innocent, Bollywood love and romance. Where the reacculturation to the Indian culture through Bollywood is specifically useful, is in its power to influence the third generation of British Sikhs in relation to their identity projects (Ustuner and Holt, 2007) as Non Resident Indians (Prasad, 2003). Evident from the fieldnotes young third generation British Sikhs became highly self reflexive as they were exposed to scenes from Bollywood movies and questioned their own identity and goals in life. They became highly aware of the importance of their ethnic culture and identity. Third generation British Sikhs were aware of the crucial role of Bollywood in reconnecting them with the Indian culture.

Another important theme that emerged was the role of Bollywood movies in bringing the family together. Bollywood films were consumed and experienced as families and then reflected on as a family (Dudrah, 2006). Though there was an intergenerational conflict between the second generation, India born parents and the third generation, UK born children, Bollywood was used by the second generation to keep their children in touch with the Indian culture. In fact mothers often used the consumption of Bollywood movies to encourage their third generation children to resist acculturation to the Western world and maintain their Indian identity.

The third and final theme to materialize was the role of Bollywood in enabling young British Sikhs to become aware of their diasporic consciousness and therefore understand their hybrid, East/West identities as UK born British Sikhs. The Western and British culture was the dominant culture in the lives of young British Sikhs, however through exposure to Bollywood movies, they learnt about the significance of the Indian culture in their lives and identity. Through exposure to the Bollywood film medium they learnt that they did not have to choose either the Western or Eastern culture and were very aware of their diasporic consciousness and the transcultural mixtures. Young British Sikhs learnt that they were in fact able to adopt traits and characteristics of both the Eastern and Western cultures, therefore enabling them to comprehend and construct hybrid identities they were comfortable with as British Sikhs.

REFERENCES

Arnould, E. J. and Wallendorf, M. (1994), "Market Oriented Ethnography: Interpretation Building and Marketing Strategy Formulation", *Journal of Marketing Research*, Vol 31, No. 4, pp. 484-504.

Askegaard, S., Arnould, E. J. and Kjeldgaard, D. (2005), "Postassimilationist Ethnic Consumer Research: Qualifications and Extensions", *Journal of Consumer Research*, Vol 32, No.1, pp. 160-170.

Cresswell, J. (2007), *Qualitative Inquiry and Research design: Choosing among Five Approaches*, Thousand Oaks, CA: Sage.

Dudrah, R. K., (2006), *Bollywood: Sociology Goes to the Movies*, India, New Delhi: Sage.

Gill J. and Johnson P. (2002), *Research Methods for Managers*, London: Paul Chapman Publishing Ltd.

Hindustanlink.com. (2009), Hindustanlink. Retrieved 28th November 2009, from http://www.hindustanlink.com.

Jairath, Vinod. (1984), "In Search of Roots – the Indian Scientific Community", *Contributions to Indian Sociology*, May, Vol.18, Number 1, pp. 109-130.

Kozinets, R. V. (2002), "The Field Behind the Screen: Using Netnography for Marketing Research in Online Communities", *Journal of Marketing Research*, Vol 39, February, pp. 61-72.

Mehta, Monika (2005), "Globalizing Bombay Cinema: Reproducing the Indian State and Family", *Cultural Dynamics*, Vol. 17, p.135.

Nitsch, Thomas. (1987), "Social Economics: The Search For Identity to Quest for Roots; or, Social Economics: The First 100 Years (or so)", *International Journal of Social Economics*, Vol. 14, Issue 6, p.70.

Oswald, L. (1999) "Culture Swapping: Consumption and the Ethnogenesis of Haitian Immigrants", *Journal of Consumer Research*, Vol 25, March, pp. 303-318.

Penaloza, L. N. (1989), "Immigrant Consumer Acculturation" *Advances in Consumer Research*, Vol 16, pp. 110-118.

Peñaloza, L. (1994), "Atravesando Fronteras/Border Crossings: An Ethnographic Account of The Consumer Acculturation of Mexican Immigrants", *Journal of Consumer Research*, Vol 21, June, pp. 32-54.

Prasad, M. (2000), *Ideology of the Hindi Film: A Historical Construction*, New Delhi: Oxford University Press.

Punathambekar, Aswin. (2005), "Bollywood in the Indian-American diaspora: Mediating a transitive logic of cultural citizenship", *International Journal of Cultural Studies*, Vol. 8, pp.151-173.

Rajadhyaksha, Ashish. (2003), "The Bollywoodization of the Indian Cinema: Cultural Nationalism in a Global Arena", in Preben Kaarsholm ed. City Flicks: Cinema, Urban Worlds ad Modernities in India and Beyond, *Inter-Asia Cultural Studies*, April, Vol.4, Number 1,

Russell, Dale. (2007), "Consumers Tripping Over Their Roots", *Advances in Consumer Research*, Vol.34, pp. 387-390.

Spiggle, S. (1994), "Analysis and Interpretation of Qualitative Data in Consumer Research", *Journal of Consumer Research*, Vol 21, December, pp. 491-503.

Strauss, A. and Corbin, J.(1990), *Basics of Qualitative Research: Grounded Theory Procedures and Techniques*, London: Sage.

Ustuner, T. and Holt, D. B. (2007), "Dominated Consumer Acculturation: The Social Construction of Poor Migrant Women's Consumer Identity Projects in a Turkish Squatter", *Journal of Consumer Research*, Vol 34, No.1, pp. 41-56.

Wamwara-Mbugua,Wakiuru, L., Cornwell, B. T. and Boller, G. (2006), "Triple Acculturation: The Role of African Americans in the Consumer Acculturation of Kenyan Immigrants", *Advances in Consumer Research*, Vol 33, pp. 428.

You make me feel bad about myself: Shaken self-view through observing a merged other act inconsistent with one's self-view

Ali Faraji-Rad, BI Norwegian School of Management, Norway

Imagine Nick, a PhD student who has a strong belief that eating healthy is an important attribute that one should possess and truly believes that he actually possesses that attribute.One day, on his way to the cafeteria, Nick sees his friend Jeff, another PhD student at Nick's department to whom he really identifies, carrying a big bucket of French fries and toasted chicken in one hand and a big Coke in the other. How would this observation affect Nick's choice (healthy vs. unhealthy) in the cafeteria?

The consensus in persuasion literature is that similarity of one individual to another increases the propensity of him being influenced by the other person. Therefore, it would be reasonable to predict that in the previous scenario Nick would be influenced by Jeff and take an unhealthy snack in the cafeteria. Yet, we suggest that exactly due to the high degree of merged identity between Nick and Jeff, Nick is more likely to choose a healthy food in contradiction to the above-mentioned prediction.

People have the motivation to maintain a positive and consistent self-view (Aronson 1999). Therefore, any temporal threat to this self-view could result in motivation to restore this confidence (Gao, Wheeler, and Shiv 2009). For example, if someone believes that he has a healthy life-style, by reminding him that he had junk food yesterday, we would be able to shake his self-view confidence and create the motivation in him to restore his self-view by choosing a healthy snack next time. In this research, building on the spyglass-self model (Goldstein and Cialdini 2007) and merged identity theory (Aron et al. 1991) we propose that we necessarily need not remind an individual of his *own* self-view inconsistent behavior. The threat to self-view could be created by merely observing a merged-other behave in self-view inconsistent behavior. And this will result in changed behavior to restore one's own self-confidence. In the scenario above, when Nick sees Jeff, a merged other, indulge in unhealthy eating behavior; he automatically makes a self-perception that he *himself* is an unhealthy eater. But this inference is contrary to Nick's self-view and therefore it is a threat to his self-image. To restore his self-image, he will be more inclined to buy a healthy snack at the cafeteria.

Feeling of merged identity can be enhanced by perspective taking (Cialdini t al. 1997). A number of studies support this notion (Ku, Wang, andGalinsky 2010;Goldstein and Cialdini2007). Based on this evidence, we propose that participants high in chronic belief of health consciousness, when instructed to take the perspective of another individual, will showhigher preference for healthy products if they see that individual engage in unhealthy eating behavior. As the sense of merged identity is necessary for the effects of shaken self-view to emerge, we propose that this effect will not be observed in non-perspective taking individuals. Also, participants who do not see health-consciousness as central to their self-view, do not feel any treat to their self by observing a merged other act in unhealthy manner.

Design and procedure:One hundred and fifty one online panel members participated in a 2-group (perspective taker vs. observer) study for a fixed payment of 0.75$ and also "a chance to be included in a lottery for a price of around 15$". Perspective taking was manipulated between subjects and attitude towards healthy eating was measured as a continuous-measure for all participants.

First, under the disguise of a study on personalities and lifestyles, participants completed a 20-item questionnaire. Three of these items were of interest to us and were related to healthy eating andwere averaged to come up with a single measure for health consciousness ($\alpha=$ 0.864). As the next step, participants had to "read a transcript of an interview and to answer some questions about he interviewee" (always the same sex as participant). Depending on the condition, half of the participants were given perspective taking instructions and the other half did not get any particular instructions on how to read the interview. Perspective taking instructions and the interview were adopted (and slightly modified) from the ones previously used by Goldstein and Cialdini(2007). The interview was ostensibly a transcript of an audio recording and included some questions that the interviewee answered with generic responses. In the answer to the last question the interviewee showed unhealthy eating behavior.Then, participants wrote down three first thoughts that came to their mind about the interviewee. Then, they had to indicate their preference for either a 56 oz. bag of M&M or a black Fisher Space Pen (to receive incase they won the lottery). Also, they were (truly) informed that both products are worth around 15 dollars.

A logistic regression on choice data showed a significant interaction between perspective taking and health consciousness (B=-0.61, Wald=3.975, p= 0.046),a simple effect of health consciousness (B= 0.847, Wald=12.6, p= 0.000) and a non-significant effect of perspective taking (B=2.32, Wald=2.61, p>.106). Therefore, our hypothesis was supported by the data. To illustrate the difference between the conditions, we performed a median split on the health consciousness measure and calculated the percentage of participants who chose the M&M over the pen in each of the four conditions. In the non-perspective taking condition the health consciousparticipants chose the M&M 47% of the time while the non-health conscious participants chose it 50% of the time. However in the perspective taking condition the non-health conscious participants chose the M&M 58% of the time compared to only 26% of the health conscious participants who chose the M&M.

Further experiments are already on the way to further establish the effect and also to shed light on the process. The authors are currently running an experiment with a manipulation of merged identity other than perspective taking.

REFERENCES

Aron, A., Aron, E. N., Tudor, M., & Nelson, G. (1991). Close relationships as including other in the self. *Journal of Personality and Social Psychology, 60*(2), 241-253.

Aronson, E. (1999).Dissonance, Hypocrisy, and the Self-Concept. In E. Harmon-Jones & J. Mills (Eds.), *Cognitive Dissonance: Progress on a pivotal theory in social psychology* (pp. 103-126).

Cialdini, R. B., Brown, S. L., Lewis, B. P., Luce, C., &Neuberg, S. L. (1997). Reinterpreting the empathy-altruism relationship: when one into one equals oneness. *Journal of personality and social psychology, 73*(3), 481-94.

Gao, L., Wheeler, S. C., &Shiv, B. (2009). The "Shaken Self": Product Choices as a Means of Restoring Self-View Confidence. *Journal of Consumer Research, 36*(1), 29-38.

Goldstein, N. J., &Cialdini, Robert B. (2007). The spyglass self: a model of vicarious self-perception. *Journal of personality and social psychology, 92*(3), 402-17.

Ku, G., Wang, C. S., &Galinsky, A. D. (2010). Perception through a perspective-taking lens: Differential effects on judgment and behavior. *Journal of Experimental Social Psychology, 46*(5), 792-798.

More Ambient Scent, Less Product Scent?

Fan Liu, University of Central Florida, USA

Scent literature has shed light on ambient scent and product scent. As described by Orth and Bourrain (2005), ambient scent is scent or odor that is not emanating from a particular object but is present in the environment (Spangenberg et al., 1996), whereas product-specific scent derives from the product itself. According to Krishna et al. (2010), scent research has focused primarily on the effects of ambient scent on consumer evaluations, but they emphasize instead the effects of product scent on memory enhancement. It could be explained as memory for odors is assumed to have a unique system (Zucco 2003). Morrin and Ratneshwar (2000, 2003, 2010) find that ambient scent improves recall and recognition of familiar and unfamiliar brands and the retrieval of brand memory, while product scent has a stronger effect on memory enhancement due to the fact that scent-related associations are focusing on a single subject.

The project attempts to bridge the gap between ambient scent and product scent, except that scent intensity is the key variable in the manipulations, not in the position to support the findings of Spangenberg, Crowley and Henderson (1996) that only the presence or absence (not the nature or intensity) of a scent affects evaluations and behaviors. The importance of intensity should derive from individual differences, sensitivity to scent (STS) (Cupchik, Phillips, and Truong 2005). An importance question is rooted: with or without the presence of ambient scent, how differently would consumers choose scented product?

This research aims to create a framework linking ambient scent with product scent. Individuals' STS and temperature in the stores as moderators, are found to predict how the intensity of ambient scent influences consumers' attitudes and choice of scented products. Need for Stimulation (NFS) is proposed to be the underlying mechanism for variety seeking behaviors of product scent (McAlister and Pessemier 1982; Menon and Kahn 1995). Based on Menon and Kahn (1995) who are in line with previous researchers developing their theories out of Optimum Stimulation Level (OSL), when the environment provides low (high) stimulation below (above) OSL, the individual desires for increasing (decreasing) stimulation and seeks (avoids) variety and novelty. Thus, NFS (consumer actual stimulation minus OSL) refers to the tendency to maintain OSL, otherwise, simulation seeking (avoidance) will rise in order to reduce or augment incoming stimulation (Sales 1971). In the system of Stimulus Intensity Modulation, the augmenters amplify stimulus intensity, the reducers attenuate the intensity, and the moderates have no effect on the intensity (Sales 1971). Align with Sales's strength-of-the-nervous-system but not the formulation of Zuckerman that argues augmenters (reducers) are high (low) in sensation seeking, Goldman, Kohn and Hunt (1983) prove that high sensation seekers tend to be reducers, lacking sensitivity to weak stimulation (low sensitivity also means strong nervous system). This paper is more prone to apply this strength-of-the-nervous-system so as to explain the effect of ambient scent intensity on variety seeking behavior of product scent. That is to say, individuals with low STS have strong olfactory systems and high NFS, hence tend to be variety seekers. On the contrary, those with high STS have weak olfactory systems, need less stimulation and tend to seek less variety.

In Study 1, three groups of people are expected out of measuring individual differences on STS: low STS, high STS with pleasant disposition, and high STS with unpleasant disposition (neglected in the experiment). In the absence (presence) of ambient scent, STS is positively (negatively) related to variety seeking behaviors of product scent. As the ambient scent intensity increases, consumers with high STS show a greater reduction in variety seeking than those with low STS, while NFS decreases in both groups. In addition, it is hypothesized that temperature is likely to moderate the effect, as NFS could be changeable. This intuitive assumption comes from the cold and warm types of fragrance illustrated by Milotic (2003). In the cold condition, the olfactory system is stronger with increasing NFS that leads to increasing variety seeking, whereas the warm condition tends to weaken the olfactory system with lower NFS and less variety seeking. Study 2 is a 2 (ambient scent intensity: absence vs. moderate presence) x 2 (STS: high vs. low) x 2 (temperature: cold vs. warm) factorial design. In the absence (presence) of ambient scent, warmness is more likely to increase (decrease) NFS, resulting in variety seeking (avoidance) behaviors as well as supporting the results of study 1.

The research hypotheses will be empirically tested by involving undergraduate students in laboratory settings. Completion of data collection is expected by December 2011. Analysis of variance will be utilized to analyze the data and a completed manuscript is expected by April 2011. The implications of this research will advance both theoretical and managerial knowledge in scent, in light of growing concerns about scent research and marketing.

REFERENCES

Cupchik, Gerald, Krista Phillips, and Henhuy Truong (2005), "Sensitivity to the cognitive and affective qualities of odours," *Cognition & Emotion,* 19 (1), 121-31.

Goldman, Danny, Paul M. Kohn, and Robert W. Hunt (1983), "Sensation seeking, augmenting-reducing, and absolute auditory threshold: A strength-of-the-nervous-system perspective," *Journal of Personality and Social Psychology,* 45 (2), 405-11.

Krishna, Aradhna (2010), *Sensory marketing: Research on the sensuality of products* In Krishna A. (Ed.), New York, NY US: Routledge/Taylor & Francis Group.

Krishna, Aradhna, May O. Lwin, and Maureen Morrin (2010), "Product scent and memory," *Journal of Consumer Research,* 37 (1), 57-67.

Milotic, Daniel (2003), "The impact of fragrance on consumer choice," *Journal of Consumer Behaviour,* 3 (2), 179-91.

Morrin, Maureen, and S. Ratneshwar (2003), "Does it make sense to use scents to enhance brand memory?" *Journal of Marketing Research (JMR),* 40 (1), 10-25.

Orth, Ulrich R., and Aurelie Bourrain (2005), "Ambient scent and consumer exploratory behaviour: A causal analysis," *Journal of Wine Research,* 16 (2), 137-50.

Orth, Ulrich R., and Aurelie Bourrain (2005), "Optimum stimulation level theory and the differential impact of olfactory stimuli on consumer exploratory tendencies," *Advances in Consumer Research,* 32 (1), 613-9.

Sales, Stephen M. (1971), "Need for stimulation as a factor in social behavior," *Journal of Personality and Social Psychology,* 19 (1), 124-34.

Sales, Stephen M., Raymond M. Guydosh, and William Iacono (1974), "Relationship between "strength of the nervous system" and the need for stimulation," *Journal of Personality and Social Psychology,* 29 (1), 16-22.

Spangenberg, Eric A., Ayn E. Crowley, and Pamela W. Henderson (1996), "Improving the store environment: Do olfactory cues affect evaluations and behaviors?" *Journal of Marketing,* 60 (2), 67-80.

Steenkamp, Jan-Benedict E. M., and Hans Baumgartner (1992), "The role of optimum stimulation level in exploratory consumer behavior," *Journal of Consumer Research,* 19 (3), 434-48.

Zucco, Gesualdo M. (2003), "Anomalies in cognition: Olfactory memory," *European Psychologist,* 8 (2), 77-86.

The Tense of the Question Matters: Asking about the Past Leads to Personally Typical Future Behavior

Kate E. Min, Duke University, USA
Tanya L. Chartrand, Duke University, USA
Gavan J. Fitzsimons, Duke University, USA

How likely are you to visit the gym in the coming week? How often did you visit the gym in the past week? Both of these questions are about visiting the gym, but the key difference is that the former asks about visits intended in the future whereas the latter asks about visits already made in the past. According to existing research, when you are asked about future intentions to visit the gym, you are more likely to visit the gym more often than if you were not asked. That is, you are more likely to behave in the socially desirable way and align with social norms. However, extant research does not address what happens to your subsequent gym attendance when you are asked about your past gym visits. In the present research, we theorized that being asked about your past gym visits (or lack thereof) will lead you to go to the gym as frequently (or infrequently) as you did in the past. In other words, your subsequent gym visits will be aligned with how often you typically visit the gym, or what is personally typical for you.

Research has demonstrated that the simple act of asking future intention questions leads to biased responses on the part of respondents (e.g., Simmons, Bickart, and Lynch 1993) and it can even change the underlying behavior itself (e.g., Morwitz, Johnson, and Schmittlein 1993; Sherman 1980). This phenomenon has been referred to as the "question-behavior effect," (for a review, see Sprott, Spangenberg, Block, Fitzsimons, Morwitz, and Williams 2006) although it was originally referred to as the "self-erasing nature of errors of prediction" (Sherman 1980) and later referred to as "self-prophecy" (Spangenberg & Greenwald, 1999) and "mere-measurement" (Morwitz, Johnson, and Schmittlein 1993). This robust phenomenon has been demonstrated for a wide range of socially normative (desirable and undesirable) behaviors, including increasing voter registration and turnout (Greenwald, Carnot, Beach, and Young 1987), increasing volunteering for a charitable organization (Sherman 1980; Williams, Fitzsimons, and Block 2004), reducing cheating in a college classroom (Spangenberg and Obermiller 1996), and reducing gender stereotyping (Spangenberg and Greenwald 1999). Past research has repeatedly demonstrated that the simple act of answering a question about socially normative behaviors causes behavioral change aligned with social norms.

Still, it is questionable whether questions always lead to behavioral change aligned with social norms. Past research has shown that individuals align to social norms after answering questions about their future behaviors. However, in the present research, we predict and find that individuals align with personally typical behavior after answering questions about their past behaviors. We argue that this is because asking individuals about past behaviors (but not future behaviors) simply reminds them of the various past instances in which they have engaged (or not) in the target behavior and makes salient how typical it is for them to engage in that behavior. This thought of personally typical behavior then directs behavior accordingly (studies 1 and 2). We test this mechanism for the observed effects (study 3). If it is the case that asking about past behaviors makes salient what is personally typical and then aligns behavior in that way, then it should be possible to wipe out the effect when we make the discrepancy between what is personally typical and socially normative clear. Thus, we test for this possibility. We find that even when individuals are asked about their behavior in the past (and reminded of what they have typically done in the past), simply informing them that what is personally typical is not socially normative (i.e., they are doing "worse" than the average peer) leads their behavior to be more socially normative (than personally typical).

In three studies, we demonstrate that asking about future intentions to engage in behavior alters subsequent behavior differently than being asked about behavior already engaged in in the past. While extant research on the effect of questions on behavior has typically focused on asking about *future* behaviors, the present research raises the issue of asking about *past* behaviors. Our data suggest that asking about the past has significant behavioral consequences for the respondent, namely that asking about the past leads the respondent to engage in behavior one typically engages in (personally typical behavior). Furthermore, we provide support that the observed effects are due to a "consistency" mechanism whereby individuals strive to be consistent with thoughts they have about a behavior and their actual behavior.

Although our focus was on asking about the past, these findings raise the broader issue of how mental travel has consequences for what thoughts are made salient in the mind and ultimately actual behavior. As theorized by construal level theory (Liberman and Trope 2008), an event, object, or target of any sort can be removed from one's sense of immediate experience through psychological distance, with time being one dimension. Thus, an event that is to occur in the far future is experienced differently than one that is to occur in the near future. It would be interesting to test whether psychological distance from an event (near future vs. distant future) would alter behavior differently. One possibility is that asking about the distant future is construed in an abstract manner and corresponds more to abstract information, such as social norms, ultimately leading to behavior aligned with social norm. In contrast, asking about the near future may be construed in a concrete manner and correspond more to concrete information, such as behavior one normally engages in (what is personally typical), eventually leading one to engage in personally typical behavior.

In sum, the present findings contribute to the literature on how asking questions has behavioral consequences by identifying that the tense of the question matters: Asking about the past leads to personally typical future behavior. Importantly, providing feedback that one's personally typical behavior is not the social norm and providing information on the social norm, alters behaviors to be aligned with social norms. More broadly, this research provides a unique perspective on the power of social influence.

REFERENCES

Greenwald, Anthony G., Catherine G. Carnot, Rebecca Beach, and Barbara Young (1987), "Increasing Voting Behavior by Asking People if They Expect to Vote," *Journal of Applied Psychology,* 72 (2), 315-18.

Liberman, Nira and Yaacov Trope (2008), "The Psychology of Transcending the Here and Now," *Science,* 322, 1201-05.

Morwitz, Vicki, G., Eric Johnson, and David Schmittlein (1993), "Does Measuring Intent Change Behavior?" *Journal of Consumer Research,* 20 (1), 46-61.

Sherman, Steven J. (1980), "On the Self-Erasing Nature of Errors of Prediction," *Journal of Personality and Social Psychology,* 39, 211-21.

Simmons, Carolyn J., Barbara A. Bickart, and John G. Lynch (1993), "Capturing and Creating Public Opinion in Survey Research," *Journal of Consumer Research,* 20 (2), 316-329.

Spangenberg, Eric R. and Carl Obermiller (1996), "To Cheat or Not to Cheat: Reducing Cheating by Requesting Self-Prophecy," *Marketing Education Review,* 6 (3), 95-103.

Spangenberg, Eric R. and Anthony G. Greenwald (1999), "Social Influence by Requesting Self-Prophecy," *Journal of Consumer Psychology,* 8 (1), 61-89.

Sprott, Eric R., David E. Spangenberg, Lauren G. Block, Gavan J. Fitzsimons, Vicki G. Morwitz, and Patti Williams (2006), "The Question-Behavior Effect: What We Know and Where We Go From Here," *Social Influence,* 1 (2), 128-37.

Williams, Patti, Gavan J. Fitzsimons, and Lauren G. Block (2004), "When Consumers Don't Recognize 'Benign' Intentions Questions as Persuasion Attempts," *Journal of Consumer Research,* 31 (3), 540-550.

Don't Lose Your Edge: The Subculture Hard-Core as Prevention-Focused Consumers

Sommer Kapitan, University of Texas at San Antonio, USA
Kristin Trask, University of Texas at San Antonio, USA

Western society no longer revolves around town hall meetings and church socials (Belk, 1985). In the modern consumer society, instead, those in need of social interaction self-select into identity subgroups that become part social, part image-projection, and at their base, material-driven. In a subculture of consumption - formed around any brand or consumption activity, from riding Harley Davidson motorcycles and skateboarding to quilting bees, rock-climbing, kayaking, and listening to heavy metal - the "hard-core" members at the center of the subculture are the opinion leaders. They are the cultural disseminators who strictly set, maintain and adhere to a code of conduct for their group and enforce its upkeep among junior members (Fox 1987). As keepers of the faith, the hard-core are role models for the aspirant peripheral culture and probationary soft-core members who revolve around their leadership (Schouten & McAlexander 1995).

Aspiring, fringe members and those among the mainstream who are lured into the periphery of any subculture of consumption are hopeful about their possible entry into the hard-core. Their reverence and adulation of the hard-core supports the concentric structure of the subculture (Fox 1987). In this way, hard-core members operate with a prevention focus in their subculture (Higgins 1998) are sensitive to the duties and obligations of maintaining values, are on guard for negative outcomes for themselves, and may eject non-followers formally or via social ostracizing. Their role is of vigilant avoidance, which Semin, Higgins, Gil de Montes and Valencia (2005) associate with regulatory focus. Fringe members and peripheral aspirants flirting with the subculture of consumption are by definition hopeful and aspiring, sensitive to what Semin et al. (2005) note is the positive outcome orientation and eager approach of the promotion-focused strategy. Semin et al. chart responses to the different goals-based language strategies of prevention- and promotion-focused individuals that sheds insight into research on consumption subcultures and brand communities: Prevention-focused consumers are more responsive to concrete, avoidance language, whereas promotion-focused consumers are more responsive to abstract, approach-oriented language.

Since individuals speak in different ways depending on their goals, consumers are more influenced by wording that matches their goal-focus. This is especially the case in a subculture formed around a particular brand or an activity dominated by a few specialty brands. Those in the outer rings of membership are hopeful, and need encouragement from brands to pursue those hopes and rise to the ideals of the subcultures. Those in the hard-core inner circle no longer need such encouragement to stay with the brand or consumption activity, but instead are focused on the penalties of losing touch with the group or their responsibilities now that they are at the top of their game.

In this research, we hypothesize that advertising must reflect prevention language to achieve the most influence among the hard-core in any consumption subculture. Advertisements must also reflect promotion language for beginner-level products to gain market share with new converts.

Is abstract, aspiration language enough to influence all members of the subculture—especially if advertising is framed to evoke the wonderment peripheral parties have for the endurance, uniqueness, or values displayed by the subculture (Schouten & McAlexander 1995)? The literature shows further evidence to support our prediction that abstract language is not enough for members of the hard-core inner circle. Maheswaran, Sternnthal, and Gurhan-Cali (1996) find that experts only lend higher evaluations to advertisements that catalog both benefit and attribute features. Only novices, like Adidas' enthusiastic new running converts, respond positively to broad, unsupported statements like "cushioning for an amazingly smooth ride."

Thus, we predict that while abstract language may have a positive influence on the hard-core, concrete language with specific prevention orientation will engender the most favorable response from the hard-core.

In fall 2010, we assessed how members of the "gym rat" campus recreation center subculture— those who report going the most to the center and taking advantage of the machines, basketball courts, classes, and outdoor trips— respond to advertisements for a new fitness class. The 196 lab respondents (55% male, mean age=23.4) were randomly assigned to the abstract-language (i.e., "the new class works all your muscles to tone and sculpt your physique. Feel better, look better. Guaranteed") or the concrete-language (i.e., the class "combines CrossFit training with powerlifting to improve your BMI and stamina. Visible results, guaranteed") version of the advertisement, then asked to evaluate their interest in attending the class as well as their intent to recommend the class to other students. We find a significant difference between how hard-core users view the ad versus aspiring users, $F(1, 194)=9.34$, $p<.01$. Aspirant or fringe users expressed more interest in attending the advertised class when the language was abstract ($M=4.38$) versus concrete ($M=3.12$), whereas hard-core gym rats preferred the class when expressed in concrete terms ($M=4.71$) vs. abstract ($M=4.29$). Simple effects tests show that there is no significant difference between preference for abstract language, which confirms our hypothesis that hard-core users still respond positively to abstract, promotion-focused language. However, they respond significantly more to concrete language advertisements.

Our next step takes this examination beyond the lab setting to explore how members of subcultures of consumption become initiated into a subculture, and what activities (focused on key purchase moments) keep them engaged and invested with the subculture. We are conducting a study of newcomers to the triathlon community, charting their training, goals, and purchase behaviors via online diaries to capture what levels of engagement result in subsequent subculture-specific purchasing behavior (from technical gear to health food). In addition, semi-structured interviews with elite, hard-core runners are planned to understand how a member of the running subculture identifies worthy events, recognizes a runner, and incidentally reveals purchase behavior. Our hypotheses revolve around investment: Once members of a subculture reach a certain purchase threshold (i.e.,$100 for a pair of technical shoes, $1,000 for a respectable canoe or kayak, $1,000 for a top-of-the-line sewing machine), they are "in" the subculture and can work toward becoming hard-core with increasingly specialized purchases.

REFERENCES

Belk, Russell W (1985), "Trait Aspects of Living in the Material World," *Journal of Consumer Research,* 12 (3), 265-280

Fox, Kathryn Joan (1987), "Real Punks and Pretenders: The Social Organization of a Counterculture," *Journal of Contemporary Ethnography*, 16 (October), 344-370.

Higgins, E. Tory (1998), "Promotion and Prevention: Regulatory Focus as a Motivational Principle," *Advances in Experimental Social Psychology*, 30, 1-46.

Maheswaran, Durairaj, Brian Sternthal, and Zeynep Gurhan-Canli (1996), "Impact and Acquisition of Consumer Expertise," *Journal of Consumer Psychology*, 5 (2), 115-33.

Schouten, John W. and McAlexander, James H. (1995), "Subcultures of Consumption: An Ethnography of the New Bikers," *Journal of Consumer Research*, 22 (June), 43-61.

Semin, Gun R., Tory Higgins, Lorena Gil de Montes, Yvette Estourget, and Jose F. Valencia (2005), "Linguistic Signatures of Regulatory Focus: How Abstraction Fits Promotion More Than Prevention." *Journal of Personality and Social Psychology*, 89 (1), 36-45.

Is your Product in the Right Place? The Effect of Objects' Elongation and Spatial Disposition on Size Perception

Soumaya Cheikhrouhou, Concordia University, Canada
Bianca Grohmann, Concordia University, Canada

Product packaging is a key source of information consumers use to make choices and inferential judgments about products (Greenleaf and Raghubir 2008). Consumers rarely read volume labels or unitary prices (Yang and Raghubir 2005). They rely instead on visual cues in product assessment and are subject to evaluation biases. Raghubir and Krishna (1999) and Wansink and Van Ittersum (2003) find support for an elongation bias, that is, a positive and consistent bias in size estimation as elongation (i.e., ratio of height to width) increases. However, both the process underlying the elongation bias and its boundaries still remain unexplored.

Based on past work in experimental psychology (Goto et al. 2007; Marr 1977; Quinlan and Humphreys 1993; Sutherland 1968), this research seeks to demonstrate, through five studies, that the positive effect of elongation on size perception stems from a combination of assimilation/contrast judgments and a spatial disposition bias. We propose that when comparing the size of two identically-sized two-dimensional items, people first try to detect both their similar and discriminant geometrical dimensions. If no difference in the length of the two dimensions is apparent (i.e., assimilation), individuals are expected to perceive them as identical. If a difference between the two figures on the length of one dimension (e.g., height) is perceptible (i.e., contrast) while no noticeable difference appears on the other dimension (i.e., assimilation), individuals are expected to base their size assessment on the contrasting dimension solely. It is argued that side by side presentation favours the adoption of such a process where the height dimension is contrasted and the width is assimilated, which simplifies decision making. When objects are presented side by side, this process leads to the elongation bias reported in past literature. When objects are presented one above the other, width dimension is likely to contrast at low elongation difference between objects and the elongation effect is expected to be reversed.

When both dimensions' lengths contrast, the simpler assimilation/contrast mechanism does not allow for size assessment and more complex processing is needed. First, individuals are expected to fruitlessly try to use both dimensions in a compensatory manner, thus leading to no difference in choice share. When a significant difference between elongations exists and the easier assimilation/contrast processing cannot be used, another heuristic is likely to be adopted. We propose that the spatial disposition of objects triggers the salience of one dimension, leading to a hypothesized "spatial disposition bias" where horizontal presentation, for instance, increases salience of width. It is argued that this bias operates progressively as differences between the dimensions of the two objects increase, until the object presenting the longer salient dimension will be more often selected as the bigger one (i.e., the wider object in side by side presentation and the taller one in a one above the other presentation).

In study 1 (n=51), participants were shown ten pairs of rectangles of identical size and presented side by side, successively and in a random order. Each pair contained a baseline figure, which elongation ($EL_{BF}=1.5$) remained unchanged, and a manipulated figure, which elongation (EL_{MF}=1.6, 1.7, 1.8, 1.9, 2, 2.1, 2.2, 2.3, 2.4, and 2.5) varied. Participants were instructed to select the bigger figure in each pair. As expected, a positive effect of elongation on size perception was found when EL_{MF}=1.6, a level close to the baseline figure, thus illustrating the initial assimilation/contrast processing. Choice share (CS_{MF}) was significantly different from 50% (CS_{MF} =78.43%, Z=2.75, p<.01). At EL_{MF}=2.5, this effect was reversed, as hypothesized (CS_{MF}= 27.45%, Z=2.17, p<.05), reflecting the spatial disposition bias.

In study 2 (n=52), participants evaluated the same pairs, but rotated by 90 degrees. Choice share for the same figure but rotated significantly dropped from 78.43% in study 1 (EL_{MF}=1.6) to 36% in study 3 (EL_{MF}=1/1.6). Similar to study 1, the more elongated figure (which is the baseline figure here) was significantly more often chosen than 50% when EL_{MF}=1/1.7 (CS_{BF}=75%, Z=2.43, p=.01) and less often selected when EL_{MF}=1/2.4 (CS_{BF}=26.92%, Z=2.21, p<.05).

In study 3 (n=50), participants saw the same pairs presented one above the other. As expected, the elongation positive effect was reversed. At EL_{MF}=1.7 for instance, the choice share for the same more elongated figure dropped from 62.75% in study 1 to 20% in study 3 (Z=2.93, p<.01). Starting EL_{MF}=2, although steadily increasing as elongation increases, choice share for the more elongated figure was significantly different from 50%.

In study 4 (n=50), participants evaluated the same pairs of study 2, but presented one above the other. Again, the elongation effect significantly reversed when EL_{MF}=1/2.5 (CS_{MF}=28%, Z=2.05, p<.05).

Finally, in study 5 (n=50), study 1 results were replicated with a shampoo bottle image, for the sake of generalizability. The positive effect of elongation on size perception was found when EL_{MF}=1.6 (CS_{MF}=72%, Z=2, p<.05). This effect reversed more rapidly than with rectangles (starting EL_{MF}=2: CS_{MF}= 18%, Z=3.16, p<.01).

In conclusion, the elongation bias holds only for levels close to the baseline elongation, when objects are presented side by side (study 1). This effect is reversed at higher levels of elongation due to the hypothesized spatial disposition bias. When objects are rotated by 90 degrees in study 2, the more elongated object in study 1 became the less elongated one. Shifts in choice shares replicate the elongation bias and its boundaries demonstrated in study 1. When objects are presented one above the other (study 3), contrasting width led to a negative effect of elongation at lower levels of elongation difference, which disappeared at higher levels due to the absence of one contrasting dimension. These results were also found after a 90 degrees rotation (study 4). The elongation bias and its reversal were replicated with a more complex shape, where the effect reversed more rapidly than with the rectangular shape in study 5, as expected. These findings add to the cognitive psychology and consumer behavior literatures. They have critical managerial implications in terms of packaging, visual display merchandising, and positioning.

REFERENCES

Goto, Takuo, Ichiro Uchiyama, Akira Imai, Shin'ya Takahashi, Takashi Hanari, Shinji Nakamura, and Hiroyuki Kobari (2007), "Assimilation and Contrast in Optical Illusions," *Japanese Psychological Research*, 49 (1), 33–44.

Greenleaf, Eric, and Priya Raghubir (2008), "Geometry in the Marketplace," in *Visual Marketing*, eds. Michel Wedel and Rik Pieters, Lawrence Erlbaum Associates, 113-142.

Marr, David (1977), "Analysis of Occluding Contour," *Proceedings of The Royal Society*, London (B), 197, 441-475.

Quinlan, Philip T., and Glyn W. Humphreys (1993), "Perceptual Frames of Reference and Two-dimensional Shape Recognition: Further Examination of Internal Axes," *Perception*, 22, 1343-1364.

Raghubir, Priya, and Aradhna Krishna (1999), "Vital Dimensions: Biases in Volume Estimates," *Journal of Marketing Research*, 36 (3), 313-326.

Sutherland, N. S. (1968), *"Outlines of a Theory of Visual Pattern Recognition in Animals and Man,"* Proceedings of the Royal Society *(Series B)*, 17 (1024), 297-317.

Wansink, Brian, and Koert Van Ittersum (2003), "Bottoms Up! The Influence of Elongation on Pouring and Consumption Volume," *Journal of Consumer Research*, 30 (3), 455-463.

Yang, Sha, and Priya Raghubir (2005), "Can Bottles Speak Volumes? The Effect of Package Shape on How Much to Buy," *Journal of Retailing*, 81 (October), 269–281.

Would Petty Crime Be More Acceptable In The Red Light District? The Effect Of Conceptual Fluency On Moral Judgment

Tine De Bock, Ghent University, Belgium
Mario Pandelaere, Ghent University, Belgium
Patrick Van Kenhove, Ghent University, Belgium

Moral judgments have traditionally been considered as the result of rational and deliberate reasoning processes (e.g., Jones, 1991). More recently, however, scholars have argued that moral decision making is also influenced by intuitive factors (e.g., Reynolds, 2006). Like many other judgments, moral judgments are guided by not only rational thought, but also by feelings that are present at the time of judgment (Schwarz & Clore, 2007). One important class of feelings which influence people's judgments involves metacognitive experiences, which are the experiences that arise during information processing. Conceptual and perceptual fluency are a specific instance of what is called processing fluency (Tulving & Schacter, 1990), a metacognitive experience which refers to the subjective experience of ease versus difficulty while processing information and stimuli. Experiencing fluency evokes a positive affective state which people attribute to the judgmental stimuli they are evaluating (Winkielman, et al., 2003). In particular, perceptual fluency refers to the ease with which people perceive and identify the physical characteristics of stimuli, which can be enhanced through for example figure-ground contrast (e.g., Reber, Winkielman, & Schwarz,

1998). A stimulus is conceptually fluent when its mental representation is easier to activate due to the semantic relatedness with the context in which the stimulus appears (e.g., Whittlesea, 1993).

Considering the role of feelings in moral judgment, we expect feelings that stem from conceptual fluency to affect these moral judgments. In particular, a context associated with something *good* activates the concept of *good* which, in turn, should render the processing of good behavior (i.e., moral behavior) more conceptually fluent. In contrast, a context associated with something *bad* activates the concept of *bad* which should make it easier to process bad behavior (i.e., immoral behavior). The resulting enhanced conceptual fluency (i.e., good behavior in a good context; bad behavior in a bad context) should result in enhanced processing fluency which, in turn, triggers a positive affective state. This positive affect leads subsequently to a more positive evaluation of the good and bad (i.e., moral and immoral) behavior at hand. In sum, people should judge a given moral or immoral behavior more positively when the valence of the context in which the behavior is evaluated matches the valence of the target behavior.

In the current paper, conceptual fluency was manipulated by means of a match versus non-match between the valence (negative vs. positive) of consumer behaviors to be evaluated, and the valence (negative vs. positive) of the background color on which these behaviors were described. In the first study, participants viewed descriptions of (im)moral consumer behaviors on either a red (negative valence) or green (positive valence) background color. We used the colors red and green as these two colors are often used as cues signaling bad and good, respectively (e.g., Dijksterhuis & Smith, 2002). Findings reveal that immoral behaviors were perceived as more acceptable when described on a red (vs. green) background color while the opposite was true for moral behaviors. In the second study, instead of using the "moral colors" red and green, we relied on two colors that were initially perceived as neutral but which were endowed with either a negative or positive valence. Results of this second study confirm those of the first: A match between the valence of the behavior to be evaluated and the valence of the background color on which the behavior appears, renders processing more conceptually fluent. The resulting enhanced processing fluency translates into a positive affective state and, subsequently, a more positive evaluation of the (im)moral consumer behavior at hand.

These results contribute to the literature in at least two respects. First, while moral judgments are traditionally considered to result from rational deliberation, our findings add to the emerging stream of research that shows that these judgments are also affected by more intuitive elements (e.g., Haidt, 2001). Second, most research dealing with processing fluency focused on perceptual fluency. Although perceptual and conceptual fluency are independent, distinct constructs, with each their own unique antecedents and consequences (e.g., Lee, 2002), processing fluency is typically studied through manipulations that trigger perceptual fluency. Nevertheless, processing fluency can also be conceptually driven. While the impact of perceptual fluency has been investigated on a wide array of domains, research on conceptual fluency has been limited (Lee & Labroo, 2004). Our findings therefore add to the limited literature on conceptual fluency. Further, to the best of our knowledge, this is the first research that operationalizes conceptual fluency through a *valence* match between a stimulus and its context, rather than through a semantic association.

Conceptual fluency may also underlie some other recent findings testifying to the impact of intuitive elements in the moral domain. For instance, conceptual fluency may explain why darkness increases dishonesty and self-interested behavior (Zhong, Bohns & Gino, 2010). In particular, Zhong et al. (2010) found that participants in a room with slightly dimmed lighting cheated more and, consequently, earned more undeserved money than those in a well-lit room. As darkness is often related to badness (Meier, Robinson, & Clore, 2004), dishonest behavior may be deemed more acceptable in a dark room than in a well-lit room (for reasons of conceptual fluency). This may have led to a more positive rate of dishonest behavior.

Given the omnipresent and far-ranging consequences of moral judgment (Hofmann & Baumert, 2010), it is highly important to gain a more comprehensive insight into the various aspects that might influence these moral judgments. This paper shows that conceptual fluency may affect the acceptability of (im)moral behaviors. In addition, our studies show that conceptual fluency may lead to paradoxical effects. For instance, messages to deter undesirable behavior may inadvertently render that behavior more acceptable if some message elements carry a negative connotation (e.g., when written in a red font). In addition, undesirable behavior, like petty crime, may be more likely if the physical environment is evaluated negatively (e.g., Bronx or Red light district). An important goal for future research might be to identify physical elements that promote or prevent (im)moral behavior due to their evaluative connotation.

REFERENCES

Dijksterhuis, A., & Smith, P.K. (2002). Affective habituation: Subliminal exposure to extreme stimuli decreases their extremity. *Emotion*, *2*(2), 203-214.

Haidt, J. (2001). The emotional dog and its rational tail: A social intuitionist approach to moral judgment. *Psychological Review*, *108*(4), 814-834.

Hofmann, W., & Baumert, A. (2010). Immediate affect as a basis for intuitive moral judgment: An adaptation of the affect misattribution procedure. *Cognition and Emotion*, *24*(3), 522-535.

Jones, T.M. (1991). Ethical decision making by individuals in organizations: An issue-contingent model. *Academy of Management Review*, *16*(2), 366-395.

Lee, A.Y. (2002). Effects of implicit memory on memory-based versus stimulus-based brand choice. *Journal of Marketing Research*, *39*(4), 440-454.

Lee, A.Y., & Labroo, A.A. (2004). The effect of conceptual and perceptual fluency on brand evaluation. *Journal of Marketing Research*, *41*(2), 151-165.

Meier, B.P., Robinson, M.D., & Clore, G.L. (2004). Why good guys wear white: Automatic inferences about stimulus valence based on brightness. *Psychological Science*, *15*(2), 82-87.

Reber, R., Winkielman, P., & Schwarz, N. (1998). Effects of perceptual fluency on affective judgments. *Psychological Science*, *29*(1), 45-48.

Reynolds, S.J. (2006). A neurocognitive model of the ethical decision-making process: Implications for study and practice. *Journal of Applied Psychology*, *91*(4), 737-748.

Schwarz, N., & Clore, G. L. (2007). Feelings and phenomenal experiences. In E. T. Higgins & A. Kruglanski (Eds.), *Social psychology. Handbook of basic principles* (2nd ed.; pp. 385-407). New York: Guilford.

Tulving, E., & Schacter, D.L. (1990). Priming and human memory systems. *Science, 247*(4940), 301-306.

Whittlesea, B.W.A. (1993). Illusions of familiarity. *Journal of Experimental Social Psychology: Learning, Memory, and Cognition, 19*(6), 1235-1253.

Winkielman, P., Schwarz, N., Fazendeiro, T., & Reber, R. (2003). The hedonic marking of processing fluency: Implications for evaluative judgment. In J. Musch & K.C. Klauer (Eds.), *The psychology of evaluation: Affective processes in cognition and emotion* (pp. 189-217). Mahwah, NJ: Erlbaum Associations, Inc..

Zhong, C.B., Bohns, V.K., & Gino, F. (2010). Good lamps are the best police: Darkness increases dishonesty and self-interested behavior. *Psychological Science, 21*(3), 311-314.

Social Exclusion and Consumer Product Preferences

Jessie Wang, Indiana University, USA
Shuoyang Zhang, Colorado State Univeristy, USA

Human beings have fundamental needs to feel included and to belong to social groups (Baumeister and Leary 1995). Prior research indicates that socially excluded people have an increased desire to reconnect (Maner et al. 2007). The impact of social exclusion on consumption has attracted consumer researchers' interests in recent years. Mead et al. (2011) suggest that people use consumption to seek potential affiliation when they are excluded. Specifically, the experience of social exclusion increases people's tendency to conform to their potential affiliations' consumption preferences in order to seek inclusion. In the current research, we take a closer look at consumers' reaction to social exclusion and examine whether their conformity behavior is product domain specific.

We propose that excluded consumers conform to their potential affiliations' product preferences only in the value-expressive product domain, and not in the utilitarian product domain. Previous studies have shown that people make inferences about others' social identity and preferences based on their product preferences and purchase decisions (Belk, Bahn, and Mayer 1982; Calder and Burnkrant 1977; Holman 1981). However, people do not infer identities equally in all product domains (Shavitt and Nelson 1999; Berger and Heath, 2007; Belk, 1981). Instead, people are more likely to make inferences or to communicate with others through product preferences in the value-expressive product domain rather than in the utilitarian product domain (Shavitt and Nelson 1999; Berger and Heath, 2007). Mead at al., (2011) have found that high self-monitors align their product preferences to potential affiliations' preferences but not low self-monitors. We thus predict that when excluded consumers are high in self-monitoring they are more likely to conform in the value-expressive domain, to infer identity while seeking inclusion from their potential affiliation, but not in the utilitarian domain.

METHOD

Study 1 was a 3 (social exclusion: exclusion vs. acceptance vs. control) x 2 (product domain: value-expressive vs. utilitarian) x 2 (self-monitoring: high vs. low) mixed factorial design. Social exclusion and self-monitoring were between-subject factors; while product domain was a within-subject factor. The social exclusion manipulation was adopted from Gardner et al. (2000). Participants arrived in the lab for ostensibly separate studies, and they were randomly assigned to one of the three essay conditions: social exclusion, social acceptance, or neutral control. Participants were told to engage in a memory task and asked to write an essay of a personal experience when they either felt excluded, accepted or neutral (a lunch experience). Participants were then led to believe they were engaging in a separate study that was interested in their momentary feelings. They responded to a mood measure using the positive and negative affect schedule (PANAS) scale (Watson, Clark, and Tellegen 1988), which served as our manipulation check on social exclusion.

Following the mood measure, participants were led to believe that the next study was a product evaluation study and they would complete it with an assigned partner. They then were given a sheet that indicates their partners' product preferences on a series of 12 sample products. They were also told that their response would be revealed to the partner before the face to face meeting (Mead et al. 2011). After reading their partners' product preferences, all the participants were asked to choose one of two options for 12 product sets, including 6 in the value-expressive and 6 in the utilitarian domain. The order of the product categories is randomized. For example, in the utilitarian product domain, participants were given choices between two brands of bike light that have similar functionality. In the value-expressive product domain, participants are given choices between two music genres.

After the product evaluation task, participants were told to engage in one more independent study before meeting their partners. All participants were led to believe that the purpose of the next study was to find out how people feel about themselves in relationships with others. We used Snyder and Gangestad (1986)'s revised self-monitoring scale to measure people's self-monitoring levels. Finally, participants were debriefed and released.

RESULTS

74 undergraduate students in a public university participated in exchange for partial course credit. We used the number of participants conformed in each product category as the dependent measure. Consistent with our hypothesis, we found that in the social exclusion condition significantly more participants who are high self-monitors conform to their partners' product preferences in the value-expressive product domain compared to low self-monitors. We did not find such difference in utilitarian product domain.

CONCLUSION

In the current research, we investigate excluded consumers' conformity behavior in different product domains. We identified that consumers' desire to reconnect is more likely to be satisfied in the value-expressive domain. Our finding adds to the current literature by suggesting that excluded consumers selectively align their product preferences to their potential affiliations' in the specific product domain that communicates their identity most effectively. In future studies, we plan to use different social exclusion manipulation methods to test the robustness of the hypothesis in the first study. We also intend to further explore excluded consumers' consumption behaviors in addition to conformity in the value expressive product domain.

REFERENCES

Baumeister, Roy F. and Mark R. Leary (1995), "The Need to Belong: Desire for Interpersonal Attachments as a Fundamental Human Motivation," Psychological Bulletin, 117 (3), 497-529.

Maner, Jon K., C. Nathan DeWall, Roy F. Baumeister, and Mark Schaller (2007), "Does Social Exclusion Motivate Interpersonal Reconnection? Resolving the "Porcupine Problem," Journal of Personality and Social Psychology, 92 (1), 42-55.

Mead, Nicole L., Roy F. Baumeister, Tyler F. Stillman, Catherine D. Rawn, and Kathleen D. Vohs (2011), "Social Exclusion Causes People to Spend and Consume Strategically in the Service of Affiliation," *Journal of Consumer Research*, 37(5), 902-19.

Calder, Bobby J. and Robert E. Burnkrant (1977), "Interpersonal Influence on Consumer Behavior: An Attribution Theory Approach," *Journal of Consumer Research*, 4 (June), 29–38.

Belk, Russell W., Kenneth D. Bahn, and Robert N. Mayer (1982), "Developmental Recognition of Consumption Symbolism," Journal of Consumer Research, 9 (June), 4–17.

Holman, Rebecca H. (1981), "Product as Communication: A Fresh Appraisal of a Venerable Topic," in Review of Marketing, ed. Ben M. Eris and Kenneth J. Boering, Chicago: American Marketing Association, 106–19.

Shavitt, Sharon and Michelle R. Nelson (1999), "The Social Identity Function in Person Perception: Communicated Meanings of Product Preferences," in *Why We Evaluate: Function of Attitudes*, ed. Gregory R. Maio and James M. Olson, Mahwah, NJ: Erlbaum, 37–57.

Berger, Jonah and Chip Heath (2007), "Where Consumers Diverge from Others: Identity-Signaling and Product Domains," *Journal of Consumer Research*, 34 (August), 121–34.

Belk, Russell W. (1981), "Determinants of Consumption Cue Utilization in Impression Formation: An Associational Deviation and Experimental Verification," in *Advances in Consumer Research*, Vol. 8, ed. Kent Monroe, Ann Arbor, MI: Association for Consumer Research.

Gardner, Wendi L., Cynthia L. Pickett, and Marilynn B. Brewer (2000), "Social Exclusion and Selective Memory: How the Need to Belong Influences Memory for Social Events, *"Personality and Social Psychology Bulletin,* 26 (4), 486-96.

Snyder, Mark and Steve Gangestad (1986), "On the Nature of Self-Monitoring: Matters of Assessment, Matters of Validity," *Journal of Personality and Social Psychology*, 51 (1), 121-139.

Doing non-transcendent go green: the moderating role of identity on value-behavior relationship.

Diego Costa-Pinto, Reims Management School, France
Adilson Borges, Reims Management School, France
Walter Nique, UFRGS, Brazil
Márcia Herter, Reims Management School, France

VALUES–BEHAVIOR AND THE MODERATING ROLE OF IDENTITY-BASED MOTIVATION

Values are preceded by culture, society and personality, and extant research has shown that value leads to behavioral outcomes (Rokeach, 1973; Schwartz, 1992, 1994). Although numerous empirical studies support a value–behavior relation (e.g., Rokeach, 1973; Schwartz, 1996) the variability of this relationship may be impacted by facilitating or impeding factors, such as construal level (Torelli and Kaikati, 2009). According to situated social cognition perspective, cognition and action are dynamically shaped by contexts (Schwarz, 2007, 2009). In this sense, we argue that the value–behavior relation maybe affected by evoked identities.

Identity-based motivation is the readiness to engage in identity-congruent action (Oyserman, 2007), using identity-congruent mindsets in making sense of the world (Oyserman *et al.*, 2009). As part of the self-concept, the identity presents a basis for making predictions about oneself and about others' response to the self. Personal identities focus on traits, characteristics and goals that are not connected to a social group. The salience of a personal identity facilitates one to construe the situation in terms of values that are relevant to the self, leading to value-congruent judgments and behaviors (Oyserman, 2009). In contrast, when the social identity is salient, the self is contextualized and linked to a social group, which in turn downplay the personal values and increase in-group conformity (Briley, 2001).

DOING NON-TRANSCENDENT PEOPLE GO GREENER

The present study examines the interactional effect of identity and self-transcendence values on green consumption. We suggest that the fit between values and evoked identities can influence green consumption of non-transcendent values. Specifically, we expect that in social (vs. personal) identity situation, people will increase their pro-social evaluations and intentions. This mechanism will change values influence on behavior, doing non-transcendence values take into green consumption.

One hundred and fifty three participants were randomly assigned to one of the four conditions of a 2 values (transcendent vs. non-transcendent) x 2 identities (personal vs. social) between-subjects design. In this study, evoked identities were manipulated using as priming, similarities and differences between family and friends – SDFF (Oyserman and Lee, 2007). Values were chronically accessed by values index: transcendence ($\alpha = 0.714$) - Non-transcendent values ($\alpha = 0.640$; Schwartz, 1992). Transcendence and non-transcendence values were obtained by median split of composite values index. The main dependent variable is the preference for green products. This DV has been computed by asking subjects to indicate their preference for a green or a non-green option for three product categories (batteries, lamp and backpack) (adapted from Griskevicius *et al.*, 2010).

Manipulation checks were made by self-construal index (Singelis, 1994). A 2x2 ANOVA interaction between values and identity for the manipulation checks was significant (F (1.154) = 6:35, p <.05).

Results show that values and identity have an interactional effect on green consumption, as predicted (F (1, 153) = 10.36, $p<$ .01). As expected, when personal identity was salient, transcendent participants reported more green consumption than non-transcendent participants ($M_{transcendent}$ = 4.92, $M_{non\text{-}transendent}$ = 3.48; $p<.001$). More interesting though, when social identity was salient, participants in both transcendent and non-transcendent values reported similar green consumption intention (M_t = 4.69, M_{nt} = 4.56; *n.s.*). That is, in a social identity, congruent and incongruent values took into more green consumption.

IMPLICATIONS

Our findings indicate the hypothesized moderating role of identity on value-behavior relationship. First, we show that identity salience can change values influence on behavior, increasing green consumption in non-transcendent values condition. In doing so, provide new evidence for values-behavior relation strengthen or weaken factors, using identity-based motivation as a boundary condition (Briley and Wyer, 2001; Torelli and Kaikati, 2009).

Second, although past research indicates that values-behavior congruence will lead to action-readiness (Allen *et al.*, 2008), our results demonstrate that people can take action even under incongruent values-behavior situations. Specifically, we show that non-transcendent values can increase green consumption, when the social identity is activated.

Third, we highlight a new path for research, the value-identity-behavior approach. Specifically, we suggest that personal identity salience reinforce the role that values will have on intention formation. In contrast, social identity reinforces social context, increasing social action-readiness. That can result in more positive green consumption even when values and behavior are incongruent.

One alternative explanation for this mechanism is that social identity can place in evidence the social values systems (Rohan, 2000), increasing social value priorities attachment. Further studies can investigate this possibility.

REFERENCES

Allen, M. W., Gupta, R. and Monnier, A. (2008) "The Interactive Effect of Cultural Symbols and Human Values on Taste Evaluation", *Journal of Consumer Research: An Interdisciplinary Quarterly,* 35(2), 294-308.

Briley, D. A. and Wyer, R. S. (2001) "Transitory determinants of values and decisions: The utility (or nonutility) of individualism and collectivism in understanding cultural differences", *Social Cognition,* 19(3), 197-227.

Fraj, E. and Martinez, E. (2006) "Environmental values and lifestyles as determining factors of ecological consumer behaviour: an empirical analysis", *Journal of Consumer Marketing,* 23(3), 133-144.

Griskevicius, V., Tybur, J. M. and Van den Bergh, B. (2010) "Going green to be seen: Status, reputation, and conspicuous conservation", *Journal of personality and social psychology,* 98(3), 392-404.

Oyserman, D. (2009) "Identity-based motivation and consumer behavior", *Journal of Consumer Psychology,* 19(3), 276-279.

Oyserman, D. and Lee, S. W. S. (2007) "Priming" culture": Culture as situated cognition".

Oyserman, D., Sorensen, N., Reber, R. and Chen, S. X. (2009) "Connecting and separating mind-sets: Culture as situated cognition", *Journal of personality and social psychology,* 97(2), 217-235.

Rohan, M. J. (2000) "A rose by any name? The values construct", *Personality and Social Psychology Review,* 4(3), 255.

Rokeach, M. (1973) "The nature of human values".

Schwartz, S. (1996) "Value priorities and behavior: Applying a theory of integrated value systems", *The psychology of values,* 8, 1-24.

Schwartz, S. H. (1992) "Universals in the content and structure of values: Theoretical advances and empirical tests in 20 countries", *Advances in experimental social psychology,* 25(1), 1-65.

Schwartz, S. H. (1994) "Are there universal aspects in the structure and contents of human values?", *Journal of social issues,* 50(4), 19-45.

Schwartz, S. H. (2007) "Universalism values and the inclusiveness of our moral universe", *Journal of Cross-Cultural Psychology,* 38(6), 711.

Schwartz, S. H. and Rubel-Lifschitz, T. (2009) "Cross-national variation in the size of sex differences in values: effects of gender equality", *Journal of personality and social psychology,* 97(1), 171-185.

Singelis, T. M. (1994) "The measurement of independent and interdependent self-construals", *Personality and Social Psychology Bulletin,* 20(5), 580.

Torelli, C. J. and Kaikati, A. M. (2009) "Values as predictors of judgments and behaviors: The role of abstract and concrete mindsets", *Journal of Personality and Social Psychology,* 96(1), 231-247.

Going green for friends, family or community?
How different levels of subject norms and identity influence green behavior.

Márcia Herter, Reims Management School, France
Diego Costa-Pinto, Reims Management School, France
Adilson Borges, Reims Management School, France
Walter Nique, UFRGS, Brazil

This paper has two main goals. First, this study aims to examine how the interaction between identity and different subjective norms influences the green behavior. Specifically, it is expected that green behavior, typically a social behavior, produce larger effects in social (vs. personal) identity, because it activates subjective norms. Second, we analyze how different subjective norms influence green behavior. In this sense we investigate whether people go green for friends, family or community.

IDENTITY-BASED MOTIVATION AND SUBJECTIVE NORMS

The identity-based motivation model (IBM) provides an integrative review of how the identity active processes and content (Oyserman, 2009). In this sense, people interpret situations and problems in ways that are congruent with the activated (personal or social) identity. Subjective norms regulate behavior and act as informal social controls (Ajzen, 1991). However, according to the identity-based motivation (IBM), the influence of subjective norms on behavior can be intensified or weakened depending on the evoked identity (Oyserman, 2009). As consequence, when personal identity is evoked, people are less prone to be influenced by norms. However, when the social identity is evoked, norms will present a great importance on behavior. Thus, it is expect that identity has a moderating role in influencing subjective norms.

SUBJECTIVE NORMS LEVELS

Prior research suggests that the self is composed by different levels of inclusion (Markus and Kitayama, 1991). In this sense, Harb and Smith (2008) extend the concept of self-construal (independent and interdependent), suggesting four different layers of the self (personal, relational, collective and humanity). These four levels of self-inclusion can have different importance in consumer decisions.

In this study we investigated how relational and collective subjective norms influence green behavior. According to Goldstein *et al.* (2008) it is expected that relational norms (family and friends) will be more influential on the green behavior than collective norms (community).

In contrast, construal level theory predicts that individuals in an abstract construal were more inclined to perceive their relevant high-level goals (Freitas *et al.*, 2009). In this sense, conversely to Goldstein *et al.* (2008) proposition, people would engage on green behavior when abstract norms are salient (collective vs. relational norms). Then, how these different levels of subject norms and identity influence green behavior?

RESULTS

One hundred and fifty nine participants were randomly assigned to one of four conditions in a 2 (subjective norms: high and low) x 2 (identities: social and personal) design. Three different ANOVA's 2x2 were performed for each of the different subjective norms (friends, family and community). In this study, evoked identities were primed through similarities and differences between family and friends task – SDFF (Oyserman and Lee, 2007). Subjective norms were chronically accessed by green subjective norms items (Van Birgelen *et al.*, 2008). High and low subjective norms were obtained by median split of each norm. The main dependent variable (DV) is the behavioral choice between recycled and regular paper. This measure was obtained when participants chose the second questionnaire booklet between a green or a non-green paper option. The interaction of identity and subjective norms in the choice of paper (recycled) was performed using generalized linear models (GLM) binomial distribution in a logistic function.

First, we analyzed the interaction between identity and relational norms. In contrast to expectations, the interaction between identity and friends norms (Wald χ^2 (1) =.78; *ns*) and between identity and family norms (Wald χ^2 (1) =.78; *ns*) were not significant.

Second, we analyzed the interactional effect of identity and collective norms. Results provide support for this interaction (Wald χ^2 (1) =4.42; *p*<.05). As expected, when a personal identity was salient, community norms had not impacted green behavior (M_{high} = 0.64, M_{low} = 0.68; *ns*). Conversely, when social identity was salient, high norms participants reported more green behavior than low norms participants (M_{high} = 0.84, M_{low} = 0.59; *p*<.01).

CONCLUSIONS

Our findings indicate the hypothesized moderating role of identity on subjective norms activation. Specifically, we show that social identity (vs. personal identity) activates the influence of subjective norms on green behavior.

In addition we investigated how different subjective norms can influence the green behavior. In contrast with predicted by theory (Goldstein *et al.*, 2008), we found that collective (vs. relational) social norms were more influential on the green behavior. In our results, subjective norms were more effective for the layers more distant to the self, increasing the use of recycled paper.

A proposed mechanism for that is social identity activates social goals, making the choice to help the environment something relevant to the communitarian goals (Briley and Wyer, 2001). In one hand, the effects of relational norms (family and friends) would occur in situations where the green behavior could improve the social image for closer social identity. On the other hand collective norms will be more important for green behavior than relational norms because is a typical pro-social behavior. This could be the reason why collective (vs. relational norms) were more important on increasing green behavior.

These unexpected results can open space for new interpretations. One alternative suggested mechanism is that social identity takes into more abstract way of thinking (Eyal *et al.*, 2008). Moreover, Torelli and Kaikati (2009) found that and abstract (and not a concrete) mindset led participants to engage in behaviors that were consistent with an abstract mindset. Then, we expect that the interaction between an abstract identity (social) and an abstract norm (collective) could lead into more green behavior. Further studies can investigate this possibility.

REFERENCES

Ajzen, I. (1991) "The theory of planned behavior", *Organizational behavior and human decision processes,* 50(2), 179-211.

Briley, D. A. and Wyer, R. S. (2001) "Transitory determinants of values and decisions: The utility (or nonutility) of individualism and collectivism in understanding cultural differences", *Social Cognition,* 19(3), 197-227.

Eyal, T., Sagristano, M. D., Trope, Y., Liberman, N. and Chaiken, S. (2009) "When values matter: Expressing values in behavioral intentions for the near vs. distant future", *Journal of Experimental Social Psychology,* 45(1), 35-43.

Freitas, A. L., Clark, S. L., Kim, J. Y. and Levy, S. R. (2009) "Action-construal levels and perceived conflict among ongoing goals: Implications for positive affect", *Journal of Research in Personality,* 43(5), 938-941.

Goldstein, N. J., Cialdini, R. B. and Griskevicius, V. (2008) "A room with a viewpoint: Using social norms to motivate environmental conservation in hotels", *Journal of Consumer Research,* 35(3), 472-482.

Harb, C. and Smith, P. B. (2008) "Self-Construals Across Cultures", *Journal of Cross-Cultural Psychology,* 39(2), 178.

Markus, H. R. and Kitayama, S. (1991) "Culture and the self: Implications for cognition, emotion, and motivation", *Psychological review,* 98(2), 224.

Oyserman, D. (2009) "Identity-based motivation and consumer behavior", *Journal of Consumer Psychology,* 19(3), 276-279.

Oyserman, D. and Lee, S. W. S. (2007) "Priming culture: Culture as situated cognition".

Torelli, C. J. and Kaikati, A. M. (2009) "Values as predictors of judgments and behaviors: The role of abstract and concrete mindsets", *Journal of Personality and Social Psychology,* 96(1), 231-247.

van Birgelen, M., Semeijn, J. and Keicher, M. (2009) "Packaging and proenvironmental consumption behavior", *Environment and Behavior,* 41(1), 125.

When Vices Make You Feel Less Guilty Than Virtues: The Discarding of Vice and Virtue Products

Olivia (Wan-Ting) Lin, Texas A&M University, USA

Most people (93%) are guilty of abandoning products they have purchased but never used (Wansink, Basel, and Amjab 2000). Living in this materialistic society, consumers make daily decisions not only about buying and consuming products but also about disposing of them. Depending on the price and the type of the product, consumers may form differential perceptions and feelings toward its disposal. For instance, discarding a jar of spoiled Russian caviar usually induces more regret than dumping a dozen of rotten chicken eggs. As manifested by the sunk cost psychology (Arkes and Blumer 1985), missing the opportunity benefits of the $300 caviar is generally more painful than failing to reap the benefits of the $3 chicken eggs. However, is trashing a $10 pack of cigarettes the same as discarding a $10 bottle of vitamins? This research investigates if consumers perceive and feel differently about the disposal of two relative goods: a vice (product with immediate benefits and delayed costs) and a virtue (product with immediate costs and delayed benefits) (Wertenbroch 1998). We propose that the discarding of a vice induces less guilt than that of a virtue because the former can be justified as "good riddance" while the latter is regarded as "bad rubbish."

While haste makes waste, so does procrastination. Purchase impulsiveness and consumption procrastination can create huge waste. Owing to their present-biased preferences, consumers are vulnerable to making impulse purchases of vices and putting off the consumption of virtues (e.g., Ainslie 1975; Milkman, Rogers, and Bazerman 2009; Read, Loewenstein, and Kalyanaraman 1999). Thus, decisions regarding the disposal of expired virtues and vices can often confront consumers, who knowingly defer or negligently forget consuming the products, or simply fail to use them because of competing alternatives. For example, many people do their grocery shopping on weekends but barely use their perishables during the week because they are too tired or too busy to cook after work (Jones 2004). Not surprisingly, they eventually find virtues (e.g., broccolis, cabbage sprouts, grapefruits, etc.), vices (e.g., bacon, butter, cake, etc.), or other things go bad in their refrigerators. In fact, "as *much as 25% of the food we bring into our homes is wasted. So a family of four that spends $175 a week on groceries squanders more than $40 worth of food each week and $2,275 a year,*" estimated Bloom (2010) based on various studies such as the three-decade-long Garbage Project of the University of Arizona. Arkes and Blumer (1985) claim that people fall for the sunk cost fallacy because they do not want to be or appear to be wasteful. Aversion to waste is widely assumed to prevail among consumers (Arkes 1996; Bolton and Alba 2007) because of economic, environmental, religious, ethical, psychological, or other reasons (Lastovicka et al. 1999; DeYoung 1986). Nevertheless, wasteful consumption of foods and other goods remains a tough global challenge (UNEP 2011).

This research first adopts a "refrigerator cleaning" scenario to test if consumers feel differential when finding a bag of rotten grapefruits (expired virtue) and a box of stale chocolate cake (expired vice) in their refrigerators. We employ a within-subject experimental design in which the sequence of the products is counterbalanced. For checking the effects of different price levels, we randomly assigned our college student participants to three price conditions. The first condition provides no price information, while the second (third) indicates $5 ($10) for each product. We ask our participants to imagine being in the scenario, answer Likert-scale questions about their guilt levels for the discarding of each product, and then explain why they feel so in an open-ended question. They also rate how enjoyable or beneficial they normally think about the consumption of fresh grapefruits and chocolate cakes. After rating their preference for some filler pictures for distraction purposes, participants are presented a grocery shopping scenario and are asked their intention for purchasing grapefruits or chocolate cakes. Finally, participants respond to some basic demographic questions and are thanked for their participation.

Our results show that consumers generally feel less guilty about the disposal of a vice than that of a virtue. Guilt levels do not vary significantly across the three price levels or account for the variances of repurchase intention. Perceived hedonic (e.g., enjoyable) and utilitarian (e.g., beneficial) values do predict the guilt level and the repurchase intention. The more consumers perceive the product as enjoyable or beneficial, the higher their guilt levels for its discarding and the stronger their repurchase intentions for the product.

Belk (1988) argues that consumers' possessions play an important role in shaping their self-concept. Consumers may acquire (Richins 1994) or discard (Roster 2001) products to express or reinforce their sense of self. Hence, in the parlance of mental accounting theory, both virtue and vice buyers may regret their monetary loss. However, vice buyers may mentally label the expired vice as "good riddance", something that was harmful and had better be thrown away. Some of the vice discarders might even feel a slight joy because of the illusion that they might have exerted self-control to resist the consumption of the vice. Conversely, virtue buyers may label the expired virtue as "bad rubbish", something that was valuable and beneficial and should not have ended up in a trash bin. Virtue buyers may regret their consumption procrastination, waste of money and resources, and failure to reap the benefits of the virtue product. A purchase decision, originally intended to better the consumers' *actual selves*, seems to expose their failure to live up to their *ought selves* and push them farther away from their *ideal selves*. As a result, a vice discarder feels less guilty than does a virtue discarder although they both paid the same price to acquire the products.

REFERENCES

Ainslie, George (1975), "Specious Reward: A Behavioral Theory of Impulsiveness and Impulse Control," *Psychological Bulletin*, 82, 463–96.

Arkes, Hal R. (1996), "The Psychology of Waste," *Journal of Behavioral Decision Making*, 9 (3), 213-24.

Arkes, Hal R. and Catherine Blumer (1985), "The Psychology of Sunk Cost," *Organizational Behavior and Human Decision Processes,* 35, 124-40.

Belk, Russell W. (1988), "Possessions and the Extended Self," *Journal of Consumer Research*, 15 (2), 139-68.

Bloom, Jonathan (2010), American Wasteland: How America Throws Away Nearly Half of Its Food, Cambridge, Mass. : Da Capo Press.

Bolton, Lisa E., and Joseph W. Alba (2007), "When Less is More: Consumer Aversion to Waste," under review.

DeYoung, Raymond (1986), "Encouraging Environmentally Appropriate Behavior: The Role of Intrinsic Motivation," *Journal of Environmental Systems,* 15 (4), 281–291.

Jones, Timothy (2004), "The Value of Food Loss in the American Household, Bureau of Applied Research in Anthropology," *A Report to Tilia Corporation*, San Francisco, California.

Lastovicka, John L., Lance A. Bettencourt, Renée Shaw Hugher, and Ronald J. Kuntze (1999), "Lifestyle of the Tight and Frugal: Theory and Measurement," *Journal of Consumer Research,* 26 (1), 85-98.

Milkman, Katherine L., Todd Rogers, Max H. Bazerman (2009), "Highbrow Films Gather Dust: Time-Inconsistent Preferences and Online DVD Rentals," *Management Science*, 55 (6), 1047-59.

Read, Daniel, George Loewenstein, and Shobana Kalyanaraman (1999), "Mixing Virtue and Vice: Combining the Immediacy Effect and the Diversification Heuristic," *Journal of Behavioral Decision Making*, 12, 257-73.

Richins, Marsha L. (1994), "Valuing Things: The Public and Private Meanings of Possessions," *Journal of Consumer Research*, 21, 504-21.

Roster, Catherine A. (2001), "Letting Go," *Advances in Consumer Research B2 - Advances in Consumer Research*, 425-30.

UNEP (2011), "Waste," *United Nations Environmental Programme*, http://www.unep.org/climateneutral/Topics/Waste/tabid/156/Default.aspx.

Wansink, Brian, S. Adam Brasel, and Steven Amjad (2000), "The Mystery of the Cabinet Castaway: Why We Buy Products We Never Use," *Journal of Family and Consumer Sciences*, 92 (1), 104-7.

Wertenbroch, Klaus (1998), "Consumption Self-Control by Rationing Purchase Quantities of Virtue and Vice," *Marketing Science,* 17, 317-37.

Facets of Distress Tolerance as Predictors of Buying in Response to Self-esteem Threats

Paul Rose, Southern Illinois University Edwardsville, USA
Dan Segrist, Southern Illinois University Edwardville, USA

Many people use buying as a means of coping with emotionally-distressing events. One type of emotionally-distressing event that may be particularly likely to lead to buying is self-esteem threat. Buying can serve important identity-regulation functions (Dittmar, 2004) and an enormous social psychological literature suggests that threats to self-esteem lead to defensive responses (e.g., Tesser, 2001). In consumerist cultures in particular, "retail therapy" may be used to restore a desired identity following self-threat.

One purpose of the present study is to identify who might be especially prone to buying in response to threatened self-esteem. Our focus was on individual differences in distress tolerance, a variable that has begun to attract attention in the addictions literature because of observations that some people use substances as a means of coping with negative emotions. Simons and Gaher (2005) define distress tolerance as "the capacity to experience and withstand negative psychological states" (p. 83). They further conceptualize distress tolerance as encompassing four facets—tolerance, regulation, appraisal, and absorption. Tolerance refers to the degree to which an individual considers aversive emotions intolerable and unmanageable. Regulation involves a tendency to engage in behaviors to avoid or distract oneself from distress. Appraisal is an individual's perception of the acceptability of negative emotions and self-perceived ability to deal with them. Absorption refers to the degree to which an individual becomes preoccupied with and dominated by aversive emotions.

To support the prevention and treatment of excessive buying problems, we focused our analysis of self-threat-induced buying on the facets of distress tolerance. By doing so, we hoped to identify specific, malleable beliefs that might promote or inhibit self-threat-induced buying. Of the facets, it seemed to us that *regulation* would be a particularly important predictor because people who believe that action must be immediately taken to alleviate distress might be most prone to making rash purchases in order to feel better.

METHOD

One-hundred-fifty-eight college students (70% female) wrote about two personal events from the last year, a minor self-esteem threat and a major self-esteem threat. (Order of these two event descriptions, which were adapted from Campbell, Baumeister, Dhavale & Tice, 2003, was counterbalanced. We asked about both event types to explore the generalizability of effects across experience intensity.) Participants then reported (within a table that listed numerous post-event coping behaviors) the degree to which they bought things to make themselves feel better (1 = not at all, 7 = very much). After several filler measures, participants completed the 15-item Simons and Gaher (2005) Distress Tolerance Scale, which includes tolerance, regulation, appraisal, and absorption subscales.

RESULTS

Because participants described a major and a minor self-esteem threat and what they did to make themselves feel better after these events, major vs. minor event was treated as a within-participants factor. The distress tolerance subscales were between-participants factors. Thus, the results were analyzed with a mixed-model, hierarchical multiple regression analysis (Judd, 2000). Order of event description (major event first vs. minor event first) and sex were entered in a first block but neither of these predictors was significant. Tolerance (β = -.17), absorption (β = .24), appraisal (β = .11) and regulation (β = .29) were added in a second block. Absorption produced an unexpected marginally significant main effect (p = .07) and, as predicted, regulation produced a significant main effect (p = .01). Interaction terms for appraisal (β = -.28) and regulation (β = .21) approached significance (.05 > p's <.06) because the associations between the appraisal and regulation predictors and self-threat-induced buying varied in strength across major and minor events. (Unexpectedly, the association between appraisal and buying in response to a minor self-esteem threat was strong enough to reach significance, β = .21, p = .04. We hesitate to interpret this finding because it is not clear why appraisal should matter only when a self-threat is minor.) However, the slopes for appraisal and (most importantly) regulation were uniformly positive. The most noteworthy results for understanding buying in response to self-threat, therefore, are the marginally significant main effect of absorption and the significant main effect of regulation.

DISCUSSION

Averaging across major and minor events, the regulation facet of distress tolerance (i.e., the belief that distress must be alleviated through urgent action) emerged as an important predictor of buying in response to self-esteem threat. Lynch and Mizon (2011) have pointed out that the appraisal, absorption, and tolerance components of distress tolerance focus on internal cognitive and emotional processes but regulation focuses on behavior—"the tendency to act with urgency to avoid feeling upset" (p. 61). The emergence of regulation as a significant predictor suggests that some consumers with excessive buying problems may be helped by learning to think of occasional self-esteem threats as normal life events rather than crises. They may also be helped by learning that if quick action really is necessary to feel better, there are healthier options than making rash purchases (such as seeking social support).

Future research may confirm that absorption, which was a marginally significant predictor in our analysis, also plays an important role in self-threat-induced buying. It may be that some consumers feel so overwhelmed by threats to their self-esteem that they struggle to think of the many coping options available to them. If this is true, consumers with excessive buying problems may benefit from practicing more flexible thinking (e.g., "I feel terrible about myself, but I can call my friend or get some exercise rather than going shopping").

REFERENCES

Campbell, W. K., Baumeister, R. F., Dhavale, D., & Tice, D. M. (2003). Responding to major threats to self-esteem: A preliminary, narrative study of ego-shock. *Journal of Social and Clinical Psychology, 22,* 79-96.

Dittmar, H. (2004). Are you what you have? *The Psychologist, 17,* 206-210.

Judd, C. M. (2000). Everyday data analysis in social psychology. In H. T. Reis & C. M. Judd (Eds.), *Handbook of Research Methods in Social and Personality Psychology* (pp. 370-392). New York, NY: Cambridge.

Lynch, T. R., & Mizon, G. A. (2011). Distress overtolerance and distress intolerance: A behavioral perspective. In M. J. Zvolensky, A. Bernstein, & A. A. Vujanovic (Eds.), *Distress Tolerance: Theory, Research and Clinical Applications* (pp. 52-79). New York, NY: Guilford.

Simons, J. S., & Gaher, R. M., (2005). The Distress Tolerance Scale: Development and validation of a self-report measure. *Motivation and Emotion, 29,* 83 – 102.

Tesser, A. (2001). On the plasticity of self-defense. *Current Directions in Psychological Science, 10,* 66-69.

The Fluency of Consumer Incidental Emotion on Nine-Ending Prices

Shih-Chieh Chuang, National Chung Cheng University, Taiwan
Yin-Hui Cheng, National Taichung University of Education, Taiwan
Chia-Jung Chang, National Chung Cheng University, Taiwan
Molly Chien-Jung Huang, National Chung Cheng University, Taiwan

Previous studies on nine-ending prices have focused on level effect, which results in an underestimation of the magnitude perception of a price and leads consumers to lower purchase intentions (e.g., Manning and Sprott 2009). However, level effect can only explain the degree of influence on nine-ending effect, but can not explain the reasons why some studies showed inversing results on purchasing intentions. In order to clarify such condition, researchers consider that price-image and quality-image effect may be regarded as other possible reasons. In these studies, researchers merely focus on the influence of cognitive effort, but ignore the importance of incidental emotion.

Therefore, first, this article argues that the asymmetric effects of positive and negative emotion on nine-ending prices influence the level effect via the cognitive processing of information. People experiencing a positive emotion are likely to engage in high processing fluency, and will ignore, or give very little attention to the ending digits of a price. For example, an item priced at $2.99 will be viewed as priced at $2.00. In contrast, people experiencing a negative emotion may engage in effortful and low processing fluency of information, which results in highly accurate price cognition. In the case noted above, such individuals will perceive the price to be $2.99 rather than $2.00.

Second, this emotional effect will also produce image effects that influence purchase intention related to nine-ending prices. Positive emotion is associated with price image effects and negative emotion is associated with quality image effects. When people experience a positive emotion, a high processing fluency will induce them to recall various pleasant events in and view an event in a positive way. In other words, they will view a nine-ending price as the retailer giving a small amount back to the consumer (price image effect), and providing therefore an opportunity to buy the product for less, which will greatly increase their purchase intention. In contrast, when experiencing a negative emotion, consumers will view the nine-ending price as a signal of inferior quality or an indicator of the quality loss (quality image effect), which will reduce their purchase intention. In order to demonstrate our hypotheses, four studies are investigated.

Study 1: 1a and 1b

The purpose of Study 1a is to test whether prices ending in different digits (rightmost effect) results in different purchase intentions in consumers experiencing positive/negative emotional states that are induced by the recalling method adapted from Smith and Ellsworth (1985). In order to extend the generalizability of our findings, Study 1b further explores if the different emotional induction method adapted from Forgas and Ciarrochi (2001) has the same influence on leftmost effect, and demonstrates the mediating role of processing fluency.

Both of Studies 1a and 1b use 3 (emotion: positive, neutral and negative) x 2 (digit: nine, zero) between-subjects designs. A total of 240 undergraduate students from a large southern university are randomly assigned to Studies 1a and 1b, and are paid $5.

As we expected, no matter what emotional induction methods are used, the analysis reveals a significantly robust effect of incidental emotion on both of rightmost and leftmost effect. Besides, the mediation analysis of processing fluency is also supported.

Study 2

The purpose of Study 2 is first to examine the moderating role of processing fluency manipulated by writing down two or ten reasons adapted from Novemsky et al. (2007). Second, Study 2 tests if consumers with positive (negative) emotions will evaluate the extent of the perceived monetary gain is greater (less) than the extent of the perceived quality loss.

Study 2 use 3 (emotion: positive, neutral and negative) x 2 (digit: nine, zero) x 2 (fluency: high, low) between-subjects designs. A total of 240 undergraduate students from a large southern university are randomly assigned to Study 2, and are paid $5 for their participation. As expected, the analysis proves all of the inference.

Study 3

According to the results of Studies 1a, 1b, and 2, one possible question may occur: Do all positive or negative emotions have the same influence on nine-ending price effect? To solve this question, Study 3 manipulates certainty versus uncertainty emotions as Tiedens and Linton (2001). Besides, quantitative estimations developed by Bizer and Schindler (2005) with the nine-ending prices are also examined to avoid two major causes of failures in research into the nine-ending pricing effect. These two causes are high variation among open-ended responses in free-recall tasks and unrealistic conditions.

Therefore, Study 3 uses 2 (valance: positive, negative) x 2 (certainty: certainty, uncertainty) x 2 (digit: nine, zero) between-subjects designs to examine the inference. A total of 160 undergraduate students from a large southern university are randomly assigned to Study 3.

As expected, the analysis demonstrates that the differences of quantitative estimations for individuals in the certain emotion condition induced high processing fluency are greater than in uncertain emotion condition induced low processing fluency, when people have positive emotions, compared to those who have negative emotions. Combined with the results of Studies 1a, 1b, and 2, incidental emotion undoubtedly can be classified as an important role on the nine-ending price effect.

REFERENCES

Bizer, George Y. and Robert M. Schindler (2005), "Direct Evidence of Ending-digit Drop-off in Price Information Processing," *Psychology and Marketing,* 22(October), 771-783.

Forgas, Joseph P. and Joseph Ciarrochi (2001), "On Being Happy and Possessive: The Interactive Effects of Mood and Personality on Consumer Judgments," *Psychology and Marketing,* 18(1), 239-260.

Manning, Kenneth C. and David E. Sprott (2009), „Price endings, left-digit effects, and choice," *Journal of Consumer Research,* 36, 328-35.

Novemsky, Nathan, Ravi Dahr, Norbert Schwarz, and Itamar Simonson (2007), "Preference fluency in choice," *Journal of Marketing Research,* 44, 347-356.

Smith, Craig A. and Phoebe C. Ellsworth (1985), "Patterns of Cognitive Appraisal in Emotion," Journal of Personality and Social Psychology, 48(4), 813-838.

Tiedens, Larissa Z. and Susan Linton (2001), "Judgment under emotional certainty and uncertainty: The effects of specific emotions on information processing," *Journal of Personality and Social Psychology,* 81, 973-988.

The Influence of Humor on Sharing

Caleb Warren, Bocconi University, Italy
Jonah Berger, University of Pennsylvania, USA

Consumers frequently share content through email, text messages, Facebook, Twitter, and other forms of social media (Allsop, Bassett, and Hopkins 2007). Because social transmission has a powerful influence on attitudes, product adoption, and sales (Asch 1956; Chevalier and Mayzlin 2006; Godes and Mayzlin 2009), understanding why some content is shared and other content is not is important for marketers and consumers researchers.

We investigate if and when humor influences the likelihood that something is shared. There are at least two reasons to suspect that humor increases sharing. First, consumers share content as a way to build and maintain social relationships, and research suggests that humor is an effective way to invite further social interaction (Martin 2007). Second, humor typically involves a positive emotional response to potentially negative stimuli (McGraw and Warren 2010; Ramuchandran 1998; Veatch 1998). Consequently, humorous content may be shared more both because negative information attracts more attention than positive information (Baumeister et al. 2001) and because consumers are more likely to share content that elicits positive rather than negative emotions (Berger and Milkman 2011).

The benign violation theory argues that humor occurs when a violation simultaneously seems benign (Warren and McGraw 2010). Violations are threats to your beliefs about how things should be (Veatch 1998). They include threats to physical well-being (e.g., attacks), self-concept (e.g., insults), social norms (e.g., flatulence), cultural norms (e.g., not wearing pants), linguistic norms (e.g., unusual accents), and moral norms (e.g., bestiality). In order to be humorous, violations must simultaneously seem benign, or okay. Three factors that increase the benignity of a violation are: (1) alternate norms suggesting the violation is acceptable, (2) weak commitment to the violated belief, and (3) psychological distance from the violation (McGraw and Warren 2010). We predict that the violation severity (i.e., the extent to which something seems wrong) and benignity (i.e., the extent to which it seems okay) of content jointly determine its humorousness and that more humorous content is more frequently shared than less humorous content.

Our first study investigated the relationship between violation severity, humor, and sharing in a sample of Youtube videos. Importantly, these videos are psychologically distant. Most are hypothetical and nearly all portray other people at some other place and time. Consequently, we suspected that the videos would seem benign and that the ones depicting more severe violations would be funnier and, thus, shared more often (i.e., have a high number of views) than videos depicting milder violations.

We assembled a sample of 76 videos by using two generic pronouns as search words on youtube.com: "the" and "a." Trained coders rated the level of humor ($\alpha = .694$) and violation severity ($\alpha = .751$) in each of the videos. The number of views was highly skewed, so we took its log as the main dependent variable. As hypothesized, videos with more severe violations were seen as more humorous (b = .46) and were shared more frequently (b = .36). Further analysis using Preacher and Hayes's (2008) bootsrapping algorithm shows that humor mediated the effect of violation severity on sharing (mean indirect effect = .31; 95% CI = .14 to .61).

While these results indicate that more severe violations are shared more, this strategy may not apply when content feels psychologically closer. When psychologically close, severe violations may be difficult to see as benign, and, thus, seem less humorous than milder violations (McGraw and Warren 2010; McGraw et al. 2011). Consequently, violation severity might decrease the virality of psychologically close content, like a text message from a friend.

We tested this by asking 93 student participants to rate the violation severity, humor, and their likelihood of sharing several text messages posted on a website (socially distant condition) or sent by a friend (socially close condition). As expected, when the texts were ostensibly from a friend, milder violations (e.g., "tell me why there is a bowl of oatmeal from starbucks in my purse") were seen as more humorous ($M = 5.3$ vs. 2.1) and were more likely to be shared ($M = 4.0$ vs. 1.9) than severe violations (e.g., "He waited till after we had sex to tell me he had herpes… Ugh I hate being drunk"). However, when the texts were ostensibly on a website, there was little difference between the mild and severe violations on perceived humor ($M = 3.4$ vs. 2.6) or sharing ($M = 2.9$ vs. 2.5). We suspect that unlike the Youtube videos in the previous studies, the severe text messages may not have seemed benign even at a distance.

Another important question is *when* does humor increase sharing? Because perceptions about what is wrong (i.e, a violation) and what is okay (i.e., benign) vary considerably across individuals, not all consumers share the same sense of humor. Consequently, the recipients of shared content may not find the same things humorous as the sender, and this is especially likely when the recipient and sender are dissimilar. Recipients may fail to perceive humor in transmitted online content either because they do not perceive a violation (benign content) or because they perceive a violation that does not seem benign (malign violation). Because the costs of sharing a failed humor attempt are likely higher for malign violations than for benign content (Warren and McGraw 2011), we suspect that consumers will be hesitant to share severe violations with dissimilar recipients even when they personally consider the violations humorous. Thus, we also plan to investigate whether the recipient of the shared content moderates the relationship between humor and sharing.

Consumers often share content that they find humorous, and humor depends on the consumer's perception that a violation is benign. Consequently, the severity of a portrayed violation, the consumer's psychological distance, and the consumer's similarity to the intended recipient jointly influence the likelihood that something is shared.

REFERENCES

Allsop, Dee T., Bryce R. Bassett, and James A. Hoskins (2007), "Word-of-Mouth Research: Principles and Applications," Journal of Advertising Research, 47, 388-411.

Asch, Solomon E. (1956), "Studies of Independence and Conformity: A Minority of One Against a Unanimous Majority," Psychological Monographs, 70 (416).

Baumeister, Roy F., Ellen Bratslavsky, Catrin Finkenauer, and Kathleen D. Vohs (2001), "Bad Is Stronger Than Good," *Review of General Psychology*, 5, 323-70.

Berger, Jonah and Katherine L. Milkman (2011), "Social Transmission, Emotion, and the Virality of Online Content," Working paper.

Chevalier, Judith A. and Dina Mayzlin (2006), "The Effect of Word of Mouth on Sales: Online Book Reviews," Journal of Marketing Research, 43, 345-354.

Godes, David and Dina Mayzlin (2009), "Firm-Created Word-of-Mouth Communication:Evidence from a Field Test," Marketing Science, 28, 721-739.

Martin, Rod A. (2007), *The Psychology of Humor: An Integrative Approach*, Burlington, MA: Elsevier Academic Press.

McGraw, A. Peter and Caleb Warren (2010), "Benign Violations: Making Immoral Behavior Funny," *Psychological Science*, 21 (August), 1141-49.

---, Caleb Warren, Lawrence E. Williams and Bridget Leonard (2011), "Too Close For Comfort or Too Far to Care? Finding Humor in Distant Tragedies and Close Mishaps." Working paper.

Ramachandran, V. S. (1998), "The Neurology and Evolution of Humor, Laughter, and Smiling: The False Alarm Theory," *Medical Hypotheses*, 51, 351-54.

Veatch, T. C. (1998), "A Theory of Humor," *Humor-International Journal of Humor Research*, 11 (May), 161-215.

Warren, Caleb and A. Peter McGraw (2011), "Benign Marketing Violations: How and When Humorous Marketing Hurts Brands," Working paper.

Can I Pay More?: The Moderating Effect of Gender and Self-Esteem Following Consumer Rejection

Hamed Aghakhani, University of Manitoba, Canada
Kelley Main, University of Manitoba, Canada
Fang Wan, University of Manitoba, Canada

Human beings look to communicate with others and to belong to a group. Unfortunately, though, there are many situations that make people feel rejected and, therefore, feel pain and sadness (Blackhart 2009). Rejection occurs when a person is deliberately excluded by a group (Blackhart 2009). Some cosumer researchers demonstrated that rejected consumers are more conservative with their spending (Baumeister et al. 2005), but others evidenced that excluded consumers spend their money more selectively and more lavishly (Mead et al., 2011). Excluded consumers tend to spend more for products that are more symbolic and enhance their group membership. Further, excluded people are willing to spend money on products that enhance their feeling of acceptance and attractiveness (Baumeister et al. 2005, Mead et al. forthcoming). The goal of this research is to investigate the boundary conditions of whether exclusion affects spending positively and negatively. We particularly examined the moderating effects of self esteem and gender, two understudied factors in prior research.

The literature reveals that consumers use their money to impress others and as a way to enhance their status with friends and other groups (Ariely and Levav 2000; Berger and Heath, 2007). This idea leads excluded persons to spend their money to gain social status, so there is a trade-off between one's social well-being and one's monetary well-being (Baumeiseter and Leary, 1995). Also from the literature, it is known that social exclusion reduces a person's level of self-regulation (Baumiester et al., 2005). Based on this, it is presumed that impaired self-regulation leads to spending money unwisely. Although higher levels of self-esteem do not guarantee better performance and success, people with higher self-esteem have greater self-regulation (Baumiester et al., 2005). From the previous research, it is known that social exclusion can lead to a decrease in self-regulation (Baumeister et al. 2005) and lower levels of self-regulation may lead consumers to spend more.

In addition to the effects self-esteem may have on consumer's spending following rejection, the literature suggests gender may also play a moderating role. Research on gender differences with respect to positive and negative emotions revealed that men and women have equal levels of happiness towards stimuli (Myers 1993), but regarding sadness, it seems that women are more willing to show sadness and negative emotions than men (Fujita, Diener and Sandvik 1991). In addition women not only show more negative emotions regarding unpleasant events, but also have a greater tendency to ruminate in comparison to men, therefore causing difficulties in solving current problems (Nolen-Hoeksema, Larson and Grayson 1999). When consumers are rejected, this negative event requires a solution, a way to repair one's negative feelings. Therefore, it is expected that women will be more likely than men to experience negative emotion following a rejecting event. However, this response is expected to be moderated by self-esteem.

Therefore, it is expected that when women with higher self-esteem face rejection, they will try to boost their negative emotion by spending money for products, but women with lower self-esteem will be less likely to make a significant attempt to overcome this negative emotion through spending. In comparison with women, the influence of rejection on men will be attenuated.

EXPERIMENT

This study was a 2 (rejection: yes vs. no) × 2 (Self-esteem: high vs. low) × 2 (gender: female vs. male) between-subjects design with a total of 155 participants (49% Male and 51% Female). Rejection was manipulated by asking participants to imagine an interaction with a salesclerk where they were going to buy a jacket and all participants receive a store credit card offer from clerk. Half of the participants were told that they applied for the store credit card and then after a few minutes the clerk tells them they were rejected (rejection) and the other half of participants were told that they decided not to apply for the store credit card (no rejection). Self-esteem was measured through a self-report scale (Rosnberg 1965). Individuals were categorized as high or low in self-esteem by a median split. The dependent variable was participant's willingness to pay for a small household appliance (a toaster).

The results showed a significant main effect of self-esteem *(M_{high}= 21.64, M_{low}=17.62, F(1,154)=5.222, p<.02)*, and a marginally significant effect of gender *(M_{male}=32.080, M_{women}=36.06, F(1,154)=3.57, p<.061)*. The results also revealed marginally significant interaction between self-esteem and rejection *(F(1,155)=3.656, p<.058)*, self-esteem and gender *(F(1,155)=3.606, p<.060)*, and a marginally significant three way interaction *(F(1,155)=3.635, p<.059)*. Further simple effect analysis revealed no interaction effect for men (p>.9), but a significant interaction for women *(F(1,80)=6.055, p<.016)*. As expected women with high self-esteem were willing to pay a higher price for the appliance, whereas low self-esteem women showed no significant difference in the amount of money they were willing to pay.

GENERAL DISCUSSION

The present research contributes to the literature by demonstrating the interactive effects of gender and self-esteem on consumer spending behavior. Future research in this area can examine other product categories in addition to examining the effects of rejection on people's risky behavior (e.g.: investing in the stock market). Furthermore it is important to compare the effects of rejection with exclusion and inclusion as well as comparing different types of rejection (e.g.: interpersonal vs. romantic) and the subsequent influence on consumer behavior.

REFERENCES

Ariely, Dan and Jonathan Levav (2000), "Sequential Choice in Group Settings: Taking the Road Less Traveled and Less Enjoyed," *Journal of Consumer Research*, 27 (December), 279– 90.

Baumeister, Roy F., C. Nathan DeWall, Natalie J. Ciarocco, and Jean M. Twenge (2005), "Social Exclusion Impairs Self-Regulation," *Journal of Personality and Social Psychology,* 88 (4), 589-604.

_____, and Mark R. Leary (1995), "The Need to Belong: Desire for Interpersonal Attachments as a Fundamental Human Motivation," *Psychological Bulletin,* 117 (3), 497-529.

Berger Jonah and Chip Heath (2007), "Where Consumers Diverge from Others: Identity- Signaling and Product Domains," *Journal of Consumer Research,* 34 (August), 121–34.

Blackhart, Ginette C., B. C. Nelson, M. L. Knowles, & R. F. Baumeister (2009), "Rejection Elicits Emotional Reactions but Neither Causes Immediate Distress nor Lowers Self-Esteem: A Meta-Analytic Review of 192 Studies on Social Exclusion," *Personality and Social Psychology Review,* 13, 269.

Brebner, John (2003), "Gender and Emotions," *Personality and Individual Differences,* 34, 387-94.

Fujita, F., E. Diener, and E. Sandvik (1991), "Gender Differences in Negative Affect and Well-being: the Case for Emotional Intensity," Journal of Personality and Social Psychology, 61, 427-434.

Mead, Nicole L., Roy. F. Baumeister, Tyler F. Stillman, Catherine D. Rawn, and Kathleen D. Vohs (2011), "Social Exclusion Causes People to Spend and Consume Strategically in the Service of Affiliation," *Journal of Consumer Research,* 37, 902-919.

Myers, D. G. (1993). The pursuit of happiness. London: Aquarian Press.

Nolen-Hoeksema, Susan, Judith Larson, and Carla Grauson (1999), "Explaining the Gender Difference in Depressive Symptoms," *Journal of Personality and Social Psychology*, 5, 1061-72.

Rosenberg, M. (1965), Society and the adolescent self-image. Princeton, NJ: Princeton University Press.

Moral dynamics in consumer behavior – the moderating effect of ethical frameworks

Gert Cornelissen, Universitat Pompeu Fabra, Spain
Michael Bashshur, Universitat Pompeu Fabra, Spain
Julian Rode, Universidad Autónoma de Barcelona, Spain
Marc Le Menestrel, Universitat Pompeu Fabra, Spain

The ethical dimension of consumption has gained prominence in the light of the ecological and economical crisis we currently suffer. In recent years, the dynamics of moral behavior has received much attention, including in marketing and consumer behavior literature (e.g., Khan & Dhar, 2006; Mazar, Amir, & Ariely, 2008). Moral balancing (Nisan, 1991), refers to the observation that engaging in a moral behavior at one point in time reduces the likelihood of doing so in a subsequent situation (Effron, Cameron, & Monin, 2009; Merritt, Effron, & Monin, 2010; Sachdeva, Iliev, & Medin, 2009). For example, after committing to helping a foreign student, participants in a study donated less money to charity (Khan & Dhar, 2006). Other studies, however, demonstrate the opposite phenomenon, something we can refer to as moral consistency. For example, in a study by Gino, Norton, and Ariely (in press), participants who wore counterfeit sunglasses were more likely to cheat on a number of tasks, compared to participants who wore branded sunglasses. These examples show that previous behavior may have opposite effects on current decisions. In the current paper, we investigate whether the ethical frameworks or mindsets one uses – thinking of moral behavior in terms of consequences versus in terms of rules or principles – moderates whether initial behavior will lead to moral balancing or moral consistency.

Two prominent frameworks in (Western) moral philosophy are deontological and consequentialist ethics. We predict that an outcome-based mindset (i.e., consequentialism) favors a moral balancing effect. Thinking in terms of outcomes allows the individual to make tradeoffs involving the moral self, which may demand acting in the interest of others, and immediate self-interest, and make flexible computations regarding the current status of the moral self. After choosing an ethical course of action which benefitted mostly others, the individual feels licensed to compensate and benefit the self. On the other hand, we expect that rule-based thinking (i.e., deontology) will favor a moral consistency effect. In general, rules are less flexible to be traded off with selfish benefits (Baron & Spranca, 1997; Tetlock, Kristel, Elson, Green, & Lerner, 2000). Inconsistency regarding following (ethical) rules would threaten an individual's personal integrity (Festinger, 1957). Therefore, we predict that individuals, when in a rule-based mindset, are more likely to behave morally consistent.

To test this hypothesis, we asked our participants to remember an episode in the past in which they did an (un)ethical thing. By defining ethics in terms of consequences or rules we brought them in a consequential or deontological mindset. We then observed whether participants subsequently behaved consistent with the act they recollected from their past, or whether they showed a balancing effect. We manipulated Ethical Framework (deontological versus consequential) and Valence of an initial act (positive or negative). To do so, we asked half of our participants to remember an episode in the past where they did something ethical, and we asked the others to think about something unethical they did. Half of the individuals in each group were instructed to think about a behavior that was (un)ethical "*because it benefitted/hurt other people*" (i.e., the Consequential condition). The others thought about a behavior that was (un)ethical "*because you did (not) do your duty to follow an ethical norm or principle*" (i.e., the deontological condition).

As a dependent measure, we used a modified Prisoner's Dilemma Game (PDG; Smeesters, Warlop, Van Avermaet, Corneille, & Yzerbyt, 2003). We performed a two-way ANOVA with Moral Framework (deontological versus consequential) and Valence of the recollected behavior (positive or negative) as between-subject factors and number of coins given in the PDG as the dependent variable using. We did not find a main effect of Moral Framework or Valence, but we did find a significant interaction effect of both factors ($F(1, 87) = 9.53$, $p < 0.01$). When participants were successfully instructed to be in a consequentialist mindset, they gave more coins in the PDG if they recalled a moment in the past in which they behaved unethically ($M = 2.89$, $SD = 1.71$) than those who recollected an ethical act ($M = 1.77$, $SD = 1.97$; $F(1, 87) = 5.05$, $p < 0.03$). In other words, those participants who were in an outcome-based mindset showed a moral balancing effect. When participants were brought into a deontological mindset, they gave more coins in the PDG if they had recollected an ethical act ($M = 2.74$, $SD = 1.52$) than when the recalled an unethical act ($M = 1.71$, $SD = 1.24$; $F(1, 87) = 4.48$, $p < 0.04$). In other words, these participants showed a moral consistency effect. For participants who were asked to remember an ethical act in the past, those who were in a consequentialist mindset gave less yellow coins than those in a deontological mindset ($F(1, 87) = 3.89$, $p = 0.05$). For participants who were asked to remember an unethical act in the past, those who were in a consequentialist mindset gave more yellow coins than those in a deontological mindset ($F(1, 87) = 5.72$, $p < 0.01$).

The study supported our hypothesis that a consequentialist, outcome-based mindset leads to moral balancing and a deontological, rule-based thinking mindset leads to moral consistency. This finding provides an interesting suggestion to explain the inconsistent findings in the recent literature on moral dynamics. Many of these articles indeed employ a rather consequential definition of ethical behavior, and therefore may present a somewhat distorted view on the moral dynamics of everyday life. In some cases an individual's behavior might be preceded by rule-based reasoning about how to interpret their previous behavior.

REFERENCES

Baron, J., & Spranca, M. (1997). Protected Values. *Organizational Behavior and Human Decision Processes, 70*(1), 1-16.

Effron, D. A., Cameron, J. S., & Monin, B. (2009). Endorsing Obama licenses favoring Whites. *Journal of experimental social psychology, 45*(3), 590-593.

Festinger, L. (1957). *A theory of cognitive dissonance*: Stanford University Press.

Khan, U., & Dhar, R. (2006). Licensing Effect in Consumer Choice. *Journal of Marketing Research, 43*(2), 259-266.

Mazar, N., Amir, O., & Ariely, D. (2008). The Dishonesty of Honest People: A Theory of Self-Concept Maintenance. *Journal of Marketing Research, 45*(6), 633-644.

Merritt, A. C., Effron, D. A., & Monin, B. (2010). Moral Self-Licensing: When Being Good Frees Us to Be Bad. *Social and Personality Psychology Compass, 4*(5), 344-357.

Nisan, M. (1991). The Moral Balance Model:Theory and Research Extending Our Understanding of Moral Choice and Deviation In W. M. Kurtines & J. L. Gewirtz (Eds.), *Handbook of Moral Behavior and Development* (Vol. 3). Hillsdale, New Jersey: Lawrence Erlbaum Associates.

Sachdeva, S., Iliev, R., & Medin, D. L. (2009). Sinning Saints and Saintly Sinners. *Psychological Science, 20*(4), 523-528.

Smeesters, D., Warlop, L., Van Avermaet, E., Corneille, O., & Yzerbyt, V. (2003). Do not prime hawks with doves: The interplay of construct activation and consistency of social value orientation on cooperative behavior. *Journal of Personality and Social Psychology, 84*(5), 972-987.

Tetlock, P. E., Kristel, O. V., Elson, S. B., Green, M. C., & Lerner, J. S. (2000). The psychology of the unthinkable: Taboo trade-offs, forbidden base rates, and heretical counterfactuals. *Journal of Personality and Social Psychology, 78*(5), 853-870.

Status-relevant cues and conspicuous consumption – the moderating role of prenatal androgen exposure

Xavier Palacios, Universitat Pompeu Fabra, Spain
Gert Cornelissen, Universitat Pompeu Fabra, Spain

Consumer psychologists have suggested that individual differences exist between people regarding their need to display status (Stenstrom et al., 2010), and some of them seem to be grounded in biological mechanisms (Miller et al., 2007; Griskevicius et al., 2007). We investigated how status-relevant experiences influence an individual's need to display status. We contrasted two types of status-relevant experiences. Both provoke the activation of a status goal, but in one case the goal of attaining a dominant status was achieved (i.e., football supporters vicariously experiencing a victory of their preferred team; Bernhart et al., 1998), and in another such a goal remained unsatisfied (i.e., individuals on their way to the beach). We also tested the moderating effect of exposure to prenatal androgens on the response to these experiences. In previous studies, Digit Ratio (i.e., the ratio of the length of the index finger (2D) compared to the ring finger (4D); DR) has been negatively related to the prenatal level of testosterone (Manning, 2002; Hönekopp et al., 2007). Low DR is associated with more competitive and dominant behaviors in humans (Manning, 2002; Millet, 2009). Therefore, we expect that the effect of status-relevant experiences on status oriented behavior will be more pronounced in low DR individuals.

In a first study, we randomly approached 51 individuals on their way to ($N = 19$), or going home from ($N = 32$), a popular beach, located in the vicinity of a large size cosmopolitan city. Their age varied from 15 to 47 ($M = 26$, $SD = 10.9$); 29 participants were male and 22 were female. We expected those who are on their way to the beach to anticipate being exposed to "hot stimuli" (Van den Berg, 2008). The anticipation of such a mating cue activates a goal to display status (Jansens et al., 2010). We measured participants' goal to display status using a visual recognition task. An activated goal leads to a perceptual "readiness" to recognize those items that may help the individual to achieve that goal (Roskos-Ewoldsen and Fazio, 1992). Therefore it is assumed that a higher need to display status will lead to faster recognition of luxury consumer products. Participants were asked to look at ten displays which appeared on the screen for 1 second. Each display contained five different products, one of which was a luxury product. After being exposed to each display, participants were given the time to write down which objects they had recognized.

Based on the number of luxury products that participants recognized, we created an index for the *Goal to Display Status*. We performed a two-way ANCOVA on this index including the discrete variable Status Cue (on the way to the beach versus going away from the beach), and the continuous variable DR as predictors. The analysis revealed a marginal interaction effect between the presence of a Status Cue and DR ($F(1, 43) = 3.36$, $p = 0.07$). In the control condition, we do not find a correlation between DR and attention to luxury products ($r(29) = 0.07$, *ns*), whereas there was a correlation when participants are going towards the beach ($r(16) = -0.48$, $p < 0.05$). This suggests that when a status cue is present, those with a lower DR have a larger need to display status, resulting in recognizing more luxury products.

In a second study, we tested whether we would replicate the pattern of data of Study 1 in a context where the status-relevant experience provides a satisfaction of the status goal. We invited 56 university students to participate in a lab experiment (23 males and 33 females). Half of our participants viewed a compilation of videos in which their favorite football team won an important match against their strongest rival (Madrigal et al., 2008). It has been shown that the testosterone level of football supporters increase when they see their favorite team win (Carré, 2009). Previous research has further demonstrated that testosterone levels influence the tendency to display status through the purchase of luxury products (Janssens et al, 2010). In the control condition, participants did not see any video. Then participants in both conditions completed the recognition task we used in Study 1. We performed a two-way ANOVA on this *Goal to Display Status* index including the variables Status Cue (video versus no video) and DR (high versus low). We find an interaction effect of both variables on the proportion of luxury products recognized ($F(1,37) = 7.26$, $p = 0.01$). In the control condition, participants with a low DR ($M = 0.17$, $SD = 0.06$) indentified fewer luxury products than those with a high DR ($M = 0.21$, $SD = 0.03$). The effect was marginally significant ($F(1,37) = 3.50$, $p < 0.07$). In the Status Cue condition, after being exposed to the two videos, participants with a low DR ($M = 0.21$, $SD = 0.06$) see more luxury products than those with a high DR ($M = 0.17$, $SD = 0.05$). This difference was marginally significant ($F(1,37) = 3.83$, $p < 0.06$). The status cue had a significant effect on participants with a low DR ($F(1,37) = 4.00$, $p = 0.05$). After being exposed to the status cue, they recognized more luxury products than in the control condition. The reverse is true for participants with a low DR. After being exposed to the status cue they recognized less luxury products than in the control condition. This effect was only marginally significant ($F(1,37) = 3.30$, $p < 0.08$).

In both studies an individual difference variable (i.e., exposure to prenatal androgens) moderated the effect of status cues on individual's tendency to achieve and display status. Our findings suggest that cues that activate a status goal, whether or not the status goal is satisfied, increase the need to achieve and display status, but only for individuals who received higher levels of prenatal androgens. Follow-up studies that extend these findings are currently ongoing and will be completed by the date of the conference.

REFERENCES

Bernhardt, P. C., Dabbs, J. M., Jr., Fielden, J. A., & Lutter, C. D. (1998). Testosterone changes during vicarious experiences of winning and losing among fans at sporting events. Physiology and Behavior, 65, 59-62.

Carré, J.M. (2009). No place like home: Testosterone responses to victory depend on game location American Journal of Human Biology, 21: 3, 392–394.

Griskevicius, V., Tybur, J. M., Sundie, J. M., Cialdini, R. B., Miller, G. F., & Kenrick, D. T. (2007). Blatant benevolence and conspicuous consumption: When romantic motives elicit costly displays. J. Personality and Social Psychology.

Hönekopp, J., Bartholdt, L., Beier, L. and Liebert, A. (2007) Second to fourth digit length ratio (2D:4D) and adult sex hormone levels: New data and a meta-analytic review. Psychoneuroendocrinology, 32:4, 313-321.

Janssens, K., Pandelaere, M., Van den Bergh, B., Millet, K., Lens, I. and Roe, K. (2010), Can buy me love: Mate attraction goals lead to perceptual readiness for status products, Journal of Experimental Social Psychology, Article in Press.

Miller, G. F., Tybur, J., & Jordan, B. (2007). Ovulatory cycle effects on tip earnings by lap-dancers: Economic evidence for human estrus? Evolution and Human Behavior.

Millet, K. (2009). Low second-to-fourth-digit ratio might predict success among high-frequency financial traders because of a higher need for achievement. Proceedings of the National Academy of Sciences of the United States of America, 106 (11), E30.

Millet, K. (2010). An interactionist perspective on the relation between 2D:4D and behavior: An overview of (moderated) relationships between 2D:4D and economic decision making. Personality and Individual Differences.

Madrigal, R., Dalakas, V. (2008). Consumer psychology of sport: More than just a game. In Haugtvert,C.P., Herr, P.M., & Kardes, F.R. (Eds.), Handbook of consumer psychology, (pp. 857-876).

Manning J.T (2002). Digit Ratio: a pointer to fertility, behaviour, and health. In Rutgers University Press New Brunswick :Rutgers University Press.

Stenstrom, E., Saad, G., Nepomuceno, M.V., and Mendenhall, Z. (2010). Testosterone and domain-specific risk: Digit ratios (2D:4D and rel2) as predictors of recreational, firisk: D, and social risk-taking behaviors. Personality and Individual Differences, August 2010.

Multicomponent Bundle Pricing: Partitioned or Consolidated Presentation?

Marit Gundersen Engeset, Buskerud University College, Norway
Birger Opstad, Buskerud University College, Norway

Product bundling is a pervasive marketing strategy across industries. Managers choose between two forms of price presentations; assign price tags for each item (partitioned pricing), or present the bundle with one single price tag (consolidated pricing). Economic theory predicts that price presentation should not affect evaluation as long as the total price is identical. However, a growing body of literature shows that price presentation influence consumer evaluation of product bundles (Hamilton and Srivastava 2008). Bundles with partitioned price presentations are preferred over identical offerings with consolidated presentations (Chakravarti et al. 2002), but a variety of context factors may influence how consumers attend to and process price information (Suri and Monroe 1999), and partitioned pricing may not be the optimal strategy in every situation. In this research we build on the empirical law of sensation (Stevens 1985) and propose that the size of the bundle (i.e., number of items) will moderate the effect of price presentation on evaluation. This law states that a percentage change in objective magnitude leads to the same percentage change in subjective magnitude – implying that estimations increase at a slower rate than do actual magnitudes. When presented with a bundled offering, consumers will evaluate its price relative to an expected price – and following the law of sensations, it is likely that the expected price will be relatively smaller for bigger bundles. When the price is partitioned, the consumer will evaluate the offering relative to the expected price for each individual item which will be more accurate than if they are to compare the actual price to an expected price for a consolidated bundle. When presented with an offering, the consumer is likely to evaluate the offering more positively if its price is perceived as equal to or lower than the expected price. Hence, we propose that consumers will evaluate a partitioned offering more favorably than a consolidated offering, and that this effect will be stronger for larger bundles.

We report two experiments testing our predictions. In the first experiment 67 participants were presented with a vacation offering consisting of 2 (small bundle) or 6 (large bundle) products, and the prices were given as one price tag (consolidated) or individual tags (partitioned). Then they evaluated the offering on a 3-item scale (α=.92). The results showed a marginally significant difference in evaluation depending on bundle size (M_{small}=4.39, M_{large}=3.79; $F(1, 66) = 3.39$, $p <.1$), and no difference in evaluation depending on price presentation ($M_{consolidated} = 3.85$, $M_{partitioned} = 4.33$, $F = 2.15$, NS). We found a significant effect of the size x presentation interaction on evaluation ($F(1, 66) = 4.75$, $p <.05$). For the large bundle, the partitioned offering was evaluated best ($M_{partitioned} = 4.77$, $M_{consolidated} = 3.27$), while there was no difference in evaluation for the small bundle ($M_{partitioned} = 4.69$, $M_{consolidated} = 4.71$). These results support our predictions that bundle size moderates the effect of price presentation on evaluation. We proposed that this effect would be due to relatively lower price expectations for larger bundles. In experiment 2 the price was not presented up front, instead 70 participants were asked to guess the price of either the consolidated offering (guess one price) or the partitioned offering (guess one price for each product in the bundle). After guessing the price, they evaluated the offering on the 3-item scale (α= .90), and after answering questions about demographics, they were informed about the actual price and asked to evaluate the offering again. Average relative difference between actual and expected price was calculated to form a measure of discrepancy from actual price for each offering. Difference in average discrepancy depending on price presentation was marginally significant ($M_{consolidated} = 33\%$, $M_{partitioned} = 22\%$, $F(1,69) = 3.93$, $p <.05$), but there were no difference in discrepancy depending on bundle size ($M_{large} = 32\%$, $M_{small} = 23\%$, $F(1,69) = 2.39$, NS). We found a significant effect of size x presentation interaction on discrepancy ($F(1,69) = 4.06$, $p < .05$). The actual price for the large bundle was NOK 7476, and there was a big difference in average price guessed depending on price presentation ($M_{consolidated} =$ NOK 4667, $M_{partitioned} =$ NOK 7800). For the small bundle, the actual price was NOK 4820, and the differences in guessed price was smaller ($M_{consolidated} =$ NOK 4027, $M_{partitioned} =$ NOK 5441). This supports our predictions that prices are expected to be lower for consolidated than partitioned offerings, and that this effect will be stronger for larger bundles. We expected participants to evaluate the offering with their expected price in mind. There was a significant size x presentation interaction effect on evaluation ($F(1,69) = 4.70$, $p < .05$), for the large bundle, the partitioned offering was evaluated lower than the consolidated ($M_{consolidated} = 5.02$, $M_{partitioned} = 3.96$), for the small bundle the difference in evaluation was much smaller and in the opposite direction ($M_{consolidated} = 5.00$, $M_{partitioned} = 5.36$). To see how the price expectations in turn affected evaluation after the price was disclosed, participants were presented with the actual price and again asked to evaluate the offerings on the same 3-item scale (α= .93). We performed a repeated measures test to test the difference in evaluation from before and after price disclosure, and found a significant effect of the presentation x time of evaluation effect on evaluation ($F(1,69) = 21.24$, $p < .01$). For the consolidated presentation, evaluation changed substantially ($M_{price\ not\ disclosed}$=5.01 to $M_{price\ disclosed} = 3.39$), while the change in evaluation of the partitioned presentation was only marginal ($M_{price\ not\ disclosed}$=4.61 to $M_{price\ disclosed} = 4.63$).

When marketing product bundles managers need to decide whether to present the offering with partitioned or consolidated prices. The results presented here shows that bundle size is an important factor to consider when deciding on price presentation. We need more research to understand the mechanisms and how it affects evaluation across product categories, with different bundle sizes and in situations where consumers are not asked to reflect on the price at all.

REFERENCES

Chakravarti, Dipankar., Rajan Krish, Pallab Paul, and Joydeep Srivastava (2002), " Partitioned Presentation of Multicomponent Bundle Prices: Evaluation, Choice, and Underlying Processing Effects," *Journal of Consumer Psychology* , 12 (3), 215-229.

Stevens, Stanely Smith (1986), *Psychophysics: Introduction to its Perceptual, Neural, and Social Prospects.* Oxford: Transaction Books.

Suri, Rajneesh and Kent B. Monroe (1999), "Consumer Prior Purchase Intentions and their Evaluation of Savings on Product Bundles," in *Optimal Bundling. Marketing Strategies for Improving Economic Performance,* eds Ralph Fuerder, Andreas Hermann, and Georg Wuebker, New York: Springer-Verlag, 177-194.

Hamilton, Rebecca W., and Joydeep Srivastava (2008), "When 2+2 Is Not the Same as 1+3: Variations in Price Sensitivity Across Components of Partitioned Prices," *Journal of Marketing Research*, 45 (August), 450-461.

Affect Evaluation or Regulation in Visual Art Consumption?
The Influence of Pure and Mixed Emotions

Jianping Liang, Sun Yat-sen University, China
Zengxiang Chen, Ph.D., Nankai University, China

Imagine that you are watching two visual art pieces in an art exhibition. One is about a happy person and the other is about an upset person. Which one would you like better? Would you have different opinions when you are in positive (e.g., feeling strong) or negative (feeling upset) emotions incidentally? More importantly, would you react differently when you have pure positive/negative emotion or mixed emotions (feeling upset and strong at the same time)?

Previous research seems to have partial and mixed answers to the above questions. Affect evaluation theories, including affect-as-information (Schwarz and Clore 1983) and emotion-congruency effect (Bower 1981, Isen et al., 1978), argue that people have higher evaluation of an object that has positive (negative) emotional valence when they are in positive (negative) emotions. However, affect regulation theories (Andrade and Cohen 2007, Andrade 2005) propose that people tend to maintain their positive emotions and they will try to repair any negative emotions. Thus, people have higher evaluation of an object that has positive emotional valence even if they are in negative emotions.

Some recent studies provided supportive evidence to affect evaluation theories. For example, Martin et al. (1997) found that a story is evaluated more favorably when consumers have feelings that match the story's emotional valence, because a sad (happy) story is supposed to make consumers feel sad (happy), which is consistent with the affect-as-information effect. Kim, Park and Schwarz (2010) found that consumers have higher evaluation of vacation products with adventurous (serene) appeals when they are in excited (peaceful) than peaceful (excited) emotion, which is consistent with the emotion-congruency effect. Nevertheless, Martin et al. (1997) only studied pure *happy vs. sad* emotion *during* a *verbal* consumption experience, and Kim, Park and Schwarz (2010) only studied two pure *positive* emotions *before* direct consumption experience.

On the other hand, some other recent studies found supportive evidence to affect regulation theories. In particular, Agrawal and Duhachek (2010) found that because of a defensive processing to reduce the existing negative emotion, it was less effective to use compatible appeals in advertisements, which elicit the same emotion (e.g., shame or guilt) as the one experienced by consumers. However, Agrawal and Duhachek (2010) only used two pure *negative* emotions.

It is important to note that in most of our daily life, it is much more common to experience mixed emotions than pure positive or negative emotions. In addition, as Hagtvedt and Patrick (2008) found, visual art has a content-independent spillover effect in product evaluations. Thus, it is unclear whether visual art consumption experiences per se would be different from its spillover effect and from the verbal consumption experiences in this context. Therefore, this paper attempts to explore (1) whether *affect evaluation* theories could predict consumers' reactions *during visual art* consumption when emotions are *pure* positive or negative; and (2) whether *mixed* emotions may lead to *affect regulation* so that consumers react more favorably to visual arts with positive emotions instead of negative emotions. To the best of our knowledge, this is the first paper to investigate the effects of mixed emotions, in particular, feeling upset and strong simultaneously, on experiential consumption.

STUDY ONE

In Study One, we wanted to test whether affect evaluation theories or affect regulation theories could predict experiential consumptions on visual art. Thus, we ran a 2 (emotion: upset vs. happy) X 2 (consumption experience: upset vs. happy) between-subjects design experiment. After manipulating their emotions, participants were asked to appreciate one of two paintings (i.e., the manipulation of consumption experience on paintings with upset vs. happy valence), which the participants have not seen before. Then participants were asked to complete a questionnaire, including the control (e.g., whether they have seen the painting before, whether they like paintings, etc.) and dependent variables, as well as manipulation checks.

We found that when participants were upset (happy), they spent more time and effort to appreciate, and have better evaluations of the upset ("happy") painting. In other words, participants were more likely to have better consumption experiences when their emotions were congruent with the paintings' emotional valence, which is consistent with the affect evaluation theories.

STUDY TWO

In Study Two, we wanted to test whether mixed emotions, in particular, feeling upset (negative emotion) and feeling strong (positive emotion) at the same time, will make consumers have the same consumption experiences as the pure positive emotion (i.e., feeling strong) will do. This result will be consistent with affect regulation theories, because participants may be discomfort with mixed emotions and they want to get rid of the negative emotions instead of the positive emotions. We ran a 2 (emotion: mixed vs. strong) X 2 (consumption experience: upset vs. happy) between-subjects experiment. Similar procedures were used as in Study One.

We found that when participants were in mixed emotions, they spent more time and effort to appreciate, and have better evaluations of the "happy" painting than the "upset" painting. This result is consistent with the situation when participants were in pure positive emotion, and is also consistent with the affect regulation theories.

REFERENCES

Andrade, Eduardo B. (2005), "Behavioral Consequences of Affect: Combining Evaluative and Regulatory Mechanisms," *Journal of Consumer Research*, 32 (December), 355-362.

Andrade, Eduardo B. and Joel B. Cohen (2007), "On the Consumption of Negative Feelings," *Journal of Consumer Research*, 34 (October), 283–300.

Agrawal, Nidhi and Adam Duhachek (2010), "Emotional Compatibility and the Effectiveness of Antidrinking Messages: A Defensive Processing Perspective on Shame and Guilt," *Journal of Marketing Research*, Vol. XLVII, April, 263-273.

Bower, Gordon H. (1981), "Mood and Memory," *American Psychologist*, 36 (2), 129–48.

Hagtvedt, Henrik and Vanessa M. Patrick (2008), "Art Infusion: The Influence of Visual Art on the Perception and Evaluation of Consumer Products," *Journal of Marketing Research*, 45 (June), 379-89.

Isen, A. M., T. E. Shalker, M. S. Clark and L. Karp (1978), "Affect, Accessibility of Material in Memory, and Behavior: A Cognitive Loop?" *Journal of Personality and Social Psychology*, 36, 1-12.

Kim Hakkyun, Kiwan Park and Norbert Schwarz (2010), "Will This Trip Really Be Exciting? The Role of Incidental Emotions in Product Evaluation", *Journal of Consumer Research*, Vol. 36, April, 983-991.

Martin, Leonard L., Teresa Abend, Constantine Sedikides, and Jeffrey D. Green (1997), "How Would I Feel If . . .? Mood as Input to a Role Fulfillment Evaluation Process," *Journal of Personality and Social Psychology*, 73 (2), 242–53.

Schwarz, Norbert and Gerald L. Clore (1983), "Mood, Misattribution, and Judgments of Well-Being: Informative and Directive Functions of Affective States," *Journal of Personality and Social Psychology*, 45 (3), 513–23.

With a Little Help from my Friends: Friends Reduce Excessive Consumption by Promoting Self-Control

Eline L.E. de Vries, University of Groningen
Debra Trampe, University of Groningen
Bob M. Fennis, University of Groningen

Failures to override impulses lie at the heart of many problematic consumer behaviors. Failures to control impulses to eat unhealthy food, drink alcohol or smoke cigarettes for instance (Friese, Hofmann, and Wiers 2011), but also failures to resist impulses to buy. The continuous proximity of consumption temptations constitutes what we term a *buyogenic environment*. By provoking irresistible consumption impulses, this buyogenic environment composes a serious challenge to the exercise of self-control of consumers (Faber and Vohs 2011; Hoch and Loewenstein 1991). Especially for consumers with self-regulatory deficits, the buyogenic environment makes it extremely difficult to inhibit consumption impulses, resulting in excessive consumption. In its extreme case, such difficulties with inhibiting consumption impulses can lead to adverse consequences for both the individual and others (Faber and Vohs 2011).

Given that consumption behaviors like shopping and dining almost never happen in a social vacuum, it is surprising that little research has examined the role of close friendship on excessive consumption. After all, friends have been consistently linked to good mental and physical health (Cohen and Wills 1985; Hawkley et al. 2003) and just ordinary, day-to-day activities with friends have been found to be sufficient to be of beneficial influence (Lakey and Orehek 2011).

In the present research we conceptualize excessive consumption as a form of self-regulatory failure. The interplay between irresistible consumption impulses evoked by the buyogenic environment and insufficient self-control strength to inhibit these impulses, results into excessive consumption. In four experiments we show that the (psychological) presence of a friend reduces excessive consumption, by enhancing the capacity to inhibit (consumption) impulses when confronted with (consumption) temptations. In addition, we demonstrate that this beneficial influence of friendship on self-control is the result of a dual process; improved self-control as a result of both reduced impulses and conserved self-control strength.

The first study was a scenario study and observed that among individuals classified as compulsive buyers (Ridgway, Kukar-Kinney, and Monroe 2008), the presence of a close friend reduced both the buying urge and buying intention. That is, when compulsive buyers were asked to imagine themselves in a shopping situation, their buying urge and intention to buy a desirable pair of jeans that were on sale, was significantly lower when they imagined being accompanied by a close friend (M_{urge} = 5.06; $M_{intention}$ = 5.00) compared to when they imagined being alone (M_{urge} = 5.74; $M_{intention}$ = 5.89).

The second study (N = 106; all female) confirmed that self-regulatory processes underlie our findings of study 1, by demonstrating that the *actual* presence of a friend enhances compulsive buyers' self-control. Compulsive buyers who were in the actual presence of a close friend had significantly less difficulty with suppressing impulses (i.e., made significantly fewer errors on the Color Word Stroop Task, M = 0.00) compared to compulsive buyers that performed the task alone (M = 0.41) or in the presence of a stranger (M = 0.36). In fact, the presence of a friend enhanced the self-control of compulsive buyers to a 'normal' level, i.e. comparable to the self-control of non-compulsive buyers who were alone.

In the last two studies we generalized our findings to consumers not chronically, like compulsive buyers, but temporarily prone to self-regulatory failure by resource depletion (Faber and Vohs 2011). Moreover, study 3A showed that the beneficial influence of friends generalizes to a behavioral measure of self-control, i.e. candy consumption. In both studies, participants in the friendship condition were first primed with friendship, by asking them to write about a close friendship. Participants in the control condition were asked to write about the manufacturing process of a wooden table. Next, participants were depleted by performing an e-circling task or not.

After the friendship and depletion manipulation, participants in study 3A (N = 80; 37 female, 43 male) were tempted by a bowl filled with M&Ms, from which they could consume as much as they desired. Results showed that while depleted consumers ate more candy (M = 18.54 grams) than non depleted consumers in the control condition (M = 11.86), depleted consumers ate significantly less candy after being primed with friendship (*M* = 11.31). Although friendship had no influence on non-depleted consumers, friendship thus enhanced self-control of depleted consumers. Reminding people of friendship seemed to conserve their self-control strength.

Finally, if excessive consumption is the result of the interplay between self-control strength and impulse strength, the most effective intervention to reduce excessive consumption may be one that improves both factors (Friese et al. 2011). In study 3B (N = 80; 34 female, 46 male) we show that reminding people of friendship is such an intervention.

After the friendship and depletion manipulation, participants in study 3B first received an Implicit Association Test to measure their impulse strength towards hedonic products (Friese et al. 2011; Wiers et al. 2011). Subsequently, their willingness-to-pay (WTP) regarding these products was measured.

In line with Vohs and Faber (2007), participants depleted of their self-regulatory resources showed higher WTP for hedonic products than non-depleted participants. However, depleted participants reminded of friendship did not show this increase in WTP. Moreover, the relationship between depletion and friendship on WTP was mediated by impulse strength as measured by the IAT. Again friendship had no influence on non-depleted consumers.

The present research shows that the (psychological) presence of a friend reduces excessive consumption, and gives insight in the underlying process. By influencing both sides of the self-control struggle, i.e. conserving self-control strength and reducing impulse strength, the (psychological) presence of a friend satisfies an important condition for effective intervention (Friese et al. 2011). Friendship did not influence the self-control of non-compulsive and non-depleted individuals, suggesting that it only promotes self-control of individuals with self-regulatory deficits, either at the trait or state level (i.e. compulsive buyers or depleted consumers respectively). Non-compulsive and non-depleted consumers do not need much help in situations requiring self-control; they were capable of resisting temptations themselves. For the other consumers however, the (psychological) presence of a friend seems a valuable buffer against the temptations from our buyogenic environment.

REFERENCES

Cohen, Sheldon, and Thomas A. Wills (1985), "Stress, Social Support, and the Buffering Hypothesis," *Psychological Bulletin,* 98 (2), 310-57.

Faber, Ronald J., and Kathleen D. Vohs (2011), "Self-Regulation and Spending: Evidence from Impulsive and Compulsive Buying," in *Handbook of self-regulation: Research, theory, and applications (2nd ed.).* Edited by K. D. Vohs, R. F. Baumeister, K. D. Vohs et al. New York, NY US: Guilford Press, 537-50.

Friese, Malte, Wilhelm Hofmann, and Reinout W. Wiers (2011), "On Taming Horses and Strengthening Riders: Recent Developments in Research on Interventions to Improve Self-Control in Health Behaviors," *Self & Identity,* 10 (3), 336-51.

Hawkley, Louise C., Mary H. Burleson, Gary G. Berntson, and John T. Cacioppo (2003), "Loneliness in Everyday Life: Cardiovascular Activity, Psychosocial Context, and Health Behaviors," *Journal of Personality and Social Psychology,* 85 (1), 105-20.

Hoch, Stephen J., and George F. Loewenstein (1991), "Time-Inconsistent Preferences and Consumer Self-Control," *Journal of Consumer Research,* 17 (4), 492-507.

Lakey, Brian, and Edward Orehek (2011), "Relational Regulation Theory: A New Approach to Explain the Link Between Perceived Social Support and Mental Health," *Psychological Review,* 118 (3), 482-95.

Ridgway, Nancy M., Monika Kukar-Kinney, and Kent B. Monroe (2008), "An Expanded Conceptualization and a New Measure of Compulsive Buying," *Journal of Consumer Research,* 35 (4), 622-39.

Vohs, Kathleen D., and Ronald J. Faber (2007), "Spent Resources: Self-regulatory Resource Availability Affects Impulse Buying," *Journal of Consumer Research,* 33 (4), 537-47.

Wiers, Reinout W., Carolin Eberl, Mike Rinck, Eni S. Becker, and Johannes Lindenmeyer (2011), "Retraining Automatic Action Tendencies Changes Alcoholic Patients' Approach Bias for Alcohol and Improves Treatment Outcome," *Psychological Science,* 22 (4), 490-7.

Mere Exposure Effect in Sponsorship?
A Field Investigation Involving a Highly Familiar Brand

Jean-Luc Herrmann, Université Paul Verlaine-Metz, CEREFIGE, France
Mathieu Kacha, Université Paul Verlaine-Metz, CEREFIGE, France
Björn Walliser, Université de Nancy, CEREFIGE, France
Jonathan Dedonder, Université Catholique de Louvain, Belgium
Olivier Corneille, Université Catholique de Louvain, Belgium

Does a sponsorship influence decisions about a sponsor brand for people unable to recall that they were exposed to it? And is this mere exposure effect observed for prominent, highly familiar, brands that can afford to sponsor widely broadcasted events (e.g., Olympus for the US Open tennis tournament)? Mere exposure studies provide abundant evidence that repeated exposure to a stimulus may increase its liking without its recall (e.g., Bornstein 1989; Monahan, Murphy and Zajonc 2001). However, most of these studies were conducted in the lab with students and/or involved low-familiarity, fictive or novel brands and ads stimuli. Among a very few field studies that examined mere exposure effects of sponsorship in naturalistic environments (e.g., Bennet 1999), none involved highly familiar brands. Hence, it is currently unclear whether a sponsorship may influence decisions about a highly familiar brand in the absence of recall of this sponsoring brand.

To our knowledge, this research is one of the first to investigate this possibility. In order to secure statistical power, it involved a large sample of 1084 visitors of an international Tennis Tournament. Measures were collected for brand recall and brand preference, along with two additional factors, which we reasoned might qualify the effects: consumer status (consumer or non-consumer of the brand) and choice condition (free or comparative choice). We anticipated that mere exposure effects could be observed for a highly familiar brand, at least for non-consumers of the brand who can be assumed to have relatively weak attitudes about this brand. We also reasoned that comparative choices might disrupt fluency effects of sponsorship exposure (and so be detrimental to mere exposure effects).

METHOD

Data collection took place during an international tennis tournament. The research focuses on one of the 10 official sponsors of the event, an extremely familiar brand of mineral water present on the court. During this event, face-to-face interviews were conducted with a sample of more than one thousand visitors on site. The control group ($n=276$) interviews took place before the spectators had entered the stadium. Interviews for the larger experimental group ($n=808$) took place inside the arena, after the respondents attended one or several matches. No respondent was exposed to any sponsorship stimulus during the interviews.

Within each group, respondents were randomly assigned to a free or comparative choice condition. In the first condition, respondents were asked to mention which brands they would consider choosing if they were in need of mineral water. In the second condition, respondents were asked the same question, but this time they were presented with a list of 16 highly familiar mineral water brands (including the target brand). Purchase consideration for other product categories were measured as filler decisions preceding a free recall test of the sponsors. Respondents were also asked whether they were consumers of the brand or not.

RESULTS

The mere exposure effect was assessed by considering respondents who failed to mention the brand as a sponsor ($n=995$). Among those, brand consumers were more likely to choose the brand than non-consumers, $\chi^2(1)=169.06$, $p<.001$. More importantly, exposure to the sponsoring brand almost doubled the probability of choosing it among non-consumers making a free choice, $\chi^2(1)=4.271$, $p<.04$. No such mere exposure effect was observed for brand consumers, or for non-consumers making a comparative choice (all $ps = ns$).

DISCUSSION

While previous mere exposure studies generally involved lab experiments with students and/or exposure to fictive or low-familiarity stimuli and ads (e.g., Janiszewski 1988; Karremans, Stroebe and Klaus 2006; Olson and ThjØmØe 2003; Shapiro, MacInnis and Heckler 1997), the present field research shows that mere exposure effects of sponsorship may be observed in naturalistic settings for prominent brands. This original finding importantly suggests that measures of sponsorship recall traditionally used in marketing may fail to fully capture the effectiveness of sponsorship.

Of interest too, these effects were limited to non-consumers of the brand making a free choice. Hence, these effects may be observed whenever non-consumers of a brand think of which brand to purchase, but may not be observed when they make choices in front of supermarket shelves or internet sites displaying the target brand among competitors (at least in the short-term). Theoretical reasons for this may be (1) that mere exposure effects only influence individuals who have no strong established preferences about the target stimulus (Bornstein 1989), and (2) that non-consumers engage in an analytic processing of the respective brands' merits when choosing a sponsoring brand among competitors. Such analytic processing mode typically disrupts fluency effects (Whittlesea and Price 2001).

The present findings suggest that sponsorship may affect consumer choices through processes that are more subtle and implicit than deliberate inferences made about the brand or explicit reminders of it (Cornwell, Weeks and Roy 2005). However, one should be careful in concluding about the unconscious nature of the present effects. It is likely that spectators watching the matches paid at least shallow attention to the sponsor, too shallow to guarantee its spontaneous recall, but strong enough to secure its encoding in memory (see also Ferraro, Bettman and Chartrand 2009). There is strong evidence that fluency resulting from mere exposure increases both liking and familiarity, which are dissociated only when individuals apply different processing strategies (i.e., holistic versus analytic) for evaluative and recognition tasks (e.g., Whittlesea and Price 2001; Willems, Salmon and Van der Linden 2008).

In sum, the present field research provides original evidence (1) that sponsoring may influence consumer decisions in naturalistic environments even without explicit recall of a highly familiar sponsor, and (2) that the latter effect is constrained by the status of the consumer and the nature of the choice.

REFERENCES

Bennett, R. (1999), "Sports sponsorship, spectator recall and false consensus" *European Journal of Marketing, 33*, 291-313.

Bornstein, R. F. (1989), "Exposure and affect: overview and meta-analysis of research, 1968-1987", *Psychological Bulletin, 106*, 265-289.

Cornwell, B. T., Weeks, C. S. and Roy, D. P. (2005), "Sponsorship-linked marketing: opening the black box", *Journal of Advertising, 34*, 21-42.

Ferraro, Rosellina, Bettman James R. and Chartrand, Tanya L. (2009), "The Power of Strangers: The Effect of Incidental Consumer Brand Encounters on Brand Choice", *Journal of Consumer Research*, Vol. 35, 5 (February), 729-41.

Janiszewski. C. (1988), "Preconscious processing effects: The independence of attitude formation and conscious thought", *Journal of Consumer Research, 15*, 199-209.

Karremans, J. C., Stroebe,W. and Klaus J. (2006), "Behond Vicary's fantasies: The impact of subliminal priming and brand choice", *Journal of Experimental Social Psychology, 42,* 792-798.

Monahan, J. L., Murphy S. T. and Zajonc R.B. (2000), "Subliminal mere exposure: specific general and diffuse effects", *Psychological Science, 11,* 462-466.

Olson, E. L. and ThjØmØe, H. M. (2003), "The effects of peripheral exposure to information on brand performance", *European Journal of Marketing, 37*, 243-255.

Shapiro, S., MacInnis D. J. and Heckler S. E. (1997), "The effect of incidental ad exposure on the formation consideration sets", *Journal of Consumer Research, 24*, 94-104.

Whittlesea, B. and Price J. (2001), "Implicit/Explicit memory versus analytic/nonanalytic processing: Rethinking the mere exposure effect", *Memory & Cognition, 29*, 234–246.

Willems, S., Salmon E. and Van Der Linden M. (2008), "Implicit/Explicit memory dissociation in Alzheimer's disease: the consequence of inappropriate processing?", *Neuropsychology, 22*, 710-717.

Zajonc, R. B. (1968), "Attitudinal effects of mere exposure", *Journal of Personality and Social Psychology, 9*, 1-27.

Is More Always Better?
Examining the Effects of Highly Attentive Service

Hean Tat Keh, Beijing University, China
Maggie Wenjing Liu, Tsinghua University, China
Lijun Zhang, Beijing University, China

The services marketing literature generally indicates that attentive, friendly, and personalized services can help improve customer satisfaction (Bitner, 1990; Bitner, Booms, & Mohr, 1994; Hui, Au, & Fock, 2004; Price, Arnould & Tierney, 1995; Surprenant & Solomon, 1987). Some researchers even suggest that firms should attempt to transcend customer expectations by delighting them (Oliver, Rust, & Varki, 1997; Rust & Oliver, 2000). Consequently, it has become imperative for many service firms to invest in customer-focused procedures or programs in order to create more competitive service offerings (Lemmink & Mattsson, 2002), and some of them are even willing to go the extra mile in serving customers. For example, the wait staff of many restaurants is trained to get to know their customers, frequently drop by customer tables and enquire if things were going well (Scanlon, 1998).

The underlying assumption is that such outwardly concern for consumers and personalization would be well received. Yet, some customers may find such efforts to be overwhelming and disruptive of their service experience. As observed by Solomon, Surprenant, Czepiel, and Gutman (1985, p. 107), "greater personalization of service does not necessarily result in a more positive service expectation." Indeed, there is considerable anecdotal evidence suggesting that, rather than increasing customer satisfaction, highly attentive service may lead to customer complaints, dissatisfaction, and even switching behavior. This raises the paradox that more attentive service is not always better. From the perspective of the organization, Schneider, Paul, and White (1998) suggest that an overemphasis on service quality for end users may be detrimental to the organization in the long-term as overemphasis on a single constituent will be in conflict with the expectations and demands of other constituents such as employees and shareholders.

The literature in related areas indicates that too much of a good thing may not always turn out well. For instance, in the context of product choices, Iyengar and Lepper (2000) challenge the popular notion that "the more choice, the better." They find that consumers faced with extensive choices may find them to be initially more appealing but are subsequently less satisfied with their choices compared with those in the limited-choice condition. Similarly, when manufacturers put too many features into a product, it can be overwhelming for consumers and result in "feature fatigue" (Thompson, Hamilton, & Rust, 2005). We expect the effects of highly attentive service to be analogous to such choice overload effects.

Our review of the literature yields surprisingly little insight into the paradox of highly attentive service (see Estelami & De Maeyer, 2002). Questions on how customers respond to highly warm or generous service attention, and to what extent should firms attend to their customers, have not been systematically addressed. Knowing the answers would be relevant and important for both managerial practice and marketing scholars. Accordingly, our objective in this research is to understand the nature of highly attentive service and how it affects customers' responses and evaluations of service providers. As little has been done in this area, we use a two-phase research design in conducting this study (Creswell, 1994). We first perform an exploratory qualitative research to define the concept of highly attentive service from the perspective of the customer. Based on the dimensions identified, we then proceed to conduct two experiments to better understand customers' response mechanisms. Specifically, we address the following research questions:

1.   How do customers define or perceive highly attentive service?

2.   How does highly attentive service influence customer affective response and evaluation of the provider?

3.   Do customers' characteristics and situational factors influence their affective response and evaluation of highly attentive services?

Based on the related literature and content analysis of our qualitative study, we establish a conceptual model of highly attentive service and develop the relevant hypotheses. We conduct two experiments to test the model. Finally, we discuss the results, the theoretical and managerial implications, and conclude with the limitations of this study and directions for further research.

We contribute to the literature by expanding the scope of investigation beyond monetary generosity. As the literature is sparse on the "attentiveness fatigue" problem, our exploratory study on the nature and consequences of highly attentive service fills a major theoretical void. The main results of our empirical analysis are that highly attentive services have an inverted U-shaped relationship with customer satisfaction, and this relationship is partially mediated by customers' affect and moderated by customers' need for interaction. These findings are new to the literature, and impel us to reconsider the received wisdom of providing services that exceed the desired level (Zeithaml, Berry, & Parasuraman, 1993, 1996).

Specifically, our results confirm the affective satisfaction model (Oliver, 1993; Westbrook, 1987; Westbrook & Oliver, 1991); service attributes influence customer satisfaction both directly and indirectly via positive and negative affects. While past research highlights the effect of positive affect on satisfaction (Lemmink & Mattsson, 2002; Price, Arnould, & Tierney, 1995), our study reveals the crossover effects between service attributes and positive and negative affects simultaneously. Our factor analysis elicits one positive affect, "warmth," and two types of negative affects, "pressure" and "sadness/anger." This is in line with Russell's (1980) "circumplex model of affect," which posits two dimensions of affective structure, pleasure/displeasure and arousal/boredom. In our three-factor affect model, "warmth" and "sadness/anger" are almost polar opposites on the same continuum, and are independent of (orthogonal to) "pressure." Additionally, we find that while both negative affects, "pressure" and "sadness/anger," are evoked by unfavorable service attentiveness conditions, the underlying mechanisms are different. Results show that "pressure" is more likely to be evoked by highly attentive services, but "sadness/anger" is not significantly different for either excessive or too little attention.

REFERENCES

Allen, C. T., Machleit, K. A., & Kleine, S. S. (1992). A comparison of attitudes and emotions as predictors of behavior at diverse levels of behavioral experience. *Journal of Consumer Research*, 18 (March), 493-504.

Arnould, E. J., & Price, L. L. (1993). River magic: extraordinary experience and the service encounter. *Journal of Consumer Research*, 20 (June), 24-45.

Baron, R. M., & Kenny, D. A. (1986). The moderator-mediator variable distinction in social psychological research: conceptual, strategic, and statistical considerations. *Journal of Personality and Social Psychology*, 51 (6), 1173-1182.

Bitner, M. J. (1990). Evaluating service encounters: the effects of physical surroundings and employee responses. *Journal of Marketing*, 54 (Apr.), 57-71.

---, Booms, B. H., & Mohr, L. A. (1994). Critical service encounters: the employee's viewpoint, *Journal of Marketing*, 58 (Oct.), 95-106.

---, ---, & Tetreault, M. S. (1990). The service encounter: diagnosing favorable and unfavorable incidents. *Journal of Marketing*, 54 (January), 95-106.

Creswell, J. W. (1994). *Research design: qualitative and quantitative approaches*. CA: Sage.

Dabholkar, P. A. (1996). Consumer evaluations of new technology-based self-service options: an investigation of alternative models of service quality. *International Journal of Research in Marketing*, 13, 29-51.

---, & Bagozzi, R. (2002). An attitudinal model of technology-based self-service: moderating effects of consumer traits and situational factors. *Journal of the Academy of Marketing Science*, 30(3), 184-201.

Dillon, W. R., & Goldstein, M. (1984). *Multivariate analysis: methods and applications*. New York: John Wiley and Sons.

Dubé-Rioux, L. (1990). The power of affective reports in predicting satisfaction judgments. *Advances in Consumer Research*, 17, 571-576.

Edell, J., & Burke, M. C. (1987). The power of feelings in understanding advertising effects. *Journal of Consumer Research*, 14 (December), 421-433.

Estelami, H., & De Maeyer, P. (2002). Customer reactions to service provider overgenerosity. *Journal of Service Research*, 4 (3), 205-216.

Havlena, W. J., & Holbrook, M. B. (1986). The varieties of consumption experience: comparing two typologies of emotion in consumer behavior. *Journal of Consumer Research*, 13 (December), 394-404.

Holsti, O. R. (1968). Content analysis. In G. Lindzey & E. Aronson (Ed.), *The handbook of social psychology: research methods*, Vol. 2, (pp. 596-692) MA: Addison-Wesley.

Hui, M. K., Au, K., & Fock, H. (2004). Reactions of service employees to organization–customer conflict: A cross-cultural comparison. *International Journal of Research in Marketing*, 21 (2), 107-121.

Iyengar, S. S., & Lepper, M. R. (2000). When choice is demotivating: can one desire too much of a good thing. *Journal of Personality and Social Psychology*, 79 (6), 995-1006.

Johnson, M. & Zinkhan, G. M. (1991). Emotional responses to a professional service encounter. *Journal of Services Marketing*, 5 (2), 5-16.

Kassarjian, H. H. (1977). Content analysis in consumer research. *Journal of Consumer Research*, 4 (June), 8-18.

Keaveney, S. M. (1995). Customer switching behavior in service industries: an exploratory study. *Journal of Marketing*, 59 (April), 71-82.

Lemmink, J. & Mattsson, J. (2002). Employee behavior, feelings of warmth and customer perception in service encounters. *International Journal of Retail & Distribution Management*, 30 (1), 18-33.

Liljander, V. & Strandvik, T. (1997). Emotions in service satisfaction. *International Journal of Service Industry Management*, 8 (2), 148-169.

Malhotra, N. K. (2007). *Marketing research: an applied orientation* (5th ed). Prentice Hall.

Meuter, M. L., Ostrom, A. L., Roundtree, R. J., & Bitner, M. J. (2000). Self-service technologies: understanding consumer satisfaction with technology-based service encounters," *Journal of Marketing*, 64 (3), 50-64.

Oliver, R. L. (1980). A cognitive model of the antecedents and consequences of satisfaction decisions. *Journal of Marketing Research*, 17 (November), 460-469.

--- (1981). Measurement and evaluation of satisfaction process in retail settings. *Journal of Retailing*, 57 (3), 25-48.

--- (1993). Cognitive, affective, and attribute bases of the satisfaction response. *Journal of Consumer Research*, 20 (December), 418-430.

--- (1994). Conceptual issues in the structural analysis of consumption emotion, satisfaction, and quality: evidence in a service setting," *Advances in Consumer Research*, (21), 16-22.

---, & Burke, R. R. (1999). Expectation processes in satisfaction formation: a field study. *Journal of Service Research*, 1 (3), 196-214.

---, Rust, R. T., & Varki, S. (1997). Customer delight: foundations, findings, and managerial insight. *Journal of Retailing*, 73 (3), 311-336.

Ostrom, A. L., & Iacobucci, D. (1995). Consumer trade-offs and the evaluation of services. *Journal of Marketing*, 59 (1), 17-28.

Phillips, D. M., & Baumgartner, H. (2002). The role of consumption emotions in the satisfaction response. *Journal of Consumer Psychology*, 12 (3), 243-252.

Price, L. L., Arnould, E. J., & Deibler. S. L. (1995). Customers' emotional responses to service encounters: the influence of the service provider. *International Journal of Service Industry Management*, 6 (3), 34-63.

---, ---, & Tierney, P. (1995). Going to extremes: managing service encounters and assessing provider performance. *Journal of Marketing*, 59 (April), 83-97.

Russell, J. A. (1980). A circumplex model of affect. *Journal of Personality and Social Psychology*, 39 (December), 1161-1178.

Rust, R. T., & Oliver, R. L. (2000). Should we delight the customer? *Journal of the Academy of Marketing Science*, 28 (1), 86-94.

Scanlon, N. L. (1998). *Quality restaurant service guaranteed: a training outline*, New York, NY: Wiley.

Schneider, B., Paul, M. C. & White, S. S. (1998). Too much of a good thing: a multiple-constituency perspective on service organization effectiveness. *Journal of Service Research*, 1 (1), 93-102.

Smith, A. K., & Bolton, R. N. (2002). The effect of customers' emotional responses to service failure on their recovery effort evaluations and satisfaction judgments. *Journal of the Academy of Marketing Science*, 30 (1), 5-23.

Soley, L., Teel, J. E. Jr., & Reid, L. N. (1980). A comparison of influences on fixed and grid radio advertising rates. *Journal of Advertising*, 9 (Fall), 15-19.

Solomon, M. R., Surprenant, C. F, Czepiel, J. A., & Gutman, E. G. (1985). A role theory perspective on dyadic interactions: the service encounter. *Journal of Marketing*, 49 (Winter), 99-111.

Surprenant, C. F., & Solomon, M. R. (1987). Predictability and personalization in the service encounter. *Journal of Marketing*, 51 (April), 73-80.

Thompson, D. V., Hamilton, R. W., & Rust, R. T. (2005). Feature fatigue: when product capabilities become too much of a good thing. *Journal of Marketing Research*, 42 (4), 431-442.

Westbrook, R. A. (1987). Product/consumption-based affective responses and postpurchase processes. *Journal of Marketing Research*, 24 (August), 258-270.

---, & Oliver, R. L. (1981). Developing better measures of consumer satisfaction: some preliminary results. *Advances in Consumer Research*, 94-99.

---, & ---. (1991). The dimensionality of consumption emotion patterns and consumer satisfaction. *Journal of Consumer Research*, 18 (June), 84-91.

Zeithaml, V. A., Berry, L. L., & Parasuraman, A. (1993). The nature and determinants of customer expectations of service. *Journal of the Academy of Marketing Science*, 21 (1), 1-12.

---, ---, & ---. (1996). The behavioral consequences of service quality. *Journal of Marketing*, 60 (2), 31-46.

---, Parasuraman, A., & Berry, L. L. (1985). Problems and strategies in service marketing. *Journal of Marketing*, 49 (Spring), 33-46.

Humorous Complaining

Christina Kan, University of Colorado, USA
Caleb Warren, Bocconi University, Italy
A. Peter McGraw, University of Colorado, USA

"I should have flown with someone else or gone by car… 'cause United breaks guitars."

When United Airlines was unresponsive to David Carroll's complaint, he did what consumers are increasingly doing – he turned to the Internet. But rather than taking a strictly negative tone, the little-known musician and owner of a Taylor guitar broken during a United flight created a music video parody, "United Breaks Guitars." His humorous complaint became an Internet sensation, spurring international media coverage and an immediate response from United (Deighton and Kornfeld 2010).

Marketers, consumer researchers, and consumers know the power of complaints. Negative word-of-mouth, a complaint about a product or service directed toward other consumers, can have significant detrimental effects on brand attitudes and sales (Chevalier and Mayzlin 2006; Mizerski 1982). For example, United's stock dropped 10% after Carrol's video went viral (Deighton and Kornfeld 2010).

Although a complaint by its nature is the expression of a negative experience, we highlight that not all complaints are strictly negative. A simple internet search illustrates how some complaints have a humorous element (e.g., ATT steals oranges; Comcast technician sleeping on my couch). We introduce the concept of humorous complaining and differentiate it from strict complaints by investigating its audience, antecedents, and implications.

To derive our predictions, we draw on a theory that proposes that humor occurs when a violation is simultaneously perceived as benign (McGraw and Warren 2010). A violation refers to anything that threatens one's belief about how things should be (Veatch 1998). Violations are seen as benign when the perceived threat also seems okay. Play fighting and tickling are prototypical examples of benign violations: both are physically threatening but harmless attacks (Gervais and Wilson 2005). In a similar manner, we suspect that unlike serious complaints, which only highlight a violation committed by a firm, humorous complaints also involve an element that makes the violation seem benign.

We present two studies that explore how the audience, antecedents, and consequences of humorous complaints differ from serious complaints.

1) Audience. Consistent with anecdotal evidence in the marketplace, we investigate whether consumers are more likely to complain humorously to other consumers rather than the offending firm or third party agencies. Consumers typically complain to firms and third party agencies in order to motivate reparative actions. Because humor softens criticism by suggesting the violation is benign (Keltner et al. 2001; McGraw and Warren 2010), humorous complaints may be less likely than serious complaints to prompt action. Thus, consumers should be more likely to direct humorous complaints to other consumers rather than firms or third-party agencies.

We randomly assigned members (*N*=83) of an online survey panel to imagine themselves in a hypothetical scenario depicting either an extreme or a mild customer service violation at a restaurant. In the extreme violation scenario, the patron receives the wrong order, the food is completely overcooked, and the waiter, who is very rude, does not rectify the mistake. In the mild violation scenario, the food is mildly overcooked, and the waiter eventually brings the correct order.

We asked participants how likely they would be to complain, both humorously and seriously (order counterbalanced), about their experience to the following audiences (1=Very Unlikely, 7 = Very Likely): 1) other consumers in person, 2) other consumers via the Internet, 3) the firm, and 4) a third party agency. Although participants were likely to complain seriously directly to the firm (*M*=3.9), they were significantly more likely to complain humorously to other consumers, either in person (*M*=4.2) or via the Internet (*M*=3.4), than to a third party agency (*M*=1.8) or the firm (*M*=1.6).

2) Antecedents. In accordance with the benign violation theory, we expect that humor will be more prevalent in mildly negative than extremely negative experiences. Extremely negative experiences are less likely to be perceived as benign making it more difficult for consumers to complain about them in a humorous manner (McGraw et al. 2011).

We asked participants who read about the negative restaurant experience how easy or difficult it would be to recount their experiences in a humorous manner (1=Very Difficult, 7=Very Easy). Participants who read about a mildly negative experience reported that it would be easier to complain in a humorous manner than participants who read about an extremely negative experience (M_{mild}=4.83, $M_{extreme}$=3.91).

3) Consequences. Because humor is attention getting, enjoyable, and memorable (Alden, Mukherjee and Hoyer 2000; Eisend 2009), we suspect that humorous complaints are more likely to go viral than serious complaints.

We asked 63 undergraduate students to read either a serious or humorous version of a letter complaining about a bank's poor service. This letter was selected based on a search conducted by members of an online panel (*N*=50) asked to submit an example of the funniest consumer complaint that they could find on the Internet. Two research assistants blind to the study's hypothesis ranked the written complaints based on their humor and selected the letter with the average highest ranking. One of the assistants then rewrote the complaint letter highlighting the same reasons but removing any humorous content.

Subjects read either the humorous or the serious version of the complaint. As expected, participants found the humorous version of the letter significantly more humorous than the serious version ($M_{humorous}$=4.9, $M_{non-humorous}$=2.1). Importantly, participants also enjoyed the humorous version significantly more ($M_{humorous}$=4.9, $M_{non-humorous}$=3.0) and, as a result, were more likely to share this version with other consumers ($M_{humorous}$=3.6, $M_{non-humorous}$=2.6; indirect effect (a x b) = .67, 95% CI = .19 to 1.29).

Our findings suggest that firms should be wary of consumers complaining humorously about their products and services. The spread of humorous complaints is more difficult for firms to control than the spread of serious complaints not only because the humorous complaints tend to be directed at other consumers, but also because their enjoyable nature makes them more likely to be circulated, thereby increasing the number of consumers exposed to negative information about the firm.

REFERENCES

Alden, Dana L., Ashesh Mukherjee, and Wayne D. Hoyer (2000), "The Effects of Incongruity, Surprise and Positive Moderators of Perceived Humor in Television Advertising," *Journal of Advertising*, 29 (Summer), 1-15.
Chevalier, Judith A. and Dina Mayzlin (2006), "The Effect of Word of Mouth on Sales: Online Book Reviews," *Journal of Marketing Research*, 43 (August), 345-54.
Deighton, John and Leora Kornfeld (2010), *United Breaks Guitars (Case Study)*, Boston: Harvard Business Publishing.
Eisend, Martin (2009), "A Meta-Analysis of Humor in Advertising," *Journal of the Academy of Marketing Science*, 37 (Summer), 191-203.
Gervais, Matthew and David S. Wilson (2005), "The Evolution and Functions of Laughter and Humor: A Synthetic Approach," *Quarterly Review of Biology*, 80 (Dec), 395-430.
Keltner, Dacher, Lisa Capps, Ann M. Kring, Randall C. Young, and Erin A. Heerey (2001), "Just Teasing: A Conceptual Analysis and Empirical Review," *Psychological Bulletin*, 127 (2), 229-48.
McGraw, A. Peter and Caleb Warren (2010), "Benign Violations: Making Immoral Behavior Funny," *Psychological Science*, 21 (August), 1141-49.
McGraw, A. Peter, Caleb Warren, Lawrence E. Williams and Bridget Leonard (2011), "Finding Humor in Distant Tragedies and Close Mishaps." working paper, Marketing Department, Leeds School of Business, University of Colorado at Boulder, Boulder, CO 80309.
Mizerski, Richard W. (1982), "An Attribution Explanation of the Disproportionate Influence of Unfavorable Information," *Journal of Consumer Research*, 9 (December), 301-10.
Veatch, Tom C. (1998), "A Theory of Humor," *Humor-International Journal of Humor Research*, 11 (May), 161-215.

In the Aftermath of an Earthquake: The Interactive Role of Self-construal and Victim Group-Status in Charitable Behavior

Rod Duclos, Hong KongThe Hong Kong University of Science & Technology, Hong Kong
Alixandra Barasch, Wharton, University of Pennsylvania, USA

When a natural disaster strikes a community, consumers often face countless appeals to donate time or money to help the victims. Only a small percentage of people who view these advertisements, however, will investigate the cause further, and an even smaller percentage will end up offering resources to aid the rescue and rebuilding efforts. What factors influence whether individuals will help victims of natural disasters and other disadvantaged populations? The present research attempts to answer this question by investigating the interactive effects of self-construal and victim origin on prosocial behavior.

Fundamental to people's emotional and cognitive responses, self-construal characterizes the extent to which one considers oneself separate from vs. connected with others (Markus and Kitayama 1991). Hence, individuals vary on the self construal continuum from inter dependent to independent (Singelis 1994, Stapel and Koomen 2001). Because the *interdependent* self is more meaningful in the context of social relationships or as part of a larger social unit, one might expect interdependent (independent) individuals to be more (less) generous when faced with calls for help. Consistent with this view, several studies found positive correlations between interdependence and charitable behavior (Moorman and Blakely 2006; Eckstein 2001; Skarmeas and Shabbir 2011).

Drawing from work in psychology, we contrast from the above view and argue that interdependent individuals may not necessarily be more connected to or generous toward others. Much self-construal research has indeed underscored the importance of group status (*in* vs. *out*) for the interdependent self (Markus and Kitayama 1991; Iyengar and Lepper 1999; Kitayama et al. 1997). I.e., interdependent individuals are more motivated to integrate themselves with and meet the expectations of others, but only when these others are considered *relevant* (e.g., family members, peers, significant groups; Heine and Lehman 1997).

Accordingly, the present study investigates the interaction of self-construal and victim group-status on donation behavior. We propose that, when individuals are faced with a plea to support victims of a severe earthquake, victims' status (in- vs. out-group) will interact with donors' self-concept. Specifically, we predict that victims' group-status should influence interdependents' willingness to help more than independents' (since the latter see themselves as more separate from others, regardless of group-status).

Design & procedures. To test these propositions, we randomly assigned 112 students from a large East Asian university to one of four conditions. Our experiment followed a 2 (Self-construal: Independent vs. Interdependent) by 2 (Victim status: In- vs. Out-group) between-subjects design. To manipulate self-construal, we asked participants to complete an alleged emotional empathy questionnaire. To this effect, subjects read a short story written either in the first person (e.g., I, my, me) or in the inclusive plural form (e.g., we, our, us) before completing a series of manipulation checks intended to assess their ensuing self-construal orientation and mood.

Next, participants viewed an appeal from "Global Relief", a fictitious charity collecting money to help victims of earthquakes. Vivid in nature, the advertisement featured death toll statistics (e.g., "over 100,000 killed and 1 million others homeless"), a description of the victims' needs (e.g., "food and medicine for vulnerable children and devastated families"), and the pictures of two suffering victims underneath the text. The ad concluded by asking participants to visit the charity's website to make a donation.

Since our sample was composed almost exclusively of south-east Chinese, we manipulated victims' status by featuring pictures from the recent Sichuan (in-group) vs. Haiti (out-group) earthquakes. Of note, the pictures included in each advertisement were identical in every aspect except, of course, race. I.e., based on pretests, the victims depicted in our ads matched in all regards (e.g., age, gender, apparent suffering, etc). This was further confirmed through multiple affect-related manipulation checks.

Results. An analysis of variance on participants' willingness to help revealed no main effects (Fs < 1, NS) but a significant crossover interaction ((F1, 111) = 5.333, p = .023). On average, independents were neither more nor less likely to donate than interdependents. Similarly, Haitian victims were neither more nor less likely than their Sichuan counterparts to elicit donations. Follow-up contrast analyses, however, revealed that, while victims' origin did not seem to matter for independents (F (1 ,111) = 1.294, p = NS), it did so for interdependents (F (1 ,111) = 4.542, p = .0353). That is, whereas independent participants were just as likely to make a donation regardless of victims' origin, interdependent participants donated significantly more to in-group (i.e., Sichuan) than to out-group (i.e., Haitian) victims. Of note, this simple effect was driven by interdependents' increased generosity toward Sichuan victims (F (1 ,111) = 3.040, p = .084), not their reduced benevolence toward Haitians (F (1 ,111) = 2.319, NS). Also of note, these findings were not driven by affective considerations. Indeed, none of our manipulation checks (e.g., PANAS, sadness, anxiety, depression, nervousness, mood, etc) revealed any main effect or interaction capable of explaining our results.

So to account for these findings, we next turned to cognitive aspects of decision-making. Building on Duclos et al. (2011), we tested whether participants' beliefs about happiness and prosocial behavior could mediate the interaction described above. Following Baron and Kenny's (1986) four-step approach to mediated moderation, we were able to confirm that participants' willingness to assist earthquake victims depended on the interactive influences of self-construal and victims' group-status, and this interaction was mediated by the degree to which participants believed that helping others promotes happiness (Sobel test: z = 1.609, p = .1).

By highlighting the interactive effects of self-construal orientation and victim group-status on donation behavior, the present study bridges the gap between and offers novel theoretical insights for two important and burgeoning research areas. Furthermore, by identifying the mediating role of cognitions vs. affect in consumers' decision to donate money, our findings provide charities actionable insights into the psychology of donors (e.g., matching recipients of help to donors' profile in interdependent contexts, highlighting the happiness derived from helping others). Hence, for its contributions to both theory and practice, we believe this poster would be of interest to a wide audience at ACR.

REFERENCES

Baron, R.M. & Kenny, D.A. (1986), "The Moderator-Mediator variable distinction", in Social Psychological research: Conceptual, strategic, and statistical considerations. Journal of Personality and Social Psychology, 51, 1173-1182.

Duclos, Bettman, Bloom, and Zauberman (2011), "Charitable Giving: How Ego-Threats Impact Donations of Time and Money," Working Paper.

Eckstein, Susan (2001), "Community as gift-giving: Collectivistic roots of volunteerism," American Sociological Review, 66 (Dec), 829-851.

Heine, Steven J. and Darrin R. Lehman (1997), "The cultural construction of self-enhancement: An examination of group-serving biases," Journal of personality and social psychology, 72 (6), 1268-1283.

Iyengar, Sheena S. and Mark R. Lepper (1999), "Rethinking the Value of Choice: A Cultural Perspective on Intrinsic Motivation," Journal of Personality and Social Psychology, 76 (3), 349-366.

Kitayama, Shinobu, Hazel Rose Markus, Hisaya Matsumoto, and Vinai Norasakkunit (1997), "Individual and collective processes in the construction of the self: Self enhancement in the United States and self-criticism in Japan," Journal of Personality and Social Psychology, 72 (6), 1245-67.

Markus, Hazel Rose and Shinobu Kitayama (1991), "Culture and the self: Implications for cognition, emotion, and motivation," Psychological Review, 98 (2), 224-53.

Moorman, Robert H. and Gerald L. Blakely (2006), "Individualism-collectivism as an individual difference predictor of organizational citizenship behavior," Journal of Organizational Behavior, 16 (2), 829-851.

Singelis, Theodore M. (1994), "The Measurement of Independent and Interdependent Self-Construals," Personality and Social Psychology Bulletin, 20 (5), 580-591.

Skarmeas, Dionysis and Haseeb Shabbir (2011), "Relationship quality and giving behaviour in the UK fundraising sector: Exploring the antecedent roles of religiosity and self-construal," European Journal of Marketing, 45 (5).

Stapel, Diederik A. and Willem Koomen (2001), "I, we, and the effects of others on me: Self-construal level moderates social comparison effect," Journal of Personality and Social Psychology, 80, 766-781.

The Endowment Effect: Deciding for Oneself versus Deciding for Others

Shih-Chieh Chuang, National Chung Cheng University, Taiwan
Yin-Hui Cheng, National Taichung University, Taiwan
Sui-Min Wang, National Chung Cheng University, Taiwan
Kuo-shu Hwang, National Yunlin University of Science and Technology, Taiwan

Research into the individual decision-making process has examined potential gains or losses, measured relative to the individual's status quo position (Kahneman & Tversky, 1979), and found that sellers tend to overvalue objects relative to buyers. Thaler (1980) and Kahneman, Knetsch, and Thaler (1990) call this tendency to place a larger value on an item that is in one's possession the "endowment effect." The essential idea is that individuals are more reluctant to lose something they own than they are to gain something they do not. Hence, although buyers generally value goods objectively, due to seller behavior (Inder & O'Brien, 2003), there is a discrepancy between the minimum price a seller will accept and the maximum price a buyer will pay. Given the importance of the endowment effect in everyday economic behavior, it is expected that people's perceptions of that effect may be equally important.

In recent years, business transactions appear to occur more frequently when self-other differences exist, as such differences influence consumer behavior. Much of the research on the endowment effect has focused on the valuations an individual makes for him or herself. It has generally failed to address how it affects valuations made for others and whether there are self-other differences. Making decisions for others is quite common. For example, parents regularly make decisions for their children, and friends frequently make decisions for one another. Thus, it is important to identify the factors that differentiate decisions made for oneself from those made for others. Also of interest is whether the endowment effect is larger or smaller on business transactions in which sellers and buyers make decisions for others. The research reported herein examines both issues. The findings of this study will also contribute to the literature on the influence of psychophysical properties by providing a better understanding of the factors that mediate the effects of self-other differences on willingness to accept (WTA) and willingness to pay (WTP). It is founded on the premise that knowledge of self-other differences concerning perceived stimuli may arise from the different valuation levels that are due to varying degrees of personal involvement in the decision-making process. The study's findings will also facilitate assessment of the psychological underpinnings of ownership and the effects of the self-other discrepancy on the endowment effect. An understanding of these mechanisms will not only identify the factors determining the self-other differences that appear to follow a trade-off strategy between sellers and buyers, but also provide direction for marketers interested in increasing the transaction amount gained. If individuals are capable of correctly predicting others' needs and desires, then these predictions may well affect the decisions they make during the transaction process.

Building on the concepts of perceived ownership and the features of focus, the authors predict that individuals will make decisions for another person differently than they will for themselves, thus eliminating the disparity between the selling and buying price. They also employ the theory of self-other differences to determine whether sellers and buyers are differentially sensitive to item changes and, if so, whether this difference in sensitivity depends on the presence of a market price.

In the first study, 136 university students (68 of whom were male) were given a coffee mug and asked to estimate the price they would be willing to pay/accept for it in the self and other conditions. The experimenter asked participants in the self condition: "If you were to sell/buy this coffee mug , how much would you be willing to accept/pay for it?" A similar question was asked of those in the other condition: "If you were to sell/buy this coffee mug for a friend, how much would you be willing to accept/pay for it?" Results supported the hypothesis that the selling price will decrease and the buying price increase when one is acting on behalf of another (and that the opposite will be true when one is acting on one's own behalf).

In the second study, we investigated the proposed perceived ownership and features of focus effects could account for the observed decrease in the endowment effect in the others condition. Thus, this study employed a 2 (role: seller versus buyer) × 2 (valence features: positive versus negative) × 2 (target person: self-focused frame versus others-focused frame) design, with the first and third factors varying between participants and the second within participants. Results from this study indicate that the participants were more likely to consider positive features when they were acting as a seller for themselves than when they were acting as a buyer. In addition, we found that perceived ownership and the features of focus work together to partially mediate the relationship between the endowment effect and the effect of trading for others,

In the final study, the aim of broadening our knowledge of the "other" on whose behalf a transaction is made. It tested whether the level of intimacy between owner and seller/buyer influences the endowment effect and whether this influence depends on the presence of a reference price. The participants were told that they were taking part in an experimental auction. A description of self-other differences was given in each of the eight experimental conditions, with each participant presented with a different version of the screen, that is, one of the four self-other conditions: valuing the object for oneself, for a family member, for a friend, or for a stranger. They were then asked to provide a selling/buying price. Results showed that the endowment effect on the estimation varies with the level of intimacy of the relationship the seller/buyer has with the target other, although the difference is less in the presence of a reference price.

To conclude, the results of three studies demonstrate the existence of differing perceptions of the self-other discrepancy among buyers and sellers. More specifically, we hypothesized that when valuation outcomes are explicitly framed in terms of seller/buyer gains and losses, consumers are more loss-averse when acting for themselves rather than others in contexts involving losses. The endowment effect does appear to reflect self-other biases, thereby providing us with a deeper understanding of the mental processes involved. Our results also have implications for social psychology and prospect theory, as they identify the greater hedonic impact of losses, although this impact is lessened in situations in which one is acting on behalf of another. The effect found in the others condition was inconsistent with the expectations of status quo reference dependence and loss aversion, although that in the self condition was consistent with them, as no endowment effect was observed. It is clear that individuals' perceptions of others' behavior are closely linked to their valuations of the selling price. These findings are important for the transactions of market that can help seller and buyer to improve asymmetric information and biased information integration, solve the lemon problem, and ensure a more successful experience by enhancing trade-offs and interpersonal mechanisms.

REFERENCES

Inder, B., & O'Brien, T. (2003). The endowment effect and the role of uncertainty. *Bulletin of Economic Research*, 55, 289–301

Kahneman, D., &. Tversky, A. (1979). Prospect theory: An analysis of decision under risk. *Econometrica* 47, 263–29

Kahneman, D., Knetsch J., & Thaler, R. (1990). Experimental tests of the endowment effect and the coase theorem, *Journal of Political Economy*, 98, 1325–1348.

Thaler, R. (1980). Tnward a positive theory of cons5meR chgice. *Jotrnal of Economic Behavior and Organization, 1,* 39–60.

How to Motivate People: The Influence of Perceived Goal Progress on Construal Level

Jooyoung Park, University of Iowa, USA
William M. Hedgcock, University of Iowa, USA

The primary purpose of this study is to understand the relationship between perceived goal progress and mental construal. Previous studies on self-regulation have investigated the relationship between goal progress and subsequent goal pursuit. However, the studies have not examined how goal progress influences individuals' information processing. Our findings of the relationship between goal progress and construal level suggest that people can more easily process information and be persuaded by messages construed at different levels depending on goal progress.

CONCEPTUAL BACKGROUND

Construal level theory suggests that people construe (represent) an object or event at different levels. For example, people can describe reading either in terms of a low-level aspect ("following lines of print") or a high-level aspect ("gaining knowledge").

In the context of consumer behavior, Labroo and Patrick (2008) showed that construal level is influenced by moods. They hypothesized that positive moods signal that all is currently well and allow people to see the big picture. They found that positive moods evoke an abstract construal level and that participants in a positive mood prefer a product when its benefits are described in an abstract manner rather than in a concrete manner.

Previous studies on the relationship between moods and goal progress suggest that positive affect compared to negative affect reduces persistence in focal goal and increases cognitive flexibility and attention toward novel stimuli (Dreishbach and Goschke 2004). Also, Louro, Pieters, and Zeelenberg (2007) proposed that people tend to have positive moods when they experience significant goal progress.

These studies suggest that significant goal progress can evoke positive moods and in turn increase cognitive flexibility and construal level. Accordingly, we predict that greater goal progress can produce positive moods and thus increase construal level.

METHODOLOGY

Perceived goal progress is frequently manipulated through social comparison (e.g., Fishbach, Dhar, and Zhang 2006). Using a goal of keeping in shape, we predict that a comparison to a low social standard (1 hour of exercise) suggests that one has successfully pursued the goal, whereas a comparison to a high social standard (10 hours of exercise) suggests that one did not successfully pursue the goal. Following previous studies (e.g., Fishbach and Dhar 2005), we informed our participants that prior participants answered only the first question, and we were reusing their paper. When they received their booklet, participants were asked to first report the amount of time they had spent working out during the previous week. On the following page, they found a fictitious participant's answer for the amount of time he or she had spent working out (either 1 hour or 10 hours). Then, participants reported their perceived goal progress.

Louro et al. (2007) measured positive and negative moods about individuals' progress using eight items (e.g., I feel "proud of myself," "good about myself," "regretful," I am "happy with myself," "satisfied with myself," "ashamed with myself," and "angry with myself"). We used the items on 7-point scales ranging from not at all (1) to very much (7).

Researchers often use a classification task to measure construal level based on the premise that an abstract, higher-level construal leads to broader, more inclusive categories (Liberman, Sagristano, and Trope 2002). Following previous research, we asked participants to classify twenty-five items for each of two scenarios (i.e., going camping and organizing a yard sale). Last, they reported age, gender, and the importance of the goal of keeping in shape.

FINDINGS

Seventy-seven undergraduate students participated in the study (forty-nine were males). We first compared perceived progress depending on the manipulation (a high versus a low social standard) using t-test. Consistent with our expectations, participants who were exposed to a low social standard (1 hour, $M = 4.41$) perceived greater goal progress than those exposed to a high social standard (10 hour, $M = 3.65$) ($t(75) = 1.998$, $p = .049$). Also, participants under the low standard condition (camping trip, M = 5.16; yard sale, $M = 5.24$) used a fewer number of categories than participants under the high standard condition (camping trip, $M = 6.13$; yard sale, $M = 6.53$); camping trip, $t(75) = -.2.306$, $p = .024$; yard sale, $t(75) = -2.884$; $p = .005$). Similarly, we found consistent results from correlation analyses. The correlation between social standards and the number of categories (camping trip, $r = .257$, $p = .024 < .05$; yard sale, $r = .316$, $p=.005$) suggests that a lower social standard leads to a fewer number of categories (a higher construal level) than a higher social standard. Following Louro et al. (2007), we combined positive and negative moods into a single index (i.e., the difference between positive and negative moods, positive scores indicate net positive moods). We found significant correlation between standard and moods ($r = -.276$, $p = .015$) and between progress and moods ($r = .383$, $p = .001$). However, we did not find significant relationship between moods and construal level (camping trip, $r = -.113$, $p = .328$; yard sale, $r = .109$, $p = .343$).

DISCUSSION

Lee et al. (2009) showed that fit between individuals' regulatory focus and the construal level of a message can enhance engagement in information processing and in turn lead to processing fluency and intensified reactions. In this study, we found that greater goal progress increases construal level. This implies that individuals are likely to construe information at different levels depending on goal progress and that different messages represented either at a high or a low construal level can be more influential in goal pursuit. In the subsequent studies, we intend to examine the persuasiveness of messages focusing on different construal levels depending on goal progress. Different from our expectation, we did not find a mediating role of moods in the relationship between goal progress and construal level. This may suggest goal progress may expand individuals' cognitive flexibility and thus increase construal level. We will elaborate on the underlying processes in subsequent studies.

REFERENCES

Dreisbach, Gesine and Thomas Goschke (2004), "How Positive Affect Modulates Cognitive Control: Reduced Perseveration at the Cost of Increased Distractibility," *Journal of Experimental Psychology: Learning, Memory, and Cognition*, 30(2), 343-353.

Fishbach, Ayelet and Ravi Dhar (2005), "Goals as Excuses or Guides: The Liberating Effect of Perceived Goal Progress on Choice, "*Journal of Consumer Research*, 32 (3), 370 - 377.

Labroo, Aparna A. and Vanessa M. Patrick (2009), "Why a Positive Mood Helps Seeing the Big Picture," *Journal of Consumer Research*, 35 (5), 800-809.

Lee, Angela Y., Punam Keller, and Brian Sternthal (2010), "Value from Regulatory Construal Fit," *Journal of Consumer Research*, 36 (5), 735-747.

Liberman, Nara, Michael D. Sagristano, and Yaacov Trope (2002), "The Effect of Temporal Distance on Level of Mental Construal," *Journal of Experimental Social Psychology*, 38 (6), 523 - 534.

Louro, Maria J., Rik Pieters, and Marcel Zeelenberg (2007), "Dynamics of Multiple-Goal Pursuit," *Journal of Personality and Social Psychology*, 93 (2), 174–193.

Do People Spend More in a Crowded Store?
A Field Experiment on Control Deprivation and Compensatory Spending

Charlene Chen, Columbia University, USA
Leonard Lee, Columbia University, USA
Andy Yap, Columbia University, USA

Desire for control over the environment is a fundamental human motive (White, 1959). Violation of this need provokes distress that initiates efforts to reassert control (Skinner, 1996). Recent research has shown that people might compensate for their perceived lack of control through an increase in acquisition behaviors to feel a sense of ownership and control (Chen, Lee, & Yap, 2011). The current study extends this research by investigating whether control deprivation induced by a crowded supermarket could affect buying and spending behaviors similarly. Crowding in retail settings has been found to diminish one's sense of control because it frustrates one's shopping goals of moving freely and locating products (Langer & Saegart, 1977). Hence, we expected shoppers in a crowded (vs. uncrowded) store to buy and spend more.

Another goal of this experiment was to demonstrate that control restoration in the crowded store would attenuate these effects, thus strengthening our confidence that loss of control indeed drives increased purchasing behavior. In a study by Langer and Saegert (1977), participants given information about the psychological effects of being in crowded situations (e.g., physiological arousal) did not exhibit the same decrements on a simulated shopping task in a crowded store as those who were not given such information. The authors argued that information provision raises people's control of the situation by allowing them to anticipate the onset of the stressor and to initiate cognitive preparation (see also Schmidt & Keating, 1979). In our experiment, a similar intervention was introduced to alleviate control deprivation caused by crowding. We predicted that giving shoppers information related to retail store environments (e.g., crowding) would reverse their tendency to buy and spend more in a crowded store.

METHODOLOGY

Regular shoppers were recruited during crowded and uncrowded periods at the entrance of a supermarket, and were given a $3-coupon for participating. Based on communication with the store, we were able to ascertain beforehand time intervals in the afternoon that were either crowded or uncrowded. Shoppers in crowded periods were randomly assigned to either receive or not receive any intervention before shopping. Those that received the intervention were given this information: "Research studies in the area of marketing have shown that retail store environments can influence consumers' shopping behavior. Certain characteristics of a store like crowding for example can cause customers to shop differently." Overall, there were three conditions: (a) uncrowded; (b) crowded and no information was given (no-info); and (c) crowded and information was given (info). All shoppers were told to redeem their coupons and answer a survey regarding their experiences after shopping. Eighteen shoppers did not redeem the coupon and were removed from the sample (non-redemption rates were equivalent across conditions). The final sample comprised 57 shoppers (22 males) between 18-70 years of age (M=29.79; SD=15.79).

RESULTS

To analyze the data, we conducted planned contrast tests comparing the crowded/no-info condition with the other two conditions. A contrast weight sequence of 2, -1, -1 was used for all outcome variables (sense of control, number of items bought, expenditure, and number of utilitarian items bought) across: the crowded/no-info, uncrowded, and crowded/info conditions (respectively). Crowded/no-info shoppers perceived lower control over their environment (M=3.59; SD=2.06; n=17) than uncrowded shoppers (M=4.90; SD=1.25; n=20) and crowded/info shoppers (M=4.50; SD=1.67; n=20), t(54)=2.30, p<.05. Therefore, crowding did reduce perceived control but this was prevented when shoppers received the information.

Support was obtained for our prediction that crowded/no-info shoppers would buy and spend more than shoppers in the other conditions. Crowded/no-info bought more items (M=6.12; SD=5.72) than uncrowded shoppers (M=2.80; SD=1.58) and crowded/info shoppers (M=3.30; SD=1.81), t(54)=3.09, p<.005. They also spent more money (M=\$17.28; SD=15.49) than uncrowded shoppers (M=\$7.04; SD=4.62) and crowded/info shoppers (M=\$8.34; SD=5.14), t(54)=3.53, p<.005. Two independent raters classified each product purchased by participants as "utilitarian", "hedonic", or "either utilitarian or hedonic" (Kappa=.72). For each participant, the quantity of items in each category was computed. Crowded/no-info shoppers bought significantly more utilitarian products (M=4.12; SD=4.40) than uncrowded shoppers (M=1.55; SD=1.28) and crowded/info shoppers (M=1.90; SD=1.62), t(54)=3.07, p<.005. The contrast test did not show any significant difference in number of hedonic products purchased, p=.83. Controlling for emotions and shopper characteristics (e.g., buying more because of long queues) did not alter the results.

DISCUSSION

Lacking control in crowded situations without an opportunity to restore it through information provision led shoppers to buy more and spend more. A finding by Chen et al. that control-deprived individuals tend to buy more utilitarian products was also replicated in this study. According to these authors, such products are typically viewed as means to certain ends, and thus help people feel that they are accomplishing some intended effect on the environment. In this experiment, shoppers who were not given the information bought more utilitarian products when the store was crowded. Shoppers in crowded situations who had the chance to regain it through information provision however resembled shoppers in the uncrowded situations in what they bought and spent. Hence, the current findings support our claim that control motivation underlies our effects.

Shopping opportunities in contemporary life makes buying a convenient channel for compensating for one's lack of control. While prudent use of this strategy may be helpful for control-deprived individuals, frequent employment may result in excessive spending. From a policy standpoint, shoppers should be informed that certain retail environments (e.g., crowding) can instill feelings of control loss that in turn may propel them to increase their purchasing.

REFERENCES

Chen, C.Y., Lee, L., & Yap, A.J. (2011). *Seeking a sense of control in buying.* Unpublished manuscript.

Langer, E.J., & Saegert, S. (1977). Crowding and cognitive control. *Journal of Personality and Social Psychology, 35,* 175-182.

Skinner, E.A. (1996). A guide to constructs of control. *Journal of Personality and Social Psychology, 71,* 549-570.

Schmidt, D.E., & Keating, J.P. (1979). Human crowding and personal control: An integration of the research. *Psychological Bulletin, 86,* 680-700.

White, R.W. (1959). Motivation reconsidered: The concept of competence. *Psychological Review, 66,* 297-335.

Should Santa Still Wear Red? Investigating the Effects of Color on Impulsive Buying Behavior

Liangyan Wang, Antai Management School, Shanghai Jiao Tong University, China
Dante M. Pirouz, The Richard Ivey School of Business,University of Western Ontario, Canada
Xinan Zhang, Antai Management School, Shanghai Jiao Tong University

Impulsiveness or impulsivity has long been extensively studied as a general trait by psychologists, educators and criminologists (Rook and Fisher 1995; Eysenck and McGurk 1980). Accordingly, to a large extent, impulsive buying behavior has been examined involving with long-term predisposed factors such as norms (Rook and Fisher 1995), cultural orientations (Kacen and Lee 2002), and fashion-involvement and lifestyle (Park et al., 2006). Scant research has empirically examined the environmental cue's impact on consumers' impulsive buying behavior. Also, large body of research on impulse buying has been studied in the developed western contexts. Attempting to fill the gaps in this area of consumer behavior, this research, contrast to prior research involving with predisposition factors, aims to examine the impact of brief exposure to color (blue vs. red) on impulsive buying behavior in China- a developing country recently with much transitions and many new international market experiences.

Color is ubiquitous in people's life. And it influences human perception, cognition and behavior (Meth and Zhu 2009; Elliot et al 2007). As to research studying color topics, most of them have focused on "two of the three primary colors-red versus blue (green)" (P.1226, Meth and Zhu 2009). Elliot et al 2007 demonstrated that prior to an anagram test, participants briefly exposed to red performed worse than those briefly exposed to green. Meth and Zhu 2009 suggested that short exposure to red (versus blue) could enhance performance on detail-oriented (versus creative) cognitive tasks. Gorn et al 2004 found that participants who were exposed to the blue background screen perceived the page download as quicker than did participants exposed to the red background screen. The empirically examined consequence differences between brief exposure to red versus blue (green) result from different learned associations, which are likely to activate different motivations (approach vs. avoidance) and possibly different levels of relaxations (Meth and Zhu 2009; Elliot et al 2007; Gorn et al 2004). In line with prior research, we propose that compared to individuals briefly exposed to red, individuals briefly exposed to blue have higher impulsive buying intent in general.

Two experimental studies were conducted among several hundred subjects to test our hypothesis using both online and traditional paper-and-pencil surveys. In experiment 1, 68 participants were randomly assigned to one of the two between-subjects experimental conditions: the red condition or the blue condition. The study was conducted by an experimenter blind to the experimental hypothesis. Impulsive purchase decision served as the dependent measure. The impulsive purchase decision measure was used and justified by Rook and Fishier 2004. An imaginary shopping situation was provided and participants were asked to make a purchase choice out of five purchase decision alternatives ranging from low to high impulsiveness. Participants assigned to the red condition filled up a survey printed in red paper whereas participants assigned to the blue condition filled up a survey printed in blue paper. The two groups were asked to fill in the paper-and-pencil survey starting with some filler questions first, followed by the dependent measure and demographic information. A unifactorial (color condition: red vs. blue) between subjects analysis of covariance was conducted on impulsive purchase decision. The analysis revealed an effect of color on impulsive purchase decision, $F(1, 66)=5.10$, $p<.05$. More specifically, consistent with our hypothesis, participants in the blue condition achieved higher impulsiveness on specific impulsive purchase decision (means=3.16 vs. 2.44).

In experiment 2, we verified our findings by conducting an online survey. Rather than to fill up a paper-and-pencil survey respectively in red or blue, 122 participants were randomly assigned to fill up an online survey respectively with blue or red computer background screen. The procedure was similar with the first experiment. Similarly a unifactorial (color condition: red vs. blue) between subjects analysis of covariance revealed an effect of color on impulsive purchase decision, means=2.87 vs. 2.45; $F(1, 120)=3.71$, $p=.05$.

In sum, in this study, through two experiments, conducted among almost 200 participants, we consistently found that color (blue vs. red) did influence individual's impulsive buying behavior. Specifically, compared to individuals briefly exposed to red, individuals briefly exposed to blue had higher impulsive buying intent. The findings suggest that color can serve as an important environmental cue that has large impact on consumer impulsive buying behavior. Our findings contribute to the literatures both on consumer impulsive buying behavior and color psychology. Also our findings have practical implications on how to help retailing stores to create an environment to enhance consumer impulsive buying and also bring up the question that whether Santa Clause still wears red in the large shopping malls when the shopping spree season comes.

REFERENCES

Elliot, A.J., Maier, M.A., Moller, A.C.; Friedman, R. and J. Meinhardt (2007), "Color and Psychological Functioning: The Effect of Red on Performance Attainment," *Journal of Experimental Psychology: General*, 136(1), 154-168.

Eysenck, Sybil B., P. R. Pearson, G. Easting, and J. F. Allsopp (1985), "Age Norms for Impulsiveness, Venturesomeness and Empathy in Adults," *Personality and Individual Differences,* 6(5), 613-619.

Gorn Gerald J., A. Chattopadhyay, J. Sengupta, and S. Tripathi (2004), "Waiting for the Web: How Screen Color Affects Time Perception," *Journal of Marketing Research*, May, 215-225.

Kacen, J. J. and J. A. Lee (2002), "The Influence of Culture on Consumer Impulsive Buying Behavior", *Journal of Consumer Psychology,* 12(2), 163-176.

Ravi, Meth and Rui Zhu (2009), "Blue or Red? Exploring the Effect of Color on Cognitive Task Performances," *Science* (323), 1226-1229.

Park, E. J., Kim, E. Y. and Forney, J. C. (2006),"A Structural model of Fashion-oriented Impulse Buying Behavior", *Journal of Fashion Marketing and Management*, 10 (4), 433-446.

Rook, Dennis W. and Robert J. Fisher (1995), "Normative Influences on Impulsive Buying Behavior," *Journal of Consumer Research*, 22, 305-313.

The Influence of Framing and Processing Fluency on the Estimates of Conjunctive Events

Ahmad Daryanto, Lancaster University, UK
Peter Hampson, Northumbria University, UK

Many events in life constitute conjunctive events (e.g., getting tenure). A conjunctive event consists of more than simple event (e.g., getting a paper published). The likelihood of a conjunctive event is the probability that all simple events occur. Past research has examined how people interpret the probability occurence of the conjunctive events (e.g., Bar-Hillel, 1972; Brockner et al. 2002; Mandel, 2008). For instance, Bar Hillel (1973) has found that people overestimate the likelihood of conjunctive events. Research by Brockner et al. (2002) demonstrates that promotion-focused individuals may do better at estimating conjunctive events than prevention-focused individuals. The present research aims at extending the previous research. We posit that estimates of a conjunctive event may be affected by the framing of its simple events (i.e., gain e.g., accepted vs. loss, e.g., not rejected) and the effect is mediated by processing fluency. We aim at making contribution to framing and consumer decision making literature.

Recent research has examined a strict refocusing framing effect (Mandel, 2008), which refers to the description of a conjunctive event as consisting a series of simple event framed as either a gain or loss (e.g., two acceptances out of three paper submissions or its complementarity of one rejection out of three paper submissions). Despite extant research on framing, strict refocusing framing effect was paid little attention. The main aim of the present research is to examine the effect of strict refocusing framing on the estimation of conjunctive events.

SIGNIFICANCE AND IMPLICATIONS OF THE RESEARCH

In this study, we examine how people's judgment on the probability of a conjunctive event influences their subsequent inference (e.g., after successfully getting five papers accepted what is the probability of getting tenure?). Our study demonstrates that a conjunctive event that contains series of success events was judged more probable if they were supported with positive evidence, whereas its complementary event that contains a series of failure events was judged more probable if they were supported with negative evidence. We provide support for our theory in empirical setting involving hypothetical scenarios. We study the role of processing fluency as a cognitive mechanism of the strict refocusing framing effect and test the prediction in more naturalistic settings.

To test our prediction, we designed a 2×2 between-subjects experiment in which we manipulate frame (success vs. failure) and base rate information (33% vs. 67%). This prediction was tested in a study involving hypothetical scenarios. A total of 104 undergraduates (49 men and 55 women) participated in the study. Participants in the success condition read information about the chance of selling a product in the first week of employment of a new sales person who has never participated in a sales training program before joining a company. Next, they read a paragraph about Linda, who is a new employee of a company X. During the first week of her employment, she has contacted six customers where four of them had decided to buy one unit product each from Linda (coded as event A). Participants in the failure condition read the negation of event A (i.e., two of them had decided not to buy from Linda. In all four conditions, the probabilities of the events are exact, which can be calculated from binomial theorem. After reading the scenario, participants indicated their subjective probability regarding the chance that Linda had participated in a sales training program before joining the company by putting a cross (X) in a single line mark as 0% or never in one end and 100% or certain in the other end. These responses were transformed to probabilities by taking the ratio of the length of the marked line from origin with the total length of the line. We also included items for measuring message processing, and processing fluency using 7-point scale, anchored by strongly disagree [1] and strongly agree [7].

RESULTS

With regard to frame, the results show a non-significant difference between the gain (M_{LOSS} = 0.53, SD=0.17) and loss (M_{LOSS} = 0.61, (t(97)=0.165, p>0.05). With regard to base rate, the results show a significant difference between the low base rate ($M_{p=0.33}$ = 0.61, SD=0.17) and high base rate ($M_{p=0.67}$ = 0.53, SD=0.17, (t(97)=2.12, p<0.05). This result highlights respondents' subjective judgments were affected by the base rate, i.e., the chance of occurrence of one event. A 2(frame: gain, loss) x 2(base rate: p=0.33, p=0.67) ANOVA revealed the frame x base rate interaction on the subjective probability judgment (F(1,99)=4.7, p=0.036). Contrast analysis shows that, albeit the four events are equally likely, participants' subjective judgment is higher when presented with event A (i.e., where the probability of making one success is low and the information regarding Linda's performance is described in gain) than its negation of event ~A (i.e., where the probability of making one failure is low and information regarding Linda's performance is described in loss). In contrast, participants' subjective judgment were higher when they read event ~B (i.e., where the probability of making one failure is low and the information regarding Linda's performance is described as a loss) than event B (i.e., where the probability of making one success is high and the information regarding Linda's performance is described as a gain).To examine the role of processing fluency as a potential mediator of the framing effect, a structural equation model was developed. Our results confirmed our hypotheses.

GENERAL DISCUSSION

Our study examines people's subjective probability judgment on the estimates of conjunctive events that consists of an independent series of simple events. The results of our empirical study confirm our prediction and extend previous findings of Brockner (2002) and Mandel (2008). Further research is needed to generalize the findings to another consumer research setting (e.g., estimates of resolving product complaints after filing five complaints).

REFERENCES

Brockner, Joel, Srikanth Paruchuri, Lorraine Chen Idson, and E. Tory Higgins (2002), 'Regulatory Focus and the Probability Estimates of Conjunctive and Disjunctive Events,' Organizational *Behavior and Human Decision Processes*, 87(1), 5-24.

Bar-Hillel, M. (1973), "On the subjective probability of conjunctive events," *Organizational Behavior and Human Performance*, 9, 396-406.

Mandel, David. R. (2008). " Violations of coherence in subjective probability: A representational and assessment processes account," *Cognition*, 106(1), 130-156.

Why Retail Therapy Works: It is Choice, Not Acquisition, That Primarily Alleviates Sadness

Beatriz Pereira, University of Michigan, USA
Scott Rick, University of Michigan, USA

People often engage in shopping activities when feeling sad. Indeed, folk wisdom suggests that negative affect can be healed by going shopping, a phenomenon labeled as retail therapy (Underhill 1999, Gardner and Rook 1988, Atalay and Meloy 2011). Although it is increasingly clear that sadness stimulates spending (e.g., Cryder et al. 2008; Lerner, Small and Loewenstein 2004), it is less clear whether and why shopping actually helps to alleviate negative affect.

Answering the question of whether retail therapy "works" is complicated by the fact that the shopping experience consists of several components (e.g., browsing, choosing, acquiring, and consuming), some of which may be more hedonically influential than others. Previous qualitative work in marketing suggests that consumers might shop in an effort to regain a sense of control over their life (e.g., Pavia and Mason 2004), which is somewhat ironic given that the act of spending while sad is itself often viewed as a loss of self-control (cf. Faber and

Vohs 2004). Nevertheless, this work suggests that it is the act of choosing whether or how to spend, rather than the acquisition of products, that primarily alleviates sadness. The primary focus of our work is to show experimentally that choosing repairs sadness. If that is the case, we can argue that the choice component of retail therapy contributes to the alleviation of sadness, whereas mere acquisition does not.

Indeed, prior work suggests that small amounts of choice can be energizing and hedonically beneficial (e.g., Botti and Iyengar 2004; Moller, Deci, and Ryan 2006). However, none of this prior work has examined whether choice alleviates negative affect. Moreover, much of this work compares choice conditions to conditions that arguably highlight the absence of choice (e.g., by informing participants that someone else has made a choice on their behalf, or that the outcome was randomly determined). Thus, a secondary purpose of our work is to provide a more conservative test of the hedonic benefits of choice, by comparing choice conditions to conditions that do not highlight absence of choice.

To examine whether choice can help to reduce sadness, we conducted two experiments that induced sadness and then manipulated whether or not participants made monetarily consequential choices. In Experiment 1A, 41 participants learned that they would receive $1 in exchange for watching a sad video clip. The clip, from *The Champ*, portrayed a boy watching his mentor die, and is a common sadness induction (e.g., Gross and Levenson 1995). In the No Choice condition, participants watched the full three-minute clip uninterrupted. In the Choice condition, participants watched the first two minutes, and then the computer gave them the choice to stop watching (and return their $1 to the experimenter) or to continue watching (and keep their $1). Participants subsequently rated their current level of sadness (and other emotions) on a modified Positive and Negative Affect Schedule (PANAS; Watson, Clark and Tellegen 1988). The three items of interest were averaged to form a sadness index ("sad", "blue", and "depressed", $\alpha = 0.88$). Only two participants chose to stop watching the video. (Their data are excluded from the analyses.)

As predicted, reported sadness was significantly lower in the Choice condition than in the No Choice condition (3.54 vs. 4.71, $t(37)$ = 2.12, $p < .05$, $d = 0.68$). Participants with a chance to exert control reported lower levels of sadness than participants who did not have a choice, even though both groups performed a sadness induction of equal content and duration. No significant differences were found in the other emotions. Although the results are consistent with our hypothesis, Experiment 1A cannot rule out an artifactual explanation, namely that it was the interruption in the video (rather than the opportunity to choose) that helped to alleviate sadness. In Experiment 1B we told all participants that we were studying how people respond to emotional flip clips when there is an interruption in the clip, but gave only half of them the choice to stop watching in the intermission. Similar to Experiment 1A, the results showed that participants in the Choice condition reported lower levels of sadness. The replication suggests that the benefits of choosing observed in study 1 were not an artifact of an interruption. It also suggests that the reduction in reported sadness is not due to distraction.

To speak more directly to the effectiveness of retail therapy, Experiment 2 examined whether choosing between money and products can be similarly healing. Sadness was induced by showing all 77 participants the clip from *The Champ*. Next, we told participants that they would receive a small reward as a thank-you for participating. In the No Choice conditions, participants either learned that they would receive $2.50 or a shot glass emblazoned with their school's logo. Participants were not made aware that there were two possible rewards or that their reward was randomly determined. In the Choice condition, participants chose whether they wanted to receive the cash or the glass. (Participants were only slightly, and not significantly, more likely to choose the glass than the cash.) Finally, participants rated their current feelings on the modified PANAS.

Consistent with our prediction, the ANOVA revealed a significant main effect of choice ($F(1,73) = 3.98$, $p < .05$). Pooling across gift type, sadness index ($\alpha = .88$) was significantly lower when participants chose their gift than when their gift was assigned (2.91 vs. 3.75; $t(75)$ = 2.06, $p < .05$; $d = .47$). The main effect of gift type and the interation were non-significant. Consistent with our hypothesis, the opportunity to exert a choice in a consumption domain yielded lower reported levels of sadness, regardless of whether a product or cash was chosen.

Taken together, the results suggest that shopping can help to alleviate sadness. Specifically, it appears that choosing, rather than merely acquiring, is the primary healing component of retail therapy. Although retail therapy can surely be taken to dangerous extremes, our results suggest that moderate amounts of shopping might actually be an effective emotion regulation strategy, and not a failure of self-control.

REFERENCES

Atalay, A. Selin and Margaret G. Meloy (forthcoming), "Retail therapy: A strategic effort to improve mood", *Psychology and Marketing.*

Botti, Simona and Sheena Iyengar (2004), "The Psychological Pleasure and Pain of Choosing: When People Prefer Choosing at the Cost of Subsequent Outcome Satisfaction", *Journal of Personality and Social Psychology,* 87 (3), 312-326.

Cryder, Cynthia, Jennifer Lerner, James Gross and Ronald Dahl (2008), "Misery is not Miserly: Sad and Self-Focused Individuals Spend More", *Psychological Science,* 19 (6), 525-530.

Gardner, M. P. and D. Rook (1988), "Effects of impulsive purchases on consumers' affective states", *Advances in Consumer Research,* XV, 127-130, Provo, UT: Association for Consumer Research.

Gross, James J. and Robert W. Levenson (1995), "Emotion Elicitation Using Films", *Cognition and Emotion,* 9 (1), 87-108.

Lerner, Jennifer, Deborah Small, and George Loewenstein (2004), "Heart Strings and Purse Strings: Carryover Effects of Emotions on Economic Decisions", *Psychological Science,* 15 (5), 337-341.

Moller, Arlen, Edward Deci, and Richard Ryan (2006), "Choice and ego-depletion: The moderating role of autonomy", *Personality and Social Psychology Bulletin,* 32 (8), 1024-1036.

Pavia, Teresa and Mason, Marlys (2004), "The Reflexive Relationship between Consumer Behavior and Adaptive Coping", *Journal of Consumer Research,* 31, 441-454.

Vohs, Kathleen, and Ronald Faber (2007), "Spent Resources: Self-Regulatory Resource Availability Affects Impulse Buying", *Journal of Consumer Research,* 33, 537-547.

Underhill, Paco (1999), "Why We Buy: The Science of Shopping", New York: Simon & Schuster.

Watson, David, Lee Anna Clark and Auke Tellegen (1988), "Development and Validation of Brief Measures of Positive and Negative Affect: The PANAS Scales", *Journal of Personality and Social Psychology,* 54 (6), 1063-1070.

No Good Deed Goes Unpunished:
Citing Sources in Print Advertisement Claims

Catherine Armstrong Soule, University of Oregon, USA
Leslie Koppenhafer, University of Oregon, USA

Discovering how to best protect consumers from deception in the marketplace has steadily increased in importance to business practitioners, government policy, and academics in the consumer behavior field. The Federal Trade Commission current requires advertisers to have factual data to justify all claims made in print advertisements (for example, "Brand XYZ is 77% more effective than the leading competitor"), but it is not necessary for that information to actually be present in the copy of the ad. However, many media companies, such as Hearst Publications and Time Inc., now require companies to print this claim citation information in order to assist consumers in making correct judgments about the real meaning of claims. Some companies are also voluntarily including this "fine print" in order to appear more trustworthy to consumers. This research investigates whether these well-intentioned actions may in reality be harmful to these forthright companies by inadvertently and erroneously increasing consumers' perceptions of deception.

Advertisements that make claims without substantiating the source of the information are deceptive, according to many experts on the subject (Boush, Friestad, and Wright 2009). This can be viewed as a case of omission, which is the act of failing to include relevant information, such as context, sample sizes, and/or where and when the supporting data were collected that a consumer needs in order to correctly interpret the claim (Boush et al. 2009) Also, these types of advertising claims often include numerical information presented in a conditional probability (such as 77% improvement) that is meaningless without more information and is very difficult for most individuals to interpret (Gigerenzor 2002). This research aims to provide direction for the important societal need of teaching consumers to recognize and protect against deceptive marketing attempts and make better marketplace decisions. Consumers must learn to protect themselves in both low and high financial risk scenarios. While consumers are more involved in high financial risk situations and are more likely to engage in more in depth processing by definition (Evans 2003), inexpensive purchases are made much more frequently and therefore in totality also have the potential to cause serious harm to consumers in the long run.

Two issues explored in this research are the effects of advertising skepticism and innumeracy on consumer perceptions of deception. Individuals naturally develop skepticism towards marketing attempts throughout their lives which can be seen as a protection mechanism against deception (Friedman, 1998; Obermiller and Spangenberg 2005). Knowing that consumers are rightfully skeptical of ad claims, truthful advertisers often seek to provide additional information to overcome the initial distrust (Ford, Smith, and Swasy 1990). Unfortunately, skepticism has been shown to decrease trust in advertisements regardless of the content or actual truthfulness (Koslow 2000). Adding to the problems arising from skepticism, people's inability to process numbers in a meaningful way, or statistically illiteracy, can also lead to distrust of claims which contain numbers (Sowey 2003). We expect individuals with high advertising skepticism to perceive higher levels of deception (H_{1a}) and those with low numeracy skills to perceive higher levels of deception (H_{1b}).

After examining how individual differences influence deception perception, our main interest was to examine how the presence of source citations affected perceptions of deception. We expect, contrary to common wisdom and current advertising practice, consumers to perceive higher levels of perceived deception when the advertiser provides source citation (H_2).

Data were obtained via a lab experiment from undergraduate university students in exchange for course credit (n=110, 42% female). The experiment was a 2 (source citation present/absent) x 2 (financial risk low/high) between subjects design. Participants randomly viewed one of two advertisements for headphones, one with a conditional probability claim ("77% improvement in sound quality") and no source citation and the other with the same claim with an asterisk and fine print citing the scientific research to prove the claim. Half the subjects were told the headphones cost $34.99 (low financial risk) and the other half were told the cost was $199.99 (high financial risk). The participants evaluated the ad on the dimensions of purchase intent, attitude toward the product and advertisement, claim and source credibility and perceived deceptiveness. Participants also completed separate scales for individual difference measures on skepticism, financial risk and innumeracy.

H_{1a} was not supported, since level of skepticism towards advertising was not a significant predictor of perceived deception level ($F_{cha}(1,105)=0.186$, $p=0.770$). Supporting H_{1b}, score on the numeracy scale was a significant predictor of perceived deception level, with those answering more questions correctly perceiving less deception ($F_{cha}(1,104)=7.578$, $p=0.007$). This indicates that an ability to actually understand a number used in a claim and how advertisers arrived at that number in the citation increases consumer ability to detect deception.

An ANOVA was used to test H2 and partial support was found. There was no significant main effect for source citation ($F(1,108)=0.360$, $p=0.550$) or financial risk ($F(1,108)=0.139$, $p=0.710$), but the interaction was significant ($F(1,106)=4.019$, $p=0.048$). When the product was less expensive, those in the condition with correct source citation perceived higher levels of deception, but when the product was more expensive, those in the source citation absent condition correctly perceived more deception.

Our findings regarding skepticism and innumeracy are encouraging for consumers. Because high skepticism did not increase perceived deception, there is less reason to be concerned that marketplace deception teaching interventions are detrimental. Also, numeracy findings indicate that teaching consumers probability and other basic math skills could be extremely helpful in increasing accuracy in detecting deception. Perhaps more importantly, knowing that differences exist in interpretation of source citation depending on the financial risk involved with the advertised product has serious implications for researchers and practitioners. Requiring source citation for all products, while well-intentioned, may actually be detrimental to honest marketers.

REFERENCES

Boush, David, Marian Friestad and Peter Wright (2009), *Deception In The Marketplace*, New York, NY: Psychology Press.

Evans, Jonathon (2003), In Two Minds: Dual-Process Accounts of Reasoning. *Trends in Cognitive Sciences, 7(10),* 454-59.

Friedman, Monroe (1998), "Coping With Consumer Fraud: The Need For a Paradigm Shift," *Journal of Consumer Affairs*, 32(1): 1-12.

Ford, Gary, T., Darlene B. Smith, and John L. Swasy (1990), "Consumer Skepticism of Advertising Claims: Testing Hypotheses From Economics of Information," *Journal of Consumer Research,* 16(*4*): 433-41.

Gigerenzer, Gary (2002), *Calculated Risks: How to Know When Numbers Deceive You.* New York, NY: Simon & Schuster.

Koslow, Scott (2000) "Can The Truth Hurt? How Honest and Persuasive Advertising Can Unintentionally Lead to Increased Consumer Skepticism," *Journal of Consumer Affairs,* 34(*2*): 245-67.

Obermiller, Carl, Eric Spangenberg, and Douglas L. MacLachlan (2005), "Ad Skepticism: The Consequences of Disbelief," *Journal of Advertising* 34(*3*): 7-17.

Sowey, Eric R. (2003), "The Getting of Wisdom: Teaching Statisticians to Enhance Their Clients' Numeracy. *The American Statistician,* 57(*2*), 89-93.

Green Consumption and Materialism among Young Consumers

Liyanage Perera, Melbourne University, Australia

Jill Klein, Melbourne University, Australia

Green consumption refers to environmentally conscious consumption (Autioet al. 2009 ; Gilget al. 2005 ; Stern 2000) and has recently gained significant scholarly attention due to environmental issues such as climate change. Some of these studies are concerned with the relationship between materialism and green consumption and provide mixed findings. Materialism – the excessive regard for worldly possessions, and the accumulation of possessions to gain happiness (Belk 1984 ; Belk 2001 ; Kasseret al. 2004 ; Richins 2004 ; Richins & Dawson 1992) - is thought to be negatively associated with green consumption (Kilbourne & Pickett 2008). Some argue that green consumers hold postmaterialistic values (Inglehart 1995) which relate to simplistic life styles (Richins & Dawson 1992). There is, however, no consistent findings on the relationship between materialism or postmaterialism and green consumption (i.e.,Dietzet al. 1998 ; Dunlap & York 2008).

SELF EXPRESSION AND MATERIALISM

A close scrutiny of studies on materialism shows that consumers express a 'sense of self' through consumer materials (Ahuvia 2005 ; Belk 1988 ; Dolfsma 2004 ; Giddens 1991 ; Kleineet al. 1995 ; McCracken 1986 ; Oyserman 2009). More recent studies also relate green consumption to the formation and expression of consumer identities (Connolly & Prothero 2008 ; Horton 2003 ; Soron 2010). Andreou (2010) theoretically argues that materialism is not antithetical to green consumption as happiness from materialistic consumption relies on an emotional, not material level. Furthermore, green consumption conveys a 'costly signal' and therefore there is a strong association between high social status and green consumption (Griskeviciuset al. 2010).

Building on the above research, we argue materialism may not be negatively related to green consumption. Green consumers expect and enjoy emotional benefits such as self expression and social interaction through their consumption (i.e.,Bourdieu & Nice 1984 ; Holt 1995 ; McCracken 1986), regardless of whether they are materialists or postmaterialists (Douglas & Isherwood 1996). Thus, the purpose of this scholarship is to explore the emotional benefits or symbolic reproductions of green consumption.

Young consumers have often been criticized for their materialistic consumption (Miles 2000 ; O'Shaughnessy & O'Shaughnessy 2007). Criticisms of young consumers' understanding of the environmental impacts of their consumption (Autio & Heinonen 2004), or the extent to which they actually engage in green consumption (Hume 2009) coexist in the literature with characterizations of young consumers as socially, culturally and environmentally conscious consumers (Sheahan 2009 ; Sullivan & Heitmeyer 2008). These contradictory findings suggest the need for further study of young consumers' green consumption. To this end, we investigate: What does it mean to a young consumer to be a green consumer? And, how does he/she engage in green consumption practices?

METHODOLOGICAL CONSIDERATION AND ANALYSIS

Twenty photo-elicited, semi-structured interviews ranging from 1.5-3 hours were conducted with young consumers (aged between 19-25 years) in a large Australian city. Purposive and snowball sampling techniques were used to ensure respondent diversity and gain access to 'information *rich*' cases of youth engaged in environmental groups, activism and consumption practices (Patton 2002). The interviews were audio recorded and transcripts were made. Line-by-line analysis was completed after the first 12 interviews to refine the interview protocol for subsequent cases. After analyzing all the interviews thematic categories (Strauss & Corbin 1990) were derived and tested with respondents in member check interviews.

FINDINGS: THE MEANING OF GREEN CONSUMPTION

Green consumption among young consumers is constructed as having an awareness of each stage of production and consumption cycles, and concern about environmental problems such as climate change. Drastically withdrawing from environmentally destructive consumption through adoption of a green lifestyle is considered important. Respondents described green consumption as a conscience-driven consumption practice, which predominantly moves them away from making 'new' mass-market commodity purchases and towards alternative consumption practices. In unavoidable purchase occasions, they use mobile phone applications to access information about environmentally unfriendly production and consumption practices. Green consumption with a positive appeal (i.e., a means of fun, happiness, social networking and adventure) instead of a negative appeal (i.e., restricted or controlled consumption) is preferred.

1. Connection to Nature

Our informants frequently engage in activities related to the natural environment both individually and collectively (i.e., bushwalking, camping). They enjoy the connectedness with the natural environment and strive to participate in sustainable practices that maintain ecological balance (i.e., permaculture). Thus, they discursively construct themselves as *contributors* to ecological balance instead of *consumers* which usually conveys the meaning of being a passive *end user* (i.e.,Firat & Venkatesh 1995).

2. Expression of the self

Engaging in green consumption helps these young consumers to express their identities as environmentally conscious individuals. Since the meaning of green consumption among them is constructed through awareness of environment-related issues, they try to value being highly informed and share information with other individuals similarly engaging in green consumption. They perceive climate change problems as a massive phenomenon that is somewhat overwhelming. By engaging in green consumption they see themselves as people who deal with this massive phenomenon (Connolly & Prothero 2008 ; Giddens 1991).–

3. Social costs of green consumption

Informants believe that green consumption is yet to be practiced by mainstream society. They describe difficult experiences in social interactions, in which they are criticized for their green consumption. Criticisms from friends and family lead to feelings of disconnection, and informants navigate a difficult balance between self-expression and accusations that they are preaching to others. While some informants try to avoid associating with non-green consumers, some make compromises to keep up with mainstream consumer expectations (i.e., wearing second-hand t-shirts with a leading brand).

4. Empowered consumption

These consumers try remove themselves from existing market systems through (1) not making new purchases and trying to grow, make or build whatever they need (2) boycotting popular supermarkets, buying from farmers' markets or engaging in *dumpster diving* (procuring goods that have been thrown away), (3) staying updated with environmental issues through information technologies and (4) finding alternative exchange methods (i.e., clothing swaps, barter systems among friends). They are also skeptical about green labeled products and perceived them as profit-driven corporate *greenwashing*. By avoiding *greenwashed consumption*, these consumers enjoy a greater amount of power and control over their personal consumption in being able to act against environmentally unfavorable marketing practices. However, consistent with previous studies (i.e.,Autio,et al. 2009 ; Clevelandet al. 2005), anxiety about not being able to make a significant positive impact on environmental sustainability is common among these consumers.

DISCUSSION AND CONCLUSION

We found that the meaning of green consumption among young consumers involves being aware of every aspect of consumption/production cycles through critical information processing. Our interpretive analysis revealed green consumption is practiced as a means of self-expression, identity performance and has positive associations, such as having fun, being happy, social networking and engaging in adventurous activities (i.e.,Andreou 2010 ; Autio,et al. 2009). Enjoying the positive connotations of green consumption, such as discovering alternative means of consumption, taking challenges, enjoying the natural environment, contributing to sustaining the ecological balance and feeling empowered by withdrawing from existing market systems seems to be more prominent for our informants than negative connotations, such as limiting, restricting or controlling consumption.

REFERENCES

Ahuvia, A. C.(2005).Beyond the extended self: loved objects and consumers' identity narratives.*Journal of Consumer Research,*32:1,171-184.

Andreou, C.(2010).A shallow route to environmentally friendly happiness: why evidence that we are shallow materialists need not be bad news for the environment (alist).*Ethics, Place & Environment,*13:1,1-10.

Autio, M., & Heinonen, V.(2004).To Consume or Not to Consume?*Young,*12:2,137.

Autio, M., Heiskanen, E., & Heinonen, V.(2009).Narratives of 'green'consumers-the antihero, the environmental hero and the anarchist. *Journal of Consumer Behaviour,*8:1,40-53.

Belk, R. W. (1984). Three Scales to Measure Constructs Related to Materialism:Reliability,Validity, ad Relationships to Measures of Happiness. In P. Thomas Kinner, UT:Association for Consumer Research (Ed.), *Advances in Consumer Research* (Vol. 11, pp. 291-297).

Belk, R. W.(1988).Possessions and the extended self.*Journal of Consumer Research,*15:2,139.

Belk, R. W.(2001).Materialism and you.*Journal of Research for Consumers,*1:1,

Bourdieu, P., & Nice, R.(1984).Distinction: A social critique of the judgement of taste.Harvard Univ Pr

Cleveland, M., Kalamas, M., & Laroche, M.(2005).Shades of green: linking environmental locus of control and pro-environmental behaviors. *Journal of Consumer Marketing,*22:4,198-212.

Connolly, J., & Prothero, A.(2008).Green Consumption: Life-politics, risk and contradictions.*Journal of Consumer Culture,*8:1,117.

Dietz, T., Stern, P. C., & Guagnano, G. A.(1998).Social structural and social psychological bases of environmental concern.*Environment and Behaviour,*30:4,450.

Dolfsma, W.(2004).Consuming Symbolic Goods: Identity & Commitment-Introduction.*Review of Social Economy,*62:3,275-277.

Douglas, M, & Isherwood, B.(1996).*The world of goods.*Routledge

Dunlap, R. E., & York, R.(2008).The globalization of environmental concern and the limits of the postmaterialist values explanation: evidence from four multinational surveys.*Sociological Quarterly,*49:3,529-563.

Firat, A. F., & Venkatesh, A.(1995).Liberatory postmodernism and the reenchantment of consumption.*Journal of Consumer Research,*239-267.

Giddens, A.(1991).*Modernity and self-identity: Self and society in the late modern age.*Stanford Univ Pr

Gilg, A., Barr, S., & Ford, N.(2005).Green consumption or sustainable lifestyles? Identifying the sustainable consumer.*Futures,*37:6,481-504.

Griskevicius, V., Tybur, J. M., & Van den Bergh, B.(2010).Going green to be seen: Status, reputation, and conspicuous conservation.*Journal of personality and social psychology,*98:3,392.

Holt, D. B.(1995).How consumers consume: a typology of consumption practices.*The Journal of Consumer Research,*22:1-16.

Horton, D.(2003).Green distinctions: the performance of identity among environmental activists1.*Sociological Review,*51:s2,63-77.

Hume, M.(2009).Compassion without action: Examining the young consumers consumption and attitude to sustainable consumption.*Journal of World Business,*

Inglehart, R.(1995).Public support for environmental protection: Objective problems and subjective values in 43 societies.*PS: Political Science and Politics,*28:1,57-72.

Kasser, T., Ryan, R. M., Couchman, C. E., & Sheldon, K. M.(2004).Materialistic values: Their causes and consequences.*Psychology and consumer culture: The struggle for a good life in a materialistic world,*11-28.

Kilbourne, W., & Pickett, G.(2008).How materialism affects environmental beliefs, concern, and environmentally responsible behavior.*Journal of Business Research,*61:9,885-893.

Kleine, S. S., Kleine, REIII., & Allen, C. T.(1995).How is a possession" me" or" not me"? Characterizing types and an antecedent of material possession attachment.*Journal of Consumer Research,*22:3,327.

McCracken, G.(1986).Culture and consumption: A theoretical account of the structure and movement of the cultural meaning of consumer goods.*Journal of Consumer Research,*13:1,71.

Miles, S.(2000).*Youth lifestyles in a changing world.*Open Univ Pr

O'Shaughnessy, J., & O'Shaughnessy, N. J.(2007).Reply to criticisms of marketing, the consumer society and hedonism.*European Journal of Marketing,*41:1/2,7-16.

Oyserman, D.(2009).Identity-based motivation: Implications for action-readiness,procedural-readiness, and consumer behavior.*Journal of Consumer Psychology,*19:3,250-260.

Patton, M. Q.(2002).*Qualitative research and evaluation methods.*Sage

Richins, M. L, & Dawson, S.(1992).A consumer values orientation for materialism and its measurement: Scale development and validation. *Journal of Consumer Research,*19:3,303.

Richins, M. L.(2004).The material values scale: Measurement properties and development of a short form.*Journal of Consumer Research,*31:1,209-219.

Sheahan, P.(2009).*Generation Y: Thriving and surviving with generation Y at work.*National Centre for Vocational Education Research (NCVER)

Soron, D.(2010).Sustainability, self-identity and the sociology of consumption.*Sustainable Development,*18:3,172-181.

Stern, P.C.(2000).Toward a Coherent Theory of Environmentally Significant Behaviour.*Journal of Social Issues,*56:3,407-424.

Strauss, A. L., & Corbin, J.(1990).*Basics of qualitative research.*Sage Newbury Park, CA

Sullivan, P., & Heitmeyer, J.(2008).Looking at Gen Y shopping preferences and intentions: exploring the role of experience and apparel involvement.*International Journal of Consumer Studies,*32:3,285-295.

Doers Conform, Perceivers Counteract:
The Effect of Synchrony on Uniqueness Seeking

Xianchi Dai, The Chinese University of Hong Kong, China
Ping Dong, The Chinese University of Hong Kong, China

In our daily life, we come across synchronous activities (e.g. chorus, dancing, marching, and so on) very often. Given the ubiquity of these behaviors, it is surprising that little is known in the existing literature how it affects subsequent behavior. In this paper we try to answer the following questions: 1) how does interpersonal synchrony with others affect subsequent uniqueness seeking behavior? 2) Is the effect the same for doers and for perceivers of the synchronous behavior? In answering these questions, we also try to understand the processes underlying these behaviors.

Synchronized behaviors refer to behaviors or actions that are matched in time (Hove and Risen, 2009). Acting in synchrony with others requires individuals to surrender self-centered behaviors and fit into group norm, which in fact imposes a pressure towards people's behavioral freedom. Thus, after engaging in synchronized behavior, a reactance may occur (Brehm 1966; Brehm and Brehm 1981), which leads to greater uniqueness seeking (i.e., the opposite of conformity). Similarly, watching a group of people's synchrony behavior may also elicit a feeling of "forced uniformity" from the observers' perspective. We thus predict the same effect for the perceivers. On the other hand, synchrony has been shown to enhance group cohesion and subsequently strengthens social attachment, fosters cooperation within groups (Haidt 2007; Wiltermuth and Heath 2009; Hove and Risen 2009). As a consequence, those who engage in synchronous behavior would be more likely to conform.

These two forces thus make opposite predictions regarding the effect of synchrony on subsequent preferences. For the doers who engage in interpersonal synchrony, the two forces jointly affect their preferences. We predict that the force that leads to conformity would be stronger and thus dominate the opposite force (i.e., the reactance). Thus, doers would be less uniqueness seeking after engaging in synchronous behavior than after engaging in non-synchronous behavior. The situation is quite different for the perceivers. Perceivers also experience a sense of threat after seeing synchrony, but they do not engage in any action that could increase conformity. That is, for them the psychological reactance would still persist but the action induced conformity would be absent. Thus, perceivers would be more uniqueness seeking after seeing synchronous behavior than after seeing non synchronous behavior. Furthermore, when the synchronous behavior is perceived to be a result of forced choice rather than free choice, the levels of psychological reactance should be higher. Thus, after forced (versus freely chosen) synchronous behavior, people's preference for uniqueness would be stronger as a consequence of stronger psychological reactance.

Two studies were conducted to test the predictions and the underlying mechanism that governs the different synchrony effect for doers and perceivers. Study 1 was a 2 (synchrony: synchrony vs. non-synchrony) x 2 (role: doer vs. perceiver) between-subjects design.

Undergraduate students from a major Hong Kong university were recruited to participate in the experiment. The students participated in the study in a group of 10-12 people. Participants in each group were randomly assigned to be either doers or perceivers. Doers were instructed to do some exercises and perceivers simply observe the doers' behavior. The groups were randomly decided to be either synchrony group or non-synchrony group. In the synchrony group, all the doers were instructed to do the exercise synchronously; whereas in the non-synchrony group, all the doers were instructed to do the same exercise, but they were not instructed to do them synchronously. After this task, participants moved to a second task, in which they were asked to make several choices of different product categories. In each choice, they were presented with three brands, each with different market share. For example, in a typical choice, option (A) was preferred by around 65% of people, option (B) was preferred by around 25% of people, and option (C) was owned by around 10% of people. Participants' choice were coded as 1, 2, or 3 depending on which option they chose (1 = brand with highest market share; 3 = brand with lowest market share). The sum of these numbers formed a uniqueness seeking index (the higher the score, the higher is the uniqueness seeking motivation). The results confirmed our prediction. Perceivers were more uniqueness seeking under synchrony condition than under non-synchrony condition. Conversely, doers were less uniqueness seeking under synchrony condition than under non-synchrony condition

Study 2 manipulated the perceived freedom of choices of the doers acting in synchrony with each other to detect the source of "synchrony reactance". The study adopted a 2 (role: doer vs. perceiver) x 2 (choice freedom: forced choice vs. free choice) full factorial design. Similar to study 1, the students participated in the study in a group of 10-12 persons and were randomly assigned to be perceivers or doers. In this study all the doers were instructed to do the exercise synchronously. The doers were randomly assigned to the forced or free choice conditions. In the forced choice condition, participants were required to do the exercise synchronously. In the free choice condition, the participants were asked to choose from two tasks: the synchrony task, or an essay writing task in which they were asked to write an essay of about 500 words on "The Individual and the Cosmos in Renaissance Philosophy." All the participants in the free choice condition actually chose to do the synchrony task (which is identical to the one in the forced choice condition). Perceivers were either instructed that the doers were required to do the synchrony task, or that the doers chose to do the synchrony task. The measure of uniqueness seeking was identical to that in study 1. Again, the results were consistent with our prediction. First, perceivers showed stronger preference for unique options than doers. Second, those in the forced choice condition demonstrated stronger preference for uniqueness than those in the free choice condition – this conclusion was true for both doers and perceivers. These results suggest that reactance due to threat to behavioral freedom was the process underlying such effects.

REFERENCES

Bem, Darryl J. (1972), "Self Perception Theory," in *Advances in Experimental Social Psychology*, Vol. 6, ed. L. Berkowitz, New York: Academic Press, 1–62.

Brehm, J. W. (1966), *A Theory of Psychological Reactance*. Academic Press.

Brehm, S. S. and Brehm, J. W. (1981), *Psychological Reactance: A Theory of Freedom and Control*. Academic Press.

Haidt, J. (2007), "The New Synthesis in Moral Psychology," *Science*, 316, 998-1002.

Hove, Michael. J. and Risen, Jane. L. (2009), "It's All in the Timing: Interpersonal Synchrony Increases Affiliation," *Social Cognition*, 27, 949-961.

Wiltermuth, Scott. S. and Heath, Chip. (2009), "Synchrony and Cooperation," *Psychological Science*, 20, 1-5.

When One's Death Awareness Involves Others: The Role of Relationship Closeness in Luxury Consumption

Shuoyang Zhang, Colorado State University, USA
Aditi Grover, Plymouth State University, USA

Death is a reality of life. While people are fundamentally aware of death, there coexists an inherent will to survive. Terror Management Theory (Greenberg et al. 1986, 1994) posits that people manage these conflicting thoughts (and associated emotions) to maintain order, continuity, and permanence.

While research has shown that reminder of death or mortality salience can significantly impact human behavior (Niemiec et al. 2010), one's awareness of death has never been investigated in the relationship context in terms of how one connects to others. According to evolutionary theory, individuals do not so much attempt to ensure their own welfare and survival as to ensure the welfare and survival of their genes, which are collectively shared with others (Cialdini et al. 1997; Hamilton's 1964). Therefore, one's relationship with others inevitably plays a role when one has the awareness of death.

The purpose of the current study is to examine how relationship closeness influences consumers' attitude toward luxury goods when they experience death anxiety. Specifically, we propose: a) in general, people with close relationships are less likely to consume luxury goods than people with weak relationships; b) under mortality salience, people with close relationships are even less likely to consumer luxury goods than people with weak relationships. This study contributes to the literature by emphasizing the role of relationship closeness in luxury consumption under the condition of mortality salience.

Hypotheses Development

Mortality salience has been found to induce intense feelings of anxiety and terror. To buffer against this death-related anxiety, people attempt to live up to their cultural values or norms there-by increasing their self-esteem (Greenberg et al. 1986) and value. In fact, prior research has demonstrated that under conditions of mortality salience people are more likely to show preference towards high status (vs. low status) products (Mandel and Heine 1999).

When individuals experience a strong relationship, the perceived closeness could indicate relationship cues—kinship, friendship, similarity, and familiarity—that signal relatively high genetic commonality (Rushton, Russell, and Wells 1984). They are less likely to be threatened by the mortality salience due to the sense of gene overlap and continuity carried by the close other. Research has shown that when people feel close the other, the enhanced closeness could arise from attachment and perspective taking that causes the expansion of the self into the other (Aron, Aron, and Smollan 1992). Because their need for permanence is met by their connection with close others, they are less likely to rely on luxury consumption to maintain self-esteem comparing with people with weak relationships. More specifically, people in weak relationships are more likely to meet their need for self-preservation through more favorable attitudes and intentions towards luxury products (Mandel and Heine 1999).

METHOD

The experiment will use a 2 (mortality salience vs. control) * 2 (close friend vs. acquaintance) between-participants design. Participants are randomly assigned to one of the four experiment conditions using Qualtrics in a behavioral lab.

Participants are told that the experiment session involves several unrelated studies. They are let to believe that the purpose of the first study was to understand their feelings about death. Following Greenberg et al. (1997)'s procedure, mortality salience is induced by two open-ended questions: "Please briefly describe the emotions that the thought of your own death arouses in you" and "Jot down as specifically as you can, what you think will happen to you when you physically die." Participants in the control condition answer the same questions concerning taking a difficult exam. Previous research has shown that mortality salience effects mainly occur after distraction from conscious thought about death (Greenberg et al 1994), therefore participant are asked to proceed to the next study, which intends to understand their interpersonal relationships.

Following the approach of Starzyk et al. (2006), participants read one of the two sets of instructions that asked them to choose someone to focus on during the study. In the *strong* relationship condition, participants choose someone with whom they have a strong relationship, for example, a close friend. In the *weak* relationship condition, participants choose someone with whom they have a weak relationship, for example, a casual acquaintance. Participants are asked to indicate the chosen person's initials, age, and gender, how long they had known the person, and the kind of relationship they had with the person. With this person in mind, they answer some questions that intended to measure the strength of the tie that they have with the chosen person, including the Inclusion of Other in the Self (IOS) scale (Aron et al. 1992), the adapted Subjective Closeness Index and the Relationship Closeness Inventory (RCI) (Berscheid, Snyder, and Omoto1989), and the Personal Acquaintance Measure (PAM) (Starzyk et al. 2006).

Participants then precede to the last study to collect their product evaluations. While participants review a series of luxury products, the initials of their chosen person show up in the background to strengthen the manipulation of relationship closeness. Participants respond to three 10-point semantic scales to reveal their attitude about the product: bad/good, negative/positive, unfavorable/favorable. They also indicate their likelihood of buying the product and recommending the product, each on a 10-point scale: very unlikely/very likely.

CONCLUSION

People are often reminded of death—either due to natural or man-made causes. People are also social animals who are embedded in their relationship networks all the time. Therefore, it is important to understand how people respond to mortality salience in the context of relationship closeness. Our research demonstrates that people's attitudes and intentions toward luxury goods depend on how salient people are aware of death as well as how close people are connected with others.

REFERENCES:

Aron, Arthur, Elaine N. Aron, and Danny Smollan (1992), "Inclusion of Other in the Self Scale and the Structure of Interpersonal Closeness," *Journal of Personality and Social Psychology*, 63 (4), 596-612.

Berscheid, Ellen, Mark Snyder, and Allen M. Omoto (1989), "The Relationship Closeness Inventory: Assessing the Closeness of Interpersonal Relationships," *Journal of Personality and Social Psychology*, 57 (5), 792-807.

Cialdini, Robert. B., Stephanie L. Brown, Brian P. Lewis, Carol Luce, and Steven L. Neuberg (1997), "Reinterpreting the Empathy-Altruism Relationship: When One into One Equals Oneness," *Journal of Personality and Social Psychology*, 73 (3), 481-94.

Greenberg, Jeff, Tom Pyszczynski, and Sheldon Solomon (1986), "The Causes and Consequences of a Need for Self-Esteem: a Terror Management Theory," In Roy F. Baumeister (Ed.), *Public Self and Private Self,* New York: Springer-Verlag, 189-212.

Greenberg, Jeff, Tom Pyszczynski, Sheldon Solomon, Linda Simon (1994), "Role of Consciousness and Accessibility of Death-Related Thoughts in Mortality Salience Effects. *Journal of Personality and Social Psychology*, 67(4), 627–37.

Hamilton, William D. (1964), "The Genetic Evolution of Social Behavior," *Journal of Theoretical Biology*, 7(1), 1-52.

Mandel, Naomi and Steven J. Heine (1999), "Terror Management and Marketing: He Who Dies with the Most Toys Wins," *Advances in Consumer Research*, 26(1), 527–32.

Niemiec, Christopher P., Kirk Warren Brown, Todd B. Kashdan, Philip J. Cozzolino, William E. Breen, Chantal Levesque-Bristol, and Richard M. Ryan (2010), "Being Present in the Face of Existential Threat: The Role of Trait Mindfulness in Reducing Defensive Responses to Mortality Salience," *Journal of Personality and Social Psychology*, 99(2), 344-65.

Rushton, J. Philippe, Robin J. H. Russell, and Pamela A. Wells (1984), "Genetic Similarity Theory: Beyond Kin Selection," *Behavior Genetics*, 14(3), 179-93.

Starzyk, Katherine B., Ronald R. Holden, Leandre R. Fabrigar, and Tara K. MacDonald (2006), "The Personal Acquaintance Measure: A Tool for Appraising One's Acquaintance with Any Person," *Journal of Personality and Social Psychology*, 90 (5), 833-47.

Increased Sensitivity to Specific Disabilities via Matched Psychomotor Experience

Ab Litt, Stanford University, USA
Taly Reich, Stanford University, USA

More than 30% of US adults suffer from at least one basic-actions difficulty or complex-activity limitation, including 61% of those 65 and older (Centers for Disease Control and Prevention, 2010). As populations age worldwide, the proportion of individuals living with physical, sensory, mental-capacity, and illness-related disabilities is rising even further. It is thus of both current and growing importance for products, services, and environments to incorporate accessibility features which ensure they can be used by as many people as possible.

Accessibility accommodations can increase costs to deliver products and services that all consumers must bear, whether or not they themselves would currently benefit from them (e.g., adding wheelchair-lifts to buses, manufacturing foods in special facilities free of common allergens). It is therefore valuable that able-bodied people be able to understand, empathize with, and better appreciate and maintain sensitivity to challenges those afflicted with disabilities face in navigating their daily lives. How can we increase consumers' motivation to help improve the lives and lessen obstacles faced by the disabled, such as via increased willingness to pay to incorporate accessibility accommodations into products and services?

We demonstrate that consumers' incidental psychomotor actions and experiences can increase their sensitivity to *specifically aligned* disabilities, manifesting itself in increased willingness-to-pay to add product-accessibility accommodations. By "aligned" we mean in the sense that the psychomotor experience of having to walk up and down a flight of stairs matches with sensitivity to mobility disabilities, versus having to squint and struggle to read a blurred text matches with vision disabilities. This result builds on growing research showing that motor actions or simulations, such as pulling products toward oneself, can alter judgments and feelings (e.g., Hung & Labroo, 2011; Labroo & Nielsen, 2010). We show such effects of a completely novel nature—induced sensitivity to others' disabilities specifically matched to one's own incidental psychomotor experience. Whereas Bargh et al. (1996) showed that priming elderly stereotypes caused individuals to walk slower, we propose that essentially reversed effects might also hold: that the motor behavior of walking slowly might influence thoughts and feelings regarding the elderly.

STUDY METHOD

Part 1 of the experiment was described as investigating the effects of change of location on task completion. Participants moved up and down three times from the basement to the third-floor of a building, completing a word-puzzle at each location. Participants either took the elevator up and down each time (*n*=21), or walked up and down three flights of stairs each time (*n*=20).

In part 2, participants were asked to report their willingness-to-pay "to allow for features and enhancements to various goods and services that would make them more useful and appealing to different groups of people". For each, they indicated the maximum percentage above regular price they would be willing to pay extra to make possible the proposed change to the product. Each of the cases (presented in random order) involved adding an accommodation for a specific disability or usability-need:

- providing a Braille version of a textbook (*vision*, % above book price)
- adding wheelchair-ramp access to the main entrance of your favorite restaurant (*mobility*, % above average meal price)
- a museum hiring guides who can communicate in sign language (*hearing*, % above admission price)
- producing a DVD of a popular movie with closed captioning in multiple languages (*linguistic*, % above DVD price)
- producing a candy bar with nut-free processes and facilities for the benefit of those with allergies (*health condition*, % above candy price)
- adding a sensor system to a furnace that could remind those with dementia to turn off the gas, and/or alert a caregiver of unlit gas (*cognitive*, % above furnace price)

These primary DVs of interest were encountered among some unrelated filler questions. Afterwards, participants also reported on one-to-nine scales of how physically tired they felt, and how difficult or physically demanding they found moving around between the different locations in the change of scenery portion of the study.

RESULTS

In debriefing, no participants reported awareness or guessing of our manipulation, experimental intentions, or hypotheses. For the mobility-related accessibility accommodation (wheelchair access), participants in the Stairs condition reported a significantly higher willingness-to-pay than those in the Elevator condition (M_S=16.16 vs. M_E=10.86; $t(39)$=2.14, p=.04). However, no such differences were observed for any of the other accessibility accommodation measures (*t*'s< .58, *p*'s>.56). Thus, walking up and down the stairs (relative to taking the elevator) induced a higher premium that able-bodied consumers were willing to pay to specifically help those with mobility disabilities, but not those with other needs.

Participants in the two conditions did not report any difference in how tired they felt (M_S=3.65 vs. M_E=3.05; $t(39)$=.89, p=.38), but those in the Stairs condition did report the experiment to be more physically difficult/demanding (M_S=3.10 vs. M_E=1.67; $t(39)$=2.89, p=.01). There was a marginal correlation between this measure and the wheelchair-ramp WTP measure (r=.289, p=.07), though with this small sample the Sobel test of mediation of stairs/elevator condition by felt difficulty was not significant (z=1.04,p=.29).

ONGOING WORK AND EXTENSIONS

In follow-up studies we are exploring new psychomotor manipulations to test for specific sensitivity-induction to other forms of disability: for example, reading blurry text and specific sensitivity to visual disability, listening to muffled sound and sensitivity to hearing disabilities, and performing difficult memory tasks and sensitivity to cognitive and memory impairments. We are also planning more investigation of the underlying process for this effect—is it due to induced *empathy* or *sympathy* for those with aligned disabilities, higher attention to semantic content associated with preceding psychomotor experience, or some other mechanism? To test possible explanations as well as explore other practical consequences, we are also developing an expanded array of dependant measures. For instance, participants' perceptions of how difficult it is to live with various disabilities, how easy/difficult they find imagining living with various disabilities, implicit measures of their sensitivity to disabilities, and measures with real consequences (e.g., soliciting donations to charities helping those with specific disabilities).

REFERENCES

Bargh, J. A., Chen, M., & Burrows, L. (1996). Automaticity of social behavior: direct effects of trait construct and stereotype activation on action. *Journal of Personality and Social Psychology, 71*(2), 230-244.

Centers for Disease Control and Prevention (2010). *Summary Health Statistics for U.S. Adults: National Health Interview Survey, 2009.* DHHS Publication No. (PHS) 2011-1577: Hyattsville, MD, August 2010.

Hung, I. W. & Labroo, A. A. (2011). From firm muscles to firm willpower: understanding the role of embodied cognition in self-regulation. *Journal of Consumer Research*, forthcoming.

Labroo, A. A. & Nielsen, J. H. (2010). Half the thrill is in the chase: twisted inferences from embodied cognitions and brand evaluation. *Journal of Consumer Research, 37*(1), 143-158.

Investigating the Effects of Multiple Country of Origins Label

Yupin Patara, Chulalongkorn University, Thailand

Kent B Monroe, University of Richmond and University of Illinois at Urbana Champaign, USA

Research on the influence of a product's country of origin has been based on the premise that country of origin as an external cue, similar to brand name and price, has an influence on consumers' product evaluations and willingness to buy (Verleigh and Steenkamp, 1999). However, the role of the *country of ingredients origin* as an extrinsic cue has not been studied previously.

The main research questions in the preliminary stage are: -- (1) How do consumers utilize the ingredient country of origin information along with *brand and price* when evaluating products' quality? (2) How do consumers evaluate "Made in …" label if various ingredients of the product were made in multiple countries?

CONCEPTUALIZATION AND THEORETICAL FRAMEWORK

When consumers are uncertain about the quality of products, they may use extrinsic cues to judge the quality claims made by the sellers (Monroe 2003). A product's *brand name* is a cue for customers representing images that they have formed about the brand and may be used as an indicator of quality (Rao and Monroe 1989). Brucks, Zeithaml and Naylor (2000) find that when price is paired with a consistent brand cue, the quality evaluation is enhanced. Chao (1989) finds the same enhancement when pairing price with positive country of origin brand.

According to cue consistency theory (Slovic 1966; Maheswaran and Chaiken 1991; Miyazaki, Grewal, and Goodstein 2000) when a set of cues is consistent each cue will reinforce a subsequent judgment. If a brand name is capable of signaling quality, then the presence of country of origin as an additional signal to endorse and signal the primary brand's product quality may enhance quality perceptions. It is because they provide enhancing impact and are likely to be used jointly in overall evaluations.

Similarly, *country of origin* cues can also influence consumers' quality perceptions and their confidence in the quality of the product. People form an initial concept of a product on the basis of its country of origin and this concept once formed can influence how information about the product's specific attributes is interpreted (Hong and Wyer 1990).

On the other hand, inconsistent cues may signal contradictory information. Moreover, evaluations with inconsistent cues may depend upon some consistent subset of the inconsistent cues. Consumers may focus on the negative cue and anchor their perceptions of quality based more on the negative cues (Ahluwalia 2002; Campbell and Goodstein 2001).

RESEARCH DESIGN

Utilizing cues consistency theory as the conceptual basis for the research, three experimental between subjects studies using three different products are planned to examine how multiple extrinsic cues to influence consumers' perceptions of product quality and value and their behavioral intentions.

Study 1 is a 2 (Price: high and low) x 2 (Certification: yes and no) x 2 (Ingredient Origin: USA and China) between subjects, factorial design.

Study 2 is a 2 (Price: high and low) x 2 (Brand Familiarity: high and low) x 2 (Ingredient Origin: USA and China) between subjects, factorial design.

Study 3 is a 2 (Price: high and low) x 3 (Ingredient Origin: 100% USA, 50% USA 50% China, 100% China) between subjects, factorial design.

PRELIMINARY RESULTS

Study 1 Results -- Manipulation check results indicate that price (Low = 3.67, High = 6.28; F (168) – 3.54, p<.05) and ingredient origin (China = 3.59, USA = 6.62; F (168) = 3.26, p<.05) were manipulated as intended. The hypothesized effect from H1 reveals a significant price x ingredient origin information interaction on perceived quality (F (170) = 6.95, p<.001, see figure 4). We found no mean differences for the inconsistent conditions relative to price and ingredient origin pairing (F <1, NSP). The effect of either cue will be stronger when paired with a consistent (i.e., High price/ Strong country of ingredient origin) versus inconsistent cue (i.e., High price/ Weak country of ingredient origin or Low price/ Strong country of ingredient origin.)

Study 2 Results -- Manipulation check results indicate that brand (Low familiarity = 5.28, High familiarity = 6.28; F (162) = 10.19, p<.001) and ingredient origin (China = 3.50, USA = 6.74; F (162) = 3.08, p<.03) were manipulated as intended. The hypothesized effect from H2 reveals a significant brand x ingredient origin information interaction on perceived quality (F (162) = 5.51, p<.01, see figure 5). We found no mean differences for the inconsistent conditions relative to brand and ingredient origin pairing (F <1, NSP). The effect of either cue will be stronger when paired with a consistent (i.e., Highly familiar brand/ Weak country of ingredient origin) versus inconsistent cue (i.e., High price/ Weak country of ingredient origin or Low price/ Strong country of ingredient origin.)

Study 3 Results -- Manipulation check results indicate that price (Low = 4.53, High = 7.40; F (1,151) = 8.69, p<.01) and ingredient origin (100% China = 3.52, 50% China and 50% USA = 5.22, USA = 6.56; t (150) = 1.88, p=0.03) were manipulated as intended. The hypothesized effect from H3 reveals that when the brand is highly familiar cobranded with a reputable certification agency, an increase in proportion of ingredients from a strong country of origin will result in an increase in the perception of quality (t (150) = 3.83, p<0.001), increase in the perception of value (t (150) = 4.73, p<0.001), and willingness to buy (t (150) = 1.88, p<0.05).

DISCUSSION

Study 1 and 2 provide strong support for the consistency hypotheses. The target cue is a stronger predictor of perceived quality when paired with a consistent versus an inconsistent alternative cues. Study 3 provide support for the proportion of the ingredient origin hypotheses that when the brand is highly familiar cobranded with a reputable certification agency, an increase in proportion of ingredients from a strong country of origin will result in an increase in the perception of quality, value and willingness to buy.

REFERENCES

Carey, John (2007), "Not Made in China," *Business Week*, July, 41-43.

Hong, Sung-Tai and Robert S. Wyer (1990), "Determinants of Product Evaluation: Effects of the Time Interval between Knowledge of a Product's Country-of-origin and Information about Its Specific Attributes," *Journal of Consumer Research*, 17 (December), 277-88.

Hong, Sung-Tai and Dong Kyoon Kang (2006), "Country-of-Origin Influences on Product Evaluations: The Impact of Animosity and Perceptions of Industriousness Brutality on Judgments of Typical and Atypical Products," *Journal of Consumer Psychology*, 16 (3), 232-39.

Miyazaki, Anthony D., Dhruv Grewal and Ronald C. Goodstein (2005), "The Effect of Multiple Extrinsic Cues on Quality Perceptions: A Matter of Consistency," *Journal of Consumer Research*, 32 (March), 146-53.

Monroe, Kent B. (2003), *Pricing: Making Profitable Decisions*, 3rd ed., Boston, MA: McGraw-Hill/Irwin.

Rao, Akshay R. and Kent B. Monroe (1989), "The Effect of Price, Brand Name, and Store Name on Consumers' Perceptions of Quality," *Journal of Marketing Research*, 26 (August), 351-57.

Slovic, Paul (1966), "Cue-Consistency and Cue-Utilization in Judgment," *The American Journal of Psychology*, 79 (3), 427-34.

Urbany, Joel E., Ajit Kaicker, and Melinda Smith-de Borrero (1996), "Transaction Utility Effects When Quality is Uncertain," *Journal of the Academy of Marketing Science*, 25 (1), 45-55.

Verlegh Peeter W.J. and Steenkamp Jan-Benedict E.M. (1999), "A Review and Meta-Analysis of Country-of-Origin Research," *Journal of Economic Psychology*, 20, 521-46.

The Different Effects of Lay Theory of Gender Differences on Gift Shopping Behavior

Jianping Liang, Sun Yat-sen Business School, Sun Yat-sen University, China

If you want to buy a gift, what kinds of attributes of a gift would you look for? Would you look for different kinds of attributes if you want to buy a gift for a person with the same vs. different gender from yours? More importantly, does it matter whether you naively believe that males (females) prefer functionality (aesthetics) over aesthetics (functionality)? Would the extent to which you hold these naive beliefs matter? What is the psychological mechanism of such a naive theory on our behavior? Does it matter if we buy a product for ourselves and for others?

Previous research indicates that people may have a stereotypical perception that male (female) consumers prefer functionality (form) over form (functionality), and as a result, the access of such a stereotypical perception may influence male and female consumers' choice behavior (Liang and Murray 2010). However, Liang and Murray (2010) only conducted an in-depth interview to examine the potential relationships between such a stereotypical perception and choice behavior. We still have no much more knowledge about this stereotypical perception.

According to Dweck (1996), this stereotypical perception may be considered as a lay theory, also called implicit theory, which is a framework for meaning-constructions, a naive or lay system of beliefs that ordinary consumers use in daily life to interpret and evaluate the world around them, including events and experiences (No et al. 2008; Mukhopadhyay and Yeung 2010). Based on No et al. (2008), a similar lay theory of gender differences on preferences of functionality and aesthetics could be proposed. In particular, some consumers have the "essentialist theory of gender" that the gender difference is biologically based and historically invariant. In contrast, the other consumers have the "social constructionist theory of gender" that the gender differences are not deep-seated and inalterable disposition but alterable social constructions. Similarly, most research on the behavioral effects of lay theories by Dweck (see Dweck 1999) makes categorizations of "incremental theories" (i.e., beliefs that people have malleable quantities of ability and intelligence improvable through effort) and "entity theorists" (i.e., beliefs that people have fixed quantities of ability and intelligence that cannot be improved) (Mukhopadhyay and Yeung

2010). Based on the above categorization, Mukhopadhyay and Johar (2005) identify two theoretically orthogonal dimensions: the quantum (limited or unlimited amount of ability) and the changeability (fixed or malleable over time). Subsequently, they further draw distinction on four types of lay theories: limited-fixed, limited-malleable, unlimited-fixed, and unlimited-malleable. In this paper, we investigated these four types of lay theories of gender differences in responses to functionality and aesthetics, and their different impacts on consumers' gift shopping behavior. Interestingly, we found that the different gift shopping behaviors result from lay theories instead of actual preferences. In other words, the lay theories only influence consumers' gift shopping behavior for others but NOT for shopping behavior for themselves.

STUDY ONE

In this study, we recruited one hundred and seventy-five volunteer consumers at a large shopping mall and asked them to complete a short survey about their gifting shopping behavior during the Christmas and New Year holiday in 2010, a busy time of gift shopping for many consumers. In particular, we asked them whether they have shopped or are planning to shop for one gift recently, what the gift was or would be, the gender and age of the person who would receive the gift. Then they were asked to indicate whether they focus more on the functionality or aesthetics of the gift in an 11-point scale. Subsequently, they completed a questionnaire on the measure of the limited/unlimited (two items) and fixed/malleable (two items) lay theories of gender differences in responding to functionality and aesthetics in seven-point scales anchored by "strongly disagree/strongly agree" adapted from Mukhopadhyay and Johar (2005) and Mukhopadhyay and Yeung (2010). Finally, they answered some demographic questions related to age, gender, etc. We also took record of the day and time when they completed the survey. The types of gifts were mentioned in a variety of product categories, including cell phone, necklace, clothes, shoes, MP3, laptop, mug, gloves, backpack, handbag, wallet, etc.

We found that *limited-fixed* male theorists on functionality who believe that females have limited and fixed ability to functionality are more likely to focus on aesthetics instead of functionality when choosing a gift for females. *Limited-malleable* male theorists on functionality focus more highly on functionality instead of aesthetics when choosing a gift for females.

However, *limited-malleable* female theorists on functionality who believe that females have limited and malleable ability to functionality are more likely to focus on aesthetics instead of functionality when choosing a gift for females. *Unlimited-malleable* female theorists on functionality focus more highly on functionality instead of aesthetics when choosing a gift for females.

STUDY TWO

This study aims to investigate the influence of lay theories on product choices consumers make for themselves. It is possible that male (female) consumers choose a gift that reflects their lay theories because their actual preferences influence their decision. Hence, in Study Two, we wanted to test this consideration, which may pose as an alternative explanation for the findings in Study One.

As in Study One, we measured the four types of lay theories. We also asked the degree to which participants pay attention to the functionality and aesthetics of a series of 10 product categories when they shop for products for THEMSELVES, including jackets, jeans, shoes, backpacks, wallets/purses, digital cameras, cell phones, laptops, watches, and table lamps. Interestingly, we found that the four types of lay theorists, limited-fixed, limited-malleable, unlimited-fixed, and unlimited-malleable theorists have no significant different preferences for functionality and aesthetics when they shop for these products for themselves. Therefore, it seems that lay theory of gender differences does not influence the actual shopping behavior for consumers themselves.

REFERENCES

Dweck, Carol S. (1996), "Implicit Theories as Organizers of Goals and Behavior," in *The Psychology of Action: Linking Cognition and Motivation to Behavior*, Peter M. Gollwitzer and John A. Bargh, eds. NewYork: The Guildford Press, 69–90.

——— (1999), Self Theories: Their Role in Motivation, Personality and Development. Philadelphia: Taylor and Francis.

Liang, Jianping and Kyle B. Murray (2010), "Gender Differences in Responding to Form and Function," in Darren W. Dahl, Gita V. Johar and Stijn M. J. van Osselaer (eds.), *Advances in Consumer Research,* Vol. XXXVIII.

Mukhopadhyay, Anirban and Gita V. Johar (2005), "Where There Is aWill, Is There aWay? Effects of Lay Theories of Self-Control on Setting and Keeping Resolutions," *Journal of Consumer Research*, 31 (March), 779–86.

Mukhopadhyay, Anirban and Catherine W. M. Yeung (2010), "Building Character: Effects of Lay Theories of Self-Control on the Selection of Products for Children," *Journal of Marketing Research*, Vol. XLVII, April, 240-250.

No, Sun, Ying-yi Hong, Hsin-Ya Liao, Kyoungmi Lee, Dustin Wood, Melody Manchi Chao (2008), "Lay Theory of Race Affects and Moderates Asian Americans' Responses Toward American Culture," *Journal of Personality and Social Psychology*, Vol. 95, No. 4, 991-1004.

The Road Traveled, the Road Ahead, or Simply on the Road? When Progress Framing Affects Motivation in Goal Pursuit

Jacob H. Wiebenga, Department of Marketing, Faculty of Economics and Business, University of Groningen, the Netherlands
Bob M. Fennis, Department of Marketing, Faculty of Economics and Business, University of Groningen, the Netherlands

Most of our behavior starts with goal setting through which we get involved in goal pursuit (Locke and Latham, 1990). After this initial step we monitor our progress toward these goals, such as rewards in loyalty programs (Fishbach and Dhar, 2005). Progress can be conceived as the distance traveled from the initial state to the present state (i.e. work-done) and/or the remaining distance from the present state toward the end state (i.e. work-left; Carver and Scheier, 1998). Although both frames imply one another and thus are logically equivalent, research on their impact on motivation in goal pursuit has failed to yield unequivocal results. The present work seeks to extend previous research by examining when progress framing affects motivation in goal pursuit.

In essence, information on goal progress can only be perceived as 'diagnostic' when it is construed in relation to an initial state that is removed from the presence and some end state that is not yet attained. Under these conditions, information on progress may affect motivation in goal pursuit because it informs people on the accomplished and remaining distance and thus on the attainability of the goal and on the investments already made in order to attain it (Koo and Fishbach, 2008).

However, there is reason to assume that these effects of progress framing on motivation in goal striving will not hold for all people in all circumstances. That is, in order to have an effect, it requires that people actively relate information about where they are now to an initial state and/or to an end state, both of which are distant from the here and now (Bar-Anan, Liberman, and Trope, 2006). We propose that this tendency to actively relate progress information to distal states removed from the presence may be a function of people's construal level (Trope and Liberman, 2010).

Thus, since progress cues inform people of the distance traveled from the initial state and/or the distance left to attain the end state, and since perceiving such goal distances as meaningful in goal pursuit requires people to actively transcend the here and now, it follows that if progress framing has an effect on motivation in goal pursuit it will mainly have so under high, rather than low construal level conditions when people have an abstract, rather than concrete mindset.

EXPERIMENT 1

Experiment 1 was designed to test the hypothesis that the effect of progress framing on motivation is stronger for people induced with an abstract (vs. concrete) mindset. One hundred and fourteen undergraduate students were randomly assigned to the condition of a 2 x (progress framing: work-left vs. work-done) x 2 (construal level: abstract vs. concrete) between-participants design. We used a letter identification task (Navon, 1977) to vary participants' construal levels. Next, the manipulation of progress framing was administered as an evaluation task of a loyalty program (cf. Koo and Fishbach, 2008), followed by measuring participants' motivation in goal pursuit.

Motivation was submitted to a 2 x 2 ANOVA with progress framing and construal level as independent variables. No main effect of construal level ($F(1,110) = 1.45$, *n.s.*) or progress framing ($F(1,110) = 2.59$, *n.s.*) was observed. However, the progress framing by construal level interaction was significant ($F(1,110) = 7.52$, $p = .007$). More specifically, under conditions of an abstract mindset, goal progress framed as work done produced higher motivation levels ($M = 4.00$; $F(1,110) = 9.46$, $p = .003$) than progress framed as work left ($M = 2.89$). For participants with a concrete mindset, type of progress framing failed to affect motivation in goal pursuit ($M_{\text{work-done}} = 3.61$ vs. $M_{\text{work-left}} = 3.90$; $F(1,110) = 1.19$, n.s.).

EXPERIMENT 2

A key objective for the second study was to provide converging evidence, by using a trait measure of construal level. In addition, Experiment 2 sought to directly test the psychological process assumed to underlie the proposed effects.

A sample of one hundred twenty four loyalty card members were randomly assigned to a design with progress framing (work-done vs. work-left) as a between-subjects factor, and construal level as a continuous individual difference variable. The first part pertained to the manipulation of progress framing, presented as an evaluation task of a loyalty program, albeit with a different set-up than the one used in Experiment 1. This was followed by measures of perceived goal distance and motivation. For the second part, participants completed the trait construal level measure (BIF; Vallacher and Wegner, 1989).

A regression analysis with progress framing and construal level as the independent variables and motivation as the dependent variable replicated our findings from Experiment 1. Furthermore, the main effect of construal level on perceived goal distance was significant ($\beta = .18$, $t(120) = 1.98$, $p = .05$), in that people with a more abstract mindset perceived goal distance as larger. Additionally, a significant progress framing by construal level interaction was found ($\beta = -.27$, $t(120) = -2.91$, $p = .004$). In order to test for moderated mediation, we performed a simultaneous regression analysis in which the interaction, goal distance, and the progress framing and construal level main effect terms served as predictors for motivation. The results showed that the effect of the interaction disappeared ($t < 1$), whereas perceived goal distance remained a strong predictor ($\beta = -.66$, $t(119) = -9.37$, $p < .001$).

GENERAL DISCUSSION

In two experiments we found that both state and chronic differences in experienced construal level modulate the impact of progress framing on motivation to pursue a reward in loyalty programs, such that type of framing only affected motivation of people with an abstract, but not a concrete mindset. Under these conditions, progress framed in terms of work-done produced increased motivation compared to a work-left frame. Moreover, perceived goal distance was found to mediate the impact of progress framing on motivation for individuals with an abstract, but not a concrete mindset. As such, the present work aids in resolving inconsistencies in the literature on the motivational impact of goal progress information, by identifying conditions where progress cues affect motivation and when they do not.

REFERENCES

Bar-Anan, Yoav, Nira Liberman, and Yaacov Trope (2006), "The Association between Psychological Distance and Construal level: Evidence from an Implicit Association Test," *Journal of Experimental Psychology: General,* 135 (4), 609-22.

Carver, Charles S., and Michael F. Scheier (1998), *On the self-regulation of behavior,* NY US: Cambridge University Press.

Fishbach, Ayelet, and Ravi Dhar (2005), "Goals as Excuses or Guides: The Liberating Effect of Perceived Goal Progress on Choice," *Journal of Consumer Research,* 32 (3), 370-7.

Koo, Minjung, and Ayelet Fishbach (2008), "Dynamics of Self-Regulation: How (Un)accomplished Goal Actions Affect Motivation," *Journal of Personality and Social Psychology,* 94 (2), 183-95.

Locke, Edwin A., and Gary P. Latham (1990), *A Theory of Goal Setting & Task Performance,* Englewood Cliffs, NJ US: Prentice-Hall, Inc.

Navon, David (1977), "Forest before Trees: The Precedence of Global Features in Visual Perception," *Cognitive Psychology,* 9 (3), 353-83.

Trope, Yaacov, and Nira Liberman (2010), "Construal-Level Theory of Psychological Distance," *Psychological Review,* 117 (2), 440-63.

Vallacher, Robin R., and Daniel M. Wegner (1989), "Levels of Personal Agency: Individual Variation in Action Identification," *Journal of Personality and Social Psychology,* 57 (4), 660-71.

The Configuration and Interplay of Consumer Practices within Consumer-Constituted Communities in Kenya

Fredah Mwiti, Lancaster University, United Kingdom
Dr. Maria Piacentini, Lancaster University, United Kingdom
Dr. Andrew Pressey, Lancaster University, United Kingdom

This paper explores the interplay and configuration of practices as enacted by consumers within the context of 'Chama', a form of consumer-constituted community in Kenya. 'Chama' is the specific word used to refer to collectives very similar to the Rotating Savings and Credit Associations (ROSCAs), and is the term to be used in this paper to refer to ROSCA and other similar collectives. The roles of the Chama (and the rotating pot inherent therein) in enabling members to interact as consumers and fulfill their need to be part of a community (Cova 1997), to engage in consumption practices and ultimately meet varied consumption goals, position it as a fitting context to highlight how consumer practices emerge on a bedrock of such social-historically patterned collectives. The study is hence considered to fall within the consumer culture theory domain (Arnould and Thompson, 2005).

CONSUMER COMMUNITIES LITERATURE

Within consumer behavior literature, an increasing number of studies now focus on ways in which consumers organize themselves into social collectives or communities to meet various consumption goals. Such studies have been placed in the context of brand communities, both on virtual and physical space (e.g. Muniz Jnr and O'Guinn 2001) and consumer tribes (e.g. Cova et al. 2007). This literature has been useful in illuminating how such groups emerge and are maintained, and how different consumer practices consequently emerge (Schau et al, 2009). These studies have however been limited to western contexts, and there is a paucity of studies highlighting consumer-based collectives in non-western developing country contexts, and especially Africa. Despite their absence in consumer literature however, these collective do exist, albeit in different forms from those discussed in western contexts. Whereas brand communities and consumer tribes are 'market-facing' and constituted around marketplace resources and brands (Schau et al, 2009), those in non-western contexts are constituted along non-commercial lines, and are significantly influenced by the socio-historical structures within which they are (re)produced (Johnson 2004). These non-market based non-western forms of collectives are however understudied, and the study seeks to fill in this gap.

The study draws on the precepts of Actor Network Theory, which considers the interaction of both human and non-human elements key in the constitution of entities (Latour 2005). This is because existing literature on Chama presents it as an entity consisting of a number of elements including human participants, documents used (constitutions, rules and regulations); objects (the pot representing consumer savings, consumer durables acquired by participant); or actions (attending meetings, entertaining) (Ardener 1964). By using ANT lens to analyze these interactions it is possible to account for outcomes that impact on consumer behaviour.

THE STUDY

This was a pilot study which employed an interpretivist perspective in order to understand the consumer environment and their lived experiences (Holbrook and O'Shaughnessy, 1988). Consistent with similar studies focusing on consumer communities (Schouten and McAlexander 1995) ethnographic methods were used, employing multiple data collection methods which included participant observation, individual as well as group interviews, informal conversations and photographs. In total, three Chama meetings were attended in participants' homes; one with an urban middle-class group of professionals, one with a semi-urban group of affluent women and one with women from the slum area. The findings revealed three practices consistent across the three groups.

The first set, maintenance practices, revolved around activities that ensured that the Chama was constantly performed and maintained. For instance, in order to distribute saved funds, consumer participants met in one of their homes and feasted together. It was clear that the social benefits gained from entertaining and interacting with others during such meetings was more important for the consumers than receiving the funds. This is consistent with what Holt (1995) refers to as consumption as play, where consumers interact purely for autotelic purposes.

Support practices also emerged as important, as the participating consumers were actively involved in offering support to others in the group during occasions such as death of a loved one, birth, weddings and even during job losses. Such benevolent acts emanate from practices in the wider society in which members of the community participate in collective efforts to assist those facing misfortunes, in what is referred to as 'Harambee' in Kenya (Johnson 2004). As part of this practice for instance, members engaged in shopping activities, which required certain skills in identifying the appropriate items for the particular cause being supported. As posited by Warde (2005) to be a competent 'practitioner' requires one to possess the requisite goods and services, as well as the skills and competencies to be able to appropriate and deploy them as per the conventions of the practice.

Also prevalent were consumption control practices. Consumer self-control was highlighted as a significant reason for participating in Chama, as the consumers needed discipline to save for future purchases benefited from the collective support in Chama to do so. Some of the less affluent women indicated that they would go hungry on some nights in order to set aside some money for the Chama pot, as failure to do this incurred heavy fines from the others. Control was also enforced on how the funds saved were spent. In some instances, the group would buy household utensils for the consumer rather than give them the savings to enforce discipline. Chama hence acts as a pre-commitment avenue (Ambec and Treich, 2005) but not for necessarily to control hedonic consumption (Hirschman and Holbrook 1982), but to reinforce goal-oriented and deliberate consumption practices.

CONCLUSION

The study reveals that Chama is a conduit in which a number of practices interact to produce outcomes that are of interest to consumer research. As evidenced, consumption opportunities arise, consumption behaviours are patterned and practices (and practitioners) are configured, social and cultural capital necessary for consumer practice are accrued and demonstrated, and ultimately consumption goals are met. By focusing on the Chama context the contribution has been in revealing that consumer collectives can be formed and thrive outside brand influence, reinforced by society-wide norms and practices that have implications for consumer behaviour.

REFERENCES

Ardener, S. (1964) Comparative Study of Rotating Credit Associations, *Journal of the Royal Anthropological Institute, 94,* 201-229.

Arnould, E. J. and Thompson, C. J. (2005) Consumer Culture Theory: Twenty Years of Research, Journal of Consumer Research, 31(4), 868-882.

Cova, B. (1997) Community and Consumption towards a Definition of the "Linking Value" of Products or Services, *European Journal of Marketing,* 31(3/4), 297-319.

Cova, B., Kozinets, R., V. and Shankar, A. (2007) Tribes, Inc.: The New World of Tribalism in Cova, B., Kozinets, R., V. and Shankar, A., eds., *Consumer Tribes,* Oxford: Elsevier.

Hirschman, Elizabeth C. and Morris B. Holbrook (1982), "Hedonic Consumption: Emerging Concepts, Methods and Propositions," Journal of Marketing. 46 (Summer), 92-101.

Holbrook, Morris B. and O'Shaughnessy, John (1988), On the Scientific Status of Consumer Research and the Need for an Interpretive Approach to Studying Consumption Behavior, *Journal of Consumer Research*, 15 (December) 398-402

Holt, D. B. (1995) How Consumers Consume: A Typology of Consumption Practices, *Journal of Consumer Research,* 22(1), 1-16.

Johnson, S. (2004) Gender Norms in Financial Markets: Evidence from Kenya, *World Development,* 32(8), 1355-1374.

Latour, B. (2005) *Reassembling the Social, An Introduction to Actor-Network-Theory,* Oxford: Oxford University Press.

Muniz Jnr, A. M. and O'Guinn, T. (2001) Brand Community, *Journal of Consumer Research,* 27(March), 412-432.

Schau, H. J., Muniz Jr, A. M. and Arnould, E., J. (2009) How Brand Community Practices Create Value, *Journal of Marketing,* 73(September), 30-51.

Schouten, J. W. and McAlexander, J. (1995) Subculture of Consumption: An Ethnography of the New Bikers, *Journal of Consumer Research,* 22(March), 43-61.

Warde, A. (2005) Consumption and Theories of Practice, *Journal of Consumer Culture,* 5(2), 131–153.

The Importance of Multisensory Integration to Understand Products Appreciation: fMRI Study

Laura Romoli, Illycaffè S.P.A., Italy
Furio Suggi Liverani, Illycaffè S.P.A., Italy
Piero Paolo Battaglini, University of Trieste, Italy

It is well known that flavour is a psychological construct. Flavour, in fact, is an example of multisensory integration, because is a taste/odour combination. Rarely individual components are perceived independently. Manifestations of interactions include smell/taste confusions, attribution of taste properties to odours, and the enhancement and suppression of taste by such odours. Moreover, food is characterized by visual properties, above all colour. Colour, in fact, has a profound effect on the perception of odors (1).

In everyday life the existence of cross-modal association between vision and olfaction is obvious; if you are in a market and suddenly noticed a wonderful smell of ripe strawberries you would look for a fruit that was red rather than a fruit that was orange. Even if these associations between vision and olfaction would appear obvious, to date little research has attempted to investigate this potentially important topic. Gottfried et al (2) has shown that the presentation of visual stimuli can influence olfactory information processing; but what it is known about the contrary? Could a smell stimulus influence visual perception?

To address this complex topic, it is important to understand which is the role of higher-level cognitive factor in the appreciation and comprehension of a smell or a taste stimulus.

In this study, we investigated, with the fMRI technique, how the citrus aroma is processed by the brain, at the cortical level. There is a large amount of study in psychophysical literature underlying the cross-modal association between colors and odors. Many of the odors that we come across everyday life can be readily described by means of colors. But, what happen into our brain when we smell the citrus aroma? Does the brain elaborate the aroma just as a smell stimulus, or elaborate also others perceptual characteristics of it? We address this issue, investigating 13 healthy subjects with fMRI technique while they were sniffing the citrus aroma.

MATERIALS & METHODS

2 stimuli were chosen in this experiment: citrus fruit and neutral (pure air).

The experiment consisted of 3 sessions of about 10 min duration each; each sessions consisted of alternation of citrus aroma and pure air.

Participants received 2 seconds of aroma's stimulation directly in their nose through 2 polythene tubes converging in a facial mask. Subjects were previously instructed to do not move and pay attention to the aroma, trying to recognize it. Timing, amount and order of presentation were controlled by an fMRI compatible, computerized, olfactometer.

Imaging was conducted using a 1,5 Tesla fMRI scanner at the Radiology Unit of Cattinara Hospital, Trieste.

The fMRI data were analysed using SPM5 package. The images were first corrected to remove the effects of subject's moving whilst in the MR scanner; then the brain images for each subject were morphed to make them all the same shape; finally we carried out statistical analysis to detect the particular effect that we were interested in (e.g. smelling citrus aroma compared with smelling neutral).

The analyses were conducted for citrus aroma compared to neutral during the timing in which subjects received the aroma and the few seconds immediately after.

RESULTS & DISCUSSION

We demonstrated that citrus aroma stimulate cerebral regions according to its semantic characteristics; citrus is an edible stimulus, generally associated with the orange or the lemon; it is extremely scented. This stimulus is characterized by the colour, varying from orange to yellow (all nuances belonging to the same family of colour); in fact citrus is a typical example of colour-material colour.

Specifically, while subjects were receiving the stimulus, the brain's response is characterized by the perceptual aspects, especially visual: MNI coordinates: right/left BA 17 and 18, right middle occipital gyrus, left BA 2/1; these areas are involved in the elaboration of visual and somatosensory aspects of stimuli, specifically BA 17 is the primary visual cortex involved in the elaboration of colour, and BA 18 is the secondary visual cortex involved in the elaboration of shape and implicated, also, in visual imagery.

In the "after" period, corresponding to the few seconds after the olfactory stimulation, the cerebral response changes, becoming canonical for a smell stimulus, involving the left superior frontal gyrus and the left middle frontal gyrus, both areas involved in the cortical elaboration of familiar odours.

CONCLUSIONS

To date, all previous studies of colour-odor correspondences have required participants to make explicit matches between specific colours and particular odors (3;4), or how chromatic stimuli modulate odor response in the human brain (1), whereas in the present study, we demonstrated how a odor stimulus could produce a brain activation typically associated to visual stimuli while subjects are sniffing the aroma. These results, even if preliminary, underlying how certain aspects of a product could work as synesthetic cues in the human brain. This interest in odor-visual interactions is an example of areas where future research might be directed, particularly in terms of implications for the study of individual differences, the role of mental imagery, the promise of more neurocognitive approaches, and the need for more consideration of the multy-sensory interactions of our senses on consumption behavior.

REFERENCES

(1) Osterbauer, et al. 2005. J. Neurophysiol. 93, 3434-3441
(2) Gottfried et al. 2003. Neuron, 39, 375-386.
(3) Schifferstein et al. 2004. Perception, 33, 1249-1266.
(4) Gilbert et al. 1996. Am. J. Psychol. 109, 335-351.

The Influence of Self-construal on Managing Conflicting Saving and Spending Goals

Wei Lu, Shanghai Jiao Tong University, China
Li Pan, Shanghai Jiao Tong University, China
Liangyan Wang, Shanghai Jiao Tong University, China

We propose that independent and interdependent differ on how they manage conflicting goals. We demonstrate interdependent are more likely to highlight saving in two sequential choices, while independent are more likely to adopt balancing mode by preferring spending first and intending to achieve the saving goal at next opportunity.

Researchers in North America often focus on how to help consumers to succeed in their personal saving goals (e.g., Bayuk, Janiszewski, and Leboeuf 2010; Loibl 2009). However, contrary to North American's difficulty in saving money, economic growth of some countries has long been hindered by their residents' high saving rates, such as China. So understanding what factors account for such big difference in saving and spending across countries would be of great importance to governments, financial service firms and consumers. In this research we suggest that individuals with different self-construals (independent vs. interdependent) differ on how they manage conflicting saving and spending goals, which in turn leads to the difference described above.

Consumers often have spending goal and saving goal at the same time. Saving is a goal with more virtue, which can provide people with financial safety. Spending is a temptation which can provide immediate satisfaction to consumers. Pursuing either one of them could not completely abandon the other. We have to save money while constantly spend. When managing two conflicting goals, people can highlight one goal and continue to behave in the same way consistent with this focal goal, or they might also balance between two goals and their behavior varies (Fishbach and Dhar 2008). Highlighting a focal goal in two sequential choices would benefit the pursuing of the focal goal, while balancing the focal goal and temptation by preferring the tempting option that can provide immediate satisfaction first and intending to choose a goal option at the next opportunity would probably hurt the achieving of the focal goal, as people might constantly postpone the goal-congruent choices (Fishbach and Zhang 2008).

Research on cross-cultural differences suggest that individuals with an interdependent self-construal might be better at handling intrapersonal conflict and mixed emotions than those with an independent self-construal (Hong and Lee 2010; Kyoungmi and Shavitt 2004; Williams and Aaker 2002). And conflicting vice and virtuous goals are often associated with ambivalence and mixed emotions (Emmons and King 1988), which would make consumers feel a lot of tension and give in to the buying impulse (Rook 1987). It's possible that the advantage of interdependent on coping with intrapersonal conflict and mixed emotions makes them less torn by the temptation and better focus on the more important goal. Findings from Zhang and Shrum (2009) also suggested that individuals with interdependent self-construal exhibited less impulsive consumption tendencies than those with independent self-construal. In line with prior research, we propose that when managing conflicting saving and spending goals, individuals with interdependent self-construal would be more likely to adopt a highlighting mode, while individuals with independent self-construal are more likely to adopt a balancing mode.

Two experimental studies were conducted to test our hypothesis using both chronic and situational self-construals. In experiment 1, we tested whether chronic self-construals resulted in different managing mode when facing conflicting goals. 217 Full-time MBA students were asked to imagine that they were trying hard to save money now and could save about one third of their monthly income. However, both this month and next month there would be a product on sale they like equally, which will make them save nothing that month. Respondents were asked to choose whether they would buy or not buy the product specifically this month and next month. Then respondents' self-construals were measured (Singelis 1994). Demographic information, such as personal and household incomes, is also recorded at the end of the survey. 51 (53) participants were classified as independence-dominated (interdependence-dominated) whose independence (interdependence) score fell above the median and whose interdependence (independence) score fell below the median. ANOVA analysis with self-construal as a between-subjects factor and time-order choice as a within-subjects factor showed that there was a main effect of time order ($p<0.05$) and no main effect of self-construal. More specifically to our hypothesis, the interaction between self-construal and time order is significant ($p<0.05$). Further analysis showed that respondents are less likely to choose not to buy the product (behavior consistent with the saving goal) in this month (32.7%) than in next month (44.2%) ($p<0.05$). Among individuals with interdependent self-construal, respondents' intention to choose behavior consistent with their saving goal did not differ between this month (43.4%) and next month (43.4%), a pattern that indicates highlighting saving. While among individuals with independent self-construal, significantly less respondents chose saving goal this month (21.6%) than next month (45.1%) ($p<0.01$), a pattern that indicates balancing saving and spending by preferring immediate satisfaction and intending to pursue the saving goal later. And as to this month's choice, significantly more individuals with interdependent self-construal (43.4%) chose to save than those with independent self-construal(21.6%) ($p<0.05$).

In the second experiment, we verified our findings by situationally activating individuals' self-construals. The procedure was similar with the first experiment, except that rather than measured, independent or interdependent self-construal was primed at the very beginning of the experiment. We used the same Chinese priming materials used by Sui and Han (2007). 97 adult college students were asked to circulate all the pronouns in a travel story. The same text was presented with almost all of the pronouns being either independent pronouns (e.g. I) or interdependent pronouns (e.g. we) to prime the two selves. The result is similar as those in experiment 1 with approaching significance ($p<0.10$), except that the main effect of time-order is not significant.

In sum, the two studies both demonstrated that individuals with independent self-construal are more likely to adopt a balancing mode and individuals with interdependent self-construal are more likely to adopt a highlighting mode when facing conflicting saving sand spending goals. Our new findings contribute to the literature both on self-construal and goal system theory. Also our findings have practical implications on how to encourage spending in those countries with high saving rate and how to help consumers to save in those countries with low saving rate.

REFERENCES

Bayuk, Julia Belyavsky, Chris Janiszewski, and Robyn A Leboeuf (2010), "Letting Good Opportunities Pass Us By: Examining the Role of Mind-Set During Goal Pursuit," *The Journal of Consumer Research*, 37 (4), 570-83.

Emmons, Robert A. and Laura A. King (1988), "Conflict among Personal Strivings: Immediate and Long-Term Implications for Psychological and Physical Well-Being," *Journal of Personality and Social Psychology*, 54 (6), 1040-48.

Fishbach, Ayelet and Ravi Dhar (2008), "Dynamics of Goal-Based Choice: Toward an Understanding on How Goals Commit Versus Liberate Choice," in *Handbook of Consumer Psychology*, ed. Curtis P.. Haugtvedt, Paul M.. Herr and Frank R.. Kardes, New Yok: Psychological Press.

Fishbach, Ayelet and Ying Zhang (2008), "Together or Apart: When Goals and Temptations Complement Versus Compete," *Journal of Personality & Social Psychology*, 94 (4), 547-59.

Hong, Jiewen and Angela Y. Lee (2010), "Feeling Mixed but Not Torn: The Moderating Role of Construal Level in Mixed Emotions Appeals," *Journal of Consumer Research*, 37 (2), 456-72.

Kyoungmi, Lee and Sharon Shavitt (2004), "The Influence of Cultural Thinking Style on Evaluative Processes," *Advances in Consumer Research*, 31 (1), 451-53.

Loibl, Cäzilia (2009), "Loosening the Belt: On the Effects of Goal-Conflict Situations on Regular Savings," *International Journal of Consumer Studies*, 33 (4), 448-55.

Rook, DW (1987), "The Buying Impulse," *Journal of Consumer Research*, 14 (2), 189-99.

Shefrin, Hersh M. and Richard H. Thaler (1988), "The Behavioral Life-Cycle Hypothesis," *Economic Inquiry*, 26 (4), 609.

Singelis, TM (1994), "The Measurement of Independent and Interdependent Self-Construals," *Personality and Social Psychology Bulletin*, 20 (5), 580.

Sui, J. and S. H. Han (2007), "Self-Construal Priming Modulates Neural Substrates of Self-Awareness," *Psychological Science*, 18, 861-66.

Williams, P. and J.L. Aaker (2002), "Can Mixed Emotions Peacefully Coexist?," *Journal of Consumer Research*, 28 (4), 636-49.

Zhang, Yinlong and L. J. Shrum (2009), "The Influence of Self-Construal on Impulsive Consumption," *Journal of Consumer Research*, 35 (838-50.

Do health claims always lead to obesity? The role of consumers' lay theories about low-nutrients food in quality and quantity estimation

Pierrick Gomez, Reims Management School and Université Paris Dauphine, France

Past research has indicated that consumers' evaluation of health claims is prone to bias. These judgments errors affect both quality and quantity estimation of food products. For example, when making inferences from nutrition information, consumers tend to overestimate the health benefits of food products (Roe, Levy and Derby, 1999). Thus, consumers tend to rate higher a product on other nutrition attribute when a health claim is displayed. Recent research has also pointed to the role of health halos, created by health claims or food stereotyping, in calories overestimation (Chandon and Wansink, 2007; Chernev and Gal, 2010).

The impact of low-fat claims has often been studied in past research (e.g., Chandon and Wansink, 2006; Finkelstein and Fishbach, 2010). To our knowledge, the effect of low-sugar claims has not yet been addressed. However, there is a differential perception between fat and sugar. Fat is perceived as an unhealthy ingredient whereas sugar is strongly associated to hedonic pleasure (Fischler, 2001). One can argue that low-fat claims may reduce anticipated consumption guilt whereas low sugar claims may decrease anticipated consumption pleasure. For this reason, we suggest that low-sugar claims lead less to judgment errors in quantity estimation. This research highlights the underlying role of lay theories about low-nutrients food. We suggest that people can subscribe to the view that low-nutrients food is associated with healthiness or to the view that low-nutrients food and tastiness are inversely correlated. We examine this in three field studies.

In study 1, we tested our basic proposition. Ninety eight people (N=98, 27 years old, male 51%, 22.3 BMI) took part to the survey. Our objective was twofold: to demonstrate that people hold lay theory about low-nutrients food and to test the difference of perception between sugar and fat. People tend to believe (those who rated their agreement from 5 to 7 on a 7 points scale) that low-nutrients food are less pleasurable (65.3%), have bad taste (44.8%), are healthier than regular food (38.8%) and are food that can help them to overcome weight problem (55.1%). This is initial evidence supporting the prevalence of our lay theories about low-nutrients food. It should be noted that difference has been found among dieters and people who believe that healthiness and tastiness are negatively correlated. Results revealed that high fat foods are perceived to be less healthy (t=-5.957; p<0.001) and less tasty than high sugar foods (t=-6.626; p<0.001).

Study 2 was designed to test whether estimation of nutrition quality and quantity decisions differs when the product is labeled as "low sugar". Respondents were 86 students recruited to participate in a survey on consumer food preferences (N=86, female 52%, age 20, BMI 21.4). Participants were assigned to one of three conditions and saw low-sugar cookies, low-fat cookies or regular cookies. Consistent with our hypothesis, analysis revealed that participants who saw cookies labeled as low-sugar claim (vs. regular) believed that it was healthier (8.291; p<0.01) but intended to consume it less frequently (F=13.492; p<0.001). This result may occur because of a decrease of anticipated consumption pleasure when participants are exposed to a low-sugar label (F=7.964; p<0.01). Further analysis show that anticipated consumption pleasure induces lower frequency of consumption (r=-0.466; p<0.01) and higher perceived serving-size (r=0.28; p<0.05).

Study 3 tested whether lay theories about low-nutrients food may reverse this finding. Following past research on lay beliefs (e.g. Mukhopadhyay & Johar, 2005), participants (N=148, 56% male, 32 years old, BMI 22.6) read a paragraph, based on available scientific information, which either stated that low-nutrients food are useful to reduce calories intake (low-nutrients food=healthy belief) or that nutrients-reducing technology diminishes food tastiness (low-nutrients food=untasty belief). As expected, respondents who read the low-nutrients food=healthy passage (vs. low-nutrients food=untasty) are more likely to believe that low-nutrients food help people to manage their weight (F=5.276; p<0.05) and less likely to believe that low-nutrients food are pleasurable (F=4.958; p<0.05). Then, the experimental task involved estimating the calories content and appropriate consumption (frequency consumption and appropriate serving size) of low-sugar and low-fat cookies. Our results show that low-nutrients labelling do not influence consumers' estimation of nutrition quality and quantity. The results revealed a significant main effect of lay beliefs about low-nutrients food. Respondents in the low-nutrients food=healthy condition tend to overestimate the number of calories of cookies (by 26 calories or 35%; F=4.257; p<0.05) and the amount they believe to be an appropriate serving-size (by 27%; F=4.023; p<0.05). Importantly, lay conception of low-nutrients food affect anticipated consumption pleasure. Confirming our supposition, anticipated pleasure (marginally so, F=3.600; p=0.06) is higher in the low-nutrients food=healthy condition (vs. low-nutrients food=untasty condition). Again, analysis revealed that lower anticipated consumption pleasure decrease perceived serving-size (r=0.29; p<0.01) and frequency of use estimation (r=-0.31; p<0.01). The data further show that dieters intend to consume more frequently low-nutrients food if they had read the unhealthy article than the untasty one (F=4.568; p<0.05).

Across three studies, we provide evidence that people hold mainly two lay conceptions of low-nutrients food and that these beliefs may underlie the difference of perception between low-fat and low-sugar food products. Thus, low-sugar labels reduce frequency of consumption because of a decrease of anticipated consumption pleasure. The accessibility of these beliefs can be influenced and affect people's perception of health claims.

REFERENCES:

Chandon, Pierre and Brian Wansink (2007), "Is Obesity Caused by Calorie Underestimation? A Psychophysical Model of Meal Size Estimation", *Journal of Marketing Research*, *44* (1), 84-99.

Chernev, Alexander and David Gal (2010), "Categorization Effects in Value Judgments: Averaging Bias in Evaluating Combinations of Vices and Virtues", *Journal of Marketing Research*. *47* (4), 738-747.

Finkelstein, Stacey R. and Ayelet Fishbach (2010), "When Healthy Food Makes You Hungry", *Journal of Consumer Research*, *37* (3), 357-367.

Fischler Claude (2001), *L'Homnivore*, 3rd edition, Paris, Odile Jacob.

Mukhopadyay Anirban and Gita Johar (2005), "Where There Is a Will, Is There a Way? Effects of Lay Theories of Self-Control on Setting and Keeping Resolutions", *Journal of Consumer Research*, 2005, 31, 4 (2), 779-786.

Roe, Brian, Alan S. Levy and Brenda M. Derby (1999), "The Impact of Health Claims on Consumer Search and Product Evaluation Outcomes: Results from FDA Experimental Data", *Journal of Public Policy and Marketing*, *18* (1), 89-105.

Wansink, Brian and Pierre Chandon (2006), "Can Low Fat Nutrition Labels Lead to Obesity?", *Journal of Marketing Research*, *43* (4), 605-617.

Are modern Chinese getting more materialistic? – A study of materialism with longitude and cross-cultural comparisons

Chunyan Xie, Stord/Haugesund University College, Norway
Richard P. Bagozzi, University of Michigan, USA
Zhi Yang, Hunan University, China
Ping Wu, University of Michigan, USA

China, as one of the fast-growing developing economies, has experienced strong economic development in recent years. The up-surging materialism brought forth by the economic growth in China has attracted attentions from both practitioners and academics. However, most existent research on materialism has been conducted in Western, developed economies dominated by individualistic values. Few studies on materialism in developing economies are available in the literature. Although there has been some recent attention to the historic rise of consumer culture and materialism in China (Clunas 1991), both the popular and scholarly prototypes of materialism is either Western European or American. Some researchers have also explored cultural variation in materialism to some degree (Ger and Belk, 1996), but there is still a surprising lack of highly culture-specific understandings of materialism. Therefore, a challenging for both practitioners and academics is how to understand the materialism phenomenon in countries with fast-growing economies and dominant collective values (e.g., China).

The aim of this study is to understand the materialism tendency in modern China. We look for answers to such questions as "Is the current Chinese generation becoming more materialistic than the earlier generation?" and "Are they becoming more materialistic than their Western counterparts?" To do so, we first applied the Model of Goal-directed Behavior (MGB) (Perugini and Bagozzi 2001)) to examine the decision making process of people's actual choice between materialist and non-materialist lifestyles. Then, we developed cognitive schemas to map the motivations underlying such choices. In order to explore how rapid economic growth influences materialism tendencies, we conduct a longitude comparison of cognitive schemas between two samples of Chinese respondents with a ten-year period difference (Year 1998 vs. Year 2008). Finally, a cross-cultural comparison of cognitive schemas between Chinese and American respondents was conducted in order to understand how modern Chinese differ from their Western counterparts in materialism tendencies.

THEORY

Materialism is defined as "a set of centrally held beliefs about the importance of possessions in one's life" (Richins and Dawson, 1992). It has been treated as general values that are presumed to apply universally across contexts. Richins and Dawson (1992) measured three dimensions of materialism: acquisition centrality, acquisition as the pursuit of happiness, possession-defined success. Further, some researchers explored cultural variation in materialism (Ger and Belk 1996) and claimed people from collective cultures are less materialistic than those from individual cultures. Inglehart (1990) also argued that materialism relates to affluence: materialism will peak and begin to decline after a certain level of affluence is reached and lower order needs have been met.

In this study, instead for studying materialism as general values, we investigate an actual choice between materialistic vs. non-materialistic lifestyles. The model of goal-directed behavior (MGB), an extension of the theory of planned behavior (TPB), was applied to capture the decision making process. In the MGB, anticipated positive and negative emotions and past behavior are included in addition to attitudes, subjective norms, and perceived behavioral control. Further, desire is added as the mediator between all antecedents and intentions, and functions as the central motivational process transforming reasons for acting into actual decisions to act.

Cognitive schemas were further developed to map the motivations underlying such lifestyle choices. Cognitive schemas are "learned, internalized patterns of though-feeling that mediate both the interpretation of on-going experience and the reconstruction of memories" (Strauss 1992). We argue the motives constitute the reasons for behavior and justify or rationalize one's chosen behavior. They are presented in a hierarchical cognitive schema, connected through means-ends linkages.

METHOD

Two waves of survey were conducted. The first was conducted in both China and US in Year 1998. Respondents from two Chinese Universities in South-eastern China and from one US University in Middle-West answered a qualitative motive elicitation part in the questionnaire and provided motives for choosing between a materialistic vs. a non-materialist lifestyle. 330 complete questionnaires were obtained in China and 362 in US. The second wave of survey was conducted in one Chinese University in Southern China in Year 2008, where 322 complete questionnaires were collected. The survey included an identical qualitative part for eliciting motives for lifestyle choice and a quantitative inventory of closed-ended questions measuring variable in the MGB.

RESULTS

The finding from the MGB (Year 2008) showed that in the decision making process of lifestyle choices, subjective norms, anticipated positive emotions and perceived behavioral control are significant predictors of desire and intentions to pursue a materialistic lifestyle for Chinese respondents. On the other hand, desire and intentions to pursue a non-materialistic lifestyle were significantly affected by attitudes, anticipated positive emotions and perceived behavioral control. In order to understand why social norms are important for Chinese respondents to choose a materialist lifestyle, we developed cognitive schemas to further explore their motivations underlying the choices. The results of t-tests also provided preliminary evidence supporting the argument that motives and linkages between motives in cognitive schemas can impact variables in the MGB for both Chinese materialists and non-materialists.

We also got interesting results from a longitude comparison of Chinese materialists over a ten-year period with rapid economic growth (Year 1998 vs. Year 2008). The cognitive schemas of Chinese materialists have become more well-defined as their affluence increase over time. While personal motives remained relatively stable over time, social motives are more contingent on economic development. A cross-cultural comparison of Chinese materialists with their American counterparts showed that Chinese materialists not only have a more complex structure of social motives but also have some unique motives such as socially defined success.

REFERENCE

Clunas, Craig (1991), *Superfluous Things: Material Culture and Social Status in Early Modern China*, Urbana, IL: University of Illinois Press.

Ger, Güliz and Russell Belk (1996), "Cross-cultural differences in materialism", *Journal of Economic Psychology,* 17(1), 55-77.

Inglehart, Ronald (1990), *Cultural Shift in Advanced Industrial Society*, Princeton, NJ: Princeton University Press.

Perugini, Marco and Richard P. Bagozzi (2001), "The role of desires and anticipated emotions in goal-directed behaviours: Broadening and deepening the theory of planned behavior," *British Journal of Social Psychology*, 40(1), 79-98.

Richins, Marsha L. and Scott Dawson (1992), "A Consumer Values Orientation for Materialism and Its Measurement: Scale Development and Validation," *Journal of consumer research*, 19, 303-316.

Strauss, Claudia (1992), "Models and motives," In R.G. D' Andrade & C. Strauss (Eds.), *Human motives and cultural models,* 45-58. Cambridge: Cambridge University Press.

Transcultural Tourism: Role of Cultural Metaphors in Enhancing Destination Image

Esi Abbam Elliot, University of Illinois at Chicago, USA
Benet DeBerry Spence, University of Illinois at Chicago, USA
Hernan Casakin, Ariel University Centre of Samaria

In recent times, immigration and globalization has resulted in a *transcultural* consumer era (Penaloza, 1994) that calls for enriching transcultural attractions to enhance destination image. *Transculture* is a new sphere of cultural development that transcends the borders of traditional cultures (Epstein, 2009). A destination's image is the "composite of various products (attractions) and attributes woven into a total impression" (MacKay and Fesenmaeir, 1997, p. 2). This paper investigates transcultural tourism as an alternative to conventional cultural tourism. The paper considers the use of cultural metaphors to influence consumer mental models, which in turn enhances their perception of the destination image. *Cultural metaphors* are associations that convey shared beliefs and understandings of a particular society (Gannon, 2002). The term metaphor refers to associations that relate abstract concepts to physical things and are used to construct conceptual understandings (Lakoff and Johnson, 1980). The symbolic anthropological construal of metaphor is grounded in cultural images (Hirschman 2007) and has been noted for its ability to create new mental models and to overcome entrenched perspectives (Barret & Cooperrider, 1990). Consumers' mental models are structures of meaning, which includes beliefs and feelings, activated when a consumption situation takes place (Christensen and Olson, 2002).

This study makes three theoretical contributions. First, this study examines how transcultural metaphors enhance the destination image. A number of studies have examined cultural tourism and the enhancement of destination image such as iconic structures (e.g. Thakara, 2002), megaevents (e.g. Allen et al., 2002), thematisation (e.g. (e.g. Arnould and Price, 1993; Joy and Sherry, 2003; Hughes, 2000) and heritage mining (e.g. Russo, 2002). However, there have been minimal studies that diverge from the traditional cultural tourism to discover other non-conventional ways of leveraging culture to enhance the destination image. This study diverges from the traditional cultural tourism perspective to investigate transcultural tourism that enhances destination image by leading consumers to transcend cultural differences and to incorporate new concepts and visions from alternative cultures. This is important because according to Richards and Wilson (2005), consumers are increasingly searching for alternatives to traditional cultural tourism.

Second, this study considers how metaphors can be used to transcend consumer mental models. A number of researchers have examined metaphors and their effects on consumer mental models (e.g. Zaltman and Coulter, 1995; Christensen and Olson, 2002). These studies have exposed the fact that metaphors assist in shaping consumer mental models. However, "what about transformative experiences that falls outside the range of consumer mental models?" The current study addresses this gap by introducing the concept of mental model transcendence. Transcendence is "the capacity of individuals to stand outside of their immediate sense of time and place to view life from a larger, more objective perspective" (Piedmont 1999, p.988). We argue that incorporation of transcultural perspectives has a potential to lead to a transcendent state that falls outside of existing mental models.

Third, this study extends the role of cultural metaphors. Some studies have also been conducted on the role of cultural metaphors as a consumer research tool (e.g. Denny and Sunderland, 2005). Others have examined the role of cultural metaphors in understanding cultural differences (e.g. Gannon, 2002). Although these studies have exposed the fact that cultural metaphors are tools for understanding cultural complexities, they do not explain how the cultural metaphors lead to consumer mental model transcendence. The introduction of mental model transcendence in this paper extends the current literature to include a transcendent experience in the mental models of consumers that is made possible by transcultural metaphors. It also captures the psychological perspectives embedded in transcultural interactions and acknowledges the importance of these perspectives in understanding consumer behavior.

To examine consumer use of cultural metaphors, the investigation was conducted with artisans as well as American tourists in the Pilsen Mexican community in Chicago. A qualitative approach, in the form of phenomenological interviews, observations and photography, was adopted to address the research objectives. The Pilsen community, with a rich cultural heritage, predominantly Latino is selected for the investigation. Three thematic dimensions are discovered that explain the concept of mental model transcendence. These are: 1) an awareness of a transcultural identity 2) an awakening to a sense of self, and 3) an inspiration of universal ideals. We utilize Teichart et al's (2006) theory on metaphor roles and Fauconnier and Turner's (2002) Blending theory to inform our argument. While Teichart et al's (2006) theory of how metaphors influence and alter mental models is crucial to our argument, we extend it to accommodate the process of mental model transcendence evident in our data.

REFERENCES

Arnould Eric J. and Linda L. Price (1993), "River Magic: Extraordinary Experience and the Extended Service Encounter," *The Journal of Consumer Research*, 20 (June), 24-45.

Denny, R. M., and P. L. Sunderland (2005), "Researching Cultural Metaphors in Action: Metaphors of Computing Technology in Contemporary U.S. life" *Journal of Business Research* 58 (October), 1456– 1463.

Epstein M. (2009), "Transculture: A Broad Way between Globalism and Multiculturalism, *American Journal of Economics and Sociology,* 68 (January) 327-351.

Fauconnier, Gilles and Mark Turner (2002), "The Way We Think," New York: Basic.

Hirschman E.C. (2007), "Metaphors in the Marketplace" *Marketing Theory,* 7 (March), 227-248.

Joy, Annamma and John F. Sherry Jr. (2003), "Speaking of Art as Embodied Imagination: A Multisensory Approach to Understanding Aesthetic Experience," *Journal of Consumer Research*, 30 (Sept), 259 - 282.

Lakoff, George and Mark Johnson (1980), "Metaphors we live by", *Chicago University Press*, Chicago.

Penaloza, Lisa (1994), "Altravesando Fronteras/Border Crossings: A Critical Ethnographic Exploration of The Consumer Acculturation Of Mexican Immigrants," *Journal of Consumer Research*, 21 (June), 32-54.MacKay and Fesenmaeir, 1997, p. 2

Piedmont, Ralph L (1999), "Does Spirituality Represent the Sixth Factor of Personality? Spiritual Transcendence and the Five-factor Model," *Journal of Personality*, 67: 985–1013.

Teichert, Thorsten, Iwan Von Wartburg and Russell Braterman (2006), "Tacit Meaning in Disguise: Hidden Metaphors in New Product Development and Market Making," *Business Horizons* 49:451-461

Zaltman, Gerald and Robin H. Coulter (1995), "Seeing The Voice of The Customer: Metaphor-Based Advertising Research", *Journal of Advertising Research*, 35, 35–51.

The Power of One in Mindful Consumer Behavior

Nada Nasr Bechwati, Bentley University, USA
Imad Baalbaki, American University of Beirut, Lebanon

The purpose of this research is to (1) introduce *mindful consumer behavior* and (2) identify the underlying mechanisms, i.e., what drives consumers to behave mindfully or mindlessly. We define mindful consumers as individuals who, in all stages of consumer behavior, are aware of themselves, their communities and the society at large and behave in ways that contribute to the well-being of all these entities. The concept of well-being goes beyond instant satisfaction to involve good health, sustainability including financial sustainability, social responsibility and self-actualization.

Mindful consumer behavior involves an internal facet and an external one. The internal facet pertains to the individual such as her/his health, financial sustainability, and happiness. The external facet is related to the environment and society at large. Hence, issues related to nutrition, exercise, medical information and treatments, budgeting and frugality are all examples of internal aspects. Consuming in a socially responsible way including going green and donating for noble causes are examples of external aspects. The two are not unrelated. For instance, a mindful spending might enable a consumer to have the ability to donate money to support those in need.

Mindful consumer behavior can be practiced at all stages of consumption. The stages of consumer behavior include acquisition, consumption including possession and maintenance, and disposal of goods and services (Hoyer and MacInnis 2010). At the acquisition stage, consumers can be mindful while making product and brand choices and, e.g., choose healthy food, environmentally friendly goods and be cautious about the way they invest their time and money. At the consumption stage, mindful consumers consume moderately, share, and take care of their possessions. Finally, consumers can recycle, donate and pass possessions to others at the disposal stage.

To understand what drives conscious consumer behavior, we draw on research in sociology, psychology and social psychology. We argue that consumers' tendency to behave mindfully is contingent on their (1) temporal focus, and (2) perception of self-efficacy.

Temporal focus is *"the attention individuals devote to thinking about the past, present, and future."* (Shipp et al. 2009). The concept is important because it affects how people incorporate perceptions about past experiences, current situations, and future expectations into their attitudes, cognitions and behavior (Zimbardo & Boyd 1999). Mindful behavior usually involves thinking about the future and the consequences of one's actions such as over-eating or consuming a particular product. Strathman et al. (1994) demonstrated that the extent to which people consider distant vs. immediate consequences of potential behaviors impact these behaviors. Hence, we expect the following:

H₁: *Individuals who tend to focus on the future behave more mindfully as consumers than individuals who tend to focus on the present or the past.*

Self-efficacy refers to one's perception that s/he is can make enough difference (Kinnear, Taylor and Ahmed 1974). Studies show that making individuals believe they can make a difference results in them behaving more actively such as voting and sharing their opinions publically (Crain et al. 1987), acting in a more environmentally conscious manner (Roberts 1996; Webster 1975), and resisting overeating (Kinard, Webster and White 2007). On the other hand, fatalistic individuals do not do much as they believe that their lives are driven by fate, i.e., predetermined (Zimbardo & Boyd 1999). Mindful behavior involves making decisions while inherently believing that these decisions impact one's life and others'. Hence, we propose:

H$_2$: *The higher consumers' perception of self efficacy the more likely they are to behave mindfully.*

In Study 1, we survey consumers in two phases separated by four weeks. In the first phase, we measure participants' tendency to behave as mindful consumers on all aspects of mindfulness and in all stages of consumer behavior. One month later, we measure the same participants' temporal focus and perceptions of their ability to make a difference as well as possibly relevant variables such as locus of control, ability to restrain desires, and values. To measure mindful consumer behavior, we build on the internal and external facets in our definition and draw on several scales to design a 49-item 7-point Likert-type scale.

One hundred and one undergraduate students at a Northeastern university participated in both phases of Study 1. An exploratory factor analysis of the 49 items designed to measure different aspects of mindful consumer behavior revealed the following twelve dimensions: (1) concern for the environment, (2) making the most of one's possessions, (3) contributing through donations and choice of socially responsible firms, (4) passing on used possessions to others, (5) minimizing waste in consumption, (6) concern for one's health, (7) concern for one's wealth, (8) cautious buying, (9) sharing possessions with others, (10) concern for impact of actions on other humans, (11) interest in exercising, and (12) interest in healthy eating.

To test our hypotheses we conduct a series of regression analyses. Contrary to our expectations in H$_1$, our findings reveal a non-significant role for temporal focus on the future in mindful consumer behavior except for the three dimensions pertaining to minimizing waste in consumption, passing on used possessions to others and interest in exercising. The weak role of temporal focus on the future could be attributed to temporal discounting (Critchfield and Kollins 2001). Our results, however, lend strong support to H$_2$. Running stepwise regressions with dimensions of mindful behavior as the dependent variables and a set of variables including temporal focus, self-efficacy, locus of control, materialism, ability to restrain desires, and Kahle's (1984) list of values as our independent variables resulted in significant models containing self-efficacy. Interestingly, for most of the dependent variables pertaining to the external facet of mindful behavior such as effect on other humans, sharing, and concern for the environment, self-efficacy was the only significant predictor in the regression models.

In the second study, we run an experiment to further examine the impact of self-efficacy on mindful consumer behavior. We manipulate self-efficacy through priming and empowering participants. We also have participants make choices reflecting mindful (or mindless) consumer behavior. Results from Study 2 should be ready for sharing at the Conference.

REFERENCES

Crain, W. Mark, Leavans, Donald R. and Lynn Abbot (1987), "Voting and Not Voting at the Same Time; Why and When Do People Vote?" *Public Choice*, 53(3), 221-230.

Critchfield, Thomas S. and Scott H. Kollins (2001), "Temporal Discounting: Basic Research and the Analysis of Socially Important Behavior," *Journal of Applied Behavior Analysis*, 34(1), 101-122.

Hoyer, Wayne D. and Deborah J. MacInnis (2010), "Consumer Behavior," Fifth Edition Mason, Ohio: South-Western Cengage Learning.

Kahle, Lynn R. (1984), "The Values of Americans: Implications for Consumer Adaptation," In R. E. Pitts and A. Woodside (Eds.), *Personal Values and Consumer Psychology*, pp. 77-86, Lexington, MA: Lexington Books.

Kinard, Brian, Webster, Cynthia and Allyn White (2008), "A Comparison of Advertising, Social, and Cognitive Predictors of Overeating Behavior," *Advances in Consumer Research*, 35, 563-569.

Kinnear, Thomas C., Taylor, James R. and Sadrudin A. Ahmed (1974), "Ecologically Concerned Consumers: Who Are They?" *Journal of Marketing*, 38(2), 20-24.

Roberts, James A. (1996) "Green Consumers in the 1990s: Profile and Implications for Advertising," *Journal of Business Research*, 36(3), 217-231.

Shipp, Abbie J., Edwards, Jeffery R. and Schurer Lambert, Lisa (2009), "Conceptualization and Measurement of Temporal Focus: The Subjective Experience of the Past, Present, and Future," *Organizational Behavior and Human Decision Processes*, 110, 1-22.

Strathman, Alan, Gleicher, Faith, Boninger, David S. and C. Scott Edwards (1994), "The Consideration of Future Consequences: Weighing Immediate and Distant Outcomes of Behavior," *Journal of Personality and Social Psychology*, 66(4), 742-752.

Webster, Frederick E. (1975), "Determining the Characteristics of the Socially Conscious Consumer," *Journal of Consumer Research*, 2(3), 188-196.

Zimbardo, Philip G. and John N. Boyd (1999), "Putting Time in Perspective: A Valid, Reliable Individual-Difference Metric," *Journal of Personality and Social Psychology*, 77(6), 1271-1288.

The Effect of Color on Cognitive Resource Depletion

Dante Pirouz, University of Western Ontario, USA

Liangyan Wang, Antai Management School, Shanghai Jiao Tong University

Much of what consumers see – advertising, packaging, brand logos, products, websites, retail environments – are imbued with color. Given the ubiquitous nature of color, there is a wide range of research on the physics and physiology of color and visual processing (Elliot et al. 2007). However, there has been relatively little attention given in the consumer behavior literature to the effect of color on behavior, despite the fact that color is a key executional decision of marketing managers, product designers, and creative directors. Thus, there remain a number of unanswered questions regarding the effects of color on behavior and more specifically on consumer behavior (Fehrman and Fehrman 2004; Whitfield and Wiltshire 1990). Understanding how color hue influences risky choices by consumers would provide an important contribution to theory in addition to allowing for a better understanding of consumer behavior in general (Bellizzi and Hite 1992; Gorn et al. 1997).

This research investigates whether differences in color hue – defined as the wavelength or actual pigment or color visually perceived, such as red, blue, green and yellow (Gorn et al. 1997; Valdez and Mehrabian 1994) – lead to changes in behavior related to risky choices in the consumption domain. More specifically, this research investigates the question of whether exposure to red or blue stimuli in a realistic format (advertising in a magazine) will result in cognitive resource depletion, which in turn leads to an increased preference for risky choices.

Recent research has demonstrated that color may influence cognitive performance. For example, Mehta and Zhu (2009) examined the effect of color hue on approach and avoidance behavior. Red has been shown to increase vigilance and attention to detail and avoidance motivation (Elliot et al. 2007; Mehta and Zhu 2009), while blue has been shown to increase relaxation, creative thinking and approach motivation (Gorn et al. 2004; Mehta and Zhu 2009) consistent with regulatory focus theory (Higgins 1997; Higgins 1998).

Additionally, there has been some evidence in the literature that avoidance motivation can instigate a cognitive resource depletion effect (Hamilton et al. 2010; Trawalter and Richeson 2006). Resource depletion results from the exertion of limited cognitive resources in the process of self-regulation to resist tempting stimuli and/or behavioral impulses. The literature has demonstrated a robust resource depletion effect in a number of different consumer domains including impulsive purchasing (Baumeister 2002; Vohs and Faber 2007), eating (Hofmann et al. 2007) and financial decision making (Oaten and Cheng 2007) among others. This study tests whether exposure to color hue and the subsequent activation of an avoidance motivation results in an exertion of self-regulatory maintenance resulting in cognitive resource depletion – a theoretical connection that has not yet been established in the literature and which could have profound managerial and public policy implications.

Building on the theoretical model outlined by Elliot and Maier (2007), the empirical work of Mehta and Zhu (2009), and cognitive resource depletion (Baumeister and Heatherton 1996; Muraven and Baumeister 2000), this research examines whether color hue in the form of red or blue can impair cognitive processing and if so how this exposure impacts subsequent behavior. A key construct will be cognitive resource depletion, defined as a limited capacity for and a subsequent weakness in exerting willpower and resisting temptations for risk in unrelated domains (Baumeister 2002; Baumeister et al. 1998). This research extends the current theory on the effects of hue on behavior by determining whether the effects lead to cognitive resource depletion, which may lead to risky behaviors such as smoking and unhealthy eating.

METHOD

The study was a two (color hue: red vs. blue) x two (cognitive load: high vs. low) between-subjects experimental design. Participants were exposed to a mock magazine format and asked for their opinion on a new magazine being launched. Each page of the magazine was surrounded by either a red or blue background panel with saturation and value held constant. It has been stressed that saturation and value must be controlled when examining the effects of color hue on behavior because they have been shown to have their own distinctive psychological effects (Elliot et al. 2007). The dependent variables were a 7-point measure of urge to smoke cigarettes (Choi et al. 1997) and a 7-point measure of preference for unhealthy over healthy snack foods modified from the measure used in Vohs and Faber (2007). Four hundred seventy five participants aged 18-28 years old took part in the study for partial course credit.

RESULTS

The study results show that exposure to red (vs. blue) stimuli resulted in a higher urge to smoke cigarettes and a higher preference for unhealthy over healthy snack foods. These results indicate a cognitive resource depletion effect. There was no effect for the cognitive load moderator. Additional studies are currently ongoing to determine if this effect is mediated by regulatory focus using a response time measure for solving approach or avoidance anagrams (Mehta and Zhu 2009) and whether the effect is moderated by any personality traits such as need for cognition (Cacioppo et al. 1984).

IMPLICATIONS

The results of this study contribute theoretically to the current literature by testing whether the connection between color hue exposure and the activation of regulatory focus motivation leads to cognitive resource depletion effects. This research also has potentially important practical implications. Marketing managers will have a better understanding of the effect of color hue in advertising, product packaging, product design and the subsequent effects of consumer behavior. In addition, for product categories where regulatory control over marketing materials is being considered – such as for tobacco, alcohol, or pharmaceuticals – or for health campaigns that strive to promote or deter consumers from risky behaviors, there may be some benefit to utilizing particular color hues in order to facilitate self-regulatory control.

REFERENCES

Baumeister, Roy F. (2002), "Yielding to Temptation: Self-Control Failure, Impulsive Purchasing, and Consumer Behavior," *Journal of Consumer Research*, 28 (4), 670.

Baumeister, Roy F., Ellen Bratslavsky, Mark Muraven, and Diane M. Tice (1998), "Ego depletion: Is the active self a limited resource?," *Journal of Personality & Social Psychology*, 74 (5), 1252-65.

Baumeister, Roy F. and Todd F. Heatherton (1996), "Self-Regulation Failure: An Overview," *Psychological Inquiry*, 7 (1), 1-15.

Bellizzi, Joseph A. and Robert E. Hite (1992), "Environmental Color, Consumer Feelings, and Purchase Likelihood," *Psychology & Marketing*, 9 (5), 347-63.

Cacioppo, John T., Richard E. Petty, and Kao Chuan Feng (1984), "The Efficient Assessment of Need for Cognition," *Journal of Personality Assessment*, 48 (3), 306.

Choi, Won S., John P. Pierce, and Arthur J. Farkas (1997), "A new measure of the smoking uptake continuum," *Annals of Behavioral Medicine*, 16, S078.

Elliot, Andrew J. and Markus A. Maier (2007), "Color and Psychological Functioning," *Current Directions in Psychological Science*, 16 (5), 250-54.

Elliot, Andrew J., Arlen C. Moller, Ron Friedman, Markus A. Maier, and Jorg Meinhardt (2007), "Color and Psychological Functioning: The Effect of Red on Performance Attainment," *Journal of Experimental Psychology*, 136 (1), 154-68.

Fehrman, Kenneth .R. and Cherie Fehrman (2004), *Color: The secret influence* (2nd ed. ed.). Upper Saddle River, NJ: Prentice Hall.

Gorn, Gerald J., Amitava Chattopadhyay, Jaideep Sengupta, and Shashank Tripathi (2004), "Waiting for the Web: How Screen Color Affects Time Perception," *Journal of Marketing Research*, VLI (May, 2004), 215-25.

Gorn, Gerald J., Amitava Chattopadhyay, Tracey Yi, and Darren W. Dahl (1997), "Effects of Color As an Executional Cue in Advertising: They're in the Shade," *Management Science*, 43 (10), 1387-400.

Hamilton, Ryan, Kathleen Vohs, Anne-Laure Sellier, and Tom Meyvis (2010), "Being of Two Minds: Switching Mindsets Exhausts Self-Regulatory Resources " *Organizational Behavior and Human Decision Processes*, forthcoming.

Higgins, E. T. (1997), "Beyond pleasure and pain," *American Psychologist*, 52, 1280-300.

---- (1998), "*Promotion and prevention: Regulatory focus as a motivational principle*," in Advances in Experimental Social Psychology, M.P. Zanna, Ed. Vol. 30. San Diego, CA: Academic Press.

Hofmann, Wilhelm, Wolfgang Rauch, and Bertram Gawronski (2007), "And deplete us not into temptation: Automatic attitudes, dietary restraint, and self-regulatory resources as determinants of eating behavior," *Journal of Experimental Social Psychology*, 43 (3), 497-504.

Mehta, Ravi and Rui Zhu (2009), "Blue or Red? Exploring the Effect of Color on Cognitive Task Performances," *Science*, 1169144.

Muraven, Mark and Roy F. Baumeister (2000), "Self-Regulation and Depletion of Limited Resources: Does Self-Control Resemble a Muscle?," *Psychological Bulletin*, 126 (2), 247-59.

Oaten, Megan and Ken Cheng (2007), "Improvements in self-control from financial monitoring," *Journal of Economic Psychology*, 28 (4), 487-501.

Trawalter, Sophie and Jennifer A. Richeson (2006), "Regulatory focus and executive function after interracial interactions," *Journal of Experimental Social Psychology*, 42 (3), 406-12.

Valdez, Patricia and Albert Mehrabian (1994), "Effects of Color on Emotion," *Journal of Experimental Psychology*, 123 (4), 394-409.

Vohs, Kathleen D. and Ronald J. Faber (2007), "Spent Resources: Self-Regulatory Resource Availability Affects Impulse Buying," *Journal of Consumer Research*, 33 (4), 537-47.

Whitfield, T.W. and T.J. Wiltshire (1990), "Color psychology: a critical review," *Genetic, Social and General Psychology Monographs*, 116, 387-412.

Consumer Usage of Green Products

Ying-ching Lin, National Dong-Hua University, Taiwan
Chiu-chi Angela Chang, Shippensburg University, USA
Jyun-jhih Huang, National Dong-Hua University, Taiwan

Prior research has extensively explored the consumer motivation for *acquiring* green products, as well as how to orchestrate marketing programs to influence consumer purchase of green products (e.g., Bonini & Oppenheim, 2008; Griskevicius, Tybur, and de Bergh, 2010). Extending the marketing literature, the focus of the present research is on consumer *usage* of green products. We define green products investigated in this study to be those in product categories where strength is a major determinant of product choice and where there is a possibility of over-using without consumers' realizing it.

What determines the usage amount of a green product? Prior research has suggested factors, such as package size, container shape, and partitioning, that can influence the amount of consumption (e.g., Wansink, 1996; Cheema & Soman, 2008). In contrast, the present research proposes that the status of a green product itself is an influential heuristic cue for determining its usage. In fact, there is evidence to suggest that the status or type of a product may relate to its usage. For example, Scott, Nowlis, and Mandel (2009) suggest that consumers overuse the ultra-concentrated product relative to the regular-strength version. Along similar lines, we propose that consumers see green products differently and make differential inferences about them compared to regular products. Recent research provides some evidence to support this assertion. Aaker, Vohs, and Mogilner (2010) show that consumers hold stereotypical views of organizations: nonprofits are perceived as being warmer than for-profits, whereas for-profits are perceived as being more competent than nonprofits. The emphasis of green products on the environment or social cause may be regarded as more of a signal of generosity, trustworthiness, and sincerity, but less of a signal of competency, efficiency, and effectiveness (cf. Aaker et al., 2010). Such impressions on green products may decrease perceptions of product performance, which, in turn, may increase the product usage amount to compensate for the perceived low-effectiveness and still achieve the end-goal. Furthermore, Luchs, Naylor, Irwin, and Raghunathan (2010) argue that consumers infer a positive association between ethicality and gentleness and a negative association between ethicality and strength. Therefore, in product categories in which strength-related attributes are valued, products advertised as being green and/or ethical could be a liability because of their low perceived strength or effectiveness. The above reasoning leads to our hypothesis that consumers may use a larger amount of a green product relative to its regular counterpart in order to make up for its low level of effectiveness.

To overcome the perception of green products being less effective, a logical strategy is to boost their perceived effectiveness. Prior research has demonstrated that an endorsement by a highly credible source can boost a nonprofit's perceived competence and result in a greater willingness to buy from a not-for-profit organization (Aaker et al., 2010). A highly credible source of information, such as *Consumer Reports*, also influences consumers' product usage, as evidenced in the decreased over-use of ultra-concentrated detergent (Scott et al., 2009). When explicit information about product strength such as a product guarantee is provided, consumers rely less on inferences of a negative relationship between ethicality and strength and they will have a more favorable attitude toward ethical products (Luchs et al., 2010). Therefore, we hypothesize that providing information on the product effectiveness should mitigate the usage amount of green products.

Three studies were designed to test our research hypotheses. Both studies 1A and 1B had a one factor (product type: green versus regular) between-subjects design. In study 1A, product type was manipulated by the presence or absence of a green/eco label. In study 1B, brand names were used to manipulate a green (Green Angel) versus a regular (Dr. Strong) product. The participants in study 1A were asked to evaluate a glass cleaner product and presented with a description of a window cleaning task. Similarly, the participants in study 1B were asked to evaluate a toilet bowl cleaner and presented with a toilet cleaning task description. Study 2, where a dish-washing task was involved, had a 2 (product type: green versus regular) x 2 (product effectiveness cue: endorsement versus no endorsement) between-subjects design. While product label colors (green versus red) conveyed a green versus regular product dish-washing detergent, the presence or absence of an endorsement from *Consumer Reports* represented the presence or absence of a product effectiveness cue, respectively. In all studies, participants gave their estimates regarding the number of times they thought they would press the nozzle of the cleaning product in order to get the task done. In addition, participants rated their perceptions of product effectiveness, attitude toward the product, purchase intentions, as well as their attitude toward the environment (Dunlap & Van Liere, 1978).

The results of the three studies show that consumers use more of a green product, compared with its conventional counterpart, in order to accomplish a given task. In addition, consumers exhibit differences in their usage of a green versus a regular product. Consumers who have a more favorable environmental attitude overuse a green product, while consumers who have a less favorable environmental attitude don't. This phenomenon of using more of a green than a regular product is driven by consumers' perception of a product's effectiveness. Consequently, when the perceived effectiveness of a green product is boosted by a credible endorsement, the discrepancy between green and regular product usage disappears.

This research advances the understanding of consumer usage of green products in several ways. First, extending the literature on product usage, this work demonstrates that product type influences product usage amount. Consumers have a stereotypical association of green versus regular products. These perceptions affect the product usage. Second, this work demonstrates an unintended, potentially detrimental, and nuanced effect of green products, that is, product overuse. In addition, this work uncovers a somewhat unexpected effect of environmental attitude: high (versus low) environmental attitude consumers actually use more of a green product. Finally, our findings demonstrate that supplying explicit information about a product's effectiveness has an effect on that product's usage as well (cf. Luchs et al. 2010).

REFERENCES

Aaker, J., Vohs, K. D., & Mogilner, C. (2010). Nonprofits are seen as warm and for-profits as competent: Firm stereotypes matter. *Journal of Consumer Research, 37*, 224-237.

Bonini, S., & Oppenheim, J. (2008). Cultivating the green consumer. *Stanford Social Innovation Review, 6*, 56-61.

Cheema, A., & Soman, D. (2008). The effect of partitions on controlling consumption. *Journal of Marketing Research, 45*, 665-675.

Dunlap, R. E., & Van Liere, K. D. (1978). The new environmental paradigm: A proposed measuring instrument and preliminary results. *The Journal of Environmental Education, 9*, 10–19.

Griskevicius, V., Tybur, J. M., & den Bergh, B. (2010). Going green to be seen: Status, reputation, and conspicuous conservation. *Journal of Personality and Social Psychology, 98*, 392-404.

Luchs, M. G., Naylor, R. W., Irwin, J. R., & Raghunathan, R. (2010). The sustainability liability: Potential negative effects of ethicality on product preference. *Journal of Marketing, 74*, 18-31.

Scott, M. L., Nowlis, S. M., & Mandel, N. (2009). Consumer usage of ultra-concentrated products. In A. L. McGill & S. Shavitt (Eds.), *Advances in Consumer Research, Vol. 36* (pp. 195-197). Duluth, MN: Association for Consumer Research.

Wansink, B. (1996). Can package size accelerate usage volume? *Journal of Marketing, 60*, 1-13.

Expressive Oriented Relationships:
A New Type of Commercial Friendships

Bryan R. Johnson, Creighton University, USA
William T. Ross, University of Connecticut, USA
Robin Coulter, University of Connecticut, USA

CONCEPTUALIZATION & THEORY

The development of relationships between firms and their customers has received considerable attention in the marketing literature. Interestingly, these relationships are not always limited to traditional commercial relationships. For example, in response to Bagozzi's (1995) call for marketing scholars to identify additional types of relationships fundamental to marketing, Price and Arnould (1999) identified a new and important type of marketing relationship – "commercial friendships." These relationships, which are characterized as friendships that form between customers and a firm's representatives over time, as a result of economic transactions, move beyond the boundaries of traditional commercial relationships.

Interestingly, commercial friendships that develop as a result of ongoing economic exchanges (Price and Arnould 1999) aren't the only type of commercial friendships operating between consumers and representatives of firms in the marketplace. As demonstrated by DiMaggio and Louche (1998), friendship relationships oftentimes exist between consumers and firm representatives, before a single transaction ever takes place. Such occurrences, in which consumers draw upon pre-existing friendship ties with a firm's employees to make purchases, represent a new and important type of commercial friendship.

Surprisingly, this type of pre-existing commercial friendship has not been examined in the marketing literature. Accordingly, the purpose of this study is to investigate this new class of marketing relationships and demonstrate how such relationships impact consumption. Identifying and explicating the use of alternative types of commercial friendships provides a valuable backdrop against which other types of marketing relationships can be juxtaposed and understood. The framework that emerges from this study highlights important similarities and differences among the different types of friendships used in consumption contexts, which ultimately reveals important ways marketing relationships can be conceptualized, studied, and managed.

To demonstrate the impact of this new category of commercial friendships on consumption, and to develop a framework for understanding these friendships in the context of other marketing relationships, we draw upon social capital theory. Social capital theory asserts that individuals obtain benefits or returns as a result of their relationships with others (Lin 2001; Portes 1998). Social capital theory highlights how differences in the nature and the structure of relationships create diversity in outcomes resulting from their use. Given fundamental differences between the types of relationships used in the marketplace, social capital theory provides an effective and robust theoretical framework for understanding the friendships examined in this study.

METHOD

To investigate, explain, and develop this new category of commercial friendships in the context of existing marketing relationships, we utilized the grounded theory approach (Glaser and Strauss 1967; Strauss and Corbin 1998). We conducted semi-structured depth interviews with 26 U.S. consumers, yielding 122 consumption experiences. Participants were purposively selected according to established theoretical sampling techniques (Charmaz 2006; Glaser and Strauss 1967; Strauss and Corbin 1998). To ensure that the developing theory and framework were grounded in the data, we adhered to the constant comparative approach (Glaser and Strauss 1967). Finally, to establish trustworthiness, we conducted member checks with all study participants, as advocated in previous research (Belk, Sherry, and Wallendorf 1988; Lincoln and Guba 1985).

FINDINGS & DISCUSSION

As alluded to previously, our analysis of participants' experiences reveals an exciting new category of commercial friendships used by consumers. Our data identify important differences between this new type of commercial friendship and previously documented commercial friendships (Price and Arnould 1999). Our analysis highlights *instrumentality* (Lin, Dean, and Ensel 1981), which represents the extent to which relationships are *instrumental* or *expressive*, as a key factor distinguishing different types of commercial friendships. Conceptually, *instrumental* relationships are those in which relationships are used to achieve an end that is distinguishable from the relationship itself, such as making a purchase. Alternatively, *expressive* relationships serve as both the means and the end and do not have any extrinsic purpose beyond the relationship itself, as in the case of friendship (Lin et al. 1981).

Participants' experiences reveal that, by their very nature, commercial friendships involve both *instrumental* and *expressive* characteristics. Consequently, we develop a relationship continuum, anchored by *instrumental* and *expressive* motives at the extremes, to model these dynamic relationships. Using this framework, our analysis highlights the importance of conceptualizing commercial friendships according to their *instrumental orientation* or their *expressive orientation*, in order to account for the dynamic underlying factors driving these relationships.

Drawing upon this framework, our analysis also reveals that the nature of commercial friendships, at the time they are initially established, anchors the relationships as they develop and evolve in the future. Our data demonstrate that relationships that begin *instrumentally* will continue to be dominated by the *instrumental* dimension over time. Although they may move toward the *expressive* end of the continuum, they rarely make the jump and become *expressive oriented* commercial friendships. Alternatively, relationships that begin as *expressive* relationships, and are later introduced into consumption contexts, continue to be dominated by the *expressive* dimension of the relationship. Although they may move toward the *instrumental* end of the continuum and receive important consumption related benefits, they rarely become *instrumental oriented* commercial friendships, due to consumers' efforts to compartmentalize, maintain, and protect their *expressive* relationships. These differences, ultimately derived from the nature of the relationships at the time of their inception, frame the way consumers perceive, categorize, and use their relationships for consumption purposes, even as the relationships fluctuate and operate at different points along the relationship continuum over time.

CONCLUSION

The identification and examination of a new class of commercial friendships illuminates important theoretical differences underlying the various types of relationships between consumers and firm representatives. This study demonstrates the importance of conceptualizing commercial friendships as multi-dimensional phenomena that are both determined and constrained by *instrumental* and *expressive* components. Interestingly, we find that the nature of the relationships, at the time they are established, has a lasting and powerful impact. Ultimately, identifying the underlying features of these friendships has important implications regarding how consumers perceive their relationships with firms and how they use them for consumption purposes. Additionally, explicating these relationships also reveals important ways firms might manage customers engaged in *instrumental oriented* and *expressive oriented* marketing relationships.

REFERENCES

Bagozzi, Richard P. (1995), "Reflections on Relationship Marketing in Consumer Markets," Journal of the Academy of Marketing Science, 23 (4), 272.

Belk, Russell W., John F. Sherry, and Melanie Wallendorf (1988), "A Naturalistic Inquiry Into Buyer and Seller Behavior at A Swap Meet," Journal of Consumer Research, 14 (4), 449-70.

Charmaz, Kathy (2006), Constructing Grounded Theory. Thousand Oaks, CA: Sage.

DiMaggio, Paul and Hugh Louch (1998), "Socially Embedded Consumer Transactions: For What Kinds of Purchases Do People Most Often Use Networks?" American Sociological Review, 63 (5), 619.

Glaser, Barney G. and Anselm Strauss (1967), "The Constant Comparative Method of Qualitative Analysis," in The Discovery of Grounded Theory: Strategies for Qualitative Research. Chicago, IL: Aldine.

Lin, Nan (2001), Social Capital: A Theory of Social Structure and Action (1 ed.). Cambridge: Cambridge University Press.

Lin, Nan, Alfred Dean, and Walter M. Ensel (1981), "Social Support Scales: A Methodological Note," Schizophrenia Bulletin, 7(1), 73-89.

Lincoln, Yvonna S. and Egon G. Guba (1985), "Designing a Naturalistic Inquiry," in Naturalistic Inquiry, Yvonna S. Lincoln and Egon G. Guba, Eds. Beverly Hills, CA: Sage.

Portes, Alejandro (1998), "Social Capital: Its Origins and Applications in Modern Sociology," Annual Review of Sociology, 24, 1-24.

Price, Linda L. and Eric J. Arnould (1999), "Commerical Friendships: Service Provider--Client Relationships in Context," Journal of Marketing, 63 (4), 38-56.

Strauss, Anselm and Juliet Corbin (1998), Basics of Qualitative Research: Techniques and Procedures for Developing Grounded Theory (2nd ed.). Thousand Oaks, CA: Sage.

Impact of Mortality Salience on Advertising Effectiveness in a Commercial Pod

Priyamvadha Rangan, University of Kansas, USA
Surendra N. Singh, University of Kansas, USA
Mark J. Landau, University of Kansas, USA
Jungsil Choi, University of Kansas, USA

A crucial media planning consideration is the nature of the program itself, as the program context influences the effectiveness of embedded advertising, with the context effect being maximal for the first ad in the ensuing commercial pod and minimal for the last ad in the pod (Murry, Lastovicka and Singh 1992). Terror management theory (Greenberg, Pyszczynski and Solomon 1986) posits that humans' innate desire for perpetual life, coupled with awareness of their mortality, creates the potential for existential anxiety. Conscious death-related thoughts instigate proximal defenses (e.g., thought suppression/denial of one's vulnerability to death; Arndt, Allen and Greenberg 2001), whereas nonconscious but accessible death-related thoughts activate distal defenses (e.g., cultural worldview bolstering; Pyszczynski, Greenberg and Solomon 1999).

Recent research in marketing (Liu and Smeesters 2010) induced mortality salience (hereafter, MS) by exposing participants to epochal news coverage (9/11 terror attacks). MS-inducing programs caused participants to prefer domestic brands over foreign brands; due to enhanced patriotism. However, the authors do not find MS effects on ad evaluation. They suggest that ad evaluations are affected by program-induced mood, and since MS does not affect mood, MS will not influence ads. Based on extant literature, we expect program-induced mood effects to be independent of program-induced MS effects, in that moods influence the first few commercials in the pod, while program-induced distal MS effects manifest themselves on the later commercials.

We investigate whether (a) archetypal death-depicting television programs trigger death-related thoughts and whether these vary over an ensuing commercial pod, (b) if and when death-related thoughts turn from being conscious to nonconscious in the pod, and (c) do distal defenses impact advertising effectiveness in the pod, and if so, what is the process mechanism? We conducted three studies. Local news from an affiliate was recorded and edited before each study. The first three-and-a-half minutes of the MS and control videos contained information on local governance etc. The last one-and-a-half minutes of the MS video contained death-related information while the control video contained sports information. Pre-tests were done to select filler ads for all studies and the target ad for the third study.

Study 1: One factor, four-level between-subjects design was used with MS-content and ads at three pod positions: beginning (MS_{BEG}), middle (MS_{MID}), and end (MS_{END}) and a control condition. Death thought accessibility (DTA; Greenberg et al. 1994) was measured after stimulus exposure. Results showed that DTA in control condition (M_{CON} = 1.55) was similar to MS_{MID} (M_{MID} = 1.52, p = 1) but lower than at MS_{BEG} (M_{BEG} = 2.2, p = .026) and MS_{END} (M_{END} = 2.15, p = .044).

Study 2: Six-level between-subjects design was used with MS-content and ads at five pod positions: MS_{BEG}, after one ad (MS_1), after two ads (MS_2), MS_{MID}, and MS_{END}, and a control condition. Participants completed a thought-listing exercise (Greenberg et al. 1994), the Emotional Lability Inventory (ELI; Greenberg et al. 2000), and PANAS after stimulus exposure. Results showed that number of death-related thoughts in the control condition (M_{CON} = .07) was comparable to MS_{MID} (M_{MID} = .52, p = .095) and MS_{END} (M_{END} = .47, p = .161) but lower than other pod positions (ps < .001). ELI scores at MS_{END} (M_{END} = 5.83) were similar to control condition (M_{CON} = 6.01, p = .941), but lower than other pod positions (ps < .05). Positive and negative affect did not vary across conditions.

Study 3: 5 (MS: MS_{BEG}, MS_1, MS_2, MS_{MID}, MS_{END}) x 2 (AdType: Foreign vs. Domestic) + 2 (Control: Foreign vs. Domestic) between-subjects design was used. Participants viewed the video and then saw one of two ads varying *only* in the country-of-origin information in the headline, and completed DTA, attitude toward the ad and attitude toward the brand measures. There was only a treatment main effect for DTA (F (5,288) = 4.61, p < .001). Contrasts showed that DTA followed the first study's pattern. There was only an interaction effect for attitude toward the ad (F (5,288) = 2.86, p = .015). The foreign ad was rated lower than domestic ad only at end of pod (F (1, 288) = 7.5, p = .007); ps > .14 in other positions. Moderated mediation (Preacher, Rucker and Hayes 2007) showed that DTA mediated relationship between program context and attitude toward the ad for foreign ad, but not domestic ad. ANOVA results for attitude toward the brand were similar to attitude toward the ad. A multiple step, multiple mediator model (Hayes, Preacher and Myers 2010) showed that the relationship between program context and attitude toward the brand was mediated by attitude toward the ad via DTA. To summarize, we demonstrate that quotidian violent television programming makes mortality salient, triggering death-related thoughts over the ensuing pod. We find that death-related thoughts are of a conscious nature at the front of the pod and become nonconscious but accessible at the end of the pod. Further, distal defenses against death-related thoughts are activated only at the end of the pod—advertisements for foreign brands are negatively evaluated over advertisements for domestic brands—driven by nonconscious but accessible death-related thoughts.

REFERENCES

Greenberg, Jeff, Pyszczynski, Tom and Solomon, Sheldon (1986), "The Causes and Consequences of a Need for Self-Esteem: A Terror Management Theory," in Public Self and Private Self, R. F. Baumeister, Ed. New York: Springer-Verlag, 189-212.

---, ---, ---, Simon, Linda and Breus, Michael (1994), "Role of Consciousness and Accessibility of Death-Related Thoughts in Mortality Salience Effects," Journal of Personality and Social Psychology, 67 (4), 627-637.

---, Arndt, Jamie, Simon, Linda, Pyszczynski, Tom and Solomon, Sheldon (2000), "Proximal and Distal Defenses in Response to Reminders of One's Mortality: Evidence of a Temporal Sequence," Personality and Social Psychology Bulletin, 26 (1), 91-99.

Hayes, Andrew F., Preacher, Kristopher J. and Myers, Teresa A. (2010). Mediation and the estimation of indirect effects in political communication research: In E. P. Bucy & R. Lance Holbert (Eds.), Sourcebook for political communication research: Methods, measures, and analytical techniques. New York: Routledge, 434-465.

Liu, Jia and Smeesters, Dirk (2010), "Have You Seen the News Today? The Effect of Death-Related Media Contexts on Brand Preferences," Journal of Marketing Research, 47 (April), 251-262.

Murry, John P., Lastovicka, John L. and Singh, Surendra N. (1992), "Feeling and Liking Responses to Television Programs: An Examination of Two Explanations for Media-Context Effects," Journal of Consumer Research, 18 (March), 441-451.

Preacher, Kristopher J., Rucker, Derek D. and Hayes, Andrew F. (2007), "Assessing Moderated Mediation Hypothesis: Theory, Methods and Prescriptions," Multivariate Behavioral Research, 42 (1), 185-227.

Pyszczynski, Tom, Greenberg, Jeff and Solomon, Sheldon (1999), "A Dual-Process Model of Defense Against Conscious and Unconscious Death-Related Thoughts: An Extension of Terror Management Theory," Psychological Review, 106 (4), 835-845.

Fourteen Research Ideas in Behavioral Pricing

Robert Schindler, Rutgers University - Camden, USA

Price is unique among marketing variables in at least two ways. First, it is the marketing variable that "harvests" the benefits created by all the others (Nagle and Holden 1995). This gives price a crucial managerial relevance that makes one wonder why courses in pricing are not more prominent in the business school curriculum. Second, its numerical nature makes price explicit and specific to a degree unmatched by any of the other marketing-mix variables (Schindler 2007). This gives the study of how consumers deal with price an extraordinary theoretical potential – the price side of things being so clear and concrete, the habits and limitations of the consumer can emerge in bold relief.

As I have been reviewing behavioral pricing research during my writing of a new pricing textbook, some particular examples of needed work in pricing-related consumer behavior have become apparent. Thinking of the many young researchers at the ACR conference, I feel it is an appropriate setting for encouraging needed research. Below are fourteen ideas that I have selected as promising opportunities for making a difference in the practice of pricing as well as in approaching more fundamental behavioral questions. It is my hope that these ideas will at least stimulate thinking in these important research areas.

1. Prospect theory suggests that framing a loss as a gain foregone reduces its negative impact. Nagle and Holden (1995) have suggested that this is illustrated by retail advertisements, often seen around April, that suggest consumers use their income tax refund to purchase a product. Is this type of advertising appeal effective?

2. Hoch and Loewenstein (1991) have found that sensory proximity can lead a quantity to be considered part of one's status quo. Could this be applied to the "dangling" of discounts commonly seen in price advertising? If dangling causes an offered discount to become part of one's "endowment," then passing up the discount could feel like a painful loss.

3. Terms such as "price points" and "price lining" are commonly used, but have received relatively little academic attention. Is the use of a small number of price points effective as means of price simplification? A recall measure could be used to test this. Are such price simplification methods more likely to be used by retailers whose prices are low?

4. Bobinski, Cox, and Cox (1996) have shown that a retailer's advertised reasons for a price decrease affect consumers. Given the commonness of price decreases and increases, it seems that further study of possible "price rationales" and their effects would be of considerable interest.

5. Sundaram, Mitra, and Webster (1998) have found that a large proportion of consumer word-of-mouth communication concerns price. Because consumer word-of-mouth communication is so important, it would be interesting to know what price information is being shared. A study of this could be carried out using consumer reviews posted on the Internet.

6. Determining the items most influential in affecting a retailer's price image is an important practical problem. There is need to build on the past research (e.g., Desai and Talukdar 2003) to develop methods to determine such "price exemplars."

7. For many years, discounts greater than five percent were illegal in Germany (Trumbull 2000). This suggests it might be interesting to carry out a comparison of pricing laws between cultures. Findings could bear on cultural universals in price fairness perceptions.

8. It is recognized that "natural monopolies," such as the delivery of electricity to homes, justify exceptions to free-market economics. Healthcare is not such a natural monopoly, but it does seem to have some difficulties with a free-market system. Could one factor be the consumer's extreme sensitivity to healthcare quality differences? For example, would people find it acceptable for price to determine who gets treatment from the best doctors?

9. Research on price promotions has tended to focus on decision processes. There seems to be a lack of research regarding decision consequences, such as whether price promotions lead people to buy things that they don't really use. For example, does the extent of a consumer's deal proneness correlate with the amount of clutter and unused items in his/her home?

10. Although there has been much written on ethics and social responsibility in pricing, there has been little academic work on the social-responsibility aspects of price promotions. More research seems needed on the role of price promotions in (1) compulsive buying, (2) over-spending, (3) borrowing, and (4) product or purchase dissatisfaction.

11. Most prices are either round numbers (e.g., $5.00) or just below round numbers (e.g., $4.99). What about all the rest of the numbers? Recently, Thomas, Simon, and Kadiyali (2010) have studied such "sharp-number" prices in real estate transactions, but what about other product categories? What questions may be evoked in consumers' minds from sharp-number prices?

12. In addition to early work on the importance of perceived risk in the consumer's use of price to indicate quality, a recent study has found evidence of more "price reliance" in countries with greater levels of risk aversion (Volckner and Hofmann 2007). It may be time to look more carefully at the role of perceived risk in supporting high prices. For example, might willingness to pay a higher price be more sensitive than measures of persuasion in assessing the effectiveness of a fear appeal?

13. Recent evidence for effects of superstitious causation (e.g., Risen and Gilovich 2008) raises the question of whether such a phenomenon may have some role in consumers' price-quality associations. Paying a premium could give consumers a sense of good luck toward receiving high quality. For example, would respondents feel more likely to win a high-quality version of a product if they paid more for the chance?

14. There has recently been some work on the practice of "pay what you want" pricing (e.g., Kim, Natter, and Spann 2009). It would be interesting to study the oldest and most common use of this practice – i.e., in the financial support of religious organizations.

REFERENCES

Bobinski, George, Dena Cox, and Anthony Cox (1996), "Retail 'Sale' Advertising, Perceived Retailer Credibility, and Price Rationale," *Journal of Retailing*, 72 (3), 291-306.

Desai, Kalpesh K. and Debabrata Talukdar (2003), "Relationship Between Product Groups' Price Perceptions, Shopper's Basket Size, and Grocery Store's Overall Store Price Image," *Psychology & Marketing*, 20 (10), 903-933.

Hoch, Stephen J. and George F. Loewenstein (1991), "Time-Inconsistent Preferences and Consumer Self-Control," *Journal of Consumer Research*, 17 (March), 492-507.

Kim, Ju-Young, Martin Natter, and Martin Spann (2009), "Pay What You Want: A New Participative Pricing Mechanism," *Journal of Marketing*, 73 (January), 44-58.

Risen, Jane L. and Thomas Gilovich (2008), "Why People Are Reluctant to Tempt Fate," *Journal of Personality and Social Psychology*, 95 (2), 297-307.

Nagle, Thomas T. and Reed K. Holden (1995), *The Strategy and Tactics of Pricing*, 2nd edition, Englewood Cliffs, NJ: Prentice Hall.

Schindler, Robert M. (2007), "What Prices Reveal About the Mind," Keynote address, Fordham University Behavioral Pricing Conference, September 28-29, New York City.

Sundaram, D. S., Kaushik Mitra, and Cynthia Webster (1998), "Word-of-Mouth Communications: A Motivational Analysis," *Advances in Consumer Research*, 25, 527-531.

Thomas, Manoj, Daniel H. Simon, and Vrinda Kadiyali (2010), "The Price Precision Effect: Evidence from Laboratory and Market Data," *Marketing Science*, 29 (January-February), 175-190.

Trumbull, J. Gunnar (2000), "Divergent Paths of Product Market Regulation in France and Germany, 1970-1990," in *Handbook of Global Economic Policy*, Stuart S. Nagle, ed., New York: Marcel Dekker, 435-462.

Volckner, Franziska and Julian Hofmann (2007), "The Price-Perceived Quality Relationship: A Meta-Analytic Review and Assessment of its Determinants," *Marketing Letters*, 18, 181-196.

Thanks for Nothing: The Dark Side of Gratitude

Waylon McGill, University of Houston, USA
Vanessa Patrick, University of Houston, USA

Despite significant public interest in gratitude (Emmons & McCullough 2003), researchers have only recently begun to rigorously examine this complex emotion (Emmons & McCullough 2003, Emmons & Crumpler 2000, McCullough et al. 2002, Bartlett & De Steno 2006). This research has identified a host of positive effects of gratitude that range from improving subjective well-being (Emmons & McCullough 2003), strengthening interpersonal relationships (Lambert et al. 2010) and promoting prosocial behavior (Froh, Bono & Emmons 2010). One question that seems to have been overlooked in the extant research is whether there is a downside to experiencing gratitude. The present research explores this question.

THEORETICAL FOUNDATION

Gratitude is a low arousal, positively valenced emotion, similar to happiness, and is characterized as having two key components (McCullough et al. 2001): (1) the person must believe that they have received a benefit to which they were not entitled, and, (2) the beneficiary must attribute responsibility for the benefit to an external source (Solomon 1977).

Emotions are frequently differentiated based on their specific action tendencies (Frijda 1986). Negative emotions can be seen as indicating that there is something wrong with the environment and that a person needs to take action to correct it. Fear, for example, mobilizes resources to escape or defend oneself, while anger promotes aggression. Conversely, positive emotions have less well-defined, non-specific action tendencies (Fredrickson & Branigan 2005). Positive affect has been found to promote inclusive thinking (Fredrickson and Branigan 2005), facilitate self-control (Tice et al. 2007) and enhance motivation (Isen & Reeve 2005).

Do all positive emotions have these same effects? The central thesis of the current research is that gratitude is actually likely to result in *decreased* motivation towards future oriented outcomes compared to a similar positive emotion like happiness. We hypothesize since gratitude is tied to a very specific outcome ("I am grateful for X"), it is a relatively more specific emotion than happiness, and consequently the experience of gratitude is likely to induce more concrete construals than happiness. Prior research has demonstrated that happiness results in the adoption of more abstract construals, which mediates the influence of happiness on the preference for future benefits (Labroo & Patrick 2008). Since concrete construals are associated with a more proximal focus, we expect that gratitude would decrease motivation for future oriented outcomes compared to happiness.

Prior research has demonstrated that emotions bias individuals' expectations regarding future outcomes. Specifically, people tend to overestimate the probability of events occurring that are consistent with the emotional state they are experiencing (Wright & Bower 1992). Accordingly, we posit that grateful people are more likely to overestimate the probability of receiving similar unearned benefits to those for which they are grateful in the future than are happy people. In other words, we hypothesize that the effects of gratitude on motivation for future oriented outcomes is domain-specific.

SUMMARY OF HYPOTHESES

We propose the following hypotheses:
1. Grateful individuals are less motivated to pursue future oriented goals than happy individuals.
2. The effect of gratitude (versus happiness) on the motivation to pursue future goals is mediated by construal level.
3. The effects of gratitude on motivation to adopt a future orientation are domain-specific.

Specifically, grateful individuals are more likely to expect to receive unearned future benefits within the domain for which they are grateful than happy individuals.

EXPERIMENTS

We propose two experiments to empirically investigate these hypotheses.

Experiment 1 will test hypotheses 1 and 3. Subjects will read the following statement(s). "When thinking about their health many people feel grateful (happy). Please indicate the extent to which you feel this way, and provide a list of reasons why your health makes you feel this way." A 7-point Likert scale will be used, and subjects will be given 5 minutes to provide reasons for their response. Upon completion they will be asked to read a health communication promoting an HPV vaccine, how it is transmitted and the risks associated with it. They will then be asked to indicate on 7-point Likert scales 1) How effective they think the communication is, 2) the likelihood that they themselves will get vaccinated, and, 3) The likelihood that they will contract the virus if they do not get vaccinated. Dependent variable (2) will assess the motivation to engage in future oriented behavior, while (3) will assess the extent to which grateful (versus happy) individuals expect future benefits for which they are not responsible.

Experiment 2 will be similar to experiment 1, but will be a 2 (gratitude versus happiness) x2 (health versus family) full factorial design designed to test hypotheses 1-3. Participants will undergo the same affect induction procedure used in experiment 1, but half the respondents will give reasons why they feel grateful (happy) when thinking about their family instead of their health. They will then see the same health communication and be given the same brief questionnaire followed by Vallacher and Wegner's (1989) personal agency questionnaire (BIF). These trait differences may be used to study differences in abstract versus concrete construals (e.g., Freitas et al. 2001; Levy, Freitas, and Salovey 2002). Construal level scores will then be calculated using the standard procedure. We would expect that grateful participants would reveal relatively more concrete construal levels than happy participants, and that construal level would mediate the influence of grateful (happy) participants on motivation to engage in future oriented behavior and the extent to which grateful (versus happy) individuals expect future benefits for which they are not responsible. We also expect that these effects will be domain-specific, such that this influence will be stronger for participants reflecting on being grateful about their health (versus family).

CONCLUSION

The purpose of this research is not to condemn gratitude, which we acknowledge as an important and adaptive emotion. Rather, it is simply to provide balance to an overwhelmingly positive body of literature on gratitude. Further, we believe that by if someone thinks about how their gratitude makes them feel in a more general sense, this negative effect of gratitude can be reversed by activating more abstract construals.

Transnational tourists consuming hyper-masculinity in the Dominican Republic: 'All inclusive'?

Nacima Ourahmoune, Reims management school (RMS), France

In locations around the world, sex tourism is a booming business. The Dominican Republic has experienced very rapid socio-cultural and economic change due to the development of tourism. The Island has become the leading destination for tourists in the Caribbean. This has a tremendous impact on local populations in terms of consumption (from the structure of purchases to brand awareness). On the other hand, western consumers in their vast majority adopt the "All inclusive" offer as a form of vacation where they maximize recreation/leisure, pleasure and exotic fantasy in huge closed resorts where everything is presented as free (in fact pre-paid…). Prostitution is often quoted as a strong motive for the choice of this destination. "Although prostitution may involve an immoral exploitation of human beings (Hirschman 1991; Truong 1990), and sex slavery certainly does so (Aisbett and Malan 1993; Hornblower 1993; Sherrill 1993), the patronage of prostitutes is plausibly the oldest form of consumer behavior. Nevertheless, prostitution has been studied to a very limited degree by consumer researchers (Ostergaard 1993)" (Belk, 1994). This research project is an attempt to research the intersection of transnational consumption behaviors and (gender) power relations.

Kamala Kempadoo (1999) suggests sex tourism provides a clear example of how power relationships are perpetuated between North/South countries through globalization processes. In this perspective, Caribbean countries are forced into marketing their beaches and also their bodies as commodities to the tourist markets of North America and Europe as the Caribbean becomes a tropical playground for the globally powerful to explore their racialized fantasies.

More specifically, previous anthropological research has been carried out in the Dominican Republic. Denise Brennan (2004) considers why Dominican and Haitian women move to the town of Sosúa to pursue sex work and describes how sex tourists, primarily Europeans, come to Sosúa to buy sex cheaply and live out racial fantasies. Illuminating the complex world of Sosúa's sex business in rich detail, Brennan (2004) draws on extensive interviews not only with sex workers and clients, but also with others who facilitate and benefit from the sex trade. She weaves these voices into an analysis of Dominican economic and migration histories to consider the opportunities—or lack thereof—available to poor Dominican women. She shows how these women, local actors caught in a web of global economic relations, try to take advantage of the foreign men who are in Sosúa. Through her detailed study of the lives and working conditions of the women in Sosúa's sex trade, Brennan (2004) raises important questions about women's power, control, and opportunities in a globalized economy.

This research pursues this effort by examining other aspects not touched on by Brennan's research. Unlike a body of research that tackled specifically sex workers' representations in the Caribbean, the author locates this study in the context of crowded, close, safe, family resorts in Punta Cana. I specifically investigate Local men/ Tourist female interactions in the context of those resorts. Escaping usual images of female sex workers or the interactions of young male "beach boys" with aged female tourists, the research shows how it is difficult to untangle the phenomenon of prostitution from "romance tourism" when young female tourists are involved in relationships with Dominican males working in the tourism industry.

The author conducted an ethnographic research over 4 years, with over 20 weeks in the field. More specifically, a group of Dominicans who are part of the Animation staff in a typical local resort - was investigated (over 2 years, 7 weeks). The author shared activities with informants (local dances, discos, visits to native towns/family…), performed observations, in-depth interviews (with 15 Dominicans and 12 female tourists). Also, a semiotic analysis of hundreds of pictures taken in the field helped enrich the findings.

We specifically focus here on gender relations between female tourists and local male hotel staff. Those relationships raise issues of performing and consuming the body mediated by the "all inclusive" offer.

The findings show elements that reinforce power logics in both economic and racial terms in the context of local/tourists interactions. In particular a "day and night" theme emerged from the field showing how far the dominance is important while Dominican males are at work, serving client's expectations with the necessary distance to be maintained with them. In contrast, at night, when tourists and locals gather in discos as clients, relationships are complexified in terms of power logics.

For instance, Dominican male agency is emphasized through romances with young tourists. Various respondents' discourses and behaviors show how rivalry between male tourists and male locals is expressed in the reversed context of female tourists consuming the racialized fantasy of Black or Latin hyper-masculinity.

Bodies, possessions and brands are manipulated as signs to convey specific discourses on sex, gender, ethnicity and social status. At a macro-level tourism is an obligation for the Caribbean to survive against the Global North. The narratives displayed rely on four S's of tourism advertising: Sun, Sand, Sea and Sex. Those images of The Garden of Eden and old fantasies of tropical paradise and constructions of radical difference are fundamental in understanding what fuels sex tourism and drives Caribbean consumers to sell their bodies to transnational/global consumers. At a micro-level, intimate interactions between tourists and locals reveal the reproduction of power relations while male Dominicans also show a sense of agency trying to take advantage of this situation by both emulating white male consumers and exaggerating stereotypes of hyper-masculinity. The findings aim at both contributing to the literature on transnational consumers and the growing research area in masculinity in our field.Selected Bibliography

REFERENCES

Albuquerque K. (1998), Sex, Beach Boys, and Female Tourists in the Caribbean, *Sexuality and Culture*, 2:87-111.

Belk R. W. (1994), Prostitution and AIDS in Thailand: sexual consumption a time of crisis, in *Asia Pacific Advances in Consumer Research*, Volume 1: 288-290.

Brennan D. (2004), *What's Love Got to Do With It? Transnational Desires and Sex Tourism in the Dominican Republic*, Durham and London: Duke University Press.

Cabezas A. L. (2004), Between Love and Money: Sex, Tourism, and Citizenship in Cuba and the Dominican Republic, *Signs,* 29(4): 987-1015.

Campbell Sh., Perkins A., and Mohammed P. (1999), "Come to Jamaica and Feel All Right": Tourism and the Sex Trade. In *Sun, Sex, and Gold: Tourism and Sex Work in the Caribbean*. Kamala Kempadoo, Ed. Lanham, MD: Rowman and Littlefield Publishers.

Canterbury D. (2005), Globalization, Inequality and Growth in the Caribbean, *Canadian Journal of Development Studies*, 26(4): 847-866.

Clarke C. (1983), Review: Colonialism and Its Social and Cultural Consequences in the Caribbean, *Journal of Latin American Studies*, 15(2):491-503.

Henshall M. (2005) Uncertain Images: Tourism Development and Seascapes of the Caribbean, In *Seductions of Place: Geographical Perspectives on Globalization and Touristed Landscapes*. Carolyn Cartier and Alan A. Lew, Eds. New York: Routledge.

Herold E., Garcia R., DeMoya T. (2001), Female Tourists and Beach Boys: Romance or Sex Tourism?, *Annals of Tourism Research*, 28(4): 2001.

Kaur Puar J. (2002), Circuits of Queer Mobility: Tourism, Travel, and Globalization, *GLQ*, 8(1-2):101-137

Kamala K. (2004), *Sexing the Caribbean: Gender, Race and Sexual Labor*, New York: Routledge.

Knippers Black, Jan 1997 Responsibility Without Authority: the Growing Burden for Women in the Caribbean. Review of Social Economy LV(2):235-242.

Lowry L. L. (1993) Sun, Sand, Sea & Sex; A Look at Tourism Advertising Through the Decoding and Interpretation of Four Typical Tourism Advertisements. Society of Travel and Tourism Educatiors Annual Conference, Miami, Florida, *Proceedings of Research and Academic Papers*, Volume V: 183-204.

Mullings B. (1999), Globalization, Tourism, and the International Sex Trade, In *Sun, Sex, and Gold: Tourism and Sex Work in the Caribbean*, Kamala Kempadoo, Ed. Lanham, MD: Rowman and Littlefield Publishers.

O'Connell D., Sanchez Taylor J. J. (1999), Fantasy Islands: Exploring the Demand for Sex Tourism, In *Sun, Sex, and Gold: Tourism and Sex Work in the Caribbean*, Kamala Kempadoo, Ed. Lanham, MD: Rowman and Littlefield Publishers.

Opperman, Martin 1999 Sex Tourism. Annals of Tourism Research 26(2): 251-266

Pattullo P. (2005), *Last Resorts: The Cost of Tourism in the Caribbean*, 2nd Edition, New York: Monthly Review Press.

Pruitt D. and LaFont S. (1995), For Love and Money: Romance Tourism in Jamaica, *Annals of Tourism Research*, 22:422-40.247-272.

Sanchez Taylor J. (2000), Tourism and 'Embodied' Commodities: Sex Tourism in the Caribbean, In *Tourism and Sex: Culture, Commerce and Coercion*, Stephen Clift and Simon Carter Eds. London; New York: Pinter.

Sanchez Taylor J. (2001), Dollars are a Girl's Best Friend? Female Tourists' Sexual Behavior in the Caribbean. *Sociology,* 35(3): 749-764

Shankar G. (1999), Where the Present is Haunted by the Past: Disarticulating Colonialism's Legacy in the Caribbean, *Cultural Dynamics*, 11:57-87.

Shawe, R. (2001), Fantasy Voyages: An Exploration of White Males' Participation in the Costa Rican Sex Tourism Industry, *The Berkeley McNair Research Journal*, 81-91.

Sharpe J., Pinto S. (2006) The Sweetest Taboo: Studies of Caribbean Sexualities; A Review Essay, *Signs: Journal of Women in Culture and Society*, 32(1):247-274

Sheller M. (2004), Natural Hedonism: the Invention of Caribbean Islands as Tropical Playgrounds, In *Tourism in the Caribbean*, Timothy Duval ed. London: Routledge.

Wonders N. A. and Michalowski R. (2001), Bodies, Borders, and Sex Tourism in a Globalized World: A Tale of Two Cities - Amsterdam and Havana, *Social Problems,* 48(4):545-71.

The effects of a brand recall on the recalled brand and its competitors

Sheila Goins, University of Iowa, USA
Catherine Cole, University of Iowa, USA
DongWoo Ko, University of Iowa, USA

THEORETICAL BACKGROUND

In prior research, manufacturer's reputation influences the extent to which consumers use extrinsic cues to make inferences (Purohit and Srivastava 2001, Dawar and Pillutal 2000). When reputation is good, consumers utilize negative information to revise attitudes, but when reputation is low, consumers don't revise their attitudes, because they interpret negative extrinsic cues as evidence consistent with their negative attitudes. So we expect that:

H1: *Product quality will moderate the effect of a recall on consumer brand evaluations such that when a low quality brand is recalled there will be no change in evaluations, but when a high quality brand is recalled there will be a decline in evaluations.*

Prior research examines how a firm's announcements affect the reputations of competitors (Goins and Gruca 2008). These competitive effects depend on the intensity of competitive rivalry. When competitive rivalry is high (e.g. brands are made from the same inputs), competitive effects are stronger than when competitive rivalry is low (e.g. brands are made from different inputs). Product quality may moderate further these competitive effects. When high quality brands are recalled, consumer may revise their judgments about low quality brands *upward*, especially if the brands are made from the same inputs. But, if low quality products are recalled, consumers may view the recall as confirming evidence about the known difference between high quality and low quality brands, regardless of whether inputs are shared or unique. We specify:

H2: *Shared inputs will moderate the competitive effect such that when a low quality brand is recalled, there will be no changes in the evaluations of the high quality brand, but when a high quality brand is recalled, the large positive increase in the evaluations of the low quality brand will be stronger when inputs are shared than when inputs are unique.*

EXPERIMENT 1

To test H1, we use a 3 level (recall condition: no recall, high quality brand recall and low quality brand recall) between subjects design, with 134 undergraduate participants randomly assigned to read one of three versions of a new camping e-magazine. The third section of the e-magazine contained reviews of fictional carabiners, describing one carabiner, made by the fictional F&G Company, as high quality and described another, made by the fictional QRB Company, as low quality. Then participants read about product recalls. In the control condition, they read about two recalls, but in the experimental conditions, participants read about an additional recall in which either F&G or QRB recalled their carabiners. As they were reading each section, respondents answered questions about the products and the e-magazine. At the end, participants again rated the quality of the reviewed products.

RESULTS

The pattern of results for the manipulation check suggests that we successfully manipulated carabiner quality. To test H1, the final carabiner evaluations were analyzed separately using one-way analysis of covariance variance (ANCOVA) with one between subjects factor (recall condition with three levels no recall, F&G carabiner recall and QRB carabiner recall), one covariate (initial evaluation) and the final carabiner evaluation. By including the initial evaluation of the brand, as a covariate, we are able to study judgment revision after a brand recall (As done by Pham and Muthukrishan 2002).

In the ANCOVA for the high quality carabiner evaluations, the covariate (first evaluations ($F(1,129)=14.18$, $p<.01$)) and the recall conditions $F(2,129)=4.8$, $p<.01$) were significant. Specifically, the F&G high quality carabiner evaluations are lower after the F&G carabiner is recalled than after there is no recall (4.01 vs. 3.60, $t=2.60$, $p<.01$). Similarly, in the ANNCOVA for the low quality carabiner evaluations, the covariate (first evaluations ($F(1,129)=87.56$, $p<.01$) and the recall conditions were significant (($F2,129)=4.97$, $p<.01$). However, there is not a significant decline in QRB carabiner evaluations after the QRB brand is recalled when compared to the evaluations in the no recall condition. Consequently, consistent with H1, product quality moderates the effects of a product recall such that when a high quality brand is recalled, there is a large negative effect on brand evaluations, but when a low quality brand is recalled, there is no effect of on low quality brand evaluations.

EXPERIMENT 2

We investigate whether the intensity of competitive rivalry and product quality moderate the competitive effects (H2). We use the same methodology as in Experiment 1, but manipulate competitive rivalry in the recall announcement. Participants either learned that inputs for all carabiner manufacturers are the same or that they are unique. Our experimental design is a one way design with 5 conditions (QRB recall-inputs shared; QRB recall inputs unique, F&G recall-inputs shared, F&G recall inputs unique, no recall).

Consistent with H2, shared inputs moderate the interaction between product quality and competitive effects. When competitive rivalry is high (inputs are shared), the evaluations of the low quality carabiners are *higher* when the high quality carabiner is recalled than in the no recall condition (5.39 vs. 4.34, $t=2.33$, $p<.02$). However, this same competitive effect is not observed in the unique inputs conditions. Additionally as stated in H2, a low quality brand recall does not affect the evaluations of a high quality brand, whether inputs are unique or shared.

DISCUSSION AND FUTURE RESEARCH DIRECTIONS

We find evidence that brand quality is critical in understanding brand recall effects. We find that lower quality brands suffer less than higher quality brands. Additionally, we find that brand quality moderates competitive effects so that when a high quality brand is recalled, the low quality brand evaluation increases, but only if inputs are shared and when a low quality brand is recalled, there is no change in high quality brand evaluations. In a 3rd planned study, we will consider the effects of a recall on other brands in the same brand family (transfer effects).

BIBLIOGRAPHY

Dawar, Niraj and Madan M. Pillutla (2000), "Impact Of Product-Harm Crises On Brand Equity: The Moderating Role Of Consumer Expectations," Journal of Marketing Research, 37(May), 215-226.

Goins, Sheila and Thomas Gruca (2008), "Understanding Competitive and Contagion Effects of Layoff Announcements," Corporate Reputation Review, 11(1):12-34.

Pham, Michael Tuan and A.V. Muthukrishnan (2002)," Search and Align in Judgment Revision: Implications for Brand Positioning, " *Journal of Marketing Research,* 39(1), 18-30.

Purohit, D. and Srivastava, J. (2001), "Effect of manufacturer reputation, retailer reputation and product warranty on consumer judgments of product quality: A cue diagnosticity framework," *Journal of Consumer Psychology*, 10, 123-134.

Twice the Vice

Lauren Trabold, Baruch College, CUNY Graduate Center, USA
Lauren Block, Baruch College, USA

Extant literature has often studied consumer goal pursuit, particularly in the area of self-control. This stream of research has frequently examined the pattern of consumer behavior when a person is faced with a choice between a goal-consistent and a goal-inconsistent option. Research has suggested that consumers establish a reference point based upon their self-control goal to which each choice option is compared in order to determine which choice is most consistent with their goal (Hoch and Lowenstein, 1991). Research has also studied consumers' affective response, suggesting that the choice of a goal inconsistent option will yield feelings of guilt and a goal consistent option will yield feelings of satisfaction and self-efficacy (Giner-Sorolla, 2001; Ramanathan and Williams, 2007). A common operationalization of this choice is in the context of a health goal, in which a person is given a choice between an unhealthy and healthy option such as chocolate cake and fruit salad. Given a reference point of healthiness, the fruit salad is clearly the goal-consistent choice and the chocolate cake, the goal inconsistent choice. Not surprisingly, greater guilt is experienced when a consumer chooses the chocolate cake rather than the fruit salad. Anticipation of guilt will be a driving factor in a person's ensuing willpower. Consumers make judgments about their own willpower and self-efficacy based upon their previous consumption decisions and regularly use past decisions as a precedent for how to behave when faced with a similar situation (Benabou and Tirole, 2004). If a consumer acts inconsistently with his/her goal, he/she not only risk relying on such indiscretions in the future as a precedent for further indulgence, but also will experience immediate feelings of guilt.

The current study seeks to extend this literature by observing how consumers will make a decision when they are not given an opportunity to behave consistently with their goal. Specifically, we observe the way that consumers will utilize different decision strategies to make a choice when faced with two equally goal-inconsistent options (e.g., a consumer with a health goal faced with a choice between two decadent desserts). Literature suggests that consumer choice may differ dependent upon the decision strategy used, namely, whether they select the option they want or reject the option they don't want (Shafir, 1993). By presenting two equivalently goal-inconsistent options, we hypothesize that without a goal-relevant reference point by which to compare the options, consumers will decide based upon their preference; we explore whether or not instructions to select or reject from the goal-inconsistent options will moderate whether consumers choose their least or most preferred option. We anticipated that consumers should reject their favorite item immediately and thus choose their least preferred option, whereas selection may encourage them to rationalize that each option is equally goal-inconsistent and therefore allow them to justify choosing their favorite option. Moreover, we expected participants to feel less guilt when consuming their less-preferred option relative to those consuming their favorite option. Thus, while consumers in this situation are faced with imminent goal failure, they may be able to establish a reference point that will allow them to minimize their guilt.

We conducted a 2 (goal: self-control vs. indulgence) x 2(decision strategy: select vs. reject) between subjects study. All subjects were asked to rank order a list of 10 desserts based on preference and were subsequently given a choice between their first and second ranked items. Prior to making a choice, subjects were either asked to imagine a scenario about dieting to fit into a new outfit for your high school reunion (self-control goal) or to imagine a scenario in which they are pampering themselves prior to their high school reunion and have decided to indulge at a restaurant (indulgence goal). Additionally, participants were randomly assigned to make their decision by either selecting ("Please select the dessert you want to order") or rejecting ("Please reject the dessert you do NOT want to order") one of the options. Nutrition information provided suggested that the two desserts were approximately equivalent in caloric value. After making their choice, participants were asked a variety of questions including how guilty they felt for their choice.

Findings thus far have strongly supported our hypotheses. Analysis revealed a mediated moderation suggesting that the influence of goal type (self-control or indulgence) on choice is moderated by the subjects' decision strategy (select or reject) ($p < .05$) and the influence of rejecting on those with a self-control goal on choice is mediated by feelings of guilt ($p < .01$). Subjects with a self-control goal (vs. an indulgence goal) that rejected the dessert they did not want (vs. selected the dessert they did want) were significantly more likely to choose their less preferred dessert option than those in the other three experimental conditions. Interestingly, these subjects also perceived their choice to be less indulgent ($p < .01$), although study instructions clearly indicated that the caloric value was approximately equal. Notably, these participants also experienced less post-consumption guilt over their goal failure than subjects in the other three conditions.

Our study provides an interesting account in which consumers are able to minimize their guilt in the face of imminent self-control goal failure by using a rejection strategy, ultimately resulting in the counterintuitive choice of a less preferred, yet equally goal inconsistent option.

REFERENCES

Benabou, Roland and Jean Tirole (2004), "Willpower and Personal Rules," *Journal of Personal Economy*, 112 (4), 848-886.

Giner-Sorolla, Roger (2001), "Guilty Pleasures and Grim Necessities: Affective Attitudes in Dilemmas of Self-Control," *Journal of Personality and Social Psychology*, 80 (2), 206-221.

Hoch, Stephen J. and George F. Lowenstein (1991), "Time Inconsistent Preferences and Consumer Self-Control," *Journal of Consumer Research*, 17 (4), 492-507.

Ramanathan, Suresh and Patti Williams (2007), "Immediate and Delayed Emotional Consequences of Indulgence: The Moderating Influence of Personality Type on Mixed Emotions," *Journal of Consumer Research*, 34, 212-223.

Shafir, Eldar (1993), "Choosing Versus Rejecting - Why Some Options Are Both Better And Worse Than Others," *Memory & Cognition*, 21 (4), 546-56.

Differences in Brand-Related User-Generated Content Across Three Social Media Sites: An Inductive Content Analysis

Andrew N. Smith, York University, Canada
Eileen Fischer, York University, Canada
Chen Yongjian, York University, Canada

Consumers today are spending more time on social media sites than ever before (Radwanick 2011). As they engage with these sites – including Facebook, Twitter, and YouTube – many become involved in the process of creating, modifying, and consuming user-generated content (UGC). UGC is an increasingly important means through which consumers express themselves and communicate with others online (boyd and Ellison 2008); it may be thought of as published content that demonstrates a degree of creative effort that is produced "outside of professional routines and practices" (OECD 2007; Kaplan and Haenlein 2010, 61). Facebook 'wall' posts, status updates, and posted photos, tweets on Twitter, and consumer-produced videos and comments on YouTube are some of the many forms UGC takes on. UGC may be facilitated by firms, or produced more spontaneously by consumers (Berthon, Pitt & Campbell 2008; Christodoulides 2009), while occasionally referencing brands and products.

Academic marketing research on UGC, while still nascent (Burmann 2010), has investigated a number of aspects of UGC, including motivations behind its creation (Daugherty, Eastin and Bright 2008), its value to firms (Dhar and Chang 2009; JPRM09), and its connection to brand communities (Muñiz and Schau 2007). Daugherty, Eastin and Bright's (2008) work is distinct in that it incorporates data about multiple types of UGC, such as videos, pictures, audio, and blogs, whereas other marketing studies typically examine a single type of UGC, or UGC originating from a particular site. However, as their focus is on motivations to produce UGC, Daugherty, Eastin and Bright (2008) provide limited insight into the distinctive characteristics of the UGC that is created in different social media channels; moreover, their focus is not exclusively on brand-related UGC, arguably the form of greatest interest to marketing and consumer researchers. Our study thus goes beyond prior research to compare and contrast the content of brand-related UGC posted on three of the most popular social media sites: Facebook, Twitter, and YouTube. Our work builds on prior research to make two valuable contributions. First, it provides a grounded framework that illuminates similarities and differences in the content that consumers create when they make posts that refer to brands. Second, it helps us to better understand how specific social media may influence or shape the brand-related messages that consumers create (cf. McLuhan 1964).

Facebook, Twitter and YouTube were chosen for this research because they are among the most popular social media sites for consumers and marketers, and because they belong to different social media niches: Facebook is a social network; Twitter is a microblogging application; and, YouTube is a content community. Each site encourages UGC of different forms, from 140-character tweets to posted photos to 8-minute videos. The data for this study consists of 600 brand-related UGC posts – 200 from each of Facebook, Twitter, and Youtube – for two brands: Lululemon and American Apparel. The posts, which were published between June, 2010 and January, 2011, were selected at random from Google search results for: 'brand' on 'site": (e.g.) 'Facebook.com'. The two brands were selected because they generate enough interest from consumers to be featured in UGC, and are in the same category: clothing manufacturing and retailing. Moreover, one brand (Lululemon) has had no major scandals or challenges, while the other (American Apparel) has come under negative scrutiny for various reasons. The project comprised three steps. Initially, a coding scheme was created inductively by the three authors who analyzed posts on each medium for both brands. The main dimensions for coding (all binary, except for valence) were whether the post reflected: consumer self-promotion; brand centrality of either Lululemon or American Apparel; presence of multiple brands; communications directed to the company; communications responding to company actions; information about the brand; and/or valenced evaluations of the brand.

Next, each post was manually coded by an independent coder, and one member of the research team, using the inductively developed coding scheme. Intercoder reliability, as calculated using Perreault and Leigh's (1989) formula, was approximately 0.9, falling within the accepted range of 0.8 to 1.0; any discrepancies in coding were examined and adjudicated by a second member of the research team.

Finally, coding frequencies were tabulated, and statistical differences were assessed using Chi-square tests. Prior to testing for differences between content on the three media sites, Chi-square analyses were run between brands, along each of the coded dimensions, to test for homogeneity. Since between-brand differences were detected, comparisons across the three media sites were run separately for the posts for the two brands.

Our findings reveal a number of differences in UGC across the three channels. For example, consumer self-promotion was most common in YouTube UGC and least common in Twitter UGC, reinforcing YouTube's slogan of 'Broadcast Yourself.' Across both brands, YouTube UGC was least likely to focus centrally on the brand of interest and was most likely to feature it alongside a constellation of other brands. For Lululemon, Youtube UGC was least likely to be used to communicate with the company (for American Apparel, no form of UGC was used to communicate with the company, which may reflect the ambivalent attitude that many consumers have with the brand's founder, and the company's social media engagement strategy). For both brands, YouTube was least likely to be used to respond to some company action made online or offline. These findings convey that, while the medium is not, strictly speaking, the message, the different social media sites and their unique cultures foster variance in the brand-related content generated by the consumers who use each medium. Our research offers other scholars a preliminary scheme upon which they may build when seeking to understand differences in brand-related UGC, and insights into the factors (characteristics of medium, as well as the perceptions and actions of the company) that shape UGC in particular ways.

REFERENCES

Berthon, Pierre, Leyland Pitt and Colin Campbell (2008), "Ad Lib: When Customers Create the Ad," *California Management Review*, 50 (4), 6-30.

Boyd, Danah M. and Nicole B. Ellison (2008), "Social Network Sites: Definition, History, and Scholarship," *Journal of Computer-Mediated Communication*, 13, 210-230.

Burgess, Jean and Joshua Green (2009), *YouTube (Digital Media and Society Series)*. Cambridge, UK: Polity Press.

Burmann, Christoph (2010), "A Call for 'User-Generated Branding'," *Journal of Brand Management*, 18 (1), 1-4.

Christodoulides, George (2009), "Branding in the Post-Internet Era," *Marketing Theory*, 9 (1), 141-144.

Dhar, Vasant and Elaine A. Chang (2009), "Does Chatter Matter? The Impact of User-Generated Content on Music Sales," *Journal of Interactive Marketing*, 23, 300-307.

Daugherty, Terry, Matthew S. Eastin, and Laura Bright (2008), "Exploring Consumer Motivations for Creating User-Generated Content," *Journal of Interactive Advertising*, 8 (2), 16-25.

Ghose, Anindya and Panagiotis Ipeirotis (2010), "The EconoMining Project at NYU: Studying the Economic Value of User-Generated Content on the Internet," *Journal of Revenue and Pricing Management*, 8 (2/3), 241-246.

Jansen, Bernard J., Mimi Chang, Kate Sobel, and Abdur Chowdury (2009), "Twitter Power: Tweets as Electronic Word of Mouth," *Journal of the American Society for Information Science and Technology*, 60 (11), 2169-2188.

Kaplan, Andreas M. and Michael Haenlein (2010), "Users of the World, Unite! The Challenges and Opportunities of Social Media," *Business Horizons*, 53, 59-68.

MacLuhan, Marshall (1964), *Understanding Media: The Extensions of Man.* Mentor: New York.

Marwick, Alice E. and danah boyd (2011), "I Tweet Honestly, I Tweet Passionately: Twitter Users, Context Collapse, and the Imagined Audience," *New Media & Society*, 13 (1), 114-133.

Muñiz, Albert M. (Jr.) and Hope Jensen Schau (2007), "Vigilante Marketing and Consumer-Created Communications," *Journal of Advertising*, 36 (3), 35-50.

OECD (2007), *Participative Web and User-Created Content: Web 2.0, Wikis, and Social Networking*. Paris: Organisation for Economic Co-operation and Development.Perrault , William D. (Jr.) and Laurence E. Leigh (1989), "Reliability of Nominal Data Based on Qualitative Judgments," *Journal of Marketing Research*, XXVI (May), 135-148.

Radwanick, Sarah (2011), "U.S. Digital Year in Review 2010: A Recap of the Year in Digital Media," *ComScore Inc. White Paper*, February. Accessible at: http://www.comscore.com/Press_Events/Presentations_Whitepapers/2011/2010_US_Digital_Year_in_Review

Shape-Shifters: Exploring Dynamic Culture Through The Shaping of Bicultural Identity

Akon Ekpo, University of Illinois at Chicago, USA

The growing number of individuals with mixed cultural identities in the global workforce and consuming market has given rise to the awareness of and opportunities to understand biculturals and their role in the global market. Bicultural individuals are typically described as people who have internalized two cultures to the extent that both cultures are alive inside of them (Hong, Morris, Chiu, & Benet-Martinez, 2000). They are people who have deeply internalized, and operate fluidly between, two or more distinct cultural meaning systems, inherently carrying with them critical intercultural adaptability skills that guide their thoughts, feelings, and subsequently their behavior (M. Brannen, Garcia, & Thomas, 2009; Hong, et al., 2000). However, the small number of studies on biculturalism in the international marketing and management contexts have mainly focused on the adaptability skills, cultural knowledge, and metacognitions of bicultural individuals (M. Y. Brannen, 2009), assuming a fairly static perspective of culture.

Even though biculturalism is relatively new to the international marketing field, it has been examined more so from the social psychology discipline. Hong et al.'s (2000) study on Westernized Chinese students in Hong Kong found that cultural icons have the ability to prime bicultural individuals, in which a particular cultural identity is readily accessible and promote cultural frame switching (Hong, et al., 2000). Furthermore, Briley & Wyer (2001) found that even though chronically accessible cultural values and norms may influence a particular cultural identity, transitory situational factors may also activate cultural values that may be inconsistent with a person's cultural inclinations (Briley & Wyer Jr, 2001); furthermore, these activated cultural values may impact individuals' judgment or decision behaviors. Benet-Martinez et al (2002) empirically examined how bicultural individuals managed and negotiated their dual cultural identities, and found that Chinese-American biculturals who perceived their cultural identities as compatible (high bicultural identity integration or BII) responded in culturally congruent ways to cultural cues (Benet-Martinez, Leu, Lee, & Morris, 2002). However, Chinese-American biculturals who perceived their cultural identities as oppositional (low BII) exhibited a reverse priming effect (i.e. responded to cultural cues that were directly inconsistent with cultural norms). Finally, Lau-Gesk (2003) found that biculturals responded favorably to values-promoting appeals that were congruent with the activated cultural disposition; and the response differed among individuals based on whether they tended to compartmentalize or blend the two cultures (Lau-Gesk, 2003). Taken together, these studies suggest the need for a more *dynamic* view of culture.

To explore this dynamic perspective, this study proposes to understand meaning making of the bicultural identity. Specifically, the aim here is to understand the meanings bicultural consumers attach to their social identity through food consumption, in an effort to illustrate how one's culture is shaped by the socio-cultural environment. Studies have shown that food consumption is at the heart of most ethnic cultures and carries cultural meanings (Wallendorf & Reilly, 1983). However, unlike prior studies that focus on cultural meanings of food, this study focuses on the (consumption) experience to understand meanings of the bicultural identity. Because experiences are inherently dynamic, by focusing on bicultural consumers' consumption experiences, this study is able to capture the dynamic nature of culture. As such, this study seeks to understand how bicultural consumers make sense of their consumption experience by exploring their meaning interpretations to which they act/react in constructing their identities.

Meaning making has a long history in consumer research in which the investigator attempts to get at the how's and why's of consumer behavior. Meaning making is the process by which consumers interpret and make sense of their environment. It provides an understanding of the environment from the consumer's perspective. Understanding meanings are important because they provide the individual with a framework to which people then act/react. In this sense, meanings are causal. Much of the research has focused on the meanings of monocultural consumers, who may see things differently than bicultural consumers. Given the prevalence of bicultural individuals, it is important to understand the perspectives of these individuals as they have gone under researched, and may paint an incomplete picture of the importance of the consumption context in consumer behavior. Therefore, this study has theoretical implications for understanding culture as dynamic (versus static), provide deeper understanding of biculturals as it relates to their consumption experiences, and highlights the potential differences and similarities between different types of consumers.

To begin to explore the research objectives, a small pilot study of two bicultural informants (both non-American born, 1 African and 1 Hispanic descent) was conducted using structured interviews, lasting 2 to 2-1/2 hours each, participation during consumption with informants, observations (of food orders, interactions within social setting, site descriptions), and informant diaries (their thoughts, reasons for consuming particular foods, and feelings about their consumption experiences), over the course of two months. Observational data was collected at the sites where informants consumed and/or prepared food, which included: restaurants, at the homes of the informant, and cafeterias/cafes. Preliminary findings showed that informants' food consumption experiences were colored by the social environment, in which interactions with others in the consumption setting invoked cultural values and customs from their respective cultures. During these experiences informants described how the consumption environment invoked fond memories of being "at home" (i.e. native country), being amongst friends and family back home, having pride in one's culture, and dreaming of going back home. During their consumption experiences, both informants described how they became more aware of their ability to function in both the American and non-American cultures and that their sense of self "shifted" depending on the consumption setting.

While this study is still in its preliminary stages, these finding suggest some evidence that the shifts between cultures by bicultural individuals are invoked through the social context and the interactions amongst individuals within the consumption setting. This shifting between cultures paints a more dynamic picture of culture that is driven by social cues in as much by psychological cues. Although identity and identification has been studied as an internal (cognitive) process, it is equally (if not more) an external interaction (i.e. social) process as well.

REFERENCES

Benet-Martinez, V., Leu, J., Lee, F., & Morris, M. (2002). Negotiating biculturalism: Cultural frame switching in biculturals with oppositional versus compatible cultural identities. *Journal of Cross-Cultural Psychology, 33*(5), 492.

Brannen, M., Garcia, D., & Thomas, D. (2009). *Biculturals as natural bridges for intercultural communication and collaboration.* Paper presented at the 2009 International Workshop on Intercultural Collaboration (IWIC), New York, NY, USA.

Brannen, M. Y. (2009). Culture in Context: New Theorizing for Today's Complex Cultural Organization. In C. Nakata (Ed.), *Beyond Hofstede: Culture Frameworks for Global Marketing and Management.* New York: Palgrave.

Briley, D., & Wyer Jr, R. (2001). Transitory determinants of values and decisions: The utility (or nonutility) of individualism and collectivism in understanding cultural differences. *Social Cognition, 19*(3: Special issue), 197-227.

Hong, Y., Morris, M., Chiu, C., & Benet-Martinez, V. (2000). Multicultural minds: A dynamic constructivist approach to culture and cognition. *American Psychologist, 55*(7), 709-720.

Lau-Gesk, L. (2003). Activating culture through persuasion appeals: An examination of the bicultural consumer. *Journal of Consumer Psychology, 13*(3), 301-315.

Wallendorf, M., & Reilly, M. D. (1983). Ethnic Migration, Assimilation, and Consumption. *The Journal of Consumer Research, 10*(3), 292-302.

Nestle and Tastle: The Effect of Phonetic Similarity in Brand Name Innovation

Ann Kronrod, Massachusetts Institute of Technology, USA
Tina M. Lowrey, University of Texas at San Antonio, USA
Mark Nespoli, University of Texas at San Antonio, USA

Selection of an effective brand name is perhaps one of the most important decisions a marketing manager must make. Of course, there are many factors that affect such a decision (product category, cultural connotations, competition, etc.) One that is sometimes overlooked is phonetic sound. Past research has shown that how a brand name sounds can have a profound effect on how it is perceived and evaluated. For example, research by Chisnall (1974); Lowrey, et al. (2003); Myers-Levy et al., (1994); and Peterson and Ross (1972) has demonstrated that perceived phonetic fit between brand name and product category can increase product recall, preference, and inference.

Oftentimes, managers, especially those of international brands, prefer to select names that have no meaning in any language so as to avoid any unintended connotations. The focus of this research is to examine the effects that phonetic similarity and familiarity can have on the preference and evaluation of such "non-word" brand names. Kohli, Harich, and Leuthesser (2005) found that repeated exposure to a non-word brand name increases evaluations of its quality and other attributes (perhaps due to Zajonc's "mere exposure effect," 1968). Likewise, a number of studies have shown that when presented with a name similar to their own, that name is preferred by people more than less similar names (Jiang, et al., 2010; Burger, et al., 2004; Gueguen, 2003; and Brendl, et al., 2005).

Research on linguistic innovation proposes the Optimal Innovation Hypothesis (Giora, Fein, Kronrod et al 2004), according to which an optimally innovative stimulus that induces a novel response while allowing for the recovery of a salient one (Giora, 1997b, 2003) would be rated as more pleasing than both a more and less familiar stimulus. We test this hypothesis in relation to brand name innovation, predicting that new, non-word brand names that are highly similar to or highly distant from non-word brand names of disliked products will elicit more negative evaluations in terms of liking and WOM and purchase intentions than those that are moderately similar. Similarly, when a familiar, non-word brand name is associated with a negative attribute of a firm, we predict that a moderately similar variant would elicit more negative evaluations than more similar and distant variants and vice versa when the familiar non-word brand name is associated with a positive firm attribute.

PRETEST

A set of 30 non-word brand names were generated, each with a similar, a moderate, and a distant variant. Participants rated the original names for familiarity and valence and listed any thoughts that came to mind when they thought about each. The originals were then paired with each of their three variants, and the pairs were then rated for similarity. The ten originals (and their variants) that best exhibited the expected pattern in terms of similarity (highly similar, moderately similar, and distantly similar), were neutral in valence, and roughly equivalent in terms of familiarity; were selected for use in Studies 1 and 2.

STUDY 1

Familiarity with originals was manipulated via repeated, randomized exposure (four times each) and completion of three cognitive ordering tasks. Participants then rated their level of familiarity as a manipulation check. They then rated each of the variants in randomized order for degree of liking, purchase likelihood, and likelihood of recommendation to a friend. Of the 30 variants, they then selected the 10 they believed to: (a) belong to the most credible companies, (b) represent the most enjoyable products, (c) last the longest, (d) be the most popular, and (e) be the finalists they would recommend to a company to have as finalists for the perfect brand name. Participants then completed involvement and innovativeness scales, as well as PANAS. As expected, similarity elevated positive attitudes towards the new brand name in terms of liking, credibility evaluation, WOM intention and purchase intention.

STUDY 2

The 10 original brand names employed in Study 1 were divided into two groups, positive and negative, according to one of three attributes of the firm: the use of environmentally-friendly (unfriendly) materials, ethical (corrupt) management practices, and an excellent (poor) return policy. The same overall procedure from Study 1 was implemented. Supporting the Optimal Innovation Hypothesis, Repeated-measures ANOVAs revealed an inverted U-shaped pattern, where for liked names, highly similar and highly distant variants were significantly less favored in terms of liking, purchase intention and WOM intention, compared to moderately similar variants of these brands. For disliked names, however, a U-shape relationship emerged, with the moderately similar variants being significantly less favored than the highly similar and the highly distant variants of these brand names.

SUMMARY

This research is an attempt to clarify the question of brand name innovation in marketplace. Highly-controlled experimental design allows us to evaluate the contribution of new brand name similarity to a familiar brand name. We find that new brand names that are moderately similar to familiar liked brand names receive higher evaluations in terms of liking and WOM and purchase intentions than those that are both more close and distant phonetically (optimal innovation effect). However, when the familiar brand name is associated with a negative firm attribute, the effect is reversed, with the moderately similar new brand name being less favored than both the phonetically close and distant new brand names. In continuation to this line of research we will employ a field experiment design to validate our laboratory results in more realistic conditions.

REFERENCES

Brendl, C. Miguel, Amitava Chattopadhyay, Brett W. Pelham, and Mauricio Carvallo (2005), "Name Letter Branding: Valence Transfers When Product Specific Needs Are Active," *Journal of Consumer Research*, 32 (3), 405-15.

Burger, Jerry M., Nicole Messian, Shebani Patel, Alicia del Prado, and Carmen Anderson (2004), "What a Coincidence! The Effects of Incidental Similarity on Compliance," *Personality and Social Psychology Bulletin*, 30 (1), 35-43.

Chisnall, Peter M. (1974), "Aluminum Household Foil in the Common Market: Research for an Effective Brand Name," *Journal of Management Studies*, 11 (1), 246-55.

Gioria, Rachel (1997), "Understanding Figurative and Literal Language: The Graded Salience Hypothesis," *Cognitive Linguistics*, 7 (1), 183-206.

Gioria, Rachel (2003), *On Our Mind: Salience, Context and Figurative Language*, New York, NY: Oxford University Press.

Gioria, Rachel, Ofer Fein, Ann Kronrod, Idit Elnatan, Noa Shuval, and Adi Zur (2004), "Weapons of Mass Distraction: Optimal Innovation and Pleasure Ratings," *Metaphor and Symbol*, 19 (2), 115-41.

Gueguen, Nicolas (2003), "Help in the Web: The Effect of the Same First Name between the Sender and the Receptor in a Request Made by Email.," *Journal of Consumer Research*, 53 (3), 459-66.

Jiang, Lan, Joandrea Hoegg, Darren W. Dahl, and Amitava Chattopadhyay (2010), "The Persuasive Role of Incidental Similarity on Attitudes and Purchase Intentions in a Sales Context," *The Journal of Consumer Research*, 36 (5), 778-91.

Kohli, Chiranjeev S., Katrin R. Harich, and Lance Leuthesser (2005), "Creating Brand Identity: A Study of Evaluation of New Brand Names," *Journal of Business Research*, 58 (11), 1506-15.

Lowrey, Tina M., L.J. Shrum, and Tony M. Dubitsky (2003), "The Relation between Brand-Name Linguistic Characteristics and Brand-Name Memory," *Journal Of Advertising*, 32 (3), 7-17.

Meyers-Levy, Joan, Therese A. Louie, and Mary T. Curren (1994), "How Does the Congruity of Brand Names Affect Evaluations of Brand Name Extensions?," *Journal of Applied Psychology*, 79 (1), 46-53.

Peterson, Robert A. and Ivan Ross (1972), "How to Name New Brands," *Journal of Advertising Research*, 12 (6), 29-34.

Zajonc, Robert B. (1968), "Attitudinal Effects of Mere Exposure," *Journal of Personality and Social Psychology*, 9 (2), 1-27.

More than New, Creative Design Solution: Factors Necessary for Delivering a Creative Design in the New Product Development Process

JaeHwan Kwon, University of Iowa, USA
Moonkyu Lee, Yonsei University, South Korea
Hae-Ryong Kim, KonKuk University, South Korea

Many companies are struggling with successful new products development. As pointed out by Brethauer (2002), only a small percentage of new products released into the market are successful, and the creative design of a product is one of the most critical elements in the successful launching of a new product. The importance of creative design in new products has often been emphasized. Nevertheless, surprisingly little research has examined design creativity in the NPD process. In the present research, we explore the factors influencing design creativity of a new product and their relationships.

Although previous studies emphasized the relationship between firm- (e.g., market orientation)/project-level (e.g., team characteristics) variables and creativity in the NPD context (**Im and Workman, 2004; Sethi, Smith, and Park, 2001), the role of individual-level variables has not been considered.** In this study, we adopt a designer's ability factor as an independent variable and the output, design creativity, as dependent variable. So that we can answer our research question: do creative designers necessarily translate into creative designs?

In today's business, the design solutions of new products come from the interactions of individual designers (Kristensson and Norlander, 2003). Thus, we follow the view proposed by Burroughs and Mick (2004); we adopt the person-situation perspective from social psychology (e.g., Higgins, 1990). Specifically, this research focuses on defining the roles of the three person-based variables (analogical thinking ability, perceived length of experience, and self-confidence) and one situation-based variable (team culture).

Our hypotheses are as follows:

H_1: *Higher analogical thinking ability of a designer will increase the design creativity of a new product.*

H_2: *Higher self-confidence to produce a creative design will increase design creativity.*

H_3: *Self-confidence will mediate a positive relationship between analogical thinking ability and design creativity.*

H_4: *The effect of analogical thinking ability on self-confidence will be stronger when a designer's perceived length of experience is higher rather than lower.*

H_5: *The effect of self-confidence on design creativity will be stronger when team culture encourages creativity.*

This study has two different parts: one experiment with 164 design school students and another with 164 consumers. In the first part, we measure all independent variables and collect each participant's photocopy of the design output from his/her previous team project. In the second part of the study, another group of participants (consumers) is asked to evaluate the design creativity of the photocopies (dependent variables). As a result, this study is able to be free from the effect of common method bias. Also, in this way, design creativity of a new product can be examined from a consumer's perspective, not from a designer's perspective.

Upon analysis, we first conducted two-stage regression analysis to test the mediating effect of self-confidence between ATA (analogical thinking ability) and design creativity. Support for the mediating effect was expected to emerge in the last procedure of four consecutive regression procedures. ATA positively affected self-confidence (Procedure 1: $\beta = .492$, $t = 7.193$, $p < .001$), and both ATA and self-confidence positively influenced design creativity (Procedure 2: $\beta = .394$, $t = 5.462$, $p < .001$, and Procedure 3: $\beta = .356$, $t = 4.852$, $p < .001$). In the Procedure 4, however, the coefficient of ATA was insignificant ($\beta = -.005$, $t = -.553$, p, NS), while that of self-confidence was significant ($\beta = .136$, $t = 3.699$, $p < .001$). It was, therefore, substantiated that self-confidence has a full mediating effect between ATA and design creativity. Consequently, H_2 and H_3 were supported, but H_1 was rejected.

For testing H_4—the moderating effect of PLE (perceived length of experience) between ATA and self-confidence, Aiken and West's (1991) regression analysis was conducted. Actual length of experience was included as a control variable. Support for our predictions was emerged in the form of interaction between ATA and PLE ($\beta = .252$, $t = 3.355$, $p < .001$). Also, the effect of ATA on self-confidence was significant ($\beta = .675$, $t = 5.839$, $p < .001$), while the effect of PLE was not ($\beta = -.063$, $t = -1.068$, NS). Thus, it was proven that the effect of ATA on self-confidence was greater when PLE was higher rather than lower.

H_5 (the moderating effect of team culture between self-confidence and design creativity) was proven true through beta-slope tests. The effect of self-confidence on design creativity was greater when team culture was individuality-oriented, as opposed to collectivity-oriented ($t = 2.137$, $p < .05$).

The present study extends our understanding of the underlying process in which design creativity can be promoted both by the individual designer's traits and perceptions and by the design team's culture during NPD projects. Our findings contribute to research on creativity in broader contexts, as well as to on the qualified context of design creativity in the NPD. Most of the extant research on creativity has focused on the effect of analogical thinking ability on person's creativity, not on the outcome of creative process. By examining the effect of analogical thinking ability on the creativity of an outcome, we show that the ability has more direct relationship with an outcome. More importantly, we find that self-confidence should be accompanied for a creative outcome. Given that the most likely response to a new idea will be extremely negative, one needs high self-confidence to believe that he or she is right and that the rest of the world is wrong (Martindale, 1989).

However, there was little empirical evidence to the extent that individual differences in self-confidence affect creativity of an outcome. In the current study, we demonstrate that self-confidence is motivated by analogical thinking ability, and that it facilitates creative outcome.

This research also shows that both person and situation variables affect creativity in NPD settings. Burroughs and Mick (2004) showed that both influence creativity in the problem-solving settings. By extending the applicable settings, we suggest that research on creativity be approached from the person-situation perspective.

Individual Differences in Interpersonal Touch: Development of the "Comfort with Interpersonal Touch" Scale

Joann Peck, University of Wisconsin - Madison, USA
Andrea Webb, University of Wisconsin - Madison, USA

Communication is one of the cornerstones of the marketing field. While the marketing literature has heavily investigated various communication strategies between channel members, consumers, etc., nonverbal communication, specifically communication through touch, is often neglected. We often think of organizations or business units as forming alliances and partnerships, but it is really *individuals* who are interacting to form these relationships. This underscores the criticality of understanding individual preferences in communication, especially as it relates to the sense of touch.

The sense of touch can influence product decisions (McCabe and Nowlis 2003; Peck and Childers 2003a,b, 2006; Peck and Shu 2009); yet, we know relatively little about interpersonal touch, especially as it varies across individuals and cultures. This paper seeks to develop a measure of individual difference in touch, the Comfort with Interpersonal Touch (CIT) Scale. This paper is the foundation for a larger stream of research to investigate cultural- and business-specific interpersonal touch norms.

Previous research has shown that interpersonal touch can be persuasive and can greatly influence our perceptions. Some researchers suggest that more than half of the variability of response in interpersonal communication can be attributed to nonverbal factors such as touch (Mehrabian 1981). In a study done by Fisher, Rytting, and Heslin (1976), a university library clerk inadvertently touched the hand of students, and those who were touched rated the librarian, as well as the university's library facilities, more positively than those who were not touched. This effect was found even for students who hadn't noticed the touch. Interpersonal touch has also been shown to increase compliance. Hornik (1992) had an in-store marketer touch customers lightly on the upper arm, and those touched were found to be more compliant in both sampling and buying a new product. In related research, individuals who were asked to sign a petition were found to be more compliant if they were briefly touched (Willis and Hamm 1980), and shoppers who were touched were more willing to participate in mall intercept interviews (Hornik and Ellis 1988). Previous studies also show that restaurant servers who briefly touched customers received larger tips than servers who did not touch (Crusco and Wetzel 1984; Hornik 1992; Stephen and Zweigenhaft 1986). Thus, brief interpersonal touch in social exchanges can have significant effects on our perceptions. However, like product touch, some individuals are more comfortable with both touching and being touched in a social situation. We expect this individual difference to moderate the persuasive effects of interpersonal touch. As yet, there is no comprehensive scale to measure an individual's comfort with interpersonal touch.

We believe that there are five latent dimensions that underlie an individual's comfort with interpersonal touch. First is the source of the touch initiation. That is, we propose a distinction between one's comfort with touching someone else and comfort with being touched by someone else. Second, one's relationship to the other individual likely influences the perception of touch (friends, family, coworkers, etc.). Third, perceptions of touch are likely altered due to the gender of the individuals involved. Norms surrounding male-to-male touch have more variance than female-to-female or opposite gender touch. In order to understand a culture's idiosyncratic touch norms, we need to include both the gender of the person touching and the gender of the person being touched. Fourth is the type of touch. There is likely a difference between a handshake, a hug, a touch on the arm, etc. in how comfortable an individual is with the touch. Finally, the fifth dimension is the context in which the touch occurs. Whether individuals are greeting each other, saying good-bye, mid-conversation, etc. the acceptance of touch will likely vary. These five dimensions are captured in the items that were developed for the CIT Scale.

Peck and Childers (2003) developed the 'Need for Touch' (NFT) scale to identify individual differences in preference for haptic information. The 12-item NFT scale consists of two dimensions, instrumental, the outcome-directed touch in which we touch to gain more information about an object, and autotelic, the touch that is for sensory pleasure in which touch is an end in itself. The NFT scale is tailored toward product touch, which is why we believe that CIT is capturing a different aspect of touch, namely, interpersonal touch. A pre-study was conducted to ensure that the CIT construct is significantly different from the NFT construct. A pre-study was conducted with 325 undergraduate students in which we used a preliminary 11-item scale (a= .92) to measure CIT. The CIT scale and the NFT scale (a = .92) were correlated at .34 (p < .001) thus supporting the distinctness of these two constructs.

In order to more accurately capture the CIT construct, 63 scale items were developed to capture the predicted underlying five dimensions. The scale was administered to a sample of 382 undergraduate students to provide preliminary estimates for reliability and scale structure. The CIT construct was measured using a 7-point Likert scale ranging from strongly disagree to strongly agree.

Long-run future research plans involve multi-national studies of interpersonal touch in business settings. Currently, we are fostering relationships in 5 different countries in order to collect data using this CIT scale. This collaboration will allow us to understand how business practice is affected by interpersonal touch across high and low touch cultures.

We anticipate that this research will contribute greatly to the marketing field. The sense of touch or haptics has been studied, as it related to product purchases; however, there is currently no available measure that captures individual differences in comfort with interpersonal touch. Managerially, this research should inform negotiation and persuasion across cultures. For example, a culture or person comfortable with interpersonal touch may find it offensive if touch is not initiated. Conversely, the result could be true if a person is not comfortable with touch. Regarding theory development, this proposed scale will also allow for future research in the interpersonal touch domain and will support cross-cultural understanding of nonverbal communication norms.

REFERENCES

Crusco, April H. and Christopher G. Wetzel (1984), "The Midas Touch: The Effects of Interpersonal Touch on Restaurant Tipping," *Personality and Social Psychology Bulletin*, 10, 512-517.

Fisher, Jeffery D., Marvin Rytting, and Richard Heslin (1976), "Hands Touching Hands: Affective and Evaluative Effects of an Interpersonal Touch," *Sociometry, 39* (4), 416-421.

Hornik, Jacob (1992), "Tactile Stimulation and Consumer Response," *Journal of Consumer Research, 19*(3), 449.

Hornik, Jacob and Shmuel Ellis (1988), "Strategies to Secure Compliance for a Mall Intercept Interview," *Public Opinion Quarterly*, 52 (4), 539-551.

McCabe, Deborah Brown and Stephen M. Nowlis (2003), "The Effect of Examining Actual Products or Product Descriptions on Consumer Preference," *Journal of Consumer Psychology*, 13 (4), 431-439.

Mehrabian, Albert. (1981), Silent Messages: Implicit Communication of Emotions and Attitudes (2nd ed.), Belmont, CA: Wadsworth.

Peck, Joann and Terry L. Childers (2003), "To Have and To Hold: The Influence of Haptic Information on Product Judgments," *Journal of Marketing*, April 67 (2), 35-48.

Peck, Joann and Terry L. Childers (2003), "Individual Differences in Haptic Information Processing: On the Development, Validation, and Use of the 'Need for Touch' Scale," *Journal of Consumer Research*, 30 (3), 430-442.

Peck, Joann and Terry L. Childers (2006), "If I Touch It I have to Have it: Individual and Environmental Influences on Impulse Purchasing," *Journal of Business Research*, 59, 765-769.

Peck, Joann and Suzanne Shu (2009), "The Effect of Mere Touch on Perceived Ownership," *Journal of Consumer Research*, 36(3), 434-447.

Stephen, Renee and Richard L. Zweigenhaft (1986), "The Effect on Tipping of a Waitress Touching Male and Female Customers," *Journal of Social Psychology, 126*(1), 141.

Willis, Frank N. and Hellen K. Hamm (1980), "The Value of Interpersonal Touch in Securing Compliance," *Journal of Nonverbal Behavior*, 5(1), 49-55.

Good Bye, Old Self! - The Transformation of Self-Identity

Woo Jin Choi, Texas A&M University, USA
Ji Yun Kang, Texas State University, USA

Individuals may, at times, experience the transformation of their identities. For example, when students graduate from college, they may adopt a new identity as an employee of a company while, simultaneously, leaving behind their former identity as a student. Another example is that of a woman taking her husband's surname after marriage, and thereby becoming "Mrs. Man" (Penfield 1987, p.118). In this case, a woman is expected to adopt a new identity while submerging or burying her former identity (Penfield 1987). Given that one's name is strongly and personally related to one's self-identity (Penfield 1987), a surname change could cause a significant identity transformation. In this research, we investigate the courses of identity transformation after taking on a new surname and, how this affects the consumption behavior of female consumers.

Past research on social identity suggests that people have multiple identities but only those identities that are salient at a given moment influence one's consumption behavior (Escalas and Bettman 2003, 2005; White and Dhal 2007). This stream of research has shown that consumers tend to have more positive attitudes toward products that are associated with their social identities (e.g., student identity, female identity, organization identity, political affiliations, etc.) when that certain identity is salient (Forehand, Deshpandé, and Reed 2002; Reed 2004). For example, Reed (2004) showed that people are more willing to purchase an interpersonal telecommunication product that enables them to stay connected with their families when their family identity is salient. While extant research has focused on *which identity* exerts an effect on consumers' brand preferences and choices, little is known about how one is influenced during *the transformation of self-identity* and, more importantly, how this change influences consumers' brand preferences and choices.

While the traditional practice of marital surnaming still continues, the social status of women has dramatically improved as they have increasingly been taking on social roles traditionally assumed by men (Damhorst, Miller-Spillman, and Michelman 2005). Consequently, women are now more likely to 'acquire' or 'choose' their social identity as independent individuals, in contrast to the past in which women were expected to passively 'accept' their social identity given to them upon marriage to their husbands. In their research on marital name change, Kline, Stafford, and Miklosovic (1996) revealed that the self-perception that a maiden name can be equated with one's self-identity strongly influences a woman's decision to adopt her married name. Other studies also suggest that females who retain their maiden name after marriage place great emphasis on their self-identities, and they tend to be concerned that the name change might bring about the loss of their self-identities (Arliss 1991; Dralle and Mackiewicz 1981; Scanzoni and Scanzoni 1988). Therefore, it is plausible that women who adopt their married names might experience a sense of loss in regard to their self-identity, since these women may still have a feeling of attachment toward their maiden names—a symbol that represents their independence, as well as their long-time ties to their families.

An interesting question that arises next is, how can this nostalgia for their former name/identity influence consumers' brand evaluations and product choices? We expect that newly-wed female consumers will favor products that are associated with their former identity as 'single women' because of their affection for their maiden name. Defining one's self in terms of consumption behavior is more relevant when an identity is inchoate, or in other words, when an individual begins playing a new, unfamiliar role (Solomon and Rabolt 2009). It is thus likely that the sense of loss women experience in regard to their maiden names will decrease over time, because they will gradually become accustomed to their new names and their new social roles. Therefore, the effect of a former identity will be a decay function.

We conducted a pretest to investigate whether the feeling of nostalgia toward a maiden name/single identity decreases as the length of a marriage increases. Thirty-nine females who spoke English and were U.S. residents participated in this study through MTurk for payment. The results showed that those who had been married less than five years experienced a feeling of nostalgia for their maiden names to a greater extent than those who had been married for more than five years. Therefore, the data supports our premise of the decaying effect of a former identity with time. We are now in the process of conducting a series of studies to test our predictions (a) in in-depth interviews with five married females and (b) in a survey.

The contributions of this research are as follows. First, to the best of our knowledge, the current work takes the first step in focusing on how individuals respond to the extinction phase of their former identities and the adoption of new social identities. Insights into the manner in which people respond to both former and new identities would expand our understanding of the influence of social identity on cognition and behavior. Therefore, the current research unlocks the door extending this line of research on the transformation of self-identify and to a further understanding of its effect on consumer behavior. In addition to theoretical contributions, this study has practical implications in that it could provide marketing practitioners with strategic ideas for targeting consumers in the identity transformation period, such as new persuasion points and appropriate timing of the persuasion points.

REFERENCES

Arliss, Laurie P., (1991), Gender Communication, Englewood Cliffs, NJ: Prince Hall.

Damhorst, Mary. L, Kimberly A. Miller-Spillman, and Susan O. Michelman (2005), *The Meanings of Dress*, New York: Fairchild Publications.

Dralle, Penelope W. and Kathelynne Mackiewicz (1981), "Psychological Impact of Women's Name Change at Marriage: Literature Review and Implication for Future Study," *American Journal of Family Therapy*, 9, 50-5.

Forehand, Mark R., Rohit Deshpandé, and Americus Reed II (2002), "Identity Salience and the Influence of Activation of the Social Self-Schema on Advertising Response*,*" *Journal of Applied Psychology*, 87 (6), 1086-99.

Escalas, Jennifer Edson and James R. Bettman (2003), "You Are What They Eat: The Influence of Reference Groups on Consumers' Connections to Brands," *Journal of Consumer Psychology*, 13 (3), 339-48.

_____ and _____ (2005), "Self-Construal, Reference Groups, and Brand Meaning," *Journal of Consumer Research*, 32 (3), 378-89.

Kline, Susan L., Laura Stafford and Jill C. Miklosovic (1996), "Women's Surnames: Decisions, Interpretations and Associations with Relational Qualities*,*" *Journal of Social and Personal Relationships*, 13 (4), 539-617.

Penfield, Joyce (1987), "Surnaming: The Struggle for Personal Identity," in *Women and Language in Transition*, New York, NY: State University of New York, 117-29.

Reed, Americus II (2004), "Activating the Self-Importance of Consumer Selves: Exploring Identity Salience Effects on Judgments," *Journal of Consumer Research*, 31 (September), 286-95.

Scanzoni, Letha D. and John Scanzoni (1988), *Men, Women, and Change: A Sociology of Marriage and Family*, New York: McGraw Hill.

Solomon, Michael, and Nancy J. Rabolt (2009), *Consumer Behavior in Fashion,* Upper Saddle River, NJ: Pearson Prentice Hall.

White, Kate and Darren Dahl (2007), "Are All Out-Groups Created Equal? Consumer Identity and Dissociative Influence," *Journal of Consumer Research*, 34 (December), 525-36.

Affect, Cognition, and Consumer Charity: The Moderating Role of Social Distance

Joseph Paniculangara, University of Central Florida, USA
Xin He, University of Central Florida, USA

Charitable donation is important in transformative consumer research. This paper investigates the use of affect versus cognition in consumer donation and its interaction with social distance. We demonstrate that affect-driven consumers tend to donate more than cognition-driven consumers. In addition, the difference between affect-driven and cognition-driven consumers is more evident with greater social distance between the donating consumer and the recipient of her charity. This interactive effect is due to the differences in goals pursued by different types of consumers.

A consummatory goal is particularly relevant for affect-driven consumers (Millar and Tesser, 1986). Motivated by the consummatory goal, people engage in behavior that is intrinsically rewarding (Holbrook and Hirschman, 1982; Pham 1998). Past research shows that when a consummatory goal is made salient, people tend to make decisions based on affect (Pham 1998). In charitable donations, the consummatory goal may be manifested as maximizing "warm-glow" utility (Andreoni, 1989). In such cases, donors are primarily interested in the intrinsic satisfaction stemming from their behavior of donation of resources.

In contrast, an instrumental goal is important for cognition-driven consumers (Millar and Tesser, 1986). Such a goal is secondary - while the behavior may not be rewarding in itself, the undertaking may help to achieve another goal (Millar and Tesser, 1986). Pham (1998) shows that an instrumental goal decreases the use of affect in arriving at decisions. In the context of donation, an instrumental goal may be manifested as a desire to contribute to causes similar to "public-goods" and consequent utility (Andreoni, 1989). That is, donors may sometimes contribute so as to derive utility that comes from consumption of the cause donated to. For example, a donation made to National Public Radio (NPR) may be made to ensure adequate funding for NPR to continue broadcasting.

We argue that the consummatory goal of enhancing "warm-glow" utility and the instrumental goal of increasing the provision of "public-goods" may be differentially influenced by the social distance between donor and recipient. Social distance refers to the degree of social similarity and social connection between oneself and another (Trope, Liberman and Wakslak, 2007). While social distance is known to be an important factor in the donation literature (Winterich, Mittal and Ross, 2009), its interaction with "warm-glow" and "public-goods" types of utilities is unclear. We reason that as social distance increases, cognition-driven donors may find it increasingly difficult to derive the "public-goods" type of utility given their instrumental goals. Consumers may not donate to a radio station at greater distance as it is unlikely that they will listen to its broadcast. In contrast, affect-driven donors may continue to satisfy their consummatory goal because they derive "warm-glow" utility regardless of the social distance between them and the recipient. For example, donating to help a starving child in a far-off community will still provide them with "warm-glow" as much as will donating to help a child in their immediate social circle. This reasoning leads to our prediction that the gap between affect-driven and cognition-driven consumers in donation becomes pronounced as the social distance between the consumer and the recipient increases. More formally,

Hypothesis: The beneficial effect of greater reliance on affect rather than cognition will be exacerbated when the donor and recipient are separated by greater social distance and attenuated when the donor and recipient are separated by lesser social distance. An interaction will exist between the relative use of affect and cognition and social distance in donation.

Support for the above hypothesis was found in three experiments with undergraduate students as participants. The stimulus for the first experiment was adapted from the work of Kogut and Ritov (2007). Participants were asked for their hypothetical donation to assist a group of either American or Indian tourists lost on an island in the Indian Ocean after the 2004 tsunami. In this manipulation physical distance is held constant. Participants reported their relative use of affect versus cognition in their decision about the donation using the five-item scale from Shiv and Fedorikhin (1999). The dependent variable was the amount out of $10 they would have donated if they were compensated with that amount for their participation. The interaction between social distance and the relative use of affect versus cognition was marginally significant, such that at closer social distance the use of affect versus cognition made little difference to the proposed donation. Whereas at greater social distance the use of affect versus cognition led to significant differences in the proposed donation. The stimulus for the second experiment was modified so that participants contemplated hypothetical donations to help either American or Russian tourists. This was done to rule out a possible confound of India not having similar resources as the USA. There was a significant interaction between the relative use of affect versus cognition and social distance. The third experiment was designed to address possible criticism of the first two experiments as not involving actual donation. Undergraduates who received ten extra points for research participation in their introductory marketing class (graded on 1,000 points) were asked how many points out of the ten they would donate to help either a marketing or a nursing student who was unable to participate in the extra credit session. Following completion of the questionnaire, participants were debriefed and reassured that they would receive their ten points. Again, a significant interaction between the relative use of affect versus cognition and social distance was found.

In three studies we find that affect-driven consumers tend to donate more and this effect is pronounced in situations of greater social distance. These results contribute to our understanding of charitable behavior, in terms of the roles of affect and cognition as well as the moderating effect of social distance. Our findings may help not-for-profit organizations that seek to maximize donations, especially those facing the difficult situation of donors reducing donations if they perceive greater social distance to the potential recipient (Burnstein, Crandall and Kitayama, 1994). This research indicates that it may be in the interest of such organizations to induce more reliance on affect by donors.

REFERENCES

Andreoni, James (1989), "Giving with Impure Altruism: Applications to Charity and Ricardian Equivalence", *Journal of Political Economy*, 97 (6), 1447-1458.

Burnstein, Eugene, Christian Crandall and Shinobu Kitayama (1994), "Some neo-Darwinian Decision Rules for Altruism: Weighing Cues for Inclusive Fitness as a Function of the Biological Importance of the Decision", *Journal of Personality and Social Psychology*, 67 (5), 773-789.

Holbrook, Morris B. and Elizabeth C. Hirschman (1982), "The Experiential Aspects of Consumption: Consumer Fantasies, Feelings and Fun", *Journal of Consumer Research*, 9 (2), 132-140.

Kogut, Tehila and Ilana Ritov (2007), "'One of Us': Outstanding Willingness to Help Save a Single Identified Compatriot", *Organizational Behavior and Human Decision Processes*, 104, 150 -157.

Millar, Murray G. and Abraham Tesser (1986), "Effects of Affective and Cognitive Focus on the Attitude-Behavior Relation", *Journal of Personality and Social Psychology*, 51 (2), 270-276.

Pham, Michel Tuan (1998), "Representativeness, Relevance and the Use of Feelings in Decision Making", *Journal of Consumer Research*, 25, 144-159.

Shiv, Baba and Alexander Fedorikhin (1999), "Heart and Mind in Conflict: The Interplay of Affect and Cognition in Consumer Decision Making", *Journal of Consumer Research*, 26, 278- 292.

Trope, Yaacov, Nira Liberman and Cheryl Wakslak (2007), "Construal Levels and Psychological Distance: Effects on Representation, Prediction, Evaluation, and Behavior", *Journal of Consumer Psychology*, 17 (2), 83-95.

Winterich, Karen Page, Vikas Mittal and William T. Ross Jr. (2009), "Donation Behavior toward In-groups and Out-groups: The Role of Gender and Moral Identity", *Journal of Consumer Research*, 36, 199-214.

Boycotters Who Don't Boycott:
Attitude-Behavior Inconsistency in an Anti-Consumption Movement

Juan Wan, Ivey School of Business, UWO, Canada
Aimee Huff, Ivey School of Business, UWO, Canada

Consider the following fictional story: Walking across their university campus in Beijing, two Chinese girls, Hsing-yi and Linlin, encounter a group of senior students trying to gather support for a campus-wide boycott on Japanese products in protest of recent actions by a Japanese car company. The seniors are encouraging other students to demonstrate their commitment to the boycott by signing their names on a large flag. Hsing-yi and Linlin consider joining the movement, which would require them to refrain from buying Japanese products for six months, but also realize this would be difficult because they both believe Japanese products are high quality and very popular. Hsing-yi was born in a city that suffered under the Japanese invasion during World War II, and she quickly decides to participate in the boycott because of this historical and personal connection. Linlin, however, was originally less compelled by the senior students' claims that Japanese products should be boycotted, but feels pressure to join after Hsing-yi signed the flag and after seeing the hundreds of other signatures on the flag. She finally commits to the boycott. Within a few weeks, however, Hsing-yi and Linlin are surprised to discover that they each have bought a Japanese camera. Even though Hsing-yi had deliberated much longer over her purchase of a Japanese camera than Linlin did, they both made conscious decisions to break their boycott commitments. Ultimately, each girl was swayed in her purchase behavior by the high quality of Japanese cameras.

This phenomenon occurs regularly in China; Chinese students frequently organize boycotts of Japanese products, and encourage others to commit to the movement. However, it is equally common for students to purchase the boycotted Japanese brands and products. In this paper, we refer to consumers who do not behave consistently with their boycott commitments as *pseudo-boycotters*, and we seek to understand why they break from their boycott commitments. We develop a conceptual model of pseudo-boycotter behavior to explain why these consumers publically commit to anti-consumption behavior and later engage in behavior that is explicitly contradictory to their public commitment. We draw from literature on explicit and implicit attitudes (Wilson, Lindsey, and Schooler 2000; Gawronski and Bodenhausen 2006) to suggest that an underlying, favorable attitude toward the boycott target can override the conscious, explicit negative attitude toward the boycott target in a purchase situation. We suggest that boycotters' motivations to join the boycott can influence the salience of the explicit negative attitude toward the boycott target (Epley and Gilovich 1999), such that some boycotters (i.e., those motivated by social pressure) are not strongly influenced by their negative attitudes at the time of purchase. Other boycotters (i.e., those who were motivated to join by a desire for intrinsic satisfaction) experience salient, competing attitudes at the time of purchase (Kozinets and Handelman 1998), but the purchase context activates their consumer role (McLeod and Lively 2003), which boosts the underlying, favorable attitude toward the boycott target and directs purchase behavior. In the actual purchasing context, where self-interested behavior is cued, the consequences of being a boycotter become blurry while those of being a consumer (e.g., perceived usefulness of the products, low cost of the products) become more salient, which consequently triggers purchase behaviors that are congruent with the consumer role (Callero 1994; Pillutla and Chen 1999).

In the preliminary phase of data collection, we conducted semi-structured depth interviews with seven undergraduate students at a large Chinese university. We found that students do hold a stable and favorable implicit attitude toward Japanese products. However, when asked to describe their motivations for participating in boycotts, many reasons emerged, including social pressure from friends and personal desires. Regardless of the reasons for participation, our informants revealed explicitly negative attitudes toward Japanese companies by stating that Japanese companies deserve boycotts. Furthermore, many informants revealed that they did purchase Japanese product again within the boycott period, and they usually felt disappointed with themselves in the post-purchase period. However – and, perhaps, more interestingly – they did not feel the same way when purchasing, because they believed they were making the correct purchase decision. This preliminary data validates our conceptual framework. Based on these results, a series of experiments has been designed to further investigate the underlying mechanisms. Initial boycott commitment and motivations will be contrasted with subsequent behavior in a real purchasing condition. In this second phase of the research, we extend the context into a general boycotting situation, aiming to show that this phenomenon is not culturally specific and that it has broader implications for consumer behavior.

The theoretical contributions of our research are twofold. First, most traditional research focuses on the motivations of boycott participations, and the consequences of boycotts (Garrett 1987). Assuming that the attitudes and behaviors of boycotters will directly influence the effectiveness of boycotts, we focus on the individual boycotters – specifically, the pseudo-boycotters whose attitudes and behaviors are inconsistent with the boycott objectives. Second, our work dovetails with research on socially responsible consumption, where behavioral intention is influenced by the trade-offs between prosocial and individual outcomes – which are in opposition (Moisander 2007). Some research has shown that while prosocial and consumer interests are both salient in a consumption context, consumption choices are necessarily individual choices, and therefore social concerns tend to play an insignificant role when decisions need to satisfy immediate, personal needs (Warlop, Smeesters, and VandenAbeele 2000). We extend this research by accounting for this phenomenon in an anti-consumption context.

The model developed in this paper may be of use to two types of managers: those who manage boycotts, and those who manage the firms that are targeted by boycotts. Boycott organizers may find ways to reinforce the boycott objectives in ways that make the explicit, negative attitudes salient at the time of purchase – although we suggest that, even when salient, these explicit attitudes are overridden by the activation of the consumer role.Managers of the boycotted targets may find tactics to attenuate the effects of boycotts by activating the consumer role and the positive, implicit attitudes at the point of purchase.

REFERENCES

Callero, Peter L. (1994), "From Role-Playing to Role-Using: Understanding Role as a Resource," *Social Psychology Quarterly*, 57 (3), 228-43.
Epley, Nicholas and Thomas Gilovich (1999), "Just Going Along: Nonconscious Priming and Conformity to Social Pressure," *Journal of Experimental Social Psychology*, 35 (6), 578-89.

Garrett, Dennis E. (1987), "The Effectiveness of Marketing Policy Boycotts: Environmental Opposition to Marketing," *Journal of Marketing*, 51 (2), 46-57.

Gawronski, Bertram and Galen V. Bodenhausen (2006), "Associative and Propositional Processes in Evaluation: An Integrative Review of Implicit and Explicit Attitude Change," *Psychological Bulletin*, 132 (5), 692-731.

Kozinets, Robert V. and Jay M. Handelman (1998), "Ensouling Consumption: A Netnographic Exploration of Boycotting Behavior," in *Advances in Consumer Research*, Vol. 25, ed. J. Alba and W. Hutchinson: Association for Consumer Research, 475-80.

McLeod, Jane D. and Kathryn J. Lively (2003), "Social Structure and Personality," in *Handbook of Social Psychology*, ed. John D. DeLamater, New York: Plenum Publishers.

Moisander, Johanna (2007), "Motivational Complexity of Green Consumerism," *International Journal of Consumer Studies*, 31 (4), 404-09.

Pillutla, Madan M. and Xiao-Ping Chen (1999), "Social Norms and Cooperation in Social Dilemmas: The Effects of Context and Feedback," *Organizational Behavior and Human Decision Processes*, 78 (2), 81-103.

Warlop, Luk, Dirk Smeesters, and Piet VandenAbeele (2000), "On Selling Brotherhood Like Soap: Influencing Everyday Disposal Decisions," in *The Why of Consumption: Contemporary Perspectives on Consumer Motives, Goals, and Desires*, ed. S. Ratneshwar, David Glen Mick and Cynthia Huffman, London: Routledge.

Wilson, Timothy D., Samuel Lindsey, and Tonya Y. Schooler (2000), "A Model of Dual Attitudes," *Psychological Review*, 107 (1), 101-26.

The Bidirectional Relation between Number and Location

Fengyan Cai, The Chinese University of Hong Kong, China
Hao Shen, The Chinese University of Hong Kong, China
King-man Hui, The Chinese University of Hong Kong, China

The number-location association refers to the fact that people spontaneously think that large numbers should be located at the top or on the right hand side of a display, whereas small numbers should be put at the bottom or on the left side (Wood and Fischer 2008-Dehaene, Bossini and Giraux 1993;Zorzi, Priftis and Umilta 2002; see Fias and Fischer 2005 for review).

Extant literature already provides preliminary evidence for the existence of the number-location association. For example, Dehaene, Bossini and Giraux(1993) presented a number at a fixation, and then asked subjects to judge whether the number was odd or even by pressing the assigned response key. They found that participants responded to larger numbers faster when the assigned response key was on the right (vs. left) hand side, and that the reverse pattern was true for small numbers.

However, extant research usually focuses on uni-directional relation between number and location—from numerical magnitude to location. This paper proposes and demonstrates that there is a bidirectional relation between number and location. First, we will examine the impact of numerical magnitude on people's memory about location in study 1. Secondly, we will test whether location can bias people's numerical estimation in study 2.

STUDY 1: IMPACT OF NUMERICAL MAGNITUDE ON MEMORY

ABOUT LOCATON

The number-location association will be automatically activated when numbers are presented (Dehaene, Bossini and Giraux 1993). Research on spatial memory has shown that when participants can not clearly recall locations, they will use other source of information to help them recall (Huttenlocher, Hedges, Corrigan and Crawford 2004; Huttenlocher, Hedges and Duncan 1991). Accordingly, if people can not clearly recall the locations of numbers, the activated number-location association may serve as an additional source of information. As a result, recalled location of large number may be biased rightward whereas recalled location of small number may be biased leftward.

METHOD

Forty college students took part in this study in exchange for HK\$ 20. Participants firstly watched a slide show in which each number was shown for one second and followed by one second blank screen. The horizontal location of those numbers varied but the vertical location remained the same. After all stimuli (6 small numbers<1, 2, 3, 4, 5, 6>, 6 large numbers<999, 996, 997, 995, 998, 989>) were shown, participants saw each number again in the order they originally saw them, one at a time, at the center of the slide. Then, participants were asked to recall the location of each number by checking one of the fifteen boxes that located from left to the right on the screen.

RESULTS

The main dependent variable we used was the difference between the recalled location and original location. For both original location and recalled location, small code numbers represented locations near to the left side of the slide while large code numbers represented locations near to the right side. Therefore, we expect that for large numbers, the difference between recalled location and original location would be larger than 0; for small numbers, the difference would be smaller than 0.

The results showed a significant main effect of the category of stimulus ($F(1,80)=22.72$, $p<.001$). As expected, for large numbers, the difference ($M=1.85$) was significantly higher than zero ($t(40)=5.92$, $p<.001$); for small numbers, the difference ($M=-1.10$) was significantly lower than zero ($t(40)=-3.42$, $p<.001$). Therefore, our expectation got supported.

STUDY 2: THE EFFECT OF LOCATION ON NUMERICAL ESTIMATION

Perceptual symbols system theory suggests that people often behave like as though perceptual associations are literal (Barsalou 1999; Barsalou 2008). People's judgment and decision are consequently biased by the perceptual factors in those associations (Schuber 2005; Nelson and Simmons 2009). For example, because of the association between cardinal direction and vertical position—"North is up", people feel that heading north is going uphill, and hence expect that northbound travel(vs. southbound) will take longer time. Accordingly, we expect that people might treat the association between number and location literally. As a result, once the number-location association is activated, people's numerical estimation could be biased by location. Specifically, we assumed that a large (small) number will be more accessible in people's mind when they estimate the amount of products that are presented on the right (left) side of a screen.

METHOD

Eighty college students were told that we are interested in their memory ability and were asked to remember anything that appeared on the wall. On this pretense, participants were sequentially exposed to a pile of books and a pile of balls on the wall. The order of the two pictures was counterbalanced. Each picture was either displayed on the left or right side of the wall. Participants were given 1second to look at each picture. After that, they were asked to estimate the number of books and balls. As a manipulation check, they were also asked to indicate the location of each picture by circling "left" or "right".

RESULTS

98% of participants correctly recalled the locations of the pictures. The results of repeated measure ANOVA revealed a significant main effect of location on estimation ($F (1, 78) = 7.20$, $p < .05$). The estimated amount of objects was significantly higher when objects was presented on the right hand side ($M=17.53$) than when it was presented on the left hand side ($M=14.84$). This finding demonstrated that location could bias people's numerical estimation in an assimilation way.

This paper may contribute to extant literature in two different ways. First, it demonstrates an undocumented bidirectional relation between number and location. Second, much of extant literature only demonstrated that the number-location association could influence how fast or accurate a judgment was made. This research demonstrates that the number-location association can bias not only the process by which a judgment is made but also the judgment outcome itself.

REFERENCES

Barsalou, Lawrence (1999), "Perceptual Symbol Systems," *Behavioral and Brain Sciences*, 22(4), 637-60.
_____ (2008), "Grounded Cognition," *Annual Review of Psychology*, 59, 617-45.
Dehaene, Stanislas, Serge Bossini and Pascal Giraux (1993), "The Mental Representation of Parity and Number Magnitude," *Journal of Experimental Psychology*, 122 (3), 371-96.
Fias, Wim and Martin H. Fischer (2005) "Spatial Representation of Numbers," in *Handbook of Mathematical Cognition*, ed. Campbell JID, New York: Psychology Press, 43-54.
Huttenlocher, Janellen, Larry V. Hedges, Bryce Corrigan, and L. Elizabeth Crawford (2004), "Spatial Categories and the Estimation of Location," *Cognition*, 93(1), 75-97.
Huttenlocher, Janellen, Larry V. Hedges and Susan Duncan (1991), "Categories and Particulars: Prototype Effects in Estimating Spatial Location," *Psychological Review*, 98(3), 352-76.
Nelson, Leif D. and Joseph P. Simmons (2009), "On Southbound Ease and Northbound Fees: Literal Consequences of Metaphoric Link between Vertical Position and Cardinal Direction," *Journal of Marketing Research*, forthcoming.
Schubert, Thomas W.(2005), "Your Highness: Vertical Positions as Perceptual Symbols of Power," *Journal of Personality and Social Psychology*, 89(1), 1-21.
Wood, Guilherme and Martin H. Fischer (2008), "Numbers, Space, and Action—From Finger Counting to the Number Line and Beyond," *Cortex*, 44(4), 353-8.
Zorzi, Marco, Konstantinos Priftis and Carlo Umiltà (2002), "Brain Damage: Neglect Disrupts the Mental Number Line," *Nature*, 417, 138-9.

When Under Cognitive Load, Extraverts Generate More False Memories but Introverts Generate Fewer False Memories

Daniel Rubin, CUNY Graduate Center, USA
Paul M. Connell, SUNY Stony Brook, USA

A considerable body of research has demonstrated that confabulations are relatively common with respect to memory for advertisements and consumption experiences (e.g., Bernstein & Loftus, 2009; Braun, 1999; Schlosser, 2006). Despite this attention, we still know very little about the intraindividual processes that lead to false memory formation. The purpose of this research was to explore the potential situational and dispositional boundary conditions for the formation of false memories.

The need for such a model has been suggested by prior false memory research, such as that of Schlosser (2006), who found that virtual object interactivity has the potential to increase accurate memory, while simultaneously increasing imagined attributes, or false memories. False memories of product attributes may lead to dissatisfaction as consumers may mistakenly expect product benefits despite the fact that they were never advertised. This research suggests that marketers should make an effort to better understand the conditions under which a false memory is most likely to occur, as false recall of product attributes can have a dramatic negative impact on customers' satisfaction levels. Studying false memories should be a priority when it is considered that they have actually been shown to impact ones' behavior. Bernstein and Loftus (2009) found that it was possible to convince people that as children a particular food had made them ill. The participants that adopted this false memory had altered food preferences and showed avoidance to the food used in the study. False memory research can enhance the protection of consumers from ads with a greater likelihood of generating false memories as well as prevent misguided campaigns that will harm an organization by leading to customer dissatisfaction.

We predicted there to be an interaction between processing resource availability and an individual's level of extraversion on the generation of false memories. It was theorized that constraining processing resources during encoding would inhibit participants from mentally rehearsing the semantic associations between provided words. In terms of memory accuracy, we envisioned that this would result in a decided advantage for introverts who we believe normally rely on a rote memorization tactic. Extraverts on the other hand, we believe to be more conversation oriented, thus the connections between words or their semantic associations are focal to extraverts during the encoding of new information. Going under the assumption that introverts and extraverts use unique processes for memorization, we believe that extraverts use a conversation oriented encoding process that facilitates more accurate memory and encoding when processing resources are not constrained. The advantages of this process are however limited by a heavier reliance on cognitive resources and thus vanish when these resources are occupied by other tasks. We predicted that extraverts would show an increase in false memory formation under a cognitive load because they would be forced to rely upon a less resource intensive rote memorization process for which they are neither accustomed to, nor as adept at as introverts.

This experiment was conducted using 126 college undergraduates as participants. Processing resources were constrained by having an experimental group memorize a 7-digit number, while a control group was given a 2-digit number. Afterwards, participants were presented with six lists of words, each of which contained 15 terms that were conceptually linked (Deese, 1959; Roediger & McDermott, 1995). Participants were then asked to freely recall the terms immediately after viewing each individual list. A false memory was recorded if a non-given word was provided during free recall. After the memorization tasks were completed, participants completed the big-five personality inventory (Digman, 1990), which included items measuring extraversion, using a five-point Likert scale.

Analysis of the data revealed a significant 2-way interaction of extraversion and cognitive load on the formation of false memory, but not on correct recall. At a baseline level (i.e., with unconstrained processing resources), introverts generated more false memories than extraverts. When processing resources were constrained, this relationship is inverted, and extraverts generated significantly more false memories. Under a high cognitive load introverts had directionally fewer false memories, thought this reduction was only nearly significant. This suggests that introverts are more skillful rote memorizers, and that forcing them to rely on their natural process may improve memory accuracy in certain situations.

In summary, we believe that introverts tend to rely on rote memorization to encode new information and are thus less likely to mentally rehearse the semantic associations between words. In addition, we believe that extraverts generated significantly more false memories when processing resources were constrained because their natural conversation oriented memorization process, which focuses on the semantic associations between words, is inhibited. Because they are forced to use a process that they are not accustomed to during encoding they have greater difficulty source monitoring during recall. This explains the significant increase in false memory formation that we observe among extraverts in the high load condition. Additional studies are planned to further test this hypothesized psychological process driving the effect.

REFERENCES

Bernstein, Daniel M., and Elizabeth Loftus (2009), "The Consequences of False Memories for Food Preferences and Choices," *Perspectives on Psychological Science*, 4 (2), 135-39.

Braun, Kathryn A. (1999), "Postexperience Advertising Effects on Consumer Memory," *Journal of Consumer Research*, 25 (4), 319–34.

Deese, James (1959). "On the Prediction of Occurrence of Particular Verbal Intrusions in   Immediate Recall," *Journal of Experimental Psychology*, 58 (1), 17–22.

Digman, J. M. (1990), "Personality Structure: Emergence of the Five-factor Model," Annual Review of Psychology, 41, 417-40.

Roediger, Henry L. and Kathleen B. McDermott (1995), "Creating False Memories: Remembering Words Not Presented in Lists," *Journal of Experimental Psychology: Learning, Memory, and Cognition*, 21 (4), 803–14.

Schlosser, Ann E. (2006), "Learning Through Virtual Product Experience: The Role of Imagery on True versus False Memories," *Journal of Consumer Research*, 33 (3), 377-83.

Understanding Sustainable Decision-Making of Young Consumers

Silke Speidel, University of Leipzig, Germany
Andre Marchand, Bauhaus-University of Weimar, Germany

Sustainable consumption is already a permanent element in the public debate and will become more important in the future (Sanne 2002), particularly when several exhaustible raw materials run out. Thus the competence of making the 'right' sustainable decisions might become one of the most important issues of future consumer generations. The most accepted model for operationalizing sustainability is currently the "triple bottom line", which postulates that sustainability is based on environmental, social and economic dimensions (Elkington 1998). However, existing empirical studies of sustainable consumption usually focus only one of the three aspects, like environmental aspects (Cornelissen et al. 2008), social aspects (Jackson 2008) or economic aspects (Kumar et al. 2011). When approached this way, it has not yet been sufficiently analyzed how the different and sometimes even conflicting aspects of sustainable decisions influence each other, which makes an integrative approach necessary. This study aims to understand how all three aspects of sustainability are taken into account when judging sustainable consuming decisions.

METHOD

A grounded theory approach (Corbin and Strauss 2008) was used for analysis and further data collection. Data was collected from high school students aged 16 to 18 from different high schools. This age group is old enough to make their own consumption decisions, but influenced by both their peer group and adults (parents, teacher etc.). These young consumers make interesting interviewees, as the idea of sustainability has been around ever since they have been able to make consumption decisions and they are closest to the future generations, whose rights sustainability acknowledges. The students were interviewed individually with a hypothetical decision situation concerning sustainable consumption and a set of predefined questions. The protagonist in the described situation desires a certain cell phone which to his/her knowledge has been or could have been produced in a problematic way. The problems addressed include child labor, working conditions in Least-Developed Countries, endangered species, and precarious working conditions in industrial nations. The situation was presented by orally explaining the circumstances of the decision situation and handing out cards with information the protagonist was said to possess. The word 'sustainable' was neither used in the description of the situation nor in the question, in order to avoid misunderstandings due to another concept of sustainability on the part of the interviewee. After the initial advice to the protagonist, for which the interviewees had to give reasons, they were asked about the assumed perspectives of different stakeholders mentioned on the cards, on hypothetical situations of every consumer acting the same way, and on possible solutions for the addressed problems.

PRELIMINARY RESULTS

Young consumers present themselves as perfectly willing to take environmental, social and economic issues into account when making consumption decisions as long as they can do so without noticeably modifying their patterns of consumption, especially if they perceive the modification as cutting back the standard of living to which they are accustomed. They display different ways of escaping a decision situation where their attitudes would possibly conflict with their preferred actions, such as reducing the problem on one particular product, breaking the situation down into one or more dilemmas, or arguing that they cannot make a difference anyway.

Although they get the information that every product of a certain kind comes with a particular (environmental, social, or economic) 'drawback' in the information cards, they try to solve the problem first by turning to another product of the same kind, thereby ignoring the information given. It seems that they expect to find a solution within consumption rather than in resisting a certain desire for consumption. When they are confronted again with the information that the particular 'drawback' exists for every product of that kind, they tend to break the more complex situation down into one or more dilemmas (e.g. protecting the environment vs. securing jobs), which often allows them to use one of the lines of argumentation to justify their preferred actions (e.g. buying a certain product). A young person's self-efficacy as a consumer in a certain situation might also influence the decision, as consumer behavior will only be adjusted according to what is perceived to be 'sustainable' if a person's actions are expected to make an ever so slight difference.

Furthermore, if sustainable development "seeks to meet the needs and aspirations of the present without compromising the ability to meet those of the future" (World Commission on Environment and Development 1987), a consumer's idea of man will influence what they think those "needs and aspirations" of the present and future generations are. What young consumers perceived as needs in industrial nations often differed from what they perceived as needs in Least-Developed Countries, e.g. they acknowledged that a consumer in an industrial nation has the need or at least the legitimate aspiration for a new cell phone, whereas they argued that consumers in Least-Developed Countries would not need a cell phone but food, concluding that (from their point of view) selling cell phones in Least-Developed Countries makes no sense.

CONCLUSIONS AND FUTURE RESEARCH

Since judging the sustainability of consuming decisions is challenging for consumers due to the possibly conflicting nature of the environmental, social and economic dimensions of sustainability, education for sustainable development should address this topic. Further data collection, e.g. in form of interviews with consumers who show sustainable consumption patterns in one area of life or the other, shall help to clarify the different levels of competence that consumers show when deciding about sustainable consumption. Based on the results from qualitative research, scales shall be developed to measure the complex competence of sustainable consumption in future analysis.

REFERENCES

Corbin, Juliet M. and Anselm L. Strauss (2008), *Basics of Qualitative Research: Techniques and Pocedures for Developing Grounded Theory*, Thousand Oaks, CA: Sage.

Cornelissen, Gert, Mario Pandelaere, Luk Warlop and Siegfried Dewitte (2008), "Positive Cueing: Promoting Sustainable Consumer Behavior by Cueing Common Environmental Behaviors as Environmental," *International Journal of Research in Marketing*, 25 (1), 46-55.

Elkington, John (1998), "Partnerships from Cannibals with Forks: The Triple Bottom Line of 21st-Century Business," *Environmental Quality Management*, 8 (1), 37-51.

Jackson, Tim (2008), "Live Better by Consuming Less? Is There a 'Double Dividend' in Sustainable Consumption?" *Journal of Industrial Ecology*, 9 (1-2), 19-36.

Kumar, V., Eli Jones, Rajkumar Venkatesan and Robert P. Leone (2011), "Is Market Orientation a Source of or Simply the Cost of Competing?" *Journal of Marketing*, 75 (1), 16-30.

Sanne, Christer (2002), "Willing Consumers – or Locked-in? Policies for a Sustainable Consumption," *Ecological Economics*, 42 (1-2), 273-87.

World Commission on Environment and Development (1987*), Report of the World Commission on Environment and Development: Our Common Future*, A/42/427 (Part I, No. 49), Oslo, Norway, http://www.un-documents.net/wced-ocf.htm.

Which Rejection Makes Brand Yearning Stronger? The Impact of Consumer Exclusion, Brand Exclusion, and Ego-Defensive Goals on Brand Evaluations

Fang Wan, University of Manitoba, Canada
Namita Bhatnagar, University of Manitoba, Canada

One of the key strategies within niche branding involves the construction of perceived exclusivity and membership to desirable cliques through brand use (e.g., for *Harley-Davidson*). Mike Jeffries, the CEO of the fashion label *Abercrombie and Fitch* made comments that the retailer only hires and markets to cool, good-looking individuals, and that a lot of people don't, and cannot, belong to A&F (a likely reference to those that are unattractive, overweight, and therefore undesirable; Denizet-Lewis 2006). This is indicative of niche branding strategy at play. Though it has been found that exclusivity in brand membership engenders brand commitment and loyalty amongst *existing* consumers (McAlexander, Schouten, & Koenig 2002; Muniz & O'Guinn 2001), the impact on *future* consumers is not as clear—specifically, it is not well understood whether brand exclusivity would result in heightened desire or felt alienation within consumers desirous of joining a community of brand users. This is the central issue examined in our research.

Specifically, we study the direct and joint effects of two types of perceived exclusion on aspiring consumers' felt alienation and brand evaluations—i.e., (a) exclusion by a target brand (or its management team), and (b) exclusion by its existing consumers. Research in the areas of ostracism and scarcity effects provides evidence for dual effects of social exclusion—fortified yearning for group membership when ostracized (e.g., Williams, Cheung, & Choi 2000) and strengthened desire for products that are restricted in access (e.g., Cialdini 1993; Verhallen & Robben 1994) on the one hand, coupled with greater anti-social attitudes and aggressive behaviors toward those engaged in social ostracism on the other (e.g., Twenge et al. 2001; Gaertner & Iuzzini 2005).

We therefore started out by testing these two competing effects (positive vs. negative) of brand and co-consumer exclusion using a 2 (*co-consumer* exclusion vs. control) by 2 (*brand* exclusion vs. control) between-subjects experimental design in Study 1. Participants, recruited from a local university, were asked to imagine scenarios pertaining to their experiences at a hypothetical event organized by a network of prestigious university graduates. Consumer exclusion was manipulated by the treatment participants purportedly received at the networking event: in the co-consumer exclusion condition, participants were told that the other members snubbed and ignored them; in the control condition, no such information was provided. Brand exclusion was manipulated by the presence or absence of granted network membership after the event: in the brand exclusion condition, participants were told they were denied membership; in the control condition, they were granted membership to the network. Significant interaction effects of the manipulated variables on brand evaluations ($F(1,145) = 4.82$, $p<.05$) and felt alienation ($F(1,145) = 10.81$, $p<.001$) were found.

Planned contrasts revealed that brand exclusion (vs. control) lowers brand evaluations and intensifies felt alienation in the absence of co-consumer exclusion. However, where co-consumer exclusion does occur, brand exclusion has no significant effect. Additional contrasts revealed that with perceived brand exclusion, co-consumer exclusion (vs. control) positively affects brand evaluations but has no impact on felt alienation. Finally, felt alienation also mediated the relationship between the manipulated variables and brand evaluations. These findings of study 1 present a more complex picture of brand exclusion than previously hypothesized. Brand exclusion appears more detrimental to future consumers' brand evaluations than co-consumer exclusion (supporting a negative effect of social exclusion). The presence of both brand and co-consumer exclusion, however, makes brand evaluations more favorable (supporting a positive effect of social exclusion).

We conducted Study 2 to uncover moderators of the negative effects of brand exclusion. Specifically, we examined whether co-consumer inclusion (i.e., when future consumers feel included or welcomed by existing consumers) can counteract the negative effect of brand exclusion (vs. control). A 2 (brand control vs. brand exclusion) by 2 (consumer inclusion vs. consumer exclusion) between-subjects design was adopted. Findings suggest the negative effect of brand exclusion (vs. control) cannot be eliminated via co-consumer inclusion. Findings of Study 2 revealed the relative weight of brand vs. co-consumer exclusions in shaping consumers' brand experience. That is, brand exclusion is a diagnostic factor to evoke consumers' feelings of alienation. This negative brand experience is not affected by how co-consumers treat target consumers.

Study 3 was conducted to further delineate the underlying mechanism of the negative effect of brand exclusion on brand experience. We propose that brand exclusion (vs. co-consumer exclusion) can activate a self-defending goal, which leads to consumers' negative brand evaluations. We adopted self-affirmation procedure (Sherman 1988) to test this proposition. That is, when individuals are given positive feedbacks on a task, they would receive an ego boost. In this case, they will be less likely to engage in self defensive strategy when their self views are threatened. In our research context, we expect that consumers' self view is threatened more severely by brand exclusion (vs. co-consumer exclusion). Furthermore, when consumers receive an ego boost (vs. control), they will evaluate the brand less negatively even though a brand alienates consumers. Therefore, we further argue that consumers' self view mediates the relationship between brand alienation and brand evaluation. We conducted a 2 (brand exclusion, co-consumer exclusion) by 2 (ego-boost, control) between-subjects factorial design. ANOVA analyses yielded supportive findings.

We contribute to branding literature by examining a brand-exclusivity effect from the perspective of aspiring consumers (Kirmani, Sood, & Bridges 1999), and by providing evidence that brand exclusion may activate an ego-defensive goal which lower brand evaluations. We also look at the previously unexamined role of co-consumer exclusion in buffering negative brand exclusion effects.

REFERENCES

Cialdini, Robert B. (1993), *Influence: The Psychology of Persuasion*, revised edition, New York: Quill.

Denizet-Lewis, Benoit (2006), "The Man behind Abercrombie & Fitch," http://www.salon.com/mwt/feature/2006/01/24/jeffries/index3.html.

Gaertner, Lowell and Jonathan Iuzzini (2005), "Rejection and Entitativity: A Synergistic Model of Mass Violence," in Kipling D. Williams, Joseph P. Forgas, and William von Hippel (Eds.), *The Social Outcast: Ostracism, Social Exclusion, Rejection, and Bullying*, New York: Psychology Press.

Kirmani, Amna, Sanjay Sood, and Sheri Bridges (1999), "The Ownership Effect in Consumer Responses to Brand Line Stretches," *Journal of Marketing*, 63 (1), 88-101.

McAlexander, James H., John W. Schouten, and Harold F. Koenig (2002), "Building Brand Community," *Journal of Marketing*, 66 (January), 38-54.

Muniz, Albert M., Jr. and Thomas C. O'Guinn (2001), "Brand Community," *Journal of Consumer Research*, 27 (March), 412-32.

Twenge, Jean M., Roy F. Baumeister, Dianne M. Tice, and Tanja S. Stucke (2001), "If You Can't Join Them, Beat Them: Effects of Social Exclusion on Aggressive Behavior," *Journal of Personality and Social Psychology*, 81, 1058–69.

Williams, Kipling D., Christopher K. T. Cheung, and Wilma Choi (2000), "Cyberostracism: Effects of Being Ignored Over the Internet," *Journal of Personality and Social Psychology*, 79, 748-62.

Verhallen, Theo M. and Henry S. Robben (1994), "Scarcity and Preference: An Experiment on Unavailability and Product Evaluation," *Journal of Economic Psychology*, 15 (June), 315-31.

What do single female baby boomers fear? Planning for their post-retirement housing

Foula Kopanidis, RMIT University, Australia
Linda Robinson, RMIT University, Australia
Mike Reid, RMIT University, Australia

The post-retirement housing market is expanding due to strong demand drivers including changing demographics such as greater longevity; universal access to healthcare; affluence within the population; and greater acceptance of alternative living arrangements (Beer, Faulkner and Gabriel, 2006). These trends are seen across Australia many industrialised nations including the United States of America, New Zealand, Italy, Japan, France and Canada experiencing similar patterns (Kim, Kim and Kim, 2003). For example, the number of Americans aged 65 and over is expected to increase from 35 million in 2000 to 40 million in 2010. As the baby boomer cohort matures and moves into retirement between 2011 and 2029, many will consider future accommodation options (Furlong, 2007).

As a viable and sustainable segment, baby boomers will become the largest driver of consumer demand for post retirement housing over the next four decades. Critical to marketers in developing strategies is understanding how baby boomers' will influence housing markets. However, while there has been a great deal of research examining post-retirement economic well-being among baby boomers (Sanders and Porterfield, 2010) few studies have explored the decision-making process related to post-retirement housing (Huang, 2011). In addition, there are still relatively few reviews published in major marketing journals about the effects of an aging baby boomer cohort on consumer decision making, public policy and marketing practice (see Yoon, Cole and Lee, 2009). Compounding this, few studies have considered two potentially important contributing factors of gender and marital status. According to U.S. Census data, the number of female householders has increased in recent decades from over five million in 1970 to 14 million in 2006 (U.S. Census Bureau 2006). Thus, with the proportion of female baby boomers entering retirement single, a reasonable question to ask is, how do these women plan for post-retirement housing, and what factors influence the decision making process in planning for a change in post-retirement housing?

This research employs the theory of planned behaviour (TPB) model to estimate the intention of single female baby boomers to change their housing situation post-retirement. In particular, we explore the impact of psychological barriers on retirement planning to generate a better understanding of decision making process for considering and planning for changes to housing post-retirement. The specific objectives of the study were to (a) use a modified TPB model to examine their attitudes and intentions on post-retirement housing decision making; and (b) identify the effects of psychological barriers on post-retirement housing decision making.

A total of 703 Australian single female baby boomers were surveyed regarding their attitudes and intentions in relation to their post-retirement housing. The questionnaire included measures of attitude towards housing change, social norms, perceived behavioural control, intention to change housing, advice seeking behaviour and general attitudes towards retirement as well as demographic items. All items included in the current investigation were derived from the TPB framework (Fishbein and Ajzen, 1975) and theoretical considerations regarding possible attitude and psychological barriers to retirement planning (Topa et al., 2009). Exploratory as well as confirmatory factor analyses were used to assess the reliability of all measures. The model was then tested using structural equation modelling analysis to estimate the effect of psychological barriers to retirement planning on intentions to change housing post-retirement and advice-seeking behaviour.

The results show that subjective norms (t=9.145, $p<.01$) and perceived behavioural control (t=10.738, $p<.01$) have significant direct effects on single female baby boomers intention to change housing post-retirement as well as advice-seeking behaviour (t=6.692, $p<.01$ and t=3.282, $p<.01$ respectively). The respondents' attitude towards this change (t=1.850, $p<.1$) and their general attitude towards retirement (t=2.428, $p<.01$) also both had significant effects on determining their intention. These findings are consistent with previous work on post-retirement housing (Huang, 2011). However, the absolute magnitude of the standardized path coefficients indicate that attitude towards a change in housing has the lowest direct effect on intention to change. The data revealed that the general attitude towards retirement *not* attitude towards a change in post-retirement housing was the salient factor in both intention to change housing post-retirement and advice-seeking behaviour of single female baby boomers. When the respondents attitude towards retirement revealed negative views to post-retirement planning, for example 'retirement is too far away to be bothered thinking about', there was a negative direct effect on both intention to change housing post-retirement as well as advice-seeking behaviour. Furthermore, this general attitude towards retirement completely mediates the relationship between perceived barriers to a change in post-retirement housing and both advice seeking and intention to change post-retirement housing. This suggests that behaviour-specific psychological barriers of single female baby boomers are not directly related to the actual intention to perform or the actual performance of that behaviour, such as retirement planning and related advice-seeking, but rather act through a general predisposition towards the larger object, in this case retirement.

In conclusion, this study suggests that for single female baby boomers, their general attitude towards retirement is a salient factor in the application of the TPB in the context of post-retirement housing decisions. Pertinent to achieving a greater understanding of how single female baby boomers are planning their post-retirement housing, is the examination of psychological barriers to retirement planning. This study provides insights into what is driving post-retirement housing planning, or lack therefore, in this cohort. Such information allows marketers and public policy makers to develop and communicate housing retirement planning products and services offerings specific to this demographic.

REFERENCES

Beer, Andrew, Debbie Faulkner and Michelle Gabriel (2006) "21st Century Housing Careers and Australia's Housing Future: A Literature Review," Australian Housing and Urban Research Institute, Melbourne.

Fishbein, Martin and Icek Ajzen (1975), *Belief, attitude, intention, and behavior: An introduction to theory and research*, Addison-Wesley Pub. Co.: Reading, Mass.

Furlong, M. (2007), *Turning Silver into Gold: How to Profit in the New Baby Boomer Marketplace*, Financial Times Press: Upper Saddle River, NJ.

Huang, Hui-Chun (2011), "Factors Influencing Intention to Move into Senior Housing," *Journal of Applied Gerontology*, (January), 1-22.

Kim, Sung-hyuk, Hong-bumm Kim and Woo Gon Kim, (2003), "Impacts of senior citizens' lifestyle on their choices of elderly housing", *Journal of Consumer Marketing*, 20 (3), 210-226.

Sanders, Cynthia K. and. Porterfield Shirley L (2010), "The Ownership Society and Women: Exploring Female Householders' Ability to Accumulate Assets," *Journal of Family and Economic Issues*, 31(1), 90-106.

Topa, Gabriela, Juan Antonio Moriano, Marco Depolo, Carlos-Maria Alcover, and J. Francisco Morales (2009), "Antecedents and Consequences of Retirement Planning and Decision-Making: A Meta-Analysis and Model," *Journal of Vocational Behaviour*, 75 (August), 38-55

U.S. Census Bureau (2006). Current Population Survey, March and Annual Social and Economic Supplements, 2006 and earlier, Retrieved February 19, 2011, from: http://www.census.gov/population/www/socdemo/hh-fam.html

Yoon, Carolyn, Catherine A. Cole and Michelle P. Lee (2009), "Consumer Decision Making and Aging: Current Knowledge and Future Directions," *Journal of Consumer Psychology*, 19 (January), 2–16.

What's important depends upon how I see us:
The influence of self-construal on choice and advice-giving

Jason Stornelli, University of Michigan, USA
Richard Gonzalez, University of Michigan, USA
Carolyn Yoon, University of Michigan, USA

Consumers are often faced with the task of making recommendations about products and services to others; explosive growth in online reviews, brand communities, and social networks has made sharing recommendations more common than ever before. Yet, although much marketing research has examined choices for the self, we know relatively little about how individuals consider marketing features when choosing for others.

Research examining advice-giving shows that advisors use a weighting strategy that is more lexicographic, placing emphasis on one attribute when recommending jobs, courses and volunteering opportunities. Conversely, when choosing for the self, the difficulty of making tradeoffs and foregoing valued attributes leads to more equal weighting patterns (Kray & Gonzalez 1999; Kray 2000).

We broaden the scope of this framework in two ways. First, in contrast to Kray & Gonzalez, who explored decisions that are central to personal identity, we examine the model's effectiveness in a less identity-centric and broader product/service context. Additionally, we examine the role of self-construal – how the self is defined in relation to others – in this process. As recommendation networks become more global with the growth of online interaction, we need to study how culture impacts attribute weighting (Park 2008). Changes in self-construal generate two opposing hypotheses regarding attribute weighting for self-choices versus other-choices.

First, a self-other merging perspective (e.g. Aron et al. 1991) argues that collective self-construals promote a shared sense of resources, perspectives, and characteristics between the self and close others. This perspective suggests that self-other differences in attribute weights should be *attenuated* when the decision-maker operates under a collective (vs. independent) self-construal.

Conversely, the ability and motivation to engage in perspective-taking varies by culture, suggesting that collectivism may *enhance* differences in self-other attribute weighting structures. For instance, Cohen, Hoshino-Browne and Leung (2007; see also Wu & Keysar 2007) argue that Asian-Americans are more likely to use attention toward the background, habits, and feelings of others when understanding the world, compared to Euro-Americans who rely on egocentric projection. However, it remains unclear whether these results are driven by self-construal or other cultural norms, and if they would also apply to a choice context, particularly in light of research demonstrating that the links between agency, preferences, and choice are inconsistent across cultures (Savani, Markus & Conner 2010).

Thus, we predict that,

H1: *When making product/service choices, decision-makers are more likely to assign greater weight to one attribute when making a recommendation to others, compared to when they are making a choice for themselves.*

H2a: *This self-other difference will be attenuated when the decision-maker is operating under a collective self-construal due to self-other merging, or;*

H2b: *This self-other difference will be enhanced when the decision-maker is operating under a collective self-construal due to improved perspective-taking.*

METHOD

Two factors were varied between-subjects (n=91): self-construal [individual/collective] and choice target [self/other]. Participants began by completing two self-construal primes: pronoun-circling and Sumerian Warrior (Oyserman & Lee 2008; Gardner, Gabriel & Lee 1999). Respondents then read a scenario about choosing an apartment for themselves or recommending an apartment for a close friend of the same gender, and chose between two apartments described on three dimensions (rent, neighborhood, and in-unit laundry). The attribute structure allowed inference of the weighting strategy (Kray & Gonzalez 1999; Kray 2000). The *equal weighting* alternative was an apartment that maximized utility on two dimensions (the cost of rent and the washer/dryer), while the *lexicographic* alternative maximized utility on one dimension (the safety of the neighborhood). Thus, by observing the selection of the lexicographic alternative, we can infer that participants are giving greater weight to safety at the expense of the other two attributes. Conversely, the selection of the equal weighting alternative suggests participants maximize value on the greatest number of attributes.

RESULTS/DISCUSSION

Results support the perspective-taking hypothesis. A logistic regression yielded a significant omnibus interaction of self-construal and choice target: $Z = -1.99$, $p < 0.05$. More importantly, planned contrasts within each self-construal condition indicated that the choice target impacted choice patterns differentially. When respondents were primed with a collective self-construal, they preferred the lexicographic alternative when choosing for a friend, and the equal weighting alternative when choosing for themselves. This self-other difference in choice pattern was significant: $Z = 2.38$, $p < 0.05$. Conversely, there was no significant difference in self-other choices under an independent self-construal ($Z = -0.37$, $p = n.s.$). The equal weighting alternative was preferred for both self-choices and recommendations to others.

Two follow-up studies are underway. It is possible that, rather than differentially weighting attributes for self-versus-other choices, collectivist participants preferred lower rent for themselves and a safer neighborhood for a friend. Risk judgments are impacted by culture (e.g. Weber & Hsee 1998; Hsee & Weber 1999) and the judgment target (e.g. Raghubir & Menon 1998), so choice may have been influenced by the judged likelihood of one's ability to absorb financial obligations or of a dangerous event in the less-attractive neighborhood. Further, Luce (1999) argues that certain attributes, including safety, generate more loss aversion. Participants in the collective/self condition may be more attuned to this consideration and hesitant to recommend less-desirable neighborhoods. Thus, we employ a flipped attribute pattern, where the lexicographic apartment maximizes rent utility, and the equal weighting option maximizes utility from the neighborhood and washer/dryer. We measure risk perception, decision difficulty, and decision importance.

In a second follow-up, we change the attribute structure to infer weights differently. Participants choose between gyms that maximize one dimension (aesthetics or travel distance). When collective decision-makers give advice, we expect one option to garner a greater choice share because a disproportionate degree of weight is placed on the focal attribute. In contrast, both collective advisors and independent choosers/advisors should display choice shares closer to parity.

Additional follow-up studies are also in progress to explore whether the mechanism is affective or cognitive in nature.

This package provides an exciting advance in our understanding of the ways in which people weight attributes when choosing for another person, and begin to shed a brighter light on mechanisms underlying cultural differences in perspective-taking.

REFERENCES

Aron, Arthur, Elaine N. Aron, Michael Tudor & Greg Nelson (1991), "Close Relationships as Including Other in the Self," *Journal of Personality and Social Psychology, 60*(2), 241-253.

Cohen, Dov, Etsuko Hoshino-Browne, & Angela K.-y. Leung (2007), "Culture and the structure of personal experience: Insider and outsider phenomenologies of the self and social world," *Advances in Experimental Social Psychology, 39*, 1-67.

Gardner, Wendi L., Shira Gabriel & Angela Y. Lee (1999), ""I" Value Freedom, but "We" Value Relationships: Self-Construal Priming Mirrors Cultural Differences in Judgment," *Psychological Science, 10*(4), 321-326.

Hsee, Christopher K. & Elke U. Weber (1999), "Cross-National Differences in Risk Preference and Lay Predictions," *Journal of Behavioral Decision Making, 12*, 165-179.

Kray, Laura J. & Richard Gonzalez (1999), "Differential Weighting in Choice versus Advice: I'll do this, you do that," *Journal of Behavioral Decision-Making, 12*, 207-217.

Kray, Laura J. (2000), "Contingent Weighting in Self-Other Decision-Making," *Organizational Behavior and Human Decision Processes, 83*(1), 82-106.

Luce, Mary Frances (1998), "Choosing to Avoid: Coping with Negatively Emotion-Laden Consumer Decisions," *Journal of Consumer Research, 24*(4), 409-433.

Oyserman, Daphna & Spike W.S. Lee (2008), "Does Culture Influence What and How We Think? Effects of Priming Individualism and Collectivism," *Psychological Bulletin, 134*(2), 311-342.

Park, C. Whan (2008), "An Extraordinary Journal for Extraordinary Ideas," *Journal of Consumer Psychology, 18*(4), 239-241.

Raghubir, Priya & Geeta Menon (1998), "AIDS and Me, Never the Twain Shall Meet: The Effects of Information Accessibility on Judgments of Risk and Advertising Effectiveness," *Journal of Consumer Research, 25*(June), 52-63.

Savani, Krishna, Hazel Rose Markus & Alana L. Conner (2008), "Let Your Preference Be Your Guide? Preferences and Choices Are More Tightly Linked for North Americans Than for Indians," *Journal of Personality and Social Psychology, 95*(4), 861-876.

Weber, Elke U. & Christopher Hsee (1998), "Cross-Cultural Differences in Risk Perception, but Cross-Cultural Similarities in Attitudes," *Management Science,* 44(9), 1205-1217.

Wu, Shali & Boaz Keysar (2007), "The Effect of Culture on Perspective Taking," *Psychological Science, 18*(7), 600-606.

Effects of Legibility of Text in Product Descriptions on Price Perceptions

Rajneesh Suri, Drexel University, USA
Chiranjeev Kohli, Cal State Fullerton, USA
Dhruv Grewal, Babson College, USA
Shan Feng, Drexel University, USA

Marketing often needs to engage consumers and hold their attention in likable ways. It is not surprising then that retailers like Trader Joe's use creative point-of-sale materials with fancy calligraphy, a merchandising technique that not only provides product details but also capture consumers' attention by its uniqueness. Pieters and Wedel (2004) showed that advertisers aiming to maximize attention to their communications should consider devoting more space to its text, but also asserted that the extent to which such effects were caused by text layout (e.g., font type) was not well understood. The focus of the present study is whether typeface used to present product information affects attention to different text elements (price and product attributes).

Several recent studies provide evidence confirming that words are identified during reading by discriminating the underlying structure of their component letters. In particular, Sanocki (1987) showed that the visual cues readers use to derive the underlying structure of letters, and the rules they implement to achieve this, are adjusted according to the typeface in which text appears. Based on this research and evidence that individuals have limited visual attention (Wolfe, Cave and Franzel 1989), we predict that when typeface consumes greater cognitive resources, it results in increased attention to product details using that text at the expense of price information. Integrating this underlying process and the concept of working memory capacity (Hambrick and Engle 2002) and left-digit effect in number processing (Thomas and Morwitz 2005), we predict that consumers when processing product information presented in a harder to read typeface will pay greater attention to product attributes than if they were presented information in a relatively easy to read typeface. Because consumers' attentional resources are limited, increasing attention to an element in a communication maybe at the expense of other elements. Consequently recall of price information in more difficult to read typeface will be distorted and consumers will truncate numbers in a price (say $29.58) and recall a lower price (e.g., $20.08) than when price was presented in an easier to read typeface.

Pretests led to the selection of two typefaces that were either easy (Helvetica) or hard (Bradley) to read. Two studies then collected initial evidence for whether legibility of such typeface affected processing of attribute information and a distortion of price recall. In study 1, materials were presented on computer stations in a behavioral laboratory and participants (55 undergraduate students) were included in a lottery to stimulate their engagement with the task. The study was conducted as part of a larger study and the software randomly presented product information for two products using these two typefaces. At the conclusion of the study, participants completed a working memory task adapted from Hambrick and Engle (2002). Results revealed that participants committed fewer errors recognizing attributes when product descriptions were presented in the harder to read typeface. Furthermore, such a pattern of errors was explained by participants' working memory capacity; those with lower working memory capacity showed greater errors.

Though study 1 showed differences in the scrutiny of product attributes described in the two typefaces, the effects of this closer examination of attributes on recall of price information was not measured. Study 2 assessed both processing of product attributes, as well as price recall for the target product. Using the same typefaces as in study 1, four versions of the target description were created. These versions differed in whether product descriptions accompanied price in the same or a contrasting typeface. Similar to study 1, working memory capacity of participants (111 undergraduate students) was also measured. The results were interesting and revealed that the harder to read typeface resulted in a greater distortion of price recall, supporting not only a parallel visual search by consumers (Wolfe, Cave and Franzel 1989), but also left digit-effects on price recall. Furthermore, these main effects were qualified by a significant interaction effect of typeface and working memory capacity, with differences between the typefaces on price recall becoming non-significant for those with high working memory capacity. Consistent with study1, the harder to read typeface also increased accuracy of processing product attributes.

Though Nelson (1985) endorsed a complexity in advertising as it "slows down the reader making things more difficult to take in" (p. 115), others suggest that complexity hurts advertising because it makes people pay less attention to the brand (Pieters Wedel and Batra 2010). The initial evidence from this research shares kinship with the latter research and shows a superior effect of harder-to-read typeface on consumers' recognition of product attributes, but a weaker recall of the accompanying price. These results add not only to our understanding of how consumers conduct visual search, but also how consumers' attention to product descriptions compromises their attention to price.

REFERENCES:

Hambrick, D. Z., and R. W. Engle (2002), "Effects of domain knowledge, working memory capacity, and age on cognitive performance: An investigation of the knowledge-is-power hypothesis," *Cognitive Psychology*, 44, 339-384.

Nelson, Roy Paul (1985), *The Design of Advertising*, 5th ed.Dubuque, IA: Wm. C. Brown Publishers.

Pieters, Rik and Michel Wedel (2004), "Attention Capture and Transfer in Advertising: Brand, Pictorial and Text-Size Effects," *Journal of Marketing*, 68 (April), 35-50.

____, ____, and Rajeev Batra (2010), "Stopping Power of Advertising: Measures and Effects of Visual Complexity," *Journal of Marketing*, 74 (September), 48-60.

Sanocki, T. (1987). "Visual knowledge underlying letter perception: Font-specific, schematic tuning," *Journal of Experimental Psychology: Human Perception and Performance,* 13,267-278.

Thomas, Manoj and Vicki Morwitz (2005), "Penny Wise and Pound Foolish: The Left-Digit Effect in Price Cognition," *Journal of Consumer Research,* 32 (June), 54–64.

Wolfe, J. M., K. R. Cave, and S. L. Franzel (1989), "Guided search: An alternative to the feature integration model for visual search," *Journal of Experimental Psychology: Human Perception and Performance, 15,* 419– 433.

The Neural Correlates of Buying: Implications for Marketing

Kristin Wiggs, University of Iowa, USA
Kanchna Ramchandran, University of Iowa, USA
Daniel Tranel, University of Iowa, USA
Levin Irwin, University of Iowa, USA

The emerging field of neuromarketing attempts to apply "neuroscientific methods to analyze and understand human behaviour in relation to markets and marketing exchanges"(Lee, Broderick, & Chamberlain, 2007). This field has touched on the brain systems associated with the processing of advertisements, as well as those associated with the predictability of choice, pleasure, and reward in the context of buying/ shopping (Lee et al., 2007). The current research expands on this through preliminary exploration of brain systems that may be associated with impulse buying, compulsive buying, and shopping ruminations. We hypothesized that the prefrontal cortex (PFC) and temporal (TL)/ parietal lobes (PL) (with projections from reward processing circuitry) would be differentially implicated in impulse buying, compulsive buying, and shopping ruminations. The medial prefrontal cortex has been previously implicated in collecting behaviors (Anderson, Damasio, & Damasio, 2005) and hence we hypothesized that compulsive buying behavior and excessive shopping ruminations may be associated with the PFC. Sections of the TL and PL have been associated with impulse control/temporal discounting since they receive projections from the subcortical reward processing circuitry, and we hypothesized that they would be associated with impulse buying (Raab, Elger, Neuner, & Weber, 2010; Richards, Zhang, Mitchell, & de Wit, 1999).

Utilizing the neuroscientific research approach of the lesion method, we recruited 36 participants (from the University of Iowa, Lesion Patient Registry) with single, stable, well-characterized brain lesions to the PFC *(N=10)*, TL *(N=10)*, PL *(N=4)* as target groups as well as the occipital lobe (OL) *(N=12)*, as a brain damaged comparison group. These participants and their collaterals (a close relative), were administered a Shopping Behavior Questionnaire, which we created, based on other well validated questionnaires (Ridgway, Kukar-Kinney & Monroe, 2008) in order to assess the dimensions of impulse buying, compulsive buying, shopping ruminations and their life consequences. Each statement in the questionnaire was rated on two scales. The first scale was a Likert scale from 1 (strongly disagree) to 7 (strongly agree). The second scale was used to ascertain whether there was change in shopping behavior after the participant's brain lesion, ranging from a large decrease to large increase with an option of no change. Following these statements, a second section of the questionnaire assessed family history of compulsive/impulsive buying. In addition, usage, overall time, and access to the Internet and television were assessed. Transportation access and means (for shopping), as well as various financial questions (to ascertain income and financial control) were also asked. Only collaterals were asked if they had taken any steps or measures to curb the participant's spending. Twenty-three participants (63%) identified a collateral. Three participants were unable to respond via phone and data was solely collected from their collaterals. The research study was executed as phone based interviews, lasting approximately 15 minutes per participant/collateral.

Based on data drawn from participant self-ratings on the questionnaire, our preliminary analyses (ANOVA) have indicated that the PFC and the TL/PL are differentially implicated in buying behaviors. Not only the PFC (as we had hypothesized), but the TL and PL as well were associated with compulsive shopping behaviors, as the self-ratings ($p= 0.0256$) and change scores (after brain lesion) ($p=0.1179$) were significantly higher than the OL comparison group. In the case of impulse buying, however, only the TL and PL (as hypothesized) were implicated and the self-rating ($p=0.0232$) and change scores ($p= 0.0048$) were significantly higher than the OL and PFC groups. In the case of excessive shopping ruminations, the TL and PL groups were significantly higher in self-ratings ($p=0.0107$) and change scores ($p=0.1647$) than the PFC and OL groups. This is interesting since one would assume that the PFC, with its prior association with collecting behavior and compulsive shopping behavior (from our dataset), would also be associated with excessive shopping ruminations, but this was not the case in our dataset. This indicates that compulsive buying need not always be preceded or accompanied by perseverative cognitions or thoughts about shopping. Strong correlations existed between the PL/TL groups' excessive shopping ruminations and (a) lying about the time or money spent shopping to friends or family (.77), (b) having difficulty controlling the amount of time spent thinking about shopping (.72), and (c) having to obtain new lines of credit to increase or maintain shopping habits (.72).

Additionally, we also note that although a few individual participants did report decreases in buying behavior or ruminations after the onset of brain damage, no brain lesion group demonstrated a pattern of such decrease. While our target groups spent significantly less time on the Internet than the OL comparison group, t-tests revealed that there were no significant differences between our target and comparison groups in financial resources, financial control, or transportation access.

The brain lesions of a subset of these participants have been mapped. Thus, the next step in data analysis would be to map the region of maximum overlay within each target group to identify those regions within the PFC, TL and PL (for example, medial PFC, hippocampus, insula) that may shed more light on specific regions and how their explicit functions contribute to these buying behaviors.

Thus our data indicate that compulsive buying may be associated with both prefrontal and temporal and parietal lobes, while shopping ruminations and impulse buying are unique to only temporal and parietal lobes. These preliminary findings may have implications for the field of marketing in further delineating the neural substrates underlying buying behavior. Thus, consumers that impulsively shop need not be compulsive shoppers and vice versa. Based on the nature of a product, particular shopping contexts, and susceptibility to advertisements, this distinction may be relevant to marketers.

REFERENCES

Anderson, S. W., Damasio, H., & Damasio, A. R. (2005). A neural basis for collecting behavior in humans. *Brain, 128,* 201-212.

Black, D. W. (2007). Compulsive buying disorder: A review of the evidence. *CNS Spectrums, 12*(2), 124-132.

Hollander, E., Berlin, H. A., & Stein, D. J. (2011). Impulse-control disorders not elsewhere classified. *Essentials of Psychiatry, 3,* 271-292.

Lee, N., Broderick, A. J., & Chamberlain, L. (2007). What is 'neuromarketing'? A discussion and agenda for future research. *International Journal of Psychophysiology, 63*(2), 199-204.

Raab, G., Elger, C. E., Neuner, M., & Weber, B. (2010). The neural basis of compulsive buying. In Müller, A. & Mitchell, J. E., *Compulsive buying: Clinical foundations and treatment* (63-86). New York, NY: Routledge/Taylor & Francis Group.

Richards, J. B., Zhang, L., Mitchell, S. H., & de Wit, H. (1999). Delay or probability discounting in a model of impulsive behavior: effect of alcohol. *Journal of the Experimental Analysis of Behavior, 71*(2), 121-143.

Ridgway, N. M., Kukar-Kinney, M., & Monroe K. B. (2008). An expanded Conceptualization and a New Measure of Compulsive Buying. *Journal of Consumer Research, 35,* 622-639.

The Influence of Goal Publicity on Goal-Consistent Behaviors

Yuchen Hung, National University of Singapore, Singapore
Xiuping Li, National University of Singapore, Singapore
Catherine Yeung, National University of Singapore, Singapore

People are encouraged to share with the world the goals they want to achieve. For example, World Wild Fund for Nature (WWF) encourages its supporters to "show off "commitments to a better environment by buying its logoed products. But how does publicizing one's goal affect one's subsequent behaviors? Several theory mechanisms predict that goal publicity motivates goal-consistent behaviors. First, people may do so because of social pressure. Nyer and Dellande (2010) show that weight losers in a weight management center achieved their stated targets when they posted their targets in bulletin. Second, goal publicity may increase goal-consistent behaviors because of an increase in intrinsic motivation. Publicizing one's opinion is shown to increase commitment to the stated position. This is because one attachments self to the public attitude so that one enacts one's belief (Ahluwalia, 2000). In fact, publicizing one's opinion is typically used as commitment manipulations (Nyer and Dellande, 2010). If so, one should attach a greater goal importance when the goal is public, and experience high motivation to carry out goal-consistent behaviors.

In addition, goal publicity may change self perception. Tice (1992) shows self presentation in public changes self concept. The reason is overt behaviors call the individuals' attention to certain aspects or potentialities of the self, which are then highly accessible and exert a powerful influence on subsequent self-assessment. Goal pursuers are typically associated with certain traits, and the associated traits may be incorporated to oneself concept due to goal publicity. For example, academic pursuers are associated with intelligence. Announcing an academic goal may lead one to see oneself as more intelligent. The change in self perception may self script associated with the goal highly accessible (Schlenker , Dlugolecki and Doherty, 1994), and increase goal enactment.

The above analyses suggest that when a goal becomes public, people are likely to internalize it and act upon it when opportunity arises. However, previous research has overlooked the distinctive values that goal achievement delivers. These values may fall into two categories, utilitarian- and symbolic-related. The distinction between utilitarian and symbolic values is well documented in consumer research. Researchers have shown that consumers consider purchasing decisions based on utilitarian values or symbolic values of products (Shavitt, 1990). Consumer needs are classified as functional needs or symbolic needs (Park, Jaworski and McInnis 1986). The functional needs are related to specific and practical problems, whereas symbolic needs are related to self image and social identification (Subodh Bhat, 1998). The distinctive values that one focuses on goal achievement predict different consequences of goal publicity. When symbolic value is highlighted, goal publicity communicates a desirable self image to others attainment. The communication of such a desirable self image may give a sense of temporary goal completion, thus decrease motivation for subsequent goal-consistent behaviors. In contrast, when utilitarian value is highlighted, the communication of a desirable self image should make one internalize the goal importance and motivate its enactment. Therefore, goal publicity should affect goal-consistent behaviors differently as a function of the values under consideration.

EXPERIMENTS & RESULTS

To test this hypothesis, we conducted a 2 (goal framing: symbolic vs. utilitarian) by 2 (publicizing: publicizing vs. not publicizing) between-subjects design in Experiment 1. The students were instructed to think of how academic success expressed who they were (vs. how academic success benefited them) in symbolic (vs. utilitarian) priming. Their answers were read by experimenter in the publicizing condition, but not read in the not publicizing condition. One week later, they were contacted via email and asked to report the time that they spent on studying in their own time in the past one week. The results were consistent with our hypothesis. The two-way interaction was significant (F (1, 114) = 4.31, p = .04). When symbolic values were considered, the studying time was significantly lower among students who publicized their goal than among those who did not publicize (F (1,114) = 3.86, p =.05). In contrast, when utilitarian values were considered, the studying time was not different between publicizing and not-publicizing conditions (F (1, 114) = 1.09, p = .30).

Experiment 2 examined a different goal, environmentally friendly. Similar to experiment 1, the participants were instructed to think of how being environmental expressed who they were (vs. how being environmental benefited them) in symbolic (vs. utilitarian) priming. Their answers were (not) read by experimenter in the (not) publicizing condition. Afterwards, they read an article from World Wild Fund for Nature

(WWF) on responsible consumption of seafood. The participants were instructed to read the article as they would read it in the newspaper and rate its overall persuasiveness. The article contained information on the ecological impact of overfishing and guideline of seafood consumption. The guideline categorized 18 fish into 3 consumption categories, which were "recommended", "think twice" or "avoid", according to the level of extinction. After reading the article, the participants were presented with a comprehension task, in which they identified the category to which the 18 fish belonged. Motivated individuals should exert more effort on goal-consistent information and remember the information to a better extent. Thus, the number of correct answers was indicative of their motivation of goal pursuit. The results showed that the two-way interaction of goal prime and publicizing was significant (F (1, 70) = 7.73, p= .007). The number of correct answers was lower in symbolic, publicizing condition than in symbolic, not publicizing (F (1, 70) = 4.83, p= .03), indicating publicizing symbolic goal decreased motivation. The reverse was found when participants considered the utilitarian value of environmental goal. Participants answered more answers correctly in the publicizing condition than in the not publicizing condition (F (1, 70) = 2.99, p= .09).

CONCLUSION

Past research has shown publicizing one's goal motivates people for goal achievement. Building on past research, the studies show that that goal publicity does not always increases goal-consistent behaviors. Goal publicity may decreases goal-consistent behaviors when the symbolic value of goal achievements was considered. In two experiments, we demonstrated divergent behavioral consequences of goal publicity when symbolic versus non-symbolic values were salient. The results showed that publicizing academic goal reduced time spent on studying, and publicizing environmental goal lowered attention paid to environmental information when symbolic value was highlighted. We established the contingency of goal publicity and its enactment.

Illusory Control as a Determinant of Ambiguity Seeking

Liang Song, National University of Singapore, Singapore
Yih Hwai Lee, National University of Singapore, Singapore

People generally tend to avoid taking risks with vaguely specified probabilities. This tendency, termed as *ambiguity aversion*, has been found robust in a variety of contexts, such as risky gambling, medical, or insurance decisions (Camerer and Weber 1992). Despite the robustness of ambiguity aversion, *ambiguity seeking* was also observed. Many theories have been put forward to explain what affected people's attitudes towards ambiguity, especially what might lead to ambiguity seeking (e.g., Heath and Tversky 1991; Kuhn 1997). The current research examined two new situational variables that contributed to ambiguity seeking, and pointed out a new psychological process.

Study 1 examined the effect of temporal distance on ambiguity seeking in gambling decisions. We propose that, when a gamble is played in distant future, as compared to near future, people may demonstrate greater ambiguity seeking. If illusory control is the underlying mechanism, ambiguity seeking should be reflected in terms of the judged winning likelihood. To test these hypotheses, we modified the classic Ellsberg's experimental paradigm (Ellsberg 1961) and asked participants to guess the color of a ball that would be drawn from some bottle(s) for a \$2 prize. Ambiguity was defined as uncertainty about a probability (Frisch and Baron 1988) and operationalized in many past research as a range of interval (e.g., Curley and Yates 1985; Kuhn 1997). Following this definition, participants in one condition (i.e. the condition with ambiguous probability) saw two bottles: one was described as containing 30 - 50% more white marbles than blue marbles, and the other 40% more blue marbles than white marbles. A die would be tossed to decide from which bottle the ball would be drawn. In comparison, participants in the other condition (e.g. the condition with precise probability) were presented with one bottle that was described as containing 50% white and 50% blue marbles. Temporal distance was manipulated by telling half of the participants that the ball would be drawn in 5 minutes and the other half of the participants that it would be drawn on the next day. Then they guessed the color and estimated their own probability of winning. Consistent with our hypothesis, the estimated winning likelihood was greater in response to the 1-day delay than to the 5-minute delay when the gamble was described ambiguously (0.58 vs. 0.47, $p < .001$); however, this tendency diminished greatly when the gamble was described precisely (0.53 vs. 0.51, $p = .413$).

Study 2 examined how having an option to select a product item from a chosen product influence ambiguity seeking. To illustrate, in the marketplace, consumers usually either get to select an item amongst similar SKU (e.g., picking up a box of vacuum cleaner amongst similar ones at the store floor) or have to rely on a store assistant to get an item for them (e.g., there is only 1 display item for each SKU on the store floor and the store assistant have to retrieve available stock from the store storage).We propose that consumers who are allowed to freely pick up a product from many others, as compared to those who are not allowed to do so, may demonstrate greater ambiguity-seeking towards product information that may be amenable to illusory control. We tested these hypotheses in a lab which simulated a marketplace setting. Participant entered a lab one at a time and was asked to make a choice between two brands of MP4 based on constructed product information. Ambiguity was manipulated by varying the "failure rate" product information. To explain, in one condition, failure rate of brand-B was given as range from 10-26%; in the other condition, failure rate of brand-B was given precisely as 18% (which was the center of 10-26%). Failure rate of brand-A was 22% in both conditions. Ratings for two other non-failure-rate attributes (e.g., sound quality) were also calibrated to make the two brands relatively comparable. To manipulate how participants pick up a product, in one condition, ten real items of each brand were displayed together on the table, and participants were allowed to pick up any item as their choice. In the other condition, only one item of each brand was displayed on the table, and participants were told that once they made a choice, the shop assistant (i.e. the experimenter) would get them another box of the same item from the storage (participants were told there are 10 "available stock" available). All participants then indicated their choice, relative preference (measured from 1- "definitely prefer brand-A" to 10-"definitely prefer brand-B") and estimated the failure rate of the product they would get. As predicted, allowing participants to pick up an item, compared to not allowing them to do so, led to a greater preference towards (and also greater choice over) brand-B when its failure rate was described ambiguously (6.58 vs. 5.09, $p < .05$), but not when it was described precisely (5.40 vs. 5.92, $p = .49$). More importantly, the estimated failure rate fully mediated the interactive effect between probability format and way of choosing on consumers' preference judgments, supporting our argument about illusory control as the underlying mechanism.

Overall, this research adds to our understanding by revealing the underlying psychological causes of both ambiguity seeking behavior and illusory control perception.

REFERENCES

Camerer, C. and M. Weber (1992), "Recent Developments in Modeling Preferences: Uncertainty and Ambiguity," *Journal of Risk and Uncertainty*, 5 (4), 325-70.

Curley, S.P. and J.F. Yates (1985), "The Center and Range of the Probability Interval as Factors Affecting Ambiguity Preferences," *Organizational Behavior and Human Decision Processes*, 36 (2), 273-87.

Ellsberg, D. (1961), "Risk, Ambiguity, and the Savage Axioms," *The Quarterly Journal of Economics*, 75 (4), 643-69.

Frisch, D. and J. Baron (1988), "Ambiguity and Rationality," *Journal of Behavioral Decision Making*, 1 (3), 149-57.

Heath, C. and A. Tversky (1991), "Preference and Belief: Ambiguity and Competence in Choice under Uncertainty," *Journal of Risk and Uncertainty*, 4 (1), 5-28.

Kuhn, Kristine M. (1997), "Communicating Uncertainty: Framing Effects on Responses to Vague Probabilities," *Organizational Behavior and Human Decision Processes*, 71 (1), 55-83.

You're Shady: The Effect of Pupil Obscuration on Consumers' Perceived Trust

Hamed Aghakhani, University of Manitoba, Canada
Kelley Main, University of Manitoba, Canada
Nick Turner, University of Manitoba, Canada

Research on eye contact has revealed that the most important cue in determining whether one is perceived as lying is a lack of eye contact (Sporer and Schwandt 2007). In contrast, direct eye contact results in greater perceived intimacy, attraction and trust (Burgoon et al. 1985) and greater perceptions of friendliness (Beebe 1974). While an averted eye gaze is believed to be a strong cue of deception, a prolonged gaze can be seen as threatening (Bayliss and Tipper 2006). However to date, the literature has focused only on comparisons of direct versus indirect eye contact with no consideration of eye contact with one's pupil obscured. The goal of the current research is to understand how the physical obscuration of a person's eyes (by wearing shaded or darkened glasses) affects others' perceptions of that person. In particular, we are interested in observing the effects of wearing shaded eyeglasses on other people's trust judgements of the wearer. Utilizing the theory of spontaneous trait transference (Winter and Uleman 1984) wherein people rely on automatically elicited inferences when making social judgments to interpret the behaviors of others, we expect that wearing shaded eyeglasses may result in the "shady" trait to transfer to the wearer, thereby reducing the previously demonstrated positive effects of direct eye contact. It is hypothesized that even when recipients are able to see the pupils of the person wearing shaded eyeglasses, some degree of distrust is expected based on the partial obscuration. We also propose that status of the person wearing the glasses moderates this effect. In particular, it is expected that wearing shady glasses does not affect those high in status and instead lower status individuals with shaded glasses are perceived as more distrusted. Two experiments examine these hypotheses.

EXPERIMENTS

Study 1 examined the main effect of pupil obscuration on perceived trust. This study was a 2 (participant gender: male vs. female) x 4(level of shade: clear, low, medium, full) x 2(model gender: male vs. female) plus 1(clear indirect eye gaze) between subjects design (N= 343). Participants were given a picture of a person with eyeglasses. The lenses of the glasses were tinted with computer software to vary from completely clear to fully shaded. Then participants asked to indicate their level of trust towards the target on seven items measuring trust that were mixed in with various other traits. The results revealed a main effect of model gender (M_{male}=2.99, M_{female}=3.22, $F(1,326)$=4.066 , p=.045) and a main effect of the level of shade (M_{clear}=3.40, $_{Mlow}$ = 3.11, M_{med}= 2.62, M_{full}=2.61 and $M_{indirect\ gaze}$=3.50, $F(4, 326)$=15.084, p=.000). These results reveal that people have less trust in a person wearing shaded eyeglasses even when there is a direct eye contact and the recipients are able to see the pupils of the communicator. The gender of the person wearing the glasses reveals that recipients have less trust in men as compared to women. Participants' gender had no effect. Post-hoc tests of the effects of different degrees of shading revealed that people have the highest trust in a person wearing clear eyeglasses and this trust decreases as the darkness of the lenses increases. The findings also show that even a picture with an indirect eye gaze with clear glasses had higher trust as compared with shaded glasses.

In experiment 2, we sought to extend the finding of the previous study by examining the status of the model as a potential moderator of recipient's perceived trust. In addition, we examined whether the model gender effect was a result of the attractiveness of the model. A 2(model gender: male vs. female) x 3(level of shade: low, medium, high) x 2(status: high vs. low) between subjects design (N= 236) was conducted. Status was manipulated through a paragraph that accompanied the photo indicating that the person featured in the photo did/did not win a prestigious award.

The results replicate the main effect of shade (p=.049) and model gender (M_{male}=3.908, M_{female}=4.259, p=.001) on perceived trust using the same items as Study 1. Results also indicate a significant two way interaction of shade and status ($F(2.224)$=2.43, p=.09) and a significant three way interaction of shade, model gender and status ($F(2,224)$= 4.69, p=.01). It is found that people have the least perceived trust in a lower status person who has shaded glasses (M=3.671) in comparison to those with low (M=4.20) or medium (M=4.12) shaded glasses. In contrast wearing shaded glasses does not affect perceived trust in a high status person. The results for model attractiveness showed no difference between the two models (p>.5).

GENERAL CONCLUSION

This research makes two major contributions to the field. First, in contradiction to results demonstrating that direct eye contact increases friendliness (Burgoon, Coker, and Coker 1986), this research found a boundary condition under which eye contact has no positive effect, specifically when there is a physical obscuration of the pupil. The second contribution of this research is the extension of the gazing literature above and beyond eye gaze or contact to demonstrate the importance of no barrier to one's pupils. The outcome of this research has direct implications for the marketing field, especially in a sales context. Many sales agents wear prescription photochromic glasses that will appear shaded depending on the time of day and lighting in the store. The current research suggests that this will lead to lower perceived trust in the agent, and perhaps may even influence evaluations of the store.

REFERENCES

Bayliss, A., S. Tipper (2006), "Predictive Gaze Cues and Personality Judgments," *Psychological Science*, 17, 514-520.

Beebe, S. A. (1974), "Eye contact: A Nonverbal Determinant of Speaker Credibility," *Speech Teacher*, 23, 21-25.

Burgoon, J., D. Coker, R. Coker (1986), "Communicative Effects of Gaze Behavior: A Test of Two Contrasting Explanation," *Human Communication Research*, 12, 495-524.

Burgoon, J., V. Manusov, P. Mineo, and J. Hale (1985), 'Effects of Eye Gaze on Hiring, Credibility, Attraction and Relational Message Interpretation," *Journal of Nonverbal Behavior*, 9, 133-146.

Sporer, S. L., B. Schwandt (2007), "Moderators of Nonverbal Indicators of Deception: A Meta-analytic Synthesis," *Psychology, Public Policy, and Law, 13*(1), 1-34.

Winter, L., & Uleman, J. S. (1984). When are social judgments made? Evidence for the spontaneousness of trait inferences. Journal of Personality and Social Psychology, 47, 237–252.

The Effects of Labeling on Prosocial Behavior

Zoe F. Rogers, Baruch College & The Graduate Center, CUNY, USA

Pragya Mathur, Baruch College, CUNY, USA

Labeling is a common persuasion tactic that involves suggesting to someone that they possess a specific attribute with the intention of influencing their behavior in ways corresponding to that attribute (Reingen & Bearden, 1983). For example, labeling an individual as a responsible voter can lead to increased voting behavior (Tybout & Yalch, 1980). In this investigation, we examine the impact of labeling on the effectiveness of charity appeals.

Most of the labeling literature in marketing involves positive labels (Moore, Bearden, & Teel, 1985), while few have considered negative labels, with the exception of Steele (1975) who found that negative (vs. positive) name-calling resulted in increased helping behavior. The potential effectiveness of negative labels can be understood in terms of the "shaken self" perspective (Gao, Wheeler, & Shiv, 2008), in which negative labels are understood as threatening a strongly held self-view, leading to behavior contrary to the label in attempts to restore confidence in this self-view.

The effectiveness of many persuasion techniques is often determined by the activation of an individual's persuasion knowledge, which is much more likely when an individual engages in thorough elaboration on the persuasion attempt (Friestad & Wright, 1994). Positive labeling is more effective when elaborative processing of the label is prevented (Cornelissen et al., 2007), while the impact of elaboration level on negative labels has not been examined.

Labeling is not only impacted by elaboration level, but also by content of the appeal, specifically whether it is self-focused (focused on the benefits to the self) or other-focused (focused on the benefits to others). This distinction corresponds to perceivers' underlying altruistic or egoistic motivations to engage in prosocial behavior (Wilson, 2000). Engaging in helping behavior for altruistic reasons is perceived as more appropriate behavior and serves as a norm to guide behavior in our society (White & Peloza, 2009).

Therefore, we hypothesized that in low elaboration conditions, those who are negatively labeled and who view the other-benefit appeal will have the highest giving intentions. Other-focused behavior is the *most* generous behavior people can display and is thus the most effective way in which to restore confidence in a "shaken" self-view. For those who are positively labeled, we did not expect any impact of the content of the appeal on giving intentions.

Study one was conducted using a 2 (valence of label: negative vs. positive) X 2 (accuracy motivation: high vs. low) X 2 (type of appeal: self vs. other) between-subjects design. First, respondents received the elaboration manipulation, which involved responding to two scenarios either with general opinions (low accuracy) or more thorough consideration (high accuracy), a manipulation used effectively by Agrawal & Maheswaran (2005). Participants then reported their opinions about different people, after which the computer "evaluated" the responses and provided (fictitious) feedback containing the (randomly assigned) "generous" or "not generous" label. This procedure has been shown by Strenta and Dejong (1981) to create convincing labels. Participants then viewed the appeal for "Hearing Loss Research" donations featuring either self-benefit or other-benefit ad copy. Participants evaluated the advertisement on several dimensions and indicated giving intentions.

A 2 X 2 X 2 ANOVA on label valence, accuracy motivation, and type of appeal revealed a significant three-way interaction ($F (1,177) = 4.09$, $p < .05$). In the low accuracy conditions, individuals who viewed the other-benefit appeal reported higher giving intentions when positively (vs. negatively) labeled ($M = 4.71$, $M = 4.0$; $p = ns$). In the high accuracy condition, individuals who viewed the self-benefit appeal reported higher giving intentions when positively (vs. negatively) labeled ($M = 5.17$, $M = 4.36$; $p = ns$). The results of this study indicate that when little elaboration occurred, those who were labeled as "generous" and viewed the other-benefit appeal responded with the highest giving intentions. When high elaboration occurred, those who were labeled as "generous" and viewed the self-benefit appeal responded with the highest giving intentions. These unexpected findings will be addressed in a future study.

A second study further examined negative labels using a different operationalization of elaboration, relevance of the appeal. When a message is self-relevant, an individual scrutinizes the message more thoroughly in order to judge the information more confidently (Maheswaran & Chaiken, 1991). When there is little relevance of the appeal, those who view the other-benefit (vs. self-benefit) appeal should be more willing to give, as these individuals are more likely to depend upon the "altruistic giving" norm discussed above to guide their behavior.

This study was conducted using a 2 (self-relevance: high vs. low) X 2 (type of appeal: self vs. other) between-subjects design. The procedure was the same as that of study 1, with two exceptions: (a) all participants were negatively labeled, and (b) participants viewed the appeal from the perspective of either someone who has never known anyone with hearing loss (low self-relevance) or someone who had a family member recently diagnosed with hearing loss (high self-relevance).

A 2 X 2 ANOVA on self-relevance and type of appeal revealed a significant interaction ($F(1, 66) = 3.110$, $p = .05$), as well as a main effect of the type of appeal ($M_{\text{Other-Benefit Appeal}} = 5.36$ vs. $M_{\text{Self-Benefit Appeal}} = 4.70$; $p = .08$). Decomposing the two-way interaction revealed that in the low-relevance condition, the individuals who viewed the other- (vs. self-) benefit appeal reported significantly higher giving intentions ($M = 5.63$, $M = 4.25$; $p < .01$). Additionally, respondents who viewed the self-benefit appeal reported significantly higher giving intentions in the high (vs. low) relevance condition ($M = 5.19$, $M = 4.25$; $p = .05$).

This research contributes to the labeling literature by comparing the relative effectiveness of positive and negative labels, as well as demonstrating the impact of content of the appeal on the effectiveness of labeling. Future research will further examine positive labels and their relationship with content of the appeal to better understand the findings of our first study. We will also consider cultural variables in order to examine the effectiveness of labels when used worldwide.

REFERENCES

Agrawal, N. & Maheswaran, D. (2005). Motivated reasoning in outcome-bias effects. *Journal of Consumer Research, 31(4),* 798-805.

Cornelissen, G., Dewitte, S., Warlop, L., & Yzerbyt, V. (2007). Whatever people say I am, that's what I am: Social labeling as a social marketing tool. *International Journal of Research in Marketing, 24,* 278-288.

Friestad, M. & Wright, P. (1994). The persuasion knowledge model: How people cope with persuasion attempts. *Journal of Consumer Research, 21,* 1-31.

Gao, L., Wheeler, S.C. & Shiv, B. (2008). The "shaken self": Product choices as a means of restoring self-view confidence. *Journal of Consumer Research, 36,* 29-38.

Maheswaran, D. & Chaiken, S. (1991). Promoting systematic processing in low-motivation settings: Effect of incongruent information on processing and judgment. *Journal of Personality and Social Psychology, 61(1),* 13-25.

Moore, E.M., Bearden, W.O., & Teel, J.E. (1985). Use of labeling and assertions of dependency in appeals for consumer support. *Journal of Consumer Research, 12,* 90-96.

Reingen, P.H. & Bearden, W.O. (1983). Salience of behavior and the effects of labeling. *Advances in Consumer Research (10),* 51-55.

Steele, C.M. (1975). Name-calling and compliance. *Journal of Personality and Social Psychology, 31(2),* 361-369.

Strenta, A. & Dejong, W. (1981). The effect of a prosocial label on helping behavior. *Social Psychology Quarterly, 44(2),* 142-147.

Tybout, A.. & Yalch, R.F. (1980). The effect of experience: A matter of salience? *Journal of Consumer Research, 6,* 406-413.

White, K. & Peloza, J. (2009). Self-benefit versus other-benefit marketing appeals: Their effectiveness in generating charitable support. *Journal of Marketing, 73,* 109-124.

Wilson, J. (2000). Volunteering. *Annual Review of Sociology, 26,* 215-240.

How Mindset Influences Consumer Decisions: Investigating the Role of Mental Imagery and Affective Responses

Cheng Qiu, University of Hong Kong, China

Consumers may process incoming product information using different cognitive procedures. In some cases they may focus on abstract issues relating to values or end benefits (e.g., the effects brought by a product). In other cases they may focus on concrete aspects of the process (e.g., the process of consuming a product). The former can be referred to as an abstract mindset and the latter, a concrete mindset (Freitas, Gollwitzer, and Trope 2004). The activation of different mindsets may be influenced by individual difference such as age and culture (Hong and Lee 2010), psychological distance such as whether things happen in near or distant future (see Trope and Liberman 2010 for a review of construal level theory), and situational factors that induce a certain mindset temporarily (Escalas and Luce 2004; Torelli and Kaikati 2009).

Once a mindset is activated, it would have profound influence on people's responses. Previous research shows that an abstract mindset may shift people's focus to the desirable aspects whereas a concrete mindset may highlight feasibility concerns when people consider whether to carry out an activity (Eyal et al. 2004; Liberman and Trope 1998). While this finding bears important implications for many consumer decisions, there are also plenty of daily purchase or consumption decisions which involve few feasibility concerns. Under such situations, will mindsets still influence consumer decisions? Why or why not? This research is aimed to address these questions.

This research proposes that people in a concrete (vs. abstract) mindset are more interested in hedonic products when detailed product description is provided. This is because when consumers encounter such products, their focus on concrete processes and contextual information would facilitate the construction of vivid mental simulation of consuming the product, especially if there is sufficient product information that provides enough materials for mental simulation. When the consumption imagery becomes more accessible in memory, consumers have more favorable responses to the product (Petrova and Cialdini 2005). Moreover, such mental imagery may elicit positive affective responses (MacInnis and Price 1987), which also enhance consumer judgments. Therefore, we expect that a concrete (vs. abstract) mindset may lead to greater intention to try products involving immediate, desirable experiences (e.g., nice fruit dessert) when detailed product information is provided (e.g., product picture). However, when product information is very limited, consumers may lack sufficient information for generating consumption imagery, regardless of their mindset. This would become a boundary condition where a concrete mindset may not enhance consumer judgments. Experiment 1 tested these hypotheses.

Experiment 1. This experiment adopted a 2 (mindset: concrete vs. abstract) x 2 (product information: picture vs. no-picture) between-subjects design. 110 participants were induced to be in a certain mindset by completing a task under the pretense of psychology research on actions and goals. In the abstract mindset condition, they were instructed to write about why they carry out several actions such as improving leadership skills, which shifted their focus to end benefits. Participants in the concrete mindset condition were instructed to write about how they carry out those actions, which shifted their focus to concrete processes (adapted from Freitas, Gollwitzer, and Trope 2004). Thereafter, they proceed to an ostensibly unrelated product survey in which they assessed several products. The target product was a fruit dessert. In the picture condition, participants saw a picture of a fruit dessert and indicated their interest in having it, whereas in the no-picture condition, participants were simply asked to indicate how interested they were in having a fruit dessert. The main dependent variable was measured on a seven-point scale ranging from "not interested at all (1)" to "very interested (7)". An ANOVA analysis reveals a main effect of product information (picture vs. no-picture; $F(1,106) = 18.92, p < .001$) and an interaction between product information and mindset ($F(1,106) = 6.27, p = .01$). Consistent with our prediction, when participants saw the product picture, they were more interested in trying the product if they were in a concrete mindset (M = 5.97) than if they were in an abstract mindset (M = 5.08; $F(1,106) = 4.31, p < .05$). However, when they did not see the product picture, the difference between concrete mindset condition (M = 3.89) and abstract mindset condition (M = 4.52; $F(1,106) = 2.14$, NS) diminished. Another set of planned comparisons show that when participants were in a concrete mindset, they were more interested in trying the product if they saw the product picture (M = 5.97) than if they did not (M = 3.89; $F(1,106) = 24.37, p < .001$); the difference diminished when participants were in an abstract mindset (5.08 vs. 4.52, $F(1,106) = 1.64$, NS). The findings provide preliminary support to our hypotheses.

Experiments are planned to further investigate the mechanism underlying the mindset effect. The next experiment would examine different types of hedonic products to improve generalizability, collect measures of imagery generation and affective responses to validate the mechanism, and study the possible moderating role of individual difference in imagery ability. A third experiment would examine the potential moderating role of the affective nature of consumption, which would help further pin down the mechanism. Note the fruit dessert studied in experiment 1 is desirable in terms of both consumption experience and end benefits. However, some products may bring desirable end benefits but entail negative consumption experience (e.g., using insect killer). If the proposed mindset effect is simply due to the accessibility of consumption imagery, a concrete (vs. abstract) mindset should be more likely to trigger mental imagery and lead to more favorable responses regardless of the affective nature of usage experience. However, if the affective responses elicited by the consumption imagery matter, a concrete (vs. abstract) mindset may result in greater interest/less interest in products involving pleasant/unpleasant usage experience.

To summarize, this research will complement previous research to offer a more comprehensive understanding of the mindset effect. The research will also investigate new mechanisms through which mindset may influence consumer judgments, namely, the generation of consumption mental imagery and the affective responses toward the mental imagery.

REFERENCES

Escalas, Jennifer Edson, and Mary Frances Luce (2004), "Understanding the Effects of Process-Focused versus Outcome-Focused Thought in Response to Advertising," Journal of Consumer Research, 31 (Sept), 274-285.

Eyal, Tal, Nira Liberman, Yaacov Trope, and Eva Walther (2004), "The Pros and Cons of Temporally Near and Distant Action," Journal of Personality and Social Psychology, 86 (6), 781-795.

Freitas, Antonio L., Peter Gollwitzer, and Yaacov Trope (2004), "The Influence of Abstract and Concrete Mindsets on Anticipating and Guiding Other's Self Regulatory Efforts," Journal of Experimental Social Psychology, 40 (6), 739-752.

Hong, Jiewen and Angela Y. Lee (2010), "Feeling Mixed but Not Torn: The Moderating Role of Construal Level in Mixed Emotions Appeals," Journal of Consumer Research, 37 (Oct), 456-472.

Liberman, Nira and Yaacov Trope (1998), "The Role of Feasibility and Desirability Considerations in Near and Distant Future Decisions: A Test of Temporal Construal Theory," Journal of Personality and Social Psychology, 75 (1), 5-18.

MacInnis, Deborah J. and Linda L. Price (1987), "The Role of Imagery in Information Processing: Review and Extensions," Journal of Consumer Research, 13 (March), 473-491.

Petrova, Petia K. and Robert B. Cialdini (2005), "Fluency of Consumption Imagery and the Backfire Effects of Imagery Appeals," Journal of Consumer Research, 32 (Dec), 442-452.

Torelli, Carlos J. and Andrew M. Kaikati (2009), "Values ad Predictors of Judgments and Behaviors: The Role of Abstract and Concrete Mindsets," Journal of Personality and Social Psychology, 96 (1), 231-247.

Trope, Yaacov and Nira Liberman (2010), "Construal-Level Theory of Psychological Distance," Psychological Review, 117 (2), 440-463.

The Perception of lower and higher Price-Thresholds: Implications from Consumer Neuroscience

Marc Linzmajer, Zeppelin University, Germany
Mirja Hubert, Zeppelin University, Germany
Marco Hubert, Zeppelin University, Germany
Peter Kenning, Zeppelin University, Germany

The investigation of optimal pricing has a long tradition in marketing and already yielded important contributions to our understanding of consumer behavior (Lowe and Alpert 2010; Mazumdar, Raj and Sinha 2005; Ofir 2004). Behavioral pricing research and theories (e.g., adaption-level theory, assimilation-contrast theory) have shown consumers to have lower and upper price-thresholds, represented by an inverted U-shaped price-acceptability-function (Helson 1964; Monroe 1973, 1990; Rao and Sieben 1992; Sherif and Hovland 1961; Winer 1988). Whereas prices below a lower price-threshold may signal suspect product quality, prices above an upper threshold may be considered as too expensive (Monroe 1973). The idea of lower and upper price-thresholds and, in between, an acceptable price range, are widely accepted and integrated in most theoretical accounts in pricing research (e.g., Kalwani and Yim 1992; Kalyanaram and Winer 1995, Lichtenstein, Bloch and Black 1988; Mazumdar and Jun 1992). Moreover, recent neuroscientific studies show the effect of different price levels on brain activation and decision-making (Knutson et al. 2007; Plassmann, O'Doherty and Rangel 2007).

However, the reason *why* consumers tend to have lower and upper price-thresholds and *how* the acceptable price range is processed in the consumers' brain remains mainly unclear. Against this background, we applied functional magnetic resonance imaging (fMRI) in order to investigate if there are neural activation patterns that correspond to a lower-, optimal-, and upper-price-threshold. Based on the theories we assumed, that people will not only accept prices from the optimal price range more often compared to prices below or above the price-thresholds, but that they will also exhibit different neural activation patterns during the perception of optimal versus low/high prices.

In a preliminary study, 127 participants were asked for their individual price-settings (too cheap, cheap, expensive or too expensive) for different variations of one FMCG. According to van Westendorp (1976) we extracted a lower- (.88 monetary units (MU) and upper price-threshold (.99 MU) as well as a (fictive) optimal price (.96 MU). In order to have more variance in the fMRI-study, we took the lower-price-threshold and subtracted 5%, 10%, and 25%. Accordingly we added 5%, 10% and 25% to the upper-price-threshold. Therefore we got a lower threshold-range from .66 to .84 MU, an optimal range from .88 to .96 MU and an upper threshold-range from 1.04 to 1.24 MU. In our fMRI-study, we measured the brain activity of 29 subjects (M_{age} =42.24 years; SD=4.22) during the perception of the price-product combinations extracted from our preliminary study. The task-design followed Knutson et al. (2007). Thus, we first showed participants a picture of a product (4 seconds), followed by the price information (4 seconds), and a decision-phase where they had to indicate their purchase intention (1="yes"/0="no"). In total, participants evaluated 90 product-price combinations. The study was executed on a 3T scanner (Magnetom Trio, SIEMENS). The data set consisted of 36 transversal slices of 3.6 mm thickness without a gap, FOV 230 mm x 230 mm, acquired matrix 64 x 64, that is, isotropic voxels with 3.6 mm edge length. Contrast parameters were TR=3000 ms, TE=50 ms, flip angle=90°. Within the group analysis a one-sample t-test was applied based on the individual contrasts of the lower price-thresholds versus the optimal prices as well as upper price-thresholds versus the optimal prices.

Preliminary results confirmed our assumption of an upper-price-threshold. Only 2.4% of prices within the upper-price-threshold-range were accepted by our participants compared to 31.5% accepted prices within the optimal range (χ^2 = 261, 277; p<.001). Also, the fMRI-data confirmed these results. The contrasting of high prices versus the optimal price range exhibited higher activity changes in the insula, the DLPFC (BA46), the superior frontal cortex (BA8), the anterior and posterior cingulate cortex (ACC/PCC). Activity in the insula has often been associated with the "price pain" and negative emotions (e.g., uncertainty, pain, anger) (Eisenberger and Lieberman, 2004; Knutson et al., 2007; Sanfey et al., 2003). Furthermore, our results indicate that the decision becomes more complex for prices above the upper-price-threshold, because the prefrontal areas (BA46, BA8) as well as the ACC/PCC are frequently associated with reflective processes, decision-making and conflict monitoring (Bechara 2005; Ridderinkhof et al. 2004; Sanfey et al. 2003; Volz, Schubotz and Cramon 2005) Additionally high prices led to higher activity changes in regions associated with memory retrieval and semantic/visual processing such as the hippocampus or the inferior frontal gyrus (BA 45) (Gabrieli, Poldrack and Desmond 1998; Squire 1992). However, our results did not confirm the assumption of a lower threshold. Prices below the lower-price-threshold-range were significantly more accepted (64. 8%) than prices within the optimal range (31.5 %) (χ^2 = 193,595; p<.001). Furthermore, prices below the lower-price-threshold did not lead to activity changes in regions associated with negative emotions such as the insula. Rather they lead higher activity changes in the middle temporal gyrus (BA 22), and the caudate nucleus. These results provide some evidence that lower prices are perceived as more rewarding than optimal prices (Delgado et al. 2003; Haruno and Kawato 2006). However, there is also no linear relationship between higher prices and activity changes in the insula. We only found higher activity changes in the insula for prices above the upper-price threshold. Contrasting the optimal price range versus the lower prices did not reveal activity changes in this brain region.

Our results provide some evidence and are in line with research on a revision of the inverted U-shaped price-acceptance-function. Based on the stimulus material from the FMCG-segment in this study, it might be that the price-quality relationship is stronger when higher-priced products are used (Völckner and Hofmann 2007). Therefore, a lower price threshold might come into play when the price-perceived quality relationship is stronger. But indeed, there already exists some theoretical evidence against a lower-price-threshold: first, economic theory presumes a decreasing demand function implying that, in general, consumers find lower price more acceptable (Monroe and Lee 1999). Second, observation of consumer behavior in the marketplace shows that some consumers actively seek out lower prices. In fact, the discount-retail formats addressing these needs are often very successful. Third, the commonly used direct-questioning-method (Monroe 1990) may be inherently biased, potentially directing consumers to indicate a lower price threshold when, in fact, it may not exist. The prevalent usage of this methodology in academic and applied research may have contributed to overlooking the possibility of the existence of only one threshold for some consumers or products.

REFERENCES:

Bechara, Antoine (2005), "Decision Making, Impulse Control and Loss of Willpower to Resist Drugs: A Neurocognitive Perspective," *Nature Neuroscience*, 8 (November), 1458-463.

Delgado, M.R., Locke, H.M, Stenger, V.A., and Fiez, J.A (2003), "Dorsal striatum responses to reward and punishment: Effects of valence and magnitude manipulations," *Cognitive, Affective, and Behavioral Neuroscience*, 3, 27-38.

Eisenberger, Naomi I. and Matthew D. Lieberman (2004), „Why rejection hurts: a common neural alarm system for physical and social pain," *Trends in Cognitive Sciences*, Vol. 8 (7), 294-300.

Gabrieli, John D., Russell A. Poldrack, and John E. Desmond (1998), "The role of left prefrontal cortex in language and memory," *PNAS*, 95(3), 906-913.

Helson, Harry (1964), *Adaption-Level Theory*, New York: Harper & Row.

Kalwani, Manohar U. and Chi-Ki Yim (1992), "Consumer Price and Promotion Expectations: An Experimental Study," *Journal of Marketing Research*, Vol. 29, 90-100.

Haruno, M. and Kawato, M. (2006), "Different Neural Correlates of Reward Expectation and Reward Expectation Error in the Putamen and Caudate Nucleus During Stimulus-Action-Reward Association Learning," *Journal of Neurophysiology*, 95, 948-59.

Kalyanaram, Gurumurthy and Russell S. Winer (1995), "Empirical Generalizations from Reference Price Research," *Marketing Science*, Vol. 14, 161-169.

Knutson, Brian, Scott Rick, G. Elliott Wimmer, Drazen Prelec, and George Loewenstein (2007), "Neural Predictors of Purchase," *Neuron*, 53 (January), 147-56.

Lichtenstein, Donald R., Peter H. Bloch and William C. Black (1988), "Correlates of Price Acceptability," *Journal of Consumer Research*, Vol. 15, 243-252.

Lowe, Ben and Frank Alpert (2010), "Pricing Strategy and the Formation and Evolution of Reference Price Perceptions in New Product Categories," *Psychology and Marketing*, Vol. 27, 846-873.

Mazumdar, Tridib and Sung Y. Jun (1992), "Effects of price Uncertainty on Consumer Purchase Budget and Price Thresholds," *Marketing Letters*, Vol. 3, 323-330.

Mazumdar, Tridib, S. P. Raj and Indrajit Sinha (2005), "Reference Price Research: Review and Propositions," *Journal of Marketing*, Vol. 69, 84-102.

Monroe, Kent B. (1973), "Buyers Subjective Perceptions of Price," *Journal of Marketing Research*, Vol. 8, 460-464.

Monroe, Kent B. (1990), *Pricing: Making Profitable Decisions*, 2nd ed., New York: Mc Graw-Hill.

Monroe, Kent B. and Angela Lee (1999), "Remembering versus knowing: Issues in Buyers' Processing of Price Information," *Journal of the Academy of Marketing Science*, Vol. 27, 207-225.

Ofir, Chezy (2004), "Reexamining Latitude of Price Acceptability and Price Thresholds: Predicting Basic Consumer Reaction to Price," *Journal of Consumer Research*, Vol. 30, 612-621.

Plassmann, Hilke, John O'Doherty, and Antonio Rangel (2007), "Orbitofrontal Cortex Encodes Willingness to Pay in Everyday Economic Transactions," *The Journal of Neuroscience*, 27 (37), 9984-988

Rao, Akshay R. and Wanda A. Sieben (1992), "The Effect of Prior Knowledge on Price Acceptability and the Type of Information Examined," *Journal of Consumer Research*, Vol. 19, 256-270.

Ridderinkhof, K. Richard, Markus Ullsperger, Eveline A. Crone, and Sander Nieuwenhuis (2004), "The Role of the Medial Frontal Cortex in Cognitive Control," *Science*, 306 (5695), 443-47.

Sanfey, Alan G., James K. Rilling, Jessica A. Aronson, Leigh E. Nystrom, and Jonathan D. Cohen (2003), "The Neural Basis of Economic Decision-Making in the Ultimatum Game," *Science*, 300 (5626), 1755-758.

Sherif, Muzafer and Carl I. Hovland (1961), *Social Judgment*, New Haven, CT: Yale University Press.

Squire, Larry R. (1992), "Memory and the hippocampus: A synthesis from findings with rats, monkey, and humans," *Psychological Review*, 99 (2), 195-231.

Volz, Kirsten G., Ricarda I.Schubotz, and D. Yves Cramon (2005), "Variants of uncertainty in decision-making and their neural correlates," *Brain Research Bulletin*, 67 (5), 403-412.

Völckner, Franziska and Julian Homann (2007), "The price-perceived quality relationship: A meta-analytic review and assessment of its determinants," *Marketing Letters*, Vol. 18, 181-196.

VanWestendorp, Peter H. (1976), "NSS-Price Sensitivity Meter (PSM) – a new approach to study consumer perception of price," *Proceedings of the ESOMAR Congress*, Venice.

Winer, Russell S. (1986), "A Reference Price Model of Brand Choice for Frequently Purchased Products," *Journal of Consumer Research*, Vol. 13, 250-257.

The Effects of Mastery on Subjective Utility

Irene Scopelliti, Carnegie Mellon University, USA
George Loewenstein, Carnegie Mellon University, USA

Motivation to achieve and to improve skills is an important characteristic of mankind and a strong driver of behavior, even if it is not related to any immediate physical reward. Human beings engage and put enormous amounts of effort in a wide variety of activities just to prove themselves they are capable of doing them and of improving their performance. In such activities, the mastery of the task appears to be a reward in itself, since it reflects one's control over the environment (White 1959). Mastery motivation has been defined as a psychological force (a disposition) that stimulates a person in a focused and persistent manner to attempt to master a skill or task that is at least moderately challenging for her (Morgan, Harmon, and Maslin-Cole 1990, 319).

Bentham (1781) included mastery, in the form of *pleasures of skill*, i.e., the pleasures derived by being good at an activity, in its original broad theory of utility. Mastery generates pleasure because it entails a sense of control over the environment, of goal achievement, and often a state of flow (Rozin 1999; Frijda 2002; Kubovy 1999; Csikszentmihalyi 1991). However, partly because of the difficulties encountered in formalizing its contribution to utility in decision theoretic terms (Loewenstein 1999), mastery has been overlooked even in the most recent refinements of utility theory. Nevertheless, the empirical observation that it is pleasurable to engage in an activity one is good at, no matter how useless it might be, while it is typically aversive to do something one is incompetent at, no matter how instrumental the activity (Loewenstein 1999), seems to legitimate the inclusion of this non-consumption form of utility within economic models.

In one experiment we manipulate mastery in mathematical problem solving (high vs. low) and assess its effects on persistence at (measured as the time spent and as the number of non-mandatory problems solved), and enjoyment (self-report measures) of the activity. In addition, we examine how the experience of high vs. low mastery affects the hypothetical choice between scenarios describing the two conditions (high-mastery with a low payoff and low-mastery with a high payoff). Subjects in the high-mastery condition (i.e., confronted with a set of mathematical problems that they can solve correctly almost in toto) spent more time, solved more problems and enjoyed more the activity than subjects in the low-mastery condition (i.e., confronted with a set mathematical problems of which they can solve correctly only a small fraction), despite in the latter condition they received a higher payoff per problem solved than in the former. However, results also show that these effects are not reflected in the hypothetical choice made by subjects between the two conditions: subjects that have experienced high mastery show a greater preference toward the low mastery condition (that gives a higher payoff) than subjects that have experienced low mastery, thus underestimating the impact of high mastery on their experienced utility compared to the pleasure of money. A reason could be that subjects in the high-mastery condition think of mastery as their natural state, and lack the ability to imagine how miserable low mastery would feel.

The results of this study provide initial insights on how mastery influences subjective utility by making a task being perceived as more enjoyable and by inducing subjects to work longer. From a social standpoint, it would be beneficial that people do something they master, since they would be more productive and happier than people that do something they are not good at. However, results also suggest that often people may choose activities they do not master because they give more weight to the materialistic utility of alternative options, disregarding non-consumption aspects of utility such as the pleasure of mastery.

REFERENCES

Bentham, Jeremy (1781) *An Introduction to the Principles of Morals and Legislation*, available online at http://www.constitution.org/jb/pml.htm.

Csikszentmihalyi, Mihaly (1991) *Flow: The psychology of optimal experience.* New York: Harper & Row Publishers.

Frijda, Nico H. (2002) "The nature of pleasure," in J. A. Bargh and D. K. Apsley (Eds.), *Unraveling the Complexities of Social Life: A Festschrift in Honor of Robert B. Zajonc*, Washington: American Psychological Association, 71–94.

Kubovy, Mauro (1999) "On the pleasures of the mind," In D. Kahneman, E. Diener, & N. Schwarz (Eds.), *Well-being: The Foundations of Hedonic Psychology.* New York: Russell Sage Foundation, 134-154.

Loewenstein, George (1999) "Because It Is There: The Challenge of Mountaineering... For Utility Theory," *Kyklos*, 52, 315-44.

Rozin, Paul (1999) "Preadaptation and the puzzles and properties of pleasure," In D. Kahneman, E. Diener & N. Schwarz (Eds.). *Well-being: The Foundations of Hedonic Psychology.* New York: Russell Sage Foundation, 109-133.

White, Robert W. (1959) "Motivation reconsidered: The concept of competence," *Psychological Review*, 66, 297-333.

Value Co-Creation in Subsistence Markets: An Empirical Study

Esi Abbam Elliot, University of Illinois at Chicago, USA
Benet DeBerry-Spence, University of Illinois at Chicago, USA

There is increasing interest in changing customers' role from passive adopters of product-services to equal partners in the process of adding value (Reichwald et al., 2003). One manifestation of this interest is value co-creation. Value co-creation has been defined as collaboration between a firm-provider and its customers to jointly create value (Vargo and Lusch, 2004, 2008; Prahalad and Ramaswami, 2004; Payne et al., 2007). Value is defined here as benefits eventually obtained by the customer through its involvement and assessment when using or consuming product-services (Holbrook and Batra, 1987). Recently, firm-providers such as Lego, Skype and E-bay, are engaging in value co-creation with their customers in the design and marketing of their products. Value co-creation activities are identified as a) collaboration, which refers to the firm relating to its customer as an equal and joint partner in the co-creation process (Lusch et al., 2007), b) dialogical interaction, which refers to interactivity, deep engagement, and the ability and willingness to act on both sides (Prahalad and Ramaswami, 2004) c) learning processes for both the firm-provider and the customer (Payne et al, 2008) and d) creative processes (e.g. Potts et al., 2008). Taken together, this body of work reveals the complexity and dynamism inherent to value co-creation.

Yet, existing research does not address a number of essential perspectives. First, value co-creation is a dyadic process, yet it has been studied primarily from the firm-provider's perspective; that is, most studies have focused on the customer's involvement in the firm's value creation. But what about the customer's perspective of the firm-provider's involvement in the customer's value creation? This perspective is important since value co-creation is a dyadic process and as such both the firm-providers' and the customers' viewpoints should be considered. Second, studies on value co-creation have been limited to business-to-consumer markets. Only recently has this work been extended to business-to-business markets (e.g., Ng et al., 2010). These studies, however, have mostly considered value co-creation between large firms.

How then is value co-created with micro-entrepreneurs (MEs), which form a large percentage of customers in many business markets? This consideration is important because value co-created with consumers or large firms may be different from value co-created with micro-entrepreneurs. Third, value co-creation has mostly been based on markets characterized by strong business infrastructures. A question that arises is: How does value co-creation occur between firm-providers and customers operating in markets characterized by weak business infrastructure (e.g., subsistence markets)? Business infrastructure significant impacts not only on how value is co-created, but also the type(s) of value that is co-created. For example whilst value for a business customer in a Western market might be convenience, value for the micro-entrepreneur in African markets might be an enhanced ability to leverage social networks.

In addition to these perspectives, studies on value co-creation have acknowledged the importance of socio-cultural factors (e.g. Penaloza and Venkatesh, 2006). Socio-cultural refers to traditional and social systems including values, norms and activities. With few exceptions (e.g. London, 2007; Simanas et al., 2008), however, theorizing has been limited to empirical studies based on Western markets, which have very different socio-cultural factors than most subsistence markets. Additionally, they have different environmental circumstances (i.e. environmental hostilities) from their Western counterparts. For example, subsistence markets, unlike more developed economies, have limited access to capital, technology, technical and managerial skills (Henriques and Herr, 2008). Arguably, it becomes obvious that incorporating non-Western markets is vital to gaining a global perspective and a more comprehensive understanding of value co-creation.

As such, the purpose of the dissertation is to address two critical research questions. First, how do firms (service providers) and micro-entrepreneur customers (customer-MEs) operating in subsistence markets engage in value co-creation? And what are the types of value they co-create? A subset question is how do socio-cultural and environmental factors impact the value co-creation process? An outcome of this research will be a working model of value co-creation. The context for this investigation is financial services firms and customer-MEs in Ghana, West Africa. Given that Ghana is ranked among the top ten reformers on the ease of doing business in Africa (World Bank report on Doing Business, 2007), it seems an ideal platform in which to investigate theories of value co-creation. Furthermore, due to the liberalized economy of Ghana, relationships between financial services firms and micro-enterprises are improving (Aryeetey, 2003). To address the research objectives, a qualitative approach, in the form of phenomenological interviews and observations will be used for the study. Phenomenological interviews are well suited for the study because they produce extraordinary depth and richness of data and enable the researcher to "understand phenomena from the perspective of those who experience it" (Cope, 2005, p.17). They also unveil the essence of participant experiences and uncover the reasons behind these experiences (Sanders, 1982).

Findings from this study will extend theories of value co-creation. Additionally, they will contribute to current research streams on creativity and learning and more specifically may be applied to theories of collateral learning (i.e. learning together to build the knowledge base of each partner) and relational-based creativity.

REFERENCES

Cope, J. (2005). Researching entrepreneurship through phenomenological inquiry: Philosophical and methodological issues, *International Small Business Journal*, 23(2): 159-183.
London, T. (2007). A base-of-the-pyramid perspective on poverty alleviation. *William Davidson Institute*, Working Paper.
Lusch, R. F., Vargo, S. L., & O'Brien, M. (2007). Competing through service: insights from service–dominant logic. *Journal of Retailing*, 83(1), 5–18.
Payne, A.. Storbacka, K. & Frow, P. (2008). Managing the co-creation of value. *Journal of the Academy of Marketing Science*, 36: 83-96.
Peñaloza, L. & Venkatesh, A. (2006). Further evolving the new dominant logic of Marketing: From Services to the Social Construction of Markets, *Marketing Theory*, 6 (3), 299-316.
Prahalad, C. K. & Ramaswamy, V. (2004). Co-Creation experiences: The next practice in value creation," *Journal of Interactive Marketing*, 18 (3), 5-14.
Vargo, S.L. & Lusch, R. F. (2004). Evolving to a new dominant logic for marketing. *Journal of Marketing*, 68 (1), 1-17.

Time Pressure, Choice Overload and Well-Being Decision Deferral

Carlos Rossi, PPGA/EA/UFRGS, Brazil
Kenny Basso, PPGA/EA/UFRGS, Brazil
Amanda Lima, PPGA/EA/UFRGS, Brazil
Mariana Rosa, PPGA/EA/UFRGS, Brazil
Danielle Machado, PPGA/EA/UFRGS, Brazil

The studies about time, behavior and consumption are acquiring a growing importance on the scientific agenda, highlighting time pressure as the main subject (Dhar and Nowlis, 1999; Ackerman and Gross, 2003; Suri and Monroe, 2003; Lin et al., 2008). The pressure felt is linked to the perception of being unable to devote sufficient time to the chosen activities. The lack of time could affect the well-being choices, since the individual may postpone activities linked to well-being and the improvement of life quality because of the time pressure and busy life in big cities. Based on this, we develop our study within well-being choice context, verifying when time pressure and choice overload could affect well-being decision deferral.

By relating time pressure to deferral, Dhar and Nowlis (1999) found that deferral is lower when the individual feels time pressure, since the customers may change the way they process information. Consumers under time pressure use an effortless non-compensatory decision strategy (Dhar and Nowlis, 1999). The use of decision non-compensatory rules facilitates the choice, and decreases the likelihood of choice deferral (Payne *et al.*, 1988).

In addition, an aspect that may change the way that an individual makes a choice and may interfere in deferral decision is the complexity of decision making (Tversky and Shafir, 1992), in which the conflict between the alternatives can cause consumer deferral. With increasing complexity of the sets of alternatives the individuals may choose to defer the decision to a future moment (Jessup *et al.*, 2009), or not choose to prevent a possible negative outcome (Anderson, 2003). Then, in a well-being context, under time pressure, individuals exposed to a larger choice set will postpone the decision. We predict, based on a prospect theory (Kahneman and Tversky, 1979), that the perceived losses in the larger set will be greater than those of the smaller set, and therefore the likelihood of choice deferral will be higher to individuals under time pressure and larger choice set. We assume that choice overload will moderate the effect of time pressure on choice deferral.

To test this, the experimental design was a 2 (with or without time pressure) by 2 (two or six alternatives in the choice set) between subjects, with 153 undergraduate students (57.5% female, age average of 26).

Before showing the scenario, we instigated the participants to think about his/her daily routine. In the scenario, participants received information about a research presented by a fictitious European health magazine, which praised the benefits of therapy for well-being. Then a program developed by the government that offered free treatment service to the population was presented. To participate in this program, it was necessary to choose the therapist. If the participant did not make his/her choice among the therapists, then he/she could choose to defer. In the time pressure conditions we show time count decreasing and inform a time limit to take a decision. To manipulate choice overload, we presented two or six therapists to each participant.

Checking the manipulations, the increase of the number of therapists increases the difficulty to make a decision (M_2=2.22, M_6=2.86, F=25.09, df=1, p<.01), and under time pressure condition the pressure felt by subjects was higher ($M_{no-time}$=2.13, $M_{time-pressure}$=3.17, F=37.64, df=1, p<.01).

Our analysis indicates a significant interaction between time pressure and number of alternatives (Wald $\chi^2(1)$=4.15, p<.05). In the two alternatives set, we found that participants were more likely to defer without time pressure (35.3%) than with time pressure (17.2%, $\chi^2(1)$=10.25, p<.01), which confirms the results found by Dhar and Nowlis (1999). However, under time pressure subjects in the six alternatives condition (40.5%) choose deferral more than subjects in the two alternatives (17.2%, $\chi^2(1)$=12.57, p<.01), which confirms our assumption that choice overload moderates the effect of time pressure on deferral. In addition, there are no differences in the amount of deferral between six alternative set without time pressure (35.3%) and six alternative set with time pressure (40.5%, $\chi^2(1)$=.21, p=.64).

Although time pressure reduces the focus on negative information, diminishing the choice deferral, the increase of the quantity of alternatives in the choice set may be linked to the increase of the feeling of loss, since more alternatives represent more chances to make the wrong choice. The interaction between time pressure and choice overload evidences that the perceived losses suppress the effect of time pressure on choice deferral, since the more evident the losses the higher the risk associated to the choice, which is why the individual chooses to defer. The risk in this study was associated to the commitment to the experimental public health program and the time spent to participate. This result integrates the field of research suggested by Scheibehenne *et al.* (2010), and supports the assumption that time pressure interacts with a number of alternatives causing choice deferral.

We suppose that the type of information active in the subject, may reduce the risk in the decision. The information active before the decision drives the choice (deferral or not) since the information is congruent with the decision to be made (Laran, 2010). Based on this, we consider that our scenario may induce the individual to reflect about self-controlled past decisions (e.g. work), which could enable him/her to take an indulgent decision (Laran, 2010) in the experiment, choosing deferral under time pressure and with six alternatives. Therefore, we suggest to follow this study with the manipulation of the type of information prime in the subject, expecting that no differences will be found between two and six alternatives under time pressure.

Additionally, the type of decision (in this case, the opportunity to choose a therapist) may influence the interaction between time pressure and choice overload, and then have an impact on the choice deferral. So, a hedonic set choice may be more attractive and the effects of time pressure suppress the effects of choice overload, while an instrumental one may be more influenced by the choice overload effects. Hence we suggest that future studies manipulate the type of decision and the type of product or service involved in the choice set.

REFERENCES

Ackerman, David S., and Barbara L. Gross, (2003), "So Many Choices, So Little Time: Measuring the Effects of Free Choice and Enjoyment on Perception of Free Time, Time Pressure and Time Deprivation," *Advances in Consumer Research*, Vol. 30, ed. Punam Anand Keller, Dennis Rook, GA: Association for Consumer Research, 290-294.

Anderson, Christopher J. (2003), "The Psychology of Doing Nothing: Forms of Decision Avoidance Result From Reason and Emotion," *Psychological Bulletin*, 129 (1), 139-167.

Dhar, Ravi, and Stephen M. Nowlis (1999), "The Effect of Time Pressure on Consumer Choice Deferral," *Journal of Consumer Research*, 25 (4), 369-384.

Jessup, Ryan K., Elizabeth S. Veinott, Peter M. Todd, and Jerome R. Busemeyer (2009), "Leaving the Store Empty-Handed: Testing Explanations for the Too- Much-Choice Effect Using Decision Field Theory," *Psychology and Marketing*, 26 (3), 299-320.

Kahneman, Daniel, and Amos Tversky (1979), "Prospect Theory: An Analysis of Decision Under Risk," *Econometrica*, 47 (2), 263-290.

Laran, Juliano (2010), "Choosing your future: temporal distance and the balance between self-control and indulgence," *Journal of Consumer Research*, 36 (6), 1002-1015.

Lin, Chien-Huang, Ya-Chung Sun, Shih-Chieh Chuang and Hung-Jen Su (2008), "Time Pressure and the Compromise and Attraction Effects in Choice," Advances in Consumer Research, Vol. 35, ed. Angela Y. Lee, Dilip Soman, GA: Association for Consumer Research, 348-352.

Payne, John W., James R. Bettman, and Eric J. Johnson (1988), "Adaptive Strategy Selection in Decision Making," *Journal of Experimental Psychology: Learning, Memory, and Cognition*, 14 (3), 534-552.

Scheibehenne, Benjamin, Rainer Greifeneder, and Peter M. Todd (2010), "Can There Ever Be Too Many Options? A Meta-Analytic Review of Choice Overload," *Journal of Consumer Research*, 37 (3), 409–425.

Suri, Rajneesh, and Kent B. Monroe (2003), "The Effects of Time Constraints on Consumers' Judgments of Prices and Products," *Journal of Consumer Research,* 30 (1), 92-104.

Tversky, Amos, and Eldar Shafir (1992), "Choice under Conflict: The Dynamics of Deferred Decision," *Psychological Science,* 3 (6), 358-361.

Images of Attractive Women Make Young Females Behave Virtuously

Xiuping Li, National University of Singapore, Singapore

Meng Zhang, Chinese University of Hong Kong, China

Images of sexy women are ubiquitous in daily life. Prior research has focused on the negative effect of these stimuli on other women. For example, women engaging in upward social comparison with images of physically more attractive women might demonstrate a lower level of self-satisfaction and a higher rate of self-destructive behavior, such as an eating disorder (Grogan, 2008; Cattarin et al. 2000). In this paper, we test how such kinds of stimuli would affect females' social interaction. Drawing on prior research which shows that the positive relationship between physical attractiveness and social popularity is a strong and internalized belief for women (Brouwers, 1990; Diener, Wolsic, and Fujita 1995), we propose that exposure to pictures of attractive women leads other women to behave more pro-socially in unrelated tasks. This might occur for two reasons. First, when physical attractiveness, as a source of gaining favorable social impressions and acceptance by others, is under threat from the sight of images of ideally-shaped women, other women may become more motivated to gain such favorable impressions by engaging in desirable behavior. This is consistent with the view of self-affirmation theory (Liu and Steele, 1986), which proposes that when one's integrity or adequacy is being challenged, one will strive to "protect" it by employing other means of achieving integrity or adequacy. Second, the presence of attractive women may prime a motivation to gain social popularity due to the strong association between the two concepts for females. We investigated our predictions in three experiments.

EXPERIMENT 1: GREEN PRODUCT CHOICE

All participants were college female students aged from 18 to 24 recruited from a large university in Asia. Experiment 1 (N = 87) examined participants' choices of green products. Participants were randomly assigned to three conditions (sexy women, landscape, and baseline). In the first two conditions, they were asked to select the best picture out of eight that they thought fit for the cover of either a *fashion* magazine (sexy women condition) or a *travel* magazine (landscape condition). All participants were then asked to indicate their preference of battery brand from a choice of two. Brand A was described as "lasting for longer hours" and brand B as "being the most environmentally friendly." The prices were the same. As predicted, participants in the attractive women condition were more likely to select brand B (53%) than those in the other two conditions (16% for baseline and 28% for landscape condition, χ^2 (1, N = 87) = 9.17, p < .01). The other two conditions did not differ (χ^2 (1, N = 57) = 1.20, p = .27).

EXPERIMENT 2: PROSOCIAL BEHAVIOR

Experiment 2 (N = 132) examined whether the changes in women's preference for green products were merely driven by viewing "human pictures", which could have heighted concern about social values. We included a condition in which some participants viewed pictures of average-looking women. The participants were randomly assigned into three picture conditions. The conditions of attractive women and landscapes employed the same set of pictures as in experiment 1, while in the average-looking women condition, participants were asked to select a picture of an average-looking woman to appear on the cover of a *life* magazine. Pretesting showed that the pictures of average-looking women were evaluated as less attractive than those of sexy women (N = 60; p < .001).

Afterwards, participants were asked to play nine decomposed games in which they needed to allocate points between themselves and a stranger. These games are a widely used technique for measuring social value orientation (Van Lange et al.1997). Based on the established criteria, participants were categorized as *pro-socials* if they chose six or more "pro-social options" (maximizing a stranger's welfare). As predicted, after viewing pictures of landscapes or average-looking women, 26% and 30% of the participants were *prosocials* (p = .69). However, after viewing pictures of attractive women, the percentage of *prosocials* significantly increased to 51% (χ^2s > 4.13, ps < .05).

EXPERIMENT 3: ADVERTISEMENT COPY AND PURCHASE INTENTION

Experiment 3 (N=105) had a 2 (pictures: attractive women or landscapes) × 2 (ad frame: self-benefit or other-benefit) between-subject design. After selecting the picture, participants viewed an advertisement for a new vacuum cleaner. The two advertisement frames differed only in the taglines. In the *self-benefit* condition, the tagline read "Great News for Your Ears," whereas in the *other-benefit* condition, it read "Great News for Your Neighbor's Ears." The participants were asked to indicate their intention to buy this product if they were shopping for a new vacuum cleaner on a scale ranging from 1 (not likely at all) to 7 (very likely).

As predicted, an interaction was observed (F(1, 101) = 5.75, p < .05). After viewing the pictures of landscapes, the participants indicated a higher intention to buy when the advertisement emphasized benefit to the self rather than others (M = 5.28 vs. 4.23; F(1, 101) = 8.23, p < .01). However, after viewing pictures of attractive women, participants' preference for the other-benefit advertisement increased; there were no differences between the two advertisement conditions (M = 5.20 vs. 5.42; p = .59).

Taken together, the results of three experiments support our prediction that exposure to pictures of attractive women as those portrayed in mass media will enhance other women's pro-social behavior in unrelated tasks. These results are interesting and worth future investigation. For instance, responses of women from different demographic groups should be explored.

REFERENCES

Brouwers, M. (1990). Treatment of body image among women with bulimia nervosa. *Journal of Counseling and Development, 69*, 144-147.

Cattarin, J.A., Thompson, J.K., Thomas, C., & Williams, R. (2000). Body image, mood and televised images of attractiveness: The role of social comparison. *Journal of Social Clinical Psychology*, 19, 220-239.

Diener, E., Wolsic, B., & Fujita, F. (1995). Physical attractiveness and subjective well-being. *Journal of Personality and Social Psychology*, 69, 120-129.

Grogan, S. (2008). *Body image: Understanding body dissatisfaction in men, women and children.* London: Routledge, Taylor and Francis group.

Liu, T. J., & Steele, C. M. (1986). Attributional analysis as self-affirmation. *Journal of Personality and Social Psychology*, *51*, 531-540

Rosenberg, M. (1965). Society and the adolescent self-image. Princeton, NJ: Princeton University Press.

Van Lange, P. A. M., Otten, W., De Bruin, E. M. N., & Joireman, J. A. (1997). Development of prosocial, individualistic, and competitive orientations: Theory and preliminary evidence. *Journal of Personality and Social Psychology*, 73, 733-746

My Heart Longs for More: The Role of Emotions in Assortment Size Preferences

Yangjie Gu, London Business School, UK
Aylin Aydinli, London Business School, UK

Past research has documented the factors that influence consumer choice among assortments, such as the decision flexibility (McAlister and Pessemier 1982), the probability of a match between consumers' preferences and the available alternatives (Lancaster 1990), availability of ideal point (Chernev 2003), the anticipated cognitive effort in making a choice (Huffman and Kahn 1998) and the nature of decision process (Chernev 2006). This research has mainly focused on the cognitive processes used in the construction of assortment size preferences.

In this paper, we investigate the role of emotions in influencing consumers' assortment-size preferences. In particular, we explore whether decisions based on affective versus cognitive processes may influence preferences for assortment size. Prior research has shown that emotional system is holistic (Epstein 1994). Accordingly, we argue that while evaluating the assortment, people who engage in such holistic processing may focus more on judging the overall features of the choice set. Research has shown that individuals who perform global evaluations favour high variety (Ratner, Kahn and Kahnman 1999). Compared to smaller assortments, larger assortments may therefore provide greater "fit" to the desire for more variety. Hence, we argue that people who make feeling-based choices would be more satisfied with a large assortment than a small assortment.

In contrast, people who are more likely to engage in cognitive processing may experience less "fit" from the large assortment compared to people who engage in affective processing. As a consequence, the difference in preference for large versus smaller assortment is mitigated when people are making reason-based choices. The predicted effect of different types of processing strategies on preference for large assortments versus smaller assortments was tested in three studies by using both individual difference measure and indirect manipulation of likelihood of reliance on feelings.

In study 1, we provided participants a scenario where they were asked to consider purchasing a DVD at an entertainment store that either provided a selection of 24 movies (small-set condition) or a selection of 60 movies (large-set condition). We measured (1) their satisfaction with the assortment and (2) their dispositional tendency to rely on their feelings as opposed to their reason and logic by using the 10-item version of the Rational-Experiential Inventory (Epstein et al. 1996). As hypothesized, for participants who are inclined to adopt affective thinking styles, those in the large-set condition were more satisfied with their assortment than those in the small-set condition. Conversely, this difference in satisfaction was not significant for those who adopted cognitive processing.

Study 2 was designed to replicate the effect found in Study 1 by manipulating the degree of reliance on affective processing. This study was a 2 (assortments size: small vs. large) x 2 (cognitive load: high vs. low) between-subjects design. We provided participants a scenario in which they were asked to select a coffee for their friend from either a selection of 12 options (small-set condition) or a selection of 36 options (large-set condition). In order to induce different degrees of reliance on affective system, we used the cognitive load manipulation (Shiv and Fedorikhin 1999), where participants were asked to memorize either a 2-digit code (low-load condition), or a 10-digit code (high-load condition) and to reproduce the code at the end of the study. Prior research has demonstrated that choice under cognitive load limits cognitive capacity, thus generating a greater degree of reliance on affective system than choice under low cognitive load (Lieberman et al. 2002). Accordingly, we predicted that participants who memorized 10-digit (vs. 2-digit) code are likely to rely more on their affective system while making decisions. Consistent with our hypothesis, when their cognitive capacities were constrained and therefore had to rely on affective system, participants in the large-set condition were more satisfied with the selection of coffees than those in the small-set condition. However, this difference in satisfaction was not significant for low-load participants who relied on affective system less.

Study 3 was designed in order to test the underlying mechanism, as well as to replicate the effect demonstrated in Study 1 and Study 2. This study was a 2 (assortments size: small vs. large) x 2 (cognitive load: high vs. low) between-subjects design. Similar to Study 2, reliance on feelings was operationalized by manipulating participants' cognitive capacities. Participants were asked to select a snack for their friend either from a selection of 36 snacks (large-set condition) or a selection of 12 snacks (small-set condition). At the end of the study, participants answered some questions about (1) their satisfaction with the assortments they were given; and (2) desire for variety. Replicating the previous findings, the results showed that high-load participants who were confronted with large assortments were more satisfied with their snack selection than those who were confronted with smaller assortments. Mediation analysis showed that the desire for variety mediates the effect of the choice-set size on satisfaction with the selection, in the context of making either feeling-based or reason-based choices.

To summarize, we found that the reliance on affective processes boosts individuals' preference for larger assortments as opposed to smaller assortments. However, this difference in preferences is mitigated when individuals rely on cognitive processes. Study 1 and Study

2 have demonstrated the main effect. Study 3 has provided the process evidence: A large assortment provides a better "fit" to the desire for variety seeking that is triggered by the emotional processing, thereby inducing greater satisfaction, compared to a smaller assortment.

REFERENCES

Chernev, Alexander (2003), "When More Is Less and Less Is More: The Role of Ideal Point Availability and Assortment in Consumer Choice," *Journal of Consumer   Research*, 30 (September), 170-183.

_____ (2006), "Decision Focus and Consumer Choice among Assortments," *Journal of Consumer Research*, 33 (June), 50-59.

Epstein, Seymour (1994), "Integration of the Cognitive and the Psychodynamic Unconscious," *American Psychologist*, 49 (8), 709–24.

Epstein, Seymour, Rosemery Pacini, Veronika Denes-Raj, and Harriet Heier (1996), "Individual differences in Intuitive-Experiential and Analytical-Rational Thinking Styles," *Journal of Personality and Social Psychology*, 71 (2), 390-405.

Lancaster, Kelvin (1990), "The Economics of Product Variety: A Survey," *Marketing Science*, 9 (Summer), 189-206.

Lieberman, Matthew D., Ruth Gaunt, Daniel T. Gilbert, and Yaacov Trope (2002), "Reflexion and Reflection: A Social Cognitive Neuroscience Approach to Attributional Inference," in *Advances in Experimental Social Psychology*, Vol. 34,   ed. Mark P. Zanna, San Diego: Academic Press, 199–249.

McAlister, Leigh (1982), "A Dynamic Attribute Satiation Model of Variety-Seeking Behavior," *Journal of Consumer Research*, 9 (September), 141-151.

Ratner, Rebecca K., Barbara E. Kahn, and Daniel Kahneman (1999), "Choosing Less Preferred Experiences for the Sake of Variety," *Journal of Consumer Research*, 26 (1), 1-15.

Shiv, Baba and Alexander Fedorikhin (1999), "Heart and Mind in Conflict: The Interplay of Affect and Cognition in Consumer Decision Making," *Journal of Consumer Research*, 26 (December), 278–92.

Dispositional Greed: Scale Development and Validation

Goedele Krekels, Department of Marketing, Ghent University, Belgium
Mario Pandelaere, Department of Marketing, Ghent University, Belgium
Bert Weijters, Department of Marketing & Sales, Vlerick Leuven Gent Management School

BACKGROUND AND PURPOSE

Greed is often invoked as an explanation for non-cooperative behavior in economic games (Stanley & Ume, 1998), as a driving force in resource exploitation (Ludwig et al, 1993) and is considered as intrinsic in a materialistic lifestyle (Belk, 1985). Despite this view of greed as a fundamental motive, no empirical research has been conducted to investigate causes and consequences of greed. Related to this, it is not clear why people differ in how greedy they are. To investigate these issues, a measure for dispositional greed - or greed as an individual behavior caused by internal characteristics - is develop to investigate the extent to which various factors covary with greed.

We first engaged in a thorough review of the philosophical and psychological literature concerning greed and conducted focus group research to identify different associations with 'greed' that may serve as the foundation for the development and individual difference measure of greed. In a second step an initial item pool of 60 items was generated based on theoretical assumptions, on operationalizations of theoretically related constructs in previous studies, like materialism (Richins and Dawson, 1992), envy (Belk, 1995) and greed avoidance (Lee and Ashton, 2004), and on population sampling, thus enhancing face validity. Furthermore, the response format was determined based on response tendencies and social desirability literature. The item pool and response format were both judged by laypersons for face and content validity, and the response format was assessed by a measurement expert. Moreover, the scale items and question wording were checked by a professional copy editor to ensure wording clarity, wording redundancy and correct meaning of the items. This resulted in an initial item pool of 60 questions attributed to five latent dimensions, of which three were highly related. These dimensions were: wanting more than is merely needed; insatiability; joy and pleasure from owning much; greed for status, wealth and power; and the use of ethically questionable methods to gain more.

METHOD

Pilot testing was used as an item-trimming procedure and to obtain initial estimates of reliability and validity. Given that the scale will be administered to further samples for refinement, a pilot study can reduce the number of items that do not meet certain psychometric criteria in an initial pool to a more manageable number. Also, items can be assessed initially for internal consistency, means, variances, average inter-item correlation and factor structure. Therefore, as part of a bigger questionnaire, the greed scale was administered among 400 Caucasian Americans (200 males, M age = 44.5, SD = 12.4).

RESULTS

An exploratory factor analysis was conducted for trimming and retaining items for the final scale. This EFA was used to reveal items that load poorly in terms of magnitude on an intended factor or load highly on more than one factor. The useful sample of this pilot study was 318. Factor interpretation took all items into account with loadings greater than 0.35. The requirements for the measures of sampling adequacy were met: KMO was 0.884 and Bartlett's Test of Sphericity was highly significant at $p < 0.001$. Items which violated the criteria of anti-image correlations greater than 0.5, high inter-item correlations through item-wording redundancy, high cross loadings on different factors or low factor loadings were eliminated from the factor solution. The cumulative percentage of total variance explained by the final factor solution was 63%. Three factors were retained: insatiability, materialistic greed and unethical greed, measured by 10, 15 and 7 items respectively and with Cronbach's Alphas of 0.89, 0.83 and 0.78, respectively.

On this refined item pool, an initial confirmatory factor analysis was conducted. Bearing in mind that more studies have to be executed before finalizing the scale, an initial test of internal consistency and validity was deemed useful as a detection of initial items that may threaten the dimensionality of the scale. The factor structure derived from the EFA and from theory showed a manageable initial fit. After deletion of items with highly correlated residual errors or low squared multiple correlations the model had a decent fit: the χ^2/Df ratio was 1.997, the Goodness-of-fit index was 0.89, the Non Normed Fit Index was 0.96 and the Standardized RMR was 0.056. The Root Mean Square Approximation was only 0.059 but the threshold of 0.05 fell within the 90% confidence interval and had an upper confidence interval limit of 0.067. Discriminant analysis showed that all three greed constructs were significantly different and they had adequate composite reliability indices: 0.84 (insatiability, 7 items), 0.87 (materialistic greed, 10 items) and 0.79 (unethical greed, 5 items), respectively.

RELEVANCE

This model still has to be tested profoundly through further studies on several samples of relevant populations and additional item analysis and estimates of validity across studies have to be executed. Nonetheless, this initial study shows that this scale should be reliable and valid. Next the scale will be used to gain insight in greed. First, more research will be executed investigating what it means to be greedy, why people differ in how greedy they are, and how the concept of greed is linked to other psychological traits such as materialism, egoism and individualism. Second, when we have a better understanding of the effects and motives for greed, experiments will be set up to gain further insight into the nature of greed and to see how greed affects economic decisions. Specifically we will explore whether greed necessarily leads to uncooperative decision making in economic games, and if so, how these effects differ from those due to (anticipated) envy.

LITERATURE

Balot RK (2001) Greed and Injustice in Classical Athens, Princeton: Princeton university press, 280 p.

Belk RW (1985) Materialism: Trait Aspects of Living in the Material World. *Journal of Consumer Research, 12*, 265–80.

Insko A, Schopler J, Hoyle RH, Dardis GJ & Graetz KA (1990) Individual-Group Discontinuity as a Function of Fear and Greed Chester. *Journal of Personality and Social Psychology*, 1, 68-79.

Lee K & Ashton MC (2004) The HEXACO Personality Inventory: A new measure of the major dimensions of personality. *Multivariate Behavioral Research*, 39, 329-358.

Ludwig D, Hilborn R, & Walters C (1993) Uncertainty, resource exploitation and conservation: lessons from history. *Ecological Applications*, 4, 548-549.

Rand A (1964). The virtues of selfishness. New York: Signet, 173p.

Richins ML & Dawson S (1992) A consumer values orientation for materialism and its measurement: scale development and validation. *Journal of Consumer Research*, 19, 303–316.

Robertson AF (2001) Greed : gut feelings, growth, and history, Cambridge : Polity press, 277 p.

Stanley TD & Tran U (1998) Economics Students Need not be Greedy: fairness and the ultimatum game. *Journal of Socio-Economics*, 27, 657–664.

Why Does Guilt Lead to Self-punishment?
A Deterrence Account

Liang Song, National University of Singapore, Singapore
Xiuping Li, National University of Singapore, Singapore
Gita Venkataramani Johar, Columbia University, USA

The self-punishment triggered by the feeling of guilt has been documented in the literature. For example, it has been found that participants who cheated in an earlier task tended to impose a higher intensity of electronic shock to themselves later in an unrelated task (Wallington 1973). Similarly, Nelissen and Zeelenberg (2009) manipulated guilt via fairness concern and found that people in the guilt condition tended to allocate more penalty points to themselves later on. However, seeking unpleasant experience voluntarily seems to contradict with the hedonistic assumptions (e.g., seeking pleasure but avoiding pain), and such a behavior has been explained with the motivation to reduce guilt feelings via self-punishment. In other words, it has been suggested that people carry out the "eye for an eye" philosophy even for their own wrongdoings and want to balance out the wrong for which they felt responsible by punishing themselves. Self-punishment thus is predicted to restore moral balance and resolve the negative experience of guilt (Lindsay-Hartz, De Rivera, and Mascolo 1995). This view focuses on the affect-regulatory function of self-punishment.

However, we propose that people can have the intention to "prolong" their negative experience via self-punishment to protect the goal that they have failed (which elicits guilt). This view focuses on the strategic motivational function of guilt and is referred to as the "deterrence" account.

The position that self-punishment is viewed as a motivational device for future successes is consistent with the "feeling-is-for-doing" approach (Zeelenberg and Pieters 2006). According to this approach, emotion facilitates behavior that is aimed to address the concern reflected in an emotion. As guilt, a self-conscious emotion, arises when one's behavior violates norms or goals that guide our behavior, it will be associated with an unsatisfied goal when such as an emotion is experienced (e.g., Berndsen et al. 2004). In most situations, people do not have opportunities to satisfy the goal. Alternatively, they might be in a mind of seeking ways to "protect" the failed goals by strategically choosing to stay in negative states. We argue that self-punishment may occur as a way to make the failed goal more likely to be achieved in the future.

If as we argue that self-punishment (e.g., forgoing pleasure experience) is a strategic behavior to protect one's goal, those who experience guilt should be more likely to demonstrate a tendency to engage in self-punishing behavior when and only when participants are motivated to achieve the failed goal. Thus, we will find more self-punishing behavior when participants are persistent with their goals (Study 1), when the failed goal is more accessible in their mind when they make decisions (Study 2), or when they believe that self-punishment is useful in achieving their goals (Study 3).

In study 1, goal persistence was primed with a "sentence unscrambling task", and guilt was elicited with a recall task. All participants recalled an experience where they did not spend their own money prudently and felt responsible for their decisions. After that, self-punishment was assessed with a "news reading task" where participants chose one piece of news among two: one about a baby who died because of child abuse, the other about how to take an enjoyable vacation. As predicted, when experiencing guilt, participants who were persistent with their goals were more likely to pick up the sad news than participants who were less persistent with their goals (72.2% vs. 38.9%, $p < .05$).

Study 2 extended the findings of Study 1 in three aspects. First, a different goal violation scenario was employed to elicit guilt: failure in academic performance. Second, rather than goal persistence, participants' chronic achievement motivation was measured and used as the moderator (Hart and Albarracín 2009). Third, self-punishment was measured more directly. Participants indicated the amount of penalty they wanted to allocate to themselves for giving a wrong guess. Supporting the "deterrence" account, guilty participants allocated significantly more penalty points to themselves than did non-guilty participants only when chronic achievement motivation was high (2.81 vs. 1.45, $p = .001$), but not when it was low (1.24 vs. 1.59, $p = .373$).

Study 3 further supported the "deterrence" account by showing the moderating role of individual beliefs regarding whether self-punishment is a good way for goal achievement. It found that participants were more willing to forgo pleasant experiences in response to guilt (than non-guilt) only when they regarded self-punishment as useful in achieving their goals. Belief regarding the instrumentality of self-punishment was assessed with 3 items (e.g., "Self-punishment for one's goal failure makes one remember the failed goal better"; Cronbach's $\alpha = 0.77$). Guilt was manipulated as in study 2, and self-punishment was assessed with two scenario questions (e.g. forgoing a coupon of dinning at a five-star restaurant, accepting a concert ticket from a close friend). Results hold for both combined and separate responses.

Overall, this research added to the growing body of research on self-conscious emotions by looking at the strategic motivational function of guilt.

REFERENCES

Berndsen, Mariëtte, Mariëtte Joop van der Plight, Bertjan Doosje, and Antony S. R. Manstead (2004), "Guilt and Regret: The Determining Role of Interpersonal and Intrapersonal Harm," *Cognition & Emotion*, 18 (1), 55-70.

Hart, W. and D. Albarracín (2009), "The Effects of Chronic Achievement Motivation and Achievement Primes on the Activation of Achievement and Fun Goals," *Journal of Personality and Social Psychology*, 97 (6), 1129.

Lindsay-Hartz, J., J. De Rivera, and M.F. Mascolo (1995), "Differentiating Guilt and Shame and Their Effects on Motivation," in *Self-Conscious Emotions: The Psychology of Shame, Guilt, Embarrassment, and Pride*, ed. J. P. Tangney and K. W. Fischer, New York: The Guilford Press.

Wallington, Sue A. (1973), "Consequences of Transgression: Self-Punishment and Depression," *Journal of Personality & Social Psychology*, 28 (1), 1-7.

Zeelenberg, Marcel and Rik Pieters (2006), "Feeling Is for Doing: A Pragmatic Approach to the Study of Emotions in Economic Behavior," in *Social Psychology and Economics*, ed. D. De Cremer, M. Zeelenberg and K. Murnighan, Mahwah, NJ: Erlbaum, 117-37.

Individualism, Collectivism, and Goal-Oriented Saving

Zhenfeng Ma, University of Ontario Institute of Technology, Canada
Terry Wu, University of Ontario Institute of Technology, Canada
Zhiyong Yang, University of Texas, USA
Tamotsu Nakamura, Kobe University, Japan

Domestic savings rate in the United States is persistently lower than that in some East Asian countries such as Japan. The United States and East Asia also differ markedly on an important cultural dimension, namely individualism (vs. collectivism). The United States is characterized by higher individualism and lower collectivism than are East Asian countries (Hofstede 1980). It may be tempting to posit that individualism is associated with lower propensity to save than is collectivism. In this research, we show that chronically salient or situationally primed individualism is actually associated with a higher propensity for goal-oriented saving than is collectivism, provided that the saving is for self-enhancing rather than self-indulging purposes.

Hypotheses. People often save money for a specific purpose. We recognize two distinct types of saving in terms of their purposes. The first type involves saving for self-enhancement, such as saving for a better education or career. The other type relates to saving for self-indulgence, such as saving for a vacation or a luxury car. The dichotomy between the self-enhancing and self-indulging goals is akin to the dichotomy between virtues and vices (Dhar and Wertenbroch 2000).

We expect that people high in individualist value (the "individualists") have a higher propensity to save for self-enhancing purposes than do those high in collectivist value ("collectivists"). Such differential propensity to save for self-enhancement can be explained by the difference in self-orientation associated with the individualists versus the collectivists. The individualists define the self as an autonomous entity separated from others, whereas the collectivists view the self as part of a social network and connected with others (Markus and Kitayama 1991). Because of their orientation toward the self, the individualists will attach more importance to goals that hold high stakes for self-enhancement (Markus and Kitayama 1991). Consequently, the individualists will be motivated to save for self-enhancing goals, especially when saving is the only means for achieving such goals. By contrast, the collectivists insist on self-others connection and show pervasive attentiveness to the relevant others. Research has shown that the perception of an extended social network can serve as a psychological "cushion" against financial risks (but not other types of risks such as physical risks) (Hsee and Weber 1999; Mandel 2003). Because of this cushion effect, the collectivists will be more tolerant of financial uncertainties and consequently are less motivated to save for personally significant goals compared with the individualists. However, the individualists and the collectivists will not differ in their propensity to save for self-indulging purposes. This is because self-indulgence is not more pertinent to the goal orientation of the individualists versus the collectivists and is thus unlike to induce differential propensity to save between the individualists and the collectivists.

H1: *The individualists have a higher propensity to save for self-enhancing purposes than do the collectivists, whereas the individualists and the collectivists do not differ in their propensity to save for self-indulging purposes.*

People often need to resist myopic temptations to prematurely dip into their savings in order to fulfill their savings plan. Because the individualists have a strong motivation to fulfill their savings plan for self-enhancing purposes, they will be less likely to yield to myopic temptations when following through such a plan than will the collectivists. However, the individualists and the collectivists will not differ in their ability to resist myopic temptations when saving for self-indulging purposes, because the motivation to save for such purposes does not differ between the two groups of individuals in the first place.

H2: *The individualists have a higher propensity to resist myopic temptations than do the collectivists when saving for self-enhancing purposes; the individualists and the collectivists do not differ in their propensity to resist myopic temptations when saving for self-indulging purposes.*

METHODS AND RESULTS

The hypotheses were tested through three experiments, in which individualism (collectivism) was manipulated through either situational prime or culture. In experiment 1, we manipulated individualism (vs. collectivism) through situational prime. The experiment features a 2 (prime: individualism vs. collectivism) × 2 (purpose of saving: self-enhancing vs. self-indulging) design. Participants were 190 undergraduate students in a Canadian university. We first primed individualist or collectivist values using a scenario about a tennis match (Aaker and Lee 2001). Participants then imagined a scenario in which they made decisions on how much to save out of a fixed amount of personal income for an anticipated job transition (self-enhancement) or for a vacation (self-indulgence). Consistent with hypothesis 1, the individualists saved more than the collectivists for job transition ($p < .05$), whereas the collectivists saved directionally more than the individualists for a vacation. The same findings were replicated in experiment 2, using different prime for individualism (collectivism) (Trafimow, Triandis, and Goto 1991) and different stimuli for purpose of saving (education vs. vacation).

Experiment 3 is a cross-country study, which features a 2 (country: US vs. Japan) × 2 (purpose of saving: self-enhancing vs. self-indulging) design. Participants were 300 undergraduate students from a US university and 300 undergraduate students from a Japanese university. Purpose of saving was manipulated as previously. After indicating the amount of savings, participants imagined a scenario in which their most favourite musician has come to town to stage a live concert. Temptation for immediate gratification was measured in terms of the amount of money they would spend out of their savings to buy a concert ticket. Consistent with hypothesis 1, the US participants reported a higher savings rate than did their Japanese counterparts for job transition ($p < .05$), but the two groups did not differ in their savings for the vacation. Furthermore, the US participants showed a higher tendency to resist myopic temptation than did the Japanese participants when saving for self-enhancing purposes, as indicated by the lower amount of money they spent on the concert ticket ($p < .05$). However, the tendency to resist temptation did not differ between the US and the Japanese participants when saving for a vacation. Thus, hypothesis 2 was supported.

DISCUSSION

Our findings show that individualism (vs. collectivism) promotes goal-oriented saving behavior, provided that the saving is for self-enhancing purposes. So far, we have focused on decision contexts where the saving is for relatively short-term goals and saving is the only means of achieving the goals. In the next step, we will investigate whether the individualists' relatively high propensity to save for self-enhancement will persist when alternative means for obtaining financial resources (e.g., borrowing) is available, or when the saving is for long-term goals.

REFERENCES

Aaker, Jennifer L. and Angela Y. Lee (2001), "'I' Seek pleasures and 'We' Avoid Pains: The Role of Self-Regulatory Goals in Information Processing and Persuasion," *Journal of Consumer Research*, 28 (June), 33-49.

Dhar, Ravi and Klaus Wertenbrauch (2000), "Consumer Choice between Hedonic and Utilitarian Goods," *Journal of Marketing Research,* 37 (February), 60-71,

Hofstede, Geert. (1980). *Culture's Consequences: International Differences in Work-Related Values*. Newbury Park, CA: Sage.

Hsee, Christopher K. and Elke U. Weber (1999), "Cross-National Differences in Risk Preference and Lay Predictions," *Journal of Behavioral Decision Making*, 12 (June), 165-179.

Mandel, Naomi (2003), "Shifting Selves and Decision Making: The Effects of Self-Construal Priming on Consumer Risk-Taking," *Journal of Consumer Research*, 30 (June), 30-40.

Markus, Hazel and Shinobu Kitayama (1991), "Culture and the Self: Implications for Cognition, Emotion, and Motivation," *Psychological Review*, 98 (April), 224-53.

Social Stratification and Luxury Consumption Value: Classifying Complaint Types of Korean Luxury Consumers

Su Yeon Kim, Yonsei University, South Korea
Ae-Ran Koh, Yonsei University, South Korea

This study was conducted in reference to two intertwining socio-cultural phenomena in Korea; (a) various and stratified motivational values of luxury clothing consumptions and (b) diversified types of post-purchase complaints against luxury clothing. Consumers' high/low levels of cultural and economic capitals were applied as the major determinants of perceived luxury consumption value. Since there have been limited studies regarding distinguishing complaint types based on consumer's economic & cultural class, this study might present a widen approach to conceptualize social value-oriented complaining types.

Complaint types of Korean consumers are various due to the different values they impose on luxury, and after all, due to the disparity of culture they are involved. The nation could not have had long-lasting dominant culture since 1910. After undergoing Japanese occupations and Korean War, there had been sudden social change through democratic labor movements. The rapid economic development gave rise to the sudden wealth, and barriers to the excess of luxury fashion products have been lowered due to the increase of wealth-creation opportunities in a variety of social statuses.

Social stratification refers to the prevailing structure of inequality within a society, and the relationship between social class and consumption value is the subject of a debate in sociological literature. In Bourdieu(1986)'s point of view, the arrogation of distinction showing off economic power and cultural distancing is actively used by dominant social classes as a means of symbolically demonstrating their superiority. Luxury clothing functions as code allowing for social distinctions and individual's ability to determine the fashion reflects their capitals. This study adopts the two conceptual forms of capitals, economic & cultural, to analyze the antecedent factors of luxury consumers' complaining propensity.

The major purpose of this qualitative study is to develop a conceptual framework of categorizing the complaint types of economically and culturally stratified Korean luxury consumers. To allocate individual consumers by stratus, the researcher originated 2X2 matrix utilizing the distinctive 2 levels of economic and cultural capitals that Bourdieu (1986) articulated as the major basis of social classes. Thus, divided 4 social groups are characterized as luxury clothing consumers (1) with higher level of economic and cultural capitals, (2) with higher economic capital but lower cultural capital, (3) with lower economic capital but higher cultural capital, and (4) with lower economic and cultural capitals.

Additional purpose of this ethnographic research is to establish 'capital scales' to measure high/low levels of economic and cultural capitals in Korean society. The standards for high/low levels of economic capital will be partially set up by the monthly income figures of the affluent and the middle-income classes released by The Korea National Statistical Office (2009) imposing the lower limit of $9,023 for group 1 and 2, $3,176 for group 3 and 4. Origin of wealth and means of wealth accumulation will be further investigated through in-depth interviews, by checking if they inherited a fortune or earned sudden money.

The high/low levels of cultural capital will be established through observing respondents' embodied state of cultural capital, i.e., opinion, attitude, tone of voice, typical body- movements, taste in culture (food, clothing, music, painting, exhibition, social activities), and mannerism. Bourdieu(1986)'s concept of legitimate cultural taste, e.g., frequency of attending culture exhibition, activities, and purchasing objectified state of cultural goods, is to be modified to fit Korean cultural contexts.

This study used grounded theory methodology to explore Korean luxury consumers' hidden and fundamental complaining intentions, which were constructed by socially symbolic luxury consumption values based on the hierarchically divided social contexts. Respondents of this study are Korean luxury clothing complainers who are clearly identified as each of the 4 class groups. Since this research is in the working paper stage, up to the present, 24 cases were interviewed using a snow-ball sampling. Observations and in-depth interviews were carried out during four months from March, 2010 to June, 2011.

The classified 4 groups were named as (1) 'high class elite', (2) 'parvenus' (3) 'low income cultural elite', and (4) 'low class luxury seeker'. Luxury consumption values for each group were characterized as (1) 'individuality': seeking differentiated clothing for individual distinction, (2) 'conspicuousness': having preference on well-recognized luxury brands, (3) 'hedonism': exploring various taste-suiting clothing for self-satisfaction, and (4) 'conformity': causing excessive consumption to meet ideal group norms. These 4 types of luxury consumption value distinctively influenced each group's complaint motivations respectively, such as (1) uniqueness of design, special services, (2) social recognitions, (3) design-related dissatisfaction, (4) exchange, refunds, and compensations. Complaint types of 4 groups were determined by their motivations, and classified as (1) expressing their opinion mildly on their ways to shop (2) direct aggressive voice complaint (3) complaint with preparations, taking plans to do actions, (4) website posting, negative word of mouth, and sabotage.

Group 1 with high cultural capitals chose to complain mildly, and they could successfully communicate their dissatisfactions. Whereas, group 2 with less cultural capital, with poorly restrained manners in complaining, failed delivering what she demanded but expressing her anger. Both group 1 and 3, with high cultural capital asked for unique and better design. While group 1 complained based on their beliefs regarding the brand's artistic accomplishment, group 3 required compensations in return to their design-related dissatisfactions. Group 3's demands for the financial compensations were due to their lower level of economic capitals which leads to their high sensitiveness on price.

The level of economic capitals, however, was not the direct indicator of the level of price consciousness. Group 2, who accumulated sudden wealth and spend far more money on luxury clothing than other groups, seemed even more price sensitive than the other groups with less economic capitals, and group 4, who perceived relatively lower subjective value of money, refused to voice out. Instead, Group 1,2, and 3, who held relatively higher capitals than group 4 tended to exhibit greater self-confidence, and they were more willing to take risks and had positive attitude toward complaining.

REFERENCES

Bourdieu, P. (1986) *The forms of capital*. In J. Richardson (Ed.) Handbook of Theory and Research for the Sociology of Education, Greenwood:NY.

Chan, T. W. & Goldthorpe, J. H. (2007). Social stratification and cultural consumption The visual arts in England. *Poetics, 35*(1), 168-190.

Hirschman, A. O. (1970). *Exit, voice and loyalty: Responses to decline in firms, organizations and states*. Harvard University Press: Cambridge, MA.

Lee, S. & Jang, Y. (2009). Cultural capital and classification of taste for citizens of Seoul: a case of leisure activity associated with theater performance. *International journal of urban sciences* 1(1). 62-83.

McCracken, G. (1988) *Culture and consumption: New approaches to the symbolic character of consumer goods and activities*. Bloomington: Indiana.

Neap, H. S. & Celik, T. (1999). Value of a product: A definition. *International journal of value-based management*, 12(2), 181-191.

Richins, M. L. (1982). An Investigation of consumers' attitude toward complaining. *Advances in Consumer Research, 9(1)*. 502-506.

Singh, J. & Wilkes, R.E. (1996), When consumers complain: a path analysis of the key antecedents of consumer complaint response estimates. *Academy of Marketing Science*, 24(4), 350-365.

Wiedmann, K., Hennings, N. & Siebels, A. (2009). Value-based segmentation of luxury consumption behavior. *Psychology & Marketing*, 26(7). 625-651.

To relate or not to relate – How feature relatedness contributes to product value

Valentin Gattol, Delft University of Technology, The Netherlands
Maria Sääksjärvi, Delft University of Technology, The Netherlands
Tripat Gill, University of Ontario Institute of Technology, Canada
Jan P. L. Schoormans, Delft University of Technology, The Netherlands

INTRODUCTION AND CONCEPTUAL FRAMEWORK

New product concepts are often the result of combining features of two or more existing product concepts into one product. In most combinations one of the parent products can be considered the 'base' to which another product or part of another product (e.g., a single feature) is added. The present research examines new products where a single new feature is added to a base product. Building on Gill (2008) we propose that the fit between a given base product and the newly added feature can be better or worse, depending on consumers' consumption goals. Consumption goals are defined as benefits that consumers seek in a consumption context (Gill 2008; Huffman and Houston 1993). They may differ according to dimensions such as (1) hedonic–utilitarian (i.e., whether a product offers experiential or functional benefits) and (2) feature relatedness (i.e., whether or not a new feature offers benefits related to a product's core). While the effect of fit between the hedonic versus utilitarian consumption goals of the base and the added new feature has been examined previously (e.g., Gill 2008), we investigate the role of feature relatedness in determining the value of new product concepts.

Gill (2008) showed that the nature of the fit in the hedonic versus utilitarian consumption goals of the base and the new feature can have a differential effect on overall incremental product value. Specifically that for products with a utilitarian base, adding an incongruent hedonic feature improved overall product value perceptions more than adding a congruent utilitarian feature. In contrast, for products with a hedonic base, adding an incongruent utilitarian feature improved overall product value much less than adding a congruent hedonic feature. In other words, fit/congruence of consumption goals of the added feature is more valuable for a hedonic base product, but incongruence is more valuable for a utilitarian base product.

In the present research we investigate the second aspect of fit of consumption goals: namely, the extent to which the added new feature is *related* vs. *unrelated* to the base product's core functionality. Consumption goals are *related* when a newly added feature enhances the core benefits in the base product (e.g., an improved battery increases the talk time on a cell phone). Consumption goals are *unrelated* when the new feature does not influence the core benefits in the base (e.g., a scratch-resistant screen does not affect the talk time of a cell phone). We propose that increases in product value of a base with an added new feature can be explained more accurately by also accounting for the effect of feature relatedness in addition to the fit on hedonic/utilitarian goals. More specifically, we predict that adding a new feature that is related to the core benefits of the base product will increase overall incremental value more than adding a new feature that is unrelated. Additionally, we expect that feature relatedness would explain changes in incremental value over and above those based on the fit between the hedonic versus utilitarian consumption goals of the new feature and the base.

METHOD AND RESULTS

We tested our predictions in a 2 (type of base: hedonic vs. utilitarian) x 2 (type of new feature: hedonic vs. utilitarian) x 2 (new feature relatedness: related vs. unrelated) factorial design. Two hundred and ninety-eight students from a mid-sized University participated in the experiments. All stimuli were pretested in order to match them as closely as possible with the proposed factor levels. In each condition participants read a scenario in which a new feature was added to either a hedonic base (mp3 player) or a utilitarian base (business smartphone). The newly added feature was either hedonic or utilitarian and (in addition) either related or unrelated to the product core feature/functionality. Overall incremental value (OIV) and incremental willingness to spend money (IWTSM) served as our main dependent variables (both measured on 7-point bipolar scales). The data was analyzed by means of two factorial ANOVAs for each dependent variable. We found a significant main effect of feature relatedness for both OIV, $F(1, 290) = 6.00$, $p = .02$, $\eta_p^2 = .02$, and IWTSM, $F(1, 291) = 4.94$, $p = .03$, $\eta_p^2 = .02$. That is, related new features increased both OIV and IWTSM more compared to unrelated features. In addition, we obtained a significant main effect of type of new feature (hedonic/utilitarian) for OIV, $F(1, 290) = 4.33$, $p = .04$, $\eta_p^2 = .02$, but not for IWTSM, $F(1, 291) = .95$, $p = .33$. OIV increased more when a hedonic (vs. utilitarian) new feature was added, however there were no differences in terms of IWTSM. Interestingly, there was a significant interaction for OIV between feature relatedness and type of base product, $F(1, 290) = 8.85$, $p < .01$, $\eta_p^2 = .03$, and between feature relatedness and type of new feature, $F(1, 290) = 6.78$, $p = .01$, $\eta_p^2 = .02$. The first interaction showed that related new features (vs. unrelated ones) improved OIV for the hedonic but not for the utilitarian base product. The second interaction showed that relatedness improved OIV when the added new feature was utilitarian but not so when it was hedonic (for hedonic features the OIV remained high irrespective of relatedness).

CONCLUSIONS

Our results show that both related (as opposed to unrelated) and hedonic (as opposed to utilitarian) new features contribute to overall incremental product value. From a company's perspective, adding a new feature that is utilitarian (as opposed to hedonic) is least advantageous. However, if a new utilitarian feature is added, it should be related to a product's core feature/functionality. In short: hedonic-new features lead to an increase in product value, even when unrelated; however, utilitarian new features must always be related to yield a similar increase in product value.

REFERENCES

Gill, T. (2008), "Convergent Products: What Functionalities Add More Value to the Base?," *Journal of Marketing*, 72 (2), 46-62.
Huffman, C. and M. J. Houston (1993), "Goal-Oriented Experiences and the Development of Knowledge," *Journal of Consumer Research*, 20 (2), 190-207.\

When Would Extroversion in Me Come Out?
Personality Paradox in Different Contexts

Alisara Charinsarn, JDBA Program, Thammasat University, Thailand
Kritsadarat Wattanasuwan, Thammasat University, Thailand

Why some quiet people become sociable when they are in the online social network? Why some shy people become talkative when they are with close friends and family? If this is the case, these personality traits such as being introvert or extrovert are not intrinsic, sustainable, over time, and across different situations like what the traditional personality trait theory stated. How could this be possible?

The situation affects how people behave (Belk 1975). The big five personality can be variant across situations (Fennis et al. 2005). People can have multiple self-concepts across time (Kelly and Rodriguez 2006).

The Interactional Personality model (Lewin 1935) believes that the personality or the behavior we can observe is a result of the interaction between the person him/herself and the situation. This is in line with what Wattanasuwan and Elliott (1999) explain that the life history of a person and the social situation together form a meaning of a person's experience (Wattanasuwan and Elliott 1999). Zayas et al. (2002) mentioned that "human behaviors commonly attributed to the individual are inseparable from the context in which they occur: Some behaviors may not be meaningful or even observable without placing individuals within contexts, particularly those that involve interpersonal relations" (Zayas et al. 2002) (p.852).

One important and interesting aspect is that the other person we interact with is a type of situation (Zayas et al., 2002). Goffmann wrote that people change in the society because of the presence of another person (Goffman 1956).

In this paper, we focus on the introvert/extrovert personality paradox when interacting with different situations.

Introvert is defined as "reserved, quiet, shy, and distant" (Karkoulian et al. 2009)(p.74). Manning and Ray (1993) did a research on shyness and proposed that shyness is situational. It can be activated or deactivated by situation (Manning and Ray 1993).

Extrovert is defined as associable, active, talkative, person-oriented, optimistic, fun-loving and affectionate (McCrae and Costa 1987). Interestingly, prior research found that there is an association between the latent trait and extroversion (Maij-de Meij et al. 2005).

We believe that the latent extrovert trait will become dominant when a person perceives that the situation is secure, that is, when it is lack of 'perceived subjective discomfort (arises from interacting with the situation)'.

'Subjective discomfort' is a type of 'interaction anxiety' or 'contingent interaction' (Pilkonis, 1977). In other words, whether this discomfort will occur or not depends on the situation. Pilkonis (1977) explained that people speak less and try to avoid the situation when they feel anxious about the interaction.

'Fear of negative evaluation' is a kind of subjective discomfort (Pilkonis 1977) which is in line with Shepperd and Arkin (1990) that how an anxious person present him/herself is not to seek approval, but to 'avoid disapproval' (Shepperd and Arkin 1990).

People who are generally shy or introvert might lack of trust in the social interaction, and therefore, perceive the subjective risk more than extrovert people (Manning and Ray 1993). It is possible that introvert could have higher subjective risk and is more selective in whom to reveal information (Maij-de Meij et al. 2005). When people perceive that the subjective risk is higher, they are less likely to reveal information (Omarzu 2000).

The online environment is a great example of reduced subjective discomfort because it is lack of physical presence, it facilitates the sense of control, and it can be anonymous.

An introvert likes to reflect and think on one's own rather than talking and thinking with the group. Being online, one does not have to immediately respond to other person on the spot like in face-to-face context (McKenna and Bargh 2000), and therefore feels more control.

The virtual world makes it possible for people to be anonymous. When one is anonymous, one is de-individualized. As a result, the influence of self decrease while the influence of the context increase (Johnson and Downing 1979). People do not have to confine themselves in the boundary of their real life such as their family, their responsibility, or even their self (Haraway 1991; Haraway 1997). Young et al. mentioned that anonymity helps shy people to feel safe and secure in the social interaction (Chak and Leung 2004), and therefore a comfortable arena for them to express.

Online environment is found to reduce social anxiety (McKenna and Bargh 2000). Those who are shy or have anxiety find internet an outlet that they can express, which they cannot do so in the offline world (Tosun and Lajunen 2009). The online context is an alternative playground which is like a laboratory which one can try out different personality without any risk (McKenna and Bargh 2000; Turkle 1995).

We employ the interpretive approach using both offline ethnography and online netnography. This method allows us to investigate the complex nature of human beings. The contrast online/offline context is selected as the site of study to explore the paradox personality.

Our initial findings suggested that there is dynamism between the virtual and the real world. An introvert student at school becomes extrovert in the online game. Likewise, a quiet office worker becomes an opinion leader in a political chat room.

Personality paradox is found when looking across different contexts. We seek to further explore how the online and offline world shape this personality contradiction.

REFERENCES

Belk, Russell W. (1975), "The Objective Situation as a Determinant of Consumer Behavior," *Advances in Consumer Research*(January 1, 1975).

Chak, Katherineand Leung, Louis. (2004), "Shyness and Locus of Control as Predictors of Internet Addiction and Internet Use," *CyberPsychology & Behavior*, 7(5), 559-570.

Fennis, Bob M., Pruyn, Ad Th H., and Maasland, Mascha. (2005), "Revisiting the Malleable Self: Brand Effects on Consumer Self-Perceptions of Personality Traits," *Advances in Consumer Research*, 32(1), 371-377.

Goffman, Erving. (1956). Teh Presentation of Self in Everyday Life, New York: Doubledayu.

Haraway, Donna J. (1991). Simians, Cyborgs, and Women: The Reinventing of Nature, New York: Routledge.

_____. (1997). Modest_Witness@Second_Millennium.Femaleman_Meets_Oncomousetm: Feminism and Technoscience, New York: Routledge.

Johnson, R.D.and Downing, L.L. (1979), "Deindividuation and Valence of Cues: Effects on Prosocial and Antisocial Behavior," *Journal of the Personality and Social Psychology*, 76, 349-366.

Karkoulian, Silva, Messarra, Leila, and Sidani, Mohamad. (2009), "Correlates of the Bases of Power and the Big Five Personality Traits: An Empirical Investigation," *Journal of Organizational Culture, Communications and Conflice*, 13(2).

Kelly, Anita E.and Rodriguez, Robert R. (2006), "Publicly Committing Oneself to an Identity," *Basic & Applied Social Psychology*, 28(2), 185-191.

Lewin, K. (1935). A Dynamic Theory of Personality, New York: McGraw-Hill.

Maij-de Meij, Annette M., Kelderman, Henk, and van der Flier, Henk. (2005), "Latent-Trait Latent-Class Analysis of Self-Disclosure in the Work Environment," *Multivariate Behavioral Research*, 40(4), 435-459.

Manning, Philipand Ray, George. (1993), "Shyness, Self-Confidence, and Social Interaction," *Social Psychology Quarterly*, 56(3), 178-192.

McCrae, RRand Costa, PT. (1987), "Validation of the Five-Factor Model of Personality across Intruments and Observers," *Journal of Personality and Social Psychology*, 81-90.

McKenna, Katelyn, Y. A.and Bargh, John A. (2000), "Plan 9 from Chyberspace: The Implications of the Internet for Personalityh and Social Psychology," *Personality and Social Psychology Review*, 4(1), 57-75.

Omarzu, J. (2000), "A Disclosure Decision Model: Determining How and When Individuals Will Self-Disclose," *Personality and Social Psychological Review*, 4, 174-185.

Pilkonis, Paul A. (1977), "Shyness, Public and Private, and Its Relationship to Other Measures of Social Behavior," *Journal of Personality*, 45(4), 585.

Shepperd, J.and Arkin, R. (1990). "Shyness and Self-Presentation", in W. R. Crozier, (ed.), *Shyness and Embarrassment: Perspectives from Social Psychology*. Cambridge: Cambridge University Press.

Tosun, Leman Pinarand Lajunen, Timo. (2009), "Why Do Young Adults Develop a Passion for Internet Activities? The Associations among Personality, Revealing "True Self" on the Internet, and Passion for the Internet," *CyberPsychology & Behavior*, 12(4), 401-406.

Turkle, Sherry. (1995). Life on the Screen: Identity in the Age of the Internet, New York: Simon & Schuster.

Wattanasuwan, Kritsadaratand Elliott, Richard. (1999), "The Buddhist Self and Symbolic Consumption: The Consumption Experience of the Teenage Dhammakaya Buddhists in Thailand," *Advances in Consumer Research*, 26.

Zayas, Vivian, Shoda, Yuichi, and Ayduk, Ozlem N. (2002), "Personality in Context: An Interpersonal Systems Perspective," *Journal of Personality*, 70(6), 851-900.

Great Expectations and Charity: Studying the Effect of Unexpected Schemas on Charitable Behavior

Geetanjali Saluja, HKUST, Hong Kong
Rod Duclos, HKUST, Hong Kong

Whereas the last decade has seen more extreme adverse meteorological conditions than any comparable period before, scientists predict this trend will only worsen in years to come due to global warming. Hence, as the frequency and severity of natural disasters striking the planet are expected to rise (e.g., earthquakes, tsunamis, floods, etc), nonprofit organizations will have no choice but to increasingly turn to the more fortunate among us to plea for help. And with the proliferation of causes, charities face today fierce competition. Indeed, in the US alone, thousands of charitable organizations are officially registered with the Internal Revenue Service (IRS) and actively vying for donors and resources. Critical for these organizations, then, is to understand *why* and *how* consumers decide to help others. The present research attempts to address this question by examining the influence of embodied cognitions (i.e., ideas, thoughts, concepts shaped by aspects of the body) on prosocial behavior. So doing, we also examine the impact of unexpected environmental influences on charitableness.

Lakoff and Johnson (1999) have proposed that concrete experiences (e.g., temperature) ground abstract concepts (e.g., affection). A study by Zhong et al. (2008) has shown that social exclusion can induce an experience of psychological coldness. Ijzerman et al. (2009) have also explored the effects of temperature on perception of social proximity. Hence, drawing on the above, we propose that feeling warm (cold) may foster (impede) one's charitable orientation.

Design & procedures. To test this proposition, we randomly assigned 94 students from a large East Asian university to one of four conditions. To manipulate body temperature, we asked participants to drink (under the pretence of a taste-test) either hot, cold, cool (i.e., room temperature) or no (i.e., control) tea before completing a series of manipulation checks. Among other things, these checks prompted participants to rate their respective beverage in terms of taste, smell, and temperature. Next, in a seemingly unrelated survey administered on behalf of the Facilities Management Office (FMO), we asked participants of all four conditions to estimate the temperature of the room in which they were as well as how hot/cold and how comfortable they felt. Lastly to control for any potential mood effect, we asked participants to complete the PANAS scales, an exhaustive measure of affect/emotions by Watson et al. (1988).

To assess charitableness, we asked participants to review an appeal from "Global Relief", an alleged charity collecting money to help the victims of a recent earthquake that struck China's Sichuan province. Vivid in nature, the advertisement featured death toll statistics (e.g., "over 100,000 killed and 1 million others homeless"), a description of the victims' needs (e.g., "food and medicine for vulnerable children and devastated families"), and the pictures of suffering victims underneath the text. The ad concluded by asking participants to visit the charity's website to make a donation.

Results. An analysis of variance and follow-up contrast analyses on our manipulation checks suggest that our manipulation was unequally successful. Indeed, whereas participants in the hot tea condition did report feeling warmer than their counterparts in the cool, cold, and control conditions, the latter three conditions did not differ from one another. Hence, participants in the cold tea condition did not feel any colder than subjects in the cool and control conditions.

Pertaining to our hypothesis, we found that participants in the cool condition (M = $155) pledged donating strikingly more than their counterparts in the hot (M = $74), cold (M = $106), and control (M = $69) conditions (F (3, 90) = 4.061, p = .009). Follow-up contrast analyses further confirmed that the latter three groups did not differ from one another.

These results are quite surprising. Indeed, whereas we expected participants in the hot tea condition to donate most, we found instead that these participants donated neither more nor less than subjects in the cold and control conditions. Rather, subjects in the cool-tea condition exhibited the most generosity toward victims of the Sichuan earthquake.

To make sense of these surprising yet very significant results, we took a closer look at our manipulation checks and proceeded by elimination. One at a time, we examined whether body temperature (i.e., how cold/hot I feel), liking of the beverage's taste, liking of the beverage's smell, personal comfort, or affect (i.e., PANAS scores) could account for our findings. Unfortunately, none of these factors provided a viable explanation.

Discussion. Drinking cool tea (as opposed to hot, cold, or no tea at all) led our participants to subsequently donate strikingly more in favor of earthquake victims. Contrary to what one might expect, this boost in charitableness cannot be readily explained by subjective feelings of body warmth or overall enjoyment of the beverage. To understand this puzzling phenomenon, follow-up experiments are now investigating the role that schemas and expectations might have played in our findings. Tea is traditionally served hot or cold/iced. Few would indeed make/ buy hot or cold tea to let it sit until it reaches room temperature before drinking it. From this simple observation, we derived the hypothesis that schema-inconsistent experiences might subsequently foster a sense of openness in consumers. Greater openness, in turn, might give way to greater empathy, compassion, and charitableness. Preliminary results from follow-up experiments seem to support this view.

This paper highlights the importance of understanding various cognitive constructs and processes, and the possible effect of these processes on charitable behavior. To our knowledge, this paper is one of the first to explore the link between schema-based expectations and prosocial behavior. Hence, for its potential contributions to both theory and practice, we believe this poster would be of interest to a wide audience at ACR.

REFERENCES:

Duclos, Bettman, Bloom, and Zauberman (2010), "Charitable Giving: How Ego Threats Impact Donations of Time and Money".

Dewall, C. Nathan, Baumeister, Roy F., Gailliot, Matthew T. and Maner, Jon K. (2008), "Depletion Makes the Heart Grow Less Helpful: Helping as a function of Self-Regulatory Energy and Genetic Relatedness", *Personality and Social Psychology Bulletin*, 34, 1653-1662.

Barsalou, Lawrence W. (1999), "Perceptual Symbol Systems", *Behavioral and Brain Sciences*, 22, 577-660.

Watson, David, Lee Anna Clark, and Auke Tellegen (1988), "Development and Validation of Brief Measures of Positive Affect and Negative Affect: The PANAS Scales," *Journal of Personality and Social Psychology*, Vol. 54, No. 6, 1063-1070.

Zhong, Chen-Bo and Leonardelli, Geoffrey J. (2008), "Cold and Lonely: Does Social Exclusion Literally Feel Cold?", *Psychological Science*, Vol. 19, No. 9, 838-842

Ijzerman, Hans and Semin, Gün R. (2009), "The Thermometer of Social Relations: Mapping Social Proximity on Temperature", *Psychological Science*, Vol. 20, No.10, 1214-1220

Less is More: Positional Concerns are stronger in Inevaluable Domains

Tess Bogaerts, Ghent University, Belgium
Mario Pandelaere, Ghent University, Belgium

Positional concern is the extent to which one is concerned about one's status or position in one's reference group. To measure positional concerns, Solnick and Hemenway (1998) developed the Positional Concern Questionnaire (PCQ), in which respondents have to indicate for a number of domains which of two outcomes they would prefer. One of the options is always superior from an absolute point of view but inferior from a relative point of view (e.g. working in a company in which one earns USD 50,000 but others earn USD 60,000). The second option is superior from a relative point of view but inferior from an absolute point of view (e.g. working in a company in which one earns USD 40,000 but others earn USD 30,000). As people become more concerned about their position, they are more likely to choose the second option in which one is the better off in *relative* terms. A number of studies indicate that positional concern may vary across domains (Solnick & Hemenway, 1998, 2005). We propose that the domain differences in positional concern are due to differences in the inherent evaluability of the domains involved.

Inherent evaluability refers to whether people have an innate reference system to assess the value of an outcome (Hsee & Zhang, 2010). For instance, if people take a sip from a cup of coffee, they know immediately whether or not it is too hot because people have an innate reference system to evaluate temperature. Temperature is therefore an inherently evaluable quantity (Hsee & Zhang, 2010). In contrast, a woman who receives a diamond engagement ring may want to compare her ring to that of her friends in order to assess the love of her future spouse. Diamond value is an inherently inevaluable quantity (Hsee & Zhang, 2010) as people cannot judge how valuable a diamond is without an external reference system. We suggest that relative position is more important for inherently inevaluable domains.

The PCQ was developed to measure differences between *people* in positional concern. While some people routinely care about their position, others do not. Correspondingly, the former exhibit positional concern in a host of domains, the latter do not. The (in)evaluability framework not only allows predicting for which domains people are more likely to display positional concern, but also when people are more likely to differ from one another. We expect that most people do not care for relative position for inherently evaluable domains. So, the impact of individual differences on positional concerns should be moderated by the evaluability of the domain involved.

To test this idea, we focused on an individual difference variable that may be associated with positional concern, namely envy. Considering that envy entails a negative feeling that is triggered when others do better than oneself, envy-prone people should not want others to outperform them. In the PCQ, envy should thus be associated with the tendency to prefer a positional outcome over an absolute one.

In a first study, 400 US citizens participated in an online study in return for a participation fee. First, we used the PCQ to measure concerns regarding relative standing. To measure envy, we administered a 7-point scale (1 = strongly disagree, 7 = strongly agree) which contained 9 items (α = .61) based on the envy dimension from Belk's materialism scale (Belk, 1985; Ger & Belk, 1995). Finally, we used the AB identification survey developed by Hsee and Yang (in press) to identify whether a given domain is inherently evaluable (type A) or inherently inevaluable (type B).

To test whether domain evaluability and envy predict positional concern, we ran a multilevel logistic regression with choice of relative option as binary dependent variable. The inverse relationship between positional concerns and domain evaluability was clearly significant (B = -1.620, SD = .156, p < .001). The more a domain is inherently inevaluable, the more people prefer to be better off from a relative point of view. Moreover, results revealed a significant main effect of envy (B = .156, SD = .064, p = .014) and a significant interaction effect between envy and domain evaluability (B = -.612, SD = .205, p = .003) on positional concerns. Consistent with the hypothesis, we found that positional concerns are stronger in inherently inevaluable domains, and even more so for envy-prone people.

In a second study, we investigated what happens if people have a third option in the PCQ, in which everyone in society is equal (e.g. working in a company in which one earns USD 50,000 and others also earn USD 50,000). Another 400 US citizens participated in this second online study in return for a participation fee. Afterwards, we ran a multilevel regression with positional concern as ordinal dependent variable. Consistent with the first study, we found a significant inverse relationship between domain evaluability and the tendency to choose a positional outcome (B = -1.750, SD = .153, p < .001). Choosing the positional outcome over an absolute or an equal one is more likely if one is envious (B = .489; SD = 0,120; p < .001), envy especially predicts positional choosing in inherently inevaluable domains (B = -.463; SD = 0,184; p = .012). Taken together, we found that domain evaluability is a strong predictor of people's tendency to choose a positional outcome, and moderates the impact of individual differences in envy on positional concern.

The contribution of this article is threefold. First, it provides an explanation of the difference in positional concern across domains. Second, it shows that the (in)evaluability framework could be applied to choices people make. Third, this research contributes to a better understanding of positional concern on both an individual level and domain specific level. Consistent with an interactionist point of view, this article shows that dispositions interact with situations to shape behavior. To arrive at an even better understanding of positional concerns, additional research is being conducted to investigate the effect of domain evaluability and other dispositions on people's inclination to choose a positional outcome.

REFERENCES

Hsee, C.K., & Yang, A.X. (forthcoming). The AB Identification Survey: Identifying Absolute versus Relative Determinants of Happiness. Paper presented at the Association for Consumer Research conference. Jacksonville, 7-10/10/2010.

Hsee, C.K. & Zhang, J. (2010). General Evaluability Theory. *Perspectives on Psychological Science, 5*(4), 343-355.

Solnick, S., & Hemenway, D. (1998). Is more always better? A survey on positional concerns *Journal of Economic Behavior and Organization, 37*, 373-383.

Solnick, S., & Hemenway, D. (2005). Are positional concerns stronger in some domains than in others? *American Economic Review, 95*, 147-151.

On the Question of Altruism vs. Self-Interest in Ethical Consumption, And On Why This Question Might Not Really Matter

Joachim Scholz, Queen's University, Canada
Jay M. Handelman, Queen's University, Canada

Do consumers consume ethically because they truly care for the well-being of others or out of more selfishly oriented desires to be perceived in a favorable light? Previous research has pointed towards the predominance of identity projects in anti-consumption practices (Cherrier 2009). For example, consumers boycott companies to express their individuality and for moral self-realization (Kozinets and Handelman 1998), and consumer activists construct morally superior identities (Kozinets and Handelman 2004). In these accounts, ethical behavior is presented as rooted in self-interested concerns of self-transformation or the creation of hero identities (Cherrier 2009).

Other investigations have explored self-scarifying caring dimension of consumption (Thompson 1996) and how sharing has a component of care for others (Belk 2010). Research on citizen consumerism has extended these caring orientations into non-family contexts without exploring in detail the interplay between self-interested desires for favorable identities and desires to benefit the well-being of distant others (McGinnis and Gentry 2009).

When does caring for others become self-serving through establishing a caring identity? We suggest that questions like this, which call for the disentanglement of altruistic and selfish motives, are ill-posed, since they are based on the assumption that each individual is a separated entity apart from other people (Gergen 2009). While this understanding is certainly dominant in contemporary Western culture, an alternative view of the self that is based on the assumption that everyone is connected to everyone and everything else (Capra 1996) has become more influential over recent years due to a growing awareness of the interconnections in our physical world (e.g., ecological systems, social networks; Rifkin 2009)

Rather than continuing the quest of disentangling "true altruism" from "self-interest" and the related quest of drawing boundaries between self-interest and caring for others, we argue that our understanding of ethical consumerism would be advanced by taking into account different perspectives of the self and how relationships between self and others are conceptualized (i.e., separated self vs. interconnected self). Specifically, the purpose of our research is to expose beliefs of interconnectedness in consumer activists' narratives and to explore how this worldview allows consumers to care for the wellbeing of others.

We conducted a netnography of various webpages associated with the Transition Movement (TM). Four major webpages that serve as global info and discussion hubs of the TM served as our main data source.

We found the beliefs of *interconnectedness* to be a hotly debated issue within the TM. Those who subscribed to these beliefs frequently rejected the atomistic view of individuals (e.g., "a shift in consciousness" that "gives the lie to old-paradigm notions of the isolated, competitive self") and instead saw their own well-being as dependent on and "inseparable from the well being of all the people, plants, and creatures that we affect and that affect us". Furthermore, we registered a second theme of *individual empowerment*. Based on beliefs that the current state of the world is an outcome of the cascading effects of interconnected relationships and choices, members of the TM located responsibility for the world as well as the power to change the world in everyone's personal reach (e.g., "taking responsibility for our individual power to create the world"). Such localization of responsibility was connected with an awareness to avoid vilifying others (e.g., corporations or mainstream consumers) as 'evil', in part out of a realization that the world can be changed on the level of positive, individual connections among individuals.

Our findings contribute to the ethical consumption literature by questioning the core assumptions of separated individuals when analyzing why and how people engage in caring consumption. But more broadly, our study complements and extends recent explorations of the relational self (e.g., Epp and Price 2008) by addressing the question to "what extent the self is best conceptualized as extended [...] versus part of an organic unity with others and the environment" (Belk 2010, p. 728). As we demonstrate in this research, some consumers indeed adopt the latter perspective, which has implications for why they care for others, how they relate their caring consumption to their self-interest, and how they attempt to create social change. Last, our finding that members of the TM transcend dualistic notions of 'good' versus 'evil' point towards the possibility that such dualisms may be only a structural feature of identity construction (Luedicke, Thompson, and Giesler 2010) if the self is conceptualized as separated from others, but less so when people adopt an understanding of the self as being interconnected with other people and with the natural world at large.

REFERENCES

Belk, Russell W. (2010), "Sharing," *Journal of Consumer Research*, 36 (February), 715-734.
Cherrier, Hélène (2009), "Anti-Consumption Discourses and Consumer-Resistant Identities," *Journal of Business Research*, 62, 181-190.
Gergen, Kenneth J. (2009), *Relational Being: Beyond Self and Community*, Oxford: Oxford University Press
Kozinets, Robert V. and Jay Handelman (1998), "Ensouling Consumption: A Netnographic Exploration of the Meaning of Boycotting Behavior," *Advances of Consumer Research*, 25, 475-480.
Kozinets, Robert V. and Jay Handelman (2004), "Adversaries of Consumption: Consumer Movements, Activism, and Ideology," *Journal of Consumer Research*, 31 (December), 691-704.
Luedicke, Marius K., Craig J. Thompson, and Markus Giesler (2010), "Consumer Identity Work as Moral Protagonism: How Myth and Ideology Animate a Brand-Mediated Moral Conflict," *Journal of Consumer Research*, 36 (April), 1016-1032.
McGinnis, Lee P. and James W. Gentry (2009), "Underdog Consumption: An Exploration into Meanings and Motives," *Journal of Business Research*, 62, 191-199.
Rifkin, Jeremy (2009), *The Empathic Civilization: The Race to Global Consciousness In A World In Crisis*, New York:Penguin.
Thompson, Craig J. (1996), "Caring Consumers: Gendered Consumption Meanings and the Juggling Lifestyle," *Journal of Consumer Research*, 22 (March), 388-407.

Artistic Stylistic Properties of Fashion Luxury Advertisements

Jennifer Zarzosa, New Mexico State University, USA
Cuauhtemoc Luna-Nevarez, New Mexico State University, USA

Visual consumption is a critical attribute of the experience economy. The visual past is critical as it influences a vocabulary of representation. Traditions of art history inform how consumers relate to the visual world, affecting advertising imagery and creative techniques (Schroeder 2002). Through sophisticated visual rhetoric, advertising images become part of a convention-based symbolic system (Scott 1994). Cultural knowledge allows for a learned system of pictorial conventions. Thus, a symbol theory of pictures is needed for complex visual consumption (McCracken 1987). Furthermore, the theory of visual literacy proposes analogical representation does not need obvious visual similarity between the image and what the image is about. Additionally, the lack of explicitness of visual syntax allows advertisers to convey persuasive messages (Messaris 1998).

Fashion photography has shifted stylistically since the 1960s due to cultural and historical changes. Specifically, style was reinterpreted in terms of the new economy. Fashion photography featured the liberated woman in many distinct images: the working girl who replaced couture with prêt-à-porter and the active girl who favored active wear to formal wear. The new rather than the well-made became preferred, thus, making innovation rather than quality signifiers of style (Bruzzi and Gibson 2000). With this change, the "look" of style, its vocabulary, its iconography, were reversed; low became high.

Fashion photography creates a historical document that captures a given period. It is a vehicle for circulating new patterns of consumption tied to evolving notions of the self. Early fashion photography created a visual fantasy to which women could aspire, and which fashion photography still pursues. Only after the art movements of surrealism, realism, and modernism was the fantasy notion challenged. Modernism influenced fashion photography with graphic and geometric styles while surrealism inspired dream-like images. Realism inspired a less formal approach where models were depicted in movement. Brutal realism portrayed images of melancholy and anxiety, using images that resembled snapshots with a glamorous setting. The School of London Style stripped the fantasies of the fashion industry and presented the reality of everyday life in a defiant anti-glamour style (Bruzzi and Gibson 2000).

The purpose of this study is to identify artistic stylistic properties of fashion luxury advertisements. The dimensions of style can be examined to evaluate brand identity-related styles by using four perceptual dimensions: complexity, representation, movement, and potency (Schmitt and Simonson 1997). The dimension of complexity places style on a continuum from simple to complex. Minimalism, on one end of the spectrum, strives for simplicity of structure and form while ornamentalism possesses complexity and multiple meanings. Representation explores the depiction of reality on a continuum of realism to abstraction. Realism is the depiction of the world of objects and human beings. Conversely, abstraction does not represent any objects in the contemporary real world. Movement is placed on a continuum from dynamic to static. The style dimension of potency refers to whether an identity comes across as loud and strong, or soft and weak.

Coherent themes provide mental anchors and reference points that are a crucial to aesthetics. The thematic stylistic property of protoypicality is the degree to which an object is representative of a category. In most cases, consumers respond more favorably to objects that are highly prototypical as they are more familiar. However, some consumers prefer novelty as seen in non- prototypical images (Veryzer and Hutchinson 1998). The postmodern thematic elements of pastiche and hyper-reality are also investigated. Pastiche refers to irony, parody, and imitation. Hyper-reality involves the loss of a sense of authenticity and the becoming real of what was originally a simulation (Brown 1995).

An exploratory content analysis approach was used to reveal how stylistic properties evolve. A pretest of eight hundred and twelve fashion luxury advertisements that advertise apparel and leather goods and accessories were sampled. *Vogue* magazine was selected as it offers high fashion accessibility while reaching one out of ten American women. September and February issues were chosen which aligns with the fall and spring collections. The sample captured ads from1995 to 2000 and 2005 to 2010 in order to compare two decades. Forty fashion luxury brands were selected from the luxury fashion brands index (Okonkwo 2007). Two students coded the fashion luxury advertisements and a coding book was included with detailed instructions and visual examples of each variable along with the code sheet.

Fashion luxury advertisements during 1995-2000 exhibited the following perceptual dimensions of style: minimalism (85%), realism (91%), static movement (86%), and soft and weak potency (86%). Interestingly, advertisements during 2005- 2010 also featured the same dimensions of style: minimalism (53%), realism (84%), static movement (76%), and soft and weak potency (68%). Currently, the artistic stylistic properties support a traditional classical visual style, which is characterized by simplicity, realism, static movement, and lack of color. However, there is an increasing trend towards the ornamental, abstract, dynamic, and loud and strong styles. The postmodern thematic stylistic properties of hyper-reality and pastiche respectively increased 30% and 10%. During 1995- 2000, 63% of ads had no or low prototypicality while 39% had no or low prototypicality during 2005-2010. Although, there was a decrease, there are still a considerable number of ads that lack prototypicality suggesting the social construct of fashion luxury is evolving as it is based on historical and cultural conditions influenced by the broad cultural production system of artistic movements. There are parallels between the artistic movements and advertising. Consumers view advertisements as a cultural text with distinct cultural codes of branding, therefore, advertisers need to understand the meaning based representation system in order to create powerful campaigns.

The study is designed to contribute to the literature in multiple ways. First, the study examines the social and cultural antecedents for contemporary visual culture. Secondly, the study illustrates a negotiated concept of luxury that is culturally derived. Thirdly, the study identifies visual creative techniques and execution tactics. The objective is to show a sociohistoric pattern of visual consumption influenced by the social structure of artistic movements, which shapes consumption choices and behaviors.

REFERENCES

Brown, Stephen (1995), *Postmodern Marketing*. London, UK: Routledge
Bruzzi, Stella, and Pamela Church Gibson (2000), "Fashion Cultures: Theories, Explorations, and Analysis," London: Routledge.

McCracken, Grant (1986), "Culture and Consumption: A Theoretical Account of the Structure: A Theoretical Account of the Structure and Movement of the Cultural Meaning of Consumer Goods." *Journal of Consumer Research*, 13 (1), 71-84.

Messaris, Paul (1998), Visual aspects of media literacy. *Journal of Communication*, 48, 70-80.

Okonkwo, Uche (2007), *Luxury Fashion Branding: Trends, Tactics, Techniques*. London: Palgrave MacMillan

Schmitt, Bernd and Alex Simonson (1997), *Marketing Aesthetics*. New York: The Free Press.

Schroeder, Jonathan E. (2002), *Visual consumption*. London: Routledge.

Scott, Linda M. (1994), "Images in Advertising: The Need for a Theory of Visual Rhetoric," *Journal of Consumer Research*, 21 (2), 252-273.

Veryzer, Robert W. & J. Wesley Hutchinson (1998), "The influence of unity and prototypicality on aesthetic responses to new product designs," *Journal of Consumer Research*, 24 (4), 374-394.

When the Same Objects Mean Completely Different Things That Unite Us All

Joachim Scholz, Queen's University, Canada
Jay M. Handelman, Queen's University, Canada

The role of special objects in the construction of identities is one of the most central concepts in consumer research (Arnould and Thompson 2005). While previous research has focused on the relations between special possessions and either individual identities (Kleine, Kleine, and Allen 1995) or collective identities (Belk 1992), more recent research stresses the importance of considering objects through the lens of dynamic interplays between individual, relational, and collective identities. For example, Epp and Price (2008) assert (but do not empirically test) that a single activity that is symbolic for a collective identity (e.g., family) can incorporate a diversity of meanings to the individual members of the collective. Going beyond the context of family identities, the purpose of the current research is to empirically explore how special objects help consumers to negotiate tensions that may arise when they seek affiliation in a consumption community and strive to maintain their autonomous identities at the same time.

We examine this question through ethnographic research of the engineering student community at our university. This community resembles more typical consumption communities in that a variety of special objects, most notably a jacket called the "Golden Party Armor" (GPA), are central to this community. Over the last two years, we have visited various community events and have been exposed to many GPAs during our daily commute over campus. In addition to observational research, we conducted on-site and in-depth interviews with several members of the community.

We find that students use the GPA to negotiate individual and collective identities. Four interrelated themes emerged through interpretive analysis. *(1) GPA as a community symbol*: The GPA is heavily invested with shared meanings, and wearing the GPA enables students to be a part of the community. On a more collective level, wearing the GPA also sets the engineering community apart from other faculties and thereby provides collective identities for our informants. *(2) Imbuing individualized meanings:* Our informants achieve individuality within their community through physically altering their jacket. Almost all jackets we observed over the last two years have physical alterations in forms of color, bars, and badges. The combination of such additions make each jacket unique. On a more psychological level, we also found our interview partners to achieve individuality within their community by using their jacket as a "scrapbook" to collect individualizing memories and experiences. Through its inclusion in core community events (e.g., slamming the jacket, dyeing the jacket purple, kicking the jacket over the campus, and having cars rolling over the jacket), each jacket becomes a transcript of ones own personal history with the community. *(3) Standing out without falling outside:* All GPAs have certain features (e.g., the university crest) that reaffirm the communal character of the jacket. Beyond this, community members adhere to firm rules and norms how to individualize their jackets (e.g., which and where badges can be added). In our fieldwork, we hardly ever came across jackets that break with these codes. Even more surprising, we found that some interview partners did not bother to sew on all the badges they had, even if these badges represented important achievements within their community. We interpret such foregone opportunities to highlight individual uniqueness as attempts to emphasize the shared meaning of the jacket for the sake of safeguarding one's communal identity. *(4) Enabling individualization through enacting community:* It is interesting to note that opportunities to individualize one's GPA are provided through community traditions. For example, dyeing one's jacket purple offers opportunities for individualized experiences (e.g., the act of purpling, or how the purple color fades away) while at the same time the shared rituals reaffirms the community and increases the communal character of the jacket. This link between individuality and community is apparent in how students connect their enactment of a community ritual (i.e., either "kicking home" their jacket as a first year student or interfering with such efforts as an upper year student) with both notions of experiencing community and collecting unique experiences.

In sum, our study demonstrates how community members embed individualized meanings into a shared community symbol while emphasizing and reaffirming – not sacrificing – its shared meanings. In other words, the 'same object', by becoming a 'completely different thing' in everybody's own mind, allows community members to feel like individuals, but by being still the 'same object' it also 'unites' these individuals in a community.

We believe that these findings advance our understanding of the meaning of objects and of the nature of object-person relationships. Specifically, we point out how objects can take on different meanings at any singular moment in time (Epp and Price 2010) and how objects allow consumers to negotiate conflicts that can arise from an interplay of various levels of identities (Epp and Price 2008). Previous research exploring multiple layers of meanings emphasizes the relative freedom consumers enjoy in constructing individualized meanings (Hirschman 2001), but also that some meanings are institutionalized as a shared "canon" (Kozinets 2001). However, this research does not pay attention to the interplay between individual and collective identities and therefore curtails our understanding of the dynamic nature of subject-object relationships: By only adopting an individual identity perspective, one fails to recognize how shared meanings are preserved and becomes prone to misinterpret members' safeguarding activities as sign domination (Murray 2002). On the other hand, by only adopting a communal identity perspective, one easily neglects the individualized meanings of symbols in favor of their shared core meanings (Belk and Costa 1998). Recognizing the interplay between being an individual and being a community member allows for a much more dynamic and holistic understanding of special objects.

REFERENCES

Arnould, Eric J. and Craig J. Thompson (2005), "Consumer Culture Theory (CCT): Twenty Years of Research," *Journal of Consumer Research, 31* (March), 868-82.

Belk, Russel W. (1992), "Moving Possessions: An Analysis Based on Personal Documents from the 1847–1869 Mormon Migration," *Journal of Consumer Research, 19* (December), 339-61.

Belk, Russell W. and Janeen Arnold Costa (1998), "The Mountain Man Myth: A Contemporary Consuming Fantasy," *Journal of Consumer Research, 25* (December), 218-41.

Epp, Amber M. and Linda L. Price (2008), "Family Identity: A Framework of Identity Interplay in Consumption Practices," *Journal of Consumer Research, 35* (June), 50-70.

Epp, Amber M. and Linda L. Price (2010), "The Storied Life of Singularized Objects: Forces of Agency and Network Transformation," *Journal of Consumer Research, 36* (February),820-837.

Hirschman, Elizabeth C. (2001), "When Expert Consumers Interpret Textual Products: Applying Reader-Response Theory to Television Programs," *Consumption, Markets and Culture, 2* (3), 233-335.

Kleine, Susan Schultz, Robert E. Kleine III, and Chris T. Allen (1995), "How Is a Possession 'Me' or 'Not Me'? Characterizing Types and an Antecedent of Material Possession Attachment," *Journal of Consumer Research, 22* (December), 327–43.

Kozinets 2001), "Utopian Enterprise: Articulating the Meanings of Star Trek's Culture of Consumption," *The Journal of Consumer Research, 28* (June), 67-88.

Murray, Jeff B. (2002), "The Politics of Consumption: A Re-Inquiry on Thompson and Haytko's (1997) "Speaking of Fashion"," *Journal of Consumer Research, 29* (December), 427-440.

This Time (Again) Consumption May Not Unite Us

Cagri Yalkin, King's College, UK
Sinasi Ozgur Mumcu, Galatasaray University, Turkey

This paper aims to explore the ideological and social tensions that soap operas exported by a developing country engenders in other developing countries, and hence to extend the resistance literature in marketing as suggested by Izberk-Bilgin (2010) through the use of qualitative research.   In-depth interviews with international relations experts and media professionals as well collated material from the press provided preliminary insights and clarified the context, as explained below. Izberk-Bilgin (2010) pointed out the need to expand the geographical boundaries of research on resistance beyond the Western world. While she suggested studying the tensions and reactions to Western goods in developing countries as a starting point, this study will examine the tensions created by and reactions to (immaterial) goods originating from developing countries in developing countries, extending Thompson and Arsel's (2004) local-local work. Although a number of scholars have studied the tensions in developing countries by exploring consumer desire for Western products (e.g. Belk 1988; Eckhardt and Houston 2002; Ger, Belk, and Lascu 1993), the reactions to goods exported by one developing country to another have not been studied within the resistance literature in marketing.

Thompson and Arsel (2004) develop the notion of hegemonic brandscape which is "a cultural system of servicescapes that are linked together and structured by discursive, symbolic, and competitive relationships to a dominant experiential brand" (p.632). They use this notion to study how Starbucks structures local coffee shops and the anti-Starbucks discourse. Similarly, it is suggested here, based on the interviews with international relations experts and media practitioners, and on material in the media, that a hegemonic cultural goods space exists which consists of production and consumptionscapes that are structured around relationships to soap operas exported from a dominant country. The dominant country in this study is Turkey, for reasons explained below.

Ahmet Davutoglu (2001), in his 2001 book *Strategic Depth* (SD), argues that geographic depth transcends the artificial breakdown of ancient ties in the Middle East. SD aims, for example, to reunite Urfa(Turkey) and Aleppo(Syria), or the whole Mesopotamia which disintegrated after the collapse of the Ottoman Empire. SD claims that this reunification does not have any irredentist or imperial agenda and that Turkey's relations with former Ottoman regions are reminiscent of Japan's influence over Eastern Pacific region (Davutoglu 2001). This tightening of relationships comes with the baggage of spreading Turkey's cultural and economic influence over Ottoman cultural sphere (countries formerly included in the Empire territory), as is also acknowledged by Davutoglu (2001). One of the hallmarks of this cultural influence has been that of exporting the currently very popular Turkish soap operas (such as Gumus, known as *Noor*) to other countries in this sphere.

Within these hegemonic production and consumptionscapes, there are different discourses that are produced by both the consumers in the host countries (e.g. Syria, Egypt, etc.) and the guest country (Turkey), as is gathered from the preliminary interviews and the media (e.g. Apikian 2010, Bilbassy-Charters 2010): *"The (Anonymous) Media Group is good at this, since they are the producer company. They get their share of success… always running pieces about how people in those countries buy licensed t-shirts of the series, how the royal family there is friendly with the actors"* (interview, news editor in a national Turkish TV channel, 37, male). Further complicating the terrain are competing constructions in the media. In addition, there are competing discourses around how these TV series are received, consumed, and resisted in the host countries. What can be classified as the celebratory approach to this import/export of soap operas lies within the market-bound perspective of resistance (e.g. Firat and Venkatesh 1995). Some (Baraka 2009, Gokcek 2010) suggest that the popularity of the soaps is drawing the Arabic and Turkish people together after years of mutually held prejudice. The non-celebratory approach, provided by interviews with two editors form the media and two international relations experts, however still market-bound, resonates with Marx's (1844/1973) and Horkheimer and Adorno's (1944/2000) views on resistance which are centered around the concepts of enslavement, cultural imperialism (Tomlinson 2002), hegemony, and at times, misogyny.

Davutoglu (2001) suggests that the Western civilisation no longer has the monopoly over humanity's accumulation of experience. SD asserts that in order to contribute to that accumulation of experience, Turkey, as the centre of the last non-Western civilisation basin, can use its Islamic-Ottoman legacy to influence the interaction of civilisations (Davutoglu 2001) and give the Western civilisation an opportunity to cope with cultural plurality (Davutoglu 2002). By presenting Turkey as the centre of the last non-Western basin, SD is rooting Turkey as the potentially hegemonic party which is also accentuated by the Ottoman rule's heritage. It is suggested here that Turkey emerges as the hegemonic power both because of this conceptualisation and is perceived as such by some accounts (Buccianti 2010), therefore casting the import of its immaterial cultural goods as hegemonic, if not culturally imperial. How consumers in both the host countries and Turkey perceive and negotiate the export of these goods is the ultimate concern of this paper.

Just as Thompson and Arsel (2004) report different manifestations of the desire to experience the local, it is expected that consumers will have built more than one discourse about the hegemonic cultural presence of Turkish soap operas. Do the consumption of soap operas challenge the practices in the host countries as is suggested by some accounts (i.e. the values communicated through the television series challenging religious values and norms) or structure the reactions of local media production companies (Sakr 2007, Baraka 2009, Thompson and Arsel 2004)? What form of resistance is practiced by different agents such as those that view the series as *'wicked and evil'* (see Hammond 2009) or by left-wingers who perceive the phenomenon as *"politically insignificant markers of the relationship between Turkey and Arabs"* (interview, international relations expert, 30, female, Egyptian)? It is suggested here that opinions of the consumers of these soap operas be consulted to better understand the "…issues of national sovereignty, preservation of national idiosyncrasies, and authenticity and ownership of cultural products… [that] may arise in cross-cultural examinations… revealing previously unexplored motivations and forms of resistance" (Izberk-Bilgin 2010, p.316).

REFERENCES

Apikian, Jonathan (2010), "The Perception of Turkey in the Middle East: Soap Opera Diplomacy?," *The Middle East Blog*, http://www.cipe.org/blog/?p=4985

Baraka, Mohamed (2009), "Awash with Turkish Soap," *Al-Ahram Weekly Online*, 930(15 - 21 January) http://weekly.ahram.org.eg/2009/930/ee2.htm.

Belk, Russell W. (1988), "Third world consumer culture," in *Marketing and Development: Toward a Broader Dimension,* ed. E. Kumcu and A.F. Firat, Greenwich: JAI Press, 103–27.

Bilbassy-Charters, Nadia (2010), "Leave it to Turkish Soap Operas to Conquer Hearts and Minds," *Foreign Policy Blogs*, http://mideast.foreignpolicy.com/posts/2010/04/15/leave_it_to_turkish_soap_operas_to_conquer_hearts_and_minds

Buccianti, Alexandra (2010), "Dubbed Turkish Soap Operas Conquering the Arab World: Social Liberation or Cultural Alienation?," *Arab Media&Society*, 10(Spring), http://www.arabmediasociety.org/index.php?article=735&p=0.

Davutoglu, Ahmet (2001), *Stratejik Derinlik: Turkiye'nin Uluslararasi Konumu*, Kure Yayinlari, Istanbul.

Davutoglu, Ahmet (2002), *Kuresel Bunalim*, Kure Yayinlari, Istanbul.

Eckhardt, Giana M. and Michael J. Houston (2002), "Cultural Paradoxes Reflected in Brand Meaning: McDonald's in Shanghai, China," *Journal of International Marketing*, 10(2), 68-82.

Firat, Fuat A. and Alladi Venkatesh (1995), Liberatory Postmodernism and the Reenchantment of Consumption, *Journal of Consumer Research*, 22(December), 239-267.

Ger, Güliz, Russell W. Belk, and Dana N. Lascu (1993), "The Development of Consumer Desire in Marketing and Developing Economies: The Cases of Romania and Turkey," in *Advances in Consumer Research,* eds. L. McAlister and M.L. Rothschild, Provo, UT: Association for Consumer Research, 102–107.

Gokcek, Mustafa (2010), "Arabs and Turks: How They Have Drawn Closer," *Middle East Institute Viewpoints*, 6-8.

Hammond, Andrew (2009), "Reading Lohaidan in Riyadh: Media and the Struggle for Judicial Power in Saudi Arabia," *Arab Media & Society*, 2009(Winter), http://www.arabicmediasociety.com/?article=702#_edn3.

Horkheimer, Max and Theodor W. Adorno (1944/2000), "The Culture Industry: Enlightenment as Mass Deception," in *The Consumer Society Reader*, eds. J.B. Schor and D.B. Holt, New York: New Press, 3-19.

Izberk-Bilgin, Elif (2010), "An Interdisciplinary review of Resistance to Consumption, Some Marketing Interpretations, and Future Research Suggestions," *Consumption Markets & Culture,* 13 (September), 299–323.

Marx, Karl (1867/1976), *Capital*, London: Penguin.

Murison, Alexander (2006), "The Strategic Depth Doctrine of Turkish Foreign Policy", *Middle Eastern Studies,* 42 (November), 945-55.

Sakr, Naomi (2007), *Arab Television Today*, London: IB Tauris.

Thompson, Craig J. and Zeynep Arsel (2004), "The Starbucks brandscape and consumers' (anticorporate) experiences of glocalization," *Journal of Consumer Research,* 31(December), 631–42.

Tomlinson, John (2002), *Cultural Imperialism: A Critical Introduction*, London: Continuum.

Consumers' Commitment to Spend

Chrissy Mitakakis, Baruch College, USA
Keith Wilcox, Babson College, USA
Lauren Block, Baruch College, USA

In Western culture and society, emphasis has been placed on necessities, which are considered moral and ethical obligations, and are generally more important in the hierarchy of needs (Kivetz and Simonson 2002). As a result, much prior research has documented the lower status of luxuries and indulgences (as compared to necessities) and has found that individuals tend to select necessities over indulgences (i.e., saving for college over going on a cruise; Kivetz and Simonson 2002; Maslow 1970). Furthermore, research has also found that in order to avoid the mental angst and guilt most often associated with the consumption of indulgences, consumers utilize various justifying mechanisms to rationalize spending on indulgences.

Although previous research has shown that people use precommitments or effort in order to justify the consumption of an indulgence, most of this research has focused on people's commitment to consume a single indulgence. Alternatively, the current research examines the question of whether individuals can commit to the act of spending, such that they continue to spend until an initial indulgence goal has been satisfied. Thus, we propose that the commitment to spend on an indulgence activate individuals' indulgence goals. We do not expect these effects to occur when individuals initially commit to a necessity, nor when a subsequent item that is presented to individuals whose indulgence goal has been activated is non-indulgent.

We test these predictions in a series of experimental studies. For our first study, we sought to examine whether individuals do indeed have a commitment to spend. Participants were given a hypothetical scenario where they had seen an advertisement in the newspaper for a particular product. We provided participants with a picture and description of this product, for which half were told it was an indulgent item (sunglasses) while the other half were told it was a necessity item (laptop). All participants were told that they had committed to purchasing this product, which cost $499, upon seeing the advertisement. Participants were then told that upon arriving at the store, they found out that the item was discounted by $50. Next, participants encountered a second item, which was either an indulgent item (scarf) or a necessity (flashdrive). They proceeded to answer a series of questions, including how likely they would be to purchase this second product and several self-report measures. In addition, we measured reward-seeking tendencies using the behavioral approach system subscale in order to assess whether our proposed effect might be stronger for individuals with particularly strong reward-seeking tendencies (Carver and White 1990). Results support our hypotheses; participants who were told that they had committed to spending on an indulgent first product were more likely to buy the second product when it was an indulgent product than when it was a necessity product. Furthermore, we did not find a greater likelihood of purchase of a second item, regardless of its type, when participants initially committed to spending on a necessity product. Importantly, we also found a significant three-way interaction of first product, second product, and BAS reward responsiveness, such that effects were especially pronounced for individuals who had relatively high reward-seeking tendencies.

In our second study (currently underway), we seek to generalize the findings from Study 1, as well as provide stronger evidence for individuals' commitment to spend. Similar to our previous study, we gave participants a hypothetical shopping scenario which included either a necessity or indulgent product. Importantly, we told participants that once they arrived at the store to purchase this item, they found out it was out of stock. Participants were then told about a second product that they could purchase instead, which was varied to be either an indulgent item or a necessity, and asked about their likelihood of purchasing this second item. We reason that participants who are firstly presented with an indulgent item will commit to spending, such that they will therefore be more likely to purchase the subsequent item when it is an indulgent item rather than a necessity. We do not, however, expect individuals to be very likely to purchase the second item when it is a necessity, nor when they were initially committed to spending on a necessity item (regardless of the second item type).

Finally, in our third study, we will examine whether the nature of our effect is in fact driven by an indulgence goal. If so, then we expect to see our effect moderated when individuals are given other, different category opportunities to satisfy an activated indulgence goal. We will provide participants with a hypothetical shopping scenario similar to the one in our previous two studies. We will tell participants that they have committed to spending on an initial product (i.e., either an indulgent or necessity product), and then inform them that the product is out of stock. Next, we will present participants with an allegedly separate study, in which they will be given a choice task that will include a series of dessert options ranging in indulgence. We expect that participants who were initially committed to spend yet denied the opportunity to purchase an indulgent product to be more likely to choose the most indulgent dessert than those who initially committed to spending on a necessity product.

In conclusion, our research finds initial evidence for individuals' commitment to spend. Interestingly, we do not find this effect to hold when individuals initially commit to spending on a necessity, therefore providing initial evidence that an indulgence goal may be driving individuals' commitment to spend. Our results can have important implications for consumers' behavior with regard to their commitment to spend. In particular, our findings may lend insight into particular situations that consumers often encounter during the consumption of indulgences (i.e., discounts), and specifically the consequences these situations can have on consumer behavior leading to overspending and debt. Therefore, future research may find it worthwhile to explore how consumers' commitment to spend can be prevented or lessened through alternate means (i.e., fulfilling the indulgence goal through non-monetary ways).

REFERENCES

Carver, Charles. S., and White, Teri. L. (1994), "Behavioral Inhibition, Behavioral Activation, and Affective Responses to Impending Reward and Punishment: The BIS/BAS Scales," *Journal of Personality and Social Psychology*, 67, 319-333.

Kivetz, Ran, and Itamar Simonson (2002), "Self Control for the Righteous: Toward a Theory of Precommitment to Indulgence*,*" *Journal of Consumer Research*, 29 (2), 199-217.

Maslow, Abraham H. (1970), *Motivation and Personality*, 2d ed. New York: Harper & Row.

Objectification and Consumer Choice

Chrissy Mitakakis, Baruch College, USA
Sankar Sen, Baruch College, USA
Stephen Gould, Baruch College, USA

Prior research has examined the effects of media on people's attitudes and behaviors. In particular, researchers have found that one of the most prominently imposed values and beliefs from the media has been the objectified view of the human body (Monro and Huon 2005). Such research has mainly focused on the negative consequences that often result from the exposure to stereotypical and objectified cultural standards, and has found that the internalization of these pervasive social standards can lead to adverse effects in many domains of endeavor (Stice et al. 1994). For example, researchers have found that the constant exposure to objectification has been associated with severe, long-lasting consequences such as depression, sexual dysfunction, and eating disorders. In addition, because Western media emphasizes objectified views of the female "ideal" much more than that of the male, the effects of objectification are often especially dire for females compared to those for males.

As a result, many researchers have attempted to understand females' process of internalization of objectification, and have come up with empirically validated theoretical accounts and explanations. One such construct, termed objectification theory, posits that in Western society, the female body is regarded as a sexual object that is to be looked at and evaluated (Fissel and Lafreniere 2006; Fredrickson and Roberts 1997; Moradi, Dirks, and Matteson 2005). According to this theory, the female body is "treated as a body (or collection of body parts) valued predominantly for its use (or consumption) by others," (Frederickson and Roberts 1997, 174). Consequently, females come to internalize this "observer" position of themselves, and therefore view their bodies as objects for visual inspection and evaluation, in a process termed self-objectification (Calogero 2004; Fiissel and Lafreniere 2006). In addition to the long-term effects often produced by objectification, self-objectification has also been associated with more immediate consequences, such as the decline of peak motivational states and flow experiences because of the conditioned responses of shame when failing to meet societally constructed ideals. Additionally, these feelings of shame have also been shown to lead to momentary decreases in cognitive ability (Fredrickson and Roberts 1997; Moradi et al. 2005).

Given the potential of self-objectification to cause immediate, negative consequences for females, it can be argued that objectification can affect decision processes. Research in behavioral decision making suggests that consumer preferences are not always defined, but are instead constructed during a choice task (Novemsky et al. 2007). Oftentimes, consumers base their decisions on the apparent ease or difficulty surrounding the choice. While this subjective experience of ease or difficulty can be the result of the choice process itself, it can also be an outcome of external circumstances that are unrelated to the choice (Novemsky et al. 2007). Regardless of the source of difficulty, however, consumers often attempt to reduce the resulting feelings of discomfort and conflict through the choice process itself, by choosing a cognitively easier, more easily defensible compromise option. The current research proposes that the momentary experience of self-objectification will act as a source of difficulty for females during the choice process. This, in turn, will lead to an increase in the choice of the compromise option among females (but not males).

In our first study, we examined the proposed effect of objectification on female consumers' choice through a hypothetical shopping scenario. We gave all participants a word scramble task, which has been utilized in prior objectification research (Roberts and Gettman 2004), in which they had to rearrange four out of five words to form a coherent sentence,. Half of the participants received all neutral words (i.e., "sat to they town drove"), while the other half received words relating to objectification (i.e., "was hear unshapely she really"). After the word scramble task, participants were told to imagine that they were shopping for a camera. Following our manipulation, participants were given a choice set of three cameras varying in dimensions and price (Novemsky et al. 2007), and asked to carefully examine the options and select one.

Results confirm our hypothesis. We found a main effect of condition ($F(1, 268) = 9.30, p < .01$), such that choice of a compromise option was greater for the objectification condition ($M = 36\%$) than for the control condition ($M = 17\%$). In addition, results also demonstrate a significant main effect of gender ($F(1, 268) = 13.47, p < .01$), as choice for the compromise option was greater for females ($M = 34\%$) than for males ($M = 15\%$). Further analyses also indicate a significant condition by gender interaction ($F(1,268) = 4.19, p<.05$). Planned follow-up contrasts showed a significant effect for female participants in the objectification condition, as these participants choose the compromise option more than females in the control condition ($M = 47\%$ versus $M = 21\%$; $F(1, 268) = 16.00, p < .01$). Furthermore, we also found that females in the objectification condition chose the compromise option more than males in the objectification condition ($M = 47\%$ versus 7%; $F(1, 268) = 16.47, p<.01$). Based on our findings, Study 2 (currently in progress) examines the effect of objectification on consumer choice in greater detail, by attempting to determine the underlying process (i.e., the nature of the proposed difficulty during choice) that may be driving the effects we observed in Study 1.

Our research contributes to the literature by examining the effect of a rather common phenomenon on consumer choice. This paper demonstrates that objectification can lead to choice of a compromise option for those most vulnerable to its consequences, namely, females. In addition, given that we did not find any effect of objectification on males' choice process, we argue that the effects of objectification are much more pronounced for females because of the implications of the female gender role in society. Thus, we offer new insight about the effect of objectification within the choice domain. Future research might also examine whether the effects of objectification on choice might vary for different types of products.

REFERENCES

Calogero, Rachel M. (2004), "A Test of Objectification Theory: The Effect of the Male Gaze on Appearance Concerns in College Women," *Psychology of Women Quarterly*, 28, 16-21.

Fiissel, Dorrie L. and Kathryn D. Lafreniere (2006), "Weight Control Motives for Cigarette Smoking: Further Consequences of the Sexual Objectification of Women?" *Feminism & Psychology*, 16(3), 327-344.

Fredrickson, Barbara L., Tomi-Ann Roberts, Stephanie M. Noll, Diane M. Quinn, and Jean M. Twenge (1998), "That Swimsuit Becomes You: Sex Differences in Self-Objectification, Restrained Eating, and Math Performance," *Journal of Personality and Social Psychology,* 75(1), 269-284.

Monro, Fiona and Gail Huon (2005), "Media-Portrayed Idealized Images, Body Shame, and Appearance Anxiety," *International Journal of Eating Disorders*, 38(1), 85-90.

Moradi, Bonnie, Danielle Dirks and Alicia V. Matteson (2005), "Roles of Sexual Objectification Experiences and Internalization of Standards of Beauty in Eating Disorder Symptomatology: A Test and Extension of Objectification Theory," *Journal of Counseling Psychology,* 52(3), 420-428.

Novemsky, Nathan, Ravi Dhar, Norbert Schwarz and Itamar Simonson (2007), "Preference Fluency in Choice," *Journal of Marketing Research*, 44(August), 347-56.

Stice, Eric, Erika Schupak-Neuberg, Heather E. Shaw and Richard I. Stein (1994), "Relation of Media Exposure to Eating Disorder Symptomatology: An Examination of Mediating Mechanisms," *Journal of Abnormal Psychology,* 103(4), 836-840.

A Test of Universality of the Relationship between Self-Construal and Impulsive Consumption: the case of Russia

Alexander Jakubanecs, Institute for Research in Economics and Business, Norway
Olga Patosha, State University Higher School of Economics, Russia

Impulsive consumption plays an important role in consumer behavior being a major driver of sales across many industries (Vohs and Faber 2007). Furthermore, research has shown effects of the cultural dimension of self-construal type on impulsiveness (Zhang and Shrum 2009; Chen et al. 2005). However, since the connection between self-construal and impulsive consumption has been investigated primarily within and between the North American and a number of Asian cultures e.g. (Chen et al. 2005; Zhang and Shrum 2009) the question remains whether the connection is universal. Russia particularly presents an interesting subject of research since impulsiveness as well as recklessness has often been mentioned as Russian cultural traits both by Western and Russian researchers (Dicks 1952; Inkeles, Hanfmann et al. 1961; Peabody, Shmelev et al. 1994; Peabody and Shmelyov 1996). At the same time, Russia historically has had a collectivist societal structure (Miller 1960; Toltz 2001) and is often classified as collectivist in the extant research (Hofstede 1991). Thus, we may expect to find a different relationship between self-construal and impulsiveness in the Russian context. This research has important implications for cross-cultural research in impulsive consumption and universality of consumer behavior theories.

SELF-CONSTRUAL AND IMPULSIVE CONSUMPTION

Independent self-construal implies loose connection to other members of society while interdependent implies close connection (Triandis 1995). Impulsiveness is usually defined as greater accessibility of hedonic compared to self-regulation goals (Shiv and Fedorikhin 1999). Cross-cultural differences in impulsive consumption have been documented with independent self-construal positively influencing impulsive consumption and consumer impatience and interdependent negatively both on individual and inter-cultural levels (Chen et al. 2005; Trafimow et al. 1991). Furthermore, peer presence can be expected to enhance chronic cultural patterns (Zajonc 1965).

RUSSIAN CULTURAL TRAITS

Extant research on Russian culture has shown it to be considerably less developed in capacity for self-regulation that is very typical of other Northern peoples (Dicks 1952; Inkeles et al. 1961). This characteristic has been documented both through qualitative research e.g. (Inkeles et al. 1961) and through self-ratings (Peabody and Shmelyov 1996). Self-ratings have shown Russians to be considerably more impulsive, reckless and rash compared to a range of other cultures e.g. American, German, British and Japanese (Peabody et al. 1994; Peabody and Shmelyov 1996). Traditionally experiencing these tendencies, albeit evaluated negatively by the members of the culture, has been socially acceptable and not associated with guilt or remorse after the experience.

HYPOTHESES

Weakly developed self-regulation and thus impulsiveness are widely spread syndromes in the Russian culture that are socially acceptable (Dicks 1952; Peabody and Shmelyov 1996). Therefore we postulate that peer presence may increase impulsiveness in both self-construals, albeit in different ways. Independents will be concerned with their unique identity which can be also expressed through impulsive consumption. This predisposition can be enhanced by peer presence. Thus, the interaction of independent self-construal with peer presence will be manifested in attitudes towards impulsive consumption.

Group norms are important for interdependents (Triandis 1995). However, since impulsive behavior and consumption in Russia are socially acceptable, although not necessarily encouraged, we should not see the interaction of interdependent self-construal with peer presence on the attitudes. Yet, as interdependent self-construal is chronic in the Russian culture and impulsiveness is a cultural syndrome, we should observe this interaction on the level of internal state, i.e. level of impulsiveness. Thus,

H1: There will be positive effects of peer presence on consumption attitudes for independent self-construal.

H2: There will be positive effects of peer presence on state of impulsiveness for interdependent self-construal, but not on consumption attitudes.

Further, impulsiveness is such a central cultural trait that it should be less subject to variations in value orientations (e.g. unique identity vs. group norms). Thus, it will be less dependent on the type of primed self-construal. Therefore:

H3: The main effect of self-construal on impulsive consumption will be insignificant.

Since both impulsiveness and recklessness are chronic cultural traits we expect impulsiveness and risk preferences to be interrelated and both to influence impulsive consumption. Therefore, the effects of impulsiveness on consumption are likely to be moderated by risk preferences.

METHODOLOGY

The study built on the methodology by Zhang and Shrum (2009). In both the pretest and the main study participants were undergraduate students of Moscow's Higher School of Economics. 90% were ethnic Russians. A pretest to elicit impulsiveness of several consumption scenarios has been conducted (N=107). The main study was run using the alcohol consumption scenario, 2(type of primed self-construal) X 2(peer presence)(N=118). The scenario focused on going to a café to have an alcoholic drink. Peer presence was manipulated by referring to going on one's own vs. going with friends. Consumption attitudes were measured by three items: good/bad, positive/negative, like/dislike. Self-construal cognitions were measured by 6-item scale (Hamilton and Biehal 2005), impulsiveness by 10-item scale (Puri 1996), risk preferences by 12-item scale (Weber et al. 2002) and affect by 10-item scale (Pham et al. 2001). All items were measured by 7-point Likert scales.

RESULTS

Manipulation of self-construal was significant (F(1,117=10.68,p<0.001). The 2x2 interaction was significant for immediate alcohol consumption attitudes (F(1,117=4.18,p<0.01). In support of H1 there was a positive effect of interaction of peer presence with independent self-construal on consumption (M=4.37 vs. M=3.23 (no peer presence); t(59)=2.37,p<0.03). The interaction with interdependent self-construal was insignificant (M=3.60 vs. M=3.43 (no peer presence);t(55)=0.33,p=.74).

The 2x2 interaction was significant for state of impulsiveness (F(1,117=2.18,p<0.09). There was only a tendency of a positive interaction of peer presence with interdependent self-construal on impulsiveness (M=-0.10 vs. M=0.43;t(55)=-1.01,p=0.32) (the smaller value means stronger impulsiveness). Thus, H2 receives only mixed support. No interaction was shown for independent self-construal (M=-.57 vs. M=-.60,t(59)=.09,p=.93).

The main effect of self-construal on consumption attitude was insignificant (F<1) in support of H3.

Regressions confirmed H3. Effect of impulsiveness on consumption was positive (β=-.248,p<.01), its effect on risk preferences was also positive (β=-.227,p<.02). When both impulsiveness and risk preferences were included in the regression on consumption, both were significant (β=-.164,p<.07; β=.354,p<.001).The effect of impulsiveness was significantly reduced, which implies moderating effect of risk attitudes. General affect, alcohol knowledge, experience and gender were not significantly related to the variables in the study. The effect of 2x2 manipulations on risk preferences was insignificant contrary to extant research (Hamilton and Biehal 2005).

CONCLUSIONS

Our findings indicate results partially diverging from extant research e.g.(Chen et al. 2005; Zhang and Shrum 2009). Priming self-construal does not enhance or suppress impulsive consumption in the Russian context, contrary to the literature. According to extant research self-regulation is relatively weakly developed among Russians (Peabody and Shmelyov 1996). Priming self-construal does not appear to change these entrenched predispositions. Interdependent self-construal which is chronic (Dicks 1952) for Russians does not significantly interact with peer presence, both for impulsiveness and consumption attitudes. However, there are tendencies for positive effects which can become significant with other scenarios of impulsive consumption.

At the other hand, we see positive effects of the peer condition for independent self-construal on impulsive consumption which suggest potential universality of this relationship. Furthermore, priming self-construal does not change risk preferences which also deviates from the existing research (Hamilton and Biehal 2005). Risk preferences are closely related to impulsiveness which is different from other research (Zhang and Shrum 2009), but in line with the literature on the Russian culture.

The results have to be confirmed by further tests on other types of impulsive consumption before being conclusive. However, the findings point to possible cultural specificity of the relationship between self-construal and impulsive consumption. Majority of fundamental consumer behavior theories have been tested primarily in North America and parts of Asia. Our results warrant caution in generalizing established theories to other parts of the world, particularly to nations characterized by potentially culture-specific traits.

REFERENCES

Chen, H. P., S. Ng, and A. R. Rao (2005), "Cultural differences in consumer impatience," Journal of Marketing Research, 42 (3), 291-301.

Dicks, H. V. (1952), "Observations on Contemporary Russian Behavior," Human Relations, 5, 111-74.

Hamilton, R. W. and G. J. Biehal (2005), "Achieving your goals or protecting their future? The effects of self-view on goals and choices," Journal of Consumer Research, 32 (2), 277-83.

Hofstede, G. (1991), Cultures and Organizations, Software of the Mind: McGraw-Hill.

Inkeles, Alex, Eugenia Hanfmann, and Helen Beier (1961), "Modal Personality and Adjustment to the Soviet Socio-Political System," in Studying Personality Cross-Culturally, Bert Kaplan, Ed. New York, Evanston, and London: Harper & Row.

Miller, Wright (1960), Russians as People. London: Phoenix House.

Peabody, D., A. G. Shmelev, M. K. Andreeva, and A. E. Gramenitskii (1994), "A Psychosemantic Analysis of Stereotypes of the Russian Character," Russian Education and Society, 36 (10), 75-94.

Peabody, D. and A. G. Shmelyov (1996), "Psychological characteristics of Russians," European Journal of Social Psychology, 26 (3), 507-12.

Pham, M. T., J. B. Cohen, J. W. Pracejus, and G. D. Hughes (2001), "Affect monitoring and the primacy of feelings in judgment," Journal of Consumer Research, 28 (2), 167-88.

Puri, Radhika (1996), "Measuring and Modifying Consumer Impulsiveness: A Cost-Benefit Accessibility Framework," Journal of Consumer Psychology, 5 (2), 87.

Shiv, B. and A. Fedorikhin (1999), "Heart and mind in conflict: The interplay of affect and cognition in consumer decision making," Journal of Consumer Research, 26 (3), 278-92.

Toltz, Vera (2001), Inventing the Nation: Russia. London: Arnold.

Trafimow, D., H. C. Triandis, and S. G. Goto (1991), "Some Tests of the Distinction Between the Private Self and the Collective Self," Journal of Personality and Social Psychology, 60 (5), 649-55.

Triandis, H. C. (1995), Individualism and collectivism. Boulder, CO: Westview.

Vohs, K. D. and R. J. Faber (2007), "Spent resources: Self-regulatory resource availability affects impulse buying," Journal of Consumer Research, 33 (4), 537-47.

Weber, E. U., A. R. Blais, and N. E. Betz (2002), "A domain-specific risk-attitude scale: Measuring risk perceptions and risk behaviors," Journal of Behavioral Decision Making, 15 (4), 263-+.

Zajonc, R. B. (1965), "Social Facilitation," Science, 149 (July 16), 269-74.

Zhang, Y. L. and L. J. Shrum (2009), "The Influence of Self-Construal on Impulsive Consumption," Journal of Consumer Research, 35 (5), 838-50.

Like 'Em or Leave 'Em: Prior Beliefs and Correspondent Inferences Spark Endorser Effectiveness

Sommer Kapitan, University of Texas at San Antonio, USA
David H. Silvera, University of Texas at San Antonio, USA
Maria L. Cronley, Miami Univeristy, USA

Does a celebrity endorser's reputation precede him or her into the endorsement context? Since the advancement of source attractiveness and credibility models (McGuire 1969, Miller 1970), the literature has questioned whether the use of a famous face in advertising buys lasting attention and access to consumers. Existing models indicate that a match-up between endorser and product features is necessary (Kahle and Homer 1985), and that advertisers must weigh meanings the endorser brings to the product (McCracken 1989). Yet if reputation and image factor into the endorsement context, how do consumers' prior beliefs about an endorser impact endorser effectiveness?

We suggest that, depending on personal inclinations to engage with a message, prior beliefs about an endorser become a processing filter for messages. What happens when consumers are triggered to think carefully about product endorsers? The default tendency is for observers to make correspondent inferences (Gilbert and Malone 1995) that endorsers promote products because they like, value, and actually use the product. We propose that attributions are a key mechanism for endorser effectiveness, and that they can lead to source effectiveness via shallow or deep processing. Mehta (1994) argues that advertising responses to celebrities are only found in shallow processing encounters. Her study finds that consumers viewing celebrity-endorsed commercials generate thoughts about the source that cannibalize thoughts about the product or brand, yet still lead to positive evaluations (Mehta 1994). Kang and Herr (2006), however, argue that source information is also encoded as product arguments. We suggest that endorser characteristics always impact persuasion, but that the influence of the endorser is either direct—via simple reliance on source characteristics and shallow processing—or indirect, as a result of deep processing and a preferential search for information that supports consumers' prior beliefs about the celebrity.

Under shallow processing, research suggests that correspondence bias should occur. This is positive for celebrity endorsers, since a default correspondent inference is that celebrities promote products because they truly believe in the products. Yet this finding has only been demonstrated with positive or neutral endorsers (i.e., Cronley, Kardes, Goddard and Houghton 1999). For disliked endorsers, consistent with existing research on source effects, the endorser takes on the role of a product argument. In this way, prior beliefs about a celebrity endorser spur properly motivated consumers to engage more deeply with the message. We expect resulting inferences about the endorser to turn on the valence of those prior beliefs.

Our goal was to understand how endorser likeability cues processing when consumers face environmental stimuli and are motivated to engage with promotional messaging. We hypothesize that non-motivated consumers will process likeability as a heuristic, but that motivated individuals will use prior beliefs about an endorser as a deep processing cue when situational information is made salient. 127 participants viewed one of two advertisements for sunglasses. The advertisements were identical aside from featuring two different celebrity endorsers. The endorsers were closely matched on demographic characteristics and pre-tested as high (rapper and actor Will Smith) and low likeability (rapper Kanye West). Similar to previous research, (Cronley et al. 1999; Silvera and Austad 2004), we also provided information about whether the endorser was paid or not for his endorsement. After viewing the ad and receiving payment information, participants completed measures of correspondent inferences about the endorser's true liking for the product and their attitudes toward the product, the advertisement, and the endorser, then completed the Need for Cognitive Closure scale (NFCC; Webster and Kruglanski 1994) to capture their motivation to engage with the advertising message. The final design was thus 2 (likeability: liked vs. disliked) x 2 (fee: paid vs. unpaid) x 2 (NFCC; high or low). Confirming our pre-test results, Will Smith was viewed as significantly more likeable than Kanye West, indicating that the likeability manipulation was successful.

A 3-way (likeability x fee x NFCC) ANOVA predicting correspondent inferences indicated significant main effects such that both unpaid and likeable endorsers produced stronger correspondent inferences, in addition to a marginally significant 3-way interaction between pay, likeability, and NFCC ($F(1,126) = 3.20$, $p < .08$). To further explore this interaction, 2-way (NFCC x likeability) ANOVAs were conducted separately for paid and unpaid endorsers. In the unpaid condition, results indicated a simple source effect—stronger correspondent inferences were made about the likeable than the unlikeable endorser ($F(1,55)=4.33$, $p<.05$), with no main effect or interactions with NFCC (F's<1). In the paid condition, a similar main effect for likeability was observed ($F(1,64)=7.25$, $p<.01$), but this main effect was qualified by a likeability by NFCC interaction ($F(1,64)=10.03$, $p<.005$). Further breaking down this interaction indicated that likeability had no impact on correspondent inferences for high NFCC participants ($F<1$), but that likeability increased correspondent inferences for low NFCC participants ($F(1,33)=19.44$, $p<.001$).

These results suggest that two distinct evaluation processes operate depending on information about payment of the endorser. When participants received salient payment information, they appear to have engaged in simple source-based processing—they trusted the likeable endorser more, and this was not moderated by their motivation to process information carefully (i.e., NFCC). When participants were told that the endorser was unpaid, their reasoning process appears to be more complex—unmotivated (high NFCC) participants showed no source effects, but highly motivated (low NFCC) participants showed the strongest source effects of any group. This suggests that low NFCC participants engaged in a deeper processing in which they accessed their pre-existing attitudes toward the endorser and used them to guide processing of ad-related information.

Why do we care about correspondent inference processes? In the present study, correspondent inferences were significantly correlated with attitudes toward both the advertisement ($r(127) = .41$, $p < .001$) and the product ($r(127) = .45$, $p < .001$). The role of prior beliefs, when cued by environmental information such as an endorser's salary, thus can have an important impact on evaluations of both promotion and product. In short, reputation impacts endorsed advertising via both heuristic and systematic thought processing.

REFERENCES

Cronley, Maria L., Frank R. Kardes, Perilou Goddard, and David C. Houghton (1999), "Endorsing Products for the Money: The Role of Correspondence Bias in Celebrity Advertising," in *Advances in Consumer Research* Vol. 26, eds. Eric J. Arnould and Linda M. Scott, Provo, UT : Association for Consumer Research, 627-631.

Folkes, Valerie S. (1988), "Recent Attribution Research in Consumer Behavior: A Review and New Directions," *Journal of Consumer Research*, 14 (March), 548-565.

Khale, Lynn R. and Homer, Pamela M. (1985), "Phyiscal Attractiveness of the Celebrity Endorser: A Social Adaptation Perspective," *Journal of Consumer Research,* 11 (March), 954-961.

McCracken, Grant (1989), "Who is the Celebrity Endorser? Cultural Foundation of the Endorsement Process," *Journal of Consumer Research*, 16 (December), 310-321.

McGuire, William J. (1969), "The Nature of Attitudes and Attitude Change," in *The Handbook of Social Psychology* (2nd ed.. Vol. 3), eds. Gardner Lindzey and Elliot Aronson, Reading, MA: Addison-Wesley, 136-314.

Miller, Arthur G. (1970), "The Role of Phsyical Attractiveness in Impression Formation," *Pscyhonomic Science*, 19 (4), 241-243.

Silvera, David H. and Benedikte Austad (2004), "Factor predicting the effectiveness of celebrity endorsement advertisements," *European Journal of Marketing*, 38 (11/12), 1509-1526.

Sparkman, Richard M. (1982), "The Discounting Principle in the Perception of Advertising," in *Advances in Consumer Research* Vol. 9, ed. Andrew Mitchell, Ann Arbor, MI: Association for Consumer Research, 277-280.

Webster, D. M., and Arie W. Kruglanski (1994), "Individual Differences in Need for Cognitive Closure." *Journal of Personality and Social Psychology*, 67 (6),1049-1062.

What You Smell Affects What You Like
How Incidental Scents Can Affect Product Preference By Eliciting Emotion

Elise Riker, Arizona State University, USA
Andrea Morales, Arizona State University, USA
Stephen Nowlis, Washington University in St. Louis, USA

The sense of smell is commonly overlooked amid the five senses, but recently the human nose has been getting popular press on its unexpected emotional power and connection with memories. How might this power be harnessed in the marketplace? We propose that the scent-evoked emotions and memories affect consumers' choices, making a particular subset of products and services more attractive in subsequent decisions.

Scents associated with emotional experiences can evoke the same emotion by its mere presence. Past research has shown that the scent of eugenol, associated with dental procedures, induces fear for those who fear the dentist (Robin et al., 1998). It is interesting that the scent alone, independent of other dentist-related cues, is sufficient to elicit a strong negative emotion, but only for those with painful associated memories. Beyond eliciting associations, smell has the power to reactivate the original emotional experience.

Several reasons have been suggested for this connection between scent and emotion. First, the two areas of the brain that respond to and evaluate odors, the amygdala and the orbitofrontal cortex, are also closely connected to processing of emotion in the brain (Hamman, 2003). The olfactory system's close synaptic distance connects easily and quickly with emotional context, requiring little cognitive mediation (Bone and Ellen, 1999). Emotions and scents can thus be encoded without conscious effort. Additionally, scents generally have less interference than do other stimuli (Herz, 2004), due, in part, to the immense number of differentiated smells. With over 10,000 scents, a unique scent may be encountered and encoded with a distinct emotional experience.

Past research on ambient scent suggests that congruency, or correspondence among store elements, increases evaluations (Mitchell et al., 1995, Spangenberg et al., 2005). However, prior work has focused on the semantic match, rather than the match between consumers' specific emotional states and product evaluations (for an exception, see Griskevicius et al., 2010). We focus on the emotional congruency of the scent and product choices, based on product-in-use and associated memories.

Specifically, we propose that a scent-induced discrete emotion will increase attraction to products that 'match' with that emotion, or to those products that enable consumers to carry out the action tendencies evoked by that emotion. In this study, we investigate a light, sweet smell that is unique to baby products (lotions, shampoos, etc.), and propose that this scent will induce nurturant love via consumers' associations with caring for helpless infants. 'Nurturant love' is defined as feelings of love and concern for another's well-being, particularly of kin, and compassion toward those that are dependent (Griskevicius et al., 2010). We hypothesize that these feelings will increase the evaluations of family-focused products and services, cute products, and services that involve the vulnerable or express compassion. In contrast, a general positive affect induced by a pleasant scent should increase evaluations of all products across categories, as seen in past research (Chebat and Michon 2003).

Study 1 consists of two parts. In the first part, we exposed participants to either the target scent or the control scent under the guise of a new product evaluation. Participants evaluated a product sample on a variety of dimensions, with the product scent evaluated last. Participants completed part 2 of the experiment as an ostensibly unrelated study on general product and service evaluations, including emotionally-congruent products (e.g. grape tomatoes, baby carrots, nurturing cat food, Goldfish crackers, Cracker Barrel dinner, and Disneyland vacation) and emotionally-incongruent products in similar product categories (e.g. beefsteak tomato, Quilted Northern toilet paper, Brawny paper towels, RA Sushi dinner, Vegas vacation, rat trap). Participants then reported their emotional state during the study.

Results showed that the baby scent increased evaluations of the nurturant-love-congruent products as compared to the control scent (4.84 versus 4.32), and this difference was significant ($F(1,40) = 4.56$, $p = .035$). To ensure that the baby smell did not increase evaluations across the board, emotionally-incongruent products were selected that were similar in product categories or kinds to the emotionally-congruent products, but were purposely not consistent with actions associated with the emotion (i.e., not family-friendly or cute). A comparative index showed no significant differences ($F(1,40) = .58$, $p = .48$), although the control condition produced directionally higher index evaluations (4.60 versus 4.78). This indicates that the baby scent did not increase general product evaluations, but selectively enhanced evaluations for emotionally-congruent products.

Subject's emotional states support our explanation of the role of emotions. We expected that the 'baby' scented shampoo would evoke feelings of nurturing, love, and compassion, while the control scented shampoo was expected to evoke general positive affect without activating specific emotions. Using self-reports of love and compassion as a proxy for nurturant love, we found stronger emotions reported in the baby condition (6.18) than the control condition (4.93) and this difference was marginally significant ($F(1,40) = 4.56$ $p = .073$). There were no significant differences for general positive emotions (i.e., good, happy, and positive), indicating that the scents produced comparable generally positive feelings.

Study 1 also eliminated familiarity and liking of the scents as potential explanations; no significant differences were found on either measure. To further validate the results, Study 2 addressed other possible emotions or associations that could be elicited by the scent, such as romantic love or priming 'baby' in general, resulting in increased preference for romantic or baby related products respectively. Neither product types were found to be affected by the target scent. Study 3 addressed the role of scent identification in eliciting the desired emotions. Because scents can be ambiguous and difficult to interpret when unidentified (Herz, 2003), we wanted to see what differences resulted from upfront identification of the scent as 'baby' or left as a general personal care product scent.

By connecting recent findings on emotions in psychology with sensory marketing, this research demonstrates that an incidentally encountered olfactory cue can increase perceptions of emotionally-congruent offerings. Scents created as part of a branding identity become entangled with the emotional memories that consumers create as they use the brand, and thus the scent activates that powerful emotional connection.

REFERENCES

Bone, Paula Fitzgerald and Pam Scholder Ellen (1999), "Scents in the Marketplace: Explaining a Fraction of Olfaction," *Journal of Retailing*, 75(2) 243–262.

Chebat, Jean-Charles, and Richard Michon (2003), "Impact of Ambient Odors on Mall Shoppers' Emotions, Cognition, and Spending: A Test of Competitive Causal Theories," *Journal of Business Research* (56) 529-539.

Griskevicius, Vladas, Michelle N. Shiota, and Samantha L. Neufeld (2010), "Influence of Different Positive Emotions on Persuasion Processing: A Functional Evolutionary Approach" *Emotion* 10(2) 190-206.

Hamann, Stephan (2003), "Nosing in on the Emotional Brain," *Nature Neuroscience* 6(2) 106-108.

Herz, Rachel S. (2003), "The Effect of Verbal Context on Olfactory Perception," *Journal of Experimental Psychology*, 132 (4) 595-606.

Herz, Rachel S. (2004) "A Naturalistic Analysis of Autobiographical Memories Triggered by Olfactory Visual and Auditory Stimuli," *Chemical Senses* (29) 217-224.

Mitchell, Deborah J., Barbara E. Kahn, and Susan C. Knasko (1995), "There's Something in the Air: Effects of Congruent or Incongruent Ambient Odor on Consumer Decision Making" *Journal of Consumer Research* 22 (September) 229-238.

Robin, O., O. Alaoui-Ismali, A. Dittmar, and E. Vernet-Maury (1998), "Emotional Responses Evoked by Dental Odors: An Evaluation from Autonomic Parameters" *Journal of Dental Research* 77(8) 1638-1646.

Spangenberg, E.R., A.E. Crowley, P.W. Henderson (1996), "Improving the Store Environment: Do Olfactory Cues Affect Evaluations and Behaviors?" *Journal of Marketing* 60 (April) 67-80.

A Subtle Sense of Specialness Triggers Feelings of Uniqueness

Jiska Eelen, KULeuven, Belgium

Kobe Millet, VU Amsterdam, Netherlands

Luk Warlop, KULeuven, Belgium, Norwegian School of Management, Norway

Would you feel awkward and uncomfortable or rather special and intrigued when you do not feel your usual self? Gao, Wheeler and Shiv (2009) have suggested that unfamiliar actions may shake one's self and lower self-confidence. Also, research about familiarity would suggest that unfamiliar stimuli are not fluently processed and hence disliked (Winkielman et al. 2003). Yet we propose that people may actually like what is unknown and different, and that doing something unfamiliar can activate the goal to stand out of the clutter. Recent research by Wood (2010) points in this direction. Wood found that people who experienced life changes were more likely to be attracted to new or unfamiliar options. Of interest to our research, Maimaran and Wheeler revealed that exposure to novel visual arrays of geometrical shapes made people choose more unique products (2008). We predict that performing an unfamiliar action will result in a similar effect, namely trigger a goal to be unique and make people choose more unique products. Also we predict that this effect will be moderated by initial feelings of uniqueness. For consumers who have a chronic need for expressing uniqueness, we expect our manipulation to have no effect. Momentary affective states can have an impact on judgments, but when people are made aware of the source they correct for it (Pham 1998; Schwarz and Clore 1983). In line with affect-as-information theory, we predict that unfamiliar actions need to be subtle in order to impact behavior. In three studies we find evidence for these hypotheses.

In Study 1, right-handers performed a task with their dominant right hand (i.e., usual) or nondominant left hand (i.e., unusual). After several filler tasks, participants filled in the consumers' need for uniqueness scale (Tian, Bearden, and Hunter 2001) on a 5-point Likert scale. A one-way ANOVA with hand used as the independent variable and need for uniqueness (Cronbach's alpha = .94) as the dependent variable was marginally significant ($F(1,68) = 3.53$, $p = .06$). There was a tendency for participants who used their left hand to score higher on need for uniqueness ($M = 2.66$) than participants who used their right hand during the choice task ($M = 2.39$).

One way for consumers to communicate their uniqueness through the choices they make, is by buying scarce products (Lynn and Harris 1997). In Study 2 we made participants (all right-handers) choose between four different boxes of chocolates of which one was labeled as "limited edition". First they performed a computer task with their left (unusual) or right (usual) hand. In a logistic regression with choice (0 = not unique, 1 = unique) as a dependent variable, and hand used (left vs. right) as a discrete between-subjects variable and NFU as a continuous between-subjects variable, we found a significant two-way interaction ($\chi^2(1, N = 99) = 4.16$, $p = .04$). Doing the usual task, low NFU participants (M_{NFU} - $1SD$) seemed less likely to choose the unique product ($\hat{P} = .19$) than high NFU participants (M_{NFU} + $1SD$, $\hat{P} = .42$) ($\beta = .73$, $\chi^2(1, N = 99) = 3.28$, $p = .07$). Doing the unusual task, NFU was not significant, but the probability to choose the scarce product for low NFU participants increased from 19% (usual task) to 49% ($\chi^2(1, N = 99) = 4.16$, $p = .04$). Also this chance was not different from high NFU participants who did the usual task ($\hat{P} = .42$, $\beta = .43$, $\chi^2(1, N = 99) = .24$, $p = .63$).

In our third study we generalized our findings to a different unfamiliar task (i.e., performing a task with a new technological device, namely a touch screen). In a control condition participants performed a computer task with the mouse, whereas in the "unusual" conditions participants had to touch the screen to indicate their choices. In the explicitly unusual condition we drew people's attention to the specialness of the task. Our dependent measure was the extent to which people chose different travel destinations than a majority of students of whom they saw the choices while responding to the survey. In the implicitly unusual condition, participants preferred unique travel destinations more ($M = 3.94$, $SE = .19$) than in the control condition ($M = 3.25$, $SE = .19$, $t(79) = 2.53$, $p = .01$), and in the explicitly unusual condition ($M = 3.38$, $SE = .19$, $t(79) = 2$, $p < .05$). There were no differences between the control condition and the explicitly special condition ($t(79) = .50$, $p = .62$).

Our research shows that doing unfamiliar tasks boosts people to stand out of the clutter. Performing a task with the nondominant hand made people feel more unique and choose products that are scarce in the marketplace. We demonstrated that a subtle situational cue boosted people's goal to be unique to the level of people who have this goal chronically activated. Using a new technological device led people to prefer more unique travel destinations. When people's attention was drawn to the task specialness, it no longer affected behavior. Perceptions of difficulty did not affect our results. Neither did self-esteem or self-awareness mediate our findings. This suggests that encountering an unfamiliar situation does not always lower people's self-views, as suggested by Gao et al (2009). Rather it may induce an open mind-set and break habitual behavioral patterns and promote novel options (Wood 2010). Future research should investigate whether unusual situational cues affect decision making processes more broadly. As suggested above, it is possible that unfamiliar situations make people more open-minded. As such, unfamiliar situations may also induce higher levels of variety-seeking, or even creativity. Our research may have considerable practical implications. If change is not always disliked, then shopping aisles for instance, may be reorganized once in a while to break consumers' habitual shopping patterns. Also websites may be visited more thoroughly when updated from time to time. However it remains an open question how subtle changes should be and whether too obvious changes result in opposite patterns of choice.

REFERENCES

Gao, Leilei, Christian S. Wheeler, and Baba Shiv (2009), "The "Shaken Self": Product Choices as a Means of Restoring Self-View Confidence," *Journal of Consumer Research*, 36 (1), 29-38.

Lynn, Michael and Judy Harris (1997), "Individual Differences in the Pursuit of Self-Uniqueness through Consumption," *Journal of Applied Social Psychology*, 27, 1861-83.

Maimaran, Michal and Christian S. Wheeler (2008), "Circles, Squares, and Choice: The Effect of Shape Arrays on Uniqueness and Variety Seeking," *Journal of Marketing Research*, 45 (6), 731-40.

Pham, Michel Tuan (1998), "Representativeness, Relevance, and the Use of Feelings in Decision Making," *Journal of Consumer Research*, 25 (2), 144-59.

Schwarz, Norbert and Gerald L. Clore (1983), "Mood, Misattribution, and Judgments of Well-Being: Informative and Directive Functions of Affective States," *Journal of Personality and Social Psychology*, 45 (3), 513-23.

Tian, Kelly Tepper, William O. Bearden, and Gary L. Hunter (2001), "Consumers' Need for Uniqueness: Scale Development and Validation," *Journal of Consumer Research*, 28 (1), 50-66.

Winkielman, Piotr, Norbert Schwarz, Tedra A. Fazendeiro, and Rolf Reber (2003), "The Hedonic Marking of Processing Fluency: Implications for Evaluative Judgment," in *The Psychology of Evaluation: Affective Processes in Cognition and Emotion.*, ed. Jochen Musch and Karl Christoph Klauer, Mahwah, NJ: Lawrence Erlbaum, 189-217.

Wood, Stacy (2010), "The Comfort Food Fallacy: Avoiding Old Favorites in Times of Change," *Journal of Consumer Research*, 36 (6), 950-63.

Shifting Away From Discomfort: Managing Difficult Decisions Through Reconstruals

Stephanie M. Carpenter, University of Michigan, USA
J. Frank Yates, University of Michigan, USA
Stephanie D. Preston, University of Michigan, USA
Lydia Chen, University of Michigan, USA

Research on pre-decisional coherence shifting (Simon, Krawezyk, & Holyoak, 2004; see also pre-decisional distortion; Russo, Meloy, & Medvec, 1998) indicates that changes in the desirability and importance of choice alternative features begins prior to making a choice, rather than following the choice. Proposed mechanisms for why coherence shifting occurs, however, have been limited. Evidence suggests that difficult decisions that are likely to create cognitive dissonance (see Cooper, 2007, for a review) are associated with a heightened arousal state or a feeling of discomfort (Croyle & Cooper, 1983). This research sought to determine whether feature conflict arising from lacking a clearly dominant option produces a feeling of discomfort, which, in turn, produces a motivating need or desire to reduce this discomfort. We propose that coherence shifting reduces decision conflict, which reduces discomfort.

In the present study, we predicted that coherence shifting would resolve feelings of discomfort that are experienced when an individual must make a difficult choice between two competing alternatives, each of which includes both positive and negative attributes. We hypothesized that those individuals who coherence shift more would feel less physiological arousal and would self-report the decision as being less difficult.

To test these hypotheses, 59 university undergraduates participated individually in a computerized study using an established coherence shift paradigm (Simon et al., 2004) and physiological measures. One method for measuring physiological arousal is the skin conductance response (SCR), which is measured by attaching electrodes to the palm of the hand to detect slight changes in skin perspiration that reflect sympathetic activation. A seminal study on cognitive dissonance and skin conductance response (Croyle & Cooper, 1983) indicated that cognitive dissonance increased SCR, and that resolving cognitive dissonance weakened the high arousal state. In our study, individuals were informed that they would be participating in a physiological study on decision making, and skin conductance response electrodes were attached to the palm of each participant's non-dominant hand. Participants were randomly assigned to either a control condition, which served to replicate previous evidence of coherence shifting (Simon et al., 2004), or a justification condition, where participants were asked to imagine that eventually they would be justifying their decision to a close other. The justification condition was added to ensure that participants would take the decision task seriously, and also to determine if there were effects of being asked to imagine justifying the decision to a close other (Lerner & Tetlock, 1999). All participants rated the desirability of a number of possible job attributes, and then weighted how important these attributes were in an average decision context. Participants were then shown the attributes of two possible job offers that varied on the dimensions of commute time, salary, office space, and vacation package. After viewing the job offers, participants rated the desirability of the attributes and weighted attribute importance a second time. Participants then indicated their choice leaning. An interim task was given prior to participants making their final choice, followed by a third rating of attribute desirability and weighted importance.

Results indicated that the justification condition did not interact significantly with the final choices or degree of coherence shifting, and justification condition effects were not included in subsequent analyses on coherence shifting. Participants in the control condition, however, had higher overall SCR across the study blocks ($p<.05$) than those in the imagined justification condition. This plausibly occurred because individuals who are not prompted to justify their choices are less successful at reducing discomfort. Such an explanation is consistent with research on accountability that suggests when people know they will be held accountable for their decisions, they make decisions that they expect will meet the approval of those to whom they are accountable. This process is thought to reduce the cognitive effort necessary for making complex decisions or difficult tradeoffs (see Lerner & Tetlock, 1999, for a review).

In the studies conducted by Simon et al. (2004), coherence shifting was measured as a change in the attribute desirability and importance ratings at each time point to be consistent with the preferred option that was eventually chosen. We replicated these general findings that individuals shift their desirability and importance ratings toward their final choice leanings. Analyses were conducted by dividing participants into three groups based on the degree of coherence shifting, with the dependent variables representing SCR during the maximal decision window of 2000ms–3000ms. Results indicated that participants with high levels of coherence shifting on importance weightings also had significantly lower SCR ($p<.05$) across study blocks. Coherence shifting on the importance weightings was also negatively correlated with the perceived difficulty of the decision ($r=-.262$, $p=.045$), indicating that those who coherence shifted more perceived the decision as less difficult. Correlations between desirability and importance also increased over time ($p<.05$) such that participants' evaluations on the two dimensions became more consistent with each attribute re-rating. Analyses were next conducted to measure coherence shifting with respect to the specific attributes. These revealed that participants who changed their importance weights the most also had significantly lower SCR ($p<.05$) across blocks, and that degree of coherence shifting with respect to the job offer attributes correlated significantly with decision difficulty for both the desirability ratings (*r*=-.36, *p*=.005) and the importance weightings (*r*=-.53, *p*<.05). These results were consistent with our predictions that participants who coherence shift more resolve feelings of discomfort and perceived decision difficulty that arise from not having a dominant choice option.

These data provide initial evidence for our proposed model of feature conflict leading to feelings of discomfort, which some individuals resolve through the use of pre-decisional coherence shifting. Additional research is being conducted to further establish the proposed causal sequencing. In the present study, those who coherence shifted less exhibited higher physiological arousal, while those who coherence shifted more exhibited lower physiological arousal. These findings shed light on the basic mechanisms underlying decision making and have implications for how consumers make decisions in difficult decision contexts when there is no objectively correct choice.

REFERENCES

Cooper, J. (2007). *Cognitive dissonance: Fifty years of a classic theory.* London: Sage.

Croyle, R. T., & Cooper, J. (1983). Dissonance arousal: Physiological evidence. *Journal of Personality and Social Psychology, 45*, 782-791.

Lerner, J. S., & Tetlock, P. E. (1999). Accounting for the effects of accountability. *Psychological Bulletin, 125*, 255-275.

Russo, E. J., Meloy, M. G., & Medvec, V. H. (1998). Pre-decisional distortion of product information. *Journal of Marketing Research, 35*, 438-452.

Simon, D., Krawezyk, D. C., & Hoyoak. K. J. (2004). Construction of preferences by constraint satisfaction. *Psychological Science, 15*, 331-336.

Too Much Information?
How Expertise Disclosures Affect the Persuasiveness of Online Consumer Reviews

Soyean (Julia) Kim, Boston University, USA
Barbara Bickart, Boston University, USA
Frederic Brunel, Boston University, USA

Online word-of-mouth (WOM) via consumer-generated product reviews has a significant impact on consumers' purchase decisions (e.g., Chevalier and Mayzlin 2006; Godes and Mayzlin 2004). In this context, information exchange is typically among strangers, and readers can learn about reviewers only through reviewers' own disclosure of their identity, expertise, and product involvement. Thus, source-related disclosures function as one cue through which readers can evaluate the usefulness of the review and thus, the persuasiveness of the message.

Identity-related disclosures can be important determinants of the persuasiveness of a review (e.g., Forman, Ghose, and Wisenfeld 2008; Naylor, Lamberton, and Norton 2011). Our research builds on this earlier work by focusing on the effect of expertise-related disclosures on the persuasiveness of an online review. Specifically, we test the hypothesis that in some situations, too many expertise-related disclosures can reduce the persuasive impact of a message.

LITERATURE

Recent research has focused on the role of identity-related disclosures on the persuasive impact of an online consumer review. For example, Forman et al. (2008) found a positive relationship between the presence of identity-related information in a review and product sales. Naylor et al. (2011) demonstrated that when limited or ambiguous identity-related information is provided in a review, consumers automatically infer that the reviewer has preferences similar to their own. Thus, a review with no identity-related information is often as persuasive as one that includes similar identity information.

Both of these papers focus on identity-related disclosures, such as age, gender or geography. Our research focuses on disclosures related to reviewer expertise. In general, we expect that expertise-related disclosures will increase perceptions of source credibility and thus the persuasiveness of the review (e.g., McGuire 1969). While expertise-related disclosures should increase perceptions of source credibility, expertise disclosures could also reduce perceptions of similarity between the source and the message recipient. Thus, we expect that the impact of the number of expertise-related disclosures on persuasion will depend on the consumers' level of product category knowledge. Specifically, for high knowledge consumers, the number of expertise-related disclosures in a review will increase source credibility and judgments about the evaluated product will be assimilated toward the evaluation provided in the review. On the other hand, for low knowledge consumers, high levels of expertise-related disclosure may reduce perceptions of similarity. If the message recipient infers that he/she is different than the message source, then they may use the review information as a standard of comparison or anchor, in which case the product evaluation would be contrasted from the evaluation provided in the review. Thus, a review containing more expertise-related disclosures will be less persuasive for low product knowledge consumers.

METHOD

To test these hypotheses, we conducted an experiment where the number of expertise-related disclosures and level of expertise represented by these disclosures were manipulated, and participants' self-reported product category knowledge was measured. Undergraduate students (n = 176) participated for course credit. Participants read three online reviews about a specific pair of running shoes. A photo of the shoes was provided, followed by the reviews. The first two reviews were seen by all participants. These reviews were mixed, mentioning some positive and some negative features of the shoes and included a rating of three out of five stars. These reviews did not include any disclosures or identification information about the reviewers.

The third review was favorable, mentioning all positive attributes and a rating of five out of five stars. The structure of this review varied across participants. Specifically, we varied the number of disclosures included in the review (one vs. three) and the level of expertise suggested by the disclosures (expert vs. novice). We used a pre-test to select three novice (e.g., "I am a new runner") and three expert (e.g., "I am a lifelong runner") disclosures. In the high disclosure condition, the review included either three novice or three expert disclosures, while in the low disclosure condition only one novice or expert disclosure was included, and we counterbalanced across the three disclosures in each group.

After reading the target review, we measured brand attitudes. We then measured participant's perceived similarity to the target reviewer, and perceptions of this reviewer's expertise and trustworthiness. The analyses below are based on the top and bottom 40% of respondents on the product category knowledge measure.

RESULTS AND DISCUSSION

Our predictions suggest a three-way interaction between number of disclosures, expertise of the disclosures and participants' product category knowledge. This interaction is significant ($F1,128 = 6.20$, $p < .01$). For participants *low* in product category knowledge, when the reviewer makes only one disclosure, brand attitudes do not differ by the expertise of that disclosure ($p > .29$). Consistent with our predictions, when the reviewer makes three disclosures, brand attitudes are higher when these disclosures indicate that the reviewer is a novice ($M = 3.44$) versus an expert ($M = 2.95$), $F1,128 = 3.76$, $p < .055$. In contrast, for participants *high* in product category knowledge, one disclosure has more influence on brand attitudes than does three disclosures. Specifically, brand attitudes are more favorable when the reviewer makes one novice disclosure ($M = 3.31$) versus one expert disclosure ($M = 2.87$), $F1,128 = 2.75$, $p < .10$. When the review includes three disclosures, brand attitudes do not vary by the expertise of the disclosure ($p > .39$). The participant's perceived similarity to the reviewer mediates these results.

These findings suggest that for lower knowledge consumers, source similarity has a larger effect on the persuasive impact of a message than that of source expertise, and that more disclosures allow low knowledge consumers to identify similar reviewers. High knowledge consumers seem to infer that a source is similar when disclosures are limited, and appear to discount reviews as the number of disclosures increases, regardless of the expertise suggested by those disclosures. In other words, for both low knowledge and high knowledge consumers, increasing the number of expertise-related disclosures can reduce the persuasive impact of a review.

REFERENCES

Chevalier, Judith A and Dina Mayzlin (2006), "The Effect of Word of Mouth on Sales: Online Book Reviews," *Journal of Marketing Research*, 43 (3), p.345-54

Forman, Chris, Anindya Ghose, and Batia Wiesenfeld (2008), "Examining the Relationship Between Reviews and Sales: The Role of Reviewer Identity Disclosure in Electronic Markets," *Information Systems Research*, 19 (3), p. 291-313

Godes, David and Dina Mayzlin (2004), "Using Online Conversations to Study Word-of-Mouth Communication," *Marketing Science*, 23 (4), p. 545-60

McGuire, William J.: The Nature of Attitudes and Attitude Change, in *Handbook of Social Psychology*, 2nd ed., G. Lindzey and E. Aronson, eds., Addison-Wesley, Cambridge, MA. 1969, p. 135-214.

Naylor, Rebecca Walker, Cait Poynor Lamberton, and David A. Norton (2011), "Seeing Ourselves in Others: Reviewer Ambiguity, Egocentric Anchoring, and Persuasion," *Journal of Marketing Research*, forthcoming

That tastes awful, unless I hear it tastes good – The impact of informational social influence on conflicting evaluations

Andrew Bryant, The George Washington University, USA
Kashef Majid, The George Washington University, USA
Vanessa Perry, The George Washington University, USA

In today's marketplace consumers are becoming increasingly reliant on the judgments of others in order to form their subject evaluations. For example, when determining if a movie is good or bad the consumer can view the ratings given by other users, or when sampling a new drink the consumer recalls that in a national taste test nine out of 10 consumers preferred the drink over the current market leader. Instances such as these are but a few examples where the prior judgments made by an anonymous group of consumers can exert a powerful effect on the judgment of the target.

Deutsch and Gerard (1955, 629) conceptualize this effect as information social influence where the individual "accepts information obtained from another as evidence about reality." The term should not be confused with a normative social influence that refers to "an influence to conform to the positive expectations of another" (Deutsch and Gerard 1955, 629). Under informational influence the individual has no pressure to conform while under the normative influence the individual's judgments are motivated by a desire to conform to the judgments of others. The present paper focuses on the impact that informational influence can have on the judgments of consumers. Specifically, whether the impact of informational social influence can increase how a poor product is evaluated or decrease how a good product is evaluated.

Prior work has done well to demonstrate that a positive informational social influence can positively impact the evaluations consumers have (Cohen and Golden 1972) and a negative influence can have the reverse effect (Pincus and Waters 1977). However, what is less clear is the interplay between the type of informational social influence and the quality of the product. Specifically, what impact does a positive (negative) informational influence effect have on a poor (good) quality product? Furthermore, the presence of competing signals, a positive informational influence and one's own subjective taste can create a state of dissonance (Festinger 1957). In order to move away from this state of dissonance, consumers often attempt to resolve this conflict through further evaluation (Sengupta and Johar 2001). Therefore, it is likely that when consumers are faced with competing information they will be more likely to want to try the product again to move away from their state of dissonance.

Using an experimental methodology we tested whether a positive or negative informational social influence would either enhance or decrease the perceptions of sweet (or bitter) tasting drink. A total of 105 undergraduate students from a large Mid-Atlantic private university participated in the study in exchange for bonus course credit. Participants were divided into one of six cells for our 2 (sweet tasting vs. bitter tasting) x 3 (positive vs. negative information social influence vs. no informational influence) between subjects design.

An unsweetened guava juice concentrate was mixed according to the directions and the flavor was either enhanced using a sweetener (sweet) or made to taste worse using lemon juice (bitter). A pre-test found that the sweeter drink was rated as more pleasant than the bitter drink (MSweet = 4.22 vs. MBitter = 2.94, F(1, 40) = 11.22, $p < .01$). Participants in the study were randomly divided into one of the six cells and told that they would be sampling a new type of drink. The drink was given to participants in a clear plastic cup with no markings. Before sampling the juice, the participants' attention was directed to a whiteboard that contained previous students' flavor ratings of the drink displayed in a stem and leaf style tick mark chart similar to the manipulation used by Cohen and Golden (1972). The tick marks were skewed to the top of the whiteboard under the positive informational influence condition and then inverted under the negative informational social influence condition.

Each participant was given approximately four ounces of the juice mixture and asked to fill out a questionnaire. Two seven point measures; Pleasant (*anchored by Unpleasant to Pleasant*) and Willingness to Try Again (*anchored by Never to Very Likely*) were used as the main dependent variables of interest. Once the study was over, participants were debriefed as to the true nature of the experiment and asked not to discuss the study with anyone.

Results were analyzed using an Analysis of Variance (ANOVA). Participants who received the sweet tasting juice were not impacted by the informational social influence effects; however, those that received the bitter tasting juice were significantly impacted by the social influence manipulation. Those who tasted the bitter juice and viewed the ratings given by others felt the pleasantness of the drink was significantly higher than those who were making their judgments without any social influence effects (MInformation_Positive = 4.10 vs. MNo_Information = 2.94, F(1, 37) = 12.25, $p < .01$). This finding indicates that the positive informational influence effect can increase the evaluation of a poor product. Furthermore, the in-congruency between the positive informational influence and the bitter tasting drink caused consumers to want to try the drink again (MInformation_Positive = 4.10 vs. MNo_Information = 2.61, F(1, 37, $p < .001$) which indicates that not only can informational social influence impact subjective consumer evaluations but it may also impact repeat behaviors.

Our study explores the interplay between informational social influence and evaluations of products. Our results suggest that an unpleasant product can be given a more favorable evaluation if consumers are made aware that other consumers had previously evaluated the product favorably. We also provide an avenue for further investigation by identifying the impact that conflicting signals can have on future intentions. In summary, we question the familiar adage, if everybody did it would you?

REFERENCES

Cohen, Joel B. and Ellen Golden (1972), "Informational Social Influence and Product Evaluations," *Journal of Applied Psychology*, 56(1), 54-59.
Deutsch, Morton and Harold B. Gerard (1955), "A Study of Normative and Informational Social Influence upon Individual Judgment," *Journal of Abnormal and Social Psychology*, 51, 629-636.
Festinger, Leon A. (1957), *A Theory of Cognitive Dissonance*, Stanford, CA: Stanford University Press.
Pincus, Steven and L. K. Waters (1977), "Informational Social Influence and Product Quality Judgments," *Journal of Applied Psychology*, 62(5), 615-619.
Sengupta, Jaideep and Gita Venkataramani Johar (2001), "Effects of Inconsistent Attribute Information on the Predictive Value of Product Attitudes: Toward a Resolution of Opposing Perspectives," *The Journal of Consumer Research*, 1 (June), 39-56.

The Price of Love: the Gifting Behaviors of Insecure Lovers

Weixing Ma, University of Houston, USA

Love is in the giver, not the gift. (William Sloan Coffin)

In the romantic dyad relationship, to love and to be loved may not always strike the perfect balance. If a person is more in love with or more devoted to his or her lover, he or she may feel insecure in the relationship. Purchasing and giving gifts to one's romantic partner is one of the most important and common ways to show one's love and nurture the intimate relationship. The average American spent about $100 on Valentine's Day in recent years, which was equivalent to almost one third of their entire Christmas shopping spending (Paul 2009). While the early research generally regard gift giving as an economic exchange process based on reciprocity motivation (e.g., Mauss 1925; Sherry 1983), Belk and Coon (1993) turned to the romantic love model within the agapic love paradigm to explain lovers' gifting behaviors, and found it to be a necessary addition to the economic exchange model. Nevertheless, they still viewed gift giving as an instrumental act designed to accomplish a goal such as gaining the recipient's love (Belk and Coon 1993). Particularly in an unbalanced romantic dyad, the motivation of an insecure lover trying to gain more "love" and secure feelings, may be manifested by the way he or she gives gifts for his or her beloved one.

In Sherry (1983)'s influential study of consumer gift giving in anthropological perspective, gift-giving is viewed as a continuous cycle of reciprocities. One important factor that is associated with satisfaction in a relationship is the reward level of the resources exchanged in the relationship (cf. Sprecher 1998).Notably, gift giving is a way of reinforcing relationships that are highly valued but insecure such as the kinship ties weakened by distance (Caplow 1982). In the romantic relationship, gifts are used to enhance self-attractiveness and self-esteem

(Mick and DeMoss 1990) or express feelings of love towards one's significant other (Cheal 1987). Research on dating gift giving shows that such gifts can also serve as a diagnostic cue for people to assess the intensity of a partner's love (Belk and Cook 1991). These instrumentalities of gift-giving naturally lead us to ask when and how people may develop different gifting strategies. Initial evidence has shown that gift giving patterns do evolve along different stages of a romantic relationship, e.g. often starting from the "gift-showering" at the early stage to "becoming unnecessary" at the mature stage (Joy 2001).

Existing literature has primarily focused on the desired recipients' influence as the origin of gift givers' gifting behaviors. For example, Otnes et al. (1993) integrated the study of recipient influences within the research on gift-selection behavior and explored how givers themselves actually view recipients and then examine how these perceptions influence actual gift-selection practices. Similarly, Ruth et al. (1999) investigated how the recipient's perceptions of the existing relationship, the gift, and his or her emotional reactions converge to affect relationship realignment. In this research, we propose a different perspective to consider givers' motivation of gaining feelings of security as the origin of their gifting behaviors. More specifically, we propose that the need to feel secure in the relationship will influence (1) how often an insecure lover gives gifts to his or her lover, (2) what kind of gifts he or she is inclined to purchase, and (3) how much is his or her willingness to pay for the chosen gift.

We first conducted an exploratory study to probe the gifting behaviors of lovers. Semi-structured interviews with 18 subjects who were in romantic relationship uncovered the following gifting patterns: (1) people tended to spend more time and effort in gift giving during courtship; what's more, they tended to focus on more hedonic items as their gift choice; (2) once the relationship settled down, people tended to reduce gift-giving to only occasion based (e.g. birthday) and holiday based gifting, and they tended to choose more functional or utilitarian items as gifts; (3) gifting was one of the most common means to please one's romantic partner; (4) when people felt less secure in the relationship, they thought of purchasing a gift more often, and they indeed did so. These findings support that in general, the power structure of a romantic relationship influences people's gifting behaviors.

We also conducted an experiment to investigate whether level of felt security in a romantic relationship has impact on people's choice of gift items. We randomly primed subjects (N=125) using scrambled sentence task with either feeling secure or feeling insecure in a relationship. Subsequently, the subjects primed as feeling insecure were more likely to select hedonic or discretionary items from the given list of gift choices compared to the subjects primed as secure (budget was controlled for; 85.6% vs. 57%, p<.01). Additionally, we plan to conduct a second experiment to test the difference in the willingness-to-pay for a desired gift item when subjects are subliminally primed with either feeling secure or insecure.

Meanwhile, a 3-month event-contingent diary study (N=38) is under way (confidentiality was assured through study's administrative procedure). Each time a subject gives a gift to his or her romantic partner, (s)he is instructed to record the experience following an agenda of topics specified in the journal kit as well as filling out a set of scale items adapted from the Relationship Assessment Scale (RAS, Hendrick 1988), the commitment scale (Lund 1985) and Braiker and Kelley (1979)'s love scale. This longitudinal study aims to gather further evidence of how level of felt security influences a lover's gifting behaviors along the evolving relationship.

We aim to contribute to the literature by demonstrating that in a romantic dyad relationship, an insecure lover is more likely to engage in more frequent gift giving to his or her beloved one, is more likely to select hedonic or discretionary items as gift choice, and is willing to pay more for a desired gift item. We also identify managerial and public policy implications that stem from these findings.

REFERENCES

Belk, Russell W. and Gregory S. Coon (1991), "Can't Buy Me Love: Dating, Money, and Gifts," *Advances in Consumer Research*, ed. Rebecca H. Holman and Michael R. Solomon, Provo, UT: Association for Consumer Research, 18, 521-527.

Belk, Russell W. and Gregory S. Coon (1993), "Gift Giving as Agapic Love: An Alternative to the Exchange Paradigm Based on Dating Experiences," *Journal of Consumer Research*, 20 (December), 393-417.

Braiker, Harriet B. and Harold H. Kelley (1979), "Conflict in the Development of Close Relationships," in *Social Exchange in Developing Relations*, ed. Robert Burgess and Ted Hudson, New York: Academic Press, 135-168.

Caplow, Theodore (1982), "Christmas Gifts and Kin Networks," *American Sociological Review*, 47 (June), 383-392.

Cheal, David (1987), "'Showing Them You Love Them': Gift Giving and the Dialectic of Intimacy," *Sociological Review*, 35 (February), 151-169.

Hendrick, Susan (1988), "A Generic Measure of Relationship Satisfaction," *Journal of Marriage and the Family*, 50, 93-98.

Joy, Annamma (2001), "Gift Giving in Hong Kong and the Continuum of Social Ties," *Journal of Consumer Research*, 28 (September), 239-256.

Lund, Mary (1985), "The Development of Investment and Commitment Scales for Predicting Continuity of Personal Relationships," *Journal of Social and Personal Relationships*, 2, 3-23.

Mauss, Marcel (1925), *The Gift: Form and Functions of Exchange in Archaic Societies*, New York: Norton.

Mick, David Glen and Michelle DeMoss (1990), "Self-Gifts: Phenomenological Insights from Four Contexts," *Journal of Consumer Research*, 17 (December), 322-332.

Otnes, Cele, Tina M. Lowrey and Young Chan Kim (1993), "Gift Selection for Easy and Difficult Recipients: A Social Roles Interpretation," *Journal of Consumer Research*, 20 (September), 229-244.

Paul Jason (2009), "Valentine's Day Shoppers Expected to Spend Less in 2009," *USA Today*, February 12, 1:28pm.

Ruth, Julie A., Cele C. Otnes and Frédéric F. Brunel (1999), "Gift Receipt and the Reformulation of Interpersonal Relationships," *Journal of Consumer Research*, 25 (March), 385-402.

Sherry, John F., Jr. (1983), "Gift-Giving in Anthropological Perspective," *Journal of Consumer Research*, 10 (September), 147-168.

Sprecher, Susan (1998), "The Effect of Exchange Orientation on Close Relationships," *Social Psychology Quarterly*, 61 (September), 220-231.

Do I Listen to You When You are Not Like Me?
The Effects of Priming Self Construal on the Influence of Others

Mina Kwon, University of Illinois, USA
Rashmi Adaval, HKUST, Hong Kong

Consumers are constantly exposed to ads where a similar or dissimilar source advocates the use of a product. People spontaneously compare themselves with these spokespersons and assimilate when they think of similarities or contrast away from them when they think of dissimilarities (Mussweiler 2003). Yet, the conditions in which these comparisons occur are unclear.

Research on source similarity presents mixed evidence with some suggesting that similarity can increase persuasion (Brock 1965; Woodside and Davenport 1974) and other work showing that this is not always the case (Leavitt and Kaigler-Evans 1975). Such discrepancies imply that the same source could have different effects depending on the recipients' frame of mind. We propose that self construal might be a critical factor that has been ignored.

Self construal pertains to how one sees oneself in relation to others; either independent of them or interdependent on them (Triandis 1989; Hofstede 1980). Although these differences might be chronic, self construal can also be primed (Brewer and Gardner 1996; Oyserman, Sorensen, Bergen, and Chen 2009). We suggest that one's self construal can influence whether people see themselves in relation to the source or not and this plays a role in how the message from the source is processed and the impact it has.

When a communication is presented, participants who have an interdependent self construal are more likely to assess if they are similar to the source or not. In contrast, participants who have an independent self construal might be more likely to see themselves as independent of any person or group. Thus, they may not engage in this assessment. We conducted two experiments to examine the effect of self construal on how much one takes into account information provided by similar or dissimilar others.

96 participants participated in Study 1. First, participants' self construal was manipulated by asking them to circle the pronouns "I" or "we" (Brewer and Gardner 1996). Then, as part of a different task, each participant read two product testimonials. Both came from the same source; a student with a gender neutral name who belonged to either their home university (similar source) or from a different university (dissimilar source). The two testimonials described the spokesperson's reactions to products that were either favorable or unfavorable. Participants then indicated how good the product was and indicated how similar they felt to the source (Aron, Aron, and Smolan 1992).

As expected, participants who were primed with "I" indicated that they felt further apart from the spokesperson (M = 3.13) whereas those who were primed with "we" reported feeling closer to the spokesperson (M = 3.68), $F_{dir}(1, 92) = 2.74$, p < .05.

Results suggest that when participants are primed with "I", the effect of product information (favorable vs. unfavorable) on participants' judgments does not depend on source similarity (M_{diff} = 3.32 vs. 3.39 for similar and dissimilar source), F < 1. However, when participants are primed with "we" the impact of product information on these judgments is greater when it comes from a source that is similar to them (M_{diff} = 4.17) than when it comes from a source that is dissimilar to them (M_{diff} = 2.25), F(1, 48) = 4.90, p < .05. This difference in means is confirmed by a marginally significant 3-way interaction involving the three variables, F(1, 92) = 2.63, (p = .10).

Although Study 1 shows that self construal determines the extent to which one takes into account information provided by the source, it is unclear if cognitive procedures activated by other tasks can override such effects. Experiment 2, investigates this issue.

Study 2 employed a 2x2x2x2 between subject design with procedures similar to Study 1, but with an additional comparison prime in the beginning. First, 208 participants were given a word task in which they were asked to compare pairs of objects (e.g., dog and cat) and asked to rate either how dissimilar or how similar they are (Xu and Wyer 2008). Then, participants were primed to think of themselves as independent or interdependent (using the "I" or "we" pronoun circling task). They then evaluated a testimonial from a similar or dissimilar source. The source described the product as having favorable or unfavorable features. Participants were then asked to indicate how good the product was and how persuaded they were by the message. They also indicated how similar they felt to the spokesperson.

Participants primed to think about similarities reported that they felt the spokesperson was more similar to them (M = 5.93) than those who were primed to think about differences (M = 5.03), $F_{dir}(1,191) = 7.26$, p <.01. Participants who were given product information from a similar spokesperson rated this person as more similar to them (M = 5.80) than those who were told that this information came from a dissimilar source (M = 5.18), $F_{dir}(1.191) = 3.42$, p < .05.

Consistent with study 1, the effect of product information on judgments was the same for participants with an independent self construal and source similarity did not matter. The additional task to induce a cognitive procedure to think about commonalities and differences had no effect on these participants (F < 1). In contrast, this task had an effect on participants primed with an interdependent self construal. The effect of product information on judgments was stronger when participants were thinking of commonalities rather than differences and was independent of source similarity. Thus, participants who had an interdependent self construal attempted to see commonalities and differences between themselves and the source if the prior task activated these procedures overriding the effects of source similarity. A three-way interaction of self-construal, commonality and difference prime and product information F(1, 200) = 4.05, p < .05 that was not contingent on where the source came from (F < 1) confirmed this pattern.

This research suggests that consideration of self construal might help clarify ambiguities in previous research findings on the effects of source similarity.

REFERENCES

Aron, A., E. Aron, and D. Smolan (1990), "Assessing closeness as including other in the self: The IOS Scale. Paper presented at the International Conference on Personal Relationships, Oxford, England.

Brewer, M. B., and W. Gardner (1996), "Who is this "we"? Levels of collective identity and self representations," *Journal of Personality and Social Psychology*, 71, 83–93.

Brock, T.C. (1965), "Communicator-recipient similarity and decision change," *Journal of Personality and Social Psychology*, 1(6), 650-654.

Hofstede, G. (1980), Culture's consequences. Beverly Hills, CA: Sage.

Leavitt, Clark and Karen Kaigler-Evans (1975), "Mere Similarity Versus Information Processing: An Investigation of Source and Message Interaction," Communication Research, 2, 300-306.

Mussweiler, Thomas (2003), "Comparison Processes in Social Judgment: Mechanisms and Consequences," Psychological Review, 110 (3), 472–89.

Oyserman, Sorensen, Bergen, and Chen (2009), "Connecting and separating mind-sets: Culture as situated cognition," Journal of Personality and Social Psychology. 97(2), 217-235.

Triandis (1989), "The self and social behavior in differing cultural contexts," Psychological Review, 96 (3), 506-520.

Woodside, A.G. and Davenport Jr. JW (1974), "The effect of salesman similarity and expertise on consumer purchasing behavior," Journal of Marketing Research, 6, 198-202.

Xu, Alison Jing and Robert S. Wyer (2008), "The Comparative Mind-set: From Animal Comparisons to Increased Purchase Intentions," Psychological Science, 19 (September), 859-864.

Shaping Product Perceptions

Tanuka Ghoshal, Indian School of Business, India
Peter Boatwright, Carnegie Mellon University, USA

Academic researchers reiterate the importance of product design and aesthetics as an opportunity for differential advantage in the marketplace (Creusen and Schoormans 2005, Bloch 1995). There has been a recent upsurge in academic interest in product design aesthetics, and some of this work includes studying how aesthetic stimuli are processed (Reimann et al 2010), how aesthetics impact perceived functionality (Hoegg, Alba and Dahl 2010) etc. In the current research we attempt to isolate and investigate the impact of product shape, arguably a more subtle component of product design. We firstly investigate whether people have preferences for certain kinds of shapes for different types of products for which shape is not related to product functionality. We then try to establish whether there is transference of the positive attitude towards aesthetically appealing shapes to perceived functional and/or hedonic benefits of the product. We finally investigate how product shape influences perceptions, and whether the influence of shape occurs at a conscious or non-conscious level.

Preference for specific shapes. Given that a vast majority of products and packages in the marketplace are rectangular (Raghubir and Greenleaf 2006) a question that naturally arises is whether consumers in general prefer products with angular shapes as opposed to curvaceous shapes, despite evidence from psychology that people tend to prefer curved objects to angular objects (Bar and Neta 2005). Photographs of various common hedonic (examples: car, mp3 player) as well as utilitarian products (examples: teapot, external hard drive, sports bottle) that are typically available in both curvilinear and angular forms, were converted into outline diagrams using a software so that there were no obvious differences in design other than the outer shape of the products. These line drawings were evaluated by subjects, as part of a "Product Prototype Evaluation study". The angular and curvilinear versions of each product were pretested to be equivalent on prototypicality (Reber, Schwarz and Winkielman 2004). We find that across the range of products we tested, the curvilinear form is preferred over the angular by a vast majority of respondents. "Visual pleasure" is the most common spontaneous reason provided for the preference, and in an upcoming study, response times will be measured to see whether higher perceptual fluency for curvilinear shapes drives this preference (Reber, Schwarz and Winkielman 2004).

Shape and perceived functionality. There is a fair amount of research evidencing that shape of a container can impact perceived quantity perceptions and consumption (Raghubir and Greenleaf 2006, Yang and Raghubir 2005, Wansink and Ittersum 2005), but the specific role of aesthetically pleasing shape(s) in influencing product perceptions has received limited attention. We study whether superior functional and/or hedonic benefits are attributed to aesthetically preferred shapes, for products where shape should not be associated with functionality. We have evidence that visually appealing shapes are associated with perceived superior functional benefits (example: a curvilinear car is perceived to be more fuel-efficient than a more angular (boxy) car, a curvilinear external hard drive is perceived to have more capacity than an angular shaped one), and/or perceived superior hedonic benefits (example: curvilinear teapot perceived to be "better suited for party"). This will be further explored with a larger range of utilitarian and hedonic products.

The nonconscious role of shape. In a third study we set out to investigate whether the influence of product shape may be at a less conscious level than we imagine. We showed subjects two prototype products belonging to the same category, one curvilinear in shape and the other angular. The products shared one common attribute specification, were individually superior to the other product on a second attribute, and were individually inferior on a third attribute. (The latter two attributes were pretested to be equally important). A control group evaluated the same pair of products with the same attribute specifications but without any pictures (no difference on visual appeal). Subjects were asked to evaluate the importance of the three given attributes for the purchase decision-making process for that category. The hypothesis was that the attribute on which the aesthetically appealing shaped (curvilinear) product is superior would be deemed to be of higher importance as compared to the control group. We find preliminary support for our hypothesis in several product categories, and are currently working on generalizing these results to different kinds of product categories.

In summary, in this research we investigate in what manner product shape impacts decision-making, and whether apart from conscious visual aesthetic preferences, there are nonconscious impacts of aesthetically pleasing shapes on perceived functionality, or whether there is nonconscious rationalization of visual pleasure by awarding higher importance to other functional aspects.

REFERENCES

Bar Moshe, and Neta Maital (2006), "Humans prefer curved visual objects,"*Psychological Science* 17(8), 645–648.

Bloch, Peter H. (1993), "Seeking the Ideal Form: Product Design and Consumer Response," Journal of Marketing, 59(3), 16-29.

Creusen, M.E.H. and J.P.L. Schoormans (2005), "The Different Roles of Product Appearance in Consumer Choice," *Journal of Product Innovation Management*, 22(1), 63-81.

Hoegg, JoAndrea, Joseph W. Alba and Darren W. Dahl (2010), "The Good, the Bad, and the Ugly: Influence of Aesthetics on Product Feature Judgments," *Journal of Consumer Psychology*, 20 (4), 419-430.

Reimann, Martin, Judith Zaichkowsky, Carolin Neuhaus, Thomas Bender and Bernd Weber (2010), "Aesthetic Package Design: A Behavioral, Neural, and Psychological Investigation," *Journal of Consumer Psychology*, 20 (4), 419-430.

Raghubir, Priya and Eric A. Greenleaf (2006), "Ratios in Proportion: What Should the Shape of the Package Be?" *Journal of Marketing*, 70 (2), 95-107.

Reber, Rolf, Norbert Schwarz and Winkielman, Piotr (2004), " Processing Fluency and Aesthetic Pleasure: Is Beauty in the Perceiver's Processing Experience?" *Personality and Social Psychology Review*, 8(4), 364-382.

Wansink, Brian and Koert van Ittersum (2005), "Shape of Glass and Amount of Alcohol Poured: Comparative Study of Effect of Practice and Concentration," *BMJ – British Medical Journal*, 331:7531 (December 24) 1512-1514.

Yang, Sha and Priya Raghubir (2005), "Can bottles speak volumes? The effect of package shape on how much to buy," *Journal of Retailing* 81 (4), 269-281.

The Relationship between Brand Personality and Self Construal

Jenny Jiao, University of Iowa, USA

Irwin Levin, University of Iowa, USA

This paper examines the sincere and exciting dimensions of brand personality and individual differences which prior work on consumer-brand relationship has overlooked. The aim of this research is to provide insight in the previously stated question about consumer–brand relationships. The major question is how individual difference affects consumer-brand relationships by attaching to different kinds of brand personalities. This research examines the extent to which Aaker's (1997) structure of personality attributes is associated with individual difference (either independent or interdependent individual).

This study defines brand personality as the set of human personality traits that are both relevant and associated with brands (Aaker, 1997). Thus it includes such characteristics as gender, age, socioeconomic class and human personality traits as warmth, concern and sentimentality (Aaker, 1996). For example, Coca Cola is classic but Pepsi is young; Victoria's Secret tends to be feminine and sexy in comparison to Jockey; Disney tents to be young and fun when compared to Yellow Stone National Park.

Brand personality is a vehicle for the consumer to express different aspects of self (Aaker 1997; Belk 1988; Escalas and Bettman 2005; Johar, Sengupta, and Aaker 2005). Previous research suggested that a person's personality could influence consumer behavior, and consumer's personality traits could influence their shopping styles or strategies (Horton 1979). Furthermore, researchers have suggested that brand personality could help differentiate brands (e.g., Crask and Laskey 1990), identify personal meaning for the consumer and to determine brand equity (Aaker 1991). But little research is known about how individual difference influences consumer-brand relationship by attaching to different kinds of brand personalities. This study tries to fill up the gap between individual difference and brand personality.

This study will focus on capturing *exciting and sincere* brand personalities. Among Aaker's five dimensions of Brand Personality Scale, exciting and sincere brand personalities appear to capture much of the variance in personality ratings of brands (Aaker, 1997). Exciting and sincere brand personalities are particularly important because they map onto the key three ideals that Fletcher et al. (1999) note as being important in interpersonal relationships: warmth, vitality, and status (Swaminathan& Stilley, 2009). *Exciting* brand personalities try to achieve differentiation through unique and irrelevant advertising (e.g., Dr. Pepper and BMW). *Sincere* brand personalities have been pursued by companies which wish to build a warmer, trustful and responsible brand image (e.g., Coca-cola and Ford).

Independent individuals regard themselves as independent from others in order to express their unique attributes (Johnson, 1985; Marsella et al., 1985), this view of the self derives from the belief that each person's configuration of internal attributes are whole and unique (Johnson, 1985). *Interdependent individuals* view the relationship between the self and others features the person not as separate from the social context; they view themselves as part a group. Individuals with an interdependent self-construal are motivated to find a way to "fit in with relevant others, fulfill and create obligation", and in general to become part of various interpersonal relationships (Markus and Kitayama, 1991).

Consumers are known to form a strong relationship with their brands to express their identities (Escalas & Bettman, 2005; Reed, 2004). Therefore, we hypothesize that individuals would have different motivations to be attached to a certain brand. An independent individual should be motivated by an exciting brand that allow expression of his important self-defining, and validate his inner attributes. In contrast, an interdependent individual should be motivated to those actions that enhance or foster one's relatedness or connection to others, maintain harmony with social context and adjust oneself to the social group. Sincere brands fit interdependent individuals' needs by allowing one to be connected to the social context and convey a sense of belonging.

Across two studies we test the overall hypothesis that consumers with an independent self construal are more likely to have a higher brand attachment and brand attitude toward exciting brands than sincere brands. We also tested how brand information type influences the consumer brand relationship.

In study 1, 119 participants were randomly assigned to one of two conditions in a 2 (brand personality: sincere vs. exciting). Instead of manipulating self construal, we used Singels' (1994) Independent Self-Construal scale to measure independent and interdependent self construal. Participants were asked to view a Win detergent ad which manipulated the brand personality and provide their reactions to it. We chose Win detergent because based on the pretest, it is not a very exiting or sincere brand, and participants have a very low familiarity with win detergent. Brand personality was manipulated via taglines and brand elements and pictures to convey either a sincere or an exciting brand personality.

The pretest confirmed that participants who *were exposed* to the exciting ad rated the brand as significantly more exciting than sincere (*Mexciting= 3.89, Msincere=3.09; t= -2.58, p<0.005*).

The result showed that generally the exciting brands are rated higher than the sincere brands on consumer-brand relationship *(Mexciting= 2.86, Msincere=2.44; t=-2.20, p<0.015)*, that's because our participants are undergraduate students who are their age of 20s. 2 (brand personality: exciting brand vs. sincere brand) * 2 (individual difference: independent individual vs. interdependent individual) ANOVA revealed a significant interaction between brand personality and self construal (F (1, 116) =3.89, p<0.02). As we predicted, an independent self prefers the exciting brands than the sincere brands.

However, this consumer-brand relationship might change depending on the advertising's type. Study 2 examined the commercial information type and brand personality because we are also interested in examining how the commercial information type influences consumer brand relationship. 183 participants were randomly assigned to one of the following 4 conditions: 2 (Brand personality: sincere vs. exciting) *2 (Commercial information type: attractive vs. professional). Brand personality was manipulated as the same way in study 1, commercial information type was manipulated by conveying difference source of information providers and information contents. For example, in the attractive information condition, the Win detergent information was provided by a Mom from Iowa City, starting with "I saw Tim Gunn endorse this product on a talk show. I bought and tried; now I love it;" but in the professional condition, the information was provided by an expert, starting with "The new product, is 100% biodegradable, and doesn't contain brighteners, phosphates, or dyes." The resulted showed a significant two-way interaction between brand personality and information (F(1, 170) =4.62, p<0.005) , which means consumers have a higher brand attitude toward a sincere brand if the product information is framed in an attractive way than professional way.

This prediction is consistent with self-congruity theory (e.g., Sirgy 1982), which suggests that consumers feel more connected, and are more likely to purchase brands whose personality matches consumers' self-concept. This study tries to demonstrate that distinct views of the self will lead to different consumer-brand relationship with exciting and sincere brands. It has important implications for companies who wish to build a strong relationship with consumers, the independent individuals prefer the exciting brands but the interdependent individuals prefer the sincere brands. We also showed this consumer-brand relationship might change depending on the advertising's type. Future research could focus on investigating whether there are any circumstances under which consumers are more likely to choose brands that mismatch their self-concept. Furthermore, it would be interesting to investigate whether self-construal moderates how consumers respond to transgressions from exciting vs. sincere brands (e.g., Aaker, Fournier and Brasel 2004)

REFERENCES:

Aaker, J. L. (2000), "Accessibility or diagnosticity? Disentangling the influence of culture on persuasion processes and attitudes," Journal of Consumer Research, 26 (4), 340-57.

---- (1997), "Dimensions of brand personality," Journal of Marketing Research, 34 (3), 347-56.

---- (1999), "The malleable self: The role of self-expression in persuasion," Journal of Marketing Research, 36 (1), 45-57.

Aaker, J. L., V. Benet-Martinez, and J. Garolera (2001), "Consumption symbols as carriers of culture: A study of Japanese and Spanish brand personality constructs," Journal of Personality and Social Psychology, 81 (3), 492-508.

Aaker, J. L., A. M. Brumbaugh, and S. A. Grier (2000), "Nontarget markets and viewer distinctiveness: The impact of target marketing on advertising attitudes," Journal of Consumer Psychology, 9 (3), 127-40.

Aaker, J. L. and A. Y. Lee (2001), ""I" seek pleasures and "we" avoid pains: The role of self-regulatory goals in information processing and persuasion," Journal of Consumer Research, 28 (1), 33-49.

---- (2006), "Understanding regulatory fit," Journal of Marketing Research, 43 (1), 15-19.

Aaker, J., Fournier, S., & Brasel, S.A. (2004), "When good brands do bad?" Journal of Consumer Research, 31 (1), 1-16.

Aggarwal, P. (2004), "The effects of brand relationship norms on consumer attitudes and behavior," Journal of Consumer Research, 31 (1), 87-101.

Briley, D. A. and J. L. Aaker (2006), "Bridging the culture chasm: Ensuring that consumers are healthy, wealthy, and wise," Journal of Public Policy & Marketing, 25 (1), 53-66.

Caprara, G. V., C. Barbaranelli, and G. Guido (2001), "Brand personality: How to make the metaphor fit?," Journal of Economic Psychology, 22 (3), 377-95.

Crask, M. R. and H. A. Laskey (1990), "A Positioning-Based Decision-Model for Selecting Advertising Messages," Journal of Advertising Research, 30 (4), 32-38.

Escalas, J. E. and J. R. Bettman (2005), "Self-construal, reference groups, and brand meaning," Journal of Consumer Research, 32 (3), 378-89.

---- (2003), "You are what they eat: The influence of reference groups on consumers' connections to brands," Journal of Consumer Psychology, 13 (3), 339-48.

Fournier, S. (1998), "Consumers and their brands: Developing relationship theory in consumer research," Journal of Consumer Research, 24 (4), 343-73.

Johar, G. V., J. Sengupta, and J. L. Aaker (2005), "Two roads to updating brand personality impressions: Trait versus evaluative inferencing," Journal of Marketing Research, 42 (4), 458-69.

Johnson, F. (1985). The Western concept of self. In A. Marsella, G. DeVos, & F. L. K. Hsu (Eds.), Culture and self London: Tavistock

Horton, R. L. (1979), "Some Relationships between Personality and Consumer Decision-Making," Journal of Marketing Research, 16 (2), 233-46.

Markus, H. R. and S. Kitayama (1991), "Culture and the Self - Implications for Cognition, Emotion, and Motivation," Psychological Review, 98 (2), 224-53.

Swaminathan, V., K. M. Stilley, and R. Ahluwalia (2009), "When Brand Personality Matters: The Moderating Role of Attachment Styles," Journal of Consumer Research, 35 (6), 985-1002.

Uh-Oh, This Might Hurt Our Bottom Line: Consumer and Company Reactions to Product Harm Crises

R. Justin Goss, University of Texas at San Antonio, USA
David H. Silvera, University of Texas at San Antonio, USA
Daniel Laufer, Yeshiva University, USA
Kate Gillespie, University of Texas at Austin, USA
Ashley Arsena, University of Texas at San Antonio, USA

Product harm crises, "discrete, well publicized occurrences wherein products are found to be defective or dangerous" (Siomkos and Kurzbard 1994), can cause damage to both the financials and reputation of a company. Research suggests that an important determinant of the amount of damage the company incurs is the degree to which consumers blame the company for the crisis. Blame attributions for product-harm crises can have a variety of negative consequences for the company, including reduced consumer satisfaction with the product, increased consumer complaints, and desire for refunds. These findings suggest that blame attributed to a company in association with a product-harm crisis will negatively affect attitudes toward the brand, purchase intentions, and recommendations relative to the company's products. The current research attempts to identify factors that can potentially influence blame attributions by observers of a product-harm crisis. Specifically, we investigated the roles severity of the crisis, familiarity of the involved brand, post-crisis company reactions, and personal vulnerability of observers of the product-harm crisis have in determining blame attributions.

Much of our understanding of the mechanisms underlying blame attributions comes from social psychology; in particular, social psychology research related to the defensive attribution hypothesis offers some potential insights into these mechanisms. The defensive attribution hypothesis posits that when an incident results in a more severe outcome and/or observers feel more personal vulnerability in relation to that incident, more blame will be attributed to a potentially responsible party (Shaver 1970). Further, outcome severity is an important feature of product failures and product-harm crises in marketing contexts. For example, minor product defects have a small effect on consumers, whereas major defects (e.g., contaminated drinks or cars that tend to roll over on turns) can lead to catastrophe. The present research examines the applicability of the defensive attribution framework to product harm crises, and also adds several variables that the marketing literature suggests might moderate blame to the company, most notably familiarity of the brand involved in the crisis and the content of the company's public response to the crisis. In three studies, participants read a product harm scenario in which the severity of the product harm crisis was manipulated, after which participants were asked to make a series of judgments in relation to the product harm crisis including the amount of blame attributed to the company, personal vulnerability, severity of the crisis, future purchase intentions, and attitudes toward the company involved.

The three experiments used similar methods. Participants were asked to read a fictitious newspaper article about a product harm crisis. Severity of the crisis (Experiments 1-3) and familiarity of the involved brand (Experiment 2) were manipulated using different versions of the article. In Experiment 3, participants were also presented with a press release that manipulated the company's reaction to the crisis. Subsequent to the manipulations, participants were asked to respond to measures assessing blame, feelings of vulnerability, and perceived severity.

Experiment 1 developed a preliminary model testing the impact of severity and other relevant variables on blame attributions in a product-harm crisis about tires. Results showed that blame to the company is positively related to both severity of the product harm crisis and participants' feelings of personal vulnerability in relation to the product-harm crisis. Further, instead of personal vulnerability predicting blame to the company directly, personal vulnerability only influenced blame indirectly through its relation with perceived severity. Blame to the company was also negatively related to attitudes toward the brand, which were in turn related to purchase and recommendation intentions.

Experiment 2 tested the interaction between brand familiarity and severity. For the low severity crisis, brand familiarity had no impact on blame to the company; for the high severity crisis, participants ascribed significantly more blame to the company when the brand was unfamiliar than when the brand was familiar. These results indicate that familiar brands are more resistant to the negative effects of a product harm crisis than unfamiliar brands.

Experiment 3 investigated how an unfamiliar brand can similarly protect itself against negative effects of product harm crises based on the company's media response to the crisis. Analyses revealed a significant 2 (severity: low vs. high) x 4 (press release: no press release vs. apology vs. accepting responsibility vs. blaming the victim) ANOVA interaction predicting blame to the company involved in the product harm crisis. Specifically, compared to the no press release control condition, (a) a company apology resulted in increased blame to the company regardless of the severity of the crisis, (b) the company taking responsibility for the crisis and promising to fix the problem resulted in less blame for a low severity crisis but more blame for a high severity crisis, and (c) blaming the victims in the crisis resulted in decreased blame to the company regardless of the severity of the crisis. The reduction in blame to the company, when the company blamed victims, was larger for a low severity than for a high severity crisis. These results suggest that the best way for an unknown company to avoid blame is to use media communications to try to deflect blame to victims of the product-harm crisis. This might be something of a catch-22 situation, however, as it seems unlikely that consumers who were harmed in the crisis will respond favorably to such a media policy.

Across three experiments, results indicated that blame to the company was positively related to feelings of personal vulnerability and the severity of the crisis, familiar brands are more resistant to the negative effects of a product harm crisis, and companies that respond by shifting the blame to the victim of a product harm crisis are most able to keep their reputations intact. Future studies aim to investigate potential moderators and outcomes of the victim-blaming strategy and the impact public interest groups and legislative changes have on blame attributions after a product harm crisis.

REFERENCES

Davies, Martin F. (1997), "Belief Persistence after Evidential Discrediting: The Impact of Generated versus Provided Explanations on the Likelihood of Discredited Outcomes." *Journal of Experimental Social Psychology*, 33 (November), 561-78.

Jones, Edward E. and Richard E. Nisbett (1972), "The Actor and the Observer: Divergent Perceptions of the Causes of Behavior," in *Attribution: Perceiving the Causes of Behavior,* eds. Edward E. Jones, David E. Kanouse, Harold H. Kelley, Richard. E. Nisbett, Stuart Valins, and Bernard Weiner, Morristown, NJ: General Learning Press, 79-94.

Shaver, Kelly G. (1970), "Defensive Attribution: Effects on Severity and Relevance on the Responsibility Assigned for an Accident, *Journal of Personality and Social Psychology,* 14 (2), 101-13.

Siomkos, George J. and Gary Kurzbard (1994), "The Hidden Crisis in Product-harm Crisis Management," *European Journal of Marketing,* 28 (2), 30-41.

Effects of Green Products on Price Perceptions

R. Justin Goss, University of Texas at San Antonio, USA
David H. Silvera, University of Texas at San Antonio, USA
Daniel Laufer, Yeshiva University, USA
Kate Gillespie, University of Texas at Austin, USA
Ashley Arsena, University of Texas at San Antonio, USA

Desire to buy green products, although far from being a fad, has not always resulted in product purchase. For instance, sale of hybrid cars, long considered as fuel efficient and green, only accounted for 3.5 percent of the cars sold in the US market in 2010 (www.hybridcars.com). Similarly, in the American cleaning products segment, though companies such as Seventh Generation and San Francisco's Method Products have been making natural cleaning products for years, their combined sales amount to only 1% (Information Resources Inc.). Highlighting this as a worldwide trend, Mckinsey and Company's global poll reported that only 33% of those surveyed had bought a green product during the previous year even though 87% expressed strong interest in purchasing green products (Bonnini and Oppenheim 2008). A goal of this research is to explore this lack of 'interest-to-sales' conversion in green products.

Price is often cited as one of the inhibitors of green product purchase (Ewing 2009) although some consumer surveys point to consumer willingness to pay a premium for the same (Environmental Leader 2007). This raises an interesting question pertaining to how consumers may trade-off green aspects of a product when assessing its price (Bonnini and Oppenheim 2008). Specifically, we begin by asking if consumers expect to pay relatively higher price for green products.

Furthermore, companies often try to get around the cost of developing completely green products by joining the green bandwagon by promoting traditional offerings in their lineup as somewhat or partially green alternatives (e.g., Toshiba's A600 laptops running on low voltage; HP desktop PCs featuring AMD's 'Cool 'n' Quiet' processors). In the recent past only few companies worked on plans to increase their offerings of completely green products (e.g. Toyota Prius). A second issue, then, is to understand if consumers process price information differently for complete and partially green products. Finally, given the gap between interest and actual purchase, will consumers' motivation to purchase a product differentially influence the way they process such higher prices when products under consideration area) completely green products and b)with few green attributes (i.e. partially green)?

Though past research on information processing proposes that consumers are cognitive misers (Shugan 1980), the idea also embodies that efficient information processors must strike a balance between minimizing their processing efforts and maximizing their judgmental confidence. Maheswaran and Chaiken (1991) proposed the *sufficiency principle* which suggests that consumers cannot be completely confident that their judgments are correct and can only hope to achieve some level of confidence (sufficiency threshold), which is benchmarked against their desired level of confidence. Based on this principle consumers would step up their efforts to systematically process information when less effortful heuristic mode confers insufficient judgment confidence; a discrepancy in product attribute information would encourage consumers to scrutinize the given information. Integrating these conclusions with research on consumers' use of price as a dual cue to infer quality (Miyazaki, Grewal and Goodstein 2005) and assess monetary sacrifice (Monroe 2003), we predict that participants who are motivated to process information will use a relatively high price of a green product, irrespective of whether it is completely or partially green to conclude that it requires a high monetary sacrifice. In low motivation conditions, a completely green product would be processed heuristically and its high price will be used more to infer that it is of high quality. More importantly, we predict that despite low motivation to process information, a partially green product at a high price will be processed systematically, and its price will lead to perceptions of a high monetary sacrifice.

A series of three studies examined this issue. In Study 1, using semantic association task and implicit association test (Greenwald, Nosek and Banaji 2003), we confirmed differences in associations between products described as completely and partially green. In study 2, participants were first provided with a description of a green product and an average price (P) for a similar conventional product. Participants then indicated their willingness to pay (WTP) for the green product. Three products, tote bag, metallic water bottle and jump drive, were randomly presented to the participants. The results revealed a significant price appreciation [(WTP- P) / P; 28% - 177%] for the green products over their conventional counterparts affirming the perceived expensiveness of such products.

Study 3 tested our predictions by examining how a relatively expensive ($399.99) environmentally friendly printer described as either completely green (all green attributes) or partially green (one green attribute) will be perceived by participants with different processing goals towards its purchase (low vs. high motivation). The results revealed that in high motivation conditions, printers were perceived high on monetary sacrifice irrespective of the number of green attributes associated with them. Also in low motivation conditions, the printer was perceived less expensive when it was described as completely green. More interesting was the result that in low motivation conditions, description for the partially green printer was processed systematically and it was perceived expensive compared to the completely green printer.

Overall, the results seem to suggest that consumers with no assigned purchasing goals were willing to pay more for a green versus a comparable conventional product. Assigning purchase responsibility for a product enhanced attention to its price and the evaluation of its monetary sacrifice was not impacted by the number of green attributes used to describe that product. In low motivation conditions, participants relied less on price to assess monetary sacrifice but more to infer product quality when its description was dominated by green attributes. However inconsistency between its high price and a few green attributes, i.e., partially green product, resulted in a heightened attention to price which was then used to infer that the product required a high monetary sacrifice. Hence, though green products are perceived as expensive (DeBare 2008), the results suggest that "greenness" of a product is a cue which when diluted, as in case of partially green products, may reduce consumers' willingness to pay high prices.

REFERENCES

Bonini, Sheila and Jeremy Oppenheim (2008), "Cultivating the Green Consumer", *Stanford Social Innovation Review,* Fall 2008.

Ball, Jeffrey (2009), "Environment (A Special Report)-What Price, Green? AutoNation's Mike Jackson and Edelman's Richard Edelman on how to get consumers out of gas guzzlers", *The Wall Street* Journal *(Eastern Edition)*. New York, N.Y.: Mar 9, 2009. pg. R.4.

Dolliver, Mark (2008),"Deflating a Myth", *Brand Week,* May 12, pp 30.

DeBare, Ilana (2008), "Clorox expects greenbacks from green cleaners," *San Francisco Chronicle*, January (14th), A1 Environment Leader (http://www.environmentalleader.com/2007/10/18/two-thirds-of-people-will-pay-premium-for-green-products/

Ewing, Jack (2009), "Diamler: The Dawning of the Age of Electric Cars," *Bloomburg Business Week,* July, 20, 2009. (http://www.businessweek.com/globalbiz/content/jul2009/gb20090720_943294_page_2.htm)

Greenwald, A. G., Nosek, B. A., & Banaji, M. R. (2003), "Understanding and using the Implicit Association Test: I. An improved scoring algorithm," *Journal of Personality and Social Psychology*, 85, 197–216.

Maheswaran, Durairaj and Shelly Chaiken (1991), "Promoting Systematic Processing in Low-Motivation Settings: Effect of Incongruent Information on Processing and Judgment," *Journal of Personality and Social Psychology*, 61 (1), 13-25.

Miyazaki, Anthony D., Dhruv Grewal, and Ronald C. Goodstein (2005), "The Effect of Multiple Extrinsic Cues on Quality Perceptions: A Matter of Consistency", *Journal of Consumer Research* 32 (June): 146-153.

Monroe, Kent B. (2003), *Pricing: Making Profitable Decisions*. Burr Ridge, IL: McGraw-Hill/Irwin.

Shugan, Steven M. (1980), "The Cost of Thinking," *Journal of Consumer Research* 7 (September): 99-111.

Loyalty Can Engender Blind Acceptance:
Brand Identification and Brand Identity Fit in Co-branding

Na Xiao, University of Winnipeg, Canada

Fang Wan, University of Manitoba, Canada

Brand identity is considered to be one of the most important drivers of a successful brand. Emerging research defines brand identity as a cultural meaning system that resonates with target consumers' lifestyles, dreams, and goals (Thompson, Rindfleisch, and Arsel, 2006). Brands with strong identities make it easier for consumers to identify with, to internalize brand values, and therefore foster a strong bonding between consumers and brands (de Chernatony 1999, 2006). As a result, brands can eventually become important means, tools and symbols for consumers to employ to express values and identities, or become an extended part of consumers themselves (Mittal, 2006; Fournier, 1995).

Existing research has explored how brand concept fit and product category fit can affect the success of brand alliances. Therefore, attitude will be more positive when brand concept fit or product category fit than misfit (e.g., Aaker and Keller 1990; Park et al. 1991; Simonin and Ruth 1998) whereas "brand identity fit" is rarely examined in this context. We argue that brand identity is an important dimension to gauge the fit between brand partners other than brand concept (Park et al. 1991; Simonin and Ruth 1998). Brand identity is the cultural meaning system co-created, shared and perceived by consumers whereas brand concept is brand meaning engineered and crafted by corporations. Therefore, our focal concern is how brand identity fit between brand partners affects the success of their alliance and how identification with a focal brand moderates the effect of brand identity fit on attitude toward brand alliance. Specifically, we address 1) how the fit or misfit of the brand identities of two partners affect consumers' attitude towards the brand alliance and 2) how loyal consumers of the focal brand reconcile with the misfit with co-brand, if there is any. This research addresses these issues in a co-branding context where two parent brands are aligned to create a single product or service.

To address these research questions, we tested how identification with a focal brand moderates the impact of brand identity fit on the attitude toward brand alliance and found that consumers with high identification with a focal brand tend to tolerate brand identity misfit in a brand alliance (Study 1). We employed qualitative depth interviews and identified two coping strategies loyal consumers of original brand employ to reconcile with the misfit between the original brand and the co-brand (Study 2). Lastly, we examined the effect of different coping strategies on loyal consumers' attitude towards the brand alliance (Study 3).

Study 1. Study 1 was designed to test how identification with a focal brand moderates the relationship between brand identity fit and attitude towards the brand alliance and loyalty of the target brand. We first conducted a pretest to identify brand alliance pairs which have either a high or low identity fit. In a pretest of 30 participants, Apple had the highest rating on the dimension of anti-status quo and rebellious (M=4.00) among all selected brands. Among the brand partners, Intel had significantly lower rating on this dimension (M=2.73, p<.05) and Nintendo had similar rating compared to Apple (M=3.98, p>.05). In addition, the perceived fit between Apple and Intel is lower than between Apple and Nintendo (4 vs. 4.78, p<.05). Therefore, we selected Apple and Intel alliance as the brand alliance with low brand identity fit and Apple and Nintendo as high brand identity fit.

In the study, eighty four Apple users were asked to indicate their identification with Apple brand on 5 items (Bhattacharya et al., 1995). Next, they read a fictitious press release announcing the collaboration of Apple and Intel (or Nintendo). They were asked to rate the identity fit between the two brands, their attitudes of the brand alliance. Regression of identification (a continuous variable) and identity fit (high vs. low) on the attitude toward brand alliance was significant (beta =.43, p<.05). We found that when consumers have strongly identified themselves with Apple brand, their attitude toward brand alliance is not affected by whether brand partner is a fit or misfit with Apple brand (M=5.45 vs. 4.98, F<1). However, when consumers have low identification with Apple brand, they evaluated low fit pair (Apple+Intel) more favorably than high fit pair (Apple+Nintendo) (M=5.93 vs. 4.72, $F_{(1, 80)}$=6.86, p<.05). Our post-hoc study discovered that consumers highly identifying themselves with Apple demonstrated a halo effect. In other words, their emotional bonding with Apple carried over to its brand partners regardless of their fit, therefore they do not discriminate brand alliance with low brand identity fit. In contrast, with low identification with Apple brand, consumers' attitude toward brand alliance is driven by the functional benefit of the partner. In this case, Intel made the computer run faster whereas consumers did not know in what way Nintendo could benefit Apple, therefore, they rated brand alliance more positively in a brand identity misfit condition.

Study 2. Study 2 set out to understand the halo effect uncovered in Study 1. That is, when a brand partner has a low brand identity fit with the focal brand, how do loyal consumers reconcile with the misfit and evaluate the brand alliance positively? Depth interviews (one to two hours) with six Apple loyal Mac users (basic themes can present themselves within six interviews, Guest et al., 2006) were conducted. Through thematic analysis, we found that informants felt that Apple's brand identity was impaired because Intel had been mainly associated with PCs. This indicates that loyal Apple brand users in Study 1 recognized the identity misfit between Apple and Intel but they were just tolerant of the misfit. In addition, we uncovered two coping strategies informants employed to buttress their support of Apple brand vis-à-vis the misfit co-branding efforts: "decoupling" (as in Ahluwalia, 2000, subjectively and blatantly dismiss the negative impact of Intel on Apple brand) and "biased assimilation" (subjectively boost evaluation of Intel so that it can be assimilated into positive associations of Apple brand).

Taking findings of Study 1 and Study 2 together, we propose that when brand identity fit is low, *decoupling* is more effective than *biased assimilation* at defending, or maintaining the positive attitudes of the brand alliance. However, when brand identity fit is high, coping strategies may not affect brand alliance evaluation because both the positive association with the original brand and the brand identity fit can drive up the evaluation of the brand alliance. We tested this proposition in Study 3.

Study 3. A 2 (coping strategy: decoupling vs. biased assimilation) by 2 (fit: low vs. high, measured factor) between-subject design was adopted. Eighty six Apple users participated in the study. They read a "new product release" announcing the brand alliance between Apple and Intel and then were provided with comments by online consumers on the brand alliance (coping strategies were manipulated by whether comments from peer consumers demonstrate decoupling or biased assimilation strategies). Then subjects responded to a survey measuring their attitude toward the brand alliance and the perceived fit between Apple and Intel (7 items, adapted from Taylor and Bearden 2002). Regression yielded a significant interaction between coping strategies and fit on attitude towards the brand alliance (beta=-.42, *p*<.05). To extrapolate the interaction, we classified perceived fit into low and high groups based on median split. Our propositions were confirmed that when the perceived fit was low, attitude towards brand alliance was more positive when a decoupling strategy (vs. biased assimilation) was activated (M=5.08 v.s. 4.22; F(1,41)= .66, p<.05). However, when the perceived fit was high, coping strategy had no impact ($M_{decoupling}$=5.19 vs. M_{biased}=5.47, F(1,39)= .17, p>.05).

This research discovered that whether brand identity fit/misfit affects attitudes towards brand alliances depends on how consumers identify themselves with the focal brand. Specifically, loyal consumers are tolerant of brand identity misfit in brand alliance due to the halo effect and due to the biased assimilation strategy (vs. decoupling) they adopt to maintain their loyalty. However, for consumers with low brand identification, brand identity fit is not a diagnostic cue for their evaluation of the brand alliance as they do not really understand the nuanced meaning of the focal brand and can accidentally favor brand alliance with brand identity misfit.

REFERENCES

Aaker, David A., Keller, Kevin Lane (1990), "Consumer Evaluations Of Brand Extensions", Journal of Marketing. 54 (1), p. 27-42

Ahluwalia, Rohini (2000), "Examination of psychological processes underlying resistance to persuasion", Journal of Consumer Research, 27 (2), 217-233

Bhattacharya, C. B., Hayagreeva Rao, and Mary A. Glynn (1995), "Understanding the bond of identification: An investigation of its correlates among art museum members," Journal of Marketing, 59 (4), 46.

De Chernatony, Leslie, Susan Cottam, Susan Segal-Horn (2006), "Communicating Services Brands' Values Internally and Externally" The Service Industries Journal. 26, 8, 819

De Chernatony, Leslie, Riley, Francesca Dall Olmo (1999), "Experts' views about defining services brands and the principles of services branding", Journal of Business Research. 46, 2, 181

Einwiller, Sabine, Alexander Fedorikhin, Allison R Johnson, Michael A Kamins (2006), "Enough Is Enough! When Identification No Longer Prevents Negative Corporate Associations", Academy of Marketing Science. 34 (2), 185-195

Fournier, Susan (1998), "Consumers and Their Brands: Developing Relationship Theory in Consumer Research", Journal of Consumer Research, 24(Mar), 343-374

Guest, Greg, Arwen Bunce, and Laura Johnson (2006), "How Many Interviews Are Enough? An Experiment with Data Saturation and Variability," Field Methods, 18 (1), 59–82.

Mittal, Banwari (2006), "I, Me, and Mine-How Products Become Consumers' Extended Selves," Journal of Consumer Behaviour, 5 (Nov/Dec), 550-563

Park, C. Whan, Milberg, Sandra, Lawson, Robert (1991), "Evaluation of Brand Extensions: The Role of Product Feature", Journal of Consumer Research, 18 (2), 185-194

Simonin, Bernard L, Julie A Ruth (1998). "Is a company known by the company it keeps? Assessing the spillover effects of brand alliances on consumer brand attitudes", Journal of Marketing Research, 35 (1), 30-43

Taylor, V.A. and Bearden, W.O. (2002), "The effects of price on brand extension evaluations: the moderating role of extension similarity", Journal of the Academy of Marketing Science, Vol. 30 No. 2, pp. 131-40.

Thompson, Craig J, Aric Rindfleisch, Zeynep Arsel(2006), "Emotional Branding and the Strategic Value of the Doppelganger Brand Image", Journal of Marketing, 70(Jan), 50-64

White, Katherine, Darren W Dahl (2007), "Are All Out-Groups Created Equal? Consumer Identity and Dissociative Influence", Journal of Consumer Research. 34(4), 525

Picture Yourself...: The Effect of Personal Imagery on Pragmatic / Ideal Trade-offs

MengHsien (Jenny) Lin, Iowa State University, USA
Laura Smarandescu, Iowa State University, USA

In order to understand consumers' judgments and preferences researchers must first determine what inputs are attended externally or retrieved from memory and understand how these inputs are weighted in decision outcomes. Construal-level theory provides a theoretical framework that explains how psychological distance alters the mental representation of these inputs and the weights that are attributed to "high-level" and "low-level" criteria.

THEORETICAL BACKGROUND

Liberman and Trope (1998) first introduced construal level–theory (CLT) to explain how temporal distance affects the mental representations individuals have for events. CLT suggests that individuals use concrete, low-level construals to represent near events, and abstract, high-level construals to represent temporally distant events. Liberman and Trope (1998) suggest that a high construal level activation is linked with a subordinate purpose, the "why" of the activity, such as getting a good education, whereas in a low construal level activation, the focus is placed on "how" to do the activity, such as reading a textbook.

So far the notion of psychological distance has been explored in relation to spatial distance (i.e., spatially close vs. far), social distance (i.e., self vs. others), or in relation to an event's probability of occurrence (i.e., frequent vs. less frequent). Fujita et al. (2006) show that people who believed that characters in a film were spatially distant used more abstract language in describing the events in the movie. In a social distance domain, a higher level of dissimilarity is considered to be a higher construal level (Liviatan et al. 2008), as individuals view distant others at a more abstract level than similar others. Research that looked at how individuals perceive events with different occurrence likelihood shows that events with a lower occurrence probability are perceived at a greater psychological distance than events that have a higher probability of occurring (Chandran and Menon 2004).

A form of psychological distance that has been examined less in relation to consumer decisions and behavior is related to the notion of personal perspective and self-imagery. Bem (1972) suggests that perspective affects individuals' attributions of cause for a behavior. Observers tend to understand an actor's behavior as a function of the actor's disposition, where visual focus is on the actor. In comparison, actors tend to understand their own behavior as a function of the situation, where the situation is focal for the actor (Jones and Nisbett 1971; Storms 1973). People use visual perspective to picture past events, with effects on emotions, self-judgment and behavior (Ashworth and van Boven 2007; McIsaac and Eich 2002; Robinson and Swanson 1993). Libby et al. (2007) found that people who pictured themselves voting in a third-person perspective not only adopted a stronger mindset before voting, but they were significantly more likely to vote in the election. The present research investigates the effects of psychological distance in the form of personal perspective on individual preference judgments. Hence, we investigate how taking a first vs. third person personal perspective may highlight different aspects of options and influence preference for pragmatic and ideal considerations.

Consistent with previous studies on personal perspective (Libby et al. 2007; Libby and Eibach 2002), we conceptualize that a first-person mental perspective would be represented at a lower construal level. We hypothesize that individuals taking a first person perspective will make preference judgments based on more concrete and pragmatic reasons. In comparison, individuals primed with a third person mindset may construe the same activity at a more abstract higher construal level. Hence, we propose that purchase decisions made under this context would be based on more idealistic rather than pragmatic reasoning.

This paper is organized as follows. Study 1 examines how perceived psychological distance cued by a personal perspective manipulation affects how individuals weigh pragmatic and ideal dimensions in choice. Study 2 investigates the moderating effect of individual differences in self-orientation (i.e., pragmatic vs. value orientation).

Study 1

Sixty-three undergraduate students participated in a consumer preference study. The study design was a 2 (personal perspective: first, third) × 1 between subjects design. Following the personal perspective manipulation, individuals were presented with a consumer choice scenario. The choice task presented two types of light bulbs, one described with ideal attributes (e.g., energy savings, recyclable) and the other with pragmatic attributes (e.g., lifespan, natural light). Individuals primed with a third person mindset were more likely to choose the light bulb described with ideal features (63%), consistent with a mindset favoring more abstract, higher construal level features. Individuals who were primed with a first person mindset favored the option described with more pragmatic considerations (61%), a marginally significant relationship ($c^2_{(1, 63)} = 3.57, p = .059$).

Study 2

Study 2 was a 2 (personal perspective: first, third) × 2 (self-orientation: pragmatic/ ideal based on a median split) between subjects design. Individuals were randomly assigned to one of the two personal perspective conditions, indicated their preference between two banks (Bank A: pragmatic attributes vs. Bank B: ideal/ value attributes), and rated their self-orientation using a 4-item scale (Liberman and Trope

1998). The preference judgment was concerned with the strength of preference for bank A vs. bank B. The analysis revealed a significant interaction between personal perspective and self-orientation on preference for a bank (β = .416, t (53)= 2.22; p < .05). In a third person perspective, and when the individual was more idealistic than pragmatic, preference for bank B increased by .41.

CONCLUSION

Through two studies we show that predictions of CLT theory are supported in the personal perspective domain. As hypothesized, a first person perspective is associated with less perceived psychological distance, more concrete judgments, and greater weight attributed to pragmatic considerations. On the other hand, individuals primed with a third person mindset make judgments based on more abstract and idealistic attributes. This present study contributes and extends previous findings on construal level theory and suggests a causal role of mental imagery in determining future purchase behavior.

REFERENCES

Ashworth Laurence and Leaf Van Boven (2007), "Looking Forward, Looking Back: Anticipation is More Evocative than Retrospection," *Journal of Experimental Psychology, 136(2)*, 289-300.

Bem Daryle J. (1972), "Self-Perception Theory," in *Advances in Experimental Social Psychology* Vol. 6, ed. Leonard Berkowitz, New York, NY: Academic Press, 1-62.

Chandran Sucharita and Geeta Menon (2004), "When a Day Means More Than a Year: Effects of Temporal Framing on Judgments of Health Risk," *Journal of Consumer Research,* 31(September), 375-89.

Fujitsu Kentaro, Marlone D. Henderson, Juliana Eng, Yaacov Trope, and Nira Liberman (2006), "Spatial Distance and Mental Construal of Social Events," *Psychological Science,* 17(4), 278-82.

Jones Edward E. and Richard E. Nisbett (1971), "The Actor and the Observer: Divergent Perceptions of the Cause of Behavior," in *Attribution: Perceiving the Cause of Behavior Vol. 13,* ed. Edward E. Jones, David E. Kanouse, Harold H. Kelley, Richard E. Nisbett, Stuart Valins and Bernard Weiner, New York, NY: General Learning Press, 79-94.

Libby Lisa K. and Richard P. Eibach (2002), "Looking Back in Time: Self-Concept Change Affects Visual Perspective in Autobiographical Memory," *Journal of Personality and Social Psychology,* 82(2), 167-79.

Libby Lisa K., Eric M. Shaeffer, Richard P. Eibach, and Jonathan A. Slemmer (2007), "Picture Yourself at the Polls: Visual Perspective in Mental Imagery Affects Self-Perception and Behavior," *Psychological Science,* 18(3), 199-203.

Liberman Nira, Michael D. Sagristano, and Yaacov Trope (2002), "The Effect of Temporal Distance on Level of Construal," *Journal of Experimental Social Psychology,* 38(6), 523-35.

Liberman Nira and Yaacov Trope (1998), "The Role of Feasibility and Desirability Considerations in Near and Distant Future Decisions: A Test of Temporal Construal Theory," *Journal of Personality and Social Psychology,* 75(1), 5-18.

Liviatan Ido, Yaacov Trope, and Nira Liberman (2008), "Interpersonal Similarity as a Social Distance Dimension: Implications for Perception of Others' Actions," *Journal of Experimental Social Psychology,* 44(5), 1256-69.

McIsaac Heather K. and Eric Eich (2002), "Vantage Point in Episodic Memory," *Psychonomic Bulletin & Review,* 9(1), 146-50.

Robinson John A. and Karen L. Swanson (1993), "Field and Observer Modes of Remembering" *Memory,* 1(3), 169-84.

Thomas, M., Sucharita Chandran, and Yaacov Trope (2006), "The Effects of Temporal Distance on Purchase Construal," Unpublished manuscript, Cornell University.

Trope Yaacov, Nira Liberman, and Cheryl Wakslak (2007), "Construal Levels and Psychological Distance: Effects on Representation, Prediction, Evaluation and Behavior," *Journal of Consumer Psychology,* 17(2), 83-95.

Temporal Distance and the Endowment Effect

Dongwoo Ko, University of Iowa, USA
William Hedgcock, University of Iowa, USA
Catherine Cole, University of Iowa, USA

Research on the endowment effect has identified factors which enhance or mitigate the effect such as duration of ownership (Strahilevitz and Loewenstin, 1998), and information processing differences between sellers and buyers (Nayakankuppam and Misha, 2005). But these studies have primarily involved immediate transactions between sellers and buyers. An interesting question emerges about whether the endowment effect will be observed for temporally distant transactions. The main purpose of my research is to examine how the temporal distance of transactions influences customers' evaluations of products by comparing buyers' willingness to pay and sellers' willingness to accept in the present and in the future.

THEORETICAL FRAMEWORK

The mechanisms underlying the endowment effect and temporal construal level theory (Liberman & Trope, 1998) suggest different underlying processes for temporally different transactions. Prior studies have found buyers and sellers have different cognitive perspectives during transactions. Sellersfocus on their products while buyers focus on their money. These different cognitive perspectives induce price gaps between sellers and buyers and increase loss aversion. However, if events are in the far distance, sellers' and buyers' cognitive perspectives may change. When sellers conduct transactions in the present, they think about the feasibility of the transaction. Sellers may describe actions and transactions in terms of how they will attach a value to the product. However, if the transaction is in the future, the primary purpose of the transaction will be weighted relatively more than the subordinate feature of the action. For sellers, the main purpose of the transaction will be obtaining money, whereas for buyers the main purpose will be to acquire the product. Thus, aspects of the "why" identification will lead sellers and buyers to change their cognitive perspectives, which will decrease the endowment effect. The willingness to accept will decrease because the sellers' cognitive perspective will move from the product to money; in contrast, willingness to pay will increase because buyers will give more weight to the products when the transaction is expected in the far future. Specified hypothesis are as follows:

H1. As temporal psychological distance increases, the price difference between sellers and buyers will decrease.

H1a. When a transaction is temporally distant, buyers will be willing to pay a higher price than when a transaction is temporally close.

H1b. When a transaction is temporally distant, sellers will be willing to accept a lower price than when a transaction is temporally close.

H2. Temporal distance will affect sellers and buyers' cognitive perspectives

H2a. When a transaction is temporally distant, sellers' cognitive perspective will be more on the cash than product. Whereas when a transaction is temporally near, sellers' cognitive perspective will be more on the product than cash.

H2b. When a transaction is temporally distant, buyers' cognitive perspective will be more on the product than cash. Whereas when a transaction is temporally near, buyers' cognitive perspective will be more on the cash than product.

STUDY 1

The main objective of this experiment is to examine whether temporal distance affects people's willingness to pay and accept. In the experiment, subjects were divided into two groups—sellers and buyers—as well as into two different situations involving near and distant transactions, resulting in a 2 (buyers vs. sellers) x 2 (near distance vs. far distance) between subjects design. The participants were 74 undergraduate marketing students. The experiments were conducted via a paper and pencil survey. As subjects sat down, they found a pen which they used throughout the study. Participants were told the research was part of a new product development study. Participants were randomly assigned to the buyer or seller roles by a coin toss. Temporal distance was manipulated by giving two different transaction situations: today and a month from today. Respondents were asked what price they would pay or what price they would accept (depending on their role). The 2(role) X 2(time) between subject ANOVA on price revealed a significant main effect for role ($F(1, 65)= 7.873, <.007$) and a significant two way interaction effect between role and temporal distance ($F(1, 65) =5.710, <.020$). The interaction was significant because the price gap between sellers and buyers in the present (seller - buyer : 1.69 -.998) was greater than the same price gap in the future (seller - buyer: 1.535-1.2974). As temporal distance increases, buyers' willingness to pay increased ($t=-1.748, <.09$) and sellers' willingness to accept decreased ($t=2.204, <.051$), consistent with H1.

In order to examine the underlying process, respondents' thought listings were analyzed using the Standardized median rank difference (SMRD) between money and pen. SMRD is defined as 2(MRP-MRM)/n where MRP = median rank of product thought type in a participant's sequence, MRM = median rank of money thought type in a participant's sequence, and n=total number of thoughts in respondents' sequence (Johnson et al., 2006). Analysis yields the variable, "thought type", which approaches 1 if subjects give more value to the product and approaches -1 if subjects give more value to the money.

A 2 (role) X 2 (time) between subjects ANOVA on thought type revealed the only significant factor was the two way interaction between role and time ($F(1, 65) – 7.547, <.008$). This occurred because under near transaction condition, sellers thought more about products, while buyers thought more about money (0.7086, -.4792). On the other hands, when the transaction was expected in the future, sellers gave more value on money than product, while buyers gave value more on product than money (-.3033, .2474). This is consistent with H2.

We believe this is the first study that demonstrates the endowment effect changes depending on whether transactions are temporally near or distant. We show the cognitive focus of sellers and buyers changes as transaction distance changes. These results raise interesting questions about whether construal level influences customers' willingness to pay and sellers' willingness to accept without temporal distance manipulation. We are currently running studies to see whether alternative construal level manipulations influence the endowment effect.

REFERENCE

Johnson, E. J., Häubl, G., & Keinan, A. (2007). Aspects of endowment: A query theory account of loss aversion for simple objects, Journal of Experimental Psychology 33(3).

Liberman, N., & Trope, Y. (1998). The role of feasibility and desirability considerations in near and distant future decisions: A test of temporal construal theory. Journal of Personality and Social Psychology, 75, 5–18

Nayakankuppam. D., & Mishra. H (2005). The endowment effect: rose-tinted and dark-tinted glasses. Journal of Consumer Research, 32(Dec).

Strahilevitz, M. A. & Loewenstein, G. (1998). The effect of ownership history on the valuation of objects. Journal of Consumer Research, 25 (December), 276–89.

The Two-Sided Mirror: How Correcting For Diagnosticity Impacts Social Comparisons With Advertisement Models

Abigail Schneider, University of Colorado, USA
Susan Jung Grant, University of Colorado, USA

The impact of featuring idealized models versus realistic depictions of people in advertisements has been a topic of much debate in both the consumer literature (Richins 1991; Smeesters, Mussweiler, and Mandel 2010) and society (www.campaignforrealbeauty.com). Much of this research has focused on the detrimental effects of idealized images on satisfaction with the self (Richins 1991), on resulting distortions of body image (Rothblum 1990), or on the diminished judgment of the attractiveness of others (Kenrick and Gutierres 1980).

As a stand against the adverse effects of idealized models, Dove launched its Campaign for Real Beauty in 2004, casting women of all shapes and sizes in its advertising. Yet, the actual effect of these "real" women models on women's self-esteem is debatable. For instance, Smeesters et al. (2010) find that "real beauty" advertising may not enhance consumers' self-esteem, suggesting that the potential persuasive impact of Dove's ads may be limited.

Our research seeks to extend this work and address when "real beauty" ads are effective in evoking social comparison that leads to enhanced perceptions of attractiveness (contrast) or average perceptions of attractiveness (assimilation). We then explore the role of a more diagnostic standard of comparison in women's assessments of their own attractiveness when exposed to ads featuring idealized models versus everyday people.

We report findings from a study in which women rate themselves as being less attractive after seeing advertisements featuring idealized models but rate themselves as being more attractive after exposure to advertisements featuring more realistic images of everyday women. We then reverse this effect and suggest that it is moderated through assessments of diagnosticity for social comparison.

The literature suggests that an assimilation-contrast framework is relevant to self-assessments of attractiveness. Richins (1991) suggests that consumers viewing an advertisement spontaneously engage in social comparison (Festinger 1954; Gilbert, Giesler, and Morris 1995) and relate to the model by assimilating to the model's level of attractiveness or contrasting away. With assimilation, the model's attractiveness becomes incorporated into the consumer's self-perception. With contrast, the model's attractiveness becomes a standard against which a comparison is made. People may also correct for such judgments (DeCoster and Claypool 2004) and, thereby, "mentally undo" assimilation or contrast. However, because the diagnosticity of the comparison, or the appropriateness of the target as an object of comparison, is only considered after the comparison is made (Gilbert et al. 1995), it is possible for people to make nondiagnostic comparisons that they then correct (Gilbert et al. 1995, p. 227). One way of "mentally undoing" the comparison is to consider the diagnosticity of the comparison standard and to re-evaluate based on a more diagnostic source.

We conducted a 2 (advertising: model vs. real people) x 2 (referent group: non-salient peers vs. salient peers) factorial design. Participants were 102 female undergraduate students from a large Western US university who participated in exchange for partial course credit.

Upon entering the lab, participants were told that they would be completing separate studies related to college female undergraduates' opinions about health and beauty advertisements and about a potential dating service that would be piloted on campus. Participants received a booklet containing six ads, three of which were ads featuring either models or real people and three of which were filler ads showing only products. Participants first wrote a few sentences about their initial reactions to the ads and then rated the ads on various dimensions (e.g. "How much do you like this advertisement?" "How attractive do you think the featured model is?").

Students then read about a dating service that would ostensibly target the college market and hence sought feedback from college students. Afterwards, they rated their own attractiveness, as well as the attractiveness of the typical female on their campus. The order of rating constituted the manipulation of referent group salience. In the non-salient referent condition participants rated their own attractiveness first. In the salient-referent condition, participants rated the attractiveness of the typical female undergraduate before rating their own attractiveness.

A two-way ANOVA revealed a significant interaction between advertising type and referent-group salience on ratings of self-attractiveness ($F(1,98)=16.12$, $p<.0001$). When assessing themselves without a referent group, participants felt less attractive when they viewed model ads (M=4.96) than when they viewed real people ads (M=5.44). This effect was reversed when participants assessed their own attractiveness with a referent group (after being asked about the typical female undergraduate student). Participants judged themselves as less attractive when they viewed real people ads (M =4.63) than when they viewed model ads (M=5.52). Planned contrasts showed that all four pairwise comparisons are significant (all Fs>4.00; all ps<.05).

In summary, when people rate their own attractiveness first, they demonstrate a contrast effect when viewing real and ideal models; however, when they rate their peers' attractiveness first, they demonstrate an assimilation effect with the real and ideal models. We theorize that the introduction of a diagnostic referent group, such as other female undergraduates, influences correction. Thus, when participants saw model ads and were then reminded of the typical undergraduate, the contrast effect was deemed to be extreme, not diagnostic. When correcting for the influence of a non-diagnostic comparison, participants could still justify elevated self-attractiveness ratings. Alternatively, when participants saw real people ads and were then reminded of the typical undergraduate, the comparison was deemed to be appropriate and diagnostic. When taking into account a diagnostic comparison, participants had no justification for inflating judgments of their own attractiveness and thus, ratings were lower.

We propose a second study to explore this explanation. Because correcting for diagnosticity requires cognitive resources (Gilbert et al. 1995), we expect that those who rate others' attractiveness first but are under cognitive load will demonstrate a contrast effect similar to the one observed for those who rate themselves first; however, those who rate others first but are not under cognitive load will continue to demonstrate assimilation. Thus, we propose a 2 (advertising: model vs. real people) x 2 (referent group: non-salient peers vs. salient peers) x 2 (cognitive resources: load vs. no load) factorial design.

REFERENCES:

DeCoster, Jamie and Heather M. Claypool (2004), "A Meta-Analysis of Priming Effects on Impression Formation Supporting a General Model of Informational Biases," *Personality and Social Psychology Review,* 8 (1), 2-27.

Festinger, Leon (1954), "A theory of social comparison processes," *Human Relations,* 7, 117-140.

Gilbert, Daniel T., R. Brian Giesler, and Kathryn A. Morris (1995), "When Comparisons Arise," *Journal of Personality and Social Psychology,* 69 (August), 227-236.

Kenrick, Douglas T., and Sara E. Gutierres (1980), "Contrast Effects and Judgments of Physical Attractiveness: When Beauty Becomes a Social Problem," *Journal of Personality and Social Psychology, 38,* 131-140.

Richins, Marsha L. (1991), "Social Comparison and the Idealized Images of Advertising," *Journal of Consumer Research,* 18(June), 71-83.

Rothblum, E. (1990). "Women and Weight: Fad and Fiction," *Journal* of *Psychology,* 124, 5-24.

Smeesters, Dirk, Thomas Mussweiler, and Naomi Mandel (2010), "The Effects of Thin and Heavy Media Images on Overweight and Underweight Consumers:

Social Comparison Processes and Behavioral Implications," *Journal of Consumer Research,* 36(April), 930-949.

Is Older Wiser?
Effects of Expertise and Aging on Experiential Learning

Ashley Goerke, Temple University, USA
Eric Eisenstein, Temple University, USA
Ayalla Ruvio, Temple University, USA

Consumers often need to learn the relationship between an unobservable outcome of interest and observable attributes. For example, antique shoppers appraise items; used car buyers must learn how car attributes affect price; gift-givers must learn the preferences of those to whom they give gifts; and in general, consumers constantly make decisions that are based on their predictions of quality, price, value, and liking. In this research, we investigate the costs and benefits of having developed expertise, both recently (based on training) and over a lifetime of consumer learning and decision making (for products that are highly familiar), and we compare the costs and benefits of expertise against the greater processing speed of more youthful subjects.

Prior research has presented a mixed view of expertise, with some researchers demonstrating costs of expertise (Camerer & Johnson, 1991; Wood & Lynch, 2002) and others showing benefits (Alba & Hutchinson, 1987; Hutchinson & Eisenstein, 2008; Meyer, 1987). As a general rule, people develop expertise from their repeated experiences in markets. Based on this, we posit that a lifetime of encountering products, developing fair market price and quality judgments about these products, and filing away this information for use at a later date, could be categorized as a form of experiential learning (EL) expertise, which increases with age.

Consumers often use previously paid or encountered prices as a reference for the evaluation of price expectations when dealing with frequently purchased goods (Kalyanaram & Winer, 1995). However, developing price referents is increasingly more complicated in situations where consumers have little or no previous experience with the product or product category. Price predictions for novel products that are associated with multi-attribute learning tasks have shown to produce generally conservative, implicit, rules associated with each attribute in just a few trials (Shirai & Meyer, 1997). However, as previously alluded to, the overall level of respondent accuracy in these trials is poor. While most consumer learning research focuses on conditions under which learning is inhibited (Howard & Howard, 2001; Wood & Lynch, 2002), and circumstances under which learning can be improved (Huffman & Houston, 1993; West, 1996), it has generally failed to address the inhibitory or enhancing conditions in an experiential context. In response, this study aims to bring these learning strategies, more recently identified in the consumer learning literature, into the EL paradigm in order to improve respondent performance on price and preference prediction tasks.

Consumer Learning and Age.

This study takes a unique interest into the differences in learning performance between senior citizens and their Generation Y counterparts. The U.S. Administration on Aging estimates that by the year 2030 the number of Americans over the age of 65 will more than double, to nearly 72 million people. Acknowledging the senior market's power due to high proportions of discretionary income and increased leisure time, and compounding this with the impending exponential growth the market is about to endure, it is critical to gain insight into the differences in how this consumer group learns about products.

Studies have suggested that experience feeds into knowledge, and that older adults may use non-traditional cognitive skills when performing difficult tasks (Baltes et al. 1995; Hedden, Lautenschlager, & Park, 2005). In contrast, much of the geriatric literature has demonstrated a cognitive decline associated with age (Hedden & Gabrieli, 2004) including reductions in processing speed and the ability to encode information into short term memory (Craik, 1994). These deficits lend themselves to the prediction that performance on EL tasks will decrease with age due to seniors' decreased ability to quickly process the information, identify and remember patterns and relationships, and ultimately encode the recognized associations into short term memory to serve as a reference point throughout the task. Considering the substantial support for either prediction, proposition 1 serves as an exploratory inquisition:

> **Proposition 1:** Evidence for the increase in EL expertise will be supported by senior respondents outperforming undergraduate respondents on price prediction tasks, holding the environment constant.

The Advantage of Environmental Cueing.

While several cognitive psychology studies have shown the advantage of prior knowledge on subsequent learning (Alba & Hutchinson, 1987), recent consumer research has shown some evidence in dispute of this claim (Wood & Lynch, 2002). Given the poor performance of experts when an environmental change was not cued, the authors posited a lack of motivation at the point of information encoding as the cause of inferior learning. As this motivation was adjusted using an environmental cue, experts paid more attention and performed better on the learning task than their novice counterparts (Wood & Lynch, 2002). This research focuses on whether cueing environmental change in an experiential context, will improve the respondents' performance on the multi-attribute learning task across generations.

> **Proposition 2:** The existence of a cue about a change in relationships between attributes will increase respondents' rate of EL, in comparison to before the cued environmental change.

Goal Oriented Learning and the Impact of Emotion.

Consumers direct their information acquisition toward goal-relevant feature information, therefore retaining more information associated with their purchase goal and ignoring the goal irrelevant information (Huffman & Houston, 1993). Older consumers focus more attention on, and retain more information from, emotionally charged information (Levanthal, 1990). This is empirically attributed to the relatively stable condition of the emotional processing centers of the brain throughout later life (Hedden & Gabrieli, 2004). This literature suggests that introducing goal directedness to the EL paradigm should increase performance across both groups, and additionally, the use of an emotionally charged goal may further increase the performance of senior citizens on the learning task.

> **Proposition 3:** The introduction of goal directedness to the learning task, will increase performance when predictive attributes are goal relevant.

> **Proposition 4:** The introduction of an emotionally charged goal will increase senior's performance on the learning task to a greater degree than their generation Y counterparts, when predictive attributes are goal relevant.

Study design is complete and analysis of preliminary results should commence shortly.

REFERENCES

Alba, Joseph W. and Wesley J. Hutchinson (1987), "Dimensions of Consumer Expertise," *Journal of Consumer Research,* 13(March), 411-54.

Baltes, Paul B. Ursula M. Staudinger, Andreas Maercker and Jacqui Smith (1995), "People Nominated as Wise: A Comparative Study of Wisdom Related Knowledge," *Psychology and Aging,* 10(2), 155-66.

Camerer, Colin F. and Eric J. Johnson (1991), "The Process-Performance Paradox in Expert Judgement: How Can Experts Know So Much and Predict So Badly?" In *Toward a General Theory of Expertise: Prospects and Limits,* eds. K. Anders Ericsson and Jacqui Smith, New York: Cambridge University Press, 195-217.

Craik, Fergus I.M. (1994), "Memory Changes in Normal Aging," *Current Directions in Psychological Science,* 3, 155-58.

Hedden, Trey and John D.E. Gabrieli (2004), "Insights into the Ageing Mind: A View from Cognitive Neuroscience," *Neuroscience,* 5(February), 87-96.

Hedden, Trey, Gary Lautenschlager, and Denise C. Park (2005), "Contributions of Processing Ability and Knowledge to Verbal Memory Tasks across the Adult Lifespan," *The Quarterly Journal of Experimental Psychology,* 58(1).

Howard, Darlene V., and James H. Howard (2001), "When it does hurt to try: Adult age differences in the effects of instructions on implicit pattern learning," *Psychonomic Bulletin & Review,* 8(4), 798-805.

Huffman, Cynthia and Michael J. Houston (1993), "Goal-Oriented Experiences and the Development of Knowledge," *Journal of Consumer Research,* 20(September), 190-207.

Hutchinson, J. Wesley and Eric M. Eisenstein (2008), "Consumer Learning and Expertise" In *The Handbook of Consumer Psychology,* eds. Curtis P. Haugtvedt, Paul M. Herr and Frank R. Kardes, New York, NY: Lawrence Erlbaum Associates, 103-31.

Kalyanaram, Gurumurthy and Russel S. Winer (1995), "Emperical Generalizations from Reference Price Research," *Journal of Marketing Science,* 14(3), 161-69.

Levanthal, Richard C. (1990), "Aging Consumers and their Effects on the Marketplace," *The Journal of Consumer Marketing,* 14(4).

Meyer, Robert (1987), "The Learning of Multiattribute Judgment Policies," *Journal of Consumer Research,* 14(2), 155-73.

Shirai, Miyuri and Robert Meyer (1997), "Learning and the Cognitive Algebra of Price Expectations," *Journal of Consumer Psychology,* 6(4), 365-88.

West, Pat M. (1996), "Predicting Preferences: An Examination of Agent Learning," *Journal of Consumer Research,* 23(June), 68-80.

Wood, Stacy and John G. Lynch (2002), "Prior Knowledge and Complacency in New Product Learning," *Journal of Consumer Research,* 29(December), 416-26.

Price Comparisons as Information about Personal Competence and Relational Value: The Influence on Perceived Fairness

Lindsay McShane, Queens University, Canada
Laurence Ashworth, Queens University, Canada

It is not uncommon for consumers to pay different prices for the same product (Elmaghraby and Keskinocak 2003). Fairness research, however, indicates that not all of these price discrepancies are equally unfair. Work based on equity theory finds that price unfairness is affected by consumers' perceptions of their inputs (Darke and Dahl 2003). Other research shows that fairness is affected by perceptions of the firms' role in causing the unfairness (e.g. motive, intent, responsibility) (Campbell 1999; Vaidyanathan and Aggarwal 2003). Largely absent, however, is consideration of the self-threatening nature of unfair treatment. We suggest that one reason why unfavorable price discrepancies are considered so unfair is because they can threaten aspects of consumers' self-concept. We examine the role of two types of self-threat that we think are important in (un)fairness judgments: threats to personal competence and threats to relational value.

People want to be seen as competent and valued (Jones and Pittman 1982). Such characteristics are important to individuals' self-concepts, and are often treated as components of self-esteem (Heatherton and Polivy 1991). Some have even argued that being valued by others is the *function* of self-esteem (Leary et al. 1995). We suggest that, in some cases, paying more than someone else for the same product threatens one or both of these components of self-concept. To the extent that a price inequity conveys threatening information about consumers' competence and/or relational value, we expect consumers to perceive the situation as more unfair. We examine the influence of these self-threats on fairness judgments in Study 1. In Study 2, we focus more specifically on the different sources of threats to relational value and their influence on fairness judgments.

Unfair treatment is often facilitated by consumers' credulity or naivety. We argue that these situations are likely to be particularly threatening because they undermine consumers' perceptions of personal competence. We test whether threats to personal competence influence consumer reactions to price discrepancies by varying the extent to which consumers had a choice in the purchase. When consumers have little choice, price discrepancies should have fewer implications for their competence, and therefore, we argue, be perceived as less unfair.

Price inequities can be threatening for other reasons too. Specifically, they may suggest that the consumer is not valued by their relational partners. In Study 1, we look at situations where the threat to relational value stems from what it implies about the consumer's relationship with the firm. We expect price inequities to be threatening to the extent that they communicate to the consumer that the firm does not value them. We expect price inequities to communicate this information when the firm is perceived to have deliberately charged the consumer the higher price. When the firm is not held responsible for the discrepancy, implications for the firm's opinion of the consumer should be reduced, and therefore have a diminished impact on fairness.

STUDY 1

Study 1 consisted of a 2 (Deliberate: yes, no) x 2(Choice: yes, no) experiment. In the Deliberate conditions, we manipulated whether the other consumer's lower price was the result of a deliberate action taken by the seller. In the Choice conditions we varied whether the consumer had a choice in whether to engage in the exchange.

Primary analysis revealed a main effect of Deliberate on perceived fairness and perceived relational value (Fs$(1,112)=40.72$ and 54.48, ps$<.001$ and $<.001$). Consumers perceived the situation as significantly more unfair and felt less valued when the seller's actions were deliberate (Ms$=2.78$ vs. 4.51 and Ms$=3.81$ vs. 5.46: note that in the lower numbers indicate more unfair and less valued). A Sobel test of the indirect path from deliberate to fairness via perceived relational value was significant ($z = 4.32$, $p < .001$), consistent with mediation.

The ANOVA also showed the predicted two-way interaction ($F (1, 112) =3.84$, $p=0.05$). Follow-up analyses showed that in the Deliberate condition, consumers perceived the situation as significantly less unfair and felt less incompetent when they had no choice in whether to engage in the exchange (Ms$=3.39$ vs. 2.15 and Ms$=3.71$ vs. 3.02, Fs$(1,112)=9.84$ and 6.55 and ps $<.01$ and $<.05$). The results of a Sobel test of the indirect path from Choice to fairness via perceived competence supported the prediction that threats to personal competence exacerbate perceived unfairness ($z = 2.21$, $p < .05$).

STUDY 2

Study 1 focuses on threats to relational value that stem from what the price inequity implies about the consumer's standing with the firm. Price inequities, however, may threaten the consumer's perceived relational value with regards to other relationships as well, such as friendships. The purpose of Study 2 was to investigate the influence of these threats. We predicted that threats to one's relational value in relationships external to the consumer-seller relationship would exacerbate unfairness perceptions only when the other consumer's lower price was not attributable to a mistake made by the seller.

To test these ideas we ran a 2 (Mistake: yes, no) x 2(Seller Selection: Friend, Target Consumer) experiment. Participants read that they paid $30 more than another consumer for the same product at a different online retailer. In the Mistake conditions, we varied whether the other consumer's lower price the result of a mistake made by he seller or not. For Seller Selection, we varied whether the consumer selected the online retailer or whether it was recommended by a friend. We predicted that when the price inequity was not the result of a mistake, participants would perceive the situation as particularly unfair when the seller was recommended by a friend. Here, the risk that the consumer's friend may knowingly have led the consumer to overpay may be taken by the consumer as evidence that their friend does not value their relationship. We expect this threat to relational value to exacerbate perceived unfairness.

Consistent with Study 1, an ANOVA revealed a main effect of Mistake on perceived fairness and perceived relational value (Fs$(1,67)=8.82$ and 9.58, ps$<.01$ an d $<.01$). Consumers perceived the situation as significantly more unfair and felt less valued when the seller's actions were not a mistake (Ms$=4.19$ vs. 5.14 and Ms$=3.67$ vs. 4.26). A Sobel test of the indirect path from mistake to fairness via perceived relational value supported the predicted mediation ($z = 2.67$, $p < .01$).

Follow-up analyses showed that in the Mistake condition, consumers perceived the situation as significantly more unfair and felt less valued when the seller was recommended by their friend rather than self-selected (*M*s=3.69 vs. 4.69 and *M*s=3.36 vs. 3.97, *F*s(1,67)=4.88 and 4.93 and *p*s <.01 and <.05). A Sobel test of the indirect path from Seller Selection to fairness supported the predicted mediation of perceived relational value (*z* = 2.04, *p* < .05). The results suggest that, in certain cases, external threats to relational value (i.e., those based on relationships other than the consumer's relationship with the firm) may also exacerbate perceived unfairness.

DISCUSSION

Given the negative consequences of perceived unfairness, it is important to understand why price discrepancies across consumers vary in the extent to which they are deemed unfair. This research suggests price inequities are perceived as unfair to the extent that they threaten important aspects of the self. Importantly, we identify two different self-threats, threats to personal competence and threats to relational value, that exacerbate perceived unfairness.

REFERENCES

Campbell, Margaret C. (1999), "Perceptions of Price Unfairness," *Journal of Marketing Research,* 36 (May), 187-199.

Cox, J. (2001), "Can Differential Prices be Fair?," *Journal of Product and Brand Management,* 10(5), 264-275.

Darke, P. R. and D. Dahl (2003), "Fairness and Discounts: The Subjective Value of a Bargain," *Journal of Consumer Psychology,* 13, 328-338.

Elmaghraby, W. and P. Keskinocak (2003), "Dynamic Pricing in the Presence of Inventory Considerations: Research Overview, Current Practices and Future Directions," *Management Science*, 49 (10), 1287-1309.

Heatherton, T. F., and J. Polivy (1991), "Development and Validation of a Scale for Measuring State Self-Esteem," *Journal of Personality and Social Psychology,* 60, 895-910.

Leary, M. R., E. S. Tambor, S. K. Terdal, and D. L. Downs (1995), "Self-esteem as an Interpersonal Monitor: The Sociometer Hypothesis," *Journal of Personality and Social Psychology*, 6, 518-530.

Vaidyanathan, R. and P. Aggarwal (2003), "Who is the Fairest of Them All? An Attributional Approach to Price Fairness Perceptions," *Journal of Business Research* 56, 453-463.

Does a Product Category Have a Motivational Orientation? Effects on Health Message Efficacy

Adilson Borges, Reims Management School, France
Pierrick Gomez, Reims Management School, France

Designing effective health message is important for health policy makers (Keller and Lehmann, 2008). Extant research shows that regulatory focus is a strong determinant of health message efficacy. Regulatory focus theory postulates that goal-pursuit strategies will result in fit when these strategies match the individual or situational regulatory orientation (Higgins 1998). For instance, pursuing a goal through carefully avoiding losses, highlighting safety and security will "feels right" for prevention oriented individuals, while pursuing a goal through searching for gains and avoid missing gains will match promotion oriented individuals

The persuasive power of regulatory fit results from the sense of having done the right thing – it "feels right" and a heightened motivation (Camacho, Higgins, and Luger 2003; Higgins 2002, Aaker and Lee, 2006). Thus, under prevention orientation consumers are more sensitive to health problems than under promotion orientation. Loss framed-messages are also more convincing when prevention focus is activated whereas gain-framed messages are more convincing under promotion focus (Aaker and Lee, 2004). Keller (2006) has shown that health messages are more efficient when the perceived easiness of the advocated health behavior is paired with promotion focus and when the response effectiveness is paired with prevention focus.

Regulatory fit has mainly been sustained throughout two paths (Lee and Higgins 2009). The first is when the goal pursuit strategy fits with the individual regulatory orientation. For example, subjects took an experiment where they have to choose between a pen and a coffee mug. Prevention oriented subjects using a safety strategy declared higher willingness to pay for the mug than subjects that used an eager strategy. The results were reversed for promotion subjects (Higgins et al. 2003). The second is when the message regulatory focus fits with the characteristics of the persuasion appeal. For instance, promotion oriented adolescents declare lower smoking intentions to gain (vs. non-gains) messages whereas prevention oriented subjects were more persuaded by messages stressing potential losses (instead of no-losses) (Zhao and Pechmann 2007).

We proposed that regulatory fit may be sustained trough a third path. Indeed, we suggest that product category can trigger regulatory focus (i.e, product category motivational orientation), which could create a fit with the message orientation. Past research seems to imply that a product category could prime regulatory focus. For instance, people carrying out a decision-making task related to stock market shares (a product associated with the idea of maximizing gains) tend to use a promotion strategy in a subsequent unrelated task, whereas those carrying out a decision-making task related to saving plans (a product associated with the idea of avoiding losses) have a greater tendency to use prevention strategies (Zhou and Pham, 2004). Extant research has shown that products are highly connected to the goals they serve and product categories have a motivational component (Dhar and Wertenbroch, 2000). Product category is also preferably associated to delayed or immediate gratification (Wertenbroch, 1998). In three studies, we show that product category motivational orientation and message regulatory focus interact to determine health message efficacy.

A first pre-test shows the priming effect of product category. 41 participants were randomly assigned to a category goal orientation (prevention vs. promotion). Following Aaker and Lee (2004) we use orange juice and a sunscreen cream as respectively a promotion and a prevention category. To prime regulatory focus, respondents imagined that they have to buy this product. Subjects are then asked to indicate three best strategies to face an exam (Zhou and Pham, 2004). Six strategies were presented (3 prevention and 3 promotion strategies). The results show that subjects declare more promotion (prevention) strategies after seeing the promotion (prevention) category.

The study 1 tests the persuasive effects of the fit between product category motivational orientation and the health outcome frame. Thus, we expect that an individual exposed to a prevention category should be more convinced by a prevention message whereas an individual exposed to a promotion category should be more convinced by a promotion message.

Using the same categories from the pre-test, we develop an advertising that frame the product benefits either as a health gain (promotion frame) or health loss (prevention frame). 136 participants took part in a 2 (product category: prevention vs. promotion) by 2 (message frame: gain vs. avoiding loss) between subjects design. The results show that promotion (prevention) categories increase the attitude toward the product and the purchase intention when the message frame is gain (avoiding loss).

The study 2 tests different product categories and identifies ad credibility as a mediator. We randomly selected 3 categories identified on a previous qualitative study as promotion oriented (orange juice, chocolate and yogurt) and 3 prevention oriented (sunscreen, insurance and elliptical trainer). 260 subjects told they would buy promotion categories more due to the pleasure the product provides than for the problems the product avoid. The results are reversed for prevention categories. Subjects then look at an advertising following the same structure of the study 1. The results show the same pattern as study 1. Promotion (prevention) categories increase the attitude toward the product and the purchase intention when the message frame is gain (avoiding loss). These results stand even when the subject's regulatory orientation is controlled for. Moreover, ad credibility fully mediated the fit effects on intentions.

This research shows that the product category creates fit with the message frame independently of the perceiver regulatory orientation. Product categories are used to achieve goals, and these goals become strongly associated with the category itself. The product category itself is enough to elicit the goal orientation (prevention or promotion), and the use of the right category creates fit with the message frame, increasing product evaluation trough ad credibility.

REFERENCES:

Camacho, Christopher J., E. Tory Higgins, and Lindsay Luger (2003), "Moral Value Transfer from Regulatory Fit: What Feels Right Is Right and What Feels Wrong Is Wrong," *Journal of Personality and Social Psychology*, 84 (3), 498-510.

Cesario, Joseph, Heidi Grant, and E. Tory Higgins (2004), "Regulatory Fit and Persuasion: Transfer from "Feeling Right"," *Journal of Personality and Social Psychology*, 86 (3), 388-404.

Higgins, E. Tory (1998), "Promotion and Prevention: Regulatory Focus as a Motivational Principle," in *Advances in Experimental Social Psychology*, Vol. 30, ed. Mark P. Zanna, New York NY: Academic Press, 1-46.

--- (2002), "How Self-Regulation Creates Distinct Values: Case of Promotion and Prevention Decision Making," *Journal of Consumer Psychology*, 12 (3), 177-91.

Higgins, E. Tory, Lorraine Chen Idson, Antonio L. Freitas, Scott Spiegel, and Daniel C. Molden (2003), "Transfer of Value from Fit," *Journal of Personality and Social Psychology*, 84 (6), 1140-53.

Lee, Angela Y. and Jennifer L. Aaker (2004), "Bringing the Frame into Focus: The Influence of Regulatory Fit on Processing Fluency and Persuasion.," *Journal of Personality & Social Psychology*, 86 (2), 205-18.

Lee, Angela Y. and E. Tory Higgins (2009), "The Persuasion Power of Regulatory Fit," in *Social Psychology of Consumer Behavior*, ed. Michaela Wänke, New York: Psychology Press, 319–33.

Zhao, Guangzhi and Cornelia Pechmann (2007), "The Impact of Regulatory Focus on Adolescents' Response to Antismoking Advertising Campaigns," *Journal of Marketing Research,* 44 (4), 671-87.

Fair for You and Indulgent For Me:
Product Positioning and Consumer Intentions Toward Ethical Products

Katherine White, University of Calgary, Canada
Rhiannon MacDonnell, University of Calgary, Canada
John Ellard, University of Calgary, Canada

Although the marketing literature has begun to examine the implications of justice perceptions related to *one's own* consumption experiences, less attention has been given to consumer attitudes and behaviors related to *justice received by others*. Notably, recent research has suggested that while consumers are increasingly interested in ethical, socially conscious product options (Trudel and Cotte 2009), product ethicality does not invariably lead to a positive consumer response (Luchs et al. 2010). This work suggests that the way in which the product is positioned—as an indulgence or a necessity—can influence consumer concerns for justice for others. This, in turn, can influence willingness to purchase products with ethical attributes (e.g., fair trade products).

Fair trade is a social movement that aims to set fair prices for products, alleviate poverty, and assist producers marginalized by the traditional economic model (Pelsmacker and Janssens 2007). Of particular interest from a marketing perspective is research showing that consumers are increasingly interested in ethical options such as fair trade products (Nicholls and Opal 2005). However, consumers often do not actually support fair trade options when given the opportunity to do so (Auger and Devinny 2007). Recent research finds that one reason for this is because it is not clear whether such options will resolve the observed injustice (White, MacDonnell, and Ellard 2011). Such uncertainty about the ability to resolve injustice via purchases can ironically lead to decreased support for fair trade options when communicated need on the part of producers is very high (as opposed to low). We build on this past work to examine two key variables that will influence consumer fair trade intentions, even when marketers communicate high need circumstances (i.e., very dire and unjust circumstances for producers).

First, we propose that *indulgences* increase sensitivity towards justice for others, leading consumers to favor fair trade options. We define indulgences are products "adding to pleasure or comfort but not absolutely necessary" (Hagtvedt and Patrick 2009). In this context, considering an indulgence is predicted to heighten sensitivity to justice for others for two reasons: 1) the unjust fate of the producer is highlighted (i.e., high need communications about fair trade) and 2) the privileged, and hence "undeserved" fate of the consumer is salient (i.e., consumer is considering an indulgence). Thus, indulgent products may lead the consumer to be particularly sensitive to injustice for others. Second, we examine the moderating role of individual differences in sensitivity to injustice—belief in a just world (BJW; Lipkus 1991). High BJW individuals are particularly sensitive to injustice (Rubin and Peplau 1973). Importantly, when the opportunity to help is available, those high in BJW are particularly likely to assist victims (Miller 1977). We propose that when sensitivity to injustice is most heighted—the product is an indulgence and BJW is high—Consumers will be most moved to help by purchasing fair trade.

In study 1, we test the assertion that, in the fair trade context, indulgences lead to more of a concern for justice for others. Fifty-eight undergraduates read background information to familiarize them with fair trade and to communicate high need (unfair circumstances for producers; White et al. 2011). They then read a scenario asking them to imagine a purchase of the "Dagoba" snack bar, made with fair trade cocoa. The bar was described as either an *indulgence* or a *necessity*. Participants then completed items to assess concern for justice for others and the extent to which they were focused on their own needs. As expected, participants reported greater concern for justice for others when they considering an indulgence ($M = 4.94$), rather than a necessity ($M = 3.64$; $p < .01$). Further, they were more focused on the self when the product was a necessity ($p < .01$).

In study 2, we suggest that because indulgences are particularly likely to activate justice concerns (study 1) and those high in BJW are most sensitive to injustice (Rubin and Peplau 1973), when the product is positioned as an indulgence and BJW is high, people will be most responsive to fair trade options. Further, we examine whether concern for justice for others mediates the effects. Consumers ($n = 147$) at a local market read the background information and the product manipulation (study 1). They then completed a purchase intentions measure regarding the Dagoba bar ($a = .88$). They also completed items to assess concern for justice for others ($a = .92$), general efficacy ($a = .74$), and BJW ($a = .92$; Lipkus 1991).

Regression analysis using product type, BJW, and the interaction as predictors of purchase intentions, revealed the predicted interaction ($p < .02$). Simple slopes analysis showed that when the product was an indulgence those higher in BJW reported stronger purchase intentions than those lower in BJW ($t = 2.55$, $p < .02$). However, when the product was a necessity no differences as a function of BJW emerged ($p < .40$). Bootstrapping analysis showed that justice concerns for others mediated the effects (CI: .0083-.2362), but general efficacy did not (CI: .0994-.0946).

The results demonstrate that product type can influence justice concern for others. Although intuition might suggest that indulgences would relate to a focus on the self, in study 1, consumers were more concerned about justice for others (and less focused on the self) when the product was an indulgence versus a necessity. In study 2, when the product was an indulgence, higher BJW related to more positive purchase intentions towards a fair trade product. When the product was a necessity, consumers did not demonstrate differential purchase intentions as a function of BJW. Thus, when justice concerns are heightened (the product is an indulgence and BJW is high), consumers are most likely to support fair trade products. The results further suggest that justice concerns for others are driving responses, rather than more general efficacy effects. We also make a unique contribution to the marketing and justice literatures by examining how responsiveness to the plight of others is influenced by circumstances shaping one's own deserving.

REFERENCES

Auger, Pat and Timothy M. Devinney (2007), "Does What Consumers Say Matter? The Misalignment of Preferences with Unconstrained Ethical Intentions," *Journal of Business Ethics*, 76, 361-383.

Hagtvedt, Henrik and Vanessa M Patrick (2010), "The Broad Embrace of Luxury: Hedonic Potential as a Driver of Brand Extendibility," *Journal of Consumer Psychology*.

Lipkus, Issac (1991), "The Construction and Preliminary Validation of a Global Belief in a Just World Scale and the Exploratory Analysis of the Multidimensional Belief in a Just World Scale," *Personality and Individual Differences*, 12, 1171-78.

Luchs, Michael G., Rebecca Walker Naylor, Julie R. Irwin, and Rajagopal Raghunathan (2010), "The Sustainability Liability: Potential Negative Effects of Ethicality on Product Preference, *Journal of Marketing* 74 (5), 18-31

Miller, Dale T. (1977), "Altruism and Threat to Belief in a Just World," *Journal of Experimental Social Psychology*, 13 (March), 113-24.

Nicholls, Alex and Charlotte Opal (2005), *Fair Trade: Market-Driven Ethical Consumption*. London: Sage.

Pelsmacker, Patrick and Wim Janssens (2007), "A Model for Fair Trade Buying Behavior: The Role of Perceived Quantity and Quality of Information and Product-Specific Attitudes," *Journal of Business Ethics*, 75, 361-80.

Rubin, Zick and Anne Peplau (1975), "Belief in a Just World and Reactions to Another's Lot: A Study of Participants in the National Draft Lottery," *Journal of Social Issues*, 29, 73-93.

Trudel, Remi and June Cotte (2009), "Does it Pay to Be Good?" *Sloan Management Review*, 50(2), 61-68.

White, Katherine, Rhiannon MacDonnell and John Ellard (2011), "Belief in a Just World and Consumer Intentions and Behaviors Toward Ethical Products," Working Paper, Revise and Resubmit at Journal of Marketing.

My picture, my product: Does co-creation of a usage experience lead to positive consumer outcomes?

Shanker Krishnan, Indiana University, USA
Arun Lakshmanan, SUNY Buffalo, USA
Lura Forcum, Indiana University, USA

Many modern products engage consumers as co-creators in the exchange process (Vargo and Lusch 2004) rather than being passive recipients of product benefits. One of the dominant findings from this literature is that customer co-creation often correlates with consumer elaboration (Moreau and Herd 2010). Such elaboration could take the form of visual imagery, narrative transportation or cognitive elaboration (e.g., Green and Brock 2000; Schlosser 2003; Unnava, Agrawal and Haugtvedt 1996).

Co-creation engages the consumer in an active role with the end product often a result of consumer action. For example, many websites allow consumers to manipulate and design various fashion accessories by uploading their own pictures, versus seeing images of others (from ads, catalogs). Major retailers (Wal-Mart, Carrefour) are also considering the use of virtual mirrors that allow consumers to design a specific look for some products (e.g., cosmetics). In such situations, consumers are visually transporting themselves into product use with the attendant elaboration and visual imagery. Whether such transportation (versus cognitive elaboration) moderates the effects of image use is an issue that is worthy of investigation.

A laboratory based study was conducted using a commercial online service aimed at making collages using digital pictures. The primary consumption task was the formation of collages from a set of photographs to design a vacation. Image type was manipulated by providing participants product images, product images with people, or product images with self-images. For this last condition, as the user provides images, involvement should increase. Yet, a greater degree of physical activity should lead to a stronger focus on the task and thus, attitude formation may be impeded (versus the passive conditions where the user does not provide any images). Further, when transportation imagery is engaged via a second manipulation, participants in the self-image conditions should face greater interruption to the imagery generation process (due to the necessity to perform operations upon the website/images). This interruption of the mental transportation process should lead to poorer attitudes for this group when transportation is engaged (versus not). Thus, narrative transportation should interact with the type of imagery in predicting attitudes. This hypothesis was tested using the method described below.

One hundred and sixty two undergraduate marketing students at a large Midwestern university completed the study. The experiment followed a 2 (elaboration: transportation imagery vs. cognitive) by 3 (image type) between-subjects factorial design. Each participant was provided with a fictitious spring-break travel planning scenario in which they were either asked to immerse themselves and imagine their prospective holiday vividly (transportation imagery group) or plan for their holiday as comprehensively as possible (cognitive elaboration group). Subsequently, participants were directed via the computer's web-browser to one of three versions of the website. One-third of the participants (product image) were shown a screen with 36 images of a beach vacation. A second group (product image with people) was shown 36 images of beach vacations with people in them. The third (product image with self-images) group was asked to upload up to six images of their choice from personal online accounts and their screen showed these six images along with 30 images from the experimental website.

Subjects in all conditions were simply instructed to "make a collage" depicting their ideal vacation. This collage was subsequently saved yielding a unique participant-specific collage image. Time-stamped user information was collected unobtrusively on the experimental website and logged for process analysis. Subsequently, the website directed them to the online survey containing other measures. Cognitive response protocols were also collected toward the end of the session.

The primary dependent measures for this study were attitude towards the website and vacation purchase likelihood. A two-way ANCOVA with elaboration (transportation imagery vs. cognitive) and image type (product image, product image with people, and product image with self-images) as predictors, and overall attitude toward the website as the criterion variable revealed a significant main effect for the photo condition ($F(2,148) = 4.2$; $p < .02$) This effect was qualified by a two-way interaction with the elaboration factor ($F(2,148) = 4.92$; $p < .01$). Planned contrasts revealed that within the self-image condition the transportation imagery group had *lower* attitudes compared to the cognitive elaboration group ($M_{imagery} = 17.52$, $M_{cognitive} = 15$; $t = 2.44$, $p < .02$), with other within-group comparisons not statistically significant ($ps > .2$). This finding supports our hypothesis.

Consistent with this finding, a two-way ANCOVA on participants' purchase likelihood for the vacation also revealed a main effect for the photo condition ($F(2,148) = 3.29$; $p < .04$) as well as a significant two-way interaction ($F(2,148) = 3.06$; $p < .05$). Planned contrasts revealed that within the self-image condition the imagery group had lower purchase likelihoods compared to the cognitive elaboration group ($M_{imagery} = 3.84$, $M_{cognitive} = 4.78$; $t = 2.1$, $p < .04$), with other within-group comparisons not significant ($ps > .2$). This finding also supports our core hypothesis.

Study 1 presents initial evidence that the combination of narrative transportation and self-selected images can interfere with the formation of product attitudes and willingness to buy.

We intend to continue to our investigation with two additional studies which will also be presented at ACR, should this paper be accepted.

Study 2 will involve evaluating the output of the creative process and investigating process explanations for our counter-intuitive findings. We plan on rating collages on a variety of dimensions, including creativity, overall aesthetic value, and characteristics related to the photographs chosen in the subject-selected image condition. Study 3 will explore whether varying degrees of involvement in the collage-creation process affect attitude toward the site and willingness to purchase.

REFERENCES

Green, Melanie C. and Brock, Timothy C. (2000), "The role of transportation in the persuasiveness of public narratives," *Journal of Personality and Social Psychology, 79,* 701-721.

Moreau, Page and Kelly Herd (2010), "To each his own? How comparisons with others influence consumers' evaluations of their self-designed products," *Journal of Consumer Research*, 36 (February), 806-819.

Schlosser, Ann E. (2003), "Experiencing products in the virtual world: The role of goal and imagery in influencing attitudes versus purchase intentions," *Journal of Consumer Research,* 30, 184-198.

Unnava, H. Rao, Agarwal, Sanjeev, and Haugtvedt, Curtis P. (1996), "Interactive effects of presentation modality and message-generated imagery on recall of advertising information," *Journal of Consumer Research,* 23, 81-88.

Vargo, Stephen L. and Robert F. Lusch (2004), "Evolving to a new dominant logic for marketing," *Journal of Marketing*, 68 (1),1-17.

Say No More!
Experiential Consumption and the Spoiler Effect of Positive Word of Mouth

Kendra Hart, Ivey Business School, University of Western Ontario, Canada
Mirand R. Goode, Ivey Business School, University of Western Ontario, Canada
Matthew Thomson, Ivey Business School, University of Western Ontario, Canada

People seek WOM from a trusted source as a way to anticipate and explore consumption choices (Frenzen and Davis 1990; Smith, Menon, and Sivakumar 2005). Yet, people also engage in storytelling, a form of WOM, as a way to savor prior hedonic experiences, such as vacations or other special events**.** We propose that this latter post-consumption communication can negatively impact consumers who are in the pre-consumption stage of a similar hedonic experience. We suggest that WOM in the form of storytelling can interrupt a receiver's pre-consumption fantasy, discouraging future consumption and altering choice. Specifically, receiving information about a hedonic experience from a trusted source is likely to lead to a sense of experiential demystification resulting in reduced motivation to pursue that experience.

PRE-CONSUMPTION FANTASIES AND DEMYSTIFICATION

Consumption experiences include three distinct phases: A pre-consumption phase characterized by information search and consumption fantasies; the actual consumption phase; and a post-consumption phase characterized by consumption memories and reminiscing. Pre-consumption pleasure can stem from forecasting the details of an experience and enjoying the emotional response in prospect. However, there is also utility in the curiosity and suspense that may arise prior to engaging in an experience (Knobloch-Westerwick and Keplinger 2006). Uncertainty in how an experience may unfold, followed by the thrill of discovery during an actual experience, is a hedonic reward (Quinn 2003) – one which we argue can be weakened through experiential demystification.

People in the pre-consumption phase, anticipating a consumption experience, seek WOM from a trusted source as a way to explore consumption choices. People in the post-consumption phase are often eager to share their memories. Exposure to a sender's recounting of a consumption experience demystifies speculation surrounding the receiver's impending experience. Demystification is a process that clarifies the previously uncertain and vague. We propose that this demystification of an upcoming experience serves as a story spoiler, satiating curiosity, and constraining the receiver's ability to imagine the many ways in which an experience may unfold.

To investigate the effect of demystification on consumer choice, we explore how WOM from a friend versus stranger weakens desire for a consumption experience. Individuals associate and bond with those who have similar values, tastes, and attitudes (McPherson, Smith-Lovin, and Cook 2001). We suggest this greater similarity between friends increases trust, resulting in increased demystification via smoother acceptance of the details communicated by a friend. This leads to a demotivating effect, characterized by a decreased sense of specialness surrounding the impending experience and reduced interest in pursuing the experience.

METHOD AND FINDINGS

Participants (n = 144) were asked to select one of five consumption experiences (e.g., white water rafting, hot air balloon ride) that they would like to try if given a free ticket. Next, participants were directed to envision the experience and asked to write a paragraph recording the details and expectations for their chosen experience. After a filler task, participants were randomly assigned to one of two WOM conditions, where they read a description of the selected experience and were asked to imagine that it was provided by either a friend or stranger. Participants responded to a series of scale measures to assess their expectations for the experience, as well as measures related to demystification, desire to pursue the selected experience and individual trait measures.

A series of ANOVAs, controlling for individual need for uniqueness, showed that participants exposed to WOM from a stranger estimated a greater expectation of being able to "make the experience their own" had a "greater sense of wonder" about the experience than those exposed to WOM from a friend. Participants in the friend condition reported that they expected the experience to be *more boring* and *less adventurous* than those in the stranger condition. Further, particpants in the friend condition reported that the experience would be less "special" (meaningful, special, extraordinary); and more "ordinary" (familiar, typical, run-of-the-mill). Taken together, these measures provide evidence for demystification. Interestingly, a set of contamination-like indicators emerged suggesting that the upcoming experience seemed more "tainted" (devalued, spoiled, tainted) in the friend (versus stranger) condition.

As anticipated, the WOM source (friend vs. stranger) significantly influenced participants' desire to try their selected experience. Participants who received WOM from a friend (versus stranger) were significantly more willing to switch their selected experience for an alternate option. It is important to note that these findings are not a result of altered or disconfirmed expectations for a future event. We measured the degree to which respondents thought the WOM matched their own expectations, and found that most respondents believed the WOM was highly consistent with their own expectations.

DISCUSSION

These results contribute to the extant literature on WOM, suggesting that positive WOM can have a negative impact on consumer evaluations and choice. Additionally, this research introduces the idea of demystification, an idea which has not previously been applied to experiential consumption. This initial study suggests that WOM may demystify an impending experience, and reduce consumer motivation. The effect of demystification on notions of meaningfulness and the ordinary in experiential consumption are consistent with previous research on the pleasure paradox (Wilson et al. 2005).

However, one interesting line in these results is the evaluation of an experience being "tainted" after WOM exposure. Indicators such as "tainted", "spoiled" and "polluted" suggest a contamination-like effect that begs further exploration. Physical objects touched by others leads to consumer disgust and perceived contamination, rendering the touched object impure (Argo, Dahl, and Morales 2006). We consider that perhaps, analogously, *conceptual contamination* is driven by consumer demystification, when the open-ended *idea* of potential consumption is sullied by details of another's actual consumption. Specifically, we question if conceptual contamination stems from demystification and a loss of wonderment about the impending experience, leaving the receiver feeling that the experience will be more spoiled, impure, mundane, and less his own. In essence, the impending consumption experience is contaminated for the receiver. Additional studies are underway to address the dimensions of this possible contamination.

REFERENCES

Argo, Jennifer J., Darren W. Dahl, and Andrea C. Morales (2006), "Consumer Contamination: How Consumers React to Products Touched by Others," *Journal of Marketing*, 70, 81-94.

Frenzen, Jonathan K. and Harry L. Davis (1990), "Purchasing Behavior in Embedded Markets," *Journal of Consumer Research*, 17 (1), 1-12.

Knobloch-Westerwick, Silvia and Caterina Keplinger (2006), "Mystery Appeal: Effects of Uncertainty and Resolution on the Enjoyment of Mystery," *Media Psychology*, 8, 193-212.

McPherson, Miller, Lynn Smith-Lovin, and James M. Cook (2001), "Birds of a Feather: Homophily in Social Networks," *Annual Revue of Psychology*, 27, 415-44.

Quinn, Bill (2003), "The Essence of Adventure," in *Adventure Programming*, ed. John C. Miles and Simon Priest, State College, Pennsylvania: Venture Publishing Inc.

Smith, Donnavieve, Satya Menon, and K. Sivakumar (2005), "Online Peer and Editorial Recommendations, Trust, and Choice in Virtual Markets," *Journal of Interactive Marketing*, 19 (3), 15-37.

Wilson, Timothy D., David B. Centerbar, Deborah A. Kermer, and Daniel T. Gilbert (2005), "The Pleasures of Uncertainty: Prolonging Positive Moods in Ways That People Do Not Anticipate," *Journal of Personality and Social Psychology*, 88 (1), 5-21.

The Effects of Dissociative Segment Adoption of Brand Extensions on the Evaluation of the Parent Brand

Claudio Alvarez, Boston University, USA
Remi Trudel, Boston University, USA

Brand extensions play a critical role in corporate growth strategies because they bring new sources of revenue while minimizing brand development investments. This revenue growth can be achieved by extending the brand to new customers (e.g., Porsche Panamera, Bic surfboards) or through more conservative moves within the customer base (e.g., Clorox's home cleaning products). A major concern when branching out into new customer segments is the potential negative impact on the image of the original brand, particularly when these new customers are perceived to belong to an outgroup by current customers. After all, brand managers try to maximize revenues from brand extensions without exposing the current customer and revenue base to significant risks. Despite its relevance to managers, the effect that venturing into new segments has on existing customers has been largely overlooked in the brand extension literature. The present study aims to fill this gap by investigating the potential negative effects of extending the brand into new customer segments to the parent brand.

Consumer research has provided compelling evidence for the impact of reference groups on brand evaluation. Escalas and Bettman (2005) proposed that reference groups can be an important source of brand associations, and showed that the association of a brand with a group that consumers belong to (an ingroup) leads to higher self-brand connection whereas the association with an outgroup lowers self-brand connection. White and Dahl (2007) also demonstrated that consumers tend to avoid brands associated with dissociative reference groups, not only in terms of self-brand connection but also in product evaluation and product choice tasks. In a longitudinal field study conducted by Berger and Heath (2008), students that had bought Livestrong wristbands stopped using them after they were adopted by "geek" students. Mere extension of this line of research would lead us to predict that the negative affect derived from the adoption of a brand extension by a dissociative segment (*versus* an ingroup) can transfer to the parent brand, resulting in more negative attitudes and purchase intentions.

However, the effect of reference groups is expected to vary depending on the perceived fit of the parent brand with the extension product category. Perceived fit impacts the affect transfer from the brand extension to the parent brand, as has been extensively demonstrated in experimental manipulations of brand extension failure (see Keller and Sood 2003 for a review). When the performance of the brand extension contradicts expectations derived from the parent brand, dilution effects are more likely to happen when the extension has high fit with the parent brand. In other words, brands can be largely immune from being contaminated by far extensions. We make the novel prediction that perceived fit will moderate the effect of dissociative segment adoption, so that a brand extension adoption by a dissociative segment (*versus* an ingroup) will negatively impact the parent brand when product category similarity is high, but will not have an impact when similarity is low.

To test these hypotheses, we randomly assigned 238 undergraduate students to six experimental conditions in a 2 (fit: high, low) x 3 (reference group: no information, ingroup, dissociative segment) between-subjects design. Through a series of four pretests, we defined (1) the parent brand to be American Eagle, which was familiar, moderately liked, and perceived as being characteristic of our student population (i.e., an ingroup brand); (2) the brand extensions to be backpack (high fit) and bicycle (low fit); and (3) reference group characterizations to be "men and women between 18-35 years old from middle and upper socioeconomic classes that are pursuing an undergraduate degree" (ingroup) and "men and women between 40-60 years old from a lower socioeconomic class and less than high school education" (dissociative segment).

After a brief introduction, participants were asked to imagine that American Eagle had launched a new backpack (high fit) or bicycle (low fit), and that this brand extension was being used by the ingroup or dissociative segment (no information about user profile was given in the control conditions). They were then asked about their attitudes toward the American Eagle brand and how likely they were to buy an American Eagle t-shirt, which is one of the current products sold by this brand; men and women received almost identical pictures of a white t-shirt with the American Eagle logo.

The expected two-way interaction was confirmed both for brand attitudes and likelihood of purchase. Specifically, the use of American Eagle backpacks (high fit) by a dissociative segment resulted in lower attitudes toward the parent brand and lower likelihood of purchasing American Eagle t-shirts relative to the ingroup condition. On the other hand, the use of American Eagle bicycles (low fit) by a dissociative segment did not impact attitudes toward the parent brand and resulted in even higher likelihood or purchasing an American Eagle t-shirt than the ingroup condition.

The results of this first study provide preliminary support for our hypotheses. They demonstrate that the negative affect derived from the usage of a brand extension by a dissociative segment may transfer to the parent brand when there is high fit between the parent brand and the brand extension product category. They also provide an important boundary condition for the effect of reference groups on brands, since no dilution effects emerged in low fit conditions. The implications to managers are mildly optimistic. On the one hand, managers who use brand extension as a mechanism to increase consumption within the current target market should be more careful about not extending into too dissimilar product categories. But on the other hand, if the main objective is to bring new customers to the parent brand franchise, dissimilar brand extensions may be a viable alternative (Milberg, Sinn and Goodstein 2010) that generates lower dilution risks than similar brand extensions.

REFERENCES

Berger, Jonah and Chip Heath (2008), "Who Drives Divergence? Identity Signaling, Outgroup Dissimilarity, and the Abandonment of Cultural Tastes," *Journal of Personality and Social Psychology,* 95(3), 593-607.

Escalas, Jennifer Edson and James R. Bettman (2005), "Self-Construal, Reference Groups, and Brand Meaning," *Journal of Consumer Research,* 32(3), 378-389.

Keller, Kevin Lane and Sanjay Sood (2003), "Brand Equity Dilution," *MIT Sloan Management Review,* 45(1), 12-15.

Milberg, Sandra J., Francisca Sinn and Ronald C. Goodstein (2010), "Consumer Reactions to Brand Extensions in a Competitive Context: Does Fit Still Matter?," *Journal of Consumer Research,* 37(3), 543-553.

White, Katherine and Darren W. Dahl (2007), "Are All Out-Groups Created Equal? Consumer Identity and Dissociative Influence," *Journal of Consumer Research,* 34(4), 525-536.

Understanding Design Elements in Bundles

Deny Belisle, Concordia University, Canada
H. Onur Bodur, Concordia University, Canada

Bundling strategy is widely used in today products and services markets. It refers to the selling of two or more products/services together at a single price (Stremersch and Tellis 2002). Past research suggests that the contingency level among bundled products (i.e., their complementarity, substitutability or independence) influences consumers' evaluation of the offer. On the one hand, products complementarity appears as an essential condition to building successful bundles (Guiltinan 1987). On the other hand, products substitutability is viewed as detrimental to bundle value (Venkatesh and Kamakura 2003). Despite the wide array of bundles offered in the marketplace, it is unknown whether contextual information provided with the offer such as price and image presentation formats can influence bundle attractiveness, by either highlighting products' complementarity or reducing their perceived substitutability.

Past work highlighted consumers' use of contextual information when evaluating bundles. Different contextual cues, such as the set of alternatives considered as well as their presentation format, can be used as a means to simplify information processing (e.g., Simonson and Tversky 1992). In line with this literature, we examine the influence of adopting a mixed-joint pricing strategy where the reduction is assigned to the total price of the bundle (Guiltinan 1987; Yadav and Monroe 1993) versus a mixed-leader strategy, where price reduction is applied to one of the bundled items only, on bundle attractiveness across contingency levels. We also investigate whether presenting the products under the same or in separate images affects consumers' perceived attractiveness of bundles of complements.

It is proposed here that using a mixed-joint pricing strategy is likely to emphasize complementarity among items, which essence is the joint use of products. It should therefore yield to a higher bundle attractiveness perception for bundles of complements as compared to a mixed-leader strategy. On the other hand, mixed-leader pricing strategy is expected to be beneficial to bundles of substitutes. Coherent with Blattberg and Wisniewski's (1989) findings, a mixed-leader strategy is expected to increase dissimilarity between substitutable products. Applying a reduction on only one product in a bundle composed of two equally-priced products makes the prices of these products different. As a result, products' similarity is reduced, therefore leading to a higher assessment of bundle attractiveness than when a mixed-joint strategy is adopted. Finally, these pricing strategies are not expected to differently influence the assessment of bundles of independent products.

To test our predictions, a first study was developed using a 2 (pricing strategy: mixed-joint (MJ) vs. mixed-leader (ML)) × 3 (contingency levels: complements, substitutes, independent products) between-subjects design. Three bundles of two equally-priced products differing in terms of contingency levels were chosen based on a pretest. The primary product of this triplet was identical across the three combinations. Three different add-on products determined bundles' contingency level. Each of the 150 participants evaluated one bundle offer, which was briefly presented with a picture of the products. An identical price reduction amount was applied to each bundle. However, the price reduction was presented either in a mixed-joint or in a mixed-leader format. Bundle description was immediately followed by 7-point scales measuring transaction value, willingness to buy, and discount attractiveness.

A MANOVA with transaction value, willingness to buy, and deal attractiveness as dependent variables revealed a significant multivariate interaction between price bundling strategy and products' contingency level ($F_{6,276} = 4.81$, p <.01). Items' preference and price consciousness did not have a significant influence on the dependent variables.

As expected, higher perceived transaction value ($M_{MJ} = 5.33$ vs. $M_{ML} = 4.45$; $F_{(1,46)} = 7.00$, p = .01), willingness to buy ($M_{MJ} = 5.16$ vs. $M_{ML} = 3.86$; $F_{(1,46)} = 12.02$, p < .01), and deal attractiveness ($M_{MJ} = 5.04$ vs. $M_{ML} = 4.24$; $F_{(1,46)} = 3.65$, p = .06) were reported for the bundle of complements when the identical price reduction amount was presented under a mixed-joint than under a mixed-leader format. Similarly, for the bundle of substitutes, higher perceived transaction value ($M_{MJ} = 4.21$ vs. $M_{ML} = 5.03$; $F_{(1,45)} = 4.16$, p < .05), willingness to buy ($M_{MJ} = 3.75$ vs. $M_{ML} = 4.68$; $F_{(1,45)} = 4.24$, p < .05), and deal attractiveness ($M_{MJ} = 3.33$ vs. $M_{ML} = 5.32$; $F_{(1,45)} = 23.99$, p < .01) were reported when the price reduction was presented under a mixed-leader than under a mixed-joint format. Finally, as expected, no significant difference between the two strategies was found for the bundle of independent products. These results support our predictions and suggest that price bundling strategy effectiveness depends on bundled products contingency level.

In study 2, we extend these context effects to the visual presentation of the bundle itself. Based on Fishbach and Zhang (2008), we expect that presenting products under the same image enhances their perceived complementarity more than presenting them under separate images. Therefore, presenting bundled products under a same image format is expected to lead to higher bundle perceived attractiveness than presenting products under a separate images format.

Fourty-two participants evaluated a bundle offer of complementary products presented in a mixed-joint format along with an illustration of the products that are either presented in the same photo or in two separate photos. As expected, higher perceived transaction value ($M_{SI} = 4.48$ vs. $M_{DI} = 3.68$; $F_{(1,40)} = 3.89$, p = .05), willingness to buy ($M_{SI} = 3.91$ vs. $M_{DI} = 2.93$; $F_{(1,40)} = 4.11$, p < .05), and deal attractiveness ($M_{SI} = 4.57$ vs. $M_{DI} = 3.71$; $F_{(1,40)} = 4.20$, p < .05) were found when the bundle offer was presented under a same image than a separate images format

This research provides evidence that perceived attractiveness of a bundle can be positively affected by contextual information present in the bundle offer. This is, to our knowledge, the first research that examines the impact of products' contingency level on price framing effect in a bundling context. Our results suggest that the superiority of a mixed-joint or mixed-leader strategy is contingent upon bundle composition. In addition, this research innovates by demonstrating that contextual information, not related to price (i.e., image presentation format), can also influence bundle perceived attractiveness.

REFERENCES

Blattberg, Robert C. and Kenneth J. Wisniewski (1989), "Price-Induced Patterns of Competition," *Marketing Science*, 8 (4), 291-309.

Fishbach, Ayalet and Ying Zhang (2008), "Together or Apart: When Goals and Temptations Complement versus Compete," *Journal of Personality and Social Psychology,* 94 (4), 547-559.

Guiltinan, Joseph P. (1987), "The Price Bundling of Services: A Normative Framework," *Journal of Marketing,* 51 (2), 74-85.

Simonson, Itamar and Amos Tversky (1992), "Choice in Context: Trade off Contrast and Extremeness Aversion," *Journal of Marketing Research,* 29 (3), 281-295.

Stremersch, Stefan and Gerard J. Tellis (2002), "Strategic Bundling of Products and Prices: A New Synthesis for Marketing," *Journal of Marketing,* 66 (1), 55-72.

Venkatesh R. and Wagner Kamakura (2003), "Optimal Bundling and Pricing under a Monopoly: Contrasting Complements and Substitutes from Independently Valued Products," *The Journal of Business*, 76 (2), 211-231.

Yadav, Manjit S. (1994), "How Buyers Evaluate Product Bundles: A Model of Anchoring and Adjustment," *Journal of Consumer Research,* 21 (2), 342-353.

Yadav, Manjit. S. and Kent B. Monroe (1993), "How Buyers Perceive Savings in a Bundle Price: An Examination of a Bundle's Transaction Value," *Journal of Marketing Research,* 30 (3), 350-358.

Perceived Difficulty of Manufacturing the Extension and Extension Evaluation: Do Perceptions of Complementarity and Substitutability Matter?

Vishal Bindroo, Indiana University South Bend, USA
Rajani Ganesh Pillai, North Dakota State University, USA

Brand extension – using an established brand name to enter a different product class – is frequently used by marketers to enter new categories (Aaker and Keller 1990). A good proportion of research in brand extension has focused on understanding the factors that influence consumers' attitude towards the extension product, including the perceived fit of the extension with the parent brand (Aaker and Keller 1990; Mao and Krishnan 2006). Mariadoss et al. (2010) note that despite the advances made in understanding influences on the attitudes towards the extension, a primary focus in extant research has been on the characteristics of the parent brand. In this research we extend the work of Mariadoss et al. (2010) to investigate two important characteristics of extension brands that may influence the relationship between perceived difficulty of manufacturing the extension and attitude towards the extension product: the perception of extension as complement of or substitute to the parent brand.

Perceived difficulty of manufacturing the extension (the difficulty of designing or making products in the extension category) has been shown to impact the evaluation of extension product (Aaker and Keller 1990). Mriadoss et al. (2010) investigated the often conflicting findings in literature (e.g. Aaker and Keller 1990; Bottomley and Holden 2001) to show that the relationship between perceived difficulty of manufacturing the extension and extension evaluation is not simple and linear as was often proposed, but instead is complex and non-linear. Additionally, they have called to investigate other inconsistent relationships in brand extension research. We heed this call by demonstrating that perceived complementarity and perceived substitutability of the extension product moderate the curvilinear relationship between perceived difficulty of manufacturing the extension and extension evaluation.

Perceived complementarity is defined as the extent to which the extended brand is jointly consumed with the parent brand to satisfy a specific need and perceived substitutability is defined as the extent to which the extended brand is perceived to be a substitute of the parent brand (Aaker and Keller 1990). We argue that both perceived complementarity and perceived substitutability moderate the curvilinear relationship between perceived difficulty of manufacturing the extension and evaluation of the extended product. We draw upon the literature in holistic versus analytical thinking (e.g. Monga and John 2007; Nisbett et al. 2001) to suggest that perceived complementarity of the extension product will induce consumers to use holistic thinking that encourages reliance on the context, complementarity of use, and relationships among objects to evaluate the extension (thinking style that is not primarily focused on evaluation of attributes). Further, complementarity itself becomes an additional cue in holistic thinking, aiding the evaluation of relatively less difficult to make extension that has fewer differentiating attributes. This leads to decrease in evaluation difficulty, which in turn, results in higher attitudes towards the extension. When the extension is considered to be extremely difficult to make, complementarity does not help as an additional cue in holistic thinking. It makes the evaluation of extension more difficult since the presence of so many attributes may in fact hinder successful evaluation of the extension in a holistic manner. This increase in evaluation difficulty will lead to lower attitudes towards the extension.

Unlike, complementarity, perceived substitutability will induce analytic thinking that is characterized by focus on evaluation of attributes (thinking style that is not focused on relationships and context, but rather on evaluation of attributes). Substitutable products that share several common and allignable attributes make such multiattribute evaluations more effortful and difficult, especially when there are fewer differentiating attributes as with trivial extensions. This increase in evaluation difficulty will lead to lower attitudes towards the extension. When the extension product is perceived to be extremely difficult to make, whereas, too many differentiating attributes are available for evaluation, doing so becomes even more difficult (Payne, Bettman, and Johnson 1993).

EMPIRICAL STUDY

We tested our predictions using a comprehensive database assembled by Bottomley and Holden (2001), which contains consumer perceptions of different brands and their extensions obtained from university students. In all, the comprehensive datatbase contained a total of 10,689 observations pooled from six separate data sets. The observations were generated by 9-18 evaluations of extensions per participant, as minimum of three parent brands and three brand extensions per brand were used in all the studies (cf. Mariadoss et al. 2010). All the variables in the study were measured. Perceived difficulty of manufacturing the extension (one 7-point item) and evaluation of extension (two 7-point items) was operationalized similar to Mariadoss et al. (2010). In addition, perceived complementarity and perceived substitutability were measured by one 7-point item each. Finally control variables like parent brand quality, and transferability of parent brand to extension were also measured consistent with Bottomley and Holden (2001). To control for within-respondent correlations, we estimated a mixed model as suggested by Echambadi et al. (2006) and Mariadoss et al. (2010). Results indicate support to our hypotheses that as perceived difficulty of manufacturing the extension increases, perceived complementarity significantly strengthens the relationship between perceived difficulty and extension evaluation ($\beta =0.007$, $p<.05$), whereas at extremely high levels of perceived difficulty, the relationship is significantly weakened ($\beta= -0.005$, $p< .01$). Perceived substitutability weakened the relationship between perceived difficulty and extension evaluation when extension was relatively less difficult to make ($\beta= -0.01$, $p<.05$), whereas in case of extremely difficult to make extensions ($\beta=0.001$, $p=NS$), we did not find statistical support. Thus, our predictions were largely supported, although results were clearer for complementary extensions.

DISCUSSION

This paper investigates an important research question as to whether perceived complementarity and perceived substitutability influence the relationship between perceived difficulty of manufacturing the extension and extension evaluation. We make theoretical contributions and attempt to resolve several inconsistent findings in the area of brand extension research. Further, the research has implications for managers who plan to leverage the equity of existing brand by introducing extensions that are either complements or substitutes of the parent brand. We show that complementarity helps in some cases but substitutability hurts the extension evaluation.

REFERENCES

Aaker, David . A. and Kevin L. Keller (1990), "Consumer evaluations of brand extensions," *Journal of Marketing*, 54(1), 27–41.

Bottomley, Paul. A., and Stephen J.S. Holden (2001), "Do We Really Know How Consumers Evaluate Brand Extensions? Empirical Generalizations Based on Secondary Analysis of Eight Studies," *Journal of Marketing Research*, 38(4), 494–500.

Echambadi, Raj, Inigo Arroniz, Werner Reinartz, and Junsoo Lee (2006),"Empirical Generalizations From Brand Extension Research: How Sure Are We?" International Journal of Research in Marketing, 23(6), 253-261.

Laroche, Michel., Mark Cleveland, Jasmin Bergeron, and Christine Goutaland (2003), "The Knowledge-Experience-Evaluation Relationship: A Structural Equations Modeling Test of Gender Differences," *Canadian Journal of Administrative Sciences*, 20(3), 246–259.

Mao, Huifang and Shanker Krishnan (2006), "Effects of Prototype and Exemplar Fit on Brand Extension Evaluations: A Two-Process Contingency Model," *Journal of Consumer Research*, 33(1), 41–49.

Mariadoss, Babu John, Raj Echambadi, Mark J. Arnold, and Vishal Bindroo, (2010) "An Examination of the Effects of Perceived Difficulty of Manufacturing the Extension Product on Brand Extension Attitudes," *Journal of the Academy of Marketing Science,* Volume 38, Number 6, 704-719

Monga, Alokparna B. and Deborah R. John (2007), "Cultural Differences in Brand Extension Evaluation: The Influence of Analytic versus Holistic Thinking," *Journal of Consumer Research* , 33 (March), 529-536.

Nisbett, Richard E., Kaiping Peng, Incheol Choic, and Ara Norenzayan (2001), " *Psychological Review*, 108 (April), 291-310.

Payne, John. W., James R. Bettman, and Eric J. Johnson (1993), *The Adaptive Decision Maker.* Cambridge, UK, Cambridge.

Poseurs: Understanding When Product Use is Perceived as Impression Management

Ethan Pancer, Queens University, Canada
Laurence Ashworth, Queens University, Canada

People frequently make inferences of consumers' personalities based on the products they use. The identity-signaling literature has largely assumed that observers interpret an identity signal as intended; e.g. if you ride a Harley, you are seen as rebellious. Along with emerging research (e.g. Ferraro, Kirmani, and Matherly 2010), we question this assumption and ask: What causes observers to think that a consumer is *intentionally* trying to create a certain impression? What is the effect of such motive judgments?

We know that "our possessions are a major contributor to and reflection of our identities" (Belk 1988, p. 139). This perspective has recently evolved into the identity-signaling literature, where researchers have demonstrated empirically that consumers use products to construct and express desired identities to others (e.g. Berger and Heath 2007; Escalas and Bettman 2005). In fact, we are pretty good at predicting what people will be like based on the products they use. People are able to 'read' elements of others (identities and other preferences) based on their possessions (e.g Belk, Bahn, and Mayer 1982; Gosling et al. 2002). Observers are able to form remarkably accurate impressions based on the belongings of others, even based on minimal information (Funder 2001; Gosling et al. 2002). These findings are certainly consistent with the idea that using trait-laden products allows the consumer to absorb and embody their symbolic values. So if we, as observers in the general public, believe that "you are what you eat / wear / use / consume," why would one ever believe this is not the case?

Another research stream questions the connection between a person and their products as solely identity expression. Impression management (IM) has been the subject of extensive research in both consumer behavior and social psychology (Schlenker and Weigold 1992; Leary 1995; White and Dahl 2007). This literature suggests that consumption may not always be motivated by identity expression, but is sometimes based on strategically influencing the opinions of others. Consumers have been shown to avoid products linked to dissociative reference groups (White and Dahl 2006; 2007), choose higher quality products in presence of others (Argo et al. 2005), and not use coupons to avoid looking cheap (Ashworth et al. 2005). Nevertheless, while people may able to 'read' people from their possessions, little attention has been paid to the ability to understand the intentionality and motives underlying behavior. Anecdotal evidence suggests that we do have the ability to make attributions about others as poseurs. Our research begins to examine the conditions where we question why people are using certain products, which instead, can lead to the inference that they are attempting to manipulate the image they create.

At the heart of the inference of an IM attempt is the idea that the observer believes the target is deliberately using a product in order to create a particular look. We believe that questions surrounding the target's motives for their appearance (of which an attempt to impression manage might be one) are initially inspired by product usage that cannot be explained by the situation. Observers are motivated to explain product usage when the product is seen as obviously not needed for the situation. This can be conceptualized as a product-situation discrepancy, where the central function of their product cannot be tied to elements of the situation i.e., wearing sunglasses when it is dark; using a scarf when it is warm. In these cases, the product use is seen as a little odd, not fitting with the norms of the particular situation. This discrepancy leads the researchers to the question: Which environmental cues are more suggestive of a motive of impression management versus something else?

Without other cues regarding the functional reasons for product use, observers are likely to use visible and salient cues in the environment that observers can use to deal with a product-situation discrepancy. The primary cue that is suggestive of an impression management motive is the perceived impact the image is having on others. One cause of impact is the overall positivity and extent of the impression, referred to forward as efficaciousness or efficacy of their look. If we believe that the product is responsible for making the target look good, we are likely to infer that they selected these products to create this impression.

278 university students responded to our 2 (Legitimacy of Product Use: Low vs. High) X 2 (Attractiveness of Product: Ugly vs. Attractive) X 2 (Brand Prominence: Logo Present vs. Logo Absent) between-subjects factorial design for course credit. Participants were shown an image of an individual wearing a scarf either indoors or outside, manipulating the legitimacy of scarf use. The scarf shown was either ugly or attractive (pre-tested earlier). Also, consistent with research on brand prominence (Han et al. 2010, Berger & Ward 2010), we manipulated the presence or absence of a Burberry logo.

As predicted, there was a significant interaction between legitimacy of product use and attractiveness of the product on the attribution of IM motive ($F(1,269) = 8.30, p < .01$). The target was perceived as significantly more motivated by IM concerns when they wore an attractive scarf inside (M = 4.51) compared with an ugly scarf inside (M = 3.97). When outside, a legitimate context for product use, inferences of IM motive attenuated. Interestingly, the presence of a large brand logo (M = 4.39) on the scarf was only marginally significant compared with the no logo condition (M = 4.15) ($F(1,269) = 3.26, p = .072$). This suggests that environmental cues and the efficaciousness of product use may be cues that are more suggestive of motive inferences than brand prominence. This research begins to examine the environmental cues which are suggestive of a motive of impression management. Although the target may have an appropriate functional reason for using a product in a certain context, observers may perceive a discrepancy between cues, which can ultimately lead to unintended outcomes. Future research will test cues beyond attractiveness that are suggestive of this motive as well as additional observer-related moderating variables.

REFERENCES:

Argo, Jennifer J., Darren W. Dahl, and Rajesh V. Manchanda (2005), "The Influence of a Mere Social Presence in a Retail Context," *Journal of Consumer Research*, 32 (September), 207-212.

Ashworth, Laurence, Peter R. Darke, and Mark Schaller (2005), "No one wants to look cheap: Trade-offs between social disincentives and the economic and psychological incentives to redeem coupons," *Journal of Consumer Psychology*, 15(4), 295-306.

Belk, Russell W., Kenneth D. Bahn, and Robert N. Mayer (1982), "Developmental Recognition of Consumption Symbolism," *Journal of Consumer Research, 9* (June), 4–17.

Belk, Russell W. (1988), "Possessions and the Extended Self," Journal of Consumer Research, 15 (September), 139–67.

Berger, Jonah and Chip Heath (2007), "Where Consumers Diverge from Others: Identity-Signaling and Product Domains," *Journal of Consumer Research,* 34 (August), 121–34.

Escalas, Jennifer and James R. Bettman (2005), "Self-Construal, Reference Groups, and Brand Meaning," *Journal of Consumer Research*, 32 (3), 378–89.

Ferraro, Rosellina, Amna Kirmani, and Ted Matherly (2010), "Signaling Identity Through Brands: The Role of Perceived Authenticity," in Advances in Consumer Research Volume 37, eds. Margaret C. Campbell, Jeff Inman, and Rik Pieters, Duluth, MN : Association for Consumer Research.

Funder, David C. (2001), Personality. *Annual Review of Psychology, 52,* 197–221.

Gosling, Samuel D., Sei Jin Ko, Thomas Mannarelli, and Margaret E. Morris (2002), "A Room with a Cue: Personality Judgments Based on Offices and Bedrooms," *Journal of Personality and Social Psychology*, 82(3), 379-398.

Leary, Mark (1995), Self-Presentation: Impression Management and Interpersonal Behavior, Boulder, CO: Westview Press.

Schlenker, Barry R. and Michael F. Weigold (1992), "Interpersonal processes involving impression regulation and management," *Annual Review of Psychology*, 43, 133-168.

White, Katherine and Darren W. Dahl (2006), "To Be or Not Be? The Influence of Dissociative Reference Groups on Consumer Preferences," *Journal of Consumer Psychology*, 16(4), 404-414.

White, Katherine and Darren W. Dahl (2007), "Are All Out-Groups Created Equal? Consumer Identity and Dissociative Influence," *Journal of Consumer Research*, 34 (4), 525-536.

Word-of-Mouth vs. Number-of-Mouth and the (Mis)Communication of Preferences

Samuel Bond, Georgia Tech, USA
Stephen Xihao He, Georgia Tech, USA
Talya Miron-Shatz, University of Pennsylvania, Ono Academic College, USA

Mirroring recent growth in social networks and consumer-generated content, word-of-mouth (WOM) research has regained attention in marketing theory and practice. Among various purposes served by consumer WOM, one important function is to communicate speakers' evaluations of goods or services, and this advisory role of WOM is perhaps most clearly illustrated by online product reviews. A burgeoning literature has explored the content of these communication efforts and their relation to audience inferences, persuasion, and firm performance (Chevalier and Mayzlin 2006; Weiss, Lurie, and MacInnis 2008; Schellekens, Verlegh, and Smidts 2010). In contrast, we focus on the ability of consumer WOM to perform its basic communication function. This issue is important to consumers and marketers alike, as more accurate WOM not only benefits consumer decision processing, outcomes, and satisfaction, but also enables more efficient use of WOM as a communications and feedback tool.

Consumers exchange WOM in a variety of forms varying in richness and complexity. We focus on two distinctive forms that represent opposite extremes: attribute ratings and commentary. For example, when sharing our opinions about a product online (e.g., a hotel stay), some forums allow open-ended discussion of anything deemed relevant (e.g., a description of our experience), while other forums restrict communication to ratings of specific features (e.g., cleanliness, location). Each format has distinct advantages for communicating one's opinion. Attributes are concise and easily understood; to the extent that relevant attributes are included, this format is consistent with multi-attribute utility models (Holbrook and Havlena 1988), enabling recipients to 'calculate' a sender's opinion. Commentaries are not conducive to such mental calculation and the process of verbally transcribing one's opinions is inherently noisy. However, commentary provides a far richer context offering its own advantages (e.g., West, Huber, and Min 2004; Escalas 2007). Commentaries allow speakers to express not only 'pros and cons', but also the idiosyncratic importance of those pros and cons to that speaker. In addition, commentaries aggregate components of a consumption experience to convey an overall impression, while attributes artificially separate the experience in a manner that may exaggerate single positive or negative aspects (Thaler 1985). Importantly, both these advantages are compounded for very positive or negative experiences, which often result from extreme performance on a few important dimensions. Therefore, building on prior evidence that narratives elicit stronger affective reactions (Adaval and Wyer 1998), we suggest that commentary is particularly suited to transmission of highly valenced opinions, so that any advantage of attributes over commentary in communicating evaluations will be attenuated when those evaluations are extreme.

Utilizing actual consumer reviews from a popular travel website, Study 1 examined individuals' ability to predict the hotel evaluations of reviewers. Twenty five reviews (each from a different hotel) were selected from the website using a stratified random sampling procedure. Undergraduate participants (N=109) were assigned to one of three conditions: participants in the *commentary* condition were given the body of review text to read; participants in the *attribute* condition were given the reviewers' rating of specific attributes (e.g., "service = 3/5"), and participants in the *combination* condition were given both forms of content together. Participants read reviews for five different hotels, one at a time. After reading each review, they were asked to estimate what overall rating the reviewer gave for the hotel (on a 5-pt. scale).

Communication error was calculated by taking the absolute deviation between a participant's estimate and the reviewer's overall rating. In support of our hypotheses, analysis revealed a significant interaction between information type and evaluation extremity. For hotels rated far from the mean, commentary and combination were more effective than attributes; for medium-rated hotels, attributes were more effective.

A follow-up analysis explored how the effectiveness of commentaries related to their linguistic content. Each of the 25 commentaries was analyzed using the Linguistic Inquiry and Word Count tool (Pennebaker, Booth, and Francis 2001), which categorizes words from a target script into over 70 linguistic or psychological categories. Descriptive analyses yielded interesting insights (e.g., positive emotional content greatly outnumbered negative content - Liu 2006)' surprisingly, longer reviews did not enhance communication (c.f. Mudambi and Schuff 2010). Words describing cognitive processes accounted for fully 16% of review content, and greater use of these words was a significant predictor of communication error. Moreover, cognitive process content was found to partially mediate the effect of extremity, supporting the notion that the idiosyncratic theorizing inherent to neutral evaluations is partly responsible for their greater communication error.

A defining property of WOM communication is its ability to be absorbed and retransmitted along a 'chain' of communicators. Building on the first study, we suggest that the disadvantages of commentary-based WOM make it especially unsuited to accurate retransmission. In particular, if the likelihood of commentary elements being retransmitted depends solely on their vividness than their representativeness, certain valuable elements will be "lost" as the chain progresses. Study 2 explored the implications of this property for communication effectiveness by adopting a 'telephone-game' framework (Bartlett 1932; Brown and Reingen 1987). After a screening process, one hotel review was selected from those used in Study 1. Undergraduate students (n=135) were divided into 45 different 'chains' of three participants apiece. The first member of each chain was given the original hotel review in one of three formats (*commentary, attributes*, or a *combination*), along with the reviewer's overall evaluation. After completing a short filler task, they were then asked to both reproduce the original review to the best of their ability and recall the evaluation. The next member in each chain was provided the first member's reproduced WOM, without any evaluation, and then (after a delay) asked to both reproduce it themselves and estimate the original evaluation. This process was repeated for the third member of the chain.

Decay of information was captured by the absolute difference between the original reviewer's evaluation and the estimates of each member along the chain. Analysis of decay revealed an interaction between stage and information type. Follow-up analyses showed that for *commentary* and *combination* conditions, the accuracy of review estimates fell sharply from stage-1 to stage-2, and continued to decline at stage-3. In contrast, decay in the *attribute* condition was negligible across the sequence. Examination of the reproductions themselves revealed an explanation in keeping with our arguments. Although the original evaluation was positive (4/5), reproductions in the *commentary* condition contained a disproportionate level of content that was vivid but negative (and therefore unrepresentative); in the *attribute* conditions this was not the case.

Taken together, our results provide insights regarding the utility of consumer WOM for performing a basic but critical function: communicating the speaker's preference. As such, this research represents an initial foray into a topic of growing importance to the field of consumer behavior. In addition, our findings have important implications for marketers interested in utilizing WOM to inform or influence consumer learning, choice, and satisfaction.

REFERENCES:

Adaval, Rashmi and Robert S. Wyer Jr (1998), "The Role of Narratives in Consumer Information Processing," *Journal of Consumer Psychology*, 7 (3), 207.

Bartlett, Frederic C. (1932), *Remembering: A study in experimental and social psychology*, Cambridge, England: Cambridge University Press.

Borgida, Eugene and Richard E. Nisbett (1977), "The Differential Impact of Abstract vs. Concrete Information on Decisions," *Journal of Applied Social Psychology*, 7 (3), 258-71.

Brown, Jacqueline J. and Peter H. Reingen (1987), "Social Ties and Word-of-Mouth Referral Behavior," *Journal of Consumer Research*, 14 (3), 350-62.

Chevalier, Judith A. and Dina Mayzlin (2006), "The Effect of Word of Mouth on Sales: Online Book Reviews," *Journal of Marketing Research*, 43(3), 345-54.

Escalas, Jennifer Edson (2007), "Self-Referencing and Persuasion: Narrative Transportation versus Analytical Elaboration," *Journal of Consumer Research*, 33 (4), 421-29.

Holbrook, M. B. and W. J. Havlena (1988), "Assessing the Real-to-Artificial Generalizability of Multiattribute Attitude Models in Tests of New Product Designs," *Journal of Marketing Research*, 25(1), 25-35.

Liu, Yong (2006), "Word of Mouth for Movies: Its Dynamics and Impact on Box Office Revenue," *Journal of Marketing*, 70 (3), 74-89.

Pennebaker, J. W., R.J. Booth, and M.E. Francis (2001), *Linguistic Inquiry and Word Count (LIWC): LIWC2001*, Mahwah: Lawrence Erlbaum Associates.

Schellekens, Gaby A. C., Verlegh, Peeter W. J. and Ale Smidts (2010), "Language Abstraction in Word of Mouth," *Journal of Consumer Research*, 37(2), 207-23.

Thaler, Richard (1985), "Mental Accounting and Consumer Choice," *Marketing Science*, 4 (3), 199.

Weiss, Allen M., Lurie, Nicholas H. and Deborah J. Macinnis, "Listening to Strangers: Whose Responses are Valuable, How Valuable are They, and Why?," *Journal of Marketing Research*, 45(4), 425-36.

West, P. M., Huber, Joel, and K. S. Min (2004), "Altering Experienced Utility: The Impact of Story Writing and Self-Referencing on Preferences," *Journal of Consumer Research*, 31(3), 623-30.

The Dark Side of Social Consumption:
Behavioral Addiction in the WoW Online Brand Community

Darrell Bartholomew, Oklahoma State University, USA
Marlys Mason, Oklahoma State University, USA

Past literature has revealed a dark side to consumption in terms of compulsive behaviors and addictions (Hirschman 1992; O'Guinn and Faber 1989). Such adverse consumption has typically been examined in contexts involving products with addictive physical attributes (e.g., tobacco, drugs) or in contexts where compulsive tendencies arise due to the pleasurable engagement derived from the consumption (e.g., gambling, excessive shopping, binge eating). In today's high-tech world, an excessive use of technology has prompted questions about whether some behaviors (e.g., excessive texting, online gaming) may also exhibit compulsive patterns.

Research in brand communities has also alluded to a potential dark, compulsive side that may result for some participants. Schouten and colleagues (2007 p. 366) note that, "there may be a fine line between the well-being of transcendence (flow) and the dangers of addictive escapism… it appears that one person's path to bliss may be another person's road to ruin." Virtual brand communities may pose one such threat for heightened addiction due to transcendent nature of technology and immersion in the virtual/online (rather than tangible/physical) realm.

The purpose of this research is to explore the merging of technology, transcendence, and community in heightening the potential for compulsive consumption. We examine this phenomena in the context of online gaming. Drawing upon the addiction literature and through a lens of social learning, we explore the nature and potential for compulsive consumption in the online brand community of the World of Warcraft (WoW). Using a netnographic approach (Kozinets 2006), we examine a popular blog set up for current and former gamers of WoW. This blog contains more than 2,000 anonymous entries posted over a four year period. WoW was the chosen context because it is estimated that as many as 40% of WOW players are addicted (Ahn 2007).

CONCEPTUAL BACKGROUND

Compulsive consumption is defined as, "…a response to an uncontrollable drive or desire to obtain, use, or experience a feeling, substance, or activity that leads an individual to repetitively engage in behavior that will ultimately cause harm to the individual and/or to others" (O'Guinn and Faber 1989, p. 148). Compulsive consumers may be aware of the harmful personal consequences, but are driven and 'lose control' by the psychological fulfillment derived from the consumption. Similarly, addiction is viewed as a psychological or physical dependence on something (Herie 2007), with behavioral addictions involving "an impulse-control disorder that does not involve an intoxicant" (Young 1998). Compulsive, addictive consumption may be especially difficult to break if it involves social identification with other product users/community members. For example, smoking and drinking are embedded in the norms and socialization of some groups, and ending the substance use would involve renegotiating group inclusion. New forms of consumption and community affiliation which is co-constructed through technology may be particularly prone to such behavioral addictions.

ANALYSIS

The goal of our analysis was twofold: 1) to identify how online gaming attributes and communities may contribute to the potential for compulsive behavior, and 2) to explore the nature of harmful outcomes (if any) may be occurring. Transcendent consumer experiences (TCE; Schouten et al 2007) and social learning theory are used to guide the analysis. TCE are defined as "peak" and "flow" experiences in a consumption context (Schouten, McAlexander and Koenig 2007) where individuals feel more active, alert, happy, and become highly focused and immersed in the activity. TCE can be enhanced by both the social aspect of the community and attributes of the product. Social learning (Bandura 1977) and its processes of 1) attention, 2) retention, 3) motor reproduction, and 4) motivation can shed light on how transcendent elements may built into online gaming. Table 1 highlights our findings within this framework. Table 2 then presents emergent themes in the blogs of harmful consequences stemming from compulsive involvement in the online brand community.

Attention in Game Environment	Retention through TCE
Game play is joined, game always active (real-time) leading to immersion. High quality graphics, sound and 3-D stimulate sensory engagement Game world is continuous (can never be fully explored) Game advancement is never-ending (goals/ rewards always changing)	Entering game, escapism. Enjoyment through anticipation and play Rewards in power/skill increases Attainment of high levels form of peak experience Achieving state of TCE increasingly important
Avatar Modeling Active character performing acts Customizable character reflect ideal self Race, gender uninhibited Rewards for violent acts is acceptable norm	**Social Motivation** Socialization part of game structure Team efforts to achieve game goals Game activities are socially structured Norms jointly enforced company and group Characters are part of a group identity that allows for group inclusion Stories are shared in game that motivate continuation with storyline. Tools given for documentation (record videos) and sharing game themes with others.

Table 1. Social Learning Theory Applied to Video Games

Based on these	Expressions of Harm	Consequences of Harm
Behavioral Harm	Sleep deprivation Eating deprivation Eye strain No desire to leave the game Physical aggression towards others Verbal aggression towards others Depression Trying to quit Absenteeism Neglecting school work/attendance Preoccupation with the game and virtual world	Neglect of housekeeping Poor health Poor eyesight Homebound by choice Physical abuse, violent acts w/ weapon Verbal abuse Suicide Inability to quit Loss of Jobs Lower grades, drop out of school Retaking classes Inability to concentrate on other tasks and tangible world
Social Harm	Neglecting relationships outside of game and virtual community Lying about playing Socializing in the game	Loss of relationships, divorce Child neglect Loss of Trust Loss of social activities outside game

Table 2. Signs of Addictive Gaming Behavior.

Our initial coding suggests that addictive patterns are occurring that harm both the community member and others. Our findings can be used can shed light on the harm that may be caused by some forms of brand communities and technology. We hope these insights foster new ways for envisioning and transforming emerging societal problems related to gaming and behavioral addiction that have not been addressed by the industry or the government.

REFERENCES

Ahn, Joe and Randall, George (2007). "Computer Game Addiction." in: Clemson University.
Bandura, Albert (1977). *Social Learning Theory*. Englewood Cliffs, N.J.: Prentice Hall.
Herie, Marilyn, Godden, Tim, Shenfeld, Joanne, and Kelly, Colleen (2007). "Addiction: An Information Guide." http://www.camh.net/About_Addiction_Mental_Health/Drug_and_Addiction_Information/Addiction_Information_Guide/addiction_infoguide.pdf.
Hirschman, Elizabeth C. (1992). "The Consciousness of Addiction: Toward a General Theory of Compulsive Consumption." *Journal of Consumer Research* 19 (2), 155.
Kozinets, Robert V. (2006). "Click to Connect: Netnography and Tribal Advertising." *Journal of Advertising Research* 46 (3), 279-88.

O'Guinn, Thomas C. and Ronald J. Faber (1989). "Compulsive Buying: A Phenomenological Exploration." *Journal of Consumer Research* 16 (2), 147-57.

Schouten, John W. , James H. McAlexander, and Harold F. Koenig (2007). "Transcendent Customer Experience and Brand Community." *Academy of Marketing Science* 35, 357.

Young, Kimberly S. (1998). "Internet Addiction: The Emergence of a New Clinical Disorder." *CyberPsychology & Behavior* 1 (3), 237-44.

The Role of Self-Regulatory Focus, Self-View, and Benefit Focus in Attitudes Toward Organic Brands

Ioannis Kareklas, Washington State University, USA
Jeffrey Carlson, University of Connecticut, USA

The organic food segment has experienced considerable growth over the past two decades (Organic 2010). According to the Organic Trade Association (2010), U.S. sales of organic food and beverages have grown from $1 billion in 1990 to $24.8 billion in 2009. Extant research suggests two main attitudinal and behavioral influences of organic food consumption: 1) concern for one's health (e.g., Chen 2009) and, 2) concern for the environment (e.g., Squires et al. 2001; Wandel and Bugge 1997). However, despite these influences, Hughner et al. (2007) observe that the majority of organic researchers have focused mostly on the demographic differences of consumers, at the expense of important behavioral influences (e.g., attitudes, goals, etc.). Hence, the purpose of this study is to understand how a consumer's attitudinal preferences toward organic food intersect with organic food labels in impacting consumers' organic food attitudes. Given the relative importance of the concern for one's own health and concern for the environment in regards to organic food, we test how the manipulation of such factors can interact and subsequently affect consumers' attitudes toward an organic brand.

THEORETICAL BACKGROUND

The theoretical foundations for this study stems from two areas. First, is that the view of self intersects and in influenced by broad society (see Fiske et al. 1998 for a review). This often results in an independent focus (e.g., unique individual characteristics, concern for one's health) or interdependent focus (e.g., one's self defined by others, a focus on greater good for society, etc.). The second conceptual foundation is regulatory focus theory (Higgins 1997). Aaker and Lee (2001) show promotion-focused message are more persuasive on individuals with an active, independent self-view. However, prevention-focused messages are more persuasive if an individual has an active, interdependent self-view. Given that a focus on one's self or for the environment drives organic food attitudes and purchase intention, we study how prevention and promotion-framed food messages intersect with one's active self-view. Based on Aaker and Lee's (2001) findings, one can expect promotion-framed messages to more effective with an active, independent self-view and a prevention-framed message to more effective with an active, interdependent self-view. Our study addresses how this process is impacted by the focus of the organic food labels, whether they highlights personal health benefits versus environmental benefits (a common practice in organic food labeling).

METHOD

We examined evaluations of an organic brand of milk called Farmer's Cow. While this is an existing brand sold in Connecticut, it was presented to participants at a large west coast university as "a new brand of organic milk," produced by a group of six local dairy farms, that is now available in their local grocery stores. We used a 2 (self-view prime: independent or interdependent) x 2 (benefit type: promotion or prevention) x 2 (benefit focus: personal health benefits or environmental benefits) between-subject design.

Existing research has shown that self-view and regulatory focus can be activated using a situational prime (Aaker and Williams 1998). The situational prime we used to activate the desired self-view was manipulated by using a picture focusing on an individual or group of people, accompanied by text. Regulatory-focus was manipulated through differences in text (e.g., a prevention message emphasized the presence or absence of negatives). Finally, benefit focus was manipulated by exposing half the participants to messages that focused on the environment versus a focus on personal health). All manipulations scored in the expected direction on manipulation check questions. Our dependent variable, attitude toward the brand, was measured using three seven-point scale items ($\alpha = .93$).

RESULTS

Results show a significant three-way interaction ($F (1, 188) = 8.53$, $p = .004$) between the factors. If the focus in on environment ($F (1, 101) = 5.70$, $p = .019$), a promotion-farmed message (M = 5.63, SD = 1.06) is more persuasive than a prevention-framed message (M = 5.32, SD = 1.17) with an active independent self-view. However, a prevention-farmed message (M = 5.58, SD = .70) is more persuasive than a promotion-framed message (M = 4.89, SD = 1.13) with an active interdependent self-view. If the focus in on personal-health ($F (1, 85) = 4.01$, $p = .049$), a prevention-farmed message (M = 5.54, SD = 1.10) is more persuasive than a promotion-framed message (M = 5.03, SD = 1.16) with an active independent self-view. However, a promotion-farmed message (M = 5.69, SD = .88) is more persuasive than a promotion-framed message (M = 5.59, SD = 1.49) with an active interdependent self-view.

DISCUSSION AND FUTURE RESEARCH

The results of this study make several theoretical and practical contributions. First, it extends previous works on self-view and regulatory focus and shows that promotion-framed messages are not always most persuasive with an independent self-view (or that prevention-framed message are not always most persuasive with an interdependent self-view). In other words, "I" do not always seek pleasure and "we" do not always avoid pains. Specifically, if an organic food message focuses on the environment, then "I" avoid pain and "We" seek pleasure. We do find, though, that Aaker and Lee's original finding does apply to messages that focus on personal health. This finding underscores that in an organic food context, a focus on personal health versus environmental health is important. In our next study, we are exploring the mechanism that helps explain these results. Second, we believe the results of this study can inform practitioners in the design of better organic food messages (e.g., labels). Finally, consumers' can also better understand the often overlooked forces that impact their daily purchase attitudes and decisions.

REFERENCES

Aaker, Jennifer and Angela Lee (2001), "'I' Seek Pleasures and 'We' Avoid Pains: The Role of Self-Regulatory Goals in Information Processing and Persuasion," Journal of Consumer Research, 28 (June), 33–49.

Aaker, Jennifer and Patti Williams (1998), "Empathy versus Pride: The Influence of Emotional Appeals across Cultures," Journal of Consumer Research, 25 (December), 241-261.

Chen, Mei-Fiang (2009), "Attitude toward organic foods among Taiwanese as related to health consciousness, environmental attitudes, and the mediating effects of a healthy lifestyle," *British Food Journal*, 111 (2), 165.

Fiske, Alan, Shinobu Kitayama, Hazel R. Markus, and Richard Nisbett (1998), "The Cultural Matrix of Social Psychology," in The Handbook of Social Psychology, Daniel T. Gilbert and Susan T. Fiske, Eds. Vol. 2. Boston: McGraw-Hill.

Higgins, E. Tory (1997), "Beyond pleasure and pain," *American Psychologist*, 52 (12), 1280-300.

Hughner, Renee Shaw, Pierre McDonagh, Andrea Prothero, Clifford J. Shultz, II, and Julie Stanton (2007), "Who are organic food consumers? A compilation and review of why people purchase organic food," *Journal of Consumer Behaviour*, 6 (2), 94-110.

Organic Trade Association (2010), "Industry Statistics and Projected Growth," http://www.ota.com/organic/mt/business.html.

Squires, L., B. Juric, and T. Bettina Cornwell (2001), "Level of market development and intensity of organic food consumption: cross-cultural study of Danish and New Zealand consumers," *Journal of Consumer Marketing*, 18 (5), 392-409.

Wandel, Margareta and Annechen Bugge (1997), "Environmental concern in consumer evaluation of food quality," *Food Quality and Preference*, 8 (1), 19-26.

Is Negative Brand Publicity Always Damaging? The Moderating Role of Power

David Norton, University of South Carolina, USA
Alokparna Monga, University of South Carolina, USA
William Bearden, University of South Carolina, USA

As consumers have increasing access to multiple sources for product information (e.g., blogs, television, news outlets, etc.), the ability to manage negative publicity becomes increasingly difficult. Prior research has demonstrated that consumers place more weight on negative than positive information in forming judgments (Eagly and Chaiken, 1993) showing that negative publicity can cause substantial harm. For example, the recent events surrounding British Petroleum's oil spill in the Gulf of Mexico have led to detrimental effects on the brand.

We know that negative publicity can be damaging for brands ((Menon et al. 1999; Tybout et al. 1981). Surprisingly, little research has focused on characteristics of the message recipients and how they might influence responses to negative publicity (Ahluwalia, Unnava and Burnkrant, 2000; Monga and John, 2008). In this vein, we examine the effect of consumers' power on responses to negative publicity. Power is an important characteristic to study, as it is ubiquitous and highly malleable. In many instances throughout our daily life, we may be shifting between a high power (e.g., meeting with a subordinate) and a low power (e.g., meeting with a boss) mindset. Aside from these situational variations, power is also conceptualized as an individual difference which varies across consumers (Anderson and Galinsky, 2006).

In this research, we suggest that high power individuals are less likely to be affected by negative publicity than low power individuals. Galinsky et al. (2008) find that high power people possess more freedom from influence of external forces compared to low power people. High power people are less influenced and constrained by salient information in the environment, because power increases sensitivity to internal states and increases confidence in one's own thoughts (Brinol et al., 2007). This sensitivity to internal states suggests that high power individuals may rely more on their own thoughts about the brand and are less likely to be influenced by negative publicity information, compared to low power individuals. Thus, upon exposure to negative publicity, brand evaluations of high power individuals would be more favorable than those of low power individuals.

In study 1, we test our hypothesis using a power manipulation (Galinksy et al., 2008) in a 2 Power: High, Low) x 2 (Stimuli: negative information, control) between subjects design. In the high power condition, participants wrote about a situation in which he/she controlled the ability of another person or persons to get something they wanted. In the low power condition, participants wrote about a situation in which another person controlled the ability of the participant to get something he/she wanted. Next, participants in the negative information condition were exposed to a press release stating that BMW was experiencing manufacturing problems on their new line of cars. Participants in the control condition (who served as a baseline) were not exposed to the press release. Subsequently, participants rated the BMW brand on attitude and belief scales. As expected, when exposed to the negative information, participants in the high power condition rated the brand more favorably than participants in the low power condition. In contrast, there were no differences between low and high power participants in the control condition. Further, high power participants also weighted the negative information less heavily than did low power participants.

In study 2, we examine the role of source credibility (Brinol et al., 2004). We anticipate that when negative information originates from a less credible source, high power individuals would be less susceptible to the negative publicity than low power individuals (as in our prior study). However, for a more credible source, which is likely to be a more powerful source, we expect that high power individuals would be more likely to attend to the negative publicity and their brand evaluations would decrease. As a result, differences in brand evaluations between low power and high power individuals would dissipate.

In study 2, participants were exposed to the same power manipulation as in study 1. The source of the press release was indicated as either a highly credible source (*The Wall Street Journal*) or a significantly less credible source (*The National Enquirer*). Participants in this condition were not exposed to the negative publicity. Thus, we used a 2 (Power: High, Low) x 3 (Source Credibility: High, Low, Control) between subjects design. Our results show a significant interaction between power and credibility on brand evaluations, such that in the low credibility condition high power individuals evaluate the brand higher (and weight the negative information less heavily) than low power individuals. However, this difference dissipated in the high credibility condition. Further, no differences emerged in the control condition.

In study 3 we examine the role of thought confidence (Petty et al. 2002). High power people tend to be more confident in their own thoughts and consequently place less weight on external information. If we boost the confidence of low power individuals before they are exposed to negative information, we expect that they would be less likely to rely on external information in brand evaluations. Consequently, we expect their brand evaluations of low power individuals would rise to the level of the high power individuals, thus eliminating the difference.

In study 3 participants were exposed to a confidence priming task, such that people in the high confidence condition wrote about a time they felt confident in their abilities and individuals in the low confidence condition wrote about a time they were skeptical or less confident of their abilities. Power was measured using the Sense of Power (SOP) scale (Anderson and Berdahl 2002). Thus, we used a 2 (Power: High, Low) x 3 (Confidence: High, Low, Control) between subjects design. Our results show a significant interaction between power and confidence, such that in the low confidence condition high power individuals evaluate the brand higher (and weight the negative information less heavily) than low power individuals. However, this difference dissipates in the high confidence condition, with evaluations of low power individuals rising to the level of the high power individuals. Further, no differences emerged in the control condition.

The findings in our paper contribute to the negative publicity literature and to the largely understudied area of consumer power. Prior research shows that negative publicity can adversely affect the brand. We show that this effect is more likely to happen for low power than high power consumers, except when the source of the negative information is highly credible or when the consumer's confidence is high.

REFERENCES

Anderson, Cameron and Adam D. Galinsky (2006), "Power, optimism, and risk-taking," *European Journal of Social Psychology,* 36, 511-36.

Ahluwalia, R., Burnkrant, R. E., & Unnava. H. R. (2000). Consumer response to negative publicity: The moderating role of commitment, *Journal of Marketing Research*, 37, 203-214.

Briñol, P., Petty, R. E., Valle, C., Rucker, D. D., & Becerra, A. (2007). The effects of message recipients' power before and after persuasion: A self-validation analysis. *Journal of Personality and Social Psychology, 93,* 1040-1053.

Eagly, A., & Chaiken, S. (1993). *The psychology of attitudes*, Fort Worth, TX: Harcourt Brace Jovanovich.

Galinsky, A. D., Magee, J. C., Gruenfeld, D. H, Whitson, J., & Liljenquist, K. A. (2008). Social power reduces the strength of the situation: Implications for creativity, conformity, and dissonance. *Journal of Personality and Social Psychology*, 95, 1450-1466.

Monga, A. B. and D. R. John (2008), "When Does Negative Brand Publicity Hurt? The Moderating Influence of Analytic Versus Holistic Thinking," *Journal of Consumer Psychology*, 18 (4), 320-332.

Can Colors Make Me Happy? The Effect Of Color On Mood: A Meta-Analysis

Jamie Hyodo, Pennsylvania State University, USA

Being visually-oriented creatures, color is a pervasive and encompassing feature of our visual environment. There is not a single physical thing that cannot be described by its color. Furthermore, colors have long been understood to be used as judgement criteria. Some of these judgements are widely agreed upon, such as a blue sky being a source of pleasure, but many more are personal judgements, such as favorite colors, or reactions to clothing. In these personal contexts, colors are seen to have the power to alter the meaning and value of an object.

Colors can also add meaning to objects or environments via association. For example, red is often considered a color of aggression or anger due to it also being the color of blood (Grossman 1999). These meanings may vary by culture; for example, white symbolizes mourning or death in many East Asian cultures (Ricks 1983), but happiness or purity in Australia, New Zealand, and the USA (Neal et al 2002).

Despite the potential impact of color in an exchange environment, many practitioners spend very little time or effort deciding on color. Those that do spend time making color decisions may be skewed by personal biases or weigh the aesthetic value disproportionately when compared to potential symbolism inferences.

While some researchers measure the direct effect of color on purchasing behavior (Bellizzi & Hite, 1992), many more follow the belief that the effect of color on behavior is mediated by mood. Specifically, there is a growing body of research which recognizes the effects of warm and cool colors on a range of pleasure and arousal constructs (Cheng, Wu, & Yen, 2009). This literature, however, has not been comprehensively evaluated to this point, and many of the findings have been widely varying in effect size and even effect direction in some cases. Therefore, a meta-analysis, a systematic statistical tool, will be used to quantitatively synthesize these diverse findings.

The primary purpose of this meta-analysis is to analyse the color-mood relationship, with the understanding that consumer mood can have a significant impact on behaviour. Drawing on the collective efforts of many researchers in their individual studies of color and affect, I conduct two meta-analyses, analyzing the overall effects of warm versus cool colors on both arousal and pleasure.

Following a review of the relevant literature, I will aggregate the findings of past publications in order to determine the overall effect of warm versus cool colors on the pleasure and arousal constructs. I will also use the statistical power of the combined vast quantity of data to explore the possibility of a series of moderating variables in the color-mood relationship. Finally, I will address future research needs in this area.

LITERATURE REVIEW

Research on color is part of the study of 'atmospherics.' The field of atmospherics came about as a result of earlier psychology work in the field of environmental behaviour. Environment-behavioral theory suggests that individuals interact with the environment around them, resulting in certain responses and behaviors (Lewin, 1951).

Kotler (1973) examined environmental psychology through a marketing lens when he examined the idea of the physical environment as an important part of the total consumption package. He believed that the atmosphere of a purchase environment had an effect on purchase intentions, and identified an initial set of variables which affect the perceived quality of a business atmosphere. These variables were termed 'atmospherics' (Kotler, 1973). While the concept of atmosphere had been recognized as important in service and entertainment industries, this had not been considered as a valuable feature for most other consumption and exchange environments.

Research on the influence of atmospheric variables built off of this early work to currently encompass five categories: external variables, general interior variables, layout and design variables, point-of-purchase and decoration variables, and human variables (Turley & Milliman, 2000). A prominent feature that is relevant across all five categories is color.

Color

Color is an ever-present characteristic of products as well as less intrusive elements of the exchange environment, such as lighting, decorations, themes, signage, and walls. Most consumers have a 'favorite' color and are subconsciously attracted or repelled from spaces or objects as a result of the color of these spaces and objects. Colors have also been classified as warm and cool. The descriptor 'warm' is colloquial, but is generally accepted to include the colors red, yellow, and to a lesser extent, orange. Red is the 'warmest' color. Color can be measured by wavelength within the electromagnetic spectrum, and within the visible spectrum (400-700 nm), red has the longest wavelength of any color (650 nm) (Kusterer, 2007). The descriptor 'cool' is also colloquial, and is generally accepted to include the colors blue and green. Blue is the 'coolest' color, and generally considered to be opposite to red. Blue has one of the shortest wavelengths (475 nm) (Kusterer, 2007).

While it is not wholly certain why different colors have effects on behavior, one area of research that may help to explain these effects is associative learning (Grossman & Wisenblit, 1999). This theory indicates that consumers learn color preferences for particular products or settings as a result of associations that have been formulated through their experiences (Grossman & Wisenblit, 1999). Researchers have suggested that color associations may have been formulated early in human history when man associated dark blue with night, and therefore passivity, and bright yellow with sunlight and arousal (Luscher & Scott, 1969).

While the underlying theory is not entirely certain *why* consumers react differently to different colors, much research has examined *what* various color effects may be across various contexts. Color has been studied for its effects on purchase behavior (Bellizzi & Hite, 1992), affect, (Bellizzi, Crowley, & Hasty, 1983; Bellizzi & Hite, 1992; Chebat & Morrin, 2007; Cheng et al., 2009; Countryman & Jang, 2006) and behavioral change (Etter, Cucherat, & Perneger, 2002; Garrett & Brooks, 1987). It is possible that color's relationship with affect may supersede or mediate these more specific relationships.

Affective responses to color stimuli

As can be seen above, the impact of color on affect has been one of the most widely studied areas of color research. Affective responses consist of two dimensions: arousal and pleasure (Lin, 2010). Arousal is a basic, subjective state, ranging from sleep to frantic excitement (Berlyne, 1960), while pleasure refers to the degree to which a person feels good, joyful, happy, or satisfied in the situation (Donovan & Rossiter, 1982). A recent study found that across many measures of mood, these two factors, pleasure and arousal, accounted for 80% of measured variance (Cheng et al., 2009).

Mehrabian and Russell (1973, p. 315) identified arousal-seeking tendency (AST) as "an individual's preference for an environment that is closely related to his preferred arousal level; some persons characteristically prefer calm settings, whereas others actively seek to increase their arousal by selecting novel, complex, or unpredictable settings". If different colors affect arousal and pleasure, AST may explain why affective responses to colors are not perfectly universal, and may also help explain the existence of demographic-based moderating variables on color-affect relationships.

Researchers generally agree that cool colors (such as blue) are more strongly associated with pleasure than warm colors (such as red) (e.g. Babin, Hardesty, & Suter, 2003; Bellizzi et al., 1983; Bellizzi & Hite, 1992; Moore, Stammerjohan, & Coulter, 2005), and that warm colors are more strongly associated with arousal than cool colors (e.g. Bellizzi et al., 1983; Cheng et al., 2009; Moore et al., 2005). This is because of widespread acceptance of both Bellizzi's (1983) seminal findings on the topic, and the evolutionary theory outlined above. Consquently, I hypothesize that:

H_1: Cool colors lead to affective pleasure responses more strongly than the warm colors.

H_2: Warm colors lead to affective arousal responses more strongly than the cool colors.

However, not all studies support these hypotheses. Some studies findings are counter to H_1 (e.g. Chebat & Morrin, 2007; Cheng et al., 2009), while others have findings counter to H_2 (e.g. Babin, Hardesty, & Suter, 2003; Bellizzi & Hite, 1992; Yildirim, Akalin-Baskaya, & Hidayetoglu, 2007). Therefore, potential demographic moderators such as culture, gender, and study date will be explored. Drawing on associative learning theory, it is plausible to assume that individuals of different cultural backgrounds would have different color associations. Male and female children are also often surrounded by male- or female-specific colors of toys and clothing, which may also produce different associations across gender. It is also possible that as popular media changes across time, different generations will have grown up with different color associations. Finally, it is possible that these varied findings are a result of study design differences, therefore moderators such as colors used and manipulation strength will also be examined.

METHOD

Meta-analysis is a transparent, systematic review of currently existing research which uses statistical analysis to synthesize previous quantitative results from a series of studies which employ similar variables. This synthesized data is used to determine the nature of a particular relationship between variables and will usually be drawn from studies with similar hypotheses. The goal of a meta-analysis is to understand the results of any study in the context of all the other studies by examining consistency of effect size, whether this effect size is robust across studies and, if not, to quantify the extent of the variance and consider implications (Borenstein et. al, 2009). A meta-analysis is an appropriate tool to employ here, as all studies included are experimental and quantitative in nature and examine similar independent variables (warm versus cool color stimuli) and similar dependent variables (various measures of pleasure and arousal). Furthermore, all studies examine similar theoretical constructs and as such can be compared conceptually.

In conducting this meta-analysis, I follow the steps outlined in Borenstein et. al's *Introduction to Meta-Analysis*. An initial search of Scholars Portal for 'color' OR 'colour' and 'meta-analysis' indicated that a meta-analysis on this paper's topic had not been conducted. I then conducted a literature review and selected articles for inclusion based upon pre-determined meta-analysis criteria (for criteria, see Appendix A). An initial literature search was conducted using Scholars Portal, using the terms 'color' and 'colour' as present in peer-reviewed journal articles and conference papers. Follow-up searches in the PsycINFO and Web of Science databases and reverse-tracing of reference searches were subsequently conducted. In all, these searches resulted in 16 articles which examined how colors pertain to mood or affect behavior. No other meta-analysis was found, and four authors were emailed requesting further data, one of whom provided it. As a result of these searches, seven articles were found which were included in the meta-analysis. A summary of the data in these studies can be found in Appendix B.

A comparison of mean differences was used as the standard comparison effect size for this analysis. Effect size calculations were conducted using Formula 1 from Table B10 of Lipsey and Wilson's *Practical Meta-Analysis* (2001):

Formula 1: $$ES_{sm} = \frac{\bar{X}_1 - \bar{X}_2}{s_{pooled}}$$

$$s_{pooled} = \sqrt{\frac{(n_1 - 1)s_1^2 + (n_2 - 1)s_2^2}{n_1 + n_2 - 2}}$$

While some studies provided means and standard deviations for relevant condition groups, other studies' data was presented in the form of multi-way ANOVA F-values or independent t-values. Authors of papers which reported multi-way F-values were contacted to request condition group means and standard deviations. For the studies which reported independent t-values, a mean differences effect size was calculated using either formula 2 from Table B10 for different sample sizes:

Formula 2: $$ES_{sm} = t\sqrt{\frac{n_1 + n_2}{n_1 n_2}}$$

or formula 3 from Table B10 in the case of equal sample sizes (when sample sizes were not given, equal sample sizes were assumed):

Formula 3: $$ES_{sm} = \frac{2t}{\sqrt{N}}$$

These effect sizes were then corrected for unreliability:

Formula 4: $$ES' = \frac{ES_{sm}}{\sqrt{r_{yy}}}$$

I then weighted each individual effect size for relative sample size:

Formula 5: $$w_{sm} = \frac{2n_{G1}n_{G2}(n_{G1} + n_{G2})}{2(n_{G1} + n_{G2})^2 + n_{G1}n_{G2}ES_{sm}^2}$$

A weighted mean effect size was calculated for both pleasure and arousal conditions, and Z-scores were calculated for these to determine significance.

Q was calculated for both pleasure and arousal analyses to determine heterogeneity of true study effects.

Formula 5: $$Q = \sum_{i=1}^{k} W_i Y_i^2 - \frac{\left(\sum_{i=1}^{k} W_i Y_i\right)^2}{\sum_{i=1}^{k} W_i}$$

These Qs were then compared to the degrees of freedom:

$$df = k - 1,$$ where k is the number of studies, where k is the number of studies

I have not gained the necessary data to accurately include two key study results: the Moore et al. and Middelstadt studies. The Moore et al. study used a two-way ANOVA and provided F-values. These values were used as an approximation of a one-way ANOVA. The Middelstadt study was not included in the analysis.

RESULTS

The results of the two meta-analyses incorporate over 1,000 participants each (pleasure: 1,601; arousal: 1,607). As Table 1 (calculations in Tables 2, 3) indicates, color does indeed have an effect on consumer mood as measured by pleasure. As expected, blue is seen to be more strongly associated with pleasure responses than red (Z=3.325, p<.001). Thus, H_1 was supported with an effect size of 0.168. Unexpectedly, H_2 was not supported, with an overall insignificant effect of color on mood. Arousal was still reviewed in the moderator analysis, in order to determine whether H_2 holds under select boundary conditions.

Q, a measure of chi-square distribution, was used to test for heterogeneity of data. Upon comparison of each Q to each meta-analysis' degrees of freedom, Q far exceeded the degrees of freedom for both the arousal and pleasure meta-analyses ($Q_{Arousal}$-$df_{Arousal}$ = 22.705; $Q_{Pleasure}$-$df_{Pleasure}$ = 43.167). This excess variation indicates differences in the true effect from study to study.

Table 1 - Results

	Pleasure		Arousal	
Mean effect size (ES')	0.168		0.075	
Effect direction	C > W		C > W	
Z on mean effect size	3.325		1.476	
Confidence interval	0.069	0.267	-0.174	0.024
Q	28.705		49.167	
d.f.	6		6	

In an attempt to resolve the differences shown by Q, potential moderators of culture, color selection, gender, publication date, and manipulation strength were investigated (see Appendices C and D for moderator coding).

Table 2 - Calculations: Pleasure

Article	Bellizzi et al. 1983[a]	Bellizzi & Hite 1992[b]	Babin et al. 2003[d]	Chebat & Morin 2005[b]	Moore et al. 2005	Yildirim et al. 2007[c]	Cheng et al. 2010[b]
t-value	1.71	2.45	-	-	-	-	-
F-value	-	-	-	-	1.23	-	-
$n_{1 (cool)}$	-	54	-	148	-	250	64
$n_{2 (warm)}$	-	52	-	215	-	245	64
Total N	100	106	209	363	195	495	128
Mean X_1	-	4.58	18.79	3.38	-	3.16	3.63
Mean X_2	-	3.87	17.09	3.29	-	2.75	4.50
sd_1	-	-	5.13	2.08	-	0.92	1.27
sd_2	-	-	4.97	2.14	-	0.93	1.22
s-pooled	-	-	5.05	2.11	-	0.96	1.25
ES_{sm}	0.318	0.476	0.337	0.043	0.159	0.073	0.699
ES direction	C > W	C > W	C > W	C > W	C > W	C > W	W > C
Weight	24.38	26.46	51.71	87.65	48.63	121.89	29.70
Reliability	1	0.89	1	0.91	0.91	0.68	0.95
ES'	0.318	0.505	0.337	0.045	0.167	0.089	0.717
ES' * Weight	7.75	13.35	17.43	3.95	8.11	10.79	21.30
ES'^2 * Weight	2.47	6.74	5.87	0.18	1.35	0.96	15.28

[a] t-value calculated using probability of 0.09, and df=98

[b] means based on 7 pt scale

[c] means based on 5 point scale, reverse coded to correct for direction

[d] means based on 9 point scale, summations of 3 measures

Table 3 - Calculations: Arousal

Article	Bellizzi et al. 1983	Bellizzi & Hite 1992[a]	Babin et al. 2003[c]	Chebat & Morin 2005[a]	Moore et al. 2005	Yildirim et al. 2007[b]	Cheng et al. 2010[b]
t-value	2.42	0.52	-	-	-	-	-
F-value	-	-	-	-	0.97	-	-
$n_{1 (cool)}$	-	54	-	148	-	250	64
$n_{2 (warm)}$	-	52	-	215	-	245	64
Total N	100	106	209	363	195	495	128
Mean X_1	-	4.53	10.65	4.06	0.5	2.84	2.71
Mean X_2	-	4.48	8.98	3.98	0.6	2.68	3.95
sd_1	-	-	6.08	2.43	-	0.92	1.30
sd_2	-	-	5.5	2.43	-	0.99	1.81
s-pooled	-	-	5.79	2.43	-	0.92	1.58
ES_{sm}	0.449	0.101	0.289	0.031	0.141	0.348	0.787
ES direction	W > C	C > W	C > W	C > W	W > C	C > W	W > C
Weight	24.38	26.46	51.71	87.65	48.63	121.89	29.70
Reliability	1	0.88	1	0.86	0.91	0.7	0.94
ES'	0.449	0.108	0.289	0.033	0.148	0.416	0.812
ES' * Weight	10.95	2.85	14.94	2.93	7.19	50.70	24.11
ES'^2 * Weight	4.92	0.31	4.32	0.10	1.06	21.09	19.57

[a] means based on 7 pt scale

[b] means based 5 point scale, reverse coded to correct for direction

[c] means are summations of 4 bipolar semantic differentials

MODERATORS

For each moderator, the set of studies was divided into sub-samples according to my coding of each in Appendix D. For each sub-sample, an overall weighted mean was calculated, as well as a Z-score and Q comparison.

Table 4 - Moderator Results

	Pleasure				Arousal			
	Result direction	Mean effect size	Untransformed mean effect size	Z on mean effect size	Result direction	Mean effect size	Untransformed mean effect size	Z on mean effect size
Sample Nationality								
North American	C > W	0.21	0.21	3.27	C > W	0.01	0.01	0.17
Non-North American	C > W	0.10	0.10	1.23	C > W	0.18	0.17	2.16
Color Treatment Condition								
Blue/red only	C > W	0.00	0.00	0.02	W > C	0.27	0.27	2.78
Other cool/warm	C > W	0.23	0.23	3.88	C > W	0.20	0.20	3.41
Sample Gender								
Both male and female	C > W	0.13	0.13	2.28	C > W	0.08	0.08	1.42
Female only	C > W	0.34	0.32	2.42	C > W	0.05	0.05	0.46
Publication Date								
Pre-1995	C > W	0.41	0.39	2.96	W > C	0.16	0.16	1.14
Post-1995	C > W	0.13	0.13	2.42	C > W	0.11	0.11	2.02
Manipulation Strength								
Strong manipulation	C > W	0.19	0.19	3.24	C > W	0.13	0.13	2.23
Subtle manipulation	C > W	0.10	0.10	1.10	W > C	0.07	0.07	0.76

Culture

Color associations vary by culture (Aslam, 2006). As such, it is possible that color manipulations which are tested on non-North American participants may produce unexpected results.

Arousal: Exploring different levels of arousal by culture revealed a very interesting difference in results. The North American sample showed no relationship between color and arousal, while the non-North American sample showed a significant effect size (ES = 0.18, Z = 2.16) in favor of cool colors being more arousing than warm colors, counter to H$_2$.

Pleasure: The North American sub-sample showed a mean effect size of 0.21 in favor of cool colors leading to greater pleasure than warm colors, while the non-North American sub-sample showed an insignificant effect .

Colors

Red and blue are considered opposite colors (Bellizzi & Hite, 1992). The original studies upon which my hypotheses were based drew their conclusions based largely on a comparison of red versus blue manipulations. The examination of warm versus cool colors, however, possibly 'blurs' this contrast, resulting in weaker effect sizes. Another possibility is that red and blue specifically have associative properties which lead to pleasure and arousal effects, while other warm and cool colors do not share these associations. As such, the first moderator sub-segment was limited to studies which exclusively used red versus blue, while the second sub-segment included all other studies.

Arousal: Studies using red versus blue manipulations showed a significant mean effect size of 0.27 (Z=2.78) in favor of red more strongly associating with arousal than blue. Studies using other warm versus cool comparisons, however, showed a significant mean effect size of 0.20 (Z=3.41) in favor of *cool colors* being more strongly associated with arousal than warm colors. This would appear to indicate that a) effect sizes are greater when comparing more extremely opposite warm and cool colors and b) other warm (cool) colors do not elicit arousal (disinterest) in the same way that red (blue) do.

Pleasure: Studies using red versus blue manipulations showed insignificant results. A more significant finding was that other warm versus cool color manipulations supported H$_1$ with an effect size of 0.23 (Z=3.88). Thus, while H$_2$ may not hold across the full spectrum of cool and warm colors, H$_1$ received some support from the warm/cool sub-sample.

Gender

As seen in Appendix D, some of the studies employed female-only participant groups. In one case, this was because the authors believed that the majority of shopping/purchase decisions were made by women (Bellizzi et al, 1983). It is possible that women differ from men in some cognitive or associative manner which affects their perception or interpretation of environmental colors.

Arousal: No significant results were found for either sub-sample of arousal measures when split by gender.

Pleasure: When split by sample gender, H$_1$ is seen to hold true across both sub-samples with significance. A point of interest here is the effect size for each sub-sample. For the mixed gender sub-sample, cool colors were weakly associated with pleasure at an effect size of 0.13 (Z=2.28). For the female-only sub-sample, cool colors were more strongly associated with pleasure at a medium-strength effect size of 0.34 (Z=2.42). This effect size is almost three times the mixed gender sub-sample, which might indicate that women find cool colors more pleasing than men.

Publication Date

Kreitler (Kreitler & Kreitler, 1974) notes that color associations change over time, sometimes in as little as a few years. Some studies included are over twenty years old. As such, it is possible that warm/cool color associations have shifted since then. A cut-off date of 1995 was selected due to its tangency to one of the greatest recent culturally impactful process, the widespread acceptance of the internet. It is possible that as a result of various tasks and media being replaced by the internet, traditional associations have also changed.

Arousal: When split into pre- and post-1995 sub-samples, the data reveal an interesting change of direction in effect. Pre-1995 data show that warm colors are more strongly associated with arousal at an effect size of 0.16, without significance (Z=1.14). Post-1995 data show a dramatic shift, to cool colors being more strongly associated with arousal at an effect size of 0.11 (Z=2.02). This might indicate that a shift in underlying population color associations occurred during the mid-1990s or has been consistently shifting since that time.

Pleasure: Similarly interesting results were seen when comparing pre- and post-1995 sub-sample data for pleasure. Pre-1995 sub-samples showed a mean effect size of 0.41 (Z=2.96), while post-1995 sub-samples showed a mean effect size of 0.13 (Z=2.42). While the direction of the effect (that cool colors are more strongly associated with pleasure) held true across both sub-samples, the degradation of the strength of the effect also serves to support the possibility of a shift in color effects in or since the 1990s.

Manipulation Strength

Manipulation strength is defined here as the extent to which a participant's full visual perception is impacted by a color manipulation. Manipulations such as wall color changes or entire background color tinting are considered strong, while manipulations which impact less than half of the visual environment, such as décor or wall panels, are considered subtle.

Arousal: When comparing strong versus subtle manipulation sub-samples, the strong manipulation sub-sample shows a mean effect size of 0.13 (Z=2.23). This effect runs counter to H$_2$, however, as its direction shows that cool colors elicit greater arousal than warm colors. The subtle manipulation sub-sample was in the opposite direction, but without significance. This seems to indicate that the extent to which a certain color scheme is used to elicit consumer arousal is important, as subtle color schemes do not induce arousal effects.

Pleasure: For pleasure, similar findings are noted. Both sub-samples indicate that cool colors more strongly lead to pleasure, with the strong manipulation having an effect size of 0.19 (Z=3.24) and the subtle manipulation having an insignificant effect size of 0.10 (Z=1.10). Both of these sub-samples support H$_1$. These results appear to indicate that manipulation strength is a moderator to the color-pleasure relationship, with environments requiring a dominant color to elicit a mood effect.

DISCUSSION

This meta-analysis examined two previously widely accepted beliefs: that cool environmental colors elicit a greater sense of pleasure and that warm colors elicit a greater sense of excitement or arousal. Based on the results of this meta-analysis, the first of these beliefs (H$_1$) is seen to be of weak-moderate effect size with significance (ES = 0.17, Z = 3.325), while the second (H$_2$) is shown to be not significant.

Thus, while managers have been employing warm colors in an effort to gain consumer attention, this actually may not be effective, possibly as a result of changing color associations in the general population. H_1 shows a fairly robust relationship, however, indicating that managers should feel comfortable in creating store environments which are dominated by cool colors, as these environments will likely be perceived as pleasurable by consumers.

Impact of Potential Moderators

The exploration of potential moderators led to discovery of various boundary conditions and findings that were not initially obvious.

An analysis of sample cultures led to interesting, if not entirely unexpected, results. North Americans were found to elicit pleasure from cool-color environments, while non-North Americans were found to not be significantly impacted in terms of pleasure. Non-North Americans were found to be excited by cool colors, however, while North-Americans' arousal was not significantly impacted. This finding serves to strengthen the possibility that colors' meanings are derived through association, as different cultures place different symbolic meaning on different cultures. It also serves as a reminder that it is unsafe to generalize results from a North American sample pool to an international context.

When colour manipulations were examined, red was seen to be more strongly associated with arousal than blue, while other cool colors were seen to be more arousing than other warm colors, though with a slightly weaker effect size. These results would support the idea that red is the most arousing color, but not necessarily as a result of being the warmest color. Red may simply be considered arousing as a result of red-specific color associations. While cool colors were seen to be more pleasing than warm colors, however, the color blue itself was not seen to be more pleasing than the color red. This finding also serves to show that cool and warm colors do not have universal effects, but rather it is possible that individual colors each have their own effect.

The most significant implication of gender as a moderator was that women appear to elicit more pleasure from cool colors than men. With a medium strength effect size, this finding has strong implications for businesses with a female-skewed clientele.

Analysis of study age showed that there have been changes in color effects on mood since initial color-mood studies began in the 1980s. Once-assumed relationships (that warm colors are arousing and that cool colors are pleasing) have shifted and weakened since this time, perhaps as a result of greater access to color stimuli via the internet and other forms of media. Whether or not this is leading to new color associations, or simply a diminishing of color associations, is yet to be determined.

Examination of the dominance or strength of a color stimulus produced did provided very clear results. Stronger manipulations lead to stronger effects, for both pleasure and arousal, while subtle manipulations were not seen to have any significant effect. It would appear safe to state that colors do not have impact on consumer mood unless they are presented in a dominant and perhaps overwhelming fashion. There are so many color cues surrounding modern consumers that it is unlikely that colors will even be noted unless they are made obvious to the senses.

Overall, only three conditions presented by moderator analysis supported H_2: exclusive blue/red comparison, studies conducted prior to 1995, and subtle manipulations (and only one of these conditions had significance). It appears safe to say there is not a strong enough relationship between color and arousal to be overly useful in an exchange context. When examining color's effects on pleasure, however, H_1 is seen to be robust across all but two scenarios: when examining cultures outside of North America and when exclusively comparing blue to red. This would seem to indicate that planning for environments to have cool color schemes comes at little risk.

Strengths and Weaknesses

This study employed statistical analysis to evaluate the effect of color on mood on a larger scale than has been done before. In combining the results of past studies, I was able to work with a much larger sample size, which was much more representative of the consumer spectrum than any single previous study was able to do.

This study contributes to the marketing literature by evaluating previously unexplored moderators of the color-mood relationship of gender, study age, and manipulation strength. Furthermore, it provides actionable recommendations for marketing managers regarding atmosphere design and reactions to expect from specific customer groups that are exposed to significant degrees of warm or cool colors.

Despite these contributions, this study has some notable weaknesses. Firstly, with only seven studies comprising the meta-analysis, it was not possible to examine potential interaction effects of moderators to isolate more exact boundary conditions. Also, and potentially more significantly, one of the studies is currently included in the meta-analysis on the assumption that its 2-way ANOVA F-values are equivalent to what a one-way ANOVA would result in. This study, while providing results in-line with many other studies, may be skewing results.

Directions for Future Research

Future color-mood research is needed to further explore the culture moderator – thus study showed that North Americans differ in their reactions to environmental color from non-North Americans, but this finding could be expanded by research that investigates different cultures within North America as well as more specific non-North American cultures.

The longitudinal change in color effects is one that is of great interest. Further development of the theory behind this change and monitoring of the color-pleasure/arousal relationship correlations is necessary to determine whether or not this effect is still shifting or if more recent studies have identified a 'stabilized' effect. Finally, further experiments are needed to determine the true extent of cool versus warm effects, especially regarding whether they hold across warm colors other than red. Further notable holes encountered during the process of creating this meta-analysis include examination of color hues, blended colors, and text color effects.

CONCLUSION

This meta-analysis has reaffirmed the belief that cool environmental colors can increase consumer pleasure, while rejecting the hypothesis that warm colors lead to greater excitement/arousal. The beliefs that cool colors increase pleasure and warm colors increase arousal were firmly entrenched in the color literature prior to this meta-analysis, with authors of studies which produced findings counter to these discounting their findings or indicating that their findings were outside of the true relationship boundary conditions. This meta-analysis showed that the color-arousal link is questionable, at least when considering warm versus cool colors, while also showing that the color-pleasure link, while different across conditions, is one which is robust and significant. This study also revealed a trend of shifting color effects over time. This finding bears potential significance and requires further investigation. Overall, while it is seen that colors do have an effect on mood, this effect varies by context and subject. Further, the extent and direction of these effects may also vary. Strong understanding of the extent of color effects in specific contexts, however, will undeniably be of aid to marketers operating in exchange environments.

Appendix A – Meta-Analysis Study Inclusion Criteria

Studies included in this meta-analysis were limited to those that:
- employed an experimental or quasi-experimental design
- examined different color treatment conditions (warm versus cool colors)
- measured effect of treatment conditions on mood in some manner which included measures or factors representing arousal or pleasure constructs, or constructs which could act as proxies for pleasure or arousal
- provided statistical findings
- were available via either database searches or requests from researchers
- were written or translated to English for publication

Appendix B – Individual Study Details

Study	Authors	Year	N	Participants	Study Type	Manipulation Medium	Manipulation Colors	Measures	Measurement Scale	Arousal Result Direction	Pleasure Result Direction	Mediators / Moderators	Effect Size Provided	Country
1	*Bellizzi, Joseph A.; Crowley, Ayn E.; Hasty, Ronald W.*	1983	125	Female	Lab experiment	Walls with different color panels, slides projected on these	Red, Yellow, Blue, Green, White	20-item bipolar adjective questions	7-point scale	Warm more stimulating	Cool more pleasing	-	Means and significance	USA
2	*Bellizzi, Joseph A.; Hite, Robert E.*	1992	107	Mixed gender undergraduate marketing students	Lab experiment	Color-tinted slides of furniture store	Red/Blue	18-item PAD scale	7-point scale	Blue more arousing	Blue more pleasing	-	Independent t-test	USA
3	*Moore, Robert S; Stammerjohan, Claire Allisson; Coulter, Robin A.*	2005	195	Mixed gender, undergraduate students	Lab experiment	Banner advertisement background	Red/Blue	Multiple Likert scales	9-point scale	Red more attractive	Blue more pleasing	Text color, context congruency	F-value	USA
4	*Babin, Barry J.; Hardesty, David M.; Suter, Tracy A.*	2003	209	Female	Experiment	Store interior (clothing store)	Orange/Blue	Bipolar semantic differential and Likert scales	9-point scale	Blue more exciting	Blue higher evaluation	Lighting strength, item price	Means and std. deviations	USA
5	*Chebat, Jean-Charles; Morrin, Maureen*	2005	587	Mixed gender	Cross-sectional survey	Mall décor (flowers and drapes vs plants)	Yellow&Red/ Green	Semantic differential scale	7-point scale	Blue more arousing	Blue more pleasing	Culture (French-Canadian/Anglo-Canadian)	Means and std. deviations	Canada
6	*Cheng, Fei-Fei; Wu, Chin-Shan; Yen, David C.*	2010	128	Mixed gender	Lab experiment	E-commerce web page background	Red/Blue	12-item semantic differential scale	Unspecified	Red more arousing	Red more pleasing	Music tempo	F-value	Taiwan
7	*Middelstadt, Susan E.*	1990	84	Female undergraduate students	Lab experiment	Single-product slide background	Red/Blue	6-item bipolar differential scale	7-point scale	n/a	Blue more pleasing	Product type	Means	USA
8	*Yildirim, K.; Akalin-Baskaya, A.; Hidayetoglu, M.L.*	2007	500	Mixed gender	Cross-sectional survey	Restaurant wall color	Yellow/Violet	8-item bipolar semantic scale	1-5	Violet more attractive	Violet more pleasing	Age, gender, interaction of age and gender	Means and std. deviations	Turkey

Appendix C – Moderator Variables

	Sample Nationality	Color Treatment Condition	Sample Gender	Publication Date	Manipulation Strength
1 *Bellizzi 1983*	1	2	2	1	2
2 *Bellizzi 1992*	1	1	1	1	1
3 *Moore 2005*	1	1	1	2	1
4 *Babin 2003*	1	2	2	2	1
5 *Chebat 2005*	1	2	1	2	2
6 *Cheng 2010*	0	1	1	2	1
7 *Middelstadt 1990*	1	1	2	1	1
8 *Yildirim 2007*	0	2	1	2	1

Appendix D – Moderator Coding

Sample Nationality	1 – North American
	2 – Non-North American
Color Treatment Condition	1 – Blue/red2 – Blue/non-red warm or Non-blue cool/Red or Non-blue cool/non-red warm
Sample Gender	1 – Both male and female participants
	2 – Female only
	3 – Male only
Publication Date	1 – Pre-1995
	2 – Post-1995
Manipulation Strength	1 – Strong Manipulation (full background, walls, room lighting)
	2 – Subtle Manipulation (décor, partial wall)

{{10 Bellizzi,Joseph A. 1983; 9 Bellizzi,Joseph A. 1992; 8 Babin, Barry J. 2003; 7 Chebat,J.C. 2007; 11 Cheng, Fei-Fei 2009; 15 Yildirim,K. 2007; 33 Middelstadt,Susan E. 1990; 32 Moore,Robert S. 2005}}(Moore, Stammer

References

Aslam, M. M. (2006). Are you selling the right colour? A cross-cultural review of colour as a marketing cue. *Journal of Marketing Communications, 12*(1), 15-30.

Babin, B. J., Hardesty, D. M., & Suter, T. A. (2003). Color and shopping intentions: The intervening effect of price fairness and perceived affect. *Journal of Business Research, 56*(7, pp. 541-551), July.

Bellizzi, J. A., Crowley, A. E., & Hasty, R. W. (1983). The effects of color in store design. *Journal of Retailing, 59*(1), 21-45.

Bellizzi, J. A., & Hite, R. E. (1992). Environmental color, consumer feelings, and purchase likelihood. *Psychology & Marketing, 9*(5), 347.

Berlyne, D. E. (1960). *Conflict, arousal, and curiosity.* New York, NY: McGraw-Hill.

Chebat, J. C., & Morrin, M. (2007). Colors and cultures: Exploring the effects of mall decor on consumer perceptions. *Journal of Business Research, 60*(3, pp. 189-196), March.

Cheng, F., Wu, C., & Yen, D. (2009). The effect of online store atmosphere on consumer's emotional responses - an experimental study of music and colour. *Behaviour and Information Technology, 28*(4), 323-334.

Countryman, C. C., & Jang, S. (2006). The effects of atmospheric elements on customer impression: The case of hotel lobbies. *International Journal of Contemporary Hospitality Management, 18*(7), 534-545.

Donovan, R. J., & Rossiter, J. R. (1982). Store atmosphere - an environmental psychology approach. *Journal of Retailing, 58*(1), 34-57.

Etter, J., Cucherat, M., & Perneger, T. (2002). Questionnaire color and response rates to mailed surveys - A randomized trial and a meta-analysis.

Garrett, J. C., & Brooks, C. I. (1987). Effect of ballot color, sex of candidate, and sex of college-students of voting age on their voting-behavior. *Psychological Reports, 60*(1), 39-44.

Grossman, R. P., & Wisenblit, J. Z. (1999). What we know about consumers' color choices. *Journal of Marketing Practice: Applied Marketing Science, 5*(3), 78-88.

Kotler, P. (1973). Atmospherics as a marketing tool. *Journal of Retailing, 49*(4), 48.

Kreitler, H., & Kreitler, S. (1974). Psychology of arts - reply. *Journal of Aesthetic Education, 8*(3), 145-150.

Kusterer, J. M. (2007). *What wavelength goes with a color?* Retrieved November 16, 2010, from http://eosweb.larc.nasa.gov/EDDOCS/Wavelengths_for_Colors.html

Lin, I. Y. (2010). The interactive effect of gestalt situations and arousal seeking tendency on customers' emotional responses: Matching color and music to specific servicescapes. *Journal of Services Marketing, 24*(4-5), 294-303.

Luscher, M., & Scott, I. (1969). *The luscher color test.* New York, NY: Random House.

Moore, R. S., Stammerjohan, C. A., & Coulter, R. A. (2005). Banner advertiser-web site context congruity and color effects on attention and attitudes. *Journal of Advertising, 34*(2), 71-84.

Turley, L. W., & Milliman, R. E. (2000). Atmospheric effects on shopping behavior: A review of the experimental evidence. *Journal of Business Research.Special Issue: Retail Atmospherics, 49*(2), 193-211.

Yildirim, K., Akalin-Baskaya, A., & Hidayetoglu, M. L. (2007). Effects of indoor color on mood and cognitive performance. *Building and Environment, 42*(9), 3233-3240.

Variety Leads to Satiety: Varied Meal Composition Leads to Greater Satiety

Aner Tal, Cornell University, USA
Brian Wansink, Cornell University, USA
Michael Giblin, State University of New York at Buffalo

Variety-seeking has been extensively studied in consumer research. Many studies have documented consumers showing a preference for variety for its own sake, leading researchers to treat variety as a drive (Faison 1977, Goukens et al. 2007, McAlister 1982, Menon and Kahn 1995). The drive towards variety might stem from seeking optimum stimulation-level (Menon & Kahn 1995, Raju 1980) or from attempts to fulfill self-presentation or identity needs, making the consumer appear more interesting to her fellows (Ariely & Levav 2000, Ariely & Norton 2009).

Variety-seeking tends to guide consumer choice to such extent that at times, consumers select less-preferred products that they may in fact enjoy less for the sake of variety (Ariely & Levav 2000, Ratner et al. 1999). This may potentially lead to suboptimal choices, particularly when selecting products for future consumption (Simonson 2000, 2002).

Though less attention has been given to the effects of variety once already present within purchases, the presence of variety within meals has been shown to have specifically detrimental effects on quantity people eat, leading people to eat more when offered variety than they would without variety (Raynor and Wing 2006, Wansink 2004).

Tough it may indeed lead people to eat more, due to reduced habituation and a satisfaction of the variety-seeking urge in more varied meals, it may also potentially increase satiety regardless of the amount eaten. Below, we explain the reasoning for this hypothesis.

HABITUATION, ATTENTION AND ENCODING

A considerable portion of day-to-day eating behavior tends to be mindless (Wansink 2004). Consumers can drift through a meal without registering how much they ate, relying on cues to retrospectively infer how much they've eaten (Wansink 2006).

Variety within a meal might call more attention to the meal, leading consumers to register the quantity eaten to greater extent. Generally, consumers tend to remember particular moments within experience, with "segment" endings being recorded to greater extent than other parts (Ariely and Carmon 2000, Baumgartner et al. 1997, Kahenman 2000, Schrieber and Kahneman 2000). Accordingly, when experiences are "broken" into segments, consumers process events differently, with different segments that would normally be neglected influencing evaluation. This leads segmented experiences to be evaluated differently than non-segmented experiences. (Ariely and Zauberman 2003, Nelson et al. 2009).

Relevant to our case, segmenting snacking into particular portions can alter the manner people register their meal and consequently affect when consumers think they're full (Geier, Wansink and Rozin 2011). The more segmented an experience is, the more consumers can register its discrete parts, leading them to remember eating more than they would given unsegmented experience.

Satiety is determined by a combination of physical and psychological cues (Wansink 2006). In determining how full they are, consumers rely not only on internal cues, but also on their judgment of how much they've eaten, often driven by external cues (Wansink et al. 2005, Wansink and Payne 2007). If ttention is aroused at "segmentation points" during consumption, when consumers shift from one type of food to another, consumers may be more sensitive to their physiological level of satiey. No less importantly, they may register what they eat to greater extent, leading to a memory-induced inference of quantity eaten, which would in turn result in a greater *psychologically-driven* sense of satiety.

STUDY

The study aimed to examine whether variety in a meal led to greater satiety in a naturalistic snacking situation. To this end, participants (*N*=106) were given snacks while completing unrelated questionnaires and allowed to snack as much as they wanted. Participants were randomly assigned to one of five conditions, with three conditions offering a single snack: cheese, chocolate kisses, or crackers, and two conditions offering snack combinations: cheese+chocolate or cheese+crackers.

Participants reported their satiety on a 3-item scale, the items of which were averaged to create each person's fullness score. Each person answered the 3-item scale before and after snacking. A person's level of satiety was her fullness score after snacking, and her fullness score after snacking.

Results. Participants in combo conditions reported being more full (1.63 increase in fullness from time 0) than did participants in the non-combo condition (.83). However, combo participants also ate more, in accordance with prior findings (Wansink 2004). To test whether variety led to increased satiety even controlling for quantity eaten, we ran a model of satiety as a function of being in a combo condition, with the amounts eaten of each snack as covariates. Adjusted means were virtually identical as non-adjusted means, with higher lsmeans for combo participants (1.66) than for non-combo participants (.79). Being in a combo condition had a significant effect on satiety controlling for quantity of food eaten: $F(1,60)=6.62, p=.01$.

Discussion. The current study provides an initial demonstration that eating a combination of foods, rather than one type of food, leads to greater satiety, controlling for quantity eaten. However, in the current study quantity eaten was controlled statistically, rather than experimentally. A planned follow-up study will control for quantity of food, providing participants with similar size/weight snacks of two types, either on their own (non-combo) or in combination (combo). We predict a similar finding to that in the current study, with higher satiety for people who received a combo snack.

Further followup studies will aim to get a better idea regarding the causes of enhanced satiety given variety. Specifically, we believe increased attention and encoding during the meal may underlie the effects of variety on satiation. Passage from one food item to the next may supply an attentional cue that leads to increased encoding of foods eaten during the meal. This may later serve to psychologically cue consumers that they've eaten more, leading to greater reported satiety.

Regulatory Fit, Attitudes, and Loyalty: The Interactive Effect of Chronic and Situational Regulatory Focus

Meltem Tugut, Saint Louis University, USA
Mark J. Arnold, Saint Louis University, USA
Rajani Ganesh-Pillai, North Dakota State University, USA

This research proposes that fit between consumers' chronic and situational regulatory focus enhances their evaluations of and loyalty intentions toward the promoted product. Two experiments were conducted to test the proposed regulatory fit effects in the context of a loyalty program and a favorable restaurant dining experience. Findings from both studies confirm the interactive effect of chronic and situational regulatory focus on attitudes and loyalty intentions of prevention-focused consumers.

Regulatory focus theory (Higgins 1997) posits that individuals differ in how they approach pleasure and avoid pain. These differences are manifested in two distinct regulatory orientations which govern how people pursue goals: promotion focus and prevention focus (Higgins 1997). Both self-regulation systems can be a chronic predisposition of individuals or can be situationally induced (Aaker and Lee 2001; Higgins et al. 2001; Semin et al. 2005). Promotion-focused individuals are sensitive to the presence and absence of positive outcomes (gains and non-gains), are approach motivated, and are oriented to the pursuit of accomplishment, advancement, and growth (Camacho, Higgins, and Lugar 2003; Higgins et al. 1994). On the other hand, prevention-focused people are concerned with the presence and absence of negative outcomes (losses and non-losses), are avoidance motivated, and emphasize protection, safety, and responsibility (Higgins, Shah, and Friedman 1997; Shah, Higgins, and Friedman 1998).

Central to the current research is the notion of regulatory fit. People experience regulatory fit when their strategies for goal pursuit match their regulatory orientation (Higgins 2006; Lee and Higgins 2009). Accordingly, regulatory fit has been shown to make individuals "feel right" about their actions and intensify their motivational strength during goal pursuit (Higgins 2000). In contrast, when people adopt strategies that conflict with their regulatory focus, they exhibit reduced motivation due to the resulting regulatory nonfit state (Hong and Lee 2008). These subjective experiences then transfer to individuals' subsequent evaluations of attitude objects.

Consistent with Higgins (2000) claim that regulatory fit can be applied to a broad range of orientations and goal pursuit means, extant research offers different conceptualizations and operationalizations of the phenomenon. For instance, promotion-focused consumers are more persuaded when they encounter messages emphasizing eagerness (vs. vigilance) appeals, whereas the reverse occurs for prevention-focused consumers (Keller 2006). Lee and Aaker (2004) found that individuals evaluate promotion-focused information presented in a gain frame and prevention-focused information presented in a loss frame more favorably. Similarly, promotion-focused consumers are willing to pay more for a product when they base their evaluations on feelings (vs. reasons), whereas the reverse is observed for prevention-focused consumers (Avnet and Higgins 2003). Other regulatory fit studies have reported that promotion vs. prevention focus is associated with distant vs. proximal temporal perspective (Mogilner, Aaker, and Pennington 2008), abstract vs. concrete mental representations (Lee, Keller, and Sternthal 2010) and search strategies (Pham and Chang 2010), and dejection vs. agitation emotions (Lee, Aaker, and Gardner 2000).

Above all, Haws, Dholakia, and Bearden (2010) recently called for further research examining the potential interaction between individuals' chronic and situational regulatory focus. The present research highlights this relatively less explored perspective of regulatory fit (see Zhao and Pechmann 2007 for an exception). Specifically, we test the hypothesis that fit between consumers' chronic and situational regulatory focus enhances their evaluations of and loyalty intentions toward the promoted brand. This proposition builds on past literature which indicates that the experience of regulatory fit enhances the perceived value of an object (Higgins et al. 2003) and attitudes toward a brand (Wan, Hong, and Sternthal 2009).

In particular, we posit that chronically promotion-focused consumers who are exposed to promotion-framed (vs. prevention-framed) consumption messages and experiences will express more favorable attitudes and loyalty intentions toward the focal product. Conversely, chronically prevention-focused consumers are expected to sense regulatory fit, and hence develop more favorable attitudes and intentions, when exposed to prevention-framed (vs. promotion-framed) consumption messages. We believe that chronic regulatory focus prompts individuals to selectively pay attention to messages that help them sustain their orientation. Therefore, messages that fit one's chronic regulatory focus will be perceived as more diagnostic and persuasive, leading to a state of increased satisfaction. This increased satisfaction may be one mechanism underlying the proposed regulatory fit effects.

We tested the present predictions in two studies. Study 1 examined the hypothesized fit effects in the context of a loyalty program. We used a chronic regulatory focus (promotion vs. prevention) x situational regulatory focus (promotion-framing vs. prevention-framing) between-subjects design (N = 103). While chronic regulatory focus was measured as an individual difference factor, situational regulatory focus was induced by framing the description of a loyalty program in terms of presence of positive outcomes (promotion-framing) or absence of negative outcomes (prevention-framing). The dependent variables were preference toward the loyalty program and willingness to join the program. Separate ANOVAs revealed a significant chronic regulatory focus x situational regulatory focus interaction [$F(1,92) =$ 4.62, $p<0.03$]; $F(1,92) = 4.64$, $p<0.03$]. As predicted, chronically prevention-focused consumers indicated a higher preference toward and an increased willingness to participate in the loyalty program advertised in prevention (vs. promotion) terms.

The purpose of Study 2 was to extend our earlier findings to a different consumption context, while assessing consumers' loyalty intentions. In this study (N = 247), we induced situational regulatory focus by framing the description of a favorable restaurant dining experience in either promotion or prevention terms. The dependent variables were positive word of mouth and repatronage intentions. Separate ANOVAs confirmed a significant chronic regulatory focus – situational regulatory focus fit effect and provided further support for Study 1 results [$F(1,215) = 5.48$, $p<0.03$; $F(1,215) = 8.00$, $p<0.01$]. Chronically prevention-focused consumers expressed higher levels of positive word of mouth and repatronage intentions toward the restaurant when their consumption experience emphasized attaining prevention (vs. promotion) goals. An additional ANOVA uncovered that the observed fit effects were accompanied by increased levels of satisfaction with the consumption experience [$F(1,215) = 4.23$, $p<0.05$]. Our current efforts are concentrated around studying this potential underlying mechanism in more detail.

Across two experiments, we demonstrated that when consumers detect a fit between their chronic and situational regulatory orientations, they express more favorable attitudes and loyalty intentions toward the advertised product. From a theoretical perspective, the present research offers an additional conceptualization and operationalization of the regulatory fit construct in response to Haws, Dholakia, and Bearden (2010). Consequently, the robustness of the results across two different consumption situations illustrates that the wording of promotional messages constitutes a critical factor for marketers in fostering loyalty among consumers, especially those who are chronically prevention-focused.

REFERENCES

Haws, Kelly L., Utpal M. Dholakia, and William O. Bearden (2010), "An Assessment of Chronic Regulatory Focus Measures," *Journal of Consumer Research*, 47 (October), 967–82.

Higgins, E. Tory (1997), "Beyond Pleasure and Pain," *American Psychologist*, 52 (December), 1280-300.

_____ (2000), "Making a Good Decision: Value from Fit," *American Psychologist,* 55 (November), 1217-30.

Hong, Jiewen and Angela Y. Lee (2008), "Be Fit and Be Strong: Mastering Self-Regulation through Regulatory Fit," *Journal of Consumer Research*, 34 (February), 682-95.

Lee, Angela Y. and Jennifer Aaker (2004), "Bringing the Frame into Focus: The Influence of Regulatory Fit on Processing Fluency and Persuasion," *Journal of Personality and Social Psychology*, 86 (February), 205–18.

_____, Punam Anand Keller, and Brian Sternthal (2010), "Value from Regulatory Construal Fit: The Persuasive Impact of Fit between Consumer Goals and Message Concreteness," *Journal of Consumer Research,* 36 (February), 735-47.

Mogilner, Cassie, Jennifer L. Aaker, and Ginger L. Pennington (2008), "Time Will Tell: The Distant Appeal of Promotion and Imminent Appeal of Prevention," *Journal of Consumer Research*, 34 (February), 670-81.

Pham, Michel Tuan and Hannah H. Chang (2010), "Regulatory Focus, Regulatory Fit, and the Search and Consideration of Choice Alternatives," *Journal of Consumer Research,* 37 (December), 626-40.

When Brand Symbolism Matters: A Social Identity Perspective

Hua Chang, Drexel University, USA
Daniel Korschun, Drexel University, USA

Previous research has examined the effect of brand symbolism on consumers' self concept (Grubb and Grathwohl 1967) and consumer identity (Elliott 1998). However, no research has been done on the role of brand cultural symbolism in the cross-border brand acquisition context. Based on recent studies on brand symbolism (e.g. Escalas and Bettman 2003; White and Dahl 2007) and drawing on social identity theory, we propose that consumers experience a sense of loss when a culturally symbolic brand is acquired by a foreign country, which in turn affects their brand evaluation. Further, consumers' social identity strengthens this relationship.

Brand symbolism refers to the image that a specific brand evokes in the minds of consumers (O'Cass and Frost 2002). Consumers may see a brand as a symbol, with connected meanings which define what consumers value most. Essentially, brand symbolism represents what a brand means to consumers and the emotions or feelings they attach to when purchasing and using it. Consumers may link the symbolic meanings of a brand with their personal identity and social identity, as suggested by social identity theory (Tajfel and Turner 1979). This is corroborated by the evidence found in previous research that consumers tend to use brand symbolic connections to convey meanings in three different levels: cultural level, shared social group level, and the individual level (Eastman et al. 1999).

Iconic brands are most frequently, if not always, perceived to have rich symbolic images attached to them. According to Holt (2003), iconic brands are successful because "they forged a deep connection with the culture" (p. 43). Iconic brands possess a set of symbolic properties which are unique to American culture and ideology. However, when such an iconic brand is acquired by a foreign country, its unique symbolic connections with American ideology or culture may be replaced by new associations with different culture and ideology. Onkvisit and Shaw (1987) found that consumers tend to evaluate a brand in terms of its symbolic meaning. A recent study also reveals the moderating effect of brand symbolism on consumers' evaluation of in-group and out-group brands (Escalas and Bettman 2005). Since the acquired brand will not possess its original unique symbolic meanings, consumers who were attached to the brand due to its cultural symbolism may suffer a psychological loss and will not perceive the brand as positive as before. Thus we speculate that iconic brand's cultural symbolism will affect how consumers evaluate the brand when the brand is acquired by a foreign country.

One hundred and twenty seven undergraduates were randomly assigned to 2 (priming: identity prime vs. no identity prime) X 2 (brand symbolism: iconic vs. non-iconic) between subjects experimental conditions. Participants were told that they would be completing two separate studies. The social identity priming procedure was adopted from White and Dahl (2007). Participants began to read a short scenario about a foreign company acquiring the focal brands (either iconic or non-iconic). Participants then completed a questionnaire that includes the instruments measuring brand evaluation and purchase intent, sense of loss, and their self-brand connection. Manipulation checks were done to ensure that the focal brands were perceived differently in terms of their cultural symbolic meaning.

ANOVA analysis results indicated that there was significant main effect of brand symbolism on brand evaluation and purchase intent. The interaction effects between brand symbolism and social identity on brand evaluation ($F(1,123) = 5.49$, $p < 0.05$) and purchase intent ($F(1,123) = 8.16$, $p < 0.05$) were significant. A further mediation analysis was also conducted to examine the mediating role of sense of loss in the relationship between brand symbolism and brand evaluation and purchase intent (Baron and Kenny 1986). We assessed whether the β and t values associated with the independent variables were reduced when we controlled for the effects of the mediator. The results showed that controlling the mediator noticeably attenuated the strength of the interaction of brand symbolism and social identity on brand evaluation (from $\beta =.71$, t=2.44 to $\beta =.43$, t=1.58).

The results in the study supported our prediction that when a culturally symbolic brand was acquired by a foreign country, consumers would experience a sense of loss as their attachment to the brand was replaced by a dissociative group. This relationship is stronger when consumers' social identity is primed. This study contributes to the literature by offering one of the first empirical evidence about the effect of brand cultural symbolism on brand evaluation in a cross-border brand acquisition context. Future research can examine the role of self-brand connection in the relationship between brand symbolism and brand evaluation or the three-way interaction effects between brand symbolism, social identity and self-brand connection. As companies are increasingly using brand acquisition as a strategy to enter a foreign market and create value, they have to understand how consumers view the cross-border mergers and acquisitions and react to brand acquisition.

REFERENCES

Anderson, John R. (1983), *The Architecture of Cognition*. Cambridge, MA: Harvard University Press.

Eastman, Jacqueline K. and Ronald E. Goldsmith (1999), "Status Consumption in Consumer Behavior: Scale Development and Validation," *Journal of Marketing Theory & Practice*, 7(3), 41.

Elliott, Richard (1998), "Brands as Symbolic Resources for Construction of Identity," *International Journal of Advertising*, 17(2), 131–143.

Escalas, Jennifer E. and James R. Bettman (2005), "Self-construal, Reference Groups, and Brand Meaning," *Journal of Consumer Research*, 32(3), 378-89.

Grubb, Edward L. and Harrison L. Grathwohl (1967), "Consumer Self-Concept, Symbolism and Marketing Behavior: A Theoretical Approach," *Journal of Marketing*, 31 (4), 22-27.

Holt, Douglas B. (2003), "What Becomes an Icon Most?" *Harvard Business Review*, March, 43-49.

O'Cass, Aron and Hmily Frost (2002), "Status brands: Examining the Effects of Non-Product-related Brand Associations on Status and Conspicuous Consumption," *Journal of Product and Brand Management*, 11 (2), 67-88.

Onkvisit, Sak and John J. Shaw (1987), "Standardized International Advertising: A Review and Critical Evaluation of the Theoretical and Empirical Evidence," *Columbia Journal of World Business*, 22 (Fall), 43-55.

Tajfel, Henri and John C. Turner (1979), *An Integrative Theory of Intergroup Conflict*, Monterey, CA: Brooks/Cole.

White, Katherine and Darren W. Dahl (2007), "Are All Out-Groups Created Equal? Consumer Identity and Dissociative Influence," *Journal of Consumer Research*, 34(December), 525-536.

Influence of Facial Affective Display on Social Judgments

Ze Wang, University of Central Florida, USA
Fan Liu, University of Central Florida, USA

While there is an increasing body of research on the impact of employees' affective displays on consumers' perceptions in dynamic interpersonal interactions (e.g., Lee and Lim 2010; Hennig-Thurau et al. 2006), the role of facial affective displays in static images attracted scattered attention in consumer research. This gap is surprising because the abundance of facial images in promotional materials, advertisements, and billboards suggests that marketers rely heavily on this tactic to elicit intended outcomes. For instance, a dentist may advertise with a positive affective display to highlight his/her friendliness and warmth, whereas a lawyer may use a neutral display to emphasize his/her competence and professionalism. Will a brief exposure to these facial expressions in a single still image be sufficient to form a preliminary impression of the service provider? If so, do neutral and positive affective displays differentially impact two fundamental dimensions of social judgment (i.e., warm and competence)? By addressing these questions, the current research makes an initial attempt to investigate how individuals' facial affectively display embedded in static images impact observers' evaluative judgments.

Drawing on research from social cognition and neuroscience, we posit that even a brief inspection of a facial affective display would be sufficient for observers to extract person knowledge. Face processing is automatic and spontaneous in nature, and inferences can be formed after as little as 40 ms exposure to faces (Todorov, Said, and Verosky in press). Naylor (2007) found that individuals respond to static images of unfamiliar service providers quickly and spontaneously until they form strong and reliable impressions. Interestingly, these judgments at unfamiliarity or zero-acquaintance are consensual and accurate. Adding to this line of research, the current research further examines the consequences of the automatic face processing by focusing on the influence of facial emotional expressions on warmth and competence.

We propose that neutral and positive affective displays differentially influence observers' trait inferences. Competence and warmth are two universal and fundamental dimensions of social cognition. The former refers to agency, dominance, and individualism, whereas the latter contains communality, interdependent, and collectivism (Judd et al. 2005). Research on neutral emotional expression has found evidence that restrained emotion displays reflect mastery of one's life and competence in general (Warner and Shields 2007). For instance, female managers' reacting nonemotionally to a given situation is suggestive of their ability to handle the situation, which is often associated with social power and dominance (Lewis 2000). On the other hand, research on positive affective display suggests that smiling is perceived as an indicator of affiliation or willingness to continue a current social interaction. People who express positive emotions are perceived friendlier and warmer (Barger and Grandey 2006; Hennig-Thurau et al. 2006). Therefore, we argue whereas a neutral facial display engenders perceptions of competence, a positive affective display leads to higher evaluations on warmth.

To test the aforementioned hypothesis, in Study 1, we randomly assigned participants to six conditions with increasing intensity of positive affective displays (neutral, 20 percent smile, 40 percent smile, 60 percent smile, 80 percent smile, and 100 percent smile). These experimental stimuli were facial portraits from MSFDE and NimStim databases. The results of study 1 seemed to suggest that positive affective display enhances judgments of both warmth and competence. The more intense the positive emotional display, the higher ratings on both warmth and competence dimensions. Although unexpected, this result was consistent with the extant research finding in stereotyping literature. When people judge individuals, the warmth and competence perceptions often correlate positively (halo effect), either high in both or low in both (Judd et al. 2005). Another noteworthy finding was the ceiling effect of smiling strength beyond 60 percent smile. The portrait with 60, 80, and 100 percent smiles received similar ratings on both warmth and competence.

Our first objective of Study 2 was to examine whether the facial portrait of a service provider embedded in a print ad can impact customers' judgments of his warmth and competence even before the service is actually rendered. Another objective was to test whether these evaluative judgments can further impact their downstream behavioral outcomes. In the experiment, we included three levels of affective displays (neutral, low-intensity positive affective display/60 percent smiling, and high-intensity positive affective display 100 percent smiling). Participants read a print ad of a real estate agent and subsequently indicate on 7-point scales (not at all/very much) their perceptions of the employee's warmth and competence, attitude toward the service provider, and behavioral intentions. Results of Study 2 were consistent with findings in Study 1. We found that compared to neutral emotional display, positive affective expressions enhanced both warmth and competence perceptions, which further impacted consumers' attitude toward the service provider and their intentions to use the service. Interestingly, as we moved from low-intensity to high-intensity positive affective display, consumers' ratings on service provider's competence decreased. A third study is currently in progress to better elucidate this boomerang effect.

Taken together, our findings suggest that even a brief exposure to facial affective displays embedded in static images can influence observers' social judgments about the displayer's warmth and competence. These impacts may be more complex than previously presumed or common sense predicted.

REFERENCES

Barger, Patricia B., and Alicia A. Grandey (2006), "Service with a smile and encounter satisfaction: Emotional contagion and appraisal mechanisms," *Academy of Management Journal,* 49 (6), 1229-38.

Cuddy, Amy J.C., Susan T. Fiske, and Peter Glick (In press), "Warmth and competence as universal dimensions of social perception: The stereotype content model and the BIAS map," *Advances in Experimental Social Psychology.*

Fiske, Susan T., Amy J. C. Cuddy, and Peter Glick (2007), "Universal dimensions of social cognition: Warmth and competence," *Trends in Cognitive Sciences,* 11 (2), 77-83.

Hennig-Thurau, Thorsten, Markus Groth, Michael Paul, and Dwayne D. Gremler (2006), "Are All Smiles Created Equal? How Emotional Contagion and Emotional Labor Affect Service Relationships," *Journal of Marketing,* 70 (July), 58–73.

Judd, Charles M., Laurie James-Hawkins, Vincent Yzerbyt, and Yoshihisa Kashima (2005), "Fundamental dimensions of social judgment: Understanding the relations between judgments of competence and warmth," *Journal of Personality and Social Psychology,* 89 (6), 899-913.

Macrae, C. N., Kimberly A. Quinn, Malia F. Mason, and Susanne Quadflieg (2005), "Understanding others: The face and person construal," *Journal of Personality and Social Psychology,* 89 (5), 686-95.

Lee, Yih Hwai and Elison Ai Ching Lim (2010), "When Good Cheer Goes Unrequited: How Emotional Receptivity Affect Evaluation of Expressed Emotion," *Journal of Marketing Research.*

Todorov, Alexander, Christopher P. Said, and Sara C. Verosky (In press), "Personality impressions from facial appearance," in *Handbook of face perception*, Edited by Calder, A., J. V. Haxby, M. Johnson, and G. Rhodes.Oxford University Press.

Trougakos, John P., Christine L. Jackson, and Daniel J. Beal (2010), "Service without a smile: Comparing the consequences of neutral and positive display rules," *Journal of Applied Psychology.*

Young, Steven G., and Kurt Hugenberg (2010), "Mere social categorization modulates identification of facial expressions of emotion," *Journal of Personality and Social Psychology,* 99 (6), 964-77.

Zebrowitz, Leslie A., and Joann M. Montepare (2005), "Appearance DOES matter," *Science,* 308 (5728), 1565-6.

Buying Violence: Understanding the Appeal of Violence in Popular Media

Laurence Ashworth, Queens University, Canada
Ethan Pancer, Queens University, Canada
Martin Pyle, Queens University, Canada

Violent media is extremely popular. Nearly 70% of prime-time television contains violence (National Television Violence Study, 1998), and approximately 40% of all video games are rated for violent content (Entertainment Software Association, 2009). In 2008, six of the top ten grossing movies featured substantial violence (IMDb, 2010). Although less well documented, violence is a major theme in many popular books and music. In short, violence in media is endemic. Consequently, much of the work on this topic has focused on the effects of exposure. A great deal of research purports to demonstrate a variety of negative effects of exposure to violence, although there are good reasons to question the causal link (Freedman, 2002).

One feature of violent media has remained almost completely unexplored though – the reasons for its appeal. Patterns of spending suggest that consumers enjoy violent media, but research on the topic is scant. What research has manipulated violent content and measured viewer enjoyment has shown either negative or no effects of violence (e.g. Hansen and Hansen, 1990; Sparks, Sherry, and Lubsen, 2005), consistent with Zillmann's (1998) proposition that viewing violence is actually distressing. The purpose of the current work is to examine whether violent content is attractive to consumers and why.

We suggest that violence may be appealing –not due to pleasurable reactions to the depiction of harm by one person on another – but due to the role that violence plays in satisfying other consumer goals – in particular, dominance and justice. Research in evolutionary psychology (Cummins, 1996) and fundamental human motivations (McClelland, 1985) supports the notion that dominance, especially physical dominance, is likely to be intrinsically rewarding. The ability to physically dominate others, in men in particular, is likely to confer reproductive and survival advantages that favor the selection of corresponding physical and psychological characteristics. Although not often referenced in definitions of violent content (e.g. Anderson and Bushman, 2001), domination is often central to violent encounters – the encounter typically concludes with the domination of one party by another. We argue that vicarious reactions to the domination inherent in many violent depictions are one reason for its enjoyment.

Violence can serve other functions too. One notable function, especially in media depictions, is justice. Justice is an important motive in human interactions, the achievement of which should be inherently satisfying. As such, justice may be one of the reasons for the appeal of violence. Violence that allows the satisfaction of justice should be preferred to violence enacted for other reasons. We test both of these ideas, as well as the question of whether consumers approach violence in media across three experiments.

EXPERIMENT 1

Experiment 1 was a 2 (Violence Level: High vs. Low) x 2 (Gender) between-subjects experiment designed to address the question of whether consumers preferentially approach media with violent content. We tested this by creating a synopsis of a wartime movie, loosely based on the film, "Bridge on the River Kwai", and renamed "Complicity" to disguise the origin of the movie. All participants saw the same description, which focused on the plot and meaning of the movie, but included no reference to the violent content. We also included a short review of the movie, which we varied to manipulate perceptions of the extent of violent content. The reviews were identical except for the modification of two sentences to indicate the movie included scenes of realistic violence. The primary dependent variable was the extent to which participants thought they would enjoy the movie (four items, $\alpha = .93$). An ANOVA revealed a Violence x Gender interaction ($F(1, 91) = 8.92, p < .01$) that indicated men thought they would enjoy the movie more when it appeared to be more violent ($Ms = 5.66$ vs. 4.67), whereas women thought they would enjoy it less ($Ms = 3.58$ vs. 4.39).

EXPERIMENT 2

Experiment 2 was designed to investigate the role of vicarious reactions to domination in the actual enjoyment of violent depictions. We included three experimental conditions: no violence, violence in which the protagonist dominated, and violence in which the protagonist was dominated. This resulted in a 3 (Violence) x 2 (Gender) between-subjects factorial design. Participants viewed one of three video clips of a recently released video game, "Resident Evil 5". Clips were constructed using footage from teaser-trailers, in-game cut scenes, and actual gameplay. We created a common two and half minute non-violent segment to which we interspersed one minute of additional footage corresponding to the condition. All clips were designed to be equally exciting and the latter two clips were designed to be equally violent. The final clips used the same 30 second introduction, had a common (arousing) soundtrack, and were three and a half minutes long. The primary dependent variable was attitude towards the videogame (measured by five items, $\alpha = .93$).

ANOVA revealed a Gender by Violence interaction ($F(2, 154) = 3.36, p < .05$). Follow-up analyses within gender revealed that women liked the game less when it contained *any* violence ($M_{No\ Violence} = 3.19$ vs. $M_{High\ Dominance} = 2.36$ vs. $M_{Low\ Dominance} = 2.60$; only the first mean differed from the others), whereas men liked the game less *only* when the protagonist was dominated ($Ms = 4.16$ vs. 4.34 vs. 3.56; only the latter mean differed from the former). Violent content did appear to lower attitudes, except in men when the violence portrayed high levels of protagonist domination.

EXPERIMENT 3

Experiment 3 was designed to investigate the role of justice in the enjoyment of violence. Participants read a (made-up) passage from a book that described a scene of intense violence enacted by one man on another. Violence was manipulated by providing physical details of the violent acts versus simply naming the acts (e.g. "castration" versus a description of it). We manipulated the justice motive by including a very brief reference that suggested the "victim" was responsible for the death of the enactor's wife, leading to a 2 (Violence) x 2 (Justified) x 2 (Gender) between-subjects design. The primary dependent variable was attitude towards the book (three items, $\alpha = .93$). An ANOVA revealed a marginally significant three-way interaction ($F(1, 95) = 2.81, p < .10$). Follow-up analyses indicated that within men, higher levels of violence led to more positive attitudes only when the violence was justified ($Ms = 3.60$ vs. 2.52; $F(1, 95) = 3.45, p < .07$). Within women, attitudes towards the book were uniformly low, but increased with low levels of justified violence ($Ms = 1.50$ vs. 2.59; $F(1, 95) = 6.27, p < .05$).

Overall, our results suggest that men, but not women, approach violent content in media. The violence itself, however, appears to reduce enjoyment in both men and women unless it satisfies some other motive. Both men and women enjoyed violence that satisfied the justice motive, although they responded to quite different forms of violence. Men enjoyed extreme justified violence; women only enjoyed reduced forms of justified violence. Only men enjoyed vicarious domination, although it was, at least in our experiment, equally offset by negative reactions to the violence itself.

REFERENCES

Entertainment Software Association (2009). *Essential facts*. Retrieved on 2009-05-07 from http://www.theesa.com/facts/pdfs/ESA_EF_2009.pdf

Freedman, Jonathan L. (2002), "Media Violence and Its Effect on Aggression", University of Toronto Press: Toronto, ON, CA.

Hansen, Christine H. and Ranald D. Hansen (1990), "The Influence of Sex and Violence on the Appeal of Rock Music Videos," *Communication Research*, 17(2), 212-234.

Internet Movie Database (2010). *Top Grossing Movies for 2008 in the USA*. Retrieved on 2010-01-02 from http://www.imdb.com/Sections/Years/2008/top-grossing.

National Television Violence Study (1998). Retrieved on 2010-01-02 from http://www.turnoffyourtv.com/healtheducation/violencechildren/NTVVSexecsum.pdf

Sparks, Glenn G., John Sherry, and Graig Lubsen (2005), "The Appeal of Media Violence in a Full-Length Motion Picture: An Experimental Investigation," *Communication Reports*, 18(1), 21-30.

Zillmann, Dolf (1998), "The Psychology of the Appeal of Portrayals of Violence," in *Why We Watch: The attractions of Violent Enterainment*, Jeffrey H. Goldstein ed., New York: Oxford University Press, 179-211.

I Love Your Gucci Glasses, You Have Taste vs. I Love Your Joe Glasses, You are Smart
The Role of Self Construal and Brand Status in Compliment Appreciation

Fang Wan, University of Manitoba, Canada
Hesham Fazel, University of Manitoba, Canada
Pingping Qiu, Monash University, Australia

Compliments are conducive to social interactions and communications. Little research has been done to examine the psychological underpinnings of the observed cultural differences in compliment giving and acceptance. Even more scarce attention has been given to extend research on compliments to consumer contexts and study the impact of compliments related to brand usage on consumers' evaluations and preferences of the focal brand. Our work set out to study cultural difference in compliment appreciation (Study 1) and further investigate its implications in brand usage contexts (Study 2 and 3).

CULTURAL DIFFERENCE AND COMPLIMENT APPRECIATION

Self construals are often used as a proxy to uncover cultural differences: how individuals classify or perceive themselves according to the constituted cultural values they follow (Singles & Brown, 2001). In North American culture, there is a reliance on the natural separateness of distinct persons. The normative imperative of this culture is to become independent from others and to determine and convey one's unique attributes (Markus & Kitayama, 1991, see also Triandis, 1995). However, Asians cultures have interdependent self-concepts that emphasize the connectedness between themselves and others (Morris & Peng, 1994; Hong et al., 2000). North Americans, who typically have independent self-construals, are likely to view social compliments as a matter of personal choice, indicative of compliment givers' genuine liking of self, therefore, are more likely to appreciate social compliments. Individuals with interdependent self construals view compliment givers as more likely to have ulterior motives (Park, 1998).

Therefore we propose that individuals with independent self construals are more likely to appreciate social compliments than those with interdependent self construals. We further propose that the difference in independent and interdependent individuals' reaction toward social compliments are due to perceived sincerity of the compliment givers. As a result, perceived sincerity of social compliments mediates the relationship between self construals and compliment appreciation. We test these propositions in study 1. We predict that brand status moderates the relationship of self construal and compliment appreciation. Interdependent individuals will feel less appreciative than self interdependent individuals when receiving a compliment about their low brand status (Study 2). We further propose that interdependent individuals may perceive the compliment on brand usage when brand status is low to be less sincere, which mediate the relationship of the interaction of brand status and self construal and compliment appreciation (study 3).

Study1.

Study 1 examined the impact of self construal on social compliment appreciation and the mediating role of perceived sincerity of the compliment giver. 175 undergraduate students in a major Canadian university participated in the study for course credit. They were asked to read a general compliment scenario. Then they filled out a survey measuring their appreciation of the compliment with2 items (appreciation & grateful α = .73), perceived sincerity of the compliment giver with single item and their cultural orientations with 24 items Self-construal scale (Singelis, 1994), self-independent 12 items (α = .76) and self-interdependent 12 items (α = .79).

Since our goal was to test the differences between independent and interdependent self-construal individuals; we focused on participants who score higher than the average score on either independents or interdependent and a relatively low score on the other. Accordingly, we eliminated participants who score higher (lower) than the average score on both independents and interdependent scale. This procedure enabled us to use data from 79 participants, 41 independent, 38 interdependent.

ANOVA tests on dependent variables confirmed our expectation that high independent individuals were more likely than interdependent individuals to felt more appreciated when receiving a compliment (F = 2.915, p = .09), and perceived the sincerity of the compliment giver to be higher (F = 8.292, p < .05) (Table 1a). Simple mediation analyses revealed that perceived sincerity mediated the relationship between self-construal and appreciation of social compliments (Table 1b).

Table 1a. Study 1 ANOVA Results

	Self- Construal		F value	p value
	Independent	Interdependent		
Appreciation	6.065	5.68	2.915	.09 *
Perceived sincerity	5.826	5.062	8.292	.013**

- *** <.09 Marginally Sig.**
- ****< .05**

Table 1b. Study 1 Simple Mediation Analyses

MD	Path	Step	b	SE	t	p
Perceived sincerity	1	c	.378	.221	1.707	.096
	2	a	.764	.294	2.594	.013
	3	b	.316	.106	2.980	.005
	4	c'	.161	.226	.714	.480
Soble Test:			Z		Sig (p-2tailed)	
			1.9588		**0.050**	

Study 2.

We intended to examine the moderator effect of brand high status on feeling of appreciation when receiving social compliment. In study 2 we run 2 (self construal: independent vs. interdependent) x 2 (brand status: high vs. low) experimental design. 80 university students participated in exchange for partial course credits. They were asked to read a scenario where a compliment was made about Gucci (Joe) sunglasses. The dependent variables and self construal scales were identical as in Study 1. For manipulation check, ANOVA tests on brand status variables were significant. Compared to Joe brand, Gucci is perceived to be more prestigious (F = 23.123, p = .000) and to have higher status (F = 34.351, p = .000) (Table 2a). ANOVA tests on dependent variables (appreciation) showed significant interaction effect of brand status and self construal, suggesting that independent self construal (vs. self interdependent construal) are more appreciative to compliment when they receive it on low brand status and less appreciative when they receive it on high brand status (Table 2b).

Table 2a. Study 2 Manipulation Check

	Brand status		F value	p value
	Low (Joe)	High (Gucci)		
Brand perceived to be prestigious	3.258	5.031	23.123	.000***
Brand perceived to have high status	2.849	5.250	34.351	.000***

- ****< .05**
- *****<.001**

Table 2b. Study 2 (Self-Construal * Brand Status)

Dependent variable	Brand Status* Self-Construal		F value	F value	p value
Appreciative	High	Independent	4.36	3. 107	.09*
		Interdependent	5.43		
	Low	Independent	5.9	3.50	.07*
		Interdependent	5.00		

- ****< .05**
- *****<.001**

Study 3.

We intended to examine the effect of self construal and brand status interaction on compliment appreciation and also test the mediation role of perceived sincerity. 64 undergraduate students in a major Canadian university participated in the study. We used the binary regression tool to categorize the indicators of self construal and brand status. The following is a description of the binary variables:

ANOVA test resulted in a significant interaction of brand status and self construal as in Study 2, suggesting that independent individuals are more appreciative of brand compliment than interdependent when focal brand has low status (M =5.92 vs. M =5.00). Also, our findings indicate that perceived sincerity partially mediate the relationship of self construal and brand status interaction on compliment appreciation (Table 3).

Table 3. Study 3 ANOVA Results
Mean effect

DV: Appreciation	F value	p value
Self-Construal	.037	.848
Brand Status	2.057	.158
Self-Construal * Brand Status	6.516	.014**

Simple Mediation

DV: Appreciation	F value	p value
Self-Construal	.804	.374
Brand Status	.831	.366
Self-Construal * Brand Status	5.890	.019**
Perceived sincerity	11.549	.001***

- ****< .05**
- *****<.001**

DISCUSSION

Our next step is to replicate our research with participants from different cultures. In addition, we plan to employ interpersonal encounters to add external validity to our scenario studies. Further, we will explore self construal effects on brand related variables (e.g. brand attachment, loyalty and discover if appreciation compliment effects brand relationship.

REFERENCES

Chen, R. (1993). Responding to compliments: a contrastive study of politeness strategies between American English and Chinese speakers. *Journal of Pragmatics*, 20 (1), 49–75.

Fong, M. (1998). Chinese immigrant's perceptions of semantic dimensions of direct/indirect communication in intercultural compliment interactions with North Americans. *The Howard Journal of Communications*, 9, 245-262.

Higgins, E. T. (1997). Beyond pleasure and pain. *American Psychologist, 52*, 1280-1300.

Holmes, Janet. (1986). Compliments and compliment responses in New Zealand English. *Anthropological Linguistics* 28, 485–508.

Hong, Y., Morris M., Chiu C.Y., & Benet-Martinez V. (2000). Multicultural minds: A dynamic constructivist approach to culture and cognition. American Psychologist, 55, 709–720.

Koshik, Irene A. (2002). A conversation analytic study of yes/no questions that assert their reverse polarity. *Journal of Pragmatics.* 547–571 569.

Nelson, Gayle L., Waguida, El Bakary, Mahmoud, Al-Batal. (1993). Egyptian and American compliments: a cross-cultural study. International Journal of Intercultural Relations 17, 293–313.

Manes, J . (1983). Compliments : A mirror of cultural values. In N. Wolfson & E. Judd (Eds.) , *Sociolinguistics and language acquisition* (pp . 96-102) . Rowley, MA: Newbury House.

Markus, H., & Kitayama S. (1991). Culture and the self: Implications for cognition, emotion and motivation. Psychological Review, 98, 224–253.

Morris, M. W., & Peng K.P. (1994). Culture and cause: American and Chinese attributions for social and physical events. Journal of Personality and Social Psychology, 67, 949–971.

Park, S. Y. (1998). A comparison of Korean and American gift-giving behaviors. Psychology and Marketing, 15, 577-593.

Ruth, J. A. (1996). It's the feeling that counts: Toward a framework for understanding emotion and its influence on gift-exchange processes. In C. Otnes, & R. F. Beltramini (Eds), Gift-giving: An interdisciplinary anthology (pp. 195-214). Bowling Green, OH: Bowling Green University Popular Press.

Shen, H, Wan F. and Wyer, R.S. (2010), "Cross-Cultural Differences in the Refusal to Accept a Small Gift: The Differential Influence of Reciprocity Norms on Asians and North Americans," Journal of Personality and Social Psychology.

Singelis, T. M. (1994). The measurement of independent and interdependent self-construals. Personality and Social Psychology Bulletin, 20, 580–591.

Triandis, H. C. (1995). Individualism and collectivism. Boulder, CO: Westview Press.

Tang, C. H.. Zhang, G. Q. (2009). A contrastive study of compliment responses among Australian English and Mandarin Chinese speakers. *Journal of Pragmatics*, Volume 41, Issue 2, Pages 325-345.

Wolfson, Nessa. (1981). Compliments in cross-cultural perspective. *TESOL Quarterly* 15, 117–124.

Ying, Y.W. (1996). Immigration satisfaction of Chinese Americans: An empirical examination. *Journal of Community Psychology,* 24, 3-16.

Yu, M. (2004). Interlinguistic variation and similarity in second language speech act behaviour. *The Modern Language Journal*, 88 (1), 102–119.

Unveiling the Underlying Mechanism for the Matching Effect between Construal Levels and Message Frames: How and Why Do Matches between Gain versus Loss Frames and Construal Levels Enhance Persuasion?

Yun Lee, University of Iowa, USA
Jing (Alice) Wang, University of Iowa, USA
Catherine A. Cole, University of Iowa, USA

This research investigates *how* and *why* different construal levels and different appeal frames jointly influence persuasion. We contend that individuals using high-level consturals preferentially pay attention to appeals framed by gains, whereas those using low-level construals selectively focus on appeals framed by losses, and thus this matching should impact persuasion. This perspective has yet to be investigated directly. Its consequences as well as the specific mechanism underlying these consequences are still to be unveiled. Thus, the current research addresses this gap. In what follows, we briefly review relevant literatures. We then report three sets of experiments and conclude with a brief discussion of contributions of this research.

Construal Level, Message Frames, and Functional Matching Mechanisms

Construal level theory (CLT) posits that when people use different levels of construal, they selectively include and exclude relevant or irrelevant features of an attitude object (Fujita et al. 2006a). Specifically, high-level construals preferentially capture abstract and global features of an attitude object, but low-level consturals, preferentially capture its concrete and local features.(Liberman and Trope 1998).

A closer look at the message framing literature offers some insight into how message frames are linked with different levels of construal. For example, research on message frames has demonstrated that loss frames are more persuasive when individuals process them locally (Förster and Higgins 2005), more in-depth (Block and Keller 1995; Shiv et al. 1997) and in details (Maheswaran and Meyers-Levy 1990), whereas gain frames are more persuasive when people process them globally (Förster and Higgins 2005) in less details (Maheswaran and Meyers-Levy 1990; Shiv et al. 1997).

Given these findings suggesting that gain- versus loss frames are related with the features of high- versus low-level construals, I argue that individuals using high-level construals are more likely to attend to gain-framed appeals, whereas those using low-level construals are more likely to focus on loss-framed appeals, and it influences persuasion. I refer to these predictions as the enhanced attention mechanism of the matching effect and test it across five experiments.

Experiment 1

Experiment 1 tests the hypothesis that matching high-level construals with gain frames and low-level construals with loss frames will encourage participants to pay more attention to the appeals they evaluate, and thus influence persuasion.

METHOD

I randomly assigned participants to one of the four conditions in a 2(frames: gain vs. loss) × 2 (construal level: high vs. low) between-subjects design. Participants read information about heart disease and appeals advocating a diagnostic blood test. I manipulated construal level by making the appeals either why-laden (e.g., *why* people need to take a diagnostic blood test) or how-laden (e.g., *How* to take a diagnostic blood test). I manipulated message frames by framing the appeals in terms of either gains or losses (e.g., If you (don't) take a diagnostic blood test, you can find (fail to find) out your current cholesterol level). I then asked participants to indicate their intentions to take the blood test (1 = not at all likely ~ 7 = very likely). They also indicated the extent to which they paid attention to the appeals (1=not at all ~7=very much).

RESULTS

Behavioral intentions

A 2 (framing) × 2 (construal level) ANOVA on behavioral intentions yielded a significant interaction effect ($F(1, 109) = 8.37, p < .01$). When the appeals were why-laden (high level), presenting these appeals in a gain frame was more persuasive than in a loss frame (*Mgain* = 5.30, *Mloss* = 4; $F(1, 53) = 4.17, p < .0565$), whereas when the message was how-laden (low levels), presenting these appeals in a loss frame was more persuasive than in a gain frame (*Mgain* = 4.44, *Mloss* = 5.36; ; $F(1, 56) = 4.34, p < .05$).

The mediating role of attention

Conducting a series of regression analyses (Baron and Kenny 1986) confirmed that the matching effect on behavioral intentions was mediated by attention.

The findings from experiment 1 show that attention mediates the matching effect. Experiment 2 adds processing fluency into the picture.

Experiment 2

Two objectives guide the design of experiment 2: 1) to examine the relationship between processing fluency and attention, and 2) to increase the robustness of the found effects.

METHOD

Participants were randomly assigned to one of the conditions of a 2(frames: gain vs. loss) × 2 (construal level: high vs. low) between-subjects design. For the construal level manipulation, participants were asked to write about *why* they need to improve and maintain health (high level) vs. *how* they can improve and maintain health (low level) (Freitas et al. 2004). Then they were presented with an advertisement of a fictitious printer whose ad appeals were gain vs. loss framed (e.g., Don't miss out on (Get) printing-pro for great looking documents and web-page printing!) and asked to evaluate it. They were also asked to indicate the degree to which they paid attention to the ad information and answer processing fluency items (1=hard to process, hard to understand, hard to comprehend ~7=easy to process, easy to understand, easy to comprehend).

RESULTS

Attitudes

A 2 (framing) × 2 (construal level) ANOVA on brand attitudes yielded a significant interaction effect ($F(1, 108) = 13.08, p < .001$). When participants viewed the gain-framed message under high-level construals (*Mgain* = 5.11, *Mloss* = 4.10; $F(1, 55) = 9.74, p < .005$) and when they viewed the loss-framed message under low-level construals (*Mgain* = 4.16, *Mloss* = 5.07 $F(1, 53) = 4.65, p < .05$), their brand attitudes were more favorable than any other conditons.

The relationship between processing fluency and attention

Conducting a series of regression analyses demonstrated that matches enhance attention, which in turn increases processing fluency and favorable brand attitudes.

The results from experiment 2 indicate that attention mediates the matching effect on processing fluency and on brand attitudes. Experiment 3 tests whether attention given to matching information is reflected in greater sensitivity to its argument strength (Fujita et al. 2008; Petty and Wegener 1998).

Experiment 3

The objectives of experiment 3 are: 1) to examine whether consumers under matching conditions devote greater attention to message processing and thus are more sensitive to argument strength than consumers in non-matching conditions, and 2) to increase generalizability and robustness of the found effects.

METHOD

Participants were randomly assigned to one of the conditions of a 2(frames: gain vs. loss) × 2 (construal level: high vs. low) × 2 (argument strength: strong vs. weak) between-subjects design. Participants were presented with the information about a wildlife conservation fundraising campaign. Construal level was manipulated as dedicated to protecting a specific North Atlantic Right whale, named Simmon (low level), or North Atlantic Right whales in general (high level). Argument strength was manipulated by presenting arguments that strongly or weakly endorsed the fund-raiser (e.g., 100% (50%) of your financial donation goes toward helping Simoon (North Atlantic Right whales)!). Message frames were manipulated within the stimuli (e.g., Get (Don't lose) a chance to help and save Simoon (North Atlantic Right whales)!). Then participants were asked to indicate how likely they are willing to donate (1=not at all likely ~ 7=very likely). They were also asked to answer processing fluency and attention items.

RESULTS

Willingness to donate

To test the main hypotheses, I recoded the data to reflect matches (a gain frame and high level, a loss frame and low level) and mismatches (a gain frame and low level, a loss frame and high level) between argument strength. The data were then analyzed with a 2 (match: match vs. mismatch) × 2 (argument strength: strong vs. weak) between-subjects ANOVA on willingness to donate. It yielded significant argument strength and match main effects. These main effects were qualified by a two-way interaction effect ($F(1, 141) = 13.02, p < .001$). As predicted, matches supported by weak arguments resulted in less willingness to donate than matches supported by strong arguments ($M_{match,strong} = 4.79, M_{match, weak} = 3.46; F(1, 72) = 14.64, p < .001$).

The relationship between processing fluency and attention

Running a series of regression analyses indicated that matches enhance perceived attention, and thus increases processing fluency and willingness to donate.

DISCUSSION

By demonstrating the enhanced attention mechanism underlying the matching effects between construal levels and gain versus loss frames, the current research contributes to the literatures on functional matching, message framing and construal level. This research also has managerial implications for marketing managers in that it suggests a strategic way to use message frames and construal level to enhance persuasive effectiveness.

REFERENCES

Baron, Reuben M. and David A. Kenny (1986), "The Moderator-Mediator Variable Distinction in Social Psychological Research: Conceptual, Strategic, and Statistical Considerations," *Journal of Personality and Social Psychology*, 51 (2), 1173–82.

Block, Lauren G. and Punam Anand Keller (1995), "When to Accentuate the Negative: The Effects of Perceived Efficacy and Message Framing on Intentions to Perform a Health-Related Behavior," *Journal of Marketing Research*, 32 (May), 192–203.

Förster, Jens and E. Tory Higgins (2005), "How Global Versus Local Perception Fits Regulatory Focus," *Psychological Science*, 16 (8), 631–36.

Freitas, Antonio L., Peter Gollwitzer, and Yaacov Trope (2004), "The Influence of Abstract Mindsets on Anticipating and Guiding Others' Self-regulatory Efforts," *Journal of Experimental Psychology*, 40, 739–52.

Fujita, Kentaro, Tal Eyal, Shelly Chaiken, Yaacov Trope, and Nira Liberman (2008), "Influencing Attitudes Toward Near and Distant Objects," *Journal of Experimental Social Psychology*, 44, 562–72.

Fujita, Kentaro, Yaacov Trope, Nira Liberman, and Maya Levin-Sagi (2006a), "Construal Levels and Self-Control," *Journal of Personality and Social Psychology*, 90 (3), 351–67.

Fujita, Kentaro, Marlone D. Henderson, Juliana Eng, Yaacov Trope, and Nira Liberman (2006b), "Spatial Distance and Mental Construal of Social Events," *Psychological Science*, 278–82.

Lee, Angela Y. and Aparna A. Labroo (2004), "The Effect of Conceptual and Perceptual Fluency on Brand Evaluation," *Journal of Marketing Research*, 41 (May), 151–65.

Lee, Angela Y., and Jennifer L. Aaker (2004), "Bringing the Frame Into Focus: The Influence of Regulatory Fit on Processing Fluency and Persuasion," *Journal of Personality and Social Psychology*, 86 (2), 205–18.

Lee, Angela Y., Punam Anand Keller, and Brian Sternthal (2010), "Value from Regulatory Construal Fit: The Persuasive Impact of Fit between Consumer Goals and Message Concreteness," *Journal of Consumer Research*, 36 (February), 735–47.

Liberman, Nira and Yaacov Trope (1998), "The Role of Feasibility and Desirability Considerations in Near and Distant Future Decisions: A Test of Temporal Construal Theory," *Journal of Personality and Social Psychology*, 75 (July), 5–18.

Maheswaran, Durairaj and Joan Meyers-Levy (1990), "The Influence of Message Framing and Issue Involvement," *Journal of Marketing Research*, 27 (August), 361-67.

Petty, Richard E. and Duane T. Wegener (1998), "Matching versus mismatching attitude functions: Implications for scrutiny of persuasive messages," *Personality and Social Psychology Bulletin*, 24 (3), 227–240.

Shiv, Baba, Julie A. Edell, and John W. Payne (1997), "Factors Affecting the Impact of Negatively and Positively Framed Ad Messages," *Journal of Consumer Research*, 24 (3), 285–94.

White, Katherine, Rhiannon MacDonnell, and Darren W. Dahl (2011), "It's the Mind-Set That Matters: The Role of Construal Level and Message Framing in Influencing Consumer Efficacy and Conservation Behaviors," *Journal of Marketing Research*, 48 (June), 472–85.

Disabilities and the Internet;
Understanding Consumers with Visual Impairments

William Jones, Wayne State University, USA
Terry Childers, Iowa State University, USA
Fred Morgan, Wayne State University, USA

Heralded as a great equalizer, the Internet once promised to eliminate disabling spaces by creating a barrier-free virtual "commons" where consumers of all types could interact in the marketplace. However, studies suggest that persons with disabilities are less likely to own computers, to have Internet access, and to make online purchases than persons without disabilities (Kaye, 2000a, 2000b). Moreover, online use is not automatically assured even if computers and the Internet are available. Both industry and academic web studies have shown that a substantial number of web sites are not useable by persons with disabilities since their content is not transmitted accurately, clearly, or completely (e.g., Schaefer, 2003). In fact, numerous prominent retailers have been challenged in court for web accessibility violations (Kretchmer and Carveth, 2003). These lawsuits are saddening given web-based technology's potential to achieve a sense of normalcy and facilitate shopping independence for consumers with disabilities.

Because of numerous, but addressable limitations, a sizeable market of consumers is likely to have experienced difficulties shopping online. Statistically, persons with disabilities represent 20 percent of the United States' population, collectively larger than the size of major ethnic groups (National Organization on Disability, 2005). Surprisingly, some firms argue that the market is not large enough to warrant special accommodations online (Heim, 2000). In fact, estimates of the disposable income of persons with disabilities vary from more than $176 billion (Johnson, 2000) to approximately 1 trillion (Milliman, 2002). Despite such significant potential, this substantial market has largely been overlooked both online and offline (Baker, Stephens, and Hill, 2002). To increase the welfare of all consumers, research is needed to understand the needs, behaviors, and perceptions of individuals possessing different forms of sensory, motor, and cognitive impairments. Our research was designed to provide insights on how these individuals feel toward online shopping. We first conduct a study that examines the utility and usability of online web sites across individuals possessing a broad range of disabilities. A second study examines whether online shopping can empower consumers with visual and hearing impairments to better achieve their retail shopping goals.

STUDY 1

To investigate whether online shopping experiences of consumers with disabilities differed from that of consumers without disabilities, we conducted a multi-group structural equations analysis of the Childers et al. (2001) adaption of the technology acceptance model (TAM) to groups of participants with or without disabilities. Participants were 383 participants without disabilities and 75 participants with disabilities that responded as Internet shoppers in an annual e-commerce telephone survey.

After establishing adequate reliability as well as convergent and discriminant validity of the model, we estimated the model via maximum likelihood estimation. Tests of measurement equality indicated that the measurement portion of the model was comparable across the two groups. Model fit indices meet moderate to excellent norms (Byrne 1998).

Overall, we found strong support for ease of use and usefulness as antecedents of attitudes toward online shopping irrespective of disability. Attitudes are also predictive of purchase behavior, the first study to our knowledge that has moved beyond behavioral intention to predict actual online purchase behavior. Comparing the relative effects of usefulness, we find consistent with our predictions that it is equally predictive of attitudes for consumers with and without disabilities. However, inconsistent with our predictions was that ease of use was not attenuated by mobility status. The many obstacles confronting individuals with impairments when shopping online led us to predict a weaker relationship between attitudes and ease of use among the disabled. One possibility may be that not all disabilities may face the same obstacles to online purchasing.

STUDY 2

In Study 2, we re-assess the model used in Study 1 by making model comparisons between groups of consumers with visual impairments, with hearing impairments, and without disabilities. Kaufman-Scarborough and Childers (2009) have shown previously that empowerment may be related to perceived usefulness and ease of use in online shopping environments. We therefore extend the original model by incorporating a measure psychological empowerment (Zimmerman, Israel, Schulz, and Checkoway 1992) as an antecedent of consumers' perceived usefulness and ease of use decision variables.

Overall, we find strong support for the role of empowerment in better understanding the use of online shopping by individuals with visual impairments. These results are consistent with the underlying theme of empowerment, which seemed to motivate many of the legal challenges (Study 2). Feelings of empowerment provide insight as to the importance of this personal characteristic of the disabled that leads them to possess stronger perceptions of the utility of meeting their shopping needs by engaging in online purchasing. We also find that ease of using the Internet for online shopping is related to empowerment for both groups of disabled consumers as well. However, we do not find that disability status is differentially related to ease of use as we had predicted. Different from the overall disability results of Study 1, attitudes were a stronger predictor of purchases in the non-impaired sample relative to the visually and hearing impaired with the latter two not significantly different. The direction of our empowerment findings was consistent with the premise that for those visually impaired, empowerment did not predict ease of use as strongly as found in a comparison disability group with a hearing impairment as well as for individuals without impairments.

REFERENCES

Baker, Stacey M., Stephens, Deborah L., and Hill, Ronald P. (2001), "Marketplace Experiences of Consumers with Visual Impairments: Beyond the Americans with Disabilities Act," *Journal of Public Policy & Marketing*, 20 (Fall), 297-304.

Byrne, Barbara (1998), *Structural Equations Modeling with LISREL, PRELIS, SIMPLIS. Basic Concepts, Applications, and Programming.* Mahaw, New Jersey: Lawrence Erlbaum Associates, Inc.

Childers, Terry L., Carr, Christopher L., Peck, Joann, and Carson, Stephen (2001), "Hedonic and Utilitarian Motivations for Online Retail Shopping Behavior," *Journal of Retailing*, 77 (Winter), 511-535.

Heim, J. (2000). Locking Out The Disabled: Office Buildings Have Wheelchair Ramps, TV Has Closed Captions, But Many Web Sites Are Inaccessible To People With Disabilities. Things Don't Have To Be That Way. *PC World magazine*, September, retrieved online at: www.pcworld.com.

Kaufman-Scarborough, Carol and Childers, Terry L. (2009) "Visual Impairments And Experiences Of Online Shopping: The Desire for Normalcy with Insights for Public Policy," Journal of Public Policy & Marketing, 28(1), 16-28.

Kaye, H. Stephen (2000a), Computer and Internet Use Among People with Disabilities, *Disabilities Statistics Report* (13). Washington DC: U.S. Department of Education, National Institute on Disability and Rehabilitation Research.

_____ (2000b), Disability and the Digital Divide. Washington, DC: U.S. Department of Education.

Kretchmer, S. B. & R. Carveth (2003). Analyzing Recent Americans With Disabilities Act-Based Accessible Information Technology Court Challenges, Information Technology And Disabilities, *Special Issue on Public Policy Issues: Access to Information and Information Technology,* IX (1), October,, retrieved online at: http://www.rit.edu/~easi/itd/itdv09n2/kretchmr.htm.

Milliman, R. E. (2002). Website Accessibility And The Private Sector: Disability Stakeholders Cannot Tolerate Access, Information Technology And Disabilities, Vol. VIII, 2002, Vol. VIII, No. 1 January, 2002, retrieved online at: http://www.rit.edu/~easi/itd/itdv08n2/milliman.htm.

National Organization on Disability, Frequently Asked Questions On Disability, posted On February 27, 2002; retrieved online: at www.nod.org.

Schaefer, Kelly (2003), "E-space Inclusion: A Case for the Americans with Disabilities Act in Cyberspace," *Journal of Public Policy and Marketing*, 22(Fall), 223-227.

Zimmerman, Mark, A., Barbara A. Israel, Amy Schulz and Barry Checkoway (1992), "Further Explorations in Empowerment Theory: An Empirical Analysis of Psychological Empowerment," *American Journal of Community Psychology*, 20(6), 707-727.

Unfair or Unfavorable? Social Comparisons, Attributions of Responsibility and the Spontaneous Activation of (Un)Fairness Concerns

Laurence Ashworth, Queens University, Canada
Lindsay McShane, Queens University, Canada
Svetlana Davis, Queens University, Canada

Fairness judgments are an important determinant of satisfaction and other behaviors directed towards the firm (e.g. Gregoire and Fisher, 2008). Fairness and unfairness judgments are also assumed to arise across a wide variety of different circumstances, including, for example, as a consequence of firms' service failures (e.g. rude or slow service; Tax, Brown and Chandrashekaran 1998). We question whether fairness is psychologically meaningful in these situations or if it simply reflects general dissatisfaction with the circumstances.

We argue that if explicitly asked, consumers can always form fairness judgments by assessing whether they are deserving of a given outcome or treatment. Generally speaking, they are likely to see themselves as deserving of favorable outcomes/treatments and undeserving of unfavorable ones. Thus, when consumers are asked to rate service failures, when they are unfavorable, they are likely to report them as unfair. We argue, however, that service failures do not necessarily naturally elicit fairness concerns. For instance, imagine a situation where you go to a restaurant and your server is rude. If you were explicitly asked about fairness, the extant literature suggests that you would likely indicate that the situation was relatively unfair in that you do not believe that you deserved to be treated in that way (Smith, Bolton and Wagner 1999; Tax, Brown and Chandrashekaran 1998). However, without being asked about fairness, how likely are consumers to frame the situation in terms of fairness? It seems unlikely. Taking steps to address this apparent conflict, the current research investigates a) when consumers are more or less likely to spontaneously frame a situation in terms of unfairness and b) how these spontaneous fairness judgments relate to solicited fairness judgments.

We argue that fairness violations are more likely to be spontaneously activated when deservingness concerns are salient. Deservingness assessments have been shown to be important in shaping fairness judgments (Feather 1999). Many theories of distributive justice suggest that fairness occurs when people receive in proportion to what they deserve (Adams 1965; Feather 1999). Unfairness results when that person's deservingness is violated. Although typically discussed in terms of distributive injustice, deservingness seems important in assessing service failures. We argue that being explicitly asked about fairness demands that the consumer consider whether they deserve the service failure. The result is that consumers are likely to deem service failures as unfair irrespective of whether they actually framed the situation in terms of fairness. In contrast, we argue that the spontaneous activation of fairness concerns requires that some aspect of the situation makes deservingness salient. Of interest then is what makes deservingness salient?

We predict, initially, that social comparisons make deservingness salient, thus making consumers more likely to spontaneously consider the fairness of their outcome. The logic here is that, when some other consumer receives more favorable treatment (e.g., a better price or quicker service), deservingness is activated by the presence of a clear standard for what they should have received (i.e., the same as the other consumer). We suggest that the relative concreteness of this standard increases the likelihood that the consumer will expressly consider whether they received what they deserved. We test these ideas in Study 1.

STUDY 1

In Study 1 we manipulated the presence or absence of a service failure (by varying the speed of service at a restaurant), as well as the presence or absence of social comparison information, leading to a 2 (Social Comparison Information: Yes, No) x 2 (Service Speed: Normal, Slow) between-subjects experiment. Before responding to any measures, we asked participants to list all relevant thoughts, which we coded for fairness concerns. Participants were also directly asked whether they naturally thought about fairness when reading the scenario. Finally, we asked participants to rate the extent to which the situation was unfair using standard measures.

An ANOVA showed that, when explicitly asked about fairness, participants' fairness judgments reflected both service failure and social comparison information. Specifically, social comparisons and service failures independently exacerbated perceived unfairness (Ms=3.76 vs. 5.59 and Ms=3.98 vs. 5.37, Fs$(1,153)$= 77.66 and 45.05, ps <.001). However, the thought listings indicated that participants were likely to spontaneously think about unfairness *only* when social comparison information was present ($\chi^2(1)=13.30\,p$ <.001). While the presence or absence of service failure had no effect ($\chi^2(1)=2.17\,p$ > .1). Measures of whether fairness was a spontaneous reaction to the scenario supported these results. Consumers reported being more likely to think about unfairness when social comparison information was provided (Ms=5.12 vs. 4.04, F $(1,153)$=23.0, p <.001). There was no significant difference across presence or absence of service failure (F < 1).

This study identifies a situation where reported fairness measures diverge from when consumers are likely to naturally think about unfairness. Specifically, consumers deemed service failures unfair when explicitly asked but did not naturally frame these situations in terms of fairness unless social comparison information was present. There are, however, situations where we would expect alignment between reported fairness and spontaneous thoughts. Specifically, when upward social comparison information is available, we expect elements of the exchange that exacerbate perceived unfairness to make consumers both more likely to spontaneously think about unfairness and to report the situation as more unfair when asked. We argue that attributions of seller responsibility for the service failure is one such element. We predict that the more consumers hold the seller responsible for the service failure, the more likely they are to naturally frame the situation as unfair and, when asked, to report the situation as more unfair. We explore these ideas in Study 2.

STUDY 2

In Study 2 we manipulated whether the seller was responsible for the service failure Information about another consumers' superior outcome (faster service) was always present. We measured fairness in same ways as in Study 1. An ANOVA indicated that, when explicitly asked about fairness, participants reported that they perceived the situation as more unfair when they attributed responsibility to the seller (Ms=3.44 vs. 4.64, $F(1,54)$= 7.64 p <.01). As expected, our analysis of the thought listings revealed that participants were also more likely to naturally think about unfairness in this situation ($\chi^2(1)=5.35\,p$ <.05). Finally, when directly asked, participants reported being more likely to frame this situation in terms of fairness (Ms=3.60 vs. 4.55, F $(1,53)$=5.05 and p <.05).

DISCUSSION

This research takes initial steps to identify certain conditions under which consumers are likely to naturally think about fairness violations (e.g., presence of social comparison information) and how these relate to reported fairness perceptions. This research suggests that while fair can be applied to a wide range of situations, doing so may entail thinking about the situation differently than how consumers naturally do. Finally, although previous research suggests that service failures such as inattentive service are by definition unfair, our research shows that, depending on the situation, consumers may not consider fairness a relevant construct.

REFERENCES

Adams, J. (1965). Inequity in Social Exchange. *Chapter in Advances in Experimental Social Psychology*, Vol. 2. Ed. L. Berkowitz. New York, NY: Academic Press, 267-299.

Feather, N. (1999). Values, Achievement, and Justice. *Plenum, New York*.

Grégoire, Y. and R., Fisher (2008). Customer betrayal and retaliation: when your best customers become your worst enemies. *Journal of the Academy of Marketing Science*, 36:2, 247-261.

Smith, A., Bolton, R. and Wagner, J. (1999). A Model of Customer Satisfaction with Service Encounters Involving Failure and Recovery. *Journal of Marketing Research*, XXXVI, 356-372.

Tax, S., Brown, S. and Chandrashekaran, M. (1998). Customer Evaluations of Service Complaint Experiences: Implications for Relationship Marketing. *Journal of Marketing*, 62, 60-76.

The Dissociative Nature of Product Enthusiasts

Jeffrey Lee, Harvard Business School, USA

Decades of consumer research have led to the conclusion that fans are an integral part of a product's success. Fans can make up a substantial proportion of a product customer base, and serve as a reliable source of revenue in both good times and bad. Acknowledging the importance of strong consumer supporters, a significant body of literature in branding research has focused on brand loyalty and how to increase it (Jacoby and Chestnut, 1978; Dick and Basu, 1994). Aside from providing a steady stream of consumers, efforts to promote consumer loyalists can also lead to the development of "brand ambassadors" and increased positive word-of-mouth (Godes, 2004) for the given product or brand (Godes, 2004). Furthermore, the development of brand communities (Muniz and O'Guinn, 2001) can result in a network of supporters who reinforce each others' positive opinions of the brand, which can further strengthen brand loyalty among these consumers.

Given that extant literature on the many positive effects of consumer loyalists, it seems that marketing practitioners should always generate as much enthusiasm for their products and brands as possible. Yet some recent research suggests that fans of a product can ironically have a negative impact on other consumers in terms of their likelihood of purchase (Naylor et al., 2011). Specifically, this research suggests that when non-fans are perceived to be dissimilar, consumers are less likely to purchase items from a brand relative to when fans are similar, heterogeneous or ambiguous. In a similar vein, my project also explores how fans can affect non-fans. I focus on heterogeneity among fans, in terms of their interest level towards a given product. As opposed to a "fan" of a product, I define consumers as "product enthusiasts" when they exhibit a relatively high level of interest in a product.

Intuitively, one might expect the high-levels of interest from product enthusiasts to positively influence other consumers' adoption of a product. Yet if the enthusiasm of product enthusiasts is perceived to be extreme, it is possible that their highly-positive opinions could be discounted, or even worse, result in reactance such that the product's diffusion is negatively impacted. Some behavioral decision research suggests that the extreme opinions of others are merely ignored in final decision-making (Harries et al., 2004). However, because products can be signals of identity tied to associative and dissociative groups (Dahl and White, 2007), strong opinions by product enthusiasts can result in dissociative inferences about the fans of the product. In this case, these extremely positive opinions would not be ignored; rather, product enthusiasts could ironically cause reactance against the product from non-fans.

I conducted four studies to test the effects of product enthusiasts on other consumers' purchase considerations. In Study 1, I recruited 90 subjects to complete a survey on a hypothetical new cell-phone. I provided subjects with a distribution of the interest levels of ten of their friends and acquaintances towards this new cell-phone. In one of the three conditions, subjects were told that all ten network ties were "slightly interested" in the cell-phone, whereas in the other two conditions, subjects were told that one of the ties was either "moderately interested" (the fan condition) or "extremely interested" (the product-enthusiast condition). Participant ratings of their own interest in the new cell-phone varied marginally across conditions, $F(2, 86) = 2.810$, $p < .066$. However, subsequent planned comparisons indicated that participants' interest-level ratings in the product-enthusiast condition ($M = 2.00$, $SD = 0.617$) were significantly lower than the other two conditions, $t(86) = 2.356$, $p < 0.021$.

Study 2 extends the results of Study 1 by providing subjects with real-world information about a television show. In one condition, subjects are merely provided with a description of the show (control condition), whereas in the second condition, subjects are presented with information about product enthusiasts of the show. Subjects were significantly less likely to watch the television show ($t(45) = 3.448$, $p < 0.00$), the pilot episode, ($t(45) = 3.220$, $p < 0.00$), and the first season ($t(45) = 3.156$, $p < 0.00$) in the product-enthusiast condition relative to the control condition.

Study 3 replicates Study 2, except that subjects are provided with information about a hypothetical television show, and a comparison is made between fans and product enthusiasts to test for potential mediators of the latter group's negative influence. Subjects were significantly less likely to become eventual fans of the television show ($t(84) = 2.782$, $p < 0.007$) in the product enthusiast condition relative to the fan condition. A mediation analysis indicated that the negative impact of the product-enthusiast is mediated by the dissociative nature of the product enthusiast (Sobel z = -2.5117, $p < .012$). This supports the account that product-enthusiasts are dissociative, and that their positive opinions of the product are not merely ignored, but factored *negatively* into other consumers' judgments of the focal product.

In Study 4, I tested the possibility that the dissociative perception of product-enthusiasts is moderated by the life-cycle of the producing brand. Specifically, brands that are more established may be more successful in accommodating product-enthusiasts, because they provide legitimacy for the product in ways that new brands cannot. Study 4 replicates the design of Study 2 in new water bottles, and varies whether the brand is positioned under an established brand or not. A 2 (control versus product-enthusiast) X 2 (established versus un-established brand) between-subjects ANOVA revealed that product-enthusiasts lowered subjects' likelihood of purchasing the water bottle in the un-established brand condition, but not the established brand condition. The predicted interaction between product enthusiasm and established branding was marginally significant, $F(1, 114) = 3.244$, $p < 0.07$.

Collectively, these findings suggest that product-enthusiasts can negatively impact a product's adoption (Studies 1 and 2), that this effect is explained by the dissociative element of these enthusiasts (Study 3). Furthermore, this effect is most pronounced when the producing brand is less established (Study 4). This implication of these results is that practitioners need to be careful in managing product enthusiasts to maintain their ability to attract potential new consumers.

Physical States Effects on Judgment

Consumers are often affected by a variety of physical states (Mobini et al. 1997, Loewenstein 1996). Being hungry or tired may affect the way consumers judge and choose among products (Read and Leeuwen 1998). The way a product would be experienced varies according to consumers' physical states. For instance, if you're hungry, food may appear tastier. In other words, the experience of consuming a product is imagined as it would be given the consumer's current state (Gilbert et al. 2002).

These judgmental biases are typically regarded as being errors. However, they may in fact be adaptive by helping immediate action calibration. By considering how current physical states would affect consumption experiences, consumers can make choices that are appropriate to their current state. It is when stretching current experiences inappropriately to future states, and planning in a way that neglects temporal differences between the current time and the future time, that consumers may commit errors, and potentially make suboptimal choices (Gilbert et al. 2000, 2002).

Functional Judgment: Needing More Means Seeing Less

The reasons and mechanisms leading consumers to make biased judgments and choices of products when in particular physical states are not fully understood at this time. One potential hypothesis concerns the functional view of perception and judgment, whereby judgments are not meant to be objective, but rather to direct people towards action. Objects are not seen as they are, but in terms of the actions they afford and the goals and functions they might fulfill (Gibson 1979).

One domain in which the functional view has become increasingly accepted in the past two decades concerns pleasure and pain. Pleasure and pain are assumed to be targeted towards guiding people's actions (e.g., Carver 2001, Morris 1999). Pain alerts the person that something is wrong, and motivates avoidance or actions meant to eliminate the source of pain, whereas pleasure signifies beneficial stimuli, and is supposed to motivate approach behavior.

Pleasure and pain are at root subjective experiences. However, functional experiences may generalize to supposedly objective domains, potentially biasing judgment of such dimensions as product size or the energy provided by food. If you are tired, inclines may seem steeper and distances longer (Proffitt 2006). Similarly, other dimensions of the environment or particular stimuli in it may be distorted to reflect the manner in which they would be experienced by the consumer in their current state.

In the case of hunger, the energy food provides may be judged not objectively but rather in terms of the person's subjective energy needs. Hungry people require more energy, such that in relative terms any particular food provides less energy. Note that such a prediction would not be derived without the functional view of the biasing effects of physical state on perception and judgment. This may be reflected in consumers' evaluations of the energy provided by foods, and potentially alter consumer choices accordingly (e.g., eat more, buy more food). The studies shown here are meant to provide an initial demonstration of such biasing effects of hunger on energy estimation.

Study 1: If you haven't had breakfast, it's all diet food

Methods. Participants in this study (N=70) were students who reported normally having breakfast and lunch. They were instructed to fast for 18 hours. For analyses, we split participants to two groups according to compliance – whether or not they skipped breakfast.

Each participant rated seven different food items (which served as repeated measures). Participants rated how caloric they thought items were on a 9-point scale (from not at all caloric to very caloric).

Results. Participants who skipped breakfast (47.15) evaluated foods as more caloric (lsmean=5.66) than did participants who had eaten breakfast (lsmeans=6.01), $F(1,64)=3.89$, $p=.05$. The result supports the notion that hungry people evaluate food as being less caloric.

Study 2: Being hungry means never having to say it's fattening

The next study aimed to replicate the first study's results using a different dependent measure and measured hunger. Obtaining an effect of hunger on calorie estimation would be a stronger demonstration of the effect given the noisiness of calorie estimates. Further, hunger measures are in a way cleaner measures of people's needs or motivations than not eating, since people may be differentially hungry following a period of "fasting".

Methods. Participants in this study (N=52) were asked to estimate the number of calories in eight grocery food items. Hunger levels were measured on a 9-point scale (from not at all hungry to very hungry). Participants were split to a low and high hunger group via median split.

Results. High-hunger participants evaluated food items as containing, on average, fewer calories (596.54) than did low-hunger participants (988.62): $F(1, 50)=4.21$, $p<.05$.

GENERAL DISCUSSION

The current studies demonstrated that calorie estimates are systematically altered by people's hunger state. This prediction derived from a functional view of judgment, which maintains that people see products subjectively, in terms of the manner in which they serve current needs.

Notably, the findings contrast what would be predicted from views of motivated reasoning, according to which people see what they want to see (e.g, Balcetis and Dunning 2006). In a classic though much-disputed study in social psychology, for example, poorer kids saw coins as being larger (Bruner and Goodman 1947).

In our current view, though, people see what they *need* to see, that is, how objects supply their current needs, in subjective terms. Needing more means an object is *less*, not more, in subjective terms. Indeed, initial findings from research-in-progress by the authors shows that enhanced needs make needed objects appear *smaller*, not bigger.

Further studies will attempt to explain the mechanism behind such incorporation of subjective experiences into the manner in which participants see products. Specifically, the studies would test the role of simulations of upcoming experiences as the means by which a person's subjective experience of a product given current physical state is incorporated in judgment (Tal and Wansink 2011).

REFERENCES

Balcetis, Emily, and David Dunning (2006), "See what you want to see: Motivational infleucnes on visual perception," *Journal of Personality and Social Psychology*, 91(4), 612-625.

Bruner, Jerome, and Goodman (1947), "Value and Need as Organizing Factors in Perception," *Journal of Abnormal and Social Psychology*, 42(1), 33-44.

Carver, Charles S. (2001), "Affect and the functional bases of behavior: On the dimensional structure of affective experience," *Personality and Social Psychology Bulletin*, 5(4), 345-356.

Gilbert, Daniel, and Timothy Wilson (2000), "Miswanting: Some problems in the forecasting of future affective states," In Forgas, Joseph P. (Ed.), *Feeling and Thinking: The Role of Affect in Social Cognition*. Forgas, Cambridge University Press: NY.

Gilbert, Daniel, and Jane E. J. Ebert (2002), "Decisions and revisions: The affective forecasting of changeable outcomes," *Journal of Personality and Social Psychology*, 82(4), 503-514.

Gibson, James J. (1979), *The Ecological Approach to Visual Perception*. Houghton Mifflin: Boston.

Loewenstein, George (1996), "Out of control: Visceral influences on behavior," *Organizational Behavior and Human Decision Processes*, 65(3), 272-292.

Morris, William N. (1999), "The Mood System," in Kahneman, Daniel, Edward Diener, and Noerbert Schwarz (Eds.), *Well-Being: The Foundations of Hedonic Psychology*. Sage: New York.

Mobini, Sirous, Chambers Lucy C., and Martin R. Yeomans (1997), "Effects of hunger state on flavour pleasantness conditioning at home: Flavour-nutrient learning vs. flavour-flavour learning," *Appetite*, 48(1), 20-28.

Proffitt, Dennis R. (2006), "Embodied perception and the economy of action," *Perspectives on Psychological Science*, 1(2), 110-122.

Read, Daniel, and Barbara van Leeuwen (1998), "Predicting hunger: The effects of appetite and delay on choice," *Organizational Behavior and Human Decision Processes*, 76(2), 189-205.

Tal and Wansink 2011, "The Mind's Mouth: Simulation in Consumer Research," Manuscript in preparation.

Single-Brand Experience vs. Multiple-Brand Experience: Another perspective on consumer preference formation

Mitchell Hamilton, Syracuse University, USA
Omar Woodham, North Carolina State A&T, USA

For decades, the consumer preference formation process has fascinated marketing researchers. Though versatile in nature, consumer preference literature typically encompasses the following buyer learning constructs: prior knowledge and order-of-entry (Robinson & Fornell 1985; Carpenter & Nakamoto 1989; Kardes & Kalyanaram 1992; Kerin et al. 1992). While the marketing and psychology fields have merged together to offer a wealth of knowledge dedicated to the consumer preference formation process (Carpenter & Nakamoto 1989; Arnould 1989; Mantel & Kardes 1999), a majority of these studies assume that a consumer forms her/his preferences in the following sequence: (1st) Prior to experiencing a product, a consumer's preferences are weakly formed due to the lack of product category knowledge and the ambiguity of the ideal attribute combination; (2nd) the consumer's initial experience with the new product category typically involves the pioneering brand; and (3rd) after the initial product trial, the consumer experiences some of the competing brands while constantly updating her/his preferences.

Absent from the consumer preference formation literature is the consideration of a consumer that has only experienced a single brand, even though other competing brands exist. Occasionally, consumption habits are passed down through familial generations, whether intentionally or unintentionally. For example, a young college student that is away from home may be undeterred from her/his rigid routine of using Tide when doing laundry because "that's the brand my mother always used". Also, consider a consumer that is completely satisfied after her/his initial product trial experience and has always been a firm believer in the "if it's not broke, then don't fix it" school of thought. These types of consumers may not feel the urge to try any of the competing brands (Fournier 1998).

Would these "single-brand" consumers affect the dynamics of the traditional consumer preference formation model offered by Carpenter & Nakamoto (1989)? After all, the Merriam-Webster dictionary does define preference as, "the act, fact, or principle of giving advantages to some over others." A single-brand consumer lacks the trial experience with regards to the competing brands; therefore, a single-brand consumer could not possibly develop preferences that are as strong as or stronger than a consumer with "multiple-brand" experiences. Or could they? The current paper addresses these questions and also offers an alternative perspective on the notion of first-mover's advantage. This perspective emphasizes the combined importance of a consumer's first encounter with a particular product category and the brand encountered during this initial experience (which may or may not involve the first-mover brand). The current authors refer to this as "experienced-first advantage".

THE STUDY

The purpose of this study is to distinguish the impact of single-brand user experience on the preference formation process, from the impact of multiple-brand user experience. The authors seek to answer the following question: Who develops stronger brand preferences, consumers that have only used a single brand within a product category or consumers that have used multiple brands?

Methodology

Brand user experience is operationalized into one single-brand group (experienced-first customers) and two multiple-brand groups (win-back customers; variety-seeking customers). Subjects are naturally selected based upon the following criteria:

- Experienced-First Customer
  - Has at least five years of product usage experience within the product category
  - Has not used more than one brand within the product category
  - Currently considers himself/herself to be brand loyal

- Win-Back Customer
  - Has at least five years of product usage experience within the product category
  - Has used more than one brand within the product category
  - Currently considers himself/herself to be brand loyal

- Variety-Seeking Customer
  - Has at least five years of product usage experience within the product category

    o   Has used more than one brand within the product category

          o   Does not currently consider himself/herself to be brand loyal

The data is collected using an online survey. For each of the groups, brand preference strength is measured using two types of conjoint analyses, choice-based (a decompositional, top-down approach) and self-explicated (a compositional, bottom-up approach). Each groups' level of brand preference strength is indicated by the intra-correlation and intra-variance between the two conjoint analyses. Brand preference strength will have a positive relationship with the correlation and a negative relationship with the variance.

Findings

The preliminary results suggest that experienced-first and variety-seeking customers both form preferences that are stronger than the preferences formed by win-back customers. Furthermore, the brand preference strength of experienced-first and variety-seeking customers appear to be equally strong.

The authors posit that: (1) win-back customers are not fully satisfied with their current brand but have decided to settle upon the best option; and (2) experienced-first and variety-seeking customers are both sufficiently satisfied with their brand selections. However, further data is needed to support these claims.

REFERENCES

Arnould, Eric (1989), "Toward a Broadened Theory of Preference Formation and the Diffusion of Innovations: Cases from Zinder Province, Niger Republic," *Journal of Consumer Research*, 16 (September), 239–267.

Carpenter, Gregory S. and Kent Nakamoto (1989), "Consumer Preference Formation and Pioneering Advantage," *Journal of Marketing Research*, 26 (August), 285-98.

Fournier, Susan (1998), "Consumers and Their Brands: Develop- ing Relationship Theory in Consumer Research," *Journal of Consumer Research*, 24 (March), 343-73.

Kardes, Frank R. and Gurumurthy Kalyanaram (1992) "Order-of-Entry Effects on Consumer Memory and Judgment: An Information Integration Perspective," *Journal of Marketing Research*, 29 (August), 343-357.

Kerin, Roger A., P. Rajan Varadarajan, and Robert A. Peterson (1992), "First-Mover Advantage: A Synthesis, Conceptual Framework, and Research Propositions," *Journal of Marketing*, 56 (October), 33-52.

Mantel, Susan Powell and Frank R. Kardes (1999), "The Role of Direction of Comparison, Attribute-Based Processing, and Attitude-Based Processing in Consumer Preference," *Journal of Consumer Research*, 25 (March), 335-52.

Robinson, William T. and Claes Fornell (1985), "Sources of Market Pioneer Advantages in Consumer Good Industries," *Journal of Marketing Research*, 22 (August), 305-317.

Thomas, Jacquelyn S., Robert C. Blattberg and Edward J. Fox (2004). "Recapturing Lost Customers," *Journal of Marketing Research,* 41 (February) 31–45.

Tokman, Mert, Lenita M. Davis, and Katherine N. Lemon (2006), "The WOW factor: Creating value through win-back offers to reacquire lost customers," *Journal of Retailing*, 87 (1), 47-64.

Until Death Do Us Part: Consumer Response to Brand Elimination

Kendra Hart, Ivey Business School, University of Western Ontario, Canada

Intuition tells us that there must be some degree of disappointment for consumers when their favourite brands are gone. Researchers have demonstrated consumer relationships with brands (Fournier 1998), consumer attachment to brands (Park, Macinnis, and Priester 2006), and self-brand connections (Escalas and Bettman 2003, 2005). Clearly, brands play an important part in consumers' lives.

Although anecdotal reports of consumer response to high profile brand discontinuation exist in the popular media, there is a paucity of scholarly research in this area. There is little empirical evidence of the dimensions and breadth of consumer felt response to a brand's elimination from the marketplace. Ignorance of consumer response leads to an underdeveloped sense of the consumer mindset when looking to fill the brand void with a competitive offering. It also demonstrates a weaker understanding of the dimensions of consumer-brand relationships. This study seeks to begin to drill down on the dimensions of consumer emotional response in an effort to envisage potential consumer behavioural response.

Understanding the various dimensions, strength and causes of emotions in a consumption context can help marketers to better understand and predict resulting consumer behaviour (Watson and Spence 2007). Appraisal theories have outlined how emotions stem from cognitive appraisals individuals make about situations or events relevant to their well-being (Bagozzi, Gopinath, and Nyer 1999). Arguably, the loss of a favoured brand can be seen as affecting well-being for those who have strong ties to the brand.

METHOD

This exploratory study was conducted via an online survey with 125 respondents. Participants were asked to think about a favourite brand that they like to buy, followed by instructions to write about their history with the brand and what it means to them. Subsequently, they read a fictitious newspaper article that mentioned that the brand was going to be pulled from the marketplace shortly. Participants were then asked to write about their thoughts and feelings about this news, as well as a few open-ended questions about their relationship with the brand.

FINDINGS

Analyzing participant response to open-ended questions, informants demonstrated a wide variety of emotional response. Expectedly, a large number of consumers expressed a degree of resignation and sad acceptance. Although many respondents expressed their sorrow at losing a favored brand, and their concern about finding an adequate replacement, many displayed a sense of fatalism about the event. This response is not unexpected, given the inconvenience, but not impossibility, of replacing a dead brand.

However, a deeper analysis of the comments led to an emergent pattern of consumer response that showed three interesting dominant themes. These three themes are interralted, and consistent with important dimensions of relationships previously unexamined in the consumer-brand relationship domain.

Theme #1: Risk and Regret

"I would be really bummed because I took a risk on this brand and then I got bit in the rear because it flopped and I actually enjoyed using it"

Relationships with any partner involve a degree of vulnerability. Consumers not only run the risk of relationship dissatisfaction, but also the risk of rejection and relationship discontinuance. Analysis of consumer responses revealed themes of risk awareness and relationship regret that is consistent with research in the interpersonal domain (Bartholomew 1990).

Theme #2: Abandonment and Betrayal

"Betrayed. After all these years of devotion, they had to get rid of something that I had known and trusted and enjoyed for many years"

Trust in a relationship partner's commitment to the relationship is another element of relationship vulnerability. Research on interpersonal rejection has highlighted the impact of perceptions of abandonment and betrayal across several interpersonal domains (Shackelford and Buss 1996).

"I think they just give up and abandon their own brand"

It is interesting to note that the themes of abandonment and betrayal did not end with the consumer. Rather, respondents expressed concerns over the firm's duty to the brand itself, as well as to the customer.

Theme #3: Embarrassment and Shame

"I would be embarrassed that the thing I used for years isn't there anymore"

One last theme regards the role of shame after the end of a relationship. As in interpersonal relationships, the unwanted end of a relationship can often lead to feelings of embarrassment for the partner that is left behind, and impact the individual's willingness to pursue a new relationship (Claesson and Sohlberg 2002).

DISCUSSION

This study is a first attempt to dimensionalize and delineate consumer response to brand elimination. The results of initial data collection show that consumers have deeper reactions than mere annoyance or displeasure. Themes of relationship risk and betrayal have implications not only for firms looking to reduce their brand offerings, but for competitors seeking to build new relationships with consumers who have lost a brand. Additional, more extensive data is currently being collected in an attempt to further this research to address not only the question of consumer response but also the following: How do consumers continue on in the face of this loss and negotiate replacing the brand with a competitor? Do different types of loss lead to differences in subsequent consumer search? How do consumers continue on with other brand offered by the firm in the face of a singular elimination? This knowledge would have value for surviving brands that want to capture these consumers, as well as brand competitors.

REFERENCES

Bagozzi, Richard P., Mahesh Gopinath, and Prashanth U. Nyer (1999), "The Role and Emotions of Marketing," *Journal of the Academy of Marketing Science*, 27 (2), 184-206.

Escalas, Jennifer Edson and James R. Bettman (2003), "You Are What They Eat: The Influence of Reference Groups on Consumers' Connections to Brands," *Journal of Consumer Psychology*, 13 (3), 339-48.

Escalas, Jennifer Edson and James R. Bettman (2005), "Self-Construal, Reference Groups, and Brand Meaning," *Journal of Consumer Research*, 32 (December), 378-89.

Fournier, Susan (1998), "Consumers and Their Brands: Developing Relationsip Theory in Consumer Research," *Journal of Consumer Research*, 24 (4), 343-73.

Park, C. Whan, Deborah J. Macinnis, and Joseph Priester (2006), "Beyond Attitudes: Attachment and Consumer Behavior," *Seoul Journal of Business*, 12 (2), 4-35.

Shackelford, Todd K. and David M. Buss (1996), "Betrayal in Mateships, Friendships, and Coalitions," *Personality and Social Psychology Bulletin*, 11, 1151-64.

Watson, Lisa and Mark T. Spence (2007), "Causes and Consequences of Emotions on Consumer Behaviour," *European Journal of Marketing*, 41 (5/6), 487-511.

Rooting Value: Identity Negotiations From Juxtaposing Past and Present

Leah Carter Schneider, York University, Canada
Julia Creet, York University, Canada

The postmodern landscape hinders the formation of deep, long-lasting, and personally significant connections with others and to create a cohesive sense of self (Firat and Venkatesh, 1995; Cova 1997). Consumer research has shown that consumers utilize marketplace products, resources, discourses, and sites to form identities and to create communities and neotribes with one another both in the real world and virtual world (e.g., Thompson and Hirschman 1995; Solomon 1983; Muñiz and O'Guinn 2001; Cova 1997; Cova and Cova 2002; Kozinets 1997). Participating in marketplace communities allows individuals to express one's identity, or to adopt new identities based on desire for acceptance from the focal social group (Schouten and McAlexander 1995). Products and services that facilitate connecting individuals together, such as Facebook, are also increasingly valued in the marketplace for their linking capabilities (Cova 1997). Relationships and identity work therefore seem to be interwoven in the modern market arena, and facilitated by the adoption and use of specific market products. However, consumers may also use marketplace offerings to form alternative relationships with others beyond traditional social interactions that create opportunities for more intense identity work.

The mobility of individuals to move from place to place, as well as the myriad of identity positions offered through the marketplace, most likely contribute to some consumers experiencing continued and heightened senses of dislocation, disconnection, and identity confusion (e.g., Peñaloza 1994; Askegaard, Arnould, and Kjeldgaard 2005; Ustuner and Holt 2007). In this paper, we present and explore the rooting value, or the identity value of marketplace activities that ground a person's sense of self as individuals confront their identities. Specifically, we focus on the genealogical market, a site in which consumers learn about and form relationships with their ancestors as they build their family trees. We propose that consumer identity work is not only influenced by personal actions, choices, or preferences, but also by the process of encountering and negotiating personally relevant information and relationships discovered through market activities.

Drawing on consumer identity and consumer sociality (e.g., tribes, communities, and family) research, we aim to explore consumer identity questions that arise when consumers work to learn about their ancestors. We address questions of the motivations for individuals to undertake genealogical work, and the identity value and challenges to an individual's self-concept that genealogical findings create. In order to address the research questions, we utilize data from: (1) in-depth interviews with individual and professional genealogists, (2) netnographic data of online forums of genealogical enthusiasts and amateurs, and (3) active participant notes, as the secondary author engaged in her own genealogical quest. Using an iterative data analysis process between the two authors, common themes were generated and compared in order to identify the identity work that emerged as consumers search for their ancestors.

Preliminary findings from the data suggest that the genealogical market represents a site of intense, personal identity negotiations. Individual consumers experienced a spectrum of motivations that lead them to conduct their own genealogical work, including coping with separation and loss, such as moving away from "home" or the death of a loved one, and a desire to understand family quirks, traits, and qualities that are passed through generations. However, we found that a significant motivation for undertaking genealogical work aligned with questions about one's identity and roots. By building their family history tree, informants cultivated feelings of connection to and belonging with others whose lives directly led to and influenced their traits, quirks, physical location, and values. Stories, such as great-great grandfather's who crossed the plains in dire conditions, greatly enhanced the connection with and identity value of ancestors to the present day descendant. The sense of belonging that genealogical work generated provided informants with a redefined concept of who they are, as they then incorporated the histories, stories, and characteristics of their forefathers into their own identities. Informants' self-concepts were therefore not restricted to their own life choices, consumption decisions, occupations, and so on; rather, their self-identity was deconstructed and reorganized according to their family history.

Although the identity work that occurred at the nexus of integrating one's life to one's ancestors generally led to positive outcomes for individuals and satisfied their desire for connection with their ancestors, some consumers experienced discord and tension as a result of their genealogical findings. By perceiving family history as the roots through which personal identity is grounded, information discovered that contradicted current understanding of one's identity led to crises of identity. New information brought to light through genealogy regarding family ethnicity, living relations previously unknown to them due to infidelities, secrets, and so on, provided a catalyst for confronting one's sense of self. Having to "come to terms with" such information led to identity work that involved the rejection of family history information as a way to maintain and protect the identity or a significant redefining of self. Others engaged in critical evaluation of the self, as they renegotiated their personal identities in connection to the new information.

Thus, the rooting value of connecting past with present in the genealogical market is generated as individuals learn of, analyze, and either accept/reject family history findings. By engaging in genealogical work, consumers are able to use the past in order to root themselves in the present, either by linking themselves to their family history or by disengaging with the family history and reinforcing their personal identity as it stood prior to genealogical work. The marketplace, by engaging and enticing consumers to "find themselves" through family history, acts as an arena for centering and rooting identity to anchor points either in the past or present as consumers integrate, restructure, or attempt to maintain their personal sense of self.

REFERENCES

Askegaard, Soren, Eric Arnould and Dannie Kjeldgaard (2005), "Postassimilationist Ethnic Consumer Research: Qualifications and Extensions," *Journal of Consumer Research*, 32 (June), 160-170

Cova, Bernard (1997), "Community and consumption: Towards a definition of the "linking value" of product or service," *European Journal of Marketing*, 31 (3/4), 297-316.

Cova, Bernard and Veronique Cova (2002), "Tribal marketing: The tribalisation of society and its impact on the conduct of marketing," *European Journal of Marketing*, 36 (5/6), 595-620.

Firat, A. Fuat and Alladi Venkatesh (1995), "Liberatory Postmodernism and the Reenchantment of Consumption," *Journal of Consumer Research*, 22 (December), 239-267.

Kozinets, Robert V. (1997), "E-Tribalized Marketing: The Strategic Implications of Virtual Communities of Consumption," *European Management Journal*, 17 (3), 252-264.

Muñiz, Albert M. Jr. and Thomas C. O'Guinn (2001), "Brand Community," *Journal of Consumer Research*, 27 (March), 412-432.

Peñaloza, Lisa (1994), "Atrevasado Fronteras/Border Crossings: A Critical Ethnographic Exploration of the Consumer Acculturation of Mexican Immigrants," *Journal of Consumer Research*, 21 (June), 32-54.

Schouten, John and James McAlexander (1995), "Subcultures of Consumption: An Ethnography of the New Bikers," *Journal of Consumer Research*, 22 (June), 43-61.

Thompson, Craig J. and Elizabeth C. Hirschman (1995), "Understanding the Socialized Body: A Poststructuralist Analysis of Consumer Self-Conceptions, Body Images, and Self-Care Practices," *Journal of Consumer Research*, 22 (September), 139-153.

Ustuner, Tuba and Douglas Holt (2007), "Dominated Consumer Acculturation: The Social Construction of Poor Migrant Women's Consumer Identity Projects in a Turkish Squatter," *Journal of Consumer Research*, 34 (June), 41-56.

A Poison by Any Other Name: Aversion to Functional Food Chemicals

Aner Tal, Cornell University, USA
Brian Wansink, Cornell University, USA

In recent years a growing number of consumers has drifted away from additive-laden food and towards organic foods (Greene and Dimitri 2003). In the process, some consumers have developed an aversion to "artificial" foods (Rozin 2005). The passion for organic, additive-free foods, is a complex and understudied phenomena. One factor potentially driving the movement towards organic food is a growing belief that additives are unhealthy. This may indeed be true for some additives, but untrue for others. Consumers, however, may overgeneralize and suppose that all additives are "bad for you".

In judging a food to be less appealing due to additives contained, consumers may rely on cues leading to intuitive judgment rather than on detailed information processing, in accordance with an overall tendency for heuristic processing in the marketplace (Olshavsky and Granobis 1979, Hoyer 1984). Particular cues may associationally trigger aversive reactions to products that are perceived to be harmful due to additives contained.

One cue that may be dominant in leading consumers to perceive a product as harmful is the presence of an ingredient that sounds "chemical". Consumers may know that some chemicals are harmful, and generalize that "all chemicals are bad", similar to other learned associations such as "healthy=not tasty" (Ragunathan et al. 2006). Thus, the mere presence of a chemical-sounding ingredient may suffice to trigger reduced evaluation of a product.

Chemical-sounding names may harm product evaluation not just on relevant dimensions (e.g., health). Rather, their effects may generalize to other product dimensions. For instance, consumers may anticipate worse taste for products that contain "suspicious" additives. This may emanate from contagion from one product dimension to another, or from a generalized negative halo that imbues "chemicalized" products. Such effects might operate in similar manner to how consumers reduce evaluations of products that are touched by disgusting elements (Morales and Fitzsimons 2007).

Study 1: Chemical vs. descriptive name reduces taste evaluation

The first study aimed to test whether consumers would predict lower tastiness for snacks that were reported to have "sodium benzoate" (a food preservative) rather than "food preservative".

Method. Participants (N=52) were shown a picture of a cookie and told that the cookie contained either "food preservative" or "sodium benzoate". They were then asked to rate how tasty they think they cookie is on a taste of 1 (=not at all) to 9 (=very much).

Results. Participants rated the cookie as less tasty (M=5.3) when reading it contained "sodium benzoate" than they did when reading it contained "food preservative" (M=7), p=.001. This despite the relatively innocuous name of the preservative (reminiscent of salt, or, sound-wise, soda).

Study 2: Knowledge of chemical function doesn't undo chemical halo

The second study wanted to examine whether learning of a chemical's function would undo the negative effects of knowing a product contained it. The study also aimed to increase the generality of the previous study's findings by adding a control condition where participants were told the cookies contained "milk chocolate" rather than "food preservative". In addition, the study contained a different preservative name: "potassium sorbate". This would allow testing whether there was something special that made "sodium benzoate" abnormally lower ratings. Finally, the study contained one additional condition (for a total of 4 conditions) where the words "food preservative" were written in parentheses by the chemical additive name. This was meant to examine whether knowing the chemicals' function would undo their detrimental effects on product evaluation.

Results. There was a significant effect of condition on rated tastiness: $F(5, 100)$=3.86, p=.003. Ratings were lower for the chemical-name conditions (M=5.89) than for the non-preservative condition (M=7) and the food preservative condition (M=6.94). Note that having a food preservative *did not lower evaluations*, only having a chemical-sounding additive reduced evaluations. Further, evaluations were reduced by the chemical presence even when participants knew the function of the additives (M=5.56), p>.5.

Proposed Study: Confirmatory Processing

A followup study will aim to show that containing chemical ingredients harms not only judgment, but actual product experience and choice. Through confirmatory, top-down processing, consumers may come to experience a product as less tasty, congruent with their "chemical-induced" expectations (Ha and Hoch 1989, Shiv et al. 2005).

Further studies may demonstrate the dependence of the aversive reaction to chemical-sounding additives on heuristic processing, showing increased adverse effects of chemical sounding names under cognitive load.

In addition, studies will aim to get a better hold of the mechanisms driving the phenomena. Study 2 ruled argues against harmful effects of chemical names on product evaluations being due to unfamiliarity (not knowing what the ingredient is). Additional studies will explore whether the effects of chemical-names on evaluations are due to negative associations that are activated by chemical names.

REFERENCES

Ha Young-Won, and Stephen J. Hoch (1989), "Ambiguity, Processing Strategy, and Advertising-Evidence Interactions," *Journal of Consumer Research*, 16(3), 354-360.

Hoyer, Wayne D. (1984), "An Examination of Consumer Decision Making for Common Repeat Purchase Product," *Journal of Consumer Research*, 11(3), 822-829.

Morales, Andrea C., and Gavan J. Fitzsimons (2007), "An Examination of Consumer Decision Making for Common Repeat Purchase Product," *Journal of Marketing Research*, 44(2), 272-282.

Olshavsky, Richard W., & Granbois, Donald H. (1979), "Consumer Decision Making - Fact or Fiction?" *Journal of Consumer Research*, 6(2), 93-100.

Ragunathan Rajagopal, Walker Naylor Rebecca, and Wayne D. Hoyer (2006), "The Unhealthy = Tasty Intuition and its Effects on Taste Inferences, enjoyment, and Choice of Food Products," *Journal of Marketing*, 70(4), 170-184.

Rozin, Paul (2005), "The Meaning of "Natural": Process More Important than Content," *Psychological Science*, 16(8), 652-658.

Shiv, Baba, Ziv Carmon, and Dan Ariely (2005), "Placebo Effects of Marketing Actions: Consumers May Get What They Pay For," *Journal of Marketing Research*, 42(4), 383-393.

Mishap or Justification? Whether Segregating Losses Is Bad or Good Depends on Responsibility for the Outcome

Dilney Goncalves, IE Business School, Spain

Gains and losses can often be presented in a piecemeal format or integrated. For example, the cost of repairing a car can be broken down in each individual part and labor. Gain and loss integration versus segregation has been extensively studied under the framework of Mental Accounting theory. Mental Accounting predicts that people are happier when their gains are segregated and their losses are integrated (Thaler, 1985). Whereas the basic assumption has been well documented, especially in the gains domain, less is known about how people process integrated versus segregated outcomes, especially losses.

If negative events can be painful, they can also help people minimize the pain of a loss if they provide reasons that help justify the loss. In this research we examine a loss rationalization hypothesis whereby segregating losses yields more positive evaluations if it helps rationalize the loss but yields more negative evaluations otherwise. When people feel responsible for a loss, they may automatically and unconsciously engage in rationalization processes that make the hedonic impact of the event less severe (Gilbert et al. 1998). If people are accountable for a loss they are motivated to rationalize the loss. When losses are segregated, each component of the overall loss could potentially be a justification. Thus, a segregated loss would present more opportunities for justification than an integrated one where each individual component is a (potential) reason to justify the loss. We predict that the effect of reasons on the evaluation of losses is moderated by the motivation one has to justify the loss such that (1) for people who feel responsible for the loss, reasons help justify the loss, making it less painful and (2) for people who do not feel responsible for the loss, reasons for the loss are evaluated as mishaps, making the loss more painful.

The first study tested whether segregating the cause for a loss has an impact independent of segregating the monetary value. This study used a 2 (monetary outcome: integrated vs. segregated) X 2 (cause vs. cause) between-subjects design. Participants were recruited online and were randomly assigned to one of the four experimental conditions. They read a scenario describing a situation where they had to pay for an unexpected expense (car taxes in the first replicate and house repair in the second). In the integrated monetary frame, participants saw only the total amount (e.g., $450). In the segregated monetary frame, they saw a list of items followed by the total ($260, $90, $80, $20). Participants in the cause condition were told that they had to pay for "registration and inspection fees" and "state and CO_2 taxes." Participants in the integrated, no-cause condition were not told anything about the source of the taxes. Those in the segregated, no-cause condition were shown a list of non-descriptive items (i.e., A, B, C, D). After imagining that they were in the situation described, participants stated how unhappy they would feel with the expense on a 7-point scale anchored in "not at all unhappy" and "extremely unhappy." Planned contrasts showed that participants in the integrated, no-cause condition felt significantly less unhappy (M=4.42) than participants in the other three conditions (M=5.03; p<0.05). Furthermore, evaluations in the integrated, reasons condition (M=5.03) and the two segregated conditions ($M_{reasons}$=4.96; $M_{no-reasons}$=5.10) did not differ. This pattern replicates previous research and – in addition – shows that segregating causes has a similar effect to segregating the monetary value of the outcome.

The second study, tests the moderating role of responsibility. This study has a 2 (responsible vs. non-responsible) X 3 (completely-integrated vs. monetary-integrated vs. completely-segregated) between-subjects design. Participants in the responsible condition were told that they knowingly parked the car in a no-parking zone. Those in the non-responsible condition were told that they did so unknowingly. Participants were told that their car got towed. Those in the completely-integrated condition were told that they had to "pay $200 to recover your car." Those in the monetary-integrated condition also read "(for parking ticket and towing service)." Finally, participants in the completely-segregated condition saw "parking ticket: \$80; towing service: \$120." The dependent variable is unhappiness with the expense (as in study 1). A significant responsibility by reasons interaction ($F_{2,110}$=3.53; p<0.05) supports our prediction: whereas for non-responsible participants, reasons represented unfortunate events and increased unhappiness ($M_{completely-integrated}$=6.14; $M_{monetary-integrated}$=6.45; $M_{completely-segregated}$=6.69) whereas for responsible participants, reasons helped them rationalize and decreased unhappiness ($M_{completely-integrated}$=6.19; $M_{monetary-integrated}$ =5.58; $M_{completely-segregated}$=5.37).

A third vignette study provides preliminary evidence that if individual components cannot be used to justify the loss, segregating a loss does not make it less painful even if people are motivated to rationalize it. These two experiments suggest that reasons play an important role in how people evaluate negative outcomes. The negative impact of losses can be minimized by using appropriate description: losses should be segregated when individual components help (and there is motivation to) justify a bad decision and integrated otherwise.

Losing Sight of the Struggle:
Consumer Activism in the Age of New Media and Hypervisuality

Amanda Earley, York University, Canada

Anti-Consumerist Activism on the Web

Since the beginnings of the Internet, activists have argued that it would be the first form of mass media that would belong to the people, and would consequently have liberatory potential. It has been used for organizing, coordinating events, political education, and grassroots reportage. The study of cyberactivism is an ideal complement to ongoing discussions of consumer resistance (Kozinets and Handelman, 2004; Kozinets, 2002) and liberatory conceptions of consumer behavior (Murray and Ozanne, 1991), and brings much-needed work on new media and the politics of consumer culture into the field of consumer behavior.

There have been numerous scholarly attempts to document cyberactivist practices, including Martha McCaughey and Michael D. Ayers' edited collection which chronicles the use of cyberactivist tactics by groups ranging from first-world "hacktivists" to the Zapatistas (2003). Most of the authors in the collection take on a celebratory tone, practically declaring a new age for political organizing and democracy.

These academic activists are not in bad company, as seen in coverage of the recent Twitter revolutions in Moldova, Iran, and Egypt. Within the media studies camp, Henry Jenkins is perhaps the best known proponent of the democratizing potential of the Internet. Jenkins' analysis centers on the enormous potential in the Internet, for the political process as well as for market activity (2006). He and his colleagues have argued that the internet enables a new participatory culture defined by low barriers to entry, collaboration, social connection, and a sense that the activity is valuable (2006). Here, consumers become producers or at least "prosumers," creating content and shaping market offerings by collaborating with companies.

New Media is not, however, free from detractors, academic and otherwise. Even in the case of the Tehran "Twitter Revolution," journalists passions quickly cooled as many started to question the relationship between the Internet and politics (Moaveni, 2010; Morozov, 2009). The majority of technology scholars tend to be critical, rather than celebratory. Michael Margolis and David Resnick contested the position that the Internet will bring about a long-awaited perfect democractic society, arguing that "...ordinary politics and commercial activity have invaded and captured cyberspace. Virtual reality has grown to resemble the real world," (2000, p. 2).

Legal studies scholar Cass Sunstein took this argument one step further by explicating how, in the age of the internet, democracies are moving farther from the ideal of deliberation and closer to a direct democracy based on immediate desires. This is fueled by processes of specialization and filtering that allow individuals to radically filter what they see, hear, and consider (2000, 2007). Sunstein contends that the new political ideal is that of the consumer democracy, where free choice of goods and free movement of capital is paramount to other social goals. This ideal has infected the web, as commerce dominates in the form of shopping, advertising, and consumers' discussions of products.

Examining Consumer Cyberactivism: The Case of the Toronto G20

The substantive example of the Toronto G20 was used to examine the above debates in a real-world context. Two types of media production were examined: traditional, mainstream media representations of the events, and activist-produced media productions. The coverage was both in print and digital formats. For the digital material posted by activists, attention was paid to the communities and connections underlying the posts. That said, the project is not a full netnography, as the researcher was an observer rather than a participant observer (Kozinets, 2009).

The media representations frequently juxtaposed texts and photographs, so both discursive and visual methods were employed. That said, the vast majority of the media space was in the form of photographs, so primacy is given to the visual in the analysis. Often, the text was as small as a caption or a Facebook comment, and thus served as an aid to the visual analysis moreso than an independent cultural text.

All media were subjected to open and axial coding, as explicated by Strauss and Corbin (1998). Emmison and Smith's *Researching the Visual* (2000) and Sturken and Cartwright's *Practices of Looking* (2001) provided guidance for reading and coding the content of visual images. 87 images were analyzed for the journalistic side, and 3,450 were read for the activists. Narratives of anti-consumerism activist media production and mainstream media production emerged from this analysis.

For the journalists, two main themes emerged. The first, *practiced neutrality*, is defined by presenting a large range of actors (activists, police officers, vandals) without judgment or a political analysis. The second theme is the *creation of iconic content*. The mainstream media were responsible for taking the photographs that were the most widely circulated. Two photographs and video footage of a police car on fire quickly became the dominant representations of the protest, and were circulated widely.

Two powerful narratives emerged from the activists' photographs. The first, *journalism by other means*, refers to grassroots journalist work performed by activists. Here, activists attempt to document the events in much the same way as journalists, but with supposed improved to authenticity, politicization, and choice of events. The second narrative is that of *strategic political communications*, intended to sell audiences on a particular story. In this way, activists created "marketing content" for the movement. Such claims should be read critically in light of the media studies literature, especially Sunstein's (2000, 2007) work on channels on the Internet. Sunstein argues that such self-produced strategic communications rarely reach beyond a narrow audience that already agrees with a cause, and that the acceptance of marginal and alternative channels may further disrepute the cause.

The presentation will feature further categories of activist media production, including *anarcho-porn*, images that valorize property destruction and other anarchist protest tactics; *protest tourism*, images that replicate the tropes of tourist photography, communicating little more than "we were here;" and *documenting documentation*, wherein protestors took photographs of journalists, police, and other protestors documenting the events. This latter category is of particular interest, especially when read in the contexts of activists' distrust of mainstream media, which is argued to serve corporate interests.

REFERENCES

Emmison, Michael and Philip Smith (2000), *Researching the Visual*. Thousand Oaks, CA: Sage Publications.

Jenkins, Henry (2006). *Convergence Culture: Where Old and New Media Collide*. New York: New York University Press.

Jenkins, Henry, with Katie Clinton, Ravi Purushtoma, Alice J. Robinson, and Margaret Weigel (2006). *Confronting the Challenges of Participatory Culture: Media Education for the 21st Century*. Chicago: The MacArthur Foundation.

Kozinets, Robert V. (2009), *Netnography: Doing Research Online*. Thousand Oaks, CA: Sage Publications.

Kozinets, Robert V. (2002), "Can Consumers Escape the Market? Emancipatory Illusions

from Burning Man," *Journal of Consumer Research* 29(June), 20-38.

Kozinets, Robert V. and Jay M. Handelman (2004), "Adversaries of Consumption: Consumer Movements, Activism, Ideology," *Journal of Consumer Research* 31(Dec), 691-704.

Margolis, Michael, and David Resnick (2000). *Politics as Usual: The "Cyberspace Revolution."* Thousand Oaks, CA: Sage Publications.

McCaughey, Martha and Michael D. Ayers (2003). *Cyberactivism: Online Activism in Theory and Practice*. New York: Routledge.

Moaveni, Azadeh (2010). "Tehran in Chains," *The New York Times* online edition. Available at: http://www.nytimes.com/2010/07/18/books/review/Moaveni-t.html. Last accessed December 23, 2010.

Morozov, Evgeny (2009). "The Repurcussions of a 'Twitter Revolution,'" *The Boston Globe* online edition. Available at http://www.boston.com/bostonglobe/editorial_opinion/oped/articles/2009/06/20/the_repercussions_of_a_twitter_revolution/. Last accessed December 23, 2010.

Murray and Ozanne (1991), "The Critical Imagination: Emancipatory Interests in Consumer Research," *Journal of Consumer Research* 18(Sept), 129-144.

Strauss, Anselm, and Juliet Corbin (1998), *Basics of Qualitative Research: Techniques and Procedures for Developing Grounded Theory*. Thousand Oaks, CA: Sage Publications.

Sturken, Marita, and Lisa Cartwright (2001), *Practices of Looking: An Introduction to Visual Culture*. New York: Oxford University Press.

Sunstein, Cass (2007). *Republic 2.0*. Princeton, NJ: Princeton University Press.

Sunstein, Cass (2000). *Republic.com*. Princeton, NJ: Princeton University Press.

Ideal Affect as a Basis of Judgment in Experiential and Material Purchases

Yoon Ji Shim, Seoul National University, South Korea

Incheol Choi, Seoul National University, South Korea

Previous literatures in consumer research suggest that affect plays a crucial role in consumer decision making (Bagozzi, Gopinath, & Nyer, 1999; Cohen & Areni, 1991). Despite the emphasized role of affect in consumer behavior, most of the studies have mainly focused on how consumers' *actual affect* influences on their choices (MacInnis, Patrick, & Park, 2006); moreover, it has also not been investigated in which purchasing types consumers would make decisions primarily based on affective factors. In the present research, we investigated the role of *anticipated affect* as a basis of judgment in two different purchasing types: experiential and material purchases. The anticipated affect in the context of consumption would strongly be related to *ideal affect*, the affective states that people would like to feel (Tsai, Knutson, & Fung, 2006), in that most people might mainly anticipate positive feelings from their purchasing decisions or choices (Mellers & Mcgraw, 2001). According to Tsai (2007), ideal affect consists of two-level of arousal positive affect states: high-arousal positive affect (HAP) states such as excitement, enthusiasm, and elation and low-arousal positive affect (LAP) states such as calmness, peacefulness, and serenity, and individual differences in ideal affect may account for diverse behavioral consequences especially in mood-producing behavior.

In the present research, we hypothesized that people are likely to make different choices depending on their ideal affect that they would like to experience from purchasing behavior. More importantly, we predicted that ideal affect may play a more central role in experiential purchases where the object of which is associated with having a life experience than in material purchases where the object is possession itself (Van Boven & Gilovich, 2003) because affective experiences consumers pursue from purchasing choices would be more closely related to experiential purchases than to material purchases (Kwortnik & Ross, 2007). In order to examine these hypotheses, we conducted two main experiments.

In Study 1, we examined whether people make choices which correspond to their ideal affect more in experiential purchases than in material purchases when asked to make purchase decisions for self. We posited that people would have different ideal affect depending on their age and gender and would make purchasing choices based on their own ideal affect. In Study 2, we investigated the role of affect in purchasing situations where giving gifts for other people or recommending others to purchase products or services. We predicted that people would make decisions based on ideal affect for others whom one is intending to give a gift or suggest buying (hereafter referred to as "ideal affect for targets") rather than their own ideal affect when they make choices for other people. More importantly, we also examined whether people lay greater emphasis on affective factors when they engage in experiential purchases for others than in material purchases.

Experimental methods and procedures were exactly the same between in Study 1 and in Study 2. There were two parts of the main experiment in the present research. In the first part, participants' ideal affect scores (ideal affect scores for targets for Study 2) were measured. In the second part, after few weeks later, participants were asked to complete the option choice task. This task depicted purchasing situations where people consume various experiential and material products. We chose a total of 20 categories to which people can easily access in our daily life: 11 categories for experiential purchases such as vacation places, movies, and hobbies and 9 categories for material purchases such as shoes, alarm clocks, and USB flash drives. For each of 20 item categories, we selected two stimuli as a pair; one is for HAP option and the other is for LAP option. Participants were asked to choose only one of two options in each pair for themselves in Study 1 and for others in Study 2. By calculating the number of HAP options chosen by participants in each domain, we could examine whether people make choices based on their ideal affect in Study 1 and ideal affect for targets in Study 2.

The results of Study 1 demonstrated that people have different ideal affect depending on their ages and make purchasing choices based on their ideal affect in experiential purchases but not in material purchases when they make decisions for themselves. Consequently, the effect of participants' age on purchase decisions was partially mediated by ideal affect for self only in the experiential purchases but not in material purchases. On the other hand, the results of Study 2 confirmed that people have different ideal affect for targets depending on targets' age and gender, and more importantly, ideal affect for targets did predict choices not only in experiential purchases but also material purchases. Consequently, ideal affect for targets partially mediated the relationship between targets' age and choices in both of experiential and material purchases.

In conclusion, the overall results of the present research provide confirming evidence that people are likely to employ ideal affect as a basis of judgment and make decisions relied on it especially when they engaging in experiential consumptions regardless whether the target of purchases is self or others.

Furthermore, the interesting reversal regarding material purchases observed in Study 1 and 2 indicate that people are likely to use different strategies to make decisions for themselves and for other people especially in material purchases. Since the present research do not draw an absolute conclusion regarding why people show such self-other difference in material purchases, future studies need to be done to probe the underlying mechanism of this self-other difference. Lastly, the findings of the present research have valuable implications for the market place. For example, it will be of benefit for marketers who promote experiential goods such as tour packages and tickets for performance to understand ideal affect of their target consumers whom they intend to sell their products and to make promotions by emphasizing the affective states which will be elicited from consumer decisions. Moreover, this finding would be extended to gift-giving situations.

REFERENCES

Bagozzi, R. P., Gopinath, M., & Nyer, P. U. (1999). The role of emotions in marketing. *Journal of the Academy of Marketing Science*, 27, 184-206.

Cohen, J. B., & Areni, C. S. (1991). Affect and Consumer Behavior. In T. S. Robertson & H. H. Kassarjian (Eds.), *Handbook of Consumer Behavior*. Englewood Cliffs, NJ: Prentice Hall, 188-240.

Kwortnik, R. J. & Ross, W. T. (2007). The role of positive emotions in experiential decisions. *International Journal of Research in Marketing*, 24, 324-335.

MacInnis, D. J., Patrick, V. M., & Park, C. W. (2006). Looking through the crystal ball: Affective forecasting and misforecasting in consumer behavior. *Review of Marketing Research*, 2, 43–79.

Mellers, B. & McGraw, P. (2001). Anticipated emotions as guides to choice. *Current Directions in Psychological Science*, 10, 210-214.

Tsai, J. L. (2007). Ideal affect: Cultural causes and behavioral consequences. *Perspectives on Psychological Science*, 2, 242-259.

Tsai, J. L., Knutson, B. K., & Fung, H. H. (2006). Cultural variation in affect valuation. *Journal of Personality and Social Psychology,* 90, 288-307.

Van Boven, L., & Gilovich, T. (2003). To do or to have? That is the question. *Journal of Personality and Social Psychology,* 85, 1193-1202.

The Meaning of Border and Its Effects on Cross-Border Consumption

Emre Ulusoy, University of Texas - Pan American, USA

Even though the U.S.-Mexico border represents one of the most voluminous consumer and product traffic in the world and thus comprises a prominent context for researching cross-border mobility and consumption, that border has not attracted deserved attention among academics. Further, much of the existing research on cross-border mobility and consumption takes a modernist view and focuses on economic and rational aspects of border crossing. Few studies take alternative views (e.g., postmodernist) to examine how the profound and in-depth meanings of border affect cross-border experiences, (im)mobility and consumption. Therefore, this study examines the perceived meanings of the U.S.-Mexico border and the interplay of these meanings with consumer cross-border experiences, (im)mobility and consumption.

The term border has different meanings in different contexts, and these meanings change through time and space. In its broad sense, border is a separation of two entities from each other resulting in division, differentiation and dissimilarity. In addition to its conventional meaning, U.S-Mexico border has symbolic, socially constructed (Wonders 2006) and hyperreal meanings (Duarte-Herrera 2001). The meanings of border also vary in the process of globalization by the applications of debordering and rebordering processes (Stetter 2008) and by the engendered fragmentation of globalization (Fırat 1997).

I draw on the data collected through 37 interviews with consumers who cross the U.S.-Mexico border, some frequently and some infrequently, to understand perceived meanings of that border in the local community. Several intriguing themes emerged from the analysis. Generally speaking, consumers (re)interpret borders differently, and given their familiarity with the fluid and polysemous meanings of that border, their narratives contain paradoxical articulations of the meanings of border.

The first theme taps the paradoxical feelings of security and ambivalence. Seeking order, comfort, security, and pleasant consumption experiences, many people believe that these ideals are intimately linked to the U.S.-Mexico border. Border is thus a vital component of their everyday lives. These people also report of structural influences that the border imposes upon them, leading to discomfort, feelings of self-doubt, and stress when they get closer to the border.

The second theme is resistance against the materialization of the symbolic. Those who see the border as a means of order, security and comfort condemn the wall that the Bush administration intended to build between the U.S. and Mexico. These consumers consider the border to be crucial for maintaining order and security in the region, but allude to the proposed wall as a means of discrimination. They feel that the wall will render the symbolically 'fair' order to a visibly 'discriminatory' mechanism. Although they feel that no wall can stop them from crossing over, they fear that it will make the border more palpable and definite to local people's detriment.

The third paradoxical theme introduces the border as a symbolic obstacle and consumption as reward. Local people encounter numerous difficulties while crossing the border. They wait in lengthy lines everyday, sometimes under excruciating conditions. But once they are done crossing the border, they often indulge themselves in consumption experiences available on "the other" side. Therefore, the border is a symbolic obstacle in the way of alluring consumption time, and the act of crossing it generates a mysterious and thrilling experience. It is apparent from the narratives that such sensational swings would not be possible or the same if the border was to be removed.

The fourth theme is "border as fragmentation." Fırat (1995) argues that "fragmentation of the metanarrative allows the liberation and acceptance of indifferences, as well as putting an end to the dominance of any one regime of truth." Consistent with this argument, interviewees view (a) border as a force that symbolically maintains and intensifies these differences, and (b) globalization as a force engendering fragmentation and availing desired experiences of whatever, whenever. Postconsumers are contemporary people who produce their selves and create their images within and through meaningful experiences they seek in life primarily through consumptions (Fırat 1997). Border-crossers are prime examples of postconsumers. More specifically, Mexicans who cross the border, do so in part due to their liking for the 'American Dream' and American lifestyles. Symbolically, the border represents such ideal images.

The fifth theme is "border as a privilege." Mexicans perceive border as a privilege since, for many, being able to cross the border and experience "the other" side (the U.S.) is a privilege. Crossing over to the U.S. makes Mexicans feel special, different, or even part of a superior social class in their native communities.

The last theme is "social construction of border reality and hyperreality." Many Mexicans believe and articulate that U.S. is 'better' than Mexico in almost every aspect even when they do not see any difference between the two countries in terms of the quality and variety of products and services. Advertising and media play eminent roles in the construction of border hyperreality.

REFERENCES

Fırat, F. and Alladi Venkatesh (1995) "Liberatory Postmodernism and the Reenchantment of Consumption", *Journal of Consumer Research*, 22 (December): 239-267.

Fırat, F. (1997) "Educator Insights: Globalization of Fragmentation-A Framework for Understanding Contemporary Global Markets", *Journal of International Marketing*, 5(2): 77-86.

Duarte-Herrera, C.A. (2001) "Defining the US-Mexico Border as Hyperreality", *Estudios Fronterizos*, 2(4): 139-165.

Stetter, S. (2008) "Territories We Make and Unmake: The Social Construction of Borders in the Age of Globalization", *Harvard International Review*, Web Edition, http://hir.harvard.edu/index.php?page=browse&section=11.

Wonders, N.A. (2006) "Global Flows, Semi-Permeable Borders and New Channels of Inequality", In *Borders, Mobility, and Technologies of Control*, ed. Sharon Pickering and Leanne Weber, 63-87. Springer.

It's Smiling at Me: Satisfying Social Needs Through Consumer Products

James A. Mourey, University of Michigan, USA
Jenny G. Olson, University of Michigan, USA
Carolyn Yoon, University of Michigan, USA

Beginning with imaginary friends and teddy bears in childhood, human beings demonstrate a fundamental need for belonging that continues across the lifespan (Baumeister & Leary, 1995; Maslow, 1943). Although social needs are often fulfilled through contact with other people, it seems plausible that consumer products could fulfill similar needs. For example, consumers might purchase goods and services hoping to attain love, affection, and emotional pleasure. Rather than calling a friend when feeling lonely, a person may choose to indulge in comfort food or shop online. Seeking social need fulfillment through products may, paradoxically, serve as a detriment to interpersonal relationship development and maintenance. The objective of the current research is to explore how the consumption of products, in general, can come at the cost of social relationships when products satisfy the needs customarily fulfilled by other people.

Just how far people supplement human interactions with product interactions is a matter warranting careful study. Research suggests the possibility of consumers developing relationships with nonsocial objects that mirror interpersonal relationships (Aggarwal, 2004). Fournier (1998) identified brands as viable relationship partners where one party in the exchange is a person who receives significant social benefits.

Further evidence indicates that individuals readily perceive objects as gendered (Guthrie, 2007), brands as having personality (Aaker, 1997), and brand-related characters as human (Rook & Levy, 1999). Social exclusion may play a role in these findings, however, such that those who are craving human contact may more readily "see" people in their products. Research by Epley, Waytz, Akalis, and Cacioppo (2008) shows that people who feel more chronically disconnected from others and lonely anthropomorphize more than those who feel more connected. Indeed, individuals who are well integrated in their social networks are less likely to seek additional bonds relative to their more deprived counterparts (Baumeister & Leary, 1995).

In the present research, we examine in two studies the link between social exclusion and consumer products. We propose that when a social need exists, products may satisfy it in a way similar to people, which reduces the likelihood of seeking interpersonal fulfillment. Baumeister and Leary (1995) propose, but never empirically test, that social relationships "…should substitute for each other, to some extent, as would be indicated by effective replacement of lost relationship partners and by a capacity for social relatedness in one sphere to overcome potential ill effects of social deprivation in another sphere." We seek to demonstrate that consumers who perceive a void in affiliative bonds may be able to derive similar social benefits by forming relationships with and consuming products.

Study 1 utilized a 3(social inclusion/social exclusion/control) × 2(anthropomorphized/non-anthropomorphized product) between-subjects design. Undergraduates were randomly assigned to one of three essay conditions: social inclusion ("write about a time you felt very included by other people"), social exclusion ("a time you felt very excluded by other people), or a nonsocial negative control ("a time you did worse than expected on an academic assignment"). Participants were then presented information about iRobot's Roomba. This product was deemed appropriate because previous research indicates owners readily personalize the robot, which creates emotional engagement (Sung, Grinter, & Christensen, 2009). Participants were shown either an anthropomorphized (i.e., rotated 180 degrees from its original orientation so that it appears to be smiling) or nonanthropomorphized (i.e., rotated 90 degrees so it appears on its side) version. Aggarwal and McGill (2007) utilized a similar manipulation where they exposed participants to a picture of the front of a car that had been modified by a computer graphics professional. Specifically, the grille was positioned to be either pointing up in a smile or down in a frown. A series of rating scales followed Roomba presentation to assess product perceptions.

Results revealed a significant interaction between the two independent variables for purchase likelihood, after controlling for Roomba ownership. Means suggest that the anthropomorphized version was generally preferred among both socially included and excluded individuals, but not for those in the control condition. More importantly, socially excluded participants expressed a greater likelihood of buying the anthropomorphized Roomba over its nonanthropomorphized counterpart. A second key variable was willingness to pay for a Roomba, controlling for current ownership. Results yielded a marginally significant interaction between the two independent variables. Assessing the means revealed a similar pattern to purchase likelihood such that the socially included and excluded groups were willing to spend more money on an anthropomorphized Roomba than the control group. Conversely, the control and included groups were willing to spend noticeably more on the nonanthropomorphized Roomba compared to the socially excluded group. Taken as a whole, the socially excluded individuals are willing to pay a premium to obtain a humanlike product over its nonhuman counterpart.

Study 2 replicated Study 1 with a more heterogeneous sample and focused on social behaviors rather than product perceptions. A similar design was used: 1) individuals wrote about a time they felt either socially included or excluded (no control group), 2) viewed either an anthropomorphized or nonanthropomorphized Roomba, and 3) responded to a series of items including whether they wanted to wait alone or with others for subsequent tasks. Results yielded a significant interaction between the two independent variables in desire for social contact. Means indicate that those made to feel excluded were more likely to prefer waiting alone when presented with an anthropomorphized version of the Roomba compared to those also made to feel excluded who were presented with a nonanthropomorphized version. Presumably, the excluded individuals were able to "fill the void" when presented a humanlike product.

In sum, we find initial evidence for the idea that people's perceptions of their social inclusion and exclusion 1) influence the kinds of products they might buy, and 2) those products influence their social behaviors. Additional studies are already underway to replicate these effects with other products and to elucidate the mechanisms driving these effects. We hope future results will further support our central argument: If social needs can be satisfied through products, consumers may not seek fulfillment through other people and, therefore, increase their risk of negatively impacting real social relationships, perpetuating a cycle of consumption at the expense of social interaction.

REFERENCES

Aaker, J. L. (1997). Dimensions of brand personality. Journal of Marketing Research, 34, 347-356.

Aggarwal, P. (2004). The effects of brand relationship norms on consumer attitudes and behavior. Journal of Consumer Research, 31, 87-101.

Aggarwal, P., & McGill, A. L. (2007). Is that car smiling at me? Schema congruity as a basis for evaluating anthropomorphized products. Journal of Consumer Research, 34, 468-479.

Baumeister, R. F., & Leary, M. R. (1995). The need to belong: Desire for interpersonal attachments as a fundamental human motivation. Psychological Bulletin, 117, 497-529.

Epley, N., Waytz, A., Akalis, S., & Cacioppo, J. T. (2008). When we need a human: Motivational determinants of anthropomorphism. Social Cognition, 26, 143-155

Fournier, S. (1998). Consumers and their brands: Developing relationship theory in consumer research. Journal of Consumer Research, 24, 343-373.

Guthrie, S. (2007). Bottles are men, glasses are women: Religion, gender, and secular objects. Material Religion, 3, 14-33.

Maslow, A. H. (1943). A theory of human motivation. Psychological Review, 50, 370-396.

Rook, D. W., & Levy, S. J. (1999). Defending the dowager: Communication strategies for declining main brands. In D. W. Rook (Ed.), Brands, consumers, symbols, & research: Sidney J. Levy on marketing (pp. 171-196). Thousand Oaks, CA: Sage Publications.

Sung, J., Grinter, R. E., Christensen, H. I. (2009). "Pimp my Roomba": Designing for personalization. In S. Greenberg, S. E. Hudson, K. Hinkley, M. Ringel-Morris, and D. R. Olson (Eds.), CHI2009: Proceedings of the 27th Annual CHI Conference on Human Factors in Computing Systems (pp. 193-196). New York: Association for Computing Machinery.

"Customer prioritization: profit enhancing or threat inducing?"

Svetlana Davis, Queens University, Canada

Peter Dacin, Queens University, Canada

Customer prioritization is a widely used strategy in which a company separates customers into groupings based on an estimated life-time worth (Zeithaml, Rust, and Lemon, 2001) and gains efficiency by concentrating on serving the most profitable (high priority) customers while spending less energy and resources on low priority customers. In this research, we suggest that along with these positive outcomes, customer prioritization strategies can also lead to negative consequences. Particularly, we suggest that different offerings that are tailored to different customer groups could potentially threaten the strong self-brand connection among strongly attached customers. We further predict that as a mechanism to restore this self-brand connection, some customers with strong brand attachment will feel entitled to receive better treatment from the firm. Given that increased customer's entitlement could be costly for the companies (Butori, 2010), it is important to investigate the potential downside of customer prioritization strategies.

Customers strongly attached to brands often protect the strong connection and feeling of "oneness" that they have with the brand. However, the different treatment that occurs under a customer prioritization strategy could imply a threat to this connection. Specifically examining customers with strong brand attachment, a mismatch between their perception of the brand proximity to their self (or extended self) and the company's implied brand proximity (that is defined by high/low priority customer groupings and their corresponding treatments under customer prioritization) will be likely.

So how do customers with strong attachment protect brand proximity when the company imposes distance between the customer and the brand through prioritization strategies? We suggest that such customers will attempt to restore proximity with the brand by increasing expectations to receive better treatment from the company (which we label "entitlement"). This increase in expectations to receive better treatment will then minimize the distance between the self and the brand and allow for restoration of the brand-self proximity. That is, to maintain proximity with the brand, customers who are strongly attached to the brand will increase their feelings of entitlement to better treatment, especially when comparing the treatment they receive to corresponding treatment of customers in other priority groups (i.e. they assess the perceived treatment gap). This comparison results in increased feelings of entitlement for better treatment (due to a desire to maintain proximity with the brand).

METHOD:

The goal of this study is to show how a customer prioritization strategy in combination with strong brand attachment could result in increased feelings of threat to self brand connection, leading to feelings of increased entitlement. To achieve this goal, this study employed 2 x 2 between subject design with 2 levels of measured brand attachment (strong/weak), 2 levels of randomly assigned priority groups (high/low priority) in the context of a treatment gap (credible) assessment. This study measured entitlement as a dependent variable, while controlling for a more stable entitlement conceptualized as a personality trait.

RESULTS:

Consistent with our predictions, an ANOVA test indicated that brand attachment predicted an increase in threat to self-brand connection ($F(1) = 7.24$, $p < .05$). Furthermore, following Baron and Kenny (1986), we tested for mediation. The result showed that threat to the self brand connection fully mediated the relationship between brand attachment and entitlement, confirming that customers with strong brand attachment experience increased threat to self-brand connection compared to those that have low brand attachment (Ms=3.55 vs. 3.11, $Fs(1,264)$= 4.837 and , $ps < .05$) and this increases their entitlement (Ms=4.20 vs. 3.80, $Fs(1,264)$= 6.712 and , $ps < .05$).

DISCUSSION AND CONTRIBUTIONS:

This research shows that while the use of customer prioritization strategies promise the company higher efficiency and effectiveness (Zeithaml et al., 2001), it could also backfire in increased costs for handling customers' complaints due to an increased sense of entitlement.

Further, the literature on entitlement (e.g. Butori, 2010) has mostly been concerned with the conceptualization of entitlement as a stable personality trait. My research shows that this entitlement can also be conceptualized as situation-specific. This conceptualization holds all main distinctions of the construct itself. In particular, the entitlement is a belief that one should receive desirable treatment with little consideration of actual deservingness. Further, this entitlement can occur from the desire of customers with strong brand attachment to maintain proximity with the brand when such proximity maintenance is threatened (e.g. under conditions of a customer prioritization strategies).

While the literature on brand attachment (e.g. Park, Macinnis, Eisingerich and Iacobucci, forthcoming) suggests that strong brand attachments can offer advantages to firms (such as loyalty, brand display, readiness to pay a price premium and other benefits), this research introduces a note of caution on strong brand attachments, as it shows that such customers can also develop an increased sense of situation-specific entitlement and as a result demand special treatment which could be costly for the firm. This suggests that strong consumer-brand attachments can become a potential liability associated with customer prioritization strategies.

Finally, companies that employ prioritization strategies need to account for additional costs that could occur due to customers' increased sense of entitlement. For example, such additional costs could occur when customers complain or demand a better treatment from the company etc. Thus, while a customer prioritization strategy separates customers into different priority groupings based on the amount of worth that each customer represents for the company, my research suggests that such a separation would also benefit from consideration of brand attachment.

BIBLIOGRAPHY AND CITATIONS:

Baron and Kenny (1986) "The moderator-mediator variable distinction in social psychological research: Conceptual, strategic and statistical considerations." *Journal of Personality and Social Psychology*, 51, pg.1173-1182.

Bone (1992) "Determinants of Word-of-mouth Communications during Product Consumption," Advances in Consumer Research, 19, 579-583.

Butori (2010) "Proposition for an Improved Version of the Consumer Entitlement Inventory," *Psychology & Marketing*, 27(3), 285–298.

Grégoire and Fisher (2008) "Customer betrayal and retaliation: when your best customers become your worst enemies," *Journal of the Academy of Marketing Science* 36:2, 247-261.

Park, Macinnis, Eisingerich and Iacobucci (forthcoming) "Brand Attachment and Brand Attitude Strength: Conceptual and Empirical Differentiation of Two Critical Brand Equity Drivers," *Journal of Marketing*.

Zeithaml, Rust and Lemon (2001) "The Customer Pyramid: Creating and Serving Profitable Customers," *California Management Review*, 43 (4), 118–42.

The Interactive Effects of Self-Connection and Self-Esteem in the Affect Transfer Process of Consumer Brand Extension Evaluations

Zhuohao Chen, Warwick Business School, University of Warwick, UK
Qing Wang, Warwick Business School, University of Warwick, UK

Brand extension research has been increasingly critical as the expansion of consumers' psychological cognitive and affective boundary endows brands with more and more opportunities to enter new and distant categories. Although pioneer research asserts similarity between the parent brand and brand extension category as a key determinant of consumer brand extension evaluations (e.g. (Aaker and Keller 1990), (Park et al. 1991)), more and more brand extensions challenge this rule, e.g. Pepsi music, Virgin Cola, National Geographic garments, etc. Although such aggressive brand extensions are beyond consumers' imagination, consumers are not reluctant to accept them. On the other hand, however, Coke music, Vodafone Cola and Wall Street Journal garments would be more difficult to be accepted. A possible explanation is that the trait of excitement generates an affect transfer mechanism in which brand personality induces high-esteem consumers to be so risk-seeking in brand extension evaluation that they transfer their self-connection directly to the new product regardless of the extension distance.

Two mechanisms can be identified to understand the influence of brand personality on consumer brand extension attitude. On one hand, prior research follows a cognitive stream, arguing that a process of fit is a key mechanism of brand extension evaluation, in which perceived fit consists of three dimensions. First, category-based fit assumes that feature similarity is the basis of categorization (Tversky 1977) therefore similar category or feature (e.g., white appliance) leads to a favorable brand extension (Boush and Loken 1991). Next, further research finds consumers evaluate fit with a specific benefit or goal (Broniarczyk and Alba 1994; Martin and Stewart 2001). Specifically, similar context of usage aiming at a benefit (e.g. tooth brush and toothpaste for the benefit of dental health) increases perceived fit (Joiner 2006; Ratneshwar and Shocker 1991). Third, brand-based fit theory underlies the fit of brand image or brand concept (Park et al. 1991), which is accessible when consumers evaluate symbolic brand extensions. Here, brand-based fit is a relatively broad concept (Czellar 2003) so that brand personality fit can be viewed as a critical facet of it. In terms of this steam, consumers experience a fitting process in which the fit between brand extension category and original brand personality is evaluated. If this fit is higher, the brand extension attitude is more positive. In addition, self-connection facilitates consumer's understanding of brand personality fit in that brand affect generates relational holistic and schematic thinking (Ahluwalia 2008; Monga and John 2007) thereby fit being more easily perceived for distant extensions. If a consumer is emotionally attached to a brand, he is more likely to find such fit. In this mechanism, therefore, brand personality fit plays a mediation role between self-connection and brand extension attitude.

On the other hand, recent research in brand extension has put more attention to the affective process (e.g. (Barone and Miniard 2002; Barone et al. 2000; Yeung and Wyer Jr. 2005). Compared with cognitive evaluation, affect transfer is an abstract, schematic, symbolic and self-expressive process. Evidences show that parent brand affect can be directly transferred to brand extension attitude without mediation of perceived fit if a consumer has a high brand-elicited affect or loves the brand (Yeung and Wyer Jr. 2005). Such brand affect is usually generated by brand relationship including self-brand connection (Fournier 1998). The theoretical assumption of self-brand connection mechanism underlies that consumers are involved in a subconscious matching process when a brand personality is congruent with their self-images. The more self-brand congruity there is, the more this consumer favors the brand (Sirgy 1982), as a symbolic brand with distinct personality helps the consumer express himself and reduce the inconsistency between actual and desired self (Belk 1988). However, it is suggested that different dimensions of brand personality have asymmetric effects when a brand transgression occurs. For example, consumers tolerate a service failure of an exciting brand more than that of a sincere brand (Aaker et al. 2004). Individual attachment styles play a moderating role in self-connection as well (Swaminathan et al. 2009). Further, not all consumers follow this affect transfer process. Individual difference, particularly in personality traits such as self-esteem and self-construal, triggers the brand extension attitude formation approach (Ahluwalia 2008). We suggests that self-esteem is a moderator of the relationship between self-connection and brand extension attitude, i.e. affect transfer process. Higher self-esteem makes consumers more enthusiastic, optimistic and risk-seeking (Schaninger 1976) about aggressive brand extensions.

In summary, current research explicates the influence of brand personality and self-esteem on brand extension evaluation in three mechanisms. First, perceived fit is a mediator between self-connection and brand extension attitude. Second, self-connection influences brand extension attitude directly in the affect transfer process. Third, self-esteem moderates the affect transfer mechanism.

A pilot study was conducted in China to verify the conceptual model. Two real mobile telecommunication brands under China Mobile were used as parents brands (M-zone as exciting brand and G-tone as competent brand). Two pretests verified brand personality representations and the distance of fictitious brand extensions. In the main study, 232 students of a Chinese university were recruited to evaluate two brand extensions from eight fictitious extensions varying from low (e.g. wristwatches) to medium category fit (e.g. MP3 player and PDA) and low (PDA for M-zone and MP3 for G-tone) to high brand personality fit (e.g. MP3 for M-zone and PDA for G-tone) before they were required to report perceived fit, self-brand connection and self-esteem. Finally 461 evaluations were collected. Preliminary analysis results indicate good supports for the hypotheses. First, results of structural equation modelling confirm the baseline model, in which brand extension attitude is influenced by both brand personality fit and self-connection. Second, grouped structural models show a complete mediating model (self-connection→ perceived fit→brand extension attitude) in low self-esteem group, where the influence of self-connection on brand extension attitude was non-significant (b= .13, t=1.86, p>.05), while a partial mediating model (both self-connection→ perceived fit→ brand extension attitude and self-connection →brand extension attitude) in high self-esteem group, where self-connection has significant influence on brand extension attitude (b= .24, t=3.34, p< .001).

The results support the moderating effect of self-esteem on the affect transfer mechanism, i.e. high self-esteem triggers affect transfer in consumer brand extension evaluations. This indicates that high self-esteem may be a good predictor of affect transfer as high self-esteem consumers are more likely to judge a brand extension in terms of existing brand affect. Further research will adopt lab experiments to investigate every single mechanism, where self-esteem and self-connection will be manipulated respectively.

REFERENCES

Aaker, David A. and Kevin Lane Keller (1990), "Consumer Evaluations of Brand Extensions," Journal of Marketing, 54 (1), 27-41.

Aaker, Jennifer, Susan Fournier, and S. Adam Brasel (2004), "When Good Brands Do Bad," Journal of Consumer Research, 31 (1), 1-16.

Ahluwalia, Rohini (2008), "How Far Can a Brand Stretch? Understanding the Role of Self-Construal," Journal of Marketing Research (JMR), 45 (3), 337-50.

Barone, Michael J. and Paul W. Miniard (2002), "Mood and Brand Extension Judgments: Asymmetric Effects for Desirable Versus Undesirable Brands," Jounal of Consumer Psychology, 12 (4), 283-90.

Barone, Michael J., Paul W. Miniard, and Jean B. Romeo (2000), "The Influence of Positive Mood on Brand Extension Evaluations," Journal of Consumer Research, 26 (4), 386-400.

Belk, Russell W. (1988), "Possessions and the Extended Self," Journal of Consumer Research, 15 (2), 139-68.

Boush, David M. and Barbara Loken (1991), "A Process-Tracing Study of Brand Extension Evaluation," Journal of Marketing Research, 28 (1), 16-28.

Broniarczyk, Susan M. and Joseph W. Alba (1994), "The Importance of the Brand in Brand Extension," Journal of Marketing Research, 31 (2), 214-28.

Czellar, Sandor (2003), "Consumer Attitude toward Brand Extensions: An Integrative Model and Research Propositions," International Journal of Research in Marketing, 20 (1), 97-115.

Fournier, Susan (1998), "Consumers and Their Brands: Developing Relationship Theory in Consumer Research," Journal of Consumer Research, 24 (4), 343-73.

Joiner, Christopher (2006), "Existing Products and Brand Extension Judgments: Does Brand Category Context Matter?," Advances in Consumer Research, 33 (1), 76-81.

Martin, Ingrid M. and David W. Stewart (2001), "The Differential Impact of Goal Congruency on Attitudes, Intentions, and the Transfer of Brand Equity," Journal of Marketing Research, 38 (4), 471-84.

Monga, Alokparna Basu and Deborah Roedder John (2007), "Cultural Differences in Brand Extension Evaluation: The Influence of Analytic versus Holistic Thinking," Journal of Consumer Research, 33 (4), 529-36.

Park, C. Whan, Sandra Milberg, and Robert Lawson (1991), "Evaluation of Brand Extensions: The Role of Product Feature Similarity and Brand Concept Consistency," Journal of Consumer Research, 18 (2), 185-93.

Ratneshwar, Srinivasan and Aallan D. Shocker (1991), "Substitution in Use and the Role of Usage Context in Product Category Structures," Jounal of Marketing Research, 28 (3), 281-95.

Schaninger, Charles M. (1976), "Perceived Risk and Personality," Journal of Consumer Research, 3 (September), 95-100.

Sirgy, Joseph (1982), "Self-Concept in Consumer Behavior: A Critical Review," Jounal of Consumer Research, 9 (4), 287-300.

Swaminathan, Vanitha, Karen M. Stilley, and Rohini Ahluwalia (2009), "When Brand Personality Matters: The Moderating Role of Attachment Styles," Journal of Consumer Research, 35 (6), 985-1002.

Tversky, Amos (1977), "Features of Similarity," Psychological Review, 84 (3), 327-52.

Yeung, Catherine W. M. and Robert S. Wyer Jr. (2005), "Does Loving a Brand Mean Loving Its Products? The Role of Brand-Elicited Affect in Brand Extension Evaluations," Journal of Marketing Research (JMR), 42 (4), 495-506.

A Two-Stage Cognition Model of Online Shopping

Wei Chen, University of Connecticut, USA
Shuai Yang, University of Connecticut, USA
Sixing Chen, University of Connecticut, USA

With the development of internet marketing, more and more information with various sources and formats become available online. As a consequence, online shoppers are often faced information overload, which leads to choice deferrals (Dhar 1997; Iyengar and Lepper 2000). A recent study finds that engaging in unconscious information processing could help consumers to reduce their information overload and increase their product evaluations (Messner and Wanke 2011). Although unconscious cognition is useful in such an information rich environment, conscious processing performs better in low information context (Messner and Wanke 2011). To date the studies have mainly focused on a relatively stable information environment, i.e., the information amount is constant. By contrast, our study provides a dynamic framework of information load. Specifically, we propose a two-stage cognition model. At stage one, consumers facing lots of information will unconsciously process information, and at stage two, when information load is reduced, conscious processing will dominate. Such a two-stage method could utilize the advantages of both unconscious and conscious cognitions.

Raghubir and Krishna (1996) have proposed a two-stage approach of distance judgment, through which people develop an initial judgment unconsciously and make a conscious reevaluation later. Online shoppers could apply a similar manner that they engage in thin-slice judgments of products when they first see information, such as pictures, and then update their judgment by reviewing further information, such as textural descriptions (Peracchio and Luna 2006).

Individuals have limited capabilities to process information (Miller 1956) and a likely outcome could be the unconscious processing (Dijksterhuis 2004; Dijksterhuis and Nordgren 2006). How does unconscious processing occur in an online context? The products listed online often contain information such as pictures and some textual descriptions. Compared to textual descriptions, pictures are more salient and require less effort to process and people prefer to use such an effort-saving heuristic even if it might lead to a biased estimation (Raghubir and Krishna 1996). Consumers could associate pictures with products characteristics (Mitchell and Olson 1981). Given the fact that consumers often spend very limited time on each website (Wolfinbarger and Gilly 2001), such association is likely unconscious and consumers could use it to reduce the information load, creating a short list of product alternatives and evaluating them consciously later.

We speculate that mental contamination, i.e., unwanted thoughts generated by unconscious processing (Wilson and Brekke 1994), might result from the interaction between unconscious and conscious cognitions from two stages. To avoid or correct such mental contamination, people need to be aware of it and have motivation to correct it (Wilson and Brekke 1994). When information in the second stage of the process is consistent with that in the first stage, i.e., the product information consumers obtain from the picture is congruent with that acquired from textural description, individuals will fail to correct mental contamination due to lack of awareness. Even if the two cognitions are inconsistent, people are more likely to believe that the new propositions are false in their realm of beliefs and it is difficult to reject false propositions when their cognitive capacity is taxed (Gilbert 1991, 1993). If people who are lowly involved with the product, they are not motivated enough to correct source confusion, thus, they cannot move beyond their first judgment (Wilson and Brekke 1994). Only when consumers are highly involved with the product, they have strong motivations to conceal the truth about products, through a closer look at other information (Weisbuch and Ambady 2010). High involvement can focus their cognitive effort to comprehend product information (Celsi and Olson 1988).

Study 1 examines the relationship between information load and consumers' information processing method. Subjects are asked to choose a *soft* tissue from an assortment of tissue products that contain both pictorial and textural information. We adopt the design from Mitchell and Olson (1981) that some pictures convey the information of *softness* while others do not. Moreover, some textural descriptions explicitly state the word *soft* while others do not. The combinations of pictures and texts are randomized. For low (vs. high) information load condition, subjects are asked to choose from 5 (vs. 20) tissue products. Manipulation check indicates that subjects feel much low (vs. high) information load when choosing from 5 (vs. 20) products. Preliminary results show that when information load is low (vs. high), subjects are more likely to choose the product with *soft* explicitly stated in textural description (vs. product with a picture that conveys the idea of *softness*).

Study 2 investigates whether consumers will reduce the information load using unconscious processing and consciously process the remaining information. Subjects are asked to choose a *soft* tissue from 20 tissue products that contain both pictorial and textural information. Subjects are instructed that they can put some of the products into the *shopping cart* and make the decision later. The product information is manipulated the same as that in study 1, and we record the time subjects spend on filling the *shopping cart* and on final decision. Preliminary study suggests that at stage 1, subjects rely more on the picture to reduce the information load while at stage 2, subjects depend more on the textural description to make the choice. Also, the time subjects spend on each tissue product at stage 1 is less than that at stage 2.

Study 3 focuses on the effect of information consistency between unconscious and conscious cognitions on product choice, as well as the moderating role of involvement. The study is a 2 (information consistency: yes vs. no) by 2 (involvement: low vs. high) design. The dependent measure is subjects' purchase likelihood (7-point scale: very unlikely to very likely). The picture contains a kitten which is believed to indicate *softness* (Mitchell and Olson 1981), and in consistent (vs. inconsistent) situation, the textural descriptions explicitly state the word soft (vs. non-soft). Subjects in low (vs. high) involvement condition are told that the tissue will not (vs. will) be available in near future (Petty, Cacioppo, and Schumann 1983). The data collection is on progress and results will be reported later.

REFERENCES

Celsi, Richard L. and Jerry C. Olson (1988), "The Role of Involvement in Attention and Comprehension Processes," *Journal of Consumer Research*, 15 (September), 210-24.

Dhar, Ravi (1997), "Consumer Preference for a No-Choice Option," *Journal of Consumer Research*, 24 (September), 215-31.

Dijksterhuis, Ap (2004), "Think Different: The Merits of Unconscious Thought in Preference Development and Decision Making," *Journal of Personality and Social Psychology*, 87 (November), 586-98.

——— and Loran F. Nordgren (2006), "A Theory of Unconscious Thought," *Perspectives on Psychological Science*, 1 (June), 95-109.

Gilbert, Daniel T. (1991), "How Mental Systems Believe," *American Psychologist*, 46 (February), 107-19.

——— (1993), "The Assent of Man: Mental Representation and the Control of Belief," in *The Handbook of Mental Control*, ed. D. M. Wegner, and J. W. Pennebaker, NJ: Prentice Hall, 57-87.

Iyengar, Sheena S. and Mark R. Lepper (2000), "When Choice is Demotivating: Can One Desire Too Much of a Good Thing?" *Journal of Personality and Social Psychology*, 79 (December), 995-1006.

Messner, Claude and Michaela Wanke (2011), "Unconscious Information Processing Reduces Information Overload and Increases Product Satisfaction," *Journal of Consumer Psychology*, 21 (January), 9-13.

Miller, George A. (1956), "The Magical Number Seven, Plus or Minus Two: Some Limits on Our Capacity For Processing Information," *Psychological Review*, 63 (March), 81-97.

Mitchell, Andrew A. and Jerry C. Olson (1981), "Are Product Attribute Beliefs the Only Mediator of Advertising Effects on Brand Attitude?" *Journal of Marketing Research*, 18 (August), 318-32.

Peracchio, Laura A. and David Luna (2006), "The Role of Thin-Slice Judgments in Consumer Psychology," *Journal of Consumer Psychology*, 16 (January), 25-32.

Petty, Richard E., John T. Cacioppo, and David Schumann (1983), "Central and Peripheral Routes to Advertising Effectiveness: The Moderating Role of Involvement," *Journal of Consumer Research*, 10 (September), 135-46.

Raghubir, Priya and Aradhna Krishna (1996), "As the Crow Flies: Bias in Consumers' Map-Based Distance Judgments," *Journal of Consumer Research*, 23 (June), 26-39.

Weisbuch, M., and Nalini Ambady (2010), "Thin-slice vision," in *The Science of Social Vision*, Vol. 13, ed. R. B. Adams, N. Ambady, K. Nakayama, and S. Shimojo, NY: Oxford University Press, 228-47.

Wilson, Timothy D. and Nancy Brekke (1994), "Mental Contamination and Mental Correction: Unwanted Influences on Judgments and Evaluations," *Psychological Bulletin*, 116 (July), 117-42.

Wolfinbarger, Mary and Mary C. Gilly (2001), "Shopping Online for Freedom, Control, and Fun," *California Management Review*, 43 (Winter), 34-55.

Trust in Financial Investments: Who or What Really Counts

Christopher Ruppel, Johannes Gutenberg-University Mainz, Germany
Sabine Einwiller, Johannes Gutenberg-University Mainz, Germany

The latest upheavals in the financial markets revitalized the debate on the role of customer trust in banks and in the financial system in general and stimulated discussions as well as actions concerning stricter rules and regulations in this sector. Several studies in marketing have shown that trust in a firm or its representatives can positively impact on customers' behavior, also in the financial sector. Only few studies, however, have taken the institutional environment in which the action takes place into account. One exception is the study conducted by Grayson, Johnson and Chen (2008) who distinguish between 'narrow scope trust' referring to trust in individual firms and their representatives and 'broad scope trust' referring to system trust and generalized trust. The authors highlight the role of trust in the broader context as an antecedent and narrow scope trust as a mediator for customer satisfaction. The specific role of the consumer's trust in the banker, i.e. the person advising the financial investment decision, was however not clarified. We argue that differentiating between the bank as an organization and the advisor as a person is significant, because the personal relationship between customer and financial advisor can play a crucial role in financial decision making (e.g. Howcroft, Hewer, and Durkin 2003). To gain an extensive view on the mechanisms of trust in financial decision making, we therefore propose to differentiate between the following three objects of trust: the financial system, the bank and the financial advisor.

In developing a model of trust in financial investments we drew on attitude theories (Ajzen 1991; Fazio 1990) and former definitions of trust (Lewis and Weigert 1985; McKnight, Cummings, and Chervany 1998) according to which trust shall be conceptualized as a multidimensional construct, comprising a cognitive evaluation of the trust objects, a positive expectation as well as a behavioral intention to invest and thereby accept vulnerability (Rousseau et al. 1998). Thus, the final model comprised the three objects of trust (trust in the system, the bank and the financial advisor) and as mediating variable the customer's trusting expectation that the investment decision was good, worthwhile and low-risk (trusting expectation). The target variable was the customer's trusting behavioral intention to make an investment at the respective bank (trusting intention). As potential influencing variables on trust in the bank we tested the reputation of the bank and the familiarity and satisfaction with the bank, and as potential antecedents of trust in the advisor familiarity and satisfaction.

To test the model, an online survey was conducted among private investors between January and March 2010. Participants were recruited by tapping personal networks and applying a pyramid scheme. Participants were asked to answer the questions with respect to their latest investment. The analysis builds on 145 cases. Data were analyzed using structural equation modeling with Partial Least Squares (PLS) on account of two crucial advantages: it allows representing both formative and reflective latent constructs (Jarvis et al. 2003) and even with small sample sizes it generates robust results (Chin and Newsted 1999). Evaluation of the measurement model produced satisfying results: For reflective constructs (a) indicator reliability, (b) construct reliability (c) convergent validity and (d) discriminant validity were assessed. In the final model (a) factor loadings exceeded a minimal acceptable value of 0.7 and were significant at $p < 0.05$, (b) composite reliability was greater than 0.7, (c) the average variance extracted exceeded the threshold of 0.6 for each construct, and (d) the Fornell-Larcker-Criterion (1981) was met for each latent variable. Concerning formative constructs (here: familiarity) *multicollinearity* was investigated by the variance inflation factor, which in every case fell below the recommended threshold of 5 (Diamantopoulos et. al. 2008). Evaluation of the structural model was also supporting our model: All except two of the path coefficients were significant at $p < 0.05$. Path coefficients show that trust in the system only exerts a moderate influence on the trusting expectation ($b = 0.145$) and the trusting intention ($b = 0.103$). Strong effects, however, originate from trust in the bank and trust in the advisor. While trust in the bank exerts its influence on the trusting intention mainly through the person's trusting expectation ($b = 0.343$), trust in the advisor has the strongest direct effect on the trusting intention ($b = 0.324$). Calculating total effects reveals that trust in the advisor is the main driver of a trusting intention ($b_{tot} = 0.399$ vs. $b_{tot} = 2.88$ for trust in the bank respectively $b_{tot} = 0.148$ for trust in the system). The variable exerting the strongest influence on trust in the bank is its reputation ($b = 0.470$); familiarity was the variable most relevant for trust in the advisor ($b = 0.532$). The high predictive power of the model is indicated by R^2 values exceeding a value of 0.36 for all endogenous constructs. The corresponding Stone-Geisser test criterion Q^2 exceeding the threshold of 0 for dependent variables suggests likewise a strong predictive relevance (Chin 1998).

Our study shows that the complex phenomenon of trust demands a similarly comprehensive conceptualization. For the specific context of this research, the model reveals that although the institutional environment in which the decision takes place is relevant, however, that investing is a very personal business: While system trust only marginally influences private investors' decision making, our research suggests that trusting the person who advises the investor in his or her decision making is most important. It is important to note that the research was conducted during turbulent times, namely within the context of a dramatic financial crisis. Perceived uncertainty which was most likely enhanced by the situation might have amplified the role of trust in the advisor. Further research shall clarify the influence of situation specific uncertainty for the role of the different objects of trust in engendering a trusting expectation and intention.

REFERENCES

Ajzen, Icek (1991), "The Theory of Planned Behaviour," *Organizational Behavior and Human Decision Processes*, 50, 179-211.

Chin, Wynne W. and Peter R. Newsted (1999), "Structural Equation Modeling Analysis with Small Samples Using Partial Least Squares," in Rick Hoyle (Ed.), *Statistical Strategies for Small Sample Research* (pp. 307 – 341). Thousand Oaks, CA: Sage Publications.

Chin, Wynne W. (1998), "The Partial Least Squares Approach to Structural Equation Modeling," in George A. Marcoulides, (Ed.), *Modern Methods for Business Research* (pp. 295 – 336). Mahwah: Lawrence Erlbaum.

Diamantopoulos, Adamantios, Petra Riefler, and Katharina Roth (2008), "Advancing Formative Measurement Models", *Journal of Business Research*, 61 (12), 1203-1218.

Fazio, Russell H. (1990), "Multiple Processes by Which Attitudes Guide Behavior: The MODE Model as an Integrative Framework," in Mark P. Zanna (Ed.), *Advances in Experimental Social Psychology* (Vol. 23, pp. 75 - 109). San Diego, CA: Academic Press.

Fornell, Claes and David F. Larcker (1981), "Evaluating Structural Equation Models with Unobservable Variables and Measurement Errors," *Journal of Marketing Research*, 18 (1), 39–50.

Jarvis, Cheryl B., Scott B. MacKenzie, and Philip M. Podsakoff (2003), "A Critical Review of Construct Indicators and Measurement Model Misspecification in Marketing and Consumer Research," *Journal of Consumer Research*, 30 (September), 199-218.

Grayson, Kent, Devon Johnson, and Der-Fa R. Chen (2008), "Is Firm Trust Essential in a Trusted Environment? How Trust in the Business Context Influences Customers," *Journal of Marketing Research*, 45 (2), 241 – 256.

Howcroft, Barry, Paul Hewer, and Mark Durkin (2003), "Banker-Customer Interactions in Financial Services." *Journal of Marketing Management*, 19 (9-10), 1001 – 1020.

Lewis, J. David and Andrew Weigert (1985), "Trust as a Social Reality," *Social Forces,* 63 (4), 967 – 985.

McKnight, D. Harrison, Larry L. Cummings, and Norman L. Chervany (1998), "Initial Trust Formation in New Organizational Relationships," *Academy of Management Review*, 23 (3), 473 - 490.

Rousseau, Denise M., Sim B. Sitkin, Ronald S. Burt, and Colin Camerer (1998), "Not so Different After All: A Cross-Discipline View of Trust," *Academy of Management Review*, 23 (3), 393 – 404.

Price on the Top of the Price: Effect of Sales Tax and Product Price on Consumers' Estimates of the Total Purchase Price

Igor Makienko, Universty of Nevada, Reno, USA

If consumers are well aware of sale taxes but do not see them on price tags does this mean that they are not influenced by this universal surcharge when they estimate the total purchase price? In our research we explore the impact of sale taxes on consumers' estimations of the total purchase price in traditional retail settings and suggest that price level will moderate the impact of sale taxes on consumers' estimations of the total purchase price.

Too tired to care: the selfish impulse and the will to be fair

Sachin Banker, MIT, USA

The studies presented here aim to address the apparent conflict that exists in proposed accounts of the nature of fairness versus self-interest motives. While some neuroscientific evidence has provided support for the view that the concern for fairness relies on an emotional impulse that must be controlled in order to act in rational self-interest, other evidence has supported an opposing view that the concern for fairness is instead realized through the control of selfish impulses. The two psychological theories generated from this neural evidence were tested using ego-depletion methods and provide support for the latter view that people are in fact driven by selfish impulses that must be resisted in order to enact fair outcomes. Moreover, it is also found that more general implementation of altruistic, reciprocal, as well as efficiency norms requires the control of self-interested impulses. This evidence offers important implications regarding consumer behavior that differ dramatically from those generated by the conflicting account.

THEORETICAL BACKGROUND

In a seminal study, Sanfey et.al. (2003) had subjects play an ultimatum game while placed in an fMRI. Faced with a choice to accept or reject a proposed split of an endowment, subjects had to weigh their desire for a fair outcome against a desire for money. It was found that rejections of especially low, unfair offers was associated with activation in the anterior insula, a region of the brain thought to be involved in the representation of feelings of pain and disgust, and this finding is taken to be indicative of the fact that motives for fairness are subserved by emotional impulses that must be regulated to act in an economically normative manner.

However, in a study that had subjects play an ultimatum game while temporarily disrupting activity in the right DLPFC, an area of the brain implicated in the cognitive control of impulse, subjects actually accepted unfair offers more often (Knoch et.al. 2006). This finding runs counter to the prediction of the previous story, since if control is required to regulate the impulse to reject unfair offers, disruption should decrease rather than increase acceptances. Instead, this evidence is taken to be indicative of the fact that people are driven by selfish impulses that must be controlled to act according to social and cultural fairness norms.

Together, these neural data are suggestive of two competing psychological accounts. In particular, each view proposes a relationship between an impulse and a controlled motive. In one view, there exists an emotional impulse for fairness that must be controlled to act in rational self-interest. In the opposing view, there exists a selfish impulse that must be controlled to act in line with fairness norms. Since the relationship between neural activity and the corresponding psychological constructs remains somewhat tenuous, existing data are not conclusive about either view. Fortunately though, there are established behavioral methods of manipulating these constructs.

Theories of self-regulation provide behavioral predictions regarding the way in which controlled motives versus impulsive motives may present. In specific, the strength model of self-control posits that there exists a common and depletable self-regulatory resource that is required to overcome impulses and that can be drained in the short run through any self-regulatory act (Baumeister, Vohs, Tice 2007). For example, simply controlling one's emotions during a dramatic video can reduce scores on the seemingly unrelated task of gripping a handgrip as long as possible (Muraven, Tice, Baumeister 1998). Thus, after ego-depletion we should expect to see increases in rejections of unfair offers in an ultimatum game if the fair-impulse view is accurate and decreases in rejections if the selfish-impulse view is accurate.

EXPERIMENTAL DESIGN

A series of 4 studies were conducted, each involving an ego-depletion manipulation and incentive compatible play in well-explored economic games. Studies 1a-c observe altruistic and reciprocal behavior in the dictator game and ultimatum game, and Study 2 observes behavior in taxation games that allow a number of particular fairness concerns, including efficiency, to be distinguished.

Study 1: Depletion three-ways

In Study 1a, subjects were depleted with a forced choice task that required some subjects to choose carrots rather than cookies. If in the undepleted condition, subjects were instead forced to choose cookies over carrots. Subjects then participated in a dictator game and responded to offers in an ultimatum game. Study 1b appropriates the vicarious depletion findings from Ackerman et al (2009) and Study 1c applies a typing task manipulation previously used in Muraven et al (2006). The results of these manipulations are similar to those reported below.

The findings indicate that depleted individuals exhibit a diminished concern for altruism than their undepleted counterparts, giving on average $2.56 vs. $3.72 (t(50)=2.08, p=0.0428) in the dictator game. Selfish offers of $0 increased dramatically under depletion, from 7% to 43% (t(50)=3.38, p<0.01). In addition, it is also found that depleted individuals exhibit a diminished concern for reciprocal fairness relative to their undepleted counterparts, only rejecting unfair $1 offers 42% of the time compared to the more normal value of 68% exhibited by undepleted subjects (for $1 offers t(50)=1.87, p=0.06; for $2 offers 33% vs. 58%, t(50)=1.72, p=0.09; similar logit results).

Study 2: Taxation games

In Study 2, subjects were depleted with a typing task manipulation similar to that used in Study 1c and subsequently played the 4 taxation games in Engelmann and Strobel (2004). Findings indicate that preference for efficient allocations decreases under depletion, choosing the efficient option 18.9% of the time under depletion versus 40.7% (t(89)=-2.23, p=0.028).

IMPLICATIONS

Concern for fairness constitutes an important driver of consumer behavior. However, the current findings suggest that the tendency to rely on fairness motives depends crucially on the extent to which the consumer is able to overcome impulses in the particular situation. If for example a person were overloaded with stimuli or decisions, we would expect them to be less willing to donate to charitable causes but more willing to pay unfair prices for goods. The findings also suggest that resisting a steak for a salad would have an effect of reducing tips for the waiter or waitress.

REFERENCES

Ackerman, Josh, Noah Goldstein, Jenessa Shapiro, and John Bargh (2009) "You wear me out: the vicarious depletion of self-control," *Psychological Science*, 20 (3): 326-332.

Baumeister, Roy F., Kathleen D. Vohs, and Dianne M. Tice (2007) "The strength model of self-control," *Current Directions in Psychological Science*, 16 (6): 351-355.

Engelmann, Dirk and Martin Strobel (2004) "Inequality aversion, efficiency, and maximin preferences in simple distribution experiments," *American Economic Review*, 94 (4): 857-869.

Knoch, Daria, Alvaro Pascual-Leone, Kaspar Meyer, Valerie Treyer, and Ernst Fehr (2006) "Diminishing reciprocal fairness by disrupting the right prefrontal cortex," *Science*, 314: 829-832.

Muraven, Mark, Dianne M. Tice, and Roy F. Baumeister (1998) "Self-control as limited resource: regulatory depleteion patterns," *Journal of Personality and Social Psychology*, 74 (3): 774-789.

Muraven, Mark, Dikla Shmueli, and Edward Burkley (2006) "Conserving self-control strength," *Journal of Personality and Social Psychology*, 91 (3): 524-537.

Sanfey, Alan G., James K. Rilling, Jessica A. Aronson, Leigh E. Nystrom, and Jonathan D. Cohen (2003) "The neural basis of economic decision-making in the ultimatum game," *Science*, 300: 1755-8

Tabibnia, Golnaz, Ajay Satpute, and Matthew Lieberman (2008) "The sunny side of fairness: preference for fairness activates reward circuitry (and disregarding unfairness activates self-control circuitry)," *Psychological Science*, 19 (4): 339-347

How Does Skinny Sell?
Body Size and Pricing Effects on Advertising Effectiveness and Body Esteem

Maxim Polonsky, University of Connecticut, USA
Ioannis Kareklas, Washington State University, USA

Marketers claim that skinny models sell products well (Gillian, 2000). Research findings on exposure to thin models and advertising effectiveness are mixed. Women generally feel thin fashion models are more elegant and interesting (Martin et al., 2007), and tend to associate thin with happiness, desirability, and status (Tiggermann, 2003). On the other hand, Dittmar and Howard (2004) have shown that the exposure to thin ideals in ads may harm an individual's body esteem, and there is no difference between thin and average-size models in terms of advertising effectiveness (i.e. product and ad evaluation, and purchase intention).

When asked about most important aspects in women's life, approximately fifty percent of American females indicate their shape and weight (The Downing Street Group, LLC, 2007). For young women especially, pressures to be thin contributes to lower self-esteem, body image disturbances, and eating disorders, with as many as fifty percent of undergraduate females expressing body dissatisfaction (Bearman et al., 2006).

Research shows that between 1970–1990, the emphasis on fitness increased, and the body shape of models tended to become thinner (Guillen and Barr, 1994). The content analysis of popular fashion magazines from 1959 to 1999 found a significant decrease in models' body sizes during the 80s and 90s (Sypeck et al., 2004). Botta (1999), for example, found that exposure to thin body sizes had an influence on young female's endorsement of the ideal thin body and the likelihood to use media models to define what their own bodies should look like. The relationship between exposure to thin-ideal and body image disturbances was also demonstrated in experimental research (Bessenoff, 2006; Dittmar & Howard, 2004) and supported by two meta-analytic reviews (Grabe et al., 2008; Groesz et al., 2002).

Important moderators of the relationship between exposure to thin ideals in the media and body-related disturbances are social comparison tendency and thin-ideal internalization. Internalization of thin-ideal has been viewed as an important risk factor that contributes to developing of eating disorders. Thin-ideal internalization refers to the extent to which an individual accepts the thin-ideal standard of beauty and attractiveness as her own and engages in behaviors that supposedly help to approximate these standards (Thompson et al., 1999).

As a theory, social comparison posits that individuals compare themselves to others to determine their own relative levels of abilities (Festinger, 1954). There are two directions for social comparison: an upward comparison that is made when comparison others are perceived to be more fortunate; and a downward comparison that refers to less fortunate comparison others. Research suggests that when discrepancies between the self and the comparison standard arise, people are motivated to change the self to be more like the comparison standard. Upward comparisons in particular lead to negative moods and lower self-esteem (Gibbons & Gerard, 1989). Social comparison processes may be unintentional, environmentally imposed, and even unwanted (Lyubomirsky & Ross, 1997). Richins (1991) pointed out that that social comparison with media models has unfavorable consequences for female body esteem, since the media body ideal is unattainable. That is why women who are more likely to compare their body to media models have higher levels of body dissatisfaction and lower levels of self-esteem (Stormer & Thompson, 1996).

From the review above, the marketing dilemma is evident: images that are effective in selling products may also harm consumers. We conducted two experiments in order to investigate the dilemma closely. In the first online experiment, 145 female participants were randomly assigned into one of the three print ad body size conditions: thin, average, and plus-size. Specifically, we investigated the effects of the model body size on advertising effectiveness (attitude toward the ad, attitude toward the model, and purchase intention), as well as on body-esteem and weight lose intention. Upon login onto the website, participants were randomized into one of the three conditions and told that that they are participating in a marketing research study that explores different communication and appeal strategies (print vs. video, reading detailed information versus watching a short ad, sex appeal vs. humor, etc.) for two product categories – computers and women shoes. After completing pre-test, participants in each condition were referred to CNET.com page "Best 5 desktops" (http://reviews.cnet.com/best-desktops/?tag=leftColumnArea1.0) or similar updated page, and asked to read short one-paragraph review for each of the five computers. Next, participants were asked to answer filler questions about their liking, preference, and purchase intention for any of the reviewed computers. Upon the completion, study participants saw the experimental ad and filled a post-test questionnaire that consisted of a) questions about advertising effectiveness (e.g. ad evaluation, purchase intention, willingness to pay), and b) body-esteem scale and questions about dieting and weight loss. Participants were deceived that the later part of the post-test was an unrelated small scale survey study that will be used to design health interventions.

Our results indicate that participants in the thin condition estimated price to be higher relative to the participants in the plus-size and average conditions (F = 3.587, p < .05, means = $60, $65, and $85 for plus-size, average, and thin conditions respectively). We find a similar pattern for other advertising effectiveness variables, with the thin condition having a positive effect on willingness to pay (F = 3.317, p < .05; means = $30, $32, $38 for plus-size, average, and thin conditions respectively), attitude toward the model (F = 5.812, p < .05; means = 3.1, 3.6, 4.1) and attitude toward the ad (F = 3.17, p < .05; means = 3.2, 3.6, 4). It is important to note that the participants' purchase intention was identical in the average and thin conditions (F=3.12, p < .05; means = 2.5, 3.1, 3.1 for plus-size, average, and thin conditions).

In regards to body-related outcomes, we find that in the thin condition participants reported lower levels of body-esteem (F=3.02, p = .05) and higher desire to lose weight (F = 5.174, p < .05; means in pounds = 9, 9, 14). To summarize, in the thin model body size condition, participants viewed the ad and the model more positively, estimated the price to be higher, and were more likely to indicate their willingness to pay higher price and their purchase intention. On the other hand, this same condition made female participants feel bad about their bodies, and affected their desire to lose weight.

Our second experiment employed a between-subject 3 x 2 factorial design, investigating the effect of exposure condition (ads featuring thin models, plus-size models, and average models) and price (low and high) on the following outcomes: 1) advertising effectiveness (attitude toward the ad, purchase intention), and 2) body esteem and weight loss intention. The main difference from our Experiment 1 is the introduction of price as an independent variable. We introduce price variable because, as mentioned above, thin is associated with status. We manipulate price and attempt to investigate whether price interacts with model body size to create the perception of quality and to elicit generally more favorable attitudes toward advertisements. At the same time, we investigate how body X price interaction affects consumers' body-esteem and weight loss intentions. Our preliminary results suggest that thin body size condition loses its advertising effectiveness when paired with low price. Generally the main effect for model body size disappears virtually in every variable of interest.

REFERENCES

Bearman, K., Presnell, E. & Stice, E. (2006). The skinny on body dissatisfaction: A longitudinal study of adolescent girls and boys, *Journal of Youth and Adolescence, 35,* 229–241.

Bessenoff, G. (2006). Can the media affect us? Social comparison, Self-discrepancy, and the thin ideal. *Psychology of Women Quarterly, 30,* 239-259.

Botta, R.A. (1999). Television images and adolescent girls' body image disturbance. *Journal of Communication, 49*(2), 22-42.

Dittmar, H. & Howard, S. (2004). Thin-ideal internalization and social comparison tendency as moderators of media models' impact on women's body-focused anxiety. *Journal of Social and Clinical Psychology, 23,* 747-770.

Festinger, L. (1954). A theory of social comparison processes. *Human Relations, 7,* 117–140.

Gibbons, F.,& Gerard, M. (1989). Effects of upward and downward social comparison on mood states. *Journal of Social and Clinical Psychology, 1,* 14–31.

Gillian, A. (2000, may 31). Skinny models 'send unhealthy message'. The Guardian, p. 7.

Grabe, S., Hyde, J., & Ward, M. (2008). The role of the media in body image concerns among women: A meta-analysis of experimental and correlational studies. *Psychological Bulletin, 134 (3),* 460-476.

Groesz, L., Levine, M., & Murnen, S. (2002). The effect of experimental presentation of thin media images on body satisfaction: A meta-analytic review" *International Journal of Eating Disorders, 31(1),* 1–16

Guillen, E., & Barr, S. (1994). Nutrition, dieting, and fitness messages in a magazine for adolescent women, 1970-1990. *Journal of Adolescent Health, 15 (6),* 464-472.

Lyubomirsky, S., & Ross, L. (1997). Hedonic consequences of social comparison: A contrast of happy and unhappy people. *Journal of Personality and Social Psychology, 73,* 1141-1157.

Martin, B., Veer, E., & Pervan, S. (2007). Self-referencing and consumer evaluations of larger-sized female models: A weight locus of control perspective, ' *Marketing Letters, 18 (3),* 197-209.

Richins, M. (1991). Social comparisons and idealized images of advertising. *Journal of Consumer Research, 18(1),* 71-83.

Stormer, M., & Thompson, J. (1996). Explanations of body image disturbance: A test of maturational status, negative verbal commentary, social comparison, and sociocultural hypotheses. *International Journal of Eating Disorders, 19,* 193-202.

Sypeck, M., Gray, J., & Ahrens, A. (2004). No longer just a pretty face: Fashion magazines' depictions of ideal female beauty from 1959 to 1999. *International Journal of Eating Disorders* **36,** 342–347.

Tiggemann, M. (2003). Media exposure, body dissatisfaction and disordered eating: Television and magazines are not the same! *European Eating Disorders Review, 11,* 418-430.

The Downing Street Group, LLC (2007). The Dove report: Challenging beauty. Available at < www.campaignforrealbeauty.com/uploadedFiles/challenging_beauty.pdf>.

Thompson, K., Heinger, L., Altabe, M., & Tantleff-Dunn, S. (1999). Exacting beauty: Theory, assessment, and treatment of body image disturbance. Washington, DC: APA.

Brand Suicide? Memory and Liking of Negative Brand Names

Duncan Guest, Lugano University, Switzerland
Zachary Estes, University of Warwick, UK
Michael Gibbert, Lugano Universty, Switzerland
David Mazursky, Hebrew University, Israel

Brand names can convey important attributes of a product, and can more generally impact the brand image itself. For instance, brand names such as *Dove* and *Apple* implicitly convey positivity. However, some products are marketed with distinctly negative brand names, such as *Burn* energy drink, *Fat Bastard* chardonnay, and *Poison* perfume. What are the consequences of such negative brand names for consumer behavior? Might they bestow certain benefits that outweigh their negative connotations? We report two experiments that investigate this question. Specifically, a wealth of psychological research indicates that negative words are more memorable than neutral words, and some preliminary evidence suggests that negative stimuli become less negative with repeated exposures. We therefore predicted that, relative to neutral brand names, negative brand names would be better remembered (H1) and would become less negative with repeated presentations (H2).

Experiment 1 investigated whether negative brand names are better remembered than neutral brand names (H1). Eighty-four undergraduates viewed a series of slides containing one negative brand name (e.g., *Poison*) and one neutral name (e.g., *Obsession*), with a different novel logo presented above each brand name. Half the brand names were presented in blue font and half in red. The negative and neutral names differed in valence but were matched for word length and frequency. We then tested participants' recognition memory of (1) the brand names, (2) their color, and (3) their associated logos. Based on cognitive research, we hypothesized that negative brand names would not only be more memorable than neutral names, but also that they would evoke better memory for contextual details such as font color and logo. Results supported these predictions. Relative to neutral names, negative brand names elicited significantly better recognition ($p < .05$) of the brand (71% vs. 65%), its color (55% vs. 49%), and its associated logo (58% vs. 54%). Evidently, negative branding evokes better memory for the brand name and its contextual details (e.g., color, logo).

Experiment 2 investigated attitudes toward negative brand names. Our primary interest was whether attitudes to negative brand names would improve across exposures (H2), as some prior research suggests that emotional stimuli become less extreme with repeated exposures. Secondarily, we also varied two dimensions of negative stimuli, namely, their extremity and their arousal. Negative words can be more or less extreme, and they can be high or low in arousal. Thus, 48 undergraduates evaluated the same brand-product pairs at three different times. Hypothetical brand names varied in extremity and arousal, producing a 2 (extremity: extreme, moderate) X 2 (arousal: high, low) within-participants design, with five brand-product pairs in each condition. All brand names were paired randomly with a neutral object, such as *Hatred* chair (extreme, high), *Grief* stove (extreme, low), *Trouble* clock (moderate, high), and *Neglect* cabinet (moderate, low). At time 1 (t1), each brand-product pair appeared for 13 seconds, and respondents evaluated how much they liked it (1 = "not at all"…7 = "very much"). Participants evaluated their liking of each brand-product pair again six hours later (t2) and two weeks later (t3). At t3 participants first were given a complete list of brand and product names, and they were asked to match the brands with the products that they had seen previously.

A 2 (extreme, moderate) X 2 (high, low arousal) x 3 (t1, t2, t3) repeated measures ANOVA on liking ratings indicated that all three main effects were significant ($p < .05$). Specifically, (1) moderately negative brands were liked more than extremely negative brands, (2) highly arousing brands were liked more than less arousing brands, and (3) brands were generally liked more across times. However, these effects were qualified by two interactions. First, valence and arousal interacted, with a larger effect of arousal among moderate brands than among extreme brands. Second, arousal and time interacted, with a significant effect of time only among moderately arousing brands. Extremity and arousal both affected memory identification scores at t3 as well, with better memory for extreme brands than for moderate brands, and for highly arousing brands than for less arousing brands. Interestingly, liking and memory were not directly related: Moderate brands were liked more, but extreme brands were better remembered. Thus, as predicted, negative brands tended to become less negative across exposures. Moreover, extremity and arousal both affected liking and memory of brands and products.

In sum, negative brand names are more memorable than neutral names, and repeated exposures increase liking of negative names. This exposure effect on liking was observed among low-arousal names such as *Gloom* but not among high-arousal names such as *Torture*. Those high-arousal brand names, however, were more memorable than the low-arousal names. Thus, negative brand names may be particularly memorable, but repeated advertising may be necessary to overcome consumers' initial dislike of them. Managers therefore need to think carefully about whether the benefits gleaned from making the brand stand out at the point of sale and in memory outweigh the negative perceptions created when using a negative brand name. Furthermore, because negative brand names are evaluated worst at initial exposure, a marketing strategy should consider advertising the brand for some time prior to product release to enable consumers to overcome initial negative perceptions.

Author Index